THE GUINNESS RECORD OF THE FA CUP

For Siobhan

THE GUINNESS RECORD OF THE FA CUP

MIKE COLLETT

GUINNESS PUBLISHING

THE AUTHOR

Mike Collett missed the 1953 Matthews Cup Final only because he was born 12 days too late.
Since then, he has travelled to all five continents working as a sports writer and television
producer and has covered every World Cup since 1982 and Olympic Games since 1984.
The greatest moment in a lifetime of watching sport came when Ricky Villa scored the winning
goal for Tottenham in the replayed Centenary Cup Final against Manchester City in 1981. That
was on his birthday and he made sure he was at Wembley for that one.
He writes on soccer for The Observer and while he thinks it is now unlikely that he'll ever score
the winning goal for Spurs in the Cup Final, he is convinced that at least one of his three
children will – early next century and probably when the year ends in a '1'.
He started his career on the Hendon Times, spent a decade with United Press International and
since 1989 has been a freelance journalist and sports producer. He recently joined Reuters, the
international news agency, as a sports writer. He is a member of the Association of Football
Statisticians.

Published in Great Britain by Guinness Publishing Ltd, 33 London Road, Enfield, Middlesex

Cover design by lippa pearce design ltd

Text design and layout by Kathleen Aldridge

Typeset in Bembo and Helvetica by Ace Filmsetting Ltd, Frome, Somerset

Printed in Great Britain by The Bath Press, Bath, Avon

'Guinness' is a registered trademark of Guinness Publishing Ltd

A catalogue record for this book is available from the British Library

ISBN 0–85112–538–7

CONTENTS

PART THREE
FA Cup facts and feats

INTRODUCTION

One morning in the middle of November 1990, I received a phone call from The Observer, which was, as they say, to change my life and eventually lead to the book you are holding in your hands.

The Observer assignment was to cover the FA Cup match between Littlehampton Town of the Sussex County League and Northampton Town, then of the Fourth Division, a quintessential FA Cup First Round tie, the kind from which legends have been made for more than 120 years.

The next few days were spent researching the FA Cup exploits of the two clubs – and for my purposes Littlehampton's were very easy as this was the first time they had reached the First Round. One fact I was interested in establishing about Northampton was how many non-League clubs they had played in the Cup – and how many had they lost to.

At the time it proved an almost impossible task.

Despite phone calls to the club and dipping into a number of reference books, there was no easy way to find the answer to that particular question. Understandably, yearbooks do not publish the results of old FA Cup competitions every year and although full match details have been easily accessible since the arrival of the Rothmans Football Yearbook in 1970, it's a time-consuming job compiling a breakdown of any one theme you may need. Until now.

Now if you want to know how many times Northampton Town, or Norwich or Newcastle for that matter, have lost to non-League opposition, all you have to do is look up their record in this book and you can have your answer in one minute flat.

This then was the catalyst for the Guinness Record of the FA Cup. Although there is a lot more in it besides, this book is the first to include a complete record of every club side involved in the Competition Proper, since the FA Cup started in 1871.

And these clubs represent something of an elite group as far as English football is concerned. There are 42,000 registered clubs in England – but only the 600-plus in this book including a handful from Wales, and in the 19th century from Scotland and Northern Ireland, have actually played in the Competition Proper.

In his introduction to his England Football Fact Book, author Cris Freddi accurately summed up the immediate problems faced by anyone delving into football's dim and distant past. 'It is like digging in the remains of a lost civilisation. They didn't always write everything down . . . and when they did they didn't always write it right,' wrote Freddi, words which should serve as a warning to everyone contemplating research into football's past.

Several minefields have been crossed in order to produce this record. Details one would think of as being fairly straightforward like the dates on which matches were played, where they were played and who scored the goals, become an almost unfathomable mystery when the official records of the protagonists do not even match. Own goals, penalties and abandoned matches provide another nightmare as do, in the early days, the actual names of some of the rounds. As recently as 1981 reference books were published without the names of some of the scorers in Cup Finals themselves.

This book has set out to include as much detail about every match played in the Competition Proper, including the date, the round, the venue, the scorers and the Division or Leagues the teams were in when the match was played. I have tried to use at least two or three sources for every entry. Sometimes this has proved impossible, other times the more sources you use the more confusing the picture becomes. There are some gaps that will never be filled, but there is a great deal more that is presented for the first time ever.

Football sadly does not boast the same kind of literary tradition as cricket and until 1970 did not possess a statistical fortress like Wisden. In the course of researching the book I was informed – to my astonishment – by the secretary of one of the oldest Football League clubs that they have a huge gap in their own official records before the early 1960s, ever since a new manager came into the club – admittedly in the middle of a long decline – and took a look round at the old minute books and official records in his office.

'That's the trouble with this place,' he said, 'too busy living in the past. Take this lot out and get rid of it.'

I am reliably assured, the records have been lost for over 30 years and now, probably for ever.

It has only really been in the last decade or so that football's statistical, and to a lesser degree romantic past has been pored over, analysed and examined, and served up for the public's gaze – and the more light that can be thrown on hitherto unresearched areas, the better. There's a long way to go.

Not that the FA Cup has ever been out of the limelight for long. Every year, for nearly a century and a quarter, someone somewhere has been dreaming of winning the FA Cup – players, fans, managers, agents, hopeless romantics, incurable optimists. Despite all the recent changes in domestic football, the FA Cup remains the glamour event; ask any player what he would cherish most from his career and 99.9% reply an FA Cup winner's medal. The same percentage of fans would gladly pay a King's ransom for a Cup Final ticket.

The FA Cup defies belief and always has done. It is unbelievable to think that in the 1880s Aston Villa scratched from playing Oxford University in the FA Cup to play a Birmingham Senior Cup match instead and it is unbelievable to think that in the 1980s a team like Brighton and Hove Albion could reach the Cup Final – and very nearly win it – and yet be relegated from the old First Division in the same season. Or that a team like Wimbledon, just 11 years after leaving the Southern League, could beat Liverpool in the Cup Final.

In a recent interview for this book, the former England international Gary Stevens, who played and scored for Brighton in the 1983 Final and also played for Tottenham in the 1987 Final, summed up Brighton's schizophrenic season of a decade back saying, 'We were like two different teams, the League team and the Cup team. We obviously struggled in the League because we went down – but there were no inhibitions stopping us in the Cup. We even went to Liverpool in the fifth round when they were top and we were bottom and we beat them at Anfield.'

'The Cup changes everything for a team. It really does become just 11 against 11, players become inspired when you start dreaming of those twin towers. It's ten years since I played in my first Cup Final and six since the second, but it still brings a lump to my throat when I think I played in two Cup Finals. It still makes the hair stand up on the back of my neck, and I can still get upset by the fact that I ended up beaten in both the Cup Finals I played in.

'But that's what the Cup does to you. It is special and it is magical – and I'd still like a winner's medal, but the only way I'll get one now is by going to an auction!'

And that's the only way most of us could ever hope to get a Cup medal too. Less than 1,000 men have known the thrill of winning the FA Cup – only a comparative handful have done it more than once. Players know that if they haven't done it by the time they're 30, their chances start dwindling rapidly. An FA Cup winner's medal is a prize that has eluded some of the game's greats – Steve Bloomer, Charlie Buchan, Tom Finney, Johnny Haynes, George Best and Peter Shilton among them – and been captured by many that flitted briefly across centre-stage, or the centre-circle. They reached out once – and the Cup was there!

An article in the excellent When Saturday Comes, after the largely disappointing 1993 Cup Final and replay, suggested that Cup Final Day was no longer what it was in the 1950s, 1960s and 1970s, crowded in on all sides by the League Cup Final, FA Cup semi-finals at Wembley, a plethora of minor cup finals at Wembley and the League play-offs. That article was spot on. Times change and we must change with them – but certain traditions are worth preserving.

As a boy I always used to equate Cup Final afternoon with Christmas Day because it seemed so quiet out. When we went into the street immediately afterwards and re-enacted Denis Law scoring and then holding one hand up and throwing the ball away (1963) or Ronnie Boyce running behind the goal after scoring (1964), the very air seemed magical and still, split only by boyish shouts of joy. Perhaps kids nowadays re-enact the game on their computer screens – perhaps they don't even watch the match at all – but for those of us that do, there is still an aura and a distinction about the match that must be preserved by the FA at all costs.

Obviously, given the present leadership of the FA, sooner or later the competition will be sponsored and obviously the Final will lose the last vestiges of its ancient dignity when it goes to penalties. The FA should resist these changes with all the power it has, but one knows that these unfortunate developments will only be resisted by that body for so long.

It is still not too late for the FA to work out a plan with the relevant police authorities enabling the final to be played to its natural conclusion, and still not too late for the competition to have its integrity restored by the abolition of penalties in the earlier rounds. Is it too naive to suggest that if the FA have to give 10 days notice of the date of a replay, then surely they can give the police 12 days notice of the date of the possible second replay, 14 days notice of a third replay and 16 days notice of a fourth replay if necessary. And if the games are not needed, the police have got enough time to re-adjust their rotas accordingly. And if the recent trend continues and more and more clubs will be using their own stewards instead of police matches, surely the importance of police rotas is diminished anyway.

Back in November 1965, the question of police rotas and penalties never entered into it. But one thing was as rare then as it would be today – a report of a Wigan Athletic match on the sports pages of The Times. But this was no ordinary report and in many ways it sums up the magic of the Cup like the far more famous exploits of Stanley Matthews in 1953, Jim Montgomery in 1973 and Andy Linighan in 1993. In those days Wigan Athletic were in the Cheshire County League and on November 17, 1965 they beat Doncaster Rovers 3–1 in a first round replay.

Under the heading 'Wigan Forward "Chuffed"', The Times report is the stuff of legends. It read: 'H. Lyons was the toast of Wigan last night. Carried off on a stretcher after 20 minutes of the FA Cup first round replay against Doncaster Rovers at Wigan, he defied the pain of sprained ankle ligaments to score three goals. Lyon spent 15 minutes in the Wigan dressing-room while a doctor plied him with whisky and tablets to ease the pain.

'The prescription worked wonders. Lyon's flashing header found the back of Doncaster's net in the 57th minute. This was followed up by a volley with his strapped-up foot 15 minutes later, and then three minutes from the end he scored with another header.

'After being chaired off the field by jubilant supporters, Lyon said, "I could hardly walk when I got back on the pitch, but when the first goal went in I was chuffed. I forgot all about the pain. It just didn't seem to hurt any more."'

The man was a solid gold Cup hero. This book is dedicated to all of them.

Mike Collett
London, July 1993

BIBLIOGRAPHY

Besides the following principal sources listed here, reference was also made to thousands of match programmes and dozens of individual club handbooks and histories. A major source of information covering the period 1871–1925 can be found in the four FA Cup booklets published by the Association of Football Statisticians between May 1985 and August 1987.

Association Football, FNS Creek, 1937
Association Football, 4 volumes, editors Fabian & Green, 1960
Association Football and the Men Who Made It, Gibson & Pickford, 1906
Athletic News Football Annuals – various until the 1920s
Book of Football, 12 volumes, 1905
Book of Football, 5 volumes, 1972
By The Book, Clive Thomas, 1984
Complete Book of the Olympics, David Wallechinsky, 1992 edition
Corinthians & Cricketers, Edward Grayson, 1957
Cup Final Extra! Martin Tyler, 1981
Cup Final Story, 1946–1965, David Prole, 1966
Encyclopaedia of Association Football, Maurice Golesworthy, various editions
England Football Fact Book, Cris Freddi, 1991
English Football Internationalist's Who's Who, Douglas Lamming, 1990
FA Official Yearbooks, from 1948
Finney – A Football Legend, Paul Agnew
Football Annual, edited by Charles Alcock, various from the 1870s onwards
Football Encyclopaedia, Frank Johnstone, 1934
Football From The Goalmouth, Frank Swift, 1949 edition
Football In Sheffield, Percy M. Young, 1981
Football League Players Records, 1946–1988, Barry Hugman
Football Worlds, Stanley Rous, 1978
For The Good of the Game, The Official History of the PFA, John Harding, 1991
Forward Arsenal! Bernard Joy, 1952
Gamage's Association Football Annuals – various
Giantkillers, The, Bryon Butler, 1982
Glorious Wembley, Howard Bass, 1982
Great Soccer Stars, Jimmy Hill, 1978
Grounds For A Change, Dave Twydell, 1992
Guinness Book of Hit Singles, various editions
Guinness Book of Soccer Facts and Feats, various editions, Jack Rollin
History of the FA Amateur Cup, Bob Barton
History of Football, Morris Marples, 1954
Hotbed of Soccer, The Story of Football in the North East, Arthur Appleton, 1961
Illustrated History of Modern Britain 1783–1964, Richards and Hunt, 1965
Jackie Milburn In Black and White, Mike Kirkup, 1990
Journey To Wembley, Brian James, 1977
League Football and the Men Who Made It, Simon Inglis, 1988

Lenzel's Southern League Handbooks – various
News of the World Football Annuals – various
Non League, Bob Barton, 1985
Non League Club Directory, various editions from 1978–79, editors Tony Williams, James Wright
Non League Football Fact Book, Tony Williams, 1991
Northern Goalfields, The Official History of the Northern League, Brian Hunt, 1989
Official Illustrated History of the Football League, Bryon Butler, 1988
Official History of the FA Cup, Geoffrey Green, 1948
Official History of the Football Association, Bryon Butler, 1991
One Hundred Years of the FA Cup, Tony Pawson, 1972
Pictorial History of Soccer, Dennis Signy, 1968
Rejected FC Vols 1 & 2, Dave Twydell, 1988, 1989
Revelations of a Football Manager, Terry Neill, 1985
Rothmans Football Yearbooks, all editions since 1970–71
Soccer at War 1939–1945, Jack Rollin, 1985
Soccer: A Panorama, Brian Glanville, 1969
Southern League Football, The First 50 Years, Paul Harrison, 1989
Southern League Football, The Post War Years, Paul Harrison, 1987
Spurs Supreme, Ralph L. Finn, 1961
Stanley Matthews – The Authorised Biography, David Miller, 1989
Strange Kind of Glory, Eamon Dunphy, 1991
Sunday Chronicle Football Annual 1946–47 in particular
75 Years of Southern League Football, Lionel Francis, 1969
The Double and Before, Danny Blanchflower, 1961
There's Only One United, Geoffrey Green, 1978
Wembley Presents 25 Years of Sport, Tom Morgan, 1948
Wisden Cricket Almanacks, various
You've Got To Be Crazy, Bob Wilson, 1989

NEWSPAPERS AND MAGAZINES

Accrington Observer, Athletic News, Bexley Observer, Birmingham Daily Gazette, Blackburn Standard, Bolton Journal and Guardian, Bury Guardian, Buxton Herald, Daily Express, Daily Mirror, Daily Telegraph, Ealing Times, Eastern Daily Press, FA News, Farnham, Haslemere and Hindhead Herald, Hendon Times, Grimsby Evening Telegraph, The Footballer, Football Monthly, Football League Review, Lancashire Daily Post, Lancashire Evening Telegraph, Liverpool Echo, (London) Evening News, (London) Evening Standard, (London) Star, Manchester Evening News, Match Weekly, The News (Portsmouth), Newcastle Evening Chronicle, Non-League Football Magazine, Northern Echo, Nottingham Evening Post, The Observer, Rotherham Express, Sheffield Morning Telegraph, Shoot!, Sporting Life, The Sportsman, Sports Argus (Birmingham), Stalybridge Reporter, Soccer Star, South Wales Echo, Sunday Sportsman Racing and Football Weekend Special, Sunday Express, Sunday Times, Sunday Telegraph, The Times, Team Talk, Yorkshire Post.

ACKNOWLEDGEMENTS

Thanks are due to many people who contributed something – loaned books and programmes, offered advice, general guidance and hard facts and figures which all helped me to research and write this book.

More than anyone I am especially thankful to two people for their encouragement and help – my wife Siobhan, and John Duncan of The Guardian.

Without Siobhan's unwavering support and love this project could never have been completed. She might not have known much about Old Carthusians before I started writing this book but certainly knows a fair bit about them now.

John Duncan was there at the very beginning, shared the highs and lows and helped me through some particularly manic hours in the quest to overcome all the hurdles I had to face to reach my own Cup Final – ie getting this book completed!

The task would not have been possible either without the help of the dozens of players, former players, club secretaries, chairmen and club statisticians who also willingly helped provide information or at least pointed me in the right direction. I must have heard the expression 'I can't help you, but I think I know someone who can' a thousand times in the last few years, and my special thanks go to all those people in the non-League scene who were so generous with their time, enthusiasm and support. Professional football generally could well take a leaf out of their book.

Space does not allow me to thank all the people who have helped, but I must especially mention the following, without whom . . .

Simon Duncan and Charles Richards, my editors at Guinness; David Barber of the Football Association; Arthur Appleton, R.I. Bailey, Tony Brown, Tim Clapham, Sheila Collett, Bob Crampsey, Dennis Dickens, David Emery, Phillip Elms, Cris Freddi, Mick French, Brian Glanville, John Goodbody, Paul Harrison, Terry Howes, David Kennedy, Hyder Jawad, Tom Lewis, Richard Littlejohn, William Morgan, Ian Newton, Mike Norton, Melanie O'Toole, Liam O'Toole, Chris Oakley, Paul Plowman, Myles Palmer, Mike Pavosovic, Jack Rollin, Mick Robinson, Martin Spong, Gary Stevens, Tony Thwaites, Peter Tozer, John Treleven, Bob Vaughan.

Thanks also for the support and encouragement from Simon Kelner and Alan Hubbard and all on The Observer sports desk and the library staffs of The Observer, the Daily Express, the Newspaper Library at Colindale and Blackburn, Wimbledon, Chiswick and Lincoln.

Lastly, but not leastly thanks to Ryan, Hannah and Melissa for keeping their sticky fingers off the keyboard when at times the temptation must have been almost impossible to resist.

Tony Brown also provided the data for the club-vs-club listings appendix.

LIST OF ABBREVIATIONS

To simplify the identification of the Leagues, the original name of the competition has been used throughout. Therefore clubs belonging to the Isthmian League, for example, are always designated as IL – irrespective of the sponsor's name or the name of the League in any given year. The only exception to this rule is the GM Vauxhall Conference which has been the name of the Alliance Premier League since the 1986–87 season.

One further note: Although there was no Football League competition in the 1945–46 season and League teams were playing in the regionalised war-time League North and League South competitions, the clubs have been designated to the Football League Division they were in for the 1939–40 season, abruptly curtailed by the start of World War II.

PL .... Premier League	**HEL** .... Hellenic League	**NWC** .... North West Counties
D1 .... Football League Division 1	**IL** .... Isthmian League	**NWaC** North Wales Coastal League
D2 .... Football League Division 2	**KL** .... Kent League	**PDL**Peterborough & District League
D3 .... Football League Division 3	**LC** .... Lancashire Combination	**SAL** .... Sheffield Association League
D4 .... Football League Division 4	**LCC** .... Liverpool County	**SCL** .... Sussex County League
3N .. Football League Division 3 (N)	Combination	**SL** .... Southern League
3S .... Football League Division 3 (S)	**LL** .... Lancashire League	**SPT** .... Spartan League
	Lincs .... Lincolnshire League	**SSL** .... Surrey Senior League
AL .... Athenian League	**Lon** .... London League	**Suf** .... Suffolk County League
APL .... Alliance Premier League	**Man** . Manchester & District League	**SWL** .... South Western League
BC .... Birmingham Combination	**Met** .... Metropolitan League	**TC** .... The Combination
BDL Birmingham & District League	**MC** .... Midland Combination	**TSL** .... Tees-side League
CA .... Central Alliance	**ML** .... Midland League	**UCL** .... United Counties League
CC .... Cheshire County League	**NAll** .... Northern Alliance	**WCL** ...... West Cumberland League
CL .... Central League	**N&S** ...... Norfolk & Suffolk League	**WYL** .... West Yorkshire League
CML .... Central Midlands League	**NCoE** ..... Northern Counties (East)	**Wear** .... Wearside League
CRN .... Corinthian League	League	**★Welsh** .... Welsh League
Cumb .... Cumberland League	**NCo** ..... Northern Counties League	**WL** .... Western League
DEL .... Delphian League	**N&D** .... Nottinghamshire &	**WMRL** .... West Midlands Regional
DSL .... Derbyshire Senior League	Derbyshire Senior League	League
ECL .... Eastern Counties League	**NEL** .... North Eastern League	**YL** .... Yorkshire League
FAll .... Football Alliance	**NELC** NE Lancashire Combination	
GMVC .. GM Vauxhall Conference	**NPL** .... Northern Premier League	★ *a separate League from the newly-*
Hants .... Hampshire League	**NRL** ..... Northern Regional League	*constituted League of Wales*

A GUIDE TO THE CLUB VS CLUB RECORDS

The clubs listed in the main results section (pp. 44–520) are those who have been included in the draw for the First Round Proper of the FA Cup since the competition started. A number of clubs, like Donington School, Harrow Chequers and Preston Zingari, for example, never played a match, but were included in the draw, and so are included in this list.

With a listing as exhaustive as this going back over 120 years, some anomalies inevitably occur. It was decided to include rarely-found qualifying round match results of present-day League clubs where applicable. Generally speaking, the records for former Football League clubs list only the matches the clubs have played in the Competition Proper.

The listings for the hundreds of non-League clubs are, in the vast majority of cases, their complete records in the Competition Proper. Occasionally some of their qualifying round results are also listed, but this is usually to include a result where they beat a League team in an earlier qualifying round match, but failed to reach the Competition Proper.

Generally speaking the organisation of the FA Cup competition falls into three periods. The first, from 1871–72 until 1887–88, consisted of the Competition Proper only, with no qualifying rounds. From 1888–89 to 1924–25 the qualifying competition, which in season 1904–05

actually consisted of nine rounds, including an 'intermediate' round which involved Football League clubs, who were not finally exempted from the qualifying competition until the last re-organisation of the competition as we know it today, in 1925.

The only significant change in any competition since 1925 was in the 'transitional' 1945–46 season, the first after the Second World War when all ties from the First Round to the Sixth Round Proper were played over two legs and the results of both matches are listed, and the replays where necessary.

The club-by-club listings detail, reading across: the season each match was played in, the division or League of the club listed, the round, the date, the opposition, the division or League of the opposition, the venue, the match result, the score and the scorers.

Most of the abbreviations used are self-explanatory, but occasionally n/af appears to indicate the club was not affiliated to any League when they appeared in the FA Cup.

The brief potted histories for most clubs concentrate mainly on their FA Cup records, and the author would be delighted to hear from anyone who has any more historical information on the clubs listed here, for inclusion in any future edition of this book.

PART ONE

THE
GUINNESS
RECORD
OF THE
FA CUP

THE STORY OF
THE FA CUP

Amateur hour   1872–82

On November 11, 1871 four football matches took place that were unlike any that had ever been played before.

In west London, a team from the Civil Service turned up for their game against Barnes with only eight men. In south London, Crystal Palace laid out the welcome mat for the men from Hitchin, who had travelled across Hertfordshire and the Metropolis. Out in east London, Upton Park were playing Clapham Rovers, while in rural Berkshire, Maidenhead and Marlow, two clubs who are still rivals to this day, were meeting competitively for the first time.

Those eight teams, all of them from the south and all of them amateur, were playing themselves into history. They were taking part in the very first FA Cup matches of all.

The balls that were sent rolling across those muddy, unmarked fields have long since disappeared, but the passions, emotions and frenzies that were aroused on that distant Victorian afternoon remain as strong as ever.

These games were also the first truly 'competitive' soccer matches. A prize, a tangible reward, was waiting for the winners of this competition. It could be argued that modern soccer really began that afternoon.

Could anyone living then possibly have imagined the impact the FA Cup was going to have on the development of soccer? Could anyone in the middle of the 19th century ever have imagined the impact soccer was going to have on the national, and later the global consciousness? The men who formed the Football Association were not great social reformers like William Wilberforce or the Earl of Shaftesbury, but by their deeds they would indirectly have a huge impact on the social life of the nation – an impact felt to this day.

Football of course has been with us probably for as long as men have had feet to kick things with. The Chinese were the first to formalise the game in any way with their ancient game of T'su Chi which was more of an individual ball-control game than a team effort. The Greeks played a game called 'episkyres' and the Romans one called 'harpustum'- both more like rugby than soccer. In the Middle Ages, in Florence, Italy, the game of 'calcio' developed- a brawling, violent, colourful spectacle which is still enacted in Renaissance costumes today.

Various forms of the 'foote-ball' had been known in rural Olde Englande since long before the Middle Ages. The annual ShroveTuesday match in Derbyshire is said to date back to AD 217 when the men of Derby drove out a number of Roman soldiers from the town. From ancient times there was a Shrovetide match played in Chester, and there were others at Corfe Castle in Dorset and Scone in Perthshire. The Shrove Tuesday match at Ashbourne in Derbyshire is played to this day between the 'uppers' and 'downers' while every January 6 in north Lincolnshire the villagers of Haxey and Westwoodside engage in a brawling, heaving scrum for up to six or seven hours until one side scores a 'goal' – getting the 'ball' through the doors of the nearest pub.

Most of these ancient rural traditions have survived unaltered from the earliest times – even surviving King Edward II's proclamation early in the 14th century which banned the playing of this type of football altogether:

'Forasmuch as there is great noise in the city caused by Hustling over large balls, from which many evils may arise, which God forbid, we command and forbid on behalf of the King, on pain of imprisonment, such game to be used in the city in future.'

Two hundred years later nothing much had changed. In 1531 Sir Thomas Elyot said that football was 'nothing but beastlie furie and extreme violence deserving only to be put in perpetual silence'. And the author of 'Anatomic of Abuses in the Realme of England' published in 1583 was of the same mind:

'As concerning football playing, I proteste unto you that it may rather be called a friendlie kind of fight than a play or recreation . . . a bloody murthering practice than a fellowy sport or pastime.'

As late as 1829 a report of a 'match' in Derbyshire told of people 'falling, bleeding beneath the feet of the surrounding mob'. Clearly the gap between matches of that kind, the only kind of their day, and the type of football being played just 42 years later had been closed extremely quickly, even if the football being played on that November day in 1871 may seem hugely outdated to us today. We clearly have far more in common, in terms of playing the game at least, with our relatively athletic, dapper Victorian friends, than with the brawling mob in Derby.

By 1871 there was a clearly defined pitch, with recognisable goals, a referee and umpires, teams of 11-a-side and distinct strips. But there were no crossbars or goal-nets, free-kicks and penalties had yet to be invented and there were no markings on the pitch except for the touchlines. When the ball was kicked out of play the team who 'touched it down' first, rugby style, took the throw-in.

What had brought about this revolutionary change in little more than a generation was the influence of the public schools who helped calm the game down, taking the basic structure and purpose of the urban, folkloric working-class pastime and codifying it into a sport. It was within the courtyards and libraries, the assembly halls and dormitories, but most importantly on the playing fields, that football as we know and understand it today first put down its roots.

There had been a major change of attitude towards education for the privileged in the early part of the 19th century. The boys who went to these schools had no time for the pastimes of a country squire. They did not go horse-riding or hunting at school, and while they may have rowed later at Oxford or Cambridge, their main outdoor pursuits until then were to be found on convenient playing fields, or cloisters, or any open space within the school grounds. All that was needed was enough boys to make two teams, and a ball.

The catalyst the game needed at this stage came from Dr Thomas Arnold, the reforming educationalist at Rugby School. He helped the youngsters organise themselves and impose some discipline on the embryonic football they were playing, an adaptation of the town and village games that had been around for centuries.

So by the second or third decade of the 19th century, various forms of football had now come into being in the major public schools. At Winchester the playing field was about 80 yards long and 80 feet wide; at Eton they changed ends at half-time, but at other schools this happened after every goal was scored. The art of dribbling with the ball was much favoured by the boys at Charterhouse and Harrow where the goals were known as 'bases' and stood 150 yards apart. At Cheltenham College, the game was played with the precursor of the modern-day throw-in.

Outside of the public schools, the game was also developing in other isolated pockets like Sheffield. Some rules permitted the use of hands, others didn't. Some allowed hacking, others didn't. Quite clearly, out of this Tower of Babel there could only be one result – chaos.

It was not until 1848 that the first attempt was made to unify all of these different strands. In that year fourteen Old Boys from Rugby, Winchester, Eton, Harrow and Shrewsbury met at Cambridge and after much vexing and argument, 'The Cambridge Rules' were drafted. But the knot the Old Boys tied that year was not a secure one and soon unravelled. Before long, each school and club was playing by its own rules again.

In 1862, with the game still a decade away from capturing even a twinkle of the public's imagination, another attempt was made to unite the nation's footballers. In that year Mr J.C. Thring of Uppingham School in Rutland drafted another set of 10 rules, for what he called 'The Simplest Game'. These rules allowed no kicking of the ball in the air, and no violence. Tripping was outlawed – so was kicking at your opponent's heels. These rules also contained an early concept of today's goal-kick, as well as what can now be seen as an embryonic rugby offside law. They were widely circulated, provoked interest and some schools adopted them.

In November 1862 a match took place at Cambridge between Cambridge Old Etonians and Cambridge Old Harrovians. These strapping young Victorian gentlemen had each played by one set of rules at school – now they were meeting on a level playing field to a set of rules most of us could recognise today: 11-a-side, with an umpire from each side plus a neutral referee. The goals were 12 feet across and up to 20 feet high, and the match had a set time-limit of 75 minutes. What is more, these rules worked. They provided the basis for the revised Cambridge Rules of 1863 which in turn were the basis of the first laws of the Football Association.

In one of soccer's great masterworks, *The Book of Football*, published in 1905, one writer calculated that 5,905 years previously football had begun with Cain and Abel kicking apples about in the Garden of Eden. By his reckoning, the formation of the Football Association was long overdue.

It did, in fact, come into being at a meeting at the Freemasons Tavern in Great Queen Street, Lincolns Inn Fields, London on Monday October 26, 1863. The meeting was suggested by Ebenezer Cobb Morley, a fine player in his day and the founder of the Barnes Club in 1862. He became the FA's first secretary in 1863 and lived to see the first FA Cup Final at Wembley in 1923, dying the following year at the age of 93.

Representatives of a dozen London and suburban clubs accepted Morley's invitation. They came from Barnes, Blackheath, Blackheath Proprietory School, Charterhouse School, Crystal Palace, Crusaders, Forest of Leytonstone, Kensington School, No Names of Kilburn, Percival House, Surbiton and the War Office. There were many more clubs and schools playing football, of course, than just those represented in that upstairs oak-pannelled room in the heart of Victorian London.

There were no representatives of the game being played in Sheffield and Nottingham, and none, surprisingly, from Cambridge or public schools like Harrow, Eton and Winchester. Eleven of the 12 clubs enrolled themselves as founder members – Charterhouse bided their time – and Arthur Pember of the No Names Club was elected as chairman. The main business of the evening was to 'form an Association with the object of establishing a definite code of rules for the regulation of the game.'

Over the next six weeks the FA met six times and it was in that sixth meeting that football and rugby finally branched apart from the trunk that had given birth to them both. The Blackheath Club played their game by the Rugby rules – and they were adamant that they would not sanction any proposal that outlawed the thorny old problem of hacking or tripping. The football men would not budge, and so Blackheath left the FA. In 1871 they became founder members of the Rugby Union.

At first the FA did not attempt to impose its new 'unified' laws. Rather, it saw itself as exerting an influence on the growth of the game. By 1865, for example, its membership was still small and it had only one member in the provinces. That was the Sheffield Club, founded in 1855, the oldest in the land.

But change was not long in coming. Inter-city and inter-county representative matches were starting up, and in 1870 an event that can now be recognised as being as important as anything that had happened on the playing field up to then took place in the committee rooms of the Football Association.

Charles William Alcock was appointed as the Secretary of the Football Association. It was a post he was to hold for the next 25 years. Alcock had two brilliant ideas. He was the man who invented the FA Cup, and can also rightly be regarded as the father of international soccer, because he proposed the first internationals between England and Scotland, starting with the unofficial games in 1870 and the first official matches two years later.

Alcock, barely 30 years old and still playing football with the Wanderers club, which had evolved from Forest FC of Leytonstone, was an Old Harrovian. During his time at the school from 1855 to 1859 he had played in the 'Cock House' game – a sudden-death inter-house football competition. Alcock took the concept of that game and imagined it on a national scale – a knockout Cup competition between the FA's member clubs. He probably had a very strong hunch that his proposal would be accepted by the FA Committee when he proposed it to them on the summer evening of July 20, 1871.

The meeting had been convened in the offices of *The Sportsman* newspaper, long since demolished but which then stood down the hill from St Paul's Cathedral at the bottom of Ludgate Hill, just off Fleet Street and not far from the first headquarters of the FA at 51 Holburn Viaduct.

He put his proposal to A Stair of the Upton Park Club, the FA's Honorary Treasurer; CW Stephenson of Westminster School; JH Giffard of the Civil Service Club; D Allport of the Crystal Palace Club; MP Betts of Harrow; and Captain Francis Marindin, an officer of the Royal Engineers.

After the usual formalities had been taken care of, Charles William Alcock delivered the words that would guarantee him a place in soccer history. He asked the committee to agree 'that it is desirable that a Challenge Cup should be established in connection with the Association, for which all clubs belonging to the Association should be invited to compete.'

The tweaking of Victorian moustaches was brief and the committee agreed to the idea almost immediately. Three months later, on October 16, 1871, the 18 competition rules were drafted, but there was a disappointing response from the FA's members. By now almost 50 clubs had affiliated themselves to the FA, but only 15 wanted to take part in this latest fad. Many stayed away preferring to play friendlies, to play the game for the game's sake.

The 15 clubs that entered – and were accepted – were Barnes, Wanderers, Harrow Chequers, Civil Service, Crystal Palace, Upton Park, Clapham Rovers and Hampstead Heathens from the London area; from around the Home Counties came Hitchin, Royal Engineers, Reigate Priory, Maidenhead and Marlow; while only two clubs came from north of Hertfordshire – Queen's Park from Glasgow and Donington Grammar School from Spalding in Lincolnshire.

It wasn't much, but it was a start, even though three teams scratched before they had even played a match – Harrow Chequers, Reigate Priory and Donington School. One Harrow Chequer was still to play a major part in this first FA Cup competition but his club, formed by Harrow Old Boys, was to have something of a love-hate relationship with the FA Cup. Three times, in 1871, 1874 and again in 1875, Harrow Chequers entered the competition, and three times they scratched without ever playing a match.

But the main concern of the committee in the autumn of 1871 was not the problem of scratching but the purchase of their new FA Cup trophy. The firm of Martin, Hall and Company manufactured one in silver for a cost of £20. It stood about 18 inches high, had a footballer figurine on its lid and became known in time as 'the little tin idol'.

So the stage was set for the first round of the first FA Cup. The first goal that day was scored by Jarvis Kenrick of Clapham in their match at Upton Park. He scored another that afternoon as Clapham duly went through to the second round by winning 3–0, while Barnes beat the Civil Service 2–0 and Maidenhead beat Marlow by the same score. In south London Crystal Palace and Hitchin drew 0–0, and under the laws of this new, haphazard tournament, both teams were allowed through to the second round.

To illustrate even further just how odd this first competition was in a modern context, among the handful of clubs taking part were Queen's Park of Glasgow. The Scottish FA not yet been formed, so there seemed nothing unusual then about the Glasgow side taking part in the 'English Cup'. The FA, recognising how far Queen's Park had to travel and how much it was going to cost them, exempted them until

THE ENGLISH CUP.

The Football Association Challenge Cup trophy, ribboned and adorned with the figure of a footballer on its lid. This was the trophy which became known as 'the little tin idol' (Popperfoto)

the semi-finals where they were drawn against the Wanderers.

Queen's Park had been formed in 1867 and although playing nothing like the number of matches clubs play today, they turned up for their semi-final at Kennington Oval, home of the Surrey County Cricket Club, on March 4, 1872 with an amazing record. They had never had a goal scored against them since they were founded five years previously.

By the end of that afternoon, their defence still had not been breached. The teams drew 0–0 but as Queen's Park had only £4 in the bank before the journey to London – which was only made possible by passing the hat around – they had to return to Glasgow; unbeaten, but eliminated by default.

The rules of the time stated that all matches after the second round had to take place at Kennington and that didn't help their cause either. The thought was probably never entertained that the Wanderers should go to Glasgow for a replay. Instead, the Wanderers were in the final on a walkover, after a 1–0 win over Clapham and a 0–0 draw with Crystal Palace with both teams advancing.

Another quirk of this competition was that the Royal Engineers also reached the final after playing Crystal Palace – but the FA ruled that the Engineers and Palace would have to replay after their 0–0 draw in the semi-final. This first competition may have been shambolic but not even the FA could handle the concept of three teams playing each other in the Cup Final. In the event, the Royal Engineers won their replay 3–0 – and that was to be the nearest any side called Crystal Palace got to the Cup Final until the modern club reached Wembley 118 years later.

The first FA Cup Final took place at Kennington Oval on March 16, 1872 in front of a small but interested, principally middle-class crowd of 2,000 people who had each paid the then princely sum of one shilling (5p) to be there.

The Royal Engineers were the odds-on favourites. They had not been beaten for two years and as *The Sporting Life* reported, 'by better organisation and concentration' they ought to be able to beat the Wanderers, 'despite the acknowledged superiority of the latter...in individual excellence and skill.'

The Engineers – officers to a man, two captains and nine lieutenants – must have taken the field feeling confident in their red and blue outfits. The Wanderers had all but backed into the final with their narrow win over Clapham and goalless draws against Crystal Palace and Queen's Park. It took only a quarter of an hour for the game to be decided but as has happened so many times since this first final, the Engineers were depleted by injury and could not come back after the underdogs opened the scoring.

Lieutenant Edmund Cresswell earned himself a place in the record books when he became the first player to be injured in a Cup Final, falling awkwardly after 10 minutes and breaking his collar bone. He limped out to the wing and manfully 'stayed at his post', as it was reported at the time, but the Engineers never recovered from that setback – or the next, five minutes later.

Robert Walpole Sealey-Vidal, who had learned his soccer at Westminster School and was known as 'the prince of the dribblers', fed the ball to Morton Peto Betts. His shot beat Capt. William Merriman in the 'military goal' and the Wanderers were 1–0 up. As was then the vogue, the teams changed ends, and soon after, CW Alcock himself had the ball in the net but the goal was disallowed for handball.

For many years the records showed that the Wanderers goal was scored by 'AH Chequer' – a thinly disguised *nom de guerre* used by Betts for reasons that are no longer obvious. Betts was a member of the Harrow Chequers club which scratched against the Wanderers in the First Round, and was clearly well known to everyone in footballing circles at the time. As there was no transfer-system or rules about a player being 'cup-tied' in those days, there was no risk of him falling foul of the authorities – especially as 'the authorities', in the person of the FA's secretary CW Alcock, happened to be a team-mate.

The Cup was not presented to the winning team on the day. Instead the presentation took place three weeks later at the Wanderers Club's annual dinner in the Pall Mall Restaraunt, Charing Cross. Alcock received the Cup at seven o'clock that evening from EC Morley, the president of the FA. The ceremony took place barely a mile away from the offices of *The Sportsman* where Alcock had first proposed the competition nine months before.

The Wanderers name was the first to be inscribed on the little tin idol, and it was also the second. This was the only time when the holders, under one of the original rules of the competition, were exempt until the final – the Challenge round.

While the Wanderers bided their time playing friendlies, Oxford University made it through to the final which was played at the Amateur Athletic Ground

at Lillie Bridge in West Brompton, London, not far from where Earls Court now stands. The choice of venue was also, for this season only, the prerogative of the Cup holders – but the kick-off time was not.

The match was due to start at 11 o'clock, and as *The Sporting Life* reported in the week before the match, 'this arrangement will give those anxious to see the Boat Race ample time to reach Putney, Hammersmith or any other places on the line of the race.' Clearly, the FA Cup Final still had some way to go before it won its place in the heart of the nation.

And imagine how anxious some of the 3,000 crowd at Lillie Bridge must have been feeling that morning as the final kicked off half-an-hour behind schedule due to the late arrival of some of the players. Goals from Charles Wollaston and Arthur Kinnaird, of the long red beard and white trousers, gave the Wanderers a 2–0 victory, and secured for both men the first of the five winner's medals each was to collect over the next few years. Overall it wasn't a great day for the Dark Blues as Cambridge won the Boat Race by three lengths.

Lord Kinnaird, as he later became, played in a record nine finals, making six appearances for the Old Etonians and three for the Wanderers. He was also President of the Football Association for 33 years until his death at the age of 77 shortly before the opening of Wembley in 1923.

The first seven finals were all fought out by just four teams – the Wanderers, the Royal Engineers, Oxford University and the Old Etonians, with players like RWS Vidal and CJ Ottaway seemingly changing sides back and forth from season to season.

The Royal Engineers, based at Chatham, were probably the strongest team in the land, losing only three matches of the 86 they played between 1871 and 1875. Two of the games they did lose were the Cup Finals of 1872 and 1874, but they finally won the Cup in 1875, for the first and only time, with a 2–0 win over the Old Etonians after the competition's first drawn Final.

Absent that day was another colossus of the era, Sir Francis Marindin, known as 'the Major'. While Lord Kinnaird sported a dazzling full red beard, Marindin was also a man of his times, with a full 'Empire': moustache and a wide, expanding pair of sideburns. He was the inspiration behind the Royal Engineers, led them into the FA in 1869 and also played in their losing finals of 1872 and 1874.

Marindin sat on the committee that inaugurated the Cup in 1871 and he also helped found, and later played for, the Old Etonians. So he faced a dilemma in 1875 when the Engineers met the Old Etonians in the final. He chose the only way out and played for neither. The Major also holds another record unlikely to be beaten, of refereeing nine Cup Finals in 1880, 1884–90 and the replayed game of 1886. He was President of the FA from 1874–90 and in his 'spare' time he became the Inspector of Railways for England and also had a hand in developing London's electric lighting system.

By the mid-1870s, the number of entries to the Cup was growing. If it wasn't exactly the Cup fever of a decade later, it was certainly a move in the right direction. Sheffield became the first team from the north, apart from Queen's Park, to enter in 1874, while in 1876 Druids became the first Welsh club to take part.

Between 1876 and 1878 the number of entries grew from 32 to 43 but the Wanderers remained invincible. They became the first team to win three successive Cup Finals, and under the prevailing rules they were allowed to keep the trophy. But they handed it back to the FA with the proviso that no other team winning it three times in succession in the future could keep it either. Since then only Blackburn Rovers have done so and they have a shield in their boardroom to mark their rare achievement.

It may not have been immediately obvious, when the Wanderers were presented with the Cup after beating the Royal Engineers 3–1 at the Oval one March afternoon in 1878, that their domination of the trophy was coming to an end. The club had always drawn its best players from public school old boys, but now the public schools themselves were beginning to take more and more notice of the Cup and forming their own teams.

The Wanderers began their bid for a fourth successive victory with a match against their great rivals the Old Etonians, whom they had last met and beaten in the replayed final of 1876. This time the Etonian old boys handed out the lesson with a 7–2 hiding. The following season, on January 24, 1879, the Old Etonians beat them again in the third round. That was the last FA Cup match the Wanderers ever played. They scratched when drawn to play Rangers FC of London in 1880, and scratched again when they could not raise a team to play against a side from St Bart's Hospital in 1881. It was a sad end for 'the celebrated Wanderers', as Major Marindin used to call them.

The competition of 1878–79 is notable for three events that help illustrate the growth of the Cup. For the first time one of the finalists – Clapham Rovers – came from outside the 'big four'. Second, a team from the provinces – Nottingham Forest – reached the semi-finals for the first time; and third, a team of young working men from the Lancashire mill town of Darwen gave the Old Etonians, the eventual winners, a run for their money in the fourth round.

Given the impact teams from Lancashire were to have on the Cup in the years to come, it is ironic that the first seeds of interest in Lancashire were sown by a team from a town with a population of about 30,000 people which was to have a team in the Football League for only eight seasons and who, half-a-century later, were to lose a Cup match to Arsenal at Highbury by 11 goals to one.

Darwen's exploits in 1879 were important not just because they awakened Lancastrians to the idea of Cup football, but also because they had a couple of Scotsmen in their team – who were no doubt being paid to be there, in strict contravention of the rules of the day. Fergie Suter, a stonemason by trade, and Jimmy Love moved from Glasgow to play football in Lancashire and it is inconceivable that they were not paid for doing so.

It was to be another six years before the FA legalised professionalism, but by then the nature of the Cup and the whole shape of football in England had changed beyond recognition. Suter himself went on to play in four finals for Blackburn Rovers and pick up three winner's medals.

Darwen also helped change the rules and composition of the FA Cup. They had reached Round Four – the last six teams under the still-evolving draw system

– with a walkover against Birch of Manchester and wins over Eagley of Bolton and Remnants, an amateur side from Berkshire. They were then drawn to play the Old Etonians at the Oval. Trailing 1–5 with just 15 minutes to play, they scored four times to force a 5–5 draw. That performance still ranks as one of the Cup's greatest comebacks. Three weeks later, after public fund-raising had brought in nearly £200, the men from Darwen were back in the capital and again refused to be beaten, holding their illustrious rivals to a 2–2 draw.

The decent thing would surely have been for the Old Etonians to agree to play the third match in Lancashire, or at least somewhere closer to Darwen than the manicured lawns of Kennington Oval. But, invoking the rule which stated that all matches after the second round should be played at Kennington, the Old Etonians stood firm. A week later Darwen made a third, exhausting trip to London and were beaten 6–2.

But they had made their point. From the following season, the earlier rounds of the Cup were regionalised, and although all semi-finals and finals were still played at the Oval until 1882, more Cup matches began to be played all over the country.

Old Etonians went on to beat Clapham Rovers 1–0 in the Final on March 29, the match in which the youngest finalist of all time made his first appearance.

James Frederick McLeod Prinsep was his name and he was 17 years 245 days old when he played for Clapham Rovers – 11 days younger than Paul Allen was when he played for West Ham in the Cup Final 101 years later. Described by the writer W Unite Jones as 'one of the prettiest half-backs that ever did duty for the Rose', Prinsep was born in India on July 27, 1861. He played his one and only game for England against Scotland on April 5, 1879 when aged 17 years 252 days, to become England's youngest ever international, exactly a week after playing in the Cup Final. Prinsep had left Clapham by the time they won the Cup the following season but picked up a winner's medal when Old Carthusians beat the Old Etonians 3–0 in 1881, the last of the all-amateur finals.

On March 25, 1882, almost 10 years to the day since the Wanderers won the first FA Cup Final, Old Etonians brought the curtain down on the success of the southern amateurs. They beat Blackburn Rovers 1–0 at the Oval and after the presentations Lord Kinnaird celebrated his fifth winner's medal in his eighth final by standing on his head in front of the dignitaries in the grandstand. There were those watching who felt that the whole world as they knew it was about to be turned upside down.

The North comes to Town 1883–92

Although Kinnaird and his Old Etonian team-mates returned to the Oval the following year with a team that included six England internationals, they were beaten by the first northern side to win the Cup, Blackburn Olympic. The professions of the men who made up the Olympic team that day are worth noting. Three of them were weavers, one was a spinner, one a cotton worker, another an iron worker; there was a picture framer, a dentist's assistant, a plumber, and two who were clearly professionals. These were not men of leisure, they were working-class. The balance had tilted away from the amateurs for ever.

Blackburn Olympic were one of a number of clubs from the town that competed in the Cup around this time, and although they were soon eclipsed by the success of Blackburn Rovers, they nevertheless earn a place in the history of the Cup. Their supporters – and there were thousands of them swelling the attendance at the Oval to a record 7,000 – descended on London like a conquering army, the first time the capital had seriously been struck by an attack of Cup fever. In the week before the final, the team itself had spent time 'in strict training in Blackpool', noted *The Sportsman*.

Olympic had settled into their hotel in Richmond on the Thursday before the Cup Final to make sure they recovered from the long rail journey in good time, general principles of preparing for a Cup Final which are still used by teams today. Clearly they served Blackburn well. Legend has it that when someone in the crowd saw the Cup they shouted out, 'Is that t'Coop, why it looks like a tea kettle.' To which Sam Warburton, the Olympic captain, replied, 'Aye, it might do, but it's very welcome to Lancashire and it'll never go back to London.' Prophetic words – in the next 12 years it never went south of Birmingham, where in 1895 it was stolen from a sports shop and never recovered.

The Cup Finals of the early and mid-1880s were played out against a background of fierce feuding over the rise and eventual legalisation of paying players to play football. For a while it seemed as though the FA would split on the whole argument of professionalism, with one body administering a professional game in the

The Blackburn Rovers team which lost in the 1882 final but heralded the arrival of the Northern professional sides in the FA Cup (Popperfoto)

north and another an amateur game in the south, the situation that the breakaway sport of rugby found itself in a few years later. There was even a very strong move to form a British Football Association, but it never came to anything. Football today would probably be very different if it had.

In November 1883 Accrington had been disqualified from the Cup amid accusations of professionalism and they were disqualified a year later on the same charge. The whole issue was the subject of a heated debate in January 1884 after Preston North End drew 1–1 with the amateurs of Upton Park, one of the original 15 entrants in 1872. Upton Park protested to the FA that some of Preston's players were obviously professional.

That much was true and the Preston chairman Major William Suddell admitted it to the FA. He also told them the practice was common in the north and although Preston were disqualified from that season's competition, his argument convinced some of the more enlightened FA officials – including Charles Alcock – that nothing would stop the rise of the professional game.

The FA took another 18 months to legalise professionalism and ride out a ferocious storm that seriously threatened to sink them. The 14th Cup competition that began in the autumn of 1885, the first after professionalism was allowed, was a very different affair from the almost local get-togethers between southern gentlemen which it had been for much of its early existence.

While Blackburn Olympic had taken the Cup north for the first time in 1883, the first northern side really to embellish the trophy were Blackburn Rovers. They played in six finals in 10 seasons between 1882 and 1891 and won five of them – three in successive years from 1884–86 and the other two also in succession in 1890 and 1891.

Blackburn and the Wanderers are still the only clubs to have won the Cup three times running and Rovers still hold the record for the longest unbeaten run in the competition's history. After losing 1–0 at neighbours Darwen in a second round match on December 2, 1882, they went 24 games before losing at home to the Scottish club Renton on November 27, 1886.

Perhaps Renton felt they were exacting some sort of revenge for footballers north of the border, for two of Blackburn's three Cup Final victories, in 1884 and 1885, were over Queen's Park. By the start of the 1883–84 competition, Queen's Park had entered the English Cup eight times, but they had only ever played one match in the tournament, the 0–0 draw with the Wanderers in the 1872 semi-final. They had scratched from the competition seven times, but when they decided to play they made their mark.

Their opening two matches, against Crewe Alexandra and Manchester Football Club, resulted in wins of 10–0 and 15–0, and they carried on towards the final with wins over Oswestry (7–1), Aston Villa (6–1), Old Westminsters (1–0) and the holders Blackburn Olympic, 4–1 in the semi-final. Before the final they were the 6–4 favourites to win the Cup, but in the event goals from Joe Sowerbutts and James Forrest gave Rovers a 2–1 victory.

Forrest, who shares with CWR Wollaston of the Wanderers and Lord Kinnaird the record of five winner's medals, scored against the Scots again the following year when Blackburn won 2–0 at the Oval. In the entire history of the competition this remains the only time the same two finalists have met in successive years.

It was also Queen's Park's swan-song. Two years later, after Glasgow Rangers almost became the second Scottish side to reach the final, only failing against Aston Villa in the semis, the Scottish FA banned their clubs from taking part in the English Cup. The Irish FA, whose leading teams like Distillery, Crusaders and Linfield had all competed in the past, followed their lead, but Welsh clubs were not withdrawn by the FA of Wales and still compete to this day.

In 1886 Blackburn Rovers completed their hat-trick of victories with a replayed win over West Bromwich Albion in the first final contested by clubs who are still in existence and members of the Football League or Premier League. It was also the first time the final had been decided away from London, with the replay taking place at Derby. A snowstorm on the morning of the replay threatened the game, but by lunchtime the snow had melted. By 5 o'clock West Brom's resistance had melted too, beaten by two goals to nil.

Thousands of fans had made the trip from Birmingham to Derby for the match and according to one eyewitness account, 'the Albion supporters had in their hats a large blue card, upon which was a throstle and the words "Play up Throstles". Before the termination of the match, however, the spirits of these ardent enthusiasts were dampened to such an extent that they were glad to put the cards out of sight, their appearance being a subject more of ridicule than anything else.'

After losing in 1886 to Blackburn and again in 1887 to Aston Villa in the first all-Midlands final, the Albion were back for a third successive final in 1888 – and this time they won it, the first club to do so with an all-English team. The first 15 finals had been won by clubs from just two cities – London and Blackburn – but now teams from the Midlands and Yorkshire were beginning to make an impact.

Aston Villa first entered the Cup in the 1879–80 season, but after beating Stafford Road, a railway works team from Wolverhampton, they scratched rather than face the then-mighty Oxford University. Seven years later things were very different. By general consensus the club's glory years in the later part of the 19th century and early part of the next were founded on a rock laid by three Scots – George Ramsay and Archie Hunter, who were players, and an official, William McGregor, the father of the Football League.

It was Villa who succeeded Blackburn as Cup holders, and in the 11 seasons from 1887 to 1897 they appeared in four finals winning the Cup three times, in 1887, 1895 and 1897 when they became the last team for 64 years to win the League and Cup Double. Their 3–2 win over Everton in 1897 still ranks as one of the best finals of all time. This was Villa's golden era, as they also won the League title five times in the last seven years of the century. In 1957 they would win the FA Cup for what was then a record seventh time.

Aston Villa's Double of 1897 was in fact the second. The first team to achieve that feat was Preston North End, 'The Invincibles' of 1889 whose record in winning the first ever Football League Championship without losing a match and winning the Cup without conceding a goal is unlikely ever to be equalled.

Preston had also reached the final the previous year and in doing so set another record which is unlikely to be beaten. Their 26–0 win over Hyde on October 15, 1887 is the biggest victory ever recorded out of nearly 50,000 matches played in the FA Cup since the competition began.

In fact Preston had seemed certain to win the Cup in 1888. They scored a total of 55 goals in seven Cup matches, had not lost any match all season, and were so confident of victory over West Bromwich Albion in the final that they asked Major Marindin whether they could be pictured with the Cup before the match.

Major Marindin's poignant rejoinder has entered football folklore: 'Had you better not win it first?' he asked. West Brom beat them 2–1.

But the following season, 1888–89, the first of the Football League and the first when the FA Cup had a qualifying competition, not even West Bromwich Albion could stop them. Among West Brom's ranks at this time was one of the finest wingers of the day – William Isaiah 'Billy' Bassett. He was only 5ft 5½in tall, but was so tricky on the right wing he won 16 caps for England and spent 13 years in the West Brom first team. He served the Albion for 50 years as a player, director and chairman and was at Wembley to see them beat Birmingham in the 1931 Cup Final.

Even his undoubted brilliance on the flanks could do nothing to slow Preston's march. After disposing of Bootle (3–0), Grimsby Town (2–0) and Birmingham St Georges (2–0), Preston gained their revenge over the Cup holders with a 1–0 semi-final win at Bramall Lane, Sheffield. Their opponents in the final were Wolverhampton Wanderers, making the first of their eight appearances. While Preston had won the League, Wolves had done well too, finishing third, but they had

lost 4–0 at home to Preston the previous September and 5–2 away in October.

Preston were too hot to handle again in the final, watched by a record crowd of 22,000. Major Marindin not only refereed the game, he presented the Cup to Preston, too – something he had rightly refused to do before the final the previous year.

The Preston team, containing as it did such giants of the day as Jack Gordon, Jimmy Ross and the mesmerising John Goodall, succeeded in retaining the League Championship the following season but this was their last appearance in the Cup Final for 33 years, and they would not win the Cup again until 1938.

The start of the last decade of the 19th century witnessed the first 'Roses' Cup Final. Blackburn, with three survivors from the Cup-winning teams of the mid-eighties, were back stronger than ever and opposing them were Sheffield Wednesday, or The Wednesday as they were known until the 1920s.

Wednesday then played in the Football Alliance, a short-lived League formed a year after the Football League and one which was absorbed into the League as its Second Division in 1892. Wednesday came to the 1890 final looking for what would have been a unique 'double' – Football Alliance champions and FA Cup winners.

But on the afternoon of March 29, 1890, Wednesday were completely outplayed and lost by a then-record Cup Final margin, 6–1. William Townley scored the first Cup Final hat-trick that day, something that has been done only twice in more than a century since.

The Wednesday did set one record that year: they became the first team to reach the final after losing a match on the way. In 1946 Charlton Athletic would reach the final after losing the second leg of their two-legged third round tie against Fulham, but where Wednesday's record differs is that they were actually 'knocked out' of the Cup after losing 3–2 to Notts County in a replayed quarter-final.

The West Bromwich Albion side which won the last final to be played at the Oval, beating Aston Villa 3–0. Billy Bassett is on the far left, next to him is John Reynolds (Popperfoto)

The first quarter-final had ended in a 5–0 win for Wednesday but the match was replayed after a Notts County protest. The replay ended 3–2 to County – then Wednesday protested. So with each side having won once and protested once, a third game was played. The Wednesday concluded this farce with a 2–1 win. But both teams were to have their honour satisfied before the turn of the century. Notts County became the first team from the Second Division to win the Cup when they surprisingly beat First Division Bolton Wanderers in 1894, and Wednesday won the Cup for the first time in 1896.

A year after their record win over Wednesday, Blackburn were back at the Oval to win the Cup for a fifth time, to equal the record set by the Wanderers back in 1878. William Townley, who had scored three goals in the final the previous year, added another in the 3–1 win over Notts County while James Forrest collected his fifth winner's medal.

Blackburn's bid for what would have been a unique second hat-trick of Cup Final victories came to an abrupt end in the second round of the following season's competition. They began their defence of the Cup with a 4–1 win over Derby, with Jack Southworth, an England international and a Cup winner in both 1890 and 1891, scoring all four goals. Southworth's other great love was music and after injury forced an early retirement he became a violinist with the Halle Orchestra. No doubt he was playing a mournful tune on the night of January 31, 1892 after Blackburn were dumped out of the Cup by West Bromwich Albion. By contrast, there was nothing but sweet music for Albion in 1892, the last time the Oval was used as the venue for the Cup Final.

By this time football had established itself as the premier sport in the land. The Oval was bursting at the seams and could no longer cope with the huge crowds coming to watch the match. The first final in 1872 was watched by just 2,000. By 1892 this had increased to more than 32,000. A bigger venue was clearly needed. Even the timing of the Boat Race had become an irrelevance.

Aston Villa started as favourites to win the 1892 Cup Final and repeat their victory of 1887 over the Albion. In the end it was a one-sided contest with Albion, inspired by Billy Bassett, winning 3–0. Their third goal came from John Reynolds who was to achieve an odd double of his own three years later when he played for Aston Villa in their third final against West Bromwich Albion.

Fittingly it was Lord Kinnaird who presented what was now known as 'the paltry pot' to Albion's captain Charles Perry, one of five brothers from the same family who played for WBA in the 1880s and 1890s.

Ten years previously Kinnaird stood on his head at the end of the Cup Final. All that was left for him to do after the 1892 game was to close the Oval door and follow the road to Manchester.

To Manchester and back 1893–1915

If ever you find yourself in Wolverhampton with a little time to spare, you could do worse than go to Dudley Road or Wanderers Avenue, near the Fighting Cocks pub.

Dudley Road is a typical terraced street but above the doors of two of the houses is something not at all typical. It is the Fallowfield plaque which depicts the FA Cup and Wolverhampton Wanderers' victory over Everton in the 1893 final, played at the grounds of the Manchester Athletic Club in Fallowfield. In Wanderers Avenue a number of the houses have a replica of the Cup in stone with the names of the men that won the Cup, a constant reminder to passers-by of Wolves' first FA Cup victory.

It was a victory that captured the imagination of the country, played in front of a record crowd of 45,000 people in brilliant sunshine. Apart from the replayed final of 1886 which was staged in Derby, this was the first final scheduled to be played outside London, which, strange as it seems today, did not have a stadium thought secure and safe enough to accommodate the growing numbers who wanted to see the game.

Neither, it is obvious, was Fallowfield the ideal place to hold the match. A photograph taken on the day shows the crowd standing around the touchlines with thousands hardly able to see a thing, not unlike the scenes at Wembley exactly 30 years later. According to a report in *The Sporting Chronicle*, it was only the good-natured behaviour of the crowd that prevented what would have been football's first disaster.

The newspaper was critical of the small number of police on hand to control the numbers and noted that '. . . as it was, there were several small encounters between individual policemen and the crowd and some of the latter went home with cracked heads . . .' At one point Lord Kinnaird and the referee C.J. Hughes were debating whether to call off the Cup Final and play the game as a friendly.

By all accounts it was not a brilliant match, Wolves winning it by the only goal, scored after an hour by their skipper Harry Allen. His high, dipping, long-range shot apparently blinding Dick Williams in the Everton goal as the ball dropped out of the brilliant sunshine. Everton had started as strong favourites, especially as the week before the final they had fielded their reserves and beaten Wolves 4–2 in a Division One match.

The following year Everton's ground – then at Anfield not Goodison Park – was the venue for the final. Wolves had succumbed to Aston Villa 4–2 in the first round of their defence of the trophy, while Everton also went out in the first round to Stoke. These were the days when the north reigned supreme. The only southern clubs to make it through the qualifying rounds to the competition proper were Luton Town, Woolwich Arsenal and Reading but the northern clubs soon confirmed their supremacy. Luton went out 2–1 to Middlesbrough Ironopolis, Arsenal were beaten 2–1 by The Wednesday, while Preston North End created another record when they beat Reading 18–0, the highest victory ever by a Football League club over a non-League club. The gap between the northern professionals and the amateurs in the south was as wide as ever.

The match at Deepdale was played in deep mud, but Preston had coated their boots with a form of treacly black lead and hammered in long bars or studs to their boots to secure some kind of foothold in the awful conditions. Reading had not prepared so methodically and were literally swept off their feet. Seven goals went in in the first half, 11 in the second. It was Reading's worst-ever defeat.

But Reading in 1894 also added a lighter footnote to the history of the Cup because earlier that season they became the only club ever to win a Cup match with the winning goal scored by a prisoner on the run from his jailers.

The player in question was Jimmy Stewart who, when not playing for Reading, served as a private in the King's Own Regiment at Aldershot. He was in detention in the guardroom for a breach of discipline, but Reading desperately needed him to play in their third round qualifying match against Southampton St Mary's.

Reading's secretary at the time, Horace Walker, decided to 'persuade' the Army authorities to release Stewart for the match, and turned up at the barracks with a couple of bottles of Scotch. After getting the officer watching Stewart thoroughly inebriated, Walker secured his permission for Stewart to return to Reading for the afternoon. All went well; Stewart played, scored the winner and returned to barracks under cover of darkness that night.

But the story leaked out, Southampton were informed and they immediately protested to the FA to have the match replayed. But as there was nothing in the FA rules specifically mentioning the fact that escaped prisoners were not allowed to play for affiliated teams, the protest was rejected! In the light of what happened at Preston though, perhaps Reading got their just desserts after all.

After thumping Reading, Preston lost to Liverpool in the next round and by the time the field had thinned out to the last four there were two previous winners left, Blackburn Rovers and Sheffield Wednesday, and

A teeming cup Final crowd at the Crystal Palace around the turn of the century shows the competition beginning to capture the imagination of the public (Popperfoto)

two previous finalists, Bolton Wanderers and Notts County.

Notts County were from the Second Division and for the first time since the League was formed a team from outside the First Division won the Cup. County, formed in 1862, pre-date the FA itself by a year, but in all that long history, winning the FA Cup in 1894 remains their only major honour. James Logan became the second man to score a hat-trick in the final as Bolton were beaten 4-1.

After two years in Lancashire, the Cup Final returned to London, where, with only six exceptions (the 1915 final and the replays of 1901, 1910, 1911, 1912 and 1970) it has been decided ever since. Its new home was at Crystal Palace, the equivalent then of a late 19th-century theme park. Victorians went there for a ride on the famous 'Switchback' roller-coaster railway. There were also other recreation facilities; they took picnics and they rode bikes. For many years at Crystal Palace the Cup Final was played after the crowd had eaten their lunch or had a few beers. The atmosphere was more like Twickenham today than Wembley. The stadium was situated not far from where the modern National Sports Centre is, and should not be confused with Crystal Palace's ground at Selhurst Park.

All through the history of the Cup there are strange twists and ironies, and it seems entirely fitting that the same two teams which brought the Oval era to a close in 1892 should have opened the Crystal Palace era in 1895. The final brought together Birmingham's two greatest clubs for the third time – West Bromwich Albion and Aston Villa. To this day they are the only two sides to have met each other in three Cup Finals.

They went into the game with both sides having beaten the other once in the final, Villa winning in 1887 and West Brom in 1892, and the 1895 final can still be described as one of the best ever played. Villa won it 1-0 with a goal after about 40 seconds from inside-right Bob Chatt while thousands of the 42,560 crowd were still taking their places. Despite a tremendous Albion onslaught for the remaining 89 minutes, Villa's defence stood firm.

Villa exhibited the Cup in the shop window of William Shillcock, a boot and shoe manufacturer of Newtown Row, Birmingham, and on the night of September 11, 1895 it was stolen and never recovered. Over half-a-century later, in February 1958, the *Sunday Pictorial* led with a story from a man called Harry Burge, who had spent 46 of his 83 years in and out of jail. He confessed to stealing the Cup with two accomplices and melting it down that night to make counter-feit half-crowns. The theft was national news. Although it had been heavily insured and an exact replica was made in time for the 1896 final, Aston Villa were fined £25.

The new Cup also found a new home – Yorkshire. The Wednesday, now in the Football League, took it back to Sheffield for the first time with a 2-1 win over Wolves, and bedlam greeted its arrival in the city. The Cup was paraded through the streets after the party got off the train from London, but the *Sheffield Daily Telegraph* was very upset about the chaotic arrangements made for the Cup's homecoming.

'There was no method . . . no knowledge of what was to be done . . . It is easy to see how all this could have been avoided. Clubs such as the gay and gallant Rovers from Blackburn, with all their Cup-holding experience, would never have made such an error, and when Wednesday have won the trophy a few more times perhaps we shall have a settled programme to work to, and enthusiastic supporters of the club have a better knowledge of where to go to see their favourites.'

There was plenty of opportunity to get the logistics worked out over the next few years, with Sheffield United winning the Cup in 1899, 1902 and 1915, and Wednesday following their initial success with another victory in 1907. Between them the two sides also won the League three times in the six seasons between 1898 and 1904.

But while the Sheffield sides had undoubted success at the turn of the century, the real giants of this era were still Aston Villa, and the peak of their achievements came on April 10, 1897 when they beat Everton 3-2 to become the second club in history to win the Double.

Had it not been for a dip in their form in the 1897-98 campaign, Villa might well have won the League Championship for five successive seasons. They took the title in 1896 and 1897, and then again in 1899 and 1900, and only finished outside the top three once in seven years between 1894 and the turn of the century.

Their 1897 Double-winning side contained five men from the Cup-winning team of 1895: England internationals Howard Spencer (full-back), John Reynolds (half-back), Charlie Athersmith (winger – who, legend has it, once played a whole match taking cover from the rain under an umbrella), John Devey (centre-forward) and the Scottish international defender James Cowan.

But the Everton side was a strong one too, having finished runners-up in the League to Sunderland in 1895 and third behind Villa and Derby County in 1896. John Bell, Edgar Chadwick and Johnny Holt knew all about the Crystal Palace atmosphere having played there the week previously in the England–Scotland match. And while Villa had won the Double and lost only four out of their 30 League games, one of those had been to Everton.

The record crowd of 65,891 knew they might be in for something special and they were not disappointed. But what the crowd could not have known was that the Villa and Everton players had already seen each other for breakfast that morning. Both teams had booked, purely by chance, into the same hotel!

All the goals in Villa's 3–2 win came in a 25-minute spell in the first half. Villa took the lead after 18 minutes when Athersmith and Devey combined to set up John Campbell. The Scot's shot swerved in the wind, deceiving goalkeeper Bob Menham as it flashed inside his post. Everton replied with a delightful goal within minutes, when Scottish international Bell drew Jimmy Whitehouse from his goal and then slipped the ball into the net as the goalkeeper charged him down.

On the half-hour, with the pace increasing on the field and the tension mounting in the crowd, Everton were ahead with a free-kick from Richard Boyle leaving Whitehouse beaten. The Everton fans were cheering in delight, but almost as soon as the caps and hats thrown in the air had come back down to earth, Villa were level and then almost immediately back in front. Fred Wheldon, another of Villa's internationals, made it 2–2 and soon after that there was another goal when Jimmy Crabtree headed what proved to be the winner two minutes before half-time.

The second half was just as passionate and only a series of outstanding saves from Whitehouse stopped Everton from scoring. Never before had a team scored twice in the Cup Final and lost, and apart from Sheffield United, who lost the 1901 final after a replay, Everton were to be the last team for 38 years to score as many as two goals in the Final and return home empty-handed.

The next edition of *Association Football* magazine was fulsome in its praises. 'It was the finest final that has ever been fought,' it declared. Naturally Villa were greeted by thousands of ecstatic fans when they brought the Cup back to Birmingham the following day, but when Everton returned to Lime Street they were given a cordial, polite round of applause by a handful of well-wishers. Everton still had another decade to wait before their turn for Cup glory, while babies being born at the time would be grandparents by the time Liverpool first came home with the Cup.

There is a curious symmetry to six Cup Finals at the turn of the century, largely involving four clubs – Bury, Derby County, Sheffield United and Southampton; none of whom, it must be said, have made a lasting impact on the Cup since then.

This odd sequence really begins in 1898 when Derby County lost to Nottingham Forest in an East Midlands derby final, and then returned the following year to lose again to Sheffield United in front of a then world record crowd of 73,883. There was said to be a curse on Derby, given to them by gypsies whom the club had ordered off land that was to become the Baseball Ground. They lost all three finals they reached in those six years and were not to win the Cup until 1946.

In 1900 Bury enter the picture with a 4–0 win over Southampton, the first southern club to appear in the final since the Old Etonians in 1883. Sheffield United returned in 1901 to lose to Tottenham Hotspur and

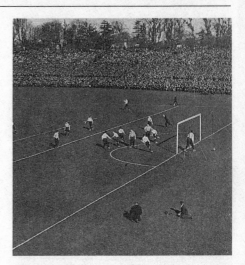

A goal for Spurs against Sheffield United in the 1901 final, which finished 2–2 in front of 110,820 at Crystal Palace (Popperfoto)

then came back again in 1902 to beat Southampton. In 1903, to round this whole period off, Bury were back in the final for a second and last time, to see off Derby County 6–0, the highest ever Cup Final victory.

In fact Bury's Cup Final aggregate of 10–0 is something of a record in itself, although when they won the Cup in 1900 the Bury paper did not consider the event worthy of its front page! Bury had finished 12th in the First Division that season and the paper complained, on an inside page, that 'Bury's Cup win was only some consolation for their poor League performance this season.'

The 1901 Cup Final is one of the most famous in history. The principal reason for this is that for the first and only time since the formation of the Football League in 1888, a team from outside the League won the Cup. Tottenham Hotspur, like Southampton, had benefited enormously from the formation of the Southern League in 1894 which enabled them to attract a higher standard of player from around the country, rather than rely merely on local talent. The Tottenham Cup-winning team of 1901 included five Scots, two Welshmen, one Irishman and three English players – and none of them came from south of the Trent. They were the first southern club to win the Cup for 19 years but they were hardly a southern team.

Tottenham had knocked out three First Division teams including Cup-holders Bury on the way to the Final, but it was Sheffield United who started the day as favourites. Although they had finished only five places off the bottom of the First Division, United, fielding nine internationals, were still capable of excellent football on their day. They had won the Championship in 1898, the Cup in 1899 and been runners-up in the League in 1900. And they had two of the game's all-time great characters in their side, the 22-stone goalkeeper Billy 'Fatty' Foulke in goal and Ernest 'Nudger' Needham at wing-half.

The interest in the match was so great it attracted a world record crowd of 110,820 people to the Crystal Palace and is the first Cup Final of which there is surviving newsreel footage. And nearly one hundred years after it was played, the fourth goal that day remains one of the most controversial ever scored in a Cup Final.

The first half ended 1–1 and five minutes into the second half, Spurs centre-forward Sandy Brown, who in scoring their first goal had become the first man ever to score in every round of the competition in the same season, added a second to make it 2–1. Within a minute United were level after a mysterious decision by the referee, Mr A Kingscott of Derby.

There are almost as many accounts of what happened as there were spectators at the match, but according to the most reliable, Bert Lipsham shot and George Clawley, the Spurs keeper, fumbled his catch. The ball dropped behind Clawley who scrambled the ball away just as United's Walter Bennett came rushing in to challenge him. The linesman immediately signalled for a corner, but the referee overruled him and gave a goal-kick. The referee then, inexplicably, changed his mind, and before the kick was taken, awarded a goal to Sheffield United which has entered the record books as scored by Bennett.

Both teams seem to have been affected by the decision, and the match ended in a tame 2–2 draw. The general feeling was that the referee was at fault and that he should have consulted his linesman, which he never did. But he was back in charge the following week when the match was replayed at Burnden Park, Bolton, a strange choice and one that was never properly explained. Only 20,470 saw the replay, the lowest attendance for a Cup Final this century. Spurs won that game 3–1 to begin their sequence of winning something when the year ends in a '1', and Sandy Brown's goal in the replay took his tally that year to 15, still the all-time record for one season.

At Tottenham's post-match banquet, the wife of the club's vice-chairman tied blue-and-white ribbons onto the Cup, often cited as the start of that particular Cup Final tradition. (But was it? Notts County's 1894 Cup-winning side, as fine looking a collection of late-Victorian sportsmen as you could wish to see, clearly have black-and-white ribbons tied to the Cup handles in their winning team group shot...)

As we have seen, Tottenham's victory was the first by a southern club for 19 years; and it was the last by a southern club until they themselves won it again 20 years later. They were the only London club to win the Cup Final at both Crystal Palace and Stamford Bridge, the two London venues used before Wembley was built in 1923.

The domination of the competition by Northern and Midland teams was so great at this time that between Tottenham's two victories, only three teams from the south – Southampton (1902), Bristol City (1909) and Chelsea (1915) – even reached the final.

Southern League Southampton, who knocked out Cup-holding Spurs in 1902, were the last non-League team to reach the Final. Even though they beat the reigning champions Liverpool 4–1 in the second round and had in full-back CB Fry one of the most outstanding footballers and all-round sportsmen (England international at both football and cricket, world-record holder in the long jump) of all time, they were beaten 2–1 by Sheffield United after a drawn game at the Crystal Palace.

Bristol City's one and only Cup Final appearance ended in more disappointment for the south. They had drawn in every round but one on their way to the final, which was their tenth Cup match of the season. Manchester United, also playing in their first Cup Final, won it 1–0 with a Sandy Turnbull goal.

Chelsea's appearance in the 'Khaki Cup Final' – the only one played during a World War – on April 24, 1915 also ended in defeat as they were beaten 3–0 by Sheffield United at Old Trafford. At the end of the game, Lord Derby, who presented the Cup, told the players, 'You have played with one another, and against one another for the Cup; now go and play with one another for England.'

James Lawrence in the Newcastle goal is beaten as Harry Hampton puts Aston Villa 1–0 up after just two minutes in the 1905 final (Popperfoto)

In this great period of Northern and Midland domination two great teams stand out – one for what they achieved, the other for what they did not.

The achievers were Aston Villa who continued in the new century where they left off in the old. After two more Cup triumphs in 1905 and 1913, they won the Cup for a sixth time in 1920, beating the record previously held by the Wanderers and Blackburn Rovers.

Their 2–0 victory over Newcastle United on April 15, 1905 was watched by another huge Cup Final crowd of 101,117. Newcastle started the match as favourites. They were League Champions and 10 days before the final had beaten Villa for the second time that season, 2–0 at home. They were also bidding, in their debut Cup Final, to become the first team since Villa eight years previously to win the Double.

But Villa's Cup-fighting tradition was legendary. After just two minutes they were a goal up through Harry Hampton, who added a second 14 minutes from time. For Newcastle, the hoodoo of playing at the Crystal Palace ground had begun.

They returned in 1906 and lost 1–0 to Everton. In 1907 they won the Championship again but lost 1–0 at home in the first round of the Cup to, of all teams, Crystal Palace, then in the Southern League. In 1908 Newcastle were back at Crystal Palace for their third Cup Final in four seasons – and lost 3–1 to Wolves, who had finished the season half-way down the Second Division.

There seemed to be no end to the curse. In 1910 they reached the final once more. Again they played a moderate Second Division side, Barnsley, and again they failed to win. But at least this time – just – they did not lose either.

Barnsley had reached the Final by avoiding First Division opposition until they beat Everton, after a replay, in the semi-final. Now with seven minutes to go in the final, the 77,000 crowd must have thought they were about to see yet another huge upset.

Barnsley had gone ahead in the 38th minute with a goal from Harry Tufnell. But with time running out on a poor game, Newcastle's Jack Rutherford, with a collection of loser's medals from 1905, 1906 and 1908, headed the equaliser. There was no extra-time then; Barnsley and Newcastle shook hands on a 1–1 draw and the final was replayed the following week at Goodison Park.

And there Newcastle finally became Cup winners for the first time with two goals from their star centre-forward Albert Shepherd; the second from the penalty spot was the first goal from a penalty in a Cup Final. According to the *Daily Mirror* though, Newcastle were desperate men, kicking anything that moved. 'It really seemed as if some of the players had deliberately gone onto the field to win at all costs,' intoned the *Mirror*, adding, 'There were cases of deliberate kicking today . . .'

After what they had been through for the past few years, one can understand their desperation.

Newcastle's was the last name to be inscribed on the trophy. Its design had been pirated and a similar Cup was being used for a tournament in Manchester, so the FA commissioned a new Cup design – the one in use today – and presented the old trophy to Lord Kinnaird to mark his 21 years as President of the FA.

So in 1911 a new Cup, made by the Bradford silversmiths Fattorini and Sons, was used for the first time. By one of those inexplicable coincidences that pepper its history, the Cup was won that year by Bradford City, the only time that either of Bradford's sides came anywhere near the Cup Final. It almost goes without saying that it was Newcastle whom they beat in the final.

If there was an omen that Bradford were going to win, it came two weeks before the final when they beat Newcastle 1–0 in the First Division. The final at the Crystal Palace was a dour affair and ended in a 0–0 draw. Newcastle, back on their old 'bogey' ground, were without Shepherd who had a broken arm and Peter McWilliam, one of the best inside-forwards of the time. Their attacks simply floundered on City's solid defence.

Four days later they could find no way through in the replay at Old Trafford either, as Jimmy Speirs scored after only 15 minutes to give Bradford City, who had been formed only eight years previously, victory. Amazingly, the day after winning the Cup, City, with four changes, beat Middlesbrough 1–0 in a First Division match.

Until 1911 only two Cup Finals, those of 1876 and 1886, had ended goalless. Now, in 1912, it was about to happen for the second successive year. No-one should have been too surprised. Barnsley, an average Second Division team but one that clearly relished a long, slow fight to the death, were back to keep the Cup in Yorkshire for a second successive season after a record six goalless draws in the earlier rounds. Three of those had been against the Cup-holders Bradford City.

The opposition was West Bromwich Albion, back in the final for the first time since losing their last duel with Aston Villa 17 years previously. The first game at the Palace ended 0–0 and after 90 minutes of the replay at Bramall Lane it was still 0–0. An unprecedented second replay looked certain, but with only two minutes of extra-time to go, the Barnsley winger Harry Tufnell evaded the Albion defenders caught out at the halfway line, and chased half the length of the field to score the winner. Like Bradford before them, Barnsley have not been back to the final since.

While Newcastle had reached five finals in seven seasons, their North-East rivals Sunderland had never been further than the last four. Sunderland's 'Team of all the Talents' had won the League Championship three times in the 1890s, but since they first entered the FA Cup in 1884, their best performances had been reaching the semi-finals in 1891 and 1895.

Despite another Championship in 1902, Sunderland's Cup record continued to be uninspiring until 1913 when, like Newcastle in 1905, they came close to winning the Double only to be denied by Aston Villa in the Cup Final. In fact the 1913 final was the only one until Liverpool played Everton in 1986 that saw the top two teams in the First Division clash in the Cup Final.

Villa's reappearance and Sunderland's first final swelled the crowd at Crystal Palace to another world record, 120,081. Fans climbed up trees, balanced precariously on poles and climbed onto roofs to see a match that fully lived up to expectation. Aston Villa's Charlie Wallace became the first person – and the last until John Aldridge in 1988 – to miss a penalty in the

Cup Final, but Villa won 1-0 with a header from Tommy Barber; exactly as Clem Stephenson, the Villa inside-right, had dreamed the night before the match.

Four days after the final the teams met again at Villa Park in the League. Sunderland's dream of the Double had died, but their Championship hopes were very much alive. Charlie Buchan, a legend on Wearside, rallied his men who drew 1–1 with the new Cup holders and stayed unbeaten to the end of the season to win the title from Villa by four points.

Aston Villa's reign as Cup-holders lasted until a replayed fourth round match the following March. Their conquerors were Burnley, who went on to record the first Cup Final victory witnessed by a reigning monarch.

The previous year King George V had been linked with another great sporting event but in altogether different circumstances when the suffragette Emily Davison threw herself under his horse in the Derby and died as a result of her injuries. But there were very few women at the 1914 Cup Final, just about 72,000 hats and caps sitting on top of 72,000 men's heads. The King, in a bowler, watched Burnley beat Liverpool 1–0 in what was the first final for both clubs and the first all-Lancashire final since 1904.

A year later the Cup Final was to be played in very different circumstances on a wet and cold day in Manchester when Sheffield United beat Chelsea, and in a way Manchester was an apt venue to bring this, the 'Crystal Palace era' of the Cup's history, to a close, because it was during this period that both Manchester City and Manchester United won the Cup for the first time.

Oddly, their wins were both inspired by the same man: Billy Meredith, the legendary Welsh wizard of the right-wing. Meredith, who always chewed a toothpick when he played, is often compared to Stanley Matthews as one of the greatest outside-rights of all time, but he was a better finisher than Matthews and scored almost 200 League and Cup goals in over 700 matches in his 30-year career.

One of those goals won the FA Cup for Manchester City when they beat Bolton 1–0 in 1904. That was his first Cup winner's medal, and his second came five years later when he played in the Manchester United team which beat Bristol City 1–0. He played in his last Cup match, a semi-final during his second spell with Manchester City, in 1924 when he was 49 years and eight months old and is the oldest player ever to appear in the competition proper. His international career lasted 25 years and he won 48 Welsh caps.

Meredith may have been a legend on the field, but he was a constant thorn in the side of authority off it. In 1905 he was the protagonist in first a bribes and then an illegal-payment scandal that led to him (with several others) being suspended by the FA and Manchester City almost destroyed as a club.

Eighteen months after helping City win the Cup, Meredith went to United. In 1909 United won the Cup with a goal from Sandy Turnbull, who had also been in City's Cup-winning side five years previously. By now Meredith and the United skipper Charlie Roberts were active members in the fight to get the Players' Union recognised by the FA and Football League. The argument raged on for 18 months and during the summer of 1909, just weeks after winning the Cup, those same players were briefly suspended by the FA, although they were reinstated by the time the 1909-10 season began.

But for Sandy Turnbull and for millions of other young men like him who had grown up at exactly the same time as football had also reached its manhood, another far bigger battle was soon raging. Turnbull, twice a Cup-winning hero, was one of those who died in the War, killed in action in France on May 3, 1917.

The Chelsea interlude 1920–22

The last Cup Final before the competition came to a halt for the First World War was played on April 24, 1915. The first one after the end of the War was on April 24, 1920 and Aston Villa's presence seemed to suggest that nothing much had changed in the intervening years.

If you had casually said at the time that Villa would win the League and the FA Cup just once more in the next 70 years your sanity would probably have been called into question. But since 1920 Aston Villa have only been back to the final twice, beaten by Newcastle in 1924 and victors over Manchester United in 1957.

The team that ran out to play Huddersfield Town at the FA Cup's temporary home of Stamford Bridge that April afternoon included four men who had played in Villa's last Cup Final in 1913: goalkeeper Sam Hardy, first capped by England in 1907; full-back Tommy Weston; and wingers Charlie Wallace, who missed the penalty in 1913, and Clem Stephenson.

Also in their line-up was a 23-year-old born a few months after Villa won the Double, who was destined for unique 'double' success of his own later in life. He was Billy Walker, who was still playing for England as late as 1933 and is the only man to have managed two different FA Cup winning teams, Sheffield Wednesday in 1935 and Nottingham Forest in 1959.

That day, as a future international, he picked up his first major honour as Villa beat Huddersfield 1–0 after extra-time. The only goal came after 100 minutes when Billy Kirton scored with a header from a corner – only he didn't realise that he was the scorer until the referee told him after the match.

Or was he? More than 70 years after that game, one of Huddersfield's players was still alive and even though he was in his nineties, he remembered the match perfectly. Jack Swann wore the No.10 shirt for Huddersfield in that final, and talking over a pint of Guinness in an Ex-Servicemen's Club in north London in 1990, he described the goal.

'We scored the only goal of that game and lost,' Swann said. 'The ball came over from the right and about four of us went up to head it . . . The ball went the wrong way right into the back of our net. The Villa players started celebrating, but I've always thought it was an own goal.'

This was the first final played at Chelsea's home of Stamford Bridge and as the competition progressed it looked more and more likely that the FA were going to be faced with a very awkward problem come the day of the final.

Crystal Palace was still requisitioned for use by the War Office, and the FA planned to move the Final back there as soon as possible. In the meantime though, a temporary home had to be found and Stamford Bridge, just a stone's throw from the site of the old Lillie Bridge ground used for the 1873 final, was chosen.

The competition's rules state that the final has to be played on a neutral ground but Chelsea, beaten finalists in 1915 and now riding high in the League, had made it through to the semi-finals. Plans were too far advanced to change the venue for the final, which meant that Chelsea, if they beat Villa in the semi-final at Bramall Lane, would be very much at home in the Cup Final. Villa spared the FA a huge dilemma, beating Chelsea 3–1.

But what about Huddersfield's 'unfair' advantage? Their semi-final win against Bristol City was at Stamford Bridge, the last time until Tottenham in 1991 that one team played the semi-final and final at the same venue. For Huddersfield, reaching their first final was an inspiring achievement by a club that – shades of Tottenham again – had faced liquidation earlier in the season. Huddersfield's day would come, but Aston Villa took the Cup back to Birmingham that year.

The second of the three Stamford Bridge finals was played on a quagmire of a pitch just after a cloudburst. It had been 20 years since a London club won the Cup and that same club was back in the final.

Since their triumph as a non-League side in 1901, Spurs had risen from the Southern League to the First Division and were strong favourites to beat Second Division Wolves. For once, the favourites lived up to their billing. The winning goal came after 55 minutes when Jimmy Dimmock maintained his balance on the slippery surface, sending his fast, low angled shot into the corner of the net, always out of reach of goalkeeper Noel George.

It has often been said that the three finals at Stamford Bridge are the 'forgotten finals', and although at the time they were as keenly fought as any other, looking back they do appear rather insignificant; mainly because of the opening of Wembley in 1923, but also because they all ended 1-0 and the last one of the three has gone down as the worst final of all time.

It ended in a win for Huddersfield who beat Preston thanks to a penalty scored by Billy Smith after 67 minutes. The only reason the match is ever mentioned at all today is because it served as a prequel for the 1938 final between Huddersfield and Preston which also ended 1–0, although Preston won that game with George Mutch's famous penalty in the last minute of extra-time.

The only other curiosity value about 1922 was that Preston's goalkeeper Jim Mitchell was an amateur who wore glasses and whose antics as Smith ran up to take the penalty – 'acting like a circus clown', according to the match reports, by waving his arms and jumping up and down – led to the law being changed whereby a goalkeeper must not move until the kick is taken.

The FA Cup competition itself was something of a dog's dinner too by the early 1920s. While the basic concept of the Cup had never changed from CW Alcock's original sudden-death idea, the competition had grown enormously. The first competition in 1871–72 had consisted of 15 teams, only twelve of whom actually played. Ten years later that figure had grown to 73, and by 1891–92 to 163. When Tottenham won the Cup for the second time in 1921, 674 clubs entered the tournament, an all-time record. Nowadays

the number of clubs accepted by the FA is around the 550-mark. So naturally the organisation of the tournament has undergone periodic changes.

Between 1896 and 1925 there were all kinds of anomalies with League clubs playing in the qualifying round, so the FA reorganised the competition for the start of the 1925–26 season, exempting all League clubs until the Competition Proper started with the First Round in November. The rules have been amended slightly now and again since then, but in the last 70 years only one current League club has played a significant part in the Qualifying Competition.

In 1932–33 Brighton & Hove Albion, then in the Third Division South, forgot to claim their exemption until the First Round. So they went into the hat for the First Qualifying round along with the likes of Courage Sports & Social FC, Leavesden Mental Hospital FC and Shoreham FC whom they despatched 12-0. They then beat Worthing, Hastings and Barnet and eventually made it all the way to the Fifth Round proper where they lost 1–0 to Second Division West Ham after a replay. They played 11 Cup matches that season, scored 43 goals and didn't even reach the quarter-finals. When they did reach the Cup Final for the first time 50 years later, they played only six games and scored just 11 goals!

When Brighton's turn did eventually come, it came of course at Wembley, which by that time had been the home of the Cup Final for 60 years.

Stamford Bridge's temporary role as the home of the Cup Final was now over, but the FA never did take the match back to Crystal Palace. Instead a much grander stage was being prepared for what was now the greatest day in the sporting life of the nation.

Wembley Stadium.

Wembley, Wembley   1923–39

If a man called Edward Watkin had succeeded in a half-baked idea he dreamt up in 1901, it is unlikely that Wembley Stadium would ever have been built.

No Twin Towers, no Abide With Me, no walk up Wembley Way, no Que Sera Sera. None of that would have existed.

Of course something else would have taken its place, but the only reason Wembley Stadium got built in the first place was because Edward Watkin failed with a plan to turn himself into England's answer to Gustav Eiffel. Mr Watkin attempted to build a 1,150-foot (350-metre) high tower to rival the Eiffel Tower in Paris. It reached a height of 200ft (61m) before the concrete foundations collapsed and the project was abandoned. Still, Watkin's Folly, as it became known, towered above the largely open countryside that was then Wembley for another 20 years. It stood exactly on the site occupied by the stadium today.

In the early twenties the Government decided to hold a British Empire Exhibition in 1924 and chose Wembley as the site with a great stadium as the centrepiece. Watkin's Folly was pulled down and work started on the stadium. It took just 300 working days to build at a cost of £750,000.

The Duke of York, who later became King George VI, cut the first turf to the right of what is now the royal entrance tunnel in January 1922 and just over a year later, the final workmen moved out. An infantry battalion and hundreds of local volunteers then marched up and down the terraces to test their strength and safety for a quarter-of-an-hour.

The Stadium opened on April 28, 1923, a year before the Exhibition itself. Its official title was The Empire Stadium and the first event staged there was the FA Cup Final between Bolton Wanderers and Second Division West Ham United. At the time it was built, Wembley was the biggest and most dramatic sports stadium in the world. And its opening day was to be unlike any other in its history.

The authorities estimated that Wembley would hold 127,000 people; but incredibly, they were also convinced that as only 53,000 had watched the previous year's Cup Final at the spartan and unwelcoming Stamford Bridge, nothing like that six-figure number would come to the match. Therefore they decided that whoever did show up would be allowed to pay at the turnstiles and gain admission.

It was a grave and almost tragic error of judgment. Cup Final day dawned bright and sunny. About a quarter of a million people woke up, saw the weather and soon got the same idea into their heads: 'Let's go to that new stadium at Wembley and see the Cup Final.'

The match was due to kick-off at 3pm, and by 1.45pm the doors were shut with 126,047 people inside. But still they came . . . swarming over railings, scaling walls and climbing over the little turnstile barriers. At 2 o'clock police stations for miles around were being mobilised, but by the time those reinforcements arrived, they could hardly do anything to stop the chaos or flow of people into the stadium.

Never before had so many people turned up to see a match. There were anywhere between 200,000–250,000 inside Wembley – and probably almost as many outside. For while the stadium was being overrun, tens of thousands more people were still arriving. The roads for miles around were jammed solid and the Bolton team were forced to abandon their coach a mile away and push and shove their way into the stadium.

King George V arrived on time at 2.45, and when he got to the Royal Box and looked out he must have thought his whole Empire had turned up for the match. There were thousands of people on the pitch. They didn't think it was all over . . . for them it hadn't even started yet.

More than three-quarters of the playing area was covered by the crowd and it looked unlikely that the match could ever be played. But out of the mayhem there emerged a saviour, as much a part of England's equine sporting mythology as Arkle, Red Rum or Desert Orchid – a 13-year-old white horse called Billy.

Billy was not the only horse at Wembley, but he was the only white one, and that was the crucial factor. Ridden by PC George Scorey, he gradually began moving the crowd back around the touchlines. It was a slow process, but the crowd responded and inch by inch the playing area was cleared. Afterwards PC Scorey explained in an interview to the BBC how he had managed it.

'As my horse picked his way onto the field, I saw nothing but a sea of heads. I thought, "We can't do it. It's impossible." But I happened to see an opening near one of the goals and the horse was very good – easing

them back with his nose and tail until we got a goal-line cleared. I told them in front to join hands and heave, and they went back step by step until we reached the line. Then they sat down and we went on like that . . . it was mainly due to the horse . Perhaps because he was white he commanded more attention. But more than that, he seemed to understand what was required of him. The other helpful thing was the good nature of the crowd.'

Eventually the playing area was cleared, but thousands in the crowd, 20 deep in places, could hardly see a thing. It was a miracle that no-one was killed, and that there were only a few injuries.

An inquiry was held into the near-disaster and the FA returned money to ticket holders who claimed never to have reached their seats. Officials also publicly said that if it had not been for PC Scorey and the white horse, the final would never have been played. But Scorey, who lived to be 82, was not a football fan. Thirty years after he saved the Cup Final, he admitted, 'I never went to another game in my life.'

The match eventually started 40 minutes late and after only two minutes Bolton were ahead. David Jack, destined to become the first £10,000 player when he moved to Arsenal, hammered in a shot so hard that it not only beat Ted Hufton in the West Ham goal but knocked down a spectator standing right behind him. He in turn brought down a section of the crowd around him like ninepins. While that goal was being scored, West Ham's right-half Jack Tresadern was trapped in the crowd, unable to get back onto the pitch after a throw-in that led to the goal.

The players stayed on the field at half-time, and eight minutes after the restart Bolton went 2–0 up when Ted Vizard crossed for John Smith to volley past Hufton, but the goal was controversial for two reasons.

First, it appeared that the ball had hit the woodwork because it immediately bounced back into play, but referee David Asson of West Bromwich ruled that it had hit the spectators behind the goal, not the crossbar, and the goal stood. West Ham then pointed to a Bolton fan they alleged had kicked the ball back out of touch into Vizard's path as he dribbled down the wing before crossing. Mr Asson pointed to the centre circle. West Ham's captain George Kay then asked the referee to abandon the match, but the Bolton skipper chimed in, 'We're doing fine, ref, we'll play until dark to finish the match if necessary.'

There were no more goals and Bolton, founder members of the Football League in 1888 and beaten in their two previous finals in 1894 and 1904, had won their first major honour. They came back to win at Wembley with unerring regularity in 1926 and 1929. They won all three finals without conceding a goal and used only 17 players in doing so.

West Ham, who gained some consolation for their Cup Final defeat by winning promotion to the First Division the following week, would not return until 1964. And any of the crowd who wished to return to Wembley for the following year's Cup Final would have to buy a ticket in advance. Ever since then, with the exception of the replayed 1982 final between Spurs and Queen's Park Rangers, every Cup Final and replay at Wembley has been all-ticket.

Familiar colours filled Wembley in the 1920s. There were the black-and-white stripes of Newcastle,

Team captains George Kay (left, West Ham) and Joe Smith (Bolton) pictured before the first Wembley final as referee David Asson looks on (Popperfoto)

and the claret-and-blue of Aston Villa. The red-and-white stripes of Sheffield United and the blue-and-white halves of Blackburn. There were new colours too – the red-and-white of Arsenal, not yet the all-conquering giants of the 1930s, and the blue-and-white of Cardiff and Portsmouth.

Old scores were settled in 1924 and 1926. First Newcastle avenged their 2-0 loss to Aston Villa in the 1905 final with a 2-0 win at Wembley. Whereas the Magpies never won a Cup Final at the Crystal Palace, here was a venue they loved. Newcastle won in 1924, 1932, 1951, 1952 and 1955. They eventually lost their unbeaten record on their sixth appearance in 1974.

Then Bolton returned in 1926 and, in the first final played under the new offside law, avenged their 1904 defeat by Manchester City with a 1-0 win in Wem-

bley's first all-Lancashire final. David Jack, scorer of Wembley's first ever goal, returned to score the winner again.

But the most famous win in the 1920s came on April 23, 1927 when Cardiff City beat Arsenal 1-0 to become the only team from outside England to win the Cup.

These were heady times when the Cardiff bluebird soared higher than ever before – or since. In 1924 Cardiff had missed out on the League championship to Huddersfield on the old goal-average rule by 0.24 of a goal. They came back from that disappointment to reach the 1925 Cup Final only to be beaten 1-0 by Sheffield United after a mistake by their wing-half Henry Wake. The headlines then were as predictable as they would be today. 'Wake Not Awake', moaned one.

But Cardiff were back again two years later and this time there was to be no slip. The sound of Abide With Me, sung at the Cup Final for the first time, and Land of My Fathers – sung for the last time – rolled down the Wembley terraces and across the stadium and inspired the Cardiff team to victory. Four of the side – which didn't include the unfortunate Wake – had played in 1925, they had knocked out the holders Bolton along the way, and they were about to make history.

The match, dubbed 'The Married Men's Final' because only three players were single, was not a classic but it was settled by one of the most famous goals in Wembley's history.

Herbert Chapman, who had masterminded Huddersfield Town's hat-trick of League wins from 1924–26, was in his first season in charge at Arsenal, who had never won a major honour. They of course became world-famous in the next decade under Chapman, but at Wembley in 1927 they were relying on a player from a bygone age. Fourteen years previously Charlie Buchan had been in the Sunderland team beaten by Villa. Now at Wembley, in the twilight of his career, he gave one final heroic display. Tall, elegant and still blessed with exquisite touch, he inspired Arsenal all afternoon, but it was all to no avail.

With 17 minutes to go, Cardiff's Scottish centre-forward Hugh Ferguson sent in a first-time shot at goal which Arsenal's (ironically) Welsh international goalkeeper Dan Lewis had covered. Lewis dropped to his knees to gather the ball with Len Davies and Sam Irving running in to challenge. At that moment Lewis turned his back, the ball slid across his chest, under his left armpit and rolled across the goal-line as he desperately tried to snatch at it. The Welsh side leapt for joy, thousands of Welshmen screamed in delight – but one Welshman just held his head in his hands.

Tom Whittaker, the Arsenal trainer, believed the ball slipped out of Lewis's arm because of the sheen on the goalkeeper's new jersey. From that day it has been an Arsenal tradition that every new goalkeeper's jersey is softened up in the wash before being worn.

That match was a turning point for both clubs. Cardiff disappeared down a valley so deep they would have to apply for re-election to the League just seven years later. Arsenal were to scale heights that no other side had ever reached and few have matched since. Their first major success came in 1930 when Herbert Chapman's old club, Huddersfield, met Herbert Chapman's new club, Arsenal, in the final.

Huddersfield had been to Wembley two years previously and had come close to the Double that season, finishing second in the League to Everton and runners-up in the Cup Final to Blackburn, whose 3–1 victory took them level with Aston Villa's record number of six wins. James Roscamp's opening goal for Blackburn that day – about 50 seconds after the kick-off – was the fastest yet scored in a Wembley Cup Final. Only one goal has ever been scored earlier – Jackie Milburn's opener after 45 seconds for Newcastle in 1955. Huddersfield's goal in the match was the first scored by a losing team for 18 years.

Huddersfield had five survivors from 1928 and Arsenal four from 1927, but it was Arsenal's new signings, the men who would carry them to greatness over the next decade, who decided the issue. This was the Arsenal of Tom Parker, Eddie Hapgood, Alex James of the baggy shorts, and David Jack, who had already won two finals with Bolton. It was the Arsenal of Joe Hulme, Cliff 'Boy' Bastin who won every

honour in the game by the time he was 21, and 'Honest Jack' Lambert, and that afternoon they were too clever for Huddersfield Town. Alex James rarely scored, but he got the opener after 16 minutes and provided the pass for Lambert to make it 2–0 two minutes from time.

It was Arsenal's first major honour and the first Cup win by a London side since Tottenham in 1921. The new decade had begun with a new name on the Cup – and a new shape in the sky. During this match the German Graf Zeppelin flew over Wembley, casting the only shadow on an otherwise perfect afternoon for half of north London, at least.

The following year's final was played in a down-pour. Wembley had witnessed its first all-Lancashire final in 1926 and now it had its first all-Midlands affair. It had to wait until 1967 for the first all-London final, while the White Rose county has never produced both Wembley finalists.

West Bromwich Albion, who had already played three finals against local rivals Aston Villa, now met another team from down the road – Birmingham, who did not add 'City' to their name until 1945. That spring Albion entered the record books by becoming the only team to win both the Cup and promotion from the old Second Division in the same season. They actually clinched promotion the Saturday after the Cup Final when they beat Charlton 3–2 in front of a then-record crowd at the Hawthorns of 52,415.

When the Baggies last played in the final in 1912 they lost to Barnsley in a replay. Their goalkeeper was Hubert Pearson, who naturally was rather disappointed with his loser's medal. His four-year-old son Harry probably didn't appreciate the full significance of what losing in a Cup Final meant then, but he did now.

Harry had followed his father's footsteps into the Albion goal and now faced Birmingham across a rain-lashed Wembley in the Cup Final of 1931. Lining up in Birmingham's goal was his cousin, the great England international Harry Hibbs, but it was to be the Pearson branch of the family rejoicing that night.

Albion scored twice through William 'Ginger' Richardson to take the Cup back to the Hawthorns for the third time. 'WG' – best remembered for the four goals in five minutes he scored against West Ham the following November – hit the winner less than a minute after Joe Bradford had equalised for Birmingham. West Brom returned to Wembley four years later as a First Division team, but lost 4–2 to Sheffield Wednesday. The Yorkshire side clinched the match with two goals from Ellis Rimmer in the last five minutes, which made him the first player since Sandy Brown of Tottenham in 1901 to have scored in every round.

There had been controversial goals before in the Cup Final but never anything like the controversy that surrounded Newcastle's opening goal in 1932. Their opponents Arsenal had powered their way back to Wembley for the third time in five years, winning every game without the need for a replay. They started their advance as they meant to go on, beating Darwen, those Cup fighters of old now playing in the Lancashire Combination, 11–1 at Highbury.

Arsenal, who became the first London side to win the League Championship the previous year with a then record haul of 66 points under the old system of two points for a win, finished as runners-up to Everton in 1932 and were to be champions again in 1933, 1934 and 1935, but they were to finish second best to the Magpies on this occasion.

Newcastle had also had a huge win on their way to the final, beating Third Division Southport 9–0 after two draws in the fourth round. But they had had a moderate season in the League, finishing 11th. Like so many teams before and since, they had reserved their best play for the Cup.

Arsenal were without the injured Alex James, but their side was full of stars and contained six survivors from the Cup-winning side of 1930. The defence looked secure with future England internationals Hapgood and George Male at the back and 'Police Constable' Herbert Roberts, the king of the stopper centre-halves, in the middle. There was Parker, Lambert and Jack, there was Bastin and James's replacement, Bob John. In contrast Newcastle looked an ordinary side, although full-back Jimmy Nelson had played for Cardiff when they beat Arsenal in 1927.

No-one was too surprised when John put Arsenal ahead after 15 minutes, but then six minutes before half-time came perhaps the most controversial goal ever scored in a Cup Final.

Newcastle inside-right Jimmy Richardson chased a long clearance down the right, slithered onto the ball and crossed it in one movement, just as it appeared to have gone a foot over the bye-line. The Arsenal defence instinctively relaxed as Richardson's cross found the unmarked Jack Allen who put it past Frank Moss and into the goal. But to the horror of the Arsenal players, the referee Percy Harper pointed to the centre-spot and awarded a goal. The players protested but their captain Tom Parker waved them back to their positions. The goal stood.

The controversial Newcastle equaliser in the 1932 final, turned in by Jack Allen. Arsenal protested that the ball had gone out of play before being crossed in (Popperfoto)

Later that day newsreel film and still photos seemed to prove the ball was out of play when Richardson crossed. The incident made the front pages of the newspapers – a rare thing for a sports story in 1932 – and arguments about the 'over-the-line goal' have raged ever since. The match was a classic, but Arsenal never recovered from that demoralising setback. Allen scored a second as Arsenal became the first team to score first in a Wembley Cup Final and lose.

In 1952 the two sides would meet in the Cup Final again, but Arsenal could not avenge that bitter defeat.

They did have plenty of time to get over their disappointment in the 1930s though, winning the Championship five times and the Cup again in 1936 when they beat Sheffield United 1–0 with a goal from Ted Drake.

But the thirties also saw Arsenal humbled in what must be regarded as the biggest upset in the history of the competition. By January 1933 the team that Chapman had built was so good it was almost unbeatable. It had been 36 years since Aston Villa last achieved the Double, but no-one doubted that this Arsenal team could do it. And when the draw for the third round of the Cup was made, nobody imagined that Walsall, halfway down the Third Division North, would give them a moment's trouble. Arsenal won their last match before the Cup-tie 9-2 against Sheffield United in the First Division. Walsall hadn't won for a month.

But Chapman was guilty of a rare yet costly error that wintry day in the middle of the Depression. He underestimated the opposition. Arsenal took the field without four regulars – Hapgood, John, Lambert and Tim Coleman, all missing through injury or illness. England winger Joe Hulme was also out of the side after a loss of form, but Chapman called in four reserves, only one of whom, Norman Sidey, had played in the first team before.

Arsenal, the southern aristocrats, who it was said had spent more on their bootlaces than Walsall had on their team, were out-fought by the poor provincial underdogs. Walsall battled for every ball, Arsenal men went flying over the surrounding wall after robust tackles, and in the end the Gunners were simply played off the park. On the hour Gilbert Alsop put Walsall 1–0 up, heading home a corner. Five minutes later Tommy Black, who was never to play another game for Arsenal and was transferred to Plymouth the following week, aimed a kick at Alsop in the box and Bill Sheppard scored from the penalty. The final score was Walsall 2, Arsenal 0. It was a sensation.

Walsall's glory did not last long as they were knocked out in the next round by Manchester City, while Arsenal went on to win the Championship. Arsenal have had a few black days in the Cup since then, losing to Peterborough, Northampton, York City and Wrexham, but never a day as black as that Saturday in the Black Country in 1933.

The final that year was the first in which the teams' shirts were numbered, Everton playing in 1–11 and Manchester City in 12–22. It was also the year that Everton completed what is an often-overlooked treble. In 1931 they won the Second Division title, in 1932 they won the League Championship, and in 1933 they won the Cup. It is a unique achievement and although the team was an outstanding one, much of its success was due to the goalscoring brilliance of Dixie Dean who in those three years played in 126 League and Cup matches for Everton and scored 123 goals, including the second in Everton's 3–0 win over City in the Cup Final of 1933.

City returned to win the Cup the following year with a 2–1 win over Portsmouth. Matt Busby, later to know both tragedy and glory with Manchester United, had been in the team beaten by Everton and this time picked up a winner's medal. The great Frank Swift, later to lose his life in the Munich air crash that almost accounted for Busby, was then a 19-year-old bundle of nerves in the City goal. He fainted with relief at the

Bill Shankly's advice was to 'close your eyes and blast it'. George Mutch does not remember aiming at goal but his penalty kick in the last minute of extra time won the Cup for Preston in 1938 (Popperfoto)

final whistle. Both of City's goals were scored by their skipper Fred Tilson, who had scored four in the semi-final when City beat Aston Villa 6–1. Tilson's winning goal was made by Alec Herd, whose son David was to play for the United side managed by Busby in the 1963 Cup Final.

But one of the most famous people on the field in that 1934 final was not a player. He was the referee, Stanley Rous. As Sir Stanley he would become the secretary of the FA and eventually the president of FIFA. His previous involvement with the Cup Final had been as a linesman in the 1926 game between Bolton and Manchester City, but now he was in charge, and very nearly made history of a different kind.

In his book, *Football Worlds*, published in 1978, Sir Stanley revealed how close he came in 1934 to sending off a player for the first time in the history of the Cup Final – something that did not happen until Durham referee Peter Willis sent off Kevin Moran of Manchester United 51 years later. Portsmouth were struggling against City and Rous noticed that John Mackie, their Northern Ireland full-back, was threatening City's England winger Eric Brook.

'I warned Mackie that he would be sent off if he carried out his threats,' wrote Sir Stanley. 'He answered me back:

"Sure, you'll never send me off at Wembley, Mr Rous."

"Try it once more and you will find I will," I told him in a tone that seemed to convince him. Certainly he gave me no more trouble, and certainly I would have sent him off if he had.'

City were to repeat their feat of losing and then winning in successive finals in the mid-1950s, but before then two other teams were going to return as winners the year after losing. The second was Charlton, losers in 1946 and winners in 1947, but first it was Preston's turn, beaten by Sunderland in 1937 but back again the following spring to beat Huddersfield Town in a repeat of the 1922 final at Stamford Bridge.

Sunderland, inspired by Raich Carter, finally won the Cup for the first time in their long history with an emphatic 3–1 win over Preston in the first Cup Final ever played in May. Preston returned the following year and won the Cup for the first time since the days of the 'Invincibles' 49 years previously. In the side was a man who in time, like Busby, would have a profound influence on football. Bill Shankly was one of four men who had lost to Sunderland in 1937 but by the end of almost two hours' play that afternoon he seemed no nearer a winner's medal.

The match, much like the previous final between the two clubs, was a drab and uneventful affair. Goalless at 90 minutes, it was still goalless a minute from the end of extra-time and the first replay in a final since 1912 looked inevitable. But the fates had one card still to play. Huddersfield had beaten Preston by a penalty in 1922 – now Preston were to do the same to them.

With a minute of extra-time remaining, Huddersfield's captain and centre-half Alf Young was adjudged to have tripped George Mutch as he came through for one last attack on goal. The foul happened at the very edge of the box – perhaps even outside the line – but the referee pointed to the spot. A bemused Mutch was handed the ball, and legend has it that Shankly went up to him and told him to close his eyes and blast it.

Mutch said after the game, 'I thought it was funny they gave the ball to me . . . an injured man. As I took my run I wondered what I was doing and why. I don't remember aiming at goal.' But his aim was true enough, the ball going in off the underside of the bar.

That match closed the book on Preston's Cup success, although they returned for the finals of 1954 and 1964. It also brought to a close the career of Joe Hulme, now playing for Huddersfield after moving from Arsenal. That day he made his fifth Cup Final appearance at Wembley, a feat not equalled until Johnny Giles played in his fifth final in 1973. But if a chapter had closed for Preston and for Hulme in 1938, it was an era that ended in 1939 when, in the last final played before the outbreak of the Second World War, there was a major upset.

Portsmouth had struggled all season against relegation while Wolves, managed by Major Frank Buckley and inspired by their future manager Stan Cullis, the skipper in those days, were in contention for the Championship. Portsmouth had only won three games away from home all season – at Derby and Sunderland in the League, and at Highbury in the FA Cup where they beat Huddersfield, the previous season's beaten finalists, 2–1 in the semi-final. What was more, exactly a month before the final Pompey had been trounced 8–2 by Middlesbrough in the First Division. In contrast Wolves had stormed into the final. Dennis Westcott had scored 11 goals on the way to Wembley, including four in the semi-final crushing of Grimsby, 5–0 at Old Trafford.

Portsmouth had lost on both their previous Wembley appearances, to Bolton in 1929 and Manchester City in 1934, and no-one except their fans gave them a chance of making it third time lucky. Maybe the influence of their manager Jack Tinn's lucky spats helped settle their nerves; perhaps they took heart when they saw the almost unrecognisably shaky signatures of the Wolves players in the Wembley visitors book when they went to sign it.

Whatever, it was the biggest upset since Blackburn beat Huddersfield 11 years previously. Wolves, to a man, never got going, gave their worst display of the season and after going a goal behind, were never in the match. Bert Barlow, a Wolves player until two months previously, scored against his old side to put Pompey ahead and the final was decided either side of half-time. Just before the interval John Anderson made it 2–0 and a minute after they restarted Barlow made it three. Dickie Dorsett, not yet 20, became the youngest player to score in a Wembley final up until that time when he pulled a goal back for Wolves, but Cliff Parker completed the rout, heading in Portsmouth's fourth with 18 minutes to play.

The Wolves players reportedly took a potion made of monkey-glands to boost their energy before the match. It is a famous Cup tale, but one strongly denied by Stan Cullis many years later. 'It was a publicity stunt,

and it never happened. Major Buckley was always interested in getting publicity for himself and for the club and that is all it was.'

The match was played in front of a crowd of 99,370, the largest at Wembley since the first final in 1923. Portsmouth became the first club from south of London to win the Cup, and they also became the holders of the trophy for the longest time in its history. It stayed in their safe-keeping until the end of the war in 1945, even surviving an enemy bombing raid.

Three-time Tangerines, Giant-killers and Geordies 1946–56

In June 1945, just three weeks after the end of the Second World War, the FA Cup organising committee met and agreed that the competition should resume the following autumn.

The Football League was not resurrected until the following year, and the FA Cup had an unusual flavour in that transitional first season after the war. From Round One until the quarter-finals, ties would be played over two legs, while matches in the qualifying round, the semi-finals and final would as usual be played on a knock-out basis.

So on September 1, 1945, just as it had back in November 1871, the FA Cup kicked off with just four matches, in the Extra Preliminary round. Aylesbury United beat Chesham 5–0, Banbury Spencer beat Headington United, later to become Oxford United, 8–1; Pressed Steel beat Morris Motors 1–0, while Uxbridge scored an 11–0 win over Lyons FC.

The 294 entries were nearly half the number that had taken part in the last competition before the war, but the important thing for millions of people was that at last life was slowly returning to normal – and there was some 'real' football to go and watch again.

There were certainly some quirky results as the Cup progressed. Aldershot beat Reading 8–6 on aggregate in the first round, and then Newport from the Isle of Wight 12–0 on aggregate in the second. Middlesbrough beat Leeds 11–6 on aggregate in the third round, while Bradford Park Avenue lost 3–1 at home to Manchester City as expected in the fourth round – then won the second leg 8–2 at Maine Road! Derby, the eventual winners, beat Brighton 10–1 on aggregate in their fifth round tie while Charlton, the eventual runners-up, beat Brentford 9–4 on aggregate in the quarter-finals.

A staggering total of 859 goals were scored in the Cup that season at an average of almost 4 per game, but one team did not score any. Portsmouth, the 1939 winners and the club who looked after the FA Cup itself all through the war, lost 1–0 on aggregate to Birmingham City.

Thousands came to every match with ground records being broken almost weekly. More than 76,000 saw the sixth round tie between Derby and Aston Villa, while in the semi-finals 80,483 watched Derby play Birmingham at Maine Road and 70,819 saw Charlton v Bolton at Villa Park. But many of the grounds were in disrepair and simply not equipped to handle such huge masses of people. On 9 March, 65,419 squeezed into every available inch of space at Burnden Park to watch Bolton's sixth round second-leg tie with Stanley Matthews' Stoke, a wall collapsed and 33 people were crushed to death. It was the worst football disaster in English history, and remained so until the Bradford fire in 1985.

But at last the final tie of a record 229 played in the competition proper took place. On April 27 the nation turned its gaze back to Wembley, turned its wireless sets on, and heard the familiar voice of Raymond Glendenning commentating on the first Cup Final for seven years.

Charlton in fact were no strangers to Wembley although this was their first appearance in the FA Cup Final. They had played in the League South Wartime Cup Finals of 1943 and 1944 and six of the team to face Derby had played in at least one of those matches. Goalkeeper Sam Bartram was in the middle of a spell in which he played in four Wembley finals in four years. He missed the 1943 Final, but played in 1944, in the 1945 match as a guest for Millwall, and for Charlton in their two FA Cup Finals of 1946 and 1947.

And the first Final after the war was one of Wembley's great finals. Nine years previously Raich Carter had helped one famous old club win the Cup for the first time when he scored one of Sunderland's goals against Preston; now he was to help another, Derby County.

Derby scored 33 goals on the way to Wembley, with Carter scoring 12 and the great Peter Doherty nine. By the end of the afternoon Derby's tally was 37, Doherty had reached double figures and the Rams had won the Cup. The Carter-Doherty partnership in attack was the cornerstone of Derby's success, but it was almost a Charlton player that gave them the Cup as with only five minutes to play, defender Bert Turner deflected the ball into his own goal and for a moment that seemed to have settled it.

But a minute later at the other end Charlton won a free-kick. Turner blasted the ball, it took a deflection off Doherty and put Charlton level. Turner became the first man – and the last until Tommy Hutchison of Manchester City in 1981 – to score for both sides in the Final.

Even before extra-time began there was another surprise when the ball burst. In one of those strange Cup coincidences, the referee, ED Smith of Cumberland, had said on the BBC the night before that he thought the odds of the ball bursting were a million to one. Someone should have had some money on it. Five days after the Wembley final Derby met Charlton in a League match and again the ball burst; and when Charlton played Burnley in the 1947 final, it burst again.

If the new ball in cricket makes things easier for bowlers, the new ball in the Cup Final certainly helped Derby, who scored three times without reply in extra-time. It was actually Charlton's second defeat in the Cup that season, as they had lost 2–1 to Fulham in the second leg of their third round match but gone through 4–3 on aggregate.

Perhaps Derby's name was destined to be on the Cup that year. Just before the final an enterprising Fleet Street journalist remembered the old story about the gypsy curse on Derby, dating back to the 1890s. The journalist, sensing a good story, took Jack Nicholas, the Derby skipper, to see a gypsy a few days before the final. He crossed her palm, she lifted the curse, and Derby won the Cup.

Charlton, like Manchester City and Preston before them, and as Manchester City, Manchester United, Arsenal and Liverpool have done since, returned to Wembley a year after losing and lifted the Cup.

Their opponents in 1947 were Second Division Burnley, whose manager Cliff Britton had been a member of Everton's winning team 14 years previously. Charlton's manager Jimmy Seed had also won a winner's medal as a player, with Tottenham in 1921, and it was Seed who drank champagne at the end as Charlton won a dour match 1–0 with a goal from Chris Duffy. Again the ball burst and again the game went into extra-time, but this was not one of Wembley's gala occasions.

The Cup Final of 1948, however, was and is still regarded, together with the final of 1953, as one of the best finals of all time. There are similarities between the two games. They both featured Blackpool and Stanley Matthews, and in both finals the eventual winners had to come from behind. In 1948 Manchester United came from 0–1 and then 1–2 down to beat Blackpool 4–2, while in 1953 Blackpool came from 1–3 down to beat Bolton 4–3. United became the first side to be behind twice in the Cup Final and win it.

The 1953 game, 'The Matthews Final', has a special place in the history books as it came in the same year as Elizabeth II was crowned, Everest was climbed and Gordon Richards won the Derby. But in 1948 it must have seemed like the match between United and Blackpool could never be bettered.

United reached the final despite having to play every match away from Old Trafford which was still being repaired after war-time bombing. They shared Maine Road with Manchester City but when both sides were drawn at home in the fourth and fifth rounds, United had to find another ground. They beat Liverpool 3–0 at Goodison Park and Charlton 2–0 at Huddersfield before they disposed of Preston 4–1 at Maine Road and Derby 3–1 in the semi-final at Hillsborough. The biggest obstacle Blackpool overcame was in the semi-final at Villa Park when a Stanley Mortensen hat-trick gave them a 3–1 win over Spurs after extra-time.

With 20 minutes to go at Wembley, Blackpool looked to have done enough to have won the Cup. Eddie Shimwell had put them ahead from the penalty spot after Allenby Chilton fouled Mortensen on 15 minutes, even though the trip looked well outside the area. Thirteen minutes later United were level when John Rowley scored, but seven minutes after that Mortensen turned in his stride and cracked the ball past Jack Crompton in the United goal to maintain his record of scoring in every round.

Both teams continued to play dazzling soccer in the second half, with Blackpool in command of the match. But then came the incident on which the match turned. Hugh Kelly, Blackpool's left-half, clashed with John Morris on the right of the penalty area. Blackpool's defence hesitated, but Morris quickly took the free-kick and John Rowley equalised.

With the score still 2–2 Mortensen thought he had won it for Blackpool, but his powerful shot, heading for the corner of the net, was tipped away at the last second by Crompton. A minute later Stan Pearson scored for United at the other end and when John Anderson drilled the ball past Joe Robinson in the Blackpool goal from 30 yards seven minutes from time, it was all over.

Blackpool returned in 1951 and lost 2–0 to Newcastle United and two Jackie Milburn goals, but the tangerine ribbons were finally tied to the Cup in 1953 when they pulled off the most famous comeback in the competition's history.

The whole country, it seemed, wanted Blackpool to win the 1953 Cup Final, even those who had never seen a football match. At 38, and after the disappointments of 1948 and 1951, surely this was Stanley Matthews' last chance for his lifelong ambition – a Cup winner's medal.

The only people who were not feeling quite so magnanimous towards Blackpool's ambitions were the Bolton team, and their fans. They were to be cast in a similiar role in 1958 when they met a Manchester United team carried to the final on a wave of post-Munich sympathy. But whereas in 1958 Bolton won, this time they lost.

The match of course has gone down in history as the Matthews Final and while his influence grew to almost mystical heights in the last 20 minutes with his marker Ralph Banks suffering from cramp, it was the other Stanley, Mortensen, who scored Wembley's first ever Cup Final hat-trick, and a strange tactical deployment by Bolton, that were as crucial in determining the final outcome.

With only 75 seconds played it was Bolton who took the lead, when the Blackpool goalkeeper George Farm let a Nat Lofthouse shot squeeze under his body. Lofthouse followed Jackie Milburn as the second man in three years to have scored in every round. But 15 minutes later Bolton's left-half Eric Bell pulled a muscle and went out to play on the wing. Harry Hassall, the inside-left, was pulled back to left-half and

Bob Langton was moved across from the wing into the centre of the attack. Despite going 3–1 ahead the Bolton side looked unbalanced and as the hot afternoon wore on and the turf sapped the energy, it was Blackpool who rose to the occasion.

Mortensen had pulled Blackpool level at 1–1 in the 35th minute, but five minutes later Bolton were back in front when Farm made another hash of a save from Bill Moir. Then when Bell, jumping off his one good leg, headed Bolton 3–1 ahead 10 minutes after half-time, the match appeared to be over.

But Mortensen pulled a goal back after 68 minutes. With Banks crippled by cramp, Matthews had the right wing to himself, sending in cross after cross. Many sailed harmlessly over the bar, but finally one did some damage. Stan Hanson went up for yet another high ball – and dropped it. Mortensen whipped it into the back of the net despite colliding with the post. Blackpool 2, Bolton 3.

Now Matthews swerved and feinted his way through the Bolton defence...but time was running out. With three minutes to go Bolton, exhausted and confounded by the wizard on the wing, were hanging on to their lead, and the Cup, by their fingertips. Then referee Mervyn Griffiths awarded a free-kick to Blackpool on the edge of the penalty area. Mortensen blasted the ball high into the net. It was 3–3, with a minute or two of injury time left.

For the last time, Matthews came down the line, going inside the helpless Banks, before rounding centre-half Malcolm Barrass. He pushed the ball to within four yards of the goal-line and then passed to Bill Perry who had made space for himself on the edge of the six-

The injured Eric Bell (6), 'jumping off his good leg', puts Bolton 3–1 up in the 1953 final before Blackpool's famous comeback which gave Stanley Matthews a Cup winner's medal at last (Popperfoto)

yard box. He turned and shot the ball home. Almost immediately it was all over. Blackpool 4, Bolton Wanderers 3, Matthews had his medal. And so at last did Eddie Shimwell, skipper Harry Johnston and Stan Mortensen, who also played in the losing finals of 1948 and 1951.

The afternoon was a special one too for Blackpool's manager Joe Smith who joined that select band of men to have played in and later managed Cup-winning teams. He had been to Wembley twice before, as a winner with Bolton in 1923 and 1926.

Sandwiched between Blackpool's first Cup Final in 1948 and their last in 1953 were the exploits of two very different clubs which captured the nation's imagination. The first was Yeovil Town, the second Newcastle United.

Yeovil's Cup run of 1949 really is the stuff of legend and their giant-killing acts through the years have gone a long way to make the Cup the special competition it is. The Somerset club had been claiming League scalps since 1924, but their only Cup match against a First Division side had ended in a crushing 6–2 defeat by Liverpool on their famous sloping pitch at The Huish in 1935.

In 1949 they reached the fourth round for the first time and were drawn at home against First Division Sunderland. At the time Yeovil were sixth from bottom of the Southern League, Sunderland eighth in Division One.

More than 15,000 watched the match and more than 100 journalists came to cover it. There was nowhere to put them, so the club borrowed some desks from the local junior school, put them down one touchline and told Fleet Street's finest to sit in them. They did, causing plenty of laughter as they squeezed into seats usually used by seven-year-olds.

And what a story they had to file. Yeovil took the lead with a goal from player-manager Alec Stock after 28 minutes, then Sunderland equalised through Barney Ramsden just after the hour. In the Sunderland side was Len Shackleton, the most expensive signing in England, but not even he could conjure up a goal – for Sunderland at least – that afternoon. After 90 minutes it was 1–1 and as Cup ties were then still being played under the Government's austerity measures to save energy and avoid lost working days following the war, extra time was played.

Just before the end of the first period, Shackleton, the 'clown prince of football', tried one trick too many. Juggling the ball on the halfway line, he sent it back towards his own goal by mistake; Wright, Yeovil's inside-left, pounced on it and passed to Bryant who scored what proved to be the winner.

In the next round Yeovil's part-timers went off to face Cup holders Manchester United, and an 80,000 crowd turned up to see if they could pull off another miracle. They couldn't. Manchester United won 8–0, but Yeovil's win over Sunderland is still remembered as one of the greatest upsets of all time.

Even today, nearly half a century on from that win, Yeovil are still making light of reputations in the Cup, and have knocked out more League teams than any other side. But for various reasons their Cup performances never secured them a place in the Football League. In the days before automatic promotion from the Conference, non-League clubs would lobby for

votes and both Peterborough and Hereford United gained League status largely through their Cup exploits.

Peterborough, 'the Posh', took few prisoners in the 1950s beating Second Division Ipswich and Lincoln amongst others, while between 1949 and 1972 when they were voted into the League, Hereford failed to reach the First Round just once. Their greatest victory came in February 1972 when they beat First Division Newcastle United at their Edgar Street ground.

In the 1970s and 1980s there were famous wins for Wimbledon, Altrincham, Telford and Blyth Spartans. In 1989 Sutton United of the Vauxhall Conference knocked out Coventry, Cup winners less than two years before.

Giant-killing is a vital ingredient of the Cup's endless magic. There *has* to be some magic. How else could you explain Vauxhall Opel (Isthmian) League Woking's 4–2 win at a club like West Bromwich Albion, whose history is older than the tournament itself? How else could a club like Chorley take apart a club like Wolves? How else could works teams like Birmingham Corporation Tramways and Farnham United Breweries get through qualifying rounds and reach the competition proper?

But one of the greatest of all non-League clubs provides only a small footnote to this story. The legendary Corinthians, formed in 1882 and at one time able to provide every player for the England side, never played in the FA Cup in their heyday because their rules prevented them from taking part in competitive matches. Yet they were more than a match for the leading professional teams of the late 19th and early 20th centuries.

In March 1904, Bury, who the previous year had won the Cup by a record margin of 6–0 over Derby County, came to London to play the Corinthians for the Sheriff of London's Shield at the Queen's Club. The Bury team contained ten of their Cup winning players – and the Corinthians beat them 10–3. In 1884 Blackburn Rovers won the first of their three successive finals. Corinthians beat them 8–1. When Blackburn won the Cup the following year, Corinthians beat them 6–0.

The Corinthians finally entered the Cup for the first time in 1922 and two years later were still good enough to beat Blackburn Rovers, then of the First Division, 1–0. Their final season in the Cup was the last before the Second World War, but by then their time had passed. The history of the competition would have been very different if they had taken part from the time of their formation.

So the Corinthian legend is something of a lost one. But while Yeovil were busy creating one of their own, Newcastle United were adding to theirs.

In 1952 they became the first team this century to win the Cup in successive seasons. A gauge of their dominance in the Cup, only matched since by Tottenham and Manchester United, was that in the five years from January 1951 to February 1956 they played 35 Cup matches, won the Cup three times and lost only three games.

Since then they have appeared in only one final – losing their 100 per cent record at Wembley to Liverpool in 1974 – but in the days of 'Wor' Jackie Milburn, the Robledo brothers, Joe Harvey and Bobby Mitchell,

Newcastle were the best Cup team in the land. The 1951 win was largely due to Milburn who scored in every round, including both the goals in a five-minute spell in the 2–0 win over Blackpool in the final.

The move that led to the second goal, one of the best scored in a Cup Final, started after a mistake by Stanley Matthews. He hit an aimless pass which was picked up by Tommy Walker who fed Ernie Taylor. Taylor back-heeled the ball into the path of Milburn, who, sprinting at full tilt, blasted the ball home on the run from 25 yards. Stan Seymour, the Newcastle manager, also made history that afternoon by becoming the first man to play for and then manage the same club in a winning Cup Final. He was a member of the Newcastle side that beat Villa in 1924. If 1953 was the Matthews Final, it is surprising that 1951 never became known as 'Milburn's Final'.

'It was definitely Milburn's match,' said Matthews a few years later, 'and his second goal was right out of this world. It was the greatest goal I have ever seen and certainly the finest ever scored at Wembley. A goal that every player dreams about . . . but how many other players would have chanced such a shot, especially in a Wembley final? Very few would have had the courage.'

The following year Newcastle faced their old adversaries Arsenal, playing in their second final in three years. In 1950 Arsenal beat Liverpool 2–0 with the oldest Cup team of all time, with an average age of 30 years 2 months. The 1950 final was also the first since the Bolton-West Ham match to have a 100,000 attendance.

The Arsenal side of 1952 was younger and fitter, but was reduced to 10 men after an early injury to Welsh international defender Walley Barnes, the first in a series of injuries in the 1950s and early 1960s that became known as the 'Wembley hoodoo'. There was to be no revenge for Arsenal. Newcastle won 1–0 with George Robledo, their Chilean-born centre-forward, scoring the only goal six minutes from time.

Newcastle's League form at this time never matched their Cup displays. Although they never finished out of the top 10 from 1949 until 1952, they slipped below mid-table in 1953 and 1954, and their League form was only moderate again when they returned to Wembley to win the Cup for the third time in five years in 1955.

In between the wins for Matthews and Milburn there was a Cup Final defeat for another giant of that era, Tom Finney. The 'Preston Plumber' is still regarded by many people as the best player that ever lived; better than George Best, better than Pele. That may or may not be so, but he did something in his career that neither Best – nor Pele! – managed in theirs: playing in the Cup Final at Wembley.

If the country had willed Matthews to his winner's medal in 1953, there was just as much neutral support for Finney in 1954. Preston had twice got to the sixth round since Finney had made his debut for them in 1946, but in 1954 they finally made it to Wembley. The previous season they had lost the title to Arsenal on goal average but their League form had slumped during the 1953-54 campaign. They had finished 11th, while their opponents in the final, West Bromwich Albion, were runners-up behind Wolves.

Although West Brom started as favourites, everyone expected Finney to dictate the play on the Wembley

wings he knew so well. Instead he had, by his own admission, the worst match he ever played for his club.

Biographer Paul Agnew, in his book *Finney – A Football Legend*, quotes Finney's memories of that Cup Final. 'Whatever the reason,' remembered Finney, 'May 1st, 1954 will always remain my worst performance. I could do little right on the day when I wanted everything to go better than ever before.'

So Finney, the Preston skipper, had a nightmare and Len Millard, his marker, virtually played him out of the game. Even so, Preston led after 51 minutes when Charlie Wayman rounded Saunders in the Albion goal to put his side 2–1 up and become the third player in four years to score in every round. But Preston's cheers were short-lived. Just after an hour Ronnie Allen scored his second of the match from the penalty spot after Tommy Docherty was judged to have pulled down Johnny Nicholls. Three minutes from time West Brom won the match with a goal from Frank Griffin. Preston, and Finney in particular, plumbed the depths of despair that day.

There was an eerie corollary to that final almost exactly 10 years to the day after. Preston, now a Second Division club, reached Wembley again in 1964. Again they were involved in a five-goal thriller and again they lost after being 2–1 up during the middle period of the match.

Preston were in fact only denied victory right at the death by two West Ham goals in the last two minutes. The Hammers had not played in the Cup Final since the first one at Wembley in 1923. Now they were back, with seven men in the team whose surnames began with the letter B, and led by a man named Bobby who was to make Wembley his second home.

Preston included a young wing-half called Howard Kendall who, 20 days before his 18th birthday, became the youngest player to appear in a Wembley Cup Final. But they had some old campaigners too. Doug Holden had played in the Bolton side beaten by Blackpool in 1953 and Alex Dawson was in the makeshift Manchester United team of 1958.

It was Holden who gave Preston the lead after 10 minutes, but a minute later another teenager, 18-year-old Johnny Sissons, became the youngest scorer at

Ronnie Allen turns away after the first of his two goals puts West Brom 1–0 up against Preston in the 1954 final (Popperfoto)

Wembley when he equalised for West Ham. Five minutes before the interval Dawson headed Preston back in front and that is how it stayed until the 89th minute when a header from Geoff Hurst put West Ham level. With only seconds remaining West Ham won it when Ronnie Boyce, running in unmarked at the far post, headed in a cross from Peter Brabrook – then ran around the back of the goal in delight.

Tom Finney had retired four years earlier in 1960 and the following year Newcastle and Preston were both relegated from the First Division. It was the end of an era; Preston have never been back in the top flight since.

Back in 1955, Newcastle were still the team to fear in the FA Cup. Before reaching Wembley though, they had a nasty fright in the semi-final against Third Division York City, only the third side from that division after Millwall (1937) and Port Vale (1954) to make it to the last four. Newcastle beat them after a replay.

Another tie earlier in the competition that year looked as if it was going to last all the way until Cup Final day itself. The third round tie between Stoke and Bury lasted for a record playing time for the competition proper of 9 hours 22 minutes, over five matches, one of which was abandoned. Stoke finally won through after a 3–2 extra time win in the fourth replay at Old Trafford – and were promptly beaten by Swansea in the fourth round five days later.

Jackie Milburn said before the eve of the 1955 final against Manchester City, 'It seems like playing a tie at home.' And he obviously felt comfortable there – within 45 seconds of the kick-off he headed the fastest ever Wembley Cup Final goal, and Newcastle, making their third appearance at Wembley in four seasons, were on their way again.

But it was City, despite the early loss of Jimmy Meadows and inspired by their Footballer of the Year Don Revie, who played the better football and deservedly equalised through Bobby Johnstone just before half-time. Then two goals in six minutes from Bobby Mitchell and George Hannah gave United the Cup. It was their sixth win, to equal the record of Aston Villa and Blackburn, and their 10th final – more than any other club.

At the end City's captain Roy Paul vowed that his side would return the following year and win the trophy – and they did. This time the Revie-plan, borrowed from the Hungarians and involving the use of Revie as a deep-lying centre-forward, worked to perfection and Birmingham City were outplayed and outfought by three goals to one. Bert Trautmann, once a German Prisoner-of-War but now Manchester City's fearless goalkeeper, unknowingly played out the last 20 minutes of the match with a broken neck.

Chasing the Double
1957–72

Manchester City's successive appearances were now to be matched by two in a row from their rivals Manchester United, the 'Busby Babes', in circumstances unparalleled in the history of the game.

In 1957 Aston Villa won the Cup for a record seventh time with a 2–1 win over United, who started the final as League Champions looking for the first Double since Villa in 1897. But the match was marred by a controversy over the sixth-minute injury to United goalkeeper Ray Wood, who was barged so heavily by Villa's outside-left Peter McParland that he broke his jaw and had to go off. He came back later as a passenger on the wing.

Centre-half Jackie Blanchflower took over in goal and Duncan Edwards replaced Blanchflower in the middle of the defence. And for more than an hour United did well to hold Villa, especially Blanchflower, who pulled off some important saves. But two goals from McParland midway through the second-half finally settled the match, Tommy Taylor's late goal for United not being enough.

Although United had lost the final and the Double, the feeling was that this young, exciting team, champions in both 1956 and 1957, had time on its side and could win more honours in the years ahead. They had reached the semi-finals of the European Cup a few months previously and although they had lost to Real Madrid, manager Matt Busby was confident he was on the verge of producing the greatest British club side of all time. 'The only difference between us and Real Madrid was in their experience, and we shall soon acquire that,' he said.

But nine months later, on February 6, 1958, the plane bringing United back from a European Cup match in Belgrade crashed on take-off after a refuelling stop at Munich and six of the side that faced Villa were dead: the captain Roger Byrne, Eddie Colman, Duncan Edwards, Bill Whelan, Tommy Taylor and David Pegg. Centre-half Mark Jones and left-back Geoff Bent also died.

Jackie Blanchflower and Johnny Berry never played again, and goalkeeper Ray Wood's career was effectively over. Bobby Charlton and Bill Foulkes both survived the crash and were in the side that reached the final again, on a wave of unprecedented public emotion, just months after the crash.

United's first match after the disaster was on February 19, 1958 when they beat Sheffield Wednesday 3–0 in a fifth round tie before 60,000 emotional souls at Old Trafford. United reached Wembley with further wins over West Brom and Second Division Fulham who they beat 5–3 in the semi-final after a 2–2 draw.

They played in that final with Stan Crowther, hurriedly signed from Aston Villa, and Ernie Taylor, a Cup winner with Newcastle in 1951 and Blackpool in 1953, who were given permission to play for United by the FA even though they were cup-tied. Crowther in fact had played against United in the 1957 final.

But Bolton were the better team on the day and two goals from Nat Lofthouse finally brought the curtain down on United's dreams. Bolton's 2–0 win at Wembley was their fourth and so far last victory. They had used only 17 players winning their three finals in the 1920s. Manchester United had used 20 players in successive finals. They would have to wait a few more years for their next Cup success.

By the late 1950s and early 1960s football was undergoing one of its periodic moultings, shedding one skin and growing another. Equipment was changing, balls and boots were being made of lighter materials;

shorts were getting shorter; the maximum wage was abolished, balls had stopped bursting like party balloons and Johnny Haynes started earning £100 a week.

There had always been great characters in the game, but now they seemed to be more famous, advertising products like breakfast cereals and turning up on TV. Footballers were beginning to receive the kind of adulation until now reserved for film stars.

There were great teams to watch too – Wolves won the League in 1958 and 1959 scoring more than 100 goals each time. The race for the title in 1960 was the closest for years with Burnley pipping Wolves to the title by a point and so depriving them of the Double as well. Wolves beat Blackburn Rovers, reduced to 10 men after Dave Whelan broke his leg, 3–0 in one of the poorest ever Cup Finals five days later.

The 1961 Final between Tottenham Hotspur and Leicester City wasn't a great match either, but it made soccer history because by winning it 2–0, Spurs became the first team this century to win both League and Cup in the same year.

Tottenham Hotspur's famous Double-winning side of 1961, pictured with the two trophies. They retained the FA Cup the following year (Popperfoto)

Spurs created record after record that season, which they opened with 11 straight wins. They were not beaten until their 17th match and won 31 out of their 42 League games. They won a record number of 16 away matches and lost only seven games – two of those in the last three matches with the championship already sewn up and the Cup Final approaching.

In goal for Leicester that afternoon of May 6, 1961 was a young man named Gordon Banks. He was to have his moments of glory at Wembley but he was powerless to stop goals from Bobby Smith and Terry Dyson, midway through the second half, winning the match for Spurs.

And so at the end of 90 minutes Danny Blanchflower climbed the 39 steps to the Royal Box and took the Cup from the Duchess of Kent. He had already had one memorable little chat with her before the match started.

After she had been introduced to the Leicester players, the Duchess came across to meet the Spurs team. She then turned to Blanchflower and said to him, 'The other team have their names on their tracksuits.'

Blanchflower, quick as a flash replied, 'Yes, but we know each other.' It was quite a day for Blanchflower.

He ended it looking down Shirley Bassey's throat after she claimed she couldn't sing at Tottenham's Savoy Hotel reception because of tonsilitis.

Spurs came back the next year to emulate Newcastle's feat of a decade earlier by winning the Cup in successive seasons. The final against Burnley was an altogether different affair from the match against Leicester. Spurs had beaten Burnley in the semi-finals on the way to Wembley in 1961, and in 1962 the two teams had been locked in a battle for the title with Alf Ramsey's Ipswich who eventually beat them both.

Now the old rivals were facing each other in the final. The Tottenham team showed two changes from the Double-winning side, Les Allen and Terry Dyson making way for Terry Medwin and Jimmy Greaves, who had joined Tottenham the previous December in a £99,999 move back to England from AC Milan. Greaves had already scored 21 goals in 22 League games for Tottenham and another eight goals in six Cup matches. Within three minutes of the start he had made it nine in seven.

Burnley were a fine side, captained by Jimmy Adamson and with the cultured Irish genius Jimmy McIlroy – being watched by the Sampdoria manager – always capable of creating a chance out of nothing. But the game was won and lost five minutes after half-time when Jimmy Robson equalised for Burnley with the 100th Cup Final goal at Wembley and Bobby Smith made it 2–1 for Tottenham a minute later with the 101st. Ten minutes from time Blanchflower sent Adam Blacklaw the wrong way from the penalty spot and soon after that made his familiar walk up the steps to receive the Cup from the Queen.

Remarkably, for the third time in three seasons the two sides faced each other in the Cup. But now in the third round in 1963 it was Burnley's turn, and on a snowbound White Hart Lane pitch in January they became the first team to beat Spurs in the Cup for three years, winning 3–0.

That match was played on a Wednesday afternoon during the longest round in the history of the competition. The 'big freeze' winter of 1963 virtually brought football to a standstill for two months. The third round took from January 5 until March 11 – 66 days – to complete and included 261 postponements. For the only time the Cup Final, originally due to be played on May 4, was moved back until May 25.

After all the postponements and disruptions two teams did finally emerge from the Wembley tunnel – one team in form and one a 'ragged rabble', as one newspaper described them. The form team were Leicester City, fourth-placed finishers in Division One. The rabble were Manchester United, who had narrowly avoided relegation to Division Two.

But it was United who won the first final played under the new roof built as part of the refurbishment of the stadium for the 1966 World Cup Finals. They did so largely because Denis Law had the type of game that earned him the nickname 'The King'. He opened the scoring after half-an-hour and then terrorised a Leicester defence in which Gordon Banks had a rare off-day.

David Herd, whose father Alec had played with the United manager Matt Busby for Manchester City in the finals of 1933 and 1934, scored twice to give United their first honour of the 1960s, a decade that would

climax for them on this same Wembley pitch five years later with a win over Benfica in the European Cup Final. Bobby Charlton and Bill Foulkes, the only men who played in both the 1957 and 1958 finals, gained Cup winner's medals against Leicester. It was the start of a golden era for Busby's latest team.

In the 68 competitions played from the end of the 'Old Boy' era in 1882 until 1960, London clubs won the Cup just six times, Arsenal winning it three times, Spurs twice and Charlton once. Compare that with 24 Lancashire victories, 19 from the Midlands, 10 from Yorkshire, seven from the North East and one each from Wales and Hampshire.

But in the 33 finals since 1961, London clubs have been the most successful with 14 wins, followed by Lancashire with 13. Since 1961 the Cup has only been won by Midlands sides twice (West Brom in 1968, Coventry 1987) and once each by a club from Yorkshire (Leeds 1972), the North East (Sunderland 1973), Hampshire (Southampton 1976) and East Anglia (Ipswich 1978). For four seasons from 1979 to 1982 the Cup never moved out of the capital with two wins for Spurs and one each for Arsenal and West Ham.

If the trend started with Tottenham in the early 1960s, it was maintained by West Ham beating Preston 3–2 in 1964. Tottenham won again when they beat Chelsea 2–1 in the first all-London final at Wembley in 1967. Chelsea maintained the capital's momentum with their first Cup victory over Leeds in 1970.

The West Ham win in 1964 was the start of a remarkable Wembley hat-trick for the Hammers skipper Bobby Moore, who in 1964 lifted the FA Cup, in 1965 the European Cup-Winners Cup and in 1966 the World Cup itself with England.

But it was a little Cornishman playing for a team

Ian St John (second from right) celebrates his extra-time winning goal in the 1965 final against Leeds United (Popperfoto)

from Lancashire who was responsible for the most thrilling victory of that decade, Everton's 3–2 win over Sheffield Wednesday in 1966. It was the first time since Blackpool in 1953 that a team had come from two goals down to win the Cup. No-one has done it since.

Before looking to Everton's win it is worth turning the clock back a year to 1965 and Liverpool's first FA Cup final victory.

This was the start of Liverpool's 25-year reign as the kings of English, and ultimately, if briefly, European soccer. Bill Shankly, who went to Anfield in 1959, rebuilt a Liverpool side that had sunk into the Second Division in 1954. By the time it re-emerged in 1962 it was nearly ready to take on the world.

In 1964 Liverpool won the title for the first time since 1947 and the following year they were preparing to face Inter Milan in the semi-finals of the European Cup when they came to Wembley to meet Leeds United, under Don Revie, in the FA Cup Final. They did not get past Inter but Ian St John headed the extra-time goal that gave them a 2–1 win over Leeds for their first Cup success. A new chant was now boomed by Kopites around Wembley: 'Ee-ay-adio, we've won the Cup.'

In 1966 it was Everton's turn, and it had been a very long wait. Everton had won the League in 1963, Liverpool matched them in 1964. Liverpool had won the Cup in 1965, and had already clinched the Championship in 1966 by the time Everton faced Sheffield Wednesday at Wembley which was soon to host the World Cup Finals.

No Yorkshire side had won the Cup since Wednesday in 1935. Everton hadn't won it since 1933 and after 57 minutes it looked as though Wednesday had done enough to settle the argument. Goals from Jim McCalliog after only four minutes and David Ford (57) left Everton trailing 2–0.

But suddenly Everton hit back. Before the match, their manager Harry Catterick had caused a major surprise when he dropped centre-forward Fred Pickering, a crowd favourite, and played instead a young reserve called Mike Trebilcock, signed from Plymouth on New Year's Eve 1965.

Trebilcock, whose name and profile were not even in the Cup Final programme, had only played in seven League matches for Everton and one cup match, the semi-final against Manchester United, but Catterick thought he would do a better job than Pickering. Later he explained, 'Fred was popular and could score goals, but he'd been injured and had gone off the boil a bit. Trebilcock was a first rate goal-poacher. I always felt his sharpness would show.'

So it did. For almost an hour Everton had been second best with the Wednesday defence totally in control. But a minute after Wednesday's second, their armour was breached when Trebilcock drove past Ron Springett who had just blocked a Derek Temple header. One of the greatest ever Cup fightbacks had begun. Five minutes later it was 2–2. Sam Ellis, the Wednesday centre-half, weakly headed an Alex Scott free-kick and Trebilcock lashed the ball into the net.

Ten minutes from time came another of those Cup Final goals that defy belief. A long punt upfield should have been easily trapped by the Wednesday left-half Gerry Young, standing near the halfway line. But the ball rolled under his foot and Temple was onto it in an instant. Springett advanced, it was one-against-one, Temple shot and the ball flashed into the corner of the net. Everton had won 3–2.

From 1964 when West Ham beat Preston, ten successive finals were won by just one-goal margins. Following Liverpool's win in 1965, Everton's in 1966 and Spurs' in 1967, West Bromwich Albion maintained the sequence with a 1–0 extra-time win over Everton in 1968. Manchester City, champions the previous year, sent Leicester to their fourth FA Cup defeat at Wembley with a solitary Neil Young goal. It was all gloom for Leicester that year. They were relegated to the Second Division as well.

It was an odd coincidence that two of England's greatest ever goalkeepers, Gordon Banks (1961 and 1963) and Peter Shilton (1969), both played in losing Cup Finals for Leicester in the sixties. Shilton is the youngest goalkeeper ever to play in a Wembley Cup Final, but despite a career that brought him a world record number of 125 England caps and almost every other honour in the game, that was his one and only FA Cup Final.

The sequence of single-goal margins continued well into the seventies. In 1970 Chelsea beat Leeds 2–1 in a replay at Old Trafford after Wembley's first drawn final; in 1971 Arsenal beat Liverpool 2–1 to win the Double; in the Centenary final of 1972 Leeds beat Arsenal 1–0 and then the following year they lost 1–0 to Sunderland who became the first Second Division winners since West Brom in 1931. The sequence ended in 1974 when Liverpool beat Newcastle 3–0.

There was another coincidental thread running through the finals at this time, besides the obvious involvement of Leeds United, a club which had never even played in the final until 1965. It was more a question of wise heads on still-sprightly shoulders.

In 1969 Manchester City's win was masterminded by manager Joe Mercer, a Cup winner with Arsenal in 1950. Don Revie, a winner as a player with Manchester City in 1956, became a winning manager with Leeds in 1972, while in 1973 Bob Stokoe joined their ranks. He was in the Newcastle team that won the Cup in 1955; now he set off on another run across the Wembley turf to embrace Jim Montgomery, his goalkeeper, whose brilliance had preserved Sunderland's hold on the Cup after Ian Porterfield's famous goal.

Oddly however, the man behind only the second Double of the century was never a professional player. Bertie Mee had become Arsenal's manager in the mid-sixties after serving as the team's physiotherapist. Together with his first lieutenant at Highbury Don Howe, Mee built a team that never knew when it was beaten.

That point was never better illustrated than in the semi-final against Stoke at Hillsborough on March 27, 1971. Arsenal were trailing 0–2 at half-time and Stoke seemed set for the first Cup Final in their 108-year history. But the Gunners fought back. With a minute to play they were still 2–1 down when Peter Storey beat Gordon Banks with a penalty. Arsenal destroyed Stoke in the replay. A year later they met Stoke again in the semi-final, and again beat them after a replay.

Arsenal knew all about chasing lost causes that spring. On March 20, with only eight League games to play, Leeds were six points clear in the Championship race. But Revie's team faltered on the run-in, Arsenal picked up 27 points from a maximum 30 in their last 15 matches and clinched the title at Tottenham, of all places, five days before the Cup Final. Suddenly the Double looked a possibility, but there could be hardly be a tougher obstacle to their doing it.

Liverpool had also reached Wembley the hard way, coming from a goal down against Everton in the semi-final at Old Trafford. This Liverpool team also gave little away; they had conceded just one goal on their way to the final and with Ray Clemence in goal, Tommy Smith in defence, youngsters like Larry Lloyd and Steve Heighway, and the experienced John Toshack and Ian Callaghan up front, they were a formidable force.

But Arsenal were just as uncompromising. Goals from Ray Kennedy, later to join Liverpool, John Radford and George Graham had carried Arsenal to the title, while their captain Frank McLintock, a Wembley loser with Leicester in the Cup Finals of 1961 and 1963, and with Arsenal in the League Cup Finals of 1968 and 1969, inspired his team to the heights.

It was goalless after 90 minutes, but Liverpool struck the opening goal in extra-time when Heighway beat Bob Wilson at the near post with a left-foot drive. Bill Shankly said before the match that if Liverpool scored first they would win – but he was wrong. Arsenal equalised 10 minutes later with an untidy goal at first credited to Graham but after TV replays given to Eddie Kelly, who became the first substitute to score in the final.

Charlie George, scorer of the winning goal in the 1971 final that gave Arsenal the Double, celebrates with skipper Frank McLintock and Ray Kennedy (Popperfoto)

Just when it appeared that for the second successive year the final would end in a draw, Charlie George gave the ghosts of Herbert Chapman, Alex James and David Jack something to cheer. He cracked home the winner past a despairing Ray Clemence from just inside the penalty area. The Double belonged to Highbury. George lay down on the Wembley turf, arms aloft, and soaked up the adulation.

Arsenal were back in 1972, the Centenary year of the FA Cup, with Geoff Barnett in goal for Bob Wilson and Alan Ball, signed from Everton for a then record fee of £200,000, taking Ray Kennedy's place. A poor start to the season had ultimately cost them their title and they finished fifth in the League, which was still unfinished by Cup Final day.

Leeds were in with a chance of matching Arsenal's Double achievement but their final First Division match was not until 48 hours after the Final, at Wolverhampton on the Monday night. Liverpool were also in contention for the title. Their final game was at Arsenal, also on the Monday. Derby, top of the table, had finished their fixtures and were already relaxing on holiday in Spain.

So the 1972 Final was played out against the intriguing possibility that Arsenal could emulate Newcastle and Tottenham by returning to Wembley to retain the trophy, or that Leeds United could clinch the first half of the Double.

In the event, a poor final was settled by a solitary goal from Allan Clarke, a loser with Leicester in 1969 and Leeds in 1970. Instead of emulating Newcastle and Spurs, Arsenal became the first team to return to Wembley as Cup holders and lose.

So Leeds had completed one half of the Double. Could they also join the immortals? Manager Don Revie banned all celebrations after the final and allowed them to drink only orange juice. They went to Wolverhampton needing just a draw for the title – and lost 2–1. On the same night Liverpool's 0–0 draw at Arsenal cost them their chance of the title – so Derby,

sunbathing in Spain, became League champions for the first time.

Leeds' best chance of winning the Double had gone and their disappointments, in the Cup at least, were to continue.

Underdogs on top   1973–80

The Leeds team that Don Revie built was the most powerful in the country in the late 1960s and early 1970s. From the time of their first Cup Final appearance in 1965 until Revie left to become the England manager in July 1974, they were always in contention for the major prizes, but too often finished second best.

Their second Cup Final appearance in 1970 ended in disappointment, just as their first had done five years earlier against Liverpool. Leeds met Chelsea on April 11, 1970, the earliest date for a Cup Final for 73 years to help world champions England prepare for their defence of the World Cup in Mexico where the tournament started on May 31. The fact that the final was not resolved until April 29 rather defeated the object, however.

The first game was played on a Wembley pitch that looked more like the Sahara as it was largely covered in sand. The Horse of the Year Show the previous year had badly damaged the turf. The match ended in a 2–2 draw with Jack Charlton and Peter Houseman scoring first-half goals to make it 1–1 and then Mick Jones of Leeds and Ian Hutchinson of Chelsea scoring in the last six minutes of normal time.

Jones put Leeds ahead in the replay at Old Trafford too, but on a night of high drama and tension Chelsea fought back to win, with a magnificent diving header from Peter Osgood – joining the select band of men to have scored in every round – and a late second from David Webb after one of Hutchinson's famous long throws, right into the jaws of the Leeds defence.

Leeds came back time and again – in the Cup, in Europe and in the League. In 1974 Revie took them to the Championship for the second time, and the year after he left they reached the European Cup Final but lost controversially to Bayern Munich in Paris. If losing to the Germans, then in the middle of their hat-trick of European Cup wins, was always a possibility and could not be classed as a major upset, the same could not be said of two famous Cup reverses Leeds suffered in the early seventies.

The first ranks as one of the biggest shocks in the Cup's history. It happened on February 13, 1971 and it was Colchester United 3, Leeds United 2. At the time Leeds were three points clear at the top of the First Division and Colchester in the middle of Division Four. Six of the Colchester team were over 30 including Ray Crawford, 34, a member of the Ipswich side that won the title in 1962 but now fast approaching retirement.

Crawford predicted before the match that he would score, and he did – twice – while Colchester's manager Dick Graham said that if his side won he would scale the walls of Colchester Castle afterwards. A few days later, he kept his word.

Colchester were given absolutely no hope against the likes of Norman Hunter, Jack Charlton, Johnny Giles, Allan Clarke et al. Billy Bremner was injured and missed the debacle, and could only watch in amazement as Colchester led 3–0 after 55 minutes with two goals from Crawford and the other from Dave Simmons. Leeds pulled two back in the last half-an-hour through Hunter and Giles, but Colchester held on for a memorable victory.

Leeds' second great Cup failure came on a far grander stage than Layer Road in Colchester. It happened at Wembley Stadium where they lost to Second Division Sunderland in the 1973 Cup Final. This result also ranks as one of the greatest Cup shocks of all time, and possibly the greatest Cup Final upset.

Leeds were appearing in the final for the third time in four years, had finished third in the First Division and no-one – save a few romantics on Wearside – gave Sunderland the faintest hope of winning. Earlier in the season they had been faced with relegation to the Third Division, but their season had changed around with the appointment of Bob Stokoe as manager. Their outstanding achievement on the way to the final was beating Arsenal in the semi-final at Hillsborough. The fans knew Stokoe had turned their club around. They refused to leave the ground after the final until he came back on the pitch and took their salute.

The Leeds team was full of international stars, Johnny Giles was playing in his fifth Wembley Cup Final, they were the Cup holders, and surely destined in Wembley's 50th anniversary year to match Newcastle and Tottenham by winning the Cup in successive seasons.

But they didn't. After 30 minutes they went 1–0 down to a goal scored by Ian Porterfield who killed a clearance on his left thigh and then swung to crack the ball into the roof of the net with his right foot. Leeds surged back but were denied time and time again by the Sunderland defence, at the heart of which the future England international Dave Watson towered majestically. None of the Sunderland team had a full cap.

With 20 minutes to go came the moment Leeds probably realised they would never win the match, the moment when Jim Montgomery made his 'double save', now more famous than many a Cup-winning goal.

Paul Reaney centred from the right, and Trevor Cherry dived to head the cross home. Montgomery made a diving save, but the ball flew out to Peter Lorimer, the man reputed to have the hardest shot in soccer. He blasted the ball for what seemed a certain goal, but Montgomery changed direction, twisted himself in mid-air, and diverted the ball onto the underside of the bar. It then bounced clear and Sunderland held on to win the Cup for the first time since 1937. No Second Division side had won the Cup for 42 years. When Sunderland next reached the Cup Final in 1992, again as a Second Division club, the save was replayed countless times on television. It looked just as incredible almost 20 years on.

Bobby Kerr, who at 5ft 4½ in was Sunderland's captain and the smallest man on the field, told a funny story after the game which proves that referees are probably human.

'Towards the end my nerves were shot to bits. The ball was pinging around our area and I was convinced we had another four or five minutes to hold on. As Ken Burns (the referee) ran by I asked him how long there was to go. He just gave me a big grin and said, "It's alright, Bobby, you've won it." Twenty seconds later he blew the whistle, and we had.'

The North-East was represented again the following year but Newcastle were unable to match Sunderland's success when they surrendered their record of never having lost at Wembley. This was Newcastle's 11th final, a record at the time but one since overtaken by Arsenal.

Leeds United skipper Billy Bremner (left) can only watch as Sunderland enjoy their big upset in the 1973 final (Popperfoto)

Opposing them were Liverpool – and Newcastle hardly got a look-in. Malcolm Macdonald came to Wembley looking to become only the 10th player to score in every round of the Cup, but he never had a shot on goal until 12 minutes from the end of a game that by then Newcastle were losing 2–0 after goals from Kevin Keegan and Steve Heighway. Keegan added another two minutes from time to give Liverpool the biggest Final win for 14 years.

Playing out on the turf that day was the third great side that Bill Shankly had created at Liverpool but it was to be the last that Shankly put together. A few weeks after the final he suddenly announced his retirement as manager. At the end of the final two fans got down on their hands and knees and kissed Shankly's feet. They had a lot to thank him for.

During the first 41 years at Wembley there had only ever been six Second Division teams in the Cup Final. That all changed in the 1970s and although the pace has slackened over the last decade, a side reaching the Final from outside the top flight is no longer the huge shock it used to be.

Sunderland were the first to prove that perhaps the gap between the top clubs and the rest was closing when they beat Leeds in 1973. In 1975 Second Division Fulham reached the final and lost to West Ham, but the following year Second Division Southampton emulated Sunderland's achievement by winning the Cup when they beat Manchester United, and in 1980 West Ham did the same when they beat Arsenal. Every one of those victories was by 1–0. Since then Queen's Park Rangers in 1982 and Sunderland in 1992 have both reached the final only to lose, but it is West Ham's Cup record that is inextricably linked with the Second Division.

In 1923 they reached the final as a Second Division team. In 1964, in their second final, they played Second Division Preston. In 1975 the Hammers won the Cup for a second time, beating Second Division Fulham, and in 1980, their third victory, they themselves were in the Second Division.

Fulham, perhaps, were the most surprising Cup Finalists of the last two decades and they needed 11 matches to get to Wembley, which included three against Hull in the third round, four against Nottingham Forest in the fourth round and two against Birmingham City in the semi-final. In fact Fulham reached the final without actually winning a game on their own pitch.

This was only the second all-London final at Wembley, and it contained some of the great characters of the capital's soccer scene. Billy Bonds, Frank Lampard and Trevor Brooking were in the West Ham side, while playing for Fulham were two men in the twilight of their careers: Bobby Moore, 34, who had led West Ham to their previous Cup Final victory in 1964, and Alan Mullery, 33, who had been in the Tottenham side which won the Cup in 1967.

Fulham were managed by a man who knew all about Cup romance, Alec Stock, the player-manager when Yeovil dumped mighty Sunderland out of the Cup in 1948. But there wasn't much romance about the 1975 Final, an uneventful match which ended 2–0 to West Ham. Both goals were scored by Alan Taylor, who had still been playing for Fourth Division Rochdale the previous Christmas.

It was the last final in which neither side used a substitute. Just one per team was allowed then, and the man wearing the No.12 shirt for West Ham, Bobby Gould, would have to wait another 13 years for his day in the sun. He was to manage Wimbledon to Cup glory in 1988.

The 1970s ended with some familiar names doing battle at Wembley – Liverpool, Arsenal and Manchester United – but two clubs who had never won the trophy before finally got their names inscribed on the silver plinth.

At the turn of the century Southampton were among the top Cup-fighters in the country, reaching the final as a Southern League team but losing in both 1900 and 1902. It had been a long wait for their next appearance. Lawrie McMenemy had built a side that really was – that old football cliché – the right blend of youth and experience.

Mick Channon, Peter Osgood, Peter Rodrigues and Jim McCalliog provided most of the experience, and three of them had played in the Cup Final before. Osgood scored Chelsea's winner in the replayed final of 1970, Rodrigues was in the Leicester side beaten by Manchester City in 1969, while McCalliog, a former Manchester United player, had scored for Sheffield Wednesday when they lost in 1966 to Everton.

Tommy Docherty, the manager of the Chelsea team beaten by Tottenham in 1967, was in the process of building a fine, attacking side at Old Trafford with Gordon Hill and Steve Coppell playing like old-fashioned wingers. The side was an inexperienced one with an average age of only 24, but they were still odds-on favourites to dispense with the South Coast underdogs. But as so often, the giant was slain. A goal seven minutes from time from Bobby Stokes settled the match. United, who had chased Cup and League honours all season, were left empty-handed. For now.

Docherty's side were back a year later featuring eight of the team that faced Southampton, nine if substitute David McCreery is included. And while they had been odds-on favourites to beat Southampton in 1976, this time Liverpool were not only expected to beat them, but also clinch a unique Treble of League, FA Cup and European Cup.

This was one of the great finals and it was decided in a five-minute spell just after half-time. Stuart Pearson scored for United, Jimmy Case equalised with a tremendous shot from the edge of the box two minutes later, and while the Liverpool fans were still celebrating, United went back in front with an untidy goal, a shot from Lou Macari which took a widely arcing deflection off Jimmy Greenhoff to plant itself in the back of Ray Clemence's net.

Liverpool, the champions, were going to have to wait for the League and Cup Double, and when Martin Buchan went up to collect the Cup he also wrote his name into the record books as the first player to captain Scottish and English FA Cup winning teams. He had previously skippered Aberdeen when they won the Scottish Cup in 1970.

This was United's day – and more poignantly, Tommy Docherty's day. He had lost as a player with Preston in 1954 and as a manager with Chelsea in 1967 and United in 1976. Now, in his eighth Wembley match including internationals for Scotland, he was a winner for the first time.

Early the following morning The Doc went for a jog in Hyde Park and apparently, just by Speakers' Corner, it hit him. He had finally won the Cup, and started to do cartwheels in celebration. It was his final hurrah as United's manager. On July 3, just six weeks later, Docherty was sacked for 'a breach of contract'. He had been having an affair with the wife of the club's physio. 'I must be the first football manager to be sacked for falling in love,' mused Docherty afterwards.

Liverpool may have been devastated by that Cup Final defeat, but they rallied. Four days after losing to United at Wembley the club had one of its greatest nights, beating Borussia Mönchengladbach 3–1 in Rome to become only the second English side to become the Champions of Europe. The other one? Manchester United of course.

A young man in a blue-and-white striped shirt, who would create history for Manchester United in the 1980s and 90s, helped knock United out of the Cup the following season. Bryan Robson was then playing for West Bromwich Albion and was in the side that beat United 3–2 in a replayed fourth round match. West Brom reached the semi-final for a then record 18th time but went down 3–1 to Ipswich at Highbury.

Ipswich had never been in the final before. Only once had they ever reached the semi-final, but managed by the future England boss Bobby Robson and inspired by a brilliant display from Clive Woods, Ipswich 'murdered' Arsenal 1–0 with the winning goal scored by Roger Osborne 13 minutes from time. He was so overcome by 'sunstroke and emotion' after scoring, he had to go off. Ipswich hit the woodwork three times and were denied further goals by a superb display in goal from Pat Jennings.

It was another dreadful disappointment for Malcolm Macdonald, now with Arsenal, a loser in 1974 who had also been in the Newcastle team beaten by Manchester City in the 1976 League Cup Final. But there was a defiant – and accurate – message from Arsenal's manager Terry Neill at the end of the game.

'We are a young team, we've got a bright future and we will be back,' said Neill afterwards and he was right. Arsenal in fact became the first club to play in three successive Wembley finals. They came back in 1979 to beat Manchester United 3–2 and returned again in 1980 when they went down to a Trevor Brooking goal in a 1–0 defeat by West Ham.

One man in their 1979 side was making history of his own. Brian Talbot played for the winning Ipswich team against Arsenal in 1978 and then played for the winning Arsenal team in 1979 to become the first man this century to play for different winning teams in successive years.

He was also involved in one of the game's mysteries – the identity of Arsenal's first goalscorer; but he, rather than Alan Sunderland, was ultimately credited with the shot that put Arsenal 1–0 ahead. Although this was another of Wembley's great, emotional occasions, most of the emotion was contained in the last five minutes when three of the goals were scored. The match itself was rather ordinary until then.

Frank Stapleton, later to win winner's medals with United, had doubled Arsenal's lead just before half-time and with only five minutes to play neither side had added to the scoreline. Arsenal looked safe. Terry Neill – who always denied this was a mistake – now took off David Price and brought on the youngster Steve Walford.

Arsenal, as their defenders had done back in 1932, collectively seemed to relax, believing their task was over and that Neill had sent Walford on for a sentimental run-out with the game safely won. At that moment their concentration went. Joe Jordan turned Steve Coppell's free-kick back into the middle and Gordon McQueen scored for United.

Two minutes later United, unbelievably, were level. Sammy McIlroy took a pass from Coppell, shimmied past David O'Leary and Walford, and squeezed home the equaliser. It was 2–2. The Arsenal players looked at each other in utter despair and bewilderment. Wembley was a sea of Manchester United red and white. Surely United had saved themselves and forced extra-time.

There was less than a minute to play when Arsenal scored the winner straight from the kick-off. The goal was made by Liam Brady who gave a magnificent midfield performance and said later, 'I was so tired I dreaded the thought of extra-time so I tried to take the ball into their half.' He succeeded, pushing the ball through to Graham Rix whose cross was slid home by Sunderland.

It was an astonishing finale, and McIlroy summed up the awful feeling for the United players and supporters. 'It was like picking eight draws and then finding the pools coupon still in your pocket,' he said.

The following day was the hottest of the year in London as Arsenal paraded the Cup through Islington in front of around 200,000 people. That evening when Terry Neill brought home football's most famous trophy, his young daughters said to him, 'What's that grubby old thing?' Soon afterwards they were giving the FA Cup a good wash – in their neighbour's swimming pool.

Civic receptions for London Cup winners now became something of a habit. West Ham had theirs the following year when they beat Arsenal with a Trevor

Alan Sunderland (left) can hardly believe it as his 89th-minute winner has just capped the most incredible finish there has ever been to an FA Cup final (Allsport/Tony Duffy)

Brooking header at Wembley – only about the third goal Brooking remembered ever getting with his head.

But Arsenal were just about physically and mentally exhausted by the time that final was played on May 10.

Between April 12 and May 1 they had met Liverpool four times in what seemed to be a never-ending semi-final series. After drawing 0–0 at Hillsborough and 1–1 twice after extra-time at Villa Park, Arsenal at last made it through to the final with a 1–0 win in the third replay at Coventry thanks to a Brian Talbot goal. At the same time they were advancing in the European Cup-Winners Cup and were due to face Valencia in Brussels four days after the final.

A few weeks before the 1980 Cup Final Brian Clough wrote in an article that 'Trevor Brooking floats like a butterfly – and stings like one....' but it was Brooking who delivered the knockout blow to Arsenal, heading home in the 13th minute. Paul Allen, at 17 years 256 days, became the youngest player to have played in a Wembley final and the youngest Cup finalist for 101 years. He cried tears of joy at the end.

But unlike Liverpool who three years before had lost in the Cup Final and then gone on to win a prize in Europe, Arsenal were a spent force. Their long season had taken its toll and Valencia beat them on penalties to win the Cup-Winners Cup four days later.

Arsenal rewrote the record books with their five finals between 1971 and 1980. Only the Wanderers in the 1870s and Newcastle United between 1905 and 1911 had ever appeared in so many finals in a shorter time-span. Pat Rice became the first and so far only man to play in five Wembley finals for the same team and Arsenal equalled Newcastle's record of 11 final appearances.

For the next two years the other side of north London were going to be doing the crowing.

Replay on Thursday   1981–83

In 1978, just after the World Cup Finals in Argentina, Tottenham pulled off one of the most audacious transfer coups in British soccer history when they signed the Argentinians Osvaldo Ardiles and Ricardo Villa from Huracan and Racing Club respectively. Ardiles had played in the World Cup winning team, while Villa had made a couple of appearances as substitute as Argentina fought their way to the final.

On the day he signed for Tottenham, Ardiles said, 'My big ambition is to play for Totting-ham (*as he always pronounced it*) in the Cup Final at Wembley.' Three years later Ossie's dream came true.

Tottenham in fact played at Wembley seven times in 15 months between May 1981 and August 1982, but it was their performance in the replayed Centenary Final against Manchester City that lives brightest in the memory.

All the omens pointed to a Spurs victory. The year ended in a '1', and it was the Chinese Year of the Cockerel. It had been 14 years since their last Cup Final appearance, and apart from a difficult semi-final against their old Cup rivals Wolves which they won after a replay at Highbury – Villa scoring with a stunning 25-yard shot in their 3–0 win – their path to Wembley was a relatively smooth one.

Their new strike force of Steve Archibald and Garth Crooks had scored 46 goals between them going into the final and, inspired by Ardiles and Glenn Hoddle in midfield and with the driving force of skipper Steve Perryman behind them, Tottenham, managed by the dour Yorkshireman Keith Burkinshaw, could match any team in the country on their day.

But Manchester City would be no pushovers. They had also powered their way into the final with wins over Crystal Palace (4–0), Norwich (6–0) and Peterborough (1–0) setting them on their course. They took Everton apart in a sixth round replay in front of 52,000 at Maine Road and then reached Wembley by beating Ipswich 1–0 in the semi-finals.

While Burkinshaw had been building his team at Tottenham for almost three years, Manchester City had been transformed in half a season. The previous October, City chairman Peter Swales sacked manager Malcolm Allison and coach Tony Book – City's captain the last time they won the Cup in 1969 – and four days later the Norwich manager John Bond moved to Maine Road. In his first match in charge City lost 1–0 at home to Birmingham and were bottom of the table without a win in 12 matches.

Curiously their revival started in their next match, a 3–1 win over Spurs. City were revitalised as Bond strengthened his side by signing Bobby McDonald and Tommy Hutchison from Coventry and the tenacious Gerry Gow from Bristol City. By the time of the Cup Final all thoughts of relegation had disappeared. Now they were thinking of Europe.

The first match on a grey, overcast day was something of an anti-climax for both teams and supporters, and ended in Wembley's first drawn final for 11 years. Tommy Hutchison scored with a header for City in the first half and then late in the game he deflected a Glenn Hoddle free-kick past Joe Corrigan for Spurs' equaliser. Not since Bert Turner in 1946 had the same player scored for both sides in the final. There was no breakthrough in extra-time and so the teams would meet again in the first replay at Wembley the following Thursday.

One feature of that first match had been the substitution of Villa after 68 minutes and his long, mournful walk back to the dressing-room, reminiscent of another long, slow walk taken by the Argentinian captain Antonio Rattin, sent off at Wembley playing against England in the 1966 World Cup quarter-final. Rattin never got another chance at Wembley but Villa did and how he took it.

The replay was only seven minutes old when Villa lashed in the opening goal to put Tottenham 1–0 up. Three minutes later City were level with a superb shot by Steve Mackenzie giving Tottenham's goalkeeper Milija Aleksic no chance. Today it is largely forgotten and rarely shown on television. But it was a goal good enough to win any match.

Five minutes after half-time, City took the lead for the second time over the two games when Dave Bennett was sandwiched between two Tottenham defenders and referee Keith Hackett awarded a penalty. No penalty had ever been missed in a Wembley final and Kevin Reeves ensured he was not going to be the first to do so, placing his kick wide of Aleksic.

It was now that Tottenham began to play their best football of the final and with 20 minutes left they drew level. Hoddle lofted a pass that caught the City players coming out with Archibald onside and moving in on goal. He couldn't control it properly but the ball ran to Crooks, who equalised.

With 76 minutes played Ricky Villa not only played himself into Tottenham folklore but guaranteed himself a place in the history of England's greatest competition. It was the kind of goal that would look dazzling scored in a Sunday League parks match – but to decide the 100th Cup Final, under the floodlights in the first ever Wembley replay, it was as magical a moment as any in the history of the FA Cup.

The goal was begun by Tony Galvin who took a long ball out of the Spurs defence and with a 20-yard pass found Villa, 35 yards out from goal. The route to goal was well policed by City defenders but Villa was not to be deterred. Inside him, Hoddle, and then Archibald, were screaming for the ball. But the tall, bearded Argentinian ignored them.

He closed in on the penalty area, with Garth Crooks stepping back out of his way. Then he quickened his pace, going past Tommy Caton and then swerving past Ray Ranson. He cut back inside and beat the covering Caton again, then went past Ranson. With Nicky Reid chasing back to cover and Corrigan and Caton converging on him, Villa still had control of the ball. At the precise moment that Corrigan spread himself to smother the ball, Villa shot, the ball went through his legs and into the net.

Villa, who had just run 35 yards with the ball, now ran 60 yards without it, sprinting across to the Spurs bench in ecstasy. City were a beaten team and Spurs were Cup winners for the sixth time in their sixth appearance, a new unbeaten record.

In 1951 and 1952 Newcastle won the Cup, in 1961 and 1962 Spurs won the Cup, and in 1982 Spurs again retained the Cup. Their opponents this time were Second Division Queen's Park Rangers managed by Terry Venables, who had played for Spurs when they won the Cup in 1967 and who would manage Spurs to victory in 1991. But Tottenham took the field without the two Argentinians who had done so much to inspire the victory 12 months previously.

Tottenham had already played in one final at Wembley that season when they were beaten 3–1 in the League Cup by Liverpool, and in fact for most of the season they were chasing four trophies – the League Championship, the FA Cup, the European Cup-Winners Cup and the League Cup.

But by the time they reached the Cup Final on May 22, it was the only trophy they still had a chance of capturing. A combination of the Falklands War and Argentina's preparations for the 1982 World Cup Finals meant that neither Ardiles nor Villa played in the final. Ray Clemence, who had joined Spurs from Liverpool the previous summer, was now in goal and Spurs started as the hot favourites.

After a goalless 90 minutes the game went into extra-time. Hoddle broke the deadlock with only 10 minutes remaining but Terry Fenwick, later to become a Spurs player himself, headed the equaliser. A Hoddle penalty after only six minutes of the replay finally settled the 1982 final. Like the five Wembley penalty takers before him, Hoddle safely converted his spot-

Ricky Villa (centre) has just opened the scoring in the 1981 Cup final replay. He went on to score a brilliant winner as Spurs beat Manchester City 3–2 (Allsport)

kick, but the match never reached the heights attained in the 1981 replay.

The 1982 final also saw the start of an unhappy little sequence which the FA later changed their rules to try and prevent. Three times in three years the captain of one of the finalists was suspended from the match. In 1982 the QPR captain Glenn Roeder played in the first match, but was suspended from the replay. In 1983 Steve Foster, the Brighton captain, was ruled out of the final but played in the replay, while in 1984 Watford's skipper Wilf Rostron missed his team's match against Everton. In each case the team with the suspended skipper failed to win the Cup.

After Spurs had won the Cup in 1961 and 1962, Manchester United followed them as winners in 1963. Now history was to repeat itself. Spurs' reign as Cup-holders ended in a fifth round match at Everton who in turn lost to Manchester United, and it was United who went all the way to victory in 1983.

United had three survivors from the team that lost to Arsenal in 1979 – goalkeeper Gary Bailey and defenders Gordon McQueen and Arthur Albiston. They also now had Frank Stapleton, who played against them in 1979, leading their attack. With the England captain Bryan Robson, his international team-mate Ray Wilkins and the Irish international teenager Norman Whiteside in their ranks, they were far too strong in the end for Brighton and Hove Albion who ended the season relegated to the Second Division.

United had only conceded one goal on the way to Wembley, against Arsenal in a 2–1 semi-final win at Villa Park, but Brighton had proved they could raise their game when it mattered. They beat Liverpool 2–1 at Anfield in the fifth round, the winning goal coming from Jimmy Case, for so long a Liverpool player.

Brighton flew high on the way to Wembley in another, more unorthodox way too. At the time their main sponsor was the airline company British Caledonian and they flew from Brighton to Wembley and back by helicopter.

Manchester United were well and truly brought down to earth after only 14 minutes when Gordon Smith headed the South Coast club ahead. The Brighton fans had a penchant for sporting huge outsize foam hands and thousands of these were raised in triumph as Wembley braced itself for yet another upset. But United, who had lost in the League Cup Final to Liverpool two months previously, rallied and started to control the match. They deservedly equalised after 55 minutes through Frank Stapleton and went ahead with a wonderful curling shot from Ray Wilkins 18 minutes from time.

With only three minutes to go, and Brighton seemingly beaten, Gary Stevens saved them when he made it 2–2 and forced extra-time. But the greatest drama was still to come. There were only seconds of the 120 minutes left to play when Brighton got one last golden opportunity to win the match. Mick Robinson forced his way through the defence and set up what looked like an easy chance for Smith. Surely he was going to score the winner.

The radio commentator thought so too – '. . . and Smith must score . . .' he said – but Smith didn't. Gary Bailey saved his shot with his legs and Manchester United were reprieved. Smith played in six cup finals for Glasgow Rangers and in 1978 scored the winner

against Celtic in the last minute of extra-time in the Scottish League Cup Final. But south of the border, and especially on the South Coast, it's that miss that has made him famous. Naturally, there's a Brighton fanzine called 'And Smith Must Score'.

Smith recalls: 'I remember going off at half-time and seeing my name on the scoreboard with the score at 1–0 and thinking to myself that if we were going to win it, it would have to stay like that. The underdogs only ever won 1–0 in the final. That would have been great. People said to me later, "If only you had done the business at the end," but these things happen. For me the main thing was to have taken part. It was the highlight of my career, despite playing in six cup finals for Rangers in Scotland.'

So for the third successive year, the Cup Final went to a replay. Brighton had their skipper Steve Foster back after suspension but they were never really in the game. Two goals from Bryan Robson and another before the break from Norman Whiteside gave United the biggest half-time lead in a Cup Final since 1900. A second-half penalty – the third in three years – was converted by the Dutchman Arnold Muhren to give United the biggest ever Cup Final win at Wembley, 4–0. Whiteside became the youngest player to score in a Wembley final and for one sprightly old man there was good cause to celebrate. United had won the Cup for the fifth time on Sir Matt Busby's 74th birthday.

Merseyside at Wembley 1984–89

If Sir Matt was the man who built United, then future England manager Graham Taylor was the man who put Watford on the footballing map – with more than a little help from his rock star chairman Elton John.

Elton, who was born Reginald Dwight in 1947 just a stone's throw from Wembley in Pinner, was not the first member of his family to be connected with the Cup Final. In 1959 his uncle Roy Dwight was a member of the Nottingham Forest team which beat Luton 2–1 to win the Cup.

Young Reg from Pinner grew up a Watford fan, but it wasn't until the mid-1970s when he was already established as one of the world's great rock stars that he began to get involved with his favourite club, now well-established as Fourth Division also-rans.

Elton's masterstroke was persuading Graham Taylor to come to Vicarage Road as manager, and between them they helped transform not only the team but the club as well. With the experience of Bertie Mee, the man who led Arsenal to the Double in 1971, Watford made rapid progress and in 1983 they finished second behind Liverpool in the title race. Now they were in their first ever Cup Final. Their previous best in the Cup was a semi-final appearance against Chelsea in 1970 which they lost 5–1.

In the 1984 semi, Watford themselves were the hot favourites against Third Division Plymouth Argyle. They duly won that game 1–0 at Villa Park to face a side which had also undergone something of a transformation.

For Everton, the season had started poorly, but once they signed the Scottish international striker

Andy Gray from Wolves in November for £250,000, things began to happen at Goodison Park. 'That was the turning point of our season,' remembered Everton manager Howard Kendall. 'He set the whole place bubbling and gave the team's confidence a boost.'

Like Tottenham in 1982 and Manchester United in 1983, Everton also reached the League Cup Final, and like Spurs and United, they lost to Liverpool. Everton, though, had gone down only after a replay at Maine Road. Now they were to go one better and win the FA Cup for the first time since 1966. Goals from Graeme Sharp and Andy Gray gave Everton a deserved 2–0 victory. Elton, who had cried tears of emotion at the start of the afternoon, was left in tears at the end too – but he would be back, and so would Everton. Elton returned for a concert at the stadium on June 30, while Everton came back to play in the Cup Finals of 1985 and 1986 but lost both times.

Everton came to Wembley the following year as League Champions, looking for the first Double since 1971 and also in the hunt for the never-achieved Treble of English Cup and League and European trophy in the same season. In 1977 Liverpool won the League and the European Cup, but were beaten in the Cup Final by Manchester United, thus dashing their hopes of the Treble. Now United were to do the same to Everton.

Howard Kendall's side had stormed to their first Championship for 15 years, finishing 13 points clear of the field. Three days before the Cup Final they won the European Cup-Winners Cup Final beating Rapid Vienna 3–1 in Rotterdam. For good measure they had played Manchester United three times already that season without losing and had beaten them 5–0 in the League the previous October.

This Everton side, with Peter Reid and Paul Bracewell running the midfield, simply never knew when they were beaten. With five minutes left in their semi-final against Luton at Villa Park, they were trailing 1–0. Then Kevin Sheedy drove in a free-kick to equalise and Derek Mountfield scored the winner in extra-time.

United had had a relatively easy passage to the semi-finals with wins over Bournemouth, Coventry, Blackburn and West Ham. But then came two titanic struggles with Liverpool, first a 2–2 draw at Goodison Park and then a replay at Maine Road. There, second-half goals from Bryan Robson and Mark Hughes gave United a 2–1 win to spoil the possibility of the first all-Merseyside final – for a year at least.

So the two Lancashire giants converged on Wembley for what everyone hoped would be a classic between two of the finest teams in the country. And everyone needed a lift. The previous week the Bradford fire disaster had claimed more than 50 lives.

The match itself turned out to be a dour affair which only came to life with the dismissal of Manchester United defender Kevin Moran. After 78 minutes referee Peter Willis of County Durham, a retired police inspector, sent Moran off for a late tackle on Reid. It was the first time in 116 Cup Final matches stretching back 113 years that anyone had been sent off. United were down to 10 men – and suddenly started playing like 20.

The game went into extra-time and with only 10 minutes to play, Norman Whiteside, still only 18, scored a Cup Final goal for the second time in three years. His curling left-foot shot from the right edge of the penalty area deceived Neville Southall in the Everton goal and United had achieved a famous 1–0 victory. Moran had to wait several weeks before receiving his winner's medal.

Eight of the United team, including substitute Mike Duxbury, had played in the winning team against Brighton two years previously. A year later, six Everton players were back at Wembley for their third successive Cup Final: Kevin Ratcliffe, Gary Stevens – not the same one that had played for Brighton – Derek Mountfield, Peter Reid, Trevor Steven and Graeme Sharp.

Only Arsenal had played in three successive Wembley finals before and they had only emerged as winners once. Everton had to overcome fairly formidable opposition to go one better than that. They had to beat the League Champions. They happened to be Liverpool.

Liverpool had been through a difficult year. On May 29, 1985 their supporters had rioted before the European Cup Final against Juventus at the Heysel Stadium in Brussels, causing the deaths of 39 innocent people, almost all of them Juventus fans. The incident brought worldwide condemnation for England and the English game. The FA withdrew all English clubs from European competition, UEFA later banned them as well, and the Heysel disaster, coming as it did just 18 days after the Bradford fire, caused many people to question the state of the game.

The day after the tragedy Liverpool announced that Kenny Dalglish was taking over from Joe Fagan as the club's player-manager, and it was Dalglish's inspiration both as a man and a player that helped Liverpool regain their self-respect.

At the start of the 1985–86 season though, it looked as if the title race was going to be all over by Christmas and that Manchester United were going to win it. The Cup holders opened the season with 10 straight wins. By the second week of January they were still the only team to have topped the table all season, but then they started to falter. Everton led the standings in February and March, before Liverpool went top for the first time as late as March 31. But once there, they were never dislodged. If United started the season in invincible form, Liverpool ended it the same way, winning 11 of their last 12 matches, including the last seven in a row, and clinching the title with a 1–0 win over Chelsea at Stamford Bridge. The scorer of the only goal – player-manager Kenny Dalglish.

So a week later, and for the first time since 1913, the teams that finished first and second in the Championship met in the Cup Final, in the first all-Merseyside Cup Final between Liverpool and Everton. It wasn't the first time the teams had met at Wembley though. As well as the 1984 League Cup Final which ended 0–0, they had met again in August 1984 in the Charity Shield which ended in a 1–0 win for Everton.

And now, after 57 minutes of what was dubbed 'The Friendly Final', it looked as though Everton were going to maintain their unbeaten record at Wembley against Liverpool. There had never been any segregation of fans in Merseyside derby matches at either Anfield or Goodison, and now at Wembley the red and blue colours mixed into one another all around the

Norman Whiteside celebrates his extra-time winner against champions Everton in the 1985 final. Former Evertonian John Gidman is just as delighted (Popperfoto)

Further goals from Rush and the South African-born Craig Johnston finally sealed Liverpool's historic victory, while the architect of the whole performance had been the Danish brick outhouse otherwise known as Jan Molby. Dalglish became the first player-manager in history to take his side to the Double. Everton had had their chances to win, but had been denied them. At the end Liverpool fans chanted, 'We love you Everton, we do.' It was small consolation.

In 1989 the two teams met in the final again. The 1986 final had been an emotional occasion played out against the memory of the Heysel disaster the previous year, but Cup Final day in 1989 was to be unlike any other day in English soccer's history. Hopefully there will never be another day like it in the future.

On April 15, 1989 Liverpool were due to play Nottingham Forest for the second straight year in the Cup semi-final at Hillsborough. They had beaten Forest 2–1 the previous year to reach the Cup Final where, with a second Double in their grasp, they lost unexpectedly to Wimbledon. Now there was talk of another Double. But all the talk ended as the disaster at the Leppings Lane end of Hillsborough, the Liverpool fans' end, unfolded. At the end of that afternoon 95 people had died in the worst disaster in British sporting history.

The semi-final had actually been in progress for six minutes but was immediately abandoned as the full horror of what was happening behind the wretched fences became known.

Liverpool did not play another match until May 3. The players and the relatives of the victims were united in a sorrow that not only enveloped the city but the entire nation. Anfield was turned into a shrine of remembrance with the penalty area at the Kop End covered in thousands and thousands of bouquets of flowers. It was a moving, terrible time.

The semi-final was replayed on May 7 at Old Trafford and there was only ever going to be one winner. Liverpool beat Nottingham Forest 3–1 and would play Everton in the Final.

But a major decision had had to be taken – whether or not to postpone the Final to the start of the following season, or whether in fact, even to play it at all. In the end, the FA, in consultation with Liverpool, decided the match should go ahead as scheduled. The programme for the Cup Final on May 20 carried a black-bordered message from Bert Millichip, the Chairman of the FA, who wrote:

'In years to come the memory of today's match, and in a sense the importance attached to its outcome, will pale to insignificance when compared to the memory of the day when 95 supporters lost their lives at the semi-final tie at Hillsborough.

'The Football Association was faced with the choice of calling off the competition or continuing in what clearly would be difficult circumstances. We believe that we made the right decision, not only as a memorial to those who died, but as a means of providing concrete support for those left to grieve their passing.'

John Aldridge gave Liverpool the lead after four minutes of the final, but the match really came to life in a brief period just before the end of normal time and just after the start of extra-time. First, Everton substitute Stuart McCall equalised in the 89th minute to force the extra period. Then Ian Rush, who came on

ground. Cars left Liverpool on the morning of the match and drove down the M6 and M1 with red scarves flying out of one window and blue ones out of the other. Just a year on from the Heysel disaster, more than 400 million people watching around the world in 40 countries got a different view of English soccer. The fans chanted in unison, 'Merseyside, Merseyside', and there was only a handful of arrests. A 40-a-side match between the fans in the stadium car park provided an interesting appetiser before the main event.

For most of the first hour of the match it was the Everton fans who looked like they would be celebrating. A mistake by Dalglish had allowed Peter Reid to feed Gary Lineker after 28 minutes and the England striker duly put Everton ahead. But suddenly, as so often happens in this story, the ghostly vision of Lord Kinnaird standing on his head floated across the decades – and turned this game upside down too.

As Hugh McIlvanney wrote in the following day's *Observer*, 'Everton are obliged to believe that Liverpool were simply destined to make history at Wembley yesterday by becoming only the third club this century to complete the Double of the League Championship and victory in the FA Cup Final. How else can the losers rationalise a match in which they went a goal ahead and achieved an almost disdainful superiority for nearly an hour and yet finished the day comprehensively beaten and all but demoralised?'

Once Ian Rush had scored the equaliser after 57 minutes, Everton must have known the fates were against them. In the six years since he had joined Liverpool from Chester in April 1980, Rush had scored in 120 matches for Liverpool and they hadn't lost in any of those. This was Goalscoring Match No.121 and they didn't lose this one either.

Lest we forget. The scene of the Hillsborough tragedy at Liverpool's semi-final in 1989 (Allsport/David Cannon)

as a substitute for John Aldridge, made it 2–1 in the 94th minute, but eight minutes later McCall equalised again to become the first substitute to score twice in the Cup Final. He didn't keep that unique record for long though, because two minutes later Rush turned the ball past Neville Southall for the winner.

So Liverpool had won the Cup and six days later they met Arsenal at Anfield in the Championship decider. Liverpool had not lost in the League since New Year's Day and only needed a point, or at the very worst a 1–0 defeat, and they would be champions.

As if the nerves of all concerned with Liverpool had not been stretched and jangled enough over the previous six weeks, it was Arsenal who carried the Championship crown out of Liverpool's grasp and back to London for the first time since they themselves won the Double in 1971. Michael Thomas's goal, with virtually the last kick of the last game of the season, gave the Gunners a 2–0 win.

Arsenal thus became the second London team to deny Liverpool the Double in little over a year. Twelve months previously Liverpool had gone to Wembley as Champions and the hottest favourites since Leeds in 1973 to win the Cup against unfancied opposition.

And there weren't many who fancied Wimbledon in any shape or form that spring. The Dons had risen from non-League football to the First Division in only 11 seasons and in the main they had got there playing 'Route One' soccer – a rather less sophisticated brand of the POMO (position of maximum opportunity) system employed by Watford earlier in the decade. Basically it involved a big boot upfield, cutting out the pretty stuff in the middle, with the intention of causing mayhem in the opposing defence. By and large it worked for the Dons whose team spirit was based on an 'all for one and one for all' credo that really did bring them some unlikely victories.

But they didn't have many fans, and they didn't have all that many admirers. On the morning of the match several newspapers carried hysterical headlines that suggested the world as we know it would end if Wimbledon won the Cup.

The condemnation of Wimbledon's playing style was as biased and uninformed as it could be, with much of Fleet Street, before and after the final, fawning pathetically to Liverpool. Wimbledon might not have been pretty to watch, but they deserved their famous victory. They were lucky when Peter Beardsley had a goal ruled out by an impatient referee who blew too quickly after a trip on Beardsley when he clearly had maintained advantage, but apart from that the Dons made their own luck.

Lawrie Sanchez scored with a well-worked header shortly before half-time and even when Liverpool had a golden opportunity to pull themselves back into the match, they blew it. In the 61st minute the referee Brian Hill ruled that Clive Goodyear had tripped Aldridge in the penalty box, though TV replays clearly showed afterwards that Goodyear had played the ball and not touched the man.

But a penalty it was. All seven Cup Final penalties taken at Wembley had been converted. No-one had missed a Cup Final penalty since 1913. Aldridge, who usually kicked his penalties to the goalkeeper's left, did so again this time. Dave Beasant, the first goalkeeper ever to captain a Cup Final side, had studied Aldridge's spot-kicks on video and knew just where this one was going. He dived to his left and beat the ball away.

Half-an-hour later Beasant went up to get the Cup. Wimbledon were the 42nd team to have won it. But there was a sad postscript to their victory. Just over a year later, on July 15, 1989, Laurie Cunningham, who came on as a second-half substitute for Alan Cork, was killed in a car crash in Spain.

Wimbledon followed Coventry as a new name on the old trophy. In 1987 Coventry ended their 104-year wait for a major honour when they ended Tottenham's 100 per cent record in the Cup Final.

Coventry had advanced to Wembley with wins over Bolton (3–0), Manchester United (1–0), Stoke (1–0), Sheffield Wednesday (3–1) and Leeds, then in the Second Division, who put up a determined fight in the semi-final at Hillsborough before Coventry won 3–2 in extra-time. The team had been put together by manager John Sillett and managing director George Curtis, who played more than 500 matches for Coventry in the 1950s and 1960s. Apart perhaps from Cyrille Regis, it was a team without stars, but with an indefatigable spirit which they were to prove conclusively on the afternoon of May 16, 1987.

Their opponents, Tottenham, had won all of their seven previous Cup Finals. But from the moment they stripped off their tracksuits they could have been forgiven for thinking this was not going to be their day. Some of the players had shirts with their sponsors' name on the front – and others didn't.

Still, Tottenham quickly forgot about their sartorial ineptitude and took the lead after only two minutes with a superb headed goal from Clive Allen, whose father Les had been in the Spurs team when they won the Double in 1961. Clive later briefly played against Spurs for QPR in the 1982 final but came off injured early in the match. This was his 49th goal of the season and it seemed only a matter of time before he would get his 50th that afternoon. But it never came.

Instead Coventry pulled level through Dave Bennett seven minutes later. Bennett, like Allen, had played against Spurs in a Cup Final and lost when he was in the Manchester City team in 1981. Bennett would get his revenge later that afternoon by running round Wembley with the Cup.

Tottenham had not gained their Cup reputation stretching back 86 years for no reason. They had three survivors from the team that won the Cup in 1982 – goalkeeper Ray Clemence, playing in his fifth Cup Final, Chris Hughton and Glenn Hoddle, while Ossie Ardiles, Hughton and Hoddle had all been in the 1981 Cup winning team. Also in the side was Clive Allen's cousin Paul, the youngest Wembley Cup Finalist when he played with West Ham in 1980, and the England internationals Chris Waddle, Gary Mabbutt and Steve Hodge. It was Mabbutt who put Tottenham back in front shortly before half-time.

Hoddle, the most skilful player England had produced in a generation, was playing in his last match for Tottenham after a 12-year career at White Hart Lane but had a poor game, tightly marshalled by Lloyd McGrath. Tottenham may have been leading but they were never truly in control and when Keith Houchen equalised for Coventry midway through the second half with a fabulous diving header, the writing was on the wall for Spurs, even if it wasn't on half their shirts.

The final moved into extra-time and was decided six minutes later when a cross-cum-shot from Lloyd McGrath took a deflection off Mabbutt and flew over Clemence into the back of the Spurs goal. History could not save Spurs now and Coventry held on for the final 24 minutes to take the Cup back to the Midlands for the first time since West Bromwich Albion 19 years before.

The usual suspects   1990–93

At the start of the 1990s, four familiar names were back on the trophy. Manchester United won the Cup in 1990 for a seventh time to equal the record jointly held by Aston Villa and Spurs. They beat Crystal Palace, managed by Steve Coppell who played for United in the finals of 1976 and 1977, in a replay after an amazing 3-3 draw which saw another goalscoring double from a substitute, Ian Wright of Crystal Palace. When Bryan Robson collected the Cup from the Duke of Kent he became the first man to captain a side to three victories at Wembley.

In 1991 Tottenham made history by winning the first FA Cup semi-final played at Wembley when they beat Arsenal 3–1, and then returned the following month to win the Cup for a record eighth time with a 2–1 extra-time win over Nottingham Forest. It escaped no-one's attention that the year ended in '1' again, although for Paul Gascoigne, the brilliant yet indisciplined midfield genius whose stupendous free-kick had set up Spurs' victory in the semi-final, Cup Final day ended in hospital after his infamous 'tackle' on Forest's Gary Charles. For Tottenham's captain the final was especially poignant. It was Gary Mabbutt's own goal that gave Coventry their 3–2 win in 1987 – now in 1991 his pressure forced Forest's Des Walker to head into his own goal for Spurs' winner.

It was the last first-class match Gascoigne played in Tottenham's colours, and for a while it looked like being one of the last matches that Tottenham Hotspur might ever play. Faced with debts of around £20 million, they drifted close to extinction before being taken over by Terry Venables, their former manager and player, and Alan Sugar, a wealthy businessman.

In 1992 Liverpool returned to Wembley after becoming the first side to reach the final by winning a penalty shoot-out in the semi-final against Second Division Portsmouth. Liverpool then had an almost routine 2–0 victory against Sunderland, also from the Second Division, in the Final, the Wearsiders unable to repeat the kind of heroics that brought their predecessors a famous win against Leeds in 1973.

Liverpool won with goals from Michael Thomas, the player who denied them the League and Cup Double in 1989, and Ian Rush, whose fifth Cup Final goal was an all-time record. Their captain Mark Wright became the first man to hold up the new FA Cup – an exact replica of the trophy made in 1911.

But Liverpool did not hold onto the trophy for long. In a major upset, they were knocked out of the Cup in the third round the following season by those great Cup fighters of old, Bolton Wanderers. Everton had been knocked out by Wimbledon and so for the first time since 1951 neither of the Merseyside giants survived the third round.

North London, by contrast, watched Arsenal and Spurs head for a showdown in the semi-final at Wembley for the second time in three years. A goal from the Gunners' skipper Tony Adams settled the issue in Arsenal's favour to put them into the Cup Final for a record 12th time. The other semi-final, also staged at Wembley after much agonising by the FA, was another closely fought local derby with Sheffield Wednesday beating Sheffield United 2–1 after extra time.

A poor final petered out at 1–1, Ian Wright heading Arsenal in front and David Hirst replying for Wednesday, and until the dying moments of the replay it seemed that the FA Cup Final would be decided by

Ian Wright scores for Arsenal in the 1993 replay, his fourth Cup final goal in four appearances (Allsport/Shaun Botterill)

penalties for the first time. Ian Wright, inevitably, had scored for Arsenal in the first half. Chris Waddle equalised with a deflected shot in the second period, and the stalemate lasted until the very last minute of extra time. Then with seconds left to play, Arsenal's Andy Linighan headed the winner from a corner to take the Cup back to Highbury after 14 years.

The 1993 Final was the first since the reorganisation of the Football League and the introduction of the FA Premier League. The English game had reached another of its periodic turning points and doubtless soon there will be others. It can only be a matter of time before the Cup Final *is* decided on penalties, and one day the final will probably be contested by two teams outside the highest echelon of English football. Perhaps a British Cup with Rangers and Celtic – and even Queen's Park – might replace it, or maybe a non-League side will come through from the qualifying round to win it.

When Cup Final Day is over, the tens of thousands of fans lucky enough to get tickets leave the Wembley area following yellow, red or blue route lines drawn on a map in the programme to help them onto the main roads and motorways and away from the Wembley area. Thousands more take the tube or overground train into London.

But probably none, except for those who might live there, ever take the Metropolitan Line stops from Wembley Park to Harrow-on-the-Hill and make the short walk to Harrow School.

It was there, just a couple of miles from the site of the modern-day Stadium, that Charles Alcock, the man who invented the FA Cup, went to school and first got the idea for the Cup by watching the Cock House game.

If the wind is blowing in the right direction, you can hear the roar of the Cup Final crowd in Harrow – a roar that probably even reaches Charles Alcock, the man who invented it all.

Presuming he can get a ticket, wherever he may be.

PART TWO

THE
GUINNESS
RECORD
OF THE
FA CUP

CLUB-BY-CLUB
CUP RESULTS

ABERDARE ATHLETIC

Originally formed: 1893 as Aberdare Town; Reformed as Aberdare Athletic 1920. Members Football League 1922-27. **First competed in FA Cup:** 1912 **Record Win:** 4-0 vs Cardiff Albion, Prelim Rd, 25.9.1920 **Record Defeat:** 1-9 vs Exeter City, 1st round, 26.11.1927 **Best Performances:** 1st round (modern day 3rd round) 1923, 1924, 3rd Round 1926

1922-23	3S	5q **Newport Co** (H) 1-1; 5qr **Newport Co** (A) 1-1aet; **Newport Co** at Ninian Park 2-1; 6q **Carlisle U** (H) 0-0; 6qr **Carlisle** (A) 2-1						
		1	13.1.23	**Preston NE**	D1	H	L	1-3	Brown
1923-24	3S	4q **Torquay U** (A) 0-0; 4qr **Torquay U** (H) 4-0; 5q **Reading** (H) 1-0; 6q **Walsall** (H) 1-0						
		1	12.1.24	**West Ham**	D1	A	L	0-5
1924-25	3S	4q **Newport Co** (H) 0-0; 4qr **Newport Co** (A) 0-3						
1925-26	3S	1	28.11.25	**Bristol R**	3S	H	W	4-1	Barwood, Barnham 3
		2	12.12.25	**Luton T**	3S	H	W	1-0	Smith
		3	9.1.26	**Newcastle U**	D1	A	L	1-4	Taylor
1926-27	3S	1	27.11.26	**Exeter C**	3S	A	L	0-3
1927-28	SL	1	26.11.27	**Exeter C**	3S	A	L	1-9	Watts

ACCRINGTON FC

Formed 1878. Founder member of the Football League 1888. Disbanded January 1896 **Best FA Cup performance:** 2nd Round, 1890, 1891, 1892, 1893 **Record Win:** 11-0 vs Rossendale, 1st round, 15.10.1887 **Record defeat:** 0-5 vs Blackburn R, 1st round replay, 9.2.1889

1881-82		1	29.10.81	**Queen's Park, Glasgow**		H	*walkover*	
		2	26.11.81	**Darwen**		A	L	1-3	Yates
1882-83		1	4.11.82	**Blackburn Olympic**		A	L	3-6	Brown, Bamber, Yates
1883-84		1	10.11.83	**Blackpool St John's**		H	W	4-0	Hacking, Bryce 2, Hargreaves
		2	26.11.83	**Blackburn Park Road**		A	W	3-2	Harper og, Hargreaves, MacBeth
		Accrington disqualified for professionalism						
1884-85		1	11.10.84	**Southport**		H	W	3-0	
		Accrington disqualified for professionalism						
1885-86		1	17.10.85	**Witton**		H	W	5-4	F.Wood 2, Deakin, Hargreaves, Wade
		2	21.11.85	**Darwen Old Wanderers**		A	L	1-2	Whittaker
1886-87		1	30.10.86	**Renton**		A	L	0-1	
1887-88		1	15.10.87	**Rossendale**		H	W	11-0	Lofthouse 3, Bonar, Yates, Conway 2, Fecitt 4
		2	5.11.87	**Burnley**		H	W	3-2	Conway, Bonar, Lofthouse
		3	26.11.87	**Blackburn R**		H	L	1-3	Yates
1888-89	D1	1	2.2.89	**Blackburn R**	D1	H	D	1-1	Wilkinson
		1r	9.2.89	**Blackburn R**	D1	H	L	0-5	
1889-90	D1	1	25.1.90	**WBA**	D1	H	W	3-0	Entwistle 2, Barbour
		2	1.2.90	**Sheffield W**	D1	A	L	1-2	A.Wilkinson
1890-91	D1	1	17.1.91	**Bolton W**	D1	H	D	2-2	Whitehead, Kirkham
		1r	24.1.91	**Bolton W**	D1	H	W	5-1	Gallocher, Kirkham, Whitehead, Pendergast, an other
		2	31.1.91	**Wolverhampton W**	D1	H	L	2-3aet	Pendergast, Kirkham
1891-92	D1	1	16.1.92	**Crusaders**		A	W	4-1	Haworth, Thomson, Kirkham, Whitehead
		2	6.2.92	**Sunderland**	D1	H	L	1-3	Whitehead
1892-93	D1	1	21.1.93	**Stoke**	D1	H	W	2-1	Cookson, H.Lea
		2	4.2.93	**Preston NE**	D1	H	L	1-4	H.Lea
1893-94	LL	1	27.1.94	**Sunderland**	D1	A	L	0-3	
1894-95	LC	1	13.10.94	**Bacup**	LL	H	L	0-4	
1895-96	LC	1	5.10.95	**West Manchester**	LL	A	L	1-5	Cunliffe

ACCRINGTON STANLEY

Formed 1893 as a seperate club to Accrington. 1921 Reformed. Resigned from Football League March 1962 but were not wound-up until December 1963. Reformed as Accrington FC December 1963, wound-up January 1966. 1968 Reformed as Accrington Stanley (1968). Currently playing in the Northern Premier (HFS Loans) League **Best FA Cup Performance:** 4th round 1927, 1937, 1959. In Competition Proper: **Record FA Cup Win:** 7-0 vs Spennymoor U, 2nd round, 8.12.1928 **Record FA Cup Defeat:** 1-7 vs Blackburn R, 1st round, 15.1.1910

1896-97	NELC	1q **Carlisle C** walkover; 2q **Chorley** (H) 0-5
1897-98	NELC	1q **Carlisle C** (A) 4-0; 2q **Horwich** (A) 1-3
1898-99	NELC	1q **Oswaldtwistle R** (A) 4-2; 2q **Frizington White Star** (H) 8-0; 3q **South Shore** (A) 1-5
1899-00	NELC	P **Blackburn Park Rd** (A) 0-3
1900-01	LC	*did not enter*
1901-02	LC	1q **Nelson** (H) 2-1; 2q **Oswaldtwistle R** (H) 1-1; 2qr **Oswaldtwistle R** (A) 2-0; 3q **Darwen** (A) 1-2
1902-03	LC	1q **Bacup** (H) 5-0; 2q **Rossendale U** (H) 1-0; 3q **Manchester U** (A) 0-7
1903-04	LC	1q **Padiham** (A) 0-0; 1qr **Padiham** (H) 4-0; 2q **Nelson** (H) 2-1; 3q **Southport** (H) 0-1
1904-05	LC	3q **Blackpool** (H) 1-4

A C C R I N G T O N   S T A N L E Y

Season	Comp	Round	Date	Opponent	Div	H/A	Res	Score	Scorers
1905-06	LC	P Nelson (H) 7-0; 1q Burnley Belvedere (H) 5-0; 2q Padiham (A) 4-1; Int. Burton U (A) 0-3							
1906-07	LC	5q West Norwood (A) 9-1							
		1	12.1.07	Crewe Alex	BDL	A	D	1-1	Randall
		1r	16.1.07	Crewe Alex		H	W	1-0	Sheridan
		2	2.2.07	Bradford C	D2	A	L	0-1	
1907-08	LC	P Chorley (A) 1-2							
1908-09	LC	P Rochdale (A) 5-3; 1q Rossendale U (H) 2-0; 2q Darwen (H) 3-1; 3q Colne (H) 1-1; 3qr Colne (A) 2-2aet *abandoned – bad light*; 3q 2r Colne 1-0 (at Burnley); 4q Northern Nomads (H) 0-2							
1909-10	LC	4q Haslingden (A) 4-3; 5q Brentford (H) 1-0							
		1	15.1.10	Blackburn R	D1	A	L	1-7	Bradley
1910-11	LC	4q Haslingden (A) 1-0; 5q Torquay T (H) 4-0							
		1	14.1.11	Wolverhampton W	D2	A	L	0-2	
1911-12	LC	4q Carlisle U (H) 3-0; 5q Walsall (A) 1-2							
1912-13	LC	4q Rochdale (A) 1-6							
1913-14	LC	4q Stalybridge C (A) 0-2							
1914-15	LC	P Adlington (H) 1-1; Pr Adlington (H) 2-3							
1919-20	LC	1q Nelson (A) 1-2							
1920-21	LC	1q Fleetwood (A) 0-8							
1921-22	3N	4q Nelson (H) 0-1							
1922-23	3N	5q Halifax T (H) 1-1; 5qr Halifax T (A) 0-1							
1923-24	3N	5q Rochdale (H) 1-0; 6q Wrexham (H) 1-0							
		1	12.1.24	Charlton A	3S	H	D	0-0	
		1r	17.1.24	Charlton A		A	L	0-1	
1924-25	3N	5q New Brighton (A) 0-0; 5qr New Brighton (H) 3-2; 6q Chesterfield (H) 1-0							
		1	10.1.25	Portsmouth	D2	H	L	2-5	R.Thompson 2 (1p)
1925-26	3N	1	28.11.25	Wrexham	3N	H	W	4-0	Jepson 3, Rooks
		2	12.12.25	Blyth Spartans	NEL	H	W	5-0	Gummery, Jepson 3, Powell
		3	9.1.26	Bolton W	D1	A	L	0-1	
1926-27	3N	1	27.11.26	Rochdale	3N	H	W	4-3	Gee (p), Clarkson 2, Martin
		2	11.12.26	Chilton Colliery	NEL	A	W	3-0	Gee, Clarkson, Martin
		3	8.1.27	Exeter C	3S	A	W	2-0	Clarkson, Martin
		4	29.1.27	Chelsea	D2	A	L	2-7	Powell, Wyper
1927-28	3N	1	26.11.27	Lincoln C	3N	H	L	2-5	Clarkson, Parkin
1928-29	3N	1	24.11.28	South Shields	3N	H	W	2-1	Parkin, Parry
		2	8.12.28	Spennymoor U	NEL	H	W	7-0	Jepson 3, Parry 2, McLoughlin 2
		3	12.1.29	Bournemouth	3S	H	D	1-1	Jepson
		3r	16.1.29	Bournemouth		A	L	0-2	
1929-30	3N	1	30.11.29	Rochdale	3N	H	W	3-1	Jepson 2, Armstrong (p)
		2	14.12.29	Bristol R	3S	A	L	1-4	Ferguson
1930-31	3N	1	29.11.30	Lancaster T	LC	H	W	3-1	Agar 2, Abel
		2	13.12.30	Torquay U	3S	H	L	0-1	
1931-32	3N	1	28.11.31	Rotherham U	3N	A	D	0-0	
		1r	2.12.31	Rotherham U		H	W	5-0	Williamson 3, Watson, Agar
		2	12.12.31	Halifax T	3N	A	L	0-3	
1932-33	3N	1	26.11.32	Hereford U	BDL	H	W	2-1	Maycock, Price (p)
		2	10.12.32	Aldershot	3S	H	L	1-2	Johnson
1933-34	3N	1	25.11.33	Scunthorpe U	ML	A	D	1-1	Kelly
		1r	29.11.33	Scunthorpe U		H	W	3-0	Lennox, Cheetham 2
		2	9.12.33	Bristol R	3S	H	W	1-0	Cheetham
		3	13.1.34	Millwall	D2	A	L	0-3	
1934-35	3N	1	24.11.34	Mansfield T	3N	A	L	1-6	Brown
1935-36	3N	1	30.11.35	Darlington	3N	A	L	2-4	Reynolds, Brown
1936-37	3N	1	28.11.36	Wellington T	BDL	H	W	3-1	Mortimer, Mee, Reynolds
		2	12.12.36	Tunbridge Wells R	KL	H	W	1-0	Mee
		3	16.1.37	Blackburn R	D2	A	D	2-2	Mortimer 2
		3r	20.1.37	Blackburn R		H	W	3-1aet	Mortimer 2, Rivers
		4	30.1.37	Manchester C	D1	A	L	0-2	
1937-38	3N	1	27.11.37	Lancaster T	LC	H	D	1-1	Moir
		1r	1.12.37	Lancaster T		A	D	1-1	Curran
		1 2r	6.12.37	Lancaster T at Preston			W	4-0	Curran 2, O'Grady, Andrews
		P	11.12.37	Crystal P	3S	H	L	0-1	
1938-39	3N	1	26.11.38	Hartlepools U	3N	A	L	1-2	Alexander
1945-46	3N	1 1L	17.11.45	Chorley	LC	A	L	1-2	Keeley
		1 2L	24.11.45	Chorley		H	W	2-0	Rothwell, Hudson
		2 1L	8.12.45	Oldham A	3N	A	L	1-2	Hudson
		2 2L	15.12.45	Oldham A		H	W	3-1	Hudson, Shipman og, Rothwell
		3 1L	5.1.46	Manchester U	D1	H	D	2-2	Conroy, Keeley

ACCRINGTON STANLEY

Season	Div	Round	Date	Opponent	Opp Div	H/A	Res	Score	Scorers
	3 2L		9.1.46	Manchester U		A	L	1-5	Keeley
1946-47	3N	1	30.11.46	Doncaster R	3N	A	D	2-2	Conroy, Keeley
		1r	4.12.46	Doncaster R		H	L	0-5	
1947-48	3N	1	29.11.47	Stockport Co	3N	A	L	1-3	T.Butler
1948-49	3N	1	27.11.48	Hull C	3N	A	L	1-3	Webster
1949-50	3N	1	26.11.49	Hartlepools U	3N	H	L	0-1	
1950-51	3N	1	25.11.50	Wrexham	3N	A	L	0-1	
1951-52	3N	1	24.11.51	Chester	3N	H	L	1-3	Watkinson
1952-53	3N	1	22.11.52	Horden Colliery W.	NEL	A	W	2-1	Watkinson
		2	6.12.52	Mansfield T	3N	H	L	0-2	
1953-54	3N	1	21.11.53	Blyth Spartans	NEL	A	W	1-0	Cocker
		2	12.12.53	Tranmere R	3N	H	D	2-2	Eastham, Musgrave (p)
		2r	16.12.53	Tranmere R		A	L	1-5	Brydon
1954-55	3N	1	20.11.54	Creswell Colliery	CA	H	W	7-1	Devlin 2, Scott 2, Wright, Brydon, Cocker
		2	11.12.54	Millwall	3S	A	L	2-3	Scott, Bodle
1955-56	3N	1	19.11.55	Wrexham	3N	H	W	3-1	Stewart 2, Wright
		2	10.12.55	Darlington	3N	A	W	1-0	Dick
		3	7.1.56	Liverpool	D2	A	L	0-2	
1956-57	3N	1	17.11.56	Morecambe	LC	H	W	4-1	Scott, Stones 2, Dick
		2	8.12.56	Oldham A	3N	H	W	2-1	Stewart 2
		3	5.1.57	Bournemouth	3S	A	L	0-2	
1957-58	3N	1	16.11.57	Wrexham	3N	A	W	1-0	Stewart (p)
		2	7.12.57	Carlisle U	3N	A	D	1-1	Mulkerrin
		2r	11.12.57	Carlisle U		H	W	3-2	J.Anders 3
		3	4.1.58	Bristol C	D2	H	D	2-2	Stewart, Byrom
		3r	7.1.58	Bristol C		A	L	1-3	Sowden
1958-59	D3	1	15.11.58	Workington	D4	H	W	5-1	Scott 3, H.Anders, Stewart
		2	6.12.58	Buxton	CC	H	W	6-1	Scott 2, J.Anders 3, Tighe
		3	10.1.59	Darlington	D4	H	W	3-0	J.Anders, Stinson, Scott
		4	24.1.59	Portsmouth	D1	H	D	0-0	
		4r	28.1.59	Portsmouth		A	L	1-4	Scott
1959-60	D3	1	14.11.59	Mansfield T	D3	H	L	1-2	Tighe
1960-61	D4	1	5.11.60	Barrow	D4	H	W	2-1	Swindells 2
		2	30.11.60	Mansfield T	D4	H	W	3-0	Swindells, Hudson, Duff
		3	7.1.61	Preston NE	D1	A	D	1-1	Duff
		3r	9.1.61	Preston NE		H	L	0-4	
1961-62	D4	1	4.11.61	Stockport Co	D4	A	W	1-0	Pickup
		2	25.11.61	Hartlepools U	D4	A	L	1-2	Irving

Accrington Stanley (1968)

Season	Div	Round	Date	Opponent	Opp Div	H/A	Res	Score	Scorers
1992-93	NPL	1	14.11.92	Gateshead	GMVC	H	W	3-2	Beck 3
		2	5.12.92	Crewe A	D3	H	L	1-6	Cooper
			played at Blackburn						

ACTON

Formed 1874. Played home matches at Gunnersbury Lane, Acton, west London. Used the King's Head pub as their dressing room.

Season	Round	Date	Opponent	H/A	Res	Score	Scorers
1879-80	1	8.11.79	Old Carthusians	H	L	0-4	
1880-81	1	13.11.80	Kildare	H	D	1-1	
	1r	20.11.80	Kildare	A	W	5-0	
	2	11.12.80	Reading Abbey	A	L	1-2	Lacey
1881-82	1	29.10.81	Finchley	H	D	0-0	
	1r	12.10.81	Finchley	A	W	4-0	
	2	3.12.81	Maidenhead	A	L	1-2aet	R. Grey
1882-83	1	4.11.82	Windsor Home Park	A	L	0-3	
1883-84	1	10.11.83	Upton Park	H	L	0-2	
1884-85	1	8.11.84	Old Carthusians	H	L	1-7	
1885-86	1	31.10.85	Old Brightonians	A	L	1-2	

ADDLESTONE & WEYBRIDGE TOWN

Formed 1979 on merger between Addlestone and Weybridge. **First competed in FA Cup:** Addlestone 1925; Weybridge 1926. Folded 1985.

Season	Div	Round	Date	Opponent	Opp Div	H/A	Res	Score	Scorers
1980-81	SL	1	22.11.80	Brentford	D3	H	D	2-2	Morris, Donaldson
			played at Griffin Park						
		1r	25.11.80	Brentford		A	L	0-2	

ALDERSHOT

Formed 1926 as Aldershot Town. Became Aldershot 1931. Folded March 1992. Reformed in 1992 as Aldershot Town and re-entered senior football as members of the Isthmian (Diadora) League. **First competed in FA Cup:** 1927. **Best FA Cup performance:** 5th round, 1933, 1979. **Record FA Cup Win:** 11-1 vs Kingstonian, 4th qual rd, 16.11.1929. In competition proper: 7-0 vs Chelmsford, 1st round, 28.11.1931 and Newport (IOW), 2nd round, 1st leg, 8.12.1945 **Record FA Cup Defeat:** 0-7 vs Swindon Town 3rd round, 8.1.1983

Season	Lg	Rd	Date	Opponent	Comp	H/A	W/D/L	Score	Scorers
1927-28	SL	1	26.11.27	QPR	3S	H	-	0-1	
				abandoned because of fog					
		1	30.11.27	QPR		H	W	2-1	Collins, Martin
		2	10.12.27	Peterborough & Fletton U	SL	A	L	1-2	Martin
1929-30	SL	1	30.11.29	Northampton T	3S	H	L	0-1	
1930-31	SL	1	29.11.30	Peterborough & Fletton U	SL	H	W	4-1	Thorn 3, Williams
		2	13.12.30	Gillingham	3S	A	W	3-1	Thorn 2, Edgar
		3	10.1.31	Bradford PA	D2	H	L	0-1	
as Aldershot									
1931-32	SL	1	28.11.31	Chelmsford	Lon	H	W	7-0	Thorn 3, Hopkins, Stevenson, Middleton, McDougall
		2	12.12.31	Crook T	NEL	H	D	1-1	Thorn
		2r	16.12.31	Crook T		A	L	0-1	
1932-33	3S	1	26.11.32	Clapton O	3S	A	W	1-0	Fishlock
		2	10.12.32	Accrington S	3N	A	W	2-1	White, Lane
		3	14.1.33	Bristol R	3S	H	W	1-0	Lane
		4	28.1.33	Millwall	D2	H	W	1-0	Fishlock
		5	18.2.33	Derby Co	D1	A	L	0-2	
1933-34	3S	1	25.11.33	Cardiff C	3S	A	D	0-0	
		1r	29.11.33	Cardiff C		H	W	3-1	Lee, White, Smithson
		2	9.12.33	Gainsborough T	ML	A	W	2-0	Proud, Lee
		3	13.1.34	Crystal P	3S	A	L	0-1	
1934-35	3S	1	24.11.34	Bournemouth	3S	H	W	4-0	Williams, Bunch, Black, McDougall
		2	8.12.34	Barrow	3N	A	W	2-0	Williams, Bunch
		3	12.1.35	Reading	3S	H	D	0-0	
		3r	16.1.35	Reading		A	L	1-3	G.Summerbee
1935-36	3S	1	30.11.35	Clapton O	3S	A	D	0-0	
		1r	4.12.35	Clapton O		H	L	0-1	
1936-37	3S	1	28.11.36	Millwall	3S	H	L	1-6	E.Smith og
1937-38	3S	1	27.11.37	Dulwich H	IL	A	W	2-1	Court, Egan
		2	11.12.37	Rotherham U	3N	A	W	3-1	Egan, Court, Kilsby
		3	8.1.38	Notts Co	3S	H	L	1-3	Court
1938-39	3S	1	26.11.38	Guildford C	SL	H	D	1-1	Egan
		1r	30.11.38	Guildford C		A	W	4-3	Ray 2, Proud, Chalmers
		2	10.12.38	Runcorn	CC	A	L	1-3	Ray
1945-46	3S	1 1L	17.11.45	Reading	3S	A	L	1-3	Brooks
		1 2L	24.11.45	Reading		H	W	7-3	Brooks 5, Glidden og, Fitzgerald
		2 1L	8.12.45	Newport IOW	Hants	H	W	7-0	Brooks 5, Hobbs, Hold
		2 2L	15.12.45	Newport IOW		A	W	5-0	Brooks, Ray, Fitzgerald 2, Sumerbee
		3 1L	5.1.46	Plymouth A	D2	H	W	2-0	Hobbs, Brooks
		3 2L	9.1.46	Plymouth A		A	W	1-0	Hold
		4 1L	26.1.46	Brighton & HA	3S	A	L	0-3	
		4 2L	30.1.46	Brighton & HA		H	L	1-4	White
1946-47	3S	1	30.11.46	Cheltenham T	SL	H	W	4-2	Hobbs, Brooks, Hassell 2
			14.12.46	Bournemouth	3S	A	L	2-4	White, Griffiths
1947-48	3S	1	29.11.47	Bromsgrove R	BC	H	W	2-1	Wainwright og, Sherwood
		2	13.12.47	Swindon T	3S	H	D	0-0	
		2r	20.12.47	Swindon T		A	L	0-2	
1948-49	3S	1	27.11.48	Ipswich T	3S	A	–	0-1	
				abandoned after 63 minutes					
		1	4.12.48	Ipswich T		A	W	3-0	Rawcliffe, Sherwood, White
		2	11.12.48	Chester	3N	H	W	1-0	White
		3	8.1.49	Gateshead	3N	A	L	1-3	Sinclair
1949-50	3S	1	26.11.49	Weymouth	SL	A	D	2-2	Rogers, Sinclair
		1r	30.11.49	Weymouth		H	L	2-3	McNichol, Rogers (p)
1950-51	3S	1	25.11.50	Bromley	AL	H	D	2-2	Menzies, Flint
		1r	29.11.50	Bromley		A	W	1-0	Woodward
		2	9.12.50	Bournemouth	3S	H	W	3-0	Flint, Gormley, Woodward
		3	10.1.51	Bristol R	3S	A	L	1-5	Woodward
1951-52	3S	1	24.11.51	Tonbridge	SL	A	D	0-0	
		1r	28.11.51	Tonbridge		H	W	3-2aet	Raine, Billington, Flint
		2	15.12.51	Buxton	CC	A	L	3-4	Gormley, Jefferson, Flint

ALDERSHOT

1952-53	3S	1	22.11.52	**Millwall**	3S	H	D	0-0
		1r	27.11.52	**Millwall**		A	L	1-7	Flint
1953-54	3S	1	21.11.53	**Wellington T**	CC	H	W	5-3	McCulloch 2, Laird, Menzies, Gaynor
		2	12.12.53	**Peterborough U**	ML	A	L	1-2	Lacey
1954-55	3S	1	20.11.54	**Chelmsford C**	SL	H	W	3-1	Menzies, Cheney 2
		2	11.12.54	**Hartlepools U**	3N	A	L	0-4
1955-56	3S	1	19.11.55	**Yeovil**	SL	A	D	1-1	Lacey
		1r	23.11.55	**Yeovil**		H	D	1-1aet	Billington
		1 2r	28.11.55	**Yeovil** at Southampton			W	3-0	L.Gaynor, Lacey 2
		2	10.12.55	**Reading**	3S	A	D	2-2	Billington, Menzies
		2r	14.12.55	**Reading**		H	W	3-0aet	J.Gaynor, L.Gaynor, Lacey
		3	7.1.56	**Barnsley**	D2	H	L	1-2	Flint
1956-57	3S	1	17.11.56	**Hereford U**	SL	A	L	2-3	Costello 2
1957-58	3S	1	16.11.57	**Worcester C**	SL	H	D	0-0
		1r	21.11.57	**Worcester C**		A	D	2-2aet	Flint, Lacey
		1 2r	25.11.57	**Worcester C** at St Andrews			W	3-2aet	Henry, Jackson, Lacey
		2	7.12.57	**Coventry C**	3S	H	W	4-1	Lacey 3, Walters
		3	4.1.58	**Portsmouth**	D1	A	L	1-5	Lacey
1958-59	D4	1	15.11.58	**Swindon T**	D3	A	L	0-5
1959-60	D4	1	14.11.59	**Kings Lynn**	SL	A	L	1-3	Mundy
1960-61	D4	1	5.11.60	**Notts Co**	D3	H	W	2-0	Lawlor 2
		2	26.11.60	**Colchester U**	D3	H	W	3-1	Kirkup 3
		3	7.1.61	**Shrewsbury T**	D3	H	D	1-1	Lawlor (p)
		3r	11.1.61	**Shrewsbury T**		A	D	2-2aet	Tyrer, Stepney
		3 2r	16.1.61	**Shrewsbury T** at Villa Park			W	2-0	Henry, Stepney
		4	28.1.61	**Stoke C**	D2	A	D	0-0
		4r	1.2.61	**Stoke C**		H	D	0-0aet
		4 2r	6.2.61	**Stoke C** at Molineux			L	0-3
1961-62	D4	1	4.11.61	**Tunbridge Wells U**	SL	H	W	3-1	Norris, Hasty 2
		2	25.11.61	**Brentford**	D3	H	D	2-2	Woan, Matthews
		2r	28.11.61	**Brentford**		A	L	0-2
1962-63	D4	1	3.11.62	**Brentford**	D4	H	W	1-0	Woan
		2	24.11.62	**Port Vale**	D3	A	L	0-2
1963-64	D4	1	16.11.63	**Sutton U**	IL	A	W	4-0	Fogg 2, Towers 2
		2	7.12.63	**Torquay U**	D4	A	W	3-2	Fogg, Priscott 2
		3	4.1.64	**Aston Villa**	D1	A	D	0-0
		3r	8.1.64	**Aston Villa**		H	W	2-1	Towers, Palethorpe
		4	25.1.64	**Swindon T**	D2	H	L	1-2	Priscott
1964-65	D4	1	14.11.64	**Dartford**	SL	A	D	1-1	Chamberlain
		1r	17.11.64	**Dartford**		H	W	1-0	Kearns
		2	5.12.64	**Reading**	D3	H	L	1-3	Burton
1965-66	D4	1	13.11.65	**Wellingborough T**	UCL	H	W	2-1	Priscott, Kearns
		2	4.12.65	**Walsall**	D3	H	L	0-2
1966-67	D4	1	26.11.66	**Torquay U**	D3	H	W	2-1	Kearns, A.Smith og
		2	16.1.67	**Reading**	D3	H	W	1-0	Howarth
		3	28.1.67	**Brighton & HA**	D3	H	D	0-0
		3r	1.2.67	**Brighton & HA**		A	L	1-3	Walton
1967-68	D4	1	13.12.67	**Reading**	D3	A	L	2-6	Walker, Howarth
1968-69	D4	1	17.11.68	**Dartford**	SL	A	L	1-3	Howarth
1969-70	D4	1	15.11.69	**Margate**	SL	A	W	7-2	Brown 3, Howarth 3, Gowans
		2	6.12.69	**Bristol R**	D3	H	W	3-1	Howarth 2, Brown
		3	3.1.70	**Huddersfield T**	D2	A	D	1-1	Walker
		3r	12.1.70	**Huddersfield T**		H	W	3-1	Melia 2 (1p), Gowans
		4	24.1.70	**Carlisle U**	D2	A	D	2-2	Howarth, Jopling
		4r	28.1.70	**Carlisle U**		H	L	1-4	Howarth
1970-71	D4	1	21.11.70	**Hendon**	IL	A	W	2-0	Howarth 2
		2	12.12.70	**Bristol R**	D3	H	D	1-1	Brown
		2r	15.12.70	**Bristol R**		A	W	3-1	Howarth, Giles, Melia
		3	2.1.71	**Liverpool**	D1	A	L	0-1
1971-72	D4	1	24.11.71	**Alvechurch**	MC	H	W	4-2	Brodie 2, Hunt og, Sydenham
		2	11.12.71	**Reading**	D4	A	L	0-1
1972-73	D4	1	18.11.72	**Southend U**	D3	A	W	2-0	Melledew, Brodie
		2	9.12.72	**Watford**	D3	H	L	0-2
1973-74	D3	1	24.11.73	**Dagenham**	IL	A	W	4-0	Dean 2, Brodie, Howarth
		2	15.12.73	**Cambridge U**	D3	H	L	1-2	Howarth
1974-75	D3	1	23.11.74	**Brighton & HA**	D3	A	L	1-3	Brodie
1975-76	D3	1	22.11.75	**Wealdstone**	SL	H	W	4-3	Richardson, Morissey (p), Howarth 2

ALDERSHOT

	2	13.12.75	Bishop's Stortford	IL	H	W	2-0	Warnock, Morrissey
	3	3.1.76	Lincoln C	D4	H	L	1-2	Howarth
1976-77 D4	1	20.11.76	Portsmouth	D3	H	D	1-1	McGregor
	1r	23.11.76	Portsmouth		A	L	1-2	McGregor
1977-78 D4	1	26.11.77	Reading	D4	A	L	1-3	McGregor
1978-79 D4	1	25.11.78	Weymouth	SL	H	D	1-1	Crosby
	1r	29.11.78	Weymouth		A	W	2-0	Shanahan, Dungworth
	2	16.12.78	Barking	IL	A	W	2-1	Dungworth, Shanahan
	3	9.1.79	Sheffield U	D2	A	D	0-0	
	3r	15.1.79	Sheffield U		H	W	1-0	Dungworth (p)
	4	30.1.79	Swindon T	D3	H	W	2-1	Dungworth 2
	5	20.2.79	Shrewsbury T	D3	H	D	2-2	Dungworth 2
	5r	26.2.79	Shrewsbury T		A	L	1-3aet	Dungworth
1979-80 D4	1	24.11.79	Exeter C	D3	H	W	4-1	Crosby, Jopling, Brodie, Giles og
	2	15.12.79	Hereford U	D4	A	W	2-1	Marshall og, Needham
	3	5.1.80	Everton	D1	A	L	1-4	McGregor
1980-81 D4	1	22.11.80	Oxford U	D3	A	L	0-1	
1981-82 D4	1	21.11.81	Leytonstone & Ilford	IL	H	W	2-0	Garwood 2
	2	15.12.81	Oxford U	D3	H	D	2-2	Brodie, McDonald
	2r	30.12.81	Oxford U		A	L	2-4	Robinson, French
1982-83 D4	1	20.11.82	Wimborne	WL	H	W	4-0	Banton 2 (1p), Sanford, Brodie
	2	11.12.82	Portsmouth	D3	A	W	3-1	Briley, Banton 2
	3	8.1.83	Swindon T	D4	A	L	0-7	
1983-84 D4	1	19.11.83	Worcester C	APL	H	D	1-1	Burvill
	1r	21.11.83	Worcester C		A	L	1-2	Banton
1984-85 D4	1	17.11.84	Newport Co	D3	A	D	1-1	McDonald (p)
	1r	20.11.84	Newport Co		H	W	4-0	Banton, Foley 2, McDonald (p)
	2	8.12.84	Burton Albion	NPL	H	L	0-2	
1985-86 D4	1	16.11.85	Plymouth A	D3	A	L	0-1	
1986-87 D4	1	15.11.86	Torquay U	D4	H	W	1-0	King (p)
	2	6.12.86	Colchester U	D4	H	W	3-2	Wignall, Foyle 2
	3	10.1.87	Oxford U	D1	H	W	3-0	Smith, Burvill, Barnes
	4	31.1.87	Barnsley	D2	H	D	1-1	Foyle
	4r	3.2.87	Barnsley		A	L	0-3	
1987-88 D3	1	14.11.87	Sutton U	GMVC	A	L	0-3	
1988-89 D3	1	19.11.88	Hayes	IL	H	W	1-0	McDonald
	2	10.12.88	Bristol C	D3	H	D	1-1	McDonald (p)
	2r	13.12.88	Bristol C		A	D	0-0aet	
	2 2r	20.12.88	Bristol C		H	D	2-2aet	Randall, Claridge
	2 3r	22.12.88	Bristol C		A	L	0-1	
1989-90 D4	1	18.11.89	Cambridge U	D4	H	L	0-1	
1990-91 D4	1	17.11.90	Tiverton T	WL	H	W	6-2	Stewart, Henry 2, Williams, Puckett, Randall
	2	8.12.90	Maidstone U	D4	H	W	2-1	Puckett, Stewart
	3	5.1.91	West Ham	D2	H	D	0-0	
			played at Upton Park					
	3r	16.1.91	West Ham		A	L	1-6	Randall
1991-92 D4	1	16.11.91	Enfield	IL	H	L	0-1	

ALFRETON TOWN

Originally formed 1921, reformed 1959. **First entered FA Cup:** 1922. **League club beaten:** Lincoln C

1924-25 CA	5q	Lincoln C (3N) H 1-0; 6q Port Vale (D2) H 2-8						
1969-70 ML	1	15.11.69	Barrow	D3	H	D	1-1	Bate
	1r	17.11.69	Barrow		A	D	0-0aet	
	1 2r	20.11.69	Barrow at Chesterfield			D	2-2aet	Ford, Woodward (p)
	1 3r	24.11.69	Barrow at Preston			L	0-2	
1973-74 ML	1	24.11.73	Blyth Spartans	NL	H	D	0-0	
	1r	28.11.73	Blyth Spartans		A	L	1-2	Ford

ALTON TOWN

First entered FA Cup: 1950. Currently in the Hampshire League and known as Alton Town Bass

1972-73 Hants 1		18.11.72	Newport Co	D4	A	L	1-5	Morton

ALTRINCHAM

Formed 1891. **First entered FA Cup:** 1906. **FA Challenge Trophy Winners:** 1978, 1986. **Runners-Up:** 1982. **League clubs defeated:** Birmingham C, Blackpool (2), Chester, Crewe A, Hartlepool U, Lincoln C, Rochdale (2), Rotherham, Scunthorpe U (2), Sheffield U, Tranmere, York C **FA Cup Final connection:** Tommy Docherty, who played for Preston in the 1954 Cup Final and later managed Manchester United in two Cup Finals, managed Altrincham for a brief spell in the late 1980s

1921-22	CC	4q	**Tranmere R** (3N) H 4-4; 4qr **Tranmere R** A 4-2; 5q **Southport** (3N) A 0-3						
1933-34	CC	1	25.11.33	**Gainsborough T**	ML	A	L	0-1	
1963-64	CC	1	16.11.63	**Wrexham**	D3	H	–	1-2	Taberner
				abandoned after 76 minutes – fog					
		1	20.11.63	**Wrexham**		H	D	0-0	
		1r	26.11.63	**Wrexham**		A	L	0-3	
1965-66	CC	1	13.11.65	**Scarborough**	ML	H	W	6-0	Connolly, Swindells 5
		2	8.12.65	**Rochdale**	D4	A	W	3-1	Swindells, Campbell, Connolly
		3	22.1.66	**Wolverhampton W**	D2	A	L	0-5	
1967-68	CC	1	9.12.67	**Grantham**	ML	A	W	3-0	Peters, Lister, Farmer og
		2	6.1.68	**Barrow**	D3	H	L	1-2	Lister
1968-69	NPL	1	16.11.68	**Crewe A**	D3	H	L	0-1	
1971-72	NPL	1	23.11.71	**Rossendale U**	CC	A	L	0-1	
1972-73	NPL	1	18.11.72	**Notts Co**	D3	H	L	0-1	
1973-74	NPL	1	24.11.73	**Hartlepool**	D4	H	W	2-0	Dickinson, Windsor
		2	15.12.73	**Blackburn R**	D3	A	D	0-0	
		2r	19.12.73	**Blackburn R**		H	L	0-2	
1974-75	NPL	1	23.11.74	**Scunthorpe U**	D4	A	D	1-1	J.Hughes
		1r	25.11.74	**Scunthorpe U**		H	W	3-1	Morris, Davison, J.Hughes
		2	14.12.74	**Gateshead**	NPL	H	W	3-0	J.Hughes, R.Hughes, Morris
		3	4.1.75	**Everton**	D1	A	D	1-1	J.Hughes
		3r	7.1.75	**Everton** at Old Trafford		H	L	0-2	
1975-76	NPL	1	22.11.75	**Halifax**	D3	A	L	1-3	Moore
1976-77	NPL	1	20.11.76	**Rotherham U**	D3	A	L	0-5	
1978-79	NPL	1	25.11.78	**Southport**	NPL	H	W	4-3	Johnson 2, Bailey, Rogers
		2	16.12.78	**Droylesden**	CC	A	W	2-0	Johnson, Brooke
		3	10.1.79	**Tottenham H**	D1	A	D	1-1	Johnson
		3r	16.1.79	**Tottenham H** at Maine Road		H	L	0-3	
1979-80	APL	1	24.11.79	**Crewe A**	D4	H	W	3-0	Rogers, Whitbread, Wilson
		2	15.12.79	**Rotherham U**	D3	A	W	2-0	Bailey, Howard
		3	5.1.80	**Orient**	D2	H	D	1-1	Whitbread
		3r	9.1.80	**Orient**		A	L	1-2	Johnson
1980-81	APL	1	22.11.80	**Burscough**	CC	A	W	2-1	Johnson, Rogers
		2	13.12.80	**Scunthorpe U**	D4	A	D	0-0	
		2r	15.12.80	**Scunthorpe U**		H	W	1-0	Davison (p)
		3	3.1.81	**Liverpool**	D1	A	L	1-4	Heathcote (p)
1981-82	APL	1	21.11.81	**Sheffield U**	D4	A	D	2-2	Rogers 2
		1r	23.11.81	**Sheffield U**		H	W	3-0	Howard 2, Heathcote
		2	12.12.81	**York C**	D4	A	D	0-0	
		2r	2.1.82	**York C**		H	W	4-3	Goulding, Rogers, Whitbread 2
		3	18.1.82	**Burnley**	D3	A	L	1-6	Howard
1982-83	APL	1	20.11.82	**Rochdale**	D4	H	W	2-1	Davison, Howard
		2	11.12.82	**Huddersfield T**	D3	H	L	0-1	
1983-84	APL	1	19.11.83	**Frickley A**	APL	A	W	1-0	Gardner
		2	10.12.83	**Darlington**	D4	A	D	0-0	
		2r	14.12.83	**Darlington**		H	L	0-2	
1984-85	APL	1	17.11.84	**Blackpool**	D4	A	W	1-0	Fagan
		2	8.12.84	**Doncaster R**	D3	A	L	1-3	Bennett
1985-86	APL	1	16.11.85	**Chorley**	NPL	A	W	2-0	Reid, Anderson
		2	7.12.85	**Blackpool**	D3	A	W	2-1	Reid, Anderson
		3	14.1.86	**Birmingham C**	D1	A	W	2-1	Ellis, Hopkins
		4	25.1.86	**York C**	D3	A	L	0-2	
1986-87	GMVC	1	15.11.86	**Frickley A**	GMVC	A	D	0-0	
		1r	18.11.86	**Frickley A**		H	W	4-0	Anderson, Farrelly, Reid, Bishop
		2	6.12.86	**Telford U**	GMVC	A	L	0-1	
1987-88	GMVC	1	14.11.87	**Wigan A**	D3	H	L	0-2	
1988-89	GMVC	1	19.11.88	**Lincoln C**	D4	H	W	3-2	Timmons, Ellis 2
		2	10.12.88	**Halifax T**	D4	H	L	0-3	
1990-91	GMVC	1	18.11.90	**Huddersfield T**	D3	H	L	1-2	Rowlands
1992-93	GMVC	1	14.11.92	**Chester**	D2	A	D	1-1	Comstive og

1r	25.11.92	Chester		H	W	2-0	Harris, Freeman
2	5.12.92	Port Vale	D2	H	L	1-4	Dyson

ALVECHURCH

Formed 1929. First entered FA Cup: 1968. Folded (possibly temporarily) 1992. Cup Final connection: A former club of Alan Smith, who played in the 1993 final for Arsenal. League club beaten: Exeter C

1971-72 MC	1	24.11.71	Aldershot	D4	A	L	2-4	Palmer, Hope
1973-74 WMRL	1	24.11.73	Exeter C	D4	A	W	1-0	Allner
	2	15.12.73	Kings Lynn	SL	H	W	6-1	Lawrence 2, Palmer, Edwards 2, Lyne (p)
	3	5.1.74	Bradford C	D4	A	L	2-4	Lawrence, Horne

AMATEUR ATHLETIC CLUB (AAC)

Home ground was Lillie Bridge, West Brompton, London, venue for the second Cup Final

1873-74	1	Clapham R	A	*scratched*	

ANDOVER

Formed 1883. First entered FA Cup: 1898. FA Cup Final connection: Former Andover player Nigel Spackman played for Liverpool in the 1988 Cup Final

1962-63 SL	1	3.11.62	Gillingham	D4	H	L	0-1	

ANNFIELD PLAIN

Formed 1890. First entered FA Cup: 1906. Record crowd of 7,200 vs Southport, 1928. Exactly half that number – 3,600 – saw the match between the same two clubs 36 years later

1926-27 NEL	1	27.11.26	Chilton Colliery	NEL	H	L	2-4	Jones, Roots
1928-29 NEL	1	24.11.28	Southport	3N	H	L	1-4	Ferguson
1964-65 Wear	1	14.11.64	Southport	D4	A	L	1-6	Lawson

APSLEY

Formed 1885. First entered FA Cup: 1901. Changed name to Hemel Hempstead 1947

1938-39 Spt	1	26.11.38	Bromley	AL	A	L	1-2	Hook

ARGONAUTS

1879-80	1	8.11.79	Hotspur		A	D	1-1	Gore
	1r	15.11.79	Hotspur		H	L	0-1	

ARNOLD

Formed 1928 as Arnold St Marys. First Entered FA Cup: 1928. Merged with Arnold Kingswell 1989 and now play as Arnold Town. Based in Nottinghamshire

1967-68 ML	1	9.12.67	Bristol R	D3	H	L	0-3	
1977-78 ML	1	26.11.77	Port Vale	D3	H	D	0-0	
	1r	28.11.77	Port Vale		A	L	2-5	Brockhurst, Livesey

ARSENAL

Formed 1886 as Dial Square. 1886-1893 Royal Arsenal; 1893-1914 Woolwich Arsenal; 1914 Arsenal. FA Cup and League Double 1971. FA Cup Winners: 1930, 1936, 1950, 1971, 1979, 1993. Runners-Up: 1927, 1932, 1952, 1972, 1978, 1980. Record FA Cup Win: 12-0 vs Ashford, 1st qual rd, 14.10.1893. In Competition Proper: 11-1 vs Darwen, 3rd round, 9.1.1932. Record FA Cup Defeat: 0-6 vs Sunderland 1st round, 21.1.1893; Derby Co, 1st round, 28.1.1899; West Ham, 3rd round 1st leg, 5.1.1946

as Royal Arsenal

1889-90	1q Lyndhurst (H) 11-0; 2q Thorpe, Norwich (A) 2-2aet; 2qr Thorpe, Norwich (H) walkover; 3q Crusaders (H) 5-2aet; 4q Swifts (H) 1-5
1890-91	1	17.1.91	Derby Co	D1	H	L	1-2	Offer
1891-92	1	16.1.92	Small Heath	FAII	A	L	1-5	Davie
1892-93	1q Highland Lt Infantry (H) 3-0; 2q City Ramblers (H) 10-1; 3q Millwall A (H) 3-2; 4q Clapton (H) 3-0
	1	21.1.93	Sunderland	D1	A	L	0-6	

A R S E N A L

as Woolwich Arsenal

1893-94	D2	1q **Ashford U** (H) 12-0; 2q **Clapton Orient** (H) 6-2; 3q **Millwall A** (H) 2-0; 4q **2nd Scots Guards** (A) 2-1aet					
		1	27.1.94 **Sheffield W**	D1	H	L	1-2	Elliott
1894-95	D2	1	2.2.95 **Bolton W**	D1	A	L	0-1
1895-96	D2	1	1.2.96 **Burnley**	D1	A	L	1-6	O'Brien
1896-97	D2	4q **Leyton** (H) 5-0; 5q **Chatham** (H) 4-0; Int **Millwall** (A) 2-4					
1897-98	D2	3q **St Albans** (H) 9-0; 4q **Sheppey U** (H) 3-0; 5q **New Brompton** (H) 4-2					
		1	29.1.98 **Burnley**	D2	A	L	1-3	Brock
1898-99	D2	1	28.1.99 **Derby Co**	D1	H	L	0-6
1899-00	D2	3q **New Brompton** (H) 1-1; 3qr **New Brompton** (A) 0-0; 3q 2r **New Brompton** at Millwall 2-2; 3q 3r **New Brompton** at Tottenham 1-1; 3q 4r **New Brompton** at Gravesend 0-1					
1900-01	D2	Int **Darwen** (A) 2-0					
		1	9.2.01 **Blackburn R**	D1	H	W	2-0	Tennant, Low
		2	23.2.01 **WBA**	D1	H	L	0-1
1901-02	D2	Int **Luton T** (H) 1-1; Int R **Luton T** (A) 2-0					
		1	25.1.02 **Newcastle U**	D1	H	L	0-2
1902-03	D2	Int **Brentford** (A) 1-1; Int R **Brentford** (H) 5-0					
		1	7.2.03 **Sheffield U**	D1	H	L	1-3	W.Anderson
1903-04	D2	Int **Bristol R** (A) 1-1; Int R **Bristol R** (H) 1-1; Int 2r **Bristol R** at Tottenham 1-0					
		1	6.2.04 **Fulham**	SL	H	W	1-0	Shanks
		2	20.2.04 **Manchester C**	D1	H	L	0-2
1904-05	D1	1	4.2.05 **Bristol C**	D2	H	D	0-0
		1r	8.2.05 **Bristol C**		A	L	0-1
1905-06	D1	1	13.1.06 **West Ham**	SL	H	D	1-1	Sharp (p)
		1r	18.1.06 **West Ham**		A	W	3-2	Ducat, Satterthwaite, Garbutt
		2	3.2.06 **Watford**	SL	H	W	3-0	Freeman, Coleman, Fitchie
		3	24.2.06 **Sunderland**	D1	H	W	5-0	Garbutt 2, Fitchie, Sands, Coleman
		4	10.3.06 **Manchester U**	D2	A	W	3-2	Freeman 2, Coleman
		SF	31.3.06 **Newcastle U**	D1		L	0-2
		played at Victoria Ground, Stoke					
1906-07	D1	1	12.1.07 **Grimsby T**	D2	A	D	1-1	Garbutt
		1r	16.1.07 **Grimsby T**		H	W	3-0	Satterthwaite, Sands, Garbutt
		2	2.2.07 **Bristol C**	D1	H	W	2-1	Hynds, Kyle
		3	23.2.07 **Bristol R**	SL	H	W	1-0	Neave
		4	9.3.07 **Barnsley**	D2	A	W	2-1	Satterthwaite, Neave
		SF	23.3.07 **Sheffield W**	D1		L	1-3	Garbutt
		played at St Andrew's Birmingham					
1907-08	D1	1	11.1.08 **Hull C**	D2	H	D	0-0
		1r	16.1.08 **Hull C**		A	L	1-4	Kyle
1908-09	D1	1	16.1.09 **Croydon Common**	SL	A	D	1-1	Fitchie
		1r	20.1.09 **Croydon Common**		H	W	2-0	Raybould, Ducat
		2	6.2.09 **Millwall**	SL	H	D	1-1	Lewis
		2r	10.2.09 **Millwall**		A	L	0-1
1909-10	D1	1	15.1.10 **Watford**	SL	H	W	3-0	Lewis 2, McKellar
		2	5.2.10 **Everton**	D1	A	L	0-5
1910-11	D1	1	14.1.11 **Clapton Orient**	D2	A	–	1-0	McEachrane
		abandoned after 55 minutes					
		1	16.1.11 **Clapton Orient**		A	W	2-1	Chalmers, Hoare
		2	4.2.11 **Swindon T**	SL	A	L	0-1
1911-12	D1	1	13.1.12 **Bolton W**	D1	A	L	0-1
1912-13	D1	1	11.1.13 **Croydon Common**	SL	A	D	0-0
		1r	15.1.13 **Croydon Common**		H	W	2-1	Duncan, Graham
		2	1.2.13 **Liverpool**	D1	H	L	1-4	Lewis
1913-14	D2	1	10.1.14 **Bradford City**	D1	A	L	0-2

as Arsenal

1914-15	D2	1	9.1.15 **Merthyr Town**	SL	H	W	3-0	King 3
		2	30.1.15 **Chelsea**	D1	A	L	0-1
1919-20	D1	1	10.1.20 **Rochdale**	CL	H	W	4-2	Rutherford, Groves, Graham, Pagnam
		2	31.1.20 **Bristol C**	D2	A	L	0-1
1920-21	D1	1	8.1.21 **QPR**	D3	A	L	0-2
1921-22	D1	1	7.1.22 **QPR**	3S	H	D	0-0
		1r	11.1.22 **QPR**		A	W	2-1	Graham (p), Milne
		2	28.1.22 **Bradford PA**	D2	A	W	3-2	White 2, Blyth
		3	18.2.22 **Leicester C**	D2	H	W	3-0	White 2, Rutherford
		4	4.3.22 **Preston NE**	D1	H	D	1-1	White
		4r	8.3.22 **Preston NE**		A	L	1-2aet	Blyth
1922-23	D1	1	13.1.23 **Liverpool**	D1	A	D	0-0

		1r	17.1.23	**Liverpool**		H	L	1-4	Turnbull
1923-24	D1	1	12.1.24	**Luton T**	3S	H	W	4-1	Blyth, Woods, Turnbull, Milne
		2	2.2.24	**Cardiff C**	D1	A	L	0-1	
1924-25	D1	1	14.1.25	**West Ham**	D1	A	D	0-0	
		1r	21.1.25	**West Ham**		H	D	2-2aet	Brain 2
		1 2r	26.1.25	**West Ham** at Stamford Bridge			L	0-1	
1925-26	D1	3	9.1.26	**Wolverhampton W**	D2	A	D	1-1	Brain
		3r	13.1.26	**Wolverhampton W**		H	W	1-0	Baker
		4	30.1.26	**Blackburn R**	D1	H	W	3-1	Haden, Brain, Hope og
		5	20.2.26	**Aston Villa**	D1	A	D	1-1	Buchan
		5r	24.2.26	**Aston Villa**		H	W	2-0	Paterson, Brain
		6	6.3.26	**Swansea T**	D2	A	L	1-2	Mackie
1926-27	D1	3	8.1.27	**Sheffield U**	D1	A	W	3-2	Brain, Buchan, Hulme
		4	29.1.27	**Port Vale**	D2	A	D	2-2	Buchan, Brain
		4r	2.2.27	**Port Vale**		H	W	1-0	Buchan
		5	19.2.27	**Liverpool**	D1	H	W	2-0	Brain, Buchan
		6	5.3.27	**Wolverhampton W**	D2	H	W	2-1	Blyth, Butler
		SF	26.3.27	**Southampton**	D2		W	2-1	Hulme, Buchan
				played at Stamford Bridge					
		F	23.4.27	**Cardiff C**	D1 WEMBLEY		L	0-1	
1927-28	D1	3	14.1.28	**WBA**	D2	H	W	2-0	Brain, Hulme
		4	28.1.28	**Everton**	D1	H	W	4-3	Hulme 2, Brain, Buchan
		5	18.2.28	**Aston Villa**	D1	H	W	4-1	Brain 2, Lambert, Hulme
		6	3.3.28	**Stoke C**	D2	H	W	4-1	Blyth 2, Hoar 2
		SF	24.3.28	**Blackburn R**	D1		L	0-1	
				played at Filbert Street					
1928-29	D1	3	12.1.29	**Stoke C**	D2	H	W	2-1	Brain, Hulme
		4	26.1.29	**Mansfield T**	ML	H	W	2-0	Jack, Peel
		5	16.2.29	**Swindon T**	3S	A	D	0-0	
		5r	20.2.29	**Swindon T**		H	W	1-0	Brain
		6	2.3.29	**Aston Villa**	D1	A	L	0-1	
1929-30	D1	3	11.1.30	**Chelsea**	D2	H	W	2-0	Lambert, Bastin
		4	25.1.30	**Birmingham**	D1	H	D	2-2	Bastin, Jack
		4r	29.1.30	**Birmingham**		A	W	1-0	Baker (p)
		5	15.2.30	**Middlesbrough**	D1	A	W	2-0	Lambert, Bastin
		6	1.3.30	**West Ham**	D1	A	W	3-0	Lambert 2, Baker
		SF	22.3.30	**Hull C**	D2		D	2-2	Jack, Bastin
				played at Elland Road					
		SFr	26.3.30	**Hull C**			W	1-0	Jack
				played at Villa Park					
		F	26.4.30	**HUDDERSFIELD TOWN**	D1 WEMBLEY		W	2-0	James, Lambert
1930-31	D1	3	10.1.31	**Aston Villa**	D1	H	D	2-2	Lambert, Jack
		3r	14.1.31	**Aston Villa**		A	W	3-1	Hulme 2, Jack
		4	24.1.31	**Chelsea**	D1	A	L	1-2	Bastin
1931-32	D1	3	9.1.32	**Darwen**	LC	H	W	11-1	Bastin 4, Jack 3, Lambert 2, Hulme 2
		4	23.1.32	**Plymouth A**	D2	H	W	4-2	Lambert 2, Hulme, Roberts og
		5	13.2.32	**Portsmouth**	D1	A	W	2-0	Bastin, Hulme
		6	27.2.32	**Huddersfield T**	D1	A	W	1-0	Roberts
		SF	12.3.32	**Manchester C**	D1		W	1-0	Bastin
				played at Villa Park					
		F	23.4.32	**Newcastle U**	D1 WEMBLEY		L	1-2	John
1932-33	D1	3	14.1.33	**Walsall**	3N	A	L	0-2	
1933-34	D1	3	13.1.34	**Luton T**	3S	A	W	1-0	Dunne
		4	27.1.34	**Crystal P**	3S	H	W	7-0	Dunne 2, Bastin 2, Beasley 2, Birkett
		5	17.2.34	**Derby Co**	D1	H	W	1-0	Jack
		6	3.3.34	**Aston Villa**	D1	H	L	1-2	Dougall
1934-35	D1	3	12.1.35	**Brighton & HA**	3S	A	W	2-0	Hulme, Drake
		4	26.1.35	**Leicester C**	D1	A	W	1-0	Hulme
		5	16.2.35	**Reading**	3S	A	W	1-0	Bastin
		6	2.3.35	**Sheffield W**	D1	A	L	1-2	Catlin og
1935-36	D1	3	11.1.36	**Bristol R**	3S	A	W	5-1	Bastin 2, Drake 2, Bowden
		4	25.1.36	**Liverpool**	D1	A	W	2-0	Bowden, Hulme
		5	15.2.36	**Newcastle U**	D2	A	D	3-3	Bowden 2, Hulme
		5r	19.2.36	**Newcastle U**		H	W	3-0	Bastin 2 (2p), Beasley
		6	29.2.36	**Barnsley**	D2	H	W	4-1	Beasley 2, Bowden, Bastin (p)
		SF	21.3.36	**Grimsby T**	D1		W	1-0	Bastin
				played at Huddersfield					

ARSENAL

Season	Div	Rd	Date	Opponent		Venue	W/L/D	Score	Scorers
		F	25.4.36	**SHEFFIELD UNITED**	D2 WEMBLEY		W	1-0	Drake
1936-37	D1	3	16.1.37	**Chesterfield**	D2	A	W	5-1	Drake 2, Kirchen 2, Davidson
		4	30.1.37	**Manchester U**	D1	H	W	5-0	Bastin, Davidson, Drake, Kirchen, Brown og
		5	20.2.37	**Burnley**	D2	A	W	7-1	Drake 4, Crayston, Bastin, Kirchen
		6	6.3.37	**WBA**	D1	A	L	1-3	Bastin
1937-38	D1	3	8.1.38	**Bolton W**	D1	H	W	3-1	Bastin 2, Kirchen
		4	22.1.38	**Wolverhampton W**	D1	A	W	2-1	Kirchen, Drake
		5	12.2.38	**Preston NE**	D1	H	L	0-1	
1938-39	D1	3	7.1.39	**Chelsea**	D1	A	L	1-2	Bastin
1945-46	D1	3 1L	5.1.46	**West Ham**	D2	A	L	0-6	
		3 2L	9.1.46	**West Ham**		H	W	1-0	Cumner
1946-47	D1	3	11.1.47	**Chelsea**	D1	A	D	1-1	McPherson
		3r	15.1.47	**Chelsea**		H	D	1-1	Rooke
		3 2r	20.1.47	**Chelsea** at Tottenham			L	0-2	
1947-48	D1	3	10.1.48	**Bradford PA**	D2	H	L	0-1	
1948-49	D1	3	8.1.49	**Tottenham H**	D2	H	W	3-0	McPherson, Roper, Lishman
		4	29.1.49	**Derby Co**	D1	A	L	0-1	
1949-50	D1	3	7.1.50	**Sheffield W**	D2	H	W	1-0	Lewis
		4	28.1.50	**Swansea T**	D2	H	W	2-1	Logie, Barnes (p)
		5	11.2.50	**Burnley**	D1	H	W	2-0	Lewis, D.Compton
		6	4.3.50	**Leeds U**	D2	H	W	1-0	Lewis
		SF	18.3.50	**Chelsea**	D1		D	2-2	Cox, L.Compton
			played at Tottenham						
		SFr	22.3.50	**Chelsea**			W	1-0aet	Cox
			played at Tottenham						
		F	29.4.50	**LIVERPOOL**	D1 WEMBLEY		W	2-0	Lewis 2
1950-51	D1	3	6.1.51	**Carlisle U**	3N	H	D	0-0	
		3r	11.1.51	**Carlisle U**		A	W	4-1	Lewis 2, Logie, Goring
		4	27.1.51	**Northampton T**	3S	H	W	3-2	Lewis 2, Roper
		5	10.2.51	**Manchester U**	D1	A	L	0-1	
1951-52	D1	3	12.1.52	**Norwich C**	3S	A	W	5-0	Lishman 2, Logie, Goring, Roper
		4	2.2.52	**Barnsley**	D2	H	W	4-0	Lewis 3, Lishman
		5	23.2.52	**Leyton Orient**	3S	A	W	3-0	Lishman 2, Lewis
		6	8.3.52	**Luton T**	D2	A	W	3-2	Cox 2, Milton
		SF	5.4.52	**Chelsea**	D1		D	1-1	Cox
		SFr	7.4.52	**Chelsea**			W	3-0	Cox 2, Lishman
			both matches played at Tottenham						
		F	3.5.52	**Newcastle U**	D1 WEMBLEY		L	0-1	
1952-53	D1	3	10.1.53	**Doncaster R**	D2	H	W	4-0	Lishman, Holton, Logie, Roper
		4	31.1.53	**Bury**	D2	H	W	6-2	Holton, Lishman, Logie, Milton, Roper, T.Daniel og
		5	14.2.53	**Burnley**	D1	A	W	2-0	Holton, Lishman
		6	28.2.53	**Blackpool**	D1	H	L	1-2	Logie
1953-54	D1	3	9.1.54	**Aston Villa**	D1	H	W	5-1	Roper 2, Holton, Logie, Milton
		4	30.1.54	**Norwich C**	3S	H	L	1-2	Logie
1954-55	D1	3	8.1.55	**Cardiff C**	D1	H	W	1-0	Lawton
		4	29.1.55	**Wolverhampton W**	D1	A	L	0-1	
1955-56	D1	3	7.1.56	**Bedford T**	SL	H	D	2-2	Tapscott, Groves
		3r	12.1.56	**Bedford T**		A	W	2-1aet	Groves, Tapscott
		4	28.1.56	**Aston Villa**	D1	H	W	4-1	Tapscott 2, Groves, Charlton
		5	18.2.56	**Charlton A**	D1	A	W	2-0	Groves, Bloomfield
		6	3.3.56	**Birmingham C**	D1	H	L	1-3	Charlton
1956-57	D1	3	5.1.57	**Stoke C**	D2	H	W	4-2	Herd 2, Tapscott, Haverty
		4	26.1.57	**Newport Co**	3S	A	W	2-0	Tapscott, Herd
		5	16.2.57	**Preston NE**	D1	A	D	3-3	Clapton, Herd, Dunn og
		5r	19.2.57	**Preston NE**		H	W	2-1	Dodgin, Herd
		6	2.3.57	**WBA**	D1	A	D	2-2	Herd, Charlton
		6r	5.3.57	**WBA**		H	L	1-2	Holton
1957-58	D1	3	4.1.58	**Northampton T**	3S	A	L	1-3	Clapton
1958-59	D1	3	10.1.59	**Bury**	D3	A	W	1-0	Herd
		4	24.1.59	**Colchester U**	D3	A	D	2-2	Groves 2
		4r	28.1.59	**Colchester U**		H	W	4-0	Herd 2, Julians, Evans (p)
		5	14.2.59	**Sheffield U**	D2	H	D	2-2	Evans (p), Julians
		5r	18.2.59	**Sheffield U**		A	L	0-3	
1959-60	D1	3	9.1.60	**Rotherham U**	D2	A	D	2-2	Julians, Williams og
		3r	13.1.60	**Rotherham U**		H	D	1-1aet	Bloomfield
		3 2r	18.1.60	**Rotherham U** at Hillsborough			L	0-2	
1960-61	D1	3	7.1.61	**Sunderland**	D2	A	L	1-2	Herd

ARSENAL

1961-62	D1	3	6.1.62	**Bradford C**	D4	H	W	3-0	Charles 2, Lawlor og
		4	31.1.62	**Manchester U**	D1	A	L	0-1	
1962-63	D1	3	30.1.63	**Oxford U**	D4	H	W	5-1	Baker 2, Strong 2, MacLeod
		4	12.3.63	**Sheffield W**	D1	H	W	2-0	MacLeod, Strong
		5	16.3.63	**Liverpool**	D1	H	L	1-2	MacLeod
1963-64	D1	3	4.1.64	**Wolverhampton W**	D1	H	W	2-1	Strong, Baker
		4	25.1.64	**WBA**	D1	A	D	3-3	MacLeod, Armstrong, Baker
		4r	29.1.64	**WBA**		H	W	2-0	Armstrong, Strong
		5	15.2.64	**Liverpool**	D1	H	L	0-1	
1964-65	D1	3	9.1.65	**Darlington**	D4	A	W	2-0	Radford, Armstrong
		4	30.1.65	**Peterborough U**	D3	A	L	1-2	Radford
1965-66	D1	3	22.1.66	**Blackburn R**	D1	A	L	0-3	
1966-67	D1	3	28.1.67	**Bristol R**	D3	A	W	3-0	Graham, Neilson, Armstrong
		4	18.2.67	**Bolton W**	D2	A	D	0-0	
		4r	22.2.67	**Bolton W**		H	W	3-0	Radford 3
		5	11.3.67	**Birmingham C**	D2	A	L	0-1	
1967-68	D1	3	27.1.68	**Shrewsbury T**	D3	A	D	1-1	Radford
		3r	30.1.68	**Shrewsbury T**		H	W	2-0	Sammels, Jenkins
		4	17.2.68	**Swansea T**	D4	A	W	1-0	Gould
		5	9.3.68	**Birmingham C**	D2	H	D	1-1	Radford
		5r	12.3.68	**Birmingham C**		A	L	1-2	Gould
1968-69	D1	3	4.1.69	**Cardiff C**	D2	A	D	0-0	
		3r	7.1.69	**Cardiff C**		H	W	2-0	Armstrong, Gould
		4	25.1.69	**Charlton A**	D2	H	W	2-0	Sammels, Robertson
		5	12.2.69	**WBA**	D1	A	L	0-1	
1969-70	D1	3	3.1.70	**Blackpool**	D2	H	D	1-1	Radford
		3r	15.1.70	**Blackpool**		A	L	2-3	Sammels, Radford
1970-71	D1	3	6.1.71	**Yeovil T**	SL	A	W	3-0	Radford 2, Kennedy
		4	23.1.71	**Portsmouth**	D2	A	D	1-1	Storey (p)
		4r	1.2.71	**Portsmouth**		H	W	3-2	George, Simpson, Storey (p)
		5	17.2.71	**Manchester C**	D1	A	W	2-1	George 2
		6	6.3.71	**Leicester C**	D2	A	D	0-0	
		6r	15.3.71	**Leicester C**		H	W	1-0	George
		SF	27.3.71	**Stoke C**	D1		D	2-2	Storey 2 (1p)
			played at Hillsborough						
		SFr	31.3.71	**Stoke C**			W	2-0	Graham, Kennedy
			played at Villa Park						
		F	8.5.71	**LIVERPOOL**	D1	WEMBLEY	W	2-1aet	Kelly, George
1971-72	D1	3	15.1.72	**Swindon T**	D2	A	W	2-0	Armstrong, Ball
		4	5.2.72	**Reading**	D4	A	W	2-1	Rice, Morgan og
		5	26.2.72	**Derby Co**	D1	A	D	2-2	George 2
		5r	29.2.72	**Derby Co**		H	D	0-0aet	
		5 2r	13.3.72	**Derby Co** at Filbert Street			W	1-0	Kennedy
		6	18.3.72	**Orient**	D2	A	W	1-0	Ball
		SF	15.4.72	**Stoke C**	D1		D	1-1	Armstrong
			played at Villa Park						
		SFr	19.4.72	**Stoke C**			W	2-1	George, Radford
			played at Goodison Park						
		F	6.5.72	**Leeds U**	D1	WEMBLEY	L	0-1	
1972-73	D1	3	13.1.73	**Leicester C**	D1	H	D	2-2	Kennedy, Armstrong
		3r	17.1.73	**Leicester C**		A	W	2-1	Radford, Kelly
		4	3.2.73	**Bradford C**	D4	H	W	2-0	Ball, George
		5	24.2.73	**Carlisle U**	D2	A	W	2-1	Ball, McLintock
		6	17.3.73	**Chelsea**	D1	A	D	2-2	Ball, George
		6r	20.3.73	**Chelsea**		H	W	2-1	Ball (p), Kennedy
		SF	7.4.73	**Sunderland**	D2		L	1-2	George
			played at Hillsborough						
		3/4	18.8.73	**Wolverhampton W**	D1	H	L	1-3	Hornsby
1973-74	D1	3	5.1.74	**Norwich C**	D1	A	W	1-0	Kelly
		4	26.1.74	**Aston Villa**	D2	H	D	1-1	Kennedy
		4r	30.1.74	**Aston Villa**		A	L	0-2	
1974-75	D1	3	4.1.75	**York C**	D2	H	D	1-1	Kelly
		3r	7.1.75	**York C**		A	W	3-1aet	Kidd 3
		4	25.1.75	**Coventry C**	D1	A	D	1-1	Ball
		4r	29.1.75	**Coventry C**		H	W	3-0	Armstrong 2, Matthews
		5	15.2.75	**Leicester C**	D1	H	D	0-0	
		5r	19.2.75	**Leicester C**		A	D	1-1aet	Radford

Season	Div	Round	Date	Opponent	Opp Div	Venue	W/D/L	Score	Scorers
		5 2r	24.2.75	Leicester C		A	W	1-0aet	Radford
		6	8.3.75	West Ham	D1	H	L	0-2	
1975-76	D1	3	3.1.76	Wolverhampton W	D1	A	L	0-3	
1976-77	D1	3	8.1.77	Notts Co	D2	A	W	1-0	Ross
		4	29.1.77	Coventry C	D1	H	W	3-1	Macdonald 2, Stapleton
		5	26.2.77	Middlesbrough	D1	A	L	1-4	Macdonald
1977-78	D1	3	7.1.78	Sheffield U	D2	A	W	5-0	Macdonald 2, Stapleton 2, O'Leary
		4	28.1.78	Wolverhampton W	D1	H	W	2-1	Sunderland, Macdonald
		5	18.2.78	Walsall	D3	H	W	4-1	Stapleton 2, Macdonald, Sunderland
		6	11.3.78	Wrexham	D3	A	W	3-2	Macdonald, Sunderland, Young
		SF	8.4.78	Orient	D2		W	3-0	Macdonald 2, Rix
				played at Stamford Bridge					
		F	6.5.78	Ipswich T	D1	WEMBLEY	L	0-1	
1978-79	D1	3	6.1.79	Sheffield W	D3	A	D	1-1	Sunderland
		3r	9.1.79	Sheffield W		H	D	1-1aet	Brady
		3 2r	15.1.79	Sheffield W at Filbert Street			D	2-2aet	Brady, Sunderland
		3 3r	17.1.79	Sheffield W at Filbert Street			D	3-3aet	Stapleton 2, Young
		3 4r	22.1.79	Sheffield W at Filbert Street			W	2-0	Gatting, Stapleton
		4	27.1.79	Notts Co	D2	H	W	2-0	Young, Talbot
		5	26.2.79	Nottingham F	D1	A	W	1-0	Stapleton
		6	19.3.79	Southampton	D1	A	D	1-1	Price
		6r	21.3.79	Southampton		H	W	2-0	Sunderland 2
		SF	31.3.79	Wolverhampton W	D1		W	2-0	Stapleton, Sunderland
				played at Villa Park					
		F	12.5.79	MANCHESTER U	D1	WEMBLEY	W	3-2	Talbot, Stapleton, Sunderland
1979-80	D1	3	5.1.80	Cardiff C	D2	A	D	0-0	
		3r	8.1.80	Cardiff C		H	W	2-1	Sunderland 2
		4	26.1.80	Brighton & HA	D1	H	W	2-0	Nelson, Talbot
		5	16.2.80	Bolton W	D1	A	D	1-1	Stapleton
		5r	19.2.80	Bolton W		H	W	3-0	Sunderland 2, Stapleton
		6	8.3.80	Watford	D2	A	W	2-1	Stapleton 2
		SF	12.4.80	Liverpool	D1		D	0-0	
				played at Hillsborough					
		SFr	16.4.80	Liverpool			D	1-1aet	Sunderland
		SF 2r	28.4.80	Liverpool			D	1-1aet	Sunderland
				both matches played at Villa Park					
		SF 3r	1.5.80	Liverpool			W	1-0	Talbot
				played at Highfield Rd					
		F	10.5.80	West Ham	D2	WEMBLEY	L	0-1	
1980-81	D1	3	3.1.81	Everton	D1	A	L	0-2	
1981-82	D1	3	2.1.82	Tottenham H	D1	A	L	0-1	
1982-83	D1	3	8.1.83	Bolton W	D2	H	W	2-1	Davis, Rix
		4	29.1.83	Leeds U	D2	H	D	1-1	Sunderland
		4r	2.2.83	Leeds U		A	D	1-1aet	Rix
		4 2r	9.2.83	Leeds U		H	W	2-1	Woodcock, Rix
		5	19.2.83	Middlesbrough	D2	A	D	1-1	Rix
		5r	28.2.83	Middlesbrough		H	W	3-2	Talbot, Woodcock, Davis
		6	12.3.83	Aston Villa	D1	H	W	2-0	Woodcock, Petrovic
		SF	16.4.83	Manchester U	D1		L	1-2	
				played at Villa Park					
1983-84	D1	3	7.1.84	Middlesbrough	D2	A	L	2-3	Woodcock, Nicholas
1984-85	D1	3	5.1.85	Hereford U	D4	A	D	1-1	Woodcock
		3r	22.1.85	Hereford U		H	W	7-2	Mariner 2, Talbot 2, Nicholas, Anderson, Woodcock
		4	26.1.85	York C	D3	A	L	0-1	
1985-86	D1	3	4.1.86	Grimsby T	D2	A	W	4-3	Nicholas 3, Rix
		4	25.1.86	Rotherham U	D3	H	W	5-1	Allinson 2 (1p), Robson, Rix, Nicholas
		5	15.2.86	Luton T	D1	A	D	2-2	Allinson, Rocastle
		5r	3.3.86	Luton T		H	D	0-0aet	
		5 2r	5.3.86	Luton T		A	L	0-3	
1986-87	D1	3	10.1.87	Reading	D2	A	W	3-1	Nicholas 2, Hayes (p)
		4	31.1.87	Plymouth A	D2	H	W	6-1	Anderson 2, Nicholas, Davis, Quinn, Rocastle
		5	21.2.87	Barnsley	D2	H	W	2-0	Hayes (p), Nicholas
		6	14.3.87	Watford	D1	H	L	1-3	Allinson
1987-88	D1	3	9.1.88	Millwall	D2	H	W	2-0	Hayes, Rocastle
		4	30.1.88	Brighton & HA	D3	A	W	2-1	Richardson, Groves
		5	20.2.88	Manchester U	D1	H	W	2-1	Smith, Duxbury og
		6	12.3.88	Nottingham F	D1	H	L	1-2	Rocastle

1988-89	D1	3	8.1.89 **West Ham**	D1	A	D	2-2	Merson 2
		3r	11.1.89 **West Ham**		H	L	0-1	
1989-90	D1	3	6.1.90 **Stoke C**	D2	A	W	1-0	Quinn
		4	27.1.90 **QPR**	D1	H	D	0-0	
		4r	31.1.90 **QPR**		A	L	0-2	
1990-91	D1	3	5.1.91 **Sunderland**	D1	H	W	2-1	Smith, Limpar
		4	27.1.91 **Leeds U**	D1	H	D	0-0	
		4r	30.1.91 **Leeds U**		A	D	1-1aet	Limpar
		4 2r	13.2.91 **Leeds U**		H	D	0-0aet	
		4 3r	16.2.91 **Leeds U**		A	W	2-1	Merson, Dixon
		5	27.2.91 **Shrewsbury T**	D3	A	W	1-0	Thomas
		6	9.3.91 **Cambridge U**	D3	H	W	2-1	Campbell, Adams
		SF	14.4.91 **Tottenham H**	D1		L	1-3	Smith
			played at Wembley					
1991-92	D1	3	4.1.92 **Wrexham**	D4	A	L	1-2	Smith
1992-93	PL	3	3.1.93 **Yeovil T**	GMVC	A	W	3-1	Wright 3
		4	25.1.93 **Leeds U**	PL	H	D	2-2	Parlour, Merson
		4r	3.2.93 **Leeds U**		A	W	3-2aet	Wright 2, Smith
		5	13.2.93 **Nottingham F**	PL	H	W	2-0	Wright 2
		6	6.3.93 **Ipswich T**	PL	A	W	4-2	Adams, Wright (p), Whelan og, Campbell
		SF	4.4.93 **Tottenham H**	PL		W	1-0	Adams
			played at Wembley					
		F	15.5.93 **Sheffield W**	PL	WEMBLEY	D	1-1aet	Wright
		Fr	20.5.93 **SHEFFIELD W**		WEMBLEY	W	2-1aet	Wright, Linighan

ASHFORD TOWN

Formed 1930. **First entered FA Cup:** 1930. **Record against League Clubs:** Played 7, Lost 7

1934-35	KL	1	24.11.34 **Clapton O**	3S	H	L	1-4	French
1958-59	KL	1	15.11.58 **Crystal P**	D4	H	L	0-1	
1959-60	SL	1	14.11.59 **Brentford**	D3	A	L	0-5	
1960-61	SL	1	5.11.60 **Gillingham**	D4	H	L	1-2	White
1961-62	SL	1	4.11.61 **Wycombe W**	IL	A	D	0-0	
		1r	8.11.61 **Wycombe W**		H	W	3-0	White, Clayton, Shepherd
		2	25.11.61 **QPR**	D3	H	L	0-3	
1966-67	SL	1	26.11.66 **Cambridge C**	SL	H	W	4-1	Soutar 2, Roberts 2
		2	10.1.67 **Swindon T**	D3	A	L	0-5	
1974-75	SL	1	27.11.74 **Walsall**	D3	H	L	1-3	Hold

ASHINGTON

Formed 1883. Football League member 1921-1929. **First entered FA Cup:** 1888 **Best FA Cup Performance:** 3rd round, 1927. FA Amateur Cup semi-finalists 1974. **Cup Final connection:** Birthplace of Bobby and Jack Charlton and their cousin Jackie Milburn who played in nine Cup finals between them

1921-22	3N	4q **Close Works** (H) 6-0; 5q **Leadgate Park** (H) 2-1; 6q **Stalybridge C** (H) 1-0						
		1	7.1.22 **Millwall**	3S	A	L	2-4	Robertson 2
1922-23	3N	5q **Blyth Spartans** (A) 1-2						
1923-24	3N	4q **Bishop Auckland** (A) 2-1; 5q **Carlisle U** (H) 2-0; 6q **Hartlepools U** (H) 2-1						
		1	12.1.24 **Aston Villa**	D1	H	L	1-5	Robertson
1924-25	3N	4q **Hartlepools U** (A) 0-0; 4qr **Hartlepools U** (H) 2-0; *Ashington disqualified for ineligible player*						
1925-26	3N	1	2.12.25 **Durham C**	3N	A	L	1-4	Roberton
1926-27	3N	1	27.11.26 **Stockton**	NL	A	W	2-1	Watson, Randall
		2	11.12.26 **Nelson**	3N	H	W	2-1	Randall, Johnson
		3	8.1.27 **Nottingham F**	D2	H	L	0-2	
1927-28	3N	1	26.11.27 **Crewe A**	3N	A	D	2-2	Bell 2
		1r	30.11.27 **Crewe A**		H	L	0-2	
1928-29	3N	1	24.11.28 **Wigan B**		A	L	0-2	
1929-30	NEL	1	30.11.29 **Rotherham U**	3N	A	L	0-3	
1950-51	NEL	1	25.11.50 **Halifax T**	3N	A	W	3-2	Gibson, Simpson, Scott
		2	9.12.50 **Rochdale**	3N	H	L	1-2	Skeen
1952-53	NEL	1	22.11.52 **Tranmere R**	3N	A	L	1-8	Wort
1961-62	NCo	1	4.11.61 **Chester**	D4	A	L	1-4	Lackenby

ASHTON UNITED

Formed 1878. **First entered FA Cup:** 1893. Currently playing in Northern Premier (HFS Loans) League

1952-53	Man	1	22.11.52 **Halifax T**	3N	A	D	1-1	Diamond
		1r	25.11.52 **Halifax T**		H	L	1-2	Diamond
1955-56	LC	1	19.11.55 **Southport**	3N	A	L	1-6	Mather

ASTLEY BRIDGE

Played at Astley Bridge, Bolton. Used the Lamb Inn pub near the playing field as their dressing room.

1880-81	1	30.10.80 **Eagley**	H	W	4-0	Curran, Foole, Moore, Smith
	2	18.12.80 **Turton**	H	L	0-3	
1881-82	1	29.10.81 **Turton**	H	D	2-2	Smith, AN Other
	1r	12.11.81 **Turton**	A	D	1-1	
	1 2r	19.11.81 **Turton** at Great Lever		D	3-3	
	1 3r	26.11.81 **Turton**	A	L	0-2	
1882-83	1	28.10.82 **Northwich Victoria**	A	L	2-3	Swimby 2
1883-84	1	20.10.83 **Great Lever**	A	L	1-4	
1884-85	1	**Bolton Association**		scratched		
1885-86	1	10.10.85 **Southport**	H	W	3-2	
	2	18.11.85 **Preston NE**	A	L	3-11	
1886-87	1	23.10.86 **Burnley**	H	D	3-3	
	1r	30.10.86 **Burnley**	A	D	2-2	
		FA disqualified Burnley after protest				
	2	**Darwen**		scratched		
1887-88	1	15.10.87 **Hurst**	A	L	3-5	
		FA disqualified Hurst after protest				
	2	5.11.87 **Halliwell**	H	L	0-4	

ASTON SHAKESPEARE

Short-lived Birmingham based amateur club

1887-88	1	8.10.87 **Burton W**	H	L	2-3	
		FA ordered replay after protest				
	1r	**Burton W**		walkover		
	2	5.11.87 **Wolverhampton W**	A	L	0-3	

ASTON UNITY

Formed 1874. Birmingham amateurs who played their home matches at the Lower Grounds, Aston

1882-83	1	**bye**				
	2	2.12.82 **Birmingham St Georges**	H	W	3-1	
	3	6.1.83 **Aston Villa**	A	L	1-3	Wilson
1883-84	1	10.11.83 **Stafford Rd,Wolverhampton**	A	L	1-5	
1884-85	1	1.11.84 **Birmingham St Georges**	H	L	0-5	
1885-86	1	31.10.85 **WBA**	A	L	1-4	
1886-87	1	30.10.86 **Derby Co**	H	L	1-4	
1887-88	1	15.10.87 **Small Heath Alliance**	A	L	1-6	

ASTON VILLA

Formed 1874. Founder members of the Football League 1888. **First entered FA Cup:** 1879. **FA Cup and League Double** 1897. **FA Cup Winners:** (7 times) 1887, 1895, 1897, 1905, 1913, 1920, 1957. **FA Cup Runners-Up:** 1892, 1924. **Record FA Cup Win:** 13-0 vs Wednesbury Old Athletic, 1st round, 30.10.1886. **Record FA Cup Defeat:** 1-8 vs Blackburn R, 16.2.1889

1879-80	1	13.12.79 **Stafford Road**	A	D	1-1	Andy Hunter
	1r	24.1.80 **Stafford Road**	H	W	3-2	Mason 2, Law
	2	**Oxford University**		scratched		
1880-81	1	4.12.80 **Nottingham F**	A	W	2-1	Andy Hunter, Vaughton
	2	12.2.81 **Notts Co**	A	W	3-1	Andy Hunter 2, Archie Hunter
	3	19.2.81 **Stafford Rd**	H	L	2-3	Vaughton 2
1881-82	1	5.11.81 **Nottingham F**	H	W	4-1	Whateley 2, Brown 2
	2	**bye**				
	3	31.12.81 **Notts Co**	H	D	2-2	Davis, Whateley
	3r	7.1.82 **Notts Co**	A	D	2-2aet	Brown, Archie Hunter
	3 2r	14.1.82 **Notts Co**	H	W	4-1	Hunter, Whateley, Brown, Dawson
	4	21.1.82 **Wednesbury OA**	A	L	2-4	Vaughton, Archie Hunter
1882-83	1	21.10.82 **Walsall Swifts**	H	W	4-1	Brown 2, Vaughton, Andy Hunter

		2	18.11.82	**Wednesbury OA**		H	W	4-1	Harvey, Archie Hunter, Whateley, Vaughton
		3	6.1.83	**Aston Unity**		H	W	3-1	Davis, Vaughton, Archie Hunter
		4	27.1.83	**Walsall Town**		H	W	2-1	Vaughton, Brown
		5	13.3.83	**Notts Co**		A	L	3-4	Archie Hunter, Whateley, Brown
1883-84		1	10.11.83	**Walsall Swifts**		A	W	5-1	Archie Hunter 2, Roberts, Phillips og, Vaughton
		2	1.12.83	**Stafford Rd**		A	W	5-1	Brown 2, Archie Hunter 2, Whateley
		3	29.12.83	**Wednesbury OA**		A	W	7-4	Brown 2, Whateley, Vaughton 3, Archie Hunter
		4	19.1.84	**Queens Park, Glasgow**		A	L	1-6	Vaughton
1884-85		1	3.11.84	**Wednesbury Town**		H	W	4-1	Arthur Brown 2, Archie Hunter, Albert Brown
		2	6.12.84	**Walsall Town**		A	W	2-0	Whateley, Archie Hunter
		3	3.1.85	**WBA**		H	D	0-0	
		3r	12.1.85	**WBA**		A	L	0-3	
1885-86		1	17.10.85	**Walsall Town**		A	W	5-0	Archie Hunter, Davis, Vaughton, Albert Brown, Arthur Brown
		2	14.11.85	**Derby Co**		A	L	0-2	
1886-87		1	30.10.86	**Wednesbury OA**		H	W	13-0	Hodgetts 3, Loach 2, Davis, Archie Hunter 3, Albert Brown 3, Burton
		2	20.11.86	**Derby Midland**		H	W	6-1	Loach 2, Hodgetts, Archie Hunter, Albert Brown 2
		3	11.12.86	**Wolverhampton W**		H	D	2-2	Hunter, Hodgetts
		3r	15.1.87	**Wolverhampton W**		A	D	1-1aet	Albert Brown
		3 2r	22.1.87	**Wolverhampton W**		A	D	3-3aet	Vaughton, Davis, Albert Brown
		3 3r	29.1.87	**Wolverhampton W**		H	W	2-0	Dawson, Hunter
		4		bye					
		5	5.2.87	**Horncastle**		H	W	5-0	Davis, Albert Brown 3, Hunter
		6	12.2.87	**Darwen**		H	W	3-2	Dawson, Hunter, Hodgetts
		SF	5.3.87	**Glasgow Rangers**			W	3-1	Hunter 2, Albert Brown
			played at Crewe						
		F	2.4.87	**WBA**			W	2-0	Hodgetts, Hunter
			played at Kennington Oval						
1887-88		1	15.10.87	**Oldbury Town**		A	W	4-0	Albert Brown 2, Hunter, Allen
		2	5.11.87	**Small Heath**		A	W	4-0	Green 2, Allen, Albert Brown
		3		bye					
		4	17.12.87	**Shankhouse**		A	W	9-0	Hunter 2, Hodgetts, Allen 2, Green 2, Albert Brown 2
		5	7.1.88	**Preston NE**		H	L	1-3	Hunter
1888-89	D1	1	2.2.89	**Witton**		H	W	3-2	Allen, Hunter, Green
		2	16.2.89	**Derby Co**	D1	H	W	5-3	Hunter 2, Hodgetts 2, Brown
		3	2.3.89	**Blackburn R**	D1	A	L	1-8	Hodgetts
1889-90	D1	1	18.1.90	**South Shore**		A	W	4-2	Hodgetts 2, Allen, Dickson
		2	1.2.90	**Notts County**	D1	A	L	1-4	Hodgetts
1890-91	D1	1	17.1.91	**Casuals**		H	W	13-1	Hodgetts 4, L.Campbell 3, McKnight 2, A.Brown 2, Graham 2
		2	31.1.91	**Stoke**	FAll	A	L	0-3	
1891-92	D1	1	16.1.92	**Heanor Town**		H	W	4-1	Hodgetts 3, J.Devey
		2	30.1.92	**Darwen**	D1	H	W	2-0	J.Devey, Hodgetts
		3	13.2.92	**Wolverhampton W**	D1	A	W	3-1	L.Campbell, Athersmith, J.Devey
		SF	27.2.92	**Sunderland**	D1		W	4-1	J.Devey 2, Hodgetts 2
			played at Bramall Lane						
		F	9.3.92	**WBA**	D1		L	0-3	
			played at Kennington Oval						
1892-93	D1	1	21.1.93	**Darwen**	D2	A	L	4-5	J.Devey, Cowan, Athersmith, J.Brown
1893-94	D1	1	27.1.94	**Wolverhampton W**	D1	H	W	4-2	J.Devey 2, Chatt, Cowan
		2	10.2.94	**Sunderland**	D1	A	D	2-2aet	Cowan, Hodgetts
		2r	21.2.94	**Sunderland**	D1	H	W	3-1	Athersmith, Hodgetts, Chatt
		3	24.2.94	**Sheffield W**	D1	A	L	2-3aet	Chatt 2
1894-95	D1	1	2.2.95	**Derby Co**	D1	H	W	2-1	Devey, Smith
		2	16.2.95	**Newcastle U**	D2	H	W	7-1	Dorrell 2, Russell, Devey 2, Athersmith 2
		3	2.3.95	**Nottingham F**	D1	H	W	6-1	Chatt 2, Smith 2, Russell, Cowan
		SF	16.3.95	**Sunderland**	D1	H	W	2-1	Smith 2
			played at Ewood Park						
		F	20.4.95	**WBA**	D1		W	1-0	Chatt
			played at Crystal Palace						
1895-96	D1	1	1.2.96	**Derby Co**	D1	A	L	2-4	Burton, Hodgetts
1896-97	D1	1	30.1.97	**Newcastle U**	D2	H	W	5-0	Athersmith, Wheldon 2, Smith, White og
		2	13.2.97	**Notts Co**	D2	H	W	2-1	Wheldon, Campbell
		3	27.2.97	**Preston NE**	D1	A	D	1-1	Campbell
		3r	3.3.97	**Preston NE**		H	D	0-0	
		3 2r	10.3.97	**Preston NE** at Bramall Lane			W	3-2	Athersmith 2, Campbell
		SF	20.3.97	**Liverpool**	D1		W	3-0	Cowan 2, Athersmith
			played at Bramall Lane						

Season	Div	Round	Date	Opponent	Comp	Venue	Result	Score	Scorers
		F	10.4.97	**EVERTON**	D1		W	3-2	Campbell, Wheldon, Crabtree
				played at Crystal Palace					
1897-98	D1	1	29.1.98	**Derby Co**	D1	A	L	0-1	
1898-99	D1	1	28.1.99	**Nottingham F**	D1	A	L	1-2	Johnson
1899-00	D1	1	27.1.00	**Manchester C**	D1	A	D	1-1	Devey
		1r	31.1.00	**Manchester C**		H	W	3-0	Garraty 2, Wheldon
		2	10.2.00	**Bristol City**	SL	A	W	5-0	Devey 4, Garraty
		3	24.2.00	**Millwall Ath**	SL	A	D	1-1	Wheldon
		3r	28.2.00	**Millwall Ath**		H	D	0-0aet	
		3 2r	5.3.00	**Millwall Ath** at Reading			L	1-2	Johnson
1900-01	D1	1	26.1.01	**Millwall Ath**	SL	H	W	5-0	Johnson 3, Devey, Smith
		2	23.2.01	**Nottingham F**	D1	H	D	0-0	
		2r	27.2.01	**Nottingham F**		A	W	3-1aet	Athersmith, Cowan, Garraty
		3	23.3.01	**Small Heath**	D2	A	D	0-0	
		3r	27.3.01	**Small Heath**		H	W	1-0aet	Garraty
		SF	6.4.01	**Sheffield U**	D1		D	2-2	Garraty, Devey
				played at Nottingham					
		SFr	11.4.01	**Sheffield U**			L	0-3	
				played at Derby					
1901-02	D1	1	25.1.02	**Stoke**	D1	A	D	2-2	Garraty 2
		1r	29.1.02	**Stoke**		H	L	1-2aet	Garraty
1902-03	D1	1	7.2.03	**Sunderland**	D1	H	W	4-1	Bache, Johnson 2, Pearson
		2	21.2.03	**Barnsley**	D2	H	W	4-1	McLuckie 3, Johnson
		3	7.3.03	**Tottenham H**	SL	A	W	3-2	McLuckie 2, Johnson
		SF	21.3.03	**Bury**	D1		L	0-3	
				played at Goodison Park					
1903-04	D1	1	6.2.04	**Stoke**	D1	A	W	3-2	Brawn (p), Leake, Bache
		2	20.2.04	**Tottenham H**	SL	A	–	1-0	Bache
				abandoned on 20 minutes after crowd invasion					
		2r	25.2.04	**Tottenham H**	SL	H	L	0-1	
1904-05	D1	1	4.2.05	**Leicester Fosse**	D2	H	W	5-1	Bache 2, Hampton, Leake, Hall
		2	18.2.05	**Bury**	D1	H	W	3-2	Bache, Garraty, Hampton
		3	4.3.05	**Fulham**	SL	H	W	5-0	Pearson, Hampton 2, Bache, Hall
		SF	25.3.05	**Everton**	D1		D	1-1	Hall
				played at Stoke					
		SFr	29.3.05	**Everton**			W	2-1	Hampton, Garraty
				played at Nottingham					
		F	15.4.05	**NEWCASTLE U**	D1		W	2-0	Hampton 2
				played at Crystal Palace					
1905-06	D1	1	13.1.06	**King's Lynn**	N&S	H	W	11-0	Millington 4, Hall 3, Garraty 2, Pearson, Wilkes
		2	3.2.06	**Plymouth A**	SL	H	D	0-0	
		2r	7.2.06	**Plymouth A**		A	W	5-1	Garraty 2, Garratt, Bache, Hampton
		3	24.2.06	**Manchester U**	D2	A	L	1-5	Hall
1906-07	D1	1	12.1.07	**Burnley**	D2	A	W	3-1	Bache 2, Cantrell
		2	2.2.07	**Bolton W**	D1	A	L	0-2	
1907-08	D1	1	11.1.08	**Stockport Co**	D2	H	W	3-0	Wallace, Bache, A.Logan
		2	1.2.08	**Hull C**	D2	H	W	3-0	Hall 2 (1p), Hampton
		3	23.2.08	**Manchester U**	D1	H	L	0-2	
1908-09	D1	1	16.1.09	**Nottingham F**	D1	A	L	0-2	
1909-10	D1	1	15.1.10	**Oldham A**	D2	A	W	2-1	Bache, Hall
		2	5.2.10	**Derby Co**	D2	H	W	6-1	Hampton 3, Wallace, Bache, Scattergood og
		3	19.2.10	**Manchester C**	D2	H	L	1-2	Gerrish
1910-11	D1	1	14.1.11	**Portsmouth**	SL	A	W	4-1	Hampton 2, Bache, Thompson og
		2	4.2.11	**Manchester U**	D1	A	L	1-2	Henshall
1911-12	D1	1	13.1.12	**Walsall**	BDL	H	W	6-0	Henshall 2, Hampton 2, Bache, Wallace
		2	3.2.12	**Reading**	SL	H	D	1-1	Hampton
		2r	7.2.12	**Reading**		A	L	0-1	
1912-13	D1	1	15.1.13	**Derby Co**	D1	A	W	3-1	Halse 2, Hampton
		2	1.2.13	**West Ham**	SL	H	W	5-0	Halse 2, Morris, Hampton, Stephenson
		3	22.2.13	**Crystal Palace**	SL	H	W	5-0	Halse 2, Stephenson 2, Bache
		4	8.3.13	**Bradford PA**	D2	A	W	5-0	Hampton 3, Halse, Stephenson
		SF	29.3.13	**Oldham A**	D1		W	1-0	Stephenson
				played at Ewood Park					
		F	19.4.13	**SUNDERLAND**	D1		W	1-0	Barber
				played at Crystal Palace					
1913-14	D1	1	10.1.14	**Stoke**	SL	H	W	4-0	Stephenson 2, Hampton 2
		2	31.1.14	**Exeter C**	SL	A	W	2-1	Hampton 2

	3	21.2.14 **WBA**	D1	H	W	2-1	Bache, Hampton
	4	7.3.14 **Sheffield W**	D1	A	W	1-0	Edgley
	SF	28.3.14 **Liverpool**	D1		L	0-2	
		played at Tottenham					
1914-15 D1	1	9.1.15 **Exeter C**	SL	H	W	2-0	C.Stephenson, Bache
	2	30.1.15 **Manchester C**	D1	A	L	0-1	
1919-20 D1	1	10.1.20 **QPR**	SL	H	W	2-1	Walker 2
	2	31.1.20 **Manchester U**	D1	A	W	2-1	Stephenson, Walker
	3	21.2.20 **Sunderland**	D1	H	W	1-0	Stpehenson
	4	6.3.20 **Tottenham H**	D2	A	W	1-0	Clay og
	SF	27.3.20 **Chelsea**	D1		W	3-1	Walker 2, Edgley
		played at Bramall Lane					
	F	24.3.20 **HUDDERSFIELD T**	D2		W	1-0aet	Kirton
		played at Stamford Bridge					
1920-21 D1	1	8.1.21 **Bristol C**	D2	H	W	2-0	C.Stephenson (p), Walker
	2	29.1.21 **Notts Co**	D2	A	D	0-0	
	2r	2.2.21 **Notts Co**		H	W	1-0	Walker
	3	19.2.21 **Huddersfield T**	D1	H	W	2-0	Walker 2
	4	7.3.21 **Tottenham H**	D1	A	L	0-1	
1921-22 D1	1	7.1.22 **Derby Co**	D2	H	W	6-1	Walker 3, Kirton 2, Dickson
	2	28.1.22 **Luton T**	3S	H	W	1-0	Walker
	3	18.2.22 **Stoke**	D2	A	D	0-0	
	3r	22.2.22 **Stoke**		H	W	4-0	Dickson 3, Walker
	4	4.3.22 **Notts Co**	D2	A	D	2-2	Dickson 2
	4r	8.3.22 **Notts Co**		H	L	3-4	Dickson 2, Walker
1922-23 D1	1	13.1.23 **Blackburn R**	D1	H	L	0-1	
1923-24 D1	1	12.1.24 **Ashington**	3N	A	W	5-1	Walker 2, Page og, Capewell, Blackburn
	2	2.2.25 **Swansea T**	3S	A	W	2-0	Capewell 2
	3	23.2.25 **Leeds U**	D2	H	W	3-0	Capewell 2, Walker
	4	8.3.25 **WBA**	D1	A	W	2-0	Capewell, Dorrell
	SF	29.3.25 **Burnley**	D1		W	3-0	York 2, Kirton
		played at Bramall Lane					
	F	26.4.25 **Newcastle U**	D1 WEMBLEY	L		0-2	
1924-25 D1	1	10.1.25 **Port Vale**	D2	H	W	7-2	Capewell 4, Walker 3
	2	31.1.25 **Swansea T**	3S	A	W	3-1	Walker 2, York
	3	21.2.25 **WBA**	D1	A	D	1-1	Walker
	3r	25.2.25 **WBA**		H	L	1-2	Phoenix
1925-26 D1	3	9.1.26 **Hull C**	D2	A	W	3-0	Capewell 2, York
	4	30.1.26 **WBA**	D1	A	W	2-1	Walker, Kirton
	5	20.2.26 **Arsenal**	D1	H	D	1-1	Kirton
	5r	24.2.26 **Arsenal**		A	L	0-2	
1926-27 D1	3	8.1.27 **Cardiff C**	D1	A	L	1-2	Dorrell
1927-28 D1	3	14.1.28 **Burnley**	D1	A	W	2-0	Walker, Beresford
	4	28.1.28 **Crewe Alex**	3N	H	W	3-0	Cook 3
	5	18.2.28 **Arsenal**	D1	A	L	1-4	Cook
1928-29 D1	3	12.1.29 **Cardiff C**	D1	H	W	6-1	Beresford 2, Tate, Dorrell, Waring, York
	4	26.1.29 **Clapton Orient**	D2	H	D	0-0	
	4r	30.1.29 **Clapton Orient**		A	W	8-0	Waring 3, Swales, Dorrell, York, Cook, Beresford
	5	16.2.29 **Reading**	D2	A	W	3-1	Waring 2, Dorrell
	6	2.3.29 **Arsenal**	D1	H	W	1-0	Waring
	SF	23.3.29 **Portsmouth**	D1		L	0-1	
		played at Highbury					
1929-30 D1	3	11.1.30 **Reading**	D2	H	W	5-1	Houghton 2, Brown, Walker (p), York
	4	25.1.30 **Walsall**	3S	H	W	3-1	Walker 2, Brown
	5	15.2.30 **Blackburn R**	D1	H	W	4-1	Brown 3 (1p), Beresford
	6	1.3.30 **Huddersfield T**	D1	H	L	1-2	Brown (p)
1930-31 D1	3	10.1.31 **Arsenal**	D1	A	D	2-2	Brown, Walker
	3r	14.1.31 **Arsenal**		H	L	1-3	Waring
1931-32 D1	3	9.1.32 **WBA**	D1	A	W	2-1	Houghton, Brown
	4	23.1.32 **Portsmouth**	D1	A	D	1-1	Beresford
	4r	27.1.32 **Portsmouth**		H	L	0-1	
1932-33 D1	3	14.1.33 **Bradford C**	D2	A	D	2-2	Mandley, Brown
	3r	18.1.33 **Bradford C**		H	W	2-1	Brown, Tate
	4	28.1.33 **Sunderland**	D1	H	L	0-3	
1933-34 D1	3	13.1.34 **Chesterfield**	3N	A	D	2-2	Cunliffe 2
	3r	17.1.34 **Chesterfield**		H	W	2-0	Astley, Beresford
	4	27.1.34 **Sunderland**	D1	H	W	7-2	Astley 4, Houghton 3

		5	17.2.34	Tottenham H	D1	A	W	1-0	Astley
		6	3.3.34	Arsenal	D1	A	W	2-1	Astley, Houghton
		SF	17.3.34	Manchester C	D1		L	1-6	Astley
			played at Huddersfield						
1934-35	D1	3	12.1.35	Bradford C	D2	H	L	1-3	Hamilton og
1935-36	D1	3	11.1.36	Huddersfield T	D1	H	L	0-1	
1936-37	D2	3	16.1.37	Burnley	D2	H	L	2-3	Houghton, Broome
1937-38	D2	3	8.1.38	Norwich C	D2	A	W	3-2	Houghton, Haycock, Iverson
		4	22.1.38	Blackpool	D1	H	W	4-0	Houghton, Broome, Shell, Starling
		5	12.2.38	Charlton A	D1	A	D	1-1	Shell
		5r	16.2.38	Charlton A		H	D	2-2	Broome, Shell
		5 2r	21.2.38	Charlton A at Highbury			W	4-1	Broome 3, Haycock
		6	6.3.38	Manchester C	D1	H	W	3-2	Shell, Broome, Haycock
		SF	26.3.38	Preston NE	D1		L	1-2	Shell
			played at Bramall Lane						
1938-39	D1	3	7.1.39	Ipswich T	3S	H	D	1-1	Allen
		3r	11.1.39	Ipswich T		A	W	2-1	Haycock 2
		4	21.1.39	Preston NE	D1	A	L	0-2	
1945-46	D1	3 1L	5.1.46	Coventry C	D2	A	L	1-2	Smith
		3 2L	8.1.46	Coventry C		H	W	2-0	Smith, Goffin
		4 1L	26.1.46	Millwall	D2	A	W	4-2	Edwards 2, Goffin, Smith
		4 2L	28.1.46	Millwall		H	W	9-1	Broome 3, Goffin 2, Parkes, Edwards, Smith, Iverson
		5 1L	9.2.46	Chelsea	D1	A	W	1-0	Broome
		5 2L	12.2.46	Chelsea		H	W	1-0	Goffin
		6 1L	2.3.46	Derby Co	D1	H	L	3-4	Edwards, Iverson, Broome
		6 2L	9.3.46	Derby Co		A	D	1-1	Broome
1946-47	D1	3	11.1.47	Burnley	D2	A	L	1-5	Graham
1947-48	D1	3	10.1.48	Manchester U	D1	H	L	4-6	Edwards 2, Smith, Dorsett (p)
1948-49	D1	3	8.1.49	Bolton W	D1	H	D	1-1aet	Ford
		3r	15.1.49	Bolton W		A	D	0-0aet	
		3 2r	17.1.49	Bolton W		H	W	2-1aet	Edwards, H.Smith
		4	29.1.49	Cardiff C	D2	H	L	1-2	Dorsett
1949-50	D1	3	7.1.50	Middlesbrough	D1	H	D	2-2	Gibson, Dorsett (p)
		3r	11.1.50	Middlesbrough		A	D	0-0aet	
		3 2r	16.1.50	Middlesbrough at Elland Road			L	0-3	
1950-51	D1	3	6.1.51	Burnley	D1	H	W	2-0	Thompson, L.Smith
		4	27.1.51	Wolverhampton W	D1	A	L	1-3	Dixon
1951-52	D1	3	12.1.52	Newcastle U	D1	A	L	2-4	Dixon 2
1952-53	D1	3	10.1.53	Middlesbrough	D1	H	W	3-1	Dixon, Thompson, Gibson
		4	31.1.53	Brentford	D2	H	D	0-0	
		4r	4.2.53	Brentford		A	W	2-1	Walsh, Thompson
		5	14.2.53	Rotherham U	D2	A	W	3-1	Walsh 2, Goffin
		6	28.2.53	Everton	D2	H	L	0-1	
1953-54	D1	3	9.1.54	Arsenal	D1	A	L	1-5	McParland
1954-55	D1	3	8.1.55	Brighton & HA	3S	A	D	2-2	Thompson 2
		3r	10.1.55	Brighton & HA		H	W	4-2	Lockhart 2, Southren, Thompson
		4	29.1.55	Doncaster R	D2	A	D	0-0	
		4r	2.2.55	Doncaster R		H	D	2-2aet	Thompson 2
		4 2r	7.2.55	Doncaster R at Maine Road			D	1-1aet	Thompson
		4 3r	14.2.55	Doncaster R at Hillsborough			–	0-0	
			abandoned after 90 minutes – bad light						
		4 4r	15.2.55	Doncaster R at the Hawthorns			L	1-3	Dixon
1955-56	D1	3	7.1.56	Hull C	D2	H	D	1-1	McParland
		3r	12.1.56	Hull C		A	W	2-1	Dixon, Sewell
		4	28.1.56	Arsenal	D1	A	L	1-4	Dixon
1956-57	D1	3	5.1.57	Luton T	D1	A	D	2-2	Dixon, McParland
		3r	7.1.57	Luton T		H	W	2-0	Dixon 2
		4	26.1.57	Middlesbrough	D2	A	W	3-2	Pace, Smith, Dixon
		5	16.2.57	Bristol C	D2	H	W	2-1	Pace, Sewell
		6	2.3.57	Burnley	D1	A	D	1-1	McParland
		6r	6.3.57	Burnley		H	W	2-0	Dixon, McParland
		SF	23.3.57	WBA	D1		D	2-2	McParland 2
			played at Molineux						
		SFr	28.3.57	WBA			W	1-0	Myerscough
			played at St Andrews						
		F	4.5.57	MANCHESTER UTD	D1	WEMBLEY	W	2-1	McParland 2
1957-58	D1	3	4.1.58	Stoke C	D2	A	D	1-1	McParland

	3r	8.1.58	Stoke C		H	D	3-3	Sewell, Lynn, Hitchens
	3 2r	13.1.58	Stoke C at Molineux			L	0-2	
1958-59	D1	3	10.1.59	Rotherham U	D2	H	W	2-1	Sewell, Hitchens
	4	24.1.59	Chelsea	D1	A	W	2-1	Hitchens, Myerscough
	5	14.2.59	Everton	D1	A	W	4-1	Wylie 3, McParland
	6	28.2.59	Burnley	D1	H	D	0-0	
	6r	3.3.59	Burnley		A	W	2-0	McParland 2
	SF	14.3.59	Nottingham F	D1		L	0-1	
		played at Hillsborough						
1959-60	D2	3	9.1.60	Leeds U	D1	H	W	2-1	McParland, Wylie
	4	30.1.60	Chelsea	D1	A	W	2-1	McParland, Thompson
	5	20.2.60	Port Vale	D3	A	W	2-1	Hitchens, Thompson
	6	12.3.60	Preston NE	D1	H	W	2-0	Hitchens, McParland
	SF	26.3.60	Wolverhampton W	D1		L	0-1	
		played at the Hawthorns						
1960-61	D1	3	7.1.61	Bristol R	D2	A	D	1-1	Thompson
	3r	9.1.61	Bristol R		H	W	4-0	Thompson 2, Hitchens 2
	4	28.1.61	Peterborough U	D4	A	D	1-1	Banham og
	4r	1.2.61	Peterborough U		H	W	2-1	McParland 2
	5	18.2.61	Tottenham H	D1	H	L	0-2	
1961-62	D1	3	6.1.62	Crystal Palace	D3	H	W	4-3	Burrows 2, McParland, Dougan
	4	27.1.62	Huddersfied T	D2	H	W	2-1	Hale, Crowe
	5	17.2.62	Charlton A	D2	H	W	2-1	Dougan, Burrows
	6	10.3.62	Tottenham H	D1	A	L	0-2	
1962-63	D1	3	16.1.63	Bristol C	D3	A	D	1-1	Burrows (p)
	3	7.3.63	Bristol C		H	W	3-2	Burrows, Baker, Thompson
	4	11.3.63	Manchester U	D1	A	L	0-1	
1963-64	D1	3	4.1.64	Aldershot	D4	H	D	0-0	
	3r	8.1.64	Aldershot		A	L	1-2	Hateley
1964-65	D1	3	9.1.65	Coventry C	D2	H	W	3-0	Hateley 2, MacLeod
	4	30.1.65	Sheffield U	D1	A	W	2-0	Hateley, Stobart
	5	20.2.65	Wolverhampton W	D1	H	D	1-1	Hateley
	5r	24.2.65	Wolverhampton W		A	D	0-0aet	
	5 2r	1.3.65	Wolverhampton W at the Hawthorns		L	1-3	Park
1965-66	D1	3	22.1.66	Leicester C	D1	H	L	1-2	Woosnam
1966-67	D1	3	28.1.67	Preston NE	D2	A	W	1-0	Roberts
	4	18.2.67	Liverpool	D1	A	L	0-1	
1967-68	D2	3	27.1.68	Millwall	D2	H	W	3-0	Godfrey, Anderson, Woodward
	4	17.2.68	Rotherham U	D2	H	L	0-1	
1968-69	D2	3	4.1.69	QPR	D1	H	W	2-1	Godfrey, Martin
	4	25.1.69	Southampton	D1	A	D	2-2	Godfrey, Hole
	4r	29.1.69	Southampton		H	W	2-1	Broadbent, Martin
	5	12.2.69	Tottenham H	D1	A	L	2-3	Hole, Broadbent
1969-70	D2	3	3.1.70	Charlton A	D2	H	D	1-1	Martin
	3r	12.1.70	Charlton A		A	L	0-1	
1970-71	D3	1	21.11.70	Torquay U	D3	A	L	1-3	Aitken
1971-72	D3	1	20.11.71	Southend U	D4	A	L	0-1	
1972-73	D2	3	13.1.73	Everton	D1	A	L	2-3	Vowden, Evans
1973-74	D2	3	5.1.74	Chester	D4	H	W	3-1	Morgan 2, Nicholl
	4	26.1.74	Arsenal	D1	A	D	1-1	Morgan
	4r	30.1.74	Arsenal		H	W	2-0	Morgan, Evans
	5	16.2.74	Burnley	D1	A	L	0-1	
1974-75	D2	3	4.1.75	Oldham A	D2	A	W	3-0	Little, Nicholl, Graydon
	4	25.1.75	Sheffield U	D1	H	W	4-1	Leonard 2, Nicholl, Graydon
	5	15.2.75	Ipswich T	D1	A	L	2-3	McDonald, Evans
1975-76	D1	3	3.1.76	Southampton	D2	A	D	1-1	Gray
	3r	7.1.76	Southampton		H	L	1-2aet	Graydon
1976-77	D1	3	8.1.77	Leicester C	D1	A	W	1-0	Gray
	4	29.1.77	West Ham	D1	H	W	3-0	Deehan 2, Mortimer
	5	26.2.77	Port Vale	D3	H	W	3-0	Nicholl, Deehan, Little
	6	19.3.77	Manchester U	D1	A	L	1-2	Little
1977-78	D1	3	7.1.78	Everton	D1	A	L	1-4	Gray
1978-79	D1	3	6.1.79	Nottingham F	D1	A	L	0-2	
1979-80	D1	3	4.1.80	Bristol R	D2	A	W	2-1	Cowans, Shaw
	4	26.1.80	Cambridge U	D2	A	D	1-1	Donovan
	4r	30.1.80	Cambridge U		H	W	4-1	Donovan 2, Little, Evans
	5	16.2.80	Blackburn R	D3	A	D	1-1	Geddis

		5r	20.2.80	Blackburn R		H	W	1-0	Evans
		6	8.3.80	West Ham	D2	A	L	0-1	
1980-81	D1	3	3.1.81	Ipswich T	D1	H	L	0-1	
1981-82	D1	3	5.1.82	Notts Co	D1	A	W	6-0	Geddis 3, Cowans (p), Shaw, Richards og
		4	23.1.82	Bristol C	D3	A	W	1-0	Shaw
		5	13.2.82	Tottenham H	D1	A	L	0-1	
1982-83	D1	3	8.1.83	Northampton T	D4	A	W	1-0	Walters
		4	29.1.83	Wolverhampton W	D2	H	W	1-0	Withe
		5	19.2.83	Watford	D1	H	W	4-1	Shaw, Morley, Gibson, Cowans
		6	12.3.83	Arsenal	D1	A	L	0-2	
1983-84	D1	3	7.1.84	Norwich C	D1	H	D	1-1	Withe
		3r	11.1.84	Norwich C		A	L	0-3	
1984-85	D1	3	5.1.85	Liverpool	D1	A	L	0-3	
1985-86	D1	3	4.1.86	Portsmouth	D2	A	D	2-2	Birch, Kerr
		3r	13.1.86	Portsmouth		H	W	3-2aet	Stainrod 2, Evans
		4	25.1.86	Millwall	D2	H	D	1-1	Hodge
		4r	29.1.86	Millwall		A	L	0-1	
1986-87	D1	3	10.1.87	Chelsea	D1	H	D	2-2	Cooper, Hunt
		3r	21.1.87	Chelsea		A	L	1-2	Hunt
1987-88	D2	3	9.1.88	Leeds U	D2	A	W	2-1	Gray, McInally
		4	31.1.88	Liverpool	D1	H	L	0-2	
1988-89	D1	3	7.1.89	Crewe Alex	D4	A	W	3-2	Platt, Gage, McInally
		4	28.1.89	Wimbledon	D1	H	L	0-1	
1989-90	D1	3	6.1.90	Blackburn R	D2	A	D	2-2	Olney, Ormondroyd
		3r	10.1.90	Blackburn R		H	W	3-1	Ormondroyd, Daley, May og
		4	27.1.90	Port Vale	D2	H	W	6-0	Platt, Birch 2, Olney, Gray 2
		5	17.2.90	WBA	D2	A	W	2-0	Mountfield, Daley
		6	14.3.90	Oldham A	D2	A	L	0-3	
1990-91	D1	3	5.1.91	Wimbledon	D1	H	D	1-1	Gray
		3r	9.1.91	Wimbledon		A	L	0-1aet	
1991-92	D1	3	5.1.92	Tottenham H	D1	H	D	0-0	
		3r	14.1.92	Tottenham H		A	W	1-0	Yorke
		4	5.2.92	Derby Co	D2	A	W	4-3	Yorke 3, Parker
*		5	16.2.92	Swindon T	D2	A	W	2-1	Yorke, Froggatt
		6	8.3.92	Liverpool	D1	A	L	0-1	
1992-93	PL	3	2.1.93	Bristol R	D1	H	D	1-1	Cox
		3r	20.1.93	Bristol R		A	W	3-0	Saunders 2, Houghton
		4	23.1.93	Wimbledon	PL	H	D	1-1	Yorke
		4r	3.2.93	Wimbledon		A	D	0-0aet	

Wimbledon won 6-5 on penalties

ATHERSTONE UNITED

Formed 1979. First entered FA Cup: 1979.

1987-88	SL	1	14.11.87	VS Rugby	SL	A	D	0-0	
		1r	17.11.87	VS Rugby		H	L	0-2	
1990-91	SL	1	17.11.90	Fleetwood	NPL	H	W	3-1	Parker 3
		2	12.12.90	Crewe A	D3	A	L	0-1	
1991-92	SL	1	16.11.91	Hereford U	D4	H	D	0-0	
		1r	26.11.91	Hereford U		A	L	0-3	

ATTERCLIFFE

Formed 1870, home matches played at Brightside Lane, Sheffield.

1886-87	1	30.10.86	Staveley		A	L	0-7	
1887-88	1	15.10.87	Sheffield Heeley		A	L	0-9	

AVELEY

Formed 1927. First entered FA Cup: 1954. Currently playing in Isthmian (Diadora) League

1970-71	AL	1	21.11.70	Yeovil T	SL	A	L	0-1	

AYLESBURY UNITED

Formed 1897 by merger of Aylesbury Night School FC and Aylesbury Printing Works. First entered FA Cup: 1897. Cup Final Connection:

Former player Ray Mabbutt is the father of Gary Mabbutt who played in the 1987 and 1991 Cup Finals for Tottenham. Former manager Trevor Gould is the brother of Bobby Gould, Wimbledon's manager when they won the Cup in 1988. **League club beaten:** Southend U

1951-52	Del	1	24.11.51	Watford	3S	H	L	0-5	
1985-86	SL	1	16.11.85	Slough T	IL	A	D	2-2	Botterill, Hercules
		1r	19.11.85	Slough T		H	L	2-5	Campbell 2
1986-87	SL	1	15.11.86	Bath C	GMVC	A	L	2-3	Hercules, Botterill (p)
1987-88	SL	1	14.11.87	Bristol C	D3	A	L	0-1	
1988-89	GMVC	1	19.11.88	Waterlooville	SL	A	W	4-1	Hercules 2, Boyland 2
		2	10.12.88	Sutton U	GMVC	H	L	0-1	
1989-90	IL	1	18.11.89	Southend U	D4	H	W	1-0	Donegal
		2	9.12.89	Northampton T	D3	A	D	0-0	
		2r	13.12.89	Northampton T		H	L	0-1aet	
1990-91	IL	1	17.11.90	Walsall	D4	H	L	0-1	
1991-92	IL	1	16.11.91	Kidderminster H	GMVC	A	W	1-0	Davies
		2	7.12.91	Hereford U	D4	H	L	2-3	Hercules 2
1992-93	IL	1	14.11.92	WBA	D2	A	L	0-8	

BANBURY UNITED

Originally formed as Banbury Spencer. **First entered FA Cup:** 1934. Reformed as Banbury United 1965

1947-48	BC	1	29.11.47	Colchester U	SL	A	L	1-2	North
1961-62	BDL	1	4.11.61	Shrewsbury T	D3	A	L	1-7	Redding
1972-73	SL	1	18.11.72	Barnet	SL	H	L	0-2	
1973-74	SL	1	24.11.73	Northampton T	D4	H	D	0-0	
		1r	29.11.73	Northampton T		A	L	2-3	Gregory og, Haynes

BANGOR CITY

Formed 1876. **First entered FA Cup:** 1896. Currently playing in the League of Wales **FA Challenge Trophy:** Runners-Up 1984. **Welsh FA Cup winners:** 1889, 1896, 1962 **League Clubs Beaten:** Wrexham, Rochdale **Cup Final Connection:** Former Bangor player Neville Southall played in three Cup Finals for Everton

1951-52	CC	1	24.11.51	Southport	3N	H	D	2-2	Wyles, Higgins
		1r	27.11.51	Southport		A	L	0-3	
1952-53	CC	1	22.11.52	Southport	3N	A	L	1-3	Glaister
1960-61	CC	1	5.11.60	Wrexham	D4	H	W	1-0	D.Jones
		2	26.11.60	Southport	D4	H	D	1-1	Hunt
		2r	29.11.60	Southport		A	L	1-3	Gryba
1963-64	CC	1	16.11.63	Barrow	D4	A	L	2-3	Kinsella 2
1964-65	CC	1	14.11.64	York C	D4	A	L	1-5	Pitchford
1966-67	CC	1	26.11.66	Mansfield T	D3	A	L	1-4	Conde
1968-69	NPL	1	16.11.68	Morecambe	NPL	H	L	2-3	Conde 2
1969-70	NPL	1	15.11.69	Kirkby T	LC	H	W	6-0	Grant 2, Jackson, Morton, Broadhead, Lucas (p)
		2	6.12.69	York C	D4	H	D	0-0	
		2r	9.12.69	York C		A	L	0-2	
1970-71	NPL	1	21.11.70	Darlington	D4	A	L	1-5	Grant
1971-72	NPL	1	20.11.71	Bolton W	D3	A	L	0-3	
1972-73	NPL	1	18.11.72	Rochdale	D3	A	W	2-1	Brodie, Marsden
		2	9.12.73	York C	D4	H	L	2-3	Marsden, Morton
1983-84	APL	1	19.11.83	Northwich Vic	APL	A	D	1-1	Howat
		1r	22.11.83	Northwich Vic		H	W	1-0	Urquhart (p)
		2	10.12.83	Blackpool	D4	H	D	1-1	Urquhart
		2r	13.12.83	Blackpool		A	L	1-2	Urquhart (p)
1984-85	NPL	1	17.11.84	Tranmere R	D4	H	D	1-1	Urquhart (p)
		1r	20.11.84	Tranmere R		A	L	0-7	

BARKING

Formed 1880. **First entered FA Cup:** 1905. **League clubs beaten:** Oxford United **FA Amateur Cup:** Runners-up 1927

1926-27	AL	1	27.11.26	Gillingham	3S	H	D	0-0	
		1r	1.12.26	Gillingham		A	L	0-2	
1928-29	AL	1	26.11.28	Exeter C	3S	A	L	0-6	
1978-79	IL	1	25.11.78	Yeovil T	SL	A	W	1-0	Key
		2	16.12.78	Aldershot	D4	H	L	1-2	Ashford
1979-80	IL	1	24.11.79	Oxford U	D3	H	W	1-0	Brothers
		2	15.12.79	Reading	D3	A	L	1-3	Dingwall
1981-82	IL	1	21.11.81	Bideford	WL	A	W	2-1	Hillman, Key

	2	15.12.81	Gillingham	D3	A	D	1-1	Hillman
	2r	2.1.82	Gillingham at Gillingham		H	L	1-3aet	Anderson
1983-84 IL	1	19.11.83	Farnborough	IL	H	W	2-1	Crown 2
	2	10.12.83	Plymouth A	D3	A	L	1-2	Groom

BARNES

Formed 1862 by Ebenezer Cobb Morley, the first secretary of the FA. One of the original 15 FA Cup entrants. Their home ground was a field near the White Hart pub.

1871-72	1	11.11.71	Civil Service		H	W	2-0	Dunnage, P.Weston
	2	23.12.71	Hampstead Heathens		H	D	1-1	AC Highton
	2r	6.1.72	Hampstead Heathens		A	L	0-1	
1872-73	1	19.10.72	South Norwood		H	L	0-1	
1873-74	1	25.10.73	1st Surrey Rifles		A	D	0-0	
	1r	8.11.73	1st Surrey Rifles		H	W	1-0	Hudson
	2	22.11.73	Oxford University		A	L	0-2	
1874-75	1	24.10.74	Upton Park		A	W	3-0	Hudson, Morice, Soden
	2	21.11.74	Wanderers		A	L	0-5	
1875-76	1	30.10.75	Reigate Priory		A	L	0-1	
1876-77	1		Old Etonians				walkover	
	2	9.12.76	Upton Park		A	L	0-1	
1877-78	1		St Mark's				walkover	
	2	15.12.77	Marlow		H	W	3-1	Ainslie 2, Dorling
	3	12.1.78	Wanderers		A	D	1-1	Ainslie
	3r	26.1.78	Wanderers		A	L	1-4	Weston
1878-79	1	19.10.78	Maidenhead		H	D	1-1	Dorling
	1r	9.11.78	Maidenhead		A	W	4-0	Wylie 2, Chamberlain, Hudson
	2	4.1.79	Upton Park		H	W	3-2	Johnstone 2, Chamberlain
	3	2.2.79	Oxford University		A	L	1-2	Dorling
1880-81	1	16.10.80	Herts Rangers		A	L	0-6	
1881-82	1	29.10.81	Rochester		H	W	3-1	
	2	3.12.81	Old Carthusians		A	L	1-7	Sibbs
1882-83	1	28.10.82	Brentwood		H	L	2-4	
1883-84	1	*did not enter*						
1884-85	1	1.11.84	Brentwood		A	L	0-2	
1885-86	1	31.10.85	Lancing		H	L	1-7	

BARNET

Formed 1888. Known as Barnet Alston 1906-1919. **First entered FA Cup:** 1911 **FA Challenge Trophy:** Runners-up 1972. **FA Amateur Cup:** Winners 1946. Runners-Up 1948, 1959 **League Clubs beaten as a non-League club:** Newport County, Northampton Town **Record FA Cup Win:** 6-1 vs Newport County, 1st round, 21.11.1970 **Record FA Cup Defeat:** 2-9 vs Southend United, 2nd round, 14.12.1946

1925-26 AL	1	28.11.25	Brentford	3S	A	L	1-3	Donnelly og
1926-27 AL	1	27.11.26	Brighton & HA	3S	A	L	0-3	
1931-32 AL	1	28.11.31	QPR	3S	H	L	3-7	Finch, Marchant, MacDonald
1933-34 AL	1	25.11.33	Cheltenham	BC	A	L	1-5	Richardson
1945-46 AL	1 1L	17.11.45	QPR	3S	H	L	2-6	Reilly, Hawkins
	1 2L	24.11.45	QPR		A	L	1-2	Finch
1946-47 AL	1	30.11.46	Sutton U	AL	H	W	3-0	Hawkes, Phipps, Finch (p)
	2	14.12.46	Southend U	3S	H	L	2-9	Phipps 2
1948-49 AL	1	4.12.48	Exeter C	3S	H	L	2-6	Kelleher, Phipps
1954-55 AL	1	20.11.54	Southampton	3S	H	L	1-4	Rudolf
1959-60 AL	1	14.11.59	Salisbury	WL	A	L	0-1	
1961-62 AL	1	4.11.61	Weymouth	SL	A	L	0-1	
1964-65 AL	1	14.11.64	Cambridge U	SL	H	W	2-1	D.Harding, Finch
	2	5.12.64	Enfield	IL	A	D	4-4	Morris, Figg 2 (1p), Finch
	2r	8.12.64	Enfield		H	W	3-0	Figg, Finch 2
	3	9.1.65	Preston NE	D2	H	L	2-3	Figg, White
1965-66 SL	1	13.11.65	Dartford	SL	H	L	0-2	
1967-68 SL	1	13.12.67	Hereford U	SL	A	L	2-3	Eason, Searle
1968-69 SL	1	16.11.68	Brentwood T	SL	H	D	1-1	Meadows
	1r	18.11.68	Brentwood T		A	L	0-1	
1969-70 SL	1	15.11.69	Walton & Hersham	AL	A	W	1-0	Meadows
	2	6.12.69	Sutton U	IL	H	L	0-2	
1970-71 SL	1	21.11.70	Newport Co	D4	H	W	6-1	George 3, Fergusson og, Powell, Adams
	2	12.12.70	Slough T	AL	A	W	1-0	Eason

		3	5.1.71	Colchester U	D4	H	L	0-1	
1971-72	SL	1	20.11.71	Kettering	SL	A	W	4-2	Embery 2, Eason 2
		2	11.12.71	Torquay U	D3	H	L	1-4	Flatt
1972-73	SL	1	18.11.72	Banbury U	SL	A	W	2-0	Powell, Eason
		2	9.12.72	Bilston T	WMRL	H	D	1-1	Fascione
		2r	11.12.72	Bilston T		A	W	1-0	Powell
		3	13.1.73	QPR	D2	A	D	0-0	
		3r	16.1.73	QPR		H	L	0-3	
1977-78	SL	1	26.11.77	Peterborough U	D3	H	L	1-2	Brown
1978-79	SL	1	25.11.78	Woking	IL	H	D	3-3	Oliver, Cleary 2 (1p)
		1r	28.11.78	Woking		A	D	3-3aet	Brown, Fairbrother 2
		1 2r	5.12.78	Woking at Brentford			L	0-3	
1980-81	APL	1	22.11.80	Minehead	SL	H	D	2-2	Walker og, Hughes (p)
		1r	25.11.80	Minehead		A	W	2-1	Roberts 2
		2	13.12.80	Peterborough U	D4	H	L	0-1	
1981-82	APL	1	21.11.81	Harlow T	IL	A	D	0-0	
		1r	24.11.81	Harlow T		H	W	1-0	Sargent
		2	15.12.81	Wycombe W	IL	H	W	2-0	Foody, Barnes
		3	2.1.82	Brighton & HA	D1	H	D	0-0	
		3r	5.1.82	Brighton & HA		A	L	1-3	Sargent
1982-83	APL	1	30.11.82	Carshalton A	IL	A	L	0-4	
1983-84	APL	1	19.11.83	Bristol R	D3	H	D	0-0	
		1r	22.11.83	Bristol R		A	L	1-3	Evans
1984-85	APL	1	17.11.84	Plymouth A	D3	A	L	0-3	
1987-88	GMVC	1	14.11.87	Hereford U	D4	H	L	0-1	
1989-90	GMVC	1	18.11.89	Bristol C	D3	A	L	0-2	
1990-91	GMVC	1	17.11.90	Chelmsford	SL	H	D	2-2	Bull, Willis
		1r	21.11.90	Chelmsford		A	W	2-0	Clarke, Willis
		2	7.12.90	Northampton T	D4	H	D	0-0	
		2r	12.12.90	Northampton T		A	W	1-0	Clarke
		3	5.1.91	Portsmouth	D2	H	L	0-5	
1991-92	D4	1	16.11.91	Tiverton T	WL	H	W	5-0	Bull, Naylor, Carter, Evans, Showler
		2	7.12.91	Enfield	IL	A	W	4-1	Bull, Carter 3
		3	5.1.92	Charlton A	D2	A	L	1-3	Carter
1992-93	D3	1	14.11.92	Bournemouth	D2	A	D	0-0	
		1r	25.11.92	Bournemouth		H	L	1-2	Carter

BARNSLEY

Formed 1887 as Barnsley St Peters. Barnsley 1899. **First entered FA Cup:** 1893. **FA Cup Winners:** 1912. **FA Cup Runners-up:** 1910. **Record FA Cup Win:** 8-0 vs Leeds AFC, 2nd qual rd, 1894-95. In Competition Proper: 6-0 vs Blackpool, 1st round replay, 20.1.1910. **Record FA Cup Defeat:** 1-8 vs Derby County, 1st round, 30.1.1897

1893-94		1q **Gainsborough T** (H) 4-5						
1894-95		1q **Grantham R** (H) 3-1; 2q **Leeds AFC** (H) 8-0; 3q **Mexborough T** (A) 1-1; 3qr **Mexborough T** (H) 1-0; 4q **Worksop T** (H) 3-1
		1	2.2.95	**Liverpool**	D1	H	L	1-2aet	Cutts
			FA ordered replay after protest
		1r	11.2.95	**Liverpool**		A	L	0-4	
1895-96	ML	1q **Rotherham T** (A) 1-1; 1qr **Rotherham T** (H) 3-7
1896-97	ML	3q **Hunslet** (H) 3-2; 4q **Sheffield Club** (H) 2-1; 5q **Lincoln C** (A) 2-1
		1	30.1.97	**Derby Co**	D1	A	L	1-8	Smith
1897-98	ML	3q **Mexborough T** (A) 1-2
1898-99	D2	2q **Wombwell** (A) 1-0; 3q **Gainsborough T** (A) 2-2; 3qr **Gainsborough T** (H) 4-0; 4q **Doncaster R** (A) 1-2
1899-00	D2	3q **Lincoln C** (H) 1-0; 4q **Grimsby T** (A) 2-3
1900-01	D2	3q **Doncaster R** (H) 2-1; 4q **Lincoln C** (H) 1-0; 5q **Chesterfield** (H) 1-5
1901-02	D2	3q **Gainsborough T** (H) 1-0; 4q **Ilkeston T** (A) 4-2; 5q **Lincoln C** (H) 0-0; 5qr **Lincoln C** (A) 1-3aet
1902-03	D2	3q **Belper T** (A) 4-1; 4q **Chesterfield** (H) 3-2; 5q **Gainsborough T** (H) 3-2; Int **Swindon T** (H) 4-0
		1	7.2.03	**Lincoln C**	D2	H	W	2-0	Bennett, Welch
		2	21.1.03	**Aston Villa**	D1	A	L	1-4	Lees
1903-04	D2	Int **Grimsby T** (A) 0-2
1904-05	D2	6q **Burslem Port Vale** (H) 0-0; 6qr **Burslem Port Vale** (A) 2-1; Int **Plymouth A** (A) 0-2
1905-06	D2	4q **Earlestown** (A) 2-0
		1	13.1.06	**Crewe Alex**	BDL	A	D	1-1	Stacey
		1r	18.1.06	**Crewe Alex**		H	W	4-0	Stacey, Wilkinson, Helliwell, Wall
		2	3.2.06	**Liverpool**	D1	A	L	0-1	
1906-07	D2	1	12.1.07	**Nottingham F**	D2	A	D	1-1	Helliwell
		1r	17.1.07	**Nottingham F**		H	W	2-1	Helliwell, Hall

		2	2.2.07	**Portsmouth**	SL	H	W	1-0	O'Donnell
		3	23.2.07	**Bury**	D1	H	W	1-0	Powell
		4	9.3.07	**W.Arsenal**	D1	H	L	1-2	O'Donnell
1907-08	D2	1	11.1.08	**Plymouth A**	SL	A	L	0-1	
1908-09	D2	1	16.1.09	**Everton**	D1	A	L	1-3	Lillycrop
1909-10	D2	1	15.1.10	**Blackpool**	D2	A	D	1-1	Tufnell
		1r	20.1.10	**Blackpool**		H	W	6-0	Lillycrop 2, Tufnell 2, Gadsby, Boyle
		2	5.2.10	**Bristol R**	SL	H	W	4-0	Forman, Utley, Bartrop, Gadsby
		3	19.2.10	**WBA**	D2	H	W	1-0	Tufnell
		4	5.3.10	**QPR**	SL	H	W	1-0	Bartrop
		SF	26.3.10	**Everton**	D1		D	0-0	
			played at Elland Road						
		SFr	1.4.10	**Everton**			W	3-0	Gadsby, Forman, Tufnell
			played at Old Trafford						
		F	23.4.10	**Newcastle U**	D1		D	1-1	Tufnell
			played at Crystal Palace						
		Fr	28.4.10	**Newcastle U**			L	0-2	
			played at Goodison Park						
1910-11	D2	1	14.1.11	**Watford**	SL	A	W	2-0	Boyle, Lillycrop
		2	4.2.11	**Burnley**	D2	A	L	0-2	
1911-12	D2	1	13.1.12	**Birmingham**	D2	A	D	0-0	
		1r	22.1.12	**Birmingham**		H	W	3-0	Tufnell, Lillycrop 2
		2	3.2.12	**Leicester F**	D2	H	W	1-0	Lillycrop
		3	24.2.12	**Bolton W**	D1	A	W	2-1	Lillycrop, Whiteside og
		4	9.3.12	**Bradford C**	D1	H	D	0-0	
		4r	13.3.12	**Bradford C**		A	D	0-0	
		4 2r	18.3.12	**Bradford C** at Elland Road			D	0-0aet	
		4 3r	21.3.12	**Bradford C** at Bramall Lane			W	3-2aet	Travers, Lillycrop 2
		SF	30.3.12	**Swindon T**	SL		D	0-0	
			played at Stamford Bridge						
		SFr	3.4.12	**Swindon T**			W	1-0	Bratley
			played at Meadow Lane, Nottingham						
		F	20.4.12	**WBA**	D1		D	0-0	
			played at Crystal Palace						
		Fr	24.4.12	**WBA**			W	1-0aet	Tufnell
			played at Bramall Lane						
1912-13	D2	1	11.1.13	**Gillingham**	SL	A	D	0-0	
		1r	16.1.13	**Gillingham**		H	W	3-1	Tufnell, Lillycrop 2
		2	1.2.13	**Blackburn R**	D1	H	L-	2-3	Moore, Tufnell
1913-14	D2	1	10.1.14	**Liverpool**	D1	A	D	1-1	Travers
		1r	14.1.14	**Liverpool**		H	L	0-1	
1914-15	D2	1	9.1.15	**Everton**	D1	A	L	0-3	
1919-20	D2	1	10.1.20	**WBA**	D1	A	W	1-0	Fletcher
		2	31.1.20	**Plymouth A**	SL	A	L	1-4	Downs
1920-21	D2	1	8.1.21	**Bradford C**	D1	A	L	1-3	Fletcher
1921-22	D2	1	7.1.22	**Norwich C**	D3	H	D	1-1	Spoors
		1r	11.1.22	**Norwich C**		A	W	2-1	Hine, Fletcher
		2	28.1.22	**Oldham A**	D1	H	W	3-1	Fletcher 2, Wainscoat
		3	18.2.22	**Preston NE**	D1	H	D	1-1	Fletcher
		3r	22.2.22	**Preston NE**		A	L	0-3	
1922-23	D2	1	13.1.23	**Swindon T**	3S	A	D	0-0	
		1r	18.1.23	**Swindon T**		H	W	2-0	Hine, Wainscoat
		2	3.2.23	**Sheffield W**	D2	A	L	1-2	Baines
1923-24	D2	1	12.1.24	**Brighton & HA**	3S	H	D	0-0	
		1r	16.1.24	**Brighton & HA**		A	L	0-1	
1924-25	D2	1	10.1.25	**Millwall**	3S	A	D	0-0	
		1r	15.1.25	**Millwall**		H	W	2-1	Fletcher, Kelly,
		2	31.1.25	**Bradford C**	D2	H	L	0-3	
1925-26	D2	1	28.11.25	**Northampton T**	3S	A	L	1-3	Fletcher
1926-27	D2	3	8.1.27	**Crewe Alex**	3N	H	W	6-1	Tilson, Fletcher 3, Eaton, Curran
		4	29.1.27	**Swansea T**	D2	H	L	1-3	Eaton
1927-28	D2	3	14.1.28	**Port Vale**	D2	A	L	0-3	
1928-29	D2	3	12.1.29	**Blackburn R**	D1	A	L	0-1	
1929-30	D2	3	11.1.30	**Bradford PA**	D2	H	L	0-1	
1930-31	D2	3	10.1.31	**Bristol C**	D2	H	W	4-1	Proudfoot, Gibbs, Curran, Harvey
		4	24.1.31	**Sheffield W**	D1	H	W	2-1	Harvey, Curran
		5	14.2.31	**Wolverhampton W**	D2	H	L	1-3	Henderson

1931-32	D2	3	9.1.32	Southport	3N	H	D	0-0	
		3r	12.1.32	Southport		A	L	1-4	Ashton
1932-33	3N	3	14.1.33	Luton T	3S	H	D	0-0	
		3r	18.1.33	Luton T		A	L	0-2	
1933-34	3N	1	25.11.33	Halifax T	3N	A	L	2-3	Andrews 2
1934-35	D2	3	12.1.35	Preston NE	D1	A	D	0-0	
		3r	16.1.35	Preston NE		H	L	0-1	
1935-36	D2	3	11.1.36	Birmingham	D1	H	D	3-3	Hine 2, Ashton
		3r	15.1.36	Birmingham		A	W	2-0	Hine, Waring
		4	25.1.36	Tranmere R	3N	A	W	4-2	Waring, Hine, Ashton, Fisher
		5	15.2.36	Stoke C	D1	H	W	2-1	Gallacher, Hine
		6	29.2.36	Arsenal	D1	A	L	1-4	Gallacher
1936-37	D2	3	16.1.37	Walsall	3S	A	L	1-3	Hamill
1937-38	D2	3	8.1.38	Southend U	3S	A	D	2-2	Asquith, Barlow
		3r	12.1.38	Southend U		H	W	3-1	Barlow, Hunt 2
		4	22.1.38	Manchester U	D2	H	D	2-2	Bokas, Fisher
		4r	26.1.38	Manchester U		A	L	0-1	
1938-39	3N	3	7.1.39	Stockport Co	3N	H	L	1-2	McGarry
1945-46	D2	3 1L	5.1.46	Newcastle U	D2	A	L	2-4	Harvey og, Pallister
		3 2L	9.1.46	Newcastle U		H	W	3-0	Wilson, Smith, Baxter
		4 1L	26.1.46	Rotherham U	3N	H	W	3-0	Kelly, Smith, G.Robledo
		4 2L	31.1.46	Rotherham U		A	L	1-2	Pallister
		5 1L	9.2.46	Bradford PA	D2	H	L	0-1	
		5 2L	13.2.46	Bradford PA		A	D	1-1	G.Robledo
1946-47	D2	3	11.1.47	Huddersfield T	D1	A	W	4-3	Smith, Asquith, Bennett, Baxter
		4	25.1.47	Preston NE	D1	A	L	0-6	
1947-48	D2	3	10.1.48	Manchester C	D1	A	L	1-2	Wright
1948-49	D2	3	8.1.49	Blackpool	D1	H	L	0-1	
1949-50	D2	3	7.1.50	Stockport Co	3N	A	L	2-4	Wright, Griffiths
1950-51	D2	3	6.1.51	Northampton T	3S	A	L	1-3	McCormack
1951-52	D2	3	12.1.52	Colchester U	3S	H	W	3-0	McMorran, Jarman, Wood
		4	2.2.52	Arsenal	D1	A	L	0-4	
1952-53	D2	3	10.1.53	Brighton & HA	3S	H	W	4-3	Kaye, Taylor 2, McMorran
		4	31.1.53	Plymouth A	D2	A	L	0-1	
1953-54	3N	1	21.11.53	York C	3N	H	W	5-2	Kaye, Lumley, Bartlett 2, Chappell
		2	12.12.53	Norwich C	3S	A	L	1-2	Brown
1954-55	3N	1	20.11.54	Wigan A	LC	H	W	3-2	Bartlett, Lumley 2
		2	11.12.54	Gateshead	3N	A	D	3-3	Wood, Kaye, Bartlett
		2r	16.12.54	Gateshead		H	L	0-1	
1955-56	D2	3	7.1.56	Aldershot	3S	A	W	2-1	Brown 2
		4	28.1.56	Blackburn R	D2	H	L	0-1	
1956-57	D2	3	5.1.57	Port Vale	D2	H	D	3-3	Kaye 2, Bartlett
		3r	7.1.57	Port Vale		A	W	1-0	Hayward og
		4	26.1.57	Cardiff C	D1	A	W	1-0	Bartlett
		5	16.2.57	Nottingham F	D2	H	L	1-2	Kaye
1957-58	D2	3	4.1.58	Hull C	3N	A	D	1-1	Smith
		3r	8.1.58	Hull C		H	L	0-2	
1958-59	D2	3	10.1.59	Brentford	D3	A	L	0-2	
1959-60	D3	1	14.11.59	Bradford C	D3	H	D	3-3	Barber, Bartlett, Beaumont (p)
		1r	18.11.59	Bradford C		A	L	1-2	Beaumont
1960-61	D3	1	5.11.60	Gateshead	NCL	A	D	0-0	
		1r	9.11.60	Gateshead		H	W	2-0	Bartlett, Beaumont
		2	26.11.60	Bradford C	D3	A	W	2-1	Bartlett 2
		3	7.1.61	Reading	D3	A	D	1-1	Tindill
		3r	11.1.61	Reading		H	W	3-1	Oliver, Tindill, Bartlett
		4	1.2.61	Huddersfield T	D2	A	D	1-1	Oliver
		4r	6.2.61	Huddersfield T		H	W	1-0	Wood
		5	18.2.61	Luton T	D2	H	W	1-0	Lunn
		6	4.3.61	Leicester C	D1	A	D	0-0	
		6r	8.3.61	Leicester C		H	L	1-2aet	Oliver
1961-62	D3	1	4.11.61	West Auckland T	NL	A	D	3-3	Oliver 2, Swindells
		1r	8.11.61	West Auckland T		H	W	2-0	Swindells, Smillie
		2	25.11.61	Carlisle U	D4	H	L	1-2	Swindells
1962-63	D3	1	3.11.62	Rhyl	CC	H	W	4-0	Kerr 2, Leighton, O'Hara (p)
		2	24.11.62	Chesterfield	D4	H	W	2-1	Oliver 2
		3	15.1.63	Everton	D1	H	L	0-3	
1963-64	D3	1	16.11.63	Stockport Co	D4	H	W	1-0	Byrne

		2	7.12.63	Rochdale	D4	H	W	3-1	Kerr 2, Leighton
		3	4.1.64	Scunthorpe U	D2	A	D	2-2	O'Hara, Byrne
		3r	7.1.64	Scunthorpe U		H	W	3-2aet	O'Hara, Byrne 2
		4	25.1.64	Bury	D2	H	W	2-1	Gallagher og, Kerr
		5	15.2.64	Manchester U	D1	H	L	0-4	
1964-65	D3	1	14.11.64	Netherfield	LC	A	W	3-1	Byrne, Kerr, Graham
		2	5.12.64	Chester	D4	H	L	2-5	Byrne, Senior
1965-66	D4	1	13.11.65	Lincoln C	D4	A	W	3-1	Bettany, Kerr (p), Earnshaw
		2	4.12.65	Grimsby T	D3	H	D	1-1	Kerr
		2r	8.12.65	Grimsby T		A	L	0-2	
1966-67	D4	1	26.11.66	Southport	D4	H	W	3-1	Evans, Thomas 2
		2	7.1.67	Port Vale	D4	H	D	1-1	Hewitt
		2r	16.1.67	Port Vale		A	W	3-1	Sherratt og, Bettany, Hewitt (p)
		3	28.1.67	Cardiff C	D2	H	D	1-1	Evans
		3r	31.1.67	Cardiff C		A	L	1-2	Thomas
1967-68	D4	1	9.12.67	Chesterfield	D4	A	L	0-2	
1968-69	D3	1	16.11.68	Rochdale	D4	H	D	0-0	
		1r	18.11.68	Rochdale		A	W	1-0	Dean
		2	7.12.68	Darlington	D4	A	D	0-0	
		2r	10.12.68	Darlington		H	W	1-0	Winstanley
		3	4.1.69	Leicester C	D1	H	D	1-1	Evans
		3r	8.1.69	Leicester C		A	L	1-2	Layden (p)
1969-70	D3	1	15.11.69	Darlington	D4	A	D	0-0	
		1r	18.11.69	Darlington		H	W	2-0	Dean, Graham
		2	6.12.69	Barrow	D3	H	W	3-0	Loyden 2, Robson
		3	3.1.70	Mansfield T	D3	A	L	2-3	Dean, Evans
1970-71	D3	1	21.11.70	Bradford PA	NPL	H	W	1-0	Dean (p)
		2	12.12.70	Rhyl	CC	A	D	0-0	
		2r	15.12.70	Rhyl		H	D	1-1aet	Lea
		2 2r	21.12.70	Rhyl		H	L	0-2	
1971-72	D3	1	20.11.71	Rochdale	D3	A	W	3-1	Winstanley 2, Seal
		2	11.12.71	Chesterfield	D3	H	D	0-0	
		2r	15.12.71	Chesterfield		A	L	0-1	
1972-73	D4	1	18.11.72	Halifax T	D3	H	D	1-1	Lea
		1r	21.11.72	Halifax T		A	L	1-2	Kemp og
1973-74	D4	1	24.11.73	Chesterfield	D3	A	D	0-0	
		1r	28.11.73	Chesterfield		H	W	2-1	Manning 2
		2	15.12.73	Bradford C	D4	H	D	1-1	Butler
		2r	19.12.73	Bradford C		A	L	1-2	Brown
1974-75	D4	1	23.11.74	Halifax T	D3	H	L	1-2	Brown
1975-76	D4	1	22.11.75	Marine	CC	A	L	1-3	Butler
1976-77	D4	1	20.11.76	Boston U	NPL	H	W	3-1	Joicey 3 (1p)
		2	11.12.76	Port Vale	D3	A	L	0-3	
1977-78	D4	1	26.11.77	Huddersfield T	D4	H	W	1-0	Warnock
		2	17.12.77	Grimsby T	D4	A	L	0-2	
1978-79	D4	1	25.11.78	Worksop T	NPL	H	W	5-1	Clarke, Riley, Bell, Reed 2
		2	16.12.78	Rotherham U	D3	H	D	1-1	Clarke
		2r	9.1.79	Rotherham U		A	L	1-2	Forrest og
1979-80	D3	1	24.11.79	Hartlepool U	D4	H	W	5-2	Clarke, Glavin 2, Aylott, Lester
		2	18.12.79	Chester	D3	A	L	0-1	
1980-81	D3	1	22.11.80	Chester	D3	A	W	2-1	Cooper, Bank s
		2	13.12.80	Rotherham U	D3	A	W	1-0	Parker
		3	3.1.81	Torquay U	D4	H	W	2-1	Parker 2
		4	24.1.81	Enfield	IL	H	D	1-1	Aylott
		4r	28.1.81	Enfield at Tottenham		A	W	3-0	Aylott 2, Glavin
		5	14.2.81	Middlesbrough	D1	A	L	1-2	Lester
1981-82	D2	3	5.1.82	Blackpool	D4	H	L	0-2	
1982-83	D2	3	8.1.83	Bradford C	D3	A	W	1-0	Glavin
		4	29.1.83	Cambridge U	D2	A	L	0-1	
1983-84	D2	3	7.1.84	Sheffield W	D2	A	L	0-1	
1984-85	D2	3	5.1.85	Reading	D3	H	W	4-3	R. Futcher, Owen 2(1p), Joyce
		4	26.1.85	Brighton & HA	D2	H	W	2-1	Owen, R. Futcher
		5	4.3.85	Southampton	D1	A	W	2-1	Agnew, Owen (p)
		6	10.3.85	Liverpool	D1	H	L	0-4	
1985-86	D2	3	13.1.86	Bury	D3	A	L	0-2	
1986-87	D2	3	10.1.87	Caernarfon T	NPL	A	D	0-0	
		3r	26.1.87	Caernarfon T		H	W	1-0	Wylde

		4	31.1.87	Aldershot	D4	A	D	1-1	Agnew
		4r	3.2.87	Aldershot		H	W	3-0	May 2, Thomas
		5	21.2.87	Arsenal	D1	A	L	0-2	
1987-88	D2	3	9.1.88	Bolton W	D4	H	W	3-1	Broddle 2, Beresford
		4	30.1.88	Birmingham C	D2	H	L	0-2	
1988-89	D2	3	7.1.89	Chelsea	D2	H	W	4-0	Thomas, Agnew 2, Currie
		4	28.1.89	Stoke C	D2	A	D	3-3	Currie 2, MacDonald
		4r	31.1.89	Stoke C		H	W	2-1	MacDonald, Cooper
		5	18.2.89	Everton	D1	H	L	0-1	
1989-90	D2	3	6.1.90	Leicester C	D2	A	W	2-1	Currie, Lowndes
		4	27.1.90	Ipswich T	D2	H	W	2-0	Taggart, Cooper
		5	18.2.90	Sheffield U	D2	A	D	2-2	Smith, Cooper
		5r	21.2.90	Sheffield U		H	D	0-0aet	
		5 2r	5.3.90	Sheffield U		H	L	0-1aet	
1990-91	D2	3	6.1.91	Leeds U	D1	H	D	1-1	Deehan
		3r	9.1.91	Leeds U		A	L	0-4	
1991-92	D2	3	4.1.92	Norwich C	D1	A	L	0-1	
1992-93	D1	3	13.1.93	Leicester C	D1	A	D	2-2	Whitlow og, Redfearn
		3r	20.1.93	Leicester C		H	D	1-1aet	Archdeacon
				Barnsley won 5-4 on penalties					
		4	24.1.93	West Ham	D1	H	W	4-1	Rammell 3, Redfearn
		5	13.2.93	Manchester C	PL	A	L	0-2	

BARNSTAPLE TOWN

Formed 1895. **First entered FA Cup:** 1948. Record crowd of 6,200 vs Bournemouth, 1954

1951-52	WL	1	24.11.51	Folkestone	KL	H	D	2-2	Pickard, Godbeer
		1r	28.11.51	Folkestone		A	L	2-5	Hayward, Granville
1954-55	WL	1	20.11.54	Bournemouth	3S	H	L	1-4	Stocker
1959-60	WL	1	14.11.59	Exeter	D4	H	L	0-4	
1972-73	WL	1	18.11.72	Bilston	WMRL	H	L	0-2	

BARROW

Formed 1901. **Members of the Football League:** 1921-1972 **FA Challenge Trophy Winners:** 1990 **Best performances in FA Cup:** 3rd round eight times

1905-06	LC	1	13.1.06	Bradford C	D2	A	L	2-3	Lawrenson, McBeath
1912-13	LC	1	15.1.13	Bradford PA	D2	A	D	1-1	Pinkey
		1r	22.1.13	Bradford PA at Bradford			L	0-1	
1921-22	3N	4q Lancaster T (H) 2-2; 4qr Lancaster T (A) 0-1							
1922-23	3N	4q Workington (H) 1-0; 5q Stockport Co (H) 3-2; 6q Bath C (H) 2-2; 6qr Bath C (A) 0-2							
1923-24	3N	4q Carlisle U (H) 1-2							
1924-25	3N	4q Darwen (H) 1-0; 5q Wrexham (H) 4-0; 6q Gillingham (A) 0-0; 6qr Gillingham (H) 1-1aet; 6q 2r Gillingham 1-1 (at Molineux); 6q 3r Gillingham 1-1 (at Highbury); 6q 4r Gillingham 2-1 (at Millwall)							
		1	10.1.25	Blackpool	D2	A	D	0-0	
		1r	14.1.25	Blackpool		H	L	0-2	
1925-26	3N	1	28.11.25	New Brighton	3N	A	L	0-2	
1926-27	3N	1	1.12.26	Wigan B	3N	A	D	2-2	Tilbrook 2
		1r	6.12.26	Wigan B		H	L	0-1	
1927-28	3N	4q Workington (A) 1-3							
1928-29	3N	1	24.11.28	York C	ML	A	W	1-0	Ferrari
		2	8.12.28	Mansfield T	ML	H	L	1-2	Ferrari
1929-30	3N	1	30.11.29	Newark T	ML	H	W	1-0	Patton
		2	14.12.29	Stockport Co	3N	A	L	0-4	
1930-31	3N	1	29.11.30	Lincoln C	3N	A	L	3-8	Millar 2, Moon
1931-32	3N	1	28.11.31	Doncaster R	3N	H	D	3-3	Littler 2, Suggett
		1r	3.12.31	Doncaster R		A	D	1-1aet	Littler
		1 2r	7.12.31	Doncaster R at Maine Road			D	1-1aet	Tinnion
		1 3r	9.12.31	Doncaster R at Elland Road			L	0-1aet	
1932-33	3N	1	26.11.32	Gateshead	3N	H	L	0-1	
1933-34	3N	1	25.11.33	Doncaster R	3N	H	W	4-2	Shankly 3, Roberts
		2	9.12.33	Bristol C	3S	A	L	1-3	Murray
1934-35	3N	1	24.11.34	Doncaster R	3N	A	W	2-0	Robinson 2
		2	8.12.34	Aldershot	3S	H	L	0-2	
1935-36	3N	1	30.11.35	Wrexham	3N	H	W	4-1	Foster (p), Reid, Robinson, Dunkerle

Season	Div	Rd	Date	Opponent	Comp	H/A	Result	Score	Scorers
		2	14.12.35	Bournemouth	3S	A	L	2-5	Reid 2
1936-37	3N	1	28.11.36	Mansfield T	3N	H	L	0-4	
1937-38	3N	1	27.11.37	Crewe Alex	3N	H	L	0-1	
1938-39	3N	1	26.11.38	Lincoln C	3N	A	L	1-4	Harris
1945-46	3N	1 1L	17.11.45	Netherfield	LC	H	W	1-0	McIntosh
		1 2L	24.11.45	Netherfield		A	D	2-2	Clarke, Hull
		2 1L	8.12.45	Carlisle U	3N	H	W	4-2	Clarke 3, Dunnigan
		2 2L	15.12.45	Carlisle U		A	W	4-3	Clarke 3, McIntosh
		3 1L	5.1.46	Manchester C	D2	A	L	2-6	Clarke 2
		3 2L	10.1.46	Manchester C		H	D	2-2	Clarkson, McIntosh
1946-47	3N	1	30.11.46	Halifax T	3N	H	D	0-0	
		1r	4.12.46	Halifax T		A	L	0-1aet	
1947-48	3N	1	29.11.47	Carlisle U		H	W	3-2	Mullen, Burnett 2
		2	13.12.47	Runcorn	CC	A	W	1-0	Livingstone
		3	10.1.48	Chelsea	D1	A	L	0-5	
1948-49	3N	1	27.11.48	Rochdale at Oldham	3N	A	D	1-1aet	McIntosh (p)
		1	4.12.48	Rochdale		H	W	2-0	Collins, Livingstone
		2	11.12.48	Notts Co	3S	H	L	2-3	Miller 2
1949-50	3N	1	26.11.49	Southport	3N	A	D	1-1	Gordon
		1r	1.12.49	Southport		H	L	0-1	
1950-51	3N	1	25.11.50	Carlisle U	3N	A	L	1-2	King
1951-52	3N	1	24.11.51	Chesterfield	3N	H	L	0-2	
1952-53	3N	1	22.11.52	York C	3N	A	W	2-1	Hannah, Gordon
		2	6.12.52	Millwall	3S	H	D	2-2	Gordon, McLaren
		2r	10.12.52	Millwall		A	L	1-4	Gordon
1953-54	3N	1	21.11.53	Spennymoor U	NEL	A	W	3-0	Gordon 3
		2	12.12.53	Great Yarmouth T	ECL	H	W	5-2	Gordon 2, A.Keen, McLaren, Collins
		3	9.1.54	Swansea T	D2	H	D	2-2	J.Keen, McLaren
		3r	14.1.54	Swansea T		A	L	2-4	Gordon, Collins
1954-55	3N	1	20.11.54	Darlington	3N	H	D	1-1	Glover
		1r	24.11.54	Darlington		A	L	1-2	Ormond
1955-56	3N	1	19.11.55	Crewe A	3N	H	D	0-0	
		1r	23.11.55	Crewe A		A	W	3-2aet	Proctor, Godwin, Roberts
		2	10.12.55	Tranmere R	3N	A	W	3-0	Roberts 2, Ormond
		3	7.1.56	Sheffield U	D1	A	L	0-5	
1956-57	3N	1	17.11.56	Chester	3N	A	D	0-0	
		1r	22.11.56	Chester		H	W	3-1	Birch, J.Keen, Callaghan
		2	8.12.56	Chesterfield	3N	A	L	1-4	J.Keen
1957-58	3N	1	16.11.57	Stockport Co	3N	A	L	1-2	Callaghan
1958-59	D4	1	15.11.58	Notts Co	D3	A	W	2-1	Roberts, McCreadie
		2	6.12.58	Hartlepools U	D4	H	W	2-0	Robertson 2
		3	10.1.59	Wolverhampton W	D1	H	L	2-4	Robertson, J.Keen
1959-60	D4	1	14.11.59	York C	D3	A	L	1-3	Murdoch
1960-61	D4	1	5.11.60	Accrington S	D4	A	L	1-2	Lowes
1961-62	D4	1	4.11.61	Wrexham	D4	A	L	2-3	Dixon, Kemp
1962-63	D4	1	3.11.62	Buxton	CC	A	D	2-2	Clark, Darwin (p)
		1r	5.11.62	Buxton		H	W	3-1	Darwin (p), Dixon, Hale
		2	24.11.62	Wrexham	D3	A	L	2-5	Wright, Dixon
1963-64	D4	1	16.11.63	Bangor C	CC	H	W	3-2	Darwin, Thomson, Clark
		2	7.12.63	Chester	D4	A	W	2-0	Maddison, Hale
		3	4.1.64	Swansea T	D2	A	L	1-4	Anderson
1964-65	D4	1	14.11.64	Grimsby T	D3	H	D	1-1	Clifton og
		1r	17.11.64	Grimsby T		A	D	2-2aet	Tait, Worthington
		1 2r	23.11.64	Grimsby T at Old Trafford			L	0-2	
1965-66	D4	1	13.11.65	Grimsby T	D3	H	L	1-2	Mulholland
1966-67	D4	1	26.11.66	Rochdale	D4	A	W	3-1	Field 2, McCarthy
		2	7.1.67	Tranmere R	D4	H	W	2-1	McAdams, J.King (og)
		3	28.1.67	Southampton	D1	H	D	2-2	McAdams, Mulholland
		3r	1.2.67	Southampton		A	L	0-3	
1967-68	D3	1	9.12.67	Oldham A	D3	H	W	2-0	Harrison, Hartland
		2	6.1.68	Altrincham	CC	A	W	2-1	McGarry 2
		3	27.1.68	Leicester C	D1	H	L	1-2	Storf
1968-69	D3	1	16.11.68	Goole T	NPL	A	W	3-1	Mulvaney 2, McLean
		2	7.12.68	Stockport Co	D3	A	L	0-2	
1969-70	D3	1	15.11.69	Alfreton	ML	A	D	1-1	Hartland
		1r	17.11.69	Alfreton		H	D	0-0aet	
		1 2r	20.11.69	Alfreton at Chesterfield			D	2-2aet	Garbett, Knox

BARROW

Season	Div	Rnd	Date	Opponent		H/A	Res	Score	Scorers
		1 3r	24.11.69	**Alfreton** at Preston			W	2-0	Knox, Fletcher
		2	6.12.69	**Barnsley**	D3	A	L	0-3	
1970-71	D4	1	21.11.70	**Lincoln C**	D4	A	L	1-2	Hartland
1971-72	D4	1	20.11.71	**Darlington**	D4	H	L	0-2	
1976-77	NPL	1	20.11.76	**Goole T**	NPL	H	L	0-2	
1988-89	NPL	1	19.11.88	**Rotherham U**	D4	A	L	1-3	Carroll
1990-91	GMVC	1	17.11.90	**Bishop Auckland**	NPL	A	W	1-0	Burgess
		2	12.12.90	**Whitley Bay**	NPL	A	W	1-0	Gilmour
		3	5.1.91	**Bolton W**	D3	A	L	0-1	

BARRY TOWN

Changed name to Barri 1992 and now playing in the League of Wales. **First entered FA Cup:** 1911. **Welsh FA Cup winners:** 1955

Season	Div	Rnd	Date	Opponent		H/A	Res	Score	Scorers
1929-30	SL	1	30.11.29	**Dagenham T**	Lon	H	D	0-0	
		1r	4.12.29	**Dagenham T**		A	W	1-0	Jones
				played at Upton Park					
		2	16.12.29	**Brighton & HA**	3S	A	L	1-4	Ward
1934-35	SL	1	24.11.34	**Northampton T**	3S	H	L	0-1	
1951-52	SL	1	24.11.51	**Newport Co**	3S	A	L	0-4	
1961-62	SL	1	4.11.61	**QPR**	D3	H	D	1-1	Sheffield
		1r	6.11.61	**QPR**		A	L	0-7	
1984-85	Welsh	1	17.11.84	**Reading**	D3	H	L	1-2	Love

BARTON ROVERS

Formed 1898. **FA Vase Runners-Up:** 1978. Based in Bedford.

Season	Div	Rnd	Date	Opponent		H/A	Res	Score	Scorers
1980-81	IL	1	22.11.80	**Torquay U**	D4	A	L	0-2	

BASFORD ROVERS

Formed 1878. Home ground was at Marmion Road, Nottingham and the club used the Pear Tree Inn as their changing room.

Season	Rnd	Date	Opponent		H/A	Res	Score	Scorers
1886-87	1	30.10.86	**Notts Co**		A	L	0-13	
1887-88	1	15.10.87	**Lincoln Albion**		H	W	3-2	
	2		**Notts Co**				*scratched*	

BASINGSTOKE TOWN

Formed 1897. **First entered FA Cup:** 1902. **Record attendance:** 4,091 vs Northampton, 1971

Season	Div	Rnd	Date	Opponent		H/A	Res	Score	Scorers
1971-72	SL	1	20.11.71	**Northampton T**	D4	H	L	1-5	Brown
1989-90	IL	1	17.11.89	**Bromsgrove R**	SL	H	W	3-0	Clarkson 2, Webb
		2	9.12.89	**Torquay U**	D4	H	L	2-3	Blankley, Clarkson

BATH CITY

Formed 1889. **First entered FA Cup:** 1890. **Record crowd:** 18,020 vs Brighton 1960. **League Clubs Beaten:** Barrow, Cardiff C, Crystal P, Exeter (2), Merthyr Town, Millwall, Newport County, Notts Co, Southend U. Their 9-0 win over Nunhead in 1931 is the joint highest victory by one non-League club over another since the competition was reorganised in 1925

Season	Div	Rnd	Date	Opponent		H/A	Res	Score	Scorers
1920-21	SL	5q	**Merthyr Town** (3S) A 0-0; 5qr **Merthyr Town** H 1-0; 6q **Leytonstone** A 1-1, H 2-0						
		1	8.1.21	**Hull C**	D2	A	L	0-3	
1922-23	SL	5q	**Exeter C** (3S) A 2-1; 6q **Barrow** (3N) A 2-2, H 2-0						
		1	13.1.22	**Wigan B**	3N	A	L	1-4	Dore
1927-28	SL	1	26.11.27	**Southall**	AL	H	W	2-0	Shepherd 2
		2	10.12.27	**London Caledonians**	IL	A	L	0-1	
1929-30	SL	1	30.11.29	**Tunbridge Wells R**	SL	A	W	3-1	Brittain, Alsop, Compton
		2	14.12.29	**Coventry C**	3S	A	L	1-7	Brittain
1931-32	SL	1	28.11.31	**Nunhead**	IL	H	W	9-0	Rhodes og, Mulley og, Guyan 5, Whipp, McCartney
		2	12.12.31	**Crystal P**	3S	H	W	2-1	Rowson, McCartney
		3	9.1.32	**Brentford**	3S	A	L	0-2	
1933-34	SL	1	25.11.33	**Charlton A**	3S	H	D	0-0	
		1r	29.11.33	**Charlton A**		A	L	1-3	McMillan
1934-35	SL	1	24.11.34	**Guildford C**	SL	A	W	2-1	Coombs, McMillan
		2	8.12.34	**Boston U**	ML	H	W	2-1	Coombs, Prentice

Season	Lge	Rnd	Date	Opponent	Div	Ven	Res	Score	Scorers
		3	12.1.35	Norwich C	D2	A	L	0-2	
1936-37	SL	1	28.11.36	Tunbridge Wells R	SL	H	L	1-2	Buckley
1945-46	SL	1 1L	17.11.45	Cheltenham T	SL	H	W	3-2	Simmons, Browne, Farringdon
		1 2L	24.11.45	Cheltenham T		A	W	2-0	Brown, McConnon
		2 1L	8.12.45	Lovell's Athletic	Welsh	A	L	1-2	Woods
		2 2L	15.12.45	Lovell's Athletic		H	L	2-5	Farrington 2
1952-53	SL	1	22.11.52	Southend U	3S	H	W	3-1	Ellison, Snook 2
		2	6.12.52	Grimsby T	3N	A	L	0-1	
1953-54	SL	1	21.11.53	Walsall	3S	H	L	0-3	
1957-58	SL	1	16.11.57	Exeter C	3S	H	W	2-1	Boseley, Pickard
		2	7.12.57	Yeovil T	SL	A	L	0-2	
1958-59	SL	1	15.11.58	Colchester U	D3	A	L	0-2	
1959-60	SL	1	14.11.59	Millwall	D4	H	W	3-1	Wilshire, Fleming, Meadows
		2	5.12.59	Notts Co	D4	A	W	1-0	O'Neil
		3	9.1.60	Brighton & HA	D2	H	L	0-1	
1960-61	SL	1	5.11.60	Swindon T	D3	A	D	2-2	Wilshire, Fleming
		1r	10.11.60	Swindon T		H	L	4-6	Fleming 2, Book, O'Neil
1963-64	SL	1	16.11.63	Maidenhead	AL	A	W	2-0	Cartwright, Sanderson
		2	7.12.63	Wimbledon	IL	A	D	2-2	Willis og, Cartwright
		2r	12.12.63	Wimbledon		H	W	4-0	Sanderson, Fleming, Owen, Cartwright
		3	4.1.64	Bolton W	D1	H	D	1-1	Owens
		3r	8.1.64	Bolton W		A	L	0-3	
1964-65	SL	1	14.11.64	QPR	D3	A	L	0-2	
1965-66	SL	1	13.11.65	Newport Co	D4	H	W	2-0	Denton 2
		2	4.12.65	Bournemouth	D3	A	L	3-5	Denton 2, Horton
1966-67	SL	1	26.11.66	Sutton U	IL	H	W	1-0	Lofty
		2	7.1.66	Brighton & HA	D3	H	L	0-5	
1974-75	SL	1	23.11.74	Wimbledon	SL	A	L	0-2	
1977-78	SL	1	26.11.77	Plymouth A	D3	H	D	0-0	
		1r	29.11.77	Plymouth A		A	L	0-2	
1985-86	APL	1	16.11.85	Farnborough T	IL	A	W	4-0	Chandler, Palmer (p), Ricketts, Bodin
		2	7.12.85	Peterborough U	D4	A	L	0-1	
1987-88	GMVC	1	14.11.87	Chelmsford C	SL	A	W	2-1	Payne, Grimshaw
		2	5.12.87	Welling U	GMVC	A	W	1-0	Singleton
		3	9.1.88	Mansfield	D3	A	L	0-4	
1988-89	SL	1	19.11.88	Grays A	IL	H	W	2-0	Singleton 2
		2	10.12.88	Welling	GMVC	H	D	0-0	
		2r	14.12.88	Welling		A	L	2-3	Payne, Smith
1989-90	SL	1	19.11.89	Fulham	D3	H	D	2-2	Freegard, Randall
		1r	22.11.89	Fulham		A	L	1-2	Smart
1992-93	GMVC	1	14.11.92	Cardiff C	D3	A	W	3-2	Withey, Gill, Vernon
		2	6.12.92	Northampton T	D3	H	D	2-2	Smart, Randall
		2r	15.12.92	Northampton T		A	L	0-3	

BEDFORD TOWN

Originally formed 1908. Original Bedford Town club folded 1982. Reformed 1989. **First entered FA Cup:** 1910. Played at the famous Eyrie Ground. **League clubs beaten:** Brighton, Exeter, Newcastle (D2), Norwich, Oxford, Watford

Season	Lge	Rnd	Date	Opponent	Div	Ven	Res	Score	Scorers
1934-35	UCL	1	24.11.34	Dartford	SL	H	L	2-3	Carr 2
1951-52	SL	1	24.11.51	Swindon T	3S	A	L	0-2	
1953-54	SL	1	21.11.53	Weymouth	SL	A	L	0-2	
1954-55	SL	1	20.11.54	Dorchester T	WL	A	L	0-2	
1955-56	SL	1	19.11.55	Leyton	AL	H	W	3-0	Farquhar, Adey, Staroscik
		2	10.12.55	Watford	3S	H	W	3-2	Steel, Staroscik 2
		3	7.1.56	Arsenal	D1	A	D	2-2	Steel, Moore
		3r	12.1.56	Arsenal		H	L	1-2aet	Yates
1956-57	SL	1	17.11.56	Norwich C	3S	H	W	4-2	Chrichton, Murray 2, Reid
		2	8.12.56	Reading	3S	A	L	0-1	
1959-60	SL	1	14.11.59	Gillingham	D4	H	L	0-4	
1962-63	SL	1	3.11.62	Cambridge U	SL	H	W	2-1	Hukin, Wright
		2	24.11.62	Gillingham	D4	A	L	0-3	
1963-64	SL	1	16.11.63	Weymouth	SL	A	D	1-1	Fahy
		1r	21.11.63	Weymouth		H	W	1-0	Miles
		2	7.12.63	Chelmsford C	SL	A	W	1-0	Miles
		3	4.1.64	Newcastle U	D2	A	W	2-1	Fahy, McKinney og
		4	25.1.64	Carlisle U	D4	H	L	0-3	

1965-66	SL	1	13.11.65	**Exeter C**	D3	A	W	2-1	Hall, Bailey
		2	4.12.65	**Brighton & HA**	D3	A	D	1-1	Brown
		2r	6.12.65	**Brighton & HA**		H	W	2-1	Hall, Paton
		3	22.1.66	**Hereford U**	SL	H	W	2-1	Hall 2
		4	12.2.66	**Everton**	D1	H	L	0-3	
1966-67	SL	1	26.11.66	**Wycombe W**	IL	A	D	1-1	Fogg
		1r	30.11.66	**Wycombe W**		H	D	3-3aet	Sturrock 2 (1p), Skinn
		1 2r	5.12.66	**Wycombe W**		A	–	1-1	Paton
				abandoned after 90 minutes – ground unfit					
		1 3r	8.12.66	**Wycombe W**		H	W	3-2	Rundle og, Riley, Fogg
		2	11.1.67	**Oxford U**	D3	A	D	1-1	Fogg
		2r	16.1.67	**Oxford U**		H	W	1-0	Sturrock
		3	26.1.67	**Peterborough U**	D3	H	L	2-6	Cooley, Fogg
1975-76	SL	1	22.11.75	**Wycombe W**	IL	A	D	0-0	
		1r	24.11.75	**Wycombe W**		H	D	2-2aet	Phillips, Folds
		1 2r	1.12.75	**Wycombe W**		A	L	1-2	Markham
1981-82	SL	1	21.11.81	**Wimbledon**	D3	H	L	0-2	

BEDLINGTON UNITED

Competed in FA Cup from 1919-1932

1926-27	NEL	1	27.11.26	**Bishop Auckland**	NL	H	W	1-0	Spry
		2	11.12.26	**Carlisle U**	NEL	A	L	0-4	

BEIGHTON MINERS WELFARE

Competed in FA Cup 1948-1958

1952-53	YL	1	22.11.52	**Wrexham**	3N	H	L	0-3	
				played at Rotherham					

BELPER TOWN

Formed 1883. **Best performance since 1888:** 4th qualifying round, 1964-65. Now play in Northern Counties East League.

1887-88		1	15.10.87	**Sheffield Wednesday**	H	L	2-3

BEXLEY UNITED

First entered FA Cup: 1963. Disbanded 1976

1963-64	SL	1	16.11.63	**Wimbledon**	IL	H	L	1-5	Johnson

BIDEFORD

Formed 1946. **First entered FA Cup:** 1948. **Record crowd:** 6,000 vs Gloucester City, 4th qualifying round, 1960.

1964-65	WL	1	14.11.64	**Colchester U**	D3	A	D	3-3	Court, Bennett, Penny (p)
		1r	18.11.64	**Colchester U**		H	L	1-2	Bennett
1973-74	SL	1	24.11.73	**Bristol R**	D3	H	L	0-2	
1977-78	WL	1	26.11.77	**Portsmouth**	D3	A	L	1-3	Wingate
1981-82	WL	1	21.11.81	**Barking**	IL	H	L	1-2	Brown

BILLINGHAM SYNTHONIA

Formed 1923. **First entered FA Cup:** 1934. When Synthonia won the Northern League in 1951 they did not concede one goal at home.

1948-49	NL	1	27.11.48	**Crewe A**	3N	A	L	0-5	
1949-50	NL	1	26.11.49	**Stockport Co**	3N	A	L	0-3	
1951-52	NL	1	24.11.51	**Scunthorpe U**	3N	A	L	0-5	
1956-57	NL	1	17.11.56	**Carlisle U**	3N	A	L	1-6	Duffy
1957-58	NL	1	16.11.57	**Boston U**	ML	A	L	2-5	Taylor 2
1987-88	NL	1	14.11.87	**Halifax T**	D4	H	L	2-4	Allen, Hewitt
				played at Hartlepool					
1989-90	NL	1	18.11.89	**Lincoln C**	D4	A	L	0-1	

BILSTON TOWN

Formed 1895. **First entered FA Cup:** 1908. **Cup Final Connection:** Former Bilston player Stan Crowther played in the 1957 and 1958 Finals for Aston Villa and Manchester United.

1968-69	WMRL	1	16.11.68 **Halifax T**	D4	H	L	1-3	Silwood (p)
1972-73	WMRL	1	18.11.72 **Barnstaple**	WL	A	W	2-0	Cooper, Cope
		2	9.12.72 **Barnet**	SL	A	D	1-1	Langford
		2r	11.12.72 **Barnet**		H	L	0-1	

BIRCH, MANCHESTER

1878-79	1	**Darwen**		scratched

BIRMINGHAM CALTHORPE

Formed 1873. Played on fields at Bristol Road, Calthorpe, Birmingham

1879-80	1	25.10.79 **Maidenhead**	A	L	1-3	Rushell
1880-81	1	11.11.80 **Grantham**	H	L	1-2	
1881-82	1	**Notts Co**		scratched		
1882-83	1	28.10.82 **Birmingham St Georges**	A	L	1-4	
1883-84	1	10.11.83 **Walsall Town**	H	L	0-9	

BIRMINGHAM CITY

Formed 1875 as Small Heath Alliance. 1888 Small Heath. 1905 Birmingham. 1945 Birmingham City. **FA Cup Runners-Up:** 1931, 1956. **Record FA Cup Win:** 10-0 vs Druids, 4th qualifying round, 9.11.1898. **Record FA Cup Defeat:** 0-6 vs Wednesbury OA, 2nd round, 3.12.1881; vs Tottenham H, 6th round replay, 12.4.1967

As Small Heath Alliance

1881-82	1	17.10.81 **Derby Town**	H	W	4-1	Slater 2, Hards, A.James
	2	3.12.81 **Wednesbury OA**	A	L	0-6	
1882-83	1	bye				
	2	11.11.82 **Stafford Road Works**	H	D	3-3	Slater 2, T.James
	2r	18.11.82 **Stafford Road Works**	A	L	2-6	Stanley, Hards
1883-84	1	20.10.83 **Birmingham Excelsior**	H	D	1-1	A.James
	1r	11.11.83 **Birmingham Excelsior**	A	L	2-3	A.James, Stanley
1884-85	1	8.11.84 **Birmingham Excelsior**	A	L	0-2	
1885-86	1	31.10.85 **Burton Wanderers**	H	W	9-2	Stanley 4, Davenport 2, Evetts, A.James, Morris
	2	14.11.85 **Darwen**	H	W	3-1	Felton, Morris, Stanley
	3	12.12.85 **Derby Co**	H	W	4-2	Stanley 2, Hill, Davenport
	4	bye				
	5	16.1.86 **Davenham**	A	W	2-1	Figures, Davenport
	6	13.2.86 **Redcar**	H	W	2-0	Davenport 2
	SF	6.3.86 **WBA** at Aston Lower Grounds		L	0-4	
1886-87	1	30.10.86 **Birmingham St G**	H	L	1-3	Price
1887-88	1	15.10.87 **Aston Unity**	H	W	6-1	Smith 2, W.Dixon 2, Figures, Stanley
	2	5.11.87 **Aston Villa**	H	L	0-4	

as Small Heath

1888-89		1q bye; 2q **Burslem Port Vale** (H) 3-2; 3q **Leek** (H) 4-0; 4q **Burton W** (H) 9-0					
	1	2.2.89 **WBA**	D1	H	L	2-3	Hill 2
1889-90 FAll		2q **Oldbury T** (A) 3-1; 3q **Wednesbury OA** (A) 5-1; 4q **Walsall TS** (H) 4-0					
	1	18.1.90 **Clapton O**		H	W	3-1	Stanley 2, W.Devey
	2	1.2.90 **Wolverhampton W**	D1	A	L	1-2	W.Devey
1890-91 FAll		1q **Hednesford T** (H) 8-0; 2q **Wednesbury OA** (A) 2-0 *Small Heath disqualified for playing an unregistered player*					
1891-92 FAll		1q **Leicester F** (A) 6-2; 2q **Burton W** (A) 1-1; 2qr **Burton W** (H) 2-1; 3q **Burton Swifts** (H) 4-2					
		4q **Brierley Hill All** (H) 6-2					
	1	16.1.92 **Royal Arsenal**		H	W	5-1	Hallam 2, Wheldon 2, Walton
	2	30.1.92 **Sheffield W**	FAll	A	L	0-2	
1892-93	D2	1	21.1.93 **Burnley**	D1	A	L	0-2	
1893-94	D2	1	27.1.94 **Bolton W**	D1	H	L	3-4	Hallam, Mobley, Wheldon
1894-95	D1	1	2.2.95 **WBA**	D1	H	L	1-2	Walton
1895-96	D1	1	1.2.96 **Bury**	D1	H	L	1-4	Lewis
1896-97	D2	1	30.1.97 **Notts Co**	D2	H	L	1-2	Walton
1897-98	D2		3q **Port Vale** (A) 1-2					
1898-99	D2		3q **Chirk** (H) 8-0; 4q **Druids** (H) 10-0; 5q **Burslem Port Vale** (H) 7-0					
		1	28.1.99 **Manchester C**	D2	H	W	3-2	McRoberts 2, Abbott

		2	11.2.99	**Stoke**	D1	A	D	2-2	Robertson, Wharton
		2r	15.2.99	**Stoke**		H	L	1-2	Inglis
1899-00	D2	3q **Oswestry Utd** (H) 10-2; 4q **Wrexham** (H) 6-1; 5q **Walsall** (H) 0-0; 5qr **Walsall** (A) 0-2							
1900-01	D2	1	9.2.01	**Stoke**	D1	A	D	1-1	Main
		1r	13.2.01	**Stoke**		H	W	2-1aet	Bennett, Wharton
		2	23.2.01	**Burnley**	D2	H	W	1-0	McMillan
		3	23.3.01	**Aston Villa**	D1	H	D	0-0	
		3r	27.3.01	**Aston Villa**		A	L	0-1	
1901-02	D1	1	7.2.02	**Portsmouth**	SL	A	L	1-2	McRoberts
1902-03	D2	1	7.3.03	**Derby Co**	D1	A	L	1-2	Windridge
1903-04	D1	Int	12.12.03	**Manchester U**	D2	A	D	1-1	Wassell
		Int R	16.12.03	**Manchester U**		H	D	1-1aet	Leonard
		Int 2r	21.12.03	**Manchester U** at Bramall Lane			D	1-1aet	Field
		Int 3r	11.1.04	**Manchester U** at Hyde Road			L	1-3	Athersmith
1904-05	D1	1	4.2.05	**Portsmouth**	SL	H	L	0-2	
as Birmingham									
1905-06	D1	1	13.1.06	**Preston NE**	D1	H	W	1-0	Beer
		2	3.2.06	**Stoke**	D1	A	W	1-0	W.H.Jones
		3	24.2.06	**Tottenham H**	SL	A	D	1-1	Harper
		3r	28.2.06	**Tottenham H**		H	W	2-0aet	Green, Mounteney
		4	10.3.06	**Newcastle U**	D1	H	D	2-2	Green, W.H.Jones
		4r	14.3.06	**Newcastle U**		A	L	0-3	
1906-07	D1	1	12.1.07	**Liverpool**	D1	A	L	1-2	Green (p)
1907-08	D1	1	11.1.08	**WBA**	D2	A	D	1-1	W.H.Jones
		1r	15.1.08	**WBA**		H	L	1-2	Eyre
1908-09	D2	1	16.1.09	**Portsmouth**	SL	H	L	2-5	Chapple (p), King
1909-10	D2	1	15.1.10	**Leicester F**	D2	H	L	1-4	Lappin
1910-11	D2	1	14.1.11	**Oldham Ath**	D1	H	D	1-1	Hall (p)
		1r	17.1.11	**Oldham Ath**		A	L	0-2	
1911-12	D2	1	13.1.12	**Barnsley**	D2	H	D	0-0	
		1r	22.1.12	**Barnsley**		A	L	0-3	
1912-13	D2	1	11.1.13	**Manchester C**	D1	A	L	0-4	
1913-14	D2	1	10.1.14	**Southend U**	SL	H	W	2-1	Duncan 2
		2	31.1.14	**Huddersfield T**	D2	H	W	1-0	Morgan
		3	23.2.14	**QPR**	SL	H	L	1-2	Duncan
1914-15	D2	1	9.1.15	**Crystal P**	SL	H	D	2-2	AW Smith (p), Eyre
		1r	16.1.15	**Crystal P** at St Andrews		H	W	3-0aet	Gibson, Tinkler, AW Smith
		2	30.1.15	**Brighton & HA**	SL	A	D	0-0aet	
		2r	6.2.15	**Brighton & HA**		H	W	3-0	Gibson, Morgan, AW Smith
		3	20.2.15	**Oldham A**	D1	H	L	2-3	Gibson, Hodges
1919-20	D2	1	10.1.20	**Everton**	D1	H	W	2-0	Burkinshaw, Whitehouse
		2	31.1.20	**Darlington**	NEL	H	W	4-0	Whitehouse 3, Millard
		3	21.2.20	**Liverpool**	D1	A	L	1-2	Barton
1920-21	D2	1	8.1.21	**Luton T**	3S	A	L	1-2	Barton
1921-22	D2		*failed to enter*						
1922-23	D1	1	13.1.23	**Huddersfield T**	D1	A	L	1-2	Bradford
1923-24	D1	1	12.1.24	**Huddersfield T**	D1	A	L	0-1	
1924-25	D1	1	10.1.25	**Chelsea**	D2	H	W	2-0	Briggs 2
		2	31.1.25	**Stockport Co**	D2	H	W	1-0	Harris
		3	21.2.25	**Liverpool**	D1	A	L	1-2	Briggs
1925-26	D1	3	9.1.26	**Grimsby T**	3N	H	W	2-0	Russell, Briggs
		4	30.1.26	**South Shields**	D2	A	L	1-2	Bradford (p)
1926-27	D1	3	8.1.27	**Manchester C**	D2	A	W	4-1	Bradford, Islip, Crosbie, Briggs
		4	29.1.27	**Southampton**	D2	A	L	1-4	Briggs
1927-28	D1	3	14.1.28	**Peterborough & Fletton**	SL	H	W	4-3	Bradford 3, Davies
		4	28.1.28	**Wrexham**	3N	A	W	3-1	Davies 2, Randle (p)
		5	18.2.28	**Manchester U**	D1	A	L	0-1	
1928-29	D1	3	12.1.29	**Manchester C**	D1	H	W	3-1	Bradford 2, Briggs
		4	26.1.29	**Chelsea**	D2	A	L	0-1	
1929-30	D1	3	11.1.30	**Bolton W**	D1	H	W	1-0	Morrall
		4	25.1.30	**Arsenal**	D1	A	D	2-2	Briggs 2
		4r	29.1.30	**Arsenal**		H	L	0-1	
1930-31	D1	3	10.1.31	**Liverpool**	D1	A	W	2-0	Curtis, Bradford
		4	24.1.31	**Port Vale**	D2	H	W	2-0	Bradford 2
		5	14.2.31	**Watford**	3S	H	W	3-0	Curtis 2, Bradford
		6	28.2.31	**Chelsea**	D1	H	D	2-2	Bradford, Curtis
		6r	4.3.31	**Chelsea**		A	W	3-0	Bradford 2, Firth

Season	Div	Round	Date	Opponent		Venue	Result	Score	Scorers
		SF	14.3.31	Sunderland	D1		W	2-0	Curtis 2
			played at Elland Road						
		F	25.4.31	WBA	D2 WEMBLEY		L	1-2	Bradford
1931-32	D1	3	9.1.32	Bradford C	D2	H	W	1-0	Bradford
		4	23.1.32	Grimsby T	D1	A	L	1-2	Bradford
1932-33	D1	3	14.1.33	Preston NE	D2	H	W	2-1	Gregg, Grosvenor
		4	28.1.33	Blackburn R	D1	H	W	3-0	Curtis 2, Haywood
		5	18.2.33	Middlesbrough	D1	A	D	0-0	
		5r	22.2.33	Middlesbrough		H	W	3-0	Gregg, Haywood, Curtis
		6	4.3.33	West Ham	D2	A	L	0-4	
1933-34	D1	3	13.1.34	Sheffield U	D1	H	W	2-1	Robertson, Haywood
		4	27.1.34	Charlton A	3S	H	W	1-0	Morrall
		5	17.2.34	Leicester C	D1	H	L	1-2	Haywood
1934-35	D1	3	12.1.35	Coventry C	3S	H	W	5-1	Harris 3, Mangnall, Guest
		4	26.1.35	Southampton	D2	A	W	3-0	White, Fillingham, Guest
		5	21.2.35	Blackburn R	D1	A	W	2-1	White, Whiteside og
		6	6.3.35	Burnley	D2	A	L	2-3	Jones, White
1935-36	D1	3	11.1.36	Barnsley	D2	A	D	3-3	White, Jones, Harris
		3r	15.1.36	Barnsley		H	L	0-2	
1936-37	D1	3	16.1.37	Stoke	D1	A	L	1-4	Morris
1937-38	D1	3	8.1.38	Blackpool	D1	H	L	0-1	
1938-39	D1	3	7.1.39	Halifax T	3N	H	W	2-0	Jennings, Phillips
		4	21.1.39	Chelmsford C	SL	H	W	6-0	Harris 2, Madden 2, Brown, Jennings
		5	11.2.39	Everton	D1	H	D	2-2	Madden 2
		5r	15.2.39	Everton		A	L	1-2	Harris

as Birmingham City

Season	Div	Round	Date	Opponent		Venue	Result	Score	Scorers
1945-46	D2	3 1L	5.1.46	Portsmouth	D2	H	W	1-0	Flewin og
		3 2L	9.1.46	Portsmouth		A	D	0-0	
		4 1L	26.1.46	Watford	3S	H	W	5-0	Mulraney 3, Jones, Bodle
		4 2L	30.1.46	Watford		A	D	1-1	Jones
		5 1L	9.2.46	Sunderland	D1	A	L	0-1	
		5 2L	13.2.46	Sunderland		H	W	3-1	Jones 2, Mulraney
		6 1L	2.3.46	Bradford PA	D2	A	D	2-2	Dougall, Jones
		6 2L	9.3.46	Bradford PA		H	W	6-0	Dougall 2, Bodle 2, Mulaney 2
		SF	23.3.46	Derby Co	D1		D	1-1	Mulraney
			played at Hillsborough						
		SFr	27.3.46	Derby Co			L	0-4aet	
			played at Maine Road						
1946-47	D2	3	11.1.47	Fulham	D2	A	W	2-1	Jones, Dorman
		4	25.1.47	Portsmouth	D1	H	W	1-0	Harris
		5	8.2.47	Manchester C	D2	H	W	5-0	Trigg 2, Bodle, Mitchell (p), Mulraney
		6	1.3.47	Liverpool	D1	A	L	1-4	Mitchell (p)
1947-48	D2	3	10.1.48	Notts Co	3S	H	L	0-2	
1948-49	D1	3	8.1.49	Leicester C	D2	H	D	1-1	Roberts
		3r	15.1.49	Leicester C		A	D	1-1aet	Bodle
		3 2r	17.1.49	Leicester C		H	L	1-2	Dorman
1949-50	D1	3	7.1.50	Swansea T	D2	A	L	0-3	
1950-51	D2	3	6.1.51	Manchester C	D2	H	W	2-0	Stewart, Higgins
		4	27.1.51	Derby Co	D1	A	W	3-1	Stewart, Trigg, Smith
		5	10.2.51	Bristol C	3S	H	W	2-0	Stewart, Trigg
		6	24.2.51	Manchester U	D1	H	W	1-0	Higgins
		SF	10.3.51	Blackpool	D1		D	0-0	
			played at Maine Road						
		SFr	14.3.51	Blackpool			L	1-2	Smith
			played at Goodison Park						
1951-52	D2	3	12.1.52	Fulham	D1	A	W	1-0	Briggs
		4	2.2.52	Leyton O	3S	H	L	0-1	
1952-53	D2	3	14.1.53	Oldham A	3N	A	W	3-1	Murphy 3
		4	31.1.53	Sheffield U	D2	A	D	1-1	Purdon
		4r	4.2.53	Sheffield U		H	W	3-1	Murphy 2, Wardle
		5	14.2.53	Chelsea	D1	A	W	4-0	Purdon 2, Trigg, Murphy
		6	28.2.53	Tottenham H	D1	H	D	1-1	Wardle
		6r	4.3.53	Tottenham H		A	D	2-2aet	Ferris, Boyd
		6 2r	9.3.53	Tottenham H at Molineux			L	0-1	
1953-54	D2	3	9.1.54	Wolverhampton W	D1	A	W	2-1	Murphy, Rowley
		4	30.1.54	Ipswich T	3S	A	L	0-1	
1954-55	D2	3	8.1.55	Hull C	D2	A	W	2-0	Kinsey, Brown

	4	29.1.55 **Bolton W**	D1	H	W	2-1	Govan, Wheeler og
	5	19.2.55 **Doncaster R**	D2	H	W	2-1	Brown 2
	6	12.3.55 **Manchester C**	D1	H	L	0-1	
1955-56 D1	3	7.1.56 **Torquay U**	3S	A	W	7-1	Brown 3, Murphy 2, Kinsey, Astall
	4	28.1.56 **Leyton O**	3S	A	W	4-0	Brown 2, Murphy, Finney
	5	18.2.56 **WBA**	D1	A	W	1-0	Murphy
	6	3.3.56 **Arsenal**	D1	A	W	3-1	Astall, Murphy, Brown
	SF	17.3.56 **Sunderland**	D1		W	3-0	Kinsey, Astall, Brown
		played at Hillsborough					
	F	5.5.56 **Manchester C**	D1	WEMBLEY	L	1-3	Kinsey
1956-57 D1	3	5.1.57 **Carlisle U**	3N	A	D	3-3	Murphy 2, Astall
	3r	9.1.57 **Carlisle U**		H	W	4-0	Brown 2, Kinsey, Astall
	4	26.1.57 **Southend U**	3S	A	W	6-1	Govan 3, Murphy, Cox, Lawler og
	5	16.2.57 **Millwall**	3S	A	W	4-1	Kinsey 2, Govan, Brown
	6	2.3.57 **Nottingham F**	D2	H	D	0-0	
	6r	6.3.57 **Nottingham F**		A	W	1-0	Murphy
	SF	23.3.57 **Manchester U**	D1		L	0-2	
		played at Hillsborough					
1957-58 D1	3	8.1.58 **York C**	3N	A	L	0-3	
1958-59 D1	3	25.1.59 **Middlesbrough**	D2	A	W	1-0	Harris og
	4	28.1.59 **Fulham**	D2	H	D	1-1	Jackson
	4r	4.2.59 **Fulham**		A	W	3-2	Hooper 2, Larkin
	5	14.2.59 **Nottingham F**	D1	H	D	1-1	Astall
	5r	18.2.59 **Nottingham F**		A	D	1-1aet	Gordon
	5 2r	23.2.59 **Nottingham F** at Filbert Street			L	0-5	
1959-60 D1	3	9.1.60 **Watford**	D4	A	L	1-2	Hooper
1960-61 D1	3	7.1.61 **Nottingham F**	D1	A	W	2-0	Singer 2
	4	28.1.61 **Rotherham U**	D2	H	W	4-0	Singer 2, Neal, Harris
	5	18.2.61 **Leicester C**	D1	H	D	1-1	Harris (p)
	5r	22.2.61 **Leicester C**		A	L	1-2	Harris
1961-62 D1	3	6.1.62 **Tottenham H**	D1	H	D	3-3	Harris 2, Leek
	3r	10.1.62 **Tottenham H**		A	L	2-4	Harris, Leek
1962-63 D1	3	5.3.63 **Bury**	D2	H	D	3-3	Leek, Harris, Lynn (p)
	3r	7.3.63 **Bury**		A	L	0-2	
1963-64 D1	3	4.1.64 **Port Vale**	D3	H	L	1-2	Beard
1964-65 D1	3	9.1.65 **West Ham**	D1	A	L	2-4	Jackson, Thwaites
1965-66 D2	3	22.1.66 **Bristol C**	D2	H	W	3-2	Vowden 2, Thompson
	4	12.2.66 **Leicester C**	D1	H	L	1-2	Thwaites
1966-67 D2	3	28.1.67 **Blackpool**	D1	H	W	2-1	Vowden, Thompson
	4	18.2.67 **Rotherham U**	D2	A	D	0-0	
	4r	21.2.67 **Rotherham U**		H	W	2-1	Hockey, Bridges
	5	11.3.67 **Arsenal**	D1	H	W	1-0	Vowden
	6	8.4.67 **Tottenham H**	D1	H	D	0-0	
	6r	12.4.67 **Tottenham H**		A	L	0-6	
1967-68 D2	3	27.1.68 **Halifax T**	D4	A	W	4-2	Pickering, Vowden, Bridges, Beard
	4	17.2.68 **Leyton O**	D3	H	W	3-0	Vowden 2, Bridges
	5	9.3.68 **Arsenal**	D1	A	D	1-1	Vowden
	5r	12.3.68 **Arsenal**		H	W	2-1	Bridges 2
	6	30.3.68 **Chelsea**	D1	H	W	1-0	Pickering
	SF	27.4.68 **WBA**	D1		L	0-2	
		played at Villa Park					
1968-69 D2	3	4.1.69 **Lincoln C**	D4	H	W	2-1	Pickering, Robinson
	4	25.1.69 **Sheffield W**	D1	A	D	0-0	
	4r	28.1.69 **Sheffield W**		H	W	2-1	Pickering, Beard
	5	11.2.69 **Manchester U**	D1	H	D	2-2	Beard, Robinson (p)
	5r	24.2.69 **Manchester U**		A	L	2-6	Greenhoff, Summerill
1969-70 D2	3	3.1.70 **Chelsea**	D1	A	L	0-3	
1970-71 D2	3	2.1.71 **Huddersfield T**	D1	A	D	1-1	Summerill (p)
	3r	5.1.71 **Huddersfield T**		H	L	0-2	
1971-72 D2	3	18.1.72 **Port Vale**	D3	H	W	3-0	Francis 2, Hynd
	4	5.2.72 **Ipswich T**	D1	H	W	1-0	Latchford
	5	26.2.72 **Portsmouth**	D2	H	W	3-1	Latchford 2 Hatton
	6	18.3.72 **Huddersfield T**	D1	H	W	3-1	Page, Latchford, Hatton
	SF	15.4.72 **Leeds U**	D1		L	0-3	
		played at Hillsborough					
	3/4	5.8.72 **Stoke C**	D1	H	D	0-0	
		Birmingham won 4-3 on penalties					

BIRMINGHAM CITY

1972-73	D1	3	13.1.73	Swindon T	D2	A	L	0-2	
1973-74	D1	3	5.1.74	Cardiff C	D2	H	W	5-2	Latchford 2, Hatton 2, Francis
		4	26.1.74	QPR	D1	A	L	0-2	
1974-75	D1	3	4.1.75	Luton T	D1	A	W	1-0	Kendall
		4	25.1.75	Chelsea	D1	A	W	1-0	Burns
		5	15.2.75	Walsall	D3	H	W	2-1	Hatton, Burns
		6	8.3.75	Middlesbrough	D1	H	W	1-0	Hatton
		SF	5.4.75	Fulham	D2		D	1-1	Gallagher
			played at Hillsborough						
		SFr	9.4.75	Fulham			L	0-1aet	
			played at Maine Road						
1975-76	D1	3	3.1.76	Portsmouth	D2	A	D	1-1	Francis
		3r	6.1.76	Portsmouth		H	L	0-1	
1976-77	D1	3	8.1.77	Portsmouth	D3	H	W	1-0	Kendall
		4	29.1.77	Leeds U	D1	H	L	1-2	Burns
1977-78	D1	3	7.1.78	Wigan Ath	NPL	H	W	4-0	Francis 2, Bertschin 2
		4	1.2.78	Derby Co	D1	A	L	1-2	Bertschin
1978-79	D1	3	6.1.79	Burnley	D2	H	L	0-2	
1979-80	D2	3	5.1.80	Southampton	D1	H	W	2-1	Bertschin, Gallagher
		4	26.1.80	Middlesbrough	D1	H	W	2-1	Gemmill (p), Bertschin
		5	16.2.80	Tottenham H	D1	A	L	1-3	Bertschin
1980-81	D1	3	3.1.81	Sunderland	D1	H	D	1-1	Bertschin
		3r	7.1.81	Sunderland		A	W	2-1	Bertschin, Evans
		4	24.1.81	Coventry C	D1	A	L	2-3	Worthington (p), Ainscow
1981-82	D1	3	2.1.82	Ipswich T	D1	H	L	2-3	Worthington (p), Curbishley
1982-83	D1	3	8.1.83	Walsall	D3	A	D	0-0	
		3r	11.1.83	Walsall		H	W	1-0aet	Summerfield
		4	29.1.83	Crystal P	D2	A	L	0-1	
1983-84	D1	3	6.1.84	Sheffield U	D3	A	D	1-1	Wright (p)
		3r	10.1.84	Sheffield U		H	W	2-0	Harford, Wright (p)
		4	28.1.84	Sunderland	D1	A	W	2-1	Kuhl, Harford
		5	18.2.84	West Ham	D1	H	W	3-0	Hopkins, Rees, Wright (p)
		6	10.3.84	Watford	D1	H	L	1-3	Terry og
1984-85	D2	3	5.1.85	Norwich C	D1	H	D	0-0	
		3r	23.1.85	Norwich C		A	D	1-1aet	Wright
		3 2r	26.1.85	Norwich C		H	D	1-1aet	Geddes
		3 3r	28.1.85	Norwich C		A	L	0-1	
1985-86	D1	3	14.1.86	Altrincham	GMVC	H	L	1-2	Hopkins
1986-87	D2	3	10.1.87	Ipswich T	D2	A	W	1-0	Mortimer
		4	31.1.87	Walsall	D3	A	L	0-1	
1987-88	D2	3	9.1.88	Gillingham	D3	A	W	3-0	Williams, Handysides, Greenall og
		4	30.1.88	Barnsley	D2	A	W	2-0	Rees, Wigley
		5	20.2.88	Nottingham F	D1	H	L	0-1	
1988-89	D2	3	7.1.89	Wimbledon	D1	H	L	0-1	
1989-90	D3	1	17.11.89	Leyton O	D3	A	W	1-0	Sturridge
		2	9.12.89	Colchester U	D4	A	W	2-0	Gleghorn 2
		3	6.1.90	Oldham A	D2	H	D	1-1	Gleghorn
		3r	10.1.90	Oldham A		A	L	0-1	
1990-91	D3	1	17.11.90	Cheltenham T	GMVC	H	W	1-0	Sturridge
		2	12.12.90	Brentford	D3	H	L	1-3	Aylott
1991-92	D3	1	16.11.91	Torquay U	D3	A	L	0-3	
1992-93	D1	1	15.11.92	Reading	D2	A	L	0-1	

BIRMINGHAM CLUB

1879-80	1		Panthers			*walkover*	
	2	19.1.80	Oxford University		A	L	0-6

BIRMINGHAM CORPORATION TRAMWAYS

Works team that entered the FA Cup for nearly 40 years from 1911. Known as Birmingham City Transport FC 1938–50

1934-35	BC	1	24.11.34	Workington	NEL	A	L	0-2

BIRMINGHAM EXCELSIOR

Formed 1876. Played at Witton Fields. **Cup Final Connection:** John and Harry Devey later played in four Cup Finals between them for Aston Villa

1883-84	1	20.10.83	Small Heath Alliance	A	D	1-1	
	1r	10.11.83	Small Heath Alliance	H	W	3-2	
	2	1.12.83	Derby Midland	H	D	1-1	Barlow
	2r	15.12.83	Derby Midland	A	L	1-2	
1884-85	1	8.11.84	Small Heath Alliance	H	W	2-0	J.Devey, H.Devey
	2	6.12.84	Birmingham St Georges	A	D	2-2	
	2r	20.12.84	Birmingham St Georges	H	L	0-2	
1885-86	1	31.10.85	Derby Midland	A	L	1-2	
1886-87	1	30.10.86	Derby Midland	H	D	3-3	
	1r	13.11.86	Derby Midland	A	L	1-2	
1887-88	1	15.10.87	Warwick County	H	W	4-1	
			FA ordered replay after protest				
	1r	22.10.87	Warwick County	A	W	5-0	
	2		bye				
	3	26.11.87	Great Bridge Unity	A	L	1-2	

BIRMINGHAM SOUTHFIELD

| 1887-88 | 1 | 15.10.87 | Burton Swifts | A | L | 0-7 |

BIRMINGHAM ST GEORGES

Formed 1875. Also known as Mitchell St George's. Played at Fentham Road, Birchfield **Cup Final Connection:** Among former St Georges' players were Dennis Hodgetts and John Devey who both played in Cup Finals for Aston Villa.

1881-82		1	5.11.81	Wednesbury OA		A	L	1-9	
1882-83		1	28.10.82	Birmingham Calthorpe		H	W	4-1	
		2	2.12.82	Aston Unity		A	L	1-3	
1883-84		1	10.11.83	Wednesbury Old Athletic		A	L	0-5	
1884-85		1	1.11.84	Aston Unity		A	W	5-0	Green 3, Hodgetts, 1 other
		2	6.12.84	Birmingham Excelsior		H	D	2-2	
		2r	20.12.84	Birmingham Excelsior		A	W	2-0	
		3	10.1.85	Walsall Swifts		H	L	2-3	Hodgetts 2
1885-86		1	31.10.85	Derby Co		A	L	0-3	
1886-87		1	30.10.86	Small Heath Alliance		A	W	3-1	Meakin 2, Harrison
		2	20.11.86	Derby Co		A	W	2-1	Rogers, 1 other
		3	11.12.86	Walsall Town		A	W	7-2	Brown 3, Breeze 2, Meakin, Rogers
		4	15.1.87	WBA		H	L	0-1	
1887-88		1	15.10.87	Walsall Town		A	W	2-1	Harrison, Hunt
		2	5.11.87	WBA		A	L	0-1	
1888-89		1	2.2.89	Long Eaton Rangers		H	W	3-2	Blackham, Harrison, J.Devey
		2	16.2.89	Halliwell		A	W	3-2	J.Devey 2, Harrison
		3	2.3.89	Preston NE	D1	A	L	0-2	
1889-90	FAll	1	18.1.90	Notts Co	D1	H	D	4-4	J.Devey 3, Richards
		1r	25.1.90	Notts Co		A	L	2-6	Marshall, Richards
1890-91	FAll	1	24.1.91	Crusaders		A	W	2-0	Davis, Shaw
		2	31.1.91	WBA	D1	H	L	0-3	
1891-92	FAll	1	16.1.92	Sunderland Albion	FAll	A	W	2-1	Marshall, 1 other
				FA ordered replay, match only lasted one hour					
		1r	23.1.92	Sunderland Albion		A	L	0-4	

BISHOP AUCKLAND

Formed 1886 as Auckland Town. The most successful and famous amateur Cup team of the 20th century. Won the FA Amateur Cup 10 times and were runners-up eight times. Northern League Champions 19 times. **First entered FA Cup:** 1889. Former Liverpool manager Bob Paisley played for Bishop Auckland. **League Clubs beaten:** Crystal Palace, Ipswich, Tranmere Rovers

1905-06	NL	1	13.1.06	Wolverhampton W	D1	H	L	0-3	
1909-10	NL	1	15.1.10	Bradford PA	D2	A	L	0-8	
1926-27	NL	1	27.11.26	Bedlington U	NEL	H	L	0-1	
1935-36	NL	1	30.11.35	Kidderminster H	BDL	A	L	1-4	Stephenson (p)
1945-46	NL	1 1L	17.11.45	Willington	NL	A	W	5-0	Clapham, Richardson 3, Anderson

	1 2L	24.11.45	Willington		H	L	0-2	
	2 1L	8.12.45	York C	3N	H	L	1-2	Tait
	2 2L	15.12.45	York C		A	L	0-3	
1946-47 NL	1	30.11.46	Rochdale	3N	A	L	1-6	Rutherford
1947-48 NL	1	29.11.47	Chester	3N	A	L	1-3	Farrer
1950-51 NL	1	25.11.50	York C	3N	H	D	2-2	Davison, Edwards
	1r	29.11.50	York C		A	L	1-2	McIlvenny
1951-52 NL	1	24.11.51	Blyth Spartans	NEL	A	L	1-2	McIlvenny
1952-53 NL	1	22.11.52	Selby T	YL	A	W	5-1	Armstrong 2, McIlvenny 3
	2	6.12.52	Coventry C	3S	H	L	1-4	Nimmins
1954-55 NL	1	20.11.54	Kettering T	SL	H	W	5-1	Major, Dickson 2, Oliver 2
	2	11.12.54	Crystal P	3S	A	W	4-2	Edwards, Major 3
	3	8.1.55	Ipswich T	D2	A	D	2-2	Oliver, McKenna
	3r	12.1.55	Ipswich T		H	W	3-0	McKenna 2, Major
	4	29.1.55	York C	3N	H	L	1-3	Edwards
1955-56 NL	1	19.11.55	Durham C	NL	H	W	3-1	Barnwell, Oliver, Lewin
	2	10.12.55	Scunthorpe U	3N	H	D	0-0	
	2r	15.12.55	Scunthorpe U		A	L	0-2	
1956-57 NL	1	17.11.56	Tranmere R	3N	H	W	2-1	Edwards, Bradley
	2	8.12.56	Rhyl	CC	A	L	1-3	Thursby
1957-58 NL	1	16.11.57	Bury	3N	H	D	0-0	
	1r	19.11.57	Bury		A	L	1-4	O'Connell
1958-59 NL	1	15.11.58	Tranmere R	3N	A	L	1-8	Brown
1960-61 NL	1	5.11.60	Bridlington Tr	YL	H	W	3-2	O'Connell, Gowland, Sharp
	2	26.11.60	Stockport Co	D4	A	L	0-2	
1966-67 NL	1	26.11.66	Blyth Spartans	NL	H	D	1-1	Siddle
	1r	30.11.66	Blyth Spartans		A	D	0-0aet	
	1 2r	5.12.66	Blyth Spartans at Roker Park			D	3-3aet	Roughley, J.Barker, McClelland
	1 3r	8.12.66	Blyth Spartans at Roker Park			W	4-1	McClelland, J.Barker, Armstrong 2
	2	7.1.67	Halifax T	D4	H	D	0-0	
	2r	10.1.67	Halifax T		A	L	0-7	
1974-75 NL	1	23.11.74	Morecambe	NPL	H	W	5-0	Boylan 3, Shoulder, Leigh og
	2	14.12.74	Preston NE	D3	H	L	0-2	
1981-82 NL	1	21.11.81	Nuneaton B	SL	H	W	4-1	Cross 2, Foster, D.Newton
	2	2.1.82	Carlisle U	D3	A	–	0-0	
		Abandoned after 69 minutes – waterlogged pitch						
	2	9.1.82	Carlisle U at Workington	D3	A	L	0-1	
1987-88 NL	1	14.11.87	Blackpool	D3	H	L	1-4	Pearson
1989-90 NPL	1	17.11.89	Tow Law Town	NL	H	W	2-0	Grant, Healey
	2	9.12.89	Crewe A	D3	A	D	1-1	Healey (p)
	2r	13.12.89	Crewe A		H	L	0-2	
1990-91 NPL	1	17.11.90	Barrow	GMVC	H	L	0-1	

BISHOP AUCKLAND CHURCH INSTITUTE

Formed 1882 and absorbed by Bishop Auckland FC in 1892

1886-87	1	23.10.86	Middlesbrough	H	L	0-1
1887-88	1	15.10.87	Elswick Rangers	A	D	3-3aet
	1r	22.10.87	Elswick Rangers	H	L	0-2

BISHOP'S STORTFORD

Formed 1874. **First entered FA Cup:** 1924. Last winners of Amateur Cup 1974 **FA Challenge Trophy Winners:** 1981. **League Club Beaten:** Reading. **Cup Final Connection:** John Radford played in Arsenal's winning Cup Final team in 1971 and for Bishop's Stortford at Wembley ten years later when they won the FA Trophy

1970-71 AL	1	21.11.70	Reading	D3	A	L	1-6	Deveaux
1972-73 IL	1	18.11.72	Enfield	IL	A	D	1-1	Francis
	1r	21.11.72	Enfield		H	W	1-0	Dear
	2	9.12.72	Peterborough U	D4	H	D	2-2	Leakey (p), Lawrence
	2r	11.12.72	Peterborough U		A	L	1-3	Francis
1974-75 IL	1	23.11.74	Leatherhead	IL	H	D	0-0	
	1r	26.11.74	Leatherhead		A	L	0-2	
1975-76 IL	1	22.11.75	Dartford	SL	A	W	4-1	P.Watson 3, McKenzie
	2	13.12.75	Aldershot	D3	A	L	0-2	
1981-82 IL	1	21.11.81	Sutton U	IL	H	D	2-2	Worrell, Clarke

		1r	24.11.81	Sutton U		A	L	1-2	Clarke
1982-83	IL	1	20.11.82	Reading	D3	A	W	2-1	Sullivan, Worrell
		2	11.12.82	Slough	IL	A	W	4-1	Lynch 3, Simmonds
		3	8.1.83	Middlesbrough	D2	A	D	2-2	Bradford 2
		3r	11.1.83	Middlesbrough		H	L	1-2	Lynch
1984-85	IL	1	17.11.84	Brentford	D3	A	L	0-4	
1985-86	IL	1	16.11.85	Peterborough U	D4	H	D	2-2	Hardy 2
		1r	20.11.85	Peterborough U		A	L	1-3	Flynn
1986-87	IL	1	15.11.86	Colchester U	D4	H	D	1-1	Fergusson
		1r	18.11.86	Colchester U		A	L	0-2	

BLACKBURN LAW

Formed 1881. Played at the Raven's Wing Ground, Blackburn. This was the only FA Cup match they ever played.

1881-82	1	5.11.81	Bootle		A	L	1-2	

BLACKBURN OLYMPIC

Formed 1876 and originally played at the Hole-In-The-Wall Ground, Blackburn **FA Cup Winners:** 1883. Did not compete in the FA Cup after 1888.

1880-81	1	30.10.80	Sheffield FC	A	L	3-4	Lever, 3 others
1881-82	1	29.10.81	Darwen	A	L	1-3	Weseley
1882-83	1	4.11.82	Accrington	H	W	6-3	Wilson 3, J.Yates 2, Weseley
	2	9.12.82	Lower Darwen	H	W	8-1	Wilson 2, Hunter, Matthews, 4 others
	3	16.12.82	Darwen Ramblers	H	W	8-0	Matthews, 7 others
	4	3.2.83	Church	H	W	2-0	Wilson, 1 other
	5	24.2.83	Druids	H	W	4-1	Costley 2, Yates, 1 other
	SF	17.3.83	Old Carthusians		W	4-0	Dewhurst, Wilson, Matthews, Costley
		played at Whalley Range, Manchester					
	F	31.3.83	OLD ETONIANS		W	2-1aet	Matthews, Costley
		played at Kennington Oval						
1883-84	1	13.10.83	Darwen Ramblers	H	W	5-1	Matthews 2, Yates 2, Dewhurst
	2	1.12.83	Darwen	A	W	2-1aet	Matthews, 1 other
	3		bye				
	4	19.1.84	Old Wykehamists	H	W	6-0	Dewhurst 2, Yates, Costley, 1 other, own goal
	5	9.2.84	Northwich Victoria	H	W	9-1	Matthews 2, Yates, Dewhurst, Parker, own goal, 2 others
	SF	1.3.84	Queens Park, Glasgow		L	1-4	Costley
		played at Trent Bridge						
1884-85	1	11.10.84	Oswaldtwistle R	H	W	12-0	Parker 4, Whitehead 3, Costley, Dewhurst, 3 others
	2	6.12.84	Blackburn R	A	L	2-3	Parker, 1 other
1885-86	1	31.10.85	Church	H	L	1-3	
1886-87	1	23.10.86	Partick Thistle, Scotland	H	L	1-3	
1887-88	1		bye				
	2	5.11.87	Blackburn R	A	L	1-5	Hothersall

BLACKBURN PARK ROAD

Formed 1875. Played at Audley Lane, Blackburn

1881-82	1	29.10.81	Blackburn R	A	L	1-9	Nuttall
1882-83	1	21.10.82	Darwen	A	L	1-4	
1883-84	1	27.10.83	Clitheroe Low Moor	H	W	6-0	Holden 3, Grimshaw, Holt, Mackereth
	2	24.11.83	Accrington	H	L	2-3	Holden, Slater
1884-85	1		Clitheroe Low Moor			scratched	
1885-86	1	17.10.85	Third Lanark	A	L	2-4	
1886-87	1	9.10.86	Cliftonville	H	D	2-2	Nuttall, Reynolds
	1r	23.10.86	Cliftonville	A	L	2-7	
1887-88	1	8.10.87	Distillery	H	W	2-1	Fish, Pomfrey
	2		*Blackburn scratched, Distillery re-instated after protest*				

BLACKBURN ROVERS

Formed 1875. Founder Members of the Football League 1888. Still hold record for **longest unbeaten run in the FA Cup:** 24 matches from Dec 1883 until Dec 1886. **FA Cup Winners:** (6 times) 1884, 1885, 1886, 1890, 1891, 1928. **FA Cup Runners-Up:** 1882, 1960. **Record FA Cup Win:** 11-0 vs Rossendale United, 1st round, 13.10.1884. **Record FA Cup Defeat:** 0-6 vs Nottingham Forest, 3rd round, 31.1.1880

1879-80	1	1.11.79	Tyne Association	H	W	5-1	Brown 2, Lewis, J.Duckworth
	2	6.12.79	Darwen	H	W	3-1	Brown 2, J.Hargreaves

	3	31.1.80 **Nottingham F**	A	L	0-6	
1880-81	1	30.10.80 **Sheffield Providence**	H	W	6-2	Hornby, Brown 2, R.Birtwistle, A.Birtwistle, J.Hargreaves
	2	18.12.80 **Sheffield W**	A	L	0-4	
1881-82	1	29.10.81 **Blackburn Park Rd**	H	W	9-1	Brown 2, J.Douglas, Wilson og, Avery, og, J.Hargreaves, Strachan 2
	2	19.11.81 **Bolton W**	H	W	6-2	Avery, McIntyre 2, Brown 2, Sharples
	3	**bye**				
	4	30.1.82 **Darwen**	H	W	5-1	J.Hargreaves 2, Brown, J.Duckworth 2
	5	11.2.82 **Wednesbury OA**	H	W	3-1	Lofthouse, Avery, Strachan
	SF	6.3.82 **Sheffield W**		D	0-0	
		played at Huddersfield				
	SFr	15.3.82 **Sheffield W**		W	5-1	J.Hargreaves, Avery, J.Douglas, og, Suter
		played at Manchester				
	F	25.3.82 **Old Etonians**		L	0-1	
		played at Kennington Oval				
1882-83	1	23.10.82 **Blackpool**	H	W	11-1	Brown 4, Barton 3, J.Duckworth 2, Suter, Avery
	2	2.12.82 **Darwen**	A	L	0-1	
1883-84	1	20.11.83 **Southport**	H	W	7-0	J.Douglas 2, Lofthouse, J.Duckworth, Sowerbutts, Avery 2
	2	1.12.83 **South Shore**	A	W	7-0	Avery 2, Suter, J.Sowerbutts 2, J.Douglas, McIntyre
	3	24.12.83 **Padiham**	H	W	3-0	Brown, Connell og, Strachan
	4	19.1.84 **Staveley**	H	W	5-1	Brown 4, Sowerbutts
	5	9.2.84 **Upton Park**	A	W	3-0	Inglis, Lofthouse 2
	SF	1.3.84 **Notts Co**		W	1-0	Lofthouse
		played at Aston Lower Grounds, Birmingham				
	F	29.3.84 **QUEENS PARK, GLASGOW**		W	2-1	Sowerbutts, Forrest
		played at Kennington Oval				
1884-85	1	13.10.84 **Rossendale**	H	W	11-0	Fecitt 4, Barton 3, Sowerbutts 2, Brown, A.Birtwistle
	2	6.12.84 **Blackburn Olympic**	H	W	3-2	Fecitt 2, Sowerbutts
	3	22.12.84 **Witton**	H	W	5-1	Forrest, Brown, Sowerbutts, Lofthouse, Fecittm
	4	19.1.85 **Romford**	H	W	8-0	Fecitt 2, Rostron, J.Douglas, Sowerbutts 2, 2 ogs
	5	**bye**				
	6	21.2.85 **WBA**	A	W	2-0	Lofthouse, J.Douglas
	SF	7.3.85 **Old Carthusians**		W	5-1	Brown 2, Sowerbutts 2, Lofthouse
		played at Trent Bridge				
	F	4.5.85 **QUEENS PARK, GLASGOW**		W	2-0	Forrest, Brown
		played at Kennington Oval				
1885-86	1	24.10.85 **Clitheroe**	A	W	2-0	J.Douglas, unknown
	2	21.11.85 **Oswaldtwistle R**	H	W	1-0	McIntyre
	3	5.12.85 **Darwen Old Wanderers**	H	W	6-1	Sowerbutts 2, Brown 2, Fecitt, Lofthouse
	4	23.1.86 **Staveley**	H	W	7-1	Lofthouse 2, Fecitt 2, Walton 2, Sowerbutts
	5	**bye**				
	6	27.2.86 **Brentwood**	A	W	3-1	Fecitt, Walton 2
	SF	13.3.86 **Swifts**		W	2-1	Walton, Strachan
		played at Derby Cricket Ground				
	F	3.4.86 **West Bromwich Albion**		D	0-0	
		played at Kennington Oval				
	Fr	10.4.86 **WEST BROMWICH ALBION**		W	2-0	Sowerbutts, Brown
		played at the Racecourse Ground, Derby				
1886-87	1	**Halliwell**		walkover		
	2	20.11.86 **Renton**	A	D	2-2aet	Walton, unknown
	2r	27.11.86 **Renton**	H	L	0-2	
1887-88	1	**Bury**		walkover		
	2	5.11.87 **Blackburn Olympic**	H	W	5-1	Rushton, Chadwick, Gill og, Jack Southworth, Townley
	3	26.11.87 **Accrington**	A	W	3-1	Chadwick 2, Walton
	4	**bye**				
	5	7.1.88 **Darwen**	A	W	3-0	Heyes, Jack Southworth, Townley
	6	28.1.88 **Derby Junction**	A	L	1-2	Jack Southworth
1888-89 D1	1	2.2.89 **Accrington**	D1 A	D	1-1	*unknown*
	1r	9.2.89 **Accrington**	H	W	5-0	Haresnape 2, Walton, Townley, Barton,
	2	**Swifts**		walkover		
	3	2.3.89 **Aston Villa**	D1 H	W	8-1	Haresnape 3, Jack Southworth 4, og
	SF	16.3.89 **Wolverhampton W**	D1	D	1-1	Haresnape
		played at Crewe				
	SFr	23.3.89 **Wolverhampton W**		L	1-3	Townley
		played at Crewe				
1889-90 D1	1	18.1.90 **Sunderland**	H	W	4-2aet	Townley 2, Campbell, Barton
	2	1.2.90 **Grimsby T**	FAll H	W	3-0	Arnold, Ogilvie og, Jack Southworth

BLACKBURN ROVERS

Season		Rd	Date	Opponent		Venue	Res	Score	Scorers
		3	15.2.90	Bootle	FAll	A	W	7-0	Walton 3, Jack Southworth 2, Forbes, Townley
		SF	8.3.90	Wolverhampton W	D1		W	1-0	Jack Southworth
			played at Racecourse Ground, Derby						
		F	29.3.90	SHEFFIELD W	FAll		W	6-1	Townley 3, Walton, Jack Southworth, Lofthouse
			played at Kennington Oval						
1890-91	D1	1	17.1.91	Middlesbrough Iron.		A	W	2-1aet	Jack Southworth, Hall
		1	24.1.91	Middlesbrough Iron.		A	W	3-0	Hall 2, Stevenson og
		2	31.1.91	Chester		H	W	7-0	Jack Southworth 3, Hall, Townley, Taylor og, unknown
		3	14.2.91	Wolverhampton W	D1	H	W	2-0	Baugh og, Fletcher og
		SF	28.2.91	WBA	D1		W	3-2	Jack Southworth, Hall, unknown
			played at Stoke						
		F	21.3.91	NOTTS CO	D1		W	3-1	Dewar, Jack Southworth, Townley
			played at Kennington Oval						
1891-92	D1	1	16.1.92	Derby Co	D1	H	W	4-1	Jack Southworth 4
		2	30.1.92	WBA	D1	A	L	1-3	Townley
1892-93	D1	1	21.1.93	Newton Heath	D1	H	W	4-0	Campbell 2, Sawers 2
		2	4.2.93	Northwich Victoria	D2	H	W	4-1	Bowdler, Campbell, Sawers, Jack Southworth
		3	18.2.93	Sunderland	D1	H	W	3-0	Jack Southworth 2, Bowdler
		SF	4.3.93	Wolverhampton W	D1		L	1-2	Taylor
			played at the Town Ground, Nottingham						
1893-94	D1	1	27.1.94	WBA	D1	A	W	3-2	Calvey, Chippendale, Forrest
		2	10.2.94	Newton Heath	D1	A	D	0-0aet	
		2r	17.2.94	Newton Heath		H	W	5-1	Calvey, Chippendale, Haydock, Whitehead 2
		3	24.2.94	Derby Co	D1	A	W	4-1	Haydock 3, Townley
		SF	10.3.94	Notts Co	D2		L	0-1	
			played at Bramall Lane						
1894-95	D1	1	2.2.95	Burton W	D2	A	W	2-1	Haydock 2
		2	16.2.95	Everton	D1	A	D	1-1	Forrest
		2r	20.2.95	Everton		H	L	2-3	Keslo og, Gordon
1895-96	D1	1	1.2.96	WBA	D1	H	L	1-2	Turnbull
1896-97	D1	1	30.1.97	Sheffield U	D1	H	W	2-1	Booth, Dewar
		2	13.2.97	Wolverhampton W	D1	H	W	2-1	Wilkie, Dewar
		3	27.2.97	Everton	D1	A	L	0-2	
1897-98	D1	1	29.1.98	Everton	D1	A	L	0-1	
1898-99	D1	1	28.1.99	Liverpool	D1	A	L	0-2	
1899-00	D1	1	27.1.00	Portsmouth	SL	A	D	0-0	
		1r	1.2.00	Portsmouth		H	D	1-1aet	Hulse
		1 2r	5.2.00	Portsmouth at Villa Park			W	5-0	Blackburn 3, Hulse 2
		2	17.2.00	Preston NE	D1	A	L	0-1	
1900-01	D1	1	9.2.01	W.Arsenal	D2	A	L	0-2	
1901-02	D1	1	1.2.02	Derby Co	D1	H	L	0-2	
1902-03	D1	1	7.2.03	Sheffield W	D1	A	D	0-0	
		1r	12.2.03	Sheffield W		H	W	1-0	Monks
		2	21.2.03	Derby Co	D1	A	L	0-2	
1903-04	D1	1	6.2.04	Liverpool	D1	H	W	3-1	Watson, Bowman, Dewhurst
		2	20.2.04	Nottingham F	D1	H	W	3-1	Dewhurst, Bowman, Blackburn
		3	5.3.04	Derby Co	D1	A	L	1-2	Dewhurst
1904-05	D1	1	4.2.05	Sheffield W	D1	H	L	1-2	Blackburn
1905-06	D1	1	13.1.06	Stoke	D1	A	L	0-1	
1906-07	D1	1	12.1.07	Manchester C	D1	H	D	2-2	Martin, Wolsenholme
		1r	16.1.07	Manchester C		A	W	1-0	Martin
		2	2.2.07	Tottenham H	SL	H	D	1-1	Martin
		2r	7.2.07	Tottenham H		A	D	1-1aet	Bracegirdle
		2 2r	11.2.07	Tottenham H at Villa Park			L	1-2	Latheron
1907-08	D1	1	11.1.08	Leicester F	D2	A	L	0-2	
1908-09	D1	1	16.1.09	Notts Co	D1	A	W	1-0	Latheron
		2	6.2.09	Chelsea	D1	H	W	2-1	Cameron, Latheron
		3	20.2.09	Manchester U	D1	A	L	1-6	Davies
1909-10	D1	1	15.1.10	Accrington S	LC	H	W	7-1	Chapman 2, Aitkenhead, Latheron 2, Anthony
		2	5.2.10	Bradford C	D1	A	W	2-1	Aitkenhead 2
		3	19.2.10	Newcastle U	D1	A	L	1-3	Anthony
1910-11	D1	1	14.11.11	Southend U	SL	H	W	5-1	Latheron 2, Bradshaw (p), Aitkenhead, Thompson og
		2	4.2.11	Tottenham H	D1	H	D	0-0	
		2r	9.2.11	Tottenham H		A	W	2-0	Bradshaw, Davies
		3	25.2.11	Middlesbrough	D1	A	W	3-0	Simpson 2, Smith
		4	11.3.11	West Ham	SL	A	W	3-2	Latheron, Simpson, Davies
		SF	25.3.11	Bradford C	D1		L	0-3	

BLACKBURN ROVERS

			played at Bramall Lane					
1911-12	D1	1	13.1.12 **Norwich C**	SL	H	W	4-1	Simpson 2, Chapman 2
		2	3.2.12 **Derby Co**	D2	A	W	2-1	Orr, Chapman
		3	24.2.12 **Wolverhampton W**	D2	H	W	3-2	Chapman, Aitkenhead 2
		4	9.3.12 **Manchester U**	D1	A	D	1-1	Aitkenhead
		4r	14.3.12 **Manchester U**		H	W	4-2aet	Simpson, Aitkenhead, Chapman 2
		SF	30.3.12 **WBA**	D1		D	0-0	
			played at Anfield					
		SFr	3.4.12 **WBA**			L	0-1aet	
			played at Sheffield					
1912-13	D1	1	18.1.13 **Northampton T**	SL	H	W	7-2	Simpson, Latheron, Aitkenhead 3, Orr 2
		2	1.2.13 **Barnsley**	D2	A	W	3-2	Shea, Bradshaw (p), Aitkenhead
		3	22.2.13 **Reading**	SL	A	W	2-1	Latheron, Anthony
		4	8.3.13 **Burnley**	D2	H	L	0-1	
1913-14	D1	1	10.1.14 **Middlesbrough**	D1	H	W	3-0	Aitkenhead 3
		2	31.1.14 **Bury**	D2	H	W	2-0	Shea 2
		3	21.2.14 **Manchester C**	D1	H	L	1-2	Aitkenhead
1914-15	D1	1	9.1.15 **Swansea T**	SL	A	L	0-1	
1919-20	D1	1	10.1.20 **Wolverhampton W**	D2	H	D	2-2	Reilly, Dawson
		1r	15.1.20 **Wolverhampton W**		A	L	0-1	
1920-21	D1	1	8.1.21 **Fulham**	D2	H	D	1-1	Dawson
		1r	13.1.21 **Fulham**		A	L	0-1	
1921-22	D1	1	7.1.22 **Southport**	3N	H	D	1-1	Rodgers
		1r	17.1.22 **Southport**		A	W	2-0	Rodgers 2
		2	28.1.22 **Swindon T**	3S	A	W	1-0	Rollo (p)
		3	18.2.22 **Huddersfield T**	D1	H	D	1-1	Hodkinson
		3r	22.2.22 **Huddersfield T**		A	L	0-5	
1922-23	D1	1	13.1.23 **Aston Villa**	D1	A	W	1-0	Bond (p)
		2	3.2.23 **South Shields**	D2	A	D	0-0	
		2r	8.2.23 **South Shields**		H	L	0-1	
1923-24	D1	1	12.1.24 **Corinthians** at Crystal Palace		A	L	0-1	
1924-25	D1	1	10.1.25 **Oldham A**	D2	H	W	1-0	McKay
		2	31.1.25 **Portsmouth**	D2	H	D	0-0	
		2r	4.2.25 **Portsmouth**		A	D	0-0aet	
		2 2r	9.2.25 **Portsmouth** at Highbury			W	1-0	Crisp
		3	21.2.25 **Tottenham H**	D1	A	D	2-2	Hulme, McKay
		3r	26.2.25 **Tottenham H**		H	W	3-1	Campbell, Puddefoot,Hulme
		4	7.3.25 **Blackpool**	D2	H	W	1-0	Puddefoot
		SF	28.3.25 **Cardiff C**	D1		L	1-3	McKay
			played at Meadow Lane					
1925-26	D1	3	9.1.26 **Preston NE**	D2	H	D	1-1	Holland
		3r	14.1.26 **Preston NE**		A	W	4-1	Dixon 2, Rigby 2
		4	30.1.26 **Arsenal**	D1	A	L	1-3	Harper
1926-27	D1	3	8.1.27 **Southport**	3N	A	L	0-2	
1927-28	D1	3	14.1.28 **Newcastle U**	D1	H	W	4-1	Puddefoot, Mitchell 2, Thornewell
		4	28.1.28 **Exeter C**	3S	A	D	2-2	Roscamp, Rigby
		4r	2.2.28 **Exeter C**		H	W	3-1aet	Roscamp, Mitchell, Puddefoot
		5	18.2.28 **Port Vale**	D2	H	W	2-1	Roscamp, Mitchell
		6	3.3.28 **Manchester U**	D1	H	W	2-0	Puddefoot 2
		SF	24.3.28 **Arsenal**	D1		W	1-0	Roscamp
			played at Filbert Street					
		F	21.4.28 **HUDDERSFIELD T**	D1 WEMBLEY		W	3-1	Roscamp 2, McLean
1928-29	D1	3	12.1.29 **Barnsley**	D2	H	W	1-0	Healless
		4	26.1.29 **Derby Co**	D1	H	D	1-1	Bourton
		4r	30.1.29 **Derby Co**		A	W	3-0	Roscamp, Bourton, McLean
		5	16.2.29 **Bury**	D1	H	W	1-0	Bourton
		6	2.3.29 **Bolton W**	D1	H	D	1-1	Hutton
		6r	6.3.29 **Bolton W**		A	L	1-2	Campbell (p)
1929-30	D1	3	11.1.30 **Northampton T**	3S	H	W	4-1	Cunliffe, Imrie (p), McLean, J.Bruton
		4	25.1.30 **Everton**	D1	H	W	4-1	McLean, Bourton, J.Bruton, Cunliffe
		5	15.2.30 **Aston Villa**	D1	A	L	1-4	Bourton
1930-31	D1	3	10.1.31 **Walsall**	3S	H	D	1-1	L.Bruton
		3r	15.1.31 **Walsall**		A	W	3-0	Puddefoot, Cunliffe, L.Bruton
		4	24.1.31 **Bristol R**	3S	H	W	5-1	Puddefoot, J.Bruton, L.Bruton 3
		5	14.2.31 **Chelsea**	D1	A	L	0-3	
1931-32	D1	3	19.1.32 **Burton T**	BDL	A	W	4-0	J.Bruton 2, Cunliffe
		4	23.1.32 **Derby Co**	D1	A	L	2-3	Britton, Cunliffe

Season	Div	Rd	Date	Opponent	Opp Div	H/A	Result	Score	Scorers
1932-33	D1	3	14.1.33	Lincoln C	D2	A	W	5-1	Dix, T.McLean (p), Cunliffe 2, Bruton
		4	28.1.33	Birmingham	D1	A	L	0-3	
1933-34	D1	3	13.1.34	Manchester C	D1	A	L	1-3	J.Bruton
1934-35	D1	3	12.1.35	Middlesbrough	D1	A	D	1-1	Talbot
		3r	17.1.35	Middlesbrough		H	W	1-0	Milne
		4	26.1.35	Liverpool	D1	H	W	1-0	Milne
		5	21.2.35	Birmingham	D1	H	L	1-2	Beattie
1935-36	D1	3	11.1.36	Bolton W	D1	H	D	1-1	Halsall
		3r	15.1.36	Bolton W		A	W	1-0aet	Thompson
		4	3.2.36	Bradford C	D2	A	L	1-3	Thompson
1936-37	D2	3	16.1.37	Accrington S	3N	H	D	2-2	Craven og, Fraser
		3r	20.1.37	Accrington S		A	L	1-3	Calladine
1937-38	D2	3	8.1.38	Tottenham H	D2	A	L	2-3	Sale, Guest
1938-39	D2	3	7.1.39	Swansea T	D2	H	W	2-0	Clarke, Chivers
		4	21.1.39	Southend U	3N	H	W	4-2	Butt 2, Clarke, Weddle
		5	11.2.39	Sunderland	D1	A	D	1-1	Butt
		5r	16.2.39	Sunderland		H	D	0-0aet	
		5 2r	20.2.39	Sunderland at Hillsborough			W	1-0aet	Guest
		6	4.3.39	Huddersfield T	D1	A	D	1-1	Weddle
		6r	9.3.39	Huddersfield T		H	L	1-2	Butt
1945-46	D2	3 1L	5.1.46	Bolton W	D1	A	L	0-1	
		3 2L	9.1.46	Bolton W		H	L	1-3	Wyles
1946-47	D1	3	11.2.47	Hull C	3N	H	D	1-1	McClelland
		3r	16.2.47	Hull C		A	W	3-0	McClelland, Rogers 2
		4	25.2.47	Port Vale	3S	H	W	2-0	Rogers, Baldwin
		5	8.3.47	Charlton A	D1	A	L	0-1	
1947-48	D1	3	10.1.48	West Ham	D2	H	D	0-0	
		3r	17.1.48	West Ham		A	W	4-2	McClelland 2, Murphy, Graham
		4	24.1.48	Southampton	D2	A	L	2-3	Campbell, McClelland
1948-49	D2	3	8.1.49	Hull C	3N	A	L	1-2aet	Graham
1949-50	D2	3	7.1.50	Liverpool	D1	H	D	0-0	
		3r	11.1.50	Liverpool		A	L	1-2	Edds
1950-51	D2	3	6.1.51	Bristol C	3S	A	L	1-2	Wharton
1951-52	D2	3	12.1.52	Nottingham F	D2	A	D	2-2	Crossan, Holmes
		3r	16.1.52	Nottingham F		H	W	2-0	Holmes, Nightingale
		4	2.2.52	Hull C	D2	H	W	2-0	Nightingale, Wharton
		5	23.2.52	WBA	D1	H	W	1-0	Eckersley (p)
		6	8.3.52	Burnley	D1	H	W	3-1	Nightingale, Holmes, Glover
		SF	29.3.52	Newcastle U	D1		D	0-0aet	
			played at Hillsborough						
		SFr	2.4.52	Newcastle U			L	1-2	Quigley
			played at Elland Road						
1952-53	D2	3	10.1.53	Luton T	D2	A	L	1-6	McLuckie
1953-54	D2	3	9.1.54	Bristol R	D2	A	W	1-0	Quigley
		4	30.1.54	Hull C	D2	H	D	2-2	Berry og, Quigley
		4r	4.2.54	Hull C		A	L	1-2	Briggs
1954-55	D2	3	8.1.55	Swansea T	D2	H	L	0-2	
1955-56	D2	3	7.1.56	Northampton T	3S	A	W	2-1	Briggs 2
		4	28.1.56	Barnsley	D2	A	W	1-0	Smith
		5	18.2.56	West Ham	D2	A	D	0-0	
		5r	23.2.56	West Ham		H	L	2-3	Langton (p), Smith
1956-57	D2	3	5.1.57	Everton	D1	A	L	0-1	
1957-58	D2	3	4.1.58	Rotherham U	D2	A	W	4-1	Douglas, Dobing 3
		4	29.1.58	Everton	D1	A	W	2-1	Dobing, Meagan og
		5	15.2.58	Cardiff C	D2	A	D	0-0	
		5r	20.2.58	Cardiff C		H	W	2-1	McGrath, Douglas
		6	1.3.58	Liverpool	D2	H	W	2-1	Clayton, MacLeod
		SF	22.3.58	Bolton W	D1		L	1-2	Dobing
			played at Maine Road						
1958-59	D1	3	10.1.59	Leyton O	D2	H	W	4-2	Johnston, MacLeod, Vernon, Dobing
		4	28.1.59	Burnley	D1	H	L	1-2	Dobing
1959-60	D1	3	9.1.60	Sunderland	D2	A	D	1-1	Dobing
		3r	13.1.60	Sunderland		H	W	4-1	Vernon 2, MacLeod, Bimpson
		4	30.1.60	Blackpool	D1	H	D	1-1	McGrath
		4r	3.2.60	Blackpool		A	W	3-0	Dobing 2, Dougan
		5	20.2.60	Tottenham H	D1	A	W	3-1	Woods, Bimpson 2
		6	12.3.60	Burnley	D1	A	D	3-3	Douglas (p), Dobing, McGrath

Season	Div	Round	Date	Opponent	Opp	H/A	Result	Score	Scorers
		6r	16.3.60	Burnley		H	W	2-0	Dobing, MacLeod
		SF	26.3.60	Sheffield W	D1		W	2-1	Dougan 2
			played at Maine Road						
		F	7.5.60	Wolverhampton W	D1 WEMBLEY		L	0-3	
1960-61	D1	3	7.1.61	Chesterfield	D3	A	D	0-0	
		3r	11.1.61	Chesterfield		H	W	3-0	Douglas, Dobing 2
		4	28.1.61	Bolton W	D1	A	D	3-3	MacLeod 2, Dougan
		4r	1.2.61	Bolton W		H	W	4-0	Dobing 2, Douglas 2
		5	18.2.61	Sheffield U	D2	A	L	1-2	Crowe
1961-62	D1	3	6.1.62	Brighton & HA	D2	A	W	3-0	Byrom, Ratcliffe, Pickering
		4	27.1.62	Stoke C	D2	A	W	1-0	Douglas (p)
		5	7.2.62	Middlesbrough	D2	H	W	2-1	Pickering, Lawther
		6	10.3.62	Fulham	D1	A	D	2-2	Thomas, Douglas
		6r	14.3.62	Fulham		H	L	0-1	
1962-63	D1	3	5.3.63	Middlesbrough	D2	H	D	1-1	Pickering
		3r	11.3.63	Middlesbrough		A	L	1-3	Byrom
1963-64	D1	3	4.1.64	Grimsby T	D2	H	W	4-0	Pickering, McEvoy 3
		4	25.1.64	Fulham	D1	H	W	2-0	Pickering, McEvoy
		5	15.2.64	Oxford U	D4	A	L	1-3	Ferguson
1964-65	D1	3	9.1.65	Leicester C	D1	A	D	2-2	Harrison, Douglas
		3r	14.1.65	Leicester C		H	L	1-2	Byrom
1965-66	D1	3	22.1.66	Arsenal	D1	H	W	3-0	McEvoy 2, Byrom
		4	12.2.66	West Ham	D2	A	D	3-3	Byrom 3
		4r	16.2.66	West Ham		H	W	4-1	McEvoy 3, Byrom
		5	5.3.66	Norwich C	D2	A	D	2-2	Byrom, Jones
		5r	9.3.66	Norwich C		H	W	3-2	McEvoy, Darling, Harrison
		6	26.3.66	Sheffield W	D1	H	L	1-2	Byrom
1966-67	D2	3	28.1.67	Carlisle U	D2	H	L	1-2	Connelly
1967-68	D2	3	27.1.68	Swindon T	D3	A	L	0-1	
1968-69	D2	3	4.1.69	Stockport Co	D3	H	W	2-0	Connelly, Fryatt
		4	25.1.69	Portsmouth	D2	H	W	4-0	Fryatt, Darling 3
		5	24.2.69	Manchester C	D1	H	L	1-4	Fryatt
1969-70	D2	3	3.1.70	Swindon T	D2	H	L	0-4	
1970-71	D2	3	2.1.71	Everton	D1	A	L	0-2	
1971-72	D3	1	20.11.71	Port Vale	D3	H	D	1-1	Fazackerley
		1r	22.11.71	Port Vale		A	L	1-3	Field (p)
1972-73	D3	1	18.11.72	Lincoln C	D4	A	D	2-2	Napier, Field
		1r	27.11.72	Lincoln C		H	W	4-1	McNamee, Field 3
		2	12.12.72	Crewe Alex	D4	H	L	0-1	
1973-74	D3	1	24.11.73	Willington T	NL	A	D	0-0	
		1r	3.12.73	Willington T		H	W	6-1	Field, O'Mara 2, Napier, Garbett, Parkes
		2	15.12.73	Altrincham	NPL	H	D	0-0	
		2r	19.12.73	Altrincham		A	W	2-0	Napier, Field (p)
		3	5.1.74	Everton	D1	A	L	0-3	
1974-75	D3	1	23.11.74	Matlock T	NPL	A	W	4-1	Martin, Beamish 2, Parkes
		2	14.12.74	Darlington	D4	H	W	1-0	Oates
		3	4.1.75	Bristol R	D2	H	L	1-2	Martin
1975-76	D2	3	3.1.76	Luton T	D2	A	L	0-2	
1976-77	D2	3	8.1.77	Charlton A	D2	A	D	1-1	Svarc
		3r	12.1.77	Charlton A		H	W	2-0	Byrom, Parkes
		4	29.1.77	Orient	D2	H	W	3-0	Waddington, Parkes, Byrom
		5	26.2.77	Derby Co	D1	A	L	1-3	Todd og
1977-78	D2	3	7.1.78	Shrewsbury T	D3	H	W	2-1	Mitchell, Brotherston
		4	28.1.78	Orient	D2	A	L	1-3	Metcalfe
1978-79	D2	3	10.1.79	Millwall	D2	A	W	2-1	Brotherston, Radford
		4	27.1.79	Liverpool	D1	A	L	0-1	
1979-80	D3	1	24.11.79	Kidderminster H	SL	A	W	2-0	Crawford, Craig
		2	17.12.79	Stafford R	APL	H	W	2-0	Crawford, McKenzie
		3	5.1.80	Fulham	D2	H	D	1-1	Crawford
		3r	15.1.80	Fulham		A	W	1-0	Crawford
		4	26.1.80	Coventry C	D1	H	W	1-0	Crawford
		5	16.2.80	Aston Villa	D1	H	D	1-1	Evans og
		5r	20.2.80	Aston Villa		A	L	0-1	
1980-81	D2	3	3.1.81	Notts Co	D2	A	L	1-2	Burke
1981-82	D2	3	2.1.82	WBA	D1	A	L	2-3	Garner 2
1982-83	D2	3	8.1.83	Liverpool	D1	H	L	1-2	Garner
1983-84	D2	3	6.1.84	Chelsea	D2	H	W	1-0	Brotherston

		4	28.1.84	Swindon T	D4	A	W	2-1	Garner, Keeley
		5	17.2.84	Southampton	D1	H	L	0-1	
1984-85	D2	3	4.1.85	Portsmouth	D2	A	D	0-0	
		3r	26.1.85	Portsmouth		H	W	2-1	Quinn 2
		4	30.1.85	Oxford U	D2	A	W	1-0	Quinn
		5	15.2.85	Manchester U	D1	H	L	0-2	
1985-86	D2	3	4.1.86	Nottingham F	D1	A	D	1-1	Thompson
		3r	13.1.86	Nottingham F		H	W	3-2	Lowey, Brotherston, Thompson
		4	25.1.86	Everton	D1	A	L	1-3	Van den Hauwe og
1986-87	D2	3	10.1.87	Portsmouth	D2	A	L	0-2	
1987-88	D2	3	9.1.88	Portsmouth	D1	H	L	1-2	Garner
1988-89	D2	3	7.1.89	Welling U	GMVC	A	W	1-0	Hildersley
		4	28.1.89	Sheffield W	D1	H	W	2-1	Garner, Finnigan
		5	18.2.89	Brentford	D3	H	L	0-2	
1989-90	D2	3	6.1.90	Aston Villa	D1	H	D	2-2	Stapleton, Sellars
		3r	10.1.90	Aston Villa		A	L	1-3	Kennedy
1990-91	D2	3	5.1.91	Liverpool	D1	H	D	1-1	Garner
		3r	8.1.91	Liverpool		A	L	0-3	
1991-92	D2	3	4.1.92	Kettering T	GMVC	H	W	4-1	Speedie, Newell 2, Cowans
		4	4.2.92	Notts Co	D1	A	L	1-2	Newell
1992-93	PL	3	2.1.93	Bournemouth	D2	H	W	3-1	Ripley 2, Newell
		4	23.1.93	Crewe A	D3	A	W	3-0	Wegerle, Newell, Moran
		5	13.2.93	Newcastle U	D1	H	W	1-0	Wegerle
		6	6.3.93	Sheffield U	PL	H	D	0-0	
		6r	16.3.93	Sheffield U		A	D	2-2aet	Livingstone, Newell

Sheffield United won 5-3 on penalties

BLACKHALL COLLIERY

Competed in the FA Cup from 1931-1958

1951-52	NEL	1	24.11.51	Workington	3N	H	L	2-5	Ford, Mason

BLACKPOOL

Formed 1887. Merged with South Shore on December 12, 1899. **FA Cup Winners:** 1953. **FA Cup Runners-Up:** 1948, 1951. **Record FA Cup Win:** 8-1 vs Oswaldtwistle R, 2nd qualifying round, 1892. **Record FA Cup Defeat:** 0-6 vs Barnsley, 1st round replay, 20.1.1910

1891-92	LL	1q Higher Walton (A) 5-4; 2q Fleetwood R (H) 4-2; 3q Bury (A) 5-5; 3qr Bury (H) 4-3; 4q Newton Heath (A) 4-3					
		1	16.1.92	Sheffield U	NL	H	L	0-3	
1892-93	LL	1q Heywood Central (A) 4-3; 2q Oswaldtwistle R (H) 8-1; 3q Fleetwood R (A) 3-1; 4q Rossendale (H) 2-1					
		1	21.1.93	Sheffield U	D2	H	L	1-3	E.Parkinson
1893-94	LL	1q South Shore (A) 1-2						
1894-95	LL	1q Chorley (H) 3-2; 2q Rossendale (A) 1-2						
1895-96	LL	2q Bacup (A) 2-1; 3q South Shore (A) 2-1; 4q Rossendale (A) 4-2						
		1	1.2.96	Burton Swifts	D2	H	W	4-1	Martin, Stirzaker, Wallace, Wilson
		2	15.2.96	Bolton W	D1	H	L	0-2	
1896-97	D2	3q Darwen (A) 0-1abnd; 3qr Darwen (A) 2-1; 4q Chorley (A) 1-0; 5q Newton Heath (A) 2-2; 5qr Newton Heath (H) 1-2					
1897-98	D2	3q Darwen (A) 2-3						
1898-99	D2	1q Southport Central (A) 2-2; 1qr Southport Central (H) 1-2					
1899-00	LL	3q Southport Central (A) 0-2						
1900-01	D2	3q Blackburn Park Rd (A) 1-0; 4q Darwen (A) 1-2					
1901-02	D2	3q Southport Central (A) 0-0; 3qr Southport Central (H) 0-0; 3q 2r Southport Central 1-2 at Preston					
1902-03	D2	1q Black Lane Temperance (H) 4-1; 2q Rochdale (H) 0-1					
1903-04	D2	3q Workington (A) 4-2; 4q Southport Central (A) 0-3					
1904-05	D2	3q Accrington S (A) 4-1; 4q Southport Central (H) 3-0; 5q Nelson (H) 1-0; 6q Stafford R (H) 2-2; 6qr Stafford R (A) 3-0; Int Bristol C (A) 1-2					
1905-06	D2	1	13.1.06	Crystal P	SL	H	D	1-1	Hancock
		1r	17.1.06	Crystal P		A	D	1-1aet	Threlfall
		1 2r	22.1.06	Crystal P at Villa Park			W	1-0	Francis
		2	3.2.06	Sheffield U	D1	A	W	2-1	Hancock 2
		3	24.2.06	Newcastle U	D1	A	L	0-5	
1906-07	D2	1	12.1.07	West Ham	SL	A	L	1-2	Grundy
1907-08	D2	1	11.1.08	Manchester U	D1	A	L	1-3	Grundy
1908-09	D2	1	16.1.09	Hastings & St L	SL	H	W	2-0	Threlfall, Whalley
		2	6.2.09	Newcastle U	D1	A	L	1-2	Weston
1909-10	D2	1	15.1.10	Barnsley	D2	H	D	1-1	Wolstenholme
		1r	20.1.10	Barnsley		A	L	0-6	

Season	Div	Round	Date	Opponent		H/A	Res	Score	Scorers
1910-11	D2	1	14.1.11	Manchester U	D1	A	L	1-2	Clennell
1911-12	D2	1	13.1.12	Crewe A	CL	A	D	1-1	Milne
		1r	17.1.12	Crewe A		H	–	2-1	Cahill, Wolstenholme
			abandoned after 61 minutes due to a blizzard						
		1r	22.1.12	Crewe A		H	D	2-2aet	Wolstenholme, Quinn
		1 2r	25.1.12	Crewe A at Maine Road			W	2-1	Cowie, Bainbridge
1912-13	D2	1	11.1.13	Tottenham H	D1	A	D	1-1	Charles
		1r	16.1.13	Tottenham H		H	L	1-6	Charles
1913-14	D2	1	10.1.14	Gillingham	SL	A	L	0-1	
1914-15	D2	1	9.1.15	Sheffield U	D1	H	L	1-2	Sibbald
1919-20	D2	1	10.1.20	Derby Co	D1	H	D	0-0	
		1r	14.1.20	Derby Co		A	W	4-1	Charles, Sibbald, Lane 2
		2	31.1.20	Preston NE	D1	A	L	1-2	Quinn
1920-21	D2	1	8.1.21	Darlington	NEL	A	D	2-2	Barrass, Ratcliffe
		1r	12.1.21	Darlington		H	W	2-1	McGinn, Ratcliffe
		2	29.1.21	Southend U	D3	A	L	0-1	
1921-22	D2	1	7.1.22	Watford	3S	H	L	1-2	Bedford
1922-23	D2	1	13.1.23	Derby Co	D2	A	L	0-2	
1923-24	D2	1	12.1.24	Sheffield U	D1	H	W	1-0	White
		2	2.2.24	Southampton	D2	A	L	1-4	Bedford
1924-25	D2	1	10.1.25	Barrow	3N	H	D	0-0	
		1r	14.1.25	Barrow		A	W	2-0	Streets, Bedford
		2	31.1.25	Bradford PA	3N	A	D	1-1	Meredith
		2r	4.2.25	Bradford PA		H	W	2-1	Streets, Meredith
		3	21.2.25	West Ham	D1	A	D	1-1	Bedford
		3r	25.2.25	West Ham		H	W	3-0	Bedford 2, Meredith
		4	7.3.25	Blackburn R	D1	A	L	0-1	
1925-26	D2	3	9.1.26	Swansea T	D2	H	L	0-2	
1926-27	D2	3	8.1.27	Bolton W	D1	H	L	1-3	Tremelling
1927-28	D2	3	14.1.28	Oldham A	D2	H	L	1-4	Neal
1928-29	D2	3	12.1.29	Plymouth A	3S	A	L	0-3	
1929-30	D2	3	11.1.30	Stockport Co	3N	H	W	2-1	Browell 2
		4	25.1.30	Hull C	D2	A	L	1-3	Hampson
1930-31	D1	3	10.1.31	Hull C	3N	A	W	2-1	Hampson, Upton
		4	24.1.31	Southport	3N	A	L	1-2	Downes
1931-32	D1	3	9.1.32	Newcastle U	D1	H	D	1-1	Hampson
		3r	13.1.32	Newcastle U		A	L	0-1	
1932-33	D1	3	14.1.33	Port Vale	D2	H	W	2-1	McClelland, Hampson
		4	28.1.33	Huddersfield T	D1	H	W	2-0	McClelland, Douglas
		5	18.2.33	Sunderland	D1	A	L	0-1	
1933-34	D2	3	13.1.34	Cheltenham T	BC	A	W	3-1	Bussey, Watson, Doherty
		4	27.1.34	Stoke C	D1	A	L	0-3	
1934-35	D2	3	12.1.35	Leicester C	D1	A	L	1-2	Hall
1935-36	D2	3	11.1.36	Margate	SL	H	W	3-1	Finan, Watmough, W.Jones
		4	25.1.36	Fulham	D2	A	L	2-5	Finan 2
1936-37	D2	3	16.1.37	Luton T	3S	A	D	3-3	Finan, Middleton, Watmough
		3r	20.1.37	Luton T		H	L	1-2	Finan
1937-38	D1	3	8.1.38	Birmingham	D1	A	W	1-0	Jones
		4	22.1.38	A.Villa	D2	A	L	0-4	
1938-39	D1	3	7.1.39	Sheffield U	D2	H	L	1-2	Lewis
1945-46	D1	3 1L	5.1.46	Wrexham	3N	A	W	4-1	Buchan, Mortensen, Blair, Dodds
		3 2L	9.1.46	Wrexham		H	W	4-1	Dodds 3, O'Donnell
		4 1L	26.1.46	Middlesbrough	D1	H	W	3-2	Mortensen 2, Dodds
		4 2L	30.1.46	Middlesbrough		A	L	2-3	H.O'Donnell, Mortensen
		4r	4.2.46	Middlesbrough at Elland Road			L	0-1aet	
1946-47	D1	3	11.1.47	Sheffield W	D2	A	L	1-4	Mortensen
1947-48	D1	3	10.1.48	Leeds U	D2	A	W	4-0	Dick, McIntosh 2, Mortensen
		4	24.1.48	Chester	3N	H	W	4-0	Shimwell, Mortensen 2, Johnston
		5	7.2.48	Colchester U	SL	H	W	5-0	Munro, McIntosh 2, Mortensen 2
		6	28.2.48	Fulham	D2	A	W	2-0	Mortensen, McIntosh
		SF	13.3.48	Tottenham H	D2		W	3-1aet	Mortensen 3
			played at Villa Park						
		F	24.4.48	Manchester U	D1 WEMBLEY		L	2-4	Shimwell (p), Mortensen
1948-49	D1	3	8.1.49	Barnsley	D2	A	W	1-0	Mortensen
		4	29.1.49	Stoke C	D1	A	D	1-1aet	Mortensen
		4r	5.2.49	Stoke C		H	L	0-1	
1949-50	D1	3	7.1.50	Southend U	3S	H	W	4-0	Slater 3, Mortensen

	4	28.1.50	Doncaster R	3N	H	W	2-1	McIntosh, McKnight
	5	11.2.50	Wolverhampton W	D1	A	D	0-0	
	5r	15.2.50	Wolverhampton W		H	W	1-0	Mortensen
	6	4.3.50	Liverpool	D1	A	L	1-2	Mortensen
1950-51 D1	3	6.1.51	Charlton A	D1	A	D	2-2	Perry, Mortensen
	3r	10.1.51	Charlton A		H	W	3-0	Mortensen 2, Mudie
	4	27.1.51	Stockport Co	3N	H	W	2-1	Mortensen, Mudie
	5	10.2.51	Mansfield T	3N	H	W	2-0	Mudie, Brown
	6	24.2.51	Fulham	D1	H	W	1-0	Brown (p)
	SF	10.3.51	Birmingham C	D2		D	0-0	
		played at Maine Road						
	SFr	14.3.51	Birmingham C at Goodison Park			W	2-1	Mortensen, Perry
	F	28.4.51	Newcastle U	D1 WEMBLEY		L	0-2	
1951-52 D1	3	12.1.52	West Ham	D2	A	L	1-2	Johnston
1952-53 D1	3	10.1.53	Sheffield W	D1	A	W	2-1	Matthews, Taylor
	4	31.1.53	Huddersfield T	D2	H	W	1-0	Garrett
	5	14.2.53	Southampton	D2	H	D	1-1	Perry
	5r	18.2.53	Southampton		A	W	2-1	Brown, Horton og
	6	28.2.53	Arsenal	D1	A	W	2-1	Taylor, Brown
	SF	21.3.53	Tottenham H	D1		W	2-1	Perry, Mudie
		played at Villa Park						
	F	2.5.53	BOLTON W	D1 WEMBLEY		W	4-3	Hassall og, Mortensen 2, Perry
1953-54 D1	3	9.1.54	Luton T	D2	H	D	1-1	Mortensen
	3r	13.1.54	Luton T		A	D	0-0aet	
	3 2r	18.1.54	Luton T at Villa Park			D	1-1aet	Cummins
	3 3r	25.1.54	Luton T at Molineux			W	2-0aet	Perry, Stephenson
	4	30.1.54	West Ham	D2	A	D	1-1	Brown
	4r	3.2.54	West Ham		H	W	3-1	Perry 2, Brown
	5	20.2.54	Port Vale	D3	A	L	0-2	
1954-55 D1	3	8.1.55	York C	3N	H	L	0-2	
1955-56 D1	3	7.1.56	Manchester C	D1	A	–	1-1	Taylor
		abandoned after 56 minutes - fog						
	3	11.1.56	Manchester C		A	L	1-2	Perry
1956-57 D1	3	5.1.57	Bolton W	D1	A	W	3-2	Mudie 2, Durie
	4	26.1.57	Fulham	D2	H	W	6-2	Mudie 4, Lampe og, Durie
	5	16.2.57	WBA	D1	H	D	0-0	
	5r	20.2.57	WBA		A	L	1-2	Perry
1957-58 D1	3	4.1.58	West Ham	D2	A	L	1-5	H.Kelly (p)
1958-59 D1	3	10.1.59	Southampton	D2	A	W	2-1	Charnley 2
	4	24.1.59	Bristol C	D2	A	D	1-1	Charnley
	4r	28.1.59	Bristol C		H	W	1-0	Durie
	5	14.2.59	WBA	D1	H	W	3-1	Charnley 2, Durie
	6	28.2.59	Luton T	D1	H	D	1-1	Charnley
	6r	4.3.59	Luton T		A	L	0-1	
1959-60 D1	3	9.1.60	Mansfield T	D3	H	W	3-0	Durie 3
	4	30.1.60	Blackburn R	D1	A	D	1-1	Kaye
	4r	3.2.60	Blackburn R		H	L	0-3	
1960-61 D1	3	7.1.61	Scunthorpe U	D2	A	L	2-6	Mudie, Charnley
1961-62 D1	3	6.1.62	WBA	D1	H	D	0-0	
	3r	10.1.62	WBA		A	L	1-2	Hauser
1962-63 D1	3	4.3.63	Norwich C	D2	A	D	1-1	McPhee
	3r	6.3.63	Norwich C		H	L	1-3aet	Quinn
1963-64 D1	3	4.1.64	WBA	D1	A	D	2-2	Charnley, Jones og
	3r	8.1.64	WBA		H	L	0-1	
1964-65 D1	3	11.1.65	Stoke C	D1	A	L	1-4	Ball
1965-66 D1	3	22.1.66	Manchester C	D2	H	D	1-1	James
	3r	24.1.66	Manchester C		A	L	1-3	Charnley
1966-67 D1	3	28.1.67	Birmingham C	D2	A	L	1-2	Vowden, Thomson
1967-68 D2	3	27.1.68	Chesterfield	D4	H	W	2-1	Neale og, Green
	4	17.2.68	Sheffield U	D1	A	L	1-2	Skirton
1968-69 D2	3	4.1.69	Coventry C	D1	A	L	1-3	Brown
1969-70 D2	3	3.1.70	Arsenal	D1	A	D	1-1	Hutchison
	3r	15.1.70	Arsenal		H	W	3-2	Suddick, Pickering, Burns
	4	24.1.70	Mansfield T	D3	H	L	0-2	
1970-71 D1	3	2.1.71	West Ham	D1	H	W	4-0	Green 2, Craven, Mowbray
	4	23.1.71	Hull C	D2	A	L	0-2	
1971-72 D2	3	15.1.72	Chelsea	D1	H	L	0-1	

1972-73	D2	3	13.1.73	Bradford C	D4	A	L	1-2	Suddick (p)
1973-74	D2	3	5.1.74	Southampton	D1	A	L	1-2	Dyson
1974-75	D2	3	4.1.75	Plymouth A	D3	A	L	0-2	
1975-76	D2	3	3.1.76	Burnley	D1	H	W	1-0	Bentley
		4	24.1.76	Southampton	D2	A	L	1-3	Alcock
1976-77	D2	3	8.1.77	Derby Co	D1	H	D	0-0	
		3r	19.1.77	Derby Co		A	L	2-3	Walsh, Spence
1977-78	D2	3	7.1.78	WBA	D1	A	L	1-4	Hatton
1978-79	D3	1	25.11.78	Lincoln C	D3	H	W	2-1	McEwan (p), Chandler
		2	16.12.78	Bury	D3	A	L	1-3	Kellow
1979-80	D3	1	24.11.79	Wigan A	D4	H	D	1-1	McEwan
		1r	28.11.79	Wigan A		A	L	0-2	
1980-81	D3	1	22.11.80	Fleetwood	CC	H	W	4-0	Entwistle, Morris, Hockaday
		2	13.12.80	Doncaster R	D4	A	L	1-2	Williams
1981-82	D4	1	21.11.81	Horden CW	NL	A	W	1-0	Harrison
				played at Hartlepool					
		2	2.1.82	Kettering T	APL	A	W	3-0	Harrison, Wann, Morris
		3	5.1.82	Barnsley	D2	A	W	2-0	Bamber, Morris
		4	23.1.82	QPR	D2	H	D	0-0	
		4r	26.1.82	QPR		A	L	1-5	Entwistle
1982-83	D4	1	20.11.82	Horwich RMI	NWC	H	W	3-0	Pashley, Bamber, Deary (p)
		2	11.12.82	Preston NE	D3	A	L	1-2	Brockbank
1983-84	D4	1	19.11.83	Gainsborough T	NPL	A	W	2-0	Mercer, McNiven
		2	10.12.83	Bangor C	APL	A	D	1-1	Mercer
		2r	13.12.83	Bangor C		H	W	2-1	Stewart, Deary
		3	7.1.84	Manchester C	D2	H	W	2-1	McNiven, McNab og
		4	28.1.84	Oxford U	D3	A	L	1-2	Mercer
1984-85	D4	1	17.11.84	Altrincham	APL	H	L	0-1	
1985-86	D3	1	16.11.85	Lincoln C	D3	A	W	1-0	West og
		2	7.12.85	Altrincham	APL	H	L	1-2	Stewart
1986-87	D3	1	15.11.86	Middlesbrough	D3	A	L	0-3	
1987-88	D3	1	14.11.87	Bishop Auckland	NL	A	W	4-1	Morgan, Madden (p), Taylor 2
		2	6.12.87	Northwich V	GMVC	A	W	2-0	Madden, Walwyn
		3	9.1.88	Scunthorpe U	D4	A	D	0-0	
		3r	12.1.88	Scunthorpe U		H	W	1-0	Madden
		4	30.1.88	Manchester C	D2	H	D	1-1	Sendall
		4r	3.2.88	Manchester C		A	L	1-2	Deary
1988-89	D3	1	19.11.88	Scunthorpe U	D4	H	W	2-1	Cunningham, Garner
		2	10.12.88	Bury	D3	H	W	3-0	Cunningham, Garner, Deary
		3	7.1.89	Bournemouth	D2	H	L	0-1	
1989-90	D3	1	18.11.89	Bolton W	D3	H	W	2-1	Eyres, Garner
		2	9.12.89	Chester C	D3	H	W	3-0	Brook, Burgess, Owen
		3	6.1.90	Burnley	D4	H	W	1-0	Methven
		4	27.1.90	Torquay U	D4	H	W	1-0	Owen
		5	18.2.90	QPR	D1	H	D	2-2	Groves, Eyres
		5r	21.2.90	QPR		A	D	0-0aet	
		5 2r	26.2.90	QPR		A	L	0-3	
1990-91	D4	1	17.11.90	Grimsby T	D3	H	W	2-0	Groves, Garner
		2	10.12.90	Huddersfield T	D3	A	W	2-0	Groves, Jackson og
		3	5.1.91	Tottenham H	D1	H	L	0-1	
1991-92	D4	1	15.11.91	Grimsby T	D2	H	W	2-1	Groves, Bamber
		2	7.12.91	Hull C	D3	H	L	0-1	
1992-93	D2	1	14.11.92	Rochdale	D3	H	D	1-1	Mitchell
		1r	25.11.92	Rochdale		A	L	0-1aet	

BLACKPOOL ST JOHNS

Formed around 1877. A forerunner of Blackpool FC, played at Masheters Field.

| 1882-83 | | 1 | 23.10.82 | Blackburn Rovers | | A | L | 1-11 | Whiteside |
| 1883-84 | | 1 | 10.11.83 | Accrington | | A | L | 0-4 | |

BLUE STAR

Formed 1930. Based in Newcastle. **FA Vase Winners:** 1978. Now known as Newcastle Blue Star

| 1984-85 | Wear | 1 | 17.11.84 | York C | D3 | A | L | 0-2 | |

BLYTH SPARTANS

Formed 1899. **First entered FA Cup:** 1909. Sponsored by Viz magazine 1992-93 **League Clubs Beaten:** Ashington, Chesterfield, Crewe A, Gillingham, Hartlepools U, Stockport Co, Stoke C

1922-23	NEL	5q	**Ashington** (3N) (H) 2-1; 6q **Gillingham** (3S) (A) 4-1					
		1	13.1.23	**Stoke**	D1	H	L	0-3
1925-26	NEL	1	28.11.25	**Hartlepools U**	3N	H	D	2-2	Green, Park
		1r	2.12.25	**Hartlepools U**		A	D	1-1aet	Fletcher
		1 2r	7.12.25	**Hartlepools U** at Newcastle			D	1-1aet	Bell
		1 3r	9.12.25	**Hartlepools U** at Sunderland			W	2-1	Fenwik, Flether
		2	12.12.25	**Accrington S**	3N	A	L	0-5
1931-32	NEL	1	28.11.31	**Lancaster T**	LC	A	W	3-0	Bunch, Smith, Ellis
		2	12.12.31	**Bournemouth**	3S	A	L	0-1
1934-35	NEL	1	24.11.34	**Stockport Co**	3N	H	D	1-1	Kennedy
		1r	28.11.34	**Stockport Co**		A	L	1-4	Robinson
1935-36	NEL	1	30.11.35	**Gainsborough Tr**	ML	A	L	1-3	Hickman
1936-37	NEL	1	28.11.36	**Wrexham**	3N	H	L	0-2
1937-38	NEL	1	27.11.37	**Doncaster R**	3N	A	L	0-7
1951-52	NEL	1	24.11.51	**Bishop Auckland**	NL	H	W	2-1	Herman, Turney
		2	15.12.51	**Tranmere R**	3N	A	D	1-1	Penrose
		2r	19.12.51	**Tranmere R**		H	–	1-1	Scott
			abandoned after 105 minutes – bad light					
		2 2r	3.1.52	**Tranmere R** at Carlisle			D	2-2aet	Fenwick, Scott,
		2 3r	7.1.52	**Tranmere R** at Everton			L	1-5	Turney
1953-54	NEL	1	21.11.53	**Accrington S**	3N	H	L	0-1
1954-55	NEL	1	20.11.54	**Boston U**	ML	A	D	1-1	Hogg
		1r	24.11.54	**Boston U**		H	W	5-4	Hogg 2, Gair 2, Weatherspoon
		2	11.12.54	**Torquay U**	3S	H	L	1-3	Hogg
1956-57	NEL	1	17.11.56	**Ilkeston T**	ML	A	W	5-1	Linacre, McHale, Turney, Langland 2
		2	8.12.56	**Hartlepools U**	3N	H	L	0-1
1958-59	ML	1	15.11.58	**Morecambe**	LC	A	W	2-1	Turney, Potts
		2	6.12.58	**Stockport Co**	D3	H	L	3-4	Reay, F.Potts, Clempson og
1959-60	ML	1	14.11.59	**Wrexham**	D3	A	L	1-2	Turney
1960-61	NCo	1	5.11.60	**Mansfield T**	D4	A	L	1-3	Caronn
1961-62	NCo	1	4.11.61	**Hartlepools U**	D4	A	L	1-5	Lodge
1962-63	NEL	1	3.11.62	**Morecambe**	LC	H	W	2-1	R.Smith, A.Smith
		2	24.11.62	**Carlisle U**	D3	H	L	0-2
1963-64	NEL	1	16.11.63	**Chester**	D4	A	L	2-3	Robson, A.Smith
1966-67	NL	1	26.11.66	**Bishop Auckland**	NL	A	D	1-1	Mason
		1r	30.11.66	**Bishop Auckland**		H	D	0-0aet
		1 2r	5.12.66	**Bishop Auckland** at Roker Park			D	3-3aet	Evans 2, Orrick
		1 3r	8.12.66	**Bishop Auckland** at Roker Park			L	1-4	Orrick
1971-72	NL	1	20.11.71	**Crewe Alex**	D4	A	W	1-0	Slane
		2	11.12.71	**Stockport Co**	D4	H	W	1-0	Young
		3	15.1.72	**Reading**	D4	H	D	2-2	Nixon, Alder
		3r	19.1.72	**Reading**		A	L	1-6	B.Wagstaff og
1973-74	NL	1	24.11.73	**Alfreton T**	ML	A	D	0-0
		1r	28.11.73	**Alfreton T**		H	W	2-1	Pink, Alder
		2	15.12.73	**Grimsby T**	D3	A	D	1-1	Slane
		2r	19.12.73	**Grimsby T**		H	L	0-2
1974-75	NL	1	23.11.74	**Preston NE**	D3	H	D	1-1	Dagless
		1r	26.11.74	**Preston NE**		A	L	1-5	Scott
1977-78	NL	1	26.11.77	**Burscough**	CC	H	W	1-0	Mutrie
		2	17.12.77	**Chesterfield**	D3	H	W	1-0	Jones
		3	7.1.78	**Enfield**	IL	H	W	1-0	Shoulder
		4	6.2.78	**Stoke C**	D2	A	W	3-2	Johnson 2, S.Carney
		5	18.2.78	**Wrexham**	D3	A	D	1-1	Johnson
		5r	27.2.78	**Wrexham** at Newcastle		H	L	1-2	Johnson
1978-79	NL	1	25.11.78	**York C**	D4	A	D	1-1	Johnson (p)
		1r	28.11.78	**York C**		H	L	3-5aet	Shoulder 2 (2p), Davies
1979-80	NL	1	24.11.79	**Mansfield T**	D3	H	L	0-2
1980-81	NL	1	22.11.80	**Burton A**	NPL	H	W	2-1	P.Walker, Mutrie
		2	13.12.80	**Hull C**	D3	A	D	1-1	Mutrie
		2r	16.12.80	**Hull C**		H	D	2-2aet	Mutrie, Young
		2 2r	22.12.80	**Hull C** at Elland Road			L	1-2	Mutrie (p)
1981-82	NL	1	21.11.81	**Walsall**	D3	H	L	1-2	Rafferty
1992-93	NL	1	14.11.92	**Southport**	NPL	H	L	1-2	Howie

BOGNOR REGIS TOWN

Formed 1883. **First entered FA Cup:** 1908. **League clubs beaten:** Swansea C, Exeter C

1972-73	SL	1	18.11.72	Colchester U	D4	A	L	0-6	
1984-85	IL	1	17.11.84	Swansea C	D3	A	D	1-1	Cooper
		1r	21.11.84	Swansea C		H	W	3-1	P.Pullen 2, Clements
		2	7.12.84	Reading	D3	A	L	2-6	Poole, P.Pullen
1985-86	IL	1	16.11.85	Enfield	APL	A	W	2-0	Cooper, Clements
		2	7.12.85	Gillingham	D3	A	L	1-6	Cooper (p)
1986-87	IL	1	15.11.86	Slough T	IL	A	D	1-1	Crumplin
		1r	17.11.86	Slough T		H	L	0-1	
1987-88	IL	1	14.11.87	Torquay U	D4	H	L	0-3	
1988-89	IL	1	19.11.88	Exeter C	D4	H	W	2-1	P.Pullen, Guille
		2	10.12.88	Cambridge U	D4	H	L	0-1	

BOLLINGTON

Formed 1875. Played at the Garden Street Ground, and changed at the Royal Oak pub

| 1885-86 | 1 | 24.10.85 | Oswestry | H | L | 0-5 |
| 1886-87 | 1 | 30.10.86 | Oswestry | H | L | 2-8 |

BOLTON ASSOCIATION

1883-84	1	3.11.83	Bradshaw	H	W	5-1	Bentley, Harper, Murray , Walker, 1 other
	2	1.12.83	Bolton Wanderers	A	L	0-3	
1884-85	1		Astley Bridge		*walkover*		
	2	22.11.84	Darwen Old Wanderers	A	L	2-7	

BOLTON OLYMPIC

Formed 1876. Played in the Tonge area of Bolton

| 1882-83 | 1 | 4.11.82 | Eagley | H | L | 4-7 | Haslam, Austin, og, 1 other |
| 1883-84 | 1 | 10.11.83 | Bolton Wanderers | A | L | 0-9 | |

BOLTON WANDERERS

Formed 1874. Founder Members of the Football League 1888. **FA Cup Winners:** 1923, 1926, 1929, 1958. **FA Cup Runners Up:** 1894, 1904, 1953. **Record FA Cup Win:** 13-0 vs Sheffield United, 2nd round, 1.2.1890. **Record FA Cup Defeat:** 1-9 vs Preston North End, 2nd round, 10.12.1887

1881-82	1	22.10.81	Eagley	H	D	5-5	Atherton, Gleaves, Struthers, 2 ogs
	1r	12.11.81	Eagley	A	W	1-0	Steel
	2	19.11.81	Blackburn R	A	L	2-6	Atherton, Struthers
1882-83	1	4.11.82	Bootle	H	W	6-1	Struthers 5, Steel
	2	30.11.82	Liverpool Ramblers	H	W	3-0	Struthers 2, og
	3	6.1.83	Druids	A	D	0-0	
	3r	22.1.83	Druids	H	D	1-1aet	Atherton
	3 2r	29.1.83	Druids at Wrexham Racecourse		L	0-1	
1883-84	1	10.11.83	Bolton Olympic	H	W	9-0	Struthers 3, Steel 2, Davenport, Gleaves, Howarth, Scholes
	2	1.12.83	Bolton Association	H	W	3-0	Steel 2, Struthers
	3	29.12.83	Irwell Springs	H	W	8-1	Davenport 2, Fallon 2, Steel 2, Struthers, og
	4	19.1.84	Notts Co	A	D	2-2aet	Davenport, Fallon
	4r	2.2.84	Notts Co	H	L	1-2	Vaughan
1884-85	1		Preston Zingari		*both teams withdrew*		
1885-86	1	17.10.85	Eagley	H	W	6-0	Fallon 2, Gregory, Hough, Bullough, og
	2	21.11.85	Rawtenstall	A	D	3-3	*Scorers unknown.*
		FA disqualified Rawtenstall for professionalism					
	3	5.12.85	Preston NE	H	L	2-3	Davenport, Struthers
		FA disqualified Preston for professionalism. Bolton reinstated					
	4		Bye				
	5		Old Westminsters				
		FA disqualified Bolton for professionalism					
1886-87	1	30.10.86	South Shore	H	W	5-3	Davenport 2, Hewitson, Struthers, Howarth
	2	13.11.86	Third Lanark	A	W	3-2	Hewitson 2, Struthers

	3	11.12.86 **Darwen**		A	L	3-4	Davenport, Howarth, Struthers
1887-88	1	15.10.87 **Everton**		H	W	1-0	Roberts
		FA ordered replay after Bolton player declared ineligible					
	1r	29.10.87 **Everton**		A	D	2-2	Brogan, Roberts
	1 2r	12.11.87 **Everton**		H	D	1-1	Brogan
	1 3r	19.11.87 **Everton**		A	L	1-2	Davenport
		FA disqualified Everton for ineligible players and reinstated Bolton					
	2	10.12.87 **Preston NE**		A	L	1-9	Howarth
1888-89 D1		1q **Hurst** (A) 0-0; 1qr **Hurst**, walkover; 2q **West Manchester** (H) 9-0; 3q **Linfield, Belfast** (A) 0-4					
1889-90 D1	1	18.1.89 **Distillery, Belfast**		H	W	10-2	Weir 4, Cassidy, Davenport 2, '2 scrimmages'
	2	1.2.89 **Sheffield U**		H	W	13-0	Cassidy 5, Weir 4, Brogan 3, Robinson
	3	15.2.89 **Preston NE**	D1	A	W	3-2	Weir 2, Brogan
	4	8.3.89 **Sheffield W** Perry Barr			L	1-2	McNee
1890-91 D1	1	24.1.90 **Accrington**	D1	A	L	1-5	Cassidy
1891-92 D1	1	16.1.91 **Sheffield W**	FAll	A	L	1-2	Munro
		Match replayed after protest over ground being unfit					
	1r	23.1.91 **Sheffield W**		A	L	1-4	Jones
1892-93 D1	1	21.1.93 **Wolverhampton W**	D1	H	D	1-1aet	Wilson
	1r	28.1.93 **Wolverhampton W**		A	L	1-2	McNee
1893-94 D1	1	27.1.94 **Small Heath**	D2	A	W	4-3	Cassidy 2, Wilson 2
	2	10.2.94 **Newcastle U**	D2	A	W	2-1	Hughes, Turner
	3	24.2.94 **Liverpool**	D2	H	W	3-0	Dickenson 2, Cassidy
	SF	10.3.94 **Sheffield W**	D1		W	2-1	Bentley 2
		played at Fallowfield, Manchester					
	F	31.3.94 **Notts Co**	D2		L	1-4	Cassidy
		played at Goodison Park					
1894-95 D1	1	2.2.95 **Woolwich Arsenal**	D2	H	W	1-0	Jones
	2	16.2.95 **Bury**	D2	H	W	1-0	Cassidy
	3	2.3.95 **Sunderland**	D1	A	L	1-2	Cassidy
1895-96 D1	1	1.2.96 **Crewe A**	D2	A	W	4-0	Brown, Gunn, Tannahill, Wright
	2	15.2.96 **Blackpool**	LL	A	W	2-0	Cassidy, Wright
	3	29.2.96 **Bury**	D1	H	W	2-0	Wright, Gunn
	SF	21.3.96 **Sheffield W**	D1		D	1-1	Tannahill
		played at Goodison Park					
	SFr	28.3.96 **Sheffield W**			L	1-3	Tannahill
		played at Nottingham					
1896-97 D1	1	30.1.97 **Grimsby T**	D2	A	D	0-0	
	1r	8.2.97 **Grimsby T**		H	D	3-3aet	Cassidy, Thomson, Jones
	1 2r	11.2.97 **Grimsby T** at Bramall Lane			W	3-2	Joyce 2, Jones
	2	13.2.97 **Derby Co**	D1	A	L	1-4	Brown
1897-98 D1	1	29.1.98 **Luton T**	D2	A	W	1-0	Cassidy
	2	12.2.98 **Manchester C**	D2	H	W	1-0	T.Miller
	3	26.2.98 **Southampton**	SL	H	D	0-0	
	3r	2.3.98 **Southampton**		A	L	0-4	
1898-99 D1	1	28.1.99 **Wolverhampton W**	D1	A	D	0-0	
	1r	1.2.99 **Wolverhampton W**		H	L	0-1	
1899-00 D2	1	27.1.00 **Sheffield W**	D2	A	L	0-1	
1900-01 D1	1	9.2.01 **Derby Co**	D1	H	W	1-0	L.Bell
	2	23.2.01 **Reading**	SL	H	L	0-1	
1901-02 D1	1	25.1.02 **Wolverhampton W**	D1	A	W	2-0	Williams, og
	2	8.2.02 **Sheffield U**	D1	A	L	1-2	McKie
1902-03 D1	1	7.2.03 **Bristol C**	D2	H	L	0-5	
1903-04 D2	1	6.2.04 **Reading**	SL	A	D	1-1	Marsh
	1r	10.2.04 **Reading**			W	3-2	Freebairn, Marsh, Yenson
	2	20.2.04 **Southampton**	SL	H	W	4-1	Marsh 2, White 2
	3	5.3.04 **Sheffield U**	D1	A	W	2-0	Marsh, Yenson
	SF	19.3.04 **Derby Co**	D1		W	1-0	Taylor
		played at Molineux					
	F	23.4.04 **Manchester C**	D1		L	0-1	
		played at Crystal Palace					
1904-05 D2	1	4.2.05 **Bristol R**	SL	H	D	1-1	Marsh
	1r	8.2.05 **Bristol R**		A	W	3-0	Stokes, Shephard, Pudon og
	2	18.2.05 **Manchester C**	D1	A	W	2-1	Shepherd, White
	3	4.3.05 **Newcastle U**	D1	H	L	0-2	
1905-06 D1	1	13.1.06 **Middlesbrough**	D1	A	L	0-3	
1906-07 D1	1	12.1.07 **Brighton & HA**	SL	H	W	3-1	Stokes, Clifford, Shepherd
	2	2.2.07 **Aston Villa**	D1	H	W	2-0	Shepherd 2

Season	Rnd	Date	Opponent	Comp	Venue	W/D/L	Score	Scorers
	3	23.2.07	**Everton**	D1	A	D	0-0	
	3r	27.2.07	**Everton**		H	L	0-3	
1907-08 D1	1	11.1.08	**Woking**	WS	H	W	5-0	Cameron, Stokes, Owen, White, McEwan
	2	1.2.08	**Notts Co**	D1	A	D	1-1	McEwan
	2r	5.2.08	**Notts Co**		H	W	2-1aet	Cameron,White
	3	22.2.08	**Everton**	D1	H	D	3-3	Marsh 3
	3r	26.2.08	**Everton**		A	L	1-3aet	Greenhalgh
1908-09 D2	1	16.1.09	**WBA**	D2	A	L	1-3	Hunter
1909-10 D1	1	15.1.10	**Stockport Co**	D2	A	L	1-4	Hogan
1910-11 D2	1	14.1.11	**Chesterfield**	ML	H	L	0-2	
1911-12 D1	1	13.1.12	**Woolwich Arsenal**	D1	H	W	1-0	Smith
	2	3.2.12	**Blackpool**	D2	H	W	1-0	Bentley
	3	24.2.12	**Barnsley**	D2	H	L	1-2	Smith
1912-13 D1	1	11.1.13	**Oldham A**	D1	A	L	0-2	
1913-14 D1	1	10.1.14	**Port Vale**		H	W	3-0	Smith, Donaldson, Lillycrop
	2	31.1.14	**Swindon T**	SL	H	W	4-2	Smith 3, Jones
	3	21.2.14	**Burnley**	D1	A	L	0-3	
1914-15 D1	1	9.1.15	**Notts Co**	D1	H	W	2-1	Smith, Hilton
	2	30.1.15	**Millwall A**	SL	H	D	0-0aet	
	2r	6.2.15	**Millwall A**		A	D	2-2aet	Vizard, Smith (p)
	2 2r	13.2.15	**Millwall A**		H	W	4-1	Jones 2, Vizard 2
	3	20.2.15	**Burnley**	D1	H	W	2-1aet	Smith 2
	4	6.3.15	**Hull C**	D2	H	W	4-2	Smith 2 (2p), Vizard, Jones
	SF	27.3.15	**Sheffield U**	D1		L	1-2	Smith
		played at Ewood Park						
1919-20 D1	1	10.1.20	**Chelsea**	D1	H	L	0-1	
1920-21 D1	1	8.1.21	**Preston NE**	D1	A	L	0-2	
1921-22 D1	1	7.1.22	**Bury**	D2	H	W	1-0	Vizard
	2	28.1.22	**Manchester C**	D1	H	L	1-3	Roberts
1922-23 D1	1	13.1.23	**Norwich C**	3S	A	W	2-0	J.Smith, JR Smith
	2	3.2.23	**Leeds U**	D2	H	W	3-1	Jack 2, J.Smith
	3	24.2.23	**Huddersfield T**	D1	A	D	1-1	Jack
	3r	28.2.23	**Huddersfield T**		H	W	1-0	Jack
	4	10.3.23	**Charlton A**	3S	A	W	1-0	Jack
	SF	24.3.23	**Sheffield U**	D1		W	1-0	Jack
		played at Old Trafford						
	F	28.4.23	**WEST HAM**	D2 WEMBLEY		W	2-0	Jack, JR Smith
1923-24 D1	1	12.1.24	**Hull C**	D2	A	D	2-2	JR Smith, Jack
	2	16.1.24	**Hull C**		H	W	4-0	JR Smith 2, Jack 2
	3	2.2.24	**Liverpool**	D1	H	L	1-4	JR Smith
1924-25 D1	1	10.1.25	**Huddersfield T**	D1	H	W	3-0	Jack, J.Smith (p), Vizard
	2	31.1.25	**Tottenham H**	D1	A	D	1-1	J.Smith
	2r	4.2.25	**Tottenham H**		H	L	0-1	
1925-26 D1	3	9.1.26	**Accrington S**	3N	H	W	1-0	Jack
	4	30.1.26	**Bournemouth**	3S	A	D	2-2	JR Smith, Jack
	4r	3.2.26	**Bournemouth**		H	W	6-2	J Smith 2, JR Smith 2, Boston, Jack
	5	20.2.26	**South Shields**	D2	H	W	3-0	J Smith (p), Jack, JR Smith
	6	6.3.26	**Nottingham F**	D2	A	D	2-2	Butler 2
	6r	10.3.26	**Nottingham F**		H	D	0-0aet	
	6 2r	15.3.26	**Nottingham F** at Old Trafford			W	1-0	J.Smith
	SF	27.3.26	**Swansea T**	D2		W	3-0	J.Smith 2 (1p), Baggett
		played at White Hart Lane						
	F	24.4.26	**MANCHESTER C**	D1 WEMBLEY		W	1-0	Jack
1926-27 D1	3	8.1.27	**Blackpool**	D2	A	W	3-1	JR Smith 3
	4	29.1.27	**Leeds U**	D1	A	D	0-0	
	4r	2.2.27	**Leeds U**		H	W	3-0	Wright, Jack, JR Smith
	5	19.2.27	**Cardiff C**	D1	H	L	0-3	
1927-28 D1	3	14.1.28	**Luton T**	3S	H	W	2-1	Butler, Smith
	4	28.1.28	**Stoke C**	D2	A	L	2-4	Round, Murphy
1928-29 D1	3	12.1.29	**Oldham A**	D2	H	W	2-0	Gibson, Blackmore
	4	26.1.29	**Liverpool**	D1	A	D	0-0	
	4r	30.1.29	**Liverpool**		H	W	5-2aet	Blackmore 2, Butler, McClelland, Gibson
	5	16.2.29	**Leicester C**	D1	A	W	2-1	Seddon, Blackmore
	6	2.3.29	**Blackburn R**	D1	A	D	1-1	Blackmore
	6r	6.3.29	**Blackburn R**		H	W	2-1	Butler 2
	SF	23.3.29	**Huddersfield T**	D1		W	3-1	Butler, Gibson, Blackmore
		played at Anfield						

Season	Round	Date	Opponent	Div	Venue	H/A	W/L/D	Score	Scorers
	F	27.4.29	**PORTSMOUTH**	D1	WEMBLEY		W	2-0	Butler, Blackmore
1929-30 D1	3	11.1.30	**Birmingham**	D1		A	L	0-1	
1930-31 D1	3	10.1.31	**Carlisle U**	3N		H	W	1-0	Blackmore
	4	24.1.31	**Sunderland**	D1		H	D	1-1	Blackmore
	4r	27.1.31	**Sunderland**			A	L	1-3	Blackmore
1931-32 D1	3	9.1.32	**Preston NE**	D2		A	D	0-0	
	3r	13.1.32	**Preston NE**			H	L	2-5	Blackmore, Gibson
1932-33 D1	3	14.1.33	**Charlton A**	D2		A	W	5-1	Cook 2, T.Griffiths, Gibson, Milsom
	4	28.1.33	**Grimsby T**	D2		H	W	2-1	T.Griffiths, Butler
	5	18.2.33	**Manchester C**	D1		H	L	2-4	Westwood, Milsom
1933-34 D2	3	13.1.34	**Halifax T**	3N		H	W	3-1	Cook 2, Westwood
	4	27.1.34	**Brighton & HA**	3S		A	D	1-1	Westwood
	4r	31.1.34	**Brighton & HA**			H	W	6-1	Milsom 3, Westwood, GT Taylor, Cameron
	5	17.2.34	**Liverpool**	D1		A	W	3-0	GT Taylor, Milsom, Westwood
	6	3.3.34	**Portsmouth**	D1		H	L	0-3	
1934-35 D2	3	12.1.35	**Northampton T**	3S		A	W	2-0	Milsom, Cook
	4	26.1.35	**Plymouth A**	D2		A	W	4-1	Milsom 2, Westwood, Rae og
	5	16.2.35	**Tottenham H**	D1		A	D	1-1	Atkinson
	5r	20.2.35	**Tottenham H**			H	D	1-1aet	Westwood
	5 2r	25.2.35	**Tottenham H** Villa Park				W	2-0	Westwood, Walton
	6	2.3.35	**Everton**	D1		A	W	2-1	Eastham, Milsom
	SF	16.3.35	**WBA**	D1			D	1-1	Walton
		played at Elland Road							
	SFr	20.3.35	**WBA**				L	0-2	
		played at Victoria Ground, Stoke							
1935-36 D1	3	11.1.36	**Blackburn R**	D1		A	D	1-1	Woods
	3r	14.1.36	**Blackburn R**			H	L	0-1aet	
1936-37 D1	3	16.1.37	**West Ham**	D2		A	D	0-0	
	3r	20.1.37	**West Ham**			H	W	1-0	Halford
	4	30.1.37	**Norwich C**	D2		H	D	1-1	Westwood
	4r	4.2.37	**Norwich C**			A	W	2-1aet	Anderson, Milsom
	5	20.2.37	**Manchester C**	D1		H	L	0-5	
1937-38 D1	3	8.1.38	**Arsenal**	D1		A	L	1-3	Carruthers
1938-39 D1	3	7.1.39	**Middlesbrough**	D1		A	D	0-0	
	3r	11.1.39	**Middlesbrough**			H	D	0-0aet	
	3 2r	16.1.39	**Middlesbrough** at Elland Rd				L	0-1	
1945-46 D1	3 1L	5.1.46	**Blackburn R**	D2		H	W	1-0	Moir
	3 2L	9.1.46	**Blackburn R**			A	W	3-1	Westwood 2, Hunt
	4 1L	26.1.46	**Liverpool**	D1		H	W	5-0	Westwood 3, Lofthouse 2
	4 2L	30.1.46	**Liverpool**			A	L	0-2	
	5 1L	9.2.46	**Middlesbrough**	D1		H	W	1-0	Westwood
	5 2L	13.2.46	**Middlesbrough**			A	D	1-1	Hunt
	6 1L	2.3.46	**Stoke C**	D1		A	W	2-0	Westwood 2
	6 2L	9.3.46	**Stoke C**			H	D	0-0	
	SF	23.3.46	**Charlton A**	D1			L	0-2	
		played at Villa Park							
1946-47 D1	3	11.1.47	**Stockport Co**	3N		H	W	5-1	Lofthouse 2, Geldard, Barrass, Woodward
	4	25.1.47	**Manchester C**	D2		H	D	3-3	Lofthouse, Barrass, Wrigglesworth
	4r	29.1.47	**Manchester C**			A	L	0-1	
1947-48 D1	3	10.1.48	**Tottenham H**	D2		H	L	0-2aet	
1948-49 D1	3	8.1.49	**Aston Villa**	D1		A	D	1-1aet	Bradley
	3r	15.1.49	**Aston Villa**			H	D	0-0aet	
	3 2r	17.1.49	**Aston Villa**			A	L	1-2aet	Lofthouse
1949-50 D1	3	7.1.50	**Coventry C**	D2		A	W	2-1	Lofthouse, Langton
	4	28.1.50	**Leeds U**	D2		A	D	1-1	Lofthouse
	4r	1.2.50	**Leeds U**			H	L	2-3aet	Lofthouse, McShane
1950-51 D1	3	6.1.51	**York C**	3N		H	W	2-0	Lofthouse, Langton
	4	27.1.51	**Newcastle U**	D1		A	L	2-3	Moir 2
1951-52 D1	3	12.1.52	**WBA**	D1		A	L	0-4	
1952-53 D1	3	14.1.53	**Fulham**	D2		H	W	3-1	Holden, Moir, Lofthouse
	4	31.1.53	**Notts Co**	D2		H	D	1-1	Lofthouse
	4r	5.2.53	**Notts Co**			A	D	2-2	Moir 2
	4 2r	9.2.53	**Notts Co** at Hillsborough				W	1-0	Lofthouse
	5	16.2.53	**Luton T**	D2		A	W	1-0	Lofthouse
	6	28.2.53	**Gateshead**	3N		A	W	1-0	Lofthouse
	SF	21.3.53	**Everton**	D2			W	4-3	Lofthouse 2, Moir, Holden
		played at Maine Road							

Season	Rd	Date	Opponent	Div	Venue	Res	Score	Scorers
	F	2.5.53	Blackpool	D1 WEMBLEY		L	3-4	Moir, Bell, Lofthouse
1953-54 D1	3	9.1.54	Liverpool	D1	H	W	1-0	Moir
	4	30.1.54	Headington U	SL	A	W	4-2	Moir, Parry, Lofthouse, Stevens
	5	20.2.54	Portsmouth	D1	H	D	0-0	
	5r	24.2.54	Portsmouth		A	W	2-1	Moir 2
	6	13.3.54	Sheffield W	D1	A	D	1-1	Moir (p)
	6r	17.3.54	Sheffield W		H	L	0-2	
1954-55 D1	3	8.1.55	Millwall	3S	H	W	3-1	Moir 2 (1p), Parry
	4	29.1.55	Birmingham C	D2	A	L	1-2	Moir
1955-56 D1	3	7.1.56	Huddersfield T	D1	H	–	0-0	
			abandoned after 47 minutes					
	3	11.1.56	Huddersfield T		H	W	3-0	Lofthouse, Stevens, Neill
	4	28.1.56	Sheffield U	D1	H	L	1-2	Hartle
1956-57 D1	3	5.1.57	Blackpool	D1	H	L	2-3	Hennin (p), Gubbins
1957-58 D1	3	4.1.58	Preston NE	D1	A	W	3-0	Parry 2, Stevens
	4	25.1.58	York C	3N	A	D	0-0	
	4r	29.1.58	York C		H	W	3-0	Allcock 2, Birch
	5	15.2.58	Stoke C	D2	H	W	3-1	Lofthouse, Stevens, Parry
	6	1.3.58	Wolverhampton W	D1	H	W	2-1	Stevens, Parry
	SF	22.3.58	Blackburn R	D2		W	2-1	Gubbins 2
			played at Maine Road					
	F	3.5.58	MANCHESTER U	D1 WEMBLEY		W	2-0	Lofthouse 2
1958-59 D1	3	10.1.59	Scunthorpe U	D2	A	W	2-0	Lofthouse 2
	4	24.1.59	Wolverhampton W	D1	A	W	2-1	Lofthouse, Parry (p)
	5	14.2.59	Preston NE	D1	H	D	2-2	Birch, Parry
	5r	18.2.59	Preston NE		A	D	1-1aet	Holden
	5 2r	23.2.59	Preston NE at Ewood Park			W	1-0	Lofthouse
	6	28.2.59	Nottingham F	D1	A	L	1-2	Birch
1959-60 D1	3	9.1.60	Bury	D3	A	D	1-1	Parry
	3r	14.1.60	Bury		H	W	4-2aet	Parry 2, Stevens, Birch
	4	30.1.60	WBA	D1	A	L	0-2	
1960-61 D1	3	7.1.61	Hull C	D3	A	W	1-0	Stevens
	4	28.1.61	Blackburn R	D1	H	D	3-3	Stanley (p), McAdams, Stevens
	4r	1.2.61	Blackburn R		A	L	0-4	
1961-62 D1	3	6.1.62	Manchester U	D1	A	L	1-2	Stevens
1962-63 D1	3	6.3.63	Sheffield U	D1	A	L	1-3	Lee
1963-64 D1	3	4.1.64	Bath C	SL	A	D	1-1	Lee
	3r	8.1.64	Bath C		H	W	3-0	Taylor, Lee (p), Davies
	4	25.1.64	Preston NE	D2	H	D	2-2	Deakin 2
	4r	27.1.64	Preston NE		A	L	1-2	Edwards
1964-65 D2	3	9.1.65	Workington	D3	H	W	4-1	Davies 2, Hill, Butler
	4	30.1.65	Preston NE	D2	A	W	2-1	Lee (p), Davies
	5	20.2.65	Liverpool	D1	H	L	0-1	
1965-66 D2	3	22.1.66	WBA	D1	H	W	3-0	Lee 2, Bromley
	4	12.2.66	Preston NE	D2	H	D	1-1	Davies
	4r	14.2.66	Preston NE		A	L	2-3	Lee, Davies
1966-67 D2	3	28.1.67	Crewe A	D4	H	W	1-0	Lee (p)
	4	18.2.67	Arsenal	D1	H	D	0-0	
	4r	22.2.67	Arsenal		A	L	0-3	
1967-68 D2	3	27.1.68	Nottingham F	D1	A	L	2-4	Taylor, Hulme
1968-69 D2	3	4.1.69	Northampton T	D3	H	W	2-1	Fletcher, Greaves
	4	25.1.69	Bristol R	D3	H	L	1-2	Williams
1969-70 D2	3	3.1.70	Watford	D2	H	L	1-2	Greaves
1970-71 D2	3	2.1.71	York C	D4	A	L	0-2	
1971-72 D3	1	20.11.71	Bangor C	NPL	H	W	3-0	Ritson (p), Nicholson, Duffy
	2	11.12.71	Rossendale U at Bury	CC	A	W	4-1	Greaves 3, Byrom
	3	15.1.72	Torquay U	D3	H	W	2-1	Hunt, Greaves
	4	5.2.72	Chelsea	D1	A	L	0-3	
1972-73 D3	1	18.11.72	Chester	D4	H	D	1-1	Byrom
	1r	22.11.72	Chester		A	W	1-0	G.Jones
	2	9.12.72	Shrewsbury T	D3	H	W	3-0	Phllips, Lee, Ritson
	3	13.1.73	Charlton A	D3	A	D	1-1	Lee
	3r	17.1.73	Charlton A		H	W	4-0	Greaves 2, Nicholson, G.Jones
	4	3.2.73	Cardiff C	D2	H	D	2-2	G.Jones, Ritson
	4r	7.2.73	Cardiff C		A	D	1-1aet	G.Jones
	4 2r	12.2.73	Cardiff C at Hawthorns			W	1-0	Lee
	5	24.2.73	Luton T	D2	H	L	0-1	

1973-74 D2	3	6.1.74	**Stoke C**	D1	H	W	3-2	Byrom 3
	4	26.1.74	**Southampton**	D1	A	D	3-3	Byrom 2, G.Jones (p)
	4r	30.1.74	**Southampton**		H	L	0-2aet	
1974-75 D2	3	4.1.75	**WBA**	D2	H	D	0-0	
	3r	8.1.75	**WBA**		A	L	0-4	
1975-76 D2	3	3.1.76	**Brentford**	D4	A	D	0-0	
	3r	6.1.76	**Brentford**		H	W	2-0	Whatmore 2
	4	24.1.76	**Huddersfield T**	D4	A	W	1-0	Reid
	5	14.2.76	**Newcastle U**	D1	H	D	3-3	G.Jones, P.Jones, Allardyce
	5r	18.2.76	**Newcastle U**		A	D	0-0aet	
	5 2r	23.2.76	**Newcastle U** at Elland Rd			L	1-2	G.Jones
1976-77 D2	3	8.1.77	**West Ham**	D1	A	L	1-2	Waldron
1977-78 D2	3	7.1.78	**Tottenham H**	D2	A	D	2-2	Greaves (p), Whatmore
	3r	10.1.78	**Tottenham H**		H	W	2-1aet	Ritson, G.Jones
	4	6.2.78	**Mansfield T**	D2	H	W	1-0	Worthington
	5	27.2.78	**Middlesbrough**	D1	A	L	0-2	
1978-79 D1	3	9.1.79	**Bristol C**	D1	A	L	1-3	Smith
1979-80 D1	3	5.1.80	**Sunderland**	D2	A	W	1-0	Whatmore
	4	26.1.80	**Halifax T**	D4	H	W	2-0	Greaves, Whatmore
	5	16.2.80	**Arsenal**	D1	H	D	1-1	Allardyce
	5r	19.2.80	**Arsenal**		A	L	0-3	
1980-81 D2	3	3.1.81	**Nottingham F**	D1	A	D	3-3	Hoggan 2, Whatmore
	3r	6.1.81	**Nottingham F**		H	L	0-1aet	
1981-82 D2	3	2.1.82	**Derby Co**	D2	H	W	3-1	Gowling, Foster, Thompso
	4	23.1.82	**Crystal P**	D2	A	L	0-1	
1982-83 D2	3	8.1.83	**Arsenal**	D1	A	L	1-2	Whatmore
1983-84 D3	1	19.11.83	**Tranmere R**	D4	A	D	2-2	Joyce, Chandler (p)
	1r	22.11.83	**Tranmere R**		H	W	4-1aet	Chandler 2(1p), Rudge, Caldwell
	2	10.12.83	**Mansfield T**	D4	H	W	2-0	Foster, Rudge
	3	7.1.84	**Sunderland**	D1	H	L	0-3	
1984-85 D3	1	17.11.84	**Hull C**	D3	A	L	1-2	Foster
1985-86 D3	1	16.11.85	**Wrexham**	D4	A	L	1-3	Thompson (p)
1986-87 D3	1	15.11.86	**Halifax T**	D4	A	D	1-1	Oghani
	1r	18.11.86	**Halifax T**		H	D	1-1aet	Caldwell
	1 2r	24.11.86	**Halifax T**		A	W	3-1	Thompson, Caldwell, Gavin
	2	6.12.86	**Tranmere R**	D4	H	W	2-0	Caldwell, Thompson
	3	10.1.87	**Coventry C**	D1	A	L	0-3	
1987-88 D4	1	14.11.87	**Burnley**	D4	A	W	1-0	Thomas (p)
	2	5.12.87	**Wrexham**	D4	A	W	2-1	Thomas 2
	3	9.1.88	**Barnsley**	D2	A	L	1-3	Stevens
1988-89 D3	1	19.11.88	**Chesterfield**	D3	H	D	0-0	
	1r	28.11.88	**Chesterfield**		A	W	3-2	Stevens, Storer, Darby
	2	10.12.88	**Port Vale**	D3	H	L	1-2	Keeley
1989-90 D3	1	18.11.89	**Blackpool**	D3	A	L	1-2	Crombie
1990-91 D3	1	17.11.90	**Wittton Alb**		A	W	2-1	Darby, Comstive
	2	11.12.90	**Chesterfield**	D4	A	W	4-3	Reeves, Philliskirk, Thompson, Storer
	3	5.1.91	**Barrow**	GMVC	H	W	1-0	Philliskirk
	4	26.1.91	**Manchester Utd**	D1	A	L	0-1	
1991-92 D3	1	17.11.91	**Emley** at Huddersfield	NPL	A	W	3-0	Reeves 2, Philliskirk
	2	7.12.91	**Bradford C**	D3	H	W	3-1	Burke, Reeves, Philliskirk
	3	4.1.92	**Reading**	D3	H	W	2-0	Philliskirk
	4	25.1.92	**Brighton & HA**	D2	H	W	2-1	Walker, Philliskirk (p)
	5	16.2.92	**Southampton**	D1	H	D	2-2	Walker, Green
	5r	26.2.92	**Southampton**		A	L	2-3aet	Walker, Darby
1992-93 D2	1	14.11.92	**Sutton Coldfield T**	SL	H	W	2-1	Reeves, Walker
	2	5.12.92	**Rochdale**	D3	H	W	4-0	McAteer, McGinlay 2, Walker
	3	3.1.93	**Liverpool**	PL	H	D	2-2	McGinlay, Seagraves
	3r	15.1.93	**Liverpool**		A	W	2-0	McGinlay, Walker
	4	24.1.93	**Wolverhampton W**	D1	A	W	2-0	Green, McGinlay
	5	13.2.93	**Derby Co**	D1	A	L	1-3	Walker

BOOTLE

Formed 1878 as Bootle St John's. Were (very) briefly the top club in Liverpool in the 1880s. As a Second Division club in 1892-93 they beat amateurs Gorton Villa 10-0 in a qualifying round match. The current Bootle club in the North West Counties League dates from 1953.

1881-82	1	5.11.81	**Blackburn Law**		H	W	2-1	Smith, Turner

	2	3.12.81	Turton		A	L	0-4	
1882-83	1	4.11.82	Bolton Wanderers		A	L	1-6	Robertson
1886-87	1	16.10.86	Great Lever		H	L	2-4	
1887-88	1	15.10.87	Workington		H	W	6-0	Lewis 2, Wilding 2, Anderson, Morris
	2	5.11.87	South Shore		H	D	1-1	Veitch
	2r	12.11.87	South Shore		A	W	3-0	Anderson, Hastings, Lewis
	3	26.11.87	Higher Walton		A	W	6-1	Hastings 4, Anderson, Morris
	4	17.12.87	Great Bridge Unity		A	W	2-1	
	5	7.1.88	Old Carthusians		A	L	0-2	
1888-89	1	2.2.89	Preston NE		H	L	0-3	
1889-90 FAll	1	18.1.90	Sunderland Albion	FAll	H	L	1-3	Jamieson

FA disqualified Sunderland Albion for ineligible players

	2	1.2.90	Derby Midland	ML	H	W	2-1	Galbraith, Woods
	3	15.2.90	Blackburn R	D1	H	L	0-7	
1890-91 FAll	1q **Carlisle** (A) 6-1; 2q **Newton Heath** (H) 2-1; 3q **Halliwell** (A) 3-4							
1891-92 FAll	1	16.1.92	Darwen	FL	H	L	0-2	
1892-93 D2	1q **Gorton Villa** (H) 10-0; 2q **Liverpool Caledonians** (H) 2-3							

BOREHAMWOOD

Formed 1948 following the merger of Borehamwood Rovers and the exotically named "Royal Retournez". **First entered FA Cup:** 1970

1973-74 AL	1	24.11.73	Southend U	D3	A	L	0-3
1977-78 IL	1	26.11.77	Swindon T	D3	H	D	0-0
	1r	29.11.77	Swindon T		A	L	0-2

BOSTON UNITED

Originally formed as Boston Town and reformed as Boston United in 1934. **First entered the FA Cup:** 1887. **FA Challenge Trophy Runners-up:** 1985 **League Clubs beaten:** Bradford PA, Crewe A, Derby Co, Hartlepool, Southport

Boston Town

1887-88	1	15.10.87	Gainsborough T		A	L	0-7	
1925-26 ML	1	28.11.25	Mansfield T	ML	H	W	5-2	Doran, Porter, Clarke, Jenkinson, Miller
	2	12.12.25	Bradford PA	D3	H	W	1-0	Doran
	3	9.1.26	Sunderland	D1	A	L	1-8	Porter
1926-27 ML	1	27.11.26	Northampton T	3S	H	D	1-1	Wainwright
	1r	2.12.26	Northampton T		A	L	1-2	Menlove
1932-33 ML	1	26.11.32	Darlington	3N	A	L	0-1	

as Boston United

1934-35 ML	1	24.11.34	Darwen	LC	A	W	2-1	Bungay, Marshall
	2	8.12.34	Bath C	SL	A	L	1-2	Bungay
1935-36 ML	1	30.11.35	Crewe A	3N	A	L	2-4	McConnell, Bungay
1936-37 ML	1	28.11.36	Spennymoor U	NEL	H	D	1-1	Notley
	1r	2.12.36	Spennymoor U		A	L	0-2	
1952-53 ML	1	22.11.52	Oldham A	3N	H	L	1-2	Kurz
1953-54 ML	1	21.11.53	Scunthorpe U	3N	A	L	0-9	
1954-55 ML	1	20.11.54	Blyth Spartans	NEL	H	D	1-1	Wilkins
	1r	24.11.54	Blyth Spartans		A	L	4-5	Lowder 2, Hazeldine 2
1955-56 ML	1	19.11.55	Northwich V	CC	H	W	3-2	Whitfield 2, Wilkins
	2	10.12.55	Derby Co	3N	A	W	6-1	Wilkins 2, Hazeldine 3, Birbeck
	3	7.1.56	Tottenham H	D1	A	L	0-4	
1956-57 ML	1	17.11.56	Bradford PA	3N	H	L	0-2	
1957-58 ML	1	16.11.57	Billingham Syn	NL	H	W	5-2	Graver 4, Lewis
	2	7.12.57	Darlington	3N	A	L	3-5	Graver, Hukin 2
1958-59 SL	1	15.11.58	Chester	D4	A	L	2-3	Hukin 2
1962-63 ML	1	3.11.62	King's Lynn	SL	H	L	1-2	Bull
1967-68 WMRL	1	9.12.67	Corby T	SL	A	W	3-0	Bowers, Rayner, Robinson
	2	6.1.68	Leyton O	D3	H	D	1-1	Wood og
	2r	15.1.68	Leyton O		A	L	1-2	Thompson
1970-71 NPL	1	21.11.70	Southport	D4	A	W	2-0	Bates, Mackay
	2	12.12.70	York C	D4	H	L	1-2	Bates
1971-72 NPL	1	20.11.71	Ellesmere Port	NPL	A	W	3-0	Wilkinson, Svarc, Coates
	2	11.12.71	Hartlepool	D4	H	W	2-1	Smith, Froggart
	3	15.1.72	Portsmouth	D2	H	L	0-1	
1972-73 NPL	1	18.11.72	Lancaster C	NPL	H	L	1-2	Froggart
1973-74 NPL	1	24.11.73	Hayes	IL	H	D	0-0	
	1r	28.11.73	Hayes		A	W	2-1aet	Tewley, Froggart

BOSTON UNITED

	2	15.12.73	Hitchin T	IL	H	W	1-0	Conde
	3	5.1.74	Derby Co	D1	A	D	0-0	
	3r	9.1.74	Derby Co		H	L	1-6	Conde
1974-75	NPL 1	23.11.74	Chesterfield	D3	A	L	1-3	Tewley
1975-76	NPL 1	22.11.75	Lincoln C	D4	H	L	0-1	
1976-77	NPL 1	20.11.76	Barnsley	D4	A	L	1-3	Daley
1978-79	NPL 1	25.11.78	Tranmere R	D3	A	L	1-2	Mayes
1980-81	APL 1	22.11.80	Rotherham U	D3	H	L	0-4	
1981-82	APL 1	21.11.81	Kettering T	APL	H	L	0-1	
1982-83	APL 1	20.11.82	Crewe A	D4	H	W	3-1	Lumby, Cook 2
	2	11.12.82	Sheffield U	D3	H	D	1-1	Lumby
	2r	14.12.82	Sheffield U		A	L	1-5	Henderson og
1983-84	APL 1	19.11.83	Bury	D4	H	L	0-3	
1985-86	APL 1	16.11.85	Runcorn	APL	A	D	2-2	Casey, Nuttell
	1r	20.11.85	Runcorn		H	D	1-1aet	Gilbert
	1 2r	25.11.85	Runcorn		A	L	1-4	Gilbert
1986-87	GMVC 1	15.11.86	Runcorn	GMVC	A	D	1-1	Fee
	1r	19.11.86	Runcorn		H	L	1-2aet	Lissaman (p)
1990-91	GMVC 1	17.11.90	Wycombe W	GMVC	H	D	1-1	Cavell
	1r	21.11.90	Wycombe W		A	L	0-4	

BOTWELL MISSION (HAYES)

Formed 1909 as Botwell Mission, renamed Hayes in 1930. **First entered FA Cup:** 1919. Also see Hayes

1927-28	Spt 1	30.11.27	Peterborough & Fletton	SL	H	L	3-4	Treasure 3

AFC BOURNEMOUTH

Formed 1899. Played as Boscombe FC 1899-1923 and played against Bournemouth FC in the FA Cup. Became Bournemouth and Boscombe Athletic in 1923 and changed name to AFC Bournemouth in 1971. **Best FA Cup performance:** 6th round, 1957. **Record FA Cup Win:** 11-0 vs Margate 1st round, 20.11.1971 when Ted MacDougall scored an FA Cup (competition proper) record of nine goals in one match. **Record FA Cup Defeat:** 0-7 vs Sheffield Wednesday, 4th round, 23.1.1932 and vs Burnley 3rd round replay, 25.1.1966

as Boscombe FC

1909-10   Hants P **Bournemouth Gasworks** (A) 0-0; Pr **Bournemouth Gas.** (A) 2-1; 3q **Poole** (A) 2-3

1910-11   Hants 1q **Weymouth** (A) 4-3; 2q **Poole** (A) 0-0; 2qr **Poole** (A) 4-1; 3q **Torquay T** (A) 0-1

1911-12   Hants *did not enter*

1912-13   Hants P **Portland** (H) 6-0; 1q **Gosport U** (A) 1-1; 1qr **Gosport** (H) 7-1; 2q **Basingstoke** (H) 3-1; 3q **1st Kings Rifles** (H) 0-0;
3qr **1st Kings Rifles** (A) 0-1

1913-14   Hants P **Royal Engineers, Aldershot** (A) 2-0; 1q **Cowes** (A) 3-2; 2q **Bournemouth FC** (H) 0-1

1914-15   Hants P RC **Artillery** walkover; 1q **Bournemouth Tramways** (H) 3-0; 2q **Thorneycrofts Ath** (A) 6-1; 3q **Cowes** (A) 1-0;
4q **Welton R** (A) 2-1; 5q **Brentford** (H) 0-0; 5qr **Brentford** (A) 1-0; 6q **Bristol R** (A) 0-3

1919-20   Hants P **Poole & St Marys** (H) 9-0; 1q **Basingstoke** (A) 0-1

1920-21   SL   1q **Blandford** (H) 1-1; 1qr **Blandford** (A) 1-2

1921-22   SL   P **Royal Artillery Gosport** (H) 2-0; 1q **Bournemouth FC** (A) 0-0; 1qr **Bournemouth FC** (H) 6-0; 2q **Thorneycroft Woolston** (H) 1-0;
3q **Harland & Wolffs** (A) 3-2; 4q **Torquay U** (A) 1-0; 5q **Swansea T** (A) 0-5

1922-23   SL   P **Blandford** (H) 3-0; 1q **Bournemouth Tramways** (A) 2-1; 2q **Sholing Ath** (H) 2-1; 3q **Gosport Ath** (H) 4-0; 4q **Exeter C** (A) 0-0;
4qr **Exeter C** (H) 1-3

as Bournemouth & Boscombe Athletic

1923-24   3S   P **Portsea Gas Company** – *scratched*

1924-25   3S   4q **Yeovil & Petters U** (A) 2-3

1925-26	3S	1	28.11.25	Merthyr T	3S	H	W	3-0	Eyre, Maidment, Stringfellow
		2	12.12.25	Brentford	3S	A	W	2-1	Stringfellow, Eyre
		3	9.1.26	Reading	3S	H	W	2-0	Eyre 2
		4	30.1.26	Bolton W	D1	H	D	2-2	Stringfellow, Roberts
		4r	3.2.26	Bolton W		A	L	2-6	Butt, Eyre
1926-27	3S	1	27.11.26	Swindon T	3S	H	D	1-1	Hayward
		1r	29.11.26	Swindon T		A	W	4-3	Eyre 2, Taylor 2
		2	11.12.26	Bristol C	3S	A	D	1-1	Stringfellow
		2r	15.12.26	Bristol C		H	W	2-0	Eyre 2
		3	8.1.27	Liverpool	D1	H	D	1-1	Taylor
		3r	12.1.27	Liverpool		A	L	1-4	Eyre
1927-28	3S	1	26.11.27	Coventry C	3S	A	D	2-2	Pike 2
		1r	30.11.27	Coventry C		H	W	2-0	Pike, Eyre
		2	10.12.27	Bristol R	3S	H	W	6-1	Taylor 2, Clifford 2, Miles, Eyre
		3	14.1.28	Sheffield W	D1	A	L	0-3	
1928-29	3S	1	24.11.28	Poole T	SL	A	W	4-1	Clifford, Eyre 2, Cherrett

Season	Div	Rnd	Date	Opponent	Lg	H/A	W/D/L	Score	Scorers
		2	8.12.28	Guildford C	SL	A	W	5-1	Hayward, Eyre 4
		3	12.1.29	Accrington Stanley	3N	A	D	1-1	Clifford
		3r	16.1.29	Accrington Stanley		H	W	2-0	Clifford, Bryce
		4	26.1.29	Watford	3S	H	W	6-4	Bryce, Cherrett Eyre 3, Clifford
		5	16.2.29	West Ham	D1	H	D	1-1	Graham
		5r	20.2.29	West Ham		A	L	1-3	Hayward (p)
1929-30	3S	1	30.11.29	Torquay U		H	W	2-0	Beswick, Eyre
		2	14.12.29	Caernarfon	Welsh	A	D	1-1	Beswick
		2r	18.12.29	Caernarfon		H	W	5-2	Edwards og, Eyre 2, Boswick, Price
		3	11.1.30	Fulham	3S	A	D	1-1	Eyre
		3r	15.1.30	Fulham		H	L	0-2	
1930-31	3S	1	29.11.30	Walsall		A	L	0-1	
1931-32	3S	1	28.11.31	Northfleet	KL	H	D	1-1	White
		1r	2.12.31	Northfleet		A	W	1-0	Webb
		2	12.12.31	Blyth Spartans	NEL	H	W	1-0	Hayward
		3	9.1.32	Halifax T	3N	A	W	3-1	Beswick 2, Eyre
		4	23.1.32	Sheffield W	D1	A	L	0-7	
1932-33	3S	1	26.11.32	Torquay U	3S	A	D	0-0	
		1r	30.11.32	Torquay U		H	D	2-2aet	Eyre 2
		1 2r	5.12.32	Torquay U at Ashton Gate			L	2-3	Tennant og, Russell
1933-34	3S	1	25.11.33	Hayes	AL	H	W	3-0	Surtees, White 2
		2	9.12.33	Tranmere R	3N	H	L	2-4	Russell 2
1934-35	3S	1	24.11.34	Aldershot	3S	A	L	0-4	
1935-36	3S	1	30.11.35	Walthamstow Ave	AL	A	D	1-1	Parris
		1r	4.12.35	Walthamstow Ave		H	W	8-1	Chalmers 3, Parris 3, Barrow, Burgin
		2	14.12.35	Barrow	3N	H	W	5-2	Parris 3, Barrow, Riley
		3	11.1.36	Bradford C	D2	A	L	0-1	
1936-37	3S	1	28.11.36	Harwich & Parkestone	ECL	H	W	5-1	Marsden 2, Harris, Riley, Kilcar
		2	12.12.36	Mansfield T	3N	A	W	3-0	Parris 2, Riley
		3	16.1.37	Everton	D1	A	L	0-5	
1937-38	3S	1	27.11.37	Dartford	SL	H	D	0-0	
		1r	1.12.37	Dartford		A	W	6-0	Millar, Chalmers 2, Collins og, Whittam 2
		2	11.12.37	Newport Co	3S	A	L	1-2	Miller
1938-39	3S	1	26.11.38	Bristol C	3S	H	W	2-1	Elliott, Langley
		2	10.12.38	Bristol R	3S	A	W	3-0	Elliott, Langley 2
		3	17.1.39	Leeds U	D1	A	L	1-3	Fletcher
1945-46	3S	1 1L	17.11.45	Lovells Athletic	Welsh	A	L	1-4	Thomas
		1 2L	24.11.45	Lovells Athletic		H	W	3-2	Paton, J.Thomas 2
1946-47	3S	1	30.11.46	Exeter C	3S	H	W	4-2	Gallacher, Tunnicliffe, Kirkham (p), Paton
		2	14.12.46	Aldershot	3S	H	W	4-2	Tagg, Kirkham 2, Mcdonald
		3	11.1.47	Derby Co	D1	H	L	0-2	
1947-48	3S	1	29.11.47	Guildford C	SL	H	W	2-0	Milligan, McDonald
		2	13.12.47	Bradford C	3N	H	W	1-0	Blair
		3	10.1.48	Wolverhampton W	D1	H	L	1-2	Milligan
1948-49	3S	3	8.1.49	Manchester U	D1	A	L	0-6	
1949-50	3S	3	7.1.50	Bradford PA	D2	A	W	1-0	Cross
		4	28.1.50	Northampton T	3S	H	D	1-1	Weigh
		4r	2.2.50	Northampton T		A	L	1-2	Cross
1950-51	3S	1	25.11.50	Colchester U	3S	H	W	1-0	Boxshall
		2	9.12.50	Aldershot	3S	A	L	0-3	
1951-52	3S	1	24.11.51	Southend U	3S	A	L	1-6	Stroud
1952-53	3S	1	22.11.52	Ipswich T	3S	A	D	2-2	Cheney, Harrison
		1r	26.11.52	Ipswich T		H	D	2-2aet	Rees og, Cross
		1 2r	1.12.52	Ipswich T at Highbury			L	2-3	Eyre 2
1953-54	3S	1	21.11.53	Southampton	3S	A	D	1-1	Fidler
		1r	25.11.53	Southampton		H	W	3-1	Fidler, Stephens, Cheney
		2	12.12.53	Scunthorpe U	3N	A	L	0-1	
1954-55	3S	1	20.11.54	Barnstaple	WL	A	W	4-1	Hunt, Harrison 2, Siddall
		2	11.12.54	Oldham Ath	3N	H	W	1-0	Allen
		3	8.1.55	WBA	D1	H	L	0-1	
1955-56	3S	1	19.11.55	Reading	3S	A	L	0-1	
1956-57	3S	1	17.11.56	Burton Albion	BDL	H	W	8-0	Wright og, Lyons, Bedford, Norris 3, Newsham 2
		2	8.12.56	Swindon T	3S	A	W	1-0	Cutler
		3	5.1.57	Accrington Stanley	3N	H	W	2-0	Norris, Bedford
		4	26.1.57	Wolverhampton W	D1	A	W	1-0	Cutler
		5	16.2.57	Tottenham H	D1	H	W	3-1	Norris, Newsham, Stiffle
		6	2.3.57	Manchester U	D1	H	L	1-2	Bedford

BOURNEMOUTH

1957-58	3S	1	16.11.57	Oswestry T	BDL	A	W	5-1	Dowsett, Bedford 3, Burgess
		2	7.12.57	Northampton T	3S	A	L	1-4	Norris
1958-59	D3	1	15.11.58	Tooting & Mitcham	IL	A	L	1-3	Burgess
1959-60	D3	1	14.11.59	Walthamstow Ave	IL	A	W	3-2	Evans, Brown, Bumstead
		2	5.12.59	Enfield	AL	A	W	5-1	Bumstead 3, Dowsett, Arnott
		3	9.1.60	York C	D3	H	W	1-0	Southren
		4	30.1.60	Bradford C	D3	A	L	1-3	Lawlor og
1960-61	D3	1	5.11.60	Exeter C	D4	A	D	1-1	Bumstead
		1r	9.11.60	Exeter C		H	W	3-1	Bolton, Bumstead, Evans
		2	26.11.60	Yeovil T	SL	H	W	3-1	Bolton, Weller, Smith
		3	7.1.61	Burnley	D1	A	L	0-1	
1961-62	D3	1	4.11.61	Margate	SL	H	L	0-3	
1962-63	D3	1	3.11.62	Coventry C	D3	A	L	0-1	
1963-64	D3	1	16.11.63	Bristol R	D3	H	L	1-3	Crickmore
1964-65	D3	1	14.11.64	Gravesend & N	SL	H	W	7-0	Hodgson 3, Bolton, Bumstead, Coxon, Groves
		2	5.12.64	Bristol C	D3	H	L	0-3	
1965-66	D3	1	13.11.65	Weymouth	SL	H	D	0-0	
		1r	17.11.65	Weymouth		A	W	4-1	Crickmore, Archer (p), Coughlin 2
		2	4.12.65	Bath C	SL	H	W	5-3	Naylor, Coughlin 3, Hodgson
		3	22.1.66	Burnley	D1	H	D	1-1	Archer
		3r	25.1.66	Burnley		A	L	0-7	
1966-67	D3	1	26.11.66	Welton R	WL	H	W	3-0	Weller 2, Hold
		2	7.1.67	QPR	D3	A	L	0-2	
1967-68	D3	1	9.12.67	Northampton T	D3	H	W	2-0	Bolton (p), Hole
		2	6.1.68	Walthamstow Ave	IL	A	W	3-1	K.White, Pound 2
		3	27.1.68	Liverpool	D1	H	D	0-0	
		3r	30.1.68	Liverpool		A	L	1-4	Hughes og
1968-69	D3	1	16.11.68	Bury Town	Met	A	D	0-0	
		1r	20.11.68	Bury Town		H	W	3-0	Hold, Bolton, Heffer og
		2	7.12.68	Bristol R	D3	H	D	0-0	
		2r	10.12.68	Bristol R		A	L	0-1	
1969-70	D3	1	15.11.69	Luton T	D3	H	D	1-1	Hartley
		1r	18.11.69	Luton T		A	L	1-3	White
1970-71	D4	1	21.11.70	Oxford C	IL	A	D	1-1	MacDougall
		1r	23.11.70	Oxford C		H	W	8-1	MacDougall 6, Longhorn, Rowles
		2	12.12.70	Yeovil T	SL	H	L	0-1	

as AFC Bournemouth

1971-72	D3	1	20.11.71	Margate	SL	H	W	11-0	MacDougall 9 (1p), Cave, Machin
		2	11.12.71	Southend U	D4	H	W	2-0	Boyer, MacDougall
		3	15.1.72	Walsall	D3	A	L	0-1	
1972-73	D3	1	18.11.72	Cambridge U	D4	H	W	5-1	Clark 2, Gibson, Groves, Boyer
		2	9.12.72	Colchester U	D4	H	D	0-0	
		2r	11.12.72	Colchester U		A	W	2-0	Clark, Boyer
		3	13.1.73	Newcastle U	D1	A	L	0-2	
1973-74	D3	1	24.11.73	Charlton A	D3	H	W	1-0	Boyer
		2	15.12.73	Watford	D3	A	W	1-0	Cave
		3	5.1.74	Orient	D2	A	L	1-2	Powell
1974-75	D3	1	23.11.74	Southwick	SCL	H	W	5-0	Goddard 3, Greenhalgh, Hague
		2	14.12.74	Wycombe W	IL	A	D	0-0	
		2r	18.12.74	Wycombe W		H	L	1-2	Goddard
1975-76	D4	1	22.11.75	Sutton U	IL	A	D	1-1	Ashworth
		1r	26.11.75	Sutton U		H	W	1-0	Ashworth
		2	13.12.75	Hereford U	D3	H	D	2-2	Ashworth, Goddard
		2r	17.12.75	Hereford U		A	A	0-2	
1976-77	D4	1	20.11.76	Newport Co	D4	H	D	0-0	
		1r	23.11.76	Newport Co		A	L	0-3	
1977-78	D4	1	26.11.77	Colchester U	D3	A	D	1-1	Howarth
		1r	29.11.77	Colchester U		H	D	0-0aet	
		1 2r	5.12.77	Colchester U		H	L	1-4	Barton
1978-79	D4	1	25.11.78	Hitchin T	IL	H	W	2-1	Massey (p), M.Butler
		2	16.12.78	Wimbledon	D4	A	D	1-1	MacDougall
		2r	28.12.78	Wimbledon		H	L	1-2aet	MacDougall
1979-80	D4	1	24.11.79	Peterborough U	D4	A	W	2-1	Chard og, Evanson
		2	15.12.79	Colchester U	D3	A	L	0-1	
1980-81	D4	1	22.11.80	Wycombe W	IL	A	W	3-0	Massey, Morgan 2
		2	13.12.80	Charlton A	D3	A	L	1-2	Webb
1981-82	D4	1	21.11.81	Reading	D3	H	W	1-0	Funnell

BOURNEMOUTH

		2	12.12.81	**Dorchester T**	SL	A	D	1-1	Funnell
		2r	15.12.81	**Dorchester T**		H	W	2-1aet	Crawford, Williams
		3	2.1.82	**Oxford U**	D3	H	L	0-2	
1982-83	D3	1	20.11.82	**Southend U**	D3	H	L	0-2	
1983-84	D3	1	19.11.83	**Walsall**	D3	H	W	4-0	Thompson, Beck, Morgan, Lee
		2	13.12.83	**Windsor & Eton**	IL	A	D	0-0	
		2r	19.12.83	**Windsor & Eton**		H	W	2-0	Beck, Thompson
		3	7.1.84	**Manchester U**	D1	H	W	2-0	Graham, Thompson
		4	31.1.84	**Middlesbrough**	D2	A	L	0-2	
1984-85	D3	1	17.11.84	**Kettering T**	APL	A	D	0-0	
		1r	20.11.84	**Kettering T**		H	W	3-2	Savage, Russell, Thrower og
		2	8.12.84	**Dartford**	APL	A	D	1-1	Savage
		2r	11.12.84	**Dartford**		H	W	4-0	Williams, Savage (p), Russell, Rafferty
		3	5.1.84	**Manchester U**	D1	A	L	0-3	
1985-86	D3	1	16.11.85	**Dartford**	APL	H	D	0-0	
		1r	19.11.85	**Dartford**		A	W	2-0	Clarke, Newson
		2	7.12.85	**Dagenham**	APL	H	W	4-1	O'Driscoll, Thompson, Brown, Clarke
		3	4.1.86	**Wigan A**	D3	A	L	0-3	
1986-87	D3	1	15.11.86	**Fareham T**	SL	H	W	7-2	Aylott, Richards 2, Puckett 3, Davies og
		2	6.12.86	**Orient**	D4	H	L	0-1	
1987-88	D2	3	9.1.88	**Brighton & HA**	D3	A	L	0-2	
1988-89	D2	3	7.1.89	**Blackpool**	D3	A	W	1-0	Blissett
		4	28.1.89	**Hartlepool U**	D4	A	D	1-1	Blissett (p)
		4r	31.1.89	**Hartlepool U**		H	W	5-2	Baker og, Stokes og, Newson, Morrell, Cooke
		5	18.2.89	**Manchester U**	D1	H	D	1-1	Aylott
		5r	22.2.89	**Manchester U**		A	L	0-1	
1989-90	D2	3	6.1.90	**Sheffield U**	D2	A	L	0-2	
1990-91	D3	1	17.11.90	**Gillingham**	D4	H	W	2-1	Teale, Jones
		2	8.12.90	**Hayes**	IL	H	W	1-0	Brooks
		3	5.1.91	**Chester**	D3	A	W	3-2	Jones 2, Ekoku
		4	26.1.91	**Portsmouth**	D2	A	L	1-5	Fereday
1991-92	D3	1	16.11.91	**Bromsgrove R**	SL	H	W	3-1	Bond, Mundee 2
		2	7.12.91	**Brentford**	D3	H	W	2-1	Quinn 2
		3	4.1.92	**Newcastle U**	D2	H	D	0-0	
		3r	14.1.92	**Newcastle U**		A	–	0-0	
				abandoned after 17 minutes – fog					
		3 2r	22.1.92	**Newcastle U**		A	D	2-2aet	Wood, Bond
				Bournemouth won 4-3 on penalties					
		4	5.2.92	**Ipswich T**	D2	A	L	0-3	
1992-93	D2	1	14.11.92	**Barnet**	D3	H	D	0-0	
		1r	25.11.92	**Barnet**		A	W	2-1	Lovell, Mundee
		2	5.12.92	**Cheltenham T**	SL	A	D	1-1	Shearer
		2r	16.12.92	**Cheltenham T**		H	W	3-0	Mundee, McGorry, Morgan
		3	2.1.93	**Blackburn R**	PL	A	L	1-3	Ekoku

BOURNEMOUTH ROVERS

Formed 1873. Played at Dean Park and Malmesbury Park, Bournemouth

1884-85		1	1.11.84	**Old Westminsters**		A	L	0-6	
1885-86		1		**Old Etonians**			*scratched*		
1886-87		1		**Chatham**			*scratched*		

BRADFORD CITY

Formed 1903. Originally a Rugby League club known as Manningham. **FA Cup Winners:** 1911, first winners of new trophy, made in Bradford. **Record FA Cup Win:** 11-3 vs Walker Celtic, 1.12.1937. **Record FA Cup Defeat:** 0-5 vs Burnley (1960); Newcastle U (1963), Tottenham (1970)

1903-04	D2		1q Rockingham Colliery (H) 6-1; 2q **Mirfield U** (H) 3-1; 3q **Worksop** (H) 5-0; 4q **Chesterfield** (A) 1-2						
1904-05	D2		6q **Sunderland WE** (H) 9-0						
		1	14.1.05	**Millwall A**	SL	H	L	1-4	Conlin
1905-06	D2		Int **Darlington** (A) 4-0						
		1	13.1.06	**Barrow**	LC	H	W	3-2	Smith 2, Bennett
		2	3.2.06	**Wolverhampton W**	D1	H	W	5-0	Clarke, McGeachan, Robinson, Smith, Conlin
		3	24.2.06	**Everton**	D1	A	L	0-1	
1906-07	D2	1	12.1.07	**Reading**	SL	A	W	2-0	Bartlett, Hall
		2	2.2.07	**Accrington S**	LC	H	W	1-0	Penman
		3	23.2.07	**Liverpool**	D1	A	L	0-1	

BRADFORD CITY

1907-08	D2	1	11.1.08	**Wolverhampton W**	D2	H	D	1-1	Handley
		1r	15.1.08	**Wolverhampton W**		A	L	0-1	
1908-09	D1	1	19.1.09	**Workington**	NEL	H	W	2-0	Robinson, Hanger
		2	6.2.09	**WBA**	D2	A	W	2-1	Pennington og, Hardman
		3	20.2.09	**Sunderland**	D1	H	L	0-1	
1909-10	D1	1	15.1.10	**Notts Co**	D1	H	W	4-2	O'Rourke 2, Bond, Speirs
		2	5.2.10	**Blackburn R**	D1	H	L	1-2	O'Rourke
1910-11	D1	1	14.1.11	**New Brompton**	SL	A	W	1-0	Bond
		2	4.2.11	**Norwich C**	SL	H	W	2-1	Speirs, Logan
		3	25.2.11	**Grimsby T**	ML	H	W	1-0	Bond
		4	11.3.11	**Burnley**	D2	H	W	1-0	Thompson
		SF	25.3.11	**Blackburn R**	D1	H	W	3-0	O'Rourke, Devine, Thompson
		F	22.4.11	**Newcastle U**	D1		D	0-0	
			played at Crystal Palace						
		Fr	26.4.11	**NEWCASTLE U**			W	1-0	Speirs
			played at Old Trafford						
1911-12	D1	1	13.1.12	**QPR**	SL	A	D	0-0	
		1r	18.1.12	**QPR**		H	W	4-0	Walden 3, Logan
		2	3.2.12	**Chelsea**	D2	H	W	2-0	Bond, Logan
		3	24.2.12	**Bradford PA**	D2	A	W	1-0	O'Rourke
		4	9.3.12	**Barnsley**	D2	A	D	0-0	
		4r	13.3.12	**Barnsley** at Elland Road			D	0-0aet	
		4 2r	21.3.12	**Barnsley** at Bramall Lane			L	2-3aet	Speirs, Devine
1912-13	D1	1	11.1.13	**Newcastle U**	D1	A		0-0	
			abandoned 45 minutes – gale						
			16.1.13	**Newcastle U**		A	L	0-1	
1913-14	D1	1	10.1.14	**Woolwich Arsenal**	D1	H	W	2-0	Bond 2
		2	31.1.14	**Millwall A**	SL	A	L	0-1	
1914-15	D1	1	9.1.15	**Darlington**	NEL	A	W	1-0	Shepherd
		2	30.1.15	**Middlesbrough**	D1	H	W	1-0	Bond
		3	20.2.15	**Norwich C**	SL	H	D	1-1aet	Shepherd
		3r	27.2.15	**Norwich C**		A	D	0-0aet	
		3 2r	3.3.15	**Norwich C** at Lincoln			W	2-0	McDonald, Bond (p)
		4	6.3.15	**Everton**	D1	H	L	0-2	
1919-20	D1	1	10.1.20	**Portsmouth**		H	–	2-2	Bond, McIlvenny
			abandoned 63 minutes – waterlogged pitch						
			17.1.20	**Portsmouth**		H	W	2-0	Fox, Goldthorpe
		2	31.1.20	**Sheffield U**	D1	H	W	2-1	Goldthorpe, Logan
		3	21.2.20	**Preston NE**	D1	A	W	3-0	Bond 2 (1p), Goldthorpe
		4	6.3.20	**Bristol C**	D2	A	L	0-2	
1920-21	D1	1	8.1.21	**Barnsley**	D2	H	W	3-1	Howson, Bond (p), Marsh
		2	29.1.21	**Tottenham H**	D1	A	L	0-4	
1921-22	D1	1	7.1.22	**Walsall**	3N	A	D	3-3	Howson 2, Hibbert
		1r	11.1.22	**Walsall**		H	W	4-0	Hibbert, Howson 2, Logan
		2	28.1.22	**Notts Co**	D2	H	D	1-1	Bond (p)
		2r	1.2.22	**Notts Co**		A	D	0-0aet	
		2 3r	6.2.22	**Notts Co** at Bramall Lane			L	0-1	
1922-23	D2	1	13.1.23	**Manchester U**	D2	H	D	1-1	Duckett (p)
		1r	17.1.23	**Manchester U**		A	L	0-2	
1923-24	D2	1	12.1.24	**Liverpool**	D1	A	L	1-2	Logan
1924-25	D2	1	10.1.25	**Derby Co**	D2	A	W	1-0	Rhodes
		2	31.1.25	**Barnsley**	D2	A	W	3-0	Cheetham 2, Rigby
		3	21.2.25	**Southampton**	D2	A	L	0-2	
1925-26	D2	3	9.1.26	**Nottingham F**	D2	A	L	0-1	
1926-27	D2	3	8.1.27	**Derby Co**	D1	H	L	2-6	Cheetham, McMillan
1927-28	3N	1	26.11.27	**Workington**	NEL	H	W	6-0	Cairns, Moore, Richardson 2, Burkinshaw 2
		2	10.12.27	**Rothertham U**	3N	H	L	2-3	Harvey, Richardson
1928-29	3N	1	24.11.28	**Doncaster R**	3N	H	W	4-1	Moore 3, Randall
		2	8.12.28	**Tranmere R**	3N	H	W	1-0	Moore
		3	12.1.29	**Stockport Co**	3N	H	W	2-0	Mitchell, Barkas
		4	26.1.29	**Portsmouth**	D1	A	L	0-2	
1929-30	D2	3	11.1.30	**Southampton**	D2	H	W	4-1	Cairns, Cochrane 2, Moore
		4	25.1.30	**Wrexham**	3N	A	D	0-0	
		4r	27.1.30	**Wrexham**		H	W	2-1	Cochrane, Whitehurst
		5	15.2.30	**Huddersfield T**	D1	A	L	1-2	Cochrane
1930-31	D2	3	14.1.31	**Middlesbrough**	D1	A	D	1-1	Moore
		3r	19.1.31	**Middlesbrough**		H	W	2-1	Scrivens, Peel

Season	Div	Rd	Date	Opponent		Venue	Result	Score	Scorers
		4	24.1.31	Wolverhampton W	D2	H	D	0-0	
		4r	28.1.31	Wolverhampton W		A	L	2-4	Cairns 2
1931-32	D2	3	9.1.32	Birmingham	D1	A	L	0-1	
1932-33	D2	3	14.1.33	Aston Villa	D1	H	D	2-2	Watmough, Bauld
		3r	18.1.33	Aston Villa		A	L	1-2	Hallows
1933-34	D2	3	13.1.34	West Ham	D2	A	L	2-3	Hallows, Spence
1934-35	D2	3	12.1.35	Aston Villa	D1	A	W	3-1	Hallows, Keetley 2
		4	26.1.35	Stockport Co	3N	H	D	0-0	
		4r	31.1.35	Stockport Co		A	L	2-3aet	Hallows, Spence
1935-36	D2	3	11.1.36	Bournemouth	3S	H	W	1-0	Jeffries
		4	3.2.36	Blackburn R	D1	H	W	3-1	Travis 2, Hallows
		5	15.2.36	Derby Co	D1	H	L	0-1	
1936-37	D2	3	16.1.37	York C	3N	H	D	2-2	Travis, Gallon
		3r	20.1.37	York C		A	L	0-1	
1937-38	3N	1	27.11.37	Walker Celtic	NEL	A	D	1-1	Deakin
		1r	1.12.37	Walker Celtic		H	W	11-3	Deakin 4 (1p), Bartholomew 4, Bagley, Whittingham, Cooke
		2	11.12.37	Wrexham	3N	A	W	2-1	Bartholomew 2
		3	8.1.38	Chesterfield	D2	H	D	1-1	Deakin
		3r	12.1.38	Chesterfield		A	D	1-1aet	Bartholomew
		3 2r	17.1.38	Chesterfield at Bramall Lane			L	0-2	
1938-39	3N	1	26.11.38	Chester	3N	A	L	1-3	Hinsley
1945-46	3N	1 1L	17.11.45	Notts Co	3S	A	D	2-2	Murphy 2
		1 2L	24.11.45	Notts Co		H	L	1-2	Pickles
1946-47	3N	1	30.11.46	Gateshead	3N	A	L	1-3	G.Murphy
1947-48	3N	1	29.11.47	Gateshead	3N	H	W	3-1	McGill, Neilson 2
		2	13.12.47	Bournemouth	3S	A	L	0-1	
1948-49	3N	1	4.12.48	Doncaster R	3N	H	W	4-3	Brown, Shearer 2 (1p), Hawksworth
		2	11.12.48	New Brighton	3N	H	D	0-0	
		2r	18.12.48	New Brighton		A	L	0-1	
1949-50	3N	1	26.11.49	Fleetwood	LC	H	W	9-0	Carr 4, W.Price 3 (1p), McGill, Ward
		2	10.12.49	Southport	3N	A	L	1-2	W.Price
1950-51	3N	1	25.11.50	Oldham A	3N	H	D	2-2	McGill, W.Price
		1r	28.11.50	Oldham A		A	L	1-2	Carr
1951-52	3N	1	24.11.51	Carlisle U	3N	H	W	6-1	Millar 2, Carr 2, Williamson (p), Twentyman og
		2	15.12.51	Bradford PA	3N	A	L	2-3	Millar, Greenhoff
1952-53	3N	1	22.11.52	Rhyl A	CC	H	W	4-0	Close 2, Ward 2
		2	6.12.52	Ipswich T	3S	H	D	1-1	Close
		2r	10.12.52	Ipswich T		A	L	1-5	Williamson
1953-54	3N	1	21.11.53	Crewe Alex	3N	A	D	0-0	
		1r	25.11.53	Crewe Alex		H	L	0-1	
1954-55	3N	1	20.11.54	Mansfield T	3N	H	W	3-1	Robb (p), Squires 2
		2	11.12.54	Merthyr Tydfil	SL	H	W	7-1	Tunnicliffe 2, Chapman 2, Duthie 2, Chew
		3	8.1.55	Brentford	3S	A	D	1-1	Lambert
		3r	12.1.55	Brentford		H	D	2-2aet	Robb, Bakes
		3 2r	20.1.55	Brentford at Highbury			L	0-1	
1955-56	3N	1	19.11.55	Oldham A	3N	H	W	3-1	Walsh, Kelly 2
		2	10.12.55	Worksop T	ML	H	D	2-2	Webb, Kelly
		2r	15.12.55	Worksop T		A	L	0-1	
1956-57	3N	1	17.11.56	Derby Co	3N	A	L	1-2	Simm
1957-58	3N	1	16.11.57	Scarborough	ML	H	W	6-0	Samuels, D.Jackson, Webb, Marshall 3
		2	7.12.57	Chester	3N	A	D	3-3	D.Jackson 2, Samuels
		2r	11.12.57	Chester		H	W	3-1	Boyle, Samuels, Lawlor
		3	4.1.58	Scunthorpe U	3N	A	L	0-1	
1958-59	D3	1	15.11.58	Mansfield T	D3	A	W	4-3	D.Jackson, McCole 3
		2	6.12.58	Bradford PA	D4	A	W	2-0	McCole 2
		3	10.1.59	Brighton & HA	D2	A	W	2-0	D.Jackson, Stokes
		4	24.1.59	Preston NE	D1	A	L	2-3	McCole, Lawlor
1959-60	D3	1	14.11.59	Barnsley	D3	A	D	3-3	Stokes 2, Reid
		1r	18.11.59	Barnsley		H	W	2-1	Rea, Stokes
		2	5.12.59	Rochdale	D4	A	D	1-1	Stokes
		2r	9.12.59	Rochdale		H	W	2-1	Stokes 2
		3	9.1.60	Everton	D1	H	W	3-0	D.Jackson, Reid, Stokes
		4	30.1.60	Bournemouth	D3	H	W	3-1	D.Jackson, Stokes 2
		5	20.2.60	Burnley	D1	H	D	2-2	Webb, Stokes
		5r	23.2.60	Burnley		A	L	0-5	
1960-61	D3	1	5.11.60	Scarborough	NCo	H	D	0-0	
		1r	9.11.60	Scarborough		A	W	3-1aet	Hockey, Smith 2

106

Season	Div	Rd	Date	Opponent	Comp	H/A	Res	Score	Scorers
		2	26.11.60	Barnsley	D3	H	L	1-2	Webb
1961-62	D4	1	4.11.61	York C	D4	H	W	1-0	Layne
		2	25.11.61	Hull C	D3	A	W	2-0	Layne, Webb
		3	6.1.62	Arsenal	D1	A	L	0-3	
1962-63	D4	1	3.11.62	Oldham A	D4	A	W	5-2	P.Bircumshaw 3, Devitt, Harland (p)
		2	24.11.62	Gateshead	NRL	H	W	3-2	Harland, McCole, P.Bircumshaw
		3	7.3.63	Newcastle U	D2	H	L	1-6	Kelly
1963-64	D4	1	16.11.63	Port Vale	D3	H	L	1-2	D.Price
1964-65	D4	1	14.11.64	Scarborough	ML	A	L	0-1	
1965-66	D4	1	13.11.65	Darlington	D4	A	L	2-3	Ellam, Rodon
1966-67	D4	1	26.11.66	Port Vale	D4	H	L	1-2	Hall
1967-68	D4	1	9.12.67	Wrexham	D4	H	W	7-1	Bannister 2, Aimson 2, Rackstraw, Swallow, Hall
		2	6.1.68	Bury	D3	H	L	2-3	Bannister, Hall
1968-69	D4	1	16.11.68	Chester	D4	H	L	1-2	Bannister
1969-70	D3	1	15.11.69	Grimsby T	D4	H	W	2-1	Leighton, Corner
		2	6.12.69	Lincoln C	D4	H	W	3-0	Middleton 2, Hall
		3	3.1.70	Tottenham H	D1	H	D	2-2	England og, Stowell
		3r	7.1.70	Tottenham H		A	L	0-5	
1970-71	D3	1	21.11.70	Macclesfield T	NPL	H	W	3-2	Bannister (p), Middleton, Corner
		2	12.12.70	Lincoln C	D4	A	D	2-2	Bannister, Corner
		2r	16.12.70	Lincoln C		H	D	2-2aet	Corner, Bannister
		2 2r	21.12.70	Lincoln C at Doncaster			L	1-4	Corner
1971-72	D3	1	20.11.71	Wrexham	D3	A	L	1-5	O'Neill
1972-73	D4	1	18.11.72	Grantham	SL	H	W	3-0	Ingram, Oates, Johnston
		2	9.12.72	Tranmere R	D3	H	W	2-1	Gilliver, Brown
		3	13.1.73	Blackpool	D2	H	W	2-1	Ingram 2
		4	3.2.73	Arsenal	D1	A	L	0-2	
1973-74	D4	1	24.11.73	Workington	D4	H	W	2-0	Gilliver, Ingram (p)
		2	15.12.73	Barnsley	D4	A	D	1-1	Ingram
		2r	19.12.73	Barnsley		H	W	2-1	Cooke, Brown
		3	6.1.74	Alvechurch	WMRL	H	W	4-2	Ham, Baker, Oates, Ingram (p)
		4	26.1.74	Luton T	D2	A	L	0-3	
1974-75	D4	1	23.11.74	Hartlepool	D4	A	L	0-1	
1975-76	D4	1	22.11.75	Chesterfield	D3	H	W	1-0	Hutchins
		2	13.12.75	Rotherham U	D3	A	W	3-0	Cooke, Ingram 2
		3	3.1.76	Shrewsbury T	D3	A	W	2-1	Cooke, Hutchins
		4	24.1.76	Tooting & Mitcham	IL	H	W	3-1	Hutchins 2, Middleton
		5	23.2.76	Norwich C	D1	A	W	2-1	Hutchins, McGinley
		6	6.3.76	Southampton	D2	H	L	0-1	
1976-77	D4	1	20.11.76	Walsall	D3	A	D	0-0	
		1r	24.11.76	Walsall		H	L	0-2	
1977-78	D3	1	26.11.77	Crewe Alex	D4	H	L	0-1	
1978-79	D4	1	25.11.78	Port Vale	D4	H	W	1-0	Dolan (p)
		2	16.12.78	Stockport Co	D4	A	L	2-4	Cooke, Dolan
1979-80	D4	1	24.11.79	Brandon U	NAll	A	W	3-0	Gallagher, Martinez, McNiven
			played at Spennymoor						
		2	15.12.79	Darlington	D4	A	W	1-0	Baines
		3	5.1.80	Carlisle U	D3	A	L	2-3	Baines, Dolan (p)
1980-81	D4	1	22.11.80	Port Vale	D4	A	L	2-4	Wood, Chapman
1981-82	D4	1	21.11.81	Scunthorpe U	D4	A	L	0-1	
1982-83	D3	1	20.11.82	Port Vale	D4	A	W	1-0	Campbell
		2	11.12.82	Mansfield T	D4	A	D	1-1	Gray
		2r	15.12.82	Mansfield T		H	W	3-2	Campbell, Lester, McNiven
		3	8.1.83	Barnsley	D2	H	L	0-1	
1983-84	D3	1	19.11.83	Wigan A	D3	H	D	0-0	
		1r	28.11.83	Wigan A		A	L	2-4	Hawley, Haire
1984-85	D3	1	17.11.84	Tow Law Town	NL	H	W	7-2	McCall, Hendrie, Campbell 2, Goodman 3
		2	8.12.84	Mansfield T	D4	H	W	2-1	Campbell, Abbott
		3	5.1.85	Telford U	APL	A	L	1-2	Haire
1985-86	D2	3	4.1.86	Ipswich T	D1	A	D	4-4	Goodman, Abbott 2 (1p), Hendrie
		3r	13.1.86	Ipswich T at Elland Road		H	L	0-1aet	
1986-87	D2	3	10.1.87	Oldham A	D2	A	D	1-1	McCall
		3r	19.1.87	Oldham A		H	W	5-1	Hendrie 2, Ormondroyd 2, Ellis
		4	31.1.87	Everton	D1	A	L	0-1	
1987-88	D2	3	9.1.88	Wolverhampton W	D4	H	W	2-1	Hendrie, Ellis
		4	30.1.88	Oxford U	D1	H	W	4-2	Kennedy (p), McCall, Evans, Hendrie
		5	20.2.88	Portsmouth	D1	A	L	0-3	

1988-89	D2	3	7.1.89	Tottenham H	D1	H	W	1-0	Mitchell
		4	28.1.89	Hull C	D2	H	L	1-2	Leonard
1989-90	D2	3	7.1.90	Charlton A	D1	A	D	1-1	Tinnion (p)
		3r	10.1.90	Charlton A		H	L	0-3	
1990-91	D3	1	17.11.90	Shrewsbury T	D3	H	D	0-0	
		1r	21.11.90	Shrewsbury T		A	L	1-2	Jewell
1991-92	D3	1	16.11.91	Bury	D3	A	W	1-0	Tinnion
		2	7.12.91	Bolton W	D3	A	L	1-3	Tinnion
1992-93	D2	1	14.11.92	Preston NE	D2	H	D	1-1	Jewell
		1r	25.11.92	Preston NE		A	W	5-4	McCarthy 2, Blake, Tinnion (p), Jewell
		2	6.12.92	Huddersfield T	D2	H	L	0-2	

BRADFORD PARK AVENUE

Formed 1907. Members of the Football League 1908-1970. Disbanded 1974. Reformed 1988 and currently play in North West Counties League. Their **record FA Cup victory** of 11-0 in a 2nd qualifying round tie was achieved by the Reserves as the first team were playing a League match on the same day. The FA fined Park Avenue £50 for not fielding their strongest side.

1908-09	D2	1q		South Kirkby Coll. (H) 8-1; 2q Denby Dale (A) 11-0; 3q Heckmondwike walkover; 4q Mexborough (H) 6-0					
				5q Croydon Common (H) 1-2					
1909-10	D2	1	15.1.10	Bishop Auckland	NL	H	W	8-0	Newton 3, McClarence, Smith 2, Reeves 2
		2	5.2.10	Sunderland	D1	A	L	1-3	Reeves
1910-11	D2	1	14.1.11	QPR	SL	H	W	5-3	Turnbull 2, Little 2, Logan
		2	4.2.11	Darlington	NEL	A	L	1-2	Thackeray
1911-12	D2	1	13.1.12	Nottingham F	D2	A	W	1-0	Reeves
		2	3.2.12	Portsmouth	SL	H	W	2-0	Reeves, Simpson
		3	24.2.12	Bradford C	D1	H	L	0-1	
1912-13	D2	1	15.1.13	Barrow	LC	H	D	1-1	Smith
		1r	22.1.13	Barrow at Bradford		A	W	1-0	Smith
		2	1.2.13	Wolverhampton W	D2	H	W	3-0	Smith 2, Little
		3	22.2.13	Sheffield W	D1	H	W	2-1	Smith, Howie
		4	8.3.13	A.Villa	D1	H	L	0-5	
1913-14	D2	1	10.1.14	Reading	SL	H	W	5-1	Bauchop 3, Smith, McCandless
		2	31.1.14	Sheffield U	D1	A	L	1-3	Smith
1914-15	D1	1	9.1.15	Portsmouth	SL	H	W	1-0	Smith
		2	30.1.15	Bury	D2	A	W	1-0	Bauchop
		3	20.2.15	Sheffield U	D1	A	L	0-1aet	
1919-20	D1	1	10.1.20	Nottingham F	D2	H	W	3-0	McLean, Bauchop, Turnbull
		2	31.1.20	Castleford T		H	W	3-2	Little, McLean 2
		3	23.2.20	Notts Co	D1	A	W	4-3	McLean 2, McCandless, Bauchop
		4	6.3.20	Chelsea	D1	A	L	1-4	Little
1920-21	D1	1	8.1.21	Clapton O	D2	H	W	1-0	Burkinshaw
		2	29.1.21	Huddersfield T	D1	H	L	0-1	
1921-22	D2	1	7.1.22	Sheffield W	D2	H	W	1-0	Batten
		2	28.1.22	Arsenal	D1	H	L	2-3	McLean, Bauchop
1922-23	3N	1	13.1.23	Everton	D1	A	D	1-1	Peel
		1r	17.1.23	Everton		H	W	1-0	McLean
		2	3.2.23	Plymouth A	3S	A	L	1-4	Fell
1923-24	3N	1	12.1.24	Swindon T	3S	A	L	0-4	
1924-25	3N	5q		Wigan Borough (A) 1-0; 6q Crook T (A) 4-0					
		1	10.1.25	Middlesbrough	D2	H	W	1-0	Turnbull
		2	31.1.25	Blackpool	D2	H	D	1-1	Hubbert
		2r	14.2.25	Blackpool		A	L	1-2	Scattergood (p)
1925-26	3N	1	28.11.25	Lincoln C	3N	H	D	2-2	McDonald 2
		1r	2.12.25	Lincoln C		A	D	1-1aet	McDonald
		1 2r	7.12.25	Lincoln C at Bramall Lane			W	2-1	Peel 2
		2	12.12.25	Boston T	ML	A	L	0-1	
1926-27	3N	1	27.11.26	Walsall	3N	A	L	0-1	
1927-28	3N	1	26.11.27	Nelson	3N	A	W	3-0	Cartwright 2, Hawes
		2	10.12.27	Southport	3N	H	L	0-2	
1928-29	D2	3	12.1.29	Hull C	D2	A	D	1-1	Parris
		3r	16.1.29	Hull C		H	W	3-1	Davis, Atherton, McLean
		4	26.1.29	Plymouth A	3S	A	W	1-0	Davis
		5	16.2.29	WBA	D2	A	L	0-6	
1929-30	D2	3	11.1.30	Barnsley	D2	A	W	1-0	Quantrill
		4	25.1.30	Derby Co	D1	A	D	1-1	Harwood
		4r	29.1.30	Derby Co		H	W	2-1	Millership, Davis

Season	Div	Rd	Date	Opponent		H/A	Result	Score	Scorers
		5	15.2.30	Sheffield W	D1	A	L	1-5	McLean
1930-31	D2	3	10.1.31	Aldershot T	SL	A	W	1-0	Scott
		4	24.1.31	Burnley	D2	H	W	2-0	McMillan, Rhodes
		5	14.2.31	Southport	3N	A	L	0-1	
1931-32	D2	3	9.1.32	Cardiff C	3S	H	W	2-0	Harwood, Rhodes
		4	23.1.32	Northampton T	3S	H	W	4-2	Leedham, Harwood, Dickinson, Davis
		5	13.2.32	Watford	3S	A	L	0-1	
1932-33	D2	3	14.1.33	Plymouth A	D2	H	W	5-1	Dickinson, Robertson 2, Robson 2
		4	28.1.33	Brighton & HA	3S	A	L	1-2	Robson
1933-34	D2	3	13.1.34	Stoke C	D1	A	L	0-3	
1934-35	D2	3	12.1.35	Leeds U	D1	A	L	1-4	Suggett
1935-36	D2	3	11.1.36	Workington	NEL	H	W	3-2	Lewis, Nolan, Doran
		4	29.1.36	WBA	D1	H	D	1-1	Wesley
		4r	3.2.36	WBA		A	D	1-1aet	Meek
		4 2r	10.2.36	WBA at Old Trafford			W	2-0	Nolan, Doran
		5	15.2.36	Tottenham H	D2	H	D	0-0	
		5r	17.2.36	Tottenham H		A	L	1-2	Nolan
1936-37	D2	3	16.1.37	Derby Co	D1	H	L	0-4	
1937-38	D2	3	8.1.38	Newport Co	3S	H	W	7-4	Martin, Henson 4, Lewis 2
		4	22.1.38	Stoke C	D1	H	D	1-1	Wesley
		4r	26.1.38	Stoke C		A	W	2-1	Stabb, Henson
		5	12.2.38	Sunderland	D1	A	L	0-1	
1938-39	D2	3	7.1.39	Wolverhampton W	D1	A	L	1-3	Gallon
1945-46	D2	3 1L	5.1.46	Port Vale	3S	H	W	2-1	Downie, Gibbons
		3 2L	7.1.46	Port Vale		A	D	1-1	Gibbons
		4 1L	26.1.46	Manchester C	D2	H	L	1-3	Gibbons
		4 2L	30.1.46	Manchester C		A	W	8-2	Gibbons 4, Dix 2, Knott, Farrell
		5 1L	9.2.46	Barnsley	D2	A	W	1-0	Shackleton
		5 2L	13.2.46	Barnsley		H	D	1-1	Gibbons
		6 1L	2.3.46	Birmingham C	D2	H	D	2-2	Hallard, Dix
		6 2L	9.3.46	Birmingham C		A	L	0-6	
1946-47	D2	3	11.1.47	Manchester U	D1	H	L	0-3	
1947-48	D2	3	10.1.48	Arsenal	D1	A	W	1-0	Elliott
		4	24.1.48	Colchester U	SL	A	L	2-3	Elliott, Ainsley
1948-49	D2	3	8.1.49	Newcastle U	D1	A	W	2-0	Downie, McIlvenny
		4	29.1.49	Manchester U	D1	A	D	1-1aet	Henry
		4r	5.2.49	Manchester U		H	D	1-1aet	Farrell
		4 2r	7.2.49	Manchester U		A	L	0-5	
1949-50	D2	3	7.1.50	Bournemouth	3S	H	L	0-1	
1950-51	3N	1	25.11.50	Chester	3N	A	W	2-1	Elliott, Deplidge
		2	9.12.50	Millwall	3S	A	D	1-1	Crosbie
		2r	13.12.50	Millwall		H	L	0-1	
1951-52	3N	1	24.11.51	York C	3N	A	D	1-1	Crosbie
		1r	28.11.51	York C		H	D	1-1aet	Lyons
		1 2r	3.12.51	York C at Elland Road			W	4-0	Haines 2, Turner, Crosbie
		2	15.12.51	Bradford C	3N	H	W	3-2	Turner 2, Lyons
		3	12.1.52	Sheffield W	D2	H	W	2-1	Turner 2
		4	12.2.52	Leeds U	D2	A	L	0-2	
1952-53	3N	1	22.11.52	Rochdale	3N	H	W	2-1	Haines, Lyons
		2	6.12.52	Gateshead	3N	H	L	1-2	Smith
1953-54	3N	1	21.11.53	Selby T	YL	A	W	2-0	Dunlop, Pickard
		2	12.12.53	Cambridge U	ECL	A	W	2-1	Pickard, Whitaker
		3	9.1.54	Manchester C	D1	H	L	2-5	Pickard, Beattie
1954-55	3N	1	20.11.54	Southport	3N	H	W	2-0	Adey, Wright
		2	11.12.54	Southend U	3S	H	L	2-3	McLaren, Miles
1955-56	3N	1	19.11.55	Rhyl A	CC	A	W	3-0	Brickley, Ward, Houghton
		2	10.12.55	Workington	3N	H	W	4-3	Houghton 2, Whitaker, Ward
		3	7.1.56	Middlesbrough	D2	H	L	0-4	
1956-57	3N	1	17.11.56	Boston U	ML	A	W	2-0	Kendall, Smith
		2	8.12.56	Peterborough U	ML	A	L	0-3	
1957-58	3N	1	16.11.57	Oldham A	3N	A	L	0-2	
1958-59	D4	1	15.11.58	Gateshead	D4	A	W	4-1	Buchanan 2, Atkinson, Booth
		2	6.12.58	Bradford C	D3	H	L	0-2	
1959-60	D4	1	14.11.59	Scarborough	ML	H	W	6-1	Buchanan 4, Allan 2
		2	5.12.59	South Shields	ML	A	W	5-1	Allan 2, Harvey 2, Buchanan
		3	9.1.60	Chelsea	D1	A	L	1-5	Allan
1960-61	D4	1	5.11.60	York C	D4	A	D	0-0	

BRADFORD PA

		1r	9.11.60	**York C**		H	L	0-2
1961-62	D3	1	4.11.61	**Port Vale**	D3	H	L	0-1
1962-63	D3	1	3.11.62	**Halifax T**	D3	A	L	0-1
1963-64	D4	1	16.11.63	**Heanor T**	ML	H	W	3-1	Evans, Atkinson, Flynn
		2	7.12.63	**Oldham A**	D3	A	L	0-2
1964-65	D4	1	14.11.64	**Doncaster R**	D4	H	L	2-3	Fryatt, Hector
1965-66	D4	1	13.11.65	**Hull C**	D3	H	L	2-3	Lightowler, Hector
1966-67	D4	1	26.11.66	**Witton A**	CC	H	W	3-2	Symonds, Robinson, Waddell
		2	11.1.67	**Workington**	D3	H	W	3-1	Symonds 2, Madden
		3	28.1.67	**Fulham**	D1	H	L	1-3	Robinson
1967-68	D4	1	9.12.67	**Grimsby T**	D3	A	D	1-1	Down
		1r	11.12.67	**Grimsby T**		H	W	4-1	Lloyd 2, Ham, Down
		2	6.1.68	**Tranmere R**	D3	H	L	2-3	Ham, Pritchard og
1968-69	D4	1	16.11.68	**Stockport Co**	D3	A	L	0-3
1969-70	D4	1	15.11.69	**South Shields**	NPL	A	L	1-2	Brannan
1970-71	NPL	4q	**Washington** (A) 3-0					
		1	21.11.70	**Barnsley**	D3	A	L	0-1

BRADSHAW

Formed 1878. Played at Rigby Fields, Bradshaw, near Bolton

1883-84	1	3.11.83	**Bolton Association**	A	L	1-5
1884-85	1	11.10.84	**Darwen**	A	L	0-11
1885-86	1	31.10.85	**Hurst**	A	L	1-3

BRANDON UNITED

Formed 1972 as Rostrons FC after a waste-paper company where most of the founders were employed.Became Brandon United 1974. Based in Durham.

1979-80	NAII	1	24.11.79	**Bradford C**	D4	H	L	0-3
				played at Spennymoor				
1988-89	NL	1	19.11.88	**Doncaster R**	D4	A	D	0-0
		1r	22.11.88	**Doncaster R** at Doncaster		H	L	1-2	Calvert

BRENTFORD

Formed 1889. **FA Cup best performance:** 6th round, 1938, 1946, 1949, 1989. **FA Cup Record Win:** 8-0 vs Uxbridge, 3rd qual rd, 1903-04; In competition proper: 7-0 vs Windsor & Eton, 1st round, 20.11.1982. **FA Cup Record Defeat:** 1-7 vs Manchester U, 3rd round, 14.1.1928

1897-98	Lon	1q **1st Coldstream Guards** (H) 6-1; 2q **3rd Grenadier Guards** (H) 1-1; 2qr **3rd Grenadier Guards** (A) 1-4
1898-99	SL	3q **Clapton** (A) 1-6
1899-00	SL	3q **Richmond Association** (H) 1-2
1900-01	SL	3q **Maidenhead** (A) 3-1; 4q **Richmond Association** (A) 0-1
1901-02	SL	3q **Marlow** (A) 3-0; 4q **Shepherds Bush** (H) 2-3 after abandoned match;
1902-03	SL	3q **Oxford C** (A) 2-2; 3qr **Oxford C** (H) 5-4; 4q **Southall** (H) 5-0; 5q **Shepherds Bush** (H) 2-2; 5qr **Shepherds Bush** (A) 1-1;
		5q 2r **Shepherds Bush** 1-0 at Kensal Rise; Int **Woolwich Arsenal** (H) 1-1; Int r **Woolwich Arsenal** (A) 0-5
1903-04	SL	3q **Uxbridge** (H) 8-0; 4q **Oxford C** (A) 3-1; 5q **Wycombe W** (A) 4-1; Int **Plymouth A** (H) 1-1; Int r **Plymouth A** (A) 1-4
1904-05	SL	6q **QPR** (A) 2-1; Int **Reading** (H) 1-1; Int r **Reading** (A) 0-2
1905-06	SL	4q **Wycombe W** (H) 4-0

		1	13.1.06	**Bristol C**	D2	H	W	2-1	Corbett 2
		2	3.2.06	**Lincoln C**	D2	H	W	3-0	Parsonage, Underwood, Corbett
		3	24.2.06	**Liverpool**	D1	A	L	0-2
1906-07	SL	1	12.1.07	**Glossop**	D2	H	W	2-1	Corbett, Pentland (p)
		2	2.2.07	**Middlesbrough**	D1	H	W	1-0	Hagan
		3	23.2.07	**Crystal P**	SL	A	D	1-1	Hagan
		3r	27.2.07	**Crystal P**		H	L	0-1
1907-08	SL	1	11.1.08	**Carlisle U**	LC	A	D	2-2	Bowman, Corbett
		1r	15.1.08	**Carlisle U**		H	L	1-3aet	Tomlinson
1908-09	SL	1	16.1.09	**Gainsborough T**	D2	H	W	2-0	Richards 2
		2	6.2.09	**Nottingham F**	D1	A	L	0-1
1909-10	SL	4q **Luton T** (H) 2-1; 5q **Accrington S** (A) 0-1						
1910-11	SL	1	14.1.11	**Preston NE**	D1	H	L	0-1
1911-12	SL	4q **Kings Royal Rifles** (H) 1-1; 4qr **Kings Royal Rifles** (H) 4-1; 5q **Southend U** (A) 1-0						
		1	13.1.12	**Crystal P**	SL	H	D	0-0
		1r	17.1.12	**Crystal P**		A	L	0-4

Season	Div	Round	Date	Opponent		Venue	Result	Score	Scorers
1912-13	SL	4q **Watford** (H) 0-0; 4qr **Watford** (A) 1-5							
1913-14	SL	4q **Luton Clarence** (H) 1-0; 5q **Southend U** (H) 1-1; 5qr **Southend U** (A) 0-2							
1914-15	SL	4q **Nunhead** (A) 1-0; 5q **Boscombe** (A) 0-0; 5qr **Boscombe** (H) 0-1							
1919-20	SL	1	1.10.20	**Huddersfield T**	D2	A	L	1-5	Morris
1920-21	D3	1	8.1.21	**Huddersfield T**	D1	H	L	1-2	King
1921-22	3S	5q **Dulwich Hamlet** (H) 3-1; 6q **Shildon** (H) 1-0							
		1	7.1.22	**Tottenham H**	D1	H	L	0-2	
1922-23	3S	5q **Maidstone U** (A) 0-0; 5qr **Maidstone U** (H) 4-0; 6q **Merthyr Town** (H) 0-1							
1923-24	3S	5q **Botwell Mission** (A) 1-1; 5qr **Botwell Mission** (H) 2-0; 6q **Portsmouth** (H) 1-1; 6qr **Portsmouth** (A) 0-1aet							
1924-25	3S	5q **St Albans C** (A) 3-5							
1925-26	3S	1	28.11.25	**Barnet**	AL	H	W	3-1	J.Lane, Whitton, Graham
		2	12.12.25	**Bournemouth**	3S	H	L	1-2	Whitton
1926-27	3S	1	27.11.26	**Clapton**	IL	A	D	1-1	Anderson
		1r	1.12.26	**Clapton**		H	W	7-3	Watkins 3, J.Lane 2, Hendren 2
		2	11.12.26	**Gillingham**	3S	H	D	1-1	Hendren
		2r	15.12.26	**Gillingham**		H	W	1-0	Dearn
		3	8.1.27	**Oldham A**	D2	A	–	1-2	Watkins
				abandoned after 73 minutes – fog					
		3r	10.1.27	**Oldham A**		A	W	4-2	Allen 3, Watkins
		4	29.1.27	**West Ham**	D1	A	D	1-1	J.Lane
		4r	2.2.27	**West Ham**		H	W	2-0	J.Lane, Allen
		5	19.2.27	**Reading**	D2	A	L	0-1	
1927-28	3S	3	14.1.28	**Manchester U**	D1	A	L	1-7	Jones og
1928-29	3S	1	24.11.28	**Brighton & HA**	3S	H	W	4-1	J.Lane 2, Drinnan, Sherlaw
		2	8.12.28	**Plymouth A**	3S	H	L	0-1	
1929-30	3S	1	30.11.29	**Southend U**	3S	A	L	0-1	
1930-31	3S	1	29.11.30	**Ilford**	IL	A	W	6-1	W.Lane 3, J.Lane 3
		2	13.12.30	**Norwich C**	3S	H	W	1-0	J.Lane
		3	10.1.31	**Cardiff C**	D2	H	D	2-2	Berry, W.Lane
		3r	14.1.31	**Cardiff C**		A	W	2-1	W.Lane, J.Lane
		4	24.1.31	**Portsmouth**	D1	H	L	0-1	
1931-32	3S	1	28.11.31	**Tunbridge Wells R**	KL	A	D	1-1	Burns
		1r	2.12.31	**Tunbridge Wells R**		H	W	2-1	W.Lane, Burns
		2	12.12.31	**Norwich C**	3S	H	W	4-1	W.Lane 2, Robson, Berry
		3	9.1.32	**Bath C**	SL	H	W	2-0	W.Lane, Berry
		4	23.1.32	**Manchester C**	D1	A	L	1-6	W.Lane
1932-33	3S	1	26.11.33	**Reading**	3S	A	L	2-3	Scott, Holliday
1933-34	D2	3	13.1.34	**Hull C**	D2	A	L	0-1	
1934-35	D2	3	12.1.35	**Plymouth A**	D2	H	L	0-1	
1935-36	D1	3	11.1.36	**Leicester C**	D2	A	L	0-1	
1936-37	D1	3	16.1.37	**Huddersfield T**	D1	H	W	5-0	Reid 2 (1p), McCulloch 2, Holliday
		4	30.1.37	**Derby Co**	D1	A	L	0-3	
1937-38	D1	3	8.1.38	**Fulham**	D2	H	W	3-1	Reid, Holliday, McCulloch
		4	22.1.38	**Portsmouth**	D1	H	W	2-1	Wilson (p), McCulloch
1938-39	D1	3	7.1.39	**Newcastle U**	D2	H	L	0-2	
1945-46	D1	3 1L	5.1.46	**Tottenham H**	D2	A	D	2-2	Durrant, Thomas
		3 2L	10.1.46	**Tottenham H**		H	W	2-0	Hopkins 2
		4 1L	26.1.46	**Bristol C**	3S	A	L	1-2	Townsend
		4 2L	31.1.46	**Bristol C**		H	W	5-0	McAloon 3, Durrant, Guy og
		5 1L	9.2.46	**QPR**	3S	A	W	3-1	McAloon, Durrant, Hopkins
		5 2L	14.2.46	**QPR**		H	D	0-0	
		6 1L	2.3.46	**Charlton A**	D1	A	L	3-6	McAloon 2, Durrant
		6 2L	9.3.46	**Charlton A**		H	L	1-3	Scott
1946-47	D1	3	11.1.47	**Cardiff C**	3S	H	W	1-0	Townsend
		4	25.1.47	**Leicester C**	D2	H	D	0-0	
		4r	30.1.47	**Leicester C**		A	D	0-0	
		4 2r	3.2.47	**Leicester C** at Villa Park			L	1-4	Scott
1947-48	D2	3	10.1.48	**Rotherham U**	3N	A	W	3-0	Dawson, Gibbons, Buchanan
		4	24.1.48	**Middlesbrough**	D1	H	L	1-2	Girling
1948-49	D2	3	8.1.49	**Middlesbrough**	D1	H	W	3-2aet	Harper, Monk, McKennon
		4	29.1.49	**Torquay U**	3S	H	W	1-0	McKennan
		5	12.2.49	**Burnley**	D1	H	W	4-2	McKennan 2, Gibbons, Monk
		6	26.2.49	**Leicester C**	D2	H	L	0-2	
1949-50	D2	3	7.1.50	**Chelsea**	D1	H	L	0-1	
1950-51	D2	3	6.1.51	**Stockport Co**	3N	A	L	1-2	Paton
1951-52	D2	3	12.1.52	**QPR**	D2	H	W	3-1	Coote, Paton, Sperrin
		4	2.2.52	**Luton T**	D2	A	D	2-2	Sperrin 2

Season	Div	Rnd	Date	Opponent	OppDiv	H/A	Res	Score	Scorers
		4r	6.2.52	Luton T		H	D	0-0aet	
		4 2r	18.2.52	Luton T at Highbury			L	2-3aet	Dare 2
1952-53	D2	3	10.1.53	Leeds U	D2	H	W	2-1	Ledgerton, Lawton
		4	31.1.53	A.Villa	D1	A	D	0-0	
		4r	4.2.53	A.Villa		H	L	1-2	Lawton
1953-54	D2	3	9.1.54	Hull C	D2	H	D	0-0	
		3r	14.1.54	Hull C		A	D	2-2aet	Dudley, Rainford
		3 2r	18.1.54	Hull C at Doncaster			L	2-5	Sperrin, Bloomfield
1954-55	3S	1	20.11.54	Nuneaton Borough	BDL	H	W	2-1	Dare, Stobbart
		2	11.12.54	Crook Town	NL	H	W	4-1	Stobbart 2, Rainford, Towers
		3	8.1.55	Bradford C	3N	H	D	1-1	Dudley
		3r	12.1.55	Bradford C		A	D	2-2aet	Dare, Dudley
		3 2r	20.1.55	Bradford C at Highbury			W	1-0	Dare
		4	29.1.55	Newcastle U		A	L	2-3	Stobbart, Rainford
1955-56	3S	1	19.11.55	March T	ECL	H	W	4-0	Stobbart 2, Towers (p), Francis
		2	10.12.55	Leyton O	3S	A	L	1-4	Taylor
1956-57	3S	1	17.11.56	Guildford C	SL	H	W	3-0	Morton og, Taylor, Newcombe
		2	8.12.56	Crystal P	3S	H	D	1-1	Taylor
		2r	12.12.56	Crystal P		A	L	2-3aet	Towers, Francis
1957-58	3S	1	16.11.57	Millwall	3S	A	L	0-1	
1958-59	D3	1	15.11.58	Exeter C	D4	H	W	3-2	Towers, Francis, Rainford
		2	6.12.58	Kings Lynn	SL	H	W	3-1	Towers 3
		3	10.1.59	Barnsley	D2	H	W	2-0	Towers, Francis
		4	24.1.59	WBA	D1	A	L	0-2	
1959-60	D3	1	14.11.59	Ashford T	SL	H	W	5-0	Francis 4, Towers
		2	5.12.59	Exeter C	D4	A	L	1-3	Francis
1960-61	D3	1	5.11.60	Watford	D3	A	D	2-2	Francis 2
		1r	8.11.60	Watford		H	L	0-2	
1961-62	D3	1	4.11.61	Oxford U	SL	H	W	3-0	Edgley 2, Summers
		2	25.11.61	Aldershot	D4	A	D	2-2	Edgley, Francis
		2r	28.11.61	Aldershot		H	W	2-0	Edgley, Brooks
		3	6.1.62	Leyton O	D2	H	D	1-1	Summers
		3r	8.1.62	Leyton O		A	L	1-2	Higginson
1962-63	D4	1	3.11.62	Aldershot	D4	A	L	0-1	
1963-64	D3	1	16.11.63	Margate	SL	H	D	2-2	Block, Dick
		1r	20.11.63	Margate		A	W	2-0	Ward 2
		2	7.12.63	Gravesend & N	SL	H	W	1-0	Block
		3	4.1.64	Middlesbrough	D2	H	W	2-1	Dick, McAdams
		4	25.1.64	Oxford U	D4	A	D	2-2	Block, Ward
		4r	28.1.64	Oxford U		H	L	1-2	Mcadams
1964-65	D3	1	14.11.64	Wisbech T	SL	A	W	2-0	Bonson, Cobb
		2	5.12.64	Notts Co	D4	H	W	4-0	Cobb 2, Bonson, Fielding
		3	9.1.65	Burnley	D1	A	D	1-1	Lazarus
		3r	12.1.65	Burnley		H	L	0-2	
1965-66	D3	1	13.11.65	Yeovil T	SL	H	W	2-1	Fielding 2
		2	4.12.65	Reading	D3	A	L	0-5	
1966-67	D4	1	26.11.66	Chelmsford C	SL	H	W	1-0	Docherty (p)
		2	7.1.67	Leyton O	D3	A	D	0-0	
		2r	10.1.67	Leyton O		H	W	3-1	Docherty 2, Richardson
		3	28.1.67	Sunderland	D1	A	L	2-5	Docherty 2
1967-68	D4	1	9.12.67	Guildford C	SL	H	–	1-2	Myers
			abandoned after 53 minutes – snow						
		1	14.12.67	Guildford C		H	D	2-2	Docherty, Myers
		1r	18.12.67	Guildford C		A	L	1-2	Myers
1968-69	D4	1	16.11.68	Woking	IL	H	W	2-0	Fenton, Ross
		2	7.12.68	Watford	D3	A	L	0-1	
1969-70	D4	1	15.11.69	Plymouth A	D3	H	D	0-0	
		1r	19.11.69	Plymouth A		A	L	0-2	
1970-71	D4	1	21.11.70	Gillingham	D3	H	W	2-1	Docherty, Dawson
		2	12.12.70	Walsall	D3	H	W	1-0	Cross
		3	2.1.71	Workington	D4	A	W	1-0	Docherty
		4	23.1.71	Cardiff C	D2	A	W	2-0	Graham, Docherty
		5	13.2.71	Hull C	D2	A	L	1-2	Ross
1971-72	D4	1	20.11.71	Swansea C	D3	A	D	1-1	O'Mara
		1r	22.11.71	Swansea C		H	L	2-3	Ross, O'Mara
1972-73	D3	1	18.11.72	Yeovil T	SL	A	L	1-2	Allen
1973-74	D4	1	24.11.73	Plymouth A	D3	A	L	1-2	Allen

BRENTFORD

1974-75	D4	1	23.11.74	**Slough T**	IL	A	W	4-1	Woon 2, Graham, Simmons
		2	14.12.74	**Brighton & HA**	D3	A	L	0-1	
1975-76	D4	1	22.11.75	**Northampton T**	D4	H	W	2-0	Sweetzer 2
		2	13.12.75	**Wimbledon**	SL	A	W	2-0	Johnson 2 (1p)
		3	3.1.76	**Bolton W**	D2	H	D	0-0	
		3r	6.1.76	**Bolton W**		A	L	0-2	
1976-77	D4	1	20.11.76	**Chesham U**	IL	H	W	2-0	French, Cross
		2	11.12.76	**Colchester U**	D4	A	–	0-0	
			abandoned after 62 minutes – ice						
		2	20.12.76	**Colchester U**		A	L	2-3	Rolph, Fraser
1977-78	D4	1	26.11.77	**Folkestone & Shepway**	SL	H	W	2-0	Phillips 2
		2	17.12.77	**Swindon T**	D3	A	L	1-2	Phillips (p)
1978-79	D3	1	25.11.78	**Exeter C**	D3	A	L	0-1	
1979-80	D3	1	24.11.79	**Swindon T**	D3	A	L	1-4	Smith
1980-81	D3	1	22.11.80	**Addlestone & Weybridge**	SL	A	D	2-2	Booker, Funnell (p)
			played at Griffin Park						
		1r	25.11.80	**Addlestone & Weybride**		H	W	2-0	Crown, Funnell
		2	13.12.80	**Fulham**	D3	A	L	0-1	
1981-82	D3	1	21.11.81	**Exeter C**	D3	H	W	2-0	Bowen 2
		2	16.12.81	**Colchester U**	D4	H	D	1-1	G. Roberts
		2r	30.12.81	**Colchester U**		A	L	0-1	
1982-83	D3	1	20.11.82	**Windsor & Eton**	IL	A	W	7-0	Mahoney 3, Hurlock 2, McNichol, Joseph
			played at Griffin Park						
		2	11.12.82	**Swindon T**	D4	A	D	2-2	Bowen, G.Roberts
		2r	14.12.82	**Swindon T**		H	L	1-3aet	G.Roberts
1983-84	D3	1	19.11.83	**Dagenham**	APL	A	D	2-2	Joseph, P.Roberts
		1r	22.11.83	**Dagenham**		H	W	2-1	Mahoney, G.Roberts
		2	10.12.83	**Wimbledon**	D3	H	W	3-2	Kamara, G.Roberts, Joseph
		3	7.1.84	**Gillingham**	D3	A	L	3-5	G.Roberts, Hurlock, Cassells
1984-85	D3	1	17.11.84	**Bishops Stortford**	IL	H	W	4-0	Alexander 2, Cassells 2
		2	8.12.84	**Northampton T**	D4	H	D	2-2	Alexander, Cassells (p)
		2r	11.12.84	**Northampton T**		A	–	0-0	
			abandoned after 26 minutes – fog						
		2r	17.12.84	**Northampton T**		A	W	2-0	Hurlock, Cassells
		3	5.1.85	**Oldham A**	D2	A	L	1-2	Kamara
1985-86	D3	1	16.11.85	**Bristol R**	D3	H	L	1-3	Evans
1986-87	D3	1	3.12.86	**Bristol R**	D3	A	D	0-0	
		1r	6.12.86	**Bristol R**		H	W	2-0	Stevens 2
		2	9.12.86	**Cardiff C**	D4	A	L	0-2	
1987-88	D3	1	14.11.87	**Brighton & HA**	D3	H	L	0-2	
1988-89	D3	1	19.11.88	**Halesowen T**	SL	H	W	2-0	Evans, Sinton
		2	10.12.88	**Peterborough U**	D4	A	D	0-0	
		2r	14.12.88	**Peterborough U**		H	W	3-2	Cadette, Cockram, Smillie
		3	7.1.89	**Walsall**	D2	A	D	1-1	Jones
		3r	10.1.89	**Walsall**		H	W	1-0	Cockram
		4	28.1.89	**Manchester C**	D2	H	W	3-1	Blissett 2, Jones
		5	18.2.89	**Blackburn R**	D2	A	W	2-0	Blissett 2
		6	18.3.89	**Liverpool**	D1	A	L	0-4	
1989-90	D3	1	18.11.89	**Colchester U**	D4	H	L	0-1	
1990-91	D3	1	17.11.90	**Yeovil T**	GMVC	H	W	5-0	Holdsworth 2, Blissett, May, Jones
		2	12.12.90	**Birmingham C**	D3	A	W	3-1	Blissett, Godfrey, Jones
		3	5.1.91	**Oldham A**	D2	A	L	1-3	Holdsworth
1991-92	D3	1	18.11.91	**Gillingham**	D3	H	D	3-3	Holdsworth 2, Blissett
		1r	26.11.91	**Gillingham**		A	W	3-1	Holdsworth 2, Sealy
		2	7.12.91	**Bournemouth**	D3	A	L	1-2	Bates
1992-93	D1	3	2.1.93	**Grimsby T**	D1	H	L	0-2	

BRENTWOOD

Essex-based amateur club

1878-79	1	9.11.78	**Pilgrims**	H	L	1-3	Sparham
1879-80	1	1.11.79	**South Norwood**	A	L	2-4	Groves, Sparham
1880-81	1	6.11.80	**Old Etonians**	H	L	0-10	
1881-82	1	17.10.81	**Great Marlow**	A	L	1-3	Bowen
1882-83	1	28.10.82	**Barnes**	A	W	4-2	
	2	2.12.82	**Old Etonians**	A	L	1-2	Rumball

1883-84	1	3.11.83	Hanover U		A	W	6-1	Abott 2, Evelyn, Morice, Powell 2
	2		bye					
	3	29.12.83	Romford		A	W	4-1	Britten 3, Evelyn
	4	19.1.83	Northwich Victoria		A	L	0-3	
1884-85	1	8.11.84	Barnes		H	W	2-0	Crossley, Evelyn
	2	6.12.84	Old Etonians		H	D	2-2	Evelyn, Rose
	2r	20.12.84	Old Etonians		A	L	1-6	Bretton
1885-86	1	31.10.85	Maidenhead		H	W	3-0	
	2	14.11.85	Lancing Old Boys		H	W	6-1	
	3		bye					
	4	2.1.86	South Reading		A	W	3-0	Marchand 2, Morice
	5	30.1.86	Burslem Port Vale		A	D	1-1	Evelyn
	5r	13.2.86	Burslem Port Vale		H	D	3-3	Britten, Moore, AN Other
	5 2r		Burslem Port Vale					walkover
	6	27.2.86	Blackburn R		H	L	1-3	Britten

BRENTWOOD TOWN

No connection with earlier Brentwood Club. **First competed in FA Cup:** 1965. Merged with Chelmsford City in 1970. **League Club beaten:** Reading

1968-69	SL	1	16.11.68	Barnet	SL	A	D	1-1	Stevenson
		1r	18.11.68	Barnet		H	W	1-0	Stevenson
		2	7.12.68	Southend	D4	A	L	1-10	Stratton
1969-70	SL	1	15.11.69	Reading	D3	H	W	1-0	Halliday
		2	6.12.69	Hendon	IL	A	W	2-0	O'Connell, Halliday
		3	12.1.70	Northampton T	D4	H	L	0-1	

BRIDGWATER TOWN

Original Bridgwater Club **first competed in FA Cup** in 1901. Bridgwater Town formed 1948. **First entered FA Cup:** 1949. Folded 1983. Club reformed 1984 and currently play in Somerset Senior League

1960-61	WL	1	5.11.60	Hereford U	SL	H	W	3-0	Rice, Burr 2
		2	26.11.60	Oxford U	SL	A	L	1-2	Burr
1961-62	WL	1	4.11.61	Weston-super-Mare	WL	H	D	0-0	
		1r	9.11.61	Weston-super-Mare		A	W	1-0	Irons
		2	25.11.61	Crystal P	D3	H	L	0-3	
1963-64	WL	1	16.11.63	Luton T	D3	H	L	0-3	
1971-72	WL	1	20.11.71	Reading	D4	H	L	0-3	

BRIDLINGTON TOWN

Formed 1926. Known as Bridlington Central until 1959. **FA Vase Winners:** 1993. Runners-up 1990

1960-61	YL	1	5.11.60	Bishop Auckland	NL	A	L	2-3	Pudsey, Head
1991-92	NPL	1	16.11.91	York C	D4	H	L	1-2	Stephenson

BRIERLEY HILL ALLIANCE

First entered the FA Cup in 1891 and only made it to the competition proper once. Disbanded 1981

1961-62	BDL	1	4.11.61	Grantham	ML	H	W	3-0	Richardson, Thomas 2
		2	25.11.61	Shrewsbury T	D3	A	L	0-3	

BRIGG BRITANNIA

1880-81	1	16.10.80	Turton	A	L	0-5	
1881-82	1	5.11.81	Sheffield FC	A	L	0-8	
1882-83	1		Nottingham F			scratched	

BRIGG TOWN

Formed 1864. Last reached the Competition Proper over a century ago. Currently play in Northern Counties East League.

1879-80	1	25.10.79	Turton	A	L	0-7	
1880-81	1	13.11.80	Darwen	A	L	0-8	
1881-82	1	5.11.81	Grantham	A	L	0-6	

BRIGHTON & HOVE ALBION

Formed 1900. Note their odd record for the 1932-33 season. **FA Cup Runners Up:** 1983. **FA Cup Record Win:** 14-0 vs Brighton Ath, 1st qual rd, 1902-03. In competition proper: 10-1 vs Wisbech, 1st round, 13.11.1965. **FA Cup Record Defeat:** 2-7 vs Norwich C, 1st round, 30.11.1946

Season	Lg	Rd	Date	Opponent		Opp Lg	H/A	Result	Score	Scorers
1901-02		P		**Brighton Ath** (H) 6-2; 1q **Eastbourne** (H) 3-1; 2q **Hastings** (H) 5-0; 3q **Clapton** (H) 2-3						
1902-03				1q **Brighton Ath** (H) 14-0; 2q **Shoreham** (A) 2-0; 3q **Grays U** (H) 5-5; 3qr **Grays U** (A) 3-0; 4q **Ilford** (A) 0-1						
1903-04	SL			3q **W.Ham** (A) 0-4						
1904-05	SL			3q **Shoreham** (H) 7-1; 4q **Gillingham** (A) 1-0; 5q **Ilford** (H) 5-1; 6q **West Ham** (A) 2-1						
				Int. **Bristol R** (H) 1-2						
1905-06	SL			4q **Glossop** (A) 1-0						
		1	13.1.06	**Swindon T**		SL	H	W	3-0	Hall, Yates 2
		2	3.2.06	**Middlesbrough**		D1	H	D	1-1	J.Kennedy
		2r	7.2.06	**Middlesbrough**			A	D	1-1aet	Joynes
		2 2r	12.2.06	**Middlesbrough** at Bramall Lane				L	1-3	Hulme
1906-07	SL	1	12.1.07	**Bolton W**		D1	A	L	1-3	Smith
1907-08	SL	1	11.1.08	**Preston NE**		D1	H	D	1-1	Hall
		1r	16.1.08	**Preston NE**			A	–	2-1	Hall 2
				abandoned after 112 minutes – fog						
		1 2r	20.1.08	**Preston NE** at Stamford Bridge				W	1-0	Wombwell
		2	1.2.08	**Liverpool**		D1	A	D	1-1	Hall
		2r	5.2.08	**Liverpool**			H	L	0-3	
1908-09	SL	1	16.1.09	**Manchester U**		D1	A	L	0-1	
1909-10	SL	1	15.1.10	**Southampton**		SL	H	L	0-1	
1910-11	SL	1	14.1.11	**Leeds C**		D2	A	W	3-1	Jones 2, Smith
		2	4.2.11	**Coventry C**		SL	H	D	0-0	
		2r	8.2.11	**Coventry C**			A	L	0-2	
1911-12	SL	1	13.1.12	**Darlington**		NEL	A	L	1-2	Haworth
1912-13	SL	1	15.1.13	**Portsmouth**		SL	A	W	2-1	Higham, Webb
		2	1.2.13	**Everton**		D1	H	D	0-0	
		2r	5.2.13	**Everton**			A	L	0-1	
1913-14	SL	1	10.1.14	**Oldham A**		D1	A	D	1-1	Jones
		1r	14.1.14	**Oldham A**			H	W	1-0aet	Booth
		2	31.1.14	**Clapton O**		D2	H	W	3-1	Webb 2, Jones
		3	21.2.14	**Sheffield W**		D1	A	L	0-3	
1914-15	SL	1	9.1.15	**Lincoln C**		D2	H	W	2-1	Longstaff, Jones
		2	30.1.15	**Birmingham**		D2	H	D	0-0aet	
		2r	6.2.15	**Birmingham**			A	L	0-3	
1919-20	SL			6q **Luton T** (H) 0-1						
1920-21	D3	1	8.1.21	**Oldham A**		D1	H	W	4-1	Coomber, Marsh 2, Doran
		2	29.1.21	**Cardiff C**		D2	H	D	0-0	
		2r	2.2.21	**Cardiff C**			A	L	0-1	
1921-22	3S	1	7.1.22	**Sheffield U**		D1	H	W	1-0	Little
		2	28.1.22	**Huddersfield T**		D1	H	D	0-0	
		2r	1.2.22	**Huddersfield T**			A	L	0-2	
1922-23	3S	1	13.1.23	**Corinthians**		–	H	D	1-1	Neil
		1r	17.1.23	**Corinthians** at Crystal P				D	1-1aet	Cook
		1 2r	22.1.23	**Corinthians** at Stamford Bridge				W	1-0	Cook
		2	3.2.23	**W.Ham**		D2	H	D	1-1	Cook
		2r	7.2.23	**W.Ham**			A	L	0-1	
1923-24	3S	1	12.1.24	**Barnsley**		D2	A	D	0-0	
		1r	16.1.24	**Barnsley**			H	W	1-0	Hopkins
		2	2.2.24	**Everton**		D1	H	W	5-2	Little, Neil, Cook 3
		3	23.2.24	**Manchester C**		D1	H	L	1-5	Little
1924-25	3S	1	10.1.25	**Watford**		3S	A	D	1-1	Hopkins
		1r	14.1.25	**Watford**			H	W	4-3	Dennison 3, Hopkins
		2	31.1.25	**Southampton**		D2	A	L	0-1	
1925-26	3S	1	28.11.25	**Watford**		3S	H	D	1-1	Little
		1r	2.12.25	**Watford**			A	L	0-2	
1926-27	3S	1	27.11.26	**Barnet**		AL	H	W	3-0	Jennings 2, Cook
		2	11.12.26	**Watford**		3S	A	W	1-0	Cook
		3	8.1.27	**Sheffield W**		D1	A	L	0-2	
1927-28	3S	1	30.11.27	**Watford**		3S	A	W	2-1	James, Cook
		2	10.12.27	**Northampton T**		3S	A	L	0-1	
1928-29	3S	1	24.11.28	**Brentford**		3S	A	L	1-4	Kirkwood
1929-30	3S	1	30.11.29	**Peterborough & F.Utd**		SL	H	W	4-0	Farrell, Kirkwood 2, Smith
		2	14.12.29	**Barry T**		SL	H	W	4-1	Smith 2, Kirkwood, Thompson

		3	11.1.30	**Grimsby T**	D1	H	D	1-1	Dutton
		3r	14.1.30	**Grimsby T**		A	W	1-0	Vallance
		4	25.1.30	**Portsmouth**	D1	A	W	1-0	Vallance
		5	15.2.30	**Newcastle U**	D1	A	L	0-3	
1930-31	3S	3	10.1.31	**Leicester C**	D1	A	W	2-1	Smith 2
		4	26.1.31	**Watford**	3S	A	L	0-2	
1931-32	3S	1	28.11.31	**Folkestone**	SL	A	W	5-2	Farrwell, Wilson, Attwood, Smith, Kirkwood
		2	12.12.31	**Doncaster R**	3N	H	W	5-0	Wilson, Kirkwood, Attwood 2, Farrell
		3	9.1.32	**Port Vale**	D2	H	L	1-2	Attwood
1932-33	3S								

1q **Shoreham** (H) 12-0; 2q **Worthing** (H) 7-1; 3q **Hastings** (A) 9-0; 4q **Barnet** (A) 4-0 *Brighton failed to claim exemption

		1	26.11.32	**Crystal P**	3S	A	W	2-1	Thompson, Attwood
		2	10.12.32	**Wrexham**	3N	H	D	0-0	
		2r	14.12.32	**Wrexham**		A	W	3-2	Smith, Walker, Farrell
		3	14.1.33	**Chelsea**	D1	H	W	2-1	Attwood, Wilson
		4	28.1.33	**Bradford PA**	D2	H	W	2-1	Attwood, Smith
		5	18.2.33	**West Ham**	D2	H	D	2-2	Wilkinson, Attwood
		5r	22.2.33	**West Ham**		A	L	0-1	
1933-34	3S	3	13.1.34	**Swindon T**	3S	H	W	3-1	Short. Walker, Farrell
		4	27.1.34	**Bolton W**	D2	H	D	1-1	Wilkinson
		4r	31.1.34	**Bolton W**		A	L	1-6	Finney og
1934-35	3S	1	24.11.34	**Folkestone**	SL	H	W	3-1	Smith, Jepson, Brown
		2	8.12.34	**QPR**	3S	A	W	2-1	Brown, Farrell
		3	12.1.35	**Arsenal**	D1	H	L	0-2	
1935-36	3S	1	30.11.35	**Cheltenham T**	SL	H	D	0-0	
		1r	4.12.35	**Cheltenham T**		A	W	6-0	Law 3, Stephens 2, Farrell
		2	14.12.35	**Scarborough**	ML	A	D	1-1	Farrell
		2r	18.12.35	**Scarborough**		H	W	3-0	Law, Farrell, Darling
		3	11.1.36	**Fulham**	D2	A	L	1-2	Farrell
1936-37	3S	1	28.11.36	**QPR**	3S	A	L	1-5	Davie
1937-38	3S	1	27.11.37	**Tunbridge Wells R.**	KL	H	W	5-1	Davie 3, Wilson, Farrell
		2	11.12.37	**South Liverpool**	LC	A	D	1-1	Wilson
		2r	15.12.37	**South Liverpool**		H	W	6-0	Davie 4, Stephens, Farrell
		3	8.1.38	**Bury**	D2	A	L	0-2	
1938-39	3S	1	26.11.38	**Yeovil & Petters U**	SL	A	L	1-2	Marriott
1945-46	3S	1 1L	17.11.45	**Romford**	IL	H	W	3-1	Davie 2, Hindley
		1 2L	24.11.45	**Romford**		A	D	1-1	Stephens
		2 1L	8.12.45	**Walthamstow Ave**	IL	A	D	1-1	Longdon
		2 2L	15.12.45	**Walthamstow Ave**	H		W	4-2	Longdon, Stephens, Wilson, Davie
		3 1L	5.1.46	**Norwich C**	3S	A	W	2-1	Stephens, Moore
		3 2L	9.1.46	**Norwich C**		H	W	4-1	Chase, Davie (2), Stephens
		4 1L	26.1.46	**Aldershot**	3S	H	W	3-0	Davie 3
		4 2L	30.1.46	**Aldershot**		A	W	4-1	Davie 2, Chase, Stephens
		5 1L	9.2.46	**Derby Co**	D1	H	L	1-4	Willems
		5 2L	13.2.46	**Derby Co**		A	L	0-6	
1946-47	3S	1	30.11.46	**Norwich C**	3S	A	L	2-7	Hindley, Darling
1947-48	3S	1	29.11.47	**Trowbridge**	WL	A	D	1-1aet	Willard
		1r	6.12.47	**Trowbridge**		H	W	5-0	Hacking, Sim, Chapman 2, James (p)
1948-49	3S	1	27.11.48	**Newport Co**	3S	A	L	1-3	Tennant
1949-50	3S	1	26.11.49	**Ipswich T**	3S	A	L	1-2	Tennant
1950-51	3S	1	25.11.50	**Tooting & Mitcham**	AL	A	W	3-2	Mansell, Tennant, McNicholl
		2	9.12.50	**Ipswich T**	3S	H	W	2-0	Mansell, Thompson
		3	6.1.51	**Chesterfield**	D2	H	W	2-1	Bennett, McNichol
		4	27.1.51	**Bristol C**	3S	A	L	0-1	
1951-52	3S	1	24.11.51	**Bristol C**	3S	H	L	1-2	Bennett
1952-53	3S	1	22.11.52	**Yeovil T**	SL	A	W	4-1	Howard, Owen 2, Tennant
		2	6.12.52	**Norwich C**	3S	H	W	2-0	Bennett 2
		3	10.1.53	**Barnsley**	D2	A	L	3-4	Owens, Howard, Reed
1953-54	3S	1	21.11.53	**Coventry C**	3S	H	W	5-1	Addinall 2, Leadbetter, Howard, Tennant
		2	12.12.53	**Wrexham**	3N	A	D	1-1	Leadbetter
		2r	16.12.53	**Wrexham**		H	D	1-1aet	Gordon
		2 2r	21.12.53	**Wrexham** at Selhurst Park			L	1-3	Sirrell
1954-55	3S	1	20.11.54	**Tunbridge Wells U**	KL	H	W	5-0	Leadbetter, Gordon, Gilberg 2, Tennant
		2	11.12.54	**Norwich C**	3S	A	D	0-0	
		2r	15.12.54	**Norwich C**		H	W	5-1	Tennant, Mundy 2, Leadbetter, Howard
		3	8.1.55	**Aston Villa**	D1	H	D	2-2	Moore, Munday
		3r	10.1.55	**Aston Villa**		A	L	2-4	Foreman, Wilson
1955-56	3S	1	19.11.55	**Newport Co**	3S	H	W	8-1	Harburn 4, Foreman 3, Howard

Season	Div	Round	Date	Opponent	Comp	H/A	Result	Score	Scorers
		2	10.12.55	Norwich C	3S	H	L	1-2	Langley
1956-57	3S	1	17.11.56	Millwall	3S	H	D	1-1	Wilson
		1r	19.11.56	Millwall		A	L	1-3	Langley (p)
1957-58	3S	1	16.11.57	Walsall	3S	H	W	2-1	Sexton 2
		2	7.12.57	Norwich C	3S	A	D	1-1	Foreman
		2r	11.12.57	Norwich C		H	L	1-2	Foreman
1958-59	D2	3	10.1.59	Bradford C	D3	H	L	0-2	
1959-60	D2	3	9.1.60	Bath C	SL	A	W	1-0	Tiddy
		4	30.1.60	Rotherham U	D2	A	D	1-1	Thorne
		4r	3.2.60	Rotherham U		H	D	1-1aet	Thorne
		4 2r	8.2.60	Rotherham U at Highbury			W	6-0	Curry 3, Jones, Thorne 2
		5	20.2.60	Preston NE	D1	A	L	1-2	Wilson (p)
1960-61	D2	3	7.1.61	Derby Co	D2	H	W	3-1	McNeill, Laverick, Windross
		4	28.1.61	Burnley	D1	H	D	3-3	Bertolini, McNicol, Windross
		4r	31.1.61	Burnley		A	L	0-2	
1961-62	D2	3	6.1.62	Blackburn R	D1	H	L	0-3	
1962-63	D3	1	3.11.62	Southend U	D3	A	L	1-2	Cooper
1963-64	D4	1	16.11.63	Colchester U	D3	H	L	0-1	
1964-65	D4	1	14.11.64	Bristol C	D3	A	L	0-1	
1965-66	D3	1	13.11.65	Wisbech T	SL	H	W	10-1	Livesey 3, Smith 2, Cassidy 2, Howell og, Goodchild, Collins
		2	4.12.65	Bedford T	SL	H	D	1-1	Gould
		2r	6.12.65	Bedford T		A	L	1-2	Morgan og
1966-67	D3	1	26.11.66	Newport Co	D4	A	W	2-1	Turner, Whittington
		2	7.1.67	Bath C	SL	A	W	5-0	Turner, Whittington 2, Tawse 2
		3	28.1.67	Aldershot	D4	A	D	0-0	
		3r	1.2.67	Aldershot		H	W	3-1	Whittington, Napier, Livesey
		4	18.2.67	Chelsea	D1	H	D	1-1	Turner
		4r	22.2.67	Chelsea		A	L	0-4	
1967-68	D3	1	13.12.67	Southend U	D4	H	W	1-0	K.Napier
		2	6.1.68	Swansea T	D4	A	L	1-2	Hickman
1968-69	D3	1	16.11.68	Kidderminster H	WMRL	H	D	2-2	Livesey, Lawton
		1r	20.11.68	Kidderminster H		A	W	1-0	K.Napier
		2	7.12.68	Northampton T	D3	H	L	1-2	K.Napier
1969-70	D3	1	15.11.69	Enfield	IL	H	W	2-1	Gilliver 2
		2	6.12.69	Walsall	D3	H	D	1-1	Dawson
		2r	9.12.69	Walsall		A	D	1-1aet	Dawson
		2 2r	15.12.69	Walsall at Coventry			D	0-0aet	
		2 3r	17.12.69	Walsall at Fulham			L	1-2	Lawton
1970-71	D3	1	21.11.70	Cheltenham	SL	H	W	4-0	Gilliver, O'Sullivan, K.Napier (p), Woffinden
		2	12.12.70	Hereford U	SL	A	W	2-1	Lawton, K.Napier
		3	2.1.71	Cardiff C	D2	A	L	0-1	
1971-72	D3	1	20.11.71	Hillingdon Borough	SL	H	W	7-1	Spearitt, K.Napier 2, O'Sullivan 2, Ryan og, Murray
		2	11.12.71	Walsall	D3	H	D	1-1	Irvine
		2r	14.12.71	Walsall		A	L	1-2	K.Napier
1972-73	D2	3	13.1.73	Chelsea	D1	H	L	0-2	
1973-74	D3	1	24.11.73	Walton & Hersham	IL	A	D	0-0	
		1r	28.11.73	Walton & Hersham		H	L	0-4	
1974-75	D3	1	23.11.74	Aldershot	D3	H	W	3-1	Binney 2, Mellor
		2	14.12.74	Brentford	D4	H	W	1-0	Binney
		3	4.1.75	Leatherhead	IL	H	L	0-1	
1975-76	D3	1	22.11.75	Watford	D4	A	W	3-0	Martin, Binney 2
		2	13.12.75	Gillingham	D3	A	W	1-0	Fell
		3	3.1.76	Southend U	D3	A	L	1-2	Binney
1976-77	D3	1	20.11.76	Crystal P	D3	H	D	2-2	Ward, Mellor
		1r	23.11.76	Crystal P		A	D	1-1aet	Mellor
		1 2r	6.12.76	Crystal P at Stamford Bridge			L	0-1	
1977-78	D2	3	7.1.78	Scarborough	NPL	H	W	3-0	Ward, Potts, Horton
		4	31.1.78	Notts Co	D2	H	L	1-2	Towner
1978-79	D2	3	9.1.79	Wolverhampton W	D1	H	L	2-3	Lawrence, Ryan
1979-80	D1	3	5.1.80	Mansfield T	D3	A	W	2-0	Ryan, Clarke
		4	26.1.80	Arsenal	D1	A	L	0-2	
1980-81	D1	3	3.1.81	Manchester U	D1	A	D	2-2	Horton, Ritchie
		3r	7.1.81	Manchester U		H	L	0-2	
1981-82	D1	3	2.1.82	Barnet	APL	A	D	0-0	
		3r	5.1.82	Barnet		H	W	3-1	Thomas, Case, McNab (p)
		4	23.1.82	Oxford U	D3	H	L	0-3	

BRIGHTON HA

1982-83	D1	3	8.1.83	Newcastle U	D2	H	D	1-1	Ritchie
		3r	12.1.83	Newcastle U		A	W	1-0	Ward
		4	29.1.83	Manchester C	D1	H	W	4-0	Case, Smillie, Robinson 2
		5	20.2.83	Liverpool	D1	A	W	2-1	Ryan, Case
		6	12.3.83	Norwich C	D1	H	W	1-0	Case
		SF	16.4.83	Sheffield W	D2		W	2-1	Case, Robinson
				played at Highbury					
		F	21.5.83	Manchester U	D1 WEMBLEY		D	2-2aet	Smith, Stevens
		Fr	26.5.83	Manchester U		WEMBLEY	L	0-4	
1983-84	D2	3	7.1.84	Swansea C	D2	H	W	2-0	McQuillan og, Connor
		4	29.1.84	Liverpool	D1	H	W	2-0	Ryan, Connor
		5	18.2.84	Watford	D1	A	L	1-3	Wilson (p)
1984-85	D2	3	5.1.85	Hull C	D3	H	W	1-0	Hutchings
		4	26.1.85	Barnsley	D2	A	L	1-2	Ryan
1985-86	D2	3	4.1.86	Newcastle U	D1	A	W	2-0	Young, Saunders
		4	25.1.86	Hull C	D2	A	W	3-2	Saunders, Connor 2
		5	15.2.86	Peterborough U	D4	A	D	2-2	Saunders, Jacobs
		5r	3.3.86	Peterborough U		H	W	1-0	Saunders
		6	8.3.86	Southampton	D1	H	L	0-2	
1986-87	D2	3	10.1.87	Sheffield U	D2	A	D	0-0	
		3r	21.1.87	Sheffield U		H	L	1-2	Jasper
1987-88	D3	1	14.11.87	Brentford	D3	A	W	2-0	Nelson 2 (1p)
		2	5.12.87	Northampton T	D3	A	W	2-1	Bremner, Nelson
		3	9.1.88	Bournemouth	D2	H	W	2-0	Rougvie, Nelson
		4	30.1.88	Arsenal	D1	H	L	1-2	Nelson
1988-89	D2	3	7.1.89	Leeds U	D2	H	L	1-2	Curbishley (p)
1989-90	D2	3	6.1.90	Luton T	D1	H	W	4-1	Dublin, Nelson, Codner, Curbishley
		4	27.1.90	Oldham A	D2	A	L	1-2	Barham
1990-91	D2	3	5.1.91	Scunthorpe U	D4	H	W	3-2	Barham 2, Gurinovich
		4	26.1.91	Liverpool	D1	A	D	2-2	Small (p), Byrne
		4r	30.1.91	Liverpool		H	L	2-3aet	Small, Byrne
1991-92	D2	3	4.1.92	Crawley T	SL	H	W	5-0	Gall, Walker, Chapman 2 (1p), Meade
		4	25.1.92	Bolton W	D3	A	L	1-2	Meade
1992-93	D2	1	14.11.92	Hayes	IL	H	W	2-0	Kennedy, Codner
		2	5.12.92	Woking	GMVC	H	D	1-1	Kennedy
		2r	16.12.92	Woking		A	W	2-1	Codner, Crumplin
		3	2.1.93	Portsmouth	D1	H	W	1-0	Edwards
		4	23.1.93	Manchester U	PL	L		0-1	

BRISTOL CITY

Formed 1894 as Bristol South End. Bristol City 1897. **FA Cup Runners-Up:** 1909. **FA Cup Record Win:** 11-0 vs Chichester City, 1st round, 5.11.1960. **FA Cup Record Defeat:** 0-5 vs Preston 1935, 0-5 vs Brentford 1946, 1-6 vs Sunderland 1964. Welsh Cup winners 1934

As Bristol South End

1895-96		P **Slough** (H) 5-1; 1q **Marlow** (H) 0-1
1896-97		1q **Bedminster** (H) 2-4

As Bristol City

1897-98	SL	1q **Clifton** (H) 9-1; 2q **Trowbridge Town** (A) 5-2; 3q **Southampton** (A) 0-2						
1898-99	SL	3q **Cowes** (A) 5-0; 4q **Bristol St George** (A) 1-0; 5q **Reading** (H) 3-2						
		1	28.1.99	Sunderland	D1	H	L	2-4	Finnerham, Langham
1899-00	SL	1	27.1.00	Stalybridge R	LL	H	W	2-1	Blessington, Jones
		2	10.2.00	Aston Villa	D1	A	L	1-5	Jones
1900-01	SL	Int **Reading** (A) 1-1; Int r **Reading** (H) 0-0aet; Int 2r **Reading** 1-2 at Swindon						
1901-02	D2	3q **Bristol East** (H) 5-1; 4q **Bristol R** (A) 1-1aet; 4qr **Bristol R** (H) 2-3						
1902-03	D2	Int **Middlesbrough** (H) 3-1						
		1	7.12.02	Bolton W	D1	A	W	5-0	Banks 3, Dean, Wombwell
		2	21.1.03	Tottenham H	SL	A	L	0-1	
1903-04	D2	Int **New Brompton** (A) 1-1; Int r **New Brompton** (H) 5-2						
		1	6.2.04	Sheffield U	D1	A	L	1-3	Hosie
1904-05	D2	Int **Blackpool** (H) 2-1						
		1	4.2.05	W.Arsenal	D1	A	D	0-0	
		1r	8.2.05	W.Arsenal		H	W	1-0	Dean
		2	18.2.05	Preston NE	D1	H	D	0-0	
		2r	23.2.05	Preston NE		A	L	0-1	
1905-06	D2	1	13.1.06	Brentford	SL	A	L	1-2	Maxwell
1906-07	D1	1	12.1.07	Leeds C	D2	H	W	4-1	Gilligan 2, Maxwell 2

Season	Div	Round	Date	Opponent	Comp	H/A	Res	Score	Scorers
		2	2.2.07	W. Arsenal	D1	A	L	1-2	Gilligan
1907-08	D1	1	11.1.08	Grimsby T	D2	H	D	0-0	
		1r	15.1.08	Grimsby T		A	L	1-2	Hilton
1908-09	D1	1	16.1.09	Southampton	SL	H	D	1-1	Rippon
		1r	20.1.09	Southampton		A	W	2-0	Hardy, Rippon (p)
		2	6.2.09	Bury	D1	H	D	2-2	Burton, Gilligan
		2r	10.2.09	Bury		A	W	1-0	Gilligan
		3	20.2.09	Norwich C	SL	H	W	2-0	Burton, Rippon
		4	6.3.09	Glossop	D2	A	D	0-0	
		4r	10.3.09	Glossop		H	W	1-0	Gilligan
		SF	27.3.09	Derby Co	D2		D	1-1	Rippon (p)
				played at Stamford Bridge					
		SFr	31.3.09	Derby Co			W	2-1	Hardy, Rippon
				played at St Andrews, Birmingham					
		F	24.4.09	Manchester U	D1		L	0-1	
				played at Crystal Palace					
1909-10	D1	1	15.1.10	Liverpool	D1	H	W	2-0	Burton, Rippon
		2	5.2.10	WBA	D2	H	D	1-1	Gilligan
		2r	9.2.10	WBA		A	L	2-4	Gilligan, Staniforth
1910-11	D1	1	14.1.11	Crewe A	BDL	H	L	0-3	
1911-12	D2	1	13.1.12	Northampton T	SL	A	L	0-1	
1912-13	D2	1	15.1.13	Liverpool	D1	A	L	0-3	
1913-14	D2	1	10.1.14	QPR	SL	A	D	2-2	Picken, Pullan (og)
		1r	14.1.14	QPR		H	L	0-2aet	
1914-15	D2	1	9.1.15	Cardiff C	SL	H	W	2-0	Burton 2
		2	30.1.15	Everton	D1	A	L	0-4	
1919-20	D2	1	10.1.20	Grimsby T	D2	A	W	2-1	Howarth 2
		2	31.1.20	Arsenal	D1	H	W	1-0	Howarth
		3	21.2.20	Cardiff C	SL	H	W	2-1	Howarth, Neesam
		4	6.3.20	Bradford C	D1	H	W	2-0	Harris 2
		SF	27.3.20	Huddersfield T	D2		L	1-2	Howarth
				played at Stamford Bridge					
1920-21	D2	1	8.1.21	Aston V	D1	A	L	0-2	
1921-22	D2	1	7.1.22	Nottingham F	D2	H	D	0-0	
		1r	11.1.22	Nottingham F		A	L	1-3	Bown
1922-23	3S	1	13.1.23	Wrexham	3N	H	W	5-1	Fairclough 3, Paul, Walker
		2	3.2.23	Derby Co	D2	H	L	0-3	
1923-24	D2	1	12.1.24	Norwich C	3S	A	W	1-0	Smailes
		2	2.2.24	Sheffield W	D2	A	D	1-1	Pocock
		2r	6.2.24	Sheffield W		H	W	2-0	Walsh 2
		3	23.2.24	Cardiff C	D1	A	L	0-3	
1924-25	3S	1	10.1.25	Bristol R	3S	A	W	1-0	Walsh
		2	31.1.25	Liverpool	D1	H	L	0-1	
1925-26	3S	3	9.1.26	WBA	D1	A	L	1-4	Pocock
1926-27	3S	1	27.11.26	Merthyr T	3S	A	W	2-0	Foster, Paul
		2	11.12.26	Bournemouth	3S	H	D	1-1	Martin
		2r	15.12.26	Bournemouth		A	L	0-2	
1927-28	D2	3	14.1.28	Tottenham H	D1	H	L	1-2	Martin
1928-29	D2	3	12.1.29	Liverpool	D1	H	L	0-2	
1929-30	D2	3	11.1.30	Derby Co	D1	A	L	1-5	Williams
1930-31	D2	3	10.1.31	Barnsley	D2	A	L	1-4	Vials
1931-32	D2	3	9.1.32	Notts Co	D2	A	D	2-2	Elliott 2
		3r	13.1.32	Notts Co		H	W	3-2	Williams 2, Elliott
		4	23.1.32	Watford	3S	A	L	1-2	Elliott
1932-33	3S	1	26.11.32	Romford	AL	H	W	4-0	Bowen 3, Loftus
		2	10.12.32	Tranmere R	3N	H	D	2-2	Keating, Loftus
		2r	14.12.32	Tranmere R		A	L	2-3	Bowen, Loftus
1933-34	3S	1	25.11.33	Kingstonian	IL	A	W	7-1	Brinton 2, Heale 2, Reed 2, Riley
		2	9.12.33	Barrow	3N	H	W	2-1	Cainey, Riley
		3	13.1.34	Derby Co	D1	H	D	1-1	Scriven
		3r	17.1.34	Derby Co		A	L	0-1	
1934-35	3S	1	24.11.34	Gillingham	3S	H	W	2-0	Landells 2
		2	8.12.34	Rotherham U	3N	A	W	2-1	Loftus
		3	12.1.35	Bury	D2	H	D	1-1	Harston
		3r	16.1.35	Bury		A	D	2-2aet	Harston, Hodge
		3 2r	21.1.35	Bury at Villa Park			W	2-1	Hodge 2
		4	26.1.35	Portsmouth	D1	A	D	0-0	

Season	Div	Rd	Date	Opponent	Comp	H/A	Res	Score	Scorers
		4r	30.1.35	Portsmouth		H	W	2-0	Harston, Hodge
		5	16.2.35	Preston NE	D1	H	D	0-0	
		5r	25.2.35	Preston NE		A	L	0-5	
1935-36	3S	1	30.11.35	Crystal P	3S	H	L	0-1	
1936-37	3S	1	28.11.36	Newport Co	3S	A	L	0-3	
1937-38	3S	1	27.11.37	Enfield	AL	H	W	3-0	Haycox 2, Hockaday (og)
		2	11.12.37	Cardiff C	3S	A	D	1-1	Brain (p)
		2r	15.12.37	Cardiff C		H	L	0-2	
1938-39	3S	1	26.11.38	Bournemouth	3S	A	L	1-2	Peters
1945-46	3S	1 1L	17.11.45	Yeovil & Petters U	SL	A	D	2-2	Artus, Curran
		1 2L	24.11.45	Yeovil & Petters U		H	W	3-0	Chilcott 2, Curran
		2 1L	8.12.45	Bristol R	3S	H	W	4-2	Morgan 2, Clark, Williams
		2 2L	15.12.45	Bristol R		A	W	2-0	Clark, Thomas
		3 1L	5.1.46	Swansea T	D2	H	W	5-1	Clark 3, Bentley, Chilcott
		3 2L	10.1.46	Swansea T		A	D	2-2	Chilcott, Williams
		4 1L	26.1.46	Brentford	D1	H	W	2-1	Hargreaves, Williams
		4 2L	31.1.46	Brentford		A	L	0-5	
1946-47	3S	1	30.11.46	Hayes	AL	H	W	9-3	Clark 4, Williams 2, Chilcott, Hargreaves, Thomas
		2	14.12.46	Gillingham	SL	H	L	1-2	Clark
1947-48	3S	1	29.11.47	Dartford	SL	A	D	0-0aet	
		1r	6.12.47	Dartford		H	W	9-2	Clark 3, Townsend 3, Williams 3
		2	13.12.47	Crystal P	3S	H	L	0-1aet	
1948-49	3S	1	27.11.48	Crystal P	3S	A	W	1-0aet	Townsend
		2	11.12.48	Swansea T	3S	H	W	3-1	Barney, Boxshall, Townsend
		3	8.1.49	Chelsea	D1	H	L	1-3	Clark
1949-50	3S	1	26.11.49	Nottingham F	3S	A	L	0-1	
1950-51	3S	1	25.11.50	Gloucester C	SL	H	W	4-0	Guy, Peacock, Rodgers, Rogers
		2	9.12.50	Wrexham	3N	H	W	2-1	Rogers, Williams
		3	6.1.51	Blackburn R	D2	H	W	2-1	Rodgers 2
		4	27.1.51	Brighton & HA	3S	H	W	1-0	Clark (p)
		5	10.2.51	Birmingham C	D2	A	L	0-2	
1951-52	3S	1	24.11.51	Brighton & HA	3S	A	W	2-1	Atyeo 2
		2	15.12.51	Colchester U	3S	A	L	1-2	Rodgers
1952-53	3S	1	22.11.52	Coventry C	3S	A	L	0-2	
1953-54	3S	1	21.11.53	Torquay U	3S	A	W	3-1	Micklewright 2, Atyeo
		2	12.12.53	Rhyl A	CC	A	W	3-0	Atyeo, Micklewright, Williams
		3	9.1.54	Rotherham U	D2	H	L	1-3	Atyeo
1954-55	3S	1	20.11.54	Southend U	3S	H	L	1-2	Rodgers
1955-56	D2	3	7.1.56	Everton	D1	A	L	1-3	Atyeo
1956-57	D2	3	5.1.57	Rotherham U	D2	H	W	4-1	Atyeo 2, Curtis, Hinshelwood
		4	26.1.57	Rhyl	CC	H	W	3-0	Atyeo 2, Etheridge
		5	16.2.57	Aston Villa	D1	A	L	1-2	Atyeo
1957-58	D2	3	4.1.58	Accrington S	3N	A	D	2-2	Curtis, Hinshelwood
		3r	7.1.58	Accrington S		H	W	3-1	Atyeo 2, Curtis
		4	25.1.58	Notts Co	D2	A	W	2-1	Etheridge, Hinshelwood
		5	15.2.58	Bristol R	D2	H	L	3-4	Burden, Etheridge, Watkins
1958-59	D2	3	19.1.59	Doncaster R	D3	A	W	2-0	Tindill, Watkins
		4	24.1.59	Blackpool	D1	H	D	1-1	Tindill
		4r	28.1.59	Blackpool		A	L	0-1	
1959-60	D2	3	9.1.60	Charlton A	D2	H	L	2-3	Atyeo, Cavanagh
1960-61	D3	1	5.11.60	Chichester C	SCL	H	W	11-0	Atyeo 5, Adrian Williams 3, Tait, R.Williams, Bailey og
		2	26.11.60	Kings Lynn	SL	A	D	2-2	Atyeo, Rogers
		2r	29.11.60	Kings Lynn		H	W	3-0	Rogers 2, Atyeo
		3	7.1.61	Plymouth A	D2	A	W	1-0	R.Williams
		4	28.1.61	Leicester C	D1	A	–	0-0	
				abandoned at halftime – waterlogged pitch					
		4	31.1.61	Leicester C	D1	A	L	1-5	Norman og
1961-62	D3	1	4.11.61	Hereford U	SL	H	D	1-1	Tait
		1r	8.11.61	Hereford U		A	W	5-2	Atyeo 2, Etheridge, Tait, R.Williams
		2	25.11.61	Dartford	SL	H	W	8-2	Tait 3, Derrick 2, Atyeo, Connor, Rogers
		3	6.1.62	Walsall	D2	H	D	0-0	
		3r	9.1.62	Walsall		A	L	1-4	Derrick
1962-63	D3	1	3.11.62	Wellington T	SL	H	W	4-2	Atyeo 2, Derrick, Etheridge (p)
		2	24.11.62	Wimbledon	IL	H	W	2-1	Clark 2
		3	16.1.63	Aston Villa	D1	H	D	1-1	Clark
		3r	7.3.63	Aston Villa		A	L	2-3	Etheridge, R.Williams
1963-64	D3	1	16.11.63	Corby T	SL	A	W	3-1	Clark, Low, Williams

Season	Div	Round	Date	Opponent	Comp	Venue	Result	Score	Scorers
		2	7.12.63	Exeter C	D4	A	W	2-0	Atyeo 2
		3	4.1.64	Doncaster R	D4	A	D	2-2	Atyeo, Clark
		3r	7.1.64	Doncaster R		H	W	2-0	Atyeo, Hooper (p)
		4	25.1.64	Sunderland	D2	A	L	1-6	Hooper
1964-65	D3	1	14.11.64	Brighton & HA	D4	H	W	1-0	Savino
		2	5.12.64	Bournemouth	D3	A	W	3-0	Sharpe 2, Clarke
		3	9.1.65	Sheffield U	D1	H	D	1-1	Ford (p)
		3r	11.1.65	Sheffield U		A	L	0-3	
1965-66	D2	3	22.1.66	Birmingham C	D2	A	L	2-3	Bush, Low
1966-67	D2	3	28.1.67	Halifax T	D4	A	D	1-1	Peters
		3r	31.1.67	Halifax T		H	W	4-1	Crowe 2, Down, Peters
		4	18.2.67	Southampton	D1	H	W	1-0	Bush
		5	11.3.67	Tottenham H	D1	A	L	0-2	
1967-68	D2	3	27.1.68	Bristol R	D3	H	D	0-0	
		3r	30.1.68	Bristol R		A	W	2-1	Crowe, Galley
		4	17.2.68	Middlesbrough	D2	A	D	1-1	Garland
		4r	20.2.68	Middlesbrough		H	W	2-1	Connor, Galley
		5	9.3.68	Leeds U	D1	A	L	0-2	
1968-69	D2	3	4.1.69	West Ham U	D1	A	L	2-3	Galley, Skirton
1969-70	D2	3	3.1.70	Chester	D4	A	L	1-2	Skirton
1970-71	D2	3	11.1.71	Southampton	D1	A	L	0-3	
1971-72	D2	3	15.1.72	Preston NE	D2	A	L	2-4	Spiring, Wilson
1972-73	D2	3	13.1.73	Portsmouth	D2	A	D	1-1	Gould
		3r	16.1.73	Portsmouth		H	W	4-1	Gould, Gow (p), Sweeney, Tainton
		4	3.2.73	Wolverhampton W	D1	A	L	0-1	
1973-74	D2	3	5.1.74	Hull C	D2	H	D	1-1	Merrick
		3r	8.1.74	Hull C		A	W	1-0	Tainton
		4	26.1.74	Hereford U	D3	A	W	1-0	Merrick
		5	16.2.74	Leeds U	D1	H	D	1-1	Fear
		5r	19.2.74	Leeds U		A	W	1-0	Gillies
		6	9.3.74	Liverpool	D1	H	L	0-1	
1974-75	D2	3	4.1.75	Sheffield U	D1	A	L	0-2	
1975-76	D2	3	3.1.76	Coventry C	D1	A	L	1-2	Brolly
1976-77	D1	3	8.1.77	Ipswich T	D1	A	L	1-4	Fear
1977-78	D1	3	7.1.78	Wrexham	D3	H	D	4-4	Mabbutt 2, Cormack, Ritchie
		3r	9.1.78	Wrexham		A	L	0-3	
1978-79	D1	3	9.1.79	Bolton W	D1	H	W	3-1	Gow, Ritchie, Rodgers
		4	29.1.79	Crystal P	D2	A	L	0-3	
1979-80	D1	3	5.1.80	Derby Co	D1	H	W	6-2	Garland 2, Pritchard 2, Mann, Whitehead
		4	26.1.80	Ipswich T	D1	H	L	1-2	Whitehead
1980-81	D2	3	3.1.81	Derby Co	D2	A	D	0-0	
		3r	7.1.81	Derby Co		H	W	2-0	Mabbutt, Ritchie
		4	24.1.81	Carlisle U	D3	A	D	1-1	Mabbutt
		4r	28.1.81	Carlisle U		H	W	5-0	Mabbutt 2, Ritchie 2 (1p) Mann
		5	14.2.81	Nottingham F	D1	A	L	1-2	Mabbutt
1981-82	D3	1	20.11.81	Torquay U	D4	H	D	0-0	
		1r	26.11.81	Torquay U		A	W	2-1	Mann 2
		2	15.12.81	Northampton T	D4	H	W	3-0	Harford 2, Tainton
		3	6.1.82	Peterborough U	D4	A	W	1-0	Chandler
		4	23.1.82	Aston V	D1	H	L	0-1	
1982-83	D4	1	20.11.82	Orient	D3	A	L	1-4	Johnson
1983-84	D4	1	19.11.83	Corinthian Casuals	IL		D	0-0	
			played at Dulwich Hamlet						
		1r	23.11.83	Corinthian Casuals		H	W	4-0	Pritchard 3, Riley
		2	10.12.83	Bristol R	D3	A	W	2-1	Hirst, Ritchie
		3	8.1.84	Notts Co	D1	A	D	2-2	Crawford, Ritchie
		3r	10.1.84	Notts Co		H	L	0-2	
1984-85	D3	1	7.11.84	Fisher A	SL	A	W	1-0	Riley
		2	8.12.84	Bristol R	D3	H	L	1-3	Halliday
1985-86	D3	1	17.11.85	Swindon T	D4	A	D	0-0	
		1r	20.11.85	Swindon T		H	W	4-2	Neville 3, Riley
		2	7.12.85	Exeter C	D4	H	L	1-2	Walsh (p)
1986-87	D3	1	15.11.86	VS Rugby	SL	H	W	3-1	Hutchinson, Marshall, Walsh
		2	6.12.86	Bath C	GMVC	H	D	1-1	Neville
		2r	9.12.86	Bath C		A	H	3-0	Owen 2 (1p), Neville
			played at Ashton Gate						
		3	10.1.87	Plymouth A	D2	H	D	1-1	Riley

Season	Div	Round	Date	Opponent		H/A	Res	Score	Scorers
		3r	19.1.87	Plymouth A		A	L	1-3aet	Marshall
1987-88	D3	1	14.11.87	Aylesbury U	SL	H	W	1-0	Caldwell
		2	5.12.87	Torquay U	D4	H	L	0-1	
1988-89	D3	1	19.11.88	Southend U	D3	H	W	3-1	Walsh, McGarvey, Shutt
		2	10.12.88	Aldershot	D3	A	D	1-1	Shutt
		2r	13.12.88	Aldershot		H	D	0-0aet	
		2 2r	20.12.88	Aldershot		A	D	2-2aet	Shutt, Newman (p)
		2 3r	22.12.88	Aldershot		H	W	1-0	Shutt
		3	7.1.89	Hartlepool U	D4	A	L	0-1	
1989-90	D3	1	18.11.89	Barnet	GMVC	H	W	2-0	Taylor, Turner
		2	9.12.89	Fulham	D3	H	W	2-1	Taylor, Wimbleton (p)
		3	6.1.90	Swindon T	D2	H	W	2-1	Taylor, Newman
		4	27.1.90	Chelsea	D1	H	W	3-1	Turner 2, Gavin
		5	17.2.90	Cambridge U	D4	H	D	0-0	
		5r	21.2.90	Cambridge U		A	D	1-1aet	Taylor
		5 2r	27.2.90	Cambridge U		A	L	1-5	Taylor
1990-91	D2	3	5.1.91	Norwich C	D1	A	L	1-2	Allison
1991-92	D2	3	4.1.92	Wimbledon	D1	H	D	1-1	Barton og
		3r	14.1.92	Wimbledon		A	W	1-0	May
		4	25.1.92	Leicester C	D2	A	W	2-1	Bent, Dziekanowski
		5	15.2.92	Nottingham F	D1	A	L	1-4	Dziekanowski
1992-93	D1	3	19.1.93	Luton T	D1	A	L	0-2	

BRISTOL ROVERS

Formed 1883. **Best FA Cup performance:** 6th round, 1951, 1958. **Record FA Cup Win:** 15-1 vs Weymouth, 3rd qual rd, 17.11.1900. In Competition Proper: 6-0 vs Merthyr Tydfil, 1st round, 14.11.1987. **Record FA Cup Defeat:** 1-8 vs QPR, 1st round, 27.11.1937, 1-8 vs Southampton, 5th qual rd, 1897-98

Season	Div	Round	Date	Opponent		H/A	Res	Score	Scorers
1895-96	WL	P	Warmley (H) 0-2						
1896-97	WL	1q	Newbury T (A) 1-1; 1qr Newbury T (H) 2-1; 2q Bristol St G. (H) 1-0; 3q RA Portsmouth, scratched						
1897-98	BDL	1q	Warmley (A) 0-0; 1qr Warmley (H) 6-2; 2q Bedminster (H) 3-2; 3q Eastleigh (H) 2-0; 4q Cowes (H) 6-2; 5q Southampton (A) 1-8						
1898-99	BDL	3q	Reading (H) 0-1						
1899-00	SL	3q	Eastleigh (H) 5-0; 4q Portsmouth (H) 1-1; 4qr Portsmouth (A) 0-4						
1900-01	SL	3q	Weymouth (H) 15-1; 4q Swindon T (H) 5-1; 5q Luton T (A) 2-1						
		1	1.2.01	Reading	SL	A	L	0-2	
1901-02	SL	3q	Weymouth Whiteheads (H) 5-0; 4q Bristol C (H) 1-1aet; 4qr Bristol C (A) 3-2; 5q Swindon T (A) 1-0						
		Int	Millwall A (A) 1-1; IntR Millwall A (H) 1-0						
		1	25.1.02	Middlesbrough	D2	A	D	1-1	Jones
		1r	29.1.02	Middlesbrough		H	W	1-0	Becton
		2	28.2.02	Stoke	D1	H	L	0-1	
1902-03	SL	Int	Millwall A (H) 2-2; IntR Millwall A 0-0abnd; Int 2r Millwall A 0-2 at Villa Park						
1903-04	SL	Int	W.Arsenal (H) 1-1; IntR W.Arsenal (A) 1-1; Int 2r W.Arsenal 0-1 at Tottenham						
1904-05	SL	Int	Brighton & HA (A) 2-1						
		1	4.2.05	Bolton W	D2	A	D	1-1	Dunn
		1r	8.2.05	Bolton W		H	L	0-3	
1905-06	SL	1	13.1.06	Sheffield W	D1	A	L	0-1	
1906-07	SL	1	12.1.07	QPR	SL	H	D	0-0	
		1r	14.1.07	QPR		A	W	1-0	Clark
		2	2.2.07	Millwall A	SL	H	W	3-0	Jarvie, Clark, Hutchinson
		3	23.2.07	W.Arsenal	D1	H	L	0-1	
1907-08	SL	1	11.1.08	Northampton T	SL	A	W	1-0	Smith
		2	3.2.08	Chesterfield	D2	H	W	2-0	Clarke 2
		3	22.2.08	Southampton	SL	A	L	0-2	
1908-09	SL	1	16.1.09	Burnley	D2	H	L	1-4	Peplow
1909-10	SL	1	15.1.10	Grimsby T	D2	A	W	2-0	Peplow, Rodgers
		2	5.2.10	Barnsley	D2	A	L	0-4	
1910-11	SL	1	14.1.11	Hull C	D2	H	D	0-0	
		1r	19.1.11	Hull C		A	L	0-1aet	
1911-12	SL	1	13.1.12	Portsmouth	SL	H	L	1-2	A.Hughes
1912-13	SL	1	11.1.13	Notts Co	D1	H	W	2-0	Shervey, Roe
		2	3.2.13	Norwich C	SL	H	D	1-1	Brogan
		2r	6.2.13	Norwich C		A	D	2-2	Peplow, Roe
		2 2r	10.2.13	Norwich C at Stamford Bridge			W	1-0	Shervey
		3	22.2.13	Everton	D1	H	L	0-4	
1913-14	SL	1	10.1.14	Preston NE	D1	A	L	2-5	Shervey 2
1914-15	SL	6q	Bournemouth (H) 3-0						

Season		Round	Date	Opponent	Comp	Venue	Res	Score	Scorers
		1	16.1.15	Southend U	SL	H	D	0-0	
		1r	20.1.15	Southend U		A	L	0-3	
1919-20	SL	6q Northampton T (A) 2-2; 6qr Northampton T (H) 3-2							
		1	10.1.20	Tottenham H	D2	H	L	1-4	Crompton
1920-21	D3	6q Worksop T (H) 9-0							
		1	8.1.21	Tottenham H	D1	A	L	2-6	Walter, Norton
1921-22	3S	5q Exeter C (H) 0-0; 5qr Exeter C (A) 2-0; 6q Swansea T (A) 0-2							
1922-23	3S	5q Reading (A) 1-0; 6q Stalybridge C (A) 0-0; 6qr Stalybridge C (H) 1-2							
1923-24	3S	5q Exeter C (A) 2-2; 5qr Exeter C (H) 0-1							
1924-25	3S	5q Yeovil & Petters U (A) 4-2; 6q Weymouth (H) 0-0; 6qr Weymouth (A) 2-0							
		1	10.1.25	Bristol C	3S	H	L	0-1	
1925-26	3S	1	28.11.25	Aberdare A	3S	A	L	1-4	Lofthouse
1926-27	3S	1	27.11.26	Torquay U	SL	A	D	1-1	Barrett
		1r	1.12.26	Torquay U		H	W	1-0	Williams
		2	11.12.26	Charlton A	3S	H	W	4-1	Culley 2, Barrett, Evans
		3	8.1.27	Portsmouth	D2	H	D	3-3	Culley 2, Clennell
		3r	12.1.27	Portsmouth		A	L	0-4	
1927-28	3S	1	26.11.27	Walsall	3S	H	W	4-2	Williams 2, Douglas, Culley
		2	10.12.27	Bournemouth	3S	A	L	0-1	
1928-29	3S	1	24.11.28	Wellingborough T	UCL	H	W	2-1	Rotherham (p), Murray
		2	8.12.28	Crystal P	3S	A	L	1-3	Phillips
1929-30	3S	1	30.11.29	Nunhead	IL	A	W	2-0	Britton, Phillips
		2	14.12.29	Accrington S	3N	H	W	4-1	Reay 2, Forbes, Phillips
		3	11.1.30	Clapton O	3S	A	L	0-1	
1930-31	3S	1	29.11.30	Merthyr T	SL	H	W	4-1	Attwood, Dix, Forbes, Hamilton
		2	13.12.30	Stockport Co	3N	H	W	4-2	Forbes 2, Ball, Dix
		3	10.1.30	QPR	3S	H	W	3-1	Dennis 2 (2ps), Attwood
		4	24.1.30	Blackburn R	D1	A	L	1-5	Dix
1931-32	3S	1	28.11.31	Gillingham	3S	H	W	5-1	Dix, Townrow, Oakton, Cook, Russell
		2	12.12.31	Tranmere R	3N	A	L	0-2	
1932-33	3S	1	26.11.32	Cardiff C	3S	A	D	1-1	Jackson
		1r	30.11.32	Cardiff C		H	W	4-1	Eyres, McNestry, Jackson, F.Townrow
		2	10.12.32	Gillingham	3S	H	D	1-1	Irving (p)
		2r	14.12.32	Gillingham		A	W	3-1	Eyres, Jackson, McKay
		3	14.1.33	Aldershot	3S	A	L	0-1	
1933-34	3S	1	25.11.33	Folkestone	SL	A	D	0-0	
		1r	29.11.33	Folkestone		H	W	3-1	Taylor, McNestry, McKay
		2	9.12.33	Accrington S	3N	A	L	0-1	
1934-35	3S	1	24.11.34	Harwich & P	ECL	H	W	3-0	Smith, McNestry, Prout
		2	8.12.34	Dartford	SL	A	W	1-0	McNestry (p)
		3	12.1.35	Manchester U	D2	H	L	1-3	McNestry
1935-36	3S	1	30.11.35	Northampton T	3S	H	D	0-0	
		1r	4.12.35	Northampton T		H	W	3-1	Prout 2, A.Taylor
		2	14.12.35	Oldham A	3N	A	D	1-1	Houghton
		2r	18.12.35	Oldham A		H	W	4-1	A.Taylor 3, Houghton
		3	4.1.36	Arsenal	D1	H	L	1-5	Houghton
1936-37	3S	1	28.11.36	Corinthians		A	W	2-0	Harris 2
		2	12.12.36	Southport	3N	H	W	2-1	Harris, McArthur
		3	16.1.37	Leicester C	D2	A	L	2-5	Butterworth, McArthur
1937-38	3S	1	27.11.37	QPR	3S	H	L	1-8	Pendergast
1938-39	3S	1	26.11.38	Peterborough U	ML	H	W	4-1	Tolland 2, Curran, Spivey
		2	10.12.38	Bournemouth	3S	H	L	0-3	
1945-46	3S	1 1L	17.11.45	Swindon T	3S	A	L	0-1	
		1 2L	24.11.45	Swindon T		H	W	4-1	Butterworth 2, Mills, Clarke
		2 1L	8.12.45	Bristol C	3S	A	L	2-4	Mills, Whitfield
		2 2L	15.12.45	Bristol C		H	L	0-2	
1946-47	3S	1	30.11.46	Merthyr T	SL	A	L	1-3	Lambden
1947-48	3S	1	29.11.47	Leytonstone	IL	H	W	3-2	Baldie, Lambden, Morgan
		2	13.12.47	New Brighton	3N	H	W	4-0	Morgan 2, McArthur, Lambden
		3	10.1.48	Swansea T	3S	H	W	3-0	Wookey, Lambden, Morgan
		4	24.1.48	Fulham	D2	A	L	2-5	McArthur, Petherbridge
1948-49	3S	1	27.11.48	Walsall	3S	A	L	1-2	Lambden
1949-50	3S	1	26.11.49	Swindon T	3S	A	L	0-1	
1950-51	3S	1	25.11.50	Llanelli	SL	H	D	1-1	Petherbridge
		1r	28.11.50	Llanelli		A	D	1-1aet	Bush
		1 2r	5.12.50	Llanelli at Ninian Park			W	3-1aet	Pitt, Petherbridge, Bradford
		2	9.12.50	Gillingham	3S	H	D	2-2	Bush, Lambden

123

		2r	13.12.50	Gillingham		A	D	1-1aet	Gough
		2 2r	18.12.50	Gillingham at Tottenham			W	2-1	Bradford, Warrem (p)
		3	10.1.51	Aldershot	3S	H	W	5-1	Lambden 3, Roost, Petherbridge
		4	27.1.51	Luton T	D2	A	W	2-1	Lambden, Petherbridge
		5	10.2.51	Hull C	D2	H	W	3-0	Lambden, Watling 2
		6	24.2.51	Newcastle U	D1	A	D	0-0	
		6r	28.2.51	Newcastle U		H	L	1-3	Bradford
1951-52	3S	1	24.11.51	Kettering T	SL	H	W	3-1	Lambden 2, Bradford
		2	15.12.51	Weymouth	SL	H	W	2-0	Lambden, Petherbridge
		3	12.1.52	Preston NE	D1	H	W	2-0	Lambden, Bradford
		4	2.2.52	Southend U	3S	A	L	1-2	Bradford
1952-53	3S	1	22.11.52	Leyton O	3S	A	D	1-1	Bradford
		1r	24.11.52	Leyton O		H	W	1-0	Roost
		2	6.12.52	Peterborough U	ML	A	W	1-0	Lambden
		3	10.1.53	Huddersfield T	D2	A	L	0-2	
1953-54	D2	3	9.1.54	Blackburn R	D2	H	L	0-1	
1954-55	D2	3	8.1.55	Portsmouth	D1	H	W	2-1	Bradford, Roost
		4	29.1.55	Chelsea	D1	H	L	1-3	Pitt (p)
1955-56	D2	3	7.1.56	Manchester U	D1	H	W	4-0	Biggs 2, Meyer, Bradford
		4	28.1.56	Doncaster R	D2	H	D	1-1	Hooper (p)
		4r	31.1.56	Doncaster R		A	L	0-1	
1956-57	D2	3	5.1.57	Hull C	3N	A	W	4-3	Bradford 2, Ward, Biggs
		4	26.1.57	Preston NE	D1	H	L	1-4	Hooper (p)
1957-58	D2	3	4.1.58	Mansfield T	3N	H	W	5-0	Hooper 2, Biggs, Ward, Petherbridge
		4	25.1.58	Burnley	D1	H	D	2-2	Hale, Shannon og
		4r	28.1.58	Burnley		A	W	3-2	Sykes, Ward 2
		5	15.2.58	Bristol C	D2	A	W	4-3	Meyer, Sykes, Ward, Bradford
		6	1.3.58	Fulham	D2	A	L	1-3	Bradford
1958-59	D2	3	10.1.59	Charlton A	D2	H	L	0-4	
1959-60	D2	3	9.1.60	Doncaster R	D4	H	D	0-0	
		3r	12.1.60	Doncaster R		A	W	2-1	Biggs, Ward
		4	30.1.60	Preston NE	D1	H	D	3-3	Biggs 2, Smith og
		4r	2.2.60	Preston NE		A	L	1-5	Hooper
1960-61	D2	3	7.1.61	A.Villa	D1	H	D	1-1	Biggs
		3r	9.1.61	A.Villa		A	L	0-4	
1961-62	D2	3	8.1.62	Oldham A	D4	H	D	1-1	Sykes
		3r	10.1.62	Oldham A		A	L	0-2	
1962-63	D3	1	3.11.62	Port Vale	D3	H	L	0-2	
1963-64	D3	1	16.11.63	Bournemouth	D3	A	W	3-1	Brown, Biggs (p), Stone
		2	7.12.63	Coventry C	D3	A	W	2-1	Bradford, Jarman
		3	4.1.64	Norwich C	D2	H	W	2-1	Jarman, Bradford
		4	25.1.64	Manchester U	D1	A	L	1-4	Crerand og
1964-65	D3	1	14.11.64	Walsall	D3	A	W	2-0	Stone, R.Jones
		2	5.12.64	Weymouth	SL	H	W	4-1	Jarman 2, Hamilton, Munro
		3	9.1.65	Stockport Co	D4	H	D	0-0	
		3r	11.1.65	Stockport Co		A	L	2-3	R.Mabbutt, R.Jones
1965-66	D3	1	13.11.65	Reading	D3	A	L	2-3	Hillard, R.Jones
1966-67	D3	1	26.11.66	Oxford C	IL	A	D	2-2	Davis (p), Lamb og
		1r	29.11.66	Oxford C		H	W	4-0	Biggs 3, Ronaldson
		2	7.1.67	Luton T	D4	H	W	3-2	Williams, Jarman, Davis
		3	28.1.67	Arsenal	D1	H	L	0-3	
1967-68	D3	1	9.12.67	Arnold T	ML	A	W	3-0	W.Jones, Jarman, Smith og
		2	6.1.68	Wimbledon	SL	A	W	4-0	Biggs 2, W.Jones, Ronaldson
		3	27.1.68	Bristol C	D2	A	D	0-0	
		3r	30.1.68	Bristol C		H	L	1-2	Taylor
1968-69	D3	1	16.11.68	Peterborough U	D4	H	W	3-1	Stanton, R.Mabbutt, Graydon
		2	7.12.68	Bournemouth	D3	A	D	0-0	
		2r	10.12.68	Bournemouth		H	W	1-0	Graydon
		3	4.1.69	Kettering T	SL	H	D	1-1	Graydon
		3r	7.1.69	Kettering T		A	W	2-1	S.Taylor, Gammon og
		4	25.1.69	Bolton W	D2	A	W	2-1	W.Jones 2
		5	12.2.69	Everton	D1	A	L	0-1	
1969-70	D3	1	15.11.69	Telford U	SL	A	W	3-0	R.Jones, Graydon, Stubbs
		2	6.12.69	Aldershot	D4	A	L	1-3	Stubbs
1970-71	D3	1	21.11.70	Fulham	D3	A	W	2-1	Gilbert 2
		2	12.12.70	Aldershot	D4	A	D	1-1	Jarman
		2r	15.12.70	Aldershot		H	L	1-3	Stubbs

Season	Rd	Date	Opponent	Comp	Venue	Res	Score	Scorers
1971-72	D3	1	20.11.71 Telford U	SL	H	W	3-0	Bannister 2, Godfrey
		2	11.12.71 Cambridge U	D4	H	W	3-0	Taylor, Bannister, Godfrey
		3	15.1.72 Leeds U	D1	A	L	1-4	Allan
1972-73	D3	1	18.11.72 Hayes	IL	A	L	0-1	
1973-74	D3	1	24.11.73 Bideford	SL	A	W	2-0	Warboys, Bannister
		2	15.12.73 Northampton T	D4	A	W	2-1	Warboys, Fearnley
		3	6.1.74 Nottingham F	D2	A	L	3-4	Prince, Dobson, Rudge
1974-75	D2	3	4.1.75 Blackburn R	D3	A	W	2-1	Fearnley, Bannister
		4	27.1.75 Derby Co	D1	A	L	0-2	
1975-76	D2	3	1.1.76 Chelsea	D2	A	D	1-1	Warboys
		3r	3.1.76 Chelsea		H	L	0-1	
1976-77	D2	3	8.1.77 Nottingham F	D2	A	D	1-1	D.Williams
		3r	11.1.77 Nottingham F		H	D	1-1aet	Warboys
		3 2r	18.1.77 Nottingham F at Villa Park			L	0-6	
1977-78	D2	3	7.1.78 Sunderland	D2	A	W	1-0	Gould
		4	28.1.78 Southampton	D2	H	W	2-0	Randall 2
		5	18.2.78 Ipswich T	D1	H	D	2-2	Williams 2
		5r	28.2.78 Ipswich T		A	L	0-3	
1978-79	D2	3	9.1.79 Swansea C	D3	A	W	1-0	White
		4	5.2.79 Charlton A	D2	H	W	1-0	White
		5	26.2.79 Ipswich T	D1	A	L	1-6	White
1979-80	D2	3	4.1.80 A.Villa	D1	H	L	1-2	Barrowclough
1980-81	D2	3	3.1.81 Preston NE	D2	A	W	4-3	G.Mabbutt, Barrowclough, Barrett, G.Williams
		4	24.1.81 Southampton	D1	A	L	1-3	G.Williams
1981-82	D3	1	21.11.81 Fulham	D3	H	L	1-2	D.Williams (p)
1982-83	D3	1	20.11.82 Wycombe W	IL	H	W	1-0	Stephens
		2	11.12.82 Plymouth A	D3	H	D	2-2	D.Williams 2
		2r	20.12.82 Plymouth A		A	L	0-1	
1983-84	D3	1	19.11.83 Barnet	APL	A	D	0-0	
		1r	22.11.83 Barnet		H	W	3-1	Holloway, Barrett, Slatter
		2	10.12.83 Bristol C	D4	H	L	1-2	Stephens
1984-85	D3	1	17.11.84 King's Lynn	SL	H	W	2-1	D.Williams, Adams og
		2	8.12.84 Bristol C	D3	A	W	3-1	O'Connor, Randall 2
		3	5.1.85 Ipswich T	D1	H	L	1-2	Holloway
1985-86	D3	1	16.11.85 Brentford	D3	A	W	3-1	Penrice, White, Francis
		2	7.12.85 Swansea C	D3	A	W	2-1	Morgan (p), White
		3	4.1.86 Leicester C	D1	H	W	3-1	Stevenson, Morgan 2
		4	25.1.86 Luton T	D1	A	L	0-4	
1986-87	D3	1	3.12.86 Brentford	D3	H	D	0-0	
		1r	6.12.86 Brentford		A	L	0-2	
1987-88	D3	1	14.11.87 Merthyr T	SL	H	W	6-0	Penrice 3, White 2, Meacham
		2	5.12.87 VS Rugby	SL	A	D	1-1	Meacham
		2r	17.12.87 VS Rugby		H	W	4-0	Penrice, Alexander, White, Reece
		3	9.1.88 Shrewsbury T	D2	A	L	1-2	Penrice
1988-89	D3	1	20.11.88 Fisher A	GMVC	H	W	3-0	Jones, Penrice, Holloway (p)
		2	10.12.88 Kettering T	GMVC	A	L	1-2	Reece
1989-90	D3	1	18.11.89 Reading	D3	H	D	1-1	Reece
		1r	21.11.89 Reading		A	D	1-1aet	Mehew
		1 2r	27.11.89 Reading		H	L	0-1	
1990-91	D2	3	5.1.91 Crewe Alex	D3	H	L	0-2	
1991-92	D2	3	5.1.92 Plymouth A	D2	H	W	5-0	Alexander, Saunders 4
		4	5.2.92 Liverpool	D1	H	D	1-1	Saunders
		4r	11.2.92 Liverpool		A	L	1-2	Saunders
1992-93	D1	3	2.1.93 Aston Villa	PL	A	D	1-1	Browning
		3r	20.1.93 Aston Villa		H	L	0-3	

BROMLEY

Formed 1892. **First entered FA Cup:** 1897. FA Amateur Cup Winners: 1911, 1938, 1949

Season	Rd	Date	Opponent	Comp	Venue	Res	Score	Scorers
1937-38	AL	1	27.11.37 Kings Lynn	ECL	A	W	4-0	Brown 2, Horsnall, Holbrook
		2	11.12.37 Scarborough	ML	A	L	1-4	Brown
1938-39	AL	1	26.11.38 Apsley	SPT	H	W	2-1	Timorthy, Thomas
		2	10.12.38 Lincoln C	3N	A	L	1-8	Reece
1945-46	AL	1 1L	17.11.45 Slough U	CRN	H	–	2-1	Scott, Coulsen
			abandoned after 80 minutes					
		1 1Lr	21.11.45 Slough U		H	W	6-1	Scott 2, Viles, Ruddy, Crowther, Reece

	1 2L	24.11.45	**Slough U**		A	L	0-1	
	2 1L	8.12.45	**Watford**	3S	H	L	1-3	Ruddy
	2 2L	15.12.45	**Watford**		A	D	1-1	Coulson
1947-48	AL 1	29.11.47	**Reading**	3S	H	D	3-3aet	Brown 2, Hopper
	1r	6.12.47	**Reading**		A	L	0-3	
1949-50	AL 1	26.11.49	**Watford**	3S	H	L	1-2	J.Jones
1950-51	AL 1	25.11.50	**Aldershot**	3S	A	D	2-2	G.Brown 2
	1r	29.11.50	**Aldershot**		H	L	0-1	
1951-52	AL 1	24.11.51	**Torquay U**	3S	A	L	2-3	Dunmall, Jones
1976-77	IL 1	20.11.76	**Swindon T**	D3	A	L	0-7	

BROMSGROVE ROVERS

Formed 1885. **First entered FA Cup:** 1910

1947-48	BC 1	29.11.47	**Aldershot**	3S	A	L	1-2	Cave
1949-50	BC 1	26.11.49	**Hereford U**	SL	A	L	0-3	
1950-51	BC 1	25.11.50	**Hereford U**	SL	H	L	1-3	Davenport
1956-57	BDL 1	17.11.56	**Tooting & Mitcham**	IL	A	L	1-2	Jakeman
1986-87	SL 1	15.11.86	**Newport Co**	D3	H	L	0-1	
1988-89	SL 1	19.11.88	**Welling**	GMVC	A	L	0-3	
1989-90	SL 1	17.11.89	**Basingstoke**	IL	A	L	0-3	
1991-92	SL 1	16.11.91	**Bournemouth**	D3	A	L	1-3	O'Meara (p)

BRONDESBURY

Formed 1869. Played in north London.

1873-74	1	11.10.73	**Royal Engineers**	A	L	0-5	
1874-75	1	31.10.74	**Oxford University**	A	L	0-6	

BRUSH SPORTS, LOUGHBOROUGH

First entered the FA Cup: 1946. Became Loughborough United in 1960 and folded in 1963

1946-47	N&D 1	30.11.46	**Southend U**	3S	H	L	1-6	Coleman
1951-52	BDL 1	24.11.51	**Weymouth**	SL	H	L	2-3	A.Naylor, Allen

BUCKINGHAM TOWN

Formed 1883. **First entered the FA Cup:** 1950

1984-85	UCL 1	17.11.84	**Orient**	D3	H	L	0-2

BURNLEY

Formed 1882. Founder Member of Football League 1888. **FA Cup Winners:** 1914. **FA Cup Runners Up:** 1947, 1962. **Record FA Cup Win:** 9-0 vs Crystal Palace, 2nd round replay, 10.2.1909; vs New Brighton, 4th round, 26.1.1957 and vs Penrith, 1st round, 17.11.1984. **Record FA Cup Defeat:** 0-11 vs Darwen Old Wanderers 1st round, 17.10.1885.

1885-86		1	17.10.85	**Darwen Old Wanderers**		A	L	0-11	
				Burnley fielded their reserves					
1886-87		1	23.10.86	**Astley Bridge**		A	D	3-3	Place Snr, 2 others
		1r	30.10.86	**Astley Bridge**		H	D	2-2	
				FA disqualified Burnley after protest					
1887-88		1	15.10.87	**Darwen Old W**		H	W	4-0	Friel, McFettridge, 2 others
				Replay ordered after protest					
		1r		**Darwen Old W**			walkover		
		2	5.11.87	**Accrington**		A	L	2-3	
1888-89	D1	1	2.2.89	**Old Westminsters**		H	W	4-3	Gallocher 2, Lang, W.Brady
		2	16.2.89	**WBA**	D1	A	L	1-5	Gallocher
1889-90	D1	1	18.1.90	**Sheffield U**		A	L	1-2	Bury
1890-91	D1	1	17.1.91	**Crewe A**	FAll	H	W	4-2aet	Lambie, Oswald, McLardie, Hill
		2	31.1.91	**Notts Co**	D1	A	L	1-2	McLardie
1891-92	D1	1	23.1.92	**Everton**	D1	A	W	3-1	Hill 2, Nicol
		2	30.1.92	**Stoke C**	D1	H	L	1-3	Hill
1892-93	D1	1	21.1.93	**Small Heath**	D2	H	W	2-0	McNab, Hill
		2	4.2.93	**Sheffield W**	D1	A	L	0-1	
1893-94	D1	1	27.1.94	**Notts Co**	D2	A	L	0-1	

Season	Div	Round	Date	Opponent		Venue	W/D/L	Score	Scorers
1894-95	D1	1	2.2.95	Newcastle Utd	D2	A	L	1-2	Bowes
1895-96	D1	1	1.2.96	Woolwich Arsenal	D2	H	W	6-1	Place Jnr 2, Robertson 2, Nicol, Place Snr
		2	15.2.96	Stoke	D1	H	D	1-1	'Scrimmage'
		2r	20.2.96	Stoke		A	L	1-7	Bowes
1896-97	D1	1	30.1.97	Sunderland	D1	A	L	0-1	
1897-98	D2	1	29.1.98	Woolwich Arsenal	D2	H	W	3-1	Taylor, Place Jnr, Ferguson
		2	12.2.98	Burslem Port Vale	ML	H	W	3-0	Bowes, Beveridge, Ross
		3	26.3.98	Everton	D1	H	L	1-3	Place jnr
1898-99	D1	1	28.1.99	Sheffield U	D1	H	D	2-2	Toman, Bowes
		1r	2.2.99	Sheffield U		A	L	1-2	Ross (p)
1899-00	D1	1	27.1.00	Bury	D1	H	L	0-1	
1900-01	D2	1	9.2.01	Newton Heath	D2	A	D	0-0	
		1r	13.2.01	Newton Heath		H	W	7-1	Morrison 2, Jenkinson 2, Mole, Bannister, Taylor
		2	23.2.01	Small Heath	D2	A	L	0-1	
1901-02	D2	Int	14.12.01	Bishop Auckland	NL	A	W	3-2	Hogan 2, Barron
		1	25.1.02	Walsall	ML	A	L	0-1	
1902-03	D2	1	13.12.02	Reading	SL	A	L	0-1	
1903-04	D2	3q	Keswick (H) 8-0; 4q Darwen (A) 0-2						
1904-05	D2	Int	14.1.05	Lincoln C	D2	H	D	1-1	Marshall
		Int R	18.1.05	Lincoln C		A	L	2-3	J.Smith, Marshall
1905-06	D2	1	13.1.06	Tottenham H	SL	A	L	0-2	
1906-07	D2	1	12.1.07	Aston Villa	D1	H	L	1-3	Whittaker
1907-08	D2	1	11.1.08	Southampton	SL	A	L	1-2	Bell
1908-09	D2	1	16.1.09	Bristol R	SL	A	W	4-2	Ogden 3, R.Smith
		2	6.2.09	Crystal P	SL	A	D	0-0	
		2r	10.2.09	Crystal P		H	W	9-0	R.Smith 3, Abbott 2, Cretney 2, Smethams, Moffat
		3	20.2.09	Tottenham H	D2	A	D	0-0	
		3r	24.2.09	Tottenham H		H	W	3-1	Ogden, R.Smith, Abbott
		4	6.3.09	Manchester U	D1	H	–	1-0	Ogden
			abandoned after 72 minutes						
		4	10.3.09	Manchester U		H	L	2-3	Ogden 2
1909-10	D2	1	15.1.10	Manchester U	D1	H	W	2-0	Green, Smethams
		2	5.2.10	Sunderland	D1	A	L	0-2	
1910-11	D2	1	14.1.11	Exeter C	SL	H	W	2-0	Morley, Mayson
		2	4.2.11	Barnsley	D2	H	W	2-0	Morley, Green
		3	25.2.11	Coventry C	SL	H	W	5-0	Green 2, Mayson 2, Watson,
		4	11.3.11	Bradford C	D1	A	L	0-1	
1911-12	D2	1	13.1.12	Fulham	D2	A	L	1-2	Freeman
1912-13	D2	1	15.1.13	Leeds C	D2	A	W	3-2	Boyle (p), Lindley, Freeman
		2	1.2.13	Gainsborough T	ML	H	W	4-1	Hodgson 2, Freeman, Boyle (p)
		3	22.2.13	Middlesbrough	D1	H	W	3-1	Freeman 2, Hodgson
		4	8.3.13	Blackburn R	D1	A	W	1-0	Boyle (p)
		SF	29.3.13	Sunderland	D1		D	0-0	
			played at Bramall Lane						
		SFr	2.4.13	Sunderland at St Andrews			L	2-3	Freeman, Boyle
1913-14	D1	1	10.1.14	South Shields	Wear	H	W	3-1	Lindley 2, Freeman
		2	31.1.14	Derby Co	D1	H	W	3-2	Hodgson 3
		3	21.2.14	Bolton W	D1	H	W	3-0	Freeman, Hodgson, Halley
		4	7.3.14	Sunderland	D1	A	D	0-0	
		4r	11.3.14	Sunderland		H	W	2-1	Lindley, Hodgson
		SF	28.3.14	Sheffield U	D1		D	0-0	
			played at Old Trafford						
		SFr	1.4.14	Sheffield U at Goodison Park			W	1-0	Boyle
		F	25.4.14	LIVERPOOL	D1	Crystal P	W	1-0	Freeman
1914-15	D1	1	9.1.15	Huddersfield T	D2	H	W	3-1	Freeman, Kelly, Thorpe
		2	30.1.15	Southend U	SL	H	W	6-0	Freeman 2, Kelly, Watson, Boyle (p), Thorpe
		3	20.2.15	Bolton W	D1	A	L	1-2aet	Hodgson
1919-20	D1	1	10.1.20	Thorneycrofts	Hants	A	D	0-0	
			played at Fratton Park						
		1r	13.1.20	Thorneycrofts		H	W	5-0	Lindsay 3, Nesbitt, Cragg
		2	31.1.20	Sunderland	D1	H	D	1-1	Kelly
		2r	4.2.20	Sunderland		A	L	0-2	
1920-21	D1	1	8.1.21	Leicester C	D2	A	W	7-3	Anderson 5, Kelly, Cross
		2	29.1.21	QPR	D3	H	W	4-2	Kelly 2, Anderson 2
		3	19.2.21	Hull C	D2	A	L	0-3	
1921-22	D1	1	7.1.22	Huddersfield T	D1	H	D	2-2	Anderson, Mosscrop
		1r	11.1.22	Huddersfield T		A	L	2-3	Kelly, Boyle

Season	Div	Round	Date	Opponent		H/A	Res	Score	Scorers
1922-23	D1	1	13.1.23	Sunderland	D1	A	L	1-3	Anderson
1923-24	D1	1	12.1.24	South Shields	D2	H	W	3-2	Kelly 2, Cross
		2	2.2.24	Fulham	D2	H	D	0-0	
		2r	7.2.24	Fulham		A	W	1-0aet	Cross
		3	23.2.24	Huddersfield T	D1	H	W	1-0	Weaver
		4	8.3.24	Swindon T	3S	A	D	1-1	Weaver
		4r	12.3.24	Swindon T		H	W	3-1	Beel 2, Weaver
		SF	29.3.24	Aston Villa	D1		L	0-3	
				played at Bramall Lane					
1924-25	D1	1	10.1.25	Everton	D1	A	L	1-2	Roberts
1925-26	D1	3	9.1.26	Cardiff C	D1	A	D	2-2	Beel 2
		3r	13.1.26	Cardiff C		H	L	0-2	
1926-27	D1	3	8.1.27	Grimsby T	D2	H	W	3-1	Bruton, Beel, Page
		4	29.1.27	Fulham	D2	A	W	4-0	Beel 2, Page, Bruton
		5	19.2.27	Chelsea	D2	A	L	1-2	Cross
1927-28	D1	3	14.1.28	Aston Villa	D1	H	L	0-2	
1928-29	D1	3	12.1.29	Sheffield U	D1	H	W	2-1	Beel, Page
		4	26.1.29	Swindon T	3S	H	D	3-3	Devine, Page, McCluggage
		4r	30.1.29	Swindon T		A	L	2-3	Beel, Devine
1929-30	D1	3	11.1.30	Sheffield W	D1	A	L	0-1	
1930-31	D2	3	10.1.31	Manchester C	D1	H	W	3-0	Prest, McCluggage, Jenkins
		4	24.1.31	Bradford PA	D2	A	L	0-2	
1931-32	D2	3	9.1.32	Derby Co	D1	H	L	0-4	
1932-33	D2	3	14.1.33	Swindon T	3S	A	W	2-1	Harker, C.Smith
		4	28.1.33	Sheffield U	D1	H	W	3-1	C.Smith, Mee 2
		5	18.2.33	Chesterfield	D2	H	W	1-0	Hancock
		6	4.3.33	Manchester C	D1	H	L	0-1	
1933-34	D2	3	13.1.34	Bury	D2	H	D	0-0	
		3r	17.1.34	Bury		A	L	2-3	C.Smith, Richmond
1934-35	D2	3	12.1.35	Mansfield T	3N	H	W	4-2	Hancock 2, G.Brown, C.Smith
		4	26.1.35	Luton T	3S	H	W	3-1	G.Brown, C.Smith, Hancock
		5	16.2.35	Nottingham F	D2	A	D	0-0	
		5r	19.2.35	Nottingham F		H	W	3-0	Robinson, Hancock, G.Brown
		6	2.3.35	Birmingham	D1	H	W	3-2	Hornby 2, Hancock
		SF	16.3.35	Sheffield W	D1		L	0-3	
				played at Villa Park					
1935-36	D2	3	11.1.36	Sheffield U	D2	H	D	0-0	
		3r	16.1.36	Sheffield U		A	L	1-2	Hancock
1936-37	D2	3	16.1.37	Aston Villa	D2	A	W	3-2	Toll 2, Brocklebank
		4	30.1.37	Bury	D1	H	W	4-1	Stein, Toll, Brocklebank, Fletcher
		5	20.2.37	Arsenal	D1	H	L	1-7	Richardson
1937-38	D2	3	8.1.38	Sheffield W	D2	A	D	1-1	Stein
		3r	11.1.38	Sheffield W		H	W	3-1	Brocklebank 2, Hornby
		4	22.1.38	Chesterfield	D2	A	L	2-3	Miller, Robson
1938-39	D2	3	7.1.39	Notts Co	3S	A	L	1-3	Brocklebank
1945-46	D2	3 1L	5.1.46	Stoke C	D1	A	L	1-3	Morris
		3 2L	7.1.46	Stoke C		H	W	2-1	Jackson, Kippax
1946-47	D2	3	11.1.47	Aston Villa	D1	H	W	5-1	Morris 2, Harrison 2, Potts
		4	25.1.47	Coventry C	D2	H	W	2-0	Chew, Potts
		5	8.2.47	Luton T	D2	A	D	0-0	
		5r	11.2.47	Luton T		H	W	3-0	Harrison 3
		6	1.3.47	Middlesbrough	D1	A	D	1-1	Morris
		6r	4.3.47	Middlesbrough		H	W	1-0aet	Morris
		SF	29.3.47	Liverpool	D1		D	0-0aet	
				played at Ewood Park					
		SFr	12.4.47	Liverpool at Maine Road			W	1-0	Harrison
		F	26.4.47	Charlton A	D1 WEMBLEY		L	0-1aet	
1947-48	D1	3	10.1.48	Swindon T	3S	H	L	0-2	
1948-49	D1	3	8.1.49	Charlton A	D1	H	W	2-1aet	McLaren, Clarke
		4	29.1.49	Rotherham U	3N	A	W	1-0	Spencer
		5	12.2.49	Brentford	D2	A	L	2-4	Attwell, Bray
1949-50	D1	3	7.1.50	Notts Co	3S	A	W	4-1	Spencer, Attwell, Potts, Wilson
		4	28.1.50	Port Vale	3S	H	W	2-1	Spencer, Hays
		5	11.2.50	Arsenal	D1	A	L	0-2	
1950-51	D1	3	6.1.51	Aston Villa	D1	A	L	0-2	
1951-52	D1	3	12.1.52	Hartlepools U	3N	H	W	1-0	Shanon
		4	2.2.52	Coventry C	D2	H	W	2-0	Holden, Elliott

B U R N L E Y

Season	Div	Rd	Date	Opponent	Opp	H/A	Result	Score	Scorers
		5	23.2.52	Liverpool	D1	H	W	2-0	Morris, Shannon
		6	8.3.52	Blackburn R	D2	A	L	1-3	Chew
1952-53	D1	3	10.1.53	Portsmouth	D1	A	D	1-1	Stephenson
		3r	13.1.53	Portsmouth		H	W	3-1	McIlroy, Shannon, Elliott
		4	31.1.53	Sunderland	D1	H	W	2-0	Holden 2
		5	14.2.53	Arsenal	D1	H	L	0-2	
1953-54	D1	3	9.1.54	Manchester U	D1	H	W	5-3	Shannon 2, Holden, McIlroy, Gry
		4	30.1.54	Newcastle U	D1	H	D	1-1	Pilkington
		4r	3.2.54	Newcastle U		A	L	0-1	
1954-55	D1	3	8.1.55	Sunderland	D1	A	L	0-1	
1955-56	D1	3	7.1.56	Bury	D2	A	–	2-2	McKay 2
			abandoned 65 minutes						
			10.1.56	Bury		A	W	1-0	Gray
		4	28.1.56	Chelsea	D1	H	D	1-1	McKay
		4r	1.2.56	Chelsea		A	D	1-1aet	Pilkington
		4 2r	6.2.56	Chelsea at St Andrews			D	2-2aet	McIlroy, McKay
		4 3r	13.2.56	Chelsea at Highbury			D	0-0aet	
		4 4r	15.2.56	Chelsea at White Hart Lane			L	0-2	
1956-57	D1	3	5.1.57	Chesterfield	3N	H	W	7-0	Lawson 4, Cheesebrough 2, Pilkington
		4	26.1.57	New Brighton	LC	H	W	9-0	McIlroy 3, Lawson 3, Newlands, Cheesebrough, Pilkington
		5	16.2.57	Huddersfield T	D2	A	W	2-1	Lawson, Cheesebrough
		6	2.3.57	Aston Villa	D1	H	D	1-1	Aldis og
		6r	6.3.57	Aston Villa		A	L	0-2	
1957-58	D1	3	4.1.58	Swansea T	D2	H	W	4-2	McIlroy 2, Newlands, Cheesebrough
		4	25.1.58	Bristol R	D2	A	D	2-2	Pointer, Connelly
		4r	28.1.58	Bristol R		H	L	2-3	McIlroy, Pointer
1958-59	D1	3	14.1.59	Stockport Co	D3	A	W	3-1	Pointer 2, Pilkington
		4	28.1.59	Blackburn R	D1a	A	W	2-1	Robson, McIlroy
		5	14.2.59	Portsmouth	D1	H	W	1-0	Adamson
		6	28.2.59	Aston Villa	D1	A	D	0-0	
		6r	3.3.59	Aston Villa		H	D	0-2	
1959-60	D1	3	9.1.60	Lincoln C	D2	A	D	1-1	Pointer
		3r	12.1.60	Lincoln C		H	W	2-0	McIlroy, Pilkington
		4	30.1.60	Swansea T	D2	A	D	0-0	
		4r	2.2.60	Swansea T		H	W	2-1	Robson 2
		5	20.2.60	Bradford C	D3	A	D	2-2	Connelly 2
		5r	23.2.60	Bradford C		H	W	5-0	Pointer 2, Robson 2, Connelly
		6	12.3.60	Blackburn R	D1	H	D	3-3	Pointer, Pilkington, Connelly
		6r	16.3.60	Blackburn R		A	L	0-2	
1960-61	D1	3	7.1.61	Bournemouth	D3	H	W	1-0	Connelly
		4	28.1.61	Brighton & HA	D2	A	D	3-3	Miller, Pointer, Robson
		4r	31.1.61	Brighton & HA		H	W	2-0	Miller, Robson
		5	18.2.61	Swansea T	D2	H	W	4-0	Robson 2, Pointer, Connelly
		6	4.3.61	Sheffield W	D1	A	D	0-0	
		6r	7.3.61	Sheffield W		H	W	2-0	McIlroy, Robson
		SF	18.3.61	Tottenham H	D1		L	0-3	
			played at Villa Park						
1961-62	D1	3	6.1.62	QPR	D3	H	W	6-1	Harris 2, Elder, Connelly, McIlroy, Ingham og
		4	30.1.62	Leyton O	D2	H	D	1-1	Harris
		4r	6.2.62	Leyton O		A	W	1-0	Miller
		5	17.2.62	Everton	D1	H	W	3-1	Miller, Connelly, Robson
		6	10.3.62	Sheffield U	D1	A	W	1-0	Pointer
		SF	31.3.62	Fulham	D1		D	1-1	Connelly
			played at Villa Park						
		SFr	9.4.62	Fulham at Filbert Street			W	2-1	Robson 2
		F	5.5.62	Tottenham H	D1 WEMBLEY		L	1-3	Robson
1962-63	D1	3	16.1.63	Tottenham H	D1	A	W	3-0	Connelly, Lochhead, Harris
		4	26.1.63	Liverpool	D1	H	D	1-1	Connelly
		4r	20.2.63	Liverpool		A	L	1-2aet	Elder
1963-64	D1	3	4.1.64	Rotherham U	D2	H	D	1-1	Lochhead
		3r	7.1.64	Rotherham U		A	W	3-2	Lochhead, Connelly, Towers
		4	25.1.64	Newport Co	D4	H	W	2-1	Morgan, Connelly
		5	15.2.64	Huddersfield T	D2	H	W	3-0	Pointer, Lochhead, Atkins og
		6	29.2.64	West Ham	D1	A	L	2-3	Connelly, Pointer
1964-65	D1	3	9.1.65	Brentford	D3	H	D	1-1	Irvine
		3r	12.1.65	Brentford		A	W	2-0	Irvine 2

BURNLEY

Season	Div	Round	Date	Opponent	Comp	H/A	Res	Score	Scorers
		4	30.1.65	Reading	D3	A	D	1-1	Lochhead
		4r	2.2.65	Reading		H	W	1-0	Lochhead
		5	20.2.65	Manchester U	D1	A	L	1-2	Lochhead
1965-66	D1	3	22.1.66	Bournemouth	D3	A	D	1-1	Irvine
		3r	25.1.66	Bournemouth		H	W	7-0	Lochhead 5, Irvine, Harris
		4	12.2.66	Tottenham H	D1	A	L	3-4	Irvine 3
1966-67	D1	3	28.1.67	Everton	D1	H	D	0-0	
		3r	31.1.67	Everton		A	L	1-2	Irvine
1967-68	D1	3	27.1.68	West Ham U	D1	H	L	1-3	Casper
1968-69	D1	3	4.1.69	Derby Co	D2	H	W	3-1	Casper 2, Blant
		4	25.1.69	Liverpool	D1	A	L	1-2	Latcham
1969-70	D1	3	3.1.70	Wolverhampton W	D1	H	W	3-0	O'Neill, Dobson, Casper
		4	24.1.70	Chelsea	D1	A	D	2-2	Dobson 2
		4r	27.1.70	Chelsea		H	L	1-3aet	Coates
1970-71	D1	3	11.1.71	Oxford U	D2	A	L	0-3	
1971-72	D2	3	15.1.72	Huddersfield T	D1	H	L	0-1	
1972-73	D2	3	13.1.73	Liverpool	D1	H	D	0-0	
		3r	16.1.73	Liverpool		A	L	0-3	
1973-74	D1	3	5.1.74	Grimsby T	D3	A	W	2-0	Newton, Hankin
		4	26.1.74	Oldham A	D3	A	W	4-1	Dobson 2, Fletcher, James
		5	16.2.74	Aston Villa	D2	H	W	1-0	Fletcher
		6	9.4.74	Wrexham	D3	H	W	1-0	Casper
		SF	30.4.74	Newcastle U	D1		L	0-2	
			played at Hillsborough						
1974-75	D1	3	4.1.75	Wimbledon	SL	H	L	0-1	
1975-76	D1	3	3.1.76	Blackpool	D2	A	L	0-1	
1976-77	D2	3	8.1.77	Lincoln C	D3	H	D	2-2	Noble, Fletcher
		3r	12.1.77	Lincoln C		A	W	1-0	Fletcher
		4	29.1.77	Port Vale	D3	A	L	1-2	Flynn (p)
1977-78	D2	3	7.1.78	Everton	D1	H	W	1-0	Fletcher
		4	31.1.78	Chelsea	D1	A	L	2-6	Fletcher, Kindon
1978-79	D2	3	9.1.79	Birmingham C	D1	A	W	2-0	Morley, James
		4	21.2.79	Sunderland	D2	H	D	1-1	Thompson
		4r	26.2.79	Sunderland		A	W	3-0	Ingham, Fletcher, Kindon
		5	28.2.79	Liverpool	D1	A	L	0-3	
1979-80	D2	3	5.1.80	Stoke C	D1	H	W	1-0	Dobson
		4	26.1.80	Bury	D3	A	L	0-1	
1980-81	D3	1	22.11.80	Scarborough	APL	H	W	1-0	Hamilton
		2	13.12.80	Port Vale	D4	H	D	1-1	Potts
		2r	16.12.80	Port Vale		A	L	0-2	
1981-82	D3	1	21.11.81	Runcorn	APL	H	D	0-0	
		1r	24.11.81	Runcorn		A	W	2-1	McGee 2
		2	2.1.82	Bury	D4	A	D	1-1	Taylor
		2r	4.1.82	Bury		H	W	2-1aet	Steven, Hamilton
		3	18.1.82	Altrincham	APL	H	W	6-1	Hamilton 3, Taylor 2, Steven
		4	23.1.82	Shrewsbury T	D2	A	L	0-1	
1982-83	D2	3	8.1.83	Carlisle U	D2	A	D	2-2	Taylor, Wharton
		3r	11.1.83	Carlisle U		H	W	3-1	Flynn, Stevens, Laws (p)
		4	29.1.83	Swindon T	D4	H	W	3-1	Hamilton 2, Steven
		5	19.2.83	Crystal P	D2	A	D	0-0	
		5r	28.2.83	Crystal P		H	W	1-0	Taylor (p)
		6	12.3.83	Sheffield W	D2	H	D	1-1	Cassidy
		6r	15.3.83	Sheffield W		A	L	0-5	
1983-84	D3	1	19.11.83	Hyde U	NPL	H	W	2-0	Reeves, Waldron
		2	10.12.83	Chesterfield	D4	A	D	2-2	Dobson, Reeves
		2r	19.12.83	Chesterfield		H	W	3-2	Hamilton 2, Reeves
		3	7.1.84	Oxford U	D3	H	D	0-0	
		3r	11.1.84	Oxford U		A	L	1-2	Hamilton
1984-85	D3	1	17.11.84	Penrith at Turf Moor	NWC	A	W	9-0	Hird 3(1p), Taylor 3, Powell 2, Grewcock
		2	8.12.84	Halifax T	D4	H	W	3-1	Hird, Devine, Biggins
		3	5.1.85	Wimbledon	D2	A	L	1-3	Devine
1985-86	D4	1	16.11.85	Nuneaton B	APL	A	W	3-2	Devine 2, Malley
		2	7.12.85	Rotherham U	D3	A	L	1-4	Parker
1986-87	D4	1	15.11.86	Telford U	GMVC	A	L	0-3	
1987-88	D4	1	14.11.87	Bolton W	D4	H	L	0-1	
1988-89	D4	1	19.11.88	Chester C	D3	H	L	0-2	
1989-90	D4	1	18.11.89	Stockport Co	D4	H	D	1-1	White (p)

BURNLEY

	1r	22.11.89	Stockport Co		A	W	2-1	O'Connell, Futcher
	2	9.12.89	Scunthorpe U	D4	A	D	2-2	Deary, Mumby
	2r	12.12.89	Scunthorpe U		H	D	1-1aet	Eli
	2 2r	18.12.89	Scunthorpe U		H	W	5-0	Eli 2, Futcher 2, Hardy
	3	6.1.90	Blackpool	D3	A	L	0-1	
1990-91 D4	1	17.11.90	Stafford R	GMVC	A	W	3-1	Collymore og, White, Mumby
	2	12.12.90	Stoke C	D3	H	W	2-0	Francis, White
	3	6.1.91	Manchester C	D1	H	L	0-1	
1991-92 D4	1	16.11.91	Doncaster R	D4	H	D	1-1	Davis
	1r	27.11.91	Doncaster R		A	W	3-1	Harper 2, Eli
	2	7.12.91	Rotherham U	D4	H	W	2-0	Conroy, Lancashire
	3	4.1.92	Derby Co	D2	H	D	2-2	Harper, Eli
	3r	14.1.92	Derby Co		A	L	0-2	
			abandoned after 76 minutes – fog					
	3r	25.1.92	Derby Co		A	L	0-2	
1992-93 D2	1	14.11.92	Scarborough	D3	H	W	2-1	Conroy, Curran og
	2	5.12.92	Shrewsbury T	D3	H	D	1-1	Conroy
	2r	15.12.92	Shrewsbury T		A	W	2-1	Pender, Conroy
	3	2.1.93	Sheffield U	PL	A	D	2-2	Heath 2
	3r	12.1.93	Sheffield U		H	L	2-4	Heath, Monington

BURSCOUGH

Formed 1946. **First entered FA Cup:** 1947

1959-60 LC	1	14.11.59	Crewe A	D4	H	L	1-3	J.Jones
1977-78 CC	1	26.11.77	Blyth Spartans	NL	A	L	0-1	
1979-80 CC	1	24.11.79	Sheffield U	D3	H	L	0-3	
			played at Bramall Lane					
1980-81 CC	1	22.11.80	Altrincham	APL	H	L	1-2	Perry

BURTON ALBION

Formed 1950. **First entered FA Cup:** 1951. **FA Challenge Trophy Runners-up** 1987. **League clubs beaten:** Halifax T, Aldershot. **Cup Final Connection:** Ian Hutchinson, who played for Chelsea in the 1970 final, started his career at Burton Albion

1955-56 BDL	1	19.11.55	Wycombe W	IL	A	W	3-1	Hughes, Bullock, Bowering
	2	10.12.55	Halifax T	3N	A	D	0-0	
	2r	14.12.55	Halifax T		H	W	1-0	Barker
	3	7.1.56	Charlton A	D1	A	L	0-7	
1956-57 BDL	1	17.11.56	Bournemouth	3S	A	L	0-8	
1965-66 SL	1	13.11.65	Corby T	SL	A	L	3-6	Aston, Round 2
1977-78 SL	1	26.11.77	Wrexham	D3	A	L	0-2	
1979-80 NPL	1	24.11.79	Bury	D3	H	L	0-2	
1980-81 NPL	1	22.11.80	Blyth Spartans	NL	A	L	1-2	Kent
1983-84 NPL	1	19.11.83	Windsor & Eton	IL	H	L	1-2	Dolby
1984-85 NPL	1	17.11.84	Staines	IL	H	W	2-0	Mell, Newton
	2	8.12.84	Aldershot	D4	A	W	2-0	Simmons, Mell
	3	5.1.85	Leicester C at Derby	D1	H	L	1-6	Vaughan
			FA ordered match to be replayed behind closed doors following coin-throwing incident					
	3r	16.1.85	Leicester C at Coventry			L	0-1	
1987-88 SL	1	14.11.87	York C	D3	A	D	0-0	
	1r	18.11.87	York C		H	L	1-2	Groves (p)

BURTON SWIFTS

Formed 1870s as Burton Outward Star. Changed name to Burton Swifts 1883. Merged with Burton Wanderers to form Burton United, 1901. Disbanded 1910

1885-86	1	31.10.85	Wednesbury Old Athletic		A	L	1-5	
1886-87	1	30.10.86	Crossell's Brewery		H	L	0-1	
1887-88	1	15.10.87	Birmingham Southfield		H	W	7-0	
	2	5.11.87	Great Bridge Unity		H	L	2-5	
1888-89			1q **Leek** (H) 1-3aet					
1889-90			2q **Great Bridge Unity** (H) 5-3aet; 3q **Walsall TS** (H) 1-6					
1890-91 TC			2q **Sheffield U** (H) 2-1 *FA disqualified Burton for playing unregistered player*					
1891-92 FAII			2q **Walsall TS** (A) 4-2; 3q **Small Heath** (A) 2-4					

1892-93 D2   P   **Singers FC, Coventry** (H) 3-0; 1q **Burslem Port Vale** (A) 2-0; 2q **Leek** (A) 3-0; 3q **Walsall TS** (A) 3-1
             4q **Burton Wanderers** (H) 3-2
             1   21.1.93 **Preston NE**   D1   A   L   2-9   Dewey, Emery
1893-94 D2   1q **Burslem Port Vale** (A) 4-3aet; 2q **Brierley Hill Alliance** (A) 1-3
1894-95 D2   2q **Stourbridge** (H) 3-2; 3q **Burton Wanderers** (A) 2-5
1895-96 D2   1q **Wellington St G.** (A) 6-1; 2q **Burslem Port Vale** (A) 1-1; 2qr **Burslem Port Vale** (H) 1-0
             3q **Singers FC, Coventry** (A) 2-0; 4q **Wrockwardine Wood** (H) 3-1
             1   1.2.96 **Blackpool**   LL   A   L   1-4
1896-97 D2   3q **Wrockwardine Wood** (H) 6-0; 4q **Walsall TS** (A) 1-1; 4qr **Walsall TS** (H) 1-0aet; 5q **Burslem Port Vale** (A) 3-2
             1   30.1.97 **Liverpool**   D1   A   L   3-4   Evans, Wyllie, 1 other
1897-98 D2   3q **Stourbridge** (H) 0-2
1898-99 D2   2q **Coalville T** (H) 4-1; 3q **Ilkeston T** (H) 4-2; 4q **Chesterfield** (H) 1-0
             5q **Heanor T** (H) 0-0; 5qr **Heanor T** (A) 0-1
1899-00 D2   3q **Kettering T** (H) 8-2; 4q **Leicester F** (A) 1-3
1900-01 D2   3q **Newstead Byron** (H) 2-2; 3qr **Newstead Byron** (A) 4-0; 4q **Hinckley** (A) 4-1; 5q **Kettering T** (H) 1-2

BURTON TOWN

First entered the FA Cup: 1923. **League clubs beaten:** Gateshead, York C

1931-32	BDL	1	28.11.31	**Wigan Borough**			walkover	
		2	12.12.31	**Gateshead**	3N	H	W 4-1	Boswell 2, Causer, Reay
		3	9.1.32	**Blackburn R**	D1	H	L 0-4	
1934-35	BDL	1	24.11.34	**York C**	3N	H	L 2-3	Corbett, Mills
1935-36	ML	1	30.11.35	**York C**	3N	A	W 5-1	Narol 2, McPhall, Bowater, Loftus
		2	14.12.35	**Southend U**	3S	A	L 0-3	
1936-37	ML	1	28.11.36	**Wigan A**	CC	H	W 5-1	Bridges 2, Hewitson 2, Jeavons
		2	12.12.36	**Darlington**	3N	H	L 1-2	Bridges
1937-38	ML	1	27.11.37	**Rotherham U**	3N	H	D 1-1	Lowry
		1r	29.11.37	**Rotherham U**		A	L 0-3	

BURTON UNITED

Formed 1901 by the amalgamation of Burton Swifts and Burton Wanderers. Disbanded 1910

1901-02 D2   3q **Whitwick White Cross** (A) 3-0; 4q **Northampton T** (H) 0-0 abnd; 4q **Northampton T** (H) 0-0
             4qr **Northampton T** (A) 0-2
1902-03 D2   1q **Sutton T** walkover; 2q **Newhall Red Rose** walkover; 3q **Northampton T** (H) 2-0
             4q **Kettering T** (H) 3-1; 5q **Wellingborough T** (H) 5-1; Int **Manchester U** (H) 1-1
             Int r **Manchester U** (A) 1-3
1903-04 D2   1q **Gresley R** (H) 2-0; 2q **Hinckley T** (H) 2-2; 2qr **Hinckley T** (A) 5-1; 3q **Kettering T** (H) 3-0
             4q **Whitwick White Cross** (A) 5-2; 5q **Leicester F** (H) 1-1; 5qr **Leicester F** (A) 2-2abnd
             5qr **Leicester F** 2-0 at Derby; Int **Burslem Port Vale** (A) 0-3
1904-05 D2   3q **Northampton T** (H) 2-3
1905-06 D2   4q **Accrington S** (H) 3-0
             1   13.1.06 **Millwall**   SL   A   L   0-1
1906-07 D2   5q **Bishop Auckland** (H) 6-0
             1   12.1.07 **New Brompton**   SL   H   D   0-0
             1r   16.1.07 **New Brompton**   A   –   0-0
                  abandoned after 100 minutes
             1 2r 21.1.07 **New Brompton** at Fulham   L   0-2

BURTON WANDERERS

Formed 1871. Merged with Burton Swifts to form Burton United, 1901. Disbanded 1910.

1885-86		1	31.10.85	**Small Heath Alliance**		A	L 2-9	
1886-87		1	30.10.86	**West Bromwich Albion**		A	L 0-5	
1887-88		1	15.10.87	**Aston Shakespeare**		A	W 3-2	
				FA ordered replay after protest				
		1r		**Aston Shakespeare**			scratched	
1893-94	ML	1q **Leek** (H) 9-0; 2q **Old Hill Wanderers** (H) 5-0; 3q **Hednesford T** (H) 7-2; 4q **Brierley Hill All.** (H) 2-1						
		1	27.1.94	**Stockport Co**	TC	A	W 1-0	Moore
		2	10.2.94	**Notts Co**	D2	H	L 1-2	Adrian Capes
1894-95	D2	1q **Walsall** (H) 3-0; 2q **Brierley Hill All.** (H) 3-1; 3q **Burton Swifts** (H) 5-2; 4q **Old Hill W** (H) 5-0						
		1	2.2.95	**Blackburn R**	D1	H	L 1-2	Arthur Capes
1895-96	D2	1	1.2.96	**Sheffield U**	D1	H	D 1-1	Brown

		1r	6.2.96	Sheffield U		A	L	0-1	
1896-97	D2	1	30.1.97	Everton	D1	A	L	2-5	T.Arkesden

BURY

Formed at a public meeting, April 24, 1885. **FA Cup Winners:** 1900, 1903. **FA Cup Record Win:** 12-1 vs Stockton, 1st round replay, 2.2.1897.
FA Cup Record Defeat: 0-6 vs Leeds U, 3rd round, 22.1.1966.

Season	Div	Rnd	Date	Opponent	OppDiv	H/A	Res	Score	Scorers
1887-88		1		Blackburn R					*scratched*
1891-92	LL			1q Witton (H) 3-1; 2q Heywood Central (A) 2-1; 3q Blackpool (H) 5-5; 3qr Blackpool (A) 3-4					
1892-93	LL			1q Southport (H) 9-0; 2q Stockport Co (H) 8-1; 3q Rossendale (A) 1-7					
1893-94	LL			1q Nelson (A) 3-2aet; 2q Rossendale (A) 2-1; 3q Fleetwood R (H) 2-0; South Shore (A) 1-3aet					
1894-95	D2	1	2.2.95	Leicester Fosse	D2	H	W	4-2	Henderson 2, Lee, Plant
		2	16.2.95	Bolton W	D1	A	L	0-1	
1895-96	D1	1	1.2.96	Small Heath	D1	A	W	4-1	Henderson, Millar 2, Barr
		2	15.2.96	Newcastle U	D2	A	W	3-1	Henderson, Millar, Plant
		3	29.2.96	Bolton W	D1	A	L	0-2	
1896-97	D1	1	30.1.97	Stockton	NL	A	D	0-0	
		1r	2.2.97	Stockton		H	W	12-1	Millar 4, Wylie 3, Henderson 2, Hendry, Ross, Wilson og
		2	13.2.97	Everton	D1	A	L	0-3	
1897-98	D1	1	29.1.98	Stoke C	D1	H	L	1-2	Plant
1898-99	D1	1	28.1.99	Heanor T	ML	A	W	3-0	Bennett, Sagar 2
		2	11.2.99	WBA	D1	A	L	1-2	Pray
1899-00	D1	1	27.1.00	Burnley	D1	A	W	1-0	Sagar
		2	10.2.00	Notts Co	D1	A	D	0-0	
		2r	14.2.00	Notts Co		H	W	2-0	Pray, Sagar
		3	24.2.00	Sheffield U	D1	A	D	2-2	McLuckie, Wood
		3r	1.3.00	Sheffield U		H	W	2-0	Plant, Richards
		SF	24.3.00	Nottingham F	D1		D	1-1	Pray
			played at Victoria Ground, Stoke						
		SFr	29.3.00	Nottingham F			W	3-2aet	McLuckie, Richards, Sagar
			played at Bramall Lane						
		F	21.4.00	SOUTHAMPTON		SL	W	4-0	McLuckie 2, Wood, Plant
			played at Crystal Palace						
1900-01	D1	1	9.2.01	Sheffield W	D1	A	W	1-0	Wood
		2	23.2.01	Tottenham H	SL	A	L	1-2	McLuckie
1901-02	D1	1	25.1.02	WBA	D2	H	W	5-1	Sagar 3, Thorpe, Wood
		2	8.2.02	Walsall	ML	A	W	5-0	Sagar 2, Gray, Ross, Wood
		3	22.2.02	Southampton	SL	H	L	2-3	Ross, Sagar
1902-03	D1	1	7.2.03	Wolverhampton W	D1	H	W	1-0	Richards
		2	21.2.03	Sheffield U	D1	A	W	1-0	Sagar
		3	7.3.03	Notts Co	D1	H	W	1-0	Lindsay
		SF	21.3.03	Aston Villa	D1		W	3-0	Richards, Sagar, Spencer og
			played at Goodison Park						
		F	18.4.03	DERBY CO	D1		W	6-0	Ross, Sagar, Leeming 2, Wood, Plant
			played at Crystal Palace						
1903-04	D1	1	6.2.04	Newcastle U	D1	H	W	2-1	Swann, Sagar
		2	20.2.04	Sheffield U	D1	H	L	1-2	Sagar
1904-05	D1	1	4.2.05	Notts Co	D1	H	W	1-0	Sagar
		2	18.2.05	Aston Villa	D1	A	L	2-3	Lindsay, Simpson
1905-06	D1	1	13.1.06	Nottingham F	D1	H	D	1-1	Kilbourne
		1r	17.1.06	Nottingham F		A	L	2-6	Dow, Murphy
1906-07	D1	1	12.1.07	Oxford C		A	W	3-0	Bevan 2, Kay
		2	2.2.07	New Brompton	SL	H	W	1-0	Gildea
		3	23.2.07	Barnsley	D2	A	L	0-1	
1907-08	D1	1	11.1.08	Millwall	SL	H	W	2-1	Currie, Hibbert
		2	1.2.08	Wolverhampton W	D2	A	L	0-2	
1908-09	D1	1	16.1.09	Kettering T		H	W	8-0	Lindsay, Dewhurst, MacIntosh 3, Hibbert 2, Duffy
		2	6.2.09	Bristol C	SL	A	D	2-2	Hibbert 2
		2r	10.2.09	Bristol C		H	L	0-1	
1909-10	D1	1	15.1.10	Glossop	D2	H	W	2-1	Dewhurst, Hibbert
		2	5.2.10	Leicester Fosse	D2	A	L	2-3	Hibbert, Currie
1910-11	D1	1	14.1.11	Newcastle U	D1	A	L	1-6	Currie
1911-12	D1	1	13.1.12	Millwall	SL	H	W	2-1	Cannon, Duffy
		2	3.2.12	Everton	D1	A	D	1-1	Kay
		2r	8.2.12	Everton		A	L	0-6	
1912-13	D2	1	11.1.13	Southampton	SL	A	D	1-1	Peake

Season	Div	Round	Date	Opponent		H/A	Res	Score	Scorers
		1r	15.1.13	Southampton		H	W	2-1	Peake 2
		2	1.2.13	Crystal P	SL	A	L	0-2	
1913-14	D2	1	10.1.14	Hull C	D2	A	D	0-0	
		1r	14.1.14	Hull C		H	W	2-1	Peake 2
		2	31.1.14	Blackburn R	D1	A	L	0-2	
1914-15	D2	1	9.1.15	Plymouth A	SL	H	D	1-1	Lythgoe
		1r	16.1.15	Plymouth A		A	W	2-1	Peake, Connor
		2	30.1.15	Bradford PA	D1	H	L	0-1	
1919-20	D2	1	10.1.20	Stoke C	D2	H	W	2-0	Lomes, Hird
		2	31.1.20	West Ham	D2	A	L	0-6	
1920-21	D2	1	8.1.21	Swansea T	D3	A	L	0-3	
1921-22	D2	1	7.1.22	Bolton W	D1	A	L	0-1	
1922-23	D2	1	13.1.23	Luton T	3S	H	W	2-1	McCrae, Bullock
		2	3.2.23	Stoke C	D1	H	W	3-1	Bullock, Aitken, Quinn
		3	24.2.23	Southampton	D2	H	D	0-0	
		3r	28.2.23	Southampton		A	L	0-1	
1923-24	D2	1	12.1.24	Derby Co	D2	A	L	1-2	Ball
1924-25	D1	1	10.1.25	Sunderland	D1	H	L	0-3	
1925-26	D1	3	9.1.26	Rotherham U	3N	A	W	3-2	Porter, Ball, Matthews
		4	30.1.26	Millwall	3S	H	D	3-3	Matthews, Bullock, Ball
		4r	4.2.26	Millwall		A	L	0-2	
1926-27	D1	3	8.1.27	Swansea T	D2	A	L	1-4	Amos
1927-28	D1	3	14.1.28	Charlton A	3S	A	D	1-1	Ball
		3r	18.1.28	Charlton A		H	W	4-3	Amos, Vernon 2, Ball (p)
		4	28.1.28	Manchester U	D1	H	D	1-1	Ball
		4r	1.2.28	Manchester U		A	L	0-1	
1928-29	D1	3	12.1.29	Darlington	3N	A	W	6-2	Gale 2, Smith 2, Ball, Bullock
		4	26.1.29	Manchester U	D1	A	W	1-0	Amos
		5	16.2.29	Blackburn R	D1	A	L	0-1	
1929-30	D2	3	11.1.30	Huddersfield T	D1	H	D	0-0	
		3r	15.1.30	Huddersfield T		A	L	1-3	Amos
1930-31	D2	3	10.1.31	Torquay U	3S	H	D	1-1	Hope
		3r	14.1.31	Torquay U		A	W	2-1aet	Smith, Robbie
		4	24.1.31	Exeter C	3S	H	L	1-2	Robbie
1931-32	D2	3	9.1.32	Swansea T	D2	H	W	2-1	Lindsay 2
		4	23.1.32	Sheffield U	D1	H	W	3-1	Robbie, Lindsay, Amos
		5	13.2.32	Stoke C	D2	H	W	3-0	Amos 2, Robbie
		6	27.2.32	Manchester C	D1	H	L	3-4	Smith, Robbie, Amos
1932-33	D2	3	14.1.33	Nottingham F	D2	H	D	2-2	Amos, Vernon
		3r	18.1.33	Nottingham F		A	W	2-1	Smith, Eagleston
		4	28.1.33	Everton	D1	A	L	1-3	Vernon
1933-34	D2	3	13.1.34	Burnley	D2	A	D	0-0	
		3r	17.1.34	Burnley		H	W	3-2	Vernon 2, Robbins
		4	27.1.34	Swansea T	D2	H	D	1-1	Robbie
		4r	1.2.34	Swansea T		A	L	0-3	
1934-35	D2	3	12.1.35	Bristol C	3S	A	D	1-1	Earl
		3r	16.1.35	Bristol C		H	D	2-2aet	Blyth, Robinson
		3 2r	21.1.35	Bristol C at Villa Park			L	1-2	Chalmers
1935-36	D2	3	11.1.36	Darlington	3N	A	W	3-2	Jones, Chalmers 2
		4	25.1.36	Leeds U	D1	A	–	1-2	Buttery
				abandoned after 74 minutes – fog					
		4	29.1.36	Leeds U		A	L	2-3	Matthews 2
1936-37	D2	3	16.1.37	QPR	3S	H	W	1-0	Graham
		4	30.1.37	Burnley	D2	A	L	1-4	Whitfield (p)
1937-38	D2	3	8.1.38	Brighton & HA	3S	H	W	2-0	Bargh, Davies
		4	22.1.38	Manchester C	D1	A	L	1-3	Acquroff
1938-39	D2	3	7.1.39	Fulham	D2	A	L	0-6	
1945-46	D2	3 1L	5.1.46	Rochdale	3N	H	D	3-3	Halton 2, Davies
		3 2L	8.1.46	Rochdale		A	W	4-2	Tomkins, Jones, Moss, Davies
		4 1L	26.1.46	Sunderland	D1	A	L	1-3	McGill
		4 2L	29.1.46	Sunderland		H	W	5-4aet	Davies, Roberts 3, Jones
1946-47	D2	3	11.1.47	Southampton	D2	A	L	1-5	Halton (p)
1947-48	D2	3	10.1.48	Leicester C	D2	A	L	0-1	
1948-49	D2	3	8.1.49	Yeovil T	SL	A	L	1-3	Massart
1949-50	D2	3	7.1.50	Rotherham U	3N	H	W	5-4	Bardsley, Bellis, Whitworth 2, Massart
		4	28.1.50	Derby Co	D1	H	D	2-2	Hazlett, Massart
		4r	1.2.50	Derby Co		A	L	2-5	Bodle, Bellis

Season	Div	Rd	Date	Opponent		Venue	Result	Score	Scorers
1950-51	D2	3	6.1.51	Newcastle U	D1	A	L	1-4	W.Griffiths (p)
1951-52	D2	3	12.1.52	Rotherham U	D2	A	L	1-2	Bodie
1952-53	D2	3	10.1.53	Grimsby T	3N	A	W	3-1	Daniel, Fletcher, Imlach
		4	31.1.53	Arsenal	D1	A	L	2-6	Walton, Gleadall
1953-54	D2	3	9.1.54	Chesterfield	3N	A	L	0-2	
1954-55	D2	3	8.1.55	Stoke C	D2	H	D	1-1	Daniel
		3r	12.1.55	Stoke C		A	–	1-1	Daniel
			abandoned after 112 minutes – snowstorm						
		3 2r	17.1.55	Stoke C at Goodison Pk			D	3-3aet	Simm, Pearson, Tilley
		3 3r	19.1.55	Stoke C at Anfield			D	2-2aet	Kelly, Daniel
		3 4r	24.1.55	Stoke C at Old Trafford			L	2-3aet	Daniel 2
1955-56	D2	3	7.1.56	Burnley	D1	H	–	2-2	Neilson, Lawson
			abandoned after 65 minutes						
		3	9.1.56	Burnley		H	L	0-1	
1956-57	D2	3	5.1.57	Portsmouth	D1	H	L	1-3	Kelly
1957-58	3N	1	16.11.57	Bishop Auckland	NL	A	D	0-0	
		1r	19.11.57	Bishop Auckland		H	W	4-1	Parker 2, Thursby og, Reid
		2	7.12.57	Scunthorpe U	3N	A	L	0-2	
1958-59	D3	1	15.11.58	York C	D4	H	–	0-0	
			abandoned after 60 minutes						
		1	18.11.58	York C		H	W	1-0	Mercer
		2	6.12.58	Chester	D4	A	D	1-1	Parker
		2r	9.12.58	Chester		H	W	2-1	Watson, Lovie
		3	10.1.59	Arsenal	D1	H	L	0-1	
1959-60	D3	1	14.11.59	Hartlepools	D4	H	W	5-0	Hubbard, Holden, Watson, Jackson 2
		2	5.12.59	Oldham A	D4	H	W	2-1	Hubbard, Watson
		3	9.1.60	Bolton W	D1	H	D	1-1	Higgins og
		3r	13.1.60	Bolton W		A	L	2-4aet	Calder, Watson
1960-61	D3	1	5.11.60	Tranmere R	D3	A	L	0-1	
1961-62	D2	3	6.1.62	Sheffield U	D1	H	D	0-0	
		3r	10.1.62	Sheffield U		A	D	2-2aet	Beaumont, Jones
		3 2r	15.1.62	Sheffield U at Hillsborough			L	0-2	
1962-63	D2	3	5.3.63	Birmingham C	D1	A	D	3-3	Griffin 2, Eastham
		3r	7.3.63	Birmingham C		H	W	2-0	Calder, Griffin
		4	13.3.63	Manchester C	D1	A	L	0-1	
1963-64	D2	3	4.1.64	Yeovil T	SL	A	W	2-0	Jones 2
		4	25.1.64	Barnsley	D3	A	L	1-2	Bartley
1964-65	D2	3	9.1.65	Crystal P	D2	A	L	1-5	Claxton
1965-66	D2	3	22.1.66	Leeds U	D1	A	L	0-6	
1966-67	D2	3	28.1.67	Walsall	D3	H	W	2-0	Jones, Parry
		4	18.2.67	Swindon T	D3	A	L	1-2	Lowes
1967-68	D3	1	9.12.67	Hartlepools U	D4	A	W	3-2	Jones, Lindsay, Drysdale og
		2	6.1.68	Bradford C	D4	A	W	3-2	Owen, Collins, Farrell
		3	27.1.68	Leyton Orient	D3	A	L	0-1	
1968-69	D2	3	4.1.69	Huddersfield T	D2	H	L	1-2	Jones
1969-70	D3	1	15.11.69	Mansfield T	D3	H	D	2-2	Kerr 2 (1p)
		1r	19.11.69	Mansfield T		A	L	0-2	
1970-71	D3	1	21.11.70	Grimsby T	D4	A	W	1-0	White
		2	12.12.70	Notts Co	D4	H	D	1-1	Jones
		2r	21.12.70	Notts Co		A	L	0-3	
1971-72	D4	1	20.11.71	Lincoln C	D4	A	W	2-1	Jones 2
		2	11.12.71	Workington T	D4	A	W	3-1	McDermott, Murray, Jones
		3	15.1.72	Rotherham U	D3	H	D	1-1	Connelly
		3r	19.1.72	Rotherham U		A	L	1-2	Murray
1972-73	D4	1	18.11.72	Doncaster R	D4	A	L	1-3	Robson
1973-74	D4	1	21.11.73	Tranmere R	D3	A	L	1-2	Spence
1974-75	D3	1	23.11.74	Southport	D4	H	W	4-2	Spence 2, Duffey 2
		2	14.12.74	Grimsby T	D3	A	D	1-1	Duffey
		2r	17.12.74	Grimsby T		H	W	2-1	Spence, Duffey
		3	4.1.75	Millwall	D2	H	D	2-2	Hamstead, Williams
		3r	7.1.75	Millwall		A	D	1-1aet	Thomson
		3 2r	13.1.75	Millwall at West Bromwich			W	2-0	Riley, Duffey
		4	25.1.75	Mansfield T	D4	H	L	1-2	Hamstead
1975-76	D3	1	22.11.75	Doncaster R	D4	H	W	4-3	Riley, Hamstead, Rowland 2
		2	13.12.75	Spennymoor U	NL	H	W	3-0	Kennedy, Buchan, Adams og
		3	3.1.76	Middlesbrough	D1	A	D	0-0	
		3r	6.1.76	Middlesbrough		H	W	3-2	McIlwraith, Hulme, Rowland

BURY

Season	Div	Rd	Date	Opponent	Comp	H/A	Res	Score	Scorers
		4	24.1.76	Leicester C	D1	A	L	0-1	
1976-77	D3	1	20.11.76	Workington	D4	H	W	6-0	Woolfall 2, Rowlands, Phillips, McIlwraith, Hatton
		2	14.12.76	Shrewsbury T	D3	H	D	0-0	
		2r	21.12.76	Shrewsbury T		A	L	1-2	Phillips
1977-78	D3	1	26.11.77	Sheffield W	D3	A	L	0-1	
1978-79	D3	1	25.11.78	Wigan Ath	D4	A	D	2-2	Gregory, Brown og
		1r	28.11.78	Wigan Ath		H	W	4-1	Gregory 2, Kennedy, Wilson (p)
		2	16.12.78	Blackpool	D3	H	W	3-1	Lugg, Gregory 2
		3	9.1.79	Orient	D2	A	L	2-3	Gregory, Beamish
1979-80	D3	1	24.11.79	Burton Albion	NPL	A	W	2-0	Madden, Hilton
		2	15.12.79	York C	D4	H	D	0-0	
		2r	18.12.79	York C		A	W	2-0	Hilton, Madden
		3	5.1.80	Rochdale	D4	A	D	1-1	Whitehead
		3r	21.1.80	Rochdale		H	W	3-2	Johnson 2, Wilson
		4	26.1.80	Burnley	D2	H	W	1-0	Whitehead
		5	16.2.80	Liverpool	D1	A	L	0-2	
1980-81	D4	1	22.11.80	Darlington	D4	A	W	2-0	Jakub, Butler
		2	13.12.80	Lincoln C	D4	H	W	2-0	Hilton, Mullen
		3	3.1.81	Fulham	D3	H	D	1-1	Hilton
		3r	6.1.81	Fulham		A	D	0-0aet	
		3 2r	12.1.81	Fulham at West Bromwich			L	0-1	
1981-82	D4	1	21.11.81	Tranmere R	D4	A	D	1-1	Madden
		1r	24.11.81	Tranmere R		H	W	3-1	Madden 2, Johnson
		2	2.1.82	Burnley	D3	H	D	1-1	Madden
		2r	4.1.82	Burnley		A	L	1-2aet	Johnson
1982-83	D4	1	20.11.82	York C	D4	A	L	1-3	Hilton
1983-84	D4	1	19.11.83	Boston U	APL	A	W	3-0	Entwistle 2, Madden
		2	10.12.83	Scunthorpe U	D3	A	L	0-2	
1984-85	D4	1	17.11.84	Preston NE	D3	A	L	3-4	Entwistle, Madden, Ross
1985-86	D3	1	16.11.85	Chester	D4	H	W	2-0	Young, Kerr
		2	7.12.85	Tranmere R	D4	A	D	1-1	Madden
		2r	10.12.85	Tranmere R		H	W	2-1	Valentine, Ross (p)
		3	13.1.86	Barnsley	D2	H	W	2-0	Owen, Jakub
		4	25.1.86	Reading	D3	A	D	1-1	Young
		4r	28.1.86	Reading		H	W	3-0	Madden 2, Dixon
		5	5.3.86	Watford	D1	A	D	1-1	Bramhall
		5r	8.3.86	Watford		H	L	0-3	
1986-87	D3	1	15.11.86	Preston NE	D4	A	L	1-5	Flynn
1987-88	D3	1	14.11.87	Scunthorpe U	D4	A	L	1-3	McIlroy
1988-89	D3	1	19.11.88	Guisborough	NL	A	W	1-0	Parkinson
			played at Middlesbrough						
		2	10.12.88	Blackpool	D3	A	L	0-3	
1989-90	D3	1	18.11.89	Rotherham U	D3	A	D	0-0	
		1r	21.11.89	Rotherham U		H	L	1-2	Bishop
1990-91	D3	1	17.11.90	Chorley	NPL	A	L	1-2	Mauge
1991-92	D3	1	16.11.91	Bradford C	D3	H	L	0-1	
1992-93	D3	1	14.11.92	Witton Albion	GMVC	H	W	2-0	Knill (p), Robinson (p)
		2	2.1.93	Wigan A	D2	H	W	1-0	Mauge
		3	5.1.93	Manchester U	PL	A	L	0-2	

BURY TOWN

Formed 1872. **First entered FA Cup:** 1900 as Bury St Edmunds

Season	Div	Rd	Date	Opponent	Comp	H/A	Res	Score	Scorers
1968-69	Met	1	16.11.68	Bournemouth	D3	H	D	0-0	
		1r	20.11.68	Bournemouth		A	L	0-3	

BUXTON

Formed 1877. **First entered FA Cup:** 1891. **Cup Final Connection:** Former Buxton player Ian Greaves played for Manchester United in the 1958 Cup Final. **League club beaten:** Aldershot

Season	Div	Rd	Date	Opponent	Comp	H/A	Res	Score	Scorers
1951-52	CC	1	24.11.51	Rawmarsh Welfare	SAL	A	W	4-1	Machin 3, Crossley
		2	15.12.51	Aldershot	3S	H	W	4-3	Carter, Tomlinson, Machent, White
		3	12.1.52	Doncaster R	D2	A	L	0-2	
1958-59	CC	1	15.11.58	Crook T	NL	H	W	4-1	Calderbank 2, Duggins 2
		2	6.12.58	Accrington S	D3	A	L	1-6	Duggins

BUXTON

1962-63	CC	1	3.11.62	**Barrow**	D4	H	D	2-2	Farmer, Robinson og
		1r	5.11.62	**Barrow**		A	L	1-3	Riley

CAERNARFON TOWN

Formed 1876 as Caernarfon Athletic. **First entered FA Cup:** 1929 as Caernarfon Athletic. **League clubs beaten:** Darlington, Stockport Co, York C

1929-30	Welsh1		30.11.29	**Darlington**	3N	H	W	4-2	Smith 2, Taylor, Sutton
		2	14.12.29	**Bournemouth**	3S	H	D	1-1	Smith
		2r	18.12.29	**Bournemouth**		A	L	2-5	Smith, Murray
as Caernarfon Town									
1986-87	NPL	1	15.11.86	**Stockport Co**	D4	H	W	1-0	Salmon
		2	6.12.86	**York C**	D3	H	D	0-0	
		2r	9.12.86	**York C**		A	W	2-1	Salmon, Craven
		3	10.1.87	**Barnsley**	D2	H	D	0-0	
		3r	26.1.87	**Barnsley**		A	L	0-1	

CAERNARFON WANDERERS

Formed 1885. Home ground was Bryn Sciont and the players used the Eagles Hotel as changing rooms.

1886-87		1	30.10.86	**Stoke**		A	L	1-10

CAIUS COLLEGE, CAMBRIDGE

Caius twice entered the FA Cup after Cambridge University had decided not to compete any further, but they scratched both times. Nottingham Forest then, as now, would have been expected to beat a college side.

1880-81		1	**Nottingham F**	*scratched*
1881-82		1	**Dreadnought**	*scratched*

CAMBRIDGE CITY

Formed 1908 as Cambridge Town. 1952 Cambridge City. **First entered FA Cup:** 1919

1946-47	Spt	1	30.11.46	**Swindon T**	3S	A	L	1-4	Wood
1948-49	Spt	1	27.11.48	**Walthamstow Ave**	IL	A	L	2-3	Chapman, Ferguson
as Cambridge City									
1966-67	SL	1	26.11.66	**Ashford T**	SL	A	L	1-4	McVittie

CAMBRIDGE UNITED

Formed 1919 as Abbey United. 1951 Cambridge United. **First entered FA Cup:** 1927 **Best FA Cup Performances:** 6th round, 1990, 1991 **Record FA Cup Win:** 10-0 vs Potton United, 4th qualifying round, 4.10.1969 **Record FA Cup Defeat:** (as Abbey United) 0-8 vs Cambridge Town, 22.9.1945, 0-8 vs Wisbech Town, preliminary round replay, 1949-50; as Cambridge United, several by four goal margins. **League Clubs beaten as a Non-League club:** Newport County

1953-54	ECL	1	21.11.53	**Newport Co**	3S	H	D	2-2	Stevens, Crowe
		1r	26.11.53	**Newport Co**		A	W	2-1	Saward, Stevens
		2	12.12.53	**Bradford PA**	3N	H	L	1-2	Whittaker (p)
1954-55	ECL	1	20.11.54	**Torquay U**	3S	A	L	0-4	
1962-63	SL	1	3.11.62	**Bedford T**	SL	A	L	1-2	Howell
1963-64	SL	1	16.11.63	**Chelmsford C**	SL	H	L	0-1	
1964-65	SL	1	14.11.64	**Barnet**	AL	A	L	1-2	Day
1970-71	D4	1	21.11.70	**Enfield**	IL	A	W	1-0	Hollett
		2	12.12.70	**Colchester U**	D4	A	L	0-3	
1971-72	D4	1	20.11.71	**Weymouth**	SL	H	W	2-1	Collins, Hollett
		2	11.12.71	**Bristol R**	D3	A	L	0-3	
1972-73	D4	1	18.11.72	**Bournemouth**	D3	A	L	1-5	Collins
1973-74	D3	1	24.11.73	**Gillingham**	D4	H	W	3-2	Simmons 3
		2	15.12.73	**Aldershot**	D3	A	W	2-1	Simmons 2
		3	6.1.74	**Oldham A**	D3	H	D	2-2	Wood og, Eades
		3r	8.1.74	**Oldham A**		A	D	3-3aet	Ferguson, Simmons, Watson
		3 2r	14.1.74	**Oldham A** at Nottingham F			L	1-2	Simmons
1974-75	D4	1	23.11.74	**Hitchin T**	IL	A	D	0-0	
		1r	26.11.74	**Hitchin T**		H	W	3-0	Cassidy 2, Shinton
		2	14.12.74	**Hereford U**	D3	H	W	2-0	Watson 2

	3	4.1.75	**Mansfield T**	D4	A	L	0-1	
1975-76	D3	1	22.11.75	**Leatherhead**	IL	A	L	0-2	
1976-77	D4	1	20.11.76	**Colchester U**	D4	H	D	1-1	Fallon
	1r	24.11.76	**Colchester U**		A	L	0-2	
1977-78	D3	1	26.11.77	**Lowestoft T**	ECL	A	W	2-0	Biley 2
	2	17.12.77	**Plymouth A**	D3	A	L	0-1	
1978-79	D2	3	6.1.79	**Shrewsbury T**	D3	A	L	1-3	Biley
1979-80	D2	3	5.1.80	**Chesham U**	IL	A	W	2-0	Gibbins, Reilly
	4	26.1.80	**Aston Villa**	D1	H	D	1-1	Turner
	4r	30.1.80	**Aston Villa**		A	L	1-4	Spriggs
1980-81	D2	3	3.1.81	**Norwich C**	D1	A	L	0-1	
1981-82	D2	3	2.1.82	**Doncaster R**	D3	A	L	1-2	Taylor
1982-83	D2	3	8.1.83	**Weymouth**		H	W	1-0	Reilly
	4	29.1.83	**Barnsley**	D2	H	W	1-0	Mayo
	5	19.2.83	**Sheffield W**	D2	H	L	1-2	Turner
1983-84	D2	3	7.1.84	**Derby Co**	D2	H	L	0-3	
1984-85	D3	1	17.11.84	**Peterborough U**	D4	H	L	0-2	
1985-86	D4	1	16.11.85	**Dagenham**	APL	A	L	1-2	Crown
1986-87	D4	1	15.11.86	**Exeter C**	D4	A	D	1-1	Crown
	1r	19.11.86	**Exeter C**		H	W	2-0	Dowman, Biley
	2	7.12.86	**Maidstone**	GMVC	A	L	0-1	
1987-88	D4	1	14.11.87	**Farnborough T**	IL	H	W	2-1	Beattie, Benjamin
	2	5.12.87	**Yeovil T**	IL	H	L	0-1	
1988-89	D4	1	19.11.88	**Woking**	IL	A	W	4-1	Reilly 2, Croft 2
	2	10.12.88	**Bognor Regis T**	IL	A	W	1-0	Chapple
	3	7.1.89	**Plymouth A**	D2	A	L	0-2	
1989-90	D4	1	18.11.89	**Aldershot**	D4	A	W	1-0	Taylor
	2	9.12.89	**Woking**	IL	H	W	3-1	Cheetham, Leadbitter, Taylor
	3	6.1.90	**Darlington**	GMVC	H	D	0-0	
	3r	9.1.90	**Darlington**		A	W	3-1	Taylor, Philpott, Dublin
	4	27.1.90	**Millwall**	D1	A	D	1-1	Taylor
	4r	30.1.90	**Millwall**		H	W	1-0	Thompson og
	5	17.2.90	**Bristol C**	D3	A	D	0-0	
	5r	21.2.90	**Bristol C**		H	D	1-1aet	Dublin
	5 2r	27.2.90	**Bristol C**		H	W	5-1	Leadbitter, Philpott, Dublin 2, Taylor
	6	10.3.90	**Crystal P**	D1	H	L	0-1	
1990-91	D3	1	17.11.90	**Reading**	D3	H	W	2-1	Atkins (p), Marmon
	2	7.12.90	**Fulham**	D3	A	D	0-0	
	2r	11.12.90	**Fulham**		H	W	2-1	Kimble (p), Dublin
	3	5.1.91	**Wolverhampton W**	D2	A	W	1-0	Leadbitter
	4	26.1.91	**Middlesbrough**	D2	H	W	2-0	Taylor 2
	5	16.2.91	**Sheffield W**	D2	H	W	4-0	Dublin 2, Philpott, Taylor
	6	9.3.91	**Arsenal**	D1	A	L	1-2	Dublin
1991-92	D2	3	4.1.92	**Coventry C**	D1	A	D	1-1	Dublin
	3r	14.1.92	**Coventry C**		H	W	1-0	Hurst og
	4	25.1.92	**Swindon T**	D2	H	L	0-3	
1992-93	D1	3	13.1.93	**Sheffield W**	PL	H	L	1-2	Heathcote

CAMBRIDGE UNIVERSITY

Formed to play by the Cambridge Rules 1848. Played at Parker's Piece, famous open land in Cambridge which is still used for sport and recreation.

1873-74	1	25.10.73	**South Norwood**		H	W	1-0	Hurrell
	2	29.11.73	**Clapham Rovers**		A	D	1-1	Mitford
	2r	20.12.73	**Clapham Rovers**		H	L	1-4	Roberts
1874-75	1	14.11.74	**Crystal Palace**		A	D	0-0	
	1r	21.11.74	**Crystal Palace**		H	W	2-1	Simpson, 1 other
	2	5.12.74	**Royal Engineers**		H	L	0-5	
1875-76	1		**Civil Service**			*walkover*		
	2	11.12.75	**Reigate Priory**		A	W	8-0	Cole 4, Roffey 2, Sparham, Steel
	3	31.1.76	**Oxford University**		H	L	0-4	
1876-77	1		**High Wycombe**			*walkover*		
	2	16.12.76	**Clapham Rovers**		H	W	2-1	Hughes, 1 other
	3	3.2.77	**Rochester**			W	4-0	Hughes 2, Prior, Widnell
	4	17.2.77	**Royal Engineers**			W	1-0	Hargreaves
	SF	20.3.77	**Wanderers**			L	0-1	
		played at Kennington Oval						

1877-78		1	2.11.77 **Southall Park**		H	W	3-1	Churchill 2, A.Lyttleton
		2	8.12.77 **Maidenhead**		H	W	4-2aet	Jarvis, Steel, Styan, Wild
		3	2.2.78 **Old Harrovians**			D	2-2	Hill, Styan
		3r	9.2.78 **Old Harrovians**			D	2-2aet	Steel, Styan
		3 2r	16.2.78 **Old Harrovians**			L	0-2	
1878-79		1	9.11.78 **Herts Rangers**		H	W	2-0	Harvey, Wild
		2	4.12.78 **South Norwood**		H	W	3-0	Jarvis, Martin, Wild
		3	2.2.79 **Clapham Rovers**			L	0-1aet	
1879-80		1	13.11.79 **Royal Engineers**		A	L	0-2	

CANNON FC

1886-87		1		**Old Foresters**		*scratched*

CANTERBURY CITY

Formed 1947. **First entered FA Cup:** 1948.

1964-65	SL	1	14.11.64 **Torquay U**	D4	H	L	0-6
1968-69	SL	1	16.11.68 **Swindon T**	D3	A	L	0-1

CARDIFF CITY

Formed 1899 as Riverside FC. 1908 Cardiff City. **First entered FA Cup:** 1910. **FA Cup Winners:** 1927. **FA Cup Runners-up** 1925. **Welsh FA Cup Winners:** 22 times. **Record FA Cup Win:** 8-0 vs Enfield, 1st round, 28.11.1931. **Record FA Cup Defeat:** 1-6 vs Aston Villa, 3rd round, 12.1.1929

1910-11	SL	1q **Merthyr Town** (H) 0-1						
1911-12	SL	P **Cardiff Corinthians** (H) 3-0; 1q **Mardy** (H) 2-0; 2q **Merthyr T** (A) 1-1; 2qr **Merthyr T** (H) 1-2						
1912-13	SL	1q **Merthyr T** (A) 5-1; 2q **Pontypridd** (H) 2-1; 3q **Llanelli** (A) 4-1; 4q **Exeter** (H) 5-1; 5q **Southend U** (H) 0-3						
1913-14	SL	4q **Swansea T** (A) 0-2						
1914-15	SL	1	9.1.15 **Bristol C**	D2	A	L	0-2	
1919-20	SL	1	10.1.20 **Oldham A**	D1	H	W	2-0	West, J.Evans
		2	31.1.20 **Wolverhampton W**	D2	A	W	2-1	Smith, Beare
		3	21.2.20 **Bristol C**	D2	A	L	1-2	Beare
1920-21	D2	1	8.1.21 **Sunderland**	D1	A	W	1-0	Beare
		2	29.1.21 **Brighton & HA**	D3	A	D	0-0	
		2r	2.2.21 **Brighton & HA**		H	W	1-0	Cashmore
		3	19.2.21 **Southampton**	D3	A	W	1-0	Gill
		4	5.3.21 **Chelsea**	D1	H	W	1-0	Cashmore
		SF	19.3.21 **Wolverhampton W**	D2		D	0-0	
			played at Anfield					
		SFr	23.3.21 **Wolverhampton W**			L	1-3	Keenor (p)
			played at Old Trafford					
1921-22	D1	1	7.1.22 **Manchester Utd**	D1	A	W	4-2	L.Davies, Nash, Clennell
		2	28.1.22 **Southampton**	3S	A	D	1-1	Gill
		2r	1.2.22 **Southampton**		H	W	2-0	Gill, Clennell
		3	18.2.22 **Nottingham F**	D2	H	W	4-1	L.Davies 2, Gill, Clennell
		4	4.3.22 **Tottenham H**	D1	H	D	1-1	L.Davies
		4r	9.3.22 **Tottenham H**		A	L	1-2	Gill
1922-23	D1	1	13.1.23 **Watford**	3S	H	D	1-1	J.Evans
		1r	17.1.23 **Watford**		A	D	2-2	L.Davies, Clennell
		1 2r	22.1.23 **Watford** at Villa Park			W	2-1	L.Davies, H.Evans
		2	3.2.23 **Leicester C**	D2	A	W	1-0	L.Davies
		3	24.2.23 **Tottenham H**	D1	H	L	2-3	J.Evans (p), Gill
1923-24	D1	1	12.1.24 **Gillingham**	3S	H	D	0-0	
		1r	16.1.24 **Gillingham**		A	W	2-0	Gill, L.Davies
		2	2.2.24 **Arsenal**	D1	H	W	1-0	Gill
		3	23.2.24 **Bristol C**	D2	H	W	3-0	Gill 2, Clennell,
		4	8.3.24 **Manchester C**	D1	A	D	0-0	
		4r	12.3.24 **Manchester C**		H	D	0-1aet	
1924-25	D1	1	10.1.25 **Darlington**	3N	H	D	0-0	
		1r	14.1.25 **Darlington**		A	D	0-0aet	
		1 2r	19.1.25 **Darlington** at Anfield			W	2-0	L.Davies, W.Davies
		2	31.1.25 **Fulham**	D2	H	W	1-0	L.Davies
		3	21.2.25 **Notts County**	D1	A	W	2-0	Nicholson, Gill
		4	7.3.25 **Leicester C**	D2	H	W	2-1	Beadles, W.Davies

		SF	28.3.25	**Blackburn R**	D1		W	3-1	Nicholson, Gill, Beadles
			played at Meadow Lane						
		F	25.4.25	**Sheffield U**	D1 WEMBLEY		L	0-1	
1925-26	D1	3	9.1.26	**Burnley**	D1	A	D	2-2	Cassidy, L.Davies
		3r	13.1.26	**Burnley**		H	W	2-0	Ferguson 2
		4	30.1.26	**Newcastle U**	D1	H	L	0-2	
1926-27	D1	3	8.1.27	**Aston Villa**	D1	H	W	2-0	L.Davies, Curtis
		4	29.1.27	**Darlington**	D2	A	W	2-0	McLachlan, Ferguson
		5	19.2.27	**Bolton W**	D1	A	W	2-0	Ferguson (p), L.Davies
		6	5.3.27	**Chelsea**	D2	A	D	0-0	
		6r	9.3.27	**Chelsea**		H	W	3-2	Irving, L.Davies, Ferguson (p)
		SF	26.3.27	**Reading**	D2		W	3-0	Ferguson 2, Wake
			played at Molineux						
		F	23.4.27	**ARSENAL**	D1 WEMBLEY		W	1-0	Ferguson
1927-28	D1	3	14.1.28	**Southampton**	D2	H	W	2-1	Ferguson, L.Davies
		4	28.1.28	**Liverpool**	D1	H	W	2-1	McLachlan, Nelson
		5	18.2.28	**Nottingham F**	D2	A	L	1-2	Ferguson
1928-29	D1	3	12.1.29	**Aston Villa**	D1	A	L	1-6	Hardy
1929-30	D2	3	11.1.30	**Liverpool**	D1	A	W	2-1	L.Davies 2
		4	25.1.30	**Sunderland**	D1	A	L	1-2	L.Davies
1930-31	D2	3	10.1.31	**Brentford**	3S	A	D	2-2	Jones, Valentine
		3r	14.1.31	**Brentford**		H	L	1-2	Robbins
1931-32	3S	1	28.11.31	**Enfield**	AL	H	W	8-0	Keating 3, O'Neill 2, Emmerson 2, Harris
		2	12.12.31	**Clapton O**	3S	H	W	4-0	McCambridge, Keating, Emmerson, Broadbent og
		3	9.1.31	**Bradford PA**	D2	A	L	0-2	
1932-33	3S	1	26.11.32	**Bristol R**	3S	H	D	1-1	Harris
		1r	30.11.32	**Bristol R**		A	L	1-4	McCambridge
1933-34	3S	1	25.11.33	**Aldershot**	3S	H	D	0-0	
		1r	29.11.33	**Aldershot**		A	L	1-3	Hill
1934-35	3S	1	24.11.34	**Reading**	3S	H	L	1-2	W.Lewis
1935-36	3S	1	30.11.35	**Dartford**	SL	H	L	0-3	
1936-37	3S	1	28.11.36	**Southall**	Athn	H	W	3-1	Walton, Talbot, Pugh
		2	12.12.36	**Swindon T**	3S	H	W	2-1	Granville, Prescot
		3	16.1.37	**Grimsby T**	D1	H	L	1-3	Melaniphy
1937-38	3S	1	27.11.37	**Northampton T**	3S	A	W	2-1	Collins 2
		2	11.12.37	**Bristol C**	3S	H	D	1-1	Turner
		2r	15.12.37	**Bristol C**		A	W	2-0	Collins 2
		3	8.1.38	**Charlton A**	D1	A	L	0-5	
1938-39	3S	1	26.11.38	**Cheltenham T**	SL	A	D	1-1	Prescott
		1r	30.11.38	**Cheltenham T**		H	W	1-0	Prescott
		2	10.12.38	**Crewe A**	3N	H	W	1-0	Talbot
		3	7.1.39	**Charlton A**	D1	H	W	1-0	Walton
		4	21.1.39	**Newcastle U**	D2	H	D	0-0	
		4r	25.1.39	**Newcastle U**		A	L	1-4	Pugh
1945-46	3S	3 1L	5.1.46	**WBA**	D2	H	D	1-1	Allen
		3 2L	9.1.46	**WBA**		A	L	0-4	
1946-47	3S	3	11.1.47	**Brentford**	D1	A	L	0-1	
1947-48	D2	3	10.1.48	**Sheffield W**	D2	H	L	1-2	Rees
1948-49	D2	3	8.1.49	**Oldham A**	3N	A	W	3-2	Hollyman 2, Allen
		4	29.1.49	**Aston Villa**	D1	A	W	2-1	Hollyman, Rees
		5	12.2.49	**Derby Co**	D1	A	L	1-2	Stevenson
1949-50	D2	3	7.1.50	**WBA**	D1	H	D	2-2	E.Evans, G.Williams
		3r	11.1.50	**WBA**		A	W	1-0	Edwards
		4	28.1.50	**Charlton A**	D1	A	D	1-1	E.Evans
		4r	1.2.50	**Charlton A**		H	W	2-0	E.Evans 2
		5	11.2.50	**Leeds U**	D2	A	L	1-3	Sherwood (p)
1950-51	D2	3	6.1.51	**West Ham**	D2	A	L	1-2	Grant
1951-52	D2	3	12.1.52	**Swindon T**	3S	H	D	1-1	Grant
		3r	15.1.52	**Swindon T**		A	L	0-1	
1952-53	D1	3	10.1.53	**Halifax T**	3N	A	L	1-3	W.Baker
1953-54	D1	3	9.1.54	**Peterborough U**	ML	H	W	3-1	Ford 2, Northcott
		4	30.1.54	**Port Vale**	3N	H	L	0-2	
1954-55	D1	3	8.1.55	**Arsenal**	D1	A	L	0-1	
1955-56	D1	3	7.1.56	**Leeds U**	D2	A	W	2-1	Hitchens, McSeveney
		4	28.1.56	**West Ham**	D2	A	L	1-2	Ford
1956-57	D1	3	5.1.57	**Leeds U**	D1	A	W	2-1	Stockin, McSeveney
		4	26.1.57	**Barnsley**	D2	H	L	0-1	

1957-58	D2	3	4.1.58	**Leeds U**	D1	A	W	2-1	Harrington, Nugent
		4	25.1.58	**Leyton O**	D2	H	W	4-1	Bishop og, Walsh, Bonson 2
		5	15.2.58	**Blackburn R**	D2	H	D	0-0	
		5r	20.2.58	**Blackburn R**		A	L	1-2	Hewitt
1958-59	D2	3	10.1.59	**Plymouth A**	D3	A	W	3-0	Hewitt (p), Reyolds, Bonson
		4	24.1.59	**Norwich C**	D3	A	L	2-3	Hewitt, Bonson
1959-60	D2	3	9.1.60	**Port Vale**	D3	H	L	0-2	
1960-61	D1	3	7.1.61	**Manchester C**	D1	H	D	1-1	Tapscott
		3r	11.1.61	**Manchester C**		A	D	0-0aet	
		3 2r	16.1.61	**Manchester C** at Highbury			L	0-2	
1961-62	D1	3	10.1.62	**Middlesbrough**	D2	A	L	0-1	
1962-63	D2	3	18.2.63	**Charlton A**	D2	A	L	0-1	
1963-64	D2	3	4.1.64	**Leeds U**	D2	H	L	0-1	
1964-65	D2	3	9.1.65	**Charlton A**	D2	H	L	1-2	Tapscott
1965-66	D2	3	26.1.66	**Port Vale**	D4	H	W	2-1	King, Hole
		4	12.2.66	**Southport**	D4	A	L	0-2	
1966-67	D2	3	28.1.67	**Barnsley**	D4	A	D	1-1	Bird
		3r	31.1.67	**Barnsley**		H	W	2-1	Johnston (p), King
		4	18.2.67	**Manchester C**	D1	H	D	1-1	Williams
		4r	22.2.67	**Manchester C**		A	L	1-3	Johnston (p)
1967-68	D2	3	27.1.68	**Stoke C**	D1	A	L	1-4	Jones
1968-69	D2	3	4.1.69	**Arsenal**	D1	H	D	0-0	
		3r	7.1.69	**Arsenal**		A	L	0-2	
1969-70	D2	3	3.1.70	**York C**	D4	A	D	1-1	Swallow og
		3r	7.1.70	**York C**		H	D	1-1aet	Toshack
		3 2r	15.1.70	**York C** at St Andrews			L	1-3aet	King
1970-71	D2	3	2.1.71	**Brighton & HA**	D3	H	W	1-0	King
		4	23.1.71	**Brentford**	D4	H	L	0-2	
1971-72	D2	3	15.1.72	**Sheffield U**	D1	A	W	3-1	Murray, Woodruff, Carver
		4	9.2.72	**Sunderland**	D2	H	D	1-1	King
		4r	14.2.72	**Sunderland**		A	D	1-1aet	Clark
		4 2r	16.2.72	**Sunderland** at Maine Rd			W	3-1	Clark, Woodruff, Kellock
		5	26.2.72	**Leeds U**	D1	H	L	0-2	
1972-73	D2	3	13.1.73	**Scunthorpe U**	D3	A	W	3-2	Kellock, McCulloch, Phillips
		4	3.2.73	**Bolton W**	D3	A	D	2-2	Kellock, Phillips
		4r	7.2.73	**Bolton W**		H	D	1-1aet	McCulloch
		4 2r	12.2.73	**Bolton W** at Hawthorns			L	0-1	
1973-74	D2	3	5.1.74	**Birmingham C**	D1	A	L	2-5	Impey, McCulloch
1974-75	D2	3	4.1.75	**Leeds U**	D1	A	L	1-4	Showers
1975-76	D3	1	22.11.75	**Exeter C**	D4	H	W	6-2	Alston 3, Reece 2, Evans
		2	13.12.75	**Wycombe W**	IL	H	W	1-0	Evans
		3	3.1.76	**Orient**	D2	A	W	1-0	Alston
		4	24.1.76	**Southend U**	D3	A	L	1-2	Evans
1976-77	D2	3	8.1.77	**Tottenham H**	D1	H	W	1-0	Sayer
		4	29.1.77	**Wrexham**	D3	H	W	3-2	Giles, Sayer, Buchanan
		5	26.2.77	**Everton**	D1	H	L	1-2	Evans
1977-78	D2	3	7.1.78	**Ipswich T**	D1	H	L	0-2	
1978-79	D2	3	9.1.79	**Swindon T**	D3	A	L	0-3	
1979-80	D2	3	5.1.80	**Arsenal**	D1	H	D	0-0	
		3r	8.1.80	**Arsenal**		A	L	1-2	Buchanan
1980-81	D2	3	3.1.81	**Leicester C**	D1	A	L	0-3	
1981-82	D2	3	2.1.82	**Manchester C**	D1	A	L	1-3	Maddy
1982-83	D3	1	20.11.83	**Wokingham T**	IL	A	D	1-1	Tong
		1r	23.11.83	**Wokingham T**		H	W	3-0	Jones, Hemmerman, Ingram
		2	11.12.83	**Weymouth**	APL	H	L	2-3	Gibbins, Hemmerman
1983-84	D2	3	7.1.84	**Ipswich T**	D1	H	L	0-3	
1984-85	D2	3	21.1.85	**Gillingham**	D3	A	L	1-2	Withey
1985-86	D3	1	16.11.85	**Exeter C**	D4	A	L	1-2	Stevenson
1986-87	D4	1	15.11.86	**Ton Pentre**	Welsh	A	W	4-1	Marustik 2, Wimbleton, Wheeler
		2	9.12.86	**Brentford**	D3	H	W	2-0	Wimbleton, Bartlett
		3	10.1.87	**Millwall**	D2	A	D	0-0	
		3r	20.1.87	**Millwall**		H	D	2-2aet	Vaughan, Marustik
		3 2r	26.1.87	**Millwall**		H	W	1-0	Pike
		4	31.1.87	**Stoke C**	D2	A	L	1-2	Wimbleton
1987-88	D4	1	14.11.87	**Peterborough U**	D4	A	L	1-2	Bartlett
1988-89	D3	1	19.11.88	**Hereford U**	D4	H	W	3-0	Bartlett, Tupling, Gilligan
		2	11.12.88	**Enfield**	GMVC	A	W	4-1	Wimbleton (p), Lynex, Gilligan 2

		3	7.1.89	**Hull C**	D2	H	L	1-2	Gilligan
1989-90	D3	1	17.11.89	**Halesowen**	SL	H	W	1-0	Pike
		2	9.12.89	**Gloucester C**	SL	H	D	2-2	Scott 2
		2r	12.12.89	**Gloucester C**		A	W	1-0	Scott
		3	6.1.90	**QPR**	D1	H	D	0-0	
		3r	10.1.90	**QPR**		A	L	0-2	
1990-91	D4	1	17.11.90	**Hayes**	IL	H	D	0-0	
		1r	21.11.90	**Hayes** at Brentford		A	L	0-1	
1991-92	D4	1	16.11.91	**Swansea**	D3	A	L	1-2	Pike
1992-93	D3	1	14.11.92	**Bath C**	GMVC	H	L	2-3	Millar, Blake

CARLISLE UNITED

Formed 1903 following merger of Carlisle Red Rose and Shaddongate United. **First entered FA Cup:** 1904. **Best FA Cup performance:** 6th round, 1975. **Record FA Cup win:** 9-1 vs Windermere, 2nd qualifying round, 19.10.1907; 8-0 vs Arlecdon Red Rose 2nd qualifying round, 22.10.1921 **Record FA Cup Defeat:** four defeats by five goal margins

1904-05		1q **Workington** (H) 2-2; 1qr **Workington** (A) 1-3							
1905-06	LC	1q **Red Rose** (H) 3-0; 2q **Barrow** (A) 2-4							
1906-07	NEL	2q **Wigtown Harriers** (H) 3-1; 3q **Barrow** (A) 2-1; 4q **Southport Central** (H) 0-4							
1907-08	LC	P **Carlisle C** (H) 1-0; 1q **Lancaster T** (A) 4-1; 2q **Windermere** (H) 9-1; 3q **Workington** (A) 3-2; 4q **Darlington** (H) 7-0;							
		5q **Southend U** (H) 4-0							
		1	11.1.08	**Brentford**	SL	H	D	2-2	Powell 2
		1r	15.1.08	**Brentford**		A	W	3-1aet	McAteer, Robinson 2
		2	1.2.08	**Grimsby T**	D2	A	L	2-6	McAteer, Maher
1908-09	LC	5q **Coventry C** (A) 1-1; 5qr **Coventry C** (H) 1-1; 5q 2r **Coventry C** 3-1 at Hyde Road, Manchester							
		1	16.1.09	**Fulham**	D2	A	L	1-4	Sanderson
1909-10	LC	4q **Tonge** (H) 1-0; 5q **Mexborough T** (A) 0-0; 5qr **Mexborough T** (H) 4-0							
		1	15.1.10	**West Ham U**	SL	A	D	1-1	Carter
		1r	20.1.10	**West Ham U**		A	L	0-5	
1910-11	NEL	4q **Newburn** (H) 3-0; 5q **Crewe Alex** (A) 1-1; 5qr **Crewe Alex** (H) 3-4							
1911-12	NEL	4q **Accrington Stanley** (A) 0-3							
1912-13	NEL	4q **Barrow** (A) 1-4							
1913-14	NEL	1q **Lancaster T** (A) 0-0; 1qr **Lancaster T** (H) 4-2; 2q **Frizington** (H) 2-1; 3q **Lowca** (H) 7-1; 4q **Southport Central** (H) 2-1;							
		5q **Glossop** (A) 1-4							
1914-15	NEL	1q **Barrow St Mary's** (H) 4-1; 2q **Lancaster T** (H) 3-1; 3q **Frizington** (A) 1-3							
1919-20	NEL	1q **Wigton Harriers** (H) 8-1; 2q **Cleator Moor Celtic** (H) 6-1; 3q **Frizington** (H) 3-1; 4q **Barrow** (A) 0-0; 4qr **Barrow** (H) 1-0;							
		5q **South Liverpool** (A) 1-3							
1920-21	NEL	1q **Frizington** (H) 3-1; 2q **Barrow** (A) 1-1; 2qr **Barrow** (H) 1-0aet; *Barrow awarded the tie after protest*							
1921-22	NEL	P **Vickerstown** (H) 5-0; 1q **Penrith** (H) 6-1; 2q **Arlecdon Red Rose** (H) 8-0; 3q **Cleator Moor Celtic** (H) 2-0;							
		4q **Stalybridge C** (H) 0-0; 4qr **Stalybridge C** (A) 2-3							
1922-23	NEL	4q **Fleetwood** (H) 7-1; 5q **Felling Colliery** (H) 6-0; 6q **Aberdare A** (A) 0-0; 6qr **Aberdare A** (H) 1-2							
1923-24	NEL	4q **Barrow** (A) 2-1; 5q **Ashington** (A) 0-2							
1924-25	NEL	1q **Workington** (A) 2-1; 2q **Cleator Moor Celtic** (A) 5-1; 3q **Egremont** (A) 6-2; 4q **Bishop Auckland** (H) 0-1							
1925-26	NEL	4q **Workington** (H) 3-1							
		1	28.11.25	**Chilton Colliery**	NAll	H	L	0-2	
1926-27	NEL	4q **Whitehaven A** (H) 7-1							
		1	27.11.26	**Hartlepool U**	3N	H	W	6-2	Sinclair, A.Pigg, Ward, Hamilton, Graham 2
		2	11.12.26	**Bedlington U**	NEL	H	W	4-0	Smiles 2, A.Pigg 2
		3	8.1.27	**Wolverhampton**	D2	A	L	0-1	
1927-28	NEL	4q **Lancaster T** (A) 2-0							
		1	26.11.27	**Doncaster R**	3N	H	W	2-1	Ward, McConnell
		2	10.12.27	**Wrexham**	3N	A	L	0-1	
1928-29	3N	1	24.11.28	**Wrexham**		A	W	1-0	Ward
		2	8.12.28	**Lincoln C**	3N	H	L	0-1	
1929-30	3N	1	30.11.29	**Halifax T**	3N	H	W	2-1	McConnell, McLeod
		2	14.12.29	**Crewe A**	3N	H	W	4-2	Hutchinson 2, Watson, Cape
		3	11.1.30	**Everton**	D1	H	L	2-4	McConnell, Watson
1930-31	3N	1	29.11.30	**New Brighton**	3N	H	W	3-1	Maskill, McConnell 2
		2	13.12.30	**Tunbridge Wells R**	KL	H	W	4-2	Hutchinson 2, McConnell 2
		3	10.1.31	**Bolton**	D1	A	L	0-1	
1931-32	3N	1	28.11.31	**Yorkshire Amateurs**	YL	A	W	3-1	Richmond, McConnell, Sharpe
		2	12.12.31	**Darlington**	3N	H	L	0-2	
1932-33	3N	1	26.11.32	**Denaby U**	ML	H	W	1-0	Slinger
		2	10.12.32	**Hull C**	3N	H	D	1-1	Felton
		2r	15.12.32	**Hull C**		A	L	1-2aet	White
1933-34	3N	1	25.11.33	**Wrexham**	3N	H	W	2-1	Stevenson, Slinger

Season	Div	Rd	Date	Opponent		H/A	Res	Score	Scorers
		2	9.12.33	Cheltenham T	BDL	H	L	1-2	Slinger
1934-35	3N	1	24.11.34	Wigan Athletic	CC	H	L	1-6	Ranson
1935-36	3N	1	30.11.35	Tranmere R	3N	A	L	0-3	
1936-37	3N	1	28.11.36	Stockport Co	3N	H	W	2-1	Mantle, McArdle
		2	12.12.36	Clapton Orient	3S	H	W	4-1	McArdle 2, James, O'Grady
		3	16.1.37	Swansea T	D2	A	L	0-1	
1937-38	3N	1	27.11.37	Tranmere R	3N	A	L	1-2	Leach
1938-39	3N	1	26.11.38	Walsall	3S	A	L	1-4	Hammill
1945-46	3N	1 1L	17.11.45	North Shields	NEL	H	W	5-1	Adamson, Hamilton 2, Clarke, Cape
		1 2L	24.11.45	North Shields		A	W	3-2	Hamilton, Douglas, Clarke
		2 1L	8.12.45	Barrow	3N	A	L	2-4	Cape 2
		2 2L	15.12.45	Barrow		H	L	3-4	Adamson, Clarke, Dellow
1946-47	3N	1	30.11.46	Runcorn	CC	H	W	4-0	Dougal, Iceton 2, Broadis
		2	14.12.46	South Liverpool	CC	A	W	3-2	Iceton 2, Moir
		3	11.1.47	Sheffield U	D1	A	L	0-3	
1947-48	3N	1	29.11.47	Barrow	3N	A	L	2-3	Broadis, Lindsay
1948-49	3N	1	27.11.48	New Brighton	3N	A	L	0-1	
1949-50	3N	1	26.11.49	Lincoln C	3N	H	W	1-0	Dick
		2	10.12.49	Swindon T	3S	H	W	2-0	Lindsay 2
		3	7.1.50	Leeds U	D2	H	L	2-5	Lindsay, Dick
1950-51	3N	1	25.11.50	Barrow	3N	H	W	2-1	McCue, Turner
		2	9.12.50	Southport	3N	A	W	3-1	Lindsay, Turner 2
		3	6.1.51	Arsenal	D1	A	D	0-0	
		3r	11.1.51	Arsenal		H	L	1-4	McCue
1951-52	3N	1	24.11.51	Bradford C	3N	A	L	1-6	Brown
1952-53	3N	1	22.11.52	Scunthorpe U	3N	A	L	0-1	
1953-54	3N	1	21.11.53	Southport	3N	A	L	0-1	
1954-55	3N	1	20.11.54	Stockport C	3N	A	W	1-0	Bond
		2	11.12.54	Watford	3S	H	D	2-2	Whitehouse, Ashman
		2r	15.12.54	Watford		A	L	1-4	Ashman
1955-56	3N	1	19.11.55	Darlington	3N	A	D	0-0	
		1r	22.11.55	Darlington		H	D	0-0aet	
		1 2r	28.11.55	Darlington at Newcastle			L	1-3	Kinloch
1956-57	3N	1	17.11.56	Billingham Synthonia	NL	H	W	6-1	Garvie 3, Ackerman 2, Broadis
		2	8.12.56	Darlington	3N	H	W	2-1	Ackerman 2
		3	5.1.57	Birmingham C	D1	H	D	3-3	Ackerman 3
		3r	9.1.57	Birmingham C		A	L	0-4	
1957-58	3N	1	16.11.57	Rhyl	CC	H	W	5-1	Ackerman (p), Bond 2, Broadis 2
		2	7.12.57	Accrington Stanley	3N	H	D	1-1	Ackerman
		2r	11.12.57	Accrington Stanley		A	L	2-3	Johnston, Ackerman
1958-59	D4	1	15.11.58	Heanor T	CA	A	W	5-1	Ackerman 2, Mooney, Fletcher 2
		2	6.12.58	Chesterfield	D3	H	D	0-0	
		2r	9.12.58	Chesterfield		A	L	0-1	
1959-60	D4	1	14.11.59	Rochdale	D4	A	D	2-2	McGill, Walker
		1r	17.11.59	Rochdale		H	L	1-3	Devlin
1960-61	D4	1	5.11.60	Chester	D4	A	W	1-0	Bevan
		2	26.11.60	Port Vale		A	L	1-2	Walker
1961-62	D4	1	4.11.61	Darlington	D4	A	W	4-0	Whitelaw 2, Brayton, Walker
		2	25.11.61	Barnsley	D3	A	W	2-1	Walker, Taylor
		3	8.1.62	Wolverhampton W	D1	A	L	1-3	R.Thompson
1962-63	D3	1	3.11.62	Hartlepool U	D4	A	W	2-1	Thomson og, Brayton
		2	24.11.62	Blyth Spartans	NEL	A	W	2-0	Walker, Brayton
		3	29.1.63	Gravesend & N	SL	H	L	0-1	
1963-64	D4	1	16.11.63	York C	D4	A	W	5-2	Livingstone, McIlmoyle, Kirkup, Davies (p), Taylor
		2	7.12.63	Gateshead	NRL	H	W	4-3	McIlmoyle 3, Taylor
		3	4.1.64	QPR	D3	H	W	2-0	Livingstone, McIlmoyle
		4	25.1.64	Bedford T	SL	A	W	3-0	Kirkup, Livingstone, Davies (p)
		5	15.2.64	Preston NE	D2	A	L	0-1	
1964-65	D3	1	14.11.64	Crook T	NL	A	L	0-1	
1965-66	D2	3	22.1.66	Crystal P	D2	H	W	3-0	McConnell, Welsh, Wilson
		4	12.2.66	Shrewsbury T	D3	A	D	0-0	
		4r	15.2.66	Shrewsbury T		H	D	1-1aet	Dolbie og
		4 2r	21.2.66	Shrewsbury T at Preston			L	3-4aet	Balderstone, Wilson, Carlin
1966-67	D2	3	28.1.67	Blackburn R	D2	A	W	2-1	Wilson, Carlin
		4	18.2.67	Ipswich T	D2	A	L	0-2	
1967-68	D2	3	27.1.68	Newcastle U	D1	A	W	1-0	Murray
		4	17.2.68	Everton	D1	H	L	0-2	

Season	Div	Rnd	Date	Opponent	Opp Div	H/A	Res	Score	Scorers
1968-69	D2	3	4.1.69	Chelsea	D1	A	L	0-2	
1969-70	D2	3	3.1.70	Nottingham F	D1	A	D	0-0	
		3r	6.1.70	Nottingham F		H	W	2-1	Murray, McVitie
		4	24.1.70	Aldershot	D4	H	D	2-2	Hatton, Balderstone
		4r	28.1.70	Aldershot		A	W	4-1	Murray, McVitie, Caldwell, Barton
		5	7.2.70	Middlesbrough	D2	H	L	1-2	Winstanley
1970-71	D2	3	11.1.71	Southend U	D4	A	W	3-0	Owen, Hatton 2
		4	23.1.71	Tottenham H	D1	H	L	2-3	Martin, Owen
1971-72	D2	3	15.1.72	Tottenham H	D1	A	D	1-1	Bowles
		3r	18.1.72	Tottenham H		H	L	1-3	Martin
1972-73	D2	3	13.1.73	Huddersfield T	D2	H	D	2-2	Gorman, Laidlaw
		3r	16.1.73	Huddersfield T		A	W	1-0	Dolan og
		4	3.2.73	Sheffield U	D1	H	W	2-1	Martin, Delgado
		5	24.2.73	Arsenal	D1	H	L	1-2	Martin
1973-74	D2	3	5.1.74	Sunderland	D2	H	D	0-0	
		3r	9.1.74	Sunderland		A	W	1-0	Martin
		4	26.1.74	Liverpool	D1	A	D	0-0	
		4r	29.1.74	Liverpool		H	L	0-2	
1974-75	D1	3	4.1.75	Preston NE	D3	A	W	1-0	Laidlaw
		4	25.1.75	WBA	D2	H	W	3-2	Clarke, Laidlaw, Owen
		5	15.2.75	Mansfield T	D4	A	W	1-0	Owen
		6	8.3.75	Fulham	D2	H	L	0-1	
1975-76	D2	3	3.1.76	WBA	D2	A	L	1-3	Wile og
1976-77	D2	3	8.1.77	Matlock T	NPL	H	W	5-1	Rafferty 2, McVitie, Clarke, Bonnyman
		4	29.1.77	Liverpool	D1	A	L	0-3	
1977-78	D3	1	26.11.77	Stafford Rangers	NPL	H	W	2-0	Rafferty 2
		2	17.12.77	Chester	D3	H	W	3-1	Rafferty 2, McVitie
		3	7.1.78	Manchester U	D1	H	D	1-1	McDonald
		3r	11.1.78	Manchester U		A	L	2-4	Tait, Rafferty
1978-79	D3	1	25.11.78	Halifax T	D4	H	W	1-0	Lumby
		2	16.12.78	Hull C	D3	H	W	3-0	Lumby, McCartney (p), Kemp
		3	10.1.79	Ipswich T	D1	A	L	2-3	Tait, Kemp
1979-80	D3	1	24.11.79	Hull C	D3	H	D	3-3	Bonnyman (p), Ludlam, Bannon
		1r	28.11.79	Hull C		A	W	2-0	Winstanley, Bonnyman
		2	15.12.79	Sheffield W	D3	H	W	3-0	Staniforth, Beardsley, Ludlum
		3	5.1.80	Bradford C	D4	H	W	3-2	Bonnyman (p), Ludlum, Hoolickin
		4	26.1.80	Wrexham	D2	H	D	0-0	
		4r	29.1.80	Wrexham		A	L	1-3	Bonnyman
1980-81	D3	1	22.11.80	Workington	NPL	A	D	0-0	
		1r	1.12.80	Workington		H	W	4-1	Brown 2, Beardsley 2
		2	13.12.80	Walsall	D3	H	W	3-0	Brown, Beardsley 2
		3	3.1.81	Mansfield T	D4	A	D	2-2	Bannon, Bird og
		3r	6.1.81	Mansfield T		H	W	2-1	Beardsley, MacDonald
		4	24.1.81	Bristol C	D2	H	D	1-1	Coady
		5	28.1.81	Bristol C		A	L	0-5	
1981-82	D3	1	21.11.81	Darlington	D4	A	D	2-2	Staniforth, Robson
		1r	24.11.81	Darlington		H	W	3-2	Robson, Beardsley, Bannon
		2	2.1.82	Bishop Auckland	NL	H	–	0-0	
				abandoned after 69 minutes – waterlogged pitch					
		2	9.1.82	Bishop Auckland at Workington			W	1-0	Lee
		3	23.1.82	Huddersfield T	D3	H	L	2-3	Bannon, Robson
1982-83	D2	3	8.1.83	Burnley	D2	H	D	2-2	Bannon, Poskett
		3r	11.1.83	Burnley		A	L	1-3	Poskett
1983-84	D2	3	7.1.84	Swindon T	D4	H	D	1-1	Ashurst
		3r	10.1.84	Swindon T		A	L	1-3	Shoulder (p)
1984-85	D2	3	5.1.85	Dagenham	APL	H	W	1-0	Poskett
		4	26.1.85	Leicester C	D1	A	L	0-1	
1985-86	D2	3	13.1.86	QPR	D1	H	W	1-0	Cooke
		4	25.1.86	Peterborough	D4	A	L	0-1	
1986-87	D3	1	15.11.86	Notts Co	D3	A	D	1-1	Bishop
		1r	18.11.86	Notts Co		H	L	0-3	
1987-88	D4	1	14.11.87	Macclesfield T	GMVC	A	L	2-4	Hetherington, Fulbrook
1988-89	D4	1	19.11.88	Telford U	GMVC	A	D	1-1	Walsh
		1r	22.11.88	Telford U		H	W	4-1	Saddington, Fitzpatrick, Gorman (p), Halpin
		2	10.12.88	Scarborough	D4	A	W	1-0	Richards og
		3	7.1.89	Liverpool		H	L	0-3	
1989-90	D4	1	18.11.89	Wrexham	D4	H	W	3-0	Sendall, Proudlock 2

	2	9.12.89	**Wigan Athletic**	D3	A	L	0-2
1990-91 D4	1	17.11.90	**Wigan Athletic**	D3	A	L	0-5
1991-92 D4	1	16.11.91	**Crewe Alex**	D4	H	D	1-1	Watson
	1r	26.11.91	**Crewe Alex**		A	L	3-5aet	Barnsley (2p), Fyfe
1992-93 D3	1	14.11.92	**Wigan A**	D2	A	L	1-3	Arnold

CARSHALTON ATHLETIC

Formed 1903. **First entered FA Cup:** 1946. **Cup Final Connection:** Ernie Taylor, who played in three Cup Finals for Newcastle U (1951), Blackpool (1953) and Manchester United (1958) started his career at Carshalton.

1969-70 AL	1	15.11.69	**Hendon**	IL	A	L	3-5	Burnham 2, Cadman
1982-83 IL	1	20.11.82	**Barnet**	APL	H	W	4-0	Dark, Lewington 2, Tuite
	2	11.12.82	**Torquay U**	D4	A	L	1-4	Lewington
1987-88 IL	1	23.11.87	**Welling U**	GMVC	A	L	2-3	Kane, Riley

CASTLEFORD TOWN

Competed in the FA Cup from 1919-1937

1919-20	1	10.1.20	**Hednesford T**	BDL	H	W	2-0	Howson, Gedney
	2	31.1.20	**Bradford PA**	3N	A	L	2-3	Howson, Dyer

CASUALS

Formed 1883. Played on Wandsworth Common near the Surrey Hotel. Merged with the Corinthians in 1939 to form Corinthian-Casuals. **FA Amateur Cup winners:** 1936; Runners-up 1894

1884-85	1	8.11.84	**South Reading**		A	L	1-4	
1885-86	1	31.10.85	**Swifts**		A	L	1-7	
1886-87	1	23.10.86	**Dulwich**		H	L	2-4	
1887-88	1		**Millwall Rovers**			scratched		
1890-91	1	17.1.91	**Aston Villa**	D1	A	L	1-13	A.G.Topham
1892-93	1	21.1.92	**Nottingham F**	FAII	A	L	0-4	

See also Corinthian-Casuals

CHARLTON ATHLETIC

Formed 1905. **First entered FA Cup:** 1914 **FA Cup Winners:** 1947. **FA Cup Runners-up** 1946. **Record FA Cup Win:** 7-0 vs Burton Albion, 3rd round, 7.1.1956 **Record FA Cup Defeat:** 0-6 vs Wrexham, 3rd round, 5.1.1980

1914-15 SS	1q **Dartford** (A) 0-0; 1qr **Dartford** (A) 1-2
1919-20 KL	P **Sittingbourne** (A) 2-7
1920-21 SL	P **Catford Southend** (H) 6-0; 1q **Margate** (A) 0-0; 1qr **Margate** (H) 3-1; 2q **Maidstone** (H) 1-1; 2qr **Maidstone** (A) 0-2
1921-22 3S	did not compete
1922-23 3S	5q **Northampton T** (H) 2-0; 6q **Darlington** (H) 2-1

1922-23 3S	1	13.1.23	**Manchester C**	D1	A	W	2-1	Goodman, Whalley
	2	3.2.23	**Preston NE**	D1	H	W	2-0	Goodman, S.Smith
	3	24.2.23	**WBA**	D1	H	W	1-0	Goodman
	4	10.3.23	**Bolton W**	D1	H	L	0-1	
1923-24 3S	1	12.1.24	**Accrington S**	3N	A	D	0-0	
	1r	16.1.24	**Accrington S**		H	W	1-0	Hannaford
	2	2.2.24	**Wolverhampton W**	3N	H	D	0-0	
	2r	7.2.24	**Wolverhampton W**		A	L	0-1	
1924-25 3S	5q **Dulwich Hamlet** (H) 4-0; 6q **QPR** (A) 1-1; 6qr **QPR** (H) 1-2
1925-26 3S	1	28.11.25	**Windsor & Eton**	AL	H	W	4-2	Millard 3, McCrorie
	2	12.12.25	**QPR**	3S	H	D	1-1	Pigg og
	2r	17.12.25	**QPR**		H	W	1-0	McGinn
	3	9.1.26	**Huddersfield T**	D1	H	L	0-1	
1926-27 3S	1	27.11.26	**Woking**	IL	A	W	3-1	J.Rankin, Cairns, Tricker
	2	11.12.26	**Bristol R**	3S	A	L	1-4	J.Rankin
1927-28 3S	1	26.11.27	**Merthyr T**	3S	A	D	0-0	
	1r	30.11.27	**Merthyr T**		H	W	2-1	Sherlaw, J.Horton
	2	10.12.27	**Kettering T**	SL	H	D	1-1	J.Horton
	2r	15.12.27	**Kettering T**		A	W	2-1	Biswell 2
	3	14.1.28	**Bury**	D1	H	D	1-1	Biswell
	3r	18.1.28	**Bury**		A	L	3-4	W.Welsh 2, Biswell

1928-29	3S	1	24.11.28	Peterborough & F Utd	SL	A	W	2-0	Whitlow 2
		2	8.12.28	Northfleet U	SL	A	W	5-1	Astley 2, Rowe og, Whitlow 2
		3	12.1.29	Portsmouth	D1	A	L	1-2	J.Rankin
1929-30	D2	3	11.1.30	QPR	3S	H	D	1-1	Astley
		3r	16.1.30	QPR		A	W	3-0	Lennox, J.Horton, Astley
		4	25.1.30	Middlesbrough	D1	A	D	1-1	Pugsley
		4r	29.1.30	Middlesbrough		H	D	1-1	Lennox
		4 2r	3.2.30	Middlesbrough at Maine Road			L	0-1aet	
1930-31	D2	3	10.1.31	WBA	D2	A	D	2-2	Wyper, Astley
		3r	14.1.31	WBA		H	D	1-1aet	Astley
		3 2r	19.1.31	WBA at Villa Park			L	1-3	Lennox
1931-32	D2	3	9.1.32	West Ham	D1	H	L	1-2	J.Horton
1932-33	D2	3	14.1.33	Bolton W	D1	H	L	1-5	G.Robinson
1933-34	3S	1	25.11.33	Bath C	SL	A	D	0-0	
		1r	29.11.33	Bath C		H	W	3-1	Pearce, Hobbis, JT Smith
		2	9.12.33	Gillingham	3S	H	W	1-0	Pearce
		3	13.1.34	Port Vale	D2	H	W	2-0	Pearce, Hobbis
		4	27.1.34	Birmingham	D1	A	L	0-1	
1934-35	3S	1	24.11.34	Exeter C	3S	H	D	2-2	Wilkinson, R.Allen
		1r	28.11.34	Exeter C		A	L	2-5	Wilkinson, R.Allen
1935-36	D2	3	11.1.36	Clapton O	3S	A	L	0-3	
1936-37	D1	3	16.1.37	Coventry C	D2	A	L	0-2	
1937-38	D1	3	8.1.38	Cardiff C	3S	H	W	5-0	G.Robinson, Bassett og, Boulter, Owens 2
		4	22.1.38	Leeds U	D1	H	W	2-1	G.Tadman 2
		5	12.2.38	A.Villa	D2	H	D	1-1	G.Robinson
		5r	16.2.38	A.Villa		A	D	2-2	R.Brown 2
		5 2r	21.2.38	A.Villa at Highbury			L	1-4	G.Tadman
1938-39	D1	3	7.1.39	Cardiff C	3S	A	L	0-1	
1945-46	D1	3 1L	5.1.46	Fulham	D2	H	W	3-1	Duffy, Fell, D.Welsh
		3 2L	7.1.46	Fulham		A	L	1-2	M.Tadman
		4 1L	26.1.46	Wolverhampton W	D1	H	W	5-2	Duffy 2, A.Turner, G.Robinson, Fell
		4 2L	30.1.46	Wolverhampton W		A	D	1-1	Morris og
		5 1L	9.2.46	Preston NE	D1	A	D	1-1	A.Turner
		5 2L	13.2.46	Preston NE		H	W	6-0	Duffy 3, A.Turner 2, Fell
		6 1L	2.3.46	Brentford	D1	H	W	6-3	Brown, Duffy, A.Turner 2, D.Welsh 2
		6 2L	9.3.46	Brentford		A	W	3-1	Duffy, D.Welsh, A.Turner
		SF	23.3.46	Bolton W	D1		W	2-0	Duffy 2
				played at Villa Park					
		F	27.4.46	Derby Co	D1 WEMBLEY		L	1-4aet	H.Turner
1946-47	D1	3	11.1.47	Rochdale	3N	H	W	3-1	Lancelotte, Duffy 2
		4	25.1.47	WBA	D2	A	W	2-1	Duffy, W.Robinson
		5	8.2.47	Blackburn R	D1	H	W	1-0	Dawson
		6	1.3.47	Preston NE	D1	H	W	2-1	Duffy, Hurst
		SF	29.3.47	Newcastle U	D2		W	4-0	D.Welsh 2, Dawson, Hurst
				played at Elland Road					
		F	26.4.47	BURNLEY	D2 WEMBLEY		W	1-0aet	Duffy
1947-48	D1	3	10.1.48	Newcastle U	D2	H	W	2-1	W.Robinson, Revell
		4	24.1.48	Stockport Co	3N	H	W	3-0	Revell (p), C.Vaughan, Staniforth og
		5	7.2.48	Manchester U	D1	A	L	0-2	
				played at Huddersfield					
1948-49	D1	3	8.1.49	Burnley	D1	A	L	1-2aet	O'Linn
1949-50	D1	3	7.1.50	Fulham	D1	H	D	2-2	Hurst 2
		3r	11.1.50	Fulham		A	W	2-1	D'Arcy, C.Vaughan
		4	28.1.50	Cardiff C	D2	H	D	1-1	C.Vaughan
		4r	1.2.50	Cardiff C		A	L	0-2	
1950-51	D1	3	6.1.51	Blackpool	D1	H	D	2-2	Revell (p), P.Croker
		3r	10.1.51	Blackpool		A	L	0-3	
1951-52	D1	3	12.1.52	Luton T	D2	A	L	0-1	
1952-53	D1	3	10.1.53	Hull C	D2	A	L	1-3	Leary
1953-54	D1	3	9.1.54	Portsmouth	D1	A	D	3-3	Leary, Ayre 2
		3r	14.1.54	Portsmouth		H	L	2-3aet	Leary, Kiernan
1954-55	D1	3	8.1.55	Rochdale	3N	A	W	3-1	Kiernan, Hammond, Hurst
		4	29.1.55	WBA	D1	A	W	4-2	E.Firmani (p), Ayre 3
		5	19.2.55	Wolverhampton W	D1	A	L	1-4	Hewie
1955-56	D1	3	7.1.56	Burton A	BDL	H	W	7-0	Kiernan 2, Gauld, Leary 3, Hurst
		4	28.1.56	Swindon T	3S	H	W	2-1	Hunt og, C.Hammond
		5	18.2.56	Arsenal	D1	H	L	0-2	

1956-57	D1	3	5.1.57	Middlesbrough	D2	A	D	1-1	JJ Ryan
		3r	10.1.57	Middlesbrough		H	L	2-3	Leary, Barnard og
1957-58	D2	3	4.1.58	Huddersfield T	D2	A	D	2-2	Summers, JJ Ryan
		3r	8.1.58	Huddersfield T		H	W	1-0	JJ Ryan
		4	25.1.58	Fulham	D2	A	D	1-1	JJ Ryan
		4r	29.1.58	Fulham		H	L	0-2	
1958-59	D2	3	10.1.59	Bristol R	D2	A	W	4-0	Lawrie 2, R.White, Summers
		4	24.1.59	Everton	D1	H	D	2-2	Summers, Lawrie
		4r	28.1.59	Everton		A	L	1-4aet	Lawrie
1959-60	D2	3	9.1.60	Bristol C	D2	A	W	3-2	Lawrie 3
		4	30.1.60	Wolverhampton W	D1	A	L	1-2	Summers
1960-61	D2	3	7.1.61	Tottenham H	D1	A	L	2-3	Leary, Lawrie
1961-62	D2	3	6.1.62	Scunthorpe U	D2	H	W	1-0	Kinsey
		4	27.1.62	Derby Co	D2	H	W	2-1	Matthews, Kinsey
		5	17.2.62	A.Villa	D1	A	L	1-2	Kinsey
1962-63	D2	3	18.2.63	Cardiff C	D2	H	W	1-0	Glover
		4	6.3.63	Chelsea	D2	H	L	0-3	
1963-64	D2	3	4.1.64	West Ham	D1	A	L	0-2	
1964-65	D2	3	9.1.65	Cardiff C	D2	A	W	2-1	Haydock, M.Bailey
		4	30.1.65	Middlesbrough	D2	H	D	1-1	Kenning
		4r	1.2.65	Middlesbrough		A	L	1-2	Matthews
1965-66	D2	3	22.1.66	Preston NE	D2	H	L	2-3	Singleton og, Tocknell
1966-67	D2	3	28.1.67	Sheffield U	D1	H	L	0-1	
1967-68	D2	3	27.1.68	Coventry C	D1	A	L	0-3	
1968-69	D2	3	4.1.69	Crystal P	D2	H	D	0-0	
		3r	8.1.69	Crystal P		A	W	2-0	Treacy 2
		4	25.1.69	Arsenal	D1	A	L	0-2	
1969-70	D2	3	3.1.70	A.Villa	D2	A	D	1-1	Treacy
		3r	12.1.70	A.Villa		H	W	1-0	Gregory
		4	24.1.70	QPR	D2	H	L	2-3	Riddick, Gregory
1970-71	D2	3	2.1.71	Hull C	D2	A	L	0-3	
1971-72	D2	3	15.1.72	Tranmere R	D3	H	D	0-0	
		3r	17.1.72	Tranmere R		A	L	2-4	Treacy 2
1972-73	D3	1	18.11.72	Tonbridge	SL	A	W	5-0	Flanagan, Horsfield, Peacock 2, Gilchrist og
		2	12.12.72	Walsall	D3	A	W	2-1	P.Davies, Horsfield
		3	13.1.73	Bolton W	D3	H	D	1-1	Curtis (p)
		3r	17.1.73	Bolton W		A	L	0-4	
1973-74	D3	1	24.11.73	Bournemouth	D3	A	L	0-1	
1974-75	D3	1	23.11.74	Chelmsford C	SL	A	W	1-0	Horsfield
		2	14.12.74	Peterborough U	D3	A	L	0-3	
1975-76	D2	3	3.1.76	Sheffield W	D3	H	W	2-1	Peacock, Warman
		4	24.1.76	Portsmouth	D2	H	D	1-1	R.Curtis (p)
		4r	27.1.76	Portsmouth		A	W	3-0	Powell, Flanagan, Hope
		5	14.2.76	Wolverhampton W	D1	A	L	0-3	
1976-77	D2	3	8.1.77	Blackburn R	D2	H	D	1-1	Burman
		3r	12.1.77	Blackburn R		A	L	0-2	
1977-78	D2	3	7.1.78	Notts Co	D2	H	L	0-2	
1978-79	D2	3	9.1.79	Maidstone U	SL	H	D	1-1	Flanagan
		3r	15.1.79	Maidstone U		A	W	2-1	D.Campbell, Robinson
		4	5.2.79	Bristol R	D2	A	L	0-1	
1979-80	D2	3	5.1.80	Wrexham	D2	A	L	0-6	
1980-81	D3	1	22.11.80	Harlow T	IL	A	W	2-0	Robinson, Hales
		2	13.12.80	Bournemouth	D4	H	W	2-1	P.Walsh, Hales
		3	3.1.81	Plymouth A	D3	A	W	2-1	Powell, Hales
		4	24.1.81	Fulham	D3	A	W	2-1	Shaw, Hales
		5	14.2.81	Ipswich T	D1	A	L	0-2	
1981-82	D2	3	2.1.82	Orient	D2	A	L	0-1	
1982-83	D2	3	8.1.83	Ipswich T	D1	A	L	2-3	Robinson, Hales
1983-84	D2	3	7.1.84	Colchester U	D4	A	W	1-0	Phillips og
		4	28.1.84	Watford	D1	H	L	0-2	
1984-85	D2	3	5.1.85	Tottenham H	D1	A	D	1-1	Aizlewood
		3r	23.1.85	Tottenham H		H	L	1-2	Moore (p)
1985-86	D2	3	5.1.86	West Ham	D1	H	L	0-1	
1986-87	D1	3	10.1.87	Walsall	D3	H	L	1-2	Stuart
1987-88	D1	3	9.1.88	West Ham	D1	A	L	0-2	
1988-89	D1	3	7.1.89	Oldham A	D2	H	W	2-1	Crooks, Williams
		4	28.1.89	Kettering T	GMVC	H	W	2-1	Williams, Lee

	5	18.2.89	West Ham	D1	H	L	0-1
1989-90 D1	3	7.1.90	Bradford C	D2	H	D	1-1	Jones
	3r	10.1.90	Bradford C		A	W	3-0	Lee, Williams, Jones
	4	27.1.90	WBA	D2	A	L	0-1
1990-91 D2	3	5.1.91	Everton	D1	H	L	1-2	Dyer
1991-92 D2	3	5.1.92	Barnet	D4	H	W	3-1	Gatting, Leaburn, Grant
	4	26.1.92	Sheffield U	D1	H	D	0-0
	4r	5.2.92	Sheffield U		A	L	1-3	Gatting
1992-93 D1	3	2.1.93	Leeds U	PL	A	D	1-1	Nelson
	3r	13.1.93	Leeds U		H	L	1-3	Pitcher (p)

CHATHAM

Formed 1882. Originally played at Great Lines in Chatham, the old stomping ground of the Royal Engineers. Now known as Chatham Town and playing in the Kent League.

1882-83	1		bye					
	2	2.12.82	Hendon		A	L	1-2	*scorer unknown*
1883-84	1	3.11.83	Old Westminsters		A	L	0-3
1884-85	1		Windsor Home Park		*walkover*
	2	6.12.84	Hendon		H	W	1-0	Collins
	3	3.1.85	Hanover Utd		A	W	2-0	*scorers unknown*
	4	24.1.85	Lower Darwen		H	W	1-0	McLeod
	5	7.2.85	Old Carthusians		H	L	0-3
1885-86	1	31.10.85	Old Carthusians		H	L	0-2
1886-87	1		Bournemouth Rovers		*walkover*
	2	20.11.86	Hotspur FC		H	W	1-0	*scorer unknown*
	3	11.12.86	Old Foresters		H	L	1-4	*scorer unknown*
1887-88	1	15.10.87	Luton Town		H	W	5-3	Mcleod 3, C.Hibbard 2
	2	5.11.87	Royal Engineers		H	W	3-1	*scorers unknown*
	3	26.11.87	Crusaders		A	L	0-4
1888-89	1	2.2.89	South Shore		H	W	2-1	Hobart, Conquer
	2	16.2.89	Nottingham F		H	D	1-1aet	Hibbard
	2r	23.2.89	Nottingham F		A	D	2-2aet	Hibbard 2
	2 2r	28.2.89	Nottingham F at the Oval			W	3-2	Bathurst, Hibbard, Prall
	3	2.3.89	WBA	D1	H	L	1-10	Bryan
1913-14 KL	1	10.1.14	Sunderland	D1	A	L	0-9
1925-26 KL	1	28.11.25	Sittingbourne	KL	H	L	0-3
1926-27 KL	1	27.11.26	St Albans C	IL	H	W	3-1	Anderson og, Potter 2
	2	11.12.26	Norwich C	3S	A	L	0-5
1927-28 SL	1	26.11.27	Kettering T	SL	A	L	0-2
1928-29 SL	1	24.11.28	Norwich C	3S	A	L	1-6	Brookes

CHELMSFORD

A seperate club to Chelmsford City

1931-32 Lon	1	28.11.31	Aldershot	SL	A	L	0-7

CHELMSFORD CITY

Formed 1938. Merged with Brentwood Town 1970. **League Clubs beaten:** Darlington, Oxford United, Southampton

1938-39 SL	1	26.11.38	Kidderminster H	BDL	H	W	4-0	Wood, Palethorpe 3
	2	10.12.38	Darlington	3N	H	W	3-1	Coulter, Palethorpe, Landolla
	3	7.1.39	Southampton	D2	H	W	4-1	Carnaby og, Coulter 2, Wright
	4	21.1.39	Birmingham	D1	A	L	0-6
1945-46 SL	1 1L	17.11.45	Northampton T	3S	A	L	1-5	Foreman
	2 2L	24.11.45	Northampton T		H	L	0-5
1948-49 SL	1	27.11.48	Weymouth	WL	A	L	1-2	McClelland
1949-50 SL	1	26.11.49	Leytonstone	IL	A	W	2-1	McCormack, Gowers
	2	10.12.49	Ipswich T	3S	H	D	1-1	Hurst
	2r	14.12.49	Ipswich T		A	L	0-1aet
1950-51 SL	1	25.11.50	Tonbridge	SL	H	D	2-2	Plunkett 2
	1r	29.11.50	Tonbridge		A	W	1-0aet	Plunkett
	2	9.12.50	Mansfield T	3N	H	L	1-4	Dicker
1954-55 SL	1	20.11.54	Aldershot	3S	A	L	1-3	Boxshall

CHELMSFORD CITY

1958-59	SL	1	15.11.58	Worcester C	SL	H	D	0-0	
		1r	20.11.58	Worcester C		A	L	1-3	Smith
1959-60	SL	1	14.11.59	Crystal P	D4	A	L	1-5	Phillips
1960-61	SL	1	5.11.60	Port Vale	D3	H	L	2-3	Barnard 2
1961-62	SL	1	4.11.61	Kings Lynn	SL	H	L	1-2	Hatshell
1962-63	SL	1	3.11.62	Shrewsbury T	D3	H	L	2-6	Nicholas, Hatshell
1963-64	SL	1	16.11.63	Cambridge U	SL	A	W	1-0	Nicholas
		2	7.12.63	Bedford T	SL	H	L	0-1	
1964-65	SL	1	14.11.64	Notts Co	D4	A	L	0-2	
1966-67	SL	1	26.11.66	Brentford	D4	A	L	0-1	
1967-68	SL	1	9.12.67	Oxford U	D3	H	D	3-3	Butcher 2, Pulley
		1r	13.12.67	Oxford U		A	D	3-3aet	Butcher, Shreeves (p), Pulley
		1 2r	18.12.67	Oxford U at Brentford			W	1-0	Cassidy
		2	6.1.68	Colchester U	D3	H	L	0-2	
1968-69	SL	1	16.11.68	Grantham	ML	A	L	1-2	Coughlin (p)
1969-70	SL	1	15.11.69	Hereford U	SL	H	L	1-2	Andrews (p)
1970-71	SL	1	21.11.70	Crawley T	SL	A	D	1-1	Ferry
		1r	23.11.70	Crawley T		H	W	6-1	Butcher 3, Price, Thornle, Stevenson (p)
		2	12.12.70	Torquay U	D3	H	L	0-1	
1972-73	SL	1	18.11.72	Hillingdon B	SL	H	W	2-0	Woolcott 2
		2	9.12.72	Telford U	SL	H	W	5-0	Woolcott 3, Peterson, Lewis
		3	13.1.73	Ipswich T	D1	H	L	1-3	Woolcott
1973-74	SL	1	24.11.73	Watford	D3	A	L	0-1	
1974-75	SL	1	23.11.74	Charlton A	D3	H	L	0-1	
1983-84	SL	1	19.11.83	Wycombe W	IL	H	D	0-0	
		1r	21.11.83	Wycombe W		A	W	2-1	Bishop, Anderson
		2	10.12.83	Gillingham	D3	A	L	1-6	Bishop (p)
1985-86	SL	1	16.11.85	Weymouth	APL	H	W	1-0	Poutney
		2	7.12.85	Wycombe W	APL	A	L	0-2	
1986-87	SL	1	15.11.86	Woking	IL	A	D	1-1	Wilkins
		1r	17.11.86	Woking		H	W	2-1	Cowley, Dennehy
		2	6.12.86	Gillingham	D3	A	L	0-2	
1987-88	SL	1	14.11.87	Bath C	GMVC	H	L	1-2	Wilkins
1990-91	SL	1	17.11.90	Barnet	GMVC	A	D	2-2	Jarvis, Baptiste
		1r	21.11.90	Barnet		H	L	0-2	

CHELSEA

Formed 1905 and elected to the Football League (Divsion 2) the same year. **FA Cup Winners:** 1970; **FA Cup Runners-Up:** 1915, 1967. **FA Cup Record Win:** 9-1 vs Worksop, 1st round, 31.1.1908. **FA Cup Record Defeat:** 0-6 vs Sheffield W, 2nd round replay, 5.2.1913; 1-7 vs Crystal Palace 3rd qualifying round, 16.1.1906

1905-06	D2	1q 1st **Grenadiers** (H) 6-1; 2q **Southern U** (A) 1-0; 3q **Crystal P** (A) 1-7						
1906-07	D2	1	12.1.07	Lincoln C	D2	A	D	2-2	Kirwan, Whitehouse
		1r	16.1.07	Lincoln C		H	L	0-1aet	
1907-08	D1	1	11.1.08	Worksop T	ML	H	W	9-1	Hilsdon 6, Windridge 2, Bridgeman
		2	1.2.08	Manchester U	D1	A	L	0-1	
1908-09	D1	1	16.1.09	Hull C	D2	A	D	1-1	Hilsdon
		1r	20.1.09	Hull C		H	W	1-0	Warren
		2	6.2.09	Blackburn R	D1	A	L	1-2	Hilsdon
1909-10	D1	1	15.1.10	Hull C	D2	H	W	2-1	Brawn, Williams
		2	5.2.10	Tottenham H	D1	H	L	0-1	
1910-11	D2	1	4.1.11	Leyton	SL	H	D	0-0	
		1r	19.1.11	Leyton		A	W	2-0	Downing, Hilsdon
		2	4.2.11	Chesterfield T	ML	A	W	4-1	Woodward 2, Whittingham 2
		3	25.2.11	Wolverhampton W	D2	A	W	2-0	Freeman, Woodward
		4	13.3.11	Swindon T	SL	H	W	3-1	Whittingham 2, Bridgeman
		SF	25.3.11	Newcastle U	D1		L	0-3	
			played at St Andrews						
1911-12	D2	1	13.1.12	Sheffield U	D1	H	W	1-0	Dodd
		2	3.2.12	Bradford C	D1	A	L	0-2	
1912-13	D1	1	11.1.13	Southend U	SL	H	W	5-2	Whittingham 4, Woodward (p)
		2	1.2.13	Sheffield W	D1	H	D	1-1	Whittingham
		2r	5.2.13	Sheffield W		A	L	0-6	
1913-14	D1	1	10.1.14	Millwall A	SL	A	D	0-0	
		1r	14.1.14	Millwall A		H	L	0-1	
1914-15	D1	1	9.1.15	Swindon T	SL	H	D	1-1	Thomson

CHELSEA

		1r	16.1.15	**Swindon T** at Stamford Bridge		A	W	5-2aet	Thomson 3, Ford, McNeill
		2	30.1.15	**W.Arsenal**	D2	H	W	1-0	Halse
		3	20.2.15	**Manchester C**	D1	A	W	1-0	Thomson
		4	6.3.15	**Newcastle U**	D1	H	D	1-1aet	Thomson
		4r	13.3.15	**Newcastle U**		A	W	1-0aet	Ford
		SF	27.3.15	**Everton**	D1		W	2-0	Croal, Halse
			played at Villa Park						
		F	24.4.15	**Sheffield U**	D1		L	0-3	
			played at Old Trafford						
1919-20	D1	1	10.1.20	**Bolton W**	D1	A	W	1-0	Croal
		2	31.1.20	**Swindon T**	SL	H	W	4-0	McNeill 2, Cock, Ford
		3	21.2.20	**Leicester C**	D2	H	W	3-0	Browning, Cock, Ford
		4	6.3.20	**Bradford PA**	D1	H	W	4-1	Sharp 2, Wilding, Logan
		SF	27.3.20	**Aston Villa**	D1		L	1-3	Croal
			played at Bramall Lane						
1920-21	D1	1	8.1.21	**Reading**	D3	A	D	0-0	
		1r	12.1.21	**Reading**		H	D	2-2aet	Cock, Croal
		1 2r	16.1.21	**Reading**		H	W	3-1	Wilding, Ferris, Sharp
		2	29.1.21	**Swindon T**	D3	A	W	2-0	Cock 2
		3	19.2.21	**Plymouth A**	D3	A	D	0-0	
		3r	24.2.21	**Plymouth A**		H	D	0-0aet	
		3 2r	28.2.21	**Plymouth A** at Ashton Gate			W	2-1	Croal, McNeill
		4	5.3.21	**Cardiff C**	D2	A	L	0-1	
1921-22	D1	1	7.1.22	**WBA**	D1	A	L	2-4	Bell, Ford
1922-23	D1	1	13.1.23	**Rotherham Co**	D2	H	W	1-0	Armstrong
		2	3.2.23	**Southampton**	D2	H	D	0-0	
		2r	7.2.23	**Southampton**		A	L	0-1	
1923-24	D1	1	12.1.24	**Southampton**	D2	H	D	1-1	Wilson
		1r	16.1.24	**Southampton**		A	L	0-2	
1924-25	D2	1	10.1.25	**Birmingham**	D1	A	L	0-2	
1925-26	D2	3	9.1.26	**Plymouth A**	D3	A	W	2-1	Turnbull, McNeill
		4	30.1.26	**Crystal P**	D3	A	L	1-2	Thain
1926-27	D2	3	8.1.27	**Luton T**	D3	H	W	4-0	Thain 2, Turnbull 2
		4	29.1.27	**Accrington S**	3N	H	W	7-2	Turnbull 3, Thain 2, Wilson 2
		5	19.2.27	**Burnley**	D1	H	W	2-1	Wilding, Thain
		6	5.3.27	**Cardiff C**	D1	H	D	0-0	
		6r	9.3.27	**Cardiff C**		A	L	2-3	Priestley, Turnbull
1927-28	D2	3	14.1.28	**Wolverhampton W**	D2	A	L	1-2	Brown
1928-29	D2	3	12.1.29	**Everton**	D1	H	W	2-0	Thompson, Miller
		4	27.1.29	**Birmingham**	D1	H	W	1-0	Miller
		5	16.2.29	**Portsmouth**	D1	H	D	1-1	Law
		5r	20.2.29	**Portsmouth**		A	L	0-1	
1929-30	D2	3	11.1.30	**Arsenal**	D1	A	L	0-2	
1930-31	D1	3	10.1.31	**West Ham**	D1	A	W	3-1	Jackson 2, Wade og
		4	24.1.31	**Arsenal**	D1	H	W	2-1	Bishop, Mills
		5	14.2.31	**Blackburn R**	D1	H	W	3-0	Cheyne, Mills, Law (p)
		6	28.2.31	**Birmingham**	D1	A	D	2-2	Jackson, Crawford
		6r	4.3.31	**Birmingham**		H	L	0-3	
1931-32	D1	3	9.1.32	**Tranmere R**	3N	A	D	2-2	Gallacher 2
		3r	13.1.32	**Tranmere R**		H	W	5-3	Law, Jackson, Pearson, Mills, Gallacher
		4	23.1.32	**West Ham**	D1	H	W	3-1	Mills 2, Gallacher
		5	13.2.32	**Sheffield W**	D1	A	D	1-1	Law
		5r	17.2.32	**Sheffield W**		H	W	2-0	Mills, Miller
		6	27.2.32	**Liverpool**	D1	A	W	2-0	Gallacher, Pearson
		SF	12.3.32	**Newcastle U**	D1		L	1-2	Gallacher
			played at Huddersfield						
1932-33	D1	3	14.1.33	**Brighton & HA**	3S	A	L	1-2	Barber
1933-34	D1	3	13.1.34	**WBA**	D1	H	D	1-1	Gregg
		3r	17.1.34	**WBA**		A	W	1-0	Gallacher
		4	27.1.34	**Nottingham F**	D2	H	D	1-1	Priestley
		4r	31.1.34	**Nottingham F**		A	W	3-0	Gallacher 2, Gibson
		5	17.2.34	**Stoke C**	D1	A	L	1-3	Oakton
1934-35	D1	3	12.1.35	**Luton T**	3S	H	D	1-1	Argue
		3r	16.1.35	**Luton T**		A	L	0-2	
1935-36	D1	3	11.1.36	**Norwich C**	D2	A	D	1-1	Mitchell
		3r	15.1.36	**Norwich C**		H	W	3-1	Bambrick 3
		4	25.1.36	**Plymouth A**	D2	H	W	4-1	Bambrick 2, Burgess, Barraclough

	5	19.2.36	Fulham	D2	H	D	0-0	
	5r	24.2.36	Fulham		A	L	2-3	Barraclough 2
1936-37	D1	3	16.1.37	Leeds U	D1	H	W	4-0	Spencer 2, Mills, Argue
	4	30.1.37	Millwall	3S	A	L	0-3	
1937-38	D1	3	8.1.38	Everton	D1	H	L	0-1	
1938-39	D1	3	7.1.39	Arsenal	D1	H	W	2-1	Argue 2
	4	21.1.39	Fulham	D2	H	W	3-0	Payne, Hanson, Argue
	5	11.2.39	Sheffield W	D2	H	D	1-1	Burgess
	5r	13.2.39	Sheffield W		A	D	0-0aet	
	5 2r	20.2.39	Sheffield W at Highbury			W	3-1	Burgess 2, Payne
	6	4.3.39	Grimsby T	D1	H	L	0-1	
1945-46	D1	3 1L	5.1.46	Leicester C	D2	H	D	1-1	Lawton
	3 2L	10.1.46	Leicester C		A	W	2-0	Williams, Goulden
	4 1L	26.1.46	West Ham	D2	H	W	2-0	Spencer, Machin
	4 2L	30.1.46	West Ham		A	L	0-1	
	5 1L	9.2.46	Aston Villa	D1	H	L	0-1	
	5 2L	12.2.46	Aston Villa		A	L	0-1	
1946-47	D1	3	11.1.47	Arsenal	D1	H	D	1-1	Walker
	3r	15.1.47	Arsenal		A	D	1-1	Lawton
	3 2r	20.1.47	Arsenal at Tottenham			W	2-0	Lawton 2
	4	25.1.47	Derby Co	D1	H	D	2-2	Williams, Lawton
	4r	30.1.47	Derby Co		A	L	0-1	
1947-48	D1	3	10.1.48	Barrow	3N	H	W	5-0	Armstrong 2, Gordon, Campbell, Bowie
	4	24.1.48	Manchester C	D1	A	L	0-2	
1948-49	D1	3	8.1.49	Bristol C	3S	A	W	3-1	Bentley 2, Jones
	4	29.1.49	Everton	D1	H	W	2-0	Bowie, Williams
	5	12.2.49	WBA	D2	A	L	0-3	
1949-50	D1	3	7.1.50	Brentford	D2	A	W	1-0	Bowie
	4	28.1.50	Newcastle U	D1	H	W	3-0	Billington 2, Campbell
	5	11.2.50	Chesterfield	D2	A	D	1-1	Bowie
	5r	15.2.50	Chesterfield		H	W	3-0	Bentley 2, Billington
	6	4.3.50	Manchester U	D1	H	W	2-0	Campbell, Bentley
	SF	18.3.50	Arsenal	D1		D	2-2	Bentley 2
		played at Tottenham						
	SFr	22.3.50	Arsenal			L	0-1aet	
		played at Tottenham						
1950-51	D1	3	9.1.51	Rochdale	3N	A	W	3-2	Bentley 2, Billington
	4	27.1.51	Exeter C	3S	A	D	1-1	Williams
	4r	31.1.51	Exeter C		H	W	2-0	Smith 2
	5	10.2.51	Fulham	D1	H	D	1-1	Bentley
	5r	14.2.51	Fulham		A	L	0-3	
1951-52	D1	3	12.1.52	Chester	3N	H	D	2-2	Armstrong, Gray
	3r	16.1.52	Chester		A	W	3-2aet	Smith, Bentley, Lee og
	4	2.2.52	Tranmere R	3N	H	W	4-0	Bentley 2, Armstrong, Jones
	5	23.2.52	Leeds U	D2	A	D	1-1	Smith
	5r	27.2.52	Leeds U		H	D	1-1aet	D'Arcy
	5 2r	3.3.52	Leeds U at Villa Pk			W	5-1	Smith 3, Gray, Bentley
	6	8.3.52	Sheffield U	D2	A	W	1-0	Bentley
	SF	5.4.52	Arsenal	D1		D	1-1	Gray
		played at Tottenham						
	SFr	7.4.52	Arsenal			L	0-3	
		played at Tottenham						
1952-53	D1	3	10.1.53	Derby Co	D1	A	D	4-4	Bentley, McNichol, Parsons, Armstrong
	3r	14.1.53	Derby Co		H	W	1-0	Parsons
	4	31.1.53	WBA	D1	H	D	1-1	Bentley
	4r	4.2.53	WBA		A	D	0-0aet	
	4 2r	9.2.53	WBA at Villa Pk			D	1-1aet	Bentley
	4 3r	11.2.53	WBA at Highbury			W	4-0	Bentley 2, Campbell, Parsons
	5	14.2.53	Birmingham C	D2	H	L	0-4	
1953-54	D1	3	9.1.54	WBA	D1	A	L	0-1	
1954-55	D1	3	8.1.55	Walsall	3S	H	W	2-0	O'Connell, Stubbs
	4	29.1.55	Bristol R	D2	A	W	3-1	Parsons, Bluntstone, McNicholl
	5	19.2.55	Notts Co	D2	A	L	0-1	
1955-56	D1	3	7.1.56	Hartlepool U	3N	A	W	1-0	Moore og
	4	28.1.56	Burnley	D1	A	D	1-1	Parsons
	4r	1.2.56	Burnley		H	D	1-1aet	Bluntstone
	4 2r	6.2.56	Burnley at St Andrew's			D	2-2aet	P.Sillett, Bentley

Season	Div	Round	Date	Opponent		Venue	Result	Score	Scorers
		4 3r	13.2.56	**Burnley** at Highbury			D	0-0aet	
		4 4r	15.2.56	**Burnley** at Tottenham			W	2-0	Lewis, Tindall
		5	18.2.56	**Everton**	D1	A	L	0-1	
1956-57	D1	3	5.1.57	**Leyton Orient**	D2	A	W	2-0	Brabrook, McNicholl
		4	25.1.57	**Tottenham H**	D1	A	L	0-4	
1957-58	D1	3	4.1.58	**Doncaster R**	D2	A	W	2-0	McNicholl 2
		4	25.1.58	**Darlington**	3N	H	D	3-3	McNicholl, Tindall, Lewis
		4r	29.1.58	**Darlington**		A	L	1-4	McNicholl
1958-59	D1	3	19.1.59	**Newcastle U**	D1	A	W	4-1	Gibbs, Greaves, Mortimer, Cliss
		4	24.1.59	**Aston Villa**	D1	H	L	1-2	Greaves
1959-60	D1	3	9.1.60	**Bradford PA**	D4	H	W	5-1	Brabrook 2, Greaves, Livesey, Bluntstone
		4	30.1.60	**Aston Villa**	D2	H	L	1-2	P.Sillett (p)
1960-61	D1	3	7.1.61	**Crewe Alex**	D4	H	L	1-2	Bluntstone
1961-62	D1	3	6.1.62	**Liverpool**	D2	A	L	3-4	Tambling 2, Bridges
1962-63	D2	3	5.1.63	**Tranmere R**	D4	A	D	2-2	Tambling, Bridges
		3r	30.1.63	**Tranmere R**		H	W	3-1	Venables, Bridges, Moore
		4	6.3.63	**Charlton A**	D2	H	W	3-0	Mulholland, Murray, Tambling
		5	16.3.63	**Manchester U**	D1	A	L	1-2	Sorrell
1963-64	D1	3	4.1.64	**Tottenham H**	D1	A	D	1-1	Murray
		3r	8.1.64	**Tottenham H**		H	W	2-0	Murray, Tambling
		4	25.1.64	**Huddersfield T**	D2	H	L	1-2	Tambling
1964-65	D1	3	9.1.65	**Northampton T**	D2	H	W	4-1	Bridges 2, Tambling, Foley og
		4	30.1.65	**West Ham**	D1	A	W	1-0	Tambling
		5	20.2.65	**Tottenham H**	D1	H	W	1-0	Bridges
		6	6.3.65	**Peterborough**	D3	H	W	5-1	Tambling 2, Bridges, Hollins, Murray
		SF	27.3.65	**Liverpool**	D1		L	0-2	
			played at Villa Park						
1965-66	D1	3	22.1.66	**Liverpool**	D1	A	W	2-1	Tambling, Osgood
		4	12.2.66	**Leeds U**	D1	H	W	1-0	Tambling
		5	5.3.66	**Shrewsbury T**	D3	H	W	3-2	Bridges 2, Graham
		6	26.3.66	**Hull C**	D3	H	D	2-2	Graham, Tambling
		6r	31.3.66	**Hull C**		A	W	3-1	Tambling 2, Graham
		SF	23.4.66	**Sheffield Wed**	D1		L	0-2	
			played at Villa Park						
1966-67	D1	3	28.1.67	**Huddersfield T**	D2	A	W	2-1	Houseman, Tambling
		4	18.2.67	**Brighton & HA**	D3	A	D	1-1	Tambling
		4r	22.2.67	**Brighton & HA**		H	W	4-0	Tambling 2, Young, Baldwin
		5	11.3.67	**Sheffield U**	D1	H	W	2-0	Tambling, Hateley
		6	8.4.67	**Sheffield W**	D1	H	W	1-0	Baldwin
		SF	29.4.67	**Leeds U**	D1		W	1-0	Hateley
			played at Villa Park						
		F	20.5.67	**Tottenham H**	D1 WEMBLEY		L	1-2	Tambling
1967-68	D1	3	27.1.68	**Ipswich T**	D2	H	W	3-0	Birchenall 2, Tambling
		4	17.2.68	**Norwich C**	D2	H	W	1-0	Cooke
		5	9.3.68	**Sheffield W**	D1	A	D	2-2	Tambling, Baldwin
		5r	12.3.68	**Sheffield W**		H	W	2-0	Tambling, Osgood
		6	30.3.68	**Birmingham C**	D2	A	L	0-1	
1968-69	D1	3	4.1.69	**Carlisle U**	D2	H	W	2-0	Osgood, Tambling
		4	25.1.69	**Preston NE**	D2	A	D	0-0	
		4r	29.1.69	**Preston NE**		H	–	2-0	Hutchinson, Birchenall
			abandoned after 72 minutes – floodlight failure						
		4r	3.2.69	**Preston NE**		H	W	2-1	Webb, Cooke
		5	12.2.69	**Stoke C**	D1	H	W	3-2	Osgood 2, Birchenall
		6	1.3.69	**WBA**	D1	H	L	1-2	Webb
1969-70	D1	3	3.1.70	**Birmingham C**	D2	H	W	3-0	Hutchinson 2, Osgood
		4	24.1.70	**Burnley**	D1	H	D	2-2	Hollins, Osgood
		4r	27.1.70	**Burnley**		A	W	3-1aet	Houseman 2, Baldwin
		5	7.2.70	**Crystal P**	D1	A	W	4-1	Osgood, Dempsey, Hutchinson, Houseman
		6	21.2.70	**QPR**	D2	A	W	4-2	Osgood 3, Webb
		SF	14.3.70	**Watford**	D2		W	5-1	Webb, Osgood, Houseman 2, Hutchinson
			played at Tottenham						
		F	11.4.70	**Leeds U**	D1 WEMBLEY		D	2-2aet	Houseman, Hutchinson
		Fr	29.4.70	**LEEDS U** at Old Trafford			W	2-1aet	Osgood, Webb
1970-71	D1	3	2.1.71	**Crystal P**	D1	A	D	2-2	Osgood, Baldwin
		3r	6.1.71	**Crystal P**		H	W	2-0	Baldwin, Houseman
		4	23.1.71	**Manchester C**	D1	H	L	0-3	
1971-72	D1	3	15.1.72	**Blackpool**	D2	A	W	1-0	Dempsey

CHELSEA

Season	Div	Round	Date	Opponent		H/A	Res	Score	Scorers
		4	5.2.72	Bolton W	D3	H	W	3-0	Cooke, Houseman, Hollins (p)
		5	26.2.72	Orient	D2	A	L	2-3	Webb, Osgood
1972-73	D1	3	13.1.73	Brighton & HA	D2	A	W	2-0	Osgood 2
		4	3.2.73	Ipswich T	D1	H	W	2-0	Garner 2
		5	24.2.73	Sheffield W	D2	A	W	2-1	Osgood, Garner
		6	17.3.73	Arsenal	D1	H	D	2-2	Hollins, Osgood
		6r	20.3.73	Arsenal		A	L	1-2	Houseman
1973-74	D1	3	5.1.74	QPR	D1	H	D	0-0	
		3r	15.1.74	QPR		A	L	0-1	
1974-75	D1	3	4.1.75	Sheffield W	D2	H	W	3-2	Droy 2, Garland
		4	25.1.75	Birmingham C	D1	H	L	0-1	
1975-76	D2	3	1.1.76	Bristol R	D2	H	D	1-1	Garner
		3r	3.1.76	Bristol R		A	W	1-0	Swain
		4	24.1.76	York C	D2	A	W	2-0	Garner, Hutchinson
		5	14.2.76	Crystal P	D3	H	L	2-3	R.Wilkins, Wicks
1976-77	D2	3	8.1.77	Southampton	D2	A	D	1-1	Locke
		3r	12.1.77	Southampton		H	L	0-3aet	
1977-78	D1	3	7.1.78	Liverpool	D1	H	W	4-2	Walker 2, Finniestone, Langley
		4	31.1.78	Burnley	D2	H	W	6-2	Droy, Wicks, Swain (p), Walker, Langley, R.Wilkins
		5	18.2.78	Orient	D2	A	D	0-0	
		5r	27.2.78	Orient		H	L	1-2	Roffey og
1978-79	D1	3	15.1.79	Manchester U	D1	A	L	0-3	
1979-80	D2	3	14.1.80	Wigan A	D4	H	L	0-1	
1980-81	D2	3	3.1.81	Southampton	D1	A	L	1-3	Lee
1981-82	D2	3	18.1.82	Hull C	D4	H	D	0-0	
		3r	21.1.82	Hull C		A	W	2-0	Bumstead, Mayes
		4	23.1.82	Wrexham	D2	H	D	0-0	
		4r	26.1.82	Wrexham		A	D	1-1aet	Mayes
		4 2r	1.2.82	Wrexham		A	W	2-1	Droy, Mayes
		5	13.2.82	Liverpool	D1	H	W	2-0	Rhoades-Brown, Lee
		6	6.3.82	Tottenham H	D1	H	L	2-3	Mayes, Fillery
1982-83	D2	3	8.1.83	Huddersfield T	D3	A	D	1-1	Mayes
		3r	12.1.83	Huddersfield T		H	W	2-0	Bumstead, Fillery
		4	29.1.83	Derby Co	D2	A	L	1-2	Fillery
1983-84	D2	3	7.1.84	Blackburn R	D2	A	L	0-1	
1984-85	D1	3	5.1.85	Wigan A	D3	H	D	2-2	Nevin, Speedie
		3r	26.1.85	Wigan A		A	W	5-0	Dixon 4 (1p), Speedie
		4	4.2.85	Millwall	D3	H	L	2-3	Spackman, Canoville
1985-86	D1	3	4.1.86	Shrewsbury T	D2	A	W	1-0	Speedie
		4	26.1.86	Liverpool	D1	H	L	1-2	Speedie
1986-87	D1	3	10.1.87	Aston Villa	D1	A	D	2-2	Bumstead, Speedie
		3r	21.1.87	Aston Villa		H	W	2-1	Durie, Hazard (p)
		4	1.2.87	Watford	D1	A	L	0-1	
1987-88	D1	3	9.1.88	Derby Co	D1	A	W	3-1	McAllister, Dixon, Wegerle
		4	30.1.88	Manchester U	D1	A	L	0-2	
1988-89	D2	3	7.1.89	Barnsley	D2	A	L	0-4	
1989-90	D1	3	6.1.90	Crewe Alex	D3	H	D	1-1	Clarke
		3r	10.1.90	Crewe Alex		A	W	2-0	Dixon 2
		4	27.1.90	Bristol C	D3	A	L	1-3	K.Wilson
1990-91	D1	3	5.1.91	Oxford U	D2	H	L	1-3	Dixon
1991-92	D1	3	4.1.92	Hull C	D3	A	W	2-0	Jones, Wise
		4	26.1.92	Everton	D1	H	W	1-0	Allen
		5	15.2.92	Sheffield U	D1	H	W	1-0	Stuart
		6	9.3.92	Sunderland	D2	H	D	1-1	Allen
		6r	18.3.92	Sunderland		A	L	1-2	Wise
1992-93	PL	3	13.1.93	Middlesbrough	PL	A	L	1-2	Mohan og

CHELTENHAM TOWN

Formed 1892. **First entered FA Cup:** 1914. The late Ted Croker, the FA's former Chief Executive was the club's president. **League Clubs beaten:** Carlisle United

Season		Round	Date	Opponent		H/A	Res	Score	Scorers
1933-34	BC	1	25.11.33	Barnet	AL	H	W	5-1	Payne 2, Knight 2, Yarwood
		2	9.12.33	Carlisle U	3N	A	W	2-1	Smith, Bradley og
		3	13.1.34	Blackpool	D2	H	L	1-3	Payne
1935-36	SL	1	30.11.35	Brighton & HA	3S	A	D	0-0	
		1r	4.12.35	Brighton & HA		H	L	0-6	

1937-38	SL	1	27.11.37	Watford	3S	A	L	0-3	
1938-39	SL	1	26.11.38	Cardiff C	3S	H	D	1-1	Prior
		1r	30.11.38	Cardiff C		A	L	0-1	
1945-46	SL	1 1L	17.11.45	Bath C	SL	A	L	2-3	Edwards, Goring
		1 2L	24.11.45	Bath C		H	L	0-2	
1946-47	SL	1	30.11.46	Aldershot	3S	A	L	2-4	Crowe 2
1947-48	SL	1	29.11.47	Street	WL	H	W	5-0	Crowe, Goring 3, Tadman
		2	13.12.47	Hull C	3N	A	L	2-4	Green, Goring
1950-51	SL	1	25.11.50	Reading	3S	A	L	1-3	Crowe
1956-57	SL	1	17.11.56	Reading	3S	H	L	1-2	McAllister
1959-60	SL	1	14.11.59	Watford	D4	H	D	0-0	
		1r	17.11.59	Watford		A	L	0-3	
1962-63	SL	1	3.11.62	Enfield	AL	H	L	3-6	Palmer, Mitchinson, McCool
1968-69	SL	1	16.11.68	Watford	D3	H	L	0-4	
1969-70	SL	1	15.11.69	Oxford C	IL	H	L	0-2	
1970-71	SL	1	21.11.70	Brighton & HA	D3	A	L	0-4	
1974-75	SL	1	23.11.74	Wycombe W	IL	A	L	1-3	Lewis (p)
1987-88	GMVC	1	14.11.87	Wolverhampton W	D4	A	L	1-5	Angell
1990-91	GMVC	1	17.11.90	Birmingham C	D3	A	L	0-1	
1992-93	SL	1	14.11.92	St Albans C	IL	A	W	2-1	Willetts (p), Purdie
		2	5.12.92	Bournemouth	D2	H	D	1-1	Warren
		2r	16.12.92	Bournemouth		A	L	0-3	

CHESHAM

1885-86	1	31.10.85	Luton Wanderers		A	L	2-3	Ayres, Culverhouse

CHESHAM GENERALS

1886-87	1	30.10.86	Lyndhurst		H	W	4-2
	2	20.11.86	Old Etonians		H	L	1-7
1887-88	1	15.10.87	Watford Rovers		H	W	4-2
		replay ordered after protest					
	1r	22.10.87	Watford Rovers		H	L	1-3

CHESHAM UNITED

Formed 1919, amalgamation of Chesham (1885) and Chesham Generals (1885). Some sources give earlier founding date of 1885. **FA Amateur Cup Runners-up** 1968

1966-67	AL	1	26.11.66	Enfield	IL	A	L	0-6	
1968-69	AL	1	16.11.68	Colchester U	D4	A	L	0-5	
1976-77	IL	1	20.11.76	Brentford	D4	A	L	0-2	
1979-80	IL	1	24.11.79	Minehead	SL	A	W	2-1	Woolfrey, Dodd
		2	19.12.79	Merthyr T	SL	H	D	1-1	Woolfrey
		2r	22.12.79	Merthyr T		A	W	3-1	Rosser og, Horastead, Watt
		3	5.1.80	Cambridge U	D2	H	L	0-2	
1982-83	IL	1	20.11.82	Yeovil T	APL	H	L	0-1	

CHESTER CITY

Formed 1884 and played as Chester until changing to Chester City 99 years later. **Best FA Cup performance:** 5th round, 1977, 1980. **FA Cup Record Win:** 10-1 vs Lostock Gralam, Pr rd, 1927-28. In competition proper: 6-1 vs Darlington, 1st round, 25.11.1933; 5-0 vs Crewe A, 1st round, 1964. 5-0 vs Runcorn, 1st round, 1978. **FA Cup Record Defeat:** 0-7 vs Blackburn R, 2nd round, 31.1.1891. **Welsh FA Cup Winners:** 1908, 1933, 1947. **Cup Final Connection:** Ian Rush, who has scored more goals in Cup Finals than anyone else started his career at Chester.

1886-87	1		bye				
	2	20.11.86	Goldenhill		H	W	1-0	Turner
		FA disqualified Chester following protest					
1887-88	1	15.10.87	Davenham		H	L	2-3aet	Higginson, 1 other
1888-89	1q Macclesfield (H) 2-2, Chester awarded tie; 2q Over Wanderers (H) 5-1; 3q Vale of Llangollen (H) 5-1; 4q Wreham (H) 2-3
1889-90	1q Over Wanderers (H) 2-0; 2q Burslem Port Vale (H) 1-0; 3 q Chester St Oswalds (A) 3-0; 4q Crewe Alexandra (H) 2-1
	1	18.1.90	Lincoln C	ML	A	L	0-2
1890-91	TC	1q Chester St Oswalds (A) 6-0; 2q Northwich Victoria (H) 2-0; 3q Nantwich T (A) 5-4; 4q Cliftonville (H) walkover
	1	17.1.91	Lincoln C	ML	H	W	1-0	Roberts
	2	31.1.91	Blackburn R	D1	A	L	0-7
1891-92	TC	2q Wrexham (H) 2-4

1892-93	TC	1q **Stanley** (A) 4-1; 2q **Prescot** (H) 2-1; 3q **Liverpool Caledonians** (A) 2-3						
1893-94	TC	2q **Macclesfield** (A) 1-6						
1894-95	TC	1q **Macclesfield** (H) 1-2						
1895-96	TC	1q **Port Sunlight** (A) 5-1; 2q **Middleton** (H) 0-3						
1896-97	TC	1q **Middleton** (A) 2-3						
1897-98	TC	1q **Stockport Co** (A) 0-2						
1898-99	TC	1q **Wrexham** (A) 2-3						
1899-00	TC	*did not enter*						
1900-01	TC	*did not enter*						
1901-02	TC	1q **Birkenhead** (A) 1-1; 1qr **Birkenhead** (H) 5-4 *tie awarded to Birkenhead after protest*						
1902-03	TC	*did not enter*						
1903-04	TC	*did not enter*						
1904-05	TC	*did not enter*						
1905-06	TC	1q **Northern Nomads** (H) 2-0; 2q **Chirk** (A) 0-2						
1906-07	TC	*did not enter*						
1907-08	TC	1q *Tranmere R* (H) 0-4						
1908-09	TC	1q **Druids** (H) 4-1; 2q **Wellington T** (H) 3-1; 3q **Wrexham** (H) 1-3						
1909-10	TC	P *Tranmere R* (A) 0-6						
1910-11	LC	P **Druids** (A) 3-1; 1q **Wrexham** (H) 3-0; 2q **New Brighton Tower** (A) 3-1; 3q **Witton Albion** (H) 7-1; 4q **Crewe Alexandra** (A) 3-4						
1911-12	LC	1q **Shrewsbury T** (H) 6-1; 2q **Northern Nomads** (H) 4-0; 3q **Wrexham** (A) 4-1; 4q **Stockport Co** (H) 1-4						
1912-13	LC	P **Wrexham** (A) 0-2						
1913-14	LC	P **Nantwich T** (A) 5-3; 1q **Tranmere R** (H) 2-1; 2q **Port Vale** (H) 2-5						
1914-15	LC	1q **Ormskirk** (H) 2-0; 2q **Tranmere R** (A) 1-5						
1919-20	CC	P **Nantwich T** (A) 0-5						
1920-21	CC	*did not enter*						
1921-22	CC	P **Machynlleth** (H) 7-0; 1q **Lostock Gralam** (H) 2-0; 2q **Harrowby** bye (A) W; 3q **Northwich Victoria** (A) 3-3;						
		3qr **Northwich Victoria** (H) 1-0 ; 4q **Crewe Alexandra** (A) 1-1; 4qr **Crewe Alexandra** (H) 1-2						
1922-23	CC	P **New Brighton** (A) 2-4						
1923-24	CC	P **Ellesmere Port C** (H) 1-0; 1q **Lostock Gralam** (H) 5-1; 2q Ellesmere Port T (A) 1-2						
1924-25	CC	P **Witton Albion** (A) 0-2						
1925-26	CC	P **Llandudno** (A) 0-0; Pr **Llandudno** (H) 2-1; 1q **Sandbach** (H) 2-0; 2q **Witton Albion** (H) 2-2; 2qr **Witton Albion** (A) 4-2;						
		3q **Mold** (H) 2-2; 3qr **Mold** (A) 0-5						
1926-27	CC	P **Llandudno** (A) 0-2						
1927-28	CC	P **Lostock Gralam** (H) 10-1; 1q **Winsford U** (H) 4-0; 2q **Bangor C** (A) 0-1						
1928-29	CC	P **Northwich Victoria** (A) 1-3						
1929-30	CC	*did not enter*						
1930-31	CC	*did not enter*						
1931-32	3N	1	28.11.31	**Hartlepools U**	3N	H	W	4-1	Hedley 2, Valentine, Bennett
		2	12.12.31	**Darwen**	LC	A	L	1-2	Murray og
1932-33	3N	1	26.11.32	**Rotherham U**	3N	H	W	4-0	Mantle, Wyper 3
		2	10.12.32	**Yeovil & Petters U**	SL	H	W	2-1	Cresswell, Hedley
		3	14.1.33	**Fulham**	D2	H	W	5-0	Mercer, Hedley 4
		4	28.1.33	**Halifax T**	3N	H	D	0-0	
		4r	2.2.33	**Halifax T**		A	L	2-3aet	Mantle 2
1933-34	3N	1	25.11.33	**Darlington**	3N	H	W	6-1	Mantle 2, Armes 3, Cresswell
		2	9.12.33	**Southend**	3S	A	L	1-2	Cresswell
1934-35	3N	1	24.11.34	**Dinnington A**	SAL	H	W	3-1	Whittam, Kelly, Wallbanks
		2	8.12.34	**Clapton O**	3S	A	W	3-1	Cresswell, Kelly, Wallbanks
		3	12.1.35	**Nottingham F**	D2	H	L	0-4	
1935-36	3N	1	30.11.35	**Gateshead**	3N	H	W	1-0	Cresswell
		2	14.12.35	**Reading**	3S	H	D	3-3	Cresswell 2, Wrightson
		2r	18.12.35	**Reading**		A	L	0-3	
1936-37	3N	3	16.1.37	**Doncaster R**	D2	H	W	4-0	Gale, Alderson, Sargeant, Wrightson
		4	30.1.37	**Coventry C**	D2	A	L	0-2	
1937-38	3N	3	8.1.38	**Leeds U**	D1	A	L	1-3	Gale
1938-39	3N	1	26.11.38	**Bradford C**	3N	H	W	3-1	Horsman, Hinsley og, Pendergast
		2	10.12.38	**Hull C**	3N	H	D	2-2	Horsman, Gregg
		2r	15.12.38	**Hull C**		A	W	1-0	Horsman
		3	7.1.39	**Coventry C**	D2	H	W	1-0	Pendergast
		4	21.1.39	**Sheffield W**	D2	A	D	1-1	Sanders
		4r	25.1.39	**Sheffield W**		H	D	1-1aet	Hanford og
		4 2r	30.1.39	**Sheffield W** at Maine Rd			L	0-2	
1945-46	3N	3 1L	5.1.46	**Liverpool**	D1	H	L	0-2	
		3 2L	9.1.46	**Liverpool**		A	W	2-1	Astbury
1946-47	3N	3	11.1.47	**Plymouth A**	D2	H	W	2-0	Astbury, Burden
		4	25.1.47	**Stoke C**	D1	H	D	0-0	
		4r	29.1.47	**Stoke C**		A	L	2-3	Hamilton, Yates

1947-48	3N	1	29.11.47	**Bishop Auckland**	NL	H	W	3-1	Yates, Burden 2
		2	13.12.47	**Tranmere R**	3N	A	W	1-0	Burden
		3	10.1.48	**Crystal P**	3S	A	W	1-0	Burden
		4	24.1.48	**Blackpool**	D1	A	L	0-4	
1948-49	3N	1	27.11.48	**Hartlepools U**	3N	A	W	3-1	Williamson, Harrigan, Forsyth
		2	11.12.48	**Aldershot**	3S	A	L	0-1	
1949-50	3N	1	26.11.49	**Goole T**	ML	H	W	4-1	Jackson 3, Burgess
		2	10.12.49	**Exeter C**	3S	A	L	0-2	
1950-51	3N	1	25.11.50	**Bradford PA**	3N	H	L	1-2	Coffin
1951-52	3N	1	24.11.51	**Accrington S**	3N	A	W	2-1	Fletcher, Kirkpatrick
		2	15.12.51	**Leyton**	AL	H	W	5-2	Dixon og, Moremont 2, Astbury, Jones
		3	12.1.52	**Chelsea**	D1	A	D	2-2	Coffin, Greenwood og
		3r	16.1.52	**Chelsea**		H	L	2-3aet	Willemse og, Coffin
1952-53	3N	1	22.11.52	**Hartlepools U**	3N	H	L	0-1	
1953-54	3N	1	21.11.53	**Stockport Co**	3N	A	L	2-4	Windle, Molyneux
1954-55	3N	1	20.11.54	**Gateshead**	3N	A	L	0-6	
1955-56	3N	1	19.11.55	**Chesterfield**	3N	A	L	0-1	
1956-57	3N	1	17.11.56	**Barrow**	3N	H	D	0-0	
		1r	22.11.56	**Barrow**		A	L	1-3	Turner
1957-58	3N	1	16.11.57	**Gateshead**	3N	H	W	4-3	Jepson, Mason, Pearson, Foulkes
		2	7.12.57	**Bradford C**	3N	H	D	3-3	Jepson 3
		2r	11.12.57	**Bradford C**		A	L	1-3	Jepson
1958-59	D4	1	15.11.58	**Boston U**	SL	H	W	3-2	Bullock, Boston, Pearson
		2	6.12.58	**Bury**	D3	H	D	1-1	Webster
		2r	9.12.58	**Bury**		A	L	1-2	Hunt
1959-60	D4	1	14.11.59	**Tranmere R**	D3	A	W	1-0	Kelly
		2	5.12.59	**Mansfield T**	D3	A	L	0-2	
1960-61	D4	1	5.11.60	**Carlisle U**	D4	H	L	0-1	
1961-62	D4	1	4.11.61	**Ashington**	NCL	H	W	4-1	Davies 2, Morris, Jones
		2	25.11.61	**Morecambe**	LC	H	L	0-1	
1962-63	D4	1	3.11.62	**Tranmere R**	D4	H	L	0-2	
1963-64	D4	1	16.11.63	**Blyth Spartans**	NEL	H	W	3-2	Lee 2, Morris
		2	7.12.63	**Barrow**	D4	H	L	0-2	
1964-65	D4	1	14.11.64	**Crewe A**	D4	H	W	5-0	Talbot 3, Metcalf 2 (1p)
		2	5.12.64	**Barnsley**	D3	A	W	5-2	Metcalf 3 (1p), Humes, Morris
1965-66	D4	1	13.11.65	**Chesterfield**	D4	A	W	2-0	Metcalf, Humes
		2	4.12.65	**Wigan A**	CC	H	W	2-1	Morris, Humes
		3	22.1.66	**Newcastle U**	D1	H	L	1-3	Morris
1966-67	D4	1	26.11.66	**Middlesbrough**	D3	H	L	2-5	Metcalf, Morris
1967-68	D4	1	9.12.67	**Port Vale**	D4	A	W	2-1	Metcalf, Hancox
		2	6.1.68	**Chesterfield**	D4	H	L	0-1	
1968-69	D4	1	16.11.68	**Bradford C**	D4	A	W	2-1	Dearden, Talbot
		2	7.12.68	**Lincoln C**	D4	H	D	1-1	Dearden
		2r	11.12.68	**Lincoln C**		A	L	1-2	Jones
1969-70	D4	1	15.11.69	**Halifax T**	D3	A	D	3-3	Tarbuck 2, Dearden
		1r	19.11.69	**Halifax T**		H	W	1-0	Dearden
		2	6.12.69	**Doncaster R**	D3	H	D	1-1	Tarbuck
		2r	9.12.69	**Doncaster R**		A	W	2-0	Webber, Dearden
		3	3.1.70	**Bristol C**	D2	H	W	2-1	Webber 2
		4	24.1.70	**Swindon T**	D2	A	L	2-4	Cheetham, Lang
1970-71	D4	1	21.11.70	**Preston NE**	D3	A	D	1-1	Tarbuck
		1r	24.11.70	**Preston NE**		H	W	1-0	Loyden
		2	12.12.70	**Crewe A**	D4	H	W	1-0	Turner
		3	2.1.71	**Derby Co**	D1	H	L	1-2	Webber
1971-72	D4	1	20.11.71	**Mansfield T**	D3	H	D	1-1	McHale
		1r	22.11.71	**Mansfield T**		A	L	3-4	Loyden, Kennedy, Draper
1972-73	D4	1	18.11.72	**Bolton W**	D3	A	D	1-1	Hollis
		1r	22.11.72	**Bolton W**		H	L	0-1	
1973-74	D4	1	24.11.73	**Telford U**	SL	H	W	1-0	Grummett
		2	15.12.73	**Huddersfield T**	D3	H	W	3-2	Owens, James, Draper
		3	5.1.74	**Aston Villa**	D2	A	L	1-3	James
1974-75	D4	1	23.11.74	**Rotherham U**	D4	A	L	0-1	
1975-76	D3	1	22.11.75	**Darlington**	D4	A	D	0-0	
		1r	26.11.75	**Darlington**		H	W	2-0	Moore, Redfern
		2	13.12.75	**Shrewsbury T**	D3	A	L	1-3	Edwards
1976-77	D3	1	20.11.76	**Hartlepool**	D4	H	W	1-0	Edwards
		2	11.12.76	**Grimsby T**	D3	A	W	1-0	Howat

CHESTER CITY

Season	Div	Rd	Date	Opponent		Venue	Res	Score	Scorers
		3	8.1.77	Southend U	D4	A	W	4-0	Howat, I.Edwards 3
		4	29.1.77	Luton T	D2	H	W	1-0	I.Edwards
		5	26.2.77	Wolverhampton W	D2	A	L	0-1	
1977-78	D3	1	26.11.77	Darlington	D4	H	W	4-1	Crossley 3, Kearney
		2	17.12.77	Carlisle U	D3	A	L	1-3	Crossley
1978-79	D3	1	25.11.78	Runcorn	NPL	H	D	1-1	Phillips
		1r	28.11.78	Runcorn		A	W	5-0	Mellor 2, Jones, Phillips, Howat
		2	16.12.78	Darlington	D4	A	L	1-2	Mellor
1979-80	D3	1	24.11.79	Workington	NPL	H	W	5-1	Henderson 2, Sutcliffe, Jones, Rush
		2	18.12.79	Barnsley	D3	H	W	1-0	Raynor (p)
		3	5.1.80	Newcastle U	D2	A	W	2-0	Henderson, Rush
		4	26.1.80	Millwall	D3	H	W	2-0	Storton, Rush
		5	16.2.80	Ipswich T	D1	A	L	1-2	Jones
1980-81	D3	1	22.11.80	Barnsley	D3	H	L	1-2	Birch
1981-82	D3	1	21.11.81	Penrith	NL	A	L	0-1	
1982-83	D4	1	20.11.82	Northwich Victoria	APL	H	D	1-1	Lane
		1r	22.11.82	Northwich Victoria		A	L	1-3	Williams

as Chester City

Season	Div	Rd	Date	Opponent		Venue	Res	Score	Scorers
1983-84	D4	1	19.11.83	Chesterfield	D4	H	L	1-2	Holden
1984-85	D4	1	17.11.84	Darlington	D4	A	L	2-3	Fox, Holden
1985-86	D4	1	16.11.85	Bury	D3	A	L	0-2	
1986-87	D3	1	15.11.86	Rotherham U	D3	H	D	1-1	Bennett (p)
		1r	17.11.86	Rotherham U		A	D	1-1aet	Kelly
		1 2r	24.11.86	Rotherham U		H	W	1-0	Croft
		2	6.12.86	Doncaster R	D3	H	W	3-1	Bennett (p), Graham, Houghton
		3	10.1.87	Wrexham	D4	A	W	2-1	Bennett 2
		4	31.1.87	Sheffield W	D1	H	D	1-1	Kelly
		4r	4.2.87	Sheffield W		A	L	1-3	Bennett
1987-88	D3	1	14.11.87	Runcorn	GMVC	H	L	0-1	
1988-89	D3	1	19.11.88	Burnley	D4	A	W	2-0	Dale, Benjamin
		2	10.12.88	Huddersfield T	D3	A	L	0-1	
1989-90	D3	1	18.11.89	Macclesfield	GMVC	A	D	1-1	Painter
		1r	21.11.89	Macclesfield		H	W	3-2	Abel (p), Butler, Croft
		2	9.12.89	Blackpool	D3	A	L	0-3	
1990-91	D3	1	17.11.90	Doncaster R	D4	H	D	2-2	Bennett, Dale
		20.11.90	Doncaster R		A	W	2-1aet	Dale, Painter
1991-92	D3	1	15.11.91	Guiseley	NPL	H	W	1-0	Barrow
		2	7.12.91	Crewe A	D4	A	L	0-2	
1992-93	D2	1	14.11.92	Altrincham	GMVC	H	D	1-1	Ryan
		1r	25.11.92	Altrincham		A	L	0-2	

CHESTER ST OSWALDS

One of many amateur clubs that played in and around the Chester area in the 1880s

Season		Rd	Date	Opponent		Venue	Res	Score
1887-88		1	15.10.87	Chirk		A	L	1-4

CHESTERFIELD

Formed 1866, the fourth oldest League club after Stoke, Notts County and Nottingham Forest. Originally known as Chesterfield Municipal. 1919-1922 Chesterfield Town. 1922-present Chesterfield. **Best FA Cup Performance:** 5th round, 1933, 1938, 1950. **Record FA Cup Win:** 11-1 vs Dronfield Woodhouse, Pr rd, 1920-21. In competition proper: 5-0 vs Wath Athletic, 1st rd, 28.11.1925. **Record FA Cup Defeat:** 1-8 vs West Ham, 1st round, 1st round, 10.1.1914; 0-7 vs Burnley 3rd round, 5.1.1957

as Chesterfield Municipal

Season			
1892-93		1q **Gainsborough T** (A) 2-4 abnd; 1q **Gainsborough T** (A) 0-4	
1893-94		1q **Matlock T** (A) 3-0; 2q **Derby Junction** (H) 4-0; 3q **Heanor T** (A) 1-3	
1894-95		1q **Clay Cross Town** (H) 3-0; 2q **Matlock T** (H) 3-1; 3q **Buxton** (H) 4-0; 4q **Long Eaton Rangers** (A) 1-1; 4qr **Long Eaton R** (H) 3-0	

		1	2.2.95	Middlesbrough	NL	A	L	0-4

1895-96		1q **Eckington Works** (H) 1-0; 2q **Long Eaton Rangers** (H) 2-1; 3q **Heanor T** (H) 3-0; 4q **Ilkeston** (H) 2-0

		1	1.2.96	Newcastle U	D2	H	L	0-4

1896-97	ML	3q **Swadlicote** (H) 1-1; 3qr **Swadlicote** (A) 5-1; 4q **Heanor T** (H) 0-2
1897-98	ML	3q **Long Eaton Rangers** (A) 2-3
1898-99	ML	3q **Swadlicote** (H) 8-0; 4q **Burton Swifts** (A) 0-1
1899-00	D2	1q **Ilkeston T** (A) 2-1; 2q **Stapleford T** (H) 5-2; 3q **Heanor T** (H) 6-1; 4q **Hunslet** (H) 6-0; 5q **Grimsby T** (A) 2-3
1900-01	D2	3q **Hunslet** (H) 8-3; 4q **Newark** (A) 5-0; 5q **Barnsley** (A) 5-1; Int **Walsall** (H) 3-0

		1	9.2.01	Kettering	SL	A	D	1-1	Munday

	1r	13.2.01	**Kettering**		H	L	1-2aet	Gooing
1901-02	D2		Int **Reading** (A) 0-2				
1902-03	D2		3q **Newark** (H) 6-0; 4q **Barnsley** (A) 2-3				
1903-04	D2		3q **Lincoln C** (A) 2-0; 4q **Bradford C** (H) 2-1; 5q **Gainsborough T** (H) 0-2				
1904-05	D2		6q **Stockport Co** (H) 2-0; Int **Portsmouth** (H) 0-0; Int R **Portsmouth** (A) 0-2				
1905-06	D2	1	13.1.06 **Clapton O**	D2	A	D	0-0	
		1r	17.1.06 **Clapton O**		H	W	3-0	Dyal, Marples (p), Munday
		2	3.2.06 **Everton**	D1	A	L	0-3	
1906-07	D2	1	12.1.07 **Derby Co**	D1	A	D	1-1	Banner
		1r	16.1.07 **Derby Co**		H	–	1-2	Marples
			abandoned after 114 minutes – bad light				
		1r	21.1.07 **Derby Co** at Trent Bridge			L	0-4	
1907-08	D2		5q **St Helens R** (A) 4-1				
		1	11.1.08 **Stockton**	NL	H	W	4-0	Logan, Sprott, Munday, Marples (p)
		2	1.2.08 **Bristol R**	SL	A	L	0-2	
1908-09	D2		5q **Rotherham T** (H) 3-0				
		1	16.1.09 **Glossop**	D2	H	L	0-2	
1909-10	ML		4q **Cradley Heath St Lukes** (H) 2-1; 5q **Crewe Alex** (H) 5-2				
		1	15.1.10 **Fulham**	D2	H	D	0-0	
		1r	19.1.10 **Fulham**		A	L	1-2	Bovill
1910-11	ML		4q **Desborough Town** (A) 6-1; 5q **Rotherham T** (A) 2-1				
		1	14.1.11 **Bolton W**	D2	A	W	2-0	EJ Revill 2
		2	4.2.11 **Chelsea**	D2	A	L	1-4	EJ Revill
1911-12	ML		4q **Ripley Town Athletic** (A) 1-2				
1912-13	ML		4q **Sutton Town** (H) 2-1; 5q **Watford** (H) 3-1				
		1	18.1.13 **Nottingham F**	D2	H	L	1-4	Donald
1913-14	ML		4q **Shirebrook** (A) 1-1; 4qr **Shirebrook** (H) 2-0; 5q **North Shields** (A) 1-1; 5qr **North Shields** (H) 8-2				
		1	10.1.14 **West Ham U**	SL	A	L	1-8	Edgerton
1914-15	ML		4q **Rotherham T** (A) 4-2; 5q **Gainsborough T** (A) 0-0; 5qr **Gainsborough T** (H) 3-1; 6q **Goole T** (A) 0-2				
as Chesterfield Town
1919-20	ML		P **Clay Cross Town** (H) 4-0; 1q **Ilkeston U** (H) 2-1; 2q **South Normanton Col.** (H) 5-0 *Chesterfield disqualified for fielding ineligible player*				
1920-21	ML		P **Dronfield Woodhouse** (H) 11-1; 1q **Clay Cross T** (H) 2-1; 2q **Ilkeston U** (A) 0-0; 2qr **Ilkeston U** (H) 1-0; 3q **Staveley T** (A) 0-2				
1921-22	3N		4q **Irthlingborough T** (H) 3-0; 5q **Walsall** (A) 0-2				
as Chesterfield
1922-23	3N		4q **Lincoln C** (H) 2-0; 5q **Higham Ferrers T** (H) 4-4; 5qr **Higham Ferrers T** (A) 1-0; 6q **Worksop T** (A) 0-1				
1923-24	3N		5q **Worksop T** (A) 2-0; 6q **Grimsby T** (H) 0-0; 6qr **Grimsby T** (A) 0-2				
1924-25	3N		5q **Grimsby T** (A) 2-1; 6q **Accrington Stanley** (A) 0-1				
1925-26	3N	1	28.11.25 **Wath Athletic**	ML	A	W	5-0	Cookson 2 (1p), Fisher, Roseboom, Whitfield
		2	12.12.25 **Worksop T**	ML	A	W	2-1	Whitfield, Hopkinson
		3	9.1.26 **Clapton Orient**	D2	H	L	0-1	
1926-27	3N	1	27.11.26 **Mexborough Town A**	ML	H	–	0-0	
			abandoned at half-time due to fog				
		1	1.12.26 **Mexborough Town A**		H	W	2-1	Roseboom, Cookson
		2	11.12.26 **Doncaster R**	3N	A	W	1-0	Cookson
		3	8.1.27 **Fulham**	D2	A	L	3-4	Roseboom 2, Ralphs
1927-28	3N	1	26.11.27 **Darlington**	3N	A	L	1-4	Roseboom
1928-29	3N	1	24.11.28 **Rochdale**	3N	H	W	3-2	Sam Taylor, Roseboom (p), Neale
		2	8.12.28 **Gainsborough T**	ML	A	W	3-2	Roseboom, Yarwood, JW Lee
		3	12.1.29 **Huddersfield T**	D1	H	L	1-7	Wadsworth og
1929-30	3N	1	30.11.29 **Southport**	3N	A	D	0-0	
		1r	4.12.29 **Southport**		H	W	3-2	JW Lee, Sam Taylor, Little og
		2	14.12.29 **Port Vale**	3N	H	W	2-0	Sam Taylor, Bullock
		3	11.1.30 **Middlesbrough**	D1	H	D	1-1	Sam Taylor
		3r	15.1.30 **Middlesbrough**		A	L	3-4	JW Lee 2, S.J.Tayor
1930-31	3N	1	29.11.30 **Notts Co**	3S	H	L	1-2	Pynegar
1931-32	D2	3	9.1.32 **Nottingham F**	D2	H	W	5-2	Abel 2, Ruddy 2, JW Lee
		4	23.1.32 **Liverpool**	D1	H	L	2-4	Ruddy, Abel
1932-33	D2	3	14.1.33 **Sheffield W**	D1	A	D	2-2	Lee, Cook
		3r	18.1.33 **Sheffield W**		H	W	4-2	Cook, Abel, Lee, Bacon
		4	28.1.33 **Darlington**	3N	A	W	2-0	Austin, Lee
		5	18.2.33 **Burnley**	D2	H	L	0-1	
1933-34	3N	3	13.1.34 **Aston Villa**	D1	H	D	2-2	Hughes, Cook
		3r	17.1.34 **Aston Villa**		A	L	0-2	
1934-35	3N	3	12.1.35 **Swindon Town**	3S	A	L	1-2	Dawson
1935-36	3N	1	30.11.35 **Southport**	3N	H	W	3-0	Spence 2 (1p), Harvey
		2	14.12.35 **Walsall**	3N	H	D	0-0	
		2r	19.12.35 **Walsall**		A	L	1-2	Hamilton

Season	Div	Rnd	Date	Opponent		Opp Div	Venue	Result	Score	Scorers
1936-37	D2	3	16.1.37	Arsenal		D1	H	L	1-5	Sliman (p)
1937-38	D2	3	8.1.38	Bradford C		3N	A	D	1-1	Clifton
		3r	12.1.38	Bradford C			H	D	1-1aet	Spence
		3 2r	17.1.38	Bradford C	at Bramall Lane			W	2-0	Ponting, Clifton
		4	22.1.38	Burnley		D2	H	W	3-2	Ponting (2), Spence
		5	12.2.38	Tottenham H		D2	H	D	2-2	Clifton, Sliman
		5r	16.2.38	Tottenham H			A	L	1-2	Ponting
1938-39	D2	3	7.1.39	Southend U		3S	H		1-1	Spedding
				abandoned after 73 minutes – fog						
		3	11.1.39	Southend U			H	D	1-1	Lyon
		3r	16.1.39	Southend U			A	L	3-4aet	Lyon, Hughes, Milburn (p)
1945-46	D2	3 1L	5.1.46	York C		3N	H	D	1-1	Roberts
		3 2L	9.1.46	York C			A	L	2-3aet	Dooley, Roberts
1946-47	D2	3	11.1.47	Sunderland		D1	H	W	2-1	Ottewell, Milligan
		4	25.1.47	Middlesbrough		D1	A	L	1-2	Swinscoe
1947-48	D2	3	10.1.48	Derby Co		D1	A	L	0-2	
1948-49	D2	3	8.1.49	Wolverhampton W		D1	A	L	0-6	
1949-50	D2	3	7.1.50	Yeovil T		SL	H	W	3-1	Costello 2, Thompson
		4	28.1.50	Middlesbrough		D1	H	W	3-2	Dale, Merron, Costello
		5	11.2.50	Chelsea		D1	H	D	1-1	Thompson
		5r	15.2.50	Chelsea			A	L	0-3	
1950-51	D2	3	6.1.51	Brighton & HA		3S	A	L	1-2	Booker
1951-52	3N	1	24.11.51	Barrow		3N	A	W	2-0	Wislon, Marron
		2	15.12.51	Norwich C		3S	A	L	1-3	Marron
1952-53	3N	1	22.11.52	Workington		3N	H	W	1-0	Westcott
		2	6.12.52	Shrewsbury T		3S	A	D	0-0	
		2r	10.12.52	Shrewsbury T			H	L	2-4	Smith, Westcott
1953-54	3N	1	21.11.53	Gainsborough T		ML	A	W	4-1	Marsden 2, Edwards, Hatton
		2	12.12.53	Southend U		3S	A	W	2-1	Smith, Keating
		3	9.1.54	Bury		D2	H	W	2-0	Marsden 2
		4	30.1.54	Sheffield W		D1	A	D	0-0	
		4r	3.2.54	Sheffield W			H	L	2-4	Marsden, Whiteside
1954-55	3N	1	20.11.54	Hartlepool U		3N	A	L	0-1	
1955-56	3N	1	19.11.55	Chester		3N	H	W	1-0	Sowden
		2	10.12.55	Hartlepool U		3N	H	L	1-2	Smith
1956-57	3N	1	17.11.56	South Shields		NEL	A	D	2-2	Burrell, Smith
		1r	21.11.56	South Shields			H	W	4-0	Cunliffe, Smallwood, Capel (p), Sowden
		2	8.12.56	Barrow		3N	H	W	4-1	Capel (p), Smallwood, Sowden, Blakey
		3	5.1.57	Burnley		D1	A	L	0-7	
1957-58	3N	1	16.11.57	York C		3N	A	L	0-1	
1958-59	D3	1	15.11.58	Rhyl		CC	H	W	3-0	Hutchinson, Frear, Steele
		2	6.12.58	Carlisle U		D4	A	D	0-0	
		2r	10.12.58	Carlisle U			H	W	1-0	Frear
		3	10.1.59	Colchester U		D3	A	L	0-2	
1959-60	D3	1	14.11.59	South Shields		ML	A	L	1-2	Lewis
1960-61	D3	1	5.11.60	Doncaster R		D4	H	D	3-3	Foley, Smallwood 2
		1r	9.11.60	Doncaster R			A	W	1-0	Foley
		2	26.11.60	Oldham A		D4	H	D	4-4	Havenhand 2, Maddison, Foley
		2r	29.11.60	Oldham A			A	W	3-0	Rackstraw 2, Gilbert
		3	7.1.61	Blackburn R		D1	H	D	0-0	
		3r	11.1.61	Blackburn R			A	L	0-3	
1961-62	D4	1	4.11.61	Doncaster R		D4	A	W	4-0	Kerry, Lovie, Rackstraw, Lunn
		2	25.11.61	Oldham A		D4	H	D	2-2	Broadhurst, Rackstraw
		2r	29.11.61	Oldham A			A	L	2-4aet	Lovie, Lunn
1962-63	D4	1	3.11.62	Stockport Co		D4	H	W	4-1	Frear, Poole 2, Meredith
		2	24.11.62	Barnsley			A	L	1-2	Poole
1963-64	D4	1	16.11.63	Crook Town		NL	A	W	2-1	McQuarrie, J.Beresford
		2	7.12.63	Netherfield		LC	A	D	1-1	Scott
		2r	11.12.63	Netherfield			H	W	4-1	Clarke (p), McQuarrie, Rackstraw, Holt og
		3	4.1.64	Oxford U		D4	A	L	0-1	
1964-65	D4	1	4.11.64	South Shields		NRL	H	W	2-0	Stringfellow, Commons
		2	5.12.64	York C		D4	H	W	2-1	Stringfellow, Moor og
		3	9.1.65	Peterborough U		D3	H	L	0-3	
1965-66	D4	1	13.11.65	Chester		D4	H	L	0-2	
1966-67	D4	1	26.11.66	Wrexham		D4	A	L	2-3	Randall, Stark
1967-68	D4	1	9.12.67	Barnsley		D4	H	W	2-0	Hollett, Wilson
		2	6.1.68	Chester		D4	A	W	1-0	Wilson

CHESTERFIELD

		3	27.1.68	Blackpool	D2	A	L	1-2	Hollett
1968-69	D4	1	16.11.68	Skelmersdale U	CC	H	W	2-0	Moss, Randall
		2	7.12.68	Wrexham	D4	H	W	2-1	Moss 2
		3	4.1.69	Portsmouth	D2	A	L	0-3	
1969-70	D4	1	15.11.69	Tranmere R	D3	A	L	0-3	
1970-71	D3	1	21.11.70	Halifax T	D3	H	W	2-0	Moss 2
		2	12.12.70	Workington	D4	H	D	0-0	
		2r	16.12.70	Workington		A	L	2-3	Fenoughty, Moss
1971-72	D3	1	20.11.71	Oldham A	D3	H	W	3-0	Randall 2, Moss
		2	11.12.71	Barnsley	D3	A	D	0-0	
		2r	15.12.71	Barnsley		H	W	1-0	Moss
		3	15.1.72	Stoke C	D1	A	L	1-2	Randall
1972-73	D3	1	18.11.72	Rhyl	CC	H	W	4-2	Ferris, McHale (p) Downes, Bell
		2	9.12.72	Grimsby T	D3	A	D	2-2	Downes, Ferris
		2r	13.12.72	Grimsby T		H	L	0-1	
1973-74	D3	1	24.11.73	Barnsley	D4	H	D	0-0	
		1r	28.11.73	Barnsley		A	L	1-2	Large
1974-75	D3	1	23.11.74	Boston U	NPL	H	W	3-1	Shanahan, Moss 2
		2	14.12.74	Doncaster R	D4	H	W	1-0	Moss
		3	4.1.75	Sunderland	D2	A	L	0-2	
1975-76	D3	1	22.11.75	Bradford C	D4	A	L	0-1	
1976-77	D3	1	20.11.76	Scunthorpe U	D4	A	W	2-1	McEwan, Jones
		2	11.12.76	Walsall	D3	H	D	1-1	Darling
		2r	14.12.76	Walsall		A	D	0-0aet	
		2 2r	21.12.76	Walsall at Derby County			L	0-1	
1977-78	D3	1	26.11.77	Halifax T	D4	H	W	1-0	Fern
		2	17.12.77	Blyth Spartans	NL	A	L	0-1	
1978-79	D3	1	25.11.78	Darlington	D4	A	D	1-1	Flavell
		1r	6.12.78	Darlington		H	L	0-1	
1979-80	D3	1	24.11.79	Grimsby T	D3	A	D	1-1	Walker
		1r	27.11.79	Grimsby T		H	L	2-3	Green, Salmons
1980-81	D3	1	22.11.80	Wigan A	D4	A	D	2-2	Wilson, Green
		1r	25.11.80	Wigan A		H	W	2-0	Salmons, Tartt
		2	13.12.80	Sheffield U	D3	A	D	1-1	Birch (p)
		2r	16.12.80	Sheffield U		H	W	1-0	Simpson
		3	3.1.81	Peterborough U	D4	A	D	1-1	Crawford
		3r	6.1.81	Peterborough U		H	L	1-2	Hunter
1981-82	D3	1	21.11.81	Preston NE	D3	H	W	4-1	Bonnyman 2, Henderson, Walker
		2	12.12.81	Huddersfield T	D3	H	L	0-1	
1982-83	D3	1	20.11.82	Peterborough U	D4	H	D	2-2	Walker 2
		1r	24.11.82	Peterborough U		A	L	1-2	Walker
1983-84	D4	1	19.11.83	Chester C	D4	A	W	2-1	Newton 2
		2	10.12.83	Burnley	D3	H	D	2-2	Birch (p), Newton
		2r	19.12.83	Burnley		A	L	2-3	Bellamy, Birch (p)
1984-85	D4	1	17.11.84	Whitby Town	NL	A	W	3-1	Kendal, Brown, Newton
		2	8.12.84	Walsall	D3	A	L	0-1	
1985-86	D3	1	16.11.85	Tranmere R	D4	A	D	2-2	Batty, Henderson
		1r	18.11.85	Tranmere R		H	L	0-1	
1986-87	D3	1	15.11.86	Walsall	D3	A	L	0-2	
1987-88	D3	1	15.11.87	Notts Co	D3	A	D	3-3	Travis 2, Waller
		1r	17.11.87	Notts Co		H	L	0-1	
1988-89	D3	1	19.11.88	Bolton W	D3	A	D	0-0	
		1r	28.11.88	Bolton W		H	L	2-3	Morris 2
1989-90	D4	1	18.11.89	Shrewsbury T	D3	A	W	3-2	Waller, Gunn (p), Plummer
		2	9.12.89	Huddersfield T	D3	H	L	0-2	
1990-91	D4	1	17.11.90	Spennymoor U	NCoE	H	W	3-2	Caldwell, Potts og, Barnes
		2	11.12.90	Bolton W	D3	H	L	3-4	Morris, Cooke, Caldwell
1991-92	D4	1	16.11.91	Darlington	D3	A	L	1-2	Cooke
1992-93	D3	1	14.11.92	Macclesfield	GMVC	A	D	0-0	
		1r	25.11.92	Macclesfield		H	D	2-2aet	Turnbull, Williams (p)

Macclesfield won 3-2 on pens

CHICHESTER CITY

Founded 1873. **First entered FA Cup:** 1927

1960-61	SCL	1	5.11.60	Bristol C	D3	A	L	0-11

CHILTON COLLIERY RECREATION ATH.

Formed 1919. **Competed in the FA Cup** 1923-1937. **League club beaten:** Rochdale. Disbanded late 1940s

1925-26	NAII	1	28.11.25	**Carlisle U**	NEL	A	W	2-0	Shephard, Scutt
		2	12.12.25	**Rochdale**	3N	H	D	1-1	Catterick
		2r	17.12.25	**Rochdale**		A	W	2-1	Martin, Thomson
		3	9.1.26	**South Shields**	D2	A	L	0-3	
1926-27	NEL	1	27.11.26	**Annfield Plain**	NEL	A	W	4-2	Bowran 4
		2	11.12.26	**Accrington S**	3N	H	L	0-3	

CHIPPENHAM TOWN

Formed 1873. **First entered FA Cup:** 1898.

1951-52	WL	1	24.11.51	**Leyton**	AL	A	L	0-3	

CHIRK

Formed 1877. **Competed in FA Cup** 1884–1924. **Welsh Cup winners:** 1887, 1888, 1890, 1892, 1894

1884-85	1	25.10.84	**Davenham**		H	W	4-2	
	2	29.11.84	**Wrexham**		H	W	4-1	Griffiths, Povey, 2 others
	3	10.1.85	**Druids**		A	L	1-4	Povey
1885-86	1	24.10.85	**Burslem Port Vale**		A	L	0-3	
1886-87	1	23.10.86	**Hartford St Johns**		H	W	8-1	
	2	13.11.86	**Northwich Victoria**		A	D	0-0	
	2r	20.11.86	**Northwich Victoria**		H	W	3-0	Owen 2, Williams
	3		**Goldenhill**				walkover	
	4		**bye**					
	5	22.1.87	**Darwen**		H	L	1-2	W.Owen
1887-88	1	15.10.87	**Chester St Oswalds**		H	W	4-1	
	2	5.11.87	**Shrewsbury Town**		H	W	10-2	G.Griffiths 3, W.Owen 4, Rogers, Williams, og
	3	19.11.87	**Davenham**		A	D	2-2	
	3r	26.11.87	**Davenham**		H	W	6-1	
	4		**bye**					
	5	31.12.87	**Derby Junction**		H	L	0-1	

CHORLEY

Formed 1883. **First entered FA Cup:** 1894. **Cup Final Connection:** Paul Mariner, who played in Ipswich Town's winning team in 1978, started his career with Chorley. **League clubs beaten:** Accrington S, Wolves, Bury

1899-00	LL	1	27.1.00	**Notts Co**	D1	A	L	0-6	
1938-39	LC	1	26.11.38	**Horden CW**	NEL	A	D	1-1	Ward
		1r	30.11.38	**Horden CW**		H	L	1-2	Wright
1945-46	LC	1 1L	17.11.45	**Accrington S**	3N	H	W	2-1	Haworth, Harrison
		1 2L	24.11.45	**Accrington S**		A	L	0-2	
1963-64	LC	1	16.11.63	**Rochdale**	D4	A	L	1-2	Wroth
1978-79	CC	1	25.11.78	**Scarborough**	NPL	H	L	0-1	
1985-86	NPL	1	16.11.85	**Altrincham**	APL	H	L	0-2	
1986-87	NPL	1	15.11.86	**Wolverhampton W**	D4	H	D	1-1	Moss
				played at Bolton					
		1r	18.11.86	**Wolverhampton W**		A	D	1-1aet	Moss
		1 2r	24.11.86	**Wolverhampton W**			W	3-0	Cooper 2, Edwards
				played at Bolton					
		2	6.12.86	**Preston NE**	D4	H	D	0-0	
				played at Blackburn					
		2r	9.12.86	**Preston NE**		A	L	0-5	
1987-88	NPL	1	14.11.87	**Hartlepool U**	D4	H	L	0-2	
1990-91	NPL	1	17.11.90	**Bury**	D3	H	W	2-1	Aspinall, Moss
		2	11.12.90	**Shrewsbury T**	D3	A	L	0-1	

CHURCH FC

Formed 1874. Played at Spring Hill, Accrington.

1882-83	1	2.9.82	**Clitheroe**		H	W	5-0	Illingworth 2, Smith 3
	2		**bye**					

	3	6.1.83	Darwen	H	D	2-2	Crawford, 1 other
	3r	20.1.83	Darwen	A	W	2-0	
	4	3.2.83	Blackburn Olympic	A	L	0-2	
1883-84	1	27.10.83	Darwen	A	D	2-2	Gregson 2
	1r	3.11.83	Darwen	H	L	0-1	
1884-85	1	18.10.84	Hurst	H	W	3-2	
	2	6.12.84	South Shore	A	W	3-2	
	3	3.1.85	Southport	H	W	10-0	
	4	17.1.85	Darwen	H	W	3-0	Holden 2, 1 other
	5		bye				
	6	14.2.85	Old Carthusians	H	L	0-1	
1885-86	1	31.10.85	Blackburn Olympic	A	W	3-1	
	2		Third Lanark, Scotland			walkover	
	3	12.12.85	Rossendale	H	W	5-1	
	4		bye				
	5	16.1.86	Swifts	H	L	2-6	Beresford, 1 other
1886-87	1	23.10.86	Rawtenstall	H	D	1-1	
	1r	13.11.86	Rawtenstall	A	W	7-1	
	2	20.11.86	Glasgow Rangers	A	L	1-2	Beresford
1887-88	1		Cliftonville			walkover	
	2	5.11.87	Darwen	A	L	0-2	

CIVIL SERVICE

Formed 1870. Played at Richmond Athletic Ground

1871-72	1	11.11.71	Barnes	A	L	0-2	
1872-73	1	19.10.72	Royal Engineers	A	L	0-3	
1873-74	1		Maidenhead			scratched	
1874-75	1		Harrow Chequers			walkover	
	2	14.11.74	Shropshire Wanderers	A	L	0-1	
1875-76			Cambridge University			scratched	

CLACTON TOWN

Formed 1892. **First entered FA Cup:** 1920.

1960-61	SL	1	5.11.60	Southend U	D3	H	L	1-3	Clark

CLAPHAM ROVERS

Formed 1869. One of the 15 original entrants in the FA Cup competition in 1871. Played most of their home matches on Clapham Common, Tooting Bec Common and Wandsworth Common. **FA Cup Winners:** 1880; **FA Cup Runners-up** 1879

1871-72	1	11.11.71	Upton Park	A	W	3-0	Kenrick 2, Thompson
	2	16.12.71	Wanderers	H	L	1-3	
1872-73	1		Hitchin			walkover	
	2	23.11.72	Oxford University	H	L	0-3	
1873-74	1		Amateur Athletic Club			walkover	
	2	15.11.73	Cambridge University	H	D	1-1	
	2r	29.11.73	Cambridge University	A	D	1-1	Kenrick
	2 2r	20.12.73	Cambridge University	H	W	4-1	E.Field 2, Kenrick, St.Quintin
	3	17.1.74	Sheffield FC	H	W	2-1	Buchanan, Holden
		played at Peterborough					
	SF	28.2.74	Oxford University		L	0-1	
		played at Kennington Oval					
1874-75	1	7.11.74	Panthers	H	W	3-0	
	2	5.12.74	Pilgrims	H	W	2-0	Bevington, Field
	3	30.1.75	Royal Engineers		L	2-3	Bevington, 1 other
1875-76	1		Hitchin			walkover	
	2	18.12.75	Leyton	H	W	12-0	Geaves 3, Hunter 2, Bevington, 2og, Birkett, Buchanan, Smith, Stanley
	3	29.1.76	Old Etonians		L	0-1	
1876-77	1	11.11.76	Reigate Priory	H	W	5-0	Birkett, Buchanan, Cazenov, Hunter, Taylor
	2	16.12.76	Cambridge University	A	L	1-2	Fox
1877-78	1	27.10.77	Grantham	A	W	2-0	Mackern, W.Taylor
	2	22.12.77	Swifts	H	W	4-0	Buchanan 2, Holden, Sedgwick

CLAPHAM ROVERS

	3	2.2.78	Oxford University		L	2-3	Birkett, Rawson
1878-79	1		Finchley		*walkover*		
	2	7.12.78	Forest School	H	W	10-1	Payne 2, Scott 2, Smith 2, Stanley, Giles, Growse
	3	2.2.79	Cambridge University		W	1-0aet	Growse
	4	8.3.79	Swifts		W	8-1	Bailey 2, Scott 2, Rawso, Stanley, og, 1 other
	SF		bye				
	F	29.3.79	Old Etonians at Kennington Oval		L	0-1	
1879-80	1	8.11.79	Romford	H	W	7-0	
	2	20.12.79	South Norwood	A	W	4-1	Stanley 2, Lloyd-Jones, Sparks
	3	17.1.80	Pilgrims		W	7-0	Sparks 3, Barry 2, Lloyd-Jones, Stanley
	4	14.2.80	Hendon		W	2-0	Lloyd-Jones 2
	5	21.2.80	Old Etonians		W	1-0	Lloyd-Jones
	SF		bye				
	F	10.4.80	OXFORD UNIV at Kennington Oval		W	1-0	Lloyd-Jones
1880-81	1	13.11.80	Finchley	H	W	15-0	
	2		bye				
	3	8.1.81	Swifts	H	W	2-1	Ram, Wollaston
	4	12.2.81	Upton Park	A	W	5-4	Ram 2, Barry 2, Sparks
	5	19.3.81	Old Carthusians	A	L	1-3aet	Lloyd-Jones
1881-82	1	5.11.81	Old Etonians	A	D	2-2	Payne, Taylor
	1r	19.11.81	Old Etonians	H	L	0-1	
1882-83	1	4.11.82	Kildare	H	W	3-0	Pawson 2, og
	2	2.12.82	Hanover Utd	H	W	7-1	Ram 3, Coles, Holden-Whit, Howard-Maclean, Lloyd-Jones
	3	6.1.83	Windsor Home Park	A	W	3-0	Ram 2, Howard-Maclean
	4		bye				
	5	20.2.83	Old Carthusians	A	L	3-5	Pawson 2, Lloyd-Jones
1883-84	1		Kildare		*walkover*		
	2	1.12.83	Rochester	H	W	7-0	Kerr 4, Poulton 3
	3	22.12.83	Swifts	H	L	1-2	Oxley
1884-85	1	8.11.84	Hendon	H	D	3-3	
	1r	22.11.84	Hendon	A	L	0-6	
1885-86	1	31.10.85	1st Surrey Rifles	H	W	12-0	
	2		bye				
	3		South Reading		*disqualified*		
1886-87	1	30.10.86	Old Brightonians	H	L	0-6	

CLAPTON

Formed 1878. Have played at their famous Spotted Dog Ground in Forest Gate since their formation. **First entered FA Cup:** 1884. **FA Amateur Cup Winners:** 1907, 1909, 1915, 1924, 1925; **Runners-up:** 1905

1884-85		1	1.11.84	Romford		A	L	2-3	Davies, Jackson
1885-86		1	24.10.85	Hendon		A	W	4-0	
		2	21.11.85	South Reading		H	D	1-1	
		2r		South Reading		*disqualified*			
1886-87		1	23.10.86	Crusaders		H	L	0-5	
1887-88		1	15.10.86	Old Westminsters		A	L	1-4	
1889-90		1	18.1.90	Small Heath	FAll	A	L	1-3	Burns
1890-91		1	17.1.91	Nottingham F	FAll	H	L	0-14	
			match played at Upton Park						
1925-26	IL	1	28.11.25	Norwich C	3S	H	W	3-1	Massey 2, McNeill
		2	12.12.25	Ilford	IL	H	W	1-0	Munden
		3	9.1.26	Swindon T	3S	H	L	2-3	Munden, Massey
			played at Upton Park						
1926-27	IL	1	27.11.26	Brentford	3S	H	D	1-1	Morgan
		1r	1.12.26	Brentford		A	L	3-7	Osborn 2, Massey
1927-28	IL	1	30.11.27	Luton T	3S	A	L	0-9	
1957-58	IL	1	16.11.57	QPR	3S	H	D	1-1	Bennett
		1r	18.11.57	QPR		A	L	1-3	Brewster

CLARENCE FC

Formed 1876. Played at Battersea Park, London

1879-80	1	1.11.79	Pilgrims		A	L	2-3	T.Stone, Wilmshurst
1880-81	1	30.10.80	Great Marlow		A	L	0-6	

CLEATOR MOOR CELTIC

Formed 1908. **First entered FA Cup:** 1919.

1950-51	WCL	1	25.11.50	Tranmere R	3N	H	L	0-5
				played at Workington				

CLEETHORPES TOWN

Entered the FA Cup: 1886-1929

1886-87	1	30.10.86	Mellors, Nottingham	H	W	2-1
	2	20.11.86	Lockwood Brothers	H	L	1-4
1887-88	1	15.10.87	Grimsby T	H	L	0-4

CLIFTONVILLE, BELFAST

Formed 1879. **Northern Ireland Cup Winners:** 8 times; **Runners-up** 8 times. One of three Irish teams to play in the FA Cup Proper

1886-87	1	9.10.86	Blackburn Park Rd	A	D	2-2	Dobbin, Turner
	1r	23.10.86	Blackburn Park Rd	H	W	7-2	
	2	13.11.86	Great Lever	A	W	3-1	
	3	4.12.86	Partick Thistle	H	L	0-11	
1887-88	1		Church FC			scratched	

CLITHEROE

Formed 1879. Played at the Waterloo Field and at Church Meadow, Clitheroe

1882-83	1	2.9.82	Church FC	A	L	0-5	
1883-84	1	10.11.83	South Shore	H	D	3-3	
	1r	24.11.83	South Shore	A	L	2-3	Bell, 1 other
1884-85	1		Witton			scratched	
1885-86	1	24.10.85	Blackburn R	H	L	0-2	

CLITHEROE LOW MOOR

Formed 1879. Played at Deek Field, Clitheroe

1883-84	1	27.10.83	Blackburn Park Rd	A	L	0-6
1884-85	1		Blackburn Park Rd			walkover
	2	22.11.84	Southport	A	L	1-3
1885-86	1	24.10.85	Rossendale	A	L	2-6

CLYDESDALE

1875-76	1		South Norwood		scratched

COLCHESTER UNITED

Formed 1937. Won FA Challenge Trophy and GM Vauxhall Conference Double 1992 **Best FA Cup Performance** – beating Leeds in 1971 to reach the 6th round. **Record FA Cup Win:** 7-1 vs Yeovil Town, 3rd round, 11.12.1958; 7-1 vs Woodford Town 4th qualifying round, 1950. **Record FA Cup Defeat:** 0-5 vs Reading, 1st round, 30.11.1946; 0-5 vs Blackpool, 5th round 7.2.1948; 0-5 vs Everton, 6th round, 6.3.1971

1938-39	SL	1	26.11.38	Folkestone	SL	A	L	1-2	Leslie
1945-46	SL	4q Wisbech T (A) 0-5							
1946-47	SL	1	30.11.46	Reading	3S	A	L	0-5	
1947-48	SL	1	29.11.47	Banbury Spencer	BC	H	W	2-1	Brown, Curry
		2	13.12.47	Wrexham	3N	H	W	1-0	Curry
		3	10.1.48	Huddersfield T	D1	H	W	1-0	Curry
		4	24.1.48	Bradford PA	D2	H	W	3-2	Curry 2, Cutting
		5	7.2.48	Blackpool	D1	A	L	0-5	
1948-49	SL	1	27.11.48	Reading	3S	H	–	1-1	Curry
			abandoned after 35 minutes – fog						
		1	4.12.48	Reading		H	L	2-4	Cater 2
1949-50	SL	4q Wealdstone (A) 0-1							

Season	Div	Round	Date	Opponent		H/A	Result	Score	Scorers
1950-51	3S	4q	Woodford T (A) 7-1						
		1	25.11.50	Bournemouth	3S	A	L	0-1	
1951-52	3S	1	24.11.51	Port Vale	3S	H	W	3-1	Keeble, Scott, Elder
		2	15.12.51	Bristol C	3S	H	W	2-1	Scott, Davidson
		3	12.1.52	Barnsley	D2	A	L	0-3	
1952-53	3S	1	22.11.52	Weymouth	SL	A	D	1-1	Targett og
		1r	27.11.52	Weymouth		H	W	4-0	Targett og, McKim, Edwards 2
		2	6.12.52	Llanelli	SL	H	W	3-2	Barlow, Church, McCurley
		3	10.1.53	Rotherham U	D2	A	D	2-2	McCurley 2
		3r	15.1.53	Rotherham U		H	L	0-2	
1953-54	3S	1	21.11.53	Millwall	3S	H	D	1-1	McCurley
		1r	23.11.53	Millwall		A	L	0-4	
1954-55	3S	1	20.11.54	Reading	3S	A	D	3-3	Birch, Grice, McKim
		1r	25.11.54	Reading		H	L	1-2	Elder
1955-56	3S	1	19.11.55	Torquay U	3S	A	L	0-2	
1956-57	3S	1	17.11.56	Southend U	3S	H	L	1-4	McCurley
1957-58	3S	1	16.11.57	Wisbech T	ML	A	L	0-1	
1958-59	D3	1	15.11.58	Bath C	SL	H	W	2-0	Plant, Langman
		2	6.12.58	Yeovil T	SL	H	D	1-1	Plant
		2r	11.12.58	Yeovil T		A	W	7-1	Langman 4, Williams, McLeod 2
		3	10.1.59	Chesterfield	D3	H	W	2-0	Evans, Langman
		4	24.1.59	Arsenal	D1	H	D	2-2	Langman, J.Evans
		4r	28.1.59	Arsenal		A	L	0-4	
1959-60	D3	1	14.11.59	QPR	D3	H	L	2-3	McCurley, Wright
1960-61	D3	1	5.11.60	Maidenhead	CRN	H	W	5-0	Bobby Hunt 2, Langman 2, Williams
		2	26.11.60	Aldershot	D4	A	L	1-3	Hill
1961-62	D4	1	4.11.61	Peterborough U	D3	A	D	3-3	Abrey, Wright, Bobby Hunt
		1r	6.11.61	Peterborough U		H	D	2-2aet	King, Bobby Hunt
		1 2r	13.11.61	Peterborough U at Norwich			L	0-3	
1962-63	D3	1	3.11.62	Wimbledon	IL	A	L	1-2	King
1963-64	D4	1	16.11.63	Brighton	D4	A	W	1-0	Bobby Hunt
		2	7.12.63	QPR	D3	H	L	0-1	
1964-65	D3	1	14.11.64	Bideford T	WL	H	D	3-3	Salisbury, Longbottom, Trevis
		1r	18.11.64	Bideford		A	W	2-1	Connolly, Stark
		2	5.12.64	Torquay U	D4	A	L	0-2	
1965-66	D4	1	13.11.65	QPR	D3	H	D	3-3	Blackwood 2, Hall
		1r	17.11.65	QPR		A	L	0-4	
1966-67	D3	1	26.11.66	Gainsborough T	ML	A	W	1-0	Hall
		2	7.1.67	Peterborough U	D3	H	L	0-3	
1967-68	D3	1	12.12.67	Torquay U	D3	A	D	1-1	Barlow
		1r	18.12.67	Torquay U		H	W	2-1	Trevis 2
		2	6.1.68	Chelmsford	SL	H	W	2-0	McKechnie, Stratton
		3	27.1.68	WBA	D1	H	D	1-1	Stratton
		3r	31.1.68	WBA		A	L	0-4	
1968-69	D4	1	16.11.68	Chesham U	AL	H	W	5-0	Light 2, Hall 2, Price
		2	7.12.68	Exeter C	D4	H	L	0-1	
1969-70	D4	1	15.11.69	Newport Co	D4	A	L	1-2	Ferguson
1970-71	D4	1	21.11.70	Ringmer	SCL	H	W	3-0	Crawford 3
		2	12.12.70	Cambridge U	D4	H	W	3-0	Jones, Garvey, Gilchrist
		3	5.1.71	Barnet	SL	A	W	1-0	McMahon
		4	23.1.71	Rochdale	D3	A	D	3-3	Crawford 2, Lewis
		4r	25.1.71	Rochdale		H	W	5-0	Lewis, Simmons, Parry og, Crawford, Mahon
		5	13.2.71	Leeds U	D1	H	W	3-2	Crawford 2, Simmons
		6	6.3.71	Everton	D1	A	L	0-5	
1971-72	D4	1	20.11.71	Shrewsbury T	D3	H	L	1-4	Hall
1972-73	D4	1	18.11.72	Bognor Regis Town	SL	H	W	6-0	Simmons 3, Mogan, Hall, Foley
		2	9.12.72	Bournemouth	D3	A	D	0-0	
		2r	11.12.72	Bournemouth		H	L	0-2	
1973-74	D4	1	24.11.73	Peterborough U	D4	H	L	2-3	Mahon, Harford
1974-75	D3	1	23.11.74	Watford	D3	A	W	1-0	Froggatt
		2	14.12.74	Leatherhead	IL	A	L	0-1	
1975-76	D3	1	22.11.75	Dover	SL	H	D	3-3	Leslie, Dominey, Smith
		1r	26.11.75	Dover		A	L	1-4	Packer (p)
1976-77	D4	1	20.11.76	Cambridge U	D4	A	D	1-1	Packer (p)
		1r	24.11.76	Cambridge U		H	W	2-0	Garwood, Leslie
		2	11.12.76	Brentford	D4	H	–	0-0	

abandoned after 62 minutes – icebound pitch

COLCHESTER UNITED

	2	20.12.76	Brentford		H	W	3-2	Allinson, Froggat, Packer (p)
	3	8.1.77	Kettering	SL	A	W	3-2	Froggatt, Garwood 2
	4	29.1.77	Derby Co	D1	H	D	1-1	Garwood
	4r	2.2.77	Derby Co		A	L	0-1	
1977-78 D3	1	26.11.77	Bournemouth	D4	H	D	1-1	Gough
	1r	29.11.77	Bournemouth		A	D	0-0aet	
	1 2r	5.12.77	Bournemouth		A	W	4-1	Dowman, Garwood 3
	2	17.12.77	Watford	D4	A	L	0-2	
1978-79 D3	1	25.11.78	Oxford U	D3	H	W	4-2	Gough 3, Foley
	2	16.12.78	Leatherhead	IL	A	D	1-1	Gough
	2r	18.12.78	Leatherhead		H	W	4-0	Lee, Gough, Dowman 2
	3	9.1.79	Darlington	D4	A	W	1-0	Hodge
	4	27.1.79	Newport Co	D4	A	D	0-0	
	4r	5.2.79	Newport Co		H	W	1-0	Gough
	5	20.2.79	Manchester U	D1	H	L	0-1	
1979-80 D3	1	24.11.79	Plymouth A	D3	H	D	1-1	Rowles
	1r	27.11.79	Plymouth A		A	W	1-0aet	Allinson
	2	15.12.79	Bournemouth	D4	H	W	1-0	Rowles
	3	5.1.80	Reading	D3	A	L	0-2	
1980-81 D3	1	22.11.80	Portsmouth	D3	H	W	3-0	Lee, Allinson, Bremner
	2	13.12.81	Yeovil T	APL	H	D	1-1	Wignall
	2r	17.12.81	Yeovil T		A	W	2-0	Lee, Bremner
	3	3.1.81	Watford	D2	H	L	0-1	
1981-82 D4	1	21.11.81	Newport Co	D3	H	W	2-0	Leslie, Adcock
	2	16.12.81	Brentford	D3	A	D	1-1	Allinson
	2r	30.12.81	Brentford		H	W	1-0	McNichol og
	3	4.1.82	Newcastle U	D2	A	D	1-1	Wignall
	3r	18.1.82	Newcastle U		H	L	3-4aet	Cook, Allinson 2 (2ps)
1982-83 D4	1	20.11.82	Torquay U	D4	H	L	0-2	
1983-84 D4	1	19.11.83	Torquay U	D4	A	W	2-1	Bowen 2
	2	10.12.83	Wealdstone	APL	H	W	4-0	Bowen 3, Houston
	3	7.1.84	Charlton A	D2	H	L	0-1	
1984-85 D4	1	17.11.84	Southend U	D4	A	D	2-2	Irving, Houston
	1r	21.11.84	Southend U		H	W	3-2aet	Adcock, Pennyfather og, Groves
	2	8.12.84	Gillingham	D3	H	L	0-5	
1985-86 D4	1	16.11.85	Wycombe W	APL	A	L	0-2	
1986-87 D4	1	15.11.86	Bishops Stortford	IL	A	D	1-1	T.English
	1r	17.11.86	Bishops Stortford		H	W	2-0	T.English, Adcock
	2	6.12.86	Aldershot	D4	A	L	2-3	T.English, Grenfell
1987-88 D4	1	14.11.87	Tamworth	WMRL	H	W	3-0	Wilkins, Tempest, Chatterton (p)
	2	5.12.87	Hereford U	D4	H	W	3-2	Chatterton, Wilkns, Hill
	3	11.1.88	Plymouth A	D2	A	L	0-2	
1988-89 D4	1	19.11.88	Fulham	D3	A	W	1-0	Walsh
	2	10.12.88	Swansea C	D3	H	D	2-2	Hedman, Wilkins
	2r	13.12.88	Swansea C		A	W	3-1	Hedman, Walsh, Wilkins
	3	7.1.89	Shrewsbury T	D2	A	W	3-0	Walsh, Pratley og, Allinson
	4	28.1.89	Sheffield U	D3	A	D	3-3	Hicks, Hill, Hetzke
	4r	31.1.89	Sheffield U		H	L	0-2	
1989-90 D4	1	18.11.89	Brentford	D3	A	W	1-0	Bennett
	2	9.12.89	Birmingham C	D3	H	L	0-2	
1990-91 GMVC	1	17.11.90	Reading	D3	H	W	2-1	Atkins (p), Marmon
	2	12.12.90	Leyton O	D3	H	D	0-0	
	2r	17.12.90	Leyton O		A	L	1-4	Masters
1991-92 GMVC	4q	26.10.91	Burton A	SL	H	W	5-0	McDonough (p), McGavin 2, Restarick, Kinsella
	1	16.11.91	Exeter C	D3	H	D	0-0	
	1r	26.11.91	Exeter C		A	D	0-0aet	
			Exeter C won 4-2 on pens					
1992-93 D3	1	14.11.92	Slough T	GMVC	H	W	4-0	Sorrell, Bennett 2, Ball
	2	5.12.92	Gillingham	D3	A	D	1-1	McGavin
	2r	16.11.92	Gillingham		H	L	2-3	Ball 2

COLWYN BAY

Formed 1886. **First entered FA Cup:** 1928. Currently play in Northern Premier (HFS Loans) League

1987-88 NWC	1	14.11.87	Northwich Victoria	GMVC	A	L	0-1	

CONGLETON TOWN

Formed 1901. **First entered FA Cup:** 1906

| 1989-90 | NPL | 1 | 18.11.89 **Crewe Alex** | D3 | A | L | 0-2 | |

CONSETT

Formed 1899. **First entered FA Cup:** 1928. Currently play in the Northern League.

| 1958-59 | ML | 1 | 15.11.58 **Darlington** | D4 | A | L | 0-5 | |

CORBY TOWN

Formed 1948 out of original Stewarts and Lloyds club formed 1935, **Stewarts and Lloyds first entered FA Cup:** 1937. **Cup Final Connection:** Len Chalmers, who played for Leicester City in the 1961 Cup Final was a former Corby player. **League club beaten:** Luton T

1954-55	ML	1	20.11.54 **Watford**	3S	H	L	0-2	
1963-64	SL	1	16.11.63 **Bristol C**	D3	H	L	1-3	Crawley
1964-65	SL	1	14.11.64 **Hartlepool U**	D4	H	L	1-3	Wright
1965-66	SL	1	13.11.65 **Burton A**	SL	H	W	6-3	Goodall 2, Riley, Haazs, Garden 2 (1p)
		2	4.12.65 **Luton T**	D4	H	D	2-2	Jagger, Goodall
		2r	7.12.65 **Luton T**		A	W	1-0	Goodall
		3	22.1.66 **Plymouth A**	D2	A	L	0-6	
1967-68	SL	1	9.12.67 **Boston U**	WMRL	H	L	0-3	

CORINTHIAN CASUALS

Formed 1939 by the merger of the Casuals and Corinthian clubs. **First entered FA Cup as Corinthian Casuals:** 1964. **Cup Final Connection:** Cup Final commentator Martin Tyler is among their former players. **FA Amateur Cup:** Runners-up 1956

1965-66	IL	1	13.11.65 **Watford**	D3	H	L	1-5	Phillips
1983-84	IL	1	19.11.83 **Bristol C**	D4	H	D	0-0	
			played at Dulwich Hamlet					
		1r	23.11.83 **Bristol C**		A	L	0-4	

CORINTHIANS

The Corinthians hold a unique place in the English game. During their heyday they were the top amateur side in the country, but they did not play in a League or in any competitve matches. They were founded in 1882 and would probably have won the FA Cup several times if their own rules had not barred them from taking part. They finally entered the Cup in 1922 and were were exempted from the early rounds until 1933. They merged with Casuals FC in 1939. **League clubs beaten:** Blackburn R, Walsall, Norwich C

1922-23	1	13.1.23 **Brighton & HA**	3S	A	D	1-1	Creek
	1r	17.1.23 **Brighton & HA**		H	D	1-1aet	Howell
		played at Crystal Palace					
	1 2r	22.1.23 **Brighton & HA**			L	0-1	
		played at Stamford Bridge					
1923-24	1	12.1.24 **Blackburn R**	D1	H	W	1-0	Doggart
		played at Crystal Palace					
	2	2.2.24 **WBA**	D1	A	L	0-5	
1924-25	1	10.1.25 **Sheffield U**	D1	A	L	0-5	
1925-26	3	9.1.26 **Manchester C**	D1	H	D	3-3	Creek 2, Hegan
	3r	14.1.26 **Manchester C**		A	L	0-4	
1926-27	3	8.1.27 **Walsall**	3N	A	W	4-0	Ashton 2, Creek, Hegan
	4	29.1.27 **Newcastle U**	D1	H	L	1-3	Ashton
		played at Crystal Palace					
1927-28	3	14.1.28 **New Brighton**	3N	A	L	1-2	Hartley
1928-29	3	12.1.29 **Norwich C**	3S	A	W	5-0	Ashton 3, Doggart, Stone
	4	26.1.29 **West Ham U**	D1	A	L	0-3	
1929-30	3	11.1.30 **Millwall**	D2	H	D	2-2	Robins, Ashton
	3r	15.1.30 **Millwall**		A	D	1-1aet	Robins
	3 2r	20.1.30 **Millwall**			L	1-5	Doggart
		played at Stamford Bridge					
1930-31	3	10.1.31 **Port Vale**	D2	H	L	1-3	Doggart
1931-32	3	9.1.32 **Sheffield U**	D1	A	L	1-2	Fabian
1932-33	3	14.1.33 **West Ham U**	D2	H	L	0-2	

1934-35	1	24.11.34	Watford	3S	A	L	0-2	
1935-36	1	30.11.35	Reading	3S	A	L	3-8	Charlton 2, Whewell (p)
1936-37	1	28.11.36	Bristol R	3S	H	L	0-2	
1937-38	1	27.11.37	Southend U	3S	H	L	0-2	
1938-39	1	26.11.38	Southend U	3S	A	L	0-3	

COVENTRY CITY

Formed 1883 as Singers FC. Coventry City 1898. **FA Cup Winners:** 1987. **Record FA Cup Win:** 7-0 vs Scunthorpe United, 1st round, 24.11.1934. **Record FA Cup Defeat:** 2-11 vs Berwick Rangers (Worcester) 2nd qualifying round, 1901

As Singers FC

1892-93		P	**Burton Swifts** (A) 0-3				
1893-94		1q	**Redditch** (H) 1-4				
1894-95			*did not enter*				
1895-96	BDL	1q	**Hereford Thistle** (H) 6-1; 2q **Kidderminster H** (A) 0-0; 2qr **Kidderminster H** (H) 2-1; 3q **Burton Swifts** (H) 0-2				
1896-97	BDL	2q	**Stourbridge** (A) 2-4				
1897-98	BDL	1q	**Wrockwardine Wood** (A) 0-1				

As Coventry City

1898-99	BDL	1q	**Hereford T** (H) 0-0; 1qr **Hereford T** (A) 0-1				
1899-00	BDL	1q	**Stourbridge** (A) 0-5				
1900-01	BDL	3q	**Oswestry U** *scratched*				
1901-02	BDL	2q	**Berwick R (Worcester)** (A) 2-11				
1902-03	BDL	3q	**Aberaman** (H) 3-1; 4q **Stafford R** (H) 5-2; 5q **Kidderminster H** (H) 2-2; 5qr **Kidderminster H** (A) 2-4				
1903-04	BDL	3q	**Walsall** (H) 2-4				
1904-05	BDL	1q	**Halesowen** (H) 2-2; 1qr **Halesowen** (H) 3-2; 2q **Walsall** (H) 2-0; 3q **Stafford R** (A) 2-3				
1905-06	BDL	1q	**Worcester C** (H) 0-3				
1906-07	BDL		*did not enter*				
1907-08	BDL	1q	**Brierly Hill All** (A) 6-2; 2q **Darlaston** (H) 7-1; 3q **Bilston** (A) 2-1abnd; 3q **Bilston** (H) 2-1; 4q **Worcester C** (H) 2-0;				
			5q **Oswestry U** (A) 2-2; 5qr **Oswestry U** (H) 2-0; 6q **Bishop Auckland** (H) 7-1				
		1	11.1.08 **Crystal P**	SL	H	L	2-4	Warren, Lewis
1908-09	SL	5q	**Carlisle U** (H) 1-1; 5qr **Carlisle U** (A) 1-1aet; 5q 2r **Carlisle U** 1-3 at Hyde Road, Manchester				
1909-10	SL	4q	**Wrexham** (H) 3-0; 5q **Kettering T** (A) 5-0				

		1	15.1.10	**Preston NE**	D1	A	W	2-1	Hendren, Buckle
		2	5.2.10	**Portsmouth**	SL	A	W	1-0	Chaplin
		3	19.2.10	**Nottingham F**	D1	H	W	3-1	Warren 2, Smith
		4	3.3.10	**Everton**	D1	H	L	0-2	
1910-11	SL	1	14.1.11	**Sheffield W**	D1	A	W	2-1	Smith, Buckle
		2	4.2.11	**Brighton & HA**	SL	A	D	0-0	
		2r	9.2.11	**Brighton & HA**		H	W	2-0	Parkes, Tickle
		3	25.2.11	**Burnley**	D2	A	L	0-5	
1911-12	SL	1	13.1.12	**Southampton**	SL	A	W	2-0	Turnbull, Parkes
		2	3.2.12	**Manchester U**	D1	H	L	1-5	Jones
1912-13	SL	1	11.1.13	**Manchester U**	D1	A	D	1-1	Mitchell
		1r	16.1.13	**Manchester U**		H	L	1-2	Parkes
1913-14	SL	4q	**Port Vale** (A) 1-3					
1914-15	SL	6q	**Glossop** (A) 1-3					
1919-20	D2	1	10.1.20	**Luton T**	SL	A	D	2-2	Walker, Jones
		1r	15.1.20	**Luton T**		H	L	0-1	
1920-21	D2	6q	**Rochdale** (H) 1-1; 6qr **Rochdale** (A) 1-2					
1921-22	D2	5q	**Rotherham Co** (A) 1-1; 5qr **Rotherham Co** (H) 1-0; 6q **Southport** (A) 0-1					
1922-23	D2	5q	**New Brighton** (A) 0-3					
1923-24	D2	5q	**Tranmere R** (H) 2-2; 5qr **Tranmere R** (A) 2-3					
1924-25	D2	5q	**Walsall** (A) 2-1; 6q **Nelson** (A) 1-0					
		1	10.1.25	**Notts Co**	D1	H	L	0-2	
1925-26	3N	1	28.11.25	**Worksop T**	ML	A	L	0-1	
1926-27	3S	1	27.11.26	**Kettering T**	SL	A	W	3-2	Dunne, Herbert 2
		2	11.12.26	**Lincoln C**	3N	H	D	1-1	J.Ramage
		2r	15.12.26	**Lincoln C**		A	L	1-2	Gaffney
1927-28	3S	1	26.11.27	**Bournemouth**	3S	H	D	2-2	Bird, P.Ramage
		1r	30.11.27	**Bournemouth**		A	L	0-2	
1928-29	3S	1	24.11.28	**Fulham**	3S	H	L	1-4	Starsmore
1929-30	3S	1	30.11.29	**Norwich C**	3S	A	D	3-3	Loughlin 2, Richards
		1r	4.12.29	**Norwich C**		H	W	2-0	Loughlin, Widdowson
		2	14.12.29	**Bath C**	SL	H	W	7-1	Loughlin 2, Lake 2, Widdowson, Pick, Dinsdale
		3	11.1.30	**Sunderland**	D1	H	L	1-2	Loughlin
1930-31	3S	1	29.11.30	**Northampton T**	3S	A	W	2-1	Lake, Bowden

Season	Div	Rd	Date	Opponent	Opp Div	Venue	Result	Score	Scorers
		2	13.12.30	Exeter C	3S	A	D	1-1	Phillips
		2r	18.12.30	Exeter C		H	W	1-2	Bowden
1931-32	3S	1	28.11.31	Clapton O	3S	H	D	2-2	Bourton, Lake
		1r	2.12.31	Clapton O		A	L	0-2	
1932-33	3S	1	26.11.32	Guildford	SL	A	W	2-1	Bourton, Woolhouse
		2	10.12.32	Reading	3S	A	D	2-2	Bourton, Lake
		2r	15.12.32	Reading		H	D	3-3	Bourton, Lake, Davison
		2 2r	19.12.32	Reading at Stamford Bridge			L	0-1	
1933-34	3S	1	25.11.33	Crewe A	3N	H	W	3-0	Baker 2, Lauderdale
		2	9.12.33	Rotherham U	3N	A	L	1-2	Lake
1934-35	3S	1	24.11.34	Scunthorpe U	ML	H	W	7-0	Birtley 2, Lauderdale 2, Bourton, Jones, Liddle
		2	8.12.34	Hartlepools U	3N	A	W	4-0	Bourton 2, Jones, Birtley
		3	12.1.35	Birmingham	D1	A	L	1-5	Jones
1935-36	3S	1	30.11.35	Scunthorpe U	ML	H	D	1-1	Lake
		1r	9.12.35	Scunthorpe U		A	L	2-4	Bourton 2
1936-37	D2	3	16.1.37	Charlton A	D1	H	W	2-0	Lake 2
		4	30.1.37	Chester	3N	H	W	2-0	Mason 2 (1p)
		5	20.2.37	WBA	D1	H	L	2-3	Jones, Brown
1937-38	D2	3	8.1.38	York C	3N	A	L	2-3	Brown 2
1938-39	D2	3	7.1.39	Chester	3N	A	L	0-1	
1945-46	D2	3 1L	5.1.46	Aston Villa	D1	H	W	2-1	Barratt, Simpson
		3 2L	8.1.46	Aston Villa		A	L	0-2	
1946-47	D2	3	11.1.47	Newport Co	D2	H	W	5-2	Lowrie 3, Roberts, Ashall
		4	25.1.47	Burnley	D2	A	L	0-2	
1947-48	D2	3	10.1.48	Walsall	3S	H	W	2-1	Warner 2
		4	24.1.48	Luton T	D2	A	L	2-3	Lockhart (p), Dearson
1948-49	D2	3	8.1.49	Torquay U	3S	A	L	0-1	
1949-50	D2	3	7.1.50	Bolton W	D1	H	L	1-2	Alderton
1950-51	D2	3	6.1.51	Sunderland	D1	A	L	0-2	
1951-52	D2	3	12.1.52	Leicester C	D2	A	D	1-1	Allen
		3r	14.1.52	Leicester C		H	W	4-1	Roberts, Chisholm, Lockhart 2
		4	2.2.52	Burnley	D1	A	L	0-2	
1952-53	3S	1	22.11.52	Bristol C	3S	H	W	2-0	Brown, P.Hill
		2	6.12.52	Bishop Auckland	NL	A	W	4-1	Dorman, Waldock, Johnson, Marshall
		3	10.1.53	Plymouth A	D2	A	L	1-4	Warner
1953-54	3S	1	21.11.53	Brighton & HA	3S	A	L	1-5	Dorman
1954-55	3S	1	20.11.54	Northampton T	3S	A	W	1-0	Kirk
		2	11.12.54	Scunthorpe U	3N	H	W	4-0	Harvey, Lee, Capel 2
		3	8.1.55	Huddersfield T	D1	A	D	3-3	Lee, Capel 2
		3r	13.1.55	Huddersfield T		H	L	1-2aet	Moore
1955-56	3S	1	19.11.55	Exeter C	3S	H	L	0-1	
1956-57	3S	1	17.11.56	Swindon T	3S	A	L	1-2	McPherson
1957-58	3S	1	16.11.57	Walthamstow Ave	IL	H	W	1-0	McPherson
		2	7.12.57	Aldershot		A	L	1-4	P.Hill
1958-59	D4	1	16.11.58	Weymouth	SL	A	W	5-2	P.Hill 2, Straw 2, Boxley
		2	7.12.58	Plymouth A	D3	H	L	1-3	Straw
1959-60	D3	1	14.11.59	Southampton	D3	H	D	1-1	Straw
		1r	18.11.59	Southampton		A	L	1-5	Daley
1960-61	D3	1	5.11.60	Worcester C	SL	A	W	4-1	Farmer 2, Myerscough 2
		2	26.11.60	QPR	D3	A	W	2-1	Straw, Cockell og
		3	7.1.61	Liverpool	D2	A	L	2-3	Straw, Myerscough
1961-62	D3	1	4.11.61	Gillingham	D4	H	W	2-0	Hewitt, Satchwell
		2	25.11.61	King's Lynn	SL	H	L	1-2	Hindle og
1962-63	D3	1	3.11.62	Bournemouth	D3	H	W	1-0	Whitehouse
		2	24.11.62	Millwall	D3	A	D	0-0	
		2r	27.11.62	Millwall		H	W	2-1	Barr, Whitehouse
		3	7.3.63	Lincoln C	D4	A	W	5-1	Jackson og, Whitehouse, Bly, Barr, Farmer
		4	13.3.63	Portsmouth	D2	A	D	1-1	Hale
		4r	16.3.63	Portsmouth		H	D	2-2aet	Whitehouse 2
		4 2r	19.3.63	Portsmouth at Tottenham			W	2-1	Bly, Whitehouse
		5	25.3.63	Sunderland	D2	H	W	2-1	Bruck, Curtis
		6	30.3.63	Manchester U	D1	H	L	1-3	Bly
1963-64	D3	1	16.11.63	Trowbridge	SL	A	W	6-1	Hudson 3, Rees, Kearns, Prosser og
		2	7.12.63	Bristol R	D3	H	L	1-2	Hale
1964-65	D2	3	9.1.65	Aston Villa	D1	A	L	0-3	
1965-66	D2	3	22.1.66	Swindon T	D3	A	W	2-1	Rees, Trollope og
		4	12.2.66	Crewe A	D4	A	D	1-1	Rees

Season	Div	Round	Date	Opponent		H/A	W/D/L	Score	Scorers
		4r	14.2.66	Crewe A		H	W	4-1	Hudson 2, Farmer (p), Mitten
		5	5.3.66	Everton	D1	A	L	0-3	
1966-67	D2	3	28.1.67	Newcastle U	D1	H	L	3-4	Gibson, Rees, McNamee (og)
1967-68	D1	3	27.1.68	Charlton A	D2	H	W	3-0	Baker, Hannigan, Carr
		4	17.2.68	Tranmere R	D3	H	D	1-1	Rees
		4r	21.2.68	Tranmere R		A	L	0-2	
1968-69	D1	3	4.1.69	Blackpool	D2	H	W	3-1	Machin, Curtis, Shepherd
		4	25.1.69	Everton	D1	A	L	0-2	
1969-70	D1	3	7.1.70	Liverpool	D1	H	D	1-1	Martin
		3r	12.1.70	Liverpool		A	L	0-3	
1970-71	D1	3	11.1.71	Rochdale	D3	A	L	1-2	Hunt
1971-72	D1	3	15.1.72	WBA	D1	A	W	2-1	Rafferty, Chilton
		4	5.2.72	Hull C	D2	H	L	0-1	
1972-73	D1	3	13.1.73	Orient	D2	A	W	4-1	Alderson 2, Carr, Hutchison
		4	3.2.73	Grimsby T	D3	H	W	1-0	Coop (p)
		5	24.2.73	Hull C	D2	H	W	3-0	Alderson, Stein
		6	17.3.73	Wolverhampton W	D1	A	L	0-2	
1973-74	D1	3	5.1.74	Sheffield W	D2	A	D	0-0	
		3r	8.1.74	Sheffield W		H	W	3-1	Cross, Hutchison, Coop (p)
		4	27.1.74	Derby Co	D1	H	D	0-0	
		4r	30.1.74	Derby Co		A	W	1-0aet	Cross
		5	16.2.74	QPR	D1	H	D	0-0	
		5r	19.2.74	QPR		A	L	2-3	Cross 2
1974-75	D1	3	4.1.75	Norwich C	D2	H	W	2-0	Alderson, LLoyd
		4	25.1.75	Arsenal	D1	H	D	1-1	Alderson
		4r	29.1.75	Arsenal		A	L	0-3	
1975-76	D1	3	3.1.76	Bristol C	D2	H	W	2-1	Cross, Merrick og
		4	24.1.76	Newcastle U	D1	H	D	1-1	Murphy
		4r	28.1.76	Newcastle U		A	L	0-5	
1976-77	D1	3	8.1.77	Millwall	D2	H	W	1-0	McDonald
		4	29.1.77	Arsenal	D1	A	L	1-3	Hutchison
1977-78	D1	3	7.1.78	Middlesbrough	D1	A	L	0-3	
1978-79	D1	3	9.1.79	WBA	D1	H	D	2-2	Blair, Green
		3r	15.1.79	WBA		A	L	0-4	
1979-80	D1	3	5.1.80	Oldham A	D2	A	W	1-0	Hutchison
		4	26.1.80	Blackburn R	D3	A	L	0-1	
1980-81	D1	3	3.1.81	Leeds U	D1	A	D	1-1	Thomas
		3r	6.1.81	Leeds U		H	W	1-0	Thompson
		4	24.1.81	Birmingham C	D1	H	W	3-2	Daly 2 (1p), Blair
		5	14.2.81	Tottenham H	D1	A	L	1-3	English
1981-82	D1	3	2.1.82	Sheffield W	D2	H	W	3-1	Hunt 2, Hateley
		4	23.1.82	Manchester C	D1	A	W	3-1	Hunt, Hateley, Bodak
		5	13.2.82	Oxford U	D3	H	W	4-0	Thompson 2, Hateley 2
		6	6.3.82	WBA	D1	A	L	0-2	
1982-83	D1	3	8.1.83	Worcester C	APL	H	W	3-1	Whitton 2 (1p), Hateley
		4	29.1.83	Norwich C	D1	H	D	2-2	Roberts, Thompson
		4r	2.2.83	Norwich C		A	L	1-2aet	Hateley
1983-84	D1	3	7.1.84	Wolverhampton W	D1	H	D	1-1	Withey
		3r	10.1.84	Wolverhampton W		A	D	1-1aet	Pike
		3 2r	16.1.84	Wolverhampton W		H	W	3-0	Withey 2, Hunt
		4	30.1.84	Sheffield W	D2	A	L	2-3	Gibson 2
1984-85	D1	3	5.1.85	Manchester C	D2	H	W	2-1	Gibson 2
		4	26.1.85	Manchester U	D1	A	L	1-2	Gibson
1985-86	D1	3	4.1.86	Watford	D1	H	L	1-3	Kilcline
1986-87	D1	3	10.1.87	Bolton W	D3	H	W	3-0	Downs, Regis, Bennett
		4	31.1.87	Manchester U	D1	A	W	1-0	Houchen
		5	21.2.87	Stoke C	D2	A	W	1-0	Gynn
		6	14.3.87	Sheffield W	D1	A	W	3-1	Regis, Houchen 2
		SF	12.4.87	Leeds U	D2		W	3-2aet	Gynn, Houchen, Bennett
				played at Hillsborough					
		F	16.5.87	TOTTENHAM H	D1	WEMBLEY	W	3-2aet	Bennett, Houchen, Mabbutt og
1987-88	D1	3	9.1.88	Torquay U	D4	H	W	2-0	Kilcline (p), Regis
		4	30.1.88	Watford	D1	H	L	0-1	
1988-89	D1	3	7.1.89	Sutton U	GMVC	A	L	1-2	Phillips
1989-90	D1	3	6.1.90	Northampton T	D3	A	L	0-1	
1990-91	D1	3	5.1.91	Wigan A	D3	H	D	1-1	Gynn
		3r	9.1.91	Wigan A		A	W	1-0	Gynn

		4	26.1.91	Southampton	D1	H	D	1-1	Kilcline
		4r	29.1.91	Southampton		A	L	0-2	
1991-92	D1	3	4.1.92	Cambridge U	D2	H	D	1-1	Borrows (p)
		3r	14.1.92	Cambridge U		A	L	0-1	
1992-93	PL	3	13.1.93	Norwich C	PL	A	L	0-1	

COVENTRY SPORTING

Formed 1946. **First entered FA Cup** under their original name of Coventry Amateurs 1950. Folded 1989

1975-76	WMRL	1	22.11.75	Tranmere R	D4	H	W	2-0	Gallagher 2
		2	13.12.75	Peterborough U	D3	H	L	0-4	

Both matches played at Highfield Road

COWLAIRS

Formed 1876. One of the seven Scottish clubs to compete in the FA Cup. Based at Springburn, in the north of Glasgow. Folded 1896

1886-87	1	23.10.86	Darwen Old Wanderers	A	W	4-1	
	2	20.11.86	Rossendale	A	W	10-2	Clelland 4, Bishop 2, og, 3 others
	3	4.12.86	Glasgow Rangers	A	L	2-3	

CRAWLEY TOWN

Formed 1896. **First entered FA Cup:** 1959

1970-71	SL	1	21.11.70	Chelmsford C	SL	H	D	1-1	Basey
		1r	23.11.70	Chelmsford C		A	L	1-6	Griffiths
1971-72	SL	1	20.11.71	Exeter C	D4	H	D	0-0	
		1r	24.11.71	Exeter C		A	L	0-2	
1991-92	SL	1	4.1.92	Brighton & HA	D2	A	L	0-5	

CRESWELL COLLIERY

Entered the FA Cup 1921-1964

1954-55	CA	1	20.11.54	Accrington S	3N	A	L	1-7	Atkin

CREWE ALEXANDRA

Formed 1877. **FA Cup Best Performance:** semi-finals 1888. **Record FA Cup Win:** 9-0 vs Northwich Vic, 3rd qual rd, 1889-90. In competition proper: 5-0 vs Druids, 1st round, 15.10.1887. **Record FA Cup Defeat:** 2-13 vs Tottenham H, 4th round replay, 3.2.1960

1883-84	1	6.10.83	Queens Park, Glasgow	H	L	0-10	
1884-85	1	8.11.84	Oswestry	H	W	2-1	Watkins 2
	2	6.12.84	Queens Park, Glasgow	A	L	1-2	Taylor
			match abandoned after torrential downpour 48 minutes but result stood				
1885-86	1	31.10.85	Stoke	A	D	2-2	Snelson, 1 other
	1r	7.11.85	Stoke	H	W	1-0aet	'scrimmage'
	2	21.11.85	Oswestry	A	D	1-1	Payne
	2r		Oswestry				walkover
	3	12.12.85	Davenham	A	L	1-2	Cross
1886-87	1	23.10.86	Wrexham	A	W	4-1	Pearson 2, Payne, Price
	2	20.11.86	Stoke	H	W	6-4aet	Payne 3, Ellis, Nelson 2
	3		bye				
	4	29.1.87	Leek	H	L	0-1	
1887-88	1	15.10.87	Druids	H	W	5-0	Osborne, Payne, Price, others 2
	2	5.11.87	Northwich Victoria	A	W	1-0	Price
	3	bye					
	4	10.12.87	Swifts	H	D	2-2	Payne, Price
	4r	17.12.87	Swifts	A	L	2-3	Tinsley 2
			FA ordered match to be replayed after protest about the size of the goals				
	4 2r	31.12.87	Swifts at Derby Cricket Gd		W	2-1	Pearson, Price
	5	7.1.88	Derby Co	H	W	1-0	Pearson
	6	28.1.88	Middlesbrough	A	W	2-0	Ellis, Price
	SF	18.2.88	Preston NE at Anfield		L	0-4	
1888-89	1	2.2.89	Halliwell	A	D	2-2aet	E.Payne 2
	1r	9.2.89	Halliwell	H	L	1-5	A.Payne
1889-90	FAll	3q	Northwich Victoria (H) 9-0; 4q Chester (A) 1-2				

(171)

Season	Comp	Round	Date	Opponent	Div	Venue	Result	Score	Scorers
1890-91	FAll	1	17.1.91	Burnley	D1	A	L	2-4aet	Lewis 2
1891-92	FAll	3q		Wrexham (H) 3-1; 4q Northwich Victoria (H) 1-2 *FA ordered match to be replayed*; 4qr Northwich Victoria (H) 6-2					
		1	16.1.92	Wolverhampton W	D1	A	D	2-2aet	
		1r	23.1.92	Wolverhampton W		H	L	1-3	Pearson
1892-93	D2	1q		Stourbridge (A) 0-1					
1893-94	D2	2q		Northwich Victoria (A) 1-0; 3q Macclesfield (H) 3-2; 4q Stockport Co (A) 0-0 aet; 4qr Stockport Co (H) 1-2					
1894-95	D2	1q		Newtown (A) 3-1; 2q Fairfield (H) 3-6					
1895-96	D2	P		Tranmere R (H) 2-1; 1q Stalybridge Rovers (H) 3-1; 2q Wrexham (A) 3-3aet; 2qr Wrexham (H) 5-2; 3q Middleton (A) 4-0;					
				4q Fairfield (A) 2-2; 4qr Fairfield (H) 4-3					
		1	1.2.96	Bolton Wanderers	D1	H	L	0-4	
1896-97	TC	3q		Buckley (H) 3-1 abnd; 3q Buckley (H) 1-0; 4q Fairfield (A) 0-4					
1897-98	TC	3q		Wrexham (H) 4-1; 4q New Brighton Tower (H) 1-1; 4qr New Brighton T (A) 1-4					
1898-99	LL	3q		South Liverpool (H) 4-1; 4q Glossop (A) 0-1					
1899-00	LL	3q		Wigan Co (H) 3-1; 4q Port Vale (H) 2-2; 4qr Port Vale (A) 1-3					
1900-01	LL	3q		Stalybridge Rovers (H) 3-0; 4q Stockport Co (A) 3-1; 5q Nantwich T (H) 5-1; Int Kettering (A) 0-1					
1901-02	BDL	3q		Stalybridge Rovers (A) 2-0; 4q Stockport Co (A) 0-1 abnd; 4qr Stockport Co (A) 2-3					
1902-03	BDL	3q		Glossop (H) 0-3					
1903-04	BDL	3q		Burslem Port Vale (H) 0-0; 3qr Burslem Port Vale (A) 1-2					
1904-05	BDL	3q		Wrexham (H) 0-3					
1905-06	BDL	4q		Darwen (H) 2-0					
		1	13.1.06	Barnsley	D2	H	D	1-1	Goldie
		1r	18.1.06	Barnsley		A	L	0-4	
1906-07	BDL	5q		Paulton R (A) 1-0					
		1	12.1.07	Accrington Stanley	LC	H	D	1-1	Cope
		1r	16.1.07	Accrington Stanley		A	L	0-1	
1907-08	BDL	5q		Rotherham T (H) 1-1; Rotherham T (A) 1-2					
1908-09	BDL	5q		Workington (A) 1-4					
1909-10	BDL	4q		Lincoln C (H) 2-1; 5q Chesterfield (A) 2-5					
1910-11	BDL	4q		Chester (H) 4-3; 5q Carlisle U (H) 1-1; 5qr Carlisle U (A) 4-3					
		1	14.1.11	Bristol C	D1	A	W	3-0	Mason, King, Chapple
		2	4.2.11	Grimsby T	ML	H	L	1-5	Chapple
1911-12	CL	4q		Darlaston (A) 5-0; 5q Merthyr Town (H) 4-0					
		1	13.1.12	Blackpool	D2	H	D	1-1	Fiske og
		1r	17.1.12	Blackpool		A	–	1-2	Millward
				abandoned after 61 minutes – blizzard					
		1r	22.1.12	Blackpool		A	D	2-2aet	Jukes, Smith
		1 2r	25.1.12	Blackpool at Maine Rd			L	1-2	Smith
1912-13	CL	4q		Walsall (A) 1-2					
1913-14	CL	4q		Dudley (H) 2-1; 5q Gainsborough Trinity (A) 0-2					
1914-15	CL	4q		Port Vale (H) 1-1; 4qr Port Vale (A) 2-5					
1919-20	CL	3q		South Liverpool (H) 1-3					
1920-21	CI	4q		Eccles U (A) 0-2					
1921-22	3N	4q		Chester (H) 1-1; 4qr Chester (A) 2-1; 5q Wrexham (A) 0-5					
1922-23	3N	4q		New Brighton (A) 1-1; 4qr New Brighton (H) 0-1					
1923-24	3N	5q		Stockport Co (A) 0-1					
1924-25	3N	4q		Tranmere R (A) 1-1; 4qr Tranmere R (H) 0-2					
1925-26	3N	1	28.11.25	Tranmere R	3N	A	D	0-0	
		1r	2.12.25	Tranmere R		H	W	2-1aet	Jones, Mackay
		2	12.12.25	Wigan Borough	3N	H	D	2-2	Lovat, Jones
		2r	16.12.25	Wigan Borough		A	L	1-2	Lovatt
1926-27	3N	1	1.12.26	Northern Nomads		H	W	4-1	Jackson og, Kay 2, Brown
		2	11.12.26	Wigan Borough	3N	H	W	4-1	Morris, Cotton 2, Brown
		3	8.1.27	Barnsley	D2	A	L	1-6	Brown
1927-28	3N	1	26.11.27	Ashington	3N	H	D	2-2	Richardson og, Wareham
		1r	30.11.27	Ashington		A	W	2-0	Ralphs, Ireland
		2	10.12.27	Stockport Co	3N	H	W	2-0	Owen, Kay
		3	14.1.28	London Caledonians	IL	A	W	3-2	Owen 2, Shaw
				played at Stamford Bridge					
		4	28.1.28	Aston Villa	D1	A	L	0-3	
1928-29	3N	1	24.11.28	Gainsborough T	ML	A	L	1-3	Pither
1929-30	3N	1	30.11.29	Nelson	3N	A	W	3-0	Owen, Green, Gorringe
		2	14.12.29	Carlisle U	3N	A	L	2-4	Scullion, Gorringe
1930-31	3N	1	29.11.30	Jarrow	NEL	H	W	1-0	French
		2	13.12.30	QPR	3S	A	L	2-4	French, Rouse
1931-32	3N	1	28.11.31	Gainsborough T	ML	H	D	2-2	Swindells, Deacon
		1r	2.12.31	Gainsborough T		A	L	0-1	
1932-33	3N	1	26.11.32	Crook T	NEL	H	W	4-0	Swindells 2, Deacon 2

Season	Div	Round	Date	Opponent	Comp	Venue	Res	Score	Scorers
		2	10.12.32	Darlington	3N	H	L	0-2	
1933-34	3N	1	25.11.33	Coventry C	3S	A	L	0-3	
1934-35	3N	1	24.11.34	Walsall	3N	H	L	1-2	Mustard
1935-36	3N	1	30.11.35	Boston U	ML	H	W	4-2	Wood, Swindells, Waring 2
		2	14.12.35	Gillingham	3S	H	W	2-1	Black, Waring
		3	11.1.36	Sheffield W	D1	H	D	1-1	Rigby
		3r	15.1.36	Sheffield W		A	L	1-3	Swindells
1936-37	3N	1	28.11.36	Rochdale	3N	H	W	5-1	Dyer 2, Nicol 2, Swindells
		2	12.12.36	Hartlepools U	3N	H	D	1-1	Dyer
		2r	16.12.36	Hartlepools U		A	W	2-1	Waring, Swindells
1937-38	3N	1	27.11.37	Barrow	3N	A	W	1-0	Essex
		2	11.12.37	New Brighton	3N	H	–	1-0	Foster
			abandoned after 84 minutes						
		2	15.12.37	New Brighton		H	D	2-2	Cobourne, Foster
		2r	20.12.37	New Brighton		A	L	1-4	Blake
1938-39	3N	1	26.11.38	Oldham A	3N	A	D	2-2	Foster, Gilchrist
		1r	30.11.38	Oldham A		H	W	1-0	Johnson
		2	10.12.38	Cardiff C	3S	A	L	0-1	
1945-46	3N	1L	17.11.45	Wrexham	3N	H	W	4-2	Haywood, Boothway 2, Shaw
		1 2L	24.11.45	Wrexham		A	L	0-3	
1946-47	3N	1	30.11.46	Rotherham U	3N	A	L	0-2	
1947-48	3N	1	29.11.47	South Shields	NEL	H	W	4-1	Ferris, Finan, Harrigan, Taylor
		2	13.12.47	Workington	NEL	A	W	2-1	Meaney, Harrigan
		3	10.1.48	Sheffield U	D1	H	W	3-1	Finan 2, Jones
		4	24.1.48	Derby Co	D1	H	L	0-3	
1948-49	3N	1	27.11.48	Billingham Synthonia	NL	H	W	5-0	Basford 4, Meaney
		2	11.12.48	Millwall	3S	H	W	3-2	McCormick, Mitcheson 2
		3	8.1.49	Sunderland	D1	H	L	0-2	
1949-50	3N	1	26.11.49	Darlington	3N	A	D	2-2	Phillips 2
		1r	30.11.49	Darlington		H	W	1-0aet	Mitcheson
		2	10.12.49	Oldham A	3N	H	D	1-1	Mullard
		2r	13.12.49	Oldham A		A	D	0-0	
		2 2r	19.12.49	Oldham A at Maine Road		L	0-3		
1950-51	3N	1	25.11.50	North Shields	NEL	H	W	4-0	McGuigan 2, Travis, Basford
		2	9.12.50	Plymouth A	3S	H	D	2-2	Meaney, Travis
		2r	13.12.50	Plymouth A		A	L	0-3	
1951-52	3N	1	24.11.51	Lincoln C	3N	H	L	2-4	Smith 2
1952-53	3N	1	22.11.52	Gateshead	3N	A	L	0-2	
1953-54	3N	1	21.11.53	Bradford C	3N	H	D	0-0	
		1r	25.11.53	Bradford C		A	W	1-0	Chapman
		2	12.12.53	Walsall	3S	A	L	0-3	
1954-55	3N	1	20.11.54	Oldham A	3N	A	L	0-1	
1955-56	3N	1	19.11.55	Barrow	3N	A	D	0-0	
		1r	23.11.55	Barrow		H	L	2-3aet	Rolfe, Samuels
1956-57	3N	1	17.11.56	Wrexham	3N	H	D	2-2	Connor, Williams
		1r	20.11.56	Wrexham		A	L	1-2	Connor
1957-58	3N	1	16.11.57	Hull C	3N	A	L	1-2	Whiston
1958-59	D4	1	15.11.58	South Shields	ML	H	D	2-2	Colbridge, Llewellyn
		1r	19.11.58	South Shields		A	L	0-5	
1959-60	D4	1	14.11.59	Burscough	LC	A	W	3-1	Keery (p), Riley, Llewellyn
		2	5.12.59	Stockport Co	D4	A	D	0-0	
		2r	9.12.59	Stockport Co		H	W	2-0	Wheatley 2
		3	9.1.60	Workington	D4	H	W	2-0	LLewellyn
		4	30.1.60	Tottenham H	D1	H	D	2-2	M.Jones, Llewellyn
		4r	3.2.60	Tottenham H		A	L	2-13	Coleman, Llewellyn
1960-61	D4	1	5.11.60	Rochdale	D4	H	D	1-1	Coleman
		1r	8.11.60	Rochdale		A	W	2-1	Riley, Stark
		2	29.11.60	Halifax T	D3	A	D	2-2	Stark, Jones
		2r	5.12.60	Halifax T		H	W	3-0	Foster 2, Wheatley
		3	7.1.61	Chelsea	D1	A	W	2-1	Stark, Wheatley
		4	28.1.61	Tottenham H	D1	A	L	1-5	Tighe
1961-62	D4	1	4.11.61	Lincoln C	D3	H	W	2-0	Lord, Riley
		2	25.11.61	Port Vale	D3	H	D	1-1	McGill
		2r	27.11.61	Port Vale		A	L	0-3	
1962-63	D4	1	3.11.62	Scarborough	NEL	H	D	1-1	Tighe
		1r	7.11.62	Scarborough		A	W	3-2aet	Lord, Wheatley, Haydock
		2	24.11.62	York C	D4	A	L	1-2	Lord

CREWE ALEXANDRA

Season	Div	Rd	Date	Opponent		Venue	Result	Score	Scorers
1963-64	D3	1	16.11.63	Hull C	D3	A	D	2-2	Wheatley. Ewing
		1r	20.11.63	Hull C		H	L	0-3	
1964-65	D4	1	14.11.64	Chester	D4	A	L	0-5	
1965-66	D4	1	13.11.65	Scunthorpe U	D3	H	W	3-0	King, Kane, Wheatley (p)
		2	4.12.65	South Shields	NRL	H	W	3-1	Gowans, Bradshaw, Kane
		3	22.1.66	Folkestone T	SL	A	W	5-1	Sandiford, Barnes, Gowans 2, King
		4	12.2.66	Coventry C	D2	H	D	1-1	Curtis og
		4r	14.2.66	Coventry C		A	L	1-4	Sandiford (p)
1966-67	D4	1	26.11.66	Grimsby T	D3	H	D	1-1	Regan
		1r	30.11.66	Grimsby T		A	W	1-0	Gowans
		2	7.1.67	Darlington	D3	H	W	2-1	Barnes, Mahoney
		3	28.1.67	Bolton W	D2	A	L	0-1	
1967-68	D4	1	13.12.67	Halifax T	D4	A	L	2-3	Tarbuck, Archer
1968-69	D3	1	16.11.68	Altrincham	NPL	A	W	1-0	Emerson
		2	7.12.68	Halifax T	D4	A	D	1-1	Hollett
		2r	11.12.68	Halifax T		H	L	1-3	Hollett
1969-70	D4	1	15.11.69	Doncaster R	D3	A	D	1-1	Turner
		1r	19.11.69	Doncaster R		H	L	0-1	
1970-71	D4	1	21.11.70	Doncaster R	D3	H	D	0-0	
		1r	24.11.70	Doncaster R		A	W	3-1	Bowles, Tewley, Morrissey
		2	12.12.70	Chester	D4	A	L	0-1	
1971-72	D4	1	20.11.71	Blyth Spartans	NL	H	L	0-1	
1972-73	D4	1	18.11.72	Stafford Rangers	NPL	H	W	1-0	Bradshaw
		2	9.12.72	Blackburn R	D3	A	W	1-0	Manning
		3	13.1.73	Luton T	D2	A	L	0-2	
1973-74	D4	1	24.11.73	Scarborough	NPL	H	D	0-0	
		1r	28.11.73	Scarborough		A	L	1-2	Nicholls
1974-75	D4	1	23.11.74	Gateshead	NPL	H	D	2-2	Reed, Wain
		1r	25.11.74	Gateshead		A	L	0-1aet	
1975-76	D4	1	22.11.75	Rotherham U	D3	A	L	1-2	Bevan
1976-77	D4	1	20.11.76	Preston NE	D3	H	D	1-1	Lugg
		1r	23.11.76	Preston NE		A	D	2-2aet	D.Davies 2
		1 2r	29.11.76	Preston NE at Anfield			L	0-3	
1977-78	D4	1	26.11.77	Bradford C	D3	A	W	1-0	D.Davies
		2	17.12.77	Scarborough	NPL	H	D	0-0	
		2r	21.12.77	Scarborough		A	L	0-2	
1978-79	D4	1	25.11.78	Nuneaton Borough	SL	A	W	2-0	Coyne, Bowles
		2	16.12.78	Hartlepools U	D4	H	L	0-1	
1979-80	D4	1	24.11.79	Altrincham	APL	A	L	0-3	
1980-81	D4	1	22.11.80	Mossley	NPL	A	L	0-1	
1981-82	D4	1	21.11.81	Willenhall T	WMRL	A	W	1-0	Scott
		2	2.1.82	Scunthorpe U	D4	H	L	1-3	Haslegrave
1982-83	D4	1	20.11.82	Boston U	APL	A	L	1-3	Palios
1983-84	D4	1	19.11.83	Rochdale	D4	A	L	0-1	
1984-85	D4	1	17.11.84	Northwich Victoria	APL	A	L	1-3	King
1985-86	D4	1	16.11.85	Derby Co	D3	A	L	1-5	Micklewhite og
1986-87	D4	1	15.11.86	York C	D3	A	L	1-3	Platt
1987-88	D4	1	14.11.87	Lincoln C	GMVC	A	L	1-2	Macowat
1988-89	D4	1	19.11.88	Stafford Rangers	GMVC	A	D	2-2	Fishenden, Cronin
		1r	22.11.88	Stafford Rangers		H	W	3-2	Murphy 2, Fishenden
		2	10.12.88	Runcorn	GMVC	A	W	3-0	Gardiner, Fishenden, R.Edwards
		3	7.1.89	Aston Villa	D1	H	L	2-3	Gardiner, Keown og
1989-90	D3	1	18.11.89	Congleton	NPL	H	W	2-0	Cutler, Sussex
		2	9.12.89	Bishop Auckland	NPL	H	D	1-1	Murphy (p)
		2r	13.12.89	Bishop Auckland		A	W	2-0	Sussex
		3	6.1.90	Chelsea	D1	A	D	1-1	Walters
		3r	10.1.90	Chelsea		H	L	0-2	
1990-91	D3	1	17.11.90	Lincoln C	D4	A	W	4-1	Callaghan, Gardiner, McKearney, Ward
		2	12.12.90	Atherstone	SL	H	W	1-0	Sussex
		3	5.1.91	Bristol R	D2	A	W	2-0	Carr, Hignett
		4	26.1.91	Rotherham U	D3	H	W	1-0	Hignett
		5	16.2.91	West Ham	D2	A	L	0-1	
1991-92	D4	1	16.11.91	Carlisle U	D4	A	D	1-1	Hignett
		1r	26.11.91	Carlisle U		H	W	5-3aet	Walters, Naylor 2, Gardiner, Barnsley og
		2	7.12.91	Chester	D3	H	W	2-0	Hignett, Naylor
		3	6.1.92	Liverpool	D1	H	L	0-4	
1992-93	D3	1	14.11.92	Wrexham	D3	H	W	6-1	Hignett 4, McKearney 2

	2	5.12.92	**Accrington S**	NPL	A	W	6-1	Carr, Naylor 2, Whalley 2, Clarkson
	3	12.1.93	**Marine**	NPL	H	W	3-1	McKearney, Edwards, Clarkson
	4	23.1.93	**Blackburn R**	PL	H	L	0-3	

CROOK TOWN

Formed 1894, reformed 1943. **First entered FA Cup:** 1898. **FA Amateur Cup Winners:** 1901, 1954, 1959, 1962, 1964. **League clubs beaten:** Stockport Co, Carlisle U

1926-27	NL	1	27.11.26	**Workington**	NEL	A	W	2-1	Richardson, Colman
		2	11.12.26	**Southport**	3N	A	L	0-2	
1927-28	NL*	1	26.11.27	**Rochdale**	3N	A	L	2-8	Mitchell, Duffy
1931-32	NEL	1	28.11.31	**Stockport Co**	3N	H	W	3-1	Ferguson, Cook 2
		2	12.12.31	**Aldershot**	SL	A	D	1-1	Studdick
		2r	16.12.31	**Aldershot**		H	W	1-0	Cook
		3	9.1.32	**Leicester C**	D1	A	L	0-7	
1932-33	NEL	1	26.11.32	**Crewe Alex**	3N	A	L	0-4	
1954-55	NL	1	20.11.54	**Stanley U**	NL	H	W	5-3	Harrison 2, Armstrong, Taylor, McMillan
		2	11.12.54	**Brentford**	3S	A	L	1-4	Appleby
1955-56	NL	1	19.11.55	**Derby Co**	3N	H	D	2-2	McMillan, Harrison
		1r	23.11.55	**Derby Co**		A	L	1-5	Harrison
1957-58	NL	1	16.11.57	**Workington**	3N	A	L	1-8	Coates
1958-59	NL	1	15.11.58	**Buxton**	CC	A	L	1-4	Eley
1959-60	NL	1	14.11.59	**Matlock T**	CA	H	D	2-2	O'Connell, McMillan
		1r	19.11.59	**Matlock T**		A	W	1-0	Keating
		2	5.12.59	**York C**	D3	H	L	0-1	
1962-63	NL	1	3.11.62	**Hull C**	D3	A	L	4-5	Bowron, Cocking 2, Garbutt
1963-64	NL	1	16.11.63	**Chesterfield**	D4	H	L	1-2	Weir
1964-65	NL	1	14.11.64	**Carlisle U**	D3	H	W	1-0	Brown
		2	2.12.64	**Oldham A**	D3	H	L	0-1	
1965-66	NL	1	13.11.65	**Gateshead**	NRL	A	L	2-4	Brown 2
1976-77	NL	1	20.11.76	**Nuneaton Bor**	SL	H	L	1-4	White

* suspended from playing League matches

CROSSWELL'S BREWERY, OLDBURY

Never entered the FA Cup again after losing 14-0 to Wolves

1886-87		1	30.10.86	**Burton Swifts**		A	W	1-0	
		2	13.11.86	**Wolverhampton W**		H	L	0-14	

CROYDON

Formed 1953 as Croydon Amateurs. 1974 Croydon. **First entered FA Cup:** 1967

1979-80	IL	1	24.11.79	**Wycombe W**	IL	A	W	3-0	R.Ward, Constable, A.Ward
		2	15.12.79	**Millwall**	D3	H	D	1-1	R.Ward
				played at Crystal Palace					
		2r	18.12.79	**Millwall**		A	L	2-3	Constable 2 (1p)

CROYDON COMMON

Formed 1897. Croydon Common were the only team in the Southern League who did not continue after the First World War. Folded 1917. **Cup final connection:** seven Croydon Common players appeared in Cup finals

1908-09	SL	5q	**Bradford PA** (A) 2-1						
		1	16.1.09	**Woolwich Arsenal**	D1	H	D	1-1	MacDonald
		1r	20.1.09	**Woolwich Arsenal**		A	L	0-2	
1910-11	SL	1	14.1.11	**Grimsby T**	ML	A	L	0-3	
				FA ordered match to be replayed					
		1r	26.1.11	**Grimsby T**		A	L	1-8	Wardlow
1911-12	SL	1	13.1.12	**Leicester F**	D2	H	D	2-2	Yenson, Wood
		1r	22.1.12	**Leicester F**		A	L	1-6	Yenson
1912-13	SL	1	11.1.13	**W.Arsenal**	D1	H	D	0-0	
		1r	15.1.13	**W.Arsenal**		A	L	1-2	Newton
1914-15	SL	1	9.1.15	**Oldham A**	D1	H	L	0-3	

CRUSADERS FC

Formed 1877 and played at Essex County Cricket Ground at Leyton

1886-87	1	23.10.86	Clapton		A	W	5-0	
	2	13.11.86	Old Carthusians		A	L	2-4	
1887-88	1	15.10.87	Tooting		H	W	9-0	
	2	29.10.87	Old Wykehamists		A	W	3-2	
	3	26.11.87	Chatham		H	W	4-0	
	4	7.12.87	Sheffield W		H	L	0-1	
1890-91	1	24.1.90	Birmingham St Georges		H	L	0-2	
1891-92	1	16.1.91	Accrington		H	L	1-4	Connell

CRYSTAL PALACE (1)

Original amateur club formed 1861. One of the 15 original entrants in the inaugural FA Cup of 1871-72. This Crystal Palace has no connection with the present day club and folded before the modern Crystal Palace was formed in 1905.

1871-72	1	11.11.71	Hitchin		H	D	0-0	
			Both teams qualified for second round					
	2	16.12.71	Maidenhead		H	W	3-0	Bouch, Chenery, LLoyd
	3	20.1.72	Wanderers		A	D	0-0	
			Both teams qualified for semi-finals					
	SF	17.2.72	Royal Engineers			D	0-0	
			played at Kennington Oval					
	SFr	9.3.72	Royal Engineers			L	0-3	
			played at Kennington Oval					
1872-73	1	19.10.72	Oxford University		A	L	2-3	Armitage, Soden
1873-74	1	9.10.73	Swifts		A	L	0-1	
1874-75	1	14.11.74	Cambridge University		H	D	0-0	
	1r	21.11.74	Cambridge University		A	L	1-2	Fleet
1875-76	1	6.11.75	105th Regiment		A	D	0-0	
	1r	20.11.75	105th Regiment		H	W	3-0	EP Barlow, Neame, CP Smith
	2	11.12.75	Wanderers		A	L	0-3	

CRYSTAL PALACE (2)

Formed 1905. The modern day Crystal Palace FC was founded in 1905 and is not connected with the amateur Crystal Palace club which played in the FA Cup from 1871-75. FA Cup Runners-up: 1990. FA Cup Record Win: 7-0 vs Luton Town, 3rd round, 16.1.1929; 7-0 vs Clapham, 1st qual rd, 1905-06. FA Cup Record Defeat: 0-9 vs Burnley, 2nd round replay, 10.2.1909; 4-11 vs Manchester City, 5th round, 20.2.1926.

1905-06	SL	1q Clapham (H) 7-0; 2q Grenadier Guards (A) 3-0; 3q Chelsea (H) 7-1; 4q Luton T (H) 1-0						
		1	15.1.06	Blackpool	D2	A	D	1-1	Harker
		1r	19.1.06	Blackpool		H	D	1-1aet	Birnie
		1 2r	22.1.06	Blackpool at Villa Park			L	0-1	
1906-07	SL	5q Rotherham Co (H) 4-0						
		1	12.1.07	Newcastle U	D1	A	W	1-0	Astley
		2	2.2.07	Fulham	SL	A	D	0-0	
		2r	6.2.07	Fulham		H	W	1-0	Woodger
		3	23.2.07	Brentford	SL	H	D	1-1	Harker
		3r	27.2.07	Brentford		A	W	1-0	Roberts
		4	9.3.07	Everton	D1	H	D	1-1	Astley
		4r	13.3.07	Everton		A	L	0-4	
1907-08	SL	1	11.1.08	Coventry C	SL	A	W	4-2	Woodger 2, Roberts, Davies
		2	1.2.08	Plymouth A	SL	A	W	3-2	Swann, Roberts, Smith
		3	22.2.08	Grimsby T	D2	A	L	0-1	
1908-09	SL	1	16.1.09	Wolverhampton W	D2	A	D	2-2	Bauchop 2
		1r	21.1.09	Wolverhampton W		H	W	4-2aet	Garratt, Lawrence, Bauchop, Needham
		2	6.2.09	Burnley	D2	H	D	0-0	
		2r	10.2.09	Burnley		A	L	0-9	
1909-10	SL	1	15.1.10	Swindon T	SL	H	L	1-3	Payne
1910-11	SL	1	14.1.11	Everton	D1	H	L	0-4	
1911-12	SL	1	13.1.12	Brentford	SL	A	D	0-0	
		1r	17.1.12	Brentford		H	W	4-0	Smith, Hewitt, Hanger, Harker
		2	3.2.12	Sunderland	D1	H	D	0-0	
		2r	7.2.12	Sunderland		A	L	0-1	
1912-13	SL	1	11.1.13	Glossop NE	D2	H	W	2-0	Smith, Williams
		2	1.2.13	Bury	D2	H	W	2-0	Smith, Davies

	3	22.2.13	Aston Villa	D1	A	L	0-5	
1913-14 SL	1	10.1.14	Norwich C	SL	H	W	2-1	Hewitt, Smith
	2	31.1.14	West Ham	SL	A	L	0-2	
1914-15 SL	1	9.1.15	Birmingham		A	D	2-2	Davies, Middleton
	1r	16.1.15	Birmingham at St Andrews		A	L	0-3	
1919-20 SL	1	10.1.20	Newcastle U	D1	A	L	0-2	
1920-21 D3	1	8.1.21	Manchester C	D1	H	W	2-0	Menlove, Bateman
	2	29.1.21	Hull C	D2	H	L	0-2	
1921-22 D2	1	7.1.22	Everton	D1	A	W	6-0	Conner 2, Menlove 2, Whibley, Wood
	2	28.1.22	Millwall Ath	3S	H	D	0-0	
	2r	1.2.22	Millwall Ath		A	L	0-2	
1922-23 D2	1	13.1.23	QPR	3S	A	L	0-1	
1923-24 D2	1	12.1.24	Tottenham H	D1	H	W	2-0	Morgan 2
	2	2.2.24	Notts Co	D1	H	D	0-0	
	2r	6.2.24	Notts Co		A	D	0-0aet	
	2 2r	10.2.24	Notts Co at Villa Park			D	0-0aet	
	2 3r	18.2.24	Notts Co at Villa Park			W	2-1	Hoddinott, Hand
	3	23.2.24	Swindon T	3S	H	L	1-2	Whitworth
1924-25 D2	1	10.1.25	South Shields	D2	H	W	2-1	Blakemore, Whitworth
	2	31.1.25	Hull C	D2	A	L	2-3	Hoddinott, Groves
1925-26 3S	3	9.1.26	Northampton T	3S	A	D	3-3	Cherrett 2, Blakemore
	3r	13.1.26	Northampton T		H	W	2-1	Cherrett 2
	4	30.1.26	Chelsea	D2	H	W	2-1	Cherrett, Hawkins
	5	20.2.26	Manchester C	D1	A	L	4-11	Cherrett 2, Clarke, McCracken
1926-27 3S	1	27.11.26	Norwich C	3S	H	D	0-0	
	1r	2.12.26	Norwich C		A	L	0-1	
1927-28 3S	1	26.11.27	Dartford	SL	A	W	3-1	Hopkins 2, Smith
	2	10.12.27	Swindon T	3S	A	D	0-0	
	2r	14.12.27	Swindon T		H	L	1-2	Hopkins
1928-29 3S	1	24.11.28	Kettering T	SL	H	W	2-0	Butler, Clarke
	2	8.12.28	Bristol R	3S	H	W	3-1	Harry, Charlton, Havelock
	3	12.1.29	Luton T	3S	A	D	0-0	
	3r	16.1.29	Luton T		H	W	7-0	Havelock 3, Wilde, Griffith, Butler, Hamilton
	4	26.1.29	Millwall	D2	A	D	0-0	
	4r	30.1.29	Millwall		H	W	5-3	Butler 3, Griffiths, Harry
	5	16.2.29	Huddersfield T	D1	A	L	2-5	Griffiths, Charlton (p)
1929-30 3S	3	11.1.30	Leeds U	D1	A	L	1-8	Simpson
1930-31 3S	1	29.11.30	Taunton T	WL	H	W	6-0	Simpson 3, Clarke, Greener, Butler
	2	13.12.30	Newark T	ML	H	W	6-0	Simpson 4, Butler, Clarke
	3	10.1.31	Reading	D2	H	D	1-1	Butler
	3r	14.1.31	Reading		A	D	1-1aet	Clarke
	3 2r	19.1.31	Reading at Stamford Bridge			W	2-0	Clarke, Simpson
	4	24.1.31	Everton	D2	H	L	0-6	
1931-32 3S	1	28.11.31	Reading	3S	A	W	1-0	Clarke
	2	12.12.31	Bath C	SL	A	L	1-2	Simpson
1932-33 3S	1	26.11.32	Brighton & HA	3S	H	L	1-2	Simpson
1933-34 3S	1	25.11.33	Norwich C	3S	H	W	3-0	Roberts, Manders, Turner
	2	9.12.33	Stockport Co	3N	A	W	2-1	Simpson, Manders
	3	13.1.33	Aldershot	3S	H	W	1-0	Manders
	4	27.1.33	Arsenal	D1	A	L	0-7	
1934-35 3S	1	28.11.34	Yeovil	SL	A	L	0-3	
1935-36 3S	1	30.11.35	Bristol C	3S	A	W	1-0	Dawes
	2	14.12.35	Margate	SL	A	L	1-3	Blackman
1936-37 3S	1	28.11.36	Southend U	3S	H	D	1-1	Birtley
	1r	2.12.36	Southend U		A	L	0-2	
1937-38 3S	1	27.11.37	Kettering T	UCL	H	D	2-2	Gillespie, Davies
	1r	2.12.37	Kettering T		A	W	4-0	Pritchard 2, Blackman, Waldron
	2	11.12.37	Accrington S	3N	A	W	1-0	Owens
	3	8.1.38	Liverpool	D1	H	D	0-0	
	3r	12.1.38	Liverpool		A	L	1-3aet	Waldron
1938-39 3S	1	26.11.38	QPR	3S	H	D	1-1	Blackman
	1r	28.11.38	QPR		A	L	0-3	
1945-46 3S	3 1L	5.1.46	QPR	3S	A	D	0-0	
	3 2L	9.1.46	QPR		H	D	0-0aet	
	3r	16.1.46	QPR at Fulham			L	0-1	
1946-47 3S	3	11.1.47	Newcastle U	D2	A	L	2-6	Naylor 2
1947-48 3S	1	29.11.47	Port Vale	3S	H	W	2-1	Farrington, Clough

Season	Div	Rd	Date	Opponent	Opp Div	Venue	Result	Score	Scorers
		2	13.12.47	Bristol C	3S	A	W	1-0aet	Robson
		3	10.1.48	Chester	3N	H	L	0-1	
1948-49	3S	1	27.11.48	Bristol C	3S	H	L	0-1aet	
1949-50	3S	1	26.11.49	Newport Co	3S	A	L	0-3	
1950-51	3S	1	25.11.50	Millwall	3S	H	–	0-0	
				abandoned after 34 minutes – fog					
		1	29.11.50	Millwall		H	L	1-4	Kelly
1951-52	3S	1	24.11.51	Gillingham	3S	H	L	0-1	
1952-53	3S	1	22.11.52	Reading	3S	H	D	1-1	Rainford
		1r	26.11.52	Reading		A	W	3-1	Fell 2, Rainford
		2	6.12.52	Finchley	AL	A	–	1-3	Burgess
				abandoned after 61 minutes – fog					
		2	10.12.52	Finchley		A	L	1-3	Thomas
1953-54	3S	1	21.11.53	Great Yarmouth	ECL	A	L	0-1	
1954-55	3S	1	20.11.54	Swindon T	3S	A	W	2-0	Hanlon, Randall
		2	11.12.54	Bishop Auckland	NL	H	L	2-4	Choules, Thomas
1955-56	3S	1	19.11.55	Southampton	3S	H	D	0-0	
		1r	23.11.55	Southampton		A	L	0-2	
1956-57	3S	1	17.11.56	Walthamstow A	IL	H	W	2-0	Murray, Cooper
		2	8.12.56	Brentford	3S	A	D	1-1	Pierce
		2r	12.12.56	Brentford		H	W	3-2aet	Pierce 3
		3	5.1.57	Millwall	3S	A	L	0-2	
1957-58	3S	1	16.11.57	Margate	KL	A	W	3-2	Deakin 3
		2	7.12.57	Southampton	3S	H	W	1-0	Berry
		3	4.1.58	Ipswich T	D2	H	L	0-1	
1958-59	D4	1	15.11.58	Ashford T	KL	A	W	1-0	Collins
		2	6.12.58	Shrewsbury T	D4	H	D	2-2	Deakin 2
		2r	11.12.58	Shrewsbury T		A	D	2-2aet	Byrne 2
		2 2r	15.12.58	Shrewsbury T at Molineux			W	4-1	Collins, Byrne, Deakin
		3	10.1.59	Sheffield U	D2	A	L	0-2	
1959-60	D4	1	14.11.59	Chelmsford C	SL	H	W	5-1	Byrne 3, Woan, Sexton
		2	5.12.59	Margate	SL	A	D	0-0	
		2r	9.12.59	Margate		H	W	3-0	Roche 2, Woan
		3	9.1.60	Scunthorpe U	D2	A	L	0-1	
1960-61	D4	1	5.11.60	Hitchin	AL	H	W	6-2	Gavin 2, Uphill 2, Byrne, Heckman
		2	26.11.60	Watford	D3	H	D	0-0	
		2r	29.11.60	Watford		A	L	0-1	
1961-62	D3	1	4.11.61	Portsmouth	D3	H	W	3-0	Heckman 2, Byrne
		2	25.11.61	Bridgewater T	WL	A	W	3-0	Heckman 2, Smillie
		3	6.1.61	Aston Villa	D1	A	L	3-4	Byrne 2, Uphill
1962-63	D3	1	3.11.62	Hereford U	SL	H	W	2-0	Wood, Werge
		2	24.11.62	Mansfield T	D4	H	D	2-2	Burridge, Allen (p)
		2r	26.11.62	Mansfield T		A	L	2-7	Summersby, Phillips og
1963-64	D3	1	16.11.63	Harwich & P	ECL	H	W	8-2	Holton 3, Allen 2, Burridge, Sewell, Howe
		2	7.12.63	Yeovil T	SL	A	L	1-3	Wood
1964-65	D2	3	9.1.65	Bury	D2	H	W	5-1	Holton 3, Burnside, Wood
		4	30.1.65	Southampton	D2	A	W	2-1	Holton, Smith
		5	20.2.65	Nottingham F	D1	H	W	3-1	Burnside, Burridge, Holton
		6	10.3.65	Leeds U	D1	H	L	0-3	
1965-66	D2	3	22.1.66	Carlisle U	D2	A	L	0-3	
1966-67	D2	3	28.1.67	Leeds U	D1	A	L	0-3	
1967-68	D2	3	27.1.68	Walsall	D3	A	D	1-1	White
		3r	31.1.68	Walsall		H	L	1-2	Byrne
1968-69	D2	3	4.1.69	Charlton A	D2	A	D	0-0	
		3r	8.1.69	Charlton A		H	D	0-2	
1969-70	D1	3	3.1.70	Walsall	D3	H	W	2-0	Gregg og, Blyth
		4	24.1.70	Tottenham H	D1	A	D	0-0	
		4r	28.1.70	Tottenham H		H	W	1-0	Queen
		5	7.2.70	Chelsea	D1	H	L	1-4	Hoy
1970-71	D1	3	2.1.71	Chelsea	D1	H	D	2-2	McCormick, Birchenall
		3r	6.1.71	Chelsea		A	L	0-2	
1971-72	D1	3	15.1.72	Everton	D1	H	D	2-2	Wallace 2
		3r	18.1.72	Everton		A	L	2-3	Tambling 2
1972-73	D1	3	13.1.73	Southampton	D1	H	W	2-0	Rogers, Cooke
		4	3.2.73	Sheffield W	D2	A	D	1-1	Craven
		4r	6.2.73	Sheffield W		H	D	1-1aet	Phillip
		4 2r	19.2.73	Sheffield W at Villa Park			L	2-3aet	Payne, Rogers

CRYSTAL PALACE

Season	Div	Round	Date	Opponent	Opp Div	H/A	Result	Score	Scorers
1973-74	D2	3	5.1.74	Wrexham	D3	H	L	0-2	
1974-75	D3	1	27.11.74	Tooting & Mitcham	IL	A	W	2-1	P.Hinshelwood, Whittle
		2	14.12.74	Plymouth A	D3	A	L	1-2	Swindlehurst
1975-76	D3	1	22.11.75	Walton & Hersham	IL	H	W	1-0	Kemp
		2	13.12.75	Millwall	D3	A	D	1-1	Swindlehurst
		2r	16.12.75	Millwall		H	W	2-1	Kemp, Taylor (p)
		3	3.1.76	Scarborough	NPL	A	W	2-1	Taylor, Evans
		4	24.1.76	Leeds U	D1	A	W	1-0	Swindlehurst
		5	14.2.76	Chelsea	D2	A	W	3-2	Taylor 2, Chatterton
		6	6.3.76	Sunderland	D2	A	W	1-0	Whittle
		SF	3.4.76	Southampton	D2		L	0-2	
				played at Stamford Bridge					
1976-77	D3	1	20.11.76	Brighton & HA	D3	A	D	2-2	Evans, Harkouk
		1r	23.11.76	Brighton & HA		H	D	1-1aet	Harkouk
		1 2r	6.12.76	Brighton & HA at Stamford Bridge			W	1-0	Holder
		2	11.12.76	Enfield	IL	H	W	4-0	Swindlehurst 2, Silkman, P.Hinshelwood
		3	8.1.77	Liverpool	D1	A	D	0-0	
		3r	11.1.77	Liverpool		H	L	2-3	P.Hinshelwood, Graham
1977-78	D2	3	2.1.78	Hartlepool U	D4	A	L	1-2	Chatterton
1978-79	D2	3	9.1.79	Middlesbrough	D1	A	D	1-1	Walsh
		3r	15.1.79	Middlesbrough		H	W	1-0	Sansom
		4	29.1.79	Bristol C	D1	H	W	3-0	Nicholas, Fenwick, Kember
		5	26.2.79	Wolverhampton W	D1	H	L	0-1	
1979-80	D1	3	5.1.80	Swansea C	D3	A	D	2-2	Kember, Walsh
		3r	8.1.80	Swansea C		H	D	3-3aet	Hinshelwood, Fenwick, Hilaire
		3 2r	14.1.80	Swansea C at Ninian Park			L	1-2	Boyle
1980-81	D1	3	3.1.81	Manchester C	D1	A	L	0-4	
1981-82	D2	3	2.1.82	Enfield	APL	A	W	3-2	Hilaire 2, Price
		4	23.1.82	Bolton W	D2	H	W	1-0	Cannon (p)
		5	13.2.82	Orient	D2	H	D	0-0	
		5r	16.2.82	Orient		A	W	1-0	Smillie
		6	6.3.82	QPR	D2	A	L	0-1	
1982-83	D2	3	8.1.83	York C	D4	H	W	2-1	Lovell, Langley
		4	29.1.83	Birmingham C	D1	H	W	1-0	Edwards
		5	19.2.83	Burnley	D2	H	D	0-0	
		5r	28.2.83	Burnley		A	L	0-1	
1983-84	D2	3	7.1.84	Leicester C	D1	H	W	1-0	Gilbert
		4	28.1.84	West Ham	D1	H	D	1-1	McCulloch
		4r	31.1.84	West Ham		A	L	0-2	
1984-85	D2	3	5.1.85	Millwall	D3	A	D	1-1	Mahoney
		3r	23.1.85	Millwall		H	L	1-2	Aylott
1985-86	D2	3	6.1.86	Luton T	D1	H	L	1-2	Taylor
1986-87	D2	3	11.1.87	Nottingham F	D1	H	W	1-0	Irvine
		4	31.1.87	Tottenham H	D1	A	L	0-4	
1987-88	D2	3	9.1.88	Newcastle U	D1	A	L	0-1	
1988-89	D2	3	7.1.89	Stoke C	D2	A	L	0-1	
1989-90	D1	3	6.1.90	Portsmouth	D2	H	W	2-1	Thomas, Gray (p)
		4	27.1.90	Huddersfield T	D3	H	W	4-0	Bright 2, Hopkins, Salako
		5	17.2.90	Rochdale	D4	H	W	1-0	Barber
		6	10.3.90	Cambridge U	D4	H	W	1-0	Thomas
		SF	8.4.90	Liverpool	D1		W	4-3aet	Bright, O'Reilly, Gray, Pardew
				played at Villa Park					
		F	12.5.90	Manchester U	D1 WEMBLEY		D	3-3aet	Wright 2, O'Reilly
		F	17.5.90	Manchester U	WEMBLEY		L	0-1	
1990-91	D1	3	6.1.91	Nottingham F	D1	H	D	0-0	
		3r	21.1.91	Nottingham F		A	D	2-2aet	Wright, Salako
		3 2r	28.1.91	Nottingham F		A	L	0-3	
1991-92	D1	3	4.1.92	Leicester C	D2	A	L	0-1	
1992-93	PL	3	2.1.93	Hartlepool U	D2	A	L	0-1	

DAGENHAM

Formed 1949. **First entered FA Cup:** 1952. **FA Amateur Cup Runners-up:** 1970, 1971 **FA Challenge Trophy Winners:** 1980; **Runners-up:** 1977. Merged with Redbridge Forest to form Dagenham and Redbridge, 1992. See also Ilford, Leytonstone. Note Redbridge Forest never reached the FA Cup proper. **League Club beaten:** Cambridge United

Season	Div	Round	Date	Opponent	Opp Div	H/A	Result	Score	Scorers
1967-68	AL	1	9.12.67	Tonbridge	SL	H	W	1-0	Greene

		2	6.1.68	**Reading**	D3	A	D	1-1	Morris
		2r	15.1.68	**Reading**		H	L	0-1	
1969-70	AL	1	15.11.69	**Sutton U**	IL	H	L	0-1	
1970-71	AL	1	21.11.70	**Margate**	SL	H	W	2-0	Dear, Smith
		2	12.12.70	**Southend U**	D4	A	L	0-1	
1971-72	AL	1	20.11.71	**Walsall**	D3	A	L	1-4	Moore
1973-74	IL	1	24.11.73	**Aldershot**	D3	H	L	0-4	
1977-78	IL	1	26.11.77	**Walsall**	D3	A	L	0-1	
1978-79	IL	1	25.11.78	**Watford**	D3	A	L	0-3	
1980-81	IL	1	22.11.80	**Gillingham**	D3	A	L	1-2	Kidd
1981-82	APL	1	21.11.81	**Yeovil T**	APL	H	D	2-2	Burton 2
		1r	25.11.81	**Yeovil T**		A	W	1-0aet	Stewart
		2	30.12.81	**Millwall**	D3	H	L	1-2	Stein
1982-83	APL	1	20.11.82	**Gillingham**	D3	A	L	0-1	
1983-84	APL	1	19.11.83	**Brentford**	D3	H	D	2-2	Dunwell, Smith
		1	22.11.83	**Brentford**		A	L	1-2	Rhoden
1984-85	APL	1	19.11.84	**Swindon T**	D4	H	D	0-0	
1985-86	APL	1	16.11.85	**Cambridge U**	D4	H	W	2-1	Sullivan, Scott
		2	7.12.85	**Bournemouth**	D3	A	L	1-4	Cox
1987-88	GMVC	1	14.11.87	**Maidstone U**	GMVC	H	L	0-2	
1988-89	IL	1	19.11.88	**Sutton U**	GMVC	H	L	0-4	
as Dagenham and Redbridge									
1992-93	GMVC	1	14.11.92	**Leyton O**	D2	H	L	4-5	Broom, Conner, Butterworth, Cavell

DAGENHAM TOWN

First entered FA Cup: 1929. A separate club from Dagenham FC – folded before Second World War

1929-30	Lon	1	30.11.29	**Barry T**	SL	A	D	0-0
		1r	4.12.29	**Barry T**		H	L	0-1
			played at Upton Park					

DARLINGTON

Formed 1883. **GM Vauxhall Conference Champions** 1990. **FA Cup Best Performance:** 5th round, 1958. **FA Cup Record Win:** 13-1 vs Scarborough, 2nd qual rd, 24.10.1891. In competition proper: 7-2 vs Evenwood Town, 1st round, 17.11.1956. **FA Cup Record Defeat:** 0-8 vs Grimsby T, 2nd round, 21.11.1885

1885-86		1		**bye**					
		2	21.11.85	**Grimsby T**		A	L	0-8	
1886-87		1	30.10.86	**Horncastle**		A	L	0-2	
1887-88		1	15.10.87	**Gateshead**		A	W	3-0	Brooks, H.Hope, Stabler
		2	5.11.87	**Elswick Rangers**		H	W	4-3aet	Rogers, 3 others
		3	26.11.87	**Shankhouse**		H	L	0-2	
1888-89		1q **Birtley** (A) 0-2aet
1889-90	NL	1q **Darlington St Augustines** (A) 0-5
1890-91	NL	2q **Darlington West End**, walkover; 3q **Middlesbrough** (A) 0-2 *Middlesbrough disqualified for playing ineligible player*; 4q **Middlesbrough Ironopolis** (A) 0-6; *FA ordered replay after protest*; 4qr **Middlesbrough Ironopolis** (A) 0-3
1891-92	NL	1q **Port Clarence** (H) 3-0; 2q **Scarborough** (H) 13-1; 3q **Leeds Albion**, walkover; 4q **Middlesbrough Ironopolis** (H) 0-3
1892-93	NL	1q **Scarborough** walkover; 2q **Darlington St Augustines** (H) 5-1; 3q **Hurworth**, walkover; 4q **Stockton** (H) 1-5
1893-94	NL	1q **Willington A** (A) 0-1
1894-95	NL	1q **Darlington St Augustines** (H) 7-0; 2q **Stockton** (H) 2-0; 3q **Middlesbrough** (H) 0-1
1895-96	NL	P **Tow Law T** (A) 1-3
1896-97	NL	3q **Blyth S** (H) 7-1; 4q **Stockton** (H) 1-3
1897-98	NL	3q **Stockton** (A) 0-3
1898-99	NL	3q **Bishop Auckland** (A) 1-4
1899-00	NL	P **Tow Law T** (H) 2-0; 1q **Crook T** (A) 1-1; 1qr **Crook T** (H) 2-3
1900-01	NL	P **Tow Law T** (H) 3-0; 1q **Darlington St Augustines** (A) 1-1; 1qr **Darlington St Augustines** (H) 4-1; 2q **Bishop Auckland** (A) 0-3
1901-02	NL	P **Leadgate Park** (A) 0-3
1902-03	NL	P **Leadgate Park** (A) 5-0; 1q **Tow Law T** (A) 1-1; 1qr **Tow Law T** (H) 1-2
1903-04	NL	1q **Darlington St Augustines** (H) 7-3; 2q **Bishop Auckland** (H) 5-2; 3q **Sunderland Royal** (A) 2-4
1904-05	NL	3q **Morpeth Harriers** (A) 6-0; 4q **Bishop Auckland** (A) 1-3
1905-06	NL	4q **Bradford C** (H) 0-4
1906-07	NL	P **Eldon Albion** (H) 2-1; 1q **South Bank** (A) 0-6
1907-08	NL	1q **South Bank** (H) 2-0; 2q **Darlington St Augustines** (A) 2-0; 3q **Skinningrove U** (H) 6-0; 4q **Carlisle U** (A) 0-7
1908-09	NEL	1q **Scarborough** (H) 3-2; 2q **West Hartlepool Exp** (H) 4-0; 3q **South Bank** (A) 0-1
1909-10	NEL	P **Horden Athletic** (A) 1-1; Pr **Horden Athletic** (H) 2-0; 1q **West Hartlepool Exp** (H) 2-1; 2q **Hartlepools U** (H) 1-0; 3q **South Bank** (A) 2-3

1910-11	NEL	1q Hartlepools U (H) 1-1; 1qr Hartlepools U (A) 1-0; 2q Wingate Albion (H) 1-1; 2qr Wingate Albion (H) 3-3;					
		2q 2r Wingate Albion (H) 2-1; 3q Bishop Auckland (H) 2-0; 4q Shildon (H) 5-3; 5q Blackwell Colliery (A) 6-1					
		1	14.1.11	Sheffield U	D1	A	W	1-0	Fraser
		2	4.2.11	Bradford PA	D2	H	W	2-1	Curnock, Dodds
		3	25.2.11	Swindon T	SL	H	L	0-3	
1911-12	NEL	4q Shildon (H) 6-0; 5q North Shields (A) 2-1					
		1	13.1.12	Brighton & HA	SL	H	W	2-1	Donnelly, Fraser
		2	3.2.12	Northampton T	SL	H	D	1-1	Donnelly
		2r	8.2.12	Northampton T		A	L	0-2	
1912-13	NEL	4q North Shields (H) 0-0; 4qr North Shields (A) 4-0; 5q Rochdale (A) 1-1; 5qr Rochdale (H) 0-1					
1913-14	NEL	4q Stockton (H) 4-1; 5q Port Vale (A) 2-2; 5qr Port Vale (H) 1-2 abnd; 5qr Port Vale 1-2 (at Sheffield)					
1914-15	NEL	4q South Bank (A) 4-0; 5q Sunderland Rovers (A) 1-1; 5qr Sunderland R (H) 3-0; 6q London Caledonians (A) 1-0					
		1	9.1.15	Bradford C	D1	H	L	0-1	
1919-20	NEL	4q South Bank (H) 4-2; 5q Bishop Auckland (H) 9-2; 6q Norwich C (H) 5-0					
		1	14.1.20	Sheffield W	D1	H	D	0-0	
		1r	19.1.20	Sheffield W		A	W	2-0	Stevens, Healey
		2	31.1.20	Birmingham	D2	A	L	0-4	
1920-21	NEL	6q Blyth Spartans (H) 4-0					
		1	8.1.21	Blackpool	D2	H	D	2-2	Healey 2
		1r	12.1.21	Blackpool		A	L	1-2	Travis
1921-22	3N	5q Durham C (A) 2-0; 6q Merthyr Town (A) 0-0; 6qr Merthyr T (H) 1-0					
		1	7.1.22	Manchester C	D1	A	L	1-3	Healey
1922-23	3N	5q Bishop Auckland (A) 2-1; 6q Charlton A (A) 1-2					
1923-24	3N	5q Leadgate Park (A) 1-1; 5qr Leadgate Park (H) 1-0; 6q Southport (H) 3-0					
		1	12.1.24	Wolverhampton W	3N	A	L	1-3	Hooper
1924-25	3N	5q Durham C (H) 3-1; 6q Reading (A) 1-0					
		1	10.1.25	Cardiff C	D1	A	D	0-0	
		1r	14.1.25	Cardiff C		H	D	0-0aet	
		1 2r	19.1.25	Cardiff C at Anfield			L	0-2	
1925-26	D2	1	28.11.25	Horden A	Wear	A	W	3-2	Brown 2, Jackson
		2	12.12.25	New Brighton	3N	A	L	0-2	
1926-27	D2	3	8.1.27	Rhyl	Welsh	H	W	2-1	Little, Ruddy
		4	29.1.27	Cardiff C	D1	H	L	0-2	
1927-28	3N	1	26.11.27	Chesterfield	3N	H	W	4-1	Ruddy 3, Lees
		2	10.12.27	Rochdale		H	W	2-1	Ruddy 2
		3	14.1.28	Liverpool	D1	A	L	0-1	
1928-29	3N	1	24.11.28	New Brighton	3N	H	W	3-0	Cochrane, Lees 2
		2	10.12.28	Scarborough	ML	A	D	2-2	Lowe 2
		2r	12.12.28	Scarborough		H	W	2-1	Eden, Dickson
		3	12.1.29	Bury	D1	H	L	2-6	Eden 2
1929-30	3N	1	30.11.29	Caernarfon	Welsh	A	L	2-4	Wellock 2
1930-31	3N	1	29.11.30	Southport	3N	A	L	2-4	Halliday, Vine
1931-32	3N	1	28.11.31	Walsall	3N	H	W	1-0	Wellock
		2	12.12.31	Carlisle U	3N	A	W	2-0	Hurst, Grieve
		3	9.1.32	Northampton T	3S	H	D	1-1	Mitchell
		3r	14.1.32	Northampton T		A	L	0-2	
1932-33	3N	1	26.11.32	Boston T	ML	H	W	1-0	Waugh
		2	10.12.32	Crewe A	3N	H	W	2-0	Hurst, Johnson
		3	14.1.33	QPR	3S	H	W	2-0	Hurst, Johnson
		4	28.1.33	Chesterfield	D2	H	L	0-2	
1933-34	3N	1	25.11.33	Chester	3N	A	L	1-6	Alderson
1934-35	3N	1	24.11.34	Gateshead	3N	A	W	4-1	Best 2, Edgar, Middleton
		2	8.12.34	Stockport Co	3N	A	L	2-3	Eden, Best
1935-36	3N	1	30.11.35	Accrington S	3N	H	W	4-2	Anderson, Best, Towers, Reed
		2	14.12.35	Stalybridge C	CC	A	W	1-0	Best
		3	11.1.36	Bury	D2	H	L	2-3	Reed, Alderson
1936-37	3N	1	28.11.36	Halifax T	3N	A	W	2-1	Stanger, Towers
		2	12.12.36	Burton T	ML	A	W	2-1	Brattisford, Brown
		3	16.1.37	Dartford	SL	A	W	1-0	Lowery
		4	30.1.37	WBA	D1	A	L	2-3	Brattisford 2
1937-38	3N	1	27.11.37	Scarborough	ML	H	L	0-2	
1938-39	3N	1	26.11.38	Stalybridge C	CC	H	W	4-0	Feeney 3, Birley
		2	10.12.38	Chelmsford C	SL	A	L	1-3	Alderson
1945-46	3N	1 1L	17.11.45	Stockton	NEL	H	W	2-0	Clarke 2
		1 2L	24.11.45	Stockton		A	W	4-1	Harrison 2, Towers, Sykes
		2 1L	8.12.45	Gateshead	3N	H	L	2-4	Towers, Varty
		2 2L	15.12.45	Gateshead		A	W	2-1	Harrison 2

1946-47	3N	1	30.11.46	Gainsborough T	ML	A	W	2-1	Clarke 2
		2	14.12.46	Hull C	3N	H	L	1-2	Stubbs
1947-48	3N	1	29.11.47	Hartlepools U	3N	A	L	0-1	
1948-49	3N	1	27.11.48	Tranmere R	3N	A	W	3-1	Bower 2, Quinn
		2	11.12.48	Leyton O	3S	H	W	1-0	Milner
		3	8.1.49	Rotherham U	3N	A	L	2-4	Ward 2
1949-50	3N	1	26.11.49	Crewe A	3N	H	D	2-2	Brown 2
		1r	30.11.49	Crewe A		A	L	0-1	
1950-51	3N	1	25.11.50	Rotherham U	3N	H	L	2-7	Murray, Steel
1951-52	3N	1	24.11.51	Grimsby T	3N	A	L	0-4	
1952-53	3N	1	22.11.52	Grimsby T	3N	H	L	2-3	Murray, Davison
1953-54	3N	1	21.11.53	Port Vale	3N	H	L	1-3	Robson
1954-55	3N	1	20.11.54	Barrow	3N	A	D	1-1	Davies
		1r	24.11.54	Barrow		H	W	2-1	Davis, Spuhler
		2	11.12.54	Walthamstow Ave	IL	A	W	3-0	Spuhler, Dunlop Furphy
		3	8.1.55	Hartlepools U	3N	A	D	1-1	Houlahan
		3r	12.1.55	Hartlepools U		H	D	2-2aet	Walsh, Houlahan
		3 2r	17.1.55	Hartlepools U at Ayresome Park			L	0-2	
1955-56	3N	1	19.11.55	Carlisle U	3N	H	D	0-0	
		1r	22.11.55	Carlisle U		A	D	0-0aet	
		1 2r	28.11.55	Carlisle U at St James's Park			W	3-1	Rutherford, Bell, Furphy
		2	10.12.55	Accrington S	3N	H	L	0-1	
1956-57	3N	1	17.11.56	Evenwood T	NL	H	W	7-2	Bell, Morton 3, Forster, Tulip 2
		2	8.12.56	Carlisle U	3N	A	L	1-2	Davis
1957-58	3N	1	16.11.57	Rochdale	3N	A	W	2-0	Harbertson 2
		2	7.12.57	Boston U	ML	A	W	5-3	Harbertson 2 (1p), Carr 3
		3	4.1.58	Norwich C	3S	A	W	2-1	Harbetson, Moran
		4	25.1.58	Chelsea	D1	A	D	3-3	Harbertson, Carr, Morton
		4r	29.1.58	Chelsea		H	W	4-1	Harbertson, Carr, Moran 2
		5	15.2.58	Wolverhampton W	D1	A	L	1-6	Bell
1958-59	D4	1	15.11.58	Wrexham	D3	A	W	2-1	McGrath 2
		2	6.12.58	Halifax T	D3	A	D	1-1	McGrath
		2r	10.12.58	Halifax T		H	W	3-0	Morton, Carr, Bell
		3	10.1.59	Accrington S	D3	A	L	0-3	
1959-60	D4	1	14.11.59	Prescot Cables	LC	H	W	4-0	Fletcher og, Redfearn, Poole, Morton
		2	5.12.59	Doncaster R	D4	A	L	2-3	Milner, Carr
1960-61	D4	1	5.11.60	Grimsby T	D3	H	W	2-0	Robson 2
		2	26.11.60	Hull C	D3	H	D	1-1	Baxter
		2r	28.11.60	Hull C		A	D	1-1aet	Baxter
		2 2r	5.12.60	Hull C at Elland Road		–		1-1	Rayment
				match abandoned at 90 minutes – ground unfit					
		2 3r	12.12.60	Hull C at Doncaster			D	0-0 aet	
		2 4r	15.12.60	Hull C at Middlesbrough			L	0-3	
1961-62	D4	1	4.11.61	Carlisle U	D4	H	L	0-4	
1962-63	D4	1	3.11.62	Lincoln C	D4	A	D	1-1	Lawton
		1r	7.11.62	Lincoln C		H	L	1-2	Lawton
1963-64	D4	1	16.11.63	Gateshead	NRL	H	L	1-4	Lawton
1964-65	D4	1	14.11.64	Scunthorpe U	D3	A	W	2-1	Lawton, Burlison
		2	5.12.64	Hartlepools U	D4	A	D	0-0	
		2r	9.12.64	Hartlepools U		H	W	4-1	Lawton 2, Maltby 2 (1p)
		3	9.1.65	Arsenal	D1	H	L	0-2	
1965-66	D4	1	13.11.65	Bradford C	D4	H	W	3-2	Cummings, Greener, Conlon
		2	4.12.65	Oldham A	D3	H	L	0-1	
1966-67	D3	1	26.11.66	Stockport Co	D4	H	D	0-0	
		1r	29.11.66	Stockport Co		A	D	1-1aet	Hellawell
		1 2r	5.12.66	Stockport Co at Elland Road			W	4-2	Conlon 2, Fidler, Hellawell
		2	7.1.67	Crewe A	D4	A	L	1-2	Ratcliffe
1967-68	D4	1	13.12.67	Shrewsbury T	D3	A	L	0-3	
1968-69	D4	1	16.11.68	Grimsby T	D4	H	W	2-0	Hale, Robson
		2	7.12.68	Barnsley	D3	H	D	0-0	
		2r	10.12.68	Barnsley		A	L	0-1	
1969-70	D4	1	15.11.69	Barnsley	D3	H	D	0-0	
		1r	18.11.69	Barnsley		A	L	0-2	
1970-71	D4	1	21.11.70	Bangor	NPL	H	W	5-1	Graham, Hale, Gauden 2, Harding
		2	12.12.70	Rochdale	D3	H	L	0-2	
1971-72	D4	1	20.11.71	Barrow	D4	A	W	2-0	Peddelty, Sproates
		2	11.12.71	Port Vale	D3	A	L	0-1	

Season	Div	Rd	Date	Opponent	Opp Div	H/A	Res	Score	Scorers
1972-73	D4	1	18.11.72	Wrexham	D3	H	D	1-1	Sinclair
		1r	21.11.72	Wrexham		A	L	0-5	
1973-74	D4	1	24.11.73	Scunthorpe U	D4	A	L	0-1	
1974-75	D4	1	23.11.74	Workington	D4	H	W	1-0	Sinclair
		2	14.12.74	Blackburn R	D3	A	L	0-1	
1975-76	D4	1	22.11.75	Chester	D3	H	D	0-0	
		1r	26.11.75	Chester		A	L	0-2	
1976-77	D4	1	20.11.76	Scarborough	NPL	A	D	0-0	
		1r	22.11.76	Scarborough		H	W	4-1	Rowles 3, Seal
		2	15.12.76	Sheffield W	D3	H	W	1-0	Ferguson
		3	8.1.77	Orient	D2	H	D	2-2	Seal 2
		3r	11.1.77	Orient		A	D	0-0aet	
		3 2r	17.1.77	Orient at Tottenham			L	0-3	
1977-78	D4	1	26.11.77	Chester	D3	A	L	1-4	Craig
1978-79	D4	1	25.11.78	Chesterfield	D3	H	D	1-1	Ferguson
		1r	6.12.78	Chesterfield		A	W	1-0	Ferguson
		2	16.12.78	Chester	D3	H	W	2-1	Craig, Ferguson
		3	9.1.79	Colchester U	D3	H	L	0-1	
1979-80	D4	1	24.11.79	Huddersfield T	D4	H	D	1-1	Stalker
		1r	27.11.79	Huddersfield T		A	W	1-0	Stalker
		2	15.12.79	Bradford C	D4	H	L	0-1	
1980-81	D4	1	22.11.80	Bury	D4	H	L	0-2	
1981-82	D4	1	21.11.81	Carlisle U	D3	H	D	2-2	Speedie, Walsh
		1r	24.11.81	Carlisle U		A	L	1-3	Smith
1982-83	D4	1	20.11.82	Scunthorpe U	D4	H	L	0-1	
1983-84	D4	1	19.11.83	Mossley	NPL	H	W	5-0	Barton, Walsh 3, McLean
		2	10.12.83	Altrincham	APL	H	D	0-0	
		2r	14.12.83	Altrincham		A	W	2-0	Todd, Walsh
		3	7.1.84	Maidstone	APL	H	W	4-1	Davies, Walsh, Cartwright, McLean
		4	28.1.84	Plymouth A	D3	A	L	1-2	Todd
1984-85	D4	1	17.11.84	Chester C	D4	H	W	3-2	Airey 2, MacDonald
		2	8.12.84	Frickley Ath	APL	H	W	1-0	Lloyd
		3	5.1.85	Middlesbrough	D2	A	D	0-0	
		3r	8.1.85	Middlesbrough		H	W	2-1	MacDonald, Lloyd
		4	29.1.85	Telford U	APL	H	D	1-1	Forster
		4r	4.2.85	Telford U		A	L	0-3	
1985-86	D3	1	16.11.85	Rochdale	D4	A	L	1-2	Hicks og
1986-87	D3	1	16.11.86	Mansfield T	D3	H	W	2-1	Ward, Graham og
		2	6.12.86	Wigan Ath	D3	H	L	0-5	
1987-88	D4	1	14.11.87	Sunderland	D3	A	L	0-2	
1988-89	D4	1	19.11.88	Notts Co	D3	H	L	1-2	Leonard og
1989-90	GMVC	4q	28.10.89	Runcorn	GMVC	H	W	4-2	Borthwick, Corner (p), McJannet, Stephens
		1	18.11.89	Northwich Victoria	GMVC	H	W	6-2	Cork, McJannet, Corner 2, Toman, Anderson
		2	9.12.89	Halifax T	D4	H	W	3-0	Coverdale, McJannet, Borthwick
		3	6.1.90	Cambridge U	D4	A	D	0-0	
		3r	9.1.90	Cambridge U		H	L	1-3	McJannet
1990-91	D4	1	17.11.90	York C	D4	H	D	1-1	Gill
		1r	19.11.90	York C		A	L	0-1	
1991-92	D3	1	16.11.91	Chesterfield	D4	H	W	2-1	Ellison (p), Smith
		2	17.12.91	Hartlepool U	D3	H	L	1-2	Toman
1992-93	D3	1	14.11.92	Hull C	D2	H	L	1-2	Dobie

DARTFORD

Formed 1888. **First entered FA Cup:** 1896. **FA Trophy Runners-up:** 1974 **League Clubs beaten:** Cardiff City, Aldershot

Season	Div	Rd	Date	Opponent	Opp Div	H/A	Res	Score	Scorers
1927-28	SL	1	26.11.27	Crystal Palace	3S	H	L	1-3	Thomson
1932-33	SL	1	26.11.32	Yeovil & Petters U	SL	H	D	0-0	
		1r	1.12.32	Yeovil & Petters U		A	L	2-4	Hunt 2
1933-34	SL	1	25.11.33	Northfleet U	KL	A	W	2-0	Phillips, Haley
		2	9.12.33	Swindon T	3S	A	L	0-1	
1934-35	SL	1	24.11.34	Bedford T	UCL	A	W	3-2	Meads 2, Starsmore
		2	8.12.34	Bristol R	3S	H	L	0-1	
1935-36	SL	1	30.11.35	Cardiff C	3S	A	W	3-0	Harron, Mercer, Meads
		2	14.12.35	Gainsborough T	ML	H	W	4-0	Dell 3, Meads
		3	11.1.36	Derby Co	D1	A	L	2-3	Dell, Harron
1936-37	SL	1	28.11.36	Peterborough U	ML	H	W	3-0	Gardiner, Meads 2

DARTFORD

	2	12.12.36	**Shildon**	NL	A	W	3-0	Meads, Moseley 2
	3	16.1.37	**Darlington**	3N	H	L	0-1	
1937-38 SL	1	27.11.37	**Bournemouth**	3S	A	D	0-0	
	1r	1.12.37	**Bournemouth**		H	L	0-6	
1947-48 SL	1	29.11.47	**Bristol C**	3S	H	D	0-0aet	
	1r	6.12.47	**Bristol C**		A	L	2-9	Gibbons 2
1948-49 SL	1	27.11.48	**Leyton O**	3S	H	L	2-3	Viles 2
1950-51 SL	1	25.11.50	**Guildford C**	SL	A	W	5-1	Jefferies, Kelly 2, Butler, Shallcross
	2	9.12.50	**Reading**	3S	A	L	0-4	
1961-62 SL	1	4.11.61	**Exeter C**	D4	A	D	3-3	Taylor 2, White
	1r	8.11.61	**Exeter C**		H	W	2-1	Fletcher, Taylor
	2	25.11.61	**Bristol C**	D3	A	L	2-8	Fletcher, Pacey
1962-63 SL	1	3.11.62	**Yeovil T**	SL	A	L	2-3	Ripley, Pacey
1964-65 SL	1	14.11.64	**Aldershot**	D4	H	D	1-1	Sitford
	1r	17.11.64	**Aldershot**		A	L	0-1	
1965-66 SL	1	13.11.65	**Barnet**	SL	A	W	2-0	Stepney, Dennis
	2	4.12.65	**Port Vale**	D4	A	L	0-1	
1968-69 SL	1	16.11.68	**Aldershot**	D4	A	W	3-1	Sitford, Burns (p), Ripley
	2	7.12.68	**Kettering T**	SL	A	L	0-5	
1974-75 SL	1	23.11.74	**Plymouth A**	D3	H	L	2-3	Henderson 2
1975-76 SL	1	22.11.75	**Bishops Stortford**	IL	H	L	1-4	Reeves
1976-77 SL	1	20.11.76	**Tooting & Mitcham**	IL	A	L	2-4	Greenhalgh, Brown
1978-79 SL	1	25.11.78	**AP Leamington**	SL	H	L	1-2	Jones
1982-83 SL	1	20.11.82	**Worthing**	IL	A	L	1-2	Lazarus
1983-84 SL	1	19.11.83	**Millwall**	D3	A	L	1-2	Simmonds (p)
1984-85 APL	1	17.11.84	**Metropolitan Police**	IL	A	W	3-0	Burman, Cowley, Borg
	2	8.12.84	**Bournemouth**	D3	H	D	1-1	Robinson
	2r	11.12.84	**Bournemouth**		A	L	1-4	Dingwall
1985-86 APL	1	16.11.85	**Bournemouth**	D3	A	D	0-0	
	1r	19.11.85	**Bournemouth**		H	L	0-2	
1986-87 SL	1	15.11.86	**Enfield**	GMVC	H	D	1-1	Robinson
	1r	18.11.86	**Enfield**		A	L	0-3	
1988-89 SL	1	19.11.88	**Kettering T**	GMVC	A	L	1-2	Taylor (p)
1989-90 SL	1	17.11.89	**Exeter C**	D4	H	D	1-1	Hessenthaler
	1r	22.11.89	**Exeter C**		A	L	1-4	Johnson

DARWEN

Formed 1870. Reformed 1899. Currently playing in the North West Counties League. Members of Football League 1891–99

1877-78	1	7.11.77	**Manchester**		H	W	3-0	Lewis, 2 others
	2	29.12.77	**Sheffield FC**		A	L	0-1	
1878-79	1		**Manchester Birch**			walkover		
	2	7.12.78	**Eagley**		H	D	0-0	
	2r	21.12.78	**Eagley**		A	W	4-1	Love 2, Gledhill, Marshall
	3	30.1.79	**Remnants**		A	W	3-2aet	Love 2, Bury
	4	13.2.79	**Old Etonians**		A	D	5-5	Love, og, 3 others
	4r	8.3.79	**Old Etonians**		A	D	2-2aet	Clerke, Whitfield
	4 2r	15.3.79	**Old Etonians**		A	L	2-6	Marshall, F.Suter
		all three matches played at Kennington Oval						
1879-80	1	25.10.79	**Eagley**		A	W	1-0	Rostron
	2	6.12.79	**Blackburn R**		A	L	1-3	E.Suter
1880-81	1	13.11.80	**Brigg**		H	W	8-0	Rostron 3, Marshall, Moorhouse, 3 others
	2	18.12.80	**Sheffield FC**		A	W	5-1	Bury 2, Rostron, 2 others
	3		**bye**					
	4	5.2.81	**Sheffield W**		H	W	5-2	Bury 3, Rostron 2
	5	5.3.81	**Romford**		H	W	15-0	Kirkham 3, Marshall 3, Mellor 3, Rostron 3, Bury, 2 others
	SF	26.3.81	**Old Carthusians**			L	1-4	Marshall
		played at Kennington Oval						
1881-82	1	29.10.81	**Blackburn Olympic**		H	W	3-1	Bury, Rostron, Towers
	2	26.11.81	**Accrington**		H	W	3-0	Rostron 2, Marshall
	3	17.12.81	**Turton**		H	W	4-1	Kirkham, Marshall, Rostron, Towers
	4	30.1.82	**Blackburn R**		A	L	1-5	own goal
1882-83	1	21.10.82	**Blackburn Park Rd**		H	W	4-1	
	2	2.12.82	**Blackburn R**		H	W	1-0	Mellor
	3	6.1.83	**Church FC**		A	D	2-2	Ashton, Marshall
	3r	20.1.83	**Church FC**		H	L	0-2	

D A R W E N

1883-84		1	27.10.83	Church FC		H	D	2-2	
		1r	3.11.83	Church FC		A	W	1-0	
		2	1.12.83	Blackburn Olympic		H	L	1-2 aet	
1884-85		1	11.10.84	Bradshaw		H	W	11-0	Kenyon 2, Owers, 8 others
		2	22.10.84	Fishwick Ramblers		A	W	2-0	Kenyon, Walsh
		3		bye					
		4	17.1.85	Church FC		A	L	0-3	
1885-86		1	31.10.85	Junction St School, Derby		H	D	2-2	
		1r	7.11.85	Junction St School, Derby		H	W	4-0	
		2	21.11.85	Small Heath Alliance		A	L	1-3	
1886-87		1	30.10.86	Heart of Midlothian		H	W	7-1	Nightingale 4, Broughton, Rostron, Slater
		2		Astley Bridge			walkover		
		3	11.12.86	Bolton W		H	W	4-3	Rostron, 3 others
		4		bye					
		5	22.1.87	Chirk		A	W	2-1	Rostron 2
		6	12.2.87	Aston Villa		A	L	2-3	Rostron, Slater
1887-88		1	15.10.87	Rawtenstall		A	W	3-1	
		2	5.11.87	Church FC		H	W	2-0	
		3	26.11.87	Witton		H	D	1-1	Shorrock
		3r	3.12.87	Witton played at Blackburn			W	2-0	Dimmock, Shorrock
		4	17.12.87	Notts Rangers		H	W	2-1	Smith 2, Shorrock
		5	7.1.88	Blackburn R		H	L	0-3	
1890-91	FAll	1	17.1.91	Kidderminster	BDL	H	W	3-1	Marsden 2, Atkins og
			replay ordered after protest						
		1r	24.1.91	Kidderminster		H	W	13-0	Nightingale 2, Entwistle 2, Marsden, Owen, J.Smith, R.Smith, 5 others
		2	31.1.91	Sunderland	D1	H	L	0-2	
1891-92	D1	1	16.1.92	Bootle	FAll	A	W	2-0	Alexander, Wade
		2	30.1.92	Aston Villa	D1	A	L	0-2	
1892-93	D2	1	21.1.93	Aston Villa	D1	H	W	5-4	Entwistle 3, McAvoy, Sutherland
		2	4.2.93	Grimsby T	D2	H	W	2-0	Sutherland, Wade
		3	18.2.93	Wolverhampton W	D1	A	L	0-5	
1893-94	D1	1	27.1.94	Derby Co	D1	A	L	0-2	
1894-95	D2	1	2.2.95	Wolverhampton W	D1	H	D	0-0	
		1r	6.2.95	Wolverhampton W		A	L	0-2	
1895-96	D2	1	1.2.96	Grimsby T	D2	H	L	0-2	
1896-97	D2	3q	Blackpool (H) 1-0 abnd; 3q Blackpool (H) 1-2						
1897-98	D2	3q	Blackpool (H) 3-2; 4q Chorley (H) 2-2; 4qr Chorley (A) 0-0						
			4q2r Chorley 2-1 at Blackburn; 5q Wigan Co (H) 1-1; 5qr Wigan Co (A) 0-4						
1898-99	D2	3q	Wigan Co (H) 1-5						
1931-32	LC	1	28.11.31	Peterborough & Fletton	SL	H	W	4-1	Dale 2, Crompton, Quigley
		2	12.12.31	Chester	3N	H	W	2-1	Preedy 2
		3	9.1.32	Arsenal	D1	A	L	1-11	Dale
1932-33	LC	1	26.11.32	Halifax T	3N	A	L	0-2	
1933-34	LC	1	25.11.33	Gateshead	3N	A	L	2-5	Preedy, Cooper
1934-35	LC	1	24.11.34	Boston U	ML	H	L	1-2	Reid
1935-36	LC	1	30.11.35	Scarborough	ML	A	L	0-2	

LOWER DARWEN

Formed 1877. Played at Ley's Meadow, Darwen and changed at the Railway Inn

1882-83	1	28.10.82	Irwell Springs	H	W	5-2	RT Duckworth 4, Brindle
	2	9.12.82	Blackburn Olympic	A	L	1-8	Marsden
1883-84	1	31.10.83	Padiham	A	L	1-3	
1884-85	1	11.10.84	Halliwell	H	W	4-1	
	2		bye				
	3	20.12.84	Darwen Old Wanderers	H	W	4-2	
	4	24.1.85	Chatham	A	L	0-1	
1885-86	1	31.10.85	Oswaldtwistle	A	L	1-3	

DARWEN OLD WANDERERS

Formed 1879.

1884-85	1	11.10.84	Higher Walton	A	D	1-1	
	1r	8.10.84	Higher Walton	H	W	4-1	

		29.11.84	Bolton Association	H	W	7-2	
	2	20.12.84	Lower Darwen	A	L	2-4	
1885-86	3	17.10.85	Burnley	H	W	11-0	
	1		*Burnley fielded their reserves*				
	2	21.11.85	Accrington	H	W	2-1	
	3	5.12.85	Blackburn R	A	L	1-6	
1886-87	1	23.10.86	Cowlairs	H	L	1-4	
1887-88	1	15.10.87	Burnley	A	L	0-4	
			replay ordered after protest				
	1r		Burnley			*scratched*	

DARWEN RAMBLERS

Formed 1878. Played at the Hill House Ground

1882-83	1	14.10.82	South Shore	H	W	5-2	
	2	2.12.82	Haslingden	H	W	3-2	
	3	16.12.82	Blackburn Olympic	A	L	0-8	
1883-84	1	13.10.83	Blackburn Olympic	A	L	1-5	T.Kenyon
1884-85	1	1.11.84	Fishwick Ramblers	H	L	1-2	

DAVENHAM

Formed 1879. Played home matches in the grounds of Davenham School, Northwich. Welsh FA Cup runners-up 1887

1883-84	1	10.11.83	Macclesfield	H	W	2-0	
	2	24.11.83	Northwich Victoria	A	L	1-5	Earlham
1884-85	1	25.10.84	Chirk	A	L	2-4	
1885-86	1	31.10.85	Goldenhill	H	W	2-1	
	2	21.11.85	Macclesfield	H	W	8-1	
	3	12.12.85	Crewe Alex	H	W	2-1	Holland, Plant
	4		bye				
	5	16.1.86	Small Heath Alliance	H	L	1-2	Brooks
1886-87	1	30.10.86	Burslem Port Vale	H	D	1-1aet	
	1r	13.11.86	Burslem Port Vale	A	L	0-3	
1887-88	1	15.10.87	Chester	A	W	3-2aet	Stringer, 2 others
	2	5.11.87	Wrexham	A	W	2-1	Rowbottom, 1 other
	3	19.11.87	Chirk	H	D	2-2	
	3r	26.11.87	Chirk	A	L	1-6	

DENABY UNITED

Formed 1895. **First entered FA Cup:** 1900. **Cup final connection:** Sam Cowan, who played in three Cup finals for Manchester City, was a former Denaby United player

1927-28	ML	1	26.11.27	Southport	3N	H	L	2-3	Kelly 2
1932-33	ML	1	26.11.32	Carlisle U	3N	A	L	0-1	
1958-59	ML	1	15.11.58	Oldham A	D4	H	L	0-2	

DENTON

Formed 1880. Played at Chapel Green, Denton, Manchester

1887-88	1		South Shore			*scratched*

DERBY COUNTY

Formed 1884. Founder Members of the Football League 1888. **FA Cup Winners:** 1946; **Runners-up:** 1898, 1899, 1903. **Record FA Cup Win:** 8-1 vs Barnsley St Peters, 1st round, 30.1.1897. **Record FA Cup Defeat:** 2-11 vs Everton, 1st round, 18.1.1890

1884-85	1	8.11.84	Walsall T	H	L	0-7	
1885-86	1	31.10.85	Birmingham St G.	H	W	3-0	Smith, Spilsbury, Evans
	2	14.11.85	Aston Villa	H	W	2-0	Smith, Evans
	3	12.12.85	Small Heath	A	L	2-4	Evans 2
1886-87	1	30.10.86	Aston Unity	A	W	4-1	Evans 2, L.Cooper, Knox
	2	20.11.86	Birmingham St G.	A	L	1-2	Bakewell
1887-88	1	15.10.87	Staveley	A	W	2-1	Monks 2
	2	5.11.87	Ecclesfield	H	W	6-0	Spilsbury 3, Williamson, Bakewell, Needham
	3	26.11.87	Owlerton	H	W	6-2	Spilsbury 3, Needham 2, Nash

	4		bye				
	5	7.1.88	**Crewe A**		A	L	0-1
1888-89 D1	1	2.2.89	**Derby Junction**		H	W	1-0	Higgins
	2	16.2.89	**Aston Villa**	D1	A	L	3-5	Cooper 2, L.Plackett
1889-90 D1	1	18.1.90	**Everton**	D1	H	L	2-11	J.Goodall 2
1890-91 D1	1	17.1.91	**Royal Arsenal**		A	W	2-1	Cooper, McMillan
	2	31.1.91	**Sheffield W**	FAII	H	L	2-3	Bakewell, J.Goodall
1891-92 D1	1	16.1.92	**Blackburn R**	D1	A	L	1-4	Storer
1892-93 D1	1	21.1.93	**Sheffield W**	D1	A	L	2-3aet	J.Goodall, Bloomer
		FA ordered match to be replayed because of protests						
	1	30.1.93	**Sheffield W**		H	W	1-0	J.Goodall
		FA ordered match to be replayed because of protests						
	1	2.2.93	**Sheffield W**		A	L	2-4	J.Goodall, Little
1893-94 D1	1	27.1.94	**Darwen**	D1	H	W	2-0	J.Goodall, McMillan
	2	10.2.94	**Leicester F**	ML	A	D	0-0	
	2r	17.2.94	**Leicester F**		H	W	3-0	Allan, McMillan, Francis
	3	24.2.94	**Blackburn R**	D1	H	L	1-4	McMillan
1894-95 D1	1	2.2.95	**Aston Villa**	D1	A	L	1-2	J.Goodall
1895-96 D1	1	1.2.96	**Aston Villa**	D1	H	W	4-2	Bloomer 2, Miller 2
	2	15.2.96	**Newton Heath**	D2	A	D	1-1	Bloomer
	2r	19.2.96	**Newton Heath**		H	W	5-1	Miller 3, Bloomer, McQueen
	3	29.2.96	**WBA**	D1	H	W	1-0	A.Goodall
	SF	21.3.96	**Wolverhampton W**			L	1-2	Bloomer
		played at Perry Barr, Birmingham						
1896-97 D1	1	30.1.97	**Barnsley**	ML	H	W	8-1	Bloomer 3, Fisher 2, J.Goodall, A.Goodall, McQueen
	2	13.2.97	**Bolton W**	D1	H	W	4-1	Bloomer 3, Fisher
	3	27.2.97	**Newton Heath**	D2	H	W	2-0	Bloomer, McQueen
	SF	20.3.97	**Everton**	D1		L	2-3	A.Goodall, J.Goodall
		played at Stoke						
1897-98 D1	1	29.1.98	**Aston Villa**	D1	H	W	1-0	McQueen
	2	12.2.98	**Wolverhampton W**	D1	A	W	1-0	Leonard
	3	26.2.98	**Liverpool**	D1	H	D	1-1	Stevenson
	3r	2.3.98	**Liverpool**		A	W	5-1	Boag 3, Bloomer 2
	SF	19.3.98	**Everton**	D1		W	3-1	Bloomer 2, J.Goodall
		played at Molineux						
	F	16.4.98	**Nottingham F**	D1		L	1-3	Bloomer
		played at Crystal Palace						
1898-99 D1	1	28.1.99	**W.Arsenal**	D2	A	W	6-0	Bloomer 2, Boag 2, MacDonald, Allen
	2	11.2.99	**Wolverhampton W**	D1	H	W	2-1	Allen, MacDonald
	3	25.2.99	**Southampton**	SL	A	W	2-1	Bloomer, MacDonald
	SF	18.3.99	**Stoke**	D1		W	3-1	Bloomer 3
		played at Molineux						
	F	15.4.99	**Sheffield U**	D1		L	1-4	Boag
		played at Crystal Palace						
1899-00 D1	1	27.1.00	**Sunderland**	D1	H	D	2-2	A.Goodall (p), Boag
	1r	31.1.00	**Sunderland**		A	L	0-3	
1900-01 D1	1	9.2.01	**Bolton W**	D1	A	L	0-1	
1901-02 D1	1	1.2.02	**Blackburn R**	D1	A	W	2-0	Warren 2
	2	8.2.02	**Lincoln C**	D2	A	W	3-1	Warren 3
	3	22.2.02	**Portsmouth**	SL	A	D	0-0	
	3r	27.2.02	**Portsmouth**		H	W	6-3	Bloomer 3, Warren 2, Boag
	SF	15.3.02	**Sheffield U**	D1		D	1-1	Warren
		played at the Hawthorns						
	SFr	20.3.02	**Sheffield U at Molineux**			D	1-1	Wombwell
	SF2r	27.3.02	**Sheffield U**			L	0-1	
		played at the City Ground, Nottingham						
1902-03 D1	1	7.2.03	**Small Heath**	D2	H	W	2-1	Boag, Warrington
	2	21.2.03	**Blackburn R**	D1	H	W	2-0	Bloomer, Warrington
	3	7.3.03	**Stoke C**	D1	H	W	3-0	Warren, Davis, Warrington
	SF	21.3.03	**Millwall Ath**	SL		W	3-0	Warren, Boag, Richards
		played at Villa Park						
	F	18.4.03	**Bury**	D1		L	0-6	
		played at Crystal Palace						
1903-04 D1	1	6.2.04	**Portsmouth**	SL	A	W	5-2	Bloomer 2, Warren, Richards, Davis
	2	20.2.04	**Wolverhampton W**	D1	H	D	2-2	Warren 2
	2r	24.2.04	**Wolverhampton W**		A	D	2-2aet	Bloomer, Richards
	2 2r	29.2.04	**Wolverhampton W at Villa Park**			W	1-0	Bloomer

Season	Div	Rnd	Date	Opponent		H/A	Res	Score	Scorers
		3	5.3.04	Blackburn R	D1	H	W	2-1	Warrington, Bloomer
		SF	19.3.04	Bolton W	D2		L	0-1	
			played at Molineux						
1904-05	D1	1	4.2.05	Preston NE	D1	H	L	0-2	
1905-06	D1	1	13.1.06	Kettering T	UCL	H	W	4-0	J.Davis, Hall, Warren (p), Fletcher
		2	3.2.06	Newcastle U	D1	H	D	0-0	
		2r	7.2.06	Newcastle U		A	L	1-2	Orr og
1906-07	D1	1	12.1.07	Chesterfield	D2	H	D	1-1	Ransford
		1r	16.1.07	Chesterfield		A	–	2-1	Long, Ransford
			abandoned after 114 minutes because of bad light						
		1r	21.1.07	Chesterfield at Trent Bridge			W	4-0	Long, A.Wood, Bentley, Morris
		2	2.2.07	Lincoln C	D2	H	W	1-0	Bentley
		3	23.2.07	WBA	D2	A	L	0-2	
1907-08	D2	1	11.1.08	Liverpool	D1	A	L	2-4	Bentley (p), Bevan
1908-09	D2	1	16.1.09	Northampton T	SL	A	D	1-1	Bentley
		1r	20.1.09	Northampton T		H	W	4-2	Bentley 2, Davis, Thompson
		2	6.2.09	Leicester F	D1	A	W	2-0	Bentley (p), Trueman
		3	20.2.09	Plymouth A	SL	H	W	1-0	Bentley
		4	6.3.09	Nottingham F	D1	H	W	3-0	Bentley 3
		SF	27.3.09	Bristol C	D1		D	1-1	Garry
			played at Stamford Bridge						
		SFr	31.3.09	Bristol C			L	1-2	Davis
			played at St Andrews						
1909-10	D2	1	15.1.10	Millwall A	SL	H	W	5-0	Hall 2, Bentley, Davis, Barnes
		2	5.2.10	Aston Villa	D1	A	L	1-6	Bauchop
1910-11	D2	1	14.1.11	Plymouth A	SL	H	W	2-1	Bloomer, Barnes
		2	4.2.11	WBA	D2	H	W	2-0	Bauchop, Bloomer
		3	25.2.11	Everton	D1	H	W	5-0	Bloomer 2 (1p), Bentley, Barnes, Bauchop
		4	13.3.11	Newcastle U	D1	A	L	0-4	
1911-12	D2	1	13.1.12	Newcastle U		H	W	3-0	Bauchop, Richards, Leonard
		2	3.2.12	Blackburn R	D1	H	L	1-2	Bloomer (p)
1912-13	D1	1	15.1.13	Aston Villa	D1	H	L	1-3	Bloomer
1913-14	D1	1	10.1.14	Northampton T	SL	H	W	1-0	Moore
		2	31.1.14	Burnley	D1	A	L	2-3	Barnes, Waugh
1914-15	D1	1	9.1.15	Leeds C	D2	H	L	1-2	Fordham
1919-20	D1	1	10.1.20	Blackpool	D2	A	D	0-0	
		1r	14.1.20	Blackpool		H	L	1-4	Burton
1920-21	D1	1	8.1.21	Middlesbrough	D1	H	W	2-0	Murray, Burton
		2	29.1.21	Wolverhampton W	D2	H	D	1-1	Thornewell
		2r	3.2.21	Wolverhampton W		A	L	0-1	
1921-22	D2	1	7.1.22	Aston Villa	D1	A	L	1-6	Moore
1922-23	D2	1	13.1.23	Blackpool	D2	H	W	2-0	Moore, Lyons
		2	3.2.23	Bristol C	3S	A	W	3-0	Moore 2, Lyons (p)
		3	24.2.23	Sheffield W	D2	H	W	1-0	Moore
		4	10.3.23	Tottenham H	D1	A	W	1-0	Galloway
		SF	24.3.23	West Ham	D2		L	2-5	Moore, Henderson og
			played at Stamford Bridge						
1923-24	D2	1	12.1.24	Bury	D2	H	W	2-1	Murphy, Whitehouse
		2	2.2.24	Newcastle U	D1	H	D	2-2	Storer 2
		2r	6.2.24	Newcastle U		A	D	2-2aet	Galloway, Mooney og
		2 2r	11.2.24	Newcastle U at Bolton			D	2-2aet	Galloway, Thornewell
		2 3r	13.2.24	Newcastle U at Newcastle			L	3-5	Galloway 2, Storer
1924-25	D2	1	10.1.25	Bradford C	D2	H	L	0-1	
1925-26	D2	3	9.1.26	Portsmouth	D2	H	D	0-0	
		3r	13.1.26	Portsmouth		A	D	1-1aet	Bedford
		3 2r	18.1.26	Portsmouth at Filbert St			W	2-0	Thornewell, Bromage
		4	30.1.26	Southend U	3S	A	L	1-4	Murphy
1926-27	D1	3	8.1.27	Bradford C	D2	A	W	6-2	Bedford 4, Whitehouse, Murphy
		4	29.1.27	Millwall	3S	H	L	0-2	
1927-28	D1	3	14.1.28	Millwall		A	W	2-1	Stephenson, Bedford
		4	28.1.28	Nottingham F	D2	H	D	0-0	
		4r	1.2.28	Nottingham F		A	L	0-2	
1928-29	D1	3	12.1.29	Notts Co	D2	H	W	4-3	Bedford 2, Whitehouse 2
		4	26.1.29	Blackburn R	D1	A	D	1-1	Bedford
		4r	30.1.29	Blackburn R		H	L	0-3	
1929-30	D1	3	11.1.30	Bristol C	D2	H	W	5-1	Stephenson 2, Barclay 2, Bedford
		4	25.1.30	Bradford PA	D2	H	D	1-1	Barclay

	4r	29.1.30	**Bradford PA**		A	L	1-2	Ramage
1930-31	D1	3	10.1.31	**Exeter C**	3S	A	L	2-3	Bowers 2
1931-32	D1	3	9.1.32	**Burnley**	D2	A	W	4-0	Neal 2, Alderman, Crooks
	4	23.1.32	**Blackburn R**	D1	H	W	3-2	Ramage 2, Bowers
	5	13.2.32	**Manchester C**	D1	A	L	0-3	
1932-33	D1	3	14.1.33	**Wolverhampton W**	D1	A	W	6-3	Bowers 3, Duncan 2, Crooks
	4	28.1.33	**Southend U**	3S	A	W	3-2	Bowers 2, Fabian
	5	18.2.33	**Aldershot**	3S	H	W	2-0	Bowers 2
	6	4.3.33	**Sunderland**	D1	H	D	4-4	Duncan 2, Ramage, Bowers
	6r	8.3.33	**Sunderland**		A	W	1-0	Ramage
	SF	18.3.33	**Manchester C**	D1		L	2-3	Fabian, Crooks
		played at Huddersfield						
1933-34	D1	3	13.1.34	**Bristol C**	3S	A	D	1-1	Nicholas
	3r	17.1.34	**Bristol C**		H	W	1-0	Bowers
	4	27.1.34	**Wolverhampton W**	D1	H	W	3-0	Bowers 2, Crooks
	5	17.2.34	**Arsenal**	D1	A	L	0-1	
1934-35	D1	3	12.1.35	**York C**	3N	A	W	1-0	Crooks
	4	26.1.35	**Swansea T**	D2	H	W	3-0	Duncan, Groves, Gallacher
	5	16.2.35	**Everton**	D1	A	L	1-3	Crooks
1935-36	D1	3	11.1.36	**Dartford**	SL	H	W	3-2	Gallacher, Crooks, Napier
	4	25.1.36	**Nottingham F**	D2	H	W	2-0	Halford, Bowers
	5	15.2.36	**Bradford C**	D2	A	W	1-0	Bowers
	6	29.2.36	**Fulham**	D2	A	L	0-3	
1936-37	D1	3	16.1.37	**Bradford PA**	D2	A	W	4-0	Napier, Astley, Duncan, Stockill
	4	30.1.37	**Brentford**	D1	H	W	3-0	Astley 3
	5	20.2.37	**Millwall**	3S	A	L	1-2	Keen
1937-38	D1	3	8.1.38	**Stoke C**	D1	H	L	1-2	Nicholas (p)
1938-39	D1	3	7.1.39	**Everton**	D1	H	L	0-1	
1945-46	D1	3 1L	5.1.46	**Luton T**	D2	A	W	6-0	Stamps 4, Crooks, Carter
	3 2L	9.1.46	**Luton T**		H	W	3-0	Carter 2, Morrison
	4 1L	26.1.46	**WBA**	D2	H	W	1-0	Doherty
	4 2L	30.1.46	**WBA**		A	W	3-1	Carter, Stamps (p), Harrison
	5 1L	9.2.46	**Brighton & HA**	3S	A	W	4-1	Doherty 2 (1p), Carter 2
	5 2L	13.2.46	**Brighton & HA**		H	W	6-0	Carter 3, Doherty 2, Crooks
	6 1L	2.3.46	**Aston Villa**	D1	A	W	4-3	Doherty 2, Carter, Crooks
	6 2L	9.3.46	**Aston Villa**		H	D	1-1	Carter
	SF	23.3.46	**Birmingham C**	D2		D	1-1	Carter
		played at Hillsborough						
	SFr	27.3.46	**Birmingham C**			W	4-0aet	Doherty 2, Stamps 2
		played at Maine Road						
	F	27.4.46	**CHARLTON A**	D1	WEMBLEY	W	4-1aet	Stamps 2, Doherty, H.Turner og
1946-47	D1	3	11.1.47	**Bournemouth**	3S	A	W	2-0	Ward, Carter
	4	25.1.47	**Chelsea**	D1	A	D	2-2	Stamps, Carter
	4r	29.1.47	**Chelsea**		H	W	1-0	Stamps
	5	8.2.47	**Liverpool**	D1	A	L	0-1	
1947-48	D1	3	10.1.48	**Chesterfield**	D2	H	W	2-0	Stamps, Harrison
	4	24.1.48	**Crewe A**	3N	A	W	3-0	Steel 2, Harrison
	5	7.2.48	**Middlesbrough**	D1	A	W	2-1	Harrison, Stamps
	6	28.2.48	**QPR**	3S	A	D	1-1aet	Steel
	6r	6.3.48	**QPR**		H	W	5-0	Stamps 2, Carter 2, Steel
	SF	13.3.48	**Manchester U**	D1		L	1-3	Steel
		played at Hillsborough						
1948-49	D1	3	8.1.49	**Southport**	3N	H	W	4-1	Harrison 2, Powell 2
	4	29.1.49	**Arsenal**	D1	H	W	1-0	Steel
	5	12.2.49	**Cardiff C**	D2	H	W	2-1	Taft, Harrison
	6	26.2.49	**Portsmouth**	D1	A	L	1-2	Stamps
1949-50	D1	3	7.1.50	**Manchester C**	D1	A	W	5-3	Stamps 3 (1p), Steel, Powell
	4	28.1.50	**Bury**	D2	A	D	2-2	Powell, Stamps
	4r	1.2.50	**Bury**		H	W	5-2	Stamps 3, Morris, Powell
	5	11.2.50	**Northampton T**	3S	H	W	4-2	McLaren 2, Morris, Powell
	6	4.3.50	**Everton**	D1	H	L	1-2	Powell
1950-51	D1	3	6.1.51	**WBA**	D1	H	D	2-2	Stamps 2
	3r	10.1.51	**WBA**		A	W	1-0	Stamps
	4	27.1.51	**Birmingham C**	D2	H	L	1-3	Lee
1951-52	D1	3	12.1.52	**Middlesbrough**	D1	A	D	2-2	Morris, Nielson
	3r	16.1.52	**Middlesbrough**		H	L	0-2	
1952-53	D1	3	10.1.53	**Chelsea**	D1	H	D	4-4	Lee, Parry, McLachlan, McLaren

			3r	14.1.53	Chelsea		A	L	0-1	
1953-54	D2	3		9.1.54	Preston NE	D1	H	L	0-2	
1954-55	D2	3		8.1.55	Manchester C	D1	H	L	1-3	Pye
1955-56	3N	1		19.11.55	Crook T	NL	A	D	2-2	Straw, Parry
		1r		23.11.55	Crook T		H	W	5-1	Straw 2, Parry 2, Pye
		2		10.12.55	Boston U	ML	H	L	1-6	Pye (p)
1956-57	3N	1		17.11.56	Bradford C	3N	H	W	2-1	Woodhead, Powell
		2		8.12.56	New Brighton	LC	H	L	1-3	Ryan
1957-58	D2	3		4.1.58	Middlesbrough	D2	A	L	0-5	
1958-59	D2	3		10.1.59	Preston NE	D1	H	D	2-2	Parry, Darwin
		3r		19.1.59	Preston NE		A	L	2-4aet	Cargill 2 (1p)
1959-60	D2	3		9.1.60	Manchester U	D1	H	L	2-4	Thompson, Barrowcliffe (p)
1960-61	D2	3		7.1.61	Brighton & HA	D2	A	L	1-3	Thompson
1961-62	D2	3		6.1.62	Leeds U	D2	A	D	2-2	Curry, Swallow
		3r		10.1.62	Leeds U		H	W	3-1	Curry 2, Bell og
		4		27.1.62	Charlton A	D2	A	L	1-2	Curry
1962-63	D2	3		4.2.63	Peterborough U	D3	H	W	2-0	Hutchinson 2
		4		4.3.63	Leyton O	D1	A	L	0-3	
1963-64	D2	3		4.1.64	Liverpool	D1	A	L	0-5	
1964-65	D2	3		9.1.65	Plymouth A	D2	A	L	2-4	Durban, Hopkinson
1965-66	D2	3		22.1.66	Manchester U	D1	H	L	2-5	Richardson (p), Upton
1966-67	D2	3		28.1.67	Norwich C	D2	A	L	0-3	
1967-68	D2	3		27.1.68	Leeds U	D1	A	L	0-2	
1968-69	D2	3		4.1.69	Burnley	D1	A	L	1-3	Durban
1969-70	D1	3		3.1.70	Preston NE	D2	A	D	1-1	Durban
		3r		7.1.70	Preston NE		H	W	4-1	Hector 2, Durban 2
		4		24.1.70	Sheffield U	D2	H	W	3-0	O'Hare 2, Durban
		5		7.2.70	QPR	D2	A	L	0-1	
1970-71	D1	3		2.1.71	Chester	D4	A	W	2-1	Wignall, Gemmill
		4		23.1.71	Wolverhampton W	D1	H	W	2-1	Hinton (p), O'Hare
		5		13.2.71	Everton	D1	A	L	0-1	
1971-72	D1	3		15.1.72	Shrewsbury T	D3	H	W	2-0	Hector 2
		4		5.2.72	Notts Co	D3	H	W	6-0	Durban 3, Robson, Hector, Hinton (p)
		5		26.2.72	Arsenal	D1	H	D	2-2	Durban, Hinton (p)
		5r		29.2.72	Arsenal		A	D	0-0aet	
		5 2r		13.3.72	Arsenal at Filbert Street			L	0-1	
1972-73	D1	3		13.1.73	Peterborough U	D4	A	W	1-0	Davies
		4		3.2.73	Tottenham H	D1	H	D	1-1	Davies
		4r		7.2.73	Tottenham H		A	W	5-3aet	Davies 3, Hector 2
		5		24.2.73	QPR	D2	H	W	4-2	Hector 3, Davies
		6		17.3.73	Leeds U	D1	H	L	0-1	
1973-74	D1	3		5.1.74	Boston U	NPL	H	D	0-0	
		3r		9.1.74	Boston U		A	W	6-1	Gemmill 3 (1p), Bourne 2, Nash
		4		27.1.74	Coventry C	D1	A	D	0-0	
		4r		30.1.74	Coventry C		H	L	0-1aet	
1974-75	D1	3		4.1.75	Orient	D2	A	D	2-2	Todd 2
		3r		8.1.75	Orient		H	W	2-1	Lee, Rioch
		4		27.1.75	Bristol R	D2	H	W	2-0	Hector, Rioch (p)
		5		18.2.75	Leeds U	D1	H	L	0-1	
1975-76	D1	3		3.1.76	Everton	D1	H	W	2-1	George 2
		4		24.1.76	Liverpool	D1	H	W	1-0	Davies
		5		14.2.76	Southend U	D3	H	W	1-0	Rioch
		6		6.3.76	Newcastle U	D1	H	W	4-2	Rioch 2, Newton, George
		SF		3.4.76	Manchester U	D1		L	0-2	
			played at Hillsborough							
1976-77	D1	3		8.1.77	Blackpool	D2	A	D	0-0	
		3r		19.1.77	Blackpool		H	W	3-2	Hales, James, George
		4		29.1.77	Colchester U	D4	A	D	1-1	Hales
		4r		2.2.77	Colchester U		H	W	1-0	James
		5		26.2.77	Blackburn R	D2	H	W	3-1	George 2 (1p), Hector
		6		19.3.77	Everton	D1	A	L	0-2	
1977-78	D1	3		7.1.78	Southend U	D4	H	W	3-2	Masson, Ryan, Young og
		4		1.2.78	Birmingham C	D1	H	W	2-1	Daly, Masson
		5		22.2.78	WBA	D1	H	L	2-3	Rioch 2
1978-79	D1	3		16.1.79	Preston NE	D2	A	L	0-3	
1979-80	D1	3		5.1.80	Bristol C	D1	A	L	2-6	Davies, Daly
1980-81	D2	3		3.1.81	Bristol C	D2	H	D	0-0	

DERBY COUNTY

	3r	7.1.81	Bristol C		A	L	0-2	
1981-82 D2	3	2.1.82	Bolton W	D2	A	L	1-3	B.Powell
1982-83 D2	3	8.1.83	Nottingham F	D1	H	W	2-0	Gemmill, Hill
	4	29.1.83	Chelsea	D2	H	W	2-1	Wilson 2
	5	19.2.83	Manchester U	D1	H	L	0-1	
1983-84 D2	3	7.1.84	Cambridge U	D2	A	W	3-0	Wilson, Plummer, McAlle
	4	1.2.84	Telford U	APL	H	W	3-2	Davison 3
	5	18.2.84	Norwich C	D1	H	W	2-1	Gemmill (p), Davison
	6	10.3.84	Plymouth A	D3	A	D	0-0	
	6r	14.3.84	Plymouth A		H	L	0-1	
1984-85 D3	1	17.11.84	Hartlepool U	D4	A	L	1-2	Buckley (p)
1985-86 D3	1	16.11.85	Crewe A	D4	H	W	5-1	Davison 2, Christie 2, Chandler (p)
	2	9.12.85	Telford U	APL	H	W	6-1	Chandler 3, Micklewhite 2, Gregory
	3	4.1.86	Gillingham	D3	A	D	1-1	Garner
	3r	13.1.86	Gillingham		H	W	3-1aet	Micklewhite, Garner, Christie
	4	25.1.86	Sheffield U	D2	A	W	1-0	Hindmarch
	5	26.2.86	Sheffield W	D1	H	D	1-1	Davison
	5r	5.3.86	Sheffield W		A	L	0-2	
1986-87 D2	3	26.1.87	Sheffield W	D1	A	L	0-1	
1987-88 D1	3	9.1.88	Chelsea	D1	H	L	1-3	Penney
1988-89 D1	3	7.1.89	Southampton	D1	H	D	1-1	Hebberd
	3r	10.1.89	Southampton		A	W	2-1aet	McMinn, Callaghan
	4	28.1.89	Watford	D2	A	L	1-2	Micklewhite
1989-90 D1	3	7.1.90	Port Vale	D2	A	D	1-1	Hebberd
	3r	10.1.90	Port Vale		H	L	2-3	Ramage, Francis
1990-91 D1	3	5.1.91	Newcastle U	D2	A	L	0-2	
1991-92 D2	3	4.1.92	Burnley	D4	A	D	2-2	Chalk, Comyn
	3r	14.1.92	Burnley		H	–	2-0	Gee, Patterson
		abandoned after 76 minutes – fog						
	3r	25.1.92	Burnley		H	W	2-0	P.Williams, Ormondroyd
	4	5.2.92	Aston Villa	D1	H	L	3-4	Gee 2, P.Williams
1992-93 D1	3	2.1.93	Stockport Co	D2	H	W	2-1	Short, Miller og
	4	23.1.93	Luton T	D1	A	W	5-1	Short, Pembridge 3, Gabbiadini
	5	13.2.93	Bolton W	D2	H	W	3-1	Short 2, Williams
	6	8.3.93	Sheffield W	PL	H	D	3-3	Nicholson, Gabiadini, Kitson
	6r	17.3.93	Sheffield W		A	L	0-1	

DERBY JUNCTION

Originally entered as Junction St School. Reached FA Cup semi-finals 1888

1884-85	1	25.10.84	WBA		H	L	1-7	Malpass
1885-86	1	31.10.85	Darwen		A	D	2-2	
	1r	7.11.85	Darwen		A	L	0-4	
1886-87	1	30.10.86	Wellington St G		A	W	1-0	
	2	20.11.86	WBA		A	L	1-2	Peach
1887-88	1	15.10.87	Derby St Lukes		H	W	3-2	
	2	5.11.87	Rotherham T		H	W	3-2	Radford 2, S.Smith
	3	19.11.87	Lockwood Brothers		H	W	2-1	
	4		bye					
	5	31.12.87	Chirk		A	W	1-0	S.Smith
	6	28.1.88	Blackburn R		H	W	2-1	Hopkins, 1 other
	SF	18.2.88	WBA			L	0-3	
		played at Stoke						
1888-89	1	2.2.89	Derby Co	D1	A	L	0-1	

DERBY MIDLAND

Formed 1881. Played on fields by the Midland Station

1883-84	1		bye					
	2	1.12.83	Birmingham Excelsior		A	D	1-1	
	2r	15.12.83	Birmingham Excelsior		H	W	2-1	Ward, G.Wignall
	3	29.12.83	Wednesbury Town		A	L	0-1	
1884-85	1	8.11.84	Wednesbury OA		H	L	1-2	
1885-86	1	31.10.85	Birmingham Excelsior		H	W	2-1	
	2	21.11.85	Walsall Swifts		H	L	1-3	

1886-87	1	30.10.86	Birmingham Excelsior		A	D	3-3	
	1r	13.11.86	Birmingham Excelsior		H	W	2-1	
	2	20.11.86	Aston Villa		A	L	1-6	Ward
1887-88	1	15.10.87	Ecclesfield		A	L	1-4	
1888-89	3q	17.11.88	Notts Co	D1	A	L	1-2	
1889-90 ML	1	18.1.90	Nottingham F	FAII	H	W	3-0	Daft, Garden, Mills
	2	1.2.90	Bootle	FAII	A	L	1-2	Garden

DERBY ST LUKES

Formed 1870. Played at Peet Street, off the New Uttoxeter Road, Derby.

1884-85	1	8.11.84	Wolverhampton W	A	D	0-0	
	1r	22.11.84	Wolverhampton W	H	W	4-2aet	
	2	6.12.84	Walsall Swifts	H	L	0-1	
1885-86	1	31.10.85	Wolverhampton W	A	L	0-7	
1886-87	1	30.10.86	Walsall Town	H	D	3-3	Hawkesworth 2, Wild
	1r	13.11.86	Walsall Town	A	L	1-6	
1887-88	1	15.10.87	Derby Junction	A	L	2-3	

DERBY TOWN

1881-82	1	5.11.81	Small Heath Alliance	A	L	1-4	Shaw

DERBYSHIRE FC

1880-81	1	4.11.80	Notts Co	A	D	4-4	Evans 2, Taylor, 1 other
	1r	27.11.80	Notts Co	H	L	2-4	Shaw, 1 other

DESBOROUGH TOWN

Formed 1896. First entered FA Cup: 1900

1926-27 UCL	1	27.11.26	Doncaster R	3N	A	–	0-0	
		match abandoned after 80 mins – fog						
	1	2.12.26	Doncaster R		A	L	0-3	

DINNINGTON ATHLETIC

Competed in FA Cup: 1921-49

1934-35 SAL	1	24.11.34	Chester	3N	A	L	1-3	Fearnley

DISTILLERY, BELFAST

Formed 1879. Winners of the Irish FA Cup, 12 times. One of three Irish teams to play in the FA Cup proper

1887-88	1	8.10.87	Blackburn Park Rd		A	L	1-2	McManus
		Distillery reinstated after protest						
	2	5.11.87	Witton		H	L	2-4	McManus, Stewart
1889-90	3q	16.11.89	Belfast YMCA			*walkover*		
	4q	7.12.89	Linfield Athletic		H	D	3-3	
	4qr	14.12.89	Linfield Athletic		A	W	5-3	
	1	18.1.90	Bolton W	FL	A	L	2-10	Reynolds, og

DONCASTER ROVERS

Formed 1879. First entered FA Cup: 1888. Best FA Cup Performance: 5th round, 1952, 1954, 1955, 1956. Record FA Cup Win: 8-1 vs Parkgate U, 3rd qual rd, 1898-99. In competition proper: 7-0 vs Blyth Spartans, 1st round, 27.11.1937. Record FA Cup Defeat: 0-8 vs Everton, 4th round, 21.1.1939. 1-9 vs Rotherham Town 1st qualifying round, 1888-89

1888-89		1q Rotherham T (H) 1-9
1889-90	M All	1q Rotherham T (A) 0-2
1890-91	M All	2q Kilnhurst (H) 4-5
1891-92	ML	1q Lincoln C (A) 1-3

DONCASTER ROVERS

1892-93 ML 1q **Mansfield T** (H) 2-0; 2q **Grimsby T** (H) 1-1aet; 2qr **Grimsby T** (H) 1-2

1893-94 ML 2q **Grantham R** (H) 1-2

1894-95 ML 1q **Mexborough** (H) 1-2

1895-96 ML 1q **Mexborough** (A) 1-1; 1qr **Mexborough** (H) 4-1; 2q **Rotherham T** (H) 0-7

1896-97 ML 3q **Sheffield Club** (A) 1-3

1897-98 ML 3q **Sheffield Club** (A) 4-0; 4q **Mexborough** (A) 0-0; 4qr **Mexborough** (H) 1-1; 4qr 2r **Mexborough** 1-1 abnd (at Bramall Lane); 4q 3r **Mexborough** 1-2 (at Barnsley)

1898-99 ML 2q **Wath-on-Dearne** (H) 6-1; 3q **Parkgate U** (H) 8-1; 4q **Barnsley** (H) 1-2

1899-00 ML 1q **Gainsborough Trinity** (A) 4-1; 2q **Newark** (H) 3-1; 3q **Grimsby T** (A) 1-3

1900-01 ML P **Rotherham T** (H) 6-1; 1q **Attercliffe** (A) 2-0; 2q **Worksop T** (A) 0-0; 2qr **Worksop T** (H) 2-1; 3q **Barnsley** (A) 1-2

1901-02 D2 3q **Royston U** (A) 3-1; 4q **Lincoln C** (A) 0-1

1902-03 D2 3q **Gainsborough Trinity** (A) 0-1

1903-04 ML 3q **Belper T** (H) 2-0; 4q **Gainsborough Trinity** (H) 0-1

1904-05 D2 3q **Mexborough T** (H) 0-0; 3qr **Mexborough T** (A) 1-3

1905-06 ML 1q **Denaby U** (A) 2-4

1906-07 ML P **Morley** (A) 4-1; 1q **Denaby U** (A) 0-0; 1qr **Denaby U** (H) 2-2; 1q 2r **Denaby U** 1-3

1907-08 ML 1q **Goole T** (H) 1-1; 1qr **Goole T** (A) 1-2

1908-09 ML 1q **Castleford T** (H) 1-1; 1qr **Castleford T** (A) 1-4

1909-10 ML 4q **Mexborough T** (H) 0-0; 4qr **Mexborough T** (A) 1-2

1910-11 ML P **Hull Day St OB** (H) 7-0; 1q **Grimsby Rovers** (H) 5-4; 2q **Mexborough T** (H) 1-0; 3q **Denaby U** (A) 1-2

1911-12 ML 1q **Castleford T** (A) 0-1

1912-13 ML P **Denaby U** (A) 2-1; 1q **Castleford T** (A) 0-2

1913-14 ML P **Goole T** (A) 1-2

1914-15 ML P **Grimsby Haycroft R** (A) 3-0; 1q **Cleethorpes** (H) 3-1; 2q **Scunthorpe U** (A) 0-1

1919-20   *did not compete*

1920-21 ML ExP **Atlas & NW** (H) 6-0; P **Wombwell** (H) 0-1

1921-22 ML ExP **Rotherham T** (H) 2-0; P **Wombwell** (A) 0-1

1922-23 ML 1q **Denaby U** (A) 0-0; 1qr **Denaby U** (A) 4-1; 2q **Mexborough T** (A) 0-0; 2qr **Mexborough T** (H) 2-1; 3q **Wath A** (H) 0-0; 3qr **Wath A** (A) 1-2

1923-24 3N P **Fryston Colliery** (H) *scratched*

1924-25 3N 4q **Mansfield T** (H) 3-2; 5q **Rotherham Co** (A) 3-2; 6q **Southport** (H) 1-0

	1	10.1.25	**Norwich C**	3S	H	L	1-2	Campbell
1925-26 3N	1	28.11.25	**Wellington T**	BDL	H	W	2-0	H.Keetley, Hargreaves
	2	12.12.25	**Rotherham U**	3N	H	L	0-2	
1926-27 3N	1	27.11.26	**Desborough T**	UCL	H	–	0-0	
		abandoned at 80 minutes because of fog						
	1	2.12.26	**Desborough T**		H	W	3-0	F.Keetley 2, T.Keetley
	2	11.12.26	**Chesterfield**	3N	H	L	0-1	
1927-28 3N	1	26.11.27	**Carlisle U**	NEL	A	L	1-2	Jepson (p)
1928-29 3N	1	24.11.28	**Bradford C**	3N	A	L	1-4	T.Keetley
1929-30 3N	1	30.11.29	**Shildon**	NEL	H	D	0-0	
	1r	4.12.29	**Shildon**		A	D	1-1aet	Robinson
	1 2r	9.12.29	**Shildon** at York			W	3-0	Paterson 2, R.Smith
	2	14.12.29	**New Brighton**	3N	H	H	1-0	Whitelaw
	3	11.1.30	**Stoke C**	D2	H	–	2-3	Batt, Bowman
		abandoned during the second half because of a snowstorm						
	3	16.1.30	**Stoke C**	D2	H	W	1-0	Whitelaw
	4	25.1.30	**Millwall**	D2	A	L	0-4	
1930-31 3N	1	29.11.30	**Rochdale**	3N	A	W	2-1	Bott, Smith
	2	13.12.30	**Notts Co**	3S	H	L	0-1	
1931-32 3N	1	28.11.31	**Barrow**	3N	A	D	3-3	Flowers, Gladwin, Bowman
	1r	3.12.31	**Barrow**		H	D	1-1aet	Smith
	1 2r	7.12.31	**Barrow** at Maine Road			D	1-1aet	Bowman
	1 3r	9.12.31	**Barrow** at Elland Road			W	1-0aet	Gladwin
	2	12.12.31	**Brighton & HA**	3S	A	L	0-5	
1932-33 3N	1	26.11.32	**Gainsborough T**	ML	H	W	4-1	Beresford, Atherton, Beynon 2
	2	10.12.32	**Northampton T**	3S	A	W	1-0	Atherton
	3	14.1.33	**Halifax T**	3N	H	L	0-3	
1933-34 3N	1	25.11.33	**Barrow**	3N	A	L	2-4	Waterston, Smith
1934-35 3N	1	24.11.34	**Barrow**	3N	H	L	0-2	
1935-36 D2	3	11.1.36	**Nottingham F**	D2	H	L	1-2	Turner
1936-37 D2	3	16.1.37	**Chester**	3N	A	L	0-4	
1937-38 3N	1	27.11.37	**Blyth Spartans**	NEL	H	W	7-0	Morgan 2, Burton, Killourghy 4.
	2	11.12.37	**Guildford C**	SL	H	W	4-0	Burton, Dutton, Malam, Killourghy
	3	8.1.38	**Sheffield U**	D2	H	L	0-2	
1938-39 3N	1	26.11.38	**New Brighton**	3N	H	W	4-2	Leyfield, Little, Dell 2
	2	10.12.38	**Gainsborough T**	ML	A	W	1-0	Dell

Season	Div	Rnd	Date	Opponent	Comp	H/A	Res	Score	Scorers
		3	10.1.39	Southport	3N	A	D	1-1	Potts
		3r	12.1.39	Southport		H	W	2-1	Dell, Malam
		4	21.1.39	Everton	D1	A	L	0-8	
1945-46	3N	1 1L	17.11.45	Rotherham U	3N	H	L	0-1	
		1 2L	24.11.45	Rotherham U		A	L	1-2	Todd
1946-47	3N	1	30.11.46	Accrington S	3N	H	D	2-2	Thompson, Dodd
		1r	4.12.46	Accrington S		A	W	5-0	Kirkcaldie 3, Todd, Jordan
1947-48	D2	3	10.1.48	Fulham	D2	A	L	0-2	
1948-49	3N	1	4.12.48	Bradford C	3N	A	L	3-4	Calverley, Antonio, Reeve
1949-50	3N	1	26.11.49	New Brighton	3N	H	W	5-1	Calverley, Tindill 2, Todd, Doherty
		2	10.12.49	Mansfield T	3N	H	W	1-0	Todd
		3	7.1.50	Reading	3S	A	W	3-2	Todd 2, Doherty
		4	28.1.50	Blackpool	D1	A	L	1-2	Doherty
1950-51	D2	3	6.1.51	Rotherham U	3N	A	L	1-2	Miller (p)
1951-52	D2	3	12.1.52	Buxton	CC	H	W	2-0	Harrison 2
		4	6.2.52	Middlesbrough	D1	A	W	4-1	Lawlor 2, Harrison, Tindill
		5	23.2.52	Portsmouth	D1	A	L	0-4	
1952-53	D2	3	10.1.53	Arsenal	D1	A	L	0-4	
1953-54	D2	3	9.1.54	Sunderland	D1	A	W	2-0	McMorran 2
		4	30.1.54	Plymouth A	D2	A	W	2-0	Tindill 2
		5	20.2.54	Leyton O	3S	A	L	1-3	McMorran
1954-55	D2	3	8.1.55	Watford	3S	A	W	2-1	Tindill 2
		4	29.1.55	Aston Villa	D1	H	D	0-0	
		4r	2.2.55	Aston Villa		A	D	2-2aet	Tindill, Mooney
		4 2r	7.2.55	Aston Villa at Maine Road			D	1-1aet	Jeffrey
		4 3r	14.2.55	Aston Villa at Hillsborough			D	0-0	
			abandoned after 90 minutes – bad light						
		4 4r	15.2.55	Aston Villa at the Hawthorns			W	3-1	Jeffrey 2, G.Walker
		5	19.2.55	Birmingham C	D2	A	L	1-2	Mooney
1955-56	D2	3	7.1.56	Nottingham F	D2	H	W	3-0	McMorran 2, Jeffrey
		4	28.1.56	Bristol R	D2	A	D	1-1	McMorran
		4r	31.1.56	Bristol R		H	W	1-0	Tindill
		5	18.2.56	Tottenham H	D1	H	L	0-2	
1956-57	D2	3	5.1.57	WBA	D1	H	D	1-1	Cavanagh
		3r	9.1.57	WBA		A	L	0-2	
1957-58	D2	3	4.1.58	Chelsea	D1	H	L	0-2	
1958-59	D3	1	15.11.58	Consett	ML	H	W	5-0	Sharp, Mooney 2, Reeson, Stephens
		2	6.12.58	Tranmere R	D3	A	W	2-1	Reeson, Callan
		3	19.1.59	Bristol C	D2	H	L	0-2	
1959-60	D4	1	14.11.59	Gainsborough T	ML	H	D	3-3	Walker 2, Chappell
		1r	18.11.59	Gainsborough T		A	W	1-0	Walker
		2	5.12.59	Darlington	D4	H	W	3-2	Sharp 2, Chappell
		3	9.1.60	Bristol R	D2	A	D	0-0	
		3r	12.1.60	Bristol R		H	L	1-2	Broadbent
1960-61	D4	1	5.11.60	Chesterfield	D3	A	D	3-3	Curtis 2 (2p), Swallow
		1r	9.11.60	Chesterfield		H	L	0-1	
1961-62	D4	1	4.11.61	Chesterfield	D4	H	L	0-4	
1962-63	D4	1	3.11.62	South Shields	NEL	A	D	0-0	
		1r	8.11.62	South Shields		H	W	2-1	Booth, Billings
		2	24.11.62	Tranmere R	D4	H	L	1-4	Booth
1963-64	D4	1	16.11.63	Tranmere R	D4	H	W	3-0	Robinson, Nibloe, Ripley
		2	7.12.63	Notts Co	D3	H	D	1-1	Booth
		2r	10.12.63	Notts Co		A	W	2-1	Broadbent (p), Hale
		3	4.1.64	Bristol C	D3	H	D	2-2	Taylor, Ripley
		3r	7.1.64	Bristol C		A	L	0-2	
1964-65	D4	1	14.11.64	Bradford PA	D4	A	W	3-2	Ricketts, Jeffrey 2
		2	5.12.64	Scarborough	ML	H	D	0-0	
		2r	9.12.64	Scarborough		A	W	2-1	Hale (p), Robinson
		3	9.1.65	Huddersfield T	D2	H	L	0-1	
1965-66	D4	1	13.11.65	Wigan A	CC	H	D	2-2	Ricketts, Kelly
		1r	17.11.65	Wigan A		A	L	1-3	Ogden
1966-67	D3	1	26.11.66	Halifax T	D4	A	D	2-2	Gilfillan, Ogden
		1r	29.11.66	Halifax T		H	L	1-3	Ogden
1967-68	D4	1	9.12.67	York C	D4	A	W	1-0	Jeffrey
		2	6.1.68	Workington	D4	H	D	1-1	Gilfillan
		2r	10.1.68	Workington		A	W	2-1	Watson, Webber
		3	27.1.68	Swansea T	D4	H	L	0-2	

Season	Div	Rnd	Date	Opponent		H/A	Result	Score	Scorers
1968-69	D4	1	16.11.68	Notts Co	D4	H	W	1-0	Jeffrey
		2	7.12.68	Southport	D3	H	W	2-1	Regan 2
		3	4.1.69	Liverpool	D1	A	L	0-2	
1969-70	D3	1	15.11.69	Crewe A	D4	H	D	1-1	Sheffield
		1r	19.11.69	Crewe A		A	W	1-0	Robertson
		2	6.12.69	Chester	D4	A	D	1-1	Johnson
		2r	9.12.69	Chester		H	L	0-2	
1970-71	D3	1	21.11.70	Crewe A	D4	A	D	0-0	
		1r	24.11.70	Crewe A		H	L	1-3	Watson
1971-72	D4	1	20.11.71	Stockport Co	D4	H	L	1-2	Uzelac
1972-73	D4	1	18.11.72	Bury	D4	H	W	3-1	Kitchen, Elwiss, Rabjohn
		2	9.12.72	Scarborough	NPL	A	W	2-1	Kitchen, Elwiss
		3	13.1.73	Reading	D4	A	L	0-2	
1973-74	D4	1	24.11.73	Lincoln C	D4	H	W	1-0	Murray (p)
		2	15.12.73	Tranmere R	D3	H	W	3-0	Kitchen, Woods, Elwiss
		3	5.1.74	Liverpool	D1	A	D	2-2	Kitchen, O'Callaghan
		3r	8.1.74	Liverpool		H	L	0-2	
1974-75	D4	1	23.11.74	Oswestry	CC	A	W	3-1	O'Callaghan, Kitchen 2
		2	14.12.74	Chesterfield	D3	A	L	0-1	
1975-76	D4	1	22.11.75	Bury	D3	A	L	2-4	Uzelac 2
1976-77	D4	1	20.11.76	Shrewsbury T	D3	H	D	2-2	Kitchen 2
		1r	23.11.76	Shrewsbury T		A	L	3-4	Miller, Kitchen, Reed
1977-78	D4	1	26.11.77	Shrewsbury T	D3	H	L	0-1	
1978-79	D4	1	25.11.78	Huddersfield T	D4	H	W	2-1	Lewis, Laidlaw
		2	16.12.78	Shrewsbury T	D3	H	L	0-3	
1979-80	D4	1	23.11.79	Port Vale	D4	A	W	3-1	Lewis, Pugh, Nimmo
		2	15.12.79	Mansfield T	D3	H	L	1-2	Nimmo
1980-81	D4	1	22.11.80	Sutton Coldfield T	WMRL	A	W	2-0	Dowd, Lally
		2	13.12.80	Blackpool	D3	H	W	2-1	Little, Mell
		3	3.1.81	Hull C	D3	A	L	0-1	
1981-82	D3	1	21.11.81	Mansfield T	D4	A	W	1-0	Douglas
		2	12.12.81	Penrith	NL	H	W	3-0	Warboys 2, Little
		3	2.1.82	Cambridge U	D2	H	W	2-1	Reilly og, Warboys
		4	23.1.82	Norwich C	D2	A	L	1-2	Dawson
1982-83	D3	1	20.11.82	Workington T	NPL	A	W	2-1	Owen, Austin
		2	11.12.82	Peterborough U	D4	A	L	2-5	I.Snodin, Mell
1983-84	D4	1	19.11.83	Mansfield T	D4	A	L	0-3	
1984-85	D3	1	17.11.84	Rochdale	D4	A	W	2-1	Philliben, G.Snodin
		2	8.12.84	Altrincham	APL	A	W	3-1	Harle, Douglas 2
		3	5.1.85	QPR	D1	H	W	1-0	Harle
		4	26.1.85	Everton	D1	A	L	0-2	
1985-86	D3	1	16.11.85	Wigan A	D3	A	L	1-4	Douglas
1986-87	D3	1	15.11.86	Whitby T	NL	A	D	2-2	Russell, Deane
		1r	18.11.86	Whitby T		H	W	3-2	Woods, Stead, Redfearn (p)
		2	6.12.86	Chester C	D3	A	L	1-3	Woods
1987-88	D3	1	14.11.87	Rotherham U	D3	H	D	1-1	Holmes
		1r	17.11.87	Rotherham U		A	L	0-2	
1988-89	D4	1	19.11.88	Brandon U	NL	H	D	0-0	
		1r	22.11.88	Brandon U at Doncaster		A	W	2-1	Dobson 2
		2	11.12.88	Sheffield U	D3	H	L	1-3	Daly
1989-90	D4	1	18.11.89	Notts Co	D3	H	W	1-0	Noteman
		2	9.12.89	Grimsby T	D4	A	L	0-1	
1990-91	D4	1	17.11.90	Chester C	D3	A	D	2-2	Gormley, Rankine
		1r	20.11.90	Chester C		H	L	1-2aet	Noteman
1991-92	D4	1	16.11.91	Burnley	D4	A	D	1-1	Rankine
		1r	27.11.91	Burnley		H	L	1-3	Whitehurst
1992-93	D3	1	14.11.92	Hartlepool U	D2	H	L	1-2	Quinlan

DONINGTON GRAMMAR SCHOOL, SPALDING

Formed 1870. Played at the 'School Grounds' in Donington. Entered the first FA Cup competition, scratched before playing a game, and never entered again.

1871-72	1	Queen's Park, Glasgow	teams could not arrange a date so both advanced to second round
	2	Queen's Park, Glasgow	scratched

DORCHESTER TOWN

Formed 1880. **First entered FA Cup:** 1949. **Cup Final Connection:** Former player Graham Roberts played in two Cup Finals for Tottenham in 1981 and 1982

1954-55	WL	1	20.11.54	Bedford T	SL	H	W	2-0	Dobson, Spink
		2	11.12.54	York C	3N	H	L	2-5	Curtis, Gale
1955-56	WL	1	19.11.55	Norwich C	3S	A	L	0-4	
1956-57	WL	1	17.11.56	QPR	3S	A	L	0-4	
1957-58	WL	1	16.11.57	Wycombe W	IL	H	W	3-2	Stroud (p), Cheney 2
		2	7.12.57	Plymouth A	3S	A	L	2-5	Barker, Stroud (p)
1959-60	WL	1	14.11.59	Port Vale	D3	H	L	1-2	Gillett
1981-82	SL	1	21.11.81	Minehead	SL	H	D	3-3	Miller, Steele 2
		1r	23.11.81	Minehead		A	W	4-0	Senior 3, Chutter
		2	12.12.81	Bournemouth	D4	H	D	1-1	Thorne
		2r	15.12.81	Bournemouth		A	L	1-2aet	Steele
1989-90	SL	1	18.11.89	Gloucester C	SL	A	L	0-1	

DOVER

Formed 1891. **First entered FA Cup:** 1894. Original club folded 1983 and reformed as Dover Athletic. **Cup final connection:** Peter Broadbent, who played for Wolves in the 1960 final spent a season at Dover before turning professional. **League club beaten:** Colchester U

1960-61	SL	1	5.11.60	Peterborough U	D4	H	L	1-4	Taylor
1971-72	SL	1	20.11.71	Guildford C	SL	A	D	0-0	
		1r	24.11.71	Guildford C		H	L	0-2	
1975-76	SL	1	22.11.75	Colchester U	D3	A	D	3-3	Coupland, Waite, Rogers
		1r	26.11.75	Colchester U		H	W	4-1	Hamshare, Coxhill (p), Coupland 2
		2	13.12.75	Southend U	D3	A	L	1-4	Housden
1981-82	SL	1	21.11.81	Oxford U	D3	H	L	0-2	

DREADNOUGHT FC

Formed 1875. Played at West Ham Park, east London

1880-81	1	13.11.80	Rochester		A	W	2-1	Wyllie, 1 other
	2	11.12.80	Old Carthusians		A	L	1-5	Wyllie
1881-82	1		Caius College, Cambridge			walkover		
	2		bye					
	3	17.12.81	Great Marlow		H	L	1-2	
1882-83	1	21.10.82	South Reading		A	L	1-2	Pettigrew
		match declared void after protest						
	1r	4.11.82	South Reading		H	L	1-2	
1883-84	1	10.11.83	Old Foresters		A	L	1-2	Fabian

DROYLESDEN

Formed 1892. **First entered FA Cup:** 1932

1976-77	CC	1	20.11.76	Grimsby T	D3	H	D	0-0	
		1r	23.11.76	Grimsby T		A	L	3-5	Haughton, Williams, Seddon
1978-79	CC	1	25.11.78	Rochdale	D4	A	W	1-0	Taylor
		2	16.12.78	Altrincham	NPL	H	L	0-2	

DRUIDS FC, RUABON, WALES

Formed 1874. The first Welsh club to compete in the FA Cup. Originally played at Plas Madoc Park, Ruabon. Welsh FA Cup winners eight times. Folded 1918. The present-day Druids United play in the Welsh National League and date from 1930

1876-77	1		Shropshire Wanderers			scratched		
1877-78	1	12.11.77	Shropshire Wanderers		H	W	1-0	
	2		Queen's Park			walkover		
	3	30.1.78	Royal Engineers		A	L	0-8	
1882-83	1	4.11.82	Oswestry		H	D	1-1	
	1r	18.11.82	Oswestry		A	W	2-0	WP Owen, 1 other
	2	9.12.82	Northwich Victoria		H	W	5-0	
	3	6.1.83	Bolton W		H	D	0-0	
	3r	22.1.83	Bolton W		A	D	1-1aet	Vaughan

	3 2r	29.1.83	**Bolton W**		W	1-0	Doughty
			played at Wrexham Racecourse				
	4	10.2.83	**Eagley**	H	W	2-1aet	Vaughan, 1 other
	5	24.2.83	**Blackburn Olympic**	A	L	1-4	
1883-84	1	10.11.83	**Northwich Victoria**	H	L	0-1	
1884-85	1	8.11.84	**Liverpool Ramblers**	H	W	6-1	Doughty, 5 others
	2	20.12.84	**Newtown**	A	D	1-1	
	2r	27.12.84	**Newtown**	H	W	6-0	
	3	10.1.85	**Chirk**	H	W	4-1	Powell 2, Doughty, 1 other
	4	24.1.85	**WBA**	A	L	0-1	
1885-86	1	31.10.85	**Stafford Rangers**	A	W	4-1	
	2	21.11.85	**Burslem Port Vale**	H	D	2-2aet	Green, 1 other
	2r	28.11.85	**Burslem Port Vale**	A	L	1-5	
1886-87	1	23.10.86	**Leek**	A	L	1-2	
1887-88	1	15.10.87	**Crewe A**	A	L	0-5	

DUDLEY TOWN

Formed 1893. **First entered FA Cup:** 1900 **Cup Final Connection:** Duncan Edwards, who played for Manchester United in the 1957 Cup Final and lost his life in the Munich Air Crash nine months later, was born in Dudley

1976-77	WMRL	1	20.11.76	**York C**	D3	H	D	1-1	Walker
		1r	23.11.76	**York C**		A	L	1-4	Molyneux (p)

DULWICH FC

First entered FA Cup: 1885

1884-85	1	8.11.84	**Pilgrims**		H	W	3-2	
	2	6.12.84	**Romford**		A	L	0-3	
1885-86	1	31.10.85	**South Reading**		H	L	1-2	
1886-87	1	30.10.86	**Casuals**		A	W	3-2	
	2	20.11.86	**Maidenhead**		A	W	3-2	
	3	11.12.86	**Great Marlow**		A	L	0-2	
1887-88	1	15.10.87	**Reading**		A	W	2-0	Quint 2
			match replayed following protests					
	1r		**Reading**		walkover			
	2	5.11.87	**Hotspur**		H	W	2-1	
	3	26.11.87	**Swifts**		H	L	1-3	

DULWICH HAMLET

Formed 1893. **First entered FA Cup:** 1919. **FA Amateur Cup Winners:** 1920, 1932, 1934, 1937 **Cup Final Connection:** Andy Gray, who played for Crystal Palace in the 1990 Cup Final, had a spell with Dulwich Hamlet

1925-26	IL	1	28.11.25	**Southend U**	3S	A	L	1-5	Nicol
1926-27	IL	1	27.11.26	**Southend U**	3S	H	L	1-4	Robbins
1927-28	IL	1	26.11.27	**Ilford**	IL	A	L	0-4	
1928-29	IL	1	24.11.28	**Merthyr Town**	3S	A	L	2-4	Holland, Kall
1929-30	IL	1	30.11.29	**Plymouth A**	3S	H	L	0-3	
1930-31	IL	1	29.11.30	**Newport Co**	3S	H	D	2-2	Smith, Hugo
		1r	4.12.30	**Newport Co**		A	L	1-4	Morrish
1932-33	IL	1	26.11.32	**Swindon T**	3S	A	L	1-4	Smith
1933-34	IL	1	25.11.33	**Newport Co**	3S	H	D	2-2	Ede, Miller
		1r	30.11.33	**Newport Co**		A	L	2-6	Jordan og, Levy
1934-35	IL	1	24.11.34	**Torquay U**	3S	H	L	1-2	Court
1935-36	IL	1	30.11.35	**Torquay U**	3S	H	L	2-3	Ready, Murray (p)
1936-37	IL	1	28.11.36	**Swindon T**	3S	A	L	0-6	
1937-38	IL	1	27.11.37	**Aldershot**	3S	H	L	1-2	Morrish
1948-49	IL	1	27.11.48	**Northampton T**	3S	A	L	1-2	Davies

DUNSTABLE TOWN

Formed 1895. **First entered FA Cup:** 1900

1956-57	Hel	1	17.11.56	**Margate**	KL	A	L	1-3	Grandham

DURHAM CITY

Formed 1918. **First entered FA Cup:** 1920. Disbanded 1938. Reformed 1949. Currently play in the Northern League

1921-22	3N	5q **Darlington** (H) 0-2					
1922-23	3N	4q **West Stanley** (H) 2-1; 5q **Hartlepools U** (H) 0-1					
1923-24	3N	P **West Stanley** (H) 2-2; Pr **West Stanley** (A) 1-1; P2r **West Stanley** (A) 1-0; 1q **Dipton U** (A) 0-1					
1924-25	3N	4q **Blyth Spartans** (H) 3-1; 5q **Darlington** (A) 1-3					
1925-26	3N	1	2.12.25 **Ashington**	3N	H	W	4-1	Stephenson 2, Johnson, Dent
		2	12.12.25 **Southport**	3N	H	L	0-3	
1926-27	3N		did not enter					
1927-28	3N	1	26.11.27 **Wrexham**	3N	H	D	1-1	Stokes
		1r	30.11.27 **Wrexham**		A	L	0-4	
1955-56	NL	1	19.11.55 **Bishop Auckland**	NL	A	L	1-3	Smith
1957-58	NL	1	16.11.57 **Spalding**	ECL	H	W	3-1	Armstrong, Ayre, Johnstone
		2	7.12.57 **Tranmere R**	3N	H	L	0-3	

Durham forgot to claim exemption from the early qualifying rounds in 1923-24

EAGLEY FC, BOLTON

Formed 1875. Played at Eagley Fields, Bolton

1878-79	1	bye				
	2	7.12.78 **Darwen**	A	D	0-0	
	2r	21.12.78 **Darwen**	A	L	1-4	Sarples
1879-80	1	25.10.79 **Darwen**	H	L	0-1	
1880-81	1	30.10.80 **Astley Bridge**	A	L	0-4	
1881-82	1	22.10.81 **Bolton Wanderers**	A	D	5-5	
	1r	12.11.81 **Bolton Wanderers**	H	L	0-1	
1882-83	1	4.11.82 **Bolton Olympic**	A	W	7-4	Eagley 2, Hardiker, Whittam, Derham, Burgess, R.Hall
	2	2.12.82 **Halliwell**	H	W	3-1	Corless 2, 1 other
	3	bye				
	4	10.2.83 **Druids**	A	L	1-2aet	
1883-84	1	13.10.83 **Halliwell**	A	W	5-2	
	2	bye				
	3	29.12.83 **Preston NE**	A	L	1-9	
1885-86	1	17.10.85 **Bolton Wanderers**	H	L	0-6	

EASINGTON COLLIERY WELFARE

Formed 1914. **First entered FA Cup:** 1932

1955-56	Wear 1	19.11.55 **Tranmere R**	3N	H	L	0-2	

EAST SHEEN

Formed 1873. Played at Sheen Common.

1887-88	1	15.10.87 **Old St Marks**	A	L	2-7	

ECCLES UNITED

Competed in FA Cup: 1920-26

1920-21	LC	1	8.1.21 **Southend U**	D3	A	L	1-5	Schofield

ECCLESFIELD

Formed 1873. Played at Fareham's Croft, Ecclesfield, Yorkshire.

1887-88	1	15.10.87 **Derby Midland**	H	W	4-1	
	2	5.11.87 **Derby Co**	A	L	0-6	

ECKINGTON WORKS

1885-86	1	19.10.85 **Sheffield Heeley**	A	L	1-2	
1887-88	1	15.10.87 **Owlerton, Sheffield**	A	L	1-2	

ELLESMERE PORT TOWN

First entered FA Cup: 1924 **Cup Final Connection:** Joe Mercer, who captained Arsenal to victory in the 1950 Cup Final, was born in and was a former player with Ellesmere Port.

1971-72	NPL	1	20.11.71	**Boston U**	NPL	H	L	0-3

ELSWICK RANGERS

1887-88	1	15.10.87	**Bishop Auckland Cl**		H	D	3-3aet	
	1r	22.10.87	**Bishop Auckland Cl**		A	W	2-0	
	2	5.11.87	**Darlington**		A	L	3-4aet	McCallum, McDonald, Nugent

ELY CITY

Formed: 1885. **First entered FA Cup:** 1955

1956-57	PDL	1	17.11.56	**Torquay U**	3S	H	L	2-6	Oliver, King

EMLEY

Formed 1903. **First entered FA Cup:** 1973

1991-92	NPL	1	17.11.91	**Bolton W** at Huddersfield	D3	H	L	0-3

ENDERBY TOWN

Formed 1900. Changed name to Leicester United in 1981

1977-78	SL	1	26.11.77	**A.P.Leamington**	SL	A	L	1-6	Cooper

ENFIELD

Formed 1893. **First entered FA Cup:** 1897. **FA Challenge Trophy Winners:** 1982, 1988 **FA Amateur Cup Winners:** 1967, 1970; **Runners-up:** 1964, 1972. **Cup Final Connection:** Peter Baker, who played for Tottenham in the 1961 and 1962 Cup Finals, started his career with Enfield **League Clubs beaten:** Aldershot, Exeter C, Hereford, Leyton Orient, Northampton Port Vale, Wimbledon (2).

1931-32	AL	1	28.11.31	**Cardiff C**	3S	A	L	0-8	
1937-38	AL	1	27.11.37	**Bristol C**	3S	A	L	0-3	
1959-60	AL	1	14.11.59	**Headington U**	SL	H	W	4-3	Thomas, McDonnell (p), Long, Lawrence
	2	5.12.59	**Bournemouth**	D3	H	L	1-5	McDonnell
1962-63	AL	1	3.11.62	**Cheltenham T**	SL	A	W	6-3	Thomas 2, Lawrence, Quail, Terry (p), Bloomfield
	2	24.11.62	**Peterborough U**	D3	A	L	0-1	
1963-64	IL	1	16.11.63	**Reading**	D3	A	D	2-2	Thomas, Broomfield
	1r	19.11.63	**Reading**		H	L	2-4aet	Thomas, Day
1964-65	IL	1	14.11.64	**Romford**	SL	A	D	0-0	
	1r	17.11.64	**Romford**		H	D	0-0aet	
	1 2r	23.11.64	**Romford** at Highbury		W	4-2		Day, Thomas 2, Howard
	2	5.12.64	**Barnet**	AL	H	D	4-4	Kingsland, Day 2 (2ps), Thomas
	2r	8.12.64	**Barnet**		A	L	0-3	
1966-67	IL	1	26.11.66	**Chesham U**	AL	H	W	6-0	Connell 3, Churchill (p), Adams, Reid
	2	7.1.67	**Watford**	D3	H	L	2-4	Williams og, Churchill
1967-68	IL	1	18.12.67	**Swansea T**	D4	A	L	0-2	
1969-70	IL	1	15.11.69	**Brighton & HA**	D3	A	L	1-2	Day (p)
1970-71	IL	1	21.11.70	**Cambridge U**	D4	H	L	0-1	
1971-72	IL	1	20.11.71	**Maidenhead U**	IL	H	W	2-0	Turley, Hill
	2	11.12.71	**Peterborough U**	D4	A	L	0-4	
1972-73	IL	1	18.11.72	**Bishops Stortford**	IL	H	D	1-1	Brooks
	1r	21.11.72	**Bishops Stortford**		A	L	0-1	
1976-77	IL	1	20.11.76	**Harwich & Parkeston**	IL	H	D	0-0	
	1r	23.11.76	**Harwich & Parkeston**		A	W	3-0	Searle, Wilson, Reeve
	2	11.12.76	**Crystal P**	D3	H	L	0-4	
1977-78	IL	1	26.11.77	**Wimbledon**	D4	H	W	3-0	Knapman, Bass, O'Sullivan
	2	17.12.77	**Northampton T**	D4	A	W	2-0	Searle 2
	3	7.1.78	**Blyth Spartans**	NL	A	L	0-1	
1978-79	IL	1	25.11.78	**Wealdstone**	SL	A	W	5-0	O'Sullivan, Searle, King 2, Wright
	2	16.12.78	**Swindon T**	D3	A	L	0-3	
1979-80	IL	1	24.11.79	**Yeovil T**	APL	H	L	0-1	

1980-81	IL	1	22.11.80	**Wembley**	IL	H	W	3-0	Holmes, Wade, Jennings
		2	13.12.80	**Hereford U**	D4	H	W	2-0	Burton 2
		3	3.1.81	**Port Vale**	D4	A	D	1-1	Bishop
		3r	6.1.81	**Port Vale**		H	W	3-0	Bishop, King, Howell
		4	24.1.81	**Barnsley**	D3	A	D	1-1	Burton
		4r	28.1.81	**Barnsley** at White Hart Lane		H	L	0-3	
1981-82	APL	1	21.11.81	**Hastings U**	SL	H	W	2-0	Oliver, Ashford
		2	15.12.81	**Wimbledon**	D3	H	W	4-1	Turner, Ironton, Oliver, Waite
		3	2.1.82	**Crystal P**	D2	H	L	2-3	Ironton, Oliver
1982-83	APL	1	20.11.82	**Newport Co**	D3	H	D	0-0	
		1r	23.11.82	**Newport Co**		A	L	2-4	Taylor, Turner (p)
1983-84	APL	1	19.11.83	**Wealdstone**	APL	A	D	1-1	Flint
		1r	22.11.83	**Wealdstone**		H	D	2-2aet	Holmes 2
		1 2r	28.11.83	**Wealdstone**		A	L	0-2	
1984-85	APL	1	17.11.84	**Exeter C**	D4	A	D	2-2	Cox (p), Ashford
		1r	20.11.84	**Exeter C**		H	W	3-0	Ironton, Taylor 2
		2	8.12.84	**Millwall**	D3	A	L	0-1	
1985-86	APL	1	16.11.85	**Bognor Regis T**	IL	H	L	0-2	
1986-87	GMVC	1	15.11.86	**Dartford**	SL	A	D	1-1	Duffield (p)
		1r	18.11.86	**Dartford**		H	W	3-0	Duffield (p), King, Keen
		2	6.12.86	**Swindon T**	D3	A	L	0-3	
1988-89	GMVC	1	19.11.88	**Leyton O**	D4	H	D	1-1	Furlong
		1r	23.11.88	**Leyton O**		A	D	2-2aet	Lewis, Howell
		1 2r	28.11.88	**Leyton O**		A	W	1-0	Lewis
		2	11.12.88	**Cardiff C**	D3	H	L	1-4	Bate
1991-92	IL	1	16.11.91	**Aldershot**	D4	A	W	1-0	Brush
		2	7.12.91	**Barnet**	D4	H	L	1-4	Robinson

EPSOM AND EWELL TOWN

Founded 1917. **First entered FA Cup:** 1926. **FA Vase Runners-up:** 1975. Played in 1933 as Epsom Town **Cup Final Connection:** Alan Pardew, who played for Crystal Palace in the 1990 Cup Final, played for Epsom at the start of his career.

1933-34	Lon	1	25.11.33	**Clapton O**	3S	A	L	2-4	Marlow, Graves

ESHER LEOPOLD

1881-82		1	5.11.81	**Old Carthusians**		A	L	0-5	

ETONIAN RAMBLERS

1882-83		1	21.10.82	**Romford**		H	W	6-2	
		2	2.12.82	**Old Carthusians**		A	L	0-7	

EVENWOOD TOWN

Founded 1890. **First entered FA Cup:** 1930. Currently play in Northern League

1956-57	NL	1	17.11.56	**Darlington**	3N	A	L	2-7	Chisen, Calbrook

EVERTON

Formed 1878. Founder Members of the Football League 1888. **FA Cup Winners:** (4 times) 1906, 1933, 1966, 1984. **FA Cup Runners-up (7 times – a record)** 1893, 1897, 1907, 1968, 1985, 1986, 1989. **FA Cup Record Win:** 11-2 vs Derby Co, 1st round, 18.1.1890. **FA Cup Record Defeat:** 0-6 vs Crystal Palace, 1st round, 7.1.1922.

1886-87		1		**Glasgow Rangers**					*scratched*
1887-88		1	15.10.87	**Bolton W**		A	L	0-1	
				FA ordered replay after Bolton player declared ineligible					
		1r	29.10.87	**Bolton W**		H	D	2-2	Farmer, Watson
		1 2r	12.11.87	**Bolton W**		A	D	1-1	Farmer
		1 3r	19.11.87	**Bolton W**		H	W	2-1	Goodie, Watson
				FA later disqualified Everton for playing ineligible players					
		2	26.11.87	**Preston NE**		A	L	0-6	
				FA declared match void. Bolton were re-instated					
1888-89	D1		*did not enter*						
1889-90	D1	1	18.1.90	**Derby Co**	D1	H	W	11-2	Brady 3, Geary 3, Milward 3, Doyle, Kirkwood

	2	3.2.90	**Stoke**	D1	A	L	2-4	Geary, Milward
1890-91	D1	1	17.1.91	**Sunderland**	D1	A	L	0-1	
1891-92	D1	1	16.1.92	**Burnley**	D1	H	L	2-4	Chadwick, Roertson
1892-93	D1	1	21.1.93	**WBA**	D1	H	W	4-1	Geary 2, Latta, Maxwell
	2	4.2.93	**Nottingham F**	D1	H	W	4-2	Milward 2, E.Chadwick, Geary
	3	18.2.93	**Sheffield W**	D1	H	W	3-0	E.Chadwick, Geary, Maxwell
	SF	4.3.93	**Preston NE**	D1		D	2-2	E.Chadwick, Gordon
			played at Bramall Lane					
	SFr	16.3.93	**Preston NE** at Ewood Park			D	0-0aet	
	SF 2r	20.3.93	**Preston NE** at Trent Bridge			W	2-1	Gordon, Maxwell
	F	25.3.93	**Wolverhampton W**	D1		L	0-1	
			played at Fallowfield, Manchester					
1893-94	D1	1	27.1.94	**Stoke**	D1	A	L	0-1	
1894-95	D1	1	2.2.95	**Southport**	LL	A	W	3-0	Bell 3
	2	16.2.95	**Blackburn R**	D1	H	D	1-1	Chadwick
	2r	20.2.95	**Blackburn R**		A	W	3-2	Chadwick 2, Hartley
	3	2.3.95	**Sheffield W**	D1	A	L	0-2	
1895-96	D1	1	1.2.96	**Nottingham F**	D1	A	W	2-0	Chadwick, Milward
	2	15.2.96	**Sheffield U**	D1	H	W	3-0	Bell, Cameron, Milward
	3	29.2.96	**Sheffield W**	D1	A	L	0-4	
1896-97	D1	1	30.1.97	**Burton W**	D2	H	W	5-2	Bell 2, Chadwick, Holt, Milward
	2	13.2.97	**Bury**	D1	H	W	3-0	Taylor 2, Milward
	3	27.2.97	**Blackburn R**	D1	H	W	2-0	Hartley 2
	SF	20.3.97	**Derby Co**	D1		W	3-2	Chadwick, Hartley, Milward
			played at Stoke					
	F	10.4.97	**Aston Villa**	D1		L	2-3	Bell, Boyle
			played at Crystal Palace					
1897-98	D1	1	29.1.98	**Blackburn R**	D1	H	W	1-0	Williams
	2	12.2.98	**Stoke**	D1	A	D	0-0	
	2r	17.2.98	**Stoke**		H	W	5-1	L.Bell 2, Cameron, Chadwick, Taylor
	3	26.2.98	**Burnley**	D2	A	W	3-1	Taylor 2, L.Bell
	SF	19.3.98	**Derby Co**	D1		L	1-3	Chadwick
			played at Molineux					
1898-99	D1	1	28.1.99	**Jarrow**	NAll	H	W	3-1	Chadwick, Proudfoot, Taylor
	2	11.2.99	**Nottingham F**	D1	H	L	0-1	
1899-00	D1	1	27.1.00	**Southampton**	SL	A	L	0-3	
1900-01	D1	1	9.2.01	**Southampton**	SL	A	W	3-1	Settle, Taylor, Turner
	2	23.2.01	**Sheffield U**	D1	A	L	0-2	
1901-02	D1	1	25.1.02	**Liverpool**	D1	A	D	2-2	J.Sharp, Young
	1r	30.1.02	**Liverpool**		H	L	0-2	
1902-03	D1	1	7.2.03	**Portsmouth**	SL	H	W	5-0	Bell 2, Abbott, Bearley, Sharp
	2	21.2.03	**Manchester U**	D2	H	W	3-1	Abbott, Booth, Taylor
	3	7.3.03	**Milwall A**	SL	A	L	0-1	
1903-04	D1	1	6.2.04	**Tottenham H**	SL	H	L	1-2	Taylor
1904-05	D1	1	2.2.05	**Liverpool**	D2	A	D	1-1	Makepeace
	1r	8.2.05	**Liverpool**		H	W	2-1	Hardman, McDermott
	2	18.2.05	**Stoke**	D1	A	W	4-0	McDermott 2, Makepeace, Settle
	3	3.3.05	**Southampton**	SL	H	W	4-0	Settle 3, McDermott
	SF	25.3.05	**Aston Villa**	D1		D	1-1	Sharp
			played at Stoke					
	SFr	29.3.05	**Aston Villa** at Trent Bridge			L	1-2	Sharp
1905-06	D1	1	13.1.06	**WBA**	D2	H	W	3-1	Hardman, Makepeace, Sharp
	2	3.2.06	**Chesterfield**	D2	H	W	3-0	Settle, Taylor, Young
	3	24.2.06	**Bradford C**	D2	H	W	1-0	Makepeace
	4	10.3.06	**Sheffield W**	D1	H	W	4-3	Bolton, Booth Sharp, Taylor
	SF	31.3.06	**Liverpool**	D1		W	2-0	Abbott Hardman
			played at Villa Park					
	F	21.4.06	**NEWCASTLE U**	D1		W	1-0	Young
			played at Crystal Palace					
1906-07	D1	1	12.1.07	**Sheffield U**	D1	H	W	1-0	Johnson og
	2	2.2.07	**West Ham**	SL	A	W	2-1	Settle, Sharp
	3	23.2.07	**Bolton W**	D1	H	D	0-0	
	3r	27.2.07	**Bolton W**		A	W	3-0	Abbot, Settle, Taylor
	4	9.3.07	**Crystal P**	SL	A	D	1-1	Taylor
	4r	13.3.07	**Crystal P**		H	W	4-0	Settle 2, Hardman, Young
	SF	25.3.07	**WBA**	D2		W	2-1	Sharp, G.Wilson
			played at Bolton					

	F	20.4.07	Sheffield W	D1		L	1-2	Sharp
		played at Crystal Palace						
1907-08	D1	1	11.1.08	Tottenham H	SL	H	W	1-0	Young
		2	1.2.08	Oldham A	D2	A	D	0-0	
		2r	5.2.08	Oldham A		H	W	6-1	Bolton 4, Abbot, Young
		3	22.2.08	Bolton W	D1	A	D	3-3	Settle 2, Bolton
		3r	26.2.08	Bolton W		H	W	3-1aet	Young 2, Settle
		4	7.3.08	Southampton	SL	H	D	0-0	
		4r	11.3.08	Southampton		A	L	2-3	Bolton, Young
1908-09	D1	1	16.1.09	Barnsley	D2	H	W	3-1	Coleman, Sharp, White
		2	6.2.09	Manchester U	D1	A	L	0-1	
1909-10	D1	1	15.1.10	Middlesbrough	D1	A	D	1-1	White
		1r	19.1.10	Middlesbrough		H	W	5-3	Freeman, Makepeace, Taylor, White, Young
		2	5.2.10	W.Arsenal	D1	H	W	5-0	Sharp 2, Barlow, Freeman, Young
		3	19.2.10	Sunderland	D1	H	W	2-0	Makepeace, Young
		4	5.3.10	Coventry C	SL	A	W	2-0	Freeman 2
		SF	26.3.10	Barnsley	D2		D	0-0	
			played at Elland Road						
		SFr	31.3.10	Barnsley at Old Trafford			L	0-3	
1910-11	D1	1	14.1.11	Crystal P	SL	A	W	4-0	Gourlay, Magner, A.Young, R.Young
		2	4.2.11	Liverpool	D1	H	W	2-1	A.Young 2
		3	25.2.11	Derby Co	D2	A	L	0-5	
1911-12	D1	1	13.1.12	Clapton O	D2	A	W	2-1	Beare, Browell
		2	3.2.12	Bury	D1	H	D	1-1	Maconnachie
		2r	8.2.12	Bury		H	W	6-0	Browell 4, Davidson, Jefferis
		3	24.2.12	Oldham A	D1	A	W	2-0	Browell 2
		4	9.3.12	Swindon T	SL	A	L	1-2	Makepeace
1912-13	D1	1	11.1.13	Stockport Co	D2	H	–	1-1	T.Browell
			abandoned 48 minutes						
			15.1.13	Stockport Co		H	W	5-1	T.Browell 3, Bradshaw, Wareing
		2	1.2.13	Brighton & HA	SL	A	D	0-0	
		2r	5.2.13	Brighton & HA		H	W	1-0	Jefferis
		3	22.2.13	Bristol R	SL	A	W	4-0	T.Browell, Fleetwood, Harris, Jefferis
		4	8.3.13	Oldham A	D1	H	L	0-1	
1913-14	D1	1	10.1.14	Glossop	D2	A	L	1-2	Bradshaw
1914-15	D1	1	9.1.15	Barnsley	D2	H	W	3-0	Galt 2, Parker
		2	30.1.15	Bristol C	D2	H	W	4-0	Clennell, Kirsopp, Parker, Wareing
		3	20.2.15	QPR	SL	A	W	2-1	Clennell, Millington og
		4	6.3.15	Bradford C	D1	A	W	2-0	Chedgzoy, Clennell
		SF	27.3.15	Chelsea	D1		L	0-2	
			played at Villa Park						
1919-20	D1	1	10.1.20	Birmingham	D2	A	L	0-2	
1920-21	D1	1	1.1.21	Stockport Co	D2	H	W	1-0	Brewster og
		2	29.1.21	Sheffield W	D2	H	D	1-1	Parker
		2r	3.2.21	Sheffield W		A	W	1-0	Crossley
		3	19.2.21	Newcastle U	D1	H	W	3-0	Crossley 2, Davies
		4	5.3.21	Wolverhampton W	D2	H	L	0-1	
1921-22	D1	1	7.1.22	Crystal P	D2	H	L	0-6	
1922-23	D1	1	13.1.23	Bradford PA	3N	H	D	1-1	Chedgzoy
		1r	17.1.23	Bradford PA		A	L	0-1	
1923-24	D1	1	12.1.24	Preston NE	D1	H	W	3-1	Chadwick, Chedgzoy, Cock
		2	2.2.24	Brighton & HA	3S	A	L	2-5	Chadwick, Cock
1924-25	D1	1	10.1.25	Burnley	D1	H	W	2-1	Chadwick 2
		2	31.1.25	Sunderland	D1	A	D	0-0	
		2r	4.2.25	Sunderland		H	W	2-1	Chadwick, Irvine
		3	21.2.25	Sheffield U	D1	A	L	0-1	
1925-26	D1	3	9.1.26	Fulham	D2	H	D	1-1	Dean
		3r	14.1.26	Fulham		A	L	0-1	
1926-27	D1	3	8.1.27	Poole T	SL	H	W	3-1	Dean, Irvine, Troop
		4	22.1.27	Hull C	D2	A	D	1-1	Virr
		4r	2.2.27	Hull C		H	D	2-2aet	Dean, Troop
		4 2r	7.2.27	Hull C at Villa Pk			L	2-3aet	Dean, Dominy
1927-28	D1	3	14.1.28	Preston NE	D2	A	W	3-0	Dean, Irvine, Ward og
		4	28.1.28	Arsenal	D1	A	L	3-4	Dean 2, Troop
1928-29	D1	3	12.1.29	Chelsea	D2	A	L	0-2	
1929-30	D1	3	11.1.30	Carlisle U	3N	A	W	4-2	Critchley 2, Dean 2
		4	25.1.30	Blackburn R	D1	A	L	1-4	Martin

Season	Div	Rd	Date	Opponent		Venue	Result	Score	Scorers
1930-31	D2	3	10.1.31	Plymouth A	D2	A	W	2-0	Dunn, Stein
		4	24.1.31	Crystal P	3S	A	W	6-0	Dean 4, Johnson, Wilde og
		5	14.2.31	Grimsby T	D1	H	W	5-3	Johnson 2, Stein 2, Dean
		6	28.2.31	Southport	3N	H	W	9-1	Dean 4, Critchley 2, Dunn 2, Johnson
		SF	14.3.31	WBA	D2		L	0-1	
				played at Old Trafford					
1931-32	D1	3	19.1.32	Liverpool	D1	H	L	1-2	Dean
1932-33	D1	3	14.1.33	Leicester C	D1	A	W	3-2	Dean, Dunn, Stein
		4	28.1.33	Bury	D2	H	W	3-1	Johnson 2, Dean
		5	18.2.33	Leeds U	D1	H	W	2-0	Dean, Stein
		6	3.3.33	Luton T	3S	H	W	6-0	Johnson 2, Stein 2, Dean, Dunn
		SF	18.3.33	West Ham	D2		W	2-1	Critchley, Dunn
				played at Molineux					
		F	29.4.33	MANCHESTER CITY	D1	WEMBLEY	W	3-0	Dean, Dunn, Stein
1933-34	D1	3	13.1.34	Tottenham H	D1	A	L	0-3	
1934-35	D1	3	12.1.35	Grimsby T	D1	H	W	6-3	Geldard 3, Stevenson 2, Cunliffe
		4	26.1.35	Sunderland	D1	A	D	1-1	Cunliffe
		4r	30.1.35	Sunderland		H	W	6-4aet	Coulter 3, Geldard 2, Stevenson
		5	16.2.35	Derby Co	D1	H	W	3-1	Coulter 2, Dean
		6	2.3.35	Bolton W	D2	H	L	1-2	Coulter
1935-36	D1	3	11.1.36	Preston NE	D1	H	L	1-3	Geldard
1936-37	D1	3	16.1.37	Bournemouth	3S	H	W	5-0	Gillick 2, Stevenson 2, Cunliffe
		4	30.1.37	Sheffield W	D1	H	W	3-0	Britton, Coulter, Dean
		5	20.2.37	Tottenham H	D2	H	D	1-1	Coulter
		5r	22.2.37	Tottenham H		A	L	3-4	Dean 2, Lawton
1937-38	D1	3	8.1.38	Chelsea	D1	A	W	1-0	Stevenson
		4	22.1.38	Sunderland	D1	H	L	0-1	
1938-39	D1	3	7.1.39	Derby Co	D1	A	W	1-0	Boyes
		4	21.1.39	Doncaster R	3N	H	W	8-0	Lawton 4, Boyes 2, Gillick, Stevenson
		5	11.2.39	Birmingham	D1	A	D	2-2	Boyes, Stevenson
		5r	15.2.39	Birmingham		H	W	2-1	Cook, Gillick
		6	4.3.39	Wolverhampton W	D1	A	L	0-2	
1945-46	D1	3 1L	5.1.46	Preston NE	D1	A	L	1-2	Catterick
		3 2L	9.1.46	Preston NE		H	D	2-2aet	Elliott, Mercer
1946-47	D1	3	11.1.47	Southend U	3S	H	W	4-2	Fielding, Jones, McIlhatton, Wainwright
		4	25.1.47	Sheffield W	D2	A	L	1-2	Wainwright
1947-48	D1	3	10.1.48	Grimsby T	D1	A	W	4-1	Wainwright 2, Dodds, Farrell
		4	24.1.48	Wolverhampton W	D1	A	D	1-1	Catterick
		4r	31.1.48	Wolverhampton W		H	W	3-2	Fielding 2, Grant
		5	7.2.48	Fulham	D2	A	D	1-1aet	Eglington
		5 r	14.2.48	Fulham		H	L	0-1	
1948-49	D1	3	8.1.49	Manchester C	D1	H	W	1-0	Higgins
		4	29.1.49	Chelsea	D1	A	L	0-2	
1949-50	D1	3	7.1.50	QPR	D2	A	W	2-0	Buckle, Catterick
		4	28.1.50	West Ham	D2	A	W	2-1	Catterick 2
		5	11.2.50	Tottenham H	D2	A	W	1-0	Wainwright
		6	4.3.50	Derby Co	D1	A	W	2-1	Buckle, Wainwright
		SF	25.3.50	Liverpool	D1		L	0-2	
				played at Maine Road					
1950-51	D1	3	6.1.51	Hull C	D2	A	L	0-2	
1951-52	D2	3	12.1.52	Leyton O	3S	A	D	0-0	
		3r	16.1.52	Leyton O		H	L	1-3	Parker
1952-53	D2	3	10.1.53	Ipswich T	3S	H	W	3-2	Hickson 2, Fielding
		4	31.1.53	Nottingham F	D2	H	W	4-1	Parker 2, Clinton, Eglington
		5	14.2.53	Manchester U	D1	H	W	2-1	Eglington, Hickson
		6	28.2.53	Aston Villa	D1	A	W	1-0	Hickson
		SF	21.3.53	Bolton W	D1		L	3-4	Parker 2, Farrell
				played at Maine Road					
1953-54	D2	3	9.1.54	Notts Co	D2	H	W	2-1	Eglington, Hickson
		4	30.1.54	Swansea T	D2	H	W	3-0	Parker 2, Hickson
		5	20.2.54	Sheffield W	D1	A	L	1-3	Hickson
1954-55	D1	3	8.1.55	Southend U	3S	H	W	3-1	Fielding, Hickson, Potts
		4	29.1.55	Liverpool	D2	H	L	0-4	
1955-56	D1	3	7.1.56	Bristol C	D2	H	W	3-1	Eglington, J.Harris, Wainwright
		4	28.1.56	Port Vale	D2	A	W	3-2	Eglington, B.Harris, Wainwright
		5	18.2.56	Chelsea	D1	H	W	1-0	Farrell
		6	3.3.56	Manchester C	D1	A	L	1-2	J.Harris

1956-57	D1	3	5.1.57	Blackburn R	D2	H	W	1-0	J.Harris
		4	26.1.57	West Ham	D2	H	W	2-1	Farrell, Gauld
		5	16.2.57	Manchester U	D1	A	L	0-1	
1957-58	D1	3	4.1.58	Sunderland	D1	A	D	2-2	Hickson 2
		3r	8.1.58	Sunderland		H	W	3-1	Keeley 2, Hickson
		4	29.1.58	Blackburn R	D2	H	L	1-2	J.Harris
1958-59	D1	3	10.1.59	Sunderland	D2	H	W	4-0	Hickson 2, J.Harris, Thomas
		4	24.1.59	Charlton A	D2	A	D	2-2	Collins, Thomas
		4r	28.1.59	Charlton A		H	W	4-1aet	Collins 2, Hickson 2
		5	14.2.59	Aston Villa	D1	H	L	1-4	Hickson
1959-60	D1	3	9.1.60	Bradford C	D3	A	L	0-3	
1960-61	D1	3	7.1.61	Sheffield U	D2	H	L	0-1	
1961-62	D1	3	6.1.62	King's Lynn	SL	W	W	4-0	Bingham, Collins, Fell, Vernon
		4	27.1.62	Manchester C	D1	H	W	2-0	Lill, Vernon
		5	17.2.62	Burnley	D1	A	L	1-3	Collins
1962-63	D1	3	15.1.63	Barnsley	D3	A	W	3-0	Harris, Stevens, Vernon
		4	29.1.63	Swindon T	D3	A	W	5-1	Vernon 2, Bingham, Gabriel, Morrissey
		5	16.3.63	West Ham	D1	A	L	0-1	
1963-64	D1	3	4.1.64	Hull C	D3	A	D	1-1	Scott
		3r	7.1.64	Hull C		H	W	2-1	Harris, Scott
		4	25.1.64	Leeds U	D2	A	D	1-1	Vernon
		4r	28.1.64	Leeds U		H	W	2-0	Gabriel, Vernon
		5	15.2.64	Sunderland	D2	A	L	1-3	Harris
1964-65	D1	3	9.1.65	Sheffield W	D1	H	D	2-2	Burgin og, Pickering
		3r	13.1.65	Sheffield W		A	W	3-0	Harvey, Pickering, Temple
		4	30.1.65	Leeds U	D1	A	D	1-1	Pickering
		4r	2.2.65	Leeds U		H	L	1-2	Pickering
1965-66	D1	3	22.1.66	Sunderland	D1	H	W	3-0	Pickering, Temple, Young
		4	12.2.66	Bedford T	SL	A	W	3-0	Temple 2, Pickering
		5	3.3.66	Coventry C	D2	H	W	3-0	Pickering, Temple, Young
		6	26.3.66	Manchester C	D2	A	D	0-0	
		6r	29.3.66	Manchester C		H	D	0-0aet	
		6 2r	5.4.66	Manchester C at Molineux			W	2-0	Pickering, Temple
		SF	23.4.66	Manchester U	D1		W	1-0	Harvey
				played at Bolton					
		F	14.5.66	SHEFFIELD W	D1 WEMBLEY W			3-2	Trebilcock 2, Temple
1966-67	D1	3	28.1.67	Burnley	D1	A	D	0-0	
		3r	31.1.67	Burnley		H	W	2-1	Young 2
		4	18.2.67	Wolverhampton W	D2	A	D	1-1	Ball
		4r	21.1.67	Wolverhampton W		H	W	3-1	Husband 2, Temple
		5	11.3.67	Liverpool	D1	H	W	1-0	Ball
		6	8.4.67	Nottingham F	D1	A	L	2-3	Husband 2
1967-68	D1	3	2.1.68	Southport	D3	A	W	1-0	Royle
		4	17.2.68	Carlisle U	D2	A	W	2-0	Husband, Royle
		5	9.3.68	Tranmere R	D3	H	W	2-0	Morrissey, Royle
		6	30.3.68	Leicester C	D1	A	W	3-1	Husband 2, Kendall
		SF	27.4.68	Leeds U	D1		W	1-0	Morrissey
				played at Old Trafford					
		F	18.5.68	WBA	D1 WEMBLEY L			0-1	
1968-69	D1	3	4.1.69	Ipswich T	D1	H	W	2-1	Hurst, Royle
		4	25.1.69	Coventry C	D1	H	W	2-0	Hurst, Royle
		5	12.2.69	Bristol C	D2	H	W	1-0	Royle
		6	1.3.69	Manchester U	D1	A	W	1-0	Royle
		SF	22.3.69	Manchester C	D1		L	0-1	
				played at Old Trafford					
1969-70	D1	3	3.1.70	Sheffield U	D2	A	L	1-2	Ball
1970-71	D1	3	2.1.71	Blackburn R	D2	H	W	2-0	Husband 2
		4	23.1.71	Middlesbrough	D2	H	W	3-0	Harvey, H.Newton, Royle
		5	13.2.71	Derby Co	D1	H	W	1-0	Johnson
		6	6.3.71	Colchester U	D4	H	W	5-0	Kendall 2, Ball, Husband, Royle
		SF	27.3.71	Liverpool	D1		L	1-2	Ball
				played at Old Trafford					
1971-72	D1	3	15.1.72	Crystal P	D1	A	D	2-2	Harvey, Whittle
		3r	18.1.72	Crystal P		H	W	3-2	Hurst, Kenyon, Scott
		4	5.2.72	Walsall	D3	H	W	2-1	Johnson, Whittle
		5	26.2.72	Tottenham H	D1	H	L	0-2	
1972-73	D1	3	13.1.73	Aston Villa	D2	H	W	3-2	Belfitt, Buckley, Harper

EVERTON

	4	3.2.73 **Millwall**	D2	H	L	0-2	
1973-74 D1	3	5.1.74 **Blackburn R**	D3	H	W	3-0	Clements, Harper, Hurst
	4	27.1.74 **WBA**	D2	H	D	0-0	
	4r	30.1.74 **WBA**		A	L	0-1	
1974-75 D1	3	4.1.75 **Altrincham**	NPL	H	D	1-1	Clements
	3r	7.1.75 **Altrincham** at Old Trafford		A	W	2-0	Latchford, Lyons
	4	25.1.75 **Plymouth A**	D3	A	W	3-1	Lyons 2, Pearson
	5	15.2.75 **Fulham**	D2	H	L	1-2	Kenyon
1975-76 D1	3	3.1.76 **Derby Co**	D1	A	L	1-2	G.Jones
1976-77 D1	3	8.1.77 **Stoke C**	D1	H	W	2-0	Lyons, McKenzie
	4	29.1.77 **Swindon T**	D3	A	D	2-2	Latchford, Mckenzie
	4r	1.2.77 **Swindon T**		H	W	2-1	Dobson, Jones
	5	26.2.77 **Cardiff C**	D2	A	W	2-1	Latchford, McKenzie
	6	19.3.77 **Derby Co**	D1	H	W	2-0	Latchford, Pearson
	SF	23.4.77 **Liverpool**	D1		D	2-2	McKenzie, Rioch
	SFr	27.4.77 **Liverpool**			L	0-3	
		both matches at Maine Road					
1977-78 D1	3	7.1.78 **Aston V**	D1	H	W	4-1	King, Latchford, McKenzie, Ross
	4	28.1.78 **Middlesbrough**	D1	A	L	2-3	Lyons, Telfer
1978-79 D1	3	10.1.79 **Sunderland**	D2	A	L	1-2	Dobson
1979-80 D1	3	5.1.80 **Aldershot**	D4	H	W	4-1	Hartford, Kidd, King, Latchford
	4	26.1.80 **Wigan A**	D4	H	W	3-0	Kidd, Latchford, McBride
	5	16.2.80 **Wrexham**	D2	H	W	5-2	Eastoe 2, Latchford, Megson, Ross
	6	8.3.80 **Ipswich T**	D1	H	W	2-1	Kidd, Latchford
	SF	12.4.80 **West Ham**	D2		D	1-1	Kidd
		played at Villa Park					
	SFr	16.4.80 **West Ham** at Elland Road			L	1-2	Latchford
1980-81 D1	3	3.1.81 **Arsenal**	D1	H	W	2-0	Sansom og, Lyons
	4	24.1.81 **Liverpool**	D1	H	W	2-1	Eastoe, Varadi
	5	14.2.81 **Southampton**	D1	A	D	0-0	
	5r	17.2.81 **Southampton**		H	W	1-0	O'Keefe
	6	7.3.81 **Manchester C**	D1	H	D	2-2	Eastoe, Ross
	6r	11.3.81 **Manchester C**		A	L	1-3	Eastoe
1981-82 D1	3	2.1.82 **West Ham**	D1	A	L	1-2	Eastoe
1982-83 D1	3	8.1.83 **Newport Co**	D3	A	D	1-1	Sheedy
	3r	11.1.83 **Newport Co**		H	W	2-1	King, Sharp
	4	30.1.83 **Shrewsbury T**	D2	H	W	2-1	Heath, Sheedy
	5	19.2.83 **Tottenham H**	D1	H	W	2-0	King, Sharp
	6	12.3.83 **Manchester U**	D1	A	L	0-1	
1983-84 D1	3	6.1.84 **Stoke C**	D1	A	W	2-0	Gray, Irvine
	4	28.1.84 **Gillingham**	D3	H	D	0-0	
	4r	31.1.84 **Gillingham**		A	D	0-0aet	
	4 2r	6.2.84 **Gillingham**		A	W	3-0	Sheedy 2, Heath
	5	18.2.84 **Shrewsbury T**	D2	H	W	3-0	Irvine, Reid, Griffin og
	6	10.3.84 **Notts Co**	D1	A	W	2-1	Gray, Richardson
	SF	14.4.84 **Southampton**	D1		W	1-0	Heath
		played at Highbury					
	F	19.5.84 **WATFORD**	D1 WEMBLEY		W	2-0	Gray, Sharp
1984-85 D1	3	5.1.85 **Leeds U**	D2	A	W	2-0	Sharp, Sheedy
	4	26.1.85 **Doncaster R**	D3	H	W	2-0	Steven, Stevens
	5	16.2.85 **Telford U**	APL	H	W	3-0	Reid, Sheedy, Steven
	6	9.3.85 **Ipswich T**	D1	H	D	2-2	Mountfield, Sheedy
	6r	13.3.85 **Ipswich T**		A	W	1-0	Sharp
	SF	13.4.85 **Luton T**	D1		W	2-1aet	Mountfield, Sheedy
		played at Villa Park					
	F	18.5.85 **Manchester U**	D1 WEMBLEY		L	0-1aet	
1985-86 D1	3	5.1.86 **Exeter C**	D4	H	W	1-0	Stevens
	4	25.1.86 **Blackburn R**	D2	H	W	3-1	Lineker 2, Van den Hauwe
	5	4.3.86 **Tottenham H**	D1	A	W	2-1	Heath, Lineker
	6	8.3.86 **Luton T**	D1	A	D	2-2	Donaghy og, Heath
	6r	12.3.86 **Luton T**		H	W	1-0	Lineker
	SF	5.4.86 **Sheffield W**	D1		W	2-1	Harper, Sharp
		played at Villa Park					
	F	10.5.86 **Liverpool**	D1 WEMBLEY		L	1-3	Lineker
1986-87 D1	3	10.1.87 **Southampton**	D1	H	W	2-1	Sharp 2
	4	31.1.87 **Bradford C**	D2	A	W	1-0	Snodin
	5	22.2.87 **Wimbledon**	D1	A	L	1-3	Wilkinson

EVERTON

Season	Div	Rnd	Date	Opponent		Div	H/A	Result	Score	Scorers
1987-88	D1	3	9.1.88	Sheffield W		D1	A	D	1-1	Reid
		3r	13.1.88	Sheffield W			H	D	1-1aet	Sharp
		3 2r	25.1.88	Sheffield W			H	D	1-1aet	Steven
		3 3r	27.1.88	Sheffield W			A	W	5-0	Sharp 3, Heath, Snodin
		4	30.1.88	Middlesbrough		D2	H	D	1-1	Sharp
		4r	3.2.88	Middlesbrough			A	D	2-2aet	Steven, Watson
		4 2r	9.2.88	Middlesbrough			H	W	2-1	Sharp, Mowbray og
		5	21.2.88	Liverpool		D1	H	L	0-1	
1988-89	D1	3	7.1.89	WBA		D2	A	D	1-1	Sheedy (p)
		3r	11.1.89	WBA			H	W	1-0	Sheedy
		4	28.1.89	Plymouth A		D2	A	D	1-1	Sheedy (p)
		4r	31.1.89	Plymouth A			H	W	4-0	Sharp 2, Nevin, Sheedy
		5	19.2.89	Barnsley		D2	A	W	1-0	Sharp
		6	19.3.89	Wimbledon		D1	H	W	1-0	McCall
		SF	15.4.89	Norwich C		D1		W	1-0	Nevin
			played at Villa Park							
		F	20.5.89	Liverpool		D1	WEMBLEY	L	2-3aet	McCall 2
1989-90	D1	3	6.1.90	Middlesbrough		D2	A	D	0-0	
		3r	10.1.90	Middlesbrough			H	D	1-1aet	Sheedy
		3 2r	17.1.90	Middlesbrough			H	W	1-0	Whiteside
		4	28.1.90	Sheffield W		D1	A	W	2-1	Whiteside 2
		5	17.2.90	Oldham A		D2	A	D	2-2	Sharp, Cottee
		5r	21.2.90	Oldham A			H	D	1-1aet	Sheedy
		5 2r	10.3.90	Oldham A			A	L	1-2aet	Cottee
1990-91	D1	3	5.1.91	Charlton A		D2	A	W	2-1	Ebbrell 2
		4	27.1.91	Woking		IL	H	W	1-0	Sheedy
		5	17.2.91	Liverpool		D1	A	D	0-0	
		5r	20.2.91	Liverpool			H	D	4-4aet	Sharp 2, Cottee 2
		5 2r	27.2.91	Liverpool			H	W	1-0	Watson
		6	11.3.91	West Ham		D2	A	L	1-2	Watson
1991-92	D1	3	4.1.92	Southend U		D2	H	W	1-0	Beardsley
		4	26.1.92	Chelsea		D1	A	L	0-1	
1992-93	PL	3	2.1.93	Wimbledon		PL	A	D	0-0	
		3r	12.1.93	Wimbledon			H	L	1-2	Watson

EXETER CITY

Formed 1904. **Best Performance in the FA Cup:** 6th round, 1931, 1981. **Record FA Cup Win:** 14-0 vs Weymouth, 1st qual rd, 1908-09. In competition proper: 9-1 vs Aberdare Athletic, 1st round, 26.11.1927. **Record FA Cup Defeat:** 2-6 vs Cardiff City, 1st round, 22.11.1975

Season	Div	Rnd	Date	Opponent		Div	H/A	Result	Score	Scorers
1908-09	SL	1q **Weymouth** (H) 14-0; 2q **Longfleet St Mary** 1-1 at Poole; 2qr **Longfleet St M.** (H) 10-1; 3q **Whiteheads Weymouth** (H) 4-0; 4q **Kingswood R** 2-0 at Bristol; 5q **Barnet A** (A) 3-0								
		1	16.1.09	Wrexham		BDL	A		1-1	Watson
		1r	20.1.09	Wrexham			H		2-1aet	Chadwick (p), McGuigan
		2	6.2.09	Plymouth A		SL	A		0-2	
1909-10	SL	4q **Nunhead** (H) 7-1; 5q **Stoke** (A) 0-0; 5qr **Stoke** (H) 1-1; 5q 2r **Stoke** 1-2 at Fulham								
1910-11	SL	4q **Reading** (A) 1-1; 4qr **Reading** (H) 1-0 after abandoned match; 5q **Nelson** (A) 4-3								
		1	14.1.10	Burnley		D2	A	L	0-2	
1911-12	SL	4q **Merthyr Town** (H) 1-1; 4qr **Merthyr Town** (A) 0-0aet; 4q 2r **Merthyr Town** 0-2 at Ashton Gate								
1912-13	SL	4q **Cardiff C** (A) 1-5								
1913-14	SL	1	10.1.14	Portsmouth		SL	A	W	4-0	Holt 2, Marshall 2
		2	31.1.14	A. Villa		D1	H	L	1-2	McCann
1914-15	SL	1	9.1.15	A.Villa		D1	A	L	0-2	
1919-20	SL	6q **Newport Co** (A) 0-1								
1920-21	D3	1	8.1.21	Watford		D3	A	L	0-3	
1921-22	3S	5q **Bristol R** (A) 0-0; 5qr **Bristol R** (H) 0-2								
1922-23	3S	4q **Bournemouth** (H) 0-0; 4qr **Bournemouth** (A) 3-1; 5q **Bath C** (H) 1-2								
1923-24	3S	4q **Newport Co** (A) 2-0; 5q **Bristol R** (H) 2-2; 5qr **Bristol R** (A) 1-0; 6q **Sittingbourne** (A) 2-0								
		1	12.1.24	Grimsby T		3N	W	1-0	Davis	
		2	2.2.24	Watford		3S	H	D	0-0	
		2r	6.2.24	Watford			A	L	0-1	
1924-25	3S	5q **Newport Co** (H) 1-1; 5qr **Newport Co** (A) 3-3aet; 5q 2r **Newport Co** 1-0 at Ashton Gate; 6q **Barnet** (H) 3-0								
		1	10.1.25	Southampton		D2	A	–	0-5	
			abandoned after 80 minutes – fog							
		1	14.1.25	Southampton			A	L	1-3	Kirk
1925-26	3S	1	28.11.25	Swansea T		D2	H	L	1-3	Compton
1926-27	3S	1	27.11.26	Aberdare A		3S	H	W	3-0	Compton 2, Purcell

	2	11.12.26	**Northampton T**	3S	H	W	1-0	McDevitt
	3	8.1.27	**Accrington Stanley**	3N	H	L	0-2	
1927-28 3S	1	26.11.27	**Aberdare A**	SL	H	W	9-1	Dent 4, Vaughan 2, Purcell 2, Compton
	2	10.12.27	**Ilford**	IL	H	W	5-3	Dent 2, Purcell 2, McDevitt
	3	14.1.28	**Rotherham U**	3N	A	D	3-3	Vaughan, Mason, Jackson (og)
	3r	18.1.28	**Rotherham U**		H	W	3-1	Vaughan 2, Purcell
	4	28.1.28	**Blackburn R**	D1	H	D	2-2	Gee (p), Mason
	4r	2.2.28	**Blackburn R**		A	L	1-3aet	Compton
1928-29 3S	1	24.11.28	**Barking T**	IL	H	W	6-0	Purcell, Doncaster, Clarke, Death, Cameron, Vango (og)
	2	8.12.28	**Torquay U**	3S	A	W	1-0	Purcell
	3	12.1.29	**Leeds U**	D1	H	D	2-2	Doncaster, Purcell
	3r	16.1.29	**Leeds U**		A	L	1-5	Doncaster
1929-30 3S	1	30.11.29	**Walsall**	3S	A	L	0-1	
1930-31 3S	1	29.11.30	**Northfleet U**	SL	A	W	3-0	Houghton, Purcell, Maitland (og)
	2	13.12.30	**Coventry C**	3S	H	D	1-1	Varco
	2r	18.12.30	**Coventry C**		A	W	2-1	Varco, Doncaster
	3	10.1.31	**Derby Co**	D1	H	W	3-2	Varco, Armfield, Houghton
	4	24.1.31	**Bury**	D2	A	W	2-1	Varco, Houghton
	5	14.2.31	**Leeds U**	D1	H	W	3-1	Armfield 2, Purcell
	6	28.2.31	**Sunderland**	D1	A	D	1-1	Houghton
	6r	4.3.31	**Sunderland**		H	L	2-4	Varco, Purcell
1931-32 3S	3	9.1.32	**Grimsby T**	D1	A	L	1-4	Woodward
1932-33 3S	1	26.11.32	**Southend U**	3S	A	D	1-1	Whitlow
	1r	30.11.32	**Southend U**		H	L	0-1	
1933-34 3S	1	25.11.33	**Northampton T**	3S	A	L	0-2	
1934-35 3S	1	24.11.34	**Charlton A**	3S	A	D	2-2	Hurst 2
	1r	28.11.34	**Charlton A**		H	W	5-2	T.Scott 2, Hurst, Wrightson, J.Scott
	2	8.12.34	**Yeovil & Petters U**	SL	A	L	1-4	Angus
1935-36 3S	1	30.11.35	**Gillingham**	3S	H	L	0-4	
1936-37 3S	1	28.11.36	**Folkestone**	SL	H	W	3-0	Keane 2, Williams
	2	12.12.36	**Walthamstow Ave**	AL	A	-	1-1	Clarke (p)
			abandoned after 65 minutes - fog					
	2	17.12.36	**Walthamstow Ave**		A	W	3-2	Williams 2, Keane
	3	16.1.37	**Oldham A**	3N	H	W	3-0	Williams 2, Smith
	4	30.1.37	**Leicester C**	D2	H	W	3-1	Williams 2, Bussey
	5	20.2.37	**Preston NE**	D1	A	L	3-5	Owen 2, F.Smith
1937-38 3S	1	27.11.37	**Folkestone**	SL	H	W	1-0	Pope
	2	11.12.37	**Hull C**	3N	H	L	1-2	Liddle
1938-39 3S	1	26.11.38	**Torquay U**	3S	A	L	1-3	Riley
1945-46 3S	1 1L	17.11.45	**Trowbridge T**	WL	A	W	3-1	Challis, Walker, Ebdon
	1 2L	24.11.45	**Trowbridge T**		H	W	7-2	Walker 4, Challis, Tickell, Atack (og)
	2 1L	8.12.45	**Newport Co**	D2	A	L	1-5	Gallagher
	2 2L	15.12.45	**Newport Co**		H	L	1-3	Crawshaw
1946-47 3S	1	30.11.46	**Bournemouth & BA**	3S	A	L	2-4	Regan, Hydes
1947-48 3S	1	29.11.47	**Northampton T**	3S	H	D	1-1aet	Bartholomew
	1r	6.12.47	**Northampton T**		A	L	0-2	
1948-49 3S	1	4.12.48	**Barnet**	AL	A	W	6-2	Smith 4, Bartholomew, Dymond
	2	11.12.48	**Hereford U**	SL	A	W	2-1	Dymond 2
	3	8.1.49	**Grimsby T**	D2	A	L	1-2	Regan
1949-50 3S	1	26.11.49	**Millwall**	3S	A	W	5-3	Smart 3, Regan, Smith
	2	10.12.49	**Chester**	3N	A	W	2-0	Regan 2 (1p)
	3	7.1.50	**Nuneaton Borough**	BC	A	W	3-0	Greenwood, Regan, Fallon
	4	28.1.50	**Liverpool**	D1	A	L	1-3	Smart
1950-51 3S	1	25.11.50	**Glastonbury**	WL	A	W	2-1	Smith, Mackay
	2	9.12.50	**Swindon T**	3S	H	W	3-0	Smith, Fallon, Mackay
	3	6.1.51	**Grimsby T**	D2	A	D	3-3	Mackay 2, McClelland
	3r	10.1.51	**Grimsby T**		H	W	4-2	McClelland 2, Smith 2
	4	27.1.51	**Chelsea**	D1	H	D	1-1	Regan
	4r	31.1.51	**Chelsea**		A	L	0-2	
1951-52 3S	1	24.11.51	**Kings Lynn**	ECL	A	W	3-1	McClelland 2, Smart
	2	15.12.51	**Ipswich T**	3S	A	L	0-4	
1952-53 3S	1	22.11.52	**Port Vale**	3N	A	L	1-2	Murphy
1953-54 3S	1	21.11.53	**Hereford U**	SL	H	D	1-1	Samuels
	1r	25.11.53	**Hereford U**		A	L	0-2	
1954-55 3S	1	20.11.54	**Milwall**	3S	A	L	2-3	Murphy, Mackay
1955-56 3S	1	19.11.55	**Coventry C**	3S	A	W	1-0	Rees
	2	10.12.55	**Hendon**	AL	H	W	6-2	Rees 2, Iggleden 2, Simpson, Murphy

Season		Round	Date	Opponent	Comp	H/A	Res	Score	Scorers
		3	7.1.56	Stoke C	D2	H	D	0-0	
		3r	9.1.56	Stoke C		A	L	0-3	
1956-57	3S	1	17.11.56	Plymouth A	3S	H	L	0-2	
1957-58	3S	1	16.11.57	Bath C	SL	A	L	1-2	Calland
1958-59	D4	1	15.11.58	Brentford	D3	A	L	2-3	Calland, Mitchell (p)
1959-60	D4	1	14.11.59	Barnstaple T	WL	H	W	4-0	Rees 2, Wilkinson, Stiffle
		2	5.12.59	Brentford	D3	H	W	3-1	Dale, Rees, Stiffle
		3	9.1.60	Luton T	D1	H	L	1-2	Daniel (og)
1960-61	D4	1	5.11.60	Bournemouth	D3	H	D	1-1	Bond
		1r	9.11.60	Bournemouth		A	L	1-3	Bond
1961-62	D4	1	4.11.61	Dartford	SL	H	D	3-3	McMillan 2, Mabey (og)
		1r	8.11.61	Dartford		A	L	1-2	Carter
1962-63	D4	1	3.11.62	Gravesend & N.	SL	A	L	2-3	Carter 2
1963-64	D4	1	16.11.63	Shrewsbury T	D3	H	W	2-1	Curtis, Anderson
		2	7.12.63	Bristol C	D3	H	L	0-2	
1964-65	D3	1	14.11.64	Hayes	AL	H	W	1-0	Ley
		2	5.12.64	Shrewsbury T	D3	H	L	1-2	Mitchell
1965-66	D3	1	13.11.65	Bedford T	SL	H	L	1-2	Curtis
1966-67	D4	1	26.11.66	Luton T	D4	H	D	1-1	Keeley
		1r	1.12.66	Luton T		A	L	0-2	
1967-68	D4	1	9.12.67	Nuneaton B	SL	A	D	0-0	
		1r	13.12.67	Nuneaton B		H	D	0-0aet	
		1 2r	18.12.67	Nuneaton B at Ashton Gate			W	1-0	Banks
		2	6.1.68	Walsall	D3	H	L	1-3	Blain (p)
1968-69	D4	1	16.11.68	Newport Co	D4	H	D	0-0	
		1r	18.11.68	Newport Co		A	W	3-1	Balson, Williams (og), Wood (og)
		2	7.12.68	Colchester U	D4	A	W	1-0	Banks
		3	4.1.69	Manchester U	D1	H	L	1-3	Banks
1969-70	D4	1	15.11.69	Fulham	D3	H	W	2-0	Corr, Banks
		2	6.12.69	Northampton T	D4	A	D	1-1	Wingate
		2r	10.12.69	Northampton T		H	D	0-0aet	
		2 2r	15.12.69	Northampton T at Swindon			L	1-2	Mitten (p)
1970-71	D4	1	21.11.70	Swansea C	D3	A	L	1-4	Wingate
1971-72	D4	1	20.11.71	Crawley T	SL	A	D	0-0	
		1r	24.11.71	Crawley T		H	W	2-0	Binney, Rowan
		2	11.12.71	Swansea C	D3	A	D	0-0	
		2r	15.12.71	Swansea C		H	L	0-1	
1972-73	D4	1	18.11.72	Walton & Hersham	IL	A	L	1-2	Stacey
1973-74	D4	1	24.11.73	Alvechurch	WMRL	H	L	0-1	
1974-75	D4	1	23.11.74	Newport Co	D4	H	L	1-2	Hodge
1975-76	D4	1	22.11.75	Cardiff C	D3	A	L	2-6	Beer, Bowker
1976-77	D4	1	20.11.76	Southend U	D4	H	D	1-1	Hatch
		1r	22.11.76	Southend U		A	L	1-2aet	Kellow
1977-78	D3	1	26.11.77	Newport Co	D4	A	D	1-1	Bowker
		1r	30.11.77	Newport Co		H	W	4-2	Roberts, Hatch, Kellow, Templeman
		2	17.12.77	Minehead	SL	A	W	3-0	Randell 2, Kellow
		3	7.1.78	Wolverhampton W	D1	H	D	2-2	Roberts, Holman
		3r	10.1.78	Wolverhampton W		A	L	1-3	Kellow
1978-79	D3	1	25.11.78	Brentford	D3	H	W	1-0	Forbes
		2	16.12.78	Maidstone U	SL	A	L	0-1	
1979-80	D3	1	24.11.79	Aldershot	D4	A	L	1-4	Neville
1980-81	D3	1	22.11.80	Leatherhead	IL	H	W	5-0	Kellow 2, Pearson, L.Roberts, Hinshelwood (og)
		2	13.12.80	Millwall	D3	A	W	1-0	P.Rogers
		3	3.1.81	Maidstone U	APL	A	W	4-2	Pullar 2, Kellow, P.Rogers
		4	24.1.81	Leicester C	D1	A	D	1-1	Pullar
		4r	28.1.81	Leicester C		H	W	3-1	Kellow 3 (1p)
		5	14.2.81	Newcastle U	D2	A	D	1-1	L.Roberts
		5r	18.2.81	Newcastle U		H	W	4-0	Hatch, Pearson, P.Roberts, M.Rogers
		6	7.3.81	Tottenham H	D1	A	L	0-2	
1981-82	D3	1	21.11.81	Brentford	D3	A	L	0-2	
1982-83	D3	1	20.11.82	Plymouth A	D3	A	L	0-2	
1983-84	D3	1	19.11.83	Maidstone U	APL	H	D	1-1	O'Connor
		1r	23.11.83	Maidstone U		A	L	1-2	Neville
1984-85	D4	1	17.11.84	Enfield	APL	H	D	2-2	Neville, Sims
		1r	20.11.84	Enfield		A	L	0-3	
1985-86	D4	1	16.11.85	Cardiff C	D3	H	W	2-1	Gale 2
		2	7.12.85	Bristol C	D3	A	W	2-1	Kellow, Crawford

		3	5.1.86 **Everton**	D1	A	L	0-1	
1986-87	D4	1	15.11.86 **Cambridge U**	D4	H	D	1-1	Viney
		1r	19.11.86 **Cambridge U**		A	L	0-2	
1987-88	D4	1	14.11.87 **Leyton O**	D4	A	L	0-2	
1988-89	D4	1	19.11.88 **Bognor Regis T**	IL	A	L	1-2	Rowbotham
1989-90	D4	1	18.11.89 **Dartford**	SL	A	D	1-1	Rowbotham (p)
		1r	22.11.89 **Dartford**		H	W	4-1	Bailey, Batty, Harrower, Neville
		2	9.12.89 **Maidstone U**	D4	A	D	1-1	Cooper
		2r	13.12.89 **Maidstone U**		H	W	3-2	Rowbotham 2, McDermott
		3	6.1.90 **Norwich C**	D1	H	D	1-1	Rowbotham
		3r	10.1.90 **Norwich C**		A	L	0-2	
1990-91	D3	1	17.11.90 **Cambridge U**	D3	H	L	1-2	Neville
1991-92	D3	1	16.11.91 **Colchester U**	GMVC	A	D	0-0	
		1r	26.11.91 **Colchester U**		H	D	0-0aet	
			Exeter won 4-2 on pens					
		2	7.12.91 **Swansea C**	D3	H	D	0-0	
		2r	17.12.91 **Swansea C**		A	W	2-1	Brown, Marshall
		3	4.1.92 **Portsmouth**	D2	H	L	1-2	Moran
1992-93	D2	1	14.11.92 **Kidderminster H**	GMVC	H	W	1-0	Moran
		2	5.12.92 **Swansea C**	D2	H	–	1-2	Dolan
			abandoned after 86 minutes – floodlight failure					
		2	15.12.92 **Swansea C**		H	L	2-5	Moran, Cook

FAIRFIELD

Entered FA Cup: 1891-1908. Manchester-based, Lancashire League champions 1895

1894-95	LL	1	2.2.95 **Sunderland**	D1	A	L	1-11	Allen

FALMOUTH

Formed 1946. **First entered FA Cup:** 1962

1962-63	SWL	1	3.11.62 **Oxford U**	D4	H	L	1-2	Penny
1967-68	SWL	1	11.12.67 **Peterborough U**	D3	A	L	2-5	Gray 2
1969-70	SWL	1	15.11.69 **Peterborough U**	D4	H	L	1-4	Ewings

FAREHAM TOWN

Formed: 1947. **First entered FA Cup:** 1955

1979-80	SL	1	24.11.79 **Merthyr T**	SL	H	L	2-3	Atkins, Warren
1985-86	SL	1	16.11.85 **Maidstone U**	APL	H	L	0-3	
1986-87	SL	1	15.11.86 **Bournemouth**	D3	A	L	2-7	Wilkes 2
1988-89	SL	1	19.11.88 **Torquay U**	D4	A	D	2-2	Maddock, Carroll
		1r	23.11.88 **Torquay U**		H	L	2-3	Carroll, Maddock

FARNBOROUGH TOWN

Formed 1967. **First entered FA Cup:** 1976. **League club beaten:** Torquay U

1980-81	IL	1	22.11.80 **Yeovil T**	APL	A	L	1-2	Parkin (p)
1983-84	IL	1	19.11.83 **Barking**	IL	A	L	1-2	Bromme
1984-85	IL	1	17.11.84 **Hereford U**	D4	A	L	0-3	
1985-86	IL	1	16.11.85 **Bath C**	APL	H	L	0-4	
1986-87	IL	1	15.11.86 **Swindon T**	D3	A	L	0-4	
1987-88	IL	1	14.11.87 **Cambridge U**	D4	A	L	1-2	Bailey
1989-90	GMVC	1	18.11.89 **Hereford U**	D4	H	L	0-1	
1990-91	SL	1	17.11.90 **Fulham**	D3	A	L	1-2	Horton
1991-92	GMVC	1	16.11.91 **Halesowen T**	SL	A	D	2-2	Hobson, Broome
		1r	26.11.91 **Halesowen T**		H	W	4-0	Read 3, Coombs(p)
		2	7.12.91 **Torquay U**	D3	A	D	1-1	Read
		2r	17.12.91 **Torquay U**		H	W	4-3	Coney, Read, Doherty, Broome
		3	4.1.92 **West Ham**	D1	H	D	1-1	Coney (p)
			played at Upton Park					
		3r	14.1.92 **West Ham**		A	L	0-1	

FARNHAM UNITED BREWERIES

Entered FA Cup: 1921-1927

1925-26	SSL	1	28.11.25	**Swindon T**		3S	H	L	1-10	Bicknell

FARNINGHAM

Formed 1872. Home ground was a mile from Farningham Road station near the Lion Hotel in Kent. Never played another FA Cup match after losing 16-0 to Wanderers which remained the record defeat until Preston beat Hyde 26-0 in 1887.

1873-74		1		**Trojans**					*scratched*	
1874-75		1	10.10.74	**Wanderers**			A	L	0-16	

FARSLEY CELTIC

Formed 1908. **First entered FA Cup:** 1928. Based in Pudsey, West Yorkshire. **Cup final connection:** former players include Paul Madeley (three finals for Leeds) and Stuart McCall (two goals for Everton in 1989 final)

1974-75	YL	1	23.11.74	**Tranmere R**		D3	H	L	0-2	

FERRYHILL ATHLETIC

Formed 1921. **First entered FA Cup:** 1923

1935-36	NL	1	30.11.35	**Oldham A**		3N	A	L	1-6	Booth
1953-54	NL	1	21.11.53	**Workington**		3N	A	L	0-3	

FINCHLEY

Formed 1874. **First entered FA Cup:** 1878. Merged with Wingate (1975) FC to form Wingate & Finchley, 1992. **League club beaten:** Crystal Palace

1878-79		1		**Clapham Rovers**					*scratched*	
1879-80		1	8.11.79	**Old Harrovians**			H	L	1-2	
1880-81		1	13.11.80	**Clapham Rovers**			A	L	0-15	
1881-82		1	29.10.81	**Acton**			A	D	0-0	
		1r	12.11.81	**Acton**			H	L	0-4	
1946-47	AL	1	30.11.46	**Port Vale**		3S	A	L	0-5	
1952-53	AL	1	22.11.52	**Kidderminster H**		SL	A	W	1-0	Ault
		2	6.12.52	**Crystal P**		3S	H	–	3-1	Robb 2, Nottage
			match abandoned after 61 minutes – fog							
		2	10.12.52	**Crystal P**			H	W	3-1	Robb, Duke, Nottage
		3	10.1.53	**Shrewsbury T**		3S	A	L	0-2	
1953-54	AL	1	21.11.53	**Southend U**		3S	H	L	1-3	Walton

FISHER ATHLETIC

Formed 1908 by the John Fisher Catholic Society in south-east London. **First entered FA Cup:** 1983

1984-85	SL	1	17.11.84	**Bristol C**		D3	H	L	0-1	
1988-89	GMVC	1	20.11.88	**Bristol R**		D3	A	L	0-3	

FISHWICK RAMBLERS

Formed 1871. Played at The Brow, Fishwick, Preston

1884-85		1	1.11.84	**Darwen Ramblers**			A	W	2-1	
		2	22.11.84	**Darwen**			H	L	0-2	
1885-86		1	31.10.85	**Halliwell**			A	L	1-2	

FLEETWOOD

First entered FA Cup: 1909. Reformed as Fleetwood Town, 1977. **FA Vase Runners-up:** 1985

1949-50	LC	1	26.11.49	**Bradford C**		3N	A	L	0-9	
1965-66	LC	1	13.11.65	**Rochdale**		D4	H	D	2-2	Robinson, Strachan
		1r	17.11.65	**Rochdale**			A	L	0-5	
1980-81	CC	1	22.11.80	**Blackpool**		D3	A	L	0-4	
1990-91	NPL	1	17.11.90	**Atherstone**		SL	A	L	1-3	Madden

FLEETWOOD RANGERS

Entered the FA Cup: 1886-1898

1886-87	1	30.10.86 Newton Heath		H	D	2-2	Wright, Fisher
		Fleetwood awarded tie as Newton Heath refused to play extra time					
	2	20.11.86 Partick Thistle, Scotland		A	L	0-7	
1887-88	1	15.10.87 West Manchester		H	W	4-1	
	2	5.11.87 Higher Walton		H	L	1-3	

FOLKESTONE

Formed 1884. **First entered FA Cup:** 1891. Folded 1990. **League clubs beaten:** Norwich C, Newport Co, Gillingham

1925-26 SL	1	28.11.25 Luton T	3S	A	L	0-3	
1929-30 SL	1	30.11.29 Clapton O	3S	A	D	0-0	
	1r	4.12.29 Clapton O		H	D	2-2aet	Brookes, Clamp
	1 2r	9.12.29 Clapton O at Highbury			L	1-4	Clamp
1930-31 SL	1	29.11.30 Sittingbourne	KL	H	W	5-3	Brookes 2, Vinall, Middleton, Weall
	2	13.12.30 Gateshead	3N	A	L	2-3	Saunders, Brooks
1931-32 SL	1	28.11.31 Brighton & HA	3S	H	L	2-5	Woodward,Cook
1932-33 SL	1	26.11.32 Norwich C	3S	H	W	1-0	Richards
	2	10.12.32 Newport Co	3S	H	W	2-1	J.Havelock 2
	3	14.1.33 Huddersfield T	D1	A	L	0-2	
1933-34 SL	1	25.11.33 Bristol R	3S	H	D	0-0	
	1r	29.11.33 Bristol R		A	L	1-3	Havelock
1934-35 SL	1	24.11.34 Brighton & HA	3S	A	L	1-3	Richardson
1935-36 SL	1	30.11.35 Romford	AL	H	D	3-3	Godling 2, Woodward
	1r	4.12.35 Romford		H	W	2-1	Murray, Woodward
	2	14.12.35 Clapton O	3S	H	L	1-2	Hobson
1936-37 SL	1	28.11.36 Exeter C	3S	A	L	0-3	
1937-38 SL	1	27.11.37 Exeter C		A	L	0-1	
1938-39 SL	1	26.11.38 Colchester U	SL	H	W	2-1	Birch og, Ashley
	2	10.12.38 Yeovil & Petters U	SL	H	D	1-1	Baker
	2r	15.12.38 Yeovil & Petters U		A	L	0-1	
1951-52 KL	1	24.11.51 Barnstaple	WL	A	D	2-2	Day, Hassell
	1r	28.11.51 Barnstaple		H	W	5-2	Day 3, Wiltshire, Himsworth
	2	15.12.51 Stockton	NEL	A	L	1-2	Himsworth
1963-64 SL	1	16.11.63 Oxford U	D4	A	L	0-2	
1965-66 SL	1	13.11.65 Gillingham	D3	A	W	2-1	Catleugh, Biggs
	2	4.12.65 Wimbledon	SL	A	W	1-0	Churms
	3	22.1.66 Crewe A	D4	H	L	1-5	Legate
1966-67 SL	1	26.11.66 Swansea T	D3	H	D	2-2	Catleugh, Ireland
	1r	29.11.66 Swansea T		A	L	2-7	Ballagher, Biggs
as Folkestone & Shepway							
1977-78 SL	1	26.11.77 Brentford	D4	A	L	0-2	
1982-83 SL	1	20.11.82 Oxford U	D3	A	L	2-5	N.Fusco (p), Plews

FOREST SCHOOL

Football team formed in late 1850s – probably 1859. Their ground was at Forest School at Snaresbrook, Epping Forest. This school team were the forerunners of the famous Wanderers

1875-76	1	6.11.75 Oxford University		A	L	0-6	
1876-77	1	4.11.76 Gresham		H	W	4-1	Crawley 2, Fairclough, Knowles
	2	29.11.76 Marlow		A	L	0-1	
1877-78	1	7.11.77 1st Surrey Rifles		A	L	0-1	
1878-79	1	2.11.78 Rochester		H	W	7-2	
	2	7.12.78 Clapham Rovers		A	L	1-10	Shaw

FORMBY

Formed 1919. **First entered FA Cup:** 1937

1973-74 CC	1	24.11.73 Oldham A	D3	H	L	0-2	

FRICKLEY ATHLETIC

Formed 1910. **First entered FA Cup:** 1910 as Frickley Colliery. Became Frickley Athletic 1974. **League club beaten:** Hartlepool

1936-37	ML	1	28.11.36	**Southport**	3N	H	L	0-2
1957-58	ML	1	16.11.57	**South Shields**	NEL	A	L	2-3	Lambert, Hargreaves
1963-64	CC	1	16.11.63	**Notts Co**	D3	A	L	1-2	Cartwright
1971-72	ML	1	20.11.71	**Rotherham U**	D3	H	D	2-2	Moran, Holland
		1r	23.11.71	**Rotherham U**		A	L	0-4
1973-74	ML	1	24.11.73	**Halifax T**	D3	A	L	1-6	Morgan
as Frickley Athletic								
1983-84	APL	1	19.11.83	**Altrincham**	APL	H	L	0-1
1984-85	APL	1	17.11.84	**Stalybridge C**	NWC	H	W	2-1	Hooley (p), Reed
		2	8.12.84	**Darlington**	D4	A	L	0-1
1985-86	APL	1	16.11.85	**Halesowen**	WMRL	H	D	1-1	Bishop
		1r	18.11.85	**Halesowen**		A	W	3-1	Bishop, Wilson, Wilcox (p)
		2	7.12.85	**Hartlepool U**	D4	A	W	1-0	Wilson
		3	4.1.86	**Rotherham U**	D3	H	L	1-3	Bishop
1986-87	GMVC	1	15.11.86	**Altrincham**	GMVC	H	D	0-0
		1r	18.11.86	**Altrincham**		A	L	0-4
1988-89	NPL	1	19.11.88	**Northwich Vic**	GMVC	H	L	0-2

FROME TOWN

Formed 1904. **First entered FA Cup:** 1906

1954-55	WL	1	20.11.54	**Leyton O**	3S	H	L	0-3

FULHAM

Formed 1879. **First entered FA Cup:** 1896. **FA Cup Runners-up:** 1975. **Record FA Cup Win:** 8-3 vs Luton Town, 1st round, 11.1.1908; 6-0 vs Wimbledon 1st round replay, 3.12.1930 6-0 vs Bury, 3rd round, 7.1.1938. **Record FA Cup Defeat:** 0-7 vs QPR, 3rd qual rd, 1900-01. In competition proper: 0-6 vs Newcastle United, semi-final, 28.3.1908.

1896-97	LON	2q	**Swanscombe** (A) 0-5					
1897-98	LON		*did not enter*					
1898-99	SL		*did not enter*					
1899-00	SL	1q	**QPR** (A) 0-3					
1900-01	SL	3q	**QPR** (A) 0-7					
1901-02	SL	P	**Chiswick** (A) 3-2; 1q **Crouch End Vampires** (A) 2-4					
1902-03	SL	P	**Civil Service** (H) 2-0; 1q **Crouch End Vampires** (H) 4-0; 2q **Willesden T** (H) 0-0; 2qr **Willesden T** (H) 5-0; 3q **Watford** (A) 1-1; 3qr **Watford** (H) 3-0; 4q **Luton Am.** (H) 4-1; 5q **Luton T** (A) 1-5					
1903-04	SL	1q	**Hampstead** (H) 3-0; 2q **Crouch End Vampires** (A) 5-0; 3q **Civil Service** (H) 3-3; 3qr **Civil Service** (A) 3-0; 4q **QPR** (A) 1-1; 4qr **QPR** (H) 3-1; 5q **West Norwood** (H) 4-0; 6q **Luton T** (H) 3-1; Int **West Ham** (A) 1-0					
		1	6.2.04	**Woolwich Arsenal**	D2	A	L	0-1
1904-05	SL	6q	**Luton T** (H) 4-0; Int **Manchester U** (A) 2-2; Int R **Manchester U** (H) 0-0; Int 2r **Manchester U** 1-0 at Villa Park					
		1	4.2.05	**Reading**	SL	H	D	0-0
		1r	8.2.05	**Reading**		A	D	0-0aet
		1 2r	13.2.05	**Reading** at Tottenham			W	1-0aet	Fraser
		2	18.2.05	**Nottingham F**	D1	H	W	1-0	Wardrope
		3	4.3.05	**Aston Villa**	D1	A	L	0-5
1905-06	SL	1	13.1.06	**QPR**	SL	H	W	1-0	Collins
		2	3.2.06	**Nottingham F**	D1	H	L	1-3	Fraser
1906-07	SL	1	12.1.07	**Stockport Co**	D2	H	D	0-0
		1r	16.1.07	**Stockport Co**		H	W	2-1	Freeman, Threlfall
		2	2.2.07	**Crystal P**	SL	H	D	0-0
		2r	6.2.07	**Crystal P**	SL	A	L	0-1
1907-08	D2	1	11.1.08	**Luton T**	SL	A	W	8-3	Dalrymple 2, Harrison 2, Millington 2, Morrison, Ross
		2	1.2.08	**Norwich C**	SL	H	W	2-1	Millington, Threlfall
		3	22.2.08	**Manchester C**	D1	A	D	1-1	Harrison
		3r	26.2.08	**Manchester C**		H	W	3-1	Ross, Harrison, Dalrymle
		4	7.3.08	**Manchester U**	D1	H	W	2-1	Harrison 2
		SF	28.3.08	**Newcastle U**	D1		L	0-6
			played at Anfield					
1908-09	D2	1	16.1.09	**Carlisle U**	NEL	H	W	4-1	Freeman 2, Millington, Collins
		2	6.2.09	**Tottenham H**	D2	A	L	0-1
1909-10	D2	1	15.1.10	**Chesterfield**	ML	A	D	0-0

Season	Rd	Date	Opponent		H/A	Res	Score	Scorers
	1r	19.1.10	Chesterfield		H	W	2-1	Dalrymple, Harrison
	2	5.2.10	Newcastle U	D1	A	L	0-4	
1910-11 D2	2	14.1.11	WBA	D2	A	L	1-4	Mouncher
1911-12 D2	1	13.1.12	Burnley	D2	H	W	2-1	Coleman, Brown
	2	3.2.12	Liverpool	D1	H	W	3-0	Coleman 2, Pearce
	3	24.2.12	Northampton T	SL	H	W	2-1	Brown 2
	4	9.3.12	WBA	D1	A	L	0-3	
1912-13 D2	1	11.1.13	Hull C	D2	H	L	0-2	
1913-14 D2	1	10.1.14	Manchester C	D1	A	L	0-3	
1914-15 D2	1	9.1.15	South Shields	NEL	A	W	2-1	Taylor, Walker
	2	30.1.15	Southampton	SL	H	L	2-3aet	Taylor, Pearce
1919-20 D2	1	10.1.20	Swindon T	SL	H	L	1-2	Hoare
1920-21 D2	1	8.1.21	Blackburn R	D1	A	D	1-1	Cock
	1r	13.1.21	Blackburn R		H	W	1-0	McDonald
	2	29.1.21	Lincoln C	ML	A	D	0-0	
	2r	7.2.21	Lincoln C		H	W	1-0	Morris
	3	19.2.21	Wolverhampton W	D2	H	L	0-1	
1921-22 D2	1	7.1.22	Plymouth A	3S	A	D	1-1	Travers
	1r	11.1.22	Plymouth A		H	W	1-0	Shea
	2	28.1.22	Leicester C	D2	A	L	0-2	
1922-23 D2	1	13.1.23	Leicester C	D2	A	L	0-3	
1923-24 D2	1	12.1.24	Llanelli	SL	H	W	2-0	Edmonds 2
	2	2.2.24	Burnley	D1	A	D	0-0	
	2r	7.2.24	Burnley		H	L	0-1aet	
1924-25 D2	1	10.1.25	Swindon T	3S	A	W	2-1	Edmonds, Richards
	2	1.2.25	Cardiff C	D1	A	L	0-1	
1925-26 D2	3	9.1.26	Everton	D1	A	D	1-1	Craig
	3r	14.1.26	Everton		H	W	1-0	White
	4	30.1.26	Liverpool		H	W	3-1	Pape 2, Penn
	5	20.2.26	Notts Co	D1	A	W	1-0	Prouse
	6	6.3.26	Manchester U	D1	H	L	1-2	Pape
1926-27 D2	3	8.1.27	Chesterfield	3N	H	W	4-3	Tonner 2, Pape, Craig
	4	29.1.27	Burnley	D1	H	L	0-4	
1927-28 D2	3	15.1.28	Stockport Co	3N	A	L	0-3	
1928-29 3S	1	24.11.28	Coventry C	3S	A	W	4-1	Temple 2, Price, Penn
	2	8.12.28	Luton T	3S	H	D	0-0	
	2r	13.12.28	Luton T		A	L	1-4	Temple
1929-30 3S	1	30.11.29	Thames	SL	H	W	4-0	Barrett 2, Penn, Avey
	2	14.12.29	Leyton	AL	A	W	4-1	Penn 2, Barrett, Hammond
	3	11.1.30	Bournemouth	3S	H	D	1-1	Penn
	3r	15.1.30	Bournemouth		A	W	2-0	Haley, Barrett
	4	25.1.30	Nottingham F	D2	A	L	1-2	Haley
1930-31 3S	1	30.11.30	Wimbledon	IL	H	D	1-1	Price
	1r	3.12.30	Wimbledon		A	W	6-0	Penn 2, Gibbons 2, Watkins, Hammond
	2	13.12.30	Halifax T	3N	H	W	4-0	Haley 2, Watkins, Hammond
	3	10.1.31	Portsmouth	D1	H	L	0-2	
1931-32 3S	1	28.11.31	Guildford C	SL	H	W	2-0	Hammond 2
	2	5.12.31	Yeovil	SL	H	D	0-0	
	2r	17.12.31	Yeovil		A	W	5-2	Newton 3, Price, Richards
	3	9.1.32	Watford	3S	A	D	1-1	Newton
	3r	14.1.32	Watford		H	L	0-3	
1932-33 D2	3	14.1.33	Chester	3N	A	L	0-5	
1933-34 D2	3	13.1.34	Liverpool	D1	A	D	1-1	Lambert
	3r	17.1.34	Liverpool		H	L	2-3aet	Hammond, Arnold
1934-35 D2	3	12.1.35	Sunderland	D1	A	L	2-3	Finch, Arnold
1935-36 D2	3	11.1.36	Brighton & HA	3S	H	W	2-1	Worsley, Hammond
	4	25.1.36	Blackpool	D2	H	W	5-2	Perry 4, Hammond
	5	19.2.36	Chelsea	D1	A	D	0-0	
	5r	24.2.36	Chelsea		H	W	3-2	Smith, Hammond, Arnold
	6	29.2.36	Derby Co	D1	H	W	3-0	Arnold, Barrett, Smith
	SF	21.3.36	Sheffield U	D2		L	1-2	Arnold
		played at Molineux						
1936-37 D2	3	16.1.37	Millwall	3S	A	L	0-2	
1937-38 D2	3	8.1.38	Brentford	D1	A	L	1-3	O'Callaghan
1938-39 D2	3	7.1.39	Bury	D2	H	W	6-0	Rooke 6
	4	21.1.39	Chelsea	D1	A	L	0-3	
1945-46 D2	3 1L	5.1.46	Charlton A	D1	A	L	1-3	Rampling

FULHAM

Season	Rd	Date	Opponent	Div	Venue	Result	Score	Scorers
	3 2L	7.1.46	Charlton A		H	W	2-1	Rooke 2
1946-47 D2	3	11.1.47	Birmingham C	D2	H	L	1-2	Watson
1947-48 D2	3	10.1.48	Doncaster R	D2	H	W	2-0	Ayres, Stevens
	4	24.1.48	Bristol R	3S	H	W	5-2	Stevens 3, Ayres 2
	5	7.2.48	Everton	D1	H	D	1-1aet	Quested
	5r	14.2.48	Everton		A	W	1-0	R.Thomas
	6	28.2.48	Blackpool	D1	H	L	0-2	
1948-49 D2	3	8.1.49	Walsall	3S	H	L	0-1	
1949-50 D1	3	7.1.50	Charlton A	D1	A	D	2-2	R.Thomas, Freeman
	3r	11.1.50	Charlton A		H	L	1-2	McDonald
1950-51 D1	3	6.1.51	Sheffield W	D1	H	W	1-0	Brennan
	4	27.1.51	Millwall	3S	A	W	1-0	Campbell
	5	10.2.51	Chelsea	D1	A	D	1-1	Campbell
	5r	14.2.51	Chelsea		H	W	3-0	Brennan 2, Stevens
	6	24.2.51	Blackpool	D1	A	L	0-1	
1951-52 D1	3	13.1.52	Birmingham C	D2	H	L	0-1	
1952-53 D2	3	14.1.53	Bolton W	D1	A	L	1-3	Mitten
1953-54 D2	3	9.1.54	Grimsby T	3N	A	D	5-5	Taylor 3, Stevens, Hill
	3r	13.1.54	Grimsby T		H	–	0-0	
			abandoned at half-time – ground waterlogged					
	3r	18.1.54	Grimsby T			W	3-1	Haynes 2, Taylor
	4	30.1.54	Leyton O	3S	A	L	1-2	Robson
1954-55 D2	3	8.1.55	Preston NE	D1	H	L	2-3	Haynes, Stevens
1955-56 D2	3	7.1.56	Notts Co	D2	A	W	1-0	Haynes
	4	28.1.56	Newcastle U	D1	H	L	4-5	Chamberlain 3, Hill
1956-57 D2	3	5.1.57	Ipswich T	3S	A	W	3-2	Stevens 2, Dwight
	4	26.1.57	Blackpool	D1	A	L	2-6	Lowe, Bentley
1957-58 D2	3	4.1.58	Yeovil	SL	H	W	4-0	Hill 2, Key, Doherty
	4	25.1.58	Charlton A	D2	H	D	1-1	Hill
	4r	29.1.58	Charlton A		A	W	2-0	Bentley, Stevens
	5	15.2.58	West Ham	D2	A	W	3-2	Dwight, Hill, Haynes
	6	1.3.58	Bristol R	D2	H	W	3-1	Stevens 2, Hill
	SF	22.3.58	Manchester U	D1		D	2-2	Stevens, Hill
			played at Villa Park					
	SFr	26.3.58	Manchester U			L	3-5	Dwight, Stevens, Chamberlain
			played at Highbury					
1958-59 D2	3	10.1.59	Peterborough U	ML	H	D	0-0	
	3r	24.1.59	Peterborough U		A	W	1-0	Johnson
	4	28.1.59	Birmingham C	D1	A	D	1-1	Hill
	4r	4.2.59	Birmingham C		H	L	2-3	Leggat, Hill
1959-60 D1	3	9.1.60	Hull C	D2	H	W	5-0	Leggat 2, Chamberlain Cook, Hill
	4	30.1.60	Leicester C	D1	A	L	1-2	Cunningham og
1960-61 D1	3	7.1.61	Newcastle U	D1	A	L	0-5	
1961-62 D1	3	6.1.62	Hartlepools U	D4	H	W	3-1	Cook 2, Key
	4	27.1.62	Walsall	D2	H	D	2-2	Cook, Henderson
	4r	30.1.62	Walsall		A	W	2-0	Lowe, Metchick
	5	17.2.62	Port Vale	D3	H	W	1-0	Langley (p)
	6	10.3.62	Blackburn R	D1	H	D	2-2	Woods og, Haynes
	6r	14.3.62	Blackburn R		A	W	1-0	Cook
	SF	31.3.62	Burnley	D1		D	1-1	Leggat
			played at Villa Park					
	SFr	9.4.62	Burnley			L	1-2	Langley
			played at Filbert Street					
1962-63 D1	3	4.2.63	West Ham	D1	A	D	0-0	
	3r	20.2.63	West Ham		H	L	1-2	Robson
1963-64 D1	3	4.1.64	Luton T	D3	H	W	4-1	Mullery, Leggat, Cook, Howfield
	4	25.1.64	Blackburn R	D1	A	L	0-2	
1964-65 D1	3	9.1.65	Millwall	D4	H	D	3-3	Stratton 2, Key
	3r	11.1.65	Millwall		A	L	0-2	
1965-66 D1	3	22.1.66	Sheffield U	D1	A	L	1-3	Dempsey
1966-67 D1	3	28.1.67	Bradford PA	D4	A	W	3-1	Clarke 2, Haynes
	4	18.2.67	Sheffield U	D1	H	D	1-1	Clarke
	4r	1.3.67	Sheffield U		A	L	1-3	Callaghan
1967-68 D1	3	27.1.68	Macclesfield T	CC	H	W	4-2	Clarke 2, Gilroy, Haynes
	4	17.2.68	Portsmouth	D2	H	D	0-0	
	4r	21.2.68	Portsmouth		A	L	0-1	
1968-69 D2	3	4.1.69	Sunderland	D1	A	W	4-1	Mullen 2, Brown, Haynes

FULHAM

Season	Round	Date	Opponent	Div	H/A	Res	Score	Scorers
	4	25.1.69	WBA	D1	H	L	1-2	Brown
1969-70 D3	1	15.11.69	Exeter C	D4	A	L	0-2	
1970-71 D3	1	21.11.70	Bristol R	D3	H	L	1-2	Johnston
1971-72 D2	3	15.1.72	QPR	D2	A	D	1-1	John Conway
	3r	18.1.72	QPR		H	W	2-1	Cross 2
	4	5.2.72	Huddersfield T	D1	A	L	0-3	
1972-73 D2	3	13.1.73	Sheffield W	D2	A	L	0-2	
1973-74 D2	3	5.1.74	Preston NE	D2	H	W	1-0	John Conway
	4	26.1.74	Leicester C	D1	H	D	1-1	Mullery
	4r	30.1.74	Leicester C		A	L	1-2aet	Barrett
1974-75 D2	3	4.1.75	Hull C	D2	H	D	1-1	Jim Conway
	3r	7.1.75	Hull C		A	D	2-2aet	Busby 2
	3 2r	13.1.75	Hull C at Filbert Street			W	1-0	Slough
	4	28.1.75	Nottingham F	D2	H	D	0-0	
	4r	3.2.75	Nottingham F		A	D	1-1aet	Dowie
	4 2r	5.2.75	Nottingham F		H	D	1-1aet	Slough
	4 3r	10.2.75	Nottingham F		A	W	2-1	Busby 2
	5	15.2.75	Everton	D1	A	W	2-1	Busby 2
	6	8.3.75	Carlisle U	D1	A	W	1-0	Barrett
	SF	5.4.75	Birmingham C	D1		D	1-1	Mitchell
		played at Hillsborough						
	SFr	9.4.75	Birmingham C			W	1-0aet	Mitchell
		played at Maine Road						
	F	3.5.75	West Ham	D1	WEMBLEY	L	0-2	
1975-76 D2	3	3.1.76	Huddersfield T	D4	H	L	2-3	Jim Conway, Busby
1976-77 D2	3	8.1.77	Swindon T	D3	H	D	3-3	Marsh, Howe, Barrett
	3r	11.1.77	Swindon T		A	L	0-5	
1977-78 D2	3	7.1.78	Burnley	D2	A	L	0-1	
1978-79 D2	3	9.1.79	QPR	D1	H	W	2-0	Margerrison, Davies
	4	31.1.79	Manchester U	D1	H	D	1-1	Margerrison
	4r	12.2.79	Manchester U		A	L	0-1	
1979-80 D2	3	5.1.80	Blackburn R	D3	A	D	1-1	Money
	3r	15.1.80	Blackburn		H	L	0-1	
1980-81 D3	1	22.11.80	Reading	D3	A	W	2-1	Davies, Mahoney
	2	13.12.80	Brentford	D3	H	W	1-0	Greenaway
	3	3.1.81	Bury	D4	A	D	1-1	Mahoney
	3r	6.1.81	Bury		H	D	0-0aet	
	3 2r	12.1.81	Bury at Hawthorns			W	1-0	Davies
	4	24.1.81	Charlton	D3	H	L	1-2	Davies
1981-82 D3	1	21.11.81	Bristol R	D3	A	W	2-1	Coney 2
	2	2.1.82	Hereford U	D4	A	L	0-1	
1982-83 D2	3	8.1.83	Oldham A	D2	A	W	2-0	Coney, Houghton
	4	29.1.83	Watford	D1	A	D	1-1	Coney
	4r	1.2.83	Watford		H	L	1-2	Lewington
1983-84 D2	3	7.1.84	Tottenham H	D1	H	D	0-0	
	3r	11.1.84	Tottenham H		A	L	0-2	
1984-85 D2	3	5.1.85	Sheffield W	D1	H	L	2-3	Houghton 2
1985-86 D2	3	13.1.86	Sheffield U	D2	A	L	0-2	
1986-87 D3	1	15.11.86	Hereford U	D4	A	D	3-3	Barnett, Marshall, Coney
	1r	24.11.86	Hereford U		H	W	4-0	Davies 2, Marshall, Coney
	2	6.12.86	Newport Co	D3	H	W	2-0	Oakes, Davies
	3	10.1.87	Swindon T	D3	H	L	0-1	
1987-88 D3	1	14.11.87	Gillingham	D3	A	L	1-2	Rosenior
1988-89 D3	1	19.11.88	Colchester U	D4	A	L	0-1	
1989-90 D3	1	19.11.89	Bath C	SL	A	D	2-2	Peters, Walker
	1r	22.11.89	Bath C		H	W	2-1	Marshall, Watson
	2	9.12.89	Bristol C	D3	A	L	1-2	Scott
1990-91 D3	1	17.11.90	Farnborough	SL	H	W	2-1	Pike, Brazil (p)
	2	7.12.90	Cambridge U	D3	H	D	0-0	
	2r	11.12.90	Cambridge U		A	L	1-2	Davies
1991-92 D3	1	15.11.91	Hayes	IL	H	L	0-2	
1992-93 D2	1	14.11.92	Northampton T	D3	A	L	1-3	Farrell

FURNESS VALE ROVERS

Season	Round	Date	Opponent		H/A	Res	Score
1886-87	1	30.10.86	Northwich Victoria		A	L	0-10

GAINSBOROUGH TRINITY

Formed 1873. **First entered FA Cup:** 1885. Member of the Football League 1896-1912 **1st round reached:** 33 times. **League clubs beaten as a non-league side:** Crewe A (2), Port Vale, Gateshead, Mansfield T

1885-86		1	24.10.85	**Grantham**		H	W	4-1	
		2	21.11.85	**Middlesbrough**		A	L	1-2	Eason
1886-87		1	30.10.86	**South Bank**		A	W	4-0	
		2	20.11.86	**Newcastle West End**		A	W	6-2	
		3	11.12.86	**Lincoln City**		H	D	2-2aet	Booth, Vamplen
		3r	24.1.87	**Lincoln City** at Bramall Lane			L	0-1	
1887-88		1	15.10.87	**Boston**		H	W	9-0	
		2	5.11.87	**Lincoln City**		A	L	1-2	Robinson
1896-97	D2	3q **Lincoln City** (A) 0-1							
1897-98	D2	3q **Park Gate** (H) 5-0; 4q **Lincoln C** (H) 5-1; 5q **Mexborough T** (A) 1-0							
		1	29.1.98	**Long Eaton Rangers**	ML	A	W	1-0	Scott
		2	12.2.98	**Nottingham Forest**	D1	A	L	0-4	
1898-99	D2	3q **Barnsley** (H) 2-2; 3qr **Barnsley** (A) 0-4							
1899-00	D2	1q **Doncaster R** (H) 1-4							
1900-01	D2	3q **Lincoln C** (A) 0-0; 3qr **Lincoln C** (H) 1-1 abandoned; 3q 2r **Lincoln C** 1-3 at Bramall Lane							
1901-02	D2	3q **Barnsley** (A) 0-1							
1902-03	D2	3q **Doncaaster R** (H) 1-0; 4q **Rotherham T** (H) 3-0; 5q **Barnsley** (A) 2-3							
1903-04	D2	3q **Mexborough T** (A) 2-0; 4q **Doncaster R** (A) 1-0; 5q **Chesterfield T** (A) 2-0; Int **Reading** (A) 0-1							
1904-05	D2	3q **Ilkeston U** (H) 4-1; 4q **Grimethorpe U** (H) 5-1; 5q **Mexborough T** (A) 1-1; 5qr **Mexborough T** (H) 7-0; 6q **Green Waves** (A) 3-1; Int **Grimsby T** (A) 0-2							
1905-06	D2	4q **Weymouth** (H) 2-1							
		1	13.1.06	**Burslem Port Vale**	D2	A	W	3-0	Langham, Morley, Foxall
		2	3.2.06	**Sunderland**	D1	A	D	1-1	Dixon
		2r	7.2.06	**Sunderland** at Roker Park		A	L	0-3	
1906-07	D2	1	12.1.07	**Luton T**	SL	H	D	0-0	
		1r	16.1.07	**Luton T**		A	L	1-2	Foxall
1907-08	D2	1	11.1.08	**Watford**	SL	H	W	1-0	Brawn
		2	1.2.08	**Stoke**	D2	A	D	1-1	Murphy
		2r	5.2.08	**Stoke**		H	D	2-2aet	Taylor, Murphy
		2 2r	10.2.08	**Stoke** at City Ground, Nottingham			L	1-3	Kitchen
1908-09	D2	5q **Northern Nomads** (H) 4-0							
		1	16.1.09	**Brentford**	SL	A	L	0-2	
1909-10	D2	1	15.1.10	**Southend U**	SL	H	D	1-1	Splevins
		1r	19.1.10	**Southend U**		A	L	0-1	
1910-11	D2	4q **Ilkeston U** (A) 0-0; 4qr **Ilkeston U** (H) 0-0aet; 4q 2r **Ilkeston U** 5-0 at Bramall Lane; 5q **Shrewsbury T** (H) 4-0							
		1	14.1.11	**Liverpool**	D1	A	L	2-3	Pattinson, Coulbeck
1911-12	D2	4q **Rotherham Co** (H) 1-0; 5q **Tunbridge Wells R** (H) 1-1; 5qr **Tunbridge Wells R** (A) 1-0							
		1	13.1.12	**West Ham**	SL	A	L	1-2	Bullivant
1912-13	ML	1	11.1.13	**South Shields**	NEL	A	–	0-1	
				abandoned at half-time					
		1	18.1.13	**South Shields**		A	W	1-0	Parker
		2	1.2.13	**Burnley**	D2	A	L	1-4	Ibbotson
1913-14	ML	1	10.1.14	**Leeds C**	D2	A	L	2-4	Ibbotson 2
1927-28	ML	1	26.11.27	**Stockton**	NL	H	W	6-0	Smith 2, Shaw 3, Bennett
		2	10.12.27	**Lincoln C**	3N	H	L	0-2	
1928-29	ML	1	24.11.28	**Crewe A**	3N	H	W	3-1	Morris 2, Keating
		2	8.12.28	**Chesterfield**	3N	H	L	2-3	Smith, Keating
1929-30	ML	1	30.11.29	**Port Vale**	3N	H	D	0-0	
		1r	4.12.29	**Port Vale**		A	L	0-5	
1930-31	ML	1	29.11.30	**Scunthorpe U**	ML	H	W	1-0	Hancock
		2	13.12.30	**Southport**	3N	H	L	0-4	
1931-32	ML	1	28.11.31	**Crewe A**	3N	A	D	2-2	Mills, Robinson
		1r	2.12.31	**Crewe A**		H	W	1-0	Green
		2	12.12.31	**Watford**	3S	H	L	2-5	O'Brien og, Robinson
1932-33	ML	1	26.11.32	**Doncaster R**	3N	A	L	1-4	Halliday
1933-34	ML	1	25.11.33	**Altrincham**	CC	H	W	1-0	Green
		2	9.12.33	**Aldershot**	3S	H	L	0-2	
1935-36	ML	1	30.11.35	**Blyth S**	NEL	H	W	3-1	Evers, Kirk, Taylor
		2	14.12.35	**Dartford**	SL	A	L	0-4	
1937-38	ML	1	27.11.37	**Port Vale**	3N	A	D	1-1	Bratley
		1r	1.12.37	**Port Vale**		H	W	2-1aet	Hall, Kirk
		2	11.12.37	**Yeovil & Petters U**	SL	A	L	1-2	Ranshaw

1938-39	ML	1	26.11.38	Gateshead	3N	H	W	2-1	Green, Hall
		2	10.12.38	Doncaster R	3N	H	L	0-1	
1945-46	ML	1 1L	17.11.45	Mansfield T	3S	A	L	0-3	
		1 2L	24.11.45	Mansfield T		H	W	4-2aet	Sampson, Curry, Curtis, Bratley
1946-47	ML	1	30.11.46	Darlington	3N	H	L	1-2	North
1948-49	ML	1	27.11.48	Witton A	CC	H	W	1-0	Moseley
		2	11.12.48	Walsall	3S	A	L	3-4	Churm, Vaux (p), Bates
1950-51	ML	1	25.11.50	Plymouth A	3S	H	L	0-3	
1951-52	ML	1	24.11.51	Witton A	CC	A	L	1-2	Robinson
1952-53	ML	1	22.11.52	Netherfield	LC	H	D	1-1	Morley
		1r	27.11.52	Netherfield		A	W	3-0	Hughes, Churm, Morley
		2	6.12.52	Newport Co	3S	A	L	1-2	Robinson
1953-54	ML	1	21.11.53	Chesterfield	3N	H	L	1-4	Churm
1959-60	ML	1	14.11.59	Doncaster R	D4	A	D	3-3	Purvis, Simpson, Haydon
		1r	18.11.59	Doncaster R		H	L	0-1	
1966-67	ML	1	26.11.66	Colchester U	D3	H	L	0-1	
1983-84	NPL	1	19.11.83	Blackpool	D4	H	L	0-2	

GATESHEAD ASSOCIATION

This Gateshead club was formed in 1883 and originally played at Bensham.

1887-88		1	15.10.87	Darlington		H	L	0-3	

GATESHEAD

The history of football in the Gateshead and South Shields areas is among the most complicated concerning senior clubs in England. Indeed the club that played in the Football League from 1919-1960 was unique in that it was the only club that moved its home from one town to another, changed its name, and still continued to play in the League without a break. But besides that club there have been four other Gateshead clubs and at least three other South Shields clubs all playing senior football this century. The records listed here are of the South Shields/Gateshead Football League club which survived until 1973. See under "South Shields" for the record of the club which was formed in 1936. This club changed its name to Gateshead United in 1974 and folded in 1977. The records of "Gateshead FC" are for the club formed in 1976 and which is now the senior club in the area.

South Shields (formed 1899)

1912-13	NEL	1	11.1.13	Gainsborough T	ML	H	–	1-0	Hogg
				abandoned at half-time					
		1	18.1.13	Gainsborough T		H	L	0-1	
1913-14	NEL	1	10.1.14	Burnley	D1	A	L	1-3	Keenlyside
1914-15	NEL	1	9.1.15	Fulham	D2	H	L	1-2	Whittingham
1919-20	D2	1	10.1.20	Liverpool	D1	H	D	1-1	Woods
		1r	14.1.20	Liverpool		A	L	0-2	
1920-21	D2	1	8.1.21	Portsmouth	D3	H	W	3-0	Maitland, Hawes, Potts og
		2	29.1.21	Luton T	D3	H	L	0-4	
1921-22	D2	1	7.1.22	Southampton	3S	A	L	1-3	Greenwell
1922-23	D2	1	13.1.23	Halifax T	3N	H	W	3-1	Oxberry, Keenlyside, Maitland
		2	3.2.23	Blackburn R	D1	H	D	0-0	
		2r	8.2.23	Blackburn R		A	W	1-0	Smith
		3	24.2.23	QPR	3S	A	L	0-3	
1923-24	D2	1	12.1.24	Burnley	D1	A	L	2-3	Crown, Greenwell
1924-25	D2	1	10.1.25	Crystal P	D2	A	L	1-2	Smith
1925-26	D2	3	9.1.26	Chilton Colliery	NAll	H	W	3-0	Trotter, Wilson, Parker
		4	30.1.26	Birmingham	D1	H	W	2-1	Smith, Thirlaway
		5	20.2.26	Bolton W	D1	A	L	0-3	
1926-27	D2	3	8.1.27	Plymouth A	3S	H	W	3-1	Smith, Oxberry, Hunter
		4	29.1.27	Sheffield W	D1	A	D	1-1	Matthewson
		4r	2.2.27	Sheffield W		H	W	1-0	Smith
		5	19.2.27	Swansea T	D2	H	D	2-2	Smith, Trotter
		5r	24.2.27	Swansea T		A	L	1-2	Parker
1927-28	D2	3	14.1.28	Middlesbrough	D1	A	L	0-3	
1928-29	3N	1	24.11.28	Accrington S	3N	A	L	1-2	Parker
1929-30	3N	1	30.11.29	Wrexham	3N	H	L	2-4	Mustard, Maycock
Gateshead AFC									
1930-31	3N	1	29.11.30	Tranmere R	3N	A	D	4-4	McNaughton 2, Barkas 2
		1r	3.12.30	Tranmere R		H	W	3-2	Charlton, Barkas 2
		2	13.12.30	Folkestone	SL	H	W	3-2	Barkas, Charlton, McNaughton
		3	10.1.31	Sheffield W	D1	H	L	2-6	Kennedy, Charlton

GATESHEAD

1931-32	3N	1	28.11.31	**Wrexham**	3N	H	W	3-2	Meek 2, Kennedy
		2	12.12.31	**Burton Town**	BDL	A	L	1-4	Welsh
1932-33	3N	1	26.11.32	**Barrow**	3N	A	W	1-0	Charlton
		2	10.12.32	**Margate**	KL	H	W	5-2	Kennedy 3, Ransom 2
		3	14.1.33	**Manchester C**	D1	H	D	1-1	Kennedy
		3r	18.1.33	**Manchester C**		A	L	0-9	
1933-34	3N	1	25.11.33	**Darwen**	LC	H	W	5-2	Leek 2, Atkin, Temple, McDermott
		2	9.12.33	**North Shields**	NEL	H	W	1-0	Wesley
		3	13.1.34	**Workington**	NEL	A	L	1-4	McDermott
1934-35	3N	1	24.11.34	**Darlington**	3N	H	L	1-4	Hamilton
1935-36	3N	1	30.11.35	**Chester**	3N	A	L	0-1	
1936-37	3N	1	28.11.36	**Notts Co**	3S	H	W	2-0	Reed, Mathieson
		2	12.12.36	**Millwall**	3S	A	L	0-7	
1937-38	3N	1	27.11.37	**Walsall**	3S	A	L	0-4	
1938-39	3N	1	26.11.38	**Gainsborough T**	ML	A	L	1-2	Miller
1945-46	3N	1 1L	17.11.45	**Hartlepools U**	3N	A	W	2-1	Cairns 2
		1 2L	24.11.45	**Hartlepools U**		H	W	6-2	Howden, McCormack 3, Cairns 2
		2 1L	8.12.45	**Darlington**	3N	A	W	4-2	Rutherford, J.Callender, Cairns, McCormack
		2 2L	15.12.45	**Darlington**		H	L	1-2	McCormack
		3 1L	5.1.46	**Rotherham U**	3N	A	D	2-2	Atkinson, Thompson
		3 2L	9.1.46	**Rotherham U**		H	L	0-2	
1946-47	3N	1	30.11.46	**Bradford C**	3N	H	W	3-1	Small 2, McCormack
		2	14.12.46	**Lancaster C**	LC	H	W	4-0	Gallon, T.Callender, McCormack, Small
		3	11.1.47	**Manchester C**	D2	A	L	0-3	
1947-48	3N	1	29.11.47	**Bradford C**	3N	H	L	1-3	Small
1948-49	3N	1	27.11.48	**Netherfield**	LC	H	W	3-0	J.Callender (p), Small, Atkinson
		2	11.12.48	**Scarborough**	ML	H	W	3-0	T.Callender, Ingham, Robinson
		3	8.1.49	**Aldershot**	3S	H	W	3-1	Kendall 2, Wilbert
		4	29.1.49	**WBA**	D2	H	L	1-3aet	J.Callender
1949-50	3N	1	26.11.49	**York C**	3N	H	W	3-1	Marley 2, Campbell
		2	10.12.49	**Newport Co**	3S	A	D	1-1	Winters
		2r	14.12.49	**Newport Co**		H	L	1-2aet	J.Callender
1950-51	3N	3	6.1.51	**Sheffield U**	D2	A	L	0-1	
1951-52	3N	1	24.11.51	**Stockport Co**	3N	A	D	2-2	T.Callender, Buchan
		1r	28.11.51	**Stockport Co**		H	D	1-1aet	Campbell
		1 2r	3.12.51	**Stockport Co** at Hillsborough			W	2-1	Thompson 2
		2	15.12.51	**Guildford C**	SL	H	W	2-0	Ingham, Winters
		3	12.1.52	**Ipswich T**	3S	A	D	2-2	Wilbert, Ingham
		3r	6.1.52	**Ipswich T**		H	D	3-3aet	J.Callender, Buchan, Johnson
		3 2r	21.1.52	**Ipswich T** at Bramall Lane			W	2-1aet	Ingham 2
		4	6.2.52	**WBA** at **Newcastle U**	D1	H	L	0-2	
1952-53	3N	1	22.11.52	**Crewe Alex**	3N	H	W	2-0	Smith, Price
		2	6.12.52	**Bradford PA**	3N	A	W	2-1	Ingham 2
		3	10.1.53	**Liverpool**	D1	H	W	1-0	Winters
		4	31.1.53	**Hull C**	D2	A	W	2-1	Ingham, Phillips og
		5	14.2.53	**Plymouth A**	D2	A	W	1-0	Winters
		6	28.2.53	**Bolton W**	D1	H	L	0-1	
1953-54	3N	1	21.11.53	**Tranmere R**	3N	H	L	1-2	Smith
1954-55	3N	1	20.11.54	**Chester**	3N	H	W	6-0	Campbell, Ingham, Anderson 2, Smith, Oliver
		2	11.12.54	**Barnsley**	3N	H	D	3-3	Ingham 2, Campbell
		2r	16.12.54	**Barnsley**		A	W	1-0	Smith
		3	8.1.55	**Tottenham H**	D1	H	L	0-2	
1955-56	3N	1	19.11.55	**Hartlepools U**	3N	A	L	0-3	
1956-57	3N	1	17.11.56	**Hull C**	3N	A	L	0-4	
1957-58	3N	1	16.11.57	**Chester**	3N	A	L	3-4	Baldridge, Ingham, J.Callender
1958-59	D4	1	15.11.58	**Bradford PA**	D4	H	L	1-4	Johnstone
1959-60	D4	1	14.11.59	**Halifax T**	D3	H	L	3-4	A.Trewick 2, Armstrong
1960-61	N Co	1	5.11.60	**Barnsley**	D3	H	D	0-0	
		1r	9.11.60	**Barnsley**		A	L	0-2	
1961-62	N Co	1	4.11.61	**Tranmere R**	D4	A	W	3-2	Lydon, McCullough, McGugan og
		2	25.11.61	**Workington**	D4	H	L	0-2	
1962-63	NRL	1	3.11.62	**Wigan A**	CC	H	W	2-1	Steele, Burridge
		2	24.11.62	**Bradford C**	D4	A	L	2-3	Steele, McKenna
1963-64	NRL	1	16.11.63	**Darlington**	D4	A	W	4-1	Lindsay 2, Steele 2
		2	7.12.63	**Carlisle U**	D4	A	L	3-4	Lindsay 2, McKenna
1965-66	NRL	1	13.11.65	**Crook T**	NL	H	W	4-2	Steele, McKenna, Mitchell (p), Rayment
		2	8.12.65	**Hull C**	D3	H	L	0-4	

GATESHEAD FC

See under "Gateshead" for an explanation of the genealogy of the various South Shields and Gateshead clubs which have appeared in the FA Cup this century. 'This' Gateshead was formed in 1976 but should not be confused with Gateshead United which folded in 1977.

Gateshead FC

1980-81	NPL	1	22.11.80	**Lincoln C**	D4	A	L	0-1	
1992-93	GMVC	1	14.11.92	**Accrington Stanley**	NPL	A	L	2-3	Lamb, Bell

GILLINGHAM

Formed 1893 as New Brompton. Gillingham 1912. **FA Cup Best Performance:** 5th round, 1970. **FA Cup Record Win:** 10-1 vs Gorleston, 1st round, 16.11.1957. **FA Cup Record Defeat:** 3-9 vs Sutton U, 4th qual rd, 1945-46. In competition proper: 1-6 vs Stoke City, 3rd round, 14.1.1928.

as New Brompton

1893-94		1q **Ilford** (A) 3-6							
1894-95		2q **Chatham T** (H) 2-0; 3q **Millwall** (H) 0-2							
1895-96	SL	1q **Millwall** (H) 0-1							
1896-97	SL	1q **Faversham** (H) 6-1; 2q **Gravesend** (A) 4-1; 3q **Northfleet U** (A) 1-3							
1897-98	SL	1q **Northfleet U** (A) 3-1; 2q **Eastbourne Swifts** (H) 2-0; 3q **Grays U** (H) 6-2; 4q **Chatham T** (H) 1-0; 5q **Woolwich Arsenal** (A) 2-4							
1898-99	SL	3q **Grays U** (H) 3-0; 4q **Sheppey U** (H) 2-1; 5q **Gravesend U** (A) 1-1; 5qr **Gravesend U** (H) 2-0							
		1	28.1.99	**Southampton**	SL	H	L	0-1	
1899-00	SL	3q **Woolwich Arsenal** (A) 1-1; 3qr **Woolwich Arsenal** (H) 0-0 aet; 3q 2r **Woolwich Arsenal** 2-2 aet (at Millwall);							
		3q 3r **Woolwich Arsenal** 1-1 (at Tottenham) 1-1; 3q 4r **Woolwich Arsenal** 1-0 aet (Gravesend); 4q **Thames Ironworks** (H) 0-0;							
		4qr **Thames Ironworks** (A) 0-2							
1900-01	SL	3q **Grays U** (A) 2-0; 4q **West Ham** (H) 1-1; 4qr **West Ham** (A) 1-4							
1901-02	SL	3q **Ilford** (H) 6-1; 4q **Clapton** (A) 2-2; 4qr **Clapton** (H) 2-0; 5q **Grays U** (H) 1-0; Int **Walsall** (A) 0-2							
1902-03	SL	3q **Clapton** (H) 2-0; 4q **Maidstone U** (A) 3-0; 5q **Ilford** (H) 4-1; Int **Glossop** (A) 1-2							
1903-04	SL	Int **Bristol C** (H) 1-1; IntR **Bristol C** (A) 2-5							
1904-05	SL	3q **Clapton** (A) 6-2; 4q **Brighton &HA** (H) 0-1							
1905-06	SL	1	13.1.06	**Northampton T**	SL	H	W	2-1	Beadsworth, Marriott
		2	3.2.06	**Southampton**	SL	H	D	0-0	
		2r	7.2.06	**Southampton**		A	L	0-1	
1906-07	SL	1	12.1.07	**Burton U**	D2	A	D	0-0	
		1r	16.1.07	**Burton U**		H	–	0-0	
			abandoned after 100 minutes						
		1 2r	21.1.07	**Burton U** at Fulham			W	2-0	Hartley 2
		2	2.2.07	**Bury**	D1	A	L	0-1	
1907-08	SL	5q **Shepherds Bush** (H) 6-0							
		1	11.1.08	**Sunderland**	D1	H	W	3-1	McGibbon 3
		2	1.2.08	**Manchester C**	D1	A	D	1-1	McGibbon
		2r	5.2.08	**Manchester C**		H	L	1-2	McGibbon
1908-09	SL	5q **Hastings U** (A) 2-2; 5qr **Hastings U** (H) 1-2							
1909-10	SL	4q **Oxford C** (H) 9-1; 5q **Rotherham T** (A) 1-0							
		1	15.1.10	**Leyton**	SL	A	D	0-0	
		1r	19.1.10	**Leyton**		H	D	2-2aet	Court, Pickett
		1 2r	24.1.10	**Leyton** at Tottenham			L	0-1	
1910-11	SL	4q **Aldershot Royal Engineers** (A) 2-2; 4qr **Aldershot RE** (H) 7-0; 5q **Catford Southend** (H) 4-1							
		1	14.1.11	**Bradford C**	D1	A	L	0-1	
1911-12	SL	4q **Croydon Common** (H) 2-0 abnd; 4qr **Croydon Common** (H) 1-2							
as Gillingham									
1912-13	SL	4q **Leyton** walkover; 5q **Spennymoor U** (A) 1-1; 5qr **Spennymoor U** (H) 3-0							
		1	11.1.13	**Barnsley**	D2	H	D	0-0	
		1r	16.1.13	**Barnsley**		A	L	1-3	Goffin
1913-14	SL	4q **Nunhead** (H) 2-0; 5q **Watford** (H) 1-0							
		1	10.1.14	**Blackpool**	D2	H	W	1-0	Leslie
		2	31.1.14	**Liverpool**	D1	A	L	0-2	
1914-15	SL	1	9.1.15	**Rochdale**	CL	A	L	0-2	
1919-20	SL	6q **Swansea T** (A) 1-1; 6qr **Swansea T** (H) 1-1; 6q 2r **Swansea T** (at Cardiff) 0-0; 6q 3r **Swansea T** (at Stamford Bridge) 3-1							
		1	10.1.20	**West Stanley**	NEL	A	L	1-3	Reid
1920-21	D3	4q **Maidstone U** (H) 1-0; 5q **Dulwich Hamlet** (H) 2-1; 6q **Northampton T** (A) 1-3							
1921-22	3S	5q **Northfleet U** (H) 0-0; 5qr **Northfleet U** (H) 3-1; 6q **St Albans C** (H) 3-1							
		1	7.1.22	**Oldham A**	D1	A	L	1-3	Howard
1922-23	3S	5q **London Caledonians** (A) 2-1; 6q **Blyth Spartans** (H) 1-4							
1923-24	3S	5q **Nunhead** (A) 6-0; 6q **Tranmere R** (H) 1-0							
		1	12.1.24	**Cardiff C**	D1	A	D	0-0	
		1r	16.1.24	**Cardiff C**		H	L	0-1	

1924-25	3S	5q **Kettering T** (A) 1-1; 5qr **Kettering T** (H) 6-2; 6q **Barrow** (A) 1-1; 6qr **Barrow** (H) 0-0; 6q 2r **Barrow** 1-1 (at Molineux);							
		6q 3r **Barrow** 1-1 at Highbury; 6q 4r **Barrow** 1-2 (at Millwall)							
1925-26	3S	1	28.11.25	**Southall**	AL	H	W	6-0	McKee, Adams og, Marshall, Brown, Berry, Rutherford
		2	12.12.25	**Southend**	3S	A	L	0-1	
1926-27	3S	1	27.11.26	**Barking**	AL	A	D	0-0	
		1r	1.12.26	**Barking**		H	W	2-0	Marshall, Brown
		2	11.12.26	**Brentford**	3S	H	D	1-1	Amos
		2r	15.12.26	**Brentford**		A	L	0-1	
1927-28	3S	1	26.11.27	**Plymouth A**	3S	H	W	2-1	Boswell, Meston
		2	10.12.27	**Southend**	3S	H	W	2-0	Wilcox 2
		3	14.1.28	**Stoke C**	D2	A	L	1-6	Wilcox
1928-29	3S	1	24.11.28	**Torquay U**	3S	H	D	0-0	
		1r	28.11.28	**Torquay U**		A	L	1-5	Poxton (p)
1929-30	3S	1	30.11.29	**Margate**	KL	H	L	0-2	
1930-31	3S	1	29.11.30	**Guildford C**	SL	H	W	7-2	Loasby 3, Cheesmur, Death 2, Beacham
		2	13.12.30	**Aldershot T**	SL	H	L	1-3	Death
1931-32	3S	1	28.11.31	**Bristol R**	3S	A	L	1-5	Bethall
1932-33	3S	1	26.11.32	**Wycombe W**	IL	H	D	1-1	Liddle
		1r	30.11.32	**Wycombe W**		A	W	4-2	Cox og, Cropper, Nicol 2
		2	10.12.32	**Bristol R**	3S	A	D	1-1	Nicol
		2r	14.12.32	**Bristol R**		H	L	1-3	Purcell
1933-34	3S	1	25.11.33	**Oxford C**	IL	A	W	5-1	Scott, Mills, Liddle, Purcell, Nicol
		2	9.12.33	**Charlton A**	3S	A	L	0-1	
1934-35	3S	1	24.11.34	**Bristol C**	3S	A	L	0-2	
1935-36	3S	1	30.11.35	**Exeter C**	3S	A	W	4-0	Tadman, Baldwin 3
		2	14.12.35	**Crewe A**	3N	A	L	1-2	Baldwin
1936-37	3S	1	28.11.36	**Ryde Sports**	Hants	A	W	5-1	Wilson, Fowler 2, Watson 2
		2	12.12.36	**Wrexham**	3N	A	L	0-2	
1937-38	3S	1	27.11.37	**Swindon T**	3S	H	L	3-4	Watson 3
1938-39	SL	4q **Tunbridge Wells Rangers** (H) 2-4							
1945-46	SL	4q **Sutton U** (H) 3-9							
1946-47	SL	4q **Guildford C** (A) 2-1							
		1	30.11.46	**Gravesend & N.**	SL	H	W	4-1	Russell 2, Briggs, Warsap
		2	14.12.46	**Bristol C**	3S	A	W	2-1	Wilson, Russell
		3	11.1.47	**Swansea T**	D2	A	L	1-4	Wilson
1947-48	SL	4q **Barnet** (H) 3-1aet							
		1	29.11.47	**Leyton O**	3S	H	W	1-0	Akers
		2	13.12.47	**Rochdale**	3N	A	D	1-1aet	Russell
		2r	20.12.47	**Rochdale**		H	W	3-0	Forrester, Wilson, Briggs
		3	10.1.48	**QPR**	3S	H	D	1-1aet	Russell
		3r	17.1.48	**QPR**		A	L	1-3	Warsap
1948-49	SL	4q **Romford** (A) 1-2aet							
1949-50	SL	4q **Guildford C** (A) 3-2							
		1	26.11.49	**Hastings U**	SL	A	W	3-1	Collins, Russell, W.Burtenshaw
		2	10.12.49	**Yeovil T**	SL	A	L	1-3	Russell (p)
1950-51	3S	1	25.11.50	**Linby Colliery**		A	W	4-1	Thomas, C.Burtenshaw, W.Burtenshaw, Jenkins
		2	9.12.50	**Bristol R**	3S	A	D	2-2	Thomas, Carr
		2r	13.12.50	**Bristol R**		H	D	1-1aet	Carr
		2 2r	18.12.50	**Bristol R** at Tottenham			L	1-2	Lewis
1951-52	3S	1	24.11.51	**Crystal P**	3S	A	W	1-0	Thomas
		2	15.12.51	**Rochdale**	3N	H	L	0-3	
1952-53	3S	1	22.11.52	**Wellington T**	CC	A	D	1-1	Forrester
		1r	26.11.52	**Wellington T**		H	W	3-0	Scarth, Forrester, Long
		2	6.12.52	**Stockport Co**	3N	A	L	1-3	Thomas
1953-54	3S	1	21.11.53	**Walthamstow Ave**	IL	A	L	0-1	
1954-55	3S	1	20.11.54	**Newport Co**	3S	H	W	2-0	Morgan, Miller
		2	11.12.54	**Reading**	3S	H	D	1-1	Durkin
		2r	13.12.54	**Reading**		A	L	3-5	Sowden, Morgan, Marks
1955-56	3S	1	19.11.55	**Shrewsbury T**	3S	H	D	1-1	Millar
		1r	24.11.55	**Shrewsbury T**		A	L	1-4	Millar
1956-57	3S	1	17.11.56	**Yiewsley**	CRN	A	D	2-2	Rigg, Morgan
		1r	20.11.56	**Yiewsley**		H	W	2-0	Morgan, Pollock
		2	8.12.56	**Newport Co**	3S	H	L	1-2	Crossan
1957-58	3S	1	16.11.57	**Gorleston**	ECL	H	W	10-1	Saunders 5, Clark 2, Fletcher 2, Morgan
		2	7.12.57	**Millwall**	3S	A	D	1-1	Fletcher
		2r	11.12.57	**Millwall**		H	W	6-1	Payne 2, Fletcher 2, Saunders, Hutton
		3	4.1.58	**Nottingham F**	D1	A	L	0-2	

Season	Div	Rd	Date	Opponent		Venue	Res	Score	Scorers
1958-59	D4	1	15.11.58	Plymouth A	D3	A	D	2-2	Patrick, Edgar
		1r	19.11.58	Plymouth A		H	L	1-4	Terry
1959-60	D4	1	14.11.59	Bedford T	SL	A	W	4-0	Albury, Terry 2, Pulley
		2	5.12.59	Torquay U	D4	H	D	2-2	Albury 2 (1p)
		2r	9.12.59	Torquay U		A	W	2-1	Terry, Hannaway
		3	9.1.60	Swansea T	D2	H	L	1-4	Griffith og
1960-61	D4	1	5.11.60	Ashford T	SL	A	W	2-1	Hughes, Shepherd
		2	26.11.60	Southend U	D3	H	W	3-2	Terry, Shepherd 2
		3	7.1.61	Leyton O	D2	H	L	2-6	Terry, Hughes (p)
1961-62	D4	1	4.11.61	Coventry C	D3	A	L	0-2	
1962-63	D4	1	3.11.62	Andover	SL	A	W	1-0	Godfrey
		2	24.11.62	Bedford T	SL	H	W	3-0	Farrall 2, Gibbs
		3	27.2.63	Port Vale	D3	H	L	2-4	Gibbs, Francis
1963-64	D4	1	16.11.63	QPR	D3	A	L	1-4	Arnott
1964-65	D3	1	14.11.64	Guildford C	SL	A	D	2-2	Riggs, Gibbs
		1r	18.11.64	Guildford C		H	W	1-0	Gibbs
		2	5.12.64	Luton T	D3	A	L	0-1	
1965-66	D3	1	13.11.65	Folkestone	SL	H	L	1-2	R.Taylor
1966-67	D3	1	26.11.66	Tamworth	WMRL	H	W	4-1	Rackstraw (p), Yeo 2, Gibbs
		2	7.1.67	Walsall	D3	A	L	1-3	Gibbs
1967-68	D3	1	18.12.67	Newport Co	D4	A	L	0-3	
1968-69	D3	1	16.11.68	Orient	D3	A	D	1-1	Smillie
		1r	20.11.68	Orient		H	W	2-1	Riddick 2
		2	7.12.68	Luton T	D3	A	L	1-3	Yeo (p)
1969-70	D3	1	15.11.69	Southend U	D4	A	D	0-0	
		1r	19.11.69	Southend U		H	W	2-1	Yeo 2
		2	6.12.69	Tamworth	WMRL	H	W	6-0	Pound, Bailey 3, Green, Smillie
		3	3.1.70	Newport Co	D4	H	W	1-0	Machin
		4	24.1.70	Peterborough U	D4	H	W	5-1	Green 2, Yeo 2, Ronaldson
		5	7.2.70	Watford	D2	A	L	1-2	Yeo
1970-71	D3	1	21.11.70	Brentford	D4	A	L	1-2	Green
1971-72	D4	1	20.11.71	Plymouth A	D3	H	W	3-2	Galvin, Wilks, Yeo
		2	11.12.71	Romford	SL	A	W	1-0	Wilks
		3	15.1.72	Swansea C	D3	A	L	0-1	
1972-73	D4	1	18.11.72	Reading	D4	H	L	1-2	Tydeman
1973-74	D4	1	24.11.73	Cambridge U	D3	A	L	2-3	Richardson, Tydeman
1974-75	D3	1	26.11.74	Hereford U	D3	A	L	0-1	
1975-76	D3	1	22.11.75	Weymouth	SL	A	W	2-0	Richardson 2
		2	13.12.75	Brighton & HA	D3	H	L	0-1	
1976-77	D3	1	20.11.76	Watford	D4	H	L	0-1	
1977-78	D3	1	26.11.77	Weymouth	SL	H	D	1-1	Westwood
		1r	30.11.77	Weymouth		A	W	1-0	Shipperley
		2	17.12.77	Peterborough U	D3	H	D	1-1	Nicholl
		2r	20.12.77	Peterborough U		A	L	0-2	
1978-79	D3	1	25.11.78	Reading	D4	H	D	0-0	
		1r	28.11.78	Reading		H	L	1-2aet	Westwood
1979-80	D3	1	24.11.79	Wimbledon	D3	H	D	0-0	
		1r	27.11.79	Wimbledon		A	L	2-4	Price
1980-81	D3	1	22.11.80	Dagenham	IL	H	W	2-1	Price, Ford
		2	13.12.80	Maidstone U	APL	H	D	0-0	
		2r	16.12.80	Maidstone U		A	D	0-0aet	
		2 2r	22.12.80	Maidstone U		H	L	0-2	
1981-82	D3	1	21.11.81	Plymouth A	D3	A	D	0-0	
		1r	24.11.81	Plymouth A		H	W	1-0	Bowman
		2	15.12.81	Barking	IL	H	D	1-1	White (p)
		2r	2.1.82	Barking at Gillingham		A	W	3-1aet	Bruce, Price, Powell
		3	5.1.82	Oldham A	D2	H	W	2-1	Kemp, White (p)
		4	23.1.82	WBA	D1	H	L	0-1	
1982-83	D3	1	20.11.82	Dagenham	APL	H	W	1-0	Cascarino
		2	11.12.82	Northampton T	D4	H	D	1-1	Johnson
		2r	14.12.82	Northampton T		A	L	2-3	Weatherley 2
1983-84	D3	1	19.11.83	AP Leamington	SL	A	W	1-0	Handford
		2	10.12.83	Chelmsford C	SL	H	W	6-1	Shaw, Weatherly 2, Sage, Mehmet, Leslie
		3	6.1.84	Brentford	D3	H	W	5-3	Cochrane, Musker, Weatherly, Leslie, Cascarino
		4	28.1.84	Everton	D1	A	D	0-0	
		4r	31.1.84	Everton		H	D	0-0aet	
		4 2r	6.2.84	Everton		H	L	0-3	

GILLINGHAM

1984-85	D3	1	17.11.84	Windsor & Eton	IL	H	W	2-1	Mehmet, Cascarino
		2	8.12.84	Colchester U	D4	A	W	5-0	Robinson, Shearer 3, Cascarino
		3	21.1.85	Cardiff C	D2	H	W	2-1	Robinson, Leslie
		4	26.1.85	Ipswich T	D1	A	L	2-3	Leslie, Sage
1985-86	D3	1	16.11.85	Northampton T	D4	H	W	3-0	Mundee og, Mehmet, Cochrane
		2	7.12.85	Bognor Regis T	IL	H	W	6-1	Cascarino 2, Robinson, Shearer, Cochrane, Hales
		3	4.1.86	Derby Co	D3	H	D	1-1	Robinson
		3r	13.1.86	Derby Co		A	L	1-3aet	Robinson
1986-87	D3	1	15.11.86	Kettering	GMVC	A	W	3-0	Robinson, Hinnigan, Kellock og
		2	6.12.86	Chelmsford C	SL	H	W	2-0	Cascarino 2
		3	19.1.87	Wigan A	D3	A	L	1-2	Greenall (p)
1987-88	D3	1	14.11.87	Fulham	D3	H	W	2-1	Lillis, Pritchard
		2	5.12.87	Walsall	D3	H	W	2-1	Lovell, Elsey
		3	9.1.88	Birmingham C	D2	H	L	0-3	
1988-89	D3	1	19.11.88	Peterborough U	D4	H	D	3-3	Lovell, Quow, Smith
		1r	23.11.88	Peterborough U		A	L	0-1aet	
1989-90	D4	1	18.11.89	Welling	GMVC	H	D	0-0	
		1r	22.11.89	Welling		A	L	0-1	
1990-91	D4	1	17.11.90	Bournemouth	D3	A	L	1-2	Crown
1991-92	D4	1	18.11.91	Brentford	D3	A	D	3-3	Walker 2, Smith
		1r	26.11.91	Brentford		H	L	1-3	Walker
1992-93	D3	1	14.11.92	Kettering T	GMVC	H	W	3-2	Clark, Crown, Forster
		2	5.12.92	Colchester U	D3	H	D	1-1	Crown
		2r	16.12.92	Colchester U		A	W	3-2	Forster, Arnott, Henry (p)
		3	2.1.93	Huddersfield T	D2	H	D	0-0	
		3r	13.1.93	Huddersfield T		A	L	1-2	Green (p)

GITANOS FC

Formed 1864. Home matches played in Battersea Park and around south London.

1873-74	1	28.10.73	Uxbridge	A	L	0-3

GLASGOW RANGERS

Formed 1873. One of the seven Scottish clubs that played in the FA Cup. Won Scottish FA Cup 26 times and reached the semi-final of the English FA Cup in 1887.

1885-86	1		Rawtenstall			scratched	
1886-87	1	30.10.86	Everton		A	W	1-0	Heggie
	2	20.11.86	Church FC		H	W	2-1	Lawrie, others 1
	3	4.12.86	Cowlairs		H	W	3-2	Fraser, Lawrie, Peacock
	4		bye					
	5	29.1.87	Lincoln C		H	W	3-0	Fraser, Lindsay, Peacock
	6	19.2.87	Old Westminsters		H	W	5-1	Lafferty, Lawrie, others 3
	SF	5.3.87	A.Villa			L	1-3	Lafferty
			played at Crewe					

GLASTONBURY

Formed 1890. **First entered FA Cup:** 1903

1950-51	WL	1	25.11.50	Exeter C	3S	H	L	1-2	Thomas

GLOSSOP (NORTH END)

Formed 1886. **First entered FA Cup:** 1895. Reformed 1919 and 1945. Members of the Football League 1899-1915. Currently play in North West Counties League.

1896-97	ML	1	30.1.97	Stoke	D1	A	L	2-5	McFarlane, Platt
1897-98	ML	3q	Aberystwyth (A) 0-1					
1898-99	D2	3q	New Brighton Tower (H) 4-2; 4q Crewe Alex (H) 1-0; 5q Stockport Co (A) 2-0					
		1	28.1.99	Newcastle U	D1	H	L	0-1	
1899-00	D1	3q	Stockport Co (H) 2-2; 3qr Stockport Co (A) 0-3					
1900-01	D2	Int	Stoke (A) 0-1					
1901-02	D2	3q	St Helens (H) 5-2; 4q Nantwich T (A) 3-1; 5q Stockport Co (H) 2-0; Int Leicester F (A) 1-0					
		1	25.1.02	Nottingham F	D1	H	L	1-3	Goddard

GLOSSOP

1902-03	D2	3q **Crewe Alex** (A) 3-0; 4q **Wrexham** (H) 4-0; 5q **St Helens** (H) 5-0; Int **New Brompton** (H) 2-1					
		1	7.2.03 **Stoke**	D1	H	L	2-3	Badenoch, Burgess
1903-04	D2	2q **Heywood** (H) *scratched*					
1904-05	D2	3q **Nantwich** (A) 2-1; 4q **Stockport Co** (H) 1-1; 4qr **Stockport Co** (A) 0-0; 4q 2r **Stockport Co** (H) 0-0; 4q 3r **Stockport Co** (A) 0-1					
1905-06	D2	4q **Brighton & HA** (H) 0-1					
1906-07	D2	5q **Newhall Swifts** (A) 2-1					
		1	12.1.07 **Brentford**	SL	A	L	1-2	McKie
1907-08	D2	5q **West Stanley** (A) 3-0					
		1	11.1.08 **Manchester C**	D1	H	D	0-0	
		1r	15.1.08 **Manchester C**		A	L	0-6	
1908-09	D2	1	6.1.09 **Chesterfield**	D2	A	W	2-0	Raine, Stapley
		2	6.2.09 **Stockport Co**	D2	A	D	1-1	Robertson
		2r	9.2.09 **Stockport Co**		H	W	1-0aet	Greechan
		3	20.2.09 **Sheffield W**	D1	A	W	1-0	Greechan
		4	6.3.09 **Bristol C**	D1	H	D	0-0	
		4r	10.3.09 **Bristol C**		A	L	0-1	
1909-10	D2	1	15.1.10 **Bury**	D1	A	L	1-2	Hoare
1910-11	D2	1	14.1.11 **Middlesbrough**	D1	A	L	0-1	
1911-12	D2	1	13.1.12 **Leeds C**	D2	A	L	0-1	
1912-13	D2	4q **Ripley** (H) 2-0; 5q **Southall** (H) 11-1					
		1	11.1.13 **Crystal P**	SL	A	L	0-2	
1913-14	D2	4q **Hinckley** (H) 5-1; 5q **Carlisle U** (H) 4-1					
		1	10.1.14 **Everton**	D1	H	W	2-1	Montgomery, Barnett
		2	31.1.14 **Preston NE**	D1	H	L	0-1	
1914-15	D2	6q **Coventry C** (H) 3-1					
		1	9.1.15 **QPR**	SL	A	L	1-2	Toward

GLOUCESTER CITY

Formed 1889. **First entered FA Cup:** 1938

1948-49	SL	1	27.11.48 **Mansfield T**	3N	A	L	0-4	
1949-50	SL	1	26.11.49 **Norwich C**	3S	H	L	2-3	Hunt 2
1950-51	SL	1	25.11.50 **Bristol C**	3S	A	L	0-4	
1989-90	SL	1	18.11.89 **Dorchester T**	SL	H	W	1-0	Talboys
		2	9.12.89 **Cardiff C**	D3	A	D	2-2	Talboys, Townsend
		2r	12.12.89 **Cardiff C**		H	L	0-1	

GOLDENHILL

Staffordshire-based amateur club which played in the Cup for three seasons

1884-85	1	18.10.84 **Wrexham**		A	L	0-1	
1885-86	1	31.10.85 **Davenham**		A	L	1-2	
1886-87	1	30.10.86 **Macclesfield**		H	W	4-2	
		replay ordered after protest					
	1r	13.11.86 **Macclesfield**		A	W	3-2	
	2	20.11.86 **Chester**		A	L	0-1	
		Chester disqualified after protest, Goldenhill re-instated					
	3	**Chirk**				*scratched*	

GOLDERS GREEN

See Hendon

GOOLE TOWN

Formed 1900. **First entered FA Cup:** 1907. **Cup Final Connection:** Tony Galvin, who played for Tottenham in the 1981 and 1982 Cup Finals started at Goole. **League club beaten:** Workington

1914-15		1	9.1.15 **Middlesbrough**	D1	A	L	3-9	Morley, Spavin, Ford
1949-50	ML	1	26.11.49 **Chester**	3N	A	L	1-4	Cutts
1951-52	ML	1	24.11.51 **Tranmere R**	3N	A	L	2-4	Kimber, Coop
1955-56	ML	1	19.11.55 **Halifax T**	3N	H	L	1-2	Steadman
1956-57	ML	1	17.11.56 **Wigan A**	LC	A	W	2-1	Handley 2
		2	8.12.56 **Workington**	3N	H	D	2-2	Handley, Iggleden
		2r	12.12.56 **Workington**		A	W	1-0	Handley

GOOLE TOWN

	3	5.1.57	Nottingham F	D2	A	L	0-6	
1957-58 ML	1	16.11.57	Scunthorpe	3N	A	L	1-2	Johnson (p)
1967-68 ML	1	9.12.67	Spennymoor U	NL	H	D	0-0	
	1r	13.12.67	Spennymoor U		A	L	1-3	Wagstaffe
1968-69 NPL	1	16.11.68	Barrow	D3	H	L	1-3	Thompson
1976-77 NPL	1	20.11.76	Barrow	NPL	A	W	2-0	Whiteley, Taylor
	2	11.12.76	Wrexham	D3	A	D	1-1	Kelly
	2r	14.12.76	Wrexham		H	L	0-1	
1977-78 NPL	1	26.11.77	Spennymoor U	NL	A	L	1-3	Thompson
1984-85 NPL	1	17.11.84	Halifax T	D4	A	L	0-2	

GORLESTON

Formed 1884. **First entered FA Cup:** 1910

1951-52 ECL	1	24.11.51	Leyton O	3S	A	D	2-2	Hunter, Chapman
	1r	29.11.51	Leyton O		H	D	0-0	
	1 2r	3.12.51	Leyton O at Highbury			L	4-5	Hunter 2, Chapman, Guy
1957-58 ECL	1	16.11.57	Gillingham	3S	A	L	1-10	Sells

GRANTHAM TOWN

Formed 1874. **First entered FA Cup:** 1877. **Cup Final Connection:** Gary Crosby, who played for Nottingham Forest in the 1991 Cup Final was signed from Grantham. **League clubs beaten:** Stockport Co, Rochdale

1877-78	1	27.10.77	Clapham Rovers		H	L	0-2	
1878-79	1	19.10.78	Sheffield FC		A	D	1-1	Hutchinson
	1r	16.11.78	Sheffield FC		H	L	1-2	Britten
1880-81	1	11.11.80	Birmingham Calthorpe		A	W	2-1	Frith, Howard
	2	11.12.80	Stafford Road		H	D	1-1	O'Dowds
	2r	16.12.80	Stafford Road		A	L	1-7	Maule
1881-82	1	5.11.81	Brigg FC		H	W	6-0	
	2	28.11.81	Staveley		A	L	1-3	
1882-83	1		Phoenix Bessemer					scratched
1883-84	1	10.11.83	Spilsby		H	W	3-2	Curtis, Bell, Lee
	2	26.11.83	Grimsby T		H	W	4-0	T.Bryan, Bell, Curtis, 1 other
	3	15.12.83	Notts Co		H	L	0-4	
1884-85	1	25.10.84	Grimsby T		H	D	1-1	
	1r	8.11.84	Grimsby T		A	L	0-1	
1885-86	1	24.10.85	Gainsborough T		A	L	1-4	
1886-87	1	23.10.86	Lincoln Lindum		A	W	1-0	
	2	13.11.86	Redcar		H	W	3-2	
	3	9.12.86	Horncastle		A	L	0-2	
1887-88	1	15.10.87	Lincoln Lindum		H	W	4-0	
	2	5.11.87	Notts Rangers		A	L	0-4	
1928-29 ML	1	24.11.28	Rhyl A	Welsh H		W	1-0	Spaven
	2	8.12.28	Wigan B	3N	A	L	1-2	Spaven
1935-36 ML	1	30.11.35	Notts Co	3S	H	L	0-2	
1945-46 ML	1 1L	17.11.45	Kettering	UCL	A	W	5-1	Searby,Ashton, Ranshaw 2, Wood
	1 2L	24.11.45	Kettering		H	D	2-2	Russell, Ranshaw
	2 1L	8.12.45	Mansfield T	3S	H	L	1-2	Searby
	2 2L	15.12.45	Mansfield T		A	L	1-2	Searby
1947-48 ML	1	29.11.47	Stockton	NEL	A	L	1-2	Searby
1949-50 ML	1	26.11.49	Wrexham	3N	A	L	1-4	McCartney
1961-62 ML	1	4.11.61	Brierley Hill All.	BDL	A	L	0-3	
1965-66 ML	1	13.11.65	Hendon	IL	H	W	4-1	Alexander 4
	2	4.12.65	Swindon T	D3	H	L	1-6	Alexander
1966-67 ML	1	26.11.66	Wimbledon	SL	H	W	2-1	Martin og, South
	2	7.1.67	Oldham A	D3	H	L	0-4	
1967-68 ML	1	9.12.67	Altrincham	CC	H	L	0-3	
1968-69 ML	1	16.11.68	Chelmsford C	SL	H	W	2-1	Tomlinson, Bly
	2	7.12.68	Swindon T	D3	H	L	0-2	
1969-70 ML	1	15.11.69	Oldham A	D4	A	L	1-3	Benskin
1970-71 ML	1	21.11.70	Stockport Co	D4	H	W	2-1	Tomlinson, Norris
	2	12.12.70	Rotherham U	D3	H	L	1-4	Nixon

GRANTHAM TOWN

1972-73	SL	1	18.11.72	Bradford C	D4	A	L	0-3
1973-74	SL	1	24.11.73	Hillingdon B	SL	A	W	4-0	Norris 2, Benskin, Horobin
		2	15.12.73	Rochdale	D3	H	D	1-1	Benskin
		2r	18.12.73	Rochdale		A	W	5-3aet	Chambers 3, Norris, Horobin
		3	5.1.74	Middlesbrough	D2	H	L	0-2
1975-76	SL	1	22.11.75	Port Vale	D3	H	D	2-2	Benskin, Norris
		1r	24.11.75	Port Vale		A	L	1-4	Norris

GRAVESEND & NORTHFLEET UNITED

See also Northfleet United. **Formed** 1946 by merger of Gravesend United (1893) and Northfleet United. **League clubs beaten:** Exeter C, Carlisle U

1946-47	SL	1	30.11.46	Gillingham	3S	A	L	1-4	Crowe
1949-50	SL	1	26.11.49	Torquay U	3S	H	L	1-3	Viles
1962-63	SL	1	3.11.62	Exeter C	D4	H	W	3-2	Williams 2, McNichol
		2	24.11.62	Wycombe W	IL	H	W	3-1	Cameron, Skingley 2
		3	29.1.63	Carlisle U	D3	A	W	1-0	Sitford
		4	12.2.63	Sunderland	D2	H	D	1-1	Skingley
		4r	18.2.63	Sunderland		A	L	2-5	McNicol, Sitford
1963-64	SL	1	16.11.63	Tooting & Mitcham U	IL	A	W	2-1	Wilkins, Easton (p)
		2	7.12.63	Brentford		A	L	0-1
1964-65	SL	1	14.11.64	Bournemouth	D3	A	L	0-7
1965-66	SL	1	13.11.65	Wimbledon	SL	A	L	1-4	Chamberlain
1978-79	SL	1	25.11.78	Wimbledon	D4	H	D	0-0
		1r	28.11.78	Wimbledon		A	L	0-1
1979-80	APL	1	24.11.79	Torquay U	D4	H	L	0-1
1980-81	APL	1	22.11.80	St Albans C	IL	H	L	1-2	Stonebridge

GRAYS ATHLETIC

Formed 1890. **First entered FA Cup:** 1912.

1952-53	CRN	1	22.11.52	Llanelli	SL	H	L	0-5
1988-89	IL	1	19.11.88	Bath C	SL	A	L	0-2

GREAT BRIDGE UNITY

Formed 1879. Played at Horseley Heath, Horseley, Tipton

1887-88		1	15.10.87	Stafford Road		A	L	1-2
			replay ordered after protest				
		1r	22.10.87	Stafford Road		H	D	1-1
		1 2r		Stafford Road			*walkover*
		2	5.11.87	Burton Swifts		A	W	5-3
		3	26.11.87	Birmingham Excelsior		H	W	2-1
		4	17.12.87	Bootle		H	L	1-2

GREAT HARWOOD

Formed 1877. **First entered FA Cup:** 1900. Folded 1978. Present day club Great Harwood Town formed 1978

1970-71	NPL	1	24.11.70	Rotherham U	D3	H	L	2-6	Beardall, Vernon

GREAT LEVER, BOLTON

Formed 1877. Played in the Woodside area of Bolton. **Cup Final Connection:** Albert Shepherd, first player to score a penalty in the Cup final (1910 replay, for Newcastle) was born in Great Lever

1882-83		1	21.10.82	Halliwell		A	L	2-3
1883-84		1	20.10.83	Astley Bridge		H	W	4-1	Hardman, Howarth, Rostron, 1 other
		2	1.12.83	Preston NE		A	L	1-4
1885-86		1		Preston NE			*scratched*
1886-87		1	16.10.86	Bootle		A	W	4-2
		2	13.11.86	Cliftonville		H	L	1-3

GREAT YARMOUTH TOWN

Formed 1897. First entered FA Cup: 1901. League club beaten: Crystal Palace

1947-48	ECL	1	29.11.47	Shrewsbury T	ML	H	L	1-4	Daynes
1952-53	ECL	1	22.11.52	Guildford C	SL	A	D	2-2	Plunkett, Keaveney
		1r	27.11.52	Guildford C		H	W	1-0	Horsfall og
		2	6.12.52	Wrexham	3N	H	L	1-2	Cutting
1953-54	ECL	1	21.11.53	Crystal P	3S	H	W	1-0	Rackham
		2	12.12.53	Barrow	3N	A	L	2-5	Plunkett 2

GRESHAM FC

Formed 1874. Played at South Hackney Common, now part of Hackney Downs. Used the Bedford Hotel in Victoria Park Road as their changing rooms.

1876-77	1	4.11.76	Forest School	A	L	1-4	
1879-80	1	1.11.79	Kildare	H	W	3-0	Cullen 2, Jeffrey
	2	20.12.79	Grey Friars	A	L	0-9	

GRESLEY ROVERS

Formed 1882. First entered FA Cup: 1896. FA Vase Runners-up: 1991

| 1930-31 | BC | 1 | 29.11.30 | York C | 3N | A | L | 1-3 | Warren |

GRETNA

Formed 1946. Became the first Scottish club to play in the competition proper for 105 years in 1991. Compete in the Northern League.

| 1991-92 | NL | 1 | 16.11.91 | Rochdale | D4 | H | D | 0-0 | |
| | | 1r | 27.11.91 | Rochdale | | A | L | 1-3 | Carruthers |

GREY FRIARS

Formed 1876. Played at The Greyhound fields, Dulwich, south London. Used The Greyhound pub as their changing rooms.

1878-79	1	9.11.78	Great Marlow	H	W	2-1	
	2	7.12.78	Minerva	H	L	0-3	
1879-80	1	8.11.79	Hanover Utd	H	W	2-1	
	2	20.12.79	Gresham	H	W	9-0	Broadhurst, Green 2, Stransham, Sharp, Kirkpatrick, own goals 2, 1 other
	3		bye				
	4	18.2.80	Royal Engineers	A	L	0-1	
1880-81	1	13.11.80	Windsor Home Park	H	D	0-0	
	1r	20.11.80	Windsor Home Park	A	W	3-1	
	2	11.12.80	Maidenhead	H	W	1-0	Thompson
	3		bye				
	4	19.2.81	Old Etonians	A	L	0-4	

GRIMSBY DISTRICT

Formed 1878. Played at Cleethorpes Road, Grimsby. A seperate club from Grimsby Town

| 1884-85 | 1 | | Middlesbrough | | | scratched | |
| 1885-86 | 1 | 17.10.85 | Lincoln Lindum | A | L | 0-4 | |

GRIMSBY TOWN

Formed 1878. FA Cup Best Performance: Semifinals, 1936 and 1939 FA Cup Record Win: 10-0 vs Boston Town, 2nd qualifying round, 24.10.1891 (in competition proper) 8-0 vs Darlington, 2nd round, 21.11.1885 FA Cup Record Defeat: 1-9 vs Phoenix Bessemer, 2nd round, 25.11.1882

1882-83	1		Queens Park, Glasgow			walkover	
	2	25.11.82	Phoenix Bessemer	H	L	1-9	Monument
1883-84	1	3.11.83	Hull T	A	W	3-1	
	2	26.11.83	Grantham	A	L	0-4	
1884-85	1	25.10.84	Grantham	A	D	1-1	Mundahl
	1r	8.11.84	Grantham	H	W	1-0	Garnham

GRIMSBY TOWN

Season	Comp	Rd	Date	Opponent		V	R	Score	Scorers
		2	6.12.84	Redcar		H	W	3-1	Garnham 2, Raynes
		3	3.1.85	Lincoln C		H	W	1-0	Mundahl
		4	24.1.85	Old Carthusians		A	L	0-3	
1885-86		1	31.10.85	Lincoln C		A	W	2-0	Sharman, Monument
		2	21.11.85	Darlington		H	W	8-0	Monument 4, Seal 3, Atkinson
		3	19.12.85	Middlesbrough Iron		A	L	1-2	Monument
1886-87		1	30.10.86	Sheffield Heeley		A	W	4-1	Pearson 3, Chapman
		2	13.11.86	Nottingham F		A	D	2-2	Garnham, Caborn og
		2r	20.11.86	Nottingham F		H	L	0-1	
1887-88		1	15.10.87	Cleethorpes		A	W	4-0	Lundie, Smith, Lee, Atkinson og
		2	26.11.87	Lincoln C		H	W	2-0	Lundie, Lee
		3	17.12.87	Old Foresters		A	L	2-4	Atkinson, Lee
1888-89	TC	1q Lincoln C (H) 1-1aet; 1qr Lincoln C (A) 1-1aet; 1q 2r Lincoln C 3-1 at Bramall Lane; 2q **Newark** (A) 4-4; 2qr **Newark** (H) 9-0; 3q **Cleethorpes** (H) 5-0							
		1	15.12.88	Sunderland A	FAll	H	W	3-1	McBeth 2, J. Taylor
		2	16.2.89	Preston NE	D1	H	L	0-2	
1889-90	FAll	1	18.1.90	Newcastle U	NL	H	W	2-1	McBeth, Black
		2	1.2.90	Blackburn R	D1	A	L	0-3	
1890-91	FAll	1q Ecclesfield (A) 2-8							
1891-92	FAll	1q Long Eaton Rangers (H) 2-1; 2q Boston T (H) 10-0; 3q **Sheffield U** (H) 1-2							
1892-93	D2	1q Attercliffe (A) 2-0; 2q Doncaster R (H) 1-1; 2qr Doncaster R (A) 2-1; 3q Gainsborough T (H) 1-0; 4q **Lincoln C** (H) 5-0							
		1	21.1.93	Stockton	NL	H	W	5-0	Mullen 2, Higgins, Ackroyd, og
		2	3.2.93	Darwen	D2	A	L	0-2	
1893-94	D2	1q Kilnhurst (H) 5-1; 2q Lincoln C (A) 5-2; 3q **Grantham R** (A) 6-2; 4q Gainsborough T (H) 6-1							
		1	27.1.94	Liverpool	D2	A	L	0-3	
1894-95	D2	1q **Lincoln C** (A) 3-0; 2q **Attercliffe** (H) 2-2; 2qr **Attercliffe** (H) 8-0; 3q **Worksop T** (H) 0-1							
1895-96	D2	1q **Staveley** (A) 5-0; 2q **Kilnhurst** (A) 4-1; 3q **Lincoln C** (A) 5-2; 4q **Rotherham T** (H) 4-0							
		1	1.2.96	Darwen	D2	A	W	2-0	Graham, Pratt
		2	15.2.96	WBA	D1	H	D	1-1	Gray
		2r	20.2.96	WBA		A	L	0-3	
1896-97	D2	1	28.1.97	Bolton W	D1	H	D	0-0	
		1r	3.2.97	Bolton W		A	D	3-3	Rogers, Bell, McCairns
		1 2r	11.2.97	Bolton W at Bramall Lane			L	2-3	Fletcher, og
1897-98	D2	1	29.1.98	Nottingham F	D1	A	L	0-4	
1898-99	D2	3q Mexborough (H) 5-0; 4q Lincoln C (H) 2-1; 5q **Barnsley** (A) 0-0; 5qr **Barnsley** (H) 2-1							
		1	28.1.99	Preston NE	D1	H	L	0-7	
1899-00	D2	3q Doncaster R (H) 3-1; 4q Barnsley (H) 3-2; 5q **Chesterfield** (H) 3-2							
		1	27.1.00	Nottingham F	D1	A	L	0-3	
1900-01	D2	Int	5.1.01	Middlesbrough	D2	H	L	0-1	
1901-02	D1	1	25.1.02	Portsmouth	SL	H	D	1-1	Appleyard
		1r	29.1.02	Portsmouth		A	L	0-2	
1902-03	D1	1	7.2.03	Newcastle U	D1	H	W	2-1	Fletcher, Ronaldson
		2	21.2.03	Notts Co	D1	H	L	0-2	
1903-04	D2	Int	12.12.03	Barnsley	D2	H	W	2-0	Hodginson, Wilkinson
		1	6.2.04	Preston NE	D2	A	L	0-1	
1904-05	D2	Int	14.1.05	Gainsborough T	D2	H	W	2-0	Reynolds, Baker
		1	4.2.05	Stoke	D1	A	L	0-2	
1905-06	D2	1	6.1.06	Newcastle U	D1	A	L	0-6	
1906-07	D2	1	12.1.07	W.Arsenal	D1	D	D	1-1	Hooper
		1r	6.1.07	W.Arsenal		A	L	0-3	
1907-08	D2	1	11.1.08	Bristol C	D1	A	D	0-0	
		1r	15.1.08	Bristol C		H	W	2-1	Lee, Blanthorne
		2	1.2.08	Carlisle	LC	H	W	6-2	Blanthorne 5, Kilbourne
		3	22.2.08	Crystal P	SL	H	W	1-0	Blanthorne
		4	7.3.08	Newcastle U	D1	A	L	1-5	Kilbourne
1908-09	D2	1	6.1.09	Stockport Co	D2	H	–	0-2	
				abandoned after 75 minutes					
		1	20.1.09	Stockport Co		H	L	0-2	
1909-10	D2	1	15.1.10	Bristol R	SL	H	L	0-2	
1910-11	ML	1	14.1.11	Croydon Common	SL	H	W	3-0	Leonard 3
				FA ordered match to be replayed					
		1	26.1.11	Croydon Common		H	W	8-1	Leonard 3, Hubbard 2, Worth 2, Springthorpe
		2	4.2.11	Crewe Alex	BDL	A	W	5-1	Hubbard 2, Gordon, Springthorpe, Leonard (p)
		3	25.2.11	Bradford C	D1	A	L	0-1	
1911-12	D2	4q Lincoln C (A) 2-3							
1912-13	D2	1	18.1.13	Sheffield W	D1	A	L	1-5	Rippon
1913-14	D2	1	10.1.14	WBA	D1	A	L	0-2	

1914-15	D2	1	9.1.15	**Northampton T**	SL	H	L	0-3	
1919-20	D2	1	10.1.20	**Bristol C**	D2	H	L	1-2	Thompson
1920-21	D3	6q	**Kettering T** (A) 4-2						
		1	8.1.21	**Norwich C**	D3	H	W	1-0	Smith (p)
		2	29.1.21	**Southampton**	D3	H	L	1-3	Storer
1921-22	3N	5q	**Kettering T** (H) 1-1; 5qr **Kettering T** (A) 2-0; 6q **Tufnell Park** (H) 1-1; 6qr **Tufnell Park** (A) 2-1						
		1	7.1.22	**Notts Co**	D2	H	D	1-1	Carmichael
		1r	12.1.22	**Notts Co**		A	L	0-3	
1922-23	3N	5q	**Worksop** T (H) 0-2						
1923-24	3N	5q	**Hinckley** (A) 3-0; 6q **Chesterfield** (A) 0-0; 6qr **Chesterfield** (H) 2-0						
		1	12.1.24	**Exeter C**	3S	A	L	0-1	
1924-25	3N	5q	**Chesterfield** (H) 1-2						
1925-26	3N	1	28.11.25	**Walsall**	3N	A	W	1-0	McKenna
		2	12.12.25	**Kettering T**	SL	A	D	1-1	Carmichael
		2r	15.12.25	**Kettering T**		H	W	3-1	Devan, Carmichael, McKenna
		3	9.1.26	**Birmingham**	D1	A	L	0-2	
1926-27	D2	1	27.11.26	**Halifax T**	3N	H	W	3-2	Pugsley (p), McKenna, Marshall
		2	11.12.26	**York C**	ML	H	W	2-1	Bestall, Robson
		3	8.1.27	**Burnley**	D1	A	L	1-3	Hardy
1927-28	D2	3	14.1.28	**Reading**	D2	A	L	0-4	
1928-29	D2	3	12.1.29	**WBA**	D2	H	D	1-1	Cooper
		3r	6.1.29	**WBA**		A	L	0-2	
1929-30	D1	3	11.1.30	**Brighton & HA**	D2	A	D	1-1	Prior
		3r	14.1.30	**Brighton & HA**		H	L	0-1	
1930-31	D1	3	10.1.31	**Scarborough**	ML	A	W	2-1	Prior, Bestall
		4	24.1.31	**Manchester U**	D1	H	W	1-0	Marshall
		5	14.2.31	**Everton**	D2	A	L	3-5	Bestall, Coleman, Marshall
1931-32	D1	3	9.1.32	**Exeter C**	3S	H	W	4-1	Glover 4
		4	23.1.32	**Birmingham**	D1	H	W	2-1	Bestall 2
		5	13.2.32	**Liverpool**	D1	A	L	0-1	
1932-33	D2	3	14.1.33	**Portsmouth**	D1	H	W	3-2	Glover 2, Dyson
		4	28.1.33	**Bolton W**	D1	A	L	1-2	Craven
1933-34	D2	3	13.1.34	**Clapton O**	3S	H	W	1-0	Glover
		4	27.1.34	**Portsmouth**	D1	A	L	0-2	
1934-35	D1	3	12.1.35	**Everton**	D1	A	L	3-6	Glover 2, Craven
1935-36	D1	3	11.1.36	**Hartlepool U**	3N	A	D	0-0	
		3r	14.1.36	**Hartlepool U**		H	W	4-1	Glover 2, Buck, Bestall
		4	25.1.36	**Port Vale**	D2	A	W	4-0	Baldry 2, Bestall, Craven
		5	15.2.36	**Manchester C**	D1	H	W	3-2	Lewis 2, Glover
		6	29.2.36	**Middlesbrough**	D1	H	W	3-1	Glover, Craven, Smailes
		SF	21.3.36	**Arsenal**	D1		L	0-1	
			played at Huddersfield						
1936-37	D1	3	6.1.37	**Cardiff C**	3S	A	W	3-1	Glover, Craven, Lewis
		4	30.1.37	**Walsall**	3S	H	W	5-1	Glover 3, Lewis, Buck
		5	20.2.37	**Wolverhampton W**	D1	H	D	1-1	Craven
		5r	24.2.37	**Wolverhampton W**		A	L	2-6	Craven, Lewis
1937-38	D1	3	8.1.38	**Swindon T**	3S	H	D	1-1	Tomlinson
		3r	12.1.38	**Swindon T**		A	L	1-2	Tomlinson
1938-39	D1	3	10.1.39	**Tranmere R**	D2	H	W	6-0	Howe 2, Beattie 2, Vincent (p), Lewis
		4	21.1.39	**Millwall**	D2	A	D	2-2	Howe 2
		4r	24.1.39	**Millwall**		H	W	3-2	Boyd, Howe, Jones
		5	11.2.39	**Sheffield U**	D2	A	A	0-0	
		5r	14.2.39	**Sheffield U**		H	W	1-0	Howe
		6	4.3.39	**Chelsea**	D1	A	W	1-0	Crack
		SF	25.3.39	**Wolverhampton W**	D1		L	0-5	
			played at Old Trafford						
1945-46	D1	3 1L	5.1.46	**Sunderland**	D1	H	L	1-3	Rodi
		3 2L	9.1.46	**Sunderland**		A	L	1-2	Moore
1946-47	D1	3	11.1.47	**Reading**	3S	A	D	2-2	Cairns 2
		3r	14.1.47	**Reading**		H	W	3-1	Cairns 2, Keeble
		4	25.1.47	**Liverpool**	D1	A	L	0-2	
1947-48	D1	3	10.1.48	**Everton**	D1	H	L	1-4	Whitfield
1948-49	D2	3	3.1.49	**Exeter C**	3S	H	W	2-1	Whitfield, Cairns
		4	29.1.49	**Hull C**	3N	H	L	2-3	Forrest, Biggs
1949-50	D2	3	7.1.50	**Luton T**	D2	A	W	4-3	Briggs 4
		4	28.1.50	**Portsmouth**	D1	A	L	0-5	
1950-51	D2	3	6.1.51	**Exeter C**	3S	H	D	3-3	Scotson, Bloomer, Mackenzie

Season	Div	Rnd	Date	Opponent		Venue	Res	Score	Scorers
		3r	10.1.51	Exeter C		A	L	2-4	Squires, Bloomer
1951-52	3N	1	24.11.51	Darlington	3N	H	W	4-0	Cairns 3, Bloomer
		2	15.12.51	Lincoln C	3N	A	L	1-3	Cairns
1952-53	3N	1	22.11.52	Darlington	3N	A	W	3-2	Johnston, Millar, Rayner
		2	6.12.52	Bath C	SL	H	W	1-0	Johnston
		3	10.1.53	Bury	D2	H	L	1-3	McCue
1953-54	3N	1	21.11.53	Rochdale	3N	H	W	2-0	Smith, Maddison
		2	12.12.53	Witton A	CC	A	D	1-1	Rayner
		2r	15.12.53	Witton A		H	W	6-1	Rayner 3, Bloomer, Wright, Maddison
		3	9.1.54	Fulham	D2	H	D	5-5	Bloomer 3, Scotson, Brice og
		3r	13.1.54	Fulham		H	–	0-0	
			abandoned at half-time – ground waterlogged						
		3r	18.1.54	Fulham		A	L	1-3	Stroud
1954-55	3N	1	20.11.54	Halifax T	3N	H	W	2-1	Hughes, Maddison
		2	11.12.54	Southampton	3S	H	W	4-1	Harbertson 2, Harrison 2
		3	8.1.55	Wolverhampton W	D1	H	L	2-5	Harrison, Stokes
1955-56	3N	1	19.11.55	Netherfield	LC	A	W	5-1	Crosbie 2, Reeson 2, Evans
		2	10.12.55	Southport	3N	A	D	0-0	
		2r	13.12.55	Southport		H	W	3-2	Priestley, Crosbie (p), Reeson
		3	7.1.56	Portsmouth	D1	A	L	1-3	Maddison
1956-57	D2	3	5.1.57	West Ham	D2	A	L	3-5	Conner, Priestley, Rafferty
1957-58	D2	3	4.1.58	Sheffield U	D2	A	L	1-5	Evans
1958-59	D2	3	10.1.59	Manchester C	D1	H	D	2-2	Cullen, Stockin
		3r	24.1.59	Manchester C		A	W	2-1	Cockerill 2
		4	28.1.59	Nottingham F	D1	A	L	1-4	Scott
1959-60	D3	1	14.11.59	Rhyl A	CC	A	W	2-1	Reynolds og, Mills og
		2	5.12.59	Wrexham	D3	H	L	2-3	Rafferty, Hunt
1960-61	D3	1	5.11.60	Darlington	D4	A	L	0-2	
1961-62	D3	1	4.11.61	Mansfield T	D4	A	L	2-3	Portwood, Rafferty
1962-63	D2	3	7.1.63	Leicester C	D1	H	L	1-3	Scott (p)
1963-64	D2	3	25.1.64	Blackburn R	D1	A	L	0-4	
1964-65	D3	1	14.11.64	Barrow	D4	A	D	1-1	Barratt
		1r	17.11.64	Barrow		H	D	2-2aet	Cockerill (p), Foster
		1 2r	23.11.64	Barrow at Old Trafford			W	2-0	Pennington, Tees
		2	5.12.64	Stockport Co	D4	A	–	0-0	
			abandoned after 50 minutes – fog						
		2	7.12.64	Stockport Co		A	L	0-1	
1965-66	D3	1	13.11.65	Barrow	D4	A	W	2-1	Tees, Foster
		2	4.12.65	Barnsley	D4	A	D	1-1	Green (p)
		2r	8.12.65	Barnsley		H	W	2-0	Tees 2
		3	22.1.66	Portsmouth	D2	H	D	0-0	
		3r	26.1.66	Portsmouth		A	W	3-1	Green 2, Tees
		4	12.2.66	Manchester C	D2	A	L	0-2	
1966-67	D3	1	26.11.66	Crewe Alex	D4	A	D	1-1	Tees
		1r	30.11.66	Crewe Alex		H	L	0-1	
1967-68	D3	1	9.12.67	Bradford PA	D4	H	D	1-1	Ross (p)
		1r	11.12.67	Bradford PA		A	L	1-4	Worthington
1968-69	D4	1	16.11.68	Darlington	D4	A	L	0-2	
1969-70	D4	1	15.11.69	Bradford C	D3	A	L	1-2	Boylen
1970-71	D4	1	21.11.70	Bury	D3	H	L	0-1	
1971-72	D4	1	20.11.71	York C	D3	A	L	2-4	Thomson 2 (2ps)
1972-73	D3	1	18.11.72	Wigan A	NPL	H	W	2-1	Brace, Boylen
		2	9.12.72	Chesterfield	D3	H	D	2-2	Hickman, Gauden
		2r	13.12.72	Chesterfield		A	W	1-0	Brace
		3	13.1.73	Preston NE	D2	H	D	0-0	
		3r	15.1.73	Preston NE		A	W	1-0	Gauden
		4	3.2.73	Coventry C	D1	A	L	0-1	
1973-74	D3	1	14.11.73	Runcorn	NPL	A	W	1-0	Barton
		2	15.12.73	Blyth S	NL	H	D	1-1	Hickman
		2r	18.12.73	Blyth S		A	W	2-0	Hickman, Hubbard
		3	5.1.74	Burnley	D1	H	L	0-2	
1974-75	D3	1	23.11.74	Huddersfield T	D3	H	W	1-0	Hutt og
		2	14.12.74	Bury	D3	H	D	1-1	Barton
		2r	17.12.74	Bury		A	L	1-2	Lewis
1975-76	D3	1	22.11.75	Gateshead U	NPL	H	L	1-3	Booth
1976-77	D3	1	20.11.76	Droylsden	CC	A	D	0-0	
		1r	23.11.76	Droylsden		H	W	5-3	Partridge 2 (1p), Gray, Lewis, Wigg

	2	11.12.76	Chester	D3	H	L	0-1	
1977-78 D4	1	26.11.77	Workington	NPL	A	W	2-0	Waters, Liddell
	2	17.12.77	Barnsley	D4	H	W	2-0	Donovan 2
	3	7.1.78	Southampton	D2	H	D	0-0	
	3r	11.1.78	Southampton		A	D	0-0aet	
	3 2r	17.1.78	Southampton at Filbert Street		L	1-4	Waters	
1978-79 D4	1	25.11.78	Hartlepool U	D4	A	L	0-1	
1979-80 D3	1	24.11.79	Chesterfield	D3	H	D	1-1	Waters
	1r	27.11.79	Chesterfield		A	W	3-2	K.Moore, Drinkell
	2	15.12.79	Sheffield U	D3	H	W	2-0	Waters, Crombie
	3	5.1.80	Liverpool	D1	A	L	0-5	
1980-81 D2	3	3.1.81	WBA	D1	A	L	0-3	
1981-82 D2	3	5.1.82	Millwall	D3	A	W	6-1	Drinkell 2, Cumming 2, Whymark, Brolly
	4	23.1.82	Newcastle U	D2	A	W	2-1	Kilmore, Drinkell
	5	13.2.82	QPR	D2	A	L	1-3	K.Moore
1982-83 D2	3	8.1.83	Scunthorpe U	D4	A	D	0-0	
	3r	11.1.83	Scunthorpe U		H	W	2-0	Waters (p), Ford
	4	29.1.83	Ipswich T	D1	A	L	0-2	
1983-84 D2	3	7.1.84	Portsmouth	D2	A	L	1-2	Drinkell
1984-85 D2	3	5.1.85	Notts Co	D2	A	D	2-2	Ford, Lund
	3r	8.1.85	Notts Co		H	W	4-2	Lund 3, Wilkinson
	4	26.1.85	Watford	D1	H	L	1-3	Foley
1985-86 D2	3	4.1.86	Arsenal	D1	H	L	3-4	Lund, Lyons, Peake (p)
1986-87 D2	3	10.1.87	Stoke C	D2	H	D	1-1	Walsh
	3r	26.1.87	Stoke C		A	D	1-1aet	K.Moore
	3 2r	28.1.87	Stoke C		A	L	0-6	
1987-88 D3	1	14.11.87	Scarborough	D4	A	W	2-1	McGarvey, North
	2	5.12.87	Halifax T	D4	H	D	0-0	
	2r	8.12.87	Halifax T		A	L	0-2	
1988-89 D4	1	19.11.88	Wolverhampton W	D3	H	W	1-0	Cockerill
	2	10.12.88	Rotherham U	D4	H	W	3-2	North, Cunnington, Russell og
	3	7.1.89	Middlesbrough	D1	A	W	2-1	North 2
	4	28.1.89	Reading	D3	H	D	1-1	North
	4r	1.2.89	Reading		A	W	2-1	Cunnington, Jobling
	5	18.2.89	Wimbledon	D1	A	L	1-3	Alexander
1989-90 D4	1	17.11.89	York C	D4	A	W	2-1	Hargreaves 2
	2	9.12.89	Doncaster R	D4	H	W	1-0	Cockerill
	3	6.1.90	Huddersfield T	D3	A	L	1-3	Gilbert
1990-91 D3	1	17.11.90	Blackpool	D4	A	L	0-2	
1991-92 D2	1	16.11.91	Blackpool	D4	A	L	1-2	Cunnington
1992-93 D1	3	2.1.93	Brentford	D1	A	W	2-0	Mendonca, Dobbin
	4	2.2.93	Swansea C	D2	A	D	0-0	
	4r	9.2.93	Swansea C		H	W	2-0	Mendonca, Gilbert
	5	13.2.93	Ipswich T	PL	A	L	0-4	

GUILDFORD CITY

Merged with Dorking in 1973 to become Guildford and Dorking United. Club folded on December 9, 1976. **League clubs beaten:** QPR, Reading, Brentford

1928-29 SL	1	24.11.28	QPR	3S	H	W	4-2	J.Smith, Hetherington 2, S.Smith
	2	8.12.28	Bournemouth	3S	H	L	1-5	J.Smith
1930-31 SL	1	29.11.30	Gillingham	3S	A	L	2-7	Coundon, William
1931-32 SL	1	28.11.31	Fulham	3S	A	L	0-2	
1932-33 SL	1	26.11.32	Coventry C	3S	H	L	1-2	Burke
1934-35 SL	1	24.11.34	Bath C	SL	H	L	1-2	Thom
1937-38 SL	1	27.11.37	Reading	3S	H	W	1-0	J.Brown
	2	11.12.37	Doncaster R	3N	A	L	0-4	
1938-39 SL	1	26.11.38	Aldershot	3S	A	D	1-1	J.Brown
	1r	30.11.38	Aldershot		H	L	3-4	R.Brown 2, J.Brown
1947-48 SL	1	29.11.47	Bournemouth	3S	A	L	0-2	
1950-51 SL	1	25.11.50	Dartford	SL	H	L	1-5	Passmore
1951-52 SL	1	24.11.51	Hereford U	SL	H	W	4-1	Baynham 2, Langley, Passmore
	2	15.12.51	Gateshead	3N	A	L	0-2	
1952-53 SL	1	22.11.52	Gt Yarmouth T	ECL	H	D	2-2	Perkins, Sutherland
	1r	27.11.52	Gt Yarmouth T		A	L	0-1	
1953-54 SL	1	21.11.53	Hastings U	SL	A	L	0-1	

GUILDFORD CITY

1956-57	SL	1	17.11.56	Brentford	3S	A	L	0-3	
1957-58	SL	1	16.11.57	Yeovil T	SL	H	D	2-2	Edwards, Devine
		1r	21.11.57	Yeovil T		A	L	0-1	
1958-59	SL	1	15.11.58	Hereford U	SL	H	L	1-2	Clarke
1964-65	SL	1	14.11.64	Gillingham	D3	H	D	2-2	Stevens, Porter
		1r	18.11.64	Gillingham		A	L	0-1	
1965-66	SL	1	13.11.65	Wycombe W	IL	H	D	2-2	Massey, Vafiadis
		1r	17.11.65	Wycombe W		A	L	0-1	
1967-68	SL	1	9.12.67	Brentford	D4	A	–	2-1	Brown, Burge
				abandoned after 53 minutes – snow					
		1	14.12.67	Brentford		A	D	2-2	Brown 2
		1r	18.12.67	Brentford		H	W	2-1	Hudson, Brown
		2	6.1.68	Newport Co	D4	H	L	0-1	
1971-72	SL	1	20.11.71	Dover	SL	H	D	0-0	
		1r	24.11.71	Dover		A	W	2-0	Malley, Burge
		2	11.12.71	Shrewsbury T	D3	A	L	1-2	Dyson
1972-73	SL	1	18.11.72	Watford	D3	A	L	2-4	Tyler, Burns
1973-74	SL	1	24.11.73	Hitchin T	IL	A	D	1-1	Westburgh
		1r	28.11.73	Hitchin T		H	L	1-4	Burge

GUISBOROUGH TOWN

Formed 1973. **FA Vase Runners-up:** 1980

1988-89	NL	1	19.11.88	Bury at Middlesbrough	D3	H	L	0-1

GUISELEY

Formed 1909. **First entered FA Cup:** 1930. **FA Vase Winners:** 1991; **Runners-up:** 1992

1991-92	NPL	1	16.11.91	Chester C	D3	A	L	0-1

HALESOWEN TOWN

Formed 1873. **First entered FA Cup:** 1899. **FA Vase Winners:** 1985, 1986. **Runners-up:** 1983

1955-56	BDL	1	19.11.55	Hendon	AL	H	L	2-4	Dugmore (p), Basterfield
1985-86	BDL	1	16.11.85	Frickley A	APL	A	D	1-1	P.Joinson
		1r	19.11.85	Frickley A		H	L	1-3	Sherwood (p)
1986-87	SL	1	15.11.86	Southend U	D4	A	L	1-4	Moss
1987-88	SL	1	14.11.87	Kidderminster H	GMVC	H	D	2-2	L.Joinson, Moss
		1r	16.11.87	Kidderminster H		A	L	0-4	
1988-89	SL	1	19.11.88	Brentford	D3	A	L	0-2	
1989-90	SL	1	18.11.89	Cardiff C	D3	A	L	0-1	
1990-91	SL	1	17.11.90	Tranmere R	D3	H	L	1-2	Flynn
1991-92	SL	1	16.11.91	Farnborough T	IL	H	D	2-2	Flynn, Hazelwood
		1r	26.11.91	Farnborough T		A	L	0-4	

HALIFAX TOWN

Formed 1911. **First entered FA Cup:** 1912. **Best FA Cup Performance:** 5th round, 1933, 1953 **Record FA Cup Win:** 12-0 vs West Vale Ramblers, 1st qualifying round, 1913-14 **Record FA Cup Defeat:** 0-5 vs Wrexham, 1st round, 29.11.1947

1911-12	ML		Did Not Enter						
1912-13	ML		P **Horsforth** (A) 4-2; 1q **Hebden Bridge** (A) 3-2; 2q **Knaresborough** (H) 6-2; 3q **S.Kirkby Colliery** (H) 6-4; 4q **Nelson** (H) 3-3; 4qr **Nelson** (A) 3-2; 5q **Walsall** (A) 0-0; 5qr **Walsall** (H) 1-0						
		1	11.1.13	QPR	SL	A	L	2-4	Roscoe, Pentland
1913-14	ML		1q **West Vale Ramblers** (H) 12-0; 2q **Rothwell** (A) 1-1; 2qr **Rothwell** (H) 6-0; 3q **Mirfield** (H) 2-0; 4q **Rotherham Co** (A) 1-1; 4qr **Rotherham Co** (H) 5-2; 5q **Norwich C** (A) 0-2						
1914-15	ML		P **Castleford T** (A) 1-2						
1919-20	ML		1q **Apperley Bridge** (H) 7-0; 2q **Castleford T** (A) 0-3						
1920-21	ML		ExP **Rowntrees** (H) 5-3; P **Liversedge** (H) 3-1; 1q **Allerton Bywater** (H) 4-1; 2q **Harrogate** (H) 1-0; 3q **Calverley** (A) 4-2; 4q **Castleford T** (A) 1-3						
1921-22	3N		Did Not Enter						
1922-23	3N		4q **Rotherham T** (H) 6-1; 5q **Accrington S** (A) 1-1; 5qr **Accrington S** (H) 1-0; 6q **Mansfield T** (A) 2-0						
		1	13.1.23	South Shields	D2	A	L	1-3	Price
1923-24	3N		5q **Peterborough & Fletton** (A) 1-0; 6q **Rotherham Co** (H) 1-0						

(231)

HALIFAX TOWN

Season	Div	Rnd	Date	Opponent	Comp	H/A	Res	Score	Scorers
		1	12.1.24	Northampton T	3N	A	D	1-1	Dixon
		1r	6.1.24	Northampton T		H	D	1-1aet	Dixon
		1 2r	21.1.24	Northampton T at Bramall Lane			W	4-2	Dixon, Wilde, Moore, Whalley
		2	2.2.24	Manchester C	D1	A	D	2-2	Moore, E.Hall
		2r	6.2.24	Manchester C		H	D	0-0aet	
		2 2r	11.2.24	Manchester C at Old Trafford			L	0-3	
1924-25	3N	5q	Rochdale (H) 0-1						
1925-26	3N	1	28.11.25	Rotherham U	3N	H	L	0-3	
1926-27	3N	1	27.11.26	Grimsby T	D2	A	L	2-3	McCafferty, Dixon
1927-28	3N	1	26.11.27	Hartlepools U	3N	H	W	3-0	Proctor, Seabrook, Coleman
		2	10.12.27	Tranmere R	3N	A	L	1-3	Seabrook
1928-29	3N	1	24.11.28	Stockport Co	3N	A	L	0-1	
1929-30	3N	1	30.11.29	Carlisle U	3N	A	L	0-2	
1930-31	3N	1	29.11.30	Mansfield T	ML	A	D	2-2	Cooper, Pape
		1r	3.12.30	Mansfield T		H	W	2-1	Cooper, Pape
		2	13.12.30	Fulham	3N	A	L	0-4	
1931-32	3N	1	28.11.31	Newark T	ML	A	D	1-1	Mays
		1r	2.12.31	Newark T		H	W	2-1	Crawford, Mays
		2	12.12.31	Accrington S	3N	H	W	3-0	McFarlane, Mays, Betteridge
		3	9.1.32	Bournemouth	3S	H	L	1-3	Betteridge
1932-33	3N	1	26.11.32	Darwen	LC	H	W	2-0	Wellock 2
		2	10.12.32	Workington	NEL	H	W	2-1	Davies, Wilson og
		3	14.1.33	Doncaster R	3N	A	W	3-0	Chambers 2, Brown
		4	28.1.33	Chester	3N	A	D	0-0	
		4r	2.2.33	Chester		H	W	3-2aet	Wellock 2, Davies
		5	18.2.33	Luton T	3S	H	L	0-2	
1933-34	3N	1	25.11.33	Barnsley	3N	H	W	3-2	Brown, Ferguson, Chambers
		2	9.12.33	Hartlepools U	3N	H	D	1-1	Brown
		2r	13.12.33	Hartlepools U		A	W	2-1aet	Brown, Cooke
		3	13.1.34	Bolton W	D2	A	L	1-3	Tunstall
1934-35	3N	1	24.11.34	Hartlepools U	3N	H	D	1-1	Atherton
		1r	28.11.34	Hartlepools U		A	L	0-2	
1935-36	3N	1	30.11.35	Rochdale	3N	H	W	4-0	Barkas 2, Betteridge 2
		2	14.12.35	Hartlepools U	3N	H	D	1-1	Valentine
		2r	18.12.35	Hartlepools U		A	D	0-0aet	
		2 2r	23.12.35	Hartlepools U at St James's Park			L	1-4aet	Cook
1936-37	3N	1	28.11.36	Darlington	3N	H	L	1-2	Valentine
1937-38	3N	1	27.11.37	York C	3N	A	D	1-1	Barkas
		1r	1.12.37	York C		H	L	0-1	
1938-39	3N	1	26.11.38	Rochdale	3N	H	W	7-3	Widdowfield 4, Wood 2, Jackson
		2	10.12.38	Mansfield T	3S	H	D	1-1	Griffiths
		2r	14.12.38	Mansfield T		A	D	3-3aet	Griffiths, Widdowfield, Wood
		2 2r	19.12.38	Mansfield T at Doncaster			D	0-0aet	
		2 3r	21.12.38	Mansfield T at Old Trafford			W	2-1aet	Widdowfield, Bungay og
		3	7.1.39	Birmingham	D1	A	L	0-2	
1945-46	3N	1 1L	17.11.45	York C	3N	H	W	1-0	Gordon
		1 2L	24.11.45	York C		A	L	2-4	Barkas 2
1946-47	3N	1	30.11.46	Barrow	3N	A	D	0-0	
		1r	4.12.46	Barrow		H	D	1-0aet	Waters
		2	14.12.46	Stockport Co	3N	H	D	1-1	Waters
		2r	18.12.46	Stockport Co		A	L	1-2	Massey
1947-48	3N	1	29.11.47	Wrexham	3N	A	L	0-5	
1948-49	3N	1	27.11.48	Scunthorpe U	ML	H	D	0-0	
		1r	6.12.48	Scunthorpe U		A	L	0-1	
1949-50	3N	1	26.11.49	Tranmere R	3N	A	L	1-2	Hindle
1950-51	3N	1	25.11.50	Ashington	NEL	H	L	2-3	Glaister, Core
1951-52	3N	1	24.11.51	Wrexham	3N	A	L	0-3	
1952-53	3N	1	22.11.52	Ashton U	LC	H	D	1-1	Holt
		1r	25.11.52	Ashton U		A	W	2-1	Lorenson, Moncrieff
		2	6.12.52	Southport	3N	H	W	4-2	Moncrieff 2, Hampson, Holt
		3	10.1.53	Cardiff C	D1	H	W	3-1	Priestley, Murphy, Moncrieff
		4	31.1.53	Stoke C	D1	H	W	1-0	Priestley
		5	14.2.53	Tottenham H	D1	H	L	0-3	
1953-54	3N	1	21.11.53	Rhyl	CC	H	D	0-0	
		1r	26.11.53	Rhyl		A	L	3-4aet	Murphy, Priestley, Haddington
1954-55	3N	1	20.11.54	Grimsby T	3N	A	L	1-2	Watkinson
1955-56	3N	1	19.11.55	Goole T	ML	A	W	2-1	Lonsdale, Watson

	2	12.12.55	**Burton A**	BDL	H	D	0-0
	2r	14.12.55	**Burton A**		A	L	0-1
1956-57 3N	1	17.11.56	**Oldham A**	3N	H	L	2-3	Hutchinson, Smith
1957-58 3N	1	16.11.57	**Mansfield T**	3N	A	L	0-2
1958-59 D3	1	15.11.58	**Southport**	D4	A	W	2-0	Tilley, South
	2	6.12.58	**Darlington**	D4	H	D	1-1	Harrison
	2r	10.12.58	**Darlington**		A	L	0-3
1959-60 D3	1	14.11.59	**Gateshead**	D4	A	W	4-3	Tilley 2, Roscoe, Smith
	2	5.12.59	**Workington**	D4	A	L	0-1
1960-61 D3	1	5.11.60	**Hartlepools U**	D4	H	W	5-1	Large, Whitelaw, Priestley, Sinclair, Blackburn
	2	29.11.60	**Crewe A**	D4	H	D	2-2	Large, Sinclair
	2r	5.12.60	**Crewe A**		A	L	0-3
1961-62 D3	1	4.11.61	**Rochdale**	D4	A	L	0-2
1962-63 D3	1	3.11.62	**Bradford PA**	D3	H	W	1-0	Redfearn
	2	24.11.62	**Lincoln C**	D4	A	L	0-1
1963-64 D4	1	16.11.63	**Workington**	D4	A	L	1-4	Granger
1964-65 D4	1	14.11.64	**South Liverpool**	LC	H	D	2-2	South, Westlake
	1r	18.11.64	**South Liverpool**		A	L	2-4	Frear, Westlake
1965-66 D4	1	13.11.65	**Southport**	D4	A	L	0-2
1966-67 D4	1	26.11.66	**Doncaster R**	D3	H	D	2-2	Hutchinson 2
	1r	29.11.66	**Doncaster R**		A	W	3-1	Parks, McCarthy, Atkins
	2	7.1.67	**Bishop Auckland**	NL	A	D	0-0
	2r	10.1.67	**Bishop Auckland**		H	W	7-0	Hutchinson 2, Taylor 2, Parks 2, Atkins
	3	28.1.67	**Bristol C**	D2	H	D	1-1	Parks
	3r	31.1.67	**Bristol C**		A	L	1-4	Hutchinson
1967-68 D4	1	13.12.67	**Crewe A**	D4	H	W	3-2	Ryden 2, Wallace
	2	6.1.68	**Scunthorpe U**	D3	H	W	1-0	Russell
	3	27.1.68	**Birmingham C**	D2	H	L	2-4	Holt, Ryden
1968-69 D4	1	16.11.68	**Bilston**	WMRL A	W	3-1	Massie, Lawther, Flower
	2	7.12.68	**Crewe A**	D3	H	D	1-1	Wallace
	2r	11.12.68	**Crewe A**		A	W	3-1	Shawcross 2, Massie
	3	4.1.69	**Swansea**	D4	A	W	1-0	Massie
	4	25.1.69	**Stoke C**	D1	A	D	1-1	Massie
	4r	28.1.69	**Stoke C**		H	L	0-3
1969-70 D3	1	15.11.69	**Chester**	D4	H	D	3-3	Atkins, Lawther, Hill
	1r	19.11.69	**Chester**		A	L	0-1
1970-71 D3	1	21.11.70	**Chesterfield**	D3	A	L	0-2
1971-72 D3	1	20.11.71	**Wigan A**	NPL	A	L	1-2	Burgin
1972-73 D3	1	18.11.72	**Barnsley**	D4	A	D	1-1	Shanahan
	1r	21.11.72	**Barnsley**		H	W	2-1	Robertson, Kemp
	2	9.12.72	**Scunthorpe U**	D3	A	L	2-3	Robertson 2
1973-74 D3	1	24.11.73	**Frickley Colliery**	ML	H	W	6-1	Gwyther 3, Ford, Hale (p), Rhodes
	2	15.12.73	**Oldham A**	D3	H	L	0-1
1974-75 D3	1	23.11.74	**Barnsley**	D4	A	W	2-1	Jones 2
	2	14.12.74	**Stafford Rangers**	NPL	A	L	1-2	Gwyther
1975-76 D3	1	22.11.75	**Altrincham**	NPL	H	W	3-2	McHale 2 (1p), Rhodes
	2	13.12.75	**Stafford Rangers**	NPL	A	W	3-1	McHale (p), Downes, Gwyther
	3	3.1.76	**Ipswich T**	D1	A	L	1-3	McHale (p)
1976-77 D4	1	20.11.76	**Stafford Rangers**	NPL	A	D	0-0
	1r	23.11.76	**Stafford Rangers**		H	W	1-0	Phelan
	2	14.12.76	**Preston NE**	D3	H	W	1-0	Lawson
	3	8.1.77	**Luton T**	D2	H	L	0-1
1977-78 D4	1	26.11.77	**Chesterfield**	D3	A	L	0-1
1978-79 D4	1	25.11.78	**Carlisle U**	D3	A	L	0-1
1979-80 D4	1	24.11.79	**Scarborough**	APL	H	W	2-0	Burke, Stafford
	2	15.12.79	**Walsall**	D4	A	D	1-1	Kennedy
	2r	18.12.79	**Walsall**		H	D	1-1aet	Harris
	2 2r	24.12.79	**Walsall**		H	W	2-0aet	Burke, Smith
	3	5.1.80	**Manchester C**	D1	H	W	1-0	Hendrie
	4	26.1.80	**Bolton W**	D1	A	L	0-2
1980-81 D4	1	22.11.80	**Hull C**	D4	A	L	1-2	Firth
1981-82 D4	1	21.11.81	**Peterborough**	D4	H	L	0-3
1982-83 D4	1	20.11.82	**North Shields**	NL	H	L	0-1
1983-84 D4	1	19.11.83	**Whitby Town**	NL	H	L	2-3	Ward, Evans
1984-85 D4	1	17.11.84	**Goole T**	NPL	H	W	2-0	Gallagher, Cook
	2	7.12.84	**Burnley**	D3	A	L	1-3	Gallagher
1985-86 D4	1	16.11.85	**Scunthorpe U**	D4	H	L	1-3	Kendall

1986-87	D4	1	15.11.86	Bolton W	D3	H	D	1-1	Longhurst
		1r	18.11.86	Bolton W		A	D	1-1aet	Brown
		1 2r	24.11.86	Bolton W		H	L	1-3	Galloway
1987-88	D4	1	14.11.87	Billingham at Hartlepool	NL	A	W	4-2	Black 2, Robinson, N.Mathews
		2	5.12.87	Grimsby T	D3	A	D	0-0	
		2r	8.12.87	Grimsby T		H	W	2-0	M.Mathews, Thornber
		3	9.1.88	Nottingham F	D1	H	L	0-4	
1988-89	D4	1	19.11.88	York C	D4	H	W	1-0	McPhilips
		2	10.12.88	Altrincham	GMVC	A	W	3-0	W.Barr, Allison 2
		3	7.1.89	Kettering	GMVC	A	D	1-1	Watson
		3r	10.1.89	Kettering		H	L	2-3	Bramhall, W.Barr
1989-90	D4	1	17.11.89	Stafford Rangers	GMVC	A	W	3-2	Fleming, Horner 2
		2	9.12.89	Darlington	GMVC	A	L	0-3	
1990-91	D4	1	17.11.90	Wrexham	D4	H	W	3-2	Norris, Graham. Juryeff
		2	11.12.90	Rotherham U	D3	A	D	1-1	Juryeff
		2r	17.12.90	Rotherham U		H	L	1-2	Norris
1991-92	D4	1	16.11.91	Witton Albion	GMVC	A	D	1-1	Hildesley
		1r	27.11.91	Witton Albion		H	L	1-2aet	Richardson
1992-93	D3	1	14.11.92	Marine	NPL	A	L	1-4	German

HALLIWELL FC

Formed 1877. Played at an open field near the Crofter's Arms, Halliwell

1882-83	1	21.10.82	Great Lever		H	W	3-2	Bell, Harper, Rhodes
	2	2.12.82	Eagley		A	L	1-3	Harper
1883-84	1	13.10.83	Eagley		H	L	2-5	
1884-85	1	11.10.84	Lower Darwen		A	L	1-4	
1885-86	1	31.10.85	Fishwick Ramblers		H	W	2-1	
	2		Hurst					*walkover*
	3	19.12.85	South Shore		H	L	1-6	
1886-87	1		Blackburn R					*scratched*
1887-88	1	15.10.87	Liverpool Stanley		A	W	5-1	
	2	5.11.87	Astley Bridge		A	W	4-0	
	3	3.12.87	Preston NE		A	L	0-4	
1888-89	1	2.2.89	Crewe A		H	D	2-2	Hewitson 2
	1r	9.2.89	Crewe A		A	W	5-1	McGuiness 2, Edge, Cross 2
	2	16.2.89	Birmingham St G		H	L	2-3	Hay, Edge
1890-91	1	17.1.91	Sheffield W		A	L	0-12	

HAMPSTEAD HEATHENS

Formed 1869. Played in the inaugural FA Cup in 1871-72 and did not enter the competition again. A junior club of the same name still plays in north London.

1871-72	1		bye					
	2	23.12.71	Barnes		A	D	1-1	Barker
	2r	6.1.72	Barnes		H	W	1-0	Leach
	3	27.1.72	Royal Engineers		A	L	0-3	

HANOVER UNITED

Formed 1873. Played at The Limes, in Barnes, south-west London. The first club believed to have used the name "United"

1879-80	1	8.11.79	Grey Friars		A	L	1-2	
1880-81	1	6.11.80	West End		A	L	0-1	
1881-82	1		bye					
	2	26.11.81	Upton Park		H	L	1-3	
1882-83	1	4.11.82	Mosquitoes		H	W	1-0	
	2	2.12.82	Clapham Rovers		A	L	1-7	
1883-84	1	3.11.83	Brentwood		H	L	1-6	
1884-85	1	8.11.84	Reading Minster		H	W	1-0	
	2	29.11.84	Old Foresters		H	W	2-1	
	3	3.1.85	Chatham		H	L	0-2	
1885-86	1	31.10.85	Romford		H	D	1-1	
	1r	7.11.85	Romford		A	L	0-3	
1886-87	1	30.10.86	Old Wykehamists		A	L	0-3	
1887-88	1	15.10.87	Old Carthusians		A	L	0-5	

HARLOW TOWN

Formed 1879. **First entered FA Cup:** 1937. **Folded:** 1992. **League clubs beaten:** Southend U, Leicester C

1979-80	IL	1	24.11.79	Leytonstone-Ilford	IL	H	W	2-1	Twigg, Fairclough
		2	15.12.79	Southend U	D3	A	D	1-1	Prosser
		2r	18.12.79	Southend U		H	W	1-0	Mann
		3	5.1.80	Leicester C	D2	A	D	1-1	Prosser
		3r	8.1.80	Leicester C		H	W	1-0	Mackenzie
		4	26.1.80	Watford	D2	A	L	3-4	Prosser, Mackenzie 2
1980-81	IL	1	22.11.80	Charlton A	D3	H	L	0-2	
1981-82	IL	1	21.11.81	Barnet	APL	H	D	0-0	
		1r	24.11.81	Barnet		A	L	0-1	

HARROW BOROUGH

Formed 1933. **First entered FA Cup:** 1967

1983-84	IL	1	19.11.83	Yeovil	APL	A	W	1-0	Duck
		2	10.12.83	Newport Co	D3	H	L	1-3	Pearce

HARROW CHEQUERS

Formed 1865. Used the Kennington Oval for their home matches, but never managed to play an FA Cup tie there.

1871-72	1		Wanderers					scratched
1874-75	1		Civil Service					scratched
1875-76	1		Leyton					scratched

HARTFORD ST JOHNS

Formed 1876. Played at Hartford, near Northwich, Chesire.

1883-84	1	10.11.83	Oswestry T		A	L	0-7
1884-85	1	8.11.84	Macclesfield		A	L	0-9
1885-86	1	24.10.85	Newtown		H	L	1-3
1886-87	1	23.10.86	Chirk		A	L	1-8

HARTLEPOOL UNITED

Formed 1908. **First entered FA Cup:** 1908. Hartlepools United, 1908-1968. Hartlepool 1968-1977; Hartlepool United 1977-present. **Best FA Cup performance:** 4th round, 1955, 1978, 1989, 1993. When Hartlepools beat St Peters Albion 10-1 in 1923, W.Smith scored seven goals, five of them before half-time. **Record FA Cup Win:** 10-1 vs St Peters Albion, 4th qualifying round, 1923. **Record FA Cup Defeat:** 0-6 vs Manchester City, 3rd round, 3.1.1976

as Hartlepools United

1908-09	NEL	1q **West Hartlepool** (H) 2-1; 2q **South Bank** (A) 2-2; 2qr **South Bank** (H) 0-2
1909-10	NEL	1q **Wingate A** (H) 6-3; 2q **Darlington** (H) 0-1
1910-11	NEL	P **Horden A** (H) 5-0; 1q **Darlington** (A) 1-1; 1qr **Darlington** (H) 0-1
1911-12	NEL	4q **North Shields A** (A) 1-2
1912-13	NEL	1q **Houghton R** (H) 3-1; 2q **Wingate A** (H) 4-1; 3q **Sunderland R** (H) 2-1; 4q **Castleford T** (H) 1-0; 5q **Gainsborough T** (A) 0-4
1913-14	NEL	P **Sunderland R** (H) 0-0; Pr **Sunderland R** (A) 2-1; 1q **Annfield Plain** (H) 6-1; 2q **Birtley** (H) 4-0; 3q **Horden A** (H) 4-0; 4q **Gateshead** (H) 0-1
1914-15	NEL	4q **Bishop Auckland** (H) 6-2; 5q **Rochdale** (A) 0-2
1919-20	NEL	4q **Bishop Auckland** (A) 0-1
1920-21	NEL	P **South Bank East End** (H) 7-0; 1q **Haverton Hill** (A) 2-2; 1qr **Haverton Hill** (H) 0-0aet; 1q 2r **Haverton Hill** 1-0 at Ayresome Pk; 2q **Scarborough T** (A) 4-1; 3q **Loftus A** (H) 2-1; 4q **Houghton R** (H) 3-0; 5q **Bishop Auckland** (H) 1-1; 5qr **Bishop Auckland** (A) 5-0; 6q **Swansea T** (A) 0-3
1921-22	3N	5q **Stalybridge C** (A) 0-2
1922-23	3N	5q **Durham C** (A) 1-0; 6q **Wrexham** (A) 0-1
1923-24	3N	4q **St Peters Albion** (H) 10-1; 5q **Shildon** (H) 3-1; 6q **Ashington** (A) 1-2
1924-25	3N	4q **Ashington** (H) 0-0; 4qr **Ashington** (A) 0-2 Ashington disqualified – ineligible player; 5q **Bishop Auckland** (H) 2-0; 6q **St Albans C** (H) 4-0

		1	10.1.25	Newcastle U	D1	A	L	1-4	S.Hardy
1925-26	3N	1	28.11.25	Blyth Spartans	NEL	A	D	2-2	S.Hardy, Best
		1r	2.12.25	Blyth Spartans		H	D	1-1aet	C.Hardy
		1 2r	7.12.25	Blyth Spartans at St James' Pk			D	1-1aet	Hunter
		1 3r	9.12.25	Blyth Spartans Roker Park			L	1-2	Wensley

1926-27	3N	1	27.11.26	Carlisle U	NEL	A	L	2-6	W.Robinson, Craig
1927-28	3N	1	26.11.27	Halifax T	3N	A	L	0-3	
1928-29	3N	1	24.11.28	Spennymoor U	NEL	A	L	2-5	T.Mordue, Duncan og
1929-30	3N	1	30.11.29	Scunthorpe U	ML	A	L	0-1	
1930-31	3N	1	29.11.30	Stockport Co	3N	H	L	2-3	Dickinson, Waller
1931-32	3N	1	28.11.31	Chester	3N	A	L	1-4	Wigham
1932-33	3N	1	26.11.32	Marine	LCC	A	W	5-2	Wigham 2, Thornton, Hewett, Dixon
		2	10.12.32	Walsall	3N	A	L	1-2	Thornton
1933-34	3N	1	25.11.33	York C	3N	A	W	3-2	Hewitt, Redwell, Wigham
		2	9.12.33	Halifax T	3N	A	D	1-1	Hardy
		2r	13.12.33	Halifax T		H	L	1-2aet	Pedwell
1934-35	3N	1	24.11.34	Halifax T	3N	A	D	1-1	Bonass
		1r	28.11.34	Halifax T		H	W	2-0	Bonass, Lindsay
		2	8.12.34	Coventry C	3S	H	L	0-4	
1935-36	3N	1	30.11.35	Mansfield T	3N	A	W	3-2	Bonass, Robertson, Procter (p)
		2	14.12.35	Halifax T	3N	A	D	1-1	Robertson
		2r	18.12.35	Halifax T		H	D	0-0aet	
		2 2r	23.12.35	Halifax T at St James's Park			W	4-1aet	Wigham 3, Robertson
		3	4.1.36	Grimsby T	D1	H	D	0-0	
		3r	11.1.36	Grimsby T		A	L	1-4	Bonas
1936-37	3N	1	28.11.36	Rotherham U	3N	A	D	4-4	Proctor (p), English, Self, Park
		1r	2.12.36	Rotherham U		H	W	2-0	Self, Scott
		2	12.12.36	Crewe A	3N	A	D	1-1	English
		2r	16.12.36	Crewe A		H	L	1-2	Self
1937-38	3N	1	27.11.37	Southport	3N	H	W	3-1	Scott, English, Embleton
		2	11.12.37	Tranmere R	3N	A	L	1-3	Hamilton og
1938-39	3N	1	26.11.38	Accrington S	3N	H	W	2-1	Woods, Self
		2	10.12.38	QPR	3S	H	L	0-2	
1945-46	3N	1 1L	17.11.45	Gateshead	3N	H	L	1-2	McMahon
		1 2L	24.11.45	Gateshead		A	L	2-6	Holland, McMahon
1946-47	3N	1	30.11.46	North Shields	NEL	H	W	6-0	Sloan 4, Scott 2
		2	14.12.46	Rochdale	3N	A	L	1-6	McMahon
1947-48	3N	1	29.11.47	Darlington	3N	H	W	1-0	Isaac
		2	13.12.47	Brighton & HA	3S	H	D	1-1	Isaac
		2r	20.12.47	Brighton & HA		A	L	1-2	Harden
1948-49	3N	1	27.11.48	Chester	3N	H	L	1-3	Price
1949-50	3N	1	26.11.49	Accrington S	3N	A	W	1-0	Owens
		2	10.12.49	Norwich C	3S	H	D	1-1	Clarke
		2r	15.12.49	Norwich C		A	L	1-5	Harden
1950-51	3N	1	25.11.50	Worcester C	SL	A	W	4-1	Burnett, Wildon, McGuigan 2
		2	9.12.50	Oldham A	3N	H	L	1-2	Stamper
1951-52	3N	1	24.11.51	Rhyl	CC	H	W	2-0	Elder, Harden
		2	15.12.51	Watford	3S	A	W	2-1	McClure, Burnett
		3	12.1.52	Burnley	D1	A	L	0-1	
1952-53	3N	1	22.11.52	Chester	3N	A	W	1-0	McClure
		2	6.12.52	Tranmere R	3N	A	L	1-2	Elder
1953-54	3N	1	21.11.53	Mansfield T	3N	H	D	1-1	Willetts
		1r	25.11.53	Mansfield T		A	W	3-0	Wildon, Richardson, W.Linacre
		2	12.12.53	Northampton T	3S	A	D	1-1	Harden
		2r	16.12.53	Northampton T		H	W	1-0	W.Linacre
		3	9.1.54	Stoke C	D2	A	L	2-6	Richardson 2
1954-55	3N	1	20.11.54	Chesterfield	3N	H	W	1-0	Richardson
		2	11.12.54	Aldershot	3S	H	W	4-0	McGuigan 2, Richardson, Willetts
		3	8.1.55	Darlington	3N	H	D	1-1	Harden
		3r	12.1.55	Darlington		A	D	2-2aet	Richardson 2
		3 2r	17.1.55	Darlington at Ayresome Park			W	2-0	Richardson, Newton
		4	29.1.55	Nottingham F	D2	H	D	1-1	Newton
		4r	2.2.55	Nottingham F		A	L	1-2aet	Stamper
1955-56	3N	1	19.11.55	Gateshead	3N	H	W	3-0	Luke 2, Lumley
		2	10.12.55	Chesterfield	3N	A	W	2-1	Luke 2
		3	7.1.56	Chelsea	D1	A	L	0-1	
1956-57	3N	1	17.11.56	Selby T	YL	H	W	3-1	Luke, Stamper, Robinson
		2	8.12.56	Blyth Spartans	NEL	A	W	1-0	Johnson
		3	5.1.57	Manchester U	D1	H	L	3-4	Stamper, Johnson, Newton
1957-58	3N	1	16.11.57	Prescot Cables	LC	H	W	5-0	Newton, P.Thompson 4
		2	7.12.57	Stockport Co	3N	A	L	1-2	Johnson
1958-59	D4	1	15.11.58	Rochdale	D3	H	D	1-1	Luke

Season	Div	Rd	Date	Opponent		Venue	Res	Score	Scorers
		1r	19.11.58	Rochdale		A	D	3-3aet	Luke 2, Johnson
		1 2r	27.11.58	Rochdale at Old Trafford			W	2-1aet	Smith, Johnson
		2	6.12.58	Barrow	D4	A	L	0-2	
1959-60	D4	1	14.11.59	Bury	D3	A	L	0-5	
1960-61	D4	1	5.11.60	Halifax T	D3	A	L	1-5	Cooper
1961-62	D4	1	4.11.61	Blyth Spartans	NC	H	W	5-1	Folland 3, Johnson, Parkes
		2	25.11.61	Accrington S	D4	H	W	2-1	Folland, McLean
		3	6.1.62	Fulham	D1	A	L	1-3	Burlison
1962-63	D4	1	3.11.62	Carlisle U	D3	A	L	1-2	McConnell og
1963-64	D4	1	16.11.63	Lincoln C	D4	H	L	0-1	
1964-65	D4	1	14.11.64	Corby T	SL	A	W	3-1	Entwistle 2, Fogarty (p)
		2	5.12.64	Darlington	D4	H	D	0-0	
		2r	9.12.64	Darlington		A	L	1-4	Fogarty
1965-66	D4	1	13.11.65	Workington	D3	H	W	3-1	McPheat 2, Brass
		2	4.12.65	Wrexham	D4	H	W	2-0	Wright, Mulvaney
		3	24.1.66	Huddersfield T	D2	A	L	1-3	Thompson
1966-67	D4	1	26.11.66	Shrewsbury T	D3	A	L	2-5	Phythian, Fogarty
1967-68	D4	1	9.12.67	Bury	D3	H	L	2-3	Bell, Wright
as Hartlepool									
1968-69	D3	1	16.11.68	Rotherham U	D3	H	D	1-1	Young
		1r	19.11.68	Rotherham U		A	L	0-3	
1969-70	D4	1	15.11.69	North Shields	NL	H	W	3-0	Bell 2, Kirk
		2	6.12.69	Wrexham	D4	H	L	0-1	
1970-71	D4	1	21.11.70	Rhyl	CC	A	L	0-1	
1971-72	D4	1	20.11.71	Scarborough	NPL	H	W	6-1	Ellis, Young 2, Warnock, Veart 2
		2	11.12.71	Boston U	NPL	A	L	1-2	Veart
1972-73	D4	1	18.11.72	Scunthorpe U	D3	H	D	0-0	
		1r	21.11.72	Scunthorpe U		A	D	0-0aet	
		1 2r	27.11.72	Scunthorpe U at Roker Pk			L	1-2aet	Veart
1973-74	D4	1	24.11.73	Altrincham	NPL	A	L	0-2	
1974-75	D4	1	23.11.74	Bradford C	D4	H	W	1-0	Honour
		2	14.12.74	Lincoln C	D4	H	D	0-0	
		2r	16.12.74	Lincoln C		A	L	0-1	
1975-76	D4	1	22.11.75	Stockport Co	D4	H	W	3-0	D.Smith, McMahon, Potter
		2	13.12.75	Marine	CC	A	D	1-1	Scaife
		2r	15.12.75	Marine		H	W	6-3	Moore 3, Johnson (p), Rowlands, Scaife
		3	3.1.76	Manchester C	D1	A	L	0-6	
1976-77	D4	1	20.11.76	Chester	D3	A	L	0-1	
as Hartlepool United									
1977-78	D4	1	26.11.77	Tranmere R	D3	A	D	1-1	T.Smith
		1r	29.11.77	Tranmere R		H	W	3-1	Newton, Ayre, Bielby
		2	17.12.77	Runcorn	NPL	H	W	4-2	Bielby, Newton 2, Poskett (p)
		3	7.1.78	Crystal P	D2	H	W	2-1	Newton 2
		4	28.1.78	Ipswich T	D1	A	L	1-4	Downing
1978-79	D4	1	25.11.78	Grimsy T	D4	H	W	1-0	Goldthorpe
		2	16.12.78	Crewe A	D4	A	W	1-0	Crumplin
		3	18.1.79	Leeds U	D1	H	L	2-6	Newton 2 (2ps)
1979-80	D4	1	24.11.79	Barnsley	D3	A	L	2-5	J.Linacre, Newton
1980-81	D4	1	22.11.80	Scunthorpe U	D4	A	L	1-3	Hampton
1981-82	D4	1	20.11.81	Wigan A	D4	A	D	2-2	P.Linacre, Newton
		1r	25.11.81	Wigan A		H	W	1-0	Newton
		2	4.1.82	Hull C	D4	A	L	0-2	
1982-83	D4	1	20.11.83	Lincoln C	D3	H	W	3-0	P.Linacre 2, Hogan
		2	11.12.82	York C	D4	H	D	1-1	Dobson
		2r	14.12.82	York C		A	L	0-4	
1983-84	D4	1	19.11.83	Rotherham U	D3	A	D	0-0	
		1r	23.11.83	Rotherham U		H	L	0-1aet	
1984-85	D4	1	17.11.84	Derby Co	D3	H	W	2-1	Taylor, Dixon
		2	8.12.84	York C	D3	H	L	0-2	
1985-86	D4	1	16.11.85	Macclesfield T	NPL	A	W	2-1	Shoulder 2
		2	7.12.85	Frickley A	APL	H	L	0-1	
1986-87	D4	1	15.11.86	Wrexham	D4	A	L	1-2	Hogan
1987-88	D4	1	14.11.87	Chorley	NPL	A	W	2-0	Gibb, Baker
		2	5.12.87	York C	D3	A	D	1-1	Baker
		2r	9.12.87	York C		H	W	3-1	Baker, Toman 2
		3	9.1.88	Luton T	D1	H	L	1-2	Toman
1988-89	D4	1	19.11.88	Wigan A	D3	H	W	2-0	Smith, Borthwick

	2	10.12.88	**Notts Co**	D3	H	W	1-0	Allon
	3	7.1.89	**Bristol C**	D3	H	W	1-0	Baker (p)
	4	28.1.89	**Bournemouth**	D2	H	D	1-1	Honour
	4r	31.1.89	**Bournemouth**		A	L	2-5	Allon, Toman
1989-90 D4	1	17.11.89	**Huddersfield T**	D3	H	L	0-2	
1990-91 D4	1	17.11.90	**Runcorn**	GMVC	A	W	3-0	Allon 3
	2	7.12.90	**Wigan A**	D3	A	L	0-2	
1991-92 D3	1	16.11.91	**Shrewsbury T**	D3	H	W	3-2	Tinkler, Johnson, Baker (p)
	2	17.12.91	**Darlington**	D3	A	W	2-1	Dalton, Honour
	3	4.1.92	**Ipswich T**	D2	A	D	1-1	Baker
	3r	15.1.92	**Ipswich T**		H	L	0-2	
1992-93 D2	1	14.11.92	**Doncaster R**	D3	A	W	2-1	Johnrose, Saville (p)
	2	6.12.92	**Southport**	NPL	H	W	4-0	Peverall, Saville 3
	3	2.1.93	**Crystal P**	PL	H	W	1-0	Saville (p)
	4	23.1.93	**Sheffield U**	PL	A	L	0-1	

HARWICH & PARKESTON

Formed 1877. First entered FA Cup: 1899. FA Amateur Cup Runers-up: 1899, 1953

1934-35 ECL	1	24.11.34	**Bristol R**	3S	A	L	0-3	
1936-37 ECL	1	28.11.36	**Bournemouth**	3S	A	L	1-5	W.Ceasar
1953-54 ECL	1	21.11.53	**Headington U**	SL	H	L	2-3	McDonagh, Pearson
1961-62 ECL	1	4.11.61	**Torquay U**	D3	A	L	1-5	Sanderson
1963-64 ECL	1	16.11.63	**Crystal P**	D3	A	L	2-8	Stevens 2
1976-77 IL	1	20.11.76	**Enfield**	IL	A	D	0-0	
	1r	23.11.76	**Enfield**		H	L	0-3	

HASLINGDEN FC

Formed 1876. Played at Rye Hill, Haslingden, Lancashire

1882-83	1		**bye**			
	2	2.12.82	**Darwen Ramblers**	A	L	2-3

HASTINGS & ST LEONARDS AMATEURS

Formed 1898. First entered FA Cup: 1901. The club is still in existence as Hastings Town and was a separate club from Hastings United.

1906-07 SL	1	12.1.07	**Norwich C**	SL	A	L	1-3	Beney
1907-08 SL	1	11.1.08	**Portsmouth**	SL	H	L	0-1	
1908-09 SL	1	6.1.09	**Blackpool**	D2	A	L	0-2	

HASTINGS UNITED

Formed 1948. First entered FA Cup: 1949. Folded 1985. Cup final connection: Kevin Ball (Sunderland 1992) was born in Hastings and played for United's youth team

1949-50 SL	1	26.11.49	**Gillingham**	SL	H	L	1-3	Moore
1953-54 SL	1	21.11.53	**Guildford C**	SL	H	W	1-0	Hillman
	2	12.12.53	**Swindon T**	3S	H	W	4-1	Hunt og, Huckstepp, Asher, Hillman
	3	9.1.54	**Norwich C**	3S	H	D	3-3	Parks 2, Girling
	3r	13.1.54	**Norwich C**		A	L	0-3	
1954-55 SL	1	20.11.54	**Hounslow T**	CRN	A	W	4-2	Burgess 2, Parks, Asher
	2	11.12.54	**Selby T**	YL	A	W	2-0	Girling, Asher
	3	8.1.55	**Sheffield W**	D1	A	L	1-2	Asher
1955-56 SL	1	19.11.55	**Southall**	AL	H	W	6-1	Burgess 2, Parks 2, Asher 2 (1p)
	2	10.12.55	**Northampton T**	3S	A	L	1-4	Asher
1956-57 SL	1	17.11.56	**Ipswich T**	3S	A	L	0-4	
1959-60 SL	1	14.11.59	**Notts Co**	D4	H	L	1-2	McCorkindale
1960-61 SL	1	5.11.60	**Northampton T**	D4	A	L	1-2	Smith
1981-82 SL	1	21.11.81	**Enfield**	APL	A	L	0-2	

HAWKS

Southern-based amateurs who soon disappeared from the Cup scene.

1877-78	1	3.11.77	**Minerva**		H	W	5-2	JR Fox, J.Hamilton, Pitman, Ram, Rumball

	2	22.12.77	**Remnants**		A	L	0-2	
1878-79	1	9.11.78	**Swifts**	·	A	L	1-2	Ram

HAYES

Formed 1909 as Botwell Mission, renamed Hayes 1930. **First entered FA Cup as Hayes:** 1930. **FA Amateur Cup Runners-up:** 1931. **League clubs beaten:** Bristol R, Cardiff C, Fulham

as Botwell Mission

1927-28	SPT	1	30.11.27	**Peterborough & Fletton**	SL	H	L	3-4	Treasure 3
as Hayes									
1931-32	AL	1	28.11.31	**Yeovil & Petters U**	SL	A	L	1-3	Caesar
1933-34	AL	1	25.11.33	**Bournemouth**	3S	A	L	0-3	
1938-39	AL	1	26.11.38	**Clapton Orient**	3S	A	L	1-3	Ward
1946-47	AL	1	30.11.46	**Bristol C**	3S	A	L	3-9	Dowse, Crout, Nolan
1964-65	AL	1	14.11.64	**Exeter C**	D3	A	L	0-1	
1972-73	IL	1	18.11.72	**Bristol R**	D3	H	W	1-0	Hatt
		2	9.12.72	**Reading**	D4	A	D	0-0	
		2r	11.12.72	**Reading**		H	L	0-1	
1973-74	IL	1	24.11.73	**Boston U**	NPL	A	D	0-0	
		1r	28.11.73	**Boston U**		H	L	1-2aet	Hutchinson
1987-88	IL	1	14.11.87	**Swansea C**	D4	H	L	0-1	
1988-89	IL	1	19.11.88	**Aldershot**	D3	A	L	0-1	
1989-90	IL	1	18.11.89	**Peterborough U**	D4	A	D	1-1	Barrowcliffe
		1r	21.11.89	**Peterborough U**		H	L	0-1	
1990-91	IL	1	17.11.90	**Cardiff C**	D4	A	D	0-0	
		1r	21.11.90	**Cardiff C** at Brentford			W	1-0	Clarke
		2	8.12.90	**Bournemouth**	D3	A	L	0-1	
1991-92	IL	1	15.11.91	**Fulham**	D3	A	W	2-0	Day, Stephen
		2	7.12.91	**Crawley**	SL	H	L	0-2	
1992-93	IL	1	14.11.92	**Brighton & HA**	D2	A	L	0-2	

HEANOR TOWN

Formed 1883. **First entered FA Cup:** 1890

1891-92	n/af	1	6.1.92	**Aston Villa**	D1	A	L	1-4	Shepherd
1893-94	n/af	1	27.1.93	**Nottingham F**	D1	A	L	0-1aet	
1896-97	ML	1	30.1.97	**Southampton St Marys**	SL	A	D	1-1	McCallum
		1r	3.2.97	**Southampton St Marys**		H	L	0-1	
1898-99	ML	1	28.1.99	**Bury**	D1	H	L	0-3	
1958-59	CA	1	15.11.58	**Carlisle U**	D4	H	L	1-5	Johnston
1963-64	ML	1	16.11.63	**Bradford PA**	D4	A	L	1-3	Fidler

HEART OF MIDLOTHIAN

Formed 1874. Scottish FA Cup Winners 5 times. One of the seven Scottish clubs that briefly played in the FA Cup.

1885-86		1		**Padiham**			*scratched*		
1886-87		1	30.10.86	**Darwen**		A	L	1-7	McKay

HEDNESFORD TOWN

Formed 1880. **First entered FA Cup:** 1891. Welsh FA Cup runners-up 1992

1919-20	BDL	1	10.1.20	**Castleford T**		A	L	0-2	

HENDON (1)

The original Hendon Club were formed in 1874. Their home ground was in Brent Street, Hendon next to the Rose and Crown pub which was demolished in 1970 to make way for a shoppng precinct.

1877-78		1	3.11.77	**Great Marlow**		A	L	0-2	
1878-79		1	9.11.78	**Reading**		A	L	0-1	
1879-80		1	8.11.79	**Old Foresters**		H	D	1-1	Williams
		1r	15.11.79	**Old Foresters**		A	D	2-2	Buck, 1 other
		1 2r	22.11.79	**Old Foresters**		H	W	3-1	Buck, H.O.Ince, Morice
		2	20.12.79	**Mosquitos**		H	W	7-1	H.O.Ince 3, Morice, J.Powell, R.Powell, og
		3		**bye**					

		14.2.80	Clapham Rovers		A	L	0-2	
	4							
1880-81	1	6.11.80	St Peters Institute		A	W	8-1	
	2	4.12.80	Old Etonians		H	L	0-2	
1881-82	1	29.10.81	Reading		A	L	0-5	
1882-83	1	4.11.82	West End		A	W	3-1	
	2	30.11.82	Chatham		H	W	2-1	
	3	6.1.83	South Reading		H	W	11-1	Clarkson 3, A.Redford 3, Coutts 2, Morton, Perry, 1 other
	4	27.1.83	Great Marlow		A	W	3-0	
	5	3.2.83	Old Etonians		H	L	2-4	
1883-84	1	10.11.83	Old Etonians		H	W	3-2	K.P.Wilson, 2 others
	2	1.12.83	Old Westminsters		A	L	1-2	
1884-85	1	8.11.84	Clapham Rovers		A	D	3-3	
	1r	22.11.84	Clapham Rovers		H	W	6-0	Ince 3, Bather, Coutts, og
	2	6.12.84	Chatham		A	L	0-1	
1885-86	1	24.10.85	Clapton		H	L	0-4	
1886-87	1	30.10.86	London Caledonians		H	L	1-2	
1887-88	1	15.10.87	Old Harrovians		H	L	2-4	

HENDON (2)

Formed 1908 as Hampstead Town. Played as Golders Green from 1933-1946. Hendon from 1946. **First entered FA Cup:** 1926. **FA Amateur Cup Winners:** 1960, 1965, 1972. **Runners-up:** 1955, 1966. **Cup Final Connection:** Denis and Leslie Compton, who played for Arsenal in the 1950 FA Cup Final, started their careers with Hendon and Denis Compton was born there. **League club beaten:** Reading

as Golders Green

1934-35	AL	1	24.11.34	Southend U	3S	A	L	1-10	Drinkwater
as Hendon									
1952-53	AL	1	22.11.52	Northampton T	3S	H	D	0-0	
			27.11.52	Northampton T		A	L	0-2	
1955-56	AL	1	19.11.55	Halesowen T	BDL	A	W	4-2	Matthews, Rawlings, Spector, Edwards
		2	10.12.55	Exeter C	3S	A	L	2-6	Spector, Avis
1960-61	AL	1	5.11.60	Oxford U	SL	H	D	2-2	Spector, Figg
		1r	9.11.60	Oxford U		A	L	2-3	Quail, Howard
1964-65	IL	1	14.11.64	Port Vale	D3	A	L	1-2	Hyde
1965-66	IL	1	13.11.65	Grantham	ML	A	L	1-4	Hyde
1966-67	IL	1	26.11.66	Reading	D3	H	L	1-3	Ashworth
1969-70	IL	1	15.11.69	Carshalton A	AL	H	W	5-3	Baker 2, Collett 2, Anderson
		2	6.12.69	Brentwood T	SL	H	L	0-2	
1970-71	IL	1	21.11.70	Aldershot	D4	H	L	0-2	
1972-73	IL	1	18.11.72	Plymouth A	D3	A	L	0-1	
1973-74	IL	1	24.11.73	Leytonstone	IL	H	W	3-0	Somers 2, Baker
		2	15.12.73	Merthyr Tydfil	SL	A	W	3-0	Baker, Phillips, Somers
		3	5.1.74	Newcastle U	D1	A	D	1-1	Haider
		3r	9.1.74	Newcastle U at Watford			L	0-4	
1975-76	IL	1	22.11.75	Reading	D4	H	W	1-0	Phillips
		2	13.12.75	Swindon T	D3	H	L	0-1	
1977-78	IL	1	26.11.77	Watford	D4	A	L	0-2	
1981-82	IL	1	21.11.81	Wycombe W	IL	H	D	1-1	Bennett
		1r	23.11.81	Wycombe W		A	L	0-2	
1988-89	IL	1	19.11.88	Reading	D3	A	L	2-4	Keen, Dowie

HENLEY FC

Formed 1871. Original ground was at Marlow Road near the Catherine Wheel pub. The club currently play in the Chiltonian League.

1879-80	1		Reading		walkover			
	2	29.11.79	Maidenead	H	L		1-3	Cooper
1880-81	1	13.11.80	Weybridge Swallows	A	L		1-3	
1881-82	1	17.10.81	Maidenhead	H	L		0-2	
1884-85	1		bye					
	2	6.12.84	Old Westminsters	A	L		0-7	

HEREFORD UNITED

Formed 1924. **First entered FA Cup:** 1925. **Entered Football League:** 1972. Legendary Cup-fighting team whose performances eventually won them a place in the Football League. **Record FA Cup Win:** 11-0 vs Thynnes Ath, Pr rd, 1947-48. In competition proper: 6-1 vs QPR, 2nd round, 7.12.1957 **Record FA Cup Defeat:** 2-7 vs Arsenal, 3rd round, 21.1.1985. **Welsh FA Cup Winners:** 1990

Season		Rd	Date	Opponent		H/A	Res	Score	Scorers
1932-33	BDL	1	26.11.32	**Accrington S**	3N	A	L	1-2	Hann
1948-49	SL	1	27.11.48	**Kidderminster H**	SL	A	W	3-0	Hogben, C.Thompson, Duggan
		2	11.12.48	**Exeter C**	3S	A	L	1-2	Thompson
1949-50	SL	1	26.11.49	**Bromsgrove R**	BC	H	W	3-0	Thompson, Clifford, Dymond
		2	10.12.49	**Weymouth**	SL	A	L	1-2	Clifford
1950-51	SL	1	25.11.50	**Bromsgrove R**	BC	A	W	3-1	Bowen, Duggan, Best
		2	9.12.50	**Newport Co**	3S	H	L	0-3	
1951-52	SL	1	24.11.51	**Guildford C**	SL	A	L	1-4	Allum
1952-53	SL	1	22.11.52	**Leyton**	AL	A	D	0-0	
		1r	27.11.52	**Leyton**		H	W	3-2	Coulson 2, Bowen
		2	6.12.52	**Scunthorpe U**	3N	H	D	0-0	
		2r	11.12.52	**Scunthorpe U**		A	L	1-2	Thompson
1953-54	SL	1	21.11.53	**Exeter C**	3S	A	D	1-1	O'Hara
		1r	26.11.53	**Exeter C**		H	W	2-0	O'Hara 2
		2	12.12.53	**Wigan A**	LC	A	L	1-4	T.Lewis
1955-56	SL	1	19.11.55	**Swindon T**	3S	A	L	0-4	
1956-57	SL	1	17.11.56	**Aldershot**	3S	H	W	3-2	Bowen, Mulgrew, Williams
		2	8.12.56	**Southend U**	3S	H	L	2-3	Bowen 2
1957-58	SL	1	16.11.57	**Newport (IOW)**	Hants	A	W	3-0	Beech, Williams 2
		2	7.12.57	**QPR**	3S	W	W	6-1	Horton 2 (2ps), Beech, Clayton, Williams, Bowen
		3	4.1.58	**Sheffield W**	D1	H	L	0-3	
1958-59	SL	1	15.11.58	**Guildford C**	SL	A	W	2-1	Morris, Hardiman
		2	6.12.58	**Newport Co**	D3	H	L	0-2	
1959-60	SL	1	14.11.59	**Newport Co**	D3	A	L	2-4	Hardiman, Beech
1960-61	SL	1	5.11.60	**Bridgewater T**	WL	A	L	0-3	
1961-62	SL	1	4.11.61	**Bristol C**	D3	A	D	1-1	Biggs
		1r	8.11.61	**Bristol C**		H	L	2-5	Daniel, Smith
1962-63	SL	1	3.11.62	**Crystal P**	D3	A	L	0-2	
1963-64	SL	1	16.11.63	**Newport Co**	D4	H	D	1-1	Dixon
		1r	18.11.63	**Newport Co**		A	L	0-4	
1964-65	SL	1	14.11.64	**Oldham A**	D3	A	L	0-4	
1965-66	SL	1	13.11.65	**Leytonstone**	IL	A	W	1-0	Punter
		2	4.12.65	**Millwall**	D3	H	W	1-0	Fogg
		3	22.1.66	**Bedford T**		A	L	1-2	Fogg
1966-67	SL	1	26.11.66	**Peterborough U**	D3	A	L	1-4	Holliday
1967-68	SL	1	13.12.67	**Barnet**	SL	H	W	3-2	Cocker, Derrick, Timms
		2	6.1.68	**Watford**	D3	A	L	0-3	
1968-69	SL	1	16.11.68	**Torquay U**	D3	H	D	0-0	
		1r	20.11.68	**Torquay U**		A	L	2-4	Charles, Scarrott
1969-70	SL	1	15.11.69	**Chelmsford C**	SL	A	W	2-1	Tyler, Lewis
		2	6.12.69	**Newport Co**	D4	A	L	1-2	Punter
1970-71	SL	1	21.11.70	**Northampton T**	D4	H	D	2-2	Jones, Owen
		1r	24.11.70	**Northampton T**		A	W	2-1	Meadows, Owen
		2	12.12.70	**Brighton**	D3	H	L	1-2	Charles
1971-72	SL	1	20.11.71	**King's Lynn**	SL	A	D	0-0	
		1r	24.11.71	**King's Lynn**		H	W	1-0	Gough
		2	11.12.71	**Northampton T**	D4	H	D	0-0	
		2r	14.12.71	**Northampton T**		A	D	2-2aet	Tyler, Owen
		2 2r	20.12.71	**Northampton T** at Hawthorns			W	2-1aet	Mallender, Tyler
		3	24.1.72	**Newcastle U**	D1	A	D	2-2	Addison, Owen
		3r	5.2.72	**Newcastle U**		H	W	2-1aet	Radford, George
		4	9.2.72	**West Ham**	D1	H	D	0-0	
		4r	14.2.72	**West Ham**		A	L	1-3	Meadows
1972-73	D4	1	18.11.72	**Torquay U**	D4	A	L	0-3	
1973-74	D3	1	24.11.73	**Torquay U**	D4	H	W	3-1	Evans, Hinch, Owen
		2	15.12.73	**Walton & Hersham**	IL	H	W	3-0	Hinch, Tyler, Jones
		3	5.1.74	**West Ham**	D1	A	D	1-1	Redrobe
		3r	9.1.74	**West Ham**		H	W	2-1	Naylor (p), Jones
		4	26.1.74	**Bristol C**	D2	H	L	0-1	
1974-75	D3	1	26.11.74	**Gillingham**	D3	H	W	1-0	Tucker
		2	14.12.74	**Cambridge U**	D4	A	L	0-2	
1975-76	D3	1	22.11.75	**Torquay U**	D4	H	W	2-0	Carter, Tucker
		2	13.12.75	**Bournemouth**	D4	A	D	2-2	McNeil, Tyler
		2r	17.12.75	**Bournemouth**		H	W	2-0	Layton, McNeil
		3	3.1.76	**York C**	D2	A	L	1-2	Layton
1976-77	D2	3	8.1.77	**Reading**	D3	H	W	1-0	Briley
		4	29.1.77	**Middlesbrough**	D1	A	L	0-4	

1977-78	D3	1	26.11.77	Wealdstone	SL	A	D	0-0	
		1r	29.11.77	Wealdstone		H	L	2-3	Sheedy, Davey
1978-79	D4	1	25.11.78	Newport Co	D4	H	L	0-1	
1979-80	D4	1	24.11.79	Northampton T	D4	H	W	1-0	Layton
		2	15.12.79	Aldershot	D4	H	L	1-2	McGrellis
1980-81	D4	1	22.11.80	Southend U	D4	A	W	1-0	Jones
		2	13.12.80	Enfield	IL	H	L	0-2	
1981-82	D4	1	21.11.81	Southend	D3	H	W	3-1	Harvey, Laidlaw, Phillips
		2	2.1.82	Fulham	D3	H	W	1-0	Laidlaw
		3	6.1.82	Scunthorpe U	D4	A	D	1-1	Showers
		3r	20.1.82	Scunthorpe U		H	W	4-1	Showers, Harvey, Overson, Phillips
		4	23.1.82	Leicester C	D2	H	L	0-1	
1982-83	D4	1	20.11.82	Portsmouth	D3	A	L	1-4	Showers
1983-84	D4	1	19.11.83	Reading	D4	A	L	0-2	
1984-85	D4	1	17.11.84	Farnborough T	IL	H	W	3-0	Kearns 2, Phillips
		2	7.12.84	Plymouth A	D3	A	D	0-0	
		2r	12.12.84	Plymouth A		H	W	2-0	Kearns, Phillips
		3	5.1.85	Arsenal	D1	H	D	1-1	Price
		3r	21.1.85	Arsenal		A	L	2-7	Kearns, Pejic
1985-86	D4	1	16.11.85	Yeovil T	IL	A	W	4-2	Carter 3, Kearns
		2	7.12.85	Reading	D3	A	L	0-2	
1986-87	D4	1	15.11.86	Fulham	D3	H	D	3-3	Kearns, Wells, Spooner
		1r	24.11.86	Fulham		A	L	0-4	
1987-88	D4	1	14.11.87	Barnet	GMVC	A	W	1-0	Stant
		2	5.12.87	Colchester U	D4	A	L	2-3	Stant, Phillips
1988-89	D4	1	19.11.88	Cardiff C	D3	A	L	0-3	
1989-90	D4	1	18.11.89	Farnborough T	GMVC	A	W	1-0	Peacock
		2	9.12.89	Merthyr T	GMVC	H	W	3-2	Robinson, MA Jones, Tester
		3	6.1.90	Walsall	D3	H	W	2-1	M Jones (p), Pejic
		4	28.1.90	Manchester U	D1	H	L	0-1	
1990-91	D4	1	17.11.90	Peterborough U	D4	H	D	1-1	Narbett
		1r	20.11.90	Peterborough U		A	L	1-2	Pejic
1991-92	D4	1	16.11.91	Atherstone U	SL	A	D	0-0	
		1r	26.11.91	Atherstone U		H	W	3-0	Lowndes, Brain 2
		2	7.12.91	Aylesbury U	IL	A	W	3-2	Fry, Heritage, Brain
		3	4.1.92	Woking	IL	A	D	0-0	
		3r	14.1.92	Woking		H	W	2-1	Narbett, Brain
		4	26.1.92	Nottingham F	D1	A	L	0-2	
1992-93	D3	1	14.11.92	Sutton U	IL	A	W	2-1	Pickard, Barton og
		2	5.12.92	Yeovil T	GMVC	A	D	0-0	
		2r	15.12.92	Yeovil T		H	L	1-2	Pickard

HERTS RANGERS

Formed about 1865, the premier club in Hertfordshire for many years. Originally played in a meadow in Langley Road, Watford, near the present-day Watford Junction Station. One of the forerunners of the present Watford FC.

1875-76	1	6.11.75	Rochester		H	W	4-0	Day 2, Gilbert, Sparks
	2	18.12.75	Oxford University		A	L	2-8	Gilbert, 1 other
1876-77	1	4.11.76	Great Marlow		H	L	1-2	
1877-78	1	3.11.77	Oxford University		A	L	2-5	
1878-79	1	9.11.78	Cambridge University		A	L	0-2	
1879-80	1	15.11.79	Minerva		H	W	2-1	Hill 2
	2		Pilgrims			scratched		
1880-81	1	6.11.80	Barnes		H	W	6-0	
	2		bye					
	3	5.2.81	Old Etonians		H	L	0-3	
1881-82	1	5.11.81	Swifts		A	L	0-4	

HEYWOOD CENTRAL

Formed 1887. Played at the Phoenix Pleasure ground, near the Britannia Hotel.

1887-88	1	15.10.87	Higher Walton		A	L	1-8

HIGHER WALTON

Formed 1882. Played at the Higher Walton ground near the Greyhound, Hotel

1884-85	1	11.10.84	Darwen Old Wanderers	H	D	1-1	
	1r	8.11.84	Darwen Old Wanderers	A	L	1-4	
1885-86	1	17.10.85	South Shore	H	L	3-4	
1886-87	1	16.10.86	Third Lanark, Scotland	A	L	0-5	
1887-88	1	15.10.87	Heywood Central	H	W	8-1	
	2	5.11.87	Fleetwood Rangers	A	W	3-1	
	3	26.11.87	Bootle	H	L	1-6	

93RD HIGHLANDERS

Formed 1872. Played in the FA Cup in 1890-91 and the following season when they were eliminated in the qualifying competition.

| 1890-91 | 1 | 17.1.91 | Sunderland Albion | FAll | A | L | 0-2 |

HIGH WYCOMBE

1873-74	1		Old Etonians			walkover	
	2	22.11.73	Maidenhead	A	L	0-1	
1874-75	1	10.10.74	Woodford Wells	A	L	0-1	
1875-76	1	10.11.75	Royal Engineers	A	L	0-15	
1876-77	1		Cambridge University			scratched	
1877-78	1	27.10.77	Wood Grange	H	W	4-0	Grange 2, Wellicombe, 1 other
	2	15.12.77	Wanderers	H	L	0-9	

HILLINGDON BOROUGH

Formed as Yiewsley FC 1872. **First entered FA Cup:** 1908. **FA Challenge Trophy Runners-up:** 1971. Club folded in mid-1980s and was reformed 1990. **League clubs beaten:** Luton T, Torquay U. **Cup Final Connection:** Jackie Milburn, who played in three Cup Finals, for Newcastle U, was player-coach 1961–3

as Yiewsley

| 1956-57 | CRN | 1 | 17.11.56 | Gillingham | 3S | H | D | 2-2 | Moore 2 |
| | | 1r | 20.11.56 | Gillingham | | A | L | 0-2 | |

as Hillingdon Borough

1969-70	SL	1	15.11.69	Wimbledon	SL	H	W	2-0	Carter, Vafiadis
		2	6.12.69	Luton T	D3	H	W	2-1	Reeve, Townend
		3	6.1.70	Sutton U	IL	H	D	0-0	
		3r	12.1.70	Sutton U		A	L	1-4	Terry
1971-72	SL	1	20.11.71	Brighton	D3	A	L	1-7	Bishop
1972-73	SL	1	18.11.72	Chelmsford C	SL	A	L	0-2	
1973-74	SL	1	24.11.73	Grantham	SL	H	L	0-4	
1976-77	SL	1	20.11.76	Torquay U	D4	A	W	2-1	Metchick, Smith
		2	11.12.76	Watford	D4	H	L	2-3	Basey, Ryan
1978-79	SL	1	25.11.78	Swansea C	D3	A	L	1-4	Williams

HINCKLEY ATHLETIC

Formed 1879. **First entered FA Cup:** 1896

1954-55	BDL	1	20.11.54	Newport (IOW)	Hants	H	W	4-3	Grant, Burnett, Taulbutt og, Perry
		2	11.12.54	Rochdale	3N	A	L	1-2	Perry
1962-63	SL	1	3.11.62	Sittingbourne	SL	H	W	3-0	S.Round 2, Lockton
		2	24.11.62	QPR	D3	A	L	2-7	Aston, S.Round

HITCHIN TOWN

Formed 1865. Their match against Crystal Palace was one of the first four FA Cup matches ever played on November 11, 1871. **Cup Final Connection:** David Pacey, who played for Luton Town in the 1959 Cup Final started his career at Hitchin.

1871-72	1	11.11.71	Crystal P		A	D	0-0	
			Both teams qualified for second round					
	2	10.1.72	Royal Engineers		H	L	0-5	
1872-73	1		Clapham Rovers			scratched		
1874-75	1	14.11.74	Maidenhead		H	L	0-1	

1875-76		1		Clapham Rovers				scratched	
1887-88		1	8.10.87	Old Wykehamists		H	L	2-5	
1953-54	AL	1	21.11.53	Peterborough U	ML	H	L	1-3	Hammond
1958-59	AL	1	15.11.58	Millwall	D4	H	D	1-1	Hammond
		1r	17.11.58	Millwall		A	L	1-2	
1960-61	AL	1	5.11.60	Crystal P	D4	A	L	2-6	Waldock, Randall
1973-74	IL	1	24.11.73	Guildford C	SL	H	D	1-1	Kettleborough
		1r	28.11.73	Guildford C		A	W	4-1	Kettleborough 2, Martin, Giggle
		2	15.12.73	Boston U	NPL	A	L	0-1	
1974-75	IL	1	23.11.74	Cambridge U	D4	H	D	0-0	
		1r	26.11.74	Cambridge U		A	L	0-3	
1976-77	IL	1	20.11.76	Weymouth	SL	A	D	1-1	Watson
		1r	23.11.76	Weymouth		H	D	2-2aet	Martin, Giggle
		1 2r	29.11.76	Weymouth at Aldershot			D	3-3aet	Watson 2, Mulkern
		1 3r	2.12.76	Weymouth at Salisbury			W	3-1	Bunker, Watson 2
		2	11.12.76	Swindon T	D3	H	D	1-1	Bunker
		2r	21.12.76	Swindon T		A	L	1-3aet	Bunker
1978-79	IL	1	25.11.78	Bournemouth	D4	A	L	1-2	Taylor

HODDESDON TOWN

Formed 1879. **First entered FA Cup:** 1884 and did not play in the competition again until 1931. **First winners of the FA Vase:** 1975. Curently play in South Midlands (Campri Leisurewear) League.

1884-85	1	1.11.84	Old Foresters		A	L	0-8	

HOLBEACH UNITED

Formed 1929. **First entered FA Cup:** 1949

1982-83	UCL	1	20.11.82	Wrexham	D3	H	L	0-4	

HORDEN COLLIERY WELFARE

First entered FA Cup: 1910. Reformed 1980. **Cup Final Connection:** Two former Horden players appeared in Cup Finals: Tom Garrett played for Blackpool in 1951 and 1953 and Richie Norman played for Leicester City in 1961.

as Horden Athletic

1925-26	Wear	1	28.11.25	Darlington	D2	H	L	2-3	Temple 2

as Horden CW

1938-39	NEL	1	26.11.38	Chorley	LC	H	D	1-1	Armes
		1r	30.11.38	Chorley		A	W	2-1	Armes 2
		2	10.12.38	Newport Co	3S	H	L	2-3	Low og, Dunmore
1948-49	NEL	1	27.11.48	Southport	3N	A	L	1-2	W.Hayward
1952-53	NEL	1	22.11.52	Accrington S	3N	H	L	1-2	Ivey
1953-54	NEL	1	21.11.53	Wrexham	3N	H	L	0-1	
1954-55	NEL	1	20.11.54	Scunthorpe U	3N	H	L	0-1	
1981-82	NL	1	21.11.81	Blackpool	D4	H	L	0-1	
				played at Hartlepool					

HORNCASTLE FC

Formed 1879. Played at The Wong, Horncastle, Lincs.

1885-86	1		Middlesbrough				scratched	
1886-87	1	30.10.86	Darlington		H	W	2-0	Allen, J.Turner
	2		bye					
	3	9.12.86	Grantham		H	W	2-0	
	4		bye					
	5	5.2.87	Aston Villa		A	L	0-5	
1887-88	1	15.10.87	Lincoln C		A	L	1-4	

HORNCHURCH

Formed 1878. Not connected with the present Hornchurch club (1923) which plays in the Isthmian (Diadora) League.

1882-83	1	28.10.82	Great Marlow		A	L	0-2	
1883-84	1	10.11.83	Great Marlow		H	L	0-9	

HORSHAM

Formed 1885. **First entered FA Cup:** 1903

1947-48	SCL	1	29.11.47	**Notts Co**	3S	A	L	1-9	Smallwood
1966-67	AL	1	26.11.66	**Swindon T**	D3	H	L	0-3	

HORWICH RMI

Formed 1896. **First entered FA Cup:** 1914

1928-29	LC	1	24.11.28	**Scarborough T**	ML	H	L	1-2	Keetley
1982-83	NWC	1	20.11.82	**Blackpool**	D4	A	L	0-3	

HOTSPUR FC

Formed 1878. Played in and around the Barnsbury area of north London. This club were not the forerunners of the modern Tottenham Hotspur club.

1879-80	1	8.11.79	**Argonauts**	H	D	1-1	Winter
	1r	15.11.79	**Argonauts**	A	W	1-0	Cherry
	2	6.12.79	**West End**	A	L	0-1	
1880-81	1	13.11.80	**Reading**	A	L	1-5	Maugham
1881-82	1	5.11.81	**Union FC**	H	W	1-0	
	2	26.11.81	**Reading Abbey**	A	W	4-1	
	3	17.12.81	**Reading Minster**	H	D	0-0	
	3r	26.12.81	**Reading Minster**	A	W	2-0	
	4	21.1.82	**Upton Park**	A	L	0-5	
1882-83	1	4.11.82	**Rochester**	A	L	0-2	
1884-85	1	8.11.84	**Uxbridge**	A	W	3-1	
	2	6.12.84	**Old Wykehamists**	H	L	1-2	Whittaker
1885-86	1	31.10.85	**Old Westminsters**	A	L	1-3	
1886-87	1	23.10.86	**Luton T**	A	W	3-1	Johnson, C.Sutton, J.Sutton
	2	20.11.86	**Chatham**	A	L	0-1	
1887-88	1		bye				
	2	5.11.87	Dulwich	A	L	1-2	

HOUNSLOW TOWN

Formed 1884. **First entered FA Cup:** 1898. **FA Amateur Cup:** Runners-up 1962. Merged with Feltham FC 1991 and now known as Feltham & Hounslow Borough

1954-55	CRN	1	20.11.54	**Hastings U**	SL	H	L	2-4	Page 2
1962-63	AL	1	3.11.62	**Mansfield T**	D4	H	D	3-3	Walsh, Somers, Bigmore
	1r	5.11.62	**Mansfield T**		A	L	2-9	Creasey (p), Black

HUCKNALL ST JOHNS

First entered FA Cup: 1893

1897-98	1	29.1.98	**Liverpool**	D1	A	L	0-2

HUDDERSFIELD TOWN

Formed 1908. **FA Cup Winners:** 1922. **Runners-up:** 1920, 1928, 1930, 1938 **Record FA Cup Win:** 11-0 vs Heckmondwike, Pr rd, 18.9.1909. In competition proper: 7-0 vs Lincoln U, 1st rd, 16.11.1991. **Record FA Cup Defeat:** 0-6 vs Sunderland, 3rd round, 7.1.1950

1909-10	ML		P **Heckmondwike** (A) 11-0; 1q **Mirfield** (H) 6-0; 2q **Rothwell White Rose** (H) 7-0; 3q **South Kirkby Colliery** (H) 5-2; 4q **Rotherham T** (H) 2-2; 4qr **Rotherham T** (A) 1-2					
1910-11	D2		1q **Horsforth** (H) 6-0; 2q **Mirfield** (H) 2-0; 3q **South Kirkby Colliery** (A) 5-1; 4q **Lincoln C** (H) 1-1; 4qr **Lincoln C** (A) 0-1					
1911-12	D2	1	13.1.12	**Manchester U**	D1	A	L	1-3	Macauley
1912-13	D2	1	15.1.13	**Sheffield U**	D1	H	W	3-1	Elliott 2, Mann
		2	2.2.13	**Swindon T**	SL	H	L	1-2	Macauley
1913-14	D2	1	10.1.14	**London Caledonians**	IL	H	W	3-0	Islip 2, Armour
		2	31.1.14	**Birmingham**	D2	A	L	0-1	
1914-15	D2	1	9.1.15	**Burnley**	D1	A	L	1-3	Fayers
1919-20	D2	1	10.1.20	**Brentford**	SL	H	W	5-1	Taylor 2, Smith, Swann, Shields
		2	31.1.20	**Newcastle U**	D1	A	W	1-0	Mann

	3	21.2.20	**Plymouth A**	SL	H	W	3-1	Taylor, Slade, Swann
	4	6.3.20	**Liverpool**	D1	H	W	2-1	Swann, Taylor
	SF	27.3.20	**Bristol C**	D2		W	2-1	Taylor 2
		played at Stamford Bridge						
	F	24.4.40	**Aston Villa**	D1		L	0-1	
		played at Stamford Bridge						
1920-21 D1	1	8.1.21	**Brentford**	D3	A	W	2-1	Islip, Wright
	2	29.1.21	**Bradford PA**	D1	A	W	1-0	Mann
	3	19.2.21	**Aston Villa**	D1	A	L	0-2	
1921-22 D1	1	7.1.22	**Burnley**	D1	A	D	2-2	Islip, Watson
	1r	11.1.22	**Burnley**		H	W	3-2	Stephenson 2, Mann
	2	28.1.22	**Brighton & HA**	3S	A	D	0-0	
	2r	1.2.22	**Brighton**		H	W	2-0	Stephenson, Richardson
	3	18.2.22	**Blackburn R**	D1	A	D	1-1	Mann
	3r	22.2.22	**Blackburn R**		H	W	5-0	Islip 2, W.H.Smith 2, Mann
	4	4.3.22	**Millwall**	3S	H	W	3-0	Stephenson 2, Islip
	SF	25.3.22	**Notts Co**	D2		W	3-1	Mann, W.H.Smith, Stephenson
		played at Turf Moor						
	F	29.4.22	**PRESTON NE**	D1		W	1-0	Smith (p)
		played at Stamford Bridge						
1922-23 D1	1	13.1.23	**Birmingham**	D1	H	W	2-1	Stephenson, C.Wilson
	2	3.2.23	**Millwall**	3S	A	D	0-0	
	2r	7.2.23	**Millwall**		H	W	3-0	C.Wilson 2, Richardson
	3	24.2.23	**Bolton W**	D1	H	D	1-1	Islip
	3r	28.2.23	**Bolton W**		A	L	0-1	
1923-24 D1	1	12.1.24	**Birmingham**	D1	H	W	1-0	Johnstone
	2	2.2.24	**Manchester U**	D2	A	W	3-0	C.Wilson 2, Stephenson
	3	23.2.24	**Burnley**	D1	A	L	0-1	
1924-25 D1	1	10.1.25	**Bolton W**	D1	A	L	0-3	
1925-26 D1	3	9.1.26	**Charlton**	3S	A	W	1-0	Goodall (p)
	4	30.1.26	**Manchester C**	D1	A	L	0-4	
1926-27 D1	3	8.1.27	**Millwall**	3S	A	L	1-3	Brown
1927-28 D1	3	14.1.28	**Lincoln C**	3N	H	W	4-2	Brown, W.H.Smith, Goodall (p), Steele
	4	28.1.28	**West Ham**	D1	H	W	2-1	Brown, Jackson
	5	18.2.28	**Middlesbrough**	D1	H	W	4-0	Steele, Brown, Jackson, W.H.Smith
	6	3.3.28	**Tottenham H**	D1	H	W	6-1	Brown 4, W.H.Smith 2
	SF	24.3.28	**Sheffield U**	D1		D	2-2aet	Jackson, Brown
		played at Old Trafford						
	SFr	26.3.28	**Sheffield U**			D	0-0aet	
		played at Goodison Park						
	SF 2r	2.4.28	**Sheffield U**			W	1-0	Jackson
		played at Maine Road						
	F	21.4.28	**Blackburn R**	D1 WEMBLEY		L	1-3	Jackson
1928-29 D1	3	12.1.28	**Chesterfield**	3N	A	W	7-1	Brown 4, Cumming 2, Jackson
	4	26.1.28	**Leeds U**	D1	H	W	3-0	Jackson 2, Smith
	5	16.2.28	**Crystal Palace**	3S	H	W	5-2	Brown 3, Smith, Kelly
	6	2.3.28	**WBA**	D2	A	D	1-1	Brown
	6r	6.3.28	**WBA**		H	W	2-1	Jackson, Kelly
	SF	23.3.28	**Bolton W**	D1		L	1-3	Jackson
		played at Anfield						
1929-30 D1	3	11.1.30	**Bury**	D2	A	D	0-0	
	3r	15.1.30	**Bury**		H	W	3-1	Jackson 3
	4	25.1.30	**Sheffield U**	D1	H	W	2-1	Jackson 2
	5	15.2.30	**Bradford C**	D2	H	W	2-1	R.Kelly, Jackson
	6	1.3.30	**Aston Villa**	D1	A	W	2-1	Smith, Jackson
	SF	22.3.30	**Sheffield W**	D1		W	2-1	Jackson 2
		played at Old Trafford						
	F	26.4.30	**Arsenal**	D1 WEMBLEY		L	0-2	
1930-31 D1	3	10.1.31	**Leeds U**	D1	A	L	0-2	
1931-32 D1	3	9.1.32	**Oldham A**	D2	A	D	1-1	Mangnall
	3r	13.1.32	**Oldham A**		H	W	6-0	Mangnall 4, McLean, Luke
	4	23.1.32	**QPR**	3S	H	W	5-0	Mangnall 2, Luke 2, Campbell
	5	13.2.32	**Preston NE**	D2	H	W	4-0	Mangnall 2, Luke, Ward og
	6	27.2.32	**Arsenal**	D1	H	L	0-2	
1932-33 D1	3	14.1.33	**Folkestone**	SL	H	W	2-0	Luke, Willingham
	4	28.1.33	**Blackpool**	D1	A	L	0-2	
1933-34 D1	3	13.1.34	**Plymouth A**	D2	A	D	1-1	McLean

Season	Div	Round	Date	Opponent	OppDiv	Venue	W/L	Score	Scorers
		3r	17.1.34	Plymouth A		H	W	6-2	Mangnall 3, Luke Bott, Mclean
		4	27.1.34	Northampton T	3S	H	L	0-2	
1934-35	D1	3	12.1.35	Portsmouth	D1	A	D	1-1	Lythgoe
		3r	6.1.35	Portsmouth		H	L	2-3	Lythgoe, Lang
1935-36	D1	3	11.1.36	Aston Villa	D1	A	W	1-0	Luke
		4	25.1.36	Tottenham H	D2	A	L	0-1	
1936-37	D1	3	6.1.37	Brentford	D1	A	L	0-5	
1937-38	D1	3	8.1.38	Hull City	3N	H	W	3-1	Lythgoe 2, Beasley
		4	22.1.38	Notts Co	3S	H	W	1-0	Beattie
		5	12.2.38	Liverpool	D1	A	W	1-0	Barclay
		6	5.3.38	York C	3N	A	D	0-0	
		6r	9.3.38	York C		H	W	2-1	E.Watson, Chivers
		SF	26.3.38	Sunderland	D1		W	3-1	Beasley, Barclay, McFadyen
			played at Ewood Park						
		F	30.4.38	Preston NE	D1	WEMBLEY	L	0-1aet	
1938-39	D1	3	11.1.39	Nottingham F	D2	H	D	0-0	
		3r	6.1.39	Nottingham F		A	W	3-0	Isaac 2, Price
		4	21.1.39	Leeds U	D1	A	W	4-2	Price 3, Barclay
		5	11.2.39	Walsall	3S	H	W	3-0	Price 2, McCall
		6	4.3.39	Blackburn R	D2	H	D	1-1	Price
		6r	9.3.39	Blackburn R		A	W	2-1	Mahon, Beasley
		SF	25.3.39	Portsmouth	D1		L	1-2	Barclay
			played at Highbury						
1945-46	D1	3 1L	5.1.46	Sheffield U	D1	H	D	1-1	Price
		3 2L	7.1.46	Sheffield U		A	L	0-2	
1946-47	D1	3	11.1.47	Barnsley	D2	H	L	3-4	Doherty 2, Bateman
1947-48	D1	3	10.1.48	Colchester U	SL	A	L	0-1	
1948-49	D1	3	8.1.49	QPR	D2	A	D	0-0aet	
		3r	15.1.49	QPR		H	W	5-0	Glazzard 2, Nightingale, McKenna, Bateman
		4	29.1.49	Newport Co	3S	A	D	3-3aet	Glazzard 2, Doherty
		4r	5.2.49	Newport Co		H	L	1-3	Metcalfe
1949-50	D1	3	7.1.50	Sunderland	D1	A	L	0-6	
1950-51	D1	3	6.1.51	Tottenham H	D1	H	W	2-0	Taylor, Glazzard
		4	27.1.51	Preston NE	D2	A	W	2-0	Metcalfe (p), Taylor
		5	10.2.51	Wolverhampton W	D1	A	L	0-2	
1951-52	D1	3	12.1.52	Tranmere R	3N	H	L	1-2	Metcalfe (p)
1952-53	D2	3	10.1.53	Bristol R	3S	H	W	2-0	Glazzard, Watson
		4	31.1.53	Blackpool	D1	A	L	0-1	
1953-54	D1	3	9.1.54	West Ham	D2	A	L	0-4	
1954-55	D1	3	8.1.55	Coventry C	3S	H	D	3-3	Glazzard 2, Watson
		3r	13.1.55	Coventry C		A	W	2-1aet	Glazzard, Watson
		4	29.1.55	Torquay U	3S	A	W	1-0	Glazzard
		5	19.2.55	Liverpool	D2	A	W	2-0	Glazzard, Hobson
		6	12.3.55	Newcastle U	D1	H	D	1-1	Glazzard
		6r	16.3.55	Newcastle U		A	L	0-2aet	
1955-56	D1	3	7.1.56	Bolton W	D1	A	–	0-0	
			Abandoned after 47 minutes						
		3	11.1.56	Bolton W		A	L	0-3	
1956-57	D2	3	5.1.57	Sheffield U	D2	H	D	0-0	
		3r	7.1.57	Sheffield U		A	D	1-1aet	Simpson
		3 2r	14.1.57	Sheffield U at Maine Rd			W	2-1	Quested, Hickson
		4	26.1.57	Peterborough U	ML	H	W	3-1	Law, Hickson, Simpson
		5	16.2.57	Burnley	D1	H	L	1-2	Hickson
1957-58	D2	3	4.1.58	Charlton A	D2	H	D	2-2	Law, Massie
		3r	8.1.58	Charlton A		A	L	0-1	
1958-59	D2	3	10.1.59	Ipswich T	D2	A	L	0-1	
1959-60	D2	3	9.1.60	West Ham	D1	H	D	1-1	Law
		3r	13.1.60	West Ham		A	W	5-1	Massie 2, Connor 2, McGarry
		4	30.1.60	Luton T	D1	H	L	0-1	
1960-61	D2	3	7.1.61	Wolverhampton W	D1	A	D	1-1	Stokes
		3r	11.1.61	Wolverhampton W		H	W	2-1	Stokes, O'Grady
		4	1.2.61	Barnsley	D3	H	D	1-1	Coddington (p)
		4r	6.2.61	Barnsley		A	L	0-1	
1961-62	D2	3	9.1.62	Rotherham U	D2	H	W	4-3	McHale 2, Massie, Kerray
		4	27.1.62	Aston Villa	D1	A	L	1-2	McHale
1962-63	D2	3	4.3.63	Manchester U	D1	A	L	0-5	
1963-64	D2	3	4.1.64	Plymouth A	D2	A	W	1-0	McHale

	4	25.1.64 **Chelsea**	D1	A	W	2-1	McHale, White
	5	15.2.64 **Burnley**	D1	A	L	0-3	
1964-65 D2	3	9.1.65 **Doncaster R**	D4	A	W	1-0	Massie
	4	30.1.65 **Swansea T**	D2	A	L	0-1	
1965-66 D2	3	24.1.66 **Hartlepools U**	D4	H	W	3-1	Quigley 2, Leighton
	4	12.2.66 **Plymouth A**	D2	A	W	2-0	Smith, Massie
	5	5.3.66 **Sheffield W**	D1	H	L	1-2	Smith
1966-67 D2	3	28.1.67 **Chelsea**	D1	H	L	1-2	Leighton
1967-68 D2	3	27.1.68 **Tranmere R**	D3	A	L	1-2	Worthington
1968-69 D2	3	4.1.69 **Bury**	D2	A	W	2-1	Hill, Nicholson
	4	25.1.69 **West Ham**	D1	H	L	0-2	
1969-70 D2	3	3.1.70 **Aldershot**	D4	H	D	1-1	Smith
	3r	12.1.70 **Aldershot**		A	L	1-3	Worthington
1970-71 D1	3	2.1.71 **Birmingham C**	D2	H	D	1-1	Hoy
	3r	5.1.71 **Birmingham C**		A	W	2-0	Krzywicki, Worthington
	4	23.1.71 **Stoke C**	D1	A	D	3-3	Worthington, Chapman, Mahoney
	4r	26.1.71 **Stoke C**		H	D	0-0aet	
	4 2r	8.2.71 **Stoke C** at Old Trafford			L	0-1	
1971-72 D1	3	15.1.72 **Burnley**	D2	A	W	1-0	Clarke
	4	5.2.72 **Fulham**	D2	H	W	3-0	J.Lawson 2, Chapman
	5	26.2.72 **West Ham**	D1	H	W	4-2	J.Lawson, Dolan, D.Smith, Worthington
	6	18.3.72 **Birmingham C**	D2	A	L	1-3	Cherry
1972-73 D2	3	13.1.73 **Carlisle U**	D2	A	D	2-2	Fairclough 2
	3r	6.1.73 **Carlisle U**		H	L	0-1	
1973-74 D3	1	24.11.73 **Wigan A**	NPL	H	W	2-0	Newton 2
	2	15.12.73 **Chester**	D4	A	L	2-3	Saunders, Gowling
1974-75 D3	1	23.11.74 **Grimsby T**	D3	A	L	0-1	
1975-76 D4	1	22.11.75 **Walsall**	D3	A	W	1-0	Belfitt
	2	13.12.75 **Port Vale**	D3	H	W	2-1	Belfitt, Baines
	3	3.1.76 **Fulham**	D2	A	W	3-2	Gray 2, Lawson
	4	24.1.76 **Bolton W**	D2	H	L	0-1	
1976-77 D4	1	20.11.76 **Mansfield T**	D3	H	D	0-0	
	1r	22.11.76 **Mansfield T**		A	L	1-2	Sidebottom
1977-78 D4	1	26.11.77 **Barnsley**	D4	A	L	0-1	
1978-79 D4	1	25.11.78 **Doncaster R**	D4	A	L	1-2	Fletcher
1979-80 D4	1	24.11.79 **Darlington**	D4	A	D	1-1	Hart
	1r	27.11.79 **Darlington**		H	L	0-1	
1980-81 D3	1	22.11.80 **Northwich V**	APL	A	D	1-1	Stanton
	1r	25.11.80 **Northwich V**		H	W	6-0	Santon 2, Robins 2, Hanvey, Laverick
	2	13.12.80 **Tranmere R**	D4	A	W	3-0	Robins 2, Stanton
	3	3.1.81 **Shrewsbury T**	D2	H	L	0-3	
1981-82 D3	1	21.11.81 **Workington**	NPL	A	D	1-1	Brown
	1r	24.11.81 **Workington**		H	W	5-0	Laverick 2, Robins, Lillis, Brown
	2	12.12.81 **Chesterfield**	D3	A	W	1-0	Cowling
	3	23.1.82 **Carlisle U**	D3	A	W	3-2	Fletcher 3
	4	26.1.82 **Orient**	D2	H	D	1-1	Austin
	4r	1.2.82 **Orient**		A	L	0-2	
1982-83 D3	1	20.11.82 **Mossley**	NPL	H	W	1-0	Brown
	2	11.12.82 **Altrincham**	APL	A	W	1-0	Stanton
	3	8.1.83 **Chelsea**	D2	H	D	1-1	Stanton
	3r	12.1.83 **Chelsea**		A	L	0-2	
1983-84 D2	3	7.1.84 **QPR**	D1	H	W	2-1	Lillis, Stonehouse
	4	1.2.84 **Notts Co**	D1	H	L	1-2	Stonehouse
1984-85 D2	3	5.1.85 **Wolverhampton W**	D2	A	D	1-1	Tempest
	3r	23.1.85 **Wolverhampton W**		H	W	3-1	Lillis 2 (1p), Pugh
	4	26.1.85 **Luton T**	D1	A	L	0-2	
1985-86 D2	3	4.1.86 **Reading**	D3	H	D	0-0	
	3r	13.1.86 **Reading**		A	L	1-2	Cowling
1986-87 D2	3	10.1.87 **Norwich C**	D1	A	D	1-1	Shearer
	3r	21.1.87 **Norwich C**		H	L	2-4	Brown (p), Cork
1987-88 D2	3	9.1.88 **Manchester C**	D2	H	D	2-2	Shearer 2
	3r	12.1.88 **Manchester C**		A	D	0-0aet	
	3 2r	25.1.88 **Manchester C**		H	L	0-3	
1988-89 D3	1	19.11.88 **Rochdale**	D4	H	D	1-1	May
	1r	28.11.88 **Rochdale**		A	W	4-3	Withe, O'Shaughnessy og, Maskell, Bent
	2	10.12.88 **Chester C**	D3	H	W	1-0	O'Regan
	3	7.1.89 **Sheffield U**	D3	H	L	0-1	

1989-90	D3	1	18.11.89	Hartlepool U	D4	A	W	2-0	Cecere 2 (2 p)
		2	9.12.89	Chesterfield	D4	A	W	2-0	Cecere (p), Maskell
		3	6.1.90	Grimsby T	D4	H	W	3-1	Smith, Maskell, Lever og
		4	27.1.90	Crystal Palace	D1	A	L	0-4	
1990-91	D3	1	17.11.90	Altrincham	GMVC	A	W	2-1	Onuora, Roberts
		2	8.12.90	Blackpool	D4	H	L	0-2	
1991-92	D3	1	16.11.91	Lincoln U	CML	H	W	7-0	O'Regan, Donovan 2, Stapleton, Roberts 2, Onuora
		2	7.12.91	Rochdale	D4	A	W	2-1	Roberts, Onuora
		3	4.1.92	Millwall	D2	H	L	0-4	
1992-93	D2	1	14.11.92	Scunthorpe U	D3	A	D	0-0	
		1r	25.11.92	Scunthorpe U		H	W	2-1aet	Barnett 2
		2	6.12.92	Bradford C	D2	A	W	2-0	Dunn, O'Regan (p)
		3	2.1.93	Gillingham	D3	A	D	0-0	
		3r	13.1.93	Gillingham		H	W	2-1	Robinson, Dunn
		4	23.1.93	Southend U	D2	H	L	1-2	Mitchell

HULL CITY

Formed 1904. **First entered FA Cup:** 1904. **Best FA Cup Performance:** semifinals, 1930. **Record FA Cup Win:** 8-1 vs Grimethorpe United, 1st qualifying round, 7.10.1905. In Competition Proper: 8-2 vs Stalybridge Celtic, 1st round, 26.11.1932 **Record FA Cup Defeat:** 0-5 vs Fulham, 3rd round, 9.1.1960

1904-05 P **Stockton** (A) 3-3; Pr **Stockton** (A) 1-4
1905-06 D2 1q **Grimethorpe U** (H) 8-1; 2q **Denaby U** (A) 2-0; 3q **Leeds C** (H) 1-1; 3qr **Leeds C** (A) 2-1; 4q **Oldham A** (H) 2-1

		1	13.1.06	Reading	SL	H	L	0-1	
1906-07	D2	1	12.1.07	Tottenham H	SL	A	D	0-0	
		1r	17.1.07	Tottenham H		H		0-0	
				abandoned after 100 minutes – bad light					
		1 2r	21.1.07	Tottenham H		A	L	0-1	
1907-08	D2	1	11.1.08	W.Arsenal	D1	A	D	0-0	
		1r	6.1.08	W.Arsenal		H	W	4-1	Shaw 2, Temple, Jack Smith
		2	1.2.08	A. Villa	D1	A	L	0-3	
1908-09	D2	1	6.1.09	Chelsea	D1	H	D	1-1	Temple
			20.1.09	Chelsea		A	L	0-1	
1909-10	D2	1	15.1.10	Chelsea		A	L	1-2	Temple
1910-11	D2	1	14.1.11	Bristol R	SL	A	D	0-0	
		1r	19.1.11	Bristol R		H	W	1-0aet	McQuillan
		2	4.2.11	Oldham A	D1	H	W	1-0	Temple
		3	25.2.11	Newcastle U	D1	A	L	2-3	Joe Smith 2
1911-12	D2	1	13.1.12	Oldham A	D1	A	D	1-1	Best
		1r	6.1.12	Oldham A		H	L	0-1	
1912-13	D2	1	11.1.13	Fulham	D2	A	W	2-0	Fazackerley, Stevens
		2	1.2.13	Newcastle U	D1	H	D	0-0	
		2r	5.2.13	Newcastle U		A	L	0-3	
1913-14	D2	1	10.1.14	Bury	D2	H	D	0-0	
		1r	14.1.14	Bury		A	L	1-2	Lee
1914-15	D2	1	9.1.15	WBA	D1	H	W	1-0	Stevens
		2	30.1.15	Northampton T	SL	H	W	2-1	Stevens 2
		3	20.2.15	Southampton	SL	A	D	2-2aet	Cameron, Lee
		3r	27.2.15	Southampton		H	W	4-0	Stevens 2, Cameron, Lee
		4	6.3.15	Bolton W	D1	A	L	2-4	Deacey, Stevens
1919-20	D2	1	14.1.20	Sunderland	D1	A	L	2-6	Stevens
1920-21	D2	1	8.1.21	Bath C	SL	H	W	3-0	Wilson, Sergeaunt, Crawford
		2	29.1.21	Crystal P	D3	A	W	2-0	Wilson, Crawford
		3	19.2.21	Burnley	D1	H	W	3-0	Brandon 2, Wilson
		4	5.3.21	Preston NE	D1	H	D	0-0	
		4r	10.3.21	Preston NE		A	L	0-1	
1921-22	D2	1	7.1.22	Middlesbrough	D1	H	W	5-0	Coverdale 2, Mills, Bleakley, Crawford
		2	28.1.22	Nottingham F	D2	A	L	0-3	
1922-23	D2	1	13.1.23	West Ham	D2	H	L	2-3	Crawford, Mills
1923-24	D2	1	12.1.24	Bolton W	D1	H	D	2-2	Martin, Mills
		1r	6.1.24	Bolton W		A	L	0-4	
1924-25	D2	1	10.1.25	Wolverhampton W	D1	H	D	1-1	Mills
		1r	15.1.25	Wolverhampton W		A	W	1-0aet	Mills
		2	31.1.25	Crystal P	D2	H	W	3-2	Mills 2, Bleakley
		3	21.2.25	Leicester C	D2	H	D	1-1	O'Brien
		3r	26.2.25	Leicester C		A	L	1-3	Hamilton

1925-26	D2	3	9.1.26	Aston Villa	D1	H	L	0-3	
1926-27	D2	3	8.1.27	WBA	D1	H	W	2-1	Cowan, Scott
		4	29.1.27	Everton	D1	H	D	1-1	Martin
		4r	2.2.27	Everton		A	D	2-2aet	Guyan, Scott
		4 2r	7.2.27	Everton at Villa Park			W	3-2aet	Whitworth, Guyan, Scott
		5	19.2.27	Wolverhampton W	D2	A	L	0-1	
1927-28	D2	3	14.1.28	Leicester C	D1	H	L	0-1	
1928-29	D2	3	12.1.29	Bradford PA	D2	H	D	1-1	McDonald
		3r	6.1.29	Bradford PA		A	L	1-3	McDonald
1929-30	D2	3	11.1.30	Plymouth A	3S	A	W	4-3	Alexander 3, Duncan
		4	25.1.30	Blackpool	D2	H	W	3-1	Alexander, Starling, Mills
		5	15.2.30	Manchester C	D1	A	W	2-1	Taylor, Mills
		6	1.3.30	Newcastle U	D1	A	D	1-1	Alexander
		6r	6.3.30	Newcastle U		H	W	1-0	Howieson
		SF	22.3.30	Arsenal	D1		D	2-2	Howieson, Duncan
			played at Elland Road						
		SFr	26.3.30	Arsenal			L	0-1	
			played at Villa Park						
1930-31	3N	3	10.1.31	Blackpool	D1	H	L	1-2	D.Duncan
1931-32	3N	1	28.11.31	Mansfield T	3S	H	W	4-1	Wainscoat 2, Speed, Munnings
		2	12.12.31	New Brighton	3N	A	W	4-0	Speed 2, Wainscoat, Munnings
		3	9.1.32	Stoke City	D2	A	L	0-3	
1932-33	3N	1	26.11.32	Stalybridge C	CC	A	W	8-2	Wainscoat 4, McNaughton, Forward, Sargeant, Hill
		2	10.12.32	Carlisle U	3N	A	D	1-1	Sargeant
		2r	15.12.32	Carlisle U		H	W	2-1aet	Wainscoat, Forward
		3	14.1.33	Sunderland	D1	H	L	0-2	
1933-34	D2	3	13.1.34	Brentford	D2	H	W	1-0	Hubbard
		4	27.1.34	Manchester C	D1	H	D	2-2	Hill, Dale og
		4r	31.1.34	Manchester C		A	L	1-4	McNaughton
1934-35	D2	3	12.1.35	Newcastle U	D2	H	L	1-5	Charlton
1935-36	D2	3	11.1.36	WBA	D1	A	L	0-2	
1936-37	3N	1	28.11.36	York C	3N	A	L	2-5	Mayson, Hubbard
1937-38	3N	1	27.11.37	Scunthorpe U	ML	H	W	4-0	MacNeill 2, Pears 2
		2	11.12.37	Exeter C	3S	A	W	2-1	Hubbard, Fryer
		3	8.1.38	Huddersfield T	D1	A	L	1-3	Pears
1938-39	3N	1	26.11.38	Rotherham U	3N	H	W	4-1	Hubbard 2, Cunliffe, Davies
		2	10.12.38	Chester	3N	A	D	2-2	Davies 2
		2r	15.12.38	Chester		H	L	0-1	
1945-46	3N		*did not compete*						
1946-47	3N	1	30.11.46	New Brighton	3N	H	D	0-0	
		1r	4.12.46	New Brighton		A	W	2-1aet	Lester, Chadwick
		2	14.12.46	Darlington	3N	A	W	2-1	Lester, Peach
		3	11.1.47	Blackburn R	D1	A	D	1-1	Cook
		3r	6.1.47	Blackburn R		H	L	0-3	
1947-48	3N	1	29.11.47	Southport	3N	H	D	1-1aet	Gallacher
		1r	6.12.47	Southport		A	W	3-2	Richardson, Reagan, McGorrighan
		2	13.12.47	Cheltenham T	SL	A	W	4-2	Richardson 3, Reagan
		3	10.1.48	Middlesbrough	D1	H	L	1-3	Murphy
1948-49	3N	1	27.11.48	Accrington S	3N	H	W	3-1	Carter 2, Jensen
		2	11.12.48	Reading	3S	H	D	0-0aet	
		2r	18.12.48	Reading		A	W	2-1	Moore 2
		3	8.1.49	Blackburn R	D2	A	W	2-1aet	Moore, Buchan
		4	29.1.49	Grimsby T	D2	A	W	3-2	Moore 2, Carter
		5	12.2.49	Stoke City	D1	A	W	2-0	Moore, Greenhalgh
		6	26.2.49	Manchester U	D1	H	L	0-1	
1949-50	D2	3	7.1.50	Southport	3N	A	D	0-0	
		3r	12.1.50	Southport		H	W	5-0	Moore, Revie, Harrison, Burbanks, Greenhalgh
		4	28.1.50	Stockport Co	3N	A	D	0-0	
		4r	2.2.50	Stockport Co		H	L	0-2	
1950-51	D2	3	6.1.51	Everton	D1	H	W	2-0	Carter, Gerrie
		4	27.1.51	Rotherham U	3N	H	W	2-0	Carter, Harrison
		5	10.2.51	Bristol R	3S	A	L	0-3	
1951-52	D2	3	12.1.52	Manchester U	D1	A	W	2-0	Harrison, Gerrie
		4	2.2.52	Blackburn R	D2	A	L	0-2	
1952-53	D2	3	10.1.53	Charlton A	D1	H	W	3-1	Horton, Jensen, Harris
		4	31.1.53	Gateshead	3N	H	L	1-2	Gerrie
1953-54	D2	3	9.1.54	Brentford	D2	A	D	0-0	

Season	Div	Round	Date	Opponent		Venue	Res	Score	Scorers
		3r	14.1.54	Brentford		H	D	2-2aet	Horton, Crosbie
		3 2r	18.1.54	Brentford at Doncaster			W	5-2	Horton 2, Crosbie 2, Ackerman
		4	30.1.54	Blackburn R	D2	A	D	2-2	Crosbie, K.Harrison
		4r	4.2.54	Blackburn R		H	W	2-1	Ackerman, Bulless
		5	20.2.54	Tottenham H	D1	H	D	1-1	Jensen
		5r	24.2.54	Tottenham H		A	L	0-2	
1954-55	D2	3	8.1.55	Birmingham C	D2	H	L	0-2	
1955-56	D2	3	7.1.56	Aston Villa	D1	A	D	1-1	Clarke
		3r	12.1.56	Aston Villa		H	L	1-2	Atkinson
1956-57	3N	1	17.11.56	Gateshead	3N	H	W	4-0	Mortensen 2, Bradbury, Cripsey
		2	8.12.56	York City	3N	H	W	2-1	Bulless 2
		3	5.1.57	Bristol R	D2	H	L	3-4	Clarke 2, Stephens
1957-58	3N	1	16.11.57	Crewe Alex	3N	H	W	2-1	Bradbury, Clarke
		2	7.12.57	Port Vale	3S	A	D	2-2	Bradbury, Davidson
		2r	9.12.57	Port Vale		H	W	4-3aet	Bradbury 2, Cleary og, Carberry og
		3	4.1.58	Barnsley	D2	H	D	1-1	Bradbury
		3r	8.1.58	Barnsley		A	W	2-0	Clarke, Bulless
		4	29.1.58	Sheffield W	D1	A	L	3-4	Bradbury, Bulless, Stephens
1958-59	D3	1	15.11.58	Stockport Co	D3	H	L	0-1	
1959-60	D2	3	9.1.60	Fulham	D1	A	L	0-5	
1960-61	D3	1	5.11.60	Sutton T	CA	H	W	3-0	Sewell, Price, Gubbins
		2	26.11.60	Darlington	D4	A	D	1-1	Price
		2r	28.11.60	Darlington		H	D	1-1aet	Chilton
		2 2r	5.12.60	Darlington at Elland Rd				1-1	Price
				abandoned at end of normal time, ground unfit					
		2 3r	12.12.60	Darlington at Doncaster			D	0-0aet	
		2 4r	15.12.60	Darlington at Ayresome Pk			W	3-0	Clarke, Gubbins, King
		3	7.1.61	Bolton W	D1	H	L	0-1	
1961-62	D3	1	4.11.61	Rhyl	CC	H	W	5-0	Chilton 2, McSeveney, Henderson, McMillan
		2	25.11.61	Bradford C	D4	H	L	0-2	
1962-63	D3	1	3.11.62	Crook T	NL	H	W	5-4	McSeveney 2, Henderson 2, Chilton
		2	24.11.62	Workington	D4	H	W	2-0	McSeveney 2
		3	11.2.63	Leyton Orient	D1	A	D	1-1	Chilton
		3r	19.2.63	Leyton Orient		H	L	0-2aet	
1963-64	D3	1	16.11.63	Crewe Alex	D3	H	D	2-2	Chilton, Shaw
		1r	20.11.63	Crewe Alex		A	W	3-0	Wilkinson 2, Henderson
		2	7.12.63	Wrexham	D3	A	W	2-0	Chilton, Henderson
		3	4.1.64	Everton	D1	H	D	1-1	Wilkinson
		3r	7.1.64	Everton		A	L	1-2	McSeveney
1964-65	D3	1	14.11.64	Kidderminster H	WMRL	A	W	4-1	Wilkinson 2, McSeveney, Heath
		2	5.12.64	Lincoln C	D4	H	D	1-1	Summers
		2r	9.12.64	Lincoln C		A	L	1-3	McSeveney
1965-66	D3	1	13.11.65	Bradford PA	D4	A	W	3-2	Houghton, Chilton, I.Butler
		2	8.12.65	Gateshead	NRL	A	W	4-0	Henderson, Wagstaff, Houghton, I.Butler
		3	22.1.66	Southampton	D2	H	W	1-0	Houghton
		4	12.2.66	Nottingham F	D1	H	W	2-0	Heath 2
		5	5.3.66	Southport	D4	H	W	2-0	Chilton 2
		6	26.3.66	Chelsea	D1	A	D	2-2	Wagstaff 2
		6r	31.3.66	Chelsea		H	L	1-3	Simpkin
1966-67	D2	3	28.1.67	Portsmouth	D2	H	D	1-1	Houghton
		3r	1.2.67	Portsmouth		A	D	2-2aet	Houghton, Chilton
		3 2r	6.2.67	Portsmouth at Coventry			L	1-3	Chilton
1967-68	D2	3	27.1.68	Middlesbrough	D2	A	D	1-1	Chilton
		3r	31.1.68	Middlesbrough		H	D	2-2aet	Wagstaff 2
		3 2r	7.2.68	Middlesbrough at York			L	0-1	
1968-69	D2	3	4.1.69	Wolverhampton W	D1	H	L	1-3	Chilton
1969-70	D2	3	3.1.70	Manchester C	D1	H	L	0-1	
1970-71	D2	3	2.1.71	Charlton A	D2	H	W	3-0	Wagstaff, Houghton, I.Butler
		4	23.1.71	Blackpool	D1	H	W	2-0	Wagstaff, Chilton
		5	13.2.71	Brentford	D4	H	W	2-1	Houghton, Chilton
		6	6.3.71	Stoke C	D1	H	L	2-3	Wagstaff 2
1971-72	D2	3	15.1.72	Norwich C	D2	H	W	3-0	Wagstaff, Butler, McGill
		4	5.2.72	Coventry C	D1	A	W	1-0	Wagstaff
			26.2.72	Stoke C	D1	A	L	1-4	Wagstaff
1972-73	D2	3	13.1.73	Stockport Co	D4	A	D	0-0	
		3r	23.1.73	Stockport Co		H	W	2-0aet	Wagstaff, Houghton
		4	3.2.73	West Ham	D1	H	W	1-0	Houghton

HULL CITY

	5	24.2.73	Coventry C	D1	A	L	0-3	
1973-74 D2	3	5.1.74	Bristol C	D2	A	D	1-1	Galvin
	3r	8.1.74	Bristol C		H	L	0-1	
1974-75 D2	3	4.1.75	Fulham	D2	A	D	1-1	Wagstaff
	3r	7.1.75	Fulham		H	D	2-2aet	Fletcher, Croft
	4	13.1.75	Fulham at Filbert Street			L	0-1	
1975-76 D2	3	3.1.76	Plymouth A	D2	H	D	1-1	Grimes
	3r	6.1.76	Plymouth A		A	W	4-1	Wood 2, Hawley, Sutton og
	4	2.2.76	Sunderland	D2	A	L	0-1	
1976-77 D2	3	8.1.77	Port Vale	D3	H	D	1-1	Nisbet
	3r	10.1.77	Port Vale		A	L	1-3aet	Hemmerman
1977-78 D2	3	7.1.78	Leicester C	D1	H	L	0-1	
1978-79 D3	1	25.11.78	Stafford R	NPL	H	W	2-1	Seargeant og, Edwards
	2	16.12.78	Carlisle U	D3	A	L	0-3	
1979-80 D3	1	24.11.79	Carlisle U		A	D	3-3	Hugh, Tait, G.Roberts
	1r	28.11.79	Carlisle U		H	L	0-2	
1980-81 D3	1	22.11.80	Halifax T	D4	H	W	2-1	Edwards 2
	2	13.12.80	Blyth S	NL	H	D	1-1	Edwards
	2r	16.12.80	Blyth S		A	D	2-2aet	Edwards, Norrie
	2 2r	22.12.80	Blyth S at Elland Road			W	2-1	Norrie, Croft
	3	3.1.81	Doncaster R	D4	H	W	1-0	Deacy
	4	24.1.81	Tottenham H	D1	A	L	0-2	
1981-82 D4	1	21.11.81	Rochdale	D4	A	D	2-2	Whitehurst, McClaren
	1r	24.11.81	Rochdale		H	D	2-2aet	Whitehurst, Swann
	1 2r	30.11.81	Rochdale at Elland Road			W	1-0	McClaren
	2	4.1.82	Hartlepool U	D4	H	W	2-0	Marwood, Mutrie
	3	18.1.82	Chelsea	D2	A	D	0-0	
	3r	21.1.82	Chelsea		H	L	0-2	
1982-83 D4	1	20.11.82	Sheffield U	D3	H	D	1-1	Kenworthy og
	1r	23.11.82	Sheffield U		A	L	0-2	
1983-84 D3	1	19.11.83	Penrith	NWC	A	W	2-0	Whitehurst, G.Roberts
	2	10.12.83	Rotherham U	D3	A	L	1-2	Flounders
1984-85 D3	1	17.11.84	Bolton W	D3	H	W	2-1	Massey, Flounders
	2	8.12.84	Tranmere R	D4	A	W	3-0	Ring, McLaren, Skipper
	3	5.1.85	Brighton & HA	D2	A	L	0-1	
1985-86 D2	3	4.1.86	Plymouth A	D3	H	D	2-2	Flounders 2
	3r	7.1.86	Plymouth A		A	W	1-0	Roberts
	4	25.1.86	Brighton & HA	D2	H	L	2-3	Roberts, McEwan
1986-87 D2	3	31.1.87	Shrewsbury T	D2	A	W	2-1	Bunn, Saville
	4	3.2.87	Swansea C	D4	A	W	1-0	Jobson
	5	21.2.87	Wigan A	D3	A	L	0-3	
1987-88 D2	3	9.1.88	Watford	D1	A	D	1-1	Roberts
	3r	12.1.88	Watford		H	D	2-2aet	Williams, Dyer
	3 2r	18.1.88	Watford		A	L	0-1	
1988-89 D2	3	7.1.89	Cardiff C	D3	A	W	2-1	Brown, Edwards
	4	28.1.89	Bradford C	D2	A	W	2-1	Whitehurst, Edwards
	5	18.2.89	Liverpool	D1	H	L	2-3	Whitehurst, Edwards
1989-90 D2	3	6.1.90	Newcastle U	D1	H	L	0-1	
1990-91 D2	3	5.1.91	Notts Co	D2	H	L	2-5	Buckley, McParland
1991-92 D3	1	16.11.91	Morecambe	NPL	A	W	1-0	Wilcox
	2	7.12.91	Blackpool	D4	A	W	1-0	Hunter
	3	4.1.92	Chelsea	D1	H	L	0-2	
1992-93 D2	1	14.11.92	Darlington	D3	A	W	2-1	Atkinson, Norton
	2	5.12.92	Rotherham U	D2	A	L	0-1	

HULL TOWN

Formed 1879. Played at open space at Argyle Street Hull, near the Nag's Head Inn.

1883-84	1	3.11.83	Grimsby T		H	L	1-3	Percy
1884-85	1	1.11.84	Lincoln C		H	L	1-5	

HUNGERFORD TOWN

Formed 1886. **First entered FA Cup:** 1924. Currently play in the Isthmian (Diadora) League

1979-80 IL	1	24.11.79	Slough T	IL	A	L	1-3	Farr

HURST FC

Formed 1879. Based in Ashton-under-Lyne.

1883-84	1	20.10.83	**Turton**		H	W	3-0	
	2	1.12.83	**Irwell Springs**		H	W	3-2	
		replay ordered after protest, but Hurst scratched						
1884-85	1	18.10.84	**Church FC**		A	L	2-3	
1885-86	1	31.10.85	**Bradshaw FC**		H	W	3-1	
	2		**Halliwell**				*scratched*	
1887-88	1	15.10.87	**Astley Bridge**		H	W	5-3	
		FA disqualified Hurst after protest						

HYDE UNITED

Formed 1885-1917 as Hyde FC. Reformed 1919 as Hyde United. **First entered FA Cup as Hyde U:** 1935. Hyde FC gained an everlasting niche in the history of the FA Cup for the one and only Cup match they ever played ended in the competition's biggest ever victory margin.

1887-88		1	15.10.87	**Preston North End**		A	L	0-26	
Hyde United									
1954-55	CC	1	20.11.54	**Workington**	3N	A	L	1-5	Hilton
1983-84	NPL	1	19.11.83	**Burnley**	D3	H	L	0-2	

ILFORD

Formed 1881. **First entered FA Cup:** 1890. **FA Amateur Cup winners:** 1929, 1930 **Runners-up:** 1936, 1958, 1974. Merged with Leytonstone to become Leytonstone-Ilford 1979. See also Leytonstone-Ilford

1925-26	IL	1	28.11.25	**London Caledonians**	IL	A	W	2-1	V.F.Welch, Adey
		2	12.12.25	**Clapton**	IL	A	L	0-1	
1927-28	IL	1	26.11.27	**Dulwich Hamlet**	IL	H	W	4-0	Drane 2, Dellow 2
		2	10.12.27	**Exeter C**	D3	A	L	3-5	Drane, Holmes 2
1928-29	IL	1	24.11.28	**Northfleet U**	SL	A	L	2-5	Craymer, Drane
1929-30	IL	1	30.11.29	**Watford**	3S	H	L	0-3	
1930-31	IL	1	29.11.30	**Brentford**	3S	H	L	1-6	Peploe
1932-33	IL	1	26.11.32	**Newport Co**	3S	A	L	2-4	Drane, Charlton og
1933-34	IL	1	25.11.33	**Swindon T**	3S	H	L	2-4	Halerow, Hellard
1936-37	IL	1	28.11.36	**Reading**	3S	H	L	2-4	Watts, Hellard
1958-59	IL	1	15.11.58	**Norwich C**	D3	A	L	1-3	Winch
1974-75	IL	1	23.11.74	**Romford**	SL	A	W	2-0	Butterfield, Turley
		2	14.12.74	**Southend U**	D3	H	L	0-2	

ILKESTON TOWN

Formed 1945. **First entered FA Cup:** 1947

1951-52	ML	1	24.11.51	**Rochdale**	3N	H	L	0-2	
1956-57	ML	1	17.11.56	**Blyth Spartans**	NEL	H	L	1-5	Marsh

IPSWICH TOWN

Formed 1878. **First entered FA Cup:** 1890. **Best FA Cup Performance:** Winners 1978 **Record FA Cup Win:** 11-0 vs Cromer, 3rd qualifying round, 31.10.1936. In competition proper: 7-0 vs Street, 1st rd, 26.11.1938. **Record FA Cup Defeat:** 1-7 vs Southampton, 3rd round, 2.2.1974

1890-91	1q **Reading** (H) 2-0; 2q **Norwich Thorpe** (A) 4-0; 3q **Huntington Co** (H) 5-2; 4q **93rd Highlanders** (H) 1-4
1891-92	1q **Old Westminsters** (A) 0-5
1892-93	1q **Old Wykehamists** (H) 4-0; 2q **Old Westminsters** (A) 1-4
1893-1929	*did not enter*
1930-31 SUF	ExP **Harwich & P** (H) 5-0; P **Leiston Works** (H) 5-2; 1q **Severalls A** (H) 6-1; 2q **Crittalls A** (H) 2-3
1931-32 SUF	P **Leiston Works** (A) 2-3
1932-33 SUF	ExP **Kirkley** (H) 0-0; ExPr **Kirkley** (A) 3-2; P **Cambridge T** (A) 2-2; Pr **Cambridge T** (H) 1-2
1933-34 SUF	ExP **Gorleston** (A) 2-3
1934-35 SUF	P **Norwich St Barnabas** (H) 3-2; 1q **Norwich YMCA** (H) 1-1; 1qr **Norwich YMCA** (H) 4-2; 2q **Frost A** (H) 2-0; 3q **Gorleston** (A) 0-2
1935-36 ECL	1q **Yarmouth T** (H) 0-0; 1qr **Yarmouth T** (A) 1-4
1936-37 SL	P **Eastern Co. U.** (H) 7-0; 1q **Stowmarket** (H) 8-0; 2q **Lowestoft T** (A) 1-1; 2qr **Lowestoft T** (H) 7-1; 3q **Cromer** (H) 11-0;

			4q **Cambridge T** (H) 2-1						
		1	28.11.36	**Watford**	3S	H	W	2-1	Bruce, Carter

Season	Div	Round	Date	Opponent	League	H/A	Result	Score	Scorers
		2	12.12.36	Spennymoor U	NEL	H	L	1-2	Carter
1937-38	SL	4q	Hoffmann A (A) 3-0						
		1	27.11.37	Yeovil & Petters U	SL	A	L	1-2	Astill
1938-39	3S	1	26.11.38	Street	WL	H	W	7-0	Chadwick 4, Davies 2, Fletcher
		2	10.12.38	Torquay U	3S	H	W	4-1	Little 2, Jones, Chadwick
		3	7.1.39	A. Villa	D1	A	D	1-1	Hutcheson
		3r	11.1.39	A. Villa		H	L	1-2	Jones
1945-46	3S	1 1L	17.11.45	Wisbech T	UCL	A	W	3-0	Little 2, Fletcher
		1 2L	24.11.45	Wisbech T		H	W	5-0	Parker 3, Price 2
		2 1L	8.12.45	QPR	3S	A	L	0-4	
		2 2L	15.12.45	QPR		H	L	0-2	
1946-47	3S	1	30.11.46	Torquay U	3S	H	W	2-0	T.Parker, S.Parker
		2	14.12.46	Walsall	3S	A	D	0-0	
		2r	18.12.46	Walsall		H	L	0-1	
1947-48	3S	1	29.11.47	Swindon T	3S	A	L	2-4	T.Parker, S.Parker
1948-49	3S	1	27.11.48	Aldershot	3S	H	–	1-0	Dempsey
			abandoned after 63 minutes						
		1	4.12.48	Aldershot		H	L	0-3	
1949-50	3S	1	26.11.49	Brighton & HA	3S	H	W	2-1	Baird, Brown
		2	10.12.49	Chelmsford C	SL	A	D	1-1	Brown
		2r	14.12.49	Chelmsford C		H	W	1-0aet	S.Parker
		3	7.1.50	West Ham	D2	A	L	1-5	S.Parker
1950-51	3S	1	25.11.50	Leyton O	3S	A	W	2-1	T.Parker, Jennings
		2	9.12.50	Brighton & HA	3S	A	L	0-2	
1951-52	3S	1	29.11.51	Merthyr Tydfil	SL	A	D	2-2	McCrory, Garneys
		1r	5.12.51	Merthyr Tydfil		H	W	1-0	Roberts
		2	15.12.51	Exeter C	3S	H	W	4-0	Garneys 2, Driver, Dobson
		3	12.1.52	Gateshead	3N	H	D	2-2	Garneys, Myles
		3r	6.1.52	Gateshead		A	D	3-3aet	Dobson 2, Roberts
		3 2r	21.1.52	Gateshead at Bramall Lane			L	1-2aet	Garneys
1952-53	3S	1	22.11.52	Bournemouth	3S	H	D	1-1	Elsworthy
		1r	26.11.52	Bournemouth		A	D	2-2aet	Elsworthy, Garneys
		1 2r	1.12.52	Bournemouth at Highbury			W	3-2	Garneys 2, Gaynor
		2	6.12.52	Bradford C	3N	A	D	1-1	Elsworthy
		2r	10.12.52	Bradford C		H	W	5-1	Brown 2, Elsworthy 2, Garneys
		3	10.1.53	Everton	D2	A	L	2-3	Brown, Garneys
1953-54	3S	1	21.11.53	Reading	3S	H	W	4-1	Garneys 2, Elsworthy, Crowe
		2	12.12.53	Walthamstow Ave	IL	H	D	2-2	Myles, Brown
		2r	16.12.53	Walthamstow Ave		A	W	1-0	Crowe
		3	9.1.54	Oldham A	D2	H	D	3-3	Myles, Reed, Garneys
		3r	12.1.54	Oldham A		A	W	1-0	Garneys
		4	30.1.54	Birmingham C	D2	H	W	1-0	Reed
		5	20.2.54	Preston NE	D1	A	L	1-6	Garneys
1954-55	D2	3	8.1.55	Bishop Auckland	NL	H	D	2-2	Reed, Garneys
		3r	12.1.55	Bishop Auckland		A	L	0-3	
1955-56	3S	1	19.11.55	Peterborough U	ML	A	L	1-3	T.Parker
1956-57	3S	1	17.11.56	Hastings U	SL	H	W	4-0	Phillips 2, Leadbetter, Garneys
		2	8.12.56	Watford	3S	A	W	3-1	Phillips 2, Garneys
		3	5.1.57	Fulham	D2	H	L	2-3	Phillips, Garneys
1957-58	D2	3	4.1.58	Crystal P	3S	A	W	1-0	McLuckie
		4	25.1.58	Manchester U	D1	A	L	0-2	
1958-59	D2	3	10.1.59	Huddersfield T	D2	H	W	1-0	Crawford
		4	24.1.59	Stoke C	D2	A	W	1-0	Rees
		5	14.2.59	Luton T	D1	H	L	2-5	Rees 2
1959-60	D2	3	9.1.60	Peterborough U	ML	H	L	2-3	Phillips, Millward
1960-61	D2	3	7.1.61	Southampton	D2	A	L	1-7	Page og
1961-62	D1	3	6.1.62	Luton T	D2	H	D	1-1	Phillips
		3r	10.1.62	Luton T		A	D	1-1aet	Elsworthy
		3 2r	15.1.62	Luton T at Highbury			W	5-1	Stephenson 2, Phillips 2, Moran
		4	27.1.62	Norwich C	D2	A	D	1-1	Leadbetter
		4r	30.1.62	Norwich C		H	L	1-2	Crawford
1962-63	D1	3	9.1.63	Mansfield T	D4	A	W	3-2	Leadbetter 3
		4	30.1.63	Leicester C	D1	A	L	1-3	Blackwood
1963-64	D1	3	4.1.64	Oldham A	D3	H	W	6-3	Baker 3, Hegan 2, Broadfoot
		4	25.1.64	Stoke C	D1	H	D	1-1	Baxter
		4r	29.1.64	Stoke C		A	L	0-1	
1964-65	D2	3	9.1.65	Swindon T	D2	A	W	2-1	Brogan 2

Season	Div	Rd	Date	Opponent		Venue	Res	Score	Scorers
		4	30.1.65	Tottenham H	D1	A	L	0-5	
1965-66	D2	3	22.1.66	Southport	D4	A	D	0-0	
		3r	25.1.66	Southport		H	L	2-3	Baker, Brogan
1966-67	D2	3	28.1.67	Shrewsbury T	D3	H	W	4-1	Hegan, Crawford, Brogan, Harper
		4	18.2.67	Carlisle U	D2	H	W	2-0	Brogan, Crawford
		5	11.3.67	Manchester C	D1	H	D	1-1	Crawford
		5r	14.3.67	Manchester C		A	L	0-3	
1967-68	D2	3	27.1.68	Chelsea	D1	A	L	0-3	
1968-69	D1	3	4.1.69	Everton	D1	A	L	1-2	O'Rourke
1969-70	D1	3	3.1.70	Manchester U	D1	H	L	0-1	
1970-71	D1	3	11.1.71	Newcastle U	D1	A	D	1-1	Mills
		3r	13.1.71	Newcastle U		H	W	2-1	Viljoen, Hill
		4	23.1.71	WBA	D1	A	D	1-1	Clarke
		4r	26.1.71	WBA		H	W	3-0	Viljoen, Clarke, Robertson
		5	13.2.71	Stoke C	D1	A	D	0-0	
		5r	16.2.71	Stoke C		H	L	0-1	
1971-72	D1	3	15.1.72	Peterborough U	D4	A	W	2-0	Hill, Viljoen
		4	5.2.72	Birmingham C	D2	A	L	0-1	
1972-73	D1	3	13.1.73	Chelmsford C	SL	A	W	3-1	Hamilton, Harper, Johnson
		4	3.2.73	Chelsea	D1	A	L	0-2	
1973-74	D1	3	5.1.74	Sheffield U	D1	H	W	3-2	Beattie 2, Hamilton
		4	26.1.74	Manchester U	D1	A	W	1-0	Beattie
		5	16.2.74	Liverpool	D1	A	L	0-2	
1974-75	D1	3	4.1.75	Wolverhampton W	D1	A	W	2-1	Viljoen, Johnson
		4	25.1.75	Liverpool	D1	H	W	1-0	Mills
		5	15.2.75	A. Villa	D2	H	W	3-2	Hamilton 2, Johnson
		6	8.3.75	Leeds U	D1	H	D	0-0	
		6r	11.3.75	Leeds U		A	D	1-1aet	Johnson
		6 2r	25.3.75	Leeds U at Leicester			D	0-0aet	
		6 3r	27.3.75	Leeds U at Leicester			W	3-2	Whymark, Woods, Hamilton
		SF	5.4.75	West Ham	D1		D	0-0	
				played at Villa Park					
		SFr	9.4.75	West Ham			L	1-2	Jennings og
				played at Stamford Bridge					
1975-76	D1	3	3.1.76	Halifax T	D3	H	W	3-1	Lambert 3
		4	24.1.76	Wolverhampton W	D1	H	D	0-0	
		4r	27.1.76	Wolverhampton W		A	L	0-1	
1976-77	D1	3	8.1.77	Bristol C	D1	H	W	4-1	Mariner 2, Gates, Whymark
		4	29.1.77	Wolverhampton W	D2	H	D	2-2	Mariner, Burley
		4r	2.2.77	Wolverhampton W		A	L	0-1	
1977-78	D1	3	7.1.78	Cardiff C	D2	A	W	2-0	Mariner
		4	28.1.78	Hartlepool	D4	A	W	4-1	Viljoen 2, Mariner, Talbot
		5	18.2.78	Bristol R	D2	A	D	2-2	Turner 2
		5r	28.2.78	Bristol R		H	W	3-0	Mills, Mariner, Woods
		6	11.3.78	Millwall	D2	A	W	6-1	Mariner 3, Burley, Talbot, Wark
		SF	8.4.78	WBA	D1		W	3-1	Talbot, Mills, Wark
				played at Highbury					
		F	6.5.78	ARSENAL	D1	WEMBLEY	W	1-0	Osborne
1978-79	D1	3	10.1.79	Carlisle U	D3	H	W	3-2	Wark, Muhren, Beattie
		4	27.1.79	Orient	D2	H	D	0-0	
		4r	30.1.79	Orient		A	W	2-0	Mariner 2
		5	26.2.79	Bristol R	D2	H	W	6-1	Brazil 2, Mills, Mariner, Muhren, Geddis
		6	10.3.79	Liverpool	D1	H	L	0-1	
1979-80	D1	3	5.1.80	Preston NE	D2	A	W	3-0	Mariner 2, Brazil
		4	26.1.80	Bristol C	D1	A	W	2-1	Wark, Mariner
		5	16.2.80	Chester	D3	H	W	2-1	Wark, Burley
		6	8.3.80	Everton	D1	A	L	1-2	Beattie
1980-81	D1	3	3.1.81	A. Villa	D1	H	W	1-0	Mariner
		4	24.1.81	Shrewsbury T	D2	H	D	0-0	
		4r	27.1.81	Shrewsbury T		A	W	3-0	Gates 2, Wark
		5	14.2.81	Charlton A	D3	H	W	2-0	Wark, Mariner
		6	7.3.81	Nottingham F	D1	A	D	3-3	Mariner, Anderson o.g, Thyssen
		6r	10.3.81	Nottingham F		H	W	1-0	Muhren
		SF	11.4.81	Manchester C			L	0-1	
				played at Villa Park					
1981-82	D1	3	2.1.82	Birmingham C	D1	A	W	3-2	Brazil 2, Wark
		4	23.1.82	Luton T	D2	A	W	3-0	Gates 2, Brazil

IPSWICH TOWN

		5	13.2.82	**Shrewsbury T**	D2	A	L	1-2	D'Avray
1982-83	D1	3	8.1.83	**Charlton A**	D2	A	W	3-2	Wark 2, Thijssen
		4	29.1.83	**Grimsby T**	D2	H	W	2-0	Osman, McCall
		5	19.2.83	**Norwich C**	D1	A	L	0-1	
1983-84	D1	3	7.1.84	**Cardiff C**	D2	A	W	3-0	Gates 3
		4	28.1.84	**Shrewsbury T**	D2	A	L	0-2	
1984-85	D1	3	5.1.85	**Bristol R**	D3	A	W	2-1	Dozzell, Brennan
		4	26.1.85	**Gillingham**	D3	H	W	3-2	Wilson, Sage og, Dozzell
		5	4.3.85	**Sheffield W**	D1	H	W	3-2	Zondervan, Burley, Sunderland
		6	9.3.85	**Everton**	D1	A	D	2-2	Wilson, Zondervan
		6r	13.3.85	**Everton**		H	L	0-1	
1985-86	D1	3	4.1.86	**Bradford C**	D2	H	D	4-4	Evans, Wilson, Brennan, D'Avray
		3r	13.1.86	**Bradford C** at Elland Road		A	W	1-0aet	Brennan
		4	25.1.86	**West Ham**	D1	A	D	0-0	
		4r	4.2.86	**West Ham**		H	D	1-1aet	Dozzell
		4 2r	6.2.86	**West Ham**		H	L	0-1aet	
1986-87	D2	3	10.1.87	**Birmingham C**	D2	H	L	0-1	
1987-88	D2	3	10.1.88	**Manchester U**	D1	H	L	1-2	Humes
1988-89	D2	3	7.1.89	**Nottingham F**	D1	A	L	0-3	
1989-90	D2	3	6.1.90	**Leeds U**	D2	A	W	1-0	Dozzell
		4	27.1.90	**Barnsley**	D2	A	L	0-2	
1990-91	D2	3	5.1.91	**Southampton**	D1	A	L	2-3	Dozzell 2
1991-92	D2	3	4.1.92	**Hartlepool U**	D3	H	D	1-1	Dozzell
		3r	15.1.92	**Hartlepool U**		A	W	2-0	Dozzell, Milton
		4	5.2.92	**Bournemouth**	D3	H	W	3-0	Dozzell, Whitton, Kiwomya
		5	16.2.92	**Liverpool**	D1	H	D	0-0	
		5r	26.2.92	**Liverpool**		A	L	2-3aet	Johnson, Dozzell
1992-93	PL	3	12.1.93	**Plymouth A**	D2	A	W	3-1	Thompson, Dozzell, Whitton (p)
		4	23.1.93	**Tranmere R**	D1	A	W	2-1	Dozzell, Guentchev
		5	13.2.93	**Grimsby T**	D1	H	W	4-0	Guentchev 3, Wark
		6	6.3.93	**Arsenal**	PL	H	L	2-4	Kiwomya, Guentchev

IRTHLINGBOROUGH TOWN

First competed in FA Cup: 1902

1906-07	UCL	1	12.1.07	**Port Vale**	D2	H	L	1-7	Barker

IRWELL SPRINGS

Formed 1879. Based in Bacup and played at the Broad Clough, near The Roebuck pub.

1882-83	1	28.10.82	**Lower Darwen**		A	L	2-5	Banham, Pickles
1883-84	1	17.11.83	**Rossendale**		A	L	2-6	
		Irwell re-instated after Rossendale disqualified for professionalism						
	2	1.12.83	**Hurst**		A	L	2-3	
		Replay ordered after protest, but Hurst scratched						
	3	29.12.83	**Bolton W**		A	L	1-8	

JARDINES LTD, NOTTINGHAM

Formed 1874. A Nottingham works team that played on a pitch at Sherwood Forest.

1887-88	1	15.10.87	**Notts Rangers**		A	L	1-10

JARROW

First entered FA Cup: 1895 and took part in the competition until 1949. **Cup Final Connection:** Alf Common (Sheffield U 1902) played for Jarrow

1898-99	NAII	1	28.1.99	**Everton**	D1	A	L	1-3	McDonald
1899-00	NAII	1	27.1.00	**Millwall Ath**	SL	H	L	0-2	
1930-31	NEL	1	29.11.30	**Crewe A**	3N	A	L	0-1	

KELLS UNITED

First entered FA Cup: 1931. Kells were a mining works club from Whitehaven.

1935-36	Cumb	1	30.11.35	**Stalybridge C**	CC	A	L	0-4

KETTERING TOWN

Formed 1880. **First entered FA Cup:** 1888. **FA Challenge Trophy Runners-up:** 1979. **League clubs beaten:** Chesterfield, Swindon T, Millwall, Swansea C, Oxford U, Bristol R, Halifax T, Maidstone U

1895-96	ML	1	1.2.96	**Newton Heath**	D2	A	L	1-2	Pell
1896-97	ML	1	30.1.97	**Newton Heath**	D2	A	L	1-5	Dixon
1898-99	ML	4q **Loughborough** (H) 2-1; 5q **Leicester Fosse** (H) 1-1; 5qr **Leicester F** (A) 2-1
		1	28.1.99	**Notts Co**	D1	A	L	0-2
1900-01	ML	1	9.2.01	**Chesterfield**	D2	H	D	1-1	McMain
		1r	13.2.01	**Chesterfield**		A	W	2-1aet	Webb, own goal
		2	23.2.01	**Middlesbrough**	D2	A	L	0-5
1905-06	UCL	1	13.1.06	**Derby Co**	D1	A	L	0-4
1908-09	UCL	1	6.1.09	**Bury**	D1	A	L	0-8
1925-26	SL	1	28.11.25	**Worcester C**	BDL	A	D	0-0
		1r	3.12.25	**Worcester C**		H	D	0-0aet
		1 2r	7.12.25	**Worcester C** at St Andrews			W	2-0	Allison, Starsmore
		2	12.12.25	**Grimsby T**	3N	H	D	1-1	Allison
		2r	15.12.25	**Grimsby T**		A	L	1-3	Cairns
1926-27	SL	1	27.11.26	**Coventry C**	3S	H	L	2-3	Chalmers, Butler
1927-28	SL	1	26.11.27	**Chatham**	SL	H	W	2-0	Simpson, Starsmore
		2	10.12.27	**Charlton A**	3S	A	D	1-1	Allison
		2r	15.12.27	**Charlton A**		H	L	1-2	Charlesworth
1928-29	SL	1	24.11.28	**Crystal P**	3S	A	L	0-2
1929-30	SL	1	30.11.29	**Newport Co**	3S	A	L	2-3	Houston, Duncan
1933-34	UCL	1	25.11.33	**QPR**	3S	A	L	0-6
1937-38	UCL	1	27.11.37	**Crystal P**	3S	A	D	2-2	Carr, Potter
		1r	2.12.37	**Crystal P**		H	L	0-4
1945-46	UCL	1 1L	17.11.45	**Grantham**	ML	H	L	1-5	Smith
		1 2L	24.11.45	**Grantham**		A	D	2-2	Smith, Malloy
1951-52	SL	1	24.11.51	**Bristol R**	3S	A	L	0-3
1953-54	SL	1	21.11.53	**Leyton O**	3S	A	L	0-3
1954-55	SL	1	20.11.54	**Bishop Auckland**	NL	A	L	1-5	Lane
1958-59	SL	1	15.11.58	**Peterborough U**	ML	A	D	2-2	Toseland, Draper
		1r	20.11.58	**Peterborough U**		H	L	2-3	Draper, Burrows
1959-60	SL	1	14.11.59	**Margate**	SL	H	D	1-1	Burrows
		1r	19.11.59	**Margate**		A	L	2-3	Toseland 2
1960-61	SL	1	5.11.60	**Wycombe W**	IL	A	W	2-1	Morrow, Walden
		2	26.11.60	**Reading**	D3	A	L	2-4	Walden, Morrow
1961-62	SL	1	4.11.61	**Swindon T**	D3	A	D	2-2	Golding, Curran (p)
		1r	8.11.61	**Swindon T**		H	W	3-0	Curran 2 (1p), Ritchie
		2	25.11.61	**Northampton T**	D3	A	L	0-3
1963-64	SL	1	16.11.63	**Millwall**	D3	H	D	1-1	Snowdon og
		1r	25.11.63	**Millwall**		A	W	3-2	Armour 2, Daldy
		2	7.12.63	**Oxford U**	D4	A	L	1-2	Curran
1964-65	SL	1	14.11.64	**Millwall**	D4	A	L	0-2
1968-69	SL	1	16.11.68	**Waterlooville**	SL	A	W	2-1	Gully, Daldy
		2	7.12.68	**Dartford**	SL	H	W	5-0	Lillis og, Gully, Daldy, Smith, Walden
		3	4.1.69	**Bristol R**	D3	A	D	1-1	Reed
		3r	8.1.69	**Bristol R**		H	L	1-2	Daldy
1969-70	SL	1	15.11.69	**Swansea T**	D4	H	L	0-2
1971-72	SL	1	20.11.71	**Barnet**	SL	H	L	2-4	King og, Jacques
1972-73	SL	1	18.11.72	**Walsall**	D3	A	D	3-3	Clayton 2, Pawley
		1r	22.11.72	**Walsall**		H	L	1-2	Pawley
1974-75	SL	1	26.11.74	**Swansea C**	D4	A	D	1-1	Atkinson
		1r	2.12.74	**Swansea C**		H	W	3-1	Pawley, Ashby (p), Clayton
		2	14.12.74	**Wimbledon**	SL	A	L	0-2
1976-77	SL	1	20.11.76	**Oxford U**	D3	H	D	1-1	Merrick
		1r	23.11.76	**Oxford U**		A	W	1-0	Dougan
		2	11.12.76	**Tooting & Mitcham U**	IL	H	W	1-0	Clayton
		3	8.1.77	**Colchester U**	D4	H	L	2-3	Clayton, Kellock
1977-78	SL	1	26.11.77	**Tilbury**	IL	A	W	1-0	Phipps
			FA declared match void as Kettering fielded ineligible player
		1	5.12.77	**Tilbury**		A	D	2-2	Kellock, Phipps
		1r	7.12.77	**Tilbury**		H	L	2-3	Kellock, Phipps
1979-80	APL	1	24.11.79	**Reading**	D3	A	L	2-4	Phipps 2
1980-81	APL	1	22.11.80	**Maidstone U**	APL	H	D	1-1	Guy

Season	Comp	Round	Date	Opponent	Div	H/A	Res	Score	Scorers
		1r	26.11.80	Maidstone U		A	D	0-0aet	
		1 2r	1.12.80	Maidstone U		A	L	1-3	Middleton
1981-82	APL	1	21.11.81	Boston U	APL	A	W	1-0	Atkins
		2	2.1.82	Blackpool	D4	H	L	0-3	
1982-83	APL	1	20.11.82	Walsall	D3	A	L	0-3	
1983-84	APL	1	19.11.83	Swindon T	D4	H	L	0-7	
1984-85	APL	1	17.11.84	Bournemouth	D2	H	D	0-0	
		1r	20.11.84	Bournemouth		A	L	2-3	Alexander, Jeffrey
1986-87	GMVC	1	15.11.86	Gillingham	D3	H	L	0-3	
1988-89	GMVC	1	19.11.88	Dartford	SL	H	W	2-1	Lewis, Griffith
		2	10.12.88	Bristol R	D3	H	W	2-1	Cooke 2
		3	7.1.89	Halifax T	D4	H	D	1-1	Griffith
		3r	10.1.89	Halifax T		A	W	3-2	Lewis, Cooke 2
		4	28.1.89	Charlton A	D1	A	L	1-2	Cooke
1989-90	GMVC	1	18.11.89	Northampton T	D3	H	L	0-1	
1991-92	GMVC	1	16.11.91	Wycombe W	GMVC	H	D	1-1	Christie
		1r	27.11.91	Wycombe W		A	W	2-0	Brown, Graham
		2	7.12.91	Maidstone U	D4	A	W	2-1	Brown, Oxbrow og
		3	4.1.92	Blackburn R	D2	A	L	1-4	Brown
1992-93	GMVC	1	14.11.92	Gillingham	D3	A	L	2-3	Brown, Hill (p)

KIDDERMINSTER HARRIERS

Formed 1886. First entered FA Cup: 1890. FA Trophy Winners: 1987. Runners-up: 1991

Season	Comp	Round	Date	Opponent	Div	H/A	Res	Score	Scorers
1890-91	BDL	1	17.1.90	Darwen	FAll	A	L	1-3	Smith
		replay ordered after protests							
		1r	24.1.91	Darwen		A	L	0-13	
1906-07	BDL	1	12.1.07	Oldham A	LC	A	L	0-5	
1935-36	BDL	1	30.11.35	Bishop Auckland	NL	H	W	4-1	Boswell 3, Salters
		2	14.12.35	Workington	NEL	A	L	1-5	Boswell
1937-38	BDL	1	27.11.37	Newport Co	3S	H	D	2-2	Salters, Buck
		1r	2.12.37	Newport Co		A	L	1-4	Birch
1938-39	BDL	1	26.11.38	Chelmsford C	SL	H	L	0-4	
1948-49	SL	1	27.11.48	Hereford U	SL	H	L	0-3	
1952-53	SL	1	22.11.52	Finchley	AL	H	L	0-1	
1964-65	WMRL	1	14.11.64	Hull C	D3	H	L	1-4	Gosling
1965-66	WMRL	1	13.11.65	Peterborough U	D3	A	L	1-2	Gilbert
1967-68	WMRL	1	9.12.67	Walthamstow Ave	IL	A	L	1-2	P.Wassall (p)
1968-69	WMRL	1	16.11.68	Brighton	D3	A	D	2-2	P.Wassall, B.Wassall
		1r	20.11.68	Brighton		H	L	0-1	
1979-80	SL	1	24.11.79	Blackburn R	D3	H	L	0-2	
1980-81	SL	1	22.11.80	Millwall	D3	H	D	1-1	Wright
		1r	25.11.80	Millwall		A	L	0-1	
1987-88	GMVC	1	14.11.87	Halesowen T	SL	A	D	2-2	Hazelwood, Woodhall
		1r	16.11.87	Halesowen T		H	W	4-0	Tuohy 2, Davies, R Jones
		2	5.12.87	Maidstone U	GMVC	A	D	1-1	Davies
		2r	7.12.87	Maidstone U		H	D	2-2aet	Tuohy, Casey
		2 2r	14.12.87	Maidstone U		H	D	0-0aet	
		2 3r	16.12.87	Maidstone U		A	L	1-2	Casey
1989-90	GMVC	1	18.11.89	Swansea C	D3	H	L	2-3	Forsyth, Bancroft
1990-91	GMVC	1	17.11.90	Woking	IL	A	D	0-0	
		1r	21.11.90	Woking		H	D	1-1aet	Davies
		1 2r	26.11.90	Woking		H	L	1-2	Lilwall
1991-92	GMVC	1	16.11.91	Aylesbury U	IL	H	L	0-1	
1992-93	GMVC	1	14.11.92	Exeter C	D2	A	L	0-1	

KILDARE FC

Formed 1877. Played at Kensal Green, in North West London. Used the Mason's Circus pub as their changing rooms.

Season	Round	Date	Opponent	H/A	Res	Score	Notes
1879-80	1	1.11.79	Gresham	A	L	0-3	
1880-81	1	13.11.80	Acton	A	D	1-1	
	1r	20.11.80	Acton	H	L	0-5	
1881-82	1	5.11.81	Royal Engineers	A	L	0-6	
1882-83	1	4.11.82	Clapham Rovers	A	L	0-3	
1883-84	1		Clapham Rovers				*scratched*

KING'S LYNN

Formed 1879. **First entered FA Cup:** 1900. **FA Amateur Cup Runners-up:** 1901. **League clubs beaten:** Aldershot, Coventry C

1905-06	N&S	1	13.1.06	**A.Villa**	D1	A	L	0-11
1937-38	ECL	1	27.11.37	**Bromley**	AL	H	L	0-4
1949-50	ECL	1	26.11.49	**Nuneaton B**	BC	A	L	1-2	Everitt
1951-52	ECL	1	24.11.51	**Exeter C**	3S	H	L	1-3	Whitelumb
1958-59	SL	1	15.11.58	**Merthyr T**	SL	H	W	2-1	Neilson, Dixon
		2	6.12.58	**Brentford**	D3	A	L	1-3	Dixon
1959-60	SL	1	14.11.59	**Aldershot**	D4	H	W	3-1	Dixon 2, Luke
		2	5.12.59	**Reading**	D3	A	L	2-4	Luke, Dixon
1960-61	SL	1	5.11.60	**Loughborough**	CA	A	D	0-0
		1r	9.11.60	**Loughborough**		H	W	3-0	Sewell, Sharp, Dixon
		2	26.11.60	**Bristol C**	D3	H	D	2-2	Sewell, Dunn
		2r	29.11.60	**Bristol C**		A	L	0-3
1961-62	SL	1	4.11.61	**Chelmsford C**	SL	A	W	2-1	Bacon, Wright
		2	25.11.61	**Coventry C**	D3	A	W	2-1	Johnson, Wright
		3	6.1.62	**Everton**	D1	A	L	0-4
1962-63	SL	1	3.11.62	**Boston U**	ML	A	W	2-1	Coates 2
		2	24.11.62	**Oxford U**	D4	H	L	1-2	Wright
1964-65	SL	1	14.11.64	**Shrewsbury T**	D3	H	L	0-1
1968-69	SL	1	16.11.68	**Southend U**	D4	A	L	0-9
1971-72	SL	1	20.11.71	**Hereford U**	SL	H	D	0-0
		1r	24.11.71	**Hereford U**		A	L	0-1
1973-74	SL	1	24.11.73	**Wimbledon**	SL	H	W	1-0	Elliott
		2	15.12.73	**Alvechurch**	WMRL	A	L	1-6	Lindsay
1984-85	SL	1	17.11.84	**Bristol R**	D3	A	L	1-2	Adams

KINGSTONIAN

Formed 1885. **First entered FA Cup:** 1919. **FA Amateur Cup Winners:** 1933. **Runners-up:** 1960

1926-27	AL	1	27.11.26	**Nunhead**	IL	A	L	0-9
1930-31	IL	1	29.11.30	**Tunbridge Wells R**	KL	A	L	0-3
1932-33	IL	1	26.11.32	**Luton T**	3S	A	D	2-2	Gibson, Birks
		1r	30.11.32	**Luton T**		H	L	2-3	Birks, Gibson
1933-34	IL	1	25.11.33	**Bristol C**	3S	A	L	1-7	Whitehead
1992-93	IL	1	14.11.92	**Peterborough U**	D1	H	D	1-1	Russell
		1r	25.11.92	**Peterborough U**		A	L	1-9	Finch
			FA ordered match to be replayed after Kingstonian goalkeeper was struck by a missile				
		1r	4.12.92	**Peterborough U**		A	L	0-1
			played at London Road, Peterborough, behind closed doors				

KIRKBY TOWN

Formed 1962. **First entered FA Cup:** 1966. Disbanded and reformed twice. Changed name to Knowsley United in 1988

1969-70	LC	1	15.11.69	**Bangor C**	NPL	A	L	0-6

LANCASTER CITY

Formed 1902 as Lancaster Town. **First entered FA Cup:** 1906. Renamed City of Lancaster, 1983. **League clubs beaten:** Barrow, Stockport Co

as Lancaster Town

1921-22	LC	4q	**Barrow** (3N) A 2-2; 4qr **Barrow** (H) 1-0; 5q **Stockport Co** (3N) H 2-0; 6q **Northampton** (3S) A 0-1				
1928-29	LC	1	24.11.28	**Lincoln C**	3N	H	L	1-3	Grass
1929-30	LC	1	30.11.29	**New Brighton**	3N	A	L	1-4	Longworth
1930-31	LC	1	29.11.30	**Accrington S**	3N	A	L	1-3	Pilkington
1931-32	LC	1	28.11.31	**Blyth Spartans**	NEL	H	L	0-3
1933-34	LC	1	25.11.33	**Stockport Co**	3N	H	L	0-1
1937-38	LC	1	27.11.37	**Accrington S**	3N	A	D	1-1	Lewitt
		1r	1.12.37	**Accrington S**		H	D	1-1	Clarke
		1 2r	6.12.37	**Accrington S** at Preston			L	0-4

as Lancaster City

1938-39	LC	1	26.11.38	**Scunthorpe U**	ML	A	L	2-4	Heaton, O'Connor
1946-47	LC	1	30.11.46	**Spennymoor U**	NEL	H	W	1-0	Downham
		2	14.12.46	**Gateshead**	3N	A	L	0-4

1947-48	LC	1	29.11.47 **Oldham A**	3N	A	L	0-6
1972-73	NPL	1	18.11.72 **Boston U**	NPL	A	W	2-1	Donegan, Cullingford
		2	9.12.72 **Notts Co**	D3	A	L	1-2	Whitbread

LANCING OLD BOYS

Team formed by old boys of Lancing School

1885-86	1	31.10.85 **Barnes**	A	W	7-1
	2	14.11.85 **Brentwood**	A	L	1-6
1887-88	1	8.10.87 **Old Etonians**	A	L	2-4

AP LEAMINGTON

Formed 1945 as Lockheed Leamington. **First entered FA Cup: 1948**

1974-75	SL	1	23.11.74 **Southend U**	D3	H	L	1-2	Lee
1975-76	SL	1	22.11.75 **Stafford R**	NPL	H	L	2-3	Keeley 2
1977-78	SL	1	26.11.77 **Enderby**	SL	H	W	6-1	Stewart, Brown 3, Cavenagh (p), Keeley
		2	17.12.77 **Southend U**	D4	H	D	0-0	
		2r	19.12.77 **Southend U**		A	L	0-4	
1978-79	SL	1	25.11.78 **Dartford**	SL	A	W	2-1	Gardner 2
		2	16.12.78 **Torquay U**	D4	H	L	0-1	
1979-80	APL	1	24.11.79 **Tranmere R**	D4	A	L	0-9	
1983-84	SL	1	19.11.83 **Gillingham**	D3	H	L	0-1	

LEATHERHEAD

Formed 1946. **First entered FA Cup: 1947. FA Challenge Trophy Runners-up: 1974. League clubs beaten:** Colchester U, Brighton, Cambridge U, Northampton T

1974-75	IL	1	23.11.74 **Bishops Stortford**	IL	A	D	0-0	
		1r	26.11.74 **Bishops Stortford**		H	W	2-0	Layers, Doyle
		2	14.12.74 **Colchester U**	D3	H	W	1-0	Doyle
		3	4.1.75 **Brighton**	D3	A	W	1-0	Kelly
		4	25.1.75 **Leicester C**	D1	H	L	2-3	McGillicuddy, Kelly
			played at Filbert St					
1975-76	IL	1	22.11.75 **Cambridge U**	D4	H	W	2-0	Batson og, Doyle
		2	13.12.75 **Tooting & Mitcham**	IL	H	D	0-0	
		2r	16.12.75 **Tooting & Mitcham**		A	–	1-1	Cooper
			abandoned after 57 minutes – icy pitch					
		2r	22.12.75 **Tooting & Mitcham**		A	L	1-2aet	Reid
1976-77	IL	1	20.11.76 **Northampton T**	D3	H	W	2-0	Doyle 2
		2	14.12.76 **Wimbledon**	SL	H	L	1-3	Reid
1977-78	IL	1	26.11.77 **Swansea C**	D4	H	D	0-0	
		1r	29.11.77 **Swansea C**		A	L	1-2	Baker
1978-79	IL	1	25.11.78 **Merthyr T**	SL	H	W	2-1	Baker, Camp
		2	16.12.78 **Colchester U**	D3	H	D	1-1	Kelly
		2r	19.12.78 **Colchester U**		A	L	0-4	
1980-81	IL	1	22.11.80 **Exeter C**	D3	A	L	0-5	

LEEDS CITY

Formed 1904. Wound-up by the FA in October 1919 following allegations of illegal payments

1904-05	WYL	1q	**Rockingham Colliery** (A) 1-3					
1905-06	D2		1q **Morley** (H) 11-0; 2q **Mexborough** (H) 1-1; 2q r **Mexborough** (A) 1-1; 2q 2r **Mexborough** (H) 3-2; 3q **Hull C** (A) 1-1; 3qr **Hull C** (H) 1-2					
1906-07	D2	1	12.1.07 **Bristol C**	D1	A	L	1-4	McLeod
1907-08	D2	1	11.1.08 **Oldham A**	D2	A	L	1-2	Parnell
1908-09	D2	1	16.1.09 **Oldham A**	D2	A	D	1-1	McLeod
		1r	20.1.09 **Oldham A**		H	W	2-0	McLeod (p), Guy
		2	6.2.09 **West Ham**	SL	H	D	1-1	Burnett
		2r	11.2.09 **West Ham**		A	L	1-2aet	Bowman
1909-10	D2	1	15.1.10 **Sunderland**	D1	A	L	0-1	
1910-11	D2	1	14.1.11 **Brighton & HA**	SL	H	L	1-3	Roberts
1911-12	D2	1	13.1.12 **Glossop**	D2	H	W	1-0	Roberts
		2	3.2.12 **WBA**	D1	H	L	0-1	

LEEDS CITY

1912-13	D2	1	15.1.13 Burnley	D2	H	D	2-3	McLeod, Foley
1913-14	D2	1	10.1.14 Gainsborough T	ML	H	W	4-2	Jackson 2, Law, McLeod
		2	31.1.14 WBA	D1	H	L	0-2	
1914-15	D2	1	9.1.15 Derby Co	D2	A	W	2-1	McLeod, Sharpe
		2	30.1.15 QPR	SL	A	L	0-1	

LEEDS UNITED

Formed 1919 after disbandonment of Leeds City. Played their first season in the Midland League. **FA Cup Winners:** 1972 **FA Cup Runners-up:** 1965, 1970, 1973 **Record FA Cup Win:** 8-1 vs Crystal Palace, 3rd round, 11.1.1930, 7-0 vs Leeds Steelworks, preliminary round, 25.9.1920 **Record FA Cup Defeat:** 2-7 vs Middlesbrough, 3rd round, second leg, 9.1.1946

1919-20	ML		*did not enter*					
1920-21	D2	1q	**Boothtown** (H) 5-2; 2q **Leeds Steelworks** (H) 7-0. Leeds withdrew					
1921-22	D2	1	7.1.22 Swindon T	3S	A	L	1-2	Swann
1922-23	D2	1	13.1.23 Portsmouth	3S	A	D	0-0	
		1r	17.1.23 Portsmouth		H	W	3-1	Whipp, Armitage, Swann
		2	3.2.23 Bolton W	D1	A	L	1-3	Swann
1923-24	D2	1	12.1.24 Stoke	D2	H	W	1-0	Harris
		2	2.2.24 West Ham	D1	A	D	1-1	Coates
		2r	6.2.24 West Ham		H	W	1-0	Whipp
		3	23.2.24 Aston Villa	D1	A	L	0-3	
1924-25	D1	1	10.1.25 Liverpool	D1	A	L	0-3	
1925-26	D1	3	9.1.26 Middlesbrough	D2	A	L	1-5	Armand (p)
1926-27	D1	3	8.1.27 Sunderland	D1	H	W	3-2	Jennings 2 (1p), Duggan
		4	29.1.27 Bolton W	D1	H	D	0-0	
		4r	2.2.27 Bolton W		A	L	0-3	
1927-28	D2	3	14.1.28 Manchester C	D2	A	L	0-1	
1928-29	D1	3	12.1.29 Exeter C	3S	A	D	2-2	Keetley, Menzies
		3r	16.1.29 Exeter C		H	W	5-1	Waisncoat, Reed, Cochrane, Keetley, Lowton og
		4	26.1.29 Huddersfield T	D1	A	L	0-3	
1929-30	D1	3	11.1.30 Crystal Palace	3S	H	W	8-1	Wainscoat 3, Jennnigs 2, White 2, Turnbull
		4	25.1.30 West Ham	D1	A	L	1-4	Jennings
1930-31	D1	3	10.1.31 Huddersfield T	D1	H	W	2-0	Hydes, Furness
		4	24.1.31 Newcastle U	D1	H	W	4-1	Furness, Wainscoat 2, Mitchell
		5	14.2.31 Exeter C	3S	A	L	1-3	Mitchell
1931-32	D2	3	9.1.32 QPR	3S	A	L	1-3	J.Milburn (p)
1932-33	D1	3	14.1.33 Newcastle U	D1	A	W	3-0	Hydes 3
		4	28.1.33 Tranmere R	3N	A	D	0-0	
		4r	1.2.33 Tranmere R		H	W	4-0	J.Milburn (p), Mahon, Cochrane, Hydes
		5	18.2.33 Everton	D1	A	L	0-2	
1933-34	D1	3	13.1.34 Preston NE	D2	H	L	0-1	
1934-35	D1	3	12.1.35 Bradford PA	D2	H	W	4-1	Hydes 2, Furness, Mahon
		4	26.1.35 Norwich C	D2	A	D	3-3	Mahon, Duggan, Cochrane
		4r	30.1.35 Norwich C		H	L	1-2	Hydes
1935-36	D1	3	11.1.36 Wolverhampton W	D1	A	D	1-1	McDougall
		3r	15.1.36 Wolverhampton W		H	W	3-1	J.Kelly, Cochrane, Duggan
		4	25.1.36 Bury	D2	H	–	2-1	Furness, Kelly
			abandoned 74 minutes – fog					
			29.1.36 Bury		H	W	3-2	Brown 2, Duggan
		5	15.2.36 Sheffield U	D2	A	L	1-3	Furness
1936-37	D1	3	16.1.37 Chelsea	D1	A	L	0-4	
1937-38	D1	3	8.1.38 Chester	3N	H	W	3-1	Buckley, Ainsley, Armes
		4	22.1.38 Charlton A	D1	A	L	1-2	Hodgson
1938-39	D1	3	17.1.39 Bournemouth	3S	H	W	3-1	Stephenson, Hargreaves, Cochrane
		4	21.1.39 Huddersfield T	D1	H	L	2-4	Hodgson, Cochrane
1945-46	D1	3 1L	5.1.46 Middlesbrough	D1	H	D	4-4	Henry, Ainsley, Hardwick og, Short
		3 2L	9.1.46 Middlesbrough		A	L	2-7	Grainger, Ainsley
1946-47	D1	3	11.1.47 WBA	D2	A	L	1-2	Ainsley
1947-48	D2	3	10.1.48 Blackpool	D1	A	L	0-4	
1948-49	D2	3	8.1.49 Newport Co	3S	H	L	1-3	Browning
1949-50	D2	3	7.1.50 Carlisle U	3N	A	W	5-2	Browning, Dudley 2, Williams, Cochrane
		4	28.1.50 Bolton W	D1	H	D	1-1	Williams
		4r	1.2.50 Bolton W		A	W	3-2aet	Dudley 2, Browning
		5	11.2.50 Cardiff C	D2	H	W	3-1	Williams, Cochrane, Iggleden
		6	4.3.50 Arsenal	D1	A	L	0-1	
1950-51	D2	3	6.1.51 Middlesbrough	D1	H	W	1-0	Browning

Season	Div	Round	Date	Opponent	Comp	H/A	Result	Score	Scorers
		4	27.1.51	Manchester U	D1	A	L	0-4	
1951-52	D2	3	12.1.52	Rochdale	3N	A	W	2-0	Kirk 2
		4	2.2.52	Bradford PA	3N	H	W	2-0	Milburn, Iggleden
		5	23.2.52	Chelsea	D1	H	D	1-1	Milburn
		5r	27.2.52	Chelsea		A	D	1-1aet	Kirk
		5 2r	3.3.52	Chelsea at Villa Pk			L	1-5	Mills
1952-53	D2	3	10.1.53	Brentford	D2	A	L	1-2	Charles
1953-54	D2	3	9.1.54	Tottenham H	D1	H	D	3-3	Iggleden, Charles, Ramsey og
		3r	13.1.54	Tottenham H		A	L	0-1	
1954-55	D2	3	8.1.55	Torquay U	3S	H	D	2-2	Kerfoot, Charles
		3r	12.1.55	Torquay U		A	L	0-4	
1955-56	D2	3	7.1.56	Cardiff C	D1	H	L	1-2	Brook
1956-57	D1	3	5.1.57	Cardiff C	D1	H	L	1-2	Charles
1957-58	D1	3	4.1.58	Cardiff C	D2	H	L	1-2	Forrest
1958-59	D1	3	10.1.59	Luton T	D1	A	L	1-5	Shackleton
1959-60	D1	3	9.1.60	Aston Villa	D2	A	L	1-2	McCole
1960-61	D2	3	7.1.61	Sheffield W	D1	A	L	0-2	
1961-62	D2	3	6.1.62	Derby Co	D2	H	D	2-2	Peyton, Charlton
		3r	10.1.62	Derby Co		A	L	1-3	McAdams
1962-63	D2	3	6.3.63	Stoke C	D2	H	W	3-1	Charlton, Reaney, Hair
		4	16.3.63	Middlesbrough	D2	A	W	2-0	Storrie, Johanneson
		5	19.3.63	Nottingham F	D1	A	L	0-3	
1963-64	D2	3	4.1.64	Cardiff C	D2	H	W	1-0	Bremner
		4	25.1.64	Everton	D1	H	D	1-1	Lawson
		4r	28.1.64	Everton		A	L	0-2	
1964-65	D1	3	9.1.65	Southport	D4	H	W	3-0	Greenhoff, Johanneson, Johnson
		4	30.1.65	Everton	D1	H	D	1-1	Storrie
		4r	2.2.65	Everton		A	W	2-1	Charlton, Weston
		5	20.2.65	Shrewsbury T	D3	H	W	2-0	Giles, Johanneson
		6	10.3.65	Crystal Palace	D2	A	W	3-0	Peacock 2, Storrie
		SF	27.3.65	Manchester U	D1		D	0-0	
			played at Hillsborough						
		SFr	31.3.65	Manchester U at City Ground, Nottingham			W	1-0	Bremner
		F	1.5.65	Liverpool	D1 WEMBLEY		L	1-2aet	Bremner
1965-66	D1	3	22.1.66	Bury	D2	H	W	6-0	Lorimer 3, Reaney, Greenhoff, Giles
		4	12.2.66	Chelsea	D1	A	L	0-1	
1966-67	D1	3	28.1.67	Crystal Palace	D2	H	W	3-0	O'Grady, Bell, Johanneson
		4	18.2.67	WBA	D1	H	W	5-0	Lorimer 2, Madeley, Belfitt 2
		5	11.3.67	Sunderland	D1	A	D	1-1	Charlton
		5r	15.3.67	Sunderland		H	D	1-1aet	Giles
		5 2r	20.2.67	Sunderland at Hull			W	2-1	Belfitt, Giles (p)
		6	8.4.67	Manchester C	D1	H	W	1-0	Charlton
		SF	29.4.67	Chelsea	D1		L	0-1	
			played at Villa Park						
1967-68	D1	3	27.1.68	Derby Co	D2	A	W	2-0	Charlton, Lorimer
		4	17.2.68	Nottingham F	D1	H	W	2-1	Jones, Giles
		5	9.3.68	Bristol C	D2	H	W	2-0	Jones, Lorimer
		6	30.3.68	Sheffield U	D1	H	W	1-0	Madeley
		SF	27.4.68	Everton	D1		L	0-1	
			played at Old Trafford						
1968-69	D1	3	4.1.69	Sheffield W	D1	A	D	1-1	Lorimer (p)
		3r	8.1.69	Sheffield W		H	L	1-3	Johanneson
1969-70	D1	3	3.1.70	Swansea T	D4	H	W	2-1	Giles, Jones
		4	24.1.70	Sutton U	IL	A	W	6-0	Clarke 4, Lorimer 2
		5	7.2.70	Mansfield T	D3	H	W	2-0	Giles, Clarke
		6	21.2.70	Swindon T	D2	A	W	2-0	Clarke 2
		SF	14.3.70	Manchester U	D1		D	0-0	
			played at Hillsborough						
		SFr	23.3.70	Manchester U at Villa Park			D	0-0aet	
		SF2r	26.3.70	Manchester U at Burnden Park, Bolton			W	1-0	Bremner
		F	11.4.70	Chelsea	D1 WEMBLEY		D	2-2aet	Charlton, Jones
		Fr	29.4.70	Chelsea at Old Trafford			L	1-2aet	Jones
1970-71	D1	3	11.1.71	Rotherham U	D3	A	D	0-0	
		3r	18.1.71	Rotherham U		H	W	3-2	Lorimer 2, Giles
		4	23.1.71	Swindon T	D2	H	W	4-0	Jones 3, Clarke
		5	13.2.71	Colchester U	D4	A	L	2-3	Hunter, Giles
1971-72	D1	3	15.1.72	Bristol R	D3	H	W	4-1	Giles 2, Lorimer 2

	4	5.2.72	**Liverpool**	D1	A	D	0-0	
	4r	9.2.72	**Liverpool**		H	W	2-0	Clarke 2
	5	26.2.72	**Cardiff C**	D2	A	W	2-0	Giles 2
	6	18.3.72	**Tottenham H**	D1	H	W	2-1	Clarke, Charlton
	SF	15.4.72	**Birmingham C**	D2		W	3-0	Jones 2, Lorimer
		played at Hillsborough
	F	6.5.72	**ARSENAL**	D1 WEMBLEY	W	1-0	Clarke
1972-73 D1	3	13.1.73	**Norwich C**	D1	A	D	1-1	Lorimer
	3r	17.1.73	**Norwich C**		H	D	1-1aet	Giles
	3 2r	29.1.73	**Norwich C** at Villa Park			W	5-0	Clarke 3, Jones, Lorimer
	4	3.2.73	**Plymouth A**	D3	H	W	2-1	Clarke, Bates
	5	24.2.73	**WBA**	D1	H	W	2-0	Clarke 2
	6	17.3.73	**Derby Co**	D1	A	W	1-0	Lorimer
	SF	7.4.73	**Wolverhampton W**	D1		W	1-0	Bremner
		played at Maine Road
	F	5.4.73	**Sunderland**	D2 WEMBLEY	L	0-1
1973-74 D1	3	5.1.74	**Wolverhampton W**	D1	A	D	1-1	Lorimer
	3r	9.1.74	**Woverhampton W**		H	W	1-0	Jones
	4	26.1.74	**Peterborough U**	D4	A	W	4-1	Lorimer, Jordan 2, Yorath
	5	16.2.74	**Bristol C**	D2	A	D	1-1	Bremner
	5r	19.2.74	**Bristol C**		H	L	0-1
1974-75 D1	3	4.1.75	**Cardiff C**	D2	H	W	4-1	E.Gray, Clarke 2, McKenzie
	4	25.1.75	**Wimbledon**	SL	H	D	0-0
	4r	10.2.75	**Wimbledon** at Selhurst Pk			1-0	Bassett og
	5	18.2.75	**Derby Co**	D1	A	W	1-0	Nish og
	6	8.3.75	**Ipswich T**	D1	A	D	0-0
	6r	11.3.75	**Ipswich T**		H	D	1-1aet	McKenzie
	6 2r	25.3.75	**Ipswich T** at Filbert Street			D	0-0aet
	6 3r	27.3.75	**Ipswich T** at Filbert Street			L	2-3	Clarke, Giles
1975-76 D1	3	3.1.76	**Notts Co**	D2	A	W	1-0	Clarke
	4	24.1.76	**Crystal Palace**	D3	H	L	0-1
1976-77 D1	3	8.1.77	**Norwich C**	D1	H	W	5-2	Clarke, Reaney, Jordan, McQueen, Hampton
	4	29.1.77	**Birmingham C**	D1	A	W	2-1	Jordan, Clarke
	5	26.2.77	**Manchester C**	D1	H	W	1-0	Cherry
	6	19.3.77	**Wolverhampton W**	D1	A	W	1-0	E.Gray
	SF	23.4.77	**Manchester U**		D1	L	1-2	Clarke
		played at Hillsborough
1977-78 D1	3	7.1.78	**Manchester C**	D1	H	L	1-2	F.Gray
1978-79 D1	3	18.1.79	**Hartlepool U**	D4	A	W	6-2	E.Gray 2, Hart, Graham, Harris, F.Gray
	4	26.2.79	**WBA** at the Hawthorns		H	D	3-3	F.Gray, Graham, Harris
	4r	1.3.79	**WBA**		A	L	0-2aet
1979-80 D1	3	5.1.80	**Nottingham F**	D1	H	L	1-4	Lloyd og
1980-81 D1	3	3.1.81	**Coventry C**	D1	H	D	1-1	Hird (p)
	3r	6.1.81	**Coventry C**		A	L	0-1
1981-82 D1	3	2.1.82	**Wolverhampton W**	D1	A	W	3-1	Hamson, Hird, E.Gray
	4	28.1.82	**Tottenham H**	D1	A	L	0-1
1982-83 D2	3	8.1.83	**Preston NE**	D3	H	W	3-0	Sheridan, Connor, Graham
	4	29.1.83	**Arsenal**	D1	A	D	1-1	Nicholas og
	4r	2.2.83	**Arsenal**		H	D	1-1aet	Butterworth
	4 2r	9.2.83	**Arsenal**		A	L	1-2	Connor
1983-84 D2	3	7.1.84	**Scunthorpe U**	D3	H	D	1-1	Wright
	3r	10.1.84	**Scunthorpe U**		A	D	1-1aet	Wright
	3 2r	16.1.84	**Scunthorpe U**		A	L	2-4	Wright, Ritchie
1984-85 D2	3	4.1.85	**Everton**	D1	H	L	0-2
1985-86 D2	3	4.1.86	**Peterborough U**	D4	A	L	0-1
1986-87 D2	3	11.1.87	**Telford U**	GMVC	A	W	2-1	Baird 2
		played at the Hawthorns
	4	3.2.87	**Swindon T**	D3	A	W	2-1	Quinn og, Baird
	5	21.2.87	**QPR**	D1	H	W	2-1	Baird, Ormsby
	6	15.3.87	**Wigan A**	D3	A	W	2-0	Stiles, Adams
	SF	12.4.87	**Coventry C**	D1		L	2-3aet	Rennie, Edwards
		played at Hillsborough
1987-88 D2	3	9.1.88	**Aston Villa**	D2	H	L	1-2	Davidson
1988-89 D2	3	7.1.89	**Brighton & HA**	D2	A	W	2-1	Baird 2
	4	28.1.89	**Nottingham F**	D1	A	L	0-2
1989-90 D2	3	6.1.90	**Ipswich T**	D2	H	D	0-1
1990-91 D1	3	6.1.91	**Barnsley**	D2	A	D	1-1	Sterland

LEEDS UNITED

	3r	9.1.91	**Barnsley**	H	W	4-0	Smith og, Chapman, McAllister, Strachan (p)
	4	27.1.91	**Arsenal**	D1 A	D	0-0	
	4r	30.1.91	**Arsenal**	H	D	1-1aet	Chapman
	4 2r	13.2.91	**Arsenal**	A	D	0-0aet	
	4 3r	16.2.91	**Arsenal**	H	L	1-2	Chapman
1991-92 D1	3	15.1.92	**Manchester U**	D1 H	L	0-1	
1992-93 PL	3	2.1.93	**Charlton A**	D1 H	D	1-1	Speed
	3r	13.1.93	**Charlton A**	A	W	3-1	Speed, Garland og, McAllister
	4	25.1.93	**Arsenal**	PL A	D	2-2	Speed, Chapman
	4r	3.2.93	**Arsenal**	H	L	2-3aet	Shutt, McAllister

LEEK FC

1884-85	1	8.11.84	**Northwich Victoria**	H	W	4-3
	2	6.12.84	**Macclesfield**	A	W	5-1
	3	3.1.85	**Queens Park, Scotland**	H	L	2-3
1885-86	1	31.10.85	**Wrexham**	H	W	6-3
	2		**Newtown**			*walkover*
	3		**Burslem Port Vale**			*scratched*
1886-87	1	23.10.86	**Druids**	H	W	2-1
	2	20.11.86	**Oswestry**	H	W	4-2
	3	11.12.86	**Burslem Port Vale**	H	D	2-2	Rider, others 1
	3r	20.1.87	**Burslem Port Vale**	A	W	3-1	Allen, Stonehewer, Vickerstaffe
	4	29.1.87	**Crewe A**	A	W	1-0	Allen
	5	5.2.87	**Old Carthusians**	H	L	0-2
1887-88	1	15.10.87	**Northwich V**	H	D	2-2
	1r	22.10.87	**Northwich V**	A	L	2-4

LEEK TOWN

Formed 1952. **First entered FA Cup:** 1956. **FA Challenge Trophy Runners-up:** 1990

1990-91 NPL	1	17.11.90	**Scarborough**	D4 A	W	2-0	Sommerville, Sutton
	2	12.12.90	**Chester C**	D3 H	D	1-1	Griffiths
	2r	17.12.90	**Chester C**	A	L	0-4	

LEICESTER CITY

Formed 1884 as Leicester Fosse. 1919 changed name to Leicester City. **FA Cup Best Performances:** Runners-up: 1949, 1961, 1963, 1969. **FA Cup Record Win:** 13-0 vs Notts Olympic, 1st qualifying round, 13.10.1894. **FA Cup Record Defeat:** 3-7 vs Burnley, 1st round, 8.1.1921 and six other four goal defeats

as Leicester Fosse

1890-91		1q **Burton W** (H) 0-4				
1891-92 ML		1q **Small Heath** (H) 2-6				
1892-93 ML		1q **Rushden** (H) 7-0; 2q **Notts Olympic** (A) 3-3aet; 2qr **Notts Olympic** (H) 7-0; 3q **Buxton** (H) 1-2				
1893-94 ML		2q **Mansfield T** (H) 1-0; 3q **Mansfield Greenhalgh** (H) 5-0; 4q **Loughborough** (A) 1-0				
	1	27.1.94	**South Shore**	H	W	2-1	Hill, Brown
	2	10.2.94	**Derby Co**	D1 H	D	0-0aet
	2r	17.2.94	**Derby Co**	A	L	0-3
1894-95 D2		1q **Notts Olympic** (H) 13-0; 2q **Kimberley** (H) 7-2; 3q **Rushden** (A) 3-2; 4q **Loughborough** (H) 1-1; 4qr **Loughborough** (A) 2-2aet; 4q 2r **Loughborough** (H) 3-0				
	1	2.2.95	**Bury**	D2 A	L	1-4	McArthur
1895-96 D2		1q **Hinckley T** (H) 4-0; 2q **Hucknall St Johns** (H) 3-1; 3q **Kimberley** (A) 3-1; 4q **Kettering T** (H) 1-2				
1896-97 D2		3q **Bulwell U** (H) 3-1; 4q **Wellingborough T** (A) 3-2; 5q **Kettering T** (A) 1-2				
1897-98 D2	1	29.1.98	**Southampton**	SL A	L	1-2	McLeod
1898-99 D2		3q **Kimberley** (H) 9-0; 4q **Rushden** (H) 2-1; 5q **Kettering T** (A) 1-1; 5qr **Kettering T** (H) 1-2				
1899-00 D2		3q **Wellingborough T** (H) 3-1; 4q **Burton Swifts** (H) 3-1; 5q **Hucknall Portland** (H) 6-1				
	1	27.1.00	**Sheffield U**	D1 A	L	0-1
1900-01 D2	1	9.2.01	**Nottingham F**	D1 A	L	1-5	Kyle
1901-02 D2		1nt **Glossop NE** (H) 0-1				
1902-03 D2		3q **Irthlingborough** (A) 1-0; 4q **Wellingborough T** (A) 1-4				
1903-04 D2		3q **Market Harborough** (H) 10-0; 4q **Wellingborough T** (A) 2-1; 5q **Burton U** (A) 1-1; 5qr **Burton U** (H) 2-2; 5q 2r **Burton U** 0-2 at Baseball Ground				
1904-05 D2		3q **Linby Church** (H) 10-1; 4q **Gresley R** (H) 5-0; 5q **Northampton T** (A) 2-2; 5qr **Northampton T** (H) 2-0; 6qr **Southall** (A) 4-0; 1nt **WBA** (A) 5-2				
	1	4.2.05	**Aston Villa**	D1 A	L	1-5	Mounteney (p)

Season	Div	Rd	Date	Opponent	OppDiv	Venue	Res	Score	Scorers
1905-06	D2	1	13.1.06	**Liverpool**	D1	A	L	1-2	Moody
1906-07	D2	1	12.1.07	**Sunderland**	D1	A	L	1-4	Bannister
1907-08	D2	1	11.1.08	**Blackburn R**	D1	H	W	2-0	Humphreys, Pollock (p)
		2	1.2.08	**Portsmouth**	SL	A	L	0-1	
1908-09	D1	1	16.1.09	**Watford**	SL	A	D	1-1	Shinton
		1r	20.1.09	**Watford**		H	W	3-1	Donnelly, Walker, RF Turner
		2	6.2.09	**Derby Co**	D2	H	L	0-2	
1909-10	D2	1	15.1.10	**Birmingham**	D2	A	W	4-1	Hubbard 2, Shinton 2
		2	5.2.10	**Bury**	D1	H	W	3-2	Threlfall 2, Owen
		3	19.2.10	**Leyton**	AL	A	W	1-0	Threlfall
		4	5.3.10	**Newcastle U**	D1	A	L	0-3	
1910-11	D2	1	14.1.11	**Southampton**	SL	H	W	3-1	Walker, Osborn, Threlfall
		2	4.2.11	**Middlesbrough**	D1	A	D	0-0	
		2r	9.2.11	**Middlesbrough**		H	L	1-2aet	Currie (p)
1911-12	D2	1	13.1.12	**Croydon Common**	SL	A	D	2-2	Mills, Humphreys
		1r	22.1.12	**Croydon Common**		H	W	6-1	Hubbard, Osborn, Humphreys 2, Hanger, og
		2	3.2.12	**Barnsley**	D2	A	L	0-1	
1912-13	D2	1	11.1.13	**Norwich C**	SL	H	D	0-0	
				abandoned after 65 minutes – snowstorm					
		1	16.1.13	**Norwich C**		H	L	1-4	Proctor
1913-14	D2	1	10.1.14	**Tottenham H**	D1	H	D	5-5	Stoodley 3, Mortimer, Currie
		1r	15.1.14	**Tottenham H**		A	L	0-2	
1914-15	D2	6q	19.12.14	**Swansea T**	SL	A	L	0-1	
as Leicester City									
1919-20	D2	1	10.1.20	**Newport Co**	SL	A	D	0-0	
		1r	15.1.20	**Newport Co**		H	W	2-0	Walker, Paterson
		2	31.1.20	**Manchester C**	D1	H	W	3-0	Douglas, Walker, T.Smith
		3	21.2.20	**Chelsea**	D1	A	L	0-3	
1920-21	D2	1	8.1.21	**Burnley**	D1	H	L	3-7	Smith, J.Roxburgh, Paterson
1921-22	D2	1	7.1.22	**Clapton O**	D2	H	W	2-0	Pynegar (p), Trotter
		2	28.1.22	**Fulham**	D2	H	W	2-0	Graham, Paterson
		3	18.2.22	**Arsenal**	D1	A	L	0-3	
1922-23	D2	1	13.1.23	**Fulham**	D2	H	W	4-0	J.Duncan 2, Smith, Graham
		2	3.2.23	**Cardiff C**	D1	H	L	0-1	
1923-24	D2	1	12.1.24	**Sheffield W**	D2	A	L	1-4	Barrett (p)
1924-25	D2	1	10.1.25	**Stoke**	D2	H	W	3-0	Duncan 2, Chandler
		2	31.1.25	**Newcastle U**	D1	A	D	2-2	Chandler 2
		2r	5.2.25	**Newcastle U**		H	W	1-0	Carr
		3	21.2.25	**Hull C**	D2	A	D	1-1	Duncan
		3r	26.2.25	**Hull C**		H	W	3-1	Chandler 3
		4	7.3.25	**Cardiff C**	D1	A	L	1-2	Duncan
1925-26	D1	3	9.1.26	**Notts Co**	D1	A	L	0-2	
1926-27	D1	3	8.1.27	**Middlesbrough**	D2	A	L	3-5	Duncan, Hine, Chandler
1927-28	D1	3	14.1.28	**Hull C**	D2	A	W	1-0	Barry
		4	28.1.28	**Reading**	D2	A	W	1-0	Adcock
		5	18.2.28	**Tottenham H**	D1	H	L	0-3	
1928-29	D1	3	12.1.29	**Lincoln C**	3N	A	W	1-0	Lochhead
		4	26.1.29	**Swansea T**	D2	H	W	1-0	Lochhead
		5	16.2.29	**Bolton W**	D1	H	L	1-2	Lochhead
1929-30	D1	3	11.1.30	**Sheffield U**	D1	A	L	1-2	Hine
1930-31	D1	3	10.1.31	**Brighton & HA**	3S	H	L	1-2	Lochhead
1931-32	D1	3	9.1.32	**Crook T**	NEL	H	W	7-0	Hine 5, Langford, Chandler
		4	23.1.32	**Port Vale**	D2	A	W	2-1	Hine, Chandler
		5	13.2.32	**Newcastle U**	D1	A	L	1-3	Lochhead
1932-33	D1	3	14.1.33	**Everton**	D1	H	L	2-3	Campbell 2
1933-34	D1	3	13.1.34	**Lincoln C**	D2	H	W	3-0	Maw, Lochhead, Paterson
		4	27.1.34	**Millwall**	D2	A	W	6-3	Smith, Chandler 2, Maw, Liddle, Lochhead
		5	17.3.34	**Birmingham**	D1	A	W	2-1	Chandler 2
		6	3.3.34	**Preston NE**	D2	A	W	1-0	Chandler
		SF	17.3.34	**Portsmouth**	D1		L	1-4	Lochhead
				played at St Andrews					
1934-35	D1	3	12.1.35	**Blackpool**	D2	H	W	2-1	Maw, Ritchie
		4	26.1.35	**Arsenal**	D1	H	L	0-1	
1935-36	D2	3	11.1.36	**Brentford**	D1	H	W	1-0	Maw
		4	25.1.36	**Watford**	3S	H	W	6-3	Maw 2, Dewis, Liddle 3
		5	15.2.36	**Middlesbrough**	D1	A	L	1-2	McNally
1936-37	D2	3	16.1.37	**Bristol R**	3S	A	W	5-2	Bowers 2, Carroll, O'Callaghan, Stubbs

	4	30.1.37	Exeter C	3S	A	L	1-3	Liddle
1937-38 D1	3	8.1.38	Mansfield T	3S	A	W	2-1	Liddle, Bowers
	4	22.1.38	Preston NE	D1	A	L	0-2	
1938-39 D1	3	7.1.39	Stoke C	D1	H	D	1-1	Dewis
	3r	11.1.39	Stoke C		A	W	2-1	Dewis, Liddle
	4	21.1.39	Wolverhampton W	D1	A	L	1-5	Bowers
1945-46 D2	3 1L	5.1.46	Chelsea	D1	A	D	1-1	Adam
	3 2L	10.1.46	Chelsea		H	L	0-2	
1946-47 D2	3	11.1.47	West Ham	D2	A	W	2-1	Adam, Dewis
	4	25.1.47	Brentford	D1	A	D	0-0	
	4r	30.1.47	Brentford		H	D	0-0	
	4 2r	3.2.47	Brentford at Villa Park			W	4-1	Griffiths, A.Smith 2, Dewis
	5	8.2.47	Newcastle U	D2	A	D	1-1	Dewis
	5r	20.2.47	Newcastle U		H	L	1-2	S.Smith (p)
1947-48 D2	3	10.1.48	Bury	D2	H	W	1-0	Lee
	4	24.1.48	Sheffield W	D2	H	W	2-1	W.Harrison, Haines
	5	7.2.48	Tottenham H	D2	A	L	2-5	W.Harrison, Lee
1948-49 D2	3	8.1.49	Birmingham C	D1	A	D	1-1	Revie (p)
	3r	15.1.49	Birmingham C		H	D	1-1aet	Griffiths
	3 2r	17.1.49	Birmingham C		A	W	2-1	J.Harrison, Revie
	4	29.1.49	Preston NE	D1	H	W	2-0	Lee (p), Griffiths
	5	12.2.49	Luton T	D2	A	D	5-5	Lee 4, Griffiths
	5r	19.2.49	Luton T		H	W	5-3	Lee 2(1p), Griffiths 2, Chisholm
	6	26.2.49	Brentford	D2	A	W	2-0	Lee, Griffiths
	SF	26.3.49	Portsmouth	D1		W	3-1	Revie 2, Chisholm
		played at Highbury						
	F	30.4.49	Wolverhampton W	D1 WEMBLEY		L	1-3	Griffiths
1949-50 D2	3	7.1.50	Sheffield U	D2	A	L	1-3	Adam
1950-51 D2	3	6.1.51	Preston NE	D2	H	D	0-3	.
1951-52 D2	3	12.1.52	Coventry C	D2	H	D	1-1	Griffiths
	3r	14.1.52	Coventry C		A	L	1-4	Dryburgh
1952-53 D2	3	10.1.53	Notts Co	D2	H	L	2-4	Rowley 2 (1p)
1953-54 D2	3	9.1.54	Middlesbrough	D1	A	D	0-0	
	3r	14.1.54	Middlesbrough		H	W	3-2	Rowley 3
	4	30.1.54	Stoke C	D2	A	D	0-0	
	4r	2.2.54	Stoke C		H	W	3-1	Morris, Small 2
	5	20.2.54	Norwich C	3S	A	W	2-1	Rowley (p), Small
	6	13.3.54	Preston NE	D1	H	D	1-1	Jackson
	6r	17.3.54	Preston NE		A	D	2-2aet	Small, Rowley
	6 2r	22.3.54	Preston NE at Hillsborough			L	1-3	Rowley
1954-55 D1	3	8.1.55	Rotherham U	D2	A	L	0-1	
1955-56 D2	3	11.1.56	Luton T	D1	A	W	4-0	Gardiner, Rowley 3
	4	28.1.56	Stoke C	D2	H	D	3-3	Rowley 2(1p), Griffiths
	4r	30.1.56	Stoke C		A	L	1-2	Rowley
1956-57 D2	3	5.1.57	Tottenham H	D1	A	L	0-2	
1957-58 D1	3	4.1.58	Tottenham H	D1	A	L	0-4	
1958-59 D1	3	10.1.59	Lincoln C	D2	H	D	1-1	Kelly
	3r	14.1.59	Lincoln C		A	W	2-0	Kelly, Hines
	4	24.1.59	Luton T	D1	H	D	1-1	McNeill
	4r	28.1.59	Luton T		A	L	1-4	Leek
1959-60 D1	3	9.1.60	Wrexham	D3	A	W	2-1	Cheesebrough, Leek
	4	30.1.60	Fulham	D1	H	W	2-1	McDonald, Wills
	5	20.2.60	WBA	D1	H	W	2-1	Walsh, Cheesebrough
	6	12.3.60	Wolverhampton W	D1	H	L	1-2	McDonald
1960-61 D1	3	7.1.61	Oxford U	SL	H	W	3-1	Walsh Leek, Riley
	4	28.1.61	Bristol C	D3	H	–	0-0	
		abandoned at half-time – waterlogged pitch						
	4	31.1.61	Bristol C	D3	H	W	5-1	Wills, Leek 2, Walsh 2
	5	18.2.61	Birmingham C	D1	A	D	1-1	Riley
	5r	22.2.61	Birmingham C		H	W	2-1	Leek 2
	6	4.3.61	Barnsley	D3	H	D	0-0	
	6r	8.3.61	Barnsley		A	W	2-1aet	Riley, Leek
	SF	18.3.61	Sheffield U	D2		D	0-0	
		played at Elland Road						
	SFr	23.3.61	Sheffield U at City Ground, Nottingham			D	0-0aet	
	SF 2r	27.3.61	Sheffield U at St Andrews			W	2-0	Walsh, Leek
	F	6.5.61	Tottenham H	D1 WEMBLEY		L	0-2	

LEICESTER CITY

Season	Div	Rnd	Date	Opponent		Div	H/A	Res	Score	Scorers
1961-62	D1	3	10.1.62	Stoke C		D2	H	D	1-1	Riley
		3r	15.1.62	Stoke C			A	L	2-5	Riley (p), Keyworth
1962-63	D1	3	7.1.63	Grimsby T		D2	A	W	3-1	Gibson 2, Keyworth
		4	30.1.63	Ipswich T		D1	H	W	3-1	Cross, Keyworth 2
		5	16.3.63	Leyton O		D1	A	W	1-0	Keyworth
		6	30.3.63	Norwich C		D2	A	W	2-0	Stringfellow, Gibson
		SF	27.4.63	Liverpool		D1		W	1-0	Stringfellow
			played at Hillsborough							
		F	25.5.63	Manchester U		D1 WEMBLEY		L	1-3	Keyworth
1963-64	D1	3	4.1.64	Leyton O		D2	H	L	2-3	Cross, Keyworth
1964-65	D1	3	9.1.65	Blackburn R		D1	H	D	2-2	Stringfellow, Roberts
		3r	14.1.65	Blackburn R			A	W	2-1	Roberts, Cross
		4	30.1.65	Plymouth A		D2	H	W	5-0	Stringfellow, Goodfellow 2, Gibson, Roberts
		5	20.2.65	Middlesbrough		D2	A	W	3-0	Cross 2, Gibson
		6	6.3.65	Liverpool		D1	H	D	0-0	
		6r	10.3.65	Liverpool			A	L	0-1	
1965-66	D1	3	22.1.66	Aston Villa		D1	A	W	2-1	Dougan, Stringfellow
		4	12.2.66	Birmingham C		D2	A	W	2-1	Sinclair, Goodfellow
		5	5.3.66	Manchester C		D2	A	D	2-2	Sinclair, Stringfellow
		5r	9.3.66	Manchester C			H	L	0-1	
1966-67	D1	3	28.1.67	Manchester C		D1	A	L	1-2	Sweenie
1967-68	D1	3	27.1.68	Barrow		D3	A	W	2-1	Sjoberg, Arrowsmith og
		4	17.2.68	Manchester C		D1	A	D	0-0	
		4r	19.2.68	Manchester C			H	W	4-3	Fern, Large 2, Nish
		5	9.3.68	Rotherham U		D2	A	D	1-1	Nish (p)
		5r	13.3.68	Rotherham U			H	W	2-0aet	Large, Stringfellow
		6	30.3.68	Everton		D1	H	L	1-3	Nish
1968-69	D1	3	4.1.69	Barnsley		D3	A	D	1-1	Glover
		3r	8.1.69	Barnsley			H	W	2-1	Fern, Glover
		4	25.1.69	Millwall		D2	A	W	1-0	Glover
		5	1.3.69	Liverpool		D1	H	D	0-0	
		5r	3.3.69	Liverpool			A	W	1-0	Lochhead
		6	8.3.69	Mansfield T		D3	A	W	1-0	Fern
		SF	29.3.69	WBA		D1		W	1-0	Clarke
			played at Hillsborough							
		F	26.4.69	Manchester C		D1 WEMBLEY		L	0-1	
1969-70	D2	3	3.1.70	Sunderland		D1	H	W	1-0	Roberts
		4	24.1.70	Southampton		D1	A	D	1-1	Farrington
		4r	28.1.70	Southampton			H	W	4-2	Lochhead 2, Farrington, Nish (p)
		5	7.2.70	Liverpool		D1	A	D	0-0	
		5r	11.2.70	Liverpool			H	L	0-2	
1970-71	D2	3	2.1.71	Notts Co		D4	H	W	2-0	Brown, Partridge
		4	25.1.71	Torquay U		D3	H	W	3-0	Glover, Partridge, Cross
		5	13.2.71	Oxford U		D2	H	D	1-1	Partridge
		5r	17.2.71	Oxford U			A	W	3-1	Brown, Fern 2
		6	6.3.71	Arsenal		D1	H	D	0-0	
		6r	15.3.71	Arsenal			A	L	0-1	
1971-72	D1	3	15.1.72	Wolverhampton W		D1	A	D	1-1	Farrington
		3r	19.1.72	Wolverhampton W			H	W	2-0	Farrington, Glover
		4	5.2.72	Orient		D2	H	L	0-2	
1972-73	D1	3	13.1.73	Arsenal		D1	A	D	2-2	Worthington, Farrington
		3r	17.1.73	Arsenal			H	L	1-2	Farrington
1973-74	D1	3	5.1.74	Tottenham H		D1	H	W	1-0	Earle
		4	26.1.74	Fulham		D2	A	D	1-1	Glover
		4r	30.1.74	Fulham			H	W	2-1	Glover, Worthington
		5	16.2.74	Luton T		D2	A	W	4-0	Earle 2, Worthington, Weller
		6	9.3.74	QPR		D1	A	W	2-0	Waters 2
		SF	30.3.74	Liverpool		D1		D	0-0	
			played at Old Trafford							
		SFr	3.4.74	Liverpool				L	1-3	Glover
			played at Villa Park							
1974-75	D1	3	13.1.75	Oxford U		D2	H	W	3-1	Worthington, Earle 2
		4	25.1.75	Leatherhead		IL	A	W	3-2	Sammels, Earle, Weller
			played at Filbert Street							
		5	15.2.75	Arsenal		D1	A	D	0-0	
		5r	19.2.75	Arsenal			H	D	1-1aet	Birchenall
		5 2r	24.2.75	Arsenal			H	L	0-1aet	

LEICESTER CITY

1975-76	D1	3	3.1.76	Sheffield U	D1	H	W	3-0	Garland 3
		4	24.1.76	Bury	D3	H	W	1-0	Lee
		5	14.2.76	Manchester U	D1	H	L	1-2	Lee
1976-77	D1	3	8.1.77	Aston Villa	D1	H	L	0-1	
1977-78	D1	3	7.1.78	Hull C	D2	A	W	1-0	Armstrong
		4	28.1.78	Walsall	D3	A	L	0-1	
1978-79	D2	3	6.1.79	Norwich C	D1	H	W	3-0	May, Weller, Henderson
		4	26.2.79	Oldham A	D2	A	L	1-3	Henderson
1979-80	D2	3	5.1.80	Harlow T	IL	H	D	1-1	Henderson
		3r	8.1.80	Harlow T		A	L	0-1	
1980-81	D1	3	3.1.81	Cardiff C	D2	H	W	3-0	Lineker, Buchanan, Melrose
		4	24.1.81	Exeter C	D3	H	D	1-1	Henderson
		4r	28.1.81	Exeter C		A	L	1-3	Melrose
1981-82	D2	3	2.1.82	Southampton	D1	H	W	3-1	Young 2, Lineker
		4	23.1.82	Hereford U	D4	A	W	1-0	May
		5	13.2.82	Watford	D2	H	W	2-0	O'Neill, Terry og
		6	6.3.82	Shrewsbury T	D2	H	W	5-2	May, Melrose 2, Lineker, Cross og
		SF	3.4.82	Tottenham H	D1		L	0-2	
			played at Villa Park						
1982-83	D2	3	8.1.83	Notts Co	D1	H	L	2-3	A.Smith, Wilson
1983-84	D1	3	7.1.84	Crystal P	D2	A	L	0-1	
1984-85	D1	3	5.1.85	Burton A	NPL	A	W	6-1	Lineker 3, A.Smith 2, Lynex
			Played at Derby. FA ordered match to be replayed behind closed doors following coin-throwing incident						
		3	16.1.85	Burton A at Coventry			W	1-0	Ramsey
		4	26.1.85	Carlisle U	D2	H	W	1-0	B.Smith
		5	19.2.85	Millwall	D3	A	L	0-2	
1985-86	D1	3	4.1.86	Bristol R	D3	A	L	1-3	McAllister (p)
1986-87	D1	3	10.1.87	QPR	D1	A	L	2-5	A.Smith, McAllister (p)
1987-88	D2	3	9.1.88	Oxford U	D1	A	L	0-2	
1988-89	D2	3	7.1.89	Manchester C	D2	A	L	0-1	
1989-90	D2	3	6.1.90	Barnsley	D2	H	L	1-2	Paris
1990-91	D2	3	5.1.91	Millwall	D2	H	L	1-2	James
1991-92	D2	3	4.1.92	Crystal P	D1	H	W	1-0	R.Smith
		4	25.1.92	Bristol C	D2	H	L	1-2	Kitson
1992-93	D1	3	13.1.93	Barnsley	D1	H	D	2-2	Thompson (p), Oldfield
		3r	20.1.93	Barnsley		A	D	1-1aet	Joachim
			Barnsley won 5-4 on penalties						

LEYTON FC

Formed as Leyton FC 1869. **First entered FA Cup** 1874. **FA Amateur Cup Winners:** 1927, 1928. Runners-up: 1929, 1934, 1937, 1952. Merged with the original Wingate (1948) FC in 1975 to become Leyton-Wingate. Reverted to original name of Leyton FC 1992

1874-75	1	14.11.74	Southall Park		A	D	0-0	
	1r	28.11.74	Southall Park		H	L	0-5	
1875-76	1		Harrow Chequers		*walkover*			
	2	18.12.75	Clapham Rovers		A	L	0-12	
1876-77	1	28.10.76	Upton Park		A	L	0-7	
1877-78	1	7.11.77	Swifts		A	L	2-3	Rawson 2
1878-79	1		South Norwood		*scratched*			
1909-10 SL	1	15.1.10	New Brompton	SL	H	D	0-0	
	1r	19.1.10	New Brompton		A	D	2-2aet	Ryder, Robertson
	1 2r	24.1.10	New Brompton at Tottenham			W	1-0	Shanks
	2	5.2.10	Stockport Co	D2	A	W	2-0	Ryder, Robertson
	3	19.2.10	Leicester Fosse	D2	A	L	0-1	
1910-11 SL	1	14.1.11	Chelsea	D2	A	D	0-0	
	1r	19.1.11	Chelsea		H	L	0-2	
1911-12 SL	1	13.1.12	Liverpool	D1	A	L	0-1	
1925-26 Lon	1	28.11.25	St Albans C	IL	H	W	1-0	Hall
	2	12.12.25	Reading	3S	A	L	0-6	
1927-28 AL	1	26.11.27	Northampton	3S	A	L	0-8	
1928-29 AL	1	24.11.28	Watford	3S	H	L	0-2	
1929-30 AL	1	30.11.29	Merthyr Tydfil	3S	H	W	4-1	G.Collins 2, Margetts, Keeble
	2	14.12.29	Fulham	3S	H	L	1-4	GD Collins
1934-35 AL	1	24.11.34	Wimbledon	IL	A	D	1-1	Lloyd
	1r	29.11.34	Wimbledon		H	L	0-1	

LEYTON FC

1951-52	AL	1	24.11.51	**Chippenham T**	WL	H	W	3-0	Goddard 2, Casey
		2	15.12.51	**Chester**	3N	A	L	2-5	Fitch, Hasley
1952-53	AL	1	22.11.52	**Hereford U**	SL	H	D	0-0	
		1r	27.11.52	**Hereford U**		A	L	2-3	Goddard, Bessex
1955-56	AL	1	19.11.55	**Bedford**	SL	A	L	0-3	

as Leyton-Wingate

1985-86	IL	1	16.11.85	**Swansea C**	D3	A	L	0-2	

LEYTON ORIENT

Formed 1881. **First entered FA Cup:** 1904. Clapton Orient until 1946. Leyton Orient 1946-1966. Orient 1966-1987. Leyton Orient 1987-present. **Best FA Cup Performance:** Semi-finals 1978 **Record FA Cup Win:** 7-1 vs Lovells Athletic, 1st round, 19.11.1955 **Record FA Cup Defeat:** 0-8 vs Aston Villa, 4th round, 30.1.1929

as Clapton Orient

1904-05	SL	P		**Enfield** (H) 4-1; 1q **Cheshunt** (A) 0-0; 1q **Cheshunt** (A) 4-1; 2q **Leytonstone** (H) 1-1; 2qr **Leytonstone** (A) 5-2; 3q **New Brompton** (H) 2-6					
1905-06	D2			1q **Felstead** (A) 1-1; 1qr **Felstead** (H) 5-1; 2q **Barking** (H) 3-1; 3q **Leyton** (A) 3-1; 4q **Clapton** (A) 2-0					
		1	13.1.06	**Chesterfield**	D2	H	D	0-0	
		1r	17.1.06	**Chesterfield**		A	L	0-3	
1906-07	D2		did not enter						
1907-08	D2			1q **Custom House** (H) 3-0; 2q **Romford** (A) 6-3; 3q **Old Newportians** (H) 5-2; 4q **Southend U** (H) 1-1; 4qr **Southend U** (A) 1-3					
1908-09	D2	1	16.1.09	**Newcastle U**	D1	A	L	0-5	
1909-10	D2	1	15.1.10	**WBA**	D2	A	L	0-2	
1910-11	D2	1	14.1.11	**Woolwich Arsenal**	D1	H	–	0-1	
				abandoned afer 55 minutes					
		1	16.1.11	**Woolwich Arsenal**		H	L	1-2	Goffin
1911-12	D2	1	13.1.12	**Everton**	D1	H	L	1-2	Bevan
1912-13	D2	1	11.1.13	**Sunderland**	D1	A	L	0-6	
1913-14	D2	1	10.1.14	**Nottingham F**	D2	H	D	2-2	McFaAdden, Jonas
		1r	14.1.14	**Nottingham F**		A	W	1-0	McFadden
		2	31.1.14	**Brighton & HA**	SL	A	L	1-3	Scott
1914-15	D2	1	9.1.15	**Millwall A**	SL	A	L	1-2	Jonas (p)
1919-20	D2	1	10.1.20	**Manchester C**	D1	A	L	1-4	J.Tonner
1920-21	D2	6q		**Port Vale** (H) 1-0					
		1	8.1.21	**Bradford PA**	D1	A	L	0-1	
1921-22	D2	1	7.1.22	**Leicester C**	D2	A	L	0-2	
1922-23	D2	1	131.23	**Millwall A**	3S	H	L	0-2	
1923-24	D2	1	12.1.24	**Swansea T**	3S	A	D	1-1	Williams
		1r	17.1.24	**Swansea T**		H	D	1-1aet	Rennox
		1 2r	21.1.24	**Swansea T** at Tottenham			L	1-2	Williams (p)
1924-25	D2	1	10.1.25	**Nottingham F**	D1	A	L	0-1	
1925-26	D2	3	9.1.26	**Chesterfield**	3N	A	W	1-0	J.Tonner
		4	30.1.26	**Middlesbrough**	D2	H	W	4-2	J.Tonner 2, Henderson, Cock
		5	20.2.26	**Newcastle U**	D1	H	W	2-0	Galbraith, Cock
		6	6.3.26	**Manchester C**	D1	H	L	1-6	Cock
1926-27	D2	3	8.1.27	**Port Vale**	D2	H	D	1-1	Dennison
		3r	12.1.27	**Port Vale**		A	L	1-5	Dennison
1927-28	D2	3	14.1.28	**Swindon T**	3S	A	L	1-2	Whipp
1928-29	D2	3	12.1.29	**Southampton**	D2	A	D	0-0	
		3r	17.1.29	**Southampton**		H	W	2-1	Dennison, Corkindale
		4	26.1.29	**Aston Villa**	D1	A	D	0-0	
		4r	30.1.29	**Aston Villa**		H	L	0-8	
1929-30	3S	1	30.11.29	**Folkestone**	SL	H	D	0-0	
		1r	4.12.29	**Folkestone**		A	D	2-2aet	Mills, Campbell
		1 2r	9.12.29	**Folkestone** at Highbury			W	4-1	Eastman, Vanner, Campbell, Grimsdell
		2	14.1.30	**Northfleet U**	SL	H	W	2-0	Grimsdell, Mills
		3	11.1.30	**Bristol R**	3S	H	W	1-0	Lyons (p)
		4	25.1.30	**Newcastle U**	D1	A	L	1-3	Mills
1930-31	3S	1	29.11.30	**Luton T**	3S	A	D	2-2	Tricker, McGinnile og
		1r	4.12.30	**Luton** T at Highbury			L	2-4	Tricker, Cropper
1931-32	3S	1	28.11.31	**Coventry C**	3S	A	D	2-2	Fletcher, Sanders
		1r	3.12.31	**Coventry C**		H	W	2-0	Tricker, Fletcher
		2	12.12.31	**Cardiff C**	3S	A	L	0-4	
1932-33	3S	1	26.11.32	**Aldershot**	3S	H	L	0-1	
1933-34	3S	1	25.11.33	**Epsom T**	Lon	H	W	4-2	Morris 2, Rigby (p), Taylor

		2	9.12.33	Walsall	3N	A	D	0-0
		2r	14.12.33	Walsall		H	W	2-0	Morris, Taylor
		3	13.1.34	Grimsby T	D2	A	L	0-1
1934-35	3S	1	24.11.34	Ashford T	KL	A	W	4-1	Halliday 2, Mayson, Ware
		2	8.12.34	Chester	3N	H	L	1-3	Halliday
1935-36	3S	1	30.11.35	Aldershot	3S	A	D	0-0
		1r	4.12.35	Aldershot		H	W	1-0	Crawford
		2	14.12.35	Folkestone	SL	A	W	2-1	McAleer, Crawford
		3	11.1.36	Charlton A	3S	H	W	3-0	H.Taylor, Foster
		4	25.1.36	Middlesbrough	D1	A	L	0-3
1936-37	3S	1	28.11.36	Torquay U	3S	H	W	2-1	H.Smith, Crawford
		2	12.12.36	Carlisle U	3N	A	L	1-4	Crawford
1937-38	3S	1	27.11.37	Torquay U	3S	A	W	2-1	Tully, Graham
		2	11.12.37	York C	3N	H	D	2-2	Lane, H.Smith
		2r	15.12.37	York C		A	L	0-1
1938-39	3S	1	26.11.38	Hayes	AL	H	W	3-1	H.Smith, Williams, Crawford
		2	10.12.38	Walsall	3S	A	L	2-4	Crawford, Williams
1945-46	3S	1 1L	17.11.45	Newport (IOW)	Hants	H	W	2-1	Gore, Parr (p)
		1 2L	24.11.45	Newport (IOW)		A	L	0-2

as Leyton Orient

1946-47	3S	1	30.11.46	Notts Co	3S	H	L	1-2	Hunt
1947-48	3S	1	29.11.47	Gillingham	SL	A	L	0-1
1948-49	3S	1	27.11.48	Dartford	SL	A	W	3-2	Connelly, Deverall, McGreachy,
		2	11.12.48	Darlington	3N	A	L	0-1
1949-50	3S	1	26.11.49	Southend U	3S	H	L	0-2
1950-51	3S	1	25.11.50	Ipswich T	3S	H	L	1-2	Rees
1951-52	3S	1	24.11.51	Gorleston	ECL	H	D	2-2	Banner (p), Blatchford
		1r	29.11.51	Gorleston		A	D	0-0
		1 2r	3.12.51	Gorleston at Highbury			W	5-4	Pacey 3, Brown 2
		2	15.12.51	Wrexham	3N	A	D	1-1	Pacey
		2r	19.12.51	Wrexham		H	W	3-2	Rees 3
		3	12.1.52	Everton	D2	H	D	0-0
		3r	16.1.52	Everton		A	W	3-1	Harris, Pacey 2
		4	2.2.52	Birmingham C	D2	A	W	1-0	Harris
		5	23.2.52	Arsenal	D1	H	L	0-3
1952-53	3S	1	22.11.52	Bristol R	3S	H	D	1-1	Pacey
		1r	24.11.52	Bristol R		A	L	0-1
1953-54	3S	1	21.11.53	Kettering T	SL	H	W	3-0	Poulton 2, Facey
		2	12.12.53	Weymouth	SL	H	W	4-0	Rees 2, Mogan, Pacey
		3	9.1.54	Tranmere R	3N	A	D	2-2	Rees, Facey (p)
		3r	14.1.54	Tranmere R		H	W	4-1	Pacey 3, Rees
		4	30.1.54	Fulham	D2	H	W	2-1	Poulton, Davies
		5	20.2.54	Doncaster R	D2	H	W	3-1	Morgan, Pacey, Burgess
		6	13.3.54	Port Vale	3N	H	L	0-1
1954-55	3S	1	20.11.54	Frome T	WL	A	W	3-0	Facey, Groves, Fitz og
		2	11.12.54	Workington	3N	H	L	0-1
1955-56	3S	1	19.11.55	Lovell's Athletic	SL	H	W	7-1	Heckman 5, Facey, Hartburn
		2	10.12.55	Brentford	3S	H	W	4-1	Heckman, Facey, Hartburn, Burgess
		3	7.1.56	Plymouth A	D2	H	W	1-0	Hartburn
		4	28.1.56	Birmingham C	D1	H	L	0-4
1956-57	D2	3	5.1.57	Chelsea	D1	H	L	0-2
1957-58	D2	3	4.1.58	Reading	3S	H	W	1-0	Johnston
		4	25.1.58	Cardiff C	D2	A	L	1-4	Julians
1958-59	D2	3	10.1.59	Blackburn R	D1	A	L	2-4	Lewis 2
1959-60	D2	3	9.1.60	Liverpool	D2	A	L	1-2	Foster
1960-61	D2	3	7.1.61	Gillingham	D4	A	W	6-2	Elwood 2, Lewis 2 (2p), Johnston, McDonald
		4	28.1.61	Southampton	D2	A	W	1-0	Gibbs
		5	18.2.61	Sheffield W	D1	H	L	0-2
1961-62	D2	3	6.1.62	Brentford	D3	A	D	1-1	Foster
		3r	8.1.62	Brentford		H	W	2-1	Foster, Elwood
		4	30.1.62	Burnley	D1	A	D	1-1	Foster
		4r	6.2.62	Burnley		H	L	0-1
1962-63	D1	3	11.2.63	Hull C	D3	H	D	1-1	Musgrove
		3r	19.2.63	Hull C		A	W	2-0aet	Musgrove, Gibbs
		4	4.3.63	Derby Co	D2	H	W	3-0	Dunmore, Elwood, Deeley
		5	16.3.63	Leicester C	D1	H	L	0-1
1963-64	D2	3	4.1.64	Leicester C		A	W	3-2	Musgrove 2, King og

LEYTON ORIENT

	4	25.1.64	West Ham	D1	H	D	1-1	Deeley
	4r	29.1.64	West Ham		A	L	0-3	
1964-65	D2	3	9.1.65	Southampton	D2	A	L	1-3	Dunmore
1965-66	D2	3	22.1.66	Norwich C	D2	H	L	1-3	Price
1966-67	D3	1	26.11.66	Lowestoft	ECL	H	W	2-1	Whitehouse, Metchick
	2	7.1.67	Brentford	D4	H	D	0-0	
	2r	10.1.67	Brentford		A	L	1-3	Metchick

as Orient

1967-68	D3	1	9.12.67	Weymouth	SL	A	W	2-0	Halom 2
	2	6.1.68	Boston	WMRL	A	D	1-1	Simpson
	2r	15.1.68	Boston		H	W	2-1	Mancini, Halom
	3	27.1.68	Bury	D3	H	W	1-0	Massey
	4	4.2.68	Birmingham C	D2	A	L	0-3	
1968-69	D3	1	16.11.68	Gillingham	D3	H	D	1-1	Bloomfield
	1r	20.11.68	Gillingham		A	L	1-2	Slater
1969-70	D3	1	15.11.69	Walsall	D3	A	D	0-0	
	1r	17.11.69	Walsall		H	L	0-2	
1970-71	D2	3	11.1.71	Sunderland	D2	A	W	3-0	Fairbrother, Dyson, Lazarus
	4	23.1.71	Nottingham F	D1	A	D	1-1	Dyson
	4r	25.1.71	Nottingham F		H	–	0-0	

abandoned at half-time, ground unfit

	4r	1.2.71	Nottingham F		H	L	0-1	
1971-72	D2	3	15.1.72	Wrexham	D3	H	W	3-0	Dyson (p), Fairbrother, Bowyer
	4	5.2.72	Leicester C	D1	A	W	2-0	Bowyer, Allen
	5	25.2.72	Chelsea	D1	H	W	3-2	Hoadley, Bullock, Fairbrother
	6	18.3.72	Arsenal	D1	H	L	0-1	
1972-73	D2	3	13.1.73	Coventry C	D1	H	L	1-4	Arber (p)
1973-74	D2	3	5.1.74	Bournemouth	D3	H	W	2-1	Fairbrother 2
	4	27.1.74	Portsmouth	D2	A	D	0-0	
	4r	29.1.74	Portsmouth		H	D	1-1aet	Fairbrother
	4 2r	5.2.74	Portsmouth at Selhurst Pk		L	0-2	
1974-75	D2	3	4.1.75	Derby Co	D1	H	D	2-2	Possee, Queen
	3r	8.1.75	Derby Co		A	L	1-2	Fairbrother
1975-76	D2	3	3.1.76	Cardiff C	D3	H	L	0-1	
1976-77	D2	3	8.1.77	Darlington	D4	A	D	2-2	Possee, Hoadley
	3r	11.1.77	Darlington		H	D	0-0aet	
	3 2r	17.1.77	Darlington at Tottenham		W	3-0	Whittle 2, Roffey
	4	29.1.77	Blackburn R	D2	A	L	0-3	
1977-78	D2	3	6.1.78	Norwich C	D1	H	D	1-1	Kitchen
	3r	16.1.78	Norwich C		A	W	1-0	Kitchen
	4	28.1.78	Blackburn R	D2	H	W	3-1	Kitchen 2, Mayo
	5	18.2.78	Chelsea	D1	H	D	0-0	
	5r	27.2.78	Chelsea		A	W	2-1	Kitchen 2
	6	11.3.78	Middlesbrough	D1	A	D	0-0	
	6r	14.3.78	Middlesbrough		H	W	2-1	Kitchen, Mayo
	SF	8.4.78	Arsenal	D1		L	0-3	

played at Stamford Bridge

1978-79	D2	3	9.1.79	Bury	D3	H	W	3-2	Kitchen 2, Chiedozie
	4	27.1.79	Ipswich T	D1	A	D	0-0	
	4r	30.1.79	Ipswich T		H	L	0-2	
1979-80	D2	3	5.1.80	Altrincham	APL	A	D	1-1	Jennings
	3r	9.1.80	Altrincham		H	W	2-1	Mayo, Jennings
	4	26.1.80	West Ham	D2	H	L	2-3	Taylor (p), Chiedozie
1980-81	D2	3	3.1.81	Luton Town	D2	H	L	1-3	Jennings
1981-82	D2	3	2.1.82	Charlton A	D2	H	W	1-0	Moores
	4	26.1.82	Huddersfield T	D3	A	D	1-1	Moores
	4r	1.2.82	Huddersfield T		H	W	2-0	Foster, Moores
	5	13.2.82	Crystal Palace	D2	A	D	0-0	
	5r	16.2.82	Crystal Palace		H	L	0-1	
1982-83	D3	1	20.11.82	Bristol C	D4	H	W	4-1	Foster, Godfery 2, Sussex
	2	11.12.82	Newport Co	D3	A	L	0-1	
1983-84	D3	1	19.11.83	Wimbledon	D3	A	L	1-2	Smith og
1984-85	D3	1	19.11.84	Buckingham T	UCL	A	W	2-0	Cornwell (p), McNeil
	2	8.12.84	Torquay U	D4	H	W	3-0	Godfery, Jones, Foster
	3	5.1.85	WBA	D1	H	W	2-1	Silkman, Cadette
	4	26.1.85	Southampton	D1	H	L	0-2	
1985-86	D4	1	16.11.85	V.S. Rugby	SL	A	D	2-2	Brooks 2 (1p),

LEYTON ORIENT

		1r	19.11.85	**V.S. Rugby**		H	W	4-1	Jones, Castle, Juryeff, Brooks
		2	7.12.85	**Slough T**	IL	H	D	2-2	Cornwell, Juryeff
		2r	10.12.85	**Slough T**		A	W	3-2	Juryeff, Godfery, Shinners
		3	6.1.86	**Oldham A**	D2	A	W	2-1	Shinners, Foster
		4	25.1.86	**Sheffield W**	D1	A	L	0-5	
1986-87	D4	1	15.11.86	**Woodford T**	SL	A	W	1-0	Foster
		2	6.12.86	**Bournemouth**	D3	A	W	1-0	Harvey
		3	10.1.87	**West Ham**	D1	H	D	1-1	Castle (p)
		3r	31.1.87	**West Ham**		A	L	1-4	Brooks

as Leyton Orient

1987-88	D4	1	14.11.87	**Exeter C**	D4	H	W	2-0	Godfery, Hull
		2	5.12.87	**Swansea C**	D4	H	W	2-0	Shinners, Comfort
		3	9.1.88	**Stockport Co**	D4	A	W	2-1	Juryeff, Shinners
		4	30.1.88	**Nottingham F**	D1	H	L	1-2	Juryeff
1988-89	D4	1	19.11.88	**Enfield**	GMVC	A	D	1-1	Ward
		1r	23.11.88	**Enfield**		H	D	2-2aet	Juryeff 2
		1 2r	28.11.88	**Enfield**		H	L	0-1	
1989-90	D3	1	18.11.89	**Birmingham C**	D3	H	L	0-1	
1990-91	D3	1	17.11.90	**Southend U**	D3	H	W	3-2	Castle 2, Nugent
		2	12.12.90	**Colchester U**	GMVC	A	D	0-0	
		2r	17.12.90	**Colchester U**		H	W	4-1	Carter, Howard, Pike, Castle
		3	5.1.91	**Swindon T**	D2	H	D	1-1	Pike
		3r	14.1.91	**Swindon T**		A	–	1-1	Dickenson
				abandoned after 54 minutes, frozen pitch					
		3r	21.1.91	**Swindon T**		A	L	0-1	
1991-92	D3	1	16.11.91	**Welling T**	GMVC	H	W	2-1	Howard, Cooper
		2	9.12.91	**WBA**	D3	H	W	2-1	Berry 2
		3	4.1.92	**Oldham A**	D1	A	D	1-1	Day
		3r	15.1.92	**Oldham A**		H	W	4-2	Harvey, Nugent 2, Castle (p)
		4	25.1.92	**Portsmouth**	D2	A	L	0-2	
1992-93	D2	1	14.11.92	**Dagenham & Redbridge**	GMVC	A	W	5-4	Howard, Whitbread, Cooper 2, Jones
		2	6.12.92	**Reading**	D2	A	L	0-3	

LEYTONSTONE

Formed 1886. **First entered FA Cup:** 1896. **FA Amateur Cup Winners:** 1947, 1948, 1968. Merged with Ilford to form Leytonstone-Ilford in 1979. Became Redbridge Forest 1989 and subsequently Dagenham-Redbridge 1992

1946-47	IL	1	30.11.46	**Walsall**	3S	H	L	1-6	Banham
1947-48	IL	1	29.11.47	**Bristol R**	3S	A	L	2-3	Bunce, Groves
1948-49	IL	1	27.11.48	**Watford**	3S	H	A	1-1	Noble
				abandoned after 63 minutes					
		1	4.12.48	**Watford**		H	W	2-1	Smith, Joseph
		2	11.12.48	**Newport Co**	3S	H	L	3-4aet	Noble 2, Kavanagh
1949-50	IL	1	26.11.49	**Chelmsford C**	SL	H	L	1-2	Noble
1951-52	IL	1	24.11.51	**Shrewsbury T**	3S	H	W	2-0	Joseph, Noble
		2	15.12.51	**Newport Co**	3S	H	D	2-2	Noble 2
		2r	20.12.51	**Newport Co**		A	L	0-3	
1952-53	IL	1	22.11.52	**Watford**	3S	H	L	0-2	
1965-66	IL	1	13.11.65	**Hereford U**	SL	H	L	0-1	
1967-68	IL	1	9.12.67	**Walsall**	D3	H	L	0-1	
1968-69	IL	1	16.11.68	**Walsall**	D3	H	L	0-1	
1973-74	IL	1	24.11.73	**Hendon**	IL	A	L	0-3	

as Leytonstone-Ilford

1979-80	IL	1	24.11.79	**Harlow T**	IL	A	L	1-2	Powell
1981-82	IL	1	21.11.81	**Aldershot**	D4	A	L	0-2	

LINBY COLLIERY

Formed 1892. **Entered FA Cup:** 1948-56. Colliery closed 1987, club still plays in Notts Alliance League

1950-51	CA	1	25.11.50	**Gillingham**	3S	H	L	1-4	Dulson

LINCOLN ALBION

Formed 1882. Played at West Common, near the Vine Inn.

| 1887-88 | 1 | 15.10.87 **Basford Rovers** | | A | L | 2-3 | |

LINCOLN CITY

Formed 1883. **Best FA Cup Performances:** 1887, 1890, 1902 when they reached the last 16 (designated by different round numbers in those years) **Record FA Cup Win:** 13-0 vs Peterborough Club, 1st qualifying round, 12.10.1895 **Record FA Cup Defeat:** 0-5 vs Grimsby T, 4th qualifying round, 10.12.1892 0-5 vs Stoke, 1st round, 11.1.1907

1884-85	1	1.11.84 **Hull T**		A	W	5-1	Fox 2, C.Newsum, H.Newsum, 1 other
	2	**bye**					
	3	3.1.85 **Grimsby T**		A	L	0-1	
1885-86	1	31.10.85 **Grimsby T**		H	L	0-2	
1886-87	1	**bye**					
	2	20.11.86 **Middlesbrough**		A	D	1-1	Slater
	2r	27.11.86 **Middlesbrough**		H	W	2-0	Gregson, Simpson
	3	11.12.86 **Gainsborough T**		A	D	2-2aet	Gregson, 1 other
	3r	24.1.87 **Gainsborough T** at Bramall Lane			W	1-0	
	4	**bye**					
	5	29.1.87 **Glasgow Rangers**		A	L	0-3	
1887-88	1	15.10.87 **Chatham**		A	L	1-5	Smart

1888-89 1q **Grimsby T** (A) 1-1aet; 1qr **Grimsby T** (H) 1-1aet; 1q 2r **Grimsby T** 1-3 at Bramall Lane

1889-90 ML 2q **Notts Olympic** (H) 2-1; 3q **Notts Rangers** (A) 7-2; 4q **Gainsborough T** (H) 5-3

| | | 1 | 18.1.90 **Chester** | | H | W | 2-0 | Mckay, Duckworth |
| | | 2 | 1.2.90 **Preston NE** | D1 | A | L | 0-4 | |

1890-91 ML 1q **Gainsborough T** (A) 3-1; 2q **Boston** (H) 9-0; 3q **Ecclesfield** (H) 3-0; 4q **Staveley** (H) 4-1

| | | 1 | 17.1.91 **Chester** | TC | A | L | 0-1 | |

1891-92 ML 1q **Doncaster R** (H) 3-1; 2q **Sheffield U** (A) 1-4

1892-93 D2 1q **Newark** (H) 3-1 abnd; 1q **Newark** (A) 4-3; 2q **Hednesford T** (A) 3-0; 3q **Rotherham T** (H) 2-0; 4q **Grimsby T** (A) 0-5

1893-94 D2 1q **Sheffield Club** (A) 2-0; 2q **Grimsby T** (H) 2-5

1894-95 D2 1q **Grimsby T** (H) 0-3

1895-96 D2 1q **Peterborough Club** (A) 13-0; 2q **Worksop T** (A) 3-0; 3q **Grimsby T** (H) 2-4

1896-97 D2 3q **Gainsborough T** (H) 1-0; 4q **Worksop T** (A) 3-3; 4qr **Worksop T** (H) 8-0; 5q **Barnsley** (H) 1-2

1897-98 D2 3q **Attercliffe** (H) 5-0; 4q **Gainsborough T** (A) 1-5

1898-99 D2 3q **Attercliffe** (H) 5-0; 4q **Grimsby T** (A) 1-2

1899-00 D2 3q **Barnsley** (A) 0-1

1900-01 D2 3q **Gainsborough Trinity** (H) 0-0; 3qr **Gainsborough T** (A) 1-1 abnd; 3qr **Gainsborough T** 3-1 at Bramall Lane; 4q **Barnsley** (A) 0-1

1901-02 D2 3q **Worksop T** (A) 4-0; 4q **Doncaster R** (H) 1-0; 5q **Barnsley** (A) 0-0; 5qr **Barnsley** (H) 3-1; Int **Newton Heath** (A) 2-1

		1	25.1.02 **Oxford C**		A	D	0-0	
		1r	29.1.02 **Oxford C**		H	W	4-0	McInnes 2, O'Donnell, 1 other
		2	8.2.02 **Derby Co**	D1	H	L	1-3	McInnes

1902-03 D2 Int **West Ham** (H) 2-0

| | | 1 | 7.2.03 **Barnsley** | D2 | A | L | 0-2 | |

1903-04 D2 3q **Chesterfield** (H) 0-2

1904-05 D2 6q **Watford** (A) 1-1; 6qr **Watford** (H) 2-1; Int **Burnley** (A) 1-1; Int R **Burnley** (H) 3-2

		1	4.2.05 **Manchester C**	D1	H	L	1-2	D. O'Donnell
1905-06	D2	1	13.1.06 **Stockport Co**	D2	H	W	4-2	Watson, Martin 2, F.Simpson
		2	3.2.06 **Brentford**	SL	A	L	0-3	
1906-07	D2	1	12.1.07 **Chelsea**	D2	H	D	2-2	E.Dixon, W.Watson
		1r	16.1.07 **Chelsea**		A	W	1-0aet	Mackin
		2	2.2.07 **Derby Co**	D1	A	L	0-1	
1907-08	D2	1	11.1.08 **Stoke**	D2	A	L	0-5	

1908-09 ML 5q **Stockton** (H) 1-0

| | | 1 | 16.1.09 **Liverpool** | D1 | A | L | 1-5 | Morris |

1909-10 D2 4q **Crewe Alex** (A) 1-2

1910-11 D2 4q **Huddersfield T** (A) 1-1; 4qr **Huddersfield T** (H) 1-0; 5q **Stoke** (A) 0-4

1911-12 CL 4q **Grimsby T** (H) 3-2; 5q **Crook T** (A) 3-2;

| | | 1 | 13.1.12 **Stockport Co** | D2 | H | W | 2-0 | McCubbin, Batty |
| | | 2 | 3.2.12 **Wolverhampton W** | D2 | A | L | 1-2 | Brindley |

1912-13 D2 4q **Rotherham Co** (A) 3-1; 5q **South Shields** (A) 0-1

| 1913-14 | D2 | 1 | 10.1.14 **Plymouth A** | SL | A | L | 1-4 | Barrell |

1914-15 D2 6q **Rotherham Co** (H) 6-0

| | | 1 | 9.1.15 **Brighton & HA** | SL | A | L | 1-2 | Egerton |
| 1919-20 | D2 | 1 | 14.1.20 **Middlesbrough** | D1 | A | L | 1-4 | Ball |

Season		Round	Date	Opponent		Venue	Result	Score	Scorers
1920-21	ML	6q		Bromley (H) 5-0					
		1	8.1.21	Millwall	D3	A	W	3-0	Rippon 2, Bretnall
		2	29.1.21	Fulham	D2	H	D	0-0	
		2r	7.2.21	Fulham		A	L	0-1	
1921-22	3N	5q		Northampton T (H) 1-2					
1922-23	3N	4q		Chesterfield (A) 0-2					
1923-24	3N	4q		Denaby U (A) 2-1; 5q Northampton T (A) 1-5					
1924-25	3N	4q		Rossington Main (H) 3-0; 5q Alfreton T (A) 0-1					
1925-26	3N	1	28.11.25	Bradford PA	3N	A	D	2-2	Havelock, Merritt
		1r	2.12.25	Bradford PA		H	D	1-1aet	McGraham
		1 2r	7.12.25	Bradford PA at Bramall Lane			L	1-2	Hooper
1926-27	3N	1	27.11.26	Rotherham U	3N	H	W	2-0	Pringle, Andrews
		2	11.12.26	Coventry C	3S	A	D	1-1	Andrews
		2r	15.12.26	Coventry C		H	W	2-1	Dinsdale, Bosberry
		3	8.1.27	Preston NE	D2	H	L	2-4	Dinsdale 2
1927-28	3N	1	26.11.27	Accrington Stanley	3N	A	W	5-2	Dinsdale 2, Pringle, Andrews, Bosberry
		2	10.12.27	Gainsborough Trinity	ML	A	W	2-0	Bosbury 2
		3	14.1.28	Huddersfield T	D1	A	L	2-4	Pringle, Dinsdale
1928-29	3N	1	24.11.28	Lancaster T	LC	H	W	3-1	Dinsdale 2, Pringle
		2	10.12.28	Carlisle U	3N	A	W	1-0	Roberts
		3	12.1.29	Leicester C	D1	H	L	0-1	
1929-30	3N	1	30.11.29	Wigan Borough	3N	H	W	3-1	Maidment 2, Thursby
		2	14.12.29	QPR	3S	A	L	1-2	Maidment
1930-31	3N	1	29.11.30	Barrow	3N	H	W	8-3	Dinsdale 4, Cartwright, Lax 2, Kitching
		2	13.12.30	Scarborough	ML	A	L	4-6	Cartwright, Lax, Dinsdale 2
1931-32	3N	1	28.11.31	Manchester Central	CC	A	W	3-0	Riley 3
		2	12.12.31	Luton T	3S	H	D	2-2	Hall 2
		2r	16.12.31	Luton T		A	L	1-4	Hall
1932-33	D2	3	14.1.33	Blackburn R	D1	H	L	1-5	Horne
1933-34	D2	3	13.1.34	Leicester C	D1	A	L	0-3	
1934-35	3N	1	24.11.34	Shildon	NL	A	D	2-2	Wilkinson 2
		1r	28.11.34	Shildon		H	W	4-0	Burke, Read 3
		2	8.12.34	Swindon T	3S	A	L	3-4	Read, Campbell, Iverson
1935-36	3N	1	30.11.35	Walsall	3N	A	L	0-2	
1936-37	3N	1	28.11.36	New Brighton	3N	H	D	1-1	Towler
		1r	2.12.36	New Brighton		A	W	3-2	Towler, Campbell, Horne
		2	12.12.36	Oldham A	3N	H	L	2-3	Towler 2
1937-38	3N	1	27.11.37	Rochdale	3N	A	D	1-1	Deacon
		1r	1.12.37	Rochdale		H	W	2-0	White, Campbell
		2	11.12.37	Mansfield T	3S	A	–	2-1	White, Towler
				abandoned after 62 minutes					
		2	15.12.37	Mansfield T		A	L	1-2	Campbell
1938-39	3N	1	26.11.38	Barrow	3N	H	W	4-1	Wilson, Hancock, Deacon, Ponting
		2	10.12.38	Bromley	AL	H	W	8-1	Clare 2, Ponting 3, Wilson, Deacon, White
		3	7.1.39	Portsmouth	D1	A	L	0-4	
1945-46	3N	1 1L	17.11.45	Yorkshire Amateurs	YL	A	L	0-1	
		1 2L	24.11.45	Yorkshire Amateurs		H	W	5-1	Cheetham 2, Marlow, Wroe, Farman og
		2 1L	8.12.45	Rotherham U	3N	A	L	1-2	Marlow
		2 2L	15.12.45	Rotherham U		H	D	1-1	Marlow
1946-47	3N	1	30.11.46	Stockton	NL	A	W	4-2	Cheetham, Hutchinson, Davies, Marlow
		2	14.12.46	Wrexham	3N	H	D	1-1	Marlow
		2r	18.12.46	Wrexham		A	D	3-3aet	Hutchinson, Cheetham 2
		2 2r	23.12.46	Wrexham at Maine Road			W	2-1	Marlow, Cheetham
		3	11.1.47	Nottingham F	D2	H	L	0-1	
1947-48	3N	1	29.11.47	Workington	NEL	H	L	0-2	
1948-49	D2	3	8.1.49	WBA	D2	H	L	0-1	
1949-50	3N	1	26.11.49	Carlisle U	3N	A	L	0-1	
1950-51	3N	1	25.11.50	Southport	3N	H	D	1-1	Graver
		1r	28.11.50	Southport		A	L	2-3	Troops, Windle
1951-52	3N	1	24.11.51	Crewe Alex	3N	A	W	4-2	Garvie, Graver, Whittle, Young
		2	15.12.51	Grimsby T	3N	H	W	3-1	Graver 2, Galbraith og
		3	12.1.52	Portsmouth	D1	A	L	0-4	
1952-53	D2	3	10.1.53	Southampton	D2	H	D	1-1	Birch
		3r	14.1.53	Southampton		A	L	1-2	Finch
1953-54	D2	3	9.1.54	Walsall	3S	H	D	1-1	Graver
		3r	14.1.54	Walsall		A	D	1-1aet	Finch
		3 2r	18.1.54	Walsall at Nottingham Forest			W	2-1	Whittle, Green (og)

	4	30.1.54	**Preston NE**	D1	H	L	0-2
1954-55 D2	3	8.1.55	**Liverpool**	D2	H	D	1-1	Munro
	3r	12.1.55	**Liverpool**		A	L	0-1aet
1955-56 D2	3	7.1.56	**Southend U**	3S	H	L	2-3	Bannan, Troops
1956-57 D2	3	5.1.57	**Peterborough U**	ML	A	D	2-2	Watson, Troops
	3r	9.1.57	**Peterborough U**		H	L	4-5	Bannan 2 (1p), Neal, Northcott
1957-58 D2	3	4.1.58	**Wolverhampton W**	D1	H	L	0-1
1958-59 D2	3	10.1.59	**Leicester C**	D1	A	D	1-1	McClelland
	3r	14.1.59	**Leicester C**		H	L	0-2
1959-60 D2	3	9.1.60	**Burnley**	D1	H	D	1-1	Herbertson
	3r	12.1.60	**Burnley**		A	L	0-2
1960-61 D2	3	7.1.61	**WBA**	D1	H	W	3-1	Graver, Linnecor, McClelland
	4	28.1.61	**Sheffield U**	D2	A	L	1-3	Graver
1961-62 D3	1	4.11.61	**Crewe Alex**	D4	A	L	0-2
1962-63 D4	1	3.11.62	**Darlington**	D4	H	D	1-1	Scanlon
	1r	7.11.62	**Darlington**		A	W	2-1	Campbell 2
	2	24.11.62	**Halifax T**	D3	H	W	1-0	Campbell
	3	7.3.63	**Coventry C**	D3	H	L	1-5	Punter
1963-64 D4	1	16.11.63	**Hartlepools U**	D4	A	W	1-0	Holmes
	2	7.12.63	**Southport**	D4	H	W	2-0	Morton, Wilkinson
	3	4.1.64	**Sheffield U**	D1	H	L	0-4
1964-65 D4	1	14.11.64	**Tranmere R**	D4	A	D	0-0
	1r	18.11.64	**Tranmere R**		H	W	1-0	Hawksby
	2	5.12.64	**Hull C**	D3	A	D	1-1	Houghton
	2r	9.12.64	**Hull C**		H	W	3-1	Houghton, Fencott, Milner
	3	9.1.65	**Rotherham U**	D2	A	L	1-5	Houghton
1965-66 D4	1	13.11.65	**Barnsley**	D4	H	L	1-3	Ellis
1966-67 D4	1	26.11.66	**Scunthorpe U**	D3	H	L	3-4	Chapman, Bonson, Grummett
1967-68 D4	1	9.12.67	**Southport**	D3	A	L	1-3	Cobb
1968-69 D4	1	16.11.68	**Macclesfield T**	CC	A	W	3-1	Kearns, Smith, Thom
	2	7.12.68	**Chester**	D4	A	D	1-1	Corner
	2r	11.12.68	**Chester**		H	W	2-1	Kearns, Smith
	3	4.1.69	**Birmingham C**	D2	A	L	1-2	Smith
1969-70 D4	1	15.11.69	**Southport**	D3	H	W	2-0	Smith, Fletcher
	2	6.12.69	**Bradford C**	D3	A	L	0-3
1970-71 D4	1	21.11.70	**Barrow**	D4	H	W	2-1	Svarc, Smith
	2	12.12.70	**Bradford C**	D3	H	D	2-2	Trevis, Svarc
	2r	16.12.70	**Bradford C**		A	D	2-2aet	Fletcher, Svarc
	2 2r	21.12.70	**Bradford C** at Doncaster			W	4-1	Freeman 2, Svarc, W.Taylor
	3	2.1.71	**Torquay U**	D3	A	L	3-4	Freeman 2, Hubbard
1971-72 D4	1	20.11.71	**Bury**	D4	H	L	1-2	Gilliver
1972-73 D4	1	18.11.72	**Blackburn R**	D3	H	D	2-2	Freeman, Bradley
	1r	27.11.72	**Blackburn R**		A	L	1-4	Smith
1973-74 D4	1	24.11.73	**Doncaster R**	D4	A	L	0-1
1974-75 D4	1	23.11.74	**Port Vale**	D3	A	D	2-2	Dulson og, Krzywicki
	1r	27.11.74	**Port Vale**		H	W	2-0	Graham, Harding
	2	14.12.74	**Hartlepool**	D4	A	D	0-0
	2r	17.12.74	**Hartlepool**		H	W	1-0	Cooper
	3	4.1.75	**Swindon T**	D3	A	L	0-2
1975-76 D4	1	22.11.75	**Boston U**	NPL	A	W	1-0	Freeman
	2	13.12.75	**Mansfield T**	D3	A	W	2-1	Branfoot, Freeman
	3	3.1.76	**Aldershot**	D3	A	W	2-1	Ward, Ellis (p)
	4	24.1.76	**WBA**	D2	A	L	2-4	Ellis (p), Fleming
1976-77 D3	1	20.11.76	**Morecambe**	NPL	H	W	1-0	Freeman
	2	11.12.76	**Nuneaton Borough**	SL	H	W	6-0	Ellis 2 (2ps), Harding, Ward, Graham 2
	3	8.1.77	**Burnley**	D2	A	D	2-2	Ward, Harding
	3r	12.1.77	**Burnley**		H	L	0-1
1977-78 D3	1	26.11.77	**Preston NE**	D3	A	L	2-3	Harding, Wigginton (p)
1978-79 D3	1	25.11.78	**Blackpool**	D3	A	L	1-2	Ward
1979-80 D4	1	24.11.79	**Sheffield W**	D3	A	L	0-3
1980-81 D4	1	22.11.80	**Gateshead**	NPL	H	W	1-0	Turner
	2	13.12.80	**Bury**	D4	A	L	0-2
1981-82 D3	1	21.11.81	**Port Vale**	D4	H	D	2-2	S.Thompson, Cammack
	1r	30.11.81	**Port Vale**		A	D	0-0aet
	1 2r	2.12.81	**Port Vale**		A	L	0-2
1982-83 D3	1	20.11.82	**Hartlepool U**	D4	A	L	0-3
1983-84 D3	1	19.11.83	**Port Vale**	D3	A	W	2-1	Jack, Shipley

	2	10.12.83	**Sheffield U**	D3	H	D	0-0	
	2r	19.12.83	**Sheffield U**		A	L	0-1	
1984-85	D3	1	17.11.84	**Telford U**	APL	H	D	1-1	Redfearn
	1r	20.11.84	**Telford U**		A	L	1-2	Walker
1985-86	D3	1	16.11.85	**Blackpool**	D3	H	L	0-1	
1986-87	D4	1	15.11.86	**Wigan Ath**	D3	A	L	1-3	Lund
1987-88	GMVC	4q	24.10.87	**Brigg T**	NCoE	H	W	4-1	McGinley 2, Cumming, Waite
	1	14.11.87	**Crewe Alex**	D4	H	W	2-1	McGinley, Cumming
	2	5.12.87	**Mansfield T**	D3	A	L	3-4	Smith, Brown, Clarke
1988-89	D4	1	19.11.88	**Altrincham**	GMVC	A	L	2-3	Davis, Sertori
1989-90	D4	1	18.11.89	**Billingham Syn.**	NL	H	W	1-0	Nicholson
	2	9.12.89	**Rochdale**	D4	A	L	0-3	
1990-91	D4	1	17.11.90	**Crewe Alex**	D3	H	L	1-4	Lormor
1991-92	D4	1	16.11.91	**Stockport Co**	D3	A	L	1-3	Lee
1992-93	D3	1	14.11.92	**Stafford R**	GMVC	H	D	0-0	
	1r	25.11.92	**Stafford R**		A	L	1-2	Costello

LINCOLN LINDUM

Formed 1868. Played at Wragby Road, Lincoln.

1885-86	1	17.10.85	**Grimsby District**	H	W	4-0
	2	21.11.85	**Redcar**	A	L	0-2
1886-87	1	23.10.86	**Grantham**	H	L	0-1
1887-88	1	15.10.87	**Grantham**	A	L	0-4

LINCOLN RAMBLERS

Formed 1878. Played at the Cowpaddle Ground

| 1887-88 | 1 | 15.10.87 | **Notts Co** | A | L | 0-9 |

LINCOLN UNITED

Formed 1938 as Lincoln Amateurs. Lincoln United 1954

| 1991-92 | CM | 1 | 16.11.91 | **Huddersfield T** | D3 | A | L | 0-7 |

LINFIELD ATHLETIC

Formed 1886. One of the three Irish teams to take part in the FA Cup proper. Won Irish FA Cup 33 times.

1888-89	3q	17.11.88	**Bolton W**	FL	H	W	4-0	
	4q	8.12.88	**Cliftonville**		A	D	3-3	
	4qr	15.12.88	**Cliftonville**		H	D	3-3	
	4q 2r	25.12.88	**Cliftonville**		H	W	7-0	
	1	2.2.89	**Nottingham Forest**		A	D	2-2aet	Pedan 2
	1r		**Nottingham Forest**				*scratched*	

LITTLEHAMPTON TOWN

Formed 1894. **First entered FA Cup:** 1912

| 1990-91 | SCL | 1 | 17.11.90 | **Northampton T** | D4 | H | L | 0-4 |

LIVERPOOL

Formed 1892. FA Cup and League Double 1986. **FA Cup Winners:** 1965, 1974, 1986, 1989, 1992. **FA Cup Runners-Up:** 1914, 1950, 1971, 1977, 1988. **FA Cup Record Win:** 9-0 vs Newtown, 2nd qualifying round, 29.10.1892. **In Competition Proper:** 8-0 vs Swansea City, 3rd round replay, 9.1.1990. **FA Cup Record Defeat:** 0-5 vs Bolton Wanderers, 4th round, 1st leg, 26.1.1946.

1892-93	LL	1q **Nantwich** (A) 4-0aet; 2q **Newtown** (H) 9-0; 3q **Northwich Victoria** (A) 1-2						
1893-94	D2	1	27.1.94	**Grimsby T**	D2	H	W	3-0	Bradshaw 2, McQue
	2	10.2.94	**Preston NE**	D1	H	W	3-2	Henderson 2, McVean
	3	24.2.94	**Bolton W**	D1	A	L	0-3	
1894-95	D1	1	2.2.95	**Barnsley St Peters**		A	W	2-1aet	McLean, Ross
			FA ordered replay after protest					
	1r	11.2.95	**Barnsley St Peters**		H	W	4-0	Bradshaw, Drummond, McVean, McQueen

Season	Div	Rd	Date	Opponent	Comp	H/A	Res	Score	Scorers
		2	16.2.95	Nottingham F	D1	H	L	0-2	
1895-96	D2	1	1.2.96	Millwall A	SL	H	W	4-1	Ross, Becton, Allan, Bradshaw
		2	15.2.96	Wolverhampton W	D1	A	L	0-2	
1896-97	D1	1	30.1.97	Burton Swifts	D2	H	W	4-3	Hannah, Allan, Cleghorn, Ross
		2	13.2.97	WBA	D1	A	W	2-1	McVean, Neill
		3	27.2.97	Nottingham F	D1	H	D	1-1	Becton
		3r	3.3.97	Nottingham F		A	W	1-0	Allan
		SF	20.3.97	A.Villa	D1		L	0-3	
			played at Bramall Lane						
1897-98	D1	1	29.1.98	Hucknall St Johns		H	W	2-0	Becton, McQue
		2	12.2.98	Newton Heath	D2	A	D	0-0	
		2r	16.2.98	Newton Heath		H	W	2-1	Wilkie, Cunliffe
		3	25.2.98	Derby Co	D1	A	D	1-1	Bradshaw
		3r	2.3.98	Derby Co		H	L	1-5	Becton
1898-99	D1	1	28.1.99	Blackburn R	D1	H	W	2-0	Cox, Allan
		2	11.2.99	Newcastle U	D1	H	W	3-1	Morgan, Raisbeck, Higgins og
		3	25.2.99	WBA	D1	A	W	2-0	Morgan, Robertson
		SF	18.3.99	Sheffield U	D1		D	2-2	Allan, Morgan
			played at Nottingham						
		SFr	23.3.99	Sheffield U			D	4-4aet	Walker, Allan, Cox, Boyle og
			played at Bolton						
		SF 2r	27.3.99	Sheffield U			–	1-0	Allan
			abandoned after halftime, played at Fallowfield						
		SF 3r	30.3.99	Sheffield U			L	0-1	
			played at Derby						
1899-00	D1	1	27.1.00	Stoke	D1	A	D	0-0	
		1r	1.2.00	Stoke		H	W	1-0	Hunter
		2	17.2.00	WBA	D1	H	D	1-1	Cox
		2r	21.2.00	WBA		A	L	1-2	Robertson
1900-01	D1	1	9.2.01	Notts Co	D1	A	L	0-2	
1901-02	D1	1	25.1.02	Everton	D1	H	D	2-2	T.Robertson (p), Hunter
		1r	30.1.02	Everton		A	W	2-0	Raisbeck, Hunter
		2	8.2.02	Southampton	SL	A	L	1-4	Fleming
1902-03	D1	1	7.2.03	Manchester U	D2	A	L	1-2	Raybould
1903-04	D1	1	6.2.04	Blackburn R	D1	A	L	1-3	Raybould
1904-05	D2	1	4.2.05	Everton	D1	H	D	1-1	Parkinson
		1r	8.2.05	Everton		A	L	1-2	Goddard
1905-06	D1	1	13.1.06	Leicester Fosse	D2	H	W	2-1	Raybould, Goddard
		2	3.2.06	Barnsley	D2	H	W	1-0	West
		3	24.2.06	Brentford	SL	H	W	2-0	Hewitt, Goddard
		4	10.3.06	Southampton	SL	H	W	3-0	Raybould 3
		SF	31.3.06	Everton	D1		L	0-2	
			played at Villa Park						
1906-07	D1	1	12.1.07	Birmingham	D1	H	W	2-1	Raybould
		2	2.2.07	Oldham A	LC	A	W	1-0	McPherson
		3	23.2.07	Bradford C	D2	H	W	1-0	Cox
		4	9.3.07	Sheffield W	D1	A	L	0-1	
1907-08	D1	1	11.1.08	Derby Co	D2	H	W	4-2	Cox, Gorman, Bradley, Parkinson
		2	1.2.08	Brighton & HA	SL	H	D	1-1	Cox
		2r	5.2.08	Brighton & HA		A	W	3-0	Bradley 2, Cox
		3	22.2.08	Newcastle U	D1	A	L	1-3	Saul
1908-09	D1	1	16.1.09	Lincoln C	ML	H	W	5-1	Orr 3, Hewitt, Parkinson
		2	6.2.09	Norwich C	SL	H	L	2-3	Cox, Robinson
1909-10	D1	1	15.1.10	Bristol C	D1	A	L	0-2	
1910-11	D1	1	14.1.11	Gainsborough T	D2	H	W	3-2	Bowyer 2, Goddard
		2	4.2.11	Everton	D1	A	L	1-2	Parkinson
1911-12	D1	1	13.1.12	Leyton	SL	H	W	1-0	Parkinson
		2	3.2.12	Fulham	D2	A	L	0-3	
1912-13	D1	1	15.1.13	Bristol C	D2	H	W	3-0	Goddard (p), Peake, Lacey
		2	1.2.13	W.Arsenal	D1	A	W	4-1	Metcalfe 3, Lacey
		3	22.2.13	Newcastle U	D1	H	D	1-1	Lacey
		3r	26.2.13	Newcastle U		A	L	0-1	
1913-14	D1	1	10.1.14	Barnsley	D2	H	D	1-1	Lacey
		1r	15.1.14	Barnsley		A	W	1-0	Lacey
		2	31.1.14	Gillingham	SL	H	W	2-0	Lacey, Ferguson
		3	21.2.14	West Ham	SL	A	D	1-1	Miller
		3r	25.2.14	West Ham		H	W	5-1	Lacey 2, Miller 2, Metcalfe

	4	7.3.14 **QPR**	SL	H	W	2-1	Sheldon, Miller
	SF	28.3.14 **A.Villa**	D1		W	2-0	Nicholl 2
		played at Tottenham					
	F	25.4.14 **Burnley**	D1		L	0-1	
		played at Crystal Palace					
1914-15	D1	1	9.1.15 **Stockport Co**	D2	H	W	3-0	Pagnam 2, Metcalfe
		2	30.1.15 **Sheffield U**	D1	A	L	0-1	
1919-20	D1	1	10.1.20 **South Shields**	D2	A	D	1-1	Lewis
		1r	14.1.20 **South Shields**		H	W	2-0	Lewis, Sheldon
		2	31.1.20 **Luton T**	SL	A	W	2-0	Lacey 2
		3	21.1.20 **Birmingham**	D2	H	W	2-0	Sheldon, T.Miller
		4	6.3.20 **Huddersfield T**	D2	A	L	1-2	T.Miller
1920-21	D1	1	8.1.21 **Manchester U**	D1	H	D	1-1	Chambers
		1r	12.1.21 **Manchester U**		A	W	2-1	Lacey, Chambers
		2	29.1.21 **Newcastle U**	D1	A	L	0-1	
1921-22	D1	1	7.1.22 **Sunderland**	D1	A	D	1-1	Forshaw
		1r	11.1.22 **Sunderland**		H	W	5-0	Forshaw 2, Chambers 2, W.Wadsworth
		2	28.1.22 **WBA**	D1	H	L	0-1	
1922-23	D1	1	13.1.23 **Arsenal**	D1	H	D	0-0	
		1r	17.1.23 **Arsenal**		A	W	4-1	Chambers 2, Johnson, McKinley (p)
		2	3.2.23 **Wolverhampton W**	D2	A	W	2-0	Johnson, Forshaw
		3	24.2.23 **Sheffield U**	D1	H	L	1-2	Chambers
1923-24	D1	1	12.1.24 **Bradford C**	D2	H	W	2-1	Chambers 2
		2	2.2.24 **Bolton W**	D1	A	W	4-1	Walsh 3, Chambers
		3	23.2.24 **Southampton**	D2	A	D	0-0	
		3r	27.2.24 **Southampton**		H	W	2-0	Chambers, Forshaw
		4	8.3.24 **Newcastle U**	D1	A	L	0-1	
1924-25	D1	1	10.1.25 **Leeds U**	D1	H	W	3-0	Shone 2, Hopkin
		2	31.1.25 **Bristol C**	3S	A	W	1-0	Rawlings
		3	21.2.25 **Birmingham**	D1	H	W	2-1	Rawlings, Shone
		4	7.3.25 **Southampton**	D2	A	L	0-1	
1925-26	D1	3	9.1.26 **Southampton**	D2	A	D	0-0	
		3r	13.1.26 **Southampton**		H	W	1-0	Forshaw
		4	30.1.26 **Fulham**	D2	A	L	1-3	Forshaw
1926-27	D1	3	8.1.27 **Bournemouth**	3S	A	D	1-1	Hodgson
		3r	12.1.27 **Bournemouth**		H	W	4-1	Chambers 3, Hopkin
		4	29.1.27 **Southport**	3N	H	W	3-1	Hodgson, Chambers, Edmed
		5	19.2.27 **Arsenal**	D1	A	L	0-2	
1927-28	D1	3	14.1.28 **Darlington**	3N	H	W	1-0	Chambers
		4	28.1.28 **Cardiff C**	D1	A	L	1-2	Edmed (p)
1928-29	D1	3	12.1.29 **Bristol C**	D2	A	W	2-0	Salisbury, Hodgson
		4	26.1.29 **Bolton W**	D1	H	D	0-0	
		4r	30.1.29 **Bolton W**		A	L	2-5aet	Lindsay, Hodgson
1929-30	D1	3	11.1.30 **Cardiff C**	D2	H	L	1-2	McPherson
1930-31	D1	3	10.1.31 **Birmingham**	D1	H	L	0-2	
1931-32	D1	3	9.1.32 **Everton**	D1	A	W	2-1	Gunson, Hodgson
		4	23.1.32 **Chesterfield**	D2	A	W	4-2	Barton 4
		5	13.2.32 **Grimsby T**	D1	H	W	1-0	Gunson
		6	27.2.32 **Chelsea**	D1	H	L	0-2	
1932-33	D1	3	14.1.33 **WBA**	D1	A	L	0-2	
1933-34	D1	3	13.1.34 **Fulham**	D2	H	D	1-1	Hodgson
		3r	17.1.34 **Fulham**		A	W	3-2aet	Hanson, Bradshaw, Roberts
		4	27.1.34 **Tranmere R**	3N	H	W	3-1	English 2, Nieuwenhuys
		5	17.2.34 **Bolton W**	D1	H	L	0-3	
1934-35	D1	3	12.1.35 **Yeovil & Petters U**	SL	A	W	6-2	Roberts 2, Hodgson 2, Nieuwenhuys, Wright
		4	26.1.35 **Blackburn R**	D1	A	L	0-1	
1935-36	D1	3	11.1.36 **Swansea T**	D2	H	W	1-0	Wright
		4	25.1.36 **Arsenal**	D1	H	L	0-2	
1936-37	D1	3	16.1.37 **Norwich C**	D2	A	L	0-3	
1937-38	D1	3	8.1.38 **Crystal P**	3S	A	D	0-0	
		3r	12.1.38 **Crystal P**		H	W	3-1aet	Shafto, Fagan (p), Collins og
		4	22.1.38 **Sheffield U**	D2	A	D	1-1	Hanson
		4r	26.1.38 **Sheffield U**		H	W	1-0	Johnson og
		5	12.2.38 **Huddersfield T**	D1	H	L	0-1	
1938-39	D1	3	7.1.39 **Luton T**	D2	H	W	3-0	Balmer 2, Paterson
		4	21.1.39 **Stockport Co**	3N	H	W	5-1	Nieuwenhuys 2, Balmer 2, Eastham
		5	11.2.39 **Wolverhampton W**	D1	A	L	1-4	Fagan (p)

LIVERPOOL

Season	Div	Round	Date	Opponent	Comp	H/A	Res	Score	Scorers
1945-46	D1	3 1L	5.1.46	Chester	3N	A	W	2-0	Liddell, Fagan
		3 2L	9.1.46	Chester		H	W	2-1	Fagan 2
		4 1L	26.1.46	Bolton W	D1	A	L	0-5	
		4 2L	30.1.46	Bolton W		H	W	2-0	Balmer, Nieuwenhuys
1946-47	D1	3	11.1.47	Walsall	3S	A	W	5-2	Balmer 2, Liddell, Done, Foulkes og
		4	25.1.47	Grismby T	D1	H	W	2-0	Stubbins, Done
		5	8.2.47	Derby Co	D1	H	W	1-0	Balmer
		6	1.3.47	Birmingham C	D2	H	W	4-1	Stubbins 3, Balmer
		SF	29.3.47	Burnley	D2		D	0-0aet	
			played at Ewood Park						
		SFr	12.4.47	Burnley			L	0-1	
			played at Maine Road						
1947-48	D1	3	10.1.48	Nottingham F	D2	H	W	4-1	Stubbins 2, Liddell, Priday
		4	24.1.48	Manchester U	D1	A	L	0-3	
			played at Goodison Park						
1948-49	D1	3	8.1.49	Nottingham F	D2	A	D	2-2aet	Fagan, Paisley
		3r	15.1.49	Nottingham F		H	W	4-0	Balmer 2, Stubbins, Payne
		4	29.1.49	Notts Co	3S	H	W	1-0	Liddell
		5	12.2.49	Wolverhampton W	D1	A	L	1-3	Done
1949-50	D1	3	7.1.50	Blackburn R	D2	A	D	0-0	
		3r	11.1.50	Blackburn R		H	W	2-1	Payne, Fagan
		4	28.1.50	Exeter C	3S	H	W	3-1	Barron, Fagan, Payne
		5	11.2.50	Stockport Co	3N	A	W	2-1	Fagan, Stubbins
		6	4.3.50	Blackpool	D1	H	W	2-1	Fagan, Liddell
		SF	25.3.50	Everton	D1		W	2-0	Paisley, Liddell
			played at Maine Road						
		F	29.4.50	Arsenal	D1 WEMBLEY		L	0-2	
1950-51	D1	3	6.1.51	Norwich C	3S	A	L	1-3	Balmer
1951-52	D1	3	12.1.52	Workington	3N	H	W	1-0	Payne
		4	2.2.52	Wolverhampton W	D1	H	W	2-1	Paisley, Done
		5	23.2.52	Burnley	D1	A	L	0-2	
1952-53	D1	3	10.1.53	Gateshead	3N	A	L	0-1	
1953-54	D1	3	9.1.54	Bolton W	D1	A	L	0-1	
1954-55	D2	3	8.1.55	Lincoln C	D2	A	D	1-1	Evans
		3r	12.1.55	Lincoln C		H	W	1-0aet	Evans
		4	29.1.55	Everton	D1	A	W	4-0	Evans 2, Liddell, A'Court
		5	19.2.55	Huddersfield T	D1	H	L	0-2	
1955-56	D2	3	7.1.56	Accrington S	3N	H	W	2-0	Liddell 2
		4	28.1.56	Scunthorpe U	3N	H	D	3-3	Liddell 2, Payne
		4r	6.2.56	Scunthorpe U		A	W	2-1aet	Liddell, Arnell
		5	18.2.56	Manchester C	D1	A	D	0-0	
		5r	22.2.56	Manchester C		H	L	1-2	Arnell
1956-57	D2	3	5.1.57	Southend U	3S	A	L	1-2	Wheeler
1957-58	D2	3	4.1.58	Southend U	3S	H	D	1-1	Smith og
		3r	8.1.58	Southend U		A	W	3-2	Molyneux, White, Rowley
		4	25.1.58	Northampton T	3S	H	W	3-1	Liddell, Bimpson, Collins og
		5	15.2.58	Scunthorpe Utd	3N	A	W	1-0	Murdoch
		6	1.3.58	Blackburn R	D2	A	L	1-2	Murdoch
1958-59	D2	3	15.1.59	Worcester C	SL	A	L	1-2	Twentyman (p)
1959-60	D2	3	9.1.60	Leyton Orient	D2	H	W	2-1	Hunt 2
		4	30.1.60	Manchester U	D1	H	L	1-3	Wheeler
1960-61	D2	3	7.1.61	Coventry C	D3	H	W	3-2	Hunt, Lewis, Harrower
		4	28.1.61	Sunderland	D2	H	L	0-2	
1961-62	D2	3	6.1.62	Chelsea	D1	H	W	4-3	St John 2, Hunt, A'Court
		4	27.1.62	Oldham A	D4	A	W	2-1	St John 2
		5	17.2.62	Preston NE	D2	H	D	0-0	
		5r	20.2.62	Preston NE		A	D	0-0aet	
		5 2r	26.2.62	Preston NE at Old Trafford			L	0-1	
1962-63	D1	3	9.1.63	Wrexham	D3	A	W	3-0	Hunt, Lewis, Melia
		4	26.1.63	Burnley	D1	A	D	1-1	Lewis
		4r	20.2.63	Burnley		H	W	2-1aet	St John, Moran (p)
		5	16.3.63	Arsenal	D1	A	W	2-1	Melia, Moran (p)
		6	30.3.63	West Ham	D1	H	W	1-0	Hunt
		SF	27.4.63	Leicester C	D1		L	0-1	
			played at Hillsborough						
1963-64	D1	3	4.1.64	Derby Co	D2	H	W	5-0	Arrowsmith 4, Hunt
		4	25.1.64	Port Vale	D3	H	D	0-0	

	4r	27.1.64	Port Vale		A	W	2-1aet	Hunt, Thompson
	5	15.2.64	Arsenal	D1	A	W	1-0	St John
	6	29.2.64	Swansea T	D2	H	L	1-2	Thompson
1964-65 D1	3	9.1.65	WBA	D1	A	W	2-1	Hunt, St John
	4	30.1.65	Stockport Co	D4	H	D	1-1	Milne
	4r	3.2.65	Stockport Co		A	W	2-0	Hunt 2
	5	20.2.65	Bolton W	D2	A	W	1-0	Callaghan
	6	6.3.65	Leicester C	D1	A	D	0-0	
	6r	10.3.65	Leicester C		H	W	1-0	Hunt
	SF	25.3.65	Chelsea	D1		W	2-0	Thompson, Stevenson (p)
			played at Villa Park					
	F	1.5.65	LEEDS U	D1 WEMBLEY	W	2-1aet	Hunt, St John
1965-66 D1	3	22.1.66	Chelsea	D1	H	L	1-2	Hunt
1966-67 D1	3	28.1.67	Watford	D3	A	D	0-0	
	3r	1.2.67	Watford		H	W	3-1	St John, Hunt, Lawler
	4	18.2.67	Aston Villa	D1	H	W	1-0	St John
	5	11.3.67	Everton	D1	A	L	0-1	
1967-68 D1	3	27.1.68	Bournemouth	D3	A	D	0-0	
	3r	30.1.68	Bournemouth		H	W	4-1	Hateley, Thompson, Hunt, Lawler
	4	17.2.68	Walsall	D3	A	D	0-0	
	4r	19.2.68	Walsall		H	W	5-2	Hateley 4, Strong
	5	9.3.68	Tottenham H	D1	A	D	1-1	Hateley
	5r	12.3.68	Tottenham H		H	W	2-1	Hunt, Smith (p)
	6	30.3.68	WBA	D1	A	D	0-0	
	6r	8.4.68	WBA		H	D	1-1aet	Hateley
	6 2r	18.4.68	WBA at Maine Road			L	1-2	Hateley
1968-69 D1	3	4.1.69	Doncaster R	D4	H	W	2-0	Hunt, Callaghan
	4	25.1.69	Burnley	D1	H	W	2-1	Smith (p), Hughes
	5	1.3.69	Leicester C	D1	A	D	0-0	
	5r	3.3.69	Leicester C		H	L	0-1	
1969-70 D1	3	7.1.70	Coventry C	D1	A	D	1-1	Graham
	3r	12.1.70	Coventry C		H	W	3-0	Ross, Thompson, Graham
	4	24.1.70	Wrexham	D4	H	W	3-1	Graham 2, St John
	5	7.2.70	Leicester C	D2	H	D	0-0	
	5r	11.2.70	Leicester C		A	W	2-0	Evans 2
	6	21.2.70	Watford	D2	A	L	0-1	
1970-71 D1	3	2.1.71	Aldershot	D4	H	W	1-0	McLaughlin
	4	23.1.71	Swansea C	D3	H	W	3-0	Toshack, St John, Lawler
	5	13.2.71	Southampton	D1	H	W	1-0	Lawler
	6	6.3.71	Tottenham H	D1	H	D	0-0	
	6r	16.3.71	Tottenham H		A	W	1-0	Heighway
	SF	27.3.71	Everton	D1		W	2-1	Evans, Hall
			played at Old Trafford					
	F	8.5.71	Arsenal	D1 WEMBLEY	L	1-2aet	Heighway
1971-72 D1	3	15.1.72	Oxford U	D2	A	W	3-0	Keegan 2, Lindsay
	4	5.2.72	Leeds U	D1	H	D	0-0	
	4r	9.2.72	Leeds U		A	L	0-2	
1972-73 D1	3	13.1.73	Burnley	D2	A	D	0-0	
	3r	16.1.73	Burnley		H	W	3-0	Toshack 2, Cormack
	4	4.2.73	Manchester C	D1	H	D	0-0	
	4r	7.2.73	Manchester C		A	L	0-2	
1973-74 D1	3	5.1.74	Doncaster R	D4	H	D	2-2	Keegan 2
	3r	8.1.74	Doncaster R		A	W	2-0	Heighway, Cormack
	4	26.1.74	Carlisle U	D2	H	D	0-0	
	4r	29.1.74	Carlisle U		A	W	2-0	Boersma, Toshack
	5	16.2.74	Ipswich T	D1	H	W	2-0	Hall, Keegan
	6	9.3.74	Bristol C	D2	A	W	1-0	Toshack
	SF	30.3.74	Leicester C	D1		D	0-0	
			played at Old Trafford					
	SFr	3.4.74	Leicester C			W	3-1	Hall, Keegan, Toshack
			played at Villa Park					
	F	4.5.74	NEWCASTLE U	D1 WEMBLEY	W	3-0	Keegan 2, Heighway
1974-75 D1	3	4.1.75	Stoke C	D1	H	W	2-0	Heighway, Keegan
	4	25.1.75	Ipswich T	D1	A	L	0-1	
1975-76 D1	3	3.1.76	West Ham	D1	A	W	2-0	Keegan, Toshack
	4	24.1.76	Derby Co	D1	A	L	0-1	
1976-77 D1	3	8.1.77	Crystal P	D3	H	D	0-0	

Season	Div	Round	Date	Opponent		Venue	Result	Score	Scorers
		3r	11.1.77	Crystal P		A	W	3-2	Heighway 2, Keegan
		4	29.1.77	Carlisle U	D2	H	W	3-0	Keegan, Toshack, Heighway
		5	26.2.77	Oldham A	D2	H	W	3-1	Keegan, Case, Neal (p)
		6	19.3.77	Middlesbrough	D1	H	W	2-0	Fairclough, Keegan
		SF	23.4.77	Everton	D1		D	2-2	McDermott, Case
			played at Maine Road						
		SFr	27.4.77	Everton			W	3-0	Neal (p), Case, R.Kennedy
			played at Maine Road						
		F	21.5.77	Manchester United	D1 WEMBLEY		L	1-2	Case
1977-78	D1	3	7.1.78	Chelsea	D1	A	L	2-4	Johnson, Dalglish
1978-79	D1	3	10.1.79	Southend U	D3	A	D	0-0	
		3r	17.1.79	Southend U		H	W	3-0	Case, Dalglish, R.Kennedy
		4	30.1.79	Blackburn R	D2	H	W	1-0	Dalglish
		5	28.2.79	Burnley	D2	H	W	3-0	Johnson 2, Souness
		6	10.3.79	Ipswich T	D1	A	W	1-0	Dalglish
		SF	31.3.79	Manchester U	D1		D	2-2	Dalglish, Hanson
			played at Maine Road						
		SFr	4.4.79	Manchester U			L	0-1	
			played at Goodison Park						
1979-80	D1	3	5.1.80	Grimsby T	D3	H	W	5-0	Johnson 3, Souness, Case
		4	26.1.80	Nottingham F	D1	A	W	2-0	Dalglish, McDermott (p)
		5	16.2.80	Bury	D3	H	W	2-0	Fairclough 2
		6	8.3.80	Tottenham H	D1	A	W	1-0	McDermott
		SF	12.4.80	Arsenal	D1		D	0-0	
			played at Hillsborough						
		SFr	16.4.80	Arsenal			D	1-1aet	Fairclough
			played at Villa Park						
		SF 2r	28.4.80	Arsenal			D	1-1aet	Dalglish
			played at Villa Park						
		SF 3r	1.5.80	Arsenal			L	0-1	
			played at Highfield Road						
1980-81	D1	3	3.1.81	Altrincham	APL	H	W	4-1	Dalglish 2, McDermott, R.Kennedy
		4	24.1.81	Everton	D1	A	L	1-2	Case
1981-82	D1	3	2.1.82	Swansea C	D1	A	W	4-0	Rush 2, Hansen, Lawrenson
		4	23.1.82	Sunderland	D1	A	W	3-0	Dalglish 2, Rush
		5	13.2.82	Chelsea	D2	A	L	0-2	
1982-83	D1	3	8.1.83	Blackburn R	D2	A	W	2-1	Hodgson, Rush
		4	29.1.83	Stoke C	D1	H	W	2-0	Dalglish, Rush
		5	20.2.83	Brighton & HA	D1	H	L	1-2	Johnson
1983-84	D1	3	6.1.84	Newcastle U	D2	H	W	4-0	Rush 2, Johnson, Robinson
		4	29.1.84	Brighton & HA	D2	A	L	0-2	
1984-85	D1	3	5.1.85	Aston Villa	D1	H	W	3-0	Rush 2, Wark
		4	27.1.85	Tottenham H	D1	H	W	1-0	Rush
		5	16.2.85	York C	D3	A	D	1-1	Rush
		5r	20.2.85	York C		H	W	7-0	Wark 3, Whelan 2, Neal, Walsh
		6	10.3.85	Barnsley	D2	A	W	4-0	Rush 3, Whelan
		SF	13.4.85	Manchester U	D1		D	2-2aet	Whelan, Walsh
			played at Goodison Park						
		SFr	17.4.85	Manchester U			L	1-2	McGrath og
			played at Maine Road						
1985-86	D1	3	4.1.86	Norwich C	D2	H	W	5-0	McDonald, Walsh, McMahon, Whelan, Wark
		4	26.1.86	Chelsea	D1	A	W	2-1	Rush, Lawrenson
		5	15.2.86	York C	D3	A	D	1-1	Molby (p)
		5r	18.2.86	York C		H	W	3-1aet	Wark, Molby, Dalglish
		6	11.3.86	Watford	D1	H	D	0-0	
		6r	17.3.86	Watford		A	W	2-1aet	Molby (p), Rush
		SF	5.4.86	Southampton	D1		W	2-0aet	Rush 2
			played at Tottenham						
		F	10.5.86	EVERTON	D1 WEMBLEY		W	3-1	Rush 2, Johnson
1986-87	D1	3	11.1.87	Luton T	D1	A	D	0-0	
		3r	26.1.87	Luton T		H	D	0-0aet	
		3 2r	28.1.87	Luton T		A	L	0-3	
1987-88	D1	3	9.1.88	Stoke C	D2	A	D	0-0	
		3r	12.1.88	Stoke C		H	W	1-0	Beardsley
		4	31.1.88	Aston Villa	D2	A	W	2-0	Barnes, Beardsley
		5	21.2.88	Everton	D1	A	W	1-0	Houghton
		6	13.3.88	Manchester C	D2	A	W	4-0	Houghton, Beardsley (p), Johnson, Barnes

LIVERPOOL

Season	Div	Round	Date	Opponent		Venue	Result	Score	Scorers
		SF	9.4.88	Nottingham F	D1		W	2-1	Aldridge 2 (1p)
		F	14.5.88	Wimbledon	D1 WEMBLEY		L	0-1	
1988-89	D1	3	7.1.89	Carlisle U	D4	A	W	3-0	McMahon 2, Barnes
		4	29.1.89	Millwall	D1	A	W	2-0	Aldridge, Rush
		5	18.2.89	Hull C	D2	A	W	3-2	Aldridge 2, Barnes
		6	18.3.89	Brentford	D3	H	W	4-0	Beardsley 2, McMahon, Barnes
		SF	15.4.89	Nottingham F	D1		–	0-0	
		The Hillsborough Disaster. Abandoned after six minutes							
		SF	7.5.89	Nottingham F			W	3-1	Aldridge 2, Laws og
		F	20.5.89	EVERTON	D1 WEMBLEY		W	3-2aet	Rush 2, Aldridge
1989-90	D1	3	6.1.90	Swansea C	D3	A	D	0-0	
		3r	9.1.90	Swansea C		H	W	8-0	Rush 3, Barnes 2, Whelan, Beardsley, Nichol
		4	28.1.90	Norwich C	D1	A	D	0-0	
		4r	31.1.90	Norwich C		H	W	3-1	Nichol, Barnes, Beardlsey
		5	17.2.90	Southampton	D1	H	W	3-0	Rush, Beardlsey, Nichol
		6	11.3.90	QPR	D1	A	D	2-2	Barnes, Rush
		6r	14.3.90	QPR		H	W	1-0	Beardsley
		SF	8.4.90	Crystal P	D1		L	3-4aet	Rush, McMahon, Barnes
		played at Villa Park							
1990-91	D1	3	5.1.91	Blackburn R	D2	A	D	1-1	Atkins og
		3r	8.1.91	Blackburn R		H	W	3-0	Houghton, Rush, Staunton
		4	26.1.91	Brighton & HA	D2	H	D	2-2	Rush 2
		4r	30.1.91	Brighton & HA		A	W	3-2aet	McMahon 2, Rush
		5	17.2.91	Everton	D1	H	D	0-0	
		5r	20.2.91	Everton		A	D	4-4aet	Beardsley 2, Rush, Barnes
		5 2r	27.2.91	Everton		A	L	0-1	
1991-92	D1	3	6.1.92	Crewe Alex	D4	A	W	4-0	McManaman, Barnes 3 (1p)
		4	5.2.92	Bristol R	D2	A	D	1-1	Saunders
		4r	11.2.92	Bristol R		H	W	2-1	McManaman, Saunders
		5	16.2.92	Ipswich T	D2	A	D	0-0	
		5r	26.2.92	Ipswich T		H	W	3-2aet	Houghton, Molby, McManaman
		6	8.3.92	Aston Villa	D1	H	W	1-0	Thomas
		SF	5.4.92	Portsmouth	D2		D	1-1aet	Whelan
		played at Highbury							
		SFr	13.4.92	Portsmouth			D	0-0aet	
		played at Villa Park. Liverpool won 3-1 on penalties							
		F	9.5.92	SUNDERLAND	D2 WEMBLEY		W	2-0	Thomas, Rush
1992-93	PL	3	3.1.93	Bolton W	D2	A	D	2-2	Winstanley og, Rush
		3r	13.1.93	Bolton W		H	L	0-2	

LIVERPOOL RAMBLERS

Formed 1862. Still in existence – as a cricket club

Season	Round	Date	Opponent		Venue	Result	Score
1882-83	1	21.10.82	Southport		H	D	1-1
	1r	4.11.82	Southport		A	W	4-0
	2	2.12.82	Bolton W		A	L	0-3
1883-84			Wrexham			scratched	
1884-85	1	8.11.84	Druids		A	L	1-6

LIVERPOOL STANLEY

Formed 1882. Home ground was in Kirkdale.

Season	Round	Date	Opponent	Venue	Result	Score
1887-88	1	15.10.87	Halliwell	H	L	1-5

LLANELLI

Formed 1896. **First entered FA Cup:** 1911

Season	Div	Round	Date	Opponent		Venue	Result	Score	Scorers
1923-24	SL	5q Merthyr Town (3S) 3-1; 6q Southend U (3S) 2-1							
		1	12.1.24	Fulham	D2	A	L	0-2	
1950-51	SL	1	25.11.50	Bristol R	3S	A	D	1-1	McInnes
		1r	28.11.50	Bristol R		H	D	1-1aet	Wallace
		1 2r	5.12.50	Bristol R at Ninian Park			L	1-3aet	Massie
1952-53	SL	1	22.11.52	Grays A	CRN	A	W	5-0	Comley, Ross, Love, Neilson, Morris
		2	6.12.52	Colchester U	3S	A	L	2-3	Morris, Neilson
1953-54	SL	1	21.11.53	Northampton T	3S	A	L	0-3	

LLOYDS FC (SITTINGBOURNE)

Entered FA Cup: 1932-49. Works team of the Lloyds paper factory

1932-33	KL	1	26.11.32 **Northampton T**	3S	A	L	1-8	Mantle

LOCKWOOD BROTHERS, SHEFFIELD

Formed 1870. Sheffield-based works team that played in the Heeley area and used the Levair Hotel on Eccleshall Road as their changing room.

1881-82	1	17.10.81 **Sheffield Heeley**	A	L	1-5	Beard
1882-83	1	4.11.82 **Macclesfield**	H	W	4-3	West, others 3
	2	2.12.82 **Sheffield Wednesday**	A	L	0-6	
1883-84	1	10.11.83 **Sheffield FC**	H	W	4-1	
	2	1.12.83 **Rotherham T**	H	W	3-1	
	3	29.12.83 **Staveley**	A	L	0-1	
1884-85	1	8.11.84 **Sheffield FC**	H	L	0-3	
1885-86	1	31.10.85 **Notts Rangers**	H	D	2-2	
	1r	7.11.85 **Notts Rangers**	A	L	0-4	
1886-87	1	30.10.86 **Long Eaton Rangers**	H	W	1-0	
	2	20.11.86 **Cleethorpes Town**	A	W	4-1	
	3	11.12.86 **Nottingham F**	H	W	2-1	
	4	bye				
	5	29.1.87 **WBA**	H	L	0-1aet	
		replay ordered following protests				
	5r	12.2.87 **WBA at Derby Cricket Gd**		L	1-2	
1887-88	1	15.10.87 **Sheffield FC**	A	W	3-1	
	2	bye				
	3	19.11.87 **Derby Junction**	A	L	1-2	

LONDON CALEDONIANS

Formed 1885. **First entered FA Cup:** 1886. Originally based at Dulwich. **FA Amateur Cup Winners:** 1923. Disbanded during World War II

1886-87	1	30.10.86 **Hendon**		A	W	2-1	
	2	20.11.86 **Old Wykehamists**		A	W	1-0	
	3	**Old Carthusians**		scratched			
1887-88	1	15.10.87 **Old Foresters**		H	L	1-6	
1912-13	IL	1	18.1.13 **Wolverhampton W**	D2	A	L	1-3	How
1913-14	IL	1	10.1.14 **Huddersfield T**	D2	A	L	0-3	
1925-26	IL	1	28.11.25 **Ilford**	IL	H	L	1-2	Allen og
1926-27	IL	1	27.11.26 **Luton T**	3S	A	L	2-4	Noble, May
1927-28	IL	1	26.11.27 **Northfleet U**	SL	A	W	1-0	McGeorge
	2	10.12.27 **Bath C**	SL	H	W	1-0	Conridge
	3	14.1.28 **Crewe A**	3N	H	L	2-3	Noble, Hamilton

LONDON OLYMPIC

1882-83	1	4.11.82 **United Hospitals**	A	L	0-3	

LONDON PAPER MILLS (DARTFORD)

Entered FA Cup 1933-1938. Club folded when factory closed in 1965

1933-34	KL	1	25.11.33 **Southend U**	3S	H	L	0-1

LONG EATON RANGERS

Formed 1882. Played at Long Eaton Recreation Ground.

1883-84	1	27.10.83 **Wolverhampton W**	A	L	1-4	
1884-85	1	8.11.84 **Sheffield W**	A	L	0-1	
1885-86	1	31.10.85 **Sheffield W**	H	W	2-0	Hexter, Winfield
	2	21.11.85 **Staveley**	H	L	1-4	
1886-87	1	30.10.86 **Lockwood Brothers**	A	L	0-1	
1887-88	1	15.10.87 **Park Grange**	H	W	6-3	
	2	5.11.87 **Sheffield W**	H	L	1-2aet	Plackett
1888-89	1	2.2.89 **Birmingham St G.**	A	L	2-3	Lowe, Locker

| 1890-91 | ML | 1 | 17.1.91 | Wolverhampton W | D1 | H | L | 1-2aet | J.Start |
| 1897-98 | ML | 1 | 29.1.98 | Gainsborough T. | ML | H | L | 0-1 | |

LOUGHBOROUGH

Founded 1886. Member of the Football League 1895-1900 and never played in the Competition Proper as a League team. Folded June 1900.

1892-93	ML	1	21.1.93 Northwich Victoria	D2	H	L	1-2	Carnelly
1895-96	D2		1q Bulwell U (H) 5-2; 2q Newstead (A) 0-0; 2qr Newstead (H) 1-0; 3q Kettering T (A) 1-2
1896-97	D2		3q Mansfield (A) 1-2
1897-98	D2		3q Bulwell U (A) 0-3
1898-99	D2		1q Mansfield (H) 4-0; 2q Rothwell TS (H) 7-0; 3q Wellingborough (H) 0-0; 3qr Wellingborough (A) 3-1; 4q Kettering (A) 1-2
1899-00	D2		3q Hinckley T (H) 1-2

LOUGHBOROUGH UNITED

Formed 1946, incorporating Brush Sports works team who took part in the FA Cup in their own right. Folded 1963.

1960-61	CA	1	5.11.60 Kings Lynn	SL	H	D	0-0	
		1r	9.11.60 Kings Lynn		A	L	0-3	
1963-64	ML	1	16.11.63 Netherfield	LC	A	L	1-6	Broadhurst

LOVELL'S ATHLETIC

Formed: 1918. First entered FA Cup: 1921. Welsh FA Cup Winners: 1948. League club beaten: Bournemouth. Folded 1969

1945-46	Welsh1	1L	17.11.45 Bournemouth	3S	H	W	4-1	Clarke 2, Williams 2
		1 2L	24.11.45 Bournemouth		A	L	2-3	Holland 2
		2 1L	8.12.45 Bath C	SL	H	W	2-1	Morgan, Williams
		2 2L	15.12.45 Bath C		A	W	5-2	Williams, Hardwicke 2, Morgan, Holland
		3 1L	5.1.46 Wolverhampton W	D1	H	L	2-4	Morgan, Hardwick
		3 2L	9.1.46 Wolverhampton W		A	L	1-8	Prangley
1955-56	SL	1	19.11.55 Leyton O	3S	A	L	1-7	Ridsdale

LOWESTOFT TOWN

Formed 1890. First entered FA Cup: 1898. FA Amateur Cup Runners-up: 1900

1926-27	N&S	1	27.11.26 Watford	3S	A	L	1-10	Hook
1938-39	ECL	1	26.11.38 Swindon T	3S	A	L	0-6	
1966-67	ECL	1	26.11.66 Leyton O	D3	A	L	1-2	Cassidy
1967-68	ECL	1	9.12.67 Watford	D3	H	L	0-1	
1977-78	ECL	1	26.11.77 Cambridge U	D3	H	L	0-2	

LUTON TOWN

Formed 1885. First entered FA Cup: 1885. FA Cup Best Performance: Runners-up: 1959. Record FA Cup Win: 15-0 vs Great Yarmouth T., 4th qualifying round, 21.11.1914. In competition proper: 9-0 vs Clapton, 1st round replay, 30.11.1927. Record FA Cup Defeat: 0-7 vs 93rd Highland Regiment, 1st qualifying round 4.10.1890. In competition proper: 0-7 vs Crystal Palace, 1st round, 16.1.1929

1885-86		1	31.10.85 Great Marlow		A	L	0-3	
1886-87		1	23.10.86 Hotspur		A	L	1-3	Ellingham
1887-88		1	15.10.87 Chatham		A	L	1-5	Deacon
1888-89			1q Reading (H) 4-0; 2q Chesham (A) 3-3; 2qr Chesham (H) 10-2; 3q Old Brightonians (A) 1-3
1889-90			2q Maidenhead (A) 2-1; 3q Old St Pauls (A) 0-4
1890-91			1q 93rd Highland Regiment (A) 0-7
1891-92			1q Swindon (H) 3-1; 2q Windsor Phoenix (H) 3-0; 3q Bedminster (A) 4-1; 4q Clifton (A) 3-0
		1	16.1.92 Middlesbrough		H	L	0-3	
1892-93			1q Old St Marks (H) 4-0; 2q Old Etonians (H) 4-2; 3q Merton Polytechnic (A) 2-4
1893-94			2q Old Westminsters (A) 1-0; 3q Norwich CEYMS (H) 5-1; 4q Sherwood Foresters (H) 2-1
		1	27.1.94 Middlesbrough Iron.	D2	A	L	1-2	Dimmock
1894-95	SL		1q City Ramblers (H) 8-2; 2q St Albans (A) 6-1; 3q Ilford (A) 2-0; 4q Tottenham H (A) 2-2; 4qr Tottenham H (H) 4-0
		1	2.2.95 Preston NE	D1	H	L	0-2	
1895-96	SL		1q Tottenham H (H) 1-2
1896-97	3q		1st Scots Guards (H) 7-0; 4q Marlow (A) 5-0; 5q Tottenham H (H) 3-0
		1	30.1.97 WBA	D1	H	L	0-1	
1897-88	D2		4q Tottenham H (A) 4-3; 5q Clapton (A) 2-0
		1	29.1.98 Bolton W	D1	H	L	0-1	

1898-99 D2 3q **Watford** (H) 2-2; 3qr **Watford** (A) 1-0; 4q **Shepherds Bush** (H) 4-3; 5q **Tottenham H** (A) 1-1; 5qr **Tottenham H** (H) 1-1;
5q2r **Tottenham** 0-2 at Tufnell Park

1899-00 D2 3q **Lowestoft** (A) 2-0; 4q **Watford** (H) 3-2; 5q **QPR** (H) 1-1; 5qr **QPR** (A) 1-4

1900-01 SL 3q **Kings Lynn** (A) 4-1; 4q **Civil Service** (H) 9-1; 5q **QPR** (H) 3-0; Int **Bristol R** (H) 0-2

1901-02 SL 1q **Aspley Guise** (H) 13-1; 2q **Bedford Queens** (H) 4-2; 3q **Lowestoft** (A) 2-1; 4q **Watford** (A) 2-1; 5q **QPR** (H) 2-0;
Int. **W.Arsenal** (A) 1-1; IntR **W.Arsenal** (H) 0-2

1902-03 SL 3q **QPR** (A) 3-0; 4q **Lowestoft** (H) 5-1; 5q **Fulham** (H) 6-1; Int. **Kidderminster** (H) 3-0

	1	7.2.03 **Millwall**	SL	A	L	0-3

1903-04 SL 3q **Hitchin** (A) 2-1; 4q **Watford** (H) 4-1; 5q **Fulham** (A) 1-3

1904-05 SL 6q **Fulham** (A) 0-4

1905-06 SL 4q **Crystal Palace** (A) 0-1

1906-07	SL	1	12.1.07 **Gainsborough T**	D2	A	D	0-0	
		1r	16.1.07 **Gainsborough T**		H	W	2-1	Warner, Brown
		2	2.2.07 **Sunderland**	D1	H	D	0-0	
		2r	6.2.07 **Sunderland**		A	L	0-1	
1907-08	SL	1	11.1.08 **Fulham**	D2	H	L	3-8	Rigate, Rankin, Moody

1908-09 SL 5q **Southend** (H) 1-1; 5qr **Southend** (A) 4-2

		1	16.1.09 **Millwall Ath**	SL	H	L	1-2	Menzies

1909-10 SL 4q **Brentford** (A) 1-2

1910-11 SL 4q **Cambridge C** (H) 9-1; 5q **Rochdale** (H) 1-1; 5qr **Rochdale** (A) 3-2

		1	14.1.11 **Northampton T**	SL	A	L	1-5	Moody
1911-12	SL	1	13.1.12 **Notts Co**	D1	H	L	2-4	Streeton, Moody

1912-13 SL 4q **Tunbridge Wells Rangers** (H) 3-0; 5q **Croydon Common** (A) 0-2

1913-14 SL 4q **Croydon Common** (H) 3-0; 5q **South Shields** (H) 0-0; 5qr **South Shields** (A) 0-2

1914-15 SL 4q **Gt Yarmouth** (H) 15-0; 5q **Oxford C** (A) 1-0; 6q **Bromley** (H) 5-1

		1	9.1.15 **Southampton**	SL	A	L	0-3	

1919-20 SL 6q **Brighton & HA** (A) 1-0

		1	10.1.20 **Coventry C**	D2	H	D	2-2	Parker, Dodd
		1r	16.1.20 **Coventry C**		A	W	1-0	Hoar
		2	31.1.20 **Liverpool**	D1	H	L	0-2	

1920-21 3S 6q **Rotherham Co** (A) 3-1

		1	8.1.21 **Birmingham**	D2	H	W	2-1	Simms, Bookman
		2	29.1.21 **South Shields**	D2	A	W	4-0	Higginbotham, Butcher 2, Simms
		3	19.2.21 **Preston NE**	D1	H	L	2-3	Higginbotham 2
1921-22	3S	1	7.1.22 **Portsmouth**	3S	A	D	1-1	Bassett
		1r	11.1.22 **Portsmouth**		H	W	2-1	Higginbotham, Hoar
		2	28.1.22 **Aston Villa**	D1	A	L	0-1	
1922-23	3S	1	13.1.23 **Bury**	D2	A	L	1-2	Tirrell (p)
1923-24	3S	1	12.1.24 **Arsenal**	D1	A	L	1-4	Green
1924-25	3S	1	10.1.25 **WBA**	D1	A	L	0-4	
1925-26	3S	1	28.11.25 **Folkestone**	SL	H	W	3-0	Reid, Littlewood, Shankly
		2	12.12.25 **Aberdare A**	3S	A	L	0-1	
1926-27	3S	1	27.11.26 **London Caledonians**	IL	H	W	4-2	Reid 2, Clark, Pointon
		2	11.12.26 **Northfleet U**	KL	H	W	6-2	Woods 3, Reid 2, Rennie
		3	8.1.27 **Chelsea**	D2	A	L	0-4	
1927-28	3S	1	30.11.27 **Clapton**	IL	H	W	9-0	Dennis 2, Woods, Yardley 4, Reid 2
		2	10.12.27 **Norwich C**	3S	H	W	6-0	Reid 3, Woods, Yardley, Dennis
		3	14.1.28 **Bolton W**	D1	A	L	1-2	Reid
1928-29	3S	1	24.11.28 **Southend U**	3S	H	W	5-1	Rennie 4, Bedford
		2	8.12.28 **Fulham**	3S	A	D	0-0	
		2r	13.12.28 **Fulham**		H	W	4-1	Yardley 2, Rennie, Bedford
		3	12.1.29 **Crystal P**	3S	H	D	0-0	
		3r	16.1.29 **Crystal P**		A	L	0-7	
1929-30	3S	1	30.11.29 **QPR**	3S	H	L	2-3	Yardley 2
1930-31	3S	1	29.11.30 **Clapton O**	3S	H	D	2-2	Rennie, Bryce
		1r	4.12.30 **Clapton O** at Highbury		A	W	4-2	McNestry, Rennie 2, Armstrong
		2	13.12.30 **Watford**	3S	A	L	1-3	Yardley
1931-32	3S	1	28.11.31 **Swindon T**	3S	A	W	5-0	McNestry, Rennie 2, Yardley 2
		2	12.12.31 **Lincoln C**	3N	A	D	2-2	Yardley 2
		2r	16.12.31 **Lincoln C**		H	W	4-1	Tait 2, Yardley, Slicer
		3	9.1.32 **Wolverhampton W**	D2	H	L	1-2	Yardley
1932-33	3S	1	26.11.32 **Kingstonian**	IL	H	D	2-2	Rennie, Tait
		1r	30.11.32 **Kingstonian**		A	W	3-2	McGinnigle, Rennie, Tait
		2	10.12.32 **Stockport Co**	3N	A	W	3-2	Kean, Rennie, Tait
		3	14.1.33 **Barnsley**	3N	A	D	0-0	
		3r	18.1.33 **Barnsley**		H	W	2-0	Rennie 2
		4	28.1.33 **Tottenham H**	D2	H	W	2-0	Alderson, Tait

Season	Div	Round	Date	Opponent		H/A	Res	Score	Scorers
		5	18.2.33	Halifax T	3N	A	W	2-0	Nelson, Tait
		6	4.3.33	Everton	D1	A	L	0-6	
1933-34	3S	3	13.1.34	Arsenal	D1	H	L	0-1	
1934-35	3S	3	12.1.35	Chelsea	D1	A	D	1-1	Bell
		3r	16.1.35	Chelsea		H	W	2-0	Ball, Roberts
		4	26.1.35	Burnley	D2	A	L	1-3	Stephenson
1935-36	3S	3	11.1.36	West Ham	D2	A	D	2-2	Ball, Roberts
		3r	15.1.36	West Ham		H	W	4-0	Ball, Crompton, Roberts, Stephenson
		4	25.1.36	Manchester C	D1	A	L	1-2	Martin
1936-37	3S	3	16.1.37	Blackpool	D2	H	D	3-3	Payne 2, Stephenson
		3r	20.1.37	Blackpool		A	W	2-1	Sloan, Roberts
		4	30.1.37	Sunderland	D1	H	D	2-2	Roberts 2
		4r	3.2.37	Sunderland		A	L	1-3	Payne
1937-38	D2	3	8.1.38	Scarborough	ML	A	D	1-1	Ferguson
		3r	12.1.38	Scarborough		H	W	5-1	Vinall 2, Ferguson, Dawes, Stephenson
		4	22.1.38	Swindon T	3S	H	W	2-1	Ferguson, Stephenson
		5	12.2.38	Manchester C	D1	H	L	1-3	Payne
1938-39	D2	3	7.1.39	Liverpool	D1	A	L	0-3	
1945-46	D2	3 1L	5.1.46	Derby Co	D1	H	L	0-6	
		3 2L	9.1.46	Derby Co		A	L	0-3	
1946-47	D2	3	11.1.47	Notts Co	3S	H	W	6-0	Billington 5, Daniel
		4	25.1.47	Swansea T	D2	H	W	2-0	Daniel, Roberts og
		5	8.2.47	Burnley	D2	H	D	0-0	
		5r	11.2.47	Burnley		A	L	0-3	
1947-48	D2	3	10.1.48	Plymouth	D2	A	W	4-2	Brennan 2, Billington 2
		4	24.1.48	Coventry C	D2	H	W	3-2	Soo, Waugh, Ottewell
		5	7.2.48	QPR	3S	A	L	1-3	Waugh
1948-49	D2	3	8.1.49	West Ham	D2	H	W	3-1	Kiernan, Arnison, Watkins
		4	29.1.49	Walsall	3S	H	W	4-0	Brennan 3, Watkins
		5	12.2.49	Leicester C	D2	H	D	5-5	Kiernan 2, Small, Brennan, Watkins
		5r	19.2.49	Leicester C		A	L	3-5	Brennan 2, Arnison
1949-50	D2	3	7.1.50	Grimsby T	D2	H	L	3-4	Kiernan, Waugh
1950-51	D2	3	6.1.51	Portsmouth	D1	H	W	2-0	Davie, Havenga
		4	27.1.51	Bristol R	3S	H	L	1-2	Watkins
1951-52	D2	3	12.1.52	Charlton A	D1	H	W	1-0	Turner
		4	2.2.52	Brentford	D2	H	D	2-2	Turner, Taylor
		4r	6.2.52	Brentford		A	D	0-0aet	
		4 2r	18.2.52	Brentford at Highbury			W	3-2aet	Taylor, Moore, Morton
		5	23.2.52	Swindon T	3S	H	W	3-1	Taylor 2, Davies
		6	8.3.52	Arsenal	D1	H	L	2-3	Moore, Mitchell (p)
1952-53	D2	3	10.1.53	Fulham	D2	H	W	6-1	Taylor 2, Pye 3, Moore
		4	31.1.53	Manchester C	D1	A	D	1-1	Pye
		4r	4.2.53	Manchester C		H	W	5-1	Turner 3, Mitchell, Little og
		5	14.2.53	Bolton W	D1	H	L	0-1	
1953-54	D2	3	9.1.54	Blackpool	D1	A	D	1-1	Cummins
		3r	13.1.54	Blackpool		H	D	0-0aet	
		3 2r	18.1.54	Blackpool at Villa Park			D	1-1aet	Cummins
		3 3r	25.1.54	Blackpool at Molineux			L	0-2aet	
1954-55	D2	3	8.1.55	Workington	3N	H	W	5-0	Turner 2, Cummins, Cullen 2
		4	29.1.55	Rotherham U	D2	A	W	5-1	Turner 3, Cummins, Cullen
		5	19.2.55	Manchester C	D1	H	L	0-2	
1955-56	D1	3	11.1.56	Leicester C	D2	H	L	0-4	
1956-57	D1	3	5.1.57	Aston Villa	D1	H	D	2-2	Davies, Turner (p)
		3r	7.1.57	Aston Villa		A	L	0-2	
1957-58	D1	3	4.1.58	Stockport Co	3N	A	L	0-3	
1958-59	D1	3	10.1.59	Leeds U	D1	H	W	5-1	Bingham 2, Morton, Gregory 2
		4	24.1.59	Leicester C	D1	A	D	1-1	Bingham
		4r	28.1.59	Leicester C		H	W	4-1	Brown 3, Gregory
		5	14.2.59	Ipswich T	D2	A	W	5-2	Pacey, Morton 2, Bingham, Gregory
		6	28.2.59	Blackpool	D1	A	D	1-1	Bingham
		6r	4.3.59	Blackpool		H	W	1-0	Brown
		SF	14.3.59	Norwich C	D3		D	1-1	Brown
				played at Tottenham					
		SFr	18.3.59	Norwich C			W	1-0	Bingham
				played at St Andrews					
		F	2.5.59	Nottingham F	D1 WEMBLEY		L	1-2	Pacey
1959-60	D1	3	9.1.60	Exeter C	D4	A	W	2-1	Turner 2

Season	Div	Rd	Date	Opponent		Venue	W/L	Score	Scorers
		4	30.1.60	Huddersfield T	D2	A	W	1-0	Gregory
		5	20.2.60	Wolverhampton W	D1	H	L	1-4	Turner
1960-61	D2	3	7.1.61	Northampton T	D4	H	W	4-0	Turner 2, Brown, Ashworth
		4	28.1.61	Manchester C	D1	H	–	2-6	Ashworth 2
			abandoned after 69 minutes – waterlogged pitch						
		4	1.2.61	Manchester C		H	W	3-1	Ashworth 2, Fleming
		5	18.2.61	Barnsley	D3	A	L	0-1	
1961-62	D2	3	6.1.62	Ipswich T	D1	A	D	1-1	Chandler
		3r	10.1.62	Ipswich T		H	D	1-1aet	Pacey
		3 2r	15.1.62	Ipswich T at Highbury			L	1-5	Ashworth
1962-63	D2	3	26.1.63	Swindon T	D3	H	L	0-2	
1963-64	D3	1	16.11.63	Bridgewater T	WL	A	W	3-0	McKechnie 2, Turner
		2	7.12.63	Reading	D3	H	W	2-1	Fairchild, Turner
		3	4.1.64	Fulham	D1	A	L	1-4	Smith
1964-65	D3	1	14.11.64	Southend U	D3	H	W	1-0	Bramwell
		2	5.12.64	Gillingham	D3	H	W	1-0	Riddick
		3	9.1.65	Sunderland	D1	H	L	0-3	
1965-66	D4	1	13.11.65	Romford	SL	A	D	1-1	Harris og
		1r	18.11.65	Romford		H	W	1-0	O'Rourke
		2	4.12.65	Corby T	SL	A	D	2-2	O'Rourke, Whittaker (p)
		2r	7.12.65	Corby T		H	L	0-1	
1966-67	D4	1	26.11.66	Exeter C	D4	A	D	1-1	Whittaker
		1r	1.12.66	Exeter C		H	W	2-0	Rioch, Pleat
		2	7.1.67	Bristol R	D3	A	L	2-3	Kevan 2
1967-68	D4	1	14.12.67	Oxford C	IL	A	W	2-1	Rioch, Buxton
			played at Kenilworth Road						
		2	6.1.68	Swindon T	D3	A	L	2-3	Allen, Whittaker (p)
1968-69	D3	1	16.11.68	Ware	AL	H	W	6-1	Potter, Slough 2, Allen 3
		2	7.12.68	Gillingham	D3	H	W	3-1	French, Harrison 2
		3	4.1.69	Manchester C	D1	A	L	0-1	
1969-70	D3	1	15.11.69	Bournemouth	D3	A	D	1-1	Collins
		1r	18.11.69	Bournemouth		H	W	3-1	Collins, Tees, MacDonald
		2	6.12.69	Hillingdon B	SL	A	L	1-2	Tees
1970-71	D2	3	2.1.71	Nottingham F	D1	A	D	1-1	MacDonald
		3r	11.1.71	Nottingham F		H	L	3-4	MacDonald 3
1971-72	D2	3	15.1.72	West Ham	D1	A	L	1-2	Givens
1972-73	D2	3	13.1.73	Crewe A	D4	H	W	2-0	Jim Ryan, Butlin
		4	3.2.73	Newcastle U	D1	A	W	2-0	Aston 2
		5	24.2.73	Bolton W	D3	A	W	1-0	Garner
		6	17.3.73	Sunderland	D2	A	L	0-2	
1973-74	D2	3	5.1.74	Port Vale	D3	A	D	1-1	Jim Ryan
		3r	9.1.74	Port Vale		H	W	4-2	Aston, Anderson 2, Jim Ryan
		4	26.1.74	Bradford C	D4	H	W	3-0	Fretwell og, Butlin, Jim Ryan
		5	16.2.74	Leicester C	D1	H	L	0-4	
1974-75	D1	3	4.1.75	Birmingham C	D1	H	L	0-1	
1975-76	D2	3	3.1.76	Blackburn R	D2	H	W	2-0	R.Futcher, Chambers
		4	24.1.76	Norwich C	D1	A	L	0-2	
1976-77	D2	3	8.1.77	Halifax T	D4	A	W	1-0	Aston
		4	29.1.77	Chester	D3	A	L	0-1	
1977-78	D2	3	7.1.78	Oldham A	D2	H	D	1-1	Fuccillo
		3r	10.1.78	Oldham A		A	W	2-1	Boersma 2
		4	31.1.78	Millwall	D2	A	L	0-4	
1978-79	D2	3	9.1.79	York C	D4	A	L	0-2	
1979-80	D2	3	5.1.80	Swindon T	D3	H	L	0-2	
1980-81	D2	3	3.1.81	Orient	D2	A	W	3-1	Moss 2, Ingram
			24.1.81	Newcastle U	D2	A	L	1-2	Ingram
1981-82	D2	3	2.1.82	Swindon T	D3	H	W	2-1	Moss, Horton
		4	23.1.82	Ipswich T	D1	H	L	0-3	
1982-83	D1	3	8.1.83	Peterborough U	D4	H	W	3-0	Horton, Hill, Walsh
		4	29.1.83	Manchester U	D1	H	L	0-2	
1983-84	D1	3	7.1.84	Watford	D1	H	D	2-2	Nwajiobi, B.Stein
		3r	10.1.84	Watford		A	L	3-4aet	Donaghy, Walsh
1984-85	D1	3	5.1.85	Stoke C	D1	H	D	1-1	Foster
		3r	9.1.85	Stoke C		A	W	3-2	Hill, Harford, Donaghy
		4	26.1.85	Huddersfield T	D2	H	W	2-0	Donaghy, B.Stein
		5	4.3.85	Watford	D1	H	D	0-0	
		5r	6.3.85	Watford		A	D	2-2aet	Nwajiobi, Hill

	5 2r	9.3.85	**Watford**		H	W	1-0	Turner
	6	13.3.85	**Millwall**	D3	H	W	1-0	B.Stein
	SF	13.4.85	**Everton**	D1		L	1-2aet	Hill
		played at Villa Park						
1985-86	D1	3	4.1.86	**Crystal Palace**	D2	A	W	2-1	B.Stein, Preece
		4	25.1.86	**Bristol R**	D3	H	W	4-0	Hill, Harford, North, Parkin og
		5	15.2.86	**Arsenal**	D1	H	D	2-2	Hill, Harford
		5r	3.3.86	**Arsenal**		A	D	0-0aet	
		5 2r	5.3.86	**Arsenal**		H	W	3-0	M.Stein, Foster, O'Leary og
		6	8.3.86	**Everton**	D1	H	D	2-2	M.Stein, Harford
		6r	12.3.86	**Everton**		A	L	0-1	
1986-87	D1	3	11.1.87	**Liverpool**	D1	H	D	0-0	
		3r	26.1.87	**Liverpool**		A	D	0-0aet	
		3 2r	28.1.87	**Liverpool**		H	W	3-0	B.Stein, Harford, Newell
		4	31.1.87	**QPR**	D1	H	D	1-1	Harford
		4r	4.2.87	**QPR**		A	L	1-2	Harford
1987-88	D1	3	9.1.88	**Hartlepool U**	D4	A	W	2-1	Weir, McDonough
		4	30.1.88	**Southampton**	D1	H	W	2-1	Allinson, B.Stein
		5	20.2.88	**QPR**	D1	A	D	1-1	Harford
		5r	24.2.88	**QPR**		H	W	1-0	Neill og
		6	12.3.88	**Portsmouth**	D1	H	W	3-1	Wilson, M.Stein, Harford
		SF	9.4.88	**Wimbledon**	D1		L	1-2	Harford
			played at Tottenham						
1988-89	D1	3	7.1.89	**Millwall**	D1	A	L	2-3	Black, Wilson (p)
1989-90	D1	3	6.1.90	**Brighton & HA**	D2	A	L	1-4	Wilson
1990-91	D1	3	5.1.91	**Sheffield U**	D1	A	W	3-1	Farrell, Elstrup 2
		4	26.1.91	**West Ham**	D1	H	D	1-1	Black
		4r	30.1.91	**West Ham**		A	L	0-5	
1991-92	D1	3	4.1.92	**Sheffield U**	D1	A	L	0-4	
1992-93	D1	3	19.1.93	**Bristol C**	D1	H	W	2-0	Gray, Hughes
		4	23.1.93	**Derby Co**	D1	H	L	1-5	Telfer

LUTON WANDERERS

Formed 1880. **First entered FA Cup:** 1884. Played at Dallow Lane, Luton near the Cricketer's Arms pub. Were a seperate club from Luton Town.

1884-85	1	8.11.84	**Old Etonians**	H	L	1-3	Ellingham
1885-86	1	31.10.85	**Chesham**	H	W	3-2	Ellingham, G.Smith, 1 other
	2	21.11.85	**Old Wykehamists**	A	L	0-10	
1886-87	1	23.10.86	**Swifts**	A	L	0-13	

LYNDHURST FC

Formed 1883. Played at Denmark Hill in South London and changed at a pub called The Fox Under The Hill.

1886-87	1	30.10.86	**Chesham Generals**	A	L	2-4	

LYTHAM FC

Formed 1880. **First entered FA Cup:** 1922. The club based in the town that houses the headquarters of the Football League only made one appearance in the Competition Proper.

1925-26	LC	1	28.11.25	**Oldham A**	D2	A	L	1-10	Leeming

MACCLESFIELD TOWN

Formed 1874. **First entered FA Cup:** 1882. **First winners of the FA Challenge Trophy:** 1970 **Runners-up:** 1989. **League clubs beaten:** Stockport Co, Carlisle U, Rotherham U, Chesterfield

1882-83	1	4.11.82	**Lockwood Brothers**	A	L	3-4	Goldthorpe, Sadler 2
1883-84	1	10.11.83	**Davenham**	A	L	0-2	
1884-85	1	8.11.84	**Hartford St Johns**	H	W	9-0	
	2	6.12.84	**Leek**	H	L	1-5	
1885-86	1	31.10.85	**Northwich Victoria**	H	W	4-1	
	2	21.11.85	**Davenham**	A	L	1-8	
1886-87	1	30.10.86	**Goldenhill**	A	L	2-4	
		FA ordered match to be replayed					
	1r	13.11.86	**Goldenhill**	H	L	2-3	

1887-88		1	15.10.87	Shrewsbury T	A	L	1-3	
1960-61	CC	1	5.11.60	Southport	D4	A	L	2-7	Bowyer (p), Bentham og
1964-65	CC	1	14.11.64	Wrexham	D4	H	L	1-2	Wilson
1967-68	CC	1	9.12.67	Stockport Co	D3	A	D	1-1	Calder
		1r	13.12.67	Stockport Co		H	W	2-1	Taberner, Fidler (p)
		2	6.1.68	Spennymoor U	NL	H	W	2-0	Taberner, Fidler
		3	27.1.68	Fulham	D1	A	L	2-4	Taberner, Fidler
1968-69	CC	1	16.11.68	Lincoln C	D4	H	L	1-3	Clay (p)
1969-70	NPL	1	15.11.69	Scunthorpe U	D4	H	D	1-1	Lyon
		1r	18.11.69	Scunthorpe U		A	L	2-4	Young, Sievewright
1970-71	NPL	1	21.11.70	Bradford C	D3	A	L	2-3	Fidler, Lyon
1975-76	NPL	1	22.11.75	Sheffield W	D3	A	L	1-3	Eccleshare
1982-83	NPL	1	20.11.82	Worcester C	APL	H	L	1-5	Long
1983-84	NPL	1	19.11.83	York C	D4	H	D	0-0	
		1r	22.11.83	York C		A	L	0-2	
1984-85	NPL	1	17.11.84	Port Vale	D4	H	L	1-2	White (p)
1985-86	NPL	1	16.11.85	Hartlepool U	D4	H	L	1-2	Askey
1987-88	GMVC	1	14.11.87	Carlisle U	D4	H	W	4-2	Hardman, Askey, Tobin, Burr
		2	6.12.87	Rotherham U	D3	H	W	4-0	Burr 3, Grant
		3	10.1.88	Port Vale	D3	A	L	0-1	
1989-90	GMVC	1	18.11.89	Chester	D3	H	D	1-1	Burr
		1r	21.11.89	Chester		A	L	2-3	Burr 2
1992-93	GMVC	1	14.11.92	Chesterfield	D3	H	D	0-0	
		1r	25.11.92	Chesterfield		A	D	2-2aet	Mitchell 2
			Macclesfield won 3-2 on penalties					
		2	5.12.92	Stockport Co	D2	H	L	0-2	

MAIDENHEAD

Formed 1869. Have competed in the FA Cup ever since its inception except for 1876-77. **Cup Final Connection:** Former Maidenhead player Lawrie Sanchez scored Wimbledon's winning goal in the 1988 Cup Final.

1871-72	1	11.11.71	Marlow	H	W	2-0	Young 2
	2	16.12.71	Crystal Palace	A	L	0-3	
1872-73	1	26.10.72	Marlow	H	W	1-0	Carter
	2	23.11.72	1st Surrey Rifles	H	W	3-0	Collings, Goulden, Hebbes
	3	21.12.72	Windsor Home Park	A	W	1-0	Hebbes
	4	3.2.73	Oxford University	A	L	0-4	
1873-74	1		Civil Service		*walkover*		
	2	22.11.73	High Wycombe	H	W	1-0	W.Wild
	3	10.12.73	Royal Engineers	A	L	0-7	
1874-75	1	14.11.74	Hitchen	A	W	1-0	Nicholls
	2	5.12.74	Reigate Priory	H	W	2-1	Burnham 2
	3	23.1.75	Old Etonians	A	L	0-1	
1875-76	1	23.10.75	Ramblers	H	W	2-0	Goulden, Price
	2	11.12.75	Old Etonians	A	L	0-8	
1877-78	1	27.10.77	Reading Hornets	H	W	10-0	F.Price, others 9
	2	8.12.77	Cambridge University	A	L	2-4aet	Mackie 2
1878-79	1	19.10.78	Barnes	A	D	1-1	Tilley
	1r	9.11.78	Barnes	H	L	0-4	
1879-80	1	25.10.79	Birmingham Calthorpe	H	W	3-1	Bassett, Blackwell, Goldsmith
	2	29.11.79	Henley	A	W	3-1	Lovegrove 2, Harris
	3		bye				
	4	14.2.80	Oxford University	A	L	0-1	
1880-81	1	13.11.80	Old Harrovians	H	D	0-0	
	1r	20.11.80	Old Harrovians	A	W	1-0	Goodchild
	2	11.12.80	Grey Friars	A	L	0-1	
1881-82	1	22.10.81	Henley	A	W	2-0	
	2	3.12.81	Acton	H	W	2-1aet	Blackwell, Green
	3		bye				
	4	14.1.82	Old Etonians	A	L	3-6	Blackwell 2, Bailey
1882-83	1	4.11.82	Old Westminsters	A	L	0-2	
1883-84	1	10.11.83	West End	H	L	0-1	
1884-85	1	8.11.84	Old Wykehamists	H	L	0-3	
1885-86	1	31.10.85	Brentwood	A	L	0-3	
1886-87	1	30.10.86	South Reading	A	W	2-0	
	2	20.11.86	Dulwich	H	L	2-3	

1887-88		1	15.10.87 **Swifts**		A	L	1-3
1960-61	CRN	1	5.11.60 **Colchester U**	D3	A	L	0-5
1962-63	CRN	1	3.11.62 **Wycombe W**	IL	H	L	0-3
1963-64	AL	1	16.11.63 **Bath C**	SL	H	L	0-2
1971-72	AL	1	20.11.71 **Enfield**	IL	A	L	0-2

MAIDSTONE UNITED

Formed 1897. **First entered FA Cup:** 1898. Promoted to the Football League in 1989. Members of the Football League: 1989-1992. Went into liquidation August 1992. **League clubs beaten as a non-league club:** Exeter C, Gillingham, Cambridge U

1974-75	SL	1	23.11.74 **Nuneaton B**	SL	A	D	2-2	Morton, McVeigh
		1r	26.11.74 **Nuneaton B**		H	W	2-0	Basey, Tough
		2	14.12.74 **Swindon T**	D3	A	L	1-3	McLaughlin og
1978-79	SL	1	25.11.78 **Wycombe W**	IL	H	W	1-0	Aitken
		2	16.12.78 **Exeter C**	D3	H	W	1-0	Hill
		3	9.1.79 **Charlton A**	D2	A	D	1-1	Coupland
		3r	15.1.79 **Charlton A**		H	L	1-2	Coupland
1980-81	APL	1	22.11.80 **Kettering**	APL	A	D	1-1	Ovard
		1r	26.11.80 **Kettering**		H	D	0-0aet	
		1 2r	1.12.80 **Kettering**		H	W	3-1	Woon 2, Newson (p)
		2	13.12.80 **Gillingham**	D3	A	D	0-0	
		2r	16.12.80 **Gillingham**		H	D	0-0aet	
		2 2r	22.12.80 **Gillingham**		A	W	2-0	Newson, Ovard
		3	3.1.81 **Exeter C**	D3	H	L	2-4	Woon, Ovard
1982-83	APL	1	20.11.82 **Weymouth**	APL	A	L	3-4	Hil, Bartley 2
1983-84	APL	1	19.11.83 **Exeter C**	D3	A	D	1-1	Newson
		1r	23.11.83 **Exeter C**		H	W	2-1	Lazarus, Dingwall
		2	10.12.83 **Worcester C**	APL	H	W	3-2	Moore, Bartley, Donn
		3	7.1.84 **Darlington**	D4	A	L	1-4	Lazarus
1985-86	APL	1	16.11.85 **Fareham T**	SL	A	W	3-0	Cugley 2, Barnes
		2	7.12.85 **Plymouth A**	D3	A	L	0-3	
1986-87	GMVC	1	15.11.86 **Welling**	GMVC	A	D	1-1	Glover
		1r	24.11.86 **Welling**		H	W	4-1	Torrance, Butler, Hatter, Galloway
		2	7.12.86 **Cambridge U**	D4	H	W	1-0	Galloway
		3	10.1.87 **Watford**	D1	A	L	1-3	Galloway
1987-88	GMVC	1	14.11.87 **Dagenham**	GMVC	A	W	2-0	Butler (p), Harrison
		2	5.12.87 **Kidderminster H**	GMVC	H	D	1-1	Rogers
		2r	7.12.87 **Kidderminster H**		A	D	2-2aet	Doherty, Pamphlett
		2 2r	14.12.87 **Kidderminster H**		A	D	0-0aet	
		2 3r	16.12.87 **Kidderminster H**		H	W	2-1	Butler 2 (1p)
		3	9.1.88 **Sheffield U**	D2	A	L	0-1	
1988-89	GMVC	1	19.11.88 **Newport Co**	GMVC	A	W	2-1	Hill, Gall
		2	10.12.88 **Reading**	D3	A	D	1-1	Sorrell
		2r	14.12.88 **Reading**		H	L	1-2	Gall
1989-90	D4	1	18.11.89 **Yeovil T**	GMVC	H	W	2-1	Gall, Barton
		2	9.12.89 **Exeter C**	D4	H	D	1-1	Elsey
		2r	13.12.89 **Exeter C**		A	L	2-3	Butler, Gall
1990-91	D4	1	17.11.90 **Torquay U**	D4	H	W	4-1	Butler 2, Osborne, Gall
		2	8.12.90 **Aldershot**	D4	A	L	1-2	Gall
1991-92	D4	1	16.11.91 **Sutton U**	IL	H	W	1-0	Thompson
		2	7.12.91 **Kettering T**	GMVC	H	L	1-2	Henry

MANCHESTER FC

Formed 1866. Played at Whalley Range, Manchester and used the Albion Hotel as their changing rooms. No connection with either Manchester City or Manchester United.

1877-78		1	7.11.77 **Darwen**		A	L	0-3	
1883-84		1	10.11.83 **Stoke**		A	W	2-1	Colhurst, Bassett
		2	1.12.83 **Queens Park, Glasgow**		A	L	0-15	

MANCHESTER CENTRAL

First entered FA Cup: 1929. Played at the old Belle Vue stadium

1929-30	LC	1	30.11.30 **Mansfield T**	ML	A	W	2-0	Roberts, Pelan
		2	14.12.29 **Wrexham**	3N	H	L	0-1	
1931-32	CC	1	28.11.31 **Lincoln C**	3N	H	L	0-3	

MANCHESTER CITY

Formed 1887 as Ardwick FC. Manchester City 1894. **FA Cup Best Performance:** Winners: 1904, 1934, 1956, 1969. Runners-up: 1926, 1933, 1955, 1981. **FA Cup Record Win:** (as Ardwick) 12-0 vs Liverpool Stanley, 1st qual.round, 4.10.1890. In competition proper: 10-1 vs Swindon Town, 4th round, 29.1.1930 9-0 vs Gateshead, 3rd round replay, 18.1.1933. **FA Cup Record Defeat:** 0-6 vs Preston NE, 1st round, 30.1.1897, 2-8 vs Bradford PA, 4th round, 2nd leg, 30.1.1946.

As Ardwick

1890-91		1q		**Liverpool Stanley** (H) 12-0; 2q **Halliwell** scratched					
1891-92	FAll	1q		**Newton Heath** (A) 1-5					
1892-93	D2	1q		**Fleetwood** (A) 1-1; 1qr **Fleetwood** (H) 0-2					
1893-94	D2	1q		**West Manchester** (A) 0-3					

As Manchester City

1894-95	D2			*did not enter*					
1895-96	D2	1q		**Oswaldtwistle** *scratched*					
1896-97	D2	1	30.1.97	**Preston NE**	D1	A	L	0-6	
1897-98	D2	1	29.1.98	**Wigan Co**	LL	H	W	1-0	Gillespie
		2	12.2.98	**Bolton W**	D1	A	L	0-1	
1898-99	D1	1	28.1.99	**Small Heath**	D2	A	L	2-3	Meredith, Gillespie
1899-00	D1	1	27.1.00	**Aston Villa**	D1	H	D	1-1	Ross
		1r	31.1.00	**Aston Villa**		A	L	0-3	
1900-01	D1	1	9.2.01	**WBA**	D1	A	L	0-1	
1901-02	D1	1	25.1.02	**Preston NE**	D2	A	–	1-1	Henderson
				abandoned in extra time					
		1r	29.1.02	**Preston NE**		H	D	0-0aet	
		1 2r	3.2.02	**Preston NE**		A	W	4-2aet	Smith 3, Morgan
		2	8.2.02	**Nottingham F**	D1	H	L	0-2	
1902-03	D2	1	7.2.03	**Preston NE**	D2	A	L	1-3	Turnbull
1903-04	D1	1	6.2.04	**Sunderland**	D1	H	W	3-2	Turnbull 2, Gillespie
		2	20.2.04	**W.Arsenal**	D2	A	W	2-0	Turnbull, Booth
		3	5.3.04	**Middlesbrough**	D1	H	D	0-0	
		3r	9.3.04	**Middlesbrough**		A	W	3-1	Livingstone, Gillespie, Turnbull
		SF	19.3.04	**Sheffield W**	D1		W	3-1	Meredith, Gillespie, Turnbull
				played at Goodison Park					
		F	23.4.04	**BOLTON W**	D2		W	1-0	Meredith
				played at Crystal Palace					
1904-05	D1	1	4.2.05	**Lincoln C**	D2	A	W	2-1	Meredith, Turnbull
		2	18.2.05	**Bolton W**	D2	H	L	1-2	Gillespie
1905-06	D1	1	13.1.06	**Sheffield W**	D1	A	L	1-4	Bannister
1906-07	D1	1	12.1.07	**Blackburn R**	D1	A	D	2-2	Dorsett, Thornley
		1r	16.1.07	**Blackburn R**		H	L	0-1	
1907-8	D1	1	11.1.08	**Glossop**	D2	A	D	0-0	
		1r	15.1.08	**Glossop**		H	W	6-0	Buchan, Wood, Dorsett, Grieve, Jones, Conlin
		2	1.2.08	**New Brompton**	SL	H	D	1-1	Jones
		2r	5.2.08	**New Brompton**		A	W	2-1	Buchan, Wood
		3	22.2.08	**Fulham**	D2	H	D	1-1	Blair
		3r	26.2.08	**Fulham**		A	L	1-3	Wood
1908-09	D2	1	16.1.09	**Tottenham H**	D2	H	L	3-4	Holford 3
1909-10	D2	1	15.1.10	**Workington**	NEL	A	W	2-1	Wynn 2
		2	5.2.10	**Southampton**	SL	A	W	5-0	Dorsett, Stewart, Jones, Conlin, Holford
		3	19.2.10	**Aston Villa**	D1	A	W	2-1	Stewart, Jones
		4	5.3.10	**Swindon T**	SL	A	L	0-2	
1910-11	D1	1	10.1.11	**Stoke**	BDL	A	W	2-1	J.Smith, Jones
		2	4.2.11	**Wolverhampton W**	D2	A	L	0-1	
1911-12	D1	1	13.1.12	**Preston NE**	D1	A	W	1-0	Wynn
		2	3.2.12	**Oldham A**	D1	H	L	0-1	
1912-13	D1	1	11.1.13	**Birmingham**	D2	H	W	4-0	Wynn 2, Hoad, Taylor
		2	1.2.13	**Sunderland**	D1	H	–	0-2	
				abandoned after 60 minutes due to dangerous overcrowding in the ground					
		2r	5.2.13	**Sunderland**		A	L	0-2	
1913-14	D1	1	10.1.14	**Fulham**	D2	H	W	2-0	Hindmarsh, Howard
		2	31.1.14	**Tottenham H**	D1	H	W	2-1	Howard, Browell
		3	21.2.14	**Blackburn R**	D1	A	W	2-1	Howard, Cartwright
		4	7.3.14	**Sheffield U**	D1	H	D	0-0	
		4r	12.3.14	**Sheffield U**		A	D	0-0	
		4 2r	16.3.14	**Sheffield U** at Villa Park		L		0-1	
1914-15	D1	1	9.1.15	**Preston NE**	D2	A	D	0-0	

Season	Div	Round	Date	Opponent	Comp	Venue	Res	Score	Scorers
		1r	16.1.15	Preston NE		H	W	3-0	Barnes 2, Hughes
		2	30.1.15	Aston Villa	D1	H	W	1-0	Cartwright
		3	20.2.15	Chelsea	D2	H	L	0-1	
1919-20	D1	1	10.1.20	Clapton O	D2	H	W	4-1	Goodwin 2, Barnes, Murphy
		2	31.1.20	Leicester C	D2	A	L	0-3	
1920-21	D1	1	8.1.21	Crystal P	D3	A	L	0-2	
1921-22	D1	1	7.1.22	Darlington	3N	H	W	3-1	Browell 3
		2	28.1.22	Bolton W	D1	A	W	3-1	Browell 2, Kelly
		3	18.2.22	Tottenham H	D1	A	L	1-2	Kelly
1922-23	D1	1	13.1.23	Charlton A	3S	A	L	1-2	Johnson
1923-24	D1	1	12.1.24	Nottingham F	D1	H	W	2-1	Roberts, Barnes
		2	2.2.24	Halifax T	3N	A	D	2-2	Hamill, Roberts
		2r	6.2.24	Halifax T		H	D	0-0aet	
		2 2r	11.2.24	Halifax T at Old Trafford			W	3-0	Roberts 2, Browell
		3	23.2.24	Brighton & HA	3S	H	W	5-1	Browell 2, Meredith, Barnes, Sharp
		4	8.3.24	Cardiff C	D1	H	D	0-0	
		4r	12.3.24	Cardiff C		A	W	1-0aet	Browell
		SF	29.3.24	Newcastle U	D1		L	0-2	
			played at St Andrews						
1924-25	D1	1	10.1.25	Preston NE	D1	A	L	1-4	Roberts
1925-26	D1	3	9.1.26	Corinthians		A	D	3-3	Hicks, Cookson, Roberts
		3r	13.1.26	Corinthians		H	W	4-0	Austin 2, Johnson, Hicks
		4	30.1.26	Huddersfield T	D1	H	W	4-0	Hicks 2, Roberts, Browell
		5	20.2.26	Crystal P	3S	H	W	11-4	Roberts 5, Browell 3, Austin, Johnson, Hicks
		6	6.3.26	Clapton O	D2	A	W	6-1	Johnson 3, Hicks, Roberts, Browell
		SF	27.3.26	Manchester U	D1		W	3-0	Browell 2, Roberts
			played at Bramall Lane						
		F	24.4.26	Bolton W	D1 WEMBLEY		L	0-1	
1926-27	D2	3	8.1.27	Birmingham	D1	A	L	1-4	Hicks
1927-28	D2	3	14.1.28	Leeds U	D2	H	W	1-0	Johnson
		4	28.1.28	Sunderland	D1	A	W	2-1	Broadhurst, Hicks
		5	18.2.28	Stoke C	D2	H	L	0-1	
1928-29	D1	3	12.1.29	Birmingham	D1	A	L	1-3	Austin
1929-30	D1	3	11.1.30	Tottenham H	D2	A	D	2-2	Toseland, Cowan
		3r	15.1.30	Tottenham H		H	W	4-1	Busby 2, Toseland, Marshall
		4	25.1.30	Swindon T	3S	A	D	1-1	Cowan
		4r	29.1.30	Swindon T		H	W	10-1	Marshall 5, Tait 3, Johnson, Brook
		5	15.2.30	Hull C	D2	H	L	1-2	Toseland
1930-31	D1	3	10.1.31	Burnley	D2	A	L	0-3	
1931-32	D1	3	9.1.32	Millwall	D2	A	W	3-2	Halliday 2, Toseland
		4	23.1.32	Brentford	3S	H	W	6-1	Tilson 3, Brook 2, Halliday
		5	13.2.32	Derby Co	D1	H	W	3-0	Marshall 2, Brook
		6	27.2.32	Bury	D2	A	W	4-3	Toseland 2, Halliday, Cowan
		SF	12.3.32	Arsenal	D1		L	0-1	
			played at Villa Park						
1932-33	D1	3	14.1.33	Gateshead	3N	A	D	1-1	Toseland
		3r	18.1.33	Gateshead		H	W	9-0	Tilson 3, Cowan 2, Busby, Barrass, McMullen, Brook
		4	28.1.33	Walsall	3N	H	W	2-0	Brook 2
		5	18.2.33	Bolton W	D1	A	W	4-2	Brook 3, Tilson
		6	4.3.33	Burnley	D2	A	W	1-0	Tilson
		SF	18.3.33	Derby Co	D1		W	3-2	Toseland, Tilson, McMullen
			played at Huddersfield						
		F	28.4.33	Everton	D1 WEMBLEY		L	0-3	
1933-34	D1	3	13.1.34	Blackburn R	D1	H	W	3-1	Brook, Toseland 2
		4	27.1.34	Hull C	D2	A	D	2-2	Brook, Herd
		4r	31.1.34	Hull C		H	W	4-1	Tilson 2, Toseland, Marshall
		5	17.2.34	Sheffield W	D1	A	D	2-2	Herd 2
		5r	21.2.34	Sheffield W		H	W	2-0	Marshall, Tilson
		6	3.3.34	Stoke C	D1	H	W	1-0	Brook
		SF	17.3.34	Aston Villa	D1		W	6-1	Tilson 4, Herd, Toseland
			played at Huddersfield						
		F	28.4.34	PORTSMOUTH	D1 WEMBLEY		W	2-1	Tilson 2
1934-35	D1	3	12.1.35	Tottenham H	D1	A	L	0-1	
1935-36	D1	3	11.1.36	Portsmouth	D1	H	W	3-1	Brook 3
		4	25.1.36	Luton T	3S	H	W	2-1	Herd, McLeod
		5	15.2.36	Grimsby T	D1	A	L	2-3	Tilson, McLeod
1936-37	D1	3	16.1.37	Wrexham	3N	A	W	3-1	Brook (p), Herd, Tilson

Season	Div	Rd	Date	Opponent	OppDiv	H/A	Res	Score	Scorers
		4	30.1.37	Accrington S	3N	H	W	2-0	Doherty, Tilson
		5	20.2.37	Bolton W	D1	A	W	5-0	Tilson, Herd 2, Brook, Doherty
		6	6.3.37	Millwall	3S	A	L	0-2	
1937-38	D1	3	8.1.38	Millwall	3S	A	D	2-2	Herd 2
		3r	12.1.38	Millwall		H	W	3-1	Herd, Heale, Brook
		4	22.1.38	Bury	D2	H	W	3-1	Whitfield og, Toseland 2
		5	12.2.38	Luton T	D2	A	W	3-1	Heale, Doherty, Nelson og
		6	5.3.38	Aston Villa	D2	A	L	2-3	Doherty, Allen og
1938-39	D2	3	12.1.39	Norwich C	D2	A	W	5-0	Herd 2, Milsom, Doherty
		4	21.1.39	Sheffield U	D2	A	L	0-2	
1945-46	D2	3 1L	5.1.46	Barrow	3N	H	W	6-2	Herd 3, Constantine 3
		3 2L	10.1.46	Barrow		A	D	2-2	Hart, Dunkley
		4 1L	26.1.46	Bradford PA	D2	A	W	3-1	SMith 2, Herd
		4 2L	30.1.46	Bradford PA		H	L	2-8	Constantine, Smith
1946-47	D2	3	11.1.47	Gateshead	3N	H	W	3-0	Westwood, Jackson, Capel
		4	25.1.47	Bolton W	D1	A	D	3-3	Black 2, Capel
		4r	29.1.47	Bolton W		H	W	1-0	Westwood
		5	8.2.47	Birmingham C	D2	A	L	0-5	
1947-48	D1	3	10.1.48	Barnsley	D2	H	W	2-1	Black, Smith
		4	24.1.48	Chelsea	D1	H	W	2-0aet	Linacre, Smith
		5	7.2.48	Preston NE	D1	H	L	0-1	
1948-49	D1	3	8.1.49	Everton	D1	A	L	0-1	
1949-50	D1	3	7.1.50	Derby Co	D1	H	L	3-5	Clarke, Black 2
1950-51	D2	3	6.1.51	Birmingham C	D2	A	L	0-2	
1951-52	D1	3	12.1.52	Wolverhampton W	D1	H	D	2-2	Meadows, Revie
		3r	16.1.52	Wolverhampton W		A	L	1-4	Clarke
1952-53	D1	3	10.1.53	Swindon T	3S	H	W	7-0	Williamson, Hart 4, Broadies, Cunliffe
		4	31.1.53	Luton T	D2	H	D	1-1	Broadis
		4r	4.2.53	Luton T		A	L	1-5	Spurdle
1953-54	D1	3	9.1.54	Bradford PA	3N	A	W	5-2	McAdams 3, Revie, Clarke
		4	30.1.54	Tottenham H	D1	H	L	0-1	
1954-55	D1	3	8.1.55	Derby Co	D2	A	W	3-1	Hayes, Revie, Barnes
		4	29.1.55	Manchester U	D1	H	W	2-0	Hayes, Revie
		5	19.2.55	Luton T	D2	A	W	2-0	Clarke 2
		6	12.3.55	Birmingham C	D2	A	W	1-0	Hart
		SF	26.3.55	Sunderland	D1		W	1-0	Clarke
			played at Villa Park						
		F	7.5.55	Newcastle U	D1	WEMBLEY	L	1-3	Johnstone
1955-56	D1	3	7.1.56	Blackpool	D1	H	–	1-1	Dyson
			abandoned after 56 minutes – fog						
		3	11.1.56	Blackpool		H	W	2-1	Johnstone, Dyson
		4	28.1.56	Southend U	3S	A	W	1-0	Hayes
		5	18.2.56	Liverpool	D2	H	D	0-0	
		5r	22.2.56	Liverpool		A	W	2-1	Dyson, Hayes
		6	4.3.56	Everton	D1	H	W	2-1	Hayes, Johnstone
		SF	17.3.56	Tottenham H	D1		W	1-0	Johnstone
			played at Villa Park						
		F	5.4.56	BIRMINGHAM C	D1	WEMBLEY	W	3-1	Hayes, Dyson, Johnstone
1956-57	D1	3	5.1.57	Newcastle U	D1	A	D	1-1	Johnstone
		3r	9.1.57	Newcastle U		H	L	4-5	Stokoe og, Johnstone 2, Fagan
1957-58	D1	3	4.1.58	WBA	D1	A	L	1-5	Hayes
1958-59	D1	3	10.1.59	Grimsby T	D2	A	D	2-2	Hayes, Barlow
		3r	24.1.59	Grimsby T		H	L	1-2	Johnstone
1959-60	D1	3	9.1.60	Southampton	D3	H	L	1-5	Barlow
1960-61	D1	3	7.1.61	Cardiff C	D1	A	D	1-1	Harrington og
		3r	11.1.61	Cardiff C		H	D	0-0aet	
		3 2r	16.1.61	Cardiff C at Highbury			W	2-0	Law, Hayes
		4	28.1.61	Luton T	D2	A	–	6-2	Law 6
			abandoned after 69 minutes – waterlogged pitch						
		4	1.2.61	Luton T		A	L	1-3	Law
1961-62	D1	3	6.1.62	Notts Co	D3	A	W	1-0	Young
		4	27.1.62	Everton	D1	A	L	0-2	
1962-63	D1	3	6.3.63	Walsall	D2	A	W	1-0	Harley
		4	13.3.63	Bury	D2	H	W	1-0	Harley
		5	16.3.63	Norwich C	D2	H	L	1-2	Oakes
1963-64	D2	3	4.1.64	Swindon T	D2	A	L	1-2	Oakes
1964-65	D2	3	9.1.65	Shrewsbury T	D3	H	D	1-1	Kevan

	3r	13.1.65	Shrewsbury T		A	L	1-3	Gray
1965-66 D2	3	22.1.66	Blackpool	D1	A	D	1-1	Crossan
	3r	24.1.66	Blackpool		H	W	3-1	Crossan, Summerbee, Doyle
	4	12.2.66	Grimsby T	D3	H	W	2-0	Cockerill og, Summerbee
	5	5.3.66	Leicester C	D1	H	D	2-2	Young 2
	5r	9.3.66	Leicester C		A	W	1-0	Young
	6	26.3.66	Everton	D1	H	D	0-0	
	6r	29.3.66	Everton		A	D	0-0aet	
	6 2r	4.4.66	Everton at Molineux			L	0-2	
1966-67 D1	3	28.1.67	Leicester C	D1	H	W	2-1	Pardoe, Doyle Pardoe
	4	18.2.67	Cardiff C	D2	A	D	1-1	Coldrick og
	4r	22.2.67	Cardiff C		H	W	3-1	Bell, Young, Crossan
	5	11.3.67	Ipswich T	D2	H	D	1-1	Young
	5r	14.3.67	Ipswich T		A	W	3-0	Summerbee 2, McNeil og
	6	8.4.67	Leeds U	D1	A	L	0-1	
1967-68 D1	3	27.1.68	Reading	D3	H	D	0-0	
	3r	31.1.68	Reading		A	W	7-0	Summerbee 3, Young, Coleman, Heslop, Bell
	4	17.2.68	Leicester C	D1	H	D	0-0	
	4r	19.2.68	Leicester C		A	L	3-4	Summerbee, Bell, Lee
1968-69 D1	3	4.1.69	Luton T	D3	H	W	1-0	Lee
	4	25.1.69	Newcastle U	D1	A	D	0-0	
	4r	29.1.69	Newcastle U		H	W	2-0	Owen, Young
	5	24.2.69	Blackburn R	D2	A	W	4-1	Lee 2, Coleman 2
	6	1.3.69	Tottenham H	D1	H	W	1-0	Lee
	SF	22.3.69	Everton	D1		W	1-0	Booth
		played at Villa Park						
	F	26.4.69	LEICESTER C	D1 WEMBLEY	W	1-0		Young
1969-70 D1	3	3.1.70	Hull C	D2	A	W	1-0	Young
	4	24.1.70	Manchester U	D1	A	L	0-3	
1970-71 D1	3	2.1.71	Wigan A	NPL	H	W	1-0	Bell
	4	23.1.71	Chelsea	D1	A	W	3-0	Bell 2, Bowyer
	5	17.2.71	Arsenal	D1	H	L	1-2	Bell
1971-72 D1	3	15.1.72	Middlesbrough	D2	H	D	1-1	Lee
	3r	18.1.72	Middlesbrough		A	L	0-1	
1972-73 D1	3	13.1.73	Stoke C	D1	H	W	3-2	Summerbee, Bell, Marsh
	4	3.2.73	Liverpool	D1	A	D	0-0	
	4r	7.2.73	Liverpool		H	W	2-0	Bell, Booth
	5	24.2.73	Sunderland	D2	H	D	2-2	Towers, Montgomery og
	5r	27.2.73	Sunderland		A	L	1-3	Lee
1973-74 D1	3	5.1.74	Oxford U	D2	A	W	5-2	Law 2, Summerbee 2, Marsh
	4	26.1.74	Nottingham F	D2	A	L	1-4	Carrodus
1974-75 D1	3	4.1.75	Newcastle U	D1	H	L	0-2	
1975-76 D1	3	3.1.76	Hartlepool	D4	H	W	6-0	Tueart 2, Booth 2, Hartford, Oakes
	4	28.1.76	Stoke C	D1	A	L	0-1	
1976-77 D1	3	8.1.77	WBA	D1	H	D	1-1	Kidd
	3r	11.1.77	WBA		A	W	1-0	Royle
	4	29.1.77	Newcastle U		A	W	3-1	D.Craig og, Royle, Owen
	5	26.2.77	Leeds U	D1	A	L	0-1	
1977-78 D1	3	7.1.78	Leeds U	D1	A	W	2-1	Barnes, Tueart
	4	31.1.78	Nottingham F	D1	A	L	1-2	Kidd
1978-79 D1	3	15.1.79	Rotherham U	D3	H	D	0-0	
	3r	17.1.79	Rotherham U		A	W	4-2	Kidd 2, Barnes, Owen
	4	25.1.79	Shrewsbury T	D3	A	L	0-2	
1979-80 D1	3	5.1.80	Halifax T	D4	A	L	0-1	
1980-81 D1	3	3.1.81	Crystal P	D1	H	W	4-0	Reeves 2, Power, Boyer
	4	24.1.81	Norwich C	D1	H	W	6-0	McDonald, Reeves, Mackenzie, Power, Gow, Bennett
	5	14.2.81	Peterborough U	D4	A	W	1-0	Booth
	6	7.3.81	Everton	D1	A	D	2-2	Power, Gow
	6r	11.3.81	Everton		H	W	3-1	McDonald 2, Power
	SF	11.4.81	Ipswich T	D1		W	1-0	Power
		played at Villa Park						
	F	9.5.81	Tottenham H	D1 WEMBLEY	D	1-1aet		Hutchinson
	Fr	14.5.81	Tottenham H	WEMBLEY	L	2-3		Mackenzie, Reeves (p)
1981-82 D1	3	2.1.82	Cardiff C	D2	H	W	3-1	Francis 2, McDonald
	4	23.1.82	Coventry C	D1	H	L	1-3	Bond
1982-83 D1	3	8.1.83	Sunderland	D1	A	D	0-0	
	3r	12.1.83	Sunderland		H	W	2-1	Cross, Hartford

MANCHESTER CITY

		4	29.1.83	Brighton & HA	D1	A	L	0-4	
1983-84	D2	3	7.1.84	Blackpool	D4	A	L	1-2	Hetzke og
1984-85	D2	3	5.1.85	Coventry C	D1	A	L	1-2	Power
1985-86	D1	3	4.1.86	Walsall	D3	A	W	3-1	Simpson 2, Davies
		4	25.1.86	Watford	D1	H	D	1-1	Davies
		4r	3.2.86	Watford		A	D	0-0aet	
		4 2r	6.2.86	Watford		H	L	1-3	Kinsey
1986-87	D1	3	10.1.87	Manchester U	D1	A	L	0-1	
1987-88	D2	3	9.1.88	Huddersfield T	D2	A	D	2-2	Brightwell, Gidman
		3r	12.1.88	Huddersfield T		H	D	0-0aet	
		3 2r	25.1.88	Huddersfield T		A	W	3-0	Hinchcliffe, White, Varadi
		4	30.1.88	Blackpool	D3	A	D	1-1	Lake
		4r	3.2.88	Blackpool		H	W	2-1	Stewart, Simpson
		5	20.2.88	Plymouth A	D2	H	W	3-1	Scott, Simpson, Moulden
		6	13.3.88	Liverpool	D1	H	L	0-4	
1988-89	D2	3	7.1.89	Leicester C	D2	H	W	1-0	McNab (p)
		4	28.1.89	Brentford	D3	A	L	1-3	Gleghorn
1989-90	D1	3	6.1.90	Millwall	D1	H	D	0-0	
		3r	9.1.90	Millwall		A	D	1-1aet	Hendry
		3 2r	15.1.90	Millwall		A	L	1-3	Lake
1990-91	D1	3	6.1.91	Burnley	D4	A	W	1-0	Hendry
		4	26.1.91	Port Vale	D2	A	W	2-1	Quinn, Allen
		5	16.2.91	Notts Co	D2	A	L	0-1	
1991-92	D1	3	4.1.92	Middlesbrough	D2	A	L	1-2	Reid
1992-93	PL	3	2.1.93	Reading	D2	H	D	1-1	Sheron
		3r	13.1.93	Reading		A	W	4-0	Sheron, Holden, Flitcroft, Quinn
		4	23.1.93	QPR	PL	A	W	2-1	White, Vonk
		5	13.2.93	Barnsley	D1	H	W	2-0	White 2
		6	7.3.93	Tottenham H	PL	H	L	2-4	Sheron, Phelan

MANCHESTER UNITED

Founded as Newton Heath 1878. Renamed Manchester United 1902. **Best FA Cup Performance:** Winners (7 times) 1909, 1948, 1963, 1977, 1983, 1985, 1990. Runners-up: 1957, 1958, 1976, 1979. **Record FA Cup Win:** 8-0 vs Yeovil, 5th round, 12.2.1949. **Record FA Cup Defeat:** 1-7 vs Burnley, 1st round replay, 13.2.1901 0-6 vs Sheffield Wednesday, 2nd round, 20.2.1904

As Newton Heath

1886-87		1	30.10.86	Fleetwood R		A	D	2-2	Doughty 2
			Newton Heath refused to play extra time, Fleetwood awarded tie						
1887-88		*did not enter*							
1888-89		*did not enter*							
1889-90	FAII	1	18.1.90	Preston NE	D1	A	L	1-6	Craig
1890-91	FAII	1q Higher Walton (H) 2-0; 2q Bootle Reserves (A) 0-1							
1891-92	FAII	1q Ardwick (H) 5-1; 2q Heywood (H) walkover; 3q South Shore (A) 2-0; 4q Blackpool (H) 3-4							
1892-93	D1	1	21.1.93	Blackburn R	D1	A	L	0-4	
1893-94	D1	1	27.1.94	Middlesbrough	D2	H	W	4-0	Donaldson 2, Farman, Peden
		2	10.2.94	Blackburn R	D1	H	D	0-0aet	
		2R	17.2.94	Blackburn R		A	L	1-5	Donaldson
1894-95	D2	1	2.2.95	Stoke	D1	H	L	2-3	Smith, Peters
1895-96	D2	1	1.2.96	Kettering T	ML	H	W	2-1	Donaldson, Smith
		2	15.2.96	Derby Co	D1	H	D	1-1	Kennedy
		2R	19.2.96	Derby Co		A	L	1-5	Donaldson
1896-97	D2	1q West Manchester (H) 7-0; 2q Nelson (H) 3-0; 3q Blackpool (H) 2-2; 3qr Blackpool (A) 2-1							
		1	30.1.97	Kettering T	ML	H	W	5-1	Cassidy 3, Donaldson 2
		2	13.2.97	Southampton	SL	A	D	1-1	Donaldson
		2r	17.2.97	Southampton		H	W	3-1	Bryant 2, Cassidy
		3	27.2.97	Derby Co	D1	A	L	0-2	
1897-98	D2	1	29.1.98	Walsall	D2	H	W	1-0	*own goal*
		2	12.2.98	Liverpool	D1	H	D	0-0	
		2r	16.2.98	Liverpool		A	L	1-2	Collinson
1898-99	D2	1	28.1.99	Tottenham H	SL	A	D	1-1	Cassidy
		1r	1.2.99	Tottenham H		H	L	3-5	Bryant 3
1899-00	D2	1q South Shore (A) 1-3							
1900-01	D2	Int Portsmouth (H) 3-0							
		1	9.2.01	Burnley	D2	H	D	0-0	
		1r	13.2.01	Burnley		A	L	1-7	Schofield

Season	Div	Rd	Date	Opponent		Venue	Result	Score	Scorers
1901-02	D2		Int **Lincoln City** (H) 1-2						
As Manchester United									
1902-03	D2		3q **Accrington S** (H) 7-0; 4q **Oswaldtwistle** (H) 3-2; 5q **Southport Central** (H) 4-1; Int **Burton U** (H) 1-1; Int r **Burton U** (H) 3-1						
		1	7.2.03	**Liverpool**	D1	H	W	2-1	Peddie 2
		2	21.2.03	**Everton**	D1	A	L	1-3	Griffiths
1903-04	D2		Int **Small Heath** (H) 1-1; Int r **Small Heath** (A) 1-1aet; Int 2r **Small Heath** 1-1aet at Bramall Lane;						
			Int 3r **Small Heath** 3-1 at Hyde Road, Manchester						
		1	6.2.04	**Notts Co**	D1	A	D	3-3	Downie, Schofield, Arkesden
		1r	10.2.04	**Notts Co**		H	W	2-1	Morrison, Pegg
		2	20.2.04	**Sheffield W**	D1	A	L	0-6	
1904-05	D2		Int **Fulham** (H) 2-2; Int r **Fulham** (A) 0-0; Int 2r **Fulham** 0-1 at Villa Park						
1905-06	D2	1	13.1.06	**Staple Hill**	WL	H	W	7-2	Beddow 3, Picken 2, Allen, Williams
		2	3.2.06	**Norwich C**	SL	H	W	3-0	Downie, Peddie, Sagar
		3	24.2.06	**A.Villa**	D1	H	W	5-1	Picken 3, Sagar 2
		4	10.3.06	**W.Arsenal**	D1	H	L	2-3	Peddie, Sagar
1906-07	D1	1	12.1.07	**Portsmouth**	SL	A	D	2-2	Picken, Wall
		2	16.1.07	**Portsmouth**		H	L	1-2	Wall
1907-08	D1	1	11.1.08	**Blackpool**	D2	H	W	3-1	Wall 2, Bannister
		2	1.2.08	**Chelsea**	D1	H	W	1-0	Sandy Turnbull
		3	22.2.08	**A.Villa**	D1	A	W	2-0	Sandy Turnbull, Wall
		4	7.3.08	**Fulham**	D2	A	L	1-2	J.Turnbull
1908-09	D1	1	16.1.09	**Brighton & HA**	SL	H	W	1-0	Halse
		2	6.2.09	**Everton**	D1	H	W	1-0	Halse
		3	20.2.09	**Blackburn R**	D1	H	W	6-1	Sandy Turnbull 3, J.Turnbull 3
		4	5.3.09	**Burnley**	D2	A	–	0-1	
			abandoned after 72 minutes						
		4	10.3.09	**Burnley**		A	W	3-2	J.Turnbull 2, Halse
		SF	27.3.09	**Newcastle U**	D1		W	1-0	Halse
			played at Bramall Lane						
		F	24.4.09	**BRISTOL CITY**	D1		W	1-0	Sandy Turnbull
			played at Crystal Palace						
1909-10	D1	1	15.1.10	**Burnley**	D2	A	L	0-2	
1910-11	D1	1	14.1.11	**Blackpool**	D2	A	W	2-1	Picken, West
		2	4.2.11	**A.Villa**	D1	H	W	2-1	Halse, Wall
		3	25.2.11	**West Ham**	SL	A	L	1-2	Sandy Turnbull
1911-12	D1	1	13.1.12	**Huddersfield T**	D2	H	W	3-1	West 2, Halse
		2	3.2.12	**Coventry C**	SL	A	W	5-1	Halse 2, West, Sandy Turnbull, Wall
		3	24.2.12	**Reading**	SL	A	D	1-1	West
		3r	29.2.12	**Reading**		H	W	3-0	Sandy Turnbull 2, Halse
		4	9.3.12	**Blackburn R**	D1	H	D	1-1	Walmsley og
		4r	14.3.12	**Blackburn R**		A	L	2-4aet	West 2
1912-13	D1	1	11.1.13	**Coventry C**	SL	H	D	1-1	Wall
		1r	16.1.13	**Coventry C**		A	W	2-1	Anderson, Roberts
		2	1.2.13	**Plymouth A**	SL	A	W	2-0	Anderson, Wall
		3	22.2.13	**Oldham A**	D1	A	D	0-0	
		3r	26.2.13	**Oldham A**		H	L	1-2	West
1913-14	D1	1	10.1.14	**Swindon T**	SL	A	L	0-1	
1914-15	D1	1	9.1.15	**Sheffield W**	D1	A	L	0-1	
1919-20	D1	1	10.1.20	**Port Vale**	D2	A	W	1-0	Toms
		2	31.1.20	**A.Villa**	D1	H	L	1-2	Woodcock
1920-21	D1	1	8.1.21	**Liverpool**	D1	A	D	1-1	Miller
		2	12.1.21	**Liverpool**		H	L	1-2	Partridge
1921-22	D1	1	7.1.22	**Cardiff C**	D1	H	L	1-4	Sapsford
1922-23	D2	1	13.1.23	**Bradford C**	D2	A	D	1-1	Partridge
		1r	17.1.23	**Bradford C**		H	W	2-0	Barber, Goldthorpe
		2	3.2.23	**Tottenham H**	D1	A	L	0-4	
1923-24	D2	1	12.1.24	**Plymouth A**	3S	H	W	1-0	McPherson
		2	2.2.24	**Huddersfield T**	D1	H	L	0-3	
1924-25	D2	1	10.1.25	**Sheffield W**	D2	A	L	0-2	
1925-26	D1	3	9.1.26	**Port Vale**	D2	A	W	3-2	Spence 2, McPherson
		4	30.1.26	**Tottenham H**	D1	A	D	2-2	Thomas, Spence
		4r	3.2.26	**Tottenham H**		H	W	2-0	Spence, Rennox
		5	20.2.26	**Sunderland**	D1	A	D	3-3	Smith 2, McPherson
		5r	24.2.26	**Sunderland**		H	W	2-1	Smith, McPherson
		6	6.3.26	**Fulham**	D2	A	W	2-1	Smith, McPherson
		SF	21.3.26	**Manchester C**	D1		L	0-3	
			played at Bramall Lane						

Season	Div	Rd	Date	Opponent	Opp	Venue	Res	Score	Scorers
1926-27	D1	3	8.1.27	Reading	D2	A	D	1-1	McPherson
		3r	12.1.27	Reading		H	D	2-2aet	Spence, Sweeney
		3 2r	17.1.27	Reading at Villa Park			L	1-2	McPherson
1927-28	D1	3	14.1.28	Brentford	3S	H	W	7-1	Hanson 4, Spence, McPherson, Johnston
		4	28.1.28	Bury	D1	A	D	1-1	Johnston
		4r	1.2.28	Bury		H	W	1-0	Spence
		5	18.2.28	Birmingham	D1	H	W	1-0	Johnston
		6	3.3.28	Blackburn R	D1	A	L	0-2	
1928-29	D1	3	12.1.29	Port Vale	D2	A	W	3-0	Spence, Hanson, Taylor
		4	26.1.29	Bury	D1	H	L	0-1	
1929-30	D1	3	11.1.30	Swindon T	3S	H	L	0-2	
1930-31	D1	3	10.1.31	Stoke C	D2	A	D	3-3	Reid 3
		3r	14.1.31	Stoke C		H	D	0-0aet	
		3 2r	19.1.31	Stoke C played at Anfield			W	4-2	Hopkinson 2, Spence, Gallimore
		4	24.1.31	Grimsby T	D1	A	L	0-1	
1931-32	D1	3	9.1.32	Plymouth A	D2	A	L	1-4	Reid
1932-33	D2	3	14.1.33	Middlesbrough	D1	H	L	1-4	Spence
1933-34	D2	3	13.1.34	Portsmouth	D1	H	D	1-1	McLenahan
		3r	17.1.34	Portsmouth		A	L	1-4	Ball
1934-35	D2	3	12.1.35	Bristol R	3S	A	W	3-1	Mutch, Bamford 2
		4	26.1.35	Nottingham F	D2	A	D	0-0	
		4r	30.1.35	Nottingham F		H	L	0-3	
1935-36	D2	3	11.1.36	Reading	3S	A	W	3-1	Manley, Mutch 2
		4	25.1.36	Stoke C	D1	A	D	0-0	
		4r	29.1.36	Stoke C		H	L	0-2	
1936-37	D1	3	16.1.37	Reading	3S	H	W	1-0	Bamford
		4	30.1.37	Arsenal	D1	A	L	0-5	
1937-38	D2	3	8.1.38	Yeovil	SL	H	W	3-0	Pearson, Baird, Bamford
		4	22.1.38	Barnsley	D2	A	D	2-2	Carey, Baird
		4r	26.1.38	Barnsley		H	W	1-0	Baird
		5	12.2.38	Brentford	D1	A	L	0-2	
1938-39	D1	3	7.1.39	WBA	D2	A	D	0-0	
		3r	11.1.39	WBA		H	L	1-5	Redwood
1945-46	D1	3 1L	5.1.46	Accrington S	3N	A	D	2-2	Smith, Wrigglesworth
		3 2L	9.1.46	Accrington S		H	W	5-1	Rowley 2, Bainbridge, Wrigglesworth, Briggs og
		4 1L	26.1.46	Preston NE	D1	H	W	1-0	Hanlon
		4 2L	30.1.46	Preston NE		A	L	1-3	Hanlon
1946-47	D1	3	11.1.47	Bradford PA	D2	A	W	3-0	Buckle, Rowley 2
		4	25.1.47	Nottingham F	D2	H	L	0-2	
1947-48	D1	3	10.1.48	A.Villa	D1	A	W	6-4	Pearson 2, Morris 2, Delaney, Rowley
		4	24.1.48	Liverpool	D1	H	W	3-0	Rowley, Morris, Mitten
				played at Goodison Park					
		5	7.2.48	Charlton A	D1	H	W	2-0	Warner, Mitten
				played at Huddersfield					
		6	28.2.48	Preston NE	D1	H	W	4-1	Mitten, Pearson 2, Rowley
				played at Maine Road					
		SF	13.3.48	Derby Co	D1		W	3-1	Pearson 3
				played at Hillsborough					
		F	24.4.48	Blackpool	D1	WEMBLEY	W	4-2	Rowley 2, Pearson, Anderson
1948-49	D1	3	8.1.49	Bournemouth	3S	H	W	6-0	Burke 2, Rowley 2, Pearson, Mitten
		4	29.1.49	Bradford PA	D2	H	D	1-1aet	Mitten
		4r	5.2.49	Bradford PA		A	D	1-1aet	Mitten
		4 2r	7.2.49	Bradford PA		H	W	5-0	Burke 2, Rowley 2, Pearson
		5	12.2.49	Yeovil T	SL	H	W	8-0	Rowley 5, Burke 2, Mitten
		6	26.2.49	Hull C	3N	A	W	1-0	Pearson
		SF	26.3.49	Wolverhampton W	D1		D	1-1aet	Mitten
				played at Hillsborough					
		SFr	2.4.49	Wolverhampton W			L	0-1	
				played at Goodison Park					
1949-50	D1	3	7.1.50	Weymouth	SL	H	W	4-0	Rowley 2, Pearson, Delaney
		4	28.1.50	Watford	3S	A	W	1-0	Rowley
		5	11.2.50	Portsmouth	D1	H	D	3-3	Mitten 2, Pearson
		5r	15.2.50	Portsmouth		A	W	3-1	Delaney, Downie, Mitten
		6	4.3.50	Chelsea	D1	A	L	0-2	
1950-51	D1	3	6.1.51	Oldham A	3N	H	W	4-1	Pearson, Aston, Whyte og, Birch
		4	27.1.51	Leeds U	D2	H	W	4-0	Pearson 3, Rowley
		5	10.2.51	Arsenal	D1	H	W	1-0	Pearson

Season	Div	Rd	Date	Opponent		H/A	Res	Score	Scorers
		6	24.2.51	Birmingham C	D2	A	L	0-1	
1951-52	D1	3	12.1.52	Hull C	D2	H	L	0-2	
1952-53	D1	3	10.1.53	Millwall	3S	A	W	1-0	Pearson
		4	31.1.53	Walthamstow Ave	AL	H	D	1-1	Lewis
		4r	5.2.53	Walthamstow Ave at Highbury		A	W	5-2	Pearson, Lewis, Rowley 2, Byrne (p)
		5	14.2.53	Everton	D2	A	L	1-2	Rowley
1953-54	D1	3	9.1.54	Burnley	D1	A	L	3-5	Viollet, Blanchflower, Taylor
1954-55	D1	3	8.1.55	Reading	3S	A	D	1-1	Webster
		3r	12.1.55	Reading		H	W	4-1	Webster 2, Viollet, Rowley
		4	29.2.55	Manchester C	D1	A	L	0-2	
1955-56	D1	3	7.1.56	Bristol R	D2	A	L	0-4	
1956-57	D1	3	5.1.57	Hartlepools U	3N	A	W	4-3	Whelan 2, Berry, Taylor
		4	26.1.57	Wrexham	3N	A	W	5-0	Whelan 2, Byrne (p), Taylor 2
		5	16.2.57	Everton	D1	H	W	1-0	Edwards
		6	2.3.57	Bournemouth	3S	A	W	2-1	Berry 2
		SF	23.3.57	Birmingham C	D1		W	2-0	Berry, Charlton
			played at Hillsborough						
		F	4.5.57	A.Villa	D1 WEMBLEY		L	1-2	Taylor
1957-58	D1	3	4.1.58	Workington	3N	A	W	3-1	Viollet 3
		4	25.1.58	Ipswich T	D2	H	W	2-0	Charlton 2
		5	19.2.58	Sheffield W	D1	H	W	3-0	Brennan 2, Dawson
		6	1.3.58	WBA	D1	A	D	2-2	E.Taylor, Dawson
		6r	5.3.58	WBA		H	W	1-0	Webster
		SF	22.3.58	Fulham	D2		D	2-2	Charlton 2
			played at Villa Park						
		SFr	26.3.58	Fulham			W	5-3	Dawson 3, Brennan, Charlton
			played at Highbury						
		F	3.5.58	Bolton W	D1 WEMBLEY		L	0-2	
1958-59	D1	3	10.1.59	Norwich C	D3	A	L	0-3	
1959-60	D1	3	9.1.60	Derby Co	D2	A	W	4-2	Goodwin, Charlton, Scanlon, Barrowcliffe og
		4	30.1.60	Liverpool	D2	H	W	3-1	Charlton 2, Bradley
		5	20.2.60	Sheffield W	D1	A	L	0-1	
1960-61	D1	3	7.1.61	Middlesbrough	D2	H	W	3-0	Cantwell, Dawson 2
		4	28.1.61	Sheffield W	D1	A	D	1-1	Cantwell (p)
		4r	1.2.61	Sheffield W		H	L	2-7	Dawson, Pearson
1961-62	D1	3	6.1.62	Bolton W	D1	A	W	2-1	Herd, Nicholson
		4	31.1.62	Arsenal	D1	H	W	1-0	Setters
		5	17.2.62	Sheffield W	D1	H	D	0-0	
		5r	21.2.62	Sheffield W		A	W	2-0	Giles, Charlton
		6	10.3.62	Preston NE	D2	A	D	0-0	
		6r	14.3.62	Preston NE		H	W	2-1	Charlton, Herd
		SF	31.3.62	Tottenham H	D1		L	1-3	Herd
			played at Hillsborough						
1962-63	D1	3	4.3.63	Huddersfield T	D2	H	W	5-0	Law 3, Quixall, Giles
		4	11.3.63	A.Villa	D1	H	W	1-0	Quixall
		5	16.3.63	Chelsea	D2	H	W	2-1	Law, Quixall
		6	30.3.63	Coventry C	D4	A	W	3-1	Charlton 2, Quixall
		SF	27.4.63	Southampton	D2		W	1-0	Law
			played at Villa Park						
		F	25.5.63	LEICESTER CITY	D1 WEMBLEY		W	3-1	Herd 2, Law
1963-64	D1	3	4.1.64	Southampton	D2	A	W	3-2	Moore, Herd, Crerand
		4	25.1.64	Bristol R	D3	H	W	4-1	Law 3, Herd
		5	15.2.64	Barnsley	D3	A	W	4-0	Law 2, Best, Herd
		6	29.2.64	Sunderland	D2	H	D	3-3	Hurley og, Charlton, Best
		6r	4.3.64	Sunderland		A	D	2-2aet	Law, Charlton
		6 2r	9.3.64	Sunderland at Huddersfield			W	5-1	Law 3 (1p), Chisnall, Herd
		SF	14.3.64	West Ham	D1		L	1-3	Law
			played at Hillsborough						
1964-65	D1	3	9.1.65	Chester	D4	H	W	2-1	Best, Kinsey
		4	30.1.65	Stoke C	D1	A	D	0-0	
		4r	3.2.65	Stoke C		H	W	1-0	Herd
		5	20.2.65	Burnley	D1	H	W	2-1	Law, Crerand
		6	10.3.65	Wolverhampton W	D1	A	W	5-3	Law 2, Herd, Best, Crerand
		SF	27.3.65	Leeds U	D1		D	0-0aet	
			played at Hillsborough						
		SFr	31.3.65	Leeds U			L	0-1	
			played at City Ground, Nottingham						

1965-66	D1	3	22.1.66	**Derby Co**	D2	A	W	5-2	Best 2, Law 2 (1p), Herd
		4	12.2.66	**Rotherham U**	D3	H	D	0-0	
		4r	15.2.66	**Rotherham U**		A	W	1-0	Connelly
		5	5.3.66	**Wolverhampton W**	D2	A	W	4-2	Law 2, Best, Herd
		6	26.3.66	**Preston NE**	D2	A	D	1-1	Herd
		6r	30.3.66	**Preston NE**		H	W	3-1	Law 2, Connelly
		SF	23.4.66	**Everton**	D1		L	0-1	
			played at Burnden Park, Bolton						
1966-67	D1	3	28.1.67	**Stoke C**	D1	H	W	2-0	Law, Herd
		4	18.2.67	**Norwich C**	D2	H	L	1-2	Law
1967-68	D1	3	27.1.68	**Tottenham H**	D1	H	D	2-2	Best, Charlton
		3r	31.1.68	**Tottenham H**		A	L	0-1aet	
1968-69	D1	3	4.1.69	**Exeter C**	D4	A	W	3-1	Fitzpatrick, Newman og, Kidd
		4	25.1.69	**Watford**	D3	H	D	1-1	Law
		4r	3.2.69	**Watford**		A	W	2-0	Law 2
		5	8.2.69	**Birmingham C**	D2	A	D	2-2	Law, Best
		5r	24.2.69	**Birmingham C**		H	W	6-2	Law 3, Kidd, Morgan, Crerand
		6	1.3.69	**Everton**	D1	H	L	0-1	
1969-70	D1	3	3.1.70	**Ipswich T**	D1	A	W	1-0	McNeil og
		4	24.1.70	**Manchester C**	D1	H	W	3-0	Morgan (p), Kidd 2
		5	7.2.70	**Northampton T**	D4	A	W	8-2	Best 6, Kidd 2
		6	21.2.70	**Middlesbrough**	D2	A	D	1-1	Sartori
		6r	25.2.70	**Middlesbrough**		H	W	2-1	Charlton, Morgan (p)
		SF	14.3.70	**Leeds U**	D1		D	0-0	
			played at Hillsborough						
		SFr	23.3.70	**Leeds U**			D	0-0aet	
			played at Villa Park						
		SF 2r	26.3.70	**Leeds U**			L	0-1	
			played at Burnden Park, Bolton						
		3/4	10.4.70	**Watford**	D2		W	2-0	Kidd 2
			played at Highbury						
1970-71	D1	3	2.1.71	**Middlesbrough**	D2	H	D	0-0	
		3r	5.1.71	**Middlesbrough**		A	L	1-2	Best
1971-72	D1	3	15.1.72	**Southampton**	D1	A	D	1-1	Charlton
		3r	19.1.72	**Southampton**		H	W	4-1aet	Best 2, Sadler, Aston
		4	5.2.72	**Preston NE**	D2	A	W	2-0	Gowling 2
		5	26.2.72	**Middlesbrough**	D2	H	D	0-0	
		5r	29.2.72	**Middlesbrough**		A	W	3-0	Morgan (p), Best, Charlton
		6	18.3.72	**Stoke C**	D1	H	D	1-1	Best
		6r	22.3.72	**Stoke C**		A	L	1-2aet	Best
1972-73	D1	3	13.1.73	**Wolverhampton W**	D1	A	L	0-1	
1973-74	D1	3	5.1.74	**Plymouth A**	D3	H	W	1-0	Macari
		4	26.1.74	**Ipswich T**	D1	H	L	0-1	
1974-75	D2	3	4.1.75	**Walsall**	D3	H	D	0-0	
		3r	7.1.75	**Walsall**		A	L	2-3aet	Daly, McIlroy
1975-76	D1	3	3.1.76	**Oxford U**	D2	H	W	2-1	Daly 2 (2pens)
		4	24.1.76	**Peterborough U**	D3	H	W	3-1	Forsyth, McIlroy, Hill
		5	14.2.76	**Leicester C**	D1	A	W	2-1	Macari, Daly
		6	6.3.76	**Wolverhampton W**	D1	H	D	1-1	Daly
		6r	9.3.76	**Wolverhampton W**		A	W	3-2aet	Pearson, B.Greenhoff, McIlroy
		SF	3.4.76	**Derby Co**	D1		W	2-0	Hill 2
			played at Hillsborough						
		F	1.5.76	**Southampton**	D2 WEMBLEY		L	0-1	
1976-77	D1	3	8.1.77	**Walsall**	D3	H	W	1-0	Hill
		4	29.1.77	**QPR**	D1	H	W	1-0	Macari
		5	26.2.77	**Southampton**	D2	A	D	2-2	Macari, Hill
		5r	8.3.77	**Southampton**		H	W	2-1	J.Greenhoff 2
		6	19.3.77	**A.Villa**	D1	H	W	2-1	Houston, Macari
		SF	23.4.77	**Leeds U**	D1		W	2-1	J.Greenhoff, Coppell
			played at Hillsborough						
		F	21.5.77	**LIVERPOOL**	D1 WEMBLEY		W	2-1	Pearson, J.Greenhoff
1977-78	D1	3	7.1.78	**Carlisle U**	D3	A	D	1-1	Macari
		3r	11.1.78	**Carlisle U**		H	W	4-2	Macari 2, Pearson 2
		4	28.1.78	**WBA**	D1	H	D	1-1	Coppell
		4r	1.2.78	**WBA**		A	L	2-3	Pearson, Hill
1978-79	D1	3	15.1.79	**Chelsea**	D1	H	W	3-0	Coppell, Grimes, J.Greenhoff
		4	31.1.79	**Fulham**	D2	A	D	1-1	J.Greenhoff

	4r	12.2.79	**Fulham**		H	W	1-0	J.Greenhoff
	5	20.2.79	**Colchester U**	D3	A	W	1-0	J.Greenhoff
	6	10.3.79	**Tottenham H**	D1	A	D	1-1	Thomas
	6r	14.3.79	**Tottenham H**		H	W	2-0	Jordan, McIlroy
	SF	31.3.79	**Liverpool**	D1		D	2-2	Jordan, B.Greenhoff
		played at Maine Road						
	SFr	4.4.79	**Liverpool**			W	1-0	J.Greenhoff
		played at Goodison Park						
	F	12.5.79	**Arsenal**	D1 WEMBLEY		L	2-3	McQueen, McIlroy.
1979-80 D1	3	5.1.80	**Tottenham H**	D1	A	D	1-1	McIlroy
	3r	9.1.80	**Tottenham H**		H	L	0-1aet	
1980-81 D1	3	3.1.81	**Brighton & HA**	D1	H	D	2-2	Duxbury, Thomas
	3r	7.1.81	**Brighton & HA**		A	W	2-0	Nicholl, Birtles
	4	24.1.81	**Nottingham F**	D1	A	L	0-1	
1981-82 D1	3	2.1.82	**Watford**	D2	A	L	0-1	
1982-83 D1	3	8.1.83	**West Ham**	D2	H	W	2-0	Coppell, Stapleton
	4	29.1.83	**Luton T**	D1	A	W	2-0	Moses, Moran
	5	19.2.83	**Derby Co**	D1	A	W	1-0	Whiteside
	6	12.3.83	**Everton**	D1	H	W	1-0	Stapleton
	SF	16.4.83	**Arsenal**	D1		W	2-1	Robson, Whiteside
		played at Villa Park						
	F	21.5.83	**BRIGHTON & HA**	D1 WEMBLEY		D	2-2aet	Stapleton, Wilkins
	Fr	26.5.83	**BRIGHTON & HA**		WEMBLEY	W	4-0	Robson 2, Whiteside, Muhren (p)
1983-84 D1	3	7.1.84	**Bournemouth**	D3	A	L	0-2	
1984-85 D1	3	5.1.85	**Bournemouth**	D3	A	W	3-0	Strachan, McQueen, Stapleton
	4	26.1.85	**Coventry C**	D1	H	W	2-1	Hughes, McGrath
	5	15.2.85	**Blackburn R**	D2	A	W	2-0	Strachan, McGrath
	6	9.3.85	**West Ham**	D1	H	W	4-2	Hughes, Whiteside 3 (1p)
	SF	13.4.85	**Liverpool**	D1		D	2-2aet	Robson, Stapleton
		played at Goodison Park						
	SFr	17.4.85	**Liverpool**			W	2-1	Robson, Hughes
		played at Maine Road						
	F	18.5.85	**EVERTON**	D1 WEMBLEY		W	1-0aet	Whiteside
1985-86 D1	3	9.1.86	**Rochdale**	D4	H	W	2-0	Stapleton, Hughes
	4	25.1.86	**Sunderland**	D2	A	D	0-0	
	4r	29.1.86	**Sunderland**		H	W	3-0	Whiteside, Olsen 2 (1p)
	5	5.3.86	**West Ham**	D1	A	D	1-1	Stapleton
	5r	9.3.86	**West Ham**		H	L	0-2	
1986-87 D1	3	19.1.87	**Manchester C**	D1	H	W	1-0	Whiteside
	4	31.1.87	**Coventry C**	D1	H	L	0-1	
1987-88 D1	3	10.1.88	**Ipswich T**	D2	A	W	2-1	D'Avray og, Anderson
	4	30.1.88	**Chelsea**	D1	H	W	2-0	Whiteside, McClair
	5	20.2.88	**Arsenal**	D1	A	L	1-2	McClair
1988-89 D1	3	7.1.89	**QPR**	D1	H	D	0-0	
	3r	11.1.89	**QPR**		A	D	2-2aet	Gill, Graham
	3 2r	23.1.89	**QPR**		H	W	3-0	McClair 2 (1p), Robson
	4	28.1.89	**Oxford U**	D2	H	W	4-0	Hughes, Bruce, J.Phillips og, Robson
	5	18.2.89	**Bournemouth**	D2	A	D	1-1	Hughes
	5r	22.2.89	**Bournemouth**		H	W	1-0	McClair
	6	18.3.89	**Nottingham F**	D1	H	L	0-1	
1989-90 D1	3	7.1.90	**Nottingham F**		A	W	1-0	Robins
	4	28.1.90	**Hereford U**	D4	A	W	1-0	Blackmore
	5	18.2.90	**Newcastle U**	D2	A	W	3-2	Robins, Wallace, McClair
	6	11.3.90	**Sheffield U**	D2	A	W	1-0	McClair
	SF	8.4.90	**Oldham A**	D2		D	3-3aet	Robson, Webb, Wallace
		played at Maine Road						
	SFr	11.4.90	**Oldham A**			W	2-1aet	McClair, Robins
		played at Maine Road						
	F	12.5.90	**CRYSTAL P**	D1 WEMBLEY		D	3-3aet	Hughes 2, Robson
	Fr	17.5.90	**CRYSTAL P**		WEMBLEY	W	1-0	Martin
1990-91 D1	3	5.1.91	**QPR**	D1	H	W	2-1	Hughes, McClair
	4	26.1.91	**Bolton W**	D3	H	W	1-0	Hughes
	5	16.2.91	**Norwich C**	D1	A	L	1-2	McClair
1991-92 D1	3	15.1.92	**Leeds U**	D1	A	W	1-0	Hughes
	4	27.1.92	**Southampton**	D1	A	D	0-0	
	4r	5.2.92	**Southampton**		H	D	2-2aet	Kanchelskis, McClair
		Southampton won 4-2 on penalties						

1992-93	PL	3	5.1.93	Bury	D3	H	W	2-0	Phelan, Gillespie
		4	23.1.93	Brighton & HA	D2	H	W	1-0	Giggs
		5	14.2.93	Sheffield U	PL	A	L	1-2	Giggs

MANSFIELD TOWN

Founded 1910. There were a number of different clubs called Mansfield Town but the current Football League club dates from 1910. **Best FA Cup performance:** 6th round, 1969. **FA Cup Record Win:** 10-1 vs Highgate, 4th qual rd, 1930-31. In competition proper: 9-2 vs Hounslow Town, 1st round replay, 5.11.1962. **FA Cup Record Defeat:** 0-8 vs Worksop T, 5th qualifying round replay, 1920-21.

1910-11	CA	P **Market Harborough** (A) 5-0; 1q **Loughborough Cen.** (H) 3-0; 2q **Basford U** (H) 2-2; 2qr **Basford U** (A) 3-1; 3q **Hinckley U** (A) 2-1; 4q **Blackwell Colliery** (H) 0-1
1911-12	CA	1q **Hinckley U** (A) 0-1
1912-13	CA	P **Notts Rangers** (H) 5-0; 1q **Netherfield R** (A) 3-2; 2q **Loughborough Cen.** (H) 5-2; 3q **Sutton T** (A) 1-3
1913-14	CA	P **Mapperley** (H) 3-1; 1q **Netherfield R** (H) 2-2; 1qr **Netherfield R** (A) 4-0; 2q **Hinckley U** (H) 1-3
1914-15	CA	P **Sutton T** (A) 0-5
1919-20	CA	P **Shirebrook** (A) 1-3
1920-21	CA	P **Sutton Junction** (H) 8-1; 1q **Hucknall Byron** (H) 2-1; 2q **Grantham T** (A) 3-1; 3q **Boots Athletic** (H) 3-0; 4q **Scunthorpe U** (A) 1-0; 5q **Worksop T** (A) 2-2; 5qr **Worksop T** (H) 0-8
1921-22	CA	P **Mansfield Colliery** (H) 8-0; 1q **Stanton Hill** (H) 6-0; 2q **Grantham T** (H) 2-0; 3q **Welbeck Colliery** (A) 2-1; 4q **Gainsborough T** (A) 2-1; 5q **Darlaston** (H) 2-0; 6q **Walsall** (H) 1-1; 6qr **Walsall** (A) 0-4
1922-23	CA	P **Langwith A** (H) 2-1; 1q **Shirebrook** (A) 3-1; 2q **Sutton Junction** (H) 3-0; 3q **Sutton T** (H) 4-1; 4q **Coalville Swifts** (A) 2-0; 5q **Wath Ath** (H) 1-0; 6q **Halifax T** (H) 0-2
1923-24	CA	1q **Shirebrook** (H) 1-1; 1qr **Shirebrook** (A) 2-4
1924-25	CA	P **Sneinton** (H) 6-1; 1q **Whitwell Colliery** (H) 7-0; 2q **Sutton Junction** (H) 3-0; 3q **Grantham T** (H) 1-0; 4q **Doncaster R** (A) 2-3
1925-26	ML	4q **Gainsborough T** (H) 2-0

1925-26	ML	1	28.11.25	Boston T	ML	A	L	2-5	Hart, Heathcote
1926-27	ML	4q **Burton T** (H) 2-1							
		1	27.11.26	Wellington T	BDL	A	W	2-1	Stamforth, Laycock
		2	11.12.26	Walsall	3N	A	L	0-2	
1927-28	ML	4q **Gainsborough T** (H) 0-5							
1928-29	ML	4q **Ardsley Ath** (A) 2-2; 4qr **Ardsley A** (H) 2-0							
		1	24.11.28	Shirebrook	ML	A	W	4-2	Morris 2, Staniforth, Kerry
		2	8.12.28	Barrow	3N	A	W	2-1	Morris 2
		3	12.1.29	Wolverhampton W	D2	A	W	1-0	McLachlan
		4	26.1.29	Arsenal	D1	A	L	0-2	
1929-30	ML	1	30.11.30	Manchester Central	CC	H	L	0-2	
1930-31	ML	4q **Highgate** (H) 10-1							
		1	29.11.30	Halifax T	3N	A	D	2-2	Devlin, Chambers
		1r	3.12.30	Halifax T		H	L	1-2	Murphy
1931-32	3S	1	28.11.31	Hull C	3N	A	L	1-4	Death
1932-33	3N	1	26.11.32	Walsall	3N	A	L	1-4	Johnson
1933-34	3N	1	25.11.33	New Brighton	3N	A	D	0-0	
		1r	29.11.33	New Brighton		H	L	3-4	Raynor, Johnson 2
1934-35	3N	1	24.11.34	Accrington S	3N	H	W	6-1	Hunt 2, Atkinson, Dellow, Johnson 2
		2	8.12.34	Tranmere R	3N	H	W	4-2	Dellow, Johnson 2, Hunt
		3	12.1.35	Burnley	D2	A	L	2-4	Hunt, Johnson
1935-36	3N	1	30.11.35	Hartlepools U	3N	H	L	2-3	Harston, Atkinson
1936-37	3N	1	28.11.36	Barrow	3N	A	W	6-0	Magnall 4 (1p), Thorogood, Thomas
		2	12.12.36	Bournemouth	3S	H	L	0-3	
1937-38	3S	1	27.11.37	Wellington T	BDL	A	W	2-1	O'Connor, Bangay
		2	11.12.37	Lincoln C	3N	H	–	1-2	Holmes
				abandoned after 62 minutes					
		2	15.12.37	Lincoln C		H	W	2-1	Holmes, Crawshaw
		3	8.1.38	Leicester C	D1	H	L	1-2	Johnston
1938-39	3S	1	26.11.38	Workington	NEL	A	D	1-1	Somerfield
		1r	30.11.38	Workington		H	W	2-1	Somerfield, Dutton
		2	10.12.38	Halifax T	3N	A	D	1-1	Somerfield
		2r	14.12.38	Halifax T		H	D	3-3aet	Dutton, Bell, Wilson
		2 2r	19.12.38	Halifax T at Doncaster			D	0-0aet	
		2 3r	21.12.38	Halifax T at Old Trafford			L	1-2aet	Somerfield
1945-46	3S	1 1L	17.11.45	Gainsborough T	ML	H	W	3-0	Harkin, Wombwell 2
		1 2L	24.11.45	Gainsborough T		A	L	2-4aet	Poole, Wombwell
		2 1L	8.12.45	Grantham	ML	A	W	2-1	Thorpe, Wombwell
		2 2L	15.12.45	Grantham		H	W	2-1	Hogg, Wombwell
		3 1L	5.1.46	Sheffield W	D2	H	D	0-0	
		3 2L	9.1.46	Sheffield W		A	L	0-5	

1946-47	3S	1	30.11.46	Northampton T	3S	A	L	0-2	
1947-48	3N	1	29.11.47	Wimbledon	IL	A	W	1-0	Cooling
		2	13.12.47	Oldham A	3N	A	W	1-0	Cooling
		3	10.1.48	Stoke C	D1	H	L	2-4	Oscroft, Butt (p)
1948-49	3N	1	27.11.48	Gloucester C	SL	H	W	4-0	Mercer 3, Oscroft
		2	11.12.48	Northampton T	3S	H	W	2-1aet	Mercer, Oscroft
		3	8.1.49	Preston NE	D1	A	L	1-2	Oscroft
1949-50	3N	1	26.11.49	Walsall	3S	H	W	4-1	Antonio, Coole (2), Steele
		2	10.12.49	Doncaster R	3N	A	L	0-1	
1950-51	3N	1	25.11.50	Walthamstow Ave	IL	H	W	1-0	Steele
		2	9.12.50	Chelmsford C	SL	A	W	4-1	Coole, Donaldson 2, Barks
		3	6.1.51	Swansea T	D2	H	W	2-0	Steele 2
		4	27.1.51	Sheffield U	D2	A	D	0-0	
		4r	31.1.51	Sheffield U		H	W	2-1aet	Steele, Ottewell
		5	10.2.51	Blackpool	D1	A	L	0-2	
1951-52	3N	1	24.11.51	Stockton	NEL	A	D	1-1	Lewis
		1r	28.11.51	Stockton		H	L	0-2	
1952-53	3N	1	22.11.52	Scarborough	ML	A	W	8-0	Watson, Marron 2, Adam 2, Fox 3
		2	6.12.52	Accrington S	3N	A	W	2-0	Fox, Adam
		3	10.1.53	Nottingham F	D2	H	L	0-1	
1953-54	3N	1	21.11.53	Hartlepools U	3N	A	D	1-1	S.Watson
		1r	25.11.53	Hartlepools U		H	L	0-3	
1954-55	3N	1	20.11.54	Bradford C	3N	A	L	1-3	Adam
1955-56	3N	1	19.11.55	Stockport Co	3N	H	W	2-0	Watkin, Jepson
		2	10.12.55	York C	3N	A	L	1-2	Darwin
1956-57	3N	1	17.11.56	Workington	3N	H	D	1-1	Murray
		1r	20.11.56	Workington		A	L	1-2	Jepson
1957-58	3N	1	16.11.57	Halifax T	3N	H	W	2-0	Chapman, Mitten (p)
		2	7.12.57	Wigan A	LC	A	D	1-1	Chapman
		2r	11.12.57	Wigan A		H	W	3-1	Mitten, Morris 2
		3	4.1.58	Bristol R	D2	A	L	0-5	
1958-59	D3	1	15.11.58	Bradford C	D3	H	L	3-4	B.Thomas, Uphill 2
1959-60	D3	1	14.11.59	Accrington S	D3	A	W	2-1	Nugent, Humble
		2	5.12.59	Chester	D4	H	W	2-0	Fitzsimmons, Jones
		3	9.1.60	Blackpool	D1	A	L	0-3	
1960-61	D4	1	5.11.60	Blyth Spartans	NCo	H	W	3-1	Fitzsimmons, Coates, Wragg
		2	30.11.60	Accrington S	D4	A	L	0-3	
1961-62	D4	1	4.11.61	Grimsby T	D3	H	W	3-2	Wagstaff, Hall 2
		2	25.11.61	Southport	D4	A	L	2-4	Stringfellow, Shaw
1962-63	D4	1	3.11.62	Hounslow	AL	A	D	3-3	Hollett 2, Wagstaff
		1r	5.11.62	Hounslow		H	W	9-2	Chapman 3, Hollett 3, Weir, Wagstaff, Askey
		2	24.11.62	Crystal P	D3	A	D	2-2	Wagstaff 2
		2r	26.11.62	Crystal P		H	W	7-2	Wagstaff 3, Long og, Askey, R.Chapman 2
		3	9.1.63	Ipswich T	D1	H	L	2-3	Hall, Askey
1963-64	D3	1	20.11.63	Oldham A	D3	A	L	2-3	R.Chapman, Hall
1964-65	D3	1	14.11.64	Oxford U	D4	A	W	1-0	Hall
		2	5.12.64	Newport Co	D4	A	L	0-3	
1965-66	D3	1	13.11.65	Oldham A	D3	H	L	1-3	MacReady
1966-67	D3	1	26.11.66	Bangor C	CC	H	W	4-1	Mitchinson, Brace, Curry 2
		2	7.1.67	Scunthorpe U	D3	H	W	2-1	Mitchinson, Brace
		3	28.1.67	Middlesbrough	D3	H	W	2-0	Brace, Curry
		4	18.2.67	Sheffield W	D1	A	L	0-4	
1967-68	D3	1	9.12.67	Tow Law Town	NL	A	–	0-0	
			abandoned at half-time						
		1	13.12.67	Tow Law Town		A	L	1-5	Melling
1968-69	D3	1	16.11.68	Tow Law Town	NL	H	W	4-1	Ledger 2, Sharkey, Keeley
		2	7.12.68	Rotherham U	D3	A	D	2-2	Sharkey, Keeley
		2r	9.12.68	Rotherham U		H	W	1-0	Ledger
		3	4.1.69	Sheffield U	D2	H	W	2-1	Roberts 2
		4	25.1.69	Southend U		H	W	2-1	Sharkey, Roberts
		5	26.2.69	West Ham	D1	H	W	3-0	Roberts, Keeley, Sharkey
		6	8.3.69	Leicester C	D1	H	L	0-1	
1969-70	D3	1	15.11.69	Bury	D3	A	D	2-2	Keeley, Stenson
		1r	19.11.69	Bury		H	W	2-0	Bates, Partridge
		2	6.12.69	Shrewsbury T	D3	A	W	2-1	Keeley, Roberts
		3	3.1.70	Barnsley	D3	H	W	3-2	Walter, Partridge, Goodfellow (p)
		4	24.1.70	Blackpool	D2	A	W	2-0	D.Jones 2

	5	7.2.70	Leeds U	D1	A	L	0-2
1970-71 D3	1	21.11.70	Wrexham	D3	H	W	2-0	Stenson, D.Roberts
	2	12.12.70	Scunthorpe U	D4	A	L	0-3
1971-72 D3	1	20.11.71	Chester	D4	A	D	1-1	Bingham
	1r	22.11.71	Chester		H	W	4-3	Bingham, Fairbrother, Thompson, Roberts (p)
	2	11.12.71	Tranmere R	D3	H	D	2-2	Thompson, Fairbrother
	2r	15.12.71	Tranmere R		A		2-4	Fairbrother 2
1972-73 D4	1	18.11.72	York C	D3	A	L	1-2	Fairbrother
1973-74 D4	1	24.11.73	York C	D3	A	D	0-0
	1r	10.12.73	York C		H	W	5-3	Thompson, C.Foster, Walker, McCaffrey, Eccles
	2	15.12.73	Scunthorpe U	D4	H	D	1-1	Eccles
	2r	18.12.73	Scunthorpe U		A	L	0-1
1974-75 D4	1	23.11.74	Wrexham	D3	H	W	3-1	Eccles 2, McCaffrey
	2	14.12.74	Wigan A	NPL	A	D	1-1	Eccles
	2r	16.12.74	Wigan A		H	W	3-1	Hodgson, O'Connor 2
	3	4.1.75	Cambridge U	D4	H	W	1-0	Clarke
	4	25.1.75	Bury	D3	A	W	2-1	McCaffrey, Clarke
	5	15.2.75	Carlisle U	D1	H	L	0-1
1975-76 D3	1	22.11.75	Wrexham	D3	H	D	1-1	Eccles
	1r	24.11.75	Wrexham		A	D	1-1aet	Eccles
	1 2r	8.12.75	Wrexham at Villa Park			W	2-1	Laverick, May og
	2	13.12.75	Lincoln C	D4	H	L	1-2	McDonald
1976-77 D3	1	20.11.76	Huddersfield T	D4	A	D	0-0
	1r	22.11.76	Huddersfield T		H	W	2-1	Randall, Eccles
	2	15.12.76	Matlock T	NPL	H	L	2-5	Matthews, C.Foster
1977-78 D2	3	7.1.78	Plymouth A	D3	H	W	1-0	Miller
	4	6.2.78	Bolton W	D2	A	L	0-1
1978-79 D3	1	25.11.78	Shrewsbury T	D3	H	L	0-2
1979-80 D3	1	24.11.79	Blyth Spartans	NL	A	W	2-0	McClelland, Allen
	2	15.12.79	Doncaster R	D4	A	W	2-1	Curtis, Austin
	3	5.1.80	Brighton & HA	D1	H	L	0-2
1980-81 D4	1	22.11.80	Rochdale	D4	H	W	3-1	Parkinson 2 (2ps), Caldwell
	2	13.12.80	Mossley	NPL	A	W	3-1	Allen (p), Thomson, Caldwell
	3	3.1.81	Carlisle U	D3	H	D	2-2	Bird, Parkinson
	3r	6.1.81	Carlisle U		A	L	1-2	Pollard
1981-82 D4	1	21.11.81	Doncaster R	D3	H	L	0-1
1982-83 D4	1	20.11.82	Stockport Co	D4	H	W	3-2	Bell, Dungworth 2
	2	11.12.82	Bradford C	D3	H	D	1-1	Dungworth (p)
	2r	15.12.82	Bradford C		A	L	2-3	Dungworth, Bell
1983-84 D4	1	19.11.83	Doncaster R	D4	H	W	3-0	Caldwell, Calderwood, Barrowclough
	2	10.12.83	Bolton W	D3	A	L	0-2
1984-85 D4	1	17.11.84	Rotherham U	D3	H	W	2-1	Caldwell, Lowery
	2	8.12.84	Bradford C	D3	A	L	1-2	Barrowclough
1985-86 D4	1	16.11.85	Port Vale	D4	H	D	1-1	Chamberlain
	1r	18.11.85	Port Vale		A	L	0-1
1986-87 D3	1	16.11.86	Darlington	D3	A	L	1-2	Foster
1987-88 D3	1	14.11.87	Preston NE	D3	A	D	1-1	Stringfellow
	1r	17.11.87	Preston NE		H	W	4-2	Cassells 2, Charles (p), Kent
	2	5.12.87	Lincoln C	GMVC	H	W	4-3	Lowery, Foster, Cassells, Kent
	3	9.1.88	Bath C	GMVC	H	W	4-0	Ryan, Withey og, Charles 2
	4	30.1.88	Wimbledon	D1	H	L	1-2	Kent
1988-89 D3	1	19.11.88	Sheffield U	D3	H	D	1-1	Kent
	1r	22.11.88	Sheffield U		A	L	1-2	Kearney
1989-90 D3	1	18.11.89	Wigan A	D3	A	L	0-0
1990-91 D3	1	17.11.90	Preston NE	D3	A	W	1-0	Kearney
	2	17.12.90	York C	D4	H	W	2-1	Charles, Wilkinson
	3	5.1.91	Sheffield W	D2	H	L	0-2
1991-92 D4	1	16.11.91	Preston NE	D3	H	–	1-1	Wilkinson
			abandoned after 32 minutes – fog
	1	27.11.91	Preston NE		H	L	0-1
1992-93 D2	1	14.11.92	Shrewsbury T	D3	A	L	1-3	Fairclough

MARCH TOWN UNITED

Formed 1885. **First entered FA Cup:** 1950

1955-56 ECL	1	19.11.55	Brentford	3S	A	L	0-4
1978-79 ECL	1	25.11.78	Swindon T	D3	A	L	0-2

MARGATE

Formed 1896. **First entered FA Cup:** 1913. Known as Thanet United 1981-1989. **League clubs beaten:** Gillingham, QPR, Crystal Palace, Bournemouth, Swansea C

1929-30	KL	1	30.11.29	Gillingham	3S	A	W	2-0	Adams, Kitto
		2	14.12.29	Northampton T	3S	A	L	0-6	
1932-33	KL	1	26.11.32	Ryde Sports		H	W	5-0	Harris, Mays, Hughes, Moran, Mayn
		2	10.12.32	Gateshead	3N	A	L	2-5	Harris, Mays
1933-34	SL	1	25.11.33	Torquay U	3S	A	D	1-1	Mays
		1r	30.11.33	Torquay U		H	L	0-2	
1935-36	SL	1	30.11.35	QPR	3S	H	W	3-1	Clare, Robbie, Lambert
		2	14.12.35	Crystal P	3S	H	W	3-1	Evans 3
		3	11.1.36	Blackpool	D2	A	L	1-3	Clare
1955-56	KL	1	19.11.55	Walsall	3S	H	D	2-2	Kelly 2
		1r	24.11.55	Walsall		A	L	1-6	Phillips
1956-57	KL	1	17.11.56	Dunstable T	Met	H	W	3-1	Bennett, Marsh, Roche
		2	8.12.56	Millwall	3S	A	L	0-4	
1957-58	KL	1	16.11.57	Crystal P	3S	H	L	2-3	Bostock, Kearns
1958-59	KL	1	15.11.58	Headington U	SL	A	L	2-3	Yeomans 2
1959-60	SL	1	14.11.59	Kettering	SL	A	D	1-1	Kearns
		1r	19.11.59	Kettering		H	W	3-2	Kearns 3
		2	5.12.59	Crystal P	D4	H	D	0-0	
		2r	9.12.59	Crystal P		A	L	0-3	
1961-62	SL	1	4.11.61	Bournemouth	D3	A	W	3-0	Roche, Blackburn, Fraser
		2	25.11.61	Notts Co	D3	H	D	1-1	Barnett
		2r	30.11.61	Notts Co		A	L	1-3	Blackburn
1962-63	SL	1	3.11.62	Millwall	D3	A	L	1-3	Jeans
1963-64	SL	1	16.11.63	Brentford	D3	A	D	2-2	Roche, Blackburn
		1r	20.11.63	Brentford		H	L	0-2	
1967-68	SL	1	13.12.67	Yeovil T	SL	A	W	3-1	Amato 2, Fahy
		2	6.1.68	Peterborough U	D3	H	L	0-4	
1968-69	SL	1	16.11.68	Northampton T	D3	A	L	1-3	Houston
1969-70	SL	1	15.11.69	Aldershot	D4	H	L	2-7	Ray, Houston
1970-71	SL	1	21.11.70	Dagenham	AL	A	L	0-2	
1971-72	SL	1	20.11.71	Bournemouth	D3	A	L	0-11	
1972-73	SL	1	18.11.72	Swansea C	D3	H	W	1-0	Jones
		2	9.12.72	Walton & Hersham	IL	A	W	1-0	Brown
		3	13.1.73	Tottenham H	D1	H	L	0-6	

MARINE

Formed 1894 as Waterloo Melville. Changed name to Marine 1903. **First entered FA Cup:** 1920 **FA Amateur Cup runners-up:** 1932. **League clubs beaten:** Barnsley, Halifax

1932-33	LCC	1	26.11.32	Hartlepools U	3N	H	L	2-5	Constantine. Jones
1945-46	LCC	1 1L	17.11.45	Stalybridge C	CC	H	W	4-0	Fenton 2, Jackson, Bretton
		1 2L	24.11.45	Stalybridge C		A	D	3-3	Bretton, Fenton, Jolliffe
		2 1L	8.12.45	Port Vale	3S	A	L	1-3	Peacock
		2 2L	15.12.45	Port Vale		H	D	1-1	Hanson
1946-47	LC	1	30.11.46	Wrexham	3N	A	L	0-5	
1947-48	LC	1	29.11.47	New Brighton	3N	A	L	0-4	
1974-75	CC	1	23.11.74	Rochdale	D4	A	D	0-0	
		1r	27.11.74	Rochdale		H	L	1-2aet	Woosey
1975-76	CC	1	22.11.75	Barnsley	D4	H	W	3-1	Burke og, Glover 2
		2	13.12.75	Hartlepool	D4	H	D	1-1	Shergold
		2r	15.12.75	Hartlepool		A	L	3-6	Edwards, P.Smith (p), Shergold
1989-90	NPL	1	17.11.89	Rochdale	D4	H	L	0-1	
				played at Anfield					
1992-93	NPL	1	14.11.92	Halifax	D3	H	W	4-1	Ward, Gautrey, Rowland, Camden
		2	5.12.92	Stafford R	GMVC	H	W	3-2	Murray 2, Gautrey
		3	12.12.92	Crewe A	D3	A	L	1-3	Johnson

MARLOW

Formed 1870 originally known as Great Marlow. The only club to have played in every FA Cup competition since it started in 1871.

1871-72		1	11.11.71	Maidenhead		A	L	0-2	

M A R L O W

1872-73	1	19.10.72	Maidenhead		A	L	0-1	
1873-74	1	9.10.73	Pilgrims		A	L	0-1	
1874-75	1	7.11.74	Royal Engineers		A	L	0-3	
1875-76	1	3.11.75	Swifts		A	L	0-2	
1876-77	1	4.11.76	Herts Rangers		A	W	2-1	
	2	29.11.76	Forest School		H	W	1-0	Cox
	3	24.1.77	Upton Park		A	D	2-2	Price, Vardy
	3r	27.1.77	Upton Park		H	L	0-1	
1877-78	1	3.11.77	Hendon		H	W	2-0	Flint 2
	2	15.12.77	Barnes		A	L	1-3	
1878-79	1	9.11.78	Greyfriars		A	L	1-2	
1879-80	1	6.11.79	Oxford University		A	D	1-1	Flint
	1r	10.11.79	Oxford University		H	L	0-1	
1880-81	1	30.10.80	Clarence		H	W	6-0	R.A. Lunnon 3, Shaw 2, Flint
	2	11.12.80	West End		H	W	4-0	J.Flint, R.A.Lunnon, R.H.Lunnon, Milward
	3		bye					
	4	19.2.81	Romford		A	L	1-2	R.H.Lunnon
1881-82	1	22.10.81	Brentwood		H	W	3-1	G.Flint 2, R.H.Lunnon
	2	30.11.81	St Bart's Hosital		H	W	2-0	R.A.Lunnon, R.H. Lunnon
	3	17.12.81	Dreadnought		A	W	2-1	Shaw
	4		Reading			walkover		
	5	14.2.82	Old Foresters		A	D	0-0	
	5r	14.2.82	Old Foresters		H	W	1-0	Shaw
	SF	4.3.82	Old Etonians Kennington Oval			L	0-5	
1882-83	1	28.10.82	Hornchurch		H	W	2-0	
	2		Reading Minster			walkover		
	3		bye					
	4	3.2.83	Hendon		H	L	0-3	
1883-84	1	10.11.83	Hornchurch		A	W	9-0	R.A.Lunnon 5, Shaw 2, Walker 2
	2	1.12.83	Swifts		A	L	0-2	
1884-85	1	8.11.84	Royal Engineers		H	W	10-1	R.H.Lunnon 2, Walker 2, R.A.Lunnon, Bailey, 4 others
	2	6.12.84	Old Carthusians		A	L	3-5	R.A.Lunnon, Pigg, Speller
1885-86	1	31.10.85	Luton Town		H	W	3-0	H.Walker 2, og
	2	21.11.85	Old Etonians		H	W	6-1	
			Old Wykehamists			scratched		
1886-87	1	23.10.86	Rochester		A	W	2-0	
	2	20.11.86	Upton Park		H	W	4-0	
	3	11.12.86	Dulwich		H	W	2-0	
	4		bye					
	5	29.1.87	Notts County		A	L	2-5	
1887-88	1	8.10.87	South Reading		H	W	4-1	
	2	5.11.87	Old Foresters		H	L	2-3aet	
1892-93	1	21.1.93	Middlesbrough Iron	NL	H	L	1-3	Shaw
1991-92	IL 1	16.11.91	WBA	D3	A	L	0-6	
1992-93	IL 1	14.11.92	Salisbury	SL	H	D	3-3	Lay, Watkins, Glasgow
	1r	5.12.92	Salisbury		A	D	2-2aet	Hannigan, Glasgow
			Marlow won 4-3 on penalties					
	2	9.12.92	VS Rugby	SL	A	D	0-0	
	2r	15.12.92	VS Rugby		H	W	2-0	Bushay, Watkins
	3	2.1.93	Tottenham H	PL	H	L	1-5	Lay
			played at White Hart Lane					

MATLOCK TOWN

Formed 1885 and competed in the FA Cup in their first season. **FA Trophy Winners:** 1975. **League club beaten:** Mansfield T

1885-86	1	17.10.85	Stafford Road		A	L	0-7	
1886-87	1	30.10.86	Wolverhampton W		A	L	0-6	
1887-88	1	15.10.87	Rotherham Town		H	L	2-3	Turner og, 1 other
1959-60	CA 1	14.11.59	Crook T	NL	A	D	2-2	Lambert (p), Boot
	1r	19.11.59	Crook T		H	L	0-1	
1974-75	NPL 1	23.11.74	Blackburn R	D3	H	L	1-4	Stuart
1975-76	NPL 1	22.11.75	Wigan A	NPL	A	L	1-4	N.Fenoughty
1976-77	NPL 1	20.11.76	Wigan A	NPL	H	W	2-0	T.Fenoughty, N.Fenoughty
	2	15.12.76	Mansfield T	D3	A	W	5-2	Goodwin, N.Fenoughty 2 (1p), Oxley, Scott
	3	8.1.77	Carlisle U	D2	A	L	1-5	Oxley
1989-90	NPL 1	18.11.89	Scunthorpe U	D4	A	L	1-4	Walker

MELLORS LIMITED, NOTTINGHAM

Formed 1883. A works team that played at Arkwright Street, Nottingham.

1885-86		1	31.10.85	**Nottingham F**		A	L	2-6	Rouse, other 1
1886-87		1	30.10.86	**Cleethorpes**		A	L	1-2	
1887-88		1	15.10.87	**Notts Olympic**		A	W	6-3aet	
			replay ordered after protest						
		1r	22.10.87	**Notts Olympic**		A	W	2-1	
		2	5.11.87	**Nottingham F**		A	L	0-2	

MERTHYR TOWN

Formed 1908. **First entered FA Cup:** 1910. Members of Football League 1922-1930. Disbanded 1934.

1913-14	SL	1	10.1.14	**Swansea T**	SL	A	L	0-2	
1914-15	SL	1	9.1.15	**Arsenal**	D2	A	L	0-3	
1922-23	3S	5q	**Swansea T** (3S) H 0-0; 5qr **Swansea T** A 1-0; 6q **Brentford** (3S) A 1-0						
		1	13.1.23	**Wolverhampton W**	D2	H	L	0-1	
1923-24	3S	5q	**Llanelli** (A) 1-3						
1924-25	3S	5q	**Weymouth** (A) 2-3						
1925-26	3S	1	28.11.25	**Bournemouth**	3S	A	L	0-3	
1926-27	3S	1	27.11.26	**Bristol C**	3S	H	L	0-2	
1927-28	3S	1	26.11.27	**Charlton A**	3S	H	D	0-0	
		1r	30.11.27	**Charlton A**		A	L	1-2	Jones
1928-29	3S	1	24.11.28	**Dulwich H**	IL	H	W	4-2	Borland, Jones, Mercer, Brown
		2	8.12.28	**Watford**	3S	A	L	0-2	
1929-30	3S	1	30.11.29	**Leyton**	AL	A	L	1-4	Woodward
1930-31	SL	1	29.11.30	**Bristol R**	3S	A	L	1-4	Williams
1932-33	SL	1	26.11.32	**QPR**	3S	H	D	1-1	Murphy
		1r	1.12.32	**QPR**		A	L	1-5	Williams

MERTHYR TYDFIL

Formed 1945. **First entered FA Cup:** 1945. A seperate club from Merthyr Town. **League club beaten:** Bristol Rovers. Welsh FA Cup winners: 1949, 1951, 1987

1946-47	SL	1	30.11.46	**Bristol R**	3S	H	W	3-1	Hallett 2, Crisp
		2	14.12.46	**Reading**	3S	H	L	1-3	Hallett
1951-52	SL	1	29.11.51	**Ipswich T**	3S	H	D	2-2	Squires, Phillips
		1r	5.12.51	**Ipswich T**		A	L	0-1	
1954-55	SL	1	20.11.54	**Wellington T**	CC	H	D	1-1	Reynolds
		1r	24.11.54	**Wellington T**		A	W	6-1	Reynolds 3, Driscoll, Jarman 2
		2	11.12.54	**Bradford C**	3N	A	L	1-7	Jarman
1958-59	SL	1	15.11.58	**Kings Lynn**	SL	A	L	1-2	Watkins
1965-66	SL	1	13.11.65	**Swindon T**	D3	A	L	1-5	Jenkins
1973-74	SL	1	24.11.73	**Weymouth**	SL	A	W	1-0	Bryant
		2	15.12.73	**Hendon**	IL	H	L	0-3	
1978-79	SL	1	25.11.78	**Leatherhead**	IL	A	L	1-2	Pratt
1979-80	SL	1	24.11.79	**Fareham T**	SL	A	W	3-2	Pratt 3
		2	19.12.79	**Chesham U**	IL	A	D	1-1	Docherty
		2r	22.12.79	**Chesham U**		H	L	1-3	Elliott
1987-88	SL	1	14.11.87	**Bristol R**	D3	A	L	0-6	
1988-89	SL	1	19.11.88	**Yeovil T**	SL	A	L	2-3	Rogers, Webley
1989-90	GMVC	1	18.11.89	**Redditch U**	SL	A	W	3-1	Thompson 2, Rodgers
		2	9.12.89	**Hereford U**	D4	A	L	2-3	Webley 2
1990-91	GMVC	1	17.11.90	**Sutton U**	GMVC	H	D	1-1	Sanderson
		1r	21.11.90	**Sutton U**		A	W	1-0	Webley
		2	8.12.90	**Woking**	IL	A	L	1-5	Haig
1992-93	GMVC	1	14.11.92	**Wycombe W**	GMVC	A	L	1-3	Rogers

METROPOLITAN POLICE

Formed 1919. **First entered FA Cup:** 1924

1931-32	SPT	1	28.11.31	**Northampton T**	3S	A	L	0-9	
1984-85	IL	1	17.11.84	**Dartford**	APL	H	L	0-3	

MEXBOROUGH TOWN

Formed 1890. **First entered FA Cup:** 1903

1885-86		1	31.10.85	Staveley		A	D	1-1
		1r		Staveley			scratched	
(as Mexborough Town Athletic)								
1926-27	ML	1	27.11.26	Chesterfield	3N	A	D	0-0
				abandoned at half-time due to fog				
		1	1.12.26	Chesterfield		A	L	1-2	Dent

MIDDLESBROUGH

Formed 1876. **FA Amateur Cup Winners:** 1895, 1898. **FA Cup Best Performance:** 6th round, 1936, 1947, 1970, 1975, 1977, 1978, 1981. **FA Cup Record Win:** 11-0 vs Scarborough, 1st qual rd, 4.10.1890. In competition proper: 9-3 vs Goole T, 1st round, 9.1.1915. **FA Cup Record Defeat:** 1-8 vs Hebburn Argyle, 3rd qual rd, 1896-97. In competition proper: 1-6 vs Sheffield W, 2nd round, 16.2.1895; 1-6 vs Southampton 3rd round, 24.2.1906; 1-6 vs Wolverhampton W, 3rd round, 16.1.1937.

1883-84		1	10.11.83	Staveley		H	L	1-4	Pringle
1884-85		1		Grimsby Distrrict			walkover		
		2	6.12.84	Newark		H	W	4-1	Borrie, Hardwick, Pringle 2
		3		bye					
		4	24.1.85	Old Etonians		A	L	2-5	Borrie, Pringle
1885-86		1		Horncastle			walkover		
		2	21.11.85	Gainsborough T		A	L	1-2	Eason
1886-87		1	30.10.86	Bishop Auckland Cl		A	W	1-0	Dennis
		2	20.11.86	Lincoln C		H	D	1-1	Borrie
		2r	27.11.86	Lincoln C		A	L	0-2	
1887-88		1	15.10.87	Whitburn		H	W	4-0	Borrie, 3 others
		2	5.11.87	South Bank		H	W	4-1	Borrie 2, EJ Wilson, Dennis
		3	26.11.87	Sunderland		H	D	2-2	McCrie, Dennis
		3r	3.12.87	Sunderland		A	L	2-4	Cochrane, 1 other
				FA disqualified Sunderland for professionalism and re-instated Middlesbrough					
		4		bye					
		5	7.1.88	Old Foresters		H	W	4-0	Borrie, Dennis, Fox, EJ Wilson
		6	28.1.88	Crewe Alex		H	L	0-2	
1888-89		1q Ecclesfield (H) 0-1							
1889-90	NL	1q South Bank (H) 3-4							
1890-91	NL	1q Scarborough (H) 11-0; 2q Darlington St Augustines (A) 4-1; 3q Darlington (H) 2-0							
		FA disqualified Middlesbrough for playing unregistered player							
1891-92	NL	1	16.1.92	Luton T		A	W	3-0	Og, Bell, Bache
		2	30.1.92	Preston NE	D1	A	L	1-2	scorer unknown
1892-93	NL	1	21.1.93	Newcastle U	NL	A	W	3-2	Black, Blyth, McKnight
		2	4.2.93	Wolverhampton W	D1	A	L	1-2aet	Black
1893-94		1q Leadgate Exiles (A) 4-2; 2q Gateshead NER (H) 2-1; 3q Tow Law (H) 3-0; 4q Willington (A) 4-1							
		1	27.1.94	Newton Heath	D1	A	L	0-4	
1894-95	NL	1q Willington (H) 2-1; 2q Howden R (H) 4-1; 3q Darlington (A) 1-0; 4q Bishop Auckland (H) 3-1							
		1	2.2.95	Chesterfield		H	W	4-0	Davidson 2, Rogers, Mullen
		2	16.2.95	Sheffield W	D1	A	L	1-6	Nelmes
1895-96	NL	1q Jarrow (A) 3-0; 2q Newcastle U (A) 1-4							
1896-97	ML	3q Hebburn Arg. (A) 1-8							
1897-98	NL	1q South Bank (A) 3-2; 2q Rendel (A) 1-0; 3q Bishop Auckland (H) 3-1; 4q Hebburn Arg. (H) 2-0; 5q Newcastle U (H) 0-2							
1898-99	NL	3q Hebburn Arg. (H) 0-1							
1899-00	D2	1q Jarrow (H) 1-2							
1900-01	D2	1q Willington A (H) 3-3; 1qr Willington A (A) 0-0; 1q 2r Willington A (H) 8-0; 2q Jarrow (H) 3-0; 3q Bishop Auckland (H) 4-0							
		1	5.1.01	Grimsby T	D2	A	W	1-0	Wilkie
		2	9.2.01	Newcastle U	D1	H	W	3-1	A.Robertson, McCowie, Wardrope
		3	23.2.01	Kettering T	ML	H	W	5-0	A.Robertson 3, McCowie, Wilkie
		4	23.3.01	WBA	D1	H	L	0-1	
1901-02	D2	1	25.1.02	Bristol R	SL	H	D	1-1	Cassidy
		1r	29.1.02	Bristol R		A	L	0-1	
1902-03	D1	1	13.12.02	Bristol C	D2	A	L	1-3	A.Robertson
1903-04	D1	1	6.2.04	Millwall A	SL	A	W	2-0	A.Brown 2
		2	20.2.04	Preston NE	D1	A	W	3-0	A.Brown 2, Atherton
		3	5.3.04	Manchester C	D1	A	D	0-0	
		3r	9.3.04	Manchester C		H	L	1-3	A.Brown
1904-05	D1	1	4.2.05	Tottenham H	SL	H	D	1-1	Astley
		1r	8.2.05	Tottenham H		A	L	0-1	

1905-06	D1	1	13.1.06	**Bolton W**	D1	H	W	3-0	Common, Hewitt, Thackeray
		2	3.2.06	**Brighton & HA**	SL	A	D	1-1	Hewitt
		2r	7.2.06	**Brighton & HA**		H	D	1-1aet	Common
		2 2r	12.2.06	**Brighton & HA** at Bramall Lane			W	3-1	Common 3
		3	24.2.06	**Southampton**	SL	A	L	1-6	RH Walker
1906-07	D1	1	12.1.07	**Northampton T**	SL	H	W	4-2	Bloomer 2, Common, Brawn
		2	2.2.07	**Brentford**	SL	A	L	0-1	
1907-08	D1	1	11.1.08	**Notts Co**	D1	A	L	0-2	
1908-09	D1	1	16.1.09	**Preston NE**	D1	A	L	0-1	
1909-10	D1	1	15.1.10	**Everton**	D1	H	D	1-1	Thackeray
		1r	19.1.10	**Everton**		A	L	3-5	Common, Cail, Bloomer
1910-11	D1	1	14.1.11	**Glossop**	D2	H	W	1-0	Cail
		2	4.2.11	**Leicester F**	D2	H	D	0-0	
		2r	9.2.11	**Leicester F**		A	W	2-1aet	Cail, Dixon
		3	25.2.11	**Blackburn R**	D1	H	L	0-3	
1911-12	D1	1	13.1.12	**Sheffield W**	D1	H	D	0-0	
		1r	25.1.12	**Sheffield W**		A	W	2-1	James, Windridge
		2	3.2.12	**West Ham**	SL	H	D	1-1	Elliott
		2r	8.2.12	**West Ham**		A	L	1-2	Elliott
1912-13	D1	1	11.1.13	**Millwall A**	SL	A	D	0-0	
		1r	15.1.13	**Millwall A**		H	W	4-1	J Carr 3 (1p), Elliott
		2	1.2.13	**QPR**	SL	H	W	3-2	Elliott 2, Eyre
		3	22.2.13	**Burnley**	D2	A	L	1-3	Eyre
1913-14	D1	1	10.1.14	**Blackburn R**	D1	A	L	0-3	
1914-15	D1	1	9.1.15	**Goole T**		H	W	9-3	J Carr 3, Elliott 3, Tinsley 3
		2	30.1.15	**Bradford C**	D1	A	L	0-1	
1919-20	D1	1	14.1.20	**Lincoln C**	D2	H	W	4-1	Elliott 3, W Carr
		2	31.1.20	**Notts Co**	D1	A	L	0-1	
1920-21	D1	1	8.1.21	**Derby Co**	D1	A	L	0-2	
1921-22	D1	1	7.1.22	**Hull C**	D2	A	L	0-5	
1922-23	D1	1	13.1.23	**Oldham A**	D1	A	W	1-0	Birrell
		2	3.2.23	**Sheffield U**	D1	H	D	1-1	AN Wilson (p)
		2r	8.2.23	**Sheffield U**		A	L	0-3	
1923-24	D1	1	12.1.24	**Watford**	3S	H	L	0-1	
1924-25	D2	1	10.1.25	**Bradford PA**	3N	A	L	0-1	
1925-26	D2	3	9.1.26	**Leeds U**	D1	H	W	5-1	McClelland 5
		4	30.1.26	**Clapton O**	D2	A	L	2-4	McClelland, Birrell
1926-27	D2	3	8.1.27	**Leicester C**	D1	H	W	5-3	Birrell 2, O Williams, Pease, Camsell
		4	29.1.27	**Preston NE**	D2	A	W	3-0	Camsell 3
		5	19.2.27	**Millwall**	3S	A	W	2-3	O Williams, Pease
1927-28	D1	3	14.1.28	**South Shields**	D2	H	W	3-0	Peacock 2, Camsell
		4	28.1.28	**Southport**	3N	A	W	3-0	Camsell 3
		5	18.2.28	**Huddersfield T**	D1	A	L	0-4	
1928-29	D2	3	12.1.29	**Walsall**	3S	A	D	1-1	Camsell
		3r	21.1.29	**Walsall**		H	W	5-1	Camsell 2, Pease 2, Williams
		4	26.1.29	**WBA**	D2	A	L	0-1	
1929-30	D1	3	11.1.30	**Chesterfield**	3N	A	D	1-1	Bruce (p)
		3r	15.1.30	**Chesterfield**		H	W	4-3	Camsell 2, Bruce 2
		4	25.1.30	**Charlton A**	D2	H	D	1-1	Muttitt
		4r	29.1.30	**Charlton A**		A	D	1-1	Bruce
		4 2r	3.2.30	**Charlton A** at Maine Road			W	1-0aet	McKay
		5	15.2.30	**Arsenal**	D1	H	L	0-2	
1930-31	D1	3	14.1.31	**Bradford C**	D2	H	D	1-1	Warren
		3r	19.1.31	**Bradford C**		A	L	1-2	Barkas og
1931-32	D1	3	9.1.32	**Portsmouth**	D1	H	D	1-1	Bruce
		3r	13.1.32	**Portsmouth**		A	L	0-3	
1932-33	D1	3	14.1.33	**Manchester U**	D2	A	W	4-1	Bruce 2, JJ Williams, Blackmore
		4	28.1.33	**Stoke C**	D2	H	W	4-1	Blackmore 2, Camsell, Baxter
		5	18.2.33	**Birmingham**	D1	H	D	0-0	
		5r	22.2.33	**Birmingham**		A	L	0-3	
1933-34	D1	3	13.1.34	**Sunderland**	D1	A	D	1-1	Camsell
		3r	17.1.34	**Sunderland**		H	L	1-2	Ferguson
1934-35	D1	3	12.1.35	**Blackburn R**	D1	H	D	1-1	JJ Williams
		3r	17.1.35	**Blackburn R**		A	L	0-1	
1935-36	D1	3	11.1.36	**Southampton**	D2	H	W	1-0	Cunliffe
		4	25.1.36	**Clapton O**	3S	H	W	3-0	Camsell 2, Cunliffe
		5	15.2.36	**Leicester C**	D2	H	W	2-1	Camsell, Forrest

Season	Div	Round	Date	Opponent	OppDiv	H/A	W/D/L	Score	Scorers
		6	29.2.36	Grimsby T	D1	A	L	1-3	Camsel
1936-37	D1	3	16.1.37	Wolverhampton W	D1	A	L	1-6	Birkett
1937-38	D1	3	8.1.38	Stockport Co	3N	H	W	2-0	Fenton 2 (1p)
		4	22.1.38	Nottingham F	D2	A	W	3-1	Mannion, Camsell, Milne
		5	12.2.38	York C	3N	A	L	0-1	
1938-39	D1	3	7.1.39	Bolton W	D1	H	D	0-0	
		3r	11.1.39	Bolton W		A	D	0-0aet	
		3 2r	16.1.39	Bolton W at Elland Road			W	1-0	Fenton
		4	21.1.39	Sunderland	D1	H	L	0-2	
1945-46	D1	3 1L	5.1.46	Leeds U	D1	A	D	4-4	Dews 2, Fenton, Murphy
		3 2L	9.1.46	Leeds U		H	W	7-2	Fenton 3, Gordon, Hardwick (p), Spuhler, Douglas
		4 1L	26.1.46	Blackpool	D1	A	L	2-3	Suart og, Spuhler
		4 2L	30.1.46	Blackpool		H	W	3-2	Fenton 2, Spuhler
		4r	4.2.46	Blackpool at Elland Road			W	1-0aet	Hardwick (p)
		5 1L	9.2.46	Bolton W	D1	A	L	0-1	
		5 2L	13.2.46	Bolton W		H	D	1-1	Fenton
1946-47	D1	3	11.1.47	QPR	3S	A	D	1-1	Fenton
		3r	15.1.47	QPR		H	W	3-1	Fenton 2, Mannion
		4	25.1.47	Chesterfield	D2	H	W	2-1	Spuhler 2
		5	8.2.47	Nottingham F	D2	A	D	2-2	Mannion, Spuhler
		6	1.3.47	Burnley	D2	H	D	1-1	Walker
		6r	4.3.47	Burnley		A	L	0-1aet	
1947-48	D1	3	10.1.48	Hull C	3N	A	W	3-1	Dobbie 2, Mannion
		4	24.1.48	Brentford	D2	A	W	2-1	Spuhler, McCormack
		5	7.2.48	Derby Co	D1	H	L	1-2	Spuhler
1948-49	D1	3	8.1.49	Brentford	D2	A	L	2-3aet	Walker, Spuhler
1949-50	D1	3	7.1.50	Aston Villa	D1	A	D	2-2	Linacre, McKennan
		3r	11.1.50	Aston Villa		H	D	0-0aet	
		3 2r	16.1.50	Aston Villa at Elland Road			W	3-0	McCrae 2, Mannion
		4	28.1.50	Chesterfield	D2	A	L	2-3	Walker, Spuhler
1950-51	D1	3	6.1.51	Leeds U	D2	A	L	0-1	
1951-52	D1	3	12.1.52	Derby Co	D1	H	D	2-2	Mannion 2
		3r	16.1.52	Derby Co		A	W	2-0	Delapenha 2
		4	6.2.52	Doncaster R	D2	A	L	1-4	Bell
1952-53	D1	3	10.1.53	Aston Villa	D1	A	L	1-3	Fitzsimons
1953-54	D1	3	9.1.54	Leiester C	D2	H	D	0-0	
		3r	14.1.54	Leicester C		A	L	2-3	Spuhler, Mannion
1954-55	D2	3	8.1.55	Notts Co	D2	H	L	1-4	Wayman
1955-56	D2	3	7.1.56	Bradford PA	3N	A	W	4-0	Scott 2, Delapenha, Wayman
		4	28.1.56	Tottenham H	D1	A	L	1-3	Scott
1956-57	D2	3	5.1.57	Charlton A	D1	H	D	1-1	Scott
		3r	10.1.57	Charlton A		A	W	3-2	Day, Clough, Fitzsimons
		4	26.1.57	Aston Villa	D1	H	L	2-3	Clough, Harris
1957-58	D2	3	4.1.58	Derby Co	D2	H	W	5-0	Peacock 2, Day, Holliday, Clough
		4	25.1.58	Stoke C	D2	A	L	1-3	Clough
1958-59	D2	3	24.1.59	Birmingham C	D1	H	L	0-1	
1959-60	D2	3	9.1.60	Sheffield W	D1	A	L	1-2	Clough
1960-61	D2	3	7.1.61	Manchester U	D1	A	L	0-3	
1961-62	D2	3	10.1.62	Cardiff C	D1	H	W	1-0	Peacock
		4	27.1.62	Shrewsbury T	D3	A	D	2-2	Peacock 2
		4r	31.1.62	Shrewsbury T		H	W	5-1	Holliday 2, Harris, Peacock, Kaye
		5	17.2.62	Blackburn R	D1	A	L	1-2	Burbeck
1962-63	D2	3	5.3.63	Blackburn R	D1	A	D	1-1	Orritt
		3r	11.3.63	Blackburn R		H	W	3-1	Peacock 2, Kaye (p)
		4	16.3.63	Leeds U	D2	H	L	0-2	
1963-64	D2	3	4.1.64	Brentford	D3	A	L	1-2	Kaye
1964-65	D2	3	9.1.65	Oldham A	D3	H	W	6-2	Irvine 3, Horsfield 2, Kaye
		4	30.1.65	Charlton A	D2	A	D	1-1	Nurse
		4r	1.2.65	Charlton A		H	W	2-1	Gibson, Masson
		5	20.2.65	Leicester C	D1	H	L	0-3	
1965-66	D2	3	22.1.66	Tottenham H	D1	A	L	0-4	
1966-67	D3	1	26.11.66	Chester	D4	A	W	5-2	O'Rourke 3, Downing, Hickton
		2	7.1.67	York C	D4	H	D	1-1	Hickton
		2r	11.1.67	York C		A	D	0-0aet	
		2 2r	16.1.67	York C at Newcastle			W	4-1	Lawson, Lugg, Horsfield, Jackson og
		3	28.1.67	Mansfield T	D3	A	L	0-2	
1967-68	D2	3	27.1.68	Hull C	D2	H	D	1-1	Crossan

	3r	31.1.68	**Hull C**		A	D	2-2aet	Horsfield
	3 2r	7.2.68	**Hull C** at York			W	1-0	Downing
	4	17.2.68	**Bristol C**	D2	H	D	1-1	Parr og
	4r	20.2.68	**Bristol C**		A	L	1-2	Hickton
1968-69 D2	3	4.1.69	**Millwall**	D2	H	D	1-1	Allen
	3r	6.1.69	**Millwall**		A	L	0-1	
1969-70 D2	3	3.1.70	**West Ham**	D1	H	W	2-1	McIlmoyle, Downing
	4	24.1.70	**York C**	D4	H	W	4-1	McMordie, G.Smith, Hickton (p), Laidlaw
	5	7.2.70	**Carlisle U**	D2	A	W	2-1	Hickton, Downing
	6	21.2.70	**Manchester U**	D1	H	D	1-1	Hickton
	6r	25.2.70	**Manchester U**		A	L	1-2	Hickton
1970-71 D2	3	2.1.71	**Manchester U**	D1	A	D	0-0	
	4	5.1.71	**Manchester U**		H	W	2-1	McIlmoyle, Downing
	5	23.1.71	**Everton**	D1	A	L	0-3	
1971-72 D2	3	15.1.72	**Manchester C**	D1	A	D	1-1	Mills
	3r	18.1.72	**Manchester C**		H	W	1-0	Hickton
	4	5.2.72	**Millwall**	D2	A	D	2-2	Hickton, Downing
	4r	8.2.72	**Millwall**		H	W	2-1	Downing, Hickton (p)
	5	26.2.72	**Manchester U**	D1	A	D	0-0	
	5r	29.2.72	**Manchester U**		H	L	0-3	
1972-73 D2	3	13.1.73	**Plymouth A**	D3	A	L	0-1	
1973-74 D2	3	5.1.74	**Grantham**	SL	A	W	2-0	Mills, Armstrong
	4	26.1.74	**Wrexham**	D3	A	L	0-1	
1974-75 D1	3	4.1.75	**Wycombe W**	IL	A	D	0-0	
	3r	7.1.75	**Wycombe W**		H	W	1-0	Armstrong (p)
	4	25.1.75	**Sunderland**	D2	H	W	3-1	Hickton 2 (2p), Murdoch
	5	15.2.75	**Peterborough U**	D3	A	D	1-1	Mills
	5r	18.2.75	**Peterborough U**		H	W	2-0	Foggon
	6	8.3.75	**Birmingham C**	D1	A	L	0-1	
1975-76 D1	3	3.1.76	**Bury**	D3	H	D	0-0	
	3r	6.1.76	**Bury**		A	L	2-3	Brine, Hickton (p)
1976-77 D1	3	8.1.77	**Wimbledon**	SL	A	D	0-0	
	3r	11.1.77	**Wimbledon**		H	W	1-0	Armsrong (p)
	4	29.1.77	**Hereford U**	D2	H	W	4-0	Armstrong 2 (1p), Souness, Willey
	5	26.2.77	**Arsenal**	D1	H	W	4-1	Mills 3, Armstrong
	6	19.3.77	**Liverpool**	D1	A	L	0-2	
1977-78 D1	3	7.1.78	**Coventry C**	D1	H	W	3-0	Mills 2, McAndrew
	4	28.1.78	**Everton**	D1	H	W	3-2	Mills 2, Mahoney
	5	27.2.78	**Bolton W**	D2	H	W	2-0	Ashcroft, Cummins
	6	11.3.78	**Orient**	D2	H	D	0-0	
	6r	14.3.78	**Orient**		A	L	1-2	Armstrong
1978-79 D1	3	9.1.79	**Crystal P**	D2	H	D	1-1	Ashcroft
	3r	15.1.79	**Crystal P**		A	L	0-1	
1979-80 D1	3	9.1.80	**Portsmouth**	D4	A	D	1-1	Cochrane
	3r	14.1.80	**Portsmouth**		H	W	3-0	Cochrane, Johnson, Armstrong
	4	26.1.80	**Birmingham C**	D2	A	L	1-2	Hodgson
1980-81 D1	3	3.1.81	**Swansea C**	D2	A	W	5-0	Hodgson 2, Ashcroft, Angus, Cochrane
	4	24.1.81	**WBA**	D1	H	W	1-0	Bailey
	5	14.2.81	**Barnsley**	D3	H	W	2-1	Proctor, Jankovic
	6	7.3.81	**Wolverhampton W**	D1	H	D	1-1	Cochrane
	6r	10.3.81	**Wolverhampton W**		A	L	1-3aet	Hodgson
1981-82 D1	3	2.1.82	**QPR**	D2	A	D	1-1	Thomson
	3r	18.1.82	**QPR**		H	L	2-3aet	Otto, Thomson
1982-83 D2	3	8.1.83	**Bishops Stortford**	IL	H	D	2-2	S Bell 2
	3r	11.1.83	**Bishops Stortford**		A	W	2-1	Shearer
	4	29.1.83	**Notts Co**	D1	H	W	2-0	Hankin, Beattie (p)
	5	19.2.83	**Arsenal**	D1	H	D	1-1	Otto
	5r	28.2.83	**Arsenal**		A	L	2-3	Shearer 2
1983-84 D2	3	7.1.84	**Arsenal**	D1	H	W	3-2	Macdonald, Sugrue, Baxter
	4	31.1.84	**Bournemouth**	D3	H	W	2-0	Sugrue
	5	18.2.84	**Notts Co**	D1	A	L	0-1	
1984-85 D2	3	5.1.85	**Darlington**	D4	H	D	0-0	
	3r	8.1.85	**Darlington**		A	L	1-2	McAndrew
1985-86 D2	3	13.1.86	**Southampton**	D1	H	L	1-3	O'Riordan
1986-87 D3	1	15.11.86	**Blackpool**	D3	H	W	3-0	Slaven 3
	2	7.12.86	**Notts Co**	D3	A	W	1-0	Hamilton
	3	10.1.87	**Preston NE**	D4	H	L	0-1	

MIDDLESBROUGH

1987-88	D2	3	9.1.88	**Sutton U**	GMVC	A	D	1-1	Pallister
		3r	12.1.88	**Sutton U**		H	W	1-0aet	Kerr
		4	30.1.88	**Everton**	D1	A	D	1-1	Kerr
		4r	3.2.88	**Everton**		H	D	2-2aet	Mowbray, Kernaghan
		4 2r	9.2.88	**Everton**		A	L	1-2	Ripley
1988-89	D1	3	7.1.89	**Grimsby T**	D4	H	L	1-2	Slaven
1989-90	D2	3	6.1.90	**Everton**	D1	H	D	0-0	
		3r	10.1.90	**Everton**		A	D	1-1aet	Parkinson
		3 2r	17.1.90	**Everton**		A	L	0-1	
1990-91	D2	3	5.1.91	**Plymouth A**	D2	H	D	0-0	
		3r	14.1.91	**Plymouth A**		A	W	2-1	Baird, Kerr
		4	26.1.91	**Cambridge U**	D3	A	L	0-2	
1991-92	D2	3	4.1.92	**Manchester C**	D1	H	W	2-1	Kernaghan, Wilkinson
		4	4.2.92	**Sheffield W**	D1	A	W	2-1	Hendrie, Wilkinson
		5	15.2.92	**Portsmouth**	D2	A	D	1-1	Kernaghan
		5r	26.2.92	**Portsmouth**		H	L	2-4	Wilkinson 2
1992-93	PL	3	13.1.93	**Chelsea**	PL	H	W	2-1	Wright, Falconer
		4	23.1.93	**Nottingham F**	PL	A	D	1-1	Falconer
		4r	3.2.93	**Nottingham F**		H	L	0-3	

MIDDLESBROUGH IRONOPOLIS

Formed 1889. Member of the Football League 1893-1894. Folded 1894.

1890-91	NL	1	17.1.91	**Blackburn R**	D1	H	L	1-2	McReddie
1891-92	NL	1	16.1.92	**Preston NE**	D1	A	–	2-2	Hughes, McNair
			abandoned due to bad weather and frost						
		1	23.1.92	**Preston NE**		A	L	0-6	
1892-93	NL	1	21.1.93	**Marlow**		A	W	3-1	Hill, McArthur, Seymour
		2	4.2.93	**Notts Co**	D1	H	W	3-2	Hill, Hughes, McArthur
		3	18.2.93	**Preston NE**	D1	A	D	2-2	Hill, McArthur
		3r	25.2.93	**Preston NE**		H	L	0-7	
1893-94	D2	1	27.1.94	**Luton T**		H	W	2-1	Hunt, Adams
		2	10.2.94	**Nottingham F**	D1	H	L	0-2	

MILLWALL

Formed 1885 as Millwall Rovers. Changed name to Millwall Athletic 1894. Millwall 1925. **Best FA Cup Performance:** Semifinals: 1900 and 1903 as a Southern League club; 1937 as Third Division South club, the first Third Division club to reach the last four. **Record FA Cup Win:** 7-0 vs Clapton, 3rd qualifying round, 28.10.1899. **In Competition Proper:** 7-0 vs Gateshead, 2nd round, 12.12.1936. **Record FA Cup Defeat:** 1-9 vs Aston Villa, 4th round, 2nd leg, 9.1.1946.

as Millwall Rovers

1887-88		1		**Casuals**			*walkover*		
		2	5.11.87	**Old Westminsters**		A	L	1-8	Oliver

1888-89 1q **Lancing Old Boys** (A) 0-4
1889-90 1q **Schorne College** (H) 0-4
1890-91 1q **Ilford** (H) 2-3
1891-92 1q **Rochester** (A) 2-1 aet; 2q **1st Highland Lt.Inf.** (H) 3-4
1892-93 1q **Folkestone** (H) 6-1; 2q **West Kent Regiment** (H) 2-0; 3q **Woolwich Arsenal** (A) 2-3

as Millwall Athletic

1893-94 1q **bye**; 2q **Ilford** (A) 3-1; 3q **Woolwich Arsenal** (A) 0-2

1894-95	SL	1q **Folkestone** (H) 5-0; 2q **Royal Engineers Tr.Bat.** (A) 4-1; 3q **New Brompton** (A) 2-0; 4q **Royal Ordnanace** (A) 3-0							
		1	2.2.95	**Sheffield U**	D1	A	L	1-3	Geddes
1895-96	SL	1q **New Brompton** (A) 1-0; 2q **Folkestone** (H) 5-0; 3q **Sheppey U** (H) 4-0; 4q **Royal Ordnance** (A) 2-1							
		1	1.2.96	**Liverpool**	D2	A	L	1-4	Geddes
1896-97	SL	3q **Sheppey U** (A) 3-3; 3qr **Sheppey U** (H) 3-1; 4q **Northfleet** (H) 6-1; 5q **Woolwich Arsenal** (H) 4-2							
		1	30.1.97	**Wolverhampton W**	D1	H	L	1-2	McKenzie
1897-98	SL	3q **Sheppey U** (H) 5-1 *match replayed by FA order*; 3q **Sheppey U** (A) 0-5							
1898-99	SL	3q **Brighton U** (H) 3-0; 4q **Gravesend U** (A) 1-3							
1899-00	SL	3q **Clapton** (H) 7-0; 4q **Chatham T** (H) 3-0; 5q **West Ham** (A) 2-1							
		1	27.1.00	**Jarrow**	NAll	A	W	2-0	Banks, Brearley
		2	17.2.00	**QPR**	SL	A	W	2-0	Gettins 2
		3	24.2.00	**Aston V**	D1	H	D	1-1	Nicol
		3r	28.2.00	**Aston V**		A	D	0-0aet	
		3 2r	5.3.00	**Aston V** at Reading			W	2-1	Banks, Gettins
		SF	24.3.00	**Southampton**	SL		D	0-0	
			played at Crystal Palace						

		SFr	28.3.00	**Southampton**			L	0-3	
			played at Reading						
1900-01	SL	1	9.3.01	**Aston V**	D1	A	L	0-5	
1901-02	SL	Int	**Bristol R** (H) 1-1; Int r **Bristol R** (A) 0-1						
1902-03	SL	Int	**Bristol R** (A) 2-2; Int r **Bristol R** (H) 0-0abnd; Int 2r **Bristol R** (at Villa Pk) 2-0						
		1	7.2.03	**Luton T**	SL	H	W	3-0	Hulse, Jones, Watkins
		2	21.2.03	**Preston NE**	D2	H	W	4-1	Gettins, Jones, Moran, Derbyshire og
		3	7.3.03	**Everton**	D1	H	W	1-0	Watkins
		SF	21.3.03	**Derby Co**	D1		L	0-3	
			played at Villa Park						
1903-04	SL	1	6.2.04	**Middlesbrough**	D1	H	L	0-2	
1904-05	SL	Int	**Bradford C** (A) 4-1						
		1	4.2.05	**Southampton**	SL	A	L	1-3	Benson og
1905-06	SL	1	13.1.06	**Burton U**	D2	H	W	1-0	Heaton
		2	3.2.06	**Sheffield W**	D1	A	D	1-1	Hunter
		2r	8.2.06	**Sheffield W**		H	L	0-3	
1906-07	SL	1	12.1.07	**Plymouth A**	SL	H	W	2-0	Dean, Milsom
		2	2.2.07	**Plymouth A**		A	L	0-3	
1907-08	SL	1	11.1.08	**Bury**	D1	A	L	1-2	Jones
1908-09	SL	1	16.1.09	**Luton T**	SL	A	W	2-1	Dean, Tellum
		2	6.2.09	**W. Arsenal**	D1	A	D	1-1	Twigg
		2r	10.2.09	**W. Arsenal**		H	W	1-0	Jones
		3	20.2.09	**Nottingham F**	D1	A	L	1-3	Shand
1909-10	SL	1	15.1.10	**Derby Co**	D2	A	L	0-5	
1910-11	SL	1	14.1.11	**Tottenham H**	D1	A	L	1-2	Martin
1911-12	SL	1	13.1.12	**Bury**	D1	A	L	1-2	Davis
1912-13	SL	1	11.1.13	**Middlesbrough**	D1	H	D	0-0	
		1r	15.1.13	**Middlesbrough**		A	L	1-4	Wilson
1913-14	SL	1	10.1.14	**Chelsea**	D1	H	D	0-0	
		1r	14.1.14	**Chelsea**		A	W	1-0	Davis
		2	31.1.14	**Bradford C**	D1	H	W	1-0	Davis
		3	21.2.14	**Sheffield U**	D1	H	L	0-4	
1914-15	SL	1	9.1.15	**Clapton O**	D2	H	W	2-1	Moody 2
		2	30.1.15	**Bolton W**	D1	A	D	0-0aet	
		2r	6.2.15	**Bolton W**		H	D	2-2aet	Davis, Moody
		2 2r	13.2.15	**Bolton W** at Bolton		A	L	1-4	Davis
1919-20	SL	1	10.1.20	**Notts Co**	D1	A	L	0-2	
1920-21	D3	1	8.1.21	**Lincoln C**	ML	H	L	0-3	
1921-22	3S	1	7.1.22	**Ashington**	3N	H	W	4-2	Taylor, Moule, Keen 2
		2	28.1.22	**Crystal P**	D2	A	D	0-0	
		2r	1.2.22	**Crystal P**		H	W	2-0	Moule, Dorsett
		3	18.2.22	**Swansea T**	3S	H	W	4-0	Keen 4
		4	4.3.22	**Huddersfield T**	D1	A	L	0-3	
1922-23	3S	1	13.1.23	**Clapton O**	D2	A	W	2-0	Hannaford 2
		2	3.2.23	**Huddersfield T**	D1	H	D	0-0	
		2r	7.2.23	**Huddersfield T**		A	L	0-3	
1923-24	3S	1	12.1.24	**WBA**	D1	H	L	0-1	
1924-25	3S	1	10.1.25	**Barnsley**	D2	H	D	0-0	
		1r	15.1.25	**Barnsley**		A	L	1-2	Lincoln
as Millwall									
1925-26	3S	3	9.1.26	**Oldham A**	D2	H	D	1-1	Chance
		3r	12.1.26	**Oldham A**		A	W	1-0	Parker
		4	30.1.26	**Bury**	D1	A	D	3-3	Amos 2 (2ps), Parker
		4r	4.2.26	**Bury**		H	W	2-0	Parker, Moule
		5	20.2.26	**Swansea T**	D2	H	L	0-1	
1926-27	3S	3	8.1.27	**Huddersfield T**	D1	H	W	3-1	Phillips, Gomm, Black.
		4	29.1.27	**Derby Co**	D1	A	W	2-0	Parker, Phillips (p)
		5	19.2.27	**Middlesbrough**	D2	H	W	3-2	Gomm, Black, Chance
		6	5.3.27	**Southampton**	D2	H	D	0-0	
		6r	9.3.27	**Southampton**		A	L	0-2	
1927-28	3S	3	14.1.28	**Derby Co**	D1	H	L	1-2	Cock
1928-29	D2	3	12.1.29	**Northampton T**	3S	H	D	1-1	Phillips (p)
		3r	17.1.29	**Northampton T**		A	D	2-2aet	Cock, Readman
		3 2r	21.1.29	**Northampton T** at Highbury			W	2-0	Landells, Cock
		4	26.1.29	**Crystal P**	3S	H	D	0-0	
		4r	30.1.29	**Crystal P**		A	L	3-5	Cock, Landells, Black
1929-30	D2	3	11.1.30	**Corinthians**		A	D	2-2	Forsyth, Phillips

	3r	15.1.30	Corinthians		H	D	1-1aet	Poxton
	3 2r	20.1.30	Corinthians at Stamford Bridge			W	5-1	Forsyth, Corkindale 2, Cock 2
	4	25.1.30	Doncaster R	3N	H	W	4-0	Hawkins 2, Corkindale, Wadsworth
	5	15.2.30	West Ham	D1	A	L	1-4	Wadsworth
1930-31 D2	3	10.1.31	Southport	3N	A	L	1-3	Poxton
1931-32 D2	3	9.1.32	Manchester C	D1	H	L	2-3	Smith, Poxton
1932-33 D2	3	14.1.33	Reading	3S	H	–	2-0	Poxton (p), Bloxham
			abandoned after 75 minutes – fog					
	3	18.1.33	Reading		H	D	1-1	Poxton
	3r	23.1.33	Reading		A	W	2-0	Bloxham, Bond
	4	28.1.33	Aldershot	3S	A	L	0-1	
1933-34 D2	3	13.1.34	Accrington S	3N	H	W	3-0	Yardley 2, Phillips
	4	27.1.34	Leicester C	D1	H	L	3-6	Phillips, Yardley 2
1934-35 3S	3	12.1.35	Wigan	CC	A	W	4-1	Yardley 2, Thorogood, Alexander
	4	26.1.35	Reading	3S	A	L	0-1	
1935-36 3S	3	11.1.36	Stoke C	D1	H	D	0-0	
	3r	15.1.36	Stoke C		A	L	0-4	
1936-37 3S	1	28.11.36	Aldershot	3S	A	W	6-1	Mangnall 4 (1p), Thorogood, Thomas
	2	12.12.36	Gateshead	3N	H	W	7-0	Mangnall, Thorogood, McCartney 2, Burditt 2, Thomas (p)
	3	16.1.37	Fulham	D2	H	W	2-0	Burditt, Mangnall
	4	30.1.37	Chelsea	D1	H	W	3-0	Burditt 2, Thorogood
	5	20.2.37	Derby Co	D1	H	W	2-1	Mangnall, McCartney
	6	6.3.37	Manchester C	D1	H	W	2-0	Mangnall 2
	SF	10.4.37	Sunderland	D1		L	1-2	Mangnall
			played at Huddersfield					
1937-38 3S	3	8.1.38	Manchester C	D1	H	D	2-2	JR Smith, Walsh
	3r	12.1.38	Manchester C		A	L	1-3	Burditt
1938-39 D2	3	11.1.39	York C	3N	A	W	5-0	McLeod 4, Rawlings
	4	21.1.39	Grimsby T	D1	H	D	2-2	McLeod 2
	4r	24.1.39	Grimsby T		A	L	2-3	Richardson, McLeod
1945-46 D2	3 1L	5.1.46	Northampton T	3S	A	D	2-2	JR Smith, Ridley
	3 2L	7.1.46	Northampton T		H	W	3-0	Smalley og, Phillips, JR Smith
	4 1L	26.1.46	Aston Villa	D1	H	L	2-4	Jinks 2
	4 2L	28.1.46	Aston Villa		A	L	1-9	JR Smith
1946-47 D2	3	11.1.47	Port Vale	3S	H	L	0-3	
1947-48 D2	3	10.1.48	Preston NE	D1	H	L	1-2	Mansfield
1948-49 3S	1	27.11.48	Tooting & Mitcham	AL	H	W	1-0	McMillen
	2	11.12.48	Crewe A	3N	A	L	2-3	Constantine 2
1949-50 3S	1	26.11.49	Exeter C	3S	H	L	3-5	Constantine, Brolly
1950-51 3S	1	25.11.50	Crystal P	3S	A	D	0-0	
			abandoned after 34 minutes – fog					
	1	29.11.50	Crystal P		A	W	4-1	Johnson, Morgan, Constantine, Neary
	2	9.12.50	Bradford PA	3N	H	D	1-1	Neary
	2r	13.12.50	Bradford PA		A	W	1-0	Morgan
	3	6.1.51	QPR	D2	A	W	4-3	Neary 2, Johnson, Constantine
	4	27.1.51	Fulham	D1	H	L	0-1	
1951-52 3S	1	24.11.51	Plymouth A	3S	H	W	1-0	White
	2	15.12.51	Scunthorpe U	3N	H	D	0-0	
	2r	20.12.51	Scunthorpe U		A	L	0-3	
1952-53 3S	1	22.11.52	Aldershot	3S	A	D	0-0	
	1r	27.11.52	Aldershot		H	W	7-1	Neary, Monkhouse 3, Shepherd 3
	2	6.12.52	Barrow	3N	A	D	2-2	Stobbart, Neary
	2r	10.12.52	Barrow		H	W	4-1	Stobbart, Shepherd 3
	3	10.1.53	Manchester U	D1	H	L	0-1	
1953-54 3S	1	21.11.53	Colchester U	3S	A	D	1-1	Stobbart
	1r	23.11.53	Colchester U		H	W	4-0	Stobbart 2, Hazlett, Neary
	2	12.12.53	Headington U	SL	H	D	3-3	Shepherd, Neary, Short
	2r	17.12.53	Headington U		A	L	0-1	
1954-55 3S	1	20.11.54	Exeter C	3S	H	W	3-2	Pacey 2, Jardine
	2	11.12.54	Accrington S	3N	H	W	3-2	Prior, Ramscar, Pacey
	3	8.1.55	Bolton W	D1	A	L	1-3	Smith
1955-56 3S	1	19.11.55	Northampton T	3S	A	L	1-4	Pacey
1956-57 3S	1	17.11.56	Brighton & HA	3S	A	D	1-1	Shepherd
	1r	19.11.56	Brighton & HA		H	W	3-1	Shepherd, Anslow 2 (2ps)
	2	8.12.56	Margate	KL	H	W	4-0	Shepherd 3, Rawson
	3	5.1.57	Crystal P	3S	H	W	2-0	Anslow, Shepherd
	4	26.1.57	Newcastle U	D1	H	W	2-1	Anslow 2

Season	Div	Round	Date	Opponent	Opp Div	H/A	Result	Score	Scorers
		5	16.2.57	Birmingham C	D1	H	L	1-4	Shepherd
1957-58	3S	1	16.11.57	Brentford	3S	H	W	1-0	Morrison
		2	7.12.57	Gillingham	3S	H	D	1-1	Shepherd
		2r	11.12.57	Gillingham		A	L	1-6	Summersby
1958-59	D4	1	15.11.58	Hitchin T	AL	A	D	1-1	Summersby
		1r	17.11.58	Hitchin T		H	W	2-1	Heckman, Hutton
		2	6.12.58	Worcester C	SL	A	L	2-5	Roche, Moyse
1959-60	D4	1	14.11.59	Bath C	SL	A	L	1-3	Wilson
1960-61	D4	1	5.11.60	Reading	D3	A	L	2-6	Burridge 2
1961-62	D4	1	4.11.61	Northampton T	D3	A	L	0-2	
1962-63	D3	1	3.11.62	Margate	SL	H	W	3-1	Terry, Jones, Haverty
		2	24.11.62	Coventry C	D3	H	D	0-0	
		2r	27.11.62	Coventry C		A	L	1-2	Jones (p)
1963-64	D3	1	16.11.63	Kettering	SL	A	D	1-1	Snowdon og
		1r	25.11.63	Kettering		H	L	2-3	Obeney, Fraser
1964-65	D4	1	14.11.64	Kettering	SL	H	W	2-0	Rowan 2
		2	5.12.64	Port Vale	D3	H	W	4-0	Julians, Nicholson og, Whitehouse 2
		3	9.1.65	Fulham	D1	A	D	3-3	Curran, Whitehouse 2
		3r	11.1.65	Fulham		H	W	2-0	Harper, Rowan
		4	30.1.65	Shrewsbury T	D3	H	L	1-2	John
1965-66	D3	1	13.11.65	Wealdstone	IL	H	W	3-1	Brown, Jacks, Rowan
		2	4.12.65	Hereford U	SL	A	L	0-1	
1966-67	D2	3	28.1.67	Tottenham H	D1	H	D	0-0	
		3r	1.2.67	Tottenham H		A	L	0-1	
1967-68	D2	3	27.1.68	Aston Villa	D2	A	L	0-3	
1968-69	D2	3	4.1.69	Middlesbrough		A	D	1-1	Possee
		3r	6.1.69	Middlesbrough		H	W	1-0	Howell
		4	25.1.69	Leicester C	D1	H	L	0-1	
1969-70	D2	3	3.1.70	Scunthorpe U	D4	A	L	1-2	Bolland
1970-71	D2	3	2.1.71	Stoke C	D1	A	L	1-2	Possee
1971-72	D2	3	15.1.72	Nottingham F	D1	H	W	3-1	Bolland (p), Smethurst, Possee
		4	5.2.72	Middlesbrough	D2	H	D	2-2	Smethurst, Possee
		4r	8.2.72	Middlesbrough		A	L	1-2	Burnett
1972-73	D2	3	13.1.73	Newport Co	D4	H	W	3-0	Burnett, Smethurst, Wood
		4	3.2.73	Everton	D1	A	W	2-0	Cripps, Wood
		5	24.2.73	Wolverhampton W	D1	A	L	0-1	
1973-74	D2	3	5.1.74	Scunthorpe U	D4	H	D	1-1	Wood
		3r	8.1.74	Scunthorpe U		A	L	0-1	
1974-75	D2	3	3.1.75	Bury	D3	A	D	2-2	Bolland (p), Hill
		3r	7.1.75	Bury		H	D	1-1aet	Summerhill
		3 2r	13.1.75	Bury at the Hawthorns			L	0-2	
1975-76	D3	1	22.11.75	Yeovil T	SL	A	D	1-1	Kitchener
		1r	25.11.75	Yeovil T		H	D	2-2aet	Salvage, Welsh
		1 2r	3.12.75	Yeovil T at Aldershot			W	1-0	Hart
		2	13.12.75	Crystal P	D3	H	D	1-1	Summerhill
		2r	16.12.75	Crystal P		A	L	1-2	Moore
1976-77	D2	3	8.1.77	Coventry C	D1	A	L	0-1	
1977-78	D2	3	7.1.78	Rotherham U	D3	A	D	1-1	Kitchener
		3r	10.1.78	Rotherham U		H	W	2-0	Lee 2
		4	31.1.78	Luton T	D2	H	W	4-0	Pearson 3, Seasman
		5	18.2.78	Notts Co	D2	H	W	2-1	Chambers (p), Walker
		6	11.3.78	Ipswich T	D1	H	L	1-6	Mehmet
1978-79	D2	3	10.1.79	Blackburn R	D2	H	L	1-2	Walker
1979-80	D3	1	24.11.79	Salisbury	SL	A	W	2-1	Mitchell, Donaldson
				played at Southampton					
		2	15.12.79	Croydon	IL	A	D	1-1	Chatterton
				played at Crystal Palace					
		2r	18.12.79	Croydon		H	W	3-2	O'Callaghan, Towner (p), Mitchell
		3	5.1.80	Shrewsbury T	D2	H	W	5-1	McKenna, Tagg, Lyons 3
		4	26.1.80	Chester	D3	A	L	0-2	
1980-81	D3	1	22.11.80	Kidderminster H	SL	A	D	1-1	Williams og
		1r	25.11.80	Kidderminster H		H	W	1-0	Chatterton
		2	13.12.80	Exeter C	D3	H	L	0-1	
1981-82	D3	1	21.11.81	Portsmouth	D3	A	D	1-1	Chatterton (p)
		1r	25.11.81	Portsmouth		H	W	3-2aet	Allardyce, Chatterton, Hayes
		2	30.12.81	Dagenham	APL	A	W	2-1	Allardyce, Chatterton
		3	5.1.82	Grimsby T	D2	H	L	1-6	Neal

1982-83	D3	1	20.11.82	**Slough T**	IL	A	L	0-1	
1983-84	D3	1	19.11.83	**Dartford**	SL	H	W	2-1	Massey, Cusack
		2	10.12.83	**Swindon T**	D4	H	L	2-3	Lovell (p), Martin
1984-85	D3	1	17.11.84	**Weymouth**	APL	A	W	3-0	Lovell (p), Bremner, Otulakowski
		2	8.12.84	**Enfield**	APL	H	W	1-0	Neal
		3	4.1.85	**Crystal P**	D2	H	D	1-1	Neal
		3r	23.1.85	**Crystal P**		A	W	2-1	Briley, Lovell
		4	4.2.85	**Chelsea**	D1	A	W	3-2	Lovell 2 (1p), John Fashanu
		5	19.2.85	**Leicester C**	D1	H	W	2-0	McLeary, John Fashanu
		6	13.3.85	**Luton T**	D1	A	L	0-1	
1985-86	D2	3	4.1.86	**Wimbledon**	D2	H	W	3-1	Lovell, John Fashanu, Walker
		4	25.1.86	**Aston Villa**	D1	A	D	1-1	McLeary
		4r	29.1.86	**Aston Villa**		H	W	1-0	John Fashanu
		5	15.2.86	**Southampton**	D1	A	D	0-0	
		5r	5.3.86	**Southampton**		H	L	0-1	
1986-87	D2	3	10.1.87	**Cardiff C**	D4	H	D	0-0	
		3r	20.1.87	**Cardiff C**		A	D	2-2aet	Leslie, Morgan
		3 2r	26.1.87	**Cardiff C**		A	L	0-1	
1987-88	D2	3	9.1.88	**Arsenal**	D1	A	L	0-2	
1988-89	D1	3	7.1.89	**Luton T**	D1	H	W	3-2	Cascarino, Carter, Sheringham
		4	29.1.89	**Liverpool**	D1	H	L	0-2	
1989-90	D1	3	6.1.90	**Manchester C**	D1	A	D	0-0	
		3r	9.1.90	**Manchester C**		H	D	1-1aet	Carter
		3 2r	15.1.90	**Manchester C**		H	W	3-1	Goddard, Sheringham 2
		4	27.1.90	**Cambridge U**	D4	H	D	1-1	Cascarino
		4r	30.1.90	**Cambridge U**		A	L	0-1	
1990-91	D2	3	5.1.91	**Leicester C**	D2	H	W	2-1	Sheringham, Stephenson
		4	26.1.91	**Sheffield W**	D2	H	D	4-4	Stephenson, Rae 2, Sheringham
		4r	30.1.91	**Sheffield W**		A	L	0-2	
1991-92	D2	3	4.1.92	**Huddersfield T**	D3	A	W	4-0	Thompson, Verveer, Rae 2
		4	5.2.92	**Norwich C**	D1	A	L	1-2	Kerr
1992-93	D1	3	13.1.93	**Southend U**	D1	A	L	0-1	

MINEHEAD

Formed 1889. **First entered FA Cup:** 1912. **League club beaten:** Swansea C

1970-71	WL	1	21.11.70	**Shrewsbury T**	D3	H	L	1-2	Bryant
1976-77	SL	1	20.11.76	**Swansea C**	D4	A	W	1-0	Leitch
		2	11.12.76	**Portsmouth**	D3	A	L	1-2	Leitch
1977-78	SL	1	26.11.77	**Wycombe W**	IL	H	W	2-0	Brown, Leitch
		2	17.12.77	**Exeter C**	D3	H	L	0-3	
1979-80	SL	1	24.11.79	**Chesham**	IL	H	L	1-2	Brown
1980-81	SL	1	22.11.80	**Barnet**	APL	A	D	2-2	Chick, Brown
		1r	25.11.80	**Barnet**		H	L	1-2	Druce
1981-82	SL	1	21.11.81	**Dorchester**	SL	A	D	3-3	Guscott, Hodgson, Darke
		1r	23.11.81	**Dorchester**		H	L	0-4	

MINERVA FC

1877-78	1	3.11.77	**Hawks**		A	L	2-5	Clegg, Duthie
1878-79	1		**105th Regiment**		*walkover*			
	2	7.12.78	**Grey Friars**		A	W	3-0	Bain, Hearn, Turner
	3	11.1.79	**Old Etonians**		A	L	2-5	Thompson, Ware
1879-80	1	15.11.79	**Herts Rangers**		A	L	1-2	Fabian

MITCHELL ST GEORGES

see Birmingham St Georges

MOLD FC

Originally formed 1874.

1925-26	Welsh 1		28.11.25	**Southport**		3N	A	L	0-1

MOOR GREEN

Formed 1906. **First entered FA Cup:** 1934

| 1979-80 | MC | 1 | 24.11.79 | **Sttafford R** | APL | A | L | 2-3 | Howell, Clamp (p) |

MORECAMBE

Formed 1920. **First entered FA Cup:** 1920. **FA Challenge Trophy Winners:** 1974. **Cup Final Connection:** Alan Taylor, who scored both goals when West Ham beat Fulham in the 1975 Cup Final, started at Morecambe. **League club beaten:** Chester

1936-37	LC	1	28.11.36	**South Liverpool**	LC	A	L	0-1	
1956-57	LC	1	17.11.56	**Accrington S**	3N	A	L	1-4	Horton
1958-59	LC	1	15.11.58	**Blyth Spartans**	ML	H	L	1-2	Borrowdale
1961-62	LC	1	4.11.61	**South Shields**	NCo	H	W	2-1	Shields og, Whitehead
		2	25.11.61	**Chester**	D4	A	W	1-0	Howarth
		3	6.1.62	**Weymouth**	SL	H	L	0-1	
1962-63	LC	1	3.11.62	**Blyth Spartans**	NEL	A	L	1-2	Whitehead
1966-67	LC	1	26.11.66	**York C**	D4	A	D	0-0	
		1r	5.12.66	**York C**		H	D	1-1aet	Lear
		1 2r	8.12.66	**York C** at Maine Road			L	0-1	
1968-69	NPL	1	16.11.68	**Bangor C**	NPL	A	W	3-2	Wroth, Porter, Lancaster (p)
		2	7.12.68	**York C**	D4	A	L	0-2	
1974-75	NPL	1	23.11.74	**Bishop Auckland**	NL	A	L	0-5	
1975-76	NPL	1	22.11.75	**Scarborough**	NPL	A	L	0-2	
1976-77	NPL	1	20.11.76	**Lincoln C**	D3	A	L	0-1	
1978-79	NPL	1	25.11.78	**Stockport Co**	D4	A	L	1-5	Towers
1979-80	NPL	1	24.11.79	**Rotherham U**	D3	H	D	1-1	McLachlan (p)
		1r	27.11.79	**Rotherham U**		A	L	0-2	
1985-86	NPL	1	16.11.85	**York C**	D3	A	D	0-0	
		1r	19.11.85	**York C**		H	L	0-2	
1991-92	NPL	1	16.11.91	**Hull C**	D3	H	L	0-1	

MORPETH HARRIERS

Northumberland-based amateurs who competed in the FA Cup 1887-1909

1887-88		1	15.10.87	**Sunderland**		A	L	2-4	
			replay ordered after protest						
		1r	22.10.87	**Sunderland**		H	L	2-3	Crackett, Waterson

MORTON RANGERS

Not a forerunner of the Scottish League club, but a London-based amateur outfit

| 1881-82 | | 1 | 5.11.81 | **Old Foresters** | | A | L | 0-3 | |

MOSQUITOES

Formed 1870. Played at the Greyhound Field, Dulwich and used the Greyhound Pub as their changing room.

1879-80		1	1.11.79	**St Peters Institute**		H	W	3-1	Davey 2, Borman
		2	20.12.79	**Hendon**		A	L	1-7	Ginger
1880-81		1	13.11.80	**Upton Park**		A	L	1-8	
1881-82		1	5.11.81	**Pilgrims**		H	D	1-1	A.Cornford
		1r	12.11.81	**Pilgrims**		A	L	0-5	
1882-83		1	4.11.82	**Hanover U**		A	L	0-1	
1883-84		1	10.11.83	**Pilgrims**		H	W	3-2	J.Cornford, others 2
		2	1.12.83	**Romford**		A	L	1-3	Soulby

MOSSLEY

Formed 1903. **First entered FA Cup:** 1948. **FA Challenge Trophy Runners-up:** 1980. **League club beaten:** Crewe A

1949-50	CC	1	26.11.49	**Witton Albion**	CC	A	W	1-0	Moss
		2	10.12.49	**Nuneaton B**	BC	A	D	0-0	
		2r	17.12.49	**Nuneaton B**		H	L	0-3	
1969-70	CC	1	15.11.69	**Stockport Co**	D3	A	D	1-1	Batty
		1r	18.11.69	**Stockport Co**		H	L	0-1	
1977-78	NPL	1	26.11.77	**Rotherham U**	D3	A	L	0-3	

1979-80	NPL	1	24.11.79	York C	D4	A	L	2-5	Smith 2
1980-81	NPL	1	22.11.80	Crewe Alex	D4	H	W	1-0	Mobley
		2	13.12.80	Mansfield T	D4	H	L	1-3	Skeete
1981-82	NPL	1	21.11.81	Stockport Co	D4	A	L	1-3	Moore
1982-83	NPL	1	20.11.82	Huddersfield T	D3	A	L	0-1	
1983-84	NPL	1	19.11.83	Darlington	D4	A	L	0-5	

NELSON FC

Formed 1881. **First entered FA Cup:** 1893. **Members of the Football League:** 1921-1931 Currently play in the NW Counties League

1921-22	3N			4q **Accrington S** (H) 1-0; 5q **Rochdale** (H) 3-2; 6q **Worksop** (ML) (A) 1-2					
1922-23	3N			4q **Rochdale** (H) 1-0; 5q **Stalybridge C** (A) 0-1					
1923-24	D2			5q **Wigan B** (A) 1-1; 5qr **Wigan B** (H) 0-1					
1924-25	3N			5q **Winsford U** (H) 4-1; 6q **Coventry C** (H) 0-1					
1925-26	3N	1	2.12.25	Wigan Borough	3N	A	L	0-3	
1926-27	3N	1	27.11.26	Stockport Co	3N	H	W	4-1	Hampson 2, Sharp, Stevenson
		2	11.12.26	Ashington	3N	A	L	1-2	Stevenson
1927-28	3N	1	26.11.27	Bradford PA	3N	H	L	0-3	
1928-29	3N			did not compete – failed to enter by deadline					
1929-30	3N	1	30.11.29	Crewe A	3N	H	L	0-3	
1930-31	3N	1	29.11.30	Workington	NEL	H	W	4-0	Raisbeck 3, Hawes
		2	13.12.30	York C	3N	H	D	1-1	Allam
		2r	17.12.30	York C		A	–	0-2	
				abandoned because of fog					
		2r	18.12.30	York C		A	L	2-3	H.Robinson, Raisbeck
1932-33	LC	1	26.11.32	Southport	3N	A	D	3-3	J.Howarth, Chadwick, Garbutt
		1r	29.11.32	Southport		H	L	0-4	
1950-51	LC	1	25.11.50	Witton Albion	CC	A	W	2-1	Burns, Cowell
		2	9.12.50	Port Vale	3S	A	L	2-3	Ward. Coates
1951-52	LC	1	24.11.51	Oldham A	3N	H	L	0-4	
1953-54	LC	1	21.11.53	Witton A	CC	A	L	1-4	Wolstanholme

NETHERFIELD

Formed 1920. **First entered FA Cup:** 1925

1945-46	LC	1 1L	17.11.45	Barrow	3N	A	L	0-1	
		1 2L	24.11.45	Barrow		H	D	2-2	Hickton, Carswell
1948-49	LC	1	27.11.48	Gateshead	3N	A	L	0-3	
1949-50	LC	1	26.11.49	North Shields	NEL	H	W	4-3	Offord, Reed, Ashworth, Ferguson
		2	10.12.49	Watford	3S	A	L	0-6	
1952-53	LC	1	22.11.52	Gainsborough T	ML	A	D	1-1	Rooke
		1r	27.11.52	Gainsborough T		H	L	0-3	
1954-55	LC	1	20.11.54	Wrexham	3N	H	D	3-3	Ferguson, Parker og, Rooke
		1r	24.11.54	Wrexham		A	L	0-4	
1955-56	LC	1	19.11.55	Grimsby T	3N	H	L	1-5	Hayes
1963-64	LC	1	16.11.63	Loughborough U	ML	H	W	6-1	Hodgson, Browwnlee 4, Lambert
		2	7.12.63	Chesterfield	D4	H	D	1-1	Brownlee
		2r	11.12.63	Chesterfield		A	L	1-4	Lambert
1964-65	LC	1	14.11.64	Barnsley	D3	H	L	1-3	Hodgson

NEWARK FC

1884-85		1	8.11.84	Spilsby		H	W	7-3	
		2	6.12.84	Middlesbrough		A	L	1-3	Huskinson
1885-86		1	31.10.85	Sheffield FC		H	L	0-3	

NEWARK TOWN

Entered FA Cup: 1928-38. Folded mid-1960s, new Newark Town formed 1989

1929-30	ML	1	30.11.29	Barrow	3N	A	L	0-1	
1930-31	ML	1	29.11.30	Rotherham U	3N	H	W	2-1	Speed 2
		2	13.12.30	Crystal P	3S	A	L	0-6	
1931-32	ML	1	28.11.31	Halifax T	3N	H	D	1-1	Hill
		1r	2.12.31	Halifax T		A	L	1-2	Hill
1933-34	ML	1	25.11.33	Tranmere R	3N	A	L	0-7	

NEW BRIGHTON

Formed 1921. **First entered FA Cup:** 1922. **Members of the Football League:** 1923-1951. Folded 1983.

1922-23	LC	4q **Crewe A** (3N) (H) 1-1; 4qr **Crewe A** (A) 1-0; 5q **Coventry C** (D2) (H) 3-0							
		1	13.1.23 **Sheffield W**	D2	A	L	0-3	
1923-24	3N	4q **Southport** (A) 1-1; 4qr **Southport** (H) 0-1							
1924-25	3N	5q **Accrington Stanley** (H) 0-0; 5qr **Accrington Stanley** (A) 2-3							
1925-26	3N	1	28.11.25 **Barrow**	3N	H	W	2-0	Dunne, Whitter
		2	12.12.25 **Darlington**	D2	H	W	2-0	Kelly 2
		3	9.1.26 **Sheffield W**	D2	H	W	2-1	Gee, Broad
		4	30.1.26 **Notts Co**	D1	A	L	0-2	
1926-27	3N	1	27.11.26 **Wrexham**	3N	A	D	1-1	Williams
		1r	1.12.26 **Wrexham**			D	2-2	Whitter, Worrall
		1 2r	6.12.26 **Wrexham** at Anfield			L	1-3	Hawksworth
1927-28	3N	1	26.11.27 **Shildon**	NEL	A	W	3-1	Whitter, Harley 2
		2	10.12.27 **Rhyl A**	Welsh	H	W	7-2	Lewis, Dixon og, Harley 4, Reid
		3	14.1.28 **Corinthians**		H	W	2-1	Whitter 2
		4	28.1.28 **Port Vale**	D2	A	L	0-3	
1928-29	3N	1	24.11.28 **Darlington**	3N	A	L	0-3	
1929-30	3N	1	30.11.29 **Lancaster T**	LC	H	W	4-1	Taylor 2, Johnson, Roscoe
		2	14.12.29 **Doncaster R**	3N	A	L	0-1	
1930-31	3N	1	29.11.30 **Carlisle U**	3N	A	L	1-3	Pither
1931-32	3N	1	28.11.31 **York C**	3N	H	W	3-1	Johnson og, Stevens 2
		2	12.12.31 **Hull C**	3N	H	L	0-4	
1932-33	3N	1	26.11.32 **Tranmere R**	3N	A	L	0-3	
1933-34	3N	1	25.11.33 **Mansfield T**	3N	H	D	0-0	
		1r	29.11.33 **Mansfield T**		A	W	4-3	Barley 3, Page
		2	9.12.33 **QPR**	3S	A	D	1-1	Barley
		2r	13.12.33 **QPR**		H	L	0-4	
1934-35	3N	1	24.11.34 **Southport**	3N	A	D	1-1	L.Carr
		1r	28.11.34 **Southport**		H	D	1-1aet	Allen
		1 2r	3.12.34 **Southport** at Goodison Park			W	2-1	Kenyon, Butler
		2	8.12.34 **York C**	3N	A	L	0-1	
1935-36	3N	1	30.11.35 **Workington**	NEL	H	L	1-3	Lawrence
1936-37	3N	1	28.11.36 **Lincoln C**	3N	A	D	1-1	Griffiths
		1r	2.12.36 **Lincoln C**		H	L	2-3	Mustard, Watters
1937-38	3N	1	27.11.37 **Workington**	NEL	H	W	5-0	Montgomery 4, Mustard
		2	11.12.37 **Crewe Alex**	3N	A	–	0-1	
			abandoned after 84 minutes					
		2	15.12.37 **Crewe Alex**		A	D	2-2	Wright, Montgomery
		2r	20.12.37 **Crewe Alex**		H	W	4-1	Ainsworth, Smith, Gilchrist og, Montgomery
		3	8.1.38 **Plymouth A**	D2	H	W	1-0	Mustard
		4	22.1.38 **Tottenham H**	D2	H	D	0-0	
		4r	26.1.38 **Tottenham H**		A	L	2-5	Hitchins og, Bulloch
1938-39	3N	1	26.11.38 **Doncaster R**	3N	A	L	2-4	Stamps, Allmark
1945-46	3N		*did not enter*					
1946-47	3N	1	30.11.46 **Hull C**	3N	A	D	0-0	
		1r	4.12.46 **Hull C**		H	L	1-2aet	Wells
1947-48	3N	1	29.11.47 **Marine**	LC	H	W	4-0	McGeachie, Ainsworth, Hope, Pendergast
		2	13.12.47 **Bristol R**	3S	A	L	0-4	
1948-49	3N	1	27.11.48 **Carlisle U**	3N	H	W	1-0	Lyon
		2	11.12.48 **Bradford C**	3N	A	D	0-0	
		2r	18.12.48 **Bradford C**		H	W	1-0	Lyon
		3	8.1.49 **Sheffield U**	D1	A	L	2-5	Carter, Latham og
1949-50	3N	1	26.11.49 **Doncaster R**	3N	A	L	1-5	Carter
1950-51	3N	1	25.11.50 **Port Vale**	3S	A	L	2-3	Carter 2
1956-57	LC	1	17.11.56 **Stockport Co**	3N	H	D	3-3	Vincent 2, Windle
		1r	20.11.56 **Stockport Co**		A	W	3-2	Burgess, Vincent, Windle
		2	8.12.56 **Derby Co**	3N	A	W	3-1	Lewis, Burgess, Vincent
		3	5.1.57 **Torquay U**	3S	H	W	2-1	Windle 2
		4	26.1.57 **Burnley**	D1	A	L	0-9	

NEW BRIGHTON TOWER

Formed 1897. **First entered FA Cup:** 1897. Member of the Football League: 1898-1901. This club folded in August 1901 and was a separate club from New Brighton FC

1897-98 LL 1 29.1.98 **WBA** D1 A L 0-2
1898-99 D2 3q **Glossop** (A) 2-4
1899-00 D2 P **Birkenhead** (H) 5-0; 1q **Wirral Railways** (H) 7-1; 2q **South Liverpool** (A) 2-3
1900-01 D2 Int **Port Vale** (A) 3-1
1 9.2.01 **Wolverhampton W** D1 A L 1-5 Hulse

NEWCASTLE UNITED

Newcastle United were formed in the summer of 1892 following the merger of Newcastle West End and Newcastle East End whose records are both listed here. **Best FA Cup Performances:** Winners (6 times) 1910, 1924, 1932, 1951, 1952, 1955. Runners-up: 1905, 1906, 1908, 1911, 1974. **Record FA Cup Win:** 9-0 vs Southport, 4th round, 1.2.1932. **Record FA Cup Defeat:** 1-7 vs Aston Villa, 2nd round, 16.2.1895.

Newcastle West End
1886-87 1 30.10.86 **Sunderland** A L 1-2aet Campbell
Match declared void by FA and replayed after protest from West End
1r 13.11.86 **Sunderland** H W 1-0 Angus
2 20.11.86 **Gainsborough Trinity** H L 2-6 Aitken, Dobson
1887-88 1 15.10.87 **Redcar** H W 5-1 Angus 2, Barker, McDonald, Nicholson
2 5.11.87 **Sunderland** A L 1-3aet McColl
1888-89 1q **Bishop Auckland** (H) 7-2; 2q **Sunderland Albion** (H) 3-5 – *match declared void by FA and replayed;*
2qr **Sunderland Albion** (H) 1-2aet
1889-90 NL 1q **Port Clarence** (H) 9-1; 2q **Birtley** (A) 2-1; 3q **South Bank** (H) 5-2; 4q **Stockton** (A) 1-0
1 18.1.90 **Grimsby T** FAll H L 1-2 McColl
1890-91 NL 1q **Elswick Rangers** (A) 5-2; 2q **Southwick** (H) 8-1; 3q **Sunderland Albion** (H) 0-3
1891-92 NL 2q **Newcastle East End** (H) 0-3
Newcastle East End
1887-88 1 15.10.87 **South Bank** A L 2-3aet W.Muir 2
1888-89 1 6.10.88 **Port Clarence** H W 3-1 Raylstone, Muir, White
2 27.10.88 **Stockton** H W 2-1 Hoban, unknown
3 17.11.88 **Sunderland** D1 A L 0-2aet
1889-90 NL 1q **Shankhouse BW** (H) 4-0; 2q **Darlington St Augustine's** (A) 1-2
1890-91 NL 2q **Bishop Auckland** (A) 2-1; 3q **Shankhouse BW** (H) 5-0; 4q **Sunderland Albion** (H) 2-2; 4qr **Sunderland Albion** (H) 0-2
1891-92 NL 1q **Tow Law T** (A) 5-1; 2q **Newcastle West End** (A) 3-0; 3q **Shankhouse BW** (H) 3-2; 4q **Bishop Auckland** (H) 7-0
1 16.1.92 **Nottingham F** FAll A L 1-2 Brown og
As Newcastle United
1892-93 NL 1 21.1.93 **Middlesbrough** NL H L 2-3 Reay, Thompson
1893-94 D2 1 27.1.94 **Sheffield U** D1 H W 2-0 Wallace 2
2 10.2.94 **Bolton W** D1 H L 1-2 Crate
1894-95 D2 1 2.2.95 **Burnley** D1 H W 2-1 Rendell 2
2 16.2.95 **Aston Villa** D1 A L 1-7 Thompson
1895-96 D2 P **Leadgate Exiles** (A) walkover; 1q **W.Hartlepool NER** (A) 8-0; 2q **Middlesbrough** (H) 4-1; 3q **Rendel** (H) 5-0; 4q **Tow Law T** (H) 4-0
1 1.2.96 **Chesterfield** A W 4-0 Wardrope 2, Aitken, Thompson
2 15.2.96 **Bury** D1 H L 1-3 Thompson
1896-97 D2 1 30.1.97 **Aston Villa** D1 A L 0-5
1897-98 D2 3q **Willington Ath** (H) 6-0; 4q **Stockton** (A) 4-1; 5q **Middlesbrough** (A) 2-0
1 29.1.98 **Preston NE** D1 A W 2-1 Peddie 2
2 12.2.98 **Southampton St Marys** SL A L 0-1
1898-99 D1 1 28.1.99 **Glossop** D2 A W 1-0 Peddie
2 11.2.99 **Liverpool** D1 A L 1-3 Peddie
1899-00 D1 1 27.1.00 **Reading** SL H W 2-1 Stevenson, Rogers
2 10.2.00 **Southampton** SL A – 0-0
Abandoned after 50 minutes – bad light
2 17.2.00 **Southampton** A L 1-4 Peddie
1900-01 D1 1 9.2.01 **Middlesbrough** D2 A L 1-3 Aitken
1901-02 D1 1 25.1.02 **W.Arsenal** D2 A W 2-0 Veitch, A.Gardner
2 12.2.02 **Sunderland** D1 H W 1-0 Orr
3 22.2.02 **Sheffield U** D1 H D 1-1 Stewart
3r 27.2.02 **Sheffield U** A L 1-2 McColl
1902-03 D1 1 7.2.03 **Grimsby T** D1 A L 1-2 McColl
1903-04 D1 1 6.2.04 **Bury** D1 A L 1-2 Templeton
1904-05 D1 1 4.2.05 **Plymouth A** SL H D 1-1 Gosnell
1r 8.2.05 **Plymouth A** A D 1-1aet Gosnell
1 2r 13.2.05 **Plymouth A** at Plumstead W 2-0 Orr 2 (1p)
2 18.2.05 **Tottenham H** SL A D 1-1 Howie
2r 22.2.05 **Tottenham H** H W 4-0 Orr 2, Appleyard, Howie
3 4.3.05 **Bolton W** D2 A W 2-0 Appleyard, Howie
SF 25.3.05 **Sheffield W** D1 W 1-0 Howie
played at Hyde Road, Manchester

Season	Div	Rd	Date	Opponent	Code	H/A	Res	Score	Scorers
		F	15.4.05	Aston Villa	D1		L	0-2	
			played at Crystal Palace						
1905-06	D1	1	13.1.06	Grimsby T	D2	H	W	6-0	Orr 2, Gosnell, Appleyard 2, J.Rutherford
		2	3.2.06	Derby Co	D1	A	D	0-0	
		2r	7.2.06	Derby Co		H	W	2-1	Appleyard, J.Rutherford
		3	24.2.06	Blackpool	D2	H	W	5-0	Orr 2, Appleyard, Gardner, Carr
		4	10.3.06	Birmingham	D1	A	D	2-2	Veitch 2 (1p)
		4r	14.3.06	Birmingham		H	W	3-0	Appleyard 2, Howie
		SF	31.3.06	W.Arsenal	D1		W	2-0	Veitch, Howie
			played at Victoria Ground, Stoke						
		F	21.4.06	Everton	D1		L	0-1	
			played at Crystal Palace						
1906-07	D1	1	12.1.07	Crystal P	SL	H	L	0-1	
1907-08	D1	1	11.1.08	Nottingham F	D1	H	W	2-0	Appleyard, Rutherford
		2	1.2.08	West Ham U	SL	H	W	2-0	Appleyard 2
		3	22.2.08	Liverpool	D1	H	W	3-1	Speedie, Appleyard, Rutherford
		4	7.3.08	Grimsby T	D2	H	W	5-1	Appleyard 3, Gardner, Vincett og
		SF	28.3.08	Fulham	D2		W	6-0	Appleyard, Gardner, Howie 2, Rutherford 2
			played at Anfield						
		F	25.4.08	Wolverhampton W	D2		L	1-3	Howie
			played at Crystal Palace						
1908-09	D1	1	16.1.09	Clapton O	D2	H	W	5-0	Anderson, Shepherd, Wilson 3
		2	6.2.09	Blackpool	D2	H	W	2-1	Howie, Rutherford
		3	20.2.09	West Ham	SL	A	D	0-0	
		3r	24.2.09	West Ham		H	W	2-1	Anderson, Shepherd (p)
		4	6.3.09	Sunderland	D1	H	D	2-2	Rutherford, Wilson
		4r	10.3.09	Sunderland		A	W	3-0	Shepherd 2, Wilson
		SF	27.3.09	Manchester U	D1		L	0-1	
			played at Bramall Lane						
1909-10	D1	1	15.1.10	Stoke	BDL	A	D	1-1	Howie
		1r	19.1.10	Stoke		H	W	2-1	Higgins, Howie
		2	5.2.10	Fulham	D2	H	W	4-0	Higgins 2, Rutherford, McCracken (p)
		3	19.2.10	Blackburn R	D1	H	W	3-1	Higgins, Howie, Rutherford
		4	5.3.10	Leicester F	D2	H	W	3-0	Wilson, Shepherd, Howie
		SF	26.3.10	Swindon T	SL		W	2-0	Stewart, Rutherford
			played at White Hart Lane						
		F	23.4.10	BARNSLEY	D2		D	1-1	Rutherford
			played at Crystal Palace						
		F	28.4.10	BARNSLEY			W	2-0	Shepherd 2 (1p)
			played at Goodison Park						
1910-11	D1	1	14.1.11	Bury	D1	H	W	6-1	Shepherd 3, Stewart, Duncan, McWilliam
		2	4.2.11	Northampton T	SL	H	D	1-1	Higgins
		2r	8.2.11	Northampton T		H	W	1-0	Shepherd (p)
		3	25.2.11	Hull C	D2	H	W	3-2	Shepherd 2, Veitch
		4	13.3.11	Derby Co	D2	H	W	4-0	Shepherd, Stewart, Rutherford, Willis
		SF	25.3.11	Chelsea	D2		W	3-0	Wilson, Shepherd, Stewart
			played at St Andrews						
		F	22.4.11	Bradford C	D1		D	0-0	
			played at Crystal Palace						
		F	26.4.11	Bradford C			L	0-1	
			played at Old Trafford						
1911-12	D1	1	13.1.12	Derby Co	D2	A	L	0-3	
1912-13	D1	1	11.1.13	Bradford C	D1	H	A	1-0	G.Wilson
			Abandoned 45 minutes – gale						
		1	16.1.13	Bradford C		H	W	1-0	G.Wilson
		2	1.2.13	Hull C	D2	A	D	0-0	
		2r	5.2.13	Hull C		H	W	3-0	Hibbert, Rutherford, Hudspeth (p)
		3	22.2.13	Liverpool	D1	A	D	1-1	Shepherd
		3r	26.2.13	Liverpool		H	W	1-0	Hudspeth (p)
		4	8.3.13	Sunderland	D1	A	D	0-0	
		4r	12.3.13	Sunderland		H	D	2-2aet	McTavish, Veitch
		4 2r	17.3.13	Sunderland		H	L	0-3	
1913-14	D1	1	10.1.14	Sheffield U	D1	H	L	0-5	
1914-15	D1	1	9.1.15	West Ham U	SL	A	D	2-2	Goodwill 2
		1r	16.1.15	West Ham U		H	W	3-2	Pailor 2, Hibbert
		2	30.1.15	Swansea T	SL	H	D	1-1	McCracken (p)
		2r	6.2.15	Swansea T		A	W	2-0	King, Pailor

Season	Div	Round	Date	Opponent		Venue	Result	Score	Scorers
		3	20.2.15	Sheffield W	D1	A	W	2-1	King, Hibbert
		4	6.3.15	Chelsea	D1	A	D	1-1aet	Goodwill
		4r	13.3.15	Chelsea		H	L	0-1aet	
1919-20	D1	1	10.1.20	Crystal P	SL	H	W	2-0	Dixon, Hall
		2	31.1.20	Huddersfield T	D2	H	L	0-1	
1920-21	D1	1	8.1.21	Nottingham F	D2	H	D	1-1	Harris
		1r	12.1.21	Nottingham F		H	W	2-0	Seymour, Harris
		2	29.1.21	Liverpool	D1	H	W	1-0	Harris
		3	19.2.21	Everton	D1	A	L	0-3	
1921-22	D1	1	7.1.22	Newport Co	3S	H	W	6-0	McDonald 2, Harris, Dixon 2, Mooney
		2	28.1.22	Preston NE	D1	A	L	1-3	Seymour
1922-23	D1	1	13.1.23	Southampton	D2	H	D	0-0	
		1r	17.1.23	Southampton		A	L	1-3	Harris
1923-24	D1	1	12.1.24	Portsmouth	3S	A	W	4-2	Seymour, Harris, J.Low, Gibson
		2	2.2.24	Derby Co	D2	A	D	2-2	McDonald 2
		2r	6.2.24	Derby Co		H	D	2-2aet	Harris, Cowan
		2 2r	11.2.24	Derby Co at Bolton			D	2-2aet	Seymour, Hudspeth (p)
		2 3r	13.2.24	Derby Co		H	W	5-3	Seymour, Harris 3, Cowan
		3	23.2.24	Watford	3S	A	W	1-0	Seymour
		4	8.3.24	Liverpool	D1	H	W	1-0	McDonald
		SF	29.3.24	Manchester C	D1		W	2-0	Harris 2
				played at St Andrews					
		F	27.4.24	ASTON VILLA	D1	WEMBLEY	W	2-0	Seymour, Harris
1924-25	D1	1	10.1.25	Hartlepools U	3N	H	W	4-1	Cowan, Harris, McDonald, McKenzie
		2	31.1.25	Leicester C	D2	H	D	2-2	McDonald (p), Cowan
		2r	5.2.25	Leicester C		A	L	0-1	
1925-26	D1	3	9.1.26	Aberdare A	3S	H	W	4-1	Cowan, Gallacher 2, Gibson
		4	30.1.26	Cardiff C	D1	A	W	2-0	Seymour 2
		5	20.2.26	Clapton O	D2	A	L	0-2	
1926-27	D1	3	8.1.27	Notts Co	D2	H	W	8-1	Gallacher 3, McDonald 3, Seymour, Urwin
		4	29.1.27	Corinthians		A	W	3-1	McDonald 2, McKay
		5	19.2.27	Southampton	D2	A	L	1-2	McDonald (p)
1927-28	D1	3	14.1.28	Blackburn R	D1	A	L	1-4	Seymour
1928-29	D1	3	12.1.29	Swindon T	3S	A	L	0-2	
1929-30	D1	3	11.1.30	York C	3N	H	D	1-1	Gallacher
		3r	15.1.30	York C		A	W	2-1	Gallacher, Hutchinson
		4	25.1.30	Clapton O	3S	H	W	3-1	J.R. Richardson 3
		5	15.2.30	Brighton & HA	3S	H	W	3-0	Gallacher 3
		6	1.3.30	Hull C	D2	H	D	1-1	Lang
		6r	5.3.30	Hull C		A	L	0-1	
1930-31	D1	3	10.1.31	Nottingham F	D2	H	W	4-0	Bedford, Hutchinson 3
		4	24.1.31	Leeds U	D1	A	L	1-4	Hutchinson (p)
1931-32	D1	3	9.1.32	Blackpool	D1	A	D	1-1	Lang
		3r	13.1.32	Blackpool		H	W	1-0	Boyd
		4	23.1.32	Southport	3N	H	D	1-1	Boyd
		4r	26.1.32	Southport		A	D	1-1aet	Boyd
		4 2r	1.2.32	Southport at Hillsborough			W	9-0	Lang, McMenemy, Cape 2, Weaver, Boyd, JR Richardson 3
		5	13.2.32	Leicester C	D1	H	W	3-1	Weaver, Lang, Allen
		6	27.2.32	Watford	3S	H	W	5-0	Allen 3, Boyd, J.R.Richardson
		SF	12.3.32	Chelsea	D1		W	2-1	Allen, Lang
				played at Huddersfield					
		F	23.4.32	ARSENAL	D1	WEMBLEY	W	2-1	Allen 2
1932-33	D1	3	14.1.33	Leeds U	D1	H	L	0-3	
1933-34	D1	3	13.1.34	Wolerhampton W	D1	A	L	0-1	
1934-35	D2	3	12.1.35	Hull C	D2	A	W	5-1	Quantick og, Bott 2, Pearson, Cairns
		4	26.1.35	Tottenham H	D1	A	L	0-2	
1935-36	D2	3	11.1.36	Walsall	3N	A	W	2-0	Connelly, J.Smith
		4	25.1.36	Sheffield W	D1	A	D	1-1	Pearson
		4r	29.1.36	Sheffield W		H	W	3-1	Bott 2, J.Smith
		5	15.2.36	Arsenal	D1	H	D	3-3	Pearson, J.Smith 2
		5r	19.2.36	Arsenal		A	L	0-3	
1936-37	D2	3	16.1.37	Preston NE	D1	A	L	0-2	
1937-38	D2	3	8.1.38	WBA	D1	A	L	0-1	
1938-39	D2	3	7.1.39	Brentford	D1	A	W	2-0	Clifton, Mooney
		4	21.1.39	Cardiff C	3S	A	D	0-0	
		4r	25.1.39	Cardiff C		H	W	4-1	Clifton, Gordon, Mooney, Park

Season	Div	Round	Date	Opponent	Opp Div	H/A	Res	Score	Scorers
		5	11.2.39	Preston NE	D1	H	L	1-2	Cairns
1945-46	D2	3 1L	5.1.46	Barnsley	D2	H	W	4-2	Milburn 2, Hair, Stubbins
		3 2L	9.1.46	Barnsley		A	L	0-3	
1946-47	D2	3	11.1.47	Crystal P	3S	H	W	6-2	Bentley, Pearson, Shackleton 2, Stobbart, Wayman
		4	25.1.47	Southampton	D2	H	W	3-1	Wayman 3
		5	8.2.47	Leicester C	D2	H	D	1-1	Shackleton
		5r	20.2.47	Leicester C		A	W	2-1	Bentley, Pearson
		6	1.3.47	Sheffield U	D1	A	W	2-0	Bentley (p), Milburn
		SF	29.3.47	Charlton A	D1		L	0-4	
			played at Elland Road						
1947-48	D2	3	10.1.48	Charlton A	D1	A	L	1-2	Pearson
1948-49	D1	3	8.1.49	Bradford PA	D2	H	L	0-2	
1949-50	D1	3	7.1.50	Oldham A	3N	A	W	7-2	Milburn 3, Mitchell, Walker 2, Houghton
		4	28.1.50	Chelsea	D1	A	L	0-3	
1950-51	D1	3	6.1.51	Bury	D2	H	W	4-1	Milburn, G.Robledo, Taylor, Walker
		4	27.1.51	Bolton W	D1	H	W	3-2	Milburn 2, Mitchell
		5	10.2.51	Stoke C	D1	A	W	4-2	Milburn, Mitchell, G.Robledo 2
		6	24.2.51	Bristol R	3S	H	D	0-0	
		6r	28.2.51	Bristol R		A	W	3-1	Crowe, Milburn, Taylor
		SF	10.3.51	Wolverhampton W	D1		D	0-0aet	
			played at Hillsborough						
		SFr	14.3.51	Wolverhampton W			W	2-1	Milburn, Mitchell
			played at Huddersfield						
		F	28.4.51	BLACKPOOL	D1	WEMBLEY	W	2-0	Milburn 2
1951-52	D1	3	12.1.52	Aston Villa	D1	H	W	4-2	Foulkes, Mitchell 2, G.Robledo
		4	2.2.52	Tottenham H	D1	A	W	3-0	Mitchell, G.Robledo 2
		5	23.2.52	Swansea T	D2	A	W	1-0	Mitchell
		6	8.3.52	Portsmouth	D1	A	W	4-2	Milburn 3, G.Robledo
		SF	29.3.52	Blackburn R	D2		D	0-0aet	
			played at Hillsborough						
		SFr	2.4.52	Blackburn R at Elland Road			W	2-1	Mitchell (p), G.Robledo
		F	3.5.52	ARSENAL	D1	WEMBLEY	W	1-0	G.Robledo
1952-53	D1	3	10.1.53	Swansea T	D2	H	–	0-0	
			abandoned after 8 minutes						
			14.1.53	Swansea T		H	W	3-0	Davies, Keeble, Mitchell
		4	31.1.53	Rotherham U	D2	H	L	1-3	Keeble
1953-54	D1	3	9.1.54	Wigan A	NPL	H	D	2-2	Broadis, Milburn
		3r	13.1.54	Wigan A		A	W	3-2	Broadis, Keeble, White
		4	30.1.54	Burnley	D1	A	D	1-1	Broadis
		4r	3.2.54	Burnley		H	W	1-0	Mitchell (p)
		5	20.2.54	WBA	D1	A	L	2-3	Milburn, Mitchell
1954-55	D1	3	8.1.55	Plymouth A	D2	A	W	1-0	Keeble
		4	29.1.55	Brentford	3S	H	W	3-2	Curry, Hannah, R.Mitchell
		5	19.2.55	Nottingham F	D2	A	D	1-1	Milburn
		5r	28.2.55	Nottingham F		H	D	2-2aet	Keeble, R.Mitchell
		5 2r	2.3.55	Nottingham F		H	W	2-1aet	Monkhouse 2
		6	12.3.55	Huddersfield T	D1	A	D	1-1	White
		6r	16.3.55	Huddersfield T		H	W	2-0aet	Keeble, R.Mitchell
		SF	26.3.55	York C	3N		D	1-1	Keeble
			played at Hillsborough						
		SFr	30.3.55	York C at Roker Park			W	2-0	Keeble, White
		F	7.5.55	MANCHESTER C	D1	WEMBLEY	W	3-1	Milburn, Mitchell, Hannah
1955-56	D1	3	7.1.56	Sheffield W	D2	A	W	3-1	Curry, Keeble, Milburn
		4	28.1.56	Fulham	D2	A	W	5-4	Casey, Keeble 2, Milburn, Stokoe
		5	18.2.56	Stoke C	D2	H	W	2-1	Curry, Mitchell
		6	3.3.56	Sunderland	D1	H	L	0-2	
1956-57	D1	3	5.1.57	Manchester C	D1	H	D	1-1	White
		3r	9.1.57	Manchester C		A	W	5-4	Curry, Tait, White 2, Casey (p)
		4	26.1.57	Millwall	3S	A	L	1-2	Tait
1957-58	D1	3	4.1.58	Plymouth A	3S	H	W	6-1	Eastham 2, R.Mitchell, White 3
		4	25.1.58	Scunthorpe U	3N	H	L	1-3	Paterson
1958-59	D1	3	19.1.59	Chelsea	D1	H	L	1-4	Eastham
1959-60	D1	3	9.1.60	Wolverhampton W	D1	H	D	2-2	Allchurch, Eastham
		3r	13.1.60	Wolverhampton W		A	L	2-4	Eastham, White
1960-61	D1	3	7.1.61	Fulham	D1	H	W	5-0	Allchurch, Neale 3, Woods
		4	1.2.61	Stockport Co	D4	H	W	4-0	Allchurch, White, Woods 2
		5	18.2.61	Stoke C	D2	H	W	3-1	Scanlon, Allchurch, McKinney (p)

Season	Div	Round	Date	Opponent	Opp Div	H/A	Result	Score	Scorers
		6	4.3.61	Sheffield U	D2	H	L	1-3	McGuigan
1961-62	D2	3	6.1.62	Peterborough U	D3	H	L	0-1	
1962-63	D2	3	7.3.63	Bradford C	D4	A	W	6-1	McGarry 2, Thomas, Hilley, Hughes 2
		4	13.3.63	Norwich C	D2	A	L	0-5	
1963-64	D2	3	4.1.64	Bedford T	SL	H	L	1-2	Anderson
1964-65	D2	3	9.1.65	Swansea T	D2	A	L	0-1	
1965-66	D1	3	22.1.66	Chester	D4	A	W	3-1	Robson, McGarry, Craig
		4	12.2.66	Sheffield W	D1	H	L	1-2	Suddick
1966-67	D1	3	28.1.67	Coventry C	D2	A	W	4-3	Davies 3, B.Robson
		4	18.2.67	Nottingham F	D1	A	L	0-3	
1967-68	D1	3	27.1.68	Carlisle U	D2	H	L	0-1	
1968-69	D1	3	4.1.69	Reading	D3	H	W	4-0	Craig, Dyson, B.Robson, Scott
		4	25.1.69	Manchester C	D1	H	D	0-0	
		4r	29.1.69	Manchester C		A	L	0-2	
1969-70	D1	3	3.1.70	Southampton	D1	A	L	0-3	
1970-71	D1	3	11.1.71	Ipswich T	D1	H	D	1-1	Mitchell
		3r	13.1.71	Ipswich T		A	L	1-2	Robson
1971-72	D1	3	24.1.72	Hereford U	SL	H	D	2-2	Tudor, Macdonald
		3r	5.2.72	Hereford U		A	L	1-2	Macdonald
1972-73	D1	3	13.1.73	Bournemouth	D3	H	W	2-0	Macdonald, Cave og
		4	3.2.73	Luton T	D2	H	L	0-2	
1973-74	D1	3	5.1.74	Hendon	IL	H	D	1-1	Howard
		3r	9.1.74	Hendon at Watford		A	W	4-0	Hibbitt, Tudor, Macdonald, McDermott (p)
		4	26.1.74	Scunthorpe U	D4	H	D	1-1	McDermott
		4r	30.1.74	Scunthorpe U		A	W	3-0	Macdonald 2, Barrowclough
		5	16.2.74	WBA	D2	A	W	3-0	Tudor, Macdonald, Barrowclough
		6	9.3.74	Nottingham F	D2	H	W	4-3	Tudor, Moncur, McDermott (p), DJ Craig

FA ordered replay after pitch invasion when Forest were leading 3-1

Season	Div	Round	Date	Opponent	Opp Div	H/A	Result	Score	Scorers
		6r	18.3.74	Nottingham F at Goodison Park			D	0-0	
		6 2r	21.3.74	Nottingham F at Goodison Park			W	1-0	Macdonald
		SF	30.3.74	Burnley	D1		W	2-0	Macdonald 2

played at Hillsborough

Season	Div	Round	Date	Opponent	Opp Div	H/A	Result	Score	Scorers
		F	4.5.74	Liverpool	D1 WEMBLEY		L	0-3	
1974-75	D1	3	3.1.75	Manchester C	D1	A	W	2-0	Nulty, Burns
		4	25.1.75	Walsall	D3	A	L	0-1	
1975-76	D1	3	3.1.76	QPR	D1	A	D	0-0	
		3r	7.1.76	QPR		H	W	2-1	T.Craig (p), Gowling
		4	24.1.76	Coventry C	D1	A	D	1-1	Gowling
		4r	28.1.76	Coventry C		H	W	5-0	Gowling, Macdonald 2, Cassidy, Burns
		5	14.2.76	Bolton W	D2	A	D	3-3	Gowling, Macdonald 2
		5r	18.2.76	Bolton W		H	D	0-0aet	
		5 2r	23.2.76	Bolton W at Elland Road			W	2-1	Gowling, Burns
		6	6.3.76	Derby Co	D1	A	L	2-4	Gowling 2
1976-77	D1	3	8.1.77	Sheffield U	D2	A	D	0-0	
		3r	24.1.77	Sheffield U		H	W	3-1	T.Craig, Burns, McCaffery
		4	29.1.77	Manchester C	D1	H	L	1-3	Gowling
1977-78	D1	3	7.1.78	Peterborough U	D3	A	D	1-1	Hudson
		3r	11.1.78	Peterborough U		H	W	2-0	T.Craig (p), Blackhall
		4	28.1.78	Wrexham	D3	H	D	2-2	Bird, Blackhall
		4r	6.2.78	Wrexham		A	L	1-4	Burns
1978-79	D2	3	16.1.79	Torquay U	D4	H	W	3-1	Robinson, Withe, Nattrass (p)
		4	27.1.79	Wolverhampton W	D1	H	D	1-1	Withe
		4r	22.2.79	Wolverhampton W		A	L	0-1	
1979-80	D2	3	5.1.80	Chester	D3	H	L	0-2	
1980-81	D2	3	3.1.81	Sheffield W	D2	H	W	2-1	Waddle 2
		4	24.1.81	Luton T	D2	H	W	2-1	Clarke, Martin
		5	14.2.81	Exeter C	D3	H	D	1-1	Shoulder
		5r	18.2.81	Exeter C		A	L	0-4	
1981-82	D2	3	4.1.82	Colchester U	D4	H	D	1-1	Varadi
		3r	18.1.82	Colchester U		A	W	4-3aet	Waddle, Varadi, Saunders, Brownlie
		4	23.1.82	Grimsby T	D2	H	L	1-2	K.Moore og
1982-83	D2	3	8.1.83	Brighton & HA	D1	A	D	1-1	McDermott
		3r	12.1.83	Brighton & HA		H	L	0-1	
1983-84	D2	3	6.1.84	Liverpool	D1	A	L	0-4	
1984-85	D1	3	6.1.85	Nottingham F	D1	A	D	1-1	Megson
		3r	9.1.85	Nottingham F		H	L	1-3	Waddle
1985-86	D1	3	4.1.86	Brighton & HA	D2	H	L	0-2	

1986-87	D1	3	21.1.87	Northampton T	D4	H	W	2-1	A.Thomas, Goddard
		4	31.1.87	Preston NE	D4	H	W	2-0	Roeder, Goddard
		5	21.2.87	Tottenham H	D1	A	L	0-1	
1987-88	D1	3	9.1.88	Crystal P	D2	H	W	1-0	Gascoigne
		4	30.1.88	Swindon T	D2	H	W	5-0	D.Jackson, Goddard, Gascoigne 2 (1p), O'Neill
		5	20.2.88	Wimbledon	D1	H	L	1-3	McDonald
1988-89	D1	3	7.1.89	Watford	D2	H	D	0-0	
		3r	10.1.89	Watford		A	D	2-2aet	Brock, Mirandinha (p)
		3 2r	16.1.89	Watford		H	D	0-0aet	
		3 3r	18.1.89	Watford		A	L	0-1aet	
1989-90	D2	3	6.1.90	Hull C	D2	A	W	1-0	O'Brien
		4	27.1.90	Reading	D3	A	D	3-3	McGhee 2, Quinn
		4r	31.1.90	Reading		H	W	4-1	McGhee 2, Quinn, Robinson
		5	18.1.90	Manchester U	D1	H	L	2-3	McGhee (p), Scott
1990-91	D2	3	5.1.91	Derby Co	D1	H	W	2-0	Quinn, Stimson
		4	13.2.91	Nottingham F	D1	H	D	2-2	Quinn, McGhee
		4r	18.2.91	Nottingham F		A	L	0-3	
1991-92	D2	3	4.1.92	Bournemouth	D3	A	D	0-0	
		3r	14.1.92	Bournemouth		H	A	0-0	
			Abandoned 17 minutes – fog						
		3r	22.1.92	Bournemouth		H	D	2-2aet	Peacock, Hunt
			Bournemouth won 4-3 on penalties						
1992-93	D1	3	2.1.93	Port Vale	D2	H	W	4-0	Peacock 2, Lee, Sheedy
		4	23.1.93	Rotherham U	D2	A	D	1-1	Lee
		4r	3.2.93	Rotherham U		H	W	2-0	Kelly, Clark
		5	13.2.93	Blackburn R	PL	A	L	0-1	

NEW CRUSADERS

Formed 1905. **First entered FA Cup:** 1905. Six Farnfield brothers played in the match against Plymouth. Based at Sidcup, Kent

1905-06		1	13.1.06	Plymouth Argyle	SL	H	L	3-6	G.Farnfield, H.Farnfield, B.Farnfield

NEWPORT COUNTY

Formed 1912. Members of the Football League 1921-1988. **Best FA Cup Performance:** 5th round, 1949. Newport County were wound up on February 27, 1989 with debts of £126,000, and were expelled from the GM Vauxhall Conference for failing to fulfil their fixtures. The club were later re-formed as Newport AFC at junior level. **Welsh FA Cup winners:** 1980

1919-20	SL	1	10.1.20	Leicester C	D2	H	D	0-0	
		1r	15.1.20	Leicester C		A	L	0-2	
1920-21	D3	4q Merthr Tydfil (H) 0-0; 4qr Merthyr Tydfil (H) 0-4							
1921-22	3S	5q **Bath C** (H) 2-0; 6q **Wrexham** (A) 0-0; 6qr **Wrexham** (H) 3-0							
		1	7.1.22	Newcastle U	D1	A	L	0-6	
1922-23	3S	5q **Aberdare A** (A) 1-1; 5qr **Aberdare A** (H) 1-1aet; 5q 2r **Aberdare A** (Ninian Park) 1-2							
1923-24	3S	4q **Exeter C** (H) 0-2							
1924-25	3S	4q **Aberdare A** (A) 0-0; 4qr **Aberdare A** (H) 3-0; 5q **Exeter C** (A) 1-1; 5qr **Exeter C** (H) 3-3aet; 5q 2r **Exeter C** (Ashton Gate) 0-1							
1925-26	3S	1	28.11.25	Weymouth	SL	A	W	1-0	Taylor
		2	12.12.25	Northampton T	3S	A	L	1-3	Drinnan
1926-27	3S	1	27.11.26	Poole T	SL	A	L	0-1	
1927-28	3S	1	26.11.27	Swindon T	3S	H	L	0-1	
1928-29	3S	1	24.11.28	Woking	IL	H	W	7-0	Young 3, Pugh 2, Reid, Gittens
		2	8.12.28	Norwich C	3S	A	L	0-6	
1929-30	3S	1	30.11.29	Kettering T	SL	H	W	3-2	Morris, Thomas, Martin
		2	14.12.29	Walsall	3S	H	L	2-3	Martin, Morris
1930-31	3S	1	29.11.30	Dulwich H	IL	A	D	2-2	Pearce 2
		1r	4.12.30	Dulwich H		H	W	4-1	Pearce, Brown, Davies, Bagley
		2	13.12.30	Walsall	3S	A	L	0-4	
1931-32	SL		*did not enter*						
1932-33	3S	1	26.11.32	Ilford	IL	H	W	4-2	Reed, Weale, Green 2
		2	10.12.32	Folkestone	SL	A	L	1-2	Weale
1933-34	3S	1	25.11.33	Dulwich H	IL	A	D	2-2	Burgess, Higgins
		1r	30.11.33	Dulwich H		H	W	6-2	Burgess 2, Taylor 2, Reynolds, Thomas
		2	9.12.33	Workington	NEL	A	L	1-3	Higgins
1934-35	3S	1	24.11.34	Swindon T	3S	A	L	0-4	
1935-36	3S	1	30.11.35	Southend U	3S	H	L	0-1	
1936-37	3S	1	28.11.36	Bristol C	3S	H	W	3-0	Duggan, Sullivan, Chadwick

Season	Div	Rd	Date	Opponent	Lge	H/A	Res	Score	Scorers
		2	12.12.36	Reading	3S	A	L	2-7	Duggan 2
1937-38	3S	1	27.11.37	Kidderminster H	BDL	A	D	2-2	Webb, Derrick
		1r	2.12.37	Kidderminster H		H	W	4-1	Brinton 3, Duggan
		2	11.12.37	Bournemouth	3S	H	W	2-1	Duggan, Derrick
		3	8.1.38	Bradford PA	D2	A	L	4-7	Duggan, Derrick, W.Owen, Hickman
1938-39	3S	1	26.11.38	Reading	3S	A	D	3-3	Hydes 2, Derrick
		1r	5.12.38	Reading		H	W	3-1	Wood 2, Hydes
		2	10.12.38	Horden Colliery W	NEL	A	W	3-2	Wood 2, Hickman
		3	7.1.39	Walsall	3S	H	L	0-2	
1945-46	D2	1 1L	17.11.45	Torquay U	3S	A	W	1-0	Derrick
		1 2L	24.11.45	Torquay U		H	D	1-1	Derrick
		2 1L	8.12.45	Exeter C	3S	H	W	5-1	Wookey, Derrick 2, Brinton, Carr
		2 2L	15.12.45	Exeter C		A	W	3-1	Hydes 2, Wilkins
		3 1L	5.1.46	Southampton	D2	A	L	3-4	Granville, Derrick, Wookey
		3 2L	10.1.46	Southampton		H	L	1-2	Owen
1946-47	D2	3	11.1.47	Coventry C	D2	A	L	2-5	Batty, Haywood
1947-48	3S	1	29.11.47	Southend U	3S	H	W	3-2	Roffi, Allen, Lewis
		2	13.12.47	Reading	3S	A	L	0-3	
1948-49	3S	1	27.11.48	Brighton & HA	3S	H	W	3-1	Parker, Comley 2
		2	11.12.48	Leytonstone	IL	A	W	4-3aet	Harper, Carr 2, Comley
		3	8.1.49	Leeds U	D2	A	W	3-1	Roffi, Carr, Comley
		4	29.1.49	Huddersfield T	D1	H	D	3-3aet	Comley, Williams, Carr
		4r	5.2.49	Huddersfield T		A	W	3-1	Carr 2, Parker
		5	12.2.49	Portsmouth	D1	A	L	2-3aet	Harper, Carr
1949-50	3S	1	26.11.49	Crystal P	3S	A	W	3-0	Comley, Payne, Griffiths
		2	10.12.49	Gateshead	3N	H	D	1-1	Harper
		2r	14.12.49	Gateshead		A	W	2-1aet	Parker, Harper
		3	7.1.50	Port Vale	3S	H	L	1-2	Comley
1950-51	3S	1	25.11.50	Walsall	3S	H	W	4-2	Parker 2, Shergold, Haywood
		2	9.12.50	Hereford U	SL	A	W	3-0	Shergold, Moore 2
		3	6.1.51	Reading	3S	H	W	3-2	Shergold, Birch, Parker
		4	27.1.51	Norwich C	3S	H	L	0-2	
1951-52	3S	1	24.11.51	Barry T	SL	H	W	4-0	Moore 3, Beattie
		2	15.12.51	Leytonstone	IL	A	D	2-2	Birch, Beattie
		2r	20.12.51	Leytonstone		H	W	3-0	Moore 2, Beattie
		3	12.1.52	Sheffield U	D2	A	L	0-2	
1952-53	3S	1	22.11.52	Walsall	3S	H	W	2-1	Moore, Beattie
		2	6.12.52	Gainsborough T	ML	H	W	2-1	Beattie, Parker
		3	10.1.53	Sheffield U	D2	H	L	1-4	Moore
1953-54	3S	1	21.11.53	Cambridge U	ECL	A	D	2-2	Thomas, Birch
		1r	26.11.53	Cambridge U		H	L	1-2	Parker
1954-55	3S	1	20.11.54	Gillingham	3S	A	L	0-2	
1955-56	3S	1	19.11.55	Brighton & HA	3S	A	L	1-8	Johnstone
1956-57	3S	1	17.11.56	Walsall	3S	A	W	1-0	Terry
		2	8.12.56	Gillingham	3S	A	W	2-1	Terry, Brown
		3	5.1.57	Southampton	3S	H	D	3-3	Hudson, Harris 2
		3r	9.1.57	Southampton		A	W	1-0	Harris
		4	26.1.57	Arsenal	D1	H	L	0-2	
1957-58	3S	1	16.11.57	Northampton T	3S	A	L	0-3	
1958-59	D3	1	15.11.58	Wisbech T	SL	A	D	2-2	Graham, McPherson
		1r	17.11.58	Wisbech T		H	W	4-1aet	McPherson, McSeveney 2, Graham
		2	6.12.58	Hereford U	SL	A	W	2-0	Graham, McPherson
		3	10.1.59	Torquay U	D4	H	D	0-0	
		3r	14.1.59	Torquay U		A	W	1-0	McPherson
		4	24.1.59	Tottenham H	D1	A	L	1-4	Hollyman
1959-60	D3	1	14.11.59	Hereford U	SL	H	W	4-2	Meyer, McPherson, McSeveney, Dixon
		2	5.12.59	Salisbury	WL	A	W	1-0	Meyer
		3	9.1.60	Tottenham H	D1	H	L	0-4	
1960-61	D3	1	5.11.60	Shrewsbury T	D3	A	L	1-4	McSeveney
1961-62	D3	1	4.11.61	Reading	D3	A	D	1-1	W.Herritty
		1r	6.11.61	Reading		H	W	1-0	W.Herritty
		2	25.11.61	Weymouth	SL	A	L	0-1	
1962-63	D4	1	3.11.62	QPR	D3	A	L	2-3	W.Herritty, Bonson
1963-64	D4	1	16.11.63	Hereford U	SL	A	D	1-1	Hunt
		1r	18.11.63	Hereford U		H	W	4-0	Hunt 3, Webster
		2	7.12.63	Watford	D3	H	W	2-0	Smith 2
		3	4.1.64	Sheffield W	D1	H	W	3-2	Bonson 2, Hunt

Season	Div	Round	Date	Opponent		H/A	Res	Score	Scorers
		4	25.1.64	Burnley	D1	A	L	1-2	Sheffield
1964-65	D4	1	14.11.64	Spalding U	ML	H	W	5-3	Frowen, Morgan, Swindells 2, Reece
		2	5.12.64	Mansfield T	D3	H	W	3-0	Sheffield 2 (1p), Smith
		3	9.1.65	Reading	D3	A	D	2-2	Swindells, Reece
		3r	11.1.65	Reading		H	L	0-1	
1965-66	D4	1	13.11.65	Bath C	SL	A	L	0-2	
1966-67	D4	1	26.11.66	Brighton & HA	D3	H	L	1-2	Thomas
1967-68	D4	1	18.12.67	Gillingham	D3	H	W	3-0	A.Williams, Hill, King (p)
		2	6.1.68	Guildford C	SL	A	W	1-0	Buck
		3	27.1.68	Southampton	D1	A	D	1-1	King (p)
		3r	30.1.68	Southampton		H	L	2-3	A.Williams, Hill
1968-69	D4	1	16.11.68	Exeter C	D4	A	D	0-0	
		1r	18.11.68	Exeter C		H	L	1-3	Buck
1969-70	D4	1	15.11.69	Colchester U	D4	H	W	2-1	White, Thomas
		2	6.12.69	Hereford U	SL	H	W	2-1	Thomas, Wood
		3	3.1.70	Gillingham	D3	A	L	0-1	
1970-71	D4	1	21.11.70	Barnet	SL	A	L	1-6	Jones
1971-72	D4	1	20.11.71	Notts Co	D3	A	L	0-6	
1972-73	D4	1	18.11.72	Alton	Hants	H	W	5-1	Harris 2, White, Brown, R.Jones (p)
		2	9.12.72	Torquay U	D4	A	W	1-0	Brown
		3	13.1.73	Millwall	D2	A	L	0-3	
1973-74	D4	1	24.11.73	Wycombe W	IL	A	L	1-3	Hooper
1974-75	D4	1	23.11.74	Exeter C	D4	A	W	2-1	White, Giles og
		2	14.12.74	Walsall	D3	H	L	1-3	Jones
1975-76	D4	1	22.11.75	Swindon T	D3	H	D	2-2	Godfrey, Parsons
		1r	25.11.75	Swindon T		A	L	0-3	
1976-77	D4	1	20.11.76	Bournemouth	D4	A	D	0-0	
		1r	23.11.76	Bournemouth		H	W	3-0	Parsons 2, Woods
		2	11.12.76	Southend U	D4	A	L	0-3	
1977-78	D4	1	26.11.77	Exeter C	D3	H	D	1-1	Goddard
		1r	30.11.77	Exeter C		A	L	2-4	Clark, Goddard
1978-79	D4	1	25.11.78	Hereford U	D4	A	W	1-0	Goddard (p)
		2	16.12.78	Worcester C	SL	H	D	0-0	
		2r	18.12.78	Worcester C		A	W	2-1	Pemberton og, Goddard
		3	9.1.79	West Ham	D2	H	W	2-1	Goddard, Woods
		4	30.1.79	Colchester U	D3	H	D	0-0	
		4r	5.2.79	Colchester U		A	L	0-1	
1979-80	D4	1	24.11.79	Portsmouth	D4	A	L	0-1	
1980-81	D3	1	22.11.80	Plymouth A	D3	A	L	0-2	
1981-82	D3	1	21.11.81	Colchester U	D4	A	L	0-2	
1982-83	D3	1	20.11.82	Enfield	APL	A	D	0-0	
		1r	23.11.82	Enfield		H	W	4-2	Tynan 3 (1p), Aldridge
		2	11.12.82	Orient	D3	H	W	1-0	Tynan (p)
		3	8.1.83	Everton	D1	H	D	1-1	Gwyther
		3r	11.1.83	Everton		A	L	1-2	Aldridge
1983-84	D3	1	20.11.83	Poole T	SL	A	D	0-0	
		1r	22.11.83	Poole T		H	W	3-1	Oakes, Aldridge, Lewis
		2	10.12.83	Harrow B	IL	A	W	3-1	Aldridge 2, Chamberlain
		3	7.1.84	Plymouth A	D3	A	D	2-2	Aldridge 2
		3r	10.1.84	Plymouth A		H	L	0-1	
1984-85	D3	1	17.11.84	Aldershot	D4	H	D	1-1	Pulis
		1r	20.11.84	Aldershot		A	L	0-4	
1985-86	D3	1	16.11.85	Southend U	D4	A	W	1-0	Mardenborough
		2	7.12.85	Torquay U	D4	H	D	1-1	Berry
		2r	10.12.85	Torquay U		A	W	3-2	Boyle, Jones, James
		3	4.1.86	Sunderland	D2	A	L	0-2	
1986-87	D3	1	15.11.86	Bromsgrove R	SL	A	W	1-0	Vinter
		2	6.12.86	Fulham	D3	A	L	0-2	
1987-88	D4	1	14.11.87	Northampton T	D3	A	L	1-2	Holtham
1988-89	GMVC 4q		29.10.88	Weymouth	GMVC	H	W	2-1	Brignull, Sanderson
		1	19.11.88	Maidstone U	GMVC	H	L	1-2	Sugrue

NEWPORT (IOW)

Formed 1888. **First entered FA Cup:** 1930. **League club beaten:** Clapton Orient

1935-36	Hants 1	30.11.35 **Yeovil & Petters U**	SL	A	W	1-0	Gardiner
	2	14.12.35 **Southall**	AL	A	L	0-8	
1945-46	Hants 1 1L	17.11.45 **Clapton O**	3S	A	L	1-2	Rose
	1 2L	24.11.45 **Clapton O**		H	W	2-0	Rose, Merritt
	2 1L	8.12.45 **Aldershot**	3S	A	L	0-7	
	2 2L	15.12.45 **Aldershot**		H	L	0-5	
1952-53	Hants 1	22.11.52 **Swindon T**	3S	A	L	0-5	
1953-54	Hants 1	21.11.53 **Swindon T**	3S	A	L	1-2	Gilfillan
1954-55	Hants 1	20.11.54 **Hinckley A**	BDL	A	L	3-4	Slade, Gilfillan 2
1956-57	Hants 1	17.11.56 **Watford**	3S	H	L	0-6	
1957-58	Hants 1	16.11.57 **Hereford U**	SL	H	L	0-3	
1958-59	Hants 1	15.11.58 **Shrewsbury T**	D4	H	D	0-0	
	1r	20.11.58 **Shrewsbury T**		A	L	0-5	

NEWTOWN FC

Formed 1875. **First entered FA Cup:** 1884. Currently play in the League of Wales. **Welsh FA Cup winners:** 1879, 1895

1884-85	1	**Stafford Rangers**			*walkover*	
	2	20.12.84 **Druids FC**	H	D	1-1	
	2r	27.12.84 **Druids FC**	A	L	0-6	
1885-86	1	24.10.85 **Hartford St Johns**	A	W	3-1	
	2	21.11.85 **Leek**			*walkover*	

NORTHAMPTON TOWN

Formed 1897. **First entered FA Cup:** 1898. **Best FA Cup Performance:** 5th round 1934, 1950, 1970. **Record FA Cup Win:** 10-0 vs Sutton T, 5th qual rd, 1907-8. In competition proper: 9-0 vs Metropolitan Police, 1st round, 28.11.1931. **Record FA Cup Defeat:** 2-8 vs Manchester United, 5th round, 7.2.1970.

1898-99		1q **Hinckley T** (A) 2-1; 2q **Wellingborough T** (A) 2-0 *FA ordered match to be replayed after protest*; 2qr **Wellingborough T** (A) 1-6					
1899-00		1q **Wellingborough T** (H) 1-2					
1900-01		3q **Hinckley T** (A) 0-2					
1901-02	SL	3q **Gresley R** (A) 2-0; 4q **Burton U** (A) 0-0abnd; 4q **Burton U** (A) 0-0; 4qr **Burton U** (H) 2-0; 5q **Kettering T** (A) 2-2; 5qr **Kettering T** (H) 2-0; Int **Darwen** (H) 4-1					
		1 25.1.02 **Sheffield U**	D1	H	L	0-2	
1902-03	SL	3q **Burton U** (A) 0-2					
1903-04	SL	3q **Wellingborough T** (A) 0-2					
1904-05	SL	3q **Burton U** (A) 3-2; 4q **Kettering T** (A) 3-0; 5q **Leicester F** (H) 2-2; 5qr **Leicester F** (A) 0-2					
1905-06	SL	4q **West Stanley** (A) 1-1; 4qr **West Stanley** (H) 3-0					
		1 13.1.06 **New Brompton**	SL	A	L	1-2	Springthorpe
1906-07	SL	5q **Southport Central** (H) 2-1					
		1 12.1.07 **Middlesbrough**	D1	A	L	2-4	Dunkerley, Watkins
1907-08	SL	5q **Sutton T** (H) 10-0					
		1 11.1.08 **Bristol R**	SL	H	L	0-1	
1908-09	SL	1 16.1.09 **Derby Co**	D2	H	D	1-1	McDiarmid
		1r 20.1.09 **Derby Co**		A	L	2-4	McCartney, Lewis
1909-10	SL	1 15.1.10 **Sheffield W**	D1	H	D	0-0	
		1r 20.1.10 **Sheffield W**		A	W	1-0	Walker
		2 5.2.10 **Nottingham F**	D1	H	D	0-0	
		2r 9.2.10 **Nottingham F**		A	L	0-1	
1910-11	SL	1 14.1.11 **Luton T**	SL	H	W	5-1	Bradshaw 2, Lessons 2, Lewis
		2 4.2.11 **Newcastle U**	D1	A	D	1-1	Bradshaw
		2r 8.2.11 **Newcastle U** at St James's Park		A	L	0-1	
1911-12	SL	1 13.1.12 **Bristol C**	D2	H	W	1-0	Lewis
		2 3.2.12 **Darlington**	NEL	A	D	1-1	King
		2r 8.2.12 **Darlington**		H	W	2-0	King, Lessons
		3 24.2.12 **Fulham**	D2	A	L	1-2	Lewis
1912-13	SL	1 18.1.13 **Blackburn R**	D1	A	L	2-7	Walden, Suttie og
1913-14	SL	1 10.1.14 **Derby Co**	D1	A	L	0-1	
1914-15	SL	1 9.1.15 **Grimsby T**	D2	A	W	3-0	Smith, Lockett, Freeman
		2 30.1.15 **Hull C**	D2	A	L	1-2	Freeman
1919-20	SL	6q **Bristol R** (H) 2-2; 6qr (A) 2-3					
1920-21	D3	6q **Gillingham** (H) 3-1					
		1 8.1.21 **Southampton**	D3	H	D	0-0	
		1r 12.1.21 **Southampton**		A	L	1-4	Lockett
1921-22	3S	5q **Lincoln C** (A) 2-1; 6q **Lancaster T** (H) 1-0					
		1 7.1.22 **Reading**	3S	H	W	3-0	Lockett 3

	2	28.1.22 **Stoke**	D2	H	D	2-2	Hewison, Lockett
	2r	2.4.22 **Stoke**		A	L	0-3	
1922-23 3S	5q **Charlton A** (A) 0-2						
1923-24 3S	5q **Lincoln C** (H) 5-1; 6q **Wigan B** (A) 6-0						
	1	12.1.24 **Halifax T**	3N	H	D	1-1	Lockett
	1r	16.1.24 **Halifax T**		A	D	1-1aet	Wood
	1 2r	21.1.24 **Halifax T** at Bramall Lane			L	2-4	Wood, Lockett
1924-25 3S	1	10.1.25 **Tottenham H**	D1	A	L	0-3	
1925-26 3S	1	28.11.25 **Barnsley**	D2	H	W	3-1	George 2, Robinson
	2	12.12.25 **Newport Co**	3S	H	W	3-1	Robinson 3
	3	9.1.26 **Crystal P**	3S	H	D	3-3	Robinson 2, Lockett
	3r	13.1.26 **Crystal P**		A	L	1-2	Pease
1926-27 3S	1	27.11.26 **Boston T**	ML	A	D	1-1	Gunnell
	1r	2.12.26 **Boston T**		H	W	2-1	Hoten, Watson
	2	11.12.26 **Exeter C**	3S	A	L	0-1	
1927-28 3S	1	26.11.27 **Leyton**	AL	H	W	8-0	Whitehurst 4, Clennell 3, Martin
	2	10.12.27 **Brighton & HA**	3S	H	W	1-0	Daly
	3	14.1.28 **Sunderland**	D1	A	D	3-3	Daly, Cowen, Wells
	3r	19.1.28 **Sunderland**		H	L	0-3	
1928-29 3S	3	12.1.29 **Millwall**	D2	A	D	1-1	Weston
	3r	17.1.29 **Millwall**		H	D	2-2aet	Hoten 2
	3 2r	21.1.29 **Millwall** at Highbury			L	0-2	
1929-30 3S	1	30.11.29 **Aldershot**	SL	A	W	1-0	Weston
	2	14.12.29 **Margate**	KL	H	W	6-0	Sissons, Hoten 3, Bowen 2
	3	11.1.30 **Blackburn R**	D1	A	L	1-4	Wells
1930-31 3S	1	29.11.30 **Coventry C**	3S	H	L	1-2	Bowen
1931-32 3S	1	28.11.31 **Met.Police**	SPT	H	W	9-0	Dawes 3, Riches, Bowen 2, Woodcock og, Wells 2
	2	12.12.31 **Southend**	3S	H	W	3-0	Dawes, Bowen, Lovett
	3	9.1.32 **Darlington**	3N	A	D	1-1	Lovett
	3r	14.1.32 **Darlington**		H	W	2-0	Lovett, Dawes
	4	23.1.32 **Bradford PA**	D2	A	L	2-4	Wells, Lovett
1932-33 3S	1	26.11.32 **Lloyds, Sittingbourne**	KL	H	W	8-1	A.Dawes 5, Mcfarlane, Wells, Dowsey
	2	10.12.32 **Doncaster R**	3N	H	L	0-1	
1933-34 3S	1	25.11.33 **Exeter C**	3S	H	W	2-0	Wells, Dowsey
	2	9.12.33 **Torquay U**	3S	H	W	3-0	A.Dawes 2, Boyle
	3	13.1.34 **Southampton**	D2	A	D	1-1	Wells
	3r	18.1.34 **Southampton**		H	W	1-0	Henson
	4	27.1.34 **Huddersfield T**	D1	A	W	2-0	Boyle, Wells
	5	17.2.34 **Preston NE**	D2	A	L	0-4	
1934-35 3S	1	24.11.34 **Barry T**	SL	A	W	1-0	Cochrane
	2	8.12.34 **Workington**	NEL	H	D	0-0	
	2r	13.12.34 **Workington**		A	W	1-0	Hobbs
	3	12.1.35 **Bolton W**	D2	H	L	0-2	
1935-36 3S	1	30.11.35 **Bristol R**	3S	H	D	0-0	
	1r	4.12.35 **Bristol R**		A	L	1-3	Deacon
1936-37 3S	1	28.11.36 **Walthamstow Ave**	AL	A	L	1-6	Hewitt
1937-38 3S	1	27.11.37 **Cardiff C**	3S	A	L	1-2	Tolland
1938-39 3S	1	26.11.38 **Watford**	3S	A	L	1-4	Tilson
1945-46 3S	1 1L	17.11.45 **Chelmsford C**	SL	H	W	5-1	Roberts, Hughes 2, Morrall 2
	1 2L	24.11.45 **Chelmsford C**		A	W	5-0	Roberts, Morrall 2, Fowler, Smith
	2 1L	8.12.45 **Notts Co**	3S	H	W	3-1	Morrall 2, Blunt
	2 2L	15.12.45 **Notts Co**		A	L	0-1	
	3 1L	5.1.46 **Millwall**	D2	H	D	2-2	Hughes, Black
	3 2L	7.1.46 **Millwall**		A	L	0-3	
1946-47 3S	1	30.11.46 **Mansfield T**	3S	H	W	2-0	Garrett, Blunt
	2	14.12.46 **Peterborough U**	ML	A	D	1-1	Garrett
	2r	19.12.46 **Peterborough U**		H	D	1-1aet	Padgett
	2 2r	23.12.46 **Peterborough U** at Coventry			W	8-1	Garrett 4, Roberts 2, Morrall 2
	3	11.1.47 **Preston NE**	D1	H	L	1-2	Roberts
1947-48 3S	1	29.11.47 **Exeter C**	3S	A	D	1-1aet	Roberts
	1r	6.12.47 **Exeter C**		H	W	2-0	Briscoe, Jenkins
	2	13.12.47 **Torquay U**	3S	H	D	1-1	Heaslegrave
	2r	20.12.47 **Torquay U**		A	L	0-2	
1948-49 3S	1	27.11.48 **Dulwich Hamlet**	IL	H	W	2-1	W.Smith, D.Smith
	2	11.12.48 **Mansfield T**	3N	A	L	1-2aet	English
1949-50 3S	1	26.11.49 **Walthamstow Ave**	IL	H	W	4-1	Mitchell 2, Dixon, McCulloch
	2	10.12.49 **Torquay U**	3S	H	W	4-2	Mitchell 3 (1p), Dixon

		3	7.1.50	Southampton	D2	H	D	1-1	McCulloch
		3r	11.1.50	Southampton		A	W	3-2	Dixon, Hughes, Candlin
		4	28.1.50	Bournemouth	3S	A	D	1-1	Mitchell
		4r	2.2.50	Bournemouth		H	W	2-1	English, McCullough
		5	11.2.50	Derby Co	D1	A	L	2-4	Dixon 2
1950-51	3S	3	6.1.51	Barnsley	D2	H	W	3-1	Murphy, Mitchell 2 (1p)
		4	27.1.51	Arsenal	D1	A	L	2-3	English 2
1951-52	3S	1	24.11.51	Norwich C	3S	A	L	2-3	Payne, Ramscar
1952-53	3S	1	22.11.52	Hendon	AL	A	D	0-0	
		1r	27.11.52	Hendon		H	W	2-0	Ramscar, Fowler
		2	6.12.52	Swindon T	3S	A	L	0-2	
1953-54	3S	1	21.11.53	Llanelli	SL	H	W	3-0	Ramscar, Fowler, Cross
		2	12.12.53	Hartlepools U	3N	H	D	1-1	Ramscar
		2r	16.12.53	Hartlepools U		A	L	0-1	
1954-55	3S	1	20.11.54	Coventry C	3S	H	L	0-1	
1955-56	3S	1	19.11.55	Millwall	3S	H	W	4-1	English 3, Hurley og
		2	10.12.55	Hastings U	SL	H	W	4-1	Draper 2, E.Smith, English
		3	7.1.56	Blackburn R	D2	H	L	1-2	English
1956-57	3S	1	17.11.56	Southampton	3S	A	L	0-2	
1957-58	3S	1	16.11.57	Newport Co	3S	H	W	3-0	Gale, N.Robinson, Mills
		2	7.12.57	Bournemouth	3S	H	W	4-1	Woan, Fowler, Hughes og, Norris og
		3	4.1.58	Arsenal	D1	H	W	3-1	Tebbutt, Leek, Hawkings
		4	25.1.58	Liverpool	D2	A	L	1-3	Hawkings
1958-59	D4	1	15.11.58	Wycombe W	IL	H	W	2-0	Kirkup, Fowler
		2	6.12.58	Tooting & Mitcham	IL	A	L	1-2	Kirkup
1959-60	D4	1	14.11.59	Torquay U	D4	A	L	1-7	Kane
1960-61	D4	1	5.11.60	Hastings U	SL	H	W	2-1	Wilson, Brown
		2	26.11.60	Romford	SL	A	W	5-1	Brown 2, Leck 3
		3	7.1.61	Luton T	D2	A	L	0-4	
1961-62	D3	1	4.11.61	Millwall	D4	H	W	2-0	Lines, Terry
		2	25.11.61	Kettering T	SL	H	W	3-0	Holton 3
		3	6.1.62	Port Vale	D3	A	L	1-3	Moran
1962-63	D3	1	3.11.62	Torquay U	D4	H	L	1-2	Everitt
1963-64	D2	3	4.1.64	Sunderland	D2	A	L	0-2	
1964-65	D2	3	9.1.65	Chelsea	D1	A	L	1-4	Foley (p)
1965-66	D1	3	22.1.66	Nottingham F	D1	H	L	1-2	Brown
1966-67	D2	3	28.1.67	WBA	D1	H	L	1-3	Foley (p)
1967-68	D3	1	9.12.67	Bournemouth	D3	A	L	0-2	
1968-69	D3	1	16.11.68	Margate	SL	H	W	3-1	Fairbrother, Roberts 2
		2	7.2.68	Brighton & HA	D3	A	W	2-1	Townsend, Hatton
		3	4.1.69	Bolton W	D2	A	L	1-2	Knox
1969-70	D4	1	15.11.69	Weymouth	SL	H	D	0-0	
		1r	19.11.69	Weymouth		A	W	3-1	Fairbrother, Rankmore 2 (1p)
		2	6.12.69	Exeter C	D4	H	D	1-1	Neal
		2r	9.12.69	Exeter C		A	D	0-0aet	
		2 2r	15.12.69	Exeter C at Swindon			W	2-1	Large, McNeill
		3	12.1.70	Brentwood	SL	A	W	1-0	Fairbrother
		4	24.1.70	Tranmere R	D3	A	D	0-0	
		4r	27.1.70	Tranmere R		H	W	2-1	Felton, Rankmore
		5	7.2.70	Manchester U	D1	H	L	2-8	McNeil, Large
1970-71	D4	1	21.11.70	Hereford U	SL	A	D	2-2	Fairbrother, McNeil
		1r	24.11.70	Hereford U		H	L	1-2	Rankmore
1971-72	D4	1	20.11.71	Basingstoke T	SL	A	W	5-1	Buchanan 2, McNeil 2, Large
		2	11.12.71	Hereford U	SL	A	D	0-0	
		2r	14.12.71	Hereford U		H	D	2-2aet	Large, Hawkins
		2 2r	20.12.71	Hereford U at the Hawthorns			L	1-2aet	Large
1972-73	D4	1	18.11.72	Peterborough U	D4	A	L	0-1	
1973-74	D4	1	24.11.73	Banbury U	SL	A	D	0-0	
		1r	29.11.73	Banbury U		H	W	3-2	Best, Robertson, Felton
		2	15.12.73	Bristol R	D3	H	L	1-2	Buchanan
1974-75	D4	1	23.11.74	Torquay U	D4	A	W	1-0	Gregory
		2	14.12.74	Rotherham U	D4	A	L	1-2	Stratford
1975-76	D4	1	22.11.75	Brentford	D4	A	L	0-2	
1976-77	D3	1	20.11.76	Leatherhead	IL	A	L	0-2	
1977-78	D4	1	26.11.77	Tooting & Mitcham	IL	A	W	2-1	Christie, Martin
		2	17.12.77	Enfield	IL	H	L	0-2	
1978-79	D4	1	25.11.78	Portsmouth	D4	A	L	0-2	

1979-80	D4	1	24.11.79 Hereford U	D4	A	L	0-1	
1980-81	D4	1	22.11.80 Peterborough U	D4	H	L	1-4	Phillips
1981-82	D4	1	21.11.81 Weymouth	APL	A	D	0-0	
		1r	24.11.81 Weymouth		H	W	6-2	Gage 2, Sandy, Carlton, Phillips, Mahoney
		2	15.12.81 Bristol C	D3	A	L	0-3	
1982-83	D4	1	20.11.82 Wimbledon	D4	H	D	2-2	Burrows, Denyer
		1r	23.11.82 Wimbledon		A	W	2-0	Coffill 2
		2	11.12.82 Gillingham	D3	A	D	1-1	Saxby
		2r	14.12.82 Gillingham		H	W	3-2	Belfon 2, Massey
		3	8.1.83 Aston Villa	D1	H	L	0-1	
1983-84	D4	1	19.11.83 Waterlooville	SL	H	D	1-1	Gage
		1r	23.11.83 Waterlooville		A	D	1-1aet	Austin
		1 2r	28.11.83 Waterlooville		H	W	2-0	O'Neill (p), Mundee
		2	10.12.83 Telford U	APL	H	D	1-1	Austin
		2r	14.12.83 Telford U		A	L	2-3	Muir, Jeffrey
1984-85	D4	1	17.11.84 VS Rugby	SL	H	D	2-2	Lee, Train
		1r	21.11.84 VS Rugby		A	W	1-0	Gage
		2	8.12.84 Brentford	D3	A	D	2-2	Lee, Train
		2r	11.12.84 Brentford		H	–	0-0	
			abandoned after 26 minutes – fog					
		2r	17.12.84 Brentford		H	L	0-2	
1985-86	D4	1	16.11.85 Gillingham	D3	A	L	0-3	
1986-87	D4	1	16.11.86 Peterborough U	D4	H	W	3-0	McGoldrick, Gilbert (p), Benjamin
		2	5.12.86 Southend U	D4	A	D	4-4	Donald, Hill 2, Benjamin
		2r	10.12.86 Southend U		H	W	3-2	Benjamin, Gilbert 2 (2ps)
		3	21.1.87 Newcastle U	D1	A	L	1-2	Hill
1987-88	D3	1	14.11.87 Newport Co	D4	H	W	2-1	Chard, Morley
		2	5.12.87 Brighton & HA	D3	H	L	1-2	Morley
1988-89	D3	1	19.11.88 Swansea C	D3	A	L	1-3	Berry
1989-90	D3	1	18.11.89 Kettering T	GMVC	A	W	1-0	Thomas
		2	9.12.89 Aylesbury	IL	H	D	0-0	
		2r	13.12.89 Aylesbury		A	W	1-0aet	Barnes
		3	6.1.90 Coventry C	D1	H	W	1-0	Berry
		4	27.1.90 Rochdale	D4	A	L	0-3	
1990-91	D4	1	17.11.90 Littlehampton T	SCL	A	W	4-0	Barnes 2, Campbell, Beavon
		2	8.12.90 Barnet	GMVC	A	D	0-0	
		2r	12.12.90 Barnet		H	L	0-1	
1991-92	D4	1	16.11.91 Crawley T	SL	A	L	2-4	Chard, Adcock
1992-93	D3	1	14.11.92 Fulham	D2	H	W	3-1	Wilkin, Brown, Terry
		2	6.12.92 Bath C	GMVC	A	D	2-2	Brown, Chard
		2r	15.12.92 Bath C		H	W	3-0	McParland, Wilkin, Bell
		3	12.1.93 Rotherham U	D2	H	L	0-1	

NORTHERN NOMADS

Formed 1900. Reformed 1947, disbanded 1985. **FA Amateur Cup Winners:** 1926. **Runners-up:** 1914. Manchester-based

1926-27		1	1.12.26 Crewe A	3N	A	L	1-4	Randle

NORTHFLEET UNITED

Formed 1890. Merged with Gravesend 1946. See also Gravesend & Northfleet United.

1925-26	KL	1	28.11.25 QPR	3S	H	D	2-2	Pilcher 2
		1r	3.12.25 QPR		A	L	0-2	
1926-27	KL	1	27.11.26 Sittingbourne	KL	A	W	3-1	Sanders 3
		2	11.12.26 Luton T	3S	A	L	2-6	Bell 2
1927-28	SL	1	26.11.27 London Caledonians	IL	H	L	0-1	
1928-29	SL	1	24.11.28 Ilford	IL	H	W	5-2	Bell 2, Sanders, Johnson 2
		2	8.12.28 Charlton A	3S	H	L	1-5	Johnson
1929-30	SL	1	30.11.29 Wimbledon	IL	A	W	4-1	Bell 2, Hopper, Howe
		2	14.1.30 Clapton O	3S	A	L	0-2	
1930-31	KL	1	29.11.30 Exeter C	3S	H	L	0-3	
1931-32	KL	1	28.11.31 Bournemouth	3S	A	D	1-1	Sparke
		1r	2.12.31 Bournemouth		H	L	0-1	
1933-34	KL	1	25.11.33 Dartford	SL	H	L	0-2	

NORTH SHIELDS

Formed 1898. **First entered FA Cup:** 1905. **FA Amateur Cup Winners:** 1969. **League team beaten:** Halifax T. Folded, then reformed 1992

Season	Comp	Round	Date	Opponent	Div	H/A	Res	Score	Scorers
1933-34	NEL	1	25.11.33	Scarborough	ML	H	W	3-0	Dryden, Cole, Forster
		2	9.12.33	Gateshead	3N	A	L	0-1	
1938-39	NEL	1	26.11.38	Stockport Co	3N	H	L	1-4	Coyde
1945-46	NEL	1 1L	17.11.45	Carlisle U	3N	A	L	1-5	Jamieson
		1 2L	24.11.45	Carlisle U		H	L	2-3	McLean, Jamieson
1946-47	NEL	1	30.11.46	Hartlepools U	3N	A	L	0-6	
1949-50	NEL	1	26.11.49	Netherfield	LC	A	L	3-4	Cooper, Pyle, McGarry
1950-51	NEL	1	25.11.50	Crewe A	3N	A	L	0-4	
1952-53	NEL	1	22.11.52	Stockport Co	3N	H	L	3-6	Wood, McKenna, Robson
1962-63	NEL	1	3.11.62	Workington	D4	H	D	2-2	Trewick, Doyle
		1r	8.11.62	Workington		A	L	2-7	Thompson, Prior
1969-70	NL	1	15.11.69	Hartlepools U	D4	A	L	0-3	
1982-83	NL	1	20.11.82	Halifax T	D4	A	W	1-0	McCaffery
		2	11.12.82	Walsall	D3	H	L	0-3	

NORTHWICH VICTORIA

Formed 1873. **First entered FA Cup:** 1882. **FA Challenge Trophy Winners:** 1984 **Runners-up:** 1983. Members of the Football League 1892-1894. **Cup Final Connection:** Billy Meredith, who played in Cup Finals for Manchester City (1904) and Manchester United (1909) also played for Northwich Victoria. **League clubs beaten as non-league team:** Rochdale, Peterborough, Watford, Chester, Crewe A

Season	Comp	Round	Date	Opponent	Div	H/A	Res	Score	Scorers
1882-83		1	28.10.82	Astley Bridge		H	W	3-2	Plant 3
		2	9.12.82	Druids		A	L	0-5	
1883-84		1	10.11.83	Druids		A	W	1-0	
		2	24.11.83	Davenham		H	W	5-1	Malham 3, Brook, Hankey
		3		bye					
		4	19.1.84	Brentwood		H	W	3-0	Atherton, Plant, Rhodes
		5	9.2.84	Blackburn Olympic		A	L	1-9	Rhodes
1884-85		1	8.11.84	Leek		A	L	3-4	
1885-86		1	31.10.85	Macclesfield		A	L	1-4	
1886-87		1	30.10.86	Furness Vale Rovers		H	W	10-0	
		2	13.11.86	Chirk		H	D	0-0	
		2r	20.11.86	Chirk		A	L	0-3	
1887-88		1	15.10.87	Leek		A	D	2-2	
		1r	22.10.87	Leek		H	W	4-2	
		2	5.11.87	Crewe A		H	L	0-1	
1892-93	D2	1	21.1.93	Loughborough T	ML	A	W	2-1	Bradshaw, Drinkwater
		2	4.2.93	Blackburn R	D1	A	L	1-4	Hargreaves
1893-94	D2	1q		bye					
		2q	4.11.93	Crewe A	D2	H	L	0-1	
1955-56	CC	1	19.11.55	Boston U	ML	A	L	2-3	Adams 2
1961-62	CC	1	4.11.61	Southport	D4	A	L	0-1	
1976-77	NPL	1	20.11.76	Rochdale	D4	A	D	1-1	Nieman
		1r	22.11.76	Rochdale		H	D	0-0aet	
		1 2r	29.11.76	Rochdale at Maine Rd			W	2-1	Smith, Collier
		2	11.12.76	Peterborough	D3	H	–	0-1	
			abandoned after 20 minutes						
		2	14.12.76	Peterborough		H	W	4-0	Smith 2, Wain (p), Swede
		3	8.1.77	Watford	D4	H	W	3-2	Swede, Wain (p), Corrigan
		4	29.1.77	Oldham at Maine Rd	D2		L	1-3	Collier
1979-80	APL	1	24.11.79	Nuneaton B	APL	A	D	3-3	Stromek, Smith 2 (1p)
		1r	26.11.79	Nuneaton B		H	W	3-0	Nieman, Collier, Smith
		2	24.12.79	Wigan A	D4	H	–	0-3	
			abandoned after 65 minutes – fog						
		2	5.1.80	Wigan A		H	D	2-2	Smith (p), Mayman
		2r	7.1.80	Wigan A		A	L	0-1	
1980-81	APL	1	22.11.80	Huddersfield T	D3	H	D	1-1	Denham
		1r	25.11.80	Huddersfield T		A	L	0-6	
1982-83	APL	1	20.11.82	Chester	D4	A	D	1-1	Wilson
		1r	22.11.82	Chester		H	W	3-1	Chesters, Ward 2
		2	11.12.82	Scunthorpe U	D4	A	L	1-2	Chesters
1983-84	APL	1	19.11.83	Bangor C	APL	H	D	1-1	Reid
		1r	22.11.83	Bangor C		A	L	0-1	

1984-85	APL	1	17.11.84	Crewe A	D4	H	W	3-1	Forshaw, Reid, Craven
		2	8.12.84	Wigan A	D3	A	L	1-2	Power
1987-88	GMVC	1	14.11.87	Colwyn Bay	NWC	H	W	1-0	Sayer (p)
		2	6.12.87	Blackpool	D3	H	L	0-2	
1988-89	GMVC	1	19.11.88	Frickley A	NPL	A	W	2-0	O'Connor, Howey og
		2	10.12.88	Tranmere R	D4	H	L	1-2	O'Connor
1989-90	GMVC	1	18.11.89	Darlington	GMVC	A	L	2-6	Hanchard, Callaghan

NORWICH CITY

Formed 1902 and entered the FA Cup that season. **Best FA Cup performance:** Semi-finals: 1959 (as a Third Division club), 1989, 1992. **Record FA Cup Win:** 8-0 vs Sutton United, 4th round, 28.1.1989. **Record FA Cup Defeat:** 0-6 vs Luton T, 2nd round, 10.12.1927; 0-6 vs Manchester C 4th round, 24.1.1981

1902-03	NSL	P	20.9.02	Lowestoft T	NSL	A	L	0-5	
1903-04	NSL	P	19.9.03	Lowestoft T	NSL	H	W	4-1	Gooch 3, Collinson
		1q Gt Yarmouth T (A) 2-1; 2q Harwich & P (A) 4-2; 3q West Norwood (H) 1-1; 3qr West Norwood scratched							
1904-05	NSL	3q Grays U (H) 0-0; 3qr Grays U (A) 2-3							
1905-06	SL	4q Sheppey U (A) 2-0							
		1	13.1.06	Tunbridge Wells R	SL	H	D	1-1	Bowman
		1r	17.1.06	Tunbridge Wells R		A	W	5-0	Ross 3, Graham 2
		2	3.2.06	Manchester U	D2	A	L	0-3	
1906-07	SL	1	12.1.07	Hastings & St Leonards	SL	H	W	3-1	Ross 2, Archer
		2	2.2.07	WBA	D2	A	L	0-1	
1907-08	SL	1	11.1.08	Sheffield W	D1	H	W	2-0	Beauchop, Allsopp
		2	1.2.08	Fulham	D2	A	L	0-2	
1908-09	SL	1	16.1.09	Reading at Stamford Bridge	SL		D	0-0	
		1r	20.1.09	Reading		A	D	1-1aet	Allsopp
		1 2r	25.1.09	Reading at Villa Park			W	3-2aet	Tomlinson, Flanagan, Allsopp
		2	6.2.09	Liverpool	D1	A	W	3-2	Tomlinson, Smith, Allsopp
		3	20.2.09	Bristol C	D1	A	L	0-2	
1909-10	SL	1	15.1.10	QPR	SL	H	D	0-0	
		1r	19.1.10	QPR		A	L	0-3	
1910-11	SL	1	14.1.11	Sunderland	D1	H	W	3-1	Hampson 2, Whiteside
		2	4.2.11	Bradford C	D1	A	L	1-2	Ingham
1911-12	SL	1	13.1.12	Blackburn R	D1	A	L	1-4	Birchall
1912-13	SL	1	11.1.13	Leicester F	D2	A	–	0-0	
		abandoned after 65 minutes – snowstorm							
		1	16.1.13	Leicester F		A	W	4-1	Osborne, Hughes, Woodlands, Wolstenholme
		2	1.2.13	Bristol R	SL	A	D	1-1	Woods
		2r	6.2.13	Bristol R		H	D	2-2aet	Woods, Sutcliffe
		2 2r	10.2.13	Bristol R at Stamford Bridge			L	0-1	
1913-14	SL	4q Walthamstow Grange (H) 6-0; 5q Halifax T (H) 2-0							
		1	10.1.14	Crystal P	SL	A	L	1-2	McDonald
1914-15	SL	1	9.1.15	Nottingham F	D2	A	W	4-1	Ritchie, Potter, Wilson, Taylor
		2	30.1.15	Tottenham H	D1	H	W	3-2	Wilson 2, Taylor
		3	20.2.15	Bradford C	D1	A	D	1-1aet	Potter
		3r	27.2.15	Bradford C		H	D	0-0aet	
		3 2r	3.3.15	Bradford C at Lincoln			L	0-2	
1919-20	SL	6q Darlington (A) 0-5							
1920-21	D3	1	8.1.21	Grimsby T	D3	A	L	0-1	
1921-22	3S	5q Metrogas London (A) 2-1; 6q Oxford C (A) 1-1; 6qr Oxford C (H) 3-0							
		1	7.1.22	Barnsley	D2	A	D	1-1	Woodhouse
		1r	12.1.22	Barnsley		H	L	1-2	Austin
1922-23	3S	5q Southend U (A) 2-2; 5qr Southend U (H) 2-1; 6q Ilford (H) 5-1							
		1	13.1.23	Bolton W	D1	H	L	0-2	
1923-24	3S	5q Folkestone T (A) 3-2; 6q Stockport Co (H) 2-0							
		1	12.1.24	Bristol C	D2	H	L	0-1	
1924-25	3S	5q Folkestone T (H) 2-0; 6q Rochdale (H) 1-0							
		1	10.1.25	Doncaster R	3N	A	W	2-1	Banks 2
		2	31.1.25	Notts Co	D1	A	L	0-4	
1925-26	3S	1	28.11.25	Clapton	IL	A	L	1-3	Jackson
1926-27	3S	1	27.11.26	Crystal P	3S	A	D	0-0	
		1r	2.12.26	Crystal P		H	W	1-0	Jackson
		2	11.12.26	Chatham	KL	H	W	5-0	Cropper 2, Jackson 2, McWhirr
		3	8.1.27	Southampton	D2	A	L	0-3	
1927-28	3S	1	26.11.27	Poole T	SL	A	D	1-1	Robinson

Season	Div	Rnd	Date	Opponent	Comp	H/A	Res	Score	Scorers
		1r	1.12.27	Poole T		H	W	5-0	Varco 3, Robinson, Moule
		2	10.12.27	Luton T	3S	A	L	0-6	
1928-29	3S	1	24.11.28	Chatham	KL	H	W	6-1	Varco 2, Hannah (p), Porter, Hooper, Rowden og
		2	8.12.28	Newport Co	3S	H	W	6-0	Varco 4, Hannah, Slicer
		3	12.1.29	Corinthians		H	L	0-5	
1929-30	3S	1	30.11.29	Coventry C	3S	H	D	3-3	Varco, Slicer, Greenwell
		1r	5.12.29	Coventry C		A	L	0-2	
1930-31	3S	1	29.11.30	Swindon T	3S	H	W	2-0	Peed 2
		2	13.12.30	Brentford	3S	A	L	0-1	
1931-32	3S	1	28.11.31	Wimbledon	IL	A	W	3-1	Thompson, Burditt, Murphy
		2	12.12.31	Brentford	3S	A	L	1-4	Burditt
1932-33	3S	1	26.11.32	Folkestone	SL	A	L	0-1	
1933-34	3S	1	25.11.33	Crystal P	3S	A	L	0-3	
1934-35	D2	3	12.1.35	Bath C	SL	H	W	2-0	Vinall, Kirchen
		4	26.1.35	Leeds U	D1	H	D	3-3	Kirchen 2, Vinall
		4r	30.1.35	Leeds U		A	W	2-1	Burditt, Vinall
		5	16.2.35	Sheffield W	D1	H	L	0-1	
1935-36	D2	3	11.1.36	Chelsea	D1	H	D	1-1	Manders
		3r	15.1.36	Chelsea		A	L	1-3	Warnes
1936-37	D2	3	16.1.37	Liverpool	D1	H	W	3-0	Vinall, Scott
		4	30.1.37	Bolton W	D1	A	D	1-1	O'Reilly
		4r	4.2.37	Bolton W		H	L	1-2aet	Manders
1937-38	D2	3	8.1.38	Aston Villa	D2	L		2-3	Coleman, Manders
1938-39	D2	3	12.1.39	Manchester C	D2	H	L	0-5	
1945-46	3S	3 1L	5.1.46	Brighton & HA	3S	H	L	1-2	Graham
		3 2L	9.1.46	Brighton & HA		A	L	1-4	Ware
1946-47	3S	1	30.11.46	Brighton & HA	3S	H	W	7-2	Eyre 5, Robinson, Johnson
		2	14.12.46	QPR	3S	H	D	4-4	Eyre 2, Johnson, Jones
		2r	18.12.46	QPR		A	L	0-2	
1947-48	3S	1	29.11.47	Merthyr Tydfil	SL	H	W	3-0	Dutton, Kinsey, Eyre
		2	13.12.47	Walsall	3S	H	D	2-2aet	Hold, Kinsey
		2r	20.12.47	Walsall		A	L	2-3	Hold, Kinsey
1948-49	3S	1	27.11.48	Wellington T	CC	W		1-0	Ashman
		2	11.12.48	Torquay U	3S	A	L	1-3	Kinsey
1949-50	3S	1	26.11.49	Gloucester C	SL	A	W	3-2	Kinsey, Jones, Ryder
		2	10.12.49	Hartlepools U	3N	A	D	1-1	Pickwick
		2r	15.12.49	Hartlepools U		H	W	5-1	Ryder 3, Kinsey, Eyre
		3	7.1.50	Portsmouth	D1	A	D	1-1	Kinsey
		3r	12.1.50	Portsmouth		H	L	0-2	
1950-51	3S	1	25.11.50	Watford	3S	H	W	2-0	Eyre, Hollis
		2	9.12.50	Rhyl	CC	A	W	1-0	Kinsey
		3	6.1.51	Liverpool	D1	H	W	3-1	Docherty 2, Eyre
		4	27.1.51	Newport Co	3S	A	W	2-0	Docherty, Dutton
		5	10.2.51	Sunderland	D1	A	L	1-3	Gavin
1951-52	3S	1	24.11.51	Northampton T	3S	H	W	3-2	Ackerman, Hollis, Kinsey
		2	15.12.51	Chesterfield	3N	H	W	3-1	Hollis, Ackerman, Gavin
		3	12.1.52	Arsenal	D1	H	L	0-5	
1952-53	3S	1	22.11.52	Tonbridge	SL	A	D	2-2	Ackerman 2
		1r	27.11.52	Tonbridge		H	W	1-0	Summers
		2	6.12.52	Brighton & HA	3S	A	L	0-2	
1953-54	3S	1	21.11.53	Yeovil T	SL	A	W	2-0	Summers 2
		2	12.12.53	Barnsley	3N	H	W	2-1	Johnston 2
		3	9.1.54	Hastings U	SL	A	D	3-3	Brennan, Hansell, Gavin
		3r	13.1.54	Hastings U		H	W	3-0	Hansell 2, Johnston
		4	30.1.54	Arsenal	D1	A	W	2-1	Johnston 2
		5	20.2.54	Leicester C	D2	H	L	1-2	Brennan
1954-55	3S	1	20.11.54	Headington U	SL	H	W	4-2	Keans 3, Pickwick
		2	11.12.54	Brighton & HA	3S	H	D	0-0	
		2r	15.12.54	Brighton & HA		A	L	1-5	Woan
1955-56	3S	1	19.11.55	Dorchester T	WL	H	W	4-0	Gordon 2, Hunt, Gavin
		2	10.12.55	Brighton & HA	3S	A	W	2-1	Hunt, Gavin
		3	7.1.56	Sunderland	D1	A	L	2-4	McCrohan, Gordon
1956-57	3S	1	17.11.56	Bedford T	SL	H	L	2-4	Hunt, Coxon
1957-58	3S	1	16.11.57	Redhill	AL	H	W	6-1	Milne 2, Gavin 2, Coxon, Hunt
		2	7.12.57	Brighton & HA	3S	H	D	1-1	Gavin
		2r	11.12.57	Brighton & HA		A	W	2-1	Gavin, Hunt
		3	4.1.58	Darlington	3N	H	L	1-2	Gavin

Season	Div	Rnd	Date	Opponent	Opp Div	H/A	Res	Score	Scorers
1958-59	D3	1	15.11.58	Ilford	IL	H	W	3-1	Brennan 2, Hill
		2	6.12.58	Swindon T	D3	A	D	1-1	Hill
		2r	11.12.58	Swindon T		H	W	1-0	Crossan
		3	10.1.59	Manchester U	D1	H	W	3-0	Bly 2, Crossan
		4	24.1.59	Cardiff C	D2	H	W	3-2	Bly 2, Crossan
		5	14.2.59	Tottenham H	D1	A	D	1-1	Allcock
		5r	18.2.59	Tottenham H		H	W	1-0	Bly
		6	28.2.59	Sheffield U	D2	A	D	1-1	Crossan
		6r	4.3.59	Sheffield U		H	W	3-2	Bly 2, Brennan
		SF	14.3.59	Luton T	D1		D	1-1	Brennan
			played at White Hart Lane						
		SFr	18.3.59	Luton T at St Andrews			L	0-1	
1959-60	D3	1	14.11.59	Reading	D3	H	D	1-1	Moran
		1r	18.11.59	Reading		A	L	1-2	Crowe
1960-61	D2	3	7.1.61	York C	D4	A	D	0-0	
		3r	11.1.61	York C		H	W	1-0	Crowe
		4	28.1.61	Scunthorpe	D2	A	W	4-1	Punton, Hill, Larkin, McCrohon
		5	18.2.61	Sunderland	D2	H	L	0-1	
1961-62	D2	3	10.1.62	Wrexham	D4	H	W	3-1	Allcock, Whitehouse, Lythgoe
		4	27.1.62	Ipswich T	D1	H	D	1-1	Allcock
		4r	30.1.62	Ipswich T		A	W	2-1	Allcock 2
		5	17.2.62	Sheffield U	D1	A	L	1-3	Hill
1962-63	D2	3	4.3.63	Blackpool	D1	H	D	1-1	Bryceland
		3r	6.3.63	Blackpool		A	W	3-1aet	Hill, Punton, Mannion
		4	13.3.63	Newcastle U	D2	H	W	5-0	Allcock 4, Mullett
		5	16.3.63	Manchester C	D1	A	W	2-1	Allcock 2
		6	30.3.63	Leicester C	D1	H	L	0-2	
1963-64	D2	3	4.1.64	Bristol R	D3	A	L	1-2	Davies
1964-65	D2	3	9.1.65	Nottingham F	D1	A	L	0-1	
1965-66	D2	3	22.1.66	Leyton O	D2	A	W	3-1	Anderson, Heath, Webb og
		4	12.2.66	Walsall	D3	H	W	3-2	Heath, Allcock, Mullett
		5	5.3.66	Blackburn R	D1	H	D	2-2	Davies 2
		5r	9.3.66	Blackburn R		A	L	2-3	Davies, Bryceland
1966-67	D2	3	28.1.67	Derby Co	D2	H	W	3-0	Kenning 2, Anderson
		4	18.2.67	Manchester U	D1	A	W	2-1	Heath, Bolland
		5	11.3.67	Sheffield W	D1	H	L	1-3	Bryceland
1967-68	D2	3	27.1.68	Sunderland	D1	H	D	1-1	Curran
		3r	31.1.68	Sunderland		A	W	1-0	Manning
		4	17.2.68	Chelsea	D1	A	L	0-1	
1968-69	D2	3	4.1.69	WBA	D1	A	L	0-3	
1969-70	D2	3	3.1.70	Wrexham	D4	H	L	1-2	Howard
1970-71	D2	3	2.1.71	Wolverhampton W	D1	A	L	1-5	Foggo
1971-72	D2	3	15.1.72	Hull C	D2	H	L	0-3	
1972-73	D1	3	13.1.73	Leeds U	D1	H	D	1-1	Cross
		3r	17.1.73	Leeds U		A	D	1-1aet	Cross
		3 2r	29.1.73	Leeds U at Villa Park			L	0-5	
1973-74	D1	3	5.1.74	Arsenal	D1	H	L	0-1	
1974-75	D2	3	4.1.75	Coventry C	D1	A	L	0-2	
1975-76	D1	3	3.1.76	Rochdale	D4	H	D	1-1	MacDougall
		3r	6.1.76	Rochdale		A	D	0-0aet	
		3 2r	13.1.76	Rochdale		H	W	2-1	MacDougall, Suggett
		4	24.1.76	Luton T	D2	H	W	2-0	Peters, Jones
		5	23.2.76	Bradford C	D4	H	L	1-2	Peters
1976-77	D1	3	8.1.77	Leeds U	D1	A	L	2-5	Suggett, Peters
1977-78	D1	3	6.1.78	Orient	D2	A	D	1-1	Gibbins
		3r	16.1.78	Orient		H	L	0-1	
1978-79	D1	3	6.1.79	Leicester C	D2	A	L	0-3	
1979-80	D1	3	5.1.80	Yeovil T	APL	A	W	3-0	Robson, Justin Fashanu, Paddon
		4	26.1.80	Wolverhampton W	D1	A	D	1-1	Bond
		4r	30.1.80	Wolverhampton W		H	L	2-3	Mendham, Bond
1980-81	D1	3	3.1.81	Cambridge U	D2	H	W	1-0	Downs
		4	24.1.81	Manchester C	D1	A	L	0-6	
1981-82	D2	3	2.1.82	Stoke C	D1	A	W	1-0	Jack
		4	23.1.82	Doncaster R	D3	H	W	2-1	Jack, Watson
		5	13.2.82	WBA	D1	A	L	0-1	
1982-83	D1	3	8.1.83	Swansea C	D1	H	W	2-1	Bertschin
		4	29.1.83	Coventry C	D1	A	D	2-2	Hareide, Barham

		4r	2.2.83 Coventry C		H	W	2-1aet	Bertschin, Roberts og
		5	19.2.83 Ipswich T	D1	H	W	1-0	Bertschin
		6	12.3.83 Brighton & HA	D1	A	L	0-1	
1983-84	D1	3	7.1.84 Aston Villa	D1	A	D	1-1	Deehan
		3r	11.1.84 Aston Villa		H	W	3-0	Channon, Mendham, Bertschin
		4	28.1.84 Tottenham H	D1	A	D	0-0	
		4r	1.2.84 Tottenham H		H	W	2-1	Van Wyck, Channon
		5	18.2.84 Derby Co	D2	A	L	1-2	Deehan
1984-85	D1	3	5.1.85 Birmingham C	D2	A	D	0-0	
		3r	23.1.85 Birmingham C		H	D	1-1aet	Haylock
		3 2r	26.1.85 Birmingham C		A	D	1-1aet	Mendham
		3 3r	28.1.85 Birmingham C		H	W	1-0	Bruce
		4	4.2.85 West Ham	D1	A	L	1-2	Donowa
1985-86	D2	3	4.1.86 Liverpool	D1	A	L	0-5	
1986-87	D1	3	10.1.87 Huddersfield T	D2	H	D	1-1	Drinkell
		3r	21.1.87 Huddersfield T		A	W	4-2	Phelan, Rosario, Drinkell, Gordon
		4	31.1.87 Wigan A	D3	A	L	0-1	
1987-88	D1	3	9.1.88 Swindon T	D2	A	D	0-0	
		3r	13.1.88 Swindon T		H	L	0-2	
1988-89	D1	3	8.1.89 Port Vale	D3	A	W	3-1	Townsend 2, Fleck
		4	28.1.89 Sutton U	GMVC	H	W	8-0	Allen 4, Fleck 3, Putney
		5	18.2.89 Sheffield U	D3	H	W	3-2	Allen (p), Gordon, Thompson og
		6	18.3.89 West Ham	D1	A	D	0-0	
		6r	22.3.89 West Ham		H	W	3-1	Allen 2, Gordon
		SF	15.4.89 Everton	D1		L	0-1	
			played at Villa Park					
1989-90	D1	3	10.1.90 Exeter C	D4	H	W	2-0	Rosario, Gordon
		4	28.1.90 Liverpool	D1	H	D	0-0	
		4r	31.1.90 Liverpool		A	L	1-3	Fleck
1990-91	D1	3	5.1.91 Bristol C	D2	H	W	2-1	Rosario, Fleck
		4	26.1.91 Swindon T	D2	H	W	3-1	Gordon, Mortensen, Fleck
		5	18.2.91 Manchester U	D1	H	W	2-1	Fleck, Gordon
		6	9.3.91 Nottingham F	D1	H	L	0-1	
1991-92	D1	3	4.1.92 Barnsley	D2	H	W	1-0	Fleck (p)
		4	5.2.92 Millwall	D2	H	W	2-1	Bowen, Fleck
		5	15.2.92 Notts Co	D1	H	W	3-0	Sutton 2, Phillips
		6	7.3.92 Southampton	D1	A	D	0-0	
		6r	18.3.92 Southampton		H	W	2-1aet	Newman, Sutton
		SF	5.4.92 Sunderland	D2		L	0-1	
			played at Hillsborough					
1992-93	PL	3	13.1.93 Coventry	PL	H	W	1-0	Beckford
		4	24.1.93 Tottenham H	PL	H	L	0-2	

NOTTINGHAM FOREST

Formed 1865, one of the four oldest clubs in the country. **Best FA Cup Performance:** Winners: 1898, 1959. Runners-up: 1991. **Record FA Cup Win:** 14-0 vs Clapton, 1st round, 17.1.1891. **Record FA Cup Defeat:** 0-5 vs Southampton, 6th round, 2nd replay, 8.4.1963.

1878-79		1	16.11.78 Notts FC		H	W	3-1	Turner, Goodyer, Smith
		2	21.12.78 Sheffield FC		H	W	2-0	Smith, Moss og
		3	18.1.79 Old Harrovians		A	W	2-0	Widdowson, Welch og
		4	25.2.79 Oxford University		A	W	2-1	Goodyer, Smith
		SF	22.3.79 Old Etonians at Kennington Oval			L	1-2	Bishop
1879-80		1	8.11.79 Notts Co		H	W	4-0	Widdowson 2, Smith 2
		2	13.12.79 Turton		A	W	6-0	Turner, Earp, Widdowson 2, Smith 2
		3	31.1.80 Blackburn R		H	W	6-0	Goodyer 2, Widdowson 2, Smith, Turner
		4	19.2.80 Sheffield FC		H	D	2-2	Smith, Widdowson
			Forest awarded tie after Sheffield's refusal to play extra time					
		5	bye					
		SF	27.3.80 Oxford University			L	0-1	
			played at Kennington Oval					
1880-81		1	Caius College Cambridge			walkover		
		2	4.12.80 Aston Villa		H	L	1-2	Widdowson
1881-82		1	5.11.81 Aston Villa		A	L	1-4	Laws og
1882-83		1	Brigg FC			walkover		
		2	2.12.82 Sheffield Heeley		H	W	7-2	Widdowson 4, Parr, Earp, Fletcher
		3	6.1.83 Sheffield W		H	D	2-2	Widdowson, Ledger og

	3r	13.1.83	Sheffield W		A	L	2-3	Parr, Earp
1883-84	1		Redcar			*walkover*	
	2	1.12.83	Notts Co		A	L	0-3	
1884-85	1	8.11.84	Rotherham Town		H	W	5-0	Unwin, Widdowson 3, Fox
	2	6.12.84	Sheffield Heeley		H	W	4-2	Billyeald, Fox 3
	3	3.1.85	Sheffield W		A	W	2-1	Lindley, Widdowson
	4	24.1.85	Swifts		A	W	1-0	Widdowson
	5		bye				
	SF	21.2.85	Queen's Park			D	1-1	Danks
		played at Derby					
	SFr	24.3.85	Queen's Park			L	0-3	
		played at Merchiston Castle School, Edinburgh					
1885-86	1	31.10.85	Mellors		H	W	6-2	Tutin 4, Fox, Danks
	2	21.11.85	Notts Olympic		H	W	4-1	Unwin 2, Leighton, Norman
	3	12.12.85	Staveley		A	L	1-2	Lindley
1886-87	1	30.10.86	Notts Olympic		H	W	3-0	Unwin, Danks, Leighton
	2	13.11.86	Grimsby T		H	D	2-2	Leighton 2
	2r	20.11.86	Grimsby T		A	W	1-0	Tutin
	3	11.12.86	Lockwood Brothers		A	L	1-2	Norman
1887-88	1	15.10.87	Notts Swifts		H	W	2-1	G.Tutin, Norman
	2	7.11.87	Mellors		H	W	2-0	Leighton 2
	3	26.11.87	Notts Co		H	W	2-1	Lindley, Burton
	4	17.12.87	Old Etonians		H	W	6-0	Fox 2, Danks 2, Norman, Lindley
	5	7.1.88	Sheffield W		H	L	2-4	Lindley, Burton
1888-89	1	2.2.89	Linfield Athletic		H	D	2-2	Norman, Burton
	1r		Linfield Athletic			*walkover*	
	2	16.2.89	Chatham		A	D	1-1aet	Lindley
	2r	23.2.89	Chatham		H	D	2-2aet	Tolley, Lindley
	2 2r	28.2.89	Chatham at Kennington Oval			L	2-3	H.Pike, Lindley
1889-90	FAII	1	18.1.90	Derby Midland		A	L	0-3	
1890-91	FAII	1	17.1.91	Clapton at Upton Park		A	W	14-0	Higgins 5, Lindley 4, McCallum 2, W.Smith 2, Shaw
	2	31.1.91	Sunderland Albion	FAII	A	D	1-1	W.Smith
	2r	7.2.91	Sunderland Albion		H	D	3-3aet	Higgins 3
	2 2r	11.2.91	Sunderland Albion at Sheffield			W	5-0	W.Smith, Higgins 2, Shaw, Lindley
	3	14.2.91	Sunderland	D1	A	L	0-4	
1891-92	FAII	1	16.1.92	Newcastle East End	NL	H	W	2-1	Higgins 2
	2	30.1.92	Sunderland Albion	NL	A	W	1-0	Higgins
	3	13.2.92	Preston NE	D1	H	W	2-0	Higgins, W.Smith
	SF	27.2.92	WBA	D1		D	1-1	Lindley
		played at Molineux					
	SFr	5.3.92	WBA			D	0-0	
		played at Molineux					
	SF 2r	9.3.92	WBA			L	2-6	Higgins 2
		played at Derby					
1892-93	D1	1	21.1.93	Casuals		H	W	4-0	Shaw, McInnes, Pike, Higgins
	2	4.2.93	Everton	D1	A	L	2-4	Pike, Shaw
1893-94	D1	1	27.1.94	Heanor T		H	W	1-0	Brodie
	2	10.2.94	Middlesbrough Iron.	D2	H	W	2-0	Brodie, Higgins
	3	24.2.94	Notts Co	D2	H	D	1-1	McInnes
	3r	3.3.94	Notts Co		A	L	1-4	McInnes
1894-95	D1	1	2.2.95	Southampton St Marys	SL	A	W	4-1	Pike, Rose 2, Carnelly
	2	16.2.95	Liverpool	D1	A	W	2-0	Stewart, McInnes
	3	2.3.95	Aston Villa	D1	A	L	2-6	Stewart, McInnes
1895-96	D1	1	1.2.96	Everton	D1	H	L	0-2	
1896-97	D1	1	30.1.97	Sheffield W	D1	A	W	1-0	Arthur Capes
	2	13.2.97	Sunderland	D1	A	W	3-1	FR Foreman 2, McInnes
	3	27.2.97	Liverpool	D1	A	D	1-1	McInnes
	3r	3.3.97	Liverpool		H	L	0-1	
1897-98	D1	1	29.1.98	Grimsby T	D2	H	W	4-0	Richards, Capes 2, McInnes
	2	13.2.98	Gainsborough T	ML	H	W	4-0	Benbow, Richards 2, McInnes
	3	26.2.98	WBA	D1	A	W	3-2	F.Foreman, Richards, Spouncer
	SF	19.3.98	Southampton	SL		D	1-1	Benbow
		played at Bramall Lane					
	SFr	24.3.98	Southampton			W	2-0	McInnes, Richards
		played at Crystal Palace					
	F	6.4.98	DERBY CO	D1		W	3-1	Capes 2, McPherson
		played at Crystal Palace					

Season	Div	Rd	Date	Opponent		H/A	Res	Score	Scorers
1898-99	D1	1	18.1.99	**Aston Villa**	D1	H	W	2-1	Capes, FR Foreman
		2	11.2.99	**Everton**	D1	A	W	1-0	FR Foreman
		3	25.2.99	**Sheffield U**	D1	H	L	0-1	
1899-00	D1	1	27.1.00	**Grimsby T**	D2	H	W	3-0	Calvey, Morris 2
		2	10.2.00	**Sunderland**	D1	H	W	3-0	Beveridge 2, Morris
		3	24.2.00	**Preston NE**	D1	A	D	0-0	
		3r	28.2.00	**Preston NE**		H	W	1-0	Capes
		SF	24.3.00	**Bury**	D1		D	1-1	Capes
				played at Stoke					
		SFr	28.3.00	**Bury**			L	2-3aet	Capes, Calvey
				played at Bramall Lane					
1900-01	D1	1	9.2.01	**Leicester Fosse**	D2	H	W	5-1	Calvey 3, Morris, FR Foreman
		2	23.2.01	**Aston Villa**	D1	A	D	0-0	
		2r	27.2.01	**Aston Villa**		H	L	1-3	Spouncer
1901-02	D1	1	25.1.02	**Glossop**	D2	A	W	3-1	Morris 2, F.Foreman
		2	8.2.02	**Manchester C**	D1	A	W	2-0	Calvey, F.Foreman
		3	22.2.02	**Stoke**	D1	H	W	2-0	F.Foreman 2
		SF	15.3.02	**Southampton**	SL		L	1-3	Calvey
				played at White Hart Lane					
1902-03	D1	1	7.2.03	**Reading**	SL	A	D	0-0	
		1r	11.2.03	**Reading**		H	W	6-3aet	Calvey 2, Morris 2, Iremonger, FR Foreman
		2	21.2.03	**Stoke**	D1	H	D	0-0	
		2r	26.2.03	**Stoke**		A	L	0-2	
1903-04	D1	1	10.2.04	**WBA**	D1	A	D	1-1	Shearman
		1r	13.2.04	**WBA**		H	W	3-1	Morris, Shearman, Spouncer
		2	20.2.04	**Blackburn R**	D1	H	L	1-3	Morris
1904-05	D1	1	4.2.05	**Sheffield U**	D1	H	W	2-0	Morris, Shearman
		2	18.2.05	**Fulham**	SL	A	L	0-1	
1905-06	D1	1	12.1.06	**Bury**	D1	A	D	1-1	Morris
		1r	17.1.06	**Bury**		H	W	6-2	Craggs, Holmes, Shearman 3, West
		2	3.2.06	**Fulham**	SL	A	W	3-1	Morris 2, West
		3	24.2.06	**Sheffield W**	D1	A	L	1-4	Spouncer
1906-07	D2	1	12.1.07	**Barnsley**	D2	H	D	1-1	Morris
		1r	17.1.07	**Barnsley**		A	L	1-2	Hughes
1907-08	D1	1	11.1.08	**Newcastle U**	D1	A	L	0-2	
1908-09	D1	1	16.1.09	**Aston Villa**	D1	H	W	2-0	Spouncer, Hooper
		2	16.2.09	**Brentford**	SL	H	W	1-0	West
		3	20.2.09	**Millwall**	SL	H	W	3-1	West 2 (1p), Hooper
		4	6.3.09	**Derby Co**	D2	A	L	0-3	
1909-10	D1	1	15.1.10	**Sheffield U**	D1	H	W	3-2	West 2, Armstrong
		2	5.2.10	**Northampton T**	SL	A	D	0-0	
		2r	9.2.10	**Northampton T**		H	W	1-0	Marrison
		3	19.2.10	**Coventry C**	SL	A	L	1-3	Morris
1910-11	D1	1	14.1.11	**West Ham U**	SL	A	L	1-2	Morris
1911-12	D2	1	13.1.12	**Bradford PA**	D2	H	L	0-1	
1912-13	D2	1	18.1.13	**Chesterfield**	ML	A	W	4-1	Gibson 3, Morris
		2	1.2.13	**Oldham A**	D1	A	L	1-5	Derrick
1913-14	D2	1	10.1.14	**Clapton O**	D2	A	D	2-2	McKnight, Bell
		1r	14.1.14	**Clapton O**		H	L	0-1	
1914-15	D2	6q	19.12.14	**Shrewsbury T**	BDL	H	W	6-1	Coleman 2, Jones 3, Lockton
		1	9.1.15	**Norwich C**	SL	H	L	1-4	Neve
1919-20	D2	1	10.1.20	**Bradford PA**	D1	A	L	0-3	
1920-21	D2	1	8.1.21	**Newcastle U**	D1	A	D	1-1	Bedford
		1r	12.1.21	**Newcastle U**		A	L	0-2	
1921-22	D2	1	7.1.22	**Bristol C**	D2	A	D	0-0	
		1r	11.1.22	**Bristol C**		H	W	3-1	Spaven 2, R.Parker
		2	28.1.22	**Hull C**	D2	H	W	3-0	Dennis, Spaven 2
		3	18.2.22	**Cardiff C**	D1	A	L	1-4	Burton
1922-23	D1	1	13.1.23	**Sheffield U**	D1	H	D	0-0	
		1r	18.1.23	**Sheffield U**		A	D	0-0aet	
		1 2r	22.1.23	**Sheffield U** at Meadow Lane			D	1-1aet	Green
		1 3r	25.1.23	**Sheffield U** at Hillsborough			L	0-1	
1923-24	D1	1	12.1.24	**Manchester C**	D1	A	L	0-2	
1924-25	D1	1	10.1.25	**Clapton O**	D2	H	W	1-0	Walker
		2	31.1.25	**West Ham**	D1	H	L	0-2	
1925-26	D2	3	9.1.26	**Bradford C**	D2	H	W	1-0	Gibson
		4	30.1.26	**Swindon T**	3S	H	W	2-0	Walker 2

	5	20.2.26	Southend U	3S	A	W	1-0	Walker
	6	6.3.26	Bolton W	D1	H	D	2-2	Stocks, Burton
	6r	10.3.26	Bolton W		A	D	0-0aet	
	6 2r	15.3.26	Bolton W at Old Trafford			L	0-1	
1926-27 D2	3	8.1.27	Ashington	3N	A	W	2-0	Burton, Stocks
	4	29.1.27	Wolverhampton W	D2	A	L	0-2	
1927-28 D2	3	14.1.28	Tranmere R	3N	H	W	1-0	Wadsworth
	4	28.1.28	Derby Co	D1	A	D	0-0	
	4r	1.2.28	Derby Co		H	W	2-0	Gibson, Stocks
	5	13.2.28	Cardiff C	D1	H	W	2-1	Thompson (p), Stocks
	6	3.3.28	Sheffield U	D1	A	L	0-3	
1928-29 D2	3	12.1.29	Swansea T	D2	H	L	1-2	Jennings
1929-30 D2	3	11.1.30	Rotherham U	3N	A	W	5-0	Dent 3, Loftus, Scott
	4	28.1.30	Fulham	3S	H	W	2-1	Loftus 2
	5	15.2.30	Sunderland	D1	A	D	2-2	Dickinson 2
	5r	19.2.30	Sunderland		H	W	3-1	Loftus, Scott, Burton
	6	1.3.30	Sheffield W	D1	H	D	2-2	Loftus, Dickinson
	6r	8.3.30	Sheffield W		A	L	1-3	Burton
1930-31 D2	3	10.1.31	Newcastle U	D1	A	L	0-4	
1931-32 D2	3	9.1.32	Chesterfield	D2	A	L	2-5	Simpson, Dickinson (p)
1932-33 D2	3	14.1.33	Bury	D2	A	D	2-2	Dickinson, J.Graham
	3r	18.1.33	Bury		H	L	1-2	Simpson
1933-34 D2	3	13.1.34	QPR	3S	H	W	4-0	Peacock 3, Simpson
	4	27.1.34	Chelsea	D1	H	D	1-1	Peacock
	4r	31.1.34	Chelsea		A	L	0-3	
1934-35 D2	3	12.1.35	Chester	3N	H	W	4-0	Race 2, Dennison, Masters
	4	26.1.35	Manchester U	D2	H	D	0-0	
	4r	30.1.35	Manchester U		A	W	3-0	Mawson, Masters, Race
	5	16.2.35	Burnley	D2	H	D	0-0	
	5r	19.2.35	Burnley		A	L	0-3	
1935-36 D2	3	11.1.36	Doncaster R	D2	A	W	2-1	Race, Peacock
	4	25.1.36	Derby Co	D1	A	L	0-2	
1936-37 D2	3	16.1.37	Sheffield U	D2	H	L	2-4	Martin 2
1937-38 D2	3	8.1.38	Southampton	D2	H	W	3-1	Martin 2, McNaughton
	4	22.1.38	Middlesbrough	D1	A	L	1-3	Martin
1938-39 D2	3	11.1.39	Huddersfield T	D1	A	D	0-0	
	3r	16.1.39	Huddersfield T		H	L	0-3	
1945-46 D2	3 1L	5.1.46	Watford	3S	H	D	1-1	Allen
	3 2L	9.1.46	Watford		A	D	1-1aet	Barks
	3r	16.1.46	Watford at White Hart Lane			L	0-1aet	
1946-47 D2	3	11.1.47	Lincoln C	3N	A	W	1-0	Rawson
	4	15.1.47	Manchester U	D1	A	W	2-0	Barks, Lyman
	5	8.2.47	Middlesbrough	D1	H	D	2-2	Scott, Mannion og
	5r	12.2.47	Middlesbrough		A	L	2-6	Barks, Edwards
1947-48 D2	3	10.1.48	Liverpool	D1	A	L	1-4	Wilkins
1948-49 D2	3	8.1.49	Liverpool	D1	H	D	2-2aet	Jones og, Scott
	3r	15.1.49	Liverpool		A	L	0-4	
1949-50 3S	1	26.11.49	Bristol C	3S	H	W	1-0	Kaile
	2	10.12.49	Stockport Co	3N	H	L	0-2	
1950-51 3S	1	24.11.50	Torquay U	3S	H	W	6-1	Johnson 3, Collindridge 2, Scott
	2	9.12.50	Rotherham U	3N	A	L	1-3	Capel
1951-52 D2	3	12.1.52	Blackburn R	D2	H	D	2-2	Capel, Scott
	3r	16.1.52	Blackburn R		A	L	0-2	
1952-53 D2	3	10.1.53	Mansfield T	3N	A	W	1-0	Ardron
	4	31.1.53	Everton	D2	A	L	1-4	Capel
1953-54 D2	3	9.1.54	Plymouth A	D2	A	L	0-2	
1954-55 D2	3	8.1.55	Sheffield U	D1	A	W	3-1	Scott, Barrett, Burkitt
	4	29.1.55	Hartlepools U	3N	A	D	1-1	Scott
	4r	2.2.55	Hartlepools U		H	W	2-1aet	Kelly (p), Wilson
	5	19.2.55	Newcastle U	D1	H	D	1-1	Small
	5r	28.2.55	Newcastle U		A	D	2-2aet	Barrett, Scott
	5 2r	1.3.55	Newcastle U		A	L	1-2aet	Wilson
1955-56 D2	3	7.1.56	Doncaster R	D2	A	L	0-3	
1956-57 D2	3	5.1.57	Goole T	ML	H	W	6-0	Barrett 3, Wilson, Baily, Higham
	4	26.1.57	Portsmouth	D1	A	W	3-1	Baily 2, Imlach
	5	16.2.57	Barnsley	D2	H	W	2-1	Wilson, Imlach
	6	2.3.57	Birmingham C	D1	A	D	0-0	

	6r	7.3.57	**Birmingham C**		H	L	0-1	
1957-58 D1	3	4.1.58	**Gillingham**	3S	H	W	2-0	Imlach, Quigley
	4	25.1.58	**WBA**	D1	A	D	3-3	Wilson 2 (1p), Imlach
	4r	29.1.58	**WBA**		H	L	1-5	Wilson
1958-59 D1	3	10.1.59	**Tooting & Mitcham**	IL	A	D	2-2	Murphy og, Gray (p)
	3r	24.1.59	**Tooting & Mitcham**		H	W	3-0	Dwight, Wilson, Imlach
	4	28.1.59	**Grimsby T**	D2	H	W	4-1	Gray 2 (1p), Whitefoot, Wilson
	5	14.2.59	**Birmingham C**	D1	A	D	1-1	Wilson
	5r	18.2.59	**Birmingham C**		H	D	1-1aet	Dwight
	5 2r	23.2.59	**Birmingham C** at Filbert St			W	5-0	Dwight 3, Gray 2 (1p)
	6	28.2.59	**Bolton W**	D1	H	W	2-1	Wilson 2
	SF	14.3.59	**Aston Villa**	D1		W	1-0	Quigley
		played at Hillsborough						
	F	2.5.59	**LUTON TOWN**	D1 WEMBLEY		W	2-1	Dwight, Wilson
1959-60 D1	3	9.1.60	**Reading**	D3	H	W	1-0	Iley
	4	30.1.60	**Sheffield U**	D2	A	L	0-3	
1960-61 D1	3	7.1.61	**Birmingham C**	D1	H	L	0-2	
1961-62 D1	3	6.1.62	**Workington**	D4	A	W	2-1	Booth, Julians
	4	27.1.62	**Sheffield W**	D1	H	L	0-2	
1962-63 D1	3	29.1.63	**Wolverhampton W**	D1	H	W	4-3	Addison, Quigley, Hockey Le Flem
	4	6.3.63	**WBA**	D1	A	D	0-0	
	4r	11.3.63	**WBA**		H	W	2-1	Addison (p), Cram og
	5	19.3.63	**Leeds U**	D2	H	W	3-0	Addison, Quigley, Hockey
	6	30.3.63	**Southampton**	D2	H	D	1-1	McKinlay
	6r	3.4.63	**Southampton**		A	D	3-3aet	Addison, Vowden 2
	6 2r	8.4.63	**Southampton** at White Hart Lane			L	0-5	
1963-64 D1	3	4.1.64	**Preston NE**	D2	H	D	0-0	
	3r	13.1.64	**Preston NE**		A	L	0-1aet	
1964-65 D1	3	9.1.65	**Norwich C**	D2	H	W	1-0	Addison
	4	30.1.65	**Sunderland**	D1	A	W	3-1	Addison, Wignall, Crowe
	5	20.2.65	**Crystal P**	D2	A	L	1-3	Wignall
1965-66 D1	3	22.1.66	**Northampton T**	D1	A	W	2-1	Wignall, Crowe
	4	12.2.66	**Hull C**	D3	A	L	0-2	
1966-67 D1	3	28.1.67	**Plymouth A**	D2	H	W	2-1	Baker, Wignall
	4	18.2.67	**Newcastle U**	D1	H	W	3-0	Barnwell, Baker, Storey-Moore
	5	11.3.67	**Swindon T**	D3	H	D	0-0	
	5r	14.3.67	**Swindon T**		A	D	1-1aet	Hindley
	5 2r	20.3.67	**Swindon T** at Villa Park			W	3-0	Lyons, Baker, Barnwell
	6	8.4.67	**Everton**	D1	H	W	3-2	Storey-Moore 3
	SF	29.4.67	**Tottenham H**	D1		L	1-2	Hennessey
		played at Hillsborough						
1967-68 D1	3	7.1.68	**Bolton W**	D2	H	W	4-2	Hilley, Baker, Wignall, Winfield
	4	17.2.68	**Leeds U**	D1	A	L	1-2	Baker
1968-69 D1	3	4.1.69	**Preston NE**	D2	A	L	0-3	
1969-70 D1	3	3.1.70	**Carlisle U**	D2	H	D	0-0	
	3r	8.1.70	**Carlisle U**		A	L	1-2	McCaffrey
1970-71 D1	3	2.1.71	**Luton T**	D2	H	D	1-1	McIntosh
	3r	11.1.71	**Luton T**		A	W	4-3	Cormack, Collier, Lyons, Rees
	4	23.1.71	**Orient**	D2	H	D	1-1	Storey-Moore (p)
	4r	25.1.71	**Orient**		A	–	0-0	
		match abandoned at halftime, ground unfit						
	4r	1.2.71	**Orient**		A	W	1-0	Collier
	5	13.2.71	**Tottenham H**	D1	A	L	1-2	Storey-Moore (p)
1971-72 D1	3	15.1.72	**Millwall**	D2	A	L	1-3	Richardson
1972-73 D2	3	13.1.73	**WBA**	D1	A	D	1-1	Galley
	3r	16.1.73	**WBA**		H	–	1-1	Lyons
		Abandoned after 80 minutes – fog						
	3r	22.1.73	**WBA**		H	D	0-0aet	
	3 2r	29.1.73	**WBA** at Filbert Street			L	1-3	Galley
1973-74 D2	3	6.1.74	**Bristol R**	D3	H	W	4-3	Martin 2, Lyall (p), Chapman
	4	27.1.74	**Manchester C**	D1	H	W	4-1	Bowyer 2, McKenzie, Lyall
	5	17.2.74	**Portsmouth**	D2	H	W	1-0	McKenzie (p)
	6	9.3.74	**Newcastle U**	D1	A	L	3-4	Bowyer, O'Kane, Lyall
		FA ordered replay after pitch invasion when Forest were leading 3-1						
	6r	18.3.74	**Newcastle U** at Goodison Park			D	0-0	
	6 2r	21.3.74	**Newcastle U** at Goodison Park			L	0-1	
1974-75 D2	3	4.1.75	**Tottenham H**	D1	H	D	1-1	Jones

Season		Round	Date	Opponent		Venue	W/D/L	Score	Scorers
		3r	8.1.75	Tottenham H		A	W	1-0	Martin
		4	28.1.75	Fulham	D2	A	D	0-0	
		4r	3.2.75	Fulham		H	D	1-1aet	Martin
		4 2r	5.2.75	Fulham		A	D	1-1aet	Robertson
		4 3r	10.2.75	Fulham		H	L	1-2	Chapman
1975-76	D2	3	1.1.76	Peterborough U	D3	H	D	0-0	
		3r	7.1.76	Peterborough U		A	L	0-1	
1976-77	D2	3	8.1.77	Bristol R	D2	H	D	1-1	Robertson (p)
		3r	11.1.77	Bristol R		A	D	1-1aet	Woodcock
		3 2r	18.1.77	Bristol R at Villa Park			W	6-0	Woodcock 2, Bowyer, Withe, Anderson, O'Hare
		4	29.1.77	Southampton	D2	H	D	3-3	Robertson 2 (1p), Woodcock
		4r	1.2.77	Southampton		A	L	1-2	Woodcock
1977-78	D1	3	7.1.78	Swindon T	D3	H	W	4-1	Woodcock 2, Withe, Robertson
		4	31.1.78	Manchester C	D1	H	W	2-1	Robertson, Withe
		5	18.2.78	QPR	D1	A	D	1-1	O'Neill
		5r	27.2.78	QPR		H	D	1-1aet	Robertson (p)
		5 2r	2.3.78	QPR		H	W	3-1	O'Neill, Woodcock 2
		6	11.3.78	WBA	D1	A	L	0-2	
1978-79	D1	3	10.1.79	Aston Villa	D1	H	W	2-0	Needham, Woodcock
		4	27.1.79	York C	D4	H	W	3-1	Lloyd, McGovern, O'Neill
		5	26.2.79	Arsenal	D1	H	L	0-1	
1979-80	D1	3	5.1.80	Leeds U	D1	A	W	4-1	Gray, Birtles, Bowyer, Robertson
		4	26.1.80	Liverpool	D1	H	L	0-2	
1980-81	D1	3	3.1.81	Bolton W	D2	H	D	3-3	Francis 2, Ponte
		3r	6.1.81	Bolton W		A	W	1-0aet	Francis
		4	24.1.81	Manchester U	D1	H	W	1-0	Francis
		5	14.2.81	Bristol C	D2	H	W	2-1	Wallace, Robertson (p)
		6	7.3.81	Ipswich T	D1	H	D	3-3	Francis, Walsh, Robertson (p)
		6r	10.3.81	Ipswich T		A	L	0-1	
1981-82	D1	3	2.1.82	Wrexham	D2	H	L	1-3	Proctor
1982-83	D1	3	8.1.83	Derby Co	D2	A	L	0-2	
1983-84	D1	3	6.1.84	Southampton	D1	H	L	1-2	Hart
1984-85	D1	3	6.1.85	Newcastle U	D1	H	D	1-1	Bowyer
		3r	9.1.85	Newcastle U		A	W	3-1	Davenport (p), Bowyer, Christie
		4	26.1.85	Wimbledon	D2	H	D	0-0	
		4r	30.1.85	Wimbledon		A	L	0-1	
1985-86	D1	3	4.1.86	Blackburn R	D2	H	D	1-1	Birtles
		3r	13.1.86	Blackburn R		A	L	2-3	Walsh, Birtles
1986-87	D1	3	11.1.87	Crystal P	D2	A	L	0-1	
1987-88	D1	3	9.1.88	Halifax T	D4	A	W	4-0	Wilson, Pearce, Plummer, Wilkinson
		4	30.1.88	Leyton O	D4	H	W	2-1	Glover, Plummer
		5	20.2.88	Birmingham C	D2	A	W	1-0	Crosby
		6	12.3.88	Arsenal	D1	A	W	2-1	Wilkinson, Rice
		SF	9.4.88	Liverpool	D1		L	1-2	Clough
			played at Hillsborough						
1988-89	D1	3	7.1.89	Ipswich T	D2	H	W	3-0	Yallop og, Gaynor, Chapman
		4	28.1.89	Leeds U	D2	H	W	2-0	Chapman, Parker
		5	19.2.89	Watford	D2	A	W	3-0	Webb, Chapman, Laws
		6	18.3.89	Manchester U	D1	A	W	1-0	Parker
		SF	15.4.89	Liverpool	D1		–	0-0	
			The Hillsborough Disaster. Abandoned after six minutes						
		SF	7.5.89	Liverpool			L	1-3	Webb
			played at Old Trafford						
1989-90	D1	3	7.1.90	Manchester U	D1	H	L	0-1	
1990-91	D1	3	6.1.91	Crystal P	D1	A	D	0-0	
		3r	21.1.91	Crystal P		H	D	2-2aet	Wilson, Pearce
		3 2r	28.1.91	Crystal P		H	W	3-0	Parker 2, Crosby
		4	11.2.91	Newcastle U	D2	A	D	2-2	Pearce, Clough
		4r	18.2.91	Newcastle U		H	W	3-0	Clough, Hodge, Parker
		5	25.2.91	Southampton	D1	A	D	1-1	Hodge
		5r	4.3.91	Southampton		H	W	3-1	Jemson 3 (1p)
		6	9.3.91	Norwich C	D1	A	W	1-0	Keane
		SF	14.4.91	West Ham	D2		W	4-0	Crosby, Keane, Pearce, Charles
			played at Villa Park						
		F	18.5.91	Tottenham H	D1 WEMBLEY		L	1-2aet	Pearce
1991-92	D1	3	4.1.92	Wolverhampton W	D2	H	W	1-0	Clough
		4	25.1.92	Hereford U	D4	H	W	2-0	Pearce, Sheringham

		5	15.2.92	**Bristol C**	D2	H	W	4-1	Llewellyn og, Clough, Pearce, Sheringham
		6	7.3.92	**Portsmouth**	D2	A	L	0-1	
1992-93	PL	3	3.1.93	**Southampton**	PL	H	W	2-1	Keane, Webb
		4	23.1.93	**Middlesbrough**	PL	H	D	1-1	Webb
		4r	3.2.93	**Middlesbrough**		A	W	3-0	Bannister, Clough, Wilson
		5	13.2.93	**Arsenal**	PL	A	L	0-2	

NOTTS COUNTY

The oldest club in the Football League, formed 1862 although recent research puts the more likely formation as 1864. Played their early matches as 'Nottingham FC'. Founder member of the Football League 1888. **Best FA Cup Performance:** Winners 1894. Runners-up: 1891. **Record FA Cup Win:** 15-0 vs Thornhill United (later Rotherham Town), 1st round, 24.10.1885. **Record FA Cup Defeat:** 1-8 vs Newcastle U, 3rd round, 8.1.1927.

1877-78	1	3.11.77	**Sheffield Club**	H	D	1-1	CL Curhsam
	1r	1.12.77	**Sheffield Club**	A	L	0-3	
1878-79	1	16.11.78	**Nottingham F**	H	L	1-3	Owen
1879-80	1	8.11.79	**Nottingham F**	A	L	0-4	
1880-81	1	4.11.80	**Derbyshire FC**	H	D	4-4	AW Curhsam, HA Cursham 2, others 1
	1r	27.11.80	**Derbyshire FC**	A	W	4-2aet	HA Cursham 2, Greenhalgh, Morse
	2		bye				
	3	12.2.81	**Aston Villa**	H	L	1-3	CL Cursham
1881-82	1		**Birmingham Calthorpe**			walkover	
	2	24.11.81	**Wednesbury Strollers**	H	W	5-2	HA Cursham 2, AW Cursham 2, Knowles og
			FA ordered replay after protest				
	2r	10.12.81	**Wednesbury Strollers**		W	11-1	HA Cursham 6, CL Cursham, CF Dobson,
			played at Derby Cricket Ground				AW Cursham 2, Bausor
	3	31.12.81	**Aston Villa**	A	D	2-2aet	Bausor 2
	3r	7.1.82	**Aston Villa**	H	D	2-2aet	Chapman, AW Cursham
	3 2r	14.1.82	**Aston Villa**	A	L	1-4	AW Cursham
1882-83	1	4.11.82	**Sheffield Club**	H	W	6-1	AW Curhsam 3, HA Cursham 2, Smith
	2		bye				
	3	27.12.82	**Phoenix Bessemer**	H	W	4-1	Gunn 2, AW Cursham, HA Cursham
	4	12.2.83	**Sheffield W**	A	W	4-1	AW Cursham 2, HA Cursham, Smith
	5	3.3.83	**Aston Villa**	H	W	4-3	HA Cursham 3, Gunn
	SF	17.3.83	**Old Etonians**		L	1-2	HA Cursham
			played at Kennington Oval				
1883-84	1	10.11.83	**Sheffield Heeley**	H	W	3-1	HA Cursham 3
	2	1.12.83	**Nottingham F**	H	W	3-0	Dixon, AW Cursham, CF Dobson
	3	15.12.83	**Grantham**	A	W	4-0	HA Cursham 2, AW Cursham, Macrae
	4	19.1.84	**Bolton W**	H	D	2-2aet	AW Cursham, Macrae
	4r	2.2.84	**Bolton W**	A	W	2-1	CF Dobson 2
	5	9.2.84	**Swifts**	H	D	1-1	HA Cursham
	5r	14.2.84	**Swifts**	A	W	1-0	HA Cursham
	SF	1.3.84	**Blackburn R**		L	0-1	
			played at Aston Grounds, Birmingham				
1884-85	1	8.11.84	**Notts Olympic**	H	W	2-0	Dixon, Emmitt
	2	6.12.84	**Staveley**	A	W	2-0	Gunn, HA Cursham
	3	3.1.85	**Sheffield Club**	H	W	5-0	HA Cursham, CF Dobson, Gunn, Jackson, Marshall
	4	24.1.85	**Walsall Swifts**	A	W	4-0	Jackson 2, Brown, Gunn
	5		bye				
	6	21.2.85	**Queens Park, Glasgow**	H	D	2-2	HA Cursham, Gunn
	6r	28.2.85	**Queens Park, Glasgow**	A	L	1-2	Jackson
			played at Derby Cricket Ground				
1885-86	1	24.10.85	**Rotherham T**	H	W	15-0	HA Cursham 4, Jackson 3, Daft 2, A.Moore 2,
							CF Dobson, Emmitt, Gunn, RJ Brown og
	2	21.11.85	**Sheffield Club**	H	W	8-0	Gunn 3, Jackson 3, HA Cursham, Daft
	3	12.12.85	**Notts Rangers**	H	W	3-0	HA Cursham 3
	4		bye				
	5	23.1.86	**South Shore**	A	L	1-2	Emmitt
1886-87	1	30.10.86	**Basford Rovers**	H	W	13-0	Burton 5, Daft 5, HA Cursham, Jackson, Slater og
	2	13.11.86	**Notts Rangers**	H	D	3-3	Burton, HA Cursham, Jackson
	2r	20.11.86	**Notts Rangers**	A	W	5-0	HA Cursham 3, Burton, Jackson
	3	11.12.86	**Staveley**	A	W	3-0	HA Cursham, Jackson, Emmitt
	4		bye				
	5	29.1.87	**Marlow**	H	W	5-2	HA Cursham 3, Jackson, Speller og
	6	19.2.87	**WBA**	H	L	1-2	HA Cursham
1887-88	1	15.10.87	**Lincoln Ramblers**	H	W	9-0	Daft 3, Moore 3, Jackson 2, Gunn

				Opponent					Scorers
		2		**Basford Rovers**				*walkover*	
		3	26.11.87	**Nottingham F**		A	L	1-2	Gunn
1888-89	D1	1q **Eckington** (H) 4-1; 2q **Beeston St Johns** (H) 4-2; 3q **Derby Midland** (H) 2-1; 4q **Staveley** (A) 3-1							
		1	2.2.89	**Old Brightonians**		H	W	2-0	C.Shelton, Moore
		2	16.2.89	**Sheffield W**		A	L	2-3	A.Shelton, Snook
1889-90	D1	1	18.1.90	**Birmingham St Georges**	FAll	A	D	4-4aet	John Oswald 2, Daft, McInnes
		1r	25.1.90	**Birmingham St Georges**		H	W	6-2	May 2, McInnes 2, Daft, John Oswald
		2	1.2.90	**Aston Villa**	D1	H	W	4-1	May 3, James Oswald
		3	15.2.90	**Sheffield W**	FAll	A	L	0-5	
			FA ordered replay after protest						
		3r	22.2.90	**Sheffield W**		A	W	3-2	Daft, John Oswald, W.Smith
			FA ordered second replay after protest						
		3 2r	3.3.90	**Sheffield W** at Racecourse Gd, Derby			L	1-2	McInnes
1890-91	D1	1	17.1.91	**Sheffield U**	ML	A	W	9-1	McGregor 4, Oswald 2, Daft, Locker, McInnes
		2	31.1.91	**Burnley**	D1	H	W	2-1	Daft 2
		3	14.2.91	**Stoke**	FAll	H	W	1-0	Locker
		SF	28.2.91	**Sunderland**	D1		D	3-3	McGregor, McInnes, Oswald
		SFr	11.3.91	**Sunderland**			W	2-0	Oswald 2
			both matches played at Bramall Lane						
		F	21.3.91	**Blackburn R**	D1		L	1-3	Oswald
			played at Kennington Oval						
1891-92	D1	1	16.1.92	**Sunderland**	D1	A	L	0-3	
			FA ordered replay after protest						
		1r	23.1.92	**Sunderland**		A	L	0-4	
1892-93	D1	1	21.1.93	**Shankhouse**		H	W	4-0	McInnes 2, Oswald 2
		2	4.2.93	**Middlesbrough Iron.**	NL	A	L	2-3	Burke, Walkerdine
1893-94	D2	1	27.1.94	**Burnley**	D1	H	W	1-0	Logan
		2	10.2.94	**Burton W**	ML	A	W	2-1	Donnelly, Logan
		3	24.2.94	**Nottingham F**	D1	A	D	1-1	Bruce
		3r	3.3.94	**Nottingham F**		H	W	4-1	Bruce 2, Donnelly, Logan
		SF	10.3.94	**Blackburn R**	D1		W	1-0	Daft
			played at Bramall Lane						
		F	31.3.94	**BOLTON W**	D1		W	4-1	Logan 3, Watson
			played at Goodison Park						
1894-95	D2	1	2.2.95	**Sheffield W**	D1	A	L	1-5	Allsopp
1895-96	D1	1	1.2.96	**Wolverhampton W**	D1	A	D	2-2	Bull 2
		1r	5.2.96	**Wolverhampton W**		H	L	3-4	Allan, Allsopp, Bull
1896-97	D2	1	30.1.97	**Small Heath**	D2	A	W	2-1	Allan, Boucher
		2	13.2.97	**Aston Villa**	D1	A	L	1-2	Murphy
1897-98	D1	1	29.1.98	**Wolverhampton W**	D1	H	L	0-1	
1898-99	D1	1	28.1.99	**Kettering**	ML	H	W	2-0	Maconnachie, Fletcher
		2	11.2.99	**Southampton**	SL	H	L	0-1	
1899-00	D1	1	27.1.00	**Chorley**	LL	H	W	6-0	Ball, Bull, Chalmers, Goss, Macconachie, McMain
		2	10.2.00	**Bury**	D1	H	D	0-0	
		2r	14.2.00	**Bury**		A	L	0-2	
1900-01	D1	1	9.2.01	**Liverpool**	D1	H	W	2-0	Morris 2
		2	23.2.01	**Wolverhampton W**	D1	H	L	2-3	Morris, Warner
1901-02	D1	1	25.1.02	**Reading**	SL	H	L	1-2	Lewis
1902-03	D1	1	7.2.03	**Southampton**	SL	H	D	0-0	
		1r	11.2.03	**Southampton**		A	D	2-2	Gee 2
		1 2r	16.2.03	**Southampton** at St Andrews			W	2-1aet	Green, Humphreys
		2	21.2.03	**Grimsby T**	D1	A	W	2-0	Green, Humphreys
		3	7.3.03	**Bury**	D1	A	L	0-1	
1903-04	D1	1	6.2.04	**Manchester U**	D2	H	D	3-3	Ross, Humphreys, Bonthron og
		1r	10.2.04	**Manchester U**		A	L	1-2	Green
1904-05	D1	1	4.2.05	**Bury**	D1	A	L	0-1	
1905-06	D1	1	13.1.06	**Sunderland**	D1	A	L	0-1	
1906-07	D1	1	12.1.07	**Preston NE**	D1	H	W	1-0	Matthews
		2	2.2.07	**Burslem Port Vale**	D2	A	D	2-2	Matthews, Humphreys
		2r	6.2.07	**Burslem Port Vale**		H	W	5-0	Emberton, Matthews 2, Humphreys, Jones
		3	23.2.07	**Tottenham H**	SL	A	W	4-0	Dean 2, Matthews, Humphreys
		4	9.3.07	**WBA**	D2	A	L	1-3	Jones
1907-08	D1	1	11.1.08	**Middlesbrough**	D1	H	W	2-0	Jones 2
		2	1.2.08	**Bolton W**	D1	H	D	1-1	Matthews
		2r	5.2.08	**Bolton W**		A	L	1-2aet	Tarplin
1908-09	D1	1	16.1.09	**Blackburn R**	D1	H	L	0-1	
1909-10	D1	1	15.1.10	**Bradford C**	D1	A	L	2-4	Jones 2

1910-11	D1	1	14.1.11	**Swindon T**	SL	A	L	1-3	Dean
1911-12	D1	1	13.1.12	**Luton T**	SL	A	W	4-2	Matthews, Cantrell, Richards, Waterall
		2	3.2.12	**Swindon T**	SL	A	L	0-2	
1912-13	D1	1	11.1.13	**Bristol R**	SL	A	L	0-2	
1913-14	D2	1	10.1.14	**Sheffield W**	D1	A	L	2-3	Flint, Peart
1914-15	D1	1	9.1.15	**Bolton W**	D1	A	L	1-2	Richards
1919-20	D1	1	10.1.20	**Millwall**	SL	H	W	2-0	Hill, McLeod
		2	31.1.20	**Middlesbrough**	D1	H	W	1-0	Cook
		3	21.1.20	**Bradford PA**	D1	H	L	3-4	Gibson, McLeod, Henshall
1920-21	D2	1	8.1.21	**WBA**	D1	H	W	3-0	Took, Stevens 2
		2	29.1.21	**Aston Villa**	D1	H	D	0-0	
		2r	2.2.21	**Aston Villa**		A	L	0-1	
1921-22	D2	1	7.1.22	**Grimsby T**	3N	A	D	1-1	Hill
		1r	12.1.22	**Grimsby T**		H	W	3-0	Cook, Hill, Henshall
		2	28.1.22	**Bradford C**	D1	A	D	1-1	Widdowson
		2r	1.2.22	**Bradford C**		H	D	0-0aet	
		2 2r	6.2.22	**Bradford C** at Bramall Lane			W	1-0	Widdowson
		3	18.2.22	**WBA**	D1	A	D	1-1	Widdowson
		3r	22.2.22	**WBA**		H	W	2-0	Cook, Hill
		4	4.3.22	**Aston Villa**	D1	H	D	2-2	Chipperfield 2
		4r	8.3.22	**Aston Villa**		A	W	4-3	Cook, Widdowson, Hill, Chipperfield
		SF	25.3.22	**Huddersfield T**	D1		L	1-3	Hill
				played at Burnley					
1922-23	D2	1	13.1.23	**Plymouth A**	3S	A	D	0-0	
		1r	17.1.23	**Plymouth A**		H	L	0-1	
1923-24	D1	1	12.1.24	**QPR**	3S	A	W	2-1	Pape, Price
		2	2.2.24	**Crystal P**	D2	A	D	0-0	
		2r	6.2.24	**Crystal P**		H	D	0-0aet	
		2 2r	10.2.24	**Crystal P** at Villa Park			D	0-0aet	
		2 3r	18.2.24	**Crystal P** at Villa Park			L	1-2	Widdowson
1924-25	D1	1	10.1.25	**Coventry C**	D2	A	W	2-0	Cock, Davis
		2	31.1.25	**Norwich C**	3S	H	W	4-0	Davis 2, Cook, Barry
		3	21.2.25	**Cardiff C**	D1	H	L	0-2	
1925-26	D1	3	9.1.26	**Leicester C**	D1	H	W	2-0	Widdowson, Taylor
		4	30.1.26	**New Brighton**	3N	H	W	2-0	Harris 2
		5	20.2.26	**Fulham**	D2	H	L	0-1	
1926-27	D2	3	8.1.27	**Newcastle U**	D1	A	L	1-8	Widdowson
1927-28	D2	3	14.1.28	**Sheffield U**	D1	H	L	2-3	Taylor, Mills
1928-29	D2	3	12.1.29	**Derby Co**	D1	A	L	3-4	Andrews 2, Haden
1929-30	D2	3	11.1.30	**West Ham**	D1	A	L	0-4	
1930-31	3S	1	29.11.30	**Chesterfield**	3N	A	W	2-1	Fenner, Taylor
		2	13.12.30	**Doncaster R**	3N	A	W	1-0	Bowman og
		3	10.1.31	**Swansea T**	D2	H	W	3-1	Andrews 2, Keetley
		4	24.1.31	**Sheffield U**	D1	A	L	1-4	Keetley
1931-32	D2	3	9.1.32	**Bristol C**	D2	H	D	2-2	Keetley 2
		3r	13.1.32	**Bristol C**		A	L	2-3	Hall, Andrews
1932-33	D2	3	14.1.33	**Tranmere R**	3N	A	L	1-2	Corkhill
1933-34	D2	3	13.1.34	**Swansea T**	D2	A	L	0-1	
1934-35	D2	3	12.1.35	**Wolverhampton W**	D1	A	L	0-4	
1935-36	3S	1	30.11.35	**Grantham**	ML	A	W	2-0	Green, Fallon
		2	14.12.35	**Torquay U**	3S	H	W	3-0	Rickard, Fallon, R.Hunt og
		3	11.1.36	**Tranmere R**	3N	H	D	0-0	
		3r	15.1.36	**Tranmere R**		A	L	3-4	Chandler, Richards, Steele
1936-37	3S	1	28.11.36	**Gateshead**	3N	A	L	0-2	
1937-38	3S	3	8.1.38	**Aldershot**	3S	A	W	3-1	Rickard, Chalmers, Gallagher
		4	22.1.38	**Huddersfield T**	D1	A	L	0-1	
1938-39	3S	3	7.1.39	**Burnley**	D2	H	W	3-1	Cooper 2, Clayton
		4	21.1.39	**Walsall**	3S	H	D	0-0	
		4r	26.1.39	**Walsall**		A	L	0-4	
1945-46	3S	1 1L	17.11.45	**Bradford C**	3N	H	D	2-2	I.McPherson, Hubbard
		1 2L	24.11.45	**Bradford C**		A	W	2-1	I.McPherson, Parker
		2 1L	8.12.45	**Northampton T**	3S	A	L	1-3	I.McPherson
		2 2L	15.12.45	**Northampton T**		H	W	1-0	Martin
1946-47	3S	1	30.11.46	**Leyton O**	3S	A	W	2-1	Cumner, Jayes
		2	14.12.46	**Swindon T**	3S	H	W	2-1	Sewell, Fallon
		3	11.1.47	**Luton T**	D2	A	L	0-6	
1947-48	3S	1	29.11.47	**Horshsam**	SCL	H	W	9-1	Lawton 3, Sewell 3, Marsh 2, Freeman

Season	Div	Rd	Date	Opponent	Comp	H/A	W/D/L	Score	Scorers
		2	13.12.47	Stockton	NEL	H	D	1-1aet	Sewell
		2r	20.12.47	Stockton at Middlesbrough		A	W	4-1	Cumner, Lawton 3
		3	10.1.48	Birmingham C	D2	A	W	2-0	Corkhill, Marsh
		4	24.1.48	Swindon T	3S	A	L	0-1	
1948-49	3S	1	27.11.48	Port Vale	3S	H	W	2-1	Lawton 2
		2	11.12.48	Barrow	3N	H	W	3-2	Lawton, Johnston 2
		3	8.1.49	Plymouth A	D2	A	W	1-0aet	Sewell
		4	29.1.49	Liverpool	D1	A	L	0-1	
1949-50	3S	1	26.11.49	Tilbury	Lon	H	W	4-0	Lawton, Sewell, Broome 2
		2	10.12.49	Rochdale	3N	A	W	2-1	Johnston, Lawton
		3	7.1.50	Burnley	D1	H	L	1-4	Johnston
1950-51	D2	3	6.1.51	Southampton	D2	H	L	3-4	Broome, Leuty, Simpson
1951-52	D2	3	12.1.52	Stockton	NEL	H	W	4-0	Broome 2, McCormack, Lawton
		4	2.2.52	Portsmouth	D1	H	L	1-3	Lawton
1952-53	D2	3	10.1.53	Leicester C	D2	A	W	4-2	Crookes, Broome, McPherson 2
		4	31.1.53	Bolton W	D1	A	D	1-1	K.McPherson
		4r	5.2.53	Bolton W		H	D	2-2aet	Jackson, K.McPherson
		4 2r	9.2.53	Bolton W at Hillsborough			L	0-1	
1953-54	D2	3	9.1.54	Everton	D2	A	L	1-2	Wylie
1954-55	D2	3	8.1.55	Middlesbrough	D2	A	W	4-1	Broadbent, Wylie 2, Wills
		4	29.1.55	Sheffield W	D1	A	D	1-1	Conwell og
		4r	3.2.55	Sheffield W		H	W	1-0aet	Jackson
		5	19.2.55	Chelsea	D1	H	W	1-0	Broadbent
		6	12.3.55	York C	3N	H	L	0-1	
1955-56	D2	3	7.1.56	Fulham	D2	H	L	0-1	
1956-57	D2	3	5.1.57	Rhyl	CC	H	L	1-3	P.Bircumshaw
1957-58	D2	3	4.1.58	Tranmere R	3N	H	W	2-0	Tucker (p), Jackson
		4	25.1.58	Bristol C	D2	H	L	1-2	Pritchard
1958-59	D3	1	15.11.58	Barrow	D4	H	L	1-2	P.Bircumshaw
1959-60	D4	1	14.11.59	Hastings U	SL	A	W	2-1	P.Bircumshaw 2
		2	5.12.59	Bath C	SL	H	L	0-1	
1960-61	D3	1	5.11.60	Aldershot	D4	A	L	0-2	
1961-62	D3	1	4.11.61	Yeovil T	SL	H	W	4-2	Withers 2, Hateley, P.Bircumshaw
		2	25.11.61	Margate	SL	A	D	1-1	Loxley
		2r	30.11.61	Margate		H	W	3-1	Bircumshaw, Hateley
		3	6.1.62	Manchester C	D1	H	L	0-1	
1962-63	D3	1	3.11.62	Peterborough U	D3	H	L	0-3	
1963-64	D3	1	16.11.63	Frickley Colliery	CC	H	W	2-1	Astle, Tait
		2	7.12.63	Doncaster R	D4	A	D	1-1	Bly
		2r	10.12.63	Doncaster R		H	L	1-2	Tait
1964-65	D4	1	14.11.64	Chelmsford C	SL	H	W	2-0	Raynor, Cavanagh
		2	5.12.64	Brentford	D3	A	L	0-4	
1965-66	D4	1	13.11.65	Southend	D3	A	L	1-3	Sheridan
1966-67	D4	1	26.11.66	Oldham A	D3	A	L	1-3	Marshall
1967-68	D4	1	9.12.67	Runcorn	CC	A	L	0-1	
1968-69	D4	1	16.11.68	Doncaster R	D4	A	L	0-1	
1969-70	D4	1	15.11.69	Rotherham U	D3	H	L	0-3	
1970-71	D4	1	21.11.70	Port Vale	D3	H	W	1-0	Crickmore (p)
		2	12.12.70	Bury	D3	A	D	1-1	Nixon
		2r	21.12.70	Bury		H	W	3-0	Hateley, Crickmore, Needham
		3	2.1.71	Leicester C	D2	A	L	0-2	
1971-72	D3	1	20.11.71	Newport Co	D4	H	W	6-0	Hateley, Cozens, Bradd, Nixon, Stubbs, Carlin
		2	11.12.71	South Shields	NPL	A	W	3-1	Masson, Cozens, Bradd
		3	15.1.72	Watford	D2	A	W	4-1	Nixon, Cozens 2, Masson
		4	5.2.72	Derby Co	D1	A	L	0-6	
1972-73	D3	1	18.11.72	Altrincham	NPL	A	W	1-0	Randall (p)
		2	9.12.72	Lancaster C	NPL	H	W	2-1	Randall (p), Bradd
		3	13.1.73	Sunderland	D2	H	D	1-1	Bradd
		3r	16.1.73	Sunderland		A	L	0-2	
1973-74	D2	3	5.1.74	WBA	D2	A	L	0-4	
1974-75	D2	3	3.1.75	Portsmouth	D2	H	W	3-1	Needham, Randall 2
		4	24.1.75	QPR	D1	A	L	0-3	
1975-76	D2	3	3.1.76	Leeds U	D1	H	L	0-1	
1976-77	D2	3	8.1.77	Arsenal	D1	H	L	0-1	
1977-78	D2	3	7.1.78	Charlton A	D2	A	W	2-0	Vintner 2
		4	31.1.78	Brighton & HA	D2	A	W	2-1	Vintner 2
		5	18.2.78	Millwall	D2	A	L	1-2	Chapman

NOTTS COUNTY

1978-79	D2	3	9.1.79 **Reading**	D4	H	W 4-2	Vintner, Hooks, Mann, Masson
		4	27.1.79 **Arsenal**	D1	A	L 0-2	
1979-80	D2	3	5.1.80 **Wolverhampton W**	D1	H	L 1-3	Hunt
1980-81	D2	3	3.2.81 **Blackburn R**	D2	H	W 2-1	Manns, Christie
		4	24.1.81 **Peterborough U**	D4	H	L 0-1	
1981-82	D1	3	5.1.82 **Aston Villa**	D1	H	L 0-6	
1982-83	D1	3	8.1.83 **Leicester C**	D2	A	W 3-2	Justin Fashanu 2, McCulloch
		4	29.1.83 **Middlesbrough**	D2	A	L 0-2	
1983-84	D1	3	8.1.84 **Bristol C**	D4	H	D 2-2	Christie 2 (1p)
		3r	10.1.84 **Bristol C**		A	W 2-0	Kilcline, McCulloch
		4	1.2.84 **Huddersfield T**	D2	A	W 2-1	Kilcline, Harkouk
		5	18.2.84 **Middlesbrough**	D2	H	W 1-0	Chiedozie
		6	10.3.84 **Everton**	D1	H	L 1-2	Chiedozie
1984-85	D2	3	5.1.85 **Grimsby T**	D2	H	D 2-2	McParland 2
		3r	8.1.85 **Grimsby T**		A	L 2-4	Harkouk, Wilkinson og
1985-86	D3	1	17.11.85 **Scarborough**	APL	H	W 6-1	Hunt, Harkouk 3, Young, McParland
		2	7.12.85 **Wrexham**	D4	H	D 2-2	Waitt 2
		2r	10.12.85 **Wrexham**		A	W 3-0	Clarke, Waitt, McParland
		3	13.1.86 **Stoke C**	D2	A	W 2-0	Waitt, McParland
		4	25.1.86 **Tottenham H**	D1	H	D 1-1	McParland
		4r	29.1.86 **Tottenham H**		A	L 0-5	
1986-87	D3	1	15.11.86 **Carlisle U**	D3	H	D 1-1	Davis
		1r	18.11.86 **Carlisle U**		A	W 3-0	Young, McParland 2
		2	7.12.86 **Middlesbrough**	D3	H	L 0-1	
1987-88	D3	1	15.11.87 **Chesterfield**	D3	H	D 3-3	Kevan, McParland, Birtles
		1r	17.11.87 **Chesterfield**		A	W 1-0	Pike (p)
		2	5.12.87 **Port Vale**	D3	A	L 0-2	
1988-89	D3	1	19.11.88 **Darlington**	D4	A	W 2-1	Thorpe, Pike
		2	10.12.88 **Hartlepool**	D4	A	L 0-1	
1989-90	D3	1	18.11.89 **Doncaster R**	D4	A	L 0-1	
1990-91	D2	3	5.1.91 **Hull C**	D2	A	W 5-2	Buckley og, Turner, O'Riordan, Bartlett, Lund
		4	26.1.91 **Oldham A**	D2	H	W 2-0	Turner, Craig Short
		5	16.2.91 **Manchester C**	D1	H	W 1-0	Lund
		6	10.3.91 **Tottenham H**	D1	A	L 1-2	O'Riordan
1991-92	D1	3	5.1.91 **Wigan A**	D3	H	W 2-0	T.Johnson, Turner
		4	4.2.91 **Blackburn R**	D2	H	W 2-1	Lund, Draper
		5	15.3.91 **Norwich C**	D1	A	L 0-3	
1992-93	D1	3	12.1.93 **Sunderland**	D1	H	L 0-2	

NOTTS OLYMPIC

Formed 1884. Played at Churchville Fields, near The Queen pub.

1884-85	1	8.11.84 **Notts County**	A	L	0-2	
1885-86	1	31.10.85 **Notts Wanderers**	H	D	2-2	
	1r	7.11.85 **Notts Wanderers**	A	W	4-1	
	2	21.11.85 **Nottingham Forest**	A	L	1-4	
1886-87	1	30.10.86 **Nottingham Forest**	A	L	0-3	
1887-88	1	15.10.87 **Mellors Ltd, Nottingham**	H	L	3-6aet	
		FA ordered replay after protest				
	1r	22.10.87 **Mellors Ltd, Nottingham**	H	L	1-2	

NOTTS RANGERS

Formed 1868. Played at the Castle Grounds, Nottingham.

1884-85	1	8.11.84 **Staveley**	A	L	1-4	H.Shelton
1885-86	1	31.10.85 **Lockwood Brothers**	A	D	2-2	
	1r	7.11.85 **Lockwood Brothers**	H	W	4-0	
	2	21.11.85 **Sheffield Heeley**	A	W	6-1	Hodder 3, Stokes 2, Saddler
	3	12.12.85 **Notts Co**	A	L	0-3	
1886-87	1	30.10.86 **Sheffield Club**	A	W	3-0	Hodder 2, Geary
	2	13.11.86 **Notts Co**	A	D	3-3	Archer, Hodder, May
	2r	20.11.86 **Notts Co**	H	L	0-5	
1887-88	1	15.10.87 **Jardines Ltd**	H	W	10-1	
	2	5.11.87 **Grantham**	H	W	4-0	
	3	**bye**				
	4	17.12.87 **Darwen**	A	L	1-3	Partington

NOTTS RANGERS

1888-89	1	2.2.89	Sheffield W	H	D	1-1	James
	1r	9.2.89	Sheffield W	A	L	0-3	

NOTTS SWIFTS

1887-88	1	15.10.87	Nottingham F	A	L	1-2	Daft

NOTTS WANDERERS

1884-85	1	8.11.84	Sheffield Heeley	A	L	0-1	
1885-86	1	31.10.85	Notts Olympic	A	D	2-2	
	1r	7.11.85	Notts Olympic	H	L	1-4	

NUNEATON BOROUGH

Formed 1937. **First entered FA Cup:** 1945. **Cup Final Connection:** Former player Trevor Peake played for Coventry City in the 1987 FA Cup Final. **League clubs beaten:** Watford, Swansea T, Oxford U

1949-50	BC	1	26.11.49	Kings Lynn	ECL	H	W	2-1	Plant 2
		2	10.12.49	Mossley	CC	H	D	0-0	
		2r	17.12.49	Mossley		A	W	3-0	Black 2, Plant
		3	7.1.50	Exeter C	3S	A	L	0-3	
1953-54	BDL	1	21.11.53	Watford	3S	H	W	3-0	Wright 2, Jessop
		2	12.12.53	QPR	3S	A	D	1-1	Davies
		2r	17.12.53	QPR		H	L	1-2	Morrow
1954-55	BDL	1	20.11.54	Brentford	3S	A	L	1-2	Jessop
1966-67	SL	1	26.11.66	Wealdstone	IL	A	W	2-0	Richards, Cutler
		2	7.1.67	Swansea T	D3	H	W	2-0	Crawley, Coughlin og
		3	28.1.67	Rotherham U	D2	H	D	1-1	Cutler
		3r	31.1.67	Rotherham U		A	L	0-1	
1967-68	SL	1	9.12.67	Exeter C	D4	H	D	0-0	
		1r	13.12.67	Exeter C		A	D	0-0aet	
		1 2r	18.12.67	Exeter C at Ashton Gate			L	0-1	
1971-72	SL	1	20.11.71	Torquay U	D3	A	L	0-1	
1972-73	SL	1	18.11.72	Telford U	SL	A	L	2-3	Gill, Harris
1974-75	SL	1	23.11.74	Maidstone U	SL	H	D	2-2	Briscoe, Lewis
		1r	26.11.74	Maidstone U		A	L	0-2	
1975-76	SL	1	22.11.75	Wimbledon	SL	H	L	0-1	
1976-77	SL	1	20.11.76	Crook T	NL	A	W	4-1	Jones 2, Briscoe, White og
		2	11.12.76	Lincoln C	D3	A	L	0-6	
1977-78	SL	1	26.11.77	Oxford U	D3	H	W	2-0	Lang, Phillips (p)
		2	17.12.77	Tilbury	IL	H	L	1-2	Vincent
1978-79	SL	1	25.11.78	Crewe A	D4	H	L	0-2	
1979-80	APL	1	24.11.79	Northwich V	APL	H	D	3-3	Pugh 3
		1r	26.11.79	Northwich V		A	L	0-3	
1981-82	SL	1	21.11.81	Bishop Auckland	NL	A	L	1-4	Jones
1984-85	APL	1	17.11.84	Scunthorpe U	D4	H	D	1-1	Hill
		1r	20.11.84	Scunthorpe U		A	L	1-2aet	Culpin
1985-86	APL	1	16.11.85	Burnley	D4	H	L	2-3	Bennyworth, Murphy
1986-87	APL	1	15.11.86	Rochdale	D4	H	L	0-3	
1992-93	SL	1	14.11.92	Woking	GMVC	A	L	2-3	Bullock, Culpin

NUNHEAD

First entered FA Cup: 1905. Their 9-0 win over Kingstonian is the joint record victory in an FA Cup match between non-League clubs since the competition was re-organised in 1925.

1926-27	IL	1	27.11.26	Kingstonian	AL	H	W	9-0	Hill 2, Sanders 2, Daniels 3, Booker, Colwell
		2	11.12.26	Poole	WL	H	L	1-2	Colwell
1929-30	IL	1	30.11.29	Bristol R	3S	H	L	0-2	
1931-32	IL	1	28.11.31	Bath C	SL	A	L	0-9	
1935-36	IL	1	30.11.35	Watford	3S	H	L	2-4	Read, Aislatt

OLD BRIGHTONIANS

Formed 1871. Played at the Greyhound Ground, Dulwich, using the Greyhound pub as their changing rooms.

1884-85	1	8.11.84	Swifts		A	L	0-3	
1885-86	1	31.10.85	Acton		H	W	2-1	
	2	21.11.85	Old Westminsters		A	L	0-3	
1886-87	1	30.10.86	Clapham R		A	W	6-0	
	2	16.11.86	Old Westminsters		H	D	1-1	
	2r	20.11.86	Old Westminsters		A	L	0-3	
1887-88	1	8.10.87	Swindon T		H	W	1-0	N.Leete
	2	5.11.87	Old Harrovians		A	W	4-0	
	3	24.11.87	Old Carthusians		A	L	0-5	
1888-89	1	2.2.89	Notts Co		A	L	0-2	

OLD CARTHUSIANS

Formed 1875. **Best FA Cup Performance:** Winners: 1881. **FA Amateur Cup Winners:** 1894, 1897. Runners-up: 1895. Played home matches at Charterhouse school

1879-80	1	8.11.79	Acton		A	W	4-0	
	2	10.1.80	Wanderers		A	L	0-1	
1880-81	1	23.10.80	Saffron Walden		H	W	7-0	Parry 4, Growse, Richards, others 1
	2	11.12.80	Dreadnought			W	5-1	Jenner 3, Richards 2
	3		bye					
	4	19.2.81	Royal Engineers			W	2-0	Wynyard, Price
	5	19.3.81	Clapham R			W	3-1aet	Page 2, Parry
	SF	26.3.81	Darwen			W	4-1	Hansell, Todd, Vincent, Wynyard
		played at Kennington Oval						
	F	9.4.81	OLD ETONIANS			W	3-0	Wynyard, Parry, Todd
		played at Kennington Oval						
1881-82	1	5.11.81	Esher Leopold		H	W	5-0	
	2	3.12.81	Barnes		H	W	7-1	Page 2, Parry 2, Wynyard 2, Richards
	3	20.12.81	Royal Engineers		H	L	0-2	
1882-83	1	21.10.82	Pilgrims		H	W	6-0	Parry 3, Last, Page, Wilson
	2	2.12.82	Etonian Ramblers		H	W	7-0	
	3	16.12.82	Old Westminsters		H	W	3-2	Page 2, Parry
	4	25.1.83	Royal Engineers		H	W	6-2	Parry 3, Cobbold 2, Page
	5	20.2.83	Clapham R		H	W	5-3	Cobbold, Last, Page, Richards, others 1
	SF	17.3.83	Blackburn Olympic			L	0-4	
		played at Whalley Range, Manchester						
1883-84	1	10.11.83	Reading Minster		A	W	10-1	Parry 5, Last 2, Escombe, King-Harman, others 1
	2	24.11.83	Old Foresters		H	L	2-7	Cobbold, Hansell
1884-85	1	8.11.84	Acton		A	W	7-1	
	2	6.12.84	Great Marlow		H	W	5-3	Cobbold 2, Last, Smith, others 1
	3		bye					
	4	24.1.85	Grimsby Town		H	W	3-0	Cobbold, Parry, own goal
	5	7.2.85	Chatham		A	W	3-0	Barmby 2, Hansell
	6	14.2.85	Church FC		A	W	1-0	Parry
	SF	7.3.85	Blackburn R			L	1-5	Barmby
		played at Trent Bridge						
1885-86	1	31.10.85	Chatham		A	W	2-0	
	2	21.11.85	Upton Park		H	W	6-0	
	3		bye					
	4		bye					
	5	23.1.86	WBA		A	L	0-1	
1886-87	1	23.10.86	Reading		H	W	2-1	Escombe, Smith
	2	13.11.86	Crusaders		H	W	4-2	
	3		London Caledonians			walkover		
	4		bye					
	5	5.2.87	Leek		A	W	2-0	
	6	2.3.87	Preston NE		H	L	1-2aet	Cobbold
1887-88	1	15.10.87	Hanover U		H	W	5-0	Price 3, Waddington, White
	2	5.11.87	Watford Rovers		A	W	3-1	Price 3
	3	24.11.87	Old Brightonians		H	W	5-0	Parry 2, Currey, Escombe, Price
	4		bye					
	5	7.1.88	Bootle		H	W	2-0	Cobbold 2
	6	28.1.88	WBA		A	L	2-4	Price 2
1888-89	1	2.2.89	Wolverhampton W	D1	A	L	3-4	Currey 2, Leman
1889-90	1	18.1.90	Wolverhampton W	D1	A	L	0-2	

OLD ETONIANS

Formed at Eton 1865. **Best FA Cup Performances:** Winners 1879, 1882. Runners-up: 1876, 1881, 1883.

1873-74	1		High Wycombe			scratched	
1874-75	1	5.11.74	Swifts	A	D	0-0	
	1r	14.11.74	Swifts	H	D	1-1	Bonsor
	1 2r	26.11.74	Swifts	H	W	3-0	
	2		bye				
	3	23.1.75	Maidenhead		W	1-0	
	SF	27.2.75	Shropshire W		W	1-0	Bonsor
	F	13.3.75	Royal Engineers		D	1-1	Bonsor
	Fr	16.3.75	Royal Engineers		L	0-2	
		semi-final and both final matches at Kennington Oval					
1875-76	1	9.11.75	Pilgrims	H	W	4-1	Bonsor, A.Lyttleton, Patton, Wilson
	2	11.22.75	Maidenhead	H	W	8-0	Patton 3, Thompson 2, Courthorpe, Griffith, og
	3	29.1.76	Clapham R		W	1-0	Bonsor
	SF	19.2.76	Oxford Univ.		W	1-0	Sturgis
	F	11.3.76	Wanderers		D	1-1	Bonsor
	Fr	18.3.76	Wanderers		L	0-3	
		semi-final and both final matches at Kennington Oval					
1876-77	1		Barnes			scratched	
1877-78		*did not enter*					
1878-79	1	9.11.78	Wanderers	A	W	7-2	Calvert, Goodhart, Lyttleton, Novelli 2, Sedgwick, own goal
	2	18.12.78	Reading	A	W	1-0	
	3	11.1.79	Minerva		W	5-2	Sturgis 3, Goodhart 2
	4	13.2.79	Darwen		D	5-5	Goodhart 3, Christian, Whitfield
	4r	8.3.79	Darwen		D	2-2aet	Clerke, Whitfield
	4 2r	15.3.79	Darwen		W	6-2	Goodhart 2, Sedgwick 2, Clerke, Whitfield
	SF	22.3.79	Nottingham F		W	2-1	Whitfield, Clerke
	F	29.3.79	CLAPHAM R		W	1-0	Clerke
		all three matches against Darwen, semi-final and final at Kennington Oval					
1879-80	1		Barnes			walkover	
	2		bye				
	3	24.1.80	Wanderers		W	3-1	Goodhart 2, Sedgwick
	4	7.2.80	West End		W	5-1	Goodhart 3, Kinnaird 2
	5	21.2.80	Clapham R		L	0-1	
1880-81	1	6.11.80	Brentwood	A	W	10-0	Goodhart 3, Whitfield 2, others 5
	2	4.12.80	Hendon	A	W	2-0	Novelli, Whitfield
	3	5.2.81	Herts Rangers		W	3-0	Anderson, Chevallier, Macauley
	4	19.2.81	Grey Friars		W	4-0	
	5	19.3.81	Stafford Road		W	2-1	Anderson, others 1
	SF		bye				
	F	9.4.81	Old Carthusians		L	0-3	
		played at Kennington Oval					
1881-82	1	5.11.81	Clapham R	H	W	2-1	Goodhart, MacAuley
	2		bye				
	3	17.12.81	Swifts		W	3-0	Dunn 2, MacAuley
	4	14.1.82	Maidenhead		W	6-3	Chitty 2, Anderson, MacAuley, Foley, others 1
	5		bye				
	SF	4.3.82	Great Marlow		W	5-0	Goodhart 3, Dunn, MacAuley
	F	25.3.82	BLACKBURN R		W	1-0	Anderson
		semi-final and final played at Kennington Oval					
1882-83	1	4.11.82	Old Foresters	H	D	1-1	Anderson
	1r	18.11.82	Old Foresters	H	W	3-1	Anderson, Dunn, Goodhart
	2	2.12.82	Brentwood	H	W	2-1	Anderson, Whitfield
	3	16.12.82	Rochester		W	7-0	
	4	24.1.83	Swifts		W	2-0	Goodhart 2
	5	3.2.83	Hendon		W	4-2	
	SF	17.3.83	Notts Co		W	2-1	MacAuley, Anderson
	F	31.3.83	Blackburn Olympic		L	1-2aet	Goodhart
		semi-final and final played at Kennington Oval					
1883-84	1	10.11.83	Hendon	A	L	2-3	
1884-85	1	8.11.84	Luton Wanderers	A	W	3-1	Chevallier 2, Whitfield
	2	6.12.84	Brentwood	A	D	2-2	Bury, Goodhart
	2r	20.12.84	Brentwood	H	W	6-1	Chevallier 2, Dunn, French, Goodhart, og
	3		bye				
	4	24.1.85	Middlesbrough	H	W	5-2	Goodhart 3, Chevallier, Marchant

			bye				
	5		bye				
	6	21.2.85	Nottingham F	H	L	0-2	
1885-86	1		Bournemouth Rovers		walkover		
	2	21.11.85	Great Marlow	A	L	1-6	
1886-87	1	30.10.86	Royal Engineers	H	W	1-0	
	2	20.11.86	Chesham Generals	A	W	7-1	
	3	11.12.86	Old Westminsters	A	L	0-3	
1887-88	1	8.10.87	Lancing Old Boys	H	W	4-2	
	2	5.11.87	Old St Marks	H	W	3-2	
	3	26.11.87	Old Westminsters	H	W	7-2	
	4	17.12.87	Nottingham Forest	A	L	0-6	

OLD FORESTERS

Formed 1876. Played at Epping Forest at Snaresbrook and used the Eagle pub as their changing room.

1877-78	1		Old Wykehamists		walkover		
	2	15.12.77	Oxford University	A	L	0-1	
1878-79	1	9.11.78	Royal Engineers	A	L	0-3	
1879-80	1	8.11.79	Hendon	A	D	1-1	
	1r	15.11.79	Hendon	H	D	2-2	Day, J.Guy
	1 2r	22.11.79	Hendon	A	L	1-3	
1880-81	1	6.11.80	Swifts	A	D	1-1	
	1r	20.11.80	Swifts	H	L	1-2	Woolley
1881-82	1	5.11.81	Morton Rangers	H	W	3-0	
	2	3.12.81	Pilgrims	H	W	3-1	
	3		bye				
	4	21.1.82	Royal Engineers	H	W	2-1	Burrows, Matthews
	5	14.2.82	Great Marlow	H	D	0-0	
	5r	18.2.82	Great Marlow	A	L	0-1	
1882-83	1	4.11.82	Old Etonians	A	D	1-1	Fairclough
	1r	18.11.82	Old Etonians	A	L	1-3	Knowles
1883-84	1	10.11.83	Dreadnought	H	W	2-1	J.Guy, Horner
	2	24.11.83	Old Carthusians	A	W	7-2	Horner 3, R.Guy, others 3
	3		bye				
	4	19.1.84	Swifts	A	L	1-2	Fairclough
1884-85	1	1.11.84	Hoddesdon	H	W	8-0	
	2	29.11.84	Hanover U	A	L	1-2	
1885-86	1	31.10.85	Royal Engineers	A	W	5-1	
	2	21.11.85	Old Harrovians	A	L	1-2	
1886-87	1		Cannon FC		walkover		
	2		bye				
	3	11.12.86	Chatham	A	W	4-1	
	4	15.1.87	Swifts	A	W	2-0	Horner, Newbery
	5	29.1.87	Preston North End	H	L	0-3	
1887-88	1	15.10.87	London Caledonians	A	W	6-1	
	2	5.11.87	Great Marlow	A	W	3-2aet	
	3		bye				
	4	17.12.87	Grimsby Town	H	W	4-2	H.Guy 2, R.Guy, Johnson
	5	7.1.88	Middlesbrough	A	L	0-4	

FA ordered replay after protest, but Old Foresters scratched after FA ordered the match to be replayed at Middlesbrough

OLD HARROVIANS

Formed 1872. Played at the Recreation Ground, Harrow.

1876-77	1	4.11.76	Royal Engineers	A	L	1-2	H.Longman
1877-78	1	7.11.77	103rd Regiment	A	W	2-0	Bevington, Betts
	2	22.12.77	1st Surrey Rifles	H	W	6-0	Bevington 2, Prior 2, Colbeck, Hadow
	3	2.2.78	Cambridge University		D	2-2	Bevington, Greaves
	3r	9.2.78	Cambridge University		D	2-2aet	Colbeck, Harvey
	3 2r	16.2.78	Cambridge University		W	2-0	Lowis, Prior
	4	9.3.78	Upton Park		W	3-1	Betts 2, Colbeck
	SF	16.3.78	Royal Engineers		L	1-2	Prior
			played at Kennington Oval				
1878-79	1	2.11.78	Southall Park	H	W	8-0	Howell 2, Lowis 2, Prior 2, Colbeck, Davidson
	2	21.12.78	Panthers	H	W	3-0	Prior 2, others 1

	3	28.1.79	Nottingham Forest		L	0-2	
1879-80	1	8.11.79	Finchley	A	W	2-1	
	2		bye				
	3	4.2.80	Royal Engineers	A	L	0-2	
1880-81	1	13.11.80	Maidenhead	A	D	0-0	
	1r	20.11.80	Maidenhead	H	L	0-1	
1881-82	1	5.11.81	Olympic FC	H	W	4-2	
	2	3.12.81	Swifts	A	L	1-7	Gray
1885-86	1		St James's		walkover		
	2	21.11.85	Old Foresters	H	W	2-1	
	3		Swifts		disqualified		
1886-87	1	30.10.86	Old Westminsters	H	L	0-4	
1887-88	1	15.10.87	Hendon	A	W	4-2	
	2	5.11.87	Old Brightonians	H	L	0-4	

OLD PHILBERDIANS, MAIDENHEAD

1880-81	1		Pilgrims		scratched	

OLD SALOPIANS

1876-77	1		Oxford University		scratched	

OLD ST MARKS

Formed 1885. Played at The Limes, in Barnes, South West London.

1887-88	1	15.10.87	East Sheen	H	W	7-2	
	2	5.11.87	Old Etonians	A	L	2-3	

OLD WESTMINSTERS

Formed 1870. No recognised home ground, they played on various pitches in and around the London area.

1882-83	1	4.11.82	Maidenhead		H	W	2-0	Allington, Bury
	2		bye					
	3	16.12.82	Old Carthusians			L	2-3	Bury, Sandwith
1883-84	1	3.11.83	Chatham		H	W	3-0	Allington 2, Jenner
	2	1.12.83	Hendon		H	W	2-1	Bain, Burridge
	3		bye					
	4	19.1.84	Wednesbury Town			W	5-0	Patrick 3, Burridge 2
	5	9.2.84	Queens Park, Glasgow			L	0-1	
1884-85	1	1.11.84	Bournemouth Rovers		H	W	6-0	Hurst 3, A.Heath, Scoones, og
	2	6.12.84	Henley		H	W	7-0	Bain 2, Hurst 2, Bailey, Janson, C.Heath
	3	3.1.85	Swifts			D	1-1	Bain
	3r	14.1.85	Swifts			D	2-2	C.Heath, Hurst
	3 2r	21.1.85	Swifts			L	1-2	C.Heath
1885-86	1	31.10.85	Hotspur FC		H	W	3-1	
	2	21.11.85	Old Brightonians		H	W	3-0	
	3	12.12.85	Romford		H	W	5-1	
	4		bye					
	5		Bolton Wanderers			walkover – FA disqualified Bolton for professionalism		
	6	13.2.86	WBA		A	L	0-6	
1886-87	1	30.10.86	Old Harrovians		A	W	4-0	
	2	16.11.86	Old Brightonians		A	D	1-1	
	2r	20.11.86	Old Brightonians		H	W	3-0	
	3	11.12.86	Old Etonians			W	3-0	
	4		bye					
	5	29.1.87	Partick Thistle			W	1-0	Bain
	6	19.2.87	Glasgow Rangers			L	1-5	Janson
1887-88	1	15.10.87	Clapton		H	W	4-1	
	2	5.11.87	Millwall Rovers		H	W	8-1	
	3	26.11.87	Old Etonians			L	2-7	
1888-89	1	2.2.89	Burnley	D1	A	L	3-4	Bedford, Phillimore, 1 other
1889-90	1	18.1.90	Stoke	D1	A	L	0-3	
1890-91	1		WBA	D1		scratched		
1891-92	1	16.1.92	WBA	D1	H	L	2-3	Sandilands, McCulloch og

OLD WYKEHAMISTS

Formed 1876. Home ground was originally in West Drayton, Middlesex.

1876-77	1		Southall Park		scratched	
1877-78	1		Old Foresters		scratched	
1883-84	1	10.11.83	Upton Park	A	W 7-0	
	2	1.12.83	Windsor Home Park	A	W 1-0	Chitty
	3		bye			
	4	19.1.84	Blackburn Olympic	A	L 0-6	
1884-85	1	8.11.84	Maidenhead	A	W 3-0	Blackburn, Fort, others 1
	2	6.12.84	Hotspur FC	A	W 2-1	Fort, Ingram
	3	3.1.85	Upton Park	H	W 2-1	
	4	17.1.85	Queen's Park, Glasgow	A	L 0-7	
1885-86	1	31.10.85	Uxbridge	H	W 5-0	
	2	21.11.85	Luton Wanderers	H	W 10-0	
	3		Great Marlow		scratched	
1886-87	1	30.10.86	Hanover U	H	W 3-0	
	2	20.11.86	London Caledonians	H	L 0-1	
1887-88	1	8.10.87	Hitchin	A	W 5-2	
	2	29.10.87	Crusaders	A	L 2-3	

OLDBURY TOWN

1887-88	1	15.10.87	Aston Villa	H	L 0-4	

OLDHAM ATHLETIC

Formed 1875 as Pine Villa FC. Oldham Athletic 1899. **Best FA Cup Performance:** semi-finals: 1913, 1990. **Record FA Cup Win:** 10-1 vs Lytham, 1st round, 28.11.1925. **Record FA Cup Defeat:** 0-6 vs Huddersfield T, 3rd round, 13.1.1932; 0-6 vs Tottenham H 3rd round, 14.1.1933.

1905-06	LC	1q **Ashton T** (H) 2-1; 2q **Fairfield** (H) 8-0; 3q **Stalybridge R** (H) 1-1; 3qr **Stalybridge R** (A) 3-1; 4q **Hull C** (A) 1-2					
1906-07	LC	1q **Hyde** (H) 5-0; 2q **Newton Heath** (H) 4-1; 3q **Buxton** (A) 3-1; 4q **Atherton Church** (A) 1-1; 4qr **Atherton Church** (H) 4-1;					
		5q **South Bank** (H) 9-1					
		1	17.1.07	Kidderminster H	BDL H	W 5-0	Hancock 2, D.Walders, Shadbolt, Brunton
		2	2.2.07	Liverpool	D1 H	L 0-1	
1907-08	D2	Int **Darwen** (H) 8-1					
		1	11.1.08	Leeds C	D2 H	W 2-1	Whaites, Newton
		2	1.2.08	Everton	D1 H	D 0-0	
		2r	5.2.08	Everton	A	L 1-6	Whaites
1908-09	D2	1	16.1.09	Leeds C	D2 H	D 1-1	Hamilton
		1r	20.1.09	Leeds C	A	L 0-2	
1909-10	D2	1	15.1.10	Aston Villa	D1 H	L 1-2	Toward
1910-11	D1	1	14.1.11	Birmingham	D2 A	D 1-1	Toward
		1r	17.1.11	Birmingham	H	W 2-0	Wilson, Woodger
		2	4.2.11	Hull C	D2 A	L 0-1	
1911-12	D1	1	13.1.12	Hull C	H	D 1-1	Wilson
		1r	16.1.12	Hull C	A	W 1-0	Woodger
		2	3.2.12	Manchester C	D1 A	W 1-0	Woodger
		3	24.2.12	Everton	D1 H	L 0-2	
1912-13	D1	1	11.1.13	Bolton W	D1 H	W 2-0	Tummon 2
		2	1.2.13	Nottingham F	D2 H	W 5-1	Kemp 2, Walters, Tummon, Woodger
		3	22.2.13	Manchester U	D1 H	D 0-0	
		3r	26.2.13	Manchester U	A	W 2-1	Gee, Toward
		4	8.3.13	Everton	D1 A	W 1-0	Gee
		SF	29.3.13	Aston Villa	D1	L 0-1	
		played at Ewood Park					
1913-14	D1	1	10.1.14	Brighton & HA	SL H	D 1-1	Donnachie
		1r	14.1.14	Brighton & HA	A	L 0-1aet	
1914-15	D1	1	9.1.15	Croydon Common	SL A	W 3-0	Wilson, Tummon, Kemp
		2	30.1.15	Rochdale	CL A	W 3-0	Kemp, Gee, Donachie
		3	20.2.15	Birmingham	D2 A	W 3-2	Kemp, Cashmore, Pilkington
		4	6.3.15	Sheffield U	D1 H	D 0-0	
		4r	13.3.15	Sheffield U	A	L 0-3	
1919-20	D1	1	10.1.20	Cardiff C	SL A	L 0-2	
1920-21	D1	1	8.1.21	Brighton & HA	3S A	L 1-4	JH Marshall
1921-22	D1	1	7.1.22	Gillingham	3S A	W 3-1	F.Broadbent 2, W Taylor

Season	Div	Round	Date	Opponent	Opp Div	Venue	Result	Score	Scorers
		2	28.1.22	Barnsley	D2	A	L	1-3	F.Broadbent
1922-23	D1	1	13.1.23	Middlesbrough	D1	H	L	0-1	
1923-24	D2	1	12.1.24	Sunderland	D1	H	W	2-1	JE Blair, Staniforth
		2	2.2.24	Swindon T	3S	A	L	0-2	
1924-25	D2	1	10.1.25	Blackburn R	D1	A	L	0-1	
1925-26	D2	1	28.11.25	Lytham		H	W	10-1	Barnes 3, Ormston 2, Pynegar 2, Watson 2, Naylor
		2	12.12.25	Stockton	NL	A	W	6-4	Watson 4, Pynegar, Wynne (p)
		3	9.1.26	Millwall	3S	A	D	1-1	Douglas
		3r	12.1.26	Millwall		H	L	0-1	
1926-27	D2	3	8.1.27	Brentford	3S	H	–	2-1	Pynegar, Watson
			abandoned after 73 minutes – fog						
		3	10.1.27	Brentford		H	L	2-4	Pynegar, Barnes
1927-28	D2	3	14.1.28	Blackpool	D1	A	W	4-1	Watson 2, Stanton, King
		4	28.1.28	Tottenham H	D1	A	L	0-3	
1928-29	D2	3	12.1.29	Bolton W	D1	A	L	0-2	
1929-30	D2	3	11.1.30	Wolverhampton W	D2	H	W	1-0	Goodier
		4	25.1.30	Sheffield W	D1	H	L	3-4	Littlewood 2, Adlam
1930-31	D2	3	10.1.31	Watford	3S	H	L	1-3	Fitton
1931-32	D2	3	9.1.32	Huddersfield T	D1	H	D	1-1	Ivill
		3r	13.1.32	Huddersfield T		A	L	0-6	
1932-33	D2	3	14.1.33	Tottenham H	D2	H	L	0-6	
1933-34	D2	3	13.1.34	Reading	3S	A	W	2-1	Rowley, Bailey
		4	27.1.34	Sheffield W	D1	H	D	1-1	Reid
		4r	31.1.34	Sheffield W		A	L	1-6	Bailey
1934-35	D2	3	12.1.35	Sheffield W	D1	A	L	1-3	Walsh
1935-36	3N	1	30.11.35	Ferryhill A	NL	H	W	6-1	Davis 2, Brunskill, Agar, Walsh, Buckley
		2	14.12.35	Bristol R	3S	H	D	1-1	Walsh
		2r	18.12.35	Bristol R		A	L	1-4	Robson
1936-37	3N	1	28.11.36	Tranmere R	3N	H	W	1-0	Davis
		2	12.12.36	Lincoln C	3N	A	W	3-2	McCormick 2, Davis
		3	16.1.37	Exeter C	3S	A	L	0-3	
1937-38	3N	1	27.11.37	Wrexham	3N	A	L	1-2	Hilton (p)
1938-39	3N	1	26.11.38	Crewe A	3N	H	D	2-2	Ferrier, Blackshaw
		1r	30.11.38	Crewe A		A	L	0-1	
1945-46	3N	1 1L	17.11.45	Southport	3N	A	W	2-1	Chapman 2
		1 2L	24.11.45	Southport		H	W	3-1	Lawton, West, Standring
		2 1L	8.12.45	Accrington S	3N	H	W	2-1	West, Standring
		2 2L	15.12.45	Accrington S		A	L	1-3	Ferrier
1946-47	3N	1	30.11.46	Tranmere R	3N	H	W	1-0	Tomlinson
		2	14.12.46	Doncaster R	3N	A	L	1-2	Bowden
1947-48	3N	1	29.11.47	Lancaster C	LC	H	W	6-0	Haddington 2, Horton, Gemmell, Wilson, Brierley
		2	13.12.47	Mansfield T	3N	H	L	0-1	
1948-49	3N	1	27.11.48	Wrexham	3N	A	W	3-0	Stock, Gemmell, Jessop
		2	11.12.48	Walthamstow A	IL	A	D	2-2aet	Tomlinson, Gemmell
		2r	18.12.48	Walthamstow A		H	W	3-1	Haddington 2, Gemmell
		3	8.1.49	Cardiff C	D2	H	L	2-3	Gemmell, Haddington
1949-50	3N	1	26.11.49	Stockton	NEL	H	W	4-0	Haddington 2, Spurdle, Gemmell
		2	10.12.49	Crewe A	3N	A	D	1-1	Jessop
		2r	13.12.49	Crewe A		A	D	0-0	
		2 2r	19.12.49	Crewe A at Maine Rd			W	3-0	Haddington 2 (1p), Spurdle
		3	7.1.50	Newcastle U	D1	H	L	2-7	Spurdle, Haddington
1950-51	3N	1	25.11.50	Bradford C	3N	A	D	2-2	Gemmell 2 (1p)
		1r	28.11.50	Bradford C		H	W	2-1	Goodfellow, Munro
		2	9.12.50	Hartlepools U	3N	A	W	2-1	Ormond, Newton og
		3	6.1.51	Manchester U	D1	A	L	1-4	Smith
1951-52	3N	1	24.11.51	Nelson	LC	A	W	4-0	McKennan 3, Gemmell
		2	15.12.51	Southend U	3S	A	L	0-5	
1952-53	3N	1	22.11.52	Boston U	ML	A	W	2-1	Clarke, McKennan
		2	6.12.52	Port Vale	3N	A	W	3-0	Gemmell 2, Ormond
		3	10.1.53	Birmingham C	D2	H	L	1-3	McKennan
1953-54	D2	3	9.1.54	Ipswich T	3S	A	D	3-3	McIlvenny 2, Clarke
		3r	12.1.54	Ipswich T		H	L	0-1	
1954-55	3N	1	20.11.54	Crewe A	3N	H	W	1-0	McShane
		2	11.12.54	Bournemouth	3S	A	L	0-1	
1955-56	3N	1	19.11.55	Bradford C	3N	A	L	1-3	Scrine
1956-57	3N	1	17.11.56	Halifax T	3N	A	W	3-2	Neale 2, Pearson
		2	8.12.56	Accrington S	3N	A	L	1-2	Neale

1957-58	3N	1	16.11.57	Bradford PA	3N	H	W	2-0	Fawley, Duffy
		2	7.12.57	Workington	3N	H	L	1-5	Murray
1958-59	D4	1	15.11.58	Denaby U	ML	A	W	2-0	Thompson 2
		2	6.12.58	South Shields	ML	H	W	2-0	Bourne, Phoenix
		3	10.1.59	Stoke C	D2	A	L	1-5	Duffy
1959-60	D4	1	14.11.59	Shildon	NL	A	D	1-1	Spurdle
		1r	17.11.59	Shildon		H	W	3-0	McGill, Bazley, Walters
		2	5.12.59	Bury	D3	A	L	1-2	Phoenix
1960-61	D4	1	5.11.60	Rhyl A	CC	A	W	1-0	Lister
		2	26.11.60	Chesterfield	D3	A	D	4-4	Lister 2, Phoenix, Johnstone
		2r	29.11.60	Chesterfield		H	L	0-3	
1961-62	D4	1	4.11.61	Shildon	NL	H	W	5-2	Lister 3, Jarvis, Johnstone (p)
		2	25.11.61	Chesterfield	D4	A	D	2-2	Lister, Colquhoun
		2r	29.11.61	Chesterfield		H	W	4-2aet	Colquhoun 2, Johnstone (p), Powell og
		3	8.1.62	Bristol R	D2	A	D	1-1	Phoenix
		3r	10.1.62	Bristol R		H	W	2-0	Colquhoun 2
		4	27.1.62	Liverpool	D2	H	L	1-2	Colquhoun
1962-63	D4	1	3.11.62	Bradford C	D4	H	L	2-5	Frizzell, Whitaker
1963-64	D3	1	20.11.63	Mansfield T	D3	H	W	3-2	Ledger, Colquhoun, Whitaker
		2	7.12.63	Bradford PA	D4	H	W	2-0	Bowie, Scoular og
		3	4.1.64	Ipswich T	D1	A	L	3-6	Lister 2, Bowie
1964-65	D3	1	14.11.64	Hereford U	SL	H	W	4-0	Colquhoun 3, Lister
		2	2.12.64	Crook T	NL	A	W	1-0	Bartley
		3	9.1.65	Middlesbrough	D2	A	L	2-6	Williams, Martin (p)
1965-66	D3	1	13.11.65	Mansfield T	D3	A	W	3-1	Holden 2, Jackson
		2	4.12.65	Darlington	D4	A	W	1-0	Dearden
		3	22.1.66	West Ham	D1	H	D	2-2	Blore 2
		3r	24.1.66	West Ham		A	L	1-2	Pennington
1966-67	D3	1	26.11.66	Notts Co	D4	H	W	3-1	Asprey, Large, Collins
		2	7.1.67	Grantham	ML	A	W	4-0	Collins 2, Wood, Bebbington
		3	28.1.67	Wolverhampton W	D2	H	D	2-2	Bebbington 2
		3r	1.2.67	Wolverhampton W		A	L	1-4	Bebbington
1967-68	D3	1	9.12.67	Barrow	D3	A	L	0-2	
1968-69	D3	1	16.11.68	Wrexham	D4	A	L	2-4	Bebbington, Chapman
1969-70	D4	1	15.11.69	Grantham	ML	H	W	3-1	Wood, Colquhoun, Bingham (p)
		2	6.12.69	South Shields	NPL	A	D	0-0	
		2r	9.12.69	South Shields		H	L	1-2	Bebbington
1970-71	D4	1	21.11.70	Rochdale	D3	A	L	0-2	
1971-72	D3	1	20.11.71	Chesterfield	D3	A	L	0-3	
1972-73	D3	1	18.11.72	Scarborough	NPL	H	D	1-1	Shaw
		1r	x2.11.72	Scaborough		A	L	1-2	Collins
1973-74	D3	1	24.11.73	Formby	CC	A	W	2-0	Jones 2
		2	15.12.73	Halifax T	D3	A	W	1-0	McVitie
		3	6.1.74	Cambridge U	D3	A	D	2-2	Lochhead, Edwards
		3r	8.1.74	Cambridge U		H	D	3-3aet	Robins 2, McVitie
		3 2r	14.1.74	Cambridge U at Nottingham Forest			W	2-1	Jones, Garwood
		4	26.1.74	Burnley	D1	H	L	1-4	Whittle (p)
1974-75	D2	3	4.1.75	Aston Villa	D2	A	L	0-3	
1975-76	D2	3	3.1.76	Sunderland	D2	A	L	0-2	
1976-77	D2	3	8.1.77	Plymouth A	D2	H	W	3-0	Whittle, Robins, Halom
		4	29.1.77	Northwich Victoria	NPL		W	3-1	Halom 2, Valentine
				played at Maine Road					
		5	26.2.77	Liverpool	D1	A	L	1-3	Shaw
1977-78	D2	3	7.1.78	Luton T	D2	A	D	1-1	Taylor
		3r	10.1.78	Luton T		H	L	1-2	Young
1978-79	D2	3	6.1.79	Stoke C	D2	–		0-2	
				abandoned at half time					
		3	17.1.79	Stoke C		A	W	1-0	Wood
		4	26.2.79	Leicester C	D1	H	W	3-1	Young 3
		5	28.2.79	Tottenham H	D1	A	L	0-1	
1979-80	D2	3	5.1.80	Coventry C	D1	H	L	0-1	
1980-81	D2	3	3.1.81	Wimbledon	D4	A	D	0-0	
		3r	6.1.81	Wimbledon		H	L	0-1	
1981-82	D2	3	5.1.82	Gillingham	D3	A	L	1-2	Heaton (p)
1982-83	D2	3	8.1.83	Fulham	D2	H	L	0-2	
1983-84	D2	3	7.1.84	Shrewsbury T	D2	A	L	0-3	
1984-85	D2	3	5.1.85	Brentford	D3	H	W	2-1	Quinn, Harrison

		4	26.1.85	Sheffield W	D1	A	L	1-5	Bowden
1985-86	D2	3	6.1.86	Orient	D4	H	L	1-2	Palmer
1986-87	D2	3	10.1.87	Bradford C	D2	H	D	1-1	McGuire
		3r	19.1.87	Bradford C		A	L	1-5	Wright
1987-88	D2	3	9.1.88	Tottenham H	D1	H	L	2-4	Wright, Cecere
1988-89	D2	3	7.1.89	Charlton A	D1	A	L	1-2	Milligan
1989-90	D2	3	6.1.90	Birmingham C	D3	A	D	1-1	Bunn
		3r	10.1.90	Birmingham C		H	W	1-0	R.Holden
		4	27.1.90	Brighton & HA	D2	H	W	2-1	McGarvey, Ritchie
		5	17.2.90	Everton	D1	H	D	2-2	Ritchie (p), Palmer
		5r	21.2.90	Everton		A	D	1-1aet	Marshall
		5 2r	10.3.90	Everton		H	W	2-1aet	Palmer, Marshall (p)
		6	14.3.90	Aston Villa	D1	H	W	3-0	R.Holden, Price og, Redfearn
		SF	8.4.90	Manchester U	D1		D	3-3aet	Barrett Marshall, Palmer
		SFr	11.4.90	Manchester U			L	1-2aet	Ritchie
			both matches played at Maine Road						
1990-91	D2	3	5.1.91	Brentford	D3	H	W	3-1	Redfearn 2 (2ps), Adams
		4	26.1.91	Notts Co	D2	A	L	0-2	
1991-92	D1	3	4.1.92	Leyton O	D3	H	D	1-1	Sharp
		3r	15.1.92	Leyton O		A	L	2-4	Adams, Palmer
1992-93	PL	3	2.1.93	Tranmere R	D1	H	D	2-2	Olney, Bernard
		3r	12.1.93	Tranmere R		A	L	0-3	

OLYMPIC FC

Formed 1869. Played at Upton Park, East London, near the Freemason's Tavern.

1887-88	1	5.11.81	Old Harrovians		A	L	2-4

OSWALDTWISTLE ROVERS

Formed 1877. Home ground was at Roe Greave Road, near the Rose and Crown pub

1884-85	1	11.10.84	Blackburn Olympic		A	L	0-12
1885-86	1	31.10.85	Lower Darwen		H	W	3-1
	2	21.11.85	Blackburn Rovers		A	L	0-1
1886-87	1	23.10.86	Witton Albion		H	L	2-3
1887-88	1	15.10.87	Witton Albion		H	L	3-4

OSWESTRY TOWN

One of the oldest clubs in the country, formed in 1860. The Victoria Ground was their home pitch from their formation until they folded in 1988. Being re-formed to compete in senior non-League football for the 1993-94 season. **Welsh FA Cup winners:** 1884, 1901, 1907

1882-83		1	4.11.82	Druids		A	D	1-1	
		1r	18.11.82	Druids		H	L	0-2	
1883-84		1	10.11.83	Hartford St John's		H	W	2-0	
		2	1.12.83	Wrexham		A	W	4-3	Roberts 3, Shaw
		3	29.12.83	Queen's Park, Glasgow		H	L	1-7	Foulkes
1884-85		1	8.11.84	Crewe A		A	L	1-2	
1885-86		1	24.10.85	Bollington		A	W	5-0	
		2	21.11.85	Crewe A		H	D	1-1	Bryan
		2r		Crewe A			scratched		
1886-87		1	30.10.86	Bollington		A	W	8-2	
		2	20.11.86	Leek		A	L	2-4	
1887-88		1	8.10.87	Vale of Llangollen		A	W	3-1	
			FA ordered replay after protest						
		1r	22.10.87	Vale of Llangollen		A	W	2-0	
		2		bye					
		3	26.11.87	Stoke		A	L	0-3	
1927-28	BDL	1	26.11.27	Stockport Co	3N	A	L	2-5	W.Jones, R.Jones
1957-58	BDL	1	16.11.57	Bournemouth	3S	H	L	1-5	Thomas
1959-60	CC	1	14.11.59	Southend U	D3	A	L	0-6	
1974-75	CC	1	23.11.74	Doncaster R	D4	H	L	1-3	Price

OVER WANDERERS

see Winsford United

OWLERTON

Formed 1869. Played at Owlerton Fields near the Crown Inn, Owlerton, Sheffield

1887-88	1	15.10.87	**Eckington Works**		H	W	2-1	
	2	5.11.87	**Sheffield Heeley**		H	W	1-0	
	3	26.11.87	**Derby Co**		A	L	2-6	Judge, other 1

OXFORD CITY

Formed 1882. **First entered FA Cup:** 1895. FA Amateur Cup Winners: 1906. Runners-up: 1903, 1913. **Cup Final Connection:** Bobby Moore, who captained West Ham when they won the FA Cup in 1964 was manager at Oxford City for a spell between 1979-1981.

1901-02	n/af	Int	14.12.01	**New Brighton Tower**	D2			*walkover*	
		1	25.1.02	**Lincoln C**	D2	H	D	0-0	
		1r	29.1.02	**Lincoln C**		A	L	0-4	
1906-07	n/af	1	12.1.07	**Bury**	D1	H	L	0-3	
1933-34	IL	1	25.11.33	**Gillingham**	3S	H	L	1-5	James
1966-67	IL	1	26.11.66	**Bristol R**	D3	H	D	2-2	Woodley, Bradbury
		1r	29.11.66	**Bristol R**		A	L	0-4	
1967-68	IL	1	9.12.67	**Luton T**	D4	H	L	1-2	Woodley
			played at Luton						
1968-69	IL	1	16.11.68	**Swansea T**	D4	H	L	2-3	Pentecost, Woodley
1969-70	IL	1	15.11.69	**Cheltenham**	SL	A	W	2-0	Oram, Woodley
		2	6.12.69	**Swansea T**	D4	H	L	1-5	Woodley
1970-71	IL	1	21.11.70	**Bournemouth**	D4	H	D	1-1	Marcham
		1r	24.11.70	**Bournemouth**		A	L	1-8	Holifield

OXFORD UNITED

Formed 1893 as Headington United. Oxford United 1960. Elected to the Football League 1962. **First entered FA Cup:** 1931. **Best FA Cup Performance:** 6th round, 1964 (as Fourth Division club), 1982. **Record FA Cup Win:** 8-0 vs Marlow, preliminary round, 13.9.1952. **In Competition Proper:** 4-0 vs Worthing, 2nd round, 11.12.1982. **Record FA Cup Defeat:** 1-8 vs Banbury Spencer, extra preliminary round, 1.9.1945 **In Competition Proper:** 1-5 vs Arsenal, 3rd round, 30.1.1963

as Headington United

1953-54	SL	1	21.11.53	**Harwich & Parkestone**	ECL	A	W	3-2	Steel, Duncan, Craig (p)
		2	12.12.53	**Millwall**	3S	A	D	3-3	Peart, Steel, Maskel
		2r	17.12.53	**Millwall**		H	W	1-0	K.Smith
		3	9.1.54	**Stockport Co**	3N	A	D	0-0	
		3r	14.1.54	**Stockport Co**		H	W	1-0	Peart
		4	30.1.54	**Bolton W**	D1	H	L	2-4	Peart, Smith
1954-55	SL	1	20.11.54	**Norwich C**	3S	A	L	2-4	Yates, K.Smith
1958-59	SL	1	15.11.58	**Margate**	KL	H	W	3-2	Jackson, Rees, Dickson
		2	6.12.58	**Peterborough U**	ML	A	L	2-4	Rees 2
1959-60	SL	1	14.11.59	**Enfield**	AL	A	L	3-4	Rivers, Mathers, Denial (p)

as Oxford United

1960-61	SL	1	5.11.60	**Hendon**	AL	A	D	2-2	Luke, Jones
		1r	9.11.60	**Hendon**		H	W	3-2	Jones, McIntosh, Love
		2	26.11.60	**Bridgwater T**	WL	H	W	2-1	Dickson, Kyle
		3	7.1.61	**Leicester C**	D1	A	L	1-3	Jones
1961-62	SL	1	4.11.61	**Brentford**	D3	A	L	0-3	
1962-63	D4	1	4.11.62	**Falmouth**	SWL	A	W	2-1	G.Atkinson, Houghton
		2	24.11.62	**Kings Lynn**	SL	A	W	2-1	Jones, Houghton
		3	30.1.63	**Arsenal**	D1	A	L	1-5	Jones
1963-64	D4	1	16.11.63	**Folkestone T**	SL	H	W	2-0	Longbottom, Peplow og
		2	7.12.63	**Kettering T**	SL	H	W	2-1	Longbottom, Calder
		3	4.1.64	**Chesterfield**	D4	H	W	1-0	Willey
		4	25.1.64	**Brentford**	D3	H	D	2-2	Calder, Willey
		4r	28.1.64	**Brentford**		A	W	2-1	Calder 2
		5	15.2.64	**Blackburn R**	D1	H	W	3-1	Jones 2, Calder
		6	29.2.64	**Preston NE**	D2	H	L	1-2	Jones
1964-65	D4	1	14.11.65	**Mansfield T**	D3	H	L	0-1	
1965-66	D3	1	13.11.66	**Port Vale**	D4	H	D	2-2	Spelman (p), Calder
		1r	15.11.66	**Port Vale**		A	L	2-3	Poole og, Calder
1966-67	D3	1	26.11.66	**Yeovil T**	SL	A	W	3-1	G.Atkinson, Harrington, Kerr
		2	11.1.67	**Bedford T**	SL	H	D	1-1	G.Atkinson
		2r	16.1.67	**Bedford T**		A	L	0-1	

OXFORD UNITED

Season	Div	Rd	Date	Opponent	Opp Div	Venue	Result	Score	Scorers
1967-68	D3	1	9.12.67	Chelmsford C	SL	A	D	3-3	Wilson og, Shuker, Clark
		1r	13.12.67	Chelmsford C		H	D	3-3aet	Skeen, Bullock, G.Atkinson
		1 2r	18.12.67	Chelmsford C at Brentford			L	0-1	
1968-69	D2	3	4.1.69	Southampton	D1	H	D	1-1	Sloan
		3r	8.1.69	Southampton		A	L	0-2	
1969-70	D2	3	3.1.70	Stoke C	D1	H	D	0-0	
		3r	7.1.70	Stoke C		A	L	2-3	G.Atkinson, Skeen
1970-71	D2	3	11.1.71	Burnley	D1	H	W	3-0	Skeen, G.Atkinson, Cassidy
		4	23.1.71	Watford	D2	H	D	1-1	Skeen
		4r	27.1.71	Watford		A	W	2-1	Skeen, C.Clarke
		5	13.2.71	Leicester C	D2	A	D	1-1	Lucas
		5r	1.2.71	Leicester C		H	L	1-3aet	R. Atkinson
1971-72	D2	3	15.1.72	Liverpool	D1	H	L	0-3	
1972-73	D2	3	13.1.73	York C	D3	A	W	1-0	Gough
		4	3.2.73	QPR	D3	H	L	0-2	
1973-74	D2	3	5.1.74	Manchester C	D1	H	L	2-5	Curran (p), G.Atkinson
1974-75	D2	3	3.1.75	Leicester C	D1	A	L	1-3	D.Clarke
1975-76	D2	3	3.1.76	Manchester U	D1	A	L	1-2	D.Clarke
1976-77	D3	1	20.11.76	Kettering T	SL	A	D	1-1	Foley
		1r	23.11.76	Kettering T		H	L	0-1	
1977-78	D3	1	26.11.77	Nuneaton B	SL	A	L	0-2	
1978-79	D3	1	25.11.78	Colchester U	D3	A	L	2-4	Foley, Seacole
1979-80	D3	1	24.11.79	Barking	IL	A	L	0-1	
1980-81	D3	1	22.11.80	Aldershot	D4	H	W	1-0	Foley
		2	13.12.80	Plymouth A	D3	A	L	0-3	
1981-82	D3	1	21.11.81	Dover	SL	A	W	2-0	Smithers, Thomas
		2	15.12.81	Aldershot	D4	A	D	2-2	Cassells 2
		2r	30.12.81	Aldershot		H	W	4-2	Cassells 3, Thomas
		3	2.1.82	Bournemouth	D4	A	W	2-0	Cassells, Thomas
		4	23.1.82	Brighton	D1	A	W	3-0	Cassells, Foley 2
		5	13.2.82	Coventry C	D1	A	L	0-4	
1982-83	D3	1	20.11.82	Folkestone T	SL	H	W	5-2	Shotton, Fogg (p), Vinter, Foley 2
		2	11.12.82	Worthing	IL	H	W	4-0	Hebberd, Foley, Vinter 2
		3	8.1.83	Torquay U	D4	H	D	1-1	Foley
		3r	12.1.83	Torquay U		A	L	1-2	Fogg (p)
1983-84	D3	1	19.11.83	Peterborough U	D4	H	W	2-0	Biggins, Mcdonald
		2	10.12.83	Reading	D4	A	D	1-1	Biggins
		2r	14.12.83	Reading		H	W	3-0	Brock, Vinter, Mcdonald
		3	7.1.84	Burnley	D3	A	D	0-0	
		3r	11.1.84	Burnley		H	W	2-1	Lawrence, Scott og
		4	28.1.84	Blackpool	D4	H	W	2-1	Macdonad 2 (2p)
		5	18.2.84	Sheffield W	D2	H	L	0-3	
1984-85	D2	3	4.1.85	Shrewsbury T	D2	A	W	2-0	McDermott, Aldridge
		4	30.1.85	Blackburn R	D2	H	L	0-1	
1985-86	D1	3	4.1.86	Tottenham H	D1	H	D	1-1	Slatter
		3r	8.1.86	Tottenham H		A	L	1-2aet	Aldridge
1986-87	D1	3	10.1.87	Aldershot	D4	A	L	0-3	
1987-88	D1	3	9.1.88	Leicester C	D2	H	W	2-0	Foyle, Saunders
		4	30.1.88	Bradford C	D2	A	L	2-4	Rhoades-Brown, Saunders (p)
1988-89	D2	3	7.1.89	Sunderland	D2	A	D	1-1	Hill
		3r	11.1.89	Sunderland		H	W	2-0	Hill 2
		4	28.1.89	Manchester U	D1	A	L	0-4	
1989-90	D2	3	6.1.90	Plymouuth A	D2	A	W	1-0	Simpson
		4	27.1.90	Southampton	D1	A	L	0-1	
1990-91	D2	3	5.1.91	Chelsea	D1	A	W	3-1	Nogan, Durnin, Magilton
		4	26.1.91	Tottenham H	D1	A	L	2-4	Foyle 2
1991-92	D2	3	4.1.92	Tranmere R	D2	H	W	3-1	Beauchamp, Magilton (p), Vickers og
		4	5.2.92	Sunderland	D2	H	L	2-3	Simpson, Penney
1992-93	D1	3	2.1.93	Swansea C	D2	A	D	1-1	Cusack
		3r	12.1.93	Swansea C		H	D	2-2aet	Magilton, Beauchamp

Swansea won 5-4 on penalties

OXFORD UNIVERSITY

Played at The Parks. **Best FA Cup Performances:** Winners 1874; Runners-up: 1873, 1877, 1880

1872-73		1	26.10.72	Crystal P		H	W	3-2	Dixon, Longman, Summer
		2	23.11.72	Clapham R		A	W	3-0	Dixon, Kirke-Smith, Ottaway

	3	9.12.72	Royal Engineers	H	W	1-0	Kirke-Smith
	4	3.2.73	Maidenhead	H	W	4-0	Dixon, Ottaway, W.Paton, Vidal
	SF		Queens Park, Glasgow		walkover		
	F	23.3.73	Wanderers		L	0-2	
	played at Lillie Bridge, South London						
1873-74	1	29.10.73	Upton Park	H	W	4-0	Hughes, Ottaway, W.Paton, Vidal
	2	22.11.73	Barnes	H	W	2-0	
	3	6.12.73	Wanderers		D	1-1	Maddison
	3r	31.1.74	Wanderers		W	1-0	Hughes
	SF	28.2.74	Clapham R		W	1-0	Vidal
	F	14.3.74	ROYAL ENGINEERS		W	2-0	Mackarness, Patton
	semi-final and Final both played at Kennington Oval						
1874-75	1	31.10.74	Brondesbury	H	W	6-0	Parry 3, Hughes 2, Cripps
	2		Windsor Home Park		walkover		
	3	30.1.75	Wanderers		W	2-1	Otter, Simpson
	SF	27.2.75	Royal Engineers		D	1-1	Bain
	SFr	5.3.75	Royal Engineers		L	0-1aet	
	both semi-final matches played at Kennington Oval						
1875-76	1	30.10.75	Forest School	H	W	6-0	Bain 2, Otter, Parry, Simpson, og
	2	18.12.75	Herts Rangers	H	W	8-2	Simpson 2, Bain, Parry, 4 others
	3	31.1.76	Cambridge University		W	4-0	Bain, Parry, 2 ogs
	SF	19.2.76	Old Etonians		L	0-1	
	played at Kennington Oval						
1876-77	1		Old Salopians		walkover		
	2	14.12.76	105th Regiment	H	W	6-1	Hills 2, Vidal 2, Bain, Todd
	3		Queen's Park, Glasgow		walkover		
	4	24.2.77	Upton Park	H	D	0-0	
	4r	10.3.77	Upton Park	A	W	1-0	Bain
	SF		bye				
	F	24.3.77	Wanderers		L	1-2aet	Waddington
	played at Kennington Oval						
1877-78	1	3.11.77	Herts Rangers	H	W	5-2	
	2	15.12.77	Old Foresters	H	W	1-0	own goal
	3	2.2.78	Clapham R	H	W	3-2	Heygate,. Otter, Parry
	4	15.2.78	Royal Engineers	A	D	3-3	
	4r	27.2.78	Royal Engineers	H	D	2-2aet	Otter 2
	4 2r	12.3.78	Royal Engineers	A	L	2-4	Crowdy, others 1
1878-79	1	2.11.78	Wednesbury Strollers	H	W	7-0	
	2	7.12.78	Royal Engineers	H	W	4-0	Childs 2, Mulholland, Page
	3	2.2.79	Barnes	H	W	2-1	Blaine, others 1
	4	25.2.79	Nottingham Forest	A	L	1-2	Blaine
1879-80	1	6.11.79	Great Marlow	H	D	1-1	Aston
	1r	10.11.79	Great Marlow	A	W	1-0	
	2	19.1.80	Birmingham Club	H	W	6-0	Guy 5, Heygate
	3		Aston Villa		walkover		
	4	14.2.80	Maidenhead		W	1-0	
	5	5.3.80	Royal Engineers		D	1-1aet	Lubbock
	5r	15.3.80	Royal Engineers		W	1-0	Childs
	SF	27.3.80	Nottingham F		W	1-0	Childs
	F	10.4.80	Clapham R		L	0-1	
	both semi-final and Final played at Kennington Oval						

PADIHAM

Formed 1877. Played their home matches near Albert Mill, Padiham, Lancs.

1883-84	1	31.10.83	Lower Darwen	H	W	3-1
	2		bye			
	3	22.12.83	Blackburn R	A	L	0-3
1885-86	1		Hearts		walkover	
	2	21.11.85	Rossendale	A	L	1-9

PANTHERS

1874-75	1	7.11.74	Clapham R	A	L	0-3
1875-76	1	6.11.75	Woodford Wells	H	W	1-0
	2		Royal Engineers		scratched	

1876-77	1	8.11.76	**Wood Grange**	H	W	3-0	E.Farquharson, others 2
	2	9.12.76	**Pilgrims**	A	L	0-1	
1877-78	1	7.11.77	**Wanderers**	A	L	1-9	E.Farquharson
1878-79	1		**Runnymede**		*walkover*		
	2	18.12.78	**Old Harrovians**	A	L	0-3	
1879-80	1		**Birmingham FC**		*scratched*		

PARK GRANGE

1887-88	1	15.10.87	**Long Eaton Rangers**	A	L	3-6	

PARTICK THISTLE

Formed 1876. One of the seven Scottish clubs that took part in the FA Cup. **Scottish FA Cup Winners** 1921; **Runners-up** 1930

1885-86	1	31.10.85	**Queens Park, Glasgow**	A	L	1-5	
1886-87	1	23.10.86	**Blackburn Olympic**	A	W	3-1	Paul 2, Johnstone
	2	20.11.86	**Fleetwood Rangers**	H	W	7-0	J.Marshall, R.Marshall, Paul, 4 others
	3	4.12.86	**Cliftonville**	A	W	11-0	Paul 4, Suter 2, Marshall, Johnstone, 3 others
	4		**bye**				
	5	29.1.87	**Old Westminsters**	A	L	0-1	

PENRITH

Formed 1894. **First entered FA Cup:** 1906. **League club beaten:** Chester

1981-82	NL	1	21.11.81	**Chester**	D3	H	W	1-0	Fell
		2	12.12.81	**Doncaster R**	D3	A	L	0-3	
1983-84	NWC	1	19.11.83	**Hull C**	D3	H	L	0-2	
1984-85	NWC	1	17.11.84	**Burnley**	D3	H	L	0-9	
			played at Turf Moor						

PETERBOROUGH & FLETTON UNITED

Formed 1923 when Peterborough City amalgamated with Fletton United. Suspended by the FA for financial irregularities and disbanded on 6 August 1932. A separate club from Peterborough United.

1927-28	SL	1	30.11.27	**Botwell Mission**	SPT	A	W	4-3	Bruton 2, McNaughton, Baker
		2	10.12.27	**Aldershot Town**	SL	H	W	3-1	McNaughton, Bruton
		3	14.1.28	**Birmingham**	D1	A	L	3-4	Bruton 2, McGuigan
1928-29	SL	1	24.11.28	**Charlton A**	3S	H	L	0-2	
1929-30	SL	1	30.11.29	**Brighton & HA**	3S	A	L	0-4	
1930-31	SL	1	29.11.30	**Aldershot Town**	SL	A	L	1-4	Hoyland
1931-32	SL	1	28.11.31	**Darwen**	LC	A	L	1-4	Willis

PETERBOROUGH UNITED

Formed 1934 after the demise of the old Peterborough & Fletton United club. **First entered FA Cup:** 1936. **Best FA Cup Performance:** 6th round, 1965. **Record FA Cup win:** 9-1 vs Rushden, 1st qualifying round, 6.10.1945, **in Competition Proper:** 7-0 vs Harlow T, 1st round, 16.11.1991. **Record FA Cup Defeat:** 1-8 vs Northampton T, 2nd round, second replay, 18.12.1946. Scored a succession of famous FA Cup wins in the 1950s and won election to the Football League in 1960.

1936-37	ML	1	28.11.36	**Dartford**	SL	A	L	0-3	
1938-39	ML	1	26.11.38	**Bristol R**	3S	A	L	1-4	Fielding
1946-47	ML	1	30.11.46	**Yeovil**	SL	A	D	2-2	Rudkin, Bayliss
		1r	5.12.46	**Yeovil**		H	W	1-0	Rudkin
		2	14.12.46	**Northampton T**	3S	H	D	1-1	Bramham
		2r	19.12.46	**Northampton T**		A	D	1-1aet	Padgett
		2 2r	23.12.46	**Northampton T** at Coventry			L	1-8	Brooksbanks
1948-49	ML	1	27.11.48	**Torquay U**	3S	H	L	0-1	
1952-53	ML	1	22.11.52	**Torquay U**	3S	H	W	2-1	Sloan, Martin
		2	6.12.52	**Bristol R**	3S	H	L	0-1	
1953-54	ML	1	21.11.53	**Hitchin T**	AL	A	W	3-1	Campbell, Taft 2
		2	12.12.53	**Aldershot**	3S	H	W	2-1	Martin, Taft
		3	9.1.54	**Cardiff C**	D1	A	L	1-3	Martin
1955-56	ML	1	19.11.55	**Ipswich T**	3S	H	W	3-1	Emery 2, Hair

	2	10.12.55	**Swindon T**	3S	A	D	1-1	Emery
	2r	15.12.55	**Swindon T**		H	L	1-2aet	Emery
1956-57	ML	1	17.11.56	**Yeovil T**	SL	A	W	3-1	Emery 2, Hails
	2	8.12.56	**Bradford PA**	3N	H	W	3-0	Emery, Hails, Donaldson
	3	5.1.57	**Lincoln C**	D2	H	D	2-2	Emery 2
	3r	9.1.57	**Lincoln C**		A	W	5-4aet	Emery, Donaldson 3, Smith
	4	26.1.57	**Huddersfield T**	D2	A	L	1-3	Shaw
1957-58	ML	1	16.11.57	**Torquay U**	3S	H	D	3-3	Emery, Donaldson 2
	1r	20.11.57	**Torquay U**		A	L	0-1	
1958-59	ML	1	15.11.58	**Kettering**	SL	H	D	2-2	Emery, Hails
	1r	20.11.58	**Kettering**		A	W	3-2aet	Emery, Hails, Reynolds og
	2	6.12.58	**Headington U**	SL	H	W	4-2	Emery 2, Hails, Rayner
	3	10.1.59	**Fulham**	D2	A	D	0-0	
	3r	24.1.59	**Fulham**		H	L	0-1	
1959-60	ML	1	14.11.59	**Shrewsbury T**	D3	H	W	4-3	Emery 2, Rayner, Smith
	2	5.12.59	**Walsall**	D4	A	W	3-2	Rayner, Smith, McNamee
	3	9.1.60	**Ipswich T**	D2	A	W	3-2	Emery 2, Raynor
	4	30.1.60	**Sheffield W**	D1	A	L	0-2	
1960-61	D4	1	5.11.60	**Dover**	SL	A	W	4-1	Emery 2, Bly, Ripley
	2	26.11.60	**Torquay U**	D3	A	W	3-1	McNamee 2, Bly
	3	7.1.61	**Portsmouth**	D2	A	W	2-1	Ripley, Hails
	4	28.1.61	**Aston Villa**	D1	H	D	1-1	Hails
	4r	1.2.61	**Aston Villa**		A	L	1-2	McNamee
1961-62	D3	1	4.11.61	**Colchester U**	D4	H	D	3-3	McNamee, Bly, Hudson
	1r	6.11.61	**Colchester U**		A	D	2-2aet	Emery, Bly
	1 2r	13.11.61	**Colchester U** at Norwich			W	3-0	Hudson 3
	2	25.11.61	**Torquay U**	D3	A	W	4-1	Hudson 2, Hails, Bly
	3	6.1.62	**Newcastle U**	D2	A	W	1-0	Bly
	4	27.1.62	**Sheffield U**	D1	H	L	1-3	Hudson
1962-63	D3	1	3.11.62	**Notts Co**	D3	A	W	3-0	Hudson 2, McNamee
	2	24.11.62	**Enfield**	AL	H	W	1-0	Hudson
	3	4.2.63	**Derby Co**	D2	A	L	0-2	
1963-64	D3	1	16.11.63	**Watford**	D3	H	D	1-1	Bell og
	1r	19.11.63	**Watford**		A	L	1-2aet	Senior
1964-65	D3	1	14.11.64	**Salisbury T**	WL	H	W	5-1	Dougan 3, Deakin, Crowe
	2	5.12.64	**QPR**	D3	A	D	3-3	Barnes, Deakin (p), McNamee
	2r	9.12.64	**QPR**		H	W	2-1aet	Deakin 2
	3	9.1.65	**Chesterfield**	D4	A	W	3-0	Dougan 3
	4	30.1.65	**Arsenal**	D1	H	W	2-1	Dougan, McNamee
	5	20.2.65	**Swansea T**	D2	H	D	0-0	
	5r	23.2.65	**Swansea T**		A	W	2-0	Deakin 2 (1p)
	6	6.3.65	**Chelsea**	D1	A	L	1-5	Crowe
1965-66	D3	1	13.11.65	**Kidderminster H**	WMRL	H	W	2-1	Deakin 2
	2	4.12.65	**Shrewsbury T**	D3	A	L	2-3	Deakin, Birks
1966-67	D3	1	26.11.66	**Hereford U**	SL	H	W	4-1	Fairbrother, Byrne, Conmy (p), Griffiths og
	2	7.1.67	**Colchester U**	D3	A	W	3-0	Watson 2, Fairbrother
	3	28.1.67	**Bedford**	SL	A	W	6-2	Watson 3, Conmy, Orr, Fairbrother
	4	18.2.67	**Sunderland**	D1	A	L	1-7	Watson
1967-68	D3	1	12.12.67	**Falmouth T**	SWL	H	W	5-2	Fairbrother 3, Brace, Byrne
	2	6.1.68	**Margate**	SL	A	W	4-0	Brace, Thompson, Deakin, Conmy
	3	27.1.68	**Portsmouth**	D2	H	L	0-1	
1968-69	D4	1	16.11.68	**Bristol R**	D3	A	L	1-3	Downes
1969-70	D4	1	15.11.69	**Falmouth T**	SWL	A	W	4-1	Hall 2, Robson, Price
	2	6.12.69	**Plymouth A**	D3	H	W	2-0	Conmy, Price
	3	3.1.70	**Rotherham U**	D3	A	W	1-0	Hall
	4	24.1.70	**Gillingham**	D3	A	L	1-5	Price
1970-71	D4	1	21.11.70	**Wimbledon**	SL	H	W	3-1	Garwood, Hall, Moss
	2	12.12.70	**Wigan A**	NPL	A	L	1-2	Moss
1971-72	D4	1	20.11.71	**Redditch**	WMRL	A	D	1-1	Price
	1r	22.11.71	**Redditch**		H	W	6-0	Price, Hall 2, Barker 2, Robson
	2	11.12.71	**Enfield**	IL	H	W	4-0	Price 2, Hall 2
	3	14.1.72	**Ipswich T**	D1	H	L	0-2	
1972-73	D4	1	18.11.72	**Northampton T**	D4	H	W	1-0	Hall
	2	9.12.72	**Bishops Stortford**	IL	A	D	2-2	Cozens, Robson
	2r	11.12.72	**Bishops Stortford**		H	W	3-1	Robson, Hall, Heath
	3	13.1.73	**Derby Co**	D1	H	L	0-1	
1973-74	D4	1	24.11.73	**Colchester U**	D4	A	W	3-2	Cozens 2, Murray

		2	15.12.73	**Wycombe W**	IL	A	W	3-1	Cozens 2, Hall
		3	5.1.74	**Southend**	D3	H	W	3-1	Cozens, Hill, Robson
		4	26.1.74	**Leeds U**	D1	H	L	1-4	Cozens
1974-75	D3	1	23.11.74	**Weymouth**	SL	H	D	0-0	
		1r	4.12.74	**Weymouth**		A	D	3-3aet	Turner, Gregory, Llewelyn
		1 2r	9.12.74	**Weymouth**		H	W	3-0	Turner, Gregory 2
		2	14.12.74	**Charlton A**	D3	A	W	3-0	Murray, Gregory, Nixon
		3	4.1.75	**Tranmere R**	D3	H	W	1-0	Bradley
		4	25.1.75	**Stafford R** at Stoke	NPL	A	W	2-1	Nixon, Gregory
		5	15.2.75	**Middlesbrough**	D1	H	D	1-1	Nixon
		5r	18.2.75	**Middlesbrough**		A	L	0-2	
1975-76	D3	1	22.11.75	**Winsford**	CC	H	W	4-1	Nixon, Gregory, Turner, Cozens
		2	13.12.75	**Coventry Sporting**	WMRL	A	W	4-0	Gregory, Hughes, Jones, D.Jones og
				played at Highfield Road					
		3	1.1.76	**Nottingham F**	D2	A	D	0-0	
		3r	7.1.76	**Nottingham F**		H	W	1-0	Nixon
		4	24.1.76	**Manchester U**	D1	A	L	1-3	Cozens
1976-77	D3	1	20.11.76	**Tranmere R**	D3	A	W	4-0	Carmichael, Moss, Cozens, Robson
		2	11.12.76	**Northwich Victoria**	NPL	A	–	1-0	Nixon
				abandoned after 20 minutes					
		2	14.12.76	**Northwich Victoria**		A	L	0-4	
1977-78	D3	1	26.11.77	**Barnet**	SL	A	W	2-1	Slough, Robson
		2	17.12.77	**Gillingham**	D3	A	D	1-1	Slough
		2r	20.12.77	**Gillingham**		H	W	2-0	Sargent, Carmichael
		3	7.1.78	**Newcastle U**	D1	H	D	1-1	Sargent
		3r	11.1.78	**Newcastle U**		A	L	0-2	
1978-79	D3	1	25.11.78	**Southend**	D3	A	L	2-3	Butlin, Anderson
1979-80	D4	1	24.11.79	**Bournemouth**	D4	H	L	1-2	Kellock
1980-81	D4	1	22.11.80	**Northampton**	D4	A	W	4-1	Robson 2, Slack, Quow
		2	13.12.80	**Barnet**	APL	A	W	1-0	Robson
		3	3.1.81	**Chesterfield**	D3	H	D	1-1	Cooke
		3r	6.1.81	**Chesterfield**		A	W	2-1	Cooke 2
		4	24.1.81	**Notts Co**	D2	A	W	1-0	Cooke
		5	14.2.81	**Manchester C**	D1	H	L	0-1	
1981-82	D4	1	21.11.81	**Halifax T**	D4	A	W	3-0	Cooke 2, Syrett
		2	2.1.82	**Walsall**	D3	H	W	2-1	Cooke, Chard
		3	6.1.82	**Bristol C**	D3	H	L	0-1	
1982-83	D4	1	20.11.82	**Chesterfield**	D3	A	D	2-2	Gynn, Clarke
		1r	24.11.82	**Chesterfield**		H	W	2-1	Gynn, Cooke
		2	11.12.82	**Doncaster R**	D3	H	W	5-2	Gynn, Cooke 2, Clarke, Quow
		3	8.1.83	**Luton T**	D1	A	L	0-3	
1983-84	D4	1	19.11.83	**Oxford U**	D3	A	L	0-2	
1984-85	D4	1	17.11.84	**Cambridge U**	D3	A	W	2-0	Kelly 2
		2	8.12.84	**Dagenham**	APL	A	L	0-1	
1985-86	D4	1	16.11.85	**Bishop's Stortford**	IL	A	D	2-2	Worrell, Hull og
		1r	20.11.85	**Bishop's Stortford**		H	W	3-1	Kowalski, Gallagher, Cassidy
		2	7.12.85	**Bath C**	APL	H	W	1-0	Gallagher
		3	4.1.86	**Leeds U**	D2	H	W	1-0	Shepherd
		4	25.1.86	**Carlisle U**	D2	H	W	1-0	Shepherd
		5	15.2.86	**Brighton**	D2	H	D	2-2	Shepherd, Kelly
		5r	3.3.86	**Brighton**		A	L	0-1	
1986-87	D4	1	16.11.86	**Northampton T**	D4	A	L	0-3	
1987-88	D4	1	14.11.87	**Cardiff C**	D4	H	W	2-1	Goodall 2
		2	5.12.87	**Sutton U**	GMVC	H	L	1-3	Lawrence
1988-89	D4	1	19.11.88	**Gillingham**	D3	A	D	3-3	Longhurst 3
		1r	23.11.88	**Gillingham**		H	W	1-0aet	Haines og
		2	10.12.88	**Brentford**	D3	H	D	0-0	
		2r	14.12.88	**Brentford**		A	L	2-3	Halsall, Cusack
1989-90	D4	1	18.11.89	**Hayes**	IL	H	D	1-1	Sterling
		1r	21.11.89	**Hayes**		A	W	1-0	Robinson
		2	9.12.89	**Swansea**	D3	A	L	1-3	Andrews
1990-91	D4	1	17.11.90	**Hereford U**	D4	A	D	1-1	Riley
		1r	20.11.90	**Hereford U**		H	W	2-1	Sterling, Riley
		2	12.12.90	**Wycombe W**	GMVC	A	D	1-1	Culpin
		2r	17.12.90	**Wycombe W**		H	W	2-0	Halsall, Culpin
		3	5.1.91	**Port Vale**	D2	A	L	1-2	Halsall
1991-92	D3	1	16.11.91	**Harlow**	IL	H	W	7-0	Cooper 2 (1p), Riley, Sterling, Halsall, Chartery, Culpin

				Reading	D3	H	D	0-0	
		2	7.12.91	Reading	D3	H	D	0-0	
		2r	17.12.91	Reading		A	L	0-1	
1992-93	D1	1	14.11.92	Kingstonian	IL	A	D	1-1	Adcock
		1r	25.11.92	Kingstonian		H	W	9-1	Philliskirk 5, Adcock 2, Cooper, Harlow og

FA ordered match to be replayed after coin-throwing incident

		1r	4.12.92	Kingstonian		H	W	1-0	Sterling
		2	9.12.92	Plymouth A	D2	A	L	2-3	Philliskirk, Sterling

PHOENIX BESSEMER, ROTHERHAM

Formed 1876. Played at Clifton Lane, Rotherham

1882-83	1		Grantham			walkover	
	2	25.11.82	Grimsby T	H	W	8-1	Marples 2, D.Willey 2, F.Thomas 2, Emmett 2
	3	27.12.82	Notts Co	A	L	1-4	Douglas

PILGRIMS FC

Formed 1870 as Clapton Pilgrims. Played in and around Walthamstow and at Hackney Downs, in east London.

1873-74	1	9.10.73	Marlow	H	W	1-0	Foley
	2	22.11.73	Sheffield Club	A	L	0-1	
1874-75	1	10.10.74	South Norwood	H	W	3-1	Good 2, others 1
	2	5.12.74	Clapham R	A	L	0-2	
1875-76	1	9.11.75	Old Etonians	A	L	1-4	T.Letchford
1876-77	1	14.10.76	Ramblers	H	W	4-1	Detmar, Elmslie, T.Letchford, Lloyd
	2	9.12.76	Panthers	H	W	1-0	Baker
	3	20.1.77	Wanderers		L	0-3	
1877-78	1	3.11.77	Ramblers	H	D	0-0	
	1r	9.11.77	Ramblers	H	W	1-0	Redwood
	2	8.12.77	Royal Engineers	A	L	0-6	
1878-79	1	9.11.78	Brentwood	A	W	3-1	Mott 2, Grieve
	2	21.12.78	Remnants	A	L	2-6	Grieve, Wohlgemuth
1879-80	1	1.11.79	Clarence	H	W	5-2	Ramsey 2, F.Last, Mott, Poland
	2		Herts Rangers			walkover	
	3	17.1.80	Clapham R		L	0-7	
1880-81	1		Old Philberdians			walkover	
	2	9.12.80	Royal Engineers	A	L	0-1	
1881-82	1	5.11.81	Mosquitoes	A	D	1-1	Scott
	1r	12.11.81	Mosquitoes	H	W	5-0	
	2	3.12.81	Old Foresters	A	L	1-3	
1882-83	1	21.10.82	Old Carthusians	A	L	0-6	
1883-84	1	10.11.83	Mosquitoes	A	L	2-3	
1884-85	1	8.11.84	Dulwich	A	L	2-3	

PLYMOUTH ARGYLE

Formed 1886 as the Argyle Athletic Club. Plymouth Argyle 1903. **Best FA Cup Performance:** semi-finals 1984. **Record FA Cup Win:** 7-0 vs Whiteheads, 1st qualifying round, 3.10.1903 **In Competition Proper:** 6-0 vs Corby T, 3rd round, 22.1.1966. **Record FA Cup Defeat:** 1-7 vs Tottenham H, 4th round, 19.1.1910

1903-04	SL	1q Whiteheads (H) 7-0; 2q Freemantle (H) 5-1; 3q Swindon T (H) 2-0; Int Brentford (A) 1-1; Int r Brentford (H) 4-1					
		1	6.2.04	Sheffield W	D1	H	D	2-2	Dalrymple, Peddie
		1r	10.2.04	Sheffield W		A	L	0-2	
1904-05	SL	Int Barnsley (H) 2-0					
		1	4.2.05	Newcastle U	D1	A	D	1-1	Dalrymple
		1r	8.2.05	Newcastle U		H	D	1-1	McLuckie
		1 2r	13.2.05	Newcastle U at Plumstead			L	0-2	
1905-06	SL	1	13.1.06	New Crusaders		A	W	6-3	Wilcox 3, Banks, Briercliffe, Saul
		2	3.2.06	Aston Villa	D1	A	D	0-0	
		2r	7.2.06	Aston Villa		H	L	1-5	Buck
1906-07	SL	1	12.1.07	Millwall Ath	SL	A	L	0-2	
1907-08	SL	1	11.1.08	Barnsley	D2	H	W	1-0	Leonard
		2	1.2.08	Crystal P	SL	H	L	2-3	Ingham, Morris
1908-09	SL	1	16.1.09	Swindon T	SL	H	W	1-0	Hindmarsh
		2	6.2.09	Exeter C	SL	H	W	2-0	Hindmarsh, Leavey
		3	20.2.09	Derby Co	D2	A	L	0-1	
1909-10	SL	1	15.1.10	Tottenham H	D1	H	D	1-1	Griffiths
		1r	19.1.10	Tottenham H		A	L	1-7	Burch

PLYMOUTH ARGYLE

1910-11	SL	1	14.1.11	Derby Co	D2	A	L	1-2	Dixon
1911-12	SL	1	13.1.12	Sunderland	D1	A	L	1-3	Burch
1912-13	SL	1	11.1.13	Preston NE	D2	H	W	2-0	McCormick, Bell
		2	1.2.13	Manchester U	D1	H	L	0-2	
1913-14	SL	1	10.1.14	Lincoln C	D2	H	W	4-1	Raymond 2, Burch, Butler
		2	31.1.14	Sunderland	D1	A	L	1-2	Bowler
1914-15	SL	1	9.1.15	Bury	D2	A	D	1-1	Bowler
		1r	16.1.15	Bury		H	L	1-2	Raymond
1919-20	SL	1	10.1.20	Reading	SL	H	W	2-0	Jack 2
		2	31.1.20	Barnsley	D2	H	W	4-1	Jack 2, Bowler 2
		3	21.2.20	Huddersfield T	D2	A	L	1-3	Jack
1920-21	3S	1	8.1.21	Rochdale	CL	H	W	2-0	Sheffield, Russell
		2	29.1.21	Swansea T	3S	A	W	2-1	Bowler, Toms
		3	19.2.21	Chelsea	D1	H	D	0-0	
		3r	24.2.21	Chelsea		A	D	0-0aet	
		3 2r	28.2.21	Chelsea at Ashton Gate			L	1-2	Toms
1921-22	3S	1	7.1.22	Fulham	D2	H	D	1-1	Baker
		1r	11.1.22	Fulham		A	L	0-1	
1922-23	3S	1	13.1.23	Notts Co	D2	H	D	0-0	
		1r	17.1.23	Notts Co		A	W	1-0	Gallogley
		2	3.2.23	Bradford PA	3N	H	W	4-1	Richardson 4
		3	24.2.23	West Ham	D2	A	L	0-2	
1923-24	3S	1	12.1.24	Manchester U	D2	A	D	0-1	
1924-25	3S	1	10.1.25	Swansea T	3S	A	L	0-3	
1925-26	3S	3	9.1.26	Chelsea	D2	H	L	1-2	Cock
1926-27	3S	3	8.1.27	South Shields	D2	A	L	1-3	Cock
1927-28	3S	1	26.11.27	Gillingham	3S	A	L	1-2	Matthews
1928-29	3S	1	4.11.28	Yeovil & Petters U	SL	H	W	4-1	Bowden 2, Leslie, Matthews
		2	8.12.28	Brentford	3S	A	W	1-0	Forbes
		3	12.1.29	Blackpool	D2	H	W	3-0	Black 3
		4	18.1.29	Bradford PA	D2	H	L	0-1	
1929-30	3S	1	30.11.29	Dulwich Hamlet	IL	A	W	4-1	Bowden 2, Black 2
		2	14.12.29	Watford	3S	A	D	1-1	Bland
		2r	18.12.29	Watford		H	W	3-0	Vidler 3
		3	11.1.30	Hull C	D2	H	L	3-4	Vidler, Leslie, Black
1930-31	D2	3	10.1.31	Everton	D2	A	L	0-2	
1931-32	D2	3	9.1.32	Manchester U	D2	H	W	4-1	Grozier 2, Vidler, Pullen
		4	23.1.32	Arsenal	D1	A	L	2-4	Vidler, Leslie
1932-33	D2	3	14.1.33	Bradford PA	D2	A	L	1-5	Leslie
1933-34	D2	3	13.1.34	Huddersfield T	D1	H	D	1-1	Cookson
		3r	17.1.34	Huddersfield T		A	L	2-6	Briggs
1934-35	D2	3	12.1.35	Brentford	D2	A	W	1-0	S.Black
		4	26.1.35	Bolton W	D2	H	L	1-4	Briggs
1935-36	D2	3	11.1.36	Stockport Co	3N	A	W	3-2	S.Black, Eggleston, Sloan
		4	25.1.36	Chelsea	D1	A	L	1-4	Vidler
1936-37	D2	3	16.1.37	Crewe A	3N	A	W	2-0	Vidler, McNeill
		4	30.1.37	Tottenham H	D2	A	L	0-1	
1937-38	D2	3	8.1.38	New Brighton	3N	A	L	0-1	
1938-39	D2	3	7.1.39	Sunderland	D1	A	L	0-3	
1945-46	D2	3 1L	5.1.46	Aldershot	3S	A	L	0-2	
		3 2L	9.1.46	Aldershot		H	L	0-1	
1946-47	D2	3	11.1.47	Chester	3N	A	L	0-2	
1947-48	D2	3	10.1.48	Luton T	D2	H	L	2-4	Dews, Thomas
1948-49	D2	3	8.1.49	Notts Co	3S	H	L	0-1	
1949-50	D2	3	7.1.50	Wolverhampton W	D1	H	D	1-1	Williams
		3r	10.1.50	Wolverhampton W		A	L	0-3	
1950-51	3S	1	25.11.50	Gainsborough T	ML	A	W	3-0	Tadman 3
		2	9.12.50	Crewe A	3N	A	D	2-2	Govan, Strauss
		2r	13.12.50	Crewe A		H	W	3-0	Dews 2, Strauss
		3	6.1.50	Wolverhampton W	D1	H	L	1-2	Dews
1951-52	3S	1	25.11.51	Millwall	3S	A	L	0-1	
1952-53	D2	3	10.1.53	Coventry C	3S	H	W	4-1	Dews, Smith, Astall, Govan
		4	31.1.53	Barnsley	D2	H	W	1-0	Govan
		5	14.2.53	Gateshead	3N	H	L	0-1	
1953-54	D2	3	9.1.54	Nottingham F	D2	H	W	2-0	McJarrow, Tadman
		4	30.1.54	Doncaster R	D2	H	L	0-2	
1954-55	D2	3	8.1.55	Newcastle U	D1	H	L	0-1	

Season	Div	Rd	Date	Opponent		H/A	Res	Score	Scorers
1955-56	D2	3	7.1.56	Leyton O	3S	A	L	0-1	
1956-57	3S	1	17.11.56	Exeter C	3S	A	W	2-0	N.Langman, Rowley
		2	8.12.56	Torquay U	3S	A	L	0-1	
1957-58	3S	1	16.11.57	Watford	3S	H	W	6-2	Barnes 2, Carter 2, Anderson, Gauld
		2	7.12.57	Dorchester T	WL	H	W	5-2	Carter 3, Penk, Gauld
		3	4.1.58	Newcastle U	D1	H	L	1-6	Carter
1958-59	D3	1	15.11.58	Gillingham	D4	H	D	2-2	Carter, Anderson
		1r	19.11.58	Gillingham		A	W	4-1	Meyer 3, Gauld
		2	6.12.58	Coventry C	D4	A	W	3-1	Carter 2, Baker
		3	10.1.59	Cardiff C	D2	H	L	0-3	
1959-60	D2	3	10.1.60	WBA	D1	A	L	2-3	Anderson, Penk
1960-61	D2	3	7.1.61	Bristol C	D3	H	L	0-1	
1961-62	D2	3	6.1.62	West Ham	D1	H	W	3-0	Carter, J.S. Williams, Maloy
		4	27.1.62	Tottenham H	D1	H	L	1-5	Anderson
1962-63	D2	3	5.1.63	WBA	D1	H	L	1-5	McAnearney
1963-64	D2	3	4.1.64	Huddersfield T	D2	H	L	0-1	
1964-65	D2	3	9.1.65	Derby Co	D2	H	W	4-2	Jones 2, Jennings, Trebilcock
		4	30.1.65	Leicester C	D1	A	L	0-5	
1965-66	D2	3	22.1.66	Corby T	SL	H	W	6-0	Bickle 3, Piper, Jackson, Jones
		4	12.2.66	Huddersfield T	D2	H	L	0-2	
1966-67	D2	3	28.1.67	Nottingham F	D1	A	L	1-2	Bloomfield
1967-68	D2	3	22.1.68	Sheffield W	D1	A	L	0-3	
1968-69	D3	1	16.11.68	Reading	D3	A	L	0-1	
1969-70	D3	1	15.11.69	Brentford	D4	A	D	0-0	
		1r	19.11.69	Brentford		H	W	2-0	Burnside, Davey
		2	6.12.69	Peterborough U	D4	A	L	0-2	
1970-71	D3	1	21.11.70	Walsall	D3	A	L	0-3	
1971-72	D3	1	20.11.71	Gillingham	D4	A	L	2-3	Reed 2
1972-73	D3	1	18.11.72	Hendon	IL	H	W	1-0	Hague
		2	9.12.72	Yeovil T	SL	A	W	2-0	Dowling, Welsh
		3	13.1.73	Middlesbrough	D2	H	W	1-0	Hinch
		4	3.2.73	Leeds U	D1	A	L	1-2	Rickard
1973-74	D3	1	24.11.73	Brentford	D4	H	W	2-1	Houston og, Mariner
		2	15.12.73	Walsall	D3	H	W	1-0	Mariner
		3	5.1.74	Manchester U	D1	A	L	0-1	
1974-75	D3	1	23.11.74	Dartford	SL	A	W	3-2	Randall 2, Mariner
		2	14.12.74	Crystal P	D3	H	W	2-1	Green, Rafferty
		3	3.1.75	Blackpool	D2	H	W	2-0	Rafferty 2
		4	24.1.75	Everton	D1	H	L	1-3	Vassallo
1975-76	D2	3	3.1.76	Hull C	D2	A	D	1-1	Rafferty
		3r	6.1.76	Hull C		H	L	1-4	Green
1976-77	D2	3	8.1.77	Oldham A	D2	A	L	0-3	
1977-78	D3	1	26.11.77	Bath C	SL	A	D	0-0	
		1r	29.11.77	Bath C		H	W	2-0	Taylor 2
		2	17.12.77	Cambridge U	D3	H	W	1-0	Johnson
		3	7.1.78	Mansfield T	D2	A	L	0-1	
1978-79	D3	1	25.11.78	Worcester C	SL	A	L	0-2	
1979-80	D3	1	24.11.79	Colchester U	D3	A	D	1-1	Hodges
		1r	27.11.79	Colchester U		H	L	0-1aet	
1980-81	D3	1	22.11.80	Newport Co	D3	H	W	2-0	Kemp, Murphy
		2	13.12.80	Oxford U	D3	H	W	3-0	Sims, Kemp, Murphy
		3	3.1.81	Charlton A	D3	H	L	1-2	Kemp
1981-82	D3	1	21.11.81	Gillingham	D3	H	D	0-0	
		1r	24.11.81	Gillingham		A	L	0-1	
1982-83	D3	1	29.11.82	Exeter C	D3	H	W	2-0	Hodges, Sims
		2	11.12.82	Bristol R	D3	A	D	2-2	Rogers, Sims
		2r	20.12.82	Bristol R		H	W	1-0	McCartney
		3	8.1.83	Watford	D1	A	L	0-2	
1983-84	D3	1	19.11.83	Southend U	D3	A	D	0-0	
		1r	22.11.83	Southend U		H	W	2-0	Stead og, Tynan
		2	10.12.83	Barking	IL	H	W	2-1	Rowe, Smith
		3	7.1.84	Newport Co	D3	H	D	2-2	Hodges, Tynan
		3r	10.1.84	Newport Co		A	W	1-0	Rogers
		4	28.1.84	Darlington	D4	H	W	2-1	Uzzell, Staniforth
		5	18.2.84	WBA	D1	A	W	1-0	Tynan
		6	10.3.84	Derby Co	D2	H	D	0-0	
		6r	14.3.84	Derby Co		A	W	1-0	Rogers

	SF	14.4.84	**Watford**	D1		L	0-1
	played at Villa Park						
1984-85 D3	1	17.11.84	**Barnet**	APL	H	W	3-0	Goodyear, Tynan, Staniforth
	2	8.12.84	**Hereford U**	D4	H	D	0-0
	2r	12.12.84	**Hereford U**		A	L	0-2
1985-86 D3	1	16.11.85	**Aldershot**	D4	H	W	1-0	Coughlin
	2	7.12.85	**Maidstone U**	APL	H	W	3-0	L.Cooper, Nelson, Summerfield
	3	4.1.86	**Hull C**	D2	A	D	2-2	Clayton, L.Cooper
	3r	7.1.86	**Hull C**		H	L	0-1
1986-87 D2	3	10.1.87	**Bristol C**	D3	A	D	1-1	Summerfield
	3r	19.1.87	**Bristol C**		H	W	3-1	Summerfield, Nelson, Tynan
	4	31.1.87	**Arsenal**	D1	A	L	1-6	Rowbotham
1987-88 D2	3	9.1.88	**Colchester U**	D4	H	W	2-0	S.Cooper, Matthews
	4	30.1.88	**Shrewsbury T**	D2	H	W	1-0	Evans
	5	20.2.88	**Manchester C**	D2	A	L	1-3	Hodges
1988-89 D2	3	7.1.89	**Cambridge U**	D4	H	W	2-0	Tynan, Summerfield
	4	28.1.89	**Everton**	D1	H	D	1-1	McCarthy
	4r	31.1.89	**Everton**		A	L	0-4
1989-90 D2	3	6.1.90	**Oxford U**	D2	H	L	0-1
1990-91 D2	3	5.1.91	**Middlesbrough**	D2	A	D	0-0
	3r	14.1.91	**Middlesbrough**		H	L	1-2	Marker (p)
1991-92 D2	3	5.1.92	**Bristol R**	D2	A	L	0-5
1992-93 D2	1	15.11.92	**Dorking**	IL	A	W	3-2	Dalton 2, Marshall
	2	9.12.92	**Peterborough U**	D1	H	W	3-2	Marshall 2, Castle
	3	12.1.93	**Ipswich T**	PL	A	L	1-3	Castle

POOLE TOWN

Formed 1880. **First entered FA Cup:** 1891. **League club beaten:** Newport Co

1926-27 SL	1	27.11.26	**Newport Co**	3S	H	W	1-0	Daws
	2	11.12.26	**Nunhead**	IL	A	W	2-1	Daws 2
	3	8.1.27	**Everton**	D1	A	L	1-3	Batten
1927-28 SL	1	26.11.27	**Norwich C**	3S	H	D	1-1	Rhodes
	1r	1.12.27	**Norwich C**		A	L	0-5
1928-29 SL	1	24.11.28	**Bournemouth**	3S	H	L	1-4	Harris
1946-47 WL	1	30.11.46	**QPR**	3S	A	D	2-2	Langley, Ames (p)
	1r	4.12.46	**QPR**		H	L	0-6
1962-63 SL	1	3.11.62	**Watford**	D3	A	D	2-2	Bellett, Osmond
	1r	6.11.62	**Watford**		H	L	1-2	Pring (p)
1966-67 SL	1	26.11.66	**QPR**	D3	A	L	2-3	Saunders, France
1983-84 SL	1	20.11.83	**Newport Co**	D3	H	D	0-0
	1r	22.11.83	**Newport Co**		A	L	1-3	Allen

PORTSMOUTH

Formed 1898. **Best FA Cup Performance:** Winners: 1939. Runners-up: 1929, 1934. **Record FA Cup Win:** 10-0 vs Ryde, 1st qualifying round, 30.9.1899 **In Competition Proper:** 7-0 vs Stockport Co, 3rd round, 8.1.1949. **Record FA Cup Defeat:** 0-5 vs Blackburn R, 1st round, second replay, 5.2.1900; 0-5 vs Everton, 1st round, 7.2.1903; 0-5 vs Tottenham H, 3rd round, 16.1.1937

1899-00 SL		1q **Ryde** (H) 10-0; 2q **Cowes** (H) 3-2; 3q **Swindon T** (H) 2-1; 4q **Bristol R** (A) 1-1; 4qr **Bristol R** (H) 4-0; 5q **Bedminster** (A) 2-1					
	1	27.1.00	**Blackburn R**	D1	H	D	0-0
	1r	1.2.00	**Blackburn R**		A	D	1-1aet	Cunliffe
	1 2r	5.2.00	**Blackburn R** at Villa Pk			L	0-5
1900-01 SL		Int **Newton Heath** (A) 0-3					
1901-02 SL		Int **Small Heath** (H) 2-1					
	1	25.1.02	**Grimsby T**	D1	A	D	1-1	Cunliffe
	1r	29.1.02	**Grimsby T**		H	W	2-0	Bedingfield, Chadwick
	2	8.2.02	**Reading**	SL	A	W	1-0	Bedingfield
	3	22.2.02	**Derby Co**	D1	H	D	0-0
	3r	27.2.02	**Derby Co**		A	L	3-6	Chadwick, Cunliffe, Smith
1902-03 SL	1	7.2.03	**Everton**	D1	A	L	0-5
1903-04 SL	1	6.2.04	**Derby Co**	D1	H	L	2-5	Whelton 2
1904-05 SL		Int **Chesterfield** (H) 0-0; Int R **Chesterfield** (H) 2-0					
	1	4.2.05	**Small Heath**	D1	A	W	2-0	Lee, S.Smith
	2	18.2.05	**Sheffield W**	D1	A	L	1-2	Cunliffe
1905-06 SL	1	13.1.06	**Southampton**	SL	A	L	1-5	Kirby
1906-07 SL	1	12.1.07	**Manchester U**	D1	H	D	2-2	Hunter, Bainbridge

			Date	Opponent				Score	Scorers
		1r	16.1.07	Manchester U		A	W	2-1	Kirby, Hunter
		2	2.2.07	Barnsley	D2	A	L	0-1	
1907-08	SL	1	11.1.08	Hastings & St L.	SL	A	W	1-0	Bellamy
		2	1.2.08	Leicester Fosse	D2	H	W	1-0	McDonald
		3	22.2.08	Stoke C	D2	H	L	0-1	
1908-09	SL	1	16.1.09	Birmingham	D2	A	W	5-2	Reid 4, McMahon
		2	6.2.09	Sheffield W	D1	H	D	2-2	Dix, Kirby
		2r	11.2.09	Sheffield W		A	L	0-3	
1909-10	SL	1	15.1.10	Shrewsbury T	BDL	H	W	3-0	Long, Bowman 2
		2	5.2.10	Coventry C	SL	H	L	0-1	
1910-11	SL	1	14.1.11	Aston Villa	D1	H	L	1-4	Long
1911-12	SL	1	13.1.12	Bristol R	SL	A	W	2-1	Louch, Jones
		2	3.2.12	Bradford PA	D2	A	L	0-2	
1912-13	SL	1	15.1.13	Brighton & HA	SL	A	L	1-2	Mounteney
1913-14	SL	1	10.1.14	Exeter C	SL	H	L	0-4	
1914-15	SL	1	9.1.15	Bradford PA	D1	A	L	0-1	
1919-20	SL	1	10.1.20	Bradford C	D1	A	–	2-2	Turner, Stringfellow
			abandoned after 63 minutes – waterlogged pitch						
		1r	17.1.20	Bradford C		A	L	0-2	
1920-21	D3	1	8.1.21	South Shields	D2	A	L	0-3	
1921-22	3S	1	7.1.22	Luton T	3S	H	D	1-1	Stringfellow
		1r	11.1.22	Luton T		A	L	1-2	Stringfellow
1922-23	3S	1	13.1.23	Leeds U	D2	H	D	0-0	
		1r	17.1.23	Leeds U		A	L	1-3	Meikle
1923-24	3S		5q London Caledonians (A) 5-1; 6q Brentford (A) 1-1; 6qr Brentford 1-0aet						
		1	12.1.24	Newcastle U	D1	H	L	2-4	Mackie, Haines
1924-25	D2	1	10.1.25	Accrington S	3N	A	W	5-2	Haines, J.Martin, Meikle, Mackie
		2	31.1.25	Blackburn R	D1	A	D	0-0	
		2r	4.2.25	Blackburn R		H	D	0-0 aet	
		2 2r	9.2.25	Blackburn R at Highbury			L	0-1	
1925-26	D2	3	9.1.26	Derby Co	D2	A	D	0-0	
		3r	13.1.26	Derby Co		H	D	1-1aet	Mackie
		3 2r| 18.1.26	Derby Co at Filbert Street				L	0-2	
1926-27	D2	3	8.1.27	Bristol R	3S	A	D	3-3	Mackie, Goodwin, Haines
		3r	12.1.27	Bristol R		H	W	4-0	Watson, Mackie, Haines, McGolgan
		4	29.1.27	Reading	D2	A	L	1-3	Haines
1927-28	D1	3	14.1.28	West Ham	D1	H	L	0-2	
1928-29	D1	3	12.1.29	Charlton A	3S	H	W	2-1	McNeil, Smith
		4	26.1.29	Bradford C	3N	H	W	2-0	Irvine, McNeil
		5	16.2.29	Chelsea	D2	A	D	1-1	Weddle
		5r	20.2.29	Chelsea		H	W	1-0	Weddle
		6	2.3.29	West Ham	D1	H	W	3-2	Smith, Cook, Weddle
		SF	23.3.29	Aston Villa	D1		W	1-0	Smith (p)
			played at Highbury						
		F	27.4.29	Bolton Wanderers	D1	WEMBLEY	L	0-2	
1929-30	D1	3	11.1.30	Preston NE	D2	H	W	2-0	Smith, Forward
		4	25.1.30	Brighton & HA	3S	H	L	0-1	
1930-31	D1	3	10.1.31	Fulham	3S	A	W	2-0	Forward, Easson
		4	24.1.31	Brentford	3S	A	W	1-0	Smith
		5	14.2.31	WBA	D2	H	L	0-1	
1931-32	D1	3	9.1.32	Middlesbrough	D1	A	D	1-1	Weddle
		3r	13.1.32	Middlesbrough		H	W	3-0	Easson 2, Worrall
		4	23.1.32	Aston Villa	D1	H	D	1-1	Thackeray
		4r	27.1.32	Aston Villa		A	W	1-0	Easson
		5	13.2.32	Arsenal	D1	H	L	0-2	
1932-33	D1	3	14.1.33	Grimsby T	D2	A	L	2-3	J.Smith, McCarthy
1933-34	D1	3	13.1.34	Manchester U	D2	A	D	1-1	Bagley
		3r	17.1.34	Manchester U		H	W	4-1	Weddle 2, McCarthy, JJ Smith
		4	27.1.34	Grimsby T	D2	H	W	2-0	Weddle, J.Smith
		5	17.2.34	Swansea T	D2	A	W	1-0	Worrall
		6	3.3.34	Bolton W	D2	A	W	3-0	Weddle, Rutherford 2
		SF	17.3.34	Leicester C	D1		W	4-1	Weddle 3, Rutherford
			played at St Andrews						
		F	28.4.34	Manchester City	D1	WEMBLEY	L	1-2	Rutherford
1934-35	D1	3	12.1.35	Huddersfield T	D1	H	D	1-1	Worrall
		3r	16.1.35	Huddersfield T		A	W	3-2	Easson, Weddle 2
		4	26.1.35	Bristol C	3S	H	D	0-0	

365

	4r	30.1.35	Bristol C		A	L	0-2	
1935-36	D1	3	11.1.36	Manchester C	D1	A	L	1-3	Worrall
1936-37	D1	3	16.1.37	Tottenham H	D2	H	L	0-5	
1937-38	D1	3	8.1.38	Tranmere R	3N	A	W	2-1	Beattie, Groves
	4	22.1.38	Brentford	D1	A	L	1-2	Parker
1938-39	D1	3	7.1.39	Lincoln C	3N	H	W	4-0	Anderson 2, Parker, Worrall
	4	21.1.39	WBA	D2	H	W	2-0	Anderson 2
	5	11.2.39	West Ham	D2	H	W	2-0	Parker, Worrall
	6	4.3.39	Preston NE	D1	H	W	1-0	Anderson
	SF	25.3.39	Huddersfield T	D1		W	2-1	Barlow, Anderson
		played at Highbury						
	F	29.4.39	WOLVERHAMPTON W	D1	WEMBLEY	W	4-1	Barlow 2, Anderson, Parker
1945-46	D1	3 1L	5.1.46	Birmingham C	D2	A	L	0-1	
	3 2L	9.1.46	Birmingham C		H	D	0-0	
1946-47	D1	3	11.1.47	Doncaster R	3N	A	W	3-2	Froggatt 2, Evans
	4	25.1.47	Birmingham C	D2	A	L	0-1	
1947-48	D1	3	10.1.48	Brighton & HA	3S	H	W	4-1	Wharton, Reid, Clarke, Harris
	4	24.1.48	Preston NE	D1	H	L	1-3	Williams og
1948-49	D1	3	8.1.49	Stockport Co	3N	H	W	7-0	Phillips 2, Harris 3, Clarke 2
	4	29.1.49	Sheffield W	D2	H	W	2-1	Harris, Phillips
	5	12.2.49	Newport Co	3S	H	W	3-2aet	Phillips 2, Froggatt
	6	26.2.49	Derby Co	D1	H	W	2-1	Clarke 2
	SF	26.3.49	Leicester C	D2		L	1-3	Harris
		played at Highbury						
1949-50	D1	3	7.1.50	Norwich C	3S	H	D	1-1	Delapenha
	3r	12.1.50	Norwich C		A	W	2-0	Reid 2 (1p)
	4	28.1.50	Grimsby T	D2	H	W	5-0	Froggatt 2, Clarke 2, Phillips
	5	11.2.50	Manchester U	D1	A	D	3-3	Clarke, Parker, Ferrier
	5r	15.2.50	Manchester U		H	L	1-3	Harris
1950-51	D1	3	6.1.51	Luton T	D2	A	L	0-2	
1951-52	D1	3	12.1.52	Lincoln C	3N	H	W	4-0	Clarke, Gaillard 2, Mundy
	4	2.2.52	Notts Co	D2	A	W	2-1	Gaillard, Mundy
	5	23.2.52	Doncaster R	D2	A	W	4-0	Harris, Phillips, Gaillard, Rouse og
	6	8.3.52	Newcastle U	D1	H	L	2-4	Gaillard, Reid
1952-53	D1	3	10.1.53	Burnley	D1	H	D	1-1	Gordon
	3r	13.1.53	Burnley		A	L	1-3	Gaillard
1953-54	D1	3	9.1.54	Charlton A	D1	H	D	3-3	Vaughan 2, Gordon
	3r	14.1.54	Charlton A		A	W	3-2aet	Harris 2, Barnard
	4	30.1.54	Scunthorpe U	3N	A	D	1-1	Harris
	4r	3.2.54	Scunthorpe U		H	D	2-2aet	Henderson 2
	4 2r	8.2.54	Scunthorpe U at Highbury			W	4-0	Froggatt 2, Harris, Henderson
	5	20.2.54	Bolton W	D1	A	D	0-0	
	5r	24.2.54	Bolton W		H	L	1-2	Gordon
1954-55	D1	3	8.1.55	Bristol R	D2	A	L	1-2	Gordon
1955-56	D1	3	7.1.56	Grimsby T	3N	H	W	3-1	Mansell, Dickinson, Harris
	4	28.1.56	WBA	D1	A	L	0-2	
1956-57	D1	3	5.1.57	Bury	D2	A	W	3-1	Harris 2, McClellan
	4	26.1.57	Nottingham F	D2	H	L	1-3	Weddle
1957-58	D1	3	4.1.58	Aldershot	3S	A	W	5-1	Gordon 2, Newman 2, Barnard
	4	25.1.58	Wolverhampton W	D1	A	L	1-5	Crawford
1958-59	D1	3	10.1.59	Swansea T	D2	H	W	3-1	Saunders, Newman, Hughes og
	4	24.1.59	Accrington Stanley	D3	A	D	0-0	
	4r	28.1.59	Accrington Stanley		H	W	4-1	Newman, Weddle, Saunders 2
	5	14.2.59	Burnley	D1	A	L	0-1	
1959-60	D2	3	9.1.60	Sheffield U	D2	A	L	0-3	
1960-61	D2	3	7.1.61	Peterborough U	D4	H	L	1-2	Wilson
1961-62	D3	1	4.11.61	Crystal P	D3	A	L	0-3	
1962-63	D2	3	26.1.63	Scunthorpe U	D2	H	D	1-1	Gordon
	3r	7.3.63	Scunthorpe U		A	W	2-1	Saunders 2
	4	13.3.63	Coventry C	D3	H	D	1-1	Saunders
	4r	16.3.63	Coventry C		A	D	2-2aet	McCann, Saunders
	4 2r	19.3.63	Coventry C at Tottenham			L	1-2	Saunders
1963-64	D2	3	4.1.64	Stoke C	D1	A	L	1-4	Saunders (p)
1964-65	D2	3	9.1.65	Wolverhampton W	D1	H	D	0-0	
	3r	12.1.65	Wolverhampton W		A	L	2-3	McClelland, Hiron
1965-66	D2	3	22.1.66	Grimsby T	D3	A	D	0-0	
	3r	26.1.66	Grimsby T		H	L	1-3	Portwood

Season	Div	Rd	Date	Opponent	Opp Div	H/A	Res	Score	Scorers
1966-67	D2	3	28.1.67	Hull C	D2	A	D	1-1	McCann
		3r	1.2.67	Hull C		H	D	2-2aet	Edwards, Pack
		3 2r	6.2.67	Hull C at Coventry			W	3-1	McCann 2 (1p), Edwards
		4	18.2.67	Tottenham H	D1	A	L	1-3	Tindall
1967-68	D2	3	27.1.68	Peterborough U	D3	A	W	1-0	Hiron
		4	17.2.68	Fulham	D1	A	D	0-0	
		4r	21.2.68	Fulham		H	W	1-0	Trebilcock
		5	9.3.68	WBA	D1	H	L	1-2	Hiron
1968-69	D2	3	4.1.69	Chesterfield	D4	H	W	3-0	Jennings 2, McCann
		4	25.1.69	Blackburn R	D2	A	L	0-4	
1969-70	D2	3	3.1.70	Tranmere R	D3	H	L	1-2	Jennings
1970-71	D2	3	2.1.71	Sheffield U	D2	H	W	2-0	Hiron, Trebilcock
		4	23.1.71	Arsenal	D1	H	D	1-1	Trebilcock
		4r	1.2.71	Arsenal		A	L	2-3	Piper, Ley
1971-72	D2	3	15.1.72	Boston U	NPL	A	W	1-0	Jennings
		4	5.2.72	Swansea C	D3	H	W	2-0	Williams og, Trebilcock
		5	26.2.72	Birmingham C	D2	A	L	1-3	Reynolds
1972-73	D2	3	13.1.73	Bristol C	D2	H	D	1-1	Piper
		3r	16.1.73	Bristol C		A	L	1-4	Hiron
1973-74	D2	3	5.1.74	Swindon T	D2	A	D	3-3	Davies, Went, Kellard (p)
		3r	9.1.74	Swindon T		H	W	1-0	Kellard
		4	27.1.74	Orient	D2	H	D	0-0	
		4r	29.1.74	Orient		A	D	1-1aet	Mellows
		4 2r	5.2.74	Orient at Selhurst Park			W	2-0	Kellard, Davies
		5	17.2.74	Nottingham F	D2	A	L	0-1	
1974-75	D2	3	3.1.75	Notts Co	D2	A	L	1-3	Marinello
1975-76	D2	3	3.1.76	Birmingham C	D1	H	D	1-1	Eames
		3r	6.1.76	Birmingham C		A	W	1-0	McGuinness
		4	24.1.76	Charlton A	D2	A	D	1-1	Piper
		4r	27.1.76	Charlton A		H	L	0-3	
1976-77	D3	1	20.11.76	Aldershot	D4	A	D	1-1	Mellows
		1r	23.11.76	Aldershot		H	W	2-1	Green, Foster
		2	11.12.76	Minehead	SL	H	W	2-1	Kemp, Kamara
		3	8.1.77	Birmingham C	D1	A	L	0-1	
1977-78	D3	1	26.11.77	Bideford	WL	H	W	3-1	Stokes, Pullar, Mellows
		2	17.12.77	Swansea C	D4	H	D	2-2	Kemp 2
		2r	20.12.77	Swansea C		A	L	1-2	Foster
1978-79	D4	1	25.11.78	Northampton T	D4	H	W	2-0	Hemmerman 2
		2	16.12.78	Reading	D4	H	L	0-1	
1979-80	D4	1	24.11.79	Newport Co	D4	H	W	1-0	Brisley
		2	18.12.79	Wimbledon	D3	A	D	0-0	
		2r	24.12.79	Wimbledon		H	D	3-3aet	Gregory, Laidlaw, Bryant
		2 2r	5.1.80	Wimbledon		A	W	1-0	Hemmerman
		3	9.1.80	Middlesbrough	D1	H	D	1-1	Brisley
		3r	14.1.80	Middlesbrough		A	L	0-3	
1980-81	D3	1	22.11.80	Colchester U	D3	A	L	0-3	
1981-82	D3	1	21.11.81	Millwall	D3	H	D	1-1	Hemmerman
		1r	25.11.81	Millwall		A	L	2-3aet	Tait, Hemmerman
1982-83	D3	1	20.11.82	Hereford U	D4	H	W	4-1	Biley 2, Rafferty 2
		2	11.12.82	Aldershot	D3	H	L	1-3	Webb
1983-84	D2	3	6.1.84	Grimsby T	D2	H	W	2-1	Hateley, Morgan
		4	28.1.84	Southampton	D1	H	L	0-1	
1984-85	D2	3	4.1.85	Blackburn R	D2	H	D	0-0	
		3r	26.1.85	Blackburn R		A	L	1-2	Kennedy
1985-86	D2	3	4.1.86	Aston Villa	D1	H	D	2-2	Blake, Dillon
		3r	13.1.86	Aston Villa		A	L	2-3aet	Stanley 2 (1p)
1986-87	D2	3	10.1.87	Blackburn R	D2	H	W	2-0	Quinn 2
		4	31.1.87	Wimbledon	D1	A	L	0-4	
1987-88	D1	3	9.1.88	Blackburn R	D2	A	W	2-1	Quinn, Dillon
		4	1.2.88	Sheffield U	D2	H	W	2-1	Dillon, Quinn
		5	20.2.88	Bradford C	D2	H	W	3-0	Blake, Quinn, Connor
		6	12.3.88	Luton T	D1	A	L	1-3	Quinn
1988-89	D2	3	7.1.89	Swindon T	D2	H	D	1-1	Quinn
		3r	10.1.89	Swindon T		A	L	0-2	
1989-90	D2	3	6.1.90	Crystal P	D1	A	L	1-2	Whittingham
1990-91	D2	3	5.1.91	Barnet	GMVC	A	W	5-0	Aspinall, Whittingham 3, Clarke
		4	26.1.91	Bournemouth	D3	H	W	5-1	Clarke, Whittingham 4

		5	16.2.91	Tottenham H	D1	H	L	1-2	Chamberlain
1991-92	D2	3	4.1.92	Exeter C	D3	A	W	2-1	Whittingham, Aspinall
		4	25.1.92	Leyton Orient	D3	H	W	2-0	Anderton 2
		5	15.2.92	Middlesbrough	D2	H	D	1-1	Whittingham
		5r	26.2.92	Middlesbrough		A	W	4-2	Clarke 2, Anderton 2
		6	7.3.92	Nottingham F	D1	H	W	1-0	McLoughlin
		SF	5.4.92	Liverpool	D1		D	1-1aet	Anderton
			at Highbury						
		SFr	13.4.92	Liverpool			D	0-0aet	
			at Villa Park, Liverpool won 3-1 on penalties						
1992-93	D1	3	2.1.93	Brighton & HA	D2	A	L	0-1	

PORT VALE

Formed 1876. Became Burslem Port Vale 1884-1911. **First entered FA Cup:** 1885. **Best FA Cup Performance:** semi-finals 1954 (as a Third Division club). **Record FA Cup Win:** In competition proper: 7-1 vs Irthlingborough, 1st round, 12.1.1907. **Record FA Cup Defeat:** 0-7 vs Small Heath Alliance, 5th qualifying round, 10.12.1898

1885-86		1	24.10.85	Chirk		H	W	3-0	
		2	21.11.85	Druids		A	D	2-2aet	Reynolds, Simpson
		2r	28.11.85	Druids		H	W	5-1	Reynolds 2, Smith 2, Simpson
		3		Leek				walkover	
		4		bye					
		5	30.1.86	Brentwood		H	D	1-1	Reynolds
		5r	13.2.86	Brentwood		A	D	3-3aet	Smith, 2 others
		5 2r		Brentwood				scratched	
1886-87		1	30.10.86	Davenham		A	D	1-1aet	
		1r	13.11.86	Davenham		H	W	3-0	
		2	20.11.86	bye					
		3	11.12.86	Leek		A	D	2-2aet	
		3r	20.1.86	Leek		H	L	1-3	
1887-88		1	15.10.87	Stoke		A	L	0-1	

1888-89		2q Small Heath Alliance (A) 2-3
1889-90		2q Chester (A) 0-1
1890-91		1q Warwick Co (A) 3-1; 2q Walsall Town Swifts (H) 2-3
1891-92		1q Burton Wanderers (H) 2-4
1892-93	D2	1q Burton Swifts (H) 0-2
1893-94	D2	1q Burton Swifts (H) 3-4aet
1894-95	D2	1q Stourbridge (A) 3-5
1895-96	D2	1q Hereford Thistle walkover; 2q Burton Swifts (H) 1-1; 2qr Burton Swifts (A) 0-1
1896-97	ML	3q Hereford walkover; 4q Stourbridge (A) 3-1; 5q Burton Swifts (H) 2-3
1897-98	ML	3q Small Heath Alliance (H) 2-1; 4q Kidderminster H walkover; 5q Burton Wanderers (H) 2-1

		1	29.1.98	Sheffield U	D1	A	D	1-1	McDonald
		1r	2.2.98	Sheffield U		H	W	2-1aet	R.Evans, Boullemier
		2	12.2.98	Burnley	D2	A	L	0-3	

1898-99	D2	3q Wellington T (H) 5-0; 4q Burton Wanderers (H) 3-0; 5q Small Heath Alliance (A) 0-7
1899-00	D2	3q Nantwich T (H) 2-0; 4q Crewe A (A) 2-2; 4qr Crewe Alex (H) 3-1; 5q Stalybridge R (H) 0-1
1900-01	D2	Int New Brighton T (H) 1-3
1901-02	D2	3q Wellington T (H) 6-0; 4q Wrexham (A) 1-2 abnd; 4q Wrexham (A) 0-0; 4qr Wrexham (H) 3-1; 5q Walsall (H) 1-2
1902-03	D2	3q Stalybridge R (H) 3-1; 4q St Helens R (A) 1-2
1903-04	D2	3q Crewe Alex (A) 0-0; 3qr Crewe A (H) 2-1; 4q Stockport Co (A) 0-0; 4qr Stockport Co (H) 6-0; 5q Nantwich T (A) 1-0; Int Burton U (H) 3-0

| | | 1 | 6.2.04 | Southampton | SL | A | L | 0-3 | |

1904-05	D2	6q Barnsley (A) 0-0; 6qr Barnsley (H) 1-2
1905-06	D2	4q Oxford C (A) 1-0

| | | 1 | 13.1.06 | Gainsborough T | D2 | H | L | 0-3 | |

| 1906-07 | D2 | 5q Swindon T (A) 2-1 |

		1	12.1.07	Irthlingborough T	UCL	A	W	7-1	Coxon 3, Dodds 2, Mountford 2
		2	2.2.07	Notts Co	D1	H	D	2-2	Beats, Mountford
		2r	6.2.07	Notts Co		A	L	0-5	

1907-1912		did not enter
as Port Vale		
1912-13	P	New Brighton T Ams (H) 7-0; 1q Northern Nomads (H) 4-1; 2q Harrowby (A) 2-0; 3q Northwich Victoria (A) 1-3
1913-14	CL	P Harrowby (H) 3-1; 1q Northern Nomads (H) 5-0; 2q Chester (A) 5-2; 3q South Liverpool (H) 5-0; 4q Coventry C (A) 3-1; 5q Darlington (H) 2-2; 5qr Darlington (A) 2-1 abnd; 5q 2r Darlington 1-0 (at Sheffield)

| | | 1 | 10.1.14 | Bolton W | D1 | A | L | 0-3 | |

| 1914-15 | CL | 4q Crewe Alex (A) 1-1; 4qr Crewe Alex (H) 5-2; 5q Swansea T (A) 0-1 |

PORT VALE

1919-20	D2	6q	**Loughborough Cor.** (H) 4-0				
		1	10.1.20 **Manchester U**	D1	H	L	0-1
1920-21	D2	6q	**Clapton Orient** (A) 0-1				
1921-22	D2	1	7.1.22 **Stoke C**	D2	H	L	2-4	Brough 2
1922-23	D2	5q	**Wrexham** (H) 0-2				
1923-24	D2	5q	**Wrexham** (A) 1-5				
1924-25	D2	5q	**Boston T** (H) 6-1; 6q **Alfreton T** (A) 8-2				
		1	10.1.25 **Aston Villa**	D1	A	L	2-7	Kirkham 2
1925-26	D2	3	9.1.26 **Manchester U**	D1	H	L	2-3	Maddock, Page
1926-27	D2	3	8.1.27 **Clapton O**	D2	A	D	1-1	Simms
		3r	12.1.27 **Clapton O**		H	W	5-1	Page, Kirkham 2, Simms, Strange
		4	29.1.27 **Arsenal**	D1	H	D	2-2	Parker og, Kirkham
		4r	2.2.27 **Arsenal**		A	L	0-1	
1927-28	D2	3	14.1.28 **Barnsley**	D2	H	W	3-0	Simms, Page, Maddock
		4	28.1.28 **New Brighton**	3N	H	W	3-0	Page, Kirkham, Anstiss
		5	18.2.28 **Blackburn R**	D1	A	L	1-2	Anstiss
1928-29	D2	3	12.1.29 **Manchester U**	D1	H	L	0-3	
1929-30	3N	1	30.11.29 **Gainsborough T**	ML	A	D	0-0	
		1r	4.12.29 **Gainsborough T**		H	W	5-0	Jennings 2, Anstiss 2, Pynegar
		2	14.12.29 **Chesterfield**	3N	A	L	0-2	
1930-31	D2	3	10.1.31 **Corinthians**	–	A	W	3-1	Roberts, Anstiss, Jennings
		4	24.1.31 **Birmingham**	D1	A	L	0-2	
1931-32	D2	3	9.1.32 **Brighton & HA**	3S	A	W	2-1	Nolan 2
		4	23.1.32 **Leicester C**	D1	H	L	1-2	Nolan
1932-33	D2	3	14.1.33 **Blackpool**	D1	A	L	1-2	Mills
1933-34	D2	3	13.1.34 **Charlton A**	3S	A	L	0-2	
1934-35	D2	3	12.1.35 **WBA**	D1	A	L	1-2	Morton
1935-36	D2	3	11.1.36 **Sunderland**	D1	A	D	2-2	Stabb, Caldwell
		3r	13.1.36 **Sunderland**		H	W	2-0	Stabb, Rhodes
		4	25.1.36 **Grimsby T**	D1	H	L	0-4	
1936-37	3N	3	13.1.37 **Sheffield W**	D1	A	L	0-2	
1937-38	3N	1	27.11.37 **Gainsborough T**		H	D	1-1	Roberts
		1r	1.12.37 **Gainsborough T**		A	L	1-2aet	Roberts
1938-39	3S	1	26.11.38 **Wrexham**	3N	A	W	2-1	Roberts 2
		2	10.12.38 **Southend U**	3S	H	L	0-1	
1945-46	3S	1 1L	17.11.45 **Wellington T**	CC	H	W	4-0	McDowall 2, Pointon, Glennoe og
		1 2L	24.11.45 **Wellington T**		A	W	2-0	McDowall, Bellis
		2 1L	8.12.45 **Marine**	LCC	H	W	3-1	Allen 2, Gregory
		2 2L	15.12.45 **Marine**		A	D	1-1	Gregory
		3 1L	5.1.46 **Bradford PA**	D2	A	L	1-2	Bellis
		3 2L	7.1.46 **Bradford PA**		H	D	1-1	Bellis
1946-47	3S	1	30.11.46 **Finchley**	AL	H	W	5-0	M.Jones, Pointon, Bellis 2, Wooton
		2	14.12.46 **Watford**	3S	A	D	1-1	M.Jones
		2r	17.12.46 **Watford**		H	W	2-1	M.Jones, Wootton
		3	11.1.47 **Millwall**	D2	A	W	3-0	Triner, Pointon 2
		4	25.1.47 **Blackburn R**	D1	A	L	0-2	
1947-48	3S	1	29.11.47 **Crystal P**	3S	A	L	1-2	Smith
1948-49	3S	1	27.11.48 **Notts Co**	3S	A	L	1-2	Martin (p)
1949-50	3S	1	26.11.49 **Wealdstone**	AL	H	W	1-0	Pinchbeck
		2	10.12.49 **Tranmere R**	3N	H	W	1-0	Pinchbeck
		3	7.1.50 **Newport Co**	3S	A	W	2-1	Allen 2
		4	28.1.50 **Burnley**	D1	A	L	1-2	Martin
1950-51	3S	1	25.11.50 **New Brighton**	3N	H	W	3-2	Aveyard 2, Pinchbeck
		2	9.12.50 **Nelson**	LC	H	W	3-2	Pinchbeck, Aveyard, Hulligan
		3	6.1.51 **Stoke C**	D1	A	D	2-2	Bennett, Pinchbeck
		3r	8.1.51 **Stoke C**		H	L	0-1	
1951-52	3S	1	24.11.51 **Colchester U**	3S	A	L	1-3	Pinchbeck
1952-53	3N	1	22.11.52 **Exeter C**	3S	H	W	2-1	Mullard, Griffiths
		2	6.12.52 **Oldham A**	3N	H	L	0-3	
1953-54	3N	1	21.11.53 **Darlington**	3N	A	W	3-1	Leake, Hayward, Cunliffe
		2	12.12.53 **Southport**	3N	A	D	1-1	Hayward
		2r	14.12.53 **Southport**		H	W	2-0	Hayward, Askey
		3	9.1.54 **QPR**	3S	A	W	1-0	Leake
		4	30.1.54 **Cardiff C**	D1	A	W	2-0	Leake, Griffiths
		5	20.2.54 **Blackpool**	D1	H	W	2-0	Leake 2
		6	13.3.54 **Leyton O**	3S	A	W	1-0	Leake
		SF	27.3.54 **WBA**	D1		L	1-2	Leake
			played at Villa Park					

Season	Div	Rd	Date	Opponent		H/A	W/D/L	Score	Scorers
1954-55	D2	3	8.1.55	West Ham	D2	A	D	2-2	Cunliffe, Smith
		3r	10.1.55	West Ham		H	W	3-1	Cunliffe, Leake, Smith
		4	29.1.55	Tottenham H	D1	A	L	2-4	Griffiths 2
1955-56	D2	3	7.1.56	Walsall	3S	A	W	1-0	Stephenson
		4	28.1.56	Everton	D1	H	L	2-3	Stephenson, Sproson
1956-57	D2	3	5.1.57	Barnsley	D2	A	D	3-3	Stephenson, Poole 2
		3r	7.1.57	Barnsley		H	L	0-1	
1957-58	3S	1	16.11.57	Shrewsbury T	3S	H	W	2-1	Wilkinson 2
		2	7.12.57	Hull C	3N	H	D	2-2	Poole, Askey
		2r	9.12.57	Hull C		A	L	3-4aet	Poole, Steele, Sproson
1958-59	D4	1	15.11.58	Torquay U	D4	A	L	0-1	
1959-60	D3	1	14.11.59	Dorchester T	WL	A	W	2-1	Poole, Barnett
		2	5.12.59	QPR	D3	A	D	3-3	Portwood, Leake, Raine
		2r	7.12.59	QPR		H	W	2-1	Barnett 2
		3	9.1.60	Cardiff C	D2	A	W	2-0	Steele, Portwood
		4	30.1.60	Scunthorpe U	D2	A	W	1-0	Portwood
		5	20.2.60	Aston Villa	D2	H	L	1-2	Jackson (p)
1960-61	D3	1	5.11.60	Chelmsford C	SL	A	W	3-2	Portwood 2, Jackson
		2	26.11.60	Carlisle U	D4	H	W	2-1	Jackson, Fidler
		3	7.1.61	Swansea T	D2	A	L	0-3	
1961-62	D3	1	4.11.61	Bradford PA	D3	A	W	1-0	Jackson
		2	25.11.61	Crewe A	D4	A	D	1-1	Longbottom
		2r	27.11.61	Crewe A		H	W	3-0	Longbottom 2, Llewellyn
		3	6.1.62	Northampton T	D3	H	W	3-1	Llewellyn 3
		4	27.1.62	Sunderland	D2	A	D	0-0	
		4r	31.1.62	Sunderland		H	W	3-1	Jackson, Poole, Longbottom
		5	17.2.62	Fulham	D1	A	L	0-1	
1962-63	D3	1	3.11.62	Bristol R	D3	A	W	2-0	Llewellyn 2
		2	24.11.62	Aldershot	D4	H	W	2-0	Llewellyn, Edwards (p)
		3	27.2.63	Gillingham	D4	A	W	4-2	Steele, Edwards, Ford, Grainger (p)
		4	13.3.63	Sheffield U	D1	H	L	1-2	Grainger
1963-64	D3	1	16.11.63	Bradford C	D4	A	W	2-1	Whalley, Richards
		2	7.12.63	Workington	D4	H	W	2-1	Steele, Bingham
		3	4.1.64	Birmingham C	D1	A	W	2-1	Sproson, Mudie
		4	25.1.64	Liverpool	D1	A	D	0-0	
		4r	27.1.64	Liverpool		H	L	1-2aet	Cheeseborough
1964-65	D3	1	14.11.64	Hendon	IL	H	W	2-1	Smith, Mitchell
		2	5.12.64	Millwall	D4	A	L	0-4	
1965-66	D4	1	13.11.65	Oxford U	D3	A	D	2-2	Sproson, Cumming
		1r	15.11.65	Oxford U		H	W	3-2	Taylor, Mudie, Hill
		2	4.12.65	Dartford	SL	H	W	1-0	Hill
		3	26.1.66	Cardiff C		A	L	1-2	Rowland
1966-67	D4	1	26.11.66	Bradford C	D4	A	W	2-1	Ritchie, Lawson
		2	7.1.67	Barnsley	D4	A	D	1-1	Hill
		2r	16.1.67	Barnsley		H	L	0-3	
1967-68	D4	1	9.12.67	Chester	D4	H	L	1-2	Goodfellow
1968-69	D4	1	16.11.68	Shrewsbury T	D3	A	D	1-1	Gough
		1r	18.11.68	Shrewsbury T		H	W	3-1	Gough, Morris, Mahon
		2	7.12.68	Workington	D4	H	D	0-0	
		2r	11.12.68	Workington		A	W	2-1	Chapman, James
		3	4.1.69	Watford	D3	A	L	0-2	
1969-70	D4	1	15.11.69	Wigan A	NPL	A	D	1-1	James
		1r	18.11.69	Wigan A		H	D	2-2aet	McLaren, Sproson
		1 2r	24.11.69	Wigan A at Old Trafford			W	1-0aet	James
		2	6.12.69	Tranmere R	D3	H	D	2-2	James, Green
		2r	8.12.69	Tranmere R		A	L	1-3	Magee
1970-71	D3	1	21.11.70	Notts Co	D4	A	L	0-1	
1971-72	D3	1	20.11.71	Blackburn R	D3	A	D	1-1	Horton
		1r	22.11.71	Blackburn R		H	W	3-1	Horton 2 (1p), Morgan
		2	11.12.71	Darlington	D4	H	W	1-0	Morgan
		3	15.1.72	Birmingham C	D2	A	L	0-3	
1972-73	D3	1	18.11.72	Southport	D4	H	W	2-1	James, Horton
		2	9.12.72	Wrexham	D3	H	W	1-0	Brodie
		3	13.1.73	West Ham	D1	H	L	0-1	
1973-74	D3	1	24.11.73	Stockport Co	D4	A	W	1-0	Summerscales
		2	15.12.73	Scarborough	NPL	H	W	2-1	Harris, Woodward
		3	5.1.74	Luton T	D2	H	D	1-1	Harris

Season	Div	Rnd	Date	Opponent		Venue	Result	Score	Scorers
		3r	9.1.74	Luton T		A	L	2-4	Mountford, Woodward
1974-75	D3	1	23.11.74	Lincoln C	D4	H	D	2-2	Bailey, Mountford
		1r	27.11.74	Lincoln C		A	L	0-2	
1975-76	D3	1	22.11.75	Grantham	SL	A	D	2-2	Brownbill 2
		1r	24.11.75	Grantham		H	W	4-1	Cullerton, Brownbill 2, Tartt
		2	13.12.75	Huddersfield T	D4	A	L	1-2	Brownbill
1976-77	D3	1	20.11.76	Southport	D4	A	W	2-1	Rogers 2
		2	11.12.76	Barnsley	D4	H	W	3-0	Williams, Griffiths, Beamish
		3	8.1.77	Hull C	D2	A	D	1-1	Beamish
		3r	10.1.77	Hull C		H	W	3-1aet	Beamish 2, Kennerley
		4	29.1.77	Burnley	D2	H	W	2-1	Tartt, Brownbill
		5	26.2.77	A.Villa	D1	A	L	0-3	
1977-78	D3	1	26.11.77	Arnold	ML	A	D	0-0	
		1r	28.11.77	Arnold		H	W	5-2	Bailey, Beamish, Ridley, Sutcliffe 2
		2	17.12.77	Walsall	D3	A	D	1-1	Beamish
		2r	19.12.77	Walsall		H	L	1-3	Beamish
1978-79	D4	1	25.11.78	Bradford C	D4	A	L	0-1	
1979-80	D4	1	23.11.79	Doncaster R	D4	H	L	1-3	Beech
1980-81	D4	1	22.11.80	Bradford C	D4	H	W	4-2	Bennett (p), N.Chamberlain 2, Beech
		2	13.12.80	Burnley	D3	A	D	1-1	Miller
		2r	16.12.80	Burnley		H	W	2-0	Farrell, M.Chamberlain
		3	3.1.81	Enfield	IL	H	D	1-1	Beech
		3r	6.1.81	Enfield		A	L	0-3	
1981-82	D4	1	21.11.81	Lincoln C	D3	A	D	2-2	N.Chamberlain, M.Chamberlain
		1r	30.11.81	Lincoln C		H	D	0-0aet	
		1 2r	2.12.81	Lincoln C		H	W	2-0	Armstrong, N.Chamberlain
		2	2.1.82	Stockport Co	D4	H	W	4-1	Moss 2, N.Chamberlain 2
		3	5.1.82	Shrewsbury T	D2	A	L	0-1	
1982-83	D4	1	20.11.82	Bradford C	D3	H	L	0-1	
1983-84	D3	1	19.11.83	Lincoln C	D3	H	L	1-2	Bright
1984-85	D4	1	17.11.84	Macclesfield	NPL	A	W	2-1	Brown, Earle
		2	7.12.84	Scunthorpe U	D4	H	W	4-1	Brown, O'Keefe (p), Bromage, I.Griffiths
		3	5.1.85	West Ham	D1	A	L	1-4	Griffiths
1985-86	D4	1	16.11.85	Mansfield T	D4	A	D	1-1	Earle
		1r	18.11.85	Mansfield T		H	W	1-0	Maguire (p)
		2	8.12.85	Walsall	D3	H	D	0-0	
		2r	10.12.85	Walsall		A	L	1-2	Brown
1986-87	D3	1	15.11.86	Stafford R	GMVC	H	W	1-0	Earle
		2	6.12.86	Walsall	D3	A	L	0-5	
1987-88	D3	1	16.11.87	Tranmere R	D4	H	W	3-1	O'Kelly, Hamson, Riley
		2	5.12.87	Notts Co	D3	H	W	2-0	Beckford, Sproson
		3	10.1.88	Macclesfield T	GMVC	H	W	1-0	Finney
		4	30.1.88	Tottenham H	D1	H	W	2-1	Walker, Sproson
		5	20.2.88	Watford	D1	H	D	0-0	
		5r	23.2.88	Watford		A	L	0-2	
1988-89	D3	1	19.11.88	Southport	NPL	A	W	2-0	Sproson, Riley
		2	10.12.88	Bolton W	D3	A	W	2-1	Futcher, Earle
		3	8.1.89	Norwich C	D1	H	L	1-3	Webb
1989-90	D2	3	7.1.90	Derby Co	D1	H	D	1-1	Beckford
		3r	10.1.90	Derby Co		A	W	3-2	Hindmarch og, Walker, Cross
		4	27.1.90	A.Villa	D1	A	L	0-6	
1990-91	D2	3	5.1.91	Peterborough U	D4	H	W	2-1	Walker (p), Beckford
		4	26.1.91	Manchester C	D1	H	L	1-2	Beckford
1991-92	D2	3	4.1.92	Sunderland	D2	A	L	0-3	
1992-93	D2	1	16.11.92	Stoke C	D2	A	D	0-0	
		1r	24.11.92	Stoke C		H	W	3-1	Foyle 2, Porter
		2	5.12.92	Altrincham	GMVC	A	W	4-1	Swan, Foyle, Taylor, Van der Laan
		3	2.1.93	Newcastle U	D1	A	L	0-4	

PRESCOT CABLES

Formed 1884. **First entered FA Cup:** 1891. Now known as Prescot AFC and playing in the NW Counties League. Based in Knowsley, Merseyside.

Season	Div	Rnd	Date	Opponent		Venue	Result	Score	Scorers
1957-58	LC	1	16.11.57	Hartlepools U	3N	A	L	0-5	
1959-60	LC	1	14.11.59	Darlington	D4	A	L	0-4	

PRESTON NORTH END

Formed 1881. Founder members of the Football League 1888. FA Cup and League Double 1889. **FA Cup Best Performance:** Winners 1889, 1938. Runners-up: 1888, 1922, 1937, 1954, 1964. **FA Cup Record Win:** 26-0 vs Hyde, 1st round, 15.10.1887 (biggest win in FA Cup history). **FA Cup Record Defeat:** 0-6 vs Charlton A, 5th round, 2nd leg, 1945-46

1883-84	1		bye				
	2	1.12.83	**Great Lever**		H	W	4-1	Belger 2, Drummond, others 1
	3	29.12.83	**Eagley**		H	W	9-1	Dewhurst 4, Russell 2, Belger, Drummond, Gordon
	4	19.1.84	**Upton Park**		H	D	1-1	Smalley
			FA disqualified Preston for professionalism				
1884-85			*did not enter*				
1885-86	1		**Great Lever**					*walkover*
	2	18.11.85	**Astley Bridge**		H	W	11-3	
	3	5.12.85	**Bolton W**		A	W	3-2	Dempsey, Dewhurst, others 1
			FA disqualified Preston for professionalism				
1886-87	1	30.10.86	**Queens Park, Scotland**		A	W	3-0	Gordon, others 2
	2	13.11.86	**Witton**		H	W	6-0	Dewhurst 4, Thomson 2
	3	22.1.87	**Renton, Scotland**		A	W	2-0	Gordon, JD Ross
	4		bye				
	5	29.1.87	**Old Foresters**		A	W	3-0	Thomson 2, own goal
	6	2.3.87	**Old Carthusians**		A	W	2-1aet	Graham, Gordon
	SF	5.3.87	**WBA**			L	1-3	Thomson
			played at Trent Bridge				
1887-88	1	15.10.87	**Hyde**		H	W	26-0	JD Ross 8, Gordon 5, Thomson 5, Drummond 3,
								Dewhurst 2, Goodall, Russell, NJ Ross
	2	26.11.87	**Everton**		H	W	6-1	Goodall 2, Dewhurst, Drummond, Gordon, JD Ross
	3	3.12.87	**Halliwell**		H	W	4-0	JD Ross 2, Dewhurst, Goodall
	4	10.12.87	**Bolton W**		H	W	9-1	JD Ross 6, Dewhurst, Goodall, Gordon
	5	7.1.88	**Aston Villa**		A	W	3-1	JD Ross, Goodall 2
	6	30.1.88	**Sheffield W**		A	W	3-1	JD Ross, Thomson 2
	SF	18.2.88	**Crewe A**			W	4-0	JD Ross, Goodall 3
			played at Anfield				
	F	24.3.88	**WBA**			L	1-2	Dewhurst
			played at Kennington Oval				
1888-89	D1	1	2.2.89	**Bootle**		A	W	3-0	Goodall, Gordon, Thomson
	2	16.2.89	**Grimsby T**		A	W	2-0	Goodall, Gordon
	3	2.3.89	**Birmingham St Georges**		H	W	2-0	Holmes, Thomson
	SF	16.3.89	**WBA**			W	1-0	Russell
			played at Bramall Lane				
	F	30.3.89	**WOLVERHAMPTON W**			W	3-0	Dewhurst, JD Ross, Thomson
			played at Kennington Oval				
1889-90	D1	1	18.1.90	**Newton Heath**		H	W	6-1	Drummond 4, JD Ross, NJ Ross
	2	1.2.90	**Lincoln C**	ML	H	W	4-0	Gillespie 2, JD Ross, NJ Ross
	3	15.2.90	**Bolton W**	D1	H	L	2-3	Pauls, Thomson
1890-91	D1	1	17.1.91	**Stoke**	FAII	A	L	0-3	
1891-92	D1	1	16.1.92	**Middlesborough Iron.**	NL	H	–	2-2	Becton, Towie
			abandoned because of unplayable, frosty pitch				
	1	23.1.92	**Middlesbrough Iron.**		H	W	6-0	JD Ross, Sharp, Becton, Stewart, Towie
	2	30.1.92	**Middlesbrough**		A	W	2-1	Gallacher, JD Ross
	3	13.2.92	**Nottingham F**	FAII	A	L	0-2	
1892-93	D1	1	21.1.93	**Burton Swifts**	D2	H	W	9-2	JD Ross 4, Beckton 3, Drummond, Gordon
	2	4.2.93	**Accrington**	D1	A	W	4-1	Becton 3, Cowan
	3	18.2.93	**Middlesbrough Iron.**	NL	H	D	2-2	Gordon, Russell
	3r	25.2.93	**Middlesbrough Iron.**		A	W	7-0	Becton 3, Cowan, JD Ross, Russell 2
	SF	4.3.93	**Everton**	D1		D	2-2	Cowan, Gordon
	SFr	16.3.93	**Everton**			D	0-0	
			both games played at Bramall Lane				
	SF 2r	20.3.93	**Everton**			L	1-2	Gordon
			played at Ewood Park				
1893-94	D1	1	27.1.94	**Reading**	n/af	H	W	18-0	Becton 6, JD Ross 6, Cowan 5, Sanders
	2	10.2.94	**Liverpool**	D2	A	L	2-3	Becton 2
1894-95	D1	1	2.2.95	**Luton T**	SL	A	W	2-0	Henderson, Sanders
	2	16.2.95	**Sunderland**	D1	A	L	0-2	
1895-96	D1	1	1.2.96	**Sunderland**	D1	A	L	1-4	Cunningham
1896-97	D1	1	30.1.97	**Manchester C**	D2	H	W	6-0	Boyd 2, Henderson 2, Orr, Stevenson
	2	13.2.97	**Stoke**	D1	H	W	2-1	Smith, Stevenson

	3	27.2.97	**Aston Villa**	D1	H	D	1-1	Stevenson
	3r	3.3.97	**Aston Villa**		A	D	0-0	
	3 2r	10.3.97	**Aston Villa** at Bramall Lane			L	2-3	Blyth
1897-98 D1	1	29.1.98	**Newcastle U**	D2	H	L	1-2	*own goal*
1898-99 D1	1	28.1.99	**Grimsby T**	D2	H	W	7-0	Pratt 4, Brown 2, Chalmers
	2	11.2.99	**Sheffield U**	D1	H	D	2-2	Brown, Halsall
	2r	16.2.99	**Sheffield U**		A	L	1-2	Brown
1899-00 D1	1	27.1.00	**Tottenham H**	SL	H	W	1-0	Stevenson
	2	17.2.00	**Blackburn R**	D1	H	W	1-0	Henderson
	3	24.2.00	**Nottingham F**	D1	H	D	0-0	
	3r	28.2.00	**Nottingham F**		A	L	0-1	
1900-01 D1	1	9.2.01	**Tottenham H**	SL	A	D	1-1	McMahon
	1r	13.2.01	**Tottenham H**		H	L	2-4	Becton, Pratt
1901-02 D2	1	25.1.02	**Manchester C**	D1	A	–	1-1	Rogers
			abandoned in extra time					
	1r	29.1.02	**Manchester C**		H	D	0-0aet	
	1 2r	3.2.02	**Manchester C**		H	L	2-4aet	Pratt, Wilcox
1902-03 D2	Int	13.12.02	**Bishop Auckland**	NL	A	W	3-1	Bond, Pearson, Wilcox
	1	7.2.03	**Manchester C**	D2	H	W	3-1	Hunter, Pearson, Smith
	2	21.2.03	**Millwall**	SL	A	L	1-4	Pearson
1903-04 D2	Int	12.12.03	**Darwen**	LC	H	W	2-1	Bond, Bell
	1	6.2.04	**Grimsby T**	D2	H	W	1-0	Wilcox
	2	20.2.04	**Middlesbrough**	D1	H	L	0-3	
1904-05 D1	1	4.2.05	**Derby Co**	D1	A	W	2-0	Bond, Bell
	2	18.2.05	**Bristol C**	D2	A	D	0-0	
	2r	23.2.05	**Bristol C**		H	W	1-0	Bourne
	3	4.3.05	**Sheffield W**	D1	H	D	1-1	Bond
	3r	9.3.05	**Sheffield W**		A	L	0-3	
1905-06 D1	1	13.1.06	**Birmingham**	D1	A	L	0-1	
1906-07 D1	1	12.1.07	**Notts Co**	D1	A	L	0-1	
1907-08 D1	1	11.1.08	**Brighton & HA**	SL	A	D	1-1	Winchester
	1r	16.1.08	**Brighton & HA**		H	–	1-2	Bond
			abandoned after 112 minutes – fog					
	1r	20.1.08	**Brighton & HA** at Stamford Bridge			L	0-1	
1908-09 D1	1	16.1.09	**Middlesbrough**	D1	H	W	1-0	Lyon
	2	6.2.09	**Sunderland**	D1	H	L	1-2	Dawson
1909-10 D1	1	15.1.10	**Coventry C**	SL	H	L	1-2	McLean
1910-11 D1	1	14.1.11	**Brentford**	SL	A	W	1-0	Rodway
	2	4.2.11	**West Ham**	SL	A	L	0-3	
1911-12 D1	1	13.1.12	**Manchester C**	D1	H	L	0-1	
1912-13 D2	1	11.1.13	**Plymouth A**	SL	A	L	0-2	
1913-14 D1	1	10.1.14	**Bristol R**	SL	H	W	5-2	Osborne 3, Barlow, Marshall
	2	31.1.14	**Glossop**	D2	A	W	1-0	Osborne
	3	21.2.14	**Sunderland**	D1	A	L	0-2	
1914-15 D2	1	9.1.15	**Manchester C**	D1	H	D	0-0	
	1r	16.1.15	**Manchester C**		A	L	0-3	
1919-20 D1	1	10.1.20	**Stockport Co**	D2	H	W	3-1	Bainbridge, Woodhouse, Roberts
	2	31.1.20	**Blackpool**	D2	H	W	2-1	Roberts 2
	3	21.2.20	**Bradford C**	D1	H	L	0-3	
1920-21 D1	1	8.1.21	**Bolton W**	D1	H	W	2-0	Rawlings, Roberts
	2	29.1.21	**Watford**	D3	H	W	4-1	Roberts 3, Woodhouse
	3	19.2.21	**Luton T**	D3	A	W	3-2	Roberts 3
	4	5.3.21	**Hull C**	D2	A	D	0-0	
	4r	10.3.21	**Hull C**		H	W	1-0	Jefferies
	SF	19.3.21	**Tottenham H**	D1		L	1-2	Clay og
			played at Hillsborough					
1921-22 D1	1	7.1.22	**Wolverhampton W**	D2	H	W	3-0	Roberts 2, Jefferies
	2	28.1.22	**Newcastle U**	D1	H	W	3-1	Rawlings, Roberts, Woodhouse
	3	18.2.22	**Barnsley**	D2	A	D	1-1	Rawlings
	3r	22.2.22	**Barnsley**		H	W	3-0	Roberts, Woodhouse 2
	4	4.3.22	**Arsenal**	D1	A	D	1-1	Jefferies
	4r	8.3.22	**Arsenal**		H	W	2-1	Roberts 2
	SF	25.3.22	**Tottenham H**	D1		W	2-1	Rawlings, Roberts,
			played at Hillsborough					
	F	29.4.22	**Huddersfield T**	D1		L	0-1	
			played at Stamford Bridge					
1922-23 D1	1	13.1.23	**Aberdare Ath**	3S	A	W	3-1	Rawlings, Roberts, Woodhouse

(373)

	2	3.2.23	**Charlton Ath**	3S	A	L	0-2	
1923-24	D1	1	12.1.24	**Everton**	D1	A	L	1-3	Rawlings
1924-25	D1	1	10.1.25	**Manchester C**	D1	H	W	4-1	Woodhouse 3, Paterson
	2	31.1.25	**WBA**	D1	A	L	0-2	
1925-26	D2	3	9.1.26	**Blackburn R**	D1	A	D	1-1	Jackson
	3r	14.1.26	**Blackburn R**		H	L	1-4	Jackson
1926-27	D2	3	8.1.27	**Lincoln C**	3N	A	W	4-2	Roberts 4
	4	29.1.27	**Middlesbrough**	D2	H	L	0-3	
1927-28	D2	3	14.1.28	**Everton**	D1	H	L	0-3	
1928-29	D2	3	12.1.29	**Watford**	3S	A	L	0-1	
1929-30	D2	3	11.1.30	**Portsmouth**	D1	A	L	0-2	
1930-31	D2	3	10.1.31	**Tottenham H**	D2	A	L	1-3	Tremelling
1931-32	D2	3	9.1.32	**Bolton W**	D1	H	D	0-0	
	3r	13.1.32	**Bolton W**		A	W	5-2	Crawford, Finney og, Harper, Wagstaffe og, Birch
	4	23.1.32	**Wolverhampton W**	D2	H	W	2-0	Rowley, Harper
	5	13.2.32	**Huddersfield T**	D1	H	L	0-4	
1932-33	D2	3	14.1.33	**Birmingham**	D1	A	L	1-2	Rowley
1933-34	D2	3	13.1.34	**Leeds U**	D1	A	W	1-0	Kelly
	4	27.1.34	**Workington**	NEL	A	W	2-1	Kelly, Fitton
	5	17.2.34	**Northampton T**	3S	H	W	4-0	McGuire og, Palethorpe 3
	6	3.3.34	**Leicester C**	D1	H	L	0-1	
1934-35	D1	3	12.1.35	**Barnsley**	D2	H	D	0-0	
	3r	16.1.35	**Barnsley**		A	W	1-0	Maxwell
	4	26.1.35	**Swindon T**	3S	A	W	2-0	Hetherington, Friar
	5	16.2.35	**Bristol C**	3S	A	D	0-0	
	5r	25.2.35	**Bristol C**		H	W	5-0	Hughes og, Maxwell 2, Fitton, Dougal
	6	2.3.35	**WBA**	D1	A	L	0-1	
1935-36	D1	3	11.1.36	**Everton**	D1	A	W	3-1	Maxwell 2, F. O'Donnell
	4	25.1.36	**Sheffield U**	D2	H	D	0-0	
	4r	30.1.36	**Sheffield U**		A	L	0-2	
1936-37	D1	3	16.1.37	**Newcastle U**	D2	H	W	2-0	Beresford, F. O'Donnell
	4	30.1.37	**Stoke C**	D1	H	W	5-1	Turner og, Dougall, F.O'Donnell 3
	5	20.2.37	**Exeter C**	3S	H	W	5-3	F.O'Donnell 3, H.O'Donnell, Beresford
	6	6.3.37	**Tottenham H**	D2	A	W	3-1	H.O'Donnell, F.O'Donnell, Dougall
	SF	10.4.37	**WBA**	D1		W	4-1	F.O'Donnell 2, Dougall 2
		played at Highbury						
	F	1.5.37	**Sunderland**	D1 WEMBLEY	L	1-3	F.O'Donnell
1937-38	D1	3	8.1.38	**West Ham**	D2	H	W	3-0	Mutch 3
	4	22.1.38	**Leicester C**	D1	H	W	2-0	Mutch, H. O'Donnell
	5	12.2.38	**Arsenal**	D1	A	W	1-0	Dougall
	6	5.3.38	**Brentford**	D1	A	W	3-0	R.Beattie 2, H. O'Donnell
	SF	26.3.38	**Aston Villa**	D2		W	2-1	H. O'Donnell, Mutch
		played at Bramall Lane						
	F	30.4.38	**HUDDERSFIELD T**	D1 WEMBLEY	W	1-0aet	Mutch (p)
1938-39	D1	3	7.1.39	**Runcorn**	CC	A	W	4-2	Milne 2, Mutch, Beattie
	4	21.1.39	**Aston Villa**	D1	H	W	2-0	White 2
	5	11.2.39	**Newcastle U**	D2	A	W	2-1	R.Beattie, Mutch
	6	4.3.39	**Portsmouth**	D1	A	L	0-1	
1945-46	D1	3 1L	5.1.46	**Everton**	D1	H	W	2-1	Humphreys og, Livesey
	3 2L	9.1.46	**Everton**		A	D	2-2aet	McIntosh, Shankly
	4 1L	26.1.46	**Manchester U**	D1	A	L	0-1	
	4 2L	30.1.46	**Manchester U**		H	W	3-1	Shankly, Livesey, McIntosh
	5 1L	9.2.46	**Charlton A**	D1	H	W	1-0	Wharton
	5 2L	13.2.46	**Charlton A**		A	L	0-6	
1946-47	D1	3	11.1.47	**Northampton T**	3S	A	W	2-1	McIntosh, McLaren
	4	25.1.47	**Barnsley**	D2	H	W	6-0	Finney 2, R.Beattie, McIntosh 2, Hamilton
	5	20.2.47	**Sheffield W**	D2	A	W	2-0	
	6	1.3.47	**Charlton A**	D1	A	L	1-2	McIntosh
1947-48	D1	3	10.1.48	**Millwall**	D2	A	W	2-1	Anders, McLaren
	4	24.1.48	**Portsmouth**	D1	A	W	3-1	McIntosh, Finney, Shankly
	5	7.2.48	**Manchester C**	D1	A	W	1-0	McIntosh
	6	28.2.48	**Manchester U**	D1	A	L	1-4	McIntosh
1948-49	D1	3	8.1.49	**Mansfield T**	3N	H	W	2-1	Finney 2
	4	29.1.49	**Leicester C**	D2	A	L	0-2	
1949-50	D2	3	7.1.50	**Watford**	3S	A	D	2-2	Brown, Finney
	3r	11.1.50	**Watford**		H	L	0-1	
1950-51	D2	3	6.1.51	**Leicester C**	D2	A	W	3-0	Wayman 2, Horton

	4	27.1.51	**Huddersfield T**	D1	H	L	0-2	
1951-52	D1	3	12.1.52	**Bristol R**	3S	A	L	0-2	
1952-53	D1	3	10.1.53	**Wolverhampton W**	D1	H	W	5-2	Finney, Wayman 3, Lewis
	4	31.1.53	**Tottenham H**	D1	H	D	2-2	Finney, Lewis
	4r	4.2.53	**Tottenham H**		A	L	0-1	
1953-54	D1	3	9.1.54	**Derby Co**	D2	A	W	2-0	Finney, Wayman
	4	30.1.54	**Lincoln C**	D2	A	W	2-0	Baxter, Wayman
	5	20.2.54	**Ipswich T**	3S	H	W	6-1	Morrison, Wayman 2, Baxter 2, Finney
	6	13.3.54	**Leicester C**	D2	A	D	1-1	Morrison
	6r	17.3.54	**Leicester C**		H	D	2-2aet	Wayman, Morrison
	6 2r	22.3.54	**Leicester C** at Hillsborough			W	3-1	Baxter, Foster, Finney
	SF	27.3.54	**Sheffield W**	D1		W	2-0	Wayman, Baxter
		played at Maine Rd						
	F	1.5.54	**WBA**	D1 WEMBLEY	L	2-3	Morrison, Wayman
1954-55	D1	3	8.1.55	**Fulham**	D2	A	W	3-2	Hatsell 2, Finney
	4	29.1.55	**Sunderland**	D1	H	D	3-3	Finney, Morrison, Foster
	4r	2.2.55	**Sunderland**		A	L	0-2	
1955-56	D1	3	7.1.56	**West Ham**	D2	A	L	2-5	T.Thompson, Finney
1956-57	D1	3	5.1.57	**Sheffield W**	D1	H	D	0-0	
	3r	9.1.57	**Sheffield W**		A	D	2-2aet	Taylor, Finney
	3 2r	14.1.57	**Sheffield W** at Goodison Pk			W	5-1	Taylor, O'Farrell, Baxter, Thompson 2
	4	26.1.57	**Bristol R**	D2	A	W	4-1	Finney 2, Dagger, Taylor
	5	16.2.57	**Arsenal**	D1	H	D	3-3	Finney 2, Thompson
	5r	19.2.57	**Arsenal**		A	L	1-2	Dagger
1957-58	D1	3	4.1.58	**Bolton W**	D1	H	L	0-3	
1958-59	D1	3	10.1.59	**Derby Co**	D2	A	D	2-2	Farrall, Hatsell
	3r	19.1.59	**Derby Co**		H	W	4-2aet	Thompson, Farrall, Mayers, Smith
	4	24.1.59	**Bradford C**	D3	H	W	3-2	Farrall, O'Farrell, Hatsell
	5	14.2.59	**Bolton W**	D1	A	D	2-2	Campbell, Thompson (p)
	5r	18.2.59	**Bolton W**		H	D	1-1aet	Smith
	5 2r	23.2.59	**Bolton W** at Ewood Pk			L	0-1	
1959-60	D1	3	9.1.60	**Stoke C**	D2	A	D	1-1	Sneddon
	3r	12.1.60	**Stoke C**		H	W	3-1	Finney, Thompson, Mayers
	4	30.1.60	**Bristol R**	D2	A	D	3-3	Sneddon, Finney, Taylor
	4r	2.2.60	**Bristol R**		H	W	5-1	Finney 2, Thompson, Taylor 2
	5	20.2.60	**Brighton & HA**	D2	H	W	2-1	Taylor, Sneddon
	6	12.3.60	**Aston Villa**	D2	A	L	0-2	
1960-61	D1	3	7.1.61	**Accrington S**	D4	H	D	1-1	T.Thompson
	3r	9.1.61	**Accrington S**		A	W	4-0	T.Thompson, P.Thompson, Sneddon, Mayers
	4	28.1.61	**Swansea T**	D2	A	L	1-2	Alston
1961-62	D2	3	6.1.62	**Watford**	D3	H	W	3-2	Biggs, Smith, Dawson
	4	27.1.62	**Weymouth**	SL	H	–	0-0	
		abandoned after 14 minutes – fog						
	4	29.1.62	**Weymouth**		H	W	2-0	Dawson, Thompson
	5	17.2.62	**Liverpool**	D2	A	D	0-0	
	5r	20.2.62	**Liverpool**		H	D	0-0aet	
	5 2r	26.2.62	**Liverpool** at Old Trafford			W	1-0	Thompson
	6	10.3.62	**Manchester U**	D1	H	D	0-0	
	6r	14.3.62	**Manchester U**		A	L	1-2	Spavin
1962-63	D2	3	5.1.63	**Sunderland**	D2	H	L	1-4	Holden
1963-64	D2	3	4.1.64	**Nottingham F**	D1	A	D	0-0	
	3r	13.1.64	**Nottingham F**		H	W	1-0aet	Kendall
	4	25.1.64	**Bolton W**	D1	A	D	2-2	Dawson 2
	4r	27.1.64	**Bolton W**		H	W	2-1	Dawson, Lawton
	5	15.2.64	**Carlisle U**	D4	H	W	1-0	Spavin
	6	29.2.64	**Oxford U**	D4	A	W	2-1	Dawson, Godfrey
	SF	14.3.64	**Swansea T**	D2		W	2-1	Dawson, Singleton
		at Villa Park						
	F	2.5.64	**West Ham**	D1 WEMBLEY	L	2-3	Holden, Dawson
1964-65	D2	3	9.1.65	**Barnet**	AL	A	W	3-2	Kendall, Godfrey, Casey og
	4	30.1.65	**Bolton W**	D2	H	L	1-2	Dawson
1965-66	D2	3	22.1.66	**Charlton A**	D2	A	W	3-2	Hannigan 2, Lee
	4	12.2.66	**Bolton W**	D2	A	D	1-1	Dawson
	4r	14.2.66	**Bolton W**		H	W	3-2	Dawson, Godfrey 2 (2ps)
	5	5.3.66	**Tottenham H**	D1	H	W	2-1	Dawson, Hannigan
	6	26.3.66	**Manchester U**	D1	H	D	1-1	Dawson
	6r	30.3.66	**Manchester U**		A	L	1-3	Singleton

1966-67	D2	3	28.1.67	Aston Villa	D1	H	L	0-1	
1967-68	D2	3	27.1.68	QPR	D2	A	W	3-1	Charnley 2, Gemmell
		4	17.2.68	Tottenham H	D1	A	L	1-3	Charnley
1968-69	D2	3	4.1.69	Nottingham F	D1	H	W	3-0	Irvine 2 (1p), Temple
		4	25.1.69	Chelsea	D1	H	D	0-0	
		4r	29.1.69	Chelsea		A	–	0-2	
				abandoned after 72 minutes - floodlight failure					
		4r	3.2.69	Chelsea		A	L	1-2	Ingram
1969-70	D2	3	3.1.70	Derby Co	D1	H	D	1-1	Lyall
		3r	7.1.70	Derby Co		A	L	1-4	Hawkins
1970-71	D3	1	21.11.70	Chester	D4	H	D	1-1	Heppolette
		1r	23.11.70	Chester		A	L	0-1	
1971-72	D2	3	15.2.72	Bristol C	D2	H	W	4-2	Lyall, Ingram, Clark 2
		4	5.2.72	Manchester U	D1	H	L	0-2	
1972-73	D2	3	13.1.73	Grimsby T	D3	A	D	0-0	
		3r	15.1.73	Grimsby T		H	L	0-1	
1973-74	D2	3	5.1.74	Fulham	D2	A	L	0-1	
1974-75	D3	1	23.11.74	Blyth Spartans	NL	A	D	1-1	Holden
		1r	26.11.74	Blyth Spartans		H	W	5-1	Holden 4, Elwiss
		2	14.12.74	Bishop Auckland	NL	A	W	2-0	Charlton, Morley
		3	4.1.75	Carlisle U	D1	H	L	0-1	
1975-76	D3	1	22.11.75	Scunthorpe U	D4	H	W	2-1	Morley (p), Elwiss
		2	13.12.75	Scarborough	NPL	A	L	2-3	Smith 2
1976-77	D3	1	20.11.76	Crewe Alex	D4	A	D	1-1	Coleman
		1r	23.11.76	Crewe Alex		H	D	2-2aet	D.Davies 2
		1 2r	29.11.76	Crewe Alex at Anfield			W	3-0	Sadler, Brown, Elwiss
		2	14.12.76	Halifax T	D4	A	L	0-1	
1977-78	D3	1	26.11.77	Lincoln C	D3	H	W	3-2	Elwiss 2, Bruce
		2	17.12.77	Wrexham	D3	H	L	0-2	
1978-79	D2	3	16.1.79	Derby Co	D1	H	W	3-0	Bruce 2, Burns
		4	12.2.79	Southampton	D1	H	L	0-1	
1979-80	D2	3	5.1.80	Ipswich T	D1	H	L	0-3	
1980-81	D2	3	3.1.81	Bristol R	D2	H	L	3-4	Houston, Bruce, McGee
1981-82	D3	1	21.11.81	Chesterfield	D3	A	L	1-4	Doyle
1982-83	D3	1	20.11.82	Shepshed Chart.	NCoE	H	W	5-1	Elliott 2, Kelly, Coleman, McAteer
		2	11.12.82	Blackpool	D4	H	W	2-1	Coleman, O'Riordan
		3	8.1.83	Leeds U	D2	A	L	0-3	
1983-84	D3	1	19.11.83	Scunthorpe U	D3	A	L	0-1	
1984-85	D3	1	17.11.84	Bury	D4	H	W	4-3	Gray, Johnson 2, Naughton
		2	8.12.84	Telford U	APL	H	L	1-4	Hunter
1985-86	D4	1	16.11.85	Walsall	D3	A	L	3-7	Thomas, Brazil, Martin
1986-87	D4	1	15.11.86	Bury	D3	H	W	5-1	Thomas 3 (1p), Jones, Williams
		2	6.12.86	Chorley	NPL	A	D	0-0	
				played at Blackburn					
		2r	9.12.86	Chorley		H	W	5-0	Thomas 3 (1p), Williams, Brazil
		3	10.1.87	Middlesbrough	D3	A	W	1-0	Hildersley
		4	31.1.87	Newcastle U	D1	A	L	0-2	
1987-88	D3	1	14.11.87	Mansfield T	D3	H	D	1-1	Atkins
		1r	17.11.87	Mansfield T		A	L	2-4	Brazil, Jemson
1988-89	D3	1	19.11.88	Tranmere R	D4	H	D	1-1	Atkins
		1r	22.11.88	Tranmere R		A	L	0-3	
1989-90	D3	1	18.11.89	Tranmere R	D3	H	W	1-0	Joyce
		2	9.12.89	Whitley Bay	NPL	A	L	0-2	
1990-91	D3	1	17.11.90	Mansfield T	D3	H	L	0-1	
1991-92	D3	1	16.11.91	Mansfield T	D4	A	–	1-1	Shaw
				abandoned after 32 minutes - fog					
		1	27.11.91	Mansfield T		A	W	1-0	Thomas
		2	7.12.91	Witton Albion	GMVC	H	W	5-1	Shaw, Swann, Senior, Flynn, Greenwood
		3	4.1.92	Sheffield W	D1	H	L	0-2	
1992-93	D2	1	14.11.92	Bradford C	D2	A	D	1-1	Fowler
		1r	25.11.92	Bradford C		H	L	4-5	Graham, Ellis, Davidson, Callaghan

PRESTON ZINGARI

| 1884-85 | | 1 | | Bolton Wanderers | | | | | |
| | | | | match not played both teams withdrew | | | | | |

QUEEN'S PARK, GLASGOW

Formed 1867. One of the seven Scottish clubs that took part in the FA Cup. **FA Cup Best Performance:** Runners-up: 1884, 1885.

1871-72	1		Donington School				
			teams could not arrange date, both advanced to Round 2				
	2		Donington School		*walkover*		
	3		bye				
	SF	5.3.72	Wanderers		D	0-0	
			played at Kennington Oval				
	SFr		Wanderers		*scratched*		
1872-73			*exempt until semi-final because of travel difficulties*				
	SF		Oxford University		*scratched*		
1876-77	1		bye				
	2		bye				
	3		Oxford University		*scratched*		
1877-78	1		bye				
	2		Druids		*scratched*		
1879-80	1		Sheffield Club		*scratched*		
1880-81	1		Sheffield Wednesday		*scratched*		
1881-82	1		Accrington		*scratched*		
1882-83	1		Grimsby T		*scratched*		
1883-84	1	6.10.83	Crewe A	A	W	10-0	Fraser 3, Christie 2, Anderson 2, Smither 2, Harrower
	2	1.12.83	Manchester FC	H	W	15-0	Anderson 4, Harrower 3, Smith 3, Fraser 2, Allan, Christie, 1 other
	3	29.12.83	Oswestry	A	W	7-1	Anderson 2, Allan, Christie, Smith, others 2
	4	19.1.84	Aston Villa	H	W	6-1	Anderson 3, Campbell, Harrower, Smith
	5	9.2.84	Old Westminsters	A	W	1-0	Allan
	SF	1.3.84	Blackburn Olympic		W	4-1	Smith 3, Watt
			played at Trent Bridge				
	F	29.3.84	Blackburn Rovers		L	1-2	Christie
			played at Kennington Oval				
1884-85	1		Stoke		*walkover*		
	2	6.12.84	Crewe A	H	W	2-1	Allan, Christie
			match abandoned after torrential downpour 48 minutes but result stood				
	3	3.1.85	Leek	A	W	3-2	
	4	17.1.85	Old Wykehamists	H	W	7-0	Anderson 2, Watt 2, Christie 2, Allan
	5		bye				
	6	21.2.85	Notts Co	A	D	2-2	Christie 2
	6r	28.2.85	Notts Co at Derby Cricket Gd		W	2-1	Arnott, Sellar
	SF	14.3.85	Nottingham F		D	1-1	Danks
			played at Derby Cricket Ground				
	SFr	28.3.85	Nottingham F		W	3-0	Sellar 2, Widdowson og
			played at Merchiston Castle School, Edinburgh				
	F	4.4.85	Blackburn Rovers		L	0-2	
			played at Kennington Oval				
1885-86	1	31.10.85	Partick Thistle	H	W	5-1	
	2		South Shore		*scratched*		
1886-87	1	30.10.86	Preston NE	H	L	0-3	

QUEENS PARK RANGERS

Formed 1885 as St Jude's Institute. Queens Park Rangers 1898. **First entered FA Cup:** 1895. **Best FA Cup Performance:** Runners-up: 1982.
Record FA Cup Win: 8-1 vs Bristol Rovers, 1st round, 27.11.1937. **Record FA Cup Defeat:** four 5-goal defeats

1895-96		1q **Old St Stephens** (H) 1-1; 1qr **Old St Stephens** (A) 0-1					
1896-97	Lon	1q **Marlow** (H) 1-3					
1897-98		P **Windsor & Eton** (H) 3-0; 1q **Wolverton LNWR** (A) 2-1; 2q **Chesham Generals** (H) 4-0; 3q **Clapton** (A) 0-1					
as Queens Park Rangers							
1898-99		P **Richmond Association** (A) 0-3					
1899-00	SL	P **London Welsh** (A) 4-2; 1q **Fulham** (H) 3-0; 2q **West Hampstead** (H) 5-0; 3q **Wandsworth** (H) 7-1; 4q **Civil Service** (H) 3-0;					
		5q **Luton T** (A) 1-1; 5qr **Luton T** (H) 4-1					
	1	27.1.00 **Wolverhampton W**	D1	H	D	1-1	Haywood
	1r	31.1.00 **Wolverhampton W**		A	W	1-0aet	Bedingfield
	2	17.2.00 **Millwall A**		SL	H	L	0-2
1900-01	SL	3q **Fulham** (H) 7-0; 4q **Watford** (A) 1-1; 4qr **Watford** (H) 4-1; 5q **Luton T** (A) 0-3					
1901-02	SL	3q **Crouch End Vampires** (H) 2-0; 4q **West Norwood** (H) 4-0; 5q **Luton T** (A) 0-2					
1902-03	SL	3q **Luton T** (H) 0-3					

1903-04	SL	3q Fulham (H) 1-1; 3qr Fulham (A) 1-3						
1904-05	SL	6q Brentford (H) 1-2						
1905-06	SL	1	13.1.06	Fulham	SL	A	L	0-1	
1906-07	SL	1	12.1.07	Bristol R	SL	A	D	0-0	
		1r	14.1.07	Bristol R		H	L	0-1	
1907-08	SL	1	11.1.08	Reading	SL	H	W	1-0	Gittins
		2	1.2.08	Swindon T	SL	A	L	1-2	Walker
1908-09	SL	1	16.1.09	West Ham	SL	H	D	0-0	
		1r	20.1.09	West Ham		A	L	0-1	
1909-10	SL	1	15.1.10	Norwich C	SL	A	D	0-0	
		1r	19.1.10	Norwich C		H	W	3-0	Steer, McNaught, Whyman
		2	5.2.10	Southend U	SL	A	D	0-0	
		2r	9.2.10	Southend U		H	W	3-2	Steer 3
		3	19.2.10	West Ham	SL	H	D	1-1	Steer
		3r	24.2.10	West Ham		A	W	1-0aet	Steer
		4	5.3.10	Barnsley	D2	A	L	0-1	
1910-11	SL	1	14.1.11	Bradford PA	D2	A	L	3-5	Steer, McKie 2
1911-12	SL	1	13.1.12	Bradford C	D1	H	D	0-0	
		1r	18.1.12	Bradford C	D1	A	L	0-4	
1912-13	SL	1	11.1.13	Halifax T	ML	H	W	4-2	Ovens, Birch, Whyman, Revill
		2	1.2.13	Middlesbrough	D1	A	L	2-3	Birch 2
1913-14	SL	1	10.1.14	Bristol C	D2	H	D	2-2	Birch, Miller
		1r	14.1.14	Bristol C		A	W	2-0aet	Birch, Gregory
		2	31.1.14	Swansea T	SL	A	W	2-1	Birch 2
		3	21.2.14	Birmingham	D2	A	W	2-1	Miller, Gregory
		4	7.3.14	Liverpool	D1	A	L	1-2	Mitchell
1914-15	SL	1	9.1.15	Glossop	D2	H	W	2-1	Miller, Birch
		2	30.1.15	Leeds C	D2	H	W	1-0	Simons
		3	20.2.15	Everton	D1	H	L	1-2	Broster
1919-20	SL	1	10.1.20	Aston Villa	D1	A	L	1-2	Birch
1920-21	D3	1	8.1.21	Arsenal	D1	H	W	2-0	Smith, Chandler
		2	29.1.21	Burnley	D1	A	L	2-4	Smith, Birch
1921-22	3S	1	7.1.22	Arsenal	D1	A	D	0-0	
		1r	11.1.22	Arsenal		H	L	1-2	Smith
1922-23	3S	1	13.1.23	Crystal P	D2	H	W	1-0	Gregory
		2	3.2.23	Wigan Borough	3N	A	W	4-2	Parker 2, Chandler, Birch
		3	24.2.23	South Shields	D2	H	W	3-0	Gregory, Parker 2
		4	10.3.23	Sheffield U	D1	H	L	0-1	
1923-24	3S	1	12.1.24	Notts Co	D1	H	L	1-2	Davies
1924-25	3S	5q Clapton (H) 4-4; 5qr Clapton (A) 2-0; 6q Charlton (H) 1-1; 6qr Charlton (A) 2-1						
		1	10.1.25	Stockport Co	D2	H	L	1-3	Myers
1925-26	3S	1	28.11.25	Northfleet U	KL	A	D	2-2	Birch 2
		1r	3.12.25	Northfleet U		H	W	2-0	Burgess, Thompson
		2	12.12.25	Charlton A	3S	H	D	1-1	Hirst
		2r	17.12.25	Charlton A		A	L	0-1	
1926-27	3S	*Failed to send in their entry form and did not compete*						
1927-28	3S	1	26.11.27	Aldershot T	SL	A	–	1-0	Neil
				abandoned because of fog					
1927-28	3S	1	30.11.27	Aldershot T		A	L	1-2	Johnson
1928-29	3S	1	24.11.28	Guildford C	SL	A	L	2-4	Goddard, Burns
1929-30	3S	1	30.11.29	Luton T	3S	A	W	3-2	Goddard, Coward, Pierce
		2	14.12.29	Lincoln C	3N	H	W	2-1	Burns 2
		3	11.1.30	Charlton A	D2	A	D	1-1	Goddard
		3r	16.1.30	Charlton A		H	L	0-3	
1930-31	3S	1	29.11.30	Thames	3S	H	W	5-0	Burns 2, Goddard 2, Rounce
		2	13.12.30	Crewe A	3N	A	W	4-2	Goddard 2, Howe, Rounce
		3	10.1.31	Bristol R	3S	A	L	1-3	Coward
1931-32	3S	1	28.11.31	Barnet	AL	A	W	7-3	Goddard 2, Coward 2, Cribb 3
		2	12.12.31	Scunthorpe U	ML	A	W	4-1	Rounce 2, Goddard 2
		3	9.1.32	Leeds U	D2	H	W	3-1	Rounce, Cribb 2
		4	23.1.32	Huddersfield T	D1	A	L	0-5	
1932-33	3S	1	26.11.32	Merthyr Town	SL	A	D	1-1	Rounce
		1r	1.12.32	Merthyr Town		H	W	5-1	Goddard 3, Marcroft, Rounce
		2	10.12.32	Torquay U	3S	A	D	1-1	Rounce
		2r	15.12.32	Torquay U		H	W	3-1	Rounce 3
		3	14.1.33	Darlington	3N	A	L	0-2	
1933-34	3S	1	25.11.33	Kettering	UCL	H	W	6-0	Brown, Emmerson 2, Blackman 2, Allen

Season	Div	Rd	Date	Opponent	Comp	H/A	Res	Score	Scorers
		2	9.12.33	New Brighton	3N	H	D	1-1	Blackman
		2r	13.12.33	New Brighton		A	W	4-0	Blackman 4
		3	13.1.34	Nottingham F	D2	A	L	0-4	
1934-35	3S	1	24.11.34	Walthamstow Ave	AL	H	W	2-0	Emmerson, Devine
		2	8.12.34	Brighton & HA	3S	H	L	1-2	Crawford
1935-36	3S	1	30.11.35	Margate	SL	A	L	1-3	Cheetham
1936-37	3S	1	28.11.36	Brighton & HA	3S	H	W	5-1	Cheetham, Fitzgerald 3 (1p) McMahon
		2	12.12.36	South Liverpool	LC	A	W	1-0	Fitzgerald
		3	16.1.37	Bury	D2	A	L	0-1	
1937-38	3S	1	27.11.37	Bristol R	3S	A	W	8-1	Fitzgerald 3, Cheetham 3, Bott 2
		2	11.12.37	Swindon T	3S	A	L	1-2	Cape
1938-39	3S	1	26.11.38	Crystal P	3S	A	D	1-1	Cheetham
		1r	28.11.38	Crystal P		H	W	3-0	Bott (p), Cheetham 2
		2	10.12.38	Hartlepools U	3N	A	W	2-0	McCarthy, Cheetham
		3	7.1.39	West Ham	D2	H	L	1-2	Cheetham
1945-46	3S	1 1L	17.11.45	Barnet	AL	A	W	6-2	Heathcote, Mallett, Neary 3, Whitehead
		1 2L	24.11.45	Barnet		H	W	2-1	Swinfen, Neary
		2 1L	8.12.45	Ipswich T	3S	H	W	4-0	Neary, Stock, Addinall 2
		2 2L	15.12.45	Ipswich T		A	W	2-0	Daniels, Addinall
		3 1L	5.1.46	Crystal P	3S	H	D	0-0	
		3 2L	9.1.46	Crystal P		A	D	0-0aet	
		3r	16.1.46	Crystal P at Fulham			W	1-0	Addinall
		4 1L	26.1.46	Southampton	D2	A	W	1-0	Addinall
		4 2L	30.1.46	Southampton		H	W	4-3	Addinall 3, Stock
		5 1L	9.2.46	Brentford	D1	H	L	1-3	Pattison
		5 2L	14.2.46	Brentford		A	D	0-0	
1946-47	3S	1	30.11.46	Poole	WL	H	D	2-2	Hatton, Pattison
		1r	4.12.46	Poole		A	W	6-0	Hatton, Mallett 2, Pattison 2, Harris
		2	14.12.46	Norwich C	3S	A	D	4-4	Mills 2, Pattison, McEwan
		2r	18.12.46	Norwich C		H	W	2-0	Mills, Hatton
		3	11.1.47	Middlesbrough	D1	H	D	1-1	Pattison
		3r	15.1.47	Middlesbrough		A	L	1-3	Boxshall
1947-48	3S	3	10.1.48	Gillingham	SL	A	D	1-1aet	Boxshall
		3r	17.1.48	Gillingham		H	W	3-1	Hartburn, Hatton, McEwan
		4	24.1.48	Stoke C	D1	H	W	3-0	Hatton 2, Ramscar
		5	7.2.48	Luton T	D2	H	W	3-1	Hatton, Boxshall, McEwan
		6	28.2.48	Derby Co	D1	H	D	1-1aet	Hartburn
		6r	6.3.48	Derby Co		A	L	0-5	
1948-49	D2	3	8.1.49	Huddersfield T	D1	H	D	0-0aet	
		3r	15.1.49	Huddersfield T		A	L	0-5	
1949-50	D2	3	7.1.50	Everton	D1	H	L	0-2	
1950-51	D2	3	6.1.51	Millwall	3S	H	L	3-4	Addinall, Parkinson 2
1951-52	D2	3	12.1.52	Brentford	D2	A	L	1-3	Shepherd
1952-53	3S	1	22.11.52	Shrewsbury T	3S	H	D	2-2	Cameron 2
		1r	27.11.52	Shrewsbury T		A	D	2-2aet	Addinall, Smith
		1 2r	1.12.52	Shrewsbury T at Villa Park			L	1-4	Smith
1953-54	3S	1	21.11.53	Shrewsbury T	3S	H	W	2-0	Hurrall 2
		2	12.12.53	Nuneaton Borough	BDL	H	D	1-1	Tomkeys
		2r	17.12.53	Nuneaton Borough		A	W	2-1	Petchey, Shepherd
		3	9.1.54	Port Vale	3N	H	L	0-1	
1954-55	3S	1	20.11.54	Walthamstow Ave	IL	H	D	2-2	Smith, Cameron
		1r	25.11.54	Walthamstow Ave		A	D	2-2aet	Fidler, Tomkeys
		1 2r	29.11.54	Walthamstow Ave at Highbury			L	0-4	
1955-56	3S	1	19.11.55	Southend U	3S	A	L	0-2	
1956-57	3S	1	17.11.56	Dorchester T	WL	H	W	4-0	Hellawell, Balogun, Locke, Cameron
		2	8.12.56	Tooting & Mitcham	IL	A	W	2-0	Balogun, Longbottom
		3	5.1.57	Sunderland	D1	A	L	0-4	
1957-58	3S	1	16.11.57	Clapton	IL	A	D	1-1	Dawson
		1r	18.11.57	Clapton		H	W	3-1	Locke, Walsh og, Longbottom
		2	7.12.57	Hereford U	SL	A	L	1-6	Dawson
1958-59	D3	1	15.11.58	Walsall	D4	A	W	1-0	Dawson
		2	6.12.58	Southampton	D3	H	L	0-1	
1959-60	D3	1	14.11.59	Colchester U	D3	A	W	3-2	Petchey, Bedford, Angell
		2	5.12.59	Port Vale	D3	H	D	3-3	Longbottom 2, Bedford
		2r	7.12.59	Port Vale		A	L	1-2	Andrews
1960-61	D3	1	5.11.60	Walthamstow Ave	IL	H	W	3-2	Bedford 3
		2	26.11.60	Coventry C	D3	H	L	1-2	Longbottom

Season	Div	Rnd	Date	Opponent		Comp		H/A	Result	Scorers
1961-62	D3	1	4.11.61	Barry T	SL		A	D	1-1	McClelland
		1r	6.11.61	Barry T			H	W	7-0	Evans 2, Collins 2, Bedford 3
		2	25.11.61	Ashford	SL		A	W	3-0	McClelland, Evans, Collins
		3	6.1.62	Burnley	D1		A	L	1-6	Evans
1962-63	D3	1	3.11.62	Newport Co	D4		H	W	3-2	Barber 2, Large
		2	24.11.62	Hinckley Ath	SL		H	W	7-2	Bedford 3, McClelland, Collins, Lazarus 2
		3	26.1.63	Swansea T	D2		A	L	0-2	
1963-64	D3	1	16.11.63	Gillingham	D4		H	W	4-1	Leary, Malcolm, Graham, Bedford
		2	7.12.63	Colchester U	D3		A	W	1-0	Leary
		3	4.1.64	Carlisle U	D4		A	L	0-2	
1964-65	D3	1	14.11.64	Bath C	SL		H	W	2-0	Leary, Collins
		2	5.12.64	Peterborough U	D3		H	D	3-3	Keen (p), R.Brady, Bedford
		2r	9.12.64	Peterborough U			A	L	1-2aet	McAdams
1965-66	D3	1	13.11.65	Colchester U	D4		A	D	3-3	Collins, L.Allen, Sanderson
		1r	17.11.65	Colchester U			H	W	4-0	Allen 2, Morgan, Sanderson
		2	4.12.65	Guildford C	SL		H	W	3-0	Hunt og, Sibley, Lazarus
		3	22.1.66	Shrewsbury T	D3		H	D	0-0	
		3r	26.1.66	Shrewsbury T			A	L	0-1	
1966-67	D3	1	26.11.66	Poole T	SL		H	W	3-2	Marsh 3
		2	7.1.67	Bournemouth	D3		H	W	2-0	Langley (p), Lazarus
		3	28.1.67	Sheffield W	D1		A	L	0-3	
1967-68	D2	3	27.1.68	Preston NE	D2		H	L	1-3	Keen
1968-69	D1	3	4.1.69	Aston Villa	D2		A	L	1-2	I.Morgan
1969-70	D2	3	3.1.70	South Shields	NPL		H	W	4-1	Marsh 2, Clarke, Ferguson
		4	24.1.70	Charlton A	D2		A	W	3-2	Marsh 2, Clarke
		5	7.2.70	Derby Co	D1		H	W	1-0	Clarke
		6	21.2.70	Chelsea	D1		H	L	2-4	Venables (p), Bridges
1970-71	D2	3	2.1.71	Swindon T	D2		H	L	1-2	Marsh (p)
1971-72	D2	3	15.1.72	Fulham	D2		H	D	1-1	Mancini
		3r	18.1.72	Fulham			A	L	1-2	Clement
1972-73	D2	3	13.1.73	Barnet	SL		H	D	0-0	
		3r	16.1.73	Barnet			A	W	3-0	Leach, Bowles, Mancini
		4	3.2.73	Oxford U	D2		A	W	2-0	Clement, Givens
		5	24.2.73	Derby Co	D1		A	L	2-4	Leach, Givens
1973-74	D1	3	5.1.74	Chelsea	D1		A	D	0-0	
		3r	15.1.74	Chelsea			H	W	1-0	Bowles
		4	26.1.74	Birmingham C	D1		H	W	2-0	Leach, Givens
		5	16.2.74	Coventry C	D1		A	D	0-0	
		5r	19.2.74	Coventry C			H	W	3-2	Givens, Thomas, Bowles
		6	9.3.74	Leicester C	D1		H	L	0-2	
1974-75	D1	3	4.1.75	Southend U	D3		A	D	2-2	Gillard, Francis
		3r	7.1.75	Southend U			H	W	2-0	Givens 2
		4	24.1.75	Notts Co	D2		H	W	3-0	Thomas, Bowles (p), Givens
		5	15.2.75	West Ham	D1		A	L	1-2	Clement
1975-76	D1	3	3.1.76	Newcastle U	D1		H	D	0-0	
		3r	7.1.76	Newcastle U			A	L	1-2	Masson
1976-77	D1	3	8.1.77	Shrewsbury T	D3		H	W	2-1	Bowles, Givens
		4	29.1.77	Manchester U	D1		A	L	0-1	
1977-78	D1	3	7.1.78	Wealdstone	SL		H	W	4-0	Givens, James, Bowles (p), Howe
		4	28.1.78	West Ham	D1		A	D	1-1	Howe
		4r	31.1.78	West Ham			H	W	6-1	Givens, Hollins, Busby 2, Bowles (p), James
		5	18.2.78	Nottingham F	D1		H	D	1-1	Busby
		5r	27.2.78	Nottingham F			A	D	1-1aet	Shanks
		5 2r	2.3.78	Nottingham F			A	L	1-3	Bowles
1978-79	D1	3	9.1.79	Fulham	D2		A	L	0-2	
1979-80	D2	3	5.1.80	Watford	D2		H	L	1-2	Hazell
1980-81	D2	3	3.1.81	Tottenham H	D1		H	D	0-0	
		3r	7.1.81	Tottenham H			A	L	1-3	Stainrod
1981-82	D2	3	2.1.82	Middlesbrough	D1		H	D	1-1	Stainrod
		3r	18.1.82	Middlesbrough			A	W	3-2aet	Stainrod 2, Neill
		4	23.1.82	Blackpool	D4		A	D	0-0	
		4r	26.1.82	Blackpool			H	W	5-1	C.Allen 4, Stainrod (p)
		5	13.2.82	Grimsby T	D2		H	W	3-1	Stainrod, C.Allen, Howe
		6	6.3.82	Crystal P	D2		H	W	1-0	C.Allen
		SF	3.4.82	WBA	D1			W	1-0	C.Allen
			played at Highbury							
		F	22.5.82	Tottenham H	D1	WEMBLEY		D	1-1aet	Fenwick

		Fr	27.5.82	Tottenham H		WEMBLEY	L	0-1	
1982-83	D2	3	8.1.83	WBA	D1	A	L	2-3	Fenwick (p), Micklewhite
1983-84	D1	3	7.1.84	Huddersfield T	D2	A	L	1-2	Gregory
1984-85	D1	3	5.1.85	Doncaster R	D3	A	L	0-1	
1985-86	D1	3	13.1.86	Carlisle U	D2	A	L	0-1	
1986-87	D1	3	10.1.87	Leicester C	D1	H	W	5-2	Fenwick 2 (1p), Lee, James, Byrne
		4	31.1.87	Luton T	D1	A	D	1-1	Fenwick (p)
		4r	4.2.87	Luton T		H	W	2-1	Fenwick, Byrne
		5	21.2.87	Leeds U	D2	A	L	1-2	Rennie og
1987-88	D1	3	9.1.88	Yeovil T	IL	A	W	3-0	Falco 2, Brock
		4	30.1.88	West Ham	D1	H	W	3-1	Pizanti, Bannister, M.Allen
		5	20.2.88	Luton T	D1	H	D	1-1	Neill
		5r	24.2.88	Luton T		A	L	0-1	
1988-89	D1	3	7.1.89	Manchester U	D1	A	D	0-0	
		3r	11.1.89	Manchester U		H	D	2-2aet	Stein, McDonald
		3 2r	23.1.89	Manchester U		A	L	0-3	
1989-90	D1	3	6.1.90	Cardiff C	D3	A	D	0-0	
		3r	10.1.90	Cardiff C		H	W	2-0	Wilkins, Wegerle
		4	27.1.90	Arsenal	D1	A	D	0-0	
		4r	31.1.90	Arsenal		H	W	2-0	Sansom, Sinton
		5	18.2.90	Blackpool	D3	A	D	2-2	Clarke 2
		5r	21.2.90	Blackpool		H	D	0-0aet	
		5 2r	26.2.90	Blackpool		H	W	3-0	Sinton, Sansom, Barker (p)
		6	11.3.90	Liverpool	D1	H	D	2-2	Wilkins, Barker
		6r	14.3.90	Liverpool		A	L	0-1	
1990-91	D1	3	7.1.91	Manchester U	D1	A	L	1-2	Maddix
1991-92	D1	3	4.1.91	Southampton	D1	A	L	0-2	
1992-93	PL	3	2.1.93	Swindon T	D1	H	W	3-0	Ferdinand 2, Penrice
		4	23.1.93	Manchester C	PL	H	L	1-2	Holloway

RAMBLERS

Formed 1874. Played at Woolwich Common and used the Perseverance Hotel as their changing rooms.

1875-76		1	23.10.75	Maidenhead		A	L	0-2	
1876-77		1	14.10.76	Pilgrims		A	L	1-4	Sang
1877-78		1	3.11.77	Pilgrims		A	D	0-0	
		1r	9.11.77	Pilgrims		A	L	0-1	
1878-79		1	2.11.78	Romford		A	L	1-3	Andrews

RAMSGATE

Formed 1946. **First entered FA Cup:** 1946

1955-56	KL	1	19.11.55	Watford	3S	A	L	3-5	Davies, McCulloch, Durkin

RANGERS FC, LONDON

Formed 1876. Played at Clapham Common and used the Invitation pub in Auckland Road, Wandsworth as their changing rooms.

1880-81		1		Wanderers		walkover	
		2		bye			
		3	9.2.81	Royal Engineers at Kennington Oval		L	0-6
1881-82		1		Romford		scratched	

RAWMARSH WELFARE

First entered FA Cup: 1930. Played at the strangely-named Hill 60 ground in Peashill Street, Rawmarsh, near Rotherham.

1951-52	SAL	1	24.11.51	Buxton	CC	H	L	1-4	Swales

RAWTENSTALL

Formed 1879. Played at Burnley Road, Rawtenstall, Lancs, near the White Lion Hotel.

1884-85		1		South Shore	scratched
1885-86		1		Glasgow Rangers	walkover

		2	21.11.85	**Bolton Wanderers**	**H**	**D**	**3-3**	
				Rawtenstall disqualified for professionalism				
1886-87		1	30.10.86	**Church**	**A**	**D**	**1-1**	
		1r	13.11.86	**Church**	**H**	**L**	**1-7**	
1887-88		1	15.10.87	**Darwen**	**H**	**L**	**1-3**	

READING

Formed 1871. **First entered FA Cup:** 1877. **Best FA Cup Performance:** semi-finals, 1927. **Record FA Cup Win:** 11-0 vs Chesham Generals, 4th qualifying round, 17.11.1900. **In Competition Proper:** 6-0 vs Leyton FC, 2nd round, 12.12.1925. **Record FA Cup Defeat:** 0-18 vs Preston NE, 1st round, 27.1.1894

1877-78		1	7.11.77	**South Norwood**	**H**	**W**	**2-0**	Field, H.Wilson og
		2	8.12.77	**Upton Park**	**A**	**L**	**0-1**	
1878-79		1	9.11.78	**Hendon**	**H**	**W**	**1-0**	Holbrook
		2	18.12.78	**Old Etonians**	**H**	**L**	**0-1**	
1879-80		1		**Henley**		*scratched*		
1880-81		1	13.11.80	**Hotspur**	**H**	**W**	**5-1**	C Field, Fuller, Holbrook, Turner, Silence
		2	18.12.80	**Swifts**	**H**	**L**	**0-1**	
1881-82		1	29.10.81	**Hendon**	**H**	**W**	**5-0**	Thompson 2, C Field, Franklin, Turner
		2	26.11.81	**West End**	**H**	**D**	**1-1**	Field
				FA disqualified West End				
		3		**bye**				
		4		**Marlow**		*scratched*		
1882-83		1		**bye**				
		2	29.11.82	**Royal Engineers**	**A**	**L**	**0-8**	
1883-84		1	10.11.83	**South Reading**	**H**	**D**	**2-2**	Lushington, Turner
		1r	17.11.83	**South Reading**	**A**	**W**	**4-0**	C.Field 2, Beacon, an other
		2	1.12.83	**West End**	**H**	**W**	**1-0**	C.Field
		3	22.12.83	**Upton Park**	**H**	**L**	**1-6**	
1884-85		1	8.11.84	**Rochester**	**H**	**W**	**2-0**	Egerton, E.Field
		2	6.12.84	**Upton Park**	**A**	**L**	**1-3**	Thompson
1885-86		1	31.10.85	**Rochester**	**A**	**L**	**1-6**	
1886-87		1	23.10.86	**Old Carthusians**	**A**	**L**	**1-2**	Murdoch
1887-88		1	15.10.87	**Dulwich**	**H**	**L**	**0-2**	
				FA ordered replay after protest				
		1r		**Dulwich**		*scratched*		

1888-89		1q Luton T (A) 0-4
1889-90		1q Old St Pauls (H) 3-4aet
1890-91		1q Ipswich T (A) 0-2
1891-92		1q **Newbury T** (H) 2-1; 2q **Southampton St Mary's (A)** 0-7, *Southampton disqualified by FA, Reading re-instated*; 3q **Clifton A** (A) 2-8
1892-93		1q **Clifton A** (H) 6-1; 2q **Uxbridge** (A) 3-2; **3q Swindon T** (A) 1-2
1893-94		1q **Warmley** (H) 3-0; 2q **Newbury T** (A) 2-1; 3q **Southampton St Marys** (H) 2-1; 4q **Swindon T** (A) 2-0
		1	27.1.94	**Preston NE**	**D1**	**A**	**L**	**0-18**	
1894-95	SL	1q **Clifton A** (A) 7-3; 2q **Southampton St Marys** (A) 2-5
1895-96	SL	1q **Bristol St Georges** (H) 7-2; 2q **Eastleigh** (H) 2-1; 3q **Southampton St Marys** (A) 0-3
1896-97	SL	3q **Bedminster** (A) 5-0; 4q **Southampton St Marys (H)** 1-4
1897-98	SL	3q **Swindon T** (H) 0-0; 4q **Swindon T (A)** 2-3
1898-99	SL	3q **Bristol R** (A) 1-0; 4q **Warmley** (H) 1-1; **4qr Warmley** (H) 3-0; 5q **Bristol C** (A) 2-3
1899-00	SL	3q **Wycombe W** (A) 8-0; 4q **Marlow** (H) 2-1; 5q **Chesham T** (H) 7-1
		1	27.1.00	**Newcastle U**	**D2**	**A**	**L**	**1-2**	Barlow
1900-01	SL	3q **Oxford C** (A) 4-0; 4q **Chesham Generals** (H) 11-0; **5q Richmond Association** (H) 2-0
		Int **Bristol C** (H) 1-1; Int r **Bristol C** (A) 0-0aet; Int 2r **Bristol C** 2-1 at Swindon							
		1	9.2.01	**Bristol R**	**SL**	**H**	**W**	**2-0**	Barnes, Pegg
		2	23.2.01	**Bolton W**	**D1**	**A**	**W**	**1-0**	A.Sharp
		3	23.3.01	**Tottenham H**	**SL**	**H**	**D**	**1-1**	Evans
		3r	28.3.01	**Tottenham H**		**A**	**L**	**0-3**	
1901-02	SL	Int **Chesterfield** (H) 2-1							
		1	25.1.02	**Notts Co**	**D1**	**A**	**W**	**2-1**	Allison, Davidson
		2	8.2.02	**Portsmouth**	**SL**	**H**	**L**	**0-1**	
1902-03	SL	Int **Burnley** (H) 1-0							
		1	7.1.03	**Nottingham F**	**D1**	**A**	**D**	**0-0**	
		1r	12.1.03	**Nottingham F**		**H**	**L**	**3-6aet**	Craggs 2, Lyon
1903-04	SL	Int **Gainsborough Trinity** (H) 1-0							
		1	6.2.04	**Bolton W**	**D2**	**H**	**D**	**1-1**	Bevan
		1r	10.2.04	**Bolton W**		**A**	**L**	**2-3**	Bevan 2
1904-05	SL	Int **Brentford** (A) 1-1; Int r **Brentford** (H) 2-0							

READING

	1	4.2.05	**Fulham**	SL	A	D	0-0	
	1r	8.2.05	**Fulham**		H	D	0-0aet	
	1 2r	13.2.05	**Fulham** at Tottenham			L	0-1aet	
1905-06 SL	1	13.1.06	**Hull C**	D2	A	W	1-0	McCafferty
	2	3.2.06	**Tottenham H**	SL	A	L	2-3	McCafferty
1906-07 SL	1	12.1.07	**Bradford C**	D2	A	L	0-2	
1907-08 SL	1	11.1.08	**QPR**	SL	A	L	0-1	
1908-09 SL	1	16.1.09	**Norwich C**	SL		D	0-0	
			played at Stamford Bridge					
	1r	20.1.09	**Norwich C**		H	D	1-1aet	Huggins
	1 2r	25.1.09	**Norwich C** at Villa Park			L	2-3aet	Wheatcroft 2
1909-10 SL	1	15.1.10	**Wolverhampton W**	D2	A	L	0-5	
1910-11 SL			4q **Exeter C** (H) 1-1; 4qr **Exeter C** (A) 0-1					
1911-12 SL			4q **Southall** (H) 7-1; 5q **Castleford T** (A) 2-1					
	1	13.1.12	**Southport Central**	CL	A	W	2-0	Lee, Andrews
	2	3.2.12	**A.Villa**	D1	A	D	1-1	Bailey
	2r	7.2.12	**A.Villa**		H	W	1-0	Foster
	3	24.2.12	**Manchester U**	D1	H	D	1-1	Bradley
	3r	29.2.12	**Manchester U**		A	L	0-3	
1912-13 SL	1	11.1.13	**Stoke**	SL	A	–	2-1	Burton
			abandoned after 25 minutes					
	1r	16.1.13	**Stoke**		A	D	2-2	Foster, Pinfield
	1 2r	22.1.13	**Stoke**		H	W	3-0	Morris, Burton, Pinfield
	2	1.2.13	**Tottenham H**	D1	H	W	1-0	Pinfield
	3	22.2.13	**Blackburn R**	D1	H	L	1-2	Bailey
1913-14 SL	1	10.1.14	**Bradford PA**	D2	A	L	1-5	Foster
1914-15 SL	1	9.1.15	**Wolverhampton W**	D2	H	L	0-1	
1919-20 SL	1	10.1.20	**Plymouth A**	SL	A	L	0-2	
1920-21 D3	1	8.1.21	**Chelsea**	D1	H	D	0-0	
	1r	12.1.21	**Chelsea**		A	D	2-2aet	Mavin, Broskon
	1 2r	17.1.21	**Chelsea**		A	L	1-3	Bailey
1921-22 3S	1	7.1.22	**Northampton T**	3S	A	L	0-3	
1922-23 3S			5q **Bristol R** (H) 0-1					
1923-24 3S			5q **Aberdare A** (A) 0-1					
1924-25 3S			4q **Erith & Belvedere** (A) 2-0; 5q **Southend U** (H) 2-1; 6q **Darlington** (H) 0-1					
1925-26 3S	1	28.11.25	**Torquay U**	SL	A	D	1-1	Messer
	1r	2.12.25	**Torquay U**		H	D	1-1aet	Davey
	1 2r	7.12.25	**Torquay U** at Ashton Gate			W	2-0	Braithwaite, Davey
	2	12.12.25	**Leyton**	Lon	H	W	6-0	Robson 2, Davey, Smith, Braithwaite 2
	3	9.1.26	**Bournemouth**	3S	A	L	0-2	
1926-27 D2	1	27.11.26	**Weymouth**	SL	H	D	4-4	Richardson 2, Johnstone 2
	1r	1.12.26	**Weymouth**		H	W	5-0	Porter, Johnstone 3, Robson
	2	11.12.26	**Southend U**	3S	H	W	3-2	Braithwaite 2, Richardson
	3	8.1.27	**Manchester U**	D1	H	D	1-1	Richardson
	3r	12.1.27	**Manchester U**		A	D	2-2aet	Richardson 2
	3 2r	17.1.27	**Manchester U** at Villa Park			W	2-1	Richardson (p), Johnstone
	4	29.1.27	**Portsmouth**	D2	H	W	3-1	Richardson, Macdonald, Johnstone
	5	19.2.27	**Brentford**	3S	H	W	1-0	Richardson
	6	5.3.27	**Swansea T**	D2	A	W	3-1	Johnstone 2, McDonald
	SF	26.3.27	**Cardiff C**	D1		L	0-3	
			played at Molineux					
1927-28 D2	3	14.1.28	**Grimsby T**	D2	H	W	4-0	Richardson 2, Batten, McDonald
	4	28.1.28	**Leicester C**	D1	H	L	0-1	
1928-29 D2	3	12.1.29	**Tottenham H**	D2	H	W	2-0	Johnstone 2
	4	26.1.29	**Sheffield W**	D1	H	W	1-0	Johnstone
	5	16.2.29	**A.Villa**	D1	H	L	1-3	Oswald
1929-30 D2	3	11.1.30	**A.Villa**	D1	A	L	1-5	Douglas
1930-31 D2	3	10.1.31	**Crystal P**	3S	A	D	1-1	Bacon
	3r	14.1.31	**Crystal P**		H	D	1-1aet	Gilhesby
	3 2r	19.1.31	**Crystal P** at Stamford Bridge			L	0-2	
1931-32 3S	1	28.11.31	**Crystal P**	3S	H	L	0-1	
1932-33 3S	1	26.11.32	**Brentford**	3S	H	W	3-2	Oxberry, McPherson, Ritchie
	2	10.12.32	**Coventry C**	3S	H	D	2-2	Bacon, McPherson
	2r	15.12.32	**Coventry C**		A	D	3-3	Liddle 2, McPherson
	2 2r	19.12.32	**Coventry C** at Stamford Bridge			W	1-0	Oxberry
	3	14.1.33	**Millwall**	D2	A	–	0-2	
			abandoned after 75 minutes - fog					

		3	18.1.33	Millwall		A	D	1-1	Pipe og
		3r	23.1.33	Millwall		H	L	0-2	
1933-34	3S	1	25.11.33	Watford	3S	A	W	3-0	McGough 2, Newton
		2	9.12.33	Sutton T	DSL	A	W	2-1	Newton, Oxberry
		3	13.1.34	Oldham A	D2	H	L	1-2	Hayhurst
1934-35	3S	1	24.11.34	Cardiff C	3S	A	W	2-1	Tait 2
		2	8.12.34	Wrexham	3N	H	W	3-0	Butler 2, Tait
		3	12.1.35	Aldershot	3S	A	D	0-0	
		3r	16.1.35	Aldershot		H	W	3-1	Tait 2, Butler
		4	26.1.35	Millwall	3S	H	W	1-0	Tait
		5	16.2.35	Arsenal	D1	H	L	0-1	
1935-36	3S	1	30.11.35	Corinthians		H	W	8-3	Tait 2, Fielding 2, Liddle 3, McGough
		2	14.12.35	Chester	3N	A	D	3-3	Tait, Liddle, Hayhurst
		2r	18.12.35	Chester		H	W	3-0	Tait, Paterson, Fielding
		3	11.1.36	Manchester U	D2	H	L	1-3	Pateman
1936-37	3S	1	28.11.36	Ilford	IL	A	W	4-2	Gregory, Tait, Fielding, Wright
		2	12.12.36	Newport Co	3S	H	W	7-2	Fielding, Watkin 4, Tait, Paterson
		3	16.1.37	Manchester U	D1	A	L	0-1	
1937-38	3S	1	27.11.37	Guildford C	SL	A	L	0-1	
1938-39	3S	1	26.11.38	Newport Co	3S	H	D	3-3	McPhee, Tait, Gledden
		1r	5.12.38	Newport Co		A	L	1-3	Tait
1945-46	3S	1 1L	17.11.45	Aldershot	3S	H	W	3-1	Edelston, Summerfield, Layton
		1 2L	24.11.45	Aldershot		A	L	3-7	McPhee 2, Summerfield
1946-47	3S	1	30.11.46	Colchester U	SL	H	W	5-0	Edelston 2, McPhee, Chitty, Barney
		2	14.12.46	Merthyr T	SL	A	W	3-1	Deverall, Barnes, Edelston
		3	11.1.47	Grimsby T	D1	H	D	2-2	McPhee, Henley
		3r	14.1.47	Grimsby T		A	L	1-3	Edelston
1947-48	3S	1	29.11.47	Bromley	AL	A	D	3-3aet	Green, Goldberg, Birchston
		1r	6.12.47	Bromley		H	W	3-0	Dix, Fisher, McPhee
		2	13.12.47	Newport Co	3S	H	W	3-0	Edelston 2, McPhee
		3	10.1.48	WBA	D2	A	L	0-2	
1948-49	3S	1	27.11.48	Colchester U	SL	A	–	1-1	McPhee
			abandoned after 35 minutes - fog						
		1	4.12.48	Colchester U		A	W	4-2	Edelston 2, McPhee, Dix
		2	11.12.48	Hull C	3N	A	D	0-0aet	
		2r	18.12.48	Hull C		H	L	1-2	McPhee
1949-50	3S	3	7.1.50	Doncaster R	3N	H	L	2-3	Blackman 2
1950-51	3S	1	25.11.50	Cheltenham T	SL	H	W	3-1	Bainbridge, Blackman 2
		2	9.12.50	Dartford	SL	H	W	4-0	Henry, Edelston, Blackman, Bainbridge
		3	6.1.51	Newport Co	3S	A	L	2-3	Blackman 2
1951-52	3S	1	24.11.51	Walsall	3S	H	W	1-0	Blackman
		2	15.12.51	Southport	3N	H	D	1-1	Henley
		2r	19.12.51	Southport		A	D	1-1aet	Brice
		2 2r	1.1.52	Southport at Villa Park			W	2-0	Henley, Hacking og
		3	12.1.52	Swansea T	D2	H	L	0-3	
1952-53	3S	1	22.11.52	Crystal P	3S	A	D	1-1	McLean
		1r	26.11.52	Crystal P		H	L	1-3	Brooks
1953-54	3S	1	21.11.53	Ipswich T	3S	A	L	1-4	Blackman
1954-55	3S	1	20.11.54	Colchester U	3S	H	D	3-3	Wheeler, Uphill, Hill og
		1r	25.11.54	Colchester U		A	W	2-1	Uphill, Mansell
		2	11.12.54	Gillingham	3S	A	D	1-1	Wheeler
		2r	13.12.54	Gillingham		H	W	5-3	Wheeler 2, Uphill 2, Chung
		3	8.1.55	Manchester U	D1	H	D	1-1	Chilton og
		3r	12.1.55	Manchester U		A	L	1-4	Uphill
1955-56	3S	1	19.11.55	Bournemouth	3S	H	W	1-0	Anderton
		2	10.12.55	Aldershot	3S	H	D	2-2	Dixon, Cross
		2r	14.12.55	Aldershot		A	L	0-3aet	
1956-57	3S	1	17.11.56	Cheltenham T	SL	A	W	2-1	Dixon 2
		2	8.12.56	Bedford T	SL	H	W	1-0	Campbell
		3	5.1.57	Wrexham	3N	A	D	1-1	Wheeler
		3r	9.1.57	Wrexham		H	L	1-2	Dixon
1957-58	3S	1	16.11.57	Swindon T	3S	H	W	1-0	Dixon
		2	7.12.57	Wisbech T	ML	H	W	2-1	Whitehouse, Dixon
		3	4.1.58	Leyton O	D2	A	L	0-1	
1958-59	D3	1	15.11.58	Watford	D4	A	D	1-1	Wheeler
		1r	19.11.58	Watford		H	L	0-2	
1959-60	D3	1	14.11.59	Norwich C	D3	A	D	1-1	Wheeler

	1r	18.11.59	Norwich C		H	W	2-1	Wheeler, Reeves
	2	5.12.59	Kings Lynn	SL	H	W	4-2	Ayre 2, Reeves (p), Wheeler
	3	9.1.60	Nottingham F	D1	A	L	0-1	
1960-61 D3	1	5.11.60	Millwall	D4	H	W	6-2	McIlvenny, Wheeler 3, Lacey, Evans
	2	26.11.60	Kettering T	SL	H	W	4-2	Lacey 3, McIlvenny
	3	7.1.61	Barnsley	D3	H	D	1-1	Whitehouse
	3r	11.1.61	Barnsley		A	L	1-3	Whitehouse
1961-62 D3	1	4.11.61	Newport Co	D3	H	D	1-1	D.Webb
	1r	6.11.61	Newport Co		A	L	0-1	
1962-63 D3	1	3.11.62	Swindon T	D3	A	L	2-4	Wheeler, Walker (p)
1963-64 D3	1	16.11.63	Enfield	IL	H	D	2-2	Allen, Wheeler
	1r	19.11.63	Enfield		A	W	4-2aet	Wheeler, D.Webb 2, Tindall
	2	7.12.63	Luton T	D3	A	L	1-2	D.Webb
1964-65 D3	1	14.11.64	Watford	D3	H	W	3-1	Walker (p), Norton, D.Webb
	2	5.12.64	Aldershot	D4	A	W	3-1	Terry 2, D.Webb
	3	9.1.65	Newport Co	D4	H	D	2-2	Spiers, D.Webb
	3r	11.1.65	Newport Co		A	W	1-0	Shreeves
	4	30.1.65	Burnley	D1	H	D	1-1	Kerr
	4r	2.2.65	Burnley		A	L	0-1	
1965-66 D3	1	13.11.65	Bristol R	D3	H	W	3-2	Terry, Allen 2
	2	4.12.65	Brentford	D3	H	W	5-0	Allen, Webb 2, Terry, Evans
	3	22.1.66	Sheffield W	D1	H	L	2-3	Thornhill, Evans
1966-67 D3	1	26.11.66	Hendon	IL	A	W	3-1	Harris, Thornhill 2
	2	16.1.67	Aldershot	D4	A	L	0-1	
1967-68 D3	1	13.12.67	Aldershot	D4	H	W	6-2	Silvester 2, Allen 2, Collins, Harris
	2	6.1.68	Dagenham	AL	H	D	1-1	Harris
	2r	15.1.68	Dagenham		A	W	1-0	Sainty
	3	27.1.68	Manchester C	D1	A	D	0-0	
	3r	31.1.68	Manchester C		H	L	0-7	
1968-69 D3	1	16.11.68	Plymouth A	D3	H	W	1-0	Henderson
	2	7.12.68	Torquay U	D3	H	D	0-0	
	2r	11.12.68	Torquay U		A	W	2-1	Harris, Silvester
	3	4.1.69	Newcastle U	D1	A	L	0-4	
1969-70 D3	1	15.11.69	Brentwood T	SL	A	L	0-1	
1970-71 D3	1	21.11.70	Bishops Stortford	AL	H	W	6-1	Habbin 3, Bell 2, Cumming
	2	12.12.70	Shrewsbury T	D3	A	D	2-2	Cumming, Williams
	2r	21.12.70	Shrewsbury T		H	W	1-0	Habbin
	3	6.1.71	Watford	D2	A	L	0-5	
1971-72 D4	1	20.11.71	Bridgwater T	WL	A	W	3-0	Prescott og, Flannigan, Cumming
	2	11.12.71	Aldershot	D4	H	W	1-0	Harman
	3	15.1.72	Blyth Spartans	NL	A	D	2-2	B.Wagstaff, Cumming (p)
	3r	19.1.72	Blyth Spartans		H	W	6-1	Harman 3, Cumming, B.Wagstaff, Habbin
	4	5.2.72	Arsenal	D1	H	L	1-2	Wagstaff
1972-73 D4	1	18.11.72	Gillingham	D4	A	W	2-1	Habbin, Dixon
	2	9.12.72	Hayes	IL	H	D	0-0	
	2r	11.12.72	Hayes		A	W	1-0	Chappell
	3	13.1.73	Doncaster R	D4	H	W	2-0	Chappell, Cummings
	4	3.2.73	Sunderland	D2	A	D	1-1	Chappell
	4r	6.2.73	Sunderland		H	L	1-3	Cumming (p)
1973-74 D4	1	24.11.73	Slough T	IL	H	W	3-0	Bromley, Hetzke, Chappell
	2	15.12.73	Southend U	D3	A	L	0-2	
1974-75 D4	1	23.11.74	Swindon T	D3	A	L	0-4	
1975-76 D4	1	22.11.75	Hendon	IL	A	L	0-1	
1976-77 D3	1	20.11.76	Wealdstone	SL	H	W	1-0	Murray
	2	11.12.76	Wycombe W	IL	A	W	2-1	Friday 2
	3	8.1.77	Hereford U	D2	A	L	0-1	
1977-78 D4	1	26.11.77	Aldershot	D4	H	W	3-1	Earles 2, Kearns
	2	17.12.77	Wealdstone	SL	A	L	1-2	Earles
1978-79 D4	1	25.11.78	Gillingham	D3	H	D	0-0	
	1r	28.11.78	Gillingham		A	W	2-1aet	Lewis, Kearney
	2	16.12.78	Portsmouth	D4	A	W	1-0	Alexander
	3	9.1.79	Notts Co	D2	A	L	2-4	Kearney 2
1979-80 D3	1	24.11.79	Kettering T	APL	H	W	4-2	Kearney 2, Heale, Kearns
	2	15.12.79	Barking	IL	H	W	3-1	Bowman (p), Sanchez, Heale
	3	5.1.80	Colchester U	D3	H	W	2-0	Earles, Heale
	4	26.1.80	Swansea C	D2	A	L	1-4	Kearney
1980-81 D3	1	22.11.80	Fulham	D3	H	L	1-2	Earles

1981-82	D3	1	21.11.81	Bournemouth	D4	A	L	0-1	
1982-83	D3	1	20.11.82	Bishops Stortford	IL	H	L	1-2	Earles
1983-84	D4	1	19.11.83	Hereford U	D4	H	W	2-0	Senior, Horrix
		2	10.12.83	Oxford U	D3	H	D	1-1	Price
		2r	14.10.83	Oxford U		A	L	0-3	
1984-85	D3	1	17.11.84	Barry T	Welsh	A	W	2-1	Beavon, Senior
		2	8.12.84	Bognor Regis T	IL	H	W	6-2	Juryeff 2, Beavon, Senior 2, White
		3	5.1.85	Barnsley	D2	A	L	3-4	Horrix (p), Senior, Crown
1985-86	D3	1	16.11.85	Wealdstone	APL	H	W	1-0	Horrix (p)
		2	7.12.85	Hereford U	D4	H	W	2-0	Senior, Horrix
		3	4.1.86	Huddersfield T	D2	A	D	0-0	
		3r	13.1.86	Huddersfield T		H	W	2-1	Senior 2
		4	25.1.86	Bury	D3	H	D	1-1	Senior
		4r	28.1.86	Bury		A	L	0-3	
1986-87	D2	3	10.1.87	Arsenal	D1	H	L	1-2	Senior
1987-88	D2	3	9.1.88	Southampton	D1	H	L	0-1	
1988-89	D3	1	19.11.88	Hendon	IL	H	W	4-2	L.Taylor 2, Elsey, Senior
		2	10.12.88	Maidstone U	GMVC	H	D	1-1	Senior
		2r	14.12.88	Maidstone U		A	W	2-1	Gernon, Senior
		3	7.1.89	Tranmere R	D4	A	D	1-1	Elsey
		3r	11.1.89	Tranmere R		H	W	2-1	Senior, Franklin
		4	28.1.89	Grimsby T	D4	A	D	1-1	Saunders og
		4r	1.2.89	Grimsby T		H	L	1-2	Moran
1989-90	D3	1	18.11.89	Bristol R	D3	A	D	1-1	Conroy
		1r	21.11.89	Bristol R		H	D	1-1aet	Senior
		1 2r	27.11.89	Bristol R		A	W	1-0	Senior
		2	9.12.89	Welling U	GMVC	H	D	0-0	
		2r	13.12.89	Welling U		A	D	1-1aet	Beavon (p)
		2 2r	19.12.89	Welling U		H	D	0-0aet	
		2 3r	22.12.89	Welling U		A	W	2-1	Moran 2
		3	6.1.90	Sunderland	D2	H	W	2-1	Jones 2
		4	27.1.90	Newcastle U	D2	H	D	3-3	Jones, Senior, Gilkes
		4r	31.1.90	Newcastle U		A	L	1-4	Senior
1990-91	D3	1	18.11.90	Colchester U	GMVC	A	L	1-2	Hicks
1991-92	D3	1	16.11.91	Slough T	GMVC	A	D	3-3	Williams, Gooding, Taylor
		1r	27.11.91	Slough T		H	W	2-1	Williams, Lovell
		2	7.12.91	Peterborough U	D3	A	D	0-0	
		2r	17.12.91	Peterborough U		H	W	1-0	Lovell
		3	4.1.92	Bolton W	D3	A	L	0-2	
1992-93	D2	1	15.11.92	Birmingham C	D1	H	W	1-0	Quinn
		2	5.12.92	Leyton O	D2	H	W	3-0	Quinn 2 (1p), Parkinson
		3	2.1.93	Manchester C	PL	A	D	1-1	Taylor
		3r	13.1.93	Manchester C		H	L	0-4	

READING ABBEY

Formed 1875. Played at King's Meadows, Reading

1880-81	1	13.11.80	St Albans		H	L	0-1	
1881-82	1	22.10.81	Woodford Bridge		A	D	1-1	Vaisley
	1r	12.11.81	Woodford Bridge		H	W	2-1	
	2	26.11.81	Hotspur		H	L	1-4	

READING HORNETS

1876-77	1	4.11.76	Swifts		A	L	0-2	
1877-78	1	27.10.77	Maidenhead		A	L	0-10	

READING MINSTER

1880-81	1	13.11.80	Romford		A	D	1-1	
	1r		Romford			scratched		
1881-82	1	22.10.81	Windsor Home Park		A	W	1-0	
	2	3.12.81	Romford		H	W	3-1	
	3	17.12.81	Hotspur		A	D	0-0	
	3r	26.12.81	Hotspur		H	L	0-2	

1882-83	1		Remnants			walkover	
	2		Great Marlow			scratched	
1883-84	1	10.11.83	Old Carthusians		H	L	1-10
1884-85	1	8.11.84	Hanover U		A	L	0-1

READING SOUTH

Formed 1879. Played at Whitby Park Farm, Reading

1882-83	1	21.10.82	Dreadnought		H	W	2-1	Callan 2
		FA ordered replay after protest					
	1r	4.11.82	Dreadnought		A	W	2-1
	2		bye				
	3	6.1.83	Hendon		A	L	1-11
1883-84	1	10.11.83	Reading		A	D	2-2
	1r	17.11.83	Reading		H	L	0-4
1884-85	1	8.11.84	Casuals		H	W	4-1
	2	6.12.84	Swifts		A	L	2-3
1885-86	1	31.10.85	Dulwich		A	W	2-1
	2		Clapton				walkover
	3		Clapham R				walkover
	4	2.1.86	Brentwood		H	L	0-3
1886-87	1	30.10.86	Maidenhead		H	L	0-2
1887-88	1	8.10.87	Great Marlow		A	L	1-4

REDCAR

First entered FA Cup: 1883. This club played in the FA Cup until 1889. Redcar FC were formed 1913 and disbanded 1922

1883-84	1		Nottingham Forest			scratched	
1884-85	1	8.11.84	Sunderland		H	W	3-1	Bulman, Harrison, Agar
	2	6.12.84	Grimsby T		A	L	1-3	Hikesley
1885-86	1	24.10.85	Sunderland		H	W	3-0	Bulman, Hikesley, Tufts
	2	21.11.85	Lincoln Lindum		H	W	2-0	
	3		bye				
	4		bye				
	5	23.1.86	Middlesbrough		H	W	2-1	Simpson, Hikesley
	6	13.2.86	Small Heath		A	L	0-2	
1886-87	1	30.10.86	Tyne Association		H	W	4-0	
	2	20.11.86	Grantham		A	L	2-3	
1887-88	1	15.10.87	Newcastle West End		A	L	1-5	Pearson

REDDITCH UNITED

Formed 1900. First entered FA Cup: 1910

1971-72	WMRL	1	20.11.71	Peterborough U	D4	H	D	1-1	Howell
		1r	22.11.71	Peterborough U		A	L	0-6	
1989-90	SL	1	18.11.89	Merthyr Tydfil	GMVC	H	L	1-3	Campbell

REDHILL

Formed 1900. First entered FA Cup: 1900

1957-58	AL	1	16.11.57	Norwich C	3S	A	L	1-6	Hills

105TH REGIMENT

Also known as the Madras Light Infantry, combined with the 51st Regiment in 1881 to form the King's Own Yorkshire Light Infantry.

1875-76	1	6.11.75	Crystal P		H	D	0-0
	1r	20.11.75	Crystal P		A	L	0-3
1876-77	1	11.11.76	1st Surrey Rifles		H	W	3-0
	2	14.12.76	Oxford University		A	L	1-6
1877-78	1	7.11.77	Old Harrovians		H	L	0-2
1878-79	1		Minerva				scratched

REIGATE PRIORY

One of the 15 original clubs to enter the FA Cup, they scratched in the first season and only won one game in the competition after that.

1871-72	1		Royal Engineers			scratched	
1872-73	1	26.10.72	Windsor Home Park	A	L	2-4	Clutton 2
1873-74	1	11.10.73	Woodford Wells	A	L	2-3	Pawle, 1 other
1874-75	1		bye				
	2	5.12.74	Maidenhead	A	L	1-2	W.Laker
1875-76	1	30.10.75	Barnes	H	W	1-0	
	2	20.11.75	Cambridge University	H	L	0-8	
1876-77	1	11.11.76	Clapham R	A	L	0-5	

REMNANTS

1877-78	1	7.11.77	St Stephen's	H	W	4-0	
	2	22.12.77	Hawks	H	W	2-0	Keyser, 1 other
	3	19.1.78	Upton Park	A	L	0-3	
1878-79	1		Unity			walkover	
	2	21.12.78	Pilgrims	H	W	6-2	Parry 4, E.Hawtrey, Keyser
	3	30.1.79	Darwen	H	L	2-3	E.Hawtrey 2
1879-80	1	15.11.79	Upton Park	H	D	1-1	Cuppage
	1r	25.11.79	Upton Park	A	L	2-5	E.Hawtrey, Cuppage
1880-81	1	13.11.80	Royal Engineers	A	D	0-0	
	1r	20.11.80	Royal Engineers	H	L	0-1	
1881-82	1	29.10.81	West End	A	L	2-3	Deare, Hughes
1882-83	1		Reading Minster			scratched	

RENTON

Formed 1873. Played at Tontine Park, Renton. One of the seven Scottish clubs that played in the FA Cup. Their victory over Blackburn on December 4, 1886 brought to an end Blackburn s record unbeaten FA Cup run of 24 matches. **Scottish FA Cup winners:** 1885, 1888. Runners-up 1875, 1886, 1895

1886-87	1	30.10.86	Accrington	H	W	1-0	Campbell
	2	20.11.86	Blackburn R	H	D	2-2	Campbell, 1 other
	2r	4.12.86	Blackburn R	A	W	2-0	Barbour, McNee
	3	22.1.87	Preston NE	H	L	0-2	

RHYL

Formed 1923. **First entered FA Cup:** 1924. Currently playing in the Manweb Cymru Alliance. Welsh FA Cup winners 1952, 1953. **League clubs beaten:** Stoke C, Wrexham, Wigan B, Halifax T, Notts Co, Hartlepool, Barnsley

1926-27	Welsh 1	27.11.26	Stoke C	3N	H	D	1-1	Hoddinott
	1r	2.12.26	Stoke C		A	D	1-1aet	Lewis
	1 2r	6.12.26	Stoke C at Old Trafford			W	2-1	Murray, Groves
	2	11.12.26	Wrexham	3N	H	W	3-1	Broad, Groves 2
	3	8.1.27	Darlington	D2	A	L	1-2	Hoddinott
1927-28	Welsh 1	26.11.27	Wigan Borough	3N	H	W	4-3	Wood, Miller, Murray 2
	2	10.12.27	New Brighton	3N	A	L	2-7	Lindsay 2 (1p)
1928-29	Welsh 1	24.11.28	Grantham	ML	A	L	0-1	
1930-31	NWC 1	29.11.30	Scarborough	ML	A	L	0-6	
1948-49	CC 1	4.12.48	Scarborough	ML	A	L	0-2	
1949-50	CC 1	26.11.49	Rochdale	3N	H	L	0-3	
1950-51	CC 1	25.11.50	Scarborough	ML	A	W	2-1	Brown, McMinn
	2	9.12.50	Norwich C	3S	H	L	0-1	
1951-52	CC 1	24.11.51	Hartlepools U	3N	A	L	0-2	
1952-53	CC 1	22.11.52	Bradford C	3N	A	L	0-4	
1953-54	CC 1	21.11.53	Halifax T	3N	A	D	0-0	
	1r	26.11.53	Halifax T		H	W	4-3aet	Valentine 2, Stafford, Hanlon
	2	12.12.53	Bristol C	3S	A	L	0-3	
1954-55	CC 1	20.11.54	Selby T	YL	A	L	1-2	Hitchen
1955-56	CC 1	19.11.55	Bradford PA	3N	H	L	0-3	
1956-57	CC 1	17.11.56	Scarborough	ML	H	W	3-2	Hughes, Russell 2
	2	8.12.56	Bishop Auckland	NL	H	W	3-1	H.Williams, Donaldson, Hughes
	3	5.1.57	Notts Co	D2	A	W	3-1	H.Williams, Hughes, Meakin
	4	26.1.57	Bristol C	D2	A	L	0-3	

1957-58	CC	1	16.11.57	Carlisle U	3N	A	L	1-5	C.Williams
1958-59	CC	1	15.11.58	Chesterfield	D3	A	L	0-3	
1959-60	CC	1	14.11.59	Grimsby T	D3	H	L	1-2	Bullock
1960-61	CC	1	5.11.60	Oldham A	D4	H	L	0-1	
1961-62	CC	1	4.11.61	Hull C	D3	A	L	0-5	
1962-63	CC	1	3.11.62	Barnsley	D3	A	L	0-4	
1970-71	CC	1	21.11.70	Hartlepool	D4	H	W	1-0	Metcalf
		2	12.12.70	Barnsley	D3	H	D	0-0	
		2r	15.12.70	Barnsley		A	D	1-1aet	Metcalf
		2 2r	21.12.70	Barnsley		A	W	2-0	E.Davies, L.Davies
		3	2.1.71	Swansea C	D3	A	L	1-6	L.Davies
1972-73	CC	1	18.11.72	Chesterfield	D3	A	L	2-4	Evans, L.Davies

RINGMER

Formed: 1910. **First entered FA Cup**: 1970

1970-71	SCL	1	21.11.70	Colchester U	D4	A	L	0-3	

ROCHDALE

Rochdale AFC was first formed in 1896 and the original club survived until January 1, 1901. Later in 1901 Rochdale Town were formed, but they folded in 1903. There was no club in existence between 1903 and 1907 when the present club were formed, playing in the FA Cup for the first time in the 1908-09 season. **Best FA Cup Performance**: 4th round, 1971. **Record FA Cup Win**: 8-2 vs Crook T, 1st round, 26.11.1927. **Record FA Cup Defeat**: 0-5 vs Colchester U, 4th round, 25.1.1971

Rochdale AFC

1896-97			*did not enter*						
1897-98			1q **Bay Moss Exchange** (A) 5-3; 2q **Horwich** (H) 1-1; 2qr **Horwich** (A) 2-6						
1898-99			2q **Middleton** (A) 2-3						
1899-00			1q **Middleton** (A) 0-2						
1900-01			1q **Rossendale U** (H) 1-0; 2q **Freetown** (A) 3-0; 3q **Workington** scratched						

Rochdale Town

1901-02			*did not enter*
1902-03			*did not enter*

Rochdale FC

1908-09	LC		1q **Accrington Stanley** (H) 3-5						
1909-10	LC		1q **Haslingden** (A) 1-3						
1910-11	LC		P **Earlestown** (H) 2-1; 1q **St Helens T** (A) 2-1; 2q **Heywood U** (A) 4-3; 3q **St Helens R** (H) 1-0; 4q **Stockport Co** (H) 0-0;						
			4qr **Stockport Co** (A) 0-0; 4q 2r **Stockport Co** (at Oldham) 1-0; 5q **Luton T** (H) 1-1; 5qr **Luton T** (A) 2-3						
1911-12	LC		4q **Barrow** (A) 0-1						
1912-13	CL		1q **Macclesfield** (A) 5-3; 2q **Newton HA** (A) 5-0; 3q **Stalybridge C** (H) 2-1; 4q **Accrington S** (H) 6-1; 5q **Darlington** (H) 1-1;						
			5qr **Darlington** (A) 1-0						
		1	11.1.13	Swindon T	SL	H	L	0-2	
1913-14	CL		4q **Barrow** (A) 0-3						
1914-15	CL		4q **Stalybridge C** (H) 3-2; 5q **Hartlepool U** (H) 2-0; 6q **Watford** (H) 2-0						
		1	9.1.15	Gillingham	SL	H	W	2-0	Walker, Hawksworth
		2	30.1.15	Oldham A	D1	A	L	0-3	
1919-20	CL		4q **Monks Hall** (H) 1-0; 5q **Stalybridge C** (H) 1-0; 6q **South Liverpool** (A) 2-1						
		1	10.1.20	Arsenal	D1	A	L	2-4	Mallalieu 2
1920-21	CL		4q **Fleetwood** (H) 1-0; 5q **Tranmere R** (H) 1-0; 6q **Coventry C** (D2) A 1-1; 6qr **Coventry C** (H) 2-1						
		1	8.1.21	Plymouth A	D3	A	L	0-2	
1921-22	3N		5q **Nelson** (A) 2-3						
1922-23	3N		4q **Nelson** (H) 0-1						
1923-24	3N		4q **Skelmersdale U** (H) 4-0; 5q **Accrington S** (A) 0-1						
1924-25	3N		5q **Halifax T** (A) 1-0; 6q **Norwich C** (A) 0-1						
1925-26	3N	1	28.11.25	West Stanley	NEL	H	–	1-1	Hughes
			abandoned at half time - ground unfit						
		1	1.12.25	West Stanley		H	W	4-0	Hughes 2, Martin (p), Ferguson
		2	12.12.25	Chilton Colliery	NAII	A	D	1-1	Ferguson
		2r	17.12.25	Chilton Colliery		H	L	1-2	Parkes
1926-27	3N	1	27.11.26	Accrington S	3N	A	L	3-4	Whitehurst 2, Bertram
1927-28	3N	1	26.11.27	Crook T		H	W	8-2	Whitehurst 4, Clenmell 3, Martin
		2	10.12.27	Darlington	3N	A	L	1-2	Bertram
1928-29	3N	1	24.11.28	Chesterfield	3N	A	L	2-3	Martin, Milsom
1929-30	3N	1	30.11.29	Accrington S	3N	A	L	1-3	Milsom
1930-31	3N	1	29.11.30	Doncaster R	3N	H	L	1-2	Cowan
1931-32	3N	1	28.11.31	Scunthorpe U	ML	A	L	1-2	Murray

Season	Div	Rd	Date	Opponent		H/A	Res	Score	Scorers
1932-33	3N	1	26.11.32	**Stockport Co**	3N	H	L	0-2	
1933-34	3N	1	25.11.33	**Sutton T**	DSL	A	L	1-2	Rigby
1934-35	3N	1	24.11.34	**Wrexham**	3N	A	L	1-4	Smith
1935-36	3N	1	30.11.35	**Halifax T**	3N	A	L	0-4	
1936-37	3N	1	28.11.36	**Crewe A**	3N	A	L	1-5	Hunt
1937-38	3N	1	27.11.37	**Lincoln C**	3N	H	D	1-1	Hunt
		1r	1.12.37	**Lincoln C**		A	L	0-2	
1938-39	3N	1	26.11.38	**Halifax T**	3N	A	L	3-7	Wynn, Duff, Goodier
1945-46	3N	1 1L	17.11.45	**Stockport Co**	3N	A	W	2-1	Brindle, Woods
		1 2L	24.11.45	**Stockport Co**		H	D	1-1	Hargreaves
		2 1L	8.12.45	**Tranmere R**	3N	A	L	1-3	Cunliffe
		2 2L	15.12.45	**Tranmere R**		H	W	3-0	Hargreaves 2, Makin
		3 1L	5.1.46	**Bury**	D2	A	D	3-3	Cunliffe 2, Reynolds
		3 2L	8.1.46	**Bury**		H	L	2-4	Hargreaves 2 (1p)
1946-47	3N	1	30.11.46	**Bishop Auckland**	NL	H	W	6-1	Woods, Hargreaves 2, Birch, Barkas, Carruthers
		2	14.12.46	**Hartlepools U**	3N	H	W	6-1	Woods 3, Carruthers 2, Cunliffe
		3	11.1.47	**Charlton A**	D1	A	L	1-3	Woods
1947-48	3N	1	29.11.47	**York C**	3N	A	W	1-0	Birch (p)
		2	13.12.47	**Gillingham**	SL	H	D	1-1aet	O'Donnell
		2r	20.12.47	**Gillingham**		A	L	0-3	
1948-49	3N	1	27.11.48	**Barrow**	3N	H	D	1-1aet	Middlebrough
				played at Oldham					
		1r	4.12.48	**Barrow**		A	L	0-2	
1949-50	3N	1	26.11.49	**Rhyl**	CC	A	W	3-0	Arthur, Connor 2
		2	10.12.49	**Notts Co**	3S	H	L	1-2	Brown
1950-51	3N	1	25.11.50	**Willington T**	NL	H	W	3-1	Whitehouse 2 (1p), Middlebrough
		2	9.12.50	**Ashington**	NEL	A	W	2-1	Livesey, Steen
		3	9.1.51	**Chelsea**	D1	H	L	2-3	Connor, Arthur
1951-52	3N	1	24.11.51	**Ilkeston**	ML	A	W	2-0	Betts 2
		2	15.12.51	**Gillingham**	3S	A	W	3-0	Tomlinson 2, Arthur
		3	12.1.52	**Leeds U**	D2	H	L	0-2	
1952-53	3N	1	22.11.52	**Bradford PA**	3N	A	L	1-2	J.Lynn (p)
1953-54	3N	1	21.11.53	**Grimsby T**	3N	A	L	0-2	
1954-55	3N	1	20.11.54	**Tranmere R**	3N	A	D	3-3	Mitcheson, Anders, Gemmill
		1r	23.11.54	**Tranmere R**		H	W	1-0	Gemmill
		2	11.12.54	**Hinckley A**	BDL	H	W	2-1	Kendall, Anders
		3	8.1.55	**Charlton A**	D1	H	L	1-3	Haines
1955-56	3N	1	19.11.55	**York C**	3N	H	L	0-1	
1956-57	3N	1	17.11.56	**Scunthorpe U**	3N	A	L	0-1	
1957-58	3N	1	16.11.57	**Darlington**	3N	H	L	0-2	
1958-59	D3	1	15.11.58	**Hartlepools U**	D4	A	D	1-1	Wainwright
		1r	19.11.58	**Hartlepools U**		H	D	3-3aet	Finney, Wainwright, Spencer
		1 2r	27.11.58	**Hartlepools U at Old Trafford**			L	1-2aet	Wainwright
1959-60	D4	1	14.11.59	**Carlisle U**	D4	H	D	2-2	Cairns, Collins
		1r	17.11.59	**Carlisle U**		A	W	3-1	Brown, Barnes, Cairns
		2	5.12.59	**Bradford C**	D3	H	D	1-1	Spencer
		2r	9.12.59	**Bradford C**		A	L	1-2	Anderson
1960-61	D4	1	5.11.60	**Crewe A**	D4	A	D	1-1	Pollitt
		1r	8.11.60	**Crewe A**		H	L	1-2	Cairns
1961-62	D4	1	4.11.61	**Halifax T**	D3	H	W	2-0	Milburn (p), Hepton
		2	25.11.61	**Wrexham**		H	L	1-2	Cairns
1962-63	D4	1	3.11.62	**York C**	D4	A	D	0-0	
		1r	6.11.62	**York C**		H	L	1-2	Phoenix
1963-64	D4	1	16.11.63	**Chorley**	LC	H	W	2-1	Watson, Richardson
		2	7.12.63	**Barnsley**	D3	A	L	1-3	Richardson
1964-65	D4	1	14.11.64	**Workington**	D3	A	L	0-2	
1965-66	D4	1	13.11.65	**Fleetwood**	LC	A	D	2-2	Lister, Sievwright
		1r	17.11.65	**Fleetwood**		H	W	5-0	Jenkins 3, Calloway, Lister
		2	8.12.65	**Altrincham**	CC	H	L	1-3	Jenkins
1966-67	D4	1	26.11.66	**Barrow**	D4	H	L	1-3	Storf
1967-68	D4	1	9.12.67	**Tranmere R**	D3	A	L	1-5	Fletcher
1968-69	D4	1	16.11.68	**Barnsley**	D3	A	D	0-0	
		1r	18.11.68	**Barnsley**		H	L	0-1	
1969-70	D3	1	15.11.69	**Workington**	D4	A	L	1-2	Whitehead
1970-71	D3	1	21.11.70	**Oldham A**	D4	H	W	2-0	Arrowsmith 2
		2	12.12.70	**Darlington**	D4	A	W	2-0	Cross, Downes
		3	11.1.71	**Coventry C**	D1	H	W	2-1	Cross, Butler

		4	23.1.71	**Colchester U**	D4	H	D	3-3	Buck 2, Ashworth
		4r	25.1.71	**Colchester U**		A	L	0-5
1971-72	D3	1	20.11.71	**Barnsley**	D3	H	L	1-3	Arrowsmith
1972-73	D3	1	18.11.72	**Bangor C**	NPL	H	L	1-2	Jenkins (p)
1973-74	D3	1	24.11.73	**South Shields**	NPL	H	W	2-0	Marsh, Brogden
		2	15.12.73	**Grantham**	SL	A	D	1-1	Brogden
		2r	18.12.73	**Grantham**		H	L	3-5aet	Taylor, Hanvey, Downes
1974-75	D4	1	23.11.74	**Marine**	CC	H	D	0-0
		1r	27.11.74	**Marine**		A	W	2-1aet	Carrick, Young
		2	14.12.74	**Tranmere R**	D3	H	D	1-1	Brears
		2r	16.12.74	**Tranmere R**		A	L	0-1
1975-76	D4	1	22.11.75	**Workington**	D4	A	D	1-1	Ferguson
		1r	25.11.75	**Workington**		H	W	2-1aet	Mounthead, Whelan
		2	13.12.75	**Gateshead**	NPL	A	D	1-1	Albeson og
		2r	16.12.75	**Gateshead**		H	W	3-1	Mountford, Morrison og, Tobin
		3	3.1.76	**Norwich C**	D1	A	D	1-1	Mullington
		3r	6.1.76	**Norwich C**		H	D	0-0aet
		3 2r	13.1.76	**Norwich C**		A	L	1-2	Mountford
1976-77	D4	1	20.11.76	**Northwich V**	NPL	H	D	1-1	Helliwell
		1r	22.11.76	**Northwich V**		A	D	0-0aet
		1 2r	29.11.76	**Northwich V at Maine Road**			L	1-2	Tarbuck
1977-78	D4	1	26.11.77	**Scarborough**	NPL	A	L	2-4	Owen 2
1978-79	D4	1	25.11.78	**Droylesden**	CC	H	L	0-1
1979-80	D4	1	24.11.79	**Scunthorpe U**	D4	H	W	2-1	Hart, Jones
		2	15.12.79	**Tranmere R**	D4	A	D	2-2	Hilditch 2
		2r	18.12.79	**Tranmere R**		H	W	2-1	Hilditch, Hart
		3	8.1.80	**Bury**	D3	H	D	1-1	O'Coughlin
		3r	21.1.80	**Bury**		A	L	2-3	Scaife 2
1980-81	D4	1	22.11.80	**Mansfield T**	D4	H	L	1-3	Jones (p)
1981-82	D4	1	21.11.81	**Hull C**	D4	H	D	2-2	Dolan, Esser
		1r	24.11.81	**Hull C**		A	D	2-2aet	Burke, Esser
		1 2r	30.11.81	**Hull C at Elland Road**			L	0-1
1982-83	D4	1	20.11.82	**Altrincham**	APL	A	L	1-2	Wellings (p)
1983-84	D4	1	19.11.83	**Crewe A**	D4	H	W	1-0	Farrell
		2	13.12.83	**York C**	D4	A	W	2-0	Johnson 2
		3	7.1.84	**Telford U**	APL	H	L	1-4	Allatt
1984-85	D4	1	17.11.84	**Doncaster R**	D3	H	L	1-2	Russell og
1985-86	D4	1	16.11.85	**Darlington**	D3	H	W	2-1	Taylor 2
		2	7.12.85	**Scunthorpe U**	D4	A	D	2-2	Taylor 2 (1p)
		2r	10.12.85	**Scunthorpe U**		H	W	2-1	Taylor, Moore
		3	9.1.86	**Manchester U**	D1	A	L	0-2
1986-87	D4	1	15.11.86	**Nuneaton Bor.**	APL	A	W	3-0	Wakenshaw, Mills, Johnson
		2	6.12.86	**Wrexham**	D4	H	L	1-4	Wakenshaw
1987-88	D4	1	14.11.87	**Wrexham**	D4	H	L	0-2
1988-89	D4	1	19.11.88	**Huddersfield T**	D3	A	D	1-1	Edmonds
		1r	22.11.88	**Huddersfield T**		H	L	3-4	Beaumont, Reid, Frain
1989-90	D4	1	17.11.89	**Marine**	NPL	A	W	1-0	Stonehouse
			played at Anfield				
		2	9.12.89	**Lincoln C**	D4	H	W	3-0	Ward, Johnson, O'Shaughnessy
		3	6.1.90	**Whitley Bay**	NPL	H	W	1-0	Johnson
		4	27.1.90	**Northampton T**	D3	H	W	3-0	O'Shaughnessy, Dawson, Goodison (p)
		5	17.2.90	**Crystal P**	D1	A	L	0-1
1990-91	D4	1	17.11.90	**Scunthorpe U**	D4	H	D	1-1	Costello
		1r	20.11.90	**Scunthorpe U**		A	L	1-2	Costello
1991-92	D4	1	16.11.91	**Gretna**	NL	A	D	0-0
		1r	27.11.91	**Gretna**		H	W	3-1	Bowden, Milner, Flounders
		2	7.12.91	**Huddersfield T**	D3	H	L	1-2	Halpin
1992-93	D3	1	14.11.92	**Blackpool**	D2	A	D	1-1	Whitehall
		1r	25.11.92	**Blackpool**		H	W	1-0aet	Reid
		2	6.12.92	**Bolton W**	D2	A	L	0-4

ROCHESTER FC

Formed 1866. Played at The Borstal Ground, near the Kings Head pub, Rochester

1875-76		1	6.11.75	**Herts Rangers**		A	L	0-4
1876-77		1	4.11.76	**Highbury Union**		H	W	5-0	G.Blackett, Gramshaw, Prall, Ramage, own goal

ROCHESTER

Season	Round	Date	Opponent		Venue	Result	Score	Scorers
	2	16.12.76	Swifts		H	W	1-0	J.Blackett
	3	3.2.77	Cambridge University		A	L	0-4	
1877-78	1	7.11.77	Upton Park		A	L	0-3	
1878-79	1	2.11.78	Forest School		A	L	2-7	
1879-80	1	15.11.79	Wanderers		H	L	0-6	
1880-81	1	13.11.80	Dreadnought		H	L	1-2	A.Henry
1881-82	1	5.11.81	Barnes		A	L	1-3	
1882-83	1	4.11.82	Hotspur		H	W	2-0	S.Henry, Jones
	2		bye					
	3	16.12.82	Old Etonians		A	L	0-6	
1883-84	1	3.11.83	Uxbridge		H	W	2-1	
	2	1.12.83	Clapham R		A	L	0-7	
1884-85	1	8.11.84	Reading		A	L	0-2	
1885-86	1	31.10.85	Reading		H	W	6-1	Mallinson 4, Mitchell, H.Prall
	2	21.11.85	Swifts		A	L	1-5	
1886-87	1	23.10.86	Great Marlow		H	L	0-2	
1887-88	1	15.10.87	Royal Engineers		A	W	3-0	
			FA ordered match to be replayed after protest					
	1r		Royal Engineers			*scratched*		

ROMFORD

Originally formed in 1876 and played at Great Mawneys, Romford. Reformed 1929. Disbanded 1977. New club formed 1992. **FA Amateur Cup runners-up:** 1949

Season		Round	Date	Opponent		Venue	Result	Score	Scorers
1878-79		1	2.11.78	Ramblers		H	W	3-1	Barnes, Lyon, Thirlwell
		2	21.12.78	Swifts		A	L	1-3	Lyon
1879-80		1	8.11.79	Clapham R		A	L	0-7	
1880-81		1	13.11.80	Reading Minster		H	D	1-1	
		1r		Reading Minster			*walkover*		
		2		bye					
		3	12.2.81	Reading Abbey		H	W	2-0	Cornell, 1 other
		4	19.2.81	Great Marlow		H	W	2-1	Cornell 2
		5	5.3.81	Darwen		A	L	0-15	
1881-82		1		Rangers FC, London			*walkover*		
		2	3.12.81	Reading Minster		A	L	1-3	
1882-83		1	21.10.82	Etonian Ramblers		A	L	2-6	
1883-84		1	3.11.83	Woodford Bridge		H	W	3-0	JA Macfarlane, Earle, Oliver
		2	1.12.83	Mosquitoes		H	W	3-1	Cornell, Earle, Goadby
		3	29.12.83	Brentwood		H	L	1-4	Cornell
1884-85		1	1.11.84	Clapton		H	W	3-2	Clark, Goadby, Oliver
		2	6.12.84	Dulwich		H	W	3-0	Oliver 2, Wright
		3		bye					
		4	17.1.85	Blackburn Rovers		A	L	0-15	
1885-86		1	31.10.85	Hanover U		A	D	1-1	
		1r	7.11.85	Hanover U		H	W	3-0	
		2		bye					
		3	12.12.85	Old Westminsters		A	L	1-5	
1932-33	AL	1	26.11.32	Bristol C	3S	A	L	0-4	
1935-36	AL	1	30.11.35	Folkestone	SL	H	D	3-3	Osborne 2, Patterson (p)
		1r	4.12.35	Folkestone		A	L	1-2aet	Thomas
1945-46	IL	1 1L	17.11.45	Brighton & HA	3S	A	L	1-3	Longton og
		1 2L	24.11.45	Brighton & HA		H	D	1-1	Bolton
1948-49	IL	1	27.11.48	Yeovil Town	SL	A	L	0-4	
1949-50	IL	1	26.11.49	Yeovil Town	SL	A	L	1-4	Jennings
1960-61	SL	1	5.11.60	Sutton U	AL	A	D	2-2	Beck og, Holmes
		1r	9.11.60	Sutton U		H	W	5-0	Holmes 2, Hencher 2 (2ps), Sanders
		2	26.11.60	Northampton T	D4	H	L	1-5	Cappi
1961-62	SL	1	4.11.61	Walthamstow Ave	IL	A	W	3-2	Lloyd, Cappi, Allison (p)
		2	25.11.61	Watford	D3	H	L	1-3	Evans (p)
1964-65	SL	1	14.11.64	Enfield	IL	H	D	0-0	
		1r	17.11.64	Enfield		A	D	0-0aet	
		1 2r	23.11.64	Enfield at Highbury			L	2-4	Coates, Brown
1965-66	SL	1	13.11.65	Luton T	D4	H	D	1-1	Barnett
		1r	18.11.65	Luton T		A	L	0-1	
1967-68	SL	1	9.12.67	Wimbledon	SL	A	L	0-3	
1971-72	SL	1	20.11.71	Witney T	Hel	A	W	3-0	King 2, Chandler

		2	11.12.71	Gillingham	D4	H	L	0-1
1974-75	SL	1	23.11.74	Ilford	IL	H	L	0-2
1975-76	SL	1	22.11.75	Tooting & Mitcham	IL	H	L	0-1

ROSSENDALE UNITED

Formed 1877 as Rossendale FC. Play at Dark Lane, New Church, near the Black Dog Inn. Reformed as Rossendale United in 1898.

1883-84		1	17.11.83	Irwell Springs		H	W	6-2	
				Rossendale disqualified for professionalism					
1884-85		1	11.10.84	Blackburn Rovers		A	L	0-11	
1885-86		1	24.10.85	Low Moor		H	W	6-2	
		2	21.11.85	Padiham		H	W	9-1	
		3	12.12.85	Church		A	L	1-5	
1887-88		1	15.10.87	Accrington		A	L	0-11	
as Rossendale United									
1971-72	CC	1	23.11.71	Altrincham	NPL	H	W	1-0	Wild (p)
		2	11.12.71	Bolton W at Bury	D3	H	L	1-4	Clay
1975-76	CC	1	22.11.75	Shrewsbury T	D3	H	L	0-1	

ROTHERHAM TOWN

Formed about 1882. **First entered FA Cup:** 1883. Members of the Football League 1893-1896. Merged with Rotherham County (previously known as Thornhill U) to form Rotherham United in 1925.

1883-84		1	10.11.83	Spital, Chesterfield	A	D	1-1	
		1r	17.11.83	Spital, Chesterfield	H	W	7-2	Douglas 2, Musson 2, Lampard 2, Kelly
		2	1.12.83	Lockwood Brothers	A	L	1-3	
1884-85		1	8.11.84	Nottingham F	A	L	0-5	
1885-86		1	24.10.85	Notts Co	A	L	0-15	
1886-87				*did not enter*				
1887-88		1	15.10.8 7	Matlock	A	W	3-2	McCormack 2, 1 other
		2	5.11.87	Derby Junction	A	L	2-3	Medley, McCormack
1888-89		1q	**Doncaster R** (A) 9-1; 2q **Owlerton** (A) 1-2					
1889-90	ML	1q	**Doncaster R** (H) 2-0; 2q **Redcar** (A) 8-1; 3q **Rotherham Swifts** (A) 0-0aet; 3qr **Rotherham Swifts** (H) 2-1; 4q **Sheffield U** (H) 2-2; 4qr **Sheffield U** (A) 1-2					
1890-91	ML	1q	**Sheffield Club** (A) 13-0; 2q **Owlerton** (A) 4-1; 3q **Beeston** (H) 6-1; **Long Eaton Rangers** (A) 1-2					
1891-92	ML	1q	**Attercliffe** (A) 2-1; 2q **Kilnhurst** (H) 5-1; 3q **Gainsborough Trinity** (A) 2-3					
1892-93	ML	1q	**Grantham R** (H) 4-0; 2q **Kilnhurst** (A) 3-0; 3q **Lincoln C** (A) 0-2					
1893-94	D2	1q	**Worksop T** (A) 2-3					
1894-95	D2	1q	**Gainsborough Trinity** (A) 1-5					
1895-96	D2	1q	**Barnsley St Peters** (H) 1-1; 1qr **Barnsley St P.** (A) 7-3; 2q **Doncaster R** (A) 7-0; 3q **Gainsborough Trinity** (A) 2-0; 4q **Grimsby T** (A) 0-4					
1907-08	ML	1	11.1.08	West Ham	SL	A	L	0-1

ROTHERHAM UNITED

Formed 1925 by the merger between Rotherham County (previously known as Thornhill United) and Rotherham Town. Thornhill United played in the FA Cup from 1901-1905 but never reached the Competition Proper. **Best FA Cup Performance:** 5th round, 1953, 1968. **Record FA Cup Win (as Rotherham United):** 6-0 vs Spennymoor U, 2nd round, 17.12.1977, 6-0 vs Wolverhampton W, 1st round, 16.11.1985. **Record FA Cup Defeat:** 0-6 vs Brighton & HA, 4th round, second replay, 8.2.1960

as Rotherham County			
1905-06	ML	1q	**Thorpe Hesley** (H) 3-1; 2q **S.Kirby Colliery** (A) 1-2
1906-07	ML	P	**S.Kirby Colliery** (A) 4-2; 1q **Elsecar Ath** (H) 2-0; 2q **Rotherham T** (H) 2-1; 3q **Hoyland T** (A) 1-0; 4q **Denaby U** (A) 0-0; 4qr **Denaby U** (H) 2-1; 5q **Crystal P** (A) 0-4
1907-08	ML	P	**Wath A** (H) 0-2
1908-09	ML	2q	**Wombwell Main** (H) 6-1; 3q **Wath Ath** (H) 5-0; 4q **Burton U** (H) 1-2
1909-10	ML	P	**Atlas & NW** (A) 3-1; 1q **Wath Ath** (A) 2-0; 2q **Elsecar** (H) 0-2
1910-11	ML	P	**Sheffield Club** (A) 9-2; 1q **Rotherham T** (A) 1-2
1911-12	ML	P	**Redfearns** (A) 2-2; Pr **Redfearns** (H) 5-0; 1q **Wath Ath** (A) 1-0; 2q **Royston M.Inst.** (H) 3-0; 3q **Rotherham T** (A) 1-0; 4q **Gainsborough Trinity** (A) 0-1
1912-13	ML	P	**Hickleton Main** (A) 4-1; 1q **Silverwood** (H) 6-0; 2q **Darfield U** (H) 5-1; 3q **Rotherham T** (H) 1-0; **Lincoln C** (H) 1-3
1913-14	ML	P	**Rawmarsh T** (H) 2-0; 1q **Kilnhurst** (H) 8-1; 2q **Wath Ath** (A) 2-2; 2qr **Wath Ath** (H) 9-1; 3q **Silverwood** (A) 2-2; 3qr **Silverwood** (H) 2-0; 4q **Halifax T** (H) 1-1; 4qr **Halifax T** (A) 2-5
1914-15	ML	6q	**Lincoln C** (A) 0-6
1919-20	D2	6q	**West Stanley** (A) 0-1

1920-21	D2	6q **Luton Town** (H) 1-3					
1921-22	D2	5q **Coventry C** (H) 1-1; 5qr **Coventry C** (A) 0-1					
1922-23	D2	1	13.1.23 **Chelsea**	D1	A	L	0-1
1923-24	3N	5q **Scunthorpe U** (A) 1-1; 5qr **Scunthorpe U** (H) 2-0; 6q **Halifax T** (A) 0-1					
1924-25	3N	5q **Doncaster R** (H) 2-3					

Rotherham County merged with Rotherham Town in 1925 to form Rotherham United

Rotherham United

Season	Div	Rd	Date	Opponent	Comp	H/A	Res	Score	Scorers
1925-26	3N	1	28.11.25	**Halifax T**	3N	A	W	3-0	Lee, Boulton, Chambers
		2	12.12.25	**Doncaster R**	3N	A	W	2-0	Pickin, Lee
		3	9.1.26	**Bury**	D1	H	L	2-3	Hammerton, Emmett
1926-27	3N	1	27.11.26	**Lincoln C**	3N	A	L	0-2	
1927-28	3N	1	26.11.27	**Spennymoor U**	NEL	A	D	1-1	Nicholson
		1r	1.12.27	**Spennymoor U**		H	W	4-2	Phillips, Lievesley 2, Hall
		2	10.12.27	**Bradford C**	3N	A	W	3-2	Lievesley, Clayton 2
		3	14.1.28	**Exeter C**	3S	H	D	3-3	Scott 2, Hemmingway
		3r	18.1.28	**Exeter C**		A	L	1-3	Scott
1928-29	3N	1	24.11.28	**Trammere R**	3N	A	L	1-2	Orr
1929-30	3N	1	30.11.29	**Ashington**	NEL	H	W	3-0	Davies 2, Sellars
		2	14.12.29	**Scunthorpe U**	ML	A	D	3-3	Cooke og, Davies 2
		2r	19.12.29	**Scunthorpe U**		H	W	5-4	Sellars 2, Lievesley 2, Orr
		3	11.1.30	**Nottingham F**	D2	H	L	0-5	
1930-31	3N	1	29.11.30	**Newark**	ML	A	L	1-2	Murden
1931-32	3N	1	28.11.31	**Accrington S**	3N	H	D	0-0	
		1r	2.12.31	**Accrington S**		A	L	0-5	
1932-33	3N	1	26.11.32	**Chester**	3N	A	L	0-4	
1933-34	3N	1	25.11.33	**South Bank St Peters**	TSL	H	W	3-2	Raynor, Hicks 2
		2	9.12.33	**Coventry C**	3S	H	W	2-1	Raynor, McConnell
		3	13.1.34	**Sheffield W**	D1	H	L	0-3	
1934-35	3N	1	24.11.34	**Spennymoor U**	NEL	H	W	2-0	Dickinson, Briggs
		2	8.12.34	**Bristol C**	3S	H	L	1-2	Fenoughty
1935-36	3N	1	30.11.35	**Wigan A**	CC	A	W	2-1	Dickinson, Bastow
		2	14.12.35	**Watford**	3S	H	D	1-1	Dickinson
		2r	18.12.35	**Watford**		A	L	0-1	
1936-37	3N	1	28.11.36	**Hartlepools U**	3N	H	D	4-4	Pedwell 2, Brown 2
		1r	2.12.36	**Hartlepools U**		A	L	0-2	
1937-38	3N	1	27.11.37	**Burton T**	ML	A	D	1-1	Smith
		1r	29.11.37	**Burton T**		H	W	3-0	Hawkins, Bramham 2
		2	11.12.37	**Aldershot**	3S	H	L	1-3	Hanson
1938-39	3N	1	26.11.38	**Hull C**	3N	A	L	1-4	Bramham
1945-46	3N	1 1L	17.11.45	**Doncaster R**	3N	A	W	1-0	Ardron
		1 2L	24.11.45	**Doncaster R**		H	W	2-1	Kearney, Nightingale
		2 1L	8.12.45	**Lincoln C**	3N	H	W	2-1	Nightingale, J.Shaw
		2 2L	15.12.45	**Lincoln C**		A	D	1-1	Ardron
		3 1L	5.1.46	**Gateshead**	3N	H	D	2-2	J.Shaw, Dawson
		3 2L	9.1.46	**Gateshead**		A	W	2-0	Kearney, Ardron
		4 1L	26.1.46	**Barnsley**	D2	A	L	0-3	
		4 2L	31.1.46	**Barnsley**		H	W	2-1	Wilson og, R.Shaw
1946-47	3N	1	30.11.46	**Crewe Alex**	3N	H	W	2-0	Wilson, Armitage
		2	14.12.46	**Scunthorpe U**	ML	H	W	4-1	Ardron 2, Wilson, R.Shaw
		3	11.1.47	**Wolverhampton W**	D1	A	L	0-3	
1947-48	3N	3	10.1.48	**Brentford**	D2	H	L	0-3	
1948-49	3N	3	8.1.49	**Darlington**	3N	H	W	4-2	Ardron 2, Grainger, Noble
		4	29.1.49	**Burnley**	D1	H	L	0-1	
1949-50	3N	3	7.1.50	**Bury**	D2	A	L	4-5	Rudd, Bower, Noble, J.Shaw
1950-51	3N	1	25.11.50	**Darlington**	3N	A	W	7-2	J.Shaw 5, Williams, Guest
		2	9.12.50	**Nottingham F**	3S	A	W	3-1	J.Shaw 3
		3	6.1.51	**Doncaster R**	D2	H	W	2-1	Williams, J.Shaw
		4	27.1.51	**Hull C**	D2	A	L	0-2	
1951-52	D2	3	12.1.52	**Bury**	D2	H	W	2-1	Guest, J.Shaw
		4	2.2.52	**Swansea T**	D2	A	L	0-3	
1952-53	D2	3	10.1.53	**Colchester U**	3S	H	D	2-2	J.Shaw 2
		3r	15.1.53	**Colchester U**		A	W	2-0	J.Shaw, Rawson
		4	31.1.53	**Newcastle U**	D1	A	W	3-1	Grainger 2, Rickett
		5	14.2.53	**Aston Villa**	D1	H	L	1-3	J.Shaw
1953-54	D2	3	9.1.54	**Bristol C**	3S	A	W	3-1	Grainger 3
		4	30.1.54	**WBA**	D1	A	L	0-4	
1954-55	D2	3	8.1.55	**Leicester C**	D1	H	W	1-0	Pell

	4	29.1.55	Luton T	D2	H	L	1-5	Guest
1955-56 D2	3	7.1.56	Scunthorpe U	3N	H	D	1-1	Grainger
	3r	12.1.56	Scunthorpe U		A	L	2-4	Farmer, Grainger
1956-57 D2	3	5.1.57	Bristol C	D2	A	L	1-4	Stephenson
1957-58 D2	3	4.1.58	Blackburn R	D2	H	L	1-4	Stephens
1958-59 D2	3	10.1.59	Aston Villa	D1	A	L	1-2	Sawyer
1959-60 D2	3	9.1.60	Arsenal	D1	H	D	2-2	Sawyer, Myerscough (p)
	3r	13.1.60	Arsenal		A	D	1-1aet	Webster
	3 2r	18.1.60	Arsenal at Hillsborough			W	2-0	Kettleborough, Sawyer
	4	30.1.60	Brighton	D2	H	D	1-1	Kirkman
	4r	3.2.60	Brighton		A	D	1-1aet	Sawyer
	4 2r	8.2.60	Brighton at Highbury			L	0-6	
1960-61 D2	3	7.1.61	Watford	D3	H	W	1-0	Houghton
	4	28.1.61	Birmingham C	D1	A	L	0-4	
1961-62 D2	3	9.1.62	Huddersfield T	D2	A	L	3-4	Houghton, Weston 2
1962-63 D2	3	20.2.63	Watford	D3	A	L	0-2	
1963-64 D2	3	4.1.64	Burnley	D1	A	D	1-1	Casper
	3r	7.1.64	Burnley		H	L	2-3	Lyons 2
1964-65 D2	3	9.1.65	Lincoln C	D4	H	W	5-1	Madden, Bennett 2, Galley 2
	4	30.1.65	Wolverhampton W	D1	A	D	2-2	Bennett, Pring
	4r	2.2.65	Wolverhampton W		H	L	0-3	
1965-66 D2	3	22.1.66	Southend U	D3	H	W	3-2	Wilcockson, Rabjohn, Bradbury og
	4	12.2.66	Manchester U	D1	A	D	0-0	
	4r	15.2.66	Manchester U		H	L	0-1	
1966-67 D2	3	28.1.67	Nuneaton Borough	SL	A	D	1-1	Chambers
	3r	31.1.67	Nuneaton Borough		H	W	1-0	Chappell
	4	18.2.67	Birmingham C	D2	H	D	0-0	
	4r	21.2.67	Birmingham C		A	L	1-2	Galley
1967-68 D2	3	27.1.68	Wolverhampton W	D1	H	W	1-0	Storrie
	4	17.2.68	Aston Villa	D2	A	W	1-0	Storrie
	5	9.3.68	Leicester C	D1	H	D	1-1	Downs
	5r	13.3.68	Leicester C		A	L	0-2aet	
1968-69 D3	1	16.11.68	Hartlepool	D3	A	D	1-1	Womble
	1r	19.11.68	Hartlepool		H	W	3-0	G.Watson 2, Storrie
	2	7.12.68	Mansfield T	D3	H	D	2-2	Gilliver
	2r	9.12.68	Mansfield T		A	L	0-1	
1969-70 D3	1	15.11.69	Notts Co	D4	A	W	3-0	Hague, Downes 2
	2	6.12.69	Workington		H	W	3-0	Downes, Swift, Fantham
	3	3.1.70	Peterborough U	D4	H	L	0-1	
1970-71 D3	1	24.11.70	Great Harwood	NPL	A	W	6-2	Watson 2, Fantham 2, Bentley, Mullen
	2	12.12.70	Grantham	ML	A	W	4-1	Watson, Hague, Fantham 2
	3	11.1.71	Leeds U	D1	H	D	0-0	
	3r	18.1.71	Leeds U		A	L	2-3	Womble, Bentley
1971-72 D3	1	20.11.71	Frickley Colliery	ML	A	D	2-2	Mullen, Bentley
	1r	23.11.71	Frickley Colliery		H	W	4-0	Bentley, Gilbert 3
	2	11.12.71	York C	D3	H	D	1-1	Gilbert
	2r	13.12.71	York C		A	W	3-2aet	Ham 2, Womble
	3	15.1.72	Bury	D4	A	D	1-1	Gilbert
	3r	19.1.72	Bury		H	W	2-1	SWift, Gilbert (p)
	4	5.2.72	Tottenham H	D1	A	L	0-2	
1972-73 D3	1	18.11.72	South Shields	NPL	H	W	4-0	Womble, Swift 2, Mielczarek
	2	9.12.72	Stockport Co	D4	H	L	0-1	
1973-74 D4	1	24.11.73	Southport	D3	H	W	2-1	Wigg, Phillips
	2	15.12.73	Wrexham	D3	A	L	0-3	
1974-75 D4	1	23.11.74	Chester	D4	H	W	1-0	Delgado
	2	4.12.74	Northampton T	D4	H	W	2-1	Wigg 2
	3	4.1.75	Stafford R	NPL	A	D	0-0	
	3r	7.1.75	Stafford R		H	L	0-2	
1975-76 D3	1	22.11.75	Crewe A	D4	H	W	2-1	Crawford, Stancliffe
	2	13.12.75	Bradford C	D4	H	L	0-3	
1976-77 D3	1	20.11.76	Altrincham	NPL	H	W	5-0	Gwyther, Finney 2, Breckin, Crawford (p)
	2	11.12.76	York C	D3	H	D	0-0	
	2r	14.12.76	York C		A	D	1-1aet	Crawford
	2 2r	21.12.76	York C		H	W	2-1aet	Crawford 2 (1p)
	3	8.1.77	Wolverhampton W	D2	A	L	2-3	Crawford 2 (1p)
1977-78 D3	1	26.11.77	Mossley	NPL	H	W	3-0	Gwyther, Finney, Phillips
	2	17.12.77	Spennymoor U	NL	H	W	6-0	Phillips 3, Crawford 2, Gwyther

	3	7.1.78	Millwall	D2	H	D	1-1	Finney
	3r	9.1.78	Millwall		A	L	0-2	
1978-79 D3	1	25.11.78	Workington	NPL	H	W	3-0	Gwyther 2, Breckin
	2	16.12.78	Barnsley	D4	A	D	1-1	Crawford
	2r	9.1.79	Barnsley		H	W	2-1	Gwyther, Phillips
	3	15.1.79	Manchester C	D1	A	D	0-0	
	3r	17.1.79	Manchester C		H	L	2-4	Breckin, Green
1979-80 D3	1	24.11.79	Morecambe	NPL	A	D	1-1	Finney
	1r	27.11.79	Morecambe		H	W	2-0	Green, Stancliffe
	2	15.12.79	Altrincham	APL	H	L	0-2	
1980-81 D3	1	22.11.80	Boston U	APL	A	W	4-0	Taylor, Moore 2, Carr
	2	13.12.80	Barnsley	D3	H	L	0-1	
1981-82 D2	3	2.1.82	Sunderland	D1	H	D	1-1	Towner
	3r	18.1.82	Sunderland		A	L	0-1	
1982-83 D2	3	8.1.83	Shrewsbury T	D2	A	L	1-2	Seasman
1983-84 D3	1	19.11.83	Hartlepool U	D4	H	D	0-0	
	1r	23.11.83	Hartlepool U		A	W	1-0aet	Kilmore
	2	10.12.83	Hull C	D3	H	W	2-1	Kilmore 2
	3	7.1.84	WBA	D1	H	D	0-0	
	3r	11.1.84	WBA		A	L	0-3	
1984-85 D3	1	17.11.84	Mansfield T	D4	A	L	1-2	Gooding
1985-86 D3	1	16.11.85	Wolverhampton W	D3	H	W	6-0	Tynan, Simmons, Gooding, Birch 2, Smith
	2	7.12.85	Burnley	D4	H	W	4-1	Birch, Trusson 2, Tynan
	3	4.1.86	Frickley Ath	APL	A	W	3-1	Gooding, Pugh, Tynan
	4	25.1.86	Arsenal	D1	A	L	1-5	Tynan
1986-87 D3	1	15.11.86	Chester	D3	A	D	1-1	Gooding (p)
	1r	18.11.86	Chester		H	D	1-1aet	Evans
	1 2r	24.11.86	Chester		A	L	0-1	
1987-88 D3	1	14.11.87	Doncaster R	D3	A	D	1-1	Dungworth (p)
	1r	17.11.87	Doncaster R		H	W	2-0	Haycock 2
	2	6.12.87	Macclesfield	GMVC	A	L	0-4	
1988-89 D4	1	19.11.88	Barrow	NPL	H	W	3-1	Williamson (p), Gordon og, Green
	2	10.12.88	Grimsby T	D4	A	L	2-3	Grealish, Dempsey (p)
1989-90 D3	1	18.11.89	Bury	D3	H	D	0-0	
	1r	21.11.89	Bury		A	W	2-1	Hazel, Evans
	2	9.12.89	Walsall	D3	A	L	0-1	
1990-91 D3	1	17.11.90	Stockport Co	D4	H	W	1-0	Dempsey
	2	11.12.90	Halifax T	D4	H	D	1-1	Goater
	2r	17.12.90	Halifax T		A	W	2-1	Evans, Johnson
	3	5.1.91	Swansea C	D3	A	D	0-0	
	3r	21.1.91	Swansea C		H	W	4-0	Dempsey, Mendonca 2, Goater
	4	26.1.91	Crewe A	D3	A	L	0-1	
1991-92 D4	1	16.11.91	Scunthorpe U	D4	A	D	1-1	Cunningham
	1r	26.11.91	Scunthorpe U		H	D	3-3aet	Page 2, Goodwin
			Rotherham won 7-6 on penalties					
	2	7.12.91	Burnley	D4	A	L	0-2	
1992-93 D2	1	14.11.92	Walsall	D3	H	W	4-0	Goodwin 2, Cunningham, Howard
	2	5.12.92	Hull C	D2	H	W	1-0	Cunningham
	3	12.1.93	Northampton T	D3	A	W	1-0	Howard
	4	23.1.93	Newcastle U	D1	H	D	1-1	Johnson
	4r	3.2.93	Newcastle U		A	L	0-2	

ROYAL ENGINEERS

Formed 1867. Their home ground was at Chatham Lines, Chatham. One of the 15 original clubs to enter the FA Cup, they were runners-up in the first FA Cup Final to Wanderers. **Best FA Cup Performance:** winners 1875. Runners-up: 1872, 1874, 1878

1871-72	1		Reigate Priory				walkover	
	2	10.1.72	Hitchin		A	W	5-0	
	3	27.1.72	Hampstead Heathens			W	3-0	
	SF	17.2.72	Crystal Palace			D	0-0	
	SFr	9.3.72	Crystal Palace			W	3-0	Renny-Tailyour 2, Mitchell
	F	16.3.72	Wanderers			L	0-1	
			both semi-final matches and the Final were played at Kennington Oval					
1872-73	1	26.10.72	Civil Service		H	W	3-0	
	2		bye					
	3	9.12.72	Oxford University		A	L	0-1	

ROYAL ENGINEERS

1873-74	1	11.10.73	Brondesbury		H	W	5-0	Addison, 4 others
	2	26.11.73	Uxbridge		H	W	2-1	
	3	10.12.73	Maidenhead		H	W	7-0	
	SF	28.1.74	Swifts			W	2-0	Renny-Tailyour 2
	F	14.3.74	Oxford University			L	0-2	
		both semi-final and Final were played at Kennington Oval						
1874-75	1	7.11.74	Great Marlow		H	W	3-0	von Donop, others 2
	2	5.12.74	Cambridge University		H	W	5-0	Mulholland, Rawson, Stafford, others
	3	30.1.75	Clapham Rovers			W	3-2	Mein, Stafford, 1 other
	SF	27.2.75	Oxford University			D	1-1	Renny-Tailyour
	SFr	5.3.75	Oxford University			W	1-0aet	Renny-Tailyour
	F	13.3.75	Old Etonians			D	1-1	Renny-Tailyour
	Fr	16.3.75	OLD ETONIANS			W	2-0	Renny-Tailyour, Stafford
		both semi-final matches and both Final matches were played at Kennington Oval						
1875-76	1	10.11.75	High Wycombe		H	W	15-0	Middlemiss 5, Rawson 5, Blackburn 2, von Donop 2, Tower
	2		Panthers			walkover		
	3	29.1.76	Swifts		H	L	1-3	Rawson
1876-77	1	4.11.76	Old Harrovians		A	W	2-1	Rawson, 1 other
	2	9.12.76	Shropshire W		H	W	3-0	Hedley, others 2
	3	20.1.77	Sheffield Club			W	1-0	Rawson
	4	17.2.77	Cambridge University			L	0-1	
1877-78	1		Union FC			walkover		
	2	8.12.77	Pilgrims		H	W	6-0	Hedley 3, others 3
	3	30.1.78	Druids		H	W	8-0	Hedley 3, Tower 2, Haynes, Lindsay, others 1
	4	15.2.78	Oxford University			D	3-3	
	4r	27.2.78	Oxford University			D	2-2aet	Bond, Haynes
	4 2r	12.3.78	Oxford University			W	4-2	Barnet, Bond, Ruck, 1 other
	SF	16.3.78	Old Harrovians			W	2-1	Barnet, Mayne
	F	23.3.78	Wanderers			L	1-3	*'scored from a rush'*
		both semi-final and Final matches were played at Kennington Oval						
1878-79	1	9.11.78	Old Foresters		A	W	3-0	
	2	7.12.78	Oxford University		A	L	0-4	
1879-80	1		bye					
	2	23.12.79	Upton Park		H	W	4-1	Learoyd 2, Paterson, others 1
	3	4.2.80	Old Harrovians			W	2-0	
	4	18.2.80	Grey Friars			W	1-0	Tanner
	5	5.3.80	Oxford University			D	1-1aet	Massey
	5r	15.3.80	Oxford University			L	0-1	
1880-81	1		bye					
	2	9.12.80	Pilgrims		H	W	1-0	Massey
	3	9.2.81	Rangers		H	W	6-0	Learoyd 2, Barnet, Burton, Wingfield-Stratford, others 1
	4	19.3.81	Old Carthusians		A	L	0-2	
1881-82	1	5.11.81	Kildare		H	W	6-0	
	2		bye					
	3	20.12.81	Old Carthusians			W	2-0	Williams, og
	4	21.1.82	Old Foresters			L	1-2	Kincaid
1882-83	1	21.10.82	Woodford Bridge		H	W	3-1	Newman, Petrie, Stafford
	2	29.11.82	Reading		H	W	8-0	Kincaid 3, Godby 2, Ruck, Stafford, others 1
	3		bye					
	4	25.1.83	Old Carthusians			L	2-6	Kincaid, Lindsay
1883-84	1	10.11.83	Windsor Home Park		A	L	3-5	Kincaid 2, Wingfield-Stratford
1884-85	1	8.11.84	Great Marlow		A	L	1-10	Stafford
1885-86	1	31.10.85	Old Foresters		H	L	1-5	
1886-87	1	30.10.86	Old Etonians		A	L	0-1	
1887-88	1	15.10.87	Rochester		H	L	0-3	
		FA ordered match to be replayed after protest						
	1r		Rochester			walkover		
	2	5.11.87	Chatham		A	L	1-3	

VS RUGBY

Formed 1956 as Valley Sports, Rugby. FA Vase Winners: 1983

1984-85	SL	1	21.11.84	Northampton T	D4	H	L	0-1	
1985-86	SL	1	16.11.85	Orient	D4	H	D	2-2	Downes 2
		1r	19.11.85	Orient		A	L	1-4	Gorman
1986-87	SL	1	15.11.86	Bristol C	D3	A	L	1-3	Lane (p)

1987-88	SL	1	14.11.87	Atherstone	SL	H	D	0-0	
		1r	17.11.87	Atherstone		A	W	2-0	Ross, Conway
		2	5.12.87	Bristol R	D3	H	D	1-1	Ingram
		2r	17.12.87	Bristol R		A	L	0-4	
1992-93	SL	1	15.11.92	Solihull B	SL	A	D	2-2	Bufton, Green
		1r	25.11.92	Solihull B		H	W	2-1	Green, Smith
		2	9.12.92	Marlow	IL	H	D	0-0	
		2r	16.12.92	Marlow		A	L	0-2	

RUNCORN

Formed 1918. **First entered FA Cup:** 1919. **Cup Final Connection:** Ian Woan, who played for Nottingham Forest in the 1991 FA Cup Final, played for Runcorn. **League clubs beaten:** Aldershot, Notts Co, Southport, Chester, Wrexham

1938-39	CC	1	26.11.38	Wellington	CC	H	W	3-0	Searth, Fitton, Mayson
		2	10.12.38	Aldershot	3S	H	W	3-1	Long, Mayson, Fitton
		3	7.1.39	Preston NE	D1	H	L	2-4	Mayson, Houghton
1946-47	CC	1	30.11.46	Carlisle U	3N	A	L	0-4	
1947-48	CC	1	29.11.47	Scunthorpe U	ML	H	W	4-2	Malam, Bailey, Coogan 2
		2	13.12.47	Barrow	3N	H	L	0-1	
1948-49	CC	1	27.11.48	York C	3N	A	L	1-2	JS Brown
1967-68	CC	1	9.12.67	Notts Co	D4	H	W	1-0	Ryan
		2	6.1.68	Southport	D3	A	L	2-4	Ryan 2
1973-74	NPL	1	24.11.73	Grimsby T	D3	H	L	0-1	
1977-78	NPL	1	26.11.77	Southport	D4	A	D	2-2	Whitbread, Lyon
		1r	28.11.77	Southport		H	W	1-0	Whitbread
		2	17.12.77	Hartlepool	D4	A	L	2-4	Spencer, Wiggett og
1978-79	NPL	1	25.11.78	Chester	D3	A	D	1-1	Keynon
		1r	28.11.78	Chester		H	L	0-5	
1981-82	APL	1	21.11.81	Burnley	D3	A	D	0-0	
		1r	24.11.81	Burnley		H	L	1-2	Seddon
1985-86	APL	1	16.11.85	Boston U	APL	H	D	2-2	Smith 2
		1r	20.11.85	Boston U		A	D	1-1aet	Carter
		1 2r	25.11.85	Boston U		H	W	4-1	Mather, Carter 2, S.Crompton
		2	7.12.85	Wigan A	D3	H	D	1-1	Mather
		2r	10.12.85	Wigan A		A	L	0-4	
1986-87	GMVC	1	15.11.86	Boston U	GMVC	H	D	1-1	Carter
		1r	19.11.86	Boston U		A	W	2-1aet	Carter (p), Rowlands
		2	6.12.86	Scunthorpe U	D4	A	L	0-1	
1987-88	GMVC	1	14.11.87	Chester C	D3	A	W	1-0	Carter
		2	5.12.87	Stockport Co	D4	H	L	0-1	
1988-89	GMVC	1	19.11.88	Wrexham	D4	H	D	2-2	Page, Anderson
		1r	22.11.88	Wrexham		A	W	3-2	Reid, Pugh, Rodwell
		2	10.12.88	Crewe A	D4	H	L	0-3	
1990-91	GMVC	1	17.11.90	Hartlepool U	D4	H	L	0-3	
1991-92	GMVC	1	15.11.91	Tranmere R	D2	H	L	0-3	

RUNNYMEDE

| 1878-79 | 1 | | Panthers | | | | *scratched* | |

RYDE SPORTS (IOW)

Formed 1888. **First entered FA Cup:** 1898. England Test cricketer Wally Hammond is a former player.

| 1932-33 | Hants 1 | | 26.11.32 | Margate | KL | A | L | 0-5 | |
| 1936-37 | Hants 1 | | 28.11.36 | Gillingham | 3S | H | L | 1-5 | Coates |

RYHOPE COLLIERY WELFARE

Formed 1898 as Ryhope Villa. **First entered FA Cup:** 1913. Merged with Sporting Club Vaux 1988

| 1967-68 | Wear 1 | | | Workington | D4 | H | L | 0-1 | |

SAFFRON WALDEN

Formed 1872. **First entered FA Cup:** 1876. Currently play in Isthmian (Diadora) League

| 1876-77 | 1 | | | Wanderers | | | | *scratched* | |

SAFFRON WALDEN

1878-79		1	30.10.78 **Upton Park**		A	L	0-5
1880-81		1	23.10.80 **Old Carthusians**		A	L	0-7

SALISBURY

Formed 1947. **First entered FA Cup:** 1948,

1955-56	WL	1	19.11.55 **Weymouth**	SL	A	L	2-3	Oakley, Prentice
1959-60	WL	1	14.11.59 **Barnet**	AL	H	W	1-0	Onslow
		2	5.12.59 **Newport Co**	D3	H	L	0-1	
1964-65	WL	1	14.11.64 **Peterborough U**	D3	A	L	1-5	Stocks
1967-68	WL	1	12.12.67 **Swindon T**	D3	A	L	0-4	
1979-80	SL	1	24.11.79 **Millwall**	D3	H	L	1-2	Hibbs
			played at Southampton					
1992-93	SL	1	14.11.92 **Marlow**	IL	A	D	3-3	Loveridge, Sanders, Fletcher
		1r	5.12.92 **Marlow**		H	D	2-2aet	Chalk, Sanders
			Marlow won 4-3 on penalties					

SAXONS

1876-77		1	4.11.76 **South Norwood**		A	L	1-4	Sharpe

SCARBOROUGH

Formed 1879. **First entered FA Cup:** 1887. **Best season:** 3rd round, 1931, 1938, 1976, 1978. FA Challenge Trophy Winners: 1973, 1976, 1977; Runners-up: 1975. **Cup Final Connection:** Colin Appleton, who played for Leicester City in the 1961 and 1963 FA Cup Finals is a former player. **Record FA Cup Win:** 6-0 vs Rhyl Athletic, 1st round, 29.11.1930. **Record FA Cup Defeat:** 0-8 vs Mansfield Town, 1st round, 22.11.1952. **League clubs beaten (as non-league club):** Lincoln, York C, Darlington, Bradford C, Oldham, Crewe A (2), Preston, Rochdale, Stockport Co

1887-88		1	15.10.87 **Shankhouse**		H	L	3-5	
1928-29	ML	1	24.11.28 **Horwich RMI**	LC	A	W	2-1	Wainwright, Glayson
		2	8.12.28 **Darlington**	3N	H	D	2-2	Glayson, Wainwright
		2r	12.12.28 **Darlington**		A	L	1-2	Glayson
1930-31	ML	1	29.11.30 **Rhyl**	NWaC	H	W	6-0	Rand 2, Hill, Palfreman 2, Small
		2	13.12.30 **Lincoln C**	3N	H	W	6-4	Palfreman, Hickman 2, Rand 2, Hill
		3	10.1.31 **Grimsby T**	D1	H	L	1-2	Palfreman
1932-33	ML	1	26.11.32 **York C**	3N	A	W	3-1	Jenkinson, Swann, Halfort
		2	10.12.32 **Southend U**	3S	A	L	1-4	Wraith
1933-34	ML	1	25.11.33 **North Shields**	NEL	A	L	0-3	
1935-36	ML	1	30.11.35 **Darwen**	LC	H	W	2-0	Boyle, Smithson
		2	14.12.35 **Brighton & HA**	3S	H	D	1-1	Smithson
		2r	18.12.35 **Brighton & HA**		A	L	0-3	
1937-38	ML	1	27.11.37 **Darlington**	3N	A	W	2-0	Nicol, Beckett
		2	11.12.37 **Bromley**	AL	H	W	4-1	Agar, Beckett, Nicol 2
		3	8.1.38 **Luton T**	D2	H	D	1-1	Barty
		3r	12.1.38 **Luton T**		A	L	1-5	Burke
1938-39	ML	1	26.11.38 **Southport**	3N	H	D	0-0	
		1r	29.11.38 **Southport**		A	L	3-5	Lister, Rivers, Hardy
1948-49	ML	1	4.12.48 **Rhyl**	CC	A	W	2-0	Langford 2
		2	11.12.48 **Gateshead**	3N	A	L	0-3	
1950-51	ML	1	25.11.50 **Rhyl**	CC	H	L	1-2	Cooling
1952-53	ML	1	22.11.52 **Mansfield T**	3N	H	L	0-8	
1953-54	ML	1	21.11.53 **Wigan Ath**	LC	A	L	0-4	
1954-55	ML	1	20.11.54 **York C**	3N	A	L	2-3	Barber, Pickard
1955-56	ML	1	19.11.55 **Workington**	3N	A	L	2-4	Michell, Parkinson (p)
1956-57	ML	1	17.11.56 **Rhyl**	CC	A	L	2-3	Parkinson, Bowman
1957-58	ML	1	16.11.57 **Bradford C**	3N	A	L	0-6	
1959-60	ML	1	14.11.59 **Bradford PA**	D4	A	L	1-6	Whittle
1960-61	NCo	1	5.11.60 **Bradford C**	3N	A	D	0-0	
		1r	9.11.60 **Bradford C**		H	L	1-3aet	Franks
1962-63	NEL	1	3.11.62 **Crewe A**	D4	A	D	1-1	Franks
		1r	7.11.62 **Crewe A**		H	L	2-3aet	Whyke, G Smith
1964-65	ML	1	14.11.64 **Bradford C**	D4	H	W	1-0	Edgar
		2	5.12.64 **Doncaster R**	D4	A	D	0-0	
		2r	9.12.64 **Doncaster R**		H	L	1-2	Cade
1965-66	ML	1	13.11.65 **Altrincham**	CC	A	L	0-6	
1970-71	NPL	1	21.11.70 **Workington**	D4	H	L	2-3	Siddle, Barmby (p)
1971-72	NPL	1	20.11.71 **Hartlepool U**	D4	A	L	1-6	Lee

SCARBOROUGH

1972-73	NPL	1	18.11.72	Oldham A	D3	A	D	1-1	Barmby
		1r	22.11.72	Oldham A		H	W	2-1	Franks, Donaghue
		2	9.12.72	Doncaster R	D4	H	L	1-2	Appleton
1973-74	NPL	1	24.11.73	Crewe A	D4	A	D	0-0	
		1r	28.11.73	Crewe A		H	W	2-1	Donaghue (p), Dunn
		2	15.12.73	Port Vale	D3	A	L	1-2	Lee
1975-76	NPL	1	22.11.75	Morecambe	NPL	H	W	2-0	Hewitt, Marshall
		2	13.12.75	Preston NE	D3	H	W	3-2	Dunn, Woodall, Marshall
		3	3.1.76	Crystal P	D3	H	L	1-2	Abbey
1976-77	NPL	1	20.11.76	Darlington	D4	H	D	0-0	
		1r	22.11.76	Darlington		A	L	1-4	Barney
1977-78	NPL	1	26.11.77	Rochdale	D4	H	W	4-2	HA Dunn, D Smith 3
		2	17.12.77	Crewe A	D4	A	D	0-0	
		2r	21.12.77	Crewe A		H	W	2-0	Woodall, Donoghue
		3	7.1.78	Brighton & HA	D2	A	L	0-3	
1978-79	NPL	1	25.11.78	Chorley	CC	A	W	1-0	HA Dunn
		2	16.12.78	York C	D4	A	L	0-3	
1979-80	APL	1	24.11.79	Halifax T	D4	A	L	0-2	
1980-81	APL	1	22.11.80	Burnley	D3	A	L	0-1	
1982-83	APL	1	20.11.82	Tranmere R	D4	A	L	2-4	Hamson 2
1985-86	APL	1	17.11.85	Notts Co	D3	A	L	1-6	Burke (p)
1987-88	D4	1	14.11.87	Grimsby T	D3	H	L	1-2	Graham
1988-89	D4	1	19.11.88	Stockport Co	D4	H	W	2-1	Brook, Cook (p)
		2	10.12.88	Carlisle U	D4	H	L	0-1	
1989-90	D4	1	18.11.89	Whitley Bay	NPL	H	L	0-1	
1990-91	D4	1	17.11.90	Leek T	NPL	H	L	0-2	
1991-92	D4	1	16.11.91	Wigan A	D3	H	L	0-2	
1992-93	D3	1	14.11.92	Burnley	D2	A	L	1-2	Mockler

SCUNTHORPE UNITED

Formed 1899. **First entered FA Cup:** 1913. **Best FA Cup Performance:** 5th round, 1958, 1970. **Record FA Cup Win:** 10-0 vs Hull Holderness, 1st qualifying round, 8.10.1922 and 10-0 vs Hull Holderness, preliminary round, 18.9.1926. In Competition Proper: 9-0 vs Boston U, 1st round, 21.11.1953. **Record FA Cup Defeat:** 0-7 vs Coventry C, 1st round, 24.11.1934

1912-13	ML	P **Brodsworth Colliery** (A) 3-2; 1q **Goole T** (H) 2-1; 2q **York C** (H) 2-2; 2qr **York C** (A) 4-5
1913-14	ML	P **Mexborough T** (A) 2-2; Pr **Mexborough T** (H) 3-0; 1q **York C** (A) 1-2
1914-15	ML	P **Hull School Old Boys** (H) 5-1; 1q **Grimsby R** (H) 4-0; 2q **Doncaster R** (H) 1-0; 3q **Goole T** (H) 1-1; 3qr **Goole T** (A) 1-5
1919-20	ML	P **Goole T** (H) 7-0; 1q **Brodsworth Colliery** (H) 2-1; 2q **Cleethorpes T** (H) 0-1
1920-21	ML	P **Hull Brunswick** (H) 6-0; 1q **Bentley Colliery** (H) 3-0; 2q **Grimsby Charltons** (A) 4-1; 3q **Brodsworth Colliery** (H) 1-1;
		3qr **Brodsworth Colliery** (A) 0-0aet; 3q 2r **Brodsworth Colliery** 3-1 at Bramall Lane; 4q **Mansfield T** (A) 0-1
1921-22	ML	P **Retford** (A) 2-1; 1q **Hull Holderness** (H) 10-0; 2q **Brodsworth Colliery** (H) 4-1; 3q **Gainsborough T** (A) 0-2
1922-23	ML	1q **Grimsby Charltons** (H) 3-0; 2q **Gainsborough T** (A) 2-1; 3q **Boston T** (A) 1-0; 4q **Worksop T** (A) 2-4
1923-24	ML	P **Grimsby Rovers** (H) 5-1; 1q **Cleethorpes T** (H) 5-0; 2q **Gainsborough T** (H) 2-0; 3q **Boston T** (H) 2-0; 4q **Rotherham T** (H) 0-0;
		4qr **Rotherham T** (A) 1-0; 5q **Rotherham Co** (H) 1-1; 5qr **Rotherham Co** (A) 0-2
1924-25	ML	P **Barton T** (H) 2-1; 1q **Boston T** (H) 0-0; 1qr **Boston T** (A) 0-3
1925-26	ML	P **Cleethorpes T** (A) 4-0; 1q **Grimsby Haycroft** (H) 5-1; 2q **Gainsborough T** (H) 2-2; 2qr **Gainsborough T** (A) 0-1
1926-27	ML	P **Hull Holderness** (H) 10-0; 1q **Grimsby Haycroft** (H) 7-2; 2q **Selby Olympia** (A) 0-0; 2qr **Selby Olympia** (H) 1-0;
		3q **Gainsborough T** (A) 3-3; 3qr **Gainsborough T** (H) 1-0; 4q **Kettering T** (H) 1-2
1927-28	ML	P **Cleethorpes T** (H) 5-2; 1q **Gainsborough T** (A) 0-3
1928-29	ML	P **Barton T** (A) 3-2; 1q **Spalding** (A) 3-0; 2q **Cleethorpes T** (H) 4-3; 3q **Boston T** (A) 1-0; 4q **Grantham** (A) 1-2
1929-30	ML	P **Selby T** (A) 3-1; 1q **Selby Olympia** (H) 1-0; 2q **Goole T** (H) 2-1; 3q **Broughton** (H) 7-0; 4q **South Kirby** (A) 6-1

		1	30.11.29	Hartlepool U	3N	H	W	1-0	Smalley
		2	14.12.29	Rotherham U	3N	H	D	3-3	Smalley, Calladine 2
		2r	19.12.29	Rotherham U		A	L	4-5	Beynon 2, Smalley, Calladine
1930-31	ML			4q **Worcester C** (H) 3-0					
		1	29.11.30	Gainsborough T	ML	A	L	0-1	
1931-32	ML			4q **Sutton Junction** (H) 7-1					
		1	28.11.31	Rochdale	3N	H	W	2-1	Hubbard, Methven
		2	12.12.31	QPR	3S	H	L	1-4	Baynam (p)
1932-33	ML			4q **Burton T** (H) 4-1					
		1	26.11.32	Workington	NEL	A	L	1-5	Tucker
1933-34	ML			1q **Selby T** (H) 4-1; 2q **Humber U** (H) 5-0; 3q **Louth** (H) 4-1; 4q **Heanor T** (H) 4-2					
		1	25.11.33	Accrington S	3N	H	D	1-1	Sumpter
		1r	30.11.33	Accrington S		A	L	0-3	
1934-35	ML			4q **Kettering T** (H) 2-2; 4qr **Kettering T** (A) 3-1					
		1	24.11.34	Coventry C	3S	A	L	0-7	

Season	Div	Round	Date	Opponent		Venue	Result	Score	Scorers
1935-36	ML	4q Denaby U (H) 4-1							
		1	30.11.35	Coventry C	3S	A	D	1-1	Snaith
		1r	9.12.35	Coventry C		H	W	4-2	Davies, Roberts, Lewis, Kilsby
		2	14.12.35	Tranmere R	3N	A	L	2-6	Lewis, Allen
1936-37	ML	4q Gainsborough Trinity (A) 1-0							
		1	28.11.36	Walsall	3S	A	L	0-3	
1937-38	ML	4q Grantham (H) 4-2							
		1	27.11.37	Hull C	3N	A	L	0-4	
1938-39	ML	1q Barton T (H) 9-1; 2q Appleby-Frodingham (H) 4-1; 3q Lysaghts Sports (H) 11-3; 4q Boston T (H) 2-1							
		1	26.11.38	Lancaster C	LC	H	W	4-2	Johnson, Nightingale, Fleetwood 2
		2	10.12.38	Watford	3S	H	L	1-2	Jones
1945-46	ML	3q Lysaghts Sports (H) 4-1; 4q Yorkshire Amateurs (H) 1-2							
1946-47	ML	P Norton Woodseats (H) 5-2; 1q Harworth Colliery (H) 5-2; 2q Rawmarsh (A) 3-0; 3q Wombwell (A) 5-2; 4q Boston T (H) 4-1							
		1	4.12.46	York C	3N	A	W	1-0	Marriott
		2	14.12.46	Rotherham U	3N	A	L	1-4	Bowers
1947-48	ML	P Sheffield FC (H) 5-1; 1q Rawmarsh (H) 8-0; 2q Denaby U (H) 1-0; 3q Norton Woodseats (H) 2-1; 4q Gainsborough T (H) 4-2							
		1	29.11.47	Runcorn	CC	A	L	2-4	Bowers, Rowney
1948-49	ML	4q Selby T (H) 2-1							
		1	4.12.48	Halifax T	3N	A	D	0-0	
		1r	6.12.48	Halifax T		H	W	1-0	Barker
		2	11.12.48	Stockport Co	3N	H	L	0-1	
1949-50	ML	4q Goole T (H) 0-0; 4qr Goole T (A) 1-3							
1950-51	3N	4q Hereford U (A) 0-1							
1951-52	3N	1	24.11.51	Billingham Synthonia	NL	H	W	5-0	Powell 2, Wallace 2, Hubbard
		2	15.12.51	Millwall	3S	A	D	0-0	
		2r	20.12.51	Millwall		H	W	3-0	Powell 2, Rudd
		3	12.1.52	Tottenham H	D1	H	L	0-3	
1952-53	3N	1	22.11.52	Carlisle U	3N	H	W	1-0	Whitfield
		2	6.12.52	Hereford U	SL	A	D	0-0	
		2r	11.12.52	Hereford U		H	W	2-1	Haigh, Whitfield
		3	10.1.53	Sunderland	D1	A	D	1-1	McGill
		3r	15.1.53	Sunderland		H	L	1-2	Daley
1953-54	3N	1	21.11.53	Boston U	ML	H	W	9-0	Jones 2, Haigh 3, Whitfield 2, Gregory, Mosby
		2	12.12.53	Bournemouth	3S	H	W	1-0	Brown
		3	9.1.54	Wrexham	3N	A	D	3-3	Bushby 2, Mosby
		3r	14.1.54	Wrexham		H	W	3-1	Gregory, Brandsword, Whitfield
		4	30.1.54	Portsmouth	D1	H	D	1-1	Jones
		4r	3.2.54	Portsmouth		A	D	2-2aet	Jones 2
		4 2r	8.2.54	Portsmouth at Highbury			L	0-4	
1954-55	3N	1	20.11.54	Horden CW	NEL	A	W	1-0	McGill
		2	11.12.54	Coventry C	3S	A	L	0-4	
1955-56	3N	1	19.11.55	Shildon	NL	H	W	3-0	Davies, Brown, Gregory
		2	10.12.55	Bishop Auckland	NL	A	D	0-0	
		2r	15.12.55	Bishop Auckland		H	W	2-0	Davies, Hubbard
		3	7.1.56	Rotherham U	D2	A	D	1-1	Brown
		3r	12.1.56	Rotherham U		H	W	4-2	Brown 3, Davies
		4	28.1.56	Liverpool	D2	A	D	3-3	Gregory, Davies 2
		4r	6.2.56	Liverpool		H	L	1-2aet	Davies
1956-57	3N	1	17.11.56	Rochdale	3N	H	W	1-0	Brown
		2	8.12.56	Wrexham	3N	H	D	0-0	
		2r	12.12.56	Wrexham		A	L	2-6aet	Gregory 2
1957-58	3N	1	16.11.57	Goole T	ML	H	W	2-1	Fletcher, Davies
		2	7.12.57	Bury	3N	H	W	2-0	Waldock, Jones
		3	4.1.58	Bradford C	3N	H	W	1-0	Haigh
		4	25.1.58	Newcastle U	D1	A	W	3-1	Haigh, Davies 2
		5	15.2.58	Liverpool	D2	H	L	0-1	
1958-59	D2	3	10.1.59	Bolton W	D1	H	L	0-2	
1959-60	D2	3	9.1.60	Crystal P	D4	H	W	1-0	Middleton
		4	30.1.60	Port Vale	D3	H	L	0-1	
1960-61	D2	3	7.1.61	Blackpool	D1	H	W	6-2	Bonson 3, Thomas 3
		4	28.1.61	Norwich C	D2	H	L	1-4	Bakes
1961-62	D2	3	6.1.62	Charlton A	D2	A	L	0-1	
1962-63	D2	3	26.1.63	Portsmouth	D2	A	D	1-1	Godfrey
		3r	7.3.63	Portsmouth		H	L	1-2	McGuigan
1963-64	D2	3	4.1.64	Barnsley	D3	H	D	2-2	Wilson, Lawther
		3r	7.1.64	Barnsley		A	L	2-3	Brownswood 2
1964-65	D3	1	14.11.64	Darlington	D4	H	L	1-2	Greener og

1965-66	D3	1	13.11.65	Crewe A	D4	A	L	0-3	
1966-67	D3	1	26.11.66	Lincoln C	D4	A	W	4-3	Smith, Burrows, Barton, Mahy
		2	7.1.67	Mansfield T	D3	A	L	1-2	Foxon
1967-68	D3	1	9.12.67	Skelmersdale U	LC	H	W	2-0	Colquhoun, Barton (p)
		2	6.1.68	Halifax T	D4	A	L	0-1	
1968-69	D4	1	16.11.68	Workington	D4	A	L	0-2	
1969-70	D4	1	15.11.69	Macclesfield T	NPL	A	D	1-1	Heath
		1r	18.11.69	Macclesfield T		H	W	4-2	Keegan 2, Rusling, Cassidy
		2	6.12.69	Stockport Co	D3	A	D	0-0	
		2r	9.12.69	Stockport Co		H	W	4-0	Cassidy, Kerr 2, Keegan
		3	3.1.70	Millwall	D2	H	W	2-1	Deere. Heath
		4	24.1.70	Sheffield W	D1	A	W	2-1	Barker, Cassidy
		5	7.2.70	Swindon T	D2	A	L	1-3	Cassidy
1970-71	D4	1	21.11.70	Tranmere R	D3	A	D	1-1	Woolmer
		1r	24.11.70	Tranmere R		H	D	0-0aet	
		1 2r	30.11.70	Tranmere R at Goodison Pk			W	1-0	Rusling
		2	12.12.70	Mansfield T	D3	H	W	3-0	Rusling 2, Kirk
		3	2.1.71	WBA	D1	A	D	0-0	
		3r	11.1.71	WBA		H	L	1-3	Deere
1971-72	D4	1	20.11.71	South Shields	NPL	A	D	3-3	Deere, Kerr 2
		1r	24.11.71	South Shields		H	L	2-3	Fletcher, Kirk
1972-73	D3	1	18.11.72	Hartlepool	D4	A	D	0-0	
		1r	21.11.72	Hartlepool		H	D	0-0aet	
		1 2r	27.11.72	Hartlepool at Roker Pk			W	2-1aet	Dawes og, Deere
		2	9.12.72	Halifax T	D3	H	W	3-2	Heath, Fletcher, Wellbourne
		3	13.1.73	Cardiff C	D2	H	L	2-3	Wellbourne, Kirk
1973-74	D4	1	24.11.73	Darlington	D4	H	W	1-0	Houghton
		2	15.12.73	Mansfield T	D4	A	D	1-1	Houghton
		2r	18.12.73	Mansfield T		H	W	1-0	Warnock
		3	5.1.74	Millwall	D2	A	D	1-1	Collier
		3r	8.1.74	Millwall		H	W	1-0	Pilling
		4	26.1.74	Newcastle U	D1	A	D	1-1	Keeley
		4r	30.1.74	Newcastle U		H	L	0-3	
1974-75	D4	1	23.11.74	Altrincham	NPL	A	D	1-1	Keeley
		1r	25.11.74	Altrincham		A	L	1-3	Collier
1975-76	D4	1	22.11.75	Preston NE	D3	A	L	1-2	Green
1976-77	D4	1	20.11.76	Chesterfield	D3	H	L	1-2	Keeley
1977-78	D4	1	26.11.77	Stockport Co	D4	A	L	0-3	
1978-79	D4	1	25.11.78	Sheffield W	D3	H	D	1-1	Pilling
		1r	28.11.78	Sheffield W		A	L	0-1	
1979-80	D4	1	24.11.79	Rochdale	D4	A	L	1-2	Pilling
1980-81	D4	1	22.11.80	Hartlepool	D4	H	W	3-1	Grimes, Green, Partridge (p)
		2	13.12.80	Altrincham	APL	H	D	0-0	
		2r	15.12.80	Altrincham		A	L	0-1	
1981-82	D4	1	21.11.81	Bradford C	D4	H	W	1-0	Cowling
		2	2.1.82	Crewe A	D4	A	W	3-1	Cowling, Telfer, Dall
		3	6.1.82	Hereford U	D4	H	D	1-1	Stewart
		3r	20.1.82	Hereford U		A	L	1-4	Grimes
1982-83	D4	1	20.11.82	Darlington	D4	A	W	1-0	Cammack
		2	11.12.82	Northwich Victoria	APL	H	W	2-1	Cowling, O'Berg
		3	8.1.83	Grimsby T	D2	H	D	0-0	
		3r	11.1.83	Grimsby T		A	L	0-2	
1983-84	D3	1	19.11.83	Preston NE	D3	H	W	1-0	Cammack (p)
		2	10.12.83	Bury	D4	H	W	2-0	Pashley og, Cammack
		3	7.1.84	Leeds U	D2	A	D	1-1	Cammack
		3r	10.1.84	Leeds U		H	D	1-1aet	Dey
		3 2r	16.1.84	Leeds U		H	W	4-2	Brolly, Cammack, Lester, Graham
		4	1.2.84	WBA	D1	A	L	0-1	
1984-85	D4	1	17.11.84	Nuneaton B	APL	A	D	1-1	Dixey og
		1r	20.11.84	Nuneaton B		H	W	2-1aet	Lester, Cammack
		2	7.12.84	Port Vale	D4	A	L	1-4	Ridley og
1985-86	D4	1	16.11.85	Halifax T	D4	A	W	3-1	Hill, Broddle, Lister
		2	7.12.85	Rochdale	D4	H	D	2-2	Graham, Hill
		2r	10.12.85	Rochdale		A	L	1-2	Broddle
1986-87	D4	1	15.11.86	Southport	NPL	H	W	2-0	Hill, Broddle
		2	5.12.86	Runcorn	GMVC	H	W	1-0	Broddle
		3	10.1.87	Tottenham H	D1	A	L	2-3	Johnson, DeMange

1987-88	D4	1	14.11.87	Bury	D3	H	W	3-1	Russell 3 (1p)
		2	5.12.87	Sunderland	D3	H	W	2-1	Taylor, Harle
		3	9.1.88	Blackpool	D3	H	D	0-0	
		3r	12.1.88	Blackpool		A	L	0-1	
1988-89	D4	1	19.11.88	Blackpool	D3	A	L	1-2	Harle (p)
1989-90	D4	1	17.11.89	Matlock T	NPL	H	W	4-1	Lillis 3, Hodkinson
		2	9.12.89	Burnley	D4	H	D	2-2	Taylor 2
		2r	12.12.89	Burnley		A	D	1-1aet	Daws
		2 2r	18.12.89	Burnley		A	L	0-5	
1990-91	D4	1	17.11.90	Rochdale	D4	A	D	1-1	Hicks
		1r	20.11.90	Rochdale		H	W	2-1	Flounders, Lillis
		2	8.12.90	Tranmere R	D3	H	W	3-2	Ward, Lillis, Flounders
		3	5.1.91	Brighton & HA	D2	A	L	2-3	Flounders (p), Bramhall
1991-92	D4	1	16.11.91	Rotherham U	D4	H	D	1-1	Helliwell
		1r	26.11.91	Rotherham U		A	D	3-3aet	Helliwell, Dawes, White
		Rotherham U win 7-6 on pens							
1992-93	D3	1	14.11.92	Huddersfield T	D2	H	D	0-0	
		1r	25.11.92	Huddersfield T		A	L	1-2aet	Buckley

SELBY TOWN

Formed 1911. **First entered FA Cup:** 1921

1952-53	YL	1	22.11.52	Bishop Auckland	NL	H	L	1-5	Benn
1953-54	YL	1	21.11.53	Bradford PA	3N	H	L	0-2	
1954-55	YL	1	20.11.54	Rhyl	CC	H	W	2-1	Campbell, Deyes
		2	11.12.54	Hastings U	SL	H	L	0-2	
1956-57	YL	1	17.11.56	Hartlepools U	3N	A	L	1-3	Clark

SHANKHOUSE

Northumberland mining village amateur side

1887-88	1	15.10.87	Scarborough		A	W	5-3	
	2		bye					
	3	26.11.87	Darlington		A	W	2-0	Matthews, Meltcalfe
	4	17.12.87	Aston Villa		H	L	0-9	
1892-93	1	21.1.93	Notts Co	D1	A	L	0-4	

SHEFFIELD FC

Also often referred to as Sheffield Club, this is the oldest club in the world. The club was formed in 1855, are still in existence, playing in the Northern Counties (East) League, but haven't reached the first round proper of the FA Cup since 1887. Their original ground was on open space at Bramall Lane and they now play at the Don Valley Stadium. Their first round replay with Shropshire Wanderers on October 17, 1873 was the only FA Cup match ever decided on the toss of a coin. FA Amateur Cup Winners: 1904. FA Vase Runners-up 1977.

1873-74	1	30.10.73	Shropshire W		H	D	0-0	
	1r	17.11.73	Shropshire W		A	D	0-0	
		Sheffield won on toss of coin						
	2	22.11.73	Pilgrims		H	W	1-0	Sorby
	3	17.1.74	Clapham R		N	L	1-2	Kirke-Smith
		match played at Peterborough						
1874-75	1		Shropshire W			scratched		
1875-76	1		Shropshire W			walkover		
	2		Upton Park			walkover		
	3	29.1.76	Wanderers		A	L	0-2	
1876-77	1		Trojans			walkover		
	2	2.12.76	South Norwood		A	W	7-0	Owen 5, Cursham, Matthews
	3	20.1.77	Royal Engineers		A	L	0-1	
1877-78	1	3.11.77	Notts Co		A	D	1-1	Cursham
	1r	1.12.77	Notts Co		H	W	3-0	Cursham 2, Matthews
	2	29.12.77	Darwen		H	W	1-0	Matthews
	3		bye					
	4	16.2.78	Wanderers		A	L	0-3	
1878-79	1	28.10.78	Grantham		H	D	1-1	Sorby
	1r	16.11.78	Grantham		A	W	2-1	J.Barber 2, J.Willey
	2	21.12.78	Nottingham Forest		A	L	0-2	
1879-80	1		Queen's Park			walkover		

	2	15.12.79	Sheffield Providence	H	D	3-3	Matthews, Moss, 1 other
	2r	29.12.79	Sheffield Providence	H	W	3-0	Cursham, Matthews, Sorby
	3		bye				
	4	19.2.80	Nottingham Forest	A	D	2-2	H.Barber, 1 other
		Sheffield disqualified for refusing to play extra-time					
1880-81	1	30.10.80	Blackburn Olympic	H	W	5-4	E.Barber, H.Barber, Sorby, og, 1 other
	2	18.12.80	Darwen	H	L	1-5	H.Barber
1881-82	1	5.11.81	Brigg Britania	H	W	8-0	Marsden 3, E.Barber, Beardshaw, J.Bradbury, others 2
	2	26.11.81	Sheffield Heeley	H	L	0-4	
1882-83	1	4.11.82	Notts Co	A	L	1-6	
1883-84	1	10.11.83	Lockwood Brothers	A	L	1-4	
1884-85	1	8.11.84	Lockwood Brothers	A	W	3-0	J.Barber, Liddall, Twining
	2	6.12.84	Spital, Chesterfield	H	W	4-1	Davy 3, E.Barber
	3	3.1.85	Notts Co	A	L	0-5	
1885-86	1	31.10.85	Newark	A	W	3-0	
	2	21.11.85	Notts Co	A	L	0-8	
1886-87	1	30.10.86	Notts Rangers	H	L	0-3	
1887-88	1	15.10.87	Lockwood Brothers	H	L	1-3	

SHEFFIELD HEELEY

Formed 1860. Played at Meersbrooke Park, Heeley, Sheffield, near the Red Lion pub

1881-82	1	17.10.81	Lockwood Brothers	H	W	5-1	Whitham 2, Ibbotson, Martin, Wild
	2	26.11.81	Sheffield Club	A	W	4-0	Whitham 3, Swallow
	3		bye				
	4	21.1.82	Sheffield Wednesday	A	L	1-3	
1882-83	1	4.11.82	bye				
	2	2.12.82	Nottingham Forest	A	L	2-7	
1883-84	1	10.11.83	Notts Co	A	L	1-3	Marsden
1884-85	1	8.11.84	Notts Wanderers	H	W	1-0	Stokes
	2	6.12.84	Nottingham Forest	A	L	1-4	Sayer
1885-86	1	19.10.85	Eckington	H	W	2-1	
	2	21.11.85	Notts Rangers	H	L	1-6	
1886-87	1	30.10.86	Grimsby T	H	L	1-4	Jackson
1887-88	1	15.10.87	Attercliffe	H	W	9-0	
	2	5.11.87	Owlerton	A	L	0-1	
1888-89	1	2.2.89	Walsall Town Swifts	A	L	1-5	A.Jackson

SHEFFIELD PROVIDENCE

Formed 1871. Played at Hyde Park, Sheffield

1879-80	1		bye				
	2	15.12.79	Sheffield Club	A	D	3-3	Brownhill, og, 1 other
	2r	29.12.79	Sheffield Club	A	L	0-3	
1880-81	1	30.10.80	Blackburn R	A	L	2-6	Hobson, A Woodcock
1881-82	1	5.11.81	Sheffield W	A	L	0-2	

SHEFFIELD UNITED

Formed 1889. **First entered FA Cup:** 1889. **Best FA Cup Performance: Winners:** 1899, 1902, 1915, 1925. **Runners-up:** 1901, 1936. **Record FA Cup Victory:** In competition proper: 5-0 vs Corinthians, 1st round, 10.1.1925; 5-0 vs Newcastle U, 1st round, 10.1.1914; 5-0 vs Barrow, 3rd round, 7.1.1956. **Record FA Cup Defeat:** 0-13 vs Bolton Wanderers, 2nd round, 1.2.1890

1889-90		1q **Scarborough** (A) 6-1; 2q **Sheffield Heeley** (A) 1-0; 3q **Sheffield Club** (H) 3-0; 4q **Rotherham T** (A) 2-2; 4qr **Rotherham T** (H) 2-1						
		1	18.1.90	Burnley	D1	H	W	2-1	Robertson, T.Wilson
		2	1.2.90	Bolton W	D1	H	L	0-13	
1890-91	ML	1q **Derby Junction** (A) 1-0; 2q **Burton Swifts** (A) 1-2; *Burton disqualified for playing unregistered player;* 3q **Matlock** (H) 3-0;						
		4q **Loughborough** (A) 6-1						
		1	17.1.91	Notts Co	D1	H	L	1-9	Calder
1891-92	NL	2q **Lincoln C** (H) 4-1; 3q **Grimsby T** (A) 2-1; 4q **Gainsborough T** (A) 1-0						
		1	16.1.92	Blackpool	LL	A	W	3-0	Wallace 2, Scott
		2	30.1.92	Wolverhampton W	D1	A	L	1-3	Dobson
1892-93	D2	1	21.1.93	Blackpool	LL	A	W	3-1	Needham 2, Hammond
		2	4.2.93	Sunderland	D1	H	L	1-3	Watson
1893-94	D1	1	27.1.94	Newcastle U	D2	A	L	0-2	
1894-95	D1	1	2.2.95	Millwall Ath	SL	H	W	3-1	Davies, R.Hil, Hammond

Season	Div	Round	Date	Opponent	Opp Div	Venue	Result	Score	Scorers
		2	16.2.95	**WBA**	D1	H	D	1-1	Davies
		2r	20.2.95	**WBA**		A	L	1-2	Watson
1895-96	D1	1	1.2.96	**Burton W**	D2	A	D	1-1	
		1r	6.2.96	**Burton W**		H	W	1-0	Needham
		2	15.2.96	**Everton**	D1	A	L	0-3	
1896-97	D1	1	30.1.97	**Blackburn R**	D1	A	L	1-2	Walls
1897-98	D1	1	29.1.98	**Burslem Port Vale**	ML	H	D	1-1	Needham (p)
		1r	2.2.98	**Burslem Port Vale**		A	L	1-2	Thickett
1898-99	D1	1	28.1.99	**Burnley**	D1	A	D	2-2	Beer 2
		1r	2.2.99	**Burnley**		H	W	2-1	Bennett, Morren
		2	11.2.99	**Preston NE**	D1	A	D	2-2	Bennett, Hedley
		2r	16.2.99	**Preston NE**		H	W	2-1	Needham 2 (1p)
		3	25.2.99	**Nottingham F**	D1	A	W	1-0	Priest
		SF	18.3.99	**Liverpool**	D1		D	2-2	Hedley, Needham
				played at Nottingham Forest					
		SFr	23.3.99	**Liverpool** at Bolton W			D	4-4	Priest 2, Beer, Bennett
		SF 2r	27.3.99	**Liverpool** at Fallowfield			–	0-1	
				abandoned after pitch invasions and encroaching darkness					
		SF 3r	30.3.99	**Liverpool** at Derby Co			W	1-0	Priest
		F	15.4.99	**DERBY CO**	D1		W	4-1	Bennett, Beer, Almond, Priest
				played at Crystal Palace					
1899-00	D1	1	27.1.00	**Leicester F**	D2	H	W	1-0	Bennett
		2	10.2.00	**Sheffield W**	D2	H	D	0-0	
		2r	17.2.00	**Sheffield W**		H	D	1-1	Almond
		2 2r	19.2.00	**Sheffield W**		A	W	2-0	Beer, Needham (p)
		3	24.2.00	**Bury**	D1	H	D	2-2	Priest, Needham (p)
		3r	1.3.00	**Bury**		A	L	0-2	
1900-01	D1	1	9.2.01	**Sunderland**	D1	A	W	2-1	Lipsham, Priest
		2	23.2.01	**Everton**	D1	H	W	2-0	Bennett 2
		3	23.3.01	**Wolverhampton W**	D1	A	W	4-0	Priest, Hedley, Bennett, og
		SF	6.4.01	**Aston Villa**	D1		D	2-2	Lipsham, Priest
				played at Nottingham Forest					
		SFr	11.4.01	**Aston Villa**			W	3-0	Priest 2, Bennett
				played at the Baseball Ground, Derby					
		F	20.4.01	**Tottenham H**	SL		D	2-2	Priest, Bennett
				played at Crystal Palace					
		Fr	27.4.01	**Tottenham H**			L	1-3	Priest
				played at Burnden Park, Bolton					
1901-02	D1	1	25.1.02	**Northampton T**	SL	A	W	2-0	Bennett, Common
		2	8.2.02	**Bolton W**	D1	H	W	2-1	Bennett, Priest
		3	22.2.02	**Newcastle U**	D1	A	D	1-1	Priest
		3r	27.2.02	**Newcastle U**		H	W	2-1	Needham, Common
		SF	15.3.02	**Derby Co**	D1		D	1-1	Hedley
				played at The Hawthorns					
		SFr	20.3.02	**Derby Co**			D	1-1aet	Priest
				played at Molineux					
		SF 2r	27.3.02	**Derby Co**			W	1-0	Priest
				played at Nottingham Forest					
		F	19.4.02	**Southampton**	SL		D	1-1	Common
				played at Crystal Palace					
		F	26.4.02	**SOUTHAMPTON**			W	2-1	Hedley, Barnes
				played at Crystal Palace					
1902-03	D1	1	7.2.03	**W.Arsenal**	D2	A	W	3-1	Hedley, E.Needham, Priest
		2	21.2.03	**Bury**	D1	H	L	0-1	
1903-04	D1	1	6.2.04	**Bristol C**	D2	A	W	3-1	Brown, Priest, Johnson
		2	20.2.04	**Bury**	D1	A	W	2-1	Parker, Bennett
		3	5.3.04	**Bolton W**	D2	H	L	0-2	
1904-05	D1	1	4.2.05	**Nottingham F**	D1	A	L	0-2	
1905-06	D1	1	13.1.06	**Manchester C**	D1	H	W	4-1	Brown 3, Lipsham
		2	3.2.06	**Blackpool**	D2	A	L	1-2	Lipsham
1906-07	D1	1	12.1.07	**Everton**	D1	A	L	0-1	
1907-08	D1	1	11.1.08	**Swindon T**	SL	A	D	0-0	
		1r	16.1.08	**Swindon T**		H	L	2-3	Brown, Lipsham
1908-09	D1	1	16.1.09	**Sunderland**	D1	H	L	2-3	Batty, Hardinge
1909-10	D1	1	15.1.10	**Nottingham F**	D1	A	L	2-3	Benson, Walton
1910-11	D1	1	14.1.11	**Darlington**	NEL	H	L	0-1	
1911-12	D1	1	13.1.12	**Chelsea**	D2	A	L	0-1	

1912-13	D1	1	15.1.13	**Huddersfield T**		A	L	1-3	Gillespie
1913-14	D1	1	10.1.14	**Newcastle U**	D1	A	W	5-0	Simmons 2, Kitchen, Gillespie, Revill
		2	31.1.14	**Bradford PA**	D2	H	W	3-1	Utley 2, Simmons
		3	21.2.14	**Millwall**	SL	A	W	4-0	Utley 2, Kitchen (p), Gillespie
		4	7.3.14	**Manchester C**	D1	A	D	0-0	
		4r	12.3.14	**Manchester C**		H	D	0-0	
		4 2r	16.3.14	**Manchester C** at Villa Park			W	1-0	Simmons
		SF	28.3.14	**Burnley**	D1		D	0-0	
				played at Old Trafford					
		SFr	1.4.14	**Burnley**			L	0-1	
				played at Goodison Park					
1914-15	D1	1	9.1.15	**Blackpool**	D2	A	W	2-1	Masterman 2
		2	30.1.15	**Liverpool**	D1	H	W	1-0	Kitchen
		3	20.2.15	**Bradford PA**	D1	H	W	1-0aet	Kitchen
		4	6.3.15	**Oldham A**	D1	A	D	0-0	
		4r	13.3.15	**Oldham A**		H	W	3-0	Kitchen 2, Fazackerley
		SF	27.3.15	**Bolton W**	D1		W	2-1	Simmons, Utley
				played at Ewood Park					
		F	24.4.15	**CHELSEA**	D1		W	3-0	Simmons, Masterman, Kitchen
				played at Crystal Palace					
1919-20	D1	1	10.1.20	**Southend U**	SL	A	W	3-0	Fazackerley 2 Milton
		2	31.1.20	**Bradford C**	D1	A	L	1-2	Johnson
1920-21	D1	1	8.1.21	**Swindon T**	D3	A	L	0-1	
1921-22	D1	1	7.1.22	**Brighton & HA**	D3	A	L	0-1	
1922-23	D1	1	13.1.23	**Nottingham F**	D1	A	D	0-0	
		1r	18.1.23	**Nottingham F**		H	D	0-0	
		1 2r	22.1.23	**Nottingham F** at Meadow Lane			D	1-1aet	Johnson
		1 3r	25.1.23	**Nottingham F** at Hillsborough			W	1-0	Gillespie
		2	3.2.23	**Middlesbrough**	D1	A	D	1-1	Sampy
		2r	8.2.23	**Middlesbrough**		H	W	3-0	Johnson, Gillespie, Sampy
		3	24.2.23	**Liverpool**	D1	A	W	2-1	Gillespie, Waugh
		4	10.3.23	**QPR**	3S	A	W	1-0	Sampy
		SF	24.3.23	**Bolton W**	D1		L	0-1	
				played at Old Trafford					
1923-24	D1	1	12.1.24	**Blackpool**	D2	A	L	0-1	
1924-25	D1	1	10.1.25	**Corinthians**		H	W	5-0	Johnson 4, Boyle
		2	31.1.25	**Sheffield W**	D2	H	W	3-2	Sampy 2, Green
		3	21.2.25	**Everton**	D1	H	W	1-0	Tunstall
		4	7.3.25	**WBA**	D1	H	W	2-0	Johnson, Tunstall
		SF	28.3.25	**Southampton**	D2		W	2-0	Tunstall, Parker og
				played at Stamford Bridge					
		F	25.4.25	**CARDIFF C**	D1 WEMBLEY		W	1-0	Tunstall
1925-26	D1	3	9.1.26	**Stockport Co**	D2	H	W	2-0	Gillespie, Boyle
		4	30.1.26	**Sunderland**	D1	H	L	1-2	Johnson
1926-27	D1	3	8.1.27	**Arsenal**	D1	H	L	2-3	Johnson, D.Mercer
1927-28	D1	3	14.1.28	**Notts Co**	D2	A	W	3-2	Johnson 2, Tunstall
		4	28.1.28	**Wolverhampton W**	D2	H	W	3-1	Johnson 2, Partridge
		5	18.2.28	**Sheffield W**	D1	A	D	1-1	Partridge
		5r	22.2.28	**Sheffield W**		H	W	4-1	Johnson 3, Partridge (p)
		6	3.3.28	**Nottingham F**	D2	H	W	3-0	Johnson, Gillespie, Partridge
		SF	24.3.28	**Huddersfield T**	D1		D	2-2aet	Johnson 2
				played at Old Trafford					
		SFr	26.3.28	**Huddersfield T**			D	0-0aet	
				played at Goodison Park					
		SF 2r	2.4.28	**Huddersfield T**			L	0-1	
				played at Maine Road					
1928-29	D1	3	12.1.29	**Burnley**	D1	A	L	1-2	Gillespie
1929-30	D1	3	11.1.30	**Leicester C**	D1	H	W	2-1	S.Gibson, Dunne
		4	25.1.30	**Huddersfield T**	D1	A	L	1-2	Dunne
1930-31	D1	3	10.1.31	**York C**	3N	H	D	1-1	S.Gibson
		3r	14.1.31	**York C**		A	W	2-0	S.Gibson, Dunne
		4	24.1.31	**Notts Co**	3S	H	W	4-1	Dunne 3, S.Gibson
		5	14.2.31	**Sunderland**	D1	A	L	1-2	Dunne
1931-32	D1	3	9.1.32	**Corinthians**		H	W	2-1	Dunne 2
		4	23.1.32	**Bury**	D2	A	L	1-3	Pickering
1932-33	D1	3	14.1.33	**Swansea T**	D2	A	W	3-2	Dunne 2, Oswald
		4	28.1.33	**Burnley**	D2	A	L	1-3	Holmes

Season	Div	Rd	Date	Opponent		Venue	Res	Score	Scorers
1933-34	D1	3	13.1.34	Birmingham	D1	A	L	1-2	Boyd
1934-35	D2	3	12.1.35	Southend U	3S	A	W	4-0	Pickering, Barton, Barclay, Pears
		4	26.1.35	WBA	D1	A	L	1-7	Pickering
1935-36	D2	3	11.1.36	Burnley	D2	A	D	0-0	
		3r	16.1.36	Burnley		H	W	2-1	Barton, Barclay
		4	25.1.36	Preston NE	D1	A	D	0-0	
		4r	30.1.36	Preston NE		H	W	2-0	Dodds, Barton
		5	15.2.36	Leeds U	D1	H	W	3-1	Pickering 2, Dodds
		6	29.2.36	Tottenham H	D2	H	W	3-1	Dodds 2, Barclay
		SF	21.3.36	Fulham	D2		W	2-1	Pickering, Bird
				played at Molineux					
		F	25.4.36	ARSENAL	D1	WEMBLEY	L	0-1	
1936-37	D2	3	16.1.37	Nottingham F	D2	A	W	4-2	Dodds 2, Ashton, Pickering
		4	30.1.37	Wolverhampton W	D1	A	D	2-2	Barton, Dodds
		4r	4.2.37	Wolverhampton W		H	L	1-2	Dodds
1937-38	D2	3	8.1.38	Doncaster R	3N	A	W	2-0	Barton, Pickering
		4	22.1.38	Liverpool	D1	H	D	1-1	Dodds
		4r	26.1.38	Liverpool		A	L	0-1	
1938-39	D2	3	7.1.39	Blackpool	D1	A	W	2-1	Hagan, Hooper
		4	21.1.39	Manchester C	D2	H	W	2-0	Pickering, Dodds
		5	11.2.39	Grimsby T	D1	H	D	0-0	
		5r	14.2.39	Grimsby T		A	L	0-1	
1945-46	D1	3 1L	5.1.46	Huddersfield T	D1	A	D	1-1	Jones
		3 2L	7.1.46	Huddersfield T		H	W	2-0	Collindridge, Brook
		4 1L	26.1.46	Stoke C	D1	A	L	0-2	
		4 2L	28.1.46	Stoke C		H	W	3-2	Collindridge 3
1946-47	D1	3	11.1.47	Carlisle U	3N	H	W	3-0	Nightingale, Hagan, Brook
		4	25.1.47	Wolverhampton W	D1	A	D	0-0	
		4r	29.1.47	Wolverhampton W		H	W	2-0	Brook, Nightingale
		5	8.2.47	Stoke C	D1	A	W	1-0	Brook
		6	1.3.47	Newcastle U	D2	H	L	0-2	
1947-48	D1	3	10.1.48	Crewe A	3N	A	L	1-3	Collindridge
1948-49	D1	3	8.1.49	New Brighton	3N	H	W	5-2	Jones 3, Hagan, Warhurst
		4	29.1.49	Wolverhampton W	D1	H	L	0-3	
1949-50	D2	3	7.1.50	Leicester C	D2	H	W	3-1	Thompson, Collindridge, Brook
		4	28.1.50	Wolverhampton W	D1	A	D	0-0	
		4r	1.2.50	Wolverhampton W		H	L	3-4	Brook 3 (1p)
1950-51	D2	3	6.1.51	Gateshead	3N	H	W	1-0	Hagan
		4	27.1.51	Mansfield T	3N	H	D	0-0	
		4r	31.1.51	Mansfield T		A	L	1-2aet	Thompson
1951-52	D2	3	12.1.52	Newport Co	3S	H	W	2-0	Brook, Ringstead
		4	2.2.52	West Ham	D2	A	D	0-0	
		4r	6.2.52	West Ham		H	W	4-2	Hawksworth 2, Ringstead, Browning
		5	23.2.52	Southend U	3S	A	W	2-1	Ringstead, Browning
		6	8.3.52	Chelsea	D1	H	L	0-1	
1952-53	D2	3	10.1.53	Newport Co	3S	A	W	4-1	Bottom 2, Browning, Ringstead
		4	31.1.53	Birmingham C	D2	H	D	1-1	Hagan
		4r	4.2.53	Birmingham C		A	L	1-3	Bannister og
1953-54	D1	3	9.1.54	Sheffield W	D1	A	D	1-1	Toner
		3r	13.1.54	Sheffield W		H	L	1-3	Hawksworth
1954-55	D1	3	8.1.55	Nottingham F	D2	H	L	1-3	Ringstead
1955-56	D1	3	7.1.56	Barrow	3N	H	W	5-0	Hoyland 2, Hawksworth, Grainger, Wragg
		4	28.1.56	Bolton W	D1	A	W	2-1	Wragg 2 (1p)
		5	18.2.56	Sunderland	D1	H	D	0-0	
		5r	22.2.56	Sunderland		A	L	0-1	
1956-57	D2	3	5.1.57	Huddersfield T	D2	A	D	0-0	
		3r	7.1.57	Huddersfield T		H	D	1-1aet	Spencer
		3 2r	14.1.57	Huddersfield T at Maine Road			L	1-2	Johnson
1957-58	D2	3	4.1.58	Grimsby T	D2	H	W	5-1	Lewis 2, Summers, Hawksworth, Howitt
		4	25.1.58	Tottenham H	D1	A	W	3-0	Pace, Russell, Hawksworth
•		5	15.2.58	WBA	D1	H	D	1-1	Lewis
		5r	19.2.58	WBA		A	L	1-4	Dudley og
1958-59	D2	3	10.1.59	Crystal P	D4	H	W	2-0	Russell 2
		4	24.1.59	Worcester C	SL	A	W	2-0	Lewis, Simpson
		5	14.2.59	Arsenal	D1	A	D	2-2	Simpson, Pace
		5r	18.2.59	Arsenal		H	W	3-0	Russell, Pace, Lewis
		6	28.2.59	Norwich C	D3	H	D	1-1	Russell

Season	Div	Round	Date	Opponent		Venue	Result	Score	Scorers
		6r	4.3.59	Norwich C		A	L	2-3	Pace, Summers
1959-60	D2	3	9.1.60	Portsmouth	D2	H	W	3-0	Pace 2, Lewis
		4	30.1.60	Nottingham F	D1	H	W	3-0	Pace 3
		5	20.2.60	Watford	D4	H	W	3-2	Pace 3
		6	12.3.60	Sheffield W	D1	H	L	0-2	
1960-61	D2	3	7.1.61	Everton	D1	A	W	1-0	Russell
		4	28.1.61	Lincoln C	D2	H	W	3-1	Russell 2, Mason
		5	18.2.61	Blackburn R	D1	H	W	2-1	Russell, Hodgson
		6	4.3.61	Newcastle U	D1	A	W	3-1	Russell 3
		SF	18.3.61	Leicester C at Elland Rd	D1		D	0-0	
		SFr	23.3.61	Leicester C at Nottingham	F		D	0-0aet	
		SF 2r	27.3.61	Leicester C at St Andrews			L	0-2	
1961-62	D1	3	6.1.62	Bury	D2	A	D	0-0	
		3r	10.1.62	Bury		H	D	2-2aet	Pace, Allchurch
		3 2r	15.1.62	Bury at Hillsborough			W	2-0	Pace 2
		4	27.1.62	Peterborough	D3	A	W	3-1	Russell 2, Pace
		5	17.2.62	Norwich C	D2	H	W	3-1	Kettleborough, Russell, Pace
		6	10.3.62	Burnley	D1	H	L	0-1	
1962-63	D1	3	6.3.63	Bolton W	D1	H	W	3-1	Kettleborough 2, Summers
		4	13.3.63	Port Vale	D3	A	W	2-1	Allchurch (p), Pace
		5	16.3.63	Southampton	D2	A	L	0-1	
1963-64	D1	3	4.1.64	Lincoln C	D4	A	W	4-0	Jones 2, Wagstaff, Hartle
		4	25.1.64	Swansea T	D2	H	D	1-1	Jones
		4r	28.1.64	Swansea T		A	L	0-4	
1964-65	D1	3	9.1.65	Bristol C	D3	A	D	1-1	Jones
		3r	11.1.65	Bristol C		H	W	3-0	Jones 2, Woodward
		4	30.1.65	A.Villa	D1	H	L	0-2	
1965-66	D1	3	22.1.66	Fulham	D1	H	W	3-1	Birchenall 2, Woodward
		4	12.2.66	Wolverhampton W	D2	A	L	0-3	
1966-67	D1	3	28.1.67	Charlton A	D2	A	W	1-0	Jones
		4	18.2.67	Fulham	D1	A	D	1-1	Jones
		4r	1.3.67	Fulham		H	W	3-1	Punton 2, Jones
		5	11.3.67	Chelsea	D1	A	L	0-2	
1967-68	D1	3	27.1.68	Watford	D3	A	W	1-0	Hill
		4	17.2.68	Blackpool	D2	H	W	2-1	Woodward, Addison
		5	9.3.68	West Ham	D1	A	W	2-1	Cliff 2
		6	30.3.68	Leeds U	D1	A	L	0-1	
1968-69	D2	3	4.1.69	Mansfield T	D3	A	L	1-2	Tudor
1969-70	D2	3	3.1.70	Everton	D1	H	W	2-1	Reece, Addison
		4	24.1.70	Derby C	D1	A	L	0-3	
1970-71	D2	3	2.1.71	Portsmouth	D2	A	L	0-2	
1971-72	D1	3	15.1.72	Cardiff C	D2	H	L	1-3	Mackenzie
1972-73	D1	3	13.1.73	Watford	D3	A	W	1-0	Eddy
		4	3.2.73	Carlisle U	D2	A	L	1-2	Dearden
1973-74	D1	3	5.1.74	Ipswich T	D1	A	L	2-3	Salmons, Currie
1974-75	D1	3	4.1.75	Bristol C	D2	H	W	2-0	Dearden, Currie
		4	25.1.75	Aston Villa	D2	A	L	1-4	Field
1975-76	D1	3	3.1.76	Leicester C	D1	A	L	0-3	
1976-77	D2	3	8.1.77	Newcastle U	D1	H	D	0-0	
		3r	24.1.77	Newcastle U		A	L	1-3	Garner
1977-78	D2	3	7.1.78	Arsenal	D1	H	L	0-5	
1978-79	D2	3	9.1.79	Aldershot	D4	H	D	0-0	
		3r	15.1.79	Aldershot		A	L	0-1	
1979-80	D3	1	24.11.79	Burscough	CC	H	W	3-0	MacPhail, Speight, Matthews
		2	15.12.79	Grimsby T	D3	A	L	0-2	
1980-81	D3	1	22.11.80	Stockport Co	D4	A	D	0-0	
		1r	25.11.80	Stockport Co		H	W	3-2	Charles, Kenworthy, Sherlock og
		2	13.12.80	Chesterfield	D3	H	D	1-1	Hatton
		2r	16.12.80	Chesterfield		A	L	0-1	
1981-82	D4	1	21.11.81	Altrincham	APL	H	D	2-2	Edwards, Hatton
		1r	23.11.81	Altrincham		A	L	0-3	
1982-83	D3	1	20.11.82	Hull C	D4	A	D	1-1	Edwards
		1r	23.11.82	Hull C		H	W	2-0	Morris, Edwards
		2	11.12.82	Boston U	APL	A	D	1-1	Edwards
		2r	14.12.82	Boston U		H	W	5-1	Young 3, Morris, Edwards
		3	8.1.83	Stoke C	D1	H	D	0-0	
		3r	12.1.83	Stoke C		A	L	2-3	Edwards, Morris (p)

SHEFFIELD UNITED

Season	Div	Round	Date	Opponent	Opp Div	Venue	W/D/L	Score	Scorers
1983-84	D3	1	19.11.83	Wrexham	D4	A	W	5-1	Edwards 4, Arnott
		2	10.12.83	Lincoln C	D3	A	D	0-0	
		2r	19.12.83	Lincoln C		H	W	1-0	Stancliffe
		3	7.1.84	Birmingham C	D1	H	D	1-1	Brazil
		3r	10.1.84	Birmingham C		A	L	0-2	
1984-85	D2	3	5.1.85	Watford	D1	A	L	0-5	
1985-86	D2	3	13.1.86	Fulham	D2	H	W	2-0	Morris 2
		4	25.1.86	Derby Co	D3	H	L	0-1	
1986-87	D2	3	10.1.87	Brighton & HA	D2	H	D	0-0	
		3r	21.1.87	Brighton & HA		A	W	2-1	Foley, Withe
		4	9.2.87	West Ham	D1	A	L	0-4	
1987-88	D2	3	9.1.88	Maidstone U	GMVC	H	W	1-0	Dempsey
		4	1.2.88	Portsmouth	D1	A	L	1-2	Philliskirk
1988-89	D3	1	19.11.88	Mansfield T	D3	A	D	1-1	Deane
		1r	22.11.88	Mansfield T		H	W	2-1	Bryson, Kenworthy og
		2	11.12.88	Doncaster R	D4	A	W	3-1	Stancliffe, Duffield, Agana
		3	7.1.89	Huddersfield T	D3	A	W	1-0	Agana
		4	28.1.89	Colchester U	D4	H	D	3-3	Todd, Deane, Bryson
		4r	31.1.89	Colchester U		A	W	2-0	Deane 2
		5	18.2.89	Norwich C	D1	A	L	2-3	Deane, Agana
1989-90	D2	3	6.1.90	Bournemouth	D2	H	W	2-0	Bryson, Agana
		4	27.1.90	Watford	D2	H	D	1-1	Ashby og
		4r	30.1.90	Watford		A	W	2-1	Deane, Stancliffe
		5	18.2.90	Barnsley	D2	H	D	2-2	Bradshaw, Bryson
		5r	21.2.90	Barnsley		A	D	0-0aet	
		5 2r	5.3.90	Barnsley		A	W	1-0aet	Agana (p)
		6	11.4.90	Manchester U	D1	H	L	0-1	
1990-91	D1	3	5.1.91	Luton T	D1	H	L	1-3	Bradhsaw
1991-92	D1	3	4.1.92	Luton T	D1	H	W	4-0	Hodges, Deane, Lake, Whitehouse
		4	26.1.92	Charlton A	D2	A	D	0-0	
		4r	5.2.92	Charlton A		H	W	3-1	Deane, Gayle, Bradshaw
		5	15.2.92	Chelsea	D1	A	L	0-1	
1992-93	PL	3	2.1.93	Burnley	D2	H	D	2-2	Hodges, Beesley
		3r	12.1.93	Burnley		A	W	4-2	Deane 3, Littlejohn
		4	23.1.93	Hartlepool U	D2	H	W	1-0	Cork
		5	14.2.93	Manchester U	PL	H	W	2-1	Hoyland, Hodges
		6	6.3.93	Blackburn R	PL	A	D	0-0	
		6r	16.3.93	Blackburn R		H	D	2-2aet	Ward 2
				Sheffield United won 5-3 on penalties					
		SF	3.4.93	Sheffield W	PL		L	1-2aet	Cork
				played at Wembley					

SHEFFIELD WEDNESDAY

Formed 1867. First entered FA Cup: 1880. **Best FA Cup Performance:** Winners 1896, 1907, 1935. Runners-up 1890, 1966, 1993. **Record FA Cup Win:** 12-0 vs Halliwell, 1st round, 17.1.1891. **Record FA Cup Defeat:** 0-5 vs Wolverhampton W, 3rd round, 2.3.1889; 1-6 vs Blackburn R FA Cup Final, 29.3.1890; 0-5 vs Everton, 3rd round replay, 27.1.1988

Season	Round	Date	Opponent	Venue	W/D/L	Score	Scorers
1880-81	1		bye				
	2	18.12.80	Blackburn R	A	W	4-0	Gregory 3, Winterbottom
	3	8.1.81	Turton	A	W	2-0	Gregory, Rhodes
	4	5.2.81	Darwen	A	L	2-5	Gregory 2
1881-82	1	5.11.81	Sheffield Providence	A	W	2-0	Cawley, Anthony
	2	28.12.81	Staveley	H	D	2-2	Rhodes, Cawley
	2r	7.1.81	Staveley	A	D	0-0	
	2 2r	9.1.81	Staveley	A	W	5-1	Rhodes 4, Cawley
	3		bye				
	4	21.1.82	Sheffield Heeley	H	W	3-1	Rhodes, Cawley, Mosforth
	5	7.2.82	Upton Park	H	W	6-0	Cawley 3, Mosforth 2, Rhodes
	SF	6.3.82	Blackburn R		D	0-0	
			played at Huddersfield				
	SFr	15.3.82	Blackburn R		L	1-5	Suter og
			played at Manchester				
1882-83	1	4.11.82	Spilsby	H	W	12-2	Gregory 5, Cawley 3, Newbould 3, Anthony
	2	2.12.82	Lockwood Bros	A	W	6-0	Gregory 2, Anthony, Newbould, Mosforth, Cawley
	3	6.1.83	Nottingham F	A	D	2-2	Gregory, Harrison
	3r	13.1.83	Nottingham F	H	W	3-2	Harrison 2, Mosforth

	4	12.2.83	Notts Co		H	L	1-4	Bentley
1883-84	1		bye					
	2	1.12.83	Staveley		A	L	1-3	Winterbottom
1884-85	1	8.11.84	Long Eaton Rangers		A	W	1-0	Cawley
	2		bye					
	3	3.1.85	Nottingham F		H	L	1-2	Sayer
1885-86	1	31.10.85	Long Eaton Rangers		A	L	0-2	
1886-87			did not compete					
1887-88	1	15.10.87	Belper		A	W	3-2	Cawley 2, Waller
	2	5.11.87	Long Eaton Rangers		A	W	2-1aet	Mosforth, Waller
	3		bye					
	4	19.12.87	Crusaders		A	W	1-0	Hiller
	5	7.1.88	Nottingham F		A	W	4-2	Ingram 3, Winterbottom
	6	30.1.88	Preston NE		H	L	1-3	Ingram
1888-89	1	2.2.89	Notts R		A	D	1-1	Thompson
	1r	9.2.89	Notts R		H	W	3-0	Dungworth 2, Cawley
	2	16.2.89	Notts Co		H	W	3-2	Ingram, Cawley, Winterbottom
	3	2.3.89	Wolverhampton W	D1	A	L	0-3	
1889-90 FAII	1	20.1.90	Swifts		H	W	6-1	Cawley 2, Mumford 2, Bennett 2
	2	1.2.90	Accrington	D1	H	W	2-1	Cawley, Winterbottom
	3	15.2.90	Notts Co	D1	H	W	5-0	Cawley 2, Ingram, Mumford, og
			FA ordered match to be replayed after protest					
	3r	22.2.90	Notts Co		A	L	2-3	Ingram, Brayshaw
			FA ordered match to be replayed after protest					
	3r	3.3.90	Notts Co at Derby Racecourse Gd			W	2-1	Cawley 2
	SF	8.3.90	Bolton W	D1		W	2-1	Mumford 2
			played at Perry Barr, Birmingham					
	F	29.3.90	Blackburn R	D1		L	1-6	Bennett
			played at Kennington Oval					
1890-91 FAII	1	17.1.91	Halliwell		H	W	12-0	Woodhouse 5, Cawley 2, R.Brandon 2, H.Brandon, Ingram, Mumford
	2	31.1.91	Derby County	D1	A	W	3-2	Hodder, H.Brandon, Winterbottom
	3	14.2.91	WBA	D1	H	L	0-2	
1891-92 FAII	1	23.1.92	Bolton W	D1	H	W	4-1	Spiksley 2, Brown, Richardson
	2	30.1.92	Small Heath		H	W	2-0	Richardson, Thompson
	3	13.2.92	WBA	D1	H	L	1-2	Richardson
1892-93 D1	1	21.1.93	Derby Co	D1	H	W	3-2aet	Spiksley 3
			FA ordered match to be replayed after protests					
	1	28.1.93	Derby Co		A	L	0-1	
			FA ordered match to be replayed after protests					
	1	2.2.93	Derby Co		H	W	4-2	Betts, Spiksley, Woodhouse, Chalmers
	2	4.2.93	Burnley	D1	H	W	1-0	Spiksley
	3	18.2.93	Everton	D1	A	L	0-3	
1893-94 D1	1	27.1.94	W.Arsenal	D2	A	W	2-1	Spiksley 2
	2	10.2.94	Stoke	D1	H	W	1-0	Woolhouse
	3	24.2.94	Aston Villa	D1	H	W	3-2aet	Spiksley 2, Woolhouse
	SF	10.3.94	Bolton W	D1		L	1-2	Woolhouse
			played at Fallowfield					
1894-95 D1	1	2.2.95	Notts Co	D2	H	W	5-1	Brash 2, Davis, Spiksley, Ferrier
	2	16.2.95	Middlesbrough	NL	H	W	6-1	Davis 3, Spiksley 2, Brady
	3	2.3.95	Everton	D1	H	W	2-0	Brady, Ferrier
	SF	16.3.95	WBA	D1		L	0-2	
			played at Derby Cricket Ground					
1895-96 D1	1	1.2.96	Southampton St Marys	SL	A	W	3-2	Brady 2, Davis
	2	15.2.96	Sunderland	D1	H	W	2-1	Bell, Spiksley
	3	29.2.96	Everton	D1	H	W	4-0	Bell 2, Brash 2
	SF	21.3.96	Bolton W	D1		D	1-1	Brash
			played at Goodison Park					
	SFr	26.3.96	Bolton W			W	3-1	Crawshaw, Davis, Spiksley
			played at the Town Ground, Nottingham					
	F	18.4.96	WOLVERHAMPTON W	D1		W	2-1	Spikesley 2
			played at Crystal Palace					
1896-97 D1	1	30.1.97	Nottingham F	D1	H	L	0-1	
1897-98 D1	1	29.1.98	Sunderland	D1	A	W	1-0	Kaye
	2	12.2.98	WBA	D1	A	L	0-1	
1898-99 D1	1	28.1.99	Stoke	D1	H	D	2-2	Earp, Crawshaw
	1r	2.2.99	Stoke		A	L	0-2	

1899-00	D2	1	27.1.00	**Bolton W**	D2	H	W	1-0	Wright
		2	10.2.00	**Sheffield U**	D1	A	D	0-0	
		2r	17.2.00	**Sheffield U**		A	D	1-1	Brash
		2 2r	19.2.00	**Sheffield U**		H	L	0-2	
1900-01	D1	1	9.2.01	**Bury**	D1	H	L	0-1	
1901-02	D1	1	25.1.02	**Sunderland**	D1	A	L	0-1	
1902-03	D1	1	7.2.03	**Blackburn R**	D1	A	D	0-0	
		1r	12.2.03	**Blackburn R**		H	L	0-1	
1903-04	D1	1	6.2.04	**Plymouth A**	SL	A	D	2-2	Wilson 2
		1r	10.2.04	**Plymouth A**		H	W	2-0	Davis, Chapman (p)
		2	20.2.04	**Manchester U**	D2	H	W	6-0	V.S. Simpson 3, Davis 2, G.Simpson
		3	5.3.04	**Tottenham H**	SL	A	D	1-1	Davis
		3r	9.3.04	**Tottenham H**		H	W	2-0	Davis, Chapman
		SF	19.3.04	**Manchester C**	D1		L	0-3	
			played at Goodison Park						
1904-05	D1	1	4.2.05	**Blackburn R**	D1	A	W	2-1	Chapman, Hemmingfield
		2	18.2.05	**Portsmouth**	SL	H	W	2-1	Stewart, Davis
		3	4.3.05	**Preston NE**	D1	A	D	1-1	Wilson
		3r	9.3.05	**Preston NE**		H	W	3-0	G.Simpson, Wilson, Stewart
		SF	25.3.05	**Newcastle U**	D1		L	0-1	
			played at Hyde Road, Manchester						
1905-06	D1	1	13.1.06	**Bristol R**	SL	H	W	1-0	G.Simpson
		2	3.2.06	**Millwall A**	SL	H	D	1-1	Stewart
		2r	8.2.06	**Millwall A**		A	W	3-0	G.Simpson, Chapman, Davis (p)
		3	24.2.06	**Nottingham F**	D1	H	W	4-1	Wilson, G.Simpson, Chapman, Stewart
		4	10.3.06	**Everton**	D1	A	L	3-4	Wilson, Bartlett, Davis (p)
1906-07	D1	1	12.1.07	**Wolverhampton W**	D2	H	W	3-2	Stewart, G.Simpson, Tummon
		2	2.2.07	**Southampton**	SL	A	D	1-1	Wilson
		2r	7.2.07	**Southampton**		H	W	3-1	Wilson, Stewart, Chapman
		3	23.2.07	**Sunderland**	D1	H	D	0-0	
		3r	27.2.07	**Sunderland**		A	W	1-0	G.Simpson
		4	9.3.07	**Liverpool**	D1	H	W	1-0	Chapman
		SF	23.3.07	**W.Arsenal**	D1		W	3-1	Wilson 2, Stewart
			played at St Andrew's						
		F	20.4.07	**EVERTON**	D1		W	2-1	Stewart, G.Simpson
			played at Crystal Palace						
1907-08	D1	1	11.1.08	**Norwich C**	SL	A	L	0-2	
1908-09	D1	1	16.1.09	**Stoke**	BDL	H	W	5-0	Wilson 2, Bradshaw 2, Chapman
		2	6.2.09	**Portsmouth**	SL	A	D	2-2	Tummon 2
		2r	11.2.09	**Portsmouth**		H	W	3-0	Brittleton, Rollinson, Wilson
		3	20.2.09	**Glossop**	D2	H	L	0-1	
1909-10	D1	1	15.1.10	**Northampton T**	SL	A	D	0-0	
		1r	20.1.10	**Northampton T**		H	L	0-1	
1910-11	D1	1	14.1.11	**Coventry C**	SL	H	L	1-2	Wilson
1911-12	D1	1	13.1.12	**Middlesbrough**	D1	A	D	0-0	
		1r	25.1.12	**Middlesbrough**		H	L	1-2	McLean
1912-13	D1	1	16.1.13	**Grimsby T**	D2	H	W	5-1	McLean 4, Brittleton
		2	1.2.13	**Chelsea**	D1	A	D	1-1	McLean
		2r	5.2.13	**Chelsea**		H	W	6-0	McLean 3, Wilson 2, Kirkman
		3	22.2.13	**Bradford PA**	D2	A	L	1-2	Kirkman
1913-14	D1	1	10.1.14	**Notts Co**	D2	H	W	3-2	J.D.Burkinshaw, L.Burkinshaw, Brittleton
		2	31.1.14	**Wolverhampton W**	D2	A	D	1-1	McLean
		2r	4.2.14	**Wolverhampton W**		H	W	1-0	Kirkman
		3	24.2.14	**Brighton & HA**	SL	H	W	3-0	McLean, Gill, J.D.Burkinshaw
		4	7.3.14	**Aston Villa**	D1	H	L	0-1	
1914-15	D1	1	9.1.15	**Manchester U**	D1	H	W	1-0	Wilson
		2	30.1.15	**Wolverhampton W**	D2	H	W	2-0	Robertson, Glennon
		3	20.2.15	**Newcastle U**	D1	H	L	1-2	McLean
1919-20	D1	1	14.1.20	**Darlington**	NEL	A	D	0-0	
		1r	19.1.20	**Darlington**		H	L	0-2	
1920-21	D2	1	8.1.21	**West Ham**	D2	H	W	1-0	Price
		2	29.1.21	**Everton**	D1	A	D	1-1	Taylor
		2r	3.2.21	**Everton**		H	L	0-1	
1921-22	D2	1	7.1.22	**Bradford PA**	D2	A	L	0-1	
1922-23	D2	1	13.1.23	**New Brighton**	LC	H	W	3-0	Binks 2, Smailes
		2	3.2.23	**Barnsley**	D2	H	W	2-1	Smailes, Binks
		3	24.2.23	**Derby Co**	D2	A	L	0-1	

1923-24	D2	1	12.1.24	Leicester C	D2	H	W	4-1	Taylor 2, Binks (p), Petrie
		2	2.2.24	Bristol C	D2	H	D	1-1	Harron
		2r	6.2.24	Bristol C		A	L	0-2	
1924-25	D2	1	10.1.25	Manchester U	D2	H	W	2-0	Hill 2
		2	31.1.25	Sheffield U	D1	A	L	2-3	Trotter 2
1925-26	D2	3	9.1.26	New Brighton	3N	A	L	1-2	Trotter
1926-27	D1	3	8.1.27	Brighton & HA	3S	H	W	2-0	Hill, Trottter
		4	29.1.27	South Shields	D2	H	D	1-1	Trotter
		4r	2.2.27	South Shields		A	L	0-1	
1927-28	D1	3	14.1.28	Bournemouth	3S	H	W	3-0	Harper 2, Seed
		4	28.1.28	Swindon T	3S	A	W	2-1	Seed, Harper
		5	18.2.28	Sheffield U	D1	H	D	1-1	Wilkinson
		5r	22.2.28	Sheffield U		A	L	1-4	Hooper
1928-29	D1	3	12.1.29	Wigan Borough	3N	A	W	3-1	Allen 2, Hooper
		4	26.1.29	Reading	D2	A	L	0-1	
1929-30	D1	3	11.1.30	Burnley	D1	H	W	1-0	Allen
		4	25.1.30	Oldham A	D2	A	W	4-3	Allen 2, Hooper, Seed
		5	15.2.30	Bradford PA	D2	H	W	5-1	Seed, Rimmer, Allen, Hooper, Bentley og
		6	1.3.30	Nottingham F	D1	A	D	2-2	Allen, Rimmer
		6r	5.3.30	Nottingham F		H	W	3-1	Seed, Allen, Burgess
		SF	22.3.30	Huddersfield T	D1		L	1-2	Hooper
			played at Old Trafford						
1930-31	D1	3	10.1.31	Gateshead	3N	A	W	6-2	Rimmer 2, Hooper, Burgess, Allen, Ball
		4	24.1.31	Barnsley	D2	A	L	1-2	Ball
1931-32	D1	3	9.1.32	Tottenham H	D2	A	D	2-2	Burgess, Rimmer
		3r	13.1.32	Tottenham H		H	W	3-1	Millership, Rimmer, Stephenson
		4	23.1.32	Bournemouth	3S	H	W	7-0	Millership 4, Burgess 3
		5	13.2.32	Chelsea	D1	H	D	1-1	Stephenson
		5r	17.2.32	Chelsea		A	L	0-2	
1932-33	D1	3	14.1.33	Chesterfield	D2	H	D	2-2	Ball 2
		3r	18.1.33	Chesterfield		A	L	2-4	Millership, Stephenson
1933-34	D1	3	13.1.34	Rotherham U	3N	A	W	3-0	Dewar, Leach, Hooper
		4	27.1.34	Oldham A	D2	A	D	1-1	Hooper
		4r	31.1.34	Oldham A		H	W	6-1	Dewar 3, Hooper, Rimmer, Burgess
		5	17.2.34	Manchester C	D1	H	D	2-2	Rimmer, Dewar
		5r	21.2.34	Manchester C		A	L	0-2	
1934-35	D1	3	12.1.35	Oldham A	D2	H	W	3-1	Palethorpe, Rimmer, Surtees
		4	26.1.35	Wolverhampton W	D1	A	W	2-1	Palethorpe, Rimmer
		5	16.2.35	Norwich C	D2	A	W	1-0	Rimmer
		6	2.3.35	Arsenal	D1	H	W	2-1	Hooper, Rimmer
		SF	16.3.35	Burnley	D2		W	3-0	Rimmer 2, Palethorpe
			played at Villa Park						
		F	27.4.35	WBA	D1	WEMBLEY	W	4-2	Rimmer 2, Palethorpe, Hooper
1935-36	D1	3	11.1.36	Crewe Alex	3N	A	D	1-1	Surtees
		3r	15.1.36	Crewe Alex		H	W	3-1	Dewar, Rimmer, Surtees
		4	25.1.36	Newcastle U	D2	H	D	1-1	Dewar
		4r	29.1.36	Newcastle U		A	L	1-3	Rimmer
1936-37	D1	3	16.1.37	Port Vale	3N	H	W	2-0	Robinson, Drury
		4	30.1.37	Everton	D1	A	L	0-3	
1937-38	D2	3	8.1.38	Burnley	D2	H	D	1-1	Millership
		3r	11.1.38	Burnley		A	L	1-3	Drury
1938-39	D2	3	7.1.39	Yeovil	SL	H	D	1-1	Robinson
		3r	12.1.39	Yeovil		A	W	2-1	Lewis, Napier
		4	21.1.39	Chester	3N	H	D	1-1	Millership
		4r	25.1.39	Chester		A	D	1-1aet	Robinson
		4 2r	30.1.39	Chester at Maine Road			W	2-0	Robinson, Hunt
		5	11.2.39	Chelsea	D1	A	D	1-1	Robinson
		5r	13.2.39	Chelsea		H	D	0-0aet	
		5 2r	20.2.39	Chelsea at Highbury			L	1-3	Fallon
1945-46	D2	3 1L	5.1.46	Mansfield T	3S	A	D	0-0	
		3 2L	9.1.46	Mansfield T		H	W	5-0	J.Thompson, Ward, Tomlinson, Aveyard, Froggatt
		4 1L	26.1.46	York C	3N	H	W	5-1	Driver 2, J.Thompson, Aveyard, Froggatt
		4 2L	30.1.46	York C		A	W	6-1	Tomlinson 3, Driver, J.Thompson, Froggatt
		5 1L	9.2.46	Stoke C	D1	A	L	0-2	
		5 2L	11.2.46	Stoke C		H	D	0-0	
1946-47	D2	3	11.1.47	Blackpool	D1	H	W	4-1	Froggatt 2, Fox, Hunt
		4	25.1.47	Everton	D1	H	W	2-1	Froggatt, Tomlinson

	5	20.2.47	Preston NE	D1	H	L	0-2	
1947-48 D2	3	10.1.48	Cardiff C	D2	A	W	2-1	Lowes, Quigley (p)
	4	24.1.48	Leicester C	D2	A	L	1-2	Lowes
1948-49 D2	3	8.1.49	Southampton	D2	H	W	2-1	Dailey, Quigley
	4	29.1.49	Portsmouth	D1	A	L	1-2	Quigley
1949-50 D2	3	7.1.50	Arsenal	D1	A	L	0-1	
1950-51 D1	3	6.1.51	Fulham	D1	A	L	0-1	
1951-52 D2	3	12.1.52	Bradford PA	3N	A	L	1-2	Dooley
1952-53 D1	3	10.1.53	Blackpool	D1	H	L	1-2	Sewell
1953-54 D1	3	9.1.54	Sheffield U	D1	H	D	1-1	Shaw
	3r	13.1.54	Sheffield U		A	W	3-1	Finney, Davies, Sewell
	4	30.1.54	Chesterfield	3N	A	D	0-0	
	4r	3.2.54	Chesterfield		A	W	4-2	Shaw 2, Sewell, Woodhead
	5	20.2.54	Everton	D2	H	W	3-1	Shaw, Sewell, Woodhead
	6	13.3.54	Bolton W	D1	H	D	1-1	Woodhead
	6r	17.3.54	Bolton W		A	W	2-0	Sewell, Shaw
	SF	27.3.54	Preston NE	D1		L	0-2	
		played at Maine Road						
1954-55 D1	3	8.1.55	Hastings U	SL	H	W	2-1	Shaw, Greensmith
	4	29.1.55	Notts Co	D2	H	D	1-1	Watson
	4r	3.2.55	Notts Co		A	L	0-1aet	
1955-56 D2	3	7.1.56	Newcastle U	D1	H	L	1-3	Gibson
1956-57 D1	3	5.1.57	Preston NE	D1	A	D	0-0	
	3r	9.1.57	Preston NE		H	D	2-2aet	Quixall, Shiner
	3 2r	14.1.57	Preston NE at Goodison Park			L	1-5	Quixall
1957-58 D1	3	4.1.58	Hereford U	SL	A	W	3-0	Froggatt 2, Shiner
	4	29.1.58	Hull C	3N	H	W	4-3	Froggatt, Shiner, Wilkinson, Davison og
	5	19.2.58	Manchester U	D1	A	L	0-3	
1958-59 D2	3	19.1.59	WBA	D1	H	L	0-2	
1959-60 D1	3	9.1.60	Middlesbrough	D2	H	W	2-1	Ellis, McAnearney (p)
	4	30.1.60	Peterborough U	ML	H	W	2-0	Craig 2
	5	20.2.60	Manchester U	D1	A	W	1-0	McAnearney (p)
	6	12.3.60	Sheffield U	D2	A	W	2-0	Wilkinson 2
	SF	26.3.60	Blackburn R	D1		L	1-2	Fantham
		played at Maine Road						
1960-61 D1	3	7.1.61	Leeds U	D2	H	W	2-0	Quinn, Ellis
	4	28.1.61	Manchester U	D1	H	D	1-1	Wilkinson
	4r	1.2.61	Manchester U		A	W	7-2	Ellis 3, Fantham 2, Finney 2
	5	18.2.61	Leyton O	D2	A	W	2-0	Fantham, Ellis
	6	4.3.61	Burnley	D1	H	D	0-0	
	6r	7.3.61	Burnley		A	L	0-2	
1961-62 D1	3	9.1.62	Swansea T	D2	H	W	1-0	Finney
	4	27.1.62	Nottingham F	D1	A	W	2-0	Craig, Ellis
	5	17.2.62	Manchester U	D1	A	D	0-0	
	5r	21.2.62	Manchester U		H	L	0-2	
1962-63 D1	3	21.2.63	Shrewsbury T	D3	A	D	1-1	Layne
	3r	7.3.63	Shrewsbury T		H	W	2-1aet	Finney, Fantham
	4	12.3.63	Arsenal	D1	A	L	0-2	
1963-64 D1	3	4.1.64	Newport Co	D4	A	L	2-3	Holliday, Finney
1964-65 D1	3	9.1.65	Everton	D1	A	D	2-2	Fantham, Quinn
	3r	13.1.65	Everton		H	L	0-3	
1965-66 D1	3	22.1.66	Reading	D3	A	W	3-2	Fantham 2, McCalliog
	4	12.2.66	Newcastle U	D1	A	W	2-1	Dobson, Mcgrath og
	5	5.3.66	Huddersfield T	D2	A	W	2-1	Ford, Usher
	6	26.3.66	Blackburn R	D1	A	W	2-1	Ford 2
	SF	23.4.66	Chelsea	D1		W	2-0	Pugh, McCalliog
		played at Villa Park						
	F	14.5.66	Everton	D1 WEMBLEY		L	2-3	McCalliog, Ford
1966-67 D1	3	28.1.67	QPR	D3	H	W	3-0	Ritchie 3
	4	18.2.67	Mansfield T	D3	H	W	4-0	Ritchie 2 Fantham, McCalliog
	5	11.3.67	Norwich C	D2	A	W	3-1	Quinn, Ford, Fantham
	6	8.4.67	Chelsea	D1	A	L	0-1	
1967-68 D1	3	27.1.68	Plymouth A	D2	H	W	3-0	Whitham, Fantham, Ritchie (p)
	4	17.2.68	Swindon T	D3	H	W	2-1	Smith, Ritchie
	5	9.3.68	Chelsea	D1	H	D	2-2	Ritchie, Megson
	5r	12.3.68	Chelsea		A	L	0-2	
1968-69 D1	3	4.1.69	Leeds U	D1	H	D	1-1	Ritchie

		3r	8.1.69	**Leeds U**		A	W	3-1	Woodall 2, Ritchie
		4	25.1.69	**Birmingham C**	D2	H	D	2-2	McCalliog, Young
		4r	28.1.69	**Birmingham C**		A	L	1-2	Young
1969-70	D1	3	3.1.70	**WBA**	D1	H	W	2-1	Whitham 2
		4	24.1.70	**Scunthorpe U**	D4	H	L	1-2	Whitham
1970-71	D2	3	2.1.71	**Tottenham H**	D1	A	L	1-4	Sunley
1971-72	D2	3	15.1.72	**Sunderland**	D2	A	L	0-3	
1972-73	D2	3	13.1.73	**Fulham**	D2	H	W	2-0	Prendergast, Joicey
		4	3.2.73	**Crystal P**	D1	H	D	1-1	Craig (p)
		4r	6.2.73	**Crystal P**		A	D	1-1aet	Sunley
		4 2r	19.2.73	**Crystal P** at Villa Park			W	3-2	Joicey 3
		5	24.2.73	**Chelsea**	D1	H	L	1-2	Coyle
1973-74	D2	3	5.1.74	**Coventry C**	D1	H	D	0-0	
		3r	8.1.74	**Coventry C**		A	L	1-3	Sunley
1974-75	D2	3	4.1.75	**Chelsea**	D1	A	L	2-3	Thompson (p) Shaw
1975-76	D3	1	22.11.75	**Macclesfield T**	NPL	H	W	3-1	Prendergast, Knighton, Proudlove
		2	13.12.75	**Wigan A**	NPL	H	W	2-0	Sunley, Nimmo
		3	3.1.76	**Charlton A**	D2	A	L	1-2	Sunley
1976-77	D3	1	20.11.76	**Stockort Co**	D4	H	W	2-0	Tynan, Wylde
		2	15.12.76	**Darlington**	D4	A	L	0-1	
1977-78	D3	1	26.11.77	**Bury**	D3	H	W	1-0	Hope
		2	17.12.77	**Wigan A**	NPL	A	L	0-1	
1978-79	D3	1	25.11.78	**Scunthorpe U**	D4	A	D	1-1	Nimmo
		1r	28.11.78	**Scunthorpe U**		H	W	1-0	Nimmo
		2	16.12.78	**Tranmere R**	D3	A	D	1-1	Leman
		2r	19.12.78	**Tranmere R**		H	W	4-0	Wylde 2, Lowey, Hornsby (p)
		3	6.1.79	**Arsenal**	D1	H	D	1-1	Johnson
		3r	9.1.79	**Arsenal**		A	D	1-1aet	Wylde
		3 2r	15.1.79	**Arsenal** at Filbert St			D	2-2aet	Hornsby 2 (1p)
		3 3r	17.1.79	**Arsenal** at Filbert St			D	3-3aet	Rushbury, Lowey, Hornsby (p)
		3 4r	22.1.79	**Arsenal** at Filbert St			L	0-2	
1979-80	D3	1	24.11.79	**Lincoln C**	D4	H	W	3-0	Smith (p), McCulloch, King
		2	15.12.79	**Carlisle U**	D3	A	L	0-3	
1980-81	D2	3	3.1.81	**Newcastle U**	D2	A	L	1-2	Pearson
1981-82	D2	3	2.1.82	**Coventry C**	D1	A	L	1-3	McCulloch
1982-83	D2	3	8.1.83	**Southend U**	D3	A	D	0-0	
		3r	11.1.83	**Southend U**		H	D	2-2aet	Smith, Megson
		3 2r	24.1.83	**Southend U**		H	W	2-1	Taylor 2
		4	29.1.83	**Torquay U**	D4	A	W	3-2	Sterland, Lyons, Megson
		5	19.2.83	**Cambridge U**	D2	A	W	2-1	Megson 2
		6	12.3.83	**Burnley**	D2	A	D	1-1	Bannister
		6r	16.3.83	**Burnley**		H	W	5-0	Shelton 2, McCulloch 2, Megson
		SF	16.4.83	**Brighton & HA**	D1		L	1-2	Mirocevic
			played at Highbury						
1983-84	D2	3	7.1.84	**Barnsley**	D2	H	W	1-0	Pearson
		4	30.1.84	**Coventry C**	D1	H	W	3-2	Sterland (p), Bannister, Shirtliff
		5	18.2.84	**Oxford U**	D3	A	W	3-0	Bannister 2, Varadi
		6	11.3.84	**Southampton**	D1	H	D	0-0	
		6r	20.3.84	**Southampton**		A	L	1-5	Shirtliff
1984-85	D1	3	5.1.85	**Fulham**	D2	A	W	3-2	Chapman 2, Sterland
		4	26.1.85	**Oldham A**	D2	H	W	5-1	Varadi 3, Chapman, Marwood
		5	4.3.85	**Ipswich T**	D1	A	L	2-3	Lyons, Varadi
1985-86	D1	3	13.1.86	**WBA**	D1	H	D	2-2	Sterland, Smith
		3r	16.1.86	**WBA**		A	W	3-2	Marwood, Chapman, Chamberlain
		4	25.1.86	**Orient**	D4	H	W	5-0	Sterland, Marwood, Blair, Thompson, Chapman
		5	26.2.86	**Derby Co**	D3	A	D	1-1	Christie og
		5r	5.3.86	**Derby Co**		H	W	2-0	Shutt 2
		6	12.3.86	**West Ham**	D1	H	W	2-1	Worthington, Shutt
		SF	5.4.86	**Everton**	D1		L	1-2	Shutt
			played at Villa Park						
1986-87	D1	3	26.1.87	**Derby Co**	D2	H	W	1-0	Bradshaw
		4	31.1.87	**Chester C**	D3	A	D	1-1	Chapman
		4r	4.2.87	**Chester C**		H	W	3-1	Chapman, Bradshaw, Abel og
		5	21.2.87	**West Ham**	D1	H	D	1-1	Shelton
		5r	25.2.87	**West Ham**		A	W	2-0	Chapman, Bradshaw
		6	14.3.87	**Coventry C**	D1	H	L	1-3	Megson
1987-88	D1	3	9.1.88	**Everton**	D1	H	D	1-1	West

SHEFFIELD WEDNESDAY

	3r	13.1.88	Everton		A	D	1-1aet	Chapman
	3 2r	25.1.88	Everton		A	D	1-1aet	Chapman
	3 3r	27.1.88	Everton		H	L	0-5	
1988-89 D1	3	7.1.89	Torquay U	D1	H	W	5-1	Jonsson, Hodgson, Varadi 2, Proctor
	4	28.1.89	Blackburn R	D2	A	L	1-2	Hirst
1989-90 D1	3	6.1.90	Wolverhampton W	D2	A	W	2-1	Shirtliff, Atkinson
	4	28.1.90	Everton	D1	H	L	1-2	Hirst
1990-91 D2	3	5.1.91	Mansfield T	D3	A	W	2-0	Shirtliff, Sheridan (p)
	4	26.1.91	Millwall	D2	A	D	4-4	Hirst, Francis, Pearson, Palmer
	4r	30.1.91	Millwall		H	W	2-0	Anderson, Hirst
	5	16.2.91	Cambridge U	D3	A	L	0-4	
1991-92 D1	3	4.1.92	Preston NE	D3	A	W	2-0	Sheridan, Bart-Williams
	4	4.2.92	Middlesbrough	D2	H	L	1-2	Hirst
1992-93 PL	3	13.1.93	Cambridge U	D1	A	W	2-1	Harkes, Bright
	4	24.1.93	Sunderland	D1	H	W	1-0	Bright
	5	13.2.93	Southend U	D1	H	W	2-0	Warhurst 2
	6	8.3.93	Derby Co	D1	A	D	3-3	Sheridan (p), Warhurst 2
	6r	17.3.93	Derby Co		H	W	1-0	Warhurst
	SF	3.4.93	Sheffield U	PL		W	2-1aet	Waddle, Bright
	F	15.5.93	Arsenal	PL WEMBLEY		D	1-1aet	Hirst
	Fr	20.5.93	Arsenal		WEMBLEY	L	1-2aet	Waddle

SHEPSHED ALBION

Formed 1890 as Shepshed Albion. Known as Shepshed Charterhouse 1975-1991. 1991 Shepshed Albion

1982-83	NCoE 1		20.11.82	Preston NE	D3	A	L	1-5	Jenas

SHILDON

Formed 1890. **First entered FA Cup:** 1898

1927-28	NEL 1		26.11.27	New Brighton	3N	H	L	1-3	Brown
1929-30	NEL 1		30.11.29	Doncaster R	3N	A	D	0-0	
		1r	4.12.29	Doncaster R		H	D	1-1aet	Trotter
		1 2r	9.12.29	Doncaster R at York			L	0-3	
1934-35	NL 1		24.11.34	Lincoln C	3N	H	D	2-2	Oliver 2
		1r	28.11.34	Lincoln C		A	L	0-4	
1936-37	NL 1		28.11.36	Stalybridge C	CC	H	W	4-2	Downing, Charlton 3
		2	12.12.36	Dartford	SL	H	L	0-3	
1955-56	NL 1		19.11.55	Scunthorpe U	3N	A	L	0-3	
1959-60	NL 1		14.11.59	Oldham A	D4	H	D	1-1	Bell
		1r	17.11.59	Oldham A		A	L	0-3	
1961-62	NL 1		4.11.61	Oldham A	D4	A	L	2-5	Sinclair, Armstrong

SHIREBROOK

Formed 1926. Nottinghamshire-based mining club. Disbanded 1939, reformed late 1940s until 1954

1927-28	ML 1		26.11.27	Tranmere R	3N	H	L	1-3	Miller
1928-29	ML 1		24.11.28	Mansfield T	ML	H	L	2-4	Bramley, Parker

SHREWSBURY TOWN

Formed 1886. **First entered FA Cup:** 1887. **Best FA Cup Performance:** 6th round, 1979, 1982. **Record FA Cup Win:** 12-0 vs Cannock T, Extra Pr rd, 7.9.1929. In competition proper: 7-1 vs Banbury Spencer, 1st round, 4.11.1961. **Record FA Cup Defeat:** 2-10 vs Chirk, 2nd round, 5.11.1887. Welsh FA Cup Winners: 6 times, runners-up three times

1887-88		1	15.10.87	Macclesfield		A	W	3-1	Pearson 3
		2	5.11.87	Chirk		A	L	2-10	Watkins, 1 other
1909-10	BDL	1	15.1.10	Portsmouth	SL	A	L	0-3	
1945-46	ML	1 1L	17.11.45	Walsall	3S	H	W	5-0	Maund 3, Bailey, Nicholls
		1 2L	24.11.45	Walsall		A	L	1-4	Nicholls
		2 1L	8.12.45	Wrexham	3N	H	L	0-1	
		2 2L	15.12.45	Wrexham		A	D	1-1	Jones
1947-48	ML	1	29.11.47	Gt Yarmouth T	ECL	A	W	4-1	Davie 2, Mulvaney 2
		2	13.12.47	Stockport Co	3N	A	–	1-1	Davie
			abandoned after 110 minutes						

		2	20.12.47	Stockport Co		A	D	2-2aet	Sheen, Argue
		2r	22.12.47	Stockport Co at Maine Road		L	2-3		Phillips, Butler
1950-51	3N			*withdrew, rather than play in the qualifying rounds following their election to the Football League*					
1951-52	3S	1	24.11.51	Leytonstone	IL	A	L	0-2	
1952-53	3S	1	22.11.52	QPR	3S	A	D	2-2	Brown, Butler
		1r	27.11.52	QPR		H	D	2-2aet	Jackson, Reagan
		1 2r	1.12.52	QPR at Villa Park			W	4-1	Brown, Jackson, Butler, Fisher
		2	6.12.52	Chesterfield	3N	H	D	0-0	
		2r	10.12.52	Chesterfield		A	W	4-1	Brown 2, Fisher, Reagan
		3	10.1.53	Finchley	AL	H	W	2-0	Roberts 2
		4	31.1.53	Southampton	D2	H	L	1-4	Jackson
1953-54	3S	1	21.11.53	QPR	3S	A	L	0-2	
1954-55	3S	1	20.11.54	Walsall	3S	A	L	2-5	Brennan, O'Donnell
1955-56	3S	1	19.11.55	Gillingham	3S	A	D	1-1	Russell
		1r	24.11.55	Gillingham		H	W	4-1aet	McCue 2, Price, Arnott
		2	10.12.55	Torquay U	3S	H	D	0-0	
		2r	14.12.55	Torquay U		A	L	1-5	O'Donnell
1956-57	3S	1	17.11.56	Weymouth	SL	A	L	0-1	
1957-58	3S	1	16.11.57	Port Vale	3S	A	L	1-2	Smith
1958-59	D4	1	15.11.58	Newport (IOW)	Hants	A	D	0-0	
		1r	20.11.58	Newport (IOW)		H	W	5-0	Russell 2, Edgley, Walter, Whitaker
		2	6.12.58	Crystal P	D4	A	D	2-2	Russell 2
		2r	11.12.58	Crystal P		H	D	2-2aet	Skeech (p), Rowley
		2 2r	15.12.58	Crystal P at Molineux			L	1-4	Russell
1959-60	D3	1	14.11.59	Peterborough	ML	A	L	3-4	Starkey 2, Rowley
1960-61	D3	1	5.11.60	Newport Co	D3	H	W	4-1	McLaughlin 2, Riggs og, Rowley
		2	26.11.60	Swindon T	D3	A	W	1-0	Rowley
		3	7.1.61	Aldershot	D4	A	D	1-1	Starkey
		3r	11.1.61	Aldershot		H	D	2-2aet	McLaughlin, Starkey
		3 2r	16.1.61	Aldershot at Villa Park			L	0-2	
1961-62	D3	1	4.11.61	Banbury Spencer	BDL	H	W	7-1	McLaughlin 2, Kenning 2, Rowley 2, Starkey
		2	25.11.61	Brierley Hill All.	BDL	H	W	3-0	Hines 2, McLaughlin
		3	9.1.62	Southport	D4	A	W	3-1	Rowley, Hines, McLaughlin
		4	27.1.62	Middlesbrough	D2	H	D	2-2	Rowley, Kenning
		4r	31.1.62	Middlesbrough		A	L	1-5	Rowley
1962-63	D3	1	3.11.62	Chelmsford C	SL	A	W	6-2	Rowley, McLaughlin 4, Clarke
		2	24.11.62	Torquay U	D4	H	W	2-1	Middleton 2
		3	21.2.63	Sheffield W	D1	H	D	1-1	Harley
		3r	7.3.63	Sheffield W		A	L	1-2aet	Rowley
1963-64	D3	1	16.11.63	Exeter C	D4	A	L	1-2	Middleton
1964-65	D3	1	14.11.64	Kings Lynn	SL	A	W	1-0	Regan
		2	5.12.64	Exeter C	D3	A	W	2-1	Regan 2
		3	9.1.65	Manchester C	D2	A	D	1-1	Ross
		3r	13.1.65	Manchester C		H	W	3-1	Dolby, Meredith, Regan
		4	30.1.65	Millwall	D4	A	W	2-1	Boardman, Meredith
		5	20.2.65	Leeds U	D1	A	L	0-2	
1965-66	D3	1	13.11.65	Torquay U	D4	H	W	2-1	Clarke 2, Broadbent
		2	4.12.65	Peterborough U	D3	H	W	3-2	Meredith 2 (1p), Clarke
		3	22.1.66	QPR	D3	A	D	0-0	
		3r	26.1.66	QPR		H	W	1-0	Meredith
		4	12.2.66	Carlisle U	D2	H	D	0-0	
		4r	15.2.66	Carlisle U		A	D	1-1aet	Ross
		4 2r	21.2.66	Carlisle U at Preston			W	4-3aet	Broadie, Broadbent, Clarke, Boardman
		5	5.3.66	Chelsea	D1	A	L	2-3	Broadbent, Clarke
1966-67	D3	1	26.11.66	Hartlepools U	D4	H	W	5-2	Clarke, Manning 2, Turner 2
		2	7.1.67	Wrexham	D4	H	W	5-1	Boardman 3, Meredith, Manning
		3	28.1.67	Ipswich T	D2	A	L	1-4	Meredith
1967-68	D3	1	13.12.67	Darlington	D4	H	W	3-0	Clarke 2, Boardman
		2	15.1.68	Tow Law Town	NL	A	D	1-1	Clarke
		2r	18.1.68	Tow Law Town		H	W	6-2	Brodie 3, Boardman, Dolby (p), McLaughlin
		3	27.1.68	Arsenal	D1	H	D	1-1	Dolby
		3r	17.2.68	Arsenal		A	L	0-2	
1968-69	D3	1	16.11.69	Port Vale	D4	H	D	1-1	Wood
		1r	18.11.69	Port Vale		A	L	1-3	Wood
1969-70	D3	1	15.11.69	Yeovil T	SL	A	W	3-2	McLaughlin, Jones og, R.Moir
		2	6.12.69	Mansfield T	D3	H	L	1-2	R.Moir
1970-71	D3	1	21.11.70	Minehead	WL	A	W	2-1	R.Moir, Andrews

Season	Div	Round	Date	Opponent	Opp Div	Venue	Result	Score	Scorers
		2	12.12.70	Reading	D3	H	D	2-2	Andrews, Clapham (p)
		2r	21.12.70	Reading		A	L	0-1	
1971-72	D3	1	20.11.71	Colchester U	D4	A	W	4-1	Andrews 3, Wood
		2	11.12.71	Guildford C	SL	H	W	2-1	Wood, R.Moir
		3	15.1.72	Derby Co	D1	A	L	0-2	
1972-73	D3	1	18.11.72	Spennymoor U	NL	A	D	1-1	Dolby
		1r	21.11.72	Spennymoor U		H	W	3-1	R.Moir, Andrews 2
		2	9.12.72	Bolton W	D3	A	L	0-3	
1973-74	D3	1	24.11.73	Wrexham	D3	A	D	1-1	Marlowe
		1r	27.11.73	Wrexham		H	L	0-1	
1974-75	D4	1	23.11.74	Wigan A	NPL	H	D	1-1	Kearney
		1r	25.11.74	Wigan A		A	L	1-2	Haywood
1975-76	D3	1	22.11.75	Rossendale U	CC	A	W	1-0	Bates
		2	13.12.75	Chester	D3	H	W	3-1	Bates 2, Durban
		3	3.1.76	Bradford C	D4	H	L	1-2	Kearney
1976-77	D3	1	20.11.76	Doncaster R	D4	A	D	2-2	Atkins, Maguire
		1r	23.11.76	Doncaster R		H	W	4-3	Maguire 3, Bates
		2	14.12.76	Bury	D3	A	D	0-0	
		2r	21.12.76	Bury		H	W	2-1	Irvine, Turner
		3	8.1.77	QPR	D1	A	L	1-2	Bates
1977-78	D3	1	26.11.77	Doncaster R	D4	A	W	1-0	Nixon
		2	17.12.77	Stockport Co	D4	H	D	1-1	Maguire
		2r	19.12.77	Stockport Co		A	W	2-1	Maguire, Lindsay
		3	7.1.78	Blackburn R	D2	A	L	1-2	Hornsby
1978-79	D3	1	25.11.78	Mansfield T	D3	A	W	2-0	Atkins, Biggins
		2	16.12.78	Doncaster R	D4	A	W	3-0	Chapman, Maguire 2
		3	6.1.79	Cambridge U	D2	H	W	3-1	Maguire, Turner, Chapman
		4	27.1.79	Manchester C	D1	H	W	2-0	Maguire, Chapman
		5	20.2.79	Aldershot	D4	A	D	2-2	Maguire, Tong
		5r	26.2.79	Aldershot		H	W	3-1aet	Biggins 2, Leonard
		6	10.3.79	Wolverhampton W	D1	A	D	1-1	Atkins (p)
		6r	13.3.79	Wolverhampton W		H	L	1-3	Keay
1979-80	D2	3	5.1.80	Millwall	D3	A	L	1-5	Maguire
1980-81	D2	3	3.1.81	Huddersfield T	D3	A	W	3-0	Topping og, Cross, Bates
		4	24.1.81	Ipswich T	D1	H	D	0-0	
		4r	27.1.81	Ipswich T		A	L	0-3	
1981-82	D2	3	5.1.82	Port Vale	D4	H	W	1-0	Bates
		4	23.1.82	Burnley	D3	H	W	1-0	Bates
		5	13.2.82	Ipswich T	D1	H	W	2-1	Cross, King
		6	6.3.82	Leicester C	D2	A	L	2-5	Bates, Keay
1982-83	D2	3	8.1.83	Rotherham U	D2	H	W	2-1	Brown 2
		4	30.1.83	Everton	D1	A	L	1-2	Cross
1983-84	D2	3	7.1.84	Oldham A	D2	H	W	3-0	Stevens, MacLaren (p), Robinson
		4	28.1.84	Ipswich T	D1	H	W	2-0	Hackett, Robinson
		5	18.2.84	Everton	D1	A	L	0-3	
1984-85	D2	3	5.1.85	Oxford U	D2	H	L	0-2	
1985-86	D2	3	4.1.86	Chelsea	D1	H	L	0-1	
1986-87	D2	3	31.1.87	Hull C	D2	H	L	1-2	Waller
1987-88	D2	3	9.1.88	Bristol R	D3	H	W	2-1	Moyes, B.Williams
		4	30.1.88	Plymouth A	D2	A	L	0-1	
1988-89	D2	3	7.1.89	Colchester U	D4	H	L	0-3	
1989-90	D3	1	18.11.89	Chesterfield	D4	H	L	2-3	McGinlay 2 (2ps)
1990-91	D3	1	17.11.90	Bradford C	D3	A	D	0-0	
		1r	21.11.90	Bradford C		H	W	2-1	Shaw 2
		2	11.12.90	Chorley	NPL	H	W	1-0	Spink
		3	5.1.91	Watford	D2	H	W	4-1	Brown, Kelly (p), Shaw 2
		4	26.1.91	Wimbledon	D1	H	W	1-0	Shaw
		5	27.2.91	Arsenal	D1	H	L	0-1	
1991-92	D3	1	16.11.91	Hartlepool U	D3	A	L	2-3	Lyne, Smith
1992-93	D3	1	14.11.92	Mansfield T	D2	H	W	3-1	Summerfield, Lyne, Williams
		2	5.12.92	Burnley	D2	A	D	1-1	Griffiths
		2r	15.12.92	Burnley		H	L	1-2	Griffiths

SHROPSHIRE WANDERERS

First entered FA Cup: 1873. Their match against Sheffield on November 17, 1873 was the only one in the history of the FA Cup to be decided by the toss of a coin.

1873-74	1	30.10.73	Sheffield Club		A	D	0-0	
	1r	17.11.73	Sheffield Club		H	D	0-0	
			Sheffield won on toss of coin					
1874-75	1		Sheffield Club			*walkover*		
	2	14.11.74	Civil Service		H	W	1-0	
	3	23.1.75	Woodford Wells			D	1-1aet	Fletcher
	3r	6.2.75	Woodford Wells			W	2-0	Randall, Fraser
	SF	27.2.75	Old Etonians at Kennington Oval			L	0-1	
1875-76	1		Sheffield Club			*scratched*		
1876-77	1		Druids			*walkover*		
	2	9.12.76	Royal Engineers		A	L	0-3	
1877-78	1	12.11.77	Druids		A	L	0-1	

SITTINGBOURNE

Formed 1881. **First entered FA Cup:** 1923

1925-26	KL	1	28.11.25	Chatham	KL	A	W	3-0	Waterall, Dowell, Thompson,
		2	12.12.25	Swindon T	3S	A	L	0-7	
1926-27	KL	1	27.11.26	Northfleet U	KL	H	L	1-3	McEly
1928-29	SL	1	24.11.28	Southall	AL	H	W	2-1	H.Wiles 2
		2	8.12.28	Walsall	3S	A	L	1-2	H.Wiles
1930-31	KL	1	29.11.30	Folkestone	SL	A	L	3-5	Handley 2, Dickie
1962-63	SL	1	3.11.62	Hinckley	SL	A	L	0-3	

SKEGNESS TOWN

Formed 1947. **First entered FA Cup:** 1948

| 1955-56 | Lincs | 1 | 19.11.55 | Worksop | ML | H | L | 0-4 | |

SKELMERSDALE UNITED

Formed 1882. **First entered FA Cup:** 1905. **FA Amateur Cup Winners:** 1971. **Runners-up:** 1967

1967-68	LC	1	9.12.67	Scunthorpe U	D3	A	L	0-2	
1968-69	CC	1	16.11.68	Chesterfield	D4	A	L	0-2	
1971-72	NPL	1	20.11.71	Tranmere R	D3	H	L	0-4	

SLOUGH TOWN

Formed 1890. **First entered FA Cup:** 1914. FA Amateur Cup: Runners-up 1973. **Cup Final Connection:** Eric Young, who played for Wimbledon when they won the 1988 FA Cup Final is a former Slough player.

as Slough United

1945-46	CRN	1 1L	17.11.45	Bromley	AL	A	–	1-2	Clarke
				match abandoned after 80 minutes					
		1 1L	21.11.45	Bromley		A	L	1-6	Clarke
		1 2L	24.11.45	Bromley		H	W	1-0	Brown

as Slough Town

1970-71	AL	1	21.11.70	Wycombe W	IL	A	D	1-1	Hobbis
		1r	24.11.70	Wycombe W		H	W	1-0	Adams (p)
		2	12.12.70	Barnet	SL	H	L	0-1	
1973-74	IL	1	24.11.73	Reading	D4	A	L	0-4	
1974-75	IL	1	23.11.74	Brentford	D4	H	L	1-4	Chatterton
1979-80	IL	1	24.11.79	Hungerford T	IL	H	W	3-1	Turl, Feely, Russell
		2	15.12.79	Yeovil T	APL	A	L	0-1	
1982-83	IL	1	20.11.82	Millwall	D3	H	W	1-0	Attrell
		2	11.12.82	Bishop's Stortford	IL	H	L	1-4	Evans
1985-86	IL	1	16.11.85	Aylesbury U	SL	H	D	2-2	Dodds, White
		1r	19.11.85	Aylesbury U		A	W	5-2	Woodley, White, Kiely, Dodds 2
		2	7.12.85	Orient	D4	A	D	2-2	Dodds, Wilson
		2r	10.12.85	Orient		H	L	2-3	White, Harris (p)
1986-87	IL	1	15.11.86	Bognor Regis T	IL	H	D	1-1	White
		1r	17.11.86	Bognor Regis T		A	W	1-0	Bateman
		2	6.12.86	Swansea C	D4	A	L	0-3	
1989-90	IL	1	18.11.89	Woking	IL	H	L	1-2	Langley
1991-92	GMVC	1	16.11.91	Reading	D3	H	D	3-3	Pluckrose, Fielder, McKinnon

		1r	27.11.91	Reading		A	L	1-2	Joseph
1992-93	GMVC	1	14.11.92	Colchester U	D3	A	L	0-4	

SOLIHULL BOROUGH

Formed 1951. **First entered FA Cup:** 1990. **Cup final connection:** Alan Smith (Arsenal 1993) is a former Solihull player

1992-93	SL	1	14.11.92	VS Rugby	SL	H	D	2-2	Canning, Carter
		1r	25.11.92	VS Rugby		A	L	1-2aet	Canning (p)

SOUTH BANK

Formed 1868. **First entered FA Cup:** 1886. **FA Amateur Cup Winners:** 1913. Runners-up: 1910, 1922. Based in Middlesbrough.

1886-87		1	30.10.86	Gainsborough T		H	L	0-4	
1887-88		1	15.10.87	Newcastle East End		H	W	3-2aet	Knox, Jones, Beattie
		2	5.11.87	Middlesbrough		A	L	1-4	Duck
1925-26	NL	1	3.12.25	Stockton	NL	H	L	1-4	Muffitt

SOUTH BANK ST PETERS

Entered FA Cup: 1933-38. Club disbanded mid-1950s but recently reformed

1933-34	TSL	1	25.11.33	Rotherham U	3N	A	L	2-3	Sherrington, Calvert

SOUTH LIVERPOOL

Formed 1934. **First entered FA Cup:** 1934. Folded, summer 1992. **Cup Final Connection:** Jimmy Case (FA Cup Finals 1977, 1983) and John Aldridge (FA Cup Finals 1988 and 1989) both played for South Liverpool. **League club beaten:** Halifax. Welsh FA Cup Winners 1939

1936-37	LC	1	28.11.36	Morecambe	LC	H	W	1-0	Roscoe
		2	12.12.36	QPR	3S	H	L	0-1	
1937-38	LC	1	27.11.37	Wigan A	CC	A	W	4-1	Houghton, Carr, G.Jones 2
		2	11.12.37	Brighton & HA	3S	H	D	1-1	Roscoe
		2r	15.12.37	Brighton & HA		A	L	0-6	
1945-46	CC	1 1L	17.11.45	Tranmere R	3N	H	D	1-1	G.Jones
		1 2L	24.11.45	Tranmere R		A	L	1-6	G.Jones
1946-47	CC	1	30.11.46	Workington	NEL	H	W	2-1	Frost 2
		2	14.12.46	Carlisle U	3N	H	L	2-3	Powell, Urmston
1964-65	LC	1	14.11.64	Halifax	D4	A	D	2-2	Eales, Watson
		1r	18.11.64	Halifax		H	W	4-2	Watson 2, Saunders, Gorman
		2	5.12.64	Workington	D3	H	L	0-2	
1965-66	LC	1	13.11.65	Wrexham	D4	A	L	1-4	Eales
1972-73	NPL	1	18.11.72	Tranmere R	D3	H	L	0-2	
1985-86	NPL	1	16.11.85	Whitby T	NL	A	L	0-1	

SOUTH NORWOOD

Formed 1871. Played at Portland Road, South Norwood, not far from where Selhurst Park is now situated.

1872-73		1	19.10.72	Barnes		A	W	1-0	Walshe
		2	23.11.72	Windsor Home Park		H	W	1-0	White
			FA ordered match to be replayed						
		2r	7.12.72	Windsor Home Park		A	L	0-3	
1873-74		1	25.10.73	Cambridge University		A	L	0-1	
1874-75		1	10.10.74	Pilgrims		A	L	1-3	
1875-76		1		Clydesdale				walkover	
		2	11.12.75	Swifts		H	L	0-5	
1876-77		1	4.11.76	Saxons		H	W	4-1	Ram 2, White 2
		2	2.12.76	Sheffield Club		H	L	0-7	
1877-78		1	7.11.77	Reading		A	L	0-2	
1878-79		1		Leyton				walkover	
		2	4.12.78	Cambridge University		A	L	0-3	
1879-80		1	1.11.79	Brentwood		H	W	4-2	Knight 2, Hamilton, Robertson
		2	20.12.79	Clapham R		A	L	1-4	

SOUTH SHIELDS

See under 'Gateshead' for an explanation of the genealogy of the various South Shields and Gateshead clubs which have appeared in the FA

SOUTH SHIELDS

Cup this century. **League clubs beaten:** Crewe (2), Chesterfield, York, Bradford PA, Oldham, Scunthorpe, Grimsby T

1947-48	NEL	1	29.11.47	Crewe A	3N	A	L	1-4	Middlesmiss
1956-57	NEL	1	17.11.56	Chesterfield	3N	H	D	2-2	Powell, Richardson
		1r	20.11.56	Chesterfield		A	L	0-4	
1957-58	NEL	1	16.11.57	Frickley Colliery	ML	H	W	3-2	Powell, Evans, Monkhouse
		2	7.12.57	York C	3N	H	L	1-3	Monkhouse (p)
1958-59	ML	1	15.11.58	Crewe A	D4	A	D	2-2	Crickett, Robson
		1r	19.11.58	Crewe A		H	W	5-0	Robson 2, Crickett 2, Monkhouse
		2	6.12.58	Oldham A	D4	A	L	0-2	
1959-60	ML	1	14.11.59	Chesterfield	D3	H	W	2-1	Powell, Robson
		2	5.12.59	Bradford PA	D4	H	L	1-5	Garbutt
1961-62	N Co	1	4.11.61	Morecambe	LC	A	L	1-2	Butler
1962-63	NEL	1	3.11.62	Doncaster R	D4	H	D	0-0	
		1r	8.11.62	Doncaster R		A	L	1-2	Smith
1964-65	NRL	1	14.11.64	Chesterfield	D4	A	L	0-2	
1965-66	NRL	1	13.11.65	York C	D3	H	W	3-1	Donoghue, Todd, Smith
		2	4.12.65	Crewe A	D4	A	L	1-3	Smith
1966-67	NRL	1	26.11.66	Workington	D3	H	L	1-4	Smith
1968-69	NPL	1	16.11.68	York C	D4	H	L	0-6	
1969-70	NPL	1	15.11.69	Bradford PA	D4	H	W	2-1	Smith 2
		2	6.12.69	Oldham A	D4	H	D	0-0	
		2r	9.12.69	Oldham A		A	W	2-1	Potter, Smith
		3	3.1.70	QPR	D2	A	L	1-4	Smith (p)
1970-71	NPL	1	21.11.70	Wigan A	NPL	H	D	1-1	Bains
		1r	23.11.70	Wigan A		A	L	0-2	
1971-72	NPL	1	20.11.71	Scunthorpe U	D4	H	D	3-3	Leask, O'Donnell 2
		1r	24.11.71	Scunthorpe U		A	W	3-2	O'Donnell, Morton, Bains
		2	11.12.71	Notts Co	D3	H	L	1-3	Bains
1972-73	NPL	1	18.11.72	Rotherham U	D3	A	L	0-4	
1973-74	NPL	1	24.11.73	Rochdale	D3	A	L	0-2	
as Gateshead United									
1974-75	NPL	1	23.11.74	Crewe A	D4	A	D	2-2	N.Smith, Wilson
		1r	25.11.74	Crewe A		H	W	1-0aet	Mutrie
		2	14.12.74	Altrincham	NPL	A	L	0-3	
1975-76	NPL	1	22.11.75	Grimsby T	D3	A	W	3-1	Common, Mutrie, Thompson
		2	13.12.75	Rochdale	D4	H	D	1-1	Guthrie
		2r	16.12.75	Rochdale		A	L	1-3	Morrison
1976-77	NPL	1	20.11.76	Wrexham	D3	A	L	0-6	

SOUTH SHORE

Formed late 1870s. Merged with Blackpool FC on December 12, 1899.

1882-83	1	14.10.82	Darwen		A	L	2-5	
1883-84	1	10.11.83	Clitheroe		A	D	3-3	
	1r	24.11.83	Clitheroe		H	W	3-2	Eaton, Elston, 1 other
	2	1.12.83	Blackburn R		H	L	0-7	
1884-85	1		Rawtenstall			walkover		
	2	6.12.84	Church FC		H	L	2-3	
1885-86	1	17.10.85	Higher Walton		A	W	4-3	
	2		Queen's Park, Glasgow			walkover		
	3	19.12.85	Halliwell		A	W	6-1	Robert Elston 2, Hall, Thackeray, others 2
	4		bye					
	5	23.1.86	Notts Co		H	W	2-1	Richard Elston, 1 other
	6	13.2.86	Swifts		H	L	1-2	Tattersall
1886-87	1	30.10.86	Bolton W		A	L	3-5	Watson, Walsh, Elston
1887-88	1		Denton			walkover		
	2	5.11.87	Bootle		A	D	1-1	
	2r	12.11.87	Bootle		H	L	0-3	
1888-89	1	2.2.89	Chatham		A	L	1-2aet	Elston
1889-90	1	18.1.90	Aston Villa	D1	H	L	2-4	Cookson 2
1893-94	LL	1	27.1.91	Leicester Fosse	ML	A	L	1-2	S.Parkinson
1898-99	LL	1	28.1.98	WBA	D1	A	L	0-8	

SOUTHALL

Formed as Southall Park 1871. **First entered FA Cup:** 1873. FA Amateur Cup Runners-up: 1925. FA Vase Runners-Up: 1986. **Cup Final Connection:** Alan Devonshire, who played for West Ham in the 1980 Cup Final started his career at Southall.

SOUTHALL

as Southall Park

1873-74	1		Wanderers				scratched	
1874-75	1	14.11.74	Leyton		H	D	0-0	
	1r	28.11.74	Leyton		A	W	5-0	
	2	5.12.74	Woodford Wells		A	L	0-3	
1875-76	1	23.10.75	Upton Park		A	L	0-1	
1876-77	1		Old Wykehamists				walkover	
	2	16.12.76	Wanderers		A	L	0-6	
1877-78	1	2.11.77	Cambridge University		A	L	1-3	
1878-79	1	2.11.78	Old Harrovians		A	L	0-8	

as Southall

1925-26	AL	1	28.11.25	Gillingham	3S	A	L	0-6	
1927-28	AL	1	26.11.27	Bath C	SL	A	L	0-2	
1928-29	AL	1	24.11.28	Sittingbourne	SL	A	L	1-2	Yates
1935-36	AL	1	30.11.35	Swindon T	3S	H	W	3-1	Leahy, Willshaw, Poxon
		2	14.12.35	Newport IOW	Hants	H	W	8-0	Willshaw 3, Graves 3, Foss, Ette
		3	11.1.36	Watford	3S	H	L	1-4	Jones
1936-37	AL	1	28.11.36	Cardiff C	3S	A	L	1-3	Leahy
1955-56	AL	1	19.11.55	Hastings U	SL	A	L	1-6	Stevens

SOUTHAMPTON

Formed 1885 as Southampton St Marys. **First entered FA Cup:** 1891. **Best FA Cup Performances:** Winners: 1976. Runners-up 1900, 1902 (both as a Southern League club). **Record FA Cup Win:** 14-0 vs Newbury, 1st qualifying round, 13.10.1894. In Competition Proper: 7-1 vs Ipswich T, 3rd round, 7.1.1961. **Record FA Cup Defeat:** 0-5 vs Manchester C, 2nd round, 5.2.1910

as Southampton St Marys

1891-92		1q **Warmley** (A) 4-1; 2q **Reading** (H) 7-0. *Southampton disqualified by FA.*						
1892-93		1q **Newbury** (H) 4-1; 2q **Maidenhead** (H) 0-4						
1893-94		1q **Uxbridge** (H) 3-1; 2q **Reading** (A) 1-2						
1894-95	SL	1q **Newbury** (H) 14-0; 2q **Reading** (H) 5-2; 3q **Marlow** (H) 7-3; 4q **Warmley** (H) 5-1						
		1	2.2.95	Nottingham F	D1	H	L	1-4	Ward
1895-96	SL	1q **Freemantle** (A) 5-1; 2q **Marlow** (H) 5-0; 3q **Reading** (H) 3-0; 4q **Uxbridge** (H) 3-0						
		1	1.2.96	Sheffield W	D1	H	L	2-3	Keay, Turner
1896-97	SL	3q **Cowes** (A) 6-0; 4q **Reading** (A) 4-1; 5q **Swindon T** (H) 8-2						
		1	30.1.97	Heanor T	ML	H	D	1-1	Turner
		1r	3.2.97	Heanor T		A	W	1-0	Farrell
		2	13.2.97	Newton Heath	D2	H	D	1-1	Turner
		2r	17.2.97	Newton Heath		A	L	1-3	Buchanan

as Southampton

1897-98	SL	3q **Bristol C** (H) 2-0; 4q **Swindon T** (A) 3-0; 5q **Eastville R** (H) 8-1						
		1	29.1.98	Leicester F	D2	H	W	2-1	Meston, Buchanan
		2	12.2.98	Newcastle U	D2	H	W	1-0	Buchanan
		3	26.2.98	Bolton W	D1	A	D	0-0	
		3r	2.3.98	Bolton W		H	W	4-0	Turner 2, Yates, Farrell
		SF	19.3.98	Nottingham F	D1		D	1-1	Haynes
			played at Bramall Lane						
		SFr	23.3.98	Nottingham F at Crystal Palace			L	0-2	
1898-99	SL	1	28.1.99	New Brompton	SL	A	W	1-0	Hartley
		2	11.2.99	Notts Co	D1	A	W	1-0	Hartley
		3	25.2.99	Derby Co	D1	H	L	1-2	Nicol
1899-00	SL	1	27.1.00	Everton	D1	H	W	3-0	Milward 2, Turner
		2	10.2.00	Newcastle U	D1	H	−	0-0	
			abandoned after 50 minutes – bad light						
			17.2.00	Newcastle U		H	W	4-1	McLeod 2, Yates, Turner
		3	24.2.00	WBA	D1	H	W	2-1	Turner, McLeod
		SF	24.3.00	Millwall	SL		D	0-0	
			played at Crystal Palace						
		SFr	28.3.00	Millwall at Elm Park, Reading			W	3-0	Milward 2, Yates
		F	21.4.00	Bury	D1		L	0-4	
			played at Crystal Palace						
1900-01	SL	1	9.2.01	Everton	D1	H	L	1-3	Chadwick
1901-02	SL	1	25.1.02	Tottenham H	SL	A	D	1-1	Bowman
		1r	1.2.02	Tottenham H		H	D	2-2aet	Chadwick, J.Turner
		1 2r	3.2.02	Tottenham H at Elm Park			W	2-1	A.Turner, Brown
		2	8.2.02	Liverpool	D1	H	W	4-1	Chadwick 2, J.Turner, Lee
		3	22.2.02	Bury	D1	A	W	3-2	Wood, Chadwick, J.Turner
		SF	15.3.02	Nottingham F	D1		W	3-1	Brown 2, Chadwick
			played at White Hart Lane						

(421)

	F	19.4.02	Sheffield U	D1	D	1-1	Wood
	Fr	28.4.02	Sheffield U		L	1-2	Brown
		both matches played at Crystal Palace					
1902-03 SL	1	7.2.03	Notts Co	D1	A	D	0-0	
	1r	11.2.03	Notts Co		H	D	2-2	J.Turner, Bell
	1 2r	16.2.03	Notts Co at St Andrews			L	1-2aet	Barlow
1903-04 SL	1	6.2.04	Burslem Port Vale	D2	H	W	3-0	J.Turner, Wood, Fraser
	2	20.2.04	Bolton W	D1	A	L	1-4	Mouncher
1904-05 SL	1	4.2.05	Millwall	SL	H	W	3-1	Bluff 2, Harrison
	2	18.2.05	Wolverhampton W	D1	A	W	3-2	Harrison 2, Bluff
	3	4.3.05	Everton	D1	A	L	0-4	
1905-06 SL	1	13.1.06	Portsmouth	SL	H	W	5-1	Brown 2, Tomlinson, Harrison, Hedley
	2	3.2.06	New Brompton	SL	A	D	0-0	
	2r	7.2.06	New Brompton		H	W	1-0	Hedley
	3	24.2.06	Middlesbrough	D1	H	W	6-1	Hedley 2, Brown 2, Tomlinson, Harrison
	4	10.3.06	Liverpool	D1	A	L	0-3	
1906-07 SL	1	12.1.07	Watford	SL	H	W	2-1	Hoskins, Mouncher
	2	2.2.07	Sheffield W	D1	H	D	1-1	Hoskins
	2r	7.2.07	Sheffield W		A	L	1-3	Hoskins
1907-08 SL	1	11.1.08	Burnley	D2	A	W	2-1	Bainbridge 2
	2	1.2.08	WBA	D2	H	W	1-0	Robertson
	3	22.2.08	Bristol R	SL	H	W	2-0	Bainbridge, Costello
	4	7.3.08	Everton	D1	A	D	0-0	
	4r	11.3.08	Everton		H	W	3-2	Costello 2, Bainbridge
	SF	28.3.08	Wolverhampton W	D2		L	0-2	
		played at Stamford Bridge					
1908-09 SL	1	16.1.09	Bristol C	D1	A	D	1-1	Jordan
	1r	20.1.09	Bristol C		H	L	0-2	
1909-10 SL	1	15.1.10	Brighton & HA	SL	A	W	1-0	McGibbon
	2	5.2.10	Manchester C	D2	H	L	0-5	
1910-11 SL	1	14.1.11	Leicester F	D2	A	L	1-3	H.Brown
1911-12 SL	1	13.1.12	Coventry C	SL	A	L	0-2	
1912-13 SL	1	11.1.13	Bury	D2	H	D	1-1	Andrews
	1r	15.1.13	Bury		A	L	1-2	Turnbull
1913-14 SL	1	10.1.14	Wolverhampton W	D2	A	L	0-3	
1914-15 SL	1	9.1.15	Luton T	SL	H	W	3-0	Andrews 2 (1p), Kimpton
	2	30.1.15	Fulham	D2	A	W	3-2aet	Jones, Andrews (p), Kimpton
	3	20.2.15	Hull C	D2	H	D	2-2aet	Andrews, Jones
	3r	27.2.15	Hull C		A	L	0-4	
1919-20 SL	1	10.1.20	West Ham	D2	H	D	0-0	
	1r	15.1.20	West Ham		A	L	1-3	Barratt
1920-21 D3	1	7.1.21	Northampton T	D3	A	D	0-0	
	1r	11.1.21	Northampton T		H	W	4-1	Dominy 2, Rawlings 2
	2	28.1.21	Grimsby T	D3	A	W	3-1	Dominy, Rawlings 2
	3	19.2.21	Cardiff C	D2	H	L	0-1	
1921-22 3S	1	7.1.22	South Shields	D2	H	W	3-1	Johnson, Rawlings, Dominy
	2	28.1.22	Cardiff C	D1	H	D	1-1	Rawlings
	2r	1.2.22	Cardiff C		A	L	0-2	
1922-23 D2	1	13.1.23	Newcastle U	D1	A	D	0-0	
	1r	17.1.23	Newcastle U		H	W	3-1	Dominy 2, Rawlings
	2	3.2.23	Chelsea	D1	A	D	0-0	
	2r	7.2.23	Chelsea		H	W	1-0	Dominy
	3	24.2.23	Bury	D2	A	D	0-0	
	3r	28.2.23	Bury		H	W	1-0	Dominy
	4	3.4.23	West Ham	D2	H	D	1-1	Elkes
	4r	14.3.23	West Ham		A	D	1-1aet	Rawlings
	4 2r	19.3.23	West Ham at Villa Park			L	0-1	
1923-24 D2	1	12.1.24	Chelsea	D1	A	D	1-1	Dominy
	1r	16.1.24	Chelsea		H	W	2-0	Dominy, Rawlings
	2	2.2.24	Blackpool	D2	H	W	3-1	Rawlings, Dominy, Price
	3	23.2.24	Liverpool	D1	H	D	0-0	
	3r	27.2.24	Liverpool		A	L	0-2	
1924-25 D2	1	10.1.25	Exeter C	3S	H	–	5-0	Dominy 2, Price 2, Parker
		abandoned after 80 minutes - fog					
	1	14.1.25	Exeter C		H	W	3-1	Dominy, Rawlings, Price
	2	31.1.25	Brighton & HA	3S	H	W	1-0	Parker (p)

		3	21.2.25	Bradford C	D2	H	W	2-0	Dominy, Harkus
		4	7.3.25	Liverpool	D1	H	W	1-0	Rawlings
		SF	28.3.25	Sheffield U	D1		A	0-2	
				played at Stamford Bridge					
1925-26	D2	3	9.1.26	Liverpool	D1	H	D	0-0	
		3r	13.1.26	Liverpool		A	L	0-1	
1926-27	D2	3	8.1.27	Norwich C	3S	H	W	3-0	Keeping, Rowley 2
		4	29.1.27	Birmingham	D1	H	W	4-1	Rowley, Rawlings 2, Harkus
		5	19.2.27	Newcastle U	D1	H	W	2-1	Rowley 2
		6	5.3.27	Millwall	3S	A	D	0-0	
		6r	9.3.27	Millwall		H	W	2-0	Rawlings 2
		SF	26.3.27	Arsenal	D1		L	1-2	Rawlings
				played at Stamford Bridge					
1927-28	D2	3	14.1.28	Cardiff C	D1	A	L	1-2	Rawlings
1928-29	D2	3	12.1.29	Clapton Orient	D2	H	D	0-0	
		3r	17.1.29	Clapton Orient		A	L	1-2	Bradford
1929-30	D2	3	11.1.30	Bradford C	D2	A	L	1-4	Rowley
1930-31	D2	3	10.1.31	Sunderland	D1	A	L	0-2	
1931-32	D2	3	9.1.32	Sunderland	D1	A	D	0-0	
		3r	13.1.32	Sunderland		H	L	2-4	Sillett, Keeping
1932-33	D2	3	14.1.33	Stoke C	D2	A	L	0-1	
1933-34	D2	3	13.1.34	Northampton T	3S	H	D	1-1	Drake
		3r	17.1.34	Northampton T		A	L	0-1	
1934-35	D2	3	12.1.35	Walsall	3N	A	W	2-1	Fishlock 2
		4	26.1.35	Birmingham	D1	H	L	0-3	
1935-36	D2	3	3.1.36	Middlesbrough	D1	A	L	0-1	
1936-37	D2	3	16.1.37	Sunderland	D1	H	L	2-3	Holt, Summers
1937-38	D2	3	8.1.38	Nottingham F	D2	A	L	1-3	Dunn
1938-39	D2	3	7.1.39	Chelmsford C	SL	A	L	1-4	Tomlinson
1945-46	D2	3 1L	5.1.46	Newport Co	D2	H	W	4-3	Bates, Bradley, McGibbon, Roper
		3 2L	10.1.46	Newport Co		A	W	2-1	McGibbon, Veck
		4 1L	26.1.46	QPR	3S	H	L	0-1	
		4 2L	30.1.46	QPR		A	L	3-4	Bradley, Bevis, Ellerington
1946-47	D2	3	11.1.47	Bury	D2	H	W	5-1	Lewis 3, Bradley, Bevis
		4	25.1.47	Newcastle U	D2	A	L	1-3	Roper
1947-48	D2	3	10.1.48	Sunderland	D1	H	W	1-0	Day
		4	24.1.48	Blackburn R	D1	H	W	3-2	Day 2, Wayman
		5	7.2.48	Swindon T	3S	H	W	3-0	Wayman, Curtis, Ithell og
		6	28.2.48	Tottenham H	D2	H	L	0-1	
1948-49	D2	3	8.1.49	Sheffield W	D2	A	L	1-2	Grant
1949-50	D2	3	7.1.50	Northampton T	3S	A	D	1-1	Scott
		3r	11.1.50	Northampton T		H	L	2-3	Wayman 2
1950-51	D2	3	6.1.51	Notts Co	D2	A	W	4-3	Brown 2, Day 2
		4	27.1.51	Sunderland	D1	A	L	0-2	
1951-52	D2	3	12.1.52	Southend U	3S	A	L	0-3	
1952-53	D2	3	10.1.53	Lincoln C	D2	A	D	1-1	Dudley
		3r	14.1.53	Lincoln C		H	W	2-1	Purves, Day
		4	31.1.53	Shrewsbury T	3S	A	W	4-1	Hoskins 2, Walker, Day
		5	14.2.53	Blackpool	D1	A	D	1-1	Horton
		5r	18.2.53	Blackpool		H	L	1-2	Walker
1953-54	3S	1	21.11.53	Bournemouth	3S	H	D	1-1	Day
		1r	25.11.53	Bournemouth		A	L	1-3	Purves
1954-55	3S	1	20.11.54	Barnet	AL	A	W	4-1	Day 2, Mulgrew 2
		2	11.12.54	Grimsby T	3N	A	L	1-4	Walker
1955-56	3S	1	19.11.55	Crystal P	3S	A	D	0-0	
		1r	23.11.55	Crystal P		H	W	2-0	Reeves, Day
		2	10.12.55	Walsall	3S	A	L	1-2	Flood
1956-57	3S	1	17.11.56	Northampton T	3S	H	W	2-0	Reeves, Mulgrew
		2	8.12.56	Weymouth	SL	H	W	3-2	Mulgrew 2, Reeves
		3	5.1.57	Newport Co	3S	A	D	3-3	Walker, Shields, Wilkins
		3r	9.1.57	Newport Co		H	L	0-1	
1957-58	3S	1	16.11.57	Walton & Hersham	AL	A	W	6-1	Reeves 4, Hoskins, Mulgrew
		2	12.12.57	Crystal P	3S	A	L	0-1	
1958-59	D3	1	15.11.58	Woking	IL	H	W	4-1	Mulgrew 2, Livesey, Paine
		2	6.12.58	QPR	D3	A	W	1-0	Rutter og
		3	10.1.59	Blackpool	D1	H	L	1-2	Reeves
1959-60	D3	1	14.11.59	Coventry C	D3	A	D	1-1	Reeves

Season	Div	Round	Date	Opponent	Opp Div	Venue	Result	Score	Scorers
		1r	18.11.59	Coventry C		H	W	5-1	Page, Simpson 2, O'Brien, Paine
		2	5.12.59	Southend U	D3	H	W	3-0	Paine 2, Reeves
		3	9.1.60	Manchester C	D1	A	W	5-1	Reeves 4, O'Brien
		4	30.1.60	Watford	D4	H	D	2-2	O'Brien 2
		4r	2.2.60	Watford		A	L	0-1	
1960-61	D2	3	7.1.61	Ipswich T	D2	H	W	7-1	O'Brien 3, Mulgrew 2, Penk, Paine
		4	28.1.61	Leyton Orient	D2	H	L	0-1	
1961-62	D2	3	6.1.62	Sunderland	D2	H	D	2-2	O'Brien 2
		3r	10.1.62	Sunderland		A	L	0-3	
1962-63	D2	3	13.2.63	York C	D4	H	W	5-0	Wimshurst, O'Brien 3, Burnside
		4	27.2.63	Watford	D3	H	W	3-1	O'Brien 2, Kirby
		5	16.3.63	Sheffield U	D1	H	W	1-0	Kirby
		6	30.3.63	Nottingham F	D1	A	D	1-1	Paine
		6r	3.4.63	Nottingham F		H	D	3-3aet	Kirby 2, Burnside
		6 2r	8.4.63	Nottingham F at Tottenham			W	5-0	Burnside 2, O'Brien 2, Wimshurst
		SF	27.4.63	Manchester U			L	0-1	
			played at Villa Park						
1963-64	D2	3	4.1.64	Manchester U	D1	H	L	2-3	Chivers, Paine
1964-65	D2	3	9.1.65	Leyton Orient	D2	H	W	3-1	Chivers, O'Brien 2
		4	30.1.65	Crystal P	D2	H	L	1-2	O'Brien
1965-66	D2	3	22.1.66	Hull C	D3	A	L	0-1	
1966-67	D1	3	28.1.67	Barrow	D4	A	D	2-2	Chivers, Davies
		3r	1.2.67	Barrow		H	W	3-0	Davies 2, Chivers
		4	18.2.67	Bristol C	D2	A	L	0-1	
1967-68	D1	3	27.1.68	Newport Co	D4	H	D	1-1	Saul
		3r	30.1.68	Newport Co		A	W	3-2	Saul, Sydenham, Channon
		4	17.2.68	WBA	D1	A	D	1-1	Saul
		4r	21.2.68	WBA		H	L	2-3	Saul, Fisher
1968-69	D1	3	3.1.69	Oxford U	D2	A	D	1-1	Davies
		3r	8.1.69	Oxford U		H	W	2-0	Paine 2
		4	25.1.69	Aston Villa	D2	H	D	2-2	McGrath, Davies
		4r	29.1.69	Aston Villa		A	L	1-2	Channon
1969-70	D1	3	3.1.70	Newcastle U	D1	A	W	3-0	Channon, Saul 2
		4	24.1.70	Leicester C	D2	H	D	1-1	Stokes
		4r	28.1.70	Leicester C		A	L	2-4	Paine, Channon
1970-71	D1	3	11.1.71	Bristol C	D2	H	W	3-0	O'Neil, Davies 2
		4	23.1.71	York C	D4	A	D	3-3	Gabriel, Channon, Davies
		4r	1.2.71	York C		H	W	3-2	O'Neil, Kirkup, Davies
		5	13.2.71	Liverpool	D1	A	L	0-1	
1971-72	D1	3	15.1.72	Manchester U	D1	H	D	1-1	Channon
		3r	19.1.72	Manchester U		A	L	1-4aet	Channon
1972-73	D1	3	13.1.73	Crystal P	D1	A	L	0-2	
1973-74	D1	3	5.1.74	Blackpool	D2	H	W	2-1	Paine, Bennett
		4	26.1.74	Bolton W	D2	H	D	3-3	Fisher, Channon, Stokes
		4r	30.1.74	Bolton W		A	W	2-0aet	Stokes 2
		5	16.2.74	Wrexham	D3	H	L	0-1	
1974-75	D2	3	4.1.75	West Ham	D1	H	L	1-2	Channon (p)
1975-76	D2	3	3.1.76	Aston Villa	D1	H	D	1-1	Fisher
		3r	7.1.76	Aston Villa		A	W	2-1aet	McCalliog 2
		4	24.1.76	Blackpool	D2	H	W	3-1	Channon 2, Stokes
		5	14.2.76	WBA	D2	A	D	1-1	Stokes
		5r	17.2.76	WBA		H	W	4-0	Channon 3 (1p), Gilchrist
		6	6.3.76	Bradford C	D4	A	W	1-0	McCalliog
		SF	3.4.76	Crystal P	D3		W	2-0	Peach (p), Gilchrist
			played at Stamford Bridge						
		F	1.5.76	MANCHESTER U	D1	WEMBLEY	W	1-0	Stokes
1976-77	D2	3	8.1.77	Chelsea	D2	H	D	1-1	Channon
		3r	12.1.77	Chelsea		A	W	3-0aet	MacDougall, Channon, Peach
		4	29.1.77	Nottingham F	D2	A	D	3-3	Ball, Channon, Osgood
		4r	1.2.77	Nottingham F		H	W	2-1	Williams, MacDougall
		5	26.2.77	Manchester U	D1	H	D	2-2	Peach (p), Holmes
		5r	8.3.77	Manchester U		A	L	1-2	Peach
1977-78	D2	3	7.1.78	Grimsby T	D4	A	D	0-0	
		3r	10.1.78	Grimsby T		H	D	0-0aet	
		3 2r	16.1.78	Grimsby T at Filbert St			W	4-1	Peach, Boyer, Holmes, MacDougall
		4	28.1.78	Bristol R	D2	A	L	0-2	
1978-79	D1	3	9.1.79	Wimbledon	D4	A	W	2-0	Boyer 2

	4	12.2.79	**Preston NE**	D2	A	W	1-0	Ball
	5	10.3.79	**WBA**	D1	A	D	1-1	Boyer
	5r	12.3.79	**WBA**		H	W	2-1aet	Peach (p), Boyer
	6	19.3.79	**Arsenal**	D1	H	D	1-1	Hayes
	6r	21.3.79	**Arsenal**		A	L	0-2	
1979-80 D1	3	5.1.80	**Birmingham C**	D2	A	L	1-2	Channon (p)
1980-81 D1	3	3.1.81	**Chelsea**	D2	H	W	3-1	Baker, Moran, Keegan
	4	24.1.81	**Bristol R**	D2	H	W	3-1	Moran 2, Williams
	5	5.2.81	**Everton**	D1	H	D	0-0	
	5r	17.2.81	**Everton**		A	L	0-1	
1981-82 D1	3	2.1.82	**Leicester C**	D2	A	L	1-3	Keegan
1982-83 D1	3	8.1.83	**Tottenham H**	D1	A	L	0-1	
1983-84 D1	3	7.1.84	**Nottingham F**	D1	A	W	2-1	Moran 2
	4	28.1.84	**Portsmouth**	D2	A	W	1-0	Moran
	5	18.2.84	**Blackburn R**	D2	A	W	1-0	Armstrong
	6	11.3.84	**Sheffield W**	D2	A	D	0-0	
	6r	20.3.84	**Sheffield W**		H	W	5-1	Williams, Oliver og, Wright, Armstrong, Moran
	SF	14.4.84	**Everton**	D1		L	0-1	
			played at Highbury					
1984-85 D1	3	5.1.85	**Sunderland**	D1	H	W	4-0	Moran 2, Curtis, Jordan
	4	26.1.85	**Orient**	D3	A	W	2-0	Jordan, Moran
	5	4.3.85	**Barnsley**	D2	H	L	1-2	Moran
1985-86 D1	3	13.1.86	**Middlesbrough**	D2	A	W	3-1	D.Wallace 3
	4	25.1.86	**Wigan A**	D3	H	W	3-0	Armstrong 2, Cockerill
	5	15.2.86	**Millwall**	D2	H	D	0-0	
	5r	3.2.86	**Millwall**		A	W	1-0	D.Wallace
	6	8.3.86	**Brighton & HA**	D2	A	W	2-0	Cockerill, Moran
	SF	5.4.86	**Liverpool**	D1		L	0-2aet	
			played at White Hart Lane					
1986-87 D1	3	10.1.87	**Everton**	D1	A	L	1-2	Hobson
1987-88 D1	3	9.1.88	**Reading**	D2	A	W	1-0	Le Tissier
	4	30.1.88	**Luton T**	D1	A	L	1-2	Clarke
1988-89 D1	3	7.1.89	**Derby Co**	D1	A	D	1-1	Statham (p)
	3r	10.1.89	**Derby Co**		H	L	1-2aet	Forrest
1989-90 D1	3	6.1.90	**Tottenham H**	D1	A	W	3-1	Le Tissier, Horne, Rod Wallace
	4	27.1.90	**Oxford U**	D2	H	W	1-0	Ruddock
	5	17.2.90	**Liverpool**	D1	A	L	0-3	
1990-91 D1	3	5.1.91	**Ipswich T**	D2	H	W	3-2	Shearer, Le Tissier 2
	4	26.1.91	**Coventry C**	D1	A	D	1-1	Shearer (p)
	4r	29.1.91	**Coventry C**		H	W	2-0	Case, Rod Wallace
	5	25.2.91	**Nottingham F**	D1	H	D	1-1	Ruddock
	5r	4.3.91	**Nottingham F**		A	L	1-3	Rod Wallace
1991-92 D1	3	4.1.92	**QPR**	D1	H	W	2-0	Wood, Le Tissier
	4	27.1.92	**Manchester U**	D1	H	D	0-0	
	4r	5.2.92	**Manchester U**		A	D	2-2aet	Gray, Shearer
			Southampton won 4-2 on penalties					
	5	16.2.92	**Bolton W**	D3	A	D	2-2	Hall 2
	5r	26.2.92	**Bolton W**		H	W	3-2aet	Shearer, Horne 2
	6	7.3.92	**Norwich C**	D1	H	D	0-0	
	6r	18.3.92	**Norwich C**		A	L	1-2aet	Ruddock
1992-93 PL	3	2.1.93	**Nottingham F**	PL	A	L	1-2	Le Tissier

SOUTHEND UNITED

Formed 1906. **Best FA Cup Best Performance:** 5th round, 1926, 1952, 1976, 1993. Old 3rd round (5th round equivalent) 1921. **Record FA Cup Win:** 10-1 vs Golders Green (later Hendon), 1st round, 24.11.1934 10-1 vs Brentwood, 2nd round, 7.12.1968. **Record FA Cup Defeat:** 0-6 vs Burnley, 2nd round, 30.1.1915

1907-08 SL	P **East Ham** (H) 3-0; 1q **Clapton** (A) 1-0; 2q **Ilford** (H) 3-1; 3q **Clapton O** (A) 1-1; 3qr **Clapton O** (H) 3-1; 4q **4th Kings Rifles** (H) 6-0; 5q **Carlisle U** (A) 0-4
1908-09 SL	P **London Caledonians** (A) 4-0; 1q **Leyton** (A) 1-0; 2q **Shoeburyness Garrison** (H) 4-0; 3q **Ilford** (A) 3-1; 4q **Cromer** (H) 2-0; 5q **Luton T** (A) 1-1; 5qr **Luton T** (H) 2-4
1909-10 SL	4q **Barnet Alston** (H) 5-2; 5q **Hastings U** (H) 4-2

	1	15.1.10	**Gainsborough Trinity**	ML	A	D	1-1	King
	1r	19.1.10	**Gainsborough Trinity**		H	W	1-0	King
	2	5.2.10	**QPR**	SL	H	D	0-0	
	2r	9.2.10	**QPR**		A	L	2-3	Sugden, Frost

1910-11	SL	4q **Enfield** (A) 3-3; 4qr **Enfield** (H) 3-1; 5q **Tunbridge Wells R** (H) 1-0					
		1	14.1.11	**Blackburn R**	D1	A	L	1-5	Curtis
1911-12	SL	4q **London Caldeonians** (A) 3-1; 5q **Brentford** (H) 0-1					
1912-13	SL	3q **Custom House** (A) 1-0; 4q **Clapton** (A) 2-1; 5q **Cardiff C** (A) 3-0					
		1	11.1.13	**Chelsea**	D1	A	L	2-5	Frost 2
1913-14	SL	4q **Tunbridge Wells R** (H) 3-0; 5q **Brentford** (A) 1-1; 5qr **Brentford** (H) 2-0					
		1	10.1.14	**Birmingham**	D2	A	L	1-2	Wiseman
1914-15	SL	1	16.1.15	**Bristol R**	SL	A	D	0-0	
		1r	23.1.15	**Bristol R**		H	W	3-0	Wiseman 2, Frost
		2	30.1.15	**Burnley**	D1	H	L	0-6	
1919-20	SL	6q **Watford** (H) 1-0					
		1	10.1.20	**Sheffield U**	D1	A	L	0-3	
1920-21	D3	6q **Hednesford T** (H) 3-1					
		1	8.1.21	**Eccles U**	LC	H	W	5-1	Myers 2, Nuttall 2, Walters
		2	29.1.21	**Blackpool**	D2	H	W	1-0	Dorsett
		3	19.2.21	**Tottenham H**	D1	H	L	1-4	Nicholls
1921-22	3S	1	7.1.22	**Worksop T**	ML	A	W	2-1	Buddery, Kettle
		2	28.1.22	**Swansea T**	3S	H	L	0-1	
1922-23	3S	4q **Sittingbourne** (A) 0-0; 4qr **Sittingbourne** (H) 4-2; 5q **Norwich C** (H) 2-2; 5qr **Norwich C** (A) 1-2					
1923-24	3S	4q **Kings Lynn** (H) 1-0; 5q **Clapton** (A) 3-1; 6q **Llanelli** (A) 1-2					
1924-25	3S	4q **London Caledonians** (H) 3-3; 4qr **London Caledonians** (A) 4-1; 5q **Reading** (A) 1-2					
1925-26	3S	1	28.11.25	**Dulwich Hamlet**	IL	H	W	5-1	Morris Shaw, Watkins, Blissett, og
		2	12.12.25	**Gillingham**	3S	H	W	1-0	Watkins
		3	9.1.26	**Southport**	3N	H	W	5-2	Smith, Shaw, Hick 2, Blissett
		4	30.1.26	**Derby Co**	D2	H	W	4-1	Andrews, Graver, Hick 2
		5	20.2.26	**Nottingham F**	D2	H	L	0-1	
1926-27	3S	1	27.11.26	**Dulwich Hamlet**	IL	A	W	4-1	Donovan 3, Hick
		2	11.12.26	**Reading**	D2	A	L	2-3	Hick, Purdy
1927-28	3S	1	26.11.27	**Wellington T**	BDL	H	W	1-0	Hick
		2	10.12.27	**Gillingham**	3S	A	L	0-2	
1928-29	3S	1	24.11.28	**Luton T**	3S	A	L	1-5	Shankly
1929-30	3S	1	30.11.29	**Brentford**	3S	H	W	1-0	Barnett
		2	14.12.29	**York C**	3N	H	L	1-4	Turnbull
1930-31	3S	1	29.11.30	**Torquay U**	3S	H	L	0-1	
1931-32	3S	1	28.11.31	**Torquay U**	3S	A	W	3-1	Shankly 2, Fowler og
		2	12.12.31	**Northampton T**	3S	A	L	0-3	
1932-33	3S	1	26.11.32	**Exeter C**	3S	H	D	1-1	Morfitt
		1r	30.11.32	**Exeter C**		A	W	1-0	Morfitt
		2	10.12.32	**Scarborough**	ML	H	W	4-1	Morfitt 3, Robson
		3	14.1.33	**Watford**	3S	A	D	1-1	Clenshaw
		3r	18.1.33	**Watford**		H	W	2-0	Morfitt, Clenshaw
		4	28.1.33	**Derby Co**	D1	H	L	2-3	Pike, Morfitt
1933-34	3S	1	25.11.33	**London Paper Mills**	KL	A	W	1-0	Fryer
		2	9.12.33	**Chester**	3N	H	W	2-1	Stevens, Barnett
		3	13.1.34	**Tranmere R**	3N	A	L	0-3	
1934-35	3S	1	24.11.34	**Golders Green**	AL	H	W	10-1	Johnson 5, Cheesmur 2, Deacon, Carr, Lane
		2	8.12.34	**Wimbledon**	IL	A	W	5-1	Johnson, Cheesmur 3, Deacon
		3	12.1.35	**Sheffield U**	D2	H	L	0-4	
1935-36	3S	1	30.11.35	**Newport Co**	3S	A	W	1-0	Lane
		2	14.12.35	**Burton T**	ML	H	W	5-0	Oswald 3, Bolan, Cheesmur
		3	11.1.36	**Tottenham H**	D2	A	D	4-4	Bolan 3, Lane
		3r	15.1.36	**Tottenham H**		H	L	1-2	Bolan
1936-37	3S	1	28.11.36	**Crystal P**	3S	A	D	1-1	Dickinson
		1r	2.12.36	**Crystal P**		H	W	2-1	Bolan, Goddard
		2	12.12.36	**York C**	3N	H	D	3-3	Lane, Willshaw, Dickinson
		2r	16.12.36	**York C**		A	L	1-2aet	Dickinson
1937-38	3S	1	27.11.37	**Corinthians**		A	W	2-0	Dickinson, Martin
		2	11.12.37	**Walthamstow Ave**	AL	A	W	1-0	Bolan
		3	8.1.38	**Barnsley**	D2	H	D	2-2	Martin, Dickinson
		3r	12.1.38	**Barnsley**		A	L	1-2	Bell
1938-39	3S	1	26.11.38	**Corinthians**		H	W	3-0	Smirke 3
		2	10.12.38	**Port Vale**	3S	A	W	1-0	Trainer
		3	7.1.39	**Chesterfield**	D2	A	–	1-1	Hague
			abandoned after 73 minutes – fog						
		3	11.1.39	**Chesterfield**		A	D	1-1	Bushby
		3r	16.1.39	**Chesterfield**		H	W	4-3aet	Bushby, Bolan, Bell 2
		4	21.1.39	**Blackburn R**	D2	A	L	2-4	Bushby, Bell

1945-46	3S	1 1L	17.11.45	Watford	3S	A	D	1-1	Smirke
		1 2L	24.11.45	Watford		H	L	0-3	
1946-47	3S	1	30.11.46	Brush Sports	N&D	A	W	6-1	Sibley, Bennett 2, Smirk, Thompson 2
		2	14.12.46	Barnet	AL	A	W	9-2	Lane 3, Thompson, Sibley 2, Bennett 2, Bunker og
		3	11.1.47	Everton	D1	A	L	2-4	Thompson, Bennett
1947-48	3S	1	29.11.47	Newport Co	3S	A	L	2-3	Bennett 2
1948-49	3S	1	4.12.48	Swansea T	3S	H	L	1-2aet	Dudley
1949-50	3S	1	26.11.49	Leyton O	3S	A	W	2-0	Wakefield 2
		2	10.12.49	Wrexham	3N	A	D	2-2	Wakefield 2
		2r	14.12.49	Wrexham		H	W	2-0	Clough, Wakefield
		3	7.1.50	Blackpool	D1	A	L	0-4	
1950-51	3S	1	29.11.50	Swindon T	3S	H	L	0-3	
1951-52	3S	1	24.11.51	Bournemouth	3S	H	W	6-1	Stubbs 2, Wakefield 2, Bird og, French
		2	15.12.51	Oldham A	3N	H	W	5-0	Wakefield 3, Stubbs, Grant
		3	12.1.52	Southampton	D2	H	W	3-0	Sibley, Stubbs, French
		4	2.2.52	Bristol R	3S	H	W	2-1	Stubbs, French
		5	23.2.52	Sheffield U	D2	H	L	1-2	Wakefield
1952-53	3S	1	22.11.52	Bath C	SL	A	L	1-3	Thompson
1953-54	3S	1	21.11.53	Finchley	AL	A	W	3-1	Sibley, McAlinden, O'Neil
		2	12.12.53	Chesterfield	3N	H	L	1-2	Dicker
1954-55	3S	1	20.11.54	Bristol C	3S	A	W	2-1	Hollis 2
		2	11.12.54	Bradford PA	3N	A	W	3-2	Hollis 3
		3	8.1.55	Everton	D1	A	L	1-3	Baron
1955-56	3S	1	19.11.55	QPR	3S	H	W	2-0	Barker, Hollis
		2	10.12.55	Weymouth	SL	A	W	1-0	Lockhart
		3	7.1.56	Lincoln C	D2	A	W	3-2	Hollis 2, McCrory
		4	28.1.56	Manchester C	D1	H	L	0-1	
1956-57	3S	1	17.11.56	Colchester U	3S	H	W	4-1	Hollis, McCrory 3
		2	8.12.56	Hereford U	SL	A	W	3-2	Thomson 2, McGuigan
		3	5.1.57	Liverpool	D2	H	W	2-1	Duthie, Thomson
		4	26.1.57	Birmingham C	D1	H	L	1-6	Hollis
1957-58	3S	1	16.11.57	Trowbridge	WL	A	W	2-0	Hollis 2
		2	7.12.57	Torquay U	3S	A	D	1-1	McCrory
		2r	11.12.57	Torquay U		H	W	2-1	Hollis, McCrory
		3	4.1.58	Liverpool	D2	A	D	1-1	McGuigan
		3r	8.1.58	Liverpool		H	L	2-3	Molyneux og, McCrory
1958-59	D3	1	15.11.58	Yeovil T	SL	H	D	0-0	
		1r	20.11.58	Yeovil T		A	L	0-1	
1959-60	D3	1	14.11.59	Oswestry	CC	H	W	6-0	McCrory, G.Jones og, Hollis 2, Price, Kellard
		2	5.12.59	Southampton	D3	A	L	0-3	
1960-61	D3	1	5.11.60	Clacton	SL	A	W	3-1	Corthine, Kellard, Houghton
		2	26.11.60	Gillingham	D4	A	L	2-3	Fryatt, Stenhouse
1961-62	D3	1	4.11.61	Watford	D3	H	L	0-2	
1962-63	D3	1	3.11.62	Brighton & HA	D3	H	W	2-1	Jones 2
		2	24.11.62	Watford	D3	H	L	0-2	
1963-64	D3	1	16.11.63	Yeovil T	SL	A	L	0-1	
1964-65	D3	1	14.11.64	Luton T	D3	A	L	0-1	
1965-66	D3	1	13.11.65	Notts Co	D4	H	W	3-1	Slack, McKinven, Bentley
		2	4.12.65	Watford	D3	H	W	2-1	Firmani 2
		3	22.1.66	Rotherham U	D2	A	L	2-3	Banks, Bentley
1966-67	D4	1	26.11.66	Watford	D3	A	L	0-1	
1967-68	D4	1	13.12.67	Brighton & HA	D3	A	L	0-1	
1968-69	D4	1	16.11.68	Kings Lynn	SL	H	W	9-0	Moore 3, Best 3, Chisnall 2, Haskins og
		2	7.12.68	Brentwood	SL	H	W	10-1	Best 5, Moore 4, Mcmillan
		3	4.1.69	Swindon T	D3	A	W	2-0	Hamilton, Best
		4	25.1.69	Mansfield T	D3	A	L	1-2	Best
1969-70	D4	1	15.11.69	Gillingham	D3	H	D	0-0	
		1r	19.11.69	Gillingham		A	L	1-2	Best
1970-71	D4	1	21.11.70	Weymouth	SL	H	W	7-0	Garner 4, Best 2, Lewis
		2	12.12.70	Dagenham	AL	H	W	1-0	Best
		3	2.1.71	Carlisle U	D2	H	L	0-3	
1971-72	D4	1	20.11.71	A.Villa	D3	H	W	1-0	Best
		2	11.12.71	Bournemouth	D3	A	L	0-2	
1972-73	D3	1	18.11.72	Aldershot	D4	H	L	0-2	
1973-74	D3	1	24.11.73	Borehamwood	AL	H	W	3-0	T.Johnson, Albeson (p), Kierstenson og
		2	15.12.73	Reading	D4	H	W	2-0	Brace, T.Johnson
		3	5.1.74	Peterborough U	D4	A	L	1-3	Moody

SOUTHEND UNITED

1974-75	D3	1	23.11.74	**AP Leamington**	SL	A	W	2-1	Guthrie, Silvester
		2	14.12.74	**Ilford**	IL	A	W	2-0	Townsend, Guthrie
		3	4.1.75	**QPR**	D1	H	D	2-2	Guthrie, Brace
		3r	7.1.75	**QPR**		A	L	0-2	
1975-76	D3	1	22.11.75	**Swansea C**	D4	H	W	2-0	Parker 2
		2	13.12.75	**Dover C**	SL	H	W	4-1	Parker, Silvester 2, Moody (p)
		3	3.1.76	**Brighton & HA**	D3	H	W	2-1	Silvester, Brace
		4	24.1.76	**Cardiff C**	D3	H	W	2-1	Parker 2
		5	14.2.76	**Derby Co**	D1	A	L	0-1	
1976-77	D4	1	20.11.76	**Exeter C**	D4	A	D	1-1	Pountney
		1r	22.11.76	**Exeter C**		H	W	2-1aet	Parker, Hadley
		2	11.12.76	**Newport Co**	D4	H	W	3-0	Hadley, Pountney, Parker
		3	8.1.77	**Chester**	D3	H	L	0-4	
1977-78	D4	1	26.11.77	**Torquay U**	D4	A	W	2-1	Parker, Fell
		2	17.12.77	**AP Leamington**	SL	A	D	0-0	
		2r	19.12.77	**AP Leamington**		H	W	4-0	Moody (p), Parker, Laverick, Morris
		3	7.1.78	**Derby Co**	D1	A	L	2-3	Parker 2
1978-79	D3	1	25.11.78	**Peterborough U**	D3	H	W	3-2	Pountney, Carmichael og, Parker
		2	16.12.78	**Watford**	D3	A	D	1-1	Parker
		2r	18.12.78	**Watford**		H	W	1-0	Polycarpou
		3	10.1.79	**Liverpool**	D1	H	D	0-0	
		3r	17.1.79	**Liverpool**		A	L	0-3	
1979-80	D3	1	24.11.79	**Wealdstone**	SL	A	W	1-0	Walker
		2	15.12.79	**Harlow T**	IL	H	D	1-1	Parker
		2r	18.12.79	**Harlow T**		A	L	0-1	
1980-81	D4	1	22.11.80	**Hereford U**	D4	H	L	0-1	
1981-82	D3	1	21.11.81	**Hereford U**	D4	A	L	1-3	Gray
1982-83	D3	1	20.11.82	**Bournemouth**	D3	A	W	2-0	Spackman og, Morgan og
		2	11.12.82	**Yeovil T**	APL	H	W	3-0	Phillips, Poutney 2
		3	8.1.83	**Sheffield W**	D2	H	D	0-0	
		3r	11.1.83	**Sheffield W**		A	D	2-2aet	Mercer, Poutney
		3 2r	24.1.83	**Sheffield W**		A	L	1-2	Cusack (p)
1983-84	D3	1	19.11.83	**Plymouth A**	D3	H	D	0-0	
		1r	22.11.83	**Plymouth A**		A	L	0-2aet	
1984-85	D4	1	17.11.84	**Colchester U**	D4	H	D	2-2	Clark, Phillips (p)
		1r	21.11.84	**Colchester U**		A	L	2-3aet	Shepherd, Phillips
1985-86	D4	1	16.11.85	**Newport Co**	D3	H	L	0-1	
1986-87	D4	1	15.11.86	**Halesowen T**	SL	H	W	4-1	Hall, McDonough 2, Cadette
		2	5.12.86	**Northampton T**	D4	H	D	4-4	Cadette 3, McDonough
		2r	10.12.86	**Northampton T**		A	L	2-3	Pennyfather, Cadette
1987-88	D3	1	14.11.87	**Walsall**	D3	H	D	0-0	
		1r	17.11.87	**Walsall**		A	L	1-2	Hall (p)
1988-89	D3	1	19.11.88	**Bristol C**	D3	A	L	1-3	Ling
1989-90	D4	1	18.11.89	**Aylesbury U**	IL	A	L	0-1	
1990-91	D3	1	17.11.90	**Leyton O**	D3	A	L	2-3	Angell 2
1991-92	D2	3	4.1.92	**Everton**	D1	A	L	0-1	
1992-93	D1	3	13.1.93	**Millwall**	D1	H	W	1-0	Collymore
		4	23.1.93	**Huddersfield T**	D2	A	W	2-1	Collymore 2
		5	13.2.93	**Sheffield W**	PL	A	L	0-2	

SOUTHPORT

Formed 1881 as Southport Central. 1894 Southport Wanderers. 1895 Southport Central. 1915 Southport Vulcan; 1919 Southport. **First entered FA Cup:** 1882. Member of the Football League: 1921-1978. **Best FA Cup Performance:** 6th round, 1931

1882-83	1	21.10.82	**Liverpool Ramblers**		A	D	1-1	
	1r	4.11.82	**Liverpool Ramblers**		H	L	0-4	
1883-84	1	20.10.83	**Blackburn R**		A	L	1-7	
1884-85	1	11.10.84	**Accrington**		A	L	0-3	
			Southport re-instated after Accrington were disqualified					
	2	22.11.84	**Clitheroe Low Moor**		H	W	3-1	Briggs, Mellor, og
	3	3.1.85	**Church FC**		A	L	0-10	
1885-86	1	10.10.85	**Astley Bridge**		A	L	2-3	
as Southport Wanderers								
1894-95	LL	1	2.2.95	**Everton**	D1	H	L	0-3	
as Southport Central								
1911-12	CL	1	13.1.12	**Reading**	SL	H	L	0-2	

SOUTHPORT

as Southport

1921-22	3N	5q **Altrincham** (H) 3-0; 6q **Coventry C** (D2) 1-0						
		1	7.1.22	**Blackburn R**	D1	A	D	1-1	Glover
		1r	12.1.22	**Blackburn R**		H	L	0-2	
1922-23	3N	5q **Wigan Borough** (H) 1-1; 5qr **Wigan Borough** (A) 1-3						
1923-24	3N	5q **Workington** (A) 2-1; 6q **Darlington** (A) 0-3						
1924-25	3N	5q **Tranmere R** (H) 1-0; 6q **Doncaster R** (A) 0-1						
1925-26	3N	1	28.11.25	**Mold**	Welsh	H	W	1-0	Sapsford
		2	12.12.25	**Durham C**	3N	A	W	3-0	Oxley 2, Sapsford
		3	9.1.26	**Southend U**	3S	A	L	2-5	Oxley, Sapsford
1926-27	3N	1	27.11.26	**Tranmere R**	3N	H	D	1-1	Sapsford
		1r	2.12.26	**Tranmere R**		A	W	2-1	Beadles, Jones
		2	11.12.26	**Crook T**	NL	H	W	2-0	Bradley 2
		3	8.1.27	**Blackburn R**	D1	H	W	2-0	White, Beadles
		4	29.1.27	**Liverpool**	D1	A	L	1-3	White
1927-28	3N	1	26.11.27	**Denaby U**	ML	A	W	3-2	Marshall, Tait 2
		2	10.12.27	**Bradford PA**	3N	A	W	2-0	Marshall, Tait
		3	14.1.28	**Fulham**	D2	H	W	3-0	Horler og, Tait 2
		4	28.1.28	**Middlesbrough**	D1	H	L	0-3	
1928-29	3N	1	24.11.28	**Annfield Plain**	NEL	A	W	4-1	Beadles 2, Mundy, Sissons
		2	8.12.28	**Stockport Co**	3N	A	L	0-3	
1929-30	3N	1	30.11.29	**Chesterfield**	3N	H	D	0-0	
		1r	4.12.29	**Chesterfield**		A	L	2-3	Allen, Cowen
1930-31	3N	1	29.11.30	**Darlington**	3N	H	W	4-2	McConnell 2, Waterston, Hills
		2	13.12.30	**Gainsborough T**	ML	A	W	4-0	Cowen, Waterston 2, Hills
		3	10.1.31	**Millwall**	D2	H	W	3-1	Hills, Cowen 2
		4	26.1.31	**Blackpool**	D1	H	W	2-1	Waterston 2
		5	14.2.31	**Bradford PA**	D2	H	W	1-0	Cowen
		6	28.2.31	**Everton**	D1	A	L	1-9	Waterston
1931-32	3N	3	9.1.32	**Barnsley**	D2	A	D	0-0	
		3r	12.1.32	**Barnsley**		H	W	4-1	Dobson, Waterston 2, Bell
		4	23.1.32	**Newcastle U**	D1	A	D	1-1	Cowen
		4r	26.1.32	**Newcastle U**		H	D	1-1aet	Cowen
		4 2r	1.2.32	**Newcastle U** at Hillsborough			L	0-9	
1932-33	3N	1	26.11.32	**Nelson**	LC	H	D	3-3	Appleby 2, Dobson
		1r	29.11.32	**Nelson**		A	W	4-0	Bell 3, Dobson
		2	10.12.32	**Swindon T**	3S	H	L	1-2	Appleby
1933-34	3N	1	25.11.33	**Workington**	NEL	A	L	0-1	
1934-35	3N	1	24.11.34	**New Brighton**	3N	H	D	1-1	Worswick
		1r	28.11.34	**New Brighton**		A	D	1-1aet	Pickering
		1 2r	3.12.34	**New Brighton** at Everton			L	1-2	Worswick
1935-36	3N	1	30.11.35	**Chesterfield**	3N	A	L	0-3	
1936-37	3N	1	28.11.36	**Frickley Colliery**	ML	A	W	2-0	Patrick 2
		2	12.12.36	**Bristol R**	3S	A	L	1-2	McCarthy
1937-38	3N	1	27.11.37	**Hartlepools**	3N	A	L	1-3	Kitchin
1938-39	3N	1	26.11.38	**Scarborough**	ML	A	D	0-0	
		1r	29.11.38	**Scarborough**		H	W	5-3	Patrick 3, Hawkins, A.Scott
		2	10.12.38	**Swindon T**	3S	H	W	2-0	Patrick 2
		3	10.1.39	**Doncaster R**		H	D	1-1	Patrick
		3r	12.1.39	**Doncaster R**		A	L	1-2	Stapleton
1945-46	3N	1 1L	17.11.45	**Oldham A**	3N	H	L	1-2	Oakes
		1 2L	24.11.45	**Oldham A**		A	L	1-3	Oakes
1946-47	3N	1	30.11.46	**Stockport Co**	3N	A	L	0-2	
1947-48	3N	1	29.11.47	**Hull C**	3N	A	D	1-1aet	Wyles
		1r	6.12.47	**Hull C**		H	L	2-3	Wyles 2
1948-49	3N	1	27.11.48	**Horden Colliery W**	NEL	H	W	2-1	Owens, Wyles
		2	11.12.48	**York C**	3N	H	D	2-2aet	Wyles, Banks
		2r	18.12.48	**York C**		A	W	2-0	Marriott, Wyles
1949-50	3N	1	26.11.49	**Barrow**	3N	H	D	1-1	Dainty
		1r	1.12.49	**Barrow**		A	L	0-1	
		2	10.12.49	**Bradford C**	3N	H	W	2-1	Meadows 2
		3	7.1.50	**Hull C**	D2	H	D	0-0	
		3r	12.1.50	**Hull C**		A	L	0-5	
1950-51	3N	1	25.11.50	**Lincoln C**	3N	A	D	1-1	Meadows
		1r	28.11.50	**Lincoln C**		H	W	3-2	Ross, Meadows, Nuttall
		2	9.12.50	**Carlisle U**	3N	H	L	1-3	Ross (p)
1951-52	3N	1	24.11.51	**Bangor C**	CC	A	D	2-2	Billingham, Livesey

		1r	27.11.51	Bangor C		H	W	3-0	Billingham, Nuttall, Livesey
		2	15.12.51	Reading	3S	A	D	1-1	Lindsay
		2r	19.12.51	Reading		H	D	1-1aet	Livesey (p)
		2 2r	1.1.52	Reading at Villa Park			L	0-2	
1952-53	3N	1	22.11.52	Bangor C	CC	H	W	3-1	Pennington, Nuttall 2
		2	6.12.52	Halifax T	3N	A	L	2-4	Hitchen, Nuttall
1953-54	3N	1	21.11.53	Carlisle U	3N	H	W	1-0	Hitchen
		2	12.12.53	Port Vale	3N	H	D	1-1	Whitworth
		2r	14.12.53	Port Vale		A	L	0-2	
1954-55	3N	1	20.11.54	Bradford PA	3N	A	L	0-2	
1955-56	3N	1	19.11.55	Ashton U	LC	H	W	6-1	Bromilow 5, Lawrenson
		2	10.12.55	Grimsby T	3N	H	D	0-0	
		2r	14.12.55	Grimsby T		A	L	2-3	Bromilow, Holmes
1956-57	3N	1	17.11.56	York C	3N	H	D	0-0	
		1r	20.11.56	York C		A	L	1-2	Prescott
1957-58	3N	1	16.11.57	Wigan A	LC	H	L	1-2	W.Phoenix
1958-59	D4	1	15.11.58	Halifax T	D3	H	L	0-2	
1959-60	D4	1	14.11.59	Workington	D4	H	D	2-2	Harrison 2 (1p)
		1r	18.11.59	Workington		A	L	0-3	
1960-61	D4	1	5.11.60	Macclesfield	CC	H	W	7-2	Blore 3, Blain 2, Griffiths, Booth
		2	26.11.60	Bangor C	CC	A	D	1-1	Hannaway
		2r	29.11.60	Bangor C		H	W	3-1	E.Jones, Blain, Blore
		3	7.1.61	Stockport Co	D4	A	L	1-3	Blore
1961-62	D4	1	4.11.61	Northwich V	CC	H	W	1-0	Blore
		2	25.11.61	Mansfield T	D4	H	W	4-2	Blain 2, Blore, Fielding
		3	9.1.62	Shrewsbury T	D3	H	L	1-3	Jones
1962-63	D4	1	3.11.62	Wrexham	D3	H	D	1-1	Cooper
		1r	7.11.62	Wrexham		A	L	2-3	Blain, Fielding
1963-64	D4	1	16.11.63	Walsall	D3	H	W	2-1	Spence, Latham
		2	7.12.63	Lincoln C	D4	A	L	0-2	
1964-65	D4	1	14.11.64	Annfield Plain	Wear	H	W	6-1	S.Taylor, Hobson og, Russell 2 (1p), Spence, Hepton
		2	5.12.64	Wrexham	D4	A	W	3-2	Russell (p), Spence
		3	9.1.65	Leeds U	D1	A	L	0-3	
1965-66	D4	1	13.11.65	Halifax T	D4	H	W	2-0	Russell 2
		2	4.12.65	Stockport Co	D4	H	D	3-3	Smith 2, Spence
		2r	13.12.65	Stockport Co		A	W	2-0	Barratt, Spence
		3	22.1.66	Ipswich T	D2	H	D	0-0	
		3r	25.1.66	Ipswich T		A	W	3-2	Spence 2, Alty
		4	12.2.66	Cardiff C	D2	H	W	2-0	Spence, Smith
		5	5.3.66	Hull C	D3	A	L	0-2	
1966-67	D4	1	26.11.66	Barnsley	D4	A	L	1-3	Fryatt
1967-68	D3	1	9.12.67	Lincoln C	D4	H	W	3-1	Redrobe 2, Andrews
		2	6.1.68	Runcorn	CC	H	W	4-2	Harkin, Redrobe, Andrews 2
		3	27.1.68	Everton	D1	H	L	0-1	
1968-69	D3	1	16.11.68	Tranmere R	D3	A	W	1-0	Spence
		2	7.12.68	Doncaster R	D4	A	L	1-2	Andrews
1969-70	D3	1	15.11.69	Lincoln C	D4	A	L	0-2	
1970-71	D4	1	21.11.70	Boston U	NPL	H	L	0-2	
1971-72	D4	1	20.11.71	Workington	D4	H	L	1-3	Dunleavy
1972-73	D4	1	18.11.72	Port Vale	D3	A	L	1-2	Provan
1973-74	D3	1	24.11.73	Rotherham U	D4	A	L	1-2	Noble (p)
1974-75	D4	1	23.11.74	Bury	D3	A	L	2-4	Sibbald (p), Russell
1975-76	D4	1	22.11.75	Spennymoor U	NL	A	L	1-4	O'Neil
1976-77	D4	1	20.11.76	Port Vale	D3	H	L	1-2	Wilson
1977-78	D4	1	26.11.77	Runcorn	NPL	H	D	2-2	Brooks, O'Neil
		1r	28.11.77	Runcorn		A	L	0-1	
1978-79	NPL	1	25.11.78	Altrincham	NPL	A	L	3-4	Nolan, Dewsnip, Whittle
1986-87	NPL	1	15.11.86	Scunthorpe U	D4	A	L	0-2	
1988-89	NPL	1	19.11.88	Port Vale	D3	H	L	0-2	
1992-93	NPL	1	14.11.92	Blyth Spartans	NL	A	W	2-1	Haw, Withers
		2	6.12.92	Hartlepool U	D2	A	L	0-4	

SOUTHWICK

Formed 1882. **First entered FA Cup:** 1890

1974-75	SCL	1	23.11.74	Bournemouth	D3	A	L	0-5	

SPALDING UNITED

Formed 1921. **First entered FA Cup:** 1921

1957-58	ECL	1	16.11.57	Durham C	NL	A	L	1-3	Jefferies
1964-65	ML	1	14.11.64	Newport Co	D4	A	L	3-5	Fox, Vest, Price

SPENNYMOOR UNITED

Formed 1901. **First entered FA Cup:** 1905. **League clubs beaten:** Hartlepools U, Southport

1927-28	NEL	1	26.11.27	Rotherham U	3N	H	D	1-1	Benstead
		1r	1.12.27	Rotherham U		A	L	2-4	Benstead, Kipling
1928-29	NEL	1	24.11.28	Hartlepools U	3N	H	W	5-2	Barkins 4, A.Middleton
		2	8.12.28	Accrington S	3N	A	L	0-7	
1932-33	NEL	1	26.11.32	Wrexham	3N	A	L	0-3	
1933-34	NEL	1	25.11.33	Walsall	3N	A	L	0-4	
1934-35	NEL	1	24.11.34	Rotherham	3N	A	L	0-2	
1936-37	NEL	1	28.11.36	Boston U	ML	A	D	1-1	Hill
		1r	2.12.36	Boston U		H	W	2-0	Wyness, Hill
		2	12.12.36	Ipswich T	SL	A	W	2-1	Wyness, Hill
		3	16.1.37	WBA	D1	A	L	1-7	Hill
1946-47	NEL	1	30.11.46	Lancaster C	LC	A	L	0-1	
1953-54	NEL	1	21.11.53	Barrow	3N	H	L	0-3	
1967-68	NL	1	9.12.67	Goole T	ML	A	D	0-0	
		1r	13.12.67	Goole T		H	W	3-1	Summerill 2, Knowles og
		2	6.1.68	Macclesfield T	CC	A	L	0-2	
1969-70	NL	1	15.11.69	Wrexham	D4	H	L	1-4	White
1972-73	NL	1	18.11.72	Shrewsbury T	D3	H	D	1-1	Banks
		1r	21.11.72	Shrewsbury T		A	L	1-3	Davies
1975-76	NL	1	22.11.75	Southport	D4	H	W	4-1	Banks 2, Mulligan, Reilly
		2	13.12.75	Bury	D3	A	L	0-3	
1977-78	NL	1	26.11.77	Goole T	NPL	H	W	3-1	Davies 2 (1p), Mulligan
		2	17.12.77	Rotherham U	D3	A	L	0-6	
1986-87	NL	1	15.11.86	Tranmere R	D4	H	L	2-3	Fowler, Mohan
1990-91	NCoE	1	17.11.90	Chesterfield	D4	A	L	2-3	Peattie, Boagey

SPILSBY

First entered FA Cup: 1880. Played at The Cricket Ground, Spilsby, Lincolnshire

1880-81	1	6.11.80	Stafford Road		H	L	0-7	
1881-82	1	29.10.81	Staveley		A	L	1-5	
1882-83	1	4.11.82	Sheffield Wednesday		A	L	2-12	B.Robinson, Barrett
1883-84	1	10.11.83	Grantham		A	L	2-3	B.Robinson, 1 other
1884-85	1	8.11.84	Newark		A	L	3-7	

SPITAL FC

Chesterfield-based amateur club.

1882-83	1	4.11.82	Wednesbury OA		H	L	1-7	Bishop
1884-85	1		bye					
	2	6.12.84	Sheffield Club		A	L	1-4	Booker

STAFFORD RANGERS

Formed 1876. **First entered FA Cup:** 1884. FA Challenge Trophy Winners: 1972, 1979. Runners-up: 1976. **Cup Final Connection:** Milija Aleksic, who played in goal for Tottenham H when they won the FA Cup Final in 1981 was a former Stafford Rangers player. **League clubs beaten:** Stockport Co, Halifax, Rotherham U, Lincoln C

1884-85		1		Newtown			scratched		
1885-86		1	31.10.85	Druids		H	L	1-4	
1972-73	NPL	1	18.11.72	Crewe A	D4	A	L	0-1	
1974-75	NPL	1	23.11.74	Stockport Co	D4	A	D	0-0	
		1r	26.11.74	Stockport Co		H	W	1-0	Albeson og
		2	14.12.74	Halifax T	D3	H	W	2-1	Cullerton, Sargeant
		3	4.1.75	Rotherham U	D4	H	D	0-0	
		3r	7.1.75	Rotherham U		A	W	2-0	Chapman, Cullerton

	4	24.1.75 **Peterborough U** at Stoke	D3	H	L	1-2	Cullerton
1975-76 NPL	1	22.11.75 **AP Leamington**	SL	A	W	3-2	Jones 2, Hughes
	2	13.12.75 **Halifax T**	D3	H	L	1-3	B.Sedden
1976-77 NPL	1	20.11.76 **Halifax T**	D4	H	D	0-0	
	1r	23.11.76 **Halifax T**		A	L	0-1	
1977-78 NPL	1	26.11.77 **Carlisle U**	D3	A	L	0-2	
1978-79 NPL	1	25.11.78 **Hull C**	D3	A	L	1-2	Wood
1979-80 APL	1	24.11.79 **Moor Green**	MC	H	W	3-2	Seddon, Howell og, Chapman
	2	17.12.79 **Blackburn R**	D3	A	L	0-2	
1980-81 APL	1	22.11.80 **Walsall**	D3	A	L	0-3	
1981-82 APL	1	21.11.81 **York C**	D4	H	L	1-2	Burr
1986-87 GMVC	1	15.11.86 **Port Vale**	D3	A	L	0-1	
1988-89 GMVC	1	19.11.88 **Crewe A**	D4	H	D	2-2	Camden 2
	1r	22.11.88 **Crewe A**		A	L	2-3	Cavell, Thacker
1989-90 GMVC	1	18.11.89 **Halifax T**	D4	H	L	2-3	Camden 2 (2ps)
1990-91 GMVC	1	17.11.90 **Burnley**	D4	H	L	1-3	Anastasi
1992-93 GMVC	1	14.11.92 **Lincoln C**	D3	A	D	0-0	
	1r	25.11.92 **Lincoln C**		H	W	2-1	Boughey, Bradshaw
	2	5.12.92 **Marine**	NPL	A	L	2-3	Berry (p), Palgrave

STAFFORD ROAD

Formed 1874. Played at Stafford Road Railway Works Recreation Ground, Wolverhampton

1879-80	1	8.11.79 **Wednesbury Strollers**		H	W	2-0	
	2	13.12.79 **Aston Villa**		H	D	1-1	
	2r	24.1.80 **Aston Villa**		A	L	1-3	Crump
1880-81	1	6.11.80 **Spilsby**		A	W	7-0	
	2	11.12.80 **Grantham**		A	D	1-1	
	2r	16.12.80 **Grantham**		H	W	7-1	
	3	**bye**					
	4	19.2.81 **Aston Villa**		A	W	3-2	Gowland 2, Crump
	5	19.3.81 **Old Etonians**		H	L	1-2	og
1881-82	1	5.11.81 **Wednesbury Strollers**		A	L	1-3	Gowland
1882-83	1	4.11.82 **Small Heath Alliance**		A	D	3-3	
	1r	18.11.82 **Small Heath Alliance**		H	W	6-2	
	2	2.12.82 **Walsall Town**		A	L	1-4	Foster
1883-84	1	10.11.83 **Aston Unity**		H	W	5-1	
	2	1.12.83 **Aston Villa**		H	L	0-5	
1884-85	1	8.11.84 **Walsall Swifts**		H	D	0-0	
	1r	17.11.84 **Walsall Swifts**		A	L	1-2	Thomas
1885-86	1	17.10.85 **Matlock**		H	W	7-0	
	2	21.11.85 **Wolverhampton W**		A	L	2-4	B.Jones, 1 other
1887-88	1	15.10.87 **Great Bridge Unity**		H	W	2-1	
		FA ordered replay after protest					
	1r	22.10.87 **Great Bridge Unity**		A	D	1-1	
	1 2r	**Great Bridge Unity**				scratched	

STAINES TOWN

Formed 1892. **First entered FA Cup:** 1904. **Cup Final Connection:** Former players Eric Young (Wimbledon 1988) and Gordon Hill (Manchester United, 1976 and 1977) both played in the FA Cup Final.

1984-85 IL	1	17.11.84 **Burton Albion**	NPL	A	L	0-2	

STALYBRIDGE CELTIC

Formed 1911. **First entered FA Cup:** 1912. Members of the Football League: 1921-1923

1921-22 3N		4q **Carlisle U** (A) 0-0; 4qr **Carlisle U** (H) 3-2; 5q **Hartlepools U** (H) 2-0; 6q **Ashington** (A) 0-1					
1922-23 3N		5q **Nelson** (H) 1-0; 6q **Bristol R** (H) 0-0; 6qr **Bristol R** (A) 2-1					
	1	13.1.23 **WBA**	D1	A	D	0-0	
	1r	17.1.23 **WBA**		H	L	0-2	
1932-33 CC	1	26.11.32 **Hull C**	3N	H	L	2-8	Hurst, Wright
1934-35 CC	1	24.11.34 **Tranmere R**	3N	A	L	1-3	Slater
1935-36 CC	1	30.11.35 **Kells U**	Cumb	H	W	4-0	Cheetham 3, Jones
	2	14.12.35 **Darlington**	3N	H	L	0-1	
1936-37 CC	1	28.11.36 **Shildon**	NL	A	L	2-4	Webster, Charles

1938-39	CC	1	26.11.38	Darlington	3N	A	L	0-4	
1945-46	CC	1 1L	17.11.45	Marine	LCC	A	L	0-4	
		1 2L	24.11.45	Marine		H	D	3-3	Webster 2, Egerton
1947-48	CC	1	29.11.47	Tranmere R	3N	A	L	0-2	
1984-85	NWC	1	17.11.84	Frickley A	APL	A	L	1-2	Stewart (p)

STALYBRIDGE ROVERS

Entered the FA Cup between 1894 and 1908.

| 1899-00 | LL | 1 | 27.1.00 | Bristol C | SL | A | L | 1-2 | Green |

STANLEY UNITED

Formed 1890. **First entered FA Cup:** 1900. **Cup final connection:** Tommy Cummings (Burnley 1962) and Geoff Strong (Liverpool 1965)

| 1954-55 | NL | 1 | 20.11.54 | Crook Town | NL | A | L | 3-5 | Bell, Hepple 2 |

STAPLE HILL

Formed 1892. Entered the FA Cup from 1895 until 1908.

| 1905-06 | WL | 1 | 13.1.06 | Manchester U | D2 | A | L | 2-7 | Tippett, G.Williams |

STAVELEY

Formed 1875. Played at the Recreation Ground, Staveley, Chesterfield

1881-82	1	29.10.81	Spilsby	H	W	5-1	Wallace 2, Beresford 2, Kenyon
	2	28.11.81	Grantham	H	W	3-1	
	3	29.12.81	Sheffield W	A	D	2-2	G.Marples, H.Marples
	3r	7.1.81	Sheffield W	H	D	0-0aet	
	3 2r	9.1.81	Sheffield W	A	L	1-5	H.Marples
1882-83	1	21.10.82	Walsall Town	A	L	1-4	Mather
1883-84	1	10.11.83	Middlesbrough	A	W	5-1	Potter, 4 others
	2	1.12.83	Sheffield W	H	W	3-1	Crookes
	3	29.12.83	Lockwood Brothers	H	W	1-0	Crookes
	4	19.1.84	Blackburn R	A	L	1-5	H.Marples
1884-85	1	8.11.84	Notts R	H	W	4-1	
	2	6.12.84	Notts Co	H	L	0-2	
1885-86	1	31.10.85	Mexborough	H	D	1-1	
	1r		Mexborough		*walkover*		
	2	21.11.85	Long Eaton R	A	W	4-1	
	3	12.12.85	Nottingham F	H	W	2-1	J.Hay, Young
	4		bye				
	5	23.1.86	Blackburn R	A	L	1-7	Needham
1886-87	1	30.10.86	Attercliffe	H	W	7-0	
	2	20.11.86	Rotherham T	H	W	4-0	Marshall, Needham, Potter, Shaw
	3	11.12.86	Notts Co	H	L	0-3	
1887-88	1	15.10.87	Derby Co	H	L	1-2	Rollinson

STOCKPORT COUNTY

Formed 1883. **First entered FA Cup:** 1892. **Best FA Cup Performance:** 5th round: 1935, 1950. **Record FA Cup Win:** 6-0 vs Barnton Rovers, 1st qualifying round, 31.10.1896. In Competition Proper: 6-2 vs West Auckland T, 1st round, 14.11.1959. **Record FA Cup Defeat:** 1-8 vs Bury, 2nd qualifying round, 29.10.1892. In Competition Proper: 0-7 vs Portsmouth, 3rd round, 8.1.1949

1892-93	TC	1q **Halliwell** (H) 4-0 *match replayed after protest*; 1q **Halliwell** (H) 4-2aet; 2q **Bury** (A) 1-8
1893-94	TC	1q **Bootle** walkover; 2q **Tranmere R** (H) 2-1; 3q **Wrexham** (H) 3-2; 4q **Crewe Alex** (H) 0-0aet; 4qr **Crewe Alex** (A) 2-1
		1 27.1.94 **Burton W** ML H L 0-1
1894-95	LL	1q **Fairfield** (H) 2-3
1895-96	LL	1q **Liverpool South End** (H) 2-0; 2q **Fairfield** (A) 1-5
1896-97	LL	1q **Barnton R** (H) 6-0; 2q **Druids** (A) 2-3
1897-98	LL	1q **Chester** (H) 2-0; 2q **Oswestry T** (H) 2-1; 3q **Rock Ferry** (H) 2-1; 4q **Aberystwyth** (H) 5-0; 5q **New Brighton Tower** (H) 0-1
1898-99	LL	3q **Ashton NE** (A) 2-2; 3qr **Ashton NE** (H) 2-0; 4q **Middleton** (H) 3-0; 5q **Glossop** (H) 0-2
1899-00	LL	3q **Glossop** (A) 2-2; 3qr **Glossop** (H) 3-0; 4q **Stalybridge R** (A) 0-2
1900-01	D2	3q **Wrexham** (H) 6-2; 4q **Crewe Alex** (H) 1-3
1901-02	D2	3q **Buxton** (A) 2-0; 4q **Crewe Alex** (H) 3-2; 5q **Glossop** (A) 0-2
1902-03	D2	1q **Stalybridge R** (H) 0-1

1903-04	D2	3q Heywood (H) 4-0; 4q Port Vale (H) 0-0; 4qr Port Vale (A) 0-6						
1904-05	ML	3q Stalybridge R (H) 2-0; 4q Glossop (A) 1-1; 4qr Glossop (H) 0-0; 4q 2r Glossop (A) 0-0; 4q 3r Glossop (H) 1-0;						
		5q Wrexham (H) 4-0; 6q Chesterfield (A) 0-2						
1905-06	D2	4q Walsall (A) 3-3; 4qr Walsall (H) 5-0						
		1	13.1.06	Lincoln C	D2	A	L	2-4	Schofield, Bardsley
1906-07	D2	1	12.1.07	Fulham	SL	A	D	0-0	
		1r	16.1.07	Fulham		A	L	1-2	Pass
1907-08	D2	1	11.1.08	Aston Villa	D1	A	L	0-3	
1908-09	D2	1	16.1.09	Grimsby T	D2	A	–	2-0	Green, Whitehouse
			abandoned after 75 minutes						
		1	20.1.09	Grimsby T		A	W	2-0	Whitehouse, Lomax
		2	6.2.09	Glossop	D2	H	D	1-1	Whitehouse
		2r	9.2.09	Glossop		A	L	0-1aet	
1909-10	D2	1	15.1.10	Bolton W	D1	H	W	4-1	Whitehouse 2, Newman, Greechan
		2	5.2.10	Leyton	SL	H	L	0-2	
1910-11	D2	4q Rochdale (A) 0-0; 4qr Rochdale (H) 0-0; 4q 2r Rochdale 0-1 (at Oldham)						
1911-12	D2	4q Chester (A) 4-1; 5q Catford Southend (H) 4-0						
		1	13.1.12	Lincoln C	CL	A	L	0-2	
1912-13	D2	4q Willenhall (A) 2-0; 5q Kings Lynn (A) 7-2						
		1	11.1.13	Everton	D1	A	–	1-1	Tatersall
			abandoned after 48 minutes						
		1	15.1.13	Everton		A	L	1-5	Maconnachie og
1913-14	D2	4q Gainsborough T (A) 2-3						
1914-15	D2	1	9.1.15	Liverpool	D1	A	L	0-3	
1919-20	D2	1	10.1.20	Preston NE	D1	A	L	1-3	Rogers
1920-21	D2	1	8.1.21	Everton	D1	A	L	0-1	
1921-22	3N	5q Lancaster T (A) 0-2						
1922-23	D2	5q Barrow (A) 2-3						
1923-24	D2	5q Crewe Alex (H) 1-0; 6q Norwich C (A) 0-2						
1924-25	D2	1	10.1.25	QPR	3S	A	W	3-1	Waterall, Blood, Simms
		2	31.1.25	Birmingham	D1	A	L	0-1	
1925-26	D2	3	9.1.26	Sheffield U	D1	A	L	0-2	
1926-27	3N	1	27.11.26	Nelson	3N	A	L	1-4	Scutt
1927-28	3N	1	26.11.27	Oswestry T	BDL	H	W	5-2	J.Smith 2 (1p), Scutt, Pearson, Duffus
		2	10.12.27	Crewe A	3N	A	L	0-2	
1928-29	3N	1	24.11.28	Halifax T	3N	H	W	1-0	Fielding
		2	10.12.28	Southport	3N	H	W	3-0	Newton 2
		3	12.1.29	Bradford C	3N	A	L	0-2	
1929-30	3N	1	30.11.29	Wellington T	BDL	A	W	4-1	Gee, Newton 2, Tompkinson
		2	14.12.29	Barrow	3N	H	W	4-0	Boardman, Newton, Lincoln 2
		3	11.1.30	Blackpool	D2	A	L	1-2	Boardman
1930-31	3N	1	29.11.30	Hartlepools U	3N	A	W	3-2	F.Newton, Lincoln, Webster
		2	13.12.30	Bristol R	3S	A	L	2-4	Lincoln, F.Newton
1931-32	3N	1	28.11.31	Crook T	NEL	A	L	1-3	Smith
1932-33	3N	1	26.11.32	Rochdale	3N	A	W	2-0	Taylor, Vincent
		2	10.12.32	Luton T	3S	H	L	2-3	Taylor, Foulkes
1933-34	3N	1	25.11.33	Lancaster T	LC	A	W	1-0	Lythgoe
		2	9.12.33	Crystal P	3S	H	L	1-2	Vincent
1934-35	3N	1	24.11.34	Blyth Spartans	NEL	A	D	1-1	Foulkes
		1r	28.11.34	Blyth Spartans		H	W	4-1	Urwin, Stevenson 2, Foulkes
		2	8.12.34	Darlington	3N	H	W	3-2	Green 2, Hill
		3	12.1.35	West Ham	D2	A	D	1-1	Barrett og
		3r	16.1.35	West Ham		H	W	1-0	Hill
		4	26.1.35	Bradford C	D2	A	D	0-0	
		4r	31.1.35	Bradford C		H	W	3-2aet	Geen, Hill 2
		5	16.2.35	WBA	D1	H	L	0-5	
1935-36	3N	3	11.1.36	Plymouth A	D2	H	L	2-3	Rae og, McNaughton
1936-37	3N	1	28.11.36	Carlisle U	3N	A	L	1-2	Still
1937-38	D2	3	8.1.38	Middlesbrough	D1	A	L	0-2	
1938-39	3N	1	26.11.38	North Shields	NEL	A	W	4-1	Bagley, Essex, Sargeant 2
		2	10.12.38	Walthamstow Ave	AL	H	D	0-0	
		2r	15.12.38	Walthamstow Ave		A	W	3-1	Sargeant 3
		3	7.1.39	Barnsley	3N	A	W	2-1	Essex, Sargeant
		4	21.1.39	Liverpool	D1	A	L	1-5	Reid
1945-46	3N	3 1L	17.11.45	Rochdale	3N	H	L	1-2	Shaw
		3 2L	24.11.45	Rochdale		A	D	1-1	Hyde
1946-47	3N	1	30.11.46	Southport	3N	H	W	2-0	Brinton, Cocker

Season	Div	Rnd	Date	Opponent	Comp	Venue	Result	Score	Scorers
		2	14.12.46	Halifax T	3N	A	D	1-1	Shaw
		2r	18.12.46	Halifax T		H	W	2-1	Earl, McCulloch
		3	11.1.47	Bolton W	D1	A	L	1-5	Walker
1947-48	3N	1	29.11.47	Accrington S	3N	H	W	3-1	Stock 2, Morris
		2	13.12.47	Shrewsbury T	ML	H	–	1-1	Barkas
			abandoned after 110 minutes						
		2	20.12.47	Shrewsbury T		H	D	2-2aet	Shaw, Glaister
		2r	22.12.47	Shrewsbury T at Maine Road			W	3-2	Glaister 2, McCulloch
		3	10.1.48	Torquay U	3S	H	W	3-0	Morris, Barkas 2
		4	24.1.48	Charlton A	D1	A	L	0-3	
1948-49	3N	1	27.11.48	Workington	NEL	A	W	3-0	Herd 2, Glaister
		2	11.12.48	Scunthorpe U	ML	A	W	1-0	Glaister
		3	8.1.49	Portsmouth	D1	A	L	0-7	
1949-50	3N	1	26.11.49	Billingham Syn	NL	H	W	3-0	McGuigan 2, Herd
		2	10.12.49	Nottingham F	3S	A	W	2-0	McGuigan, Herd
		3	7.1.50	Barnsley	D2	H	W	4-2	Cocker 2, Swinscoe, McGuigan
		4	28.1.50	Hull C	D2	H	D	0-0	
		4r	2.2.50	Hull C		A	W	2-0	Herd, Cocker
		5	11.2.50	Liverpool	D1	H	L	1-2	Herd
1950-51	3N	3	6.1.51	Brentford	D2	H	W	2-1	Cocker, Dixon
		4	27.1.51	Blackpool	D1	A	L	1-2	Black
1951-52	3N	1	24.11.51	Gateshead	3N	H	D	2-2	Oliver, Weigh
		1r	28.11.51	Gateshead		A	D	1-1aet	Weigh
		1 2r	3.12.51	Gateshead at Hillsborough			L	1-2	Glover
1952-53	3N	1	22.11.52	North Shields	NEL	A	W	6-3	Bodie 2, Connor 3, Oliver
		2	6.12.52	Gillingham	3S	H	W	3-1	Oliver, Bodie, Connor
		3	10.1.53	Walthamstow Ave	IL	A	L	1-2	Moran
1953-54	3N	1	21.11.53	Chester	3N	H	W	4-3	Clempson, Connor 3
		2	12.12.53	Workington	3N	H	W	2-1	Connor, Cushin og
		3	9.1.54	Headington U	SL	H	D	0-0	
		3r	14.1.54	Headington U		A	L	0-1	
1954-55	3N	1	20.11.54	Carlisle U	3N	H	L	0-1	
1955-56	3N	1	19.11.55	Mansfield T	3N	A	L	0-2	
1956-57	3N	1	17.11.56	New Brighton	LC	A	D	3-3	Finney, Moran 2
		1r	20.11.56	New Brighton		H	L	2-3	Finney, Daley
1957-58	3N	1	16.11.57	Barrow	3N	H	W	2-1	Davock, Wilson
		2	7.12.57	Hartlepools U	3N	H	W	2-1	Davock, Sowden
		3	4.1.58	Luton T	D1	H	W	3-0	Jackson, Holden 2
		4	25.1.58	West Ham	D2	A	L	2-3	Holden, Finney
1958-59	D3	1	15.11.58	Hull C	D3	A	W	1-0	Jackson
		2	6.12.58	Blyth Spartans	ML	A	W	4-3	Wilson, Clarke, Clempson, Jackson
		3	14.1.59	Burnley	D1	H	L	1-3	Jackson
1959-60	D4	1	14.11.59	West Auckland T	NL	A	W	6-2	Guy 2, Betts, Wilson, Davock, Ritchie
		2	5.12.59	Crewe A	D4	H	D	0-0	
		2r	9.12.59	Crewe A		A	L	0-2	
1960-61	D4	1	5.11.60	Workington	D4	H	W	1-0	Anderson
		2	26.11.60	Bishop Auckland	NL	H	W	2-0	Davock 2
		3	7.1.61	Southport	D4	H	W	3-1	Anderson 2, Wilson
		4	1.2.61	Newcastle U	D1	A	L	0-4	
1961-62	D4	1	4.11.61	Accrington S	D4	H	L	0-1	
1962-63	D4	1	3.11.62	Chesterfield	D4	A	L	1-4	Bentley
1963-64	D4	1	16.11.63	Barnsley	D3	A	L	0-1	
1964-65	D4	1	14.11.64	Wigan A	CC	H	W	2-1	Eckershall (p), Nibloe
		2	5.12.64	Grimsby T	D3	H	–	0-0	
			abandoned after 50 minutes – fog						
		2	7.12.64	Grimsby T		H	W	1-0	Hodgkinson
		3	9.1.65	Bristol R	D3	A	D	0-0	
		3r	11.1.65	Bristol R		H	W	3-2	Hodgkinson, Beaumont, Sandiford
		4	30.1.65	Liverpool	D1	A	D	1-1	White
		4r	3.2.65	Liverpool		H	L	0-2	
1965-66	D4	1	13.11.65	Tranmere R	D4	A	W	1-0	Price
		2	4.12.65	Southport	D4	A	D	3-3	Allen 2, Shawcross (p)
		2r	13.12.65	Southport		H	L	0-2	
1966-67	D4	1	26.11.66	Darlington	D3	A	D	0-0	
		1r	29.11.66	Darlington		H	D	1-1aet	Morrin
		1 2r	5.12.66	Darlington at Elland Road			L	2-4	Greener og, Sykes
1967-68	D3	1	9.12.67	Macclesfield	CC	H	D	1-1	Atkins

Season	Div	Rd	Date	Opponent	OppDiv	Venue	W/L/D	Score	Scorers
		1r	13.12.67	Macclesfield		A	L	1-2	Kevan
1968-69	D3	1	16.11.68	Bradford PA	D4	H	W	3-0	Atkins, Harley, Lowe (p)
		2	7.12.68	Barrow		H	W	2-0	Young, Atkins
		3	4.1.69	Blackburn R	D2	A	L	0-2	
1969-70	D3	1	15.11.69	Mossley	CC	H	D	1-1	Collier
		1r	18.11.69	Mossley		A	W	1-0	Rowlands
		2	6.12.69	Scunthorpe U	D4	H	D	0-0	
		2r	9.12.69	Scunthorpe U		A	L	0-4	
1970-71	D4	1	21.11.70	Grantham	ML	A	L	1-2	McMillan
1971-72	D4	1	20.11.71	Doncaster R	D4	A	W	2-1	McMillan, Lawther
		2	11.12.71	Blyth Spartans	NL	A	L	0-1	
1972-73	D4	1	18.11.72	Workington	D4	H	W	1-0	Spratt (p)
		2	9.12.72	Rotherham U	D3	A	W	1-0	Davidson
		3	13.1.73	Hull C	D2	H	D	0-0	
		3r	23.1.73	Hull C		A	L	0-2aet	
1973-74	D4	1	24.11.73	Port Vale	D3	H	L	0-1	
1974-75	D4	1	23.11.74	Stafford R	NPL	H	D	0-0	
		1r	26.11.74	Stafford R		A	L	0-1	
1975-76	D4	1	22.11.75	Hartlepool	D4	A	L	0-3	
1976-77	D4	1	20.11.76	Sheffield W	D3	A	L	0-2	
1977-78	D4	1	26.11.77	Scunthorpe U	D4	H	W	3-0	Fletcher, Massey, Fogarty
		2	17.12.77	Shrewsbury T	D3	A	D	1-1	Summerbee
		2r	19.12.77	Shrewsbury T		H	L	1-2	Prudham
1978-79	D4	1	25.11.78	Morecambe	NPL	H	W	5-1	Prudham, Bradd, Park 3
		2	16.12.78	Bradford C	D4	H	W	4-2	Fogarty, Lee, Bradd, Park
		3	1.2.79	Wrexham	D2	A	L	2-6	Lee, Park
1979-80	D4	1	24.11.79	Walsall	D4	A	L	0-2	
1980-81	D4	1	22.11.80	Sheffield U	D3	H	D	0-0	
		1r	25.11.80	Sheffield U		A	L	2-3	Coyle, Sunley
1981-82	D4	1	21.11.81	Mossley	NPL	H	W	3-1	Williams 2, Park
		2	2.1.82	Port Vale	D4	A	L	1-4	Smith
1982-83	D4	1	20.11.82	Mansfield T	D4	A	L	2-3	Williams, Park
1983-84	D4	1	19.11.83	Telford U	APL	A	L	0-3	
1984-85	D4	1	17.11.84	Walsall	D3	H	L	1-2	Taylor
1985-86	D4	1	16.11.85	Telford U	APL	H	L	0-1	
1986-87	D4	1	15.11.86	Caernarfon T	NPL	A	L	0-1	
1987-88	D4	1	14.11.87	Telford U	GMVC	A	D	1-1	Entwistle
		1r	17.11.87	Telford U		H	W	2-0	Colville, Hodkinson (p)
		2	5.12.87	Runcorn	GMVC	A	W	1-0	Colville
		3	9.1.88	Leyton O	D4	H	L	1-2	Colville
1988-89	D4	1	19.11.88	Scarborough	D4	A	L	1-2	Colville
1989-90	D4	1	18.11.89	Burnley	D4	A	D	1-1	Angell
		1r	22.11.89	Burnley		H	L	1-2	Edwards
1990-91	D4	1	17.11.90	Rotherham U	D3	A	L	0-1	
1991-92	D3	1	16.11.91	Lincoln C	D4	H	W	3-1	Gannon, Ward (og), Francis
		2	7.12.91	Wigan A	D3	A	L	0-2	
1992-93	D2	1	14.11.92	York C	D3	A	W	3-1	Todd, Francis 2
		2	5.12.92	Macclesfield	GMVC	A	W	2-0	Preece, B.Williams
		3	2.1.93	Derby Co	D1	A	L	1-2	McCourt

STOCKTON

Formed 1882. First entered FA Cup: 1888. FA Amateur Cup Winners: 1899, 1903, 1912. Folded 1975. League club beaten: Mansfield T

Season	Div	Rd	Date	Opponent	OppDiv	Venue	W/L/D	Score	Scorers
1892-93	NL	1	21.1.92	Grimsby T	D2	A	L	0-5	
1896-97	NL	1	30.1.97	Bury	D1	H	D	0-0	
		1r	2.2.97	Bury		A	L	1-12	Daniels
1903-04	NL	Int	12.12.03	Shrewsbury T	BDL	H	W	2-1	RS Foster, Payne
		1	6.2.04	Wolverhampton W	D1	H	L	1-4	Blake
1907-08	NL	1	11.1.08	Chesterfield	D2	A	L	0-4	
1925-26	NL	1	3.12.25	South Bank	NL	A	W	4-1	Harrison 2, Thompson, Longstaffe
		2	12.12.25	Oldham A	D2	H	L	4-6	Thompson 2, Smith 2
1926-27	NL	1	27.11.26	Ashington	3N	H	L	1-2	Smith
1927-28	NL	1	26.11.27	Gainsborough T	ML	A	L	0-6	
1945-46	NEL	1 1L	17.11.45	Darlington	3N	A	L	0-2	
		1 2L	24.11.45	Darlington		H	L	1-4	Middleton
1946-47	NEL	1	30.11.46	Lincoln C	3N	H	L	2-4	Glassey, Davie

STOCKTON

1947-48	NEL	1	29.11.47	Grantham	ML	H	W	2-1	Laidman 2
		2	13.12.47	Notts Co	3S	A	D	1-1aet	Leicester
		2r	20.12.47	Notts Co at Middlesbrough		H	L	1-4	Pears
1949-50	NEL	1	26.11.49	Oldham A	3N	A	L	0-4	
1951-52	NEL	1	24.11.51	Mansfield T	3N	H	D	1-1	Clarke
		1r	28.11.51	Mansfield T		A	W	2-0	Chadwick, Clarke
		2	15.12.51	Folkestone	KL	H	W	2-1	Liddle 2
		3	12.1.52	Notts Co	D2	A	L	0-4	

STOKE CITY

Formed 1863 as Stoke. Founder Members of the Football League 1888. 1925 Stoke City. **Best FA Cup Performance:** semifinals: 1899, 1971, 1972. **Record FA Cup Win:** 11-0 vs Stourbridge, preliminary round, 26.9.1914. In Competition Proper: 7-1 vs Burnley, 2nd round replay, 10.2.1896. **Record FA Cup Defeat:** 0-8 vs Wolverhampton W, 3rd round replay, 22.2.1890

as Stoke FC

1883-84		1	10.11.83	Manchester FC		H	L	1-2	Johnson
1884-85		1		Queens Park, Glasgow					*scratched*
1885-86		1	31.10.85	Crewe A		H	D	2-2	
		1r	7.11.85	Crewe A		A	L	0-1aet	
1886-87		1	30.10.86	Caernarfon W		H	W	10-1	
		2	20.11.86	Crewe A		A	L	4-6aet	Edge 2, Bennett, Conde og
1887-88		1	15.10.87	Burslem Port Vale		H	W	1-0	Lawton
		2	5.11.87	Over W		A	W	2-0	Owen, 1 other
		3	26.11.87	Oswestry		H	W	3-0	Edge, Balham, 1 other
		4		bye					
		5	7.1.88	WBA		A	L	1-4	Owen
1888-89	D1	1q	Warwick County (H) 1-2						
1889-90	D1	1	18.1.90	Old Westminsters		H	W	3-0	Gee, Ramsey, Sayer
		2	1.2.90	Everton	D1	H	W	4-2	Edge 3, Dunn
		3	15.2.90	Wolverhampton W	D1	A	L	0-4	
			FA ordered replay after protest						
		3r	22.2.90	Wolverhampton W		A	L	0-8	
1890-91	FAll	1	17.1.91	Preston NE	D1	H	W	3-0	Balham, Coupar, Turner
		2	31.1.91	Aston Villa	D1	H	W	3-0	Balham 2, Coupar
		3	14.2.91	Notts Co	D1	A	L	0-1	
1891-92	D1	1	16.1.92	Casuals		H	W	3-0	Dunn 2, Evans
		2	30.1.92	Burnley	D1	A	W	3-1	Schofield, Turner, 1 other
		3	13.2.92	Sunderland	D1	H	D	2-2aet	Turner, Schofield
		3r	20.2.92	Sunderland		A	L	0-4	
1892-93	D1	1	21.1.93	Accrington	D1	A	L	1-2	Brodie
1893-94	D1	1	27.1.94	Everton	D1	H	W	1-0	Schofield
		2	10.2.94	Sheffield W	D1	A	L	0-1	
1894-95	D1	1	2.2.95	Newton Heath	D2	A	W	3-2	Dickson 2, Robertson
		2	16.2.95	Wolverhampton W	D1	A	L	0-2	
1895-96	D1	1	1.2.96	Tottenham H	SL	H	W	5-0	A.Maxwell 2, W.Maxwell 2, Dickson
		2	15.2.96	Burnley	D1	A	D	1-1	Johnson
		2r	20.2.96	Burnley		H	W	7-1	Hyslop 4, A.Maxwell 3
		3	29.2.96	Wolverhampton W	D1	A	L	0-3	
1896-97	D1	1	30.1.97	Glossop NE	ML	H	W	5-2	W.Maxwell 3, Hingerty 2
		2	13.2.97	Preston NE	D1	A	L	1-2	W.Maxwell
1897-98	D1	1	29.1.98	Bury	D1	A	W	2-1	W.Maxwell, Hill
		2	12.2.98	Everton	D1	H	D	0-0	
		2r	17.2.98	Everton		A	L	1-5	Hill
1898-99	D1	1	28.1.99	Sheffield W	D1	A	D	2-2	Kennedy, own goal
		1r	2.2.99	Sheffield W		H	W	2-0	W.Maxwell, Schofield
		2	11.2.99	Small Heath	D2	H	D	2-2	W.Maxwell, Schofield
		2r	15.2.99	Small Heath		A	W	2-1	W.Maxwell 2
		3	25.2.99	Tottenham H	SL	H	W	4-1	Cain og, Kennedy, Turner, Johnson
		SF	18.3.99	Derby Co	D1		L	1-3	W.Maxwell
			played at Molineux						
1899-00	D1	1	27.1.00	Liverpool	D1	H	D	0-0	
		1r	1.2.00	Liverpool		A	L	0-1	
1900-01	D1	Int	5.1.01	Glossop	D2	H	W	1-0	Benbow
		1	9.2.01	Small Heath	D2	H	D	1-1	Watkins
		1r	13.2.01	Small Heath		A	L	1-2aet	Benbow
1901-02	D1	1	25.1.02	Aston Villa	D1	H	D	2-2	Holford, Johnson

Season	Div	Round	Date	Opponent		Venue	Result	Score	Scorers
		1r	29.1.02	Aston Villa		A	W	2-1aet	Higginson, Johnson
		2	8.2.02	Bristol R	SL	A	W	1-0	own goal
		3	22.2.02	Nottingham F	D1	A	L	0-2	
1902-03	D1	1	7.2.03	Glossop	D2	A	W	3-2	Capes, Watkins, Whitehouse
		2	21.2.03	Nottingham F	D1	A	D	0-0	
		2r	26.2.03	Nottingham F		H	W	2-0	Bradley, Higginson
		3	7.3.03	Derby County	D1	A	L	0-3	
1903-04	D1	1	6.2.04	Aston Villa	D1	H	L	2-3	Baddeley, Higginson
1904-05	D1	1	4.2.05	Grimsby T	D2	H	W	2-0	Baddeley, Godley
		2	18.2.05	Everton	D1	H	L	0-4	
1905-06	D1	1	13.1.06	Blackburn R	D1	H	W	1-0	Sturgess
		2	3.2.06	Birmingham	D1	H	L	0-1	
1906-07	D1	1	12.1.07	WBA	D2	A	D	1-1	Baddeley
		1r	17.1.07	WBA		H	D	2-2aet	Fielding, Arrowsmith
		1 2r	21.1.07	WBA at Villa Park			L	0-2	
1907-08	D2	1	11.1.08	Lincoln C	D2	H	W	5-0	Brown, Holford, Gallimore 3
		2	1.2.08	Gainsborough T	D2	H	D	1-1	Baddeley
		2r	5.2.08	Gainsborough T		A	D	2-2aet	Baddeley, Brown
		2 2r	10.2.08	Gainsborough T at Nottingham F			W	3-1	Watkins, Brown, Holford
		3	22.2.08	Portsmouth	SL	A	W	1-0	Holford
		4	7.3.08	Wolverhampton W	D2	H	L	0-1	
1908-09	BDL	1	16.1.09	Sheffield W	D1	A	L	0-5	
1909-10	BDL	4q Ilkeston U (H) 2-0; 5q Exeter C (H) 0-0; 5qr Exeter C (A) 1-1; 5q 2r Exeter C at Fulham								
		1	15.1.10	Newcastle U	D1	H	D	1-1	A.Baddeley
		1r	19.1.10	Newcastle U		A	L	1-2	Griffiths
1910-11	BDL	4q Worcester C (H) 7-0; 5q Lincoln C (H) 4-0								
		1	14.1.11	Manchester C	D1	H	L	1-2	A.Smith
1911-12	SL	4q Walsall (A) 1-2								
1912-13	SL	1	11.1.13	Reading	SL	H	–	2-1	Herbert, Revill
				abandoned after 25 minutes					
		1	16.1.13	Reading		H	D	2-2	Revill, A.Smith
		1r	22.1.13	Reading		A	L	0-3	
1913-14	SL	4q Shrewsbury T (H) 2-0; 5q Barrow (H) 3-1								
		1	10.1.14	Aston Villa	D1	A	L	0-4	
1914-15	SL	P Stourbridge (H) 11-0; 1q Birmingham Corporation Tramways (A) 3-2; 2q Brierley Hill Alliance (H) 1-0; 3q Walsall (A) 0-1								
1919-20	D2	1	10.1.20	Bury	D2	A	L	0-2	
1920-21	D2	1	8.1.21	Wolverhampton W	D2	A	L	2-3	Burton, Watkins
1921-22	D2	1	7.1.22	Port Vale	D2	A	W	4-2	Watkin 3, Tempest
		2	28.1.22	Northampton T	3S	A	D	2-2	Watkin 2
		2r	2.2.22	Northampton T		H	W	3-0	J.Broad 2, Tempest
		3	18.2.22	Aston Villa	D1	H	D	0-0	
		3r	22.2.22	Aston Villa		A	L	0-4	
1922-23	D1	1	13.1.23	Blyth Spartans	NEL	A	W	3-0	J.Broad 2, Nicholas
		2	3.2.23	Bury	D2	A	L	1-3	J.Broad
1923-24	D2	1	12.1.24	Leeds U	D2	A	L	0-1	
1924-25	D2	1	10.1.25	Leicester C	D2	A	L	0-3	
as Stoke City									
1925-26	D2	3	9.1.26	Wigan B	3N	A	W	5-2	Davies 2, R.johnson 3
		4	30.1.26	Swansea T	D2	A	L	3-6	Davies, Johnson, Bestwick
1926-27	3N	1	27.11.26	Rhyl A	Welsh	A	D	1-1	Wilson
		1r	2.12.26	Rhyl A		H	D	1-1aet	Davies
		1 2r	6.12.26	Rhyl A at Old Trafford			L	1-2	Davies
1927-28	D2	3	14.1.28	Gillingham	3S	H	W	6-1	Wilson 2, Williamson 2, Archibald, Bussey
		4	28.1.28	Bolton W	D1	H	W	4-2	Archibald, Davies, Wilson 2
		5	18.2.28	Manchester City	D2	A	W	1-0	Wilson
		6	3.3.28	Arsenal	D1	A	L	1-4	Wilson
1928-29	D2	3	12.1.29	Arsenal	D1	A	L	1-2	Bussey
1929-30	D2	3	11.1.30	Doncaster R	3N	A	–	3-2	Williamson, Wilson, Bussey
				abandoned during the second half because of a snowstorm					
		3	16.1.30	Doncaster R		A	L	0-1	
1930-31	D2	3	10.1.31	Manchester U	D1	H	D	3-3	Wilson, Sale 2
		3r	14.1.31	Manchester U		A	D	0-0aet	
		3 2r	19.1.31	Manchester U at Anfield			L	2-4	Archibald, Liddle
1931-32	D2	3	9.1.32	Hull C	3N	H	W	3-0	Sellars, Bussey, Mawson,
		4	23.1.32	Sunderland	D1	A	D	1-1	Mawson
		4r	28.1.32	Sunderland		H	D	1-1aet	Bussey
		4 2r	1.2.32	Sunderland at Maine Road			W	2-1aet	Mawson 2

Season	Div	Rd	Date	Opponent	Opp Div	H/A	Res	Score	Scorers
		5	13.2.32	Bury	D2	A	L	0-3	
1932-33	D2	3	14.1.33	Southampton	D2	H	W	1-0	Davies
		4	28.1.33	Middlesbrough	D1	A	L	1-4	Liddle
1933-34	D1	3	13.1.34	Bradford PA	D2	H	W	3-0	Sale, Matthews, Soo
		4	27.1.34	Blackpool	D2	H	W	3-0	Matthews, Soo, Sale
		5	17.2.34	Chelsea	D1	H	W	3-1	Matthews 2, Johnson
		6	3.3.34	Manchester C	D1	A	L	0-1	
1934-35	D1	3	12.1.35	Swansea T	D2	A	L	1-4	Matthews
1935-36	D1	3	11.1.36	Millwall	3S	A	D	0-0	
		3r	15.1.36	Millwall		H	W	4-0	Steele 3, Liddle
		4	25.1.36	Manchester U	D2	H	D	0-0	
		4r	29.1.36	Manchester U		A	W	2-0	Sale, Robson
		5	15.2.36	Barnsley	D2	A	L	1-2	Davies
1936-37	D1	3	16.1.37	Birmingham	D1	H	W	4-1	Steele 3, Johnson
		4	30.1.37	Preston NE	D1	A	L	1-5	Johnson
1937-38	D1	3	8.1.38	Derby Co	D1	A	W	2-1	Baker, Bell og
		4	22.1.38	Bradford PA	D2	A	D	1-1	Soo
		4r	26.1.38	Bradford PA		H	L	1-2	Soo
1938-39	D1	3	7.1.39	Leicester C	D1	A	D	1-1	Soo
		3r	11.1.39	Leicester C		H	L	1-2	Steele
1945-46	D1	3 1L	5.1.46	Burnley	D2	H	W	3-1	Steele 3
		3 2L	7.1.46	Burnley		A	L	1-2	Antonio
		4 1L	26.1.46	Sheffield U	D1	H	W	2-0	G.Mountford, Steele
		4 2L	28.1.46	Sheffield U		A	L	2-3	Antonio, Steele
		5 1L	9.2.46	Sheffield W	D2	H	W	2-0	Steele 2
		5 2L	11.2.46	Sheffield W		A	D	0-0	
		6 1L	2.3.46	Bolton W	D1	H	L	0-2	
		6 2L	9.3.46	Bolton W		A	D	0-0	
1946-47	D1	3	11.1.47	Tottenham H	D2	A	D	2-2	Ludford og, F.Mountford
		3r	15.1.47	Tottenham H		H	W	1-0	Matthews
		4	25.1.47	Chester	3N	A	D	0-0	
		4r	29.1.47	Chester		H	W	3-2	Steele 2, Ormston
		5	8.2.47	Sheffield U	D1	H	L	0-1	
1947-48	D1	3	10.1.48	Mansfield T	3N	A	W	4-2	Sellars, Kiernan, Steele 2
		4	24.1.48	QPR	3S	A	L	0-3	
1948-49	D1	3	8.1.49	Swindon T	3S	A	W	3-1	G.Mountford 2, Steele
		4	29.1.49	Blackpool	D1	H	D	1-1aet	F.Mountford (p)
		4r	5.2.49	Blackpool		A	W	1-0	G.Mountford
		5	12.2.49	Hull C	3N	H	L	0-2	
1949-50	D1	3	7.1.50	Tottenham H	D2	H	L	0-1	
1950-51	D1	3	6.1.51	Port Vale	3S	H	D	2-2	Mullard 2
		3r	8.1.51	Port Vale			W	1-0	Bowyer
		4	27.1.51	West Ham	D2	H	W	1-0	Bowyer
		5	10.2.51	Newcastle U	D1	H	L	2-4	Bowyer, F or G Mountford
1951-52	D1	3	12.1.52	Sunderland	D1	A	D	0-0	
		3r	15.1.52	Sunderland		H	W	3-1	McIntosh, Smyth, Malkin
		4	2.2.52	Swindon T	3S	A	D	1-1	Smyth
		4r	4.2.52	Swindon T		H	L	0-1	
1952-53	D1	3	10.1.53	Wrexham	3N	H	W	2-1	Whiston, Finney
		4	31.1.53	Halifax T	3N	A	L	0-1	
1953-54	D2	3	9.1.54	Hartlepools U	3N	H	W	6-2	Bowyer 4, Hutton, King
		4	30.1.54	Leicester C	D2	H	D	0-0	
		4r	2.2.54	Leicester C		A	L	1-3	Malkin
1954-55	D2	3	8.1.55	Bury	D2	A	D	1-1	King
		3r	12.1.55	Bury		H	–	1-1	Ratcliffe
			abandoned after 112 minutes – snowstorm						
		3 2r	17.1.55	Bury at Goodison Park			D	3-3aet	Bowyer 2, King
		3 3r	19.1.55	Bury at Anfield			D	2-2aet	King, Ratcliffe
		3 4r	24.1.55	Bury at Old Trafford			W	3-2aet	Thomson, Coleman 2
		4	29.1.55	Swansea T	D2	A	L	1-3	Malkin
1955-56	D2	3	7.1.56	Exeter C	3S	A	D	0-0	
		3r	9.1.56	Exeter C		H	W	3-0	Oscroft, Bowyer, Coleman
		4	28.1.56	Leicester C	D2	A	D	3-3	Bowyer, Graver, King
		4r	30.1.56	Leicester C		H	W	2-1	Oscroft, Graver
		5	18.2.56	Newcastle U	D1	A	L	1-2	King
1956-57	D2	3	5.1.57	Arsenal	D1	A	L	2-4	Coleman, Oscroft
1957-58	D2	3	4.1.58	Aston Villa	D1	H	D	1-1	Kelly

STOKE CITY

Season	Div	Round	Date	Opponent	OppDiv	H/A	Result	Score	Scorers
		3r	8.1.58	Aston Villa		A	D	3-3aet	Coleman, Kelly, Oscroft
		3 2r	13.1.58	Aston Villa at Molineux			W	2-0	Cairns (p), Coleman
		4	25.1.58	Middlesbrough	D2	H	W	3-1	Wilshaw 3
		5	15.2.58	Bolton W	D1	A	L	1-3	Cairns (p)
1958-59	D2	3	10.1.59	Oldham A	D4	H	W	5-1	Howitt, Asprey, Wilshaw 3
		4	24.1.59	Ipswich T	D2	H	L	0-1	
1959-60	D2	3	9.1.60	Preston NE	D1	H	D	1-1	Howitt
		3r	12.1.60	Preston NE		A	L	1-3	Bowyer
1960-61	D2	3	7.1.61	West Ham	D1	A	D	2-2	Ratcliffe, Andrew
		3r	11.1.61	West Ham		H	W	1-0	Wilshaw
		4	28.1.61	Aldershot	D4	H	D	0-0	
		4r	1.2.61	Aldershot		A	D	0-0aet	
		4 2r	6.2.61	Aldershot at Molineux			W	3-0	Wilshaw 2, Asprey
		5	18.2.61	Newcastle U	D1	A	L	1-3	King
1961-62	D2	3	10.1.62	Leicester C	D1	A	D	1-1	Mudie
		3r	15.1.62	Leicester C		H	W	5-2	Matthews, Allen, Bullock, Nibloe, Thompson
		4	27.1.62	Blackburn R	D1	H	L	0-1	
1962-63	D2	3	6.3.63	Leeds U	D2	A	L	1-3	Bebbington
1963-64	D1	3	4.1.64	Portsmouth	D2	H	W	4-1	Viollet 2, Ritchie 2
		4	25.1.64	Ipswich T	D1	A	D	1-1	McIlroy
		4r	29.1.64	Ipswich T		H	W	1-0	McIlroy
		5	15.2.64	Swansea T	D2	H	D	2-2	Matthews, McIlroy
		5r	18.2.64	Swansea T		A	L	0-2	
1964-65	D1	3	11.1.65	Blackpool	D1	H	W	4-1	Ritchie 2, Viollet 2
		4	30.1.65	Manchester U	D1	H	D	0-0	
		4r	3.2.65	Manchester U		A	L	0-1	
1965-66	D1	3	22.1.66	Walsall	D3	H	L	0-2	
1966-67	D1	3	28.1.67	Manchester U	D1	A	L	0-2	
1967-68	D1	3	27.1.68	Cardiff C	D2	H	W	4-1	Vernon, Stevenson, Burrows 2
		4	17.2.68	West Ham	D1	H	L	0-3	
1968-69	D1	3	4.1.69	York C	D4	A	W	2-0	Burrows 2
		4	25.1.69	Halifax T	D4	H	D	1-1	Dobing
		4r	28.1.69	Halifax T		A	W	3-0	Burrows, Conroy 2
		5	12.2.69	Chelsea	D1	A	L	2-3	Burrows, Dobing
1969-70	D1	3	3.1.70	Oxford U	D2	A	D	0-0	
		3r	7.1.70	Oxford U		H	W	3-2	Stevenson, Richardson 2
		4	24.1.70	Watford	D2	A	L	0-1	
1970-71	D1	3	2.1.71	Millwall	D2	H	W	2-1	Ritchie, J.Greenhoff
		4	23.1.71	Huddersfield T	D1	H	D	3-3	J.Greenhoff, Conroy, Burrows
		4r	26.1.71	Huddersfield T		A	D	0-0aet	
		4 2r	8.2.71	Huddersfield T at Old Trafford			W	1-0	J.Greenhoff
		5	13.2.71	Ipswich T	D1	H	D	0-0	
		5r	16.2.71	Ipswich T		A	W	1-0	D.Smith
		6	6.3.71	Hull C	D2	A	W	3-2	Conroy, Ritchie 2
		SF	27.3.71	Arsenal at Hillsborough	D1		D	2-2	Smith, Ritchie
		SFr	31.3.71	Arsenal at Villa Park			L	0-2	
1971-72	D1	3	15.1.72	Chesterfield	D3	H	W	2-1	Conroy, Dobing
		4	5.2.72	Tranmere R	D3	A	D	2-2	Conroy, Ritchie
		5	26.2.72	Hull C	D2	H	W	4-1	J.Greenhoff 2, Conroy, Ritchie
		6	18.3.72	Manchester U	D1	A	D	1-1	J.Greenhoff
		6r	22.3.72	Manchester U		H	W	2-1aet	Smith, Conroy
		SF	15.4.72	Arsenal at Villa Park	D1		D	1-1	Simpson og
		SFr	19.4.72	Arsenal at Goodison Park			L	1-2	J.Greenhoff (p)
		3/4	5.8.72	Birmingham C	D1	A	D	0-0	
			Birmingham won 4-3 on penalties						
1972-73	D1	3	13.1.73	Manchester C	D1	A	L	2-3	J.Greenhoff 2
1973-74	D1	3	5.1.74	Bolton W	D2	A	L	2-3	Ritchie, Haslegrave (p)
1974-75	D1	3	4.1.75	Liverpool	D1	A	L	0-2	
1975-76	D1	3	3.1.76	Tottenham H	D1	A	D	1-1	Mahoney
		3r	24.1.76	Tottenham H		H	W	2-1	Moores, Salmon (p)
		4	28.1.76	Manchester C	D1	H	W	1-0	J.Greenhoff
		5	14.2.76	Sunderland	D2	H	D	0-0	
		5r	17.2.76	Sunderland		A	L	1-2	Smith
1976-77	D1	3	8.1.77	Everton	D1	A	L	0-2	
1977-78	D2	3	7.1.78	Tilbury	IL	H	W	4-0	Cook 2, Gregory, Waddington
		4	6.2.78	Blyth Spartans	NL	H	L	2-3	Busby, Crooks
1978-79	D2	3	6.1.79	Oldham A	D2	H	–	2-0	Irvine 2
			abandoned at half-time						

	3	17.1.79	**Oldham A**		H	L	0-1
1979-80	D1	3	5.1.80	**Burnley**	D2	A	L	0-1
1980-81	D1	3	3.1.81	**Wolverhampton W**	D1	H	D	2-2	Chapman, Bracewell
	3r	6.1.81	**Wolverhampton W**		A	L	1-2	Heath
1981-82	D1	3	2.1.82	**Norwich C**	D2	H	L	0-1
1982-83	D1	3	8.1.83	**Sheffield U**	D3	A	D	0-0
	3r	12.1.83	**Sheffield U**		H	W	3-2	McAughtrie, Painter, Henderson og
	4	29.1.83	**Liverpool**	D1	A	L	0-2
1983-84	D1	3	7.1.84	**Everton**	D1	H	L	0-2
1984-85	D1	3	5.1.85	**Luton T**	D1	A	D	1-1	Painter
	3r	9.1.85	**Luton T**		H	L	2-3	Painter (p), M.Chamberlain
1985-86	D2	3	13.1.86	**Notts Co**	D3	H	L	0-2
1986-87	D2	3	10.1.87	**Grimsby T**	D2	A	D	1-1	Saunders
	3r	26.1.87	**Grimsby T**		H	D	1-1aet	Saunders
	3 2r	28.1.87	**Grimsby T**		H	W	6-0	Morgan 2, Talbot, Heath, Saunders 2
	4	31.1.87	**Cardiff C**	D4	H	W	2-1	Saunders, Heath
	5	21.2.87	**Coventry C**	D1	H	L	0-1
1987-88	D2	3	9.1.88	**Liverpool**	D1	H	D	0-0
	3r	12.1.88	**Liverpool**		A	L	0-1
1988-89	D2	3	7.1.89	**Crystal Palace**	D2	H	W	1-0	Shaw
	4	28.1.89	**Barnsley**	D2	H	D	3-3	Bamber, Berry, Beagrie
	4r	31.1.89	**Barnsley**		A	L	1-2	Bamber
1989-90	D2	3	6.1.90	**Arsenal**	D1	H	L	0-1
1990-91	D3	1	17.11.90	**Telford U**	GMVC	A	D	0-0
	1r	21.11.90	**Telford U**		H	W	1-0	Sandford
	2	12.12.90	**Burnley**	D4	A	L	0-2
1991-92	D3	1	16.11.91	**Telford U**	GMVC	H	D	0-0
	1r	26.11.91	**Telford U**		A	L	1-2	Beeston
1992-93	D2	1	16.11.92	**Port Vale**	D2	H	D	0-0
	1r	24.11.92	**Port Vale**		A	L	1-3	Sandford

STREET

Formed 1880. **First entered FA Cup:** 1899. Currently play in Somerset Senior League.

1938-39	WL	1	26.11.38	**Ipswich T**	3S	A	L	0-7
1947-48	WL	1	29.11.47	**Cheltenham T**	SL	A	L	0-5

ST ALBANS (1)

Formed 1877. Played at the Upton Ground, St Albans, near the Princess Anne pub.

1880-81	1	13.11.80	**Reading Abbey**	A	L	0-1
1881-82	1	22.10.81	**Upton Park**	A	L	0-3

ST ALBANS CITY (2)

Formed 1908. **First entered FA Cup:** 1908. **Cup Final Connection:** Former St Albans City players Joe Kinnear (Tottenham H, 1967) and John Mitchell (Fulham 1975) both appeared in FA Cup Finals. **League club beaten:** Brentford

1924-25	IL	5q	Brentford (3S) H 5-3; 6q **Hartlepools U** (A) 0-4
1925-26	IL	1	28.11.25	**Leyton**	Lon	A	L	0-1
1926-27	IL	1	27.11.26	**Chatham**	KL	A	L	1-3	Bethell
1968-69	IL	1	16.11.68	**Wealdstone**	IL	A	D	1-1	Childs (p)
	1r	19.11.68	**Wealdstone**		H	W	1-0	Neville
	2	7.12.68	**Walsall**	D3	H	D	1-1	Ratty
	2r	10.12.68	**Walsall**		A	L	1-3	Butterfield
1980-81	IL	1	22.11.80	**Gravesend & N.**	APL	A	W	2-1	Whitehead 2 (2ps)
	2	13.12.80	**Torquay U**	D4	H	D	1-1	Mayles
	2r	17.12.80	**Torquay U**		A	L	1-4	Whitehead (p)
1992-93	IL	1	14.11.92	**Cheltenham T**	SL	H	L	1-2	Duffield (p)

ST BARTS HOSPITAL

Formed 1866. Played at Battersea Park, South London.

1881-82	1		**Wanderers**		*walkover*
	2	30.11.81	**Great Marlow**	A	L	0-2

ST NEOTS TOWN

Formed 1879. **First entered FA Cup:** 1957. Folded 1988

1966-67	Met	1	26.11.66	**Walsall**	D3	A	L	0-2

ST PETER'S INSTITUTE

Formed 1877. Originally played at Battersea Park in South London and continued in one form or another until merged with Staines in 1905.

1879-80	1	1.11.79	**Mosquitoes**	A	L	1-3	Daville
1880-81	1	6.11.80	**Hendon**	H	L	1-8	

ST STEPHENS

1877-78	1	7.11.77	**Remnants**	A	L	0-4

SUNDERLAND

Formed 1879. **Best FA Cup Performance:** Winners 1937, 1973. **Runners-up:** 1913, 1992. **Record FA Cup Win:** 11-1 vs Fairfield, 1st round, 2.2.1895. **Record FA Cup Defeat:** 2-7 vs Aston Villa, 4th round, 27.1.1934

1884-85		1	8.11.84	**Redcar**		A	L	1-3	
1885-86		1	24.10.85	**Redcar**		A	L	0-3	
1886-87		1	30.10.86	**Newcastle West End**		H	W	2-1aet	Lord 2
				FA ordered replay after protest from West End					
		1r	13.11.86	**Newcastle West End**		A	L	0-1	
1887-88		1	15.10.87	**Morpeth Harriers**		H	W	4-2	Monaghan 3, Smith
				FA ordered replay after protest					
			22.10.87	**Morpeth Harriers**		A	W	3-2	Monaghan 2, Stewart
		2	5.11.87	**Newcastle West End**		H	W	3-1aet	Stewart 2, Halliday
		3	26.11.87	**Middlesbrough**		A	D	2-2	Gloag 2
		3r	3.12.87	**Middlesbrough**		H	W	4-2	Halliday, Monaghan, others 2
				Sunderland disqualified for professionalism after protest – Middlesbrough re-instated					
1888-89		2q		Elswick R (H) 5-3; 3q Newcastle East End (H) 2-0aet; 4q **Sunderland Albion** scratched					
1889-90		1	18.1.90	**Blackburn R**	D1	A	L	2-4aet	D.Hannah, Scott
1890-91	D1	1	17.1.91	**Everton**	D1	H	W	1-0	Campbell
		2	31.1.91	**Darwen**		A	W	2-0	Scott 2
		3	14.2.91	**Nottingham F**	FAll	H	W	4-0	Miller 2, Campbell 2
		SF	28.2.91	**Notts Co**	D1		D	3-3	Smith, Harvey, Campbell
		SFr	11.3.91	**Notts Co**			L	0-2	
				both matches played at Bramall Lane					
1891-92	D1	1	16.1.92	**Notts Co**	D1	H	W	3-0	Miller, Campbell, J.Hannah
				FA ordered replay after protest about frozen pitch					
			23.1.92	**Notts Co**		H	W	4-0	Hannah, Campbell 2, Smith
		2	30.1.92	**Accrington**	D1	A	W	3-1	Campbell 3
		3	13.2.92	**Stoke**	D1	A	D	2-2aet	Campbell, Miller
		3r	20.2.92	**Stoke**		H	W	4-0	Campbell, Miller, D.Hannah, J.Hannah
		SF	27.2.92	**Aston Villa**	D1		L	1-4	Scott
				played at Bramall Lane					
1892-93	D1	1	21.1.93	**Royal Arsenal**		H	W	6-0	Miller 3, Campbell 2, D.Hannah
		2	4.2.93	**Sheffield U**	D2	A	W	3-1	Campbell, Miller 2
		3	18.2.93	**Blackburn R**	D1	A	L	0-3	
1893-94	D1	1	27.1.94	**Accrington**	LL	H	W	3-0	Gillespie, J.Hannah, Wilson
		2	10.2.94	**Aston Villa**	D1	H	D	2-2aet	Gillespie, Wilson
		2r	21.2.94	**Aston Villa**		A	L	1-3	J.Hannah
1894-95	D1	1	2.2.95	**Fairfield**	LL	H	W	11-1	Miller 5, J.Hannah 3, Gillespie, McCreadie, Scott
		2	16.2.95	**Preston NE**	D1	H	W	2-0	Campbell 2
		3	2.3.95	**Bolton W**	D1	H	W	2-1	Wilson 2
		SF	16.3.95	**Aston Villa**	D1		L	1-2	J.Hannah
				played at Ewood Park					
1895-96	D1	1	1.2.96	**Preston NE**	D1	H	W	4-1	Campbell 3, Miller
		2	15.2.96	**Sheffield W**	D1	A	L	1-2	Miller
1896-97	D1	1	30.1.97	**Burnley**	D1	H	W	1-0	Morgan
		2	13.2.97	**Nottingham F**	D1	H	L	1-3	Morgan
1897-98	D1	1	29.1.98	**Sheffield W**	D1	H	L	0-1	
1898-99	D1	1	28.1.99	**Bristol C**	SL	A	W	4-2	Leslie, Crawford, Fulton, Wilson
		2	11.2.99	**Tottenham H**	SL	A	L	1-2	Fulton

S U N D E R L A N D

1899-00	D1	1	27.1.00	Derby Co	D1	A	D	2-2	Fulton, McLatchie
		1r	31.1.00	Derby Co		H	W	3-0	R.Hogg 2, W.Hogg
		2	10.2.00	Nottingham F	D1	A	L	0-3	
1900-01	D1	1	9.2.01	Sheffield U	D1	H	L	1-2	McLatchie
1901-02	D1	1	25.1.02	Sheffield W	D1	A	W	1-0	McAllister
		2	12.2.02	Newastle U	D1	A	L	0-1	
1902-03	D1	1	7.2.03	Aston Villa	D1	A	L	1-4	Bridgett
1903-04	D1	1	6.2.04	Manchester C	D1	A	L	2-3	Craggs, Buckle
1904-05	D1	1	4.2.05	Wolverhampton W	D1	H	D	1-1	Common
		1r	8.2.05	Wolverhampton W		A	L	0-1	
1905-06	D1	1	13.1.06	Notts Co	D1	H	W	1-0	Shaw
		2	3.2.06	Gainsborough T	D2	H	D	1-1	Barrie
		2r	7.2.06	Gainsborough T		H	W	3-0	Bridgett, Brown, Holley
		3	24.2.06	W.Arsenal	D1	A	L	0-5	
1906-07	D1	1	12.1.07	Leicester F	D2	H	W	4-1	Raine, McIntosh 2, Bridgett
		2	2.2.07	Luton T	SL	A	D	0-0	
		2r	6.2.07	Luton T		H	W	1-0	McIntosh
		3	23.2.07	Sheffield W	D1	A	D	0-0	
		3r	27.2.07	Sheffield W		H	L	0-1	
1907-08	D1	1	11.1.08	New Brompton	SL	A	L	1-3	Holley
1908-09	D1	1	16.1.09	Sheffield U	D1	A	W	3-2	Thomson, Hogg, Brown
		2	6.2.09	Preston NE	D1	A	W	2-1	Low, Bridgett
		3	20.2.09	Bradford C	D1	A	W	1-0	Holley
		4	6.3.09	Newcastle U	D1	A	D	2-2	Brown, Mordue
		4r	10.3.09	Newcastle U		H	L	0-3	
1909-10	D1	1	15.1.10	Leeds C	D2	H	W	1-0	Holley
		2	5.2.10	Bradford PA	D2	H	W	3-1	Low 2, Bridgett
		3	19.2.10	Everton	D1	A	L	0-2	
1910-11	D1	1	14.1.11	Norwich C	SL	A	L	1-3	Bridgett
1911-12	D1	1	13.1.12	Plymouth A	SL	H	W	3-1	Mordue 2, Bridgett
		2	3.2.12	Crystal P	SL	A	D	0-0	
		2r	7.2.12	Crystal P		H	W	1-0aet	Low
		3	24.2.12	WBA	D1	H	L	1-2	Bridgett
1912-13	D1	1	11.1.13	Clapton O	D2	H	W	6-0	Richardson 4, Holley, Mordue
		2	1.2.13	Manchester C	D1	A	–	2-0	Buchan, Richardson
				abandoned after 60 minutes due to dangerous overcrowding in the ground					
		2r	5.2.13	Manchester C		H	W	2-0	Mordue, Holley
		3	22.2.13	Swindon T	SL	H	W	4-2	Gladwin, Buchan, Richardson 2
		4	8.3.13	Newcastle U	D1	H	D	0-0	
		4r	12.3.13	Newcastle U		A	D	2-2aet	Holley, Buchan
		4 2r	17.3.13	Newcastle U		W		3-0	Holley, Buchan, Mordue
		SF	29.3.13	Burnley	D2	D		0-0	
				played at Bramall Lane					
		SFr	2.4.13	Burnley at St Andrews		W		3-2	Buchan, Mordue, Holley
		F	19.4.13	Aston Villa	D1	L		0-1	
				played at Crystal Palace					
1913-14	D1	1	10.1.14	Chatham	KL	H	W	9-0	Richardson 4, Best 2, Mordue, Buchan, Thomson
		2	31.1.14	Plymouth A	SL	H	W	2-1	Mordue, Connor
		3	21.2.14	Preston NE	D1	H	W	2-0	Buchan, Connor
		4	7.3.14	Burnley	D1	H	D	0-0	
		4r	11.3.14	Burnley		A	L	1-2	Connor
1914-15	D1	1	9.1.15	Tottenham H	D1	A	L	1-2	Mordue
1919-20	D1	1	14.1.20	Hull C	D2	H	W	6-2	Buchan 4, Travers 2
		2	31.1.20	Burnley	D1	A	D	1-1	Travers
		2r	4.2.20	Burnley		H	W	2-0	Buchan, Poole
		3	21.2.20	Aston Villa	D1	A	L	0-1	
1920-21	D1	1	8.1.21	Cardiff C	D2	H	L	0-1	
1921-22	D1	1	7.1.22	Liverpool	D1	H	D	1-1	Stannard
		1r	11.1.22	Liverpool		A	L	0-5	
1922-23	D1	1	13.1.23	Burnley	D1	H	W	3-1	Paterson 3
		2	3.2.23	WBA	D1	A	L	1-2	Buchan
1923-24	D1	1	12.1.24	Oldham A	D2	A	L	1-2	Buchan
1924-25	D1	1	10.1.25	Bury	D1	A	W	3-0	Clunas, Buchan, Rodgers
		2	31.1.25	Everton	D1	H	D	0-0	
		2r	4.2.25	Everton		A	L	1-2	Marshall
1925-26	D1	3	9.1.26	Boston T	ML	H	W	8-1	Kelly 3, Marshall 3, Halliday 2
		4	30.1.26	Sheffield U	D1	A	W	2-1	Prior, Kelly

SUNDERLAND

Season	Div	Round	Date	Opponent		Venue	W/D/L	Score	Scorers
		5	20.2.26	Manchester U	D1	H	D	3-3	Marshall, Death 2
		5r	24.2.26	Manchester U		A	L	1-2	Halliday
1926-27	D1	3	8.1.27	Leeds U	D1	A	L	2-3	Marshall, Halliday
1927-28	D1	3	14.1.28	Northampton T	3S	H	D	3-3	Wright, Hargreaves, Halliday
		3r	19.1.28	Northampton T		A	W	3-0	Halliday 2, Clunas (p)
		4	28.1.28	Manchester C	D2	H	L	1-2	Halliday
1928-29	D1	3	12.1.29	West Ham	D1	A	L	0-1	
1929-30	D1	3	11.1.30	Coventry C	3S	A	W	2-1	Gallacher, Gurney
		4	25.1.30	Cardiff C	D2	H	W	2-1	Gurney, McLean
		5	15.2.30	Nottingham F	D2	H	D	2-2	McLean, Gunson
		5r	19.2.30	Nottingham F		A	L	1-3	Eden
1930-31	D1	3	10.1.31	Southampton	D2	H	W	2-0	Eden, Urwin
		4	24.1.31	Bolton W	D1	A	D	1-1	Leonard
		4r	27.1.31	Bolton W		H	W	3-1	Connor 2, Leonard
		5	14.2.31	Sheffield U	D1	H	W	2-1	Connor, Gurney
		6	28.2.31	Exeter C	3S	H	D	1-1	Connor
		6r	4.3.31	Exeter C		A	W	4-2	Connor 2, Eden, Gurney
		SF	14.3.31	Birmingham	D1		L	0-2	
			played at Elland Road						
1931-32	D1	3	9.1.32	Southampton	D2	H	D	0-0	
		3r	13.1.32	Southampton		A	W	4-2	Vinall, Poulter 2, Shaw
		4	23.1.32	Stoke C	D2	H	D	1-1	McDougall
		4r	28.1.32	Stoke C		A	D	1-1aet	Gallacher
		4 2r	1.2.32	Stoke C *at Maine Road*			L	1-2aet	Gallacher
1932-33	D1	3	14.1.33	Hull C	3N	A	W	2-0	Gurney, Connor
		4	28.1.33	Aston Villa	D1	A	W	3-0	Gurney 3
		5	18.2.33	Blackpool	D1	H	W	1-0	Gurney
		6	25.2.33	Derby Co	D1	A	D	4-4	Gurney 2, Davis, Connor
		6r	4.3.33	Derby Co		H	L	0-1	
1933-34	D1	3	13.1.34	Middlesbrough	D1	H	D	1-1	Carter
		3r	17.1.34	Middlesbrough		A	W	2-1	Yorston, Gurney
		4	27.1.34	Aston Villa	D1	A	L	2-7	Carter, Hastings
1934-35	D1	3	12.1.35	Fulham	D2	H	W	3-2	Gurney 3
		4	26.1.35	Everton	D1	H	D	1-1	Carter
		4r	30.1.35	Everton		A	L	4-6aet	Davies, Connor 2, Gurney
1935-36	D1	3	11.1.36	Port Vale	D2	H	D	2-2	Connor, Gallacher
		3r	13.1.36	Port Vale		A	L	0-2	
1936-37	D1	3	16.1.37	Southampton	D2	A	W	3-2	Gurney, Hornby, Gallacher
		4	30.1.37	Luton T	3S	A	D	2-2	Connor, Duns
		4r	3.2.37	Luton T		H	W	3-1	Duns, Connor, Carter
		5	20.2.37	Swansea T	D2	H	W	3-0	Gurney, Duns, Caldwell og
		6	6.3.37	Wolverhampton W	D1	A	D	1-1	Duns
		6r	10.3.37	Wolverhampton W		H	D	2-2aet	Gurney, Duns
		6 2r	15.3.37	Wolverhampton W *at Hillsborough*			W	4-0	Gurney, Carter, Gallacher, Thomson
		SF	10.4.37	Millwall	3S		W	2-1	Gurney, Gallacher
			played at Huddersfield						
		F	1.5.37	PRESTON NE	D1	WEMBLEY	W	3-1	Gurney, Carter, Burbanks
1937-38	D1	3	8.1.38	Watford	3S	H	W	1-0	Duns
		4	22.1.38	Everton	D1	A	W	1-0	Gurney
		5	12.2.38	Bradford PA	D2	H	W	1-0	Duns
		6	5.3.38	Tottenham H	D2	A	W	1-0	Carter
		SF	26.3.38	Huddersfield T	D1		L	1-3	Burbanks
			played at Ewood Park						
1938-39	D1	3	7.1.39	Plymouth A	D2	H	W	3-0	Clark og, Gorman, Carter
		4	21.1.39	Middlesbrough	D1	A	W	2-0	Carter, Smeaton
		5	11.2.39	Blackburn R	D2	H	D	1-1	Hastings
		5r	16.2.39	Blackburn R		A	D	0-0aet	
		5 2r	20.2.39	Blackburn R *at Hillsborough*			L	0-1aet	
1945-46	D1	3 1L	5.1.46	Grimsby T	D1	A	W	3-1	White, Hastings 2
		3 2L	9.1.46	Grimsby T		H	W	2-1	Whitelum, Hastings
		4 1L	26.1.46	Bury	D2	H	W	3-1	Brown 2, Duns
		4 2L	29.1.46	Bury		A	L	4-5aet	White, Walshaw, Brown, Burbanks
		5 1L	9.2.46	Birmingham C	D2	H	W	1-0	Duns
		5 2L	13.2.46	Birmingham C		A	L	1-3	Brown
1946-47	D1	3	11.1.47	Chesterfield	D2	A	L	1-2aet	Robinson
1947-48	D1	3	10.1.48	Southampton	D2	A	L	0-1	
1948-49	D1	3	8.1.49	Crewe Alex.	3N	A	W	2-0	Turnbull 2

(444)

		4	29.1.49	Yeovil T	SL	A	L	1-2aet	Robinson
1949-50	D1	3	7.1.50	Huddersfield T	D1	H	W	6-0	Davis 2, Broadis 2, Shackleton 2
		4	28.1.50	Tottenham H	D2	A	L	1-5	Davis
1950-51	D1	3	6.1.51	Coventry C	D2	H	W	2-0	T.Wright, A.Wright
		4	27.1.51	Southampton	D2	H	W	2-0	Davis 2
		5	10.2.51	Norwich C	3S	H	W	3-1	Davis, Watson, T.Wright
		6	24.2.51	Wolverhampton W	D1	H	D	1-1	Davis
		6r	28.2.51	Wolverhampton W		A	L	1-3	Ford
1951-52	D1	3	12.1.52	Stoke C	D1	H	D	0-0	
		3r	14.1.52	Stoke C		A	L	1-3	McSeveney
1952-53	D1	3	10.1.53	Scunthorpe U	3N	H	D	1-1	Ford
		3r	15.1.53	Scunthorpe U		A	W	2-1	T.Wright, Ford
		4	31.1.53	Burnley	D1	A	L	0-2	
1953-54	D1	3	9.1.54	Doncaster R	D2	H	L	0-2	
1954-55	D1	3	8.1.55	Burnley	D1	H	W	1-0	Elliott
		4	29.1.55	Preston NE	D1	A	D	3-3	Purdon, Chisholm, Shackleton
		4r	2.2.55	Preston NE		H	W	2-0	Chisholm 2
		5	19.2.55	Swansea T	D2	A	D	2-2	Chisholm 2
		5r	23.2.55	Swansea T		H	W	1-0	Fleming
		6	12.3.55	Wolverhampton W	D1	H	W	2-0	Purdon 2
		SF	26.3.55	Manchester C	D1		L	0-1	
			played at Villa Park						
1955-56	D1	3	7.1.56	Norwich C	3S	H	W	4-2	Fleming 3, Elliott
		4	28.1.56	York C	3N	A	D	0-0	
		4r	1.2.56	York C		H	W	2-1	Anderson, Fleming
		5	18.2.56	Sheffield U	D1	A	D	0-0	
		5r	22.2.56	Sheffield U		H	W	1-0	Daniel
		6	3.3.56	Newcastle U	D1	A	W	2-0	Holden 2
		SF	17.3.56	Birmingham C	D1		L	0-3	
			played at Hillsborough						
1956-57	D1	3	5.1.57	QPR	3S	H	W	4-0	Elliott, Hannigan 2, Fleming
		4	26.1.57	WBA	D1	A	L	2-4	Fleming, Bingham
1957-58	D1	3	4.1.58	Everton	D1	H	D	2-2	Bingham, Frogarty
		3r	8.1.58	Everton		A	L	1-3	Fleming
1958-59	D2	3	10.1.59	Everton	D1	A	L	0-4	
1959-60	D2	3	9.1.60	Blackburn R	D1	H	D	1-1	Lawther
		3r	13.1.60	Blackburn R		A	L	1-4	O'Neill
1960-61	D2	3	7.1.61	Arsenal	D1	H	W	2-1	Anderson 2
		4	28.1.61	Liverpool	D2	A	W	2-0	Hooper, Lawther
		5	18.2.61	Norwich C	D2	A	W	1-0	Hurley
		6	4.3.61	Tottenham H	D1	H	D	1-1	McPheat
		6r	8.3.61	Tottenham H		A	L	0-5	
1961-62	D2	3	6.1.62	Southampton	D2	A	D	2-2	Anderson, Hooper (p)
		3r	10.1.62	Southampton		H	W	3-0	McPheat, Herd 2
		4	27.1.62	Port Vale	D3	H	D	0-0	
		4r	31.1.62	Port Vale		A	L	1-3	McPheat
1962-63	D2	3	5.1.63	Preston NE	D2	A	W	4-1	Sharkey 2, Fogarty, Davison
		4	12.2.63	Gravesend & N	SL	A	D	1-1	Mulhall
		4r	18.2.63	Gravesend & N		H	W	5-2	Finch og, Crossan 2, Fogarty, Sharkey
		5	25.3.63	Coventry C	D3	A	L	1-2	Crossan
1963-64	D2	3	4.1.64	Northampton T	D2	H	W	2-0	Usher, Crossan
		4	25.1.64	Bristol C	D3	H	W	6-1	Herd 2, Hurley, Sharkey, Crossan 2
		5	15.2.64	Everton	D1	H	W	3-1	McNab, Hurley, Meagan og
		6	29.2.64	Manchester U	D1	A	D	3-3	Mulhall, Crossan 2 (1p)
		6r	4.3.64	Manchester U		H	D	2-2aet	Sharkey, Setters og
		6 2r	9.3.64	Manchester U at Huddersfield			L	1-5	Sharkey
1964-65	D1	3	9.1.65	Luton T	D3	A	W	3-0	Sharkey 2, Mulhall
		4	30.1.65	Nottingham F	D1	H	L	1-3	Hood
1965-66	D1	3	22.1.66	Everton	D1	A	L	0-3	
1966-67	D1	3	28.1.67	Brentford	D4	H	W	5-2	Martin 2, Mulhall, Baxter (p), O'Hare
		4	18.2.67	Peterborough U	D3	H	W	7-1	O'Hare, Martin 3, Kerr 2, Baxter (p)
		5	11.3.67	Leeds U	D1	H	D	1-1	Martin
		5r	15.3.67	Leeds U		A	D	1-1aet	O'Hare
		5 2r	20.3.67	Leeds U at Hull			L	1-2	Gauden
1967-68	D1	3	27.1.68	Norwich C	D2	A	D	1-1	Suggett
		3r	31.1.68	Norwich C		H	L	0-1	
1968-69	D1	3	4.1.69	Fulham	D2	H	L	1-4	Kerr

Season	Div	Rnd	Date	Opponent		Venue	Res	Score	Scorers
1969-70	D1	3	3.1.70	Leicester C	D2	A	L	0-1	
1970-71	D2	3	11.1.71	Orient	D2	H	L	0-3	
1971-72	D2	3	15.1.72	Sheffield W	D2	H	W	3-0	Porterfield, Watson, Chambers
		4	9.2.72	Cardiff C	D2	A	D	1-1	Chambers
		4r	14.2.72	Cardiff C		H	D	1-1aet	Kerr
		4 2r	16.2.72	Cardiff C at Maine Rd			L	1-3	McGiven
1972-73	D2	3	13.1.73	Notts Co	D3	A	D	1-1	Watson
		3r	16.1.73	Notts Co		H	W	2-0	Watson, Tueart
		4	3.2.73	Reading	D4	H	D	1-1	Tueart
		4r	7.2.73	Reading		A	W	3-1	Watson, Tueart, Kerr
		5	24.2.73	Manchester C	D1	A	D	2-2	Horswill, Hughes
		5r	27.2.73	Manchester C		H	W	3-1	Halom, Hughes 2
		6	17.3.73	Luton T	D2	H	W	2-0	Watson, Guthrie
		SF	7.4.73	Arsenal	D1		W	2-1	Halom, Hughes
				played at Hillsborough					
		F	5.5.73	LEEDS UNITED	D1	WEMBLEY	W	1-0	Porterfield
1973-74	D2	3	5.1.74	Carlisle U	D2	A	D	0-0	
		3r	9.1.74	Carlisle U		H	L	0-1	
1974-75	D2	3	4.1.75	Chesterfield	D3	H	W	2-0	Bolton, Robson
		4	25.1.75	Middlesbrough	D1	A	L	1-3	Robson
1975-76	D2	3	3.1.76	Oldham A	D2	H	W	2-0	Holden, Robson
		4	2.2.76	Hull C	D2	H	W	1-0	Finney
		5	14.2.76	Stoke C	D1	A	D	0-0	
		5r	17.2.76	Stoke C		H	W	2-1	Holden, Robson
		6	6.3.76	C.Palace	D3	H	L	0-1	
1976-77	D1	3	8.1.77	Wrexham	D3	H	D	2-2	Holton, Holden
		3r	12.1.77	Wrexham		A	L	0-1	
1977-78	D2	3	7.1.78	Bristol R	D2	H	L	0-1	
1978-79	D2	3	10.1.79	Everton	D1	H	W	2-1	Rowell (p), Lee
		4	21.2.79	Burnley	D2	A	D	1-1	Entwhistle
		4r	26.2.79	Burnley		H	L	0-3	
1979-80	D2	3	5.1.80	Bolton W	D1	H	L	0-1	
1980-81	D1	3	3.1.81	Birmingham C	D1	A	D	1-1	Chisholm
		3r	7.1.81	Birmingham C		H	L	1-2aet	Rowell
1981-82	D1	3	2.1.82	Rotherham U	D2	A	D	1-1	Rowell
		3r	18.1.82	Rotherham U		H	W	1-0	Buckley
		4	23.1.82	Liverpool	D1	H	L	0-3	
1982-83	D1	3	8.1.83	Manchester C	D1	H	D	0-0	
		3r	12.1.83	Manchester C		A	L	1-2	Chisholm
1983-84	D1	3	7.1.84	Bolton W	D3	A	W	3-0	West, Chapman, Rowell
		4	28.1.84	Birmingham C	D1	H	L	1-2	West
1984-85	D1	3	5.1.85	Southampton	D1	A	L	0-4	
1985-86	D2	3	4.1.86	Newport Co	D3	H	W	2-0	Burley, Corner
		4	25.1.86	Manchester U	D1	H	D	0-0	
		4r	29.1.86	Manchester U		A	L	0-3	
1986-87	D2	3	10.1.87	Wimbledon	D1	A	L	1-2	Gates
1987-88	D3	1	14.11.87	Darlington	D4	H	W	2-0	Atkinson 2
		2	5.12.87	Scunthorpe U	D4	A	L	1-2	Gates
1988-89	D2	3	7.1.89	Oxford U	D2	H	D	1-1	Ord
		3r	11.1.89	Oxford U		A	L	0-2	
1989-90	D2	3	6.1.90	Reading	D3	A	L	1-2	Armstrong
1990-91	D1	3	5.1.91	Arsenal	D1	A	L	1-2	O'Leary og
1991-92	D2	3	4.1.92	Port Vale	D2	H	W	3-0	Davenport, Byrne, Atkinson
		4	25.1.92	Oxford U	D2	A	W	3-2	Byrne, Hardyman, Atkinson
		5	15.2.92	West Ham	D1	H	D	1-1	Byrne
		5r	26.2.92	West Ham		A	W	3-2	Byrne 2, Rush
		6	10.3.92	Chelsea	D1	A	D	1-1	Byrne
		6r	18.3.92	Chelsea		H	W	2-1	Davenport, Armstrong
		SF	5.4.92	Norwich C	D1		W	1-0	Byrne
				played at Hillsborough					
		F	9.5.92	Liverpool	D1	WEMBLEY	L	0-2	
1992-93	D1	3	12.1.93	Notts Co	D1	A	W	2-0	Cunnington, Goodman
		4	24.1.93	Sheffield W	PL	A	L	0-1	

SUNDERLAND ALBION

Formed 1888, a short-lived breakaway club from Sunderland FC. Folded 1892.

SUNDERLAND ALBION

1888-89		1	15.12.88	Grimsby T	TC	A	L	1-3	J.Stewart
1889-90	FAII	1	18.1.90	Bootle	FAII	A	W	3-1	Hannah, Weir, Sawers
			Bootle awarded tie as Sunderland Albion used ineligible players						
1890-91	FAII	1	17.1.90	93rd Regiment		H	W	2-0	Rae, Crozier
		2	31.1.91	Nottingham F	FAII	A	D	1-1	McClellan
		2r	7.2.91	Nottingham F		H	D	3-3aet	Hannah, Smith, McClellan
		2 2r	11.2.91	Nottingham F at Bramall Lane			L	0-5	
1891-92	FAII	1	16.1.92	Birmingham St G.	FAII	H	L	1-2	Gillespie
			FA ordered replay, match lasted only one hour						
		1r	23.1.92	Birmingham St G		H	W	4-0	Strachan 2, Gilespie, Mackie
		2	30.1.92	Nottingham F	FAII	H	L	0-1	

1ST SURREY RIFLES

Formed 1869. Home matches played at their Headquarters at Flodden Rd, Camberwell, SE London

1872-73	1	19.10.72	Upton Park		H	W	2-0	Allport, Hastie
	2	23.11.72	Maidenhead		A	L	0-3	
1873-74	1	25.10.73	Barnes		H	D	0-0	
	1r	8.11.73	Barnes		A	L	0-1	
1875-76	1	23.10.75	Wanderers		A	L	0-5	
1876-77	1	11.11.76	105th Regiment		A	L	0-3	
1877-78	1	7.11.77	Forest School		H	W	1-0	Kirkpatrick
	2	22.12.77	Old Harrovians		A	L	0-6	
1885-86	1	31.10.85	Clapham Rovers		A	L	0-12	
1886-87	1	23.10.86	Upton Park		A	L	0-9	

SUTTON COLDFIELD TOWN

Formed 1879. **Re-formed 1897. First entered FA Cup:** 1956

1980-81	WMRL	1	22.11.80	Doncaster R	D4	H	L	0-2	
1992-93	SL	1	14.11.92	Bolton W	D2	A	L	1-2	Gale

SUTTON JUNCTION

First entered FA Cup: 1906. **Cup final connection:** Henry Martin (Sunderland 1913) started his career at Sutton Junction

1911-12	CA	1	13.1.12	Swindon T	SL	A	L	0-5	

SUTTON UNITED

Formed 1898. **First entered FA Cup:** 1911. **League clubs beaten:** Aldershot, Peterborough, Coventry C

1945-46	AL	1 1L	17.11.45	Walthamstow Ave	IL	H	L	1-4	Baughan
		1 2L	24.11.45	Walthamstow Ave		A	L	2-7	Scott, Hinshelwood
1946-47	AL	1	30.11.46	Barnet	AL	A	L	0-3	
1960-61	AL	1	5.11.60	Romford	SL	H	D	2-2	Hermitage, Green
		1r	9.11.60	Romford		A	L	0-5	
1963-64	IL	1	16.11.63	Aldershot	D4	H	L	0-4	
1966-67	IL	1	26.11.66	Bath C	SL	A	L	0-1	
1969-70	IL	1	15.11.69	Dagenham	AL	A	W	1-0	Faulkner
		2	6.12.69	Barnet	SL	A	W	2-0	Howard, Drabwell
		3	6.1.70	Hillingdon Borough	SL	A	D	0-0	
		3r	12.1.70	Hillingdon Borough		H	W	4-1	Mellows, Howard, Bladon 2
		4	24.1.70	Leeds U	D1	H	L	0-6	
1975-76	IL	1	22.11.75	Bournemouth	D4	H	D	1-1	Kidd
		1r	26.11.75	Bournemouth		A	L	0-1	
1981-82	IL	1	21.11.81	Bishops Stortford	IL	A	D	2-2	Bradford og, Sunnucks
		1r	24.11.81	Bishops Stortford		H	W	2-1	Rogers, J Rains
		2	15.12.81	Swindon T	D3	A	L	1-2	Joyce
1987-88	GMVC	1	14.11.87	Aldershot	D3	H	W	3-0	McKinnon 2, Cornwell
		2	5.12.87	Peterborough U	D4	A	W	3-1	Lawrence og, Cornwell, Dennis
		3	9.1.88	Middlesbrough	D2	H	D	1-1	M Golley
		3r	12.1.88	Middlesbrough		A	L	0-1aet	
1988-89	GMVC	1	19.11.88	Dagenham	IL	A	W	4-0	McKinnon 2, Dennis, Rogers
		2	10.12.88	Aylesbury	GMVC	A	W	1-0	Dennis
		3	7.1.89	Coventry C	D1	H	W	2-1	Rains., Hanlan
		4	28.1.89	Norwich C	D1	A	L	0-8	

1989-90	GMVC 1	18.11.89	Torquay U	D4	H	D	1-1	McKinnon
	1r	22.11.89	Torquay U		A	L	0-4	
1990-91	GMVC 1	17.11.90	Merthyr Tydfil	GMVC A	D	1-1	Gill
	1r	21.11.90	Merthyr Tydfil		H	L	0-1	
1991-92	IL 1	16.11.91	Maidstone U	D4	A	L	0-1	
1992-93	IL 1	14.11.92	Hereford U	D3	H	L	1-2	Quail

SWANSEA CITY

Formed 1912 as Swansea Town. Swansea City 1970. **Best FA Cup Best Performance:** Semi-finals, 1926, 1964. Welsh FA Cup Winners: 10 times, runners-up 8 times. **Record FA Cup Victory:** 8-1 vs Caerleon Athletic, 27.9.1913. In Competition Proper: 7-2 vs Folkestone, 1st round replay, 29.11.1966. **Record FA Cup Defeat:** 0-8 vs Liverpool, 3rd round replay, 9.1.1990

as Swansea Town

1913-14	SL	P **Port Talbot** (H) 4-0; 1q **Caerleon Ath** (H) 8-1; 2q **Mid-Rhondda** (H) 1-0; 3q **Aberdare Ath** (H) 4-0; 4q **Cardiff C** (H) 2-0;								
		5q **Willington** (H) 3-0								
		1	10.1.14	Merthyr Town	SL	H	W	2-0	Weir, Ball
		2	31.1.14	QPR	SL	H	L	1-2	Greer
1914-15	SL	4q **Newport Co** (H) 1-0; 5q **Port Vale** (H) 1-0; 6q **Leicester Fosse** (H) 1-0								
		1	9.1.15	Blackburn R	D1	H	W	1-0	Benyon
		2	30.1.15	Newcastle U	D1	A	D	1-1aet	Lloyd
		2r	6.2.15	Newcastle U		H	L	0-2	
1919-20	SL	6q **Gillingham** (H) 1-1; 6qr **Gillingham** (A) 1-1; 6q 2r **Gillingham** at Ninian Pk 0-0; 6q 3r **Gillingham** at Chelsea 1-3								
1920-21	D3	6q **Hartlepools U** (H) 3-0								
		1	8.1.21	Bury	D2	H	W	3-0	Edmondson 2, Brown
		2	29.1.21	Plymouth A	D3	H	L	1-2	Edmondson
1921-22	3S	6q **Bristol R** (H) 2-0								
		1	7.1.22	West Ham	D2	H	D	0-0	
		1r	11.1.22	West Ham		A	D	1-1aet	Hole
		1 2r	16.1.22	West Ham at Bristol			W	1-0	Spottiswoode
		2	28.1.22	Southend U	3S	A	W	1-0	Jones
		3	18.2.22	Millwall	3S	A	L	0-4	
1922-23	3S	5q **Merthyr Town** (A) 0-0; 5qr **Merthyr Town** (H) 0-1								
1923-24	3S	1	12.1.24	Clapton O	D2	H	D	1-1	Smith
		1r	17.1.24	Clapton O		A	D	1-1aet	Roulson
		1 2r	21.1.24	Clapton O at Tottenham			W	2-1	Smith, S.Tonner og
		2	2.2.24	Aston Villa	D1	H	L	0-2	
1924-25	3S	1	10.1.25	Plymouth A	3S	H	W	3-0	Thompson 2, Deacon
		2	31.1.25	Aston Villa	D1	H	L	1-3	Deacon
1925-26	D2	1	28.11.25	Exeter C	3S	A	W	3-1	Thompson, Deacon, Pacey og
		2	12.12.25	Watford	3S	H	W	3-2	Nicholas, Fowler, Thompson
		3	9.1.26	Blackpool	D2	A	W	2-0	Fowler, Deacon
		4	30.1.26	Stoke C	D2	H	W	6-3	Thompson, Hole, Fowler 4
		5	22.2.26	Millwall	3S	A	W	1-0	Fowler
		6	6.3.26	Arsenal	D1	H	W	2-1	Thompson, Fowler
		SF	27.3.26	Bolton W	D1		L	0-3	
				played at White Hart Lane					
1926-27	D2	3	8.1.27	Bury	D1	H	W	4-1	Thompson 3, Deacon
		4	29.1.27	Barnsley	D2	A	W	3-1	Fowler 2, Hole
		5	19.2.27	South Shields	D2	A	D	2-2	Fowler, Deacon
		5r	24.2.27	South Shields		H	W	2-1	Deacon, Thompson
		6	5.3.27	Reading	D2	H	L	1-3	McPherson
1927-28	D2	3	14.1.28	Wrexham	3N	A	L	1-2	Hole
1928-29	D2	3	12.1.29	Nottingham F	D2	A	W	2-1	Graham og, Deacon
		4	26.1.29	Leicester C	D1	A	L	0-1	
1929-30	D2	3	11.1.30	Walsall	3S	A	L	0-2	
1930-31	D2	3	10.1.31	Notts Co	3S	A	L	1-3	Easton
1931-32	D2	3	9.1.32	Bury	D2	A	L	1-2	Gunn
1932-33	D2	3	14.1.33	Sheffield U	D1	H	L	2-3	Martin 2
1933-34	D2	3	13.1.34	Notts Co	D2	H	W	1-0	Martin
		4	27.1.34	Bury	D2	A	D	1-1	Matthews og
		4r	1.2.34	Bury		H	W	3-0	Hanford, Davies 2
		5	17.2.34	Portsmouth	D1	H	L	0-1	
1934-35	D2	3	12.1.35	Stoke C	D1	H	W	4-1	Lowry 2, Blair, Bussey
		4	26.1.35	Derby Co	D1	A	L	0-3	
1935-36	D2	3	11.1.36	Liverpool	D1	A	L	0-1	
1936-37	D2	3	16.1.37	Carlisle U	3N	H	W	1-0	Williams

Season	Div	Round	Date	Opponent	Opp Div	Venue	Res	Score	Scorers
		4	30.1.37	York C	3N	H	D	0-0	
		4r	3.2.37	York C		A	W	3-1	Williams, Henson 2
		5	20.2.37	Sunderland	D1	A	L	0-3	
1937-38	D2	3	8.1.38	Wolverhampton W	D1	H	L	0-4	
1938-39	D2	3	7.1.39	Blackburn R	D2	A	L	0-2	
1945-46	D2	3 1L	5.1.46	Bristol C	3S	A	L	1-5	Ford
		3 2L	10.1.46	Bristol C		H	D	2-2	Ford 2
1946-47	D2	3	11.1.47	Gillingham	SL	H	W	4-1	McGrory, Payne, Squires, Jones
		4	25.1.47	Luton T	D2	A	L	0-2	
1947-48	3S	3	10.1.48	Bristol R	3S	A	L	0-3	
1948-49	3S	1	4.12.48	Southend U	3S	A	W	2-1aet	Burns, O'Driscoll
		2	11.12.48	Bristol C	3S	A	L	1-3	O'Driscoll
1949-50	D2	3	7.1.50	Birmingham C	D1	H	W	3-0	I. Allchurch, Burns, Scrine
		4	28.1.50	Arsenal	D1	A	L	1-2	Scrine
1950-51	D2	3	6.1.51	Mansfield T	3N	A	L	0-2	
1951-52	D2	3	12.1.52	Reading	3S	A	W	3-0	I.Allchurch, Medwin, Bellis
		4	2.2.52	Rotherham U	D2	H	W	3-0	I.Allchurch, Scrine, Williams
		5	23.2.52	Newcastle U	D1	H	L	0-1	
1952-53	D2	3	10.1.53	Newcastle U	D1	A	–	0-0	
			abandoned after eight minutes						
		3	14.1.53	Newcastle U		A	L	0-3	
1953-54	D2	3	9.1.54	Barrow	3N	A	D	2-2	Thomas, Beech
		3r	14.1.54	Barrow		H	W	4-2	Kiley, Beech, I. Allchurch 2
		4	30.1.54	Everton	D2	A	L	0-3	
1954-55	D2	3	8.1.55	Blackburn R	D2	A	W	2-0	Medwin, Jones
		4	29.1.55	Stoke C	D2	H	W	3-1	Medwin, I.Allchurch, Griffiths
		5	19.2.55	Sunderland	D1	H	D	2-2	Charles, Medwin
		5r	23.2.55	Sunderland		A	L	0-1	
1955-56	D2	3	7.1.56	York C	3N	H	L	1-2	Griffiths
1956-57	D2	3	5.1.57	Wolverhampton W	D1	A	L	3-5	Palmer 2, I.Allchurch
1957-58	D2	3	4.1.58	Burnley	D1	A	L	2-4	Charles, Lewis
1958-59	D2	3	10.1.59	Portsmouth	D1	A	L	1-3	Charles
1959-60	D2	3	9.1.60	Gillingham	D4	A	W	4-1	B.Jones, Hughes, Williams 2
		4	30.1.60	Burnley	D1	H	D	0-0	
		4r	2.2.60	Burnley		A	L	1-2	Nurse
1960-61	D2	3	7.1.61	Port Vale	D3	H	W	3-0	L.Allchurch, Reynolds 2
		4	28.1.61	Preston NE	D1	H	W	2-1	Reynolds, R.Davies
		5	18.2.61	Burnley	D1	A	L	0-4	
1961-62	D2	3	9.1.62	Sheffield W	D1	A	L	0-1	
1962-63	D2	3	26.1.63	QPR	D3	H	W	2-0	Thomas, Reynolds
		4	4.3.63	West Ham	D1	A	L	0-1	
1963-64	D2	3	4.1.64	Barrow	D4	H	W	4-1	B.Evans, R.Evans (p), Thomas, M.Williams
		4	25.1.64	Sheffield U	D1	A	D	1-1	Thomas
		4r	28.1.64	Sheffield U		H	W	4-0	Draper 2, McLaughlin, Thomas
		5	15.2.64	Stoke C	D1	A	D	2-2	Todd 2
		5r	18.2.64	Stoke C		H	W	2-0	McLaughlin, Todd
		6	29.2.64	Liverpool	D1	A	W	2-1	McLaughlin, Thomas
		SF	14.3.64	Preston NE at Villa Park	D2		L	1-2	McLaughlin
1964-65	D2	3	9.1.65	Newcastle U	D2	H	W	1-0	McLaughlin
		4	30.1.65	Huddersfield T	D2	H	W	1-0	Kirby
		5	20.2.65	Peterborough U	D3	A	D	0-0	
		5r	23.2.65	Peterborough U		H	L	0-2	
1965-66	D3	1	13.11.65	Walsall	D3	A	L	3-6	Gregg og, Todd, McLaughlin
1966-67	D3	1	26.11.66	Folkestone	SL	A	D	2-2	McLaughlin 2
		1r	29.11.66	Folkestone		H	W	7-2	Evans, McLaughlin 3, Humphries 2, Patrick og
		2	7.1.67	Nuneaton B	SL	A	L	0-2	
1967-68	D4	1	18.12.67	Enfield	IL	H	W	2-0	B.Evans, Humphries
		2	6.1.68	Brighton & HA	D3	H	W	2-1	Allchurch, Humphries
		3	27.1.68	Doncaster R	D4	A	W	2-0	Todd, Williams
		4	17.2.68	Arsenal	D1	H	L	0-1	
1968-69	D4	1	16.11.68	Oxford C	IL	A	W	3-2	Gwyther 2, Thomas (p)
		2	7.12.68	Weymouth	SL	A	D	1-1	Screen
		2r	10.12.68	Weymouth		H	W	2-0	Biggs, Thomas
		3	4.1.69	Halifax T	D4	H	L	0-1	
1969-70	D4	1	15.11.69	Kettering	SL	A	W	2-0	H.Williams 2
		2	6.12.69	Oxford C	IL	A	W	5-1	Gwyther 4, Evans
		3	3.1.70	Leeds U	D1	A	L	1-2	Gwyther

as Swansea City

1970-71	D3	1	21.11.70	**Exeter C**	D4	H	W	4-1	Thomas 2, Evans, Gwyther
		2	12.12.70	**Telford U**	SL	H	W	6-2	Gwyther 3, Hole, L.Allchurch, H.Williams
		3	2.1.71	**Rhyl**	CC	H	W	6-1	Gwyther 3, Evans 2, Smart og
		4	23.1.71	**Liverpool**	D1	A	L	0-3	
1971-72	D3	1	20.11.71	**Brentford**	D4	H	D	1-1	Davies
		1r	22.11.71	**Brentford**		A	W	3-2	A.Williams, Gwyther, Thomas
		2	11.12.71	**Exeter C**	D4	H	D	0-0	
		2r	15.12.71	**Exeter C**		A	W	1-0	Holme
		3	15.1.72	**Gillingham**	D4	H	W	1-0	Gwyther
		4	5.2.72	**Portsmouth**	D2	A	L	0-2	
1972-73	D3	1	18.11.72	**Margate**	SL	A	L	0-1	
1973-74	D4	1	24.11.73	**Walsall**	D3	A	L	0-1	
1974-75	D4	1	26.11.74	**Kettering**	SL	H	D	1-1	Lally
		1r	2.12.74	**Kettering**		A	L	1-3	W.Evans
1975-76	D4	1	22.11.75	**Southend U**	D3	A	L	0-2	
1976-77	D4	1	20.11.76	**Minehead**	SL	H	L	0-1	
1977-78	D4	1	26.11.77	**Leatherhead**	IL	A	D	0-0	
		1r	29.11.77	**Leatherhead**		H	W	2-1	Charles, Curtis
		2	17.12.77	**Portsmouth**	D3	A	D	2-2	Curtis, K.Moore
		2r	20.12.77	**Portsmouth**		H	W	2-1	Denyer og, G.Moore
		3	7.1.78	**Walsall**	D3	A	L	1-4	R.James
1978-79	D3	1	25.11.78	**Hillingdon B**	SL	H	W	4-1	R.James, Charles 2, Waddle
		2	16.12.78	**Woking**	IL	H	D	2-2	Curtis 2
		2r	19.12.78	**Woking**		A	W	5-3aet	Curtis 3, Toshack, R.James
		3	8.1.79	**Bristol R**	D2	H	L	0-1	
1979-80	D2	3	5.1.80	**Crystal P**	D1	H	D	2-2	Toshack 2
		3r	8.1.80	**Crystal P**		A	D	3-3aet	Waddle, Giles, Toshack
		3 2r	14.1.80	**Crystal P** at Ninian Park			W	2-1	R.James, Giles
		4	26.1.80	**Reading**	D3	H	W	4-1	Giles 2, Waddle, James
		5	16.2.80	**West Ham**	D2	A	L	0-2	
1980-81	D2	3	3.1.81	**Middlesbrough**	D1	H	L	0-5	
1981-82	D1	3	2.1.82	**Liverpool**	D1	H	L	0-4	
1982-83	D1	3	8.1.83	**Norwich C**	D1	A	L	1-2	Gale
1983-84	D2	3	7.1.84	**Brighton & HA**	D2	A	L	0-2	
1984-85	D3	1	17.11.84	**Bognor Regis T**	IL	H	D	1-1	Richards
		1r	21.11.84	**Bognor Regis T**		A	L	1-3	Marustik
1985-86	D3	1	16.11.85	**Leyton-Wingate**	IL	H	W	2-0	Waddle, Williams
		2	7.12.85	**Bristol R**	D3	H	L	1-2	Burrows
1986-87	D4	1	15.11.86	**Wealdstone**	GMVC	A	D	1-1	Williams
		1r	20.11.86	**Wealdstone**		H	–	2-1	Love, McCarthy
				abandoned after 54 minutes - waterlogged pitch					
		1r	24.11.86	**Wealdstone**		H	W	4-1	Williams, Hough, McCarthy, Hutchison
		2	6.12.86	**Slough T**	IL	H	W	3-0	Pascoe, McCarthy (p), Hutchison
		3	10.1.87	**WBA**	D2	H	W	3-2	McCarthy 2, Melville
		4	3.2.87	**Hull C**	D2	H	L	0-1	
1987-88	D4	1	14.11.87	**Hayes**	IL	A	W	1-0	Pascoe
		2	5.12.87	**Leyton O**	D4	A	L	0-2	
1988-89	D3	1	19.11.88	**Northampton T**	D3	H	W	3-1	Melville, Hutchison, Wade
		2	10.12.88	**Colchester U**	D4	A	D	2-2	Coleman, Melville
		2r	13.12.88	**Colchester U**		H	L	1-3	Wade
1989-90	D3	1	18.12.89	**Kidderminster H**	GMVC	A	W	3-2	Melville 2, Davies
		2	9.12.89	**Peterborough U**	D4	H	W	3-1	Raynor (p), Chalmers 2
		3	6.1.90	**Liverpool**	D1	H	D	0-0	
		3r	9.1.90	**Liverpool**		A	L	0-8	
1990-91	D3	1	17.11.90	**Welling U**	GMVC	H	W	5-2	Gilligan (p), Connor, Legg 2, Thornber
		2	8.12.90	**Walsall**	D4	H	W	2-1	Connor, Gilligan (p)
		3	5.1.91	**Rotherham U**	D3	H	D	0-0	
		3r	21.1.91	**Rotherham U**		A	L	0-4	
1991-92	D3	1	16.11.91	**Cardiff C**	D4	H	W	2-1	Gilligan, Harris
		2	7.12.91	**Exeter C**	D3	A	D	0-0	
		2r	17.12.91	**Exeter C**		H	L	1-2	Walker
1992-93	D2	1		**bye** *(odd-number in draw created by Maidstone United folding)*					
		2	5.12.92	**Exeter C**	D3	A	–	2-1	Cornforth, Jenkins
				abandoned after 86 minutes – floodlight failure					
		2	15.12.92	**Exeter C**		A	W	5-2	West, Legg, Wimbleton, Cullen, Bowen
		3	2.1.93	**Oxford U**	D1	H	D	1-1	West

3r	12.1.93	Oxford U		A	D	2-2aet	Carnforth, Legg
	Swansea won 5-4 on penalties						
4	2.2.93	Grimsby T	D1	H	D	0-0	
4r	9.2.93	Grimsby T		A	L	0-2	

SWIFTS

Formed 1868. Slough-based amateur club whose ground was near The Dolphin pub near the town centre.

1873-74	1	18.10.73	Crystal P	H	W	1-0	Jeans
	2	22.11.73	Woodford Wells		W	2-1	EH Bambridge, Nicholls
	3		bye				
	SF	28.1.74	Royal Engineers at Kennington Oval		L	0-2	
1874-75	1	5.11.74	Old Etonians	A	D	0-0	
	1r	14.11.74	Old Etonians	H	D	1-1	Joll
	1 2r	26.11.74	Old Etonians	A	L	0-3	
1875-76	1	3.11.75	Marlow	H	W	2-0	Joll, Talbot
	2	11.12.75	South Norwood	A	W	5-0	W.Bambridge, Post, Sale, Talbot, 1 other
	3	29.1.76	Royal Engineers		W	3-1	W.Bambridge, Sale, Selwyn
	SF	26.2.76	Wanderers at Kennington Oval		L	1-2	Sale
1876-77	1	4.11.76	Reading Hornets	H	W	2-0	Joll, Rawson
	2	16.12.76	Rochester	A	L	0-1	
1877-78	1	7.11.77	Leyton	H	W	3-2	WS Bambridge 2, Short
	2	22.12.77	Clapham R	A	L	0-4	
1878-79	1	9.11.78	Hawks	H	W	2-1	WS Bambridge, Turner
	2	21.12.78	Romford	H	W	3-1	EG Bambridge 2, Parry
	3		bye				
	4	8.3.79	Clapham R	A	L	1-8	Bain
1879-80	1		West End		scratched		
1880-81	1	6.11.80	Old Foresters	H	D	1-1	
	1r	20.11.80	Old Foresters	A	W	2-1	Parke, og
	2	18.12.80	Reading	A	W	1-0	
	3	8.1.81	Clapham R	A	L	1-2	E.Wild
1881-82	1	5.11.81	Herts Rangers	H	W	4-0	EC Bambridge 4
	2	3.12.81	Old Harrovians	H	W	7-1	EC Bambridge 5, Bain, Keyser
	3	17.12.81	Old Etonians	A	L	0-3	
1882-83	1	4.11.82	Highbury Union	H	W	4-1	
	2	30.11.82	Upton Park	H	D	2-2	Parr, Thorpe
	2r	2.12.82	Upton Park	H	W	3-2	Parr 3
	3		bye				
	4	24.1.83	Old Etonians	A	L	0-2	
1883-84	1		bye				
	2	1.12.83	Marlow	H	W	2-0	EC Bambridge, Jessop
	3	22.12.83	Clapham R	H	W	2-1	EC Bambridge, Davenport
	4	19.1.84	Old Foresters	H	W	2-1	EC Bambridge, Perkins
	5	9.2.84	Notts Co	A	D	1-1	AL Bambridge
	5r	14.2.84	Notts Co	H	L	0-1	
1884-85	1	8.11.84	Old Brightonians	H	W	3-0	
	2	6.12.84	South Reading	H	W	3-2	EC Bambridge 2, others 1
	3	3.1.85	Old Westminsters	H	D	1-1	
	3r	14.1.85	Old Westminsters	A	D	2-2	Pawson, og
	3 2r	21.1.85	Old Westminsters	H	W	2-1	Brann, others 1
	4	24.1.85	Nottingham Forest	H	L	0-1	
1885-86	1		bye				
	2	21.11.85	Rochester	H	W	5-1	Bryan 2, Playford 2, Miller
	3		Old Harrovians		walkover		
	4		bye				
	5	16.1.86	Church	A	W	6-2	EC Bambridge, Brann, Smith, 3 others
	6	13.2.86	South Shore	A	W	2-1	Brann, og
	SF	13.3.86	Blackburn R		L	1-2	EC Bambridge
		played at Derby Cricket Ground					
1886-87	1	23.10.86	Luton W	H	W	13-0	
	2	20.11.86	Swindon T	H	W	7-1	EC Bambridge 3, Challen 2, Playford 2
	3		bye				
	4	15.1.87	Old Foresters	H	L	0-2	
1887-88	1	15.10.87	Maidenhead	H	W	3-1	
	2		bye				

SWIFTS

	3	26.11.87 **Dulwich**		A	W	3-1	
	4	10.12.87 **Crewe A**		A	D	2-2	EC Bambridge, Challen
	4r	17.12.87 **Crewe A**		H	W	3-2	Holden-White, Ingram, og
		FA ordered match to be replayed after protest about the size of the goals					
	4 2r	31.12.87 **Crewe A** at Derby Cricket Gd		L		1-2	EC Bambridge
1888-89	1	2.2.89 **Wrexham**		H	W	3-1	Wilson, Humphrey, Challen
	2	16.2.89 **Blackburn R**		scratched			
1889-90	4q	7.12.89 **Royal Arsenal**		A	W	5-1	
	1	18.1.90 **Sheffield W**		A	L	1-6	Challen

SWINDON TOWN

Formed 1881. **First entered FA Cup:** 1886. **Best FA Cup Performance:** semi-finals 1910, 1912 (both as a Southern League club, the last non-League club to reach the last four). **FA Cup Record Win:** 10-1 vs Farnham United Breweries, 1st round, 28.11.1925. **FA Cup Record Defeat:** 1-10 vs Manchester City, 4th round replay, 25.1.1930

1886-87	1	23.10.86 **Watford Rovers**		A	W	1-0	R.Jones
	2	20.10.86 **Swifts**		A	L	1-7	J.Thomas
1887-88	1	8.10.87 **Old Brightonians**		A	L	0-1	
1888-89	2q **Marlow** (H) 2-5						
1889-90	1q **Watford Rovers** (A) 3-5						
1890-91	1q **Maidenhead** (H) 9-0; 2q **Marlow** (H) 2-0; 3q **93rd Highlanders** (A) 0-6						
1891-92	1q **Luton T** (A) 3-4						
1892-93	1q **Cowes** (A) 2-1aet; 2q **Warmley** (H) 8-1; 3q **Reading** (H) 2-1; 4q **Marlow** (A) 0-1						
1893-94	1q **Maidenhead** (H) 4-0; 2q **Marlow** (H) 1-0; 3q **Weymouth** (A) 4-0; 4q **Reading** (H) 0-2						
1894-95 SL	1q **Bristol St G** (H) 4-2; 2q **Marlow** (A) 2-4						
1895-96 SL	1q **Trowbridge T** (A) 3-1; 2q **Warmley** (H) 2-1; 3q **Uxbridge** (A) 0-5						
1896-97 SL	3q **Uxbridge** (H) 3-2; 4q **Royal Artillery** (H) 4-1; 5q **Southampton St Marys** (A) 2-8						
1897-98 SL	3q **Reading** (A) 0-0; 3qr **Reading** (H) 3-2; 4q **Southampton St Marys** (H) 1-3						
1898-99 SL	3q **Warmley** (A) 0-1						
1899-00 SL	3q **Portsmouth** (A) 1-2						
1900-01 SL	3q **Bristol East** (H) 1-1; 3qr **Bristol East** (H) 5-0; 4q **Staple Hill** (H) 2-2; 4qr **Staple Hill** (H) 6-0; 5q **Bristol R** (A) 1-5						
1901-02 SL	3q **Yeovil Casuals** (H) 4-0; 4q **Weymouth** (H) 2-1; 5q **Bristol R** (H) 0-1						
1902-03 SL	2q **Chippenham T** (H) 5-0; 3q **Yeovil Casuals** (A) 4-0; 4q **Poole T** (H) 7-1; 5q **Whiteheads Torpedo** (A) 9-0; Int **Barnsley** (A) 0-4						
1903-04 SL	3q **Poole T** (H) 9-0; 4q **Staple Hill** (H) 5-0; 5q **Plymouth A** (A) 0-2						
1904-05 SL	3q **Whiteheads Torpedo** (H) 7-0; 4q **Longfleet St Marys** (H) 8-0; 5q **Green Waves** (A) 1-2						
1905-06 SL	5q **West Hampstead** (H) 4-0						
	1	13.1.06 **Brighton & HA**	SL	A	L	0-3	
1906-07 SL	5q **Burslem Port Vale** (H) 1-2						
1907-08 SL	1	11.1.08 **Sheffield U**	D1	H	D	0-0	
	1r	16.1.08 **Sheffield U**		A	W	3-2aet	Warburton, Tout, Johnston
	2	1.2.08 **QPR**	SL	H	W	2-1	Johnston, Warburton
	3	22.2.08 **Wolverhampton W**	D2	A	L	0-2	
1908-09 SL	1	16.1.09 **Plymouth A**	SL	A	L	0-1	
1909-10 SL	1	15.1.10 **Crystal P**	SL	A	W	3-1	Tout, Fleming, Bown
	2	2.5.10 **Burnley**	D2	H	W	2-0	Bown, Fleming
	3	19.2.10 **Tottenham H**	D1	H	W	3-2	Fleming 3
	4	5.3.10 **Manchester C**	D2	H	W	2-0	Jefferson, Bown
	SF	26.3.10 **Newcastle U**	D1		L	0-2	
		played at Tottenham					
1910-11 SL	1	14.1.11 **Notts Co**	D1	H	W	3-1	Bown 2, Fleming
	2	4.2.11 **W. Arsenal**	D1	H	W	1-0	Jefferson
	3	25.2.11 **Darlington**	NEL	A	W	3-0	Bolland, Fleming, Jefferson
	4	11.3.11 **Chelsea**	D2	A	L	1-3	Bown
1911-12 SL	1	13.1.12 **Sutton Junction**	CA	H	W	5-0	Fleming 4, Bown
	2	3.2.12 **Notts Co**	D1	H	W	2-0	Jefferson, Wheatcroft
	3	24.2.12 **West Ham**	SL	A	D	1-1	Fleming
	3r	28.2.12 **West Ham**		H	W	4-0	Glover 2ogs, Jefferson, Wheatcroft
	4	9.3.12 **Everton**	D1	H	W	2-1	Jefferson, Bown
	SF	30.3.12 **Barnsley**	D2		D	0-0	
		played at Stamford Bridge					
	SFr	3.4.12 **Barnsley**			L	0-1	
		played at Meadow Lane, Nottingham					
1912-13 SL	1	11.1.13 **Rochdale**	CL	A	W	2-0	Bown, Jefferson
	2	1.2.13 **Huddersfield T**	D2	A	W	2-1	Wheatcroft, Bown
	3	22.2.13 **Sunderland**	D1	A	L	2-4	Fleming, Wheatcroft
1913-14 SL	1	10.1.14 **Manchester U**	D1	H	W	1-0	Fleming
	2	31.1.14 **Bolton W**	D1	A	L	2-4	Batty 2

1914-15	SL	1	9.1.15	**Chelsea**	D1	A	D	1-1	Denyer
		1r	16.1.15	**Chelsea** at Stamford Bridge		A	L	2-5aet	Wheatcroft Jefferson
1919-20	SL	1	10.1.20	**Fulham**	D2	A	W	2-1	Travers 2
		2	31.1.20	**Chelsea**	D1	A	L	0-4	
1920-21	D3	1	8.1.21	**Sheffield U**	D1	H	W	1-0	Fleming
		2	29.1.21	**Chelsea**	D1	H	L	0-2	
1921-22	3S	1	7.1.22	**Leeds U**	D2	H	W	2-1	Fleming 2
		2	28.1.22	**Blackburn R**	D1	H	L	0-1	
1922-23	3S	1	13.1.23	**Barnsley**	D2	H	D	0-0	
		1r	18.1.23	**Barnsley**		A	L	0-2	
1923-24	3S	1	12.1.24	**Bradford PA**	3N	H	W	4-0	Wareing, Crossley, Denyer, Johnson
		2	2.2.24	**Oldham A**	D2	H	W	2-0	Denyer, Crossley
		3	23.2.24	**Crystal P**	D2	A	W	2-1	Wareing, Fleming
		4	8.3.24	**Burnley**	D1	H	D	1-1	Fleming
		4r	12.3.24	**Burnley**		A	L	1-3	Johnson
1924-25	3S	1	10.1.25	**Fulham**	D2	H	L	1-2	Johnson
1925-26	3S	1	28.11.25	**Farnham Utd Brew.**	SSL	A	W	10-1	Richardson 4, Johnson 3, Denyer 2, Wall
		2	12.12.25	**Sittingbourne**	KL	H	W	7-0	Richardson 4, Davies 2, Denyer
		3	9.1.26	**Clapton**	IL	A	W	3-2	Richardson 2, Moore og
				played at Upton Park					
		4	30.1.26	**Nottingham F**	D2	A	L	0-2	
1926-27	3S	1	27.11.26	**Bournemouth**	3S	A	D	1-1	Morris
		1r	29.11.26	**Bournemouth**		H	L	3-4	Thom, Wall 2
1927-28	3S	1	26.11.27	**Newport Co**	3S	A	W	1-0	Morris
		2	10.12.27	**Crystal P**	3S	H	D	0-0	
		2r	14.12.27	**Crystal P**		A	W	2-1	Morris 2
		3	14.1.28	**Clapton O**	D2	H	W	2-1	Morris 2
		4	28.1.28	**Sheffield W**	D1	H	L	1-2	Morris
1928-29	3S	3	12.1.29	**Newcastle U**	D1	H	W	2-0	Morris 2
		4	26.1.29	**Burnley**	D1	A	D	3-3	Morris 2, Denyer
		4r	30.1.29	**Burnley**		H	W	3-2	Dickenson (p), Eddleston, Morris
		5	16.2.29	**Arsenal**	D1	H	D	0-0	
		5r	20.2.29	**Arsenal**		A	L	0-1	
1929-30	3S	3	11.1.30	**Manchester U**	D1	A	W	2-0	Eddleston, Roberts
		4	25.1.30	**Manchester C**	D1	H	D	1-1	McCloy og
		4r	29.1.30	**Manchester C**		A	L	1-10	Morris
1930-31	3S	1	29.11.30	**Norwich C**	3S	A	L	0-2	
1931-32	3S	1	28.11.31	**Luton T**	3S	H	L	0-5	
1932-33	3S	1	26.11.32	**Dulwich Hamlet**	IL	H	W	4-1	Starsmore, Quinn 2, Brooks
		2	10.12.32	**Southport**	3N	A	W	2-1	Little og, Morris
		3	14.1.33	**Burnley**	D2	H	L	1-2	Munnings
1933-34	3S	1	25.11.33	**Ilford**	IL	A	W	4-2	Armstrong, Fisher, Timbrell, Flanagan
		2	9.12.33	**Dartford**	SL	H	W	1-0	Armstrong (p)
		3	13.1.34	**Brighton & HA**	3S	A	L	1-3	Helsby
1934-35	3S	1	24.11.34	**Newport Co**	3S	H	W	4-0	Fowler 3, Gunson
		2	8.12.34	**Lincoln C**	3N	H	W	4-3	Fowler 2, Bowl, Gunson
		3	12.1.35	**Chesterfield**	3N	H	W	2-1	Bowl, Fowler
		4	26.1.35	**Preston NE**	D1	H	L	0-2	
1935-36	3S	1	30.11.35	**Southall**	AL	A	L	1-3	Bowl
1936-37	3S	1	28.11.36	**Dulwich Hamlet**	IL	H	W	6-0	Hetherington, Bradley 2, Cookson, E.Jones, Fowler
		2	12.12.36	**Cardiff C**	3S	A	L	1-2	Cookson
1937-38	3S	1	27.11.37	**Gillingham**	3S	A	W	4-3	Bradley 3 (2ps), E.Jones
		2	11.12.37	**QPR**	3S	H	W	2-1	E.Jones 2
		3	8.1.38	**Grimsby T**	D1	A	D	1-1	E.Jones
		3r	12.1.38	**Grimsby T**		H	W	2-1aet	Morton, Fowler
		4	22.1.38	**Luton T**	D2	A	L	1-2	Morton
1938-39	3S	1	26.11.38	**Lowestoft T**	ECL	H	W	6-0	E.Jones, Lucas, Morton
		2	10.12.38	**Southport**	3N	A	L	0-2	
1945-46	3S	1 1L	17.11.45	**Bristol R**	3S	H	W	1-0	Emery
		1 2L	24.11.45	**Bristol R**		A	L	1-4	Francis
1946-47	3S	1	30.11.46	**Cambridge T**	SPT	H	W	4-1	Lucas 2, JW Stephens 2 (1p)
		2	14.12.46	**Notts Co**	3S	A	L	1-2	Paterson
1947-48	3S	1	29.11.47	**Ipswich T**	3S	H	W	4-2	WM Jones 2, Bell og, Lucas
		2	13.12.47	**Aldershot**	3S	A	D	0-0aet	
		2r	20.12.47	**Aldershot**		H	W	2-0	WM Jones 2
		3	10.1.48	**Burnley**	D1	A	W	2-0	Dryden, Owen
		4	29.1.48	**Notts Co**	3S	H	W	1-0	Lucas

		5	7.2.48	**Southampton**	D2	A	L	0-3
1948-49	3S	3	8.1.49	**Stoke C**	D1	H	L	1-3	Owen
1949-50	3S	1	26.11.49	**Bristol R**	3S	H	W	1-0	Owen
		2	10.12.49	**Carlisle U**	3N	A	L	0-2
1950-51	3S	1	29.11.50	**Southend U**	3S	A	W	3-0	Bain, Simner, Onslow
		2	9.12.50	**Exeter C**	3S	A	L	0-3
1951-52	3S	1	24.11.51	**Bedford T**	SL	H	W	2-0	Betteridge, Owen
		2	15.12.51	**Torquay U**	3S	H	D	3-3	Owen 2, Millar
		2r	19.12.51	**Torquay U**		A	D	1-1aet	Betteridge
		2 2r	2.1.52	**Torquay U** at Ashton Gate			W	3-1	Onslow, Bain, Owen
		3	12.1.52	**Cardiff C**	D2	A	D	1-1	Owen
		3r	16.1.52	**Cardiff C**		H	W	1-0aet	Owen
		4	2.2.52	**Stoke C**	D1	H	D	1-1	Bain
		4r	4.2.52	**Stoke C**		A	W	1-0	Millar
		5	23.2.52	**Luton T**	D2	A	L	1-3	Betteridge
1952-53	3S	1	22.11.52	**Newport (IOW)**	Hants	H	W	5-0	Lunn, Owen 3, Millar
		2	6.12.52	**Northampton T**	3S	H	W	2-0	Owen, Millar
		3	10.1.53	**Manchester C**	D1	A	L	0-7
1953-54	3S	1	21.11.53	**Newport (IOW)**	Hants	H	W	2-1	Batchelor 2
		2	12.12.53	**Hastings U**	SL	A	L	1-4	Sampson
1954-55	3S	1	20.11.54	**Crystal P**	3S	H	L	0-2
1955-56	3S	1	19.11.55	**Hereford U**	SL	H	W	4-0	Micklewright 2, Gibson, Owen
		2	10.12.55	**Peterborough U**	ML	H	D	1-1	Owen
		2r	15.12.55	**Peterborough U**		A	W	2-1aet	Micklewright, Cross
		3	7.1.56	**Worksop T**	ML	H	W	1-0	Edwards
		4	28.1.56	**Charlton A**	D1	A	L	1-2	Edwards
1956-57	3S	1	17.11.56	**Coventry C**	3S	H	W	2-1	Edwards, Richards
		2	8.12.56	**Bournemouth**	3S	H	L	0-1
1957-58	3S	1	16.11.57	**Reading**	3S	A	L	0-1
1958-59	D3	1	15.11.58	**Aldershot**	D4	H	W	5-0	Edwards, Darcy 3, Kelly
		2	6.12.58	**Norwich C**	D3	H	D	1-1	Richards
		2r	11.12.58	**Norwich C**		A	L	0-1
1959-60	D3	1	14.11.59	**Walsall**	D4	H	L	2-3	Edwards, Darcy
1960-61	D3	1	5.11.60	**Bath C**	SL	H	D	2-2	RP Hunt, Layne
		1r	10.11.60	**Bath C**		A	W	6-4	Layne 4, RP Hunt 2
		2	26.11.60	**Shrewsbury T**	D3	H	L	0-1
1961-62	D3	1	4.11.61	**Kettering T**	SL	H	D	2-2	McPherson, RA Hunt
		1r	8.11.61	**Kettering T**		A	L	0-3
1962-63	D3	1	3.11.62	**Reading**	D3	H	W	4-2	Smith, RP Hunt 2, Spiers og
		2	24.11.62	**Yeovil T**	SL	A	W	2-0	RP Hunt, Jackson
		3	26.1.63	**Luton T**	D2	A	W	2-0	Jackson 2
		4	29.1.63	**Everton**	D1	H	L	1-5	Smith
1963-64	D2	3	4.1.64	**Manchester C**	D2	H	W	2-1	Smart 2
		4	25.1.64	**Aldershot**	D4	A	W	2-1	Rogers, Atkins
		5	15.2.64	**West Ham**	D1	H	L	1-3	McPherson
1964-65	D2	3	9.1.65	**Ipswich T**	D2	H	L	1-2	Brown
1965-66	D3	1	13.11.65	**Merthyr Tydfil**	SL	H	W	5-1	East 4, Smart
		2	4.12.65	**Grantham**	ML	A	W	6-1	Weaver, Nurse, Brown, Smart 2, East
		3	22.1.66	**Coventry C**	D2	H	L	1-2	Brown
1966-67	D3	1	26.11.66	**Horsham**	AL	A	W	3-0	Rogers, Nurse, Brown
		2	10.1.67	**Ashford T**	SL	H	W	5-0	Brown, Rogers 2 (1p), Walker, Penman
		3	28.1.67	**West Ham**	D1	A	D	3-3	Rogers 2, Brown
		3r	31.1.67	**West Ham**		H	W	3-1	Penman, Rogers, Skeen
		4	18.2.67	**Bury**	D2	H	W	2-1	Morgan, Rogers
		5	11.3.67	**Nottingham F**	D1	A	D	0-0
		5r	14.3.67	**Nottingham F**		H	D	1-1aet	Walker
		5 2r	20.3.67	**Nottingham F** at Villa Park			L	0-3
1967-68	D3	1	12.12.67	**Salisbury**	WL	H	W	4-0	Penman, Terry 3
		2	6.1.68	**Luton T**	D4	H	W	3-2	Rogers 2 (1p), Heath
		3	27.1.68	**Blackburn R**	D2	H	W	1-0	Nurse
		4	17.2.68	**Sheffield W**	D1	A	L	1-2	Smart
1968-69	D3	1	16.11.68	**Canterbury C**	SL	H	W	1-0	Rogers (p)
		2	7.12.68	**Grantham**	ML	A	W	2-0	Jones, Smith
		3	4.1.69	**Southend U**	D4	H	L	0-2
1969-70	D2	3	3.1.70	**Blackburn R**	D2	A	W	4-0	Smith, Horsfield, Rogers, Butler
		4	24.1.70	**Chester**	D4	H	W	4-2	Horsfield 2, Jones, Smart
		5	7.2.70	**Scunthorpe U**	D4	H	W	3-1	Noble, Horsfield, Trollope

		6	21.2.70	Leeds U	D1	H	L	0-2	
1970-71	D2	3	2.1.71	QPR	D2	A	W	2-1	Horsfield, Noble
		4	23.1.71	Leeds U	D1	A	L	0-4	
1971-72	D2	3	15.1.72	Arsenal	D1	H	L	0-2	
1972-73	D2	3	13.1.73	Birmingham C	D1	H	W	2-0	Butler, Treacey (p)
		4	3.2.73	WBA	D1	A	L	0-2	
1973-74	D2	3	5.1.74	Portsmouth	D2	A	D	3-3	Jenkins, Moss, Trollope
		3r	9.1.74	Portsmouth		H	L	0-1	
1974-75	D3	1	23.11.74	Reading	D4	H	W	4-0	Anderson, Eastoe, Lenarduzzi og, Moss (p)
		2	14.12.74	Maidstone U	SL	H	W	3-1	Prophett, Eastoe 2
		3	4.1.75	Lincoln C	D4	H	W	2-0	Eastoe, Moss
		4	25.1.75	West Ham	D1	A	D	1-1	Eastoe
		4r	28.1.75	West Ham		H	L	1-2	Anderson
1975-76	D3	1	22.11.75	Newport Co	D4	A	D	2-2	Moss, Syrett
		1r	25.11.75	Newport Co		H	W	3-0	Love og, Trollope, Dixon
		2	13.12.75	Hendon	IL	A	W	1-0	Moss (p)
		3	3.1.76	Tooting & Mitcham	IL	H	D	2-2	Eastoe, Dixon
		3r	6.1.76	Tooting & Mitcham		A	L	1-2	Green og
1976-77	D3	1	20.11.76	Bromley	IL	H	W	7-0	McHale, Syrett 2, Moss 2, Anderson 2
		2	11.12.76	Hitchin T	IL	A	D	1-1	Dixon
		2r	21.12.76	Hitchin T		H	W	3-1aet	Syrett, Moss 2
		3	8.1.77	Fulham	D2	A	D	3-3	Anderson, Moss, McHale
		3r	11.1.77	Fulham		H	W	5-0	Anderson, Syrett 2, Moss 2
		4	29.1.77	Everton	D1	H	D	2-2	Syrett, Stroud
		4r	1.2.77	Everton		A	L	1-2	Anderson
1977-78	D3	1	26.11.77	Borehamwood	IL	A	D	0-0	
		1r	29.11.77	Borehamwood		H	W	2-0	Moss, McHale
		2	17.12.77	Brentford	D4	H	W	2-1	Prophett, McHale
		3	7.1.78	Nottingham F	D1	A	L	1-4	Moss
1978-79	D3	1	25.11.78	March Town U	ECL	H	W	2-0	Gilchrist, Bates
		2	16.12.78	Enfield	IL	H	W	3-0	Bates, Carter, Gilchrist
		3	9.1.79	Cardiff C	D2	H	W	3-0	McHale, Kamara 2
		4	30.1.79	Aldershot	D4	A	L	1-2	Rowland
1979-80	D3	1	24.11.79	Brentford	D3	H	W	4-1	Miller 2, Kamara, Carter
		2	18.12.79	Torquay U	D4	A	D	3-3	Mayes, Tucker, Rowland
		2r	22.12.79	Torquay U		H	W	3-2	Rowland, Mayes 2
		3	5.1.80	Luton T	D2	A	W	2-0	Rowland, Williams
		4	26.1.80	Tottenham H	D1	H	D	0-0	
		4r	30.1.80	Tottenham H		A	L	1-2	McHale (p)
1980-81	D3	1	22.11.80	Weymouth	APL	H	W	3-2	Mayes, Lewis, Kamara
		2	13.12.80	Wimbledon	D4	A	L	0-2	
1981-82	D3	1	21.11.81	Taunton T	WL	H	W	2-1	Pritchard 2
		2	15.12.81	Sutton U	IL	H	W	2-1	Carter, Pritchard
		3	2.1.82	Luton T	D2	A	L	1-2	Emmanuel
1982-83	D4	1	20.11.82	Wealdstone	APL	H	W	2-0	Henry, Rideout
		2	11.12.82	Brentford	D3	H	D	2-2	Lewis, Barnard
		2r	14.12.82	Brentford		A		3-1aet	Rowland, Pritchard, Batty
		3	8.1.83	Aldershot	D4	H	W	7-0	Pritchard 3, Rowland 3, Batty
		4	29.1.83	Burnley	D2	A	L	1-3	Pritchard
1983-84	D4	1	19.11.83	Kettering T	APL	A	W	7-0	Gibson, Quinn 2, Rowland, Henry, Batty
		2	10.12.83	Millwall	D3	A	W	3-2	Quinn 2, Batty
		3	7.1.84	Carlisle U	D2	A	D	1-1	Rowland
		3r	10.1.84	Carlisle U		H	W	3-1	Quinn, Batty, Rowland
		4	28.1.84	Blackburn R	D2	H	L	1-2	Quinn
1984-85	D4	1	19.11.84	Dagenham	APL	A	D	0-0	
		1r	26.11.84	Dagenham		H	L	1-2aet	Mayes
1985-86	D4	1	17.11.85	Bristol C	D3	H	D	0-0	
		1r	20.11.85	Bristol C		A	L	2-4	Ramsey, Barnard
1986-87	D3	1	15.11.86	Farnborough T	IL	H	W	4-0	Coyne, Wade, Gilligan, Baker og
		2	6.12.86	Enfield	GMVC	H	W	3-0	Wade, Bamber, Jones
		3	10.1.87	Fulham	D3	A	W	1-0	Bamber
		4	3.2.87	Leeds U	D2	H	L	1-2	Bamber
1987-88	D2	3	9.1.88	Norwich C	D1	H	D	0-0	
		3r	13.1.88	Norwich C		A	W	2-0	Bamber 2
		4	30.1.88	Newcastle U	D1	A	L	0-5	
1988-89	D2	3	7.1.89	Portsmouth	D2	A	D	1-1	Foley
		3r	10.1.89	Portsmouth		H	W	2-0	Foley, Shearer

SWINDON TOWN

		4	28.1.89	West Ham	D1	H	D	0-0	
		4r	1.2.89	West Ham		A	L	0-1	
1989-90	D2	3	6.1.90	Bristol C	D3	A	L	1-2	Shearer
1990-91	D2	3	5.1.91	Leyton O	D3	A	D	1-1	Shearer
		3r	14.1.91	Leyton O		H	–	1-1	Bodin
			abandoned after 54 minutes – frozen pitch						
		3r	21.1.91	Leyton O		H	W	1-0	White
		4	26.1.91	Norwich C	D1	A	L	1-3	White
1991-92	D2	3	4.1.92	Watford	D2	H	W	3-2	Shearer 2, Mitchell
		4	25.1.92	Cambridge U	D2	A	W	3-0	Calderwood, Shearer 2
		5	16.2.92	A.Villa	D1	H	L	1-2	Mitchell
1992-93	D1	3	2.1.93	QPR	PL	A	L	0-3	

TAMWORTH

Formed 1933. **First entered FA Cup:** 1934. **League club beaten:** Torquay U

1966-67	WMRL	1	26.11.66	Gillingham	D3	A	L	1-4	McCarthy
1969-70	WMRL	1	15.11.69	Torquay U	D3	H	W	2-1	Holmes, Jessop
		2	6.12.69	Gillingham	D3	A	L	0-6	
1970-71	WMRL	1	21.11.70	York C	D4	H	D	0-0	
		1r	23.11.70	York C		A	L	0-5	
1987-88	WMRL	1	14.11.87	Colchester	D4	A	L	0-3	
1990-91	SL	1	17.11.90	Whitley Bay	NPL	H	L	4-6	Eccleston, Smith 2, Gordon

TAUNTON TOWN

Reformed 1947. **First entered FA Cup:** 1925

1930-31	WL	1	29.11.30	Crystal P	3S	A	L	0-6	
1981-82	WL	1	21.11.81	Swindon T	D3	A	L	1-2	Hains

TELFORD UNITED

Formed 1876 as Wellington Town. Telford United 1969. **First entered FA Cup:** 1895. FA Challenge Trophy Winners: 1971, 1983, 1989. **Welsh Cup:** 1902, 1906, 1940. **Cup Final Connection:** Six men who played in FA Cup Finals later managed or coached Telford: Gordon Banks, Geoff Hurst, Alan Spavin, Ron Flowers, Johnny Hancocks and Gerry Daly. **League clubs beaten:** Wigan A, Stockport Co (twice), Northampton T, Rochdale, Lincoln C, Preston NE, Bradford C, Darlington, Burnley, Stoke C. In 1983-84 Telford beat four League teams in the FA Cup.

as Wellington Town

1925-26	BDL	1	28.11.25	Doncaster R	3N	A	L	0-2	
1926-27	BDL	1	27.11.26	Mansfield T	ML	H	L	1-2	Jones
1927-28	BDL	1	26.11.27	Southend U	3S	A	L	0-1	
1929-30	BDL	1	30.11.29	Stockport Co	3N	H	L	1-4	Prowse
1930-31	BDL	1	29.11.30	Wombwell	ML	H	D	0-0	
		1r	4.12.30	Wombwell		A	W	3-0	Capewell, Shirley, Lloyd
		2	13.12.30	Walsall	3S	H	L	2-4	Bromage, Shirley
1936-37	BDL	1	28.11.36	Accrington S	3N	A	L	1-3	Sims
1937-38	BDL	1	27.11.37	Mansfield T	3S	H	L	1-2	Griffiths
1938-39	CC	1	26.11.38	Runcorn	CC	A	L	0-3	
1945-46	CC	1 1L	17.11.45	Port Vale	3S	A	L	0-4	
		1 2L	24.11.45	Port Vale		H	L	0-2	
1946-47	CC	1	30.11.46	Watford	3S	H	D	1-1	Hopley
		1r	4.12.46	Watford		A	L	0-1	
1948-49	CC	1	27.11.48	Norwich C	3S	A	L	0-1	
1952-53	CC	1	22.11.52	Gillingham	3S	H	D	1-1	Ford
		1r	26.11.52	Gillingham		A	L	0-3	
1953-54	CC	1	21.11.53	Aldershot	3S	A	L	3-5	Skull, Davies, Turner
1954-55	CC	1	20.11.54	Merthyr Tydfil	SL	A	D	1-1	Windsor
		1r	24.11.54	Merthyr Tydfil		H	L	1-6	Antonio (p)
1962-63	SL	1	3.11.62	Bristol C	D3	A	L	2-4	Russell, Rodgers
as Telford United									
1969-70	SL	1	15.11.69	Bristol R	D3	H	L	0-3	
1970-71	SL	1	21.11.70	Walton & Hersham	AL	A	W	5-2	Owen, Harris, Jagger, Bentley, Fudge
		2	12.12.70	Swansea C	D3	A	L	2-6	Fudge, Ray
1971-72	SL	1	20.11.71	Bristol R	D3	A	L	0-3	
1972-73	SL	1	18.11.72	Nuneaton B	SL	H	W	3-2	Jones og, Fudge, Colton
		2	9.12.72	Chelmsford C	SL	A	L	0-5	

TELFORD UNITED

1973-74	SL	1	24.11.73	Chester	D4	A	L	0-1	
1982-83	APL	1	21.11.82	Wigan A	D3	A	D	0-0	
		1r	23.11.82	Wigan A		H	W	2-1	Walker, Neale
		2	11.12.82	Tranmere R	D4	H	D	1-1	Mather (p)
		2r	14.12.82	Tranmere R		A	L	1-2	Mather
1983-84	APL	1	19.11.83	Stockport Co	D4	H	W	3-0	Mather 2, Barnett
		2	10.12.83	Northampton T	D4	A	D	1-1	Burrows og
		2r	14.12.83	Northampton T		H	W	3-2	Bailey, Williams, Mather (p)
		3	7.1.84	Rochdale	D4	A	W	4-1	Edwards, Bailey, Hogan, Williams
		4	1.2.84	Derby Co	D2	A	L	2-3	Eaton, Bailey
1984-85	APL	1	17.11.84	Lincoln C	D3	A	D	1-1	Turner (p)
		1r	20.11.84	Lincoln C		H	W	2-1	Williams 2
		2	8.12.84	Preston NE	D3	A	W	4-1	Turner, McKenna, Williams 2
		3	5.1.85	Bradford C	D3	H	W	2-1	Williams, Hancock
		4	29.1.85	Darlington	D4	A	D	1-1	Williams
		4r	4.2.85	Darlington		H	W	3-0	Mather, Hogan, Alcock
		5	16.2.85	Everton	D1	A	L	0-3	
1985-86	APL	1	16.11.85	Stockport Co	D4	A	W	1-0	McGinty (p)
		2	9.12.85	Derby Co	D3	A	L	1-6	McKenna
1986-87	GMVC	1	15.11.86	Burnley	D4	H	W	3-0	Morgan, McGinty (p), McKenna
		2	6.12.86	Altrincham	GMVC	H	W	1-0	Williams
		3	11.1.87	Leeds U	D2	H	L	1-2	Williams
				played at The Hawthorns					
1987-88	GMVC	1	14.11.87	Stockport Co	D4	H	D	1-1	Biggins
		1r	17.11.87	Stockport Co		A	L	0-2	
1988-89	GMVC	1	19.11.88	Carlisle U	D4	H	D	1-1	Lloyd
		1r	22.11.88	Carlisle U		A	L	1-4	Hanchard
1989-90	GMVC	1	18.11.89	Walsall	D3	H	L	0-3	
1990-91	GMVC	1	17.11.90	Stoke C	D3	H	D	0-0	
		1r	21.11.90	Stoke C		A	L	0-1	
1991-92	GMVC	1	16.11.91	Stoke C	D3	A	D	0-0	
		1r	26.11.91	Stoke C		H	W	2-1	Benbow 2
		2	7.12.91	Wrexham	D4	H	L	0-1	

THAMES ASSOCIATION

Formed 1928. Members of the Football League 1930-1932. Folded 1932. Jimmy Dimmock, who scored the winning goal in the 1921 Cup Final scored two of Thames' three Cup goals in their short history.

1929-30	SL	1	30.11.29	Fulham	3S	A	L	0-4	
1930-31	3S	1	29.11.30	QPR	3S	A	L	0-5	
1931-32	3S	1	28.11.31	Watford	3S	H	D	2-2	Dimmock, Lennox
		1r	1.12.31	Watford		A	L	1-2	Dimmock

THIRD LANARK

Formed 1872. One of the seven Scottish clubs that took part in the FA Cup. Scottish FA Cup Winners: 1889, 1905. Runners-up: 4 times. Folded 1967.

1885-86	1	17.10.85	Blackburn Pk Rd		H	W	4-2	
	2		Church			*scratched*		
1886-87	1	16.10.86	Higher Walton		H	W	5-0	Marshall 2, McIntyre, Park, Thompson
	2	13.11.86	Bolton W		H	L	2-3	McIntyre, J.Weir

THORNEYCROFTS (WOOLSTON)

There were a number of clubs called Thorneycrofts. This one was based at Woolston, Hampshire.

1919-20	Hants	1	10.1.20	Burnley	D1	H	D	0-0	
				played at Fratton Park					
			13.1.20	Burnley		A	L	0-5	

TILBURY

Formed 1900. **First entered FA Cup:** 1927

1949-50	Lon	1	26.11.49	Notts Co	3S	A	L	0-4	
1977-78	IL	1	26.11.77	Kettering T	SL	H	L	0-1	
				FA declared match void as Kettering fielded ineligible player					

	1	5.12.77	**Kettering T**		H	D	2-2	Smith 2
	1r	7.12.77	**Kettering T**		A	W	3-2	Gray, C.Wallace, Barnett
	2	17.12.77	**Nuneaton B**	SL	A	W	2-1	C.Wallace, Gray
	3	7.1.78	**Stoke C**	D2	A	L	0-4	

TIVERTON TOWN

Formed 1920. **First entered FA Cup:** 1936

1990-91	WL	1	17.11.90	**Aldershot**	D4	A	L	2-6	Jones, Durham
1991-92	WL	1	16.11.91	**Barnet**	D4	A	L	0-5	

TONBRIDGE

Formed 1948. **First entered FA Cup:** 1948. **Cup final connection:** Malcolm Macdonald (Newcastle 1974) spent a season at Tonbridge

1950-51	SL	1	25.11.50	**Chelmsford C**	SL	A	D	2-2	Mills, Mulheron
		1r	29.11.50	**Chelmsford C**		H	L	0-1aet	
1951-52	SL	1	24.11.51	**Aldershot**	3S	H	D	0-0	
		1r	28.11.51	**Aldershot**		A	L	2-3aet	Jordan, Suttle
1952-53	SL	1	22.11.52	**Norwich C**	3S	H	D	2-2	Mulheron, Butler
		1r	27.11.52	**Norwich C**		A	L	0-1	
1967-68	SL	1	9.12.67	**Dagenham**	AL	A	L	0-1	
1972-73	SL	1	18.11.72	**Charlton A**	D3	H	L	0-5	

TON PENTRE

Formed 1935. **First entered FA Cup:** 1919.

1986-87	Welsh1	1	15.11.86	**Cardiff C**	D4	H	L	1-4	Bees

TOOTING (1)

1887-88		1	15.10.87	**Crusaders**		A	L	0-9	

TOOTING & MITCHAM UNITED

Formed 1932. **First entered FA Cup:** 1945. **Cup Final Connection:** Alex Stepney, Manchester United 1976 and 1977 FA Cup Finals, was born in Mitcham and also played for Tooting and Mitcham. **League clubs beaten:** Bournemouth, Northampton T, Swindon T

1948-49	AL	1	27.11.48	**Millwall**	3S	A	L	0-1	
1950-51	AL	1	25.11.50	**Brighton & HA**	3S	H	L	2-3	Rhodes, Parker
1956-57	IL	1	17.11.56	**Bromsgrove R**	BDL	H	W	2-1	Hasty, Bumpstead
		2	8.12.56	**QPR**	3S	H	L	0-2	
1958-59	IL	1	15.11.58	**Bournemouth**	D3	H	W	3-1	Viney 2, Slade
		2	6.12.58	**Northampton T**	D4	H	W	2-1	Viney, Hasty
		3	10.1.59	**Nottingham F**	D1	H	D	2-2	Grainger, Murphy
		3r	24.1.59	**Nottingham F**		A	L	0-3	
1963-64	IL	1	16.11.63	**Gravesend & N**	SL	H	L	1-2	Browning
1974-75	IL	1	27.11.74	**Crystal P**	D3	H	L	1-2	Grubb
1975-76	IL	1	22.11.75	**Romford**	SL	A	W	1-0	Ives
		2	13.12.75	**Leatherhead**	IL	A	D	0-0	
		2r	16.12.75	**Leatherhead**		H	–	1-1	Juneman (p)
			abandoned after 57 minutes – icy pitch						
		2r	22.12.75	**Leatherhead**		H	W	2-1aet	Juneman (p), Howell
		3	3.1.76	**Swindon T**	D3	A	D	2-2	Glover, Casey
		3r	6.1.76	**Swindon T**		H	W	2-1	Juneman, Ives
		4	24.1.76	**Bradford C**	D4	A	L	1-3	Juneman
1976-77	IL	1	20.11.76	**Dartford**	SL	H	W	4-2	Ives 2ps, Juneman, Glover
		2	11.12.76	**Kettering**	SL	A	L	0-1	
1977-78	IL	1	26.11.77	**Northampton T**	D4	H	L	1-2	Smith

TORQUAY UNITED

Formed 1898 as Torquay Town. Merged with Babbacombe FC to become Torquay United in 1921. Neither Torquay Town or Babbacombe ever reached the First Round Proper. **Best FA Cup Performance:** 4th round, 1949, 1955, 1971, 1983, 1990. **Record FA Cup Win:** 7-1 vs Northampton T., 1st round, 14.11.1959. **Record FA Cup Defeat:** 1-7 vs Birmingham C, 3rd round, 7.1.1956

1921-22	WL	P **Frome T** (H) 1-1; Pr **Frome T** (A) 3-1; 1q **Spencer Moulton** (H) 5-2; 2q **St Georges Sports** (H) 6-0; 3q **Hanham A** (H) 2-2;						
		3qr **Hanham A** (A) 3-1; 4q **Boscombe** (H) 0-1						
1922-23	SL	P **Clevedon** (H) 3-0; 1q **Welton R** (A) 2-3						
1923-24	SL	ExP **Taunton & Newton U** (A) 3-0; P **Green Waves** (A) 3-0; 1q **Coleford A** (A) 6-0; 2q **Trowbridge T** (H) 3-0;						
		3q **Yeovil & Petters** (A) 1-1; 3qr **Yeovil & Petters** (H) 2-1; 4q **Aberdare A** (H) 0-0; 4qr **Aberdare A** (A) 0-4						
1924-25	SL	P **Green Waves** (H) 2-0; 1q **Taunton & Newton U** (H) 1-1; 1q **Taunton & Newton** (A) 1-2						
1925-26	SL	4q **Yeovil & Petters** (H) 3-1						
		1	28.11.25	**Reading**	3S	H	D	1-1	Valla
		1r	2.12.25	**Reading**		A	D	1-1aet	Appleyard
		1 2r	7.12.25	**Reading** at Ashton Gate			L	0-2	
1926-27	SL	1	26.11.26	**Bristol R**	3S	H	D	1-1	Bloxham
		1r	1.12.26	**Bristol R**		A	L	0-1	
1927-28	3S	did not enter						
1928-29	3S	1	24.11.28	**Gillingham**	3S	A	D	0-0	
		1r	28.11.28	**Gillingham**		H	W	5-1	Gardiner 2, Waller, Kelly, Hemingway
		2	8.12.28	**Exeter C**	3S	H	L	0-1	
1929-30	3S	1	30.11.29	**Bournemouth & BA**	3S	A	L	0-2	
1930-31	3S	1	29.11.30	**Southend U**	3S	A	W	1-0	Trotter
		2	13.12.30	**Accrington S**	3N	A	W	1-0	Bell
		3	10.1.31	**Bury**	D2	A	D	1-1	Trotter
		3r	14.1.31	**Bury**		H	L	1-2aet	Trotter
1931-32	3S	1	28.11.31	**Southend U**	3S	H	L	1-3	Trotter
1932-33	3S	1	26.11.32	**Bournemouth**	3S	H	D	0-0	
		1r	30.11.32	**Bournemouth**		A	D	2-2aet	Bird, Tennant
		1 2r	5.12.32	**Bournemouth** at Ashton Gate			W	3-2	Stabb, Birkett, Hutchinson
		2	10.12.32	**QPR**	3S	H	D	1-1	Hutchinson
		2r	15.12.32	**QPR**		A	L	1-3	Stabb
1933-34	3S	1	25.11.33	**Margate**	SL	H	D	1-1	Kennedy
		1r	30.11.33	**Margate**		A	W	2-0	Walters, Stabb
		2	9.12.33	**Northampton T**	3S	A	L	0-3	
1934-35	3S	1	24.11.34	**Dulwich H**	IL	A	W	2-1	Prothero, Walters
		2	8.12.34	**Wigan A**	CC	A	L	2-3	Morgan, Protheroe
1935-36	3S	1	30.11.35	**Dulwich H**	IL	A	W	3-2	Daniels, Dodds, SW Hunt
		2	14.12.35	**Notts Co**	3S	A	L	0-3	
1936-37	3S	1	28.11.36	**Clapton O**	3S	A	L	1-2	Lievesly
1937-38	3S	1	27.11.37	**Clapton O**	3S	H	L	1-2	Shelley
1938-39	3S	1	26.11.38	**Exeter C**	3S	H	W	3-1	Brown, Allen, Rhodes
		2	10.12.38	**Ipswich T**	3S	A	L	1-4	Allen
1945-46	3S	1 1L	17.11.45	**Newport Co**	3S	H	L	0-1	
		1 2L	24.11.45	**Newport Co**		A	D	1-1	Conley
1946-47	3S	1	30.11.46	**Ipswich T**	3S	A	L	0-2	
1947-48	3S	1	29.11.47	**Watford**	3S	A	D	1-1aet	Hill
		1r	6.12.47	**Watford**		H	W	3-0	Conley, Shaw, Hill
		2	13.12.47	**Northampton T**	3S	A	D	1-1aet	Hill
		2r	20.12.47	**Northampton T**		H	W	2-0	Hil, Mercer
		3	10.1.48	**Stockport Co**	3N	A	L	0-3	
1948-49	3S	1	27.11.48	**Peterborough U**	ML	A	W	1-0	Lewis
		2	11.12.48	**Norwich C**	3S	H	W	3-1	Collins 2, Cameron
		3	8.1.49	**Coventry C**	D2	A	W	1-0	Cameron
		4	29.1.49	**Brentford**	D2	A	L	0-1	
1949-50	3S	1	26.11.49	**Gravesend & N**	SL	A	W	3-1	Cameron, Whitfield, Lewis
		2	10.12.49	**Northampton T**	3S	A	L	2-4	Cameron, Conley
1950-51	3S	1	25.11.50	**Nottingham F**	3S	A	L	1-6	Collins
1951-52	3S	1	24.11.51	**Bromley**	AL	H	W	3-2	Northcott, Shaw 2
		2	15.12.51	**Swindon T**	3S	A	D	3-3	Collins, Edds 2
		2r	19.12.51	**Swindon T**		H	D	1-1aet	Collins
		2 2r	2.1.52	**Swindon T** at Ashton Gate			L	1-3	Northcott
1952-53	3S	1	22.11.52	**Peterborough U**	ML	A	L	1-2	Edds
1953-54	3S	1	21.11.53	**Bristol C**	3S	H	L	1-3	Collins
1954-55	3S	1	20.11.54	**Cambridge U**	ECL	H	W	4-0	Collins, Dobbie 2, Bond
		2	11.12.54	**Blyth Spartans**	NEL	A	W	3-1	JT Smith 2, Webber
		3	8.1.55	**Leeds U**	D2	A	D	2-2	JT Smith 2
		3r	12.1.55	**Leeds U**		H	W	4-0	Collins, Dobbie, Shaw, Mills
		4	29.1.55	**Huddersfield T**	D1	H	L	0-1	
1955-56	3S	1	19.11.55	**Colchester U**	3S	H	W	2-0	S.Collins, JT SMith
		2	10.12.55	**Shrewsbury T**	3S	A	D	0-0	
		2r	14.12.55	**Shrewsbury T**		H	W	5-1	A.Collins 2, JT Smith, R.Collins, Shaw

		3	7.1.56	Birmingham C	D1	H	L	1-7	Shaw
1956-57	3S	1	17.11.56	Ely City	PDL	A	W	6-2	R.Collins 3, Shaw, Calland (?) 2
		2	8.12.56	Plymouth A	3S	H	W	1-0	R.Collins
		3	5.1.57	New Brighton	LC	A	L	1-2	R.Collins
1957-58	3S	1	16.11.57	Peterborough U	ML	A	D	3-3	Pym 2, Johnson
		1r	20.11.57	Peterborough U		H	W	1-0	Johnson
		2	7.12.57	Southend U	3S	H	D	1-1	Bond
		2r	11.12.57	Southend U		A	L	1-2	Northcott
1958-59	D4	1	15.11.58	Port Vale	D4	H	W	1-0	Mills
		2	6.12.58	Watford	D4	H	W	2-0	T.Northcott, Cox
		3	10.1.59	Newport Co	D3	A	D	0-0	
		3r	14.1.59	Newport Co		H	L	0-1	
1959-60	D4	1	14.11.59	Northampton T	D4	H	W	7-1	Bond 3, Pym 3, T.Northcott
		2	5.12.59	Gillingham	D4	A	D	2-2	Cox, Bond
		2r	9.12.59	Gillingham		H	L	1-2	Pym
1960-61	D3	1	5.11.60	Weymouth	SL	A	W	3-1	Pym, T.Northcott 2
		2	26.11.60	Peterborough U	D4	H	L	1-3	Court
1961-62	D3	1	4.11.61	Harwich & P	ECL	H	W	5-1	Pym 2 (1p), T.Northcott, Wilson og, Spencer
		2	25.11.61	Peterborough U	D3	H	L	1-4	Bond
1962-63	D4	1	3.11.62	Northampton T	D3	A	W	2-1	Handley 2
		2	25.11.62	Shrewsbury T	D3	A	L	1-2	T.Northcott
1963-64	D4	1	16.11.63	Barnet	AL	H	W	6-2	Hancock 2, T.Northcott, Swindells (p), Stubbs, Adlington
		2	7.12.63	Aldershot	D4	H	L	2-3	Pym, Jenkins
1964-65	D4	1	14.11.64	Canterbury C	SL	A	W	6-0	Cox 2, Stubbs 2, T.Northcott 2
		2	5.12.64	Colchester U	D3	H	W	2-0	Northcott, Stubbs
		3	9.1.65	Tottenham H	D1	H	D	3-3	Stubbs 3
		3r	18.1.65	Tottenham H		A	L	1-5	Stubbs
1965-66	D4	1	13.11.65	Shrewsbury T	D3	A	L	1-2	Spratt
1966-67	D3	1	26.11.66	Aldershot	D4	A	L	1-2	Clarke
1967-68	D3	1	12.12.67	Colchester U	D3	H	D	1-1	Welsh
		1r	18.12.67	Colchester U		A	L	1-2	Barnes
1968-69	D3	1	16.11.68	Hereford U	SL	A	D	0-0	
		1r	20.11.68	Hereford U		H	W	4-2	Cave 2, Benson, Bond
		2	7.12.68	Reading	D3	A	D	0-0	
		2r	11.12.68	Reading		H	L	1-2	Stubbs
1969-70	D3	1	15.11.69	Tamworth	WMRL	A	L	1-2	Rudge
1970-71	D3	1	21.11.70	Aston Villa	D3	H	W	3-1	Kitchener, Bradley og, Edwards
		2	12.12.70	Chelmsford C	SL	A	W	1-0	Rudge
		3	2.1.71	Lincoln C	D4	H	W	4-3	Cave, Rudge (p), Barnard 2
		4	25.1.71	Leicester C	D2	A	L	0-3	
1971-72	D3	1	20.11.71	Nuneaton B	SL	H	W	1-0	Tearse
		2	11.12.71	Barnet	SL	A	W	4-1	Welsh 3, Tearse
		3	15.1.72	Bolton W	D3	A	L	1-2	Tearse
1972-73	D4	1	18.11.72	Hereford U	D4	H	W	3-0	Stocks, Harrison, Twitchin
		2	9.12.72	Newport Co	D4	H	L	0-1	
1973-74	D4	1	24.11.73	Hereford U	D3	A	L	1-3	Morrall
1974-75	D4	1	23.11.74	Northampton T	D4	H	L	0-1	
1975-76	D4	1	22.11.75	Hereford U	D3	A	L	0-2	
1976-77	D4	1	20.11.76	Hillingdon B	SL	H	L	1-2	Brown
1977-78	D4	1	26.11.77	Southend U	D4	H	L	1-2	Brown
1978-79	D4	1	25.11.78	Walsall	D3	A	W	2-0	Cooper, Wilson
		2	16.12.78	AP Leamington	SL	A	W	1-0	Twitchin
		3	16.1.79	Newcastle U	D2	A	L	1-3	Lawrence
1979-80	D4	1	24.11.79	Gravesend & N	APL	A	W	1-0	Cooper
		2	18.12.79	Swindon T	D3	H	D	3-3	Sermanni, Cooper, Lawrence
		2r	22.12.79	Swindon T		A	L	2-3	Tucker og, Murphy
1980-81	D4	1	22.11.80	Barton R	IL	H	W	2-0	Weston, Cooper
		2	13.12.80	St Albans C	IL	A	D	1-1	Fell
		2r	17.12.80	St Albans C		H	W	4-1	Cooper, Fell 3 (2ps)
		3	3.1.81	Barnsley	D3	A	L	1-2	Lawrence
1981-82	D4	1	20.11.81	Bristol C	D3	A	D	0-0	
		1r	25.11.81	Bristol C		H	L	1-2	Lawrence
1982-83	D4	1	20.11.82	Colchester U	D4	A	W	2-0	Little, Cooper
		2	11.12.82	Carshalton A	IL	H	W	4-1	Anderson, Bishop 2, Wilson
		3	8.1.83	Oxford U	D3	A	D	1-1	Gallagher
		3r	12.1.83	Oxford U		H	W	2-1	Cooper, Gallagher
		4	29.1.83	Sheffield W	D2	H	L	2-3	Hughes, Bishop

1983-84	D4	1	19.11.83	**Colchester U**	D4	H	L	1-2	Curle
1984-85	D4	1	17.11.84	**Yeovil T**	APL	H	W	2-0	Laryea, Kelly
		2	7.12.84	**Orient**	D3	A	L	0-3	
1985-86	D4	1	16.11.85	**Windsor & Eton**	IL	A	D	1-1	Durham
		1r	19.11.85	**Windsor & Eton**		H	W	3-0	Walsh 2, Loram
		2	7.12.85	**Newport Co**	D3	A	D	1-1	Loram
		2r	10.12.85	**Newport Co**		H	L	2-3	Walsh 2
1986-87	D4	1	15.11.86	**Aldershot**	D4	A	L	0-1	
1987-88	D4	1	14.11.87	**Bognor Regis T**	IL	A	W	3-0	Dobson, Pearce, Gardiner
		2	5.12.87	**Bristol C**	D3	A	W	1-0	Caldwell
		3	9.1.88	**Coventry C**	D1	A	L	0-2	
1988-89	D4	1	19.11.88	**Fareham T**	SL	H	D	2-2	Joyce, Smith
		1r	23.11.88	**Fareham T**		A	W	3-2	McNichol, Smith, Loram
		2	10.12.88	**Yeovil T**	GMVC	A	D	1-1	Loram
		2r	14.12.88	**Yeovil T**		H	W	1-0	Thompson
		3	7.1.89	**Sheffield W**	D1	A	L	1-5	Edwards
1989-90	D4	1	18.11.89	**Sutton U**	GMVC	A	D	1-1	Uzzell
		1r	22.11.89	**Sutton U**		H	W	4-0	Lloyd, Smith 2, Elliott
		2	9.12.89	**Basingstoke**	IL	A	W	3-2	Elliott, Mottashed og, Loram
		3	6.1.90	**West Ham U**	D2	H	W	1-0	Hirons
		4	27.1.90	**Blackpool**	D3	A	L	0-1	
1990-91	D4	1	17.11.90	**Maidstone U**	D4	A	L	1-4	Tynan
1991-92	D3	1	16.11.91	**Birmingham C**	D3	H	W	3-0	Tynan Hall 2
		2	7.12.91	**Farnborough T**	GMVC	H	D	1-1	Loram
		2r	17.12.91	**Farnborough T**		A	L	3-4	Holmes, Loram, Colcombe
1992-93	D3	1	14.11.92	**Yeovil T**	GMVC	H	L	2-5	Foster, Herd

TOTTENHAM HOTSPUR

Formed 1882 as Hotspur FC (not connected to earlier Hotspur FC based in Barnsbury). Tottenham Hotspur 1885. FA Cup and League Double 1961. **Best FA Cup Performance:** Winners (Record 8 times) 1901 (as a Southern League club) 1921, 1961, 1962, 1967, 1981, 1982, 1991. Runners-up: 1987. **Record FA Cup Win:** 13-2 vs Crewe Alexandra, 4th round replay, 3.2.1960. **Record FA Cup Defeat:** 0-5 vs Stoke, 1st round, 1.2.1896; 1-6 vs Huddersfield T 6th round, 3.3.1928

1894-95			1q **West Herts** (H) 3-2; 2q **Wolverton** (H) 5-3; 3q **Clapton** (A) 4-0; 4q **Luton T** (H) 2-2; 4qr **Luton T** (A) 0-4						
1895-96			1q **Luton T** (A) 2-1; 2q **Vampires** (A) L 2-4 *FA declared match void because Vampires pitch was improperly marked*;						
			2qr **Vampires** (H) 2-1; 3q **Ilford** (A) 5-1; 4q **Old St Stephens** (H) 2-1						
		1	1.2.96	**Stoke**	D1	A	L	0-5	
1896-97	SL		1q **Old St Stephens** (H) 4-0; 2q **Maidenhead** (H) 6-0; 3q **Luton T** (A) 0-3						
1897-98	SL		1q **2nd Coldstream Guards** (H) 7-0; 2q **Luton T** (H) 3-4						
1898-99	SL		3q **Wolverton** (H) 4-0; 4q **Clapton** (A) 1-1; 4qr **Clapton** (H) 2-1; 5q **Luton T** (H) 1-1; 5qr **Luton T** (A) 1-1;						
			5q 2r **Luton T** at Tufnell Park 2-0						
		1	28.1.99	**Newton Heath**	D2	H	D	1-1	Joyce
		1r	1.2.99	**Newton Heath**		A	W	5-3	Jones, McNaught, Smith, Hartley, Joyce
		2	11.2.99	**Sunderland**	D1	H	W	2-1	Cameron, Bradhsaw
		3	25.2.99	**Stoke**	D1	A	L	1-4	Bradshaw
1899-00	SL	1	27.1.00	**Preston NE**	D1	A	L	0-1	
1900-01	SL	1	9.2.01	**Preston NE**	D1	H	D	1-1	Brown
		1r	13.2.01	**Preston NE**		A	W	4-2	Brown 3, Cameron
		2	23.2.01	**Bury**	D1	H	W	2-1	Brown 2
		3	23.2.01	**Reading**	SL	A	D	1-1	Kirwan
		3r	28.2.01	**Reading**		H	W	3-0	Brown 2, Copeland
		SF	8.3.01	**WBA**	D1		W	4-0	Brown 4
			played at Villa Park						
		F	20.4.01	**Sheffield U**	D1		D	2-2	Brown 2
			played at Crystal Palace						
		Fr	27.4.01	**SHEFFIELD U**			W	3-1	Smith, Brown, Copeland
			played at Burnden Park, Bolton						
1901-02	SL	1	25.1.02	**Southampton**	SL	H	D	1-1	Copeland
		1r	29.1.02	**Southampton**		A	D	2-2aet	Hughes
		1 2r	3.2.02	**Southampton** at Elm Park, Reading			L	1-2	Kirwan
1902-03	SL	1	7.2.03	**WBA**	D1	H	D	0-0	
		1r	11.2.03	**WBA**		A	W	2-0	Dryburgh (p), Woodward
		2	21.2.03	**Bristol C**	D2	H	W	1-0	Woodward
		3	7.3.03	**Aston Villa**	D1	H	L	2-3	Woodward, Copeland
1903-04	SL	1	6.2.04	**Everton**	D1	A	W	2-1	Woodward, Balmer og

Season		Round	Date	Opponent	Div	H/A	Result	Score	Scorers
		2	20.2.04	Aston Villa	D1	H	–	0-1	
			abandoned after 20 minutes after crowd invasion						
		2r	25.2.04	Aston Villa		A	W	1-0	J.Jones
		3	5.3.04	Sheffield W	D1	H	D	1-1	J.Jones
		3r	10.3.04	Sheffield W		A	L	0-2	
1904-05	SL	1	4.2.05	Middlesbrough	D1	A	D	1-1	Glen
		1r	9.2.05	Middlesbrough		H	W	1-0	O'Hagan
		2	18.2.05	Newcastle U	D1	H	D	1-1	Walton
		2r	22.2.05	Newcastle U		A	L	0-4	
1905-06	SL	1	13.1.06	Burnley	D2	H	W	2-0	Woodward, Kyle
		2	3.2.06	Reading	SL	H	W	3-2	Bull, Walton, Kyle
		3	24.2.06	Birmingham	D1	H	D	1-1	Kyle
		3r	28.2.06	Birmingham		A	L	0-2aet	
1906-07	SL	1	12.1.07	Hull C	D2	H	D	0-0	
		1r	17.1.07	Hull C		A	–	0-0	
			abandoned after 100 minutes – bad light						
		1 2r	21.1.07	Hull C		H	W	1-0	Chapman
		2	2.2.07	Blackburn R	D1	H	D	1-1	Walton
		2r	7.2.07	Blackburn R		A	D	1-1aet	Reid
		2 2r	11.2.07	Blackburn R at Villa Park			W	2-1	Walton, Reid
		3	23.2.07	Notts Co	D1	A	L	0-4	
1907-08	SL	1	11.1.08	Everton	D1	A	L	0-1	
1908-09	D2	1	16.1.09	Manchester C	D1	A	W	4-3	Morris (p), Minter 2, R.Steel
		2	6.2.09	Fulham	D2	H	W	1-0	R.Steel
		3	20.2.09	Burnley	D2	H	D	0-0	
		3r	24.2.09	Burnley		A	L	1-3	Coquet (p)
1909-10	D1	1	15.1.10	Plymouth A	SL	A	D	1-1	Humphreys
		1r	19.1.10	Plymouth A		H	W	7-1	Minter, Humphreys 3, R.Steel 2, Middlemiss 2
		2	5.2.10	Chelsea	D1	A	W	1-0	Humphreys
		3	19.2.10	Swindon T	SL	A	L	2-3	Minter, R.Steel
1910-11	D1	1	14.1.11	Millwall A	SL	H	W	2-1	Minter, Carmichael og
		2	4.2.11	Blackburn R	D1	A	D	0-0	
		2r	9.2.11	Blackburn R		H	L	0-2	
1911-12	D1	1	13.1.12	WBA	D1	A	L	0-3	
1912-13	D1	1	11.1.13	Blackpool	D2	H	D	1-1	Rance
		1r	16.1.13	Blackpool		H	W	6-1	Tattersall 2, Cantrell 2, Steel, Middlemiss
		2	1.2.13	Reading	SL	A	L	0-1	
1913-14	D1	1	10.1.14	Leicester F	D2	A	D	5-5	Walden, Minter, Cantrell, Bliss 2
		1r	15.1.14	Leicester F		H	W	2-0	Walden, Bliss
		2	31.1.14	Manchester C	D1	A	L	1-2	Bliss
1914-15	D1	1	9.1.15	Sunderland	D1	H	W	2-1	Walden, Bliss
		2	30.1.15	Norwich C	SL	A	L	2-3	Cantrell, Lansdale og
1919-20	D2	1	10.1.20	Bristol R	SL	A	W	4-1	Cantrell 3, Bliss
		2	31.1.20	West Stanley	NEL	H	W	4-0	Banks, Wilson 2, Bliss
		3	21.2.20	West Ham	D2	H	W	3-0	Grimsdell, Wilson 2
		4	6.3.20	Aston Villa	D1	H	L	0-1	
1920-21	D1	1	8.1.21	Bristol R	D3	H	W	6-2	Clay (p), Smith, Walden, Seed, Cantrell, Bliss
		2	29.1.21	Bradford C	D1	H	W	4-0	Banks, Seed 3
		3	19.2.21	Southend U	D3	A	W	4-1	Banks, Seed, Cantrill, Bliss
		4	5.3.21	Aston Villa	D1	H	W	1-0	Banks
		SF	19.3.21	Preston NE	D1		W	2-1	Bliss 2
			played at Hillsborough						
		F	23.3.21	WOLVERHAMPTON W	D2		W	1-0	Dimmock
			played at Stamford Bridge						
1921-22	D1	1	7.1.22	Brentford	3S	A	W	2-0	Seed, Cantrell
		2	28.1.22	Watford	3S	H	W	1-0	Bliss
		3	18.2.22	Manchester C	D1	H	W	2-1	Wilson, Bliss
		4	4.3.22	Cardiff C	D1	A	D	1-1	Seed
		4r	9.3.22	Cardiff C		H	W	2-1	Wilson, Dimmock
		SF	25.3.22	Preston NE	D1		L	1-2	Seed
			played at Hillsborough						
1922-23	D1	1	13.1.23	Worksop T	ML	H	D	0-0	
		1r	15.1.23	Worksop T		H	W	9-0	Seed, Lindsay 4, Handley 3, Dimmock
		2	3.2.23	Manchester U	D2	H	W	4-0	Lindsay, Handley 3
		3	24.2.23	Cardiff C	D1	A	W	3-2	Seed, Lindsay, Handley
		4	10.3.23	Derby Co	D2	H	L	0-1	
1923-24	D1	1	12.1.24	Crystal P	D2	A	L	0-2	

TOTTENHAM HOTSPUR

1924-25	D1	1	10.1.25	Northampton T	3S	H	W	3-0	Seed, Lindsay, Elkes
		2	31.1.25	Bolton W	D1	H	D	1-1	Seed
		2r	4.2.25	Bolton W		A	W	1-0	Lane
		3	21.2.25	Blackburn R	D1	H	D	2-2	Lane, Dimmock
		3r	26.2.25	Blackburn R		A	L	1-3	Dimmock
1925-26	D1	3	9.1.26	West Ham	D1	H	W	5-0	Osborne 2, Dimmock 3
		4	30.1.26	Manchester U	D1	H	D	2-2	Thompson, Lindsay
		4r	3.2.26	Manchester U		A	L	0-2	
1926-27	D1	3	8.1.27	West Ham	D1	A	L	2-3	Handley, Dimmock
1927-28	D1	3	14.1.28	Bristol C	D2	A	W	2-1	O'Callaghan, Osborne
		4	28.1.28	Oldham A	D2	H	W	3-0	O'Callaghan, Handley, Dimmock
		5	18.2 28	Leicester C	D1	A	W	3-0	O'Callaghan 2, Dimmock
		6	3.3.28	Huddersfield T	D1	A	L	1-6	O'Callaghan
1928-29	D2	3	12.1.29	Reading	D2	A	L	0-2	
1929-30	D2	3	11.1.30	Manchester C	D1	H	D	2-2	Osborne, Cook
		3r	15.1.30	Manchester C		A	L	1-4	Thompson
1930-31	D2	3	10.1.31	Preston NE	D2	H	W	3-1	Dimmock, Cook, Harper
		4	24.1.31	WBA	D2	A	L	0-1	
1931-32	D2	3	9.1.32	Sheffield W	D1	H	D	2-2	Hunt, W.Evans
		3r	13.1.32	Sheffield W		A	L	1-3	Hunt (p)
1932-33	D2	3	14.1.33	Oldham A	D2	A	W	6-0	O'Callaghan, Hunt 3, W.Evans, Brunskill og
		4	28.1.33	Luton T	3S	A	L	0-2	
1933-34	D1	3	13.1.34	Everton	D1	H	W	3-0	Hunt, Howe, W.Evans
		4	27.1.34	West Ham	D2	H	W	4-1	Hunt 2, W.Evans 2
		5	17.2.34	Aston Villa	D1	H	L	0-1	
1934-35	D1	3	12.1.35	Manchester C	D1	H	W	1-0	W.Evans
		4	26.1.35	Newcastle U	D2	H	W	2-0	GS Hunt 2
		5	16.2.35	Bolton W	D2	H	D	1-1	W.Evans
		5r	20.2.35	Bolton W		A	D	1-1aet	GS Hunt
		5 2r	25.2.35	Bolton W at Villa Park			L	0-2	
1935-36	D2	3	11.1.36	Southend U	3S	H	D	4-4	Sargent 2, Morrison 2
		3r	15.1.36	Southend U		A	W	2-1	Sargent, W.Evans
		4	25.1.36	Huddersfield T	D1	H	W	1-0	Howe
		5	15.2.36	Bradford PA	D2	A	D	0-0	
		5r	17.2.36	Bradford PA		H	W	2-1	GS Hunt 2
		6	29.2.36	Sheffield U	D2	A	L	1-3	Morrison
1936-37	D2	3	16.1.37	Portsmouth	D1	A	W	5-0	Morrison 3, Duncan, Miller
		4	30.1.37	Plymouth A	D2	H	W	1-0	McCormick
		5	20.2.37	Everton	D1	A	D	1-1	McCormick
		5r	22.2.37	Everton		H	W	4-3	Meek, Morrison 3
		6	6.3.37	Preston NE	D1	H	L	1-3	Duncan
1937-38	D2	3	8.1.38	Blackburn R	D2	H	W	3-2	Sargent, Gibbons 2
		4	22.1.38	New Brighton	3N	A	D	0-0	
		4r	26.1.38	New Brighton		H	W	5-2	Morrison 2, Gibbons 2, Lyman
		5	12.2.38	Chesterfield	D2	A	D	2-2	Gibbons, Miller
		5r	16.2.38	Chesterfield		H	W	2-1	Sargent, Morrison
		6	5.3.38	Sunderland	D1	H	L	0-1	
1938-39	D2	3	7.1.39	Watford	3S	H	W	7-1	Ward (p), Sargent, GW Hall 2, Duncan, Miller 2
		4	21.1.39	West Ham	D2	A	D	3-3	Morrison, Sargent, Duncan
		4r	30.1.39	West Ham		H	D	1-1aet	Sargent
		4 2r	2.2.39	West Ham at Highbury			L	1-2	Morrison
1945-46	D2	3 1L	5.1.46	Brentford	D1	H	D	2-2	Burgess, AE Hall
		3 2L	10.1.46	Brentford		A	L	0-2	
1946-47	D2	3	11.1.47	Stoke C	D1	H	D	2-2	Ludford, Bennett
		3r	15.1.47	Stoke C		A	L	0-1	
1947-48	D2	3	10.1.48	Bolton W	D1	A	W	2-0aet	Duquemin 2
		4	24.1.48	WBA	D2	H	W	3-1	Cox, Duquemin 2
		5	7.2.48	Leicester C	D2	H	W	5-2	Cox (p), Duquemin 3, South og
		6	28.2.48	Southampton	D2	A	W	1-0	Bennett
		SF	13.3.48	Blackpool	D1		L	1-3aet	Duquemin
			played at Villa Park						
1948-49	D2	3	8.1.49	Arsenal	D1	A	L	0-3	
1949-50	D2	3	7.1.50	Stoke C	D1	A	W	1-0	Baily
		4	28.1.50	Sunderland	D1	H	W	5-1	Walters 2, Bennett 2, Medley
		5	11.2.50	Everton	D1	A	L	0-1	
1950-51	D1	3	6.1.51	Huddersfield T	D1	A	L	0-2	
1951-52	D1	3	12.1.52	Scunthorpe U	3N	A	W	3-0	Baily, Duquemin 2

	4	2.2.52	Newcastle U	D1	H	L	0-3	
1952-53 D1	3	10.1.53	Tranmere R	3N	A	D	1-1	Bennett
	3r	12.1.53	Tranmere R		H	W	9-1	McClellan 3, Duquemin 2, Hollis 2, Baily 2
	4	31.1.53	Preston NE	D1	A	D	2-2	Withers 2
	4r	4.2.53	Preston NE		H	W	1-0	Duquemin
	5	14.2.53	Halifax T	3N	A	W	3-0	Bennett 2, Duquemin
	6	28.2.53	Birmingham C	D1	A	D	1-1	Bennett
	6r	4.3.53	Birmingham C		H	D	2-2aet	Bennett, Duquemin
	6 2r	9.3.53	Birmingham C at Molineux			W	1-0	Walters
	SF	21.3.53	Blackpool	D1		L	1-2	Duquemin
			played at Villa Park					
1953-54 D1	3	9.1.54	Leeds U	D2	A	D	3-3	Walters, Bennett 2
	3r	13.1.54	Leeds U		H	W	1-0	Bennett
	4	30.1.54	Manchester C	D1	A	W	1-0	Bennett
	5	20.2.54	Hull C	D2	A	D	1-1	Bennett
	5r	24.2.54	Hull C		H	W	2-0	Walters, Baily
	6	13.3.54	WBA	D1	A	L	0-3	
1954-55 D1	3	8.1.55	Gateshead	3N	A	W	2-0	Brooks 2
	4	29.1.55	Port Vale	D2	H	W	4-2	Gavin, Duquemin, Brooks 2
	5	19.2.55	York C	3N	A	L	1-3	Robb
1955-56 D1	3	7.1.56	Boston U	ML	H	W	4-0	Smith 2, Duquemin, Robb
	4	28.1.56	Middlesbrough	D2	H	W	3-1	Dunmore, Norman, Robb
	5	18.2.56	Doncaster R	D2	A	W	2-0	Brooks, Smith
	6	3.3.56	West Ham	D2	H	D	3-3	Harmer (p), Duquemin, Robb
	6r	8.3.56	West Ham		A	W	2-1	Harmer, Duquemin
	SF	17.3.56	Manchester C	D1		L	0-1aet	
			played at Villa Park					
1956-57 D1	3	5.1.57	Leicester C	D2	H	W	2-0	Blanchflower, Robb
	4	26.1.57	Chelsea	D1	H	W	4-0	Smith, Harmer, Medwin, Stokes
	5	16.2.57	Bournemouth	3S	A	L	1-3	Medwin
1957-58 D1	3	4.1.58	Leicester C	D1	H	W	4-0	Smith 2, Stokes, Medwin
	4	25.1.58	Sheffield U	D2	H	L	0-3	
1958-59 D1	3	10.1.59	West Ham	D1	H	W	2-0	Smith, Jones
	4	24.1.59	Newport Co	D3	H	W	4-1	Smith 2, Dunmore 2
	5	14.2.59	Norwich C	D3	H	D	1-1	Jones
	5r	18.2.59	Norwich C		A	L	0-1	
1959-60 D1	3	9.1.60	Newport Co	D3	A	W	4-0	L.Allen 2, Blanchflower, R.Smith
	4	30.1.60	Crewe A	D4	A	D	2-2	L.Allen, Jones
	4r	3.2.60	Crewe A		H	W	13-2	Harmer, Smith 4, L.Allen 5, Jones 3 (1p)
	5	20.2.60	Blackburn R	D1	H	L	1-3	Jones
1960-61 D1	3	7.1.61	Charlton A	D2	H	W	3-2	L.Allen 2, Dyson
	4	28.1.61	Crewe A	D4	H	W	5-1	Mackay, Jones, Smith, L.Allen, Dyson
	5	18.2.61	Aston Villa	D1	A	W	2-0	Jones, Neil og
	6	4.3.61	Sunderland	D2	A	D	1-1	Jones
	6r	8.3.61	Sunderland		H	W	5-0	Mackay, Smith, L.Allen, Dyson 2
	SF	18.3.61	Burnley	D1		W	3-0	Jones, Smith 2
			played at Villa Park					
	F	6.5.61	LEICESTER C	D1 WEMBLEY	W		2-0	Smith, Dyson
1961-62 D1	3	6.1.62	Birmingham C	D1	A	D	3-3	Greaves 2, Jones
	3r	10.1.62	Birmingham C		H	W	4-2	Medwin 2, L.Allen, Greaves
	4	27.1.62	Plymouth A	D2	A	W	5-1	Medwin, White, Greaves 2, Jones
	5	17.2.62	WBA	D1	A	W	4-2	Smith 2, Greaves 2
	6	10.3.62	Aston Villa	D1	H	W	2-0	Blanchflower, Jones
	SF	31.3.62	Manchester U	D1		W	3-1	Greaves, Medwin, Jones
			played at Hillsborough					
	F	5.5.62	BURNLEY	D1 WEMBLEY	W		3-1	Greaves, Smith, Blanchflower (p)
1962-63 D1	3	16.1.63	Burnley	D1	H	L	0-3	
1963-64 D1	3	4.1.64	Chelsea	D1	H	D	1-1	Dyson
	3r	8.1.64	Chelsea		A	L	0-2	
1964-65 D1	3	9.1.65	Torquay U	D4	A	D	3-3	Norman, Gilzean 2
	3r	18.1.65	Torquay U		H	W	5-1	Greaves 3, Robertson, Gilzean
	4	30.1.65	Ipswich T	D2	H	W	5-0	Greaves 3 (1p), Gilzean 2
	5	20.2.65	Chelsea	D1	A	L	0-1	
1965-66 D1	3	22.1.66	Middlesbrough	D2	H	W	4-0	Mackay 2 (1p), Saul 2
	4	12.2.66	Burnley	D1	H	W	4-3	Gilzean 3, Saul
	5	5.3.66	Preston NE	D2	A	L	1-2	Greaves
1966-67 D1	3	28.1.67	Millwall	D2	A	D	0-0	

		3r	1.2.67	Millwall		H	W	1-0	Gilzean
		4	18.2.67	Portsmouth	D2	H	W	3-1	Greaves, Gilzean 2
		5	11.3.67	Bristol C	D2	H	W	2-0	Greaves 2 (1p)
		6	8.4.67	Birmingham C	D1	A	D	0-0	
		6r	12.4.67	Birmingham C		H	W	6-0	Venables 2, Greaves 2, Saul, Gilzean
		SF	29.4.67	Nottingham F	D1		W	2-1	Greaves, Saul
		F	20.5.67	CHELSEA	D1	WEMBLEY	W	2-1	Robertson, Saul
1967-68	D1	3	27.1.68	Manchester U	D1	A	D	2-2	Chivers 2
		3r	31.1.68	Manchester U		H	W	1-0aet	Robertson
		4	17.2.68	Preston NE	D2	H	W	3-1	Greaves 2, Chivers
		5	9.3.68	Liverpool	D1	H	D	1-1	Greaves
		5r	12.3.68	Liverpool		A	L	1-2	Jones
1968-69	D1	3	4.1.69	Walsall	D3	A	W	1-0	Greaves
		4	25.1.69	Wolverhampton W	D1	H	W	2-1	Johnson, Greaves
		5	12.2.69	Aston Villa	D2	H	W	3-2	Greaves 2 (1p), England
		6	1.3.69	Manchester C	D1	A	L	0-1	
1969-70	D1	3	3.1.70	Bradford C	D3	A	D	2-2	Greaves, Morgan
		3r	7.1.70	Bradford C		H	W	5-0	Greaves 2, Pearce 2, Morgan
		4	24.1.70	Crystal P	D1	H	D	0-0	
		4r	28.1.70	Crystal P		A	L	0-1	
1970-71	D1	3	2.1.71	Sheffield W	D2	H	W	4-1	Mullery (p), Gilzean 2, Peters
		4	23.1.71	Carlisle U	D2	A	W	3-2	Gilzean, Peters, Neighbour
		5	13.2.71	Nottingham F	D1	H	W	2-1	Gilzean, Chivers
		6	6.3.71	Liverpool	D1	A	D	0-0	
		6r	16.3.71	Liverpool		H	L	0-1	
1971-72	D1	3	15.1.72	Carlisle U	D2	H	D	1-1	Gilzean
		3r	18.1.72	Carlisle U		A	W	3-1	Chivers 2, Gilzean
		4	5.2.72	Rotherham U	D3	H	W	2-0	Gilzean, Peters
		5	26.2.72	Everton	D1	A	W	2-0	Gilzean, Peters
		6	18.3.72	Leeds U	D1	A	L	1-2	Pratt
1972-73	D1	3	13.1.73	Margate	SL	A	W	6-0	Chivers 2, Knowles, Pratt, Pearce, Peters
		4	3.2.73	Derby Co	D1	A	D	1-1	Chivers
		4r	7.2.73	Derby Co		H	L	3-5aet	England (p), Gilzean, Chivers
1973-74	D1	3	5.1.74	Leicester C	D1	A	L	0-1	
1974-75	D1	3	4.1.75	Nottingham F	D2	A	D	1-1	Chivers
		3r	8.1.75	Nottingham F		H	L	0-1	
1975-76	D1	3	3.1.76	Stoke C	D1	H	D	1-1	Duncan
		3r	24.1.76	Stoke C		A	L	1-2	Perryman
1976-77	D1	3	8.1.77	Cardiff C	D2	A	L	0-1	
1977-78	D2	3	7.1.78	Bolton W	D2	H	D	2-2	Hoddle, Duncan
		3r	10.1.78	Bolton W		A	L	1-2aet	Taylor (p)
1978-79	D1	3	10.1.79	Altrincham	NPL	H	D	1-1	Taylor (p)
		3r	16.1.79	Altrincham at Maine Road		A	W	3-0	Lee 3
		4	12.2.79	Wrexham	D2	H	D	3-3	Hoddle, Jones, Roberts og
		4r	21.2.79	Wrexham		A	W	3-2aet	Jones 3
		5	28.2.79	Oldham A	D2	A	W	1-0	Perryman
		6	10.3.79	Manchester U	D1	H	D	1-1	Ardiles
		6r	14.3.79	Manchester U		A	L	0-2	
1979-80	D1	3	5.1.80	Manchester U	D1	H	D	1-1	Ardiles
		3r	9.1.80	Manchester U		A	W	1-0aet	Ardiles
		4	26.1.80	Swindon T	D3	A	D	0-0	
		4r	30.1.80	Swindon T		H	W	2-1	Armstrong 2
		5	16.2.80	Birmingham C	D2	H	W	3-1	Hoddle 2 (1p), Armstrong
		6	8.3.80	Liverpool	D1	H	L	0-1	
1980-81	D1	3	3.1.81	QPR	D2	A	D	0-0	
		3r	7.1.81	QPR		H	W	3-1	Galvin, Hoddle, Crooks
		4	24.1.81	Hull C	D3	H	W	2-0	Archibald, Brooke
		5	14.2.81	Coventry C	D1	H	W	3-1	Hughton, Ardiles, Archibald
		6	7.3.81	Exeter C	D3	H	W	2-0	Miller, Roberts
		SF	11.4.81	Wolverhampton W	D1		D	2-2aet	Archibald, Hoddle
			played at Hillsborough						
		SFr	15.4.81	Wolverhampton W			W	3-0	Crooks 2, Villa
			played at Highbury						
		F	9.5.81	Manchester C	D1	WEMBLEY	D	1-1aet	Hutchison og
		Fr	14.5.81	MANCHESTER C		WEMBLEY	W	3-2	Villa 2, Crooks
1981-82	D1	3	2.1.82	Arsenal	D1	H	W	1-0	Crooks
		4	23.1.82	Leeds U	D1	H	W	1-0	Crooks

TOTTENHAM HOTSPUR

		5	13.2.82	**Aston Villa**	D1	H	W	1-0	Falco
		6	6.3.82	**Chelsea**	D2	A	W	3-2	Archibald, Hoddle, Hazard
		SF	3.4.82	**Leicester C**	D2		W	2-0	Crooks, Wilson og
		F	22.5.82	**QPR**	D2	WEMBLEY	D	1-1aet	Hoddle
		Fr	27.5.82	**QPR**		WEMBLEY	W	1-0	Hoddle (p)
1982-83	D1	3	8.1.83	**Southampton**	D1	H	W	1-0	Hazard
		4	29.1.83	**WBA**	D1	H	W	2-1	Gibson, Crooks
		5	19.2.83	**Everton**	D1	A	L	0-2	
1983-84	D1	3	7.1.84	**Fulham**	D2	A	D	0-0	
		3r	11.1.84	**Fulham**		H	W	2-0	Roberts, Archibald
		4	28.1.84	**Norwich C**	D1	H	D	0-0	
		4r	1.2.84	**Norwich C**		A	L	1-2	Falco
1984-85	D1	3	5.1.85	**Charlton A**	D2	H	D	1-1	Crooks
		3r	23.1.85	**Charlton A**		A	W	2-1	Falco, Galvin
		4	27.1.85	**Liverpool**	D1	A	L	0-1	
1985-86	D1	3	4.1.86	**Oxford U**	D1	A	D	1-1	Chiedozie
		3r	8.1.86	**Oxford U**		H	W	2-1aet	Waddle, C.Allen
		4	25.1.86	**Notts Co**	D3	A	D	1-1	C.Allen
		4r	29.1.86	**Notts Co**		H	W	5-0	Chiedozie, C.Allen, Falco, Waddle, Hoddle
		5	4.3.86	**Everton**	D1	H	L	1-2	Falco
1986-87	D1	3	10.1.87	**Scunthorpe U**	D4	H	W	3-2	Mabbutt, Claesen, Waddle
		4	31.1.87	**Crystal P**	D2	H	W	4-0	Mabbutt, O'Reilly og, C.Allen (p), Claesen
		5	21.2.87	**Newcastle U**	D1	H	W	1-0	C.Allen (p)
		6	15.3.87	**Wimbledon**	D1	A	W	2-0	Waddle, Hoddle
		SF	11.4.87	**Watford**	D1		W	4-1	Hodge 2, C.Allen, P.Allen
			played at Villa Park						
		F	16.5.87	**Coventry C**	D1	WEMBLEY	L	2-3aet	C.Allen, Mabbutt
1987-88	D1	3	9.1.88	**Oldham A**	D2	A	W	4-2	C.Allen 2, Thomas, Waddle
		4	30.1.88	**Port Vale**	D3	A	L	1-2	Ruddock
1988-89	D1	3	7.1.89	**Bradford C**	D2	A	L	0-1	
1989-90	D1	3	6.1.90	**Southampton**	D1	H	L	1-3	Howells
1990-91	D1	3	5.1.91	**Blackpool**	D4	A	W	1-0	Stewart
		4	26.1.91	**Oxford U**	D2	H	W	4-2	Mabbutt, Lineker, Gascoigne 2
		5	16.2.91	**Portsmouth**	D2	A	W	2-1	Gascoigne 2
		6	10.3.91	**Notts Co**	D2	H	W	2-1	Craig Short og, Gascoigne
		SF	14.4.91	**Arsenal**	D1		W	3-1	Gascoigne, Lineker 2
			played at Wembley						
		F	18.4.91	**NOTTINGHAM F**	D1	WEMBLEY	W	2-1aet	Stewart, Walker og
1991-92	D1	3	5.1.92	**Aston Villa**	D1	A	D	0-0	
		3r	14.1.92	**Aston Villa**		H	L	0-1	
1992-93	PL	3	2.1.93	**Marlow** at White Hart Lane	IL	A	W	5-1	Sheringham, Barmby 2, Samways 2
		4	24.1.93	**Norwich C**	PL	A	W	2-0	Sheringham 2
		5	14.2.93	**Wimbledon**	PL	H	W	3-2	Anderton, Sheringham, Barmby
		6	7.3.93	**Manchester C**	PL	A	W	4-2	Nayim 3, Sedgley
		SF	4.4.93	**Arsenal**	PL		L	0-1	
			played at Wembley						

TOW LAW TOWN

Formed 1890. **First entered FA Cup:** 1891. **Cup Final Connection**: Harry Raw (Huddersfield 1930) and Chris Waddle, who played for Tottenham H in the 1987 Cup Final and for Sheffield Wednesday in the 1993 Final, played with Tow Law. **League club beaten:** Mansfield T

1967-68	NL	1	9.12.67	**Mansfield T**	D3	H	–	0-0	
			abandoned at half-time ground unfit						
		1	13.12.67	**Mansfield T**		H	W	5-1	Cairns, Brown 2 (1p), Henderson, Hunt
		2	15.1.68	**Shrewsbury T**	D3	H	D	1-1	Henderson
		2r	18.1.68	**Shrewsbury T**		A	L	2-6	Brown, Elliott
1968-69	NL	1	16.11.68	**Mansfield T**	D3	A	L	1-4	Hunt
1984-85	NL	1	17.11.84	**Bradford C**	D3	A	L	2-7	Blair 2
1989-90	NL	1	18.11.89	**Bishop Auckland**	NPL	A	L	0-2	

TRANMERE ROVERS

Formed 1884 as Belmont FC. Tranmere Rovers 1885. **Best FA Cup Performance:** 5th round, 1968. **Record FA Cup Win:** 13-0 vs Oswestry T, 1st qual rd, 10.10.1914. In Competition proper: 9-0 vs AP Leamington, 1st round, 24.11.1979. **Record FA Cup Defeat:** 1-9 vs Tottenham H, 3rd round replay, 14.1.1953. **Welsh FA Cup winners:** 1935

Note: In October 1919 Tranmere resigned from the Chesire County League and joined the Central League, taking over the fixtures of Leeds City Reserves after Leeds City were disbanded by the FA.

1891-92	Liv	1q **Northwich Victoria** (H) 1-5					
1892-93	LC	1q **Newtown** (A) scratched					
1893-94	LC	2q **Stockport Co** (A) 1-2					
1894-95	WDL	P **Northwich Victoria** (A) 1-3					
1895-96	LWDL	P **Crewe A** (A) 1-2					
1896-97	LWDL	2q **Warrington St Elphins** (H) 5-1; Int. **Buckley T** (A) 0-2					
1897-98	TC	*did not compete*					
1898-99	TC	*did not compete*					
1899-00	LAll	1q **South Liverpool** (A) 0-1					
1900-01	TC	1q **White Star Wanderers** (H) 0-1					
1901-02	TC	*did not compete*					
1902-03	TC	*did not compete*					
1903-04	TC	2q **Port Sunlight** (H) 3-1; 3q **Oswestry U** (H) D 2-2; 3qr **Oswestry U** (A) 1-2					
1904-05	TC	2q **Port Sunlight** (H) 1-3					
1905-06	TC	1q **Chirk** (A) 1-1; 1qr **Chirk** (H) 0-1					
1906-07	TC	1q **Wrexham** (A) 1-2					
1907-08	TC	P **Rhyl** (A) 2-0; 1q **Chester** (A) 4-0; 2q **Witton Albion** (A) 1-4					
1908-09	TC	*did not compete*					
1909-10	TC	P **Chester** (H) 6-0; 1q **Whitchurch** (H) 4-2; 2q **Oswestry U** (H) 5-1; 3q **Shrewsbury T** (H) 0-2					
1910-11	LC	1q **Witton Albion** (H) scratched					
1911-12	LC	*did not compete*					
1912-13	LC	1q **Oswestry U** (A) 4-2; 1q **Harrowby** (A) 1-2					
1913-14	LC	P **Lostock Gralam** (H) 6-1; 1q **Chester** (A) 1-2					
1914-15	LC	P **Northwich Victoria** (H) 2-2; Pr **Northwich V.** (A) 3-2; 1q **Oswestry U** (H) 13-0; 2q **Chester** (H) 5-1; 3q **Wrexham** (A) 1-1; 3qr **Wrexham** (H) 0-1					
1919-20	CC/CL	1q **Crewe A** (A) 0-1					
1920-21	CL	4q **Southport** (H) 1-0; 5q **Rochdale** (A) 0-1					
1921-22	3N	4q **Altrincham** (A) 4-4; 4qr **Altrincham** (H) 2-4					
1922-23	3N	4q **Wellington St Georges** (A) 1-2					
1923-24	3N	4q **Ellesmere Port** (H) 1-0; 5q **Coventry C** (A) 2-2; 5qr **Coventry C** (H) 3-2; 6q **Gillingham** (A) 0-1					
1924-25	3N	4q **Crewe A** (H) 1-1; 4qr **Crewe A** (A) 2-0; 5q **Southport** (H) 0-0; 5qr **Southport** (A) 0-1					
1925-26	3N	1	28.11.25 **Crewe A**	3N	H	D	0-0
		1r	2.12.25 **Crewe A**		A	L	1-2aet Proctor
1926-27	3N	1	27.11.26 **Southport**	3N	A	D	1-1 Marquis
		1r	2.12.26 **Southport**		H	L	1-2 Littlehales
1927-28	3N	1	26.11.27 **Shirebroook**	ML	H	W	3-1 Waring 2, Charlton
		2	10.12.27 **Halifax T**	3N	H	W	3-1 Bamber, Rimmer 2 (1p)
		3	14.1.28 **Nottingham F**	D2	A	L	0-1
1928-29	3N	1	24.11.28 **Rotherham U**	3N	H	W	2-1 Flanagan, Beswick
		2	8.12.28 **Bradford C**	3N	H	L	0-1
1929-30	3N	1	30.11.29 **York C**	3N	A	D	2-2 Meston, Waterston
		1r	5.12.29 **York C**		H	L	0-1
1930-31	3N	1	29.11.30 **Gateshead**	3N	H	D	4-4 Dixon 2, Urmson, Lewis
		1r	3.12.30 **Gateshead**		A	L	2-3 Watts, Urmson
1931-32	3N	1	28.11.31 **West Stanley**	NEL	H	W	3-0 Dixon, Urmson, Whitehurst
		2	12.12.31 **Bristol R**	3S	H	W	2-0 Meston, Dixon
		3	9.1.32 **Chelsea**	D1	H	D	2-2 Dixon, Watts
		3r	13.1.32 **Chelsea**		A	L	3-5 Whitehurst 2, Watts
1932-33	3N	1	26.11.32 **New Brighton**	3N	H	W	3-0 Whitehurst, Urmson, Dixon
		2	10.12.32 **Bristol C**	3S	A	D	2-2 Urmson, Whitehurst
		2r	14.12.32 **Bristol C**		H	W	3-2 Watts 2, Dixon
		3	14.1.33 **Notts Co**	D2	H	W	2-1 Urmson, Whitehurst
		4	28.1.33 **Leeds U**	D1	H	D	0-0
		4r	1.2.33 **Leeds U**		A	L	0-4
1933-34	3N	1	25.11.33 **Newark T**	ML	H	W	7-0 Bell 4, Urmson, EW Spencer 2
		2	9.12.33 **Bournemouth**	3S	A	W	4-2 Woodward 2, Bell, Pearson
		3	13.1.34 **Southend U**	3S	H	W	3-0 Urmson, Watts, Woodward
		4	27.1.34 **Liverpool**	D1	A	L	1-3 Meacock
1934-35	3N	1	24.11.34 **Stalybridge C**	CC	H	W	3-1 Baker 2, Urmson
		2	8.12.34 **Mansfield T**	3N	A	L	2-4 Burgin 2
1935-36	3N	1	30.11.35 **Carlisle U**	3N	H	W	3-0 Woodward 2, Urmson
		2	14.12.35 **Scunthorpe U**	ML	H	W	6-2 Bell 3, Urmson 2, Eden
		3	11.1.36 **Notts Co**	3S	A	D	0-0
		3r	15.1.36 **Notts Co**		H	W	4-3 MacDonald, Woodward 2, Bell
		4	25.1.36 **Barnsley**	D2	H	L	2-4 Urmson, Bell
1936-37	3N	1	28.11.36 **Oldham A**	3N	A	L	0-1
1937-38	3N	1	27.11.37 **Carlisle U**	3N	H	W	2-1 Duff, Buckley

Season	Div	Rd	Date	Opponent	Comp	H/A	Result	Score	Scorers
		2	11.12.37	Hartlepools U	3N	H	W	3-1	Waring, Dellow, Buckley
		3	8.1.38	Portsmouth	D1	H	L	1-2	Dellow
1938-39	D2	3	10.1.39	Grimsby T	D1	A	L	0-6	
1945-46	3N	1 1L	17.11.45	South Liverpool	CC	A	D	1-1	Rosenthal
		1 2L	24.11.45	South Liverpool		H	W	6-1	Atkinson, Ashcroft 2, Rosenthal, Williamson
		2 1L	8.12.45	Rochdale	3N	H	W	3-1	Atkinson, Bell, Rosenthal
		2 2L	15.12.45	Rochdale		A	L	0-3	
1946-47	3N	1	30.11.46	Oldham	3N	A	L	0-1	
1947-48	3N	1	29.11.47	Stalybridge C	CC	H	W	2-0	Bridges, Harlock
		2	13.12.47	Chester	3N	H	L	0-1	
1948-49	3N	1	27.11.48	Darlington	3N	H	L	1-3	Gould
1949-50	3N	1	26.11.49	Halifax T	3N	H	W	2-1	Wheeler, Wood
		2	10.12.49	Port Vale	3S	A	L	0-1	
1950-51	3N	1	25.11.50	Cleator Moor	WCL	A	W	5-0	Iceton 2, Williamson, Wheeler, Bainbridge
				played at Workington					
		2	9.12.50	York C	3N	A	L	1-2	Bainbridge (p)
1951-52	3N	1	24.11.51	Goole T	ML	H	W	4-2	Atkinson 3, Iceton
		2	15.12.51	Blyth Spartans	NEL	H	D	1-1	Sowden (og)
		2r	19.12.51	Blyth Spartans		A	–	1-1	Atkinson
				abandoned after 105 minutes - bad light					
		2 2r	3.1.52	Blyth Spartans at Carlisle			D	2-2aet	Rosenthal 2
		2 3r	7.1.52	Blyth Spartans at Everton			W	5-1	Tilson 2, Bainbridge, Williams, Rosenthal
		3	12.1.52	Huddersfield T	D1	A	W	2-1	Tilston, Rosenthal
		4	2.2.52	Chelsea	D1	A	L	0-4	
1952-53	3N	1	22.11.52	Ashington	NEL	H	W	8-1	Done 2, Atkinson 6
		2	6.12.52	Hartlepools U	3N	H	W	2-1	Done 2
		3	10.1.53	Tottenham H	D1	H	D	1-1	Iceton
		3r	12.1.53	Tottenham H		A	L	1-9	Done
1953-54	3N	1	21.11.53	Gateshead	3N	A	W	2-1	Done 2
		2	12.12.53	Accrington S	3N	A	D	2-2	Williams, Done
		2r	16.12.53	Accrington S		H	W	5-1	Williams 2, Done 3
		3	9.1.54	Leyton O	3S	H	D	2-2	Bainbridge, Done
		3r	14.1.54	Leyton O		A	L	1-4	Atkinson
1954-55	3N	1	20.11.54	Rochdale	3N	H	D	3-3	Done 2, Rosenthal
		1r	23.11.54	Rochdale		A	L	0-1	
1955-56	3N	1	19.11.55	Easington Colliery	Wear	A	W	2-0	Speakman 2
		2	10.12.55	Barrow	3N	H	L	0-3	
1956-57	3N	1	17.11.56	Bishop Auckland	NL	A	L	1-2	Davies
1957-58	3N	1	16.11.57	Witton Albion	CC	H	W	2-1	Williams, Eglington
		2	7.12.57	Durham City	NL	A	W	3-0	Eglington, Dodd, Williams
		3	4.1.58	Notts Co	D2	A	L	0-2	
1958-59	D3	1	15.11.58	Bishop Auckland	NL	H	W	8-1	Eglington, K.Williams 4, Green, Rowley, Finney
		2	6.12.58	Doncaster R	D3	H	L	1-2	Rowley
1959-60	D3	1	14.11.59	Chester	D4	H	L	0-1	
1960-61	D3	1	5.11.60	Bury	D3	H	W	1-0	Williams
		2	30.11.60	York C	D4	H	D	1-1	Williams
		2r	5.12.60	York C		A	L	1-2	Rowley
1961-62	D4	1	4.11.61	Gateshead	NRL	H	L	2-3	Arnell, Frye
1962-63	D4	1	3.11.62	Chester	D4	A	W	2-0	Jones, Hickson
		2	24.11.62	Doncaster R	D4	A	W	4-1	Hickson 2, Manning 2
		3	5.1.63	Chelsea	D2	H	D	2-2	King, Jones
		3r	30.1.63	Chelsea		A	L	1-3	Hickson
1963-64	D4	1	16.11.63	Doncaster R	D4	A	L	0-3	
1964-65	D4	1	14.11.64	Lincoln C	D4	H	D	0-0	
		1r	18.11.64	Lincoln C		A	L	0-1	
1965-66	D4	1	13.11.65	Stockport Co	D4	H	L	0-1	
1966-67	D4	1	26.11.66	Wigan A	CC	H	D	1-1	Parnell
		1r	28.11.66	Wigan A		A	W	1-0	Williams
		2	7.1.67	Barrow	D4	A	L	1-2	Yardley
1967-68	D3	1	9.12.67	Rochdale	D4	H	W	5-1	Yardley, Williams, Hudson 3, Fletcher
		2	6.1.68	Bradford PA	D4	A	W	3-2	Stevens, Yardley (p), McNamee
		3	27.1.68	Huddersfield T	D2	H	W	2-1	Beamish, Williams
		4	17.2.68	Coventry C	D1	A	D	1-1	A.King
		4r	21.2.68	Coventry C		H	W	2-0	Hudson, Yardley
		5	9.3.68	Everton	D1	A	L	0-2	
1968-69	D3	1	16.11.68	Southport	D3	H	L	0-1	
1969-70	D3	1	15.11.69	Chesterfield	D4	H	W	3-0	Yardley 2, Beamish

Season	Div	Rd	Date	Opponent		H/A	Res	Score	Scorers
		2	6.12.69	Port Vale	D4	A	D	2-2	Beamish, Scott
		2r	8.12.69	Port Vale		H	W	3-1	Smith (p), Scott, Broadie
		3	3.1.70	Portsmouth	D2	A	W	2-1	MacNamee, Beamish
		4	24.1.70	Northampton	D4	H	D	0-0	
		4r	27.1.70	Northampton		A	L	1-2	Smith
1970-71	D3	1	21.11.70	Scunthorpe U	D4	H	D	1-1	Gill
		1r	23.11.70	Scunthorpe U		A	D	0-0aet	
		1 2r	30.11.70	Scunthorpe U at Goodison Pk			L	0-1	
1971-72	D3	1	20.11.71	Skelmersdale U	NPL	A	W	4-0	Crossley 2, King, Moore
		2	11.12.71	Mansfield T	D3	A	D	2-2	Crossley, Storton
		2r	15.12.71	Mansfield T		H	W	4-2	Brodie, Beamish, Moore, Crossley
		3	15.1.72	Charlton A	D2	A	D	0-0	
		3r	17.1.72	Charlton A		H	W	4-2	Beamish, Storton, Crossley, Moore
		4	5.2.72	Stoke C	D1	H	D	2-2	Yeats, Beamish
		4r	9.2.72	Stoke C		A	L	0-2	
1972-73	D3	1	18.11.72	South Liverpool	NPL	A	W	2-0	Flood, Moore
		2	9.12.72	Bradford C	D4	A	L	1-2	Young
1973-74	D3	1	24.11.73	Bury	D4	H	W	2-1	Tynan, Moore
		2	15.12.73	Doncaster R	D4	A	L	0-3	
1974-75	D3	1	23.11.74	Farsley Celtic	YL	A	W	2-0	Coppell, Tynan
		2	14.12.74	Rochdale	D4	A	D	1-1	Hanvey og
		2r	16.12.74	Rochdale		H	W	1-0	Crossley
		3	4.1.75	Peterborough U	D3	A	L	0-1	
1975-76	D4	1	22.11.75	Coventry Sporting	WMRL	A	L	0-2	
				played at Highfield Rd					
1976-77	D3	1	20.11.76	Peterborough U	D3	H	L	0-4	
1977-78	D3	1	26.11.77	Hartlepool U	D4	H	D	1-1	Allen
		1r	29.11.77	Hartlepool U		A	L	1-3	James (p)
1978-79	D3	1	25.11.78	Boston Utd	NPL	H	W	2-1	McAuley, Moore
		2	16.12.78	Sheffield W	D3	H	D	1-1	Moore
		2r	19.12.78	Sheffield W		A	L	0-4	
1979-80	D4	1	24.11.79	AP Leamington	APL	H	W	9-0	Jones og, Lumby 3, O'Neill 2(1p), Evans 2, Beamish
		2	15.12.79	Rochdale	D4	H	D	2-2	Evans, Peplow
		2r	18.12.79	Rochdale		A	L	1-2	Beamish
1980-81	D4	1	22.11.80	York C	D4	H	D	0-0	
		1r	25.11.80	York C		A	W	2-1aet	Craven, Beamish
		2	13.12.80	Huddersfield T	D3	H	L	0-3	
1981-82	D4	1	21.11.81	Bury	D4	H	D	1-1	Brown
		1r	24.11.81	Bury		A	L	1-3	Williams
1982-83	D4	1	20.11.82	Scarborough	APL	H	W	4-2	Kerr, O.Brown 3
		2	11.12.82	Telford U	APL	A	D	1-1	Brown (p)
		2r	14.12.82	Telford U		H	W	2-1	Aspinall, Griffiths
		3	8.1.83	Wolverhampton W	D2	H	L	0-1	
1983-84	D4	1	19.11.83	Bolton W	D3	H	D	2-2	Aspinall, Powell
		1r	22.11.83	Bolton W		A	L	1-4aet	Allen
1984-85	D4	1	17.11.84	Bangor C	NPL	A	D	1-1	McMullen
		1r	20.11.84	Bangor C		H	W	7-0	Clayton 2, Clarke 3, Anderson, Edwards
		2	8.12.84	Hull C	D3	H	L	0-3	
1985-86	D4	1	16.11.85	Chesterfield	D3	H	D	2-2	Worthington (p), Rodaway
		1r	19.11.85	Chesterfield		A	W	1-0	Muir
		2	7.12.85	Bury	D3	H	D	1-1	Morrissey
		2r	10.12.85	Bury		A	L	1-2	Anderson
1986-87	D4	1	15.11.86	Spennymoor U	NL	A	W	3-2	Muir 3 (2ps)
		2	5.12.86	Bolton W	D3	A	L	0-2	
1987-88	D4	1	14.11.87	Port Vale	D3	H	D	2-2	Martindale, Muir
		1r	16.11.87	Port Vale		A	L	1-3	Muir
1988-89	D4	1	19.11.88	Preston NE	D3	A	D	1-1	Atkins og
		1r	22.11.88	Preston NE		H	W	3-0	Muir 3
		2	10.12.88	Northwich V	GMVC	A	W	2-1	Muir (p), Steel
		3	7.1.89	Reading	D3	H	D	1-1	Vickers
		3r	11.1.89	Reading		A	L	1-2	Muir
1989-90	D3	1	18.11.89	Preston NE	D3	A	L	0-1	
1990-91	D3	1	17.11.90	Halesowen T	SL	A	W	2-1	Morrissey, Steel
		2	8.12.90	Scunthorpe U	D4	A	L	2-3	Vickers, Irons
1991-92	D2	1	16.11.91	Runcorn	GMVC	H	W	3-0	Irons, Aldridge 2
		2	7.12.91	York C	D4	A	D	1-1	Morrissey
		2r	17.12.91	York C		H	W	2-1	Aldridge, Irons

	3	4.1.92	Oxford U	D2	A	L	1-3	Malkin
1992-93	D1	3	2.1.93	Oldham A	PL	A	D	2-2	Aldridge (p), Nevin
	3r	12.1.93	Oldham A		H	W	3-0	Vickers, Morrissey 2
	4	23.1.93	Ipswich T	PL	H	L	1-2	Nevin

TROJANS

Formed 1869 and were based at Leyton in east London using the Cowley Arms pub as their headquarters.

1873-74	1		Farningham				*walkover*	
	2		Wanderers				*scratched*	
1876-77	1		Sheffield Club				*scratched*	

TROWBRIDGE TOWN

Formed 1880. **First entered FA Cup:** 1895

1945-46	WL	1 1L	17.11.45	Exeter C	3S	H	L	1-3	Blake
		1 2L	24.11.45	Exeter C		A	L	2-7	Stratton, Powell
1947-48	WL	1	29.11.47	Brighton & HA	3S	H	D	1-1aet	Greenland
		1r	6.12.47	Brighton & HA		A	L	0-5	
1957-58	WL	1	16.11.57	Southend U	3S	H	L	0-2	
1963-64	SL	1	16.11.63	Coventry C	D3	H	L	1-6	Skeen

TUNBRIDGE WELLS RANGERS

Formed 1886. **First entered FA Cup:** 1905. The present club dates from 1967.

1905-06	KL	1	13.1.06	Norwich C	SL	A	D	1-1	L.Parke
		1r	17.1.06	Norwich C		H	L	0-5	
1929-30	KL	1	30.11.29	Bath C	SL	H	L	1-3	Millard
1930-31	KL	1	29.11.30	Kingstonian	IL	H	W	3-0	Thirlaway, Richards, Mackie
		2	13.12.30	Carlisle U	3N	A	L	2-4	Naimby, Morley
1931-32	KL	1	28.11.31	Brentford	3S	H	D	1-1	Spencer
		1r	2.12.31	Brentford		A	L	1-2	Moore
1936-37	KL	1	28.11.36	Bath C	SL	A	W	2-1	T.Dougan, Iles
		2	12.12.36	Accrington S	3N	A	L	0-1	
1937-38	KL	1	27.11.37	Brighton & HA	3S	A	L	1-5	Emerson
1938-39	KL	1	26.11.38	Walthamstow Ave	AL	A	L	1-4	Robinson

Tunbridge Wells United

1954-55	KL	1	20.11.54	Brighton & HA	3S	A	L	0-5	
1961-62	SL	1	4.11.61	Aldershot	D4	A	L	1-5	Hall

TURTON

Formed 1872. Played at Chapeltown in Bolton. One of the strong Bolton teams of the time. **Cup final connection:** Charles Sagar, who played for Bury in the 1900 and 1903 finals, joined Bury from Turton in 1898

1879-80	1	1.11.79	Brigg		H	W	7-0	H.Haworth 3, P.Toothill 2, T.Bentley, Hamer
	2	13.12.79	Nottingham Forest		H	L	0-6	
1880-81	1	16.10.80	Brigg Britannia		H	W	5-0	
	2	18.12.80	Astley Bridge		A	W	3-0	Waddicar 2, G.Haworth
	3	8.1.81	Sheffield Wednesday		H	L	0-2	
1881-82	1	29.10.81	Astley Bridge		A	D	2-2	
	1r	12.11.81	Astley Bridge		H	D	1-1	
	1 2r	19.11.81	Astley Bridge at Great Lever			D	3-3	
	1 3r	26.11.81	Astley Bridge		H	W	2-0	H.Howarth, J.Howarth
	2	3.12.81	Bootle		H	W	4-0	Bentley 2, Hamer, J.Howarth
	3	17.12.81	Darwen		A	L	1-4	J.Howarth
1883-84	1	20.10.83	Hurst		A	L	0-3	

TYNE ASSOCIATION

Amateur club based in North East which played in the FA Cup twice.

1879-80	1	1.11.79	Blackburn R		A	L	1-5	Bruce
1886-87	1	30.10.86	Redcar		A	L	0-4	

UNION FC

Formed 1873. London-based amateurs who played at Highbury Place open space, less than half-a-mile from where Arsenal play now.

1876-77	1	4.11.76 Rochester	A	L	0-5
1877-78	1	Royal Engineers			*scratched*
1881-82	1	5.11.81 Hotspur	A	L	0-1
1882-83	1	4.11.82 Swifts	H	L	1-4

UNITED HOSPITALS

Formed 1867. Played in and around London.

1882-83	1	4.11.82 London Olympic	H	W	3-0
	2	30.11.82 Windsor Home Park	A	L	1-3

UNITED LONDON SCOTTISH

1885-86	1	24.10.85 Upton Park	A	L	2-4

UNITY FC

1878-79	1	Remnants			*scratched*

UPTON PARK

Formed 1866. One of the 15 original entrants into the first FA Cup competition. Played in Upton Park and used the Spotted Dog pub as their changing room. Upton Park were stalwarts of the amateur game and were directly involved in a showdown over 'amateurism' which led to the professionals of Preston being disqualified from the Cup in 1884. Upton Park also played as the 'Great Britain' team in the 1900 Olympic Games soccer tournament in Paris. Fittingly, in light of their earlier stand on amateurism, they won the gold medal.

1871-72	1	11.11.71 Clapham R	H	L	0-3	
1872-73	1	26.10.72 1st Surrey Rifles	A	L	0-2	
1873-74	1	29.10.73 Oxford University	A	L	0-4	
1874-75	1	24.10.74 Barnes	H	L	0-3	
1875-76	1	23.10.75 Southall	H	W	1-0	
	2	Sheffield Club			*scratched*	
1876-77	1	28.10.76 Leyton	H	W	7-0	Bastard, W.Spreckley, Wild, 4 others
	2	9.12.76 Barnes	H	W	1-0	
	3	24.1.77 Marlow	H	D	2-2	Bastard, Winterbottom
	3r	27.1.77 Marlow	H	W	1-0	
	4	24.2.77 Oxford University	A	D	0-0	
	4r	10.3.77 Oxford University	A	L	0-1	
1877-78	1	7.11.77 Rochester	H	W	3-0	D.Hunter 2, J.Hunter
	2	8.12.77 Reading	H	W	1-0	
	3	19.1.78 Remnants	H	W	3-0	D.Hunter, J.Hunter, H.Williams
	4	9.3.78 Old Harrovians	A	L	1-3	J.Hunter
1878-79	1	30.10.78 Saffron Walden	H	W	5-0	Mitchell 2, J.Hunter, W.Williams, 1 other
	2	4.1.79 Barnes	A	L	2-3aet	Bastard, J.HUnter
1879-80	1	15.11.79 Remnants	A	D	1-1	EC Bambridge
	1r	25.11.79 Remnants	H	W	5-0	EC Bambridge 2, Mitchell, others 2
	2	23.12.79 Royal Engineers	A	L	1-4	Garnett-Clarke
1880-81	1	13.11.80 Mosquitoes	H	W	8-1	
	2	18.12.80 Weybridge Swallows	A	W	3-0	Mitchell, Winterbottom, Barnard
	3	bye				
	4	12.2.81 Clapham R	A	L	4-5	Mitchell, others 3
1881-82	1	22.10.81 St Albans	H	W	3-0	Bastard, Lafone, Mitchell
	2	26.11.81 Hanover U	A	W	3-1	
	3	bye				
	4	21.1.81 Hotspur	H	W	5-0	Barnett, Bastard, Mitchell, 2 others
	5	7.2.81 Sheffield Wednesday	A	L	0-6	
1882-83	1	bye				
	2	30.11.82 SWifts	A	D	2-2	Bastard, Lafone
	2r	2.12.82 Swifts	H	L	2-3	Mitchell 2
1883-84	1	10.11.83 Acton	A	W	2-0	Brearley, Hewitt
	2	bye				
	3	22.12.83 Reading	A	W	6-1	
	4	19.1.84 Preston NE	A	D	1-1	Mitchell
		Preston disqualified for professionalism				

	5	9.2.84	Blackburn Rovers	H	L	0-3	
1884-85	1	8.11.84	West End	A	D	3-3	
	1r		West End		walkover		
	2	6.12.84	Reading	H	W	3-1	Lafone, Pellatt, Bastard
	3	3.1.85	Old Wykehamists	A	L	1-2	
1885-86	1	24.10.85	United London Scottish	H	W	4-2	
	2	21.11.85	Old Carthusians	A	L	0-6	
1886-87	1	23.10.86	1st Surrey Rifles	H	W	9-0	
	2	20.11.86	Marlow	A	L	0-4	

UPTON RANGERS

1883-84	1	10.11.83	Old Wykehamists	H	L	0-7

UXBRIDGE

Formed 1871. FA Amateur Cup runners-up: 1898

1873-74	1	28.10.73	Gitanos	H	W	3-0	Clark, Turner, 1 other
	2	26.11.73	Royal Engineers	A	L	1-2	
1874-75	1		Windsor Home Park		scratched		
1883-84	1	3.11.83	Rochester	A	L	1-2	
1884-85	1	8.11.84	Hotspur	H	L	1-3	
1885-86	1	31.10.85	Old Wykehamists	A	L	0-5	

VALE OF LLANGOLLEN

1887-88	1	8.10.87	Oswestry	H	L	1-3
		FA ordered replay after protest				
	1r	22.10.87	Oswestry	H	L	0-2

VAUXHALL MOTORS

Formed 1932. First entered the FA Cup: 1945. Reformed 1963. Folded 1991

1947-48	SPT	1	29.11.47	Walsall	3S	H	L	1-2	Sharp
			played at Luton Town					

WALKER CELTIC

First entered FA Cup: 1919. Newcastle-based team.

1937-38	NEL	1	27.11.37	Bradford C	3N	H	D	1-1	Haftoe
		1r	1.12.37	Bradford C		A	L	3-11	Cotterill, Allison 2

WALSALL

Formed in 1888 when Walsall Swifts (formed 1877) and Walsall Town (formed 1879) amalgamated as Walsall Town Swifts. Walsall Swifts and Walsall Town both played in the Competition Proper (see seperate records) Walsall Town Swifts became plain Walsall in the summer of 1896.
Best FA Cup performance: 5th round 1939, 1975, 1978 Record FA Cup Win: 12-0 vs Warmley, 1st qualifying round, 27.9.1890. In Competition Proper: 6-1 vs Leytonstone, 1st round, 30.11.1946; 6-1 vs Margate 1st round replay, 24.11.1955 Record FA Cup Defeat: 0-7 vs Worcester City, 1st qualifying 11.10.1913 in Competition Proper: 0-6 vs Aston Villa, 1st round, 13.1.1912

as Walsall Town Swifts

1888-89		1	2.2.89	Sheffield Heeley		H	W	5-1	Shaw 2, Cope, Gray, Morely
		2	16.2.89	Wolverhampton W	D1	A	L	1-6	Gray
1889-90	FAII	1q Wellington St Georges (H) 3-0; 2q Warwick Co (A) 1-1aet; 2qr Warwick Co (H) 2-0; 3q Burton Swifts (A) 6-1; 4q Small Heath (A) 0-4
1890-91	FAII	1q Warmley (A) 12-0; 2q Burslem Port Vale (A) 3-2; 3q Wednesbury OA (H) 5-3; 4q Kidderminster H (A) 0-3
1891-92	FAII	1q Wednesbury OA (H) 7-2; 2q Burton Swifts (H) 2-4
1892-93	D2	1q Derby Junction (H) 1-0aet; 2q Stourbridge (H) 7-0; 3q Burton Swifts (H) 1-3
1893-94	D2	1q Wellington St Georges (A) 3-0; 2q Stourbridge (A) 3-1; 3q Brierley Hill Alliance (H) 1-2
1894-95	D2	1q Burton W (A) 0-3
1895-96	ML	1q Dresden U (H) 1-0; 2q Redditch (H) 4-0; 3q Wrockwardine Wood (A) 1-3

as Walsall FC

1896-97	D2	3q Dresden U (H) 11-0; 4q Burton Swifts (H) 1-1; 4qr Burton Swifts (A) 0-1

WALSALL

1897-98	D2	1	29.1.98	Newton Heath	D2	A	L	0-1
1898-99	D2	3q	Druids (A) 1-2					
1899-00	D2	3q	Kidderminster H (H) 6-1; 4q Wellington T (H) 2-1; 5q Small Heath (A) 0-0; 5qr Small Heath (H) 2-0					
		1	27.1.00	WBA	D1	H	D	1-1	Dailly
		1r	1.2.00	WBA		A	L	1-6	Martin (p)
1900-01	D2	3q	Shrewsbury T (A) 1-1; 3qr Shrewsbury T (H) 1-0; 4q Chirk (A) 1-0; 5q Wellington T (H) 6-0; Int Chesterfield (A) 0-3					
1901-02	ML	3q	Brierley Hill All. (A) 1-1; 3qr Brierley Hill All. (H) 2-1; 4q Berwick R, Coventry (H) 0-0; 4q Berwick R (H) 2-1; 5q Burslem Port Vale (A) 2-1; Int New Brompton (H) 2-0					
		1	25.1.02	Burnley	D2	H	W	1-0	Colley
		2	8.2.02	Bury	D1	H	L	0-5	
1902-03	ML	2q	Brierley Hill All. (H) 0-2					
1903-04	BDL	3q	Coventry C (A) 4-2; 4q Stafford R (A) 2-1; 5q Shrewsbury T (A) 0-1					
1904-05	BDL	1q	Brierley Hill All. (H) 3-0; 2q Coventry C (A) 0-2					
1905-06	BDL	4q	Stockport Co (H) 3-3; 4qr Stockport Co (A) 0-5					
1906-07	BDL	1q	Brierley Hill All. (H) 0-3					
1907-08	BDL	1q	Stafford R (H) 2-5					
1908-09	BDL	P	Worcester C (A) 2-0; 1q Kidderminster H (A) 1-2					
1909-10	BDL	P	Cannock (H) 1-2					
1910-11	BDL	P	Willenhall Swifts (H) 1-0; 1q Hednesford T (A) 3-4					
1911-12	BDL	4q	Stoke (H) 2-1; 5q Accrington S (H) 2-1					
		1	13.1.12	A.Villa	D1	A	L	0-6	
1912-13	BDL	4q	Crewe Alex (H) 2-1; 5q Halifax T (H) 0-0; 5qr Halifax T (A) 0-1					
1913-14	BDL	P	Stafford R (H) 1-0; 1q Worcester C (A) 0-7					
1914-15	BDL	ExP	Willenhall Pickwick (H) 4-0; P Cannock (H) 2-1; 1q Hednesford T (H) 3-1; 2q Cradley Heath St Lukes (H) 5-2; 3q Stoke (H) 1-0; 4q Wrexham (H) 2-1; 5q Shrewsbury T (A) 1-2					
1919-20	BDL	4q	Worcester C (H) 3-1; 5q Hednesford T (A) 2-4					
1920-21	BDL	P	Birmingham Corporation Tramways (H) 3-0; 1q Shrewsbury T (A) 0-1					
1921-22	3N	4q	Shrewsbury T (A) 1-0; 5q Chesterfield (H) 2-0; 6q Mansfield T (A) 1-1; 6qr Mansfield T (H) 4-0					
		1	7.1.22	Bradford C	D1	H	D	3-3	Butler, Groves, Reid
		1r	11.1.22	Bradford C		A	L	0-4	
1922-23	3N	5q	Wellington St Georges (A) 5-0; 6q Wigan Borough (H) 1-3					
1923-24	3N	5q	Stalybridge Celtic (H) 3-1; 6q Aberdare A (A) 0-1					
1924-25	3N	5q	Coventry C (H) 1-2					
1925-26	3N	1	28.11.25	Grimsby T	3N	H	L	0-1	
1926-27	3N	1	27.11.26	Bradford PA	3N	H	W	1-0	White
		2	11.12.26	Mansfield T	ML	H	W	2-0	White, SArvis
		3	8.1.27	Corinthians		H	L	0-4	
1927-28	3S	1	26.11.27	Bristol R	3S	A	L	2-4	White, Groves
1928-29	3S	1	24.11.28	Worcester C	BDL	H	W	3-1	Groves, N.Thompson, Gough
		2	8.12.28	Sittingbourne	SL	H	W	2-1	Gough, Moffatt
		3	12.1.29	Middlesbrough	D2	H	D	1-1	N.Thompson
		3r	21.1.29	Middlesbrough		A	L	1-5	Gough
1929-30	3S	1	30.11.29	Exeter C	3S	H	W	1-0	Roe
		2	14.12.29	Newport Co	3S	A	W	3-2	A.Walters 3
		3	11.1.30	Swansea T	D2	H	W	2-0	Eyres, A.Walters
		4	25.1.30	A.Villa	D1	A	L	1-3	Johnson
1930-31	3S	1	30.11.30	Bournemouth	3S	H	W	1-0	Eyres
		2	13.12.30	Newport Co	3S	H	W	4-0	Cooper 3, Bartley
		3	10.1.31	Blackburn R	D1	A	D	1-1	Eyres
		3r	15.1.31	Blackburn R		H	L	0-3	
1931-32	3N	1	28.11.31	Darlington	3N	A	L	0-1	
1932-33	3N	1	26.11.32	Mansfield T	3N	H	W	4-1	Lee 2, Taylor, Ball
		2	10.12.32	Hartlepool U	3N	H	W	2-1	Lee, Ball
		3	14.1.33	Arsenal	D1	H	W	2-0	Alsop, Sheppard (p)
		4	28.1.33	Manchester C	D1	A	L	0-4	
1933-34	3N	1	25.11.33	Spennymoor U	NEL	H	W	4-0	Woolhouse 2, Alsop, Sheppard
		2	9.12.33	Clapton O	3S	H	D	0-0	
		2r	14.12.33	Clapton O		A	L	0-2	
1934-35	3N	1	24.11.34	Crewe Alex	3N	A	W	2-1	Alsop 2
		2	8.12.34	Watford	3S	A	D	1-1	Alsop
		2r	13.12.34	Watford		H	W	1-0	Ball
		3	12.1.35	Southampton	D2	H	L	1-2	Alsop
1935-36	3N	1	30.11.35	Lincoln C	3N	H	W	2-0	Collins, Evans
		2	14.12.35	Chesterfield	3N	A	D	0-0	
		2r	19.12.35	Chesterfield		H	W	2-1	Richmond, Bate
		3	11.1.36	Newcastle U	D2	H	L	0-2	
1936-37	3S	1	28.11.36	Scunthorpe U	ML	H	W	3-0	Evans 3 (1p)

Season	Div	Rnd	Date	Opponent	Lg	H/A	W/D/L	Score	Scorers
		2	12.12.36	Yeovil & Petters U	SL	H	D	1-1	Woolhouse
		2r	17.12.36	Yeovil & Petters U		A	W	1-0	Bulger
		3	16.1.37	Barnsley	D2	H	W	3-1	Harwood, Evans 2
		4	30.1.37	Grimsby T	D1	A	L	1-5	Evans
1937-38	3S	1	27.11.37	Gateshead	3N	H	W	4-0	Dodd 2, Shelton, Simpson
		2	11.12.37	Watford	3S	A	L	0-3	
1938-39	3S	1	26.11.38	Carlisle U	3N	H	W	4-1	Bambrick 3, Alsop
		2	10.12.38	Clapton O	3S	H	W	4-2	Bambrick, Bulger, Simpson, Hancocks
		3	7.1.39	Newport Co	3S	A	W	2-0	Bambrick, Alsop
		4	21.1.39	Notts Co	3S	A	D	0-0	
		4r	26.1.39	Notts Co		H	W	4-0	Alsop 4
		5	11.2.39	Huddersfield T	D1	A	L	0-4	
1945-46	3S	1 1L	17.11.45	Shrewsbury T	ML	A	L	0-5	
		1 2L	24.11.45	Shrewsbury T		H	W	4-1	Mullard, Bennett, Talbot, Alsop
1946-47	3S	1	30.11.46	Leyton O	3S	A	W	6-1	Wilshaw 2, Maund, Darby, Davies 2
		2	14.12.46	Ipswich T	3S	H	D	0-0	
		2r	18.12.46	Ipswich T		A	W	1-0	Lishman
		3	11.1.47	Liverpool	D1	H	L	2-5	Kelly, Wilshaw
1947-48	3S	1	29.11.47	Vauxhall Motors	SPT	A	W	2-1	Maund, Welsh (p)
				played at Luton Town					
		2	13.12.47	Norwich C	3S	A	D	2-2aet	McGowan, Lishman
		2r	20.12.47	Norwich C		H	W	3-2	Crutchley, Wilshaw, Lishman
		3	10.1.48	Coventry C	D2	A	L	1-2	Lishman
1948-49	3S	1	27.11.48	Bristol R	3S	H	W	2-1	Chapman, Aldred
		2	11.12.48	Gainsborough T	ML	H	W	4-3	Chapman 2, Walters, Condie
		3	8.1.49	Fulham	D2	A	W	1-0	Devlin
		4	29.1.49	Luton T	D2	A	L	0-4	
1949-50	3S	1	26.11.49	Mansfield T	3N	A	L	1-4	Skidmore
1950-51	3S	1	25.11.50	Newport Co	3S	A	L	2-4	Corbett 2
1951-52	3S	1	14.11.51	Reading	3S	A	L	0-1	
1952-53	3S	1	22.11.52	Newport Co	3S	A	L	1-2	Giles
1953-54	3S	1	21.11.53	Bath C	SL	A	W	3-0	Allsopp, Dean, Morris
		2	2.12.53	Crewe Alex	3N	H	W	3-0	Holding 2, G.Jones
		3	9.1.54	Lincoln C	D2	A	D	1-1	Finlay
		3r	14.1.54	Lincoln C		H	D	1-1aet	Morris
		3 2r	18.1.54	Lincoln C at Nottingham F			L	1-2	Finlay
1954-55	3S	1	20.11.54	Shrewsbury T	3S	H	W	5-2	Richards 2, Meek, Morris, Dorman
		2	11.12.54	Wrexham	3N	A	W	2-1	Richards 2
		3	8.1.55	Chelsea	D1	A	L	0-2	
1955-56	3S	1	19.11.55	Margate	KL	A	D	2-2	Morris, McLaren
		1r	24.11.55	Margate		H	W	6-1	Walsh 3, Richards 2, McLaren
		2	10.12.55	Southampton	3S	H	W	2-1	Morris, Moore
		3	7.1.56	Port Vale	D2	H	L	0-1	
1956-57	3S	1	17.11.56	Newport Co	3S	H	L	0-1	
1957-58	3S	1	16.11.57	Brighton	3S	A	L	1-2	Tarrant
1958-59	D4	1	15.11.58	QPR	D3	H	L	0-1	
1959-60	D4	1	14.11.59	Swindon T	D3	A	W	3-2	Richards, Davies 2
		2	5.12.59	Peterborough U	ML	H	L	2-3	Richards, Billingham
1960-61	D3	1	5.11.60	Yeovil T	SL	H	L	0-1	
1961-62	D2	3	6.1.62	Bristol C	D3	A	D	0-0	
		3r	9.1.62	Bristol C		H	W	4-1	Richards 2, Taylor, Hodgkisson
		4	27.1.62	Fulham	D1	A	D	2-2	Richards 2 (1p)
		4r	30.1.62	Fulham		H	L	0-2	
1962-63	D2	3	6.3.63	Manchester C	D1	H	L	0-1	
1963-64	D3	1	16.11.63	Southport	D4	A	L	1-2	Newton
1964-65	D3	1	14.11.64	Bristol R	D3	H	L	0-2	
1965-66	D3	1	13.11.65	Swansea T	D3	H	W	6-3	Clarke 2 (1p), Summers, Kirby 2, Satchwell
		2	4.12.65	Aldershot	D4	A	W	2-0	Taylor, Clarke
		3	22.1.66	Stoke C	D1	A	W	2-0	Kirby, Clarke (p)
		4	12.2.66	Norwich C	D2	A	L	2-3	Kirby, Taylor
1966-67	D3	1	26.11.66	St Neots T	Met	H	W	2-0	Baker, Taylor
		2	7.1.67	Gillingham	D3	H	W	3-1	Taylor 2, Baker
		3	28.1.67	Bury	D2	A	L	0-2	
1967-68	D3	1	9.12.67	Leytonstone	IL	A	W	1-0	Watson
		2	6.1.68	Exeter C	D4	A	W	3-1	Meath, Watson, Simpson
		3	27.1.68	Crystal P	D2	H	D	1-1	Taylor
		3r	31.1.68	Crystal P		A	W	2-1	Simpson, Jackson

		4	17.2.68	Liverpool	D1	H	D	0-0	
		4r	19.2.68	Liverpool		A	L	2-5	Watson 2
1968-69	D3	1	16.11.68	Leytonstone	IL	A	W	1-0	Baker
		2	7.12.68	St Albans C	IL	A	D	1-1	Trevis
		2r	10.12.68	St Albans C		H	W	3-1	Gibbs og, Watson, Wilson
		3	4.1.69	Tottenham H	D1	H	L	0-1	
1969-70	D3	1	15.11.69	Orient	D3	H	D	0-0	
		1r	17.11.69	Orient		A	W	2-0	Woodward, Taylor
		2	6.12.69	Brighton & HA	D3	A	D	1-1	Bennett
		2r	8.12.69	Brighton & HA		H	D	1-1aet	Taylor
		2 2r	15.12.69	Brighton & HA at Coventry			D	0-0aet	
		2 3r	17.12.69	Brighton & HA at Fulham			W	2-1	Taylor 2
		3	3.1.70	Crystal P	D1	A	L	0-2	
1970-71	D3	1	21.11.70	Plymouth A	D3	H	W	3-0	Morris 2, Woodward
		2	12.12.70	Brentford	D4	A	L	0-1	
1971-72	D3	1	20.11.71	Dagenham	AL	H	W	4-1	Woodward, Wright, Taylor, Morris
		2	11.12.71	Brighton & HA	D3	A	D	1-1	Woodward
		2r	14.12.71	Brighton & HA		H	W	2-1	Train, Wright
		3	15.1.72	Bournemouth	D3	H	W	1-0	Wright
		4	5.2.72	Everton	D1	A	L	1-2	Evans
1972-73	D3	1	18.11.72	Kettering T	SL	H	D	3-3	Morris 2, Woodward
		1r	22.11.72	Kettering T		A	W	2-1	Atthey, C.Jones
		2	12.12.72	Charlton A	D3	H	L	1-2	Morris
1973-74	D3	1	24.11.73	Swansea C	D4	H	W	1-0	Andrews
		2	15.12.73	Plymouth A	D3	A	L	0-1	
1974-75	D3	1	27.11.74	Ashford T	SL	A	W	3-1	Buckley 2, Fry
		2	14.12.74	Newport Co	D4	A	W	3-1	Taylor, Wright, Buckley
		3	4.1.75	Manchester U	D2	A	D	0-0	
		3r	7.1.75	Manchester U		H	W	3-2aet	Wright, Buckley 2 (1p)
		4	24.1.75	Newcastle U	D1	H	W	1-0	Andrews
		5	15.2.75	Birmingham C	D1	A	L	1-2	Taylor
1975-76	D3	1	22.11.75	Huddersfield T	D4	H	L	0-1	
1976-77	D3	1	20.11.76	Bradford C	D4	H	D	0-0	
		1r	24.11.76	Bradford C		A	W	2-0	Taylor, Wright
		2	11.12.76	Chesterfield	D3	A	D	1-1	Hunter og
		2r	14.12.76	Chesterfield		H	D	0-0aet	
		2 2r	21.12.76	Chesterfield at Derby			W	1-0	Wright
		3	8.1.77	Manchester U	D1	A	L	0-1	
1977-78	D3	1	26.11.77	Dagenham	IL	H	W	1-0	Wood
		2	17.12.77	Port Vale	D3	H	D	1-1	Wood
		2r	19.12.77	Port Vale		A	W	3-1	King, Shelton, Bates
		3	6.1.78	Swansea C	D4	H	W	4-1	Buckley 3, King
		4	28.1.78	Leicester C	D1	H	W	1-0	Evans
		5	18.2.78	Arsenal	D1	A	L	1-4	Buckley
1978-79	D3	1	25.11.78	Torquay U	D4	H	L	0-2	
1979-80	D4	1	24.11.79	Stockport Co	D4	H	W	1-0	Penn, Paul
		2	15.12.79	Halifax T	D4	H	D	1-1	Buckley (p)
		2r	18.12.79	Halifax T		A	D	1-1aet	Buckley
		2 2r	24.12.79	Halifax T		A	L	0-2aet	
1980-81	D3	1	22.11.80	Stafford R	APL	H	W	3-0	Buckley, Penn, S.Waddington
		2	13.12.80	Carlisle U	D3	A	L	0-3	
1981-82	D3	1	21.11.81	Blyth Spartans	NL	A	W	2-1	Macken, Caswell
		2	2.1.81	Peterborough U	D4	A	L	1-2	Butler og
1982-83	D3	1	20.11.82	Kettering T	APL	H	W	3-0	Kearns, Preece, Buckley
		2	11.12.82	North Shields	NL	A	W	3-0	Round, Buckley, Caswell
		3	8.1.82	Birmingham C	D1	H	D	0-0	
		3r	11.1.82	Birmingham C		A	L	0-1aet	
1983-84	D3	1	19.11.83	Bournemouth	D3	A	L	0-4	
1984-85	D3	1	17.11.84	Stockport Co	D4	A	W	2-1	Shakespeare, Kelly
		2	8.12.84	Chesterfield	D4	H	W	1-0	Mower
		3	5.1.85	York C	D3	A	L	0-3	
1985-86	D3	1	16.11.85	Preston NE	D4	H	W	7-1	Naughton 3, Elliott, Childs 2, O'Kelly
		2	8.12.85	Port Vale	D4	A	D	0-0	
		2r	10.12.85	Port Vale		H	W	2-1	Cross, Hawker
		3	4.1.86	Manchester C	D1	H	L	1-3	O'Kelly (p)
1986-87	D3	1	15.11.86	Chesterfield	D3	H	W	2-0	Shakespeare, Mower
		2	6.12.86	Port Vale	D3	H	W	5-0	Shakespeare 2 (2ps), Naughton, Cross, Christie

		3	10.1.87	Charlton A	D1	A	W	2-1	Kelly, Shakespeare
		4	31.1.87	Birmingham C	D2	H	W	1-0	Cross
		5	21.2.87	Watford	D1	H	D	1-1	Christie (p)
		5r	24.2.87	Watford		A	D	4-4aet	Christie 2, Cross, Hawker
		5 2r	2.3.87	Watford		H	L	0-1	
1987-88	D3	1	14.11.87	Southend U	D3	A	D	0-0	
		1r	17.11.87	Southend U		H	W	2-1	Jones 2 (2ps)
		2	5.12.87	Gillingham	D3	A	L	1-2	Kelly
1988-89	D2	3	7.1.89	Brentford	D3	H	D	1-1	Pritchard
		3r	10.1.89	Brentford		A	L	0-1	
1989-90	D3	1	18.11.89	Telford U	GMVC	A	W	3-0	Rimmer, Bertschin, Forbes
		2	9.12.89	Rotherham U	D3	H	W	1-0	Rimmer
		3	6.1.90	Hereford U	D4	A	L	1-2	Bertschin
1990-91	D4	1	17.11.90	Aylesbury U	IL	A	W	1-0	McDonald
		2	8.12.90	Swansea C	D3	A	L	1-2	Hutchings
1991-92	D4	1	16.11.91	Yeovil T	GMVC	A	D	1-1	Tolson
		1r	27.11.91	Yeovil T		H	L	0-1aet	
1992-93	D3	1	14.11.92	Rotherham U	D2	A	L	0-4	

WALSALL SWIFTS

Formed 1877. Reached the last 16 of the FA Cup in 1885. Merged with Walsall Town to form Walsall FC in 1888.

1882-83	1	21.10.82	A.Villa	A	L	1-4	T.Farmer
1883-84	1	10.11.83	A.Villa	H	L	1-5	J.Farmer
1884-85	1	8.11.84	Stafford Rd	H	D	0-0	
	1r	11.11.84	Stafford Rd	A	W	2-1	Jefferies 2
	2	6.12.84	Derby St Lukes	A	W	1-0	Davis
	3	10.1.85	Birmingham St G	A	W	3-2	Aldridge, Morely, Richards og
	4	24.1.85	Notts Co	A	L	0-4	
1885-86	2	14.11.85	Derby Midland	A	W	3-1	Higgins, Webster 2
	3	12.12.85	Wolverhampton W	A	L	1-2	T.Farmer
1886-87		*did not enter*					
1887-88	1	15.10.87	Wolverhampton W	A	L	1-2	Higgins

WALSALL TOWN

Formed 1879. Merged with Walsall Swifts to form Walsall FC 1888.

1882-83	1	21.10.82	Staveley	A	W	4-1	Arblaster, Harrison, Hill, Tonks
	2	2.12.82	Stafford Rd	H	W	4-1	Bird 2, Bradbury 2
	3	27.1.83	A.Villa	A	L	1-2	Hill
1883-84	1	10.11.83	Birmingham Calthorpe	A	W	9-0	Bird 4, Collington 2, Brettle, Harrison, Ashe
	2	1.12.83	Wednesbury T	H	D	2-2	Arblaster 2
	2r	6.12.83	Wednesbury T	A	L	0-6	
1884-85	1	8.11.84	Derby Co	A	W	7-0	Cope 2, Bird 2, Shaw, Hunter, Ashe
	2	6.12.84	A.Villa	H	L	0-2	
1885-86	1	10.11.85	A.Villa	H	L	0-5	
1886-87	1	30.10.86	Derby St Lukes	A	D	3-3	Bradbury 2, Davis
	1r	13.11.86	Derby St Lukes	H	W	6-1	Bradbury 2, Davis 2, Cox, Wilson
	2		bye				
	3	11.12.86	Birmingham St G	H	L	2-7	Bradbury, Wilson
1887-88	1	8.12.87	Birmingham St G	H	L	1-2	Webster

WALTHAMSTOW AVENUE

Formed 1901. **First entered FA Cup:** 1921. **FA Amateur Cup Winners:** 1952, 1961 Merged with Leytonstone-Ilford to form Redbridge Forest 1989. **League clubs beaten:** Northampton T, Watford, Stockport Co, Gillingham, QPR

1930-31	AL	1	29.11.30	Watford	3S	H	L	1-5	Lewis
1934-35	AL	1	24.11.34	QPR	3S	A	L	0-2	
1935-36	AL	1	30.11.35	Bournemouth	3S	H	D	1-1	Lewis
		1r	4.12.35	Bournemouth		A	L	1-8	Vincent
1936-37	AL	1	28.11.36	Northampton T	3S	H	W	6-1	Davis 3, Magner, Vincent 2
		2	12.12.36	Exeter C	3S	H	–	1-1	Lewis
			abandoned after 65 minutes – fog					
		2	17.12.36	Exeter C		H	L	2-3	Matthews 2

WALTHAMSTOW AVENUE

1937-38	AL	1	27.11.37	Westbury U	Wilts	A	W	3-1	Magner, Lewis, Matthews
		2	11.12.37	Southend U	3S	H	L	0-1	
1938-39	AL	1	26.11.38	Tunbridge Wells R	KL	H	W	4-1	Groves, Foreman, Magner, Kitson
		2	10.12.38	Stockport Co	3N	A	D	0-0	
		2r	15.12.38	Stockport Co		H	L	1-3	Vincent
1945-46	IL	1 1L	17.11.45	Sutton U	AL	A	W	4-1	Groves, Green 3
		1 2L	24.11.45	Sutton U		H	W	7-2	Groves 4, Davsis 2, Insole
		2 1L	8.12.45	Brighton & HA	3S	H	D	1-1	Groves
		2 2L	15.12.45	Brighton & HA		A	L	2-4	Davis 2
1948-49	IL	1	27.11.48	Cambridge T	SPT	H	W	3-2	Lewis 2, Strather
		2	11.12.48	Oldham A	3N	H	D	2-2aet	Lewis, O'Connell
		2r	18.12.48	Oldham A		A	L	1-3	Butterworth
1949-50	IL	1	26.11.49	Northampton T	3S	A	L	1-4	Tyrell
1950-51	IL	1	25.11.50	Mansfield T	3N	A	L	0-1	
1952-53	IL	1	22.11.52	Wimbledon	IL	H	D	2-2	Bailey, Hall
		1r	26.11.52	Wimbledon		A	W	3-0	Lewis 2, Bailey
		2	6.12.52	Watford	3S	H	D	1-1	Croker og
		2r	10.12.52	Watford		A	W	2-1aet	Camis, Lucas
		3	10.1.53	Stockport Co	3N	H	W	2-1	Lucas 2
		4	31.1.53	Manchester U	D1	A	D	1-1	Lewis
		4r	5.2.53	Manchester U at Highbury			L	2-5	Lewis 2
1953-54	IL	1	21.11.53	Gillingham	3S	H	W	1-0	Groves
		2	12.12.53	Ipswich T	3S	A	D	2-2	R.Walker, J.Richards
		2r	16.12.53	Ipswich T		H	L	0-1	
1954-55	IL	1	20.11.54	QPR	3S	A	D	2-2	Anderson, Julians
		1r	25.11.54	QPR		H	D	2-2aet	Bee 2
		1 2r	29.11.54	QPR at Highbury			W	4-0	Julians, Paris, Anderson 2
		2	11.12.54	Darlington	3N	H	L	0-3	
1956-57	IL	1	17.11.56	Crystal P	3S	A	L	0-2	
1957-58	IL	1	16.11.57	Coventry C	3S	A	L	0-1	
1959-60	IL	1	14.11.59	Bournemouth	D3	H	L	2-3	Harvey, Lewis (p)
1960-61	IL	1	5.11.60	QPR	D3	A	L	2-3	Harvey (p), Minall
1961-62	IL	1	4.11.61	Romford	SL	H	L	2-3	Stone, Minall
1967-68	IL	1	9.12.67	Kidderminster H	WMRL	H	W	2-1	Jackson, Ford (p)
		2	6.1.68	Bournemouth	D3	H	L	1-3	Jackson

WALTON & HERSHAM

Formed 1945 when Walton FC (1896) and Hersham FC (1926) amalgamated. **First entered FA Cup:** 1907. **FA Amateur Cup Winners:** 1973. Scored memorable 4-0 win at Third Division Brighton in 1973.

1957-58	AL	1	16.11.57	Southampton	3S	H	L	1-6	Sheehan
1969-70	AL	1	15.11.69	Barnet	SL	H	L	0-1	
1970-71	AL	1	21.11.70	Telford U	SL	H	L	2-5	Longfield, Edwards
1972-73	IL	1	18.11.72	Exeter C	D4	H	W	2-1	Woffinden, Koskett
		2	9.12.72	Margate	SL	H	L	0-1	
1973-74	IL	1	24.11.73	Brighton & HA	D3	H	D	0-0	
		1r	28.11.73	Brighton & HA		A	W	4-0	Perkins, Foskett 3
		2	15.12.73	Hereford U	D3	A	L	0-3	
1975-76	IL	1	22.11.75	Crystal P	D3	A	L	0-1	

WANDERERS

Developed out of the Forest Club who were formed in 1859. Wanderers are the most famous of all the pioneering Cup teams. They were the first winners of the FA Cup in 1872, and won all five Cup Finals they played in. They disbanded at the end of the 1881-82 season. **FA Cup Winners:** 1872, 1873, 1876, 1877, 1878.

1871-72	1	11.11.71	Harrow Chequers			*walkover*	
	2	16.12.71	Clapham Rovers		A	W	3-1	Pelham, 2 others
	3	20.1.72	Crystal Palace			D	0-0	
			both clubs advanced to the next round				
	SF	5.3.72	Queens Park at Kennington Oval			D	0-0	
	SFr		Queens Park			*walkover*	
			Queen's Park scratched				
	F	16.3.72	ROYAL ENGINEERS			W	1-0	MP Betts
			played at Kennington Oval				
1872-73			*As holders Wanderers were exempt until the Final*				
	F	29.3.73	OXFORD UNIVERSITY			W	2-0	Kinnaird, Wollaston
			played at Lillie Bridge				

WANDERERS

1873-74	1		Southall			walkover	
	2		Trojans			walkover	
	3	6.12.73	Oxford University		D	1-1	Maddison
	3r	31.1.74	Oxford University		L	0-1	
1874-75	1	31.10.74	Farningham	H	W	16-0	Kingsford 5, Wollaston 4, Alcock 2, Chenery 2, Heron 2, Kenrick
	2	21.11.74	Barnes	H	W	5-0	Alcock 3, Kenrick, Wollaston
	3	30.1.75	Oxford University		L	1-2	Rawson og
1875-76	1	23.10.75	1st Surrey Rifles	H	W	5-0	Kenrick 2, Maddison 2, Alcock
	2	11.12.75	Crystal Palace	H	W	3-0	Wollaston 2, F.Heron
	3	29.1.76	Sheffield		W	2-0	F.Heron 2,
	SF	26.2.76	Swifts at Kennington Oval		W	2-1	Birley, Wollaston
	F	11.3.76	Old Etonians		D	1-1	Edwards
	Fr	18.3.76	OLD ETONIANS		W	3-0	Wollaston, Hughes 2
			both matches played at Kennington Oval				
1876-77	1	8.11.76	Saffron Walden			walkover	
	2	14.12.76	Southall Park	H	W	6-1	
	3	20.1.76	Pilgrims		W	3-0	Maddison, Wollaston, 1 other
	4		bye				
	SF	20.3.76	Cambridge University		W	1-0	Heron
			played at Kennington Oval				
	F	24.3.76	OXFORD UNIVERSITY		W	2-1aet	Kenrick, Lindsay
			played at Kennington Oval				
1877-78	1	7.11.77	Panthers	H	W	9-1	Heron 4, Wace 2, Wylie 2, Kenrick 3 ,
	2	15.12.77	High Wycombe	A	W	9-0	Wace 2, Wollaston 2, Wylie 2,, Denton, Kinnaird, og
	3	12.1.78	Barnes		D	1-1	Denton
	3r	26.1.78	Barnes		W	4-1	Kinnaird, Wollaston, Wylie, 1 other
	4	16.2.78	Sheffield		W	3-0	Denton, Wace, Wylie
	SF		bye				
	F	23.3.78	ROYAL ENGINEERS		W	3-1	Kenrick 2, Kinnaird
			played at Kennington Oval				
1878-79	1	9.11.78	Old Etonians	H	L	2-7	Kenrick, 1 other
1879-80	1	15.11.78	Rochester	A	W	6-0	
	2	10.1.79	Old Carthusians	H	W	1-0	Wace
	3	24.1.79	Old Etonians		L	1-3	Wace
1880-81	1		Rangers			scratched	
1881-82	1		St Bart's Hospital			scratched	

WARE

Formed 1892. **First entered FA Cup:** 1926.

1968-69	AL	1	16.11.68	Luton T	D3	A	L	1-6	Francis

WARWICK COUNTY

Formed 1876. Played at the County Cricket ground at Edgbaston, Birmingham. Created FA Cup history in 1888 when they became the first non-League club to beat a Football League club, defeating Stoke 2-1 in a 1st round qualifying match

1887-88	1	15.10.87	Birmingham Excelsior		A	L	1-4	
			FA ordered replay after a protest					
	1r	22.10.87	Birmingham Excelsior		H	L	0-5	

WATERLOOVILLE

Formed 1905. **First entered FA Cup:** 1966

1968-69	Hants 1	16.11.68	Kettering T	SL	H	L	1-2	Goodall
1976-77	SL 1	20.11.76	Wycombe W	IL	H	L	1-2	Robson
1983-84	SL 1	19.11.83	Northampton T	D4	A	D	1-1	Hore
	1r	22.11.83	Northampton T		H	D	1-1aet	Holland
	1 2r	28.11.83	Northampton T		A	L	0-2	
1988-89	SL 1	19.11.88	Aylesbury U	GMVC	H	L	1-4	Whittingham

WATFORD

Formed 1898. **First entered FA Cup as Watford FC** 1898. **Runners-up:** 1984. **Record FA Cup Win:** 10-0 vs Leighton CS, 3rd qualifying round, 3.11.1900 10-0 vs Bournemouth FC, 4th qualifying round, 29.11.1913. **In Competition Proper:** 10-1 vs Lowestoft T, 1st round, 27.11.1926

Record FA Cup Defeat: 0-10 vs **Wolverhampton W**, 1st round replay, 24.1.1912 The early history of the present Watford FC is a complicated one and traces its roots back to the original premier club in Hertfordshire, Herts Rangers who were originally founded in 1865. By the time the FA Cup began in 1871, the principal clubs in Watford were Herts Rangers and Watford Rovers and their records in the competition proper are included under their names. By the 1890s the two principal clubs in the town were Watford St Mary's and West Herts FC. They both entered the FA Cup, neither club reaching the competition proper. They finally merged to form Watford in 1898 which is where this record begins.

1898-99	SL	P **Chesham T** (H) 1-0; 1q **Chesham Generals** (H) 4-0; 2q **Lowestoft T** (H) 2-0; 3q **Luton T** (A) 2-2; 3qr **Luton T** (H) 0-1						
1899-00	SL	1q **Hitchin T** (H) 7-1; 2q **Wolverton LNW** (H) 1-0; 3q **Crouch End Vampires** (A) 3-0; 4q **Luton T** (A) 2-3						
1900-01	SL	3q **Leighton CS** (H) 10-0; 4q **QPR** (H) 1-1; 4qr **QPR** (A) 1-4						
1901-02	SL	3q **W.Hampstead** (A) 2-1; 4q **Luton T** (H) 1-2						
1902-03	SL	3q **Fulham** (H) 1-1; 3qr **Fulham** (A) 0-3						
1903-04	SL	3q **Redhill** (A) 6-1; 4q **Luton T** (A) 1-4						
1904-05	SL	3q **Biggleswade** (H) 7-1; 4q **Grays U** (A) 3-1; 5q **Hitchin T** (H) 2-0; 6q **Lincoln C** (H) 1-1; 6qr **Lincoln C** (A) 1-2						
1905-06	SL	4q **Southport** (H) 3-1						
		1	13.1.06 **Worcester C**	BDL	A	W	6-0	Reid 3, Richardson, Eames, Kelly
		2	3.2.06 **W.Arsenal**	D1	A	L	0-3	
1906-07	SL	5q **Stockton** (A) 2-0						
		1	12.1.07 **Southampton**	SL	A	L	1-2	Soar
1907-08	SL	1	11.1.08 **Gainsborough T**	D2	A	L	0-1	
1908-09	SL	5q **West Stanley** (H) 4-1						
		1	16.1.09 **Leicester F**	D1	H	D	1-1	Cleaver
		1r	20.1.09 **Leicester F**		A	L	1-3	Maclaine
1909-10	SL	4q **Bromley** (H) 8-1; 5q **Wycombe W** (A) 4-0						
		1	15.1.10 **W.Arsenal**	D1	A	L	0-3	
1910-11	SL	4q **Ilford** (H) 3-2; 5q **Clapton** (H) 6-0						
		1	14.1.11 **Barnsley**	D2	H	L	0-2	
1911-12	SL	4q **Custom House** (A) 5-0; 5q **Barrow** (H) 2-2; 5qr **Barrow** (A) 2-1						
		1	13.1.12 **Wolverhampton W**	D2	H	D	0-0	
		1r	24.1.12 **Wolverhampton W**		A	L	0-10	
1912-13	SL	4q **Brentford** (A) 0-0; 4qr **Brentford** (H) 5-1; 5q **Chesterfield** (A) 1-3						
1913-14	SL	4q **Bournemouth FC** (H) 10-0; 5q **Gillingham** (A) 0-1						
1914-15	SL	6q **Rochdale** (A) 0-2						
1919-20	SL	6q **Southend U** (A) 0-1						
1920-21	D3	1	8.1.21 **Exeter C**	D3	H	W	3-0	Hoddinott 2, Waterall
		2	29.1.21 **Preston NE**	D1	A	L	1-4	Hoddinott
1921-22	3S	1	7.1.22 **Blackpool**	D2	A	W	2-1	Pagnam 2
		2	28.1.22 **Tottenham H**	D1	A	L	0-1	
1922-23	3S	1	13.1.23 **Cardiff C**	D1	A	D	1-1	Pagnam
		1r	17.1.23 **Cardiff C**		H	D	2-2	Smith, Pagnam
		1 2r	22.1.23 **Cardiff C** at Villa Park			L	1-2	Stephenson
1923-24	3S	1	12.1.24 **Middlesbrough**	D1	A	W	1-0	Stephenson
		2	2.2.24 **Exeter C**	3S	A	D	0-0	
		2r	7.2.24 **Exeter C**		H	W	1-0	Poole
		3	23.2.24 **Newcastle U**	D1	H	L	0-1	
1924-25	3S	1	10.1.25 **Brighton & HA**	3S	H	D	1-1	C.White
		1r	14.1.25 **Brighton & HA**		A	L	3-4	Andrews, Pagnam, Prior
1925-26	3S	1	28.11.25 **Brighton & HA**	3S	A	D	1-1	Pagnam
		1r	2.12.25 **Brighton & HA**		H	W	2-0	Prior, Swan
		2	12.12.25 **Swansea T**	D2	A	L	2-3	Pagnam, Prior
1926-27	3S	1	27.11.26 **Lowestoft T**	N&S	H	W	10-1	Warner 3, Foster og, Swan 3, Fletcher, Daniels, Edmonds
		2	11.12.26 **Brighton & HA**	3S	H	L	0-1	
1927-28	3S	1	30.11.27 **Brighton & HA**	3S	H	L	1-2	Parker
1928-29	3S	1	24.11.28 **Leyton**	AL	A	W	2-0	McPherson, Barnett
		2	8.12.28 **Merthyr T**	3S	H	W	2-0	Barnett, McPherson
		3	12.1.29 **Preston NE**	D2	H	W	1-0	Barnett
		4	26.1.29 **Bournemouth**	3S	A	L	4-6	Barnett 2, Sheppard 2
1929-30	3S	1	30.11.29 **Ilford**	IL	A	W	3-0	McPherson 3
		2	14.12.29 **Plymouth A**	3S	H	D	1-1	Woodward
		2r	18.12.29 **Plymouth A**		A	L	0-3	
1930-31	3S	1	29.11.30 **Walthamstow Ave**	AL	A	W	5-1	James 3, Woolliscroft, Lindsay
		2	13.12.30 **Luton T**	3S	H	W	3-1	James, Woolliscroft, Barnett
		3	10.1.31 **Oldham A**	D2	A	W	3-1	Barnett, Miller, James
		4	26.1.31 **Brighton & HA**	3S	H	W	2-0	James 2
		5	14.2.31 **Birmingham**	D1	A	L	0-3	
1931-32	3S	1	28.11.31 **Thames**	3S	A	D	2-2	White 2
		1r	2.12.31 **Thames**		H	W	2-1	Lowe, Barnett
		2	12.12.31 **Gainsborough T**	ML	A	W	5-2	White 3, Lowe 2
		3	9.1.32 **Fulham**	3S	H	D	1-1	Woodward

		3r	14.1.32	**Fulham**		A	W	3-0	Lowe, James, O'Brien (p)es
		4	23.1.32	**Bristol C**	D2	H	W	2-1	Lowe, Barnett
		5	13.2.32	**Bradford PA**	D2	H	W	1-0	James
		6	27.2.32	**Newcastle U**	D1	A	L	0-5	
1932-33	3S	3	14.1.33	**Southend U**	3S	H	D	1-1	James
		3r	18.1.33	**Southend U**		A	L	0-2	
1933-34	3S	1	25.11.33	**Reading**	3S	H	L	0-3	
1934-35	3S	1	24.11.34	**Corinthians**		H	W	2-0	O'Brien, Rattray
		2	8.12.34	**Walsall**	3N	H	D	1-1	Carter
		2r	13.12.34	**Walsall**		A	L	0-1	
1935-36	3S	1	30.11.35	**Nunhead**	IL	A	W	4-2	Wright 2, Barnett, Fletcher
		2	14.12.35	**Rotherham U**	3N	A	D	1-1	Fletcher
		2r	18.12.35	**Rotherham U**		H	W	1-0	Devan
		3	11.1.36	**Southall**	AL	A	W	4-1	Barnett 3, Fletcher
		4	25.1.36	**Leicester C**	D2	A	L	3-6	McPherson 3 (1p)
1936-37	3S	1	28.11.36	**Ipswich T**	SL	A	L	1-2	Davies (p)
1937-38	3S	1	27.11.37	**Cheltenham T**	SL	H	W	3-0	Wipfler, Lewis, Jones
		2	11.12.37	**Walsall**	3S	H	W	3-0	Barnett, Johnson, Walters
		3	8.1.38	**Sunderland**	D1	A	L	0-1	
1938-39	3S	1	26.11.38	**Northampton T**	3S	H	W	4-1	Jones, Barnett, Davies, Evans
		2	10.12.38	**Scunthorpe U**	ML	A	W	2-1	Dunderdale, Jones
		3	7.1.39	**Tottenham H**	D2	A	L	1-7	Dunderdale
1945-46	3S	1 1L	17.11.45	**Southend U**	3S	H	D	1-1	Davies
		1 2L	24.11.45	**Southend U**		A	W	3-0	Lewis 2, Gray
		2 1L	8.12.45	**Bromley**	AL	A	W	3-1	Jezzard, Sheen og, Gray
		2 2L	15.12.45	**Bromley**		H	D	1-1	Gray
		3 1L	5.1.46	**Nottingham F**	D2	A	D	1-1	Blagg og
		3 2L	9.1.46	**Nottingham F**		H	D	1-1aet	Lewis
		3r	16.1.46	**Nottingham F** at Tottenham			W	1-0aet	Blagg og
		4 1L	26.1.46	**Birmingham C**	D2	A	L	0-5	
		4 2L	30.1.46	**Birmingham C**		H	D	1-1	Gray
1946-47	3S	1	30.11.46	**Wellington T**	CC	A	D	1-1	Dunderdale
		1r	4.12.46	**Wellington T**		H	W	1-0	Dunderdale
		2	14.12.46	**Port Vale**	3S	H	D	1-1	Beckett
		2r	17.12.46	**Port Vale**		A	L	1-2	R Evans
1947-48	3S	1	29.11.47	**Torquay U**	3S	H	D	1-1aet	Usher
		1r	6.12.47	**Torquay U**		A	L	0-3	
1948-49	3S	1	27.11.48	**Leytonstone**	IL	A	–	1-1	Nolan
				abandoned after 63 minutes					
		1	4.12.48	**Leytonstone**		A	L	1-2	Leslie
1949-50	3S	1	26.11.49	**Bromley**	AL	A	W	2-1	Hartburn, T.Jones
		2	10.12.49	**Netherfield**	LC	H	W	6-0	Thomas 2, Hartburn, Brown, Oliver (p), K.Richardson og
		3	7.1.50	**Preston NE**	D2	H	D	2-2	Thomas, Oliver
		3r	11.1.50	**Preston NE**		A	W	1-0	Thomas
		4	28.1.50	**Manchester U**	D1	H	L	0-1	
1950-51	3S	1	25.11.50	**Norwich C**	3S	A	L	0-2	
1951-52	3S	1	24.11.51	**Aylesbury U**	Del	A	W	5-0	Thompson 2, Haig 2, Cook
		2	15.12.51	**Hartlepools U**	3N	H	L	1-2	Thompson
1952-53	3S	1	22.11.52	**Leytonstone**	IL	A	W	2-0	Thompson 2
		2	6.12.52	**Walthamstow Ave**	IL	A	D	1-1	Meadows
		2r	10.12.52	**Walthamstow Ave**		H	L	1-2aet	Collins
1953-54	3S	1	21.11.53	**Nuneaton B**	BDL	A	L	0-3	
1954-55	3S	1	20.11.54	**Corby T**	ML	A	W	2-0	P.Walker, E.Smith
		2	11.12.54	**Carlisle U**	3N	A	D	2-2	Cook 2
		2r	15.12.54	**Carlisle U**		H	W	4-1	Cook 2, Adams, Bowie
		3	8.1.55	**Doncaster R**	D2	H	L	1-2	Cook
1955-56	3S	1	19.11.55	**Ramsgate**	KL	H	W	5-3	Hernon, Graham 3, Brown
		2	10.12.55	**Bedford T**	SL	A	L	2-3	Farquhar og, Cook
1956-57	3S	1	17.11.56	**Newport IOW**	Hants	A	W	6-0	Meadows, Graham 2, Walker, Cook 2
		2	8.12.56	**Ipswich T**	3S	H	L	1-3	Graham
1957-58	3S	1	16.11.57	**Plymouth A**	3S	A	L	2-6	Cook, Meadows
1958-59	D4	1	15.11.58	**Reading**	D3	H	D	1-1	Meadows
		1r	19.11.58	**Reading**		A	W	2-0	Gavin, Catleugh
		2	6.12.58	**Torquay U**	D4	A	L	0-2	
1959-60	D4	1	14.11.59	**Cheltenham T**	SL	A	D	0-0	
		1r	17.11.59	**Cheltenham T**		H	W	3-0	Uphill
		2	5.12.59	**Wycombe W**	IL	H	W	5-1	Uphill 2, Holton 2 (1p), McNeice

Season	Div	Round	Date	Opponent		H/A		Score	Scorers
		3	9.1.60	Birmingham C	D1	H	W	2-1	Uphill, Holton
		4	30.1.60	Southampton	D3	A	D	2-2	Holton, Page og
		4r	2.2.60	Southampton		H	W	1-0	Hartle
		5	20.2.60	Sheffield U	D2	A	L	2-3	Holton 2
1960-61	D3	1	5.11.60	Brentford	D3	H	D	2-2	Bunce, Holton
		1r	8.11.60	Brentford		A	W	2-0	Fairbrother, Benning
		2	26.11.60	Crystal P	D4	A	D	0-0	
		2r	29.11.60	Crystal P		H	W	1-0	Bunce
		3	7.1.61	Rotherham U	D2	A	L	0-1	
1961-62	D3	1	4.11.61	Southend U	D3	A	W	2-0	Gregory 2
		2	25.11.61	Romford	SL	A	W	3-1	Harmer (p), Brown, Bunce
		3	6.1.62	Preston NE	D2	A	L	2-3	Nicholas, Fairbrother
1962-63	D3	1	3.11.62	Poole T	SL	H	D	2-2	Howfield, Chung
		1r	6.11.62	Poole T		A	W	2-1	Gregory, Harris
		2	24.11.62	Southend U	D3	A	W	2-0	Harris, Chung
		3	20.2.63	Rotherham U	D2	H	W	2-0	Howfield, Harris
		4	27.2.63	Southampton	D2	A	L	1-3	Ward
1963-64	D3	1	16.11.63	Peterborough U	D3	A	D	1-1	Oliver
		1r	19.11.63	Peterborough U		H	W	2-1aet	Oliver, Livesey
		2	7.12.63	Newport Co	D4	A	L	0-2	
1964-65	D3	1	14.11.64	Reading	D3	A	L	1-3	Nicholas
1965-66	D3	1	13.11.65	Corinthian Casuals	IL	A	W	5-1	Brace 2, Welbourne, Owen 2
		2	4.12.65	Southend U	D3	A	L	1-2	Holton
1966-67	D3	1	26.11.66	Southend U	D4	H	W	1-0	Farrell
		2	7.1.67	Enfield	IL	A	W	4-2	Farrell 2, Melling, Garbett
		3	28.1.67	Liverpool	D1	H	D	0-0	
		3r	1.2.67	Liverpool		A	L	1-3	Melling
1967-68	D3	1	9.12.67	Lowestoft T	ECL	A	W	1-0	Owen
		2	6.1.68	Hereford U	SL	H	W	3-0	Eddy, Hale 2
		3	27.1.68	Sheffield U	D1	H	L	0-1	
1968-69	D3	1	16.11.68	Cheltenham T	SL	A	W	4-0	Eddy (p), Hale, Garbett, Endean
		2	7.12.68	Brentford	D4	H	W	1-0	Garbett
		3	4.1.69	Port Vale	D4	H	W	2-0	Scullion, Endean
		4	25.1.69	Manchester U	D1	A	D	1-1	Scullion
		4r	3.2.69	Manchester U		H	L	0-2	
1969-70	D2	3	3.1.70	Bolton W	D2	A	W	2-1	Endean 2
		4	24.1.70	Stoke C	D1	H	W	1-0	Franks
		5	7.2.70	Gillingham	D3	H	W	2-1	Lugg 2
		6	21.2.70	Liverpool	D1	H	W	1-0	Endean
		SF	14.3.70	Chelsea		D1	L	1-5	Garbett
			played at Tottenham						
1970-71	D2	3	6.1.71	Reading	D3	H	W	5-0	Scullion, Endean 3, Eddy (p)
		4	23.1.71	Oxford U	D2	A	D	1-1	Wigg
		4r	27.1.71	Oxford U		H	L	1-2	Wigg
1971-72	D2	3	15.1.72	Notts Co	D3	H	L	1-4	Wigg
1972-73	D3	1	18.11.72	Guildford C	SL	H	W	4-2	Wigg, Butler, Welbourne, Kenning (p)
		2	9.12.72	Aldershot	D4	H	W	2-0	Lees, Farley
		3	13.1.73	Sheffield U	D1	H	L	0-1	
1973-74	D3	1	24.11.73	Chelmsford C	SL	H	W	1-0	Morrissey
		2	15.12.73	Bournemouth	D3	H	L	0-1	
1974-75	D3	1	23.11.74	Colchester U	D3	H	L	0-1	
1975-76	D4	1	22.11.75	Brighton & HA	D3	H	L	0-3	
1976-77	D4	1	20.11.76	Gillingham	D3	A	W	1-0	Mayes
		2	11.12.76	Hillingdon B	SL	A	W	3-2	Bond (p), Mercer, Coffill
		3	8.1.77	Northwich Victoria	NPL	A	L	2-3	Mercer, Bond
1977-78	D4	1	26.11.77	Hendon	IL	H	W	2-0	Garner, Mercer
		2	17.12.77	Colchester U	D3	H	W	2-0	Jenkins, Mercer
		3	7.1.78	West Ham	D1	A	L	0-1	
1978-79	D3	1	25.11.78	Dagenham	IL	H	W	3-0	Jenkins 3
		2	16.12.78	Southend U	D3	H	D	1-1	Jenkins
		2r	18.12.78	Southend U		A	L	0-1	
1979-80	D2	3	5.1.80	QPR	D2	A	W	2-1	Bolton (p), Rostron
		4	26.1.80	Harlow T	IL	H	W	4-3	Poskett, Patching 2, Bolton
		5	16.2.80	Wolverhampton W	D1	A	W	3-0	Poskett 2, Blissett
		6	8.3.80	Arsenal	D1	H	L	1-2	Poskett
1980-81	D2	3	3.1.81	Colchester U	D3	A	W	1-0	Poskett
		4	24.1.81	Wolverhampton W	D1	H	D	1-1	Armstrong

		4r	27.1.81	Wolverhampton W		A	L	1-2	Poskett
1981-82	D2	3	2.1.82	Manchester U	D1	H	W	1-0	Lohman
		4	23.1.82	West Ham	D1	H	W	2-0	Armstrong, Callaghan
		5	13.2.82	Leicester C	D2	A	L	0-2	
1982-83	D1	3	8.1.83	Plymouth A	D3	H	W	2-0	Rostron, Blissett
		4	29.1.83	Fulham	D2	H	D	1-1	Lohman
		4r	1.2.83	Fulham		A	W	2-1	Lohman, Barnes
		5	19.2.83	A.Villa	D1	A	L	1-4	Blissett (p)
1983-84	D1	3	6.1.84	Luton T	D1	A	D	2-2	Barnes, Johnston (p)
		3r	10.1.84	Luton T		H	W	4-3aet	Callaghan, Reilly, Barnes, Johnston
		4	28.1.84	Charlton A	D2	A	W	2-0	Johnston, Reilly
		5	18.2.84	Brighton & HA	D2	H	W	3-1	Reilly, Johnston, Jackett
		6	10.3.84	Birmingham C	D1	A	W	3-1	Barnes 2, Taylor
		SF	14.4.84	Plymouth A	D3		W	1-0	Reilly
			played at Villa Park						
		F	19.5.84	Everton	D1	WEMBLEY	L	0-2	
1984-85	D1	3	5.1.85	Sheffield U	D2	H	W	5-0	Blissett 4 (1p), Taylor
		4	26.1.85	Grimsby T	D2	A	W	3-1	Blissett 2, Gilligan
		5	4.3.85	Luton T	D1	A	D	0-0	
		5r	6.3.85	Luton T		H	D	2-2aet	Taylor, Terry
		5 2r	9.3.85	Luton T		A	L	0-1	
1985-86	D1	3	4.1.86	Coventry C	D1	A	W	3-1	West 2, Jackett
		4	25.1.86	Manchester C	D1	A	D	1-1	Jackett
		4r	3.2.86	Manchester C		H	D	0-0aet	
		4 2r	6.2.86	Manchester C		A	W	3-1	Smillie, Barnes, Sterling
		5	5.3.86	Bury	D3	H	D	1-1	Barnes
		5r	8.3.86	Bury		A	W	3-0	Callaghan, West, Sterling
		6	11.3.86	Liverpool	D1	A	D	0-0	
		6r	17.3.86	Liverpool		H	L	1-2aet	Barnes
1986-87	D1	3	10.1.87	Maidstone U	GMVC	H	W	3-1	Falco 2, Allen
		4	1.2.87	Chelsea	D1	H	W	1-0	Blissett
		5	21.2.87	Walsall	D3	A	D	1-1	Bardsley
		5r	24.2.87	Walsall		H	D	4-4aet	Jackett (p), Blissett, Barnes 2
		5 2r	2.3.87	Walsall		A	W	1-0	Dornan og
		6	14.3.87	Arsenal	D1	A	W	3-1	Blissett 2, Barnes
		SF	11.4.87	Tottenham H	D1		L	1-4	Allen
			played at Villa Park						
1987-88	D1	3	9.1.88	Hull C	D2	H	D	1-1	Allen
		3r	12.1.88	Hull C		A	D	2-2aet	Jackett (p), Allen
		3 2r	18.1.88	Hull C		H	W	1-0	Allen
		4	30.1.88	Coventry C	D1	A	W	1-0	Senior
		5	20.2.88	Port Vale	D3	A	D	0-0	
		5r	23.2.88	Port Vale		H	W	2-0	Senior, Porter
		6	12.3.88	Wimbledon	D1	A	L	1-2	Allen
1988-89	D2	3	7.1.89	Newcastle U	D1	A	D	0-0	
		3r	10.1.89	Newcastle U		H	D	2-2aet	Redfearn 2 (1p)
		3 2r	16.1.89	Newcastle U		A	D	0-0aet	
		3 3r	18.1.89	Newcastle U		H	W	1-0aet	Roeder og
		4	28.1.89	Derby Co	D1	H	W	2-1	Holden, Redfearn
		5	19.2.89	Nottingham F	D1	H	L	0-3	
1989-90	D2	3	6.1.90	Wigan A	D3	H	W	2-0	Roeder, Hodges
		4	27.1.90	Sheffield U	D2	A	D	1-1	Penrice
		4r	30.1.90	Sheffield U		H	L	1-2	Porter (p)
1990-91	D2	3	5.1.91	Shrewsbury T	D3	A	L	1-4	Falconer
1991-92	D2	3	4.1.92	Swindon T	D2	A	L	2-3	Blissett 2
1992-93	D1	3	2.1.93	Wolverhampton W	D1	H	L	1-4	Nogan

WATFORD ROVERS

Formed 1881. For a brief genealogy of the Watford clubs, see Watford FC

1886-87		1	23.10.86	Swindon T		H	L	0-1	
1887-88		1	15.10.87	Chesham		A	L	2-4	
			FA ordered replay after protest						
		1r	22.10.87	Chesham		H	W	3-1	
		2	5.11.87	Old Carthusians		H	L	1-3	Coles

WATH ATHLETIC

First entered FA Cup: 1899 and took part in the competition until 1934.

1925-26	ML	1	28.11.25	**Chesterfield**	3N	H	L	0-5

WEALDSTONE

Formed 1889. **First entered FA Cup:** 1913. **FA Challenge Trophy and Alliance Premier League Double** 1985 **FA Amateur Cup Winners** 1966. **League clubs beaten:** Hereford U, Reading. **Cup final connection:** Vinny Jones (Wimbledon 1988) and Stuart Pearce (Nottingham Forest 1991) are both former Wealdstone players

1949-50	AL	1	26.11.49	**Port Vale**	3S	A	L	0-1	
1965-66	IL	1	13.11.65	**Millwall**	D3	A	L	1-3	Cooley
1966-67	IL	1	26.11.66	**Nuneaton**	SL	H	L	0-2	
1968-69	IL	1	16.11.68	**St Albans C**	IL	H	D	1-1	Lindsay (p)
		1r	19.11.68	**St Albans C**		A	L	0-1	
1975-76	SL	1	22.11.75	**Aldershot**	D3	A	L	3-4	Duck 2 (1p), Lewis
1976-77	SL	1	20.11.76	**Reading**	D3	A	L	0-1	
1977-78	SL	1	26.11.77	**Hereford U**	D3	H	D	0-0	
		1r	29.11.77	**Hereford U**		A	W	3-2	Ferry 2, Moss
		2	17.12.77	**Reading**	D4	H	W	2-1	Furphy, Duck (p)
		3	7.1.78	**QPR**	D1	A	L	0-4	
1978-79	SL	1	25.11.78	**Enfield**	IL	H	L	0-5	
1979-80	SL	1	24.11.79	**Southend U**	D3	H	L	0-1	
1982-83	APL	1	20.11.82	**Swindon T**	D4	A	L	0-2	
1983-84	APL	1	19.11.83	**Enfield**	APL	H	D	1-1	Graves
		1r	22.11.83	**Enfield**		A	D	2-2aet	Byatt (p), Graves
		1 2r	28.11.83	**Enfield**		H	W	2-0	N.Cordice, Graves
		2	10.12.83	**Colchester U**	D4	A	L	0-4	
1985-86	APL	1	16.11.85	**Reading**	D3	A	L	0-1	
1986-87	GMVC	1	15.11.86	**Swansea C**	D4	H	D	1-1	Wallace
		1r	20.11.86	**Swansea C**		A	–	1-2	Doyle (p)
			abandoned after 54 minutes – waterlogged pitch						
		1r	24.11.86	**Swansea C**		A	L	1-4	Donnellan

WEDNESBURY OLD ATHLETIC

Formed 1874. Played at Wood Green Lane, Wednesbury. Wednesbury OA's 13-0 defeat to Aston Villa in the first round of the 1886-87 competition is still Aston Villa's record win in the competition.

1881-82	1	5.11.81	**Birmingham St G**	H	W	9-1	
	2	3.12.81	**Small Heath Alliance**	H	W	6-0	Morley 3, Roberts, Reeves, 1
	3		bye				
	4	21.1.82	**Aston Villa**	A	W	4-2	G.Woodcock 2, G.Holden, Morl
	5	11.2.82	**Blackburn R**	A	L	1-3	Growcutt
1882-83	1	4.11.82	**Spital, Chesterfield**	A	W	7-1	Morley 3, Woodcock, Growcutt, G.Holden, others 1
	2	18.11.82	**Aston Villa**	A	L	1-4	Morley
1883-84	1	10.11.83	**Birmingham St G**	H	W	5-0	
	2	1.12.83	**Wolverhampton W**	H	W	4-2	Bayliss, Holden, D.Tonks 2
	3	29.12.83	**Aston Villa**	H	L	4-7	Bayliss 2, Holden, E.Tonks
1884-85	1	8.11.84	**Derby Midland**	A	W	2-1	
	2	6.12.84	**WBA**	A	L	2-4	
1885-86	1	31.10.85	**Burton Swifts**	H	W	5-1	
	2	21.11.85	**WBA**	A	L	2-3	Knight, Taylor
1886-87	1	30.10.86	**Aston Villa**	A	L	0-13	
1887-88	1	15.10.87	**WBA**	A	L	1-7	

WEDNESBURY STROLLERS

Formed 1875. Played at Wood Green Lane, Wednesbury and also at The Trapezium Ground.

1878-79	1	2.11.78	**Oxford University**	A	L	0-7	
1879-80	1	8.11.79	**Stafford Road**	A	L	0-2	
1880-81	1	30.10.80	**Aston Villa**	A	L	3-5	
1881-82	1	5.11.81	**Stafford Road**	H	W	3-1	B.Knowles, Bryan, Byrne
	2	24.11.81	**Notts Co**	A	L	3-5	Parker 2, others 1
		FA ordered replay after protest					
	2r	10.12.81	**Notts Co** at Derby Cricket Gd		L	1-11	B.Knowles

WEDNESBURY TOWN

1883-84	1	10.11.83	WBA	A	L	0-2	
1884-85	1	1.11.84	Aston Villa	A	L	1-4	

WELLING UNITED

Formed 1963. **First entered FA Cup:** 1978. Play on Bexley United's old ground

1986-87	GMVC 1	15.11.86	Maidstone U	GMVC	H	D	1-1	Abbott (p)
	1r	24.11.86	Maidstone U		A	L	1-4	Reynolds
1987-88	GMVC 1	23.11.87	Carshalton A	IL	H	W	3-2	Gaston og, Booker, Abbott
	2	5.12.87	Bath C	GMVC	H	L	0-1	
1988-89	GMVC 1	19.11.88	Bromsgrove R	SL	H	W	3-0	Booker, Robbins, White
	2	10.12.88	Bath C	SL	A	D	0-0	
	2r	14.12.88	Bath C		H	W	3-2	Robbins, Burgess, Handford
	3	7.1.89	Blackburn R	D2	H	L	0-1	
1989-90	GMVC 1	18.11.89	Gillingham	D4	A	D	0-0	
	1r	22.11.89	Gillingham		H	W	1-0	Hone
	2	9.12.89	Reading	D3	A	D	0-0	
	2r	13.12.89	Reading		H	D	1-1aet	Glover
	2 2r	19.12.89	Reading		A	D	0-0aet	
	2 3r	22.12.89	Reading		H	L	1-2	Robbins
1990-91	GMVC 1	17.11.90	Swansea C	D3	A	L	2-5	Francis, Robbins
1991-92	GMVC 1	16.11.91	Leyton O	D3	A	L	1-2	Berry

WELLINGBOROUGH TOWN

Formed 1867. **First Entered FA Cup:** 1892. **Cup final connection:** William Brown (Aston Villa 1905) played for Town

1928-29	UCL 1	24.11.28	Bristol R	3S	A	L	1-2	Shipley
1965-66	UCL 1	13.11.65	Aldershot	D4	A	L	1-2	B.Daldy

WELLINGTON ST GEORGES

Entered the FA Cup from 1886-1930

1886-87	1	30.10.86	Derby Junction	H	L	0-1	
1887-88	1	15.10.87	Over Wanderers	A	L	1-3	
1922-23		4q Tranmere R (3N) H 2-1; 5q **Walsall** (3N) A 0-5						

WELLINGTON TOWN

See Telford United

WELTON ROVERS

Formed 1887. **First entered FA Cup:** 1906

1964-65	WL 1	14.11.64	Weymouth	SL	H	D	1-1	Prosser
	1r	18.11.64	Weymouth		A	L	3-4	Henderson 2, Allen
1966-67	WL 1	26.11.66	Bournemouth	D3	A	L	0-3	

WEMBLEY

Formed 1946. **First entered FA Cup:** 1949. Geographically, the nearest senior football ground to Wembley Stadium. Psychologically it's about a million miles away

1980-81	IL 1	22.11.80	Enfield	IL	A	L	0-3

WEST AUCKLAND TOWN

Formed 1893. **First entered FA Cup:** 1905. **FA Amateur Cup:** Runners-up: 1961

1959-60	NL 1	14.11.59	Stockport Co	D4	H	L	2-6	Curtis, Carter
1961-62	NL 1	4.11.61	Barnsley	D3	H	D	3-3	Skelton, Hopper, Bloomfield (p)
	1r	8.11.61	Barnsley		A	L	0-2	

WEST BROMWICH ALBION

Formed 1879. Founder Members of the Football League 1888. **Best FA Cup Performance:** Winners: 1888, 1892, 1931, 1954, 1968. Runners-up: 1886, 1887, 1895, 1912, 1935. In 1931 WBA became the first, club to win promotion from Division Two and the Cup in the same season. **Record FA Cup Win:** 10-1 vs Chatham, 3rd round, 2.3.1889. **Record FA Cup Defeat:** 0-5 vs Leeds United, 4th round, 18.2.1967

1883-84	1	10.11.83	Wednesbury T		H	L 0-2	
1884-85	1	25.10.84	Junction St School, Derby		A	W 7-1	Bayliss 2, G.Bell 2, Aston 2, Loach
	2	6.12.84	Wednesbury OA		H	W 4-2	Aston 2, Woodhall, Taylor og
	3	3.1.85	Aston Villa		A	D 0-0	
	3r	10.1.85	Aston Villa		H	W 3-0	Loach 2, Bayliss
	4	24.1.85	Druids		H	W 1-0	Loach
	5		bye				
	6	21.2.85	Blackburn R		H	L 0-2	
1885-86	1	31.10.85	Aston Unity		H	W 4-1	T.Green 2, Woodhall 2
	2	21.11.85	Wednesbury OA		H	W 3-2	Loach 2, G.Bell
	3		bye				
	4	2.1.86	Wolverhampton W		H	W 3-1	G.Bell, T.Green, Loach
	5	23.1.86	Old Carthusians		H	W 1-0	T.Green
	6	13.2.86	Old Westminsters		H	W 6-0	Bayliss 3, G.Bell 2, Woodhall
	SF	6.3.86	Small Heath			W 4-0	Loach 2, Woodhall 2
			played at Aston Lower Grounds				
	F	3.4.86	Blackburn R			D 0-0	
			played at Kennington Oval				
	Fr	10.4.86	Blackburn R			L 0-2	
			played at The Racecourse, Derby				
1886-87	1	30.10.86	Burton W		H	W 6-0	T.Green 2, Bayliss 2, Holden, Paddock
	2	20.11.86	Derby Junction		A	W 2-1	G.Bell, Roberts
	3		bye				
	4	15.1.87	Birmingham St George's		A	W 1-0	T.Green
	5	29.1.87	Lockwood Brothers		A	1-0aet	Woodhall
			FA ordered match to be replayed after protest				
	5r	12.2.87	Lockwood Brothers at Derby Cricket Gd			2-1	T.Green, Paddock
	6	19.2.87	Notts Co		A	W 4-1	Bayliss 2, T.Green, Woodhall
	SF	5.3.87	Preston NE			W 3-1	Pearson 2, Paddock
			played at Nottingham				
	F	2.4.87	Aston Villa			L 0-2	
			played at Kennington Oval				
1887-88	1	15.10.87	Wednesbury OA		H	W 7-1	Bayliss 3, Wilson 2, Pearson, Horton
	2	5.11.87	Birmingham St Georges		A	W 1-0	Bayliss
	3	26.11.87	Wolverhampton W		H	W 2-1	Bassett, Wilson
	4		bye				
	5	7.1.88	Stoke		H	W 4-1	Bayliss 4
	6	28.1.88	Old Carthusians		H	W 4-2	Pearson 2, Wilson 2
	SF	18.2.88	Derby Junction			W 3-0	Bayliss, Wilson, Woodhall
			played at Stoke				
	F	24.3.88	PRESTON NE			W 2-1	Bayliss, Woodhall
			played at Kennington Oval				
1888-89 D1	1	2.2.89	Small Heath		A	W 3-2	W.Perry, Wilson, Pearson
	2	16.2.89	Burnley	D1	H	W 5-1	Bayliss 2, Bassett, Wilson, W.Perry
	3	2.3.89	Chatham		A	W 10-1	Wilson 3, Bayliss 2, Bassett 2, Timmins, W.Perry, Conquer og
	SF	16.3.89	Preston NE	D1		L 0-1	
			played at Sheffield				
1889-90 D1	1	18.1.90	Accrington	D1	A	L 1-3	Wilson
			FA ordered match to be replayed after protest				
	1r	25.1.90	Accrington		A	L 0-3	
1890-91 D1	1		bye				
	2	31.1.91	Birmingham St G.	FAll	A	W 3-0	Nicholls, Dyer, C.Perry
	3	14.2.91	Sheffield W	FAll	A	W 2-0	Groves, Pearson
	SF	28.2.91	Blackburn R	D1		L 2-3	Groves, Pearson
			played at Stoke				
1891-92 D1	1	16.1.92	Old Westminsters		A	W 3-2	McLeod, Pearson, Reynolds
	2	30.1.92	Blackburn R	D1	H	W 3-1	Pearson 2, Geddes
	3	13.2.92	Sheffield W	FAll	H	W 2-1	C.Perry, Nicholls
	SF	27.2.92	Nottingham F	FAll		D 1-1	Geddes
	SFr	5.3.92	Nottingham F			D 1-1	Bassett
			both matches played at Molineux				

Season	Div	Round	Date	Opponent	Opp Div	Venue	Result	Score	Scorers
		SF2r	9.3.92	Nottingham F			W	6-2	Geddes 3, Bassett, Groves, C.Perry
			played at Derby						
		F	19.3.92	ASTON VILLA	D1		W	3-0	Geddes, Nicholls, Reynolds
			played at Kennington Oval						
1892-93	D1	1	21.1.93	Everton	D1	A	L	1-4	Pearson
1893-94	D1	1	27.1.94	Blackburn R	D1	H	L	2-3	McLeod 2
1894-95	D1	1	2.2.95	Small Heath	D1	A	W	2-1	McLeod, Banks
		2	16.2.95	Sheffield U	D1	A	D	1-1	Bassett
		2r	20.2.95	Sheffield U		H	W	2-1	Hutchinson, Foulke og
		3	2.3.95	Wolverhampton W	D1	H	W	1-0	McLeod
		SF	16.3.95	Sheffield W	D1		W	2-0	Hutchinson, Williams (p)
			played at Derby						
		F	20.4.95	Aston Villa	D1		L	0-1	
			played at Crystal Palace						
1895-96	D1	1	1.2.96	Blackburn R	D1	A	W	2-1	J.Richards, W.Richards
		2	15.2.96	Grimsby T	D2	A	D	1-1	McLeod
		2r	20.2.96	Grimsby T		H	W	3-0	McLeod, W.Richards
		3	29.2.96	Derby Co	D1	A	L	0-1	
1896-97	D1	1	30.1.97	Luton T	SL	A	W	1-0	Flewitt
		2	13.2.97	Liverpool	D1	H	L	1-2	Watson
1897-98	D1	1	29.1.98	New Brighton T	LL	H	W	2-0	Garfield, Flewitt
		2	12.2.98	Sheffield W	D1	H	W	1-0	Flewitt
		3	26.2.98	Nottingham F	D1	H	L	2-3	Williams, Bassett
1898-99	D1	1	28.1.99	South Shore	LL	H	W	8-0	Bassett 3, Jones 2, W.Richards, Garfield, Barrow og
		2	11.2.99	Bury	D1	H	W	2-1	W.Richrads 2
		3	25.2.99	Liverpool	D1	H	L	0-2	
1899-00	D1	1	27.1.00	Walsall	D2	A	D	1-1	Roberts
		1r	1.2.00	Walsall		H	W	6-1	Jones 2, Brett, Roberts, Richards, Simmons
		2	17.2.00	Liverpool	D1	A	D	1-1	Simmons
		2r	21.2.00	Liverpool		H	W	2-1	Dunn, Chadburn
		3	24.2.00	Southampton	SL	A	L	1-2	Simmons
1900-01	D1	1	26.1.01	Manchester C	D1	H	W	1-0	Garfield
		2	23.2.01	W. Arsenal	D2	A	W	1-0	Garfield
		3	23.3.01	Middlesbrough	D2	A	W	1-0	Buck
		SF	8.4.01	Tottenham H	SL		L	0-4	
			played at Villa Park						
1901-02	D2	1	25.1.02	Bury	D1	A	L	1-5	Simmons
1902-03	D1	1	7.2.03	Tottenham H	SL	A	D	0-0	
		1r	11.2.03	Tottenham H		H	L	0-2	
1903-04	D1	1	6.2.04	Nottingham F	D1	H	D	1-1	Simmons
		1r	13.2.04	Nottingham F		A	L	1-3	Smith
1904-05	D2	Int	14.1.05	Leicester F	D2	H	L	2-5	Aston, Pheasant
1905-06	D2	1	13.1.06	Everton	D1	A	L	1-3	Haywood
1906-07	D2	1	12.1.07	Stoke	D1	H	D	1-1	Broad
		1r	17.1.07	Stoke		A	D	2-2aet	Rankin, Randle
		1 2r	21.1.07	Stoke at Villa Park			W	2-0	Pheasant, Dilly (p)
		2	2.2.07	Norwich C	SL	H	W	1-0	Simmons
		3	23.2.07	Derby Co	D1	H	W	2-0	Jordan, Buck
		4	9.3.07	Notts Co	D1	H	W	3-1	Jordan 2, Buck
		SF	23.3.07	Everton	D1		L	1-2	Haywood
			played at Bolton						
1907-08	D2	1	11.1.08	Birmingham	D1	H	D	1-1	Wilcox
		1r	15.1.08	Birmingham		A	W	2-1	Wilcox, Jordan
		2	1.2.08	Southampton	SL	A	L	0-1	
1908-09	D2	1	16.1.09	Bolton W	D2	H	W	3-1	Garraty, Harris (p), Buck
		2	6.2.09	Bradford C	D1	H	L	1-2	Garraty
1909-10	D2	1	15.1.10	Clapton O	D2	H	W	2-0	Pailor 2
		2	5.2.10	Bristol C	D1	A	D	1-1	Pailor
		2r	9.2.10	Bristol C		H	W	4-2	Hewitt 2, Pailor, Simpson
		3	19.2.10	Barnsley	D2	A	L	0-1	
1910-11	D2	1	14.1.11	Fulham	D2	H	W	4-1	Bowser 2, Wollaston, Lloyd
		2	4.2.11	Derby Co	D2	A	L	0-2	
1911-12	D1	1	13.1.12	Tottenham H	D1	H	W	3-0	Bowser, Deacey, Wright
		2	3.2.12	Leeds C	D2	A	W	1-0	Bowser
		3	21.2.12	Sunderland	D1	A	W	2-1	Pailor 2
		4	9.3.12	Fulham	D2	H	W	3-0	Bowser 2, Wright
		SF	30.3.12	Blackburn R	D1		D	0-0	
			played at Liverpool						

			SFr	3.4.12	**Blackburn R**			W	1-0aet	Pailor
				played at Sheffield						
			F	20.4.12	**Barnsley**	D2		D	0-0	
				played at Crystal Palace						
			Fr	24.4.12	**Barnsley**			L	0-1aet	
				played at Sheffield						
1912-13	D1	1		13.1.13	**West Ham**	SL	H	D	1-1	Wright
		1r		16.1.13	**West Ham**		A	D	2-2aet	Gregory, Bowser
		1 2r		22.1.13	**West Ham** at Stamford Bridge			L	0-3	
1913-14	D1	1		10.1.14	**Grimsby T**	D2	H	W	2-0	Edwards, Morris
		2		31.1.14	**Leeds C**	D2	A	W	2-0	Bentley, Jephcott
		3		21.2.14	**Aston Villa**	D1	A	L	1-2	Bowser
1914-15	D1	1		9.1.14	**Hull C**	D2	A	L	0-1	
1919-20	D1	1		10.1.20	**Barnsley**	D2	A	L	0-1	
1920-21	D1	1		8.1.21	**Notts Co**	D2	A	L	0-3	
1921-22	D1	1		7.1.22	**Chelsea**	D1	A	W	4-2	Blagden 2, Davies, Crisp
		2		28.1.22	**Liverpool**	D1	A	W	1-0	Davies
		3		18.2.22	**Notts Co**	D2	H	D	1-1	Davies (p)
		3r		22.2.22	**Notts Co**		A	L	0-2	
1922-23	D1	1		13.1.23	**Stalybridge C**	3N	H	D	0-0	
		1r		17.1.23	**Stalybridge C**		A	W	2-0	Davies, Morris
		2		3.2.23	**Sunderland**	D1	H	W	2-1	Morris, Jones
		3		24.2.23	**Charlton A**	3S	A	L	0-1	
1923-24	D1	1		12.1.24	**Millwall**	3S	A	W	1-0	Carter
		2		2.2.24	**Corinthians**		H	W	5-0	Morris, Reed, Carter, Davies 2 (1p)
		3		23.2.24	**Wolverhampton W**	3N	H	D	1-1	Wilson
		3r		27.2.24	**Wolverhampton W**		A	W	2-0	Wilson, Gregory
		4		8.3.24	**Aston Villa**	D1	H	L	0-2	
1924-25	D1	1		10.1.25	**Luton T**	3S	H	W	4-1	James 3, Wilson
		2		31.1.25	**Preston NE**	D1	H	W	2-0	James, Wilson
		3		21.2.25	**Aston Villa**	D1	H	D	1-1	Carter
		3r		25.2.25	**Aston Villa**		A	W	2-1	Gregory, James
		4		7.3.25	**Sheffield U**	D1	A	L	0-2	
1925-26	D1	3		9.1.26	**Bristol C**	3S	H	W	4-1	Glidden 2 (1p), Carter, Byers
		4		29.1.26	**Aston Villa**	D1	H	L	1-2	Carter
1926-27	D1	3		8.1.27	**Hull C**	D2	A	L	1-2	Howarth
1927-28	D2	3		14.1.28	**Arsenal**	D1	A	L	0-2	
1928-29	D2	3		12.1.29	**Grimsby T**	D2	A	D	1-1	Cookson
		3r		16.1.29	**Grimsby T**		H	W	2-0	Cookson, Chambers
		4		26.1.29	**Middlesbrough**	D2	H	W	1-0	Cookson
		5		16.2.29	**Bradford PA**	D2	H	W	6-0	Cookson 4, Glidden, Carter
		6		2.3.29	**Huddersfield T**	D1	H	D	1-1	Glidden
		6r		6.3.29	**Huddersfield T**		A	L	1-2	Wood
1929-30	D2	3		11.1.30	**Wrexham**	3N	A	L	0-1	
1930-31	D2	3		10.1.31	**Charlton A**	D2	H	D	2-2	Wood, Sandford
		3r		14.1.31	**Charlton A**		A	D	1-1aet	Carter
		3 2r		19.1.31	**Charlton A** at Villa Park			W	3-1	Carter, Wood, WG Richardson
		4		24.1.31	**Tottenham H**	D2	H	W	1-0	Wood
		5		14.2.31	**Portsmouth**	D1	A	W	1-0	WG Richardson
		6		28.2.31	**Wolverhampton W**	D2	H	D	1-1	WG Richardson
		6r		4.3.31	**Wolverhampton W**		A	W	2-1	Wood, WG Richardson
		SF		14.3.31	**Everton**	D2		W	1-0	Glidden
				played at Old Trafford						
		F		25.4.31	**BIRMINGHAM**	D1	WEMBLEY	W	2-1	WG Richardson 2
1931-32	D1	3		9.1.32	**Aston Villa**	D1	H	L	1-2	WG Richardson
1932-33	D1	3		14.1.33	**Liverpool**	D1	H	W	2-0	Wood, WG Richardson
		4		28.1.33	**West Ham**	D2	A	L	0-2	
1933-34	D1	3		13.1.34	**Chelsea**	D1	A	D	1-1	Robbins
		3r		17.1.34	**Chelsea**		H	L	0-1aet	
1934-35	D1	3		12.1.35	**Port Vale**	D2	H	W	2-1	Gale, WG Richardson
		4		26.1.35	**Sheffield U**	D2	H	W	7-1	WG Richardson 3, Sandford 2, Carter, Gale
		5		16.2.35	**Stockport Co**	3N	A	W	5-0	WG Richardson 2, Carter, Gale, Boyes
		6		2.3.35	**Preston NE**	D1	H	W	1-0	Gale
		SF		16.3.35	**Bolton W**	D2		D	1-1	WG Richardson
				played at Elland Road						
		SFr		20.3.35	**Bolton W**			W	2-0	WG Richardson, Sandford (p)
				played at Stoke						

Season	Div	Rd	Date	Opponent		H/A	W/D/L	Score	Scorers
		F	27.4.35	Sheffield W	D1 WEMBLEY		L	2-4	Sandford, Boyes
1935-36	D1	3	11.1.36	Hull C	D2	H	W	2-0	Wood, WG Richardson
		4	29.1.36	Bradford PA	D2	A	D	1-1	Robbins
		4r	3.2.36	Bradford PA		H	D	1-1aet	Sandford (p)
		4 2r	10.2.36	Bradford PA at Old Trafford			L	0-2	
1936-37	D1	3	16.1.37	Spennymoor U	NEL	H	W	7-1	Sandford 2, WG Richardson 2, Wood, Jones, Mahon
		4	30.1.37	Darlington	3N	H	W	3-2	WG Richardson 3
		5	20.2.37	Coventry C	D2	A	W	3-2	Boyes, Mahon 2
		6	6.3.37	Arsenal	D1	H	W	3-1	Mahon 2, WG Richardson
		SF	10.4.37	Preston NE	D1		L	1-4	Robbins
				played at Highbury					
1937-38	D1	3	8.1.38	Newcastle U	D2	H	W	1-0	WG Richardson
		4	22.1.38	York C	3N	A	L	2-3	WG Richardson, Pinder og
1938-39	D2	3	7.1.39	Manchester U	D1	H	D	0-0	
		3r	11.1.39	Manchester U		A	W	5-1	Jones 2, Witcomb, Clarke, WG Richardson
		4	21.1.39	Portsmouth	D1	A	L	0-2	
1945-46	D2	3 1L	5.1.46	Cardiff C	3S	A	D	1-1	Connelly
		3 2L	9.1.46	Cardiff C		H	W	4-0	Clarke 2, Newsome 2
		4 1L	26.1.46	Derby Co	D1	A	L	0-1	
		4 2L	30.1.46	Derby Co		H	L	1-3	Clarke
1946-47	D2	3	11.1.47	Leeds U	D1	H	W	2-1	Barlow, Walsh
		4	25.1.47	Charlton A	D1	H	L	1-2	Elliott
1947-48	D2	3	10.1.48	Reading	3S	H	W	2-0	Finch, Drury
		4	24.1.48	Tottenham H	D1	A	L	1-3	Rowley
1948-49	D2	3	8.1.49	Lincoln C	D2	A	W	1-0	Barlow
		4	29.1.49	Gateshead	3N	A	W	3-1aet	Walsh 2, A.Smith
		5	12.2.49	Chelsea	D1	H	W	3-0	Walsh 3
		6	26.2.49	Wolverhampton W	D1	A	L	0-1	
1949-50	D1	3	7.1.50	Cardiff C	D2	A	D	2-2	C.Williams, Inwood
		3r	11.1.50	Cardiff C		H	L	0-1	
1950-51	D1	3	6.1.51	Derby Co	D1	A	D	2-2	Lee, Barlow
		3r	10.1.51	Derby Co		H	L	0-1	
1951-52	D1	3	12.1.52	Bolton W	D1	H	W	4-0	Lee 2, Allen, Griffin
		4	6.2.52	Gateshead at Newcastle	3N	A	W	2-0	Allen 2
		5	23.2.52	Blackburn R	D2	A	L	0-1	
1952-53	D1	3	10.1.53	West Ham	D2	A	W	4-1	Lee, Ryan, Allen, Nicholls
		4	31.1.53	Chelsea	D1	A	D	1-1	Nicholls
		4r	4.2.53	Chelsea		H	D	0-0aet	
		4 2r	9.2.53	Chelsea at Villa Park			D	1-1aet	Dudley
		4 3r	11.2.53	Chelsea at Highbury			L	0-4	
1953-54	D1	3	9.1.54	Chelsea	D1	H	W	1-0	Greenwood og
		4	30.1.54	Rotherham U	D2	H	W	4-0	Nicholls, Allen, Ryan
		5	20.2.54	Newcastle U	D1	H	W	3-2	Allen 3
		6	13.3.54	Tottenham H	D1	H	W	3-0	Barlow, Nicholls 2
		SF	27.3.54	Port Vale	3N		W	2-1	Dudley, Allen (p)
				played at Villa Park					
		F	1.5.54	PRESTON NE	D1 WEMBLEY		W	3-2	Allen 2 (1p), Griffin
1954-55	D1	3	8.1.55	Bournemouth	3S	A	W	1-0	Williams
		4	29.1.55	Charlton A	D1	H	L	2-4	Williams 2
1955-56	D1	3	7.1.56	Wolverhampton W	D1	A	W	2-1	Griffin, Lee
		4	28.1.56	Portsmouth	D1	H	W	2-0	Lee, Allen (p)
		5	18.2.56	Birmingham C	D1	H	L	0-1	
1956-57	D1	3	5.1.57	Doncaster R	D2	A	D	1-1	Robson
		3r	9.1.57	Doncaster R		H	W	2-0	Allen 2
		4	26.1.57	Sunderland	D1	H	W	4-2	Kevan 2, Horobin, Allen (p)
		5	16.2.57	Blackpool	D1	A	D	0-0	
		5r	20.2.57	Blackpool		H	W	2-1	Kevan, Allen
		6	2.3.57	Arsenal	D1	H	D	2-2	Allen, Wills og
		6r	5.3.57	Arsenal		A	W	2-1	Whitehouse, Kevan
		SF	23.3.57	Aston Villa	D1		D	2-2	Whitehouse 2
				played at Molineux					
		SFr	28.3.57	Aston Villa			L	0-1	
				played at St Andrew's					
1957-58	D1	3	4.1.58	Manchester C	D1	H	W	5-1	Allen 2, Griffin, Barlow, Ewing og
		4	25.1.58	Nottingham F	D1	H	D	3-3	Allen, Kevan, Robson
		4r	28.1.58	Nottingham F		A	W	5-1	Kevan, Whitehouse, Griffin, Robson, Howe (p)
		5	15.2.58	Sheffield U	D2	A	D	1-1	Allen

Season	Div	Round	Date	Opponent	Opp Div	Venue	Result	Score	Scorers
		5r	19.2.58	Sheffield U		H	W	4-1	Kevan 2, Allen (p), Robson
		6	1.3.58	Manchester U	D1	H	D	2-2	Allen, Horobin
		6r	5.3.58	Manchester U		A	L	0-1	
1958-59	D1	3	19.1.59	Sheffield W	D2	A	W	2-0	Jackson, Hogg
		4	24.2.59	Brentford	D3	H	W	2-0	Kevan 2
		5	15.2.59	Blackpool	D1	A	L	1-3	Robson
1959-60	D1	3	9.1.60	Plymouth A	D2	H	W	3-2	Kevan 3
		4	30.1.60	Bolton W	D1	H	W	2-0	Jackson, Burnside
		5	20.2.60	Leicester C	D1	A	L	1-2	Kennedy
1960-61	D1	3	7.1.61	Lincoln C	D2	A	L	1-3	Burnside
1961-62	D1	3	6.1.62	Blackpool	D1	A	D	0-0	
		3r	10.1.62	Blackpool		H	W	2-1	Burnside, Smith
		4	27.1.62	Wolverhampton W	D1	A	W	2-1	Clark 2
		5	17.2.62	Tottenham H	D1	H	L	2-4	Kevan, Smith
1962-63	D1	3	5.1.63	Plymouth A	D2	A	W	5-1	Kevan 2, Smith, Cram, Newman og
		4	6.3.63	Nottingham F	D1	H	D	0-0	
		4r	11.3.63	Nottingham F		A	L	1-2aet	Smith
1963-64	D1	3	4.1.64	Blackpool	D1	H	D	2-2	Clark, Howe (p)
		3r	8.1.64	Blackpool		A	W	1-0	Fenton
		4	25.1.64	Arsenal	D1	H	D	3-3	Fenton, Kaye, Jones
		4r	29.1.64	Arsenal		A	L	0-2	
1964-65	D1	3	9.1.65	Liverpool	D1	H	L	1-2	Astle
1965-66	D1	3	22.1.66	Bolton W	D2	A	L	0-3	
1966-67	D1	3	28.1.67	Northampton T	D2	A	W	3-1	Astle, Clark, Brown
		4	18.2.67	Leeds U	D1	A	L	0-5	
1967-68	D1	3	27.1.68	Colchester U	D3	A	D	1-1	Brown (p)
		3r	31.1.68	Colchester U		H	W	4-0	Astle 2, Kaye, Clark
		4	17.2.68	Southampton	D1	H	D	1-1	Brown
		4r	21.2.68	Southampton		A	W	3-2	Astle 2, Brown
		5	9.3.68	Portsmouth	D2	A	W	2-1	Astle, Clark
		6	30.3.68	Liverpool	D1	H	D	0-0	
		6r	8.4.68	Liverpool		A	D	1-1aet	Astle
		6 2r	18.4.68	Liverpool at Maine Road			W	2-1	Astle, Clark
		SF	27.4.68	Birmingham C	D2		W	2-0	Astle, Brown
			played at Villa Park						
		F	18.5.68	EVERTON	D1	WEMBLEY	W	1-0aet	Astle
1968-69	D1	3	4.1.69	Norwich C	D2	H	W	3-0	Rees, Astle (p), Forbes
		4	25.1.69	Fulham	D2	A	W	2-1	Hartford, Rees
		5	12.2.69	Arsenal	D1	H	W	1-0	Brown
		6	1.3.69	Chelsea	D1	A	W	2-1	Brown, Astle
		SF	29.3.69	Leicester C	D1		L	0-1	
			played at Hillsborough						
1969-70	D1	3	3.1.70	Sheffield W	D1	A	L	1-2	Brown
1970-71	D1	3	2.1.71	Scunthorpe U	D4	H	D	0-0	
		3r	11.1.71	Scunthorpe U		A	W	3-1	Brown 2, Astle
		4	23.1.71	Ipswich T	D1	H	D	1-1	Suggett
		4r	26.1.71	Ipswich T		A	L	0-3	
1971-72	D1	3	15.1.72	Coventry C	D1	H	L	1-2	Brown
1972-73	D1	3	13.1.73	Nottingham F	D2	H	D	1-1	Winfield og
		3r	16.1.73	Nottingham F		A	–	1-1	Hartford
			abandoned after 80 minutes – fog						
		3r	22.1.73	Nottingham F		A	D	0-0aet	
		3 2r	29.1.73	Nottingham F at Filbert Street			W	3-1	Cantello, Hartford, Suggett
		4	3.2.73	Swindon T	D2	H	W	2-0	T.Brown, Cantello
		5	24.2.73	Leeds U	D1	A	L	0-2	
1973-74	D2	3	5.1.74	Notts Co	D2	H	W	4-0	T.Brown 3, Johnston
		4	27.1.74	Everton	D1	A	D	0-0	
		4r	30.1.74	Everton		H	W	1-0	T.Brown
		5	16.2.74	Newcastle U	D1	H	L	0-3	
1974-75	D2	3	4.1.75	Bolton W	D2	A	D	0-0	
		3r	8.1.75	Bolton W		H	W	4-0	Cantello, Wile, Shaw, Mayo
		4	25.1.75	Carlisle U	D1	A	L	2-3	T.Brown (p), Nisbett
1975-76	D2	3	3.1.76	Carlisle U		H	W	3-1	T.Brown 2 (1p), A.Brown
		4	24.1.76	Lincoln C	D4	H	W	3-2	T.Brown, Martin, B.Robson
		5	14.2.76	Southampton	D2	H	D	1-1	T.Brown
		5r	17.2.76	Southampton		A	L	0-4	
1976-77	D1	3	8.1.77	Manchester C	D1	A	D	1-1	Johnston

		3r	11.1.77	Manchester C		H	L	0-1	
1977-78	D1	3	7.1.78	Blackpool	D2	H	W	4-1	Johnston 2, Regis, T.Brown (p)
		4	28.1.78	Manchester U	D1	A	D	1-1	Johnston
		4r	1.2.78	Manchester U		H	W	3-2aet	Regis 2, T.Brown
		5	22.2.78	Derby Co	D1	A	W	3-2	Regis 2, Johnston
		6	11.3.78	Nottingham F	D1	H	W	2-0	Martin, Regis
		SF	8.4.78	Ipswich T	D1		L	1-3	T.Brown (p)
				played at Highbury					
1978-79	D1	3	9.1.79	Coventry C	D1	A	D	2-2	Cunningham, A.Brown
		3r	15.1.79	Coventry C		H	W	4-0	Batson, T.Brown 2, A.Brown
		4	26.2.79	Leeds U at the Hawthorns	D1	A	D	3-3	Cunningham, A.Brown, Regis
		4r	1.3.79	Leeds U		H	W	2-0aet	Wile, A.Brown
		5	10.3.79	Southampton	D1	H	D	1-1	A.Brown
		5r	12.3.79	Southampton		A	L	1-2aet	Cunningham
1979-80	D1	3	5.1.80	West Ham	D2	H	D	1-1	Regis
		3r	8.1.80	West Ham		A	L	1-2	T.Brown
1980-81	D1	3	3.1.81	Grimsby T	D2	H	W	3-0	B.Robson, Cowdrill, Barnes
		4	24.1.81	Middlesbrough	D1	A	L	0-1	
1981-82	D1	3	2.1.82	Blackburn R	D2	H	W	3-2	Whitehead, Mackenzie, King (p)
		4	23.1.82	Gillingham	D3	A	W	1-0	Statham
		5	13.2.82	Norwich C	D2	H	W	1-0	Regis
		6	6.3.82	Coventry C	D1	H	W	2-0	Regis, Owen
		SF	3.4.82	QPR	D2		L	0-1	
				played at Highbury					
1982-83	D1	3	8.1.83	QPR		H	W	3-2	Owen 2 (1p), Eastoe
		4	29.1.83	Tottenham H	D1	A	L	1-2	Whitehead
1983-84	D1	3	3.1.84	Rotherham U	D3	A	D	0-0	
		3r	11.1.84	Rotherham U		H	W	3-0	Thompson, Morley 2
		4	1.2.84	Scunthorpe U	D3	H	W	1-0	Forsyth
		5	18.2.84	Plymouth A	D3	H	L	0-1	
1984-85	D1	3	5.1.85	Orient	D3	A	L	1-2	Cross
1985-86	D1	3	13.1.86	Sheffield W	D1	A	D	2-2	Reilly, Statham
		3r	16.1.86	Sheffield W		H	L	2-3	Hunt, Thomas
1986-87	D2	3	10.1.87	Swansea C	D4	A	L	2-3	Anderson, Lewis og
1987-88	D2	3	9.1.88	Wimbledon	D1	A	L	1-4	Thorn og
1988-89	D2	3	7.1.89	Everton	D1	H	D	1-1	Anderson
		3r	11.1.89	Everton		A	L	0-1	
1989-90	D2	3	6.1.90	Wimbledon	D1	H	W	2-0	G.Robson, Bartlett
		4	27.1.90	Charlton A	D1	H	W	1-0	Ford
		5	17.2.90	Aston Villa	D1	H	L	0-2	
1990-91	D2	3	5.1.91	Woking	IL	L	L	2-4	West, Bradley
1991-92	D3	1	16.11.91	Marlow	IL	H	W	6-0	Strodder, Goodman, Shakespeare 2 (1p), McNally, Robson
		2	9.12.91	Leyton O	D3	A	L	1-2	Williams
1992-93	D2	1	14.11.92	Aylesbury	IL	H	W	8-0	Donovan 3, McNally, Taylor, G.Robson, Raven, Hamilton
		2	6.12.92	Wycombe W	GMVC	A	D	2-2	Bradley, Taylor
		2r	15.12.92	Wycombe W		H	W	1-0	Taylor
		3	2.1.93	West Ham	D1	H	L	0-2	

WEST END

Formed 1868. Home games were played at Wormholt Farm, Uxbridge near the Princess Alice pub in Uxbridge Road, West London.

1879-80	1			Swifts			walkover		
	2	13.12.79	Hotspur		H	W	1-0		
	3		bye						
	4	7.2.80	Old Etonians		A	L	1-5	Elmslie	
1880-81	1	6.11.80	Hanover U		H	W	1-0	Harkness	
	2	11.12.80	Marlow		A	L	0-4		
1881-82	1	29.10.81	Remnants		H	W	3-2	Elmslie 2, Black	
	2	26.11.81	Reading		A	D	1-1		
			Reading				disqualified		
1882-83	1	4.11.82	Hendon		H	L	1-3		
1883-84	1	10.11.83	Maidenhead		A	W	1-0	Cooper	
	2	1.12.83	Reading		A	L	0-1		
1884-85	1	8.11.84	Upton Park		H	D	3-3		
	1r		Upton Park				scratched		

WEST HAM UNITED

Formed 1895 as Thames Ironworks. 1900 West Ham United. **Best FA Cup Performance:** Winners: 1964, 1975, 1980. Runners-up: 1923.
Record FA Cup Win: 8-1 vs Chesterfield, 1st round, 10.1.1914. **Record FA Cup Defeat:** 0-5 vs Aston Villa, 2nd round, 1.2.1913; 0-5 vs
Tottenham H, 3rd round, 9.1.1926; 1-6 vs QPR, 31.1.1978

as Thames Ironworks

1897-98	LL	P **Redhill** (H) 3-0; 1q **Royal Engineers Training Batt** (H) 2-1; 2q **St Albans** (A) 0-2					
1898-99	SL	1q **Royal Engineers TB** (H) 2-0; 2q **Brighton U** (A) 0-0; 2qr **Brighton U** (H) 1-4					
1899-00	SL	P **Royal Engineers** (H) 6-0; 1q **Grays U** (A) 4-0; 2q **Sheppey U** (H) 4-2; 3q **Dartford** (A) 7-0; 4q **New Brompton** (A) 0-0; 4qr **New Brompton** (H) 2-0; 5q **Millwall A** (H) 1-2					

as West Ham United

1900-01	SL	3q **Olympic FC** (H) 1-0; 4q **New Brompton** (A) 1-1; 4qr **New Brompton** (H) 4-1; 5q **Clapton** (H) 1-1; 5qr **Clapton** (A) 3-2; Int **Liverpool** (H) 0-1					
1901-02	SL	3q **Leyton** (A) 1-0; 4q **Grays U** (H) 1-2					
1902-03	SL	Int **Lincoln C** (A) 0-2					
1903-04	SL	3q **Brighton & HA** (H) 4-0; 4q **Clapton** (A) 3-0; 5q **Chatham** (A) 5-0; Int.**Fulham** (H) 0-1					
1904-05	SL	6q **Brighton & HA** (H) 1-2					
1905-06	SL	1	13.1.06	**W.Arsenal**	D1	A	D	1-1	Kitchen
		1r	18.1.06	**W.Arsenal**		H	L	2-3	Bridgeman, Watson
1906-07	SL	1	12.1.07	**Blackpool**	D2	H	W	2-1	Stapley, Winterhalder
		2	2.2.07	**Everton**	D1	H	L	1-2	Stapley
1907-08	SL	1	11.1.08	**Rotherham T**	ML	H	W	1-0	Blackburn
		2	1.2.08	**Newcastle U**	D1	A	L	0-2	
1908-09	SL	1	16.1.09	**QPR**	SL	A	D	0-0	
		1r	20.1.09	**QPR**		H	W	1-0	Shea
		2	6.2.09	**Leeds C**	D2	A	D	1-1	Miller
		2r	11.2.09	**Leeds C**		H	W	2-1aet	Shea 2
		3	20.2.09	**Newcastle U**	D1	H	D	0-0	
		3r	24.2.09	**Newcastle U**		A	L	1-2	Shea
1909-10	SL	1	15.1.10	**Carlisle U**	LC	H	D	1-1	Blackburn
		1r	20.1.10	**Carlisle U**		H	W	5-0	Blackburn 2, Shea, Webb, Randall
		2	5.2.10	**Wolverhampton W**	D2	A	W	5-1	Shea 2, Webb 3
		3	19.2.10	**QPR**	SL	A	D	1-1	Webb
		3r	24.2.10	**QPR**		H	L	0-1	
1910-11	SL	1	14.1.11	**Nottingham F**	D1	H	W	2-1	Shea 2
		2	4.2.11	**Preston NE**	D1	H	W	3-0	Webb 3
		3	25.2.11	**Manchester U**	D1	H	W	2-1	Shea, Caldwell
		4	11.3.11	**Blackburn R**	D1	H	L	2-3	Butcher 2
1911-12	SL	1	3.1.12	**Gainsborough T**	D2	H	W	2-1	Webb, Harrison
		2	3.2.12	**Middlesbrough**	D1	A	D	1-1	Harrison
		2r	8.2.12	**Middlesbrough**		H	W	2-1	Ashton, Harrison
		3	24.2.12	**Swindon T**	SL	H	D	1-1	Butcher
		3r	28.2.12	**Swindon T**		A	L	0-4	
1912-13	SL	1	13.1.13	**WBA**	D1	A	D	1-1	Harrison
		1r	16.1.13	**WBA**		H	D	2-2aet	Hilsdon 2
		1 2r	22.1.13	**WBA** at Stamford Bridge			W	3-0	Hilsdon 2, Denyer
		2	1.2.13	**Aston Villa**	D1	A	L	0-5	
1913-14	SL	1	10.1.14	**Chesterfield**	ML	H	W	8-1	Puddefoot 5, Bailey, Leafe, Ashton
		2	31.1.14	**Crystal P**	SL	H	W	2-0	Bailey 2
		3	21.1.14	**Liverpool**	D1	H	D	1-1	Puddefoot
		3r	25.1.14	**Liverpool**		A	L	1-5	Puddefoot
1914-15	SL	1	9.1.15	**Newcastle U**	D1	H	D	2-2	Leafe 2
		1r	16.1.15	**Newcastle U**		A	L	2-3	Casey, Leafe
1919-20	D2	1	10.1.20	**Southampton**	SL	A	D	0-0	
		1r	15.1.20	**Southampton**		H	W	3-1	Puddefoot 2, Butcher
		2	31.1.20	**Bury**	D2	H	W	6-0	Puddefoot 3, Bailey, Butcher, Smith
		3	21.2.20	**Tottenham H**	D2	A	L	0-3	
1920-21	D2	1	8.1.21	**Sheffield W**	D2	A	L	0-1	
1921-22	D2	1	7.1.22	**Swansea T**	3S	A	D	0-0	
		1r	11.1.22	**Swansea T**		H	D	1-1aet	Watson
		1 2r	16.1.22	**Swansea T** at Ashton Gate			L	0-1	
1922-23	D2	1	13.1.23	**Hull C**	D2	H	W	3-2	Watson 2, Moore
		2	3.2.23	**Brighton & HA**	3S	A	D	1-1	Watson
		2r	7.2.23	**Brighton & HA**		H	W	1-0	Moore
		3	24.2.23	**Plymouth A**	3S	H	W	2-0	Moore, Richards
		4	10.3.23	**Southampton**	D2	A	D	1-1	Watson

	4r	14.3.23	**Southampton**		H	D	1-1aet	Watson
	4 2r	19.3.23	**Southampton** at Villa Park				1-0	Brown
	SF	24.3.23	**Derby Co**	D2		W	5-2	Brown 2, Moore 2, Ruffell
			played at Stamford Bridge					
	F	28.4.23	**Bolton W**	D1	WEMBLEY L		0-2	
1923-24 D1	1	12.1.24	**Aberdare A**	3S	H	W	5-0	Brown 2, Henderson, Moore, Williams
	2	2.2.24	**Leeds U**	D2	H	D	1-1	Kay
	2r	6.2.24	**Leeds U**		A	L	0-1	
1924-25 D1	1	14.1.25	**Arsenal**	D1	H	D	0-0	
	1r	21.1.25	**Arsenal**		A	D	2-2aet	Ruffell 2
	1 2r	26.1.25	**Arsenal** at Stamford Bridge			W	1-0	Kay
	2	31.1.25	**Nottingham F**	D1	A	W	2-0	Ruffell, Yews
	3	21.2.25	**Blackpool**	D2	H	D	1-1	Watson
	3r	25.2.25	**Blackpool**		A	L	0-3	
1925-26 D1	3	9.1.26	**Tottenham H**	D1	A	L	0-5	
1926-27 D1	3	8.1.27	**Tottenham H**	D1	H	W	3-2	Watson 3
	4	29.1.27	**Brentford**	3S	H	D	1-1	Ruffell
	4r	2.2.27	**Brentford**		A	L	0-2	
1927-28 D1	3	14.1.28	**Portsmouth**	D1	A	W	2-0	Gibbins, Ruffell
	4	28.1.28	**Huddersfield T**	D1	A	L	1-2	Gibbins
1928-29 D1	3	12.1.29	**Sunderland**	D1	H	W	1-0	Earle
	4	26.1.29	**Corinthians**		H	W	3-0	Earle, Watson, Hughes
	5	16.2.29	**Bournemouth**	3S	A	D	1-1	Yews
	5r	20.2.29	**Bournemouth**		H	W	3-1	Barrett, Yews, og
	6	2.3.29	**Portsmouth**	D1	A	L	2-3	Barrett 2
1929-30 D1	3	11.1.30	**Notts Co**	D2	H	W	4-0	Watson 2, Barrett, Gibbins
	4	25.1.30	**Leeds U**	D1	H	W	4-1	Watson 4
	5	15.2.30	**Millwall**	D2	H	W	4-1	Watson 2, Gibbins, Yews
	6	1.3.30	**Arsenal**	D1	A	L	0-3	
1930-31 D1	3	10.1.31	**Chelsea**	D1	H	L	1-3	Gibbins
1931-32 D1	3	9.1.32	**Charlton A**	D2	A	W	2-1	Watson 2
	4	23.1.32	**Chelsea**	D1	A	L	1-3	Weldon
1932-33 D2	3	14.1.33	**Corinthians**		A	W	2-0	Pollard, Watson
	4	28.1.33	**WBA**	D1	H	W	2-0	Watson, Wilson
	5	18.2.33	**Brighton & HA**	3S	A	D	2-2	Musgrave, Watson
	5r	22.2.33	**Brighton & HA**		H	W	1-0	Morton
	6	4.3.33	**Birmingham**	D1	H	W	4-0	Wilson, Morton, Pollard, Barkas og
	SF	18.3.33	**Everton** at Molineux	D1		L	1-2	Watson
1933-34 D2	3	13.1.34	**Bradford C**	D2	H	W	3-2	Watson 2, Goulden
	4	27.1.34	**Tottenham H**	D1	A	L	1-4	Watson
1934-35 D2	3	12.1.35	**Stockport Co**	3N	H	D	1-1	Mills
	3r	16.1.35	**Stockport Co**		A	L	0-1	
1935-36 D2	3	11.1.36	**Luton T**	3S	H	D	2-2	Mangnall, Ruffell
	3r	15.1.36	**Luton T**		A	L	0-4	
1936-37 D2	3	16.1.37	**Bolton W**	D1	H	D	0-0	
	3r	20.1.37	**Bolton W**		A	L	0-1	
1937-38 D2	3	8.1.38	**Preston NE**	D1	A	L	0-3	
1938-39 D2	3	7.1.39	**QPR**	D3	A	W	2-1	Foxall, Morton
	4	21.1.39	**Tottenham H**	D2	H	D	3-3	Foxall 2, Macauley
	4r	30.1.39	**Tottenham H**		A	D	1-1aet	Foxall
	4 2r	2.2.39	**Tottenham H** at Highbury			W	2-1	Foxall, Macauley
	5	11.2.39	**Portsmouth**	D1	A	L	0-2	
1945-46 D2	3 1L	5.1.46	**Arsenal**	D1	H	W	6-0	Hall 2, Wood 2, Bainbridge, Foreman
	3 2L	9.1.46	**Arsenal**		A	L	0-1	
	4 1L	26.1.46	**Chelsea**	D1	A	L	0-2	
	4 2L	30.1.46	**Chelsea**		H	W	1-0	Hall
1946-47 D2	3	11.1.47	**Leicester C**	D2	H	L	1-2	Woodgate
1947-48 D2	3	10.1.48	**Blackburn R**	D1	A	D	0-0	
	3r	17.1.48	**Blackburn R**		H	L	2-4	Parsons, Stephens
1948-49 D2	3	8.1.49	**Luton T**	D2	A	L	1-3	Wade
1949-50 D2	3	7.1.50	**Ipswich T**	3S	H	W	5-1	Woodgate 2, Gazzard, Wade, Robinson
	4	28.1.50	**Everton**	D1	H	L	1-2	McGowan
1950-51 D2	3	6.1.51	**Cardiff C**	D2	H	W	2-1	Barrett, Gazzard
	4	27.1.51	**Stoke C**	D1	A	L	0-1	
1951-52 D2	3	12.1.52	**Blackpool**	D1	H	W	2-1	Andrews, O'Farrell
	4	2.2.52	**Sheffield U**	D2	H	D	0-0	
	4r	6.2.52	**Sheffield U**		A	L	2-4	Woodgate, Gazzard

Season	Div	Rd	Date	Opponent	OppDiv	Venue	Res	Score	Scorers
1952-53	D2	3	10.1.53	WBA	D1	H	L	1-4	Kearns
1953-54	D2	3	9.1.54	Huddersfield T	D1	H	W	4-0	Hooper 2, Sexton, Dixon
		4	30.1.54	Blackpool	D1	H	D	1-1	Dixon
		4r	3.2.54	Blackpool		A	L	1-3	Sexton
1954-55	D2	3	8.1.55	Port Vale	D2	H	D	2-2	Bennett, Hooper
		3r	10.1.55	Port Vale		A	L	1-3	Hooper
1955-56	D2	3	7.1.56	Preston NE	D1	H	W	5-2	Foan 3, Dare 2
		4	28.1.56	Cardiff C	D1	H	W	2-1	Dare, Dick
		5	18.2.56	Blackburn R	D2	H	D	0-0	
		5r	28.2.56	Blackburn R		A	W	3-2	Dick 2, Hooper
		6	3.3.56	Tottenham H	D1	A	D	3-3	Dick 3
		6r	8.3.56	Tottenham H		H	L	1-2	Dare
1956-57	D2	3	5.1.57	Grimsby T	D2	H	W	5-3	Smith 2, Lewis, Dick, Musgrove
		4	26.1.57	Everton	D1	A	L	1-2	Dare
1957-58	D2	3	4.1.58	Blackpool	D1	H	W	5-1	Keeble 3, Dick 2
		4	25.1.58	Stockport Co	3N	H	W	3-2	Lewis 2, Keeble
		5	15.2.58	Fulham	D2	H	L	2-3	Grice, Bond
1958-59	D1	3	10.1.59	Tottenham H	D1	A	L	0-2	
1959-60	D1	3	9.1.60	Huddersfield T	D2	A	D	1-1	Dick
		3r	13.1.60	Huddersfield T		H	L	1-5	Musgrove
1960-61	D1	3	7.1.61	Stoke C	D2	H	D	2-2	Dunmore, Dick
		3r	11.1.61	Stoke C		A	L	0-1	
1961-62	D1	3	6.1.62	Plymouth A	D2	A	L	0-3	
1962-63	D1	3	4.2.63	Fulham	D1	H	D	0-0	
		3r	20.2.63	Fulham		A	W	2-1	Boyce, Byrne
		4	4.3.63	Swansea T	D2	H	W	1-0	Boyce
		5	16.3.63	Everton	D1	H	W	1-0	Byrne
		6	30.3.63	Liverpool	D1	A	L	0-1	
1963-64	D1	3	4.1.64	Charlton A	D2	H	W	3-0	Hurst, Brabrook, Sissons
		4	25.1.64	Leyton O	D2	A	D	1-1	Brabrook
		4r	29.1.64	Leyton O		H	W	3-0	Hurst 2, Byrne
		5	15.2.64	Swindon T	D2	A	W	3-1	Hurst 2, Byrne
		6	29.2.64	Burnley	D1	H	W	3-2	Byrne 2, Sissons
		SF	14.3.64	Manchester U	D1		W	3-1	Boyce 2, Hurst
				played at Hillsborough					
		F	2.5.64	PRESTON NE	D2	WEMBLEY	W	3-2	Sissons, Hurst, Boyce
1964-65	D1	3	9.1.65	Birmingham C	D1	H	W	4-2	Hurst 2, Byrne, Sissons
		4	30.1.65	Chelsea	D1	H	L	0-1	
1965-66	D1	3	22.1.66	Oldham A	D3	A	D	2-2	Burnett, Hurst
		3r	24.1.66	Oldham A		H	W	2-1	Hurst, Brabrook
		4	12.2.66	Blackburn R	D1	H	D	3-3	Bloomfield, Hurst, Sissons
		4r	16.2.66	Blackburn R		A	L	1-4	Hurst
1966-67	D1	3	28.1.67	Swindon T	D3	H	D	3-3	Hurst 3
		3r	31.1.67	Swindon T		A	L	1-3	Sissons
1967-68	D1	3	27.1.68	Burnley	D1	A	W	3-1	Peters 2, Dear
		4	17.2.68	Stoke C	D1	A	W	3-0	Sissons 2, Hurst
		5	9.3.68	Sheffield U	D1	H	L	1-2	Dear
1968-69	D1	3	4.1.69	Bristol C	D2	H	W	3-2	Peters 2, Hunt
		4	25.1.69	Huddersfield T	D2	A	W	2-0	Peters, Hurst
		5	26.2.69	Mansfield T	D3	A	L	0-3	
1969-70	D1	3	3.1.70	Middlesbrough	D2	H	L	1-2	Stephenson
1970-71	D1	3	2.1.71	Blackpool	D1	A	L	0-4	
1971-72	D1	3	15.1.72	Luton T	D2	H	W	2-1	Hurst, Best
		4	9.2.72	Hereford U	SL	A	D	0-0	
		4r	14.2.72	Hereford U	SL	H	W	3-1	Hurst 3
		5	26.2.72	Huddersfield T	D1	A	L	2-4	Robson, Best
1972-73	D1	3	13.1.73	Port Vale	D3	A	W	1-0	Holland
		4	3.2.73	Hull C	D2	A	L	0-1	
1973-74	D1	3	5.1.74	Hereford U	D3	H	D	1-1	Holland
		3r	9.1.74	Hereford U		A	L	1-2	Best
1974-75	D1	3	4.1.75	Southampton	D2	A	W	2-1	Lampard, Gould
		4	25.1.75	Swindon T	D3	H	D	1-1	Jennings
		4r	28.1.75	Swindon T		A	W	2-1	Brooking, Holland
		5	15.2.75	QPR	D1	H	W	2-1	Holland, Robson
		6	8.3.75	Arsenal	D1	A	W	2-0	A.Taylor 2
		SF	5.4.75	Ipswich T at Villa Park	D1		D	0-0	
		SFr	9.4.75	Ipswich T at Stamford Bridge			W	2-1	A.Taylor 2

WEST HAM UNITED

Season	Div	Round	Date	Opponent	OppDiv	H/A	Res	Score	Scorers
		F	3.5.75	FULHAM	D2	WEMBLEY	W	2-0	A.Taylor 2
1975-76	D1	3	3.1.76	Liverpool	D1	H	L	0-2	
1976-77	D1	3	4.1.77	Bolton W	D3	H	W	2-1	Jennings, Pike
		4	29.1.77	Aston Villa	D1	A	L	0-3	
1977-78	D1	3	7.1.78	Watford	D4	H	W	1-0	Robson
		4	28.1.78	QPR	D1	H	D	1-1	Bonds
		4r	31.1.78	QPR		A	L	1-6	Robson
1978-79	D2	3	9.1.79	Newport Co	D4	A	L	1-2	Robson
1979-80	D2	3	5.1.80	WBA	D1	A	D	1-1	Pearson
		3r	8.1.80	WBA		H	W	2-1	Pike, Brooking
		4	26.1.80	Orient	D2	A	W	3-2	Stewart 2 (1p), Gray og
		5	16.2.80	Swansea C	D2	H	W	2-0	Allen, Cross
		6	8.3.80	Aston Villa	D1	H	W	1-0	Stewart
		SF	12.4.80	Everton at Villa Park	D1		D	1-1	Pearson
		SFr	16.4.80	Everton at Elland Road			W	2-1	Devonshire, Lampard
		F	10.5.80	ARSENAL	D1	WEMBLEY	W	1-0	Brooking
1980-81	D2	3	3.1.81	Wrexham	D2	H	D	1-1	Stewart
		3r	6.1.81	Wrexham		A	D	0-0aet	
		3 2r	19.1.81	Wrexham		A	L	0-1aet	
1981-82	D1	3	2.1.82	Everton	D1	H	W	2-1	Bonds, Cross
		4	23.1.82	Watford	D2	A	L	0-2	
1982-83	D1	3	8.1.83	Manchester U	D1	A	L	0-2	
1983-84	D1	3	7.1.84	Wigan A	D3	H	W	1-0	Stewart
		4	28.1.84	Crystal P	D2	A	D	1-1	Swindlehurst
		4r	31.1.84	Crystal P		H	W	2-0	Barnes, Pike
		5	18.2.84	Birmingham C	D1	A	L	0-3	
1984-85	D1	3	5.1.85	Port Vale	D4	H	W	4-1	Goddard 3, Dickens
		4	4.2.85	Norwich C	D1	H	W	2-1	Stewart, Pike
		5	4.3.85	Wimbledon	D2	A	D	1-1	Cottee
		5r	6.3.85	Wimbledon		H	W	5-1	Cottee 3, Dickens, Allen
		6	9.3.85	Manchester U	D1	A	L	2-4	Allen, Hogg og
1985-86	D1	3	5.1.86	Charlton A	D2	A	W	1-0	Cottee
		4	25.1.86	Ipswich T	D1	H	D	0-0	
		4r	4.2.86	Ipswich T		A	D	1-1aet	Cottee
		4 2r	6.2.86	Ipswich T		A	W	1-0aet	Cottee
		5	5.3.86	Manchester U	D1	H	D	1-1	McAvennie
		5r	9.3.86	Manchester U		A	W	2-0	Pike, Stewart
		5 2r	12.3.86	Sheffield W	D1	A	L	1-2	Cottee
1986-87	D1	3	10.1.87	Orient	D4	A	D	1-1	Hilton
		3r	31.1.87	Orient		H	W	4-1	Parris, Keen, McAvennie, Cottee
		4	9.2.87	Sheffield U	D2	H	W	4-0	McAvennie 2, Gale, Robson
		5	21.2.87	Sheffield W	D1	A	D	1-1	McAvennie
		5r	25.2.87	Sheffield W		H	L	0-2	
1987-88	D1	3	9.1.88	Charlton A	D1	H	W	2-0	Brady, Cottee
		4	30.1.88	QPR	D1	A	L	1-3	Cottee
1988-89	D1	3	8.1.89	Arsenal	D1	H	D	2-2	Dickens, Bould (og)
		3r	11.1.89	Arsenal		A	W	1-0	Rosenior
		4	28.1.89	Swindon T	D2	A	D	0-0	
		4r	1.2.89	Swindon T		H	W	1-0	Rosenior
		5	18.2.89	Charlton A	D1	A	W	1-0	Slater
		6	18.3.89	Norwich C	D1	H	D	0-0	
		6r	22.2.89	Norwich C		A	L	1-3	Ince
1989-90	D2	3	6.1.90	Torquay U	D4	A	L	0-1	
1990-91	D2	3	5.1.91	Aldershot	D4	A	D	0-0	
			played at Upton Park						
		3r	16.1.91	Aldershot		H	W	6-1	Morley 2, Slater, Parris, Bishop, Quinn
		4	26.1.91	Luton T	D1	A	D	1-1	Parris
		4r	30.1.91	Luton T		H	W	5-0	Parris, Bishop, McAvennie, Morley 2
		5	16.2.91	Crewe Alex	D3	H	W	1-0	Quinn
		6	11.3.91	Everton	D1	H	W	2-1	Foster, Slater
		SF	14.4.91	Nottingham F	D1		L	0-4	
			played at Villa Park						
1991-92	D2	3	4.1.92	Farnborough	IL	A	D	1-1	Dicks
			played at Upton Park						
		3r	14.1.92	Farnborough		H	W	1-0	Morley
		4	25.1.92	Wrexham	D4	H	D	2-2	Dicks, Morley
		4r	4.2.92	Wrexham		A	W	1-0	Foster

	5	15.2.92	**Sunderland**	D2	A	D	1-1	Small
	5r	26.2.92	**Sunderland**		H	L	2-3	C.Allen 2
1992-93	D1	3	2.1.93	**WBA**	D2	A	W	2-0	C.Allen, Robson
		4	24.1.93	**Barnsley**	D1	A	L	1-4	Morley (p)

WEST MANCHESTER

1887-88	1	15.10.87	**Fleetwood Rangers**		A	L	1-4

WEST STANLEY

Formed 1889. First entered FA Cup: 1903. Based in Co. Durham, originally known as Oakey's Lilywhites FC. Folded 1959

1919-20	NEL	6q	**Rotherham Co** (D2) 1-0				
		1	17.1.20	**Gillingham**	SL	H	W	3-1	Walton, Bohill, Hall
		2	31.1.20	**Tottenham H**	D2	A	L	0-4	
1925-26	NEL	1	28.11.25	**Rochdale**	3N	A	–	1-1	Agar
			abandoned at half-time, ground unfit					
		1	1.12.25	**Rochdale**		A	L	0-4	
1931-32	NEL	1	28.11.31	**Tramere R**	3N	A	L	0-3	

WESTBURY UNITED

Formed 1921. First entered FA Cup: 1921

1937-38	Wilts	1	27.11.37	**Walthamstow Ave**	AL	H	L	1-3	Butler

WESTON-SUPER-MARE

Formed 1948. First entered FA Cup: 1949

1961-62	WL	1	4.11.61	**Bridgwater T**	WL	A	D	0-0	
		1r	9.11.61	**Bridgwater T**		H	L	0-1	

WEYBRIDGE SWALLOWS

1880-81	1	13.11.80	**Henley**		H	W	3-1
	2	18.12.80	**Upton Park**		H	L	0-3

WEYMOUTH

Formed 1890. First entered FA Cup: 1893. **Cup Final Connection:** Graham Roberts, played for Weymouth before appearing for Tottenham in the 1981 and 1982 Cup Finals. **League clubs beaten:** Merthyr Town, Aldershot, Shrewsbury, Newport Co, Cardiff C

1924-25	SL	5q	**Merthyr Town** (3S) H W 3-2; 6q **Bristol R** (3S) A 0-0; H 0-2				
1925-26	SL	1	28.11.25	**Newport Co**	3S	H	L	0-1	
1926-27	SL	1	27.11.26	**Reading**	D2	H	D	4-4	Caswell, Pillunger, Gibb, Rugg
		1r	1.12.26	**Reading**		A	L	0-5	
1948-49	WL	1	27.11.48	**Chelmsford C**	SL	H	W	2-1	Gallacher, Anderson
		2	11.12.48	**Yeovil**	SL	H	L	0-4	
1949-50	SL	1	26.11.49	**Aldershot**	3S	H	D	2-2	Northover, Haynes
		1r	30.11.49	**Aldershot**		A	W	3-2	Northover (p), Johnson, McGowan
		2	10.12.49	**Hereford**	SL	H	W	2-1	Haynes, Johnston
		3	7.1.50	**Manchester U**	D1	A	L	0-4	
1951-52	SL	1	24.11.51	**Brush Sports**	BDL	A	W	3-2	Massart, McCarter, Rowell
		2	15.12.51	**Bristol R**	3S	A	L	0-2	
1952-53	SL	1	22.11.52	**Colchester U**	3S	H	D	1-1	Rowell
		1r	27.11.52	**Colchester U**		A	L	0-4	
1953-54	SL	1	21.11.53	**Bedford T**	SL	H	W	2-0	Easton, Massart
		2	12.12.53	**Leyton O**	3S	A	L	0-4	
1955-56	SL	1	19.11.55	**Salisbury**	WL	H	W	3-2	Stocker 2, Hobbs
		2	10.12.55	**Southend U**	3S	H	L	0-1	
1956-57	SL	1	17.11.56	**Shrewsbury T**	3S	H	W	1-0	Henderson
		2	8.12.56	**Southampton**	3S	A	L	2-3	Easton 2
1958-59	SL	1	15.11.58	**Coventry C**	D4	H	L	2-5	Gallard 2
1960-61	SL	1	5.11.60	**Torquay U**	D3	H	L	1-2	Ayre (p)
1961-62	SL	1	4.11.61	**Barnet**	AL	H	W	1-0	Court (p)

	2	25.11.61	Newport Co	D3	H	W	1-0	Court
	3	6.1.62	Morecambe	LC	A	W	1-0	Fogg
	4	27.1.62	Preston NE	D2	A	–	0-0	
		abandoned after 14 minutes – fog						
	4	29.1.62	Preston NE		A	L	0-2	
1963-64 SL	1	16.11.63	Bedford T	SL	H	D	1-1	Robertson
	1r	21.11.63	Bedford T		A	L	0-1	
1964-65 SL	1	14.11.64	Welton R	WL	A	D	1-1	Hutchinson
	1r	18.11.64	Welton R		H	W	4-3	Hutchinson 2, Spratt, Hannigan
	2	5.12.64	Bristol R	D3	A	L	1-4	Spratt
1965-66 SL	1	13.11.65	Bournemouth	D3	A	D	0-0	
	1r	17.11.65	Bournemouth		H	L	1-4	Camp
1967-68 SL	1	9.12.67	Leyton O	D3	H	L	0-2	
1968-69 SL	1	16.11.68	Yeovil	SL	H	W	2-1	Glover (p), Bennett
	2	7.12.68	Swansea T	D4	H	D	1-1	Etteridge
	2r	10.2.68	Swansea T		A	L	0-2	
1969-70 SL	1	15.11.69	Northampton T	D4	A	D	0-0	
	1r	19.11.69	Northampton T		H	L	1-3	Allen
1970-71 SL	1	21.11.70	Southend U	D4	A	L	0-7	
1971-72 SL	1	20.11.71	Cambridge U	D4	A	L	1-2	Pound
1973-74 SL	1	24.11.73	Merthyr Tydfil	SL	H	L	0-1	
1974-75 SL	1	23.11.74	Peterborough U	D3	A	D	0-0	
	1r	4.12.74	Peterborough U		H	D	3-3aet	Oakes og, Dorrington, Brown
	1 2r	9.12.74	Peterborough U		A	L	0-3	
1975-76 SL	1	22.11.75	Gillingham	D3	H	L	0-2	
1976-77 SL	1	20.11.76	Hitchin T	IL	H	D	1-1	Robson
	1r	23.11.76	Hitchin T		A	D	2-2aet	Keirs, O'Rourke
	1 2r	29.11.76	Hitchin T at Aldershot			D	3-3aet	Courtney, McCafferty, Henderson
	1 3r	2.12.76	Hitchin T at Salisbury			L	1-3	Keirs (p)
1977-78 SL	1	26.11.77	Gillingham	D3	A	D	1-1	Courtney
	1r	30.11.77	Gillingham		H	L	0-1	
1978-79 SL	1	25.11.78	Aldershot	D4	A	D	1-1	Hawkins
	1r	29.11.78	Aldershot		H	L	0-1	
1980-81 APL	1	24.11.80	Swindon T	D3	A	L	2-3	Iannone, Dove (p)
1981-82 APL	1	21.11.81	Northampton T	D4	H	D	0-0	
	1r	24.11.81	Northampton T		A	L	2-6	Finnigan 2
1982-83 APL	1	20.11.82	Maidstone U	APL	H	W	4-3	Morrell, Peter, Bourne, Pearson
	2	11.12.82	Cardiff C	D3	A	W	3-2	Iannone, Finnegan, Pearson
	3	8.1.83	Cambridge U	D2	A	L	0-1	
1984-85 APL	1	17.11.84	Millwall	D3	H	L	0-3	
1985-86 APL	1	16.11.85	Chelmsford C	SL	H	L	0-1	

WHITBURN

Formed 1882. Folded 1973. More than 50 men born in the village of Whitburn have played for League clubs including three who played in Cup Finals: Jimmy Seed, Tottenham, 1921 and Billy Henderson and John Young, West Ham, 1923.

1887-88	1	15.10.87	Middlesbrough		A	L	0-4	

WHITBY TOWN

Formed 1896. **First entered FA Cup:** 1899. **FA Amateur Cup: Runners-up:** 1965. **League club beaten:** Halifax T

1969-70 NL	1	15.11.69	York C	D4	A	L	0-2	
1983-84 NL	1	19.11.83	Halifax T	D4	A	W	3-2	Hampton, Linacre, Sills
	2	10.12.83	Wigan A	D3	A	L	0-1	
1984-85 NL	1	17.11.84	Chesterfield	D4	H	L	1-3	Granycome
1985-86 NL	1	16.11.85	South Liverpool	NPL	H	W	1-0	Hankin
	2	7.12.85	York C	D3	A	L	1-3	Watson
1986-87 NL	1	15.11.86	Doncaster R	D3	H	D	2-2	Hedley, Graham
	1r	18.11.86	Doncaster R		A	L	2-3	Humphries og, Hedley

WHITLEY BAY

Formed 1897. **First entered FA Cup:** 1908. **League clubs beaten:** Scarborough, Preston

1989-90 NPL	1	18.11.89	Scarborough	D4	A	W	1-0	Scott
	2	9.12.89	Preston NE	D3	H	W	2-0	Robinson, Todd

WHITLEY BAY

		3	6.1.90	**Rochdale**	D4	A	L	0-1	
1990-91	NPL	1	17.11.90	**Tamworth**	SL	A	W	6-4	Briggs 2, Chandler, Barker 2, Ferris
		2	12.12.90	**Barrow**	GMVC	H	L	0-1	

WIGAN ATHLETIC

Formed 1932. **First entered FA Cup:** 1933. **Best FA Cup Performance:** 4th round, 1980, 1986 **FA Challenge Trophy Runners-up:** 1973 **Record FA Cup Win:** 6-1 vs Carlisle U, 1st round, 24.11.1934; 5-0 vs Darlington, 2nd round, 6.12.1986 **Record FA Cup Defeat:** 0-5 vs Chelsea, 3rd round replay, 26.1.1985. **League clubs beaten as non-league club:** Carlisle U, Torquay U, Southport, Doncaster R, Peterborough U, Halifax T, Shrewsbury T, York C, Sheffield W

1934-35	CC	1	24.11.34	**Carlisle U**	3N	A	W	6-1	Armes 2, Roberts 2, Scott, H.Robson
		2	8.12.34	**Torquay U**	3S	H	W	3-2	Roberts 2, Scott
		3	12.1.35	**Millwall**	3S	H	L	1-4	Roberts
1935-36	CC	1	30.11.35	**Rotherham U**	3N	H	L	1-2	Felton
1936-37	CC	1	28.11.36	**Burton T**	ML	A	L	1-5	Wallbanks
1937-38	CC	1	27.11.37	**South Liverpool**	LC	H	L	1-4	Thomas
1953-54	LC	1	21.11.53	**Scarborough**	ML	H	W	4-0	Lomax, Livesey, Hindle, Lyon
		2	12.12.53	**Hereford U**	SL	H	W	4-1	Lyon, Livesey 2, Hughes og
		3	9.1.54	**Newcastle U**	D1	A	D	2-2	Lyon, Livesey
		3r	13.1.54	**Newcastle U**		H	L	2-3	Lomax 2
1954-55	LC	1	20.11.54	**Barnsley**	3N	A	L	2-3	Penk, Hindle
1956-57	CC	1	17.11.56	**Goole T**	ML	H	L	1-2	A.McLean
1957-58	LC	1	16.11.57	**Southport**	3N	A	W	2-1	Buckle, Banks
		2	7.12.57	**Mansfield T**	3N	H	D	1-1	Hitchen
		2r	11.12.57	**Mansfield T**		A	L	1-3	Buckle
1962-63	CC	1	3.11.62	**Gateshead**	NRL	A	L	1-2	Bradbury
1964-65	CC	1	14.11.64	**Stockport Co**	D4	A	L	1-2	Lyon
1965-66	CC	1	13.11.65	**Doncaster R**	D4	A	D	2-2	Lyon, Crompton
		1r	17.11.65	**Doncaster R**		H	W	3-1	Lyon 3
		2	4.12.65	**Chester**	D4	A	L	1-2	LLewellyn
1966-67	CC	1	26.11.66	**Tranmere R**	D4	A	D	1-1	Lyon
		1r	28.11.66	**Tranmere R**		H	L	0-1	
1969-70	NPL	1	15.11.69	**Port Vale**	D4	H	D	1-1	Sutherland
		1r	18.11.69	**Port Vale**		A	D	2-2aet	Fleming, Fielding
		1 2r	24.11.69	**Port Vale at Old Trafford**			L	0-1aet	
1970-71	NPL	1	21.11.70	**South Shields**	NPL	A	D	1-1	Temple
		1r	23.11.70	**South Shields**		H	W	2-0	Temple, Todd
		2	12.12.70	**Peterborough U**	D4	H	W	2-1	Davies, Fleming (p)
		3	2.1.71	**Manchester C**	D1	A	L	0-1	
1971-72	NPL	1	20.11.71	**Halifax T**	D3	H	W	2-1	Sutherland, Oates
		2	11.12.71	**Wrexham**	D3	A	L	0-4	
1972-73	NPL	1	18.11.72	**Grimsby T**	D3	A	L	1-2	Oates (p)
1973-74	NPL	1	24.11.73	**Huddersfield T**	D3	A	L	0-2	
1974-75	NPL	1	23.11.74	**Shrewsbury T**	D4	A	D	1-1	King
		1r	25.11.74	**Shrewsbury T**		H	W	2-1	Gore, Jackson
		2	14.12.74	**Mansfield T**	D4	H	D	1-1	B.Foster og
		2r	16.12.74	**Mansfield T**		A	L	1-3	King
1975-76	NPL	1	22.11.75	**Matlock T**	NPL	H	W	4-1	Rodgers 2, Wilkinson, Worswick
		2	13.12.75	**Sheffield W**	D3	A	L	0-2	
1976-77	NPL	1	20.11.76	**Matlock T**	NPL	A	L	0-2	
1977-78	NPL	1	26.11.77	**York C**	D4	H	W	1-0	Wilkie
		2	17.12.77	**Sheffield W**	D3	H	W	1-0	Whittle
		3	7.1.78	**Birmingham C**	D1	A	L	0-4	
1978-79	D4	1	25.11.78	**Bury**	D3	H	D	2-2	Gore, Houghton
		1r	28.11.78	**Bury**		A	L	1-4	Moore
1979-80	D4	1	24.11.79	**Blackpool**	D3	A	D	1-1	Methven
		1r	28.11.79	**Blackpool**		H	W	2-0	Gore, Corrigan
		2	24.12.79	**Northwich V**	NPL	A	–	3-0	Quinn, Gore, Methven
				abandoned after 65 minutes – fog					
		2	5.1.80	**Northwich V**		A	D	2-2	Hinnigan, Gore
		2r	7.1.80	**Northwich V**		H	W	1-0	Brownbill
		3	14.1.80	**Chelsea**	D2	A	W	1-0	Gore
		4	26.1.80	**Everton**	D1	A	L	0-3	
1980-81	D4	1	22.11.80	**Chesterfield**	D3	H	D	2-2	Houghton 2
		1r	25.11.80	**Chesterfield**		A	L	0-2	
1981-82	D4	1	21.11.81	**Hartlepool U**	D4	H	D	2-2	Methven, Quinn
		1r	25.11.81	**Hartlepool U**		A	L	0-1	

WIGAN ATHLETIC

Season	Div	Rnd	Date	Opponent		H/A	W/D/L	Score	Scorers
1982-83	D3	1	21.11.82	Telford U	APL	H	D	0-0	
		1r	23.11.82	Telford U		A	L	1-2	Butler
1983-84	D3	1	19.11.83	Bradford C	D3	A	D	0-0	
		1r	28.11.83	Bradford C		H	W	4-2	Taylor 2, Bruce 2
		2	10.12.83	Whitby T	NL	H	W	1-0	Taylor (p)
		3	7.1.84	West Ham	D1	A	L	0-1	
1984-85	D3	1	17.11.84	Wrexham	D4	A	W	2-0	Langley, Newell
		2	8.12.84	Northwich V	APL	H	W	2-1	Newell, Johnson (p)
		3	5.1.85	Chelsea	D1	A	D	2-2	Jewell, Newell
		3r	26.1.85	Chelsea		H	L	0-5	
1985-86	D3	1	16.11.85	Doncaster R	D3	H	W	4-1	Lowe 2, Newell, Aspinall
		2	7.12.85	Runcorn	APL	A	D	1-1	Knowles
		2r	10.12.85	Runcorn		H	W	4-0	Methven, Newell, Jones og
		3	4.1.86	Bournemouth	D3	H	W	3-0	Methven, Kelly, Aspinall
		4	25.1.86	Southampton	D1	A	L	0-3	
1986-87	D3	1	15.11.86	Lincoln C	D4	H	W	3-1	Griffiths, Lowe 2
		2	6.12.86	Darlington	D3	A	W	5-0	Jewell 2, Campbell 2, Thompson
		3	19.1.87	Gillingham	D3	H	W	2-1	Campbell, Thompson
		4	31.1.87	Norwich C	D1	H	W	1-0	Jewell
		5	21.2.87	Hull C	D2	H	W	3-0	Thompson, Jewell, Campbell
		6	15.3.87	Leeds U	D2	H	L	0-2	
1987-88	D3	1	14.11.87	Altrincham	GMVC	A	W	2-0	Campbell, Butler
		2	5.12.87	Wolverhampton W	D4	H	L	1-3	Hilditch
1988-89	D3	1	19.11.88	Hartlepool U	D4	A	L	0-2	
1989-90	D3	1	19.11.89	Mansfield T	D4	H	W	2-0	Page, Hilditch
		2	9.12.89	Carlisle U	D4	H	W	2-0	Johnson, Griffiths
		3	6.1.90	Watford	D2	A	L	0-2	
1990-91	D3	1	17.11.90	Carlisle U	D4	H	W	5-0	Griffiths 2, Woods, Rimmer 2
		2	8.12.90	Hartlepool U	D4	H	W	2-0	Page, Griffiths
		3	5.1.91	Coventry C	D1	A	D	1-1	Patterson
		3r	9.1.91	Coventry C		H	L	0-1	
1991-92	D3	1	16.11.91	Scarborough	D4	A	W	2-0	Pilling, Worthington
		2	7.12.91	Stockport Co	D3	H	W	2-0	Griffiths, Powell
		3	5.1.92	Notts Co	D1	A	L	0-2	
1992-93	D2	1	14.11.92	Carlisle U	D3	H	W	3-1	Williams og, Dalziel og, Powell
		2	2.1.93	Bury	D3	A	L	0-1	

WIGAN BOROUGH

Members of the Football League 1921-1932. **First Entered FA Cup:** 1922. Resigned from the Football League and folded in October 1932.

Season	Div	Rnd	Date	Opponent		H/A	W/D/L	Score	Scorers
1921-22	3N		*did not enter*						
1922-23	3N		4q **Eccles U** (H) 4-0; 5q **Southport** (A) 1-1; 5qr **Southport** (H) 3-1; 6q **Walsall** (A) 3-1						
		1	13.1.23	Bath C	SL	H	W	4-1	Fare, Spencer, Dennison, Eatock
		2	3.2.23	QPR	3S	H	L	2-4	Findlay, A.Williams
1923-24	3N		5q **Nelson** (H) 1-1; 5qr **Nelson** (A) 1-0; 6q **Northampton T** (H) 0-6						
1924-25	3N		5q **Bradford PA** (H) 0-1						
1925-26	3N	1	2.12.25	Nelson	3N	H	W	3-0	Fenner, Riddell, Sayer
		2	12.12.25	Crewe A	3N	A	D	2-2	Sayer, Dickinson
		2r	16.12.25	Crewe A		H	W	2-1	Fenner 2
		3	9.1.26	Stoke C	D2	H	L	2-5	Sayer, Glover
1926-27	3N	1	1.12.26	Barrow	3N	H	D	2-2	McGuire 2
		1r	6.12.26	Barrow		A	W	1-0	Dickinson
		2	11.12.26	Crewe A	3N	A	L	1-4	Dickinson
1927-28	3N	1	26.11.27	Rhyl A	Welsh	A	L	3-4	Fenner 2, Dixon
1928-29	3N	1	24.11.28	Ashington	3N	H	W	2-0	Lievesley, Mandy
		2	8.12.28	Grantham	ML	H	W	2-1	Lievesley, Hughton
		3	12.1.29	Sheffield W	D1	H	L	1-3	Lievesley
1929-30	3N	1	30.11.29	Lincoln C	3N	A	L	1-3	Smith
1930-31	3N	1	29.11.30	Wrexham	3N	A	L	0-2	
1931-32	3N	1	28.11.31	Burton T	BDL			*scratched*	

Wigan Borough resigned from the Football League and folded.

WIGAN COUNTY

First entered FA Cup: 1897. Like Wigan Borough and later Wigan Athletic, Wigan County also played at Springfield Park.

Season	Div	Rnd	Date	Opponent		H/A	W/D/L	Score	
1897-98	LL	1	29.1.98	Manchester C	D2	A	L	0-1	

WILLENHALL TOWN

Formed 1953. **FA Vase Runners-up:** 1981

1981-82	WMRL 1		21.11.81	Crewe A	D4	H	L	0-1

WILLINGTON TOWN

Formed 1906 as Willington Temperance. Willington Town 1911. **First entered FA Cup:** 1911. **FA Amateur Cup Winners:** 1950; **Runners-up:** 1939

1945-46	NL	1 1L	17.11.45	Bishop Auckland	NL	H	L	0-5	
		1 2L	24.11.45	Bishop Auckland		A	W	2-0	Graham, Lawton
1950-51	NL	1	25.11.50	Rochdale	3N	A	L	1-3	Dodd
1973-74	NL	1	24.11.73	Blackburn R	D3	H	D	0-0	
		1r	3.12.73	Blackburn R		A	L	1-6	B.Newton (p)

WIMBLEDON

Formed 1889 as Wimbledon Old Centrals. 1905 Wimbledon FC. **First entered FA Cup:** 1906. **Best FA Cup Performance:** Winners: 1988 **FA Amateur Cup Winners:** 1963; runners-up: 1935, 1947 **Record FA Cup Win:** 15-2 vs Polytechnic FC, preliminary round, 7.2.1929. **In Competition Proper:** 7-2 vs Windsor & Eton, 1st round, 22.11.1980 **Record FA Cup Defeat:** 0-6 vs Fulham, 1st round replay, 3.12.1930

1929-30	IL	1	30.11.29	Northfleet U	SL	H	L	1-4	Dowden
1930-31	IL	1	30.11.30	Fulham	3S	A	D	1-1	Dowden
		1r	3.12.30	Fulham		H	L	0-6	
1931-32	IL	1	28.11.31	Norwich C	3S	H	L	1-3	Dowden
1934-35	IL	1	24.11.34	Leyton	AL	H	D	1-1	Batchelor
		1r	29.11.34	Leyton		A	W	1-0	Wright
		2	8.12.34	Southend U	3S	A	L	1-5	Turner
1947-48	IL	1	29.11.47	Mansfield T	3N	H	L	0-1	
1952-53	IL	1	22.11.52	Walthamstow Ave	IL	A	D	2-2	Stewart, Stannard
		1r	26.11.52	Walthamstow Ave		H	L	0-3	
1962-63	IL	1	3.11.62	Colchester U	D3	H	W	2-1	Brown, Reynolds
		2	24.11.62	Bristol C	D3	A	L	1-2	Peters og
1963-64	IL	1	16.11.63	Bexley U	SL	A	W	5-1	Brown, Reynolds 2, Williams, Keats
		2	7.12.63	Bath C	SL	H	D	2-2	Brown, Reynolds
		2r	12.12.63	Bath C		A	L	0-4	
1965-66	SL	1	13.11.65	Gravesend & N.	SL	H	W	4-1	Cooke 3, O'Rourke
		2	4.12.65	Folkestone	SL	H	L	0-1	
1966-67	SL	1	26.11.66	Grantham	ML	A	L	1-2	Cooke
1967-68	SL	1	9.12.67	Romford	SL	H	W	3-0	Hodges 2 (1p), Hobbs
		2	6.1.68	Bristol R	D3	H	L	0-4	
1969-70	SL	1	15.11.69	Hillingdon B	SL	A	L	0-2	
1970-71	SL	1	21.11.70	Peterborough U	D4	A	L	1-3	Cooke
1973-74	SL	1	24.11.73	Kings Lynn	SL	A	L	0-1	
1974-75	SL	1	23.11.74	Bath C	SL	H	W	1-0	Mahon
		2	14.12.74	Kettering T	SL	H	W	2-0	Cooke, Mahon (p)
		3	4.1.75	Burnley	D1	A	W	1-0	Mahon
		4	25.1.75	Leeds U	D1	A	D	0-0	
		4r	10.2.75	Leeds U		H	L	0-1	
				played at Selhurst Park					
1975-76	SL	1	22.11.75	Nuneaton B	SL	A	W	1-0	Connell
		2	13.12.75	Brentford	D4	H	L	0-2	
1976-77	SL	1	20.11.76	Wokingham T	IL	H	W	1-0	Connell
		2	14.12.76	Leatherhead	IL	A	W	3-1	Bryant, Marlowe 2
		3	8.1.77	Middlesbrough	D1	H	D	0-0	
		3r	11.1.77	Middlesbrough		A	L	0-1	
1977-78	D4	1	26.11.77	Enfield	IL	A	L	0-3	
1978-79	D4	1	25.11.78	Gravesend & N	SL	A	D	0-0	
		1r	28.11.78	Gravesend & N		H	W	1-0	Cork
		2	16.12.78	Bournemouth	D4	H	D	1-1	Denny
		2r	28.12.78	Bournemouth		A	W	2-1aet	Cork, Parsons
		3	9.1.79	Southampton	D1	H	L	0-2	
1979-80	D3	1	24.11.79	Gillingham	D3	A	D	0-0	
		1r	27.11.79	Gillingham		H	W	4-2	Leslie 2, Parsons, Dziadulewicz
		2	18.12.79	Portsmouth	D4	H	D	0-0	
		2r	24.12.79	Portsmouth		A	D	3-3aet	Lewington, Denny 2
		2 2r	5.1.80	Portsmouth		H	L	0-1	

1980-81	D4	1	22.11.80	Windsor & Eton	AL	H	W	7-2	M.Smith 2, Hubbick 3, Cunningham, Cork
		2	13.12.80	Swindon T	D3	H	W	2-0	Denny, Leslie
		3	3.1.81	Oldham A	D2	H	D	0-0	
		3r	6.1.81	Oldham A		A	W	1-0	Cork
		4	24.1.81	Wrexham	D2	A	L	1-2	Denny
1981-82	D3	1	21.11.81	Bedford	SL	A	W	2-0	Suddaby, Ketteridge
		2	15.12.81	Enfield	APL	A	L	1-4	Brown (p)
1982-83	D4	1	20.11.82	Northampton T	D4	A	D	2-2	Leslie, Entwistle
		1r	23.11.82	Northampton T		H	L	0-2	
1983-84	D3	1	19.11.83	Orient	D3	H	W	2-1	Cork 2
		2	10.12.83	Brentford	D3	A	L	2-3	Peters, Downes
1984-85	D2	3	5.1.85	Burnley	D3	H	W	3-1	Evans, Fishenden 2 (1p)
		4	26.1.85	Nottingham F	D1	A	D	0-0	
		4r	30.1.85	Nottingham F		H	W	1-0	Fishenden
		5	4.3.85	West Ham	D1	H	D	1-1	Evans
		5r	6.3.85	West Ham		A	L	1-5	Fishenden
1985-86	D2	3	4.1.86	Millwall	D2	A	L	1-3	Gage
1986-87	D1	3	10.1.87	Sunderland	D2	H	W	2-1	Sanchez, Hodges
		4	31.1.87	Portsmouth	D2	H	W	4-0	Fashanu 2, Blake og, Sayer
		5	21.2.87	Everton	D1	H	W	3-1	Hodges, Fashanu, Sayer
		6	15.3.87	Tottenham H	D1	H	L	0-2	
1987-88	D1	3	9.1.88	WBA	D2	H	W	4-1	Fashanu, Wise, Turner, Fairweather
		4	30.1.88	Mansfield T	D3	A	W	2-1	Cork, Phelan
		5	20.2.88	Newcastle U	D1	A	W	3-1	Gibson, Gayle, Fashanu
		6	12.3.88	Watford	D1	H	W	2-1	Young, Fashanu
		SF	9.4.88	Luton T	D1		W	2-1	Fashanu (p), Wise
				played at White Hart Lane					
		F	14.5.88	LIVERPOOL	D1	WEMBLEY	W	1-0	Sanchez
1988-89	D1	3	7.1.89	Birmingham C	D2	A	W	1-0	Gibson
		4	28.1.89	Aston Villa	D1	A	W	1-0	Jones
		5	18.2.89	Grimsby T	D4	H	W	3-1	Fashanu, Phelan, Wise
		6	19.3.89	Everton	D1	A	L	0-1	
1989-90	D1	3	6.1.90	WBA	D2	A	L	0-2	
1990-91	D1	3	5.1.91	Aston Villa	D1	A	D	1-1	McGee
		3r	9.1.91	Aston Villa		H	W	1-0aet	Cork
		4	26.1.91	Shrewsbury T	D3	A	L	0-1	
1991-92	D1	3	4.1.92	Bristol C	D2	A	D	1-1	Fashanu
		3r	14.1.92	Bristol C		H	L	0-1	
1992-93	PL	3	2.1.93	Everton	PL	H	D	0-0	
		3r	12.1.93	Everton		A	W	2-1	Fashanu, Earle
		4	23.1.93	Aston Villa	PL	A	D	1-1	Elkins
		4r	3.2.93	Aston Villa		H	D	0-0aet	
				Wimbledon won 6-5 on penalties					
		5	14.2.93	Tottenham H	PL	A	L	2-3	Dobbs, Cotterill

WIMBORNE TOWN

Formed 1878. **First entered FA Cup:** 1924. **FA Vase Winners:** 1992

1982-83	WL	1	20.11.82	Aldershot	D4	A	L	0-2	

WINDSOR & ETON

Formed 1892. **First entered FA Cup:** 1892. **Cup Final Connection:** Former player Vic Woodley played in goal for Derby County in the 1946 Cup Final.

1925-26	AL	1	28.11.25	Charlton A	3S	A	L	2-4	Norris 2
1980-81	AL	1	22.11.80	Wimbledon	D4	A	L	2-7	McCulloch, Hill
1982-83	IL	1	20.11.82	Brentford at Griffin Pk	D3	H	L	0-7	
1983-84	IL	1	19.11.83	Burton A	NPL	A	W	2-1	Hill, Baron
		2	13.12.83	Bournemouth	D3	H	D	0-0	
		2r	19.12.83	Bournemouth		A	L	0-2	
1984-85	IL	1	17.11.84	Gillingham	D3	A	L	1-2	Yates
1985-86	IL	1	16.11.85	Torquay U	D4	H	D	1-1	Woods
		1r	19.11.85	Torquay U		A	L	0-3	
1991-92	IL	1	16.11.91	Woking	IL	H	–	1-1	Gilman
				abandoned after 69 minutes – fog					
		1	26.11.91	Woking		H	L	2-4	Gilman 2

WINDSOR HOME PARK

1872-73	1	26.10.72	Reigate Priory		H	W	4-2	EH Bambridge, GF Bambridge, Gardiner, 1 other
	2	23.11.72	South Norwood		A	L	0-1	
		FA ordered replay after match failed to be completed						
	2r	7.12.72	South Norwood		H	W	3-0	Clark, Gardiner, F.Heron
	3	21.12.72	Maidenhead		H	L	0-1	
1874-75	1		Uxbridge			*walkover*		
	2		Oxford University			*scratched*		
1880-81	1	13.11.80	Grey Friars		A	D	0-0	
	1r	20.11.80	Grey Friars		H	L	1-3	
1881-82	1	22.10.81	Reading Minster		H	L	0-1	
1882-83	1	4.11.82	Acton		H	W	3-0	
	2	30.11.82	United Hospitals		H	W	3-1	
	3	6.1.83	Clapham R		A	L	0-3	
1883-84	1	10.11.83	Royal Engineers		H	W	5-3	Dear 2, Cheeseman, Harrison, Smith
	2	1.12.83	Old Wykehamists		H	L	0-1	
1884-85	1		Chatham			*scratched*		

WINSFORD UNITED

Formed 1883 and competed in FA Cup in 1888 as Over Wanderers (qv). **Cup Final Connection:** Neville Southall who played in the 1984, 1985 and 1989 FA Cup Finals for Everton is a former Winsford player.

1975-76	CC	1	22.11.75	Peterborough U	D3	A	L	1-4	Chadwick
1991-92	NPL	1	16.11.91	Wrexham	D4	A	L	2-5	Esdaile 2

WISBECH TOWN

Formed 1920. **First entered FA Cup:** 1923. **League club beaten:** Colchester U

1945-46	UCL	1 1L	17.11.45	Ipswich T	3S	H	L	0-3	
		1 2L	24.11.45	Ipswich T		A	L	0-5	
1957-58	ML	1	16.11.57	Colchester U	3S	H	W	1-0	Pye
		2	7.12.57	Reading	3S	A	L	1-2	Downie
1958-59	SL	1	15.11.58	Newport Co	D3	H	D	2-2	Marshall, Sewell
		1r	17.11.58	Newport Co		A	L	1-4aet	Pye
1959-60	SL	1	14.11.59	Wycombe W	IL	A	L	2-4	Elliott, Moore
1964-65	SL	1	14.11.64	Brentford	D3	H	L	0-2	
1965-66	SL	1	13.11.65	Brighton & HA	D3	A	L	1-10	Lawrence

WITNEY TOWN

Formed 1885. **First entered FA Cup:** 1923

1971-72	Hel	1	20.11.71	Romford	SL	H	L	0-3	

WITTON ALBION

Formed 1890. **First entered FA Cup:** 1908. **Cup final connection:** Peter Mellor, who played in goal for Fulham in the 1975 final, started his career at Witton Albion. **League club beaten:** Halifax T

1948-49	CC	1	27.11.48	Gainsborough T	ML	A	L	0-1	
1949-50	CC	1	26.11.49	Mossley	CC	H	L	0-1	
1950-51	CC	1	25.11.50	Nelson	LC	H	L	1-2	Williams
1951-52	CC	1	24.11.51	Gainsborough T	ML	H	W	2-1	Christopher, Cowden
		2	15.12.51	Workington	3N	H	D	2-2	Thompson, Dale
		2r	20.12.51	Workington		A	L	0-1	
1953-54	CC	1	21.11.53	Nelson	LC	H	W	4-1	Yearsley, McCann, Jones, Dale
		2	12.12.53	Grimsby T	3N	H	D	1-1	Yearsley
		2r	15.12.53	Grimsby T		A	L	1-6	Jones
1957-58	CC	1	16.11.57	Tranmere R	3N	A	L	1-2	Duthie
1966-67	CC	1	26.11.66	Bradford PA	D4	A	L	2-3	McDonald, Cunliffe
1990-91	NPL	1	17.11.90	Bolton W	D3	H	L	1-2	Thomas
1991-92	GMVC	1	16.11.91	Halifax T	D4	H	D	1-1	Thomas
		1r	27.11.91	Halifax T		A	W	2-1aet	Thomas, Grimshaw
		2	7.12.91	Preston NE	D3	A	L	1-5	Flynn
1992-93	GMVC	1	14.11.92	Bury	D3	A	L	0-2	

WITTON FC

Competed in the FA Cup until 1891. A seperate club from Witton Albion.

1884-85	1		Clitheroe				walkover	
	2		bye					
	3	22.12.84	Blackburn Rovers		A	L	0-5	
1885-86	1	17.10.85	Accrington		A	L	4-5	
1886-87	1	23.10.86	Oswaldtwistle R		A	W	3-2	
	2	13.11.86	Preston NE		A	L	0-6	
1887-88	1	15.10.87	Oswaldtwistle R		A	W	4-3	
	2	5.11.87	Distillery		A	W	4-2	Cunliffe 2, Hothersall, Turner
	3	26.11.87	Darwen		A	D	1-1	Horsfield
	3r	3.12.87	Darwen at Blackburn		A	L	0-2	
1888-89	1	2.2.89	Aston Villa	D1	A	L	2-3	Grimshaw, Turner

WOKING

Formed 1889. **First entered FA Cup:** 1903. **League club beaten:** WBA

1907-08	WS	1	11.1.08	Bolton W	D1	A	L	0-5	
1926-27	IL	1	27.11.26	Charlton A	3S	H	L	1-3	Price
1928-29	IL	1	24.11.28	Newport Co	3S	A	L	0-7	
1958-59	IL	1	15.11.58	Southampton	D3	A	L	1-4	Hebdon
1968-69	IL	1	16.11.68	Brentford	D4	A	L	0-2	
1978-79	IL	1	25.11.78	Barnet	SL	A	D	3-3	James, Love, Field
		1r	28.11.78	Barnet		H	D	3-3aet	Cosham, Alexander, Morton
		1 2r	5.12.78	Barnet at Brentford			W	3-0	Love, James, Morton
		2	16.12.78	Swansea C	D3	A	D	2-2	Love, Cottrell
		2r	19.12.78	Swansea C		H	L	3-5	Morton, Field, Barrett
1986-87	IL	1	15.11.86	Chelmsford C	SL	H	D	1-1	Lansley
		1r	17.11.86	Chelmsford C		A	L	1-2	Morris
1988-89	IL	1	19.11.88	Cambridge U	D4	H	L	1-4	S.Wye
1989-90	IL	1	18.11.89	Slough	IL	A	W	2-1	Buzaglo, Mulvaney
		2	9.12.89	Cambridge U	D4	A	L	1-3	Mulvaney
1990-91	IL	1	17.11.90	Kidderminster H	GMVC	H	D	0-0	
		1r	21.11.90	Kidderminster H		A	D	1-1aet	Baron
		1 2r	26.11.90	Kidderminster H		A	W	2-1	Clement, Russell
		2	8.12.90	Merthyr Tydfil	GMVC	H	W	5-1	Biggins 3, L.Wye, Buzaglo
		3	5.1.91	WBA	D2	A	W	4-2	Buzaglo 3, Worsfold
		4	27.1.91	Everton	D1	H	L	0-1	
				played at Goodison Park					
1991-92	IL	1	16.11.91	Windsor & Eton	IL	A	–	1-1	Baron
				abandoned after 69 minutes – fog					
		1	26.11.91	Windsor & Eton		A	W	4-2	Milton, Mitchell, Biggins, Friel
		2	7.12.91	Yeovil T	GMVC	H	W	3-0	Friel 3
		3	4.1.92	Hereford U	D4	H	D	0-0	
		3r	14.1.92	Hereford U		A	L	1-2aet	Pratt
1992-93	GMVC	1	14.11.92	Nuneaton B	SL	H	W	3-2	Clement, Biggins, Carroll
		2	5.12.92	Brighton & HA	D2	A	D	1-1	S.Wye
		2r	16.12.92	Brighton & HA		H	L	1-2	Senior

WOKINGHAM TOWN

Formed 1875. **First entered FA Cup:** 1958

1976-77	IL	1	20.11.76	Wimbledon	SL	A	L	0-1	
1982-83	IL	1	20.11.82	Cardiff C	D3	H	D	1-1	Torrance
		1r	23.11.82	Cardiff C		A	L	0-3	

WOLVERHAMPTON WANDERERS

Formed in 1879 when players from St Lukes (formed 1877) and Goldthorn (formed 1876) joined to form Wolverhampton Wanderers. **Best FA Cup Performances:** Winners: 1893, 1908, 1949, 1960. Runners-up: 1889, 1896, 1921, 1939. **Record FA Cup Win:** 14-0 vs Crosswell's Brewery, 2nd round, 13.11.1886. **Record FA Cup Defeat:** 0-6 vs Rotherham, 1st round, 16.11.1985.

1883-84	1	27.10.83	Long Eaton R		H	W	4-1	Brodie 2, J.Griffiths 2
	2	1.12.83	Wednesbury OA		A	L	2-4	Brodie 2

Season	Div	Rd	Date	Opponent		H/A	W/D/L	Score	Scorers
1884-85		1	8.11.84	Derby St Lukes		H	D	0-0	
		1r	22.11.84	Derby St Lukes		A	L	2-4aet	Brodie, Brazier
1885-86		1	31.10.85	Derby St Lukes		H	W	7-0	Brodie 2, H.Aston 2, H.Wood, Horton, J.Aston
		2	21.11.85	Stafford Rd		H	W	4-2	J.Aston 2, H.Aston, H.Wood
		3	12.12.85	Walsall T		H	W	2-1	Brodie, Lowder
		4	2.1.86	WBA		A	L	1-3	H.Aston
1886-87		1	30.10.86	Matlock T		H	W	6-0	Brodie 2, B.Griffiths 2, Allen, Hunter
		2	13.11.86	Crosswells Brewery		H	W	14-0	T.Hunter 4, Brodie 3, Knight 3, B.Griffiths 2, Allen, Law og
		3	11.12.86	Aston V		A	D	2-2	Brodie, B.Griffiths
		3r	15.1.87	Aston V		H	D	1-1aet	Brodie
		3 2r	22.1.87	Aston V		H	D	3-3aet	B.Griffiths 2, Knight
		3 3r	29.1.87	Aston V		A	L	0-2	
1887-88		1	15.10.87	Walsall T		A	W	2-1	Hunter, Smallwood og
		2	5.11.87	Aston Shakespeare		H	W	3-0	Hunter, Shaw, B.Griffiths
		3	26.11.87	WBA		A	L	0-2	
1888-89	D1	1	2.2.89	Old Carthusians		H	W	4-3	Wood 2, Wykes, Mason
		2	16.2.89	Walsall TS		H	W	6-1	Knight 3, Hunter, Lowder, Brodie
		3	2.3.89	Sheffield W		H	W	3-0	Wykes 2, Fletcher
		SF	16.3.89	Blackburn R	D1		D	1-1	Wykes
		SFr	23.3.89	Blackburn R			W	3-1	Allen, Hunter, Wood
			both matches played at Crewe						
		F	30.3.89	Preston NE	D1		L	0-3	
			played at Kennington Oval						
1889-90	D1	1	18.1.90	Old Carthusians		H	W	2-0	Wood 2
		2	1.2.90	Small Heath	FAll	H	W	2-1	Fletcher, Speller og
		3	15.2.90	Stoke	D1	H	W	4-0	Worrall 2, Brodie, Wood
			FA ordered match to be replayed after Stoke protest about pitch						
		3	22.2.90	Stoke		H	W	8-0	Brodie 5, Wood 2, Allen
		SF	8.3.90	Blackburn R	D1		L	0-1	
			played at Racecourse Gd, Derby						
1890-91	D1	1	17.1.91	Long Eaton R		A	W	2-1aet	Wood 2
		2	31.1.91	Accrington	D1	A	W	3-2aet	Worrall, Wood, Booth
		3	14.2.91	Blackburn R	D1	A	L	0-2	
1891-92	D1	1	16.1.92	Crewe Alex	FAll	H	D	2-2aet	Devey, Wykes
		1r	23.1.92	Crewe Alex		A	W	3-1	Baker 2, Wykes
		2	30.1.92	Sheffield U	NL	H	W	3-1	Baker 2, Topham
		3	13.2.92	Aston V	D1	H	L	1-3	Topham
1892-93	D1	1	21.1.93	Bolton W	D1	A	D	1-1aet	Johnston
		1r	28.1.93	Bolton W		H	W	2-1	Wood, Wykes
		2	4.2.93	Middlesbrough	NL	H	W	2-1aet	Wykes, Butcher
		3	18.2.93	Darwen	D2	H	W	5-0	Topham 2, Wykes, Butcher, Griffin
		SF	4.3.93	Blackburn R	D1		W	2-1	Topham, Butcher
			played at Town Ground, Nottingham						
		F	25.3.93	EVERTON	D1		W	1-0	Allen
			played at Fallowfield, Manchester						
1893-94	D1	1	27.1.94	Aston Villa	D1	A	L	2-4	Wood, Butcher
1894-95	D1	1	2.2.95	Darwen	D2	A	D	0-0	
		1r	6.2.95	Darwen		H	W	2-0	Wykes, Griffin
		2	16.2.95	Stoke	D1	H	W	2-0	Wykes 2
		3	2.3.95	WBA	D1	A	L	0-1	
1895-96	D1	1	1.2.96	Notts Co	D2	H	D	2-2	Henderson, Malpass
		1r	5.2.96	Notts Co		A	W	4-3	Wood 2, Beats, Black
		2	15.2.96	Liverpool	D2	H	W	2-0	Wood, Owen
		3	29.2.96	Stoke	D1	H	W	3-0	Tonks, Henderson, Malpass
		SF	21.3.96	Derby Co	D1		W	2-1	Tonks, Malpass
			played at Perry Barr, Birmingham						
		F	18.4.96	Sheffield W	D1		L	1-2	BLack
			played at Crystal Palace						
1896-97	D1	1	30.1.97	Millwall A	SL	A	W	2-1	Tonks, Beats
		2	13.2.97	Blackburn R	D1	A	L	1-2	Beats
1897-98	D1	1	29.1.98	Notts Co	D1	A	W	1-0	Beats
		2	12.2.98	Derby Co	D1	H	L	0-1	
1898-99	D1	1	28.1.99	Bolton W	D1	H	D	0-0	
		1r	1.2.99	Bolton W		A	W	1-0	Blackett
		2	11.2.99	Derby Co	D1	A	L	1-2	Beats
1899-00	D1	1	27.1.00	QPR	SL	A	D	1-1	Miller
		1r	31.1.00	QPR		H	L	0-1aet	

Season	Div	Round	Date	Opponent		Venue	Result	Score	Scorers
1900-01	D1	1	9.2.01	New Brighton T	D2	H	W	5-1	Wooldridge 3, Bowen 2
		2	23.2.01	Notts Co	D1	A	W	3-2	Harper 2, Beats
		3	23.3.01	Sheffield U	D1	H	L	0-4	
1901-02	D1	1	25.1.02	Bolton W	D1	A	L	0-2	
1902-03	D1	1	7.2.03	Bury	D1	A	L	0-1	
1903-04	D1	1	6.2.04	Stockton	NL	A	W	4-1	Smith 2, Wooldridge, Logan og
		2	20.2.04	Derby Co	D1	A	D	2-2	Whitehouse, Wooldridge
		2r	24.2.04	Derby Co		H	D	2-2aet	Baynham, Miller
		2 2r	29.2.04	Derby Co Villa Pk			L	0-1	
1904-05	D1	1	4.2.05	Sunderland	D1	A	D	1-1	Wooldridge
		1r	8.2.05	Sunderland		H	W	1-0	J.Smith
		2	18.2.05	Southampton	D1	H	L	2-3	J.Smith, Bevin
1905-06	D1	1	13.1.06	Bishop Auckland	NL	A	W	3-0	Baynham, Smith, Pedley
		2	3.2.06	Bradford C	D2	A	L	0-5	
1906-07	D2	1	12.1.07	Sheffield W	D1	A	L	2-3	Wooldridge, Pedley
1907-08	D2	1	11.1.08	Bradford C	D2	A	D	1-1	Shelton
		1r	15.1.08	Bradford C		H	W	1-0	Hedley
		2	1.2.08	Bury	D1	H	W	2-0	Radford 2
		3	22.2.08	Swindon T	SL	H	W	2-0	Harrison, Hedley
		4	7.3.08	Stoke	D2	A	W	1-0	Radford
		SF	28.3.08	Southampton	SL		W	2-0	Radford, Hedley
				played at Stamford Bridge					
		F	25.4.08	NEWCASTLE U	D1		W	3-1	Hunt, Hedley, Harrison
				played at Crystal Palace					
1908-09	D2	1	16.1.09	Crystal Palace	SL	H	D	2-2	Radford 2
		1r	21.1.09	Crystal Palace		A	L	2-4aet	Hedley, Radford
1909-10	D2	1	15.1.10	Reading	SL	A	W	5-0	Blunt 4, Harrison
		2	5.2.10	West Ham	SL	H	L	1-5	Wooldridge
1910-11	D2	1	14.1.11	Accrington S	LC	H	W	2-0	Hedley
		2	4.2.11	Manchester C	D1	H	W	1-0	A.Needham
		3	25.2.11	Chelsea	D2	H	L	0-2	
1911-12	D2	1	13.1.12	Watford	SL	A	D	0-0	
		1r	24.1.12	Watford		H	W	10-0	Halligan 3, J.Needham 2, Brooks 2. Hedley, Young, Harrison
		2	3.2.12	Lincoln C	CL	H	W	2-1	Hedley, Groves
		3	24.2.12	Blackburn R	D1	A	L	2-3	Halligan 2
1912-13	D2	1	18.1.13	London Cal.	IL	H	W	3-1	Halligan, J.Needham
		2	1.2.13	Bradford PA	D2	A	L	0-3	
1913-14	D2	1	10.1.14	Southampton	SL	H	W	3-0	J.Needham, Howell, Groves
		2	31.1.14	Sheffield W	D1	H	D	1-1	Howell
		2r	4.2.14	Sheffield W		A	L	0-1	
1914-15	D2	1	9.1.15	Reading	SL	A	W	1-0	Harrison
		2	30.1.15	Sheffield W	D1	A	L	0-2	
1919-20	D2	1	10.1.20	Blackburn R	D1	A	D	2-2	Richards 2
		1r	15.1.20	Blackburn R		H	W	1-0	Lea
		2	31.1.20	Cardiff C	SL	H	L	1-2	Harrison
1920-21	D2	1	8.1.21	Stoke	D2	H	W	3-2	Edmonds 2, Burrill
		2	29.1.21	Derby Co	D1	A	D	1-1	Wightman og
		2r	3.2.21	Derby Co		H	W	1-0	Richards
		3	19.2.21	Fulham	D2	A	W	1-0	Potts
		4	5.3.21	Everton	D1	A	W	1-0	Edmonds
		SF	19.3.21	Cardiff C	D2		D	0-0	
				played at Anfield					
		SFr	23.3.21	Cardiff C			W	3-0	Richards, Edmonds, Brooks
				played at Old Trafford					
		F	23.4.21	Tottenham H	D1		L	0-1	
				played at Stamford Bridge					
1921-22	D2	1	1.1.22	Preston NE	D1	A	L	0-3	
1922-23	D2	1	13.1.23	Merthyr T	3S	A	W	1-0	Fazackerley
		2	3.2.23	Liverpool	D1	H	L	0-2	
1923-24	3N	1	12.1.24	Darlington	3N	H	W	3-1	Phillipson 2, Lees
		2	2.2.24	Charlton A	3S	A	D	0-0	
		2r	7.2.24	Charlton A		H	W	1-0	Fazackerley
		3	23.2.24	WBA	D1	A	D	1-1	Fazackerley
		3r	27.2.24	WBA		H	L	0-2	
1924-25	D2	1	10.1.25	Hull C	D2	A	D	1-1	Edwards
		1r	15.1.25	Hull C		H	L	0-1aet	
1925-26	D2	3	9.1.26	Arsenal	D1	H	D	1-1	Phillipson

	3r	13.1.26	Arsenal		A	L	0-1	
1926-27 D2	3	8.1.27	Carlisle U	NEL	A	W	2-0	Lees, Weaver
	4	29.1.27	Nottingham F	D2	H	W	2-0	Phillipson, Weaver
	5	19.2.27	Hull C	D2	H	W	1-0	Lees
	6	5.3.27	Arsenal	D1	A	L	1-2	Phillipson
1927-28 D2	3	14.1.28	Chelsea	D2	H	W	2-1	Phillipson, Baxter
	4	28.1.28	Sheffield U	D1	A	L	1-3	Phillipson
1928-29 D2	3	12.1.29	Mansfield T	ML	H	L	0-1	
1929-30 D2	3	11.1.30	Oldham A	D2	A	L	0-1	
1930-31 D2	3	10.1.31	Wrexham	3N	H	W	9-1	Hartill 4, Phillips 3, J.Deacon, Hollingsworth
	4	24.1.31	Bradford C	D2	A	D	0-0	
	4r	28.1.31	Bradford C		H	W	4-2	Bottrill 2, Hartill, J.Deacon
	5	14.2.31	Barnsley	D2	A	W	3-1	Hartill, Barraclough, J.Deacon
	6	28.2.31	WBA	D2	A	D	1-1	Shaw og
	6r	5.3.31	WBA		H	L	1-2	J.Deacon
1931-32 D2	3	9.1.32	Luton T	3S	A	W	2-1	Lowton, Phillips
	4	23.1.32	Preston NE	D2	A	L	0-2	
1932-33 D1	3	14.1.33	Derby Co	D1	H	L	3-6	Crook 2, Lowton
1933-34 D1	3	13.1.34	Newcastle U	D1	H	W	1-0	Phillips
	4	22.1.34	Derby Co	D1	A	L	0-3	
1934-35 D1	3	12.1.35	Notts Co	D2	H	W	4-0	Hartill, Phillips, Brown, Martin
	4	26.1.35	Sheffield W	D1	H	L	1-2	Hartill
1935-36 D1	3	11.1.36	Leeds U	D1	H	D	1-1	Wrigglesworth
	3r	15.1.36	Leeds U		A	L	1-3	Morris
1936-37 D1	3	16.1.37	Middlesbrough	D1	H	W	6-1	Galley, Clayton, Smalley, Ashall 2, B.Jones
	4	30.1.37	Sheffield U	D2	H	D	2-2	Clayton, Johnson og
	4r	4.2.37	Sheffield U		A	W	2-1	Clayton, Ashall
	5	20.2.37	Grimsby T	D1	H	D	1-1	Galley
	5r	24.2.37	Grimsby T		H	W	6-2	Clayton 2, Ashall 2, B.Jones, Westcott
	6	6.3.37	Sunderland	D1	H	D	1-1	B.Jones
	6r	10.3.37	Sunderland		A	D	2-2aet	Galley, Thompson
	6 2r	15.3.37	Sunderland at Hillsborough			L	0-4	
1937-38 D1	3	8.1.38	Swansea T	D2	A	W	4-0	Westcott 3, B.Jones
	4	22.1.38	Arsenal	D1	H	L	1-2	B.Jones
1938-39 D1	3	7.1.39	Bradford PA	D2	H	W	3-1	Westcott 2, McIntosh
	4	21.1.39	Leicester C	D1	H	W	5-1	Westcott 2, Maguire 2, Dorsett
	5	11.2.39	Liverpool	D1	H	W	4-1	Westcott, McIntosh, Burton, Dorsett
	6	4.3.39	Everton	D1	H	W	2-0	Westcott 2
	SF	25.3.39	Grimsby T	D1		W	5-0	Westcott 4, Galley
		played at Old Trafford						
	F	29.4.39	Portsmouth	D1 WEMBLEY	L	1-4		Dorsett
1945-46 D1	3 1L	5.1.46	Lovell's A	SL	A	W	4-2	Davies 2, Galley, Crook
	3 2L	9.1.46	Lovell's A		H	W	8-1	Galley 3, Wright 2, King, Dunn, Mullen
	4 1L	26.1.46	Charlton A	D1	A	L	2-5	Chatham 2
	4 2L	30.1.46	Charlton A		H	D	1-1	Wright
1946-47 D1	3	11.1.47	Rotherham U	3N	H	W	3-0	Westcott, Hancocks, Pye
	4	25.1.47	Sheffield U	D1	H	D	0-0	
	4r	29.1.47	Sheffield U		A	L	0-2	
1947-48 D1	3	10.1.48	Bournemouth	3S	A	W	2-1	Mullen 2
	4	24.1.48	Everton	D1	H	D	1-1	Westcott
	4r	31.1.48	Everton		A	L	2-3	Westcott 2
1948-49 D1	3	8.1.49	Chesterfield	D2	H	W	6-0	Hancocks, Pye 2, Mullen, Smyth 2
	4	29.1.49	Sheffield U	D1	A	W	3-0	Hancocks 2, Dunn
	5	12.2.49	Liverpool	D1	H	W	3-1	Dunn, Smyth, Mullen
	6	26.2.49	WBA	D2	H	W	1-0	Mullen
	SF	26.3.49	Manchester U	D1		D	1-1aet	Smyth
		played at Hillsborough						
	SFr	2.4.49	Manchester U			W	1-0	Smyth
		played at Goodison Park						
	F	30.4.49	LEICESTER C	D2 WEMBLEY	W	3-1		Pye 2, Smyth
1949-50 D1	3	7.1.50	Plymouth A	D2	A	D	1-1	Smyth
	3r	11.1.50	Plymouth A		H	W	3-0	Smyth, Swinbourne, Hancocks
	4	28.1.50	Sheffield U	D2	H	D	0-0	
	4r	31.1.50	Sheffield U		A	W	4-3	Hancocks 2, Smyth, Mullen
	5	11.2.50	Blackpool	D1	H	D	0-0	
	5r	15.2.50	Blackpool		A	L	0-1	
1950-51 D1	3	6.1.51	Plymouth A	3S	A	W	2-1	Dunn, Walker

	4	27.1.51	**Aston Villa**	D1	H	W	3-1	Walker, Swinbourne, Mullen
	5	10.2.51	**Huddersfield T**	D1	H	W	2-0	Dunn 2
	6	24.2.51	**Sunderland**	D1	A	D	1-1	Walker
	6r	28.2.51	**Sunderland**		H	W	3-1	Dunn, Swinbourne, Walker
	SF	10.3.51	**Newcastle U**	D1		D	0-0aet	
		played at Hillsborough						
	SFr	14.3.51	**Newcastle U**			L	1-2	Walker
		played at Huddersfield						
1951-52 D1	3	12.1.52	**Manchester C**	D1	A	D	2-2	Broadbent, Whitfield
	3r	16.1.52	**Manchester C**		H	W	4-1	Mullen 2, Short 2
	4	2.2.52	**Liverpool**	D1	A	L	1-2	Mullen
1952-53 D1	3	10.1.53	**Preston NE**	D1	A	L	2-5	Wilshaw, Smith
1953-54 D1	3	9.1.54	**Birmingham C**	D2	H	L	1-2	Wilshaw
1954-55 D1	3	8.1.55	**Grimsby T**	3N	A	W	5-2	McDonald, Swinbourne, Smith, Wilshaw 2
	4	29.1.55	**Arsenal**	D1	H	W	1-0	Swinbourne
	5	19.2.55	**Charlton A**	D1	H	W	4-1	Wilshaw 3, Hancocks
	6	12.3.55	**Sunderland**	D1	A	L	0-2	
1955-56 D1	3	7.1.56	**WBA**	D1	H	L	1-2	Slater
1956-57 D1	3	5.1.57	**Swansea T**	D2	H	W	5-3	Bonson 2, Broadbent, Flowers, Mullen
	4	26.1.57	**Bournemouth**	3S	H	L	0-1	
1957-58 D1	3	4.1.58	**Lincoln C**	D2	A	W	1-0	Mullen
	4	25.1.58	**Portsmouth**	D1	H	W	5-1	Mason, Broadbent 2, Mullen, Rutter og
	5	15.2.58	**Darlington**	3N	H	W	6-1	Murray 3, Broadbent 2, Mason
	6	1.3.58	**Bolton W**	D1	A	L	1-2	Mason
1958-59 D1	3	10.1.59	**Barrow**	D4	A	W	4-2	Lill, Booth, Deeley 2
	4	24.1.59	**Bolton W**	D1	H	L	1-2	Hennin og
1959-60 D1	3	9.1.60	**Newcastle U**	D1	A	D	2-2	Flowers, Clamp (p)
	3r	13.1.60	**Newcastle U**		H	W	4-2	Murray, Deeley, Flowers, Horne
	4	30.1.60	**Charlton A**	D2	H	W	2-1	Horne, Broadbent
	5	20.2.60	**Luton T**	D1	A	W	4-1	Mason 2, Murray, Clamp
	6	12.3.60	**Leicester C**	D1	A	W	2-1	Broadbent, Chalmers og
	SF	26.3.60	**Aston Villa**	D2		W	1-0	Deeley
		played at the Hawthorns						
	F	7.5.60	**BLACKBURN R**	D1 WEMBLEY	W	3-0	Deeley 2, McGrath og
1960-61 D1	3	7.1.61	**Huddersfield T**	D2	H	D	1-1	Kirkham
	3r	11.1.61	**Huddersfield T**		A	L	1-2	Murray
1961-62 D1	3	8.1.62	**Carlisle U**	D4	H	W	3-1	Wharton 2, Broadbent
	4	27.1.62	**WBA**	D1	H	L	1-2	Murray
1962-63 D1	3	29.1.63	**Nottingham F**	D1	A	L	3-4	Stobart 2, Broadbent
1963-64 D1	3	4.1.64	**Arsenal**	D1	A	L	1-2	Wharton
1964-65 D1	3	8.1.65	**Portsmouth**	D2	A	D	0-0	
	3r	12.1.65	**Portsmouth**		H	W	3-2	McIlmoyle 2, Crawford
	4	30.1.65	**Rotherham U**	D2	H	D	2-2	Crawford, Flowers
	4r	2.2.65	**Rotherham U**		A	W	3-0	Woodruff, Wharton, Wagstaffe
	5	20.2.65	**Aston Villa**	D1	A	D	1-1	Woodruff
	5r	24.2.65	**Aston Villa**		H	D	0-0aet	
	5 2r	1.3.65	**Aston Villa** at the Hawthorns		W	3-1	McIlmoyle 3
	6	10.3.65	**Manchester U**	D1	H	L	3-5	McIlmoyle 2, Knowles
1965-66 D2	3	22.1.66	**Altrincham**	CC	H	W	5-0	Hunt 2, McIlmoyle, Woodruff, Dewar og
	4	12.2.66	**Sheffield U**	D1	H	W	3-0	Knowles 2, McIlmoyle
	5	5.3.66	**Manchester U**	D1	H	L	2-4	Wharton 2
1966-67 D2	3	28.1.67	**Oldham A**	D3	A	D	2-2	Thomson, Bailey
	3r	1.2.67	**Oldham A**		H	W	4-1	Woodfield, Wharton, Hunt, McIlmoyle
	4	18.2.67	**Everton**	D1	H	D	1-1	Wharton
	4r	21.2.67	**Everton**		A	L	1-3	Wharton
1967-68 D1	3	27.1.68	**Rotherham U**	D2	A	L	0-1	
1968-69 D1	3	4.1.69	**Hull C**	D2	A	W	3-1	Dougan 2, Wignall
	4	25.1.69	**Tottenham H**	D1	A	L	1-2	Wagstaffe
1969-70 D1	3	3.1.70	**Burnley**	D1	A	L	0-3	
1970-71 D1	3	2.1.71	**Norwich C**	D2	H	W	5-1	McCalliog 2, Gould 2, Hibbitt
	4	23.1.71	**Derby Co**	D1	A	L	1-2	Richards
1971-72 D1	3	15.1.72	**Leicester C**	D1	H	D	1-1	McCalliog
	3r	19.1.72	**Leicester C**		A	L	0-2	
1972-73 D1	3	13.1.73	**Manchester U**	D1	H	W	1-0	Bailey
	4	3.2.73	**Bristol C**	D2	H	W	1-0	Richards
	5	24.2.73	**Millwall**	D2	H	W	1-0	Richards
	6	17.3.73	**Coventry C**	D1	H	W	2-1	Richards, Hibbitt

	SF	7.4.73	**Leeds U**	D1		L	0-1	
		played at Maine Road						
	3/4	18.8.73	**Arsenal**	D1	A	W	3-1	Dougan 2, McCalliog
1973-74	D1	3	5.1.74	**Leeds U**	D1	H	D	1-1	Richards
	3r	9.1.74	**Leeds U**		A	L	0-1	
1974-75	D1	3	4.1.75	**Ipswich T**	D1	H	L	1-2	Richards
1975-76	D1	3	3.1.76	**Arsenal**	D1	H	W	3-0	Hibbitt, Bell, Richards
	4	24.1.76	**Ipswich T**	D1	A	D	0-0	
	4r	27.1.76	**Ipswich T**		H	W	1-0	Gould
	5	14.2.76	**Charlton A**	D2	H	W	3-0	Richards 3
	6	6.3.76	**Manchester U**	D1	A	D	1-1	Richards
	6r	9.3.76	**Manchester U**		H	L	2-3aet	Richards, Kindon
1976-77	D2	3	8.1.77	**Rotherham U**	D3	H	W	3-2	Richards. S.Daley
	4	29.1.77	**Ipswich T**	D1	A	D	2-2	Richards 2
	4r	2.2.77	**Ipswich T**	D1	H	W	1-0	Richards
	5	26.2.77	**Chester**	D3	H	W	1-0	Hibbitt
	6	19.3.77	**Leeds U**	D1	H	L	0-1	
1977-78	D1	3	7.1.78	**Exeter C**	D3	A	D	2-2	Carr, M.Daly
	3r	10.1.78	**Exeter C**		H	W	3-1	S.Daley, Hibbitt, Richards
	4	28.1.78	**Arsenal**	D1	A	L	1-2	Hibbitt
1978-79	D1	3	9.1.79	**Brighton & HA**	D2	A	W	3-2	S.Daley, Bell, Williams og
	4	27.1.79	**Newcastle U**	D2	A	D	1-1	Hibbitt
	4r	22.2.79	**Newcastle U**		H	W	1-0	Bell
	5	26.2.79	**Crystal Palace**	D2	A	W	1-0	Patching
	6	10.3.79	**Shrewsbury T**	D3	H	D	1-1	Rafferty
	6r	13.3.79	**Shrewsbury T**		A	W	3-1	Rafferty, Carr, Daniel
	SF	31.3.79	**Arsenal**	D1		L	0-2	
		played at Villa Park						
1979-80	D1	3	5.1.80	**Notts Co**	D2	A	W	3-1	Richards, Berry, Carr
	4	26.1.80	**Norwich C**	D1	H	D	1-1	Gray
	4r	30.1.80	**Norwich C**		A	W	3-2	Richards, Berry, Eves
	5	16.2.80	**Watford**	D2	H	L	0-3	
1980-81	D1	3	3.1.81	**Stoke C**	D1	A	D	2-2	Bell, Eves
	3r	6.1.81	**Stoke C**		H	W	2-1	Hibbitt, Eves
	4	24.1.81	**Watford**	D2	A	D	1-1	Richards
	4r	27.1.81	**Watford**		H	W	2-1	Richards, Parkin
	5	14.2.81	**Wrexham**	D2	H	W	3-1	Bell 2, Richards
	6	7.3.81	**Middlesbrough**	D1	A	D	1-1	Gray
	6r	10.3.81	**Middlesbrough**		H	W	3-1aet	Richards, Eves, Bell
	SF	11.4.81	**Tottenham H**	D1		D	2-2aet	Carr, Hibbitt (p)
		played at Hillsborough						
	SFr	15.4.81	**Tottenham H**			L	0-3	
		played at Highbury						
1981-82	D1	3	2.1.82	**Leeds U**	D1	H	L	1-3	Gray
1982-83	D2	3	8.1.83	**Tranmere R**	D4	A	W	1-0	Hibbitt
	4	29.1.83	**Aston Villa**	D1	A	L	0-1	
1983-84	D1	3	7.1.84	**Coventry C**	D1	A	D	1-1	Clarke
	3r	10.1.84	**Coventry C**		H	D	1-1aet	Eves
	3 2r	16.1.84	**Coventry C**		A	L	0-3	
1984-85	D2	3	5.1.85	**Huddersfield T**	D2	H	D	1-1	Pender
	3r	23.1.85	**Huddersfield T**		A	L	1-3	Ainscow
1985-86	D3	1	16.11.85	**Rotherham U**	D3	A	L	0-6	
1986-87	D4	1	15.11.86	**Chorley** at Bolton	NPL	A	D	1-1	Mutch
	1r	18.11.86	**Chorley**		H	D	1-1aet	Forman
	1 2r	24.11.86	**Chorley** at Bolton		A	L	0-3	
1987-88	D4	1	14.11.87	**Cheltenham T**	APL	H	W	5-1	Bull 3, Downing, Vaughan
	2	5.12.87	**Wigan A**	D3	A	W	3-1	Gallagher, Dennison, Robinson
	3	9.1.88	**Bradford C**	D2	A	L	1-2	Sinnott og
1988-89	D3	1	9.11.88	**Grimsby T**	D4	A	L	0-1	
1989-90	D2	3	6.1.90	**Sheffield W**	D1	H	L	1-2	Bull
1990-91	D2	3	5.1.91	**Cambridge U**	D3	H	L	0-1	
1991-92	D2	3	4.1.92	**Nottingham F**	D1	A	L	0-1	
1992-93	D1	3	2.1.93	**Watford**	D1	A	W	4-1	Holdsworth og, Downing, Mutch, Bull
	4	24.1.93	**Bolton W**	D2	H	L	0-2	

WOMBWELL TOWN

First entered FA Cup: 1920

| 1930-31 | ML | 1 | 29.11.30 | Wellington T | BDL | A | D | 0-0 |
| | | 1r | 4.12.30 | Wellington T | | H | L | 0-3 |

WOODFORD BRIDGE

Formed 1880. Played at the Woodford Bridge Field, near the White Hart pub, Woodford, Essex

1881-82	1	22.10.81	Reading Abbey	H	D	1-1	Overton
	1r	12.11.81	Reading Abbey	A	L	1-2	
1882-83	1	21.10.82	Royal Engineers	A	L	1-3	Bullard
1883-84	1	3.11.83	Romford	A	L	0-3	

WOODFORD TOWN

Formed 1937. **First entered FA Cup:** 1946

| 1986-87 | SL | 1 | 15.11.86 | Orient | D4 | H | L | 0-1 |

WOODFORD WELLS

Formed 1869. Played at Monkham Lane, Woodford, Essex

1873-74	1	11.10.73	Reigate Priory	H	W	3-2	Fraser 2, E.Beauchamp
	2	22.11.73	Swifts	A	L	1-2	R.Beauchamp
1874-75	1	31.10.74	High Wycombe	H	W	1-0	W.Spreckley
	2	5.12.74	Southall	H	W	3-0	Wild 2, Bouch
	3	23.1.75	Shropshire W	A	D	1-1aet	Powell
	3r	6.2.75	Shropshire W	H	L	0-2	
1875-76	1	6.11.75	Panthers	A	L	0-1	

WOOD GRANGE

| 1876-77 | 1 | 8.11.76 | Panthers | A | L | 0-3 |
| 1877-78 | 1 | 27.10.77 | High Wycombe | A | L | 0-4 |

WORCESTER CITY

Formed 1902. **First entered FA Cup:** 1905. **Cup Final Connection:** Ron Baynham, who played for Luton in the 1959 Cup Final is a former Worcester player. In 1959 Worcester caused a major upset when they beat Liverpool in a third round match. Roy Paul, captain of Manchester City in the 1956 final, was in the Worcester side. **League clubs beaten:** Millwall, Liverpool, Plymouth A, Wrexham, Aldershot

1905-06	BDL	1	13.1.06	Watford	SL	H	L	0-6	
1925-26	BDL	1	28.11.25	Kettering T	SL	H	D	0-0	
		1r	3.12.25	Kettering T		A	D	0-0aet	
		1 2r	7.12.25	Kettering T at St Andrews			L	0-2	
1928-29	BDL	1	24.11.28	Walsall	3S	A	L	1-3	Byers (p)
1950-51	SL	1	25.11.50	Hartlepools U	3N	H	L	1-4	Jackman
1957-58	SL	1	16.11.57	Aldershot	3S	A	D	0-0	
		1r	21.11.57	Aldershot		H	D	2-2aet	Bryceland, Knowles
		1 2r	25.11.57	Aldershot at St Andrews			L	2-3aet	Quigley, Bryceland
1958-59	SL	1	15.11.58	Chelmsford C	SL	A	D	0-0	
		1r	20.11.58	Chelmsford C		H	W	3-1	Gosling, Brown, Skuse
		2	6.12.58	Millwall	D4	H	W	5-2	Brown 2, Skuse, Knowles 2
		3	15.1.59	Liverpool	D2	H	W	2-1	Skuse, White og
		4	24.1.59	Sheffield U	D2	H	L	0-2	
1960-61	SL	1	5.11.60	Coventry C	D3	H	L	1-4	Phillips (p)
1978-79	SL	1	25.11.78	Plymouth A	D3	H	W	2-0	Phelps, Williams
		2	16.12.78	Newport Co	D4	A	D	0-0	
		2r	18.12.78	Newport Co		H	L	1-2	Phelps
1982-83	APL	1	20.11.82	Macclesfield	NPL	A	W	5-1	Moss 2, Tuohy 3
		2	11.12.82	Wrexham	D3	H	W	2-1	Moss 2
		3	8.1.83	Coventry C	D1	A	L	1-3	Moss (p)
1983-84	APL	1	19.11.83	Aldershot	D4	A	D	1-1	Moss
		1r	21.11.83	Aldershot		H	W	2-1	Moss 2

WORCESTER CITY

		2	10.12.84	Maidstone U	APL	A	L	2-3	Moss 2 (1p)
1987-88	SL	1	14.11.87	Yeovil	IL	H	D	1-1	Ferguson
		1r	18.11.87	Yeovil		A	L	0-1	

WORKINGTON

Formed 1884. **First entered FA Cup:** 1887. Members of the Football League 1951-1977

1909-10	LC	1	15.1.10	Manchester C	D2	A	L	1-2	Swan
1926-27	NEL	1	27.11.26	Crook T	NL	A	L	1-2	Gilfillan
1927-28	NEL	1	26.11.27	Bradford C	3N	A	L	0-6	
1930-31	NEL	1	29.11.30	Nelson	3N	A	L	0-4	
1932-33	NEL	1	26.11.32	Scunthorpe U	ML	H	W	5-1	Bruce 2, James, Maidment, Charlton
		2	10.12.32	Halifax T	3N	A	L	1-2	James
1933-34	NEL	1	25.11.33	Southport	3N	H	W	1-0	Stanger
		2	9.12.33	Newport Co	3S	A	W	3-1	Charlton, James, Miller
		3	13.1.34	Gateshead	3N	H	W	4-1	Lincoln 2, Charlton 2
		4	27.1.34	Preston NE	D2	H	L	1-2	Holdcroft og
1934-35	NEL	1	24.11.34	Birmingham Corp.Tram	BC	H	W	2-0	Thornton, Charlton
		2	8.12.34	Northampton T	3S	A	D	0-0	
		2r	13.12.34	Northampton T		H	L	0-1	
1935-36	NEL	1	30.11.35	New Brighton	3N	A	W	3-1	Boyd 3
		2	14.12.35	Kidderminster H	BDL	H	W	5-1	Boyd 4, Maidment
		3	11.1.36	Bradford PA	D2	A	L	2-3	Carruthers, Sewell
1937-38	NEL	1	27.11.37	New Brighton	3N	A	L	0-5	
1938-39	NEL	1	26.11.38	Mansfield	3S	H	D	1-1	Pearce
		1r	30.11.38	Mansfield		A	L	1-2	Allison
1946-47	NEL	1	30.11.46	South Liverpool	CC	A	L	1-2	Pope
1947-48	NEL	1	29.11.47	Lincoln C	3N	A	W	2-0	Armstrong, Oakes
		2	13.12.47	Crewe Alex	3N	H	L	1-2	Oakes
1948-49	NEL	1	27.11.48	Stockport Co	3N	H	L	0-3	
1951-52	3N	1	24.11.51	Blackhall Colliery	NEL	A	W	5-2	Maxfield, Simmonds, Dick, McDowall, Mullen
		2	12.12.51	Witton Albion	CC	A	D	3-3	Simmonds 2, Maxfield
		2r	20.12.51	Witton Albion		H	W	1-0	Simmonds
1952-53	3N	1	22.11.52	Chesterfield	3N	A	L	0-1	
1953-54	3N	1	21.11.53	Ferryhill Ath	NL	A	W	3-0	Stokoe, Simmonds, McAlone
		2	12.12.53	Stockport Co	3N	A	L	1-2	Cameron
1954-55	3N	1	20.11.54	Hyde U	CC	H	W	5-1	Bertolini, Whittle 3, Dailey
		2	11.12.54	Leyton O	3S	A	W	1-0	Bertolini
		3	8.1.55	Luton T	D2	A	L	0-5	
1955-56	3N	1	19.11.55	Scarborough	ML	H	W	4-2	Dailey 2, Dunlop, Whittle
		2	10.12.55	Bradford PA	3N	A	L	3-4	Mitchell, Bertolini, Dunlop
1956-57	3N	1	17.11.56	Mansfield T	3N	A	D	1-1	Dailey
		1r	20.11.56	Mansfield T		H	W	2-1	Bertolini, Dailey
		2	8.12.56	Goole T	ML	A	D	2-2	Dailey, Finlay
		2r	12.12.56	Goole T		H	L	0-1	
1957-58	3N	1	16.11.57	Crook T	NL	H	W	8-1	Brown, Bertolini 2, Kinloch, Currie 2, Purdon, Steward og
		2	7.12.57	Oldham A	3N	A	W	5-1	Robson 2, Currie, Chisholm, Purdon (p)
		3	4.1.58	Manchester U	D1	H	L	1-3	Colbridge
1958-59	D4	1	15.11.58	Accrington S	D3	A	L	1-5	Alexandra
1959-60	D4	1	14.11.59	Southport	D4	A	D	2-2	Morrison, Brownlee
		1r	18.11.59	Southport		H	W	3-0	Booth, Harburn, McGarry
		2	5.12.59	Halifax T	D3	H	W	1-0	Rollo (p)
		3	9.1.60	Crewe A	D4	A	L	0-2	
1960-61	D4	1	5.11.60	Stockport Co	D4	A	L	0-1	
1961-62	D4	1	4.11.61	Worksop T	ML	H	W	2-0	Haasz, McGarry
		2	25.11.61	Gateshead	NCo	A	W	2-0	Haasz, Kirkup
		3	6.1.62	Nottingham F	D1	H	L	1-2	McGarry
1962-63	D4	1	3.11.62	North Shields	NEL	A	D	2-2	Commons, Swindells
		1r	8.11.62	North Shields		H	W	7-2	Carr 4, Commons, Kirkup, Swindells
		2	24.11.62	Hull C	D3	A	L	0-2	
1963-64	D4	1	16.11.63	Halifax T	D4	H	W	4-1	Martin, Moran 2, Carr
		2	7.12.63	Port Vale	D3	A	L	1-2	Moran
1964-65	D3	1	14.11.64	Rochdale	D4	H	W	2-0	Carr, Moran
		2	5.12.64	South Liverpool	LC	A	W	2-0	Moran 2
		3	9.1.65	Bolton W	D2	A	L	1-4	Moran
1965-66	D3	1	13.11.65	Hartlepools	D4	A	L	1-3	Lowes

1966-67	D3	1	26.11.66	South Shields	NRL	A	W	4-1	Griffin 2 (1p), Tinnion, Oliver
		2	11.1.67	Bradford PA	D4	A	L	1-3	Oliver
1967-68	D4	1	9.12.67	Ryhope Colliery W	Wear	A	W	1-0	Spratt
		2	6.1.68	Doncaster R	D4	A	D	1-1	Tinnion
		2r	10.1.68	Doncaster R		H	L	1-2	Tinnion
1968-69	D4	1	16.11.68	Scunthorpe U	D4	H	W	2-0	Tinnion, Griffith
		2	7.12.68	Port Vale	D4	A	D	0-0	
		2r	11.12.68	Port Vale		H	L	1-2	Griffith
1969-70	D4	1	15.11.69	Rochdale	D3	H	W	2-1	Tyrer, Martin
		2	6.12.69	Rotherham U	D3	A	L	0-3	
1970-71	D4	1	21.11.70	Scarborough	NPL	A	W	3-2	Spratt 2, Goodfellow
		2	12.12.70	Chesterfield	D3	A	D	0-0	
		2r	16.12.70	Chesterfield		H	W	3-2	Goodfellow, Ogilvie, Massie
		3	2.1.71	Brentford	D4	H	L	0-1	
1971-72	D4	1	20.11.71	Southport	D4	A	W	3-1	Dunleavy og, Spencer, Goodfellow
		2	11.12.71	Bury	D4	H	L	1-3	Spratt (p)
1972-73	D4	1	18.11.72	Stockport Co	D4	A	L	0-1	
1973-74	D4	1	24.11.73	Bradford C	D4	A	L	0-2	
1974-75	D4	1	23.11.74	Darlington	D4	A	L	0-1	
1975-76	D4	1	22.11.75	Rochdale	D4	H	D	1-1	Heslop
		1r	25.11.75	Rochdale		A	L	1-2aet	Geidmintis
1976-77	D4	1	20.11.76	Bury	D3	A	L	0-6	
1977-78	NPL	1	26.11.77	Grimsby T	D4	H	L	0-2	
1978-79	NPL	1	25.11.78	Rotherham U	D3	A	L	0-3	
1979-80	NPL	1	24.11.79	Chester	D3	A	L	1-5	Diamond
1980-81	NPL	1	22.11.80	Carlisle U	D3	H	D	0-0	
		1r	1.12.80	Carlisle U		A	L	1-4	Gill
1981-82	NPL	1	21.11.81	Huddersfield T	D3	H	D	1-1	Reach
		1r	24.11.81	Huddersfield T		A	L	0-5	
1982-83	NPL	1	20.11.82	Doncaster R	D3	H	L	1-2	Gill

WORKSOP TOWN

Formed 1880. **First entered FA Cup:** 1893. **League clubs beaten:** Nelson, Grimsby T, Chesterfield, Coventry C, Bradford C

1907-08	ML	1	11.1.08	Chelsea	D1	A	L	1-9	Richardson
1921-22	ML	6q Nelson (3N) H 2-1							
		1	7.1.22	Southend U	3S	H	L	1-2	Lawrie
1922-23	ML	5q Grimsby T (3N) A 2-0; 6q Chesterfield (3N) H 1-0							
		1	13.1.23	Tottenham H	D1	A	D	0-0	
		1r	15.1.23	Tottenham H		A	L	0-9	
				played at White Hart Lane					
1925-26	ML	1	28.11.25	Coventry C	3N	H	W	1-0	Spink
		2	12.12.25	Chesterfield	3N	H	L	1-2	Tremelling
1926-27	ML	1	27.11.26	York C	ML	A	–	1-1	Tremelling
				abandoned after 70 minutes – fog					
		1	1.12.26	York C		A	L	1-4	Boulton
1955-56	ML	1	19.11.55	Skegness T	Lincs	A	W	4-0	Rooth, Dean, Scotson og, Rhodes
		2	10.12.55	Bradford C	3N	A	D	2-2	Mosby, McCall
		2r	15.12.55	Bradford C		H	W	1-0	Mosby
		3	7.1.56	Swindon T	3S	A	L	0-1	
1961-62	ML	1	4.11.61	Workington	D4	A	L	0-2	
1978-79	NPL	1	25.11.78	Barnsley	D4	A	L	1-5	Woods

WORTHING

Formed 1886. **First entered FA Cup:** 1899

1936-37	SCL	1	28.11.36	Yeovil	SL	A	L	3-4	Ockenden, Thorlby, Varndell
1982-83	IL	1	20.11.82	Dartford	SL	H	W	2-1	Lelliot, Cornwell
		2	11.12.82	Oxford U	D3	A	L	0-4	

WREXHAM

Formed 1873 (the oldest club in Wales). **Best FA Cup Performance:** 6th round, 1974, 1978. Welsh FA Cup: Winners: 21 times; Runners-up 19 times. **Record FA Cup Win:** 11-0 vs Rhyl, Extra Pr rd, 9.9.1911. In Competition Proper: 6-0 vs Gateshead, 1st round, 20.11.1976; 6-0 vs Charlton, 3rd round, 5.1.1980. **Record FA Cup Defeat:** 1-9 vs Wolverhampton W, 3rd round, 10.1.1931.

1883-84	1		**Liverpool Ramblers**			*walkover*	
	2	1.12.83	**Oswestry**	H	L	3-4	W.Davies 2, one other
1884-85	1	18.10.84	**Goldenhill**	H	W	1-0	
	2	29.11.84	**Chirk**	A	L	1-4	
1885-86	1	31.10.85	**Leek**	A	L	3-6	
1886-87	1	23.10.86	**Crewe A**	H	L	1-4	T.Roberts
1887-88	1		bye				
	2	5.11.87	**Davenham**	H	L	1-2	Groom
1888-89			1q **Davenham** (H) 3-0; 2q **Northwich Victoria** (H) 3-2; 3q **Chirk** (H) 2-1aet; 4q **Chester** (A) 3-2				
	1	2.2.89	**Swifts**	A	L	1-3	Wilding
1889-90			2q **Northwich Victoria** (A) 1-3				
1890-91	TC		2q **Nantwich Town** (H) 2-3				
1891-92	TC		2q **Chester** (A) 4-2; 3q **Crewe A** (A) 1-3				
1892-93	TC		1q **Liverpool Caledonians** (A) 1-7				
1893-94	TC		1q **Barnton Rovers** (A) 4-3aet; 2q **Nantwich T** (A) 3-2; 3q **Stockport Co** (A) 2-3				
1894-95	TC		1q **Stalybridge Rovers** (A) 3-2; 2q **Macclesfield** (H) 7-1; 3q **Glossop** (H) 1-2				
1895-96	TC		1q **Newtown** (H) 3-1; 2q **Crewe A** (H) 3-3aet; 2qr **Crewe A** (A) 2-5				
1896-97	TC		1q **Rock Ferry** (H) 0-4				
1897-98	TC		1q **Warrington St Elphins** (A) 3-0; 2q **Chirk** (A) 2-2; 2qr **Chirk** (H) 2-0; 3q **Crewe A** (A) 1-4				
1898-99	TC		1q **Chester** (H) 3-2; 2q **South Liverpool** (A) 2-4				
1899-00	TC		2q **Llandudno Swifts** (A) 2-1; 3q **Dudley T** (H) 3-2; 4q **Small Heath** (A) 1-6				
1900-01	TC		3q **Stockport Co** (A) 2-6				
1901-02	TC		2q **Chirk** (A) 2-0; 3q **Oswestry U** (A) 2-1; 4q **Port Vale** (H) 2-1abnd; 4qr **Port Vale** (H) 0-0; 4q 2r **Port Vale** (A) 1-3				
1902-03	TC		3q **Nantwich T** (H) 3-0; 4q **Glossop** (A) 0-4				
1903-04	TC		2q **Oswestry U** (A) 0-2				
1904-05	TC		3q **Crewe A** (A) 3-0; 4q **Earlestown** (A) 2-0; 5q **Stockport Co** (A) 0-4				
1905-06	BDL		P **Rhyl** (H) 1-4				
1906-07	BDL		P **Rhyl** (H) 7-0; 1q **Tranmere R** (H) 2-1; 2q **Oswestry U** (H) 3-1; 3q **Whitchurch** (H) 3-2; 4q **Kidderminster** (A) 1-2				
1907-08	BDL		1q **Oswestry U** (H) 0-1				
1908-09	BDL		P **Welshpool** (H) 6-1; 1q **Whitchurch** (A) 3-0; 2q **Nantwich T** (A) 4-2; 3q **Chester** (H) 3-1; 4q **Hednesford T** (A) 2-1;				
			5q **Oxford City** (H) 7-0				
	1	16.1.09	**Exeter C**	SL H	D	1-1	Smith
	1r	20.1.09	**Exeter C**	A	L	1-2aet	Rankin
1909-10	BDL		4q **Coventry C** (A) 0-3				
1910-11	BDL		P **Wellington St Georges** (H) 9-1; 1q **Chester** (A) 0-3				
1911-12	BDL		Ex P **Rhyl** (H) 11-0; P **Harrowby** (A) 1-1; Pr **Harrowby** walkover; 1q **Witton Albion** (H) 4-2; 2q **South Liverpool** (H) 4-3;				
			3q **Chester** (H) 1-4				
1912-13	BDL		P **Chester** (H) 2-0; 1q **Wellington T** (A) 1-1; 1qr **Wellington T** (H) 2-2; 1q 2r **Wellington T** (A) 3-0; 2q **Northwich Victoria** (A) 1-5				
1913-14	BDL		P **Witton Albion** (A) 5-0; 1q **Connah's Quay** (A) 2-1; 2q **South Liverpool** (H) 1-1; 2qr **South Liverpool** (A) 0-1				
1914-15	BDL		P **South Liverpool** (H) 2-1; 1q **Skelmersdale** (H) 2-1; 2q **Nantwich T** (H) 4-2; 3q **Tranmere Rovers** (H) 1-1;				
			3qr **Tranmere Rovers** (A) 1-0; 4q **Walsall** (A) 1-2				
1919-20	BDL		1q **Marlborough OB** (H) 8-0; 2q **Crewe A** (A) 3-3; 2qr **Crewe Alex** (H) 0-1				
1920-21	BDL		P **Northwich Victoria** (H) 3-0; 1q **Prescott W** (H) 7-0; 2q **Prescot** (H) 2-0; 3q **Buckley United** (A) 0-1				
1921-22	3N		4q **Burton All Saints** (H) 4-0; 5q **Crewe A** (H) 5-0; 6q **Newport Co** (H) 0-0; 6qr **Newport County** (A) 0-3				
1922-23	3N		5q **Port Vale** (A) 2-0; 6q **Hartlepool U** (H) 1-0				
	1	13.1.23	**Bristol City**	3S A	L	1-5	Jackson
1923-24	3N		5q **Port Vale** (H) 5-1; 6q **Accrington Stanley** (A) 0-1				
1924-25	3N		5q **Barrow** (A) 0-4				
1925-26	3N	1	28.11.25 **Accrington S**	3N A	L	0-4	
1926-27	3N	1	27.11.26 **New Brighton**	3N H	D	1-1	Miles
		1r	1.12.26 **New Brighton**	A	D	2-2	Smith, Regan
		1 2r	6.12.26 **New Brighton** at Anfield		W	3-1	Longmuir 2, Smith
		2	11.12.26 **Rhyl**	Welsh A	L	1-3	Griffiths
1927-28	3N	1	26.11.27 **Durham C**	3N A	D	1-1	Gunson
		1r	30.11.27 **Durham C**	H	W	4-0	Gunson 2, Woodhouse 2
		2	10.12.27 **Carlisle U**	3N H	W	1-0	C.Smith
		3	14.1.28 **Swansea T**	D2 H	W	2-1	Gunson, Longmuir
		4	28.1.28 **Birmingham**	D1 H	L	1-2	Thomson
1928-29	3N	1	24.11.28 **Carlisle U**	3N H	L	0-1	
1929-30	3N	1	30.11.29 **South Shields**	3N A	W	4-2	Mays 2, Woodhouse, Bamford
		2	14.12.29 **Manchester Central**	LC A	W	1-0	Mays
		3	11.1.30 **WBA**	D2 H	W	1-0	Mays
		4	25.1.30 **Bradford C**	D2 H	D	0-0	
		4r	27.1.30 **Bradford C**	A	L	1-2	Bamford
1930-31	3N	1	29.11.30 **Wigan B**	3N H	W	2-0	Taylor, Mustard
		2	13.12.30 **Wellington T**	BDL A	W	4-2	Bamford 3, Lewis
		3	10.1.31 **Wolverhampton W**	D2 A	L	1-9	Bamford

1931-32	3N	1	28.11.31	Gateshead	3N	A	L	2-3	Lewis, Bamford
1932-33	3N	1	26.11.32	Spennymoor U	NEL	H	W	3-0	Frewin, Bamford 2
		2	10.12.32	Brighton & HA	3S	A	D	0-0	
		2r	14.12.32	Brighton & HA		H	L	2-3	Bamford, Frewin
1933-34	3N	1	25.11.33	Carlisle U	3N	A	L	1-2	Bryant
1934-35	3N	1	24.11.34	Rochdale	3N	H	W	4-1	Findlay, Fryer 2, Rogers
		2	8.12.34	Reading	3S	A	L	0-3	
1935-36	3N	1	30.11.35	Barrow	3N	A	L	1-4	Fryer
1936-37	3N	1	28.11.36	Blyth Spartans	NEL	A	W	2-0	Jones, Burgon
		2	12.12.36	Gillingham	3S	H	W	2-0	Lapham, Jones
		3	16.1.37	Manchester C	D1	H	L	1-3	Burgon
1937-38	3N	1	27.11.37	Oldham A	3N	H	W	2-1	Burgon, Fraser
		2	11.12.37	Bradford C	3N	H	L	1-2	Burditt
1938-39	3N	1	26.11.38	Port Vale	3S	H	L	1-2	Burditt
1945-46	3N	1 1L	17.11.45	Crewe A	3N	A	L	2-4	Lloyd 2
		1 2L	24.11.45	Crewe Alex		H	W	3-0	Hayward, Wainwright, Jones
		2 1L	8.12.45	Shrewsbury T	ML	A	W	1-0	Hewitt
		2 2L	15.12.45	Shrewsbury T		H	D	1-1	Heywood
		3 1L	5.1.46	Blackpool	D1	H	L	1-4	Haycock
		3 2L	9.1.46	Blackpool		A	L	1-4	McLarty
1946-47	3N	1	30.11.46	Marine	LC	H	W	5-0	Boothway 4, Brown
		2	14.12.46	Lincoln C	3N	A	D	1-1	McLarty
		2r	18.12.46	Lincoln C		H	D	3-3aet	Boothway 2, McLarty
		2 2r	23.12.46	Lincoln C at Maine Road			L	1-2	Gardiner
1947-48	3N	1	29.11.47	Halifax T	3N	H	W	5-0	Beynon 2, Tunnicliffe 2, Jones
		2	13.12.47	Colchester U	SL	A	L	0-1	
1948-49	3N	1	27.11.48	Oldham A	3N	H	L	0-3	
1949-50	3N	1	26.11.49	Grantham	ML	H	W	4-1	Grainger, Sharp, Tunnicliffe, Boothway
		2	10.12.49	Southend U	3S	H	D	2-2	Tunnicliffe 2
		2r	14.12.49	Southend U		A	L	0-2	
1950-51	3N	1	25.11.50	Accrington S	3N	H	W	1-0	Beynon
		2	9.12.50	Bristol C	3S	A	L	1-2	Lawrence
1951-52	3N	1	24.11.51	Halifax T	3N	H	W	3-0	Hope 2, Bannan
		2	15.12.51	Leyton O	3S	H	D	1-1	Tunnicliffe
		2r	19.12.51	Leyton O		A	L	2-3aet	Lawrence, Bannan
1952-53	3N	1	22.11.52	Beighton Miners Wel.	YL	A	W	3-0	Hughes 2, Bannan
				played at Rotherham					
		2	6.12.52	Great Yarmouth T	ECL	A	W	2-1	Bannan 2
		3	10.1.53	Stoke C	D1	A	L	1-2	Tilston
1953-54	3N	1	21.11.53	Horden Colliery Wel.	NEL	A	W	1-0	Hughes
		2	12.12.53	Brighton & HA	3S	H	D	1-1	Bannan
		2r	16.12.53	Brighton & HA		A	D	1-1aet	Wright
		2 2r	21.12.53	Brighton & HA at Selhurst Park			W	3-1	Bannan, Richards, Hewitt
		3	9.1.54	Scunthorpe U	3N	H	D	3-3	Tapscott, Bannon 2
		3r	14.1.54	Scunthorpe U		A	L	1-3	Hubbard og
1954-55	3N	1	20.11.54	Netherfield	LC	A	D	3-3	Hewitt 2, Green
		1r	24.11.54	Netherfield		H	W	4-0	Hewitt, Jackson, Betts 2
		2	11.12.54	Walsall	3S	H	L	1-2	D.Jackson
1955-56	3N	1	19.11.55	Accrington S	3N	A	L	1-3	Richards (p)
1956-57	3N	1	17.11.56	Crewe A	3N	A	D	2-2	Thompson 2
		1r	20.11.56	Crewe A		H	W	2-1	Thompson, Hewitt
		2	8.12.56	Scunthorpe U	3N	A	D	0-0	
		2r	12.12.56	Scunthorpe U		H	W	6-2aet	Anderson, Thompson 2, Hewitt, G.Jones, D.Jones
		3	5.1.57	Reading	3S	H	D	1-1	B.Evans
		3r	9.1.57	Reading		A	W	2-1	Anderson, Hewitt
		4	26.1.57	Manchester U	D1	H	L	0-5	
1957-58	3N	1	16.11.57	Accrington S	3N	H	L	0-1	
1958-59	D3	1	15.11.58	Darlington	D4	H	L	1-2	Murray
1959-60	D3	1	14.11.59	Blyth Spartans	ML	H	W	2-1	Hewitt 2
		2	5.12.59	Grimsby T	D3	A	W	3-2	Weston 2, Jobling og
		3	9.1.60	Leicester C	D1	H	L	1-2	Weston
1960-61	D4	1	5.11.60	Bangor C	CC	A	L	0-1	
1961-62	D4	1	4.11.61	Barrow	D4	H	W	3-2	Davies, Metcalf 2
		2	25.11.61	Rochdale	D4	A	W	2-1	Metcalf, Bennion
		3	10.1.62	Norwich C	D2	A	L	1-3	Davies
1962-63	D3	1	3.11.62	Southport	D4	A	D	1-1	Whitehouse
		1r	7.11.62	Southport		H	W	3-2	R.Barnes 2, Whitehouse

		2	24.11.62	Barrow	D4	H	W	5-2	Whitehouse 3, Griffiths, R.Barnes
		3	9.1.63	Liverpool	D1	H	L	0-3	
1963-64	D3	1	16.11.63	Altrincham	CC	A	–	2-1	Metcalfe, Griffiths
				abandoned after 76 minutes – fog					
		1	20.11.63	Altrincham		A	D	0-0	
		1r	26.11.63	Altrincham		H	W	3-0	T.Jones, Metcalfe 2
		2	7.12.63	Hull C	D3	H	L	0-2	
1964-65	D4	1	14.11.64	Macclesfield	CC	A	W	2-1	McMillan 2
		2	5.12.64	Southport	D4	H	L	2-3	K.Barnes (p), King
1965-66	D4	1	13.11.65	South Liverpool	LC	H	W	4-1	King 3 (1p), Jones
		2	4.12.65	Hartlepools	D4	A	L	0-2	
1966-67	D4	1	26.11.66	Chesterfield	D4	H	W	3-2	Garrick, Lloyd, Oldfield
		2	7.1.67	Shrewsbury T	D3	A	L	1-5	McMillan
1967-68	D4	1	9.12.67	Bradford C	D4	A	L	1-7	Weston
1968-69	D4	1	16.11.68	Oldham A	D3	H	W	4-2	Griffiths 2, Moir, Kinsey
		2	7.12.68	Chesterfield	D4	A	L	1-2	Charnley
1969-70	D4	1	15.11.69	Spennymoor U	NL	A	W	4-1	Ingle, Griffiths, Kinsey, Smith
		2	6.12.69	Hartlepool	D4	A	W	1-0	Evans
		3	3.1.70	Norwich C	D2	A	W	2-1	May, Griffiths
		4	24.1.70	Liverpool	D1	A	L	1-4	R.Smith
1970-71	D3	1	21.11.70	Mansfield T	D3	A	L	0-2	
1971-72	D3	1	20.11.71	Bradford City	D3	H	W	5-1	Moir, Provan, Whittle 2, McBurney
		2	11.12.71	Wigan A	NPL	H	W	4-0	Moir, Kinsey 2, Whittle
		3	15.1.72	Orient	D2	A	L	0-3	
1972-73	D3	1	18.11.72	Darlington	D4	A	D	1-1	Tinnion
		1r	22.11.72	Darlington		H	W	5-0	Smallman 3, Thomas, Whittle
		2	9.12.72	Port Vale	D3	A	L	0-1	
1973-74	D3	1	24.11.73	Shrewsbury T	D3	H	D	1-1	Tinnion
		1r	27.11.73	Shrewsbury T		A	W	1-0	Davies
		2	15.12.73	Rotherham U	D4	A	W	3-0	Davies 2, Wilkinson og
		3	5.1.74	Crystal Palace	D2	A	W	2-0	Sutton, Smallman
		4	26.1.74	Middlesbrough	D2	H	W	1-0	Smallman
		5	16.2.74	Southampton	D1	A	W	1-0	Smallman
		6	9.3.74	Burnley	D1	A	L	0-1	
1974-75	D3	1	23.11.74	Mansfield T	D4	A	L	1-3	Whittle
1975-76	D3	1	22.11.75	Mansfield T	D3	A	D	1-1	Madden og
		1r	24.11.75	Mansfield T		H	D	1-1aet	Ashcroft
		1 2r	8.12.75	Mansfield T at Villa Park			L	1-2	Dwyer
1976-77	D3	1	20.11.76	Gateshead	NPL	H	W	6-0	Ashcroft 2, Lees, Shinton 3 (1p)
		2	11.12.76	Goole T	NPL	H	D	1-1	Whittle
		2r	14.12.76	Goole T		A	W	1-0	Shinton
		3	8.1.77	Sunderland	D1	A	D	2-2	Ashcroft, Whittle
		3r	12.1.77	Sunderland		H	W	1-0	Ashcroft
		4	29.1.77	Cardiff C	D2	A	L	2-3	Whittle, Ashcroft
1977-78	D3	1	26.11.77	Burton Albion	SL	H	W	2-0	Shinton, McNeil
		2	17.12.77	Preston NE	D3	A	W	2-0	Davis, McNeil
		3	7.1.78	Bristol C	D1	A	D	4-4	Shinton 2, Merrick og, McNeil
		3r	9.1.78	Bristol C		H	W	3-0	Thomas, McNeil, Whittle
		4	28.1.78	Newcastle U	D1	A	D	2-2	McNeil 2
		4r	6.2.78	Newcastle U		H	W	4-1	McNeil 2, Shinton, Cartwright
		5	18.2.78	Blyth Spartans	NL	H	D	1-1	McNeil
		5r	27.2.78	Blyth Spartans at Newcastle		A	W	2-1	Whittle (p), McNeil
		6	11.3.78	Arsenal	D1	H	L	2-3	McNeil, Sutton
1978-79	D2	3	1.2.79	Stockport Co	D4	H	W	6-2	Cegielski, McNeil 2, Lyons, Cartwright, Shinton
		4	12.2.79	Tottenham H	D1	A	D	3-3	Shinton, Lyons 2 (1p)
		4r	21.2.79	Tottenham H		H	L	2-3aet	Davis, McNeil
1979-80	D2	3	5.1.80	Charlton A	D2	H	W	6-0	Edwards, Vinter 3, McNeil 2
		4	26.1.80	Carlisle U	D3	A	D	0-0	
		4r	29.1.80	Carlisle U		H	W	3-1	McNeil 2, Jones
		5	16.2.80	Everton	D1	A	L	2-5	Vinter
1980-81	D2	3	3.1.81	West Ham	D2	A	D	1-1	Davis
		3r	6.1.81	West Ham		H	D	0-0aet	
		3 2r	19.1.81	West Ham		H	W	1-0aet	McNeil
		4	24.1.81	Wimbledon	D4	H	W	2-1	Fox, McNeil
		5	14.2.81	Wolverhampton W	D1	A	L	1-3	Fox
1981-82	D2	3	2.1.82	Nottingham F	D1	A	W	3-1	Dowman, Vinter, McNeil
		4	23.1.82	Chelsea	D2	A	D	0-0	

		4r	26.1.82	Chelsea		H	D	1-1aet	McNeil
		4 2r	1.2.82	Chelsea		H	L	1-2	Vinter
1982-83	D3	1	20.11.82	Holbeach U	UCL	A	W	4-0	Keay, Gregory, Savage, Muldoon
		2	11.12.82	Worcester C	APL	A	L	1-2	Hunt
1983-84	D4	1	19.11.83	Sheffield U	D3	H	L	1-5	Coleman
1984-85	D4	1	17.11.84	Wigan A	D3	H	L	0-2	
1985-86	D4	1	16.11.85	Bolton W	D3	H	W	3-1	Keay, Hencher, Cunnington
		2	7.12.85	Notts Co	D3	A	D	2-2	Gregory, Horne
		2r	10.12.85	Notts Co		H	L	0-3	
1986-87	D4	1	15.11.86	Hartlepool U	D4	H	W	2-1	Buxton, Charles
		2	6.12.86	Rochdale	D4	A	W	4-1	Steel, Massey 2, Horne
		3	10.1.87	Chester C	D3	H	L	1-2	Steel
1987-88	D4	1	14.11.87	Rochdale	D4	A	W	2-0	Carter, Buxton
		2	5.12.87	Bolton W	D4	H	L	1-2	Hinnigan
1988-89	D4	1	19.11.88	Runcorn	GMVC	A	D	2-2	Bowden, Cooper
		1r	22.11.88	Runcorn		H	L	2-3	Kearns 2
1989-90	D4	1	18.11.89	Carlisle U	D4	A	L	0-3	
1990-91	D4	1	17.11.90	Halifax T	D4	A	L	2-3	Preece 2
1991-92	D4	1	16.11.91	Winsford U	NPL	H	W	5-2	Connolly, Watkin 3, Thomas
		2	7.12.91	Telford U	GMVC	H	W	1-0	Watkin
		3	4.1.92	Arsenal	D1	H	W	2-1	Thomas, Watkin
		4	25.1.92	West Ham	D1	A	D	2-2	Phillips, L.Jones
		4r	4.2.92	West Ham		H	L	0-1	
1992-93	D3	1	14.11.92	Crewe A	D2	A	L	1-6	Bennett

WYCOMBE WANDERERS

Formed 1884. **First entered FA Cup:** 1895. **FA Amateur Cup Winners:** 1931: Runners-up: 1937 **FA Challenge Trophy Winners:** 1991, 1993.
League clubs beaten as non-league team: Newport Co, Bournemouth, Colchester U

1932-33	IL	1	26.11.32	Gillingham	3S	A	D	1-1	Simmons
		1r	30.11.32	Gillingham		H	L	2-4	Brain, Braisher
1955-56	IL	1	19.11.55	Burton Albion	BDL	H	L	1-3	Bates
1957-58	IL	1	16.11.57	Dorchester T	WL	A	L	2-3	Rockell, Reardon
1958-59	IL	1	15.11.58	Northampton T	D4	A	L	0-2	
1959-60	IL	1	14.11.59	Wisbech T	SL	H	W	4-2	Trott 2, Bates, Rockell
		2	5.12.59	Watford	D4	A	L	1-5	D.Atkins
1960-61	IL	1	5.11.60	Kettering T	SL	H	L	1-2	Thomas
1961-62	IL	1	4.11.61	Ashford T	SL	H	D	0-0	
		1r	8.11.61	Ashford T		A	L	0-3	
1962-63	IL	1	3.11.62	Maidenead	CRN	A	W	3-0	Hay, Horseman 2
		2	24.11.62	Gravesend	SL	A	L	1-3	Thomas (p)
1965-66	IL	1	13.11.65	Guildford	SL	A	D	2-2	Samuels, Worley
		1r	17.11.65	Guildford		H	L	0-1	
1966-67	IL	1	26.11.66	Bedford T	SL	H	D	1-1	Samuels
		1r	30.11.66	Bedford T		A	D	3-3aet	Bates, Horseman, Merrick
		1 2r	5.12.66	Bedford T		H	–	1-1	Sammuels
			abandoned after 90 minutes – ground unfit						
		1 3r	8.12.66	Bedford T		A	L	2-3	Horseman 2
1970-71	IL	1	21.11.70	Slough T	AL	H	D	1-1	Horseman
		1r	25.11.70	Slough T		A	L	0-1	
1973-74	IL	1	24.11.73	Newport Co	D4	H	W	3-1	Perrin 2, Evans
		2	15.12.73	Peterborough U	D4	H	L	1-3	Pritchard
1974-75	IL	1	23.11.74	Cheltenham T	SL	H	W	3-1	Horseman (p), Hallfield, Birdseye
		2	14.12.74	Bournemouth	D3	H	D	0-0	
		2r	18.12.74	Bournemouth		A	W	2-1	Horseman, Perrin
		3	4.1.75	Middlesbrough	D1	H	D	0-0	
		3r	7.1.75	Middlesbrough		A	L	0-1	
1975-76	IL	1	22.11.75	Bedford T	SL	H	D	0-0	
		1r	24.11.75	Bedford T		A	D	2-2aet	Delaney, Horseman
		1 2r	1.12.75	Bedford T		H	W	2-1	Bullock, Evans
		2	13.12.75	Cardiff C	D3	A	L	0-1	
1976-77	IL	1	20.11.76	Waterlooville	SL	A	W	2-1	Priestley, Kennedy
		2	11.12.76	Reading	D3	H	L	1-2	Pearson
1977-78	IL	1	26.11.77	Minehead	SL	A	L	0-2	
1978-79	IL	1	25.11.78	Maidstone U	SL	A	L	0-1	
1979-80	IL	1	24.11.79	Croydon	IL	H	L	0-3	

1980-81	IL	1	22.11.80	Bournemouth	D4	H	L	0-3	
1981-82	IL	1	21.11.81	Hendon	IL	A	D	1-1	Vircavs
		1r	24.11.81	Hendon		H	W	2-0	Kennedy, Glynn
		2	15.12.81	Barnet	APL	A	L	0-2	
1982-83	IL	1	20.11.82	Bristol R	D3	A	L	0-1	
1983-84	IL	1	19.11.83	Chelmsford C	SL	A	D	0-0	
		1r	22.11.83	Chelmsford C		H	L	1-2	Glynn
1985-86	APL	1	16.11.85	Colchester U	D4	H	W	2-0	West, Read
		2	7.12.85	Chelmsford C	SL	H	W	2-0	Reed, McMahon
		3	4.1.86	York C	D3	A	L	0-2	
1990-91	GMVC	1	17.11.90	Boston U	GMVC	A	D	1-1	Evans
		1r	21.11.90	Boston U		H	W	4-0	West 2, Ryan, Creaser
		2	12.12.90	Peterborough U	D4	H	D	1-1	Blackler
		2r	17.12.90	Peterborough U		A	L	0-2	
1991-92	GMVC	1	16.11.91	Kettering T	GMVC	A	D	1-1	Carroll
		1r	27.11.91	Kettering T		H	L	0-2	
1992-93	GMVC	1	14.11.92	Merthyr Tydfil	GMVC	H	W	3-1	Scott, Carroll, Stapleton
		2	6.12.92	WBA	D2	H	D	2-2	Creaser, Thompson
		2r	15.12.92	WBA		A	L	0-1	

YEOVIL TOWN

Formed 1895 as Yeovil & Petters United. 1945 Yeovil Town. Famous FA Cup giant-killers whose outstanding Cup Run was in the 1948-49 season when they reached the 5th round. **Cup Final Connection:** Alec Stock, player manager when Yeovil beat Sunderland in 1949 was Fulham's manager in the 1975 Cup Final against West Ham. **League clubs beaten:** Bournemouth (2), C Palace (2), Exeter C, Brighton, Bury, Sunderland, Southend (2), Walsall (2), Brentford, Cambridge U, Torquay U, Hereford U

1924-25	SL		4q **Bournemouth** (3S) (H) 3-2; 5q **Bristol R** (3S) (H) 2-4					
1928-29	SL	1	24.11.28	Plymouth A	D3	H	L	1-4	Rowlands
1931-32	SL	1	28.11.31	Hayes	AL	H	W	3-1	Rankin, Davin, Molloy
		2	12.12.31	Fulham	3S	A	D	0-0	
		2r	17.12.31	Fulham		H	L	2-5	Davin, McNeil
1932-33	SL	1	26.11.32	Dartford	SL	A	D	0-0	
		1r	1.12.32	Dartford		H	W	4-2	Lewis 3, Parkin
		2	10.12.32	Chester	3N	A	L	1-2	Lewis
1934-35	SL	1	24.11.34	Crystal P	3S	H	W	3-0	McNeil, Owens og, Page
		2	8.12.34	Exeter C	3S	H	W	4-1	Smith, Page, Crewe 2
		3	12.1.35	Liverpool	D1	H	L	2-6	McNeil 2
1935-36	SL	1	30.11.35	Newport (IOW)	Hants	H	L	0-1	
1936-37	SL	1	28.11.36	Worthing	SCL	H	W	4-3	Halliday, Doncaster, Payne, Attley
		2	12.12.36	Walsall	3S	A	D	1-1	Doncaster
		2r	15.12.38	Walsall		H	L	0-1	
1937-38	SL	1	27.11.37	Ipswich T	SL	H	W	2-1	Kirk, Attley
		2	11.12.37	Gainsborough T	ML	H	W	2-1	Halliday 2
		3	8.1.38	Manchester U	D2	A	L	0-3	
1938-39	SL	1	26.11.38	Brighton & HA	3S	H	W	2-1	Graham, Laing
		2	10.12.38	Folkestone	SL	A	D	1-1	Graham
		2r	15.12.38	Folkestone		H	W	1-0	Green
		3	7.1.39	Sheffield W	D2	A	D	1-1	Carter
		3r	12.1.39	Sheffield W		H	L	1-2	Green
1945-46	SL	1 1L	17.11.45	Bristol C	3S	H	D	2-2	Hamilton 2
		1 2L	24.11.45	Bristol C		A	L	0-3	
as Yeovil Town									
1946-47	SL	1	30.11.46	Peterborough	ML	H	D	2-2	Gore, Sibley (p)
		1r	5.12.46	Peterborough		A	L	0-1	
1948-49	SL	1	27.11.48	Romford	IL	H	W	4-0	Bryant 2, Hamilton, Hargreaves
		2	11.12.48	Weymouth	WL	H	W	4-0	Bryant 2, Hamilton, Hargreaves
		3	8.1.49	Bury	D2	H	W	3-1	Hargreaves, Wright, Hamilton
		4	29.1.49	Sunderland	D1	H	W	2-1aet	Stock, Bryant
		5	12.2.49	Manchester U	D1	A	L	0-8	
1949-50	SL	1	26.11.49	Romford	IL	H	W	4-1	Wright, Foulds, Mansley 2
		2	10.12.49	Gillingham	SL	H	W	3-1	Wright, Foulds, Mansley
		3	7.1.50	Chesterfield	D2	A	L	1-3	Mansley
1952-53	SL	1	22.11.52	Brighton & HA	3S	H	L	1-4	Finley
1953-54	SL	1	21.11.53	Norwich C	3S	H	L	0-2	
1955-56	SL	1	19.11.55	Aldershot	3S	H	D	1-1	Elder
		1r	23.11.55	Aldershot		A	D	1-1aet	Reid
		1 2r	28.11.55	Aldershot at Southampton			L	0-2	

1956-57	SL	1	17.11.56	Peterborough U	ML	H	L	1-3	McCaffrey
1957-58	SL	1	16.11.57	Guildford C	SL	A	D	2-2	Travis, Alexander
		1r	21.11.57	Guildford C		H	W	1-0	Travis
		2	7.12.57	Bath C	SL	H	W	2-0	Alexander, Baldwin
		3	4.1.58	Fulham	D2	A	L	0-4	
1958-59	SL	1	15.11.58	Southend U	D3	A	D	0-0	
		1r	20.11.58	Southend U		H	W	1-0	Dennis
		2	6.12.58	Colchester U	D3	A	D	1-1	Earl
		2r	11.12.58	Colchester U		H	L	1-7	Dennis
1960-61	SL	1	5.11.60	Walsall	D3	A	W	1-0	Taylor
		2	26.11.60	Bournemouth	D3	A	L	1-3	Kelly
1961-62	SL	1	4.11.61	Notts Co	D3	A	L	2-4	Taylor, Foley
1962-63	SL	1	3.11.62	Dartford	SL	H	W	3-2	Tayor, Foley, Coughin
		2	24.11.62	Swindon T	D3	H	L	0-2	
1963-64	SL	1	16.11.63	Southend U	D3	H	W	1-0	Foley
		2	7.12.63	Crystal P	D3	H	W	3-1	Taylor 2, Pound
		3	4.1.64	Bury	D2	H	L	0-2	
1965-66	SL	1	13.11.65	Brentford	D3	A	L	1-2	Harding
1966-67	SL	1	26.11.66	Oxford U	D3	H	L	1-3	Muir
1967-68	SL	1	13.12.67	Margate	SL	H	L	1-3	Vowles
1968-69	SL	1	16.11.68	Weymouth	SL	A	L	1-2	Harris
1969-70	SL	1	15.11.69	Shrewsbury T	D3	H	L	2-3	Housley, Davies
1970-71	SL	1	21.11.70	Aveley	AL	H	W	1-0	Clancy
		2	12.12.70	Bournemouth	D4	A	W	1-0	Myers
		3	6.1.71	Arsenal	D1	H	L	0-3	
1972-73	SL	1	18.11.72	Brentford	D3	H	W	2-1	Weller, Myers
		2	9.12.72	Plymouth A	D3	H	L	0-2	
1975-76	SL	1	22.11.75	Millwall	D3	H	D	1-1	Brown
		1r	25.12.75	Millwall		A	D	2-2aet	Cotton, Housley
		1 2r	3.12.75	Millwall at Aldershot			L	0-1	
1978-79	SL	1	25.11.78	Barking	IL	H	L	0-1	
1979-80	APL	1	24.11.79	Enfield	IL	A	W	1-0	Green
		2	15.12.79	Slough T	IL	H	W	1-0	Williams
		3	5.1.80	Norwich C	D1	H	L	0-3	
1980-81	APL	1	22.11.80	Farnborough T	IL	H	W	2-1	Morrall, Ritchie
		2	13.12.80	Colchester U	D3	A	D	1-1	Green
		2r	17.12.80	Colchester U		H	L	0-2	
1981-82	APL	1	21.11.81	Dagenham	APL	A	D	2-2	Green, Brown
		1r	25.11.81	Dagenham		H	L	0-1aet	
1982-83	APL	1	20.11.82	Chesham U	IL	A	W	1-0	Bell
		2	11.12.82	Southend U	D3	A	L	0-3	
1983-84	APL	1	19.11.83	Harrow B	IL	H	L	0-1	
1984-85	APL	1	17.11.84	Torquay U	D4	A	L	0-2	
1985-86	IL	1	16.11.85	Hereford U	D4	H	L	2-4	Smith, McGinlay
1987-88	IL	1	14.11.87	Worcester C	SL	A	D	1-1	Pearson
		1r	18.11.87	Worcester C		H	W	1-0	McGinlay
		2	5.12.87	Camridge U	D4	A	W	1-0	Wallace
		3	9.1.88	QPR	D1	H	L	0-3	
1988-89	GMVC	1	19.11.88	Merthyr Tydfil	SL	H	W	3-2	Wallace 2, Doherty
		2	10.12.88	Torquay U	D4	H	D	1-1	Randall
		2r	14.12.88	Torquay U		A	L	0-1	
1989-90	GMVC	1	18.11.89	Maidstone U	D4	A	L	1-2	Spencer
1990-91	GMVC	1	17.11.90	Brentford	D3	A	L	0-5	
1991-92	GMVC	1	16.11.91	Walsall	D4	H	D	1-1	Wilson
		1r	27.11.91	Walsall		A	W	1-0aet	Cooper
		2	7.12.91	Woking	IL	A	L	0-3	
1992-93	GMVC	1	14.11.92	Torquay U	D3	A	W	5-2	Batty 3 (2ps), Wilson 2
		2	5.12.92	Hereford U	D3	H	D	0-0	
		2r	16.12.92	Hereford U		A	W	2-1	Sanderson, Coates
		3	2.1.93	Arsenal	PL	H	L	1-3	Batty (p)

YORK CITY

Formed 1922. **First entered FA Cup:** 1923. **Best FA Cup Performance:** semi-finals, 1955 (as a Third Division club). **Record FA Cup Win:** 6-0 vs South Shields, 1st round, 16.11.1968. **Record FA Cup Defeat:** 0-7 vs Liverpool, 5th round replay, 20.2.1985.

1923-24	ML	ExP **Castleford & Allerton** (H) 2-1; P **Cudworth** (A) 1-0; 1q **Mexborough T** (H) 1-1; 1qr **Mexborough T** (A) 1-1aet;
		1q 2r **Mexborough T** 1-3 at Doncaster

1924-25	ML	ExP **Guiseley** (H) 1-0; P **Horsforth** (H) 7-1; 1q **Wombwell** (H) 1-2					
1925-26	ML	P **Maltby Main** (H) 5-3; 1q **Wombwell** (H) 5-0; 2q **Castleford T** (H) 3-0; 3q **Wath A** (A) 1-4					
1926-27	ML	1q **Guisborough Belmont** (H) 5-0; 2q **South Bank** (H) 4-0; 3q **Whitby U** (H) 0-0; 3qr **Whitby U** (H) 2-1; 4q **Ilkeston T** (A) 5-1					
		1	27.11.26	**Worksop T**	ML	H	–	1-1	Flood
			abandoned after 70 minutes – fog					
		1	1.12.26	**Worksop T**		H	W	4-1	Merritt 2, Rany, Harvey
		2	11.12.26	**Grimsby T**	D2	A	L	1-2	Harvey
1927-28	ML	1q **Whitby U** (H) 4-0; 2q **Scarborough** (H) 1-1; 2qr **Scarborough** (A) 4-0; 3q **Stockton Malleable** (H) 7-1; 4q **Shildon** (A) 1-1; 4qr **Shildon** (H) 1-2					
1928-29	ML	1q **Stockton** (H) 7-1; 2q **Normanby Mag** (H) 2-1; 3q **Bridlington** (H) 3-0; 4q **Jarrow** (A) 0-0; 4qr **Jarrow** (H) 2-2aet; 4q 2r **Jarrow** 3-2 at Newcastle					
		1	24.11.28	**Barrow**	3N	H	L	0-1	
1929-30	3N	4q **Scaborough** (A) 3-1					
		1	30.11.29	**Tranmere R**	3N	H	D	2-2	Fenoughty 2
		1r	5.12.29	**Tranmere R**		A	W	1-0	Fenoughty
		2	14.12.29	**Southend U**	3S	A	W	4-1	Davies, Gardiner, Fenoughty 2
		3	11.1.30	**Newcastle U**	D1	A	D	1-1	Gardiner
		3r	15.1.30	**Newcastle U**		H	L	1-2	Evans
1930-31	3N	1	29.11.30	**Gresley Rovers**	BC	H	W	3-1	Evans, Laycock, Kelly
		2	13.12.30	**Nelson**	3N	A	D	1-1	Brewis
		2r	17.12.30	**Nelson**		H	–	2-0	Laycock, Kelly
			abandoned because of fog					
		2r	18.12.30	**Nelson**		H	W	3-2	Laycock 2, Sharp
		3	10.1.31	**Sheffield U**	D1	A	D	1-1	Laycock
		3r	14.1.31	**Sheffield U**	BDL	H	L	0-2	
1931-32	3N	1	28.11.31	**New Brighton**	3N	A	L	1-3	McDonald
1932-33	3N	1	26.11.32	**Scarborough**	ML	H	L	1-3	Spooner
1933-34	3N	1	25.11.33	**Hartlepools U**	3N	H	L	2-3	Lax, Jenkinson
1934-35	3N	1	24.11.34	**Burton Town**	BDL	A	W	3-2	Hathway, Jenkins, Dando
		2	8.12.34	**New Brighton**	3N	H	W	1-0	Speed
		3	12.1.35	**Derby Co**	D1	H	L	0-1	
1935-36	3N	1	30.11.35	**Burton T**	ML	H	L	1-5	Lindsay (p)
1936-37	3N	1	28.11.36	**Hull C**	3N	H	W	5-2	Thompson 2, Agar 3
		2	12.12.36	**Southend U**	3S	A	D	3-3	Spooner, Thompson 2
		2r	16.12.36	**Southend U**		H	W	2-1aet	Comrie, Spooner
		3	16.1.37	**Bradford C**	3N	A	D	2-2	Comrie, Spooner
		3r	20.1.37	**Bradford C**		H	W	1-0	Nicol
		4	30.1.37	**Swansea T**	D2	A	D	0-0	
		4r	3.2.37	**Swansea T**		H	L	1-3	Hathway
1937-38	3N	1	27.11.37	**Halifax T**	3N	H	D	1-1	Hughes
		1r	1.12.37	**Halifax T**		A	W	1-0	Baines
		2	11.12.37	**Clapton O**	3S	A	D	2-2	Scott, Comrie
		2r	15.12.37	**Clapton O**		H	W	1-0	Hughes
		3	8.1.38	**Coventry C**	D2	H	W	3-2	Spooner, Hughes, Earl
		4	22.1.38	**WBA**	D1	H	W	3-2	Baines 3
		5	12.2.28	**Middlesbrough**	D1	H	W	1-0	Spooner
		6	5.3.38	**Huddersfield T**	D1	H	D	0-0	
		6r	9.3.38	**Huddersfield T**		A	L	1-2	Baines
1938-39	3N	3	11.1.39	**Millwall**	D2	H	L	0-5	
1945-46	3N	1 1L	17.11.45	**Halifax T**	3N	A	L	0-1	
		1 2L	24.11.45	**Halifax T**		H	W	4-2	Lee, Gledhill, Scott 2
		2 1L	8.12.45	**Bishop Auckland**	NL	A	W	2-1	Madison, Winters
		2 2L	15.12.45	**Bishop Auckland**		H	W	3-0	Winters, Brennan, Robbins
		3 1L	5.1.46	**Chesterfield**	D2	A	D	1-1	Mahon
		3 2L	9.1.46	**Chesterfield**		H	W	3-2aet	Kidd og, Winters 2
		4 1L	26.1.46	**Sheffield W**	D2	A	L	1-5	Scott
		4 2L	30.1.46	**Sheffield W**		H	L	1-6	Allen
1946-47	3N	1	14.12.46	**Scunthorpe U**	ML	H	L	0-1	
1947-48	3N	1	29.11.47	**Rochdale**	3N	H	L	0-1	
1948-49	3N	1	27.11.48	**Runcorn**	CC	H	W	2-1	Brigham, Rudd
		2	11.12.48	**Southport**	3N	A	D	2-2	Ivey, A.Patrick
		2r	18.12.48	**Southport**		H	L	0-2	
1949-50	3N	1	26.11.49	**Gateshead**	3N	A	L	1-3	Birch
1950-51	3N	1	25.11.50	**Bishop Auckland**	NL	A	D	2-2	M.Patrick, Brennen
		1r	29.11.50	**Bishop Auckland**		H	W	2-1	A.Patrick
		2	9.12.50	**Tranmere R**	3N	H	W	2-1	A.Patrick 2
		3	6.1.51	**Bolton W**	D1	A	L	0-2	

Season	Div	Rnd	Date	Opponent		H/A	Res	Score	Scorers
1951-52	3N	1	24.11.51	**Bradford PA**	3N	H	D	1-1	A.Patrick
		1r	28.11.51	**Bradford PA**		A	D	1-1aet	A.Patrick
		1 2 r	3.12.51	**Bradford PA** at Elland Road			L	0-4	
1952-53	3N	1	22.11.52	**Barrow**	3N	H	L	1-2	A.Patrick
1953-54	3N	1	21.11.53	**Barnsley**	3N	A	L	2-5	Dunmore, Fenton
1954-55	3N	1	24.11.54	**Scarborough**	ML	H	W	3-2	Wilkinson, Bottom, Spence
		2	11.12.54	**Dorchester T**	WL	A	W	5-2	Bottom 3, Wilkinson, Fenton
		3	8.1.55	**Blackpool**	D1	A	W	2-0	Storey, Fenton
		4	29.1.55	**Bishop Auckland**	NL	A	W	3-1	Storey, Bottom 2
		5	19.2.55	**Tottenham H**	D1	H	W	3-1	Wilkinson 2, Fenton
		6	12.3.55	**Notts Co**	D2	A	W	1-0	Bottom
		SF	26.3.55	**Newcastle U**	D1		D	1-1	Bottom
			played at Hillsborough						
		SFr	30.3.55	**Newcastle U**			L	0-2	
			played at Roker Park						
1955-56	3N	1	19.11.55	**Rochdale**	3N	A	W	1-0	Wilkinson
		2	10.12.55	**Mansfield T**	3N	H	W	2-1	Bottom, Hughes
		3	7.1.56	**Swansea T**	D2	A	W	2-1	Colbridge, Bottom
		4	28.1.56	**Sunderland**	D1	H	D	0-0	
		4r	1.2.56	**Sunderland**		A	L	1-2	Fenton
1956-57	3N	1	17.11.56	**Southport**	3N	A	D	0-0	
		1r	21.11.56	**Southport**		H	W	2-1	Wragg, Wilkinson
		2	8.12.56	**Hull C**	3N	A	L	1-2	Bottom
1957-58	3N	1	16.11.57	**Chesterfield**	3N	H	W	1-0	Fenton
		2	7.12.57	**South Shields**	NEL	A	W	3-1	Wilkinson 2, Bottom
		3	8.1.58	**Birmingham C**	D1	H	W	3-0	Bottom, Wragg, Wilkinson
		4	25.1.58	**Bolton W**	D1	H	D	0-0	
		4r	29.1.58	**Bolton W**		A	L	0-3	
1958-59	D4	1	15.11.58	**Bury**	D3	A	–	0-0	
			abandoned after 60 minutes						
		1	18.11.58	**Bury**		A	L	0-1	
1959-60	D3	1	14.11.59	**Barrow**	D4	H	W	3-1	Addison, Edgar, Hughes
		2	5.12.59	**Crook T**	NL	A	W	1-0	Edgar
		3	9.1.60	**Bournemouth**	D3	A	L	0-1	
1960-61	D4	1	5.11.60	**Bradford PA**	D4	H	D	0-0	
		1r	9.11.60	**Bradford PA**		A	W	2-0	Wilkinson, Addison
		2	30.11.60	**Tranmere R**	D3	A	D	1-1	Wilkinson
		2r	5.12.60	**Tranmere R**		H	W	2-1	Wilkinson 2
		3	7.1.61	**Norwich C**	D2	H	D	1-1	Hughes
		3r	11.1.61	**Norwich C**		A	L	0-1	
1961-62	D4	1	4.11.61	**Bradford C**	D4	A	L	0-1	
1962-63	D4	1	3.11.62	**Rochdale**	D4	H	D	0-0	
		1r	6.11.62	**Rochdale**		A	W	2-1	Wragg, Wilkinson
		2	24.11.62	**Crewe Alex**	D4	H	W	2-1	Wragg, Wilkinson
		3	13.2.62	**Southampton**	D2	A	L	0-5	
1963-64	D4	1	16.11.63	**Carlisle U**	D4	H	L	2-5	Wilkinson 2
1964-65	D4	1	14.11.64	**Bangor City**	CC	H	W	5-1	Provan, Aimson 3, Weddle
		2	5.12.64	**Chesterfield**	D4	A	L	1-2	Aimson
1965-66	D3	1	12.11.65	**South Shields**	NRL	A	L	1-3	Aimson (p)
1966-67	D4	1	26.11.66	**Morecambe**	LC	H	D	0-0	
		1r	5.12.66	**Morecambe**		A	D	1-1aet	Spencer
		1 2r	8.12.66	**Morecambe** at Maine Road			W	1-0	Spencer
		2	7.1.67	**Middlesbrough**	D3	A	D	1-1	Provan
		2r	11.1.67	**Middlesbrough**		H	D	0-0aet	
		2 2r	16.1.67	**Middlesbrough** at Newcastle			L	1-4	Horrey
1967-68	D4	1	9.12.67	**Doncaster R**	D4	H	L	0-1	
1968-69	D4	1	16.11.68	**South Shields**	NPL	A	W	6-0	Ross 3, MacDougall 2, Baker (p)
		2	7.12.68	**Morecambe**	NPL	H	W	2-0	MacDougall 2
		3	4.1.69	**Stoke C**	D1	H	L	0-2	
1969-70	D4	1	15.11.69	**Whitby T**	NL	H	W	2-0	Aimson, Sibbald (p)
		2	6.12.69	**Bangor C**	NPL	A	D	0-0	
		2r	10.12.69	**Bangor C**		H	W	2-0	Mahon, Boyer
		3	3.1.70	**Cardiff C**	D2	H	D	1-1	Boyer
		3r	12.1.70	**Cardiff C**		A	D	1-1aet	Taylor
		3 2r	15.1.70	**Cardiff C** at St Andrews			W	3-1aet	Swallow 2, Aimson
		4	24.1.70	**Middlesbrough**	D2	A	L	1-4	Boyer
1970-71	D4	1	21.11.70	**Tamworth**	WMRL	A	D	0-0	

	1r	23.11.70	Tamworth		H	W	5-0	Aimson 3, Boyer, Hewitt
	2	12.12.70	Boston U	NPL	A	W	2-1	Davidson, Mackie (p)
	3	2.1.71	Bolton W	D2	H	W	2-0	Davidson 2
	4	23.1.71	Southampton	D1	H	D	3-3	Hewitt, Aimson, McMahon
	4r	1.2.71	Southampton		A	L	2-3	Aimson, Johanneson
1971-72 D3	1	20.11.71	Grimsby T	D4	H	W	4-2	Rathbone og, Henderson, Swallow, McMahon
	2	11.12.71	Rotherham U	D3	A	D	1-1	Rowles
	2r	13.12.71	Rotherham U		H	L	2-3aet	McMahon, Chambers
1972-73 D3	1	18.11.72	Mansfield T	D4	H	W	2-1	Rowles, Seal
	2	9.12.72	Bangor C	NPL	A	W	3-2	Rowles, Burrows, Pollard
	3	13.1.73	Oxford U	D2	H	L	0-1	
1973-74 D3	1	24.11.73	Mansfield T	D4	H	D	0-0	
	1r	10.12.73	Mansfield T		A	L	3-5	Jones 2, Swallow
1974-75 D2	3	4.1.75	Arsenal	D1	A	D	1-1	Seal
	3r	7.1.75	Arsenal		H	L	1-3aet	Lyons
1975-76 D2	3	3.1.76	Hereford U	D3	H	W	2-1	Seal, Hosker
	4	24.1.76	Chelsea	D2	H	L	0-2	
1976-77 D3	1	20.11.76	Dudley T	WMRL	A	D	1-1	Cave
	1r	23.11.76	Dudley T		H	W	4-1	Holmes 2 (1p), Cave, Pollard
	2	11.12.76	Rotherham U	D3	A	D	0-0	
	2r	14.12.76	Rotherham U		H	D	1-1aet	Holmes (p)
	2 2r	21.12.76	Rotherham U		A	L	1-2aet	Hinch
1977-78 D4	1	26.11.77	Wigan A	NPL	A	L	0-1	
1978-79 D4	1	25.11.78	Blyth Spartans	NL	H	D	1-1	Pugh
	1r	28.11.78	Blyth Spartans		A	W	5-3aet	Ford, Clements, Wellings 2, Staniforth
	2	16.12.78	Scarborough	NPL	H	W	3-0	Faulkner, Staniforth 2
	3	9.1.79	Luton T	D2	H	W	2-0	Staniforth, Randall
	4	27.1.79	Nottingham F	D1	A	L	1-3	Wellings
1979-80 D4	1	24.11.79	Mossley	NPL	H	W	5-2	Randall, Eccles, Lorimer, Byrne, Macdonald (p)
	2	15.12.79	Bury	D3	A	D	0-0	
	2r	18.12.79	Bury		H	L	0-2	
1980-81 D4	1	22.11.80	Tranmere R	D4	A	D	0-0	
	1r	25.11.80	Tranmere R		H	L	1-2aet	Byrne
1981-82 D4	1	20.11.81	Stafford R	APL	A	W	2-1	Ford, Walwyn
	2	12.12.81	Altrincham	APL	H	D	0-0	
	2r	2.1.82	Altrincham		A	L	3-4	Pollard 2, Walwyn
1982-83 D4	1	20.11.82	Bury	D4	H	W	3-1	Hood, Ford, Walwyn
	2	11.12.82	Hartlepool U	D4	A	D	1-1	Pollard
	2r	14.12.82	Hartlepool U		H	W	4-0	Hood, Pollard, Byrne, Ford
	3	8.1.83	Crystal P	D2	A	L	1-2	Walwyn
1983-84 D4	1	19.11.83	Macclesfield	NPL	A	D	0-0	
	1r	22.11.83	Macclesfield		H	W	2-0	Sbragia, Byrne
	2	13.12.83	Rochdale	D4	H	L	0-2	
1984-85 D3	1	17.11.84	Blue Star	Wear	H	W	2-0	Walwyn, Houchen
	2	8.12.84	Hartlepool U	D4	A	W	2-0	MacPhail, Houchen
	3	5.1.85	Walsall	D3	H	W	3-0	Butler, Walwyn, Hay
	4	26.1.85	Arsenal	D1	H	W	1-0	Houchen (p)
	5	16.2.85	Liverpool	D1	H	D	1-1	Sbragia
	5r	20.2.85	Liverpool		A	L	0-7	
1985-86 D3	1	16.11.85	Morecambe	NPL	H	D	0-0	
	1r	19.11.85	Morecambe at Maine Road			W	2-0	Sbragia, Walwyn
	2	7.12.85	Whitby T	NL	H	W	3-1	Ford, Walwyn, Pearce
	3	4.1.86	Wycombe W	APL	H	W	2-0	Walwyn 2
	4	25.1.86	Altrincham	APL	H	W	2-0	Banton, Ford
	5	15.2.86	Liverpool	D1	H	D	1-1	Ford
	5r	18.2.86	Liverpool		A	L	1-3aet	Canham
1986-87 D3	1	15.11.86	Crewe A	D4	H	W	3-1	Mills, Banton, Walwyn
	2	6.12.86	Caernarfon	NPL	A	D	0-0	
	2r	9.12.86	Caernarfon		H	L	1-2	Canham
1987-88 D3	1	14.11.87	Burton A	SL	H	D	0-0	
	1r	18.11.87	Burton A		A	W	2-1	Hood (p), Mills
	2	5.12.87	Hartlepool U	D4	H	D	1-1	Wilson
	2r	9.12.87	Hartlepool U		A	L	1-3	Banton
1988-89 D4	1	19.11.88	Halifax T	D4	A	L	0-1	
1989-90 D4	1	18.11.89	Grimsby T	D4	H	L	1-2	Warburton
1990-91 D4	1	17.11.90	Darlington	D4	A	D	1-1	Canham
	1r	19.11.90	Darlington		H	W	1-0	Canham

		2	17.12.90	**Mansfield T**	D3	A	L	1-2	Pepper
1991-92	D4	1	16.11.91	**Bridlington T**	NPL	A	W	2-1	Blackstone 2
		2	7.12.91	**Tranmere R**	D2	H	D	1-1	Hall
		2r	17.12.91	**Tranmere R**		A	L	1-2	McCarthy
1992-93	D3	1	14.11.92	**Stockport Co**	D2	H	L	1-3	Canham

YORKSHIRE AMATEURS

Formed 1919. **First entered FA Cup:** 1925

1931-32	YL	1		28.11.31	**Carlisle U**	3N	H	L	1-3	S.Craven
1945-46	YL	1 1L		17.11.45	**Lincoln C**	3N	H	W	1-0	Melling
		1 2L		24.11.45	**Lincoln C**		A	L	1-5	Lyon

ARSENAL

	P	W	D	L	F	A
Aston Villa	12	6	3	3	25	13
Barnsley	4	4	0	0	12	2
Bedford T	2	1	1	0	4	3
Birmingham C	7	1	2	4	7	14
Blackburn R	4	2	0	2	5	5
Blackpool	3	0	1	2	4	6
Bolton Wan.	8	4	2	2	12	5
Bradford C	3	2	0	1	5	2
Bradford PA	2	1	0	1	3	3
Brighton &HA	3	3	0	0	6	1
Bristol C	4	1	1	2	2	3
Bristol R	3	3	0	0	9	1
Burnley	5	3	0	2	13	10
Bury	2	2	0	0	7	2
Cambridge U	1	1	0	0	2	1
Cardiff C	7	3	2	2	5	3
Carlisle U	3	2	1	0	6	2
Charlton Ath	2	2	0	0	4	0
Chelsea	13	4	5	4	17	15
Chesterfield	1	1	0	0	5	1
Colchester U	2	1	1	0	6	2
Coventry C	3	2	1	0	7	2
Croydon Com.	4	2	2	0	5	2
Crystal P	1	1	0	0	7	0
Darlington	1	1	0	0	2	0
Darwen	1	1	0	0	11	1
Derby Co.	7	2	2	3	5	11
Doncaster R	1	1	0	0	4	0
Everton	3	1	0	2	4	10
Fulham	1	1	0	0	1	0
Grimsby T	4	3	1	0	9	4
Hereford U	2	1	1	0	8	3
Huddersfield	2	2	0	0	3	0
Hull C	4	1	2	1	4	6
Ipswich T	2	1	0	1	4	3
Leeds U	11	4	6	1	13	10
Leicester C	9	5	4	0	11	4
Leyton O.	4	4	0	0	9	1
Liverpool	13	5	4	4	14	14
Luton T	6	3	2	1	10	8
Man. City	3	2	0	1	3	3
Man. Utd.	7	4	0	3	14	9
Mansfield T	1	1	0	0	2	0
Merthyr T	1	1	0	0	3	0
Middlesbro	5	2	1	2	9	10
Millwall	3	1	1	1	3	2
Newcastle U	6	1	1	4	7	10
Newport Co.	1	1	0	0	2	0
Northampton	2	1	0	1	4	5
Norwich C	3	2	0	1	7	2
Nottm Forest	3	2	0	1	4	2
Notts Co.	2	2	0	0	3	0
Oxford U	1	1	0	0	5	1
Peterborough	1	0	0	1	1	2
Plymouth Arg	2	2	0	0	10	3
Port Vale	2	1	1	0	3	2
Portsmouth	3	2	1	0	6	3
Preston NE	5	1	2	2	7	8
QPR	5	1	2	2	2	5
Reading	3	3	0	0	6	2
Rochdale	1	1	0	0	4	2
Rotherham U	4	1	2	1	8	6
Sheff. Utd.	6	3	1	2	12	10
Sheff. Wed.	12	4	5	3	18	16
Shrewsbury T	3	2	1	0	4	1
Southampton	3	2	1	0	5	2
Stoke City	8	6	2	0	18	8
Sunderland	5	2	0	3	9	11
Swansea	3	2	0	1	4	3
Swindon T	4	2	1	1	3	1
Tottenham H	9	2	0	2	5	4
Walsall	2	1	0	1	4	3
Watford	4	3	0	1	9	4
West Brom	8	2	2	4	11	12
West Ham U	12	3	4	5	12	18
Wolves	9	6	1	2	12	9
Wrexham	2	1	0	1	4	4
Yeovil T	2	2	0	0	6	1

ASTON VILLA

	P	W	D	L	F	A
Aldershot	2	0	1	1	1	2
Arsenal	12	3	3	6	13	25
Ashington	1	1	0	0	5	1
Aston Unity	1	1	0	0	3	1
Barnsley	1	1	0	0	4	1
Birmingham C	3	2	1	0	5	0
Blackburn R	7	3	2	2	12	14
Blackpool	1	1	0	0	4	0
Bolton Wan.	4	1	2	1	3	4
Bradford C	3	1	1	1	5	6
Bradford PA	1	1	0	0	5	0
Brentford	2	1	1	0	2	1
Brighton &HA	2	1	1	0	6	4
Bristol C	6	5	1	0	14	5
Bristol R	5	3	2	0	11	3
Burnley	11	6	2	3	18	11
Bury	2	1	0	1	3	5
Cambridge U	2	1	1	0	5	2
Cardiff C	3	1	0	2	8	5
Casuals	1	1	0	0	13	1
Charlton Ath	6	2	3	1	10	7
Chelsea	7	5	1	1	12	7
Chester	1	1	0	0	3	1
Chesterfield	2	1	1	0	4	2
Coventry C	3	2	0	1	6	2
Crewe Alex.	2	2	0	0	6	2
Crystal P	2	2	0	0	9	3
Darwen	3	2	0	1	9	7
Derby Co.	11	6	1	4	32	22
Derby Mid.	1	1	0	0	6	1
Doncaster R	5	0	4	1	4	6
Everton	7	3	1	3	13	13
Exeter C	2	2	0	0	4	1
Fulham	1	1	0	0	5	0
Heanor T	1	1	0	0	4	1
Horncastle	1	1	0	0	5	0
Huddersfield	5	3	0	2	6	4
Hull C	4	3	1	0	9	2
Ipswich T	4	1	1	2	5	6
King's Lynn	1	1	0	0	11	0
Leeds U	3	3	0	0	7	2
Leicester C	3	2	0	1	7	3
Leyton O.	2	1	1	0	8	0
Liverpool	6	1	0	5	3	9
Luton T	3	2	1	0	5	2
Man. City	6	2	1	3	9	12
Man. Utd.	8	2	0	6	11	20
Middlesbro	5	2	2	1	8	8
Millwall	9	4	3	2	24	8
Newcastle U	5	3	0	2	16	7
Northampton	1	1	0	0	1	0
Norwich C	3	1	1	1	4	6
Nottm Forest	9	4	1	4	16	12
Notts Co.	12	5	4	3	29	21
Oldbury T	1	1	0	0	4	0
Oldham Ath.	4	3	0	1	6	4
Peterborough	2	1	1	0	3	2
Plymouth Arg	2	1	1	0	5	1
Port Vale	4	4	0	0	18	3
Portsmouth	6	2	2	2	10	8
Preston NE	8	3	2	3	9	10
QPR	2	2	0	0	4	2
Queens Pk G	1	0	0	1	1	6
Rangers	1	1	0	0	3	1
Reading	4	2	1	1	9	4
Rotherham U	3	2	0	1	5	3
Shankhouse	1	1	0	0	9	0
Sheff. Utd.	4	2	1	1	8	6
Sheff. Wed.	2	1	0	1	3	3
South Shore	1	1	0	0	4	2
Southampton	4	1	2	1	6	6
Southend U	1	0	0	1	0	1
Stafford Rd	4	2	1	1	11	5
Stockport Co	1	1	0	0	3	0
Stoke City	10	3	4	3	18	15
Sunderland	9	7	1	1	24	11
Swansea	2	2	0	0	5	1
Swindon T	1	1	0	0	2	1
Torquay U	1	0	0	1	1	3
Tottenham H	11	4	1	6	8	12
Walsall	2	2	0	0	9	1
Walsall S	2	2	0	0	9	2
Walsall T	3	3	0	0	9	1
Watford	1	1	0	0	4	1
Wednesbry OA	4	3	0	1	26	9
Wednesbry St	1	1	0	0	5	3
Wednesbury T	1	1	0	0	4	1
West Brom	14	8	3	3	18	14
West Ham U	3	2	0	1	8	1
Wimbledon	5	0	3	2	2	4
Witton	1	1	0	0	3	2

BARNET

	P	W	D	L	F	A
Banbury U	1	1	0	0	2	0
Bilston T	2	1	1	0	2	1
Bournemouth	2	0	1	1	1	2
Brentford	1	0	0	1	1	3
Brentwood T	2	0	1	1	1	2
Brighton &HA	3	0	1	2	1	6
Bristol C	1	0	0	1	0	2
Bristol R	2	0	1	1	1	3
Cambridge U	1	1	0	0	2	1
Carshalton A	1	0	0	1	0	4
Charlton Ath	1	0	0	1	1	3
Chelmsford C	2	1	1	0	4	2
Cheltenham T	1	0	0	1	1	5
Colchester U	1	0	0	1	0	1
Dartford	1	0	0	1	0	2
Enfield	3	2	1	0	11	5
Exeter C	1	0	0	1	2	6
Harlow T	2	1	1	0	1	0
Hereford U	2	0	0	2	2	4
Kettering T	1	1	0	0	4	2
Minehead	2	1	1	0	4	3

	P	W	D	L	F	A
Newport Co.	1	1	0	0	6	1
Northampton	2	1	1	0	1	0
Peterborough	2	0	0	2	1	3
Plymouth Arg	1	0	0	1	0	3
Portsmouth	1	0	0	1	0	5
Preston NE	1	0	0	1	2	3
QPR	5	0	1	4	6	18
Salisbury	1	0	0	1	0	1
Slough T	1	1	0	0	1	0
Southampton	1	0	0	1	1	4
Southend U	1	0	0	1	2	9
Sutton U	2	1	0	1	3	2
Tiverton T	1	1	0	0	5	0
Torquay U	2	0	0	2	3	10
Walton & H	1	1	0	0	1	0
Weymouth	1	0	0	1	0	1
Woking	3	0	2	1	6	9

BARNSLEY

	P	W	D	L	F	A
Aldershot	3	2	1	0	6	2
Arsenal	4	0	0	4	2	12
Aston Villa	1	0	0	1	1	4
Barrow	1	1	0	0	3	0
Birmingham C	5	2	2	1	8	5
Blackburn R	3	0	0	3	2	5
Blackpool	4	1	1	2	7	4
Bolton Wan.	2	2	0	0	5	2
Boston	1	1	0	0	3	1
Bradford C	12	3	5	4	13	17
Bradford PA	4	1	1	2	2	3
Brentford	1	0	0	1	0	2
Brighton &HA	4	2	1	1	6	5
Bristol C	1	1	0	0	4	1
Bristol R	1	1	0	0	4	0
Burnley	1	0	0	1	0	2
Bury	3	2	0	1	3	3
Caernarvon T	2	1	1	0	1	0
Cambridge U	1	0	0	1	0	1
Cardiff C	3	1	1	1	3	3
Carlisle U	1	0	0	1	1	2
Chelsea	1	1	0	0	4	0
Chester	3	1	0	2	4	7
Chesterfield	6	2	2	2	4	5
Colchester U	1	1	0	0	3	0
Crewe Alex.	3	2	1	0	11	2
Darlington	4	2	2	0	3	0
Derby Co.	1	0	0	1	1	8
Enfield	2	1	1	0	4	1
Everton	6	1	1	4	4	10
Gateshead	4	1	2	1	5	4
Gillingham	2	1	1	0	3	1
Grimsby T	3	0	1	2	1	5
Halifax T	4	0	1	3	5	8
Hartlepool U	4	1	0	0	5	2
Huddersfield	4	3	1	0	7	4
Hull C	2	0	1	1	1	3
Ipswich T	1	1	0	0	2	0
Leeds U	2	0	1	1	1	5
Leicester C	8	2	4	2	9	9
Lincoln C	2	2	0	0	5	1
Liverpool	2	0	1	4	1	11
Luton T	3	1	1	1	1	2
Man. City	2	0	0	2	1	4

	P	W	D	L	F	A
Man. Utd.	3	0	1	2	2	7
Mansfield T	1	0	0	1	2	3
Marine	1	0	0	1	1	3
Middlesbro	1	0	0	1	1	2
Millwall	2	1	1	0	2	1
Netherfield	1	1	0	0	3	1
Newcastle U	4	1	1	2	6	7
Northampton	2	0	0	2	2	6
Norwich C	4	1	1	2	4	5
Nottm Forest	3	1	1	1	4	4
Oldham Ath.	1	1	0	0	3	1
Plymouth Arg	3	0	0	3	1	6
Port Vale	6	2	2	2	8	11
Portsmouth	1	1	0	0	1	0
Preston NE	5	0	2	3	1	11
QPR	1	1	0	0	1	0
Reading	3	2	1	0	8	5
Rhyl	4	1	2	1	5	3
Rochdale	4	3	1	0	7	2
Rotherham U	5	2	1	2	7	5
Scunthorpe U	2	1	1	0	5	4
Sheff. Utd.	3	0	2	1	2	3
Sheff. Wed.	3	1	0	2	3	4
Southampton	1	1	0	0	2	1
Southend U	2	1	1	0	4	3
Southport	3	1	1	1	4	5
Stockport Co	3	1	0	2	4	6
Stoke City	3	2	1	0	7	5
Swansea	1	0	0	1	1	3
Swindon T	4	2	2	0	3	0
Torquay U	1	1	0	0	2	1
Tranmere R	1	1	0	0	4	2
W Auckland	2	1	1	0	5	3
Walsall	1	0	0	1	1	3
Watford	1	1	0	0	2	0
West Brom	4	3	1	0	3	0
West Ham	1	1	0	0	4	1
Wigan Ath.	1	1	0	0	3	2
Wolves	1	0	0	1	1	3
Worksop T	1	1	0	0	5	1

BIRMINGHAM CITY

	P	W	D	L	F	A
Altrincham	1	0	0	1	1	2
Arsenal	7	4	2	1	14	7
Aston Unity	1	1	0	0	6	1
Aston Villa	3	0	1	2	0	5
Barnsley	5	1	2	2	5	8
Birm. Exclsr	3	0	1	2	3	6
Birm.St.Grge	1	0	0	1	1	3
Blackburn R	2	2	0	0	5	1
Blackpool	4	1	1	2	3	4
Bolton Wan.	3	2	0	1	6	5
Bradford C	1	1	0	0	1	0
Bradford PA	2	1	1	0	8	2
Brentford	1	0	0	1	1	3
Brighton &HA	2	1	1	0	3	0
Bristol C	2	2	0	0	5	2
Burnley	4	1	0	3	3	7
Burton Wan.	1	1	0	0	9	2
Bury	3	0	1	2	4	9
Cardiff C	1	1	0	0	5	2
Carlisle U	2	1	1	0	7	3

	P	W	D	L	F	A
Charlton Ath	1	1	0	0	1	0
Chelmsford C	1	1	0	0	6	0
Chelsea	8	5	1	2	13	6
Cheltenham T	1	1	0	0	1	0
Clapton	1	1	0	0	3	1
Colchester U	1	1	0	0	2	0
Coventry C	2	1	0	1	7	4
Crystal P	3	1	1	1	5	3
Darlington	1	1	0	0	4	0
Darwen	1	1	0	0	3	1
Davenham	1	1	0	0	2	1
Derby Co.	6	2	1	3	10	12
Derby Town	1	1	0	0	4	1
Doncaster R	1	1	0	0	2	1
Everton	3	1	1	1	5	4
Fulham	6	3	2	1	8	6
Gateshead	1	0	0	1	1	2
Gillingham	1	1	0	0	3	0
Grimsby T	2	1	0	1	3	2
Halifax T	2	2	0	0	6	2
Huddersfield	6	2	1	3	6	7
Hull C	1	1	0	0	2	0
Ipswich T	4	2	0	2	4	4
Leeds U	2	0	0	2	1	5
Leicester C	8	0	3	5	8	15
Leyton O.	4	3	0	1	8	1
Lincoln C	1	1	0	0	2	1
Liverpool	5	1	0	4	5	10
Luton T	2	1	0	1	2	2
Man. City	8	5	0	3	18	12
Man. Utd.	5	1	1	3	5	11
Middlesbro	5	4	1	0	7	1
Millwall	1	1	0	0	4	1
Newcastle U	2	0	1	1	2	5
Norwich C	4	0	3	1	2	3
Nottm Forest	7	2	3	2	5	8
Notts Co.	2	0	0	2	1	4
Oldham Ath.	6	1	2	3	7	9
Peterboro &F	1	1	0	0	4	3
Port Vale	3	2	0	1	6	2
Portsmouth	9	4	2	3	9	10
Preston NE	2	2	0	0	3	1
QPR	2	0	0	2	1	4
Reading	1	0	0	1	0	1
Redcar	1	1	0	0	2	0
Rotherham U	3	2	1	0	6	1
Sheff. Utd.	5	3	2	0	9	4
Sheff. Wed.	3	1	1	1	4	5
Southampton	3	2	0	1	6	5
Southend U	2	2	0	0	8	2
Stafford Rd	2	0	1	1	5	9
Stockport Co	1	1	0	0	1	0
Stoke City	6	2	2	2	8	10
Sunderland	7	5	1	1	13	5
Swansea	1	0	0	1	0	3
Swindon T	1	0	0	1	0	2
Torquay U	2	1	0	1	7	4
Tottenham H	10	1	5	4	12	21
Walsall	4	2	1	1	3	2
Watford	5	2	1	2	11	6
Wednesbury OA	1	0	0	1	0	6
West Brom	8	1	1	6	7	16
West Ham U	3	1	0	2	5	8
Wigan Ath.	1	1	0	0	4	0
Wimbledon	1	0	0	1	0	1
Wolves	2	1	0	1	3	3
Wrexham	1	1	0	0	3	1

BLACKBURN ROVERS

	P	W	D	L	F	A
Accrington	3	2	1	0	9	2
Accrington S	3	1	1	1	10	6
Altrincham	2	1	1	0	2	0
Arsenal	4	2	0	2	5	5
Aston Villa	7	2	2	3	14	12
Barnsley	3	3	0	0	5	2
Birmingham C	2	0	0	2	1	5
Blackbrn Oly	2	2	0	0	8	3
Blackburn PR	1	1	0	0	9	1
Blackpool	3	2	1	0	5	1
Blackpool SJ	1	1	0	0	11	1
Bolton Wan.	10	3	3	4	19	15
Bootle	1	1	0	0	7	0
Bournemouth	1	1	0	0	3	1
Bradford C	3	1	0	2	3	7
Brentford	1	0	0	1	0	2
Brentwood(1)	1	1	0	0	3	1
Brighton &HA	1	1	0	0	3	0
Bristol C	1	0	0	1	1	2
Bristol R	3	2	0	1	7	3
Burnley	5	2	1	2	9	7
Burton T	1	1	0	0	4	0
Burton Wan.	1	1	0	0	2	1
Bury	2	2	0	0	3	0
Cardiff C	3	1	1	1	3	4
Carlisle	1	0	0	1	1	2
Charlton Ath	3	1	1	1	3	2
Chelsea	3	2	0	1	3	4
Chester	1	1	0	0	7	0
Chesterfield	2	1	1	0	3	0
Clitheroe	1	1	0	0	2	0
Corinthian	1	0	0	1	0	1
Coventry C	1	1	0	0	1	0
Crewe Alex.	2	1	0	1	3	1
Darlington	1	1	0	0	1	0
Darwen	4	3	0	1	11	3
Darwen Old W	1	1	0	0	6	1
Derby Co.	10	4	1	5	18	16
Derby Junc.	1	0	0	1	1	2
Everton	10	2	1	7	10	18
Exeter C	2	1	1	0	5	3
Fulham	7	2	3	2	7	6
Gateshead	2	0	1	1	0	1
Grimsby T	2	2	0	0	7	0
Huddersfield	5	1	2	2	6	10
Hull C	6	2	2	2	10	7
Kettering T	1	1	0	0	4	1
Kiddrminster	1	1	0	0	2	0
Leicester C	3	0	1	2	3	6
Leyton O.	3	2	0	1	8	5
Lincoln C	3	2	1	0	11	4
Liverpool	10	3	2	5	9	13
Luton T	2	0	0	2	1	8
Man. City	5	1	1	3	6	11
Man. Utd.	8	4	2	2	17	12
Matlock T	1	1	0	0	4	1
Middlesbro	7	4	2	1	12	6
Midlsbro Irn	1	1	0	0	3	0
Millwall	1	1	0	0	2	1
Newcastle U	5	2	1	2	7	6
Northampton	3	3	0	0	13	4
Northwich V.	1	1	0	0	4	1
Norwich C	3	2	1	0	9	5

	P	W	D	L	F	A
Nottm Forest	6	3	2	1	11	12
Notts Co.	6	3	0	3	7	6
O Crthusians	1	1	0	0	5	1
O Etonians	1	0	0	1	0	1
Oldham Ath.	1	1	0	0	1	0
Oswaldtwstle	1	1	0	0	1	0
Oxford U	2	1	0	1	2	3
Padiham	1	1	0	0	3	0
Port Vale	4	2	1	1	6	5
Portsmouth	11	4	5	2	14	6
Preston NE	3	1	1	1	5	3
Queens Pk G	2	2	0	0	4	1
Reading	1	1	0	0	2	1
Renton	2	0	1	1	2	4
Romford	1	1	0	0	8	0
Rossendale U	1	1	0	0	11	0
Rotherham U	1	1	0	0	4	1
Sheff. Prov.	1	1	0	0	6	2
Sheff. Utd.	4	1	2	1	5	5
Sheff. Wed.	10	5	2	3	18	12
Shrewsbury T	1	1	0	0	2	1
South Shore	1	1	0	0	7	0
Southampton	2	0	0	2	2	4
Southend U	2	2	0	0	9	3
Southport	4	2	1	1	10	4
Stafford Rgs	1	1	0	0	2	0
Staveley	2	2	0	0	12	2
Stockport Co	1	1	0	0	2	0
Stoke City	2	1	0	1	1	1
Sunderland	7	4	3	0	14	5
Swansea	3	1	0	2	2	3
Swifts	1	1	0	0	2	1
Swindon T	4	2	0	2	3	6
Tottenham H	9	3	4	2	15	11
Tyne Assoc.	1	1	0	0	5	1
Upton Park	1	1	0	0	3	0
Walsall	2	1	1	0	4	1
Wednesbry OA	1	1	0	0	3	1
Welling U	1	1	0	0	1	0
West Brom	11	5	2	4	15	13
West Ham U	7	3	3	1	16	11
Willington	2	1	1	0	6	1
Witton	1	1	0	0	5	0

BLACKPOOL

	P	W	D	L	F	A
Altrincham	2	0	0	2	1	3
Arsenal	3	2	1	0	6	4
Aston Villa	1	0	0	1	0	4
Bangor C	2	1	1	0	3	2
Barnsley	4	2	1	1	4	7
Barrow	2	1	1	0	2	0
Birmingham C	4	2	1	1	4	3
Blackburn R	3	0	1	2	1	5
Bolton Wan.	6	3	0	3	10	12
Bournemouth	1	0	0	1	0	1
Bradford C	1	0	0	1	1	2
Bradford PA	2	1	1	0	3	2
Bristol C	2	1	1	0	2	1
Bshp Aukland	1	1	0	0	4	1
Burnley	2	2	0	0	2	0
Burton S	1	1	0	0	4	1
Bury	2	1	0	1	4	3
Charlton Ath	2	1	1	0	5	2
Chelsea	1	0	0	1	0	1
Cheltenham T	1	1	0	0	3	1

CHESTER (continued)

	P	W	D	L	F	A
Chester	2	2	0	0	7	0
Chesterfield	1	1	0	0	2	1
Colchester U	1	1	0	0	5	0
Coventry C	1	0	0	1	1	3
Crewe Alex.	3	1	2	0	5	4
Crystal P	3	1	2	0	3	2
Darlington	2	1	1	0	4	3
Derby Co.	5	1	2	2	6	6
Doncaster R	2	1	0	1	3	3
Fleetwood T	1	1	0	0	4	0
Fulham	4	3	0	1	11	7
Gainsborough	1	1	0	0	2	0
Gillingham	1	0	0	1	0	1
Grimsby T	2	2	0	0	4	1
Hastings &SL	1	1	0	0	2	0
Horden CW	1	1	0	0	1	0
Horwich RMI	1	1	0	0	3	0
Huddersfield	3	3	0	0	5	0
Hull C	4	1	0	3	3	7
Kettering T	1	1	0	0	3	0
Leeds U	1	1	0	0	4	0
Leicester C	1	0	0	1	1	2
Lincoln C	2	2	0	0	3	1
Liverpool	1	0	0	1	1	2
Luton T	8	1	5	2	9	9
Man. City	6	1	2	3	7	10
Man. Utd.	3	0	0	3	4	9
Mansfield T	3	2	0	1	5	2
Margate	1	1	0	0	3	1
Middlesbro	4	1	0	3	5	9
Newcastle U	5	0	1	4	2	11
Northwich V.	1	1	0	0	2	0
Norwich C	2	0	1	1	2	4
Oldham Ath.	1	0	0	1	1	4
Oxford U	1	0	0	1	1	2
Plymouth Arg	2	0	0	2	0	5
Port Vale	2	0	1	2	3
Preston NE	2	0	0	2	2	4
QPR	5	0	3	2	3	10
Rochdale	2	0	1	1	1	2
Scunthorpe U	4	2	1	1	5	7
Sheff. Utd.	7	2	0	5	7	13
Sheff. Wed.	2	1	0	1	3	5
Southampton	6	2	1	3	8	11
Southend U	2	1	0	1	4	1
Southport	1	0	0	1	1	2
Stockport Co	2	2	0	0	4	2
Stoke City	4	0	1	3	2	9
Sunderland	1	0	0	1	0	1
Swansea	1	0	0	1	0	2
Torquay U	1	1	0	0	1	0
Tottenham H	5	2	1	2	7	10
Watford	1	0	0	1	1	2
West Brom	8	1	3	4	8	12
West Ham U	8	3	2	3	15	12
Wigan Ath.	2	0	1	1	1	3
Wolves	2	1	1	0	1	0
Wrexham	2	2	0	0	8	2

BOLTON WANDERERS

	P	W	D	L	F	A
Accrington	2	0	1	1	3	7
Accrington S	1	1	0	0	1	0
Arsenal	8	2	2	4	5	12
Aston Villa	4	1	2	1	4	3

	P	W	D	L	F	A
Bangor C	1	1	0	0	3	0
Barnsley	2	0	0	2	2	5
Barrow	1	1	0	0	1	0
Bath C	2	1	1	0	4	1
Birmingham C	3	1	0	2	5	6
Blackburn R	10	4	3	3	15	19
Blackpool	6	3	0	3	12	10
Bolton Assoc	1	1	0	0	3	0
Bolton Oly	1	1	0	0	9	0
Bootle	1	1	0	0	6	1
Bournemouth	2	1	1	0	8	4
Bradford C	1	1	0	0	3	1
Brentford	2	1	1	0	2	0
Brighton &HA	4	3	1	0	12	4
Bristol C	2	0	0	2	1	8
Bristol R	3	1	1	1	5	3
Burnley	3	2	0	1	3	4
Bury	5	4	1	0	9	3
Cardiff C	4	1	2	1	4	5
Carlisle U	1	1	0	0	1	0
Charlton Ath	5	3	1	1	11	4
Chelsea	2	0	0	2	0	4
Chester	2	1	1	0	2	1
Chesterfield	4	2	1	1	7	7
Coventry C	2	1	0	1	2	4
Crewe Alex.	2	2	0	0	5	0
Crystal P	1	0	0	1	0	1
Darwen	1	0	0	1	3	4
Derby Co.	5	3	0	2	7	8
Distillery	1	1	0	0	10	2
Druids	3	0	2	1	1	2
Eagley	3	2	1	0	12	5
Emley	1	1	0	0	3	0
Everton	8	2	4	2	13	16
Fulham	1	1	0	0	3	1
Gateshead	2	2	0	0	4	0
Grimsby T	4	2	2	0	8	6
Halifax T	5	3	2	0	10	4
Huddersfield	6	5	1	0	12	2
Hull C	5	3	1	1	12	6
Irwell Spr.	1	1	0	0	8	1
Leeds U	5	2	2	1	9	5
Leicester C	1	1	0	0	2	1
Liverpool	11	6	2	3	22	11
Liverpool Rm	1	1	0	0	3	0
Luton T	4	3	0	1	4	2
Man. City	9	3	1	5	10	18
Man. Utd.	3	1	0	2	3	3
Mansfield T	2	2	0	0	3	0
Middlesbro	7	1	3	3	2	7
Millwall	4	2	2	0	9	4
Newcastle U	6	1	2	3	8	11
Northampton	2	2	0	0	4	1
Norwich C	3	2	1	0	5	2
Nottm Forest	7	1	3	3	9	12
Notts Co.	9	3	4	2	13	14
Oldham Ath.	2	1	0	1	2	2
Oxford U	1	1	0	0	4	0
Plymouth Arg	1	1	0	0	4	1
Port Vale	2	1	0	1	4	2
Portsmouth	4	2	1	1	4	4
Preston NE	14	4	5	5	21	30
Rawtenstall	1	0	1	0	3	3
Reading	4	2	1	1	6	4
Rochdale	1	1	0	0	4	0
Rossendale U	1	1	0	0	4	1
Scunthorpe U	1	1	0	0	2	0

	P	W	D	L	F	A
Sheff. Utd.	7	3	0	4	20	9
Sheff. Wed.	8	1	2	5	7	15
Shrewsbury T	1	1	0	0	3	0
South Shore	1	1	0	0	5	3
Southampton	7	1	3	3	11	15
Stockport Co	2	1	0	1	6	5
Stoke City	5	3	1	1	10	7
Sutton Coldfield T	1	1	0	0	2	1
Sunderland	5	1	1	3	4	9
Swansea	1	1	0	0	3	0
Swindon T	1	1	0	0	4	2
Third Lanark	1	1	0	0	3	2
Torquay U	1	1	0	0	2	1
Tottenham H	8	2	4	2	9	9
Tranmere R	3	2	1	0	8	3
Watford	1	0	0	1	1	2
West Brom	8	1	2	5	5	16
West Ham U	4	2	1	1	4	2
Witton Alb.	1	1	0	0	2	1
Woking	1	1	0	0	5	0
Wolves	8	4	2	2	10	6
Workington	1	1	0	0	4	1
Wrexham	2	1	0	1	3	4

BOURNEMOUTH

	P	W	D	L	F	A
Accrington S	3	2	1	0	5	1
Aldershot	3	1	0	2	4	9
Barnet	2	1	1	0	2	1
Barnstaple T	1	1	0	0	4	1
Barrow	1	1	0	0	5	2
Bath C	1	1	0	0	5	3
Blackburn R	1	0	0	1	1	3
Blackpool	1	1	0	0	1	0
Blyth S	1	1	0	0	1	0
Bolton Wan.	2	0	1	1	4	8
Bradford C	3	1	0	2	2	4
Bradford PA	1	1	0	0	1	0
Brentford	2	2	0	0	4	2
Brighton &HA	1	0	0	1	0	2
Bristol C	4	2	1	1	5	5
Bristol R	5	2	1	2	10	5
Bromsgrove R	1	1	0	0	3	1
Burnley	3	0	1	2	1	9
Burton Alb.	1	1	0	0	8	0
Bury Town	2	1	1	0	3	0
Caernarvon A	2	1	1	0	6	3
Cambridge U	1	1	0	0	5	1
Charlton Ath	2	1	0	1	2	2
Cheltenham T	2	1	0	1	4	1
Chester	1	1	0	0	3	2
Colchester U	7	2	3	2	5	6
Coventry C	3	1	1	1	4	3
Dagenham	1	1	0	0	4	1
Dartford	6	3	3	0	13	2
Derby Co.	1	0	0	1	0	2
Dorchester T	2	1	1	0	3	2
Enfield	1	1	0	0	5	1
Everton	1	0	0	1	0	5
Exeter C	3	2	1	0	8	4
Fareham T	1	1	0	0	7	2
Fulham	2	0	1	1	1	3
Gillingham	1	1	0	0	2	1
Gravesend &N	1	1	0	0	7	0
Guildford C	2	2	0	0	7	1
Halifax T	1	1	0	0	3	1

	P	W	D	L	F	A
Hartlepool U	2	1	1	0	6	3
Harwich & P	1	1	0	0	5	1
Hayes	2	2	0	0	4	0
Hereford U	2	0	1	1	2	4
Hitchin T	1	1	0	0	2	1
Ipswich T	4	0	2	2	6	10
Kettering T	2	1	1	0	3	2
Leeds U	1	0	0	1	1	3
Leyton O.	2	0	0	2	1	3
Liverpool	4	0	2	2	3	9
Lovells Ath.	2	1	0	1	4	6
Luton T	2	0	1	1	2	4
Man. Utd.	6	1	1	4	4	13
Mansfield T	1	1	0	0	3	0
Margate	2	1	0	1	11	3
Merthyr T	1	1	0	0	3	0
Middlesbro	1	0	0	1	0	2
Newcastle U	3	0	2	1	2	4
Newport Co.	3	0	1	2	1	5
Northampton	4	1	1	2	5	7
Northfleet U	2	1	1	0	2	1
Oldham Ath.	1	1	0	0	4	0
Oswestry T	1	1	0	0	5	1
Oxford C	2	1	1	0	9	2
Oxford U	1	0	0	1	0	2
Peterborough	1	1	0	0	2	1
Poole	1	1	0	0	4	1
Portsmouth	1	0	0	1	1	5
QPR	1	0	0	1	0	2
Reading	3	2	0	1	3	1
Scunthorpe U	1	0	0	1	0	1
Sheff. Utd.	1	0	0	1	0	2
Sheff. Wed.	2	0	0	2	0	10
Southampton	2	1	1	0	4	2
Southend U	3	1	0	2	3	8
Southwick	1	1	0	0	5	0
Spennymoor U	1	0	0	1	0	2
Sutton U	2	1	1	0	2	1
Swindon T	3	2	1	0	6	4
Tooting & M	1	0	0	1	1	3
Torquay U	4	1	2	1	6	5
Tottenham H	1	1	0	0	3	1
Tranmere R	1	0	0	1	2	4
Walsall	3	1	0	2	4	2
Walthmstw Av	4	3	1	0	15	5
Watford	2	2	0	0	7	4
Welton Rov.	1	1	0	0	3	0
West Brom	1	0	0	1	0	1
West Ham U	2	0	1	1	2	4
Weymouth	2	1	1	0	4	1
Wigan Ath.	1	0	0	1	0	3
Wimbledon	2	0	1	1	2	3
Windsor & E	2	1	1	0	2	0
Wolves	2	1	0	1	2	2
Wycombe Wan.	3	1	1	1	4	2
Yeovil T	2	1	0	1	3	2

BRADFORD CITY

	P	W	D	L	F	A
Accrington S	1	1	0	0	1	0
Alvechurch	1	1	0	0	4	2
Arsenal	3	1	0	2	2	5
Aston Villa	3	1	1	1	6	5
Barnsley	12	4	5	3	17	13
Barrow	1	1	0	0	3	2

Birmingham C	1	0	0	1	0	1
Blackburn R	3	2	0	1	7	3
Blackpool	1	1	0	0	2	1
Bolton Wan.	1	0	0	1	1	3
Bournemouth	3	2	0	1	4	2
Bradford PA	3	2	0	1	5	3
Brandon U	1	1	0	0	3	0
Brentford	3	0	2	1	3	4
Brighton &HA	1	1	0	0	2	0
Bristol C	1	0	0	1	0	2
Burnley	3	1	1	1	3	7
Bury	2	1	0	1	3	3
Carlisle U	2	1	0	1	8	4
Charlton Ath	2	0	1	1	1	4
Chelsea	1	1	0	0	2	0
Chester	4	1	1	2	8	9
Chesterfield	4	1	2	1	3	4
Crewe Alex.	3	0	1	2	0	2
Darlington	3	2	0	1	4	3
Derby Co.	4	1	0	3	4	9
Doncaster R	2	2	0	0	8	4
Everton	4	1	0	3	3	4
Fleetwood T	1	1	0	0	9	0
Gateshead	3	2	0	1	7	6
Gillingham	1	1	0	0	1	0
Grantham T	1	1	0	0	3	0
Grimsby T	2	2	0	0	3	1
Hartlepool U	1	0	0	1	0	1
Huddersfield	2	0	0	2	1	4
Hull C	2	1	0	1	3	2
Ipswich T	4	0	2	2	6	11
Lincoln C	4	1	2	1	8	8
Liverpool	2	0	0	2	1	3
Luton T	1	0	0	1	0	3
Macclesfield	1	1	0	0	3	2
Man. Utd.	2	0	1	1	1	3
Mansfield T	5	4	1	0	13	8
Merthyr Tyd.	1	1	0	0	7	1
Middlesbro	3	2	1	0	4	2
Millwall	1	0	0	1	0	1
New Brighton	2	0	1	1	0	1
Newcastle U	4	1	1	2	2	7
Norwich C	5	3	2	0	7	3
Nottm Forest	1	0	0	1	0	1
Notts Co.	6	1	3	2	8	8
Oldham Ath.	6	3	2	1	17	9
Oxford U	1	1	0	0	4	2
Port Vale	5	2	0	3	6	8
Portsmouth	3	1	0	2	2	5
Preston NE	4	2	1	1	11	8
QPR	2	1	1	0	4	0
Reading	1	1	0	0	2	0
Rhyl	1	1	0	0	4	0
Rochdale	2	1	1	0	3	2
Rotherham U	2	1	0	1	5	3
Scarborough	4	2	1	1	8	2
Scunthorpe U	2	0	0	2	0	2
Sheff. Utd.	1	1	0	0	2	1
Shrewsbury T	3	1	1	1	3	3
Southampton	3	1	0	2	4	4
Southport	1	0	0	1	1	2
Stockport Co	4	1	1	2	6	7
Sunderland	1	0	0	1	0	1
Telford U	1	0	0	1	1	2
Tooting & M	1	1	0	0	3	1
Tottenham H	4	1	1	2	3	11
Tow Law T	1	1	0	0	7	2

Tranmere R	2	2	0	0	3	1
Walker Cltc	2	1	1	0	12	4
Walsall	4	1	2	1	7	5
West Brom	1	1	0	0	2	1
West Ham U	1	0	0	1	2	3
Wigan Ath.	2	0	1	1	2	4
Wolves	6	2	2	2	10	7
Workington	3	3	0	0	10	0
Worksop T	2	0	1	1	2	3
Wrexham	5	3	1	1	12	8

BRENTFORD

	P	W	D	L	F	A
Addlestne&Wy	2	1	1	0	4	2
Aldershot	3	1	1	1	4	3
Ashford T	1	1	0	0	5	0
Aston Villa	2	0	1	1	1	2
Barnet	1	1	0	0	3	1
Barnsley	1	1	0	0	2	0
Bath C	1	1	0	0	2	0
Birmingham C	1	1	0	0	3	1
Blackburn R	1	1	0	0	2	0
Bolton Wan.	2	0	1	1	0	2
Bournemouth	2	0	0	2	2	4
Bradford C	3	1	2	0	4	3
Brighton &HA	3	1	0	2	4	4
Bristol C	3	2	0	1	8	3
Bristol R	3	1	1	1	3	3
Bshp Strtfrd	1	1	0	0	4	0
Burnley	3	1	1	1	5	5
Cardiff C	5	3	1	1	7	5
Carlisle U	2	0	1	1	3	5
Charlton Ath	2	0	0	2	4	9
Chelmsford C	1	1	0	0	1	0
Chelsea	1	0	0	1	0	1
Chesham U	1	1	0	0	2	0
Clapton	2	1	1	0	8	4
Colchester U	4	0	1	3	3	6
Crook T	1	1	0	0	4	1
Crystal P	6	0	3	3	4	10
Dagenham	2	1	1	0	4	3
Derby Co.	1	0	0	1	0	3
Exeter C	4	2	0	2	6	6
Folkestone	1	1	0	0	2	0
Fulham	2	1	0	1	3	2
Gainsborough	1	1	0	0	2	0
Gillingham	6	3	2	1	13	11
Glossop	1	1	0	0	2	1
Gravesend &N	1	1	0	0	1	0
Grimsby T	1	0	0	1	0	2
Guildford C	3	1	1	1	6	4
Halesowen T	1	1	0	0	2	0
Huddersfield	3	1	0	2	7	7
Hull C	5	0	2	3	5	10
Ilford	1	1	0	0	6	1
King's Lynn	1	1	0	0	3	1
Leeds U	1	1	0	0	2	0
Leicester C	5	0	2	3	1	7
Leyton O.	5	1	2	2	6	8
Lincoln C	1	1	0	0	3	0
Liverpool	2	0	0	2	0	6
Luton T	3	0	2	1	4	5
Man. City	2	1	0	1	4	7
Man. Utd.	2	1	0	1	3	7
March Town U	1	1	0	0	4	0
Margate	2	1	1	0	4	2

Middlesbro	4	3	0	1	7	5
Millwall	1	0	0	1	0	1
Newcastle U	2	0	0	2	2	5
Northampton	3	2	1	0	6	2
Norwich C	2	2	0	0	5	1
Nottm Forest	1	0	0	1	0	1
Notts Co.	1	1	0	0	4	0
Nuneaton B.	1	1	0	0	2	1
Oldham Ath.	3	1	0	2	6	7
Oxford U	3	1	1	1	6	4
Peterborough	2	1	1	0	3	2
Plymouth Arg	5	0	1	4	1	6
Portsmouth	2	1	0	1	2	2
Preston NE	2	0	0	2	0	4
QPR	3	2	1	0	6	2
Reading	3	0	0	3	2	9
Rotherham U	1	1	0	0	3	0
Slough T	1	1	0	0	4	1
Southend U	1	0	0	1	0	1
Stockport Co	1	0	0	1	1	2
Sunderland	1	0	0	1	2	5
Swansea	2	0	1	1	3	4
Swindon T	4	0	1	3	5	11
Torquay U	1	1	0	0	1	0
Tottenham H	3	1	1	1	4	4
Tunbridge WR	2	1	1	0	3	2
Walsall	3	2	1	0	3	1
Watford	3	0	1	2	2	5
West Brom	1	0	0	1	0	2
West Ham U	2	1	1	0	3	1
Wimbledon	2	2	0	0	5	2
Windsor & E	1	1	0	0	7	0
Wisbech T	1	1	0	0	2	0
Woking	1	1	0	0	2	0
Workington	1	1	0	0	1	0

BRIGHTON & HOVE ALBION

	P	W	D	L	F	A
Aldershot	5	4	1	0	13	3
Arsenal	3	0	0	3	1	6
Aston Villa	2	0	1	1	4	6
Barnet	3	2	1	0	6	1
Barnsley	4	1	1	2	5	6
Barry T	1	1	0	0	4	1
Bath C	2	2	0	0	6	0
Bedford T	2	0	1	1	2	3
Birmingham C	2	0	1	1	0	3
Blackburn R	1	0	0	1	0	3
Bolton Wan.	4	0	1	3	4	12
Bournemouth	1	1	0	0	2	0
Bradford C	1	0	0	1	0	2
Bradford PA	1	1	0	0	2	1
Brentford	3	2	0	1	4	4
Bristol C	3	0	0	3	1	4
Burnley	2	0	1	1	3	5
Bury	1	0	0	1	0	2
Cardiff C	3	0	1	2	0	2
Chelsea	4	1	1	2	3	8
Cheltenham T	3	2	1	0	10	0
Chesterfield	1	1	0	0	2	1
Colchester U	1	0	0	1	0	1
Corinthian	3	1	2	0	3	2
Coventry C	3	1	1	1	5	3
Crawley T	1	1	0	0	5	0
Crystal P	4	1	2	1	5	5

	P	W	D	L	F	A
Darlington	1	0	0	1	1	2
Derby Co.	3	1	0	2	4	11
Doncaster R	1	1	0	0	5	0
Enfield	1	1	0	0	2	1
Everton	3	1	1	1	5	3
Folkestone	2	2	0	0	8	3
Fulham	1	0	0	1	1	2
Gillingham	1	1	0	0	1	0
Grimsby T	2	1	1	0	2	1
Hartlepool U	2	1	1	0	3	2
Hayes	1	1	0	0	2	0
Hereford U	1	1	0	0	2	1
Hillingdon B	1	1	0	0	7	1
Huddersfield	2	0	1	1	0	2
Hull C	2	2	0	0	4	2
Ipswich T	2	1	0	1	3	2
Kiddrminster	2	1	1	0	3	2
Leatherhead	1	0	0	1	0	1
Leeds C	1	1	0	0	3	1
Leeds U	1	0	0	1	1	2
Leicester C	1	1	0	0	2	1
Leyton O.	1	1	0	0	3	1
Lincoln C	1	1	0	0	2	1
Liverpool	6	2	2	2	9	10
Luton T	1	1	0	0	4	1
Man. City	2	1	0	1	5	5
Man. Utd.	6	0	2	4	4	12
Mansfield T	1	1	0	0	2	0
Middlesbro	3	0	2	1	3	5
Millwall	2	0	1	1	2	4
Newcastle U	4	2	1	1	4	4
Newport Co.	3	2	0	1	11	5
Northampton	3	1	0	2	3	4
Norwich C	10	5	2	3	19	15
Notts Co.	1	0	0	1	1	2
Oldham Ath.	4	2	1	1	7	4
Oxford U	1	0	0	1	0	3
Peterboro &F	1	1	0	0	4	0
Peterborough	2	1	1	0	3	2
Port Vale	1	0	0	1	1	2
Portsmouth	4	3	0	1	5	5
Preston NE	4	1	2	1	4	4
QPR	2	1	0	1	3	6
Romford	2	1	1	0	4	2
Rotherham U	3	1	2	0	8	2
S Liverpool	2	1	1	0	7	1
Scarborough	3	2	1	0	7	1
Scunthorpe U	1	1	0	0	3	2
Sheff. Utd.	3	1	1	1	2	2
Sheff. Wed.	3	1	0	2	2	6
Southampton	3	0	0	3	0	4
Southend U	3	1	0	2	3	4
Swansea	2	1	0	1	3	2
Swindon T	2	2	0	0	6	1
Tooting & M	1	1	0	0	3	2
Trowbridge T	2	1	1	0	6	1
Tunbridge WR	1	1	0	0	5	1
Tunbridge WU	1	1	0	0	5	0
Walsall	7	1	4	2	7	8
Walthmstw Av	2	1	1	0	5	3
Walton & H	2	0	1	1	0	4
Watford	9	4	2	3	13	13
West Ham U	4	0	2	2	3	5
Wisbech T	1	1	0	0	10	1
Woking	2	1	1	0	3	2
Wolves	1	0	0	1	2	3
Wrexham	5	1	3	1	6	7
Yeovil & P	1	0	0	1	1	2

BRISTOL CITY

	P	W	D	L	F	A
Accrington S	2	1	1	0	5	3
Aldershot	4	1	3	0	4	3
Arsenal	4	2	1	1	3	2
Aston Villa	6	0	1	5	5	14
Aylesbury U	1	1	0	0	1	0
Barnet	1	1	0	0	2	0
Barnsley	1	0	0	1	1	4
Barrow	1	1	0	0	2	1
Bath C	2	1	1	0	4	1
Birmingham C	2	0	0	2	2	5
Blackburn R	1	1	0	0	2	1
Blackpool	2	0	1	1	1	2
Bolton Wan.	2	2	0	0	8	1
Bournemouth	4	1	1	2	5	5
Bradford C	1	1	0	0	2	0
Brentford	3	1	0	2	3	8
Brighton &HA	3	3	0	0	4	1
Bristol R	8	5	1	2	15	11
Bury	5	2	3	0	8	6
Cambridge U	3	0	2	1	2	6
Cardiff C	5	2	1	2	5	7
Carlisle U	2	1	1	0	6	1
Charlton Ath	1	0	0	1	2	3
Chelsea	2	1	0	1	4	4
Chester	2	1	0	1	1	2
Chichester C	1	1	0	0	11	0
Colchester U	1	0	0	1	1	2
Cor. Casuals	2	1	1	0	4	0
Corby T	1	1	0	0	3	1
Coventry C	2	0	0	2	1	4
Crewe Alex.	1	0	0	1	0	3
Crystal P	4	1	0	3	1	5
Dartford	3	2	1	0	17	4
Derby Co.	9	3	3	3	13	14
Doncaster R	3	2	1	0	6	2
Enfield	1	1	0	0	3	0
Everton	2	0	0	2	1	7
Exeter C	2	1	0	1	3	2
Fisher Ath.	1	1	0	0	1	0
Fulham	1	1	0	0	2	1
Gillingham	2	1	0	1	3	2
Glossop	2	1	1	0	1	0
Gloucester C	1	1	0	0	4	0
Grimsby T	3	1	1	1	3	3
Halifax T	2	1	1	0	5	2
Hartlepool U	1	0	0	1	0	1
Hayes	1	1	0	0	9	3
Hereford U	3	2	1	0	7	3
Huddersfield	1	0	0	1	1	2
Hull C	2	1	1	0	2	1
Ipswich T	2	0	0	2	2	6
King's Lynn	2	1	1	0	5	2
Kingstonian	1	1	0	0	7	1
Leeds C	1	1	0	0	4	1
Leeds U	3	1	1	1	2	3
Leicester C	2	1	0	1	3	6
Leyton O.	1	0	0	1	1	4
Liverpool	5	1	0	4	2	7
Luton T	1	0	0	1	0	2
Man. Utd.	1	1	0	0	2	1
Merthyr T	1	1	0	0	2	0
Middlesbro	2	1	1	0	3	2

	P	W	D	L	F	A
Newport Co.	1	0	0	1	0	3
Northampton	2	1	0	1	3	1
Norwich C	3	2	0	1	4	2
Nottm Forest	5	0	1	4	3	10
Notts Co.	5	2	2	1	9	9
Peterborough	1	1	0	0	1	0
Plymouth Arg	3	1	1	1	3	4
Portsmouth	4	2	2	0	7	2
Preston NE	5	0	2	3	2	10
QPR	2	0	1	1	2	4
Rhyl	2	2	0	0	6	0
Romford	1	1	0	0	4	0
Rotherham U	3	2	0	1	7	5
Sheff. Utd.	4	0	1	3	2	9
Sheff. Wed.	2	1	1	0	3	1
Southampton	4	2	1	1	4	4
Southend U	2	1	0	1	4	3
Stalybrdge R	1	1	0	0	2	1
Sunderland	2	0	0	2	3	10
Swansea	3	2	1	0	10	4
Swindon T	3	2	1	0	6	3
Torquay U	4	2	1	1	5	3
Tottenham H	3	0	0	3	1	5
Tranmere R	2	0	1	1	4	5
VS Rugby	1	1	0	0	3	1
Walsall	2	0	1	1	1	4
Watford	1	0	0	1	1	2
Wellington T	1	1	0	0	4	2
West Brom	3	0	1	2	4	9
West Ham U	1	0	0	1	2	3
Wimbledon	3	2	1	0	4	2
Wolves	1	0	0	1	0	1
Wrexham	4	2	1	1	11	9

BRISTOL ROVERS

	P	W	D	L	F	A
Aberdare Ath	1	0	0	1	1	4
Accrington S	2	1	0	1	4	2
Aldershot	5	1	1	3	8	9
Arnold	1	1	0	0	3	0
Arsenal	3	0	0	3	1	9
Aston Villa	5	0	2	3	3	11
Barnet	2	1	1	0	3	1
Barnsley	1	0	0	1	0	4
Bideford	1	1	0	0	2	0
Blackburn R	3	1	0	2	3	7
Bolton Wan.	3	1	1	1	3	5
Bournemouth	5	2	1	2	5	10
Brentford	3	1	1	1	3	3
Bristol C	8	2	1	5	11	15
Burnley	3	1	1	1	6	8
Cambridge U	1	1	0	0	3	0
Cardiff C	2	1	1	0	5	2
Charlton Ath	3	2	0	1	5	5
Chelsea	3	0	1	2	2	5
Chesterfield	1	1	0	0	2	0
Corinthian	1	1	0	0	2	0
Coventry C	1	1	0	0	2	1
Crewe Alex.	1	0	0	1	0	2
Crystal P	1	0	0	1	1	3
Dartford	1	0	0	1	0	1
Derby Co.	1	0	0	1	0	2
Doncaster R	4	1	2	1	3	3
Everton	2	0	0	2	0	5
Fisher Ath.	1	1	0	0	3	0

	P	W	D	L	F	A
Folkestone	2	1	1	0	3	1
Fulham	4	1	0	3	6	11
Gillingham	6	3	3	0	14	7
Grimsby T	1	1	0	0	2	0
Harwich & P	1	1	0	0	3	0
Hayes	1	0	0	1	0	1
Huddersfield	1	0	0	1	0	2
Hull C	4	2	1	1	7	4
Ipswich T	4	0	1	3	4	13
Kettering T	4	2	1	1	7	4
King's Lynn	1	1	0	0	2	1
Leeds U	1	0	0	1	1	4
Leicester C	2	1	0	1	5	6
Leyton O.	3	1	1	1	2	2
Leytonstone	1	1	0	0	3	2
Liverpool	2	0	1	1	2	3
Llanelli	3	1	2	0	5	3
Luton T	3	2	0	1	5	7
Man. Utd.	3	1	0	2	6	7
Mansfield T	1	1	0	0	5	0
Merthyr T	1	1	0	0	4	1
Merthyr Tyd.	2	1	0	1	7	3
Middlesbro	2	1	1	0	2	1
Millwall	1	1	0	0	3	0
New Brighton	1	1	0	0	4	0
Newcastle U	2	0	1	1	1	3
Northampton	4	3	1	0	6	2
Norwich C	4	2	2	0	6	4
Nottm Forest	4	0	2	2	5	12
Notts Co.	1	1	0	0	2	0
Nunhead	1	1	0	0	2	0
Oldham Ath.	4	1	2	1	6	5
Oxford C	2	1	1	0	6	2
Peterborough	3	3	0	0	8	2
Plymouth Arg	3	1	1	1	7	3
Port Vale	1	0	0	1	0	2
Portsmouth	4	1	1	2	6	10
Preston NE	6	2	1	3	13	20
QPR	4	2	1	1	5	9
Reading	5	0	2	3	4	8
Sheff. Wed.	1	0	0	1	0	1
Shrewsbury T	1	0	0	1	1	2
Southampton	3	1	0	2	3	5
Southend U	3	0	1	2	1	5
Southport	1	1	0	0	2	1
Stockport Co	3	1	1	1	6	5
Stoke City	1	0	0	1	0	1
Sunderland	1	1	0	0	1	0
Swansea	3	3	0	0	6	1
Swindon T	3	1	0	2	4	3
Telford U	2	2	0	0	6	0
Torquay U	2	1	1	0	2	1
Tottenham H	2	0	0	2	3	10
Tranmere R	1	0	0	1	0	2
VS Rugby	2	1	1	0	5	1
Walsall	3	2	0	1	7	4
Wellingbro T	1	1	0	0	2	1
Weymouth	2	2	0	0	6	1
Wimbledon	1	1	0	0	4	0

BURNLEY

	P	W	D	L	F	A
Accrington	1	0	0	1	2	3
Altrincham	1	1	0	0	6	1
Arsenal	5	2	0	3	10	13
Astley Brdge	1	0	1	0	3	3

	P	W	D	L	F	A
Aston Villa	11	3	2	6	11	18
Barnsley	1	1	0	0	2	0
Birmingham C	4	3	0	1	7	3
Blackburn R	5	2	1	2	7	9
Blackpool	2	0	0	2	0	2
Bolton Wan.	3	1	0	2	4	3
Bournemouth	3	2	1	0	9	1
Bradford C	3	1	1	1	7	3
Bradford PA	1	0	0	1	0	2
Brentford	3	1	1	1	5	5
Brighton &HA	2	1	1	0	5	3
Bristol R	3	1	1	1	8	6
Bury	8	3	2	3	10	8
Cardiff C	2	0	1	1	2	4
Carlisle U	2	1	1	0	5	3
Charlton Ath	2	1	0	1	2	2
Chelsea	9	0	5	4	10	19
Chester	1	0	0	1	0	2
Chesterfield	5	3	1	1	15	7
Coventry C	3	3	0	0	9	0
Crewe Alex.	1	1	0	0	4	2
Crystal P	4	2	2	0	10	0
Darwen Old W	1	0	0	1	0	11
Derby Co.	5	2	1	2	8	11
Doncaster R	2	1	1	0	4	2
Everton	6	2	1	3	10	10
Exeter C	1	1	0	0	2	0
Fulham	7	4	2	1	10	4
Gainsborough	1	1	0	0	4	1
Gateshead	2	2	0	0	6	3
Grimsby T	2	2	0	0	5	1
Halifax T	1	1	0	0	3	1
Hartlepool U	1	1	0	0	1	0
Huddersfield	7	4	1	2	13	8
Hull C	1	0	0	1	0	3
Hyde Utd.	1	1	0	0	2	0
Leeds C	1	1	0	0	3	2
Leicester C	1	1	0	0	7	3
Leyton O.	2	1	1	0	2	1
Lincoln C	4	2	2	0	6	3
Liverpool	10	3	3	4	7	11
Luton T	3	2	1	0	6	1
Man. City	3	1	0	2	3	2
Man. Utd.	6	3	1	2	17	9
Mansfield T	1	1	0	0	4	2
Middlesbro	3	2	1	0	5	2
New Brighton	1	1	0	0	9	0
Newcastle U	4	0	1	3	2	6
Newport Co.	1	1	0	0	2	1
Nottm Forest	2	1	1	0	3	0
Notts Co.	4	1	0	3	6	7
Nuneaton B.	1	1	0	0	3	2
O W'minsters	1	1	0	0	4	3
Oldham Ath.	1	1	0	0	4	1
Oxford U	3	0	1	2	1	5
Penrith	1	1	0	0	9	0
Port Vale	5	2	1	2	7	6
Portsmouth	3	2	1	0	5	2
QPR	2	2	0	0	10	3
Reading	2	1	1	0	2	1
Rotherham U	5	3	1	1	8	7
Runcorn	2	1	1	0	2	1
Scarborough	2	2	0	0	3	1
Scunthorpe U	3	1	2	0	8	3
Sheff. Utd.	12	4	4	4	16	16
Sheff. Wed.	9	2	3	4	7	13
Shrewsbury T	3	1	1	1	3	3

	P	W	D	L	F	A
Southampton	1	0	0	1	1	2
Southend U	1	1	0	0	6	0
Stafford Rgs	1	1	0	0	3	1
Stockport Co	3	2	1	0	6	3
Stoke City	7	3	1	3	9	15
Sunderland	12	3	4	5	12	13
Swansea	4	3	1	0	10	3
Swindon T	8	3	2	3	14	14
T'crfts(Wtn)	2	1	1	0	5	0
Telford U	1	0	0	1	0	3
Tottenham H	7	2	1	4	10	13
Walsall	1	0	0	1	0	1
West Brom	1	0	0	1	1	5
West Ham U	2	0	0	2	3	6
Wimbledon	2	0	0	2	1	4
Wolves	1	1	0	0	3	0

BURY

	P	W	D	L	F	A
Arsenal	2	0	0	2	2	7
Aston Villa	2	1	0	1	5	3
Barnsley	3	1	0	2	3	3
Birmingham C	3	2	1	0	9	4
Blackburn R	2	0	0	2	0	3
Blackpool	2	1	0	1	3	4
Bolton Wan.	5	0	1	4	3	9
Boston U	1	1	0	0	3	0
Bradford C	2	1	0	1	3	3
Bradford PA	1	1	0	0	1	0
Brighton &HA	1	1	0	0	2	0
Bristol C	5	0	3	2	6	8
Bshp Aukland	2	1	1	0	4	1
Burnley	8	3	2	3	8	10
Burton Alb.	1	1	0	0	2	0
Charlton Ath	2	1	1	0	5	4
Chester	3	2	1	0	5	2
Chesterfield	1	0	0	1	0	2
Chorley	1	0	0	1	1	2
Crystal P	2	0	0	2	1	7
Darlington	3	3	0	0	11	4
Derby Co.	4	1	1	2	11	9
Doncaster R	2	1	0	1	5	5
Everton	4	0	1	3	2	13
Exeter C	1	0	0	1	1	2
Fulham	4	0	2	2	1	8
Gillingham	1	1	0	0	1	0
Glossop	1	1	0	0	2	1
Grimsby T	4	3	1	0	7	3
Guisboro T	1	1	0	0	1	0
Hartlepool U	2	2	0	0	8	2
Heanor T	1	1	0	0	3	0
Huddersfield	3	0	1	2	2	5
Hull C	2	1	1	0	2	1
Kettering T	1	1	0	0	8	0
Leeds U	2	0	0	2	2	9
Leicester C	4	1	0	3	6	6
Leyton O.	2	0	0	2	2	4
Lincoln C	2	2	0	0	4	1
Liverpool	1	0	0	1	0	2
Luton T	1	1	0	0	2	1
Man. City	3	0	0	3	4	8
Man. Utd.	4	1	1	2	2	4
Mansfield T	3	0	1	2	3	6
Middlesbro	2	1	1	0	3	2
Millwall	7	3	3	1	12	10
Newcastle U	4	2	0	2	7	12

	P	W	D	L	F	A
Nottm Forest	6	2	3	1	11	13
Notts Co.	6	3	2	1	5	4
Oldham Ath.	1	1	0	0	2	1
Oxford C	1	1	0	0	3	0
Plymouth Arg	2	1	1	0	3	2
Portsmouth	1	0	0	1	1	3
Preston NE	2	0	0	2	4	9
QPR	1	1	0	0	1	0
Reading	2	1	1	0	4	1
Rochdale	4	2	2	0	11	8
Rotherham U	7	2	2	3	12	13
Scunthorpe U	3	0	0	3	1	7
Sheff. Utd.	8	3	3	2	11	9
Sheff. Wed.	2	1	0	1	1	1
Shrewsbury T	2	0	1	1	1	2
Southampton	7	2	2	3	10	11
Southport	1	1	0	0	4	2
Spennymoor U	1	1	0	0	3	0
Stockton	2	1	1	0	12	1
Stoke City	9	3	4	2	18	13
Sunderland	3	1	0	2	6	10
Swansea	5	1	1	3	4	12
Swindon T	1	0	0	1	1	2
Torquay U	2	1	1	0	3	2
Tottenham H	1	0	0	1	1	2
Tranmere R	6	2	2	2	8	7
Walsall	2	2	0	0	7	0
Watford	2	0	1	1	1	4
West Brom	2	1	0	1	6	3
West Ham U	1	0	0	1	0	6
Wigan Ath.	4	2	2	0	8	4
Witton Alb	1	1	0	0	2	0
Wolves	2	1	0	1	1	2
Workington	2	2	0	0	9	1
Yeovil T	2	1	0	1	3	3

CAMBRIDGE UNITED

	P	W	D	L	F	A
Aldershot	2	2	0	0	3	1
Arsenal	1	0	0	1	1	2
Aston Villa	2	0	1	1	2	5
Barnet	1	0	0	1	1	2
Barnsley	1	1	0	0	1	0
Bedford T	1	0	0	1	1	2
Bognor Regis	1	1	0	0	1	0
Bournemouth	1	0	0	1	1	5
Bradford PA	1	0	0	1	1	2
Bristol C	3	1	2	0	6	2
Bristol R	1	0	0	1	0	3
Chelmsford C	1	0	0	1	0	1
Chesham U	1	1	0	0	2	0
Colchester U	3	0	1	2	1	6
Coventry C	2	1	1	0	2	1
Crystal P	1	0	0	1	0	1
Dagenham	1	0	0	1	1	2
Darlington	2	1	1	0	3	1
Derby Co.	1	0	0	1	0	3
Doncaster R	1	0	0	1	1	2
Enfield	1	1	0	0	1	0
Exeter C	3	2	1	0	5	2
Farnborough	1	1	0	0	2	1
Fulham	2	1	1	0	2	1
Gillingham	1	0	0	1	0	3
Hereford U	1	1	0	0	2	0
Hitchin T	2	1	1	0	3	0
Leatherhead	1	0	0	1	0	2
Lowestoft T	1	1	0	0	2	0
Maidstone U	1	0	0	1	0	1
Mansfield T	1	0	0	1	0	1
Middlesbro	1	1	0	0	2	0
Millwall	2	1	1	0	2	1
Newport Co.	2	1	1	0	4	3
Norwich C	1	0	0	1	0	1
Oldham Ath.	3	0	2	1	6	7
Peterborough	1	0	0	1	0	2
Plymouth Arg	2	0	0	2	0	3
Sheff. Wed.	3	1	0	2	6	4
Shrewsbury T	1	0	0	1	1	3
Swindon T	1	0	0	1	0	3
Torquay U	1	0	0	1	0	4
Weymouth	2	2	0	0	3	1
Woking	2	2	0	0	7	2
Wolves	1	1	0	0	1	0

CARDIFF CITY

	P	W	D	L	F	A
Aldershot	2	0	1	1	1	3
Arsenal	7	2	2	3	3	5
Aston Villa	3	2	0	1	5	8
Barnsley	3	1	1	1	3	3
Bath C	1	0	0	1	2	3
Birmingham C	1	0	0	1	2	5
Blackburn R	3	1	1	1	4	3
Bolton Wan.	4	1	2	1	5	4
Bradford PA	1	0	0	1	0	2
Brentford	5	1	1	3	5	7
Brighton &HA	3	2	1	0	2	0
Bristol C	5	2	1	2	7	5
Bristol R	2	0	1	1	2	5
Burnley	2	1	1	0	4	2
Charlton Ath	6	2	1	3	5	9
Chelsea	3	2	1	0	4	2
Cheltenham T	2	1	1	0	2	1
Crewe Alex.	1	1	0	0	1	0
Darlington	4	2	2	0	4	0
Dartford	1	0	0	1	0	3
Derby Co.	1	0	0	1	1	2
Enfield	2	2	0	0	12	1
Everton	1	0	0	1	1	2
Exeter C	2	1	0	1	7	4
Fulham	1	1	0	0	1	0
Gillingham	3	1	1	1	3	2
Gloucester C	2	1	1	0	3	2
Grimsby T	1	0	0	1	1	3
Halesowen T	1	1	0	0	1	0
Halifax T	1	0	0	1	1	3
Hayes	2	0	1	1	0	1
Hereford U	1	1	0	0	3	0
Hull C	1	0	0	1	1	2
Ipswich T	2	0	0	2	0	5
Leeds U	7	3	0	4	8	13
Leicester C	3	2	0	1	3	4
Leyton O.	3	3	0	0	9	1
Liverpool	2	2	0	0	4	2
Man. City	8	0	4	4	4	11
Man. Utd.	1	1	0	0	4	1
Middlesbro	1	0	0	1	0	2
Millwall	3	1	2	0	3	2
Newcastle U	3	0	1	2	1	6
Northampton	1	1	0	0	2	1
Norwich C	1	0	0	1	2	3
Nottm Forest	2	1	0	1	5	3
Notts Co.	1	1	0	0	2	0
Oldham Ath.	2	2	0	0	5	2
Peterborough	2	1	0	1	4	3
Plymouth Arg	1	1	0	0	3	0
Port Vale	3	1	0	2	2	5
QPR	2	0	1	1	0	2
Reading	2	1	0	1	4	2
Scunthorpe U	1	1	0	0	3	2
Sheff. Utd.	2	1	0	1	3	2
Sheff. Wed.	1	0	0	1	1	2
Southall	1	1	0	0	3	1
Southampton	4	3	1	0	6	2
Southend U	1	0	0	1	1	2
Southport	1	0	0	1	0	2
Stoke City	2	0	0	2	2	6
Sunderland	5	2	2	1	7	5
Swansea	1	0	0	1	1	2
Swindon T	4	1	1	2	3	6
Ton Pentre	1	1	0	0	4	1
Tottenham H	4	1	1	2	5	6
Watford	3	1	2	0	5	4
West Brom	4	1	2	1	4	7
West Ham U	2	0	0	2	2	4
Weymouth	1	0	0	1	2	3
Wokingham T	2	1	1	0	4	1
Wolves	3	1	1	1	3	4
Wrexham	1	1	0	0	3	2
Wycombe Wan.	1	1	0	0	1	0

CARLISLE UNITED

	P	W	D	L	F	A
Accrington S	2	0	1	1	3	4
Aldershot	2	1	1	0	6	3
Arsenal	3	0	1	2	2	6
Barnsley	1	1	0	0	2	1
Barrow	4	1	0	3	9	12
Bedford T	1	1	0	0	3	0
Bedlington U	1	1	0	0	4	0
Billnghm Syn	1	1	0	0	6	1
Birmingham C	2	0	1	1	3	7
Blackburn R	1	1	0	0	2	0
Blyth S	1	1	0	0	2	0
Bolton Wan.	1	0	0	1	0	1
Bradford C	2	1	0	1	4	8
Brentford	2	1	1	0	5	3
Bristol C	2	0	1	1	1	6
Bshp Aukland	1	1	0	0	1	0
Burnley	2	0	1	1	3	5
Chelsea	1	0	0	1	0	2
Cheltenham T	1	0	0	1	1	2
Chester	2	2	0	0	4	1
Chesterfield	2	0	1	1	0	1
Chilton Col.	1	0	0	1	0	2
Crewe Alex.	3	1	1	1	8	8
Crook T	1	0	0	1	0	1
Crystal P	1	1	0	0	3	0
Dagenham	1	1	0	0	1	0
Darlington	8	3	3	2	12	9
Denaby Utd.	1	1	0	0	1	0
Doncaster R	1	1	0	0	2	1
Everton	2	0	0	2	1	5
Fulham	2	0	0	2	1	5
Gateshead	1	1	0	0	4	3
Gravesend &N	1	0	0	1	0	1

	P	W	D	L	F	A
Grimsby T	1	0	0	1	2	6
Halifax T	2	2	0	0	3	0
Hartlepool U	2	2	0	0	8	3
Heanor T	1	1	0	0	5	1
Huddersfield	3	1	1	1	5	5
Hull C	5	2	2	1	10	6
Ipswich T	2	0	0	2	2	5
Leeds U	1	0	0	1	2	5
Leicester C	1	0	0	1	0	1
Leyton O.	1	1	0	0	4	1
Lincoln C	2	1	0	1	1	1
Liverpool	4	0	1	3	0	8
Macclesfield	1	0	0	1	2	4
Man. Utd.	2	0	1	1	3	5
Mansfield T	3	2	1	0	5	3
Matlock T	1	1	0	0	5	1
Middlesbro	1	0	0	1	1	2
N Shields	2	2	0	0	8	3
New Brighton	2	1	0	1	3	2
Newcastle U	1	1	0	0	1	0
Nottm Forest	2	1	1	0	2	1
Notts Co.	2	0	1	1	1	4
Peterborough	1	0	0	1	0	1
Port Vale	1	0	0	1	1	2
Preston NE	2	1	0	1	1	1
QPR	2	2	0	0	3	0
Rhyl	1	1	0	0	5	1
Rochdale	2	0	1	1	3	5
Runcorn	1	1	0	0	4	0
S Liverpool	1	1	0	0	3	2
Scarborough	1	1	0	0	1	0
Scunthorpe U	1	0	0	1	0	1
Sheff. Utd.	2	1	0	1	2	4
Sheff. Wed.	1	1	0	0	3	0
Shrewsbury T	3	0	2	1	4	5
Southend U	1	1	0	0	3	0
Southport	2	1	0	1	3	2
Stafford Rgs	1	1	0	0	2	0
Stockport Co	2	2	0	0	3	1
Sunderland	2	1	1	0	1	0
Swansea	1	0	0	1	0	1
Swindon T	3	1	1	1	4	4
Telford U	2	1	1	0	5	2
Tottenham H	3	0	1	2	4	7
Tranmere R	2	0	0	2	1	5
Tunbridge WR	1	1	0	0	4	2
Walsall	2	1	0	1	4	4
Watford	2	0	1	1	3	6
West Brom	2	1	0	1	4	5
West Ham U	2	0	1	1	1	6
Wigan Ath.	4	0	0	4	2	16
Wolves	2	0	0	2	1	5
Workington	2	1	1	0	4	1
Wrexham	6	3	1	2	7	5
York C	1	1	0	0	5	2

CHARLTON ATHLETIC

	P	W	D	L	F	A
Accrington S	2	1	1	0	1	0
Arsenal	2	0	0	2	0	4
Aston Villa	6	1	3	2	7	10
Barnet	1	1	0	0	3	1
Bath C	2	1	1	0	3	1
Birmingham C	1	0	0	1	0	1
Blackburn R	3	1	1	1	2	3

	P	W	D	L	F	A
Blackpool	2	0	1	1	2	5
Bolton Wan.	5	1	1	3	4	11
Bournemouth	2	1	0	1	2	2
Bradford C	2	1	1	0	4	1
Brentford	2	2	0	0	9	4
Bristol C	1	1	0	0	3	2
Bristol R	3	1	0	2	5	5
Burnley	2	1	0	1	2	2
Burton Alb.	1	1	0	0	7	0
Bury	2	0	1	1	4	5
Cardiff C	6	3	1	2	9	5
Chelmsford C	1	1	0	0	1	0
Chelsea	1	0	0	1	0	3
Colchester U	1	1	0	0	1	0
Coventry C	2	0	0	2	0	5
Crystal P	2	1	1	0	2	0
Derby Co.	2	1	0	1	3	5
Everton	3	0	1	2	4	8
Exeter C	2	0	1	1	4	7
Fulham	7	3	2	2	11	10
Gillingham	1	1	0	0	1	0
Harlow T	1	1	0	0	2	0
Huddersfield	3	1	1	1	3	3
Hull C	2	0	0	2	1	6
Ipswich T	2	0	0	2	2	5
Kettering T	3	2	1	0	5	3
Leeds U	3	1	1	1	4	5
Leyton O.	2	0	0	2	0	4
Luton T	1	0	0	1	0	1
Maidstone U	2	1	0	1	3	2
Man. City	1	1	0	0	2	1
Man. Utd.	1	0	0	1	0	2
Merthyr T	2	1	1	0	2	1
Middlesbro	7	0	4	3	7	10
Newcastle U	2	2	0	0	6	1
Northfleet U	1	1	0	0	5	1
Notts Co.	1	0	0	1	0	2
Oldham Ath.	1	1	0	0	2	1
Peterboro &F	1	1	0	0	2	0
Peterborough	1	0	0	1	0	3
Plymouth Arg	1	1	0	0	2	1
Port Vale	1	1	0	0	2	0
Portsmouth	5	1	2	2	10	9
Preston NE	5	3	1	1	13	5
QPR	5	2	2	1	8	5
Rochdale	2	2	0	0	6	2
Scunthorpe U	1	1	0	0	1	0
Sheff. Utd.	3	0	1	2	1	4
Sheff. Wed.	1	1	0	0	2	1
Stockport Co	1	1	0	0	3	0
Swindon T	1	1	0	0	2	1
Tonbridge	1	1	0	0	5	0
Tottenham H	3	0	1	2	4	6
Tranmere R	2	0	1	1	2	4
Walsall	2	1	0	1	3	3
Watford	1	0	0	1	0	2
West Brom	7	3	2	2	11	10
West Ham U	5	0	0	5	1	9
Windsor & E	1	1	0	0	4	2
Woking	1	1	0	0	3	1
Wolves	7	1	2	4	8	13

CHELSEA

	P	W	D	L	F	A
Accrington S	1	1	0	0	7	2
Arsenal	13	4	5	4	15	17

	P	W	D	L	F	A
Aston Villa	7	1	1	5	7	12
Barnsley	1	0	0	1	0	4
Barrow	1	1	0	0	5	0
Birmingham C	8	2	1	5	6	13
Blackburn R	3	1	0	2	4	3
Blackpool	1	1	0	0	1	0
Bolton Wan.	2	2	0	0	4	0
Bradford C	1	0	0	1	0	2
Bradford PA	2	2	0	0	9	2
Brentford	1	1	0	0	1	0
Brighton &HA	4	2	1	1	8	3
Bristol C	2	1	0	1	4	4
Bristol R	3	2	1	0	5	2
Burnley	9	4	5	0	19	10
Cardiff C	3	0	1	2	2	4
Carlisle U	1	1	0	0	2	0
Charlton Ath	1	1	0	0	3	0
Chester	2	1	1	0	5	4
Chesterfield	3	2	1	0	8	2
Crewe Alex.	3	1	1	1	4	3
Crystal P	5	2	1	2	11	8
Darlington	2	0	1	1	4	7
Derby Co.	6	2	2	2	11	10
Doncaster R	1	1	0	0	2	0
Everton	6	4	0	2	7	2
Exeter C	2	1	1	0	3	1
Fulham	5	1	2	2	6	7
Grimsby T	1	0	0	1	0	1
Hartlepool U	1	1	0	0	1	0
Huddersfield	4	2	1	1	6	4
Hull C	8	5	3	0	13	5
Ipswich T	2	2	0	0	5	0
Leeds U	8	5	3	0	17	6
Leicester C	3	2	1	0	6	1
Leyton	2	1	1	0	2	0
Leyton O.	4	1	1	2	5	5
Lincoln C	2	0	1	1	2	3
Liverpool	7	4	0	3	14	11
Luton T	3	1	1	1	5	3
Man. City	3	1	0	2	1	5
Man. Utd.	5	1	0	4	3	8
Middlesbro	1	0	0	1	1	2
Millwall	4	0	1	3	2	7
Newcastle U	6	3	1	2	10	7
Northampton	1	1	0	0	4	1
Norwich C	3	2	1	0	5	2
Nottm Forest	2	1	1	0	4	1
Notts Co.	1	0	0	1	0	1
Oxford U	1	0	0	1	1	3
Peterborough	1	1	0	0	5	1
Plymouth Arg	5	3	2	0	8	3
Portsmouth	2	0	1	1	1	2
Preston NE	2	1	1	0	2	1
QPR	3	1	1	1	4	3
Reading	3	1	2	0	5	3
Rochdale	1	1	0	0	3	2
Rotherham C	1	1	0	0	1	0
Sheff. Utd.	5	4	0	1	5	3
Sheff. Wed.	13	6	5	2	18	17
Shrewsbury T	2	2	0	0	4	2
Southampton	7	0	3	4	3	11
Southend U	1	1	0	0	5	2
Stoke City	2	1	0	1	4	5
Sunderland	2	0	1	1	2	3
Swindon T	5	4	1	0	15	4
Tottenham H	7	2	1	4	7	11
Tranmere R	5	3	2	0	16	8

	P	W	D	L	F	A
Gainsborough	1	1	0	0	1	0
Gillingham	3	0	1	2	3	9
Hereford U	1	1	0	0	3	2
Huddersfield	1	1	0	0	1	0
Kettering T	1	1	0	0	3	2
Leatherhead	3	1	1	1	5	2
Leeds U	1	1	0	0	3	2
Leyton O.	2	0	1	1	1	4
Llanelli	1	1	0	0	3	0
Maidenhead U	1	1	0	0	5	0
Man. Utd.	1	0	0	1	0	1
Millwall	2	0	1	1	1	5
Newcastle U	2	0	1	1	4	5
Newport Co.	4	2	1	1	4	2
Oxford U	1	1	0	0	4	2
Peterborough	5	0	2	3	7	14
Plymouth Arg	3	1	1	1	2	3
Port Vale	1	1	0	0	3	1
Portsmouth	1	1	0	0	3	0
QPR	4	0	1	3	5	11
Reading	6	1	1	4	8	17
Ringmer	1	1	0	0	3	0
Rochdale	2	1	1	0	8	3
Rotherham U	2	0	1	1	2	4
Sheff. Utd.	2	0	1	1	3	5
Shrewsbury T	2	1	0	1	4	4
Slough T	1	1	0	0	4	0
Southend U	3	1	1	1	6	8
Swansea	2	1	1	0	5	3
Tamworth	1	1	0	0	3	0
Torquay U	6	2	1	3	5	9
Watford	3	1	0	2	1	3
Wealdstone	1	1	0	0	4	0
West Brom	2	0	1	1	1	5
Weymouth	2	1	1	0	5	1
Wimbledon	1	0	0	1	1	2
Wisbech T	1	0	0	1	0	1
Wrexham	1	1	0	0	1	0
Wycombe Wan.	1	0	0	1	0	2

COVENTRY CITY

	P	W	D	L	F	A
Aldershot	1	0	0	1	1	4
Arsenal	3	0	1	2	2	7
Aston Villa	3	1	0	2	2	6
Bath C	1	1	0	0	7	1
Birmingham C	2	1	0	1	4	7
Blackburn R	1	0	0	1	0	1
Blackpool	1	1	0	0	3	1
Bolton Wan.	2	1	0	1	4	2
Bournemouth	3	1	1	1	3	4
Brighton &HA	3	1	1	1	3	5
Bristol C	2	2	0	0	4	1
Bristol R	1	0	0	1	1	2
Bshp Aukland	1	0	0	1	4	1
Burnley	3	0	0	3	0	9
Cambridge U	2	0	1	1	1	2
Charlton Ath	2	2	0	0	5	0
Chester	2	1	0	1	2	1
Crewe Alex.	3	2	1	0	8	2
Crystal P	1	0	0	1	2	4
Derby Co.	2	1	0	1	0	0
Everton	3	0	0	3	0	7
Exeter C	3	0	1	2	2	4
Fulham	1	0	0	1	1	4

	P	W	D	L	F	A
Gillingham	1	1	0	0	2	0
Grimsby T	1	1	0	0	1	0
Guildford C	1	1	0	0	2	1
Hartlepool U	1	1	0	0	4	0
Huddersfield	2	0	1	1	4	5
Hull C	2	1	0	1	3	1
Kettering T	1	1	0	0	3	2
King's Lynn	1	0	0	1	1	2
Leeds U	3	2	1	0	5	3
Leicester C	2	1	1	0	5	2
Leyton O.	3	1	1	1	6	5
Lincoln C	3	1	1	1	7	4
Liverpool	3	0	1	2	3	7
Luton T	3	0	1	2	4	6
Man. City	2	2	0	0	5	2
Man. Utd.	6	1	1	4	6	13
Middlesbro	1	0	0	1	0	3
Millwall	3	2	1	0	3	1
Newcastle U	3	0	1	2	4	10
Newport Co.	1	1	0	0	5	2
Northampton	3	2	0	1	3	2
Norwich C	6	2	2	2	10	8
Nottm Forest	1	1	0	0	3	1
Notts Co.	1	0	0	1	0	2
Oldham Ath.	1	1	0	0	1	0
Oxford U	1	1	0	0	4	0
Plymouth Arg	2	0	0	2	2	7
Portsmouth	4	2	2	0	6	4
Preston NE	1	1	0	0	2	1
QPR	3	1	1	1	4	4
Reading	3	0	2	1	5	6
Rochdale	1	0	0	1	1	2
Rotherham U	1	0	0	1	1	2
Scunthorpe U	4	2	1	1	14	5
Sheff. Wed.	6	4	1	1	13	6
Southampton	5	1	2	2	5	9
Stoke City	1	1	0	0	1	0
Sunderland	3	1	0	2	3	5
Sutton U	1	0	0	1	1	2
Swindon T	2	1	0	1	3	3
Torquay U	2	1	0	1	2	1
Tottenham H	2	1	0	1	4	5
Tranmere R	2	0	1	1	1	3
Trowbridge T	1	1	0	0	6	1
Walsall	1	1	0	0	2	1
Walthmstw Av	1	1	0	0	1	0
Watford	2	0	0	2	1	4
West Brom	5	1	1	3	6	12
Weymouth	1	1	0	0	5	2
Wigan Ath.	2	1	0	1	2	1
Wolves	4	1	2	1	5	4
Worcester C	2	2	0	0	7	2
Worksop T	1	0	0	1	0	1

CREWE ALEXANDRA

	P	W	D	L	F	A
Accrington S	3	1	1	1	7	3
Altrincham	2	1	0	1	1	3
Ashington	2	1	1	0	4	2
Aston Villa	2	0	0	2	2	6
Atherstone U	1	1	0	0	1	0
Barnsley	3	0	1	2	2	11
Barrow	3	1	1	1	3	3
Billnghm Syn	1	1	0	0	5	0
Blackburn R	2	1	0	1	1	3

	P	W	D	L	F	A
Blackpool	3	0	2	1	4	5
Blyth S	1	0	0	1	0	1
Bolton Wan.	2	0	0	2	0	5
Boston U	2	1	0	1	5	5
Bradford C	3	2	1	0	2	0
Bristol C	1	1	0	0	3	0
Bristol R	1	1	0	0	2	0
Bishop Auckland	2	1	1	0	3	1
Burnley	1	0	0	1	2	4
Burscough	1	0	0	1	3	1
Cardiff C	1	0	0	1	0	1
Carlisle U	3	1	1	1	8	8
Chelsea	3	1	1	1	3	4
Chester	3	1	0	2	2	6
Congleton T	1	1	0	0	2	0
Coventry C	3	0	1	2	2	8
Crook T	1	1	0	0	4	0
Darlington	4	2	1	1	5	5
Davenham	1	0	0	1	1	2
Derby Co.	3	1	0	2	2	8
Doncaster R	4	1	2	1	4	3
Druids	1	1	0	0	5	0
Folkestone	1	0	0	1	5	1
Gainsborough	3	0	1	2	3	6
Gateshead	1	0	0	1	0	2
Gateshead U	2	0	1	1	2	3
Gillingham	1	1	0	0	2	1
Grimsby T	3	1	1	1	3	6
Halifax T	5	1	2	2	9	9
Halliwell	2	0	1	1	3	7
Hartlepool U	3	1	1	1	3	3
Hull C	3	0	1	2	3	7
Jarrow	1	1	0	0	1	0
Leek	1	0	0	1	0	1
Lincoln C	4	2	0	2	9	7
Liverpool	1	0	0	1	0	4
London Caley	1	1	0	0	3	2
Luton T	1	0	0	1	0	2
Marine	1	1	0	0	3	1
Middlesbro	1	1	0	0	2	0
Millwall	1	1	0	0	3	2
Mossley	1	0	0	1	0	1
N Shields	1	1	0	0	4	0
Nelson	1	1	0	0	3	0
New Brighton	2	0	1	1	3	6
Northrn Nmds	1	1	0	0	4	1
Northwich V.	2	1	0	1	2	3
Nuneaton B.	1	1	0	0	2	0
Oldham Ath.	6	1	3	2	4	7
Oswestry T	2	1	1	0	3	2
Plymouth Arg	3	0	1	2	2	7
Port Vale	2	0	1	1	1	4
Preston NE	4	0	2	2	3	10
QPR	1	0	0	1	2	4
Queens Pk G	2	0	0	2	1	12
Rochdale	4	2	1	1	8	4
Rotherham U	3	1	0	2	2	4
Runcorn	1	1	0	0	3	0
S Shields	4	2	1	1	9	9
Scarborough	6	1	3	2	5	7
Scunthorpe U	2	1	0	1	4	3
Sheff. Utd.	1	1	0	0	3	1
Sheff. Wed.	2	0	1	1	2	4
Stafford Rgs	3	2	1	0	6	4
Stockport Co	3	2	1	0	4	0
Stoke City	3	2	1	0	9	6
Sunderland	1	0	0	1	0	2

	P	W	D	L	F	A
Swifts	2	1	1	0	4	3
Tottenham H	3	0	1	2	5	20
Tranmere R	2	1	1	0	2	1
Walsall	2	0	0	2	1	5
West Ham U	1	0	0	1	0	1
Wigan Boro.	3	1	1	1	7	5
Willenhall T	1	1	0	0	1	0
Wolves	2	0	1	1	3	6
Workington	2	2	0	0	4	1
Wrexham	5	2	1	2	13	10
Wrexham Oly	1	1	0	0	4	1

CRYSTAL PALACE

	P	W	D	L	F	A
Accrington S	1	1	0	0	1	0
Aldershot	1	1	0	0	1	0
Arsenal	1	0	0	1	0	7
Ashford T	1	1	0	0	1	0
Aston Villa	2	0	0	2	3	9
Bath C	1	0	0	1	1	2
Birmingham C	3	1	1	1	3	5
Blackpool	3	0	2	1	2	3
Bolton Wan.	1	1	0	0	1	0
Brentford	6	3	3	0	10	4
Bridgwater T	1	1	0	0	3	0
Brighton &HA	4	1	2	1	5	5
Bristol C	4	3	0	1	5	1
Bristol R	1	1	0	0	3	1
Bshp Aukland	1	0	0	1	2	4
Burnley	4	0	2	2	0	10
Bury	2	2	0	0	7	1
Cambridge U	1	1	0	0	1	0
Carlisle U	1	0	0	1	0	3
Charlton Ath	2	0	1	1	0	2
Chelmsford C	1	1	0	0	5	1
Chelsea	5	2	1	2	8	11
Chester	1	0	0	1	0	1
Coventry C	1	1	0	0	4	2
Dartford	1	1	0	0	3	1
Enfield	2	2	0	0	7	2
Everton	7	1	2	4	11	20
Finchley	1	0	0	1	1	3
Fulham	2	1	1	0	1	0
Gateshead	1	1	0	0	2	1
Gillingham	1	0	0	1	0	1
Glossop	1	1	0	0	2	0
Grimsby T	1	0	0	1	0	1
Gt. Yarmouth	1	0	0	1	0	1
Hartlepool U	2	0	0	2	1	3
Harwich & P	1	1	0	0	8	2
Hereford U	1	1	0	0	1	0
Hitchin T	1	1	0	0	6	2
Huddersfield	2	1	0	1	6	5
Hull C	2	0	0	2	2	5
Ipswich T	1	0	0	1	0	1
Kettering T	3	2	1	0	8	2
Leeds U	1	0	0	3	2	14
Leicester C	2	1	0	1	1	1
Leyton O.	2	1	1	0	1	0
Liverpool	5	1	2	2	7	9
Luton T	3	1	1	1	8	2
Man. City	3	1	0	2	6	15
Man. Utd.	2	0	1	1	3	4
Mansfield T	1	1	0	1	4	9
Margate	4	2	1	1	7	5
Middlesbro	2	1	1	0	2	1
Millwall	10	2	4	4	11	16
Newark T	1	1	0	0	6	0
Newcastle U	4	1	0	3	3	9
Newport Co.	1	0	0	1	0	3
Northampton	2	1	1	0	5	4
Norwich C	4	2	1	1	5	2
Nottm Forest	5	2	2	1	6	6
Notts Co.	4	1	3	0	2	1
Plymouth Arg	2	1	0	1	4	4
Port Vale	1	1	0	0	2	1
Portsmouth	2	2	0	0	5	1
QPR	7	0	3	4	1	7
Reading	6	3	3	0	9	4
Rochdale	1	1	0	0	1	0
Scarborough	1	1	0	0	2	1
Scunthorpe U	1	1	0	0	1	0
Sheff. Utd.	1	0	0	1	0	2
Sheff. Wed.	3	0	2	1	4	5
Shrewsbury T	3	1	2	0	8	5
Southampton	6	3	1	2	5	5
Southend U	2	0	1	1	1	3
Stockport Co	1	1	0	0	2	1
Stoke City	1	0	0	1	0	1
Sunderland	3	1	1	1	1	1
Swansea	3	0	2	1	6	7
Swindon T	5	1	1	3	5	7
Taunton T	1	1	0	0	6	0
Tooting & M	1	1	0	0	2	1
Tottenham H	4	2	1	1	3	4
Walsall	3	1	1	1	4	3
Walthmstw Av	1	1	0	0	2	0
Walton & H	1	1	0	0	1	0
Watford	2	0	1	1	0	1
West Ham U	3	0	1	2	1	5
Wolves	3	1	1	1	6	5
Wrexham	1	0	0	1	0	2
Yeovil & P	1	0	0	1	0	3
Yeovil T	1	0	0	1	1	3

DARLINGTON

	P	W	D	L	F	A
Accrington S	3	1	0	2	4	6
Altrincham	2	1	1	0	2	0
Arsenal	1	0	0	1	0	2
Bangor C	1	1	0	0	5	1
Barnsley	4	0	2	2	0	3
Barrow	3	2	1	0	5	2
Birmingham C	1	0	0	1	0	4
Blackburn R	1	0	0	1	0	1
Blackpool	2	0	1	1	3	4
Boston T	1	1	0	0	1	0
Boston U	1	1	0	0	5	3
Bradford C	3	1	0	2	3	4
Bradford PA	1	1	0	0	2	1
Brighton &HA	1	1	0	0	2	1
Burton T	1	1	0	0	2	1
Bury	3	0	0	3	4	11
Caernarvon A	1	0	0	1	2	4
Cambridge U	2	0	1	1	1	3
Cardiff C	4	0	2	2	0	4
Carlisle U	8	2	3	3	9	12
Chelmsford C	1	0	0	1	1	3
Chelsea	1	1	0	0	7	4
Chester	6	2	1	3	7	15
Chesterfield	5	3	1	1	8	5

	P	W	D	L	F	A
Colchester U	1	0	0	1	0	1
Crewe Alex.	4	1	1	2	5	5
Dartford	1	1	0	0	1	0
Doncaster R	1	0	0	1	2	3
Elswick Rngr	1	1	0	0	4	3
Evenwood T	1	1	0	0	7	2
Frickley Ath	1	1	0	0	1	0
Gainsborough	1	1	0	0	2	1
Gateshead	4	2	0	2	9	10
Gateshead T	1	1	0	0	3	0
Grimsby T	5	2	0	3	6	15
Halifax T	4	3	1	0	9	2
Hartlepool U	7	1	3	3	8	9
Horden Ath.	1	1	0	0	3	2
Horncastle	1	0	0	1	0	2
Huddersfield	2	1	1	0	2	1
Hull C	7	0	4	3	5	10
Leyton O.	4	1	2	1	3	5
Lincoln C	2	0	1	1	2	3
Liverpool	1	0	0	1	0	1
Maidstone U	1	1	0	0	4	1
Man. City	1	0	0	1	1	3
Mansfield T	1	1	0	0	2	1
Middlesbro	2	1	1	0	2	1
Mossley	1	1	0	0	5	0
New Brighton	2	1	0	1	3	2
Northampton	4	0	2	2	2	6
Northwich V.	1	1	0	0	6	2
Norwich C	1	1	0	0	2	1
Notts Co.	1	0	0	1	1	2
Oldham Ath.	1	0	0	1	0	1
Plymouth Arg	1	0	0	1	1	2
Port Vale	2	0	0	2	1	4
Prescot Cbls	1	1	0	0	4	0
QPR	1	1	0	0	2	0
Rhyl	1	1	0	0	2	1
Rochdale	4	2	0	2	5	5
Rotherham U	2	0	0	2	4	11
Scarborough	5	2	2	1	8	6
Scunthorpe U	3	1	0	2	2	3
Shankhouse	1	0	0	1	0	2
Sheff. Utd.	1	1	0	0	1	0
Sheff. Wed.	3	2	1	0	3	0
Shrewsbury T	1	0	0	1	0	3
Southport	1	0	0	1	2	4
Stalybrdge C	2	2	0	0	5	0
Stockport Co	4	1	2	1	7	6
Stockton	2	2	0	0	6	1
Sunderland	1	0	0	1	0	2
Swindon T	1	0	0	1	0	3
Telford U	2	0	1	1	1	4
Tranmere R	1	1	0	0	2	1
Walsall	1	1	0	0	1	0
Walthmstw Av	1	1	0	0	3	0
West Brom	1	0	0	1	2	3
Wigan Ath.	1	0	0	1	0	5
Wolves	2	0	0	2	2	9
Workington	1	1	0	0	1	0
Wrexham	3	1	1	1	3	7

DERBY COUNTY

	P	W	D	L	F	A
Aldershot	1	1	0	0	2	0
Arsenal	7	3	2	2	11	5
Aston Unity	1	1	0	0	4	1
Aston Villa	11	4	1	6	22	32

	P	W	D	L	F	A
Barnsley	1	1	0	0	8	1
Birm.St.Grge	2	1	0	1	4	2
Birmingham C	6	3	1	2	12	10
Blackburn R	10	5	1	4	16	18
Blackpool	5	2	2	1	6	6
Bolton Wan.	5	2	0	3	8	7
Boston U	3	1	1	1	7	7
Bournemouth	1	1	0	0	2	0
Bradford C	4	3	0	1	9	4
Bradford PA	3	1	1	1	6	3
Brentford	1	1	0	0	3	0
Brighton &HA	3	2	0	1	11	4
Bristol C	9	3	3	3	14	13
Bristol R	1	1	0	0	2	0
Burnley	5	2	1	2	11	8
Bury	4	2	1	1	9	11
Cambridge U	1	1	0	0	3	0
Cardiff C	1	1	0	0	2	1
Charlton Ath	2	1	0	1	5	3
Chelsea	6	2	2	2	10	11
Chester	1	1	0	0	2	1
Chesterfield	4	2	2	0	8	2
Colchester U	2	1	1	0	2	1
Coventry C	2	0	1	1	0	1
Crewe Alex.	3	2	0	1	8	2
Crook T	2	1	1	0	7	3
Dartford	1	1	0	0	3	2
Darwen	1	1	0	0	2	0
Derby Junc.	1	1	0	0	1	0
Ecclesfield	1	1	0	0	6	0
Everton	10	3	0	7	16	25
Exeter C	1	0	0	1	2	3
Fulham	1	0	0	1	0	3
Gillingham	2	1	1	0	4	2
Hartlepool U	1	0	0	1	1	2
Kettering T	1	1	0	0	4	0
Leeds C	1	0	0	1	1	2
Leeds U	5	1	1	3	5	7
Leicester C	3	2	1	0	5	0
Leyton O.	3	1	1	1	4	6
Lincoln C	2	2	0	0	4	1
Liverpool	6	2	1	3	9	12
Luton T	3	3	0	0	14	1
Man. City	4	1	0	3	8	12
Man. Utd.	8	2	1	5	13	17
Middlesbro	5	2	1	2	6	10
Millwall	5	3	0	2	11	5
New Brighton	1	0	0	1	1	3
Newcastle U	10	2	4	4	17	21
Northampton	4	3	1	0	10	5
Norwich C	2	1	0	1	2	4
Nottm Forest	6	3	1	2	8	5
Notts Co.	2	2	0	0	10	3
Owlerton	1	1	0	0	6	2
Peterborough	2	2	0	0	3	0
Plymouth Arg	5	2	1	2	5	6
Port Vale	2	0	1	1	3	4
Portsmouth	7	3	3	1	15	8
Preston NE	7	1	2	4	9	15
QPR	4	2	1	1	10	4
Sheff. Utd.	6	2	2	2	7	7
Sheff. Wed.	8	1	2	5	9	15
Shrewsbury T	1	1	0	0	2	0
Southampton	3	2	1	0	5	3
Southend U	4	3	0	1	8	8
Southport	1	1	0	0	4	1
Staveley	1	1	0	0	2	1
Stockport Co	1	1	0	0	2	1
Stoke City	3	2	0	1	7	3
Sunderland	4	1	2	1	7	9
Swansea	1	1	0	0	3	0
Telford U	2	2	0	0	9	3
Tottenham H	3	2	1	0	7	4
Walsall T	1	0	0	1	0	7
Watford	1	0	0	1	1	2
West Brom	8	5	1	2	12	8
West Ham U	1	0	0	1	2	5
Wolves	11	6	3	2	21	13

DONCASTER ROVERS

	P	W	D	L	F	A
Accrington S	2	1	1	0	7	2
Altrincham	1	1	0	0	3	1
Arsenal	1	0	0	1	0	4
Aston Villa	5	1	4	0	6	4
Barrow	6	1	3	2	8	11
Birmingham C	1	0	0	1	1	2
Blackpool	2	1	0	1	3	3
Blyth S	1	1	0	0	7	0
Bradford C	2	0	0	2	4	8
Bradford PA	1	1	0	0	3	2
Brandon U	2	1	1	0	2	1
Brighton &HA	1	0	0	1	0	5
Bristol C	3	0	1	2	2	6
Bristol R	4	1	2	1	3	3
Burnley	2	0	1	1	2	4
Bury	2	1	0	1	5	5
Buxton	1	1	0	0	2	0
Cambridge U	1	1	0	0	2	1
Carlisle U	1	0	0	1	1	2
Chelsea	1	0	0	1	0	2
Chester	6	0	2	4	5	14
Chesterfield	5	0	1	4	3	10
Consett	1	1	0	0	5	0
Crewe Alex.	4	1	2	1	3	4
Darlington	1	1	0	0	3	2
Desborough T	1	1	0	0	3	0
Everton	2	0	0	2	0	10
Fulham	1	0	0	1	0	2
Gainsborough	4	3	1	0	9	4
Grimsby T	1	0	0	1	0	1
Guildford C	1	1	0	0	4	0
Halifax T	3	0	1	2	3	8
Hartlepool U	1	0	0	1	1	2
Huddersfield	2	1	0	1	2	2
Hull C	1	0	0	1	0	1
Leyton O.	1	0	0	1	1	3
Lincoln C	1	1	0	0	1	0
Liverpool	3	0	1	2	2	6
Mansfield T	4	2	0	2	3	5
Middlesbro	1	0	0	1	4	1
Millwall	1	0	0	1	0	4
New Brighton	3	3	0	0	10	3
Northampton	1	1	0	0	1	0
Norwich C	2	0	0	2	2	4
Nottm Forest	2	1	0	1	4	2
Notts Co.	5	3	1	1	5	3
Oldham Ath.	1	0	0	1	2	1
Oswestry T	1	1	0	0	3	1
Penrith	1	1	0	0	3	0
Peterborough	1	0	0	1	2	5
Plymouth Arg	1	1	0	0	2	0
Port Vale	1	1	0	0	3	1
Portsmouth	2	0	0	2	2	7
QPR	1	1	0	0	1	0
Reading	2	1	0	1	3	4
Rochdale	2	2	0	0	4	2
Rotherham U	6	0	1	5	3	10
S Shields(2)	2	1	1	0	2	1
Scarborough	3	2	1	0	4	2
Sheff. Utd.	2	0	0	2	1	5
Shildon	3	1	2	0	4	1
Shrewsbury T	4	0	1	3	5	10
Southport	3	2	1	0	5	3
Stockport Co	1	0	0	1	1	2
Stoke City	1	1	0	0	1	0
Sunderland	1	1	0	0	2	0
Sutton Cold.	1	1	0	0	2	0
Swansea	1	0	0	1	0	2
Tottenham H	1	0	0	1	0	2
Tranmere R	4	3	0	1	9	5
Watford	1	1	0	0	2	1
Wellington T	1	1	0	0	2	0
West Brom	2	0	1	1	1	3
Whitby T	2	1	1	0	5	4
Wigan Ath.	3	0	1	2	4	9
Workington	3	2	1	0	5	3

EVERTON

	P	W	D	L	F	A
Aldershot	1	1	0	0	4	1
Altrincham	2	1	1	0	3	1
Arsenal	3	2	0	1	10	4
Aston Villa	7	3	1	3	13	13
Barnsley	6	4	1	1	10	4
Bedford T	1	1	0	0	3	0
Birmingham C	3	1	1	1	4	5
Blackburn R	10	7	1	2	18	10
Bolton Wan.	8	2	4	2	16	13
Bournemouth	1	1	0	0	5	0
Bradford C	4	3	0	1	4	3
Bradford PA	2	0	1	1	1	2
Brighton &HA	3	1	1	1	3	5
Bristol C	2	2	0	0	7	1
Bristol R	2	2	0	0	5	0
Burnley	6	3	1	2	10	10
Burton Wan.	1	1	0	0	5	2
Bury	4	3	1	0	13	2
Cardiff C	1	1	0	0	2	1
Carlisle U	2	2	0	0	6	2
Charlton Ath	3	2	1	0	8	4
Chelsea	6	2	0	4	2	7
Chesterfield	1	1	0	0	3	0
Colchester U	1	1	0	0	5	0
Coventry C	3	3	0	0	7	0
Crystal P	7	4	2	1	20	11
Derby Co.	10	7	0	3	25	16
Doncaster R	2	2	0	0	10	0
Exeter C	1	1	0	0	1	0
Fulham	5	0	2	3	3	6
Gillingham	3	1	2	0	3	0
Glossop	1	0	0	1	1	2
Grimsby T	3	3	0	0	15	7
Hull C	6	1	3	2	8	10
Ipswich T	5	4	1	0	10	6
Jarrow	1	1	0	0	3	1
King's Lynn	1	1	0	0	4	0
Leeds U	7	4	2	1	10	4

	P	W	D	L	F	A
Leicester C	2	2	0	0	6	3
Leyton O.	3	1	1	1	3	4
Liverpool	20	6	5	9	24	34
Luton T	4	3	1	0	11	3
Man. City	10	4	3	3	12	8
Man. Utd.	8	4	0	4	7	6
Middlesbro	10	4	5	1	18	12
Millwall	2	0	0	2	0	3
Newcastle U	2	2	0	0	4	0
Newport Co.	2	1	1	0	3	2
Norwich C	1	1	0	0	1	0
Nottm Forest	5	3	0	2	12	7
Notts Co.	2	2	0	0	4	2
Oldham Ath.	7	2	3	2	12	7
Plymouth Arg	4	3	1	0	10	2
Poole	1	1	0	0	3	1
Port Vale	1	1	0	0	3	2
Portsmouth	1	1	0	0	5	0
Preston NE	8	3	3	2	14	11
QPR	2	2	0	0	4	1
Sheff. Utd.	6	2	0	4	5	6
Sheff. Wed.	19	9	5	5	35	26
Shrewsbury T	2	2	0	0	5	1
Southampton	9	5	2	2	13	8
Southend U	3	3	0	0	8	3
Southport	3	3	0	0	13	1
Stockport Co	2	2	0	0	6	1
Stoke City	7	4	1	2	15	6
Sunderland	13	6	3	4	25	16
Swansea	1	1	0	0	3	0
Swindon T	4	2	1	1	10	6
Telford U	1	1	0	0	3	0
Tottenham H	9	4	1	4	11	13
Tranmere R	1	1	0	0	2	0
Walsall	1	1	0	0	2	1
Watford	1	1	0	0	2	0
West Brom	9	4	2	3	11	7
West Ham U	9	4	1	4	12	12
Wigan Ath.	1	1	0	0	3	0
Wimbledon	4	1	1	2	3	5
Woking	1	1	0	0	1	0
Wolves	7	2	2	3	8	9

EXETER CITY

	P	W	D	L	F	A
Aberdare Ath	2	2	0	0	12	1
Accrington S	1	0	0	1	0	2
Aldershot	1	0	0	1	1	4
Alvechurch	1	0	0	1	0	1
Aston Villa	2	0	0	2	1	4
Barking T	1	1	0	0	6	0
Barnet	1	1	0	0	6	2
Barnstaple T	1	1	0	0	4	0
Bath C	1	0	0	1	1	2
Bedford T	1	0	0	1	1	2
Blackburn R	2	0	1	1	3	5
Bognor Regis	1	0	0	1	1	2
Bournemouth	3	0	1	2	4	8
Brentford	4	2	0	2	6	6
Bristol C	2	1	0	1	2	3
Burnley	1	0	0	1	0	2
Bury	1	1	0	0	2	1
Cambridge U	3	0	1	2	2	5
Cardiff C	1	0	1	0	4	7
Charlton Ath	2	1	1	0	7	4
Chelsea	2	0	1	1	1	3

	P	W	D	L	F	A
Chester	1	1	0	0	2	0
Colchester U	3	1	2	0	1	0
Coventry C	3	2	1	0	4	2
Crawley T	2	1	1	0	2	0
Dartford	4	1	2	1	9	7
Derby Co.	1	1	0	0	3	2
Enfield	2	0	1	1	2	5
Everton	1	0	0	1	0	1
Folkestone	2	2	0	0	4	0
Fulham	1	1	0	0	2	0
Gillingham	1	0	0	1	0	4
Glastonbury	1	1	0	0	2	1
Gravesend &N	1	0	0	1	2	3
Grimsby T	5	2	1	2	10	11
Hayes	1	1	0	0	1	0
Hendon	1	1	0	0	6	2
Hereford U	3	1	1	1	3	4
Hull C	1	0	0	1	1	2
Ilford	1	1	0	0	5	3
Ipswich T	1	0	0	1	0	4
Kidderminster H	1	1	0	0	1	0
King's Lynn	1	1	0	0	3	1
Leatherhead	1	1	0	0	5	0
Leeds U	3	1	1	1	6	8
Leicester C	3	2	1	0	7	3
Leyton O.	1	0	0	1	0	2
Liverpool	1	0	0	1	1	3
Luton T	3	0	1	2	2	5
Maidstone U	6	2	2	2	10	9
Man. Utd.	1	0	0	1	1	3
Millwall	3	2	0	1	8	6
Minehead	1	1	0	0	3	0
Newcastle U	2	1	1	0	5	1
Newport Co.	7	2	2	3	11	14
Northampton	7	1	3	3	4	8
Northfleet U	1	1	0	0	3	0
Norwich C	2	0	1	1	1	3
Nuneaton B.	4	2	2	0	4	0
Oldham Ath.	1	1	0	0	3	0
Plymouth Arg	3	0	0	3	0	6
Port Vale	1	0	0	1	1	2
Portsmouth	2	1	0	1	5	2
Preston NE	1	0	0	1	3	5
Rotherham U	2	1	1	0	6	4
Shrewsbury T	2	1	0	1	3	3
Southampton	1	0	0	1	1	3
Southend U	4	0	2	2	3	5
Stoke City	2	0	1	1	0	3
Sunderland	2	0	1	1	3	5
Swansea	7	1	2	4	6	14
Swindon T	1	1	0	0	3	0
Torquay U	2	1	0	1	2	3
Tottenham H	1	0	0	1	0	2
Trowbridge T	2	2	0	0	10	3
Walsall	2	0	0	2	1	4
Walthmstw Av	1	1	0	0	3	2
Walton & H	1	0	0	1	1	2
Watford	3	0	1	2	0	4
Wolves	2	0	1	1	3	5
Wrexham	2	1	1	0	3	2

FULHAM

	P	W	D	L	F	A
Arsenal	1	0	0	1	0	5
Aston Villa	1	0	0	1	0	5
Bath C	2	1	1	0	4	3

	P	W	D	L	F	A
Birmingham C	6	1	2	3	6	8
Blackburn R	7	2	3	2	6	7
Blackpool	4	1	0	3	7	11
Bolton Wan.	1	0	0	1	1	3
Bournemouth	2	1	1	0	3	1
Bradford PA	1	1	0	0	3	1
Brentford	2	1	0	1	2	3
Brighton &HA	1	1	0	0	2	1
Bristol C	1	0	0	1	1	2
Bristol R	4	3	0	1	11	6
Burnley	7	1	2	4	4	10
Bury	4	2	2	0	8	1
Cambridge U	2	0	1	1	1	2
Cardiff C	1	0	0	1	0	1
Carlisle U	2	2	0	0	5	1
Charlton Ath	7	2	2	3	10	11
Chelsea	5	2	2	1	7	6
Chester	1	0	0	1	0	5
Chesterfield	3	2	1	0	6	4
Colchester U	1	0	0	1	0	1
Coventry C	1	1	0	0	4	1
Crystal P	2	0	1	1	0	1
Derby Co.	1	1	0	0	3	0
Doncaster R	1	1	0	0	2	0
Everton	5	3	2	0	6	3
Exeter C	1	0	0	1	0	2
Farnborough	1	1	0	0	2	1
Gateshead	1	1	0	0	2	1
Gillingham	1	0	0	1	1	2
Grimsby T	2	1	1	0	8	6
Guildford C	1	1	0	0	2	0
Halifax T	1	1	0	0	4	0
Hartlepool U	1	1	0	0	3	1
Hayes	1	0	0	1	0	2
Hereford U	3	1	1	1	7	4
Huddersfield	2	0	0	2	2	6
Hull C	5	2	2	1	9	5
Ipswich T	1	1	0	0	3	2
Leicester C	5	0	1	4	3	11
Leyton	1	1	0	0	4	1
Leyton O.	1	0	0	1	1	2
Lincoln C	2	1	1	0	1	0
Liverpool	4	2	1	1	9	5
Llanelli	1	1	0	0	2	0
Luton T	4	2	1	1	13	8
Macclesfield	1	1	0	0	4	2
Man. City	3	1	1	1	4	4
Man. Utd.	6	1	2	3	9	12
Millwall	4	1	1	2	4	7
Newcastle U	4	0	0	4	4	20
Newport Co.	1	1	0	0	2	0
Northampton	2	1	0	1	3	4
Norwich C	1	1	0	0	2	1
Nottm Forest	7	2	3	2	7	8
Notts Co.	2	2	0	0	2	0
Oldham Ath.	1	1	0	0	2	0
Peterborough	2	1	1	0	1	0
Plymouth Arg	2	1	1	0	2	1
Port Vale	1	1	0	0	1	0
Portsmouth	3	0	1	2	0	3
Preston NE	2	1	0	1	3	3
QPR	4	3	1	0	6	2
Reading	4	2	2	0	3	1
Sheff. Utd.	5	0	1	4	4	11
Sheff. Wed.	3	1	0	2	3	5
Southampton	1	0	0	1	2	3
Southport	1	0	0	1	0	3

	P	W	D	L	F	A
Stockport Co	2	1	1	0	2	1
Sunderland	2	1	0	1	6	4
Swindon T	5	1	1	3	6	12
Thames	1	1	0	0	4	0
Tottenham H	3	0	1	2	0	3
Walsall	3	1	1	1	4	3
Watford	4	0	2	2	3	7
West Brom	3	0	0	3	2	9
West Ham U	4	1	1	2	4	6
Wimbledon	2	1	1	0	7	1
Wolves	1	0	0	1	0	1
Yeovil & P	2	1	1	0	5	2

GILLINGHAM

	P	W	D	L	F	A
AP Leamingtn	1	1	0	0	1	0
Aldershot	1	0	0	1	1	3
Andover	1	1	0	0	1	0
Ashford T	1	1	0	0	2	1
Barking	2	1	1	0	4	2
Barking T	2	1	1	0	2	0
Barnsley	2	0	1	1	1	3
Bedford T	2	2	0	0	7	0
Birmingham C	1	0	0	1	0	3
Blackpool	1	1	0	0	1	0
Bognor Regis	1	1	0	0	6	1
Bournemouth	1	0	0	1	1	2
Bradford C	1	0	0	1	0	1
Brentford	6	1	2	3	11	13
Brighton &HA	1	0	0	1	0	1
Bristol C	2	1	0	1	2	3
Bristol R	6	0	3	3	7	14
Burton Utd.	3	1	2	0	2	0
Bury	1	0	0	1	0	1
Cambridge U	1	0	0	1	2	3
Cardiff	3	1	1	1	2	3
Charlton Ath	1	0	0	1	0	1
Chelmsford C	2	2	0	0	8	1
Colchester U	3	2	1	0	9	3
Coventry C	1	0	0	1	0	2
Crewe Alex.	1	0	0	1	1	2
Crystal P	1	1	0	0	1	0
Dagenham	2	2	0	0	3	1
Derby Co.	2	0	1	1	2	4
Everton	3	0	2	1	0	3
Exeter C	1	1	0	0	4	0
Folkestone	1	0	0	1	1	2
Fulham	1	1	0	0	2	1
Gorleston	1	1	0	0	10	1
Gravesend &N	1	1	0	0	4	1
Guildford C	3	2	1	0	10	4
Hastings U	1	1	0	0	3	1
Hereford U	1	0	0	1	0	1
Huddersfield	2	0	1	1	1	2
Ipswich T	1	0	0	1	2	3
Kettering T	2	2	0	0	6	2
Leyton	3	0	2	1	2	3
Leyton O.	4	2	1	1	6	8
Linby Col.	1	1	0	0	4	1
Liverpool	1	0	0	1	0	2
Luton T	2	0	0	2	1	4
Maidstone U	3	0	2	1	0	2
Man. City	2	0	1	1	2	3
Margate	1	0	0	1	0	2
Millwall	2	1	1	0	7	2
Newport Co.	4	2	0	2	4	5

	P	W	D	L	F	A
Northampton	4	2	1	1	8	5
Nottm Forest	1	0	0	1	0	2
Oldham Ath.	2	1	0	1	3	4
Oxford C	1	1	0	0	5	1
Peterborough	5	1	2	2	9	8
Plymouth Arg	6	3	2	1	9	9
Port Vale	1	0	0	1	2	4
QPR	3	0	1	2	3	8
Reading	5	0	2	3	6	10
Rochdale	4	1	1	2	4	6
Romford	1	1	0	0	1	0
Ryde Sports	1	1	0	0	5	1
Shrewsbury T	2	0	1	1	2	5
Southall	1	1	0	0	6	0
Southampton	3	0	1	2	0	2
Southend U	5	3	1	1	7	4
Stockport Co	1	0	0	1	1	3
Stoke City	1	0	0	1	1	6
Sunderland	1	1	0	0	3	1
Swansea	3	0	0	3	2	9
Swindon T	1	0	0	1	3	4
Tamworth	2	2	0	0	10	1
Torquay U	4	1	2	1	5	8
W Stanley	1	0	0	1	1	3
Walsall	2	1	0	1	3	4
Walthmstw Av	1	0	0	1	0	1
Watford	2	0	0	2	1	3
Welling U	2	0	1	1	0	1
Wellington T	2	1	1	0	4	1
West Brom	1	0	0	1	0	1
Weymouth	3	2	1	0	4	1
Wigan Ath.	1	0	0	1	1	2
Wimbledon	2	0	1	1	2	4
Windsor & E	1	1	0	0	2	1
Wrexham	1	0	0	1	0	2
Wycombe Wan.	2	1	1	0	5	3
Yeovil T	1	0	0	1	1	3

GRIMSBY TOWN

	P	W	D	L	F	A
Arsenal	4	0	1	3	4	9
Barnsley	3	2	1	0	5	1
Barrow	4	2	2	0	7	4
Bath C	1	1	0	0	1	0
Birmingham C	2	1	0	1	2	3
Blackburn R	2	0	0	2	0	7
Blackpool	2	0	0	2	1	4
Blyth S	2	1	1	0	3	1
Bolton Wan.	4	0	2	2	6	8
Bradford C	2	0	0	2	1	3
Bradford PA	2	0	1	1	2	5
Brentford	1	1	0	0	2	0
Brighton &HA	2	0	1	1	1	2
Bristol C	3	1	1	1	3	3
Bristol R	1	0	0	1	0	2
Burnley	2	0	0	2	1	5
Bury	4	0	1	3	3	7
Cardiff C	1	1	0	0	3	1
Carlisle U	1	1	0	0	6	2
Chelsea	1	1	0	0	1	0
Chester	1	0	0	1	0	1
Chesterfield	4	2	2	0	7	5
Cleethorpes	1	1	0	0	4	0
Coventry C	1	0	0	1	0	1
Crewe Alex.	3	1	1	1	6	3
Croydon Com.	1	1	0	0	8	1

	P	W	D	L	F	A
Crystal P	1	1	0	0	1	0
Darlington	5	3	0	2	15	6
Darwen	2	1	0	1	2	2
Doncaster R	1	1	0	0	1	0
Droylsden	2	1	1	0	5	3
Everton	3	0	0	3	7	15
Exeter C	5	2	1	2	11	10
Fulham	2	0	1	1	6	8
Gateshead U	1	0	0	1	1	3
Grantham T	3	1	1	1	2	5
Halifax T	4	2	1	1	5	5
Hartlepool U	3	1	1	1	4	2
Huddersfield	2	1	0	1	2	3
Hull C	1	0	0	1	2	3
Hull T	1	1	0	0	3	1
Ipswich T	2	0	0	2	0	6
Kettering T	2	1	1	0	4	2
Leicester C	1	0	0	1	1	3
Leyton O.	1	1	0	0	1	0
Lincoln C	4	3	0	1	6	3
Liverpool	4	0	0	4	0	11
Luton T	1	1	0	0	4	3
Man. City	4	2	1	1	7	7
Man. Utd.	1	1	0	0	1	0
Mansfield T	1	0	0	1	2	3
Middlesbro	3	2	0	1	6	4
Millwall	3	2	1	0	11	5
Netherfield	1	1	0	0	5	1
Newcastle U	4	2	0	2	5	13
Newcastle WE	1	1	0	0	2	1
Northampton	1	0	0	1	0	3
Norwich C	1	1	0	0	1	0
Nottm Forest	5	0	1	4	3	14
Notts Co.	5	1	2	2	7	10
O Crthusians	1	0	0	1	0	3
O Foresters	1	0	0	1	2	4
Phoenix Bess	1	0	0	1	1	9
Port Vale	1	1	0	0	4	0
Portsmouth	9	2	2	5	9	18
Preston NE	5	1	1	3	1	10
QPR	1	0	0	1	1	3
Reading	5	2	2	1	8	9
Redcar	1	1	0	0	3	1
Rhyl	1	1	0	0	2	1
Rochdale	1	1	0	0	2	0
Rotherham U	1	1	0	0	3	2
Runcorn	1	1	0	0	1	0
Scarborough	2	2	0	0	4	2
Scunthorpe U	2	1	1	0	2	0
Shef. Heeley	1	1	0	0	4	1
Sheff. Utd.	4	2	1	1	4	5
Sheff. Wed.	1	0	0	1	1	5
Southampton	5	1	2	2	6	8
Southport	2	1	1	0	3	2
Stockport Co	2	0	0	2	0	3
Stockton	1	1	0	0	5	0
Stoke City	4	0	2	2	2	10
Sunderland	2	0	0	2	2	5
Sunderland A	1	1	0	0	3	1
Swansea C	2	1	1	0	2	0
Swindon T	2	0	1	1	2	3
Tranmere R	1	1	0	0	6	0
Walsall	2	2	0	0	6	1
Watford	1	0	0	1	1	3
West Brom	6	0	2	4	2	12
West Ham U	1	0	0	1	3	5
Wigan Ath.	1	1	0	0	2	1

	P	W	D	L	F	A
Wimbledon	1	0	0	1	1	3
Witton Alb.	2	1	1	0	7	2
Wolves	5	1	1	3	6	17
Workington	1	1	0	0	2	0
Wrexham	1	0	0	1	2	3

HALIFAX TOWN

	P	W	D	L	F	A
Accrington S	1	1	0	0	3	0
Altrincham	2	2	0	0	6	1
Ashington	1	0	0	1	2	3
Ashton U	2	1	1	0	3	2
Barnsley	4	3	1	0	8	5
Barrow	2	1	1	0	1	0
Billingham S	1	1	0	0	4	2
Bilston	1	1	0	0	3	1
Birmingham C	2	0	0	2	2	6
Bolton Wan.	5	0	2	3	4	10
Bournemouth	1	0	0	1	1	3
Bradford PA	1	1	0	0	1	0
Bristol C	2	0	1	1	2	5
Bshp Aukland	2	1	1	0	7	0
Burnley	1	0	0	1	1	3
Burton Alb.	2	0	1	1	0	1
Cardiff C	1	1	0	0	3	1
Carlisle U	2	0	0	2	0	3
Chester	4	1	2	1	6	6
Chesterfield	2	0	0	2	0	3
Crewe Alex.	5	2	2	1	9	9
Darlington	4	0	1	3	2	9
Darwen	1	1	0	0	2	0
Doncaster R	3	2	1	0	8	3
Frickley Col	1	1	0	0	6	1
Fulham	1	0	0	1	0	4
Gateshead	2	1	0	1	5	6
Goole T	2	2	0	0	4	1
Grimsby T	4	1	1	2	5	5
Hartlepool U	9	3	4	2	14	11
Hull C	1	0	0	1	1	2
Ipswich T	1	0	0	1	1	3
Kettering T	2	0	1	1	3	4
Lincoln C	1	0	0	1	0	1
Luton C	2	0	0	2	0	3
Man. City	4	1	2	1	3	5
Mansfield T	7	2	4	1	10	10
Marine	1	0	0	1	1	4
N Shields	1	0	0	1	0	1
Newark T	2	1	1	0	3	2
Northampton	3	1	2	0	6	4
Nottm Forest	1	0	0	1	0	4
Oldham Ath.	2	0	0	2	2	4
Peterborough	1	0	0	1	0	3
Preston NE	1	1	0	0	1	0
QPR	1	0	0	1	2	4
Rhyl	2	0	1	1	3	4
Rochdale	3	2	0	1	11	5
Rotherham U	3	0	1	2	2	6
S Liverpool	2	0	1	1	4	6
Scarborough	1	1	0	0	2	0
Scunthorpe U	5	1	1	3	4	7
Southport	3	2	0	1	6	4
Stafford Rgs	5	3	1	1	8	5
Stockport Co	3	0	1	2	2	4
Stoke City	3	1	1	1	2	4
Swansea	1	1	0	0	1	0
Tottenham H	1	0	0	1	0	3

	P	W	D	L	F	A
Tranmere R	2	0	0	2	2	5
Walsall	3	1	2	0	4	2
Whitby T	1	0	0	1	2	3
Wigan Ath.	1	0	0	1	1	2
Witton Alb.	2	0	1	1	2	3
Workington	3	1	0	2	3	6
Wrexham	3	1	0	2	3	10

HARTLEPOOL UNITED

	P	W	D	L	F	A
Accrington S	3	3	0	0	5	2
Aldershot	1	1	0	0	4	0
Altrincham	1	0	0	1	0	2
Barnsley	1	0	0	1	2	5
Barrow	1	0	0	1	0	2
Blyth S	6	2	3	1	11	7
Boston U	1	0	0	1	1	2
Bournemouth	2	0	1	1	3	6
Bradford C	1	1	0	0	1	0
Brighton &HA	2	0	1	1	2	3
Bristol C	1	1	0	0	1	0
Burnley	1	0	0	1	0	1
Bury	2	0	0	2	2	8
Carlisle U	2	0	0	2	3	8
Chelsea	1	0	0	1	0	1
Chester	4	1	0	3	3	8
Chesterfield	2	2	0	0	3	1
Chorley	1	1	0	0	2	0
Corby T	1	1	0	0	3	1
Coventry C	1	0	0	1	0	4
Crewe Alex.	3	1	1	1	3	3
Crystal P	2	2	0	0	3	1
Darlington	7	3	3	1	9	8
Derby Co.	1	1	0	0	2	1
Doncaster R	1	1	0	0	2	1
Frickley Ath	1	0	0	1	0	1
Fulham	1	0	0	1	1	3
Gateshead	3	1	0	2	6	8
Grimsby T	3	1	1	1	2	4
Halifax T	9	2	4	3	11	14
Huddersfield	2	0	0	2	1	5
Hull C	1	0	0	1	0	2
Ipswich T	3	0	1	2	2	7
Leeds U	1	0	0	1	2	6
Lincoln C	4	1	1	2	3	2
Luton T	1	0	0	1	1	2
Macclesfield	1	1	0	0	2	1
Man. City	1	0	0	1	0	6
Man. Utd.	1	0	0	1	3	4
Mansfield T	3	2	1	0	7	3
Marine	3	2	1	0	12	6
N Shields	2	2	0	0	9	0
Newcastle U	1	0	0	1	1	4
Northampton	2	1	1	0	2	1
Norwich C	2	0	1	1	2	6
Nottm Forest	2	0	1	1	2	3
Notts Co.	1	1	0	0	1	0
Oldham Ath.	1	0	0	1	1	2
Prescot Cbls	1	1	0	0	5	0
QPR	1	0	0	1	0	2
Rhyl	2	1	0	1	2	1
Rochdale	4	1	2	1	7	11
Rotherham U	6	1	3	2	7	9
Runcorn	2	2	0	0	7	2
Scarborough	1	1	0	0	6	1

	P	W	D	L	F	A
Scunthorpe U	5	0	2	3	2	6
Selby T	1	1	0	0	3	1
Sheff. U	1	0	0	1	0	1
Shrewsbury T	2	1	0	1	5	7
Southport	2	2	0	0	7	1
Spennymoor U	1	0	0	1	2	5
Stockport Co	3	1	0	2	6	5
Stoke City	1	0	0	1	2	6
Tranmere R	4	1	1	2	6	7
Walsall	1	0	0	1	1	2
Watford	1	1	0	0	2	1
Wigan Ath.	4	2	1	1	5	4
Worcester C	1	1	0	0	4	1
Workington	1	1	0	0	3	1
Wrexham	3	1	0	2	3	3

HEREFORD UNITED

	P	W	D	L	F	A
Accrington S	1	0	0	1	1	2
Aldershot	2	1	0	1	4	4
Arsenal	2	0	1	1	3	8
Atherstone U	2	1	1	0	3	0
Aylesbury U	1	1	0	0	3	2
Barnet	2	2	0	0	4	2
Bedford T	1	0	0	1	1	2
Bournemouth	2	1	1	0	4	2
Bridgwater T	1	0	0	1	0	3
Brighton &HA	1	0	0	1	1	2
Bristol C	3	0	1	2	3	7
Bromsgrove R	2	2	0	0	6	1
Cambridge U	1	0	0	1	0	2
Cardiff C	1	0	0	1	0	3
Chelmsford C	1	1	0	0	2	1
Colchester U	1	0	0	1	2	3
Crystal P	1	0	0	1	0	2
Enfield	1	0	0	1	0	2
Exeter C	3	1	1	1	4	3
Farnborough	2	2	0	0	4	0
Fulham	3	1	1	1	4	7
Gillingham	1	1	0	0	1	0
Guildford C	2	1	0	1	3	5
Kiddrminster	1	1	0	0	3	0
King's Lynn	2	1	1	0	1	0
Leicester C	1	0	0	1	0	1
Leyton	2	1	1	0	3	2
Leytonstone	1	1	0	0	1	0
Man. Utd.	1	0	0	1	0	1
Merthyr Tyd.	1	1	0	0	3	2
Middlesbro	1	0	0	1	0	4
Millwall	1	1	0	0	1	0
Newcastle U	2	1	1	0	4	3
Newport Co.	7	0	1	6	4	17
Newport(IOW)	1	1	0	0	3	0
Northampton	6	3	3	0	9	6
Nottm Forest	1	0	0	1	0	2
Oldham Ath.	1	0	0	1	0	4
Peterborough	3	0	1	2	3	7
Plymouth Arg	2	1	1	0	2	0
Portsmouth	1	0	0	1	1	4
QPR	1	1	0	0	6	1
Reading	3	1	0	2	1	4
Scunthorpe U	4	1	2	1	6	4
Sheff. Wed.	1	0	0	1	0	3
Southend U	3	2	0	1	6	4
Sutton U	1	1	0	0	2	1

	P	W	D	L	F	A
Swindon T	1	0	0	1	0	4
Torquay U	5	2	1	2	7	8
Walsall	1	1	0	0	2	1
Walton & H	1	1	0	0	3	0
Watford	1	0	0	1	0	3
Wealdstone	2	0	1	1	2	3
West Ham U	4	1	2	1	4	5
Weymouth	1	0	0	1	1	2
Wigan Ath.	1	0	0	1	1	4
Woking	2	1	1	0	2	1
Yeovil T	3	1	1	1	5	4

HUDDERSFIELD TOWN

	P	W	D	L	F	A
Aldershot	2	0	1	1	2	4
Altrincham	2	2	0	0	3	1
Arsenal	2	0	0	2	0	3
Aston Villa	5	2	0	3	4	6
Barnsley	4	0	1	3	4	7
Birmingham C	6	3	1	2	7	6
Blackburn R	5	2	2	1	10	6
Blackpool	3	0	0	3	0	5
Bolton Wan.	6	0	1	5	2	12
Bradford C	2	2	0	0	4	1
Bradford PA	1	1	0	0	1	0
Brentford	3	2	0	1	7	7
Brighton &HA	2	1	1	0	2	0
Bristol C	1	1	0	0	2	1
Bristol R	1	1	0	0	2	0
Burnley	7	2	1	4	8	13
Bury	3	2	1	0	5	2
Carlisle U	3	1	1	1	5	5
Charlton Ath	3	1	1	1	3	3
Chelsea	4	1	1	2	4	6
Chester	2	1	0	1	3	3
Chesterfield	3	3	0	0	10	1
Colchester U	1	0	0	1	0	1
Coventry C	2	1	1	0	5	4
Crystal P	2	1	0	1	5	6
Darlington	2	0	1	1	1	2
Doncaster R	2	1	0	1	2	2
Folkestone	1	1	0	0	2	0
Fulham	2	2	0	0	6	2
Gillingham	2	1	1	0	2	1
Grimsby T	2	1	0	1	3	2
Hartlepool U	2	2	0	0	5	1
Hull C	1	1	0	0	3	1
Ipswich T	1	0	0	1	0	1
Leeds U	3	2	0	1	7	4
Leyton O.	2	0	1	1	1	3
Lincoln C	1	1	0	0	4	2
Lincoln U	1	1	0	0	7	0
Liverpool	3	3	0	0	5	1
London Caley	1	1	0	0	3	0
Luton T	2	0	0	2	0	3
Man. City	4	0	2	2	2	9
Man. Utd.	3	1	0	2	4	8
Mansfield T	2	0	1	1	1	2
Middlesbro	1	1	0	0	4	0
Millwall	5	2	1	2	7	7
Mossley	1	1	0	0	1	0
Newcastle U	3	1	1	1	2	3
Newport Co.	2	0	1	1	4	6
Northampton	1	0	0	1	0	2
Northwich V.	2	1	1	0	7	1

	P	W	D	L	F	A
Norwich C	2	0	1	1	3	5
Nottm Forest	2	1	1	0	3	0
Notts Co.	3	2	0	1	5	3
Oldham Ath.	2	1	1	0	7	1
Peterborough	1	1	0	0	3	1
Plymouth Arg	5	4	1	0	13	4
Port Vale	1	1	0	0	2	1
Portsmouth	3	0	1	2	4	6
Preston NE	4	3	0	1	7	1
QPR	4	3	1	0	12	1
Reading	2	0	1	1	1	2
Rochdale	3	2	1	0	7	5
Rotherham U	1	1	0	0	4	3
Scunthorpe U	2	1	1	0	2	1
Sheff. Utd.	11	4	5	2	12	10
Sheff. Wed.	2	1	0	1	3	3
Shrewsbury T	1	0	0	1	0	3
Southend U	1	0	0	1	1	2
Stoke City	3	0	2	1	3	4
Sunderland	2	1	0	1	3	7
Swansea	1	0	0	1	0	1
Swindon T	1	0	0	1	1	2
Torquay U	1	1	0	0	1	0
Tottenham H	3	2	0	1	8	2
Tranmere R	3	1	0	2	5	4
Walsall	2	2	0	0	4	0
West Brom	2	1	1	0	3	2
West Ham U	6	3	1	2	12	11
Wigan Ath.	1	1	0	0	2	0
Wolves	5	2	2	1	7	6
Workington	2	1	1	0	6	1

HULL CITY

	P	W	D	L	F	A
Accrington S	1	1	0	0	3	1
Arsenal	4	1	2	1	6	4
Aston Villa	4	0	1	3	2	9
Barnsley	2	1	1	0	3	1
Bath C	1	1	0	0	3	0
Birmingham C	1	0	0	1	0	2
Blackburn R	6	2	2	2	7	10
Blackpool	4	3	0	1	7	3
Blyth S	3	1	2	0	5	4
Bolton Wan.	5	1	1	3	6	12
Bradford C	2	1	0	1	2	3
Bradford PA	3	1	1	1	5	6
Brentford	5	3	2	0	10	5
Brighton &HA	2	0	0	2	2	4
Bristol C	2	0	1	1	1	2
Bristol R	4	1	1	2	4	7
Burnley	1	1	0	0	3	0
Bury	2	0	1	1	1	2
Cardiff C	1	1	0	0	2	1
Carlisle U	5	1	2	2	6	10
Charlton Ath	2	2	0	0	6	1
Chelsea	8	0	3	5	5	13
Cheltenham T	1	1	0	0	4	2
Chester	2	0	1	1	2	3
Coventry C	2	1	0	1	1	3
Crewe Alex.	3	2	1	0	7	3
Crook T	1	1	0	0	5	4
Crystal P	2	2	0	0	5	2
Darlington	7	3	4	0	10	5
Doncaster R	1	1	0	0	1	0
Everton	6	2	3	1	10	8
Exeter C	1	1	0	0	2	1

	P	W	D	L	F	A
Fulham	5	1	2	2	5	9
Gateshead	3	2	0	1	9	2
Grimsby T	1	1	0	0	3	2
Halifax T	1	1	0	0	2	1
Hartlepool U	1	1	0	0	2	0
Huddersfield	1	0	0	1	1	3
Kidderminster	1	1	0	0	4	1
Leicester C	4	0	1	3	2	6
Leyton O.	2	0	1	1	1	3
Lincoln C	2	0	1	1	2	4
Liverpool	1	0	0	1	2	3
Man. City	4	1	1	2	5	8
Man. Utd.	2	1	0	1	2	1
Mansfield T	1	1	0	0	4	1
Middlesbro	5	1	2	2	9	7
Morecambe	1	1	0	0	1	0
New Brighton	3	2	1	0	6	1
Newcastle U	7	1	2	4	5	13
Northampton	1	1	0	0	2	1
Norwich C	1	1	0	0	3	0
Nottm Forest	2	1	0	1	2	3
Notts Co.	1	0	0	1	2	5
Oldham Ath.	3	1	1	1	2	2
Penrith	1	1	0	0	2	0
Plymouth Arg	5	3	2	0	12	7
Port Vale	4	1	2	1	8	9
Portsmouth	3	0	2	1	4	6
Preston NE	2	0	1	1	0	1
Reading	3	1	1	1	2	2
Rhyl	1	1	0	0	5	0
Rochdale	3	1	2	0	5	4
Rotherham U	4	2	0	2	7	4
Scunthorpe U	1	1	0	0	4	0
Sheff. Utd.	2	0	1	1	1	3
Sheff. Wed.	1	0	0	1	3	4
Shrewsbury T	1	1	0	0	2	1
Southampton	3	2	1	0	7	2
Southport	5	3	2	0	11	3
Stafford Rgs	1	1	0	0	2	1
Stalybridge C	1	1	0	0	8	2
Stockport Co	5	1	2	2	2	3
Stoke City	4	1	0	3	5	10
Sunderland	3	0	0	3	2	9
Sutton T	1	1	0	0	3	0
Swansea	1	1	0	0	1	0
Tottenham H	6	0	3	3	1	6
Tranmere R	1	1	0	0	3	0
Watford	3	0	2	1	3	4
West Brom	3	2	0	1	3	3
West Ham U	2	1	0	1	3	3
Wigan Ath.	1	0	0	1	0	3
Wolves	4	1	1	2	3	5
Workington	1	1	0	0	2	0
Wrexham	1	1	0	0	2	0

IPSWICH TOWN

	P	W	D	L	F	A
Aldershot	1	0	0	1	0	3
Arsenal	2	1	0	1	3	4
Aston Villa	4	2	1	1	6	5
Barnsley	1	0	0	1	0	2
Birmingham C	4	2	0	2	4	4
Bournemouth	4	2	2	0	10	6
Bradford C	4	2	2	0	11	6
Brighton &HA	2	1	0	1	2	3
Bristol C	2	2	0	0	6	2

	P	W	D	L	F	A
Bristol R	4	3	1	0	13	4
Bshp Aukland	2	0	1	1	2	5
Cardiff C	2	2	0	0	5	0
Carlisle U	2	2	0	0	5	2
Charlton Ath	2	2	0	0	5	2
Chelmsford C	3	2	1	0	5	2
Chelsea	2	0	0	2	0	5
Chester	1	1	0	0	2	1
Crystal P	1	1	0	0	1	0
Everton	5	0	1	4	6	10
Exeter C	1	1	0	0	4	0
Fulham	1	0	0	1	2	3
Gateshead	3	0	2	1	6	7
Gillingham	1	1	0	0	3	2
Grimsby T	2	2	0	0	6	0
Halifax T	1	1	0	0	3	1
Hartlepool U	3	2	1	0	7	2
Hastings U	1	1	0	0	4	0
Huddersfield	1	1	0	0	1	0
Leeds U	5	2	3	0	5	3
Leicester C	1	0	0	1	1	3
Leyton O.	3	2	1	0	4	1
Liverpool	5	1	1	3	3	6
Luton T	5	2	2	1	12	8
Man. City	3	0	1	2	1	5
Man. Utd.	4	1	0	3	2	5
Mansfield T	1	1	0	0	3	2
Merthyr Tyd.	2	1	1	0	3	2
Millwall	1	1	0	0	6	1
Newcastle U	2	1	1	0	3	2
Norwich C	3	0	1	2	2	4
Nottm Forest	3	1	1	1	4	6
Oldham Ath.	3	2	1	0	10	6
Peterborough	3	1	0	2	5	6
Plymouth Arg	1	1	0	0	3	1
Preston NE	2	1	0	1	4	6
QPR	2	0	0	2	0	6
Reading	1	1	0	0	4	1
Sheff. Utd.	1	1	0	0	3	2
Sheff. Wed.	1	1	0	0	3	2
Shrewsbury T	5	2	1	2	8	5
Southampton	2	0	0	2	3	10
Southport	2	0	1	1	2	3
Spennymoor U	1	0	0	1	1	2
Stoke City	5	1	2	2	2	3
Street	1	1	0	0	7	0
Swindon T	2	1	0	1	4	5
Torquay U	2	2	0	0	6	1
Tottenham H	1	0	0	1	0	5
Tranmere R	1	1	0	0	2	1
Walsall	2	0	1	1	0	1
Walthmstw Av	2	1	1	0	3	2
Watford	2	2	0	0	5	2
West Brom	3	2	1	0	7	2
West Ham U	6	0	3	3	3	9
Wisbech T	2	2	0	0	8	0
Wolves	5	1	2	2	4	5

	P	W	D	L	F	A
Bournemouth	1	1	0	0	3	1
Bradford PA	2	2	0	0	6	1
Brentford	1	0	0	1	1	2
Brighton &HA	1	1	0	0	2	1
Bristol C	3	1	1	1	3	2
Bristol R	1	1	0	0	4	1
Bury	2	2	0	0	9	2
Cardiff C	7	4	0	3	13	8
Carlisle U	1	1	0	0	5	2
Charlton Ath	3	1	1	1	5	4
Chelsea	8	0	3	5	6	17
Chester	1	1	0	0	3	1
Colchester U	1	0	0	1	2	3
Coventry C	3	0	1	2	3	5
Crystal P	4	3	0	1	14	2
Derby Co.	5	3	1	1	7	5
Everton	7	1	2	4	4	10
Exeter C	3	1	1	1	8	6
Hartlepool U	1	1	0	0	6	2
Huddersfield	3	1	0	2	4	7
Ipswich T	5	0	3	2	3	5
Liverpool	4	1	1	2	3	5
Luton T	1	0	0	1	1	5
Man. City	4	2	0	2	3	3
Man. Utd.	8	2	3	3	3	7
Mansfield T	1	1	0	0	2	0
Middlesbro	5	2	1	2	10	16
Newcastle U	2	2	0	0	7	1
Newport Co.	1	0	0	1	1	3
Norwich C	6	2	3	1	16	9
Nottm Forest	4	1	0	3	3	10
Notts Co.	1	1	0	0	1	0
Peterborough	2	1	0	1	4	2
Plymouth Arg	1	1	0	0	2	1
Portsmouth	2	1	0	1	3	1
Preston NE	2	1	0	1	3	1
QPR	2	1	0	1	3	4
Rochdale	1	1	0	0	2	0
Rotherham U	2	1	1	0	3	2
Scunthorpe U	3	0	2	1	4	6
Sheff. Utd.	2	1	0	1	2	3
Sheff. Wed.	3	0	1	2	2	6
Shrewsbury T	1	1	0	0	2	0
Southport	1	1	0	0	3	0
Stoke City	2	2	0	0	4	1
Sunderland	5	2	2	1	7	6
Sutton U	1	1	0	0	6	0
Swansea	1	1	0	0	2	1
Swindon T	4	3	0	1	9	3
Telford U	1	1	0	0	2	1
Torquay U	2	0	1	1	2	6
Tottenham H	4	1	1	2	5	6
Tranmere R	2	1	1	0	4	0
West Brom	5	2	1	2	11	7
West Ham U	3	1	1	1	3	5
Wigan Ath.	1	1	0	0	2	0
Wimbledon	2	1	1	0	1	0

	P	W	D	L	F	A
Birmingham C	8	5	3	0	15	8
Blackburn R	3	2	1	0	6	3
Blackpool	1	1	0	0	2	1
Bolton Wan.	1	0	0	1	1	2
Brentford	5	3	2	0	7	1
Brighton &HA	1	0	0	1	1	2
Bristol C	2	1	0	1	6	3
Bristol R	2	1	0	1	6	5
Burnley	1	0	0	1	3	7
Burton Alb.	1	0	0	1	0	1
Bury	4	3	0	1	6	6
Cardiff C	3	1	0	2	4	3
Carlisle U	1	1	0	0	1	0
Chelsea	3	0	1	2	1	6
Coventry C	2	0	1	1	2	5
Crook T	1	1	0	0	7	0
Croydon Com.	1	1	0	0	8	3
Crystal P	2	1	0	1	1	1
Derby Co.	3	0	1	2	0	5
Everton	2	0	0	2	3	6
Exeter C	3	0	1	2	3	7
Fulham	5	4	1	0	11	3
Grimsby T	1	1	0	0	3	1
Harlow T	2	0	1	1	1	2
Hereford U	1	1	0	0	1	0
Hull C	4	3	1	0	6	2
Ipswich T	1	1	0	0	3	1
Leatherhead	1	1	0	0	3	2
Leyton	1	1	0	0	1	0
Leyton O.	4	2	0	2	5	5
Lincoln C	4	3	1	0	7	1
Liverpool	10	2	4	4	4	8
Luton T	6	3	2	1	20	13
Man. City	8	2	2	4	10	10
Man. Utd.	2	0	0	2	2	5
Mansfield T	2	2	0	0	3	1
Middlesbro	7	2	2	3	11	11
Millwall	4	2	0	2	8	7
Newcastle U	6	1	2	3	6	11
Newport Co.	2	1	1	0	2	0
Norwich C	4	3	0	1	8	5
Nottm Forest	1	0	0	1	1	5
Notts Co.	4	1	0	3	6	9
Oldham Ath.	1	0	0	1	1	3
Oxford U	5	3	1	1	10	6
Plymouth Arg	1	1	0	0	5	0
Port Vale	1	1	0	0	2	1
Portsmouth	3	1	0	2	4	6
Preston NE	7	2	2	3	7	11
QPR	2	1	0	1	4	5
Reading	1	1	0	0	4	1
Rotherham U	3	1	1	1	3	2
Sheff. Utd.	7	2	2	3	7	6
Sheff. Wed.	2	1	0	1	3	5
Shrewsbury T	1	1	0	0	5	2
South Shore	1	1	0	0	2	1
Southampton	3	1	1	1	12	7
Stoke City	9	3	4	2	16	14
Sunderland	2	1	0	1	2	4
Swansea	1	1	0	0	1	0
Torquay U	1	1	0	0	3	0
Tottenham H	9	1	1	7	8	25
Walsall	1	0	0	1	0	1
Watford	4	3	1	0	12	5
West Brom	2	2	0	0	3	1
West Ham U	1	1	0	0	2	1
Wolves	5	1	1	3	6	11

LEEDS UNITED

	P	W	D	L	F	A
Arsenal	11	1	6	4	10	13
Aston Villa	3	0	0	3	2	7
Barnsley	2	1	1	0	5	1
Birmingham C	2	2	0	0	5	1
Blackpool	1	0	0	1	0	4
Bolton Wan.	5	1	2	2	5	9

LEICESTER CITY

	P	W	D	L	F	A
Arsenal	9	0	4	5	4	11
Aston Villa	3	1	0	2	3	7
Barnsley	8	2	4	2	9	9
Barrow	1	1	0	0	2	1

LEYTON ORIENT

	P	W	D	L	F	A
Aldershot	3	1	1	1	1	1
Altrincham	2	1	1	0	3	2
Arsenal	4	0	0	4	1	9
Ashford T	1	1	0	0	4	1
Aston Villa	2	0	1	1	0	8
Birmingham C	4	1	0	3	1	8
Blackburn R	3	1	0	2	5	8
Boston U	2	1	1	0	3	2
Bournemouth	2	2	0	0	3	1
Bradford PA	1	0	0	1	0	1
Brentford	5	2	2	1	8	6
Brighton &HA	1	0	0	1	1	3
Bristol C	1	1	0	0	4	1
Bristol R	3	1	1	1	2	2
Buckingham T	1	1	0	0	2	0
Burnley	2	0	1	1	1	2
Bury	2	2	0	0	4	2
Cardiff C	3	0	0	3	1	9
Carlisle U	1	0	0	1	1	4
Charlton Ath	2	2	0	0	4	0
Chelsea	4	2	1	1	5	5
Chester	1	0	0	1	1	3
Chesterfield	3	1	1	1	1	3
Colchester U	2	1	1	0	4	1
Coventry C	3	1	1	1	5	6
Crystal P	2	0	1	1	0	1
Dagen'm-Redbridge	1	1	0	0	5	4
Darlington	4	1	2	1	5	3
Dartford	1	1	0	0	3	2
Derby Co.	3	1	1	1	6	4
Doncaster R	1	1	0	0	3	1
Enfield	3	0	2	1	3	4
Epsom T	1	1	0	0	4	2
Everton	3	1	1	1	4	3
Exeter C	1	1	0	0	2	0
Folkestone	4	2	2	0	8	4
Frome T	1	1	0	0	3	0
Fulham	1	1	0	0	2	1
Gillingham	4	1	1	2	8	6
Gorleston	3	1	2	0	7	6
Grimsby T	1	0	0	1	0	1
Hayes	1	1	0	0	3	1
Huddersfield	2	1	1	0	3	1
Hull C	2	1	1	0	3	1
Ipswich T	3	0	1	2	1	4
Kettering	1	1	0	0	3	0
Leicester C	4	2	0	2	5	5
Liverpool	1	0	0	1	1	2
Lovells Ath.	1	1	0	0	7	1
Lowestoft T	1	1	0	0	2	1
Luton T	3	0	1	2	5	9
Man. City	2	0	0	2	2	10
Middlesbro	4	2	1	1	6	6
Millwall	2	0	0	2	1	4
Newcastle U	3	1	0	2	3	8
Newport Co.	1	0	0	1	0	1
Newport(IOW)	2	1	0	1	2	3
Northfleet U	1	1	0	0	2	0
Norwich C	3	1	1	1	3	4
Nottm Forest	6	1	2	3	5	7
Notts Co.	1	0	0	1	1	2
Oldham Ath.	3	2	1	0	7	4
Plymouth Arg	1	1	0	0	1	0
Port Vale	3	0	1	2	2	7
Portsmouth	4	0	2	2	1	5
Reading	2	1	0	1	1	3
Sheff. Wed.	2	0	0	2	0	7
Slough T	2	1	1	0	5	4
Southampton	5	2	1	2	4	6
Southend U	2	1	0	1	3	4
Stockport Co	1	1	0	0	2	1
Sunderland	2	1	0	1	3	6
Swansea	4	1	2	1	5	4
Swindon T	3	0	1	2	2	4
Torquay U	3	3	0	0	7	2
Tranmere R	2	1	1	0	6	3
VS Rugby	2	1	1	0	6	3
Walsall	5	1	2	2	4	6
Welling U	1	1	0	0	2	1
West Brom	3	2	0	1	4	4
West Ham U	5	0	2	3	5	12
Weymouth	2	2	0	0	6	0
Wimbledon	1	0	0	1	1	2
Woodford T	1	1	0	0	1	0
Workington	1	0	0	1	0	1
Wrexham	3	2	1	0	7	3

LINCOLN CITY

	P	W	D	L	F	A
Accrington S	1	1	0	0	5	2
Aldershot	1	1	0	0	2	1
Altrincham	1	0	0	1	2	3
Barnsley	2	0	0	2	1	5
Barrow	3	3	0	0	14	5
Billingham S	1	1	0	0	1	0
Birmingham C	1	0	0	1	1	2
Blackburn R	3	0	1	2	4	11
Blackpool	2	0	0	2	1	3
Boston U	1	1	0	0	1	0
Bradford C	4	1	2	1	8	8
Bradford PA	3	0	2	1	4	5
Brentford	1	0	0	1	0	3
Brighton &HA	1	0	0	1	1	2
Bromley	1	1	0	0	8	1
Burnley	4	0	2	2	3	6
Bury	2	0	0	2	1	4
Carlisle U	2	1	0	1	1	1
Chelsea	2	1	1	0	3	2
Chester	4	2	1	1	5	3
Coventry C	3	1	1	1	4	7
Crewe Alex.	4	2	0	2	7	9
Darlington	2	1	1	0	3	2
Derby Co.	2	0	0	2	1	4
Doncaster R	1	0	0	1	0	1
Fulham	2	0	1	1	0	1
Gainsborough	4	3	1	0	7	3
Gateshead(2)	1	1	0	0	1	0
Glasgow Rangers	1	0	0	1	0	3
Grimsby T	4	1	0	3	3	6
Halifax T	1	1	0	0	1	0
Hartlepool U	4	2	1	1	2	3
Horncastle	1	1	0	0	4	1
Huddersfield	1	0	0	1	2	4
Hull C	2	1	1	0	4	2
Hull T	1	1	0	0	5	1
Lancaster T	1	1	0	0	3	1
Leicester C	4	0	1	3	1	7
Liverpool	3	0	1	2	2	7
Luton T	2	0	1	1	3	6

LIVERPOOL

	P	W	D	L	F	A
Macclesfield	1	1	0	0	3	1
Man. Central	1	1	0	0	3	0
Man. City	1	0	0	1	1	2
Mansfield T	3	1	0	2	6	7
Middlesbro	3	1	1	1	4	5
Millwall	1	1	0	0	3	0
Morecambe	1	1	0	0	1	0
New Brighton	2	1	1	0	4	3
Nottm Forest	1	0	0	1	0	1
Nuneaton B.	1	1	0	0	6	0
Oldham Ath.	1	0	0	1	2	3
Oxford C	2	1	1	0	4	0
Peterborough	2	0	1	1	6	7
Plymouth Arg	1	0	0	1	1	4
Port Vale	6	2	3	1	8	7
Portsmouth	2	0	0	2	0	8
Preston NE	4	0	0	4	4	13
QPR	1	0	0	1	1	2
Rochdale	3	1	1	1	3	4
Rotherham U	4	1	1	2	5	8
Scarborough	1	0	0	1	4	6
Scunthorpe U	1	0	0	1	3	4
Sheff. Utd.	4	0	1	3	1	8
Sheff. Wed.	1	0	0	1	0	3
Shildon	2	1	1	0	6	2
Southampton	2	0	1	1	2	3
Southend U	1	0	0	1	2	3
Southport	5	2	1	2	8	7
Stafford R	2	0	1	1	1	2
Stockport Co	3	2	0	1	7	5
Stockton	1	1	0	0	4	2
Stoke City	1	0	0	1	0	5
Swindon T	2	0	0	2	3	6
Telford U	1	0	0	1	2	3
Torquay U	1	0	0	1	3	4
Tranmere R	2	1	1	0	1	0
Walsall	4	1	2	1	4	5
West Brom	3	1	0	2	5	5
Wigan Ath.	1	0	0	1	1	3
Wigan Boro.	1	1	0	0	3	1
Wolves	2	0	0	2	1	3
Workington	1	0	0	1	0	2
Wrexham	3	1	2	0	6	5
Yorkshire Am	2	1	0	1	5	2

LIVERPOOL

	P	W	D	L	F	A
Accrington S	1	1	0	0	2	0
Aldershot	1	1	0	0	1	0
Altrincham	1	1	0	0	4	1
Arsenal	13	4	4	5	14	14
Aston Villa	6	5	0	1	9	3
Barnsley	5	4	1	0	11	1
Birmingham C	5	4	0	1	10	5
Blackburn R	10	5	2	3	13	9
Blackpool	1	1	0	0	2	1
Bolton Wan.	11	3	2	6	11	22
Bournemouth	4	2	2	0	9	3
Bradford C	2	2	0	0	3	1
Brentford	2	2	0	0	6	0
Brighton &HA	6	2	2	2	10	9
Bristol C	5	4	0	1	7	2
Bristol R	2	1	0	1	3	2
Burnley	10	4	3	3	11	7
Burton S	1	1	0	0	4	3
Bury	1	1	0	0	2	0

	P	W	D	L	F	A
Cardiff C	2	0	0	2	2	4
Carlisle U	4	3	1	0	8	0
Chelsea	7	3	0	4	11	14
Chester	2	2	0	0	4	1
Chesterfield	1	1	0	0	4	2
Coventry C	3	2	1	0	7	3
Crewe Alex.	1	1	0	0	4	0
Crystal P	5	2	2	1	9	7
Darlington	1	1	0	0	1	0
Derby Co.	6	3	1	2	12	9
Doncaster R	3	2	1	0	6	2
Everton	20	9	5	6	34	24
Exeter C	1	1	0	0	3	1
Fulham	4	1	1	2	5	9
Gainsborough	1	1	0	0	3	2
Gateshead	3	1	1	1	3	2
Gillingham	1	1	0	0	2	0
Grimsby T	4	4	0	0	11	0
Hucknall SJ	1	1	0	0	2	0
Huddersfield	3	0	0	3	1	5
Hull C	1	1	0	0	3	2
Ipswich T	5	3	1	1	6	3
Leeds U	4	2	1	1	5	3
Leicester C	10	4	4	2	8	4
Leyton	1	1	0	0	1	0
Leyton O.	1	1	0	0	2	1
Lincoln C	3	2	1	0	7	2
Luton T	5	2	2	1	5	3
Man. City	5	1	2	2	5	4
Man. Utd.	12	2	4	6	13	20
Middlesbro	1	1	0	0	2	0
Millwall	2	2	0	0	6	1
Newcastle U	8	3	1	4	12	8
Northampton	1	1	0	0	3	1
Norwich C	6	2	1	3	11	10
Nottm Forest	9	6	2	1	19	8
Notts Co.	2	1	0	1	1	2
Oldham Ath.	3	3	0	0	6	2
Oxford U	1	1	0	0	3	0
Port Vale	2	1	1	0	2	1
Portsmouth	2	0	2	0	1	1
Preston NE	4	1	2	1	3	3
QPR	3	2	1	0	5	3
Scunthorpe U	3	2	1	0	6	4
Sheff. Utd.	7	1	3	3	9	11
Sheff. Wed.	1	0	0	1	0	1
Southampton	10	6	2	2	13	5
Southend U	5	2	2	1	8	5
Southport	1	1	0	0	3	1
Stockport Co	5	4	1	0	13	3
Stoke City	6	4	2	0	6	0
Sunderland	5	3	1	1	11	3
Swansea	6	4	1	1	17	2
Tottenham H	6	4	2	0	6	2
Tranmere R	1	1	0	0	3	1
Walsall	3	2	1	0	10	4
Watford	5	2	2	1	5	3
West Brom	10	3	3	4	10	11
West Ham U	4	3	1	0	9	2
Wimbledon	1	0	0	1	0	1
Wolves	5	2	0	3	6	10
Worcester C	1	0	0	1	1	2
Workington	1	1	0	0	1	0
Wrexham	2	2	0	0	6	1
Yeovil & P	1	1	0	0	6	2

LUTON TOWN

	P	W	D	L	F	A
Aberdare Ath	1	0	0	1	0	1
Arsenal	6	1	2	3	8	10
Aston Villa	3	0	1	2	2	5
Barnsley	3	1	1	1	2	1
Birmingham C	2	1	0	1	2	2
Blackburn R	2	2	0	0	8	1
Blackpool	8	2	5	1	9	9
Bolton Wan.	4	1	0	3	2	4
Bournemouth	2	1	1	0	4	2
Bradford C	1	1	0	0	3	0
Brentford	3	1	2	0	5	4
Bridgwater T	1	1	0	0	3	0
Brighton &HA	1	0	0	1	1	4
Bristol C	1	1	0	0	2	0
Bristol R	3	1	0	2	7	5
Burnley	3	0	1	2	1	6
Bury	1	0	0	1	1	2
Charlton Ath	1	1	0	0	1	0
Chatham T	1	0	0	1	1	5
Chelsea	3	1	1	1	3	5
Chester	1	0	0	1	0	1
Clapton	1	1	0	0	9	0
Corby T	2	0	1	1	2	3
Coventry C	3	2	1	0	6	4
Crewe Alex.	1	1	0	0	2	0
Crystal P	3	1	1	1	2	8
Derby Co.	3	0	0	3	1	14
Everton	4	0	1	3	3	11
Exeter C	3	2	1	0	5	2
Folkestone	1	1	0	0	3	0
Fulham	4	1	1	2	8	13
Gainsborough	2	1	1	0	2	1
Gateshead	1	1	0	0	4	0
Gillingham	2	2	0	0	4	1
Grimsby T	1	0	0	1	3	4
Halifax T	2	2	0	0	3	0
Hartlepool U	1	1	0	0	2	1
Hillingdon B	1	0	0	1	1	2
Hotspur	1	0	0	1	1	3
Huddersfield	2	2	0	0	3	0
Ipswich T	5	1	2	2	8	12
Kingstonian	2	1	1	0	5	4
Leeds U	1	1	0	0	5	1
Leicester C	6	1	2	3	13	20
Leyton O.	3	2	1	0	9	5
Lincoln C	2	1	1	0	6	3
Liverpool	5	1	2	2	3	5
London Caley	1	1	0	0	4	2
Man. City	7	2	1	4	11	11
Man. Utd.	1	0	0	1	0	2
Marlow	1	0	0	1	0	3
Middlesbro	1	0	0	1	0	3
Midlsbro Irn	1	0	0	1	1	2
Millwall	5	1	0	4	4	12
Newcastle U	2	1	0	1	3	2
Northampton	2	1	0	1	5	5
Northfleet U	1	1	0	0	6	2
Norwich C	4	2	1	1	8	3
Nottm Forest	3	0	1	2	5	7
Notts Co.	2	1	0	1	8	4
Oldham Ath.	2	1	1	0	3	2
Oxford C	1	1	0	0	2	1
Peterborough	1	1	0	0	3	0
Plymouth Arg	1	1	0	0	4	2

	P	W	D	L	F	A
Port Vale	2	1	1	0	5	3
Portsmouth	4	3	1	0	8	3
Preston NE	2	0	0	2	2	5
QPR	6	1	2	3	7	10
Reading	1	1	0	0	2	1
Romford	2	1	1	0	2	1
Rotherham U	1	1	0	0	5	1
Scarborough	2	1	1	0	6	2
Sheff. Utd.	2	1	0	1	3	5
Southampton	2	1	0	1	2	4
Southend U	2	2	0	0	6	1
Stockport Co	2	1	0	1	3	5
Stoke City	2	1	1	0	4	3
Sunderland	6	0	2	4	3	11
Swansea	1	1	0	0	2	0
Swindon T	7	4	0	3	14	10
Tottenham H	1	1	0	0	2	0
Walsall	1	1	0	0	4	0
Ware	1	1	0	0	6	1
Watford	6	1	3	2	9	11
West Brom	2	0	0	2	0	5
West Ham U	6	2	2	2	11	11
Wimbledon	1	0	0	1	1	2
Wolves	2	0	0	2	2	6
Workington	1	1	0	0	5	0

MANCHESTER CITY

	P	W	D	L	F	A
Accrington S	1	1	0	0	2	0
Arsenal	3	1	0	2	3	3
Aston Villa	6	3	1	2	12	9
Barnsley	2	2	0	0	4	1
Barrow	2	1	1	0	8	4
Birmingham C	8	3	0	5	12	18
Blackburn R	5	3	1	1	11	6
Blackpool	6	3	2	1	10	7
Bolton Wan.	9	5	1	3	18	10
Bradford PA	3	2	0	1	10	11
Brentford	2	1	0	1	7	4
Brighton &HA	2	1	0	1	5	5
Burnley	3	2	0	1	2	3
Bury	3	3	0	0	8	4
Cardiff C	8	4	4	0	11	4
Charlton Ath	1	0	0	1	1	2
Chelsea	3	2	0	1	5	1
Corinthian	2	1	1	0	7	3
Coventry C	2	0	0	2	2	5
Crystal P	3	2	0	1	15	6
Darlington	1	1	0	0	3	1
Derby Co.	4	3	0	1	12	8
Everton	10	3	3	4	8	12
Fulham	3	1	1	1	4	4
Gateshead	3	2	0	1	13	1
Gillingham	2	1	1	0	3	2
Glossop	2	1	1	0	6	0
Grimsby T	4	1	1	2	7	7
Halifax T	4	1	2	1	5	3
Hartlepool U	1	1	0	0	6	0
Huddersfield	4	2	2	0	9	2
Hull C	2	1	1	0	8	5
Ipswich T	3	2	1	0	5	1
Leeds U	4	2	0	2	3	3
Leicester C	8	4	2	2	10	10
Leyton O.	2	2	0	0	10	2
Lincoln C	1	1	0	0	2	1

	P	W	D	L	F	A
Liverpool	5	2	2	1	4	5
Luton T	7	4	1	2	11	11
Man. Utd.	4	2	0	2	5	4
Middlesbro	5	1	2	2	5	4
Millwall	7	2	3	2	10	11
Newcastle U	8	2	2	4	11	14
Norwich C	3	2	0	1	12	2
Nottm Forest	4	1	0	3	4	8
Notts Co.	2	1	0	1	1	1
Oldham Ath.	1	0	0	1	0	1
Oxford U	1	1	0	0	5	2
Peterborough	1	1	0	0	1	0
Plymouth Arg	1	1	0	0	3	1
Port Vale	1	1	0	0	2	1
Portsmouth	2	2	0	0	5	2
Preston NE	10	3	3	4	11	17
QPR	1	1	0	0	2	1
Reading	4	2	2	0	12	1
Rotherham U	2	1	1	0	4	2
Sheff. Utd.	5	0	2	3	1	7
Sheff. Wed.	3	2	1	0	7	2
Shrewsbury T	3	0	1	2	2	6
Southampton	2	1	0	1	6	5
Southend U	1	1	0	0	1	0
Stoke City	5	3	0	2	6	5
Sunderland	8	4	2	2	11	11
Swindon T	5	2	1	2	19	6
Tottenham H	12	4	2	6	19	20
Walsall	3	3	0	0	6	1
Watford	3	0	2	1	2	4
West Brom	4	1	1	2	3	7
Wigan Ath.	1	1	0	0	1	0
Wigan Co.	1	1	0	0	1	0
Wolves	3	0	1	2	3	7
Workington	1	1	0	0	2	1

MANCHESTER UNITED

	P	W	D	L	F	A
Accrington S	2	1	1	0	7	3
Arsenal	7	3	0	4	9	14
Aston Villa	8	6	0	2	20	11
Barnsley	3	2	1	0	7	2
Birmingham C	5	3	1	1	11	5
Blackburn R	8	2	2	4	12	17
Blackpool	3	3	0	0	9	4
Bolton Wan.	3	2	0	1	3	3
Bournemouth	6	4	1	1	13	4
Bradford C	2	1	1	0	3	1
Bradford PA	2	2	0	0	10	2
Brentford	2	1	0	1	7	3
Brighton &HA	6	4	2	0	12	4
Bristol C	1	1	0	0	1	0
Bristol R	3	2	0	1	7	6
Burnley	6	2	1	3	9	17
Bury	4	2	1	1	4	2
Cardiff C	1	0	0	1	1	4
Carlisle U	2	1	1	0	5	3
Charlton Ath	1	1	0	0	2	0
Chelsea	5	4	0	1	8	3
Chester	1	1	0	0	2	1
Colchester U	1	1	0	0	1	0
Coventry C	6	4	1	1	13	6
Crystal P	1	1	0	0	4	3
Derby Co.	8	5	1	2	17	13
Everton	8	4	0	4	6	7

	P	W	D	L	F	A
Exeter C	1	1	0	0	3	1
Fulham	6	3	2	1	12	9
Grimsby T	1	0	0	1	0	1
Hartlepool U	1	1	0	0	4	3
Hereford U	1	1	0	0	1	0
Huddersfield	3	2	0	1	8	4
Hull C	2	1	0	1	1	2
Ipswich T	4	3	0	1	5	2
Kettering T	2	2	0	0	7	2
Leeds U	8	3	3	2	7	3
Leicester C	2	2	0	0	5	2
Liverpool	12	6	4	2	20	13
Luton T	1	1	0	0	2	0
Man. City	4	2	0	2	4	5
Middlesbro	9	4	3	2	15	8
Millwall	1	1	0	0	1	0
Newcastle U	2	2	0	0	4	2
Northampton	1	1	0	0	8	2
Norwich C	4	1	0	3	5	7
Nottm Forest	6	1	1	4	1	7
Notts Co.	2	1	1	0	5	4
Oldham Ath.	5	2	2	1	10	7
Oxford U	2	2	0	0	6	1
Peterborough	1	1	0	0	3	1
Plymouth Arg	4	3	0	1	5	4
Port Vale	3	3	0	0	7	2
Portsmouth	6	1	3	2	11	13
Preston NE	9	5	2	2	15	13
QPR	5	3	2	0	8	3
Reading	9	4	4	1	17	9
Rochdale	1	1	0	0	2	0
Rotherham U	2	1	1	0	1	0
Sheff. Utd.	2	1	0	1	2	2
Sheff. Wed.	9	2	2	5	8	18
Southampton	11	5	5	1	19	12
Staple Hill	1	1	0	0	7	2
Stoke City	11	3	5	3	14	13
Sunderland	7	3	4	0	18	10
Swindon T	2	0	0	2	0	3
Tottenham H	12	2	5	5	15	21
Walsall	4	2	1	1	4	3
Walthmstw Av	2	1	1	0	6	3
Watford	4	2	1	1	4	2
West Brom	6	1	3	2	7	11
West Ham U	6	2	1	3	9	10
Weymouth	1	1	0	0	4	0
Wolves	7	3	2	2	14	11
Workington	1	1	0	0	3	1
Wrexham	1	1	0	0	5	0
Yeovil & P	1	1	0	0	3	0

MANSFIELD TOWN

	P	W	D	L	F	A
Accrington S	4	3	0	1	10	5
Arsenal	1	0	0	1	0	2
Bangor C	1	1	0	0	4	1
Barnsley	1	1	0	0	3	2
Barrow	2	2	0	0	6	1
Bath C	1	1	0	0	4	0
Blackpool	3	1	0	2	2	5
Blyth S	2	2	0	0	5	1
Bolton Wan.	2	0	0	2	0	3
Boston T	1	0	0	1	2	5
Bournemouth	1	0	0	1	0	3
Bradford C	5	0	1	4	8	13

	P	W	D	L	F	A
Brighton &HA	1	0	0	1	0	2
Bristol R	1	0	0	1	0	5
Burnley	1	0	0	1	2	4
Bury	3	2	1	0	6	3
Cambridge U	1	1	0	0	1	0
Carlisle U	3	0	1	2	3	5
Chelmsford C	1	1	0	0	4	1
Chester	3	2	1	0	7	4
Crystal P	2	1	1	0	9	4
Darlington	1	0	0	1	1	2
Doncaster R	4	2	0	2	5	3
Gainsborough	2	1	0	1	5	4
Gloucester C	1	1	0	0	4	0
Grantham T	2	2	0	0	4	2
Grimsby T	1	1	0	0	3	2
Halifax T	7	1	4	2	10	10
Hartlepool U	3	0	1	2	3	7
Hounslow T	1	0	1	0	12	5
Huddersfield	2	1	1	0	2	1
Hull C	1	0	0	1	1	4
Ipswich T	1	0	0	1	2	3
Leeds U	1	0	0	1	0	2
Leicester C	2	0	0	2	1	3
Lincoln C	3	2	0	1	7	6
Man. Central	1	0	0	1	0	2
Matlock T	1	0	0	1	2	5
Middlesbro	1	1	0	0	2	0
Mossley	1	1	0	0	3	1
New Brighton	2	0	1	1	3	4
Newport Co.	1	0	0	1	0	3
Northampton	1	0	0	1	2	3
Nottm Forest	1	0	0	1	0	1
Oldham Ath.	3	1	0	2	4	6
Oxford U	1	1	0	0	1	0
Plymouth Arg	1	1	0	0	2	0
Port Vale	2	0	1	1	1	2
Preston NE	5	2	1	2	7	6
Rochdale	1	1	0	0	3	1
Rotherham U	3	2	1	0	5	3
Scarborough	1	1	0	0	8	0
Scunthorpe U	4	1	1	2	3	6
Sheff. Utd.	5	2	2	1	6	5
Sheff. Wed.	4	0	1	3	0	11
Shirebrook	1	1	0	0	4	2
Shrewsbury T	3	1	0	2	3	6
Southend U	1	1	0	0	2	1
Southport	1	0	0	1	2	4
Stockport Co	2	2	0	0	5	2
Stockton	2	0	1	1	1	3
Stoke City	1	0	0	1	2	4
Swansea	1	1	0	0	2	0
Tow Law T	2	1	0	1	5	6
Tranmere R	3	1	1	1	8	8
Walsall	3	1	0	2	5	7
Walthmstw Av	1	1	0	0	1	0
Wellington T	2	2	0	0	4	2
West Ham U	1	1	0	0	3	0
Wigan Ath.	5	2	2	1	8	6
Wimbledon	1	1	0	0	2	2
Wolves	1	1	0	0	1	0
Workington	4	1	2	1	5	5
Wrexham	5	3	2	0	9	4

MIDDLESBROUGH

	P	W	D	L	F	A
Arsenal	5	2	1	2	10	9

	P	W	D	L	F	A
Aston Villa	5	1	2	2	8	8
Barnsley	1	1	0	0	2	1
Birmingham C	5	0	1	4	1	7
Blackburn R	7	1	2	4	6	12
Blackpool	4	3	0	1	9	5
Bolton Wan.	7	3	3	1	7	2
Bournemouth	1	1	0	0	2	0
Bradford C	3	0	1	2	2	4
Bradford PA	2	1	0	1	4	1
Brentford	4	1	0	3	5	7
Brighton &HA	3	1	2	0	5	3
Bristol C	2	0	1	1	2	3
Bristol R	2	0	1	1	1	2
Bshp Auk Cl	1	1	0	0	1	0
Bshp Strtfrd	2	1	1	0	4	3
Burnley	3	0	1	2	2	5
Bury	2	0	1	1	2	3
Cambridge U	1	0	0	1	0	2
Cardiff C	1	1	0	0	1	0
Carlisle U	1	1	0	0	2	1
Charlton Ath	7	3	4	0	10	7
Chelsea	1	1	0	0	2	1
Chester	1	1	0	0	5	2
Chesterfield	5	3	1	1	13	8
Coventry C	1	1	0	0	3	0
Crewe Alex.	1	0	0	1	0	2
Crystal P	2	0	1	1	1	2
Darlington	2	0	1	1	1	2
Derby Co.	5	2	1	2	10	6
Doncaster R	1	0	0	1	1	4
Everton	10	1	5	4	12	18
Gainsborough	1	1	0	0	2	1
Gateshead	1	1	0	0	3	0
Glossop	1	1	0	0	1	0
Goole T	1	1	0	0	9	3
Grantham T	1	1	0	0	2	0
Grimsby T	3	1	0	2	4	6
Hereford U	1	1	0	0	4	0
Huddersfield	1	0	0	1	0	4
Hull C	5	2	2	1	7	9
Kettering T	1	1	0	0	5	0
Leeds U	5	2	1	2	16	10
Leicester C	7	3	2	2	11	11
Leyton O.	4	1	1	2	6	6
Lincoln C	3	1	1	1	5	4
Liverpool	1	0	0	1	0	2
Luton T	1	1	0	0	3	0
Man. City	5	2	2	1	5	5
Man. Utd.	9	2	3	4	8	15
Mansfield T	1	0	0	1	0	2
Millwall	8	3	3	2	13	9
Newark	1	1	0	0	4	1
Newcastle U	2	2	0	0	6	3
Northampton	1	1	0	0	4	2
Nottm Forest	5	2	2	1	12	9
Notts Co.	6	2	0	4	4	8
O Etonians	1	0	0	1	2	5
O Foresters	1	0	0	1	0	4
Oldham Ath.	2	2	0	0	7	2
Peterborough	2	1	1	0	3	1
Plymouth Arg	3	1	1	1	2	2
Portsmouth	6	1	3	2	8	10
Preston NE	5	2	0	3	7	4
QPR	5	2	2	1	10	8
Redcar	1	0	0	1	1	2
Sheff. Utd.	2	0	1	1	1	4
Sheff. Wed.	5	2	1	2	6	10

	P	W	D	L	F	A
Shrewsbury T	2	1	1	0	7	3
South Bank	1	1	0	0	4	1
Southampton	3	1	0	2	3	9
Southport	1	1	0	0	3	0
Staveley	1	0	0	1	1	5
Stockport Co	1	1	0	0	2	0
Stoke City	2	1	0	1	5	4
Sunderland	5	1	2	2	7	8
Sutton U	2	1	1	0	2	1
Swansea	1	1	0	0	5	0
Tottenham H	4	0	1	3	2	9
Walsall	2	1	1	0	6	2
Watford	1	0	0	1	0	1
West Brom	3	1	0	2	1	2
West Ham U	3	1	1	1	4	4
Whitburn	1	1	0	0	4	0
Wimbledon	2	1	1	0	1	0
Wolves	4	0	1	3	4	12
Wrexham	1	0	0	1	0	1
Wycombe Wan.	2	1	1	0	1	0

MILLWALL

	P	W	D	L	F	A
Accrington S	2	2	0	0	6	2
Aldershot	4	2	1	1	13	3
Arsenal	3	1	1	1	2	3
Ashington	1	1	0	0	4	2
Aston Villa	9	2	3	4	8	24
Barnsley	2	0	1	1	1	2
Barrow	2	1	1	0	6	3
Bath C	1	0	0	1	1	3
Birmingham C	1	0	0	1	1	4
Blackburn R	1	0	0	1	1	2
Bolton Wan.	4	0	2	2	4	9
Bradford C	1	1	0	0	1	0
Bradford PA	2	1	1	0	2	1
Brentford	1	1	0	0	1	0
Brighton &HA	2	1	1	0	4	2
Bristol R	1	0	0	1	0	3
Burton Utd.	1	1	0	0	1	0
Bury	7	1	3	3	10	12
Cambridge U	2	0	1	1	1	2
Cardiff C	3	0	2	1	2	3
Chelsea	4	3	1	0	7	2
Chester	1	0	0	1	0	2
Colchester U	2	1	1	0	5	1
Corinthian	3	1	2	0	8	4
Coventry C	3	0	1	2	1	3
Crewe Alex.	1	0	0	1	2	3
Croydon	2	1	1	0	4	3
Crystal P	10	4	4	2	16	11
Dagenham	1	1	0	0	2	1
Dartford	1	1	0	0	2	1
Derby Co.	5	2	0	3	5	11
Doncaster R	1	1	0	0	4	0
Enfield	1	1	0	0	1	0
Everton	2	2	0	0	3	0
Exeter C	3	1	0	2	6	8
Fulham	4	2	1	1	7	4
Gateshead	1	1	0	0	7	0
Gillingham	2	0	1	1	2	7
Grimsby T	3	0	1	2	5	11
Hereford U	1	0	0	1	0	1
Hitchin T	2	1	1	0	3	2
Huddersfield	5	2	1	2	7	7
Ipswich T	1	0	0	1	1	6

	P	W	D	L	F	A
Jarrow	1	1	0	0	2	0
Kettering T	3	1	1	1	5	4
Kiddrminster	2	1	1	0	2	1
Leicester C	4	2	0	2	7	8
Leyton O.	2	2	0	0	4	1
Lincoln C	1	0	0	1	0	3
Liverpool	2	0	0	2	1	6
Luton T	5	4	0	1	12	4
Man. City	7	2	3	2	11	10
Man. Utd.	1	0	0	1	0	1
Margate	2	2	0	0	7	1
Middlesbro	8	2	3	3	9	13
Newcastle U	1	1	0	0	2	1
Newport Co.	1	1	0	0	3	0
Northampton	7	2	3	2	11	11
Norwich C	1	0	0	1	1	2
Nottm Forest	2	1	0	1	4	4
Notts Co.	2	1	0	1	2	3
O W'minsters	1	0	0	1	1	8
Oldham Ath.	2	1	1	0	2	1
Oxford U	2	0	1	1	3	4
Plymouth Arg	2	2	0	0	3	0
Port Vale	2	1	0	1	4	3
Portsmouth	2	1	1	0	4	3
Preston NE	2	1	0	1	5	3
QPR	2	2	0	0	6	3
Reading	4	1	1	2	5	8
Rotherham U	2	1	1	0	3	1
Salisbury	1	1	0	0	2	1
Scunthorpe U	5	0	2	3	2	7
Sheff. Utd.	2	0	0	2	1	7
Sheff. Wed.	4	0	2	2	5	10
Shrewsbury T	2	1	0	1	6	3
Slough T	1	0	0	1	0	1
Southampton	7	0	3	4	1	9
Southend	1	0	0	1	0	1
Southport	1	0	0	1	1	3
Stoke City	3	0	1	2	1	6
Sunderland	1	0	0	1	1	2
Swansea	2	1	0	1	4	1
Swindon T	1	0	0	1	2	3
Tooting & M	1	1	0	0	1	0
Tottenham H	3	0	1	2	1	3
Wealdstone	1	1	0	0	3	1
West Brom	1	0	0	1	0	1
West Ham U	1	0	0	1	1	4
Weymouth	1	1	0	0	3	0
Wigan Ath.	1	1	0	0	4	1
Wimbledon	1	1	0	0	3	1
Wolves	2	0	0	2	1	3
Worcester C	1	0	0	1	2	5
Yeovil T	3	1	2	0	4	3

NEWCASTLE UNITED

	P	W	D	L	F	A
Aberdare Ath	1	1	0	0	4	1
Arsenal	6	4	1	1	10	7
Aston Villa	5	2	0	3	7	16
Barnsley	4	2	1	1	7	6
Bedford T	1	0	0	1	1	2
Birmingham C	2	1	1	0	5	2
Blackburn R	5	2	1	2	6	7
Blackpool	5	4	1	0	11	2
Bolton Wan.	6	3	2	1	11	8
Bournemouth	3	1	2	0	4	2

Team	P	W	D	L	F	A
Bradford C	4	2	1	1	7	2
Bradford PA	1	0	0	1	0	2
Brentford	2	2	0	0	5	2
Brighton &HA	4	1	1	2	4	4
Bristol R	2	1	1	0	3	1
Burnley	4	3	1	0	6	2
Bury	4	2	0	2	12	7
Cardiff C	3	2	1	0	6	1
Carlisle U	1	0	0	1	0	1
Charlton Ath	2	0	0	2	1	6
Chelsea	6	2	1	3	7	10
Chester	2	1	0	1	3	3
Chesterfield	1	1	0	0	4	0
Colchester U	2	1	1	0	5	4
Corinthian	1	1	0	0	3	1
Coventry C	3	2	1	0	10	4
Crystal P	4	3	0	1	9	3
Derby Co.	10	4	4	2	21	17
Everton	2	0	0	2	0	4
Exeter C	2	0	1	1	1	5
Fulham	4	4	0	0	20	4
Glossop	1	1	0	0	1	0
Grimsby T	4	2	0	2	13	5
Hartlepool U	1	1	0	0	4	1
Hendon	2	1	1	0	5	1
Hereford U	2	0	1	1	3	4
Huddersfield	3	1	1	1	3	2
Hull C	7	4	2	1	13	5
Ipswich T	2	0	1	1	2	3
Leeds U	2	0	0	2	1	7
Leicester C	6	3	2	1	11	6
Leyton O.	3	2	0	1	8	3
Liverpool	8	4	1	3	8	12
Luton T	2	1	0	1	2	3
Man. City	8	4	2	2	14	11
Man. Utd.	2	0	0	2	2	4
Middlesbro	2	0	0	2	3	6
Millwall	1	0	0	1	1	2
Newport Co.	1	1	0	0	6	0
Northampton	3	2	1	0	4	2
Norwich C	1	0	0	1	0	5
Nottm Forest	14	5	6	3	19	17
Notts Co.	1	1	0	0	8	1
Oldham Ath.	1	0	0	0	7	2
Peterborough	3	1	1	1	3	2
Plymouth Arg	5	3	2	0	11	3
Port Vale	1	1	0	0	4	0
Portsmouth	2	2	0	0	8	2
Preston NE	5	2	0	3	6	8
QPR	2	1	1	0	2	1
Reading	4	3	1	0	13	5
Rotherham U	3	1	1	1	4	4
Scunthorpe U	3	1	1	1	5	4
Sheff. Utd.	8	3	2	3	10	12
Sheff. Wed.	7	5	1	1	13	7
Southampton	7	1	1	5	6	14
Southport	3	1	2	0	11	2
Stockport Co	1	1	0	0	4	0
Stoke City	5	4	1	0	12	6
Sunderland	7	2	3	2	8	9
Swansea	5	3	1	1	7	2
Swindon T	3	2	0	1	7	2
Torquay U	1	1	0	0	3	1
Tottenham H	5	2	1	2	8	4
Walsall	2	1	0	1	2	1
Watford	6	2	3	1	8	3
West Brom	3	1	0	2	5	4
West Ham U	5	3	2	0	9	5
Wigan Ath.	2	1	1	0	5	4
Wimbledon	1	0	0	1	1	3
Wolves	8	1	3	4	8	13
Wrexham	2	0	1	1	3	6

NORTHAMPTON TOWN

Team	P	W	D	L	F	A
Aldershot	1	1	0	0	1	0
Arsenal	2	1	0	1	5	4
Aston Villa	1	0	0	1	0	1
Aylesbury U	2	1	1	0	1	0
Banbury U	1	1	0	0	3	2
Barnet	2	0	1	1	0	1
Barnsley	2	2	0	0	6	2
Barry T	1	1	0	0	1	0
Basingstoke	1	1	0	0	5	1
Bath C	2	1	1	0	5	2
Blackburn R	3	0	0	3	4	13
Bolton Wan.	2	0	0	2	1	4
Boston T	2	1	1	0	3	2
Bournemouth	4	2	1	1	7	5
Bradford PA	1	0	0	1	2	4
Brentford	3	0	1	2	2	6
Brentwood T	1	1	0	0	1	0
Brighton &HA	3	2	0	1	4	3
Bristol C	2	1	0	1	1	3
Bristol R	4	0	1	3	2	6
Cardiff C	1	0	0	1	1	2
Chelmsford C	2	2	0	0	10	1
Chelsea	1	0	0	1	1	4
Coventry C	3	1	0	2	2	3
Crawley T	1	0	0	1	2	4
Crystal P	2	0	1	1	4	5
Darlington	4	2	2	0	6	2
Derby Co.	4	0	1	3	5	10
Doncaster R	1	0	0	1	0	1
Dulwich Ham.	1	1	0	0	2	1
Enfield	1	0	0	1	0	2
Exeter C	7	3	3	1	8	4
Fulham	2	0	1	1	4	3
Gillingham	4	1	1	2	5	8
Grimsby T	1	1	0	0	3	0
Halifax T	3	0	2	1	4	6
Hartlepool U	2	0	1	1	1	2
Hastings U	2	2	0	0	6	2
Hendon	2	1	1	0	2	0
Hereford U	6	0	3	3	6	9
Huddersfield	1	1	0	0	2	0
Hull C	1	0	0	1	1	2
Kettering T	2	2	0	0	4	0
Leatherhead	1	0	0	1	0	2
Leyton	1	1	0	0	8	0
Littlehmpton	1	1	0	0	4	0
Liverpool	1	0	0	1	1	3
Llanelli	1	1	0	0	3	0
Lloyds	1	1	0	0	8	1
Luton T	2	1	0	1	5	5
Man. Utd.	1	0	0	1	2	8
Mansfield T	2	1	0	1	3	2
Margate	2	2	0	0	9	1
Met. Police	1	1	0	0	9	0
Middlesbro	1	0	0	1	2	4
Millwall	7	2	3	2	11	11
Newcastle U	3	0	1	2	2	4
Newport Co.	3	3	0	0	8	2
Norwich C	1	0	0	1	2	3
Nottm Forest	3	0	1	2	1	3
Notts Co.	2	1	0	1	3	2
Peterborough	6	2	2	2	14	8
Port Vale	1	0	0	1	1	3
Portsmouth	1	0	0	1	0	2
Preston NE	2	0	0	2	1	6
Reading	1	1	0	0	3	0
Rochdale	1	0	0	1	0	3
Romford	1	1	0	0	5	1
Rotherham U	2	0	0	2	1	3
Sheff. Utd.	1	0	0	1	0	2
Sheff. Wed.	2	1	1	0	1	0
Southampton	7	2	3	2	7	10
Southend U	3	2	1	0	10	6
Stoke City	2	0	1	1	2	5
Sunderland	3	0	1	2	3	8
Swansea	1	0	0	1	1	3
Swindon T	1	0	0	1	0	2
Telford U	2	0	1	1	3	4
Tooting & M	2	1	0	1	3	3
Torquay U	7	3	1	3	11	14
Tottenham H	1	0	0	1	0	3
Tranmere R	2	1	1	0	2	1
VS Rugby	2	1	1	0	3	2
Walthmstw Av	2	1	0	1	5	7
Waterloovlle	3	1	2	0	4	2
Watford	1	0	0	1	1	4
West Brom	1	0	0	1	1	3
Weymouth	4	2	2	0	9	3
Wimbledon	2	1	1	0	4	2
Workington	2	1	1	0	1	0

NORWICH CITY

Team	P	W	D	L	F	A
Arsenal	3	1	0	2	2	7
Aston Villa	3	1	1	1	6	4
Barnsley	4	2	1	1	5	4
Bath C	1	1	0	0	2	0
Bedford T	1	0	0	1	2	4
Birmingham C	4	1	3	0	3	2
Blackburn R	3	0	1	2	5	9
Blackpool	2	1	1	0	4	2
Bolton Wan.	3	0	1	2	2	5
Bradford C	5	0	2	3	3	7
Brentford	2	0	0	2	1	5
Brighton &HA	10	3	2	5	15	19
Bristol C	3	1	0	2	2	4
Bristol R	4	0	2	2	4	6
Cambridge U	1	1	0	0	1	0
Cardiff C	1	1	0	0	3	2
Chatham T	2	2	0	0	11	1
Chelsea	3	0	1	2	2	5
Chesterfield	1	1	0	0	3	1
Clapton	1	0	0	1	1	3
Corinthian	1	0	0	1	0	5
Coventry C	6	2	2	2	8	10
Crystal P	4	1	1	2	2	5
Darlington	1	0	0	1	1	2
Derby Co.	2	1	0	1	4	2
Doncaster R	2	2	0	0	4	2
Dorchester T	1	1	0	0	4	0
Everton	1	0	0	1	0	3
Exeter C	2	1	1	0	3	1
Folkestone	1	0	0	1	0	1

	P	W	D	L	F	A
Fulham	1	0	0	1	1	2
Gloucester C	1	1	0	0	3	2
Grimsby T	1	0	0	1	0	1
Hartlepool U	2	1	1	0	6	2
Hastings &SL	1	1	0	0	3	1
Hastings	2	1	1	0	6	3
Huddersfield	2	1	1	0	5	3
Hull C	1	0	0	1	0	3
Ilford	1	1	0	0	3	1
Ipswich T	3	2	1	0	4	2
Leeds U	6	1	3	2	9	16
Leicester C	4	1	0	3	5	8
Leyton O.	3	1	1	1	4	3
Liverpool	6	3	1	2	10	11
Luton T	4	1	1	2	3	8
Man. City	3	1	0	2	2	12
Man. Utd.	4	3	0	1	7	5
Merthyr Tyd.	1	1	0	0	3	0
Millwall	1	1	0	0	2	1
Newcastle U	1	1	0	0	5	0
Newport Co.	2	2	0	0	8	0
Northampton	1	1	0	0	3	2
Nottm Forest	3	1	0	2	4	3
Notts Co.	2	1	0	1	3	4
Oxford U	1	1	0	0	4	2
Poole	2	1	1	0	6	1
Port Vale	1	1	0	0	3	1
Portsmouth	2	0	1	1	1	3
QPR	4	0	2	2	4	9
Reading	5	1	3	1	6	6
Redhill	1	1	0	0	6	1
Rhyl	1	1	0	0	1	0
Rochdale	3	1	2	0	3	2
Scunthorpe U	1	1	0	0	4	1
Sheff. Utd.	4	2	1	1	8	8
Sheff. Wed.	3	1	0	2	3	4
Southampton	3	1	1	1	2	4
Stoke City	1	1	0	0	1	0
Sunderland	7	2	1	4	8	11
Sutton U	1	1	0	0	8	0
Swansea	1	1	0	0	2	1
Swindon T	6	3	2	1	7	4
Tonbridge	2	1	1	0	3	2
Torquay U	1	0	0	1	1	3
Tottenham H	6	3	2	1	7	6
Tunbridge WR	2	1	1	0	6	1
Walsall	3	1	1	1	7	7
Watford	1	1	0	0	2	0
Wellington T	1	1	0	0	1	0
West Brom	3	0	0	3	0	5
West Ham U	3	1	1	1	4	3
Wigan Ath.	1	0	0	1	0	1
Wimbledon	1	1	0	0	3	1
Wolves	3	0	1	2	4	9
Wrexham	2	1	0	1	4	3
Yeovil T	2	2	0	0	5	0

NOTTINGHAM FOREST

	P	W	D	L	F	A
Arsenal	3	1	0	2	2	4
Ashington	1	1	0	0	2	0
Aston Villa	9	4	1	4	12	16
Barnsley	3	1	1	1	4	4
Birmingham C	7	2	3	2	8	5
Blackburn R	6	1	2	3	12	11

	P	W	D	L	F	A
Bolton Wan.	7	3	3	1	12	9
Bradford C	1	1	0	0	1	0
Bradford PA	2	0	0	2	0	4
Brentford	1	1	0	0	1	0
Bristol C	5	4	1	0	10	3
Bristol R	4	2	2	0	12	5
Burnley	2	0	1	1	0	3
Bury	6	1	3	2	13	11
Cardiff C	2	1	0	1	3	5
Carlisle U	2	0	1	1	1	2
Casuals	1	1	0	0	4	0
Chatham T	3	0	2	1	5	6
Chelsea	2	0	1	1	1	4
Chester	1	1	0	0	4	0
Chesterfield	2	1	0	1	6	6
Clapton	1	1	0	0	14	0
Coventry C	1	0	0	1	1	3
Crystal P	5	1	2	2	6	6
Derby Co.	6	2	1	3	5	8
Derby Mid.	1	0	0	1	0	3
Doncaster R	2	1	0	1	2	4
Everton	5	2	0	3	7	12
Fulham	7	2	3	2	8	7
Gainsborough	1	1	0	0	4	0
Gillingham	1	1	0	0	2	0
Glossop	1	1	0	0	3	1
Goole T	1	1	0	0	6	0
Grimsby T	5	4	1	0	14	3
Halifax T	1	1	0	0	4	0
Hartlepool U	2	1	1	0	3	2
Heanor T	1	1	0	0	1	0
Hereford U	1	1	0	0	2	0
Huddersfield	2	0	1	1	0	3
Hull C	2	1	0	1	3	2
Ipswich T	3	1	1	1	6	4
Leeds U	4	3	0	1	10	3
Leicester C	1	1	0	0	5	1
Leyton O.	6	3	2	1	7	5
Lincoln C	1	1	0	0	1	0
Linfield Ath	1	0	1	0	2	2
Liverpool	9	1	2	6	8	19
Lockwood B	1	0	0	1	1	2
Luton T	3	2	1	0	7	5
Man. City	4	3	0	1	8	4
Man. Utd.	6	4	1	1	7	1
Mansfield T	1	1	0	0	1	0
Mellors	2	2	0	0	8	2
Middlesbro	5	1	2	2	9	12
Midlsbro Irn	1	1	0	0	2	0
Millwall	2	1	0	1	4	4
Newcastle EE	1	1	0	0	2	1
Newcastle U	14	3	6	5	17	19
Northampton	3	2	1	0	3	1
Norwich C	3	2	0	1	3	4
Notts Co.	6	3	1	2	11	10
Notts Oly.	2	2	0	0	7	1
Notts Swifts	1	1	0	0	2	1
O Etonians	3	2	0	1	9	2
O Harrovians	1	1	0	0	2	0
Oldham Ath.	1	0	0	1	1	5
Oxford Univ.	2	1	0	1	2	2
Peterborough	2	0	1	1	0	1
Plymouth Arg	2	1	0	1	2	3
Portsmouth	3	2	0	1	4	2
Preston NE	6	2	2	2	3	4
QPR	4	2	2	0	9	3
Queens Pk G	2	0	1	1	1	4

	P	W	D	L	F	A
Reading	3	2	1	0	7	3
Rotherham T	1	1	0	0	5	0
Rotherham U	2	1	0	1	6	3
Shef. Heeley	2	2	0	0	11	3
Sheff. Utd.	11	3	3	5	11	16
Sheff. Wed.	9	2	2	5	13	21
Sheffield	2	1	1	0	4	2
Southampton	14	5	5	4	26	25
Southend U	1	1	0	0	1	0
Staveley	1	0	0	1	1	2
Stockport Co	1	0	0	1	0	2
Stoke City	3	1	1	1	2	2
Sunderland	6	4	1	1	14	9
Sunderland A	4	2	2	0	10	4
Swansea	1	0	0	1	1	2
Swifts	1	1	0	0	1	0
Swindon T	5	3	2	0	10	2
Tooting & M	2	1	1	0	5	2
Torquay U	1	1	0	0	6	1
Tottenham H	5	1	1	3	5	7
Tranmere R	1	1	0	0	1	0
Turton	1	1	0	0	6	0
Watford	4	1	2	1	5	3
West Brom	14	3	7	4	19	27
West Ham U	3	1	0	2	5	4
Wimbledon	2	0	1	1	0	1
Wolves	3	2	0	1	5	5
Workington	1	1	0	0	2	1
Wrexham	1	0	0	1	1	3

NOTTS COUNTY

	P	W	D	L	F	A
Aldershot	2	1	0	1	3	3
Altrincham	1	1	0	0	1	0
Arsenal	2	0	0	2	0	3
Aston Villa	12	3	4	5	21	29
Barrow	2	1	0	1	4	4
Basford R	1	1	0	0	13	0
Bath C	1	0	0	1	0	1
Birm.St.Grge	2	1	1	0	10	6
Birmingham C	2	2	0	0	4	1
Blackburn R	6	3	0	3	6	7
Bolton Wan.	9	2	4	3	14	13
Bradford C	6	2	3	1	8	8
Bradford PA	1	0	0	1	3	4
Brentford	1	0	0	1	0	4
Brighton &HA	1	1	0	0	2	1
Bristol C	5	1	2	2	9	9
Bristol R	1	0	0	1	0	2
Burnley	4	3	0	1	7	6
Burton Wan.	1	1	0	0	2	1
Bury	6	1	2	3	4	5
Cardiff C	1	0	0	1	0	2
Carlisle U	2	1	1	0	4	1
Charlton Ath	1	1	0	0	2	0
Chelmsford C	1	1	0	0	2	0
Chelsea	1	1	0	0	1	0
Chesterfield	3	2	1	0	6	4
Chorley	1	1	0	0	6	0
Coventry C	1	1	0	0	2	0
Crystal P	4	0	3	1	1	2
Darlington	1	1	0	0	2	1
Derby	2	1	1	0	8	6
Derby Co.	2	0	0	2	3	10
Doncaster R	5	1	1	3	3	5

Everton	2	0	0	2	2	4
Frickley Col	1	1	0	0	2	1
Fulham	2	0	0	2	0	2
Gateshead	1	0	0	1	0	2
Grantham T	2	2	0	0	6	1
Grimsby T	5	2	2	1	10	7
Hartlepool U	1	0	0	1	0	1
Hastings U	1	1	0	0	2	1
Horsham	1	1	0	0	9	1
Huddersfield	3	1	0	2	3	5
Hull C	1	1	0	0	5	2
Kettering T	1	1	0	0	2	0
Lancaster C	1	1	0	0	2	1
Leeds U	1	0	0	1	0	1
Leicester C	4	3	0	1	9	6
Leyton O.	1	1	0	0	2	1
Lincoln Ramb	1	1	0	0	9	0
Liverpool	2	1	0	1	2	1
Luton T	2	1	0	1	4	8
Man. City	2	1	0	1	1	1
Man. Utd.	2	0	1	1	4	5
Margate	2	1	1	0	4	2
Marlow	1	1	0	0	5	2
Middlesbro	6	4	0	2	8	4
Midlsbro Irn	1	0	0	1	2	3
Millwall	2	1	0	1	3	2
New Brighton	1	1	0	0	2	0
Newcastle U	1	0	0	1	1	8
Newport Co.	1	1	0	0	6	0
Northampton	2	1	0	1	2	3
Norwich C	2	1	0	1	4	3
Nottm Forest	6	2	1	3	10	11
Notts Oly.	1	1	0	0	2	0
Notts Rngrs	3	2	1	0	11	3
O Brghtnians	1	1	0	0	2	0
O Etonians	1	0	0	1	1	2
Oldham Ath.	1	1	0	0	3	3
Peterborough	2	0	0	2	0	4
Phoenix Bess	1	1	0	0	4	1
Plymouth Arg	3	1	1	1	1	1
Port Vale	5	3	1	1	10	5
Portsmouth	2	1	0	1	4	4
Preston NE	1	1	0	0	1	0
QPR	2	1	0	1	2	4
Queens Pk G	2	0	1	1	3	4
Reading	2	1	0	1	5	4
Rhyl	1	0	0	1	1	3
Rochdale	1	1	0	0	2	1
Rotherham T	1	1	0	0	15	0
Rotherham U	1	0	0	1	0	3
Runcorn	1	0	0	1	0	1
S Shields	1	1	0	0	3	1
Scarborough	1	1	0	0	6	1
Shankhouse	1	1	0	0	4	0
Shef. Heeley	1	1	0	0	3	1
Sheff. Utd.	3	1	0	2	12	8
Sheff. Wed.	7	2	1	4	12	15
Sheffield	5	3	1	1	20	5
South Shore	1	0	0	1	1	2
Southampton	5	1	2	2	7	8
Southend U	1	0	0	1	1	3
Staveley	2	2	0	0	5	0
Stockton	3	2	1	0	9	2
Stoke City	2	2	0	0	3	0
Sunderland	7	1	2	4	6	13
Swansea	2	1	0	1	3	2
Swifts	2	1	1	0	2	1

Swindon T	4	1	0	3	3	7
Tilbury	1	1	0	0	4	0
Torquay U	1	1	0	0	3	0
Tottenham H	4	1	1	2	6	8
Tranmere R	4	1	1	2	6	6
Walsall	2	0	1	1	0	4
Walsall S	1	1	0	0	4	1
Watford	1	1	0	0	4	1
Wednesbry St	1	1	0	0	11	1
West Brom	6	2	1	3	8	12
West Ham U	1	0	0	1	0	4
Wigan Ath.	1	1	0	0	2	0
Wolves	6	0	1	5	8	17
Wrexham	2	1	1	0	5	2
Yeovil T	1	1	0	0	4	2

OLDHAM ATHLETIC

	P	W	D	L	F	A
Accrington S	3	1	0	2	4	6
Aston Villa	4	1	0	3	4	6
Barnsley	1	0	0	1	1	3
Barrow	1	0	0	1	0	1
Birmingham C	6	3	2	1	9	7
Blackburn R	1	0	0	1	0	1
Blackpool	1	1	0	0	4	1
Bolton Wan.	2	1	0	1	2	2
Boston U	1	1	0	0	2	1
Bournemouth	1	0	0	1	0	1
Bradford C	6	1	2	3	9	17
Bradford PA	2	2	0	0	4	0
Brentford	3	2	0	1	7	6
Brighton &HA	4	1	1	2	4	7
Bristol R	4	1	2	1	5	6
Burnley	1	0	0	1	1	4
Bury	1	0	0	1	0	1
Cambridge U	3	1	2	0	7	6
Cardiff C	2	0	0	2	2	5
Charlton Ath	1	0	0	1	1	2
Chesterfield	5	1	2	2	10	14
Coventry C	1	0	0	1	0	1
Crewe Alex.	6	2	3	1	7	4
Crook T	1	1	0	0	1	0
Croydon Com.	1	1	0	0	3	0
Darlington	1	1	0	0	1	0
Denaby Utd.	1	1	0	0	2	0
Doncaster R	1	0	0	1	1	2
Everton	7	2	3	2	7	12
Exeter C	1	0	0	1	0	3
Ferryhill A	1	1	0	0	6	1
Formby	1	1	0	0	2	0
Fulham	1	0	0	1	0	2
Gillingham	2	1	0	1	4	3
Grantham T	2	2	0	0	7	1
Halifax T	2	2	0	0	4	2
Hartlepool U	1	1	0	0	2	1
Hereford U	1	0	0	1	0	4
Huddersfield	2	0	1	1	1	7
Hull C	3	1	1	1	2	2
Ipswich T	3	0	1	2	6	10
Kiddrminster	1	1	0	0	5	0
Lancaster C	1	1	0	0	6	0
Leeds C	3	1	1	1	3	4
Leicester C	1	1	0	0	3	1
Leyton O.	3	0	1	2	4	7
Lincoln C	1	1	0	0	3	2

Liverpool	3	0	0	3	2	6
Luton T	2	0	1	1	2	3
Lytham	1	1	0	0	10	1
Man. City	1	1	0	0	1	0
Man. Utd.	5	1	2	2	7	10
Mansfield T	3	2	0	1	6	4
Middlesbro	2	0	0	2	2	7
Millwall	2	0	1	1	1	2
Nelson	1	1	0	0	4	0
Newcastle U	1	0	0	1	2	7
Northwich V.	1	1	0	0	3	1
Nottm Forest	1	1	0	0	5	1
Notts Co.	2	1	0	1	3	3
Plymouth Arg	1	1	0	0	3	0
Port Vale	1	1	0	0	3	0
Reading	1	1	0	0	2	1
Rhyl	1	1	0	0	1	0
Rochdale	2	1	0	1	3	2
S Shields	3	1	1	1	3	2
Scarborough	2	0	1	1	2	3
Sheff. Utd.	2	0	1	1	0	3
Sheff. Wed.	5	0	1	4	7	19
Shildon	3	2	1	0	9	3
Shrewsbury T	1	0	0	1	0	3
Southend U	1	0	0	1	0	5
Southport	2	2	0	0	5	2
Stockton	2	2	0	0	10	4
Stoke City	2	1	0	1	2	5
Sunderland	2	1	0	1	2	3
Swindon T	1	0	0	1	0	2
Tottenham H	4	0	0	4	2	14
Tranmere R	4	2	1	1	4	5
Walthmstw Av	2	1	1	0	5	3
Watford	1	0	0	1	1	3
West Ham U	2	0	1	1	3	4
Wimbledon	2	0	1	1	0	1
Wolves	3	1	1	1	4	6
Workington	1	0	0	1	1	5

OXFORD UNITED

	P	W	D	L	F	A
Aldershot	4	2	1	1	7	7
Arsenal	1	0	0	1	1	5
Barking	1	0	0	1	0	1
Bedford T	2	0	1	1	1	2
Blackburn R	2	1	0	1	3	2
Blackpool	1	1	0	0	2	1
Bolton Wan.	1	0	0	1	2	4
Bournemouth	1	1	0	0	2	0
Bradford C	1	0	0	1	2	4
Brentford	3	1	1	1	4	6
Bridgwater T	1	1	0	0	2	1
Brighton &HA	1	1	0	0	3	0
Burnley	3	2	1	0	5	1
Chelmsford C	3	0	2	1	6	7
Chelsea	1	1	0	0	3	1
Chesterfield	1	1	0	0	1	0
Colchester U	1	0	0	1	2	4
Coventry C	1	0	0	1	0	4
Dover	1	1	0	0	2	0
Enfield	1	0	0	1	3	4
Falmouth T	1	1	0	0	2	1
Folkestone	2	2	0	0	7	2
Harwich & P	1	1	0	0	3	2
Hendon	2	1	1	0	5	4

	P	W	D	L	F	A
Kettering T	3	1	1	1	3	3
King's Lynn	1	1	0	0	2	1
Leicester C	5	1	1	3	6	10
Liverpool	1	0	0	1	0	3
Man. City	1	0	0	1	2	5
Man. Utd.	2	0	0	2	1	6
Mansfield T	1	0	0	1	0	1
Margate	1	1	0	0	3	2
Millwall	2	1	1	0	4	3
Norwich C	1	0	0	1	2	4
Nuneaton B.	1	0	0	1	0	2
Peterborough	2	1	0	1	4	4
Plymouth Arg	2	1	0	1	1	3
Port Vale	2	0	1	1	4	5
Preston NE	1	0	0	1	1	2
QPR	1	0	0	1	0	2
Reading	2	1	1	0	4	1
Sheff. Wed.	1	0	0	1	0	3
Shrewsbury T	1	1	0	0	2	0
Southampton	3	0	1	2	1	4
Stockport Co	2	1	1	0	1	0
Stoke City	2	1	0	1	2	3
Sunderland	3	1	1	1	5	4
Torquay U	2	0	1	1	2	3
Tottenham H	3	0	1	2	4	7
Tranmere R	1	1	0	0	3	1
Watford	2	1	1	0	3	2
Worthing	1	1	0	0	4	0
Yeovil T	1	1	0	0	3	1

PETERBOROUGH

	P	W	D	L	F	A
Aldershot	1	1	0	0	2	1
Arsenal	1	1	0	0	2	0
Aston Villa	2	0	1	1	2	3
Barnet	2	2	0	0	3	1
Bath C	1	1	0	0	1	0
Bedford T	1	1	0	0	6	2
Bournemouth	1	0	0	1	1	2
Bradford PA	1	1	0	0	3	0
Brentford	2	0	1	1	2	3
Brighton &HA	2	0	1	1	2	3
Bristol C	1	0	0	1	0	1
Bristol R	3	0	0	3	2	8
Bshp Strtfrd	4	2	2	0	10	6
Cambridge U	1	1	0	0	2	0
Cardiff C	2	1	0	1	3	4
Carlisle U	1	1	0	0	1	0
Charlton Ath	1	1	0	0	3	0
Chelsea	1	0	0	1	1	5
Chesterfield	5	3	2	0	10	5
Colchester U	5	3	2	0	14	7
Coventry Spr	1	1	0	0	4	0
Dagenham	1	0	0	1	0	1
Dartford	1	0	0	1	0	3
Derby Co.	2	0	0	2	0	3
Doncaster R	1	1	0	0	5	2
Dover	1	1	0	0	4	1
Enfield	2	2	0	0	5	0
Falmouth T	2	2	0	0	9	3
Fulham	2	0	1	1	0	1
Gillingham	5	2	2	1	8	9
Halifax T	1	1	0	0	3	0
Harlow T	1	1	0	0	7	0
Hayes	2	1	1	0	2	1
Hereford U	3	2	1	0	7	3
Hitchin T	1	1	0	0	3	1
Huddersfield	1	0	0	1	1	3
Ipswich T	3	2	0	1	6	5
Kettering T	2	1	1	0	5	4
Kiddrminster	1	1	0	0	2	1
Kingstonian	2	1	1	0	2	1
Leeds U	2	1	0	1	2	4
Lincoln C	2	1	1	0	7	6
Luton T	1	0	0	1	0	3
Man. City	1	0	0	1	0	1
Man. Utd.	1	0	0	1	1	3
Margate	1	1	0	0	4	0
Middlesbro	2	0	1	1	1	3
Newcastle U	3	1	1	1	2	3
Northampton	6	2	2	2	8	14
Northwich V.	1	0	0	1	0	4
Nottm Forest	2	1	1	0	1	0
Notts Co.	2	2	0	0	4	0
Oxford U	2	1	0	1	4	4
Plymouth Arg	2	1	0	1	4	3
Port Vale	1	0	0	1	1	2
Portsmouth	2	1	0	1	2	2
QPR	2	1	1	0	5	4
Reading	2	0	1	1	0	1
Redditch U	2	1	1	0	7	1
Rotherham U	1	1	0	0	1	0
Salisbury	1	1	0	0	5	1
Sheff. Utd.	1	0	0	1	1	3
Sheff. Wed.	1	0	0	1	0	2
Shrewsbury T	2	1	0	1	6	6
Southend U	2	1	0	1	5	4
Stafford Rgs	1	1	0	0	2	1
Sunderland	1	0	0	1	1	7
Sutton U	1	0	0	1	1	3
Swansea	3	1	1	1	3	3
Swindon T	2	0	1	1	2	3
Torquay U	6	3	1	2	12	8
Tranmere R	2	2	0	0	5	0
Walsall	2	2	0	0	5	3
Watford	2	0	1	1	2	3
Weymouth	3	1	2	0	6	3
Wigan Ath.	1	0	0	1	1	2
Wimbledon	1	1	0	0	3	1
Winsford U	1	1	0	0	4	1
Wycombe Wan.	3	2	1	0	6	2

PLYMOUTH ARGYLE

	P	W	D	L	F	A
Aldershot	3	1	0	2	1	3
Arsenal	2	0	0	2	3	10
Aston Villa	2	0	1	1	1	5
Barking	1	1	0	0	2	1
Barnet	1	1	0	0	3	0
Barnsley	3	3	0	0	6	1
Bath C	2	1	1	0	2	0
Blackpool	2	2	0	0	5	0
Bolton Wan.	1	0	0	1	1	4
Bradford PA	3	1	0	2	5	7
Brentford	5	4	1	0	6	1
Bristol C	3	1	1	1	4	3
Bristol R	3	1	1	1	3	7
Bury	2	0	1	1	2	3
Cambridge U	2	2	0	0	3	0
Cardiff C	1	0	0	1	0	3
Charlton Ath	1	0	0	1	1	2
Chelsea	5	0	2	3	3	8
Chester	1	0	0	1	0	2
Colchester U	3	1	1	1	3	2
Corby T	1	1	0	0	6	0
Coventry C	2	2	0	0	7	2
Crewe Alex.	3	2	1	0	7	2
Crystal P	2	1	0	1	4	4
Darlington	1	1	0	0	2	1
Dartford	1	1	0	0	3	2
Derby Co.	5	2	1	2	6	5
Doncaster R	1	0	0	1	0	2
Dorchester T	1	1	0	0	5	2
Dorking	1	0	0	1	0	3
Dulwich Ham.	1	1	0	0	3	0
Everton	4	0	1	3	2	10
Exeter C	3	3	0	0	6	0
Fulham	2	0	1	1	1	2
Gainsborough	1	1	0	0	3	0
Gateshead	2	0	0	2	1	4
Gillingham	6	1	2	3	9	9
Hendon	1	1	0	0	1	0
Hereford U	2	0	1	1	0	2
Huddersfield	5	0	1	4	4	13
Hull C	5	0	2	3	7	12
Ipswich T	1	0	0	1	1	3
Leeds U	1	0	0	1	1	2
Leicester C	1	0	0	1	0	5
Leyton O.	1	0	0	1	0	1
Lincoln C	1	1	0	0	4	1
Luton T	1	0	0	1	2	4
Maidstone U	1	1	0	0	3	0
Man. City	1	0	0	1	1	3
Man. Utd.	4	1	0	3	4	5
Mansfield T	1	0	0	1	0	1
Middlesbro	3	1	1	1	2	2
Millwall	2	0	0	2	0	3
New Brighton	1	0	0	1	0	1
New Crusadrs	1	1	0	0	6	3
Newcastle U	5	0	2	3	3	11
Newport Co.	3	2	1	0	5	2
Nottm Forest	2	1	0	1	3	2
Notts Co.	3	1	1	1	1	1
Oldham Ath.	1	0	0	1	0	3
Oxford U	2	1	0	1	3	1
Peterborough	2	1	0	1	3	4
Preston NE	1	0	0	1	2	0
Reading	2	1	0	1	2	1
Rochdale	1	1	0	0	2	0
Sheff. Wed.	3	0	1	2	2	7
Shrewsbury T	1	1	0	0	1	0
Southend U	2	1	1	0	2	0
Stockport Co	1	1	0	0	3	2
Sunderland	3	0	0	3	2	8
Swansea	2	1	0	1	2	4
Swindon T	1	1	0	0	1	0
Torquay U	1	0	0	1	0	1
Tottenham H	4	0	1	3	3	14
Walsall	2	1	0	1	1	3
Watford	5	2	1	2	10	6
West Brom	3	1	0	2	4	8
West Ham U	2	1	0	1	3	2
Wolves	3	0	1	2	2	6
Worcester C	1	0	0	1	0	2
Yeovil & P	1	1	0	0	4	1

PORT VALE

	P	W	D	L	F	A
Aldershot	1	1	0	0	2	0
Altrincham	1	1	0	0	4	1
Arnold	2	1	1	0	5	2
Arsenal	2	0	1	1	2	3
Aston Villa	4	0	0	4	3	18
Barnsley	6	2	2	2	11	8
Birmingham C	3	1	0	2	2	6
Blackburn R	4	1	1	2	5	6
Blackpool	2	1	0	1	3	2
Bolton Wan.	2	1	0	1	2	4
Bradford C	5	3	0	2	8	6
Bradford PA	3	1	1	1	3	3
Brentwood(1)	1	0	1	0	4	4
Brighton &HA	1	1	0	0	2	1
Bristol R	1	1	0	0	2	0
Burnley	5	2	1	2	6	7
Cardiff C	3	2	0	1	5	2
Carlisle U	1	1	0	0	2	1
Charlton Ath	1	0	0	1	0	2
Chelmsford C	1	1	0	0	3	0
Chester	1	0	0	1	1	2
Chesterfield	1	0	0	1	0	2
Chirk	1	1	0	0	3	0
Colchester U	1	0	0	1	1	3
Corinthian	1	1	0	0	3	1
Crewe Alex.	2	1	1	0	4	1
Crystal P	1	0	0	1	1	2
Darlington	2	2	0	0	4	1
Dartford	1	1	0	0	1	0
Davenham	2	1	1	0	4	1
Derby Co.	2	1	1	0	4	3
Doncaster R	1	0	0	1	1	3
Dorchester T	1	1	0	0	2	1
Druids	2	1	1	0	7	3
Enfield	2	0	1	1	1	4
Everton	1	0	0	1	2	3
Exeter C	1	1	0	0	2	1
Finchley	1	1	0	0	5	0
Fulham	1	0	0	1	0	1
Gainsborough	5	1	2	2	7	6
Gillingham	1	1	0	0	4	2
Grantham T	2	1	1	0	6	3
Grimsby T	1	0	0	1	0	4
Hendon	1	1	0	0	2	1
Huddersfield	1	0	0	1	1	2
Hull C	4	1	2	1	9	8
Irthlingboro	1	1	0	0	7	1
Leek	2	0	1	1	3	5
Leicester C	1	0	0	1	1	2
Leyton O.	3	2	1	0	7	2
Lincoln C	6	1	3	2	7	8
Liverpool	2	0	1	1	1	2
Luton T	2	0	1	1	3	5
Macclesfield	2	2	0	0	3	1
Man. City	1	0	0	1	1	2
Man. Utd.	3	0	0	3	2	7
Mansfield T	2	1	1	0	2	1
Marine	2	1	1	0	4	2
Millwall	2	1	0	1	3	4
Nelson	1	1	0	0	3	2
New Brighton	2	2	0	0	6	2
Newcastle U	1	0	0	1	0	4
Newport Co.	1	1	0	0	2	1
Northampton	1	1	0	0	3	1

Norwich C	1	0	0	1	1	3
Notts Co.	5	1	1	3	5	10
Oldham Ath.	1	0	0	1	0	3
Oxford U	2	1	1	0	5	4
Peterborough	1	1	0	0	2	1
QPR	3	2	1	0	6	4
Scarborough	1	1	0	0	2	1
Scunthorpe U	2	2	0	0	5	1
Sheff. Utd.	3	1	1	1	4	4
Sheff. Wed.	1	0	0	1	0	2
Shrewsbury T	4	2	1	1	6	4
Southampton	1	0	0	1	0	3
Southend U	1	0	0	1	0	1
Southport	5	4	1	0	9	3
Stafford Rgs	1	1	0	0	1	0
Stockport Co	2	2	0	0	5	1
Stoke City	6	1	2	3	7	9
Sunderland	5	2	2	1	7	6
Swansea	1	0	0	1	0	3
Torquay U	1	0	0	1	0	1
Tottenham H	2	1	0	1	4	5
Tranmere R	5	2	2	1	9	8
Walsall	6	1	2	3	4	11
Watford	5	1	2	2	3	6
Wealdstone	1	1	0	0	1	0
Wellington T	2	2	0	0	6	0
West Brom	2	0	0	2	2	4
West Ham U	4	1	1	2	6	8
Wigan Ath.	3	1	2	0	4	3
Workington	3	2	1	0	5	3

PORTSMOUTH

	P	W	D	L	F	A
Accrington S	3	2	1	0	9	3
Aldershot	4	2	1	1	9	6
Arsenal	3	0	1	2	3	6
Aston Villa	6	2	2	2	8	10
Barnet	1	1	0	0	5	0
Barnsley	1	0	0	1	0	1
Bideford	1	1	0	0	3	1
Birmingham C	9	3	2	4	10	9
Blackburn R	11	2	5	4	6	14
Bolton Wan.	4	1	1	2	4	4
Boston U	1	1	0	0	1	0
Bournemouth	1	1	0	0	5	1
Bradford C	3	2	0	1	5	2
Bradford PA	2	0	0	2	0	3
Brentford	2	1	0	1	2	2
Brighton &HA	4	1	0	3	5	5
Bristol C	4	0	2	2	2	7
Bristol R	4	2	1	1	10	6
Burnley	3	0	1	2	2	5
Bury	1	1	0	0	3	1
Charlton Ath	5	2	2	1	9	10
Chelsea	2	1	1	0	2	1
Chesterfield	1	1	0	0	3	0
Colchester U	1	0	0	1	0	3
Coventry C	4	0	2	2	4	6
Crystal P	2	0	0	2	1	5
Derby Co.	7	1	3	3	8	15
Doncaster R	2	2	0	0	7	2
Everton	1	0	0	1	0	5
Exeter C	2	1	0	1	2	5
Fulham	3	2	1	0	3	0
Gateshead	1	0	0	1	0	3
Grimsby T	9	5	2	2	18	9

Hastings &SL	1	1	0	0	1	0
Hereford U	1	1	0	0	4	1
Huddersfield	3	2	1	0	6	4
Hull C	3	1	2	0	6	4
Leeds U	2	0	1	1	1	3
Leicester C	3	2	0	1	6	4
Leyton O.	4	2	2	0	5	1
Lincoln C	2	2	0	0	8	0
Liverpool	2	0	2	0	1	1
Luton T	4	0	1	3	3	8
Man. City	2	0	0	2	2	5
Man. Utd.	6	2	3	1	13	11
Middlesbro	6	2	3	1	10	8
Millwall	2	0	1	1	3	4
Minehead	1	1	0	0	2	1
Newcastle U	2	0	0	2	2	8
Newport Co.	2	2	0	0	4	2
Northampton	1	1	0	0	2	0
Norwich C	2	1	1	0	3	1
Nottm Forest	3	1	0	2	2	4
Notts Co.	2	1	0	1	4	4
Peterborough	2	1	0	1	2	2
Preston NE	3	2	0	1	4	3
Reading	3	1	0	2	2	4
Scunthorpe U	5	2	3	0	10	5
Sheff. Utd.	3	2	0	1	4	4
Sheff. Wed.	4	1	1	2	5	8
Shrewsbury T	1	1	0	0	3	0
Southampton	2	0	0	2	1	6
Stockport Co	1	1	0	0	7	0
Stoke City	2	0	0	2	1	5
Swansea	5	3	1	1	9	5
Swindon T	4	1	2	1	5	6
Tottenham H	3	0	0	3	2	10
Tranmere R	2	1	0	1	3	3
West Brom	4	1	0	3	3	5
West Ham U	3	2	0	1	5	4
Wimbledon	4	1	2	1	4	7

PRESTON NORTH END

	P	W	D	L	F	A
Aberdare Ath	1	1	0	0	3	1
Accrington	1	1	0	0	4	1
Accrington S	2	1	1	0	5	1
Arsenal	5	2	2	1	8	7
Astley Brdge	1	1	0	0	11	3
Aston Villa	8	3	2	3	10	9
Barnet	1	1	0	0	3	2
Barnsley	5	3	2	0	11	1
Birm.St.Grge	1	1	0	0	2	0
Birmingham C	2	0	0	2	1	3
Blackburn R	3	1	1	1	3	5
Blackpool	2	2	0	0	4	2
Blyth S	2	1	1	0	6	2
Bolton Wan.	14	5	5	4	30	21
Bootle	1	1	0	0	3	0
Bradford C	4	1	1	2	8	11
Brentford	2	2	0	0	4	0
Brighton &HA	4	1	2	1	4	4
Bristol C	5	3	2	0	10	2
Bristol R	6	3	1	2	20	13
Bshp Aukland	1	1	0	0	2	0
Burton S	1	1	0	0	9	2
Bury	2	2	0	0	9	4
Carlisle U	2	1	0	1	1	1

	P	W	D	L	F	A
Charlton Ath	5	1	1	3	5	13
Chelsea	2	0	1	1	1	2
Chester	2	0	1	1	1	2
Chesterfield	1	0	0	1	1	4
Chorley	2	1	1	0	5	0
Coventry C	1	0	0	1	1	2
Crewe Alex.	4	2	2	0	10	3
Derby Co.	7	4	2	1	15	9
Eagley	1	1	0	0	9	1
Everton	8	2	3	3	11	14
Exeter C	1	1	0	0	5	3
Fulham	2	1	0	1	3	3
Glossop	1	1	0	0	1	0
Grimsby T	5	3	1	1	10	1
Gt. Lever	1	1	0	0	4	1
Halifax T	1	0	0	1	0	1
Halliwell	1	1	0	0	4	0
Huddersfield	4	1	0	3	1	7
Hull C	2	1	1	0	1	0
Hyde	1	1	0	0	26	0
Ipswich T	2	1	0	1	6	4
Leeds U	2	1	0	1	1	3
Leicester C	7	3	2	2	11	7
Lincoln C	4	4	0	0	13	4
Liverpool	4	1	2	1	3	3
Luton T	2	2	0	0	5	2
Man. City	10	4	3	3	17	11
Man. Utd.	9	2	2	5	13	15
Mansfield T	5	2	1	2	6	7
Middlesbro	5	3	0	2	4	7
Midlsbro Irn	3	2	1	0	15	2
Millwall	2	1	0	1	3	5
Newcastle U	5	3	0	2	8	6
Northampton	2	2	0	0	6	1
Nottm Forest	6	2	2	2	4	3
Notts Co.	1	0	0	1	0	1
O Crthusians	1	1	0	0	2	1
O Foresters	1	1	0	0	3	0
Oxford U	1	1	0	0	2	1
Plymouth Arg	1	0	0	1	0	2
Portsmouth	3	1	0	2	3	4
QPR	1	1	0	0	3	1
Queens Pk G	1	1	0	0	3	0
Reading	1	1	0	0	18	0
Renton	1	1	0	0	2	0
Runcorn	1	1	0	0	4	2
Scarborough	1	0	0	1	2	3
Scunthorpe U	2	1	0	1	2	2
Sheff. Utd.	4	0	2	2	3	6
Sheff. Wed.	9	4	3	2	15	10
Shepshed Chr	1	1	0	0	5	1
Southampton	1	0	0	1	0	1
Stockport Co	1	1	0	0	3	1
Stoke City	5	3	1	1	11	7
Sunderland	8	0	1	7	7	22
Swansea	2	1	0	1	3	3
Swindon T	1	1	0	0	2	0
Telford U	1	0	0	1	1	4
Tottenham H	11	4	2	5	16	19
Tranmere R	3	1	1	1	2	4
Upton Park	1	0	1	0	1	1
Walsall	1	0	0	1	3	7
Watford	5	2	1	2	9	7
West Brom	7	2	0	5	9	12
West Ham U	4	1	0	3	7	11
Weymouth	1	1	0	0	2	0
Whitley Bay	1	0	0	1	0	2

	P	W	D	L	F	A
Witton	1	1	0	0	6	0
Witton Alb.	1	1	0	0	5	1
Wolves	4	4	0	0	13	2
Workington	1	1	0	0	2	1

QUEENS PARK RANGERS

	P	W	D	L	F	A
Aldershot	1	0	0	1	1	2
Arsenal	5	2	2	1	5	2
Ashford T	1	1	0	0	3	0
Aston Villa	2	0	0	2	2	4
Barnet	5	4	1	0	18	6
Barnsley	1	0	0	1	0	1
Barry T	2	1	1	0	8	1
Bath C	1	1	0	0	2	0
Birmingham C	2	2	0	0	4	1
Blackpool	5	2	3	0	10	3
Bournemouth	1	1	0	0	2	0
Bradford C	2	0	1	1	0	4
Bradford PA	1	0	0	1	3	5
Brentford	3	0	1	2	2	6
Brighton &HA	2	1	0	1	6	3
Bristol C	2	1	1	0	4	2
Bristol R	4	1	1	2	9	5
Burnley	2	0	0	2	3	10
Bury	1	0	0	1	0	1
Cardiff C	2	1	1	0	2	0
Carlisle U	2	0	0	2	0	3
Charlton Ath	5	1	2	2	5	8
Chelsea	3	1	1	1	3	4
Clapton	2	1	1	0	4	2
Colchester U	4	3	1	0	11	5
Coventry C	3	1	1	1	4	4
Crewe Alex.	1	1	0	0	4	2
Crystal P	7	4	3	0	7	1
Darlington	1	0	0	1	0	2
Derby Co.	4	1	1	2	4	10
Doncaster R	1	0	0	1	0	1
Dorchester T	1	1	0	0	4	0
Everton	2	0	0	2	1	4
Fulham	4	0	1	3	2	6
Gateshead	1	1	0	0	3	0
Gillingham	3	2	1	0	8	3
Glossop	1	1	0	0	2	1
Grimsby T	1	1	0	0	3	1
Guildford C	2	1	0	1	5	4
Halifax T	1	1	0	0	4	2
Hartlepool U	1	1	0	0	2	0
Hereford U	1	0	0	1	1	6
Hinckley Ath	1	1	0	0	7	2
Huddersfield	4	0	1	3	1	12
Ipswich T	2	2	0	0	6	0
Kettering T	1	1	0	0	6	0
Leeds C	1	1	0	0	1	0
Leeds U	2	1	0	1	4	3
Leicester C	2	1	0	1	5	4
Lincoln C	1	1	0	0	2	1
Liverpool	3	0	1	2	3	5
Luton T	6	3	2	1	10	7
Man. C	1	0	0	1	1	2
Man. Utd.	5	0	2	3	3	8
Margate	1	0	0	1	1	3
Merthyr T	2	1	1	0	6	2
Middlesbro	5	1	2	2	8	10
Millwall	2	0	0	2	3	6

	P	W	D	L	F	A
New Brighton	2	1	1	0	5	1
Newcastle U	2	0	1	1	1	2
Newport Co.	1	1	0	0	3	2
Northfleet U	2	1	1	0	4	2
Norwich C	4	2	2	0	9	4
Nottm Forest	4	0	2	2	3	9
Notts Co.	2	1	0	1	4	2
Nuneaton B.	2	1	1	0	3	2
Oxford U	1	1	0	0	2	0
Peterborough	2	0	1	1	4	5
Poole T	3	2	1	0	11	4
Port Vale	3	0	1	2	4	6
Preston NE	1	0	0	1	1	3
Reading	1	1	0	0	1	0
S Liverpool	1	1	0	0	1	0
S Shields	1	1	0	0	4	1
Scunthorpe U	1	0	0	1	0	1
Sheff. Utd.	1	0	0	1	0	1
Sheff. Wed.	1	0	0	1	0	3
Shrewsbury T	7	2	3	2	9	10
Southampton	4	2	0	2	5	6
Southend U	5	2	2	1	7	6
Stockport Co	1	0	0	1	1	3
Stoke City	1	1	0	0	3	0
Sunderland	1	0	0	1	0	4
Swansea	2	1	0	1	2	3
Swindon T	4	1	0	3	6	6
Thames	1	1	0	0	5	0
Tooting & M	1	1	0	0	2	0
Torquay U	2	1	1	0	4	2
Tottenham H	4	0	2	2	2	5
Walsall	1	1	0	0	1	0
Walthmstw Av	5	2	2	1	9	10
Watford	1	0	0	1	1	2
Wealdstone	1	1	0	0	4	0
West Brom	2	1	0	1	3	3
West Ham U	9	3	3	3	14	9
Wigan Boro.	1	1	0	0	4	2
Wolves	2	1	1	0	2	1

READING

	P	W	D	L	F	A
Aldershot	11	6	2	3	24	18
Arsenal	3	0	0	3	2	6
Aston Villa	4	1	1	2	4	9
Barking	1	1	0	0	3	1
Barnsley	3	0	1	2	5	8
Barry T	1	1	0	0	2	1
Bedford T	1	1	0	0	1	0
Birmingham C	1	1	0	0	1	0
Blackburn R	1	0	0	1	1	2
Blyth S	2	1	1	0	8	3
Bognor Regis	1	1	0	0	6	2
Bolton Wan.	4	1	1	2	4	6
Bournemouth	3	1	0	2	1	3
Bradford C	1	0	0	1	0	2
Bradford PA	1	0	0	1	1	5
Brentford	3	3	0	0	9	2
Brentwood T	1	0	0	1	0	1
Bridgwater T	1	1	0	0	3	0
Bristol R	5	3	2	0	8	4
Bromley	2	1	1	0	6	3
Bshp Strtfrd	2	1	0	1	7	3
Burnley	2	0	1	1	1	2
Bury	2	0	1	1	1	4
Cardiff C	2	1	0	1	2	4

	P	W	D	L	F	A
Chelsea	3	0	2	1	3	5
Cheltenham T	2	2	0	0	5	2
Chester	2	1	1	0	6	3
Colchester U	6	4	1	1	17	8
Corinthian	1	1	0	0	8	3
Coventry C	3	1	2	0	6	5
Crystal P	6	0	3	3	4	9
Dagenham	2	1	1	0	2	1
Dartford	1	1	0	0	4	0
Doncaster R	2	1	0	1	4	3
Enfield	2	1	1	0	6	4
Fulham	4	0	2	2	1	3
Gillingham	5	3	2	0	10	6
Grimsby T	5	1	2	2	9	8
Guildford C	1	0	0	1	0	1
Hayes	2	1	1	0	1	0
Hendon	3	2	0	1	7	4
Hendon(1)	2	2	0	0	6	0
Hereford U	3	2	0	1	4	1
Hotspur	1	1	0	0	5	1
Huddersfield	2	1	1	0	2	1
Hull C	3	1	1	1	2	2
Ilford	1	1	0	0	4	2
Ipswich T	1	0	0	1	1	4
Kettering T	2	2	0	0	8	4
King's Lynn	1	1	0	0	4	2
Leicester C	1	0	0	1	0	1
Leyton	1	1	0	0	6	0
Leyton O.	2	1	0	1	3	1
Luton T	1	0	0	1	1	2
Maidstone U	2	1	1	0	3	2
Man. City	4	0	2	2	1	12
Man. Utd.	9	1	4	4	9	17
Merthyr Tyd.	1	1	0	0	3	1
Millwall	4	2	1	1	8	5
Newcastle U	4	0	1	3	5	13
Newport Co.	9	3	3	3	19	15
Northampton	1	0	0	1	0	3
Norwich C	5	1	3	1	6	6
Nottm Forest	3	0	1	2	3	7
Notts Co.	2	1	0	1	4	5
O Crthusians	1	0	0	1	1	2
O Etonians	1	0	0	1	0	1
Oldham Ath.	1	0	0	1	1	2
Oxford U	2	0	1	1	1	4
Peterborough	2	1	1	0	1	0
Plymouth Arg	2	1	0	1	1	2
Portsmouth	3	2	0	1	4	2
Preston NE	1	0	0	1	0	18
QPR	1	0	0	1	0	1
Rochester	2	1	0	1	3	6
Royal Engrs	1	0	0	1	0	8
S Norwood	1	1	0	0	2	0
S Reading	2	1	1	0	6	2
Sheff. Wed.	2	1	0	1	3	3
Shrewsbury T	2	1	1	0	3	2
Slough T	3	2	1	0	8	4
Southampton	1	0	0	1	0	1
Southend U	2	1	0	1	3	4
Southport	4	2	2	0	6	2
Stoke City	2	1	1	0	5	2
Sunderland	3	1	1	1	4	5
Sutton T	1	0	0	2	1	5
Swansea	3	1	0	2	4	8
Swifts	1	0	0	1	0	1
Swindon T	3	1	0	2	3	8
Torquay U	5	2	3	0	6	3

	P	W	D	L	F	A
Tottenham H	5	2	1	2	6	7
Tranmere R	2	1	1	0	3	2
Upton Park	3	0	0	3	2	10
Walsall	1	1	0	0	1	0
Watford	5	2	1	2	7	9
Wealdstone	3	2	0	1	3	2
Welling U	4	1	3	0	3	2
West Brom	1	0	0	1	0	2
West End	2	1	1	0	2	1
Weymouth	2	1	1	0	9	4
Wisbech T	1	1	0	0	2	1
Wolves	2	0	0	2	0	6
Wrexham	3	1	1	1	5	3

ROCHDALE

	P	W	D	L	F	A
Accrington S	2	0	0	2	4	7
Altrincham	2	0	0	2	2	5
Arsenal	1	0	0	1	2	4
Ashington	1	1	0	0	2	1
Bangor C	1	0	0	1	1	2
Barnsley	4	0	1	3	2	7
Barrow	3	0	1	2	2	6
Blackpool	2	1	1	0	2	1
Bolton W	1	0	0	1	0	4
Bradford C	2	0	1	1	2	3
Bradford PA	1	0	0	1	1	2
Bshp Aukland	1	1	0	0	6	1
Bury	4	0	2	2	8	11
Carlisle U	2	1	1	0	5	3
Charlton Ath	2	0	0	2	2	6
Chelsea	1	0	0	1	2	3
Chesterfield	1	0	0	1	2	3
Chilton Col.	2	0	1	1	2	3
Chorley	1	1	0	0	2	1
Colchester U	2	0	1	1	3	8
Coventry C	1	1	0	0	2	1
Crewe Alex.	4	1	1	2	4	8
Crook T	1	1	0	0	8	2
Crystal P	1	0	0	1	0	1
Darlington	4	2	0	2	5	5
Doncaster R	2	0	0	2	2	4
Droylsden	1	0	0	1	0	1
Fleetwood T	2	1	1	0	7	2
Gateshead U	2	1	1	0	4	2
Gillingham	4	2	1	1	6	4
Grantham T	2	0	1	1	4	6
Gretna	2	1	1	0	3	1
Grimsby T	1	0	0	1	0	2
Halifax T	3	1	0	2	5	11
Hartlepool U	4	1	2	1	11	7
Hinckley Ath	1	1	0	0	2	1
Huddersfield	3	0	1	2	5	7
Hull C	3	0	2	1	4	5
Ilkeston T	1	1	0	0	2	0
Leeds U	1	0	0	1	0	2
Lincoln C	3	1	1	1	4	3
Man. Utd.	1	0	0	1	0	2
Mansfield T	1	0	0	1	1	3
Marine	3	2	1	0	3	1
Northampton	1	1	0	0	3	0
Northwich V.	3	0	2	1	2	3
Norwich C	3	0	2	1	2	3
Notts Co.	1	0	0	1	1	2
Nuneaton B.	1	1	0	0	3	0
Oldham Ath.	2	1	0	1	2	3

	P	W	D	L	F	A
Plymouth Arg	1	0	0	1	0	2
Rhyl	1	1	0	0	3	0
S Shields	1	1	0	0	2	0
Scarborough	1	0	0	1	2	4
Scunthorpe U	7	2	2	3	9	10
Stockport Co	3	1	1	1	3	4
Sutton T	1	0	0	1	1	2
Swindon T	1	0	0	1	0	2
Telford U	1	0	0	1	1	4
Tranmere R	9	3	3	3	14	16
W Stanley	1	1	0	0	4	0
Whitley Bay	1	1	0	0	1	0
Willington	1	1	0	0	3	1
Workington	4	1	1	2	4	6
Wrexham	4	0	0	4	3	12

ROTHERHAM UNITED

	P	W	D	L	F	A
Accrington S	2	0	1	1	0	5
Aldershot	1	0	0	1	1	3
Altrincham	2	1	0	1	5	2
Arsenal	4	1	2	1	6	8
Ashington	1	1	0	0	3	0
Aston Villa	3	1	0	2	3	5
Barnsley	5	2	1	2	5	7
Barrow	1	1	0	0	3	1
Birmingham C	3	0	1	2	1	6
Blackburn R	1	0	0	1	1	4
Boston U	1	1	0	0	4	0
Bradford C	2	1	0	1	3	5
Brentford	1	0	0	1	0	3
Brighton &HA	3	0	2	1	2	8
Bristol C	3	1	0	2	5	7
Burnley	5	1	1	3	7	8
Burton T	2	1	1	0	4	1
Bury	7	3	2	2	13	12
Chester	5	1	2	2	3	7
Colchester U	2	1	1	0	4	2
Coventry C	1	1	0	0	2	1
Crewe Alex.	3	2	0	1	4	2
Darlington	2	2	0	0	11	4
Doncaster R	6	5	1	0	10	3
Exeter C	2	0	1	1	4	6
Frickley Ath	1	1	0	0	3	1
Frickley Col	2	1	1	0	6	2
Gateshead	2	1	1	0	4	2
Grantham T	1	1	0	0	4	1
Grimsby T	1	0	0	1	2	3
Gt. Harwood	1	1	0	0	6	2
Halifax T	3	2	1	0	6	2
Hartlepool U	6	2	3	1	9	7
Huddersfield	1	0	0	1	3	4
Hull C	4	2	0	2	4	7
Leeds U	2	0	1	1	2	3
Leicester C	3	1	1	1	2	3
Lincoln C	4	2	1	1	8	5
Luton T	1	0	0	1	1	5
Macclesfield	1	0	0	1	0	4
Man. City	2	0	1	1	2	4
Man. Utd.	2	0	1	1	0	1
Mansfield T	3	0	1	2	3	5
Millwall	2	0	1	1	1	3
Morecambe	2	1	1	0	3	1
Mossley	1	1	0	0	3	0
Newark T	1	0	0	1	1	2

	P	W	D	L	F	A
Newcastle U	3	1	1	1	4	4
Northampton	2	2	0	0	3	1
Nottm Forest	2	1	0	1	3	6
Notts Co.	1	1	0	0	3	0
Nuneaton B.	2	1	1	0	2	1
Peterborough	1	0	0	1	0	1
S Bank St.P	1	1	0	0	3	2
S Shields	1	1	0	0	4	0
Scunthorpe U	7	2	4	1	19	17
Sheff. Wed.	1	0	0	1	0	3
Shrewsbury T	1	0	0	1	1	2
Southend U	1	1	0	0	3	2
Southport	1	1	0	0	2	1
Spennymoor U	4	3	1	0	13	3
Stafford Rgs	2	0	1	1	0	2
Stockport Co	2	1	0	1	1	1
Sunderland	2	0	1	1	1	2
Swansea	3	1	1	1	4	3
Tottenham H	1	0	0	1	0	2
Tranmere R	1	0	0	1	1	2
Walsall	2	1	0	1	4	1
Watford	4	1	1	2	2	4
West Brom	3	0	1	2	0	7
Wigan Ath.	1	1	0	0	2	1
Wolves	6	2	1	3	11	11
Workington	2	2	0	0	6	0
Wrexham	1	0	0	1	0	3

SCARBOROUGH

	P	W	D	L	F	A
Altrincham	1	0	0	1	0	6
Bradford C	4	1	1	2	2	8
Bradford PA	1	0	0	1	1	6
Brighton &HA	3	0	1	2	1	7
Bromley	1	1	0	0	4	1
Burnley	2	0	0	2	1	3
Carlisle U	1	0	0	1	0	1
Chorley	1	1	0	0	1	0
Crewe Alex.	6	2	3	1	7	5
Crystal P	1	0	0	1	1	2
Darlington	5	1	2	2	6	8
Darwen	1	1	0	0	2	0
Doncaster R	3	0	1	2	2	4
Gateshead	1	0	0	1	0	3
Grimsby T	2	0	0	2	2	4
Halifax T	1	0	0	1	0	2
Hartlepool U	1	0	0	1	1	6
Horwich RMI	1	1	0	0	2	1
Leek T	1	0	0	1	0	2
Lincoln C	1	1	0	0	6	4
Luton T	2	0	1	1	2	6
Mansfield T	1	0	0	1	0	8
Morecambe	1	1	0	0	2	0
N Shields	1	0	0	1	0	3
Notts Co.	1	0	0	1	1	6
Oldham Ath.	2	1	1	0	3	2
Port Vale	1	0	0	1	1	2
Preston NE	1	1	0	0	3	2
Rhyl	4	2	0	2	11	5
Rochdale	1	1	0	0	4	2
Shankhouse	1	0	0	1	3	5
Southend U	1	0	0	1	1	4
Southport	2	0	1	1	3	5
Stockport Co	1	0	0	1	0	2
Tranmere R	1	0	0	1	2	4
Whitley Bay	1	0	0	1	0	1

	P	W	D	L	F	A
Wigan Ath.	2	0	0	2	0	6
Workington	2	0	0	2	4	7

SCUNTHORPE UNITED

	P	W	D	L	F	A
Accrington S	2	0	1	1	1	4
Altrincham	4	0	2	2	2	5
Barnsley	2	0	1	1	4	5
Billngham Syn	1	1	0	0	5	0
Blackpool	4	1	1	2	7	5
Bolton Wan.	1	0	0	1	0	2
Boston U	1	1	0	0	9	0
Bournemouth	1	1	0	0	1	0
Bradford C	2	2	0	0	2	0
Brighton &HA	1	0	0	1	2	3
Bshp Aukland	2	1	1	0	2	0
Burnley	3	0	2	1	3	8
Bury	3	3	0	0	7	1
Cardiff C	1	0	0	1	2	3
Carlisle U	1	1	0	0	1	0
Charlton Ath	1	0	0	1	0	1
Chesterfield	1	0	0	1	1	2
Coventry C	4	1	1	2	5	14
Crewe Alex.	2	1	0	1	3	4
Crystal P	1	1	0	0	1	0
Darlington	3	2	0	1	3	2
Gainsborough	1	0	0	1	0	1
Goole T	1	1	0	0	2	1
Grimsby T	2	0	1	1	0	2
Halifax T	5	3	1	1	7	4
Hartlepool U	5	3	2	0	6	2
Hereford U	4	1	2	1	4	6
Horden CW	1	1	0	0	1	0
Huddersfield T	2	0	1	1	1	2
Hull C	1	0	0	1	0	4
Lancaster T	1	1	0	0	4	2
Leeds U	3	1	2	0	6	4
Lincoln C	1	1	0	0	4	3
Liverpool	3	0	1	2	4	6
Macclesfield	2	1	1	0	5	3
Mansfield T	4	2	1	1	6	3
Matlock T	1	1	0	0	4	1
Millwall	5	3	2	0	7	2
Newcastle U	3	1	1	1	4	5
Northwich V.	1	1	0	0	2	1
Norwich C	1	0	0	1	1	4
Nuneaton B.	2	1	1	0	3	2
Port Vale	2	0	0	2	1	5
Portsmouth	5	0	3	2	5	10
Preston NE	2	1	0	1	2	2
QPR	1	0	0	1	1	4
Rochdale	7	3	2	2	10	9
Rotherham U	7	1	4	2	17	19
Runcorn	2	1	0	1	3	4
S Shields	2	0	1	1	5	6
Sheff. Wed.	3	1	1	1	3	6
Shildon	1	1	0	0	2	0
Skelmersdale	1	1	0	0	2	0
Southport	1	1	0	0	2	0
Stockport Co	4	1	1	2	4	4
Sunderland	3	1	1	1	4	4
Swindon T	1	0	0	1	1	3
Tottenham H	2	0	0	2	2	6
Tranmere R	5	2	2	1	7	9
Walsall	1	0	0	1	0	3

	P	W	D	L	F	A
Watford	1	0	0	1	1	2
West Brom	3	0	1	2	1	4
Workington	2	0	0	2	1	7
Wrexham	4	1	2	1	8	10

SHEFFIELD UNITED

	P	W	D	L	F	A
Aldershot	2	0	1	1	0	1
Altrincham	2	0	1	1	2	5
Arsenal	6	2	1	3	10	12
Aston Villa	4	1	1	2	6	8
Barnsley	3	1	2	0	3	2
Barrow	1	1	0	0	5	0
Birmingham C	5	0	2	3	4	9
Blackburn R	4	1	2	1	5	5
Blackpool	7	5	0	2	13	7
Bolton Wan.	7	4	0	3	9	20
Boston U	2	1	1	0	6	2
Bournemouth	1	1	0	0	2	0
Bradford C	1	0	0	1	1	2
Bradford PA	2	2	0	0	4	1
Brighton &HA	3	1	1	1	2	2
Bristol C	4	3	1	0	9	2
Burnley	12	4	4	4	16	16
Burscough	1	1	0	0	3	0
Burton Wan.	2	1	1	0	2	1
Bury	8	2	3	3	9	11
Cardiff C	2	1	0	1	2	3
Carlisle U	2	1	0	1	4	2
Charlton Ath	3	2	1	0	4	1
Chelsea	5	1	0	4	3	5
Chesterfield	2	0	1	1	1	2
Colchester U	2	1	1	0	5	3
Corinthian	2	2	0	0	7	1
Crewe Alex.	1	0	0	1	1	3
Crystal P	1	1	0	0	2	0
Darlington	1	0	0	1	0	1
Derby Co.	6	2	2	2	7	7
Doncaster R	2	2	0	0	5	1
Everton	6	4	0	2	6	5
Fulham	5	4	1	0	11	4
Gateshead	1	1	0	0	1	0
Grimsby T	4	1	1	2	5	4
Hartlepool U	1	1	0	0	1	0
Huddersfield	11	2	5	4	10	12
Hull C	2	1	1	0	3	1
Ipswich T	1	0	0	1	2	3
Leeds U	2	1	0	1	3	2
Leicester C	7	3	2	2	6	7
Lincoln C	4	3	1	0	8	1
Liverpool	7	3	3	1	11	9
Luton T	2	1	0	1	5	3
Maidstone U	1	1	0	0	1	0
Man. City	5	3	2	0	7	1
Man. Utd.	2	1	0	1	2	2
Mansfield T	5	1	2	2	5	6
Middlesbro	2	1	1	0	4	1
Millwall	2	2	0	0	7	1
New Brighton	1	1	0	0	5	2
Newcastle U	8	3	2	3	12	10
Newport Co.	2	2	0	0	6	1
Northampton	1	1	0	0	2	0
Norwich C	4	1	1	2	8	8
Nottm Forest	11	5	3	3	16	11
Notts Co.	3	2	0	1	8	12

	P	W	D	L	F	A
Oldham Ath.	2	1	1	0	3	0
Peterborough	1	1	0	0	3	1
Port Vale	3	1	1	1	4	4
Portsmouth	3	1	0	2	4	4
Preston NE	4	2	2	0	6	3
QPR	1	1	0	0	1	0
Sheff. Wed.	9	3	3	3	14	13
Southampton	4	2	1	1	5	3
Southend U	3	3	0	0	9	1
Stockport Co	3	2	1	0	5	2
Stoke City	5	2	1	2	6	7
Sunderland	7	1	1	5	7	12
Swansea	3	1	1	1	4	7
Swindon T	3	0	1	2	2	4
Tottenham H	4	2	1	1	9	6
Watford	6	4	1	1	8	9
West Brom	6	1	2	3	7	15
West Ham U	4	2	1	1	6	7
Wolves	11	3	3	5	16	18
Worcester C	1	1	0	0	2	0
Wrexham	1	1	0	0	5	1

SHEFFIELD WEDNESDAY

	P	W	D	L	F	A
Accrington	1	1	0	0	2	1
Arsenal	12	3	5	4	16	18
Aston Villa	2	1	0	1	3	3
Barnsley	3	2	0	1	4	3
Belper T	1	1	0	0	3	2
Birmingham C	3	1	1	1	5	4
Blackburn R	10	3	2	5	12	18
Blackpool	2	1	0	1	5	3
Bolton Wan.	8	5	2	1	15	7
Bournemouth	2	2	0	0	10	0
Bradford PA	4	1	0	3	7	6
Brighton &HA	3	2	0	1	6	2
Bristol C	2	0	1	1	1	3
Bristol R	1	1	0	0	1	0
Burnley	9	4	3	2	13	7
Bury	2	1	0	1	1	1
Cambridge U	3	2	0	1	4	6
Cardiff C	1	1	0	0	2	1
Carlisle U	1	0	0	1	0	3
Charlton Ath	1	0	0	1	1	2
Chelsea	13	2	5	6	17	18
Chester	5	2	3	0	8	4
Chesterfield	4	1	2	1	8	8
Coventry C	6	1	1	4	6	13
Crewe Alex.	2	1	1	0	4	2
Crusaders	1	1	0	0	1	0
Crystal P	3	1	2	0	5	4
Darlington	3	0	1	2	0	3
Darwen	1	0	0	1	2	5
Derby Co.	8	5	2	1	15	9
Everton	19	5	5	9	26	35
Fulham	3	2	0	1	5	3
Gateshead	3	1	1	1	7	4
Glossop	1	0	0	1	0	1
Grimsby T	1	1	0	0	5	1
Halliwell	1	1	0	0	12	0
Hastings U	1	1	0	0	2	1
Hereford U	1	1	0	0	1	0
Huddersfield	2	1	0	1	3	3
Hull C	1	1	0	0	4	3

	P	W	D	L	F	A
Ipswich T	1	0	0	1	2	3
Leeds U	3	2	1	0	6	2
Leicester C	2	1	0	1	5	3
Leyton O.	2	2	0	0	7	0
Lincoln C	1	1	0	0	3	0
Liverpool	1	1	0	0	1	0
Lockwood B	1	1	0	0	6	0
Long Eaton R	3	2	0	1	3	3
Macclesfield	1	1	0	0	3	1
Man. City	3	0	1	2	2	7
Man. Utd.	9	5	2	2	18	8
Mansfield T	4	3	1	0	11	0
Middlesbro	5	2	1	2	10	6
Millwall	4	2	2	0	10	5
New Brighton	2	1	0	1	4	2
Newcastle U	7	1	1	5	7	13
Newport Co.	1	0	0	1	2	3
Northampton	2	0	1	1	0	1
Norwich C	3	2	0	1	4	3
Nottm Forest	9	5	2	2	21	13
Notts Co.	7	4	1	2	15	12
Notts Rngrs	2	1	1	0	4	1
Oldham Ath.	5	4	1	0	19	7
Oxford U	1	1	0	0	3	0
Peterborough	1	1	0	0	2	0
Plymouth Arg	3	2	1	0	7	2
Port Vale	1	1	0	0	2	0
Portsmouth	4	2	1	1	8	5
Preston NE	9	2	3	4	10	15
Providence	1	1	0	0	2	0
QPR	1	1	0	0	3	0
Reading	2	1	0	1	3	3
Rotherham U	1	1	0	0	3	0
Scunthorpe U	3	1	1	1	3	3
Shef. Heeley	1	1	0	0	3	1
Sheff. Utd.	9	3	3	3	13	14
Shrewsbury T	2	1	1	0	3	2
Southampton	6	3	2	1	10	10
Southend U	4	2	2	0	6	3
Spilsby	1	1	0	0	12	2
Staveley	4	1	2	1	8	6
Stockport Co	1	1	0	0	2	0
Stoke City	6	2	2	2	8	6
Sunderland	7	4	1	2	5	5
Swansea	1	1	0	0	5	0
Swifts	1	1	0	0	6	1
Swindon T	2	2	0	0	4	2
Torquay U	2	2	0	0	8	3
Tottenham H	5	2	2	1	9	8
Tranmere R	2	1	1	0	5	1
Turton	1	1	0	0	2	0
Upton Park	1	1	0	0	6	0
West Brom	9	3	1	5	12	16
West Ham U	4	3	1	0	6	2
Wigan Ath.	2	1	0	1	2	1
Wigan Boro.	1	1	0	0	3	1
Wolves	8	6	1	1	13	9
Yeovil & P	2	1	1	0	3	2

SHREWSBURY TOWN

	P	W	D	L	F	A
Aldershot	5	1	3	1	8	8
Arsenal	3	0	1	2	1	4
Banbury Spcr	1	1	0	0	7	1

	P	W	D	L	F	A
Blackburn R	1	0	0	1	1	2
Bolton Wan.	1	0	0	1	0	3
Bradford C	3	1	1	1	3	3
Brierley HA	1	1	0	0	3	0
Bristol R	1	1	0	0	2	1
Burnley	3	1	1	1	3	3
Bury	2	1	1	0	2	1
Cambridge U	1	1	0	0	3	1
Carlisle U	3	1	2	0	5	4
Chelmsford C	1	1	0	0	6	2
Chelsea	2	0	0	2	2	4
Chester	1	1	0	0	3	1
Chesterfield	3	1	1	1	6	5
Chirk	1	0	0	1	2	10
Chorley	1	1	0	0	1	0
Colchester U	2	1	0	1	4	4
Crystal P	3	0	2	1	5	8
Darlington	1	1	0	0	3	0
Derby Co.	1	0	0	1	0	2
Doncaster R	4	3	1	0	10	5
Everton	2	0	0	2	1	5
Exeter C	2	1	0	1	3	3
Finchley	1	1	0	0	2	0
Gillingham	2	1	0	1	5	2
Gt. Yarmouth	1	1	0	0	4	1
Guildford C	1	1	0	0	2	1
Hartlepool U	2	1	0	1	7	5
Huddersfield	1	1	0	0	3	0
Hull C	1	0	0	1	1	2
Ipswich T	5	2	1	2	5	8
King's Lynn	1	1	0	0	1	0
Leeds U	1	0	0	1	0	2
Leicester C	1	0	0	1	2	5
Leytonstone	1	0	0	1	0	2
Macclesfield	1	1	0	0	3	1
Man. City	3	2	1	0	6	2
Mansfield T	3	2	0	1	6	3
Middlesbro	2	0	1	1	3	7
Millwall	2	1	0	1	3	6
Minehead	1	1	0	0	2	1
Newport Co.	1	1	0	0	4	1
Newport(IOW)	2	1	1	0	5	0
Oldham Ath.	1	1	0	0	3	0
Oxford U	1	0	0	1	0	2
Peterborough	2	1	0	1	6	6
Plymouth Arg	1	0	0	1	0	1
Port Vale	4	1	1	2	4	6
Portsmouth	1	0	0	1	0	3
QPR	7	2	3	2	10	9
Reading	2	0	1	1	2	3
Rossendale U	1	1	0	0	1	0
Rotherham U	1	1	0	0	2	1
Sheff. Wed.	2	0	1	1	2	3
Southampton	1	0	0	1	1	4
Southport	1	1	0	0	3	1
Spennymoor U	2	1	1	0	4	2
Stockport Co	5	1	3	1	8	8
Swindon T	1	1	0	0	1	0
Torquay U	4	2	1	1	5	7
Tow Law T	2	1	1	0	7	3
Walsall	3	1	0	2	8	9
Watford	1	1	0	0	4	1
Weymouth	1	0	0	1	0	1
Wigan Ath.	2	0	1	1	2	3
Wimbledon	1	0	0	1	0	1
Wolves	2	0	1	1	2	4
Wrexham	5	1	2	2	7	5

SOUTHAMPTON

	P	W	D	L	F	A
Arsenal	3	0	1	2	2	5
Aston Villa	4	1	2	1	6	6
Barnet	1	1	0	0	4	1
Barnsley	1	0	0	1	1	2
Barrow	2	1	1	0	5	2
Birmingham C	3	1	0	2	5	6
Blackburn R	2	2	0	0	4	2
Blackpool	6	3	1	2	11	8
Bolton Wan.	7	3	3	1	15	11
Bournemouth	2	0	1	1	2	4
Bradford C	3	2	0	1	4	4
Brighton &HA	3	3	0	0	4	0
Bristol C	4	1	1	2	4	4
Bristol R	3	2	0	1	5	3
Burnley	1	1	0	0	2	1
Bury	7	3	2	2	11	10
Cardiff C	4	0	1	3	2	6
Chelmsford C	1	0	0	1	1	4
Chelsea	7	4	3	0	11	3
Coventry C	5	2	2	1	9	5
Crystal P	6	2	1	3	5	5
Derby Co.	3	0	1	2	3	5
Everton	9	2	2	5	8	13
Exeter C	1	1	0	0	3	1
Fulham	1	1	0	0	3	2
Gateshead	1	1	0	0	3	1
Gillingham	3	2	1	0	2	0
Grimsby T	5	2	2	1	8	6
Heanor T	2	1	1	0	2	1
Hull C	3	0	1	2	2	7
Ipswich T	2	2	0	0	10	3
Leicester C	5	1	1	3	7	12
Leyton O.	5	2	1	2	6	4
Lincoln C	2	1	1	0	3	2
Liverpool	10	2	2	6	5	13
Luton T	2	1	0	1	4	2
Man. City	2	1	0	1	5	6
Man. Utd.	11	1	5	5	12	19
Middlesbro	3	2	0	1	9	3
Millwall	7	4	3	0	9	1
Newcastle U	7	5	1	1	14	6
Newport Co.	6	3	2	1	13	11
Northampton	7	2	3	2	10	7
Norwich C	3	1	1	1	4	2
Nottm Forest	14	4	5	5	25	26
Notts Co.	5	2	2	1	8	7
Oxford U	3	2	1	0	4	1
Port Vale	1	1	0	0	3	0
Portsmouth	2	2	0	0	6	1
Preston NE	1	1	0	0	1	0
QPR	4	2	0	2	6	5
Reading	1	1	0	0	1	0
Sheff. Utd.	4	1	1	2	3	5
Sheff. Wed.	6	1	2	3	10	10
Shrewsbury T	1	1	0	0	4	1
Southend U	2	1	0	1	3	3
Stoke City	1	0	0	1	0	1
Sunderland	9	2	2	5	11	16
Swindon T	1	1	0	0	3	0
Tottenham H	6	2	2	2	8	7
Walsall	2	1	0	1	3	3
Walton & H	1	1	0	0	6	1
Watford	4	2	1	1	7	5
West Brom	8	4	3	1	14	8
West Ham U	6	0	3	3	4	8
Weymouth	1	1	0	0	3	2
Wigan Ath.	1	1	0	0	3	0
Wimbledon	1	1	0	0	2	0
Woking	1	1	0	0	4	1
Wolves	3	1	0	2	3	7
Wrexham	1	0	0	1	0	1

SOUTHEND UNITED

	P	W	D	L	F	A
AP Leamingtn	3	2	1	0	6	1
Aldershot	1	0	0	1	0	2
Aston Villa	1	1	0	0	1	0
Aylesbury U	1	0	0	1	0	1
Barnet	1	1	0	0	9	2
Barnsley	2	0	1	1	3	4
Bath C	1	0	0	1	1	3
Birmingham C	2	0	0	2	2	8
Blackburn R	2	0	0	2	3	9
Blackpool	2	1	0	1	1	4
Borehamwood	1	1	0	0	3	0
Bournemouth	3	2	0	1	8	3
Bradford PA	1	1	0	0	3	2
Brentford	1	1	0	0	1	0
Brentwood T	1	1	0	0	10	1
Brighton &HA	3	2	0	1	4	3
Bristol C	2	1	0	1	3	4
Bristol R	3	2	1	0	5	1
Brush Sports	1	1	0	0	6	1
Burnley	1	0	0	1	0	6
Burton T	1	1	0	0	5	0
Cardiff C	1	1	0	0	2	1
Carlisle U	1	0	0	1	0	3
Chelsea	1	0	0	1	2	5
Chester	2	1	0	1	2	5
Chesterfield	3	1	1	1	6	6
Clacton T	1	1	0	0	3	1
Colchester U	3	1	1	1	8	6
Corinthian	2	2	0	0	5	0
Crystal P	2	1	1	0	3	1
Dagenham	1	1	0	0	1	0
Derby Co.	4	1	0	3	8	8
Dover	1	1	0	0	4	1
Dulwich Ham.	2	2	0	0	9	2
Eccles U	1	1	0	0	5	1
Everton	3	0	0	3	3	8
Exeter C	4	2	2	0	5	3
Finchley	1	1	0	0	3	1
Gainsborough	2	1	1	0	2	1
Gillingham	5	1	1	3	4	7
Golders Grn	1	1	0	0	10	1
Halesowen T	1	1	0	0	4	1
Harlow T	2	0	1	1	1	2
Hereford U	3	1	0	2	4	6
Huddersfield T	1	1	0	0	2	1
Ilford	1	1	0	0	2	0
King's Lynn	1	1	0	0	9	0
Leyton O.	2	1	0	1	4	3
Lincoln C	1	1	0	0	3	2
Liverpool	5	1	2	2	5	8
London Paper	1	1	0	0	4	0
Luton T	2	0	0	2	1	6
Man. City	1	0	0	1	0	1
Mansfield T	1	0	0	1	1	2
Millwall	1	1	0	0	1	0

STOCKPORT COUNTY

	P	W	D	L	F	A
Newport Co.	4	2	0	2	6	4
Northampton	3	0	1	2	6	10
Nottm Forest	1	0	0	1	0	1
Notts Co.	1	1	0	0	3	1
Oldham Ath.	1	1	0	0	5	0
Oswestry T	1	1	0	0	6	0
Peterborough	2	1	0	1	4	5
Plymouth Arg	2	0	1	1	0	2
Port Vale	1	1	0	0	1	0
QPR	5	1	2	2	6	7
Reading	2	1	0	1	4	3
Rotherham U	1	0	0	1	2	3
Scarborough	1	1	0	0	4	1
Sheff. Utd.	3	0	0	3	1	9
Sheff. Wed.	4	0	2	2	3	6
Southampton	2	1	0	1	3	3
Southport	1	1	0	0	5	2
Swansea	3	1	0	2	3	3
Swindon T	2	1	0	1	2	3
Torquay U	5	3	1	1	8	5
Tottenham H	3	0	1	2	6	10
Tranmere R	1	0	0	1	0	3
Trowbridge T	1	1	0	0	2	0
Walsall	2	0	1	1	1	2
Walthmstw Av	1	1	0	0	1	0
Watford	10	3	3	4	8	12
Wealdstone	1	1	0	0	1	0
Wellington T	1	1	0	0	1	0
Weymouth	2	2	0	0	8	0
Wimbledon	1	1	0	0	5	1
Worksop T	1	1	0	0	2	1
Wrexham	2	1	1	0	4	2
Yeovil T	4	1	1	2	3	2

	P	W	D	L	F	A
Accrington S	2	1	0	1	3	2
Aston Villa	1	0	0	1	0	3
Barnsley	3	2	0	1	6	4
Barrow	3	3	0	0	8	1
Billnghm Syn	1	1	0	0	3	0
Birmingham C	1	0	0	1	0	1
Blackburn R	1	0	0	1	0	2
Blackpool	2	0	0	2	2	4
Blyth S	4	2	1	1	9	6
Bolton Wan.	2	1	0	1	5	6
Bradford C	4	2	1	1	7	6
Bradford PA	1	1	0	0	3	0
Brentford	1	1	0	0	2	1
Bristol R	3	1	1	1	5	6
Bshp Aukland	1	1	0	0	2	0
Burnley	3	0	1	2	3	6
Burton Wan.	1	0	0	1	0	1
Caernarvon T	1	0	0	1	0	1
Carlisle U	2	0	0	2	1	3
Charlton Ath	1	0	0	1	0	3
Chester	1	1	0	0	4	2
Chesterfield	1	0	0	1	1	4
Crewe Alex.	3	0	1	2	0	4
Crook T	1	0	0	1	1	3
Crystal P	1	0	0	1	1	2
Darlington	4	1	2	1	6	7
Derby Co	1	0	0	1	0	2
Doncaster R	1	1	0	0	2	1
Everton	2	0	0	2	1	6

	P	W	D	L	F	A
Fulham	2	0	1	1	1	2
Gateshead	3	0	2	1	4	5
Gillingham	1	1	0	0	3	1
Glossop	2	0	1	1	1	2
Grantham T	1	0	0	1	1	2
Grimsby T	2	2	0	0	3	0
Halifax T	3	2	1	0	4	2
Hartlepool U	3	2	0	1	5	6
Hull C	5	2	2	1	3	2
Lancaster T	1	1	0	0	1	0
Leyton	1	0	0	1	0	2
Leyton O.	1	0	0	1	1	2
Lincoln C	3	1	0	2	5	7
Liverpool	5	0	1	4	3	13
Luton T	2	1	0	1	5	3
Macclesfield	3	1	1	1	4	3
Mansfield T	2	0	0	2	2	5
Middlesbro	1	0	0	1	0	2
Morecambe	1	1	0	0	5	1
Mossley	3	2	1	0	5	2
N Shields	2	2	0	0	10	4
Nelson	1	0	0	1	1	4
New Brighton	2	0	1	1	5	6
Newcastle U	1	0	0	1	0	4
Nottm Forest	1	1	0	0	2	0
Oswestry T	1	1	0	0	5	2
Oxford U	2	0	1	1	0	1
Plymouth Arg	1	0	0	1	2	3
Port Vale	2	0	0	2	1	5
Portsmouth	1	0	0	1	0	7
Preston NE	1	0	0	1	1	3
QPR	1	1	0	0	3	1
Rochdale	3	1	1	1	4	3
Rotherham U	2	1	0	1	1	1
Runcorn	1	1	0	0	1	0
Scarborough	1	0	0	1	1	2
Scunthorpe U	4	2	1	1	4	4
Sheff. Utd.	3	0	1	2	2	5
Sheff. Wed.	1	0	0	1	0	2
Shrewsbury T	5	1	3	1	8	8
Southport	5	3	1	1	11	6
Stafford Rgs	2	0	1	1	0	1
Telford U	4	1	1	2	3	5
Torquay U	1	1	0	0	3	0
Tranmere R	1	1	0	0	1	0
W Auckland	1	1	0	0	6	2
Walsall	2	0	0	2	1	4
Walthmstw Av	3	1	1	1	4	3
Wellington T	1	1	0	0	4	1
West Brom	1	0	0	1	0	5
West Ham U	3	1	1	1	4	4
Wigan Ath.	2	1	0	1	2	3
Workington	4	4	0	0	7	1
York C	1	1	0	0	3	1

STOKE CITY

	P	W	D	L	F	A
Accrington	1	0	0	1	1	2
Aldershot	3	1	2	0	3	0
Arsenal	8	0	2	6	8	18
Aston Villa	10	3	4	3	15	18
Barnsley	3	0	1	2	5	7
Birmingham C	6	2	2	2	10	8
Blackburn R	2	1	0	1	1	1
Blackpool	4	3	1	0	9	2
Blyth S	2	1	0	1	5	3

Bolton Wan.	5	1	1	3	7	10
Bradford PA	3	1	1	1	5	3
Bristol R	1	1	0	0	1	0
Burnley	7	3	1	3	15	9
Bury	9	2	4	3	13	18
Caernarvon W	1	1	0	0	10	1
Cardiff C	2	2	0	0	6	2
Casuals	1	1	0	0	3	0
Chelsea	2	1	0	1	5	4
Chester	2	1	1	0	3	2
Chesterfield	1	1	0	0	2	1
Coventry C	1	0	0	1	0	1
Crewe Alex.	3	0	1	2	6	9
Crystal P	1	1	0	0	1	0
Derby Co.	3	1	0	2	3	7
Doncaster R	1	0	0	1	0	1
Everton	7	2	1	4	6	15
Exeter C	2	1	1	0	3	0
Gainsborough	3	1	2	0	6	4
Gillingham	1	1	0	0	6	1
Glossop	2	2	0	0	8	4
Grimsby T	4	2	2	0	10	2
Halifax T	3	1	1	1	4	2
Hartlepool U	1	1	0	0	6	2
Huddersfield	3	1	2	0	4	3
Hull C	4	3	0	1	10	5
Ipswich T	5	2	2	1	3	2
Leeds U	2	0	0	2	1	4
Leicester C	9	2	4	3	14	16
Lincoln C	1	1	0	0	5	0
Liverpool	6	0	2	4	0	6
Luton T	2	0	1	1	3	4
Man. City	5	2	0	3	5	6
Man. Utd.	11	3	5	3	13	14
Manchester	1	0	0	1	1	2
Mansfield T	1	1	0	0	4	2
Middlesbro	2	1	0	1	4	5
Millwall	3	2	1	0	6	1
Newcastle U	5	0	1	4	6	12
Northampton	2	1	1	0	5	2
Norwich C	1	0	0	1	0	1
Nottm Forest	3	1	1	1	2	2
Notts Co.	2	0	0	2	0	3
O W'minsters	1	1	0	0	3	0
Oldham Ath.	2	1	0	1	5	2
Oswestry T	1	1	0	0	3	0
Over Wan.	1	1	0	0	2	0
Oxford U	2	1	1	0	3	2
Port Vale	6	3	2	1	9	7
Portsmouth	2	2	0	0	5	1
Preston NE	5	1	1	3	7	11
QPR	1	0	0	1	0	3
Reading	2	0	1	1	2	5
Rhyl	3	0	2	1	3	4
Sheff. Utd.	5	2	1	2	7	6
Sheff. Wed.	6	2	2	2	6	8
Southampton	1	1	0	0	1	0
Sunderland	9	2	5	2	10	12
Swansea	5	0	1	4	7	17
Swindon T	3	1	1	1	4	3
Telford U	4	1	2	1	2	2
Tilbury	1	1	0	0	4	0
Tottenham H	7	4	2	1	15	6
Tranmere R	2	1	1	0	4	2
Walsall	1	0	0	1	0	2
Watford	1	0	0	1	0	1
West Brom	4	0	2	2	4	9

West Ham U	4	2	1	1	4	5
Wigan Boro.	1	1	0	0	5	2
Wolves	7	0	1	6	5	21
Wrexham	1	1	0	0	2	1

SUNDERLAND

	P	W	D	L	F	A
Accrington	2	2	0	0	6	1
Arsenal	5	3	0	2	11	9
Aston Villa	9	1	1	7	11	24
Birmingham C	7	1	1	5	5	13
Blackburn R	7	0	3	4	5	14
Blackpool	1	1	0	0	1	0
Bolton Wan.	5	3	1	1	9	4
Boston T	1	1	0	0	8	1
Bradford C	1	1	0	0	1	0
Bradford PA	2	2	0	0	4	1
Brentford	1	1	0	0	5	2
Bristol C	2	2	0	0	10	3
Bristol R	1	0	0	1	0	1
Burnley	12	5	4	3	13	12
Bury	3	2	0	1	10	6
Cardiff C	5	1	2	2	5	7
Carlisle U	2	0	1	1	0	1
Chatham T	1	1	0	0	9	0
Chelsea	2	1	1	0	3	2
Chesterfield	2	1	0	1	3	2
Coventry C	3	2	0	1	5	3
Crewe Alex.	1	1	0	0	2	0
Crystal P	3	1	1	1	1	1
Darlington	1	1	0	0	2	0
Darwen	1	1	0	0	2	0
Derby Co.	4	1	2	1	9	7
Doncaster R	1	0	0	1	0	2
Everton	13	4	3	6	16	25
Exeter C	2	1	1	0	5	3
Fairfield	1	1	0	0	11	1
Fulham	2	1	0	1	4	6
Gainsborough	2	1	1	0	4	1
Gillingham	1	0	0	1	1	3
Gravesend &N	2	1	1	0	6	3
Grimsby T	2	2	0	0	5	2
Huddersfield	2	1	0	1	7	3
Hull C	3	3	0	0	9	2
Leeds C	1	1	0	0	1	0
Leeds U	5	1	2	2	6	7
Leicester C	2	1	0	1	4	2
Leyton O.	1	0	0	1	6	3
Liverpool	5	1	1	3	3	11
Luton T	6	4	2	0	11	3
Man. City	8	2	2	4	11	11
Man. Utd.	7	0	4	3	10	18
Middlesbro	5	2	2	1	8	7
Millwall	1	1	0	0	2	1
Morpeth H	1	1	0	0	3	2
Newcastle U	7	2	3	2	9	8
Newcastle WE	2	1	0	1	3	2
Newport Co.	1	1	0	0	2	0
Northampton	3	2	1	0	8	3
Norwich C	7	4	1	2	11	8
Nottm Forest	6	1	1	4	9	14
Notts Co.	7	4	2	1	13	6
Oldham Ath.	2	1	0	1	3	2
Oxford U	3	1	1	1	4	5
Peterborough	1	1	0	0	7	1
Plymouth Arg	3	3	0	0	8	2

	P	W	D	L	F	A
Port Vale	5	1	2	2	6	7
Preston NE	8	7	1	0	22	7
QPR	1	1	0	0	4	0
Reading	3	1	1	1	5	4
Redcar	2	0	0	2	1	6
Rotherham U	2	1	1	0	2	1
Scunthorpe U	3	1	1	1	4	4
Sheff. Utd.	7	5	1	1	12	7
Sheff. Wed.	7	2	1	4	5	5
Southampton	9	5	2	2	16	11
Stoke City	9	2	5	2	12	10
Swansea	3	2	1	0	6	2
Swindon T	1	1	0	0	4	2
Tottenham H	6	1	1	4	5	15
Watford	1	1	0	0	1	0
West Brom	3	0	0	3	4	8
West Ham U	3	1	1	1	4	4
Wimbledon	1	0	0	1	1	2
Wolves	8	2	4	2	12	9
Wrexham	2	0	1	1	2	3
Yeovil T	1	0	0	1	1	2

SWANSEA CITY

	P	W	D	L	F	A
Arsenal	3	1	0	2	3	4
Aston Villa	2	0	0	2	1	5
Barnsley	1	1	0	0	3	1
Barrow	3	2	1	0	10	5
Birmingham C	1	1	0	0	3	0
Blackburn R	3	2	0	1	3	2
Blackpool	1	1	0	0	2	0
Bognor Regis	2	0	1	1	2	4
Bolton Wan.	1	0	0	1	0	3
Brentford	2	1	1	0	4	3
Brighton &HA	2	1	0	1	2	3
Bristol C	3	0	1	2	4	10
Bristol R	3	0	0	3	1	6
Burnley	4	0	1	3	3	10
Bury	5	3	1	1	12	4
Cardiff C	1	1	0	0	2	1
Carlisle U	1	1	0	0	1	0
Colchester U	2	0	1	1	3	5
Crystal P	3	1	2	0	7	6
Derby Co.	1	0	0	1	0	3
Doncaster R	1	1	0	0	2	0
Enfield	1	1	0	0	2	0
Everton	1	0	0	1	0	3
Exeter C	7	4	2	1	14	6
Folkestone	2	1	1	0	9	4
Gateshead	2	1	1	0	4	3
Gillingham	3	3	0	0	9	2
Grimsby T	2	0	1	1	0	2
Halifax T	1	0	0	1	0	1
Hayes	1	1	0	0	1	0
Hillingdon B	1	1	0	0	4	1
Huddersfield	1	1	0	0	1	0
Hull C	1	0	0	1	0	1
Kettering T	3	1	1	1	4	4
Kidderminster	1	1	0	0	3	2
Leatherhead	2	1	1	0	2	1
Leeds U	1	0	0	1	1	2
Leicester C	1	0	0	1	0	1
Leyton O.	4	1	2	1	4	5
Leyton Wing.	1	0	0	0	2	0
Liverpool	6	1	1	4	2	17
Luton T	1	0	0	1	0	2
Mansfield T	1	0	0	1	0	2
Margate	1	0	0	1	0	1
Merthyr T	1	1	0	0	2	0
Middlesbro	1	0	0	1	0	5
Millwall	2	1	0	1	1	4
Minehead	1	0	0	1	0	1
Newcastle U	5	1	1	3	2	7
Northampton	1	1	0	0	3	1
Norwich C	1	0	0	1	1	2
Nottm Forest	1	1	0	0	2	1
Notts Co.	2	1	0	1	2	3
Nuneaton B.	1	0	0	1	0	2
Oxford C	4	2	2	0	11	6
Peterborough	3	1	1	1	3	3
Plymouth Arg	2	1	0	1	4	2
Port Vale	1	1	0	0	3	0
Portsmouth	5	1	1	3	5	9
Preston NE	2	1	0	1	3	3
QPR	2	1	0	1	3	2
Reading	3	2	0	1	8	4
Rhyl	1	1	0	0	6	1
Rotherham U	3	1	1	1	3	4
Sheff. Utd.	3	1	1	1	7	4
Sheff. Wed.	1	0	0	1	0	1
Slough T	1	1	0	0	3	0
Southend U	3	2	0	1	3	3
Stoke City	5	4	1	0	17	7
Sunderland	3	0	1	2	2	6
Telford U	1	1	0	0	6	2
Walsall	5	1	0	4	6	14
Watford	1	1	0	0	3	2
Wealdstone	2	1	1	0	5	2
Welling U	1	1	0	0	5	2
West Brom	1	1	0	0	3	2
West Ham U	5	1	2	2	2	4
Weymouth	2	1	1	0	3	1
Woking	2	1	1	0	7	5
Wolves	2	0	0	2	3	9
Wrexham	1	0	0	1	1	2

SWINDON TOWN

	P	W	D	L	F	A
Aldershot	6	4	1	1	17	3
Arsenal	4	1	1	2	1	3
Ashford T	1	1	0	0	5	0
Aston Villa	1	0	0	1	1	2
Barnsley	4	0	2	2	0	3
Bath C	2	1	1	0	8	6
Bedford T	1	1	0	0	2	0
Birmingham C	1	1	0	0	2	0
Blackburn R	4	2	0	2	6	3
Bolton Wan.	1	0	0	1	2	4
Borehamwood	2	1	1	0	2	0
Bournemouth	3	0	1	2	4	6
Bradford PA	1	1	0	0	4	0
Brentford	4	3	1	0	11	5
Brighton &HA	2	0	0	2	1	6
Bristol C	3	0	1	2	3	6
Bristol R	3	2	0	1	3	4
Bromley	1	1	0	0	7	0
Burnley	8	3	2	3	14	14
Bury	1	1	0	0	2	1
Cambridge T	1	1	0	0	4	1
Cambridge U	1	1	0	0	3	0
Canterbury C	1	1	0	0	1	0
Cardiff C	4	2	1	1	6	3
Carlisle U	3	1	1	1	4	4
Charlton Ath	1	0	0	1	1	2
Chelsea	5	0	1	4	4	15
Chester	1	1	0	0	4	2
Chesterfield	1	1	0	0	2	1
Clapton	1	1	0	0	3	2
Coventry C	2	1	0	1	3	3
Crystal P	5	3	1	1	7	5
Dagenham	2	0	1	1	1	2
Darlington	1	1	0	0	3	0
Dartford	1	1	0	0	1	0
Dulwich Ham.	2	2	0	0	10	1
Enfield	2	2	0	0	6	0
Everton	4	1	1	2	6	10
Exeter C	1	0	0	1	0	3
Farnborough	1	1	0	0	4	0
Farnham UB	1	1	0	0	10	1
Fulham	5	3	1	1	12	6
Gillingham	1	1	0	0	4	3
Grantham T	2	2	0	0	8	1
Grimsby T	2	1	1	0	3	2
Hastings U	1	0	0	1	1	4
Hendon	1	1	0	0	1	0
Hereford U	1	1	0	0	4	0
Hitchin T	2	1	1	0	4	2
Horsham	1	1	0	0	3	0
Huddersfield	1	1	0	0	2	1
Ilford	1	1	0	0	4	2
Ipswich T	2	1	0	1	5	4
Kettering T	3	1	1	1	9	5
Leeds U	4	1	0	3	3	9
Leyton O.	3	2	1	0	4	2
Lincoln C	2	2	0	0	6	3
Lowestoft T	1	1	0	0	6	0
Luton T	7	3	0	4	10	14
Maidstone U	1	1	0	0	3	1
Man. City	5	2	1	2	6	19
Man. Utd.	2	2	0	0	3	0
March Town U	1	1	0	0	2	0
Merthyr Tyd.	1	1	0	0	5	1
Millwall	1	1	0	0	3	2
Newcastle U	3	1	0	2	2	7
Newport Co.	4	3	1	0	10	2
Newport(IOW)	2	2	0	0	7	1
Northampton	1	1	0	0	2	0
Norwich C	6	1	2	3	4	7
Nottm Forest	5	0	2	3	2	10
Notts Co.	4	3	0	1	7	3
O Brghtnians	1	0	0	1	0	1
Oldham Ath.	1	1	0	0	2	0
Peterborough	2	1	1	0	3	2
Plymouth Arg	1	0	0	1	0	1
Portsmouth	4	1	2	1	6	5
Preston NE	1	0	0	1	0	1
QPR	4	3	0	1	6	6
Reading	3	2	0	1	8	3
Rochdale	1	1	0	0	2	0
Salisbury	1	1	0	0	4	0
Scunthorpe U	1	1	0	0	3	1
Sheff. Utd.	3	2	1	0	4	2
Sheff. Wed.	2	0	0	2	2	4
Shrewsbury T	1	0	0	1	0	1
Sittingborne	1	1	0	0	7	0
Southall	1	0	0	1	1	3
Southampton	1	0	0	1	0	3
Southend U	2	1	0	1	3	2

	P	W	D	L	F	A
Southport	2	1	0	1	2	3
Stoke City	3	1	1	1	3	4
Sunderland	1	0	0	1	2	4
Sutton Junc.	1	1	0	0	5	0
Sutton U	1	1	0	0	2	1
Swifts	1	0	0	1	1	7
Taunton T	1	1	0	0	2	1
Tooting & M	2	0	1	1	3	4
Torquay U	5	2	3	0	13	10
Tottenham H	3	1	1	1	4	4
Walsall	1	0	0	1	2	3
Watford	1	1	0	0	3	2
Watford R	1	1	0	0	1	0
Wealdstone	1	1	0	0	2	0
West Brom	1	0	0	1	0	2
West Ham U	9	2	4	3	14	12
Weymouth	1	1	0	0	3	2
Wimbledon	1	0	0	1	0	2
Wolves	1	0	0	1	0	2
Worksop T	1	1	0	0	1	0

TORQUAY UNITED

	P	W	D	L	F	A
AP Leamingtn	1	1	0	0	1	0
Accrington S	1	1	0	0	1	0
Aldershot	3	0	0	3	3	6
Aston Villa	1	1	0	0	3	1
Barnet	2	2	0	0	10	3
Barnsley	1	0	0	1	1	2
Barton R	1	1	0	0	2	0
Basingstoke	1	1	0	0	3	2
Birmingham C	2	1	0	1	4	7
Blackpool	1	0	0	1	0	1
Blyth S	1	1	0	0	3	1
Bognor Regis	1	1	0	0	3	0
Bolton Wan.	1	0	0	1	1	2
Bournemouth	4	1	2	1	5	6
Brentford	1	0	0	1	0	1
Bristol C	4	1	1	2	3	5
Bristol R	2	0	1	1	1	2
Bromley	1	1	0	0	3	2
Bury	2	0	1	1	2	3
Cambridge U	1	1	0	0	4	0
Canterbury C	1	1	0	0	6	0
Carshalton A	1	1	0	0	4	1
Chelmsford C	1	1	0	0	1	0
Colchester U	6	3	1	2	9	5
Coventry C	2	1	0	1	1	2
Dulwich Ham.	2	2	0	0	5	3
Ely City	1	1	0	0	6	2
Exeter C	2	1	0	1	3	2
Fareham T	2	1	1	0	5	4
Farnborough	2	0	1	1	4	5
Gillingham	4	1	2	1	8	5
Gravesend &N	2	2	0	0	4	1
Harwich & P	1	1	0	0	5	1
Hereford U	5	2	1	2	8	7
Hillingdon B	1	0	0	1	1	2
Huddersfield	1	0	0	1	0	1
Ipswich T	2	0	0	2	1	6
Leeds U	2	1	1	0	6	2
Leicester C	1	0	0	1	0	3
Leyton O.	3	0	0	3	2	7
Lincoln C	1	1	0	0	4	3
Maidstone U	1	0	0	1	1	4

	P	W	D	L	F	A
Margate	2	1	1	0	3	1
New Brighton	1	0	0	1	1	2
Newcastle U	1	0	0	1	1	3
Newport Co.	7	0	3	4	4	8
Northampton	7	3	1	3	14	11
Norwich C	1	1	0	0	3	1
Nottm Forest	1	0	0	1	1	6
Notts Co.	1	0	0	1	0	3
Nuneaton B.	1	0	0	1	0	0
Oxford U	2	1	1	0	3	2
Peterborough	6	2	1	3	8	12
Plymouth Arg	1	1	0	0	1	0
Port Vale	1	1	0	0	1	0
QPR	2	0	1	1	2	4
Reading	5	0	3	2	3	6
Sheff. Wed.	2	0	0	2	3	8
Shrewsbury T	4	1	1	2	7	5
Southend U	5	1	1	3	5	8
St. Albans C	2	1	1	0	5	2
Stockport Co	1	0	0	1	0	3
Sutton U	2	1	1	0	5	1
Swindon T	5	0	3	2	10	13
Tamworth	1	0	0	1	1	2
Tottenham H	2	0	1	1	4	8
Walsall	1	1	0	0	2	0
Watford	3	2	1	0	6	1
West Ham U	1	1	0	0	1	0
Weymouth	1	1	0	0	3	1
Wigan Ath.	1	0	0	1	2	3
Windsor & E	2	1	1	0	4	1
Yeovil T	1	0	0	1	2	5

TOTTENHAM HOTSPUR

	P	W	D	L	F	A
Altrincham	2	1	1	0	4	1
Arsenal	4	2	0	2	4	5
Aston Villa	11	6	1	4	12	8
Birmingham C	10	4	5	1	21	12
Blackburn R	9	2	4	3	11	15
Blackpool	5	2	1	2	10	7
Bolton Wan.	8	2	4	2	9	9
Boston U	1	1	0	0	4	0
Bournemouth	1	0	0	1	1	3
Bradford C	4	2	1	1	11	3
Bradford PA	2	1	1	0	2	1
Brentford	3	1	1	1	4	4
Bristol C	3	3	0	0	5	1
Bristol R	2	2	0	0	10	3
Burnley	7	4	1	2	13	10
Bury	1	1	0	0	2	1
Cardiff C	4	2	1	1	6	5
Carlisle U	3	2	1	0	7	4
Charlton Ath	3	2	1	0	6	4
Chelsea	7	4	1	2	11	7
Chesterfield	2	1	1	0	4	3
Coventry C	2	1	0	1	5	4
Crewe Alex.	3	2	1	0	20	5
Crystal P	4	1	1	2	4	3
Derby Co.	3	0	1	2	4	7
Doncaster R	1	1	0	0	2	0
Everton	9	4	1	4	13	11
Exeter C	1	1	0	0	2	0
Fulham	3	2	1	0	3	0
Gateshead	1	1	0	0	2	0
Halifax T	1	1	0	0	3	0

	P	W	D	L	F	A
Huddersfield	3	1	0	2	2	8
Hull C	6	3	3	0	6	1
Ipswich T	1	1	0	0	5	0
Leeds U	4	2	1	1	6	5
Leicester C	9	7	1	1	25	8
Liverpool	6	0	2	4	2	6
Luton T	1	0	0	1	0	2
Man. City	12	6	2	4	20	19
Man. Utd.	12	5	5	2	21	15
Margate	1	1	0	0	6	0
Marlow	1	1	0	0	5	1
Middlesbro	4	3	1	0	9	2
Millwall	3	2	1	0	3	1
New Brighton	2	1	1	0	5	2
Newcastle U	5	2	1	2	4	8
Newport Co.	2	2	0	0	8	1
Northampton	1	1	0	0	3	0
Norwich C	6	1	2	3	6	7
Nottm Forest	5	3	1	1	7	5
Notts Co.	4	2	1	1	8	6
Oldham Ath.	4	4	0	0	14	2
Oxford U	3	2	1	0	7	4
Plymouth Arg	4	3	1	0	14	3
Port Vale	2	1	0	1	5	4
Portsmouth	3	3	0	0	10	2
Preston NE	11	5	2	4	19	16
QPR	4	2	2	0	5	2
Reading	5	2	1	2	7	6
Rotherham U	1	1	0	0	2	0
Scunthorpe U	2	2	0	0	6	2
Sheff. Utd.	4	1	1	2	6	9
Sheff. Wed.	5	1	2	2	8	9
Southampton	6	2	2	2	7	8
Southend U	3	2	1	0	10	6
Stoke City	7	1	2	4	6	15
Sunderland	6	4	1	1	15	5
Swindon T	3	1	1	1	4	4
Torquay U	2	1	1	0	8	4
Tranmere R	2	1	1	0	10	2
W Stanley	1	1	0	0	4	0
Walsall	1	1	0	0	1	0
Watford	3	3	0	0	12	2
West Brom	9	5	1	3	15	11
West Ham U	10	5	3	2	26	14
Wimbledon	2	2	0	0	5	2
Wolves	4	3	1	0	8	3
Worksop T	2	1	1	0	9	0
Wrexham	2	1	1	0	6	5

TRANMERE ROVERS

	P	W	D	L	F	A
AP Leamingtn	1	1	0	0	9	0
Accrington S	2	1	1	0	7	3
Ashington	1	1	0	0	8	1
Bangor C	2	1	1	0	8	1
Barnsley	1	0	0	1	2	4
Barrow	2	0	0	2	1	5
Blyth S	4	1	3	0	9	5
Bolton Wan.	3	0	1	2	3	8
Boston U	1	1	0	0	2	1
Bournemouth	1	0	0	1	4	2
Bradford C	2	0	0	2	1	3
Bradford PA	1	1	0	0	3	2
Bristol C	2	1	1	0	5	4
Bristol R	1	1	0	0	2	0

	P	W	D	L	F	A
Bshp Aukland	2	1	0	1	9	3
Bury	6	2	2	2	7	8
Carlisle U	2	2	0	0	5	1
Charlton Ath	2	1	1	0	4	2
Chelsea	5	0	2	3	8	16
Chester	3	1	0	2	2	2
Chesterfield	3	2	1	0	6	2
Cleator Moor	1	1	0	0	5	0
Coventry C	2	1	1	0	3	1
Coventry Spr	1	0	0	1	0	2
Crewe Alex.	2	0	1	1	1	2
Darlington	1	0	0	1	1	2
Doncaster R	4	1	0	3	5	9
Durham C	1	1	0	0	3	0
Easington CW	1	1	0	0	2	0
Everton	1	0	0	1	0	2
Farsley Cltc	1	1	0	0	2	0
Gateshead	4	1	1	2	10	11
Goole T	1	1	0	0	4	2
Grimsby T	1	0	0	1	0	6
Halesowen T	1	1	0	0	2	1
Halifax T	2	2	0	0	5	2
Hartlepool U	4	2	1	1	7	6
Huddersfield	3	2	0	1	4	5
Hull C	1	0	0	1	0	3
Ipswich T	1	0	0	1	1	2
Leeds U	2	0	1	1	0	4
Leyton O.	2	0	1	1	3	6
Lincoln C	2	0	1	1	0	1
Liverpool	1	0	0	1	1	3
Mansfield T	3	1	1	1	8	8
New Brighton	1	1	0	0	3	0
Newark T	1	1	0	0	7	0
Northampton	2	0	1	1	1	2
Northwich V.	1	1	0	0	2	1
Nottm Forest	1	0	0	1	0	1
Notts Co.	4	2	1	1	6	6
Oldham Ath.	4	1	1	2	5	4
Oxford U	1	0	0	1	1	3
Peterborough	2	0	0	2	0	5
Port Vale	5	1	2	2	8	9
Portsmouth	2	1	0	1	3	3
Preston NE	3	1	1	1	4	2
Reading	2	0	1	1	2	3
Rochdale	9	3	3	3	16	14
Rotherham U	1	1	0	0	2	1
Runcorn	1	1	0	0	3	0
S Liverpool	3	2	1	0	9	2
Scarborough	1	1	0	0	4	2
Scunthorpe U	5	1	2	2	9	7
Sheff. Wed.	2	0	1	1	1	5
Shirebrook	1	1	0	0	3	1
Skelmersdale	1	1	0	0	4	0
Southend U	1	1	0	0	3	0
Southport	3	0	1	2	2	4
Spennymoor U	1	1	0	0	3	2
Stalybrdge C	2	2	0	0	5	1
Stockport Co	1	0	0	1	0	1
Stoke City	2	0	1	1	2	4
Telford U	2	1	1	0	3	2
Tottenham H	2	0	1	1	2	10
W Stanley	1	1	0	0	3	0
Wigan Ath.	2	1	1	0	2	1
Witton Alb.	1	1	0	0	2	1
Wolves	1	0	0	1	0	1

WALSALL

	P	W	D	L	F	A
Aldershot	1	1	0	0	2	0
Arsenal	2	1	0	1	3	4
Ashford T	1	1	0	0	3	1
Aston Villa	2	0	0	2	1	9
Aylesbury U	1	1	0	0	1	0
Barnsley	1	1	0	0	3	1
Bath C	1	1	0	0	2	0
Birmingham C	4	1	1	2	2	3
Blackburn R	2	0	1	1	1	4
Blyth S	1	1	0	0	2	1
Bournemouth	3	2	0	1	4	2
Bradford C	4	1	2	1	5	7
Bradford PA	1	1	0	0	1	0
Brentford	3	0	1	2	1	3
Brighton &HA	7	2	4	1	8	7
Bristol C	2	1	1	0	4	1
Bristol R	3	1	0	2	4	7
Burnley	1	1	0	0	1	0
Bury	2	0	0	2	0	7
Carlisle U	2	1	0	1	4	4
Charlton Ath	2	1	0	1	3	3
Chelsea	1	0	0	1	0	2
Chesterfield	7	4	3	0	7	2
Corinthian	1	0	0	1	0	4
Coventry C	1	0	0	1	1	2
Crewe Alex.	2	2	0	0	5	1
Crystal P	3	1	1	1	3	4
Dagenham	2	2	0	0	5	1
Darlington	1	0	0	1	0	1
Everton	1	0	0	1	1	2
Exeter C	2	2	0	0	4	1
Fulham	3	1	1	1	3	4
Gainsborough	1	1	0	0	4	3
Gateshead	1	1	0	0	4	0
Gillingham	2	1	0	1	4	3
Grimsby T	2	0	0	2	1	6
Halifax T	3	0	2	1	2	4
Hartlepool U	1	1	0	0	2	1
Hereford U	1	0	0	1	1	2
Huddersfield	2	0	0	2	0	4
Ipswich T	2	1	1	0	1	0
Kettering T	3	2	1	0	8	4
Leicester C	1	1	0	0	1	0
Leyton O.	5	2	2	1	6	4
Leytonstone	3	3	0	0	8	1
Lincoln C	4	1	2	1	5	4
Liverpool	3	0	1	2	4	10
Luton T	1	0	0	1	0	4
Man. City	3	0	0	3	1	6
Man. Utd.	4	1	1	2	3	4
Mansfield T	3	2	0	1	7	5
Margate	2	1	1	0	8	3
Middlesbro	2	0	1	1	2	6
N Shields	1	1	0	0	3	0
Newcastle U	2	1	0	1	1	2
Newport Co.	7	4	0	3	15	10
Norwich C	3	1	1	1	7	7
Notts Co.	2	1	1	0	4	0
Peterborough	2	0	0	2	3	5
Plymouth Arg	2	1	0	1	3	1
Port Vale	6	3	2	1	11	4
Preston NE	1	0	0	1	0	3
QPR	1	0	0	1	0	1
Reading	1	0	0	1	0	1

	P	W	D	L	F	A
Rotherham U	2	1	0	1	1	4
Scunthorpe U	1	1	0	0	3	0
Shef. Heeley	1	1	0	0	5	1
Shrewsbury T	3	2	0	1	9	8
Sittingborne	1	1	0	0	2	1
Southampton	2	1	0	1	3	3
Southend U	2	1	1	0	2	1
Southport	1	0	0	1	1	2
Spennymoor U	1	1	0	0	4	0
St. Albans C	2	1	1	0	4	2
St. Neots T	1	1	0	0	2	0
Stafford Rgs	1	1	0	0	3	0
Stockport Co	2	2	0	0	4	1
Stoke City	1	1	0	0	2	0
Swansea	5	4	0	1	14	6
Swindon T	1	1	0	0	3	2
Telford U	1	1	0	0	3	0
Torquay U	1	0	0	1	0	2
Tottenham H	1	0	0	1	0	1
Vauxhall Mtr	1	1	0	0	2	1
Watford	6	1	3	2	7	10
West Brom	2	0	1	1	2	7
Wolves	1	0	0	1	1	6
Worcester C	1	0	0	1	0	3
Wrexham	1	1	0	0	2	1
Yeovil & P	2	1	1	0	2	1
Yeovil T	3	0	1	2	1	3

WATFORD

	P	W	D	L	F	A
Aldershot	1	1	0	0	2	0
Arsenal	4	1	0	3	4	9
Aston Villa	1	0	0	1	1	4
Aylesbury U	1	1	0	0	5	0
Barnsley	1	0	0	1	0	2
Bedford T	1	0	0	1	2	3
Birmingham C	5	2	1	2	6	11
Blackpool	1	1	0	0	2	1
Bolton Wan.	1	1	0	0	2	1
Bournemouth	2	0	0	2	4	7
Bradford PA	1	1	0	0	1	0
Brentford	3	2	1	0	5	2
Brighton &HA	9	3	2	4	13	13
Bristol C	1	1	0	0	2	1
Bromley	3	2	1	0	6	3
Bury	2	1	1	0	4	1
Cardiff C	3	0	2	1	4	5
Carlisle U	2	1	1	0	6	3
Charlton Ath	1	1	0	0	2	0
Chelmsford C	1	1	0	0	1	0
Chelsea	2	1	0	1	2	5
Cheltenham T	4	3	1	0	10	0
Colchester U	3	2	0	1	3	1
Cor. Casuals	1	1	0	0	5	1
Corby T	1	1	0	0	2	0
Corinthian	1	0	0	1	0	2
Coventry C	2	2	0	0	4	1
Crystal P	2	1	1	0	4	0
Dagenham	1	1	0	0	3	0
Derby Co.	1	1	0	0	2	1
Doncaster R	1	0	0	1	1	2
Enfield	1	1	0	0	4	2
Everton	1	0	0	1	0	2
Exeter C	3	2	1	0	4	3
Fulham	4	2	2	0	7	3
Gainsborough	2	1	0	1	5	3

	P	W	D	L	F	A
Gillingham	2	2	0	0	3	1
Grimsby T	1	1	0	0	3	1
Guildford C	1	1	0	0	4	2
Harlow T	1	1	0	0	4	3
Hartlepool U	1	0	0	1	1	2
Hendon	1	1	0	0	2	0
Hereford U	1	1	0	0	3	0
Hillingdon B	1	1	0	0	3	2
Hull C	3	1	2	0	4	3
Ilford	1	1	0	0	3	0
Ipswich T	2	0	0	2	2	5
Leicester C	4	0	1	3	5	12
Leyton	1	1	0	0	2	0
Leytonstone	2	1	0	1	3	2
Liverpool	5	1	2	2	3	5
Lowestoft T	2	2	0	0	11	1
Luton T	6	2	3	1	11	9
Maidstone U	1	1	0	0	3	1
Man. City	3	1	2	0	4	2
Man. Utd.	4	1	1	2	2	4
Merthyr T	1	1	0	0	2	0
Middlesbro	1	1	0	0	1	0
Netherfield	1	1	0	0	6	0
Newcastle U	6	1	3	2	3	8
Newport Co.	1	0	0	1	0	2
Newport(IOW)	1	1	0	0	6	0
Northampton	1	1	0	0	4	1
Northwich V.	1	0	0	1	2	3
Norwich C	1	0	0	1	0	2
Nottm Forest	4	1	2	1	3	5
Notts Co.	1	0	0	1	1	4
Nuneaton B.	1	0	0	1	0	3
Nunhead	1	1	0	0	4	2
Oldham Ath.	1	1	0	0	3	1
Oxford U	2	0	1	1	2	3
Peterborough	2	1	1	0	3	2
Plymouth Arg	5	2	1	2	6	10
Poole T	2	1	1	0	4	3
Port Vale	5	2	2	1	6	3
Preston NE	5	2	1	2	7	9
QPR	1	1	0	0	2	1
Ramsgate	1	1	0	0	5	3
Reading	5	2	1	2	9	7
Romford	1	1	0	0	3	1
Rotherham U	4	2	1	1	4	2
Scunthorpe U	1	1	0	0	2	1
Sheff. Utd.	6	1	1	4	9	8
Shrewsbury T	1	0	0	1	1	4
Southall	1	1	0	0	4	1
Southampton	4	1	1	2	5	7
Southend U	10	4	3	3	12	8
Stoke City	1	1	0	0	1	0
Sunderland	1	0	0	1	0	1
Swansea	1	0	0	1	2	3
Swindon T	1	0	0	1	2	3
Thames	2	1	1	0	4	3
Torquay U	3	0	1	2	1	6
Tottenham H	3	0	0	3	2	12
Walsall	6	2	3	1	10	7
Walthmstw Av	3	1	1	1	7	4
Wellington T	2	1	1	0	2	1
West Ham U	2	1	0	1	2	1
Wigan Ath.	1	1	0	0	2	0
Wimbledon	1	0	0	1	1	2
Wolves	6	1	2	3	6	17
Worcester C	1	1	0	0	6	0

WEST BROMWICH ALBION

	P	W	D	L	F	A
Accrington	1	0	0	1	0	3
Arsenal	8	4	2	2	12	11
Aston Unity	1	1	0	0	4	1
Aston Villa	14	3	3	8	14	18
Aylesbury U	1	1	0	0	8	0
Barnsley	4	0	1	3	0	3
Birm.St.Grge	3	3	0	0	5	0
Birmingham C	8	6	1	1	16	7
Blackburn R	11	4	2	5	13	15
Blackpool	8	4	3	1	12	8
Bolton Wan.	8	5	2	1	16	5
Bournemouth	1	1	0	0	1	0
Bradford C	1	0	0	1	1	2
Bradford PA	4	1	2	1	8	4
Brentford	1	1	0	0	2	0
Bristol C	3	2	1	0	9	4
Burnley	1	1	0	0	5	1
Burton Wan.	1	1	0	0	6	0
Bury	2	1	0	1	3	6
Cardiff C	4	1	2	1	7	4
Carlisle U	2	1	0	1	5	4
Charlton Ath	7	2	2	3	10	11
Chatham T	1	1	0	0	10	1
Chelsea	10	4	4	2	13	11
Colchester U	2	1	1	0	5	1
Corinthian	1	1	0	0	5	0
Coventry C	5	3	1	1	12	6
Darlington	1	1	0	0	3	2
Derby Co.	8	2	1	5	8	12
Derby Junc.	3	3	0	0	12	2
Doncaster R	2	1	1	0	3	1
Druids	1	1	0	0	1	0
Everton	9	3	2	4	7	11
Fulham	3	3	0	0	9	2
Gateshead	2	2	0	0	5	1
Gillingham	1	1	0	0	1	0
Grimsby T	6	4	2	0	12	2
Huddersfield	2	0	1	1	2	3
Hull C	3	1	0	2	3	3
Ipswich T	3	0	1	2	2	7
Leeds C	2	2	0	0	3	0
Leeds U	5	2	1	2	7	11
Leicester C	2	0	0	2	1	3
Leyton O	3	1	0	2	4	4
Lincoln C	3	2	0	1	5	5
Liverpool	10	4	3	3	11	10
Lockwood B	1	1	0	0	2	1
Luton T	2	2	0	0	5	0
Man. City	4	2	1	1	7	3
Man. Utd.	6	2	3	1	11	7
Marlow	1	1	0	0	6	0
Middlesbro	3	2	0	1	2	1
Millwall	1	1	0	0	1	0
New Brghtn T	1	1	0	0	2	0
Newcastle U	3	2	0	1	4	5
Northampton	1	1	0	0	3	1
Norwich C	3	3	0	0	5	0
Nottm Forest	14	4	7	3	27	19
Notts Co.	6	3	1	2	12	8
O Crthusians	2	2	0	0	5	2
O W'minsters	2	2	0	0	9	2
Plymouth Arg	3	2	0	1	8	4

	P	W	D	L	F	A
Port Vale	2	2	0	0	4	2
Portsmouth	4	3	0	1	5	3
Preston NE	7	5	0	2	12	9
QPR	2	1	0	1	3	3
Reading	1	1	0	0	2	0
Rotherham U	3	2	1	0	7	0
Scunthorpe U	3	2	1	0	4	1
Sheff. Utd.	6	3	2	1	15	7
Sheff. Wed.	9	5	1	3	16	12
South Shore	1	1	0	0	8	0
Southampton	8	1	3	4	8	14
Spennymoor U	1	1	0	0	7	1
Stalybrdge C	2	1	1	0	2	0
Stockport Co	1	1	0	0	5	0
Stoke City	4	2	2	0	9	4
Sunderland	3	3	0	0	8	4
Swansea	1	0	0	1	2	3
Swindon T	1	1	0	0	2	0
Tottenham H	9	3	1	5	11	15
Walsall	2	1	1	0	7	2
Wednesbury OA	3	3	0	0	14	5
Wednesbury T	1	0	0	1	0	2
West Ham U	8	1	3	4	9	14
Wimbledon	2	1	0	1	3	4
Woking	1	0	0	1	2	4
Wolves	10	7	2	1	16	7
Wrexham	1	0	0	1	0	1
Wycombe W	2	1	1	0	3	2

WEST HAM UNITED

	P	W	D	L	F	A
Aberdare Ath	1	1	0	0	5	0
Aldershot	2	1	1	0	6	1
Arsenal	12	5	4	3	18	12
Aston Villa	3	1	0	2	1	8
Barnsley	1	0	0	1	1	4
Birmingham C	3	2	0	1	8	5
Blackburn R	7	1	3	3	11	16
Blackpool	8	3	2	3	12	15
Bolton Wan.	4	1	1	2	2	4
Bournemouth	2	1	1	0	4	2
Bradford C	1	1	0	0	3	2
Brentford	2	0	1	1	1	3
Brighton &HA	4	2	2	0	5	3
Bristol C	1	1	0	0	3	2
Burnley	2	2	0	0	6	3
Bury	1	1	0	0	6	0
Cardiff C	2	2	0	0	4	2
Carlisle U	2	1	1	0	6	1
Charlton Ath	5	5	0	0	9	1
Chelsea	5	1	0	4	3	9
Chesterfield	1	1	0	0	8	1
Corinthian	2	2	0	0	5	0
Crewe Alex.	1	1	0	0	1	0
Crystal P	3	2	1	0	5	1
Derby Co.	1	1	0	0	5	2
Everton	9	4	1	4	12	12
Farnborough	2	1	1	0	2	1
Fulham	4	2	1	1	6	4
Gainsborough	1	1	0	0	2	1
Grimsby T	1	1	0	0	5	3
Hereford U	4	1	2	1	5	4
Huddersfield	6	2	1	3	11	12
Hull C	2	1	0	1	3	3
Ipswich T	6	3	3	0	9	3

	P	W	D	L	F	A
Leeds C	2	1	1	0	3	2
Leeds U	3	1	1	1	5	3
Leicester C	1	0	0	1	1	2
Leyton O.	5	3	2	0	12	5
Liverpool	4	0	1	3	2	9
Luton T	6	2	2	2	11	11
Man. Utd.	6	3	1	2	10	9
Mansfield T	1	0	0	1	0	3
Middlesbro	3	1	1	1	4	4
Millwall	1	1	0	0	4	1
Newcastle U	5	0	2	3	5	9
Newport Co.	1	0	0	1	1	2
Norwich C	3	1	1	1	3	4
Nottm Forest	3	2	0	1	4	5
Notts Co.	1	1	0	0	4	0
Oldham Ath.	2	1	1	0	4	3
Plymouth Arg	2	1	0	1	2	3
Port Vale	4	2	1	1	8	6
Portsmouth	3	1	0	2	4	5
Preston NE	4	3	0	1	11	7
QPR	9	3	3	3	9	14
Rotherham T	1	1	0	0	1	0
Sheff. Utd.	4	1	1	2	7	6
Sheff. Wed.	4	0	1	3	2	6
Southampton	6	3	3	0	8	4
Stockport Co	3	1	1	1	4	4
Stoke City	4	1	1	2	5	4
Sunderland	3	1	1	1	4	4
Swansea	5	2	2	1	4	2
Swindon T	9	3	4	2	12	14
Torquay U	1	0	0	1	0	1
Tottenham H	10	2	3	5	14	26
Watford	2	1	0	1	1	2
West Brom	8	4	3	1	14	9
Wigan Ath.	1	1	0	0	1	0
Wimbledon	2	1	1	0	6	2
Wolves	1	1	0	0	5	1

WIGAN ATHLETIC

	P	W	D	L	F	A
Altrincham	1	1	0	0	2	0
Barnsley	1	0	0	1	2	3
Birmingham C	1	0	0	1	0	4
Blackpool	2	1	1	0	3	1
Bournemouth	1	1	0	0	3	0
Bradford C	2	1	1	0	4	2
Burton T	1	0	0	1	1	5
Bury	4	0	2	2	4	8
Carlisle U	4	4	0	0	16	2
Chelsea	3	1	1	1	3	7
Chester	1	0	0	1	1	2
Chesterfield	2	0	1	1	2	4
Coventry C	2	0	1	1	1	2
Darlington	1	1	0	0	5	0
Doncaster R	3	2	1	0	9	4
Everton	1	0	0	1	0	3
Gateshead	1	0	0	1	1	2
Gillingham	1	1	0	0	2	1
Goole T	1	0	0	1	1	2
Grimsby T	1	0	0	1	1	2
Halifax T	1	1	0	0	2	1
Hartlepool U	4	1	1	2	4	5
Hereford U	1	1	0	0	4	1
Huddersfield	1	0	0	1	0	2
Hull C	1	1	0	0	3	0

	P	W	D	L	F	A
Leeds U	1	0	0	1	0	2
Lincoln C	1	1	0	0	3	1
Man. City	1	0	0	1	0	1
Mansfield T	5	1	2	2	6	8
Matlock T	2	1	0	1	4	3
Millwall	1	0	0	1	1	4
Newcastle U	2	0	1	1	4	5
Northwich V.	3	2	1	0	5	3
Norwich C	1	0	0	1	1	0
Notts Co.	1	0	0	1	0	2
Peterborough	1	1	0	0	2	1
Port Vale	3	0	2	1	3	4
Rotherham U	1	0	0	1	1	2
Runcorn	2	1	1	0	5	1
S Liverpool	1	0	0	1	1	4
S Shields	2	1	1	0	3	1
Scarborough	2	2	0	0	6	0
Sheff. Wed.	2	1	0	1	1	2
Shrewsbury T	2	1	1	0	3	2
Southampton	1	0	0	1	0	3
Southport	1	1	0	0	2	1
Stockport Co	2	1	0	1	3	2
Telford U	2	0	1	1	1	2
Torquay U	1	1	0	0	3	2
Tranmere R	2	0	1	1	1	2
Watford	1	0	0	1	0	2
West Ham U	1	0	0	1	0	1
Whitby T	1	1	0	0	1	0
Wolves	1	0	0	1	1	3
Wrexham	2	1	0	1	2	4

WIMBLEDON

	P	W	D	L	F	A
Aston Villa	5	2	3	0	4	2
Bath C	3	1	1	1	3	6
Bedford T	1	1	0	0	2	0
Bexley U	1	1	0	0	5	1
Birmingham C	1	1	0	0	1	0
Bournemouth	2	1	1	0	3	2
Brentford	2	0	0	2	2	5
Bristol C	3	0	1	2	2	4
Bristol R	1	0	0	1	0	4
Burnley	2	2	0	0	4	1
Colchester U	1	1	0	0	2	1
Enfield	2	0	0	2	1	7
Everton	4	2	1	1	5	3
Folkestone	1	0	0	1	0	1
Fulham	2	0	1	1	1	7
Gillingham	2	1	1	0	4	2
Grantham T	1	0	0	1	1	2
Gravesend &N	3	2	1	0	5	1
Grimsby T	1	0	0	1	0	3
Hillingdon B	1	0	0	1	0	2
Kettering T	1	1	0	0	2	0
King's Lynn	1	0	0	1	0	1
Leatherhead	1	0	0	1	0	3
Leeds U	2	0	1	1	0	1
Leyton	2	1	1	0	2	1
Leyton O.	1	1	0	0	2	1
Liverpool	1	1	0	0	1	0
Luton T	1	1	0	0	2	1
Mansfield T	2	1	0	1	2	2
Middlesbro	2	0	1	1	0	1
Millwall	1	0	0	1	1	3
Newcastle U	1	1	0	0	3	1
Northampton	2	0	1	1	2	4

	P	W	D	L	F	A
Northfleet U	1	0	0	1	1	4
Norwich C	1	0	0	1	1	3
Nottm Forest	2	1	1	0	1	0
Nuneaton B.	1	1	0	0	1	0
Oldham Ath.	2	1	1	0	1	0
Peterborough	1	0	0	1	1	3
Portsmouth	4	1	2	1	7	4
Romford	1	1	0	0	3	0
Shrewsbury T	1	0	0	1	0	1
Southampton	1	0	0	1	0	2
Southend U	1	0	0	1	1	5
Sunderland	1	0	0	1	2	1
Swindon T	1	0	0	1	2	0
Tottenham H	2	0	0	2	2	5
Walthmstw Av	2	0	1	1	2	5
Watford	1	0	0	1	2	1
West Brom	2	1	0	1	4	3
West Ham U	2	0	1	1	2	6
Windsor & E	1	1	0	0	7	2
Woking	1	1	0	0	1	0

WOLVERHAMPTON WANDERERS

	P	W	D	L	F	A
Accrington	1	1	0	0	3	2
Accrington S	1	1	0	0	2	0
Altrincham	1	1	0	0	5	0
Arsenal	9	2	1	6	9	12
Aston Shakes	1	1	0	0	3	0
Aston Villa	12	3	5	4	17	19
Barnsley	1	1	0	0	3	1
Barrow	1	1	0	0	4	2
Birmingham C	2	1	0	1	3	3
Blackburn R	10	4	2	4	15	13
Blackpool	2	0	1	1	0	1
Bolton Wan.	8	2	2	4	6	10
Bournemouth	2	1	0	1	2	2
Bradford C	6	2	2	2	7	10
Bradford PA	2	1	0	1	3	4
Brighton &HA	1	1	0	0	3	2
Bristol C	1	1	0	0	1	0
Bshp Aukland	1	1	0	0	3	0
Burnley	1	0	0	1	0	3
Bury	2	1	0	1	2	1
Cambridge U	1	0	0	1	0	1
Cardiff C	3	1	1	1	4	3
Carlisle U	2	2	0	0	5	1
Charlton Ath	7	4	2	1	13	8
Chelsea	2	1	0	1	2	3
Cheltenham T	1	1	0	0	5	1
Chester	1	1	0	0	1	0
Chesterfield	1	1	0	0	6	0
Chorley	3	0	2	1	2	5
Coventry C	4	1	2	1	4	5
Crewe Alex.	2	1	1	0	6	3
Crosswells B	1	1	0	0	14	0
Crystal P	3	1	1	1	5	6
Darlington	2	2	0	0	9	2
Darwen	3	2	1	0	7	0
Derby Co.	11	2	3	6	13	21
Derby St.Lke	3	1	1	1	9	4
Everton	7	3	2	2	9	8
Exeter C	2	1	1	0	5	3
Fulham	1	1	0	0	1	0
Grimsby T	5	3	1	1	17	6
Huddersfield	5	1	2	2	6	7

	P	W	D	L	F	A
Hull C	4	2	1	1	5	3
Ipswich T	5	2	2	1	5	4
Leeds U	7	0	2	5	4	11
Leicester C	5	3	1	1	11	6
Lincoln C	2	2	0	0	3	1
Liverpool	5	3	0	2	10	6
London Caley	1	1	0	0	3	1
Long Eaton R	2	2	0	0	6	2
Lovells Ath.	2	2	0	0	12	3
Luton T	2	2	0	0	6	2
Man. City	3	2	1	0	7	3
Man. Utd.	7	2	2	3	11	14
Mansfield T	1	0	0	1	0	1
Matlock T	1	1	0	0	6	0
Merthyr T	1	1	0	0	1	0
Middlesbro	4	3	1	0	12	4
Millwall	2	2	0	0	3	1
New Brghtn T	1	1	0	0	5	1
Newcastle U	8	4	3	1	13	8
Norwich C	3	2	1	0	9	4
Nottm Forest	3	1	0	2	5	5
Notts Co.	6	5	1	0	17	8
O Crthusians	2	2	0	0	6	3
Oldham Ath.	3	1	1	1	6	4
Plymouth Arg	3	2	1	0	6	2
Portsmouth	4	2	1	1	9	7
Preston NE	4	0	0	4	2	13
QPR	2	0	1	1	1	2
Reading	2	2	0	0	6	0
Rotherham U	6	3	1	2	11	11
Sheff. Utd.	11	5	3	3	18	16
Sheff. Wed.	8	1	1	6	9	13
Shrewsbury T	2	1	1	0	4	2
Southampton	3	2	0	1	7	3
Stafford Rd	1	1	0	0	4	2
Stockton	1	1	0	0	4	1
Stoke City	7	6	1	0	21	5
Sunderland	8	2	4	2	9	12
Swansea	2	2	0	0	9	3
Swindon T	1	1	0	0	2	0
Tottenham H	4	0	1	3	3	8
Tranmere R	1	1	0	0	1	0
Walsall	1	1	0	0	6	1
Walsall S	2	2	0	0	4	2
Watford	6	3	2	1	17	6
Wednesbry OA	1	0	0	1	2	4
West Brom	10	1	2	7	7	16
West Ham U	1	0	0	1	1	5
Wigan Ath.	1	1	0	0	3	1

WREXHAM

	P	W	D	L	F	A
Accrington S	4	1	0	3	2	8
Altrincham	2	1	1	0	3	0
Arsenal	2	1	0	1	4	4
Bangor C	1	0	0	1	0	1
Barrow	3	2	0	1	9	8
Beighton MW	1	1	0	0	3	0
Birmingham C	1	0	0	1	1	3
Blackpool	2	0	0	2	2	8
Blyth S	4	3	1	0	7	3
Bolton Wan.	2	1	0	1	4	3
Bradford C	5	1	3	1	8	12
Brighton &HA	5	1	3	1	7	6
Bristol C	4	1	1	2	9	11
Burnley	1	0	0	1	0	1

Burton Alb.	1	1	0	0	2	0
Cardiff C	1	0	0	1	2	3
Carlisle U	6	2	1	3	5	7
Charlton Ath	1	1	0	0	6	0
Chelsea	3	0	2	1	2	3
Chester	1	0	0	1	1	2
Chesterfield	2	1	0	1	4	4
Colchester U	1	0	0	1	0	1
Crewe Alex.	5	2	1	2	10	13
Crystal P	1	1	0	0	2	0
Darlington	3	1	1	1	7	3
Durham C	2	1	1	0	5	1
Everton	1	0	0	1	2	5
Exeter C	2	0	1	1	2	3
Gateshead	2	1	0	1	6	5
Gateshead U	1	1	0	0	6	0
Gillingham	1	1	0	0	2	0
Goole T	2	1	1	0	2	1
Grantham T	1	1	0	0	4	1
Grimsby T	1	1	0	0	3	2
Gt. Yarmouth	1	1	0	0	2	1
Halifax T	3	2	0	1	10	3
Hartlepool U	3	2	0	1	3	3
Holbeach U	1	1	0	0	4	0
Horden CW	1	1	0	0	1	0
Hull C	1	0	0	1	0	2
Leicester C	1	0	0	1	1	2
Leyton O.	3	0	1	2	3	7
Lincoln C	3	0	2	1	5	6
Liverpool	2	0	0	2	1	6
Macclesfield	1	1	0	0	2	1
Man. Central	1	1	0	0	1	0
Man. City	1	0	0	1	1	3
Man. Utd.	1	0	0	1	0	5
Mansfield T	5	0	2	3	4	9
Marine	1	1	0	0	5	0
Middlesbro	1	1	0	0	1	0
Netherfield	2	1	1	0	7	3
New Brighton	3	1	2	0	6	4
Newcastle U	2	1	1	0	6	3
Norwich C	2	1	0	1	3	4
Nottm Forest	1	1	0	0	3	1
Notts Co.	2	0	1	1	2	5
Oldham Ath.	3	2	0	1	6	6
Port Vale	2	0	0	2	1	3
Preston NE	1	1	0	0	2	0
Reading	3	1	1	1	3	5
Rhyl	1	0	0	1	1	3
Rochdale	4	4	0	0	12	3
Rotherham U	1	1	0	0	3	0
Runcorn	2	0	1	1	4	5
S Liverpool	1	1	0	0	4	1
Scunthorpe U	4	1	2	1	10	8
Sheff. Utd.	1	0	0	1	1	5
Shrewsbury T	5	2	2	1	5	7
Southampton	1	1	0	0	1	0
Southend U	2	0	1	1	2	4
Southport	3	1	1	1	6	6
Spennymoor U	2	2	0	0	7	1
Stockport Co	1	1	0	0	6	2
Stoke City	1	0	0	1	1	2
Sunderland	2	1	1	0	3	2
Swansea	1	1	0	0	2	1
Swifts	1	0	0	1	1	3
Telford U	1	1	0	0	1	0
Tottenham H	2	0	1	1	5	6
Walsall	1	0	0	1	1	2

Wellington T	1	1	0	0	4	2
West Brom	1	1	0	0	1	0
West Ham U	5	1	3	1	4	4
Wigan Ath.	2	1	0	1	4	2
Wigan Boro.	1	1	0	0	2	0
Wimbledon	1	1	0	0	2	1
Winsford U	1	1	0	0	5	2
Wolves	2	0	0	2	2	12

WYCOMBE WANDERERS

	P	W	D	L	F	A
Ashford T	2	0	1	1	0	3
Barnet	1	0	0	1	0	2
Bedford T	7	1	5	1	11	11
Boston	2	1	1	0	5	1
Bournemouth	3	1	1	1	2	4
Bristol R	1	0	0	1	0	1
Burton Alb.	1	0	0	1	1	3
Cardiff C	1	0	0	1	0	1
Chelmsford C	3	1	1	1	3	2
Cheltenham T	1	1	0	0	3	1
Colchester U	1	1	0	0	2	0
Croydon	1	0	0	1	0	3
Dorchester T	1	0	0	1	2	3
Gillingham	2	0	1	1	3	5
Gravesend &N	1	0	0	1	1	3
Guildford C	2	0	1	1	2	3
Hendon	2	1	1	0	3	1
Kettering T	3	0	1	2	2	5
Maidenhead U	1	1	0	0	3	0
Maidstone U	1	0	0	1	0	1
Merthyr Tydfil	1	1	0	0	3	1
Middlesbro	2	1	1	0	1	1
Minehead	1	0	0	1	0	2
Newport Co.	1	1	0	0	3	1
Northampton	1	0	0	1	0	2
Peterborough	3	0	1	2	2	6
Reading	1	0	0	1	1	2
Slough T	2	0	1	1	1	2
Waterlooville	1	1	0	0	2	1
Watford	1	0	0	1	1	5
West Brom	2	0	1	1	2	3
Wisbech T	1	1	0	0	4	2

YORK CITY

	P	W	D	L	F	A
Altrincham	3	1	1	1	5	4
Arsenal	3	1	1	1	3	4
Bangor C	4	3	1	0	10	3
Barnsley	1	0	0	1	2	5
Barrow	3	1	0	2	4	4
Birmingham C	1	1	0	0	3	0
Blackpool	1	0	0	1	0	2
Blyth S	2	1	1	0	6	4
Bolton Wan.	4	1	1	2	4	6
Boston U	1	0	0	1	0	2
Bournemouth	1	0	0	1	0	1
Bradford C	3	1	1	1	3	3
Bradford PA	5	1	3	1	4	6
Bridlngtn Tn	1	1	0	0	2	1
Bshp Aukland	5	4	1	0	12	5
Burton Alb.	2	1	1	0	2	1
Burton T	2	1	0	1	4	7
Bury	4	1	1	2	3	4
Caernarvon T	2	0	1	1	1	2

Team	P	W	D	L	F	A		Team	P	W	D	L	F	A		Team	P	W	D	L	F	A
Cardiff C	3	1	2	0	5	3		Leyton O.	2	1	1	0	3	2		Scarborough	3	2	0	1	7	5
Carlisle U	1	0	0	1	2	5		Liverpool	4	0	2	2	3	12		Scunthorpe U	1	0	0	1	0	1
Chelsea	1	0	0	1	0	2		Luton T	1	1	0	0	2	0		Sheff. Utd.	2	0	1	1	1	3
Chesterfield	4	2	1	1	6	5		Macclesfield	2	1	1	0	2	0		Sheff. Wed.	2	0	0	2	2	11
Coventry C	1	1	0	0	3	2		Mansfield T	5	2	1	2	8	9		Southampton	3	0	1	2	5	11
Crewe Alex.	2	2	0	0	5	2		Middlesbro	5	1	2	2	4	9		Southend U	3	2	1	0	9	5
Crook T	1	1	0	0	1	0		Millwall	1	0	0	1	0	5		Southport	4	1	2	1	4	5
Crystal P	1	0	0	1	1	2		Morecambe	6	3	3	0	6	1		Stafford Rgs	1	1	0	0	2	1
Darlington	2	1	1	0	2	1		Mossley	1	1	0	0	5	2		Sockport Co	1	0	0	1	1	3
Derby Co.	1	0	0	1	0	1		Nelson	2	1	1	0	4	3		Stoke City	1	0	0	1	0	2
Doncaster R	1	0	0	1	0	1		New Brighton	2	1	0	1	2	3		Sunderland	2	0	1	1	1	2
Dorchester T	1	1	0	0	5	2		Newc. Blue S	1	1	0	0	2	0		Swansea	3	1	1	1	3	4
Dudley T	2	1	1	0	5	2		Newcastle U	4	0	2	2	3	6		Tamworth	2	1	1	0	5	0
Gateshead	1	0	0	1	1	3		Norwich C	2	0	1	1	1	2		Tottenham H	1	1	0	0	3	1
Gresley Rov.	1	1	0	0	3	1		Nottm Forest	1	0	0	1	1	3		Tranmere R	9	3	4	2	11	10
Grimsby T	3	1	0	2	6	6		Notts Co.	1	1	0	0	1	0		Walsall	1	1	0	0	3	0
Halifax T	5	2	1	2	6	5		Oxford U	1	0	0	1	0	1		West Brom	1	1	0	0	3	2
Hartlepool U	6	2	2	2	11	8		Rochdale	5	2	1	2	3	4		Whitby T	2	2	0	0	5	1
Hereford U	1	1	0	0	2	1		Rotherham U	5	0	3	2	5	7		Wigan Ath.	1	0	0	1	0	1
Huddersfield	2	0	1	1	1	2		Runcorn	1	1	0	0	2	1		Worksop T	1	1	0	0	4	1
Hull C	2	1	0	1	6	4		S Shields	3	2	0	1	10	4								

PART THREE

THE
GUINNESS
RECORD
OF THE
FA CUP

FA CUP FACTS
AND FEATS

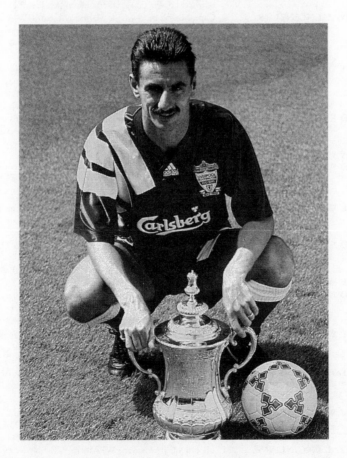

FA Cup Final Results and Line–ups

Capital letters like this [S] after a player's name signify that the player was a full international when the final was played. Small letters like this [s] signify that the player won a full cap after the final was played. Thus Billy Bremner, who was not capped until a few days after Leeds final against Liverpool in 1965, is shown as a [s] for 1965 but [S] for 1970 and thereafter.

The annotation 2–Keegan signifies that that player scored two goals in the match, while c–Robson signifies the captain. If 2–c–Robson is shown that means that Robson, the captain, scored twice.

Before 1921 Irish internationals are shown as [IRE] and after that date by [NI] and [RI]. Other countries' abbreviations used are shown at the end.

1871–72 THE WANDERERS .... 1 R. de C.Welch [e], c–CW Alcock [e], 1–MP Betts [e], AG Bonsor [e], EE Bowen, WP Crake, TC Hooman, E.Lubbock, AC Thompson, RWS Vidal [e], CHR Wollaston [e]

ROYAL ENGINEERS .... 0 Capt. Marindin, Capt. Merriman, Lieut. Addison, Lieut. Cresswell, Lieut. Mitchell, Lieut. Renny-Tailyour [s], Lieut. Rich, Lieut. Goodwyn [e], Lieut. Muirhead, Lieut. Cotter, Lieut. Bogle

1872–73 THE WANDERERS .... 2 EE Bowen, AC Thompson, R de.C.Welch [E], c–1–Hon. AF Kinnaird [S], LS Howell [E], 1–CHR Wollaston [e], JR Sturgis, Rev HH Stewart, WS Kenyon-Slaney [E], RK Kingsford [e], AG Bonsor [E]

OXFORD UNIVERSITY ..... 0 A.Kirke-Smith, AJ Leach, CC Mackarness, FH Birley [e], CJ Longman, FB Chappell-Maddison [E] HB Dixon, WB Paton, RWS Vidal [E], WE Sumner, CJ Ottaway [E]

1873–74 OXFORD UNIVERSITY ..... 2 CB Neapean, 1–CC Mackarness, FH Birley [E], FT Green [e], RWS Vidal [E], c–CJ Ottaway [E], RH Benson, 1–FJ Patton, WS Rawson [e], FB Chappell-Maddison [E], Rev AH Johnson

ROYAL ENGINEERS .... 0 Capt. Merriman, c–Major Marindin, Lieut. GW Addison, Lieut. GC Onslow, Lieut. HG Oliver, Lieut. T.Digby, Lieut. HW Renny-Tailyour [S], Lieut. HE Rawson [e], Lieut. JE Blackman [S] Lieut. AK Wood, Lieut. PG von Donop

1874–75 ROYAL ENGINEERS .... 1 Capt. Merriman, Lieut. GH Sim, Lieut. G.Onslow, Lieut. RM Ruck, Lieut. PG Von Donop, Lieut. CK Wood, Lieut. HE Rawson [E], Lieut. RH Stafford, 1–Capt. HW Renny-Tailyour [S], Lieut. Mein, Lieut. C Wingfield-Stratford [e]

OLD ETONIANS .... 1 AC Thompson, RH Benson, E.Lubbock, FH Wilson, c–Hon AF Kinnaird [S], JH Stronge, FJ Patton, CE Farmer, 1–AG Bonsor [E], CJ Ottaway [E], WS Kenyon-Slaney [E]

Replay ROYAL ENGINEERS .... 2 Unchanged. Scorers: Renny-Tailyour, Stafford

OLD ETONIANS .... 0 Capt EH Drummond-Moray, c–Hon AF Kinnaird [S], JH Stronge, T.Hammond, A.Lubbock, FJ Patton, M.Farrer, AG Bonsor [E], E.Lubbock, FH Wilson, CK Farmer

1875–76 THE WANDERERS .... 1 WDO Greig; A.Stratford [E], W.Lindsay, FB Chappell-Maddison [E], FH Birley [E], CHR Wollaston [E], H.Heron [E], F.Heron [E], 1–JH Edwards [E], J.Kenrick, T.Hughes

OLD ETONIANS .... 1 Q.Hogg; JEC Welldon, Hon.E.Lyttleton [e], AC Thompson, c–Hon. AF Kinnaird [S], C.Meysey, WS Kenyon-Slaney [E], Hon. A.Lyttleton [e], JR Sturgis, 1–AG Bonsor [E], HP Allene

Replay THE WANDERERS .... 3 Unchanged. Scorers: Wollaston, Hughes 2

OLD ETONIANS .... 0 Q.Hogg, E.Lubbock, Hon.E.Lyttleton, MG Faner, c–Hon. AF Kinnaird [S], JH Stronge, WS Kenyon-Slaney, Hon. A. Lyttleton, JR Sturgis, AG Bonsor, HP Allene

1876–77 THE WANDERERS .... 2 og–Hon. AF Kinnaird [S]; c–FH Birley [E], CA Denton, FT Green [E], H.Heron [E], TB Hughes, 1–J.Kenrick, 1–W.Lindsay [E], A Stratford [E], H.Wace [e], CWR Wollaston [E]

OXFORD UNIVERSITY ..... 1 EH Allington, J.Bain [E], OR Dunnell, JH Savory, AH Todd, EW Waddington, PH Fernandez, AF Hills [e], HS Otter, c–EH Parry [e], WS Rawson [E]. Scorer: Kinnaird og

1877–78 THE WANDERERS .... 3 J.Kirkpatrick; A.Stratford [E], W.Lindsay [E], 1–c–Hon. AF Kinnaird [S], FT Green [E], CHR Wollaston [E], H.Heron [E], JG Wylie [E], H.Wace [E], CA Denton, 2–J.Kenrick

ROYAL ENGINEERS .... 1 LB Friend; JH Cowan, WJ Morris, CB Mayne, FC Heath, CE Haynes, M.Lindsay, c–RB Hedley, FG Bond, HH Barnet [e], OE Ruck. Scorer: 'from a rush'

1878–79 OLD ETONIANS .... 1 JP Hawtrey [e], E.Christian, L.Bury [E], c–Hon. AF Kinnaird [S], E.Lubbock, 1–CJ Clerke, N.Pares, HC Goodhart [e], H.Whitfield [E], JBY Chevalier, H.Beaufoy

    CLAPHAM ROVERS .... 0 RH Birkett; c–RA Ogilvie [E], E.Field [E], NC Bailey [E], JFM Prinsep [e], FL Rawson, AJ Stanley, SW Scott, HS Bevington, EF Growse, C.Keith-Falconer

1879–80 CLAPHAM ROVERS .... 1 RH Birkett [E], c–RA Ogilvie [E], E.Field [E], V.Weston, NC Bailey [E], AJ Stanley, H.Brougham, FJ Sparkes [E], F.Barry, EA Ram, 1–C.Lloyd-Jones

    OXFORD UNIVERSITY ..... 0 PC Parr [e]; CW Wilson [E], CJS King, FAH Phillips, B.Rogers, RT Heygate (c), GB Childs, J.Eyre, FD Crowdy, EH Hill, JB Lubbock

1880–81 OLD CARTHUSIANS .... 3 LF Gillett; WH Norris, EG Colvin, JFM Prinsep [E], AJ Vintcent, WE Hansell, LM Richards, 1–WR Page, 1–EG Wynyard, 1–c–EH Parry [E], AH Todd

    OLD ETONIANS .... 0 JFP Rawlinson [e]; CW Foley, CH French, c–Hon AF Kinnaird [S], RB Farrer, RH Macauley [E], HC Goodhart [e], H.Whitfield [E], PC Novelli, WJ Anderson, JBT Chevallier

1881–82 OLD ETONIANS .... 1 JFP Rawlinson [E]; TH French, PJ de Paravicini, c–Hon AF Kinnaird [S], CW Foley, PC Novelli, ATB Dunn [e], 1–RH Macauley [E], HC Goodhart [e], JBT Chevallier, WJ Anderson

    BLACKBURN ROVERS ...... 0 R.Howarth; H.McIntyre [S], F.Suter, c–F.Hargreaves, H.Sharples, J.Hargreaves, G.Avery, J.Brown [E] T.Strachan, J.Douglas [S], J.Duckworth

1882–83 BLACKBURN OLYMPIC .... 2 T.Hacking, JT Ward, c–SA Warburton, T.Gibson, W.Astley, J.Hunter [E], T.Dewhurst, 1–A.Matthews, G.Wilson, 1–J.Crossley, J.Yates [e]

    OLD ETONIANS .... 1 JFP Rawlinson [E]; TH French, PJ de Paravicini, c–Hon.AF Kinnaird [S], CW Foley, ATB Dunn [E] HW Bainbridge, JBT Chevallier, WJ Anderson, 1–HC Goodhart [E], RH Macauley [E]

1883–84 BLACKBURN ROVERS ...... 2 Arthur [e]; Suter, Beverley [E], c–McIntyre [S], 1–Forrest [E], J.Hargreaves, Brown [E], Inglis [S] 1–Sowerbutts, Douglas [S], Lofthouse [e]

    QUEEN'S PARK .... 1 Gillespie [S]; McDonald [s], Arnott [S], Gow [s], c–Campbell [S], Allan, Harrower [S] Dr J.Smith [S], W.Anderson [S], Watt [s], 1–Christie [S]

1884–85 BLACKBURN ROVERS ...... 2 Arthur [E]; Turner, Suter, Haworth [e], McIntyre [S], 1–Forrest [E], Sowerbutts, Lofthouse [E] Douglas [S], 1–c–Brown [E], Fecitt

    QUEEN'S PARK .... 0 Gillespie [S]; Arnott [S], MacLeod, McDonald [s], c–Campbell [S], Sellar [S], Anderson [S] McWhannel, Hamilton [S], Allan, Gray [s]

1885–86 BLACKBURN ROVERS ...... 0 Arthur [E]; Turner, Suter, Heyes, Forrest [E], McIntyre [S], Douglas [S], Strachan, Sowerbutts, Fecitt, c–Brown [E]

    WEST BROMWICH A .... 0 Roberts [e]; H.Green, H.Bell, Horton, C.Perry [e], Timmins, Woodhall [e], T.Green, c–Bayliss, Loach, G.Bell

Replay BLACKBURN ROVERS ...... 2 Walton replaced Heyes. Scorers: Brown, Sowerbutts

    WEST BROMWICH A .... 0 unchanged

1886–87 ASTON VILLA .... 2 Warner; Coulton, Simonds, Yates, Dawson, Burton, Davis, Brown, 1–c–Hunter, Vaughton [E] 1–Hodgetts [e]

    WEST BROMWICH A .... 0 Roberts [E]; H.Green, Aldridge, Horton, C.Perry [e], Timmins, Woodhall [e], T.Green, c–Bayliss, Paddock, Pearson

1887–88 WEST BROMWICH A .... 2 Roberts [E]; Aldridge [e], H.Green, Horton, C.Perry [e], Timmins, 1–Woodhall [E], Bassett [e] 1–c–Bayliss, Wilson, Pearson

    PRESTON NE .... 1 Dr RH Mills–Roberts [W]; Howarth [E], Holmes [e], NJ Ross, Russell [s], Gordon, J.Ross, Goodall [E], 1–Dewhurst [E], Drummond, Graham [S]

1888–89 PRESTON NE .... 3 Dr RH Mills-Roberts [W]; Howarth [E], Holmes [E], Drummond, Russell [s], Graham [S], Gordon, Goodall [E], 1–c–Dewhurst [E], 1–Thomson, 1–J.Ross

    WOLVERHAMPTON W ..... 0 Baynton; Baugh [E], Mason [E], Fletcher [E], Allen [E], Lowder [E], Hunter, Wykes, c–Brodie [e], Wood [e], Knight

1889–90 BLACKBURN ROVERS ...... 6 JK Horne; James Southworth, Forbes [S], Barton [E], Dewar [S], Forrest [E], 1–Lofthouse [E] Campbell [S], 1–John Southworth, 1–

Walton [E], 3–Townley [E]

SHEFFIELD WED .... 1 Smith, Morley, Brayshaw [E], Dungworth, Betts [E], Waller, Ingram, Woodhouse, Bennett, 1–Mumford, Cawley

1890–91 BLACKBURN ROVERS ...... 3 Pennington; Brandon [s], c–Forbes [S], Barton [E], 1–Dewar [S], Forrest [E], Lofthouse [E] Walton, 1–John Southworth, Hall, 1–Townley [E]

NOTTS COUNTY .... 1 Thraves; Ferguson, Hendry, H.Osborne, Calderhead [S], Shelton [E], McGregror, McInnes, 1–c–Oswald [S], Locker, HB Daft [E]

1891–92 WEST BROMWICH A .... 3 Reader [e]; Nicholson, McCulloch, 1–Reynolds [E/IRE], c–C.Perry, Groves [S], Bassett [E], McLeod, 1–Nicholls, Pearson, 1–Geddes

ASTON VILLA .... 0 Warner; Evans, Cox, H.Devey, James Cowan [s], Baird, Athersmith [E], J.Devey [E], c–Dickson [S] Hodgetts [E], Campbell

1892–93 WOLVERHAMPTON W ..... 1 Rose [E]; Baugh [E], Swift, Malpass, 1–c–Allen [E], Kinsey [E], Topham [E], Wykes, Butcher, Griffin, Wood [E]

EVERTON .... 0 Williams; Kelso, Howarth [E], Boyle, Holt [E], Stewart, Latta, Gordon, Maxwell, E.Chadwick [E] Milward [E]

1893–94 NOTTS COUNTY .... 4 Toone [E]; Harper, Hendrey, Bramley, c–Calderhead [S], Shelton [E], 1–Watson, Donnelly, 3–Logan [S] Bruce [S], HB Daft [E]

BOLTON WANDERERS .... 1 Sutcliffe [E]; Somerville, c–Jones [W], Gardiner, Paton, Hughes, Tannahill, Wilson, 1–Cassidy, Bentley, Dickenson

1894–95 ASTON VILLA .... 1 Wilkes; Spencer [e], Walford, Reynolds [E/IRE], James Cowan [s], Russell, Athersmith [E] 1–Chatt, J.Devey [E], Hodgetts [E], Smith [E]

WEST BROMWICH A .... 0 Reader [E]; Williams [e], Horton, T.Perry [e], Higgins, Taggart [s], Bassett [E], McLeod, Richards, Hutchinson, Banks

1895–96 SHEFFIELD WED .... 2 Massey; Earp, Langley, Brandon, Crawshaw [E], Petrie, Brash, Brady, Bell, D Davis, 2–Spiksley [E]

WOLVERHAMPTON W ..... 1 Tennant; Baugh [E], Dunn, Owen, Malpass, Griffiths, Tanks, Henderson, Beats [e] Wood [E], 1–Black [S]

1896–97 ASTON VILLA .... 3 Whitehouse; Spencer [E], Reynolds [E/IRE], Evans, James Cowan [S], 1–Crabtree [E], Athersmith [E] J.Devey [E], 1–Campbell, 1–Wheldon [E], John Cowan

EVERTON .... 2 Menham; Meechan [S], Storrier [s], 1–Boyle, Holt [E], Stewart, Taylor [S], 1–Bell [S], Hartley, E.Chadwick [E], Milward [E]

1897–98 NOTTINGHAM FOREST ... 3 Allsop; Ritchie, Scott, c–Forman, 1–McPherson [S], Wragg, McInnes [S], Richards [E], Benbow, 2–Capes, Spouncer [e]

DERBY COUNTY .... 1 Fryer; Methven, Leiper, Cox [E], A.Goodall [ire], Turner, J.Goodall, 1–Bloomer [E], Boag, Stevenson, McQueen

1898–99 SHEFFIELD UNITED .... 4 Foulke [E]; Thickett [E], Boyle [ire], Johnson [e], Morren [E], Needham [E], 1–Bennett, 1–Beers, Hedley [e], 1–Almond, 1–Priest [e]

DERBY COUNTY .... 1 Fryer; Methven, Staley, Cox [E], Paterson, May [s], Arkesden, Bloomer [E], 1–Boag, McDonald, Allen

1899–00 BURY .... 4 Thompson; Darroch, Davidson, Pray, Leeming, Ross, Richards, 1–Wood, 2–McLuckie, Sagar [E], 1–Plant [E]

SOUTHAMPTON .... 0 Robinson [E]; Meechan [S], Durber, Meston, A.Chadwick [E], Petrie, Turner [E], Yates, Farrell, Wood [E], Milward [E]

1900–01 TOTTENHAM HOTSPUR . 2 Clawley; Erentz, Tait, Morris, Hughes [W], c–Jones [W], Smith, Cameron [S], 2–Brown, Copeland, Kirwan [IRE]

SHEFFIELD UNITED .... 2 Foulke [E]; Thickett [E], Boyle [IRE], Johnson [E], Morren [E], c–Needham [E], 1–Bennett [E], Field, Hedley [E], 1–Priest [E], Lipsham [e]

replay TOTTENHAM HOTSPUR . 3 Unchanged. Scorers: Cameron, Smith, Brown
SHEFFIELD UNITED .... 1 Unchanged. Scorer: Priest

1901–02 SHEFFIELD UNITED .... 1 Foulke [E]; Thickett [E], Boyle [IRE], c–Needham [E], Wilkinson [e], Johnson [E], Bennett [E] 1–Common [e], Hedley [E], Priest [E], Lipsham [E]

SOUTHAMPTON .... 1 Robinson [E]; CB Fry [E], Molyneux [e], Meston, Bowman, Lee [e], A.Turner [E], 1–c–Wood [E] Brown, E.Chadwick [E], J.Turner.

replay SHEFFIELD UNITED .... 2 Barnes for Bennett [E]. Scorers: Hedley, Barnes
SOUTHAMPTON .... 1 Unchanged. Scorer: Brown

The winning goal in the 1911 Cup final replay at Old Trafford, scored by Jimmy Speirs of Bradford City

1902–03 BURY .... **6** Monteith; Lindsey, McEwen, Johnstone, Thorpe, 1–c–Ross, Richards, 1–Wood, 1–Sagar [E] 2–Leeming, 1–Plant [E]

DERBY COUNTY .... **0** Fryer; Methven, Morris [W], Warren [e], A.Goodall [IRE], May [s], Warrington, York, Boag, Richards [e], Davis [e]

1903–04 MANCHESTER CITY .... **1** Hillman [E]; McMahon, Burgess [E], Frost, Hynds, Ashworth, 1–Meredith [W], Livingstone [s], Gillespie, A.Turnbull, Booth [e]

BOLTON WANDERERS .... **0** Davies; Brown, Struthers, Clifford, Greenhalgh, Freebairn, Stokes, Marsh, Yenson, White [s], Taylor

1904–05 ASTON VILLA .... **2** George [E]; c–Spencer [E], Miles, Pearson, Leake [E], Windmill, Brawn [E], Garratty [E], 2–Hampton [e], Bache [E], Hall [e]

NEWCASTLE UNITED .... **0** Lawrence [s]; McCombie [S], Carr [E], Gardner, Aitken [S], McWilliam [S], Rutherford [E], Howie [S], Appleyard, Veitch [e], Gosnell [e]

1905–06 EVERTON .... **1** Scott [IRE]; Crelley, W.Balmer [E], Makepeace [E], Taylor [S], Abbott [E], Sharp [E], Bolton, 1–Young [S], Settle [S], H. Hardman

NEWCASTLE UNITED .... **0** Lawrence [s]; McCombie [S], Carr [E], Gardner, Aitken, McWilliam [S], Rutherford [E], Howie [S], Orr [S], Veitch [E], Gosnell [E]

1906–07 SHEFFIELD WED .... **2** Lyall [S]; Layton, Burton, Brittleton [e], Crawshaw [E], Bartlett, Chapman, Bradshaw [e] Wilson [S], 1–Stewart [E], 1–Simpson

EVERTON .... **1** Scott [IRE]; W.Balmer [E], R.Balmer, Makepeace [E], Taylor [S], Abbott [E], 1–Sharp [E] Bolton, Young [S], Settle [E], H.Hardman

1907–08 WOLVERHAMPTON W ..... **3** Lunn; Jones, Collins, 1–Rev KRG Hunt [e], Wooldridge, Bishop, 1–Harrison, Shelton, 1–Hedley [E] Radford, Pedley

NEWCASTLE UNITED .... **1** Lawrence [s]; McCracken [IRE], Pudan, Gardner, Veitch [E], McWilliam [S], Rutherford [E] 1–Howie [S], Appleyard, Speedie, Wilson [S]

1908–09 MANCHESTER UNITED ... **1** Moger; Stacey, Hayes, Duckworth, c–Roberts [E], Bell, Meredith [W], Halse [e], J.Turnbull, 1–A.Turnbull, Wall [E]

BRISTOL CITY .... **0** Clay; Annan, Cottle [E], Hanlin, Wedlock [E], Spear, Staniforth, Hardy, Gilligan, Burton, Hilton

1909–10 NEWCASTLE UNITED .... **1** Lawrence [s]; McCracken [IRE], Whitson, c–Veitch [E], Low [s], McWilliam [S], 1–Rutherford [E] Howie [S], Higgins [S], Shepherd [E], Wilson [S]

BARNSLEY .... **1** Mearns; Downs [e], Ness, Glendinning, c–Boyle [e], Utley [e], 1–Tufnell, Lillycrop, Gadsby, Forman, Bartrop

replay NEWCASTLE UNITED .... **2** Carr [E] replaced Whitson. Scorer: Shepherd 2 (1p)
BARNSLEY .... **0** Unchanged

1910–11 BRADFORD CITY .... **0** Mellors; Campbell, Taylor, Robinson, Gildea, McDonald, Logan, Speirs [S], O'Rourke [S], Devine [S], Thompson

NEWCASTLE UNITED .... **0** Lawrence [S]; McCracken [IRE], Whitson, c–Veitch [E], Low [S], Willis, Rutherford [E], Jobey, Stewart [E], Higgins [S], Wilson [S]

replay BRADFORD CITY .... **1** Torrance replaced Gildea. Scorer: Speirs
NEWCASTLE UNITED .... **0** Unchanged

1911–12 BARNSLEY .... 0 Copper; Downs [e], Taylor, Glendinning, Bratley, Utley [e], Bartrop, Tufnell, Lillycrop, Travers, Moore

WEST BROMWICH A .... 0 Pearson; Cook, Pennington [E], Baddeley, Buck, McNeal [e], Jephcott, Wright, Pailor, Bowser [e], Shearman

replay **BARNSLEY** .... 1 Unchanged. Scorer: Tufnell

WEST BROMWICH A .... 0 Unchanged

1912–13 ASTON VILLA .... 1 Hardy [E]; Lyons, Weston, 1–Barber, Harrop, Leach, Wallace [E], Halse [E], Hampton [E] Stephenson [e], Bache [E]

SUNDERLAND .... 0 Butler; Gladwin, Ness, Cuggy, Thomson [S], Low, Mordue [E], Buchan [E], Richardson, Holley [E], Martin [e]

1913–14 BURNLEY .... 1 Sewell [e]; Bamford, Taylor, Halley, c–Boyle [E], Watson [E], Nesbitt, Lindley, 1–Freeman, Hodgson, Mosscrop [E]

LIVERPOOL .... 0 Campbell [e]; Longworth [e], Pursell, Fairfoul, Ferguson, MacKinley [s], Sheldon, Metcalfe, Miller [s], Lacey [IRE],Nicholl

1914–15 SHEFFIELD UNITED .... 3 Gough [e]; Cook, English, Sturgess [E], Brelsford, c–Utley [E], 1–Simmons, 1–Fazackerly, 1–Kitchen, Masterman, Evans [E]

CHELSEA .... 0 Molyneux; Bettridge, Harrow [e], Taylor, Logan [S], Walker, Ford, Halse [E], Thomson, Croal [S], McNeil

1919–20 ASTON VILLA .... 1 Hardy [E]; Smart [e], Weston, c–Ducat [E], Barson [E], Moss [e], Wallace [E], 1–Kirton [e], Walker [e], Stephenson [e], Dorrell [E]

HUDDERSFIELD T .... 0 Mutch; Wood, Bullock [e], Slade, Wilson [e], Watson, Richardson, Mann, Taylor, Swann, Islip

1920–21 TOTTENHAM HOTSPUR . 1 Hunter; Clay [E], McDonald, Smith [E], Walters, c–Grimsdell [E], Banks, Seed, Cantrell, Bliss [E], 1–Dimmock [E]

WOLVERHAMPTON W ..... 0 George; Woodward, Marshall, Gregory, Hodnett, Riley, Lea, Burrill, Edmonds, Potts, Brooks

1921–22 HUDDERSFIELD T .... 1 Mutch; Wood, Wadsworth [E], Slade, Wilson [e], Watson, Richardson, Mann, Islip, Stephenson [e], 1p–WH Smith [E]

PRESTON NE .... 0 JF Mitchell [e], Hamilton, Doolan, Duxbury, McCall [E], Williamson, Rawlings [E], Jefferis [E], Roberts [e], Woodhouse, Quinn

1922–23 BOLTON WANDERERS .... 2 Pym [e]; Haworth, Finney, Nuttall [e], Seddon [e], Jennings [W], Butler [e], 1–Jack [e], 1–JR Smith, c–Joe Smith [E], Vizard [W]

WEST HAM .... 0 Hufton [e]; Henderson, Young, Bishop [e], c–Kay, Tresadern [E], Richards [W], Brown [e], Watson [E], Moore [e], Ruffell [e]

1923–24 NEWCASTLE UNITED .... 2 Bradley; Hampson, c–Hudspeth [e], Mooney, Spencer [E], Gibson, Low, Cowan [S], 1–Harris [S], McDonald, 1–Seymour

ASTON VILLA .... 0 Jackson; Smart [E], Mort [E], Moss [E], Dr V.Milne, Blackburn [e], York [E], Kirton [E], Capewell, c–Walker [E], Dorrell [E]

1924–25 SHEFFIELD UNITED .... 1 Sutcliff; Cook, Milton, Pantling [E], King, Green [e], Mercer [E], Boyle, Johnson, c–Gillespie [NI], 1–Tunstall [E]

CARDIFF CITY .... 0 Farquharson [NI]; Nelson [S], Blair [S], Waker, c–Keenor [W], Hardy, W.Davies [W], Gill, Nicholson, Beadles [W], J.Evans

1925–26 BOLTON WANDERERS .... 1 Pym [E]; Haworth, Greenhalgh, Nuttall [e], Seddon [E], Jennings [W], Butler [E], JR Smith, 1–Jack [E], c–Joe Smith [E], Vizard [W]

MANCHESTER CITY .... 0 Goodchild; Cookson, McCloy [S], Pringle [S], Cowan [e], c–McMullan [S], Austin [E], Browell, Roberts [E], Johnson [e], Hicks

1926–27 CARDIFF CITY .... 1 Farquharson [NI]; Nelson [S], Watson [NI], c–Keenor [W], Sloan [NI], Hardy, Curtis, Irving [NI], 1–Ferguson, L.Davies [W], McLachlan

ARSENAL .... 0 Lewis [W]; Parker [E], Kennedy [NI], Baker [e], Butler [E], John [W], Hulme [E], c–Buchan [E], Brain, Blythe, Hoar

1927–28 BLACKBURN ROVERS ...... 3 Crawford; Hutton [S], Jones [E], c–Healless [E], Rankin, Campbell [e], Thornewell, Puddefoot [E], 2–Roscamp, 1–McLean, Rigby [E]

HUDDERSFIELD T .... 1 Mercer; Goodall, Barkas, Redfern, Wilson [E], Steele [S], 1–A.Jackson [S], Kelly [E], Brown [E], c–Stephenson [E], WH Smith [E]

1928–29 BOLTON WANDERERS .... 2 Pym [E]; Haworth, Finney, Kean [E], c–Seddon [E], Nuttall [E], 1–Butler [E], McClelland, 1–Blackmore, Gibson, W.Cook [s]

PORTSMOUTH .... 0 Gilfillan; Mackie [NI], Bell, Nichol, McIlwaine, Thackeray, Forward, Smith, Weddle, Watson, Cook

1929–30 ARSENAL ....2 Preedy; c–Parker [E], Hapgood [e], Baker, Seddon, John [W], Hulme [E], Jack [E], 1–Lambert, 1–James [S], Bastin [e]

HUDDERSFIELD T ....0 Turner [e]; Goodall, Spence, Naylor, c–Wilson, Campbell [E], Jackson [S], Kelly [E], Davies, Raw, WH Smith [E]

1930–31 WEST BROMWICH A........2 Pearson [e]; Shaw [e], Trentham, Magee [E], W.Richardson, Edwards, c–Glidden, Carter [E], 2–WG Richardson [e], Sandford [e]

BIRMINGHAM ....1 Hibbs [E]; Liddell, c–Barkas, Cringan, Morrall, Leslie, Briggs, Crosbie [S], 1–Bradford [E], Gregg, Curtis

1931–32 NEWCASTLE UNITED ....2 McInroy [E]; Nelson [S], Fairhurst [e], McKenzie, Davidson, Weaver [E], Boyd [s], Richardson [e], 2–Allen, McMenemy, Lang

ARSENAL ....1 Moss [e]; c–Parker [E], Hapgood [e], Jones [W], Roberts [E], Male [e], Hulme [E], Jack [E], Lambert, Bastin [E], 1–John [W]

1932–33 EVERTON ....3 Sagar [e]; Cook, Cresswell [E], Britton [e], White [E], Thomson [S], Geldard [E], 1–Dunn, 1–c–Dean [E], Johnson [E], 1–Stein

MANCHESTER CITY ....0 Langford; Cann, Dale, Busby [s], c–Cowan [E], Bray [e], Toseland, Marshall, Herd, McMullan [S], Brook [E]

1933–34 MANCHESTER CITY ....2 Swift [e]; Barnett, Dale, Busby [s], c–Cowan [E], Bray [e], Toseland, Marshall, 2–Tilson [e], Herd, Brook [E]

PORTSMOUTH....................1 Gilfillan; Mackie [NI], W.Smith, Nichol, c–Allen [E], Thackeray, Worrall [e], J.Smith, Weddle, Easson [S], 1–Rutherford

1934–35 SHEFFIELD WED ....4 Brown [E]; Nibloe [S], Catlin [e], Sharp, Millership, Burrows [E], 1–Hooper, Surtees, 1–Palethorpe, c–Starling [E], 2–Rimmer [E]

WEST BROMWICH A........2 Pearson [E]; Shaw [E], Trentham, Murphy [W], W.Richardson, Edwards, c–Glidden, Carter [E], WG Richardson [e], 1–Sandford [E], 1–Boyes

1935–36 ARSENAL ....1 Wilson; Male [E], Hapgood [E], Crayston [E], Roberts [e], Copping [E], Hulme [E], Bowden [E], 1–Drake [E], c–James [S], Bastin [E]

SHEFFIELD UNITED ....0 Smith; c–Hooper, Wilkinson, Jackson, Johnson, McPherson, Barton, Barclay [E], Dodds, Pickering [E] Williams

1936–37 SUNDERLAND ....3 Mapson; Gorman, Hall, Thomson [s], Johnson [s], McNab [S], Duns, 1–c–Carter [E], 1–Gurney [E], Gallacher [S], 1–Burbanks

PRESTON NE ....1 Burns; Gallimore, A.Beattie [S], Shankly [s], c–Tremelling, Milne, Dougal [s], Beresford [E], 1–F.O'Donnell [S], Fagan, H. O'Donnell

1937–38 PRESTON NE ....1 Holdcroft [E]; Gallimore, A.Beattie [S], Shankly [S], Smith [S], Batey, Watmough, 1p–Mutch [S], Maxwell, R.Beattie [s], H.O'Donnell

HUDDERSFIELD T ....0 Hesford; Craig, Mountford, Willingham [E], c–Young, Boot, Hulme [E], Issac, MacFadyen [S], Barclay [E], Beasley [e]

1938–39 PORTSMOUTH....................4 Walker; Morgan, Rochford, c–Guthrie, Rowe, Wharton, Worrall [E], McAlinden [NI], 1–Anderson, 1–Barlow, 2–Parker

WOLVERHAMPTON W .....1 Scott; Morris [E], Taylor, Galley [E], c–Cullis [E], Gardiner, Burton, McIntosh, Westcott, 1–Dorsett, Maguire

1945–46 DERBY COUNTY ....4 Woodley [E]; c–Nicholas, Howe [e], Bullions, Leuty, Musson, Harrison, Carter [E], 2–Stamps, 1–Doherty [NI], Duncan [S]

CHARLTON ATHLETIC ....1 Bartram; Phipps, Shreeve, 1og–1–H.Turner [W], Oakes, Johnson, Fell, Brown, AA Turner, c–Welsh [E], Duffy

1946–47 CHARLTON ATHLETIC ....1 Bartram; Croker, Shreeve, Johnson, Phipps, Whittaker, Hurst, Dawson, W.Robinson, c–Welsh [E], 1–Duffy

BURNLEY ....0 Strong; Woodruff, Mather, Attwell, c–Brown, Bray, Chew, Morris [W], Harrison, Potts, Kippax

1947–48 MANCHESTER UNITED ...4 Crompton; c–Carey [NI/IRE], Aston, 1–Anderson, Chilton [e], Cockburn [E], Delaney [S], Morris [e], 2–Rowley [e], 1–Pearson [E],Mitten

BLACKPOOL ....2 Robinson; 1p–Shimwell [e], Crosland, c–Johnston [E], Hatward, Kelly [s], Matthews [E], Munro [S], 1–Mortensen [E], Dick, Rickett

1948–49 WOLVERHAMPTON W .....3 Williams [e]; Pritchard, Springthorpe, W.Crook, Shorthouse, c–Wright [E], Hancocks [E], 1–Smyth [NI], 2–Pye [e], Dunn, Mullen [E]

LEICESTER CITY ....1 Bradley; Jelly, Scott, W.Harrison, c–Plummer, King, 1–Griffiths [W], Lee [e], J.Harrison, Chisholm, Adam

1949–50 ARSENAL .... **2** Swindin; Scott [E], Barnes [W], Forbes [S], L.Compton [e], c–
Mercer [E], Cox, Logie [s], Goring, 2–Lewis, D.Compton

LIVERPOOL .... **0** Sidlow [W]; Lambert [W], Spicer, c–Taylor [E], Hughes [e], Jones
[e], Payne, Baron, Stubbins, Fagan, Liddell [S]

1950–51 NEWCASTLE UNITED .... **2** Fairbrother; Cowell, Corbett, c–Harvey, Brennan [S], Crowe,
Walker, Taylor [e], 2–Milburn [E], G.Robledo [Ch], Mitchell [s]

BLACKPOOL .... **0** Farm; Shimwell [E], Garrett [e], c–Johnston [E], Hayward, Kelly
[s], Matthews [E], Mudie [s], Mortensen [E], Slater [e], Perry [e]

1951–52 NEWCASTLE UNITED .... **1** Simpson [s]; Cowell, McMichael [NI], c–Harvey, Brennan [S],
E.Robledo, Walker, Foulkes [W], Milburn [E], 1–G.Robledo
[Ch], Mitchell [S]

ARSENAL .... **0** Swindin; Barnes [W], L.Smith [E], Forbes [S], Daniel [W], c–
Mercer [E], Cox, Logie [s], Holton, Lishman, Roper

1952–53 BLACKPOOL .... **4** Farm [S]; Shimwell [E], Garrett [E], Fenton, c–Johnston [E],
Robinson, Matthews [E], Taylor [e], 3–Mortensen [E], Mudie [s],
1–Perry [e]

BOLTON WANDERERS .... **3** Hanson; Ball, R.Banks, Wheeler [e], Barass [E], 1–Bell, Holden
[e], 1–c–Moir [S], 1–Lofthouse [E], Hassall [E], Langton [E]

1953–54 WEST BROMWICH A .... **3** Sanders; Kennedy, c–Millard, Dudley, Dugdale, Barlow, 1–Griffin, Ryan [IRE/NI], 2(1p)–Allen [E], Nicholls [E], Lee

PRESTON NE .... **2** Thompson; Cunningham [s], Walton, Docherty [S], Marston,
Forbes, c–Finney [E], Foster, 1–Wayman, Baxter, 1–Morrison

1954–55 NEWCASTLE UNITED .... **3** Simpson [s]; Cowell, Batty, c–Scoular [S], Stokoe, Casey [NI],
White, 1–Milburn [E], Keeble, 1–Hannah, 1–Mitchell [S]

MANCHESTER CITY .... **1** Trautmann; Meadows [E], Little, Barnes, Ewing, c–Paul [W],
Spurdle, Hayes, Revie [E], 1–Johnstone [S], Fagan [RI]

1955–56 MANCHESTER CITY .... **3** Trautmann; Leivers, Little, Barnes, Ewing, c–Paul [W], 1–Johnstone
[S], 1–Hayes, Revie [E], 1–Dyson, Clarke [W]

BIRMINGHAM CITY .... **1** Merrick [E]; Hall [E], Green, Newman, Smith [e], c–Boyd, Astall
[e], 1–Kinsey [W], Brown, Murphy, Govan

1956–57 ASTON VILLA .... **2** Sims; Lynn, Aldis, Crowther, Dugdale, Saward [RI], Smith,
Sewell [E], Myerscough, c–Dixon, 2–McParland [NI]

MANCHESTER UNITED ... **1** Wood [E]; Foulkes [E], c–Byrne [E], Colman, J.Blanchflower
[NI], Edwards [E], Berry [E], Whelan [RI], 1–T.Taylor [E],
R.Charlton [e], Pegg [e]

1957–58 BOLTON WANDERERS .... **2** Hopkinson [E]; Hartle, T.Banks [e], Hennin, Higgins, Edwards,
Birch, Stevens, 2–c–Lofthouse [E] Parry [e], Holden [e]

MANCHESTER UNITED ... **0** Gregg [NI]; c–Foulkes [E], Greaves, Goodwin, Cope, Crowther,
Dawson, E.Taylor [E], R.Charlton [E], Viollet [e], Webster [W]

1958–59 NOTTINGHAM FOREST ... **2** Thomson; Whare, McDonald [S], Whitefoot, McKinlay, c–
Burkitt, 1–Dwight, Quigley, 1–Wilson, Gray, Imlach [S]

LUTON TOWN .... **1** Baynham [E]; McNally [ri], Hawkes, Groves, c–Owen [E], 1–
Pacey, Bingham [NI], Brown [S], Morton, Cummins [RI], Gregory

1959–60 WOLVERHAMPTON W ..... **3** Finlayson; Showell, Harris, Clamp [E], c–Slater [E], Flowers [E],
2–Deeley [E], Stobart, Murray, Broadbent [E], Horne

BLACKBURN ROVERS ...... **0** Leyland; Bray, Whelan, c–Clayton [E], Woods, og–McGrath
[RI], Bimpson, Dobing, Dougan [NI], Douglas [E], McLeod

1960–61 TOTTENHAM HOTSPUR . **2** Brown [S]; Baker, Henry [e], c–D.Blanchflower [NI], Norman
[e], Mackay [S], Jones [W], White [S], 1–Smith [E], Allen, 1–
Dyson

LEICESTER CITY .... **0** Banks [e]; Chalmers, Norman, McLintock [s], King, Appleton,
Riley, c–Walsh, McIlmoyle, Keyworth, Cheesebrough

1961–62 TOTTENHAM HOTSPUR . **3** Brown [S]; Baker, Henry [e], 1p–c–D.Blanchflower [NI], Norman [e], Mackay [S], Medwin [W], White [S], 1–Smith [E],
1–Greaves [E], Jones [W]

BURNLEY .... **1** Blacklaw [s]; Angus [E], Elder [NI], c–Adamson, Cummings,
Miller [E], Connelly [E], McIlroy [NI], Pointer [E], 1–Robson,
Harris [e]

1962–63 MANCHESTER UNITED ... **3** Gaskell; Dunne [RI], c–Cantwell [RI], Crerand [S], Foulkes [E],
Setters, Giles [RI], Quixall [E], 2–Herd [S], 1–Law [S], R.Charlton
[E]

LEICESTER CITY .... **1** Banks [E]; Sjoberg, Norman, McLintock [s], King, c–Appleton,
Riley, Cross, 1–Keyworth, Gibson, Stringfellow

1963–64 WEST HAM 3   Standen; Bond, Burkett, Bovington, Brown [E], c–Moore [E], Brabrook [E], 1–Boyce, Byrne [E], 1–Hurst [e], 1–Sissons

       PRESTON NE 2   Kelly [RI]; Ross, c–Lawton, Smith, Singleton, Kendall, Wilson, Ashworth, 1–Dawson, Spavin, 1–Holden [E]

1964–65 LIVERPOOL 2   Lawrence [S]; Lawler [e], Byrne [E], Strong, c–Yeats [S], Stevenson, Callaghan [e], 1–Hunt [E], 1–StJohn [S], Smith [e], Peter Thompson [E]

       LEEDS UNITED 1   Sprake [W]; Reaney [e], Bell [s], 1–Bremner [s], J.Charlton [E], Hunter [e], Giles [RI], Storrie, Peacock [E], c–Collins [S], Johanneson

1965–66 EVERTON 3   West [e]; Wright [e], Wilson [E], Gabriel [S], c–Labone [E], Harris, Scott [S], 2–Trebilcock, A.Young [S], Harvey [e], 1–Temple [E]

       SHEFFIELD WED 2   Springett [E]; Smith, c–Megson, Eustace, Ellis, G.Young [E], Pugh, Fantham [E], 1–McCalliog [s], 1–Ford, Quinn

1966–67 TOTTENHAM HOTSPUR . 2   Jennings [NI]; Kinnear [RI], Knowles [e], Mullery [E], England [W], c–Mackay [S], 1–Robertson [S], Greaves [E], Gilzean [S], Venables [E], 1–Saul

       CHELSEA 1   Bonetti [E]; A.Harris, McCreadie [S], Hollins [e], Hinton, c–R.Harris, Cooke [S], Baldwin, Hateley, 1–Tambling [E], Boyle

1967–68 WEST BROMWICH A 1   Osborne; Fraser [s], c–Williams [W], Brown [e], Talbut, Kaye (Clarke), Lovett, Collard, 1–Astle [e], Hope [s], Clark

       EVERTON 0   West [e]; Wright [e], Wilson [E], Kendall, c–Labone [E], Harvey [e], Husband, Ball [E], Royle [e], Hurst, Morrissey

1968–69 MANCHESTER CITY 1   Dowd: c–Book, Pardoe, Doyle [e], Booth, Oakes, Summerbee [E], Bell [E], Lee [E], 1–Young, Coleman

       LEICESTER CITY 0   Shilton [e]; Rodrigues [W], c–Nish [e], Roberts, Woollett, Cross, Fern, Gibson [S], Lochhead, Clarke [e], Glover (Manley)

1969–70 CHELSEA 2   Bonetti [E]; Webb, McCreadie [S], Hollins [E], Dempsey [RI], c–R.Harris (Hinton), Baldwin, 1–Houseman, Osgood [E], 1–Hutchinson, Cooke [S]

       LEEDS UNITED 2   Sprake [W]; Madeley [e], Cooper [E], c–Bremner [S], 1–J.Charlton [E], Hunter [E], Lorimer [S], Clarke [e], 1–Jones [E], Giles [RI], E.Gray [S]

replay   CHELSEA 2   unchanged. Hinton came on as substitute for Osgood. Scorers: Osgood, Webb.

       LEEDS UNITED 1   Harvey [s] replaced Sprake. No substitutions. Scorer: Jones

1970–71 ARSENAL 2   Wilson [s]; Rice [NI], McNab [E], Storey [E] (1–Kelly), c–McLintock [S], Simpson, Armstrong, Graham [s], Radford [E], Kennedy [e], 1–George [e]

       LIVERPOOL 1   Clemence [e]; Lawler [e], Lindsay [e], c–Smith [e], Lloyd [e], Hughes [E], Callaghan [E], Evans (Peter Thompson [E]), 1–Heighway [RI], Toshack [W], Hall

1971–72 LEEDS UNITED 1   Harvey [s]; Reaney [E], Madeley [E], c–Bremner [S], J.Charlton [E], Hunter [E], Lorimer [S], 1–Clarke [E], Jones [E], Giles [RI], E.Gray [S]

       ARSENAL 0   Barnett; Rice [NI], McNab [E], Storey [E], c–McLintock [S], Simpson, Armstrong, Ball [E], George [e], Radford [E] (Kennedy [e]), Graham [S]

1972–73 SUNDERLAND 1   Montgomery; Malone, Guthrie, Horswill, Watson [e], Pitt, c–Kerr, Hughes [s], Halom, 1–Porterfield, Tueart [e]

       LEEDS UNITED 0   Harvey [S]; Reaney [E], Cherry [e], c–Bremner [S], Madeley [E], Hunter [E], Lorimer [S], Clarke [E], Jones [E], Giles [RI], E.Gray [S] (Yorath [W])

1973–74 LIVERPOOL 3   Clemence [E]; Smith [E], Lindsay [e], Phil Thompson [e], Cormack [S], c–Hughes [E], 2–Keegan [E], Hall, 1–Heighway [RI], Toshack [W], Callaghan [E]

       NEWCASTLE UNITED 0   McFaul [NI]; Clark, Kennedy [e], McDermott [e], Howard, c–Moncur [S], Smith [S] (Gibb), Cassidy [NI], Macdonald [E], Tudor, Hibbitt

1974–75 WEST HAM 2   Day; McDowell, T.Taylor, Lock, Lampard [E], c–Bonds, Paddon, Brooking [E], Jennings, 2–A.Taylor, Holland

       FULHAM 0   Mellor; Cutbush, Lacy, Moore [E], Fraser, c–Mullery [E], Conway [RI], Slough, Mitchell, Busby, Barrett

1975–76 SOUTHAMPTON 1   Turner; c–Rodrigues [W], Peach, Holmes, Blyth, Steele, Gilchrist, Channon [E], Osgood [E], McCalliog [S], 1–Stokes

      MANCHESTER U 0   Stepney [E]; Forsyth [S], Houston [S], Daly [RI], B.Greenhoff [e], c–Buchan [S], Coppell [e], McIlroy [NI], Pearson [e], Macari [S], Hill [e] (McCreery [ni])

1976–77 MANCHESTER UNITED ... 2   Stepney [E]; Nicholl [NI], Albiston [s], McIlroy [NI], B.Greenhoff [E], c–Buchan [S], Coppell [e], 1–J.Greenhoff, 1–Pearson [E], Macari [S], Hill [E] (McCreery [NI])

      LIVERPOOL 1   Clemence [E]; Neal [E], Jones [W], Smith [E], Kennedy [E], c–Hughes [E], Keegan [E], 1–Case, Heighway [RI], Johnson [E] (Callaghan [E]), McDermott [e]

1977–78 IPSWICH TOWN 1   Cooper; Burley [s], c–Mills [E], 1–Osborne (Lambert), Hunter [NI], Beattie [E], Talbot [E], Wark [s], Mariner [E], Geddis, Woods

      ARSENAL 0   Jennings [NI]; c–Rice [NI], Nelson [NI], Price, Young, O'Leary [RI], Brady [RI] (Rix [e]), Hudson [E], Macdonald [E], Stapleton [RI], Sunderland [e]

1978–79 ARSENAL 3   Jennings [NI]; c–Rice [NI], Nelson [NI], 1–Talbot [E], O'Leary [RI], Young, Brady [RI], 1–Sunderland [e], 1–Stapleton [RI], Price (Walford), Rix [e]

      MANCHESTER UNITED ... 2   Bailey [e]; Nicholl [NI], Albiston [s], 1–McIlroy [NI], 1–McQueen [S], c–Buchan [S], Coppell [E], J.Greenhoff, Jordan [S], Macari [S], Thomas [W]

1979–80 WEST HAM 1   Parkes [E]; Stewart [s], Lampard [E], c–Bonds, Martin [e], Devonshire [e], Allen, Pearson [E], Cross, 1–Brooking [E], Pike

      ARSENAL 0   Jennings [NI]; c–Rice [NI], Devine [RI] (Nelson [NI]), Talbot [E], O'Leary [RI], Young, Brady [RI], Sunderland [e], Stapleton [RI], Price, Rix [e]

1980–81 TOTTENHAM HOTSPUR . 1   Aleksic; Hughton [RI], Miller, Roberts [e], c–Perryman [e], Villa [Arg] (Brooke), Ardiles [Arg], Archibald [S], Galvin [RI], Hoddle [E], Crooks. Scorer: Hutchison og

      MANCHESTER CITY 1   Corrigan [E]; Ranson, McDonald, Reid, c–Power, Caton, Bennett, Gow, Mackenzie, 1–og–Hutchison [S] (Henry), Reeves [E]

replay TOTTENHAM HOTSPUR . 3   Unchanged. no substitutions. Scorers: Villa 2, Crooks

      MANCHESTER CITY 2   Unchanged. Tueart [E] came on as substitute for McDonald. Scorers: Mackenzie, Reeves (p)

1981–82 TOTTENHAM HOTSPUR . 1   Clemence [E]; Hughton [RI], Miller, Price [W], Hazard (Brooke), c–Perryman [e], Roberts [e], Archibald [S], Galvin [ri], 1–Hoddle [E], Crooks

      QPR 1   Hucker; 1–Fenwick [e], Gillard [E], Waddock [RI], Hazell, c–Roeder, Currie [E], Flanagan, Allen [e] (Micklewhite), Stainrod, Gregory [e]

replay TOTTENHAM HOTSPUR . 1   Unchanged. Brooke came on as substitute for Hazard. Scorer: Hoddle (p)

      QPR 0   Neill replaced Roeder; Micklewhite replaced Allen. Burke came on as substitute for Micklewhite

1982–83 MANCHESTER UNITED ... 2   Bailey [e]; Duxbury [e], Moran [RI], McQueen [S], Albiston [S], Davies [w], 1–Wilkins [E], c–Robson [E], Muhren [Neth], 1–Stapleton [RI], Whiteside [NI]

      BRIGHTON & HA 2   Moseley; Ramsey (Ryan [RI]), 1–Stevens [e], Gatting, Pearce, Smillie, Case, c–Grealish [RI], Howlett [RI], Robinson [RI], 1–Smith

replay MANCHESTER UNITED ... 4   unchanged. No substitutions. Scorers: Robson 2, Whiteside, Muhren (p)

      BRIGHTON & HA 0   c–Foster [E] replaced Ramsey. No substitutions

1983–84 EVERTON 2   Southall [W]; Stevens [e], Bailey, c–Ratcliffe [W], Mountfield, Reid [e], Steven [e], Heath, 1–Sharp [s], 1–Gray [S], Richardson

      WATFORD 0   Sherwood; Bardsley, Price (Atkinson), c–Taylor, Terry, Sinnott, Callaghan, Johnston [S], Reilly, Jackett [W], Barnes [E]

1984–85 MANCHESTER UNITED ... 1   Bailey [E]; Gidman [E], Albiston [S] (Duxbury [E]), 1–Whiteside [NI], McGrath [RI], Moran [RI], c–Robson [E], Strachan [S], Hughes [W], Stapleton [RI], Olsen [Den]

United players Paul Ince (2), Mark Hughes (10), Lee Martin (3), Bryan Robson (7) and Neil Webb celebrate a goal in the 1990 final (Allsport/Simon Bruty)

EVERTON .... **0** Southall [W]; Stevens [e], Van den Hauwe [W], c–Ratcliffe [W], Mountfield, Reid [e], Steven [E], Gray [S], Sharp [s], Bracewell [e], Sheedy [RI]

1985–86 LIVERPOOL .... **3** Grobbelaar [Zim]; Lawrenson [RI], Beglin [RI], Nicol [S], Whelan [RI], c–Hansen [S], Dalglish [S], 1–Johnston, 2–Rush [W], Molby [Den], MacDonald

EVERTON .... **1** Mimms; Stevens [E] (Heath), Van den Hauwe [W], c–Ratcliffe [W], Mountfield [e], Reid [E], Steven [E], 1–Lineker [E], Sharp [S], Bracewell [E], Sheedy [RI]

1986–87 COVENTRY CITY .... **3** Ogrizovic; Phillips [W], Downs, McGrath, c–Kilcline (Rodger), Peake, 1–Bennett, Gynn, Regis [E], 1–Houchen, Pickering [E]

TOTTENHAM HOTSPUR . **2** Clemence [E]; Hughton [RI] (Claesen [Bel]), M.Thomas, Hodge [E], c–Gough [S], 1–og–Mabbutt [E], 1–C.Allen [E], P.Allen, Waddle [E], Hoddle [E], Ardiles [Arg] (Stevens [E])

1987–88 WIMBLEDON .... **1** c–Beasant [e]; Goodyear, T.Phelan [ri], Jones, Young [w], Thorn, Gibson (Scales), Cork (Cunningham [E]) Fashanu [e], 1–Sanchez [NI], Wise [e]

LIVERPOOL .... **0** Grobbelaar [Zim]; Gillespie [S], Ablett, Nicol [S], Spackman (Molby [Den]), c–Hansen [S], Beardsley [E], Aldridge [RI] (Johnston), Houghton [RI], Barnes [E], McMahon [E]

1988–89 LIVERPOOL .... **3** Grobbelaar [Zim]; Ablett, Staunton [RI] (Venison [E]), Nicol [S], c–Whelan [RI], Hansen [S], Beardsley [E], 1–Aldridge [RI] (2–Rush [W]), Houghton [RI], Barnes [E], McMahon [E]

EVERTON .... **2** Southall [W]; McDonald, Van den Hauwe [W], c–Ratcliffe [W], Watson [E], Bracewell [E] (2–McCall [s]), Nevin [S], Steven [E], Sharp [S], Cottee [E], Sheedy [RI] (Wilson [S])

1989–90 MANCHESTER UNITED ... **3** Leighton [S]; Ince [e], Martin (Blackmore [W]), Bruce, M.Phelan [e], Pallister [E] (Robins), 1–c–Robson [E], Webb [E], McClair [S], 2–Hughes [W], Wallace [E]

CRYSTAL PALACE .... **3** Martyn [e]; Pemberton, Shaw, Gray [e] (Madden), 1–O'Reilly, Thorn, Barber (2–Wright [e]) c–Thomas [e], Bright, Salako [e], Pardew

replay MANCHESTER UNITED ... **1** Sealey replaced Leighton [S]. No substitutions. Scorer: Martin

CRYSTAL PALACE .... **0** Unchanged. Wright came on as substitute for Barber, Madden substitute for Salako

1990–91 TOTTENHAM HOTSPUR . 2 Thorstvedt [Nor]; Edinburgh, Van den Hauwe [W], Sedgley, Howells, c–Mabbutt [E], 1–Stewart [e], Gascoigne [E] (Nayim), Samways (Walsh [E]), Lineker [E], P.Allen

NOTTINGHAM FOREST ... 1 Crossley; Charles [e], 1–c–Pearce [E], og–Walker [E], Chettle, Keane [RI], Crosby, Parker, Clough [E], Glover (Laws), Woan (Hodge [E])

1991–92 LIVERPOOL .... 2 Grobbelaar [Zim]; R.Jones [E], Burrows, Nicol [S], Molby [Den], c–Wright [E], Saunders [W], Houghton [RI], 1–I.Rush [W], McManaman, 1–Thomas [E]

SUNDERLAND .... 0 Norman [W]; Owers, Ball, Bennett, Rogan [NI], D.Rush (Hardyman), c–Bracewell [E], Davenport [E], Armstrong, Byrne [RI], Atkinson (Hawke)

1992–93 ARSENAL .... 1 Seaman [E], Dixon [E], Winterburn [E], Linighan, c–Adams [E], Campbell, 1–Wright [E], (O'Leary [RI]), Merson [E], Parlour (Smith [E]), Davis, Jensen [DEN]

SHEFFIELD W .... 1 Woods [E], Nilsson [SWE], Worthington [NI], Palmer [E], 1–Hirst [E], c–Anderson [E] (Hyde), Waddle [E] (Bart-Williams), Warhurst, Bright, Sheridan [RI], Harkes [USA]

replay ARSENAL .... 2 Smith [E] replaced Parlour. O'Leary [RI] came on as a substitute for Wright [E]. Scorers: Wright, Linighan

SHEFFIELD W .... 1 Wilson [RI] replaced c–Anderson [E]. Palmer was captain in the replay. Hyde came on as substitute for Wilson; Bart-Williams came on as substitute for Nilsson. Scorer: Waddle

Abbreviations: E England IRE Ireland NI Northern Ireland S Scotland W Wales Arg Argentina Bel Belgium Ch Chile Den Denmark Neth Netherlands Nor Norway Swe Sweden Zim Zimbabwe

Cup Final Venues

Since 1923 the Cup Final has been played at Wembley Stadium. The last time the Cup was not decided under the twin towers was in 1970 when the replay between Chelsea and Leeds on April 29 was staged at Old Trafford. Cup Final venues from 1872 have been as follows:

1872	Kennington Oval
1873	Lillie Bridge
1874–1892	Kennington Oval
1886	Replay at The Racecourse, Derby
1893	Fallowfield, Manchester
1894	Goodison Park, Liverpool
1895–1914	Crystal Palace
1901	Replay at Burnden Park, Bolton
1910	Replay at Goodison Park
1911	Replay at Old Trafford, Manchester
1912	Replay at Bramall Lane, Sheffield
1915	Old Trafford
1920–1922	Stamford Bridge
1923 to date	Wembley Stadium
1970	Replay at Old Trafford

FA Cup records

BIGGEST VICTORY (any round)
Preston North End 26, Hyde FC 0, FA Cup 1st round proper, 15.10.1887

BIGGEST WIN IN FA CUP FINAL
Bury 6, Derby County 0, 18.4.1903

BIGGEST WIN IN FA CUP SEMI-FINAL
Newcastle United 6, Fulham 0, at Anfield, 28.3.1908

MOST GOALS IN FA CUP MATCH
Competition Proper: 9 goals, Ted MacDougall for Bournemouth vs Margate, 1st round, 20.11.1971

Qualifying Competition: 10 goals, Chris Marron, for South Shields vs Radcliffe, preliminary round, 26.9.1947

MOST GOALS IN A SEASON
15, Sandy Brown, Tottenham Hotspur, 1900–01

MOST FA CUP GOALS IN CAREER
48, Henry Cursham, Notts County, 1880–1887
This century: 41, Denis Law for Huddersfield Town, Manchester C and Manchester U, 1957–1974

MOST FA CUP APPEARANCES
88, Ian Callaghan (Liverpool 79, Swansea C 7, Crewe Alexandra 2) 1962–1982

YOUNGEST PLAYER IN FA CUP
In any round: Andy Awford, 15 years 88 days as a substitute for Worcester C vs Borehamwood, 3rd qualifying round, 10.10.1987. Worcester C won 3–1.
In Competition Proper: Scott Endersby, 15 years 288 days, Kettering vs Tilbury, 1st round, 26.11.1977. Tilbury won the tie 3–2 after a replay.

YOUNGEST PLAYER IN AN FA CUP FINAL
James Prinsep, 17 years 245 days for Clapham Rovers vs Old Etonians, 29.3.1879
In a Wembley Cup Final: Paul Allen, 17 years 256 days for West Ham vs Arsenal, 10.5.1980

YOUNGEST CUP FINAL SCORER
Norman Whiteside, 18 years 19 days, Manchester U vs Brighton, 26.5.1983

YOUNGEST FA CUP FINAL CAPTAIN
David Nish, 21 years 212 days, Leicester C vs Manchester C, 26.4.1969

YOUNGEST FA CUP FINAL GOALKEEPER
Peter Shilton, 19 years 220 days, Leicester C vs Manchester C, 26.4.1969

OLDEST PLAYER IN FA CUP
Billy Meredith, 49 years 8 months, Manchester C vs Newcastle U, semi-final, 29.3.1924. Almost 20 years

earlier he had scored the winning goal when Manchester C beat Bolton W to win the Cup.

OLDEST PLAYER IN AN FA CUP FINAL

Walter (Billy) Hampson, 41 years 257 days, Newcastle vs Aston Villa, 26.4.1924. It is believed some players in the 1870s may have been over 40 years old when they played in the Final.

OLDEST SCORER IN WEMBLEY FINAL

Bert Turner, Charlton Athletic vs Derby County, 36 years 312 days, 27.4.1946. He also scored an own goal in the same match.

FA Cup Wins

When Wimbledon beat Liverpool in the Cup Final on May 14, 1988 they became the 42nd different team to win the Cup.

Tottenham have won the Cup a record 8 times from 9 appearances, followed by Aston Villa with 7 wins from 9 appearances and Manchester United, 7 wins from 11 appearances.

Tottenham H 8, Aston Villa 7, Manchester U 7, Blackburn R 6, Newcastle U 6, Arsenal 6, Liverpool 5, The Wanderers 5, WBA 5, Bolton W 4, Everton 4, Manchester C 4, Sheffield U 4, Wolverhampton W 4, Sheffield W 3, West Ham 3, Bury 2, Nottingham Forest 2, Old Etonians 2, Preston NE 2, Sunderland 2, Barnsley 1, Blackburn Olympic 1, Blackpool 1, Bradford C 1, Burnley 1, Cardiff C 1, Charlton A 1, Chelsea 1, Clapham R 1, Coventry C 1, Derby Co 1, Huddersfield T 1, Ipswich T 1, Leeds U 1, Notts Co 1, Old Carthusians 1, Oxford University 1, Portsmouth 1, Royal Engineers 1, Southampton 1, Wimbledon 1

Cup Final Appearances

When Crystal Palace played Manchester United in the Final on May 12, 1990, they became the 52nd different team to have appeared in the Cup Final.

Arsenal 12, Everton 11, Manchester U 11, Newcastle U 11, Liverpool 10, WBA 10, Aston Villa 9, Tottenham H 9, Blackburn R 8, Manchester C 8, Wolverhampton W 8, Bolton W 7, Preston NE 7, Old Etonians 6, Sheffield U 6, Sheffield W 6, Huddersfield T 5, The Wanderers 5, Derby Co 4, Leeds U 4, Leicester C 4, Oxford University 4, Royal Engineers 4, Sunderland 4, West Ham 4, Blackpool 3, Burnley 3, Chelsea 3, Nottingham F 3, Portsmouth 3, Southampton 3, Barnsley 2, Birmingham C 2, Bury 2, Cardiff C 2, Charlton A 2, Clapham R 2, Notts Co 2, Queens Park, Glasgow 2, Blackburn Olympic 1, Bradford C 1, Brighton & HA 1, Bristol C 1, Coventry C 1, Crystal Palace 1, Fulham 1, Ipswich T 1, Luton T 1, Old Carthusians 1, QPR 1, Watford 1, Wimbledon 1

UNBEATEN IN FINALS

Tottenham H won the first seven Finals they contested with victories in 1901, 1921, 1961, 1962, 1967, 1981 and 1982. The sequence ended when they lost 3–2 (aet) to Coventry on May 16, 1987.

The Wanderers were undefeated in all five Finals they contested (1872, 1873, 1876, 1877, 1878) and the other unbeaten finalists are:

2 – Bury (1900 and 1903)

1 – Blackburn Olympic (1883), Bradford C (1911), Coventry C (1987), Ipswich T (1978), Old Carthusians (1881), Wimbledon (1988)

FINALISTS WHO HAVE NEVER WON

4 – Leicester C (1949, 1961, 1963, 1969)

2 – Birmingham C (1931, 1956), Queen's Park, Glasgow (1884, 1885)

1 – Brighton & HA (1983), Bristol C (1909), Crystal P (1990), Fulham (1975), Luton T (1959), QPR (1982), Watford (1984)

NON-FIRST DIVISION (1888–1992) FINALISTS

When Second Division Sunderland met Liverpool in the 1992 Cup Final on May 9, they became the 23rd team from outside the First Division to reach the Final since the League was founded in 1888. Of those only eight teams have gone on to win the Cup, the last being West Ham in 1980.

1890 Sheffield Wednesday (1st, Football Alliance)
1894 Notts County (3rd, Div 2, winners)
1900 Southampton (3rd, Southern League)
1901 Tottenham Hotspur (5th, Southern League, winners)
1902 Southampton (3rd, Southern League)
1904 Bolton Wanderers (7th, Div 2)
1908 Wolverhampton W (9th, Div 2, winners)
1910 Barnsley (9th, Div 2)
1912 Barnsley (6th, Div 2, winners)
1920 Huddersfield Town (2nd, Div 2)
1921 Wolverhampton W (15th, Div 2)
1923 West Ham (2nd, Div 2)
1931 West Bromwich Albion (2nd, Div 2, winners)
1936 Sheffield United (3rd, Div 2)
1947 Burnley (2nd, Div 2)
1949 Leicester C (19th, Div 2)
1964 Preston North End (3rd, Div 2)
1973 Sunderland (6th, Div 2, winners)
1975 Fulham (9th, Div 2)
1976 Southampton (6th, Div 2, winners)
1980 West Ham (7th, Div 2, winners)
1982 Queens Park Rangers (5th, Div 2)
1992 Sunderland (18th, Div 2)

West Brom (1931) remain the only team to have won promotion from the Second Division and the FA Cup in the same season.

West Ham's four finals have all featured a club from Division Two. In 1923 and 1980 they were in the Second Division themselves while in 1964 they beat Preston and in 1975 Fulham, both in the Second Division.

RELEGATED FINALISTS

Three teams have been relegated from the First Division (1888–1992) and appeared in the Cup Final in the same season.

1926 Manchester City (lost 0–1 to Bolton)
1969 Leicester City (lost 0–1 to Manchester City)
1983 Brighton & HA (lost 0–4 to Manchester United after 2–2 draw)

In 1915 Chelsea finished one from bottom in the First Division and also reached the Cup Final but were saved from playing in the Second Division by the First World War and were not relegated. When the First Division was extended in 1919–20, Chelsea retained their place in Division One.

FROM TEARS TO JOY

The following teams all experienced the disappointment of losing the final one year, only to come back and win the Cup the following season.

1873 Oxford University (lost 2–0 to Wanderers)
1874 Oxford University (beat Royal Engineers 2–0)

1874 Royal Engineers (lost 2–0 to Oxford University)
1875 Royal Engineers (beat Old Etonians 2–0 after 1–1 draw)

1879 Clapham Rovers (lost 1–0 to Old Etonians)
1880 Clapham Rovers (beat Oxford University 1–0)

1881 Old Etonians (lost 3–0 to Old Carthusians)
1882 Old Etonians (beat Blackburn Rovers 1–0)

1887 West Bromwich Albion (lost 2–0 to Aston Villa)
1888 West Bromwich Albion (beat Preston North End 2–1)

1888 Preston North End (lost 2–1 to West Bromwich Albion)
1889 Preston North End (beat Wolverhampton Wanderers 3–0)

1901 Sheffield United (lost 3–1 to Tottenham after 2–2 draw)
1902 Sheffield United (beat Southampton 2–1 after 1–1 draw)

1933 Manchester City (lost 3–0 to Everton)
1934 Manchester City (beat Portsmouth 2–1)

1937 Preston North End (lost 3–1 to Sunderland)
1938 Preston North End (beat Huddersfield 1–0 aet)

1946 Charlton Athletic (lost 4–1 to Derby County aet)
1947 Charlton Athletic (beat Burnley 1–0 aet)

1955 Manchester City (lost 3–1 to Newcastle United)
1956 Manchester City (beat Birmingham City 3–1)

1976 Manchester United (lost 1–0 to Southampton)
1977 Manchester United (beat Liverpool 2–1)

1978 Arsenal (lost 1–0 to Ipswich)
1979 Arsenal (beat Manchester United 3–2)

1988 Liverpool (lost 1–0 to Wimbledon)
1989 Liverpool (beat Everton 3–2)

FROM JOY TO TEARS

Arsenal are the only team to have twice returned to the Final as holders and lost the Cup, an unwanted record they achieved while becoming the first team to play in three successive Wembley Cup Finals (1978–79–80).

The only other team to have played in three succesive finals, winning only in the middle year, are Old Etonians (1881–82–83).

Seven holders have lost the following year's final.

1882 Old Etonians (beat Blackburn Rovers 1–0)
1883 Old Etonians (lost 2–1 to Blackburn Olympic aet)

1906 Everton (beat Newcastle United 1–0)
1907 Everton (lost 2–1 to Sheffield Wednesday)

1910 Newcastle United (beat Barnsley 2–0 after 1–1 draw)
1911 Newcastle United (lost 1–0 to Bradford City after 0–0 draw)

1971 Arsenal (beat Liverpool 2–1 aet)
1972 Arsenal (lost 1–0 to Leeds United)

1972 Leeds United (beat Arsenal 1–0)
1973 Leeds United (lost 1–0 to Sunderland)

1979 Arsenal (beat Manchester United 3–2)
1980 Arsenal (lost 1–0 to West Ham)

1984 Everton (beat Watford 2–0)
1985 Everton (lost 1-0 to Manchester United)

SUCCESSIVE WINS

Only Wanderers and Blackburn Rovers have won the Cup three years in succession – and only four clubs have ever won the cup in successive seasons. By a strange coincidence three of them have achieved that feat more than once.

The Wanderers: 1872 and 1873; 1876, 1877 and 1878
Blackburn Rovers: 1884, 1885 and 1886; 1890 and 1891
Newcastle United: 1951 and 1952
Tottenham Hotspur: 1961 and 1962; 1981 and 1982.

SUCCESSIVE FINALS

No club has yet appeared in four successive FA Cup Finals, although Wanderers and Newcastle United both reached five finals in seven-season spells between 1872–78 and 1905–11 respectively.

The following teams have appeared in three successive finals and the (W) or (L) shows how they fared:

Wanderers: 1876 (W), 1877 (W), 1878 (W)
Old Etonians: 1881 (L), 1882 (W), 1883 (L)
Blackburn Rovers: 1884 (W), 1885 (W), 1886 (W)
West Bromwich Albion: 1886 (L), 1887 (L), 1888 (W)
Arsenal: 1978 (L), 1979 (W), 1980 (L)
Everton: 1984 (W), 1985 (L), 1986 (L)

SUCCESSIVE DEFEATS

The following clubs have lost finals in successive seasons

Old Etonians	1875, 1876
Queens Park, Glasgow	1884, 1885
West Bromwich Albion	1886, 1887
Derby County	1898, 1899
Newcastle United	1905, 1906
Manchester United	1957, 1958
Everton	1985, 1986

Derby County lost three finals in six seasons between 1898 and 1903.

SAME TIME NEXT YEAR

The only occasion that the same two teams contested the final two years running was in 1884 and 1885 when Blackburn Rovers met Queens Park, Glasgow. Blackburn won both matches, 2–1 in 1884 and 2–0 the following year.

MET BEFORE

The only clubs to have met each other in three finals are Aston Villa and West Bromwich Albion. The following lists all the repeat finals.

1872 Wanderers 1, Royal Engineers 0
1878 Wanderers 3, Royal Enginners 1

1873 Wanderers 2, Oxford University 0
1877 Wanderers 2, Oxford University 1 (aet)

1884 Blackburn Rovers 2, Queens Park, Glasgow 1	**1907** Sheffield Wednesday 2, Everton 1
1885 Blackburn Rovers 2, Queens Park, Glasgow 0	**1966** Everton 3, Sheffield Wednesday 2
1887 Aston Villa 2, West Bromwich Albion 0	**1922** Huddersfield Town 1, Preston North End 0
1892 West Bromwich Albion 3, Aston Villa 0	**1938** Preston North End 1, Huddersfield Town 0 (aet)
1895 Aston Villa 1, West Bromwich Albion 0	
1888 West Bromwich Albion 2, Preston North End 1	**1932** Newcastle United 2, Arsenal 1
1954 West Bromwich Albion 3, Preston North End 2	**1952** Newcastle United 1, Arsenal 0
1904 Manchester City 1, Bolton Wanderers 0	**1950** Arsenal 2, Liverpool 0
1926 Bolton Wanderers 1, Manchester City 0	**1971** Arsenal 2, Liverpool 1 (aet)
1905 Aston Villa 2, Newcastle United 0	**1986** Liverpool 3, Everton 1
1924 Newcastle United 2, Aston Villa 0	**1989** Liverpool 3, Everton 2 (aet)

Cup Final colours

Fashion in football strips, like in all things, comes and goes, but there are certain things that never seem to change...and if any team is looking for omens on Cup Final day they could do no worse than make sure they play in red shirts and white shorts or all red – and make sure the opposition wear all white. That perhaps was the recipe for Manchester United's success over Leicester in 1963. The majority of Cup Final winners have played in red, while more teams have lost wearing an all-white strip than any other outfit.

Since the War Arsenal have won the Cup four times – but until 1993 never in their first choice of red shirts and white sleeves, while Manchester City's four appearances since 1946 have each been in a different strip, including a rather fetching maroon and white number in 1956 and their Milanesque red and black stripes in 1969.

The only teams to wear a predominantly all-blue kit and win the final are Chelsea and Wimbledon, while the trend towards the yellow and blue look – notably worn by Arsenal and Southampton – seems to have had its hey-day . . . for now.

FA CUP WINNERS

Red Shirts, White Shorts
Nottingham Forest 1959
Manchester U 1963, 1977, 1983
   (*both matches*), 1990 (*replay*)
Arsenal (with white sleeves) 1993
   (*both matches*)

All Red
Liverpool 1965, 1974, 1986, 1989, 1992

White Shirts, Blue Shorts
Bolton Wanderers 1958
Tottenham H 1961, 1962, 1981
   (*both matches*), 1991

All White
Tottenham H 1967
West Bromwich Albion 1968
Leeds United 1972
West Ham 1980
Manchester U 1990 (*first match*)

White Shirts, Black Shorts
Derby Co 1946
Charlton Athletic 1947

Blue Shirts, White Shorts
Manchester U 1948
Everton 1966, 1984
Ipswich 1978

All Blue
Chelsea 1970
Wimbledon (*with yellow trim*) 1988

Yellow Shirts, Blue Shorts
Arsenal 1971, 1979
Southampton 1976

All Yellow
Tottenham 1982 (*both matches*)

Old Gold Shirts
Wolverhampton W (*with black shorts*) 1949, 1960
Arsenal (*with white shorts*) 1950

Tangerine Shirts, White Shorts
Blackpool 1953

Black & White Striped Shirts, Black Shorts
Newcastle U 1951, 1952, 1955

Blue & White Striped Shirts
West Bromwich Albion (*with white shorts*) 1954
Coventry City (*with black shorts*) 1987

Claret & Blue Shirts, White Shorts
West Ham 1964, 1975

Light Blue with thin Claret Stripes, White Shorts
Aston Villa 1957

Red & White Stripes, Black Shorts
Sunderland 1973

Red & Black Stripes, Black Shorts
Manchester City 1969

Maroon with white pinstripe
Manchester City 1956

RUNNERS UP

All-White
Manchester U 1957
Leicester C 1963
Leeds U 1965, 1970, 1973
Sheffield Wednesday 1966
Tottenham H 1987

White Shirts, Black Shorts
Blackpool 1948
Liverpool 1950, 1977
Luton Town 1959
Fulham 1975

White Shirts, Dark Blue Shorts
Bolton Wanderers 1953
Preston 1954, 1964
Birmingham C 1956
Sunderland 1992

Red Shirts, White Shorts
Charlton Athletic 1946
Arsenal (*with white sleeves*) 1952, 1972
Manchester United 1958, 1976, 1979
Nottingham Forest 1991

All Red
Liverpool 1971, 1988

Red Shirts, Black Shorts
QPR 1982 (*both matches*)

Blue Shirts, White Shorts
Burnley 1947
Leicester C 1949, 1961, 1969
Everton 1986, 1989

All Blue
Chelsea 1967
Brighton 1983 (*both matches*)

All Light Blue
Manchester C 1981 (*both matches*)

Light Blue Shirts, White Shorts
Manchester C 1955

Blue and White Stripes, Black Shorts
Sheffield W 1993 (*both matches*)

Blue and White Halved Shirts, White Shorts
Blackburn R 1960

Claret and Blue Shirts, White Shorts
Burnley 1962

Red and Blue Shirts, Red Shorts
Crystal Palace 1990 (*first game*)

Yellow Shirts, Blue Shorts
Everton 1968
Arsenal 1978, 1980

Yellow Shirts, Red Shorts
Watford 1984

Tangerine Shirts, White Shorts
Blackpool 1951

Black & White Stripes, Black Shorts
Newcastle U 1974

Yellow & Black Shirts, Black Shorts
Crystal Palace 1990 (*replay*)

Players in Cup Finals

A total of 1,764 different players have appeared in the 126 Cup Final matches (including replays) between 1872 and 1993.

APPEARED IN MOST CUP FINALS

9 Arthur Kinnaird	Wanderers 1873, 1877, 1878 Old Etonians 1875, 1876, 1879, 1881, 1882, 1883
5 Charles Wollaston	Wanderers 1872, 1873, 1876, 1877, 1878
James Forrest	Blackburn R 1884, 1885, 1886, 1890, 1891
Harry Wood	Wolverhampton W 1889, 1893, 1896 Southampton 1900, 1902
Jimmy Lawrence	Newcastle U 1905, 1906, 1908, 1910, 1911
Jack Rutherford	Newcastle U 1905, 1906, 1908, 1910, 1911
Colin Veitch	Newcastle U 1905, 1906, 1908, 1910, 1911
Joe Hulme	Arsenal 1927, 1930, 1932, 1936 Huddersfield 1938
Johnny Giles	Manchester U 1963 Leeds U 1965, 1970, 1972, 1973
Pat Rice	Arsenal 1971, 1972, 1978, 1979, 1980
Frank Stapleton	Arsenal 1978, 1979, 1980 Manchester U 1983, 1985
Ray Clemence	Liverpool 1971, 1974, 1977 Tottenham H 1982, 1987

Including replays Kinnaird played in 11 Cup Final matches. Forrest, Wollaston, Giles, Stapleton and Clemence played in in six Cup Final matches.

MOST FA CUP FINAL APPEARANCES AT WEMBLEY (INCLUDING REPLAYS)

6 Ray Clemence, Frank Stapleton
5 Joe Hulme, Pat Rice, Johnny Giles, Glenn Hoddle (Tottenham H), Chris Hughton (Tottenham H), Bryan Robson (Manchester U), Arthur Albiston (Manchester U) and David O'Leary (Arsenal).

Clemence and Stapleton played in five Finals and one replay. Hoddle, Hughton and Robson played in three Finals and two replays. Hulme, Rice and Giles played in five Finals. Albiston and O'Leary played in four finals and one replay.

MOST WINNER'S MEDALS

5 Charles Wollaston	Wanderers 1872, 1873, 1876, 1877, 1878
Arthur Kinnaird	Wanderers 1873, 1877, 1878 Old Etonians 1879, 1882
James Forrest	Blackburn R 1884, 1885, 1886, 1890, 1891
4 Joe Lofthouse	Blackburn R 1884, 1885, 1886, 1891

3 Twenty-six players have won three winner's medals. Those currently still playing are Bruce Grobbelaar, Steve Nicol, Ian Rush (all Liverpool) and Bryan Robson (Man United).

MOST LOSER'S MEDALS

4 Arthur Kinnaird	Old Etonians 1875, 1876, 1881, 1883
Harry Wood	Wolverhampton W 1889, 1896 Southampton 1900, 1902
Jimmy Lawrence	Newcastle U 1905, 1906, 1908, 1911
Jack Rutherford	Newcastle U 1905, 1906, 1908, 1911
Colin Veitch	Newcastle U 1905, 1906, 1908, 1911
Paul Bracewell	Everton 1985, 1986, 1989 Sunderland 1992

3 Sixteen players have collected three loser's medals. Those still playing are Kevin Ratcliffe, Graeme Sharp, Kevin Sheedy, Trevor Steven and Pat Van den Hauwe (all Everton).

Kinnaird, Wood, Lawrence, Rutherford, Veitch, Ratcliffe, Sharp, Steven and Van den Hauwe also gained winner's medals. Three of Bracewell's losing finals were against Liverpool (1986, 1989, 1992)

WINNERS MEDALS WITH DIFFERENT TEAMS

Paul Allen	West Ham U 1980	Tottenham H	1991
Francis Birley	Oxford Univ 1874	Wanderers	1876, 1877
Raich Carter	Sunderland 1937	Derby County	1946
Fred Chappell-Maddison	Oxford Univ 1874	Wanderers	1876
Ray Clemence	Liverpool 1974	Tottenham H	1982
Jim Dugdale	WBA 1954	Aston Villa	1957
Johnny Giles	Manchester U 1963	Leeds U	1972
Frederick Green	Oxford Univ 1874	Wanderers	1877, 1878
Harold Halse	Manchester U 1909	Aston Villa	1913
George Hedley	Sheffield U 1899, 1902	Wolves	1908
David Jack	Bolton W 1923, 1926	Arsenal	1930
Pat Jennings	Tottenham H 1967	Arsenal	1979

Arthur Kinnaird	Wanderers	1873, 1877, 1878	Old Etonians	1879, 1882	

			Tottenham H	1982	Liverpool	1971, 1977

Arthur Kinnaird — Wanderers — 1873, 1877, 1878 — Old Etonians — 1879, 1882

Tottenham H — 1982 — Liverpool — 1971, 1977

Stan Crowther — Aston Villa — 1957 — Manchester U — 1958

Edgar Lubbock — Wanderers — 1872 — Old Etonians — 1879
Ernie Curtis — Cardiff C — 1927 — Birmingham — 1931

Billy Meredith — Manchester C — 1904 — Manchester U — 1909
Doug Holden — Bolton W — 1958 — Preston NE — 1964

Jimmy Nelson — Cardiff C — 1927 — Newcastle U — 1932
Johnny Giles — Manchester U — 1963 — Leeds U — 1965, 1970, 1973

Peter Osgood — Chelsea — 1970 — Southampton — 1976

Stuart Pearson — Manchester U — 1977 — West Ham — 1980
Joe Hulme — Arsenal — 1930, 1936 — Huddersfield T — 1938

John Reynolds — WBA — 1892 — Aston Villa — 1895, 1897

Frank Stapleton — Arsenal — 1979 — Manchester U — 1983, 1985
David Jack — Bolton W — 1923, 1926 — Arsenal — 1932

Clem Stephenson — Aston Villa — 1913, 1920 — Huddersfield T — 1922
Pat Jennings — Tottenham H — 1967 — Arsenal — 1978, 1980

Brian Talbot — Ipswich T — 1978 — Arsenal — 1979
Tommy Johnson — Everton — 1933 — Manchester C — 1926

David Taylor — Bradford C — 1911 — Burnley — 1914
Ray Kennedy — Arsenal — 1971 — Liverpool — 1977

Ernie Taylor — Newcastle U — 1951 — Blackpool — 1953
Gary Lineker — Tottenham H — 1991 — Everton — 1986

Sandy Turnbull — Manchester C — 1904 — Manchester U — 1909
Jim McCalliog — Southampton — 1976 — Sheffield W — 1966

George Utley — Barnsley — 1912 — Sheffield U — 1915
Frank McLintock — Arsenal — 1971 — Leicester C — 1961, 1963

RWS Vidal — Wanderers — 1872 — Oxford Univ — 1874

Bobby Moore — West Ham — 1964 — Fulham — 1975
Alan Mullery — Tottenham H — 1967 — Fulham — 1975

WINNER'S MEDALS WITH DIFFERENT TEAMS IN SUCCESSIVE YEARS

Jimmy Nelson — Cardiff C — 1927 — Cardiff C — 1925 — Newcastle U — 1932

Arthur Kinnaird — Wanderers — 1878 — Old Etonians — 1879
Stuart Pearson — Manchester U — 1977 — Manchester U — 1976 — West Ham — 1980

Brian Talbot — Ipswich T — 1978 — Arsenal — 1979
Peter Rodrigues — Southampton — 1976 — Leicester C — 1969

Bill Slater — Wolverhampton — 1960 — Blackpool — 1951

LOSER'S MEDALS WITH DIFFERENT TEAMS

Frank Stapleton — Manchester U — 1983, 1985 — Arsenal — 1978, 1980

Clive Allen — QPR — 1982 — Tottenham H — 1987
Brian Talbot — Ipswich T — 1978 — Arsenal — 1980 — Arsenal — 1979

Alan Ball — Everton — 1968 — Arsenal — 1972

Bobby Barclay — Sheffield U — 1936 — Huddersfield T — 1938
Ernie Taylor — Newcastle U — 1951 — Manchester U — 1958 — Blackpool — 1953

Ted Barkas — Huddersfield — 1928 — Birmingham — 1931

John Barnes — Watford — 1984 — Liverpool — 1988
Andy Thorn — Wimbledon — 1988 — Crystal Pal. — 1990

Paul Bracewell — Everton — 1985, 1986, 1989 — Sunderland — 1992
Dennis Tueart — Sunderland — 1973 — Manchester C — 1981
Pat Van den Hauwe — Tottenham H — 1991 — Everton — 1985, 1986, 1989

Mark Bright — C Palace — 1990 — Sheffield W — 1993
Ian Wright — Arsenal — 1993 — C Palace — 1990

Charlie Buchan — Sunderland — 1913 — Arsenal — 1927

Jimmy Case — Liverpool — 1977 — Brighton & HA — 1983

Edgar Chadwick — Everton — 1893, 1897 — Southampton — 1902

PLAYED FOR AND AGAINST THE SAME TEAM IN THE CUP FINAL

	Year	Played for	Against
Allan Clarke	1969	Leeds U	1970, 1973
Clive Allen	1982	Queens Park Rangers	Tottenham H
	1987	Tottenham H	Coventry C
Ray Clemence	1971, 1977	Tottenham H	1987
Alexander Bonsor	1872	Wanderers	Royal Engineers
	1873	Wanderers	Oxford University
Alex Dawson	Manchester U	1958	Preston NE	1964
	1876	Old Etonians	Wanderers
Willie Fagan	Preston NE	1937	Liverpool	1950
Francis Birley	1873	Oxford University	Wanderers
John Goodall	Preston NE	1888	Derby County	1898
	1877	Wanderers	Oxford University
Steve Hodge	Tottenham H	1987	Nottingham F	1991
Austen Campbell	1928	Blackburn R	Huddersfield T
Doug Holden	Bolton W	1953	Preston NE	1964
	1930	Huddersfield T	Arsenal
Bob Howard	Preston NE	1888	Everton	1893
Fred Chappell-	1873	Oxford University	Wanderers
Joe Hulme	Arsenal	1927, 1932	Huddersfield T	1938
Maddison	1876	Wanderers	Old Etonians
Howard Kendall	Preston NE	1964	Everton	1968
Stan Crowther	1957	Aston Villa	Manchester U
Ray Kennedy	Arsenal	1971	Liverpool	1977
	1958	Manchester U	Bolton W
Malcolm Macdonald	Newcastle U	1974	Arsenal	1978
Steve Hodge	1987	Tottenham H	Coventry C
Terry McDermott	Newcastle U	1974	Liverpool	1977
	1991	Nottingham F	Tottenham H
Frank McLintock	Leicester C	1961, 1963	Arsenal	1972
Joe Hulme	1930	Arsenal	Huddersfield T
	1938	Huddersfield T	Preston NE
Peter Meechan	Everton	1897	Southampton	1900
Tommy Johnson	1926	Manchester City	Bolton
Alf Milward	Everton	1893, 1897	Southampton	1900
	1933	Everton	Manchester City
Ray Kennedy	1971	Arsenal	Liverpool
Henry Ness	Barnsley	1910	Sunderland	1913
	1977	Liverpool	Manchester U
Cuthbert Ottaway	Oxford Univ	1873	Old Etonians	1875
William Kenyon-	1873	Wanderers	Oxford University
Gary Stevens	Brighton & HA	1983	Tottenham H	1987
Slaney	1876	Old Etonians	Wanderers
Chris Waddle	Tottenham H	1987	Sheffield W	1993
Arthur Kinnaird	1873	Wanderers	Oxford University
Harry Wood	Wolves	1889, 1896	Southampton	1900, 1903
	1876	Old Etonians	Wanderers
	1877	Wanderers	Oxford University
	1878	Wanderers	Royal Engineers

WON WITH ONE TEAM, LOST WITH ANOTHER

Nearly 50 players have gained winners and losers medals with different teams. These are the players to have done so in Wembley finals since 1923:

	Won With		Lost With	
Paul Allen	West Ham	1980	Tottenham H	1987
	Tottenham H	1991		
John Barnes	Liverpool	1989	Watford	1984
Dave Bennett	Coventry C	1987	Manchester C	1981
Austen Campbell	Huddersfield	1930	Blackburn R	1928
Allan Clarke	Leeds U	1972	Leicester C	1969
Ray Clemence	Liverpool	1974	Tottenham H	1987

Continuing the "Played for and against" column:

Edgar Lubbock	1872	Wanderers	Royal Engineers
	1876	Old Etonians	Wanderers
Terry McDermott	1974	Newcastle U	Liverpool
	1977	Liverpool	Manchester U
Bobby Moore	1964	West Ham U	Preston NE
	1975	Fulham	West Ham U
John Reynolds	1892	WBA	Aston Villa
	1895	Aston Villa	WBA
Frank Stapleton	1979	Arsenal	Manchester U
	1983	Manchester U	Brighton & HA
	1985	Manchester U	Everton
Clem Stephenson	1920	Aston Villa	Huddersfield T
	1922	Huddersfield T	Preston NE
	1928	Huddersfield T	Blackburn R

Ernie Taylor	1951	Newcastle U	Blackpool
	1953	Blackpool	Bolton W
Albert Thompson	1872	Wanderers	Royal Engineers
	1873	Wanderers	Oxford University
	1876	Old Etonians	Wanderers
Julian Sturgis	1873	Wanderers	Royal Engineers
	1876	Old Etonians	Wanderers
Brian Talbot	1978	Ipswich T	Arsensal
	1979	Arsenal	Manchester U
	1980	Arsenal	West Ham
RWS Vidal	1872	Wanderers	Royal Engineers
	1873	Oxford University	Wanderers

PLAYED FOR THREE DIFFERENT TEAMS IN THE CUP FINAL

Only two men have played for three different teams in the Cup Final:-

Harold Halse – Manchester United 1909, Aston Villa, 1913, Chelsea 1915

Ernie Taylor – Newcastle United 1951, Blackpool 1953, Manchester United 1958

PLAYED AGAINST THE SAME OPPOSITION IN THE CUP FINAL FOR DIFFERENT TEAMS

Only 12 men have done this and only three of them won in both matches against the same opposition – Frederick Green, Jimmy Nelson and Robert Vidal.

		Playing for	Against
John Barnes	1984	Watford	Everton
	1989	Liverpool	Everton
Robert Benson	1874	Oxford University	Royal Engineers
	1875	Old Etonians	Royal Engineers
Dave Bennett	1981	Manchester City	Tottenham H
	1987	Coventry City	Tottenham H
Paul Bracewell	1986	Everton	Liverpool
	1989	Everton	Liverpool
	1992	Sunderland	Liverpool
Jimmy Case	1977	Liverpool	Manchester U
	1983	Brighton HA	Manchester U
Frederick Green	1874	Oxford University	Royal Engineers
	1878	Wanderers	Royal Engineers
Arthur Kinnaird	1875	Old Etonians	Royal Engineers
	1878	Wanderers	Royal Engineers
Edgar Lubbock	1872	Wanderers	Royal Engineers
	1875	Old Etonians	Royal Engineers
Jimmy Nelson	1927	Cardiff C	Arsenal
	1932	Newcastle U	Arsenal
James Prinsep	1879	Clapham Rovers	Old Etonians
	1881	Old Carthusians	Old Etonians
Ernie Taylor	1953	Blackpool	Bolton W
	1958	Manchester U	Bolton W
RWS Vidal	1872	Wanderers	Royal Engineers
	1874	Oxford University	Royal Engineers

SCORED FOR DIFFERENT TEAMS IN THE CUP FINAL

Not including own goals, three men have scored for different teams in the Cup Final.

George Hedley scored for Sheffield United in the 1902 replay against Southampton and for Wolverhampton Wanderers when they beat Newcastle United in 1908.

Frank Stapleton scored for Arsenal when they beat Manchester United 3-2 in 1979 and for United in their 2–2 drawn first match against Brighton in 1983.

Ian Wright scored twice as a substitute when Crystal Palace drew 3-3 with Manchester United in 1990. He scored for Arsenal when they drew 1-1 with Sheffield Wednesday in 1993 and scored again in the replay as Arsenal won 2-1.

Ian Wright (right), the third player to score for different teams in the Cup final and the first player to score twice for different teams. It took Wright just four hours of Cup Final football to score his four goals and there may be more to come (Allsport/Mike Hewitt)

FOUR CONSECUTIVE APPEARANCES

Five players appeared in four consecutive FA Cup Final matches for Wanderers – 1876 plus replay, 1877 and 1878. They were Hubert Heron, Jarvis Kenrick, William Lindsay, Alfred Stratford and Charles Wollaston.

Seven Blackburn Rovers players also appeared in four consecutive Cup Final matches in 1884, 1885, 1886 and a replay in 1886. They were Herbert Arthur, James Brown, James Douglas, James Forrest, Hugh McIntyre, Fergus Suter and Joe Sowerbutts. Brown scored a goal in all three years and all of them won three medals.

Three teams have played in four consecutive FA Cup Final matches this century – Sheffield United (1901 and replay, 1902 and replay), Newcastle United (1910 and replay, 1911 and replay), and Tottenham Hotspur (1981 and replay, 1982 and replay).

Eight Sheffield United players appeared in all four games: Billy Foulke, Harry Thickett, Peter Boyle, Harry Johnson, Ernest Needham, George Hedley, Fred Priest and Bert Lipsham.

Seven Newcastle United players appeared in all four games: Jimmy Lawrence, Billy McCracken, Colin Veitch, Wilf Low, Jack Rutherford, Alex Higgins and George Wilson.

Eight Tottenham players appeared in all four matches: Chris Hughton, Paul Miller, Graham Roberts, Steve Perryman, Steve Archibald, Tony Galvin, Glenn Hoddle and Garth Crooks. Garry Brooke set a record by appearing in three of Spurs four matches as a substitute – the only man to appear in three Cup Final matches as a sub.

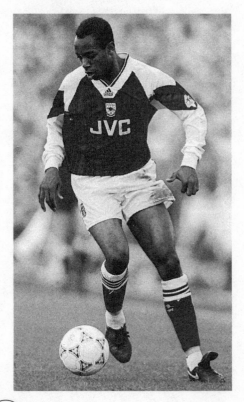

FA CUP AND AMATEUR CUP MEDALS Only two players won both FA Cup and FA Amateur Cup winners medals and both men did it in the same years.

In 1895 Tom Morren won an Amateur Cup winner's medal with Middlesbrough and in 1899 he won an FA Cup winner's medal with Sheffield United.

In 1895 Bob Chatt scored the only goal of the FA Cup Final when Aston Villa beat West Brom 1–0. In 1899, reinstated as an amateur and back at his original club, he helped Stockton beat Harwich and Parkeston 1–0 in the Amateur Cup Final at Middlesbrough.

IN THE RIGHT PLACE AT THE RIGHT TIME Some of the most famous and capped footballers of all never played in an FA Cup Final.

The list includes three men who were in England's 1966 World Cup winning team:- George Cohen (37 caps, 408 League apps), Nobby Stiles (28 caps, 413 apps) and Martin Peters (67 caps, 722 apps).

Other notable players not to make a Cup Final appearance include George Best (37 caps, 411 apps), Johnny Haynes (56 caps, 594 apps), John Charles (38 caps, 373 apps) and Terry Butcher (77 caps who has currently played more than 400 League games in both England and Scotland).

Other players have seemingly called in on one club for a short time, played in the Cup Final and moved on. This is a list of players since 1946 who only made a handful – and in one case – no League appearances during their time at a club.

	Cup Final	League Apps
Arthur Turner	Charlton 1946	0
Les Sealey	Manchester U 1990	2
Laurie Cunningham	Wimbledon 1988 (sub)	6
Alan Davies	Manchester U 1983	7 (6 +1)
Neil Price	Watford 1984	8 (7 +1)
Paul Atkinson	Watford 1984	11 (8 +3)
Mike Trebilcock	Everton 1966	11
Stan Crowther	Manchester U 1958	13
Alan Harris	Chelsea 1967	14
Jim Bullions	Derby Co 1946	17
Denis Clarke	WBA 1968 (sub)	21 (19 +2)
Cyril Robinson	Blackpool 1953	22
Ernie Taylor	Manchester U 1958	22
Milia Aleksic	Tottenham H 1981	25
Joe Robinson	Blackpool 1948	25
Gerry Gow	Manchester City 1981	26

Turner was an RAF officer and amateur inside or centre-forward who scored seven goals in nine matches as Charlton reached the first post-war Cup Final. There was no League football in the 1945–46 season and he had moved on by the time the League campaign restarted for the 1946–47 season. He later played in the League with Colchester United.

Sealey was on loan to Manchester United from Luton and became the only 'on loan' player to play in the Cup Final when he replaced Jim Leighton in the United goal for the replay against Crystal Palace. He subsequently signed for United and made a further 31 League appearance before moving to Aston Villa.

Cunningham had a short spell at Wimbledon towards the end of his career. When he came on as a substitute for Wimbledon against Liverpool in 1988 he completed a rare double as a he had also played against Liverpool for Real Madrid in the 1981 European Cup Final in Paris. He was killed in a car-crash in Spain on July 15, 1989.

Alan Davies was one of Manchester United's outstanding players when they beat Brighton over two games in 1983 and he was tipped for a bright future. But after only a handful of games he moved on to Newcastle, and had spells at Swansea City and Bradford City and loan periods at Charlton A and Carlisle U. He played 11 times for Wales. He committed suicide on February 4, 1992.

Trebilcock was signed by Everton manager Harry Catterick from Plymouth Argyle on New Year's Eve 1965. He played seven League matches before the Cup Final and made four appearances in the two seasons after it before moving on to Portsmouth and then Torquay. But he will always be remembered at Goodison for the two goals he scored in Everton's 3–2 Cup Final win over Sheffield Wednesday.

Harris was in his second spell at Chelsea. He had earlier made 70 appearances between 1960 and 1964.

Crowther joined Manchester United after the Munich air crash and spent 10 months at Old Trafford before moving on to Chelsea. He was granted special dispensation to play in the Cup for United as he had previously played for Aston Villa in the 1957–58 competition. He had played for Villa against United in the final the previous year.

Cup Final relatives

There are many instances of members of the same family playing League and Cup football and relatives, sometimes even distant ones, have appeared in the Cup Final with surprising regularity.

FATHER AND SON Peter Boyle won FA Cup winner's medals with Sheffield United in 1899 and 1902. His son Thomas Boyle won a winner's medal with Sheffield United in 1925.

Harold Johnson also won FA Cup winner's medals with Sheffield United in 1899 and 1902 and his son Harold won a winner's medal with Sheffield United in 1925. Another son, Thomas Johnson, was Sheffield United's centre-half when they lost to Arsenal in 1936.

Hubert Pearson was West Bromwich Albion's goalkeeper when they lost the FA Cup in 1912. His son Harold Pearson was West Brom's goalkeeper, gaining a winner's medal in 1931 and a runners-up medal in 1935 (*see cousins*).

Les Allen won a Cup winner's medal for Tottenham in 1961. His son Clive played against Tottenham in the 1982 Cup Final and for Tottenham in the 1987 Cup Final (*also see cousins*).

Alec Herd played for Manchester City in the 1933 and 1934 Cup Finals. His son David Herd played for Manchester United in the 1963 Cup Final. Matt Busby, who played alongside Alec Herd in 1933 and 1934, was United's manager in 1963.

Jimmy Dunn played for Everton against Manchester City in 1933. His son Jimmy played for Wolves against Leicester in 1949.

Brian Clough was the manager of the Nottingham Forest team that reached the 1991 Cup Final. His son Nigel was in the team.

Arthur Kingscott refereed the Cup finals of 1900 and 1901. His eldest son Harry refereed the 1931 Cup Final.

FATHER-IN-LAW AND SON-IN-LAW Billy Meredith won Cup winner's medals with Manchester

City in 1904 and Manchester United in 1909. His son-in-law Charlie Pringle was in the Manchester City team beaten by Bolton Wanderers in 1926.

BROTHERS There have been a number of cases of brothers playing in the Cup Final, but only one pair of brothers have played against each other in the same match. In 1874, Herbert Rawson played for the Royal Engineers and his brother William was in the Oxford University team. Oxford won 2–0.

The only pair of brothers to have played together in an FA Cup winning team and also in an international team were Frederick and Hubert Heron of the Wanderers. On March 4, 1876 they played for England against Scotland and two weeks later played for Wanderers against Old Etonians in the Cup Final. Scotland won the international 3–0 but Wanderers won the Cup Final 3–0 after a replay.

Balmer .... William and Robert Balmer played as full-backs together for Everton in their losing 1907 Cup Final to Sheffield Wednesday. William, the older brother also played in the 1906 Cup when Everton beat Newcastle.

Banks .... Ralph played for Bolton in 1953, Tommy played for Bolton in 1958. Both were left-backs.

Bell .... George and Harry Bell played for West Bromwich Albion when they lost to Blackburn Rovers in 1886.

Bennett .... Dave Bennett played in two finals against Tottenham, for Manchester City in 1981 and Coventry City in 1987. His brother Gary played for Sunderland against Liverpool in 1992.

Blanchflower ... Jackie played for Manchester United in 1957, Danny played for Tottenham in 1961 and 1962.

Bray .... John played for Manchester City in 1933 and 1934. His brother George, nine years his junior, played for Burnley in 1947.

Charlton .... Bobby played for Manchester United in 1957, 1958 and 1963, Jack played for Leeds United in 1965, 1970 and 1972.

Compton .... Denis and Leslie Compton played together for Arsenal in the 1950 Cup Final against Liverpool. Denis was also one of England's most famous Test cricketers and both Leslie and Denis played County Cricket for Middlesex.

Goodall .... Archie and John Goodall played together in the Derby beaten in 1898. John also played for Preston in 1888 and 1889, while Archie made a further appearance for Derby in 1903.

Greenhoff .... Brian and Jimmy Greenhoff followed the Comptons and the Robledos as the third pair of brothers to play together in a winning Cup Final team this century when they both played for Manchester United in 1977. Brian also played

for United in the 1976 Final, Jimmy played for United in the 1979 Final.

Hargreaves .... Fred and Jack Hargreaves played together in the Blackburn Rovers team that lost the 1882 final to Old Etonians. Jack played in the winning Blackburn side of 1884.

Harris .... Allan and Ron both played for Chelsea in 1967. Ron captained Chelsea when they beat Leeds in 1970.

Heron .... Hubert and Frederick Heron (see above) played together for Wanderers in 1876. Hubert also played in the 1877 and 1878 finals.

Horton .... Ezra and Jack both played for West Bromwich Albion. Ezra played in the finals of 1886, 1887 and 1888. Jack played in 1895.

Johnson .... Brothers Harold (1925) and Thomas (1936) both played for Sheffield United as their father had done (1899, 1902).

Lyttleton .... The Hon. Alfred and The Hon. and Rev. Edward played in the Old Etonians team beaten by Wanderers in 1876.

O'Donnell .... Frank and Hugh O'Donnell's careers spanned the Second World War. They played together in the Preston team which lost the 1937 Cup Final to Sunderland. Hugh was in the team a year later which beat Huddersfield to win the Cup.

Perry .... Five Perry brothers played for West Bromwich Albion in the 1880s and 1890s – Charles, Edward, Thomas, Walter and William. Charles played in the Finals of 1886, 1888, 1892 and 1897. Tom played in 1895.

Rawson .... Herbert and William Rawson (see above) – the only brothers to play against each other in the Cup Final when they were on opposing sides in 1874. Herbert also played in the 1875 Final, William played in 1877.

Robledo .... Edward and George Robledo of Chile played together for Newcastle in the 1952 Cup Final against Arsenal and George scored the only goal of the game. George, a Chile international, also played in the 1951 Final.

Smith .... Jack and William Smith played together in the 1934 final for Portsmouth. Jack had also played in the 1929 Pompey side beaten by Bolton.

COUSINS The most recent case of cousins playing in the Cup Final occured in 1987 when Clive and Paul Allen appeared for Tottenham. In 1931 Harry Hibbs, the England goalkeeper, was playing for Birmingham and his cousin Harold Pearson was at the other end of the field, in goal for West Bromwich Albion. (*see father and son*).

Other examples of cousins being involved in the Cup Final include:-
Dennis Stevens (Bolton Wanderers 1958) and Duncan Edwards (Manchester U 1957)

Elton John was the centre of attention as his Watford side played in the 1984 Cup Final. His uncle Roy Dwight had played in the 1959 final for Nottingham Forest (Allsport/David Cannon)

Glyn Pardoe and Alan Oakes (both played for Manchester City 1969)
Arthur Chadwick (Southampton 1900) and Edgar Chadwick (Everton 1893, 1897, Southampton 1902)
Jim Baxter and Willie Cunningham (both played for Preston NE 1954)
Jackie Milburn (Newcastle 1951, 1952 and 1955) and Bobby and Jack Charlton (*see brothers*) were second cousins. Bobby and Jack's mother Cissie was Jackie Milburn's first cousin.

UNCLES AND NEPHEWS Les Allen (Tottenham 1961) and Paul Allen (West Ham 1980, Tottenham 1987). Hubert Pearson (WBA 1912) and Harry Hibbs (Birmingham 1931). John and George Bray (see above) and John Bray (Blackburn 1960).

OTHER CONNECTIONS There are many other famous Cup Final family connections. Some of the more interesting:

Roy Dwight, who scored, and then broke his leg playing for Nottingham Forest in the 1959 Cup Final, is the uncle of singer Elton John. Elton John was the Watford chairman when they reached the Final in 1984.

Cyrille Regis, who played for Coventry when they won the Cup in 1987 is a cousin of of international sprinter John Regis who played a handful of matches for Arsenal's youth and reserve teams.

Athlete Steve Cram is one of Sunderland's most famous supporters and was accorded VIP treatment at the 1992 Cup Final. His Uncle Bobby never made it to the Cup Final but was in the Colchester team which beat Leeds 3–2 in one of the most famous giant-killing acts of all time in 1971.

Stanley Matthews' son, Stanley junior, won the Boys Singles Championship at Wimbledon in 1962. Amanda Brown, the daughter of Ken Brown, who played for West Ham in the 1964 Cup Final, was also a tennis professional.

Cliff Jones, who played for Tottenham in 1961 and 1962, is a cousin of journalist Ken Jones.

The father of Emlyn Hughes (Liverpool 1971, 1974, 1977) was a Rugby League international.

The father of Terry Dyson (Tottenham 1961) was a jockey.

George Woodhall, who played in three Cup Finals for West Bromwich Albion in 1886, 1887 and 1888, is the great-great-great-grandfather of Richie Woodhall, who won an Olympic middleweight boxing medal at Barcelona in 1992. He shouted 'Up The Baggies' on the medal rostrum.

Steve Gatting, who played for Brighton in the 1983 Final, is the brother of England Test cricketer Mike Gatting.

Cup Final Cricketers

Many professional footballers have played first-class cricket. Gary Lineker did not play first-class cricket but he did play for an invitational MCC side against Germany at Lord's in 1992. He scored one run before being dismissed. When asked about the experience afterwards, he replied, 'It's always nice to score one against the Germans . . .'

The following players all played first-class cricket and also won FA Cup winners' medals:-

Charles Alcock	Wanderers	1872	Essex
Morton Peto Betts	Wanderers	1872	Middx and Kent
Edgar Lubbock	Wanderers	1872,	Kent
	Old Etonians	1879	
William Kenyon-Slaney	Wanderers	1873	MCC
Cuthbert Ottaway	Oxford Univ	1874	Kent and Middx
Charles Nepean	Oxford Univ	1874	Middx
Francis Birley	Oxford Univ	1874	Lancs and Surrey
Henry Renny-Tailyour	Royal Engineers	1875	Kent
Herbert Whitfield	Old Etonians	1875	Sussex
Edward Wynyard	Old Carthusians	1881	Hampshire
Percy de Paravicini	Old Etonians	1882	Middx
John Goodall	Preston NE	1899	Derbys
Harry Daft	Notts County	1894	Notts
John Devey	Aston Villa	1895	Warwicks
		1897	
Ernest 'Nudger' Needham	Sheffield U	1899	Derbys
		1902	
Bill Foulke	Sheffield U	1899	Derbys
		1902	
William George	Aston Villa	1905	Warwicks
Jack Sharp	Everton	1906	Lancs
Harry Makepeace	Everton	1906	Lancs
Andy Ducat	Aston Villa	1920	Surrey
Joe Hulme	Arsenal	1930	Middx
		1936	
Ted Drake	Arsenal	1936	Hamps
Raich Carter	Sunderland	1937	Derbys
	Derby County	1946	
Denis Compton	Arsenal	1950	Middx
Leslie Compton	Arsenal	1950	Middx
Jim Standen	West Ham	1964	Worcs
Geoff Hurst	West Ham	1964	Essex

Harry Makepeace holds a unique record. He is the only man to:

● win a Cup winner's medal – Everton 1906
● win a League Championship medal – Everton 1915
● be capped as a soccer international – 4 England caps 1906–1912

- win a County Cricket Championship medal – Lancashire 1926, 1927, 1928, 1930
- and be capped as a cricket international – 4 England caps vs Australia, 1920/21

BEATEN CUP FINALISTS WHO ALSO PLAYED FIRST-CLASS CRICKET INCLUDE:-
Alfred and Edward Lyttleton (Old Etonians 1876) – Middx and Worcs
Jackie Lee (Leicester City 1949) – Leicestershire
CB (Charles) Fry (Southampton 1902) – Surrey, Sussex and Hampshire
Freddie Goodwin (Manchester United 1958) – Lancs
Don Roper (Arsenal 1952) – Hampshire
Jack Dyson (Manchester C 1956) – Lancashire
Phil Taylor (Liverpool 1950) – Gloucestershire

Cup Finalists born Outside British Isles

ARGENTINA Osvaldo Ardiles, Tottenham H 1981; Ricardo Villa, Tottenham H 1981

AUSTRALIA Joe Marston, Preston NE 1954

BELGIUM Nico Claesen, Tottenham H 1987; Pat Van den Hauwe, Everton 1985, 1986, 1989, Tottenham H 1991

BURMA Charlie Mitten, Manchester United 1948

CANADA Edward Parry, Oxford University 1877, Old Carthusians 1881; Jimmy Nicholl, Man U 1977

CEUTA (Spanish protectorate in Morocco) Nayim (Mohamed Ali Amar), Tottenham H 1991

CEYLON (Sri Lanka) Jack Butler, Arsenal 1927

CHILE Edward Robledo, Newcastle United 1952; George Robledo, Newcastle United 1951, 1952

DENMARK Jesper Olsen, Manchester United 1985; Jan Molby, Liverpool 1986, 1988, 1992; John Jensen, Arsenal 1993

FRENCH GUYANA Cyrille Regis, Coventry City 1987

GERMANY Bert Trautmann, Manchester City 1955, 1956; David Phillips, Coventry 1987 (West Germany)

INDIA Alfred Goodwyn, Royal Engineers 1872; William Kenyon-Slaney, Wanderers 1873, Old Etonians 1875, 1876; William Lindsay, Wanderers, 1876, 1877, 1878; James Prinsep, Clapham Rovers, 1879, Old Carthusians 1881

JAMAICA Bob Hazell, QPR 1982; John Barnes, Watford 1984, Liverpool 1988, 1989

MAURITIUS Herbert Rawson, Royal Engineers 1874, 1875 (brother William born in S Africa)

NETHERLANDS Arnold Muhren, Manchester United 1983

NIGERIA John Salako, Crystal Palace 1990

NORWAY Erik Thorstvedt, Tottenham H 1991

SIERRA LEONE Chris Bart-Williams, Sheffield W 1993

SINGAPORE Nigel Callaghan, Watford 1984; Eric Young, Wimbledon, 1988

SOUTH AFRICA William Rawson, Oxford University 1874, 1877; Alex Bell, Man U 1909; Bill Perry, Blackpool 1951, 1953; Albert Johanneson, Leeds U 1965; Craig Johnston, Liverpool 1986, 1988; Bruce Grobbelaar, Liverpool 1986, 1988, 1989, 1992

SWEDEN Richard Gough, Tottenham H 1987; Roland Nilsson, Sheffield W 1993

UNITED STATES John Harkes, Sheffield W 1993

Managers

The following 13 men have played in, and then managed Cup winning teams:-

	As a player	As a manager
Peter McWilliam	Newcastle U 1910	Tottenham H 1921
Billy Walker	Aston Villa 1920	Sheffield W 1935
		Nottingham F 1959
Jimmy Seed	Tottenham H 1921	Charlton A 1947
Joe Smith	Bolton W 1923	Blackpool 1953
	Bolton W 1926	
Stan Seymour	Newcastle U 1924	Newcastle U 1951
		Newcastle U 1952
Matt Busby	Manchester C 1934	Manchester U 1948
		Manchester U 1963
Bill Shankly	Preston NE 1938	Liverpool 1965
		Liverpool 1974
Joe Mercer	Arsenal 1950	Manchester C 1969
Bob Stokoe	Newcastle U 1955	Sunderland 1973
Don Revie	Manchester C 1956	Leeds U 1972
Terry Venables	Tottenham H 1967	Tottenham H 1991
Kenny Dalglish	Liverpool 1986	Liverpool 1986
		Liverpool 1989
George Graham	Arsenal 1971	Arsenal 1993

MANAGED MOST FA CUP FINAL TEAMS: Frank Watt, Newcastle U (6 times – 1905, 1906, 1908, 1910, 1911, 1924)

MANAGED MOST FA CUP WINNING TEAMS: John Nicholson, Sheffield United (3 times – 1902, 1915, 1925); Charles Foweraker, Bolton Wanderers (3 times – 1923, 1926, 1929); Bill Nicholson, Tottenham H (3 times – 1961, 1962, 1967)

YOUNGEST MANAGER The youngest FA Cup Final manager was Stan Cullis, who was 33 years 187 days old when he was in charge of the Wolverhampton Wanderers team that beat Leicester City to win the Cup in 1949. He had been in the Wolves team beaten in the 1939 FA Cup Final by Portsmouth.

MANAGER OF ENGLISH AND SCOTTISH FA CUP WINNING TEAMS Only two men have achieved this: Jimmy Cochrane (Kilmarnock 1929 and Sunderland 1937) and Alex Ferguson (Aberdeen 1982, 1983, 1984, 1986 and Manchester United 1990).

Scorers

Denis Law is universally recognised as being the highest scorer in the history of the FA Cup with 41 goals for Huddersfield, Manchester United and Manchester City in his career that lasted from 1957–1974. Law's tally would have been higher but the six goals he scored in

Brian Clough and Terry Venables lead the teams out for the 1991 FA Cup final. While Clough famously never won the FA Cup, Venables did so with Tottenham both as a player and as a manager (Allsport/David Cannon)

a match for Manchester City in 1961 were wiped from the record books when the match was abandoned.

But Henry Cursham of Notts County and England scored more Cup goals than Law. During his spell at Notts County between 1880 and 1887 he scored 48 goals in the FA Cup. A number of these were scored in rounds which were in the Competition Proper but which were regionalised until the formal introduction of the First and Second Series matches in 1886. But these matches were all in the Competition Proper. The split between the Qualifying Competition and the Competition Proper did not occur until 1888–89.

Three Cursham brothers all played for Notts County at the same time in the 1880s. AW Cursham, like Henry was an England international and scored 16 FA Cup goals for County, while CL Cursham scored three Cup goals for the club.

THE HIGHEST SCORERS IN THE FA CUP

48 ...... Henry Cursham, Notts County
41 ...... Denis Law, Huddersfield, Manchester C, Manchester U, Manchester C
39 ...... Ian Rush, Chester, Liverpool
38 ...... Allan Clarke, Walsall, Fulham, Leeds, Leicester, Barnsley

Including own goals, 255 different players have scored a total of 337 goals in FA Cup Final matches between 1872 and 1993. One goal, scored by Royal Engineers in 1878, is credited as a 'rush' and the scorer is not known. The winning team has scored 261 goals, the losers 76.

MOST GOALS SCORED IN CUP FINALS (AGGREGATE)

5 .... Ian Rush, Liverpool, 1986 (2) 1989 (2), 1992 (1)
4 .... William Townley, Blackburn R, 1890 (3), 1891
4 .... Stan Mortensen, Blackpool, 1948 (1), 1953 (3)
4 .... Ian Wright, Crystal Palace 1990 (2), 1991 (1), 1991 replay (1)

CUP FINAL HAT-TRICKS Only three men have ever scored a hat-trick in a Cup Final:-
William Townley, Blackburn Rovers 1890; Jimmy Logan, Notts County, 1894; Stan Mortensen, Blackpool 1953; Sandy Brown of Tottenham H scored three goals in the 1901 Cup Final – two in the first match, one in the replay.

SCORED IN SUCCESSIVE FINALS

Alexander Bonsor	1875 Old Etonians (1);	1876 Old Etonians (1)
Jarvis Kenrick	1877 Wanderers (1);	1878 Wanderers (2)
James Forrest	1884 Blackburn R (1);	1885 Blackburn R (1)
James Brown	1885 Blackburn R (1);	1886rBlackburn R (1)
William Townley	1890 Blackburn R (3);	1891 Blackburn R (1)
John Southworth	1890 Blackburn R (1);	1891 Blackburn R (1)
Bobby Johnstone	1955 Manchester C (1);	1956 Manchester C (1)
Bobby Smith	1961 Tottenham H (1);	1962 Tottenham H (1)

SCORED IN THREE DIFFERENT FA CUP FINAL MATCHES

Only three have achieved this: Fred Priest, Sheffield United 1899 (1), 1901 (1), 1902 replay (1) – Ian Rush, Liverpool 1986 (2), 1989 (2), 1992 (1) – Ian Wright, Crystal Palace 1990 (2), Arsenal 1993 (1), 1993 replay (1)

SCORED IN ENGLISH AND SCOTTISH FA CUP FINALS

Jack Smith is the only player to have scored in both. He scored for Kilmarnock when they beat Albion Rovers 3–2 in 1920 and for Bolton when they beat West Ham 2–0 in 1923.

FASTEST GOAL IN THE CUP FINAL Accounts of this vary, but at least four goals have been scored in the first minute of a Cup Final. Although the timings for the early years, where they are known, are unreliable, by the 1890s a far more accurate record was being kept.

Bob Chatt is credited with the only goal of the 1895 final, scored after 40 seconds. The following year Fred Spiksley scored inside a minute as Sheffield Wednesday beat Wolves 2–1.

James Roscamp scored in the first minute when Blackburn Rovers beat Huddersfield Town 3–1 at Wembley in 1928.

Jackie Milburn is generally credited with Wembley's fastest goal after 45 seconds when Newcastle beat Manchester City 3–1 in 1955.

LATE GOALS IN THE CUP FINAL No-one has scored a goal later than the second to last minute of extra-time (the 119th minute) in a Cup Final proper. George Mutch set this record with his famous penalty that gave Preston NE their 1–0 win over Huddersfield Town in 1938.

However, the latest goal to decide an FA Cup Final replay was scored in injury time at the end of extra time by Arsenal's Andrew Linighan in 1993. Referee Keren Barratt blew the final whistle 44 seconds after Linighan headed Arsenal's second goal in their 2–1 win over Sheffield Wednesday.

It was the latest goal scored in a Cup Final since the replayed final of 1912 when a goal from Harry Tufnell two minutes from the end of extra-time gave Barnsley a 1–0 win over West Bromwich Albion.

FA Cup Finals goal times and attendances

This chart shows the order in which the goals were scored in every Cup Final. Some of the times of goals scored in the early years are untraced.

date final, att, referee	1st	2nd	3rd	4th	5th	6th	7th
1872 Wanderers 1 R.Engineers 0	Betts						
March 16; 2,000; A.Stair	1–0						
1873 Wanderers 2 Oxford Univ 0	Wollaston	Kinnaird					
March 29; 3,000; A.Stair	1–0	2–0					
1874 Oxford Univ 2 R.Engineers 0	Mackarness	Patton					
March 14; 2,000; A.Stair	1–0	2–0					
1875 R.Enginners 1 Old Etonians 1	Bonsor	Renny-Tailyour					
March 13; 2,000; CW Alock aet	30 0–1	40 1–1					
Rep R.Engineers 2 Old Etonians 0	Renny-Tailyour	Stafford					
March 16; 3,000; CW Alcock	1–0	2–0					
1876 Wanderers 1 Old Etonians 1	Edwards	Bonsor					
Mar 11; 3,500; WS Buchanan aet	35 1–0	50 1–1					
1876 Wanderers 3 Old Etonians 0	Wollaston	Hughes	Hughes				
March 18; 1,500; WS Rawson	1–0	2–0	3–0				
1877 Wanderers 2 Oxford Univ 1	Kinnaird og	Kenrick	Lindsay				
March 24; 3,000; SH Wright aet	0–1	1–1	2–1				
1878 Wanderers 3 R.Engineers 1	Kenrick	'rush'	Kinnaird	Kenrick			
March 23; 4,500; SR Bastard	5 1–0	1–1	2–1	3–1			
1879 Old Etonians 1 Clapham R 0	Clerke						
March 29; 5,000; CW Alcock	65 1–0						
1880 Clapham R 1 Oxford Univ 0	Lloyd-Jones						
April 10; 6,000; Major Marindin	80 1–0						
1881 O.Carthusians 3 O.Etonians 0	Page	Wynyard	Parry				
April 9; 4,000; W.Pierce–Dix	1–0	2–0	3–0				
1882 Old Etonians 1 Blackburn R 0	Macauley						
March 25; 6,500; JC Clegg	8 1–0						
1883 Blackburn O. 2 O. Etonians 1	Goodhart	Matthews	Crossley				
Mar 31; 8,000; Major Marindin aet	30 0–1	1–1	2–1				
1884 Blackburn R 2 Queens Park 1	Sowerbutts	Forrest	Christie				
March 29; 4,000;	1–0	2–0	2–1				
1885 Blackburn R 2 Queens Park 0	Forrest	Brown					
April 4; 12,500; Major Marindin	14 1–0	58 2–0					
1886 Blackburn R 0 WBA 0							
April 3; 12,000; Major Marindin							
Rep Blackburn R 2 WBA 0	Sowerbutts	Brown					
April 10; 15,000; Major Marindin	1–0	2–0					
1887 Aston Villa 2 WBA 0	Hodgetts	Hunter					
April 2; 15,500; Major Marindin	1–0	88 2–0					
1888 WBA 2 Preston NE 1	Bayliss	Dewhurst	Woodhall				
March 24; 19,000; Major Marindin	8 1–0	52 1–1	77 2–1				
1889 Preston NE 3 Wolves 0	Dewhurst	Ross	Thompson				
March 30; 22,000; Major Marindin	15 1–0	25 2–0	70 3–0	John			
1890 Blackburn R 6 Sheffield W 1	Townley	Walton	Townley	Southworth	Mumford	Townley	Lofthouse
March 29; 20,000; Major Marindin	6 1–0	2–0	35 3–0	4–0	1–4	5–1	6–1
1891 Blackburn R 3 Notts Co 1	Dewar	John Southworth	Townley	Oswald			
March 21; 23,000; CJ Hughes	8 1–0	30 2–0	35 3–0	70 1–3			
1892 WBA 3 Aston Villa 0	Geddes	Nicholls	Reynolds				
March 19; 32,810; JC Clegg	4 1–0	27 2–0	55 3–0				
1893 Wolves 1 Everton 0	Allen						
March 25; 45,000; CJ Hughes	60 1–0						

date final, att, referee	1st	2nd	3rd	4th	5th	6th	7th
1894 Notts Co 4 Bolton W 1	Watson	Logan	Logan	Logan	Cassidy		
March 31; 37,000; CJ Hughes	18 1–0	29 2–0	67 3–0	70 4–0	87 1–4		
1895 Aston Villa 1 WBA 0	Chatt						
April 20; 42,560; J.Lewis	1 1–0						
1896 Sheffield W 2 Wolves 1	Spiksley	Black	Spiksley				
April 18; 48,836; Lt.Simpson	1 1–0	8 1–1	18 2–1				
1897 Aston Villa 3 Everton 2	Campbell	Bell	Boyle	Wheldon	Crabtree		
April 10; 65,891; J.Lewis	18 1–0	23 1–1	28 1–2	35 2–2	44 3–2		
1898 Nottm F 3 Derby Co 1	Capes	Bloomer	Capes	McPherson			
April 16; 62,017; J.Lewis	19 1–0	31 1–1	42 2–1	86 3–1			
1899 Sheffield U 4 Derby Co 1	Boag	Bennett	Beers	Almond	Priest		
April 15; 73,833; A.Scragg	12 0–1	60 1–1	65 2–1	69 3–1	89 4–1		
1900 Bury 4 Southampton 0	McLuckie	W.Wood	McLuckie	Plant			
April 21; 68,945; A.Kingscott	9 1–0	16 2–0	23 3–0	80 4–0			
1901 Tottenham H 2 Sheffield U 2	Priest	Brown	Brown	Bennett			
April 20; 110,820; A.Kingscott	10 0–1	23 1–1	51 2–1	52 2–2			
Rep Tottenham H 3 Sheffield U 1	Priest	Cameron	Smith	Brown			
April 27; 20,470; A.Kingscott	40 0–1	52 1–1	76 2–1	87 3–1			
1902 Sheffield U 1 Southampton 1	Common	H.Wood					
April 19; 76,914; T.Kirkham	55 1–0	88 1–1					
Rep Sheffield U 2 Southampton 1	Hedley	Brown	Barnes				
April 26; 33,068; T.Kirkham	2 1–0	70 1–1	79 2–1				
1903 Bury 6 Derby Co 0	Ross	Sagar	Leeming	Wood	Plant	Leeming	
April 18; 63,102; J.Adams	20 1–0	48 2–0	56 3–0	57 4–0	59 5–0	75 6–0	
1904 Manchester C 1 Bolton W 0	Meredith						
April 23; 61,374; AJ Barker	23 1–0						
1905 Aston Villa 2 Newcastle U 0	Hampton	Hampton					
April 15; 101,117; PR Harrower	2 1–0	76 2–0					
1906 Everton 1 Newcastle U 0	Young						
April 21; 75,609; F.Kirkham	75 1–0						
1907 Sheffield W 2 Everton 1	Stewart	Sharp	Simpson				
April 20; 84,594; N.Whittaker	21 1–0	38 1–1	89 2–1				
1908 Wolves 3 Newcastle U 1	Hunt	Hedley	Howie	Harrison			
April 25; 74,967; TP Campbell	40 1–0	43 2–0	73 1–2	85 3–1			
1909 Manchester U 1 Bristol C 0	Turnbull						
April 24; 71,401; J.Mason	22 1–0						
1910 Newcastle U 1 Barnsley 1	Tufnell	Rutherford					
April 23; 77,747; JT Ibbotson	37 0–1	83 1–1					
Rep Newcastle 2 Barnsley 0	Shepherd	Shepherd					
April 28; 69,000; JT Ibbotson	52 1–0	62p 2–0					
1911 Bradford C 0 Newcastle U 0							
April 22; 69,068; JH Pearson							
Rep Bradford C 1 Newcastle U 0	Speirs						
April 26; 58,000; JH Pearson	15 1–0						
1912 Barnsley 0 WBA 0							
April 20; 54,556; JR Shumacher							
Rep Barnsley 1 WBA 0 aet	Tufnell						
April 24; 38,555; JR Schumacher	118 1–0						
1913 Aston Villa 1 Sunderland 0	Barber						
April 19; 120,081; A.Adams	75 1–0						
1914 Burnley 1 Liverpool 0	Freeman						
April 25; 72,778; HS Bamlett	58 1–0						
1915 Sheffield U 3 Chelsea 0	Simmons	Fazackerley	Kitchen				
April 24; 49,557; HH Taylor	36 1–0	84 2–0	88 3–0				
1920 A.Villa 1 Huddersfield 0 aet	Kirton						
April 24; 50,018; JT Howcroft	100 1–0						
1921 Tottenham H 1, Wolves 0	Dimmock						
April 23; 72,805; S.Davies	53 1–0						
1922 Huddersfield 1 Preston NE 0	Smith						
April 29; 53,000; JWP Fowler	67p 1–0						
1923 Bolton 2 West Ham 0	Jack	JR Smith					
April 28; 126,047; DH Asson	2 1–0	53 2–0					
1924 Newcastle 2 Aston V 0	Harris	Seymour					
April 26; 91,695; WE Russell	83 1–0	85 2–0					
1925 Sheffield U 1 Cardiff 0	Tunstall						
April 25; 91,763; GN Watson	30 1–0						
1926 Bolton 1 Manchester C 0	Jack						
April 24; 91,447; I Baker	76 1–0						
1927 Cardiff 1 Arsenal 0	Ferguson						
April 23; 91,206; WF Bunnell	74 1–0						
1928 Blackburn 3 Huddersfield 1	Roscamp	McLean	Jackson	Roscamp			
April 21; 92,041; TG Bryan	1 1–0	22 2–0	55 2–1	85 3–1			
1929 Bolton 2 Portsmouth 0	Butler	Blackmore					
April 27; 92,576; A Josephs	79 1–0	87 2–0					
1930 Arsenal 2 Huddersfield 0	James	Lambert					
April 26; 92,488; T Crew	16 1–0	88 2–0					
1931 WBA 2 Birmingham 1	Richardson	Bradford	Richardson				
April 25; 92,406; AH Kingscott	25 1–0	57 1–1	58 2–1				
1932 Newcastle 2, Arsenal 1	John	Allen	Allen				
April 23; 92,298; WP Harper	15 0–1	38 1–1	72 2–1				
1933 Everton 3 Man City 0	Stein	Dean	Dunn				
April 29; 92,950; E Wood	41 1–0	52 2–0	80 3–0				

date final, att, referee	1st	2nd	3rd	4th	5th	6th	7th
1934 Man City 2 Portsmouth 1	Rutherford	Tilson	Tilson				
April 28; 93,258; SF Rous	26 0–1	73 1–1	87 2–1				
1935 Sheffield W 4 WBA 2	Palethorpe	Boyes	Hooper	Sandford	Rimmer	Rimmer	
April 27; 93,204; AE Fogg	2 1–0	21 1–1	70 2–1	75 2–2	85 3–2	89 4–2	
1936 Arsenal 1 Sheffield U 0	Drake						
April 25; 93,384; H Nattrass	75 1–0						
1937 Sunderland 3 Preston 1	F. O'Donnell	Gurney	Carter	Burbanks			
May 1; 93,495; RG Rudd	44 0–1	52 1–1	70 2–1	87 3–1			
1938 Preston 1 Huddersfield 0 aet	Mutch						
April 30; 93,497; AJ Jewell	119p 1–0						
1939 Portsmouth 4, Wolves 1	Barlow	Anderson	Parker	Dorsett	Parker		
April 29; 99,370; T Thompson	29 1–0	43 2–0	46 3–0	54 3–1	71 4–1		
1946 Derby Co 4 Charlton 1 aet	Bert Turner	Bert Turner	Doherty	Stamps	Stamps		
April 27; 98,000; ED Smith	85og 1–0	86 1–1	92 2–1	97 3–1	106 4–1		
1947 Charlton 1 Burnley 0 aet	Duffy						
April 26; 99,000; JM Wiltshire	114 1–0						
1948 Manchester U 4 Blackpool 2	Shimwell	Rowley	Mortensen	Rowley	Pearson	Anderson	
April 24; 99,000; CJ Barrick	12p 0–1	28 1–1	35 1–2	70 2–2	80 3–2	82 4–2	
1949 Wolves 3 Leicester C 1	Pye	Pye	Griffiths	Smyth			
April 30; 99,500; RA Mortimer	13 1–0	42 2–0	46 2–1	47 3–1			
1950 Arsenal 2 Liverpool 0	Lewis	Lewis					
April 29; 100,000; H Pearce	18 1–0	63 1–0					
1951 Newcastle 2 Blackpool 0	Milburn	Milburn					
April 28; 100,000; W Ling	50 1–0	55 2–0					
1952 Newcastle 1 Arsenal 0	G Robledo						
May 3; 100,000; A Ellis	84 1–0						
1953 Blackpool 4 Bolton W 3	Lofthouse	Mortensen	Moir	Bell	Mortensen	Mortensen	Perry
May 2; 100,000; M Griffiths	2 0–1	35 1–1	39 1–2	55 1–3	68 2–3	89 3–3	90 4–3
1954 WBA 3 Preston 2	Allen	Morrison	Wayman	Allen	Griffin		
May 1; 100,000; A Luty	21 1–0	22 1–1	51 1–2	63p 2–2	87 3–2		
1955 Newcastle 3 Man City 1	Milburn	Johnstone	Mitchell	Hannah			
May 7; 100,000; R Leafe	1 1–0	44 1–1	53 2–1	60 3–1			
1956 Man City 3 Birmingham C 1	Hayes	Kinsey	Dyson	Johnstone			
May 5; 100,000; A Bond	3 1–0	15 1–1	65 2–1	68 3–1			
1957 Aston V 2 Manchester U 1	McParland	McParland	Taylor				
May 4; 100,000; F Coultas	68 1–0	73 2–0	83 2–1				
1958 Bolton 2 Manchester U 0	Lofthouse	Lofthouse					
May 3; 100,000; J Sherlock	3 1–0	50 2–0					
1959 Nottingham F 2 Luton T 1	Dwight	Wilson	Pacey				
May 2; 100,000; J Clough	10 1–0	14 2–0	62 2–1				
1960 Wolves 3 Blackburn R 0	McGrath	Deeley	Deeley				
May 7; 100,000; K Howley	41og 1–0	67 2–0	88 3–0				

Norman Deeley seals Wolves' 3–0 victory over Blackburn in the 1960 final with his second goal of the game. On the goal-line is Blackburn defender Mick McGrath who was 'credited' with the opening goal (Popperfoto)

date final, att, referee	1st	2nd	3rd	4th	5th	6th	7th
1961 Tottenham H 2 Leicester 0	Smith	Dyson					
May 6; 100,000; J Kelly	70 1–0	77 2–0					
1962 Tottenham H 3 Burnley 1	Greaves	Robson	Smith	Blanchflower			
May 5; 100,000; J Finney	3 1–0	50 1–1	51 2–1	80p 3–1			
1963 Manchester U 3 Leicester 1	Law	Herd	Keyworth	Herd			
May 25; 100,000; K Aston	30 1–0	57 2–0	80 2–1	85 3–1			
1964 West Ham 3 Preston 2	Holden	Sissons	Dawson	Hurst	Boyce		
May 2; 100,000; A Holland	9 0–1	10 1–1	40 1–2	89 2–2	90 3–2		
1965 Liverpool 2 Leeds U 1 aet	Hunt	Bremner	St John				
May 1; 100,000; W Clements	93 1–0	95 1–1	113 2–1				
1966 Everton 3 Sheffield W 2	McCalliog	Ford	Trebilcock	Trebilcock	Temple		
May 14; 100,000; JK Taylor	4 0–1	57 0–2	59 1–2	64 2–2	80 3–2		
1967 Tottenham H 2 Chelsea 1	Robertson	Saul	Tambling				
May 20; 100,000; K Dagnall	40 1–0	67 2–0	85 2–1				
1968 WBA 1 Everton 0 aet	Astle						
May 18; 100,000; L Callaghan	93 1–0						
1969 Man City 1 Leicester 0	Young						
April 26; 100,000; G McCabe	24 1–0						
1970 Chelsea 2 Leeds U 2 aet	Charlton	Houseman	Jones	Hutchinson			
April 11; 100,000; E Jennings	21 0–1	41 1–1	84 1–2	86 2–2			
Rep. Chelsea 2 Leeds U 1 aet	Jones	Osgood	Webb				
April 29; 62,078; E Jennings	35 0–1	78 1–1	104 2–1				
1971 Arsenal 2 Liverpool 1 aet	Heighway	Kelly	George				
May 8; 100,000; N Burtenshaw	91 0–1	101 1–1	111 2–1				
1972 Leeds U 1 Arsenal 0	Clarke						
May 6; 100,000; DW Smith	53 1–0						
1973 Sunderland 1 Leeds U 0	Porterfield						
May 5; 100,000; K Burns	30 1–0						
1974 Liverpool 3 Newcastle U 0	Keegan	Heighway	Keegan				
May 4; 100,000; GC Kew	57 1–0	74 2–0	88 3–0				
1975 West Ham 2 Fulham 0	Taylor	Taylor					
May 3; 100,000; P Partridge	60 1–0	64 2–0					
1976 Southampton 1 Man Utd 0	Stokes						
May 1; 100,000; C Thomas	82 1–0						
1977 Man Utd 2 Liverpool 1	Pearson	Case	J.Greenhoff				
May 21; 100,000; R Matthewson	50 1–0	52 1–1	55 2–1				
1978 Ipswich T 1 Arsenal 0	Osborne						
May 6; 100,000; D Nippard	77 1–0						
1979 Arsenal 3 Manchester U 2	Talbot	Stapleton	McQueen	McIlroy	Sunderland		
May 12; 100,000; R Challis	12 1–0	43 2–0	86 2–1	88 2–2	89 3–2		
1980 West Ham 1 Arsenal 0	Brooking						
May 10; 100,000; G Courtney	13 1–0						
1981 Tottenham H 1 Man C 1 aet	Hutchison	Hutchison					
May 9; 100,000; K Hackett	29 0–1	79og 1–1					
Rep Tottenham H 3 Man C 2	Villa	Mackenzie	Reeves	Crooks	Villa		
May 14; 92,000; K Hackett	8 1–0	11 1–1	50p 1–2	70 2–2	76 3–2		
1982 Tottenham H 1, QPR 1 aet	Hoddle	Fenwick					
May 22; 100,000; C White	110 1–0	115 1–1					
Rep Tottenham H 1 QPR 0	Hoddle						
May 27; 90,000; C White	6p 1–0						
1983 Man Utd 2 Brighton 2 aet	Smith	Stapleton	Wilkins	Stevens			
May 21; 100,000; AW Grey	14 0–1	55 1–1	72 2–1	87 2–2			
Rep Man Utd 4 Brighton 0	Robson	Whiteside	Robson	Muhren			
May 26; 100,000; AW Grey	25 1–0	30 2–0	44 3–0	62p 4–0			
1984 Everton 2 Watford 0	Sharp	Gray					
May 19; 100,000; J Hunting	38 1–0	51 2–0					
1985 Man Utd 1 Everton 0 aet	Whiteside						
May 18; 100,000; P.Willis	100 1–0						
1986 Liverpool 3 Everton 1	Lineker	Rush	Johnston	Rush			
May 10; 98,000; A Robinson	28 0–1	57 1–1	63 2–1	84 3–1			
1987 Coventry 3 Tottenham 2 aet	Allen	Bennett	Mabbutt	Houchen	Mabbutt		
May 16; 98,000; N.Midgley	2 0–1	9 1–1	40 1–2	63 2–2	96og 3–2		
1988 Wimbledon 1 Liverpool 0	Sanchez						
May 14; 98,203; B Hill	37 1–0						
1989 Liverpool 3 Everton 2 aet	Aldridge	McCall	Rush	McCall	Rush		
May 20; 82,500; J Worrall	4 1–0	89 1–1	94 2–1	102 2–2	104 3–2		
1990 Man Utd 3 Crystal P 3 aet	O'Reilly	Robson	Hughes	Wright	Wright	Hughes	
May 12; 80,000; A Gunn	19 0–1	35 1–1	62 2–1	70 2–2	92 2–3	113 3–3	
Rep Man Utd 1 Crystal P 0	Martin						
May 17; 80,000; A Gunn	59 1–0						
1991 Tottenham 2 Nottm F 1 aet	Pearce	Stewart	Walker				
May 18; 80,000; R Milford	15 0–1	53 1–1	94og 2–1				
1992 Liverpool 2 Sunderland 0	Thomas	Rush					
May 9; 79,544; P.Don	47 1–0	68 2–0					
1993 Arsenal 1 Sheffield W 1 aet	Wright	Hirst					
May 15; 79,347; K.Barratt	20 1–0	61 1–1					
Rep Arsenal 2 Sheffield W 1 aet	Wright	Waddle	Linighan				
May 20; 62,267; K.Barratt	34 1–0	68 1–1	119 2–1				

Oldest and Youngest

(Note: in all cases only the players whose birthdates have been verified are included)

YOUNGEST CUP FINALISTS James Frederick McLeod Prinsep, who was born in India on July 27, 1861, played for Clapham Rovers against Old Etonians in the Cup Final on March 29, 1879, becoming the youngest ever Cup Finalist at the age of 17 years 245 days – 11 days younger than Paul Allen when he played for West Ham 101 years later.

Although he only gained a loser's medal in 1879, Prinsep collected a winner's medal two years later when he played for Old Carthusians who beat Old Etonians. He was 19 years and 256 days old.

But even then, as early as 1881 he was not the first teenager to play in two Cup Finals. That honour fell to Robert Vidal. Vidal played for Wanderers in the first two Cup Finals, of 1872 and Oxford in 1873, the first when he was 18 years 195 days old. He also played for Oxford University in the 1874 final.

The following lists the 20 youngest players to have appeared in the Cup Final before the move to Wembley in 1923.

James Prinsep .... 1879 Clapham R vs Old Etonians
          17 years 245 days
Walter Norris .... 1881 Old Carthusians vs Old Etonians
          18 years 1 day
James Ward .... 1883 Blackburn O. vs Old Etonians
          18 years 3 days
Cecil Keith-Falconer . 1879 Clapham R vs Old Etonians
          18 years 169 days
Robert Vidal .... 1872 Wanderers vs Royal Engineers
          18 years 195 days
William Sellar .... 1885 Queens Park vs Blackburn R
          18 years 195 days
Edward Growse .... 1879 Clapham R vs Old Etonians
          18 years 264 days
Joe Lofthouse .... 1884 Blackburn R vs Queens Park
          18 years 349 days
Alfred Lyttleton .... 1876 Old Etonians vs Wanderers
          19 years 33 days
William Bassett .... 1888 WBA vs Preston NE
          19 years 57 days
Billy Williams .... 1895 WBA vs Aston Villa
          19 years 90 days
Joseph Vintcent .... 1881 Old Carthusians vs Old Etonians
          19 years 148 days
William Rawson .... 1874 Oxford Univ vs Royal Engineers
          19 years 151 days
Robert Vidal .... 1873 Oxford Univ vs Wanderers
          19 years 208 days
Bertram Rogers .... 1880 Oxford Univ vs Clapham R
          19 years 228 days
James Brown .... 1882 Blackburn R vs Old Etonians
          19 years 237 days
Howard Spencer .... 1895 Aston Villa vs WBA
          19 years 240 days
William Anderson ..... 1881 Old Etonians vs Old Carthusians
          19 years 240 days
Frederick Rawson ..... 1879 Clapham R vs Old Etonians
          19 years 245 days
Percy De Paravicini ... 1882 Old Etonians vs Blackburn R
          19 years 253 days
James Prinsep .... 1881 Old Carthusians vs Old Etonians
          19 years 256 days
Evelyn Waddington .. 1877 Oxford Univ vs Wanderers
          19 years 262 days

WEMBLEY'S TEENAGERS

The following 33 players have played in Wembley FA Cup Finals in their teens. David McCreery, Malcolm Manley and Chris Bart-Williams all made their appearances as substitutes.

McCreery is the only player to have played in two Wembley FA Cup Finals as a teenager – and in both 1976 and 1977 he came on as a substitute.

John Mapson, Sunderland's goalkeeper in their winning 1937 Cup Final team, is the "oldest" teenager. He was 20 the following day.

Paul Allen .... 1980 West Ham vs Arsenal
          17 years 256 days
Howard Kendall ..... 1964 Preston vs West Ham
          17 years 345 days
Norman Whiteside . 1983 Man Utd vs Brighton
          18 years 14 days
Cliff Bastin .... 1930 Arsenal vs Huddersfield
          18 years 43 days
Alex Dawson .... 1958 Man Utd vs Bolton W
          18 years 71 days
John Sissons .... 1964 West Ham vs Preston
          18 years 215 days
Tommy Caton .... 1981 Man City vs Tottenham
          18 years 215 days
David McCreery .... 1976 Man Utd vs Southampton
          18 years 228 days
Lee Sinnott .... 1984 Watford vs Everton
          18 years 312 days
Chris Bart-Williams 1993 Sheffield W v Arsenal
          18 years 333 days
Albert Geldard .... 1933 Everton vs Man City
          19 years 18 days
Joe Royle .... 1968 Everton vs WBA
          19 years 40 days
Joe Hayes .... 1955 Man City vs Newcastle U
          19 years 106 days
Malcolm Manley .... 1969 Leicester C vs Man C
          19 years 146 days
Richard Dorsett ..... 1939 Wolves vs Portsmouth
          19 years 147 days
Steve Mackenzie .... 1981 Man City vs Tottenham
          19 years 167 days
Tommy Booth .... 1969 Man City vs Leicester C
          19 years 168 days
Warren Neill .... 1982 QPR vs Tottenham
          19 years 182 days
Graham Cross .... 1963 Leicester C vs Man U
          19 years 191 days
Bobby Charlton ..... 1957 Man Utd vs Aston Villa
          19 years 205 days
Peter Shilton .... 1969 Leicester C vs Man C
          19 years 220 days
Jim McCalliog .... 1966 Sheff Wed vs Everton
          19 years 233 days
Sam Ellis .... 1966 Sheff Wed vs Everton
          19 years 244 days
Alan Kennedy .... 1974 Newcastle vs Liverpool
          19 years 246 days
David McCreery .... 1977 Man Utd vs Liverpool
          19 years 248 days
David Bardsley .... 1984 Watford vs Everton
          19 years 251 days

Wilf Smith	1966 Sheff Wed vs Everton	19 years 253 days
Roy Keane	1991 Nottm F vs Tottenham	19 years 281 days
Ray Kennedy	1971 Liverpool vs Arsenal	19 years 284 days
Ernie Curtis	1927 Cardiff C vs Arsenal	19 years 307 days
Mervyn Day	1975 West Ham vs Fulham	19 years 311 days
Arthur Albiston	1977 Man Utd vs Liverpool	19 years 311 days
John Mapson	1937 Sunderland vs Preston	19 years 364 days

YOUNGEST WEMBLEY GOALKEEPERS

Peter Shilton set records throughout his playing career. No-one has played more League games than Shilton, and no-one has played in more internationals. His final appearance for England, against Italy on July 9, 1990, in the World Cup third-place match was his 125th appearance, an all-time world record.

Shilton was nearly 41 years old at the time, but a record he set when he was only 19 still stands. On April 26, 1969 he kept goal for Leicester City against Manchester City in the FA Cup Final, aged 19 years 220 days, and is still the youngest goalkeeper to play in an FA Cup Final at Wembley.

Despite playing in the First Division for almost a quarter of a century, that was Shilton's only FA Cup Final appearance. He ended the day with a runners-up medal after Manchester City won the match 1–0.

Peter Shilton	1969 Leicester C vs Manchester C	19 years 220 days
Mervyn Day	1975 West Ham vs Fulham	19 years 311 days
John Mapson	1937 Sunderland vs Preston	19 years 364 days

Peter Shilton, the youngest keeper to play in an FA Cup final. Seventeen years on, he clears his lines for Southampton in the 1986 semi-final which Saints lost 2–0 to Liverpool (Allsport/Michael King)

Gary Sprake	1965 Leeds U vs Liverpool	20 years 28 days
Frank Swift	1934 Manchester C vs Portsmouth	20 years 123 days
Gary Bailey	1979 Manchester U vs Arsenal	20 years 277 days
Ronnie Simpson ..	1952 Newastle U vs Arsenal	21 years 205 days
Pat Jennings	1967 Tottenham H vs Chelsea	21 years 342 days
Bob Hesford	1938 Huddersfield T vs Preston	22 years 17 days
David Harvey	1970 Leeds U vs Chelsea (R)	22 years 81 days
Eddie Hopkinson	1958 Bolton W vs Manchester U	22 years 186 days
Peter Hucker	1982 QPR vs Tottenham H	22 years 206 days
Bobby Mimms	1986 Everton vs Liverpool	22 years 210 days
David Gaskell	1963 Manchester U vs Leicester C	22 years 232 days
Ray Clemence	1971 Liverpool vs Arsenal	22 years 277 days
George Walker	1939 Portsmouth vs Wolverhampton W 22 years 344 days	
Harry Pearson	1931 WBA vs Birmingham C	22 years 352 days
Gordon West	1966 Everton vs Sheffield Wed	23 years 21 days
Ted Sagar	1933 Everton vs Manchester C	23 years 81 days

THE 20 YOUNGEST FA CUP FINALISTS

James Prinsep	1879 Clapham Rovers	17 years 245 days
Paul Allen	1980 West Ham	17 years 256 days
Howard Kendall	1964 Preston NE	17 years 345 days
Walter Norris	1881 Old Carthusians	18 years 1 day
James Ward	1883 Blackburn Rovers	18 years 3 days
Norman Whiteside	1983 Manchester U	18 years 14 days
Cliff Bastin	1930 Arsenal	18 years 43 days
Alex Dawson	1958 Manchester U	18 years 71 days
Cecil Keith-Falconer	1879 Clapham Rovers	18 years 169 days
Robert Vidal	1872 Wanderers	18 years 195 days
William Sellar	1885 Queens Park	18 years 195 days
John Sissons	1964 West Ham	18 years 215 days
Tommy Caton	1981 Manchester C	18 years 215 days
David McCreery	1976 Manchester U	18 years 228 days
Edward Growse	1879 Clapham Rovers	18 years 264 days
Lee Sinnott	1984 Watford	18 years 312 days
Chris Bart-Williams	1993 Sheffield W	18 years 333 days

Joe Lofthouse .... 1884 Blackburn Rovers
                   18 years 349 days
Albert Geldard .... 1933 Everton
                   19 years 18 days
Alfred Lyttleton .... 1876 Old Etonians
                   19 years 33 days

THE 10 OLDEST PRE-WEMBLEY CUP FINALISTS

George Baddeley .... 1912 WBA
                   38 years 11 months
Billy Evans .... 1892 Aston Villa
                   38 years 1 month
Frank Jefferis .... 1922 Preston
                   37 years 300 days
Archie Goodall .... 1903 Derby Co
                   37 years 8 months
James Kirkpatrick .... 1878 Wanderers
                   37 years 1 day
Edward Bowen .... 1873 Wanderers
                   36 years 364 days
William Merriman .... 1875 Royal Engineers
                   36 years 348 days
Jimmy Cantrell .... 1921 Tottenham H
                   36 years 10 months
Sam Hardy .... 1920 Aston Villa
                   36 years 275 days
Major Marindin .... 1874 Royal Engineers
                   35 years 317 days

Note: Some Cup Final players in the 1870s and 1880s may have been in their 40s when they played but their ages have not been verified.

WEMBLEY'S GOLDEN OLDIES

The 22 oldest players to have played in a Wembley FA Cup Final:

Billy Hampson .... 1924 Newcastle U vs Aston Villa
                   41 years 257 days
John Oakes .... 1946 Charlton A vs Derby Co
                   40 years 226 days
Ray Clemence .... 1987 Tottenham H vs Coventry C
                   38 years 284 days
Warney Cresswell ...... 1933 Everton vs Manchester C
                   38 years 175 days
Jimmy McMullan .... 1933 Manchester C vs Everton
                   38 years 34 days
Joe Mercer .... 1952 Arsenal vs Newcastle U
                   37 years 268 days
Leslie Compton .... 1950 Arsenal vs Liverpool
                   37 years 229 days
John Osborne .... 1968 WBA vs Everton
                   37 years 159 days
Stanley Matthews .... 1953 Blackpool vs Bolton W
                   37 years 152 days
George Swindin .... 1952 Arsenal vs Newcastle
                   37 years 151 days
Stan Hanson .... 1953 Bolton W vs Blackpool
                   37 years 126 days
Syd Owen .... 1959 Luton T vs Nottingham F
                   37 years 63 days
Jack Charlton .... 1972 Leeds U vs Arsenal
                   36 years 363 days
Jimmy Blair .... 1925 Cardiff C vs Sheffield U
                   36 years 349 days
Ted Vizard .... 1926 Bolton W vs Manchester C
                   36 years 321 days
Joe Smith .... 1926 Bolton W vs Manchester C
                   36 years 302 days

Viv Anderson .... 1993 Sheffield W vs Arsenal
                   36 years 260 days
Bob Kelly .... 1930 Huddersfield T vs Arsenal
                   36 years 161 days
Dick Pym .... 1929 Bolton W vs Portsmouth
                   36 years 84 days
Danny Blanchflower .. 1962 Tottenham H vs Burnley
                   36 years 84 days
Don Welsh .... 1947 Charlton A vs Burnley
                   36 years 60 days
Jack Brown .... 1935 Sheffield W vs WBA
                   36 years 39 days

OLDEST WEMBLEY GOALKEEPERS

Since the Second World War only a handful of England international goalkeepers have failed to play in the FA Cup Final at some stage during their careers.

Tottenham's Ted Ditchburn, Alan Hodgkinson of Sheffield United, Bert Williams of Wolves, Reg Matthews of Chelsea, Colin McDonald of Burnley, and Tony Waiters of Blackpool all played at Wembley for their country, but none of them made it to the Cup Final.

Other goalkeepers seem to make Wembley and the Cup Final their second home. Ray Clemence played in five Wembley Cup Finals, and made six Cup Final appearances in all, including the 1982 replay, while through the years legendary stalwarts like George Swindin, Dickie Pym, Pat Jennings and Sam Bartram all made more than one appearance while well into their thirties.

The following 23 men all played in a Wembley Cup final on or after their 31st birthdays.

Ray Clemence ..... 1987 Tottenham H vs Coventry C
                   38 years 285 days
George Swindin ... 1952 Arsenal vs Newcastle U
                   38 years 89 days
John Osborne .... 1968 WBA vs Everton
                   37 years 210 days
Stan Hanson .... 1953 Bolton W vs Blackpool
                   37 years 126 days
Dickie Pym .... 1929 Bolton W vs Portsmouth
                   36 years 85 days
George Swindin ... 1950 Arsenal vs Liverpool
                   36 years 84 days
Jack Brown .... 1935 Sheffield Wed vs WBA
                   36 years 39 days
Vic Woodley .... 1946 Derby Co vs Charlton A
                   35 years 60 days
Pat Jennings .... 1980 Arsenal vs West Ham
                   34 years 333 days
Alex Stepney .... 1977 Manchester U vs Liverpool
                   34 years 245 days
Bruce Grobbelaar . 1992 Liverpool vs Sunderland
                   34 years 216 days
Cyril Sidlow .... 1950 Liverpool vs Arsenal
                   34 years 154 days
Gil Merrick .... 1956 Birmingham C vs Manchester C
                   34 years 100 days
Tony Norman ...... 1992 Sunderland vs Liverpool
                   34 years 75 days
Arthur Goodchild . 1926 Manchester C vs Bolton W
                   34 years
Pat Jennings .... 1979 Arsenal vs Manchester U
                   33 years 335 days
Jim Sanders .... 1954 WBA vs Preston
                   33 years 300 days

Jack Fairbrother .... 1951 Newcastle U vs Blackpool
33 years 255 days
Alex Stepney .... 1976 Manchester U vs Southampton
33 years 226 days
Chris Woods .... 1993 Sheffield W vs Arsenal
33 years 187 days
Sam Bartram .... 1947 Charlton A vs Burnley
33 years 94 days
Dickie Pym .... 1926 Bolton W vs Manchester C
33 years 81 days
Ray Clemence ..... 1982 Tottenham H vs QPR
32 years 296 days
Les Sealey .... 1990 Manchester U vs Crystal P (R)
33 years 226 days
Pat Jennings .... 1978 Arsenal vs Ipswich T
32 years 229 days
Joe Corrigan .... 1981 Manchester C vs Tottenham H
32 years 177 days
Sam Bartram .... 1946 Charlton A vs Derby Co
32 years 95 days
Jim Leighton .... 1990 Manchester U vs Crystal P
31 years 292 days
Bert Trautmann ... 1955 Manchester C vs Newcastle U
31 years 197 days
Albert McInroy .... 1932 Newcastle U vs Arsenal
31 years

THE 20 OLDEST CUP FINALISTS OF ALL TIME

Billy Hampson .... 41 years 257 days
John Oakes .... 40 years 226 days
George Baddeley .... 38 years 11 months
Ray Clemence .... 38 years 284 days
Warney Cresswell .... 38 years 175 days
Jimmy McMullan .... 38 years 34 days
Billy Evans .... 38 years 1 month
Frank Jefferis .... 37 years 300 days
Joe Mercer .... 37 years 268 days
Archie Goodall .... 37 years 8 months
Leslie Compton .... 37 years 229 days
Stanley Matthews .... 37 years 152 days
George Swindin .... 37 years 151 days
Stan Hanson .... 37 years 126 days
Syd Owen .... 37 years 63 days
James Kirkpatrick .... 37 years 1 day
Edward Bowen .... 36 years 364 days
Jack Charlton .... 36 years 363 days
Jimmy Blair .... 36 years 349 days
William Merriman .... 36 years 348 days

THE 22 YOUNGEST FA CUP FINAL SCORERS AT WEMBLEY

When Norman Whiteside scored for Manchester United against Brighton in the 1983 Cup Final replay he became the youngest player ever to score in a Cup Final, and obviously the youngest to score in a Wembley Cup Final. He is also the 'sixth youngest' player to score in a Wembley Cup Final, earning that distinction when he scored in the 1985 Final to give Manchester United a 1-0 victory over Everton, the club he later joined.

The previous youngest scorer at Wembley was West Ham's John Sissons who scored in his side's win over Preston in 1964. Remarkably, Geoff Hurst and Ronnie Boyce, West Ham's other scorers in that match, all feature among the 22 youngest players to have scored in a Cup Final at Wembley.

The youngest strike force in a Cup Final hit the target in 1971 when Arsenal beat Liverpool to win the Double. Eddie Kelly, aged 20 years and 90 days, and

Charlie George, just four months older, are the youngest pair of scorers for one team in a Cup Final, with a joint age of 40 years 300 days.

But they own that record by just one week. Jim McCalliog and David Ford, who scored Sheffield Wednesday's goals in the 1966 Cup Final against Everton, had a joint age of 40 years, 307 days.

Norman Whiteside .... 1983 Manchester U vs Brighton
18 years 19 days
John Sissons .... 1964 West Ham vs Preston
18 years 215 days
Dicky Dorsett .... 1939 Wolverhampton W vs
Portsmouth 19 years 147 days
Steve Mackenzie .... 1982 Manchester C vs Tottenham H
19 years 172 days
Jim McCalliog .... 1966 Sheffield Wed vs Everton
19 years 234 days
Norman Whiteside .... 1985 Manchester U vs Everton
20 years 11 days
Gary Stevens .... 1983 Brighton vs Manchester U
20 years 56 days
Eddie Kelly .... 1971 Arsenal vs Liverpool
20 years 90 days
Joe Hayes .... 1956 Manchester C vs Birmingham C
20 years 106 days
Charlie George .... 1971 Arsenal vs Liverpool
20 years 210 days
David Ford .... 1966 Sheffield Wed vs Everton
21 years 73 days
Ronnie Boyce .... 1964 West Ham vs Preston
21 years 118 days
Mike Trebilcock .... 1966 Everton vs Sheffield Wed
21 years 166 days
Alan Taylor .... 1975 West Ham vs Fulham
21 years 170 days
Ian Hutchinson .... 1970 Chelsea vs Leeds U
21 years 250 days
Jack Dyson .... 1956 Manchester C vs Birmingham C
21 years 303 days
William 'WG' Richardson 1931 WBA vs Birmingham C
21 years 330 days
Jimmy Greaves .... 1962 Tottenham H vs Burnley
22 years 74 days
Lee Martin .... 1990 Manchester U vs Crystal P
22 years 101 days
Geoff Hurst .... 1964 West Ham vs Preston
22 years 147 days
Jimmy Robertson .... 1967 Tottenham H vs Chelsea
22 years 155 days
David Pacey .... 1959 Luton T vs Nottingham F
22 years 212 days
Frank Stapleton .... 1979 Arsenal vs Manchester U
22 years 306 days

OLDEST CUP FINAL SCORERS AT WEMBLEY

Even though the careers of players today are longer than they were in the past, it is still a relatively rare occurence for a player to score a goal in a Cup Final at Wembley after his 30th birthday. Only the 29 men listed below have done so.

It is nearly 50 years since Bert Turner became the oldest man to score in the Cup Final, and in recent years only Tommy Hutchison has come close to overhauling Turner's record or passing Danny Blanchflower and Jack Charlton in the all-time list of older scorers.

Coincidentally, both Hutchison and Turner scored for both sides and together with Gary Mabbutt of Tottenham are the only ones to do so in a Cup Final at Wembley.

Turner put through his own goal after 80 minutes to give Derby the lead and made amends 60 seconds later with Charlton's equaliser. Derby won the match 4-1 in extra time, but at least Charlton, although without Turner, returned to Wembley the following year and won the Cup.

Hutchison scored with a header to put Manchester City ahead against Spurs in the 29th minute of the 100th Cup Final on May 9, 1981 but 10 minutes from time he deflected Glenn Hoddle's free-kick into his own net for the equaliser. Tottenham went on to win the first final to be replayed at Wembley 3–2 five days later.

Bert Turner .... 1946 Charlton A vs Derby Co
  36 years 312 days
Danny Blanchflower .. 1962 Tottenham H vs Burnley
  36 years 84 days
Jack Charlton .... 1970 Leeds U vs Chelsea
  34 years 338 days
Tommy Hutchison ..... 1981 Manchester C vs Tottenham H
  33 years 229 days
Doug Holden .... 1964 Preston vs West Ham
  33 years 217 days
Arnold Muhren .... 1983 Manchester U vs Brighton (R)
  32 years 358 days
Peter Doherty .... 1946 Derby Co vs Charlton A
  32 years 326 days
Nat Lofthouse .... 1958 Bolton W vs Manchester U
  32 years 248 days
Chris Waddle .... 1993 Sheffield W vs Arsenal (R)
  32 years 157 days
Jimmy Dunn .... 1933 Everton vs Manchester C
  32 years 155 days
Bryan Robson .... 1990 Manchester U vs Crystal P
  32 years 121 days
Bob John .... 1932 Arsenal vs Newcastle U
  32 years 80 days
Charlie Wayman .... 1954 Preston vs WBA
  31 years 350 days
Stan Mortensen .... 1953 Blackpool vs Bolton W
  31 years 341 days
Trevor Brooking .... 1980 West Ham vs Arsenal
  31 years 221 days
Bill Moir .... 1953 Bolton W vs Blackpool
  31 years 13 days
Sam Tilson .... 1934 Manchester C vs Portsmouth
  31 years 9 days
Jackie Milburn .... 1955 Newcastle U vs Manchester C
  30 years 361 days
George Seymour .... 1924 Newcastle U vs Aston Villa
  30 years 345 days
Jimmy Greenhoff .... 1977 Manchester U vs Liverpool
  30 years 336 days
Andrew Linighan .... 1993 Arsenal vs Sheffield W (R)
  30 years 275 days
Bobby Mitchell .... 1955 Newcastle U vs Manchester C
  30 years 264 days
John Aldridge .... 1989 Liverpool vs Everton
  30 years 244 days
Ian Rush .... 1992 Liverpool vs Sunderland
  30 years 202 days
Bobby Gurney .... 1937 Sunderland vs Preston
  30 years 200 days
Joe Bradford .... 1931 Birmingham vs WBA
  30 years 93 days
Maldwyn Griffiths ...... 1949 Leicester C vs Wolves
  30 years 53 days
Reg Lewis .... 1950 Arsenal vs Liverpool
  30 years 53 days
Angus Morrison .... 1954 Preston vs WBA
  30 years 5 days

FA Cup Trivia (1)

BROADCASTING The 1926 Cup Final between Bolton and Manchester City was the first to be broadcast, but the only listeners were sitting in public halls in Manchester and Bolton. Radio links from Wembley to Lancashire were set up for the day, but the first real public broadcast throughout the country came the following year when Cardiff beat Arsenal.

The first final to be televised, albeit not the whole match, was the 1937 final between Sunderland and Preston.

The first final to be televised live in its entirety was the 1938 final between Preston and Huddersfield. With the exception of the 1952 final, all subsequent finals have been televised live.

The first final to be televised in colour was the 1968 final when West Bromwich Albion beat Everton.

FA CUP OUT OF ENGLAND It is widely known that when Cardiff City beat Arsenal to win the FA Cup in 1927 they became the first and only club to take the Cup out of England. But the Cup *has* been back to Wales since then.

After Manchester City won the Cup in 1956, Roy Paul, Manchester City's Welsh captain who started his working life as a coal-miner, 'borrowed' the Cup and took it on a tour of clubs and schools in the Rhondda Valley. It was the first time it had been seen in Wales since Cardiff's victory.

Newcastle United toured South Africa in 1952 and took the Cup with them.

STRANGE CUP GOAL One of the strangest goals scored in the Cup's history came in a second round match on February 8, 1902 between Lincoln and Derby County. The score was goalless at half-time. When Derby kicked off the second half, their forward and half-back lines surrounded the player with the ball preventing any Lincoln player getting near it. They guided the ball into the Lincoln goal area before Ben Warren scored the first of a hat-trick in Derby's 3–1 win.

NOTHING VENTURED....NOT MUCH GAINED In March 1950 the amateur club Banbury Spencer put forward a novel proposal to the FA which was given a polite, if quizzical examination by the authorities. Banbury proposed that a competition be set up for clubs knocked out in the early rounds of the FA Cup with a final at Wembley. The suggested name for the competition was the FA Intermediate Cup. Needless to say, it never caught on.

THE FA CUP COMES TO TOWN On November 22, 1952 three FA Cup first round matches all took place a stone's throw from each other in East London when Leyton Orient, Leytonstone and Leyton were all drawn at home. Leyton Orient, then in the southern section of the Third Division, drew 1–1 at home with Bristol Rovers; Leytonstone, then in the Isthmian League, lost 2–0 at home to Watford; and Leyton, then in the Athenian League, drew 0–0 at home with Southern League Hereford. Both Leyton Orient and Leyton lost their replays. Leyton never played another home match in the Competition Proper, while

Leytonstone did not play at home in the Competition Proper for another 13 years.

YOU ARE WHAT YOU EAT In 1926 Bolton's players openly took 'nerve powder' before their 1–0 Cup Final win over Manchester City, while in 1939 Wolves's players alledgedly took a monkey gland potion before playing Portsmouth in the final. If they did – and it is doubtful – it didn't do them much good as they lost 4–1 in one of the biggest Cup upsets of all time.

One dietary preparation that has gone out of fashion of late would seem to be that of a steak dinner with all the trappings, washed down with an egg and rum cocktail, confidently eaten by the entire King's Lynn team before their first round match with Southend in 1968. The Southern League side lost 9–0. It was King's Lynn's second huge reversal in the Cup. In 1906, then in the Norfolk and Suffolk League, they lost 11–0 to Aston Villa in another first round match, but the details of their dinner on that occasion are not known.

SEE SOUTHEND AND DIE Southend scored 19 goals in the opening two rounds of the 1968–69 competition. They beat King's Lynn 9–0 in the first round and Brentwood 10–1 in the second. Billy Best (8 goals) and Gary Moore (7) scored 15 of the 19 between them.

Southend have a habit of handing out good hidings to non-League opposition and are the only team to have scored nine goals or more in the Cup three times since the Second World War and four times since 1918. They also beat Golders Green (later Hendon) 10–1 in 1934–35 and Barnet, then of the Athenian League, 9–2 in 1946–47.

CROWDS The official record crowd for the Cup Final is 126,047 for the first Wembley final between Bolton and West Ham in 1923 – but the true attendance at that match will never be known and contemporary reports say as many as 200,000 may have been inside Wembley that afternoon.

That was the last time spectators could pay at the gate at a Cup Final, although there was cash admission available at the 1982 replay between Tottenham and Queens Park Rangers.

There have been four 100,000-plus crowds at the final:

1901 Tottenham H vs Sheffield U, Crystal Palace *110,820*
1905 Aston Villa vs Newcastle U, Crystal Palace *101,117*
1913 Aston Villa vs Sunderland, Crystal Palace *120,081*
1923 Bolton Wanderers vs West Ham, Wembley *126,047★ (★official attendance)*

The biggest crowd for an FA Cup match other than the Final itself was the 84,569 who watched the sixth round tie on March 3, 1934 between Manchester City, the eventual Cup winners, and Stoke City. Manchester City won 1–0.

BEHIND CLOSED DOORS Coincidentally, on the same date 18 years earlier an official crowd figure of 'nil' was recorded when Norwich played Bradford City in a third round second replay at Sincil Bank, Lincoln. On the afternoon of March 3, 1915 the two teams met behind locked doors so that production at a local armaments factory was not disrupted. However, it is estimated that at least 1,000 people managed to gain admittance to watch Bradford's 2–0 win.

On January 16, 1985 Leicester City played Burton Albion behind closed doors in a third round replay at Highfield Road, Coventry where the official attendance was again 'nil'. Leicester had won Burton's 'home' match at the Baseball Ground, Derby 6–1 but the FA ordered the match to be replayed because Burton's goalkeeper had been hit by a missile. Leicester won the replayed match at Coventry 1–0.

On November 25, 1992 Peterborough United beat Kingstonian 9–1 at home in a first round replay after drawing the first match 1–1. But the FA ordered the match to be replayed because Kingstonian's goalkeeper Adrian Blake had been hit by missiles. The Kingstonian manager Chris Kelly disagreed with the FA's ruling, angry that his part-timers would lose money by taking time off work to replay the match scheduled for a Friday afternoon. Kelly thought they had lost the match fair and square. Peterborough won the replay behind closed doors 1–0.

AWAY FROM HOME Manchester United's Old Trafford ground was so badly damaged by bombs during the Second World War that in the immediate post-war seasons they played their home matches at neighbouring Maine Road, and so technically at least, they became the first, and so far only, team to win Cup playing all their matches away from home.

They also set another record that season as the only team to have won the Cup by beating six First Division teams.

Arsenal achieved a remarkable record when they reached the FA Cup Final in both 1971 and 1972 without once being drawn at home in either year – although they did draw matches at Portsmouth and Leicester in 1971 and at Derby in 1972 so they did in fact play three matches at Highbury.

In a more conventional sense than Manchester United, Birmingham City became the first team to reach Wembley after being drawn away in every round, while Manchester United were the last team to reach the Cup Final in this manner in 1990.

SCORED IN EVERY ROUND The following nine players have scored in every round of the FA Cup in the same season with the total number of goals they scored on the right:

1900-01 .... Sandy Brown .... Tottenham H 15
1934-35 .... Ellis Rimmer .... Sheffield W 8
1936-37 .... Frank O'Donnell .... Preston NE 11
1947-48 .... Stan Mortensen .... Blackpool 10
1950-51 .... Jackie Milburn .... Newcastle U 8
1952-53 .... Nat Lofthouse .... Bolton W 8
1953-54 .... Charlie Wayman ..... Preston NE 7
1967-68 .... Jeff Astle .... WBA 9
1969-70 .... Peter Osgood .... Chelsea 8

SUSPENDED CUP FINAL CAPTAINS There was an unhappy sequence in the early 1980s when three captains all missed playing in the Cup Final because of suspension. In 1982 Glenn Roeder missed QPR's replay against Tottenham, in 1983 Steve Foster of Brighton missed the final against Manchester United but played in the replay and in 1984 Wilf Rostron was suspended at the time Watford played Everton. In each case their team lost.

THE VERY LONG AND WINDING ROAD...THAT DOESN'T USUALLY LEAD TO WEMBLEY

With FA Cup matches in the competition proper now decided by penalty shoot-outs at the end of extra-time if the replay ends in a draw, the long drawn out marathon Cup battles would now seem to be a thing of the past.

The following ties are unlikely to be equalled for their duration, although new records could still be set in the qualifying rounds:

Alvechurch vs Oxford City .... 1971–72 .... 4q
6 matches 11 hrs. Alvechurch won 1–0
Leyton vs Ilford .... 1924–25 .... 3q
5 matches 9 hrs 40mins Leyton won 2–0
Barrow vs Gillingham .... 1924–25 .... 6q
5 matches 9 hrs 30mins Barrow won 2–1
Stoke City vs Bury .... 1954–55 .... R3
5 matches 9 hrs 22mins Stoke won 3–2
New Brompton vs W.Arsenal ...... 1899–00 .... 3q
5 matches 9 hrs New Brompton won 1–0
Chelsea vs Burnley .... 1955–56 .... R4
5 matches 9 hrs Chelsea won 2–0
Arsenal vs Sheffield Wed .... 1978–79 .... R3
5 matches 9 hrs Arsenal won 2–0
Falmouth Town vs Bideford .... 1973–74 .... 3q
5 matches 9 hrs Bideford won 2–1
Doncaster R vs Aston Villa .... 1954–55 .... R4
5 matches 8 hrs 30mins Doncaster won 3–1
Hull C vs Darlington .... 1960–61 .... R2
5 matches 8 hrs 30mins Hull won 3–0

THIRD–FOURTH PLACE MATCHES

At the start of the 1970s it was decided to replace the traditional eve-of-final England vs Young England matches by holding a 'third-place play-off' between the losing semi-finalists. The idea was originally quite well supported, but was dropped after only a few seasons. These are the details:-

1969–70 Manchester United 2, Watford 0 at Highbury on April 10, 1970.
The first of these games attracted a crowd of 15,000 people on the night before the Cup Final and saw Brian Kidd score twice to give United victory.

1970–71 Stoke City 3, Everton 2 at Selhurst Park.
Only 5,031 people watched this match played on May 7, 1971. John Ritchie scored twice and Mike Bernard the other as Stoke won after being 2–1 down at half-time. Alan Whittle and Alan Ball scored for Everton.

1971–72 Birmingham City 0, Stoke City 0 at The Hawthorns.
Held over from the previous season and played on August 5, 1972. This was actually the first FA Cup match decided by penalties. Birmingham beat Stoke 4–3 in the shoot-out.

1972–73 Arsenal 1, Wolves 3 at Highbury.
This was also held over until the start of the following season and was played on August 18, 1973. Brendan Hornsby scored for Arsenal, Jim McCalliog and Derek Dougan (2) for Wolves.

1973–74 Leicester City 0, Burnley 1 at Filbert Street
Played on May 9, 1974, five days after the Cup Final. While 100,000 had watched Liverpool beat Newcastle at Wembley, not surprisingly only 4,000 turned up for this non-event settled by a first half goal from Ray Hankin.

MAN-OF-THE-MATCH AWARD

This was another short-lived idea at the same time as the third-fourth place play-offs. It was given by journalists after the Cup Final to the player with the most votes. Allan Clarke, who played in three finals in four years, won it twice. The trophy was sponsored by Charles Buchan's Football Monthly magazine.

1969 .... Allan Clarke .... Leicester C
1970 .... Eddie Gray .... Leeds U
1971 .... George Graham .... Arsenal
1972 .... Allan Clarke .... Leeds U
1973 .... Jim Montgomery .... Sunderland

The idea was revived by the Daily Mirror in 1993. The first winner of the new Bobby Moore trophy was Carlton Palmer of Sheffield Wednesday.

THE WEMBLEY DRESSING ROOMS

There has long been a Cup Final superstition that out of the two dressing rooms at Wembley, the South Dressing Room is the luckier one.

The superstition arose after the Second World War when Charlton, Burnley, Blackpool and Leicester all emerged from the North Dressing Room for the final – and lost. The run was broken when Arsenal had the North Dressing Room and won the 1950 Cup Final.

Of the 48 finals at Wembley since the war, the team using the 'lucky' South Dressing Room has won the Cup 34 times. Chelsea had the North Dressing Room in 1970, but as they did not win the Cup at Wembley, they are not included in this list of 'northern' winners.

There is another way of looking at this little quirk. The teams are allocated the dressing rooms on an alphabetical basis with the first-lettered team always going in the North Dressing Room. There has only been one occasion when this didn't happen, in 1964 when West Ham played Preston. Preston were given the South Dressing Room by mistake – but it didn't help them. West Ham won.

The only winners from the North Dressing Room since 1946 have been Arsenal (1950), Blackpool (1953), Aston Villa (1957), Bolton (1958), West Ham (1964), Everton (1966), Arsenal (1971) Liverpool (1974), Arsenal (1979), Everton (1984), Coventry (1987), Liverpool (1992) and Arsenal (1993).

CUP FINAL DATES

In 1963 the Cup Final was 'postponed' by the FA from the original scheduled date of May 4 to May 25 because of the 'big freeze' winter of 1962–63 which played havoc with the fixture list.

Only two other finals in the competition's history have been decided later in the year than May 25. On May 26, 1983 Manchester United beat Brighton in a replay. On May 27, 1982 Tottenham beat Queens Park Rangers in a replay and this remains the latest date in the year on which the Cup Final has been decided.

The earliest date on which the Cup Final has been played is 11 March, in 1876 when Wanderers drew 1–1 with Old Etonians.

The FA Cup Trophies

The current FA Cup trophy, first won by Liverpool in 1992, is the fourth Cup to be played for since the competition began in 1871.

The details of the trophies:-

THE FIRST FA CUP, AWARDED 1872–1895
The first FA Cup was made by the firm of Martin, Hall and Co early in 1872 and bore little relation to today's classic trophy. Made of silver, it stood less than 18 inches high, could hold little more than a couple of pints and cost £20 to manufacture. It had a footballer figurine at the top and was usually described as 'the little tin idol' or 'the insignificant pot'.

It was won by the Wanderers three years in succession (1876–78) and under the rules of the competition they were entitled to keep it, but they handed it back to the FA with the proviso that no other team could retain it if they won it three times. When Blackburn Rovers won the Cup three years running (1884–86) the FA awarded them a commemorative shield.

The last winners of the first FA Cup trophy were Aston Villa in 1895. They had the trophy put on display in the window of a football outfitters called William Shillcock whose shop was at 73, Newtown Row, Birmingham. On the night of September 11, 1895, the Cup was stolen and never recovered, despite a reward of £10 being offered for it.

Blackburn Rovers and the Wanderers each won the first Cup five times with 11 other clubs having their name engraved on it.

THE SECOND FA CUP, AWARDED 1896–1910
Sheffield Wednesday were the first winners of the new Cup in 1896 and Newcastle the last winners in 1910. There was little difference in the size and style of the second Cup to the first. This was because the silversmiths who made it, Messrs Vaughton's of Birmingham, had exact miniature replicas to work from, commissioned by Wolverhampton Wanderers when

they won the Cup in 1893. One of the Vaughton company's directors was Howard Vaughton who played for Aston Villa when they won the Cup in 1887.

In 1910 the FA discovered that the design of the Cup had been pirated and they ordered that a new one should be commissioned. The second Cup was presented to Lord Kinnaird by the Council of the Football Association to mark his 21 years as president. Aston Villa, Bury, Sheffield United and Sheffield Wednesday each won this Cup twice with seven other teams winning it once each.

THE THIRD FA CUP, AWARDED 1911–1991
The FA had the design of the third Cup registered and copyrighted, one of the best moves they ever made. The third Cup was a far more imposing trophy than the first two and today is one of the most famous sporting prizes in the world.

A large number of companies submitted designs for the new Cup, but the FA wisely chose the one submitted by Messrs Fattorini and Sons of Bradford. This Cup was 19 inches high, excluding the plinth, and weighed 175 ounces. By coincidence the first winners of the new Cup were Bradford City – the only time they reached the final. The Cup cost 50 guineas to make.

The last winners of the third Cup were Tottenham Hotspur who won this particular trophy for a record seventh time in 1991. Manchester United won it six times, Arsenal and Newcastle four times and another 29 teams also had the joy of lifting it.

THE FOURTH CUP, FIRST AWARDED 1992
The new FA Cup is an exact replica of the third trophy and the first winners were Liverpool whose name was never inscribed on the first two Cups. But on Sunday morning, May 10, 1992, just 17 hours after the team held the Cup aloft at Wembley, former Liverpool captain Phil Thompson, the club's reserve team coach, dropped the lid as he left the team's London hotel for the journey home. It smashed on the ground, was badly dented and did not fit back onto its rim properly.

FA CUP FINAL GUESTS OF HONOUR

1923	King George V,		Duke of Gloucester, Prince William, Princess Mary		Edinburgh, Duke and Duchess of Kent
	The Duke of Devonshire	1952	Sir Winston Churchill	1973	Duke of Kent
1924	Duke of York	1953	Queen Elizabeth II	1974	Princess Anne, Duke of Kent
1925	Duke of York	1954	Queen Mother, Princess Margaret	1975	Duke and Duchess of Kent
1926	King George V	1955	Princess Mary, Duke of Edinburgh	1976	Queen Elizabeth II and Duke of
1927	King George V	1956	Queen Elizabeth II		Edinburgh
1928	King George V and Queen Mary,	1957	Queen Elizabeth II and Duke of	1977	Duke and Duchess of Kent
	Duke and Duchess of York		Edinburgh	1978	Princess Alexandra
1929	Prince of Wales	1958	Queen Elizabeth II and Duke of	1979	Prince of Wales
1930	King George V		Edinburgh	1980	Duke and Duchess of Kent
1931	Duke of Gloucester	1959	Queen Elizabeth II and Duke of	1981	Queen Mother
1932	King George V and Queen Mary		Edinburgh	1981rep	Prince Michael of Kent
1933	Duke of York	1960	Duke of Gloucester	1982	Princess Anne
1934	King George V	1961	Duchess of Kent	1982rep	Duke of Kent
1935	Prince of Wales	1962	Queen Elizabeth II and Duke of	1983	Duke of Kent
1936	Sir Charles Clegg, President of the FA		Edinburgh	1983rep	Princess Michael of Kent
1937	King George VI and Queen Elizabeth	1963	Queen Elizabeth II and Duke of	1984	Duke and Duchess of Kent
1938	King George VI		Edinburgh	1985	Duke of Kent
1939	King George VI	1964	Earl of Harewood	1986	Duchess of Kent
1946	King George VI, Queen Elizabeth,	1965	Queen Elizabeth II and Duke of	1987	Duchess of Kent
	Princess Elizabeth		Edinburgh	1988	Princess of Wales
1947	Duke and Duchess of Gloucester	1966	Princess Margaret	1989	Duke and Duchess of Kent
1948	King George VI	1967	Duke and Duchess of Kent	1990	Duke and Duchess of Kent
1949	Princess Elizabeth, Duke of	1968	Princess Alexandra	1990rep	Duke and Duchess of Kent
	Gloucester	1969	Princess Anne	1991	Prince and Princess of Wales, Duke
1950	King George VI	1970	Princess Margaret		and Duchess of Kent
1951	King George VI, Queen Elizabeth,	1970rep	Sir Dr Andrew Stephen	1992	Duke and Duchess of Kent
		1971	Duke and Duchess of Kent	1993	Duke and Duchess of Kent
		1972	Queen Elizabeth II and Duke of	1993rep	Duchess of Kent

The War Years

The 1915 Cup Final between Sheffield and Chelsea, played on April 24, 1915, is unique as it is the only Cup Final played during a World War. It is known as the 'Khaki Cup Final' because of the large number of servicemen in the crowd at Old Trafford and was played on a day well in keeping with the times – the weather was bleak and murky and there was none of the exuberance from the crowd usually seen at the Cup Final. Sheffield United won the match 3–0.

It was to be the last Cup Final staged at Old Trafford until 1970, when Chelsea were again involved. Chelsea were well beaten in 1915 but contributed one unique item to FA Cup history. Their forward Bob Thomson was the only one-eyed player ever to appear in a Cup Final.

Regional tournaments were staged from the 1915–16 to the 1918–19 seasons before the return of peacetime soccer in 1919–20, but there were no 'Wartime Cup Finals' during World War One.

During World War Two there were a number of 'Cup Finals' played. The details:–

1939–40 League Cup Final West Ham 1 (Small), Blackburn R 0 *Wembley 42,399*

1940–41 League Cup Final Arsenal 1 (D.Compton), Preston NE 1 (McLaren) *Wembley 60,000*
Replay Preston 2 (R Beattie 2), Arsenal 1 (og) *Ewood Park 45,000*

1941–42 League Cup – 1L Sunderland 2 (Stubbins, Carter), Wolves 2 (Westcott 2) *Roker Park 35,000*
League Cup – 2L Wolves 4 (Rowley 2, Westcott, Broome), Sunderland 1 (Carter) *Molineux 43,038*

London Cup Final Brentford 2 (Smith 2), Portsmouth 0 *Wembley 72,000*
Cup Winners Cup Brentford 1 (Collett), Wolves 1 (Mullen) *Stamford Bridge 20,174*

1942–43 League South Cup Arsenal 7 (Lewis 4, Drake 2, D Compton), Charlton 1 (Green) *Wembley 75,000*
League North Cup –1L Blackpool 2 (Finan, Burbanks), Sheff.W 2 (Cockroft, Robinson) *Bloomfield Rd, 28,000*
League North Cup –2L Sheffield W 1 (Robinson), Blackpool 2 (Dodds, Gardner) *Hillsborough 42,657*
Cup Winners Cup Blackpool 4 (Dix, Burbanks, Dodds, Finan), Arsenal 2 (Lewis, D.Compton) *Stamford Bridge 55,195*

1943–44 League South Cup Charlton 3 (Revell 2, Welsh), Chelsea 1 (Payne pen) *Wembley 85,000*
League North Cup –1L Blackpool 2 (Dodds 2), Aston Villa 1 (Goffin) *Bloomfield Rd 28,000*
League North Cup –2L Aston Villa 4 (Bromme 2, Edwards, Iverson), Blackpool 2 (Dix, Pearson) *Villa Park 55,000*
Cup Winners Cup Aston Villa 1 (Houghton), Charlton 1 (Revell) *Stamford Bridge 38,540*

1944–45 League South Cup Chelsea 2 (McDonald, Wardle), Millwall 0, *Wembley 90,000*
League North Cup –1L Bolton 1 (Lofthouse), Manchester United 0 *Burnden Park, 40,000*
League North Cup –2L Manchester U 2 (Wrigglesworth, Bryant), Bolton 2 (Barrass 2) *Maine Rd 57,395*
Cup Winners Cup Bolton 2 (Hunt, Hamlett), Chelsea 1 (Rooke) *Stamford Bridge 35,000*

FA Cup and Non-League Clubs

NON-LEAGUE FA CUP WINNERS
Tottenham H .... (SL) 1901

NON-LEAGUE BEATEN FINALISTS
Sheffield W .... (FAll) 1890
Southampton .... (SL) 1900
Southampton .... (SL) 1902

NON-LEAGUE BEATEN SEMI–FINALISTS
Nottingham F .... (FAll) 1892
Southampton .... (SL) 1898
Millwall .... (SL) 1900
Millwall .... (SL) 1903
Southampton .... (SL) 1908
Swindon T .... (SL) 1910
Swindon T .... (SL) 1912

NON-LEAGUE CLUBS IN THE LAST EIGHT
Birmingham St Georges .... (FAll) 1889
Chatham .... (n/af) 1889
Sheffield Wednesday .... (FAll) 1889
Bootle .... (FAll) 1890
Nottingham Forest .... (FAll) 1891
Stoke .... (FAll) 1891
Sheffield Wednesday .... (FAll) 1891
Sheffield Wednesday .... (FAll) 1892
Middlesbrough Ironopolis ..... (NL) 1893
Southampton .... (SL) 1899
Tottenham H .... (SL) 1899
Reading .... (SL) 1901
Portsmouth .... (SL) 1902
Tottenham H .... (SL) 1903
Tottenham H .... (SL) 1904
Southampton .... (SL) 1905
Fulham .... (SL) 1905
Southampton .... (SL) 1906
Crystal Palace .... (SL) 1907
Coventry C .... (SL) 1910
QPR .... (SL) 1910
Swindon .... (SL) 1911
West Ham .... (SL) 1911
QPR .... (SL) 1914

Since the competition was reorganised in 1925 the best performances by non-League clubs have been the following who all reached Round 5, the last 16.

Colchester United .... (SL) 1948
Yeovil Town .... (SL) 1949
Blyth Spartans .... (NL) 1978
Telford United .... (APL) 1985

In 1919–20, Cardiff City and Plymouth Argyle, then both in the Southern League, reached the Third Round, the equivalent of today's Fifth Round, the last 16.

HIGHEST WINS BY NON-LEAGUE OVER LEAGUE CLUBS
18.11.1905   3q   7–1 Crystal Palace (SL) vs Chelsea (D2)

Left, facing page A distinguished guest at the 1944 League South Cup final at Wembley. Just two months before D-Day, General Dwight Eisenhower, Supreme Commander of the British and US Expeditionary Forces, meets the Chelsea team (Popperfoto)

24.2.1906   3   6–1 Southampton (SL) vs Middlesbrough (D1)
24.11.1934   1   1–6 Carlisle U (3N) vs Wigan A (CC)
28.11.1936   1   6–1 Walthamstow Ave (Ath) vs Northampton T (3S)
10.12.1955   1   1–6 Derby Co (3N) vs Boston U (ML)
7.12 1957   1   6–1 Hereford U (SL) vs QPR (3S)
21.11.1970   1   6–1 Barnet (SL) vs Newport Co (D4)

HIGHEST WINS BY LEAGUE OVER NON-LEAGUE CLUBS
(Note this table only includes matches in the competition proper since the formation of the Football League in 1888)

27.1.1894   1   18–0 Preston (D1) vs Reading (n/af)
17.1.1891   1   13–1 Aston Villa (D1) vs Casuals
2.2.1897   1r 12–1 Bury (D1) vs Stockton (NL)
13.1.1906   1   11–0 Aston Villa (D1) vs Kings Lynn (N&S)
5.11.1960   1   11–0 Bristol City (D3) vs Chichester C (SCL)
20.11.1971   1   11–0 Bournemouth (D3) vs Margate (SL)
2.2.1895   1   11–1 Sunderland (D1) vs Fairfield (LL)
9.1.1932   3   11–1 Arsenal (D1) vs Darwen (LC)
1.2.1937   1r 11–3 Bradford City (D2) vs Walker Celtic (NEL)
24.1.1912   1r 10–0 Wolverhampton W (D2) vs Watford (SL)

Note: Nottingham Forest's 14–0 victory over Clapton in January 1891 is still the biggest away win in the Cup since the formation of the Football League, but occurred when Nottingham Forest were members of the Football Alliance. Wolves' 14–0 win over Crosswell's Brewery in 1886 is not included as it happened two years before the League's formation.

OTHER BIG WINS: LEAGUE CLUBS AGAINST NON-LEAGUE CLUBS IN QUALIFYING ROUNDS
1.2.1889   2q   13–0 Bolton W (D1) vs Sheffield U
13.10.1894   1q   13–0 Leicester Fosse (D2) vs Notts Olympic
12.10.1895   1q   13–0 Lincoln C (D2) vs Peterborough Club
14.10.1893   1q   12–0 Woolwich Arsenal (D2) vs Ashford U
1.10.1932   1q   12–0 Brighton & HA (3S) vs Shoreham
9.12.1905   4q   12–1 Gainsborough T (D2) vs Weymouth
21.11.1896   3q   11–0 Walsall (D2) vs Dresden U
7.10.1905   1q   11–0 Leeds City (D2) vs Morley
17.10.1908   2q   11–0 Bradford PA (D2) vs Denby Dale
14.12.1912   5q   11–1 Glossop (D2) vs Southall

VICTORIES BY NON-LEAGUE CLUBS OVER THE LEAGUE CHAMPIONS
Four non-League clubs have beaten the League champions in the FA Cup.

17.1.1891 .1 ...... Stoke (FAll) 3, Preston NE 0
5.3.1900 ...3 2r .. Millwall Athletic (SL) 2, Aston Villa 1
               match played at Reading after two drawn games
8.2.1902 ...2 ...... Southampton (SL) 4, Liverpool 1
9.1.1915 ...1 ...... Swansea Town (SL) 1, Blackburn Rovers 0

Stoke's win came less than two years after Preston had won the Double – Millwall's win over Aston Villa less than three years after Villa had won the Double.

VICTORIES BY NON-LEAGUE CLUBS OVER THE CUP HOLDERS
23.2.1901 ...2 ... Tottenham H (SL) 2, Bury 1
3.2.1902 ..... 1 ... Southampton (SL) 2, Tottenham H 1
               match played at Reading after two drawn games
11.1.1908 ...1 ... Norwich City (SL) 2, Sheffield Wednesday 0
21.1.1909 ... 1r .. Crystal Palace (SL) 4, Wolverhampton W 2
               after a 2–2 draw

VICTORIES BY NON-LEAGUE CLUBS OVER FIRST DIVISION CLUBS
From the formation of the Football League in 1888 until the reorganisation of the competition in 1925, there were 83 victories by non–League clubs over Division One clubs, the majority of these recorded by Southern League clubs who regularly beat both First and Second Division Football League opposition.

The most notable victories achieved by non-Southern League clubs over Division One clubs during this period were:–

14.1.1911 ... 1 .... Bristol City 0, Crewe Alexandra (BDL) 3
14.1.1911 ... 1 .... Sheffield United 0, Darlington (NEL) 1
14.1.1920 ... 2r ... Sheffield Wednesday 0, Darlington (NEL) 2
12.1.1924 ... 1 .... Corinthians (n/af) 1, Blackburn Rovers 0

From 1924 until 1948 no non-League club defeated a First Division side. The following lists the victories by non-League clubs since 1948.

10.1.1948 .... 3 .... Colchester United (SL) 1, Huddersfield Town 0
29.1.1949 .... 4 .... Yeovil Town (SL) 2, Sunderland 1 aet
5.2.1972 .... 3r .. Hereford United (SL) 2, Newcastle United 1
4.1.1975 .... 3 .... Burnley 0, Wimbledon (SL) 1
14.1.1986 .... 3 .... Birmingham City 1, Altrincham (GMVC) 2
7.1.1989 .... 3 .... Sutton United (GMVC) 2, Coventry City 1

NON-LEAGUE VICTORIES OVER SECOND DIVISION CLUBS SINCE 1948

24.1.1948 .... 4 .... Colchester United (SL) 3, Bradford PA 2
8.1.1949 .... 3 .... Yeovil Town (SL) 3, Bury 1
12.1.1955 .... 3r .. Bishop Auckland (NL) 3, Ipswich Town 0
3.1.1957 .... 3 .... Notts County 1, Rhyl Athletic (CC) 3
9.1.1957 .... 3r .. Lincoln City 4, Peterborough United (ML) 5 aet
15.1.1959 .... 3 .... Worcester City (SL) 2, Liverpool 1
9.1.1960 .... 3 .... Ipswich Town 2, Peterborough United (ML) 3
4.1.1964 .... 3 .... Newcastle United 1, Bedford Town (SL) 2
6.2.1978 .... 4 .... Stoke City 2, Blyth Spartans (NL) 3
5.1.1980 .... 3r .. Harlow Town (IL) 1, Leicester City 0
5.1.1991 .... 3 .... West Bromwich Albion 2, Woking (IL) 4

THE TOP 10 NON-LEAGUE FA CUP RECORDS

	Seasons in Competition Proper	Rd 1	Rd 2	Rd 3	Rd 4	Rd 5
Yeovil Town	43	22	11	9	0	1
Kettering Town	34	23	7	3	1	–
Weymouth	31	21	7	2	1	–
Blyth Spartans	25	14	9	1	0	1
Altrincham	23	9	7	6	1	–
Barnet	29	20	4	5	–	–
Telford United	30	21	6	1	1	1
Enfield	25	11	11	2	1	–
Bath City	24	9	10	5	–	–
Boston United	29	20	5	4	–	–

LEAGUE CLUBS BEATEN Note: these records only include matches against clubs who were in the Football League when the tie was played.

Yeovil .... Bournemouth (1924–25 [4q] & 1970–71) C.Palace (1934–35 & 1963–64), Exeter C (1934–35), Brighton (1938–39), Bury (1948–49), Sunderland (1948–49) Southend (1958–59 & 1963–64), Walsall (1960–61) Brentford (1972–73), Cambridge United (1987–88)

Kettering .... Swindon Town (1961–62), Millwall (1963–64) Swansea City (1974–75), Oxford United (1976–77) Bristol Rovers (1988–89), Halifax Town (1988–89) Maidstone United (1991–92)

Weymouth .... Merthyr Town (1924–25 [5q]), Aldershot (1949–50) Shrewsbury Town (1956–57) Newport Co (1961–62) and Cardiff C (1982–83)

Blyth Spartans .. Ashington (1922–23 [5q], Gillingham (1922–23 [6q])

Happy faces in the dressing-room as non-league Sutton United celebrate their 2–1 win over First Division Coventry City in 1989 (Allsport)

Hartlepools U (1925–26), Crewe Alexandra (1971–72) Stockport Co (1971–72), Chesterfield (1977–78), Stoke C (1977–78)

Altrincham .... Tranmere R (1921–22 [4q]), Rochdale (1965–66 & 1982–83), Hartlepool U (1973–74), Scunthorpe United (1974–75 & 1980–81), Crewe Alexandra (1979–80), Rotherham U (1979–80), Sheffield United (1981–82), York City (1981–82), Blackpool (1984–85 & 1985–86), Birmingham City (1985–86), Lincoln City (1988–89)

Barnet .... Newport County (1970–71) and Northampton (1990–91)

Telford United .. Wigan Athletic (1982–83), Stockport Co (1983 & 1985–86), Northampton Town (1983–84) Rochdale (1983–84), Lincoln City (1984–85), Preston (1984–85), Bradford City (1984–85), Darlington (1984–85), Burnley (1986–87)

Enfield .... Wimbledon (1977–78 & 1981–82), Northampton (1977–78), Hereford U (1980–81), Port Vale (1980–81), Exeter C (1984–85), Leyton Orient (1988–89), Aldershot (1991–92)

Bath City .... Merthyr Town (1920–21 [5q], Barrow (1922–23 [6q]) Crystal Palace (1931–32), Southend (1952–53) Exeter C (1922–23 [5q] and 1957–58), Millwall (1959–60) Notts Co (1959–60), Newport Co (1965–66)

Boston United .. Bradford PA (1925–26), Derby Co (1955–56) Southport (1970–71), Hartlepools (1971–72) Crewe Alexandra (1982–83)

LEAGUE CLUBS BEATEN MOST TIMES BY NON-LEAGUE CLUBS

16 times ...... Crewe Alexandra

13 times .... Exeter City
12 times .... Rochdale, Halifax T

LEAGUE CLUBS UNBEATEN BY NON-LEAGUE OPPOSITION SINCE 1925 Arsenal, Aston Villa, Blackburn Rovers, Bolton Wanderers, Charlton, Chelsea, Everton, Fulham, Hull City, Leeds United, Manchester City, Manchester United, Middlesbrough, Nottingham Forest, Portsmouth, Tottenham H, West Ham.

CLUBS NEVER BEATEN BY NON-LEAGUE OPPOSITION Leeds U, Portsmouth, West Ham

NON-LEAGUE CLUBS WITH MOST CONSECUTIVE APPEARANCES IN ROUND ONE:
17 times .... Hereford United (1955–1972)

Hereford only failed to reach the First Round once in the 24 years between 1948 and 1972 when they were elected to the Football League. In 1954–55 they were beaten by Nuneaton in the fourth qualifying round.

15 times .... Rhyl Athletic (1948–1963)
11 times .... Wycombe Wanderers (1973–1983)
Enfield (1976–1986)
Altrincham (1978–1988)

NON-LEAGUE CLUBS TO HAVE REACHED THE FOURTH ROUND (Last 32 and beyond, or the old Second Round equivalent, since the Football League was expanded to 86 clubs in 1921. Note: Corinthians, who did not play in a League, were exempted until the third round.

Season	Club	Lge	Round	Matches played
1923–24	.. **Corinthians**		2	1 Blackburn R 1–0; 2 WBA 0–5
1925–26	.. **Corinthians**		3	3 Manchester C 3–3; 3r Manchester C 0–4
1926–27	.. **Corinthians**		4	3 Walsall 4–0; 4 Newcastle U 1–3
1928–29	.. **Corinthians**		4	3 Norwich C 5–0; 4 West Ham 0–3
	Mansfield T	ML	4	1 Shirebrook 4–2; 2 Barrow 2–1; 3 Wolverhampton W 1–0; 4 Arsenal 0–2
1933–34	.. **Workington**	NEL	4	1 Southport 1–0; 2 Newport Co 3–1; 3 Gateshead 4–1; 4 Preston NE 1–2
1938–39	.. **Chelmsford C**	SL	4	1 Kidderminster 4–0; 2 Darlington 3–1; 3 Southampton 4–1; 4 Birmingham 0–6
1947–48	.. **Colchester U**	SL	5	1 Banbury Spencer 2–1; 2 Wrexham 1–0; 3 Huddersfield T 1–0; 4 Bradford PA 3–2; 5 Blackpool 0–5
1948–49	.. **Yeovil T**	SL	5	1 Runcorn 2–1; 2 Weymouth 4–0; 3 Bury 3–1; 4 Sunderland 2–1aet; 5 Manchester U 0–8
1952–53	.. **Walthamstow A**	IL	4	1 Wimbledon 2–2, 3–0; 2 Watford 1–1, 2–1; 3 Stockport Co 2–1; 4 Manchester U 1–1, 2–5
1953–54	.. **Headington U**	SL	4	1 Harwich & P 3–2; 2 Millwall 3–3, 1–0; 3 Stockport Co 0–0, 1–0; 4 Bolton W 2–4
1954–55	.. **Bishop Auckland**	NL	4	1 Kettering 5–1; 2 Crystal P 4–2; 3 Ipswich T 2–2,3–0; 4 York 1–3
1956–57	.. **Rhyl**	CC	4	1 Scarborough 3–2; 2 Bishop Auckland 3–1; 3 Notts Co 3–1; 4 Bristol C 0–3
	New Brighton	LC	4	1 Stockport Co 3–3,3–2; 2 Derby Co 3–1; 3 Torquay U 2–1; 4 Burnley 0–9
	Peterborough U	ML	4	1 Yeovil T 3–1; 2 Bradford PA 3–0; 3 Lincoln C 2–2,5–4; 4 Huddersfield T 1–3
1958–59	.. **Worcester C**	SL	4	1 Chelmsford C 0–0, 3–1; 2 Millwall 5–2; 3 Liverpool 2–1; 4 Sheffield U 0–2
1959–60	.. **Peterborough U**	ML	4	1 Peterborough U 4–3; 2 Walsall 3–2; 3 Ipswich T 3–2; 4 Sheffield W 0–2
1961–62	.. **Weymouth**	SL	4	1 Barnet 1–0; 2 Newport Co 1–0; 3 Morecambe 1–0; 4 Preston NE 0–2
1962–63	.. **Gravesend**	SL	4	1 Exeter C 3–2; 2 Wycombe 3–1; 3 Carlisle U 1–0; 4 Sunderland 1–1, 2–5
1963–64	.. **Bedford T**	SL	4	1 Weymouth 1–1, 1–0; 2 Chelmsford 1–0; 3 Newcastle U 2–1; 4 Carlisle 0–3
1965–66	.. **Bedford T**	SL	4	1 Exeter C 2–1; 2 Brighton 1–1, 2–1; 3 Hereford 2–1; 4 Everton 0–3
1969–70	.. **Sutton U**	IL	4	1 Dagenham 1–0; 2 Barnet 2–0; 3 Hillingdon 0–0,4–1; 4 Leeds U 0–6
1971–72	.. **Hereford U**	SL	4	1 Kings Lynn 0–0, 1–0; 2 Northampton T 0–0,2–2,2–1; 3 Newcastle U 2–2, 2–1; 4 West Ham 0–0, 1–3
1974–75	.. **Wimbledon**	SL	4	1 Bath 1–0; 2 Kettering 2–0; 3 Burnley 1–0; 4 Leeds 0–0, 0–1
	Stafford R	NPL	4	1 Stockport Co 0–0, 1–0; 2 Halifax 2–1; 3 Rotherham 0–0, 2–0; 4 Peterborough 1–2
	Leatherhead	IL	4	1 Bishops Stortford 0–0,2–0; 2 Colchester 1–0; 3 Brighton 1–0; 4 Leicester C 2–3

1975–76 .. **Tooting & M.** ...... IL .... 4 ...... 1 Romford 1–0; Leatherhead 0–0,2–1; Swindon 2–2,2–1; 4 Bradford C 1–3

1976–77 .. **Northwich Vic.** .. NPL ... 4 ...... 1 Rochdale 1–1,0–0,2–1; 2 Peterborough 4–0; 3 Watford 3–2; 4 Oldham 1–3

1977–78 .. **Blyth Spartans** .... NL ..... 5 ...... 1 Burscough 1–0; 2 Chesterfield 1–0; 3 Enfield 1–0; 4 Stoke C 3–2; 5 Wrexham 1–1, 1–2

1979–80 .. **Harlow** .... IL .... 4 ...... 1 Leytonstone 2–1; 2 Southend 1–1, 1–0; 3 Leicester 1–1,1–0; 4 Watford 3–4

1980–81 .. **Enfield** .... IL .... 4 ...... 1 Wembley 3–0; 2 Hereford U 2–0; 3 Port Vale 1–1,3–0; 4 Barnsley 1–1,0–3

1983–84 .. **Telford U** .... APL ... 4 ...... 1 Stockport Co 3–0; 2 Northampton T 1–1,3–2; 3 Rochdale 4–1; 4 Derby Co 2–3

1984–85 .. **Telford U** .... APL ... 5 ...... 1 Lincoln C 1–1,2–1; 2 Preston 4–1; 3 Bradford C 2–1; 4 Darlington 1–1, 3–0; 5 Everton 0–3

1985–86 .. **Altrincham** .... GMVC 4 ...... 1 Chorley 2–0; 2 Blackpool 2–1; 3 Birmingham C 2–1; 4 York C 0–2

1988–89 .. **Sutton U** .... GMVC 4 ...... 1 Dagenham 4–0; 2 Aylesbury 1–0; 3 Coventry C 2–1; 4 Norwich C 0–8

   Kettering T .... GMVC 4 ...... 1 Dartford 2–1; 2 Bristol R 2–1; 3 Halifax 1–1,3–2; 4 Charlton 1–2

1990–91 .. **Woking** .... IL .... 4 ...... 1 Kidderminster H 0–0,1–1,2–1; 2 Merthyr T 5–1; 3 WBA 4–2; 4 Everton 0–1

MOST VICTORIES OVER LEAGUE SIDES IN ONE SEASON:

4 Telford United (APL) 1984–85 bt Lincoln, Preston, Bradford C and Darlington

3 Colchester United (SL) 1947–48 bt Wrexham, Huddersfield and Bradford PA 1–0

3 Telford United (APL) 1983–84 bt Stockport, Northampton and Rochdale

When Tottenham won the Cup as a Southern League team in 1901 they beat 4 Football League clubs; when Southampton reached the finals in 1900 and 1902 they beat 3 Football League clubs.

WORST PERFORMANCES BY A LEAGUE SIDE AGAINST NON-LEAGUE OPPOSITION

Hartlepool United, then of the Third Division North were eliminated by a non-League side four times in five seasons between 1925–26 and 1929–30.

In 1925–26 they lost to Blyth Spartans of the North Eastern League, in 1926–27 they lost to Carlisle of the same league. In 1928–29 Spennymoor, again of the North Eastern League beat them and in 1929–30 Scunthorpe then in the Midland League beat them. The only defeat at the hands of League opposition came in 1927–28 when fellow Third Division North rivals Halifax beat them.

In 1973–74 and 1974–75 Brighton were knocked out at home and without scoring a goal in successive seasons by Isthmian League teams. On November 28, 1973 Walton & Hersham won 4–0 at the Goldstone Ground after a 0–0 draw at home in a First Round match, and on January 4, 1975, Leatherhead won 1–0 at Brighton in a Third Round match.

Exeter City have been knocked out in successive seasons by a non-League club three times. In 1962 they lost to Dartford and in 1963 to Gravesend, both of the Southern League. In 1973 they lost to Walton & Hersham of the Isthmian League and in 1974 to Alvechurch of the West Midlands Regional League. In 1984 Maidstone United of the Alliance Premier beat

them, and in 1985 they went down to Enfield.

Crewe have lost 16 times to non-League opposition – although their total includes three defeats in the qualifying rounds in the 1890s when they took part as a Second Division club. They were beaten by non-league Scarborough and Gateshead in successive seasons in 1974 and 1975 and lost to non-League opposition five times in eight seasons between 1978 and 1985.

Blackpool lost in successive seasons, 1984–85 and 1985–86, to Altrincham. Merthyr Town, then in the Third Division South, also lost to non-League opposition in seasons 1923–24 and 1924–25, while Darwen were another League side knocked out by the same non-League opposition in successive years, losing to Wigan County in both 1898 and 1899.

Amateurs in the Cup Final

It is now more than a century since the strictly amateur teams of London and the Home Counties dominated the FA Cup.

From the first final in 1872 until 1881 all ten finals were all-amateur affairs, with Blackburn Rovers the first Northern professional side to reach the final in 1882 when they lost 1–0 to Old Etonians, the last 'hurrah' for the landed gentry of the day. In 1883 Blackburn Olympic beat Old Etonians to become the first Northern side to win the Cup, and the amateurs' heyday was over. The FA introduced the FA Amateur Cup in 1894 which was competed for until 1974.

Since the Cup Final moved to Wembley in 1923, only four amateur players have appeared in the Final.

1924 (Dr) Victor Milne, Aston Villa

The first amateur to play at Wembley, Victor Milne played at centre-half in the Aston Villa team beaten 2–0 by Newcastle United. He was born in 1897, the year Villa won the Cup and League double.

1946 Arthur Turner, Charlton Athletic

Not to be confused with Bert Turner who scored for both sides in the 1946 Cup Final, Arthur Turner was a 22-year-old RAF officer who played at centre-forward for Charlton in the match. He owns a unique record of being the only Cup Finalist since the Football League began in 1888 who never played in a single League match for his club. He played for Charlton during the transitional season of 1945–46 when there was no League football, but did eventually make more than 50 League appearances for Colchester after their election to the League in 1950.

1947 Peter Kippax, Burnley

Winger Peter Kippax played for Burnley in the 1947 Cup Final and a year later was in the British team that finished fourth in the soccer tournament in the 1948 Olympic Games.

1951 Bill Slater, Blackpool

In 1960 Bill Slater captained Wolves to victory in the Cup Final against Blackburn Rovers, and was also voted Footballer of the Year. It was his second Cup Final appearance. His first came in 1951, the day before his 24th birthday when he was a late call-up for the injured Allan Brown and played in the Blackpool side beaten 2–0 by Newcastle. He was still an amateur at the time, and did not turn professional until the 1953–54 season. He played for Britain in the 1952 Olympics in Helsinki, and for England won 20 amateur and 12 full international caps.

The only other amateurs to have played in the Cup Final this century are: CB Fry (Southampton 1902), Sam Ashworth (Manchester City 1904), David Davies (Bolton 1904); Harold Hardman (Everton 1906 and 1907), the Rev Kenneth Hunt (Wolverhampton W 1908) and Jim Mitchell (Preston NE 1922).

The Rev Hunt was the only amateur to score a Cup Final goal this century. He opened the scoring for Wolves when they beat Newcastle United 3–1 at the Crystal Palace. Davies and Mitchell are the only amateurs to have played in goal in Cup Finals this century. Mitchell is the only goalkeeper to have played in glasses.

FA Cup Trivia (2)

THE LONGEST UNBEATEN RUN IN FA CUP HISTORY Blackburn Rovers. 24 matches. After losing 1–0 to Darwen on December 2, 1882, Blackburn went unbeaten in their following 24 ties. The run ended when they lost 2–0 to Renton on November 27, 1886.

OTHER LONG UNBEATEN MATCH RUNS INCLUDE:

21	Arsenal	Jan 1979–May 1980
18	Tottenham H	Jan 1981–Feb 1983
17	Wanderers	Oct 1875–Nov 1878
	(does not include two byes)	
	Arsenal	Jan 1971–May 1972
16	Newcastle U	Jan 1951–Jan 1953
15	Newcastle U	Jan 1910–April 1911

14	Tottenham H	Jan 1961–Jan 1963
	Derby County	Jan 1946–Feb 1947
	Barnsley	Jan 1912–Feb 1913
	Leeds U	Jan 1972–May 1973
	WBA	Jan 1968–April 1969
13	Everton	Jan 1905–March 1906
	Sunderland	Jan 1937–March 1938
	Manchester U	Jan 1948–March 1949
	Blackpool	Jan 1953–Feb 1954
	Liverpool	Jan 1989–April 1990
12	Blackburn R	Jan 1890–Jan 1892
	Manchester U	March 1963–March 1964
	Wolverhampton W	Jan 1949–Feb 1950

THE LONGEST RUN WITHOUT A WIN Leeds United, 16 matches. After beating Bradford Park Avenue 2–0 in the fourth round on February 2, 1952, Leeds did not win another FA Cup match until March 6, 1963 when they beat Stoke City 3–1 in a third round match.

Rochdale went 13 matches without a win between 1927 and 1945. After beating Crook Town 8–2 in a first round match on November 26, 1927, Rochdale did not win another Cup match until November 17, 1945 when they beat Stockport County 2–1 in a first round, first leg match. In fact, Rochdale's win over Crook was their only FA Cup win between 1925 and 1945.

THE DOUBLE Only five teams have won the FA Cup and League Championship Double:– Preston North End 1888–89, Aston Villa 1896–97, Tottenham Hotspur 1960–61, Arsenal 1970–71, Liverpool 1985–86

THE NEAR MISSES Runners-up in both Cup and League:– Huddersfield 1927–28, Arsenal 1931–32, Wolverhampton W 1938–39, Burnley 1961–62, Leeds United 1964–65 and 1969–70, Everton 1985–86

FA Cup Winners and League runners-up:– Manchester City 1903–04, Aston Villa 1912–13, Manchester United 1947–48, West Bromwich Albion 1953–54, Wolverhampton W 1959–60, Leeds United 1971–72, Liverpool 1973–74 and 1988–89

League Champions and FA Cup runners-up Newcastle United 1904–05, Sunderland 1912–13, Manchester United 1956–57, Liverpool 1976–77 and 1987–88, Everton 1984–85

THE DOMESTIC CUP DOUBLE Arsenal are the only team to win both the major English domestic Cups in the same season. On 18 April 1993 they defeated Sheffield Wednesday 2–1 to win the Coca-Cola (League) Cup Final and on 20 May beat Wednesday again by the same score to win the FA Cup Final replay. It was also the first time that both the major domestic Cup Finals had been contested by the same teams in the same season.

THE 'QUICKEST' FA CUP WINNERS IN HISTORY Although Wanderers won the first FA Cup competition in 1871–72 by winning only one match on the way to the final and gaining a walkover in the semi-final, the time between their secound round win over Clapham Rovers and their win in the final over the Royal Engineers on March 16, 1872 was exactly three months.

But in terms of days between the playing of a team's

first match in the competition and winning the final, no team has won the Cup quicker than Manchester United in 1963. They won the final against Leicester on May 25, just 82 days after beating Huddersfield in the third round on March 4. The third round tie, originally scheduled for January 5, was postponed 12 times because of the weather during the Big Freeze.

THE LONGEST ROUND IN FA CUP HISTORY

The Third Round of the 1962–63 season was the longest in the history of the FA Cup. It was originally scheduled to be played on January 5, but only three matches went ahead then with West Brom winning 5–1 at Plymouth, Sunderland winning 4–1 at Preston and Tranmere drawing 2–2 at home to Chelsea.

The round was eventually completed on Monday, March 11 when Middlesbrough beat Blackburn Rovers 3–1 in a replay at Ayresome Park – two days after the original date of the sixth round. The round lasted 66 days. There were 22 different playing days, and a total of 261 postponements. Sixteen attemps were made to play the tie between Birmingham and Bury which was actually started once and then abandoned. When it was finally played, it went to a replay.

It was as a result of the chaos caused by the weather and especially the complete lack of soccer on January 5 that the Pools Panel was formed and they sat on four successive Saturdays through January and February to assess the results.

For the record of a round unlikely to be repeated in either its duration or the chaos it caused, this was the breakdown of the 261 postponements:-

Tie	Postponements	Date match eventually played
Lincoln v Coventry	15	March 7
Birmingham v Bury (plus one abandonment)	14	March 5
Sheffield U v Bolton	14	March 6
Walsall v Manchester C	14	March 6
Bradford C v Newcastle	12	March 7
Gillingham v Port Vale	12	Feb 27
Leeds vs Stoke	12	March 6
Manchester U v Huddersfield	12	March 4
Watford v Rotherham	12	Feb 20
Norwich v Blackpool	11	March 4
Blackburn v Middlesbrough	10	March 5
Charlton v Cardiff	10	Feb 18
Leyton Orient v Hull	10	Feb 11
Shrewsbury vs Sheffield W	10	Feb 21
Southampton v York	9	Feb 13
Arsenal v Oxford U	7	Jan 30
Derby Co v Peterborough	7	Feb 4
Swansea v QPR	7	Jan 26
West Ham v Fulham	7	Feb 4
Carlisle v Gravesend	5	Jan 29
Nottingham F v Wolves	5	Jan 29
Luton v Swindon	4	Jan 26
Portsmouth v Scunthorpe	4	Jan 26
Barnsley v Everton	2	Jan 15
Bristol C v Aston Villa	2	Jan 16
Tottenham v Burnley	2	Jan 16
Grimsby v Leicester C	1	Jan 7
Mansfield v Ipswich	1	Jan 9
Wrexham v Liverpool	1	Jan 9
Plymouth v WBA	0	Jan 5
Preston v Sunderland	0	Jan 5
Tranmere v Chelsea	0	Jan 5

Replays

Aston Villa v Bristol C	11	March 7
Scunthorpe v Portsmouth	10	March 7
Chelsea v Tranmere	5	Jan 30
Fulham v West Ham	3	Feb 20
Blackpool v Norwich	0	March 6
Bury v Birmingham	0	March 7
Hull v Leyton Orient	0	Feb 19
Middlesbrough v Blackburn	0	March 11
Sheffield W v Shrewsbury	0	March 7

Total   261

FA CUP TIES IN FOUR DIFFERENT COUNTRIES

Nottingham Forest are the only club to have been drawn to play FA Cup matches in all four home countries.

In 1885 they drew their semi-final with Queens Park at Derby and then lost the replay in the grounds of the Merchiston Castle School in Edinburgh. In February 1889 they drew 2–2 at home with Linfield in a first round match. By the time they got to Belfast for the replay, Linfield had scratched from the Cup so they played a friendly instead which Linfield won 3–1. And in February 1922 they lost 4–1 in a third round match at Cardiff City.

CUP FINALS IN FOUR COUNTRIES

Jimmy Delaney, who won a winner's medal with Manchester United in 1948, is the only man to have gained Cup winner's medals in three countries and played in Cup Finals in four countries. He also won a Cup winner's medal with Celtic in 1937 and Derry City in 1954 and gained a loser's medal when he played for Cork City in the FAI Cup Final in 1956.

'FOREIGN' CLUBS IN THE FA CUP

'Foreign', or at least non–Football Association clubs competed in the FA Cup regularly in the 1880s.

Queens Park were the most successful reaching two Cup Finals, while Glasgow Rangers reached the semi-finals in 1887. The following summer the Scottish FA banned their clubs from taking part in the English Cup. The seven Scottish clubs who competed were:– Cowlairs, Heart of Midlothian, Partick Thistle, Queens Park, Rangers, Renton and Third Lanark.

Three Irish clubs appeared in the competition proper – Cliftonville, Linfield Athletic and Belfast Distillery.

A maximum of 14 Welsh clubs can compete in the FA Cup. Cardiff City are the only club from Wales to have reached the Cup Final, losing in 1925 and winning in 1927, a year in which they also won the Welsh Cup.

WON ON THE TOSS OF A COIN

The only known instance of an FA Cup match being decided on the toss of a coin was in the first round of the 1873–74 season. Sheffield Club had drawn twice with Shropshire Wanderers and went through to the next round on the toss of a coin.

FAILING TO ENTER – REFUSING OR DECIDING NOT TO COMPETE

Entry to the FA

Cup is not automatic, as clubs have to apply each year for entry. The number of entries has grown from 15 in the first competition to a record number of 674 in the 1920–21 season and is now annually about 550 out of a total FA membership of more than 41,000 clubs.

But over the years some clubs have failed to enter, usually because someone forgot to send off the entry form, or else refused to compete. In the early days the FA were regularly called upon to settle protests and many teams were disqualified from the competition, the most notable examples of that being Preston North End and Accrington in the 1880s.

A list of the more notable examples of current League clubs missing out in the Cup:–

Aston Villa 1879–80 Villa scratched from the Cup and played in a Birmingham Senior Cup match rather than face the students of Oxford University in a second round match.

Sheffield Wednesday 1886–87 Forgot to submit their entry in time.

Everton 1888–89 Did not enter the Cup in the League's first season after being disqualified the previous season in a row over professionalism.

Sunderland 1888–89 Not a League side then but still one of the most formidable clubs in the country, Sunderland withdrew from the Cup rather than face their bitter rivals Sunderland Albion.

Leyton Orient 1906–07 Then known as Clapton Orient, failed to enter by the deadline.

Leeds United 1919–20 Following the dissolution of Leeds City, Leeds United came into being in 1920 but did not take part in the FA Cup.

Birmingham City 1921–22 Someone forget to post the entry forms.

Charlton Athletic 1921–22 Withdrew from the Cup after their election to the Football League rather than play in the qualifying rounds

Halifax Town 1921–22 Like Charlton, Halifax withdrew rather than play in the qualifying rounds

Wigan Borough 1921–22 Did not enter

Doncaster Rovers and Bournemouth 1923–24 Refused to play in the qualifying rounds after being elected to the League for the 1923–24 season. The draw for the Preliminary round of the Qualifying Competition had already been made when Bournemouth pulled out rather than play the Portsea Gas Company. Doncaster withdrew after being drawn against Fryston Colliery.

Queens Park Rangers, 1926–27 Like Birmingham in 1921, QPR forgot to enter.

Durham City 1926–27 Did not enter

Torquay United 1927–28 On election to the League, Torquay pulled out of the Cup rather than play in the qualifying rounds.

Nelson 1928–29 Failed to submit entry form by May 1 deadline.

Newport County 1931–32 Newport County did not enter following an investigation into a lottery they had been running.

Wigan Borough 1931–32 Wigan Borough of Division Three North were drawn to play Burton Town in their first round match on November 28, 1931, but Wigan folded before the match was played. Burton were given a bye into the second round, a scenario that was not to be repeated for more than 60 years.

Brighton & HA 1932–33 Entered the Cup – but forget to claim exemption from the qualifying rounds. Rather than pull out they played them – see their club section for the devastating results.

Hull City 1945–46 Did not enter because their ground was unfit following war damage.

New Brighton 1945–46 Like Hull, New Brighton's ground was not in good enough condition to stage football matches.

Shrewsbury Town 1950–51 Like Charlton, Halifax, Bournemouth, Doncaster and Torquay before them, withdrew from the Cup on election to the League rather than have to play in the qualifying rounds.

Maidstone United 1992–93 Entered the FA Cup on time, but by the time the competition got underway in November 1992 they had gone into liquidation. That left an odd number of teams in Round One, and Swansea City were awarded a bye into the next round.

In the early days of the competition clubs were continally scratching because they could not raise a team or organise their travel arrangements. It is inconceivable today but Queens Park scratched after a draw in their semi-final with with Wanderers in 1872 because they could not afford to stay on for the replay. Another example which today seems hard to credit is that of Aston Villa listed above.

Local Derbies

The first 10 Cup Finals between the amateur clubs of London and the Home Counties were all, in a sense, local derbies, but since those long-distant days there have only been 10 Cup Finals which have been real 'derbies'. They are:–

1886–87 Aston Villa	2	West Bromwich Albion	0
1891–92 West Bromwich Albion	3	Aston Villa	0
1894–95 Aston Villa	1	West Bromwich Albion	0
1930–31 West Bromwich Albion	2	Birmingham	1
1966–67 Tottenham Hotspur	2	Chelsea	1
1974–75 West Ham United	2	Fulham	0
1979–80 West Ham United	1	Arsenal	0
1981–82 Tottenham Hotspur	1	Queens Park Rangers	0
(after 1–1 draw)			
1985–86 Liverpool	3	Everton	1
1988–89 Liverpool	3	Everton	2
(aet)			

In the recent past there have been three other celebrated derbies at the semi-final stage, all played at Wembley.

On 14 April 1991 Tottenham beat Arsenal 3–1 in the first semi-final ever played at Wembley. In 1993 both semi-finals were at Wembley; Sheffield Wednesday beat Sheffield United 2–1 on 3 April and Arsenal beat Tottenham 1–0 the following day.

CUP CITIES For almost 100 years Blackburn was the only city in England to have provided a team in the Cup Final for five successive years (1882 Blackburn Rovers, 1883 Blackburn Olympic; 1884, 1885 and 1886 Blackburn Rovers). This record was not equalled until Tottenham and Queens Park Rangers met in the

1982 final, giving London at least one finalist for five successive years as well (1978 and 1979 Arsenal, 1980 West Ham and Arsenal, 1981 Tottenham, 1982 Tottenham and Queens Park Rangers). Manchester provided the finalists for four successive years in the 1950s (1955 and 1956 Manchester City, 1957 and 1958 Manchester United).

ALL LANCASHIRE FINALS 1904 Manchester C vs Bolton W; 1914 Burnley vs Liverpoool; 1926 Bolton vs Manchester C; 1933 Everton vs Manchester C; 1948 Manchester U vs Blackpool; 1953 Blackpool vs Bolton 1958 Bolton vs Manchester U; 1977 Manchester U vs Liverpool; 1985 Manchester U vs Everton

LANCASHIRE VS YORKSHIRE ('ROSES') FINALS 1890 Blackburn R vs Sheffield W; 1907 Sheffield W vs Everton; 1922 Huddersfield vs Preston 1928 Blackburn R vs Huddersfield; 1938 Preston vs Huddersfield; 1965 Liverpool vs Leeds 1966 Everton vs Sheffield W

LONDON VS LANCASHIRE FINALS 1923 Bolton vs West Ham; 1947 Charlton vs Burnley; 1950 Arsenal vs Liverpool; 1962 Tottenham vs Burnley 1971 Arsenal vs Liverpool; 1964 West Ham United vs Preston NE; 1979 Arsenal vs Manchester U 1981 Tottenham H vs Manchester C; 1988 Wimbledon vs Liverpool; 1990 Manchester United vs Crystal Palace

LONDON VS YORKSHIRE FINALS 1901 Tottenham H vs Sheffield U; 1915 Sheffield U vs Chelsea; 1930 Arsenal vs Huddersfield 1936 Arsenal vs Sheffield U; 1970 Chelsea vs Leeds U; 1972 Leeds U vs Arsenal; 1993 Arsenal vs Sheffield W.

There has never been an 'all-Yorkshire' Cup Final.

The first 15 finals were all won by teams from just two areas – London and the Home Counties, and Blackburn. Aston Villa were the first team from outside those areas to win the Cup in the 16th final in 1887.

After Old Etonians played in the 1883 final, no southern team reached the final again until Southampton 17 years later in 1900.

Following the end of the 'old boy' era in 1882, Tottenham were the first London club to win the Cup when they lifted the trophy in 1901. No London club won it again until Tottenham in 1921. Arsenal were the first London club to win at Wembley, in 1930. After Sheffield Wednesday won the Cup in 1935, no club from Yorkshire won it again until Leeds United in 1972.

CUP FINAL DERBIES THAT COULD HAVE BEEN Ever since the 1883–84 season when Blackburn Rovers and Blackburn Olympic were drawn in seperate semi-finals but only Rovers made it through to the final, there have been a number of occasions when fans held out hopes of meeting their arch-rivals in the Cup Final. Often the draw has been unkind to the fans by drawing the two rivals together in the semis, other times one team has made it through and the other hasn't.

These are the details of the Cup Final Local Derbies That Never Were.....

1883–84 Blackburn Rovers beat Notts Co 1–0 in their semi-final but Blackburn Olympic lost 4–0 to Queen's Park, Glasgow.

1896–97 Liverpool and Everton both reached the semi-finals and were kept apart in the draw. But while Everton reached the final with a 3–2 win over Derby County, Liverpool lost 3–0 to Aston Villa who went on to win the Double.

1900–01 Aston Villa and West Bromwich Albion had already met in three Cup finals in 1887, 1892 and 1895 and both reached the last four again in 1901. They were also kept apart in the draw, but Tottenham beat West Brom 4–0 and Sheffield United beat Aston Villa 3–0 after a replay.

1905–06 The prospect of Everton and Liverpool meeting in the final arose again – until they were drawn to play each other in the semi-final. Everton won 2–0 at Villa Park and went on to beat Sheffield Wednesday in the final.

1925–26 It was Manchester's turn to start dreaming of a day out at Wembley in 1926, until City and United were drawn to play each other in the semi-final at Bramall Lane. City won 3–0, but lost the final to Bolton in the third all–Lancashire final.

1927–28 Hopes of an all–Yorkshire final were dashed in 1928 when Huddersfield and Sheffield United were drawn against each other in the semi-finals. Huddersfield finally won after a second replay at Maine Road after draws at Old Trafford and Goodison Park.

1929–30 With Hull, Sheffield Wednesday and Huddersfield all in the semi-finals in 1930, another chance of an all-Yorkshire final presented itself. Arsenal beat Hull in a replay and although Huddersfield completed something of a double with their win over Wednesday just two years after they beat Sheffield United, Arsenal won the Cup.

1931–32 Two years later Arsenal and Chelsea were kept apart in the semi-finals to keep alive the possibility of the first all-London final since the end of the old amateur days 50 years previously. Arsenal beat Manchester City, but Chelsea lost to Newcastle

1935–36 Arsenal and Fulham were kept apart – so were Grimsby Town and Sheffield United. In the end Arsenal and Sheffield United got to Wembley.

1949–50 Arsenal, Chelsea, Liverpool and Everton provided the semi-finalists, and as luck had it ... Arsenal played Chelsea and Liverpool played Everton.

1951–52 Arsenal and Chelsea were drawn together again two years later, and again Arsenal got through to Wembley. In both 1950 and 1952 they needed two games to beat Chelsea, and all four games were played at White Hart Lane.

1954–55 Sunderland hadn't been in the final since 1937, Newcastle had won the Cup in both 1951 and 1952. The two North East giants reached the semi-final and were kept apart, but while Newcastle beat Third Division York City, Sunderland went down by the only goal at Villa Park to Manchester City.

1956–57 For the first time three clubs from the same city reached the semi-finals – Aston Villa West Brom and Birmingham City. Villa beat West Brom in a replay at St Andrews, but Birmingham lost to Manchester United at Hillsborough.

1961–62 For the first time in 26 years London's two representatives were kept apart in the semi-final, but while Tottenham beat Manchester United at Hillsborough, Fulham lost to Burnley after a replay at Filbert Street.

1967–68 West Brom and Birmingham both reached the semi-finals, but dreams of a replay of the 1931 final ended when they were drawn together. Naturally the game took place at Villa Park. West Brom won 1–0.

1970–71 Everton and Liverpool made it through to the last four together again, and again they faced each other. Liverpool won 2–1 at Old Trafford.

1976–77 Liverpool played Everton in the semis again. This time they beat them after a replay at Maine Road. To this day Evertonians claim they were robbed of a legitimate win in the first game when a last-minute Bryan Hamilton goal was controversially disallowed.

1977–78 Arsenal and Orient, as they then were, reached the last four. But again London's numbered balls were drawn together.

1979–80 At last Everton and Liverpool are kept apart in the semi-finals...but this time they both lose to West Ham and Arsenal respectively.

1984–85 It's now nearly 90 years since Liverpool and Everton first both qualified for the semi-finals, but still hopes of an all-Merseyside final are thwarted. Everton keep their part of the bargain by beating Luton, but Liverpool lose to Manchester United. A year later however, Everton beat Sheffield Wednesday and Liverpool beat Southampton and they finally get to meet in the final.

1990–91 Three London clubs made it to the semis for the first time – Arsenal, Tottenham and West Ham. Tottenham end Arsenal's hopes of the Double when they beat them 3–1 in the first semi-final at Wembley, but then Nottingham Forest beat West Ham to end hopes of a fifth all-London final.

1992–93 Arsenal, Tottenham, Sheffield Wednesday and Sheffield United are on course for either an all-London or the first all-Yorkshire Cup Final, but the draw puts an end to that by producing two derbies. Originally the FA announced that Arsenal would play Spurs at Wembley and the Sheffield teams would meet at Elland Road, but pressure from the Sheffield clubs and their supporters persuaded the FA to change their minds and agree to both matches being staged at Wembley. The tension and rivalry between the fans at the two matches – United played Wednesday on April 3, Arsenal met Spurs on April 4 – produced two gala occasions. Although neither match was a classic, the atmosphere at both was electric and tended to distract from the Cup Final itself six weeks later.

Cup Final Penalties

Penalty kicks were first introduced in the 1891–92 season, and it was not until 1910 that the first penalty was awarded in a Cup Final.

The following is the list of all penalties awarded in the Final:

1910 Newcastle Utd 2, Barnsley 0
Replay Albert Shepherd scored the second goal from the spot for Newcastle in the replay at Goodison Park after a 1–1 draw at Crystal Palace. He had previously put Newcastle 1–0 up in the replay and his penalty sealed Newcastle's victory.

1913 Aston Villa 1, Sunderland 0
The 1913 Final at Crystal Palace was the first between the two sides who had finished first and second in the League. It was also the first time a penalty had been awarded in the Cup Final proper.

Sunderland had won the Championship but Aston Villa foiled their bid for the Double with a 1–0 victory in the Cup Final. The match attracted a then world record crowd of 120,081 and the pressure clearly got to Villa's Charlie Wallace who became the first man to miss a Cup Final penalty when he fired wide of the goal.

1922 Huddersfield 1, Preston 0
Billy Smith was brought down and scored from the subsequent penalty to give Huddersfield their solitary FA Cup victory at Stamford Bridge in 1922.

Smith, a tall, leggy player with fine control was sent sprawling after being tackled from behind by Preston full-back Tom Hamilton. Proving that nothing is new in football, argument raged for weeks whether he was in the box or not when he was brought down. Either way, he took the penalty, shooting past Preston goalkeeper James Mitchell, the only bespectacled amateur goalkeeper to play in the final.

This final was the first to be decided on a single penalty – but 16 years later Preston avenged the loss in the most curious way..

1938 Preston 1, Huddersfield 0
George Mutch scored from the spot in the last minute of extra-time to give Preston a 1–0 victory over Huddersfield with the first Wembley Cup Final penalty. Mutch said later he closed his eyes and blasted the ball. His method worked, it came off the underside of the bar and gave Bob Hesford in the Huddersfield goal no chance.

1948 Manchester United 4, Blackpool 2
Eddie Shimwell became the first man to score a penalty in the Cup Final and end up on the losing side. After 15 minutes Stan Mortensen was tripped and Shimwell scored, putting the ball to the right of John Crompton's goal. Although United equalised through John Rowley, Blackpool were back in front by the interval, but they then conceded three second-half goals to become the first side to lead twice then lose in the Cup Final.

John Aldridge's penalty in the 1988 Cup final is saved by Wimbledon's Dave Beasant (Allsport/David Cannon)

1954 West Bromwich Albion 3, Preston 2
Ronnie Allen scored from the penalty spot midway through the second half to put Albion level. He had previously put his side ahead in the 21st minte, but Preston had come back with goals from Angus Morrison and Charlie Wayman. Frank Griffin scored Albion's late winner.

1962 Tottenham H 3, Burnley 1
Danny Blanchflower had captained Spurs to the Double the previous year and his 80th-minute penalty in 1962 clinched Spurs' second successive Cup Final victory. The penalty came after Burnley defender Tommy Cummings handled on the line. Blanchflower sent Burnley goalkeeper Adam Blacklaw the wrong way from the spot as Spurs became only the second team this century to win the Cup two years running.

1981 Tottenham H 3, Manchester C 2
Replay Kevin Reeves became the first player for 33 years to score a Cup Final penalty and finish on the losing side. The penalty came in the 50th minute of the replay when referee Keith Hackett ruled that David Bennett had been sandwiched and hauled down by Spurs defenders Paul Miller and Chris Hughton. Reeves blasted the ball past Spurs goalkeeper Milija Aleksic to put City 2–1 ahead, but goals by Garth Crooks and Ricky Villa gave Spurs victory.

1982 Tottenham H 1, Queens Park Rangers 0
Replay Glenn Hoddle, who scored Spurs' goal in the 1–1 draw in the first match, put his side 1–0 ahead after six minutes of the replay. The penalty came when Graham Roberts was tripped after a long run from his own half into the Rangers penalty area. It was only the third time in the history of the FA Cup that the final was decided by a single goal scored from the penalty spot.

1983 Manchester United 4, Brighton & HA 0
Replay Arnold Muhren became the seventh player successfully to strike home a Wembley Cup Final penalty when he scored Manchester United's fourth goal in their replay victory over Brighton. The teams had drawn the first match 2–2, but United were clear winners in Wembley's third successive replayed final – all of which included a penalty.

1988 Wimbledon 1, Liverpool 0
John Aldridge had scored 30 goals for Liverpool, including 11 penalties, as Liverpool had cantered to the First Division title. They came to the Cup Final looking for their second Double in three years and were the odds-on favourites to win, but things had gone drastically wrong as Wimbledon went ahead after 37 minutes.

Now, after 61 minutes, it looked as though the underdogs' luck had run out. Referee Brian Hill awarded Liverpool a penalty after Clive Goodyear was adjudged to have brought Aldridge down. Aldridge sent the ball high to goalkeeper Dave Beasant's left but the 6 ft 4 in goalkeeper threw up his arms to save the kick – the first goalkeeper to do so in a Wembley Cup Final.

Half-an-hour later Beasant made more Cup Final history when he became the first goalkeeping captain to receive the Cup.

1991 Tottenham H 2, Nottingham Forest 1
England captain Gary Lineker became the second player to miss a penalty in a Wembley Cup Final and only the third of all time when his 33rd-minute kick was saved by Mark Crossley, after Forest's 21-year-old goalkeeper had sent him sprawling in the box.

Lineker had dubiously had a goal disallowed 10 minutes earlier, and Forest were already 1–0 ahead. But Spurs rallied in the second half and extra time to win the Cup for a record eighth time.

The Wembley Hoodoo

When Arsenal's Welsh international full-back Walley Barnes tore his knee ligaments chasing Newcastle's Bobby Mitchell during the 1952 Cup Final, he didn't know what he was starting.

Barnes was the first victim of what became known as the Wembley Hoodoo. Between 1952 and 1965 there were nine serious injuries which left one side – usually the vanquished – either with 10 men or with the unfortunate victim hobbling out on the wing, getting the odd touch now and again but in reality a spectator.

The hoodoo was attributed to the turf itself, and in hindsight there may have been an element of truth in that. One school of thought suggests that players in the 1950s, perhaps not as fit or as agile as players today and with their heavier footwear, were more prone to have accidents on Wembley's lush turf.

Whatever the reason, the record books might show a very different story if substitutes had been allowed in the 1950s and early 1960s, but they were not permitted in competitive soccer in England until 1965. So until then, teams had to make do with 10 fully fit men, reorganise and hope for the best. There will always be injuries and accidents in all matches, but at least the jinx years of the 1950s and early 60s seem to be over.

1952 Walley Barnes, Arsenal, injured knee
Two weeks before the 1951 Cup Final Wilf Mannion broke a cheekbone while playing for England against Scotland at Wembley, the first serious incident of its kind at Wembley in the 1950s. There were no injuries in the final that year, but the jinx struck the following year.

After about 30 minutes Barnes was chasing Newcastle's Bobby Mitchell deep in Arsenal's half. He turned sharply to stay with Mitchell, but caught his studs in the turf and tore the ligaments behind his left knee. Although he limped on for a few minutes he was in too much agony and had to leave the field. Ten-man Arsenal held out for almost an hour but Newcastle won 1–0.

1953 Eric Bell, Bolton Wanderers, injured leg
After 15 minutes of the Matthews Final, Bolton's left-half Eric Bell twisted his leg and pulled a muscle that had been troubling him before the match. He went out to the wing, and although he actually scored with a header, leaping off his good leg to put Bolton 3–1 up after 55 minutes Bolton's reshuffled midfield ultimately could not cope with Matthews' inspired brilliance. Blackpool won 4–3.

1955 Jimmy Meadows, Manchester City, injured knee
The injury to Manchester City right-back Jimmy Meadows was so spookily similiar to that of Walley Barnes three years previously that it's no surprise people thought there was a hoodoo at work on Cup Final day.

Just like Barnes, Meadows was chasing a Newcastle player deep inside his own half. That Newcastle player was Bobby Mitchell, the player Barnes had been chasing in 1952. At almost exactly the same place that Barnes turned sharply, so did Meadows. And just as Barnes tore his knee ligaments, so did Meadows.

Meadows left the field just as Barnes had done, but Meadows' story had a sadder ending. Barnes recovered, but Meadows, 24, who had just won his first England cap, never played again. Newcastle won the final 3–1.

1956 Bert Trautmann, Manchester City, broken neck
A year after losing to Newcastle, Manchester City returned to Wembley and beat Birmingham City to win the Cup for the first time since 1934. All the scoring had been completed when, 15 minutes from time, City's German goalkeeper Bert Trautmann dived at the feet of Birmingham inside-forward Peter Murphy and broke his neck.

Trautmann continued playing in extreme pain, holding the posts and the goal netting to stay on his feet. The full extent of the injury was not revealed until an X-ray after the match but at least he made a full recovery from an injury that could have killed him. City won 3–1.

1957 Ray Wood, Manchester United, fractured cheekbone
No 20th-century team had won the Cup and League Double and Manchester United came to Wembley seeking to create history. The Busby Babes had already clinched the Championship and were favourites to beat an Aston Villa side that had finished 10th in the First Division. But after six minutes the fates conspired against United.

Goalkeeper Roy Wood safely gathered a header from Villa's Peter McParland, who suddenly charged at Wood in a way unthinkable today. Wood's cheekbone was fractured and his effective contribution to United's Cup-winning effort was over. Jackie Blanchflower took over in goal wearing a cap borrowed from a photographer. Wood returned to play on the wing, departed again, came back to play in goal for the final few minutes but ended with a runners-up medal as United's Double dream died. Aston Villa won 2–1.

1959 Roy Dwight, Nottingham Forest, broken leg
Roy Dwight's one and only Cup Final appearance lasted just 30 minutes, but in that time he managed to score a great goal, break his leg, and effectively end his career.

Dwight, who latterly regained fame simply for being Elton John's uncle, opened the scoring for Forest with a superb left-foot drive after 10 minutes. Forest went 2–0 up through Tommy Wilson before Dwight was injured in a collision with Luton's Brendan McNally. He finished the match having his leg set in a local hospital, listening to the commentary on the radio.

Twenty-five years after his uncle's Cup Final, Elton John was at the Cup Final in his role as Watford chairman and saw his team lose to Everton. But at least Roy Dwight earned a winner's medal as Forest became the first side with 10 men to win the Cup at Wembley.

1960 David Whelan, Blackburn Rovers, broken leg
The 1960 Cup Final was virtually decided in a three-minute spell just before half-time. Wolves, who had missed out on winning the Championship for the third successive year by just a single point, were already dominating the Final when an own goal by Blackburn's Mick McGrath gave them the lead.

If that wasn't bad enough for Rovers, a minute later left-back David Whelan made an innocuous challenge on winger Norman Deeley and broke his own right leg. Deeley scored twice in the second half, while Whelan's career was effectively over. He never played for Rovers again, and after a short spell with Crewe he knew he would never be the player he was before the injury and decided to retire. After quitting the game he went into business, built up a supermarket chain, and is now a millionaire with other business interests in the North.

1961 Len Chalmers, Leicester City, leg injury
In 1957 Manchester United's hopes of becoming the first side this century to win the Double had wilted when they lost goalkeeper Ray Wood with a fractured cheek after only six minutes. Four years later Tottenham did become the first team in modern times to win the Double – this time helped by the Wembley hoodoo afflicting their opponents.

After 19 minutes Leicester full-back Len Chalmers was injured in a tackle with Les Allen and left the field before returning to limp out the rest of the match on the left wing. In an ironic twist, when Wood was injured in 1957 Jackie Blanchflower went in goal. Four years later it was Jackie's brother Danny who lifted the Cup as Spurs won the Double.

Late goals from Bobby Smith and Terry Dyson gave Spurs a 2–0 victory over Leicester who have a Wembley hoodoo all of their own, having lost all four Cup Finals they have played there.

1965 Gerry Byrne, Liverpool, fractured collarbone
After only three minutes of the 1965 Cup Final between Liverpool and Leeds, the Leeds captain Bobby Collins collided with Liverpool full-back Gerry Byrne who sustained a broken collarbone. Byrne refused to come off and played for the next two hours with the injury. He was only the third man injured during the years of the hoodoo to play for the winning side.

On May 29, 1965 the Football League's agm approved the use of substitutes because of injury, a decision ratified by the FA on July 3, 1965. Substitutions were later allowed for any reason, and in 1987 two substitutes were allowed for the first time.

FA Cup Semi-Finals

It's one of the Cup's oldest cliches, but even so...the only people who usually do remember the beaten FA Cup semi-finalists are the fans of that defeated team. The loneliest place in football is the dressing-room of a team that has just lost the semi-final, so near yet so far from Wembley, Cup Final dreams shattered.

Probably as a result of being so close to the Final, semi-final records have also been largely overlooked so attention is quickly focused on the big day itself. So here then, are some usually hard-to-find semi-final statistics.

THE YEAR OF NO SEMI-FINALS Since the FA Cup started in 1871 there have been five occasions when only one semi-final was played (1877, 1878, 1879, 1880, 1881) when one team received a bye into the Final. But in 1873 no semi-finals at all were played.

Oxford University got a bye into the Final after Queen's Park, Glasgow scratched, while under the rules in operation in 1872–73, Wanderers were exempt until the Final having won the Cup the previous year.

CUP FINALISTS WITHOUT WINNING A SEMI-FINAL In 1871–72, Wanderers drew their semi-final 0–0 with Queen's Park, then advanced to the Final after Queen's Park scratched from the replay so they reached the Final without winning their semi-final. In 1873 and 1878 the Wanderers also reached the Final after semi-final byes.

In 1873 and 1877 Oxford University had semi-final byes while Clapham Rovers reached the Cup Finals of 1879 and 1880 after semi-final byes. Old Etonians were the last team to gain a semi-final bye in 1881.

In 1992 Liverpool became the first team to reach the Cup Final after winning a penalty shoot-out, knocking out Portsmouth after draws of 1–1 at Highbury and 0–0 at Villa Park, both after extra-time. Liverpool won the penalty shoot-out 3–1 after the second drawn game.

MOST SEMI-FINAL APPEARANCES Everton have made a record number of 22 appearances in the semi-finals, reaching the Cup Final 11 times. (For full list see page 611)

RECORD SEMI-FINAL SCORE Newcastle United 6 Fulham 0, Anfield, 28.3.1908. *Other big scores:* Manchester City 6 Aston Villa 1, Huddersfield, 17.3.1934; WBA 6 Nottingham F 2, Racecourse Ground, Derby, 9.3.1892

AGGREGATE IN ONE MATCH
8 goals ... WBA 6, Nottingham F 2, Racecourse Ground, Derby, 9.3.1892
Sheffield U 4, Liverpool 4 (replay), Burnden Park, 23.3.1899
Manchester U 5, Fulham 3 (replay), Highbury, 26.3.1958
7 goals ... West Ham 5, Derby Co 2, Stamford Bridge, 24.3.1923
Manchester C 6, Aston Villa 1, Huddersfield, 17.3.1934
Bolton W 4, Everton 3, Maine Road, Manchester, 21.3.1953
Crystal P 4, Liverpool 3, Villa Park, 8.4.1990

AGGREGATE IN ONE SEMI-FINAL TIE
13 goals .. Sheffield United vs Liverpool, 1899. The sides met four times before Sheffield United reached the Cup Final. The 13-goal total does not include the goal in the abandoned match.
18.3.1899 City Ground, Nottingham, Sheffield U 2, Liverpool 2
23.3.1899 Burnden Park, Bolton Sheffield U 4. Liverpool 4
27.3.1899 Fallowfield, Manchester Sheffield U 0, Liverpool 1 abandoned (45 minutes) after pitch invasions and darkness
30.3.1899 Baseball Ground, Derby Sheffield U 1, Liverpool 0

COMBINED AGGREGATE FROM BOTH SEMI-FINAL TIES

17 goals 1891–92 .. Aston Villa 4, Sunderland 1 (5 goals) and WBA vs Nottingham F series (see above 12 goals)

17 goals 1898–99 .. Sheffield U vs Liverpool series (see above 13 goals) and Derby County 4, Stoke 1 (4 goals)

16 goals 1989–90 .. Crystal Palace 4, Liverpool 3 (7 goals); Manchester U 3, Oldham A 3 and Manchester U 2, Oldham A 1 (9 goals)

15 goals 1957–58 .. Bolton W 2, Blackburn R 1 (3 goals); Manchester U 2, Fulham 2 and Manchester U 5, Fulham 3 (12 goals)

ABANDONED SEMI-FINALS Only two semi-finals have been abandoned. The first was on March 27, 1899 when the game between Liverpool and Sheffield United at Fallowfield was called off at half-time because of fans invading the pitch and darkness. The next was on April 15, 1989 when Liverpool's match with Nottingham Forest was called off after only six minutes as a result of the Hillsborough disaster.

THIRD DIVISION SEMI-FINALISTS Between 1920 when the Third Division was created until the reorganisation of the Football League in 1992, only six Third Division teams reached the semi-finals:- Millwall (1937), Port Vale (1954), York City (1955), Norwich City (1959), Crystal Palace (1976), Plymouth Argyle (1984). Both York City and Norwich City were knocked out in semi-final replays.

NON-LEAGUE SEMI-FINALISTS Following the formation of the Football League in 1888, the only non-League teams to reach the semi-finals have been:-

1890 .... Sheffield Wednesday (Football Alliance) – lost in the Final
1892 .... Nottingham Forest (Football Alliance)
1898 .... Southampton (Southern League)
1900 .... Southampton (Southern League) – lost in the Final
1900 .... Millwall (Southern League)
1901 .... Tottenham Hotspur (Southern League) – won the Cup
1902 .... Southampton (Southern League) – lost in the Final
1903 .... Millwall (Southern League)
1910 .... Swindon Town (Southern League)
1912 .... Swindon Town (Southern League)

SEMI-FINAL SENDINGS OFF Only five men have been sent-off in the semi-finals:- Arthur Childs (Hull City) vs Arsenal, semi-final replay at Villa Park, 26.3.1930; Mick Martin (WBA) vs Ipswich T, Highbury, 8.4.1978; Brian Kidd (Everton) vs West Ham, Villa Park, 12.4.1980; Tony Gale (West Ham) vs Nottingham Forest, Villa Park, 14.4.1991; Lee Dixon (Arsenal) vs Tottenham H, Wembley, 4.4.1993.

SEMI-FINAL SCORERS Only 11 men have scored three or more goals in one match in the 281 semi-final games played up to and including the 1992–93 season, and no-one has scored a hat-trick since 1958 when Alex Dawson scored three in Manchester United's

5–3 replay win over Fulham at Highbury. The list of semi-final hat-tricks:-

4 goals: Sandy Brown, Tottenham H 4, WBA 0, Villa Park, 8.4.1901

Fred Tilson, Manchester City 6, Aston Villa 1, Huddersfield, 17.3.1934

Dennis Westcott, Wolverhampton W 5, Grimsby T 0, Old Trafford, 25.3.1939

3 goals: Harry Goodhart, Old Etonians 5, Marlow 0, Kennington Oval, 4.3.1882

John Smith, Queens Park 4, Blackburn O 1, Trent Bridge, 1.3.1884

Alf Geddes, WBA 6, Nottingham F, 2nd replay, Racecourse Ground, Derby, 9.3.1892

Steve Bloomer, Derby Co 3, Stoke 1, Molineux, 18.3.1899

John Weddle, Portsmouth 4, Leicester C 1, St Andrews, 17.3.1934

Stan Pearson, Manchester U 3, Derby Co 1, Hillsborough, 13.3.1948

Stan Mortensen, Blackpool 3, Tottenham H 1 (aet), Villa Park, 13.3.1948

Alex Dawson, Manchester U 5, Fulham 3, replay, Highbury, 26.3.1958

Tilson's 4 for Manchester City against Aston Villa and Weddle's 3 for Portsmouth against Leicester were both scored on the same day as were Pearson and Mortensen's hat-tricks in 1948.

SEMI-FINAL JOY AND DESPAIR The Old Etonians reached the semi-final six times and made it through to the Cup Final six times – although in 1881 they gained a bye to the Final.

The Wanderers reached the semi-final five times and reached five Cup Finals – although because of walk-overs and byes they only ever played two semi-final matches.

More recently, Blackpool have a 100 per cent record in the semis, winning all three they have played in 1948, 1951 and 1953, although they needed a replay to beat Birmingham City in 1951.

Newcastle have won 11 of their 13 semi-finals, Manchester City have won eight of their 10; Huddersfield have won five out of seven, and West Ham four out of six.

Barnsley, Bury and Charlton have all appeared in two semi-finals and won both of them while Bradford City, Brighton & HA, Coventry C, QPR and Wimbledon have all won the one semi-final they have played.

In contrast, Derby County have a poor semi-final record losing nine out of 13, while Nottingham Forest also have a weak semi-final record, having played in 12 and only won three times.

Chelsea and Southampton have both lost seven of the 10 semi-finals they have played. Birmingham City, who played their first semi-final as Small Heath, have won only two of their nine semis.

Everton have lost more semi-finals than any other club – 11 – although they have also reached the Final 11 times as well.

SEMI-FINALISTS WHO HAVE NEVER REACHED THE FINAL Number of their semi-final appearances in brackets:- Millwall (3), Norwich C (3), Stoke C (3), The Swifts (3), Grimsby T (2),

Oldham A (2), Swansea C (2), Swindon T (2), Cambridge University (1), Crewe A (1), Crystal P (amateurs) (1), Darwen (1), Derby Junction (1), Rangers (1), Hull C (1), Marlow (1), Old Harrovians (1), Leyton O (1), Plymouth A (1), Port Vale (1), Reading (1), Shropshire W (1), York C (1).

ATTENDANCES The record attendance at an FA Cup semi-final is 80,407 for the replay between Derby County and Birmingham at Maine Road, Manchester on March 28, 1946. This is also the biggest crowd for a mid-week Cup game in England.

The lowest crowd for a semi-final since the war is 25,963 for the Wimbledon vs Luton Town match at White Hart Lane on April 9, 1988.

A total of 169,163 watched the four games comprising the 1980 semi-final between Arsenal and Liverpool which Arsenal finally won 1–0 after draws of 0–0, 1–1 and 1–1.

A total of 131,339 watched three semi-finals at Villa Park in April 1980. On April 12 West Ham drew with Everton in front of 47,685; on April 16 the first replay between Arsenal and Liverpool attracted 40,679 and on April 28 another 42,975 watched the second Arsenal–Liverpool replay.

In all the six semi-final matches in 1980 – two were needed to settle the Everton–West Ham tie, four to decide Arsenal vs Liverpool – attracted a total aggregate attendance of 257,568; an average of almost 43,000 at each match.

The two semi-finals at Wembley in 1993 were watched by a total of 151,627. There were 75,364 at the Sheffield derby game and 76,263 watched Arsenal and Spurs.

VENUES In all 42 different venues have been used for semi-final matches, including a school ground in Edinburgh, a ground on a racecourse in Derby, three cricket grounds, a rugby ground and Wembley Stadium.

Villa Park has played host to more semi-final matches and replays than any other ground (43), followed by Hillsborough which has staged 32 semi-final matches.

Here is the complete breakdown of all the semi-final venues. A [W] after the date means the eventual Cup winners won that particular semi-final. A [w] after the date means the semi-final was drawn but the eventual Cup winners took part in the drawn match.

LONDON

Kennington Oval 1872 (both matches and one replay), 1874 (both matches), 1875 (both matches and one replay), 1876 (both matches), 1877 [W], 1878 [W], 1879 [W], 1880, 1881 [W], 1882 [W], 1883

Crystal Palace 1900

White Hart Lane 1902, 1910 [W], 1914, 1926 [W], 1950 [w], 1950 rep [W], 1952, 1952 rep, 1959, 1970 [W], 1986 [W], 1988 [W]

Stamford Bridge 1908 [W], 1909, 1912 [w], 1920, 1923, 1925 [W], 1927, 1975 rep [W], 1976 [W], 1978

Highbury 1929, 1937, 1939 [W], 1949, 1958 rep, 1978 [W], 1981 rep [W], 1982, 1983, 1984 [W], 1992 [w]

Wembley Stadium 1991 [W], 1993 (both matches)

BIRMINGHAM

Lower Grounds, Aston 1884 [W], 1886

Perry Barr 1890, 1896

Villa Park 1901 [W], 1903, 1906 [W], 1915, 1930 rep [W], 1932, 1935 [W], 1946, 1948, 1953 [W], 1954 [W], 1955, 1956 [W], 1958, 1961 [W], 1962, 1963 [W], 1964, 1965 [W], 1966, 1967, 1968 [W], 1969 [W], 1970 rep, 1971 rep [W], 1972, 1974 rep [W], 1975 [w], 1979 [W], 1980 [w], 1980 rep, 1980 2nd rep, 1981, 1982 [W], 1983 [W], 1984, 1985, 1986, 1987, 1989, 1990, 1991, 1992 rep [W]

Hawthorns 1902 [w], 1960 [W]

St Andrews 1907 [W], 1909 rep, 1911, 1924 [W], 1934, 1957 [w], 1957 rep [W], 1959 rep, 1961 2nd rep

Villa Park has hosted few more exciting semi-finals than Luton's brave attempt to overcome all-conquering Everton in 1985. Brian Stein salutes the crowd after Ricky Hill's goal which gave the Hatters the lead (Allsport/Mike Powell)

LIVERPOOL

Anfield 1888, 1908, 1912, 1921, 1929 [W]

Goodison Park 1896 [w], 1903 [W], 1904 [W], 1914 rep [W], 1928 rep, 1949 rep [W], 1951 rep, 1972 rep, 1979 rep, 1985 [w]

MANCHESTER

Whalley Range 1882 rep, 1883

Fallowfield 1894, 1899 2nd rep [w]

Hyde Road 1905

Maine Road 1928 rep, 1946 rep [W], 1947 rep, 1950, 1951, 1953, 1954, 1958 [W], 1960, 1973, 1975 rep, 1977, 1977 rep, 1979, 1985 rep [W], 1990 [w], 1990 rep [W]

Old Trafford 1910 rep, 1914 [w], 1921 rep, 1923 [W], 1928, 1930, 1931 [W], 1939, 1968, 1971, 1974 [w], 1989 rep [W]

SHEFFIELD

Bramall Lane 1889 [W], 1891, 1891 rep, 1892, 1893, 1893 rep, 1894 [W], 1897 [W], 1898 [w], 1898 rep [W], 1900 rep [W], 1909 [W], 1911 [W], 1913, 1913 rep, 1920 [W], 1924 [W], 1926, 1938 [W]

Hillsborough 1912 rep, 1921 [W], 1922, 1946 [w], 1948 [W], 1949 [w], 1951 [w], 1952 [w], 1955 [w], 1956, 1957, 1959 [W], 1962 [W], 1963, 1964 [W], 1965, 1967 [W], 1969, 1970, 1971 [w], 1972 [W], 1973 [W], 1974, 1975, 1976, 1977 [W], 1980, 1981 [w], 1987 [W], 1988, 1989 [w], 1992

NOTTINGHAM
Trent Bridge 1884, 1885 [W], 1887

Town Ground 1893 [W], 1896 rep [W]

City Ground 1899 [w], 1901, 1902 rep [W], 1905 [W], 1961 rep, 1965 rep

Meadow Lane 1912 rep [W], 1925

DERBY
Cricket Ground 1885, 1886 [W], 1895

Racecourse Ground 1890 [W], 1892 [W]

Baseball Ground 1899 [W], 1901 rep

HUDDERSFIELD
St John's Rugby Ground 1882

Leeds Road 1932 [W], 1933, 1934 [W], 1936 [W], 1937 [W], 1951 rep [W]

CREWE
Nantwich Road 1887 [W]

Alexandra Road 1889, 1889 rep

BLACKBURN
Ewood Park 1893 rep, 1895 [W], 1913 [W], 1915 [W], 1938, 1947

BOLTON
Burnden Park 1899 rep [w], 1907, 1966, 1970 2nd rep

BURNLEY
Turf Moor 1922 [W]

COVENTRY
Highfield Road 1980 3rd rep

EDINBURGH
Merchiston Castle School Grounds 1885 rep

LEEDS
Elland Road 1910, 1930 [w], 1931, 1935, 1947 [W], 1952 rep [W], 1961, 1980 rep [W]

LEICESTER
Filbert Street 1928 [W], 1962 rep

READING
Elm Park 1900 rep

STOKE
Victoria Ground 1888 [W], 1891 [W], 1897, 1900 [w], 1905 [w], 1906, 1935 rep

SUNDERLAND
Roker Park 1955 rep [W]

WOLVERHAMPTON
Molineux 1892 [w], 1892 rep [w], 1898, 1899, 1902 rep [w], 1904, 1927 [W], 1933 [W], 1936

SEMI-FINAL APPEARANCES AT A GLANCE A guide to where current League club semi-finalists have played. The result shown in brackets refers only to the semi-final match played.

EVERTON (22 appearances – 28 matches)
Bramall Lane 1893 [d] 1893 rep [d]
Burnden Park 1907 [w] 1966 [w]
City Ground 1905 [L]
Elland Road 1910 [d] 1980 rep [L]
Ewood Park 1893 2nd rep [w]
Highbury 1984 [W]
Maine Road 1950 [L] 1953 [L]
    1977 [d] 1977 rep [L]
Molineux 1898 [L] 1933 [w]
Old Trafford 1910 [L] 1931 [L]
    1968 [w] 1971 [L]
Victoria Ground 1897 [w] 1905 [d]
Villa Park 1906 [w] 1915 [L] 1969 [L]
    1980 [d] 1985 [w] 1986 [w]
    1989 [w]

LIVERPOOL (19 apps – 29 matches, not including abandonments)
Baseball Ground 1899 3rd rep [L]
Bramall Lane 1897 [L]
Burnden Park 1899 rep [d]
City Ground 1899 [d]
Ewood Park 1947 [d]

Fallowfield 1899 2nd rep [abnd]
Goodison Park 1979 rep [L] 1985 [d]
    1988 [w] 1989 [abnd]
Hillsborough 1963 [L] 1980 [d]
Highbury 1992 [d]
Highfield Rd 1980 3rd rep [L]
Maine Road 1950 [w] 1977 [d]
    1977 rep [w] 1979 [d] 1985 rep
    [L]
Old Trafford 1971 [w] 1974 [d]
    1989 rep [w]
Villa Park 1906 [L] 1965 [w]
    1974 rep [w] 1980 rep [d]
    1980 2nd rep [d] 1990 [L]
    1992 rep [W]
White Hart Lane 1914 [w] 1986 [w]

WEST BROMWICH ALBION
(19 apps – 23 matches)
Anfield 1912 [d]
Bramall Lane 1889 [L]
Burnden Park 1907 [L]
Derby Racecourse 1892 2nd rep [w]
Elland Road 1935 [d]
Lower Gnds, Aston 1886 [w]
Highbury 1937 [L] 1978 [L] 1982 [L]
Hillsborough 1912 rep [w]
Molineux 1892 [d] 1892 rep [d]
Old Trafford 1931 [w]
St Andrews 1957 [d] 1957 rep [L]
Trent Bridge 1887 [w]
Victoria Ground 1888 [w] 1891 [L]
    1935 [w]
Villa Park 1901 [L] 1954 [w] 1968 [w]
    1969 [L]

MANCHESTER UNITED (18 apps, 26 matches)
Bramall Lane 1909 [w] 1926 [L]
Burnden Park 1966 [L]
    1970 2nd rep [L]
City Ground 1965 rep [L]
Goodison Park 1949 rep [L]
    1979 rep [w] 1985 [d]
Highbury 1958 rep [w]
Hillsborough 1948 [w] 1949 [d]
    1957 [w] 1962 [L] 1964 [L]
    1965 [d] 1970 [d] 1976 [w]
    1977 [w]
Maine Road 1979 [d] 1985 rep [w]
    1990 [d] 1990 rep [w]
Villa Park 1958 [d] 1963 [w]
    1970 rep [d] 1983 [w]

ARSENAL (18 apps, 26 matches)
Elland Rd 1930 [d]
Filbert Street 1928 [L]
Goodison Park 1972 rep [w]
Highfield Road 1980 3rd rep [w]
Hillsborough 1971 [d] 1973 [L] 1980
    [d]
Huddersfield 1936 [w]
St Andrews 1907 [L]
Stamford Bridge 1927 [w] 1978 [L]
Victoria Ground 1906 [L]
Villa Park 1930 [w] 1932 [w]
    1971 rep [w] 1972 [d] 1979 [w]
    1980 rep [d] 1980 2nd rep [d]
    1983 [L]
Wembley Stadium 1991 [L] 1993 [w]
White Hart Lane 1950 [d] 1950 rep [w]
    1952 [d] 1952 rep [w]

ASTON VILLA (17 apps, 20 matches)
Baseball Ground 1901 rep [L]
Bramall Lane 1892 [w] 1897 [w]
1920 [w] 1924 [w] 1938 [L]
City Ground 1901 [d] 1905 [w]
Ewood Park 1895 [w] 1913 [w]
Goodison Park 1903 [L]
Hawthorns 1960 [L]
Highbury 1929 [L]
Hillsborough 1959 [L]
Huddersfield 1934 [L]
Nantwich Road 1887 [w]
St Andrews 1957 [d], 1957 rep [L]
Victoria Ground 1905 [d]
White Hart Lane 1914 [L]

BLACKBURN ROVERS (16 apps,
20 matches)
Anfield 1912 [d]
Alexandra Rd, Crewe 1889 [d]
1889 rep [L]
Bramall Lane 1894 [L] 1911 [L]
Derby Cricket Gd 1886 [w]
Derby Racecourse 1890 [w]
Elland Road 1952 rep [L]
Filbert Street 1928 [w]
Hillsborough 1912 [L] 1952 [d]
Lower Gnds, Aston 1884 [w]
Maine Road 1958 [L] 1960 [W]
Meadow Lane 1925 [L]
Trent Bridge 1885 [w]
St Johns, Huddersfield 1882 [d]
Town Ground, Nottingham 1893 [L]
Whalley Range, Manchester
1882 rep [w]
Victoria Ground 1891 [w]

SHEFFIELD WEDNESDAY (16
apps, 17 matches)
Derby Cricket Gd 1895 [L]
Fallowfield 1894 [L]
Goodison Park 1896 [d] 1904 [L]
Highbury 1983 [L]
Hyde Road 1905 [L]
Maine Road 1954 [L] 1960 [L]
Old Trafford 1930 [L]
Perry Barr 1890 [w]
St Andrews 1907 [L]
St Johns, Huddersfield 1882 [d]
Town Ground, Nottingham
1896 rep [w]
Whalley Range, Manchester 1882 [L]
Villa Park 1935 [w] 1966 [w] 1986 [L]
Wembley Stadium 1993 [w]

TOTTENHAM HOTSPUR (14 apps,
15 matches)
Hillsborough 1921 [w] 1922 [L]
1962 [w] 1967 [w] 1981 [d]
Highbury 1981 rep [w]
Villa Park 1901 [L] 1948 [L] 1953 [L]
1956 [L] 1961 [L] 1982 [w]
1987 [w]
Wembley Stadium 1991 [w] 1993 [L]

DERBY COUNTY (13 apps, 17
matches)
City Ground 1902 2nd rep [L]
Hillsborough 1946 [d] 1948 [L] 1976 [L]
Huddersfield 1933 [L]
Hawthorns 1902 [d]
Maine Road 1946 rep [w]
Molineux 1898 [w] 1899 [w]
1902 rep [d] 1904 [L]
Perry Barr 1896 [L]

Stamford Bridge 1909 [d] 1923 [L]
St Andrews 1909 rep [L]
Victoria Ground 1897 [L]
Villa Park 1903 [w]

NEWCASTLE UNITED (13 apps,
16 matches)
Anfield 1908 [w]
Bramall Lane 1909 [L]
Elland Road 1947 [L] 1952 rep [w]
Hillsborough 1951 [d] 1952 [d] 1955 [d]
1974 [w]
Huddersfield 1932 [w] 1951 rep [w]
Hyde Road 1905 [w]
Roker Park 1955 rep [w]
St Andrews 1911 [w] 1924 [w]
Victoria Ground 1906 [w]
White Hart Lane 1910 [w]

**WOLVERHAMPTON
WANDERERS** (13 apps, 18 matches)
Anfield 1921 [d]
Alexandra Rd, Crewe 1889 [d],
1889 rep [w]
Derby Racecourse 1890 [L]
Goodison Park 1949 rep [w]
Hawthorns 1960 [w]
Highbury 1981 rep [L]
Hillsborough 1949 [d] 1951 [d] 1981 [d]
Huddersfield 1951 rep [L]
Maine Road 1973 [L]
Old Trafford 1921 rep [w] 1939 [w]
Perry Barr 1896 [w]
Stamford Bridge 1908 [w]
Town Ground 1893 [w]
Villa Park 1979 [L]

BOLTON WANDERERS (12 apps,
14 matches)
Anfield 1929 [w]
Ewood Park 1915 [L]
Goodison Park 1896 [d]
Elland Road 1935 [d]
Fallowfield 1894 [w]
Maine Road 1953 [w] 1958 [w]
Molineux 1904 [w]
Old Trafford 1923 [w]
Perry Barr 1890 [L]
Town Ground 1896 rep [L]
Victoria Ground 1935 rep [L]
Villa Park 1946 [L]
White Hart Lane 1926 [w]

NOTTINGHAM FOREST (12
apps, 16 matches not incl. abandoned
match)
Bramall Lane 1898 [d] 1898 rep [w]
1900 [L]
Derby Cricket Gd 1885 [L]
Derby Racecourse 1892 2nd rep [L]
Hillsborough 1959 [w] 1967 [L]
1988 [L] 1989 [abnd]
Kennington Oval 1879 [L] 1880 [L]
Merchiston Castle School, Edinburgh
1885 rep [L]
Molineux 1892 [d] 1892 rep [d]
Old Trafford 1989 rep [L]
Victoria Ground 1900 [d]
Villa Park 1991 [w]
White Hart Lane 1902 [L]

SHEFFIELD UNITED (11 apps, 20
matches not incl. abandoned match)
Baseball Ground 1899 3rd rep [w]
1901 rep [w]
Burnden Park 1899 rep [d]

City Ground 1899 [d] 1901 [d]
1902 2nd rep [w] 1961 rep [d]
Elland Road 1961 [d]
Ewood Park 1915 [w]
Fallowfield 1899 2nd rep [abnd]
Goodison Park 1914 [w] 1928 rep [d]
Hawthorns 1902 [d]
Maine Road 1928 2nd rep [L]
Molineux 1902 rep [d] 1936 [w]
Old Trafford 1914 [d] 1923 [L] 1928 [d]
Stamford Bridge 1925 [w]
St Andrews 1961 2nd rep [L]
Wembley Stadium 1993 [L]

SOUTHAMPTON (10 apps, 12
matches)
Bramall Lane 1898 [d] 1898 rep [L]
Crystal Palace 1900 [d]
Elm Park 1900 [w]
Highbury 1984 [L]
Stamford Bridge 1908 [L] 1925 [L]
1927 [L] 1976 [W]
Villa Park 1963 [L]
White Hart Lane 1902 [w] 1986 [L]

PRESTON NORTH END (10
apps, 12 matches)
Anfield 1888 [w]
Bramall Lane 1889 [w] 1893 [d]
1893 rep [d] 1938 [w]
Ewood Park 1893 2nd rep [L]
Highbury 1937 [w]
Hillsborough 1921 [L] 1922 [w]
Maine Road 1954 [w]
Trent Bridge 1887 [L]
Villa Park 1964 [w]

MANCHESTER CITY (10 apps, 10
matches)
Bramall Lane 1926 [w]
Goodison Park 1904 [w]
Huddersfield 1933 [w] 1934 [w]
St Andrews 1924 [L]
Villa Park 1932 [L] 1955 [w] 1956 [w]
1969 [w] 1981 [w]

CHELSEA (10 apps, 12 matches)
Bramall Lane 1920 [L]
Huddersfield 1932 [L]
St Andrews 1911 [L]
Villa Park 1915 [w] 1965 [L] 1966 [L]
1967 [W]
White Hart Lane 1950 [d] 1950 rep [L]
1952 [d] 1952 rep [L] 1970 [w]

BIRMINGHAM CITY (9 apps, 12
matches)
Elland Road 1931 [w]
Goodison Park 1951 rep [L]
Hillsborough 1946 [d] 1956 [w]
1957 [L] 1972 [L] 1975 [d]
Lower Gnds, Aston 1886 [L] as Small
Heath
Maine Road 1946 rep [L] 1951 [d]
1975 rep [L]
Villa Park 1968 [L]

BURNLEY (8 apps, 12 matches)
Bramall Lane 1913 [d] 1913 rep [L]
1924 [L]
Ewood Park 1947 [d]
Filbert Street 1962 rep [w]
Goodison Park 1914 rep [w]
Hillsborough 1974 [L]
Maine Road 1947 [w]
Old Trafford 1914 [d]
Villa Park 1935 [L] 1961 [L] 1962 [d]

Twice in three years in the early 1950s Arsenal and Chelsea met in the semi-finals and both times a replay was needed to settle the tie. Here the Gunners go 2–0 up in the 1952 replay at White Hart Lane, which hosted all four matches (Popperfoto)

LEEDS UNITED (8 apps, 11 matches)
Burnden Park 1970 2nd rep [w]
City Ground 1965 rep [w]
Hillsborough 1965 [d] 1970 [d]
    1972 [w] 1977 [L] 1987 [L]
Maine Road 1973 [w]
Old Trafford 1968 [L]
Villa Park 1967 [L] 1970 rep [d]

HUDDERSFIELD (7 apps, 9 matches)
Anfield 1929 [L]
Ewood Park 1938 [w]
Goodison Park 1928 rep [d]
Highbury 1939 [L]
Maine Road 1928 2nd rep [w]
Stamford Bridge 1920 [w]
Turf Moor 1922 [w]
Old Trafford 1928 [d] 1930 [w]

LEICESTER CITY (7 apps, 10 matches)
City Ground 1961 rep [d]
Elland Road 1961 [d]
Highbury 1949 [w]
Hillsborough 1963 [w]
Old Trafford 1974 [d]
St Andrews 1934 [L] 1961 2nd rep [w]
Villa Park 1969 [w] 1974 rep [L]
    1982 [L]

WEST HAM (6 apps, 8 matches)
Elland Road 1980 rep [w]
Hillsborough 1964 [w]
Molineux 1933 [L]
Stamford Bridge 1923 [w] 1975 rep [w]
Villa Park 1975 [d] 1980 [d] 1991 [L]

NOTTS COUNTY (5 apps, 6 matches)
Bramall Lane 1891 [d] 1891 rep [w]
    1894 [w]
Kennington Oval 1883 [L]

Lower Grnds, Aston 1884 [L]
Turf Moor 1922 [L]

FULHAM (5 apps, 8 matches)
Anfield 1908 [L]
Filbert Street 1962 rep [L]
Highbury 1958 rep [L]
Hillsborough 1975 [d]
Maine Road 1975 rep [w]
Molineux 1936 [L]
Villa Park 1958 [d] 1962 [d]

PORTSMOUTH (5 apps, 6 matches)
Highbury 1929 [w] 1939 [w] 1949 [L]
    1992 [d]
St Andrews 1934 [w]
Villa Park 1992 rep [L]

BLACKPOOL (3 apps, 4 matches)
Goodison Park 1951 rep [w]
Maine Road 1951 [d]
Villa Park 1948 [w], 1953 [w]

CARDIFF CITY (3 apps, 4 matches)
Anfield 1921 [d]
Meadow Lane 1925 [w]
Molineux 1927 [w]
Old Trafford 1921 rep [L]

IPSWICH TOWN (3 apps, 4 matches)
Highbury 1978 [w]
Stamford Bridge 1975 rep [L]
Villa Park 1975 [d] 1981 [L]

LUTON TOWN (3 apps, 4 matches)
St Andrews 1959 rep [w]
Villa Park 1985 [L]
White Hart Lane 1959 [d] 1988 [L]

MILLWALL (3 apps, 4 matches)
Crystal Palace 1900 [d]
Elm Park 1900 rep [L]
Huddersfield 1937 [L]
Villa Park 1903 [L]

NORWICH CITY (3 apps, 4 matches)
Hillsborough 1992 [L]
St Andrews 1959 rep [L]
Villa Park 1989 [L]
White Hart Lane 1959 [d]

STOKE CITY (3 apps, 5 matches)
Goodison Park 1972 rep [L]
Hillsborough 1971 [d]
Molineux 1898 [L]
Villa Park 1971 rep [L], 1972 [d]

WATFORD (3 apps, 3 matches)
Villa Park 1984 [w], 1987 [L]
White Hart Lane 1970 [L]

BARNSLEY (2 apps, 4 matches)
Elland Road 1910 [d]
Meadow Lane 1912 rep [w]
Old Trafford 1910 rep [w]
Stamford Bridge 1912 [d]

BRISTOL CITY (2 apps, 3 matches)
Stamford Bridge 1909 [d] 1920 [L]
St Andrews 1909 rep [w]

BURY (2 apps, 3 matches)
Bramall Lane 1900 rep [w]
Goodison Park 1903 [w]
Victoria Ground 1900 [d]

CHARLTON ATHLETIC (2 apps, 2 matches)
Elland Road 1947 [w]
Villa Park 1946 [w]

CRYSTAL PALACE (2 apps, 2 matches)
Stamford Bridge 1976 [L]
Villa Park 1990 [W]

GRIMSBY TOWN (2 apps, 2 matches)
Huddersfield 1936 [L]
Old Trafford 1939 [L]

OLDHAM (2 apps, 3 matches)
Ewood Park 1913 [L]
Maine Road 1990 [d], 1990 rep [L]

SWANSEA CITY (2 apps, 2 matches)
Villa Park 1964 [L]
White Hart Lane 1926 [L]

SWINDON TOWN (2 apps, 3 matches)
Meadow Lane 1912 rep [L]
Stamford Bridge 1912 [d]
White Hart Lane 1910 [L]

BRADFORD CITY (1 app)
Bramall Lane 1911 [w]

BRIGHTON & HA (1 app)
Highbury 1983 [w]

COVENTRY CITY (1 app)
Hillsborough 1987 [w]

CREWE ALEXANDRA (1 app)
Anfield 1888 [L]

HULL CITY (1 app, 2 matches)
Elland Road 1930 [d]
Villa Park 1930 rep [L]

LEYTON ORIENT (1 app)
Stamford Bridge 1978 [L]

PLYMOUTH ARGYLE (1 app)

Villa Park 1984 [L]

PORT VALE (1 app)
Villa Park 1954 [L]

QUEENS PARK RANGERS (1 app)
Highbury 1982 [w]

READING (1 app)
Molineux 1927 [L]

WIMBLEDON (1 app)
White Hart Lane 1988 [w]

YORK CITY (1 app, 2 matches)
Hillsborough 1955 [d]
Roker Park 1955 rep [L]

DRAWN SEMI-FINALS There have been seven occasions when both semi-finals ended in draws: 1871–72; 1899–1900; 1911–12; 1950–51; 1951–52; 1974–75; 1979–80

The 1979–80 Arsenal–Liverpool tie is the only semi-final tie that went to a third replay. The following ties were settled at the third attempt, after two replays: 1891-92 WBA vs Nottingham F; 1892-93 Everton vs Preston NE; 1898-99 Sheffield U vs Liverpool (not including abandoned match); 1901-02 Sheffield U vs Derby Co; 1927-28 Huddersfield T vs Sheffield U; 1960-61 Leicester C vs Sheffield U; 1969-70 Leeds U vs Manchester U

Strangely Sheffield United were involved in four semi-final marathons.

There have been four instances when clubs have met and drawn in their semi-final ties twice:-
Arsenal vs Chelsea 1949-50, 1951-52
Leeds vs Manchester U 1964-65, 1969-70
Arsenal vs Stoke C 1970-71, 1971-72
Manchester U vs Liverpool 1978-79, 1984-85
The same team won the replayed tie on both occasions. Arsenal beat Chelsea twice, Leeds beat Manchester United twice, Arsenal beat Stoke twice and Manchester United beat Liverpool twice.

FA Cup Trivia (3)

IF ONLY THEY KNEW... The 1923 Cup Final programme contained the following paragraph which makes interesting reading in the light of the events that unfolded on the afternoon of April 28 when Bolton played West Ham in the first Wembley Cup Final:- 'Spectators will have a fine view of the game from all points in the Stadium. They are earnestly requested to "pass right down the car" and, by squeezing as close as possible to their next-door neighbours in the standing enclosure, to give as many as possible of their fellow-enthusiasts a chance of fitting in and seeing the match.'

MEDAL MIX-UPS In 1914 the Cup Final medals bore the inscription 'English Cup' instead of 'FA Cup' due to a mistake when they were minted.

In 1992 Sunderland, beaten by Liverpool in the final, were given the winner's medals and Liverpool were given the runners-up medals. The players exchanged the medals afterwards.

In 1970 David Webb failed to collect his winner's medal after scoring the winning goal for Chelsea against Leeds. He had swapped shirts with a Leeds player and an official refused to let him go up to the directors box at Old Trafford, believing he was a Leeds player. He was given the medal in the dressing-room.

GIVING NOTHING AWAY Only three teams have reached the Cup Final without conceding a goal on the way – Preston (1889), Bury (1903) and Everton (1966). Preston won the Double in 1889 without losing a League match and without conceding a goal in the Cup. Bury and Everton also went on to win the Cup.

NAME CHECK When Tottenham won the Cup in 1901 they had players named Jones, Smith and Brown in the side. In 1921 they had a player called Smith and in 1961 and 1962 they had players called Jones, Smith and Brown again.

When Everton won the Cup in 1906 they had a player called Alex Young in the side and others called Scott and Sharp. When they won the Cup in 1966, they had another player called Alex Young in the side, and also a player called Scott. When they won the Cup in 1984, they had a Sharp in the side and he scored one of the goals in their 2–0 win over Watford.

When Sunderland played Aston Villa in 1913 they had a player called Charles Thomson in their line-up. When Sunderland played Preston in 1937 they had another Charles Thomson in the side.

Different players with the same name have played in the Cup Final surprisingly often. They include:-
John Anderson (Portsmouth 1939) and John Anderson (Manchester United 1948)
William Anderson (Old Etonians, 1881, 1882, 1883) and William Anderson (Queens Park 1884 and 1885)
Tommy Boyle (Barnsley 1910, Burnley 1914) and Tommy Boyle (Sheffield U 1925)
John Bray (Manchester C 1933, 1934) and John Bray (Blackburn R 1960)
Bill Brown (Bolton W 1904) and Bill Brown (Tottenham H 1961 and 1962)
Billy Cook (Portsmouth 1929, Sheffield U 1915, 1925) and Billy Cook (Bolton 1929)
James Cowan (Royal Engineers 1878) and James Cowan (Aston Villa 1892, 1895, 1897)
Jimmy Dunn (Everton 1933) and James Dunn (Wolverhampton W 1949)
Billy Gillespie (Manchester C 1904) and Billy Gillespie (Sheffield U 1925)
Andy Gray (Everton 1984) and Andy Gray (Crystal Palace 1990)
Billy Jennings (Bolton 1923, 1926) and Billy Jennings (West Ham 1975)

Tommy Johnson (Manchester C 1926, Everton 1933) and Tom Johnson (Sheffield U 1936)

John Jones (Tottenham H 1901) and John Jones (Wolverhampton W 1908)

William Morris (Royal Engineers 1878) and William Morris (Burnley 1947)

Frank Moss (Aston Villa 1920, 1924) and Frank Moss (Arsenal 1932)

Jimmy Nicholl (Liverpool 1914) and Jimmy Nicholl (Manchester U 1977, 1979)

Jimmy Richardson (Sunderland 1913) and Jimmy Richardson (Newcastle U 1932)

Alex Scott (Leicester C 1949) and Alex Scott (Everton 1966)

John Smith (Queens Park 1884), John Smith (Sheffield W 1890), John Smith (Bolton 1923, 1926) and John Smith (Sheffield U 1936)

Tom Smith (Tottenham H 1901), Tom Smith (Preston 1938) and Tommy Smith (Liverpool 1965, 1971, 1974, 1977)

Gary Stevens (Brighton 1983, Tottenham H 1987) and Gary Stevens (Everton 1984, 1985, 1986)

Arthur Turner (Southampton 1900, 1902) and Arthur Turner (Charlton 1946)

Billy Watson (Huddersfield 1920, 1922) and Billy Watson (Burnley 1914)

David Watson (Portsmouth 1929), Dave Watson (Sunderland 1973) and Dave Watson (Everton 1989)

Thomas Wilson (Huddersfield T 1920, 1922, 1928) and Thomas Wilson (Nottingham F 1959)

Alex Young (Everton 1906, 1907) and Alex Young (Everton 1966)

A total number of 22 Smiths have appeared in the Cup Final, 15 Browns, 14 Wilsons, 13 Taylors, 11 Jones, nine Bells, eight Allens, and eight Youngs.

But George Utley holds something of a unique record. Utley played in the 1910 and 1912 Cup Finals for Barnsley and in 1915 for Sheffield United and is the only player to have appeared in the Cup Final whose surname begins with the letter 'U'.

THE H-CONNECTION When Wolves beat Newcastle United 3–1 in the 1908 Cup Final, the Wolves goals were scored by Kenneth Hunt, George Hedley and Billy Harrison and Newcastle's goal was scored by Jimmy Howie. The four goalscorers were the only ones on the field whose surnames began with the letter 'H'.

STOKOE 2, REVIE 0 In 1955 Bob Stokoe was centre-half in the Newcastle team that beat a Manchester City team with Don Revie at centre-forward to win the Cup.

In 1973 Stokoe was the manager of Sunderland when they beat Leeds to win the Cup. His opposing manager was a familiar figure. It was Don Revie.

ER, HAVE YOU GOT A MINUTE, BOSS? An hour before the 1960 Cup Final Derek Dougan asked his Blackburn Rovers manager Dally Duncan for a transfer. Dougan played in the Rovers team beaten 3–0 by Wolves. In fact he stayed at Blackburn another 15 months before joining Aston Villa in August 1961.

FLOODLIGHTS The first FA Cup tie under floodlights was a preliminary round replay between Kidderminster Harriers and Brierley Hill Alliance on September 14, 1955. The first floodlit tie between League clubs was on November 28, 1955 when Carlisle met Darlington in a first round second replay at St James' Park, Newcastle. Darlington won 3–1.

MOST GAMES Barnsley played a record number of 12 matches and 20 hours of football to win the Cup in 1912. Half of their matches were goalless draws including one in Round 1, three in Round 4, and one in both the semi-final and final. They are the only current League side to have won the Cup and never played in the First Division (1888–1992) or Premier League.

Arsenal needed 11 matches when they won the Cup in 1979 including five in Round 3 against Sheffield Wednesday.

CLEAN SHEETS Bradford City hold the record for the number of successive clean sheets kept in the Cup. They went 12 matches without conceding a goal from Round 3 on February 25, 1911 when they beat Grimsby 1–0 until a second replay in Round 4 with Barnsley on March 21, 1912 when they lost 3–2. During the run they won the Cup on April 26, 1911 for the only time in their history.

DOING IT THE HARD WAY Only one team has won the Cup having to beat First Division opposition in every round – Manchester United in 1948. They beat Aston Villa, Liverpool, Charlton, Preston, Derby County and Blackpool.

ROUND FIGURES On January 11, 1947 eight of London's 10 League sides played at home in Round 3. In January 1992, only one London team – Charlton – was drawn at home.

In 1985–86 seven of the eight Fifth Round matches ended in draws – a record for the fifth round.

In 1986–87 for the only time in the history of the Cup, all four quarter-finals were won by the away teams. On March 14, 1987 Watford won 3–1 at Arsenal and Coventry won 3–1 at Sheffield Wednesday. On March 15, Leeds won 2–0 at Wigan and Tottenham won 2–0 at Wimbledon.

In 1992–93 all eight Fifth round matches played on February 13–14 ended in victories for the home sides.

FA Cup Final Songs

The greatest Cup Final song of all is probably 'Abide With Me' even though it hasn't appeared in the Singles Chart or, to this writer's knowledge at least, been recorded by any Cup Final team. But Wembley has always resounded to other anthems – 'You'll Never Walk Alone', 'Blowing Bubbles', 'Blaydon Races', 'Glory Glory Hallelujah', 'Good Old Arsenal' and even, courtesy of Coventry City, the Eton Boating Song.

It is now almost an unwritten rule that once a team has qualified for the Cup Final, a visit to a recording studio quickly follows. These are some of the songs that have been recorded by Cup Final teams and their position in the Singles Chart, according to the Guinness Book of British Hit Singles:-

Team	Record	Highest Place	Weeks	Entered Chart
Liverpool	*Anfield Rap (Red Machine In Full Effect)*	3	6	14.5.1988

Team	Record	Highest Place	Weeks	Entered Chart
Tottenham H	*Ossie's Dream (Spurs Are On Their Way To Wembley)*	5	8	9.5.1981
Leeds United	*Leeds United*	10	10	29.4.1972
Manchester U	*We All Follow Man Utd*	10	5	18.5.1985
Manchester U	*Glory Glory Man Utd*	13	5	21.5.1983
Everton	*Here We Go*	14	5	11.5.1985
Liverpool	*We Can Do It*	15	4	28.5.1977
Arsenal	*Good Old Arsenal*	16	7	8.5.1971
Tottenham H	*Hot Shot Tottenham*	18	5	9.5.1987
Tottenham H	*Tottenham, Tottenham*	19	7	1.5.1982
Arsenal	*Shouting for the Gunners*	28	2	11.5.1993
West Ham U	*I'm Forever Blowing Bubbles*	31	2	10.5.1975
Liverpool	*Sitting On Top Of The World*	50	2	17.5.1986
Crystal P	*Glad All Over/Where Eagles Fly*	50	2	12.5.1990
Manchester U	*Man Utd*	50	1	8.5.1976
Coventry C	*Go For It*	61	2	23.5.1987
Brighton & HA	*The Boys In The Old Brighton Blue*	65	2	28.5.1983

Those were the ones that charted, but there have been others, like Sunderland's 1973 effort 'Sunderland All The Way' with Bobby Knoxall, that never reached the charts. Among the more memorable songs was Chelsea's 1972 'Blue Is The Colour' which reached No.5 during a 12-week run in the charts, but it was recorded when Chelsea reached the Football League Cup Final, and not the FA Cup Final.

A song that didn't make the charts in 1970 was Peter Osgood, backed by the Chelsea Cup Final squad, doing a solo version of Chirpy Chirpy Cheep Cheep. There have probably been many others, whose sales were confined to a few die-hard fans, and thankfully never exposed to a wider audience.

Top Ten FA Cup Shocks

The greatest giant-killing feats in the history of the FA Cup might be considered to be the following:-

1. WALSALL 2 ARSENAL 0, JANUARY 14, 1933, ROUND 3. Arsenal were without four regulars but could still field five internationals and were expected to pulverise a Walsall team mired in the middle of Division Three North and one which had gone a month without a win. Arsenal recovered to win the first of three successive League championships but this was the worst day during manager Herbert Chapman's successful time at Highbury.

Gilbert Alsop opened the scoring after an hour and five minutes later Bill Sheppard made it 2–0 from the penalty spot. Chapman had clearly underestimated Walsall, and took swift action after the match. Tommy Black, who had never played for Arsenal until the game at Walsall, was transferred to Plymouth the following week, Charlie Walsh went to Brentford at the end of the month and Billy Warnes left for Norwich at the end of the season. Walsall lost 4–0 at Manchester City in the next round.

2. YEOVIL 2 SUNDERLAND 1, JANUARY 29, 1949, ROUND 4. The most famous victory by a non-League side over League opposition. Yeovil were lying six from bottom in the Southern League when the First Division side, including the most expensive player in the country, the £20,000 Len Shackleton, came to Somerset. But Yeovil rose to the occasion and won

2–1 with goals from Stock and an extra-time winner from Bryant. Yeovil lost 8–0 at Manchester United in the fifth round but their place in soccer history was already assured.

3. COLCHESTER UNITED 3 LEEDS UNITED 2, FEBRUARY 13, 1971, ROUND 5. Fourth Division Colchester United raced into a 3–0 lead after an hour against Don Revie's great side of the period. Leeds had been League champions in 1969, were runners-up in both the League and the Cup in 1970 and would go on to win the Cup in 1972 and reach the Final again in 1973. But they had no answer to an inspired Colchester side who scored the greatest victory in their history. Ray Crawford (2) and David Simmons scored Colchester's goals. Their run ended in the quarter-finals when they lost 5–0 at Everton.

4. HEREFORD UNITED 2 NEWCASTLE UNITED 1, FEBRUARY 5, 1972, ROUND 3 REPLAY. It is often overlooked now, but Hereford's staggering victory over Newcastle came in a replay after the Southern League side had held their First Division opponents to a 2–2 draw at St James' Park. It was the first victory by a non-League side over First Division opposition since Yeovil had beaten Sunderland 23 years previously.

Hereford had been picking off smaller League fry for the best part of 20 years but knocking out Newcastle finally won them election to the Football League in May 1972. Malcolm Macdonald had seemingly killed them off with an 84th minute goal in the replay, but Hereford replied with a spectacular goal from Ronnie Radford and won it in extra-time with a goal from Ricky George. Hereford forced West Ham to a replay in the next round before losing 3–1.

5. SUNDERLAND 1 LEEDS UNITED 0, MAY 5, 1973, CUP FINAL. Leeds were probably the hottest favourites of all time to win the Cup Final – but they hadn't bargained on goalkeeper Jim Montgomery playing the game of his life to deny them their second successive Cup win. Sunderland somehow held out after Ian Porterfield had given them a surprise lead in the first half.

6. WIMBLEDON 1 LIVERPOOL 0, MAY 14, 1988, CUP FINAL. A month before the Cup Final, Liverpool destroyed Nottingham Forest 5–0 at Anfield with a display of some of the best football ever seen from an English club side. On April 23 they clinched the Championship with a win over Tottenham and went on to finish the season having lost only two League matches. Nothing, it seemed, would stop them winning the Double for the second time in three seasons.

Wimbledon, a League side for only 11 seasons, had other ideas. They had been one of the few teams to take a point off Liverpool in the League, drawing with them the previous November, and refused to be intimidated under the Twin Towers. A Lawrie Sanchez header was the only goal of an astonishing final, best summed up for Liverpool by John Aldridge's missed penalty, the first in a Cup Final at Wembley.

7. BURNLEY 0 WIMBLEDON 1, JANUARY 4, 1975, ROUND 3. Wimbledon became the first non-League side to win away from home in the Cup against

First Division opposition since Darlington, then of the North Eastern League, beat Sheffield Wednesday in 1919–20. Burnley were seventh in the table at the time, but were thwarted by an outstanding goalkeeping display from Wimbledon's Dickie Guy. The only goal came in the 49th minute when Micky Mahon, a member of the Colchester team that had beaten Leeds in 1971, scored with a hard shot into the corner of the net.

Wimbledon's run continued with a fourth round tie against Leeds, the reigning League champions. Guy earned himself a permanent place in Cup history when he saved Peter Lorimer's 83rd minute penalty in a 0–0 draw. The replay, at Crystal Palace, was watched by 46,000 who saw Leeds win 1–0 after the future Dons manager Dave Bassett deflected the ball past Guy for the only goal of the game.

8. SUTTON UNITED 2 COVENTRY CITY 1, JANUARY 7, 1989, ROUND 3. Less than 18 months previously Coventry City had won the Cup for the first time in their history and they took the field at Gander Green Lane in Surrey against Sutton of the GM Vauxhall Conference with seven members of their Cup-winning team in their line-up. But the 8,000 fans were about to see one of the great Cup upsets. Goals from Tony Rains and Matthew Hanlan meant Sutton became only the sixth non-League club since the war to knock out a First Division club. Sutton were beaten 8–0 at Norwich in the next round.

9. DERBY COUNTY 1 BOSTON UNITED 6, DECEMBER 10, 1955, ROUND 2. Six men in the Boston United team that travelled to Derby for this famous second round tie knew all about the Baseball Ground – they were all ex-Derby County players. They were Reg Harrison, who played for Derby in the 1946 Cup Final; Geoff Hazledene and his brother Don, the Boston skipper; Ray Wilkins, Dave Miller and goalkeeper Ray Middleton. They were all seeing out their careers in the Midland League while Derby had slipped from the heights they reached just after World War II and were now in the Third Division North.

Even so, not many people in the 23,000 crowd expected anything other than a Derby win but by half-time the non-League side were 3–1 ahead and they added another three without reply in the second half. In the next round Boston lost 4–0 at Tottenham but there was a strange postscript to the Derby–Boston match years later. On January 9, 1974 Boston and Derby were drawn together again – and Derby won 6–1 at Boston in a replayed third round tie.

10. WREXHAM 2 ARSENAL, 1 JANUARY 4, 1992, ROUND 3. For the second time a lowly team whose name began with a 'W' humbled Arsenal in the Cup. For the first time the team finishing bottom of the Football League the previous season knocked out the League champions. Wrexham did it with two goals in the last eight minutes, the first a scorching free-kick equaliser from veteran Mickey Thomas who had played for Manchester United against Arsenal in the 1979 Cup Final. A second goal from Steve Watkin gave Wrexham a totally unexpected victory. They went out in the next round after losing to West Ham in a replay.

50 FA Cup Firsts

1. The First FA Cup Final
The first FA Cup final was played on March 16, 1872 when The Wanderers met Royal Engineers at the Kennington Oval in front of a 2,000 crowd who paid 1/- (5p) each for the privilege.

The Wanderers won that first final with a goal scored by Morton Peto Betts who was playing for the Wanderers under the pseudonym 'AH Chequer' as he was actually a member of the Harrow Chequers club which had scratched when due to play the Wanderers in the first round.

2. The First Goal in the History of the FA Cup
The first four matches in the history of the FA Cup were played on Saturday, November 11, 1871, and the results were:

Barnes 2, Civil Service 0
Crystal Palace 0, Hitchin 0
Maidenhead 2, Marlow 0
Upton Park 0, Clapham Rovers 3

The first goal on that historic day was scored by Jarvis Kenrick who went on to score twice in Clapham Rovers' win over Upton Park. He later played in three winning finals for The Wanderers, scoring a total of three Cup Final goals.

3. The First Club to Reach Two FA Cup Finals
The Wanderers won the first Final in 1872 and were handed a bye to the second final. In 1873 they beat Oxford Univeristy 2–0 to become also the first club to win the FA Cup in successive years.

4. The First Club to Win Three FA Cup Finals
The Wanderers won the Cup for the third time after a replay in 1876 when they beat the Old Etonians at Kennington Oval. Under the rules of the competition at the time they were entitled to keep the Cup for a third win, but handed it back to the FA.

5. The First Player to Score two goals in the FA Cup Final
Thomas Hughes, who scored two of the three goals in the 1876 replay, was the first man to score more than one goal in the final.

6. The First hat-trick in the FA Cup Final
William Townley of Blackburn Rovers scored three goals when his side beat Sheffield Wednesday, or The Wednesday as they were called at the time, 6–1 in the 1890 Cup Final at Kennington Oval.

7. The First hat-trick in a Wembley FA Cup Final
Stan Mortensen of Blackpool became the first player to score a hat-trick in a Wembley Final when his side beat Bolton Wanderers 4–3 in the Matthews Final of 1953.

8. The First own goal in the FA Cup Final
Lord Kinnaird 'achieved' this in 1877 – but the fact was lost for more than a century. Playing for the Wanderers against Oxford University he stepped over the goal-line with the ball and Oxford were credited with a goal. Conflicting newspaper reports of the time confused the issue further and until recently the result of that final was always given as Wanderers 2, Oxford University 0. Most publications now list the result as 2–1.

9. The first player to score for both sides in the FA Cup Final

Bert Turner of Charlton Athletic in 1946. With 10 minutes to play between Derby County and Charlton Athletic the score was still 0–0 and extra-time looked certain. Then Turner deflected a clearance into his own net to put Derby 1–0 ahead. Less than a minute later he equalised for Charlton with a free-kick which also took a slight defelection off Derby's Peter Doherty. It was 1–1 at the end of normal time so the match went into extra-time after all. Doherty also scored for Derby in extra-time – but it is Turner who is credited with a goal for each side. Derby won the match 4–1.

10. The First player to score a penalty in the FA Cup Final

Albert Shepherd of Newcastle United took and scored the first penalty awarded in the FA Cup Final. The goal came in the replay of the 1910 final between Newcastle and Barnsley at Goodison Park. Shepherd scored both goals as Newcastle won 2–0.

11. The First player to miss a penalty in the FA Cup Final

Charlie Wallace of Aston Villa missed a penalty in the 1913 FA Cup Final between League champions Sunderland and Villa, who finished second in the table. The 1913 final was the first between the two clubs finishing first and second in the First Division.

12. The First player to score in successive FA Cup Finals

Alexander Bonsor became the first player to score in succesive finals with goals in both 1875 and 1876 for Old Etonians. He had already played in the 1872 and 1873 finals for the Wanderers without scoring but ending up with a winner's medal both times. However, in both 1875 and 1876 the Old Etonians lost, first to the Royal Engineers and then the Wanderers.

13. The First Player to score in successive FA Cup Finals at Wembley

Bobby Johnstone of Manchester City scored in both 1955 when Manchester City lost 3–1 to Newcastle United and 1956 when City beat Birmingham 3–1.

14. The first substitute to play in an FA Cup Final

The 1967 final between Tottenham Hotspur and Chelsea was the first at which the two competing teams had named a squad of 12 men for the final – 11 players and one substitute. Tottenham's No.12 was Cliff Jones who had played in the 1961 and 1962 Cup winning teams and Chelsea's was Joe Kirkup, who two years previously had played in the West Ham side that beat TSV Munich 1860 to win the European Cup-Winners Cup at Wembley.

But neither man had the honour of being the first substitute in the Cup Final. A year later West Bromwich Albion's Derek Clarke became the first substitute used in the Cup Final when he replaced John Kaye. Albion beat Everton 1–0 with a goal from Jeff Astle.

15. The First substitute to score in the FA Cup Final

Eddie Kelly of Arsenal came on for the injured Peter Storey in the 1971 Final against Liverpool and became the first substitute to score in an FA Cup Final when he equalised for the Gunners in the 11th minute of extra

time. But the following morning the newspapers credited George Graham with the goal. It was only later that TV cameras behind the goal proved that Kelly, and not Graham, got the final touch on the ball, and the goal was credited to Kelly.

16. The first substitute to score twice in the FA Cup Final

Stuart McCall of Everton was the first – by two minutes from Ian Rush of Liverpool. Both McCall and Rush came on as substitutes during the 1989 FA Cup Final. McCall scored his first goal in the last minute of normal time to make the score 1–1 and force extra-time. Rush put Liverpool 2–1 ahead in the fourth minute of extra-time, and eight minutes later McCall scored his second to make the score 2–2 and become the first substitute to score twice in the Cup Final. Two minutes after McCall's second, Rush scored his second with sixteen minutes of extra-time remaining to become the second substitute to score two goals in the Cup Final.

17. The first all-English team to win the FA Cup

West Bromwich Albion were the first club to win the FA Cup with a team composed entirely of English-born players in 1888. Every player was locally-born and their combined wage bill was about £10 a week. Since then Bolton (1958), Manchester City (1969) and West Ham (1975) are the only other clubs to win the Cup with all-English teams.

18. The first non-English team to win the FA Cup

The Liverpool team which beat Everton to win the FA Cup Final in 1986 technically did not contain any 'English' players. Nine of the 11 players in the side were full internationals – but none of them played for England. Mark Lawrenson, who was born in Preston, played for the Republic of Ireland. Craig Johnston, who *did* play for England 'B', was born in South Africa.

The lineup with their countries was: Bruce Grobbelaar (Zimbabwe); Mark Lawrenson (Rep. Ireland), Jim Beglin (Rep. Ireland), Steve Nicol (Scotland), Ronnie Whelan (Rep. Ireland), Alan Hansen (Scotland), Kenny Dalglish (Scotland), Craig Johnston (born in South Africa), Ian Rush (Wales), Jan Molby (Denmark), Kevin Macdonald (born in Scotland).

19. The first player to play in winning Scottish and English FA Cup sides

Harry Campbell appeared in the Renton team that won the Scottish FA Cup in 1888 and played for Blackburn Rovers when they won the FA Cup two years later.

Jimmy Welford, who played for Aston Villa when they beat West Bromwich Albion 1–0 in the 1895 FA Cup Final, became the first Englishman to appear in winnng teams on both sides of the border when he played for the Celtic team which beat Rangers 2–0 in the 1899 Scottish FA Cup Final.

20. The First Player to score in every round of the Cup

Alexander (Sandy) Brown of Tottenham Hotspur became the first player to score in every round of the FA Cup when Spurs won the Cup in 1901. His total of 15 goals is still a record for one season in the competition proper.

21. The First Non-League club to reach the Cup Final

Before the foundation of the Football League in 1888, of course, all the finalists were non-league, but the first non-League side to reach the final after the formation of the League was Sheffield Wednesday, then The Wednesday, who were playing in the Football Alliance. They reached the 1890 final and lost 6–1 to Blackburn Rovers who finished third in the Football League that season. Sheffield Wednesday joined the Football League two years later.

22. The First Non-League club to win the FA Cup
Tottenham Hotspur became the first, and so far only non-League FA Cup winners since the formation of the Football League in 1888 when they won the Cup in 1901, beating Sheffield United 3–1 in a replay at Burnden Park, Bolton, after a 2–2 draw at Crystal Palace.

23. The first non-League club to beat the reigning League Champions in an FA Cup tie
Something that would seem inconceivable today has actually happened four times in the history of the FA Cup. The first occasion, however, was when Stoke, then of the Football Alliance beat Preston 3–0 in a first round match on January 17, 1891.

24. The first non-League club to beat the reigning FA Cup Holders
En route to winning the FA Cup in 1901, Tottenham Hotspur, then in the Southern League, met First Division Bury, the reigning Cup holders, in a second round match on 23 February. Spurs won the tie 2–1 and went on to win the Cup. The very next season, still a non-League side themselves and by this time Cup holders, Spurs were knocked out by Southern League opposition, losing to Southampton in the first round.

25. The First Club to win the Football League and FA Cup double
Preston North End won the inaugural Football League championship in 1888–89 without losing a match and won the FA Cup the same season without conceding a goal.

26. The first Club to finish second in the League and runners-up in the Cup in the same season
Huddersfield Town were the best team in the League in the 1920s when they won three successive titles from 1924–26. Their only success in the Cup came in 1922 when they beat Preston NE 1–0 in the last pre-Wembley Final. In 1928 they reached Wembley again were they were beaten 3–1 by Blackburn Rovers. They also finished second in the League that season behind Everton and became the first side to finish as runners-up in the race for both major honours in the same season.

27. The First Second Division Club to win the FA Cup
The Second Division of the Football League was formed for the 1892–93 season and the following year, in 1894, the first Second Division team won the FA Cup. Notts County, who finished third in the Second Division and missed out on promotion to the first by losing in the Test Matches to Liverpool, beat Bolton Wanderers 4–1 in the final at Goodison Park. Jimmy Logan scored the second FA Cup Final hat-trick.

28. The First Second Division club to be promoted and win the FA Cup in the same season
West Bromwich Albion became the first Second Divi-

sion club to win at Wembley and the first to do this Cup and promotion double when they beat Birmingham 2–1 in an all-Midland final in 1931. No side has achieved the same feat since then.

29. The First side to reach the FA Cup Final and be relegated from the First Division in the same season
Chelsea finished second from bottom of the First Division in 1914–15, the last season before the First World War. But their Cup form was in marked contrast to their League form and they reached the FA Cup Final, only to go down 3–0 to Sheffield United. But for the War, they would have been relegated, but kept their place in the First Division when it was expanded from 20 to 22 clubs in 1919.

In 1926 Manchester City finished one from bottom of the First Division and also reached the Cup Final. There was no War to save them, and they went down.

30. The First club from outside England to win the FA Cup
When Cardiff City beat Arsenal 1–0 in the 1927 Cup Final they became the first, and so far only non-English club to win the FA Cup Final. The only other non-English club to reach the final is Queen's Park, Glasgow, who finished as runners-up to Blackburn Rovers in both 1884 and 1885.

31. The First FA Cup match played on Christmas Day
By all accounts, only one FA Cup match has been played on Christmas Day and that was in 1888 when Linfield beat Cliftonville 7–0 in a fourth qualifying round second replay. On Boxing Day 1881 Hotspur FC beat Reading Minster 2–0 in a third round match.

32. The First Wembley FA Cup Final
The first Wembley FA Cup Final was played on April 28, 1923 when First Division Bolton Wanderers beat West Ham United of the Second Division 2–0. The official attendance is recorded as 126,047 but an estimated 200,000 fans were in the stadium by the time the match kicked off.

33. The First Wembley FA Cup Final goal
David Jack of Bolton scored the first FA Cup Final goal at Wembley, three minutes after the start of the match against West Ham. He also scored the fifth Wembley FA Cup final goal three years later when Bolton beat Manchester City 1–0 in 1926.

34. The first player to score two goals in a Wembley FA Cup Final
James Roscamp of Blackburn Rovers became the first man to score twice in the same Cup Final when he scored two of his side's three goals in their 3–1 win over Huddersfield Town in 1928.

35. The First player to score for the losing finalists at Wembley
Strangely, between 1910 when Newcastle beat Barnsley 2–0 in the FA Cup Final replay and 1927 when Cardiff beat Arsenal 1–0, the losing side failed to score a goal. Thus the first man to score at Wembley and end up on the losing side was Alex Jackson of Huddersfield Town, who scored his side's solitary goal when they lost 3–1 to Blackburn Rovers.

36. The First team to score first and lose the FA Cup Final at Wembley

In 1932 Bob John put Arsenal ahead against Newcastle United after 15 minutes but Newcastle came back to win the Cup 2–1 thanks to two goals from Jack Allen.

37. The First person to play in and then manage a winning FA Cup team

Peter McWilliam picked up a winner's medal as a player when Newcastle United beat Barnsley in the 1910 FA Cup Final. He was the manager of Tottenham Hotspur when they beat Wolverhampton Wanderers to win the Cup in 1921 when he became the first man to achieve this particular double.

38. The First person to play for and then manage the same club in the FA Cup Final

Only four men have ever achieved this feat and three are still actively involved in the game today – Kenny Dalglish, Terry Venables and George Graham. But the first man to perform this feat was Stan Seymour who played in the Newcastle United team which beat Aston Villa 2–0 in 1924, and then managed the club when it won the Cup in 1951 and 1952. Seymour also scored one of Newcastle's goals in 1924.

39. The First reigning monarch to attend the FA Cup Final

King George V became the first reigning monarch to attend the final when he saw Burnley beat Liverpool 1–0 in the 1914 final at Crystal Palace. He obviously enjoyed himself because he also attended the finals of 1921, 1923, 1926, 1927, 1928, 1930, 1932, and 1934.

40. The First winning team to put their ribbons on the FA Cup

One of the great traditions of the FA Cup did not actually start until the competition was almost 30 years old. But the first club to put their ribbons on the trophy

after winning it were Tottenham Hotspur at their post-match celebration in 1901. Every year before the final *both* sets of ribbons are attached to the Cup – and the losers are removed before the presentation.

41. The First Wembley FA Cup final to go to a replay

It was not until 1970 and the 42nd final that a Wembley Cup Final ended in a draw after extra-time. On April 11, 1970 Chelsea and Leeds drew 2–2, with Chelsea winning the replay 2–1 at Old Trafford. By a strange coincidence, for the first and only time, 18 top journalists were asked for their predictions in the Cup Final match programme before the match. Twelve said Chelsea would win, five voted for Leeds and only one man got it right – aptly, the gentleman from the *Sporting Life.* His name? Graham Taylor.

42. The First FA Cup Final to be replayed at Wembley

The first Wembley final to be replayed at Wembley was the 1981 Final between Tottenham Hotspur and Manchester City which Tottenham won 3–2. That was the first Final to be replayed since the Chelsea–Leeds match of 1970 but started a sequence of three successive finals – 1981, 1982 and 1983 – which all ended in draws.

43. The first player sent off in an FA Cup Final

It was not until the 116th Final match, including replays, that a player was sent off. The unlucky man was Kevin Moran of Manchester United who was dismissed by referee Peter Willis for a late tackle on Everton's Peter Reid. Manchester United, reduced to

Manchester United are unimpressed by referee Peter Willis' decision to send off Kevin Moran at Wembley in 1985, the first time a player had been dismissed in an FA Cup Final (Allsport/David Cannon)

10-men, nevertheless went on to win the FA Cup Final 1–0.

44. The first time in FA Cup history an entire round was called off due to the weather

At least one match scheduled to take place in every round of the FA Cup did so from the start of the competition in 1871 for the next 98 years. Even during the 'big freezes' of 1947 and 1963 at least some matches took place on their original dates.

But on February 8, 1969, all eight Round Five matches were postponed because of the weather.

45. The First FA Cup tie played on a Sunday

With rounds of the FA Cup now spread over three days because of broadcasting demands, it seems strange to think that until January 6, 1974, no FA Cup match had ever been played on a Sunday. The match that broke the mould was between Cambridge United and Oldham Athletic and it ended in a 2–2 draw. Ironically, it took place at the Abbey Stadium.

46. The First £1 Million Gate Receipt at the FA Cup Final

The first FA Cup Final match to produce £1 million in takings at the gate was the 1985 Final between Manchester United and Everton, which was also Britain's first £1 million gate.

The first final for which receipts are reliably known is the 1885 final which produced a gate of £442. Since then the following milestones have been reached:

First £1000 1891 Blackburn R vs Notts County (£1454)

First £10,000 1921 Tottenham H vs Wolverhampton W (£13,414)

First £100,000 1966 Everton vs Sheffield W (£109,691)

First £500,000 1978 Ipswich vs Arsenal (£500,000)

First £1m 1985 Manchester U vs Everton (£1.1m)

First £2m 1990 Manchester U vs Crystal P (£2m)

47. First Third Division side to reach the FA Cup semi-final

No side from the old Third Division of the Football League ever reached the Cup Final, but six reached the semi-finals. The first to do so were Millwall who reached the last four in 1937 where they lost 2–1 to the eventual winners, Sunderland.

48. The first team to win both the FA Cup and the FA Amateur Cup

Old Carthusians won the FA Cup in 1881 and the Amateur Cup in 1894 and 1897. Since then only Wimbledon have repeated that feat winning the Amateur Cup in the FA's Centenary Year of 1963 and the FA Cup in the Football League's Centenary Year of 1988. The FA Amateur Cup was discontinued in 1974. The only other current professional club who could emulate them are Middlesbrough who won the Amateur Cup in 1895 and 1898 but have never yet reached the final of the FA Cup.

49. The first goalkeeper to captain an FA Cup winning team

Dave Beasant of Wimbledon had a memorable day on May 14, 1988 when he became the first goalkeeper to captain his team to victory in the FA Cup. During the match he became the first goalkeeper to save a penalty in a Wembley FA Cup Final when he palmed away John Aldridge's 61st-minute spot-kick.

50. The First FA Cup penalty shoot-outs

Penalty shoot-outs were introduced to settle ties after a second drawn match from the 1991–92 season.

The first tie to be decided on penalties was the First Round match between Rotherham United and Scunthorpe United on November 26, 1991. After the first match ended in a 1–1 draw, the replay at Rotherham finished 3–3 after extra-time. Rotherham won 7–6 on penalties.

The following day Exeter City beat Colchester United 4–2 on penalties after they had drawn their two First round matches 0–0. Colchester thus became the first team to be knocked out of the Cup without conceding a goal.

The other penalty shoot-outs in the 1991–92 season came in the third round when Bournemouth beat Newcastle 4–3; in the fourth round when Southampton beat Manchester United 4–2 and in the semi-finals when Liverpool beat Portsmouth 3–1.

However, the first ever FA Cup match to be decided on penalties was a third-place play-off match between Birmingham City and Stoke City at St Andrew's on August 5, 1972. The match ended 0–0 and Birmingham won 4–3 on penalties.

THE FIRSTS OF 1993

The 1993 Cup Final between Arsenal and Sheffield Wednesday produced an unusually large number of firsts. It was the first time the same two finalists in the League Cup also met each other in the FA Cup Final in the same season. It was the first final in which the players wore their names on the back of their shirts, also done for the first time at the League Cup Final a month earlier. It was the first time that squad numbers were used rather than both teams being numbered 1–11.

Wednesday's Roland Nilsson became the first Swedish international to play in the Cup Final and his team-mate John Harkes became the first American to play in the Cup Final. Wednesday's Viv Anderson, who in 1978 became the first black player to win a full England cap, became the first black player to captain a Cup Final side. Carlton Palmer became the second in the replay, captaining Wednesday in the absence of the injured Anderson. Arsenal's Steve Morrow became the first player to receive a winner's medal at the Cup Final before the game – collecting the League Cup winner's medal he was unable to receive a month previously after being injured in the post-match celebrations. George Graham and Trevor Francis became the first two managers to collect winner's and loser's medals with their teams.

For the first time a Cup Final programme was printed with a notable omission on the cover. There was no cost price on the cover of the replay programme. And, one for the purists this, Arsenal became the first team since Tottenham 92 years previously to win the Cup from outside the Football League. Spurs were in the Southern League when they won the FA Cup in 1901, while Arsenal became the first club from the new Premier League to win the competition.

INDEX

References to photographs are
shown in italic.